THE VIRGIN BOOK OF BRITISH HIT ALBUMS

THE VIRGIN BOOK OF BRITISH HIT ALBUMS

Edited by Martin Roach

Entry biographies by
David McAleer and Matthew White

OFFICIAL

Published by Virgin Books 2009
2 4 6 8 10 9 7 5 3 1

Based on data compiled by Graham Betts

First published in Great Britain in 2009 by Virgin Books
Random House, 20 Vauxhall Bridge Road, London SW1V 2SA

www.virginbooks.com
www.rbooks.co.uk

Addresses for companies within The Random House Group Limited can be found at: www.randomhouse.co.uk/offices.htm

The Random House Group Limited Reg. No. 954009

A CIP catalogue record for this book
is available from the British Library

Trade paperback ISBN 9780753517000

Text Design: www.carrstudio.co.uk
Printed and bound in Italy by L.E.G.O.

Acknowledgements

Martin Roach would like to thank the following people for co-writing and researching the following pieces: Trevor Baker (Pete Townshend, Jeff Buckley, Mariah Carey, Thom Yorke, Flood/Youth); Brett Callwood (MC5); Kevin Cann (The Small Faces, David Bowie); Richard Carman (Chuck Berry, Phil Spector, Neil Young, Paul Weller, Madonna, Billy Fury); Ian Jones (Led Zeppelin); John Robb (Dr Dre, Public Enemy, Otis Redding, Madness, The Smiths, Jimi Hendrix, Stevie Wonder). Thanks as always to everyone at Virgin Books and the Official Charts Company. Special thanks also to Colin Hughes, Rich Carr, Ben Cracknell, to Phil Matcham for his tireless statistical work and to Dave McAleer and Matthew White for their artist bios.

Contents

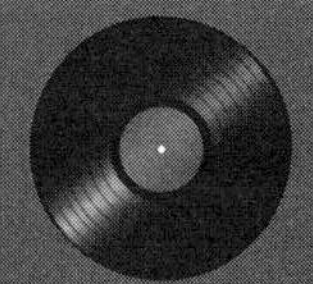

Contents

NOTABLE ALBUMS

ARTIST BIOGRAPHIES

CHART LISTINGS

How to Use this Book

KEY TO ARTIST ENTRIES

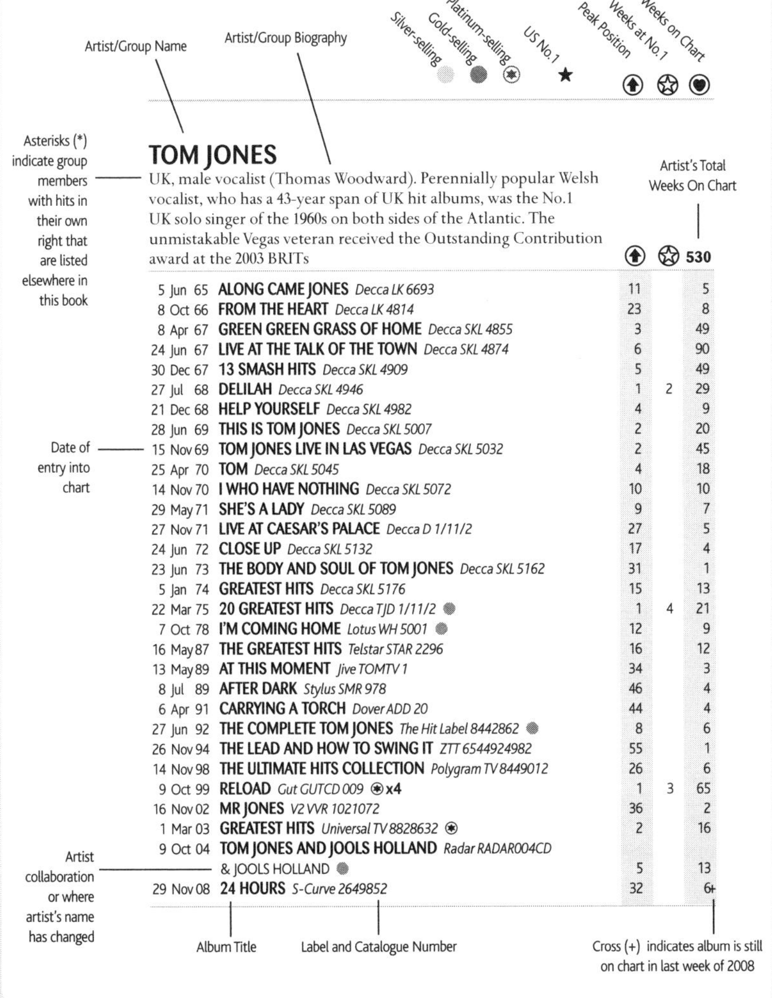

TOM JONES
UK, male vocalist (Thomas Woodward). Perennially popular Welsh vocalist, who has a 43-year span of UK hit albums, was the No.1 UK solo singer of the 1960s on both sides of the Atlantic. The unmistakable Vegas veteran received the Outstanding Contribution award at the 2003 BRITs

Date	Album	Peak	Weeks at No.1	Weeks (530)
5 Jun 65	**ALONG CAME JONES** *Decca LK 6693*	11		5
8 Oct 66	**FROM THE HEART** *Decca LK 4814*	23		8
8 Apr 67	**GREEN GREEN GRASS OF HOME** *Decca SKL 4855*	3		49
24 Jun 67	**LIVE AT THE TALK OF THE TOWN** *Decca SKL 4874*	6		90
30 Dec 67	**13 SMASH HITS** *Decca SKL 4909*	5		49
27 Jul 68	**DELILAH** *Decca SKL 4946*	1	2	29
21 Dec 68	**HELP YOURSELF** *Decca SKL 4982*	4		9
28 Jun 69	**THIS IS TOM JONES** *Decca SKL 5007*	2		20
15 Nov 69	**TOM JONES LIVE IN LAS VEGAS** *Decca SKL 5032*	2		45
25 Apr 70	**TOM** *Decca SKL 5045*	4		18
14 Nov 70	**I WHO HAVE NOTHING** *Decca SKL 5072*	10		10
29 May 71	**SHE'S A LADY** *Decca SKL 5089*	9		7
27 Nov 71	**LIVE AT CAESAR'S PALACE** *Decca D 1/11/2*	27		5
24 Jun 72	**CLOSE UP** *Decca SKL 5132*	17		4
23 Jun 73	**THE BODY AND SOUL OF TOM JONES** *Decca SKL 5162*	31		1
5 Jan 74	**GREATEST HITS** *Decca SKL 5176*	15		13
22 Mar 75	**20 GREATEST HITS** *Decca TJD 1/11/2* ●	1	4	21
7 Oct 78	**I'M COMING HOME** *Lotus WH 5001* ●	12		9
16 May 87	**THE GREATEST HITS** *Telstar STAR 2296*	16		12
13 May 89	**AT THIS MOMENT** *Jive TOMTV 1*	34		3
8 Jul 89	**AFTER DARK** *Stylus SMR 978*	46		4
6 Apr 91	**CARRYING A TORCH** *Dover ADD 20*	44		4
27 Jun 92	**THE COMPLETE TOM JONES** *The Hit Label 8442862* ●	8		6
26 Nov 94	**THE LEAD AND HOW TO SWING IT** *ZTT 6544924982*	55		1
14 Nov 98	**THE ULTIMATE HITS COLLECTION** *Polygram TV 8449012*	26		6
9 Oct 99	**RELOAD** *Gut GUTCD 009* ⊛ x4	1	3	65
16 Nov 02	**MR JONES** *V2 VVR 1021072*	36		2
1 Mar 03	**GREATEST HITS** *Universal TV 8828632* ⊛	2		16
9 Oct 04	**TOM JONES AND JOOLS HOLLAND** *Radar RADAR004CD* & JOOLS HOLLAND ●	5		13
29 Nov 08	**24 HOURS** *S-Curve 2649852*	32		6+

BIOGRAPHIES

Biographies include the nationality and category for every chart entrant.

Each entrant has at least a mini biography. The 100 acts with the most weeks on the chart (see page 290 for the top 100 chart) each have extended biographies.

Real names are included for all solo artists and, where applicable, dates of death and age of the artist at the time. "See..." links are included for soloists who also had album chart entries in other acts.

The best known line-up is listed for every group that had a Top 10 album, with the vocalist/leader mentioned first and the others following in alphabetical order. In cases where later replacements had similar success both people are named and, where applicable, the dates of death are also shown for every group/duo member listed.

Certified Awards are given by the BPI to mark unit sales to retailers. The certified awards were introduced in April 1973, based on revenue received by manufacturers. In January 1978 the qualification rules were changed and the system based on unit sales to the trade was adopted.

Silver symbol ● = 60,000 units

Gold symbol ● = 100,000 units

Platinum symbol ⊛ = 300,000 units

How to Use this Book

KEY TO COMPILATION ALBUM ENTRIES

Album Name | Catalogue Number | Silver-selling | Gold-selling | Platinum-selling | US No.1 ★ | Peak Position | Weeks at No.1 | Weeks on Chart

Date	Album	Peak Position	Weeks at No.1	Weeks on Chart
7 Sep 02	**CHILLED JAZZ** *Verve 0692092*	14		1
21 Dec 02	**THE JAZZ ALBUM 2003** *Verve 0680672*	13		2
26 Apr 03	**DIVAS OF JAZZ** *Verve 0394222*	12		3

Compilation Category | Record Label

VARIOUS ARTISTS (VIRGIN)

Date	Album	Peak Position	Weeks at No.1	Weeks on Chart
25 Jul 92	**THE GREATEST DANCE ALBUM IN THE WORLD!** *Virgin Television VTCD 13* ●	2		12
31 Oct 92	**NEW ROMANTIC CLASSICS** *Virgin Television VTCD 15* ●	7		5
17 Jul 93	**THE BEST DANCE ALBUM IN THE WORLD...EVER!** *Virgin Television VTDCD 17* ⊛x2	1	4	19
23 Oct 93	**THE SINGER AND THE SONG** *Virgin Television VTDCD 21* ●	5		6
20 Nov 93	**THE BEST DANCE ALBUM IN THE WORLD...EVER! 2** *Virgin Television VTDCD 22* ⊛	3		12
4 Dec 93	**THE BEST CHRISTMAS ALBUM IN THE WORLD...EVER!** *Virgin Television VTDCD 23* ⊛x3	2		10
29 Jan 94	**SWEET SOUL HARMONIES** *Virgin Television VTCD 20* ●	1	1	9
26 Feb 94	**DANCE TO THE MAX** *Virgin Television VTCD 24* ●	2		10
12 Mar 94	**RAP TO THE MAX** *Virgin Television VTCD 25* ●	10		4
30 Apr 94	**IN THE AIR TONIGHT** *Virgin Television VTDCD 26* ●	8		10
7 May 94	**PURE MOODS** *Virgin Television VTCD 28* ⊛x2	1	2	31
28 May 94	**DANCE TO THE MAX 2** *Virgin Television VTCD 29* ●	4		8
4 Jun 94	**THE BEST REGGAE ALBUM IN THE WORLD...EVER!** *Virgin Television VTCD 27* ⊛	4		10

Cross (+) indicates album is still on chart in last week of 2008

KEY TO INDEX ENTRIES

Album Title | Artist/Group | Peak Position | Year of Release

Album Title / Artist	Peak Position	Year of Release
ABBA ABBA	13	1976
ABBAMANIA VARIOUS ARTISTS (POLYDOR)	2	1999
THE ABBEY DOWNSIDE ABBEY MONKS & CHOIRBOYS	54	1996
ABBEY ROAD BEATLES	1	1969
ABC JACKSON FIVE	22	1970
ABDUCTION EAT STATIC	62	1993
ABOMINOG URIAH HEEP	34	1982
ABOUT A BOY – OST BADLY DRAWN BOY	6	2002
ABOUT FACE DAVID GILMOUR	21	1984
ABOUT TIME STRANGLERS	31	1995
ABOUT TIME 2 CLOCK	56	1997
ABOUT WHAT YOU KNOW LITTLE MAN TATE	27	2007
ABOVE MAD SEASON	41	1995
ABOVE THE RIM FILM SOUNDTRACK	18	1994

Editor's Note

Albums are a much more personal experience than singles. People argue about 'the greatest album ever' much more vehemently than the best single. Why is this? Possibly it's because you spend more time with an album, at home, in the car, on the train, through your headphones or in the office. In this edition of *The Virgin Book of Hit Albums*, I have tried to explore the medium in depth and from a variety of angles, to cast light across why these records have such power.

The introduction takes you behind the scenes of an album's creation to see the myriad factors that can make the difference between a hit and a miss. I've also featured a history of that most revitalised of genres, compilations, as well as a light-hearted look at some of the most delayed records of all time. Also peppered in among the statistics are analyses of some of the finest albums ever recorded, plus biographies of artists whose work makes the charts all the more entertaining.

Wherever you choose to listen to these erstwhile 'long players', the impact of a breathtaking album can be massive. Such a record can soundtrack a phase of your life, it can be the musical backdrop to relationships, jobs, travel, tragedy, joy, a multitude of experiences in life, good and bad. Albums are almost alive with personal resonance and, despite all the recent technological developments and the naysayers predicting the end of the form, a brilliant album in 2009 is still as relevant and as potent as in 1959.

Introduction

From Tranzophobia to Hell and Back Again

AS we head into the Brave New World of President Obama set against the dark clouds of the Credit Crunch, the music business is – like so many other industries – being severely afflicted by the downturn in global economic fortunes. While the fall of physical CD singles sales is well documented and is mirrored, albeit to a lesser degree, by the decline of physical album sales, there is constant speculation and discussion about that most basic of premisses: how to make an album *sell*. The fact is, when a record works, even in an economic downturn, there is money to be made. Record companies like money. Artists like success and money (in no particular order sometimes). The public like hit albums. Promoters, TV, radio, merchandisers all feed off a hit album. Despite everything, we still want new artists to emerge, albums to sell and music to be made.

But what is it exactly that makes one album work and another one fail? Why do seemingly well-crafted records sometimes fall between the cracks when other, less obviously gifted albums, sell millions? How can a brilliant album be made to sell even more after its initial sales flurry? How can a bad album be made to sell at all? For some of the answers to these questions, you have to break down the 'life of an album' into all its manifold component parts and examine which elements of this incredibly lengthy process can make the difference between a hit and a flop.

Let's start with that most battered, mistreated yet beloved of rock'n'roll companions, the humble Transit van. The legendary 'tour bus' is, in fact, a cauldron of creation, and the success or failure of an album can begin here. The unassuming van may smell of urine, beer, sweat and have witnessed a million band arguments, but it is also the place where generation after generation of classic albums enjoy their genesis.

Mega City 4, the seminal UK guitar band of the late 1980s and early 1990s, were famed for their relentless touring schedules, playing in excess of 200 gigs in most years; however, like many acts, those monotonous motorway miles and countless service station pasties also served another purpose because the band found themselves with hours to kill inside their trusty Transit van. So what did they do? Compose new material. They even honoured their long-serving vehicle by christening a new medical condition – 'Tranzophobia' – to describe the inevitable cabin fever that results from being too long in the back of a van. In calling their first album *Tranzophobia* (Number 67, June 1989), MC4 also gave us the most direct nod to the creative benefits of living in a rusty tour bus. It is the intimacy, the intensity and the boredom that create masterpieces – fuelled by the ongoing spectacle of life on the road.

Assuming a band has created an album's worth of songs on the road, they will invariably practise them in studios and rehearsal rooms; however, a tried-and-tested method is to also play them live. In their earlier days, Radiohead famously experimented song ideas out in the live arena; likewise Blur, whose critically

lauded second album, *Modern Life Is Rubbish*, evolved dramatically over the course of many live shows and a backdrop of slacker-driven grunge culture. However, it takes a brave (and self-aware) act to make their song choices for the next album in this way.

What is it exactly that makes one album work and another one fail?

Once the songs are rehearsed and road-tested, the process moves on to demo stage. Here, a band will record rough-cut versions of the prospective album songs. Typically these will act as mere guides for the more complex final studio versions; however, there are notable examples where the demo versions end up as the finished article and the purity and creative brevity of these demos can have a seismic effect on the commercial success of a record. When Dave Grohl left Nirvana following the suicide of lead singer Kurt Cobain, he chose to launch a new 'band'; in fact, what lay behind the group – Foo Fighters – was a remarkable solo effort. Grohl recorded the entire debut album in his basement and at Robert Lang's Seattle studios, playing every instrument himself (with the sole exception of one guitar line on one song). Essentially a demo, the eponymous record became a multi-million global seller, and a Number 3 record in the UK charts, and it's still going strong with 240,000 sales in the UK up to the end of 2008. Part of the record's appeal was that its stripped-bare aesthetic tapped straight into the punk/grunge mentality of so many Nirvana fans. Fearful of Grohl's newly monied and famed status tempting him to turn his back on his US hardcore roots, you could almost hear the collective sigh of relief when the Foos' debut was released and proved to be so raw.

There was a precursor within Grohl's own career – before he'd joined Cobain's band, Nirvana's debut album *Bleach* was recorded in December 1988 and January 1989 for just $606.17 with producer Jack Endino billing the band for just thirty hours of studio time in total. Elsewhere, there are plenty of precedents to Grohl's recording economy reaping rich reward for an album. US soft rockers Boston recorded the demo for their self-titled debut album (Number 11 in 1977) in lead guitarist Tom Scholz's basement. Scholz had an engineering background working for Polaroid and impressively invented his own tape system on which much of the band's debut was demoed. His genius even saw him buy an obsolete 12-track tape machine just as the 24-track successor was becoming the must-have item. His studio wizardry also extended to one home-made machine called a Power Soak, another called the Space Echo pedal, and another unit mounted in a cigar box. At the same time, Scholz had been trying to get his material heard through a live band, Mother's Milk, but he later stated this ill-fated group proved to be a mere distraction from demoing and writing.

After a raft of major record labels turned the demo songs down for a contract, the tape was sent – for the second time – to Epic Records, who signed them, with the musicians gathered around Scholz taking the name Boston. Due to the unique equipment on which the debut album songs had been created and demoed, it proved virtually impossible to replicate the sonic detail in a traditional studio. As such, to the average listener *Boston* displays almost no obvious differences from the demo that secured the band a record deal. The album has to date sold in excess of 20 million copies, making it one of the biggest-selling debuts of all time. Part of the appeal is undoubtedly the maverick approach to the demos. Incidentally,

Scholz later revealed that had the last batch of demo tapes not secured a recording contract, he was considering selling all his self-made equipment and calling time on his music dream.

By contrast to such expedient records, some albums fail long before a piece of vinyl, a CD or a download is anywhere near completion. The glory days of mid-1970s prog rock give us some of the best examples of how studio sessions can help or hinder a new album – Led Zeppelin famously enjoyed the use of 128 tracks for some of their classic albums. Such excess and the inevitable slow gestation this causes is not always a good thing for an album's sales, however. Later in this book, we look at albums that have taken far too long in the making – take a bow, Axl Rose – but suffice it to say that the longer an artist spends in the studio, the more likely it is that cyclical music fashion, record company patience and fan interest will turn against them.

With the album in the bag, there are still a myriad of reasons why the record might fail or succeed. Long before the sessions are canned and mixed, an artist will start work on the album's sleeve artwork which is, obviously, crucial to any potential success. There are endless notable examples of this, but let's use the most famous album artwork of them all: *Sgt. Pepper's Lonely Hearts Club Band* by The Beatles.

While the album itself is a landmark record, the sleeve work has become equally revered. The Grammy-winning artwork was a collaboration of several great minds – McCartney was the main thrust from within the band, working with art director Robert Fraser (himself a prominent London art dealer renowned for his expertise in modern art) plus genius pop artist/designer Peter Blake and his wife Jann Haworth. The central concept of *Sgt. Pepper's* sleeve artwork is well documented: life-size cardboard cut-outs of more than seventy famous people, with The Beatles in the guise of Sgt. Pepper's band in the foreground. The simple concept was 'People We Like'.

Like all great art, the sleeve work for *Sgt. Pepper* has been the subject of theory, conspiracy and conjecture since its release. Countless websites are dedicated to the contents, listing the medals that the band wear, the coats of arms featured, the significance of each celebrity and famous face, the artefacts shown (small statues belonging to Lennon and Harrison, a small portable TV set and a trophy) ad infinitum. Even the waxworks of mop-top-era Beatles looking at the band's name written in flowers were seen as a symbol of the passing of the early incarnation of the Fab Four into music heaven. The most poignant face on the sleeve was that of the original Beatles bass player, the late Stuart Sutcliffe. Shunning the ultimately uneconomic idea of packaging the record with pens and pencils for the record buyer to make their own collage, the album nevertheless came out with a page of cut-outs for the listener. Notably, the original artwork – a psychedelic painting by Dutch art collective The Fool – was actually used on just the initial few pressings before being dropped for the more famous cover.

With the album in the bag, there are still a myriad of reasons why the record might fail or succeed

The impact of the artwork was no doubt reinforced by the fact it was gatefold – originally the album was due to be a double-record but at the last minute the band decided they were unconvinced that enough tracks were of sufficient quality. Most notable of all the anecdotes from this seminal sleeve is the reaction of

Mae West who, when first contacted for her permission to appear on the sleeve, responded, 'What would I be doing in a lonely hearts club?' A personal letter from the admiring Beatles eventually changed her mind. The final bill for the cover was £2,868 5s/3d, approximately 100 times the average cost for an album cover in those days. And worth every penny – it is widely seen as the best album cover in history. *Sgt. Pepper* has become a highly influential album cover in its own right (aside from the album tracks), such that its influence has extended to the genre/field of album artwork in general. At the time, Frank Zappa was quick to mimic the design with his *We're Only In It For The Money* record (although legal issues forced the image inside the sleeve) and The Rutles did likewise. Even *The Simpsons* has parodied

Regardless of the truth versus the conspiracy, the art versus the commerce, such album sleeves sell records

the artistic milestone. Oasis made no secret of their Beatle-mania in the writing of their music and this was openly trumpeted with the artwork for their debut album, *Definitely Maybe*, (Number 1, September 1994). Just as with *Sgt. Pepper*, the references and items in the *Definitely Maybe* photograph have led to the Mancunian band's own rumour mill about exactly what is in the picture and for what reason. US artist Michael Cuffe is perhaps the most recent example of this Beatles album artwork becoming a cultural beacon of influence, with his poster to celebrate Barack Obama's presidency with a *Sgt. Pepper*-styled poster. As mentioned later in this book, elements of Led Zeppelin's *IV* used deliberately obtuse artwork and complex symbolism to paint a picture for a landmark record; Pink Floyd album sleeves justify their own books; and art critics have been known to pass judgement on record sleeves by the likes of Bob Dylan, The Velvet Underground and The Rolling Stones, to name but a tiny few. Regardless of the truth versus the conspiracy, the art versus the commerce, such album sleeves *sell* records.

Of course, most album sleeves are not complete without the record's title. And what's in a name? Potentially, everything. When Take That and a recovering Britney Spears decided to release an album of virtually the same name – *The Circus/Circus* – in early December 2008, there was a minor furore about who should step aside and alter their title. Neither party wanted to and, to be fair, needed to. Least of all Take That, the reformed man-band that easily charged to the top of the album charts with sales far out-stripping Britney's.

Sometimes, it isn't the existence of a similarly titled record that causes problems. Rock history has plentiful examples of album titles that probably didn't assist the artists' bank balance a great deal: The Grateful Dead's *Aoxomoxoa*, Salt 'N Pepa's *A Salt With A Deadly Pepa* (see what they did there?) and, last but not least, the record seen by many as having one of, if not, *the* longest album title ever, Fiona Apple's catchily titled *When the Pawn Hits the Conflicts He Thinks Like a King What He Knows Throws the Blows When He Goes to the Fight and He'll Win the Whole Thing 'Fore He Enters the Ring There's No Body to Batter When Your Mind Is Your Might So When You Go Solo, You Hold Your Own Hand and Remember That Depth Is the Greatest of Heights and If You Know Where You Stand, Then You'll Know Where to Land and If You Fall It Won't Matter, Cuz You Know That You're Right*. Perhaps most bizarrely of all, 50,000 people actually bought this record, sending it into the charts at Number 46 in March 2000 – imagine standing at the customer-service desk in your local record store asking some under-paid, over-bored student-on-holiday for this little beauty.

Many bands have decided that having a name for an album is a 'sell-out', an odd position perhaps given that they have usually already signed a major record deal, but it is one that bands such as Metallica and Led Zeppelin have taken. See later in this book for Led Zeppelin's 'symbol' approach, but metal-heads Metallica insisted on a similar non-titular approach with the so-called *The Black Album* in August 1991 (Number 1). With the cover featuring only the band's logo and a coiled snake, many observers took to calling this record *Metallica*. The confusion mattered little, with the record shifting in excess of 25 million copies worldwide, launching the metallers into the rock stratosphere. They are, of course, not alone, with The Beatles' plain conceptual art sleeve for their ninth album, known widely as *The White Album*. Notably, the tape version was sold in a black cover and became known jokingly as *The Black Tape* by Beatles collectors.

During one of his most tempestuous periods, in 1987, Prince had recorded an album with a completely black sleeve (bar a catalogue number in pink on the spine) and no title, but the release was shelved. Rumours suggested the artist suffered a crisis of confidence and expressed his own fear at the violent nature of the lyrics; this seems possible given Prince's notorious reputation as a driven perfectionist. Any concern about lyrical content was reportedly shared by his label Warner Brothers and the record was pulled from release schedules. Nonetheless, the mystery hyped the record's profile hugely, with other stars such as U2 saying they'd heard versions (about 100 promo copies had filtered out to Europe before the subsequent withdrawal) and it was a masterpiece. Oddly, by the time the untitled album was finally released by Warner Brothers – who were by then in a fierce legal battle with Prince – the general public response was 'what was all the fuss about?' Sales reflected this relative disinterest. In the UK album charts, the record only reached Number 36, selling 40,000 copies, 580,000 less than *Purple Rain*'s 620,000.

One final example of such obscure album titles is the brilliantly conceived *The Grey Album* by Dangermouse. This was a clever mash-up of Jay-Z's own *The Black Album* and unauthorised samples of many Beatles songs, most notably segments of *The White Album*.

Sticking with Prince for a moment, the diminutive one took the name-calling to its most (il)logical extreme when he changed his own name to first Squiggle/Symbol then 'The Artist Formerly Known as Prince' (nattily known as TAFKAP by fans). This was a decision set against a backdrop of his embittered legal row with his label, Warner Brothers, and the use of the Squiggle/Symbol was effectively intended to disown his former self and the record label he was at odds with. He wasn't the first and he won't be the last artist to launch an album with a name change: Puff Daddy/P Diddy/Diddy; Cat Stevens/Yusuf Islam (although the latter was actually his birth name).

Many bands have decided that having a name for an album is a 'sell-out'

It's important to remember that Prince is also a man who wrote the word 'Slave' on his face in protest at the row with his record label; at the same time and selling far more albums in the UK was Blur, whose drummer Dave Rowntree subsequently went on *Top Of The Pops* with the word 'wanker' written on his cheek.

Even without spontaneous name changes and record-label arguments, there is one absolutely vital aspect of the record business that can have either a catastrophic or magnificent effect on any album's prospects, and that is publicity. Successful album launches can make a massive difference; the standard idea is a signing event. Arguably one of the most frantic public appearances in history was by pop band Bros, who did various signings to general hysteria throughout 1987–8. At one such appearance at the HMV in Oxford Street, central London, to help promote their debut album *Push* (Number 2, April 1988), conservative estimates counted the number of fans – Brosettes – in attendance at around the 10,000 figure. Oxford Street had to be closed to traffic and police were called off holiday leave from all over the Greater London area. When Bros came to exit the building via their limousine, the vehicle was surrounded by thousands of screaming fans who literally tore the car's door from its hinges as it drove away. Headlines inevitably followed, as did massive album sales.

In the post-millennial age, bands and record labels are proving a little more creative in their approach than a standard record-store signing. The multi-media age has seen albums promoted virally with huge success, the obvious example being Arctic Monkeys' debut *Whatever People Say I Am, That's What I'm Not*, which has, at the time of writing, sold 1.25 million since its release in January 2006. After that innovative online PR campaign, the explosion of social-networking sites has seen the artist's blog become commonplace in promoting an album. Recent clever, entertaining and productive blogs include Mike Skinner, aka The Streets, who chronicled the complex and lengthy gestation of his 2008 album *Everything Is Borrowed* (Number 7, September 2008) with a fascinating online diary.

Where would rock 'n' roll be without scandal?

Of course, publicity that is pre-ordained can never really be as authentic and therefore as appealing to the public as pure, unadulterated *scandal*. The Sex Pistols did it, Oasis were masters, The Who's Keith Moon was without equal; where would rock 'n' roll be without scandal? Well, there'd be a lot fewer albums sold for starters ... however, genuine scandal is not something you can programme into an album schedule. So what else can you plan that helps?

Once an album has sold huge amounts of copies, it follows that awards are then often heaped upon the musician or performer who is already counting his royalties. Therefore, in analysing why some albums sell and others don't, the beneficial impact of awards such as Brits and Grammys is a little obvious and of only moderate interest. Clearly winning one of these industry-moulded awards is only going to have an upward effect on your 'units shifted' statement; however, what is fascinating are the awards given to 'breakthrough' artists or those on the more innovative edges of the form. Perhaps most notorious for this is the Mercury Music Award. Although the award is actually given for 'Best Album', it has become known for being a beacon of innovation; cynics might add that it has also become known for the question 'Who?' when nominees are announced. The awards usually take place in the autumn but nominated albums are announced the preceding July. Bands that are nominated for, or indeed win, the prize experience a large increase in album sales. Radiohead and Oasis have enjoyed several nominations but no victories; in 1994, The Prodigy, Paul Weller, Blur and Pulp all lost out to M People; Turin Brakes were nominated in 2001

> **Arctic Monkeys' debut *Whatever People Say I Am, That's What I'm Not* has, at the time of writing, sold 1.25 million since its release in 2006**

for *The Optimist* which saw a gradual and hefty sales improvement in the aftermath, despite not winning; Roni Size won in 1997 but did not go on to fulfil the maximum potential of what was seen as a glittering future; actually, the Mercury Music Awards' reputation for championing the obscure is perhaps more to do with the nominations, as a list of winners – Suede, Elbow, Franz Ferdinand, Arctic Monkeys, Dizzee Rascal, etc. – hardly reveals a lengthy catalogue of failure.

In the absence of an award cabinet crammed with trophies, there is always the ultimate publicity stunt. As harsh and cynical as this may be, the commercial reality is that one surefire way to get cracking publicity is to expire. Death is not a strategy favoured by most rock stars, at least not consciously, but it is a historical fact that shuffling off this mortal coil is a near-dead-cert (sorry) to revitalise album sales. Sometimes an artist's biggest album success comes, to put it bluntly, when they are not around to enjoy the fruits of their labours. Many established rock stars have seen exponential album sales in the aftermath of personal tragedy – Freddie Mercury, Kurt Cobain, John Lennon, Elvis Presley, Roy Orbison – but a small number of artists even achieve their first breakthrough after they have passed away. Eva Cassidy is a fine example of someone whose brilliant work and unique vocals only really came to prominence after she had succumbed to cancer. More historical figures include Buddy Holly, Ritchie Valens and The Big Bopper, who all died in a plane crash signalled by Don McLean as 'the day the music died'. The week after John Lennon was killed, his album *Double Fantasy* climbed up to Number 2 from Number 46, while his *Imagine* record re-entered the charts at Number 56. Three Beatles albums also returned to the charts that week, (*Beatles Ballads* at 40, *The Beatles 1962–1966* at 43 and *The Beatles 1967–1970* at 72).

On a more cheerful note, one rather more obvious and palatable component of any album's success is the choice of singles released from that album around the same time if not beforehand and, naturally, the videos made to promote those songs. Again, there are famous examples – Michael Jackson's status as the man behind the biggest album ever has to be at least partly attributed to the then groundbreaking video for the title track from his album, *Thriller* (Number 1, December 1982). The fact that the special effects 'transformation' of Jackson from a squeaky-clean preppy boy to a salivating werewolf might not even find its way on-to a horror spoof on *You've Been Framed* in 2008 is irrelevant. At the time, before CGI was commonplace, the video was quite startling. And the length of the video – at fourteen minutes – was previously unheard of. The image of an entire nation sitting down to watch the video's UK premiere is hard to conjure up now in an age of a seemingly infinite mass of music TV channels, but that's what his famous video did (the album's success was reinforced ably by a super-cool promo for 'Billie Jean' and other undeniably classic songs). Sixty million album sales later, who is to argue?

A hit single can revitalise an album in one short week

A hit single can revitalise an album in one short week – one artist to be the beneficiary of this undoubted phenomenon is Robbie Williams. At the time of writing, even after the relative disappointment of 2006's *Rudebox* (which sold 500,000, nearly a fifth of the amount of his best-selling album, *I've Been Expecting You*), the man from Stoke is still one of the world's biggest artists. Yet, back when he was still a fledgling solo artist, heavy drinker and most famously 'the

chubby one from Take That who left early', matters were not quite so rosy. Prior to the release of the single 'Angels', his solo career was on a knife-edge, following a string of only modest single-chart positions. Yet the potent combination of the suave black-and-white video for 'Angels' and the song itself, propelled Williams to Number 4, refuelled his album *Life Thru A Lens* to stellar sales of two million to date and singularly re-launched 'The Robster'. Over in Sherwood Forest, Bryan Adams's 'Everything I Do (I Do It For You)' – taken from the soundtrack to *Robin Hood – Prince of Thieves* – sold a trillion-squillion copies and was Number 1 for eight years; the corresponding album was also huge, shifting 1.6 million copies and peaking at Number 1. Of course, for every rule there is a counter-rule: take AC/DC, who, despite having released one of the biggest albums of all time (*Back In Black*, Number 1, August 1980), have yet to enjoy a Top Ten UK single.

On the subject of soundtracks, it is worth noting that this is another cast-iron way to assist general album sales of any artists featured on the release. Sometimes a near-afterthought can send an album's sales escalating rapidly upwards. Being used in television adverts is a proven method: 'Strange and Beautiful' from Aqualung's self-titled debut in October 2002 (Number 15) and Stiltskin's *The Mind's Eye* in October 1994 (Number 17) are both examples of albums that had little depth of material other than the advertising ditty. Film soundtracks are a more direct route to success. If a record is very closely tied to a film, then the benefits may be colossal. There are many examples to pick from, so let's use what was for many years the biggest musical film in history: *Grease*. Starring John Travolta and Olivia Newton-John, the film itself was a mammoth hit, grossing $340 million at the box office. Curiously, unlike its contemporary and equally massive musical film, *Saturday Night Fever*, the Travolta/Newton-John film was alarmingly quick to fade away. Only a year after dominating the world's charts, Travolta released an album containing a compilation of his hits from both films, which barely scraped into the US Top 200. Newton-John enjoyed a further UK Number 1 single with ELO on the track 'Xanadu', from the critically mauled film of the same name, and a ten-week stint on top of the US charts with 'Physical'. Of course, both artists have gone on to further fame but these two examples highlight the unpredictability of film tie-in albums. Other examples that have enjoyed prolonged chart stays include 1979's *The Wall* by Pink Floyd, which was then made into a 1982 film of the same name and a complex and historically revered live show. *Quadrophenia* is another sample from this genre. It doesn't always work with the official soundtrack album either – Mariah Carey's *Glitter* (Number 10, September 2001) is testament to that. But maybe that's because the film had limited commercial success.

Once on the road, an album's fortunes can change almost nightly. In the aftermath of the multiple-Grammy-winning classic, *Back To Black*, Amy Winehouse would perform one concert and her sales would go up; then she'd cancel another show at the last minute ... and her sales would go up! A rare example of an artist whose erratic touring (combined of course with a salacious private life) actually fuelled sales.

U2 were arguably already on their way to becoming global rock giants when they played Red Rocks in Denver in 1983; however, what this concert – and their legendary touring prolificacy – achieved was to position them perfectly ahead of the moment they went stratospheric, namely 1987's *The Joshua Tree*. True, it was a brilliant record rammed with classics and, even for the non-believer of stadium rock, it was a landmark album; however, by playing endless shows and managing to

AC/DC, who released one of the biggest albums of all time (*Back In Black*, Number 1, August 1980), have yet to enjoy a Top Ten UK single

perform that historically acknowledged open-air show at Red Rocks four years earlier, U2 were effectively already 'the biggest band in the world' prior to the staggering sales of *The Joshua Tree*. Rock history has countless other examples of album success stories that were made by the tour preceding them or, of course, their own promotional dates: Ziggy, Green Day's *American Idiot*, Take That's *Beautiful World* and so on; there are hundreds more. Further, sometimes a non-album gig or guest appearance can change an album's fortunes for ever. Most of the artists who performed at Sir Bob 'Give us your fucking money' Geldof's 1985 Live Aid, saw huge album sales in the days and weeks thereafter.

And yet, using U2 as a focus a little longer, a good tour can also sell a bad album. Take the highly anticipated but much-maligned *Pop*, released ten years after *The Joshua Tree*. The general critical feeling that the record was rushed was reinforced by the spate of bad reviews that saw the band's ironic take on modern consumerism being largely lost on disdainful critics. However, the record actually hit the top spot in more album charts globally than *The Joshua Tree* and the corresponding tour was a massive success financially, elongating what was otherwise an ordinary album's stay in the world's charts.

The *Pop* album was also something of a 'change in direction' – that phrase dreaded by A&R men the world over – a creative detour that may be the cause major headaches for sales figures. Take Green Day, for example: long before *American Idiot* turned them into a globe-trotting stadium punk band, their initial commercial breakthrough came with *Dookie* (Number 13, November 1994), including the blistering single, 'Basket Case'. However, by 2000's more mellow *Warning*, the change of direction and maturing of the band's personal lives from their earlier goofy prankster psyche turned the critics off en masse. In the UK, sales for the two albums were very different: *Dookie* sold 890,000 copies; *Warning* sold 260,000, although the poorer-selling record enjoyed a higher chart placing at Number 4. It's ironic then that, in 2004, an even maturer approach and socio-political theme on *American Idiot* was hailed by the same critics as one of the finest concept albums of recent years.

Getting back to the subject of live shows refuelling an album's success, it might sometimes be the case that no matter how many high-profile gigs an act plays, they are never going to enjoy chart success. In the case of G.G. Allin, classed by many as the most extreme performer in rock history, his stage shows became increasingly out of control, including watching the performer defecate and urinate – invariably thrown at/splashed towards the audience – and his numerous live jaunts were gradually shortened each time by hospital visits, broken bones, blood poisoning, spells in jail ... although his threat to commit suicide on stage never materialised. Sadly, the album charts listed in this book are not troubled by this true one-off as none of his records made the Top 100.

The opposite manifestation of this is when a tour or even a gig is so impressive that it becomes an album itself; The Who's *Live At Leeds* is widely regarded as the

A good tour can also sell a bad album

greatest live album of all time. This is something of an exception to the rule, however, as, the deluge of 'live' albums released every year is often actually little more than a quick route to fulfilling a 'final album clause' in a band's record contract.

While the band is on tour, or even still in the studio, the record label can do their part too, not just with the variety of publicity covered already. The packaging and presentation of an album can make a

huge difference. The Sex Pistols' album *Never Mind The Bollocks* (Number 1, November 1977) was famously nearly canned because at first their label could find no pressing plants that would accept the controversial work. Cue rabid headlines and handsome pre-sales. Compare this to the *X Factor* situation – albeit a single – in which Andy Peters is filmed live at the pressing plant pressing the button to manufacture the winning artist's debut CD.

Particularly loved by the artists – and loathed by the cynic – is the 'deluxe' edition of an album. Typically this will consist of the original long-player by an artist plus a new song or two that, for some reason, has recently surpassed the album's original profile and success. So for 'deluxe' read 'If we stick this hit single on the end we'll sell another million copies'. Cynical? Well, take the exceptionally gifted Amy Winehouse. When it was released as a 'deluxe' edition to include the quite brilliant collaboration with super-producer

Particularly loved by the artists – and loathed by the cynic – is the 'deluxe' edition of an album

Mark Ronson ('Valerie') the 'deluxe' edition of *Back To Black* sold 800,000 copies and reached Number 1 in its own right; the original edition has sold more, some 2.1 million copies, yet in 2008 the deluxe edition sold more copies, on its way to being that year's fourteenth best-selling album. Leona Lewis has seen a similar recent sales boost for her debut album *Spirit*, with the inclusion of her cover of Snow Patrol's 'Run' (originally a spontaneous live rendition on Radio 1s 'Live Lounge'). That debut record has subsequently hung around in the Top 75 for fifty weeks at the time of writing.

Sometimes the new material on an album needs a knee-up straight away; after Michael Jackson had pretty much ruled the music world for years, he came through a child-molestation scandal and returned with the ever-so-humble *HIStory* to monumental sales (Number 1, June 1995, the biggest multi-disc seller ever). Surely this was largely due to the inclusion of a 'greatest hits' segment to the record, rather than the decidedly ordinary new material? *HIStory* was also a good example of a launch that promised much but delivered little. Jackson had enormous statues of himself made and sent around the world, famously sailing down the Thames on a barge for which Tower Bridge was lifted. There was even a brief rumour – sadly untrue – that Tango were planning to send a sixty-foot can of their vegetable extract drink down the Thames, emblazoned with the words 'King of Pop'.

Assuming you haven't died in the course of the album's promotion, it will only be a matter of months before a record-company man is pencilling in the next long-player. Of course, when the band's previous album sells several million, each group member can earn more in a year than most people do in a lifetime. Green Day famously went from not earning enough money to register for tax, to being in the top taxation bracket within twelve months. When this happens, circumstances – and egos – change. The Transit van is replaced by a tour bus and, in the biggest bands, a tour bus *each*. Where then is the camaraderie, the chemistry needed to write the material that paid for those luxuries in the first place? So many artists have released debut albums based on their lives, be it the emotionally deprived childhoods or the violent former life of gangsta rappers, only to follow up with a record about the tedium of life as a rock star or the boredom of the road. Few do this well – Mike Skinner again (*The Hardest Way To Make An Easy Living* or much of Dr Dre and Fifty Cent's later work); most do it badly

The Sex Pistols' album *Never Mind The Bollocks*, was famously nearly canned because at first their label could find no pressing plants that would accept the controversial work

– when *Fame Academy* winner David Sneddon jumped straight to the theme and called his debut record *Seven Years Ten Weeks* (Number 5, May 2003), named after the length of his 'search' for fame, an already sceptical public tutted and turned away, leaving the record stalling. Even the genius that is Eminem occasionally fell victim to this temptation of listless self-reference after his initial breakthrough, although, in typically paradoxical style, he also peaked with a song about a pop star's stalker, 'Stan', coming from the equally introspective album *The Marshall Mathers LP*.

Part of the problem is that if a band has a big debut album they are inevitably sent out on the road to promote it mercilessly. In so doing, they have little opportunity to create new music, other than in the van itself or, worse still, in a cheap hotel; thus, when the tour nears its end and the record label need a new album, hey presto, the band haven't got enough songs. Cue second-album flop and the end of a record deal/dream. In the modern era, bands have adapted to this dynamic and have actually built recording studios *on* their tour buses – recent examples include Natasha Bedingfield and US pop heart-throbs, the Jonas Brothers, who have all kitted out their transport with state-of-the-art equipment.

Closely linked to this is that fact that the collaborative effect of writing on tour, in rehearsal rooms or moreover *as a band* is often cited as the explanation why a previously hugely successful band member cannot produce a solo album of the same stature. Examples might include Gary Barlow of Take That, members of Kiss, Black Sabbath, The Who, even some of The Beatles ... it's a long list. The regularly criticised Victoria Beckham is credited by many with releasing one of the biggest 'flop' solo albums known. The self-titled debut was the first solo effort by a Spice Girl and followed on from singles that had hardly sparked the public's imagination, but worse was to come – on its release in the first week of October 2001, the album sold only 16,000 copies in its first week, entering the chart at Number 10, which was also its highest position. To date, it has only sold 60,000 copies.

Given her massive profile and relative popularity in the glossy magazines, such starkly poor sales stats are surprising. The album dropped out of the Top 75 after two weeks (a first at that point) and sank beyond Number 250 within a month. An earlier high-profile example would be Paul McCartney, whose 1970 *McCartney* was widely seen by many observers as a huge disappointment, but to be fair, how do you follow up the biggest band in history?

So we are left with the grumbles of the millionaire artist on the so-called 'album-tour-album-tour' treadmill. Countless albums sell millions of copies due in part to some of the reasons highlighted here; many more sell disastrous quantities due also in part to these elements. There are, of course, many other aspects of the 'life of an album' that can affect its longevity (or lack of), but these are just a few key factors to contemplate. Perhaps, in an era when people are being made unemployed in their thousands and shops on the high street are lying empty, the tumbleweeds blowing through the economy in general and the music industry in particular might make a few of the more grounded musicians and performers out there a little more happy to be on a treadmill at all.

And if all this fails? If your writing, demos, artwork, promotion, launch week, singles released, tour and every other aspect of the album flounders . . . well, to quote a lyric by the late, great Wiz, lead singer of Mega City Four and co-driver of the van that inspired the term *Tranzophobia*, 'Guess I'll have to make myself alternative arrangements ... '

Every No.1 Album from 1956–2008

Includes the date of the first week at No.1 and the number of weeks at No.1

Chart Date	Album Title Artist	Weeks at No.1
28/7/56	**SONGS FOR SWINGIN' LOVERS** FRANK SINATRA	2
11/8/56	**CAROUSEL** ORIGINAL SOUNDTRACK	2
25/8/56	**SONGS FOR SWINGIN' LOVERS** FRANK SINATRA	1
1/9/56	**CAROUSEL** ORIGINAL SOUNDTRACK	4
29/9/56	**OKLAHOMA!** ORIGINAL SOUNDTRACK	2
13/10/56	**THE KING AND I** ORIGINAL SOUNDTRACK	2
27/10/56	**ROCK N ROLL STAGE SHOWS** BILL HALEY & HIS COMETS	1
3/11/56	**THE KING AND I** ORIGINAL SOUNDTRACK	1
10/11/56	**ROCK 'N' ROLL** ELVIS PRESLEY	1
17/11/56	**THE KING AND I (TIED FOR ONE WEEK)** ORIGINAL SOUNDTRACK	15
16/2/57	**HIGH SOCIETY (TIED FOR ONE WEEK)** ORIGINAL SOUNDTRACK	1
2/3/57	**THIS IS SINATRA** FRANK SINATRA	1
9/3/57	**THE KING AND I** ORIGINAL SOUNDTRACK	1
16/3/57	**THIS IS SINATRA** FRANK SINATRA	1
23/3/57	**THE KING AND I** ORIGINAL SOUNDTRACK	1
30/3/57	**THIS IS SINATRA** FRANK SINATRA	1
6/4/57	**THE KING AND I** ORIGINAL SOUNDTRACK	3
27/4/57	**THIS IS SINATRA** FRANK SINATRA	1
4/5/57	**THE KING AND I (TIED FOR ONE WEEK)** ORIGINAL SOUNDTRACK	6
8/6/57	**LOVE IS THE THING (TIED FOR ONE WEEK)** NAT 'KING' COLE	1
15/6/57	**OKLAHOMA!** ORIGINAL SOUNDTRACK	1
22/6/57	**THE KING AND I** ORIGINAL SOUNDTRACK	4
20/7/57	**THE TOMMY STEELE STORY (OST)** TOMMY STEELE	3
10/8/57	**THE KING AND I** ORIGINAL SOUNDTRACK	3
31/8/57	**THE TOMMY STEELE STORY (OST)** TOMMY STEELE	1
7/9/57	**LOVING YOU (OST)** ELVIS PRESLEY	2
21/9/57	**A SWINGIN' AFFAIR** FRANK SINATRA	7
9/11/57	**LOVING YOU (OST)** ELVIS PRESLEY	1
16/11/57	**THE KING AND I** ORIGINAL SOUNDTRACK	11
1/2/58	**PAL JOEY** ORIGINAL SOUNDTRACK	7
22/3/58	**THE KING AND I** ORIGINAL SOUNDTRACK	1
29/3/58	**PAL JOEY** ORIGINAL SOUNDTRACK	4
26/4/58	**THE DUKE WORE JEANS** ORIGINAL SOUNDTRACK	2
10/5/58	**MY FAIR LADY** ORIGINAL CAST	19
19/9/58	**KING CREOLE (OST)** ELVIS PRESLEY	7
8/11/58	**SOUTH PACIFIC** ORIGINAL SOUNDTRACK	70
20/9/59	**KING CREOLE** ELVIS PRESLEY	7
8/11/59	**SOUTH PACIFIC** ORIGINAL SOUNDTRACK	70
12/3/60	**THE EXPLOSIVE FREDDY CANNON** FREDDY CANNON	1
19/3/60	**SOUTH PACIFIC** ORIGINAL SOUNDTRACK	19
30/7/60	**ELVIS IS BACK** ELVIS PRESLEY	1
6/8/60	**SOUTH PACIFIC** ORIGINAL SOUNDTRACK	5
10/9/60	**DOWN DRURY LANE TO MEMORY LANE** ONE HUNDRED AND ONE STRINGS	5
15/10/60	**SOUTH PACIFIC** ORIGINAL SOUNDTRACK	13
14/1/61	**G.I. BLUES (OST)** ELVIS PRESLEY	7
4/3/61	**SOUTH PACIFIC** ORIGINAL SOUNDTRACK	1
11/3/61	**G.I. BLUES (OST)** ELVIS PRESLEY	3

Chart Date	Album Title Artist	Weeks at No.1
1/4/61	**SOUTH PACIFIC** ORIGINAL SOUNDTRACK	1
8/4/61	**G.I. BLUES (OST)** ELVIS PRESLEY	12
1/7/61	**SOUTH PACIFIC** ORIGINAL SOUNDTRACK	4
29/7/61	**THE BLACK AND WHITE MINSTREL SHOW** GEORGE MITCHELL MINSTRELS	4
26/8/61	**SOUTH PACIFIC** ORIGINAL SOUNDTRACK	1
2/9/61	**THE BLACK AND WHITE MINSTREL SHOW** GEORGE MITCHELL MINSTRELS	1
9/9/61	**SOUTH PACIFIC** ORIGINAL SOUNDTRACK	1
16/9/61	**THE BLACK AND WHITE MINSTREL SHOW** GEORGE MITCHELL MINSTRELS	1
23/9/61	**THE SHADOWS** SHADOWS	4
21/10/61	**THE BLACK AND WHITE MINSTREL SHOW** GEORGE MITCHELL MINSTRELS	1
28/10/61	**THE SHADOWS** SHADOWS	1
4/11/61	**I'M 21 TODAY** CLIFF RICHARD & THE SHADOWS	1
11/11/61	**ANOTHER BLACK AND WHITE MINSTREL SHOW** GEORGE MITCHELL MINSTRELS	8
6/1/62	**BLUE HAWAII (OST)** ELVIS PRESLEY	1
13/1/62	**THE YOUNG ONES (OST)** CLIFF RICHARD & THE SHADOWS	6
24/2/62	**BLUE HAWAII (OST)** ELVIS PRESLEY	17
23/6/62	**WEST SIDE STORY** ORIGINAL SOUNDTRACK	5
28/7/62	**POT LUCK** ELVIS PRESLEY	5
1/9/62	**WEST SIDE STORY** ORIGINAL SOUNDTRACK	1
8/9/62	**POT LUCK** ELVIS PRESLEY	1
15/9/62	**WEST SIDE STORY** ORIGINAL SOUNDTRACK	1
22/9/62	**THE BEST OF BALL, BARBER & BILK** KENNY BALL, CHRIS BARBER & ACKER BILK	1
29/9/62	**WEST SIDE STORY** ORIGINAL SOUNDTRACK	3
20/10/62	**THE BEST OF BALL, BARBER & BILK** KENNY BALL, CHRIS BARBER & ACKER BILK	1
27/10/62	**OUT OF THE SHADOWS** SHADOWS	3
17/11/62	**WEST SIDE STORY** ORIGINAL SOUNDTRACK	1
24/11/62	**OUT OF THE SHADOWS** SHADOWS	1
1/12/62	**ON STAGE WITH THE GEORGE MITCHELL MINSTRELS** GEORGE MITCHELL MINSTRELS	2
15/12/62	**WEST SIDE STORY** ORIGINAL SOUNDTRACK	1
22/12/62	**OUT OF THE SHADOWS** SHADOWS	1
29/12/62	**THE BLACK AND WHITE MINSTREL SHOW** GEORGE MITCHELL MINSTRELS	2
12/1/63	**WEST SIDE STORY** ORIGINAL SOUNDTRACK	1
19/1/63	**OUT OF THE SHADOWS** SHADOWS	2
2/2/63	**SUMMER HOLIDAY (OST)** CLIFF RICHARD & THE SHADOWS	14
11/5/63	**PLEASE PLEASE ME** BEATLES	30
7/12/63	**WITH THE BEATLES** BEATLES	21
2/5/64	**ROLLING STONES** ROLLING STONES	12
25/7/64	**A HARD DAY'S NIGHT** BEATLES	21
19/12/64	**BEATLES FOR SALE** BEATLES	7
6/2/65	**ROLLING STONES NO. 2** ROLLING STONES	3
27/2/65	**BEATLES FOR SALE** BEATLES	1
6/3/65	**ROLLING STONES NO. 2** ROLLING STONES	6

Chart Date	Album Title Artist	Weeks at No.1
17/4/65	**THE FREEWHEELIN' BOB DYLAN** BOB DYLAN	1
24/4/65	**ROLLING STONES NO. 2** ROLLING STONES	1
1/5/65	**BEATLES FOR SALE** BEATLES	3
22/5/65	**THE FREEWHEELIN' BOB DYLAN** BOB DYLAN	1
29/5/65	**BRINGING IT ALL BACK HOME** BOB DYLAN	1
5/6/65	**THE SOUND OF MUSIC** ORIGINAL SOUNDTRACK	10
14/8/65	**HELP** BEATLES	9
16/10/65	**THE SOUND OF MUSIC** ORIGINAL SOUNDTRACK	10
25/12/65	**RUBBER SOUL** BEATLES	8
19/2/66	**THE SOUND OF MUSIC** ORIGINAL SOUNDTRACK	10
30/4/66	**AFTERMATH** ROLLING STONES	8
25/6/66	**THE SOUND OF MUSIC** ORIGINAL SOUNDTRACK	7
13/8/66	**REVOLVER** BEATLES	7
1/10/66	**THE SOUND OF MUSIC** ORIGINAL SOUNDTRACK	18
4/2/67	**THE MONKEES** MONKEES	7
25/3/67	**THE SOUND OF MUSIC** ORIGINAL SOUNDTRACK	7
13/5/67	**MORE OF THE MONKEES** MONKEES	1
20/5/67	**THE SOUND OF MUSIC** ORIGINAL SOUNDTRACK	1
27/5/67	**MORE OF THE MONKEES** MONKEES	1
3/6/67	**THE SOUND OF MUSIC** ORIGINAL SOUNDTRACK	1
10/6/67	**SGT. PEPPER'S LONELY HEARTS CLUB BAND** BEATLES	23
18/11/67	**THE SOUND OF MUSIC** ORIGINAL SOUNDTRACK	1
25/11/67	**SGT. PEPPER'S LONELY HEARTS CLUB BAND** BEATLES	1
2/12/67	**THE SOUND OF MUSIC** ORIGINAL SOUNDTRACK	3
23/12/67	**SGT. PEPPER'S LONELY HEARTS CLUB BAND** BEATLES	2
6/1/68	**VAL DOONICAN ROCKS BUT GENTLY** VAL DOONICAN	3
27/1/68	**THE SOUND OF MUSIC** ORIGINAL SOUNDTRACK	1
3/2/68	**SGT. PEPPER'S LONELY HEARTS CLUB BAND** BEATLES	1
10/2/68	**FOUR TOPS GREATEST HITS** FOUR TOPS	1
17/2/68	**DIANA ROSS & THE SUPREMES GREATEST HITS** DIANA ROSS & THE SUPREMES	3
9/3/68	**JOHN WESLEY HARDING** BOB DYLAN	10
18/5/68	**SCOTT 2** SCOTT WALKER	1
25/5/68	**JOHN WESLEY HARDING** BOB DYLAN	3
15/6/68	**LOVE ANDY** ANDY WILLIAMS	1
22/6/68	**DOCK OF THE BAY** OTIS REDDING	1
29/6/68	**OGDEN'S NUT GONE FLAKE** SMALL FACES	6
10/8/68	**DELILAH** TOM JONES	1
17/8/68	**BOOKENDS** SIMON & GARFUNKEL	5
21/9/68	**DELILAH** TOM JONES	1
28/9/68	**BOOKENDS** SIMON & GARFUNKEL	2
12/10/68	**THE HOLLIES' GREATEST** HOLLIES	6
23/11/68	**THE SOUND OF MUSIC** ORIGINAL SOUNDTRACK	1
30/11/68	**THE HOLLIES' GREATEST** HOLLIES	1
7/12/68	**THE BEATLES (THE WHITE ALBUM)** BEATLES	7
25/1/69	**BEST OF THE SEEKERS** SEEKERS	1
1/2/69	**THE BEATLES (THE WHITE ALBUM)** BEATLES	1
8/2/69	**BEST OF THE SEEKERS** SEEKERS	1
15/2/69	**DIANA ROSS & THE SUPREMES JOIN THE TEMPTATIONS** DIANA ROSS & THE SUPREMES WITH THE TEMPTATIONS	4
15/3/69	**GOODBYE** CREAM	2
29/3/69	**BEST OF THE SEEKERS** SEEKERS	2
12/4/69	**GOODBYE** CREAM	1
19/4/69	**BEST OF THE SEEKERS** SEEKERS	1
26/4/69	**GOODBYE** CREAM	1
3/5/69	**BEST OF THE SEEKERS** SEEKERS	1
10/5/69	**ON THE THRESHOLD OF A DREAM** MOODY BLUES	2
24/5/69	**NASHVILLE SKYLINE** BOB DYLAN	4
21/6/69	**HIS ORCHESTRA HIS CHORUS HIS SINGERS HIS SOUND** RAY CONNIFF	3
12/7/69	**ACCORDING TO MY HEART** JIM REEVES	4
9/8/69	**STAND UP** JETHRO TULL	3

Chart Date	Album Title Artist	Weeks at No.1
30/8/69	**FROM ELVIS IN MEMPHIS** ELVIS PRESLEY	1
6/9/69	**STAND UP** JETHRO TULL	2
20/9/69	**BLIND FAITH** BLIND FAITH	2
4/10/69	**ABBEY ROAD** BEATLES	11
20/12/69	**LET IT BLEED** ROLLING STONES	1
27/12/69	**ABBEY ROAD** BEATLES	6
7/2/70	**LED ZEPPELIN II** LED ZEPPELIN	1
14/2/70	**MOTOWN CHARTBUSTERS VOLUME 3** VARIOUS ARTISTS	1
21/2/70	**BRIDGE OVER TROUBLED WATER** SIMON & GARFUNKEL	13
23/5/70	**LET IT BE** BEATLES	3
13/6/70	**BRIDGE OVER TROUBLED WATER** SIMON & GARFUNKEL	4
11/7/70	**SELF PORTRAIT** BOB DYLAN	1
18/7/70	**BRIDGE OVER TROUBLED WATER** SIMON & GARFUNKEL	5
22/8/70	**A QUESTION OF BALANCE** MOODY BLUES	3
12/9/70	**COSMO'S FACTORY** CREEDANCE CLEARWATER REVIVAL	1
19/9/70	**GET YER YA-YA'S OUT – THE ROLLING STONES IN CONCERT** ROLLING STONES	2
3/10/70	**BRIDGE OVER TROUBLED WATER** SIMON & GARFUNKEL	1
10/10/70	**PARANOID** BLACK SABBATH	1
17/10/70	**BRIDGE OVER TROUBLED WATER** SIMON & GARFUNKEL	1
24/10/70	**ATOM HEART MOTHER** PINK FLOYD	1
31/10/70	**MOTOWN CHARTBUSTERS VOLUME 4** VARIOUS ARTISTS	1
7/11/70	**LED ZEPPELIN 3** LED ZEPPELIN	3
28/11/70	**NEW MORNING** BOB DYLAN	1
5/12/70	**ANDY WILLIAMS GREATEST HITS** ANDY WILLIAMS	1
12/12/70	**LED ZEPPELIN 3** LED ZEPPELIN	1
19/12/70	**ANDY WILLIAMS GREATEST HITS** ANDY WILLIAMS	4
16/1/71	**BRIDGE OVER TROUBLED WATER** SIMON & GARFUNKEL	3
6/2/71	**ALL THINGS MUST PASS** GEORGE HARRISON	8
3/4/71	**HOME LOVING MAN** ANDY WILLIAMS	2
17/4/71	**MOTOWN CHARTBUSTERS VOLUME 5** VARIOUS ARTISTS	3
8/5/71	**STICKY FINGERS** ROLLING STONES	4
5/6/71	**RAM** PAUL & LINDA MCCARTNEY	2
19/6/71	**STICKY FINGERS** ROLLING STONES	1
26/6/71	**TARKUS** EMERSON, LAKE AND PALMER	1
3/7/71	**BRIDGE OVER TROUBLED WATER** SIMON & GARFUNKEL	5
7/8/71	**HOT HITS 6** VARIOUS ARTISTS	1
14/8/71	**EVERY GOOD BOY DESERVES FAVOUR** MOODY BLUES	1
21/8/71	**TOP OF THE POPS VOLUME 18** VARIOUS ARTISTS	3
11/9/71	**BRIDGE OVER TROUBLED WATER** SIMON & GARFUNKEL	1
18/9/71	**WHO'S NEXT** WHO	1
25/9/71	**FIREBALL** DEEP PURPLE	1
2/10/71	**EVERY PICTURE TELLS A STORY** ROD STEWART	4
30/10/71	**IMAGINE** JOHN LENNON & THE PLASTIC ONO BAND WITH THE FLUX FIDDLERS	2
13/11/71	**EVERY PICTURE TELLS A STORY** ROD STEWART	2
27/11/71	**TOP OF THE POPS VOLUME 20** VARIOUS ARTISTS	1
4/12/71	**LED ZEPPELIN IV (FOUR SYMBOLS)** LED ZEPPELIN	2
18/12/71	**ELECTRIC WARRIOR** T. REX	6
29/1/72	**CONCERT FOR BANGLADESH (RECORDED LIVE)** GEORGE HARRISON & FRIENDS	1
5/2/72	**ELECTRIC WARRIOR** T. REX	2

Chart Date	Album Title Artist	Weeks at No.1
19/2/72	**NEIL REID** NEIL REID	3
11/3/72	**HARVEST** NEIL YOUNG	1
18/3/72	**PAUL SIMON** PAUL SIMON	1
25/3/72	**FOG ON THE TYNE** LINDISFARNE	4
22/4/72	**MACHINE HEAD** DEEP PURPLE	2
6/5/72	**PROPHETS, SEERS AND SAGES THE ANGELS OF THE AGES ...** TYRANNOSAURUS REX	1
13/5/72	**MACHINE HEAD** DEEP PURPLE	1
20/5/72	**BOLAN BOOGIE** T. REX	3
10/6/72	**EXILE ON MAIN STREET** ROLLING STONES	1
17/6/72	**20 DYNAMIC HITS** VARIOUS ARTISTS	8
12/8/72	**20 FANTASTIC HITS** VARIOUS ARTISTS	5
16/9/72	**NEVER A DULL MOMENT** ROD STEWART	2
30/9/72	**20 FANTASTIC HITS** VARIOUS ARTISTS	1
7/10/72	**20 ALL TIME HITS OF THE 50'S** VARIOUS ARTISTS	8
2/12/72	**25 ROCKIN' AND ROLLIN' GREATS** VARIOUS ARTISTS	3
23/12/72	**20 ALL TIME HITS OF THE 50'S** VARIOUS ARTISTS	3
13/1/73	**SLAYED?** SLADE	1
20/1/73	**BACK TO FRONT** GILBERT O'SULLIVAN	1
27/1/73	**SLAYED?** SLADE	2
10/2/73	**DON'T SHOOT ME I'M ONLY THE PIANO PLAYER** ELTON JOHN	6
24/3/73	**BILLION DOLLAR BABIES** ALICE COOPER	1
31/3/73	**20 FLASHBACK GREATS OF THE SIXTIES** VARIOUS ARTISTS	2
14/4/73	**HOUSES OF THE HOLY** LED ZEPPELIN	2
28/4/73	**OOH-LA-LA** FACES	1
5/5/73	**ALADDIN SANE** DAVID BOWIE	5
9/6/73	**PURE GOLD** VARIOUS ARTISTS	3
30/6/73	**THAT'LL BE THE DAY** ORIGINAL SOUNDTRACK	7
18/8/73	**WE CAN MAKE IT** PETERS & LEE	2
1/9/73	**SING IT AGAIN ROD** ROD STEWART	3
22/9/73	**GOAT'S HEAD SOUP** ROLLING STONES	2
6/10/73	**SLADEST** SLADE	3
27/10/73	**HELLO!** STATUS QUO	1
3/11/73	**PIN-UPS** DAVID BOWIE	5
8/12/73	**STRANDED** ROXY MUSIC	1
15/12/73	**DREAMS ARE NUTHIN' MORE THAN WISHES** DAVID CASSIDY	1
22/12/73	**GOODBYE YELLOW BRICK ROAD** ELTON JOHN	2
5/1/74	**TALES FROM TOPOGRAPHIC OCEANS** YES	2
19/1/74	**SLADEST** SLADE	1
26/1/74	**AND I LOVE YOU SO** PERRY COMO	1
2/2/74	**THE SINGLES 1969-1973** CARPENTERS	4
2/3/74	**OLD NEW BORROWED AND BLUE** SLADE	1
9/3/74	**THE SINGLES 1969-1973** CARPENTERS	11
25/5/74	**JOURNEY TO THE CENTRE OF THE EARTH** RICK WAKEMAN	1
1/6/74	**THE SINGLES 1969-1973** CARPENTERS	1
8/6/74	**DIAMOND DOGS** DAVID BOWIE	4
6/7/74	**THE SINGLES 1969-1973** CARPENTERS	1
13/7/74	**CARIBOU** ELTON JOHN	2
27/7/74	**BAND ON THE RUN** PAUL MCCARTNEY & WINGS	7
14/9/74	**HERGEST RIDGE** MIKE OLDFIELD	3
5/10/74	**TUBULAR BELLS** MIKE OLDFIELD	1
12/10/74	**ROLLIN'** BAY CITY ROLLERS	1
19/10/74	**SMILER** ROD STEWART	1
26/10/74	**ROLLIN'** BAY CITY ROLLERS	1
2/11/74	**SMILER** ROD STEWART	1
9/11/74	**ROLLIN'** BAY CITY ROLLERS	2
23/11/74	**ELTON JOHN'S GREATEST HITS** ELTON JOHN	11
8/2/75	**ENGELBERT HUMPERDINCK – HIS GREATEST HITS** ENGELBERT HUMPERDINCK	3
1/3/75	**ON THE LEVEL** STATUS QUO	2
15/3/75	**PHYSICAL GRAFFITI** LED ZEPPELIN	1
22/3/75	**20 GREATEST HITS** TOM JONES	4
19/4/75	**THE BEST OF THE STYLISTICS** STYLISTICS	2
3/5/75	**ONCE UPON A STAR** BAY CITY ROLLERS	3
24/5/75	**THE BEST OF THE STYLISTICS** STYLISTICS	5
28/6/75	**VENUS AND MARS** WINGS	1
5/7/75	**HORIZON** CARPENTERS	2
19/7/75	**VENUS AND MARS** WINGS	1
26/7/75	**HORIZON** CARPENTERS	3
16/8/75	**THE BEST OF THE STYLISTICS** STYLISTICS	2
30/8/75	**ATLANTIC CROSSING** ROD STEWART	5
4/10/75	**WISH YOU WERE HERE** PINK FLOYD	1
11/10/75	**ATLANTIC CROSSING** ROD STEWART	2
25/10/75	**40 GOLDEN GREATS** JIM REEVES	3
15/11/75	**WE ALL HAD DOCTORS' PAPERS** MAX BOYCE	1
22/11/75	**40 GREATEST HITS** PERRY COMO	5
27/12/75	**A NIGHT AT THE OPERA** QUEEN	2
10/1/76	**40 GREATEST HITS** PERRY COMO	1
17/1/76	**A NIGHT AT THE OPERA** QUEEN	2
31/1/76	**THE BEST OF ROY ORBISON** ROY ORBISON	1
7/2/76	**THE VERY BEST OF SLIM WHITMAN** SLIM WHITMAN	6
20/3/76	**BLUE FOR YOU** STATUS QUO	3
10/4/76	**ROCK FOLLIES** TV SOUNDTRACK	2
24/4/76	**PRESENCE** LED ZEPPELIN	1
1/5/76	**ROCK FOLLIES** TV SOUNDTRACK	1
8/5/76	**GREATEST HITS** ABBA	9
10/7/76	**A NIGHT ON THE TOWN** ROD STEWART	2
24/7/76	**20 GOLDEN GREATS** BEACH BOYS	10
2/10/76	**BEST OF THE STYLISTICS VOLUME 2** STYLISTICS	1
9/10/76	**STUPIDITY** DR. FEELGOOD	1
16/10/76	**GREATEST HITS** ABBA	2
30/10/76	**SOUL MOTION** VARIOUS ARTISTS	2
13/11/76	**THE SONG REMAINS THE SAME** LED ZEPPELIN	1
20/11/76	**22 GOLDEN GUITAR GREATS** BERT WEEDON	1
27/11/76	**20 GOLDEN GREATS** GLEN CAMPBELL	6
8/1/77	**A DAY AT THE RACES** QUEEN	1
15/1/77	**ARRIVAL** ABBA	1
22/1/77	**RED RIVER VALLEY** SLIM WHITMAN	4
19/2/77	**20 GOLDEN GREATS** SHADOWS	6
2/4/77	**PORTRAIT OF SINATRA** FRANK SINATRA	2
16/4/77	**ARRIVAL** ABBA	9
18/6/77	**THE BEATLES LIVE AT THE HOLLYWOOD BOWL** BEATLES	1
25/6/77	**THE MUPPET SHOW** MUPPETS	1
2/7/77	**A STAR IS BORN (OST)** BARBRA STREISAND	2
16/7/77	**THE JOHNNY MATHIS COLLECTION** JOHNNY MATHIS	4
13/8/77	**GOING FOR THE ONE** YES	2
27/8/77	**20 ALL TIME GREATS** CONNIE FRANCIS	2
10/9/77	**ELVIS PRESLEY'S 40 GREATEST HITS** ELVIS PRESLEY	1
17/9/77	**20 GOLDEN GREATS** DIANA ROSS & THE SUPREMES	7
5/11/77	**40 GOLDEN GREATS** CLIFF RICHARD & THE SHADOWS	1
12/11/77	**NEVER MIND THE BOLLOCKS HERE'S THE SEX PISTOLS** SEX PISTOLS	2
26/11/77	**THE SOUND OF BREAD** BREAD	2
10/12/77	**DISCO FEVER** VARIOUS ARTISTS	6
21/1/78	**THE SOUND OF BREAD** BREAD	1
28/1/78	**RUMOURS** FLEETWOOD MAC	1
4/2/78	**THE ALBUM** ABBA	7
25/3/78	**20 GOLDEN GREATS** BUDDY HOLLY & THE CRICKETS	3
15/4/78	**20 GOLDEN GREATS** NAT 'KING' COLE	3
6/5/78	**SATURDAY NIGHT FEVER** ORIGINAL SOUNDTRACK	18
9/9/78	**NIGHT FLIGHT TO VENUS** BONEY M	4

Chart Date	Album Title Artist	Weeks at No.1
7/10/78	**GREASE** ORIGINAL SOUNDTRACK	13
6/1/79	**GREATEST HITS (1976-1978)** SHOWADDYWADDY	2
20/1/79	**DON'T WALK – BOOGIE** VARIOUS ARTISTS	3
10/2/79	**ACTION REPLAY** VARIOUS ARTISTS	1
17/2/79	**PARALLEL LINES** BLONDIE	4
17/3/79	**SPIRITS HAVING FLOWN** BEE GEES	2
31/3/79	**BARBRA STREISAND'S GREATEST HITS VOLUME 2** BARBRA STREISAND	4
28/4/79	**THE VERY BEST OF LEO SAYER** LEO SAYER	3
19/5/79	**VOULEZ-VOUS** ABBA	4
16/6/79	**DISCOVERY** ELECTRIC LIGHT ORCHESTRA	5
21/7/79	**REPLICAS** TUBEWAY ARMY	1
28/7/79	**THE BEST DISCO ALBUM IN THE WORLD** VARIOUS ARTISTS	6
8/9/79	**IN THROUGH THE OUT DOOR** LED ZEPPELIN	2
22/9/79	**THE PLEASURE PRINCIPLE** GARY NUMAN	1
29/9/79	**OCEANS OF FANTASY** BONEY M	1
6/10/79	**THE PLEASURE PRINCIPLE** GARY NUMAN	1
13/10/79	**EAT TO THE BEAT** BLONDIE	1
13/10/79	**REGGATTA DE BLANC** POLICE	4
10/11/79	**TUSK** FLEETWOOD MAC	1
17/11/79	**GREATEST HITS VOLUME 2** ABBA	3
8/12/79	**ROD STEWART – GREATEST HITS** ROD STEWART	5
12/1/80	**GREATEST HITS VOLUME 2** ABBA	1
19/1/80	**PRETENDERS** PRETENDERS	4
16/2/80	**THE LAST DANCE** VARIOUS ARTISTS	2
1/3/80	**STRING OF HITS** SHADOWS	3
22/3/80	**TEARS AND LAUGHTER** JOHNNY MATHIS	2
5/4/80	**DUKE** GENESIS	2
19/4/80	**GREATEST HITS** ROSE ROYCE	2
3/5/80	**SKY 2** SKY	2
17/5/80	**THE MAGIC OF BONEY M** BONEY M	2
31/5/80	**MCCARTNEY II** PAUL MCCARTNEY	2
14/6/80	**PETER GABRIEL** PETER GABRIEL	2
28/6/80	**FLESH AND BLOOD** ROXY MUSIC	1
5/7/80	**EMOTIONAL RESCUE** ROLLING STONES	2
19/7/80	**THE GAME** QUEEN	2
2/8/80	**DEEPEST PURPLE** DEEP PURPLE	1
9/8/80	**BACK IN BLACK** AC/DC	2
23/8/80	**FLESH AND BLOOD** ROXY MUSIC	3
13/9/80	**TELEKON** GARY NUMAN	1
20/9/80	**NEVER FOR EVER** KATE BUSH	1
27/9/80	**SCARY MONSTERS AND SUPER CREEPS** DAVID BOWIE	2
11/10/80	**ZENYATTA MONDATTA** POLICE	4
8/11/80	**GUILTY** BARBRA STREISAND	2
22/11/80	**SUPER TROUPER** ABBA	9
24/1/81	**KINGS OF THE WILD FRONTIER** ADAM & THE ANTS	2
7/2/81	**DOUBLE FANTASY** JOHN LENNON & YOKO ONO	2
21/2/81	**FACE VALUE** PHIL COLLINS	3
14/3/81	**KINGS OF THE WILD FRONTIER** ADAM & THE ANTS	10
23/5/81	**STARS ON 45** STAR SOUND	5
27/6/81	**NO SLEEP TILL HAMMERSMITH** MOTORHEAD	1
4/7/81	**DISCO DAZE AND DISCO NITES** VARIOUS ARTISTS	1
11/7/81	**LOVE SONGS** CLIFF RICHARD	5
15/8/81	**THE OFFICIAL BBC ALBUM OF THE ROYAL WEDDING** VARIOUS ARTISTS	2
29/8/81	**TIME** ELECTRIC LIGHT ORCHESTRA	2
12/9/81	**DEAD RINGER** MEAT LOAF	2
26/9/81	**ABACAB** GENESIS	2
10/10/81	**GHOST IN THE MACHINE** POLICE	3
31/10/81	**DARE!** HUMAN LEAGUE	1
7/11/81	**SHAKY** SHAKIN' STEVENS	1

Chart Date	Album Title Artist	Weeks at No.1
14/11/81	**QUEEN'S GREATEST HITS** QUEEN	4
12/12/81	**CHART HITS '81** VARIOUS ARTISTS	1
19/12/81	**THE VISITORS** ABBA	3
9/1/82	**DARE!** HUMAN LEAGUE	3
30/1/82	**LOVE SONGS** BARBRA STREISAND	7
20/3/82	**THE GIFT** JAM	1
27/3/82	**LOVE SONGS** BARBRA STREISAND	2
10/4/82	**THE NUMBER OF THE BEAST** IRON MAIDEN	2
24/4/82	**1982** STATUS QUO	1
1/5/82	**BARRY LIVE IN BRITAIN** BARRY MANILOW	1
8/5/82	**TUG OF WAR** PAUL MCCARTNEY	2
22/5/82	**COMPLETE MADNESS** MADNESS	2
5/6/82	**AVALON** ROXY MUSIC	1
12/6/82	**COMPLETE MADNESS** MADNESS	1
19/6/82	**AVALON** ROXY MUSIC	2
3/7/82	**THE LEXICON OF LOVE** ABC	4
24/7/82	**FAME** ORIGINAL SOUNDTRACK	2
7/8/82	**THE KIDS FROM FAME** KIDS FROM FAME	8
2/10/82	**LOVE OVER GOLD** DIRE STRAITS	4
30/10/82	**THE KIDS FROM FAME** KIDS FROM FAME	4
27/11/82	**THE SINGLES – THE FIRST TEN YEARS** ABBA	1
4/12/82	**THE JOHN LENNON COLLECTION** JOHN LENNON	6
15/1/83	**RAIDERS OF THE POP CHARTS** VARIOUS ARTISTS	2
29/1/83	**BUSINESS AS USUAL** MEN AT WORK	5
5/3/83	**THRILLER** MICHAEL JACKSON	1
12/3/83	**WAR** U2	1
19/3/83	**THRILLER** MICHAEL JACKSON	1
26/3/83	**THE HURTING** TEARS FOR FEARS	1
2/4/83	**THE FINAL CUT** PINK FLOYD	2
16/4/83	**FASTER THAN THE SPEED OF NIGHT** BONNIE TYLER	1
23/4/83	**LET'S DANCE** DAVID BOWIE	3
14/5/83	**TRUE** SPANDAU BALLET	1
21/5/83	**THRILLER** MICHAEL JACKSON	5
25/6/83	**SYNCHRONICITY** POLICE	2
9/7/83	**FANTASTIC!** WHAM!	2
23/7/83	**YOU AND ME BOTH** YAZOO	2
6/8/83	**THE VERY BEST OF THE BEACH BOYS** BEACH BOYS	2
20/8/83	**18 GREATEST HITS** MICHAEL JACKSON PLUS THE JACKSON FIVE	3
10/9/83	**THE VERY BEST OF THE BEACH BOYS** BEACH BOYS	1
17/9/83	**NO PARLEZ** PAUL YOUNG	1
24/9/83	**LABOUR OF LOVE** UB40	1
1/10/83	**NO PARLEZ** PAUL YOUNG	2
15/10/83	**GENESIS** GENESIS	1
22/10/83	**COLOUR BY NUMBERS** CULTURE CLUB	3
12/11/83	**CAN'T SLOW DOWN** LIONEL RICHIE	1
19/11/83	**COLOUR BY NUMBERS** CULTURE CLUB	2
3/12/83	**SEVEN AND THE RAGGED TIGER** DURAN DURAN	1
10/12/83	**NO PARLEZ** PAUL YOUNG	1
17/12/83	**NOW THAT'S WHAT I CALL MUSIC** VARIOUS ARTISTS	1
14/1/84	**NO PARLEZ** PAUL YOUNG	1
21/1/84	**NOW THAT'S WHAT I CALL MUSIC** VARIOUS ARTISTS	1
28/1/84	**THRILLER** MICHAEL JACKSON	1
4/2/84	**TOUCH** EURYTHMICS	2
18/2/84	**SPARKLE IN THE RAIN** SIMPLE MINDS	1
25/2/84	**INTO THE GAP** THOMPSON TWINS	3
17/3/84	**HUMAN'S LIB** HOWARD JONES	2
31/3/84	**CAN'T SLOW DOWN** LIONEL RICHIE	2
14/4/84	**NOW THAT'S WHAT I CALL MUSIC II** VARIOUS ARTISTS	1
19/5/84	**LEGEND – THE BEST OF BOB MARLEY & THE WAILERS** BOB MARLEY & THE WAILERS	12
11/8/84	**NOW THAT'S WHAT I CALL MUSIC III** VARIOUS ARTISTS	8

Chart Date	Album Title Artist	Weeks at No.1
6/10/84	**TONIGHT** DAVID BOWIE	1
13/10/84	**THE UNFORGETTABLE FIRE** U2	2
27/10/84	**STEELTOWN** BIG COUNTRY	1
3/11/84	**GIVE MY REGARDS TO BROAD STREET (OST)** PAUL MCCARTNEY	1
10/11/84	**WELCOME TO THE PLEASUREDOME** FRANKIE GOES TO HOLLYWOOD	1
17/11/84	**MAKE IT BIG** WHAM!	2
1/12/84	**THE HITS ALBUM/THE HITS TAPE – 32 ORIGINAL HITS** VARIOUS ARTISTS	7
19/1/85	**ALF** ALISON MOYET	1
26/1/85	**AGENT PROVOCATEUR** FOREIGNER	3
16/2/85	**BORN IN THE U.S.A.** BRUCE SPRINGSTEEN	1
23/2/85	**MEAT IS MURDER** SMITHS	1
2/3/85	**NO JACKET REQUIRED** PHIL COLLINS	5
6/4/85	**THE SECRET OF ASSOCIATION** PAUL YOUNG	1
13/4/85	**THE HITS ALBUM 2/THE HITS TAPE 2** VARIOUS ARTISTS	6
25/5/85	**BROTHERS IN ARMS** DIRE STRAITS	2
8/6/85	**OUR FAVOURITE SHOP** STYLE COUNCIL	1
15/6/85	**BOYS AND GIRLS** BRYAN FERRY	2
29/6/85	**MISPLACED CHILDHOOD** MARILLION	1
6/7/85	**BORN IN THE U.S.A.** BRUCE SPRINGSTEEN	4
3/8/85	**BROTHERS IN ARMS** DIRE STRAITS	2
17/8/85	**NOW THAT'S WHAT I CALL MUSIC 5** VARIOUS ARTISTS	1
21/9/85	**LIKE A VIRGIN** MADONNA	1
28/9/85	**HOUNDS OF LOVE** KATE BUSH	2
12/10/85	**LIKE A VIRGIN** MADONNA	1
19/10/85	**HOUNDS OF LOVE** KATE BUSH	1
26/10/85	**THE LOVE SONGS** GEORGE BENSON	1
2/11/85	**ONCE UPON A TIME** SIMPLE MINDS	1
9/11/85	**THE LOVE SONGS** GEORGE BENSON	1
16/11/85	**PROMISE** SADE	2
30/11/85	**THE GREATEST HITS OF 1985** VARIOUS ARTISTS	1
7/12/85	**NOW THAT'S WHAT I CALL MUSIC 6** VARIOUS ARTISTS	2
21/12/85	**NOW – THE CHRISTMAS ALBUM** VARIOUS ARTISTS	2
4/1/86	**NOW THAT'S WHAT I CALL MUSIC 6** VARIOUS ARTISTS	2
18/1/86	**BROTHERS IN ARMS** DIRE STRAITS	10
29/3/86	**HITS 4** VARIOUS ARTISTS	4
26/4/86	**STREET LIFE – 20 GREAT HITS** BRYAN FERRY & ROXY MUSIC	5
31/5/86	**SO** PETER GABRIEL	2
14/6/86	**A KIND OF MAGIC** QUEEN	1
21/6/86	**INVISIBLE TOUCH** GENESIS	3
12/7/86	**TRUE BLUE** MADONNA	6
23/8/86	**NOW THAT'S WHAT I CALL MUSIC 7** VARIOUS ARTISTS	5
27/9/86	**SILK AND STEEL** FIVE STAR	1
4/10/86	**GRACELAND** PAUL SIMON	5
8/11/86	**EVERY BREATH YOU TAKE – THE SINGLES** POLICE	2
22/11/86	**HITS 5** VARIOUS ARTISTS	2
6/12/86	**NOW THAT'S WHAT I CALL MUSIC 8** VARIOUS ARTISTS	6
17/1/87	**THE WHOLE STORY** KATE BUSH	2
31/1/87	**GRACELAND** PAUL SIMON	3
21/2/87	**THE PHANTOM OF THE OPERA** LONDON STAGE CAST	3
14/3/87	**THE VERY BEST OF HOT CHOCOLATE** HOT CHOCOLATE	1
21/3/87	**THE JOSHUA TREE** U2	2
4/4/87	**NOW THAT'S WHAT I CALL MUSIC 9** VARIOUS ARTISTS	5
9/5/87	**KEEP YOUR DISTANCE** CURIOSITY KILLED THE CAT	2
23/5/87	**IT'S BETTER TO TRAVEL** SWING OUT SISTER	2
6/6/87	**LIVE IN THE CITY OF LIGHT** SIMPLE MINDS	1
13/6/87	**WHITNEY** WHITNEY HOUSTON	6
25/7/87	**INTRODUCING THE HARDLINE ACCORDING TO TERENCE TRENT D'ARBY** TERENCE TRENT D'ARBY	1
1/8/87	**HITS 6** VARIOUS ARTISTS	4
29/8/87	**HYSTERIA** DEF LEPPARD	1
5/9/87	**HITS 6** VARIOUS ARTISTS	1
12/9/87	**BAD** MICHAEL JACKSON	5
17/10/87	**TUNNEL OF LOVE** BRUCE SPRINGSTEEN	1
24/10/87	**NOTHING LIKE THE SUN** STING	1
31/10/87	**TANGO IN THE NIGHT** FLEETWOOD MAC	2
14/11/87	**FAITH** GEORGE MICHAEL	1
21/11/87	**BRIDGE OF SPIES** T'PAU	1
28/11/87	**WHENEVER YOU NEED SOMEBODY** RICK ASTLEY	1
5/12/87	**NOW THAT'S WHAT I CALL MUSIC 10** VARIOUS ARTISTS	6
16/1/88	**POPPED IN SOULED OUT** WET WET WET	1
23/1/88	**TURN BACK THE CLOCK** JOHNNY HATES JAZZ	1
30/1/88	**INTRODUCING THE HARDLINE ACCORDING TO TERENCE TRENT D'ARBY** TERENCE TRENT D'ARBY	8
26/3/88	**VIVA HATE** MORRISSEY	1
2/4/88	**NOW THAT'S WHAT I CALL MUSIC 11** VARIOUS ARTISTS	3
23/4/88	**SEVENTH SON OF A SEVENTH SON** IRON MAIDEN	1
30/4/88	**THE INNOCENTS** ERASURE	1
7/5/88	**TANGO IN THE NIGHT** FLEETWOOD MAC	2
21/5/88	**LOVESEXY** PRINCE	1
28/5/88	**TANGO IN THE NIGHT** FLEETWOOD MAC	1
4/6/88	**NITE FLITE** VARIOUS ARTISTS	4
2/7/88	**TRACY CHAPMAN** TRACY CHAPMAN	3
23/7/88	**NOW THAT'S WHAT I CALL MUSIC 12** VARIOUS ARTISTS	5
27/8/88	**KYLIE – THE ALBUM** KYLIE MINOGUE	4
24/9/88	**HOT CITY NIGHTS** VARIOUS ARTISTS	1
1/10/88	**NEW JERSEY** BON JOVI	2
15/10/88	**FLYING COLOURS** CHRIS DE BURGH	1
22/10/88	**RATTLE AND HUM** U2	1
29/10/88	**MONEY FOR NOTHING** DIRE STRAITS	3
19/11/88	**KYLIE – THE ALBUM** KYLIE MINOGUE	2
3/12/88	**NOW THAT'S WHAT I CALL MUSIC 13** VARIOUS ARTISTS	3
24/12/88	**PRIVATE COLLECTION 1979-1988** CLIFF RICHARD	2
7/1/89	**NOW THAT'S WHAT I CALL MUSIC 13** VARIOUS ARTISTS	1

In 1989, various artist and cast/film soundtrack albums were separated out from the album chart. !

Chart Date	Album Title Artist	Weeks at No.1
14/1/89	**THE INNOCENTS** ERASURE	1
21/1/89	**THE LEGENDARY ROY ORBISON** ROY ORBISON	3
11/2/89	**TECHNIQUE** NEW ORDER	1
18/2/89	**THE RAW AND THE COOKED** FINE YOUNG CANNIBALS	1
25/2/89	**A NEW FLAME** SIMPLY RED	4
25/3/89	**ANYTHING FOR YOU** GLORIA ESTEFAN & MIAMI SOUND MACHINE	1
1/4/89	**LIKE A PRAYER** MADONNA	2
15/4/89	**WHEN THE WORLD KNOWS YOUR NAME** DEACON BLUE	2
29/4/89	**A NEW FLAME** SIMPLY RED	1
6/5/89	**BLAST!** HOLLY JOHNSON	1
13/5/89	**STREET FIGHTING YEARS** SIMPLE MINDS	1
20/5/89	**TEN GOOD REASONS** JASON DONOVAN	2
3/6/89	**THE MIRACLE** QUEEN	1
10/6/89	**TEN GOOD REASONS** JASON DONOVAN	2

Chart Date	Album Title Artist	Weeks at No.1
24/6/89	**FLOWERS IN THE DIRT** PAUL MCCARTNEY	1
1/7/89	**BATMAN (OST)** PRINCE	1
8/7/89	**VELVETEEN** TRANSVISION VAMP	1
15/7/89	**CLUB CLASSICS VOLUME ONE** SIMPLY RED	2
5/8/89	**CUTS BOTH WAYS** GLORIA ESTEFAN	6
16/9/89	**ASPECTS OF LOVE** LONDON STAGE CAST	1
23/9/89	**WE TOO ARE ONE** EURYTHMICS	1
30/9/89	**FOREIGN AFFAIR** TINA TURNER	1
7/10/89	**THE SEEDS OF LOVE** TEARS FOR FEARS	1
14/10/89	**CROSSROADS** TRACY CHAPMAN	1
21/10/89	**ENJOY YOURSELF** KYLIE MINOGUE	1
28/10/89	**WILD!** ERASURE	2
11/11/89	**THE ROAD TO HELL** CHRIS REA	3
2/12/89	**... BUT SERIOUSLY** PHIL COLLINS	8
27/1/90	**COLOUR** CHRISTIANS	1
3/2/90	**... BUT SERIOUSLY** PHIL COLLINS	7
24/3/90	**I DO NOT WANT WHAT I HAVEN'T GOT** SINEAD O'CONNOR	1
31/3/90	**CHANGESBOWIE** DAVID BOWIE	1
7/4/90	**ONLY YESTERDAY – RICHARD & KAREN CARPENTER'S GREATEST HITS** CARPENTERS	2
21/4/90	**BEHIND THE MASK** FLEETWOOD MAC	1
28/4/90	**ONLY YESTERDAY – RICHARD & KAREN CARPENTER'S GREATEST HITS** CARPENTERS	5
2/6/90	**VOLUME II (1990 A NEW DECADE)** SOUL II SOUL	3
23/6/90	**THE ESSENTIAL PAVAROTTI** LUCIANO PAVAROTTI	1
30/6/90	**STEP BY STEP** NEW KIDS ON THE BLOCK	1
7/7/90	**THE ESSENTIAL PAVAROTTI** LUCIANO PAVAROTTI	3
28/7/90	**SLEEPING WITH THE PAST** ELTON JOHN	5
1/9/90	**GRAFITTI BRIDGE** PRINCE	1
8/9/90	**IN CONCERT** CARRERAS DOMINGO PAVAROTTI	1
15/9/90	**LISTEN WITHOUT PREJUDICE VOLUME 1** GEORGE MICHAEL	1
22/9/90	**IN CONCERT** CARRERAS DOMINGO PAVAROTTI	4
20/10/90	**SOME FRIENDLY** CHARLATANS	1
27/10/90	**THE RHYTHM OF THE SAINTS** PAUL SIMON	2
10/11/90	**THE VERY BEST OF ELTON JOHN** ELTON JOHN	2
24/11/90	**THE IMMACULATE COLLECTION** MADONNA	9
26/1/91	**MCMCX A. D.** ENIGMA	1
2/2/91	**THE SOUL CAGES** STING	1
9/2/91	**DOUBT** JESUS JONES	1
16/2/91	**INNUENDO** QUEEN	2
2/3/91	**CIRCLE OF ONE** OLETA ADAMS	1
9/3/91	**AUBERGE** CHRIS REA	1
16/3/91	**SPARTACUS** FARM	1
23/3/91	**OUT OF TIME** R.E.M.	1
30/3/91	**GREATEST HITS** EURYTHMICS	9
1/6/91	**SEAL** SEAL	3
22/6/91	**GREATEST HITS** EURYTHMICS	1
29/6/91	**LOVE HURTS** CHER	6
10/8/91	**ESSENTIAL PAVAROTTI II** LUCIANO PAVAROTTI	2
24/8/91	**METALLICA** METALLICA	1
31/8/91	**JOSEPH AND THE AMAZING TECHNICOLOR DREAMCOAT** LONDON STAGE CAST	2
14/9/91	**FROM TIME TO TIME – THE SINGLES COLLECTION** PAUL YOUNG	1
21/9/91	**ON EVERY STREET** DIRE STRAITS	1
28/9/91	**USE YOUR ILLUSION II** GUNS N' ROSES	1
5/10/91	**WAKING UP THE NEIGHBOURS** BRYAN ADAMS	1
12/10/91	**STARS** SIMPLY RED	2
26/10/91	**CHORUS** ERASURE	1
2/11/91	**STARS** SIMPLY RED	1
9/11/91	**GREATEST HITS II** QUEEN	1
16/11/91	**SHEPHERD MOONS** ENYA	1
23/11/91	**WE CAN'T DANCE** GENESIS	1
30/11/91	**DANGEROUS** MICHAEL JACKSON	1
7/12/91	**GREATEST HITS II** QUEEN	4
4/1/92	**STARS** SIMPLY RED	5
8/2/92	**HIGH ON THE HAPPY SIDE** WET WET WET	2
22/2/92	**STARS** SIMPLY RED	3
13/3/92	**DIVINE MADNESS** MADNESS	3
3/4/92	**HUMAN TOUCH** BRUCE SPRINGSTEEN	1
10/4/92	**ADRENALIZE** DEF LEPPARD	1
17/4/92	**DIVA** ANNIE LENNOX	1
24/4/92	**UP** RIGHT SAID FRED	1
1/5/92	**WISH** CURE	1
8/5/92	**STARS** SIMPLY RED	1
16/5/92	**1992 – THE LOVE ALBUM** CARTER – THE UNSTOPPABLE SEX MACHINE	1
23/5/92	**FEAR OF THE DARK** IRON MAIDEN	1
30/5/92	**MICHAEL BALL** MICHAEL BALL	1
6/6/92	**BACK TO FRONT** LIONEL RICHIE	6
18/7/92	**U.F. ORB** ORB	1
25/7/92	**THE GREATEST HITS 1966-1992** NEIL DIAMOND	3
15/8/92	**WELCOME TO WHEREVER YOU ARE** INXS	1
22/8/92	**WE CAN'T DANCE** GENESIS	1
29/8/92	**BEST ... I** SMITHS	1
5/9/92	**KYLIE GREATEST HITS** KYLIE MINOGUE	1
12/9/92	**TUBULAR BELLS II** MIKE OLDFIELD	2
26/9/92	**THE BEST OF BELINDA VOLUME I** BELINDA CARLISLE	1
3/10/92	**GOLD – GREATEST HITS** ABBA	1
10/10/92	**AUTOMATIC FOR THE PEOPLE** R.E.M.	1
17/10/92	**SYMBOL** PRINCE & THE NEW POWER GENERATION	1
24/10/92	**GLITTERING PRIZE 81/92** SIMPLE MINDS	3
14/11/92	**KEEP THE FAITH** BON JOVI	1
21/11/92	**CHER'S GREATEST HITS: 1965-1992** CHER	1
28/11/92	**POP! THE FIRST 20 HITS** ERASURE	2
12/12/92	**CHER'S GREATEST HITS: 1965-1992** CHER	6
23/1/93	**LIVE – THE WAY WE WALK VOLUME 2: THE LONGS** GENESIS	2
6/2/93	**JAM** LITTLE ANGELS	1
13/2/93	**PURE CULT** CULT	1
20/2/93	**WORDS OF LOVE** BUDDY HOLLY & THE CRICKETS	1
27/2/93	**WALTHAMSTOW** EAST 17	1
6/3/93	**DIVA** ANNIE LENNOX	1
13/3/93	**ARE YOU GONNA GO MY WAY** LENNY KRAVITZ	2
27/3/93	**THEIR GREATEST HITS** HOT CHOCOLATE	1
3/4/93	**SONGS OF FAITH AND DEVOTION** DEPECHE MODE	1
10/4/93	**SUEDE** SUEDE	1
17/4/93	**BLACK TIE WHITE NOISE** DAVID BOWIE	1
24/4/93	**AUTOMATIC FOR THE PEOPLE** R.E.M.	1
1/5/93	**CLIFF RICHARD – THE ALBUM** CLIFF RICHARD	1
8/5/93	**AUTOMATIC FOR THE PEOPLE** R.E.M.	1
15/5/93	**REPUBLIC** NEW ORDER	1
22/5/93	**AUTOMATIC FOR THE PEOPLE** R.E.M.	1
29/5/93	**JANET** JANET JACKSON	2
12/6/93	**NO LIMITS** TWO UNLIMITED	1
19/6/93	**WHAT'S LOVE GOT TO DO WITH IT (OST)** TINA TURNER	1
26/6/93	**EMERGENCY ON PLANET EARTH** JAMIROQUAI	3
17/7/93	**ZOOROPA** U2	1
24/7/93	**PROMISES AND LIES** UB40	7
11/9/93	**MUSIC BOX** MARIAH CAREY	1
18/9/93	**BAT OUT OF HELL II – BACK INTO HELL** MEAT LOAF	1
25/9/93	**IN UTERO** NIRVANA	1
2/10/93	**BAT OUT OF HELL II – BACK INTO HELL** MEAT LOAF	1

Chart Date	Album Title Artist	Weeks at No.1
9/10/93	**VERY** PET SHOP BOYS	1
16/10/93	**BAT OUT OF HELL II – BACK INTO HELL** MEAT LOAF	1
23/10/93	**EVERYTHING CHANGES** TAKE THAT	1
30/10/93	**BAT OUT OF HELL II – BACK INTO HELL** MEAT LOAF	3
20/11/93	**BOTH SIDES** PHIL COLLINS	1
27/11/93	**BAT OUT OF HELL II – BACK INTO HELL** MEAT LOAF	5
1/1/94	**ONE WOMAN – THE ULTIMATE COLLECTION** DIANA ROSS	1
8/1/94	**EVERYTHING CHANGES** TAKE THAT	1
15/1/94	**SO FAR SO GOOD** BRYAN ADAMS	1
22/1/94	**ONE WOMAN – THE ULTIMATE COLLECTION** DIANA ROSS	1
29/1/94	**TEASE ME** CHAKA DEMUS & PLIERS	2
12/2/94	**UNDER THE PINK** TORI AMOS	1
19/2/94	**THE CROSS OF CHANGES** ENIGMA	1
26/2/94	**MUSIC BOX** MARIAH CAREY	4
26/3/94	**VAUXHALL AND I** MORRISSEY	1
2/4/94	**MUSIC BOX** MARIAH CAREY	1
9/4/94	**THE DIVISION BELL** PINK FLOYD	4
7/5/94	**PARKLIFE** BLUR	1
14/5/94	**OUR TOWN – THE GREATEST HITS OF DEACON BLUE** DEACON BLUE	2
28/5/94	**I SAY I SAY I SAY** ERASURE	1
4/6/94	**SEAL** SEAL	2
18/6/94	**REAL THINGS** TWO UNLIMITED	1
25/6/94	**EVERYBODY ELSE IS DOING IT SO WHY CAN'T WE?** CRANBERRIES	1
2/7/94	**HAPPY NATION** ACE OF BASE	2
16/7/94	**MUSIC FOR THE JILTED GENERATION** PRODIGY	1
23/7/94	**VOODOO LOUNGE** ROLLING STONES	1
30/7/94	**END OF PART ONE (THEIR GREATEST HITS)** WET WET WET	4
27/8/94	**COME** PRINCE	1
3/9/94	**END OF PART ONE (THEIR GREATEST HITS)** WET WET WET	1
10/9/94	**DEFINITELY MAYBE** OASIS	1
17/9/94	**THE THREE TENORS IN CONCERT 1994** CARRERAS DOMINGO PAVAROTTI	1
24/9/94	**FROM THE CRADLE** ERIC CLAPTON	1
1/10/94	**SONGS** LUTHER VANDROSS	1
8/10/94	**MONSTER** R.E.M.	2
22/10/94	**CROSS ROAD – THE BEST OF BON JOVI** BON JOVI	3
12/11/94	**UNPLUGGED IN NEW YORK** NIRVANA	1
19/11/94	**CROSS ROAD – THE BEST OF BON JOVI** BON JOVI	2
3/12/94	**CARRY ON UP THE CHARTS – THE BEST OF THE BEAUTIFUL SOUTH** BEAUTIFUL SOUTH	1
10/12/94	**LIVE AT THE BBC** BEATLES	1
17/12/94	**CARRY ON UP THE CHARTS – THE BEST OF THE BEAUTIFUL SOUTH** BEAUTIFUL SOUTH	6
28/1/95	**THE COLOUR OF MY LOVE** CELINE DION	6
11/3/95	**GREATEST HITS** BRUCE SPRINGSTEEN	1
18/3/95	**MEDUSA** ANNIE LENNOX	1
25/3/95	**ELASTICA** ELASTICA	1
1/4/95	**THE COLOUR OF MY LOVE** CELINE DION	1
8/4/95	**WAKE UP!** BOO RADLEYS	1
15/4/95	**GREATEST HITS** BRUCE SPRINGSTEEN	1
22/4/95	**PICTURE THIS** WET WET WET	3
13/5/95	**NOBODY ELSE** TAKE THAT	2
27/5/95	**STANLEY ROAD** PAUL WELLER	1
3/6/95	**SINGLES** ALISON MOYET	1
10/6/95	**PULSE** PINK FLOYD	2
24/6/95	**HISTORY – PAST, PRESENT AND FUTURE BOOK 1** MICHAEL JACKSON	1

Chart Date	Album Title Artist	Weeks at No.1
1/7/95	**THESE DAYS** BON JOVI	4
29/7/95	**I SHOULD COCO** SUPERGRASS	3
19/8/95	**IT'S GREAT WHEN YOU'RE STRAIGHT ... YEAH** BLACK GRAPE	2
2/9/95	**SAID AND DONE** BOYZONE	1
9/9/95	**THE CHARLATANS** CHARLATANS	1
16/9/95	**ZEITGEIST** LEVELLERS	1
23/9/95	**THE GREAT ESCAPE** BLUR	2
7/10/95	**DAYDREAM** MARIAH CAREY	1
14/10/95	**(WHAT'S THE STORY) MORNING GLORY?** OASIS	1
21/10/95	**LIFE** SIMPLY RED	3
11/11/95	**DIFFERENT CLASS** PULP	1
18/11/95	**MADE IN HEAVEN** QUEEN	1
25/11/95	**ROBSON & JEROME** ROBSON & JEROME	7
13/1/96	**(WHAT'S THE STORY) MORNING GLORY?** OASIS	6
24/2/96	**EXPECTING TO FLY** BLUETONES	1
2/3/96	**(WHAT'S THE STORY) MORNING GLORY?** OASIS	3
23/3/96	**FALLING INTO YOU** CELINE DION	1
30/3/96	**ANTHOLOGY 2** BEATLES 1	
6/4/96	**GREATEST HITS** TAKE THAT	4
4/5/96	**JAGGED LITTLE PILL** ALANIS MORISSETTE	2
18/5/96	**1977** ASH	1
25/5/96	**OLDER** GEORGE MICHAEL	3
15/6/96	**LOAD** METALLICA	1
22/6/96	**18 TIL I DIE** BRYAN ADAMS	1
29/6/96	**JAGGED LITTLE PILL** ALANIS MORISSETTE	1
6/7/96	**RECURRING DREAM – THE VERY BEST OF CROWDED HOUSE** CROWDED HOUSE	2
20/7/96	**JAGGED LITTLE PILL** ALANIS MORISSETTE	8
14/9/96	**COMING UP** SUEDE	1
21/9/96	**NEW ADVENTURES IN HI-FI** R.E.M.	1
28/9/96	**K** KULA SHAKER	2
12/10/96	**NATURAL** PETER ANDRE	1
19/10/96	**GREATEST HITS** SIMPLY RED	2
2/11/96	**BLUE IS THE COLOUR** BEAUTIFUL SOUTH	1
9/11/96	**A DIFFERENT BEAT** BOYZONE	1
16/11/96	**SPICE** SPICE GIRLS	1
23/11/96	**TAKE TWO** ROBSON & JEROME	2
7/12/96	**SPICE** SPICE GIRLS	8
1/2/97	**EVITA (OST)** MADONNA & VARIOUS ARTISTS	1
8/2/97	**GLOW** REEF	1
15/2/97	**WHITE ON BLONDE** TEXAS	1
22/2/97	**BLUR** BLUR	1
1/3/97	**ATTACK OF THE GREY LANTERN** MANSUN	1
8/3/97	**SPICE** SPICE GIRLS	1
15/3/97	**POP** U2	1
22/3/97	**SPICE** SPICE GIRLS	4
19/4/97	**DIG YOUR OWN HOLE** CHEMICAL BROTHERS	1
26/4/97	**ULTRA** DEPECHE MODE	1
3/5/97	**TELLIN' STORIES** CHARLATANS	2
17/5/97	**SPICE** SPICE GIRLS	1
24/5/97	**BLOOD ON THE DANCE FLOOR – HISTORY IN THE MIX** MICHAEL JACKSON	2
7/6/97	**OPEN ROAD** GARY BARLOW	1
14/6/97	**WU-TANG FOREVER** WU-TANG CLAN	1
21/6/97	**MIDDLE OF NOWHERE** HANSON	1
28/6/97	**OK COMPUTER** RADIOHEAD	2
12/7/97	**THE FAT OF THE LAND** PRODIGY	6
23/8/97	**WHITE ON BLONDE** TEXAS	1
30/8/97	**BE HERE NOW** OASIS	4
27/9/97	**MARCHIN' ALREADY** OCEAN COLOUR SCENE	1
4/10/97	**BE HERE NOW** OASIS	1
11/10/97	**URBAN HYMNS** VERVE	5
15/11/97	**SPICEWORLD** SPICE GIRLS	2

Chart Date	Album Title Artist	Weeks at No.1
29/11/97	**LET'S TALK ABOUT LOVE** CELINE DION	2
13/12/97	**SPICEWORLD** SPICE GIRLS	1
20/12/97	**LET'S TALK ABOUT LOVE** CELINE DION	2
3/1/98	**URBAN HYMNS** VERVE	6
14/2/98	**TITANIC (OST)** MUSIC COMPOSED AND CONDUCTED BY JAMES HORNER	1
21/2/98	**URBAN HYMNS** VERVE	1
28/2/98	**TITANIC (OST)** MUSIC COMPOSED AND CONDUCTED BY JAMES HORNER	2
14/3/98	**RAY OF LIGHT** MADONNA	2
28/3/98	**LET'S TALK ABOUT LOVE** CELINE DION	1
4/4/98	**THE BEST OF JAMES** JAMES	1
11/4/98	**THIS IS HARDCORE** PULP	1
18/4/98	**LIFE THRU A LENS** ROBBIE WILLIAMS	2
2/5/98	**MEZZANINE** MASSIVE ATTACK	2
16/5/98	**INTERNATIONAL VELVET** CATATONIA	1
23/5/98	**VERSION 2.0** GARBAGE	1
30/5/98	**BLUE** SIMPLY RED	1
6/6/98	**WHERE WE BELONG** BOYZONE	1
13/6/98	**BLUE** SIMPLY RED	1
20/6/98	**THE GOOD WILL OUT** EMBRACE	1
27/6/98	**TALK ON CORNERS** CORRS	1
4/7/98	**FIVE** FIVE	1
11/7/98	**TALK ON CORNERS** CORRS	1
18/7/98	**HELLO NASTY** BEASTIE BOYS	1
25/7/98	**JANE MCDONALD** JANE MCDONALD	3
15/8/98	**TALK ON CORNERS** CORRS	3
5/9/98	**WHERE WE BELONG** BOYZONE	2
19/9/98	**TALK ON CORNERS** CORRS	1
26/9/98	**THIS IS MY TRUTH TELL ME YOURS** MANIC STREET PREACHERS	3
17/10/98	**HITS** PHIL COLLINS	1
24/10/98	**QUENCH** BEAUTIFUL SOUTH	2
7/11/98	**I'VE BEEN EXPECTING YOU** ROBBIE WILLIAMS	1
14/11/98	**THE BEST OF 1980-1990 & B-SIDES** U2	1
21/11/98	**LADIES & GENTLEMEN – THE BEST OF GEORGE MICHAEL** GEORGE MICHAEL	8
16/1/99	**I'VE BEEN EXPECTING YOU** ROBBIE WILLIAMS	1
23/1/99	**YOU'VE COME A LONG WAY, BABY** FATBOY SLIM	4
20/2/99	**I'VE BEEN EXPECTING YOU** ROBBIE WILLIAMS	1
27/2/99	**TALK ON CORNERS** CORRS	3
20/3/99	**PERFORMANCE AND COCKTAILS** STEREOPHONICS	1
27/3/99	**13** BLUR	2
10/4/99	**TALK ON CORNERS** CORRS	1
17/4/99	**GOLD – GREATEST HITS** ABBA	1
24/4/99	**EQUALLY CURSED AND BLESSED** CATATONIA	1
1/5/99	**GOLD – GREATEST HITS** ABBA	2
15/5/99	**HEAD MUSIC** SUEDE	1
22/5/99	**THE HUSH** TEXAS	1
29/5/99	**GOLD – GREATEST HITS** ABBA	2
12/6/99	**BY REQUEST** BOYZONE	2
26/6/99	**SYNKRONIZED** JAMIROQUAI	1
3/7/99	**SURRENDER** CHEMICAL BROTHERS	1
10/7/99	**BY REQUEST** BOYZONE	7
28/8/99	**THE MAN WHO** TRAVIS	2
11/9/99	**COME ON OVER** SHANIA TWAIN	3
2/10/99	**RHYTHM AND STEALTH** LEFTFIELD	1
9/10/99	**RELOAD** TOM JONES	1
16/10/99	**COME ON OVER** SHANIA TWAIN	3
6/11/99	**STEPTACULAR** STEPS	3
27/11/99	**ALL THE WAY – A DECADE OF SONGS** CELINE DION	1
4/12/99	**STEPTACULAR** STEPS	1
11/12/99	**COME ON OVER** SHANIA TWAIN	5
15/1/00	**THE MAN WHO** TRAVIS	5

Chart Date	Album Title Artist	Weeks at No.1
19/2/00	**RISE** GABRIELLE	3
11/3/00	**STANDING ON THE SHOULDER OF GIANTS** OASIS	1
18/3/00	**THE MAN WHO** TRAVIS	2
1/4/00	**SUPERNATURAL** SANTANA	2
15/4/00	**PLAY** MOBY	5
20/5/00	**RELOAD** TOM JONES	1
27/5/00	**GREATEST HITS** WHITNEY HOUSTON	2
10/6/00	**CRUSH** BON JOVI	1
17/6/00	**RELOAD** TOM JONES	1
24/6/00	**7** S CLUB 7	1
1/7/00	**THE MARSHALL MATHERS LP** EMINEM	1
8/7/00	**ALONE WITH EVERYBODY** RICHARD ASHCROFT	1
15/7/00	**THE MARSHALL MATHERS LP** EMINEM	1
22/7/00	**PARACHUTES** COLDPLAY	1
29/7/00	**IN BLUE** CORRS	2
12/8/00	**RONAN** RONAN KEATING	2
26/8/00	**BORN TO DO IT** CRAIG DAVID	2
9/9/00	**SING WHEN YOU'RE WINNING** ROBBIE WILLIAMS	3
30/9/00	**MUSIC** MADONNA	2
14/10/00	**KID A** RADIOHEAD	2
28/10/00	**SAINTS AND SINNERS** ALL SAINTS	1
4/11/00	**GREATEST HITS** TEXAS	1
11/11/00	**ALL THAT YOU CAN'T LEAVE BEHIND** U2	1
18/11/00	**COAST TO COAST** WESTLIFE	1
25/11/00	**1** BEATLES	9
27/1/01	**GREATEST HITS** TEXAS	1
3/2/01	**CHOCOLATE STARFISH AND THE HOT DOG FLAVOURED WATER** LIMP BIZKIT	1
10/2/01	**NO ANGEL** DIDO	6
24/3/01	**SONGBIRD** EVA CASSIDY	2
7/4/01	**POPSTARS** HEAR'SAY	2
21/4/01	**JUST ENOUGH EDUCATION TO PERFORM** STEREOPHONICS	2
5/5/01	**FREE ALL ANGELS** ASH	1
12/5/01	**SURVIVOR** DESTINY'S CHILD	2
26/5/01	**REVEAL** R.E.M.	2
9/6/01	**HOT SHOT** SHAGGY	1
16/6/01	**AMNESIAC** RADIOHEAD	1
23/6/01	**THE INVISIBLE BAND** TRAVIS	4
21/7/01	**8701** USHER	1
28/7/01	**SURVIVOR** DESTINY'S CHILD	2
11/8/01	**WHITE LADDER** DAVID GRAY	1
18/8/01	**RIGHT NOW** ATOMIC KITTEN	1
25/8/01	**WHITE LADDER** DAVID GRAY	1
1/9/01	**BREAK THE CYCLE** STAIND	1
8/9/01	**IOWA** SLIPKNOT	1
15/9/01	**A FUNK ODYSSEY** JAMIROQUAI	2
29/9/01	**THE ID** MACY GRAY	1
6/10/01	**NO ANGEL** DIDO	1
13/10/01	**FEVER** KYLIE MINOGUE	2
27/10/01	**GOLD – THE GREATEST HITS** STEPS	2
10/11/01	**INVINCIBLE** MICHAEL JACKSON	1
17/11/01	**GOLD – THE GREATEST HITS** STEPS	1
24/11/01	**WORLD OF OUR OWN** WESTLIFE	1
1/12/01	**SWING WHEN YOU'RE WINNING** ROBBIE WILLIAMS	7
19/1/02	**JUST ENOUGH EDUCATION TO PERFORM** STEREOPHONICS	3
9/2/02	**COME WITH US** CHEMICAL BROTHERS	1
16/2/02	**ESCAPE** ENRIQUE IGLESIAS	2
2/3/02	**THE VERY BEST OF STING AND THE POLICE** STING / THE POLICE	2
16/3/02	**THE ESSENTIAL BARBRA STREISAND** BARBRA STREISAND	1
23/3/02	**SILVER SIDE UP** NICKELBACK	2

Chart Date	Album Title Artist	Weeks at No.1
6/4/02	**A NEW DAY HAS COME** CELINE DION	4
4/5/02	**ALL RISE** BLUE	1
11/5/02	**THE LAST BROADCAST** DOVES	2
25/5/02	**18** MOBY	1
1/6/02	**DESTINATION** RONAN KEATING	1
8/6/02	**THE EMINEM SHOW** EMINEM	5
13/7/02	**HEATHEN CHEMISTRY** OASIS	1
20/7/02	**BY THE WAY** RED HOT CHILI PEPPERS	3
10/8/02	**THE RISING** BRUCE SPRINGSTEEN	1
17/8/02	**BY THE WAY** RED HOT CHILI PEPPERS	2
31/8/02	**IMAGINE** EVA CASSIDY	1
7/9/02	**A RUSH OF BLOOD TO THE HEAD** COLDPLAY	2
21/9/02	**FEELS SO GOOD** ATOMIC KITTEN	1
28/9/02	**ILLUMINATION** PAUL WELLER	1
5/10/02	**ELV1S – 30 NUMBER 1 HITS** ELVIS PRESLEY	2
19/10/02	**FROM NOW ON** WILL YOUNG	2
2/11/02	**ONE BY ONE** FOO FIGHTERS	1
9/11/02	**A NEW DAY AT MIDNIGHT** DAVID GRAY	1
16/11/02	**ONE LOVE** BLUE	1
23/11/02	**UNBREAKABLE – THE GREATEST HITS – VOL 1.** WESTLIFE	1
30/11/02	**ESCAPOLOGY** ROBBIE WILLIAMS	6
11/1/03	**LET GO** AVRIL LAVIGNE	3
1/2/03	**JUSTIFIED** JUSTIN TIMBERLAKE	2
15/2/03	**SIMPLY DEEP** KELLY ROWLAND	1
22/2/03	**100TH WINDOW** MASSIVE ATTACK	1
1/3/03	**JUSTIFIED** JUSTIN TIMBERLAKE	2
8/3/03	**COME AWAY WITH ME** NORAH JONES	4
5/4/03	**METEORA** LINKIN PARK	1
12/4/03	**ELEPHANT** WHITE STRIPES	2
26/4/03	**A RUSH OF BLOOD TO THE HEAD** COLDPLAY	1
3/5/03	**AMERICAN LIFE** MADONNA	1
10/5/03	**JUSTIFIED** JUSTIN TIMBERLAKE	1
17/5/03	**THINK TANK** BLUR	1
24/5/03	**JUSTIFIED** JUSTIN TIMBERLAKE	3
14/6/03	**YOU GOTTA GO THERE TO COME BACK** STEREOPHONICS	1
21/6/03	**HAIL TO THE THIEF** RADIOHEAD	1
28/6/03	**FALLEN** EVANESCENCE	1
5/7/03	**DANGEROUSLY IN LOVE** BEYONCE	5
9/8/03	**MAGIC AND MEDICINE** CORAL	1
16/8/03	**ESCAPOLOGY** ROBBIE WILLIAMS	1
23/8/03	**AMERICAN TUNE** EVA CASSIDY	2
6/9/03	**PERMISSION TO LAND** THE DARKNESS	4
4/10/03	**ABSOLUTION** MUSE	1
11/10/03	**LIFE FOR RENT** DIDO	4
8/11/03	**IN TIME – THE BEST OF R.E.M. 1988–2003** R.E.M.	1
15/11/03	**GUILTY** BLUE	1
22/11/03	**LIFE FOR RENT** DIDO	1
29/11/03	**NUMBER ONES** MICHAEL JACKSON	1
6/12/03	**TURNAROUND** WESTLIFE	1
13/12/03	**FRIDAY'S CHILD** WILL YOUNG	1
20/12/03	**LIFE FOR RENT** DIDO	3
10/1/04	**FRIDAY'S CHILD** WILL YOUNG	1
17/1/04	**LIFE FOR RENT** DIDO	2
31/1/04	**CALL OFF THE SEARCH** KATIE MELUA	3
21/2/04	**FEELS LIKE HOME** NORAH JONES	2
6/3/04	**CALL OFF THE SEARCH** KATIE MELUA	3
27/3/04	**PATIENCE** GEORGE MICHAEL	1
3/4/04	**CONFESSIONS** USHER	1
10/4/04	**ANASTACIA** ANASTACIA	2
24/4/04	**GREATEST HITS** GUNS 'N' ROSES	2
8/5/04	**D12 WORLD** D12	1

Chart Date	Album Title Artist	Weeks at No.1
15/5/04	**GREATEST HITS** GUNS 'N' ROSES	1
22/5/04	**HOPES AND FEARS** KEANE	2
5/6/04	**UNDER MY SKIN** AVRIL LAVIGNE	1
12/6/04	**HOPES AND FEARS** KEANE	1
19/6/04	**NO ROOTS** FAITHLESS	1
26/6/04	**HOPES AND FEARS** KEANE	1
3/7/04	**A GRAND DON'T COME FOR FREE** THE STREETS	1
10/7/04	**SCISSOR SISTERS** SCISSOR SISTERS	1
17/7/04	**ROOM ON THE 3RD FLOOR** MCFLY	1
24/7/04	**SCISSOR SISTERS** SCISSOR SISTERS	1
31/7/04	**A GRAND DON'T COME FOR FREE** THE STREETS	1
7/8/04	**LIVE IN HYDE PARK** RED HOT CHILI PEPPERS	1
21/8/04	**ANASTACIA** ANASTACIA	1
28/8/04	**SONGS ABOUT JANE** MAROON 5	1
6/9/04	**ALWAYS OUTNUMBERED NEVER OUTGUNNED** THE PRODIGY	1
11/9/04	**THE LIBERTINES** THE LIBERTINES	1
18/9/04	**UNWRITTEN** NATASHA BEDINGFIELD	1
25/9/04	**OUT OF NOTHING** EMBRACE	1
2/10/04	**AMERICAN IDIOT** GREEN DAY	1
9/10/04	**MIND BODY AND SOUL** JOSS STONE	1
16/10/04	**AROUND THE SUN** R.E.M.	1
23/10/04	**10 YEARS OF HITS** RONAN KEATING	1
30/10/04	**GREATEST HITS** ROBBIE WILLIAMS	2
13/11/04	**IL DIVO** IL DIVO	1
20/11/04	**ENCORE** EMINEM	2
4/12/04	**HOW TO DISMANTLE AN ATOMIC BOMB** U2	3
25/12/04	**GREATEST HITS** ROBBIE WILLIAMS	2
8/1/05	**AMERICAN IDIOT** GREEN DAY	1
15/1/05	**SCISSOR SISTERS** SCISSOR SISTERS	1
22/1/05	**HOT FUSS** THE KILLERS	1
5/2/05	**PUSH THE BUTTON** CHEMICAL BROTHERS	1
12/2/05	**TOURIST** ATHLETE	1
19/2/05	**HOPES AND FEARS** KEANE	1
26/2/05	**SCISSOR SISTERS** SCISSOR SISTERS	1
5/3/05	**SOME CITIES** DOVES	1
12/3/05	**G4** G4	1
19/3/05	**THE MASSACRE** 50 CENT	1
26/3/05	**LANGUAGE.SEX.VIOLENCE.OTHER?** STEREOPHONICS	1
2/4/05	**THE DEFINITIVE COLLECTION** TONY CHRISTIE	2
16/4/05	**COUNTING DOWN THE DAYS** NATALIE IMBRUGLIA	1
23/4/05	**THE SINGLES** BASEMENT JAXX	1
30/4/05	**TROUBLE** AKON	1
7/5/05	**DEVILS AND DUST** BRUCE SPRINGSTEEN	1
14/5/05	**TROUBLE** AKON	1
21/5/05	**HEART AND SOUL** STEVE BROOKSTEIN	1
28/5/05	**FOREVER FAITHLESS – THE GREATEST HITS** FAITHLESS	1
4/6/05	**DEMON DAYS** GORILLAZ	1
11/6/05	**DON'T BELIEVE THE TRUTH** OASIS	1
18/6/05	**X & Y** COLDPLAY	4
16/7/05	**BACK TO BEDLAM** JAMES BLUNT	8
10/9/05	**WONDERLAND** MCFLY	1
17/9/05	**BACK TO BEDLAM** JAMES BLUNT	1
24/9/05	**LIFE IN SLOW MOTION** DAVID GRAY	2
8/10/05	**PIECE BY PIECE** KATIE MELUA	1
15/10/05	**YOU COULD HAVE IT SO MUCH BETTER** FRANZ FERDINAND	1
22/10/05	**TALLER IN MORE WAYS** SUGABABES	1
29/10/05	**THEIR LAW – THE SINGLES 1990-2005** THE PRODIGY	1
5/11/05	**INTENSIVE CARE** ROBBIE WILLIAMS	1
12/11/05	**FACE TO FACE** WESTLIFE	1
19/11/05	**ANCORA** IL DIVO	1
26/11/05	**CONFESSIONS ON A DANCEFLOOR** MADONNA	2

Chart Date	Album Title Artist	Weeks at No.1
10/12/05	**CURTAIN CALL – THE HITS** EMINEM	5
14/1/06	**FIRST IMPRESSIONS OF EARTH** THE STROKES	1
21/1/06	**BACK TO BEDLAM** JAMES BLUNT	1
28/1/06	**STARS OF CCTV** HARD-FI	1
4/2/06	**WHATEVER PEOPLE SAY I AM THAT'S WHAT I'M NOT** ARCTIC MONKEYS	4
4/3/06	**IN BETWEEN DREAMS** JACK JOHNSON	1
11/3/06	**CORINNE BAILEY RAE** CORINNE BAILEY RAE	1
18/3/06	**ON AN ISLAND** DAVID GILMOUR	1
25/3/06	**CORINNE BAILEY RAE** CORINNE BAILEY RAE	1
1/4/06	**JOURNEY SOUTH** JOURNEY SOUTH	1
8/4/06	**THIS NEW DAY** EMBRACE	1
15/4/06	**RINGLEADER OF THE TORMENTORS** MORRISSEY	1
22/4/06	**THE HARDEST WAY TO MAKE AN EASY LIVING** THE STREETS	1
29/4/06	**SHAYNE WARD** SHAYNE WARD	1
6/5/06	**ST ELSEWHERE** GNARLS BARKLEY	1
13/5/06	**EYES OPEN** SNOW PATROL	1
20/5/06	**STADIUM ARCADIUM** RED HOT CHILI PEPPERS	2
10/6/06	**BRIGHT IDEA** ORSON	1
17/6/06	**SMILE ... IT CONFUSES PEOPLE** SANDI THOM	1
24/6/06	**UNDER THE IRON SEA** KEANE	2
8/7/06	**LIBERATION TRANSMISSION** LOSTPROPHETS	1
15/7/06	**BLACK HOLES & REVELATIONS** MUSE	2
29/7/06	**RAZORLIGHT** RAZORLIGHT	2
12/8/06	**UNDISCOVERED** JAMES MORRISON	2
26/8/06	**BACK TO BASICS** CHRISTINA AGUILERA	1
2/9/06	**EYES OPEN** SNOW PATROL	1
9/9/06	**EMPIRE** KASABIAN	1
16/9/06	**EYES OPEN** SNOW PATROL	1
23/9/06	**FUTURESEX / LOVESOUNDS** JUSTIN TIMBERLAKE	1
30/9/06	**TA-DAH** SCISSOR SISTERS	2
14/10/06	**SAM'S TOWN** THE KILLERS	3
4/11/06	**RUDEBOX** ROBBIE WILLIAMS	1
11/11/06	**THE SOUND OF – THE GREATEST HITS** GIRLS ALOUD	1
18/11/06	**HIGH TIMES SINGLES 1992-2006** JAMIROQUAI	1
25/11/06	**TWENTY FIVE** GEORGE MICHAEL	1
2/12/06	**THE LOVE ALBUM** WESTLIFE	1
9/12/06	**BEAUTIFUL WORLD** TAKE THAT	5
20/1/07	**BACK TO BLACK** AMY WINEHOUSE	2
3/2/07	**HATS OFF TO THE BUSKERS** THE VIEW	1
10/2/07	**NOT TOO LATE** NORAH JONES	1
17/2/07	**LIFE IN CARTOON MOTION** MIKA	2
3/3/07	**BACK TO BLACK** AMY WINEHOUSE	1
10/3/07	**YOURS TRULY ANGRY MOB** KAISER CHIEFS	2
23/3/07	**DOING IT MY WAY** RAY QUINN	1
31/3/07	**BEAUTIFUL WORLD** TAKE THAT	2
14/4/07	**BECAUSE OF THE TIMES** KINGS OF LEON	2
28/4/07	**THE BEST DAMN THING** AVRIL LAVIGNE	1
5/5/07	**FAVOURITE WORST NIGHTMARE** ARCTIC MONKEYS	3
26/5/07	**MINUTES TO MIDNIGHT** LINKIN PARK	1
2/6/07	**IT WON'T BE SOON BEFORE LONG** MAROON 5	2
16/6/07	**GOOD GIRL GONE BAD** RIHANNA	1
23/6/07	**COLLECTION** TRAVELING WILBURYS	1
30/6/07	**ICKY THUMP** WHITE STRIPES	1
7/7/07	**AN END HAS A START** EDITORS	1
14/7/07	**WE ARE THE** CHEMICAL BROTHERS	1
21/7/07	**WE'LL LIVE AND DIE IN THESE TOWNS** ENEMY	1
28/7/07	**ONE CHANCE** PAUL POTTS	3
18/8/07	**MADE OF BRICKS** KATE NASH	1
25/8/07	**THE KING** ELVIS PRESLEY	1
1/9/07	**HAND BUILT BY ROBOTS** NEWTON FAULKNER	2
15/9/07	**ONCE UPON A TIME IN THE WEST** HARD-FI	1
22/9/07	**GRADUATION** KANYE WEST	1
29/9/07	**ALL THE LOST SOULS** JAMES BLUNT	1
6/10/07	**ECHOES SILENCE PATIENCE & GRACE** FOO FIGHTERS	1
13/10/07	**MAGIC** BRUCE SPRINGSTEEN	1
20/10/07	**CHANGE** SUGABABES	1
27/10/07	**PULL THE PIN** STEREOPHONICS	1
3/11/07	**THE TRICK TO LIFE** HOOSIERS	1
10/11/07	**LONG ROAD OUT OF EDEN** THE EAGLES	1
17/11/07	**BACK HOME** WESTLIFE	1
24/11/07	**SPIRIT** LEONA LEWIS	7
12/1/08	**IN RAINBOWS** RADIOHEAD	1
19/1/08	**THIS IS THE LIFE** AMY MACDONALD	1
26/1/08	**SCOUTING FOR GIRLS** SCOUTING FOR GIRLS	2
9/2/08	**19** ADELE	1
16/2/08	**SLEEP THROUGH THE STATIC** JACK JOHNSON	1
1/3/08	**JOIN WITH US** FEELING	1
8/3/08	**BACK TO BLACK (DELUXE EDITION)** AMY WINEHOUSE	1
15/3/08	**ROCKFERRY** DUFFY	5
31/3/08	**ACCELERATE** R.E.M.	1
26/4/08	**KONK** KOOKS	1
3/5/08	**AGE OF THE UNDERSTATEMENT** LAST SHADOW PUPPETS	1
10/5/08	**HARD CANDY** MADONNA	1
17/5/08	**JUMPING ALL OVER THE WORLD** SCOOTER	1
24/5/08	**HOME BEFORE DARK** NEIL DIAMOND	1
31/5/08	**WE STARTED NOTHING** TING TINGS	1
7/6/08	**HERE I STAND** USHER	1
14/6/08	**22 DREAMS** PAUL WELLER	1
21/6/08	**VIVA LA VIDA OR DEATH & ALL HIS FRIENDS** COLDPLAY	5
26/7/08	**NOW YOU'RE GONE** BASSHUNTER	1
2/8/08	**VIVA LA VIDA OR DEATH & ALL HIS FRIENDS** COLDPLAY	1
9/8/08	**GOLD – GREATEST HITS** ABBA	2
23/8/08	**THE SCRIPT** SCRIPT	2
6/9/08	**FORTH** VERVE	2
20/9/08	**DEATH MAGNETIC** METALLICA	2
4/10/08	**ONLY BY THE NIGHT** KINGS OF LEON	2
18/10/08	**DIG OUT YOUR SOUL** OASIS	1
25/10/08	**PERFECT SYMMETRY** KEANE	1
1/11/08	**BLACK ICE** AC/DC	1
8/11/08	**FUNHOUSE** PINK	1
15/11/08	**OUT OF CONTROL** GIRLS ALOUD	1
22/11/08	**THE PROMISE** IL DIVO	1
29/11/08	**SPIRIT** LEONA LEWIS	1
6/12/08	**DAY & AGE** KILLERS	1
13/12/08	**THE CIRCUS** TAKE THAT	5

BIOGRAPHIES

Biographies include the nationality and category for every chart entrant.

Each entrant has at least a mini biography. The 100 acts with the most weeks on the chart (see page 290 for the top 100 chart) each have extended biographies.

Real names are included for all solo artists and, where applicable, dates of death and age of the artist at the time. "See..." links are included for soloists who also had album chart entries in other acts.

The best known line-up is listed for every group that had a Top 10 album, with the vocalist/leader mentioned first and the others following in alphabetical order. In cases where later replacements had similar success both people are named and, where applicable, the dates of death are also shown for every group/duo member listed.

Certified Awards are given by the BPI to mark unit sales to retailers. The certified awards were introduced in April 1973, based on revenue received by manufacturers. In January 1978 the qualification rules were changed and the system based on unit sales to the trade was adopted.

Silver symbol	●	=	60,000 units
Gold symbol	●	=	100,000 units
Platinum symbol	⊛	=	300,000 units

A–D

KEY TO ARTIST ENTRIES

Artist/Group Name — Artist/Group Biography — Silver-selling — Gold-selling — Platinum-selling — US No.1 ★ — Peak Position — Weeks at No.1 — Weeks on Chart

Asterisks (*) indicate group members with hits in their own right that are listed elsewhere in this book

TOM JONES

UK, male vocalist (Thomas Woodward). Perennially popular Welsh vocalist, who has a 43-year span of UK hit albums, was the No.1 UK solo singer of the 1960s on both sides of the Atlantic. The unmistakable Vegas veteran received the Outstanding Contribution award at the 2003 BRITs

Artist's Total Weeks On Chart: 530

Date of entry into chart	Album Title / Label and Catalogue Number	Peak Position	Weeks at No.1	Weeks on Chart
5 Jun 65	**ALONG CAME JONES** *Decca LK 6693*	11		5
8 Oct 66	**FROM THE HEART** *Decca LK 4814*	23		8
8 Apr 67	**GREEN GREEN GRASS OF HOME** *Decca SKL 4855*	3		49
24 Jun 67	**LIVE AT THE TALK OF THE TOWN** *Decca SKL 4874*	6		90
30 Dec 67	**13 SMASH HITS** *Decca SKL 4909*	5		49
27 Jul 68	**DELILAH** *Decca SKL 4946*	1	2	29
21 Dec 68	**HELP YOURSELF** *Decca SKL 4982*	4		9
28 Jun 69	**THIS IS TOM JONES** *Decca SKL 5007*	2		20
15 Nov 69	**TOM JONES LIVE IN LAS VEGAS** *Decca SKL 5032*	2		45
25 Apr 70	**TOM** *Decca SKL 5045*	4		18
14 Nov 70	**I WHO HAVE NOTHING** *Decca SKL 5072*	10		10
29 May 71	**SHE'S A LADY** *Decca SKL 5089*	9		7
27 Nov 71	**LIVE AT CAESAR'S PALACE** *Decca D 1/11/2*	27		5
24 Jun 72	**CLOSE UP** *Decca SKL 5132*	17		4
23 Jun 73	**THE BODY AND SOUL OF TOM JONES** *Decca SKL 5162*	31		1
5 Jan 74	**GREATEST HITS** *Decca SKL 5176*	15		13
22 Mar 75	**20 GREATEST HITS** *Decca TJD 1/11/2* ●	1	4	21
7 Oct 78	**I'M COMING HOME** *Lotus WH 5001* ●	12		9
16 May 87	**THE GREATEST HITS** *Telstar STAR 2296*	16		12
13 May 89	**AT THIS MOMENT** *Jive TOMTV 1*	34		3
8 Jul 89	**AFTER DARK** *Stylus SMR 978*	46		4
6 Apr 91	**CARRYING A TORCH** *Dover ADD 20*	44		4
27 Jun 92	**THE COMPLETE TOM JONES** *The Hit Label 8442862* ●	8		6
26 Nov 94	**THE LEAD AND HOW TO SWING IT** *ZTT 6544924982*	55		1
14 Nov 98	**THE ULTIMATE HITS COLLECTION** *Polygram TV 8449012*	26		6
9 Oct 99	**RELOAD** *Gut GUTCD 009* ⊛ **x4**	1	3	65
16 Nov 02	**MR JONES** *V2 VVR 1021072*	36		2
1 Mar 03	**GREATEST HITS** *Universal TV 8828632* ⊛	2		16
9 Oct 04	**TOM JONES AND JOOLS HOLLAND** *Radar RADAR004CD* & JOOLS HOLLAND ●	5		13
29 Nov 08	**24 HOURS** *S-Curve 2649852*	32		6+

Artist collaboration or where artist's name has changed

Cross (+) indicates album is still on chart in last week of 2008

A

UK, male vocal/instrumental group — **10**

Date	Title / Label	Peak Position	Weeks at No.1	Weeks on Chart
28 Aug 99	**MONKEY KONG** *Tycoon 3984276952* A	62		1
16 Mar 02	**HI-FI SERIOUS** *London 0927447762* A ○	18		9

AALIYAH

US, female vocalist (Aaliyah Haughton), d. 25 Aug 2001 (age 22) — **59**

Date	Title / Label	Peak Position	Weeks at No.1	Weeks on Chart
23 Jul 94	**AGE AIN'T NOTHING BUT A NUMBER** *Jive CHIP 149* ○	23		6
7 Sep 96	**ONE IN A MILLION** *Atlantic 7567927152*	33		3
28 Jul 01	**AALIYAH** *Virgin CDVUSX 199* ⊛ ★	5		31
15 Feb 03	**I CARE 4 U** *Independiente/Blackground/Unique ISOM 37CDL* ●	4		16
16 Apr 05	**THE ULTIMATE** *Blackground/Unique/Believe SMADD895X*	32		3

ABBA

Sweden/Norway, male/female vocal group – Björn Ulvaeus, Benny Andersson, Agnetha Fältskog* & Anni-Frid Lyngstad (Frida*). The most successful act from outside the UK or US, who had eight successive UK No.1 albums. The video pioneers' four million-selling *Gold – Greatest Hits* topped the chart in 1992, 1999 and 2008 – a record-shattering feat — **957**

Date	Title / Label	Peak Position	Weeks at No.1	Weeks on Chart
8 Jun 74	**WATERLOO** *Epic EPC 80179* ○	28		2
31 Jan 76	**ABBA** *Epic EPC 80835* ●	13		10
10 Apr 76	**GREATEST HITS** *Epic EPC 69218* ⊛	1	11	130
27 Nov 76	**ARRIVAL** *Epic EPC 86018* ⊛	1	10	92
4 Feb 78	**THE ALBUM** *Epic EPC 86052* ⊛	1	7	61
19 May 79	**VOULEZ-VOUS** *Epic EPC 86086* ⊛	1	4	43
10 Nov 79	**GREATEST HITS VOLUME 2** *Epic EPC 10017* ⊛	1	4	63
22 Nov 80	**SUPER TROUPER** *Epic EPC 10022* ⊛	1	9	43
19 Dec 81	**THE VISITORS** *Epic EPC 10032* ⊛	1	3	21
20 Nov 82	**THE SINGLES – THE FIRST TEN YEARS** *Epic ABBA 10* ⊛	1	1	22
19 Nov 83	**THANK YOU FOR THE MUSIC** *Epic EPC 10043* ●	17		12
19 Nov 88	**ABSOLUTE ABBA** *Telstar STAR 2329* ●	70		7
3 Oct 92	**GOLD – GREATEST HITS** *Polydor 5170072* ⊛x13	1	8	386+
5 Jun 93	**MORE ABBA GOLD – MORE ABBA HITS** *Polydor 5193532* ⊛	13		23
7 Nov 98	**LOVE SONGS** *Polydor 5592212*	51		2
10 Nov 01	**THE DEFINITIVE COLLECTION** *Polar 5499742*	17		8
18 Nov 06	**NUMBER ONES** *Polar 1713536*	15		7
27 Jan 07	**18 HITS** *Polar 9831452*	17		21
6 Sep 08	**MORE ABBA GOLD** *Polar 1724733*	63		4

Top 3 Best-Selling Albums

	Album	Approximate Sales
1	GOLD - GREATEST HITS	4,475,000
2	GREATEST HITS	2,600,000
3	ARRIVAL	1,655,000

RUSS ABBOT

UK, male comedian/vocalist (Russell Roberts) — **16**

Date	Title / Label	Peak Position	Weeks at No.1	Weeks on Chart
5 Nov 83	**RUSS ABBOT'S MADHOUSE** *Ronco RTL 2096* ○	41		7
23 Nov 85	**I LOVE A PARTY** *K-Tel ONE 1313* ●	12		9

GREGORY ABBOTT

US, male vocalist — **5**

Date	Title / Label	Peak Position	Weeks at No.1	Weeks on Chart
10 Jan 87	**SHAKE YOU DOWN** *CBS 4500611*	53		5

ABC

UK, male vocal/instrumental group – Martin Fry, Mark Lickley, David Palmer, Stephen Singleton & Mark White — **91**

Date	Title / Label	Peak Position	Weeks at No.1	Weeks on Chart
3 Jul 82	**THE LEXICON OF LOVE** *Neutron NTRS 1* ⊛	1	4	50
26 Nov 83	**BEAUTY STAB** *Neutron NTRL 2* ●	12		13
26 Oct 85	**HOW TO BE A ZILLIONAIRE** *Neutron NTRH 3* ●	28		3
24 Oct 87	**ALPHABET CITY** *Neutron NTRH 4*	7		10
28 Oct 89	**UP** *Neutron 8386461*	58		1
21 Apr 90	**ABSOLUTELY** *Neutron 8429671* ●	7		12
24 Aug 91	**ABRACADABRA** *Parlophone PCS 7355*	50		1
4 Aug 01	**LOOK OF LOVE – THE VERY BEST OF ABC** *Mercury 5862372*	69		1

PAULA ABDUL

US, female vocalist — **51**

Date	Title / Label	Peak Position	Weeks at No.1	Weeks on Chart
15 Apr 89	**FOREVER YOUR GIRL** *Siren SRNLP 19* ⊛ ★	3		39
10 Nov 90	**SHUT UP AND DANCE** *Virgin America VUSLP 28*	40		2
27 Jul 91	**SPELLBOUND** *Virgin America VUSLP 33* ● ★	4		9
1 Jul 95	**HEAD OVER HEELS** *Virgin America CDVUS 90*	61		1

ANDY ABRAHAM

UK, male vocalist — **13**

Date	Title / Label	Peak Position	Weeks at No.1	Weeks on Chart
1 Apr 06	**THE IMPOSSIBLE DREAM** *Sony BMG 82876815372* ⊛	2		7
25 Nov 06	**SOUL MAN** *Sony BMG 88697020572*	19		6

A.B.'S

Japan, male instrumental group — **2**

Date	Title / Label	Peak Position	Weeks at No.1	Weeks on Chart
14 Apr 84	**DÉJÀ VU** *Street Sounds XKHAN 503*	80		2

ABS

UK, male vocalist/rapper (Richard Breen). See Five — **4**

Date	Title / Label	Peak Position	Weeks at No.1	Weeks on Chart
13 Sep 03	**ABSTRACT THEORY** *BMG 82876538802*	29		4

AC/DC

Australia/UK, male vocal/instrumental group – Bon Scott, d. 19 Feb 1980 (replaced by Brian Johnson), Phillip Rudd, Cliff Williams, Angus Young & Malcolm Young — **268**

Date	Title / Label	Peak Position	Weeks at No.1	Weeks on Chart
5 Nov 77	**LET THERE BE ROCK** *Atlantic K 50366* ○	17		5
20 May 78	**POWERAGE** *Atlantic K 50483* ○	26		9
28 Oct 78	**IF YOU WANT BLOOD YOU'VE GOT IT** *Atlantic K 50532* ●	13		58
18 Aug 79	**HIGHWAY TO HELL** *Atlantic K 50628* ●	8		32
9 Aug 80	**BACK IN BLACK** *Atlantic K 50735* ●	1	2	40
5 Dec 81	**FOR THOSE ABOUT TO ROCK WE SALUTE YOU** *Atlantic K 50851* ● ★	3		29
3 Sep 83	**FLICK OF THE SWITCH** *Atlantic 7801001* ●	4		9
13 Jul 85	**FLY ON THE WALL** *Atlantic 7812631* ○	7		10
7 Jun 86	**WHO MADE WHO** *Atlantic WX 57*	11		12
13 Feb 88	**BLOW UP YOUR VIDEO** *Atlantic WX 144* ●	2		14
6 Oct 90	**THE RAZOR'S EDGE** *Atco WX 364* ●	4		18
7 Nov 92	**AC/DC LIVE** *Atco 7567922152* ●	5		7
7 Oct 95	**BALLBREAKER** *East West 7559617802*	6		8
11 Mar 00	**STIFF UPPER LIP** *EMI 5256672*	12		4
25 Oct 08	**BACK IN BLACK** *Epic 5107652*	42		3
1 Nov 08	**BLACK ICE** *Columbia 88697383771* ⊛ ★	1	1	10+

ACADEMY OF ANCIENT MUSIC (CONDUCTED BY CHRISTOPHER HOGWOOD)

UK, male/female orchestra & male conductor — **2**

Date	Title / Label	Peak Position	Weeks at No.1	Weeks on Chart
16 Mar 85	**VIVALDI'S THE FOUR SEASONS** *L'oiseau Lyre 4101261*	85		2

ACCEPT

Germany, male vocal/instrumental group — **5**

Date	Title / Label	Peak Position	Weeks at No.1	Weeks on Chart
7 May 83	**RESTLESS AND WILD** *Heavy Metal International HMILP 6*	98		2
30 Mar 85	**METAL HEART** *Portrait PRT 26358*	50		1
15 Feb 86	**KAIZOKU-BAN** *Portrait PRT 54916*	91		1
3 May 86	**RUSSIAN ROULETTE** *Portrait PRT 26893*	80		1

ACE OF BASE

Sweden, female/male vocal/instrumental group – Malin, Jenny & Jonas Berggren & Ulf Ekberg — **45**

Date	Title / Label	Peak Position	Weeks at No.1	Weeks on Chart
19 Jun 93	**HAPPY NATION** *London 5177492* ⊛x2	1	2	38
2 Dec 95	**THE BRIDGE** *London 5296552*	66		1
22 Aug 98	**FLOWERS** *London 5576912* ○	15		5
27 Nov 99	**SINGLES OF THE 90S** *Polydor 5432272*	62		1

ADAM & THE ANTS

UK, male vocal/instrumental group – Adam Ant* (Stuart Goddard), Chris Hughes, Terry Lee Miall, Kevin Mooney & Marco Pirroni — **162**

Date	Title / Label	Peak Position	Weeks at No.1	Weeks on Chart
15 Nov 80	**KINGS OF THE WILD FRONTIER** *CBS 84549* ⊛	1	12	66
17 Jan 81	**DIRK WEARS WHITE SOX** *Do It RIDE 3* ●	16		29
14 Nov 81	**PRINCE CHARMING** *CBS 85268* ⊛	2		21
23 Oct 82	**FRIEND OR FOE** *CBS 25040* ADAM ANT ●	5		12
19 Nov 83	**STRIP** *CBS 25705* ADAM ANT ○	20		8
14 Sep 85	**VIVE LE ROCK** *CBS 26583* ADAM ANT	42		3

Key: ○ Silver-selling · ● Gold-selling · ⊛ Platinum-selling · ★ US No.1 · Peak Position · Weeks at No.1 · Weeks on Chart

Date	Title / Label	Peak Position	Weeks at No.1	Weeks on Chart
24 Mar 90	**MANNERS AND PHYSIQUE** *MCA MCG 6068* ADAM ANT	19		3
28 Aug 93	**ANTMUSIC – THE VERY BEST OF ADAM ANT** *Arcade ARC 3100052* ADAM ANT	6		11
15 Apr 95	**WONDERFUL** *EMI CDEMC 3687* ADAM ANT	24		2
3 Apr 99	**THE VERY BEST OF ADAM AND THE ANTS** *Columbia 4942292* ●	33		5
23 Sep 06	**THE VERY BEST OF** *Columbia 82876891242*	39		2

BRYAN ADAMS

Canada, male vocalist/guitarist. World-renowned rock singer/songwriter who has won 18 Juno awards (the Canadian equivalent of the BRITs), is the most charted Canadian act of all time in the UK and has sold more than 65 million records worldwide — **420**

Date	Title / Label	Peak Position	Weeks at No.1	Weeks on Chart
2 Mar 85	**RECKLESS** *A&M AMA 5013* ⊛x3 ★	7		115
24 Aug 85	**YOU WANT IT, YOU GOT IT** *A&M AMLH 64864*	78		5
15 Mar 86	**CUTS LIKE A KNIFE** *A&M AMLH 64919* ○	21		6
11 Apr 87	**INTO THE FIRE** *A&M AMA 3907* ●	10		21
5 Oct 91	**WAKING UP THE NEIGHBOURS** *A&M 3971641* ⊛x3	1	1	54
20 Nov 93	**SO FAR SO GOOD** *A&M 5401572* ⊛x3	1	1	55
6 Aug 94	**LIVE! LIVE! LIVE!** *A&M 3970942*	17		4
22 Jun 96	**18 TIL I DIE** *A&M 5405372* ⊛x2	1	1	40
13 Dec 97	**UNPLUGGED** *A&M 5408312* ●	19		19
31 Oct 98	**ON A DAY LIKE TODAY** *A&M 5410512* ●	11		35
27 Nov 99	**THE BEST OF ME** *A&M 4905222* ⊛	12		43
27 Jul 02	**SPIRIT – STALLION OF THE CIMARRON – OST** *A&M 4933622* ○	8		5
2 Oct 04	**ROOM SERVICE** *Polydor 9868245* ●	4		6
3 Dec 05	**ANTHOLOGY** *Polydor 9835827* ●	30		8
29 Mar 08	**11** *Polydor 1762237*	6		4

CLIFF ADAMS SINGERS

UK, male/female vocal group, Cliff Adams, d. 22 Oct 2001 (age 78) — **20**

Date	Title / Label	Peak Position	Weeks at No.1	Weeks on Chart
16 Apr 60	**SING SOMETHING SIMPLE** *Pye MPL 28013*	15		4
24 Nov 62	**SING SOMETHING SIMPLE** *Pye Golden Guinea GGL 0150*	15		2
20 Nov 76	**SING SOMETHING SIMPLE '76** *Warwick WW 5016/17*	23		8
25 Dec 82	**SING SOMETHING SIMPLE** *Ronco RTD 2087*	39		6

OLETA ADAMS

US, female vocalist/keyboard player — **34**

Date	Title / Label	Peak Position	Weeks at No.1	Weeks on Chart
26 May 90	**CIRCLE OF ONE** *Fontana 8427441* ●	1	1	26
7 Aug 93	**EVOLUTION** *Fontana 5149652*	10		7
4 Nov 95	**MOVING ON** *Fontana 5285302*	59		1

RYAN ADAMS

US, male vocalist/multi-instrumentalist — **20**

Date	Title / Label	Peak Position	Weeks at No.1	Weeks on Chart
6 Oct 01	**GOLD** *Lost Highway 1702522* ●	20		9
5 Oct 02	**DEMOLITION** *Lost Highway 1703332*	22		2
15 Nov 03	**ROCK N ROLL** *Lost Highway 9861324*	41		1
15 Nov 03	**LOVE IS HELL PART 1** *Lost Highway 9813666*	62		1
15 May 04	**LOVE IS HELL** *Lost Highway 9862325*	68		1
14 May 05	**COLD ROSES** *Mercury 9881827* & THE CARDINALS	20		2
8 Oct 05	**JACKSONVILLE CITY LIGHTS** *Lost Highway 9884907* & THE CARDINALS	59		1
7 Jul 07	**EASY TIGER** *Lost Highway 1734674*	18		2
8 Nov 08	**CARDINOLOGY** *Lost Highway 1789279* & THE CARDINALS	41		1

ADAMSKI

UK, male producer (Adam Tinley) — **16**

Date	Title / Label	Peak Position	Weeks at No.1	Weeks on Chart
9 Dec 89	**LIVEANDIRECT** *MCA MCL 1900* ○	47		11
13 Oct 90	**DOCTOR ADAMSKI'S MUSICAL PHARMACY** *MCA MCG 6107* ○	8		5

BARRY ADAMSON

UK, male producer/guitarist — **1**

Date	Title / Label	Peak Position	Weeks at No.1	Weeks on Chart
10 Aug 96	**OEDIPUS SCHMOEDIPUS** *Mute CDSTUMM 134*	51		1

KING SUNNY ADE & HIS AFRICAN BEATS

Nigeria, male vocalist/guitarist (Sunday Adeniyi) & male instrumental group — **1**

Date	Title / Label	Peak Position	Weeks at No.1	Weeks on Chart
9 Jul 83	**SYNCHRO SYSTEM** *Island ILPS 9737*	93		1

ADELE

UK, female vocalist/guitarist (Adele Adkins) — **41**

Date	Title / Label	Peak Position	Weeks at No.1	Weeks on Chart
9 Feb 08	**19** *XL Recordings XLCD313* ⊛	1	1	41

ADEVA

US, female vocalist (Patricia Daniels) — **24**

Date	Title / Label	Peak Position	Weeks at No.1	Weeks on Chart
9 Sep 89	**ADEVA** *Cooltempo ICTLP 13* ⊛	6		24

ADICTS

UK, male vocal/instrumental group — **1**

Date	Title / Label	Peak Position	Weeks at No.1	Weeks on Chart
4 Dec 82	**SOUND OF MUSIC** *Razor RAZ 2*	99		1

ADIEMUS

UK, male/female vocal/instrumental group — **22**

Date	Title / Label	Peak Position	Weeks at No.1	Weeks on Chart
1 Jul 95	**SONGS OF SANCTUARY** *Venture CDVE 925* ●	35		12
1 Mar 97	**ADIEMUS II – CANTATA MUNDI** *Venture CDVE 932* ●	15		9
24 Oct 98	**ADIEMUS III – DANCES OF TIME** *Venture CDVE 940*	58		1

LARRY ADLER

US, male harmonica player, d. 7 Aug 2001 (age 87) — **18**

Date	Title / Label	Peak Position	Weeks at No.1	Weeks on Chart
6 Aug 94	**THE GLORY OF GERSHWIN** *Mercury 5227272* ●	2		18

ADORABLE

UK, male vocal/instrumental group — **1**

Date	Title / Label	Peak Position	Weeks at No.1	Weeks on Chart
13 Mar 93	**AGAINST PERFECTION** *Creation CRECD 138*	70		1

ADVENTURES

UK, male vocal/instrumental group — **11**

Date	Title / Label	Peak Position	Weeks at No.1	Weeks on Chart
21 May 88	**THE SEA OF LOVE** *Elektra EKT 45* ○	30		10
17 Mar 90	**TRADING SECRETS WITH THE MOON** *Elektra EKT 63*	64		1

ADVERTS

UK, male/female vocal/instrumental group — **1**

Date	Title / Label	Peak Position	Weeks at No.1	Weeks on Chart
11 Mar 78	**CROSSING THE RED SEA WITH THE ADVERTS** *Bright BRL 201*	38		1

AEROSMITH

US, male vocal/instrumental group – Steven Tyler, Tom Hamilton, Joey Kramer, Joe Perry & Brad Whitford — **153**

Date	Title / Label	Peak Position	Weeks at No.1	Weeks on Chart
5 Sep 87	**PERMANENT VACATION** *Geffen WX 126* ●	37		14
23 Sep 89	**PUMP** *Geffen WX 30/GEF 24245* ●	3		26
1 May 93	**GET A GRIP** *Geffen GED 24444* ⊛ ★	2		38
12 Nov 94	**BIG ONES** *Geffen GED 24546* ⊛	7		16
22 Mar 97	**NINE LIVES** *Columbia 4850206* ○ ★	4		11
31 Oct 98	**A LITTLE SOUTH OF SANITY** *Geffen GED 25221*	36		2
24 Mar 01	**JUST PUSH PLAY** *Columbia 5015352*	7		5
8 Dec 01	**YOUNG LUST – THE ANTHOLOGY** *Universal TV 4931192* ●	32		14
3 Aug 02	**O YEAH – ULTIMATE HITS** *Sony TV 5084679* ●	6		8
10 Apr 04	**HONKIN' ON BOBO** *Columbia CK92079*	28		3
11 Nov 06	**THE VERY BEST OF** *Columbia/Geffen 88697008692*	19		16

AFGHAN WHIGS

US, male vocal/instrumental group — **3**

Date	Title / Label	Peak Position	Weeks at No.1	Weeks on Chart
16 Oct 93	**GENTLEMEN** *Blast First BFFP 90CD*	58		1
23 Mar 96	**BLACK LOVE** *Mute CDSTUMM 143*	41		2

AFI

US, male vocal/instrumental group — **4**

Date	Title / Label	Peak Position	Weeks at No.1	Weeks on Chart
22 Mar 03	**SING THE SORROW** *DreamWorks 04504482*	52		1
10 Jun 06	**DECEMBERUNDERGROUND** *Interscope 9858643* ★	16		3

AFRO CELT SOUND SYSTEM

UK/Ireland/France/Guinea, male vocal/instrumental group — **5**

Date	Title / Label	Peak Position	Weeks at No.1	Weeks on Chart
27 Jul 96	**VOLUME 1 – SOUND MAGIC** *Realworld CDRW 61* ○	59		2
8 May 99	**VOLUME 2: RELEASE** *Realworld CDRW 76*	38		3

AFTER DARK

UK, male saxophonist (Mornington Lockett) — **5**

Date	Title / Label	Peak Position	Weeks at No.1	Weeks on Chart
3 Feb 96	**LATE NIGHT SAX** *EMI TV CDEMTV 108*	18		5

AFTER THE FIRE
UK, male vocal/instrumental group — Weeks on Chart: 4

Date	Title	Label	Peak Position	Weeks at No.1	Weeks on Chart
13 Oct 79	**LASER LOVE**	*CBS 83795*	57		1
1 Nov 80	**80 F**	*Epic 84545*	69		1
3 Apr 82	**BATTERIES NOT INCLUDED**	*CBS 85566*	82		2

CHRISTINA AGUILERA
US, female vocalist — Weeks on Chart: 168

Date	Title	Label	Peak Position	Weeks at No.1	Weeks on Chart
30 Oct 99	**CHRISTINA AGUILERA**	*RCA 74321780542* ● ★	14		26
9 Nov 02	**STRIPPED**	*RCA 74321961252* ⊛x5	2		102
26 Aug 06	**BACK TO BASICS**	*RCA 82876896342* ⊛ ★	1	1	33
22 Nov 08	**KEEPS GETTING BETTER – A DECADE OF HITS**	*RCA 88697386162*	10		7+

A-HA
Norway, male vocal/instrumental group – Morten Harket, Magna Furuholmen & Pal Waaktaar — Weeks on Chart: 162

Date	Title	Label	Peak Position	Weeks at No.1	Weeks on Chart
9 Nov 85	**HUNTING HIGH AND LOW**	*Warner Brothers WX 30* ⊛x3	2		78
18 Oct 86	**SCOUNDREL DAYS**	*Warner Brothers WX 62* ⊛	2		29
14 May 88	**STAY ON THESE ROADS**	*Warner Brothers WX 166* ●	2		19
3 Nov 90	**EAST OF THE SUN, WEST OF THE MOON**	*Warner Brothers WX 378* ○	12		4
16 Nov 91	**HEADLINES AND DEADLINES – THE HITS OF A-HA**	*Warner Brothers WX 450* ⊛	12		12
26 Jun 93	**MEMORIAL BEACH**	*Warner Brothers 9362452292*	17		3
17 Jun 00	**MINOR EARTH MAJOR SKY**	*WEA 8573821832*	27		2
22 Jun 02	**LIFELINES**	*WEA 0927448492CD*	67		1
23 Apr 05	**THE DEFINITIVE SINGLES COLLECTION**	*WSM 5046783242* ○	14		10
4 Feb 06	**ANALOGUE**	*Polydor 9875415* ○	24		4

AIDEN
US, male vocal/instrumental group — Weeks on Chart: 1

Date	Title	Label	Peak Position	Weeks at No.1	Weeks on Chart
1 Sep 07	**CONVICTION**	*Victory VR349*	45		1

AIM
UK, male DJ/producer (Andy Turner) — Weeks on Chart: 1

Date	Title	Label	Peak Position	Weeks at No.1	Weeks on Chart
9 Mar 02	**HINTERLAND**	*Grand Central GCCD 112*	47		1

AIR
France, male instrumental/production duo – Jean-Benoit Dunckel & Nicolas Godin — Weeks on Chart: 88

Date	Title	Label	Peak Position	Weeks at No.1	Weeks on Chart
31 Jan 98	**MOON SAFARI**	*Virgin CDV 2848* ⊛	6		61
18 Sep 99	**PREMIERS SYMPTOMES**	*Virgin CDVX 2895* ○	12		7
11 Mar 00	**THE VIRGIN SUICIDES – OST**	*Virgin CDV 2910*	14		4
9 Jun 01	**10,000 HZ LEGEND**	*Virgin CDV 2945* ●	7		5
2 Mar 02	**EVERYBODY HERTZ**	*Virgin CDV 2956*	67		1
7 Feb 04	**TALKIE WALKIE**	*Virgin CDVX 2980* ●	2		7
17 Mar 07	**POCKET SYMPHONY**	*Virgin CDV3032*	22		3

AIR TRAFFIC
UK, male vocal/instrumental group — Weeks on Chart: 1

Date	Title	Label	Peak Position	Weeks at No.1	Weeks on Chart
14 Jul 07	**FRACTURED LIFE**	*EMI 3966332*	42		1

AIRBOURNE
Australia, male vocal/instrumental group — Weeks on Chart: 1

Date	Title	Label	Peak Position	Weeks at No.1	Weeks on Chart
9 Feb 08	**RUNNIN' WILD**	*Roadrunner RR79632*	62		1

AIRHEAD
UK, male vocal/instrumental group — Weeks on Chart: 7

Date	Title	Label	Peak Position	Weeks at No.1	Weeks on Chart
1 Feb 92	**BOING!**	*Korova 9031746792*	29		7

AKON
US (b. Senegal), male vocalist/rapper (Aliaune Thiam) — Weeks on Chart: 82

Date	Title	Label	Peak Position	Weeks at No.1	Weeks on Chart
12 Feb 05	**TROUBLE**	*Universal 2103966* ⊛	1	2	32
2 Dec 06	**KONVICTED**	*Universal UNIVB0007968022* ⊛	16		46
13 Dec 08	**FREEDOM**	*Island 1792339* ●	31		4+

ROBERTO ALAGNA/ANGELA GHEORGIU
France, male vocalist & Romania, female vocalist — Weeks on Chart: 1

Date	Title	Label	Peak Position	Weeks at No.1	Weeks on Chart
18 May 96	**DUETS & ARIAS**	*EMI Classics CDC 5561172*	42		5

ALARM
UK, male vocal/instrumental group – Mike Peters, Eddie Macdonald, Dave Sharp & Nigel Twist — Weeks on Chart: 29

Date	Title	Label	Peak Position	Weeks at No.1	Weeks on Chart
25 Feb 84	**DECLARATION**	*I.R.S. IRSA 7044* ○	6		11
26 Oct 85	**STRENGTH**	*I.R.S. MIRF 1004* ○	18		6
14 Nov 87	**EYE OF THE HURRICANE**	*I.R.S. MIRG 1023* ○	23		4
5 Nov 88	**ELECTRIC FOLKLORE LIVE**	*I.R.S. MIRMC 5001*	62		2
30 Sep 89	**CHANGE**	*I.R.S. EIRSAX 1020* ○	13		3
24 Nov 90	**STANDARDS**	*I.R.S. EIRSA 1043* ○	47		1
4 May 91	**RAW**	*I.R.S. EIRSA 1055*	33		2

ALEXANDER BROTHERS
UK, male vocal duo — Weeks on Chart: 1

Date	Title	Label	Peak Position	Weeks at No.1	Weeks on Chart
10 Dec 66	**THESE ARE MY MOUNTAINS**	*Pye Golden Guinea GGL 0375*	29		1

ALEXISONFIRE
Canada, male vocal/instrumental group — Weeks on Chart: 1

Date	Title	Label	Peak Position	Weeks at No.1	Weeks on Chart
2 Sep 06	**CRISIS**	*Hassle HOFF016CD*	72		1

ALFIE
UK, male vocal/instrumental group — Weeks on Chart: 1

Date	Title	Label	Peak Position	Weeks at No.1	Weeks on Chart
7 Apr 01	**IF YOU HAPPY WITH YOU NEED DO NOTHING**	*Twisted Nerve TN 026CD*	62		1

TATYANA ALI
US, female vocalist — Weeks on Chart: 4

Date	Title	Label	Peak Position	Weeks at No.1	Weeks on Chart
20 Feb 99	**KISS THE SKY**	*MJJ 4916512*	41		4

ALICE BAND
UK/Ireland/US, female vocal/instrumental group — Weeks on Chart: 1

Date	Title	Label	Peak Position	Weeks at No.1	Weeks on Chart
25 May 02	**THE LOVE JUNK STORE**	*Instant Karma KARMACD 4*	55		1

ALICE DEEJAY
Holland, female/male vocal/production group – Judith Pronk, Eelke Kalberg, Sebastiaan Molijn & Jurgen Rijkers (DJ Jurgen) — Weeks on Chart: 11

Date	Title	Label	Peak Position	Weeks at No.1	Weeks on Chart
29 Jul 00	**WHO NEEDS GUITARS ANYWAY**	*Positiva 5270010* ●	8		11

ALICE IN CHAINS
US, male vocal/instrumental group – Layne Staley, d. 5 Apr 2002 (replaced by William DuVall), Jerry Cantrell, Mike Inez & Sean Kinney — Weeks on Chart: 22

Date	Title	Label	Peak Position	Weeks at No.1	Weeks on Chart
24 Oct 92	**DIRT**	*Columbia 4723302* ●	42		13
5 Feb 94	**JAR OF FLIES/SAP**	*Columbia 4757132* ○ ★	4		5
18 Nov 95	**ALICE IN CHAINS**	*Columbia 4811149* ★	37		2
10 Aug 96	**MTV UNPLUGGED**	*Columbia 4843002*	20		2

ALIEN ANT FARM
US, male vocal/instrumental group — Weeks on Chart: 24

Date	Title	Label	Peak Position	Weeks at No.1	Weeks on Chart
18 Aug 01	**ANTHOLOGY**	*DreamWorks 4502932* ●	11		23
30 Aug 03	**TRUANT**	*DreamWorks 4505014*	68		1

ALIEN SEX FIEND
UK, male/female vocal/instrumental group — Weeks on Chart: 1

Date	Title	Label	Peak Position	Weeks at No.1	Weeks on Chart
12 Oct 85	**MAXIMUM SECURITY**	*Anagram GRAM 24*	100		1

ALIENS
UK, male vocal/instrumental group — Weeks on Chart: 1

Date	Title	Label	Peak Position	Weeks at No.1	Weeks on Chart
31 Mar 07	**ASTRONOMY FOR DOGS**	*EMI PETROCKLPCD001*	46		1

Silver-selling ○ Gold-selling ● Platinum-selling ⊛ US No.1 ★ — Peak Position, Weeks at No.1, Weeks on Chart

ALISHA'S ATTIC
UK, female vocal duo

Date	Title	Peak	Wks at No.1	47
23 Nov 96	**ALISHA RULES THE WORLD** *Mercury 5340272* ⊛	14		43
17 Oct 98	**ILLUMINA** *Mercury 5589912* ○	15		3
4 Aug 01	**THE HOUSE WE BUILT** *Mercury 5428542*	55		1

ALKALINE TRIO
US, male vocal/instrumental group

Date	Title	Peak	Wks at No.1	5
24 May 03	**GOOD MOURNING** *Vagrant 9801238*	32		1
4 Jun 05	**CRIMSON** *Vagrant VRUK012CD*	34		2
10 Feb 07	**REMAINS** *Vagrant VRUK044CD*	68		1
19 Jul 08	**AGONY & IRONY** *Cooperative Music/V2 88697172472*	52		1

ALL ABOUT EVE
UK, female/male vocal/instrumental group – Julianne Regan, Tim Bricheno, Andy Cousin, Mark Price & Marty Willson-Piper

Date	Title	Peak	Wks at No.1	37
27 Feb 88	**ALL ABOUT EVE** *Mercury MERH 119* ●	7		29
28 Oct 89	**SCARLET AND OTHER STORIES** *Mercury 8389651* ●	9		4
7 Sep 91	**TOUCHED BY JESUS** *Vertigo 5104611*	17		3
7 Nov 92	**ULTRAVIOLET** *MCA MCD 10712*	46		1

ALL-AMERICAN REJECTS
US, male vocal/instrumental group

Date	Title	Peak	Wks at No.1	8
9 Aug 03	**THE ALL-AMERICAN REJECTS** *DreamWorks 4504606*	50		5
8 Jul 06	**MOVE ALONG** *Interscope 9883123*	45		3

ALL ANGELS
UK, female vocal group – Daisy Chute, Melanie Nakhla, Charlotte Ritchie & Laura Wright

Date	Title	Peak	Wks at No.1	12
25 Nov 06	**ALL ANGELS** *UCJ 1709223* ●	9		8
8 Dec 07	**INTO PARADISE** *UCJ 4766199*	44		4

ALL-4-ONE
US, male vocal group

Date	Title	Peak	Wks at No.1	5
23 Jul 94	**ALL-4-ONE** *Atlantic 7567825882*	25		5

ALL SAINTS
UK/Canada, female vocal group – Natalie & Nicole Appleton (Appleton*), Melanie Blatt & Shaznay Lewis

Date	Title	Peak	Wks at No.1	98
6 Dec 97	**ALL SAINTS** *London 5560172* ⊛x5	2		71
28 Oct 00	**SAINTS & SINNERS** *London 8573852955* ⊛x2	1	1	21
17 Nov 01	**ALL HITS** *London 0927421522* ●	18		4
25 Nov 06	**STUDIO 1** *Parlophone 3784442*	40		2

ALL SEEING I
UK, male production/instrumental group

Date	Title	Peak	Wks at No.1	1
2 Oct 99	**PICKLED EGGS & SHERBET** *ffrr 3984292412*	45		1

LILY ALLEN
UK, female vocalist

Date	Title	Peak	Wks at No.1	69
29 Jul 06	**ALRIGHT, STILL** *Regal 3670282* ⊛x6	2		69

ED ALLEYNE-JOHNSON
UK, male violinist

Date	Title	Peak	Wks at No.1	1
18 Jun 94	**ULTRAVIOLET** *Equation EQCD 002*	68		1

MOSE ALLISON
US, male vocalist/pianist

Date	Title	Peak	Wks at No.1	1
4 Jun 66	**MOSE ALIVE** *Atlantic 587007*	30		1

ALLMAN BROTHERS BAND
US, male vocal/instrumental group

Date	Title	Peak	Wks at No.1	4
6 Oct 73	**BROTHERS AND SISTERS** *Warner Brothers K 47507* ★	42		3
6 Mar 76	**THE ROAD GOES ON FOREVER** *Capricorn 2637 101*	54		1

ALLSTARS
UK, female/male vocal group

Date	Title	Peak	Wks at No.1	2
25 May 02	**ALLSTARS** *Island CIDD 8116*	43		2

ALMIGHTY
UK/Canada, male vocal/instrumental group – Ricky Warwick, Pete Friesen, Floyd London & Stump Monroe

Date	Title	Peak	Wks at No.1	13
20 Oct 90	**BLOOD, FIRE AND LIVE** *Polydor 8471071*	62		1
30 Mar 91	**SOUL DESTRUCTION** *Polydor 8479611*	22		4
17 Apr 93	**POWERTRIPPIN'** *Polydor 5191042*	5		4
8 Oct 94	**CRANK** *Chrysalis CDCHRZ 6086*	15		2
30 Mar 96	**JUST ADD LIFE** *Chrysalis CDCHR 6112*	34		2

MARC ALMOND
UK, male vocalist (Peter Almond). See Soft Cell

Date	Title	Peak	Wks at No.1	40
16 Oct 82	**UNTITLED** *Some Bizzare BZA 13* MARC & THE MAMBAS	42		4
20 Aug 83	**TORMENT AND TOREROS** *Some Bizzare BIZL 4* MARC & THE MAMBAS	28		5
10 Nov 84	**VERMIN IN ERMINE** *Some Bizzare BIZL 8* MARC ALMOND & THE WILLING SINNERS	36		2
5 Oct 85	**STORIES OF JOHNNY** *Some Bizzare FAITH 1*	22		3
18 Apr 87	**MOTHER FIST AND HER FIVE DAUGHTERS** *Some Bizzare FAITH 2* & THE WILLING SINNERS	41		2
8 Oct 88	**THE STARS WE ARE** *Parlophone PCS 7324* ○	41		5
16 Jun 90	**ENCHANTED** *Parlophone PCS 7344*	52		1
1 Jun 91	**MEMORABILIA – THE SINGLES** *Mercury 8485121* SOFT CELL & MARC ALMOND	8		13
26 Oct 91	**TENEMENT SYMPHONY** *Some Bizzare WX 442*	39		3
9 Mar 96	**FANTASTIC STAR** *Some Bizzare 5286592*	54		1
16 Jun 07	**STARDOM ROAD** *Sequel SEQCD011*	53		1

ALPHABEAT
Denmark, female/male vocal/instrumental group – Stine Bramsen, Anders B, Troels Hansen, Rasmus Nagel, Anders Reinholdt & Anders SG

Date	Title	Peak	Wks at No.1	18
14 Jun 08	**THIS IS ALPHABEAT** *Charisma CASCD2014* ●	10		18

HERB ALPERT & THE TIJUANA BRASS
US, male instrumental group – Herb Alpert*, members also included Nick Ceroli, Bob Edmondson, Tonni Kalash, Lou Pagani, John Pisano, Pat Senatore & Julius Wechter

Date	Title	Peak	Wks at No.1	322
29 Jan 66	**GOING PLACES** *Pye NPL 28065/A&M AMLS 965* ★	4		138
23 Apr 66	**WHIPPED CREAM AND OTHER DELIGHTS** *Pye NPL 28058* ★	2		42
28 May 66	**WHAT NOW MY LOVE** *Pye NPL 28077/A&M AMLS 977* ★	18		17
11 Feb 67	**S.R.O.** *Pye NSPL 28088*	5		26
15 Jul 67	**SOUNDS LIKE** *A&M AMLS 900* ★	21		10
3 Feb 68	**NINTH** *A&M AMLS 905*	26		19
29 Jun 68	**BEAT OF THE BRASS** *A&M AMLS 916* ★	4		21
9 Aug 69	**WARM** *A&M AMLS 937*	30		4
14 Mar 70	**THE BRASS ARE COMIN'** *A&M AMLS 962*	40		1
30 May 70	**GREATEST HITS** *A&M AMLS 980*	8		27
27 Jun 70	**DOWN MEXICO WAY** *A&M AMLS 974*	64		1
13 Nov 71	**AMERICA** *A&M AMLB 1000*	45		1
12 Nov 77	**40 GREATEST** *K-Tel NE 1005*	45		2
17 Nov 79	**RISE** *A&M AMLH 64790* HERB ALPERT ○	37		7
4 Apr 87	**KEEP YOUR EYE ON ME** *Breakout AMA 5125* HERB ALPERT	79		3
28 Sep 91	**THE VERY BEST OF HERB ALPERT** *A&M 3971651* HERB ALPERT ○	34		3

ALT
Ireland/New Zealand/UK, male vocal/instrumental group

Date	Title	Peak	Wks at No.1	1
24 Jun 95	**ALTITUDE** *Parlophone CDPCS 7377*	67		1

ALTER BRIDGE
US, male vocal/instrumental group

Date	Title	Peak	Wks at No.1	1
20 Oct 07	**BLACKBIRD** *Universal Republic 1747403*	37		1

ALTERED IMAGES
UK, female/male vocal/instrumental group

Date	Title	Peak	Wks at No.1	40
19 Sep 81	**HAPPY BIRTHDAY** *Epic EPC 84893* ○	26		21
15 May 82	**PINKY BLUE** *Epic EPC 85665* ○	12		10
25 Jun 83	**BITE** *Epic EPC 25413*	16		9

ALTERN 8
UK, male instrumental/production duo — 4

Date	Title / Label	Peak	Wks at No.1	Wks on Chart
25 Jul 92	**FULL ON...MASK HYSTERIA** *Network TOPCD 1*	11		4

ALVIN & THE CHIPMUNKS
US, chipmunk vocal group – created by Ross Bagdasarian, Sr. (aka David Seville), d. 16 Jan 1972 (age 52) — 3

Date	Title / Label	Peak	Wks at No.1	Wks on Chart
26 Apr 08	**ALVIN AND THE CHIPMUNKS (OST)** *UMTV 4780185*	61		3

ALY & AJ
US, female vocal/instrumental duo — 1

Date	Title / Label	Peak	Wks at No.1	Wks on Chart
3 Nov 07	**INSOMNIATIC** *Hollywood 162642*	72		1

SHOLA AMA
UK, female vocalist (Mathurin Campbell) — 32

Date	Title / Label	Peak	Wks at No.1	Wks on Chart
13 Sep 97	**MUCH LOVE** *WEA 3984200202* ●	6		32

AMAZULU
UK, female/male vocal/instrumental group — 1

Date	Title / Label	Peak	Wks at No.1	Wks on Chart
6 Dec 86	**AMAZULU** *Island ILPS 9851*	97		1

AMEN CORNER
UK, male vocal/instrumental group — 8

Date	Title / Label	Peak	Wks at No.1	Wks on Chart
30 Mar 68	**ROUND AMEN CORNER** *Deram SML 1021*	26		7
1 Nov 69	**EXPLOSIVE COMPANY** *Immediate IMSP 023*	19		1

AMERICA
US/UK, male vocal/instrumental trio — 22

Date	Title / Label	Peak	Wks at No.1	Wks on Chart
22 Jan 72	**AMERICA** *Warner Brothers K 46093* ★	14		13
9 Dec 72	**HOMECOMING** *Warner Brothers K 46180*	21		5
10 Nov 73	**HAT TRICK** *Warner Brothers K 56016* ○	41		3
7 Feb 76	**HISTORY – AMERICA'S GREATEST HITS** *Warner Brothers K 56169* ○	60		1

AMERICAN MUSIC CLUB
US, male vocal/instrumental group — 3

Date	Title / Label	Peak	Wks at No.1	Wks on Chart
27 Mar 93	**MERCURY** *Virgin CDV 2708*	41		2
24 Sep 94	**SAN FRANCISCO** *Virgin CDV 2752*	72		1

AMERIE
US, female vocalist (Amerie Rogers) — 9

Date	Title / Label	Peak	Wks at No.1	Wks on Chart
14 May 05	**TOUCH** *Columbia 5201662* ○	28		6
26 May 07	**BECAUSE I LOVE IT** *Columbia 88697085222* ○	17		3

AMICI FOREVER
UK/South Africa/New Zealand, male/female vocal group — 9

Date	Title / Label	Peak	Wks at No.1	Wks on Chart
27 Sep 03	**THE OPERA BAND** *Victor 82876558822* ●	39		9

AMORPHOUS ANDROGYNOUS
UK, male instrumental/production duo. See Future Sound Of London — 1

Date	Title / Label	Peak	Wks at No.1	Wks on Chart
17 Aug 02	**FSOL PRESENTS AMORPHOUS ANDROGYNOUS: THE ISNESS** *Artful FSOLCD 101*	68		1

TORI AMOS
UK, female vocalist/pianist (Myra Amos) — 56

Date	Title / Label	Peak	Wks at No.1	Wks on Chart
18 Jan 92	**LITTLE EARTHQUAKES** *East West 7567823582* ●	14		23
12 Feb 94	**UNDER THE PINK** *East West 7567825672* ⊛	1	1	13
3 Feb 96	**BOYS FOR PELE** *East West 7567828622* ●	2		6
16 May 98	**FROM THE CHOIRGIRL HOTEL** *Atlantic 7567830952* ○	6		5
2 Oct 99	**TO VENUS AND BACK** *Atlantic 7567832422*	22		2
29 Sep 01	**STRANGE LITTLE GIRLS** *Atlantic 7567834862*	16		2
9 Nov 02	**SCARLET'S WALK** *Epic 5087829*	26		1
29 Nov 03	**TALES OF A LIBRARIAN** *Atlantic 7567932232*	74		1
5 Mar 05	**THE BEEKEEPER** *Epic 5194259*	24		2
12 May 07	**AMERICAN DOLL POSSE** *Epic 82876861402*	50		1

AMPS
US, male/female vocal/instrumental group — 1

Date	Title / Label	Peak	Wks at No.1	Wks on Chart
11 Nov 95	**PACER** *4AD CAD 5016CD*	60		1

ANASTACIA
US, female vocalist (Anastacia Newkirk) — 174

Date	Title / Label	Peak	Wks at No.1	Wks on Chart
14 Oct 00	**NOT THAT KIND** *Epic 4974122* ⊛x3	2		65
8 Dec 01	**FREAK OF NATURE** *Epic 5047572* ⊛x3	4		42
10 Apr 04	**ANASTACIA** *Epic 5134717* ⊛x4	1	3	47
19 Nov 05	**PIECES OF A DREAM** *Epic 82876731992* ⊛	6		17
8 Nov 08	**HEAVY ROTATION** *Mercury 1787307*	17		3

AND WHY NOT
UK, male vocal/instrumental group — 3

Date	Title / Label	Peak	Wks at No.1	Wks on Chart
10 Mar 90	**MOVE YOUR SKIN** *Island ILPS 9935*	24		3

AND YOU WILL KNOW US BY THE TRAIL OF DEAD
US, male vocal/instrumental group — 1

Date	Title / Label	Peak	Wks at No.1	Wks on Chart
16 Mar 02	**SOURCE TAGS AND CODES** *Interscope 4932492*	73		1

BRETT ANDERSON
UK, male vocalist. See Suede — 1

Date	Title / Label	Peak	Wks at No.1	Wks on Chart
7 Apr 07	**BRETT ANDERSON** *Drowned In Sound DISO023*	54		1

CARLEEN ANDERSON
US, female vocalist. See Brand New Heavies — 7

Date	Title / Label	Peak	Wks at No.1	Wks on Chart
13 Nov 93	**DUSKY SAPPHO EP** *Circa YRCDG 108*	38		1
18 Jun 94	**TRUE SPIRIT** *Circa CIRCDX 30* ○	12		4
2 May 98	**BLESSED BURDEN** *Circa CIRCD 35*	51		2

IAN ANDERSON
UK, male vocalist/flute player. See Jethro Tull — 1

Date	Title / Label	Peak	Wks at No.1	Wks on Chart
26 Nov 83	**WALK INTO LIGHT** *Chrysalis CDL 1443*	78		1

JON ANDERSON
UK, male vocalist. See Anderson Bruford Wakeman Howe, Jon & Vangelis, Yes — 19

Date	Title / Label	Peak	Wks at No.1	Wks on Chart
24 Jul 76	**OLIAS OF SUNHILLOW** *Atlantic K 50261* ○	8		10
15 Nov 80	**SONG OF SEVEN** *Atlantic K 50756*	38		3
5 Jun 82	**ANIMATION** *Polydor POLD 5044*	43		6

LAURIE ANDERSON
US, female vocalist/multi-instrumentalist — 8

Date	Title / Label	Peak	Wks at No.1	Wks on Chart
1 May 82	**BIG SCIENCE** *Warner Brothers K 57002*	29		6
10 Mar 84	**MISTER HEARTBREAK** *Warner Brothers 9250771*	93		2

LYNN ANDERSON
US, female vocalist — 1

Date	Title / Label	Peak	Wks at No.1	Wks on Chart
17 Apr 71	**ROSE GARDEN** *CBS 64333*	45		1

MOIRA ANDERSON
UK, female vocalist — 6

Date	Title / Label	Peak	Wks at No.1	Wks on Chart
20 Jun 70	**THESE ARE MY SONGS** *Decca SKL 5016*	50		1
5 Dec 81	**GOLDEN MEMORIES** *Warwick WW 5107* HARRY SECOMBE & MOIRA ANDERSON	46		5

SUNSHINE ANDERSON
US, female vocalist — 6

Date	Title / Label	Peak	Wks at No.1	Wks on Chart
26 May 01	**YOUR WOMAN** *Atlantic 7567930112*	39		6

ANDERSON BRUFORD WAKEMAN HOWE
UK, male vocal/instrumental group — 6

Date	Title / Label	Peak	Wks at No.1	Wks on Chart
8 Jul 89	**ANDERSON BRUFORD WAKEMAN HOWE** *Arista 209970* ○	14		6

Silver-selling ○ Gold-selling ● Platinum-selling ⊛ US No.1 ★ | Peak Position | Weeks at No.1 | Weeks on Chart

JOHN ANDERSON ORCHESTRA

Ireland, male/female orchestra — **5**

Date	Title	Label	Peak	Wks at No.1	Wks on Chart
25 Nov 95	**PAN PIPES – ROMANCE OF IRELAND**	*MCA MCD 60004* ○	56		5

PETER ANDRE

UK, male vocalist (Peter Andrea) — **33**

Date	Title	Label	Peak	Wks at No.1	Wks on Chart
12 Oct 96	**NATURAL**	*Mushroom DX 2005* ⊛	1	1	23
29 Nov 97	**TIME**	*Mushroom MUSH 18CD* ●	28		4
19 Jun 04	**THE LONG ROAD BACK**	*East West 5046738102* ○	44		1
9 Dec 06	**A WHOLE NEW WORLD**	*K&P Recordings KANDPCD1* KATIE PRICE & PETER ANDRE ●	20		5

JULIE ANDREWS

UK, female vocalist/actor (Julia Wells) — **6**

Date	Title	Label	Peak	Wks at No.1	Wks on Chart
16 Jul 83	**LOVE ME TENDER**	*Peach River JULIE 1*	63		5
2 Sep 06	**AT HER VERY BEST**	*UCJ 9842693*	70		1

ANGEL CITY

Holland, male production duo — **2**

Date	Title	Label	Peak	Wks at No.1	Wks on Chart
12 Mar 05	**LOVE ME RIGHT**	*Data DATACD5X*	44		2

ANGELIC UPSTARTS

UK, male vocal/instrumental group — **20**

Date	Title	Label	Peak	Wks at No.1	Wks on Chart
18 Aug 79	**TEENAGE WARNING**	*Warner Brothers K 50634*	29		7
12 Apr 80	**WE'VE GOTTA GET OUT OF THIS PLACE**	*Warner Brothers K 56806*	54		3
7 Jun 81	**2,000,000 VOICES**	*Zonophone ZONO 104*	32		3
26 Sep 81	**ANGELIC UPSTARTS**	*Zonophone ZEM 102*	27		7

ANGELIS

UK, male/female vocal group – Sam Adams-Nye, Natalie Grace Chua, Amy Dow, Joe Martin, Camilla Seale & Moray West — **8**

Date	Title	Label	Peak	Wks at No.1	Wks on Chart
18 Nov 06	**ANGELIS**	*Syco Music 88697019802* ⊛	2		8

ANGELS & AIRWAVES

US, male vocal/instrumental group – Tom DeLonge, David Kennedy, Matt Wachter & Adam Willard — **4**

Date	Title	Label	Peak	Wks at No.1	Wks on Chart
3 Jun 06	**WE DON'T NEED TO WHISPER**	*Geffen 9878574* ○	6		3
17 Nov 07	**I-EMPIRE**	*Geffen 1749436*	29		1

ANIMAL NIGHTLIFE

UK, male/female vocal/instrumental group — **6**

Date	Title	Label	Peak	Wks at No.1	Wks on Chart
24 Aug 85	**SHANGRI-LA**	*Island ILPS 9830*	36		6

ANIMALS

UK, male vocal/instrumental group – Eric Burdon*, Brian 'Chas' Chandler, Alan Price*, John Steel & Hilton Valentine — **86**

Date	Title	Label	Peak	Wks at No.1	Wks on Chart
14 Nov 64	**THE ANIMALS**	*Columbia 33SX 1669*	6		20
22 May 65	**ANIMAL TRACKS**	*Columbia 33SX 1708*	6		26
16 Apr 66	**MOST OF THE ANIMALS**	*Columbia 33SX 6035*	4		20
28 May 66	**ANIMALISMS**	*Decca LK 4797*	4		17
25 Sep 71	**MOST OF THE ANIMALS**	*MFP MFP 5218*	18		3

PAUL ANKA

Canada, male vocalist — **8**

Date	Title	Label	Peak	Wks at No.1	Wks on Chart
15 Oct 05	**ROCK SWINGS**	*Globe Records 9885933* ●	9		4
27 Oct 07	**CLASSIC SONGS MY WAY**	*UMTV 1747398*	13		4

ANNIHILATOR

Canada, male vocal/instrumental group — **1**

Date	Title	Label	Peak	Wks at No.1	Wks on Chart
11 Aug 90	**NEVER NEVERLAND**	*Roadrunner RR 93741*	48		1

ANOTHER LEVEL

UK, male vocal group – Mark Baron, Dane Bowers, Bobak Kianoush & Wayne Williams — **40**

Date	Title	Label	Peak	Wks at No.1	Wks on Chart
21 Nov 98	**ANOTHER LEVEL**	*Northwestside 74321582412* ⊛	13		25
25 Sep 99	**NEXUS**	*Northwestside 74321700532* ●	7		15

JONATHAN ANSELL

UK, male vocalist. See G4 — **6**

Date	Title	Label	Peak	Wks at No.1	Wks on Chart
1 Mar 08	**TENOR AT THE MOVIES**	*UCJ 1756020*	9		4
22 Nov 08	**FOREVER**	*UCJ 1779242*	32		2

ANT & DEC

UK, male vocal duo/TV presenters – Declan Donnelly & Anthony McPartlin — **31**

Date	Title	Label	Peak	Wks at No.1	Wks on Chart
19 Nov 94	**PSYCHE – THE ALBUM**	*Xsrhythm TCD 2746* PJ & DUNCAN ⊛	5		20
18 Nov 95	**TOP KATZ – THE ALBUM**	*Telstar TCD 2793* PJ & DUNCAN ●	46		8
24 May 97	**THE CULT OF ANT & DEC**	*Telstar TCD 2887*	15		3

ANTHRAX

US, male vocal/instrumental group — **23**

Date	Title	Label	Peak	Wks at No.1	Wks on Chart
18 Apr 87	**AMONG THE LIVING**	*Island ILPS 9865* ○	18		5
24 Sep 88	**STATE OF EUPHORIA**	*Island ILPS 9916* ○	12		4
8 Sep 90	**PERSISTENCE OF TIME**	*Island ILPS 9967*	13		5
20 Jul 91	**ATTACK OF THE KILLER B'S**	*Island ILPS 9980*	13		5
29 May 93	**SOUND OF THE WHITE NOISE**	*Elektra 7559614302*	14		3
1 Aug 98	**VOLUME 8 – THE THREAT IS REAL!**	*Ignition IGN 740303*	73		1

ANTI-NOWHERE LEAGUE

UK, male vocal/instrumental group — **12**

Date	Title	Label	Peak	Wks at No.1	Wks on Chart
22 May 82	**WE ARE...THE LEAGUE**	*WXYZ LMNOP 1*	24		11
5 Nov 83	**LIVE IN YUGOSLAVIA**	*I.D. NOSE 3*	88		1

ANTI-PASTI

UK, male vocal/instrumental group — **7**

Date	Title	Label	Peak	Wks at No.1	Wks on Chart
15 Aug 81	**THE LAST CALL**	*Rondelet ABOUT 5*	31		7

ANTONY & THE JOHNSONS

UK/US/Canada/Russia, male/female vocal/instrumental group — **10**

Date	Title	Label	Peak	Wks at No.1	Wks on Chart
17 Sep 05	**I AM A BIRD NOW**	*Rough Trade RTRADCD223* ●	16		10

A1

UK/Norway, male vocal group — **19**

Date	Title	Label	Peak	Wks at No.1	Wks on Chart
4 Dec 99	**HERE WE COME**	*Columbia 4961362* ●	20		8
2 Dec 00	**THE A LIST**	*Columbia 5011952* ●	14		9
8 Jun 02	**MAKE IT GOOD**	*Columbia 5082212*	15		2

APACHE INDIAN

UK, male vocalist (Steven Kapur) — **2**

Date	Title	Label	Peak	Wks at No.1	Wks on Chart
6 Feb 93	**NO RESERVATIONS**	*Island CID 8001*	36		2

APHEX TWIN

UK, male producer/multi-instrumentalist (Richard James) — **11**

Date	Title	Label	Peak	Wks at No.1	Wks on Chart
19 Mar 94	**SELECTED AMBIENT WORKS VOLUME II**	*Warp WARPCD 21*	11		3
11 Feb 95	**CLASSICS**	*R&S RS 94035CD*	24		2
6 May 95	**...I CARE BECAUSE YOU DO**	*Warp WARPCD 30*	24		2
16 Nov 96	**RICHARD D JAMES ALBUM**	*Warp WARPCD 43*	62		1
3 Nov 01	**DRUKQS**	*Warp WARPCD 92*	22		2
5 Apr 03	**26 MIXES FOR CASH**	*Warp WARPCD 102*	63		1

APOLLO FOUR FORTY

UK, male instrumental/production group — **4**

Date	Title	Label	Peak	Wks at No.1	Wks on Chart
15 Mar 97	**ELECTRO GLIDE IN BLUE**	*Stealth Sonic SSX 2440CDR*	62		1
18 Sep 99	**GETTIN' HIGH ON YOUR OWN SUPPLY**	*Epic SSX 3440CD*	20		3

APOLLO 2000

UK, male producer/multi-instrumentalist (Gordon Smith) — **2**

Date	Title	Label	Peak	Wks at No.1	Wks on Chart
27 Apr 96	**OUT OF THIS WORLD**	*Telstar TCD 2816*	43		2

FIONA APPLE

US, female vocalist (Fiona Apple Maggart) — Weeks on Chart: 1

Date	Title	Peak Position	Weeks at No.1	Weeks on Chart
11 Mar 00	**WHEN THE PAWN HITS THE CONFLICTS HE THINKS LIKE A KING WHAT HE KNOWS THROWS THE BLOWS WHEN HE GOES TO THE FIGHT AND HE'LL WIN THE WHOLE THING 'FORE HE ENTERS THE RING THERE'S NOBODY TO BATTER WHEN YOUR MIND IS YOUR MIGHT SO WHEN YOU GO SOLO YOU HOLD YOUR OWN HAND AND REMEMBER THAT DEPTH IS THE GREATEST OF HEIGHTS AND IF YOU KNOW WHERE YOU STAND THEN YOU KNOW WHERE TO LAND AND IF YOU FALL IT WON'T MATTER CUZ YOU'LL KNOW THAT YOU'RE RIGHT** *Columbia 4964282*	46		1

KIM APPLEBY

UK, female vocalist. See Mel & Kim — Weeks on Chart: 13

Date	Title	Peak Position	Weeks at No.1	Weeks on Chart
8 Dec 90	**KIM APPLEBY** *Parlophone PCS 7348* ●	23		13

APPLETON

Canada, female vocal duo – Natalie & Nicole Appleton. See All Saints — Weeks on Chart: 6

Date	Title	Peak Position	Weeks at No.1	Weeks on Chart
8 Mar 03	**EVERYTHING'S EVENTUAL** *Polydor 0651992* ○	9		6

APRIL WINE

Canada, male vocal/instrumental group — Weeks on Chart: 8

Date	Title	Peak Position	Weeks at No.1	Weeks on Chart
15 Mar 80	**HARDER...FASTER** *Capitol EST 12013*	34		5
24 Jan 81	**THE NATURE OF THE BEAST** *Capitol EST 12125*	48		3

AQUA

Denmark/Norway, male/female vocal/production group – Lene Nystrom Rasted, René Dif, Claus Norreen & Soren Nystrom Rasted — Weeks on Chart: 49

Date	Title	Peak Position	Weeks at No.1	Weeks on Chart
15 Nov 97	**AQUARIUM** *Universal UMD 85020* ⊛	6		47
11 Mar 00	**AQUARIUS** *Universal 1538102*	24		2

AQUALUNG

UK, male vocalist/producer/instrumentalist (Matt Hales) — Weeks on Chart: 6

Date	Title	Peak Position	Weeks at No.1	Weeks on Chart
12 Oct 02	**AQUALUNG** *B Unique 5046606982* ○	15		6

ARAB STRAP

UK, male vocal/instrumental duo — Weeks on Chart: 3

Date	Title	Peak Position	Weeks at No.1	Weeks on Chart
2 May 98	**PHILOPHOBIA** *Chemikal Underground CHEM 021CD*	37		3

ARCADE FIRE

Canada, male/female vocal/instrumental group – Win Butler, Regine Chassagne, William Butler, Jeremy Gara, Tim Kingsbury, Sarah Neufeld, Owen Pallett & Richard Reed Parry — Weeks on Chart: 38

Date	Title	Peak Position	Weeks at No.1	Weeks on Chart
12 Mar 05	**FUNERAL** *Rough Trade RTRADCD219* ●	33		20
17 Mar 07	**NEON BIBLE** *Sonovox 1723674* ●	2		18

ARCADIA

UK, male vocal/instrumental group. See Duran Duran — Weeks on Chart: 10

Date	Title	Peak Position	Weeks at No.1	Weeks on Chart
7 Dec 85	**SO RED THE ROSE** *Parlophone Odeon PCSD 101*	30		10

TASMIN ARCHER

UK, female vocalist — Weeks on Chart: 42

Date	Title	Peak Position	Weeks at No.1	Weeks on Chart
31 Oct 92	**GREAT EXPECTATIONS** *EMI CDEMC 3624* ●	8		42

ARCTIC MONKEYS

UK, male vocal/instrumental group – Alex Turner, Jamie Cook, Matt Helders & Andy Nicholson (replaced by Nick O'Malley) — Weeks on Chart: 83

Date	Title	Peak Position	Weeks at No.1	Weeks on Chart
4 Feb 06	**WHATEVER PEOPLE SAY I AM, THAT'S WHAT I'M NOT** *Domino WIGCD162* ⊛**x4**	1	4	45
5 May 07	**FAVOURITE WORST NIGHTMARE** *Domino WIGCD188* ⊛**x2**	1	3	38

TINA ARENA

Australia, female vocalist (Filippina Arena) — Weeks on Chart: 15

Date	Title	Peak Position	Weeks at No.1	Weeks on Chart
20 May 95	**DON'T ASK** *Columbia 4778862* ○	11		15

ARGENT

UK, male vocal/instrumental group — Weeks on Chart: 9

Date	Title	Peak Position	Weeks at No.1	Weeks on Chart
29 Apr 72	**ALL TOGETHER NOW** *Epic EPC 64962*	13		8
31 Mar 73	**IN DEEP** *Epic EPC 65475*	49		1

INDIA ARIE

US, female vocalist (India.Arie Simpson) — Weeks on Chart: 3

Date	Title	Peak Position	Weeks at No.1	Weeks on Chart
7 Jul 01	**ACOUSTIC SOUL** *Motown 137702* ○	55		3

JOAN ARMATRADING

UK (b. St Kitts), female vocalist/guitarist — Weeks on Chart: 196

Date	Title	Peak Position	Weeks at No.1	Weeks on Chart
4 Sep 76	**JOAN ARMATRADING** *A&M AMLH 64588* ●	12		27
1 Oct 77	**SHOW SOME EMOTION** *A&M AMLH 68433* ●	6		11
14 Oct 78	**TO THE LIMIT** *A&M AMLH 64732*	13		10
24 May 80	**ME MYSELF I** *A&M AMLH 64809* ●	5		23
12 Sep 81	**WALK UNDER LADDERS** *A&M AMLH 64876* ●	6		29
12 Mar 83	**THE KEY** *A&M AMLX 64912* ●	10		14
26 Nov 83	**TRACK RECORD** *A&M JA 2001*	18		32
16 Feb 85	**SECRET SECRETS** *A&M AMA 5040* ○	14		12
24 May 86	**SLEIGHT OF HAND** *A&M AMA 5130* ○	34		6
16 Jul 88	**THE SHOUTING STAGE** *A&M AMA 5211* ○	28		10
16 Jun 90	**HEARTS AND FLOWERS** *A&M 3952981*	29		4
16 Mar 91	**THE VERY BEST OF JOAN ARMATRADING** *A&M 3971221* ●	9		11
20 Jun 92	**SQUARE THE CIRCLE** *A&M 3953882*	34		2
10 Jun 95	**WHAT'S INSIDE** *RCA 74321272692*	48		2
4 Sep 04	**LOVE AND AFFECTION – CLASSICS (1975-83)** *Universal TV 9823506*	24		3

ARMOURY SHOW

UK, male vocal/instrumental group — Weeks on Chart: 1

Date	Title	Peak Position	Weeks at No.1	Weeks on Chart
21 Sep 85	**WAITING FOR THE FLOODS** *Parlophone ARM 1*	57		1

CRAIG ARMSTRONG

UK, male musical director — Weeks on Chart: 1

Date	Title	Peak Position	Weeks at No.1	Weeks on Chart
27 Apr 02	**AS IF TO NOTHING** *Melankolic CDSAD 13*	61		1

LOUIS ARMSTRONG

US, male vocalist/trumpeter, d. 6 Jul 1971 (age 69) — Weeks on Chart: 32

Date	Title	Peak Position	Weeks at No.1	Weeks on Chart
28 Jul 56	**AT THE CRESCENDO** *Brunswick LAT 8084*	4		1
22 Oct 60	**SATCHMO PLAYS KING OLIVER** *Audio Fidelity AFLP 1930*	20		1
28 Oct 61	**JAZZ CLASSICS** *Ace Of Hearts AH 7*	20		1
27 Jun 64	**HELLO DOLLY** *London HAR 8190* ★	11		6
16 Nov 68	**WHAT A WONDERFUL WORLD** *Stateside SSL 10247*	37		3
20 Feb 82	**THE VERY BEST OF LOUIS ARMSTRONG** *Warwick WW 5112*	30		3
21 May 94	**THE ULTIMATE COLLECTION** *Bluebird 74321197062*	48		3
17 Dec 94	**WE HAVE ALL THE TIME IN THE WORLD – THE VERY BEST OF LOUIS ARMSTRONG** *EMI CDEMTV 89* ●	10		12
25 Oct 03	**AT HIS VERY BEST** *UCJ 9812425*	75		1
18 Sep 04	**ELLA AND LOUIS TOGETHER** *UCJ 9867768* ELLA FITZGERALD & LOUIS ARMSTRONG	43		1

DAVID ARNOLD

UK, male composer/multi-instrumentalist — Weeks on Chart: 11

Date	Title	Peak Position	Weeks at No.1	Weeks on Chart
17 Aug 96	**INDEPENDENCE DAY (OST)** *RCA Victor 09026685642*	71		1
1 Nov 97	**SHAKEN AND STIRRED** *East West 3984207382* ○	11		9
8 Nov 08	**QUANTUM OF SOLACE (OST)** *Columbia 88697405172*	64		1

ARRESTED DEVELOPMENT

US, male/female vocal/rap/instrumental group – fronted by Headliner (Timothy Barnwell) & Speech (Todd Thomas) — Weeks on Chart: 40

Date	Title	Peak Position	Weeks at No.1	Weeks on Chart
31 Oct 92	**3 YEARS, 5 MONTHS AND 2 DAYS IN THE LIFE OF...** *Cooltempo CCD 1929* ⊛	3		34
10 Apr 93	**UNPLUGGED** *Cooltempo CTCD 33* ○	40		3
18 Jun 94	**ZINGALAMDUNI** *Cooltempo CTCD 42*	16		3

STEVE ARRINGTON

US, male vocalist — Weeks on Chart: 11

Date	Title	Peak Position	Weeks at No.1	Weeks on Chart
13 Apr 85	**DANCIN' IN THE KEY OF LIFE** *Atlantic 7812451*	41		11

Legend: ○ Silver-selling · ● Gold-selling · ⊛ Platinum-selling · ★ US No.1 · Peak Position · Weeks at No.1 · Weeks on Chart

ART OF NOISE
UK, male/female instrumental/production trio — 37

Date	Title / Label	Peak Position	Weeks at No.1	Weeks on Chart
3 Nov 84	(WHO'S AFRAID OF) THE ART OF NOISE *ZTT ZTTIQ 2* ○	27		17
26 Apr 86	IN VISIBLE SILENCE *Chrysalis WOL 2*	18		15
10 Oct 87	IN NO SENSE/NONSENSE *China WOL 4*	55		2
3 Dec 88	THE BEST OF ART OF NOISE *China 8373671*	55		3

ARTFUL DODGER
UK, male production/instrumental duo — 27

Date	Title / Label	Peak Position	Weeks at No.1	Weeks on Chart
2 Dec 00	IT'S ALL ABOUT THE STRAGGLERS *ffrr 8573859092* ●	18		27

A.S.A.P
UK, male vocal/instrumental group — 1

Date	Title / Label	Peak Position	Weeks at No.1	Weeks on Chart
4 Nov 89	SILVER AND GOLD *EMI EMC 3566*	70		1

ASH
UK, male vocal/instrumental group – Tim Wheeler, Mark Hamilton & Rick McMurray — 74

Date	Title / Label	Peak Position	Weeks at No.1	Weeks on Chart
18 May 96	1977 *Infectious INFECT 40CD* ⊛	1	1	27
17 Oct 98	NU-CLEAR SOUNDS *Infectious INFECT 060CD* ●	7		4
5 May 01	FREE ALL ANGELS *Infectious INFECT 100CD* ⊛	1	1	28
21 Sep 02	INTERGALACTIC SONIC 7'S *Infectious INFECT 120CD* ●	3		6
29 May 04	MELTDOWN *Infectious 5046732462* ●	5		8
14 Jul 07	TWILIGHT OF THE INNOCENTS *Infectious 2564698565*	32		1

ASHANTI
US, female vocalist (Ashanti Douglas) — 51

Date	Title / Label	Peak Position	Weeks at No.1	Weeks on Chart
20 Apr 02	ASHANTI *Mercury 5868302* ⊛ ★	3		36
12 Jul 03	CHAPTER II *Murder Inc 9808434* ● ★	5		8
15 Jan 05	CONCRETE ROSE *Mercury/The Inc 2103261* ●	25		7

RICHARD ASHCROFT
UK, male vocalist/multi-instrumentalist. See Verve — 48

Date	Title / Label	Peak Position	Weeks at No.1	Weeks on Chart
8 Jul 00	ALONE WITH EVERYBODY *Hut CDHUTX 63* ⊛	1	1	20
2 Nov 02	HUMAN CONDITIONS *Hut CDHUT 77* ●	3		10
4 Feb 06	KEYS TO THE WORLD *Parlophone 3545212* ⊛	2		18

ASHFORD & SIMPSON
US, male/female vocal duo — 6

Date	Title / Label	Peak Position	Weeks at No.1	Weeks on Chart
16 Feb 85	SOLID *Capitol SASH 1*	42		6

ASIA
UK, male vocal/instrumental group – John Wetton, Geoff Downes, Steve Howe* & Carl Palmer — 50

Date	Title / Label	Peak Position	Weeks at No.1	Weeks on Chart
10 Apr 82	ASIA *Geffen GEF 85577* ● ★	11		38
20 Aug 83	ALPHA *Geffen GEF 25508* ○	5		11
14 Dec 85	ASTRA *Geffen GEF 26413*	68		1

ASIAN DUB FOUNDATION
UK, male vocal/instrumental group — 6

Date	Title / Label	Peak Position	Weeks at No.1	Weeks on Chart
23 May 98	RAFI'S REVENGE *ffrr 5560062*	20		3
1 Apr 00	COMMUNITY MUSIC *ffrr 8573820422*	20		3

ASSOCIATES
UK, male vocal/instrumental duo – Billy MacKenzie, d. 22 Jan 1997, & Alan Rankine — 28

Date	Title / Label	Peak Position	Weeks at No.1	Weeks on Chart
22 May 82	SULK *Associates ASCL 1*	10		20
16 Feb 85	PERHAPS *WEA WX 9*	23		7
31 Mar 90	WILD AND LONELY *Circa 11*	71		1

RICK ASTLEY
UK, male vocalist — 72

Date	Title / Label	Peak Position	Weeks at No.1	Weeks on Chart
28 Nov 87	WHENEVER YOU NEED SOMEBODY *RCA PL 71529* ⊛x4	1	1	34
10 Dec 88	HOLD ME IN YOUR ARMS *RCA PL 71932* ⊛	8		19
2 Mar 91	FREE *RCA PL 74896* ●	9		9
14 Sep 02	GREATEST HITS *BMG 74321955122* ●	16		4
29 Oct 05	PORTRAIT *RCA 82876734312*	26		3
10 May 08	THE ULTIMATE COLLECTION *RCA 88697303802*	17		3

ASWAD
UK, male vocal/instrumental group – Brinsley Forde, Drummie Zeb (Angus Gaye) & Tony Robinson — 61

Date	Title / Label	Peak Position	Weeks at No.1	Weeks on Chart
24 Jul 82	NOT SATISFIED *CBS 85666*	50		6
10 Dec 83	LIVE AND DIRECT *Island IMA 6*	57		16
3 Nov 84	REBEL SOULS *Island ILPS 9780*	48		2
28 Jun 86	TO THE TOP *Simba SIMBALP 2*	71		3
9 Apr 88	DISTANT THUNDER *Mango ILPS 9895* ●	10		15
3 Dec 88	RENAISSANCE *Stylus SMR 866*	52		8
22 Sep 90	TOO WICKED *Mango MLPS 1054*	51		2
9 Jul 94	RISE AND SHINE *Bubblin' BUBBCD 1*	38		5
12 Aug 95	GREATEST HITS *Bubblin' BUBBCD 4*	20		3
24 Aug 02	COOL SUMMER REGGAE *Universal Music TV 0643762*	54		1

AT THE DRIVE IN
US, male vocal/instrumental group — 2

Date	Title / Label	Peak Position	Weeks at No.1	Weeks on Chart
30 Sep 00	RELATIONSHIP OF COMMAND *Grand Royal CDVUS 184*	33		2

ATB
Germany, male producer (Andre Tanneberger) — 3

Date	Title / Label	Peak Position	Weeks at No.1	Weeks on Chart
8 Apr 00	MOVIN MELODIES *Sound Of Ministry ATB CDZ1* ○	32		3

ATHLETE
UK, male vocal/instrumental group – Joel Pott, Steve Roberts, Tim Wanstall & Cary Willets — 64

Date	Title / Label	Peak Position	Weeks at No.1	Weeks on Chart
19 Apr 03	VEHICLES & ANIMALS *Parlophone 5842112* ⊛	19		32
12 Feb 05	TOURIST *Parlophone 5637040* ⊛	1	1	29
15 Sep 07	BEYOND THE NEIGHBOURHOOD *Parlophone 5031772* ●	5		3

ATHLETICO SPIZZ 80
UK, male vocal/instrumental group — 5

Date	Title / Label	Peak Position	Weeks at No.1	Weeks on Chart
26 Jul 80	DO A RUNNER *A&M AMLE 68514*	27		5

CHET ATKINS
US, male guitarist (Chester Atkins), d. 30 Jun 2001 (age 77) — 16

Date	Title / Label	Peak Position	Weeks at No.1	Weeks on Chart
18 Mar 61	THE OTHER CHET ATKINS *RCA RD 27194*	20		1
17 Jun 61	CHET ATKINS WORKSHOP *RCA RD 27214*	19		1
2 Mar 63	CARIBBEAN GUITAR *RCA RD 7519*	17		3
24 Nov 90	NECK AND NECK *CBS 4674351* & MARK KNOPFLER	41		11

ROWAN ATKINSON
UK, male comedian/actor. See Not The 9 O'Clock News Cast — 9

Date	Title / Label	Peak Position	Weeks at No.1	Weeks on Chart
7 Feb 81	LIVE IN BELFAST *Arista SPART 1150* ○	44		9

ATLANTIC STARR
US, male/female vocal/instrumental group — 19

Date	Title / Label	Peak Position	Weeks at No.1	Weeks on Chart
15 Jun 85	AS THE BAND TURNS *A&M AMA 5019*	64		3
13 Jul 85	THE ARTISTS VOLUME 2 *Street Sounds ARTIS 2* LUTHER VANDROSS/TEDDY PENDERGRASS/CHANGE/ATLANTIC STARR	45		4
11 Jul 87	ALL IN THE NAME OF LOVE *WEA WX 115*	48		12

ATOMIC KITTEN
UK, female vocal group – Natasha Hamilton, Kerry Katona (replaced by Jenny Frost) & Liz McClarnon — 83

Date	Title / Label	Peak Position	Weeks at No.1	Weeks on Chart
4 Nov 00	RIGHT NOW *Innocent CDSIN 6* ⊛	1	1	37
21 Sep 02	FEELS SO GOOD *Innocent CDSIN 10* ⊛x2	1	1	27
22 Nov 03	LADIES NIGHT *Innocent CDSIN 14* ⊛	5		11
17 Apr 04	THE GREATEST HITS *Innocent CDSIN 16* ●	5		8

ATOMIC ROOSTER
UK, male vocal/instrumental group — 13

Date	Title / Label	Peak Position	Weeks at No.1	Weeks on Chart
13 Jun 70	ATOMIC ROOSTER *B&C CAS 1010*	49		1
16 Jan 71	DEATH WALKS BEHIND YOU *Charisma CAS 1026*	12		8
21 Aug 71	IN HEARING OF ATOMIC ROOSTER *Pegasus PEG 1*	18		4

ATREYU
US, male vocal/instrumental group — 1

Date	Title / Label	Peak Position	Weeks at No.1	Weeks on Chart
8 Sep 07	LEAD SAILS PAPER ANCHOR *Roadrunner RR79572*	61		1

Silver-selling ○ Gold-selling ● Platinum-selling US No.1 ★

AU PAIRS

UK, female/male vocal/instrumental group — **10**

Date	Title	Label	Peak	Wks at No.1	Wks in Chart
6 Jun 81	PLAYING WITH A DIFFERENT SEX	*Human 1*	33		7
4 Sep 82	SENSE AND SENSUALITY	*Kamera KAM 010*	79		3

AUDIO BULLYS

UK, male vocal/production duo — **5**

Date	Title	Label	Peak	Wks at No.1	Wks in Chart
14 Jun 03	EGO WAR	*Source CDSOUR073* ○	19		3
12 Nov 05	GENERATION	*Source CDSOUR107*	33		2

AUDIOSLAVE

US, male vocal/instrumental group – Chris Cornell*, Tim Commerford, Tom Morello & Brad Wilk — **28**

Date	Title	Label	Peak	Wks at No.1	Wks in Chart
30 Nov 02	AUDIOSLAVE	*Epic/Interscope 5101302* ●	19		20
4 Jun 05	OUT OF EXILE	*Epic/Interscope 9882468* ★	5		5
16 Sep 06	REVELATIONS	*Epic/Interscope 82796977282*	12		3

AUDIOWEB

UK, male vocal/instrumental group — **1**

Date	Title	Label	Peak	Wks at No.1	Wks in Chart
9 Nov 96	AUDIOWEB	*Mother MUMCD 9604*	70		1

AUF DER MAUR

Canada, female vocalist/guitarist (Melissa Auf Der Maur). See Smashing Pumpkins — **2**

Date	Title	Label	Peak	Wks at No.1	Wks in Chart
13 Mar 04	AUF DER MAUR	*EMI 5943082CD*	31		2

PATTI AUSTIN

US, female vocalist — **1**

Date	Title	Label	Peak	Wks at No.1	Wks in Chart
26 Sep 81	EVERY HOME SHOULD HAVE ONE	*Qwest K 56931*	99		1

AUTEURS

UK, male/female vocal/instrumental group — **4**

Date	Title	Label	Peak	Wks at No.1	Wks in Chart
6 Mar 93	NEW WAVE	*Hut CDHUT 7*	35		2
21 May 94	NOW I'M A COWBOY	*Hut CDHUT 16*	27		1
16 Mar 96	AFTER MURDER PARK	*Hut DGHUT 33*	53		1

AUTOMATIC

UK, male vocal/instrumental group – Robin Hawkins, James Frost, Iwan Griffiths & Alex Pennie (replaced by Paul Mullen) — **21**

Date	Title	Label	Peak	Wks at No.1	Wks in Chart
1 Jul 06	NOT ACCEPTED ANYWHERE	*B Unique/Polydor BUN107* ●	3		20
6 Sep 08	THIS IS A FIX	*B Unique/Polydor BUN138CD*	44		1

AVALANCHES

Australia, male production group – Robbie Chater, Tony Diblasi & Darren Seltmann — **25**

Date	Title	Label	Peak	Wks at No.1	Wks in Chart
28 Apr 01	SINCE I LEFT YOU	*XL Recordings XLCD 138* ●	8		25

AVENGED SEVENFOLD

US, male vocal/instrumental group — **4**

Date	Title	Label	Peak	Wks at No.1	Wks in Chart
18 Jun 05	CITY OF EVIL	*WEA 9362486132*	63		1
10 Nov 07	AVENGED SEVENFOLD	*Warner Brothers 9362499143*	24		2
27 Sep 08	LIVE	*Warner Brothers 9362498702*	42		1

AVERAGE WHITE BAND

UK, male vocal/instrumental group – Onnie McIntyre, Roger Ball, Malcolm Duncan, Alan Gorrie, Robbie McIntosh, d. 23 Sep 1974 (replaced by Steve Ferrone), & Hamish Stuart — **50**

Date	Title	Label	Peak	Wks at No.1	Wks in Chart
1 Mar 75	AVERAGE WHITE BAND	*Atlantic K 50058* ○ ★	6		14
5 Jul 75	CUT THE CAKE	*Atlantic K 50146*	28		4
31 Jul 76	SOUL SEARCHING TIME	*Atlantic K 50272*	60		1
10 Mar 79	I FEEL NO FRET	*RCA XL 13063* ○	15		15
31 May 80	SHINE	*RCA XL 13123*	14		13
2 Apr 94	LET'S GO ROUND AGAIN – THE BEST OF AWB	*The Hit Label AHLCD 15* ○	38		3

Top 30 Acts by Weeks at No.1

Pos	Artist	Weeks at No.1
1	**BEATLES**	**174**
2	**ELVIS PRESLEY**	**63**
3	**ABBA**	**57**
4	ROLLING STONES	44
5	SHADOWS	42
6	SIMON & GARFUNKEL	40
7	CLIFF RICHARD	30
8	CARPENTERS	29
9	MADONNA	28
10	ROBBIE WILLIAMS	28
11	ELTON JOHN	28
12	ROD STEWART	27
13	SIMPLY RED	26
14	PHIL COLLINS	25
15	MICHAEL JACKSON	22
16	DAVID BOWIE	22
17	DIRE STRAITS	22
18	BOB DYLAN	22
19	QUEEN	21
20	OASIS	20
21	TAKE THAT	20
22	CELINE DION	18
23	SPICE GIRLS	18
24	BARBRA STREISAND	18
25	PAUL McCARTNEY	17
26	POLICE	17
27	GEORGE MITCHELL MINSTRELS	17
28	DIDO	17
29	DIANA ROSS	16
30	FRANK SINATRA	16

ROY AYERS
US, male vocalist/vibraphone player — 2

Date	Title	Label	Peak	Wks at No.1	Wks on Chart
26 Oct 85	YOU MIGHT BE SURPRISED	*CBS 26653*	91		2

PAM AYRES
UK, female poet — 29

Date	Title	Label	Peak	Wks at No.1	Wks on Chart
27 Mar 76	SOME OF ME POEMS AND SONGS	*Galaxy GAL 6003*	13		23
11 Dec 76	SOME MORE OF ME POEMS AND SONGS	*Galaxy GAL 6010*	23		6

CHARLES AZNAVOUR
France, male vocalist (Shanaur Aznavourian) — 21

Date	Title	Label	Peak	Wks at No.1	Wks on Chart
29 Jun 74	AZNAVOUR SINGS AZNAVOUR VOLUME 3	*Barclay 80472*	23		7
7 Sep 74	A TAPESTRY OF DREAMS	*Barclay 90003*	9		13
2 Aug 80	HIS GREATEST LOVE SONGS	*K-Tel NE 1078*	73		1

AZTEC CAMERA
UK, male vocal/instrumental group – Roddy Frame* & various session musicians — 80

Date	Title	Label	Peak	Wks at No.1	Wks on Chart
23 Apr 83	HIGH LAND HARD RAIN	*Rough Trade 47*	22		18
29 Sep 84	KNIFE	*WEA WX 8*	14		6
21 Nov 87	LOVE	*WEA WX 128*	10		43
16 Jun 90	STRAY	*WEA WX 350*	22		7
29 May 93	DREAMLAND	*WEA 4509924922*	21		2
7 Aug 99	THE BEST OF AZTEC CAMERA	*warner.esp 3984289842*	36		4

B

DEREK B
UK, male rapper (Derek Boland) — 9

Date	Title	Label	Peak	Wks at No.1	Wks on Chart
28 May 88	BULLET FROM A GUN	*Tuff Audio DRKLP 1*	11		9

ERIC B & RAKIM
US, male DJ/rap duo — 10

Date	Title	Label	Peak	Wks at No.1	Wks on Chart
12 Sep 87	PAID IN FULL	*Fourth & Broadway BRLP 514*	85		4
6 Aug 88	FOLLOW THE LEADER	*MCA MCG 6031*	25		4
7 Jul 90	LET THE RHYTHM HIT 'EM	*MCA MCG 6097*	58		1
11 Jul 92	DON'T SWEAT THE TECHNIQUE	*MCA MCAD 10594*	73		1

HOWIE B
UK, male producer (Howard Bernstein) — 1

Date	Title	Label	Peak	Wks at No.1	Wks on Chart
9 Aug 97	TURN THE DARK OFF	*Polydor 5379342*	58		1

MELANIE B
UK, female vocalist (Melanie Brown). See Spice Girls — 2

Date	Title	Label	Peak	Wks at No.1	Wks on Chart
21 Oct 00	HOT	*Virgin CDVX 2918*	28		2

B BOYS
US, male vocal/instrumental group — 1

Date	Title	Label	Peak	Wks at No.1	Wks on Chart
28 Jan 84	CUTTIN' HERBIE	*Streetwave XKHAN 501*	90		1

B*WITCHED
Ireland, female vocal group – Edele & Keavy Lynch, Lindsay Armaou & Sinéad O'Carroll — 48

Date	Title	Label	Peak	Wks at No.1	Wks on Chart
24 Oct 98	B*WITCHED	*Glow Worm 4917042* x2	3		36
30 Oct 99	AWAKE AND BREATHE	*Glow Worm 4960792*	5		12

BABES IN TOYLAND
US, female vocal/instrumental group — 3

Date	Title	Label	Peak	Wks at No.1	Wks on Chart
5 Sep 92	FONTANELLE	*Southern 185012*	24		2
3 Jul 93	PAINKILLER	*Southern 185122*	53		1

BABY ANIMALS
Australia, male vocal/instrumental group — 1

Date	Title	Label	Peak	Wks at No.1	Wks on Chart
14 Mar 92	BABY ANIMALS	*Imago PD 90580*	70		1

BABY D
UK, male/female vocal/instrumental duo – Dee Galdes-Fearon & Terry Jones — 5

Date	Title	Label	Peak	Wks at No.1	Wks on Chart
10 Feb 96	DELIVERANCE	*Systematic 8286832*	5		5

BABYBIRD
UK, male vocal/instrumental group – Stephen Jones, Huw Chadbourn, Robert Gregory, John Pedder & Luke Scott — 14

Date	Title	Label	Peak	Wks at No.1	Wks on Chart
2 Nov 96	UGLY BEAUTIFUL	*Echo ECHCD 11*	9		12
5 Sep 98	THERE'S SOMETHING GOING ON	*Echo ECHCD 024*	28		2

BABYFACE
US, male vocalist/producer (Kenneth Edmonds) — 5

Date	Title	Label	Peak	Wks at No.1	Wks on Chart
16 Nov 96	THE DAY	*Epic 4853682*	34		5

BABYLON ZOO
UK, male vocalist/multi-instrumentalist (Jas Mann) — 5

Date	Title	Label	Peak	Wks at No.1	Wks on Chart
17 Feb 96	THE BOY WITH THE X-RAY EYES	*EMI CDEMC 3742*	6		5

BABYSHAMBLES
UK, male vocal/instrumental group – Pete Doherty, Adam Ficek, Drew McConnell & Mick Whitnall — 8

Date	Title	Label	Peak	Wks at No.1	Wks on Chart
26 Nov 05	DOWN IN ALBION	*Rough Trade RTRADCD240*	10		2
16 Dec 06	THE BLINDING EP	*Regal 3799022*	62		1
13 Oct 07	SHOTTER'S NATION	*Parlophone 5086202*	5		5

BACCARA
Spain, female vocal duo — 6

Date	Title	Label	Peak	Wks at No.1	Wks on Chart
4 Mar 78	BACCARA	*RCA PL 28316*	26		6

BURT BACHARACH
US, male pianist — 48

Date	Title	Label	Peak	Wks at No.1	Wks on Chart
22 May 65	HIT MAKER – BURT BACHARACH	*London HAR 8233*	3		18
22 Jul 67	CASINO ROYALE (OST)	*RCA Victor SF 7874*	35		1
28 Nov 70	REACH OUT	*A&M AMLS 908*	52		3
27 Mar 71	PORTRAIT IN MUSIC	*A&M AMLS 2010*	5		23
10 Oct 98	PAINTED FROM MEMORY	*Mercury 5380022* ELVIS COSTELLO WITH BURT BACHARACH	32		2
5 Nov 05	AT THIS TIME	*Sony BMG 82876742832*	60		1

BACHELORS
Ireland, male vocal/instrumental trio – Con Cluskey, Declan Cluskey & John Stokes — 110

Date	Title	Label	Peak	Wks at No.1	Wks on Chart
27 Jun 64	THE BACHELORS AND 16 GREAT SONGS	*Decca LK 4614*	2		44
9 Oct 65	MORE GREAT SONG HITS FROM THE BACHELORS	*Decca LK 4721*	15		6
9 Jul 66	HITS OF THE SIXTIES	*Decca TXL 102*	12		9
5 Nov 66	BACHELORS' GIRLS	*Decca LK 4827*	24		8
1 Jul 67	GOLDEN ALL TIME HITS	*Decca SKL 4849*	19		7
14 Jun 69	WORLD OF THE BACHELORS	*Decca SPA 2*	8		18
23 Aug 69	WORLD OF THE BACHELORS VOLUME 2	*Decca SPA 22*	11		7
22 Dec 79	25 GOLDEN GREATS	*Warwick WW 5068*	38		4
2 Aug 08	I BELIEVE – THE VERY BEST OF	*Decca 5310802*	7		7

BACHMAN-TURNER OVERDRIVE
Canada, male vocal/instrumental group — 13

Date	Title	Label	Peak	Wks at No.1	Wks on Chart
14 Dec 74	NOT FRAGILE	*Mercury 9100 007* ★	12		13

BACK TO THE PLANET
UK, male/female vocal/instrumental group — 2

Date	Title	Label	Peak	Wks at No.1	Wks on Chart
18 Sep 93	MIND AND SOUL COLLABORATORS	*Parallel ALLCD 2*	32		2

Key: Silver-selling ○ · Gold-selling ● · Platinum-selling ⊛ · US No.1 ★ · Peak Position · Weeks at No.1 · Weeks on Chart

BACKBEAT
US, male vocal/instrumental group — Total weeks on chart: 2

Date	Title / Label	Peak Position	Weeks at No.1	Weeks on Chart
16 Apr 94	**BACKBEAT (OST)** *Virgin CDV 2729*	39		2

BACKSTREET BOYS
US, male vocal/instrumental group – Nick Carter, Howie Dorough, Brian Littrell, A.J. McLean & Kevin Richardson (left 2006) — Total weeks on chart: 153

Date	Title / Label	Peak Position	Weeks at No.1	Weeks on Chart
21 Sep 96	**BACKSTREET BOYS** *Jive CHIPR 169* ●	12		19
23 Aug 97	**BACKSTREET'S BACK** *Jive CHIP 186* ⊛x2	2		44
29 May 99	**MILLENNIUM** *Jive 0523222* ⊛ ★	2		56
2 Dec 00	**BLACK AND BLUE** *Jive 9221172* ● ★	13		9
10 Nov 01	**GREATEST HITS – CHAPTER ONE** *Jive 9222672* ⊛	5		18
25 Jun 05	**NEVER GONE** *Jive 82876702972* ●	11		5
10 Nov 07	**UNBREAKABLE** *Jive 88697169672*	21		2

BAD BOYS INC.
UK, male vocal group — Total weeks on chart: 6

Date	Title / Label	Peak Position	Weeks at No.1	Weeks on Chart
16 Apr 94	**BAD BOYS INC.** *A&M 5402002*	13		6

BAD COMPANY
UK, male vocal/instrumental group – Paul Rodgers*, Boz Burrell, Simon Kirke & Mick Ralphs — Total weeks on chart: 87

Date	Title / Label	Peak Position	Weeks at No.1	Weeks on Chart
15 Jun 74	**BAD COMPANY** *Island ILPS 9279* ● ★	3		25
12 Apr 75	**STRAIGHT SHOOTER** *Island ILPS 9304* ●	3		27
21 Feb 76	**RUN WITH THE PACK** *Island ILPS 9346* ●	4		12
19 Mar 77	**BURNIN' SKY** *Island ILPS 9441*	17		8
17 Mar 79	**DESOLATION ANGELS** *Swan Song SSK 59408*	10		9
28 Aug 82	**ROUGH DIAMONDS** *Swan Song SSK 59419*	15		6

BAD ENGLISH
UK/US, male vocal/instrumental group — Total weeks on chart: 2

Date	Title / Label	Peak Position	Weeks at No.1	Weeks on Chart
16 Sep 89	**BAD ENGLISH** *Epic 4634471*	74		1
19 Oct 91	**BACKLASH** *Epic 4685691*	64		1

BAD MANNERS
UK, male vocal/instrumental group — Total weeks on chart: 44

Date	Title / Label	Peak Position	Weeks at No.1	Weeks on Chart
26 Apr 80	**SKA 'N' B** *Magnet MAG 5033* ○	34		13
29 Nov 80	**LOONEE TUNES** *Magnet MAG 5038* ○	36		12
24 Oct 81	**GOSH IT'S BAD MANNERS** *Magnet MAGL 5043* ○	18		12
27 Nov 82	**FORGING AHEAD** *Magnet MAGL 5050*	78		1
7 May 83	**THE HEIGHT OF BAD MANNERS** *Telstar STAR 2229*	23		6

BAD NEWS
UK, male vocal group — Total weeks on chart: 1

Date	Title / Label	Peak Position	Weeks at No.1	Weeks on Chart
24 Oct 87	**BAD NEWS** *EMI EMC 3535*	69		1

ANGELO BADALAMENTI
US, male arranger/composer

Date	Title / Label	Peak Position	Weeks at No.1	Weeks on Chart
17 Nov 90	**MUSIC FROM 'TWIN PEAKS'** *Warner Brothers 7599263161* ●	27		25

BOOTH & THE BAD ANGEL
UK, male vocalist (Tim Booth) & US, male composer (Angelo Badalamenti). See James — Total weeks on chart: 27

Date	Title / Label	Peak Position	Weeks at No.1	Weeks on Chart
13 Jul 96	**BOOTH AND THE BAD ANGEL** *Fontana 5268522*	35		2

BADLANDS
UK, male vocal/instrumental group — Total weeks on chart: 3

Date	Title / Label	Peak Position	Weeks at No.1	Weeks on Chart
24 Jun 89	**BADLANDS** *WEA 7819661*	39		2
22 Jun 91	**VOODOO HIGHWAY** *Atlantic 7567822511*	74		1

BADLY DRAWN BOY
UK, male vocalist/producer/guitarist/pianist (Damon Gough) — Total weeks on chart: 91

Date	Title / Label	Peak Position	Weeks at No.1	Weeks on Chart
8 Jul 00	**THE HOUR OF BEWILDERBEAST** *XL Recordings TNXLCD 133* ⊛	13		47
20 Apr 02	**ABOUT A BOY – OST** *Twisted Nerve TNXLCD 152* ●	6		18
16 Nov 02	**HAVE YOU FED THE FISH?** *XL Recordings TNXLCD 156* ●	10		20
3 Jul 04	**ONE PLUS ONE IS ONE** *Twisted Nerve TNXLCD 179* ○	9		4
28 Oct 06	**BORN IN THE UK** *EMI 3740472* ○	17		2

ERYKAH BADU
US, female vocalist (Erica Wright) — Total weeks on chart: 26

Date	Title / Label	Peak Position	Weeks at No.1	Weeks on Chart
1 Mar 97	**BADUIZM** *MCA UND 53027* ●	17		25
15 Mar 08	**NEW AMERYKAH PART ONE (4TH WORLD WAR)** *Motown 1762187*	55		1

JOAN BAEZ
US, female vocalist/guitarist — Total weeks on chart: 88

Date	Title / Label	Peak Position	Weeks at No.1	Weeks on Chart
18 Jul 64	**JOAN BAEZ IN CONCERT VOLUME 2** *Fontana TFL 6033*	8		19
15 May 65	**JOAN BAEZ NO. 5** *Fontana TFL 6043*	3		27
19 Jun 65	**JOAN BAEZ** *Fontana TFL 6002*	9		13
27 Nov 65	**FAREWELL ANGELINA** *Fontana TFL 6058*	5		23
19 Jul 69	**JOAN BAEZ ON VANGUARD** *Vanguard SVXL 100*	15		5
3 Apr 71	**FIRST TEN YEARS** *Vanguard 6635 003*	41		1

PHILIP BAILEY
US, male vocalist/drummer. See Earth, Wind & Fire — Total weeks on chart: 17

Date	Title / Label	Peak Position	Weeks at No.1	Weeks on Chart
30 Mar 85	**CHINESE WALL** *CBS 26161*	29		17

ANITA BAKER
US, female vocalist — Total weeks on chart: 83

Date	Title / Label	Peak Position	Weeks at No.1	Weeks on Chart
3 May 86	**RAPTURE** *Elektra EKT 37* ⊛	13		47
29 Oct 88	**GIVING YOU THE BEST THAT I GOT** *Elektra EKT 49* ● ★	9		20
14 Jul 90	**COMPOSITIONS** *Elektra EKT 72* ●	7		9
24 Sep 94	**RHYTHM OF LOVE** *Elektra 7559615552*	14		5
1 Jun 02	**SWEET LOVE – THE VERY BEST OF ANITA BAKER** *Atlantic 8122736032*	49		2

GINGER BAKER'S AIR FORCE
UK, male vocal/instrumental group

Date	Title / Label	Peak Position	Weeks at No.1	Weeks on Chart
13 Jun 70	**GINGER BAKER'S AIR FORCE** *Polydor 2662 001*	37		1

BAKER-GURVITZ ARMY
UK, male vocal/instrumental group — Total weeks on chart: 6

Date	Title / Label	Peak Position	Weeks at No.1	Weeks on Chart
22 Feb 75	**BAKER-GURVITZ ARMY** *Vertigo 9103 201*	22		5

BALAAM & THE ANGEL
UK, male vocal/instrumental group — Total weeks on chart: 2

Date	Title / Label	Peak Position	Weeks at No.1	Weeks on Chart
16 Aug 86	**THE GREATEST STORY EVER TOLD** *Virgin V 2377*	67		2

KENNY BALL
UK, male trumpeter/vocalist — Total weeks on chart: 50

Date	Title / Label	Peak Position	Weeks at No.1	Weeks on Chart
25 Aug 62	**BEST OF BALL, BARBER AND BILK** *Pye Golden Guinea GGL 0131* KENNY BALL, CHRIS BARBER & ACKER BILK	1	2	24
7 Sep 63	**KENNY BALL'S GOLDEN HITS** *Pye Golden Guinea GGL 0209*	4		26

MICHAEL BALL
UK, male vocalist/actor — Total weeks on chart: 119

Date	Title / Label	Peak Position	Weeks at No.1	Weeks on Chart
30 May 92	**MICHAEL BALL** *Polydor 5113302* ●	1	1	10
17 Jul 93	**ALWAYS** *Polydor 5196662* ●	3		11
13 Aug 94	**ONE CAREFUL OWNER** *Columbia 4772802* ●	7		6
19 Nov 94	**THE BEST OF MICHAEL BALL** *Polygram TV 5238912* ●	25		7
27 Jan 96	**FIRST LOVE** *Columbia 4835992* ○	4		6
16 Nov 96	**THE MUSICALS** *Polygram TV 5338922* ●	20		10
7 Nov 98	**THE MOVIES** *Polygram TV 5592412* ⊛	13		17
20 Nov 99	**THE VERY BEST OF MICHAEL BALL IN CONCERT AT THE ROYAL ALBERT HALL** *Universal Music TV 5238912* ●	18		7
11 Nov 00	**THIS TIME IT'S PERSONAL** *Universal TV 1597282* ○	20		8
29 Sep 01	**CENTRE STAGE** *Universal TV 160712* ○	11		7
1 Nov 03	**A LOVE STORY** *Liberty 5919492*	41		1
6 Nov 04	**LOVE CHANGES EVERYTHING – THE ESSENTIAL** *Universal TV 9825039* ●	21		9
29 Oct 05	**MUSIC** *Universal TV 9874241* ●	11		10
11 Nov 06	**ONE VOICE** *Universal TV 1704602*	22		5
3 Nov 07	**BACK TO BACHARACH** *Universal TV 1748686*	20		5

Silver-selling ○ Gold-selling ● Platinum-selling ⊛ US No.1 ★ Peak Position Weeks at No.1 Weeks on Chart

BANANARAMA

UK, female vocal trio – Sarah Dallin, Siobhan Fahey & Keren Woodward

Date	Title	Peak	Wks at No.1	Wks (100)
19 Mar 83	**DEEP SEA SKIVING** *London RAMA 1* ○	7		16
28 Apr 84	**BANANARAMA** *London RAMA 2* ○	16		11
19 Jul 86	**TRUE CONFESSIONS** *London RAMA 3*	46		5
19 Sep 87	**WOW!** *London RAMA 4* ●	26		26
22 Oct 88	**THE GREATEST HITS COLLECTION** *London RAMA 5* ⊛x3	3		37
25 May 91	**POP LIFE** *London 8282461*	42		1
10 Apr 93	**PLEASE YOURSELF** *London 8283572*	46		1
10 Nov 01	**THE VERY BEST OF** *London 0927414992*	43		2
19 May 07	**THE GREATEST HITS & MORE MORE MORE** *WMTV WMTV054*	61		1

BANCO DE GAIA

UK, male multi-instrumentalist (Toby Marks)

Date	Title	Peak	Wks at No.1	Wks (4)
12 Mar 94	**MAYA** *Planet Dog BARKCD 3*	34		2
13 May 95	**LAST TRAIN TO LHASA** *Planet Dog BARKCD 0115*	31		2

BAND

Canada/US, male vocal/instrumental group – Robbie Robertson*, Rick Danko, d. 10 Dec 1999, Levon Helm, Garth Hudson & Richard Manuel, d. 4 Mar 1986

Date	Title	Peak	Wks at No.1	Wks (19)
31 Jan 70	**THE BAND** *Capitol EST 132*	25		11
3 Oct 70	**STAGE FRIGHT** *Capitol EA SW 425*	15		6
27 Nov 71	**CAHOOTS** *Capitol EAST 651*	41		1
30 Aug 97	**THE BAND** *Capitol 5253892*	41		1

BANDERAS

UK, female vocal/instrumental duo

Date	Title	Peak	Wks at No.1	Wks (3)
13 Apr 91	**RIPE** *London 8282471*	40		3

BANGLES

US, female vocal/instrumental group – Susanna Hoffs*, Debbi & Vicki Peterson & Michael Steele

Date	Title	Peak	Wks at No.1	Wks (105)
16 Mar 85	**ALL OVER THE PLACE** *CBS 26015*	86		1
15 Mar 86	**DIFFERENT LIGHT** *CBS 26659* ⊛	3		47
10 Dec 88	**EVERYTHING** *CBS 4629791* ⊛	5		26
9 Jun 90	**GREATEST HITS** *CBS 4667691* ⊛	4		23
4 Aug 01	**ETERNAL FLAME – THE BEST OF THE BANGLES** *Columbia STVCD 121* ○	15		7
29 Mar 03	**DOLL REVOLUTION** *Liberty 5815102*	62		1

DEVENDRA BANHART

US, male vocalist/guitarist

Date	Title	Peak	Wks at No.1	Wks (1)
1 Oct 05	**CRIPPLE CROW** *XL Recordings XLCD192*	69		1

LLOYD BANKS

US, male rapper. See G-Unit

Date	Title	Peak	Wks at No.1	Wks (12)
10 Jul 04	**THE HUNGER FOR MORE** *Interscope 9863026* ○ ★	15		10
21 Oct 06	**ROTTEN APPLE** *Interscope 1708948*	40		2

TONY BANKS

UK, male vocalist/keyboard player. See Genesis

Date	Title	Peak	Wks at No.1	Wks (7)
20 Oct 79	**A CURIOUS FEELING** *Charisma CAS 1148*	21		5
25 Jun 83	**THE FUGITIVE** *Charisma TBLP 1*	50		2

CHRIS BARBER

UK, male trombone player

Date	Title	Peak	Wks at No.1	Wks (91)
24 Sep 60	**CHRIS BARBER BAND BOX NO. 2** *Columbia 33SCX 3277*	17		1
5 Nov 60	**ELITE SYNCOPATIONS** *Columbia 33SX 1245*	18		1
12 Nov 60	**BEST OF CHRIS BARBER** *Ace Of Clubs ACL 1037*	17		1
27 May 61	**BEST OF BARBER AND BILK VOLUME 1** *Pye Golden Guinea GGL 0075* & ACKER BILK	4		43
11 Nov 61	**BEST OF BARBER AND BILK VOLUME 2** *Pye Golden Guinea GGL 0096* & ACKER BILK	8		18
25 Aug 62	**BEST OF BALL, BARBER AND BILK** *Pye Golden Guinea GGL 0131* KENNY BALL, CHRIS BARBER & ACKER BILK	1	2	24
29 Jan 00	**THE SKIFFLE SESSIONS – LIVE IN BELFAST** *Venture CDVE 945* VAN MORRISON/LONNIE DONEGAN/CHRIS BARBER	14		3

BARCLAY JAMES HARVEST

UK, male vocal/instrumental group

Date	Title	Peak	Wks at No.1	Wks (42)
14 Dec 74	**BARCLAY JAMES HARVEST LIVE** *Polydor 2683 052* ○	40		2
18 Oct 75	**TIME HONOURED GHOST** *Polydor 2383 361* ○	32		3
23 Oct 76	**OCTOBERON** *Polydor 2442 144* ○	19		4
1 Oct 77	**GONE TO EARTH** *Polydor 2442 148* ○	30		7
21 Oct 78	**BARCLAY JAMES HARVEST XII** *Polydor POLD 5006*	31		2
23 May 81	**TURN OF THE TIDE** *Polydor POLD 5040*	55		2
24 Jul 82	**A CONCERT FOR THE PEOPLE (BERLIN)** *Polydor POLD 5052*	15		11
28 May 83	**RING OF CHANGES** *Polydor POLH 3*	36		4
14 Apr 84	**VICTIMS OF CIRCUMSTANCES** *Polydor POLD 5135*	33		6
14 Feb 87	**FACE TO FACE** *Polydor POLD 5209*	65		1

SARA BAREILLES

US, female vocalist/guitarist/pianist

Date	Title	Peak	Wks at No.1	Wks (5)
28 Jun 08	**LITTLE VOICE** *Columbia 88697275552*	9		5

BARENAKED LADIES

Canada, male vocal/instrumental group

Date	Title	Peak	Wks at No.1	Wks (18)
27 Aug 94	**MAYBE YOU SHOULD DRIVE** *Reprise 9362457092*	57		1
6 Mar 99	**STUNT** *Reprise 9362469632* ●	20		16
30 Sep 00	**MAROON** *Reprise 9362478912*	64		1

GARY BARLOW

UK, male vocalist. See Take That

Date	Title	Peak	Wks at No.1	Wks (27)
7 Jun 97	**OPEN ROAD** *RCA 74321417202* ⊛	1	1	26
23 Oct 99	**TWELVE MONTHS, ELEVEN DAYS** *RCA 74321707662*	35		1

SYD BARRETT

UK, male vocalist/guitarist, d. 7 Jul 2006 (age 60). See Pink Floyd

Date	Title	Peak	Wks at No.1	Wks (1)
7 Feb 70	**MADCAP LAUGHS** *Harvest SHVL 765*	40		1

BARRON KNIGHTS

UK, male vocal/instrumental group

Date	Title	Peak	Wks at No.1	Wks (22)
2 Dec 78	**NIGHT GALLERY** *Epic EPC 83221* ●	15		13
1 Dec 79	**TEACH THE WORLD TO LAUGH** *Epic EPC 83891*	51		4
13 Dec 80	**JESTA GIGGLE** *Epic EPC 84550* ○	45		5

JOHN BARROWMAN

UK, male vocalist/actor/TV presenter

Date	Title	Peak	Wks at No.1	Wks (10)
24 Nov 07	**ANOTHER SIDE** *Sony BMG 88697188382* ●	22		6
6 Dec 08	**MUSIC MUSIC MUSIC** *Epic 88697339902*	35		4

JOHN BARRY

UK, male composer/orchestra leader (John Prendergast)

Date	Title	Peak	Wks at No.1	Wks (33)
31 Oct 64	**JAMES BOND 007 – GOLDFINGER (OST)** *United Artists ULP 1076*	14		5
29 Jan 72	**THE PERSUADERS** *CBS 64816*	18		9
22 Jun 85	**JAMES BOND 007 – A VIEW TO A KILL (OST)** *Parlophone BOND 1*	81		1
26 Apr 86	**OUT OF AFRICA (OST)** *MCA MCF 3310*	81		2
1 Aug 87	**JAMES BOND 007 – THE LIVING DAYLIGHTS (OST)** *Warner Brothers WX 111*	57		6
20 Apr 91	**DANCES WITH WOLVES (FILM SOUNDTRACK)** *Epic 4675911*	45		8
8 May 99	**THE BEYONDNESS OF THINGS** *Decca 4600092* ENGLISH CHAMBER ORCHESTRA CONDUCTED BY JOHN BARRY	67		1
31 Mar 07	**THE VERY BEST OF** *Columbia/EMI TV 88697072222*	64		1

BASEMENT JAXX

UK, male production duo – Felix Buxton & Simon Ratcliffe

Date	Title	Peak	Wks at No.1	Wks (135)
22 May 99	**REMEDY** *XL Recordings XLCD 129* ●	4		45
7 Jul 01	**ROOTY** *XL Recordings XLCD 143* ●	5		26
1 Nov 03	**KISH KASH** *XL Recordings XLCD 174* ●	17		16
2 Apr 05	**THE SINGLES** *XL Recordings XLCD187X* ⊛x2	1	1	44
16 Sep 06	**CRAZY ITCH RADIO** *XL Recordings XLCD205*	16		4

BASIA

Poland, female vocalist (Basia Trzetrzelewska). See Matt Bianco

Date	Title	Peak	Wks at No.1	Wks (4)
13 Feb 88	**TIME AND TIDE** *Portrait 4502631*	61		3
3 Mar 90	**LONDON WARSAW NEW YORK** *Portrait 4632821*	68		1

COUNT BASIE

US, male composer/band leader/pianist (William Basie), d. 26 Apr 1984 (age 79)

Date	Title	Peak Position	Weeks at No.1	Weeks on Chart
				29
16 Apr 60	**CHAIRMAN OF THE BOARD** *Columbia 33SX 1209*	17		1
23 Feb 63	**SINATRA-BASIE** *Reprise R 1008* FRANK SINATRA & COUNT BASIE	2		23
19 Sep 64	**IT MIGHT AS WELL BE SWING** *Reprise R 1012* FRANK SINATRA & COUNT BASIE & HIS ORCHESTRA	17		4
28 Oct 06	**RAY SINGS BASIE SWINGS** *Concord 7230026* RAY CHARLES & COUNT BASIE ORCHESTRA	63		1

TONI BASIL

US, female vocalist (Antonia Basilotta)

Date	Title	Peak Position	Weeks at No.1	Weeks on Chart
				16
6 Feb 82	**WORD OF MOUTH** *Radialchoice BASIL 1*	15		16

BASS-O-MATIC

UK, male multi-instrumentalist/producer (William Orbit*)

Date	Title	Peak Position	Weeks at No.1	Weeks on Chart
				2
13 Oct 90	**SET THE CONTROLS FOR THE HEART OF THE BASS** *Virgin V 2641*	57		2

SHIRLEY BASSEY

UK, female vocalist. Britain's most successful female chart artist, who has a Top 10 newly-recorded albums chart span of over 46 years. The internationally-acclaimed Welsh cabaret entertainer was made a Dame in 2000

Date	Title	Peak Position	Weeks at No.1	Weeks on Chart
				307
28 Jan 61	**FABULOUS SHIRLEY BASSEY** *Columbia 33SX 1178*	12		2
25 Feb 61	**SHIRLEY** *Columbia 33SX 1286*	9		10
17 Feb 62	**SHIRLEY BASSEY** *Columbia 33SX 1382*	14		11
15 Dec 62	**LET'S FACE THE MUSIC** *Columbia 33SX 1454* WITH THE NELSON RIDDLE ORCHESTRA	12		7
4 Dec 65	**SHIRLEY BASSEY AT THE PIGALLE** *Columbia 33SX 1787*	15		7
27 Aug 66	**I'VE GOT A SONG FOR YOU** *United Artists ULP 1142*	26		1
17 Feb 68	**TWELVE OF THOSE SONGS** *Columbia SCX 6204*	38		3
7 Dec 68	**GOLDEN HITS OF SHIRLEY BASSEY** *Columbia SCX 6294*	28		40
11 Jul 70	**LIVE AT THE TALK OF THE TOWN** *United Artists UAS 29095*	38		6
29 Aug 70	**SOMETHING** *United Artists UAS 29100*	5		28
15 May 71	**SOMETHING ELSE** *United Artists UAG 29149*	7		9
2 Oct 71	**BIG SPENDER** *Sunset SLS 50262*	27		8
30 Oct 71	**IT'S MAGIC** *Starline SRS 5082*	32		1
6 Nov 71	**THE FABULOUS SHIRLEY BASSEY** *MFP 1398*	48		1
4 Dec 71	**WHAT NOW MY LOVE** *MFP 5230*	17		5
8 Jan 72	**THE SHIRLEY BASSEY COLLECTION** *United Artists UAD 60013/4*	37		1
19 Feb 72	**I CAPRICORN** *United Artists UAS 29246*	13		11
25 Nov 72	**AND I LOVE YOU SO** *United Artists UAS 29385*	24		9
2 Jun 73	**NEVER NEVER NEVER** *United Artists UAG 29471*	10		10
15 Mar 75	**THE SHIRLEY BASSEY SINGLES ALBUM** *United Artists UAS 29728*	2		23
1 Nov 75	**GOOD, BAD BUT BEAUTIFUL** *United Artists UAS 29881*	13		7
15 May 76	**LOVE, LIFE AND FEELINGS** *United Artists UAS 29944*	13		5
4 Dec 76	**THOUGHTS OF LOVE** *United Artists UAS 30011*	15		9
25 Jun 77	**YOU TAKE MY HEART AWAY** *United Artists UAS 30037*	34		5
4 Nov 78	**25TH ANNIVERSARY ALBUM** *United Artists SBTV 601 4748*	3		12
12 May 79	**THE MAGIC IS YOU** *United Artists UATV 30230*	40		5
17 Jul 82	**LOVE SONGS** *Applause APKL 1163*	48		5
20 Oct 84	**I AM WHAT I AM** *Towerbell TOWLP 7*	25		18
18 May 91	**KEEP THE MUSIC PLAYING** *Dino DINTV 21*	25		7
5 Dec 92	**THE BEST OF SHIRLEY BASSEY** *Dino DINCD 49*	27		5
4 Dec 93	**SHIRLEY BASSEY SINGS ANDREW LLOYD WEBBER** *Premier CDDPR 114*	34		5
11 Nov 95	**SHIRLEY BASSEY SINGS THE MOVIES** *Polygram TV 5293992*	24		9
9 Nov 96	**THE SHOW MUST GO ON** *Polygram TV 5337122*	47		8
9 Sep 00	**THE REMIX ALBUM – DIAMONDS ARE FOREVER** *EMI 5258732*	62		1
25 Nov 00	**THIS IS MY LIFE – THE GREATEST HITS** *Liberty 5258742*	54		4
7 Jun 03	**THANK YOU FOR THE YEARS** *Citrus 5122722*	19		4
7 Jul 07	**GET THE PARTY STARTED** *Lock Stock & Barrel LSBRCD005*	6		5

BASSHUNTER

Sweden, male vocalist/DJ/producer (Jonas Altberg)

Date	Title	Peak Position	Weeks at No.1	Weeks on Chart
				24
26 Jul 08	**NOW YOU'RE GONE** *Hard 2 Beat H2BCD04*	1	1	24+

BAT FOR LASHES

UK, female vocalist/multi-instrumentalist (Natasha Khan)

Date	Title	Peak Position	Weeks at No.1	Weeks on Chart
				2
15 Sep 07	**FUR AND GOLD** *Echo 5020640*	48		2

MIKE BATT

UK, male vocalist/producer

Date	Title	Peak Position	Weeks at No.1	Weeks on Chart
				13
28 Oct 89	**CLASSIC BLUE** *Trax MODEM 1040* JUSTIN HAYWARD WITH MIKE BATT & THE LONDON PHILHARMONIC ORCHESTRA	47		7
5 Apr 08	**A SONGWRITERS TALE** *Dramatico DRAMCD0037*	24		6

BATTLES

US, male vocal/instrumental group

Date	Title	Peak Position	Weeks at No.1	Weeks on Chart
				1
26 May 07	**MIRRORED** *Warp WARPCD156*	70		1

BAUHAUS

UK, male vocal/instrumental group – Peter Murphy*, Daniel Ash, Kevin Haskins & David J (David Haskins)

Date	Title	Peak Position	Weeks at No.1	Weeks on Chart
				24
15 Nov 80	**IN THE FLAT FIELD** *4AD CAD 13*	72		1
24 Oct 81	**MASK** *Beggars Banquet BEGA 29*	30		5
30 Oct 82	**THE SKY'S GONE OUT** *Beggars Banquet BEGA 42*	4		6
23 Jul 83	**BURNING FROM THE INSIDE** *Beggars Banquet BEGA 45*	13		10
30 Nov 85	**1979–1983** *Beggars Banquet BEGA 64*	36		2

TOM BAXTER

UK, male vocalist/guitarist

Date	Title	Peak Position	Weeks at No.1	Weeks on Chart
				8
14 Aug 04	**FEATHER AND STONE** *Columbia 5174689*	65		3
19 Jan 08	**SKYBOUND** *Charisma CASCD2005*	12		5

BAY CITY ROLLERS

UK, male vocal group – Leslie McKeown, Eric Faulkner, Alan & Derek Longmuir & Stuart Wood

Date	Title	Peak Position	Weeks at No.1	Weeks on Chart
				136
12 Oct 74	**ROLLIN'** *Bell BELLS 244*	1	4	62
3 May 75	**ONCE UPON A STAR** *Bell SYBEL 8001*	1	3	37
13 Dec 75	**WOULDN'T YOU LIKE IT** *Bell SYBEL 8002*	3		12
25 Sep 76	**DEDICATION** *Bell SYBEL 8005*	4		12
13 Aug 77	**IT'S A GAME** *Arista SPARTY 1009*	18		4
17 Apr 04	**THE VERY BEST OF** *Bell/Arista 82876608192*	11		9

COLIN DAVIS CONDUCTING THE BBC SYMPHONY ORCHESTRA, SINGERS & CHORUS

UK, male/female orchestra

Date	Title	Peak Position	Weeks at No.1	Weeks on Chart
				7
4 Oct 69	**BBC SYMPHONY ORCHESTRA LAST NIGHT AT THE PROMS** *Philips SFM 23033*	36		1
11 Dec 82	**HIGHLIGHTS FROM LAST NIGHT AT THE PROMS '82** *K-Tel NE 1198* BBC SYMPHONY ORCHESTRA, SINGS & SYMPHONY CHORUS CONDUCTED BY JAMES LOUGHRAN	69		5
28 Feb 98	**ELGAR/PAYNE SYMPHONY NO. 3** *NMC NMCD 053* BBC SYMPHONY ORCHESTRA CONDUCTED BY ANDREW DAVIS	44		1

B.B.E.

France/Italy, male instrumental group

Date	Title	Peak Position	Weeks at No.1	Weeks on Chart
				2
28 Feb 98	**GAMES** *Positiva 4934932*	60		2

BBM

UK, male vocal/instrumental trio – Ginger Baker*, Jack Bruce* & Gary Moore*

Date	Title	Peak Position	Weeks at No.1	Weeks on Chart
				4
18 Jun 94	**AROUND THE NEXT DREAM** *Virgin CDV 2745*	9		4

BBMAK

UK, male vocal trio

Date	Title	Peak Position	Weeks at No.1	Weeks on Chart
				3
9 Jun 01	**SOONER OR LATER** *Telstar TCD 3179*	16		3

BE-BOP DELUXE

UK, male vocal/instrumental group – Bill Nelson*, Andy Clark, Simon Fox & Charlie Tumahai, d. 21 Dec 1995

Date	Title	Peak Position	Weeks at No.1	Weeks on Chart
				28
31 Jan 76	**SUNBURST FINISH** *Harvest SHSP 4053*	17		12
25 Sep 76	**MODERN MUSIC** *Harvest SHSP 4058*	12		6
6 Aug 77	**LIVE! IN THE AIR AGE** *Harvest SHVL 816*	10		5
25 Feb 78	**DRASTIC PLASTIC** *Harvest SHSP 4091*	22		5

Key: ○ Silver-selling · ● Gold-selling · ⊛ Platinum-selling · ★ US No.1 · Peak Position · Weeks at No.1 · Weeks on Chart

BE YOUR OWN PET

US, male/female vocal/instrumental group — **1**

Date	Album	Peak Position	Weeks at No.1	Weeks on Chart
8 Apr 06	**BE YOUR OWN PET** *XL Recordings XLCD193*	47		1

BEACH BOYS

US, male vocal/instrumental group – Brian Wilson*, Al Jardine, Bruce Johnston, Mike Love, Carl Wilson, d. 6 Feb 1998, & Dennis Wilson*, d. 28 Dec 1983. Arguably the most popular US group of the rock 'N' roll era, whose hits span over 40 years and whose 'Good Vibrations' single and *Pet Sounds* album are regarded as among the greatest recordings ever — **587**

Date	Album	Peak Position	Weeks at No.1	Weeks on Chart
25 Sep 65	**SURFIN' USA** *Capitol T 1890*	17		7
19 Feb 66	**BEACH BOYS PARTY** *Capitol T 2398*	3		14
16 Apr 66	**BEACH BOYS TODAY** *Capitol T 2269*	6		25
9 Jul 66	**PET SOUNDS** *Capitol T 2458*	2		39
16 Jul 66	**SUMMER DAYS (AND SUMMER NIGHTS)** *Capitol T 2354*	4		22
12 Nov 66	**BEST OF THE BEACH BOYS** *Capitol T 20865*	2		142
11 Mar 67	**SURFER GIRL** *Capitol T 1981*	13		14
21 Oct 67	**BEST OF THE BEACH BOYS VOLUME 2** *Capitol ST 20956*	3		39
18 Nov 67	**SMILEY SMILE** *Capitol ST 9001*	9		8
16 Mar 68	**WILD HONEY** *Capitol ST 2859*	7		15
21 Sep 68	**FRIENDS** *Capitol ST 2895*	13		8
23 Nov 68	**BEST OF THE BEACH BOYS VOLUME 3** *Capitol ST 21142*	8		12
29 Mar 69	**20/20** *Capitol EST 133*	3		10
19 Sep 70	**GREATEST HITS** *Capitol ST 21628*	5		30
5 Dec 70	**SUNFLOWER** *Stateside SSL 8251*	29		6
27 Nov 71	**SURF'S UP** *Stateside SLS 10313*	15		7
24 Jun 72	**CARL AND THE PASSIONS/SO TOUGH** *Reprise K 44184*	25		1
17 Feb 73	**HOLLAND** *Reprise K 54008* ○	20		7
10 Jul 76	**20 GOLDEN GREATS** *Capitol EMTV 1* ⊛	1	10	86
24 Jul 76	**15 BIG ONES** *Reprise K 54079* ○	31		3
7 May 77	**THE BEACH BOYS LOVE YOU** *Reprise K 54087*	28		1
21 Apr 79	**LA (LIGHT ALBUM)** *Caribou CRB 86081*	32		6
12 Apr 80	**KEEPING THE SUMMER ALIVE** *Caribou CRB 86109*	54		3
30 Jul 83	**THE VERY BEST OF THE BEACH BOYS** *Capitol BBTV 1867193* ⊛	1	3	17
22 Jun 85	**THE BEACH BOYS** *Caribou CRB 26378*	60		2
23 Jun 90	**SUMMER DREAMS – 28 CLASSIC TRACKS** *Capitol EMTVD 51* ⊛	2		27
1 Jul 95	**THE BEST OF THE BEACH BOYS** *Capitol CDESTVD 3* ○	25		6
16 Sep 95	**PET SOUNDS** *Fame CDFA 3298*	59		6
11 Jul 98	**GREATEST HITS** *EMI 4956962*	28		4
19 Sep 98	**ENDLESS HARMONY SOUNDTRACK** *Capitol 4963912*	56		1
21 Jul 01	**THE VERY BEST OF THE BEACH BOYS** *Capitol 5326152* ⊛	31		13
11 Jun 05	**THE PLATINUM COLLECTION** *Capitol 5713452* ○	30		5
29 Jul 06	**SOUNDS OF SUMMER – THE VERY BEST OF** *Capitol 5775802*	46		1

BEASTIE BOYS

US, male rap/vocal trio – Adam Yauch, Michael Diamond & Adam Horowitz — **95**

Date	Album	Peak Position	Weeks at No.1	Weeks on Chart
31 Jan 87	**LICENSE TO ILL** *Def Jam 450062* ● ★	7		40
5 Aug 89	**PAUL'S BOUTIQUE** *Capitol EST 2102*	44		2
4 Jun 94	**ILL COMMUNICATION** *Grand Royal CDEST 2229* ● ★	10		15
10 Jun 95	**ROOT DOWN (EP)** *Grand Royal CDEST 2262*	23		2
6 Apr 96	**THE IN SOUND FROM WAY OUT!** *Grand Royal CDEST 2281*	45		1
18 Jul 98	**HELLO NASTY** *Grand Royal 4957232* ● ★	1	1	21
4 Dec 99	**ANTHOLOGY – THE SOUNDS OF SCIENCE** *Grand Royal 5236642*	36		7
26 Jun 04	**TO THE 5 BOROUGHS** *Capitol 4733390* ● ★	2		6
19 Nov 05	**SOLID GOLD HITS** *Parlophone 3445502*	71		1

BEAT

UK, male vocal/instrumental group – Ranking Roger (Roger Charlery), Dave Wakeling, Andy Cox & David Steele — **73**

Date	Album	Peak Position	Weeks at No.1	Weeks on Chart
31 May 80	**JUST CAN'T STOP IT** *Go-Feet BEAT 001* ●	3		32
16 May 81	**WHA'PPEN** *Go-Feet BEAT 3* ○	3		18
9 Oct 82	**SPECIAL BEAT SERVICE** *Go-Feet BEAT 5*	21		6
11 Jun 83	**WHAT IS BEAT? (THE BEST OF THE BEAT)** *Go-Feet BEAT 6* ○	10		13
10 Feb 96	**BPM...THE VERY BEST OF THE BEAT** *Go-Feet 74321231952*	13		4

BEATLES

UK, male vocal/instrumental group – John Lennon*, d. 8 Dec 1980, Paul McCartney*, George Harrison*, d. 29 Nov 2001, & Ringo Starr*. The most successful group of all time with world sales of over one billion. No act has achieved more No.1 albums in the UK or the US and they are the top-selling album act in both countries — **1316**

Date	Album	Peak Position	Weeks at No.1	Weeks on Chart
6 Apr 63	**PLEASE PLEASE ME** *Parlophone PMC 1202*	1	30	70
30 Nov 63	**WITH THE BEATLES** *Parlophone PMC 1206*	1	21	51
18 Jul 64	**A HARD DAY'S NIGHT** *Parlophone PMC 1230* ★	1	21	38
12 Dec 64	**BEATLES FOR SALE** *Parlophone PMC 1240*	1	11	46
14 Aug 65	**HELP!** *Parlophone PMC 1255* ★	1	9	37
11 Dec 65	**RUBBER SOUL** *Parlophone PMC 1267* ★	1	8	42
13 Aug 66	**REVOLVER** *Parlophone PMC 7009* ★	1	7	34
10 Dec 66	**A COLLECTION OF BEATLES OLDIES** *Parlophone PMC 7016*	7		34
3 Jun 67	**SGT PEPPER'S LONELY HEARTS CLUB BAND** *Parlophone PCS 7027* ★	1	27	149
13 Jan 68	**MAGICAL MYSTERY TOUR (IMPORT)** *Capitol SMAL 2835* ★	31		2
7 Dec 68	**THE BEATLES (WHITE ALBUM)** *Apple PCS 7067/8* ★	1	8	22
1 Feb 69	**YELLOW SUBMARINE** *Apple PCS 7070*	3		10
4 Oct 69	**ABBEY ROAD** *Apple PCS 7088* ★	1	17	81
23 May 70	**LET IT BE** *Apple PXS 1* ★	1	3	59
16 Jan 71	**A HARD DAY'S NIGHT** *Parlophone PCS 3058*	30		1
24 Jul 71	**HELP!** *Parlophone PCS 3071*	33		2
5 May 73	**THE BEATLES 1962–1966** *Apple PCSP 718* ⊛	3		114
5 May 73	**THE BEATLES 1967–1970** *Apple PCSP 717* ⊛ ★	2		148
26 Jun 76	**ROCK 'N' ROLL MUSIC** *Parlophone PCSP 719* ●	11		15
21 Aug 76	**THE BEATLES TAPES** *Polydor 2683 068*	45		1
21 May 77	**THE BEATLES AT THE HOLLYWOOD BOWL** *Parlophone EMTV 4* ●	1	1	17
17 Dec 77	**LOVE SONGS** *Parlophone PCSP 721* ●	7		17
3 Nov 79	**RARITIES** *Parlophone PCM 1001* ○	71		1
15 Nov 80	**BEATLES BALLADS** *Parlophone PCS 7214* ●	17		16
30 Oct 82	**20 GREATEST HITS** *Parlophone PCTC 260* ⊛	10		30
7 Mar 87	**A HARD DAY'S NIGHT** *Parlophone CDP 7464372*	30		4
7 Mar 87	**PLEASE PLEASE ME** *Parlophone CDP 7464352*	32		4
7 Mar 87	**WITH THE BEATLES** *Parlophone CDP 7464362*	40		3
7 Mar 87	**BEATLES FOR SALE** *Parlophone CDP 7464382*	45		2
9 May 87	**REVOLVER** *Parlophone CDP 7464412*	46		12
9 May 87	**RUBBER SOUL** *Parlophone CDP 7464402*	60		5
9 May 87	**HELP!** *Parlophone CDP 7464392*	61		2
6 Jun 87	**SGT PEPPER'S LONELY HEARTS CLUB BAND** *Parlophone CDP 7464422*	3		53
5 Sep 87	**THE BEATLES (WHITE ALBUM)** *Apple CDS 7464439*	18		2
5 Sep 87	**YELLOW SUBMARINE** *Parlophone CDP 7464452*	60		1
3 Oct 87	**MAGICAL MYSTERY TOUR** *Parlophone PCTC 255*	52		1
31 Oct 87	**ABBEY ROAD** *Apple CDP 7464462*	30		11
31 Oct 87	**LET IT BE** *Parlophone CDP 7464472*	50		1
19 Mar 88	**PAST MASTERS VOLUME 1** *Parlophone CDBPM 1*	46		1
19 Mar 88	**PAST MASTERS VOLUME 2** *Parlophone CDBPM 2*	49		1
2 Oct 93	**THE BEATLES 1962–1966** *Parlophone BEACD 2511*	3		24
2 Oct 93	**THE BEATLES 1967–1970** *Parlophone BEACD 2512*	4		24
10 Dec 94	**LIVE AT THE BBC** *Apple CDS 8317962* ⊛x2	1	1	20
2 Dec 95	**ANTHOLOGY 1** *Apple CDPCSP 727* ⊛x2 ★	2		10
30 Mar 96	**ANTHOLOGY 2** *Apple CDPCSP 728* ⊛ ★	1	1	12
9 Nov 96	**ANTHOLOGY 3** *Apple CDPCSP 729* ● ★	4		11
25 Sep 99	**YELLOW SUBMARINE SONGTRACK (OST)** *Parlophone 5214812* ●	8		5
25 Nov 00	**1** *Apple 5299702* ⊛x8 ★	1	9	46
29 Nov 03	**LET IT BE – NAKED** *Apple 5957132* ●	7		7
2 Dec 06	**LOVE** *Apple 3798102* ⊛x2	3		15
3 Nov 07	**THE BEATLES 1962–1966** *Apple CDPCSP 717*	71		2

Top 3 Best-Selling Albums

		Approximate Sales
1	SGT. PEPPER'S LONELY HEARTS CLUB BAND	4,900,000
2	1	2,800,000
3	ABBEY ROAD	1,965,000

BEATMASTERS

UK, male/female production group — **10**

Date	Album	Peak Position	Weeks at No.1	Weeks on Chart
1 Jul 89	**ANYWAYYAWANNA** *Rhythm King LEFTLP 10* ○	30		10

BEATS INTERNATIONAL

UK, male/female vocal/instrumental group — **15**

Date	Album	Peak Position	Weeks at No.1	Weeks on Chart
14 Apr 90	**LET THEM EAT BINGO** *Go. Beat 8421961* ●	17		15

BEAUTIFUL SOUTH

UK, male/female vocal/instrumental group – Paul Heaton*, Briana Corrigan (replaced by Jacqui Abbott), Dave Hemingway, Dave Rotheray, Dave Stead & Sean Welch. Quirky Hull band formed from the ashes of The Housemartins whose *Best Of Collection, Carry On Up The Charts*, was 1994's second best-seller. The witty tunesmiths split up in 2007 due to "musical similarities" — **312**

Date	Album	Peak Position	Weeks at No.1	Weeks on Chart
4 Nov 89	**WELCOME TO THE BEAUTIFUL SOUTH** *Go! Discs AGOLP 16* ⊛	2		26
10 Nov 90	**CHOKE** *Go! Discs 8282331* ⊛	2		22
11 Apr 92	**0898: BEAUTIFUL SOUTH** *Go! Discs 8283102* ●	4		17
9 Apr 94	**MIAOW** *Go! Discs 8285072* ●	6		24

Date	Title	Peak Position	Weeks at No.1	Weeks on Chart
19 Nov 94	**CARRY ON UP THE CHARTS – THE BEST OF THE BEAUTIFUL SOUTH** *Go! Discs 8285722* ⊛x6	1	7	89
2 Nov 96	**BLUE IS THE COLOUR** *Go! Discs 8288452* ⊛x5	1	1	46
24 Oct 98	**QUENCH** *Go! Discs 5381662* ⊛x3	1	2	37
21 Oct 00	**PAINTING IT RED** *Go! Discs 5483352* ●	2		11
24 Nov 01	**SOLID BRONZE – GREAT HITS** *Go! Discs 5864442* ⊛	10		14
8 Nov 03	**GAZE** *Go! Discs 9865694* ○	14		3
6 Nov 04	**GOLDDIGGAS HEADNODDERS & PHOLK SONGS** *Sony Music 5186329* ○	11		3
27 May 06	**SUPERBI** *Sony BMG 82876831152*	6		5
24 Nov 07	**SOUP** *Mercury 1747147* & THE HOUSEMARTINS ⊛	15		15

BECK

US, male vocalist (David Campbell) — 84

Date	Title	Peak Position	Weeks at No.1	Weeks on Chart
2 Apr 94	**MELLOW GOLD** *Geffen GED 24634*	41		4
6 Jul 96	**O-DE-LAY** *Geffen GED 24926* ⊛	17		51
14 Nov 98	**MUTATIONS** *Geffen GED 25184*	24		6
4 Dec 99	**MIDNITE VULTURES** *Geffen 4905272* ●	19		14
5 Oct 02	**SEA CHANGE** *Geffen 4933932*	20		3
2 Apr 05	**GUERO** *Interscope 9880288* ○	15		3
19 Jul 08	**MODERN GUILT** *XL Recordings XLCD369*	9		3

JEFF BECK

UK, male vocalist/guitarist. See Yardbirds — 15

Date	Title	Peak Position	Weeks at No.1	Weeks on Chart
13 Sep 69	**COSA NOSTRA BECK – OLA** *Columbia SCX 6351*	39		1
28 Apr 73	**JEFF BECK, TIM BOGERT & CARMINE APPICE** *Epic EPC 65455* , TIM BOGERT & CARMINE APPICE	28		3
24 Jul 76	**WIRED** *CBS 86012*	38		5
19 Jul 80	**THERE AND BACK** *Epic EPC 83288*	38		4
17 Aug 85	**FLASH** *Epic EPC 26112*	83		1
27 Mar 99	**WHO ELSE?** *Epic 4930412*	74		1

VICTORIA BECKHAM

UK, female vocalist (Victoria Adams). See Spice Girls — 3

Date	Title	Peak Position	Weeks at No.1	Weeks on Chart
13 Oct 01	**VICTORIA BECKHAM** *Virgin CDV 2942*	10		3

DANIEL BEDINGFIELD

UK (b. New Zealand), male vocalist/producer — 94

Date	Title	Peak Position	Weeks at No.1	Weeks on Chart
7 Sep 02	**GOTTA GET THRU THIS** *Polydor 651252* ⊛x5	2		81
20 Nov 04	**SECOND FIRST IMPRESSION** *Polydor 9868637*	8		13

NATASHA BEDINGFIELD

UK, female vocalist — 48

Date	Title	Peak Position	Weeks at No.1	Weeks on Chart
18 Sep 04	**UNWRITTEN** *BMG 82876637022* ⊛x3	1	1	37
12 May 07	**NB** *Phonogenic 88697076452*	9		11

BEE GEES

UK, male vocal/instrumental group – Barry Gibb*, Maurice Gibb, d. 12 Jan 2003, & Robin Gibb*. The most successful family act of all time have sold more than 100 million records, enjoyed Top 10 albums and singles in every decade since the 60s and wrote and performed tracks from the world's biggest-selling soundtrack (*Saturday Night Fever*) — 422

Date	Title	Peak Position	Weeks at No.1	Weeks on Chart
12 Aug 67	**BEE GEE FIRST** *Polydor 583012*	8		26
24 Feb 68	**HORIZONTAL** *Polydor 582020*	16		15
28 Sep 68	**IDEA** *Polydor 583036*	4		18
5 Apr 69	**ODESSA** *Polydor 583049/50*	10		1
8 Nov 69	**BEST OF THE BEE GEES** *Polydor 583063*	7		22
9 May 70	**CUCUMBER CASTLE** *Polydor 2383 010*	57		2
17 Feb 79	**SPIRITS HAVING FLOWN** *RSO RSBG 001* ⊛ ★	1	2	33
10 Nov 79	**BEE GEES GREATEST** *RSO RSDX 001* ⊛ ★	6		25
7 Nov 81	**LIVING EYES** *RSO RSBG 002*	73		8
3 Oct 87	**E.S.P.** *Warner Brothers WX 83* ⊛	5		24
29 Apr 89	**ONE** *Warner Brothers WX 252*	29		3
17 Nov 90	**THE VERY BEST OF THE BEE GEES** *Polydor 8473391* ⊛x3	6		108
6 Apr 91	**HIGH CIVILIZATION** *Warner Brothers WX 417*	24		5
25 Sep 93	**SIZE ISN'T EVERYTHING** *Polydor 5199452* ●	23		13
22 Mar 97	**STILL WATERS** *Polydor 5373022* ●	2		19
19 Sep 98	**LIVE ONE NIGHT ONLY** *Polydor 5592202* ⊛x3	4		44
14 Apr 01	**THIS IS WHERE I CAME IN** *Polydor 5494582* ●	6		6
24 Nov 01	**THEIR GREATEST HITS – THE RECORD** *Polydor 5894492* ⊛x3	5		33
13 Nov 04	**NUMBER ONES** *Polydor 9868840*	7		12
10 Dec 05	**LOVE SONGS** *Polydor 9874225*	51		3
13 Oct 07	**GREATEST** *Reprise 8122799507*	35		2

BEES

UK, male vocal/instrumental group — 4

Date	Title	Peak Position	Weeks at No.1	Weeks on Chart
10 Jul 04	**FREE THE BEES** *Virgin CDV2983* ○	26		3
7 Apr 07	**OCTOPUS** *Virgin CDV3024*	26		1

LOU BEGA

Germany, male vocalist (David Lubega) — 2

Date	Title	Peak Position	Weeks at No.1	Weeks on Chart
18 Sep 99	**A LITTLE BIT OF MAMBO** *RCA 74321688612*	50		2

BEIRUT

US, male/female vocal/instrumental group — 1

Date	Title	Peak Position	Weeks at No.1	Weeks on Chart
20 Oct 07	**THE FLYING CLUB CUP** *4AD CAD2732*	69		1

BELL BIV DEVOE

US, male vocal group — 5

Date	Title	Peak Position	Weeks at No.1	Weeks on Chart
1 Sep 90	**POISON** *MCA MCG 6094*	35		5

BELLAMY BROTHERS

US, male vocal duo — 6

Date	Title	Peak Position	Weeks at No.1	Weeks on Chart
19 Jun 76	**BELLAMY BROTHERS** *Warner Brothers K 56242* ○	21		6

REGINA BELLE

US, female vocalist — 5

Date	Title	Peak Position	Weeks at No.1	Weeks on Chart
1 Aug 87	**ALL BY MYSELF** *CBS 4509981*	53		4
16 Sep 89	**STAY WITH ME** *CBS 4651321*	62		1

BELLE & SEBASTIAN

UK, male/female vocal/instrumental group – Stuart Murdoch, Isobel Campbell, Richard Colburn, Mick Cooke, Stuart David (replaced by Bobby Kildea), Chris Geddes, Stevie Jackson & Sarah Martin — 23

Date	Title	Peak Position	Weeks at No.1	Weeks on Chart
19 Sep 98	**THE BOY WITH THE ARAB STRAP** *Jeepster JPRCD 003* ●	12		6
24 Jul 99	**TIGERMILK** *Jeepster JPRCD 007*	13		4
17 Jun 00	**FOLD YOUR HANDS CHILD YOU WALK LIKE A PEASANT** *Jeepster JPRCD 010*	10		3
15 Jun 02	**STORYTELLING** *Jeepster JRPCD 014*	26		2
18 Oct 03	**DEAR CATASTROPHE WAITRESS** *Rough Trade RTRADECD 080* ●	21		3
4 Jun 05	**PUSH BARMAN TO OPEN OLD WOUNDS** *Jeepster JPRDP015*	40		1
18 Feb 06	**THE LIFE PURSUIT** *Rough Trade RTRADCD280* ○	8		4

BELLE STARS

UK, female vocal/instrumental group — 12

Date	Title	Peak Position	Weeks at No.1	Weeks on Chart
5 Feb 83	**THE BELLE STARS** *Stiff SEEZ 45* ○	15		12

BELLOWHEAD

UK, male/female vocal/instrumental group — 1

Date	Title	Peak Position	Weeks at No.1	Weeks on Chart
4 Oct 08	**MATACHIN** *Navigator 17*	73		1

BELLRAYS

US, male/female vocal/instrumental group — 1

Date	Title	Peak Position	Weeks at No.1	Weeks on Chart
18 May 02	**MEET THE BELLRAYS** *Poptones MC5069CD*	73		1

BELLY

US, female/male vocal/instrumental group – Tanya Donelly*, Fred Abong (replaced by Gail Greenwood) & Chris & Tom Gorman — 13

Date	Title	Peak Position	Weeks at No.1	Weeks on Chart
13 Feb 93	**STAR** *4AD 3002CD* ○	2		10
25 Feb 95	**KING** *4AD CADD 5004CD*	6		3

PIERRE BELMONDE

France, male panpipes player — 10

Date	Title	Peak Position	Weeks at No.1	Weeks on Chart
7 Jun 80	**THEMES FOR DREAMS** *K-Tel ONE 1077* ○	13		10

Silver-selling ○ · Gold-selling ● · Platinum-selling ⊛ · US No.1 ★ · Peak Position · Weeks at No.1 · Weeks on Chart

BELOVED
UK, male vocal/instrumental duo – Jon Marsh & Steve Waddington (replaced by Helena Marsh) — 31

Date	Title	Peak Position	Weeks at No.1	Weeks on Chart
3 Mar 90	**HAPPINESS** *East West WX 299* ●	14		14
1 Dec 90	**BLISSED OUT** *East West WX 383*	38		2
20 Feb 93	**CONSCIENCE** *East West 4509914832* ●	2		12
20 Apr 96	**X** *East West 0630133162*	25		3

BEN'S BROTHER
UK, male vocal/instrumental group — 5

Date	Title	Peak Position	Weeks at No.1	Weeks on Chart
18 Aug 07	**BETA MALE FAIRYTALES** *Relentless CDREL14*	14		5

PAT BENATAR
US, female vocalist (Patricia Andrzejewski) — 84

Date	Title	Peak Position	Weeks at No.1	Weeks on Chart
25 Jul 81	**PRECIOUS TIME** *Chrysalis CHR 1346* ★	30		7
13 Nov 82	**GET NERVOUS** *Chrysalis CHR 1396*	73		6
15 Oct 83	**LIVE FROM EARTH** *Chrysalis CHR 1451*	60		5
17 Nov 84	**TROPICO** *Chrysalis CHR 1471* ○	31		25
24 Aug 85	**IN THE HEAT OF THE NIGHT** *Chrysalis CHR 1236*	98		1
7 Dec 85	**SEVEN THE HARD WAY** *Chrysalis CHR 1507*	69		4
7 Nov 87	**BEST SHOTS** *Chrysalis PATV 1* ⊛	6		19
16 Jul 88	**WIDE AWAKE IN DREAMLAND** *Chrysalis CDL 1628* ●	11		14
4 May 91	**TRUE LOVE** *Chrysalis CHR 1805*	40		3

ERIC BENET
US, male vocalist (Eric Bennet Jordan) — 1

Date	Title	Peak Position	Weeks at No.1	Weeks on Chart
15 May 99	**A DAY IN THE LIFE** *Warner Brothers 9362473702*	67		1

CLIFF BENNETT & THE REBEL ROUSERS
UK, male vocal/instrumental group — 4

Date	Title	Peak Position	Weeks at No.1	Weeks on Chart
22 Oct 66	**DRIVIN' YOU WILD** *MFP 1121*	25		3

TONY BENNETT
US, male vocalist (Anthony Benedetto) — 78

Date	Title	Peak Position	Weeks at No.1	Weeks on Chart
29 May 65	**I LEFT MY HEART IN SAN FRANCISCO** *CBS BGP 62201*	13		14
19 Feb 66	**A STRING OF TONY'S HITS** *CBS DP 66010*	9		13
10 Jun 67	**TONY'S GREATEST HITS** *CBS SBPG 62821*	14		24
23 Sep 67	**TONY MAKES IT HAPPEN** *CBS SBPG 63055*	31		3
23 Mar 68	**FOR ONCE IN MY LIFE** *CBS SBPG 63166*	29		5
26 Feb 77	**THE VERY BEST OF TONY BENNETT – 20 GREATEST HITS** *Warwick PA 5021* ○	23		4
28 Nov 98	**THE ESSENTIAL TONY BENNETT** *Columbia 4928222* ○	49		4
5 Jul 03	**A WONDERFUL WORLD** *Columbia 5098702* & K.D. LANG	33		3
11 Nov 06	**DUETS – AN AMERICAN CLASSIC** *Sony BMG 82876809792* ●	15		8

BRENDAN BENSON
US, male vocalist/guitarist — 1

Date	Title	Peak Position	Weeks at No.1	Weeks on Chart
26 Feb 05	**THE ALTERNATIVE TO LOVE** *V2 VVR1031212*	70		1

GEORGE BENSON
US, male vocalist/guitarist. This one-time child prodigy was an award-winning jazz guitarist before transforming into a top R&B vocal song stylist. One of the few artists to win Grammy awards for both vocal and instrumental recordings — 303

Date	Title	Peak Position	Weeks at No.1	Weeks on Chart
19 Mar 77	**IN FLIGHT** *Warner Brothers K 56237* ○	19		23
18 Feb 78	**WEEKEND IN L.A.** *Warner Brothers K 66074* ○	47		1
24 Mar 79	**LIVING INSIDE YOUR LOVE** *Warner Brothers K 66085*	24		14
26 Jul 80	**GIVE ME THE NIGHT** *Warner Brothers K 56823* ⊛	3		40
14 Nov 81	**THE GEORGE BENSON COLLECTION** *Warner Brothers K 66107* ⊛	19		35
11 Jun 83	**IN YOUR EYES** *Warner Brothers 9237441* ⊛	3		53
26 Jan 85	**20/20** *Warner Brothers 9251781* ●	9		19
19 Oct 85	**THE LOVE SONGS** *K-Tel NE 1308* ⊛x2	1	2	26
6 Sep 86	**WHILE THE CITY SLEEPS** *Warner Brothers WX 55* ●	13		27
11 Jul 87	**COLLABORATION** *Warner Brothers WX 91* & EARL KLUGH	47		6
10 Sep 88	**TWICE THE LOVE** *Warner Brothers WX 160* ○	16		10
8 Jul 89	**TENDERLY** *Warner Brothers WX 263*	52		3
26 Oct 91	**MIDNIGHT MOODS – THE LOVE COLLECTION** *Telstar STAR 2450* ●	25		12
29 Jun 96	**THAT'S RIGHT** *GRP 98242*	61		1
25 Apr 98	**ESSENTIALS – THE VERY BEST OF GEORGE BENSON** *warner.esp/Jive 9548362292* ●	8		10
5 Jul 03	**THE VERY BEST OF – THE GREATEST HITS OF GEORGE BENSON** *WSM 8122736932* ⊛	4		22
27 Mar 04	**IRREPLACEABLE** *GRP 9861996*	58		1

BENTLEY RHYTHM ACE
UK, male instrumental duo — 6

Date	Title	Peak Position	Weeks at No.1	Weeks on Chart
24 May 97	**BENTLEY RHYTHM ACE** *Skint BRASSIC 5CD* ●	13		5
10 Jun 00	**FOR YOUR EARS ONLY** *Parlophone 5257322*	48		1

BERLIN
US, female/male vocal/instrumental group — 11

Date	Title	Peak Position	Weeks at No.1	Weeks on Chart
17 Jan 87	**COUNT THREE AND PRAY** *Mercury MER 101* ○	32		11

SHELLEY BERMAN
US, male comedian — 4

Date	Title	Peak Position	Weeks at No.1	Weeks on Chart
19 Nov 60	**INSIDE SHELLEY BERMAN** *Capitol CLP 1300*	12		4

LEONARD BERNSTEIN
US, male conductor/composer/pianist, d. 14 Oct 1990 (age 72) — 2

Date	Title	Peak Position	Weeks at No.1	Weeks on Chart
10 Feb 90	**BERNSTEIN IN BERLIN – BEETHOVEN SYMPHONY NO. 9** *Deutsche Grammophon 42986*	54		2

CHUCK BERRY
US, male vocalist/guitarist — 53

Date	Title	Peak Position	Weeks at No.1	Weeks on Chart
25 May 63	**CHUCK BERRY** *Pye International NPL 28024*	12		16
5 Oct 63	**CHUCK BERRY ON STAGE** *Pye International NPL 28027*	6		11
7 Dec 63	**MORE CHUCK BERRY** *Pye International NPL 28028*	9		8
30 May 64	**HIS LATEST AND GREATEST** *Pye International NPL 28037*	8		7
3 Oct 64	**YOU NEVER CAN TELL** *Pye International NPL 29039*	18		2
12 Feb 77	**MOTORVATIN'** *Chess 9288 690*	7		9

MIKE BERRY
UK, male vocalist (Michael Bourne) — 3

Date	Title	Peak Position	Weeks at No.1	Weeks on Chart
24 Jan 81	**THE SUNSHINE OF YOUR SMILE** *Polydor 2383 592*	63		3

NICK BERRY
UK, male vocalist/actor — 8

Date	Title	Peak Position	Weeks at No.1	Weeks on Chart
20 Dec 86	**NICK BERRY** *BBC REB 618*	99		1
21 Nov 92	**NICK BERRY** *Columbia 4727182* ●	28		7

BETA BAND
UK, male vocal/instrumental group — 9

Date	Title	Peak Position	Weeks at No.1	Weeks on Chart
10 Oct 98	**THE THREE E.P.'S** *Regal REG 023CD*	35		1
3 Jul 99	**THE BETA BAND** *Regal REG 030CD*	18		2
28 Jul 01	**HOT SHOTS II** *Regal REG 59CDX*	13		3
8 May 04	**HEROES TO ZEROS** *Regal REG101CD*	18		3

BEVERLEY-PHILLIPS ORCHESTRA
UK, male/female orchestra — 9

Date	Title	Peak Position	Weeks at No.1	Weeks on Chart
9 Oct 76	**GOLD ON SILVER** *Warwick WW 5018*	22		9

B-52'S
US, female/male vocal/instrumental group – Kate Pierson, Fred Schneider, Keith Strickland, Cindy Wilson & Ricky Wilson, d. 12 Oct 1985 — 70

Date	Title	Peak Position	Weeks at No.1	Weeks on Chart
4 Aug 79	**THE B-52'S** *Island ILPS 9580*	22		12
13 Sep 80	**WILD PLANET** *Island ILPS 9622*	18		4
11 Jul 81	**THE PARTY MIX ALBUM** *Island IPM 1001*	36		5
27 Feb 82	**MESOPOTAMIA** *EMI ISSP 4006*	18		6
21 May 83	**WHAMMY!** *Island ILPS 9759*	33		4
8 Aug 87	**BOUNCING OFF THE SATELLITES** *Island ILPS 9871*	74		2
29 Jul 89	**COSMIC THING** *Reprise WX 283* ⊛	8		27
14 Jul 90	**THE BEST OF THE B-52'S – DANCE THIS MESS AROUND** *Island ILPS 9959* ○	36		3
11 Jul 92	**GOOD STUFF** *Reprise 7599269432* ○	8		6
26 Apr 08	**FUNPLEX** *EMI 5197452*	73		1

BIBLE
UK, male vocal/instrumental group — 2

Date	Title	Peak Position	Weeks at No.1	Weeks on Chart
4 Jun 88	**EUREKA** *Chrysalis CHR 1646*	71		1
7 Oct 89	**THE BIBLE** *Ensign CHEN 12*	67		1

BIFFY CLYRO

UK, male vocal/instrumental trio – Simon Neil & Ben & James Johnston — 17

Date	Title / Label	Peak Position	Weeks at No.1	Weeks on Chart
28 Jun 03	**THE VERTIGO OF BLISS** *Beggars Banquet BBQCD233*	48		1
16 Oct 04	**INFINITY LAND** *Beggars Banquet BBQCD238*	47		1
16 Jun 07	**PUZZLE** *14th Floor 2564699763*	2		15

BIG AUDIO DYNAMITE

UK/US, male vocal/instrumental group — 43

Date	Title / Label	Peak Position	Weeks at No.1	Weeks on Chart
16 Nov 85	**THIS IS BIG AUDIO DYNAMITE** *CBS 26714*	27		27
8 Nov 86	**NO. 10 UPPING STREET** *CBS 4501371*	11		8
9 Jul 88	**TIGHTEN UP VOLUME 88** *CBS 4611991*	33		3
16 Sep 89	**MEGATOP PHOENIX** *CBS 4657901*	26		3
3 Nov 90	**KOOL-AID** *CBS 4674661* II	55		1
17 Aug 91	**THE GLOBE** *Columbia 4677061* II	63		1

BIG BAND

UK, male instrumental group — 1

Date	Title / Label	Peak Position	Weeks at No.1	Weeks on Chart
16 Nov 02	**SWINGIN' WITH THE BIG BAND** *Columbia STVCD 157*	62		1

BIG BEN BANJO BAND

UK, male instrumental group — 1

Date	Title / Label	Peak Position	Weeks at No.1	Weeks on Chart
17 Dec 60	**MORE MINSTREL MELODIES** *Columbia 33SX 1254*	20		1

BIG BROVAZ

UK, male/female vocal/rap/production group – Dionne, Flawless, J-Rock, Randy, Cherise Roberts & Nadia Shepherd — 35

Date	Title / Label	Peak Position	Weeks at No.1	Weeks on Chart
16 Nov 02	**NU FLOW** *Epic 5099402*	6		35

BIG COUNTRY

UK, male vocal/instrumental group – Stuart Adamson, Mark Brzezicki, Tony Butler & Bruce Watson — 149

Date	Title / Label	Peak Position	Weeks at No.1	Weeks on Chart
6 Aug 83	**THE CROSSING** *Mercury MERH 27*	3		80
27 Oct 84	**STEELTOWN** *Mercury MERH 49*	1	1	21
12 Jul 86	**THE SEER** *Mercury MERH 87*	2		16
8 Oct 88	**PEACE IN OUR TIME** *Mercury MERH 130*	9		6
26 May 90	**THROUGH A BIG COUNTRY – GREATEST HITS** *Mercury 8460221*	2		17
28 Sep 91	**NO PLACE LIKE HOME** *Vertigo 5102301*	28		2
3 Apr 93	**THE BUFFALO SKINNERS** *Compulsion CDNOIS 2*	25		2
18 Jun 94	**WITHOUT THE AID OF A SAFETY NET (LIVE)** *Compulsion CDNOIS 5*	35		1
24 Jun 95	**WHY THE LONG FACE** *Transatlantic TRACD 109*	48		2
24 Aug 96	**ECLECTIC** *Transatlantic TRACD 234*	41		1
8 Jun 02	**THE GREATEST HITS OF BIG COUNTRY AND THE SKIDS – THE BEST OF STUART ADAMSON** *Universal TV 5869892* & THE SKIDS	71		1

BIG DADDY

US, male rapper (Antonio Hardy) — 3

Date	Title / Label	Peak Position	Weeks at No.1	Weeks on Chart
30 Sep 89	**IT'S A BIG DADDY THING** *Cold Chillin' WX 305*	37		3

BIG DISH

UK, male vocal/instrumental group — 3

Date	Title / Label	Peak Position	Weeks at No.1	Weeks on Chart
11 Oct 86	**SWIMMER** *Virgin V 2374*	85		1
23 Feb 91	**SATELLITES** *East West WX 400*	43		2

BIG FUN

UK, male vocal group – Phil Creswick, Mark Gillespie & Jason John — 11

Date	Title / Label	Peak Position	Weeks at No.1	Weeks on Chart
12 May 90	**A POCKETFUL OF DREAMS** *Jive FUN 1*	7		11

BIKINI KILL/HUGGY BEAR

US, female/male vocal/instrumental group — 2

Date	Title / Label	Peak Position	Weeks at No.1	Weeks on Chart
30 Sep 89	**YEAH YEAH YEAH YEAH/OUR TROUBLED YOUTH** *Catcall TUSS 001*	12		2

MR ACKER BILK

UK, male clarinettist/vocalist/band leader — 161

Date	Title / Label	Peak Position	Weeks at No.1	Weeks on Chart
19 Mar 60	**SEVEN AGES OF ACKER** *Columbia 33SX 1205*	6		6
9 Apr 60	**ACKER BILK'S OMNIBUS** *Pye NJL 22*	14		3
4 Mar 61	**ACKER** *Columbia 33SX 1248*	17		1
1 Apr 61	**GOLDEN TREASURY OF BILK** *Columbia 33SX 1304*	11		6
27 May 61	**BEST OF BARBER AND BILK VOLUME 1** *Pye Golden Guinea GGL 0075* CHRIS BARBER & ACKER BILK	4		43
11 Nov 61	**BEST OF BARBER AND BILK VOLUME 2** *Pye Golden Guinea GGL 0096* CHRIS BARBER & ACKER BILK	8		18
26 May 62	**STRANGER ON THE SHORE** *Columbia 33SX 1407*	6		28
25 Aug 62	**BEST OF BALL, BARBER AND BILK** *Pye Golden Guinea GGL 0131* KENNY BALL, CHRIS BARBER & ACKER BILK	1	2	24
4 May 63	**A TASTE OF HONEY** *Columbia 33SX 1493*	17		4
9 Oct 76	**THE ONE FOR ME** *Pye NSPX 41052*	38		6
4 Jun 77	**SHEER MAGIC** *Warwick WW 5028*	5		8
11 Nov 78	**EVERGREEN** *Warwick PW 5045*	17		14

BILLY TALENT

Canada, male vocal/instrumental group — 1

Date	Title / Label	Peak Position	Weeks at No.1	Weeks on Chart
8 Jul 06	**BILLY TALENT II** *Atlantic 7567839412*	46		1

BIOHAZARD

US, male vocal/instrumental group — 2

Date	Title / Label	Peak Position	Weeks at No.1	Weeks on Chart
14 May 94	**STATE OF THE WORLD ADDRESS** *Warner Brothers 9362455952*	72		1
8 Jun 96	**MATA LEAO** *Warner Brothers 9362462082*	72		1

BIOSPHERE

Norway, male producer/keyboard player (Ger Jenssen) — 1

Date	Title / Label	Peak Position	Weeks at No.1	Weeks on Chart
5 Mar 94	**PATASHNIK** *Apollo AMB 3927CDX*	50		1

BIRDLAND

UK, male vocal/instrumental group — 1

Date	Title / Label	Peak Position	Weeks at No.1	Weeks on Chart
2 Mar 91	**BIRDLAND** *Lazy 25*	44		1

BIRTHDAY PARTY

Australia, male vocal/instrumental group — 3

Date	Title / Label	Peak Position	Weeks at No.1	Weeks on Chart
24 Jul 82	**JUNKYARD** *4AD CAD 207*	73		3

BIS

UK, male/female vocal/instrumental group — 1

Date	Title / Label	Peak Position	Weeks at No.1	Weeks on Chart
19 Apr 97	**THE NEW TRANSISTOR HEROES** *Wiiija WIJCD 1064*	55		1

STEPHEN BISHOP

US, male pianist — 3

Date	Title / Label	Peak Position	Weeks at No.1	Weeks on Chart
1 Apr 72	**GREIG AND SCHUMANN PIANO CONCERTOS** *Philips 6500 166*	34		3

BIZARRE

US, male rapper (Rufus Johnson). See D12 — 1

Date	Title / Label	Peak Position	Weeks at No.1	Weeks on Chart
9 Jul 05	**HANNI CAP CIRCUS** *Sanctuary Urban SANCD363*	43		1

BIZARRE INC

UK, male/female vocal/instrumental group — 2

Date	Title / Label	Peak Position	Weeks at No.1	Weeks on Chart
7 Nov 92	**ENERGIQUE** *Vinyl Solution STEAM 47CD*	41		2

BJORK

Iceland, female vocalist/multi-instrumentalist/producer (Björk Gudmundsdóttir). See Sugarcubes — 133

Date	Title / Label	Peak Position	Weeks at No.1	Weeks on Chart
17 Jul 93	**DEBUT** *One Little Indian TPLP 31CD* x2	3		69
24 Jun 95	**POST/TELEGRAM** *One Little Indian TPLP 51CD*	2		38
4 Oct 97	**HOMOGENIC** *One Little Indian TPLP 71CD*	4		13
30 Sep 00	**SELMA SONGS (OST)** *One Little Indian TPLP 151CD*	34		1
8 Sep 01	**VESPERTINE** *One Little Indian TPLP 101CD*	8		4
16 Nov 02	**GREATEST HITS** *One Little Indian TPLP 359CD*	53		2
11 Sep 04	**MEDULLA** *One Little Indian TPLP 358CD*	9		3
19 May 07	**VOLTA** *One Little Indian TPLP460CDL*	7		3

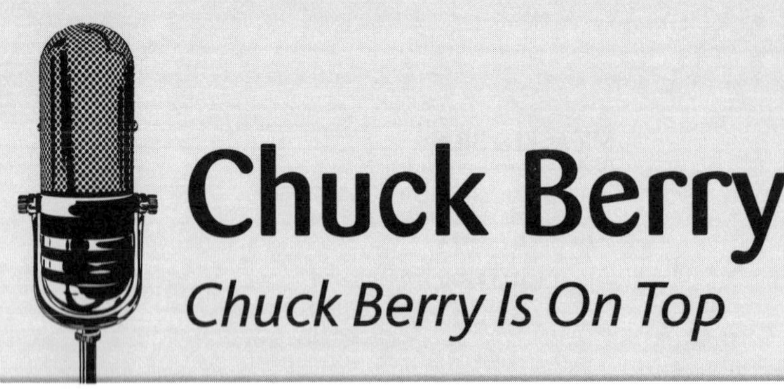

Chuck Berry

Chuck Berry Is On Top

CHUCK BERRY IS ON TOP, his third album (discounting the soundtrack album *Rock, Rock, Rock*), is also his masterpiece. It is testament to the fact that regardless of whoever 'invented' rock 'n' roll – Elvis, Jerry Lee, Little Richard – it was Chuck Berry who gave it shape, form and some of its most enduring content.

The album is like a Rosetta Stone of rock 'n' roll, a document via which 1960s, 1970s and 1980s rock can be deciphered and defined. Its clarity of vision courses through the best of everything that followed. It is included here – despite its failure to chart – as a precursor, a template for many of the albums that later did hit the official listings herein. After all, without this record, there would be no Beatles, no Rolling Stones, The Who, no Sex Pistols . . . and so on and so on. The record's best-known track, 'Johnny B. Goode', was so pivotal within popular culture that it was sent into space onboard the *Voyager I* spacecraft in 1977, intended to speak on our behalf to aliens across the galaxies about the finest aspects of the human race.

The album is like a Rosetta Stone of rock 'n' roll

The album's influence at the end of the 1950s was immense, as the initial melting pot of rock 'n' roll was still only being stirred. Half a century on, the track names are still redolent of all that has been great about the genre: 'Almost Grown', 'Carol', 'Maybellene', (already three years old and a previous chart hit), 'Sweet Little Rock and Roller', 'Roll Over Beethoven' . . . mammoth songs which all still work like beautifully made but simple Swiss watches. At least one song ('Jo Jo Gunn') spawned the name of a future group and, in 'Johnny B. Goode', many have argued that Berry produced perhaps the *definitive* pop song.

It is this song, perhaps more than any other, that typifies Chuck's gift – in a world of teen-angst pop, he tells stories. Born in a shack in the backwoods, Chuck's hero Johnny has a route out of poverty: a guitar wrapped in a sack that will some day put his name in lights. Chuck understood how to talk to his audience. His songs speak in a clear, warm voice and the stories are about girls, school and big, sleek, romantic cars – the everyday experience of American kids – and, at this juncture in the evolution of the teenager, it was all that many of their British counterparts aspired to be. Chuck's heroes and heroines have names his fans can identify with: Carol, Maybellene, Anthony, Johnny, Queenie, Jo Jo and Pedro. They're young ('almost grown', 'sweet little rock and roller', 'Anthony Boy') and, perhaps most importantly, they have *fun*.

He'd already had hits in the pop and the R&B charts, but his writing hit a new maturity on *Chuck Berry Is On Top*. A brown-skinned, handsome man (to paraphrase an early classic), Chuck wrote, performed and played guitar on all the material, a relatively unusual feat when compared to the more limited talents of some of his contemporaries. Chuck created the notes, wrote the stories, hit the tempo and found the market. Three of these songs made the Top 10: 'Let it Rock / Memphis Tennessee' (Number 6); 'No Particular Place To Go' (Number 3) and 'My Ding-A-Ling', which hit the Number 1 spot.

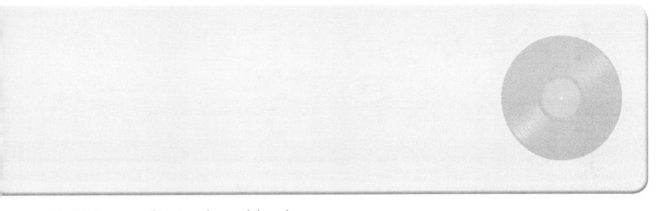

The 1950s were rushing to a close and the unknown pleasures of Beatlemania and JFK were just around the corner and, although he created further classics in the 1960s, ... *On Top* was Chuck's last hurrah in the previous decade. A jail sentence saw him behind bars when The Beatles and The Stones began their American onslaught, and by the time of his release in 1964, 'Carol' and 'Little Queenie' were well established in the Stones' canon, The Beatles had 'Roll Over Beethoven' on vinyl, and every band on the planet was playing 'Johnny B. Goode'. As the 1960s progressed, John Lennon, Keith Richards, Jimi Hendrix and Brian Wilson continued to reference this set of songs. David Bowie and Rod Stewart covered 'Around and Around' and 'Sweet Little Rock and Roller' respectively in the 1970s, while ELO forged a massive hit out of 'Roll Over Beethoven'. Such duplication was partly due to the economy of Berry's two-note guitar riffs, echoed by Johnnie Johnson's staccato piano lines, which were easily learned and copied, repetitive to just the right degree. The Beatles and The Stones owed a huge debt to the songs on this album, a debt adequately acknowledged by Keith Richards and John Lennon in particular. Even the throwaway 'Hey Pedro' found its riff reborn in a number of 1970s hits for other artists.

His songs speak in a clear, warm voice and the stories are about girls, school and big, sleek, romantic cars

Chuck's cross-over from a black to a white audience, developing the latter without losing the former, was matched by Hendrix in the 1960s and hip-hop in the 1990s – note that there is no clue in the song as to Johnny B. Goode's race – Chuck effortlessly bridged this race gap. Crusty old rockers warm up on 'Carol' and twelve-year-olds learn to riff on 'Roll Over Beethoven'. Not Buddy, not Elvis, not The Big O or Jerry Lee. Not Richard, not Fats, not Carl or Ike. *Chuck Berry Is On Top* is the definition of rock 'n' roll.

No Particular Place To Go

Silver-selling ○ Gold-selling ● Platinum-selling ⊛ US No.1 ★ Peak Position Weeks at No.1 Weeks on Chart

BLACK
UK, male vocalist (Colin Vearncombe)

		Peak	No.1	29
26 Sep 87	**WONDERFUL LIFE** *A&M AMA 5165* ⊛	3		23
29 Oct 88	**COMEDY** *A&M AMA 5222* ○	32		4
1 Jun 91	**BLACK** *A&M 3971261*	42		2

CILLA BLACK
UK, female vocalist/TV presenter (Priscilla White)

		Peak	No.1	64
13 Feb 65	**CILLA** *Parlophone PMC 1243*	5		11
14 May 66	**CILLA SINGS A RAINBOW** *Parlophone PMC 7004*	4		15
13 Apr 68	**SHER-OO** *Parlophone PCS 7041*	7		11
30 Nov 68	**THE BEST OF CILLA BLACK** *Parlophone PCS 7065*	21		11
25 Jul 70	**SWEET INSPIRATION** *Parlophone PCS 7103*	42		4
29 Jan 83	**THE VERY BEST OF CILLA BLACK** *Parlophone EMTV 38* ○	20		9
2 Oct 93	**THROUGH THE YEARS** *Columbia 4746502*	41		2
4 Oct 03	**BEGINNINGS – GREATEST HITS AND NEW SONGS** *EMI 5931812*	68		1

FRANK BLACK
US, male vocalist (Charles Thompson). See Pixies

		Peak	No.1	8
20 Mar 93	**FRANK BLACK** *4AD CAD 3004CD*	9		3
4 Jun 94	**TEENAGER OF THE YEAR** *4AD DAD 4009CD*	21		2
3 Feb 96	**THE CULT OF RAY** *Dragnet 4816472*	39		2
16 May 98	**FRANK BLACK AND THE CATHOLICS** *Play It BIAS 370CD*	61		1

MARY BLACK
Ireland, female vocalist

		Peak	No.1	10
3 Jul 93	**THE HOLY GROUND** *Grapevine GRACD 11*	58		2
16 Sep 95	**CIRCUS** *Grapevine GRACD 014*	16		4
29 Mar 97	**SHINE** *Grapevine GRACD 15*	33		3
28 Aug 99	**SPEAKING WITH THE ANGEL** *Grapevine GRACD 264*	61		1

BLACK BOX
Italy, male/female vocal/instrumental/production group

		Peak	No.1	30
5 May 90	**DREAMLAND** *Deconstruction PL 74572* ●	14		30

BLACK BOX RECORDER
UK, male/female vocal/instrumental group

		Peak	No.1	1
13 May 00	**THE FACTS OF LIFE** *Nude 16CD*	37		1

BLACK CROWES
US, male vocal/instrumental group – Chris Robinson, Jeff Cease (replaced by Marc Ford), Johnny Colt, Steve Gorman, Eddie Harsch & Rich Robinson

		Peak	No.1	34
24 Aug 91	**SHAKE YOUR MONEY MAKER** *Def American 8425151* ○	36		11
23 May 92	**THE SOUTHERN HARMONY AND MUSICAL COMPANION** *Def American 5122632* ★	2		7
12 Nov 94	**AMORICA** *American Recordings 74321241942* ○	8		4
3 Aug 96	**THREE SNAKES AND ONE CHARM** *American Recordings 74321384842*	17		3
23 Jan 99	**BY YOUR SIDE** *Columbia 4916692*	34		2
22 Jul 00	**LIVE AT THE GREEK** *SPV Recordings SPV 09172022* JIMMY PAGE & THE BLACK CROWES	39		4
19 May 01	**LIONS** *V2 VVR 1015672*	37		2
15 Mar 08	**WARPAINT** *Silver Arrow 2028611271*	52		1

BLACK DOG
UK, male instrumentalist/producer (Ken Downie)

		Peak	No.1	2
28 Jan 95	**SPANNERS** *Warp PUPCD 1*	30		2

BLACK EYED PEAS
US, male/female vocal/rap/instrumental group – Will Adams (will.i.am*), Stacy Ferguson (Fergie*), Jaime Gómez (Taboo) & Allan Pineda Lindo (apl.de.ap)

		Peak	No.1	134
30 Aug 03	**ELEPHUNK** *A&M 9860365* ⊛**x4**	3		67
11 Jun 05	**MONKEY BUSINESS** *A&M 9882184* ⊛**x3**	4		67

BLACK GRAPE
UK, male vocal/instrumental group – Shaun Ryder, Bez (Mark Berry), Kermit, Jed Lynch & Psycho

		Peak	No.1	46
19 Aug 95	**IT'S GREAT WHEN YOU'RE STRAIGHT…YEAH** *Radioactive RAD 11224* ⊛	1	2	39
22 Nov 97	**STUPID STUPID STUPID** *Radioactive RARD 11716* ●	11		7

BLACK KEYS
US, male vocal/instrumental duo

		Peak	No.1	3
18 Sep 04	**RUBBER FACTORY** *Fat Possum 03792*	62		1
12 Apr 08	**ATTACK AND RELEASE** *V2 VVR1050451*	34		2

BLACK KIDS
US, male/female vocal/instrumental group – Reggie Youngblood, Owen Holmes, Kevin Snow, Dawn Watley & Ali Youngblood

		Peak	No.1	6
19 Jul 08	**PARTIE TRAUMATIC** *Almost Gold AGUK001CD*	5		6

BLACK LABEL SOCIETY
US, male vocal/instrumental group

		Peak	No.1	1
23 Sep 06	**SHOT TO HELL** *Roadrunner RR80482*	69		1

BLACK LACE
UK, male vocal/instrumental duo – Alan Barton, d. 23 Mar 1995, & Colin Routh

		Peak	No.1	26
8 Dec 84	**PARTY PARTY – 16 GREAT PARTY ICEBREAKERS** *Telstar STAR 2250* ⊛	4		14
7 Dec 85	**PARTY PARTY 2** *Telstar STAR 2266* ○	18		6
6 Dec 86	**PARTY CRAZY** *Telstar STAR 2288*	58		6

BLACK MOUNTAIN
Canada, male vocal/instrumental group

		Peak	No.1	1
2 Feb 08	**IN THE FUTURE** *Jagjaguwar JAG130*	72		1

BLACK REBEL MOTORCYCLE CLUB
US, male vocal/instrumental group – Robert Levon Been, Peter Hayes & Nick Jago

		Peak	No.1	28
26 Jan 02	**BLACK REBEL MOTORCYCLE CLUB** *Virgin CDVUS 207* ●	25		17
6 Sep 03	**TAKE THEM ON ON YOUR OWN** *Virgin CDVUS 245* ●	3		5
3 Sep 05	**HOWL** *Echo ECHCX67* ○	14		4
12 May 07	**BABY 81** *Island/Uni-Island 1733090*	15		2

BLACK, ROCK & RON
US, male rap group

		Peak	No.1	1
22 Apr 89	**STOP THE WORLD** *Supreme SU 5*	72		1

BLACK SABBATH
UK, male vocal/instrumental group – Ozzy Osbourne*, Tommi Iommi, Terence "Geezer" Butler & Bill Ward

		Peak	No.1	221
7 Mar 70	**BLACK SABBATH** *Vertigo VO 6*	8		42
26 Sep 70	**PARANOID** *Vertigo 6360 011*	1	1	27
21 Aug 71	**MASTER OF REALITY** *Vertigo 6360 050*	5		13
30 Sep 72	**BLACK SABBATH VOLUME 4** *Vertigo 6360 071*	8		10
8 Dec 73	**SABBATH BLOODY SABBATH** *WWA WWA 005* ○	4		11
27 Sep 75	**SABOTAGE** *NEMS 9119 001* ○	7		7
7 Feb 76	**WE SOLD OUR SOUL FOR ROCK 'N' ROLL** *NEMS 6641 335* ○	35		5
6 Nov 76	**TECHNICAL ECSTASY** *Vertigo 9102 750*	13		6
14 Oct 78	**NEVER SAY DIE** *Vertigo 9102 751*	12		6
26 Apr 80	**HEAVEN AND HELL** *Vertigo 9102 752* ●	9		22
5 Jul 80	**BLACK SABBATH LIVE AT LAST** *NEMS BS 001*	5		15
27 Sep 80	**PARANOID** *NEMS NEL 6003*	54		2
14 Nov 81	**MOB RULES** *Mercury 6V02119* ○	12		14
22 Jan 83	**LIVE EVIL** *Vertigo SAB 10*	13		11
24 Sep 83	**BORN AGAIN** *Vertigo VERL 8*	4		7
1 Mar 86	**SEVENTH STAR** *Vertigo VERH 29* FEATURING TONY IOMMI	27		5
28 Nov 87	**THE ETERNAL IDOL** *Vertigo VERH 51*	66		1
29 Apr 89	**HEADLESS CROSS** *I.R.S. EIRSA 1002*	31		2
1 Sep 90	**TYR** *I.R.S. EIRSA 1038*	24		3
4 Jul 92	**DEHUMANIZER** *I.R.S. EIRSCD 1064*	28		2
12 Feb 94	**CROSS PURPOSES** *I.R.S. EIRSCD 1067*	41		1
17 Jun 95	**FORBIDDEN** *I.R.S. EIRSCD 1072*	71		1
31 Oct 98	**REUNION** *Epic 4919542*	41		1

Date	Title	Label	Peak Position	Weeks at No.1	Weeks on Chart
17 Jun 00	**THE BEST OF BLACK SABBATH**	*Metal IS RAWDD145* ●	24		6
6 Jul 02	**PARANOID**	*Castle Music ESMCD 302*	63		1

BLACK SCIENCE ORCHESTRA
UK, male production group — 1

Date	Title	Label	Peak Position	Weeks at No.1	Weeks on Chart
3 Aug 96	**WALTERS ROOM**	*Junior Boy's Own JBOCD 5*	68		1

BLACK STAR LINER
UK, male/female vocal/instrumental group — 1

Date	Title	Label	Peak Position	Weeks at No.1	Weeks on Chart
7 Sep 96	**YEMEN CUTTA CONNECTION**	*EXP EXPCD 006*	66		1

BLACK STONE CHERRY
US, male vocal/instrumental group — 2

Date	Title	Label	Peak Position	Weeks at No.1	Weeks on Chart
30 Aug 08	**FOLKLORE & SUPERSTITION**	*Roadrunner RR79402*	23		2

BLACK UHURU
Jamaica, male vocal/instrumental group — 22

Date	Title	Label	Peak Position	Weeks at No.1	Weeks on Chart
13 Jun 81	**RED**	*Island ILPS 9625*	28		13
22 Aug 81	**BLACK UHURU**	*Virgin VX 1004*	81		2
19 Jun 82	**CHILL OUT**	*Island ILPS 9701*	38		6
25 Aug 84	**ANTHEM**	*Island ILPS 9773*	90		1

BAND OF THE BLACK WATCH
UK, military band — 13

Date	Title	Label	Peak Position	Weeks at No.1	Weeks on Chart
7 Feb 76	**SCOTCH ON THE ROCKS**	*Spark SRLM 503*	11		13

BLACK WIDOW
UK, male vocal/instrumental group — 2

Date	Title	Label	Peak Position	Weeks at No.1	Weeks on Chart
4 Apr 70	**SACRIFICE**	*CBS 63948*	32		2

BLACKFOOT
US, male vocal/instrumental group — 22

Date	Title	Label	Peak Position	Weeks at No.1	Weeks on Chart
18 Jul 81	**MARAUDER**	*Atco K 50799*	38		12
11 Sep 82	**HIGHWAY SONG – BLACKFOOT LIVE**	*Atco K 50910*	14		6
21 May 83	**SIOGO**	*Atlantic 7900801*	28		3
29 Sep 84	**VERTICAL SMILES**	*Atco 790218*	82		1

BLACKstreet
US, male vocal group — 36

Date	Title	Label	Peak Position	Weeks at No.1	Weeks on Chart
9 Jul 94	**BLACKstreet**	*Interscope 6544923512* ○	35		6
21 Sep 96	**ANOTHER LEVEL**	*Interscope INTD 90071* ●	26		26
3 Apr 99	**FINALLY**	*Interscope IND 90323*	27		4

RICHARD BLACKWOOD
UK, male comedian/rapper — 2

Date	Title	Label	Peak Position	Weeks at No.1	Weeks on Chart
30 Sep 00	**YOU'LL LOVE TO HATE THIS**	*Hopefield 8573844882*	35		2

BLAKE
UK, male vocal group — 12

Date	Title	Label	Peak Position	Weeks at No.1	Weeks on Chart
17 Nov 07	**BLAKE**	*UCJ 1745108*	18		7
11 Oct 08	**AND SO IT GOES**	*UCJ 4766879*	14		5

HOWARD BLAKE CONDUCTING THE SINFONIA OF LONDON
UK, male conductor & orchestra — 12

Date	Title	Label	Peak Position	Weeks at No.1	Weeks on Chart
22 Dec 84	**THE SNOWMAN**	*CBS 71116* ●	54		12

BLANCMANGE
UK, male vocal/instrumental duo – Neil Arthur & Stephen Luscombe — 57

Date	Title	Label	Peak Position	Weeks at No.1	Weeks on Chart
9 Oct 82	**HAPPY FAMILIES**	*London SH 8552* ●	30		38
26 May 84	**MANGE TOUT**	*London SH 8554* ●	8		17
26 Oct 85	**BELIEVE YOU ME**	*London LONLP 10*	54		2

BLAZIN' SQUAD
UK, male vocal/rap group — 8

Date	Title	Label	Peak Position	Weeks at No.1	Weeks on Chart
7 Dec 02	**IN THE BEGINNING**	*East West 5046610792* ●	33		6
29 Nov 03	**NOW OR NEVER**	*East West 5046703662*	37		2

MARY J. BLIGE
US, female vocalist — 151

Date	Title	Label	Peak Position	Weeks at No.1	Weeks on Chart
20 Mar 93	**WHAT'S THE 411?**	*Uptown UPTD 10681*	53		1
17 Dec 94	**MY LIFE**	*Uptown UPTD 11156*	59		3
26 Apr 97	**SHARE MY WORLD**	*MCA MCD 11619* ● ★	8		32
28 Aug 99	**MARY**	*MCA MCD 11976* ○	5		6
8 Sep 01	**NO MORE DRAMA**	*MCA 1126322* ⊛	4		58
6 Sep 03	**LOVE & LIFE**	*Geffen 9860700* ★	8		5
24 Dec 05	**THE BREAKTHROUGH**	*Geffen 9889349* ● ★	22		30
16 Dec 06	**REFLECTIONS (A RETROSPECTIVE)**	*Geffen 1717881* ●	42		11
16 Feb 08	**GROWING PAINS**	*Geffen 1752392*	6		5

BLIND FAITH
UK, male vocal/instrumental group – Ginger Baker*, Eric Clapton*, Rick Grech & Steve Winwood* — 10

Date	Title	Label	Peak Position	Weeks at No.1	Weeks on Chart
13 Sep 69	**BLIND FAITH**	*Polydor 583059* ★	1	2	10

BLIND MELON
US, male vocal/instrumental group — 4

Date	Title	Label	Peak Position	Weeks at No.1	Weeks on Chart
22 Jan 94	**BLIND MELON**	*Capitol CDEST 2188*	53		3
19 Aug 95	**SOUP**	*Capitol CDEST 2261* ⊛	48		1

BLINK 182
US, male vocal/instrumental group – Tom DeLonge, Travis Barker & Mark Hoppus — 96

Date	Title	Label	Peak Position	Weeks at No.1	Weeks on Chart
11 Mar 00	**ENEMA OF THE STATE**	*MCA MCD 11950* ⊛	15		32
18 Nov 00	**THE MARK TOM & TRAVIS SHOW**	*MCA 1123792*	69		1
23 Jun 01	**TAKE OFF YOUR PANTS AND JACKET**	*MCA 1126712* ● ★	4		24
29 Nov 03	**BLINK 182**	*Geffen 9861408* ⊛	22		26
12 Nov 05	**GREATEST HITS**	*Geffen 9887099* ⊛	6		13

BLITZ
UK, male vocal/instrumental group — 3

Date	Title	Label	Peak Position	Weeks at No.1	Weeks on Chart
6 Nov 82	**VOICE OF A GENERATION**	*No Future PUNK 1*	27		3

BLOC PARTY
UK, male vocal/instrumental group – Kele Okereke, Russell Lissack, Gordon Moakes & Matt Tong — 61

Date	Title	Label	Peak Position	Weeks at No.1	Weeks on Chart
26 Feb 05	**SILENT ALARM**	*Wichita WEBB075CD* ⊛	3		35
10 Sep 05	**SILENT ALARM REMIXED**	*Wichita WEBB090CD*	54		1
17 Feb 07	**A WEEKEND IN THE CITY**	*Wichita WEBB120CDL* ●	2		22
8 Nov 08	**INTIMACY**	*Wichita WEBB185CD*	8		3

BLOCKHEADS
UK, male vocal/instrumental group — 3

Date	Title	Label	Peak Position	Weeks at No.1	Weeks on Chart
21 Apr 01	**BRAND NEW BOOTS AND PANTIES**	*East Central One NEWBOOTS 2CD*	44		3

BLODWYN PIG
UK, male vocal/instrumental group – Mick Abrahams, Ron Berg, Jack Lancaster, Andy Pyle — 11

Date	Title	Label	Peak Position	Weeks at No.1	Weeks on Chart
16 Apr 69	**AHEAD RINGS OUT**	*Island ILPS 9101*	9		4
25 Apr 70	**GETTING TO THIS**	*Chrysalis ILPS 9122*	8		7

BLONDIE
US, female/male vocal/instrumental group – Deborah Harry*, Clem Burke, Jimmy Destri, Chris Stein & Gary Valentine. Influential New York band who went from underground punk rock heroes to new wave pop superstars. The group, who first found fame in the UK, were inducted into the Rock and Roll Hall of Fame in 2006 — 358

Date	Title	Label	Peak Position	Weeks at No.1	Weeks on Chart
4 Mar 78	**PLASTIC LETTERS**	*Chrysalis CHR 1166* ⊛	10		54
23 Sep 78	**PARALLEL LINES**	*Chrysalis CDL 1192* ⊛	1	4	106
10 Mar 79	**BLONDIE**	*Chrysalis CHR 1165* ●	75		1
13 Oct 79	**EAT TO THE BEAT**	*Chrysalis CDL 1225* ⊛	1	1	38

Key: ○ Silver-selling · ● Gold-selling · ⊛ Platinum-selling · ★ US No.1 · Peak Position · Weeks at No.1 · Weeks on Chart

Date	Title / Label	Peak Position	Weeks at No.1	Weeks on Chart
29 Nov 80	**AUTOAMERICAN** *Chrysalis CDL 1290* ⊛	3		16
31 Oct 81	**THE BEST OF BLONDIE** *Chrysalis CDLTV 1* ⊛x2	4		40
5 Jun 82	**THE HUNTER** *Chrysalis CDL 1384*	9		12
17 Dec 88	**ONCE MORE INTO THE BLEACH** *Chrysalis CJB 2* DEBBIE HARRY & BLONDIE	50		4
16 Mar 91	**THE COMPLETE PICTURE – THE VERY BEST OF DEBORAH HARRY AND BLONDIE** *Chrysalis CHR 1817* DEBORAH HARRY & BLONDIE	3		22
29 Jul 95	**BEAUTIFUL – THE REMIX ALBUM** *Chrysalis CDCHR 6105*	25		2
25 Jul 98	**ATOMIC/ATOMIX – THE VERY BEST OF BLONDIE** *EMI 4992882* ⊛	12		34
27 Feb 99	**NO EXIT** *Beyond 74321641142* ●	3		15
2 Nov 02	**GREATEST HITS** *Chrysalis 5431052* ○	38		4
25 Oct 03	**THE CURSE OF BLONDIE** *Epic 5119219*	36		1
10 Apr 04	**PARALLEL LINES** *Fame CD 25CR01*	60		2
19 Nov 05	**GREATEST HITS** *EMI 3450542* ●	48		7

BLOOD RED SHOES

UK, male/female vocal/instrumental duo — **1**

Date	Title / Label	Peak Position	Weeks at No.1	Weeks on Chart
26 Apr 08	**BOX OF SECRETS** *Mercury 1763550*	47		1

BLOOD, SWEAT & TEARS

US/Canada, male vocal/instrumental group — **21**

Date	Title / Label	Peak Position	Weeks at No.1	Weeks on Chart
13 Jul 68	**CHILD IS THE FATHER TO THE MAN** *CBS 63296*	40		1
12 Apr 69	**BLOOD SWEAT AND TEARS** *CBS 63504* ★	15		8
8 Aug 70	**BLOOD SWEAT AND TEARS 3** *CBS 64024* ★	14		12

BLOODHOUND GANG

US, male vocal/instrumental group — **7**

Date	Title / Label	Peak Position	Weeks at No.1	Weeks on Chart
6 May 00	**HOORAY FOR BOOBIES** *Geffen 4904572*	37		7

BLOW MONKEYS

UK, male vocal/instrumental group – Bruce Howard (Dr. Robert), Mick Anker, Neville Henry & Tony Kiley — **27**

Date	Title / Label	Peak Position	Weeks at No.1	Weeks on Chart
19 Apr 86	**ANIMAL MAGIC** *RCA PL 70910* ○	21		8
25 Apr 87	**SHE WAS ONLY A GROCER'S DAUGHTER** *RCA PL 71245* ○	20		8
11 Feb 89	**WHOOPS! THERE GOES THE NEIGHBOURHOOD** *RCA PL 71858*	46		2
26 Aug 89	**CHOICES – THE SINGLES COLLECTION** *RCA PL 74191* ●	5		9

BLOWING FREE

UK, male instrumental duo – Bradley & Stewart Palmer. See Hypnosis, In Tune, Raindance, School Of Excellence — **14**

Date	Title / Label	Peak Position	Weeks at No.1	Weeks on Chart
29 Jul 95	**SAX MOODS** *Dino DINCD 106*	6		13
30 Nov 96	**SAX MOODS – VOLUME 2** *Dino DINCD 118*	70		1

BLUE

UK, male vocal group – Antony Costa, Duncan James*, Lee Ryan* & Simon Webbe* — **119**

Date	Title / Label	Peak Position	Weeks at No.1	Weeks on Chart
8 Dec 01	**ALL RISE** *Innocent CDSIN 8* ⊛x4	1	1	63
16 Nov 02	**ONE LOVE** *Innocent CDSIN 11* ⊛x4	1	1	29
15 Nov 03	**GUILTY** *Innocent CDSIN 13* ⊛x2	1	1	16
27 Nov 04	**BEST OF BLUE** *Innocent CDSINX18* ⊛	6		11

BLUE AEROPLANES

UK, male/female vocal/instrumental group — **5**

Date	Title / Label	Peak Position	Weeks at No.1	Weeks on Chart
24 Feb 90	**SWAGGER** *Ensign CHEN 13*	54		1
17 Aug 91	**BEATSONGS** *Ensign CHEN 21*	33		3
12 Mar 94	**LIFE MODEL** *Beggars Banquet BBQCD 143*	59		1

BLUE MURDER

UK, male vocal/instrumental group — **3**

Date	Title / Label	Peak Position	Weeks at No.1	Weeks on Chart
6 May 89	**BLUE MURDER** *Geffen WX 245*	45		3

BLUE NILE

UK, male vocal/instrumental group – Paul Buchanan, Robert Bell & Paul Joseph Moore — **13**

Date	Title / Label	Peak Position	Weeks at No.1	Weeks on Chart
19 May 84	**A WALK ACROSS THE ROOFTOPS** *Linn LKH 1*	80		2
21 Oct 89	**HATS** *Linn LKH 2*	12		4
22 Jun 96	**PEACE AT LAST** *Warner Brothers 9362458482*	13		4
11 Sep 04	**HIGH** *Sanctuary SANDP285* ○	10		3

BLUE OYSTER CULT

US, male vocal/instrumental group — **40**

Date	Title / Label	Peak Position	Weeks at No.1	Weeks on Chart
3 Jul 76	**AGENTS OF FORTUNE** *CBS 81385*	26		10
4 Feb 78	**SPECTRES** *CBS 86050*	60		1
28 Oct 78	**SOME ENCHANTED EVENING** *CBS 86074*	18		4
18 Aug 79	**MIRRORS** *CBS 86087*	46		5
19 Jul 80	**CULTOSAURUS ERECTUS** *CBS 86120*	12		7
25 Jul 81	**FIRE OF UNKNOWN ORIGIN** *CBS 85137*	29		7
22 May 82	**EXTRATERRESTRIAL LIVE** *CBS 22203*	39		5
19 Nov 83	**THE REVOLUTION TONIGHT** *CBS 25686*	95		1

BLUE PEARL

UK/US, male/female vocal/instrumental group — **2**

Date	Title / Label	Peak Position	Weeks at No.1	Weeks on Chart
1 Dec 90	**NAKED** *Big Life BLR LP4*	58		2

BLUE RONDO A LA TURK

UK, male vocal/instrumental group — **2**

Date	Title / Label	Peak Position	Weeks at No.1	Weeks on Chart
6 Nov 82	**CHEWING THE FAT** *Diable Noir V 2240*	80		2

BLUEBELLS

UK, male vocal/instrumental group — **15**

Date	Title / Label	Peak Position	Weeks at No.1	Weeks on Chart
11 Aug 84	**SISTERS** *London LONLP 1*	22		10
17 Apr 93	**THE BLUEBELLS – THE SINGLES COLLECTION** *London 8284052*	27		5

BLUES BAND

UK, male vocal/instrumental group — **18**

Date	Title / Label	Peak Position	Weeks at No.1	Weeks on Chart
8 Mar 80	**OFFICIAL BOOTLEG ALBUM** *Arista BBBP 101*	40		9
18 Oct 80	**READY** *Arista BB 2*	36		6
17 Oct 81	**ITCHY FEET** *Arista BB 3*	60		3

BLUES BROTHERS

US/Canada, male vocal duo/actors – John Belushi, d. 5 Mar 1982, & Dan Aykroyd — **3**

Date	Title / Label	Peak Position	Weeks at No.1	Weeks on Chart
4 Dec 04	**THE DEFINITIVE COLLECTION** *Atlantic 7567808405* ○	64		3

BLUETONES

UK, male vocal/instrumental group – Mark Morriss, Eds Chesters, Adam Devlin & Scott Morriss — **50**

Date	Title / Label	Peak Position	Weeks at No.1	Weeks on Chart
24 Feb 96	**EXPECTING TO FLY** *Superior Quality BLUE 004CD* ⊛	1	1	25
21 Mar 98	**RETURN TO THE LAST CHANCE SALOON** *Superior Quality BLUED 008* ●	10		16
27 May 00	**SCIENCE & NATURE** *Superior Quality BLUECD 014*	7		4
20 Apr 02	**THE SINGLES** *Superior Quality BLUEDD 017*	14		4
24 May 03	**LUXEMBOURG** *Superior Quality BLUE019CD*	49		1

JAMES BLUNT

UK, male vocalist/guitarist (James Blount) — **139**

Date	Title / Label	Peak Position	Weeks at No.1	Weeks on Chart
26 Mar 05	**BACK TO BEDLAM** *Atlantic 7567837525* ⊛x10	1	10	106
29 Sep 07	**ALL THE LOST SOULS** *Atlantic 7567899659* ⊛x2	1	1	33

BLUR

UK, male vocal/instrumental group – Damon Albarn, Graham Coxon* (left 2002), Alex James & Dave Rowntree. Britpop heavyweights who won four BRIT awards in 1995, including one for Best British Album (*Parklife*). After five consecutive No.1 studio albums, Albarn put the band on hold to concentrate on Gorillaz, The Good, The Bad & The Queen and Monkey — **311**

Date	Title / Label	Peak Position	Weeks at No.1	Weeks on Chart
7 Sep 91	**LEISURE** *Food FOODLP 6* ●	7		12
22 May 93	**MODERN LIFE IS RUBBISH** *Food FOODCD 9* ●	15		14
7 May 94	**PARKLIFE** *Food FOODCD 10* ⊛x4	1	1	106
23 Sep 95	**THE GREAT ESCAPE** *Food FOODCD 14* ⊛x3	1	2	47
22 Feb 97	**BLUR** *Food FOODCD 19* ⊛	1	1	65
27 Mar 99	**13** *Food FOODCD 29* ⊛	1	2	27
11 Nov 00	**BLUR: BEST OF** *Food FOODCD 33* ⊛x2	3		32
17 May 03	**THINK TANK** *Parlophone 5829972* ●	1	1	8

B M EX

UK, male production/instrumental group — **2**

Date	Title / Label	Peak Position	Weeks at No.1	Weeks on Chart
30 Jan 93	**APPOLONIA/FEEL THE DROP** *Union City UCRCD 14*	17		2

Silver-selling ○ Gold-selling ● Platinum-selling ⊛ US No.1 ★ | Peak Position | Weeks at No.1 | Weeks on Chart

BOARDS OF CANADA
UK, male instrumental/production duo

Date	Album	Peak Position	Weeks at No.1	Weeks on Chart
				4
2 Mar 02	**GEOGADDI** *Warp WARPCD 101*	21		2
29 Oct 05	**THE CAMPFIRE HEADPHASE** *Warp WARPCD123*	41		1
10 Jun 06	**TRANS CANADA HIGHWAY** *Warp WAP200CD*	63		1

BOB THE BUILDER
UK, male builder/vocalist (voiced by actor Neil Morrissey)

Date	Album	Peak Position	Weeks at No.1	Weeks on Chart
				12
13 Oct 01	**THE ALBUM** *BBC Music WMSF 60472* ●	4		12

BOBBY
US, male vocalist (Bobby Wilson)

Date	Album	Peak Position	Weeks at No.1	Weeks on Chart
				1
26 May 07	**SPECIAL OCCASION** *Def Jam B0007226CD*	68		1

ANDREA BOCELLI
Italy, male vocalist

Date	Album	Peak Position	Weeks at No.1	Weeks on Chart
				195
31 May 97	**ROMANZA** *Philips Classics 4564562* ⊛	6		25
9 May 98	**ARIA – THE OPERA ALBUM** *Philips 4620332*	33		10
13 Feb 99	**VIAGGIO ITALIANO** *Philips 4621962* ⊛	24		11
10 Apr 99	**SOGNO** *Sugar 5472212* ⊛	4		42
20 Nov 99	**SACRED ARIAS** *Philips 4626002*	20		12
23 Sep 00	**VERDI** *Philips 4646002* ○	17		10
27 Oct 01	**CIELI DE TOSCANA** *Polydor 5892452* ⊛	3		16
16 Nov 02	**SENTIMENTO** *Philips 4734102* ⊛	7		15
13 Nov 04	**ANDREA** *Universal 9867973* ●	19		7
18 Mar 06	**AMORE** *Sugar/UCJ 9876021* ●	4		14
24 Nov 07	**VIVERE – GREATEST HITS** *Sugar/UCJ 1746680* ⊛	4		20
1 Mar 08	**VIVERE – LIVE IN TUSCANY** *Sugar/UCJ 1290602*	26		5
15 Nov 08	**INCANTO** *Decca 4781071*	12		8+

BODINES
UK, male vocal/instrumental group

Date	Album	Peak Position	Weeks at No.1	Weeks on Chart
				1
29 Aug 87	**PLAYED** *Pop BODL 2001*	94		1

BODY COUNT
US, male rap/instrumental group

Date	Album	Peak Position	Weeks at No.1	Weeks on Chart
				2
17 Sep 94	**BORN DEAD** *Rhyme Syndicate RSYND 2*	15		2

ALFIE BOE
UK, male vocalist

Date	Album	Peak Position	Weeks at No.1	Weeks on Chart
				1
23 Jun 07	**ONWARD** *EMI Classics 3884292*	72		1

SUZY BOGGUSS
US, female vocalist/guitarist

Date	Album	Peak Position	Weeks at No.1	Weeks on Chart
				1
25 Sep 93	**SOMETHING UP MY SLEEVE** *Liberty CDEST 221*	69		1

C.J. BOLLAND
Belgium, male producer (Christian Jay Bolland)

Date	Album	Peak Position	Weeks at No.1	Weeks on Chart
				2
26 Oct 96	**THE ANALOGUE THEATRE** *Internal TRUCD 13*	43		2

BOLSHOI
UK, male vocal/instrumental group

Date	Album	Peak Position	Weeks at No.1	Weeks on Chart
				1
3 Oct 87	**LINDY'S PARTY** *Beggars Banquet BEGA 86*	100		1

MICHAEL BOLTON
US, male vocalist (Michael Bolotin)

Date	Album	Peak Position	Weeks at No.1	Weeks on Chart
				243
17 Mar 90	**SOUL PROVIDER** *CBS 4653431* ⊛x4	4		72
11 Aug 90	**THE HUNGER** *CBS 4601631*	44		5
18 May 91	**TIME, LOVE AND TENDERNESS** *Columbia 4678121* ⊛x4 ★	2		57
10 Oct 92	**TIMELESS (THE CLASSICS)** *Columbia 4723022* ⊛ ★	3		24
27 Nov 93	**THE ONE THING** *Columbia 4743552* ⊛	4		24
30 Sep 95	**GREATEST HITS 1985–1995** *Columbia 4810022* ⊛	2		30
22 Nov 97	**ALL THAT MATTERS** *Columbia 4885312* ●	20		7
2 May 98	**MY SECRET PASSION – THE ARIAS** *Sony Classical SK 63077*	25		5
4 Dec 99	**TIMELESS – THE CLASSICS VOLUME 2** *Columbia 4723022*	50		2
6 Apr 02	**ONLY A WOMAN LIKE YOU** *Jive 9223522*	19		2
27 Mar 04	**VINTAGE** *Universal TV 9817973*	23		2
29 Oct 05	**THE VERY BEST OF** *Columbia 82876747942* ●	18		12
2 Dec 06	**BOLTON SWINGS SINATRA** *Concord 7230038*	54		1

BOMB THE BASS
UK, male producer (Tim Simenon)

Date	Album	Peak Position	Weeks at No.1	Weeks on Chart
				16
22 Oct 88	**INTO THE DRAGON** *Rhythm King DOOD 1* ●	18		10
31 Aug 91	**UNKNOWN TERRITORY** *Rhythm King 4687740*	19		4
15 Apr 95	**CLEAR** *Fourth & Broadway BRCD 611*	22		2

BOMBALURINA FEATURING TIMMY MALLETT
UK, male/female vocal group & male vocalist/TV presenter

Date	Album	Peak Position	Weeks at No.1	Weeks on Chart
				5
15 Dec 90	**HUGGIN' AN' A KISSIN'** *Polydor 8476481* ○	55		5

BOMFUNK MCs
Finland, male DJ/rap duo

Date	Album	Peak Position	Weeks at No.1	Weeks on Chart
				2
26 Aug 00	**IN STEREO** *Epidrome 4943096*	33		2

BON JOVI
US, male vocal/instrumental group – Jon Bon Jovi*, David Bryan, Richie Sambora*, Alec John Such & Tico Torres. The stadium-packing New Jersey veterans were the biggest-selling album act of 1994 and enjoyed a string of five consecutive chart-toppers, all of which debuted at No.1. They have sold more than 120 million albums worldwide

Date	Album	Peak Position	Weeks at No.1	Weeks on Chart
				465
28 Apr 84	**BON JOVI** *Vertigo VERL 14*	71		3
11 May 85	**7800° FAHRENHEIT** *Vertigo VERL 24*	28		12
20 Sep 86	**SLIPPERY WHEN WET** *Vertigo VERH 38* ⊛x3 ★	6		123
1 Oct 88	**NEW JERSEY** *Vertigo VERH 62* ⊛x2 ★	1	2	47
14 Nov 92	**KEEP THE FAITH** *Jambco 5141972* ⊛	1	1	70
22 Oct 94	**CROSS ROAD – THE BEST OF BON JOVI** *Jambco 5229362* ⊛x5	1	5	90
1 Jul 95	**THESE DAYS** *Vertigo 5282482* ⊛x2	1	4	50
10 Jun 00	**CRUSH** *Mercury 5425622* ⊛	1	1	29
26 May 01	**ONE WILD NIGHT – LIVE 1985-2001** *Mercury 5488652* ●	2		9
5 Oct 02	**BOUNCE** *Mercury 0633952* ●	2		9
15 Nov 03	**THIS LEFT FEELS RIGHT** *Mercury 9861391* ●	4		8
1 Oct 05	**HAVE A NICE DAY** *Mercury 9884960* ●	2		9
23 Jun 07	**LOST HIGHWAY** *Mercury 1739572* ● ★	2		6

JON BON JOVI
US, male vocalist/guitarist (John Bongiovi Jr.). See Bon Jovi

Date	Album	Peak Position	Weeks at No.1	Weeks on Chart
				41
25 Aug 90	**BLAZE OF GLORY/YOUNG GUNS II (OST)** *Vertigo 8464731* ●	2		23
28 Jun 97	**DESTINATION ANYWHERE** *Mercury 5360112* ●	2		18

JOE BONAMASSA
US, male vocalist/guitarist

Date	Album	Peak Position	Weeks at No.1	Weeks on Chart
				2
8 Sep 07	**SLOE GIN** *Provogue 060283*	50		1
6 Sep 08	**LIVE – FROM NOWHERE IN PARTICULAR** *Provogue PRD72482*	45		1

BOND
Australia/UK, female instrumental group

Date	Album	Peak Position	Weeks at No.1	Weeks on Chart
				23
14 Oct 00	**BORN** *Decca 4670912* ●	16		18
16 Nov 02	**SHINE** *Decca 4734602*	26		3
18 Sep 04	**CLASSIFIED** *Decca 4756301*	32		2

GRAHAM BOND
UK, male vocalist/keyboard player, d. 8 May 1974 (age 36)

Date	Album	Peak Position	Weeks at No.1	Weeks on Chart
				2
20 Jun 70	**SOLID BOND** *Warner Brothers WS 3001*	40		2

GARY U.S. BONDS
US, male vocalist (Gary Anderson)

Date	Album	Peak Position	Weeks at No.1	Weeks on Chart
				8
22 Aug 81	**DEDICATION** *EMI America AML 3017*	43		3
10 Jul 82	**ON THE LINE** *EMI America AML 3022*	55		5

BONE THUGS-N-HARMONY
US, male rap group

Date	Album	Peak Position	Weeks at No.1	Weeks on Chart
				4
31 Aug 96	**E.1999 ETERNAL** *Epic 4810386* ★	39		3
9 Aug 97	**THE ART OF WAR** *Epic 4880802* ★	42		1

Silver-selling ○ Gold-selling ● Platinum-selling ⊛ US No.1 ★ | Peak Position | Weeks at No.1 | Weeks on Chart

BONEY M

Jamaica/Aruba/Montserrat, female/male vocal group – Liz Mitchell, Marcia Barrett, Bobby Farrell & Maizie Williams — 147

Date	Album	Peak Position	Weeks at No.1	Weeks on Chart
23 Apr 77	**TAKE THE HEAT OFF ME** *Atlantic K 50314* ○	40		15
6 Aug 77	**LOVE FOR SALE** *Atlantic K 50385* ●	60		1
29 Jul 78	**NIGHT FLIGHT TO VENUS** *Atlantic/Hansa K 50498* ⊛	1	4	65
29 Sep 79	**OCEANS OF FANTASY** *Atlantic/Hansa K 50610* ⊛	1	1	18
12 Apr 80	**THE MAGIC OF BONEY M** *Atlantic/Hansa BMTV 1* ●	1	2	26
6 Sep 86	**THE BEST OF 10 YEARS – 32 SUPERHITS** *Stylus SMR 621*	35		5
27 Mar 93	**THE GREATEST HITS** *Telstar TCD 2656*	14		10
15 Dec 01	**THE GREATEST HITS** *BMG 74321896142*	66		3
9 Dec 06	**THE MAGIC OF BONEY M** *MCI 88697034772*	48		4

BONFIRE

Germany, male vocal/instrumental group — 1

Date	Album	Peak Position	Weeks at No.1	Weeks on Chart
21 Oct 89	**POINT BLANK** *MSA ZL 74249*	74		1

GRAHAM BONNET

UK, male vocalist. See Rainbow — 3

Date	Album	Peak Position	Weeks at No.1	Weeks on Chart
7 Nov 81	**LINE UP** *Vertigo 6302 151*	62		3

BONNIE PRINCE BILLY

US, male vocalist/guitarist (Will Oldham) — 3

Date	Album	Peak Position	Weeks at No.1	Weeks on Chart
8 Feb 03	**MASTER AND EVERYONE** *Domino Recordings WIGCD121*	48		1
3 Apr 04	**SINGS GREATEST PALACE MUSIC** *Domino Recordings WIGCD140*	63		1
30 Sep 06	**THE LETTING GO** *Domino WIGCD182*	70		1

BONZO DOG DOO-DAH BAND

UK, male vocal/instrumental group — 4

Date	Album	Peak Position	Weeks at No.1	Weeks on Chart
18 Jan 69	**DOUGHNUT IN GRANNY'S GREENHOUSE** *Liberty LBS 83158*	40		1
30 Aug 69	**TADPOLES** *Liberty LBS 83257*	36		1
22 Jun 74	**THE HISTORY OF THE BONZOS** *United Artists UAD 60071*	41		2

BETTY BOO

UK, female vocalist/rapper (Alison Clarkson) — 25

Date	Album	Peak Position	Weeks at No.1	Weeks on Chart
22 Sep 90	**BOOMANIA** *Rhythm King LEFTLP 12* ⊛	4		24
24 Oct 92	**GRRR! IT'S BETTY BOO** *WEA 4509909082*	62		1

BOO RADLEYS

UK, male vocal/instrumental group – Sice (Simon Rowbottom), Timothy Brown, Martin Carr & Rob Cieka — 29

Date	Album	Peak Position	Weeks at No.1	Weeks on Chart
4 Apr 92	**EVERYTHING'S ALRIGHT FOREVER** *Creation CRECD 120*	55		1
28 Aug 93	**GIANT STEPS** *Creation CRECD 149*	17		4
8 Apr 95	**WAKE UP!** *Creation CRECD 179* ●	1	1	21
21 Sep 96	**C'MON KIDS** *Creation CRECD 194*	20		2
31 Oct 98	**KINGSIZE** *Creation CRECD 228*	62		1

BOO-YAA T.R.I.B.E.

US, male rap group — 1

Date	Album	Peak Position	Weeks at No.1	Weeks on Chart
14 Apr 90	**NEW FUNKY NATION** *Fourth & Broadway BRLP 544*	74		1

BOOGIE DOWN PRODUCTIONS

US, male rap/production group — 9

Date	Album	Peak Position	Weeks at No.1	Weeks on Chart
18 Jun 88	**BY ALL MEANS NECESSARY** *Jive HIP 63*	38		3
22 Jul 89	**GHETTO MUSIC: THE BLUEPRINT OF HIP HOP** *Jive HIP 80*	32		4
25 Aug 90	**EDUTAINMENT** *Jive HIP 100*	52		2

BOOKER T & THE M.G.s

US, male instrumental group — 5

Date	Album	Peak Position	Weeks at No.1	Weeks on Chart
25 Jul 64	**GREEN ONIONS** *London HAK 8182*	11		4
11 Jul 70	**McLEMORE AVENUE** *Stax SKATS 1031*	70		1

BOOMTOWN RATS

Ireland, male vocal/instrumental group – Bob Geldof*, Pete Briquette, Gerry Cott, Simon Crowe, Johnny Fingers (John Moylett) & Garry Roberts — 101

Date	Album	Peak Position	Weeks at No.1	Weeks on Chart
17 Sep 77	**BOOMTOWN RATS** *Ensign ENVY 1* ○	18		11
8 Jul 78	**TONIC FOR THE TROOPS** *Ensign ENVY 3* ⊛	8		44
3 Nov 79	**THE FINE ART OF SURFACING** *Ensign ENROX 11* ●	7		26
24 Jan 81	**MONDO BONGO** *Mercury 6359 042* ●	6		7
3 Apr 82	**V DEEP** *Mercury 6359 082*	64		5
9 Jul 94	**LOUDMOUTH – THE BEST OF THE BOOMTOWN RATS & BOB GELDOF** *Vertigo 5222852* & BOB GELDOF	10		3
8 May 04	**BEST OF** *Universal TV 9819145*	43		5

PAT BOONE

US, male vocalist (Charles Boone) — 12

Date	Album	Peak Position	Weeks at No.1	Weeks on Chart
22 Nov 58	**STARDUST** *London HAD 2127*	10		1
28 May 60	**HYMNS WE HAVE LOVED** *London HAD 2228*	12		2
25 Jun 60	**HYMNS WE LOVE** *London HAD 2092*	14		1
24 Apr 76	**PAT BOONE ORIGINALS** *ABC ABSD 301* ○	16		8

BOOTH & THE BAD ANGEL

UK, male vocalist (Tim Booth) & US, male composer/arranger (Angelo Badalamenti). See James — 2

Date	Album	Peak Position	Weeks at No.1	Weeks on Chart
13 Jul 96	**BOOTH AND THE BAD ANGEL** *Fontana 5268522*	35		2

BOOTY LUV

UK, female vocal duo — 3

Date	Album	Peak Position	Weeks at No.1	Weeks on Chart
29 Sep 07	**BOOGIE 2NITE** *Hed Kandi HEDK073*	11		3

BOSTON

US, male vocal/instrumental group – Brad Delp, d. 9 Mar 2007, Tom Scholz, Barry Goudreau, Sib Hashian & Fran Sheehan — 44

Date	Album	Peak Position	Weeks at No.1	Weeks on Chart
5 Feb 77	**BOSTON** *Epic EPC 81611* ●	11		20
9 Sep 78	**DON'T LOOK BACK** *Epic EPC 86057* ○ ★	9		10
4 Apr 81	**BOSTON** *Epic EPC 32038*	58		2
18 Oct 86	**THIRD STAGE** *MCA MCG 6017* ★	37		11
25 Jun 94	**WALK ON** *MCA MCD 10973*	56		1

JUDY BOUCHER

St. Vincent, female vocalist — 1

Date	Album	Peak Position	Weeks at No.1	Weeks on Chart
25 Apr 87	**CAN'T BE WITH YOU TONIGHT** *Orbitone OLP 024*	95		1

BOW WOW WOW

UK/Burma, female/male vocal/instrumental group — 38

Date	Album	Peak Position	Weeks at No.1	Weeks on Chart
24 Oct 81	**SEE JUNGLE! SEE JUNGLE! GO JOIN YOUR GANG YEAH CITY ALL OVER! GO APE CRAZY** *RCA RCALP 00273000*	26		32
7 Aug 82	**I WANT CANDY** *EMI EMC 3416*	26		6

DAVID BOWIE

UK, male vocalist/multi-instrumentalist/producer (David Jones). The groundbreaking multi-award-winner has spent longer on the album bestsellers list than any other British solo artist and holds the record for the most simultaneously charting LPs with 10 in 1983. See Tin Machine — 1026

Date	Album	Peak Position	Weeks at No.1	Weeks on Chart
1 Jul 72	**THE RISE AND FALL OF ZIGGY STARDUST AND THE SPIDERS FROM MARS** *RCA Victor SF 8287*	5		106
23 Sep 72	**HUNKY DORY** *RCA Victor SF 8244* ⊛	3		69
25 Nov 72	**THE MAN WHO SOLD THE WORLD** *RCA Victor LSP 4816*	26		22
25 Nov 72	**SPACE ODDITY** *RCA Victor LSP 4813*	17		37
5 May 73	**ALADDIN SANE** *RCA Victor RS 1001*	1	5	47
3 Nov 73	**PIN-UPS** *RCA Victor RS 1003* ●	1	5	21
8 Jun 74	**DIAMOND DOGS** *RCA Victor APLI 0576*	1	4	17
16 Nov 74	**DAVID LIVE** *RCA Victor APL 2 0771*	2		12
5 Apr 75	**YOUNG AMERICANS** *RCA Victor RS 1006* ○	2		12
7 Feb 76	**STATION TO STATION** *RCA Victor APLI 1327*	5		16
12 Jun 76	**CHANGESONEBOWIE** *RCA Victor RS 1055*	2		28
29 Jan 77	**LOW** *RCA Victor PL 12030* ○	2		18
29 Oct 77	**HEROES** *RCA Victor PL 12522*	3		18
14 Oct 78	**STAGE** *RCA Victor PL 02913* ●	5		10
9 Jun 79	**LODGER** *RCA Victor BOW LP 1* ●	4		17
27 Sep 80	**SCARY MONSTERS AND SUPER CREEPS** *RCA BOW LP 2* ⊛	1	2	32
10 Jan 81	**THE VERY BEST OF DAVID BOWIE** *K-Tel NE 1111* ⊛	3		20
17 Jan 81	**HUNKY DORY** *RCA International INTS 5064*	32		51
31 Jan 81	**THE RISE AND FALL OF ZIGGY STARDUST AND THE SPIDERS FROM MARS** *RCA International INTS 5063*	33		62
28 Nov 81	**CHANGESTWOBOWIE** *RCA BOW LP 3* ●	24		17
6 Mar 82	**ALADDIN SANE** *RCA International INTS 5067*	49		24
15 Jan 83	**RARE** *RCA PL 45406*	34		11
23 Apr 83	**LET'S DANCE** *EMI America AML 3029* ⊛	1	3	56
30 Apr 83	**PIN-UPS** *RCA International INTS 5236*	57		15

Date	Title / Label	Peak Position	Weeks at No.1	Weeks on Chart
30 Apr 83	**THE MAN WHO SOLD THE WORLD** *RCA International INTS 5237*	64		8
14 May 83	**DIAMOND DOGS** *RCA International INTS 5068*	60		14
11 Jun 83	**HEROES** *RCA International INTS 5066*	75		8
11 Jun 83	**LOW** *RCA International INTS 5065*	85		5
20 Aug 83	**GOLDEN YEARS** *RCA BOWLP 4*	33		5
5 Nov 83	**ZIGGY STARDUST – THE MOTION PICTURE** *RCA PL 84862* ⊛	17		6
28 Apr 84	**FAME AND FASHION (BOWIE'S ALL TIME GREATEST HITS)** *RCA PL 84919*	40		6
19 May 84	**LOVE YOU TILL TUESDAY** *Deram BOWIE 1*	53		4
6 Oct 84	**TONIGHT** *EMI America DB 1*	1	1	19
2 May 87	**NEVER LET ME DOWN** *EMI America AMLS 3117*	6		16
24 Mar 90	**CHANGESBOWIE** *EMI DBTV 1* ⊛	1	1	29
14 Apr 90	**HUNKY DORY** *EMI EMC 3572*	39		6
14 Apr 90	**SPACE ODDITY** *EMI EMC 3573*	64		1
14 Apr 90	**THE MAN WHO SOLD THE WORLD** *EMI EMC 3571*	66		1
23 Jun 90	**THE RISE AND FALL OF ZIGGY STARDUST AND THE SPIDERS FROM MARS** *EMI EMC 3577*	25		4
28 Jul 90	**ALADDIN SANE** *EMI EMC 3579*	43		1
28 Jul 90	**PIN-UPS** *EMI EMC 3580*	52		1
27 Oct 90	**DIAMOND DOGS** *EMI EMC 3584*	67		3
4 May 91	**YOUNG AMERICANS** *EMI EMD 1021*	54		1
4 May 91	**STATION TO STATION** *EMI EMD 1020*	57		1
7 Sep 91	**LOW** *EMI EMD 1027*	64		1
17 Apr 93	**BLACK TIE WHITE NOISE** *Arista 74321136972*	1	1	11
20 Nov 93	**THE SINGLES COLLECTION** *EMI CDEM 1512* ⊛	9		16
7 May 94	**SANTA MONICA '72** *Trident GY 002*	74		1
7 Oct 95	**OUTSIDE** *RCA 74321310662*	8		4
15 Feb 97	**EARTHLING** *RCA 74321449442*	6		4
8 Nov 98	**THE BEST OF 1969/1974** *EMI 8218492*	13		17
2 May 98	**THE BEST OF 1974/1979** *EMI 4943002*	39		2
16 Oct 99	**HOURS...** *Virgin CDV 2900*	5		5
7 Oct 00	**BOWIE AT THE BEEB** *EMI 5289582*	7		4
22 Jun 02	**HEATHEN** *Columbia 5082222*	5		18
20 Jul 02	**THE RISE AND FALL OF ZIGGY STARDUST AND THE SPIDERS FROM MARS** *EMI 5398262*	36		2
16 Nov 02	**BEST OF BOWIE** *EMI 5398212* ⊛	11		53
7 Jun 03	**ALADDIN SANE** *EMI 58030122*	53		1
27 Sep 03	**REALITY** *Columbia 5125552*	3		4
9 Oct 04	**THE RISE AND FALL OF ZIGGY STARDUST AND THE SPIDERS FROM MARS** *EMI CDP 7944002*	17		3
19 Nov 05	**THE PLATINUM COLLECTION** *EMI 3313042*	55		1
31 Mar 07	**THE BEST OF – 1980/1987** *EMI 3864782*	34		1
12 Jul 08	**LIVE SANTA MONICA '72** *EMI BOWIELIVE201072*	61		1

BOWLING FOR SOUP

US, male vocal/instrumental group — 6

Date	Title / Label	Peak Position	Weeks at No.1	Weeks on Chart
7 Sep 02	**DRUNK ENOUGH TO DANCE** *Music For Nations JIV 418192*	14		4
25 Sep 04	**HANGOVER YOU DON'T DESERVE** *Jive 82876643652*	64		1
17 Feb 07	**THE GREAT BURRITO EXTORTION CASE** *A & G Productions AGCD4*	43		1

BOX CAR RACER

US, male vocal/instrumental group — 3

Date	Title / Label	Peak Position	Weeks at No.1	Weeks on Chart
8 Jun 02	**BOX CAR RACER** *MCA 1129472*	27		3

BOXCAR WILLIE

US, male vocalist (Lecil Martin), d. 12 Apr 1999 (age 67) — 12

Date	Title / Label	Peak Position	Weeks at No.1	Weeks on Chart
31 May 80	**KING OF THE ROAD** *Warwick WW 5084*	5		12

BOY GEORGE

UK, male vocalist (George O'Dowd). See Culture Club — 15

Date	Title / Label	Peak Position	Weeks at No.1	Weeks on Chart
27 Jun 87	**SOLD** *Virgin V 2430*	29		6
13 Apr 91	**THE MARTYR MANTRAS** *More Protein CUMLP 1* JESUS LOVES YOU	60		1
2 Oct 93	**AT WORST...THE BEST OF BOY GEORGE & CULTURE CLUB** *Virgin VTCD 19* /CULTURE CLUB	24		5
12 Mar 94	**THE DEVIL IN SISTER GEORGE** *Virgin VSCDG 1490* /JESUS LOVES YOU/CULTURE CLUB	26		2
3 Jun 95	**CHEAPNESS AND BEAUTY** *Virgin CDV 2780*	44		1

BOY KILL BOY

UK, male vocal/instrumental group — 3

Date	Title / Label	Peak Position	Weeks at No.1	Weeks on Chart
3 Jun 06	**CIVILIAN** *Vertigo 9877358*	16		3

BOY MEETS GIRL

US, male/female vocal duo — 1

Date	Title / Label	Peak Position	Weeks at No.1	Weeks on Chart
4 Feb 89	**REEL LIFE** *RCA PL 88414*	74		1

MAX BOYCE

UK, male comedian/vocalist — 105

Date	Title / Label	Peak Position	Weeks at No.1	Weeks on Chart
5 Jul 75	**LIVE AT TREORCHY** *One Up OU 2033*	21		32
1 Nov 75	**WE ALL HAD DOCTOR'S PAPERS** *EMI MB 101*	1	1	17
20 Nov 76	**THE INCREDIBLE PLAN** *EMI MB 102*	9		12
7 Jan 78	**THE ROAD AND THE MILES** *EMI MB 103*	50		3
11 Mar 78	**LIVE AT TREORCHY** *One Up OU 54043*	42		6
27 May 78	**I KNOW COS I WAS THERE** *EMI MAX 1001*	6		14
13 Oct 79	**NOT THAT I'M BIASED** *EMI MAX 1002*	27		13
15 Nov 80	**ME AND BILLY WILLIAMS** *EMI MAX 1003*	37		8

BOYS

UK, male vocal group — 1

Date	Title / Label	Peak Position	Weeks at No.1	Weeks on Chart
1 Oct 77	**THE BOYS** *NEMS NEL 6001*	50		1

BOYZ II MEN

US, male vocal group – Michael McCary, Nathan & Wanya Morris & Shawn Stockman — 64

Date	Title / Label	Peak Position	Weeks at No.1	Weeks on Chart
31 Oct 92	**COOLEYHIGHHARMONY** *Motown 5300892*	7		18
24 Sep 94	**II** *Motown 5304312* ★	17		5
4 Oct 97	**EVOLUTION** *Motown 5308222* ★	12		5
23 Sep 00	**NATHAN MICHAEL SHAWN WANYA** *Universal 1592812*	54		1
16 Feb 02	**LEGACY – THE GREATEST HITS COLLECTION** *Universal 0165622*	2		20
3 Aug 02	**FULL CIRCLE** *Arista 07822147412*	56		2
17 Nov 07	**MOTOWN: HITSVILLE USA** *UMTV 1749550*	8		13

BOYZONE

Ireland, male vocal group – Ronan Keating*, Keith Duffy, Stephen Gately*, Mikey Graham & Shane Lynch — 215

Date	Title / Label	Peak Position	Weeks at No.1	Weeks on Chart
2 Sep 95	**SAID AND DONE** *Polydor 5278012* ⊛x3	1	1	58
9 Nov 96	**A DIFFERENT BEAT** *Polydor 5337422* ⊛x3	1	1	24
6 Jun 98	**WHERE WE BELONG** *Polydor 5592002* ⊛x5	1	3	55
12 Jun 99	**BY REQUEST** *Polydor 5475992* ⊛x6	1	9	57
29 Mar 03	**BALLADS – THE LOVE SONG COLLECTION** *Universal TV 0760742*	6		9
25 Oct 08	**BACK AGAIN...NO MATTER WHAT** *Polydor 1785356*	4		11+
25 Oct 08	**B-SIDES AND RARITIES** *Polydor 1787001*	34		1

Top 3 Best-Selling Albums

		Approximate Sales
1	WHERE WE BELONG	1,570,000
2	BY REQUEST	1,800,000
3	SAID AND DONE	730,000

BRAD

US, male vocal/instrumental group — 1

Date	Title / Label	Peak Position	Weeks at No.1	Weeks on Chart
15 May 93	**SHAME** *Epic 4735962*	72		1

JAMES DEAN BRADFIELD

UK, male vocalist/guitarist. See Manic Street Preachers — 2

Date	Title / Label	Peak Position	Weeks at No.1	Weeks on Chart
5 Aug 06	**THE GREAT WESTERN** *Columbia 82876857272*	22		2

PAUL BRADY

UK, male vocalist — 1

Date	Title / Label	Peak Position	Weeks at No.1	Weeks on Chart
6 Apr 91	**TRICK OR TREAT** *Fontana 8484541*	62		1

BILLY BRAGG

UK, male vocalist/guitarist (Stephen Bragg) — 91

Date	Title / Label	Peak Position	Weeks at No.1	Weeks on Chart
21 Jan 84	**LIFE'S A RIOT WITH SPY VS SPY** *Utility UTIL 1*	30		30
20 Oct 84	**BREWING UP WITH BILLY BRAGG** *Go! Discs AGOLP 4*	16		21
4 Oct 86	**TALKING WITH THE TAXMAN ABOUT POETRY** *Go! Discs AGOLP 6*	8		8

Silver-selling ○ Gold-selling ● Platinum-selling ⊛ US No.1 ★ Peak Position · Weeks at No.1 · Weeks on Chart

Date	Album	Peak Position	Weeks at No.1	Weeks on Chart
13 Jun 87	**BACK TO BASICS** *Go! Discs AGOLP 8*	37		4
1 Oct 88	**WORKERS PLAYTIME** *Go! Discs AGOLP 15*	17		4
12 May 90	**THE INTERNATIONALE** *Utility UTIL 11*	34		4
28 Sep 91	**DON'T TRY THIS AT HOME** *Go! Discs 8282791* ●	8		6
21 Sep 96	**WILLIAM BLOKE** *Cooking Vinyl COOKCD 100*	16		3
28 Jun 97	**BLOKE ON BLOKE** *Cooking Vinyl COOKCD 127*	72		1
11 Jul 98	**MERMAID AVENUE** *Elektra 7559622042* & WILCO	34		2
11 Sep 99	**REACHING TO THE CONVERTED** *Cooking Vinyl COOKCD 186*	41		2
10 Jun 00	**MERMAID AVENUE – VOLUME 2** *Elektra 7559625222* & WILCO	61		1
16 Mar 02	**ENGLAND HALF ENGLISH** *Cooking Vinyl COOKCD 222* & THE BLOKES	51		2
18 Oct 03	**MUST I PAINT YOU A PICTURE** *Cooking Vinyl COOKCD 266X*	49		1
15 Mar 08	**MR LOVE & JUSTICE** *Cooking Vinyl COOKCD452*	33		2

WILFRED BRAMBELL & HARRY H. CORBETT

UK, male vocal/TV comedy duo – Brambell, d. 18 Jan 1985, & Corbett, d. 21 Mar 1982 **34**

Date	Album	Peak Position	Weeks at No.1	Weeks on Chart
23 Mar 63	**STEPTOE AND SON** *Pye NPL 18081*	4		28
11 Jan 64	**STEPTOE AND SON** *Pye Golden Guinea GGL 0217*	14		5
14 Mar 64	**MORE JUNK** *Pye NPL 18090*	19		1

MICHELLE BRANCH

US, female vocalist/multi-instrumentalist **5**

Date	Album	Peak Position	Weeks at No.1	Weeks on Chart
27 Apr 02	**THE SPIRIT ROOM** *Maverick WB479852*	54		2
19 Jul 03	**HOTEL PAPER** *Maverick MAV 484262*	35		3

BRAND NEW HEAVIES

UK, female/male vocal/instrumental group – N'Dea Davenport (replaced by Siedah Garrett), Simon Bartholomew, Jan Kincaid & Andrew Levy **103**

Date	Album	Peak Position	Weeks at No.1	Weeks on Chart
14 Mar 92	**BRAND NEW HEAVIES** *ffrr 8283002* ○	25		16
5 Sep 92	**HEAVY RHYME EXPERIENCE VOLUME 1** *ffrr 8283352*	38		2
16 Apr 94	**BROTHER SISTER** *ffrr 8284902* ⊛	4		48
12 Nov 94	**ORIGINAL FLAVA** *Acid Jazz JAZIDCD 114*	64		1
3 May 97	**SHELTER** *ffrr 8288872* ⊛	5		33
25 Sep 99	**TRUNK FUNK – THE BEST OF THE BRAND NEW HEAVIES** *ffrr 3984291642* ○	13		3

BRAND X

UK, male vocal/instrumental group **6**

Date	Album	Peak Position	Weeks at No.1	Weeks on Chart
21 May 77	**MOROCCAN ROLL** *Charisma CAS 1126*	37		5
11 Sep 82	**IS THERE ANYTHING ABOUT** *CBS 85967*	93		1

BRANDY

US, female vocalist/actor (Brandy Norwood) **54**

Date	Album	Peak Position	Weeks at No.1	Weeks on Chart
20 Jun 98	**NEVER S-A-Y NEVER** *Atlantic 7567830392* ●	19		31
9 Mar 02	**FULL MOON** *Atlantic 7567931102* ●	9		15
10 Jul 04	**AFRODISIAC** *Atlantic 7567836332* ○	32		4
9 Apr 05	**THE BEST OF** *Atlantic 8122746612*	24		4

LAURA BRANIGAN

US, female vocalist, d. 26 Aug 2004 (age 47) **18**

Date	Album	Peak Position	Weeks at No.1	Weeks on Chart
18 Aug 84	**SELF CONTROL** *Atlantic 7801471* ○	16		14
24 Aug 85	**HOLD ME** *Atlantic 7812651*	64		4

BRASS CONSTRUCTION

US, male vocal/instrumental group **12**

Date	Album	Peak Position	Weeks at No.1	Weeks on Chart
20 Mar 76	**BRASS CONSTRUCTION** *United Artists UAS 29923* ○	9		11
30 Jun 84	**RENEGADES** *Capitol EJ 2401601*	94		1

BRATZ ROCK ANGELZ

US, female vocal/instrumental group (cartoon dolls) **4**

Date	Album	Peak Position	Weeks at No.1	Weeks on Chart
22 Oct 05	**BRATZ ROCK ANGELZ** *Universal 9884259*	42		4

BRAVERY

US, male vocal/instrumental group – Sam Endicott, Anthony Burulcich, John Conway, Mike Hindert & Michael Zakarin **11**

Date	Album	Peak Position	Weeks at No.1	Weeks on Chart
26 Mar 05	**THE BRAVERY** *Loog 9880499* ●	5		11

TONI BRAXTON

US, female vocalist **136**

Date	Album	Peak Position	Weeks at No.1	Weeks on Chart
29 Jan 94	**TONI BRAXTON** *LaFace 74321162682* ● ★	4		33
29 Jun 96	**SECRETS** *LaFace 73008260202* ⊛x2	10		81
6 May 00	**THE HEAT** *LaFace 73008260692* ●	3		19
15 Nov 03	**ULTIMATE** *Arista 82876574852*	23		3

BREAD

US, male vocal/instrumental group – David Gates*, Jim Gordon (replaced by Mike Botts, d. 9 Dec 2005), James Griffin, d. 11 Jan 2005 & Robb Royer (replaced by Larry Knechtel) **210**

Date	Album	Peak Position	Weeks at No.1	Weeks on Chart
26 Sep 70	**ON THE WATERS** *Elektra 2469 005*	34		5
18 Mar 72	**BABY I'M A-WANT YOU** *Elektra K 42100*	9		19
28 Oct 72	**THE BEST OF BREAD** *Elektra K 42115*	7		100
27 Jul 74	**THE BEST OF BREAD VOLUME 2** *Elektra K 42161*	48		1
29 Jan 77	**LOST WITHOUT YOUR LOVE** *Elektra K 52044*	17		6
5 Nov 77	**THE SOUND OF BREAD** *Elektra K 52062* ⊛	1	3	46
28 Nov 87	**THE COLLECTION – THE VERY BEST OF BREAD AND DAVID GATES** *Telstar STAR 2303* & DAVID GATES	84		2
5 Jul 97	**DAVID GATES AND BREAD: ESSENTIALS** *warner.esp/Jive 9548354082* DAVID GATES & BREAD ●	9		19
16 Sep 06	**THE SOUND OF BREAD** *Elektra/wmtv 8122747562*	18		12

BREAK MACHINE

US, male vocal group **16**

Date	Album	Peak Position	Weeks at No.1	Weeks on Chart
9 Jun 84	**BREAK MACHINE** *Record Shack SOHOLP 3*	17		16

BREAKBEAT ERA

UK, male/female drum 'N' bass trio **2**

Date	Album	Peak Position	Weeks at No.1	Weeks on Chart
11 Sep 99	**ULTRA OBSCENE** *XL Recordings XLCD 130*	31		2

BREAKS CO-OP

New Zealand, male vocal/instrumental group **1**

Date	Album	Peak Position	Weeks at No.1	Weeks on Chart
10 Jun 06	**THE SOUND INSIDE** *Parlophone 8733512*	55		1

JULIAN BREAM

UK, male guitarist/lute player **2**

Date	Album	Peak Position	Weeks at No.1	Weeks on Chart
27 Apr 96	**THE ULTIMATE GUITAR COLLECTION** *RCA Victor 74321337052*	66		2

BREATHE

UK, male vocal/instrumental group **5**

Date	Album	Peak Position	Weeks at No.1	Weeks on Chart
8 Oct 88	**ALL THAT JAZZ** *Siren SRNLP 12* ○	22		5

BREED 77

Gibraltar, male vocal/instrumental group **1**

Date	Album	Peak Position	Weeks at No.1	Weeks on Chart
15 May 04	**CULTURA** *Albert Productions JASCDUK 008*	61		1

BREEDERS

US/UK, female/male vocal/instrumental group – Kim Deal, Tanya Donelly*, Carrie Bradley, Kelley Deal, Britt Walford (replaced by Jim MacPherson) & Josephine Wiggs **10**

Date	Album	Peak Position	Weeks at No.1	Weeks on Chart
9 Jun 90	**POD** *4AD CAD 0006*	22		3
11 Sep 93	**LAST SPLASH** *4AD CAD 3014CD* ○	5		5
1 Jun 02	**TITLE TK** *4AD CAD 2205CD*	51		1
19 Apr 08	**MOUNTAIN BATTLES** *4AD CAD2803CD*	46		1

MAIRE BRENNAN

Ireland, female vocalist. See Clannad **2**

Date	Album	Peak Position	Weeks at No.1	Weeks on Chart
13 Jun 92	**MAIRE** *RCA PD 75358*	53		2

ADRIAN BRETT

UK, male flute player **11**

Date	Album	Peak Position	Weeks at No.1	Weeks on Chart
10 Nov 79	**ECHOES OF GOLD** *Warwick WW 5062* ●	19		11

PAUL BRETT

UK, male guitarist **7**

Date	Album	Peak Position	Weeks at No.1	Weeks on Chart
19 Jul 80	**ROMANTIC GUITAR** *K-Tel ONE 1079*	24		7

EDIE BRICKELL & THE NEW BOHEMIANS
US, female/male vocal/instrumental group — 19

Date	Title	Peak Position	Weeks at No.1	Weeks on Chart
4 Feb 89	**SHOOTING RUBBERBANDS AT THE STARS** *Geffen WX 215* ●	25		17
10 Nov 90	**GHOST OF A DOG** *Geffen WX 386*	63		1
3 Sep 94	**PICTURE PERFECT MORNING** *Geffen GED 24715* EDIE BRICKELL	59		1

BRIGHOUSE & RASTRICK BRASS BAND
UK, male brass band — 11

Date	Title	Peak Position	Weeks at No.1	Weeks on Chart
28 Jan 78	**FLORAL DANCE** *Logo 1001* ●	10		11

BRIGHT EYES
US, male vocalist/guitarist (Conor Oberst*) — 7

Date	Title	Peak Position	Weeks at No.1	Weeks on Chart
5 Feb 05	**I'M WIDE AWAKE IT'S MORNING** *Saddle Creek SCE72CD* ●	23		3
5 Feb 05	**DIGITAL ASH IN A DIGITAL URN** *Saddle Creek SCE73CD*	43		1
21 Apr 07	**CASSADAGA** *Polydor 1732010*	13		3

SARAH BRIGHTMAN
UK, female vocalist — 56

Date	Title	Peak Position	Weeks at No.1	Weeks on Chart
23 Mar 85	**ANDREW LLOYD WEBBER: REQUIEM** *HMV ALW 1* PLACIDO DOMINGO, SARAH BRIGHTMAN, PAUL MILES-KINGSTON, WINCHESTER CATHEDRAL CHOIR & THE ENGLISH CHAMBER ORCHESTRA CONDUCTED BY LORIN MAAZEL	4		18
17Jun 89	**THE SONGS THAT GOT AWAY** *Really Useful 8391161*	48		2
8 Aug 92	**AMIGOS PARA SIEMPRE (FRIENDS FOR LIFE)** *East West 4509902562* JOSE CARRERAS & SARAH BRIGHTMAN	53		4
11 Nov 95	**THE UNEXPECTED SONGS – SURRENDER** *Really Useful 5277022*	45		2
14 Jun 97	**TIMELESS** *Coalition 630191812*	2		21
20 Jan 01	**LA LUNA** *East West 8573859152*	37		2
14 Oct 06	**CLASSICS – THE BEST OF** *Angel CDANGE16* ●	38		3
26 Apr 08	**SYMPHONY** *Capitol 5206032*	13		4

BRILLIANT
UK, male/female vocal/instrumental group — 1

Date	Title	Peak Position	Weeks at No.1	Weeks on Chart
20 Sep 86	**KISS THE LIPS OF LIFE** *Food BRILL 1*	83		1

BRING ME THE HORIZON
UK, male vocal/instrumental group — 1

Date	Title	Peak Position	Weeks at No.1	Weeks on Chart
11 Oct 08	**SUICIDE SEASON** *Visible Noise TORMENT132*	47		1

JOHNNY BRISTOL
US, male vocalist, d. 21 Mar 2004 (age 65) — 7

Date	Title	Peak Position	Weeks at No.1	Weeks on Chart
5 Oct 74	**HANG ON IN THERE BABY** *MGM 2315 303*	12		7

BRITISH SEA POWER
UK, male vocal/instrumental group – Scott Wilkinson, Martin Noble, Neil Wilkinson & Matthew Wood — 9

Date	Title	Peak Position	Weeks at No.1	Weeks on Chart
14 Jun 03	**THE DECLINE OF BRITISH SEA POWER** *Rough Trade RTRADECD090* ●	54		1
16 Apr 05	**OPEN SEASON** *Rough Trade RTRADCD200* ●	13		4
26 Jan 08	**DO YOU LIKE ROCK MUSIC** *Rough Trade RTRADCD300*	10		4

JUNE BRONHILL & THOMAS ROUND
Australia/UK, female/male vocal duo, Bronhill, d. 24 Jan 2005 (age 75) — 1

Date	Title	Peak Position	Weeks at No.1	Weeks on Chart
18 Jun 60	**LILAC TIME** *HMV CLP 1248*	17		1

BRONSKI BEAT
UK, male vocal/instrumental group – Jimmy Somerville*, Steve Bronski & Larry Steinbachek — 69

Date	Title	Peak Position	Weeks at No.1	Weeks on Chart
20 Oct 84	**THE AGE OF CONSENT** *Forbidden Fruit BITLP 1* ⊛	4		53
21 Sep 85	**HUNDREDS AND THOUSANDS** *Forbidden Fruit BITLP 2* ●	24		6
10 May 86	**TRUTHDARE DOUBLEDARE** *Forbidden Fruit BITLP 3*	18		6
22 Sep 01	**THE VERY BEST OF JIMMY SOMERVILLE BRONSKI BEAT AND THE COMMUNARDS** *London 0927412582* JIMMY SOMERVILLE BRONSKI BEAT & THE COMMUNARDS	29		4

ELKIE BROOKS
UK, female vocalist (Elaine Bookbinder) — 223

Date	Title	Peak Position	Weeks at No.1	Weeks on Chart
18 Jun 77	**TWO DAYS AWAY** *A&M AMLH 68409* ●	16		20
13 May 78	**SHOOTING STAR** *A&M AMLH 64695* ●	20		13
13 Oct 79	**LIVE AND LEARN** *A&M AMLH 68509*	34		6
14 Nov 81	**PEARLS** *A&M ELK 1981* ⊛	2		79
13 Nov 82	**PEARLS II** *A&M ELK 1982* ⊛	5		25
14 Jul 84	**MINUTES** *A&M AML 68565*	35		7
8 Dec 84	**SCREEN GEMS** *EMI SCREEN 1* ●	35		11
6 Dec 86	**NO MORE THE FOOL** *Legend LMA 1* ●	5		23
27 Dec 86	**THE VERY BEST OF ELKIE BROOKS** *Telstar STAR 2284* ●	10		18
11 Jun 88	**BOOKBINDER'S KID** *Legend LMA 3*	57		3
18 Nov 89	**INSPIRATIONS** *Telstar STAR 2354*	58		3
13 Mar 93	**ROUND MIDNIGHT** *Castle Communications CTVCD 113*	27		4
16 Apr 94	**NOTHIN' BUT THE BLUE** *Castle Communications CTVCD 127*	58		2
13 Apr 96	**AMAZING** *Carlton Premiere 3036000282* WITH THE ROYAL PHILHARMONIC ORCHESTRA	49		2
15 Mar 97	**THE VERY BEST OF ELKIE BROOKS** *Polygram TV 5407122*	23		7

GARTH BROOKS
US, male vocalist/guitarist (Troyal Brooks) — 59

Date	Title	Peak Position	Weeks at No.1	Weeks on Chart
15 Feb 92	**ROPIN' THE WIND** *Capitol CDESTU 2162* ★	41		2
12 Feb 94	**IN PIECES** *Capitol/Liberty CDEST 2212* ● ★	2		11
24 Dec 94	**THE HITS** *Liberty CDP 8320812* ● ★	11		21
2 Dec 95	**FRESH HORSES** *Capitol CDGB 1* ●	22		6
13 Dec 97	**SEVENS** *Capitol 8565992* ● ★	34		7
28 Nov 98	**DOUBLE LIVE** *Capitol 4974242* ★	57		1
24 Nov 07	**ULTIMATE HITS** *Sony BMG 88697195522*	10		11

MEREDITH BROOKS
US, female vocalist/guitarist — 10

Date	Title	Peak Position	Weeks at No.1	Weeks on Chart
23 Aug 97	**BLURRING THE EDGES** *Capitol CDEST 2298* ●	5		10

NIGEL BROOKS SINGERS
UK, male/female choir — 17

Date	Title	Peak Position	Weeks at No.1	Weeks on Chart
29 Nov 75	**20 SONGS OF JOY** *K-Tel NE 706* ●	5		16
5 Jun 76	**20 ALL TIME EUROVISION FAVOURITES** *K-Tel NE 712*	44		1

STEVE BROOKSTEIN
UK, male vocalist — 5

Date	Title	Peak Position	Weeks at No.1	Weeks on Chart
21 May 05	**HEART & SOUL** *Syco Music 82876691852* ●	1	1	5

BROS
UK, male vocal trio – Matt & Luke Goss & Craig Logan (left 1989) — 69

Date	Title	Peak Position	Weeks at No.1	Weeks on Chart
9 Apr 88	**PUSH** *CBS 4606291* ⊛x4	2		54
28 Oct 89	**THE TIME** *CBS 4659181* ●	4		13
12 Oct 91	**CHANGING FACES** *Columbia 4688171*	18		2

BROTHER BEYOND
UK, male vocal/instrumental group – Nathan Moore, Carl Fysh, David Ben White & Francis 'Eg' White — 24

Date	Title	Peak Position	Weeks at No.1	Weeks on Chart
26 Nov 88	**GET EVEN** *Parlophone PCS 7327* ⊛	9		23
25 Nov 89	**TRUST** *Parlophone PCS 7337* ●	60		1

BROTHERHOOD
UK, male rap group — 1

Date	Title	Peak Position	Weeks at No.1	Weeks on Chart
17 Feb 96	**ELEMENTALZ** *Bite-It CDBHOOD 1*	50		1

BROTHERHOOD OF MAN
UK, male/female vocal group – Martin Lee, Lee Sheriden & Nicky & Sandra Stevens — 40

Date	Title	Peak Position	Weeks at No.1	Weeks on Chart
24 Apr 76	**LOVE AND KISSES FROM** *Pye NSPL 18490* ●	20		8
12 Aug 78	**B FOR BROTHERHOOD** *Pye NSPL 18567* ●	18		9
7 Oct 78	**BROTHERHOOD OF MAN** *K-Tel BML 7980*	6		15
29 Nov 80	**BROTHERHOOD OF MAN SING 20 NUMBER ONE HITS** *Warwick WW 5087* ●	14		8

Key: ○ Silver-selling · ● Gold-selling · ⊛ Platinum-selling · ★ US No.1 · Peak Position · Weeks at No.1 · Weeks on Chart

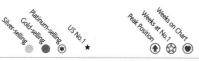

BROTHERS JOHNSON
US, male vocal/instrumental duo

Date	Album	Peak Position	Weeks at No.1	Weeks on Chart: 22
19 Aug 78	**BLAM!** *A&M AMLH 64714*	48		8
23 Feb 80	**LIGHT UP THE NIGHT** *A&M AMLK 63716*	22		12
18 Jul 81	**WINNERS** *A&M AMLK 63724*	42		2

EDGAR BROUGHTON BAND
UK, male vocal/instrumental group

Date	Album	Peak Position	Weeks at No.1	Weeks on Chart: 6
20 Jun 70	**SING BROTHER SING** *Harvest SHVL 772*	18		4
5 Jun 71	**THE EDGAR BROUGHTON BAND** *Harvest SHVL 791*	28		2

CRAZY WORLD OF ARTHUR BROWN
UK, male vocal/instrumental group – Arthur Wilton (Arthur Brown), Vincent Crane, d. 14 Feb 1989, Sean Nicholas, Carl Palmer & Drachen Theaker

Date	Album	Peak Position	Weeks at No.1	Weeks on Chart: 16
6 Jul 68	**THE CRAZY WORLD OF ARTHUR BROWN** *Track 612005*	2		16

BOBBY BROWN
US, male vocalist. See New Edition

Date	Album	Peak Position	Weeks at No.1	Weeks on Chart: 65
28 Jan 89	**DON'T BE CRUEL** *MCA MCF 3425* ⊛x2 ★	3		41
5 Aug 89	**KING OF STAGE** *MCA MCL 1886*	40		6
2 Dec 89	**DANCE…YA KNOW IT!** *MCA MCG 6074* ●	26		10
5 Sep 92	**BOBBY** *MCA MCAD 10695*	11		5
5 Aug 95	**TWO CAN PLAY THAT GAME** *MCA MCD 11334*	24		3

CHRIS BROWN
US, male vocalist

Date	Album	Peak Position	Weeks at No.1	Weeks on Chart: 47
18 Feb 06	**CHRIS BROWN** *Jive 82876768162* ○	29		6
17 Nov 07	**EXCLUSIVE** *Jive 88697160592* ⊛	3		41+

DENNIS BROWN
Jamaica, male vocalist (Clarence Brown), d. 1 Jul 1999 (age 42)

Date	Album	Peak Position	Weeks at No.1	Weeks on Chart: 6
26 Jun 82	**LOVE HAS FOUND ITS WAY** *A&M AMLH 64886*	72		6

ERROL BROWN
UK, male vocalist. See Hot Chocolate

Date	Album	Peak Position	Weeks at No.1	Weeks on Chart: 2
9 Jun 01	**STILL SEXY – THE ALBUM** *Universal TV 138162*	44		2

FOXY BROWN
US, female rapper (Inga Marchand)

Date	Album	Peak Position	Weeks at No.1	Weeks on Chart: 1
6 Feb 99	**CHYNA DOLL** *Def Jam 5589332* ★	51		1

HORACE BROWN
US, male vocalist

Date	Album	Peak Position	Weeks at No.1	Weeks on Chart: 1
6 Jul 96	**HORACE BROWN** *Motown 5306942*	48		1

IAN BROWN
UK, male vocalist/guitarist. See Stone Roses

Date	Album	Peak Position	Weeks at No.1	Weeks on Chart: 62
14 Feb 98	**UNFINISHED MONKEY BUSINESS** *Polydor 5395652* ●	4		24
20 Nov 99	**GOLDEN GREATS** *Polydor 5431412* ●	14		6
13 Oct 01	**MUSIC OF THE SPHERES** *Polydor 5891262* ●	3		5
25 Sep 04	**SOLARIZED** *Fiction 9867772* ●	7		6
1 Oct 05	**THE GREATEST** *Fiction 9872874* ●	5		16
6 Oct 07	**THE WORLD IS YOURS** *Fiction 1724664*	4		5

JAMES BROWN
US, male vocalist, d. 25 Dec 2006 (age 73)

Date	Album	Peak Position	Weeks at No.1	Weeks on Chart: 55
18 Oct 86	**GRAVITY** *Scotti Brothers SCT 57108*	85		3
10 Oct 87	**THE BEST OF JAMES BROWN – THE GODFATHER OF SOUL** *K-Tel NE 1376* ●	17		21
25 Jun 88	**I'M REAL** *Scotti Brothers POLD 5230*	27		5
16 Nov 91	**SEX MACHINE – THE VERY BEST OF JAMES BROWN** *Polydor 8458281* ●	19		22
11 May 02	**THE GODFATHER – THE VERY BEST OF** *Universal Music TV 5898412*	30		4

JOE BROWN
UK, male vocalist/guitarist

Date	Album	Peak Position	Weeks at No.1	Weeks on Chart: 55
1 Sep 62	**A PICTURE OF YOU** *Pye Golden Guinea GGL 0146* JOE BROWN & THE BRUVVERS	3		39
25 May 63	**JOE BROWN – LIVE** *Piccadilly NPL 38006*	14		8
1 Mar 08	**THE VERY BEST OF JOE BROWN** *UMTV 8823853*	14		8

ROY 'CHUBBY' BROWN
UK, male comedian/vocalist (Royston Vasey)

Date	Album	Peak Position	Weeks at No.1	Weeks on Chart: 8
25 Nov 95	**TAKE FAT AND PARTY** *Polystar 5297842* ○	29		7
7 Dec 96	**FAT OUT OF HELL** *Polystar 5370602*	67		1

SAM BROWN
UK, female vocalist

Date	Album	Peak Position	Weeks at No.1	Weeks on Chart: 30
11 Mar 89	**STOP!** *A&M AMA 5195* ●	4		18
14 Apr 90	**APRIL MOON** *A&M AMA 9014* ○	38		12

JACKSON BROWNE
US, male vocalist/guitarist/pianist

Date	Album	Peak Position	Weeks at No.1	Weeks on Chart: 42
4 Dec 76	**THE PRETENDER** *Asylum K 53048* ○	26		5
21 Jan 78	**RUNNING ON EMPTY** *Asylum K 53070* ●	28		7
12 Jul 80	**HOLD OUT** *Asylum K 52226* ★	44		5
13 Aug 83	**LAWYERS IN LOVE** *Asylum 9602681*	37		7
8 Mar 86	**LIVES IN THE BALANCE** *Asylum EKT 31*	36		7
17 Jun 89	**WORLD IN MOTION** *Elektra EKT 50*	39		2
6 Nov 93	**I'M ALIVE** *Elektra 7559615242*	35		3
9 Mar 96	**LOOKING EAST** *Elektra 7559618672*	47		1
26 Oct 02	**THE NAKED RIDE HOME** *Elektra EA627932*	53		1
16 Oct 04	**THE VERY BEST OF** *Elektra/Rhino 8122780912*	53		3
4 Oct 08	**TIME THE CONQUEROR** *Inside Recordings INR80923*	57		1

BROWNSTONE
US, female vocal group

Date	Album	Peak Position	Weeks at No.1	Weeks on Chart: 16
29 Apr 95	**FROM THE BOTTOM UP** *MJJ 4773622* ○	18		13
31 May 97	**STILL CLIMBING** *Epic 4853882*	19		3

DAVE BRUBECK
US, male pianist

Date	Album	Peak Position	Weeks at No.1	Weeks on Chart: 17
25 Jun 60	**TIME OUT** *Fontana TFL 5085* DAVE BRUBECK QUARTET	11		1
7 Apr 62	**TIME FURTHER OUT** *Fontana TFL 5161*	12		16

JACK BRUCE
UK, male vocalist/guitarist (John Asher). See Cream

Date	Album	Peak Position	Weeks at No.1	Weeks on Chart: 9
27 Sep 69	**SONGS FOR A TAILOR** *Polydor 583058*	6		9

CARLA BRUNI
Italy, female vocalist/model (Carla Gilberta Bruni Tedeschi)

Date	Album	Peak Position	Weeks at No.1	Weeks on Chart: 2
19 May 07	**NO PROMISES** *Dramatico DRAMCD0033*	65		1
26 Jul 08	**COMME SI DE RIEN N'ETAIT** *Dramatico DRAMCD0041*	58		1

PEABO BRYSON & ROBERTA FLACK
US, male vocalist (Robert Bryson) & female vocalist

Date	Album	Peak Position	Weeks at No.1	Weeks on Chart: 10
17 Sep 83	**BORN TO LOVE** *Capitol EST 7122841* ○	15		10

BT
US, male producer (Brian Transeau)

Date	Album	Peak Position	Weeks at No.1	Weeks on Chart: 5
21 Oct 95	**IMA** *Perfecto 0630123452*	45		4
4 Oct 97	**ESCM** *Perfecto 3984200652*	35		1

B2K
US, male vocal group

Date	Album	Peak Position	Weeks at No.1	Weeks on Chart: 12
5 Apr 03	**PANDEMONIUM** *Epic 5105342* ○	35		12

PATRIZIO BUANNE
Italy, male vocalist

Date	Album	Peak Position	Weeks at No.1	Weeks on Chart: 17
12 Mar 05	**THE ITALIAN** *Globe Records 9868390* ●	10		12
28 Oct 06	**FOREVER BEGINS TONIGHT** *Universal TV 1707174*	15		5

MICHAEL BUBLE
Canada, male vocalist — Weeks on Chart: 142

Date	Album	Peak	Wks at No.1	Wks on Chart
18 Oct 03	**MICHAEL BUBLE** *Reprise 9362485352* ⊛x2	6		24
29 May 04	**COME FLY WITH ME** *Reprise 9362486832*	52		2
20 Nov 04	**MICHAEL BUBLE** *Reprise 9362489162* ●	46		5
12 Feb 05	**IT'S TIME** *Reprise 9362489962* ⊛x2	4		41
11 Feb 06	**CAUGHT IN THE ACT** *Reprise 9362494442*	25		4
12 May 07	**CALL ME IRRESPONSIBLE** *Reprise 9362499989* ● ★	2		13
20 Oct 07	**CALL ME IRRESPONSIBLE – SPECIAL EDITION** *Reprise 9362499111* ⊛x3	3		53

KENNY 'DOPE' PRESENTS THE BUCKETHEADS
US, male producer (Kenny Gonzalez) — Weeks on Chart: 1

Date	Album	Peak	Wks at No.1	Wks on Chart
27 Jan 96	**ALL IN THE MIND** *Positiva CDTIVA 1010*	74		1

LINDSEY BUCKINGHAM
US, male vocalist/guitarist. See Fleetwood Mac — Weeks on Chart: 2

Date	Album	Peak	Wks at No.1	Wks on Chart
8 Aug 92	**OUT OF THE CRADLE** *Mercury 5126582*	51		1
27 Sep 08	**GIFT OF SCREWS** *Warner Brothers 9362498334*	59		1

JEFF BUCKLEY
US, male vocalist/guitarist, d. 29 May 1997 (age 30) — Weeks on Chart: 20

Date	Album	Peak	Wks at No.1	Wks on Chart
27 Aug 94	**GRACE** *Columbia 4759282*	50		8+
23 May 98	**SKETCHES FOR MY SWEETHEART THE DRUNK** *Columbia 4886612*	7		4
20 May 00	**MYSTERY WHITE BOY – LIVE 95-96** *Columbia 4979729*	8		2
4 Sep 04	**GRACE** *Columbia 5174603*	42		3+
9 Jun 07	**SO REAL – SONGS FROM JEFF BUCKLEY** *Columbia/Legacy 88697035702*	16		3

BUCKS FIZZ
UK, male/female vocal group – Jay Aston (replaced by Shelley Preston), Cheryl Baker, Bobby G (Bobby Gee) & Mike Nolan — Weeks on Chart: 81

Date	Album	Peak	Wks at No.1	Wks on Chart
8 Aug 81	**BUCKS FIZZ** *RCA RCALP 5050* ●	14		28
8 May 82	**ARE YOU READY?** *RCA RCALP 8000* ●	10		23
19 Mar 83	**HAND CUT** *RCA RCALP 6100* ○	17		13
3 Dec 83	**GREATEST HITS** *RCA PL 70022*	25		13
24 Nov 84	**I HEAR TALK** *RCA PL 70397*	66		2
13 Dec 86	**THE WRITING ON THE WALL** *Polydor POHL 30*	89		1
26 May 07	**THE VERY BEST OF** *Sony BMG 88697106452*	40		1

HAROLD BUDD, ELIZABETH FRASER, ROBIN GUTHRIE & SIMON RAYMONDE
US, male pianist & UK, male/female vocal/instrumental group (aka Cocteau Twins) — Weeks on Chart: 2

Date	Album	Peak	Wks at No.1	Wks on Chart
22 Nov 86	**THE MOON AND THE MELODIES** *4AD CAD 611*	46		2

ROY BUDD
UK, male pianist — Weeks on Chart: 1

Date	Album	Peak	Wks at No.1	Wks on Chart
19 Sep 98	**GET CARTER (OST)** *Cinephile CINCD 001*	68		1

JOE BUDDEN
US, male vocalist — Weeks on Chart: 1

Date	Album	Peak	Wks at No.1	Wks on Chart
28 Jun 03	**JOE BUDDEN** *Def Jam 9807936*	55		1

BUDGIE
UK, male vocal/instrumental group — Weeks on Chart: 10

Date	Album	Peak	Wks at No.1	Wks on Chart
8 Jun 74	**IN FOR THE KILL** *MCA MCF 2546*	29		3
27 Sep 75	**BANDOLIER** *MCA MCF 2723*	36		4
31 Oct 81	**NIGHT FLIGHT** *RCA RCALP 6003*	68		2
23 Oct 82	**DELIVER US FROM EVIL** *RCA RCALP 6054*	62		1

MUTYA BUENA
UK, female vocalist (Rosa Isabel Mutya Buena). See Sugababes — Weeks on Chart: 8

Date	Album	Peak	Wks at No.1	Wks on Chart
16 Jun 07	**REAL GIRL** *Fourth & Broadway 1734610* ●	10		8

BUENA VISTA SOCIAL CLUB
Cuba, male vocal/instrumental group — Weeks on Chart: 1

Date	Album	Peak	Wks at No.1	Wks on Chart
25 Oct 08	**AT CARNEGIE HALL** *World Circuit WCD080*	55		1

BUFFALO TOM
US, male vocal/instrumental group — Weeks on Chart: 5

Date	Album	Peak	Wks at No.1	Wks on Chart
14 Mar 92	**LET ME COME OVER** *Situation Two SITU 36CD*	49		1
9 Oct 93	**(BIG RED LETTER DAY)** *Beggars Banquet BBQCD 142*	17		3
22 Jul 95	**SLEEPY EYED** *Beggars Banquet BBQCD 177*	31		1

BUGGLES
UK, male vocal/instrumental duo — Weeks on Chart: 6

Date	Album	Peak	Wks at No.1	Wks on Chart
16 Feb 80	**THE AGE OF PLASTIC** *Island ILPS 9585*	27		6

LTJ BUKEM
UK, male DJ/producer (Danny Williamson) — Weeks on Chart: 3

Date	Album	Peak	Wks at No.1	Wks on Chart
8 Apr 00	**JOURNEY INWARDS** *Good Looking GLRAA 001*	40		3

BULLET FOR MY VALENTINE
UK, male vocal/instrumental group – Matt Tuck, Jason James, Michael Paget & Michael Thomas — Weeks on Chart: 8

Date	Album	Peak	Wks at No.1	Wks on Chart
15 Oct 05	**THE POISON** *Visible Noise TORMENT50CD* ○	21		4
9 Feb 08	**SCREAM AIM FIRE** *20-20 88697227365*	5		4

EMMA BUNTON
UK, female vocalist. See Spice Girls — Weeks on Chart: 25

Date	Album	Peak	Wks at No.1	Wks on Chart
28 Apr 01	**A GIRL LIKE ME** *Virgin CDV 2935* ●	4		12
21 Feb 04	**FREE ME** *19 9866158* ●	7		11
16 Dec 06	**LIFE IN MONO** *19 1718300*	65		2

ERIC BURDON & WAR
UK, male vocalist & US, male vocal/instrumental group. See Animals — Weeks on Chart: 4

Date	Album	Peak	Wks at No.1	Wks on Chart
3 Oct 70	**ERIC BURDON DECLARES WAR** *Polydor 2310 041*	50		2
20 Feb 71	**THE BLACK MAN'S BURDON** *Liberty LDS 8400*	25		2

TIM BURGESS
UK, male vocalist/harmonica player. See Charlatans — Weeks on Chart: 1

Date	Album	Peak	Wks at No.1	Wks on Chart
20 Sep 03	**I BELIEVE** *PIAS PIASB 099CD*	38		1

BURIAL
UK, male producer (William Bevan) — Weeks on Chart: 1

Date	Album	Peak	Wks at No.1	Wks on Chart
20 Sep 08	**UNTRUE** *Hyperdub HDBCD002*	58		1

JEAN-JACQUES BURNEL
UK, male vocalist/guitarist. See Stranglers — Weeks on Chart: 6

Date	Album	Peak	Wks at No.1	Wks on Chart
21 Apr 79	**EUROMAN COMETH** *United Artists UAG 30214*	40		5
3 Dec 83	**FIRE AND WATER** *Epic EPC 25707* DAVE GREENFIELD & JEAN-JACQUES BURNEL	94		1

BUSH
UK, male vocal/instrumental group — Weeks on Chart: 18

Date	Album	Peak	Wks at No.1	Wks on Chart
15 Jun 96	**SIXTEEN STONE** *Atlantic 6544925312*	42		3
1 Feb 97	**RAZORBLADE SUITCASE** *Interscope IND 90091* ● ★	4		12
6 Nov 99	**THE SCIENCE OF THINGS** *Polydor 4904832*	28		2
10 Nov 01	**GOLDEN STATE** *Atlantic 7567834882*	53		1

KATE BUSH
UK, female vocalist/multi-instrumentalist. Unmistakable singer/songwriter discovered by David Gilmour who became the first British female solo artist to have a UK No.1 album. Her long-awaited 2005 comeback gave her an impressive 28-year span of Top 5 albums — Weeks on Chart: 299

Date	Album	Peak	Wks at No.1	Wks on Chart
11 Mar 78	**THE KICK INSIDE** *EMI EMC 3223* ⊛	3		70
25 Nov 78	**LIONHEART** *EMI EMA 787* ⊛	6		36
20 Sep 80	**NEVER FOR EVER** *EMI EMA 7964* ●	1	1	23
25 Sep 82	**THE DREAMING** *EMI EMC 3419* ○	3		10

Date	Title / Label	Peak Position	Weeks at No.1	Weeks on Chart
28 Sep 85	**HOUNDS OF LOVE** *EMI KAB 1* ⊛x2	1	3	52
22 Nov 86	**THE WHOLE STORY** *EMI KBTV 1* ⊛x4	1	2	56
28 Jan 89	**THE SENSUAL WORLD** *EMI EMD 1010* ⊛	2		20
13 Nov 93	**THE RED SHOES** *EMI CDEMD 1047* ⊛	2		15
8 Oct 05	**HOUNDS OF LOVE** *EMI 5252392*	62		2
19 Nov 05	**AERIAL** *EMI TOCP66474* ⊛	3		15

BUSTED

UK, male vocal/instrumental trio – Charlie Simpson, James Bourne & Mattie Jay — **132**

Date	Title / Label	Peak Position	Weeks at No.1	Weeks on Chart
12 Oct 02	**BUSTED** *Universal MCD 60084* ⊛x3	2		77
29 Nov 03	**A PRESENT FOR EVERYONE** *Universal MCD 60090* ⊛x3	2		43
13 Nov 04	**LIVE – A TICKET FOR EVERYONE** *Universal MCD60096* ⊛	11		12

BERNARD BUTLER

UK, male vocalist/guitarist. See McAlmont & Butler, Suede, Tears — **19**

Date	Title / Label	Peak Position	Weeks at No.1	Weeks on Chart
9 Dec 95	**THE SOUND OF McALMONT AND BUTLER** *Hut CDHUT 32* McALMONT & BUTLER	33		8
18 Apr 98	**PEOPLE MOVE ON** *Creation CRECD 221* ○	11		8
6 Nov 99	**FRIENDS AND LOVERS** *Creation CRECD 248*	43		1
24 Aug 02	**BRING IT BACK** *Chrysalis 5399772* McALMONT & BUTLER	18		2

JONATHAN BUTLER

South Africa, male vocalist/guitarist — **14**

Date	Title / Label	Peak Position	Weeks at No.1	Weeks on Chart
12 Sep 87	**JONATHAN BUTLER** *Jive HIP 46* ●	12		11
4 Feb 89	**MORE THAN FRIENDS** *Jive HIP 70*	29		3

BUTTHOLE SURFERS

US, male vocal/instrumental group — **2**

Date	Title / Label	Peak Position	Weeks at No.1	Weeks on Chart
16 Mar 91	**PIOUHGD** *Rough Trade R 20812601*	68		1
3 Apr 93	**INDEPENDENT WORM SALOON** *Capitol CDEST 2192*	73		1

BUZZCOCKS

UK, male vocal/instrumental group — **23**

Date	Title / Label	Peak Position	Weeks at No.1	Weeks on Chart
25 Mar 78	**ANOTHER MUSIC IN A DIFFERENT KITCHEN** *United Artists UAG 30159* ○	15		11
7 Oct 78	**LOVE BITES** *United Artists UAG 30184* ○	13		9
6 Oct 79	**A DIFFERENT KIND OF TENSION** *United Artists UAG 30260*	26		3

BY ALL MEANS

US, male vocal group — **1**

Date	Title / Label	Peak Position	Weeks at No.1	Weeks on Chart
16 Jul 88	**BY ALL MEANS** *Fourth & Broadway BRLP 520*	80		1

MAX BYGRAVES

UK, male vocalist/comedian (Walter Bygraves) — **176**

Date	Title / Label	Peak Position	Weeks at No.1	Weeks on Chart
23 Sep 72	**SING ALONG WITH MAX** *Pye NSPL 18361*	4		44
2 Dec 72	**SING ALONG WITH MAX VOLUME 2** *Pye NSPL 18383* ○	11		23
5 May 73	**SINGALONGAMAX VOLUME 3** *Pye NSPL 18401* ○	5		30
29 Sep 73	**SINGALONGAMAX VOLUME 4** *Pye NSPL 18410* ○	7		12
15 Dec 73	**SINGALONGPARTY SONG** *Pye NSPL 18419* ○	15		6
12 Oct 74	**YOU MAKE ME FEEL LIKE SINGING A SONG** *Pye NSPL 18436*	39		3
7 Dec 74	**SINGALONGXMAS** *Pye NSPL 18439* ○	21		6
13 Nov 76	**100 GOLDEN GREATS** *Ronco RTDX 2019* ⊛	3		21
28 Oct 78	**LINGALONGAMAX** *Ronco RPL 2033*	39		5
16 Dec 78	**THE SONG AND DANCE MEN** *Pye NSPL 18574*	67		1
19 Aug 89	**SINGALONGAWARYEARS** *Parkfield Music PMLP 5001* ●	5		19
25 Nov 89	**SINGALONGAWARYEARS VOLUME 2** *Parkfield PMLP 5006* ●	33		6

DONALD BYRD

US, male trumpet player — **3**

Date	Title / Label	Peak Position	Weeks at No.1	Weeks on Chart
10 Oct 81	**LOVE BYRD** *Elektra K 52301*	70		3

BYRDS

US, male vocal/instrumental group – members included Roger McGuinn, Skip Battin, Gene Clark, d. 24 May 1991, Michael Clarke, d. 19 Dec 1993, David Crosby*, Chris Hillman, Gram Parsons, d. 19 Sep 1973, & Clarence White — **42**

Date	Title / Label	Peak Position	Weeks at No.1	Weeks on Chart
28 Aug 65	**MR. TAMBOURINE MAN** *CBS BPG 62571*	7		12
9 Apr 66	**TURN, TURN, TURN** *CBS BPG 62652*	11		5
1 Oct 66	**5TH DIMENSION** *CBS BPG 62783*	27		2
22 Apr 67	**YOUNGER THAN YESTERDAY** *CBS SBPG 62988*	37		4
4 May 68	**THE NOTORIOUS BYRD BROTHERS** *CBS 63169*	12		11
24 May 69	**DR. BYRD AND MR HYDE** *CBS 63545*	15		1
14 Feb 70	**BALLAD OF EASY RIDER** *CBS 63795*	41		1
28 Nov 70	**UNTITLED** *CBS 66253*	11		4
14 Apr 73	**BYRDS** *Asylum SYLA 8754*	31		1
19 May 73	**HISTORY OF THE BYRDS** *CBS 68242*	47		1

DAVID BYRNE

UK, male vocalist/multi-instrumentalist. See Talking Heads — **18**

Date	Title / Label	Peak Position	Weeks at No.1	Weeks on Chart
21 Feb 81	**MY LIFE IN THE BUSH OF GHOSTS** *E.G. EGLP 48* BRIAN ENO & DAVID BYRNE	29		8
21 Oct 89	**REI MOMO** *Warner Brothers WX 319*	52		2
14 Mar 92	**UH-OH** *Luaka Bop 7599267992*	26		5
4 Jun 94	**DAVID BYRNE** *Luaka Bop 9362455582*	44		2
19 May 01	**LOOK INTO THE EYEBALL** *Luaka Bop CDVUS 189*	58		1

MELANIE C

UK, female vocalist (Melanie Chisholm). See Spice Girls — **76**

Date	Title / Label	Peak Position	Weeks at No.1	Weeks on Chart
30 Oct 99	**NORTHERN STAR** *Virgin CDVX 2893* ⊛x3	4		69
22 Mar 03	**REASON** *Virgin CDV 2969* ●	5		4
23 Apr 05	**BEAUTIFUL INTENTIONS** *Red Girl REDGCD1*	24		2
14 Apr 07	**THIS TIME** *Red Girl REDGCD2*	57		1

C&C MUSIC FACTORY

US, male production/instrumental duo – Robert Clivilles & David Cole, d. 24 Jan 1995 — **14**

Date	Title / Label	Peak Position	Weeks at No.1	Weeks on Chart
9 Feb 91	**GONNA MAKE YOU SWEAT** *Columbia 4678141* ●	8		13
28 Mar 92	**GREATEST REMIXES VOLUME I** *Columbia 4694462*	45		1

MONTSERRAT CABALLE

Spain, female vocalist — **11**

Date	Title / Label	Peak Position	Weeks at No.1	Weeks on Chart
22 Oct 88	**FREDDIE MERCURY & MONTSERRAT CABALLE** *Polydor POLH 44* ○	15		8
8 Aug 92	**FROM THE OFFICIAL BARCELONA GAMES CEREMONY** *RCA Red Seal 9026612042* PLACIDO DOMINGO, JOSE CARRERAS & MONTSERRAT CABALLE	41		3

CABARET VOLTAIRE

UK, male vocal/instrumental group — **11**

Date	Title / Label	Peak Position	Weeks at No.1	Weeks on Chart
26 Jun 82	**2 X 45** *Rough Trade 42*	98		1
13 Aug 83	**THE CRACKDOWN** *Some Bizzare CV 1*	31		5
10 Nov 84	**MICRO-PHONIES** *Some Bizzare CV 2*	69		1
3 Aug 85	**DRINKING GASOLINE** *Some Bizzare CVM 1*	71		2
26 Oct 85	**THE COVENANT, THE SWORD AND THE ARM OF THE LAW** *Some Bizzare CV 3*	57		2

CACTUS WORLD NEWS

Ireland, male vocal/instrumental group — **2**

Date	Title / Label	Peak Position	Weeks at No.1	Weeks on Chart
24 May 86	**URBAN BEACHES** *MCA MCG 6005*	56		2

CAESARS

Sweden, male vocal/instrumental group — **2**

Date	Title / Label	Peak Position	Weeks at No.1	Weeks on Chart
7 May 05	**PAPER TIGERS** *Virgin CDVIR219*	40		2

CAGE THE ELEPHANT

US, male vocal/instrumental group — **1**

Date	Title / Label	Peak Position	Weeks at No.1	Weeks on Chart
5 Jul 08	**CAGE THE ELEPHANT** *Relentless CDRELX17*	38		1

COLBIE CAILLAT

US, female vocalist/guitarist — **3**

Date	Title / Label	Peak Position	Weeks at No.1	Weeks on Chart
20 Oct 07	**COCO** *Island 1740518*	44		3

CAJUN DANCE PARTY
UK, male/female vocal/instrumental group — Weeks on Chart: 1

Date	Title	Peak Position	Weeks at No.1	Weeks on Chart
10 May 08	**THE COLOURFUL LIFE** *XL Recordings XLCD347*	49		1

CAKE
US, male vocal/instrumental group — Weeks on Chart: 2

Date	Title	Peak Position	Weeks at No.1	Weeks on Chart
5 Apr 97	**FASHION NUGGET** *Capricorn 5328672*	53		2

J.J. CALE
US, male vocalist/guitarist (John W. Cale) — Weeks on Chart: 25

Date	Title	Peak Position	Weeks at No.1	Weeks on Chart
2 Oct 76	**TROUBADOUR** *Island ISA 50141*	53		1
25 Aug 79	**5** *Shelter ISA 5018*	40		6
21 Feb 81	**SHADES** *Shelter ISA 5021*	44		7
20 Mar 82	**GRASSHOPPER** *Shelter IFA 5022*	36		5
24 Sep 83	**NUMBER 8** *Mercury MERL 22*	47		3
26 Sep 92	**NUMBER 10** *Silvertone ORECD 523*	58		2
18 Nov 06	**THE ROAD TO ESCONDIDO** *Reprise 9362444182* & ERIC CLAPTON	50		1

CALEXICO
US, male vocal/instrumental group — Weeks on Chart: 3

Date	Title	Peak Position	Weeks at No.1	Weeks on Chart
20 May 00	**HOT RAIL** *City Slang 201532*	57		1
22 Feb 03	**FEAST OF WIRE** *City Slang 5816932*	71		1
20 Sep 08	**CARRIED TO DUST** *City Slang SLANG1051258*	55		1

MARIA CALLAS
Greece, female vocalist (Cecilia Kalogeropoulou), d. 16 Sep 1977 (age 53) — Weeks on Chart: 19

Date	Title	Peak Position	Weeks at No.1	Weeks on Chart
20 Jun 87	**THE MARIA CALLAS COLLECTION** *Stylus SMR 732*	50		7
24 Feb 96	**DIVA – THE ULTIMATE COLLECTION** *EMI CDEMTV 113*	61		1
11 Nov 00	**POPULAR MUSIC FROM TV FILM & OPERA** *EMI Classics CDC 5570622*	45		8
27 Oct 01	**ROMANTIC CALLAS – THE BEST OF** *EMI Classics CDC 5572112*	32		3

CALLING
US, male vocal/instrumental trio – Alex Band, Aaron Kamin & Nate Wood — Weeks on Chart: 29

Date	Title	Peak Position	Weeks at No.1	Weeks on Chart
29 Jun 02	**CAMINO PALMERO** *RCA 74321916102*	12		25
12 Jun 04	**TWO** *RCA 82876622622*	9		4

CAMEL
UK, male vocal/instrumental group — Weeks on Chart: 47

Date	Title	Peak Position	Weeks at No.1	Weeks on Chart
24 May 75	**THE SNOW GOOSE** *Decca SKL 5207*	22		13
17 Apr 76	**MOON MADNESS** *Decca TXS 115*	15		6
17 Sep 77	**RAIN DANCES** *Decca TXS 124*	20		8
14 Oct 78	**BREATHLESS** *Decca TXS 132*	26		1
27 Oct 79	**I CAN SEE YOUR HOUSE FROM HERE** *Decca TXS 137*	45		3
31 Jan 81	**NUDE** *Decca SKL 5323*	34		7
15 May 82	**THE SINGLE FACTOR** *Decca SKL 5328*	57		5
21 Apr 84	**STATIONARY TRAVELLER** *Decca SKL 5334*	57		4

CAMEO
US, male vocal/instrumental group – Larry Blackmon, Tomi Jenkins, Kevin Kendricks, Nathan Leftenant & Charles Singleton — Weeks on Chart: 47

Date	Title	Peak Position	Weeks at No.1	Weeks on Chart
10 Aug 85	**SINGLE LIFE** *Club JABH 11*	66		12
18 Oct 86	**WORD UP** *Club JABH 19*	7		34
26 Nov 88	**MACHISMO** *Club 836002*	86		1

ALI CAMPBELL
UK, male vocalist/guitarist. See UB40 — Weeks on Chart: 17

Date	Title	Peak Position	Weeks at No.1	Weeks on Chart
17 Jun 95	**BIG LOVE** *Kuff CDV 2783*	6		11
20 Oct 07	**RUNNING FREE** *Crumbs CRUCD1*	9		6

GLEN CAMPBELL
US, male vocalist/guitarist — Weeks on Chart: 187

Date	Title	Peak Position	Weeks at No.1	Weeks on Chart
31 Jan 70	**GLEN CAMPBELL LIVE** *Capitol SB 21444*	16		14
28 Feb 70	**BOBBIE GENTRY AND GLEN CAMPBELL** *Capitol ST 2928* BOBBIE GENTRY & GLEN CAMPBELL	50		1
30 May 70	**TRY A LITTLE KINDNESS** *Capitol ESW 389*	37		10
12 Dec 70	**THE GLEN CAMPBELL ALBUM** *Capitol ST 22493*	16		5
27 Nov 71	**GLEN CAMPBELL'S GREATEST HITS** *Capitol ST 21885*	8		113
25 Oct 75	**RHINESTONE COWBOY** *Capitol ESW 11430*	38		9
20 Nov 76	**20 GOLDEN GREATS** *Capitol EMTV 2*	1	6	27
23 Apr 77	**SOUTHERN NIGHTS** *Capitol EST 11601*	51		1
22 Jul 89	**THE COMPLETE GLEN CAMPBELL** *Stylus SMR 979*	47		4
2 Oct 99	**MY HITS AND LOVE SONGS** *Capitol 5223002*	50		1
6 Sep 08	**MEET GLEN CAMPBELL** *Capitol 2357572*	54		2

ISOBEL CAMPBELL & MARK LANEGAN
UK, female vocalist/cellist & US, male vocalist/guitarist — Weeks on Chart: 2

Date	Title	Peak Position	Weeks at No.1	Weeks on Chart
11 Feb 06	**BALLAD OF THE BROKEN SEAS** *V2 VVR1035822*	38		1
24 May 08	**SUNDAY AT DEVIL DIRT** *V2 VVR1050622*	38		1

CANIBUS
US, male rapper (Germaine Williams) — Weeks on Chart: 1

Date	Title	Peak Position	Weeks at No.1	Weeks on Chart
19 Sep 98	**CAN-I-BUS** *Universal UND 53222*	43		1

CANNED HEAT
US, male vocal/instrumental group – Bob Hite, d. 6 Apr 1981, Adolfo De La Parra, Larry Taylor, Henry Vestine, d. 20 Oct 1997 (replaced by Harvey Mandel) & Alan Wilson, d. 3 Sep 1970 — Weeks on Chart: 40

Date	Title	Peak Position	Weeks at No.1	Weeks on Chart
29 Jun 68	**BOOGIE WITH CANNED HEAT** *Liberty LBL 83103*	5		21
14 Feb 70	**CANNED HEAT COOKBOOK** *Liberty LBS 83303*	8		12
4 Jul 70	**CANNED HEAT '70 CONCERT** *Liberty LBS 83333*	15		3
10 Oct 70	**FUTURE BLUES** *Liberty LBS 83364*	27		4

FREDDY CANNON
US, male vocalist (Freddy Picariello) — Weeks on Chart: 11

Date	Title	Peak Position	Weeks at No.1	Weeks on Chart
27 Feb 60	**THE EXPLOSIVE FREDDY CANNON** *Top Rank 25/108*	1	1	11

BLU CANTRELL
US, female vocalist (Tiffany Cantrell) — Weeks on Chart: 11

Date	Title	Peak Position	Weeks at No.1	Weeks on Chart
9 Aug 03	**BITTERSWEET** *Arista 82876534042*	20		11

CAPERCAILLIE
UK/Ireland, male/female vocal/instrumental group — Weeks on Chart: 8

Date	Title	Peak Position	Weeks at No.1	Weeks on Chart
25 Sep 93	**SECRET PEOPLE** *Arista 74321162742*	40		3
17 Sep 94	**CAPERCAILLIE** *Survival 74321229112*	61		1
4 Nov 95	**TO THE MOON** *Survival SURCD 019*	41		2
20 Sep 97	**BEAUTIFUL WASTELAND** *Survival SURCD 021*	55		2

CAPPADONNA
US, male rapper (Daryl Hill) — Weeks on Chart: 1

Date	Title	Peak Position	Weeks at No.1	Weeks on Chart
4 Apr 98	**THE PILLAGE** *Epic 4888502*	43		1

CAPPELLA
Italy, male/female vocal/production group – Gianfranco Bortolotti, Rodney Bishop & Ettore Foresti (replaced by Kelly Overett) — Weeks on Chart: 9

Date	Title	Peak Position	Weeks at No.1	Weeks on Chart
26 Mar 94	**U GOT 2 KNOW** *Internal Dance CAPPC 1*	10		9

CAPTAIN
UK, male/female vocal/instrumental group — Weeks on Chart: 2

Date	Title	Peak Position	Weeks at No.1	Weeks on Chart
26 Aug 06	**THIS IS HAZELVILLE** *EMI 3708502*	23		2

CAPTAIN BEEFHEART & HIS MAGIC BAND
US, male vocal/instrumental group — Weeks on Chart: 16

Date	Title	Peak Position	Weeks at No.1	Weeks on Chart
6 Dec 69	**TROUT MASK REPLICA** *Straight STS 1053*	21		1
23 Jan 71	**LICK MY DECALS OFF BABY** *Straight STS 1063*	20		10
29 May 71	**MIRROR MAN** *Buddah 2365 002*	49		1
19 Feb 71	**THE SPOTLIGHT KID** *Reprise K 44162*	44		2
18 Sep 82	**ICE CREAM FOR CROW** *Virgin V 2337*	90		2

CAPTAIN SENSIBLE
UK, male vocalist (Ray Burns). See Damned — Weeks on Chart: 3

Date	Title	Peak Position	Weeks at No.1	Weeks on Chart
11 Sep 82	**WOMEN AND CAPTAIN FIRST** *A&M AMLH 68548*	64		3

Silver-selling ○ · Gold-selling ● · Platinum-selling ⊛ · US No.1 ★ · Peak Position · Weeks at No.1 · Weeks on Chart

CAPTAIN & TENNILLE

US, male keyboard player (Daryl Dragon) & female vocalist (Toni Tennille) **6**

Date	Album / Label	Peak Position	Weeks at No.1	Weeks on Chart
22 Mar 80	**MAKE YOUR MOVE** *Casablanca CAL 2060*	33		6

CARAVAN

UK, male vocal/instrumental group **2**

Date	Album / Label	Peak Position	Weeks at No.1	Weeks on Chart
30 Aug 75	**CUNNING STUNTS** *Decca SKL 5210*	50		1
15 May 76	**BLIND DOG AT ST. DUNSTAN'S** *BTM 1007*	53		1

CARCASS

UK, male vocal/instrumental group **2**

Date	Album / Label	Peak Position	Weeks at No.1	Weeks on Chart
6 Nov 93	**HEARTWORK** *Earache MOSH 097CD*	67		1
6 Jul 96	**SWANSONG** *Earache MOSH 160CDL*	68		1

CARDIGANS

Sweden, female/male vocal/instrumental group – Nina Persson, Lars-Olof Johansson, Bengt Lagerberg, Magnus Sveningsson & Peter Svensson **71**

Date	Album / Label	Peak Position	Weeks at No.1	Weeks on Chart
8 Jul 95	**LIFE** *Stockholm 5235562*	51		9
12 Oct 96	**FIRST BAND ON THE MOON** *Stockholm 5331172* ○	18		10
31 Oct 98	**GRAN TURISMO** *Stockholm 5590812* ⊛	8		49
5 Apr 03	**LONG GONE BEFORE DAYLIGHT** *Stockholm 0381092*	47		2
15 Mar 08	**BEST OF** *Stockholm 1747493*	32		1

MARIAH CAREY

US, female vocalist. The diva with a dynamic vocal range was named the most successful artist of the 1990s by *Billboard* magazine. She has sold over 170 million records in the US and has had more No.1 singles in the US than any other solo act **392**

Date	Album / Label	Peak Position	Weeks at No.1	Weeks on Chart
15 Sep 90	**MARIAH CAREY** *CBS 4668151* ⊛ ★	6		40
26 Oct 91	**EMOTIONS** *Columbia 4688511* ⊛	4		40
18 Jul 92	**MTV UNPLUGGED (EP)** *Columbia 4718692* ●	3		10
11 Sep 93	**MUSIC BOX** *Columbia 4742702* ⊛x5 ★	1	6	77
19 Nov 94	**MERRY CHRISTMAS** *Columbia 4773422* ●	32		7
7 Oct 95	**DAYDREAM** *Columbia 4813672* ⊛x2 ★	1	1	46
20 Sep 97	**BUTTERFLY** *Columbia 4885372* ● ★	2		27
28 Nov 98	**#1S** *Columbia 4926042* ⊛	10		32
13 Nov 99	**RAINBOW** *Columbia 4950652* ●	8		15
22 Sep 01	**GLITTER** *Virgin CDVUS 201*	10		4
15 Dec 01	**GREATEST HITS** *Columbia 5054612* ⊛	7		28
14 Dec 02	**CHARMBRACELET** *Island 0633842* ●	52		3
18 Oct 03	**THE REMIXES** *Columbia 5107542*	35		2
16 Apr 05	**THE EMANCIPATION OF MIMI** *Def Jam 9881270* ⊛x2 ★	7		43
26 Apr 08	**E=MC2** *Def Jam 1767180* ● ★	3		8
1 Nov 08	**THE BALLADS** *Columbia 88697392412*	14		10+

Top 3 Best-Selling Albums

	Album	Approximate Sales
1	MUSIC BOX	1,500,000
2	GREATEST HITS	750,000
3	NO1'S	690,000

BRANDI CARLILE

US, female vocalist/guitarist **1**

Date	Album / Label	Peak Position	Weeks at No.1	Weeks on Chart
10 May 08	**THE STORY** *RCA 88697286782*	58		1

BELINDA CARLISLE

US, female vocalist. See Go-Go's **160**

Date	Album / Label	Peak Position	Weeks at No.1	Weeks on Chart
2 Jan 88	**HEAVEN ON EARTH** *Virgin V 2496* ⊛x3	4		54
4 Nov 89	**RUNAWAY HORSES** *Virgin V 2599* ⊛	4		39
26 Oct 91	**LIVE YOUR LIFE BE FREE** *Virgin V 2680* ●	7		16
19 Sep 92	**THE BEST OF BELINDA VOLUME 1** *Virgin BELCD 1* ⊛x2	1	1	35
23 Oct 93	**REAL** *Virgin CDV 2725*	9		5
5 Oct 96	**A WOMAN AND A MAN** *Chrysalis CDCHR 6115* ●	12		5
13 Nov 99	**A PLACE ON EARTH – THE GREATEST HITS** *Virgin CDVX 2901* ●	15		6

VANESSA CARLTON

US, female vocalist **15**

Date	Album / Label	Peak Position	Weeks at No.1	Weeks on Chart
27 Jul 02	**BE NOT NOBODY** *A&M 4933672* ●	7		15

CARMEL

UK, female/male vocal/instrumental group **11**

Date	Album / Label	Peak Position	Weeks at No.1	Weeks on Chart
1 Oct 83	**CARMEL 6-TRACK (EP)** *Red Flame RFM 9*	94		2
24 Mar 84	**THE DRUM IS EVERYTHING** *London SH 8555*	19		8
27 Sep 86	**THE FALLING** *London LONLP 17*	88		1

ERIC CARMEN

US, male vocalist **1**

Date	Album / Label	Peak Position	Weeks at No.1	Weeks on Chart
15 May 76	**ERIC CARMEN** *Arista ARTY 120*	58		1

KIM CARNES

US, female vocalist **16**

Date	Album / Label	Peak Position	Weeks at No.1	Weeks on Chart
20 Jun 81	**MISTAKEN IDENTITY** *EMI America AML 3018* ★	26		16

MARY CHAPIN CARPENTER

US, female vocalist/guitarist **9**

Date	Album / Label	Peak Position	Weeks at No.1	Weeks on Chart
29 Oct 94	**STONES IN THE ROAD** *Columbia CK 64327* ○	26		5
2 Nov 96	**A PLACE IN THE WORLD** *Columbia 4851822*	36		2
5 Jun 99	**PARTY DOLL AND OTHER FAVOURITES** *Columbia 4886592*	65		1
26 May 01	**TIME SEX LOVE** *Columbia 5023542*	57		1

CARPENTERS

US, female/male vocal/instrumental duo – Karen Carpenter, d. 4 Feb 1983, & Richard Carpenter. The biggest-selling brother/sister act of all time were among the most distinctive and successful recording acts of the 1970s. *The Singles 1969 –1973* was the top-selling UK album of 1974 **620**

Date	Album / Label	Peak Position	Weeks at No.1	Weeks on Chart
23 Jan 71	**CLOSE TO YOU** *A&M AMLS 998*	23		75
30 Oct 71	**THE CARPENTERS** *A&M AMLS 63502*	12		36
15 Apr 72	**TICKET TO RIDE** *A&M AMLS 64342*	20		3
23 Sep 72	**A SONG FOR YOU** *A&M AMLS 63511*	13		37
7 Jul 73	**NOW AND THEN** *A&M AMLH 63519* ●	2		65
26 Jan 74	**THE SINGLES 1969–1973** *A&M AMLH 63601* ⊛ ★	1	17	125
28 Jun 75	**HORIZON** *A&M AMLK 64530* ●	1	5	27
23 Aug 75	**TICKET TO RIDE** *Hamlet AMLP 8001*	35		2
3 Jul 76	**A KIND OF HUSH** *A&M AMLK 64581* ●	3		15
8 Jan 77	**LIVE AT THE PALLADIUM** *A&M AMLS 68403* ●	28		3
8 Oct 77	**PASSAGE** *A&M AMLK 64703* ●	12		12
2 Dec 78	**THE SINGLES 1974–1978** *A&M AMLT 19748* ⊛	2		27
27 Jun 81	**MADE IN AMERICA** *A&M AMLK 63723* ○	12		10
15 Oct 83	**VOICE OF THE HEART** *A&M AMLX 64954* ●	6		19
20 Oct 84	**YESTERDAY ONCE MORE** *EMI/A&M SING 1* ⊛	10		26
13 Jan 90	**LOVELINES** *A&M AMA 3931*	73		1
31 Mar 90	**ONLY YESTERDAY – RICHARD & KAREN CARPENTER'S GREATEST HITS** *A&M AMA 1990* ⊛x5	1	7	82
15 Oct 94	**INTERPRETATIONS** *A&M 5402512* ●	29		10
22 Nov 97	**LOVE SONGS** *A&M 5408382* ●	47		8
9 Dec 00	**GOLD – GREATEST HITS** *A&M 4908652* ⊛	4		32
2 Dec 06	**THE ULTIMATE COLLECTION** *A&M/Polydor 9844626*	53		5

VIKKI CARR

US, female vocalist (Florencia Bisenta de Casillas Martinez Cardona) **12**

Date	Album / Label	Peak Position	Weeks at No.1	Weeks on Chart
22 Jul 67	**WAY OF TODAY** *Liberty SLBY 1331*	31		2
12 Aug 67	**IT MUST BE HIM** *Liberty LBS 83037*	12		10

PAUL CARRACK

UK, male vocalist. See Ace, Mike & The Mechanics, Squeeze **8**

Date	Album / Label	Peak Position	Weeks at No.1	Weeks on Chart
3 Feb 96	**BLUE VIEWS** *I.R.S. EIRSCD 1075*	55		7
24 Jun 00	**SATISFY MY SOUL** *Carrack-UK PCARCD 1*	63		1

JOSE CARRERAS

Spain, male vocalist **152**

Date	Album / Label	Peak Position	Weeks at No.1	Weeks on Chart
1 Oct 88	**JOSE CARRERAS COLLECTION** *Stylus SMR 860* ○	90		4
23 Dec 89	**JOSE CARRERAS SINGS ANDREW LLOYD WEBBER** *WEA WX 325* ○	42		6

Date	Title	Peak Position	Weeks at No.1	Weeks on Chart
1 Sep 90	**IN CONCERT** *Decca 4304331* LUCIANO PAVAROTTI, PLACIDO DOMINGO & JOSE CARRERAS ⦿x5	1	5	78
23 Feb 91	**THE ESSENTIAL JOSE CARRERAS** *Philips 4326921* ●	24		9
6 Apr 91	**HOLLYWOOD GOLDEN CLASSICS** *East West WX 416*	47		3
8 Aug 92	**AMIGOS PARA SIEMPRE (FRIENDS FOR LIFE)** *East West 4509902562* & SARAH BRIGHTMAN	53		4
8 Aug 92	**FROM THE OFFICIAL BARCELONA GAMES CEREMONY** *RCA Red Seal 9026612042* PLACIDO DOMINGO, JOSE CARRERAS & MONTSERRAT CABALLE	41		3
16 Oct 93	**WITH A SONG IN MY HEART** *Teldec 4509923692*	73		1
25 Dec 93	**CHRISTMAS IN VIENNA** *Sony Classical SK 53358* PLACIDO DOMINGO, DIANA ROSS & JOSE CARRERAS	71		2
10 Sep 94	**THE THREE TENORS IN CONCERT 1994** *Teldec 4509962002* CARRERAS DOMINGO PAVAROTTI WITH ORCHESTRA CONDUCTED BY ZUBIN MEHTA ⦿x2	1	1	26
3 Feb 96	**PASSION** *Erato 0630125962* ○	21		8
29 Aug 98	**THE THREE TENORS PARIS 1998** *Decca 4605002* CARRERAS DOMINGO PAVAROTTI WITH JAMES LEVINE	14		6
23 Dec 00	**THE THREE TENORS CHRISTMAS** *Sony Classical SK 89131* CARRERAS/DOMINGO/PAVAROTTI FEATURING MEHTA	57		2

DINA CARROLL

UK, female vocalist — 80

Date	Title	Peak Position	Weeks at No.1	Weeks on Chart
30 Jan 93	**SO CLOSE** *A&M 5400342* ⦿x4	2		63
26 Oct 96	**ONLY HUMAN** *Mercury 5340962* ⦿	2		13
23 Jun 01	**THE VERY BEST OF** *Mercury 5489182* ○	15		4

JASPER CARROTT

UK, male comedian/vocalist (Bob Davies) — 66

Date	Title	Peak Position	Weeks at No.1	Weeks on Chart
18 Oct 75	**RABBITS ON AND ON** *DJM DJLPS 462* ○	10		7
6 Nov 76	**CARROTT IN NOTTS** *DJM DJF 20482* ○	56		1
25 Nov 78	**THE BEST OF JASPER CARROTT** *DJM DJF 20549* ●	38		13
20 Oct 79	**THE UNRECORDED JASPER CARROTT** *DJM DJF 20560* ●	19		15
19 Sep 81	**BEAT THE CARROTT** *DJM DJF 20575* ●	13		16
25 Dec 82	**CARROTT'S LIB** *DJM DJF 20580*	80		3
19 Nov 83	**THE STUN (CARROTT TELLS ALL)** *DJM DJF 20582* ○	57		8
7 Feb 87	**COSMIC CARROTT** *Portrait LAUGH 1*	66		3

CARS

US, male vocal/instrumental group — 72

Date	Title	Peak Position	Weeks at No.1	Weeks on Chart
2 Dec 78	**CARS** *Elektra K 52088* ○	29		15
7 Jul 79	**CANDY-O** *Elektra K 52148*	30		6
6 Oct 84	**HEARTBEAT CITY** *Elektra 960296* ●	25		30
9 Nov 85	**THE CARS GREATEST HITS** *Elektra EKT 25* ●	27		19
5 Sep 87	**DOOR TO DOOR** *Elektra EKT 42*	72		2

CARTER – THE UNSTOPPABLE SEX MACHINE

UK, male vocal/instrumental duo – Leslie 'Fruitbat' Carter & James 'Jim Bob' Morrison — 40

Date	Title	Peak Position	Weeks at No.1	Weeks on Chart
2 Mar 91	**30 SOMETHING** *Rough Trade R2011 2702* ●	8		9
21 Sep 91	**101 DAMNATIONS** *Big Cat ABB 101*	29		6
1 Feb 92	**30 SOMETHING** *Chrysalis CHR 1897*	21		4
16 May 92	**1992 – THE LOVE ALBUM** *Chrysalis CCD 1946* ●	1	1	9
18 Sep 93	**POST HISTORIC MONSTERS** *Chrysalis CDCHR 7090*	5		4
26 Mar 94	**STARRY EYED AND BOLLOCK NAKED** *Chrysalis CDCHR 6069*	22		2
18 Feb 95	**WORRY BOMB** *Chrysalis CDCHRX 6096*	9		3
14 Oct 95	**STRAW DONKEY...THE SINGLES** *Chrysalis CDCHR 6110*	37		2
5 Apr 97	**A WORLD WITHOUT DAVE** *Cooking Vinyl COOKCD 120*	73		1

AARON CARTER

US, male vocalist — 8

Date	Title	Peak Position	Weeks at No.1	Weeks on Chart
28 Feb 98	**AARON CARTER** *Ultra Pop 0099572*	12		8

CARTOONS

Denmark, male/female vocal/instrumental group — 14

Date	Title	Peak Position	Weeks at No.1	Weeks on Chart
17 Apr 99	**TOONAGE** *Flex 4966922* ●	17		14

CASCADA

Germany, female/male vocal/production group – Natalie Horler, Yann Pfeiffer (Yanou) & Manuel Reuter (DJ Manian) — 51

Date	Title	Peak Position	Weeks at No.1	Weeks on Chart
17 Mar 07	**EVERY TIME WE TOUCH** *AllAround The World GLOBECD61* ⦿	2		28
15 Dec 07	**PERFECT DAY** *AATW/UMTV 1755820* ⦿	9		23

JOHNNY CASH

US, male vocalist/guitarist (J.R. Cash), d. 12 Sep 2003 (age 71). Arguably the world's best known country performer of all time. The unmistakable singer/songwriter has a 49-year span of hit albums in his homeland and a 41-year span of No.1s in the UK — 360

Date	Title	Peak Position	Weeks at No.1	Weeks on Chart
23 Jul 66	**EVERYBODY LOVES A NUT** *CBS BPG 62717*	28		1
4 May 68	**FROM SEA TO SHINING SEA** *CBS 62972*	40		1
6 Jul 68	**OLD GOLDEN THROAT** *CBS 63316*	37		2
24 Aug 68	**JOHNNY CASH AT FOLSOM PRISON** *CBS 63308*	8		53
23 Aug 69	**JOHNNY CASH AT SAN QUENTIN** *CBS 63629* ★	2		114
4 Oct 69	**GREATEST HITS VOLUME 1** *CBS 63062*	23		25
7 Mar 70	**HELLO I'M JOHNNY CASH** *CBS 63796*	6		16
15 Aug 70	**THE WORLD OF JOHNNY CASH** *CBS 66237*	5		31
12 Dec 70	**THE JOHNNY CASH SHOW** *CBS 64089*	18		6
18 Sep 71	**MAN IN BLACK** *CBS 64331*	18		7
13 Nov 71	**JOHNNY CASH** *Hallmark SHM 739*	43		2
20 May 72	**A THING CALLED LOVE** *CBS 64898*	8		11
14 Oct 72	**STAR PORTRAIT** *CBS 67201*	16		7
10 Jul 76	**ONE PIECE AT A TIME** *CBS 81416*	49		3
9 Oct 76	**THE BEST OF JOHNNY CASH** *CBS 10000*	48		2
2 Sep 78	**ITCHY FEET** *CBS 10009*	36		4
27 Aug 94	**THE MAN IN BLACK – DEFINITIVE COLLECTION** *Columbia MOODCD 35*	15		10
9 Mar 02	**MAN IN BLACK – THE VERY BEST OF** *Columbia 5063452*	39		4
6 Mar 04	**AMERICAN RECORDINGS TV – THE MAN COMES AROUND** *Lost Highway 0633392* ●	40		3
3 Dec 05	**RING OF FIRE – THE LEGEND OF JOHNNY CASH** *Columbia/UMTV 9887850* ⦿	11		33
11 Feb 06	**WALKING THE LINE – LEGENDARY SUN RECORDINGS** *Metro METRTCD805* ●	25		13
15 Jul 06	**AMERICAN V – A HUNDRED HIGHWAYS** *American/Lost Highway 862696* ● ★	9		7
3 Mar 07	**AT SAN QUENTIN** *Columbia 88697060932*	20		5

CA$HFLOW

US, male vocal/instrumental group — 3

Date	Title	Peak Position	Weeks at No.1	Weeks on Chart
28 Jun 86	**CA$HFLOW** *Club JABH 17*	33		3

CASHMERE

US, male vocal/instrumental group — 5

Date	Title	Peak Position	Weeks at No.1	Weeks on Chart
2 Mar 85	**CASHMERE** *Fourth & Broadway BRLP 503*	63		5

DAVID CASSIDY

US, male vocalist. See Partridge Family — 112

Date	Title	Peak Position	Weeks at No.1	Weeks on Chart
20 May 72	**CHERISH** *Bell BELLS 210*	2		43
24 Feb 73	**ROCK ME BABY** *Bell BELLS 218*	2		20
24 Nov 73	**DREAMS ARE NUTHIN' MORE THAN WISHES** *Bell BELLS 231* ●	1	1	13
3 Aug 74	**CASSIDY LIVE** *Bell BELLS 243* ●	9		7
9 Aug 75	**THE HIGHER THEY CLIMB** *RCA Victor RS 1012*	22		5
8 Jun 85	**ROMANCE** *Arista 206 983* ○	20		6
13 Oct 01	**THEN AND NOW** *Universal TV 0160822* ●	5		15
15 Nov 03	**A TOUCH OF BLUE** *Universal TV 9812859*	61		1
25 Nov 06	**COULD IT BE FOREVER – THE GREATEST HITS** *Sony BMG 88697020582* & THE PARTRIDGE FAMILY	52		2

EVA CASSIDY

US, female vocalist/guitarist, d. 2 Nov 1996 (age 33) — 177

Date	Title	Peak Position	Weeks at No.1	Weeks on Chart
3 Jun 00	**TIME AFTER TIME** *Blix Street G210073*	25		14
10 Feb 01	**SONGBIRD** *Blix Street G210045* ⦿x5 ★	1	2	117
31 Aug 02	**IMAGINE** *Blix Street G210075* ⦿	1	1	20
23 Aug 03	**AMERICAN TUNE** *Blix Street G210079* ●	1	1	11
24 Jul 04	**WONDERFUL WORLD** *Blix Street G210082*	11		6
6 Sep 08	**SOMEWHERE** *Blix Street G210190*	4		9

CASSIE

US, female vocalist/model (Cassandra Ventura) — 2

Date	Title	Peak Position	Weeks at No.1	Weeks on Chart
9 Sep 06	**CASSIE** *Bad Boy 7567839812*	33		2

CASSIUS

France, DJ/production duo — 2

Date	Title	Peak Position	Weeks at No.1	Weeks on Chart
6 Feb 99	**1999** *Virgin CDVIR 76*	28		2

Mariah Carey

LOOK at the history of pop music in the second half of the twentieth century and one of the main things you notice is that, decade by decade, life has become progressively easier for the vocalist. Long before rock 'n' roll, live performers had to compete, quite literally, with the volume and density of their live band. In the studio, there were no digital aids to rescue a flat note. The advancement of microphone and amplification technology helped thrust the more mellow 'crooners' into the spotlight, but ironically many of these prodigiously talented individuals were easily capable of holding their own vocally next to a big band. In the 1950s, rock 'n' roll appeared to destroy the primacy of the 'good singer' in favour of energy and enthusiasm; the 1960s took things further with garage bands and art-school experimentation meaning traditional melodies were no longer a requirement; the 1970s saw punk positively sneering at the very notion of melody and 'musicianship' and, in the 1980s, the first of a new technologically advanced generation of super-producers like Trevor Horn were determined to prove that they barely needed bands or singers to make good records at all. Then, of course, there is the Elastoplast to all post-millennial wailers – Auto-Tune software, which allows even the most dubious of vocal melodies to be made pitch-perfect.

She is a diva in the original, truest sense

It's perhaps not that surprising, then, that early in the 1990s many more purist pop fans decided that they'd had enough. Enter the arena of R&B and soul, which, at least, was far from accommodating of vocals that were anything less than sensational. All new singers had to be able to prove that they could sing, *really* sing. The original contemporary source of this trend was Whitney Houston's warbling 1992 version of 'I Will Always Love You' but of course she comes from a long line of others with outstanding voices, including Aretha Franklin, Ella Fitzgerald and an entire canon of female vocal gymnasts. Yet, perhaps of all these remarkable singers, the star who best embodied this resurgence of interest in true singing talent was Mariah Carey. She's had an absolutely astonishing run of success both in Europe and in the United States – at the time of writing she is the world's most successful female recording artist.

And it's not just her voice that put her back where stars were always supposed to belong, way out of reach of ordinary people. She has a superstar quality that makes it almost impossible to imagine her popping to the supermarket for a microwave ready meal and a bottle of Lambrusco. Jacko's the same, likewise Madonna (jaunty trips to country pubs aside). This, of course, isn't an accident. Right from the start of her recording career, Mariah was groomed by Columbia Records to be an otherworldly, celestial attraction. She is a diva in the original, truest sense. Even the biography of her early life and 'discovery' is so classically rags-to-riches that it could have been scripted by Walt Disney.

She was born on 27 March 1970, the daughter of an ex-opera singer of Irish descent, Patrica Hickey, and an Afro-Venezuelan engineer, Alfred Carey. Her parents divorced when she was three and, around the same time, she started singing, imitating her mother practising Verdi's *Rigoletto*. By the time she was eighteen, she'd already worked as a backing singer and produced a demo tape (she was frequently absent from school because of her pursuit of a music career); then, fatefully, in 1988, she met Columbia Records executive Tommy Mottola at a party. When he listened to her tape at the end of the party, so legend has it, he rushed out to look for her but she'd already gone. Nevertheless he tracked her down and, in 1990, she co-wrote and released her first album.

This part of her life is a very familiar story. Particularly the part where she and Mottola – twenty-one years her senior – became an item during the recording of her

Biggest-Selling Album			Highest	
Artist	Album	Week	Position	Approx Sales
MARIAH CAREY	MUSIC BOX	11/9/93	1	1,500,000

first album, marrying in 1993. It was part fairytale and part accident waiting to happen. But, during her first run of singles, nothing could go wrong. Her debut album *Mariah Carey* went straight in to Number 1 around the world (a Number 6 in the UK) and songs like 'Vision Of Love' introduced the vocal fireworks that she'd become famous for. With her second album, *Emotions*, things became rather tougher for a while. Although it peaked at a UK Number 4, globally it didn't do as well as her debut, commercially or critically. After she couldn't tour because of severe stage fright, there was criticism that she couldn't produce the goods live – a ludicrous suggestion in retrospect – in response, she recorded an *MTV Unplugged* album.

But, with her third studio album, *Music Box*, Mariah reached a new peak. She had her first Number 1 single in the UK with a cover of Badfinger's 'Without You', and 'Hero' became a massive hit all over the world. The album was also her first to hit the UK top spot. Her 1994 Christmas album *Merry Christmas* then became the best-selling Christmas album in history with ultra-sugary tracks like 'All I Want For Christmas Is You'.

To some fans this period of her career represents Mariah in the 'good girl' years. Her fifth album *Daydream* saw her bringing in more risqué R&B influences and duetting with rapper Ol' Dirty Bastard, to the consternation, she said at the time, of some executives at Sony. The fact that it was another huge success evidently gave her confidence because with her 1997 album *Butterfly* she attempted to break free of what she now saw as her record company's – and by implication her husband's – excessive control. She chafed at their attempts to define her public image as she wanted to show off a new, more grown-up Mariah.

This, as it so often does, mostly seemed to involve her clothes falling off in videos. The lead single from *Butterfly* saw the previously demure starlet feature in a kind of spy-fantasy video, in which she was tied to a chair in a micro-dress, before escaping and swimming away in her underwear. This period also involved a very public split from husband Tommy. This may have been where it all went wrong or it may have been a belated taste of freedom but the years that followed haven't always been easy. The £50 million Virgin were rumoured to have paid for her next contract might have helped, though.

It was part fairytale and part accident waiting to happen

The next album, *Rainbow*, was another massive hit but her semi-autobiographical 2001 film *Glitter* was a costly disaster and she was later admitted to hospital, suffering from exhaustion. A year later *Charmbracelet* was the least successful album of her career (reaching a paltry Number 52 in the UK). Luckily, Mariah's life was still following a strict, fairytale star-is-born storyline. A fall-from-grace had to be followed by a triumphant comeback and this arrived with 2005's album *The Emancipation of Mimi*. It had a new knowingness – ably assisted by producers such as The Neptunes and Kanye West – that took into account Mariah's reputation as a highly strung diva; however, it also had some of the sharpest songs of her career. The follow-up, 2007's *E=MC²*, was almost as successful and her influence on the music scene, by now, was huge.

When programmes like *Pop Idol* and *American Idol* began to appear it was almost obligatory for wannabe starlets to prove that they could climb up and down the scales over a single syllable. This became a hugely tiresome display of style over substance, for which Mariah Carey has often been blamed. Besides, Carey's five-octave vocal range was once cited as evidence that no one in the entire world could sing a higher note. So to criticise her for the latter-day and vastly inferior mimicry on most TV talent shows is very unfair. She has the voice. It would seem churlish to ask her not to use it.

CAST

UK, male vocal/instrumental group – John Power, Keith O'Neill, Liam Tyson & Peter Wilkinson — 116

Date	Title	Peak Position	Weeks at No.1	Weeks on Chart
28 Oct 95	**ALL CHANGE** *Polydor 5293122* ⊛	7		67
26 Apr 97	**MOTHER NATURE CALLS** *Polydor 5375672* ⊛	3		42
29 May 99	**MAGIC HOUR** *Polydor 5471762*	6		7

CAT POWER

US, female vocalist/guitarist/pianist (Charlyn Marshall) — 3

Date	Title	Peak Position	Weeks at No.1	Weeks on Chart
4 Feb 06	**THE GREATEST** *Matador OLE6262*	45		1
2 Feb 08	**JUKEBOX** *Matador OLE7931*	32		2

CATATONIA

UK, female/male vocal/instrumental group – Cerys Matthews*, Paul Jones, Owen Powell, Aled Richards & Mark Roberts — 125

Date	Title	Peak Position	Weeks at No.1	Weeks on Chart
12 Oct 96	**WAY BEYOND BLUE** *Blanco Y Negro 0630163052*	32		3
14 Feb 98	**INTERNATIONAL VELVET** *Blanco Y Negro 3984208342* ⊛x3	1	1	93
24 Apr 99	**EQUALLY CURSED AND BLESSED** *Blanco Y Negro 3984270942* ⊛	1	1	23
18 Aug 01	**PAPER SCISSORS STONE** *Blanco Y Negro 8573888482* ○	6		4
14 Sep 02	**GREATEST HITS** *Blanco Y Negro 0927491942*	24		2

CATHERINE WHEEL

UK, male vocal/instrumental group — 3

Date	Title	Peak Position	Weeks at No.1	Weeks on Chart
29 Feb 92	**FERMENT** *Fontana 5109032*	36		1
31 Jul 93	**CHROME** *Fontana 5180392*	58		1
16 May 98	**ADAM AND EVE** *Chrysalis 4930992*	53		1

NICK CAVE & THE BAD SEEDS

Australia/Germany, male vocal/instrumental group. See Birthday Party — 36

Date	Title	Peak Position	Weeks at No.1	Weeks on Chart
2 Jun 84	**FROM HER TO ETERNITY** *Mute STUMM 17*	40		3
15 Jun 85	**THE FIRST BORN IS DEAD** *Mute STUMM 21*	53		1
30 Aug 86	**KICKING AGAINST THE PRICKS** *Mute STUMM 28*	89		1
1 Oct 88	**TENDER PREY** *Mute STUMM 52*	67		1
28 Apr 90	**THE GOOD SON** *Mute STUMM 76*	47		1
9 May 92	**HENRY'S DREAM** *Mute CDSTUMM 92*	29		2
18 Sep 93	**LIVE SEEDS** *Mute CDSTUMM 122*	67		1
30 Apr 94	**LET LOVE IN** *Mute LCDSTUMM 123*	12		2
17 Feb 96	**MURDER BALLADS** *Mute LCDSTUMM 138* ○	8		5
15 Mar 97	**THE BOATMAN'S CALL** *Mute CDSTUMM 142*	22		3
23 May 98	**THE BEST OF NICK CAVE & THE BAD SEEDS** *Mute CDMUTEL 004*	11		4
14 Apr 01	**NO MORE SHALL WE PART** *Mute LCDSTUMM 164*	15		3
15 Feb 03	**NOCTURAMA** *Mute LCDSTUMM 207*	20		2
2 Oct 04	**ABATTOIR BLUES/THE LYRE OF ORPHEUS** *Mute CDSTUMM 233* ●	11		3
9 Apr 05	**B-SIDES AND RARITIES** *Mute CDMUTEL11*	74		1
15 Mar 08	**DIG!!! LAZARUS DIG!!!** *Mute CDSTUMM277* ○	4		3

CAVE IN

US, male vocal/instrumental group — 1

Date	Title	Peak Position	Weeks at No.1	Weeks on Chart
29 Mar 03	**ANTENNA** *RCA 82876515552*	67		1

CAVEMAN

UK, male rap group — 2

Date	Title	Peak Position	Weeks at No.1	Weeks on Chart
13 Apr 91	**POSITIVE REACTION** *Profile FILER 406*	43		2

C.C.S.

UK, male vocal/instrumental group — 5

Date	Title	Peak Position	Weeks at No.1	Weeks on Chart
8 Apr 72	**C.C.S.** *RAK SRAK 503*	23		5

CELTIC SPIRIT

Ireland/UK, male vocal/instrumental group — 1

Date	Title	Peak Position	Weeks at No.1	Weeks on Chart
31 Jan 98	**CELTIC DREAMS** *Polygram TV 5399992*	62		1

CENTRAL LINE

UK, male vocal/instrumental group — 5

Date	Title	Peak Position	Weeks at No.1	Weeks on Chart
13 Feb 82	**BREAKING POINT** *Mercury MERA 001*	64		5

CERRONE

France, male producer/multi-instrumentalist (Jean-Marc Cerrone) — 1

Date	Title	Peak Position	Weeks at No.1	Weeks on Chart
30 Sep 78	**SUPERNATURE** *Atlantic K 50431*	60		1

A CERTAIN RATIO

UK, male vocal/instrumental group — 3

Date	Title	Peak Position	Weeks at No.1	Weeks on Chart
30 Jan 82	**SEXTET** *Factory FACT 55*	53		3

PETER CETERA

US, male vocalist/guitarist. See Chicago — 4

Date	Title	Peak Position	Weeks at No.1	Weeks on Chart
13 Sep 86	**SOLITUDE/SOLITAIRE** *Full Moon 9254741*	56		4

RICHARD CHAMBERLAIN

US, male actor/vocalist (George Chamberlain) — 8

Date	Title	Peak Position	Weeks at No.1	Weeks on Chart
16 Mar 63	**RICHARD CHAMBERLAIN SINGS** *MGM C 923*	8		8

CHAMELEON

UK, male vocal/instrumental group — 4

Date	Title	Peak Position	Weeks at No.1	Weeks on Chart
25 May 85	**WHAT DOES ANYTHING MEAN? BASICALLY** *Statik STAT LP 22*	60		2
20 Sep 86	**STRANGE TIMES** *Geffen 9241191*	44		2

CHAMILLIONAIRE

US, male rapper (Hakeem Seriki) — 11

Date	Title	Peak Position	Weeks at No.1	Weeks on Chart
19 Aug 06	**THE SOUND OF REVENGE** *Universal 1705107* ●	22		11

CHAMPAIGN

US, male/female vocal/instrumental group — 4

Date	Title	Peak Position	Weeks at No.1	Weeks on Chart
27 Jun 81	**HOW 'BOUT US** *CBS 84927*	38		4

CHANGE

US, male/female vocal/instrumental group — 27

Date	Title	Peak Position	Weeks at No.1	Weeks on Chart
19 May 84	**CHANGE OF HEART** *WEA WX 5*	34		17
27 Apr 85	**TURN ON THE RADIO** *Cooltempo CHR 1504*	39		6
13 Jul 85	**THE ARTISTS VOLUME 2** *Street Sounds ARTIS 2* LUTHER VANDROSS/TEDDY PENDERGRASS/CHANGE/ATLANTIC STARR	45		4

MANU CHAO

France, male vocalist/guitarist (José-Manuel Chao) — 1

Date	Title	Peak Position	Weeks at No.1	Weeks on Chart
29 Sep 07	**LA RADIOLINA** *Because BEC5772125*	41		1

BETH NIELSEN CHAPMAN

US, female vocalist/guitarist — 1

Date	Title	Peak Position	Weeks at No.1	Weeks on Chart
12 Jun 04	**LOOK** *Sanctuary SANCD269*	63		1

MICHAEL CHAPMAN

UK, male vocalist — 1

Date	Title	Peak Position	Weeks at No.1	Weeks on Chart
21 Mar 70	**FULLY QUALIFIED SURVIVOR** *Harvest SHVL 764*	45		1

TRACY CHAPMAN

US, female vocalist/guitarist — 230

Date	Title	Peak Position	Weeks at No.1	Weeks on Chart
21 May 88	**TRACY CHAPMAN** *Elektra EKT 44* ⊛x8 ★	1	3	189
14 Oct 89	**CROSSROADS** *Elektra EKT 61* ⊛	1	1	16
9 May 92	**MATTERS OF THE HEART** *Elektra 7559612152*	19		3
6 Oct 01	**COLLECTION** *Elektra 7559627002* ⊛	3		18
2 Nov 02	**LET IT RAIN** *Elektra 7559628362*	36		2
24 Sep 05	**WHERE YOU LIVE** *Elektra 7567838032*	43		1
22 Nov 08	**OUR BRIGHT FUTURE** *Elektra 7567898212*	75		1

CHAPTERHOUSE

UK, male vocal/instrumental group — 3

Date	Title	Peak Position	Weeks at No.1	Weeks on Chart
11 May 91	**WHIRLPOOL** *Dedicated DEDLP 001*	23		3

CHAQUITO & QUEDO BRASS
UK, orchestra (Chaquito is arranger Johnny Gregory)

Date	Title	Peak	Wks No.1	Wks on Chart
				2
24 Feb 68	**THIS IS CHAQUITO** *Fontana SFXL 50*	36		1
4 Mar 72	**THRILLER THEMES** *Philips 6308 087* CHAQUITO ORCHESTRA	48		1

CHARGED GBH
UK, male vocal/instrumental group

Date	Title	Peak	Wks No.1	Wks on Chart
				1
14 Aug 82	**CITY BABY ATTACKED BY RATS** *Clay CLAYLP 4*	17		6

CHARLATANS
UK, male vocal/instrumental group – Tim Burgess*, Martin Blunt, Jon Brookes, Mark Collins & Rob Collins, d. 23 Jul 1996 (replaced by Tony Rogers)

Date	Title	Peak	Wks No.1	Wks on Chart
				119
20 Oct 90	**SOME FRIENDLY** *Situation Two SITU 30* ●	1	1	17
4 Apr 92	**BETWEEN 10TH AND 11TH** *Situation Two SITU 37CD*	21		4
2 Apr 94	**UP TO OUR HIPS** *Beggars Banquet BBQCD 147*	8		3
9 Sep 95	**THE CHARLATANS** *Beggars Banquet BBQCD 174* ●	1	1	13
3 May 97	**TELLIN' STORIES** *Beggars Banquet BBQCD 190* ⊛	1	2	28
7 Mar 98	**MELTING POT** *Beggars Banquet BBQCD 198*	4		25
30 Oct 99	**US AND US ONLY** *Universal MCD 60069* ●	2		10
22 Sep 01	**WONDERLAND** *Universal MCD 60076* ●	2		5
1 Jun 02	**SONGS FROM THE OTHER SIDE** *Beggars Banquet 2032CD*	55		1
3 Aug 02	**LIVE IT LIKE YOU LOVE IT** *Universal MCD 60080*	40		2
29 May 04	**UP AT THE LAKE** *Universal MCD60093* ○	13		6
29 Apr 06	**SIMPATICO** *Creole SANCD358*	10		2
18 Nov 06	**FOREVER – THE SINGLES** *Universal 1713091*	38		2
24 May 08	**YOU CROSS MY PATH** *Cooking Vinyl COOKCD462X*	39		1

CHARLENE
US, female vocalist (Charlene Duncan)

Date	Title	Peak	Wks No.1	Wks on Chart
				4
17 Jul 82	**I'VE NEVER BEEN TO ME** *Motown STML 12171*	43		4

RAY CHARLES
US, male vocalist/pianist/band leader (Ray Charles Robinson), d. 10 Jun 2004 (age 73)

Date	Title	Peak	Wks No.1	Wks on Chart
				82
28 Jul 62	**MODERN SOUNDS IN COUNTRY AND WESTERN MUSIC** *HMV CLP 1580* ★	6		16
23 Feb 63	**MODERN SOUNDS IN COUNTRY AND WESTERN MUSIC VOLUME 2** *HMV CLP 1613*	15		5
20 Jul 63	**GREATEST HITS** *HMV CLP 1626*	16		5
5 Oct 68	**GREATEST HITS VOLUME 2** *Stateside SSL 10241*	24		8
19 Jul 80	**HEART TO HEART – 20 HOT HITS** *London RAYTV 1*	29		5
24 Mar 90	**COLLECTION** *Arcade RCLP 101*	36		3
13 Mar 93	**RAY CHARLES – LIVING LEGEND** *Arcade ARC 946422*	48		3
25 Aug 01	**THE DEFINITIVE** *warner.esp 8122735562* ●	13		12
11 Sep 04	**GENIUS LOVES COMPANY** *Liberty 8665402* ● ★	18		16
29 Jan 05	**RAY (OST)** *Rhino 8122765402*	36		8
28 Oct 06	**RAY SINGS BASIE SWINGS** *Concord 7230026* & COUNT BASIE ORCHESTRA	63		1

TINA CHARLES
UK, female vocalist (Tina Hoskins)

Date	Title	Peak	Wks No.1	Wks on Chart
				7
3 Dec 77	**HEART 'N' SOUL** *CBS 82180* ○	35		7

CHARLES & EDDIE
US, male vocal duo – Charles Pettigrew, d. 6 Apr 2001, & Eddie Chacon

Date	Title	Peak	Wks No.1	Wks on Chart
				15
12 Dec 92	**DUOPHONIC** *Capitol CDESTU 2186* ●	19		15

CHAS & DAVE
UK, male vocal/instrumental duo – Chas Hodges & Dave Peacock

Date	Title	Peak	Wks No.1	Wks on Chart
				101
5 Dec 81	**CHAS AND DAVE'S CHRISTMAS JAMBOREE BAG** *Warwick WW 5166* ●	25		15
17 Apr 82	**MUSTN'T GRUMBLE** *Rockney 909* ○	35		11
8 Jan 83	**JOB LOT** *Rockney ROC 910* ○	59		15
15 Oct 83	**CHAS AND DAVE'S KNEES UP – JAMBOREE BAG NUMBER 2** *Rockney WW 5166* ⊛	7		17
11 Aug 84	**WELL PLEASED** *Rockney ROC 912*	27		10
17 Nov 84	**CHAS AND DAVE'S GREATEST HITS** *Rockney ROC 913* ⊛	16		10
15 Dec 84	**CHAS AND DAVE'S CHRISTMAS JAMBOREE BAG** *Rockney ROCM 001*	87		1
9 Nov 85	**JAMBOREE BAG NUMBER 3** *Rockney ROC 914* ●	15		13
13 Dec 86	**CHAS AND DAVE'S CHRISTMAS CAROL ALBUM** *Telstar STAR 2293*	37		4
29 Apr 95	**STREET PARTY** *Telstar TCD 2765* ○	3		5

CHASE & STATUS
UK, male drum 'N' bass/production duo

Date	Title	Peak	Wks No.1	Wks on Chart
				2
25 Oct 08	**MORE THAN ALOT** *Ram RAMMLP12CD*	49		2

JC CHASEZ
US, male vocalist. See N Sync

Date	Title	Peak	Wks No.1	Wks on Chart
				2
8 May 04	**SCHIZOPHRENIC** *Jive JIV537242*	46		2

CHEAP TRICK
US, male vocal/instrumental group

Date	Title	Peak	Wks No.1	Wks on Chart
				15
24 Feb 79	**CHEAP TRICK AT BUDOKAN** *Epic EPC 86083*	29		9
6 Oct 79	**DREAM POLICE** *Epic EPC 83522*	41		5
5 Jun 82	**ONE ON ONE** *Epic EPC 85740*	95		1

CHUBBY CHECKER
US, male vocalist (Ernest Evans)

Date	Title	Peak	Wks No.1	Wks on Chart
				7
27 Jan 62	**TWIST WITH CHUBBY CHECKER** *Columbia 33SX 1315*	13		4
3 Mar 62	**FOR TWISTERS ONLY** *Columbia 33SX 1341*	17		3

CHEEKY GIRLS
Romania, female vocal duo

Date	Title	Peak	Wks No.1	Wks on Chart
				7
23 Aug 03	**PARTY TIME** *Multiply MULTYCD 13* ○	14		7

CHEETAH GIRLS
US, female vocal trio

Date	Title	Peak	Wks No.1	Wks on Chart
				3
13 Jan 07	**THE CHEETAH GIRLS 2** *Walt Disney 3810472* ○	59		3

CHEMICAL BROTHERS
UK, male DJ/production duo – Tom Rowlands & Ed Simons

Date	Title	Peak	Wks No.1	Wks on Chart
				165
8 Jul 95	**EXIT PLANET DUST** *Junior Boy's Own XDUSTCD 1* ⊛	9		41
19 Apr 97	**DIG YOUR OWN HOLE** *Virgin XDUSTCD 2* ⊛	1	1	27
3 Jul 99	**SURRENDER** *Virgin XDUSTCD 4* ⊛x2	1	1	47
9 Feb 02	**COME WITH US** *Virgin XDUSTCDX 5* ●	1	1	11
4 Oct 03	**SINGLES 93-03** *Virgin XDUSTCDX 6* ●	9		7
5 Feb 05	**PUSH THE BUTTON** *Freestyle Dust XDUSTCD7* ●	1	1	18
14 Jul 07	**WE ARE THE NIGHT** *Virgin XDUSTCD8* ●	1	1	11
13 Sep 08	**BROTHERHOOD** *Virgin XDUSTCD9*	11		3

CHER
US, female vocalist (Cherilyn LaPierre). Indefatigable singer whose Farewell Tour broke the record for the highest-grossing tour ever by a female performer. *Believe*, the biggest-selling album of her career, sold 20 million copies worldwide. See Sonny & Cher

Date	Title	Peak	Wks No.1	Wks on Chart
				310
2 Oct 65	**ALL I REALLY WANT TO DO** *Liberty LBY 3058*	7		9
7 May 66	**SONNY SIDE OF CHER** *Liberty LBY 3072*	11		11
16 Jan 88	**CHER** *Geffen WX 132* ●	26		22
22 Jul 89	**HEART OF STONE** *Geffen GEF 24239* ⊛	7		82
29 Jun 91	**LOVE HURTS** *Geffen GEF 24427* ⊛x3	1	1	51
21 Nov 92	**CHER'S GREATEST HITS: 1965–1992** *Geffen GED 24439* ⊛x3	1	7	33
18 Nov 95	**IT'S A MAN'S WORLD** *WEA 0630126702* ●	10		18
7 Nov 98	**BELIEVE** *WEA 3984253192* ⊛x2	7		44
20 Nov 99	**THE GREATEST HITS** *WEA/Universal Music TV 8573804202* ⊛x2	7		24
1 Dec 01	**LIVING PROOF** *WEA 0927424632* ●	46		2
6 Dec 03	**THE VERY BEST OF** *UMTV/WSM 5046685862* ●	17		14

CHERRELLE
US, female vocalist (Cheryl Norton)

Date	Title	Peak	Wks No.1	Wks on Chart
				9
25 Jan 86	**HIGH PRIORITY** *Tabu TBU 26699*	17		9

EAGLE-EYE CHERRY
Sweden, male vocalist

Date	Title	Peak	Wks No.1	Wks on Chart
				32
1 Aug 98	**DESIRELESS** *Polydor 5372262* ●	3		29
20 May 00	**LIVING IN THE PRESENT FUTURE** *Polydor 5437442*	12		3

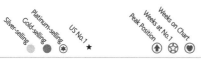

NENEH CHERRY
UK (b. Sweden), female vocalist/rapper – Neneh Karlsson — 49

Date	Title / Label	Peak Position	Weeks at No.1	Weeks on Chart
17 Jun 89	**RAW LIKE SUSHI** *Circa 8* ⊛	2		43
7 Nov 92	**HOMEBREW** *Circa CIRCD 25*	27		2
14 Sep 96	**MAN** *Hut CDHUT 38* ○	16		4

CHERRY GHOST
UK, male vocal/instrumental group – Simon Aldred, Phill Anderson, Grenville Harrop, Ben Parsons & Jim Rhodes — 6

Date	Title / Label	Peak Position	Weeks at No.1	Weeks on Chart
21 Jul 07	**THIRST FOR ROMANCE** *Heavenly HVNLP59CD* ○	7		6

CHIC
US, male/female vocal/instrumental group – Bernard Edwards, d. 18 Apr 1996, Nile Rodgers, Luci Martin, Tony Thompson & Norma Jean Wright (replaced by Alfa Anderson) — 47

Date	Title / Label	Peak Position	Weeks at No.1	Weeks on Chart
3 Feb 79	**C'EST CHIC** *Atlantic K 50565* ●	2		24
18 Aug 79	**RISQUE** *Atlantic K 50634* ○	29		12
15 Dec 79	**BEST OF CHIC** *Atlantic K 50686*	30		8
5 Dec 87	**FREAK OUT** *Telstar STAR 2319* & SISTER SLEDGE	72		3

CHICAGO
US, male vocal/instrumental group – Peter Cetera*, Terry Kath, d. 23 Jan 1978 (replaced by Bill Champlin), Robert Lamm, Lee Loughnane, James Pankow, Walter Parazaider & Danny Seraphine — 132

Date	Title / Label	Peak Position	Weeks at No.1	Weeks on Chart
27 Sep 69	**CHICAGO TRANSIT AUTHORITY** *CBS 66221* CHICAGO TRANSIT AUTHORITY	9		14
4 Apr 70	**CHICAGO** *CBS 66233*	6		27
6 Mar 71	**CHICAGO 3** *CBS 66260*	9		5
30 Sep 72	**CHICAGO 5** *CBS 69708* ★	24		2
23 Oct 76	**CHICAGO X** *CBS 86010* ○	21		11
2 Oct 82	**CHICAGO 16** *Full Moon K 99235*	44		9
4 Dec 82	**LOVE SONGS** *TV Records TVA 6*	42		8
1 Dec 84	**CHICAGO 17** *Full Moon 925060* ●	24		20
25 Nov 89	**THE HEART OF CHICAGO** *Reprise WX 328* ⊛	6		25
13 Feb 99	**THE HEART OF CHICAGO – 1967–1997** *Reprise 9362465542*	21		4
14 Sep 02	**THE CHICAGO STORY – COMPLETE GREATEST** *Rhino 8122736302* ●	11		7

CHICANE
UK, male producer/keyboard player/guitarist (Nick Bracegirdle) — 14

Date	Title / Label	Peak Position	Weeks at No.1	Weeks on Chart
1 Nov 97	**FAR FROM THE MADDENING CROWDS** *Xtravaganza 0091372EXT*	49		1
8 Apr 00	**BEHIND THE SUN** *Xtravaganza XTRAV 10CD* ●	10		8
18 Oct 08	**BEST OF 1996-2008** *Modena MODENACD3*	16		5

CHICKEN SHACK
UK, female/male vocal/instrumental group – Christine Perfect (Christine McVie*), Dave Bidwell, Alan Morley, Andy Sylvester & Stan Webb — 9

Date	Title / Label	Peak Position	Weeks at No.1	Weeks on Chart
22 Jun 68	**FORTY FINGERS FRESHLY PACKED** *Blue Horizon 763203*	12		8
15 Feb 69	**OK KEN?** *Blue Horizon 763209*	9		1

CHIEFTAINS
Ireland, male vocal/instrumental group — 27

Date	Title / Label	Peak Position	Weeks at No.1	Weeks on Chart
28 Mar 87	**JAMES GALWAY AND THE CHIEFTAINS IN IRELAND** *RCA Red Seal RL 85798* JAMES GALWAY & THE CHIEFTAINS	32		5
2 Jul 88	**IRISH HEARTBEAT** *Mercury MERH 124* VAN MORRISON & THE CHIEFTAINS	18		7
4 Feb 95	**THE LONG BLACK VEIL** *RCA 74321251672* ○	17		9
6 Mar 99	**TEARS OF STONE** *RCA Victor 09026689682*	36		4
23 Mar 02	**THE WIDE WORLD OVER** *RCA Victor 09026639172*	37		2

CHILDREN OF BODOM
Finland, male vocal/instrumental group — 1

Date	Title / Label	Peak Position	Weeks at No.1	Weeks on Chart
26 Apr 08	**BLOODDRUNK** *Spinefarm 1761283*	44		1

TONI CHILDS
US, female vocalist — 1

Date	Title / Label	Peak Position	Weeks at No.1	Weeks on Chart
22 Apr 89	**UNION** *A&M AMA 5175*	73		1

CHIMAIRA
US, male vocal/instrumental group — 1

Date	Title / Label	Peak Position	Weeks at No.1	Weeks on Chart
20 Aug 05	**CHIMAIRA** *Roadrunner RR82628*	62		1

CHIMES
UK, male/female vocal/instrumental group — 19

Date	Title / Label	Peak Position	Weeks at No.1	Weeks on Chart
23 Jun 90	**THE CHIMES** *CBS 4664811* ○	17		19

CHINA BLACK
UK, male vocal/instrumental duo — 4

Date	Title / Label	Peak Position	Weeks at No.1	Weeks on Chart
11 Mar 95	**BORN** *Wild Card 5237552*	27		4

CHINA CRISIS
UK, male vocal/instrumental group – Gary Daly, Gazza Johnson, Eddie Lundon & Kevin Wilkinson, d. 17 Jul 1999 — 68

Date	Title / Label	Peak Position	Weeks at No.1	Weeks on Chart
20 Nov 82	**DIFFICULT SHAPES AND PASSIVE RHYTHMS SOME PEOPLE THINK IT'S FUN TO ENTERTAIN** *Virgin V 2243* ○	21		18
12 Nov 83	**WORKING WITH FIRE AND STEEL – POSSIBLE POP SONGS VOLUME 2** *Virgin V 2286* ●	20		16
11 May 85	**FLAUNT THE IMPERFECTION** *Virgin V 2342* ●	9		22
6 Dec 86	**WHAT PRICE PARADISE?** *Virgin V 2410*	63		6
13 May 89	**DIARY OF A HOLLOW HORSE** *Virgin V 2567*	58		2
15 Sep 90	**CHINA CRISIS COLLECTION – THE VERY BEST OF CHINA CRISIS** *Virgin V 2613*	32		4

CHINA DRUM
UK, male vocal/instrumental group — 1

Date	Title / Label	Peak Position	Weeks at No.1	Weeks on Chart
11 May 96	**GOOSEFAIR** *Mantra MNTCD 1002*	53		1

CHINGY
US, male rapper (Howard Bailey Jr.) — 1

Date	Title / Label	Peak Position	Weeks at No.1	Weeks on Chart
29 May 04	**JACKPOT** *Capitol 5818270* ○	73		1

CHOIR OF NEW COLLEGE OXFORD/ EDWARD HIGGINBOTTOM
UK, choir & male conductor — 7

Date	Title / Label	Peak Position	Weeks at No.1	Weeks on Chart
12 Oct 96	**AGNUS DEI** *Erato 0630146342* ●	49		5
18 Apr 98	**AGNUS DEI II** *Erato 3984216592*	57		2

CHOIRBOYS
UK, male choristers — 6

Date	Title / Label	Peak Position	Weeks at No.1	Weeks on Chart
10 Dec 05	**THE CHOIRBOYS** *UCJ 9874369* ●	25		4
15 Dec 07	**CAROLS** *UCJ 1741098*	61		2

CHORDS
UK, male vocal/instrumental group — 3

Date	Title / Label	Peak Position	Weeks at No.1	Weeks on Chart
24 May 80	**SO FAR AWAY** *Polydor POLS 1019*	30		3

CHRISTIANS
UK, male vocal/instrumental group – Garry, Roger & Russell Christian & Henry Priestman — 96

Date	Title / Label	Peak Position	Weeks at No.1	Weeks on Chart
31 Oct 87	**THE CHRISTIANS** *Island ILPS 9876* ⊛x3	2		68
27 Jan 90	**COLOUR** *Island ILPS 9948* ⊛	1	1	17
10 Oct 92	**HAPPY IN HELL** *Island CID 9996*	18		3
20 Nov 93	**THE BEST OF THE CHRISTIANS** *Island CIDTV 6* ●	22		8

TONY CHRISTIE
UK, male vocalist (Tony Fitzgerald) — 33

Date	Title / Label	Peak Position	Weeks at No.1	Weeks on Chart
24 Jul 71	**I DID WHAT I DID FOR MARIA** *MCA MKPS 2016*	37		1
17 Feb 73	**WITH LOVING FEELING** *MCA MUPS 468*	19		2
31 May 75	**TONY CHRISTIE – LIVE** *MCA MCF 2703*	33		3
6 Nov 76	**BEST OF TONY CHRISTIE** *MCA MCF 2769*	28		4
5 Mar 05	**DEFINITIVE COLLECTION** *Universal TV 9827867* ⊛x2	1	2	23

Silver-selling ○ Gold-selling ● Platinum-selling ⊛ US No.1 ★ — Peak Position · Weeks at No.1 · Weeks on Chart

BRYN CHRISTOPHER
UK, male vocalist

Date	Album	Peak	No.1	Weeks
				2
20 Sep 08	**MY WORLD** *Polydor 1768516*	18		2

CHRON GEN
UK, male vocal/instrumental group

Date	Album	Peak	No.1	Weeks
				3
3 Apr 82	**CHRONIC GENERATION** *Secret SEC 3*	53		3

CHUMBAWAMBA
UK, male/female vocal/instrumental group

Date	Album	Peak	No.1	Weeks
				10
7 May 94	**ANARCHY** *One Little Indian TPLP 46CD*	29		2
4 Nov 95	**SWINGIN' WITH RAYMOND** *One Little Indian TPLP 66CDS*	70		1
13 Sep 97	**TUBTHUMPER** *EMI 4952382* ○	19		7

CHARLOTTE CHURCH
UK, female vocalist (Charlotte Reed)

Date	Album	Peak	No.1	Weeks
				71
21 Nov 98	**VOICE OF AN ANGEL** *Sony Classical SK 60957* ⊛x2	4		20
27 Nov 99	**CHARLOTTE CHURCH** *Sony Classical SK 89003* ⊛	8		10
2 Dec 00	**DREAM A DREAM** *Sony Classical SK 89459* ●	30		6
3 Nov 01	**ENCHANTMENT** *Sony Classical SK 89710* ●	24		9
23 Jul 05	**TISSUES AND ISSUES** *Sony BMG 5203462* ●	5		26

SIR WINSTON CHURCHILL
UK, male statesman, d. 24 Jan 1965 (age 90)

Date	Album	Peak	No.1	Weeks
				8
13 Feb 65	**THE VOICE OF CHURCHILL** *Decca LXT 6200*	6		8

CIARA
US, female vocalist (Ciara Harris)

Date	Album	Peak	No.1	Weeks
				25
5 Feb 05	**GOODIES** *LaFace LFC628192* ●	26		20
21 Apr 07	**EVOLUTION** *LaFace 88697056832*	17		5

GABRIELLA CILMI
Australia, female vocalist

Date	Album	Peak	No.1	Weeks
				25
12 Apr 08	**LESSONS TO BE LEARNED** *Universal 1763307* ●	8		25

CINDERELLA
US, male vocal/instrumental group

Date	Album	Peak	No.1	Weeks
				8
23 Jul 88	**LONG COLD WINTER** *Vertigo VERH 59*	30		6
1 Dec 90	**HEARTBREAK STATION** *Vertigo 8480181*	36		2

CINEMATIC ORCHESTRA
UK, male orchestra

Date	Album	Peak	No.1	Weeks
				3
25 May 02	**EVERY DAY** *Ninja Tune ZENCD 59*	54		2
19 May 07	**MA FLEUR** *Ninja Tune ZENCD122*	44		1

CISTERCIAN MONKS OF STIFT HEILIGENKR
Austria, male monastic group

Date	Album	Peak	No.1	Weeks
				14
31 May 08	**CHANT – MUSIC FOR PARADISE** *UCJ 1766016*	7		14

CITY OF PRAGUE PHILHARMONIC ORCHESTRA
Czech Republic, male/female orchestra

Date	Album	Peak	No.1	Weeks
				3
13 Sep 08	**CLASSIC FM – SONGS WITHOUT WORDS** *UCJ 1779866*	21		3

GARY CLAIL ON-U SOUND SYSTEM
UK, male vocal/instrumental group

Date	Album	Peak	No.1	Weeks
				2
4 May 91	**THE EMOTIONAL HOOLIGAN** *Perfecto PL 74965*	35		2

CLANCY BROTHERS & TOMMY MAKEM
Ireland, male vocal/instrumental group & male vocalist – Makem, d. 1 Aug 2001

Date	Album	Peak	No.1	Weeks
				5
16 Apr 66	**ISN'T IT GRAND BOYS** *CBS BPG 62674*	22		5

CLANNAD
Ireland, female/male vocal/instrumental group – Moya (Máire) Brennan*, Ciarán & Pól Brennan & Noel & Pádraig Duggan

Date	Album	Peak	No.1	Weeks
				157
2 Apr 83	**MAGICAL RING** *RCA RCALP 6072*	26		21
12 May 84	**LEGEND (MUSIC FROM ROBIN OF SHERWOOD)** *RCA PL 70188* ●	15		40
2 Jun 84	**MAGICAL RING** *RCA PL 70003*	91		1
26 Oct 85	**MACALLA** *RCA PL 70894* ●	33		24
7 Nov 87	**SIRIUS** *RCA PL 71513*	34		4
4 Feb 89	**ATLANTIC REALM (OST-TV)** *BBC REB 727*	41		3
6 May 89	**PASTPRESENT** *RCA PL 74074* ⊛	5		26
20 Oct 90	**ANAM** *RCA PL 74762* ○	14		7
15 May 93	**BANBA** *RCA 74321139612*	5		11
6 Apr 96	**LORE** *RCA 74321300802* ○	14		7
31 May 97	**THE ULTIMATE COLLECTION** *RCA 74321486742*	46		4
11 Apr 98	**LANDMARKS** *RCA 74321560072*	34		2
18 Oct 03	**THE BEST OF – IN A LIFETIME** *RCA 82876564022*	23		4
22 Mar 08	**CELTIC THEMES – THE VERY BEST OF** *Sony BMG 88697281152*	20		3

CLAP YOUR HANDS SAY YEAH
US, male vocal/instrumental group

Date	Album	Peak	No.1	Weeks
				3
4 Feb 06	**CLAP YOUR HANDS SAY YEAH** *Wichita WEBB099CDL*	26		2
10 Feb 07	**SOME LOUD THUNDER** *Wichita WEBB117CD*	45		1

ERIC CLAPTON
UK, male vocalist/guitarist. Considered a god among guitarists, the multi-Grammy-winner has remained an albums chart regular and a mega-grossing live act for five decades. He is in the Rock and Roll Hall of Fame as a soloist and as a member of both The Yardbirds and Cream. See Blind Faith, Cream, Yardbirds

Date	Album	Peak	No.1	Weeks
				577
30 Jul 66	**BLUES BREAKERS** *Decca LK 4804* JOHN MAYALL WITH ERIC CLAPTON	6		17
6 Jun 70	**ON TOUR WITH ERIC CLAPTON** *Atlantic 2400 013* DELANEY & BONNIE & FRIENDS	39		3
5 Sep 70	**ERIC CLAPTON** *Polydor 2383 021*	17		8
26 Aug 72	**HISTORY OF ERIC CLAPTON** *Polydor 2671 107*	20		6
24 Mar 73	**DEREK AND THE DOMINOS IN CONCERT** *RSO 2659 020* DEREK & THE DOMINOS	36		1
24 Aug 74	**461 OCEAN BOULEVARD** *RSO 2479 118* ● ★	3		19
12 Apr 75	**THERE'S ONE IN EVERY CROWD** *RSO 2479 132* ○	15		8
13 Sep 75	**E.C. WAS HERE** *RSO 2394 160* ○	14		6
11 Sep 76	**NO REASON TO CRY** *RSO 2479 179* ○	8		7
26 Nov 77	**SLOWHAND** *RSO 2479 201* ●	23		13
9 Dec 78	**BACKLESS** *RSO RSD 5001* ○	18		12
10 May 80	**JUST ONE NIGHT** *RSO RSDX 2* ○	3		12
7 Mar 81	**ANOTHER TICKET** *RSO RSD 5008*	18		8
24 Apr 82	**TIME PIECES – THE BEST OF ERIC CLAPTON** *RSO RSD 5010* ●	20		16
19 Feb 83	**MONEY & CIGARETTES** *Duck W 3773*	13		17
9 Jun 84	**BACKTRACKIN'** *Starblend ERIC 1*	29		16
23 Mar 85	**BEHIND THE SUN** *Duck 9251661*	8		14
6 Dec 86	**AUGUST** *Duck WX 71* ⊛	3		46
26 Sep 87	**THE CREAM OF ERIC CLAPTON** *Polydor ECTV 1* & CREAM ⊛x3	3		109
18 Nov 89	**JOURNEYMAN** *Duck WX 322* ⊛	2		34
26 Oct 91	**24 NIGHTS** *Duck WX 373* ●	17		7
12 Sep 92	**UNPLUGGED** *Duck 9362450242* ⊛x3 ★	2		90
24 Sep 94	**FROM THE CRADLE** *Duck 9362457352* ● ★	1	1	18
21 Mar 98	**PILGRIM** *Duck 9362465774* ●	6		15
26 Jun 99	**BLUES** *Polydor 5471782*	52		2
30 Oct 99	**CLAPTON CHRONICLES – THE BEST OF ERIC CLAPTON** *Duck 9362475642* ⊛	6		21
24 Jun 00	**RIDING WITH THE KING** *Reprise 9362476122* B.B. KING & ERIC CLAPTON ●	15		15
15 Jul 00	**TIME PIECES – THE BEST OF ERIC CLAPTON** *Polydor 8000142*	73		2
17 Mar 01	**REPTILE** *Reprise 9362479662* ●	7		7
16 Nov 02	**ONE MORE CAR ONE MORE RIDER** *Reprise 9362483972*	69		1
3 Apr 04	**ME AND MR JOHNSON** *Reprise 9362487302* ○	10		8
10 Sep 05	**BACK HOME** *Reprise 9362493952*	19		3
18 Nov 06	**THE ROAD TO ESCONDIDO** *Reprise 9362444182* J.J. CALE & ERIC CLAPTON	50		1
20 Oct 07	**COMPLETE CLAPTON** *Polydor 1746193*	2		15

DAVE CLARK FIVE
UK, male vocal/instrumental group – Mike Smith, d. 28 Feb 2008, Dave Clark, Lenny Davidson, Rick Huxley & Denis Payton, d. 17 Dec 2006

Date	Album	Peak	No.1	Weeks
				35
18 Apr 64	**A SESSION WITH THE DAVE CLARK FIVE** *Columbia 33SX 1598*	3		8

Key: Silver-selling ○ · Gold-selling ● · Platinum-selling ⊛ · US No.1 ★ · Peak Position · Weeks at No.1 · Weeks on Chart

Date	Title	Peak Position	Weeks at No.1	Weeks on Chart
14 Aug 65	**CATCH US IF YOU CAN** *Columbia 33SX 1756*	8		8
4 Mar 78	**25 THUMPING GREAT HITS** *Polydor POLTV 7* ●	7		10
17 Apr 93	**GLAD ALL OVER AGAIN** *EMI CDEMTV 75*	28		5
25 Oct 08	**THE HITS** *UMTV 1781774*	15		4

GARY CLARK
UK, male vocalist — Weeks on Chart: 2

Date	Title	Peak Position	Weeks at No.1	Weeks on Chart
8 May 93	**TEN SHORT SONGS ABOUT LOVE** *Circa CIRCD 23*	25		2

PETULA CLARK
UK, female vocalist — Weeks on Chart: 52

Date	Title	Peak Position	Weeks at No.1	Weeks on Chart
30 Jul 66	**I COULDN'T LIVE WITHOUT YOUR LOVE** *Pye NPL 18148*	11		10
4 Feb 67	**HIT PARADE** *Pye NPL 18159*	18		13
18 Feb 67	**COLOUR MY WORLD** *Pye NSPL 18171*	16		9
7 Oct 67	**THESE ARE MY SONGS** *Pye NSPL 18197*	38		3
6 Apr 68	**THE OTHER MAN'S GRASS IS ALWAYS GREENER** *Pye NSPL 18211*	37		1
5 Feb 77	**20 ALL TIME GREATEST** *K-Tel NE 945*	18		7
27 Apr 02	**THE ULTIMATE COLLECTION** *Sanctuary SANDD 111*	18		4
28 Jun 08	**THEN & NOW – THE VERY BEST OF PETULA CLARK** *Universal TV 5309397* ○	17		5

DAVE CLARKE
UK, male producer — Weeks on Chart: 2

Date	Title	Peak Position	Weeks at No.1	Weeks on Chart
17 Feb 96	**ARCHIVE ONE** *Bush 74321320672*	36		2

GILBY CLARKE
US, male guitarist/vocalist. See Guns N' Roses — Weeks on Chart: 1

Date	Title	Peak Position	Weeks at No.1	Weeks on Chart
6 Aug 94	**PAWNSHOP GUITARS** *Virgin CDVUS 76*	39		1

JOHN COOPER CLARKE
UK, male vocalist — Weeks on Chart: 9

Date	Title	Peak Position	Weeks at No.1	Weeks on Chart
19 Apr 80	**SNAP CRACKLE AND BOP** *Epic EPC 84083*	26		7
5 Jun 82	**ZIP STYLE METHOD** *Epic EPC 85667*	97		2

STANLEY CLARKE
US, male bass guitarist — Weeks on Chart: 2

Date	Title	Peak Position	Weeks at No.1	Weeks on Chart
12 Jul 80	**ROCK PEBBLES AND SAND** *Epic EPC 84342*	42		2

KELLY CLARKSON
US, female vocalist — Weeks on Chart: 76

Date	Title	Peak Position	Weeks at No.1	Weeks on Chart
6 Sep 03	**THANKFUL** *S 82876540882* ★	41		9
30 Jul 05	**BREAKAWAY** *RCA 82876690262* ⊛x4	3		60
7 Jul 07	**MY DECEMBER** *RCA 88697069002*	2		7

CLASH
UK, male vocal/instrumental group – Joe Strummer*, d. 23 Dec 2002, Topper Headon, Mick Jones & Paul Simonon — Weeks on Chart: 121

Date	Title	Peak Position	Weeks at No.1	Weeks on Chart
30 Apr 77	**THE CLASH** *CBS 82000* ●	12		16
25 Nov 78	**GIVE 'EM ENOUGH ROPE** *CBS 82431* ●	2		14
22 Dec 79	**LONDON CALLING** *CBS CLASH 3* ●	9		20
20 Dec 80	**SANDINISTA** *CBS FSLN 1*	19		9
22 May 82	**COMBAT ROCK** *CBS FMLN 2* ○	2		23
16 Nov 85	**CUT THE CRAP** *CBS 26601* ○	16		3
2 Apr 88	**THE STORY OF THE CLASH – VOLUME 1** *CBS 4602441* ●	7		21
16 Nov 91	**THE SINGLES COLLECTION** *Columbia 4689461*	68		2
16 Oct 99	**FROM HERE TO ETERNITY** *Columbia 4981832*	13		3
16 Oct 99	**LONDON CALLING** *Columbia 4953472*	63		1
22 Mar 03	**THE ESSENTIAL CLASH** *Columbia 05109982*	18		3
2 Oct 04	**LONDON CALLING – 25TH ANNIVERSARY** *Columbia 5179283*	26		1
16 Jun 07	**THE SINGLES** *Columbia 4953532*	13		4
18 Oct 08	**LIVE AT SHEA STADIUM** *Columbia 88697348802*	31		1

CLASSIX NOUVEAUX
UK, male vocal/instrumental group — Weeks on Chart: 6

Date	Title	Peak Position	Weeks at No.1	Weeks on Chart
30 May 81	**NIGHT PEOPLE** *Liberty LBG 30325*	66		2
24 Apr 82	**LA VERITE** *Liberty LBG 30346*	44		4

RICHARD CLAYDERMAN
France, male pianist (Philippe Pagès) — Weeks on Chart: 211

Date	Title	Peak Position	Weeks at No.1	Weeks on Chart
13 Nov 82	**INTRODUCING RICHARD CLAYDERMAN** *Decca SKL 5329* ⊛	2		64
8 Oct 83	**THE MUSIC OF RICHARD CLAYDERMAN** *Decca SKL 5333* ⊛	21		28
24 Nov 84	**THE MUSIC OF LOVE** *Decca SKL 5340* ●	28		21
1 Dec 84	**RICHARD CLAYDERMAN – CHRISTMAS** *Decca SKL 5337*	53		5
23 Nov 85	**THE CLASSIC TOUCH** *Decca SKL 5343* WITH THE ROYAL PHILHARMONIC ORCHESTRA ●	17		18
22 Nov 86	**HOLLYWOOD AND BROADWAY** *Decca SKL 5344*	28		9
28 Nov 87	**SONGS OF LOVE** *Decca SKL 5345* ●	19		13
3 Dec 88	**A LITTLE NIGHT MUSIC** *Decca Delpine 8281251*	52		5
25 Nov 89	**THE LOVE SONGS OF ANDREW LLOYD WEBBER** *Decca Delpine 8281751*	18		10
24 Nov 90	**MY CLASSIC COLLECTION** *Decca 8282281* WITH THE ROYAL PHILHARMONIC ORCHESTRA	29		7
9 Nov 91	**TOGETHER AT LAST** *Decca Delpine 5115251* & JAMES LAST ⊛	14		15
14 Nov 92	**THE VERY BEST OF RICHARD CLAYDERMAN** *Decca Delpine 8283362* WITH THE ROYAL PHILHARMONIC ORCHESTRA ○	47		5
19 Nov 94	**IN HARMONY** *Polydor 5238242* & JAMES LAST ●	28		7
25 Nov 95	**THE CARPENTERS COLLECTION** *Polygram TV 8286882*	65		2
20 Dec 97	**THE BEST OF RICHARD CLAYDERMAN** *Decca Delpine DTVCD 700*	73		1
18 Sep 99	**...WITH LOVE** *Music Collection MCITV 002*	62		1

CLAYTOWN TROUPE
UK, male vocal/instrumental group — Weeks on Chart: 1

Date	Title	Peak Position	Weeks at No.1	Weeks on Chart
21 Oct 89	**THROUGH THE EVIL** *Island ILPS 9933*	72		1

CLEOPATRA
UK, female vocal trio — Weeks on Chart: 4

Date	Title	Peak Position	Weeks at No.1	Weeks on Chart
6 Jun 98	**COMIN' ATCHA!** *WEA 3984233562* ○	20		4

CLIMAX BLUES BAND
UK, male vocal/instrumental group — Weeks on Chart: 1

Date	Title	Peak Position	Weeks at No.1	Weeks on Chart
13 Nov 76	**GOLD PLATED** *BTM BTM 1009*	56		1

CLIMIE FISHER
UK, male vocal/instrumental duo – Simon Climie & Rob Fisher, d. 25 Aug 1999 — Weeks on Chart: 38

Date	Title	Peak Position	Weeks at No.1	Weeks on Chart
13 Feb 88	**EVERYTHING** *EMI EMC 3538* ●	14		36
21 Oct 89	**COMING IN FOR THE KILL** *EMI EMC 3565*	35		2

PATSY CLINE
US, female vocalist (Virginia Hensley), d. 5 Mar 1963 (age 30) — Weeks on Chart: 28

Date	Title	Peak Position	Weeks at No.1	Weeks on Chart
19 Jan 91	**SWEET DREAMS** *MCA MCG 6003* ○	18		10
19 Jan 91	**DREAMING...** *Platinum Musix PLAT 303*	55		4
5 Sep 92	**THE DEFINITIVE PATSY CLINE 1932–1963** *Arcade ARC 94992*	11		8
6 Jul 96	**THE VERY BEST OF PATSY CLINE** *MCA MCD 11483*	21		6

CLOCK
UK, male/female vocal/rap/instrumental/production group — Weeks on Chart: 4

Date	Title	Peak Position	Weeks at No.1	Weeks on Chart
23 Sep 95	**IT'S TIME...** *Media MCD 11355*	27		2
5 Apr 97	**ABOUT TIME 2** *Media MCD 60032*	56		2

COAL CHAMBER
US, male vocal/instrumental group — Weeks on Chart: 4

Date	Title	Peak Position	Weeks at No.1	Weeks on Chart
18 Sep 99	**CHAMBER MUSIC** *Roadrunner RR 86592*	21		2
18 May 02	**DARK DAYS** *Roadrunner RR 84849*	43		2

LUIS COBOS
Spain, male conductor — Weeks on Chart: 1

Date	Title	Peak Position	Weeks at No.1	Weeks on Chart
21 Apr 90	**OPERA EXTRAVAGANZA** *Epic MOOD 12* THE ROYAL PHILHARMONIC ORCHESTRA, CHORUS ROYAL OPERA HOUSE, THE LONDON SYMPHONY ORCHESTRA	72		1

EDDIE COCHRAN

US, male vocalist/guitarist, d. 17 Apr 1960 (age 21) — 49

Date	Title	Peak	No.1	Weeks
30 Jul 60	**SINGING TO MY BABY** *London HAU 2093*	19		1
1 Oct 60	**THE EDDIE COCHRAN MEMORIAL ALBUM** *London HAG 2267*	9		12
12 Jan 63	**CHERISHED MEMORIES** *Liberty LBY 1109*	15		3
20 Apr 63	**THE EDDIE COCHRAN MEMORIAL ALBUM** *Liberty LBY 1127*	11		18
19 Oct 63	**SINGING TO MY BABY** *Liberty LBY 1158*	20		1
9 May 70	**VERY BEST OF EDDIE COCHRAN** *Liberty LBS 83337*	34		3
18 Aug 79	**THE EDDIE COCHRAN SINGLES ALBUM** *United Artists UAK 30244*	39		6
16 Apr 88	**C'MON EVERYBODY** *Liberty ECR 1*	53		3
14 Jun 08	**THE VERY BEST OF** *EMI 2122782*	31		2

BRENDA COCHRANE

Ireland, female vocalist — 14

Date	Title	Peak	No.1	Weeks
14 Apr 90	**THE VOICE** *Polydor 8431411*	14		11
6 Apr 91	**IN DREAMS** *Polydor 8490341*	55		3

JARVIS COCKER

UK, male vocalist/guitarist/keyboard player. See Pulp — 2

Date	Title	Peak	No.1	Weeks
25 Nov 06	**JARVIS** *Rough Trade RTRADCD340*	37		2

JOE COCKER

UK, male vocalist/guitarist — 74

Date	Title	Peak	No.1	Weeks
26 Sep 70	**MAD DOGS AND ENGLISHMEN** *A&M AMLS 6002*	16		8
6 May 72	**JOE COCKER/WITH A LITTLE HELP FROM MY FRIENDS** *Double Back TOOFA 1/2*	29		4
30 Jun 84	**A CIVILISED MAN** *Capitol EJ 2401391*	100		1
11 Apr 92	**NIGHT CALLS** *Capitol CDESTU 2167*	25		14
27 Jun 92	**THE LEGEND – THE ESSENTIAL COLLECTION** *Polygram TV 5154112*	4		20
17 Sep 94	**HAVE A LITTLE FAITH** *Capitol CDEST 2233* ⊛	9		15
26 Oct 96	**ORGANIC** *Parlophone CDESTD 6*	49		1
20 Feb 99	**GREATEST HITS** *EMI 4977192*	24		2
23 Oct 99	**NO ORDINARY WORLD** *Parlophone 5230912*	63		1
15 Jun 02	**RESPECT YOURSELF** *Parlophone 5396432*	51		2
26 May 07	**HYMN FOR MY SOUL** *EMI 3903732*	9		6

COCKNEY REJECTS

UK, male vocal/instrumental group — 17

Date	Title	Peak	No.1	Weeks
15 Mar 80	**GREATEST HITS VOLUME 1** *Zonophone ZONO 101*	22		11
25 Oct 80	**GREATEST HITS VOLUME 2** *Zonophone ZONO 102*	23		3
18 Apr 81	**GREATEST HITS VOLUME 3 (LIVE AND LOUD)** *Zonophone ZEM 101*	27		3

COCTEAU TWINS

UK, female/male vocal/instrumental group – Elizabeth Fraser, Robin Guthrie & Simon Raymonde — 48

Date	Title	Peak	No.1	Weeks
29 Oct 83	**HEAD OVER HEELS** *4AD CAD 313*	51		15
24 Nov 84	**TREASURE** *4AD CAD 412*	29		8
26 Apr 86	**VICTORIALAND** *4AD CAD 602*	10		7
22 Nov 86	**THE MOON AND THE MELODIES** *4AD CAD 611* HAROLD BUDD, ELIZABETH FRASER, ROBIN GUTHRIE & SIMON RAYMONDE	46		2
1 Oct 88	**BLUE BELL KNOLL** *4AD CAD 807*	15		4
29 Sep 90	**HEAVEN OR LAS VEGAS** *4AD CAD 0012*	7		5
30 Oct 93	**FOUR-CALENDAR CAFÉ** *Fontana 5182592*	13		3
27 Apr 96	**MILK & KISSES** *Fontana 5045012*	17		3
28 Oct 00	**STARS AND TOPSOIL – A COLLECTION 1982–1990** *4AD CAD2K 019CD*	63		1

COHEED & CAMBRIA

US, male vocal/instrumental group — 1

Date	Title	Peak	No.1	Weeks
3 Nov 07	**NO WORLD FOR TOMORROW** *Columbia 88697060602*	41		1

LEONARD COHEN

Canada, male vocalist/guitarist — 157

Date	Title	Peak	No.1	Weeks
31 Aug 68	**SONGS OF LEONARD COHEN** *CBS 63241*	13		71
3 May 69	**SONGS FROM A ROOM** *CBS 63587*	2		26
24 Apr 71	**SONGS OF LOVE AND HATE** *CBS 69004*	4		18
28 Sep 74	**NEW SKIN FOR THE OLD CEREMONY** *CBS 69087*	24		3
10 Dec 77	**DEATH OF A LADIES MAN** *CBS 86042*	35		5
16 Feb 85	**VARIOUS POSITIONS** *CBS 26222*	52		6
27 Feb 88	**I'M YOUR MAN** *CBS 4606421*	48		13
6 Aug 88	**GREATEST HITS** *CBS 32644*	99		1
5 Dec 92	**THE FUTURE** *Columbia 4724982*	36		3
6 Aug 94	**COHEN LIVE** *Columbia 4771712*	35		4
20 Oct 01	**TEN NEW SONGS** *Columbia 5012022*	26		3
1 Feb 03	**THE ESSENTIAL** *Columbia 4979952*	70		1
6 Nov 04	**DEAR HEATHER** *Columbia 5147682*	34		2
23 Aug 08	**ESSENTIAL** *Columbia 4979952*	57		1

MARC COHN

US, male vocalist/pianist — 23

Date	Title	Peak	No.1	Weeks
29 Jun 91	**MARC COHN** *Atlantic 7567821781*	27		20
12 Jun 93	**THE RAINY SEASON** *Atlantic 7567824912*	24		3

COLD WAR KIDS

US, male vocal/instrumental group — 5

Date	Title	Peak	No.1	Weeks
17 Feb 07	**ROBBERS & COWARDS** *V2 VVR1044142*	35		4
4 Oct 08	**LOYALTY TO LOYALTY** *V2 1781155*	68		1

COLDCUT

UK, male production duo — 5

Date	Title	Peak	No.1	Weeks
29 Apr 89	**WHAT'S THAT NOISE** *Ahead Of Our Time CCUTLP 1*	20		4
20 Sep 97	**LET US PLAY!** *Ninja Tune ZENCD 30*	33		1

COLDPLAY

UK, male vocal/instrumental group – Chris Martin, Guy Berryman, Jonny Buckland & Will Champion. Peerless tunesmiths who have racked up an average of 90 chart weeks for each of their four studio albums. Transatlantic No.1 *X&Y* was the world's bestselling album of 2005 and sold 464,471 copies in the first week in the UK (beaten only by Oasis' *Be Here Now*) — 360

Date	Title	Peak	No.1	Weeks
22 Jul 00	**PARACHUTES** *Parlophone 5277832* ⊛x7	1	1	137
7 Sep 02	**A RUSH OF BLOOD TO THE HEAD** *Parlophone 5405042* ⊛x7	1	3	114
18 Jun 05	**X & Y** *Parlophone 4747862* ⊛x8 ★	1	4	73
7 Jun 08	**LIVE 2003** *Parlophone 2269199*	46		5
21 Jun 08	**VIVA LA VIDA OR DEATH AND ALL HIS FRIENDS** *Parlophone 2121140* ⊛x2 ★	1	6	29+
6 Dec 08	**PROSPECKT'S MARCH** *Parlophone 2647371*	38		2

Top 3 Best-Selling Albums

	Approximate Sales
1 A RUSH OF BLOOD TO THE HEAD	2,690,000
2 X&Y	2,540,000
3 PARACHUTES	2,435,000

LLOYD COLE & THE COMMOTIONS

UK, male vocal/instrumental group — 92

Date	Title	Peak	No.1	Weeks
20 Oct 84	**RATTLESNAKES** *Polydor LCLP 1*	13		30
30 Nov 85	**EASY PIECES** *Polydor LCLP 2*	5		18
7 Nov 87	**MAINSTREAM** *Polydor LCLP 3*	9		20
8 Apr 89	**1984–1989** *Polydor 8377361*	14		7
3 Mar 90	**LLOYD COLE** *Polydor 8419071* LLOYD COLE	11		6
28 Sep 91	**DON'T GET WEIRD ON ME BABE** *Polydor 5110931* LLOYD COLE	21		3
23 Oct 93	**BAD VIBES** *Fontana 5183182* LLOYD COLE	38		2
7 Oct 95	**LOVE STORY** *Fontana 5285292* LLOYD COLE	27		2
23 Jan 99	**THE COLLECTION** *Mercury 5381042* LLOYD COLE	24		4

MJ COLE

UK, male producer (Matt Coleman) — 4

Date	Title	Peak	No.1	Weeks
19 Aug 00	**SINCERE** *Talkin Loud 5425792*	14		4

NAT 'KING' COLE

US, male vocalist/pianist (Nathaniel Coles), d. 15 Feb 1965 (age 45) — 153

Date	Title	Peak	No.1	Weeks
18 May 57	**LOVE IS THE THING** *Capitol LCT 6129* ★	1	1	14
19 Aug 61	**STRING ALONG WITH NAT 'KING' COLE** *Encore ENC 102*	12		9
20 Oct 62	**NAT 'KING' COLE SINGS AND THE GEORGE SHEARING QUARTET PLAYS** *Capitol W 1675* /GEORGE SHEARING QUARTET	8		7
27 Mar 65	**UNFORGETTABLE NAT 'KING' COLE** *Capitol W 20664*	11		8
7 Dec 68	**THE BEST OF NAT 'KING' COLE** *Capitol ST 21139*	5		18
5 Dec 70	**THE BEST OF NAT 'KING' COLE VOLUME 2** *Capitol ST 21687*	39		2

Silver-selling ○ Gold-selling ● Platinum-selling ⊛ US No.1 ★ — Peak Position | Weeks at No.1 | Weeks on Chart

Date	Title	Peak Position	Weeks at No.1	Weeks on Chart
27 Nov 71	**WHITE CHRISTMAS** *MFP 5224* & DEAN MARTIN	45		1
8 Apr 78	**20 GOLDEN GREATS** *Capitol EMTV 9* ⊛	1	3	37
20 Nov 82	**20 GREATEST LOVE SONGS** *Capitol EMTV 35* ⊛	7		26
26 Nov 88	**CHRISTMAS WITH NAT 'KING' COLE** *Stylus SMR 868* ●	25		9
23 Nov 91	**THE UNFORGETTABLE NAT 'KING' COLE** *EMI EMTV 61*	23		9
20 Nov 99	**THE ULTIMATE COLLECTION** *EMI 4995752* ●	26		7
15 Feb 03	**LOVE SONGS** *Capitol 05815132* ○	20		3
5 Feb 05	**THE WORLD OF NAT KING COLE** *Capitol 5606802*	51		3

NATALIE COLE

US, female vocalist — Weeks on Chart: 66

Date	Title	Peak Position	Weeks at No.1	Weeks on Chart
17 Sep 83	**UNFORGETTABLE: A MUSICAL TRIBUTE TO NAT KING COLE** *CBS 10042* JOHNNY MATHIS & NATALIE COLE	5		16
7 May 88	**EVERLASTING** *Manhattan MTL 1012* ○	62		4
20 May 89	**GOOD TO BE BACK** *EMI-USA MTL 1042* ●	10		12
27 Jul 91	**UNFORGETTABLE – WITH LOVE** *Elektra EKT 91* ● ★	11		29
26 Jun 93	**TAKE A LOOK** *Elektra 7559614962*	16		4
30 Nov 02	**ASK A WOMAN WHO KNOWS** *Verve AA3145897742*	63		1

PAULA COLE

US, female vocalist — Weeks on Chart: 1

Date	Title	Peak Position	Weeks at No.1	Weeks on Chart
26 Jul 97	**THIS FIRE** *Warner Brothers 9362464242*	60		1

DAVE & ANSIL COLLINS

Jamaica, male vocal/instrumental duo — Weeks on Chart: 2

Date	Title	Peak Position	Weeks at No.1	Weeks on Chart
7 Aug 71	**DOUBLE BARREL** *Trojan TBL 162*	41		2

EDWYN COLLINS

UK, male vocalist/guitarist. See Orange Juice — Weeks on Chart: 9

Date	Title	Peak Position	Weeks at No.1	Weeks on Chart
22 Jul 95	**GORGEOUS GEORGE** *Setanta AHOAON 058* ○	8		8
13 Sep 97	**I'M NOT FOLLOWING YOU** *Setanta SETCD 039*	55		1

JUDY COLLINS

US, female vocalist/guitarist — Weeks on Chart: 23

Date	Title	Peak Position	Weeks at No.1	Weeks on Chart
27 Feb 71	**WHALES AND NIGHTINGALES** *Elektra EKS 75010*	16		7
31 May 75	**JUDITH** *Elektra K 52019*	7		12
14 Dec 85	**AMAZING GRACE** *Elektra STAR 2265*	34		4

PHIL COLLINS

UK, male vocalist/drummer. Multi-talented singer/songwriter who successfully combined an award-winning solo career with fronting Genesis between 1981 and 1996. ... *But Seriously*, a transatlantic chart-topper, sold more than 13 million copies around the globe. See Genesis — Weeks on Chart: 879

Date	Title	Peak Position	Weeks at No.1	Weeks on Chart
21 Feb 81	**FACE VALUE** *Virgin V 2185* ⊛x5	1	3	274
13 Nov 82	**HELLO, I MUST BE GOING** *Virgin V 2252* ⊛x3	2		163
2 Mar 85	**NO JACKET REQUIRED** *Virgin V 2345* ⊛x6 ★	1	5	176
2 Dec 89	**. . .BUT SERIOUSLY** *Virgin V 2620* ⊛x8 ★	1	15	72
17 Nov 90	**SERIOUS HITS...LIVE!** *Virgin PCLP 1* ⊛x4	2		50
20 Nov 93	**BOTH SIDES** *Virgin CDV 2800* ⊛x2	1	1	21
2 Nov 96	**DANCE INTO THE LIGHT** *Face Value 0630160002* ●	4		13
17 Oct 98	**HITS** *Virgin CDV 2870* ⊛x4	1	1	52
23 Nov 02	**TESTIFY** *Face Value 5046614842* ●	15		7
12 Jun 04	**THE PLATINUM COLLECTION** *Virgin PHILCD1* ●	4		18
13 Nov 04	**LOVE SONGS** *Virgin PHILCDX2* ⊛x2	7		33

Top 3 Best-Selling Albums

	Album	Approximate Sales
1	. . .BUT SERIOUSLY	2,740,000
2	NO JACKET REQUIRED	1,940,000
3	HITS	1,590,000

WILLIE COLLINS

US, male vocalist — Weeks on Chart: 1

Date	Title	Peak Position	Weeks at No.1	Weeks on Chart
14 Jun 86	**WHERE ARE YOU GONNA BE TONIGHT?** *Capitol EST 2012*	97		1

COLOR ME BADD

US, male vocal group – Bryan Abrams, Mark Calderon, Kevin Thornton & Sam Watters — Weeks on Chart: 22

Date	Title	Peak Position	Weeks at No.1	Weeks on Chart
24 Aug 91	**C.M.B.** *Giant WX 425* ●	3		22

COLOSSEUM

UK, male vocal/instrumental group — Weeks on Chart: 14

Date	Title	Peak Position	Weeks at No.1	Weeks on Chart
17 May 69	**COLOSSEUM** *Fontana S 5510*	15		1
22 Nov 69	**VALENTYNE SUITE** *Vertigo VO 1*	15		2
5 Dec 70	**DAUGHTER OF TIME** *Vertigo 6360 017*	23		5
26 Jun 71	**COLOSSEUM LIVE** *Bronze ICD 1*	17		6

COLOUR FIELD

UK, male vocal/instrumental group — Weeks on Chart: 8

Date	Title	Peak Position	Weeks at No.1	Weeks on Chart
4 May 85	**VIRGINS AND PHILISTINES** *Chrysalis CHR 1480*	12		7
4 Apr 87	**DECEPTION** *Chrysalis CDL 1546*	95		1

COLOURBOX

UK, male vocal/instrumental group — Weeks on Chart: 2

Date	Title	Peak Position	Weeks at No.1	Weeks on Chart
24 Aug 85	**COLOURBOX** *4AD CAD 508*	67		2

SHAWN COLVIN

US, female vocalist/guitarist — Weeks on Chart: 1

Date	Title	Peak Position	Weeks at No.1	Weeks on Chart
17 Sep 94	**COVER GIRL** *Columbia 4772402*	67		1

COMIC RELIEF

UK, male/female comedians — Weeks on Chart: 8

Date	Title	Peak Position	Weeks at No.1	Weeks on Chart
10 May 86	**COMIC RELIEF PRESENTS UTTERLY UTTERLY LIVE!** *WEA WX 51*	10		8

COMMITMENTS

Ireland, male/female actor/vocal/instrumental group – Andrew Strong, Michael Aherne, Robert Arkins, Angeline Ball, Maria Doyle, Dave Finnegan, Felim Gormley, Glen Hansard, Dick Massey, Kenneth McCluskey & Johnny Murphy — Weeks on Chart: 147

Date	Title	Peak Position	Weeks at No.1	Weeks on Chart
26 Oct 91	**THE COMMITMENTS (OST)** *MCA 10286* ⊛x3	4		136
25 Apr 92	**THE COMMITMENTS VOLUME 2** *MCA MCAD 10506* ●	13		11

COMMODORES

US, male vocal/instrumental group – Lionel Richie*, William King, Ronald LaPread, Thomas McClary, Walter Orange & Milan Williams, d. 9 Jul 2006 — Weeks on Chart: 162

Date	Title	Peak Position	Weeks at No.1	Weeks on Chart
13 May 78	**COMMODORES LIVE!** *Motown TMSP 6007*	60		1
10 Jun 78	**NATURAL HIGH** *Motown STML 12087* ●	8		23
2 Dec 78	**GREATEST HITS** *Motown STML 12100* ●	19		16
18 Aug 79	**MIDNIGHT MAGIC** *Motown STMA 8032* ●	15		25
28 Jun 80	**HEROES** *Motown STMA 8034*	50		5
18 Jul 81	**IN THE POCKET** *Motown STML 12156*	69		5
14 Aug 82	**LOVE SONGS** *K-Tel NE 1171* ●	5		28
23 Feb 85	**NIGHTSHIFT** *Motown ZL 72343*	13		10
9 Nov 85	**THE VERY BEST OF THE COMMODORES – 16 CLASSIC TRACKS** *Telstar STAR 2249* ●	25		13
6 May 95	**THE VERY BEST OF THE COMMODORES** *Motown 5305472*	26		3
22 Nov 03	**THE DEFINITIVE COLLECTION** *Universal TV 9861394* LIONEL RICHIE/COMMODORES ⊛	10		33

COMMON

US, male rapper (Rasheed Lynn) — Weeks on Chart: 4

Date	Title	Peak Position	Weeks at No.1	Weeks on Chart
4 Jun 05	**BE** *Geffen 9882498*	38		2
11 Aug 07	**FINDING FOREVER** *Geffen 1742564* ★	35		2

COMMUNARDS

UK, male vocal/instrumental duo – Jimmy Somerville* & Richard Coles — Weeks on Chart: 78

Date	Title	Peak Position	Weeks at No.1	Weeks on Chart
2 Aug 86	**COMMUNARDS** *London LONLP 18* ⊛	7		45
17 Oct 87	**RED** *London LONLP 39* ⊛	4		29
22 Sep 01	**THE VERY BEST OF JIMMY SOMERVILLE BRONSKI BEAT AND THE COMMUNARDS** *London 0927412582* JIMMY SOMERVILLE BRONSKI BEAT & THE COMMUNARDS	29		4

PERRY COMO

US, male vocalist, d. 12 May 2001 (age 88) — 203

Date	Title	Peak	Wks at No.1	Wks on Chart
28 Jun 58	**WE GET LETTERS (VOL. 2)** *RCA RD 27070*	4		7
8 Nov 58	**DEAR PERRY** *RCA RD 27078*	6		5
31 Jan 59	**COMO'S GOLDEN RECORDS** *RCA RD 27100*	4		5
10 Apr 71	**IT'S IMPOSSIBLE** *RCA Victor SF 8175*	13		13
7 Jul 73	**AND I LOVE YOU SO** *RCA Victor SF 8360* ⊛	1	1	109
24 Aug 74	**PERRY** *RCA Victor APL1 0585* ●	26		3
19 Apr 75	**MEMORIES ARE MADE OF HITS** *RCA Victor RS 1005* ◌	14		16
25 Oct 75	**40 GREATEST HITS** *K-Tel NE 700* ⊛	1	6	34
3 Dec 83	**FOR THE GOOD TIMES** *Telstar STAR 2235*	41		6
17 Nov 01	**GOLD – GREATEST HITS** *RCA 74321865542*	55		2
4 Oct 03	**THE ESSENTIAL PERRY COMO** *RCA 82876560172*	54		2
5 Jun 04	**PAPA LOVES MAMBO – THE VERY BEST OF** *RCA 82876616572*	63		1

COMPULSION

Ireland/Holland, male vocal/instrumental group — 1

Date	Title	Peak	Wks at No.1	Wks on Chart
9 Apr 94	**COMFORTER** *One Little Indian TPLP 59CDL*	59		1

COMSAT ANGELS

UK, male vocal/instrumental group — 9

Date	Title	Peak	Wks at No.1	Wks on Chart
5 Sep 81	**SLEEP NO MORE** *Polydor POLS 1038*	51		5
18 Sep 82	**FICTION** *Polydor POLS 1075*	94		2
8 Oct 83	**LAND** *Jive HIP 8*	91		2

CONNELLS

US, male vocal/instrumental group — 2

Date	Title	Peak	Wks at No.1	Wks on Chart
9 Sep 95	**RING** *London 8286602*	36		2

HARRY CONNICK JR.

US, male vocalist/keyboard player — 74

Date	Title	Peak	Wks at No.1	Wks on Chart
22 Sep 90	**WE ARE IN LOVE** *CBS 4667361* ●	7		46
26 Oct 91	**BLUE LIGHT, RED LIGHT** *Columbia 4690871* ●	16		11
30 Jan 93	**25** *Columbia 4728092*	35		2
12 Jun 93	**FOREVER FOR NOW** *Columbia 4738732*	32		5
27 Aug 94	**SHE** *Columbia 4768162*	21		3
20 Mar 04	**ONLY YOU** *Columbia 5150462* ●	6		6
13 Oct 07	**MY NEW ORLEANS** *Columbia 88697144462*	63		1

RAY CONNIFF

US, male trombone player/orchestra leader, d. 12 Oct 2002 (age 85) — 96

Date	Title	Peak	Wks at No.1	Wks on Chart
28 May 60	**IT'S THE TALK OF THE TOWN** *Philips BBL 7354*	15		1
25 Jun 60	**S AWFUL NICE** *Philips BBL 7281*	13		1
26 Nov 60	**HI-FI COMPANION ALBUM** *Philips BET 101*	3		44
20 May 61	**MEMORIES ARE MADE OF THIS** *Philips BBL 7439*	14		4
29 Dec 62	**S WONDERFUL 'S MARVELLOUS** *CBS DPG 66001*	18		3
29 Dec 62	**WE WISH YOU A MERRY CHRISTMAS** *CBS BPG 62092*	12		1
16 Apr 66	**HI-FI COMPANION ALBUM** *CBS DP 66011* ●	24		4
9 Sep 67	**SOMEWHERE MY LOVE** *CBS SBPG 62740*	34		3
21 Jun 69	**HIS ORCHESTRA, HIS CHORUS, HIS SINGERS, HIS SOUND** *CBS SPR 27*	1	3	16
23 May 70	**BRIDGE OVER TROUBLED WATER** *CBS 64020* ◌	30		14
12 Jun 71	**LOVE STORY** *CBS 64294*	34		1
19 Feb 72	**I'D LIKE TO TEACH THE WORLD TO SING** *CBS 64449*	17		4

BILLY CONNOLLY

UK, male comedian/vocalist/multi-instrumentalist — 108

Date	Title	Peak	Wks at No.1	Wks on Chart
20 Jul 74	**SOLO CONCERT** *Transatlantic TRA 279* ●	8		33
18 Jan 75	**COP YER WHACK OF THIS** *Polydor 2383 310* ●	10		29
20 Sep 75	**WORDS AND MUSIC** *Transatlantic TRA SAM 32*	34		10
6 Dec 75	**GET RIGHT INTAE HIM** *Polydor 2383 368* ●	6		14
11 Dec 76	**ATLANTIC BRIDGE** *Polydor 2383 419* ◌	20		9
28 Jan 78	**RAW MEAT FOR THE BALCONY** *Polydor 2383 463* ◌	57		3
5 Dec 81	**THE PICK OF BILLY CONNOLLY** *Polydor POLTV 15* ●	23		8
5 Dec 87	**BILLY AND ALBERT** *10 Records DIX 65*	81		2

CONSOLIDATED

US, male vocal/instrumental group — 1

Date	Title	Peak	Wks at No.1	Wks on Chart
30 Jul 94	**BUSINESS OF PUNISHMENT** *London 8285142*	53		1

RUSS CONWAY

UK, male pianist (Trevor Stanford), d. 16 Nov 2000 (age 75) — 69

Date	Title	Peak	Wks at No.1	Wks on Chart
22 Nov 58	**PACK UP YOUR TROUBLES** *Columbia 33SX 1120*	9		5
2 May 59	**SONGS TO SING IN YOUR BATH** *Columbia 33SX 1149*	8		10
19 Sep 59	**FAMILY FAVOURITES** *Columbia 33SX 1169*	3		16
19 Dec 59	**TIME TO CELEBRATE** *Columbia 33SX 1197*	3		7
26 Mar 60	**MY CONCERTO FOR YOU** *Columbia 33SX 1214*	5		17
17 Dec 60	**PARTY TIME** *Columbia 33SX 1279*	7		11
23 Apr 77	**RUSS CONWAY PRESENTS 24 PIANO GREATS** *Ronco RTL 2022*	25		3

RY COODER

US, male vocalist/guitarist (Ryland Cooder) — 52

Date	Title	Peak	Wks at No.1	Wks on Chart
11 Aug 79	**BOP TILL YOU DROP** *Warner Brothers K 56691* ◌	36		9
18 Oct 80	**BORDER LINE** *Warner Brothers K 56864* ●	35		6
24 Apr 82	**THE SLIDE AREA** *Warner Brothers K 56976*	18		12
14 Nov 87	**GET RHYTHM** *Warner Brothers WX 121* ◌	75		3
9 Apr 94	**TALKING TIMBUKTU** *World Circuit WCD 040* ALI FARKA TOURE & RY COODER	44		3
5 Jul 97	**BUENA VISTA SOCIAL CLUB** *World Circuit WCD 050* ●	44		15
8 Feb 03	**MAMBO SINUENDO** *Nonesuch 7559796912* & MANUEL GALBAM	40		1
25 Jun 05	**CHAVEZ RAVINE** *Nonesuch 7559798772*	35		2
17 Mar 07	**MY NAME IS BUDDY** *Nonesuch 7559799612*	41		1

PETER COOK & DUDLEY MOORE

UK, male comedy/vocal duo – Cook, d. 9 Jan 1995; Moore, d. 28 Mar 2002 — 34

Date	Title	Peak	Wks at No.1	Wks on Chart
21 May 66	**ONCE MOORE WITH COOK** *Decca LK 4785*	25		1
18 Sep 76	**DEREK AND CLIVE LIVE** *Island ILPS 9434* DEREK AND CLIVE ◌	12		25
24 Dec 77	**COME AGAIN** *Virgin V 2094* DEREK AND CLIVE ◌	18		8

SAM COOKE

US, male vocalist, d. 11 Dec 1964 (age 33) — 52

Date	Title	Peak	Wks at No.1	Wks on Chart
26 Apr 86	**THE MAN AND HIS MUSIC** *RCA PL 87127* ●	8		27
25 Oct 03	**PORTRAIT OF A LEGEND** *Universal TV 9807446* ⊛	19		23
2 Jul 05	**PORTRAIT OF A LEGEND 1951–1964** *Abkco 9872418* ●	26		2

COOKIE CREW

UK, female rap duo — 4

Date	Title	Peak	Wks at No.1	Wks on Chart
6 May 89	**BORN THIS WAY!** *London 8281341*	24		4

COOL NOTES

UK, male/female vocal/instrumental group — 2

Date	Title	Peak	Wks at No.1	Wks on Chart
9 Nov 85	**HAVE A GOOD FOREVER...** *Abstract Dance ADLP 1*	66		2

RITA COOLIDGE

US, female vocalist — 44

Date	Title	Peak	Wks at No.1	Wks on Chart
6 Aug 77	**ANYTIME ANYWHERE** *A&M AMLH 64616* ●	6		28
6 May 78	**NATURAL ACT** *A&M AMLH 64690* KRIS KRISTOFFERSON & RITA COOLIDGE	35		4
8 Jul 78	**LOVE ME AGAIN** *A&M AMLH 64699* ◌	51		1
14 Mar 81	**THE VERY BEST OF RITA COOLIDGE** *A&M AMLH 68520* ●	6		11

COOLIO

US, male rapper (Artis Ivey Jr.) — 27

Date	Title	Peak	Wks at No.1	Wks on Chart
29 Oct 94	**IT TAKES A THIEF** *Tommy Boy TBCD 1083*	67		1
18 Nov 95	**GANGSTA'S PARADISE** *Tommy Boy TBCD 1141* ●	18		24
13 Sep 97	**MY SOUL** *Tommy Boy TBV 1180*	28		2

ALICE COOPER

US, male vocalist (Vincent Furnier) — 134

Date	Title	Peak	Wks at No.1	Wks on Chart
5 Feb 72	**KILLER** *Warner Brothers K 56005*	27		18
22 Jul 72	**SCHOOL'S OUT** *Warner Brothers K 56007*	4		20
9 Sep 72	**LOVE IT TO DEATH** *Warner Brothers K 46177*	28		7
24 Mar 73	**BILLION DOLLAR BABIES** *Warner Brothers K 56013* ★	1	1	23
12 Jan 74	**MUSCLE OF LOVE** *Warner Brothers K 56018*	34		4
15 Mar 75	**WELCOME TO MY NIGHTMARE** *Anchor ANCL 2011* ◌	19		8
24 Jul 76	**ALICE COOPER GOES TO HELL** *Warner Brothers K 56171*	23		7
28 May 77	**LACE AND WHISKY** *Warner Brothers K 56365*	33		3
23 Dec 78	**FROM THE INSIDE** *Warner Brothers K 56577*	68		3
17 May 80	**FLUSH THE FASHION** *Warner Brothers K 56805*	56		3
12 Sep 81	**SPECIAL FORCES** *Warner Brothers K 56927*	96		1

Billy Fury
The Sound Of Fury

ODD FACT: Billy Fury went to school with Ringo Starr in Liverpool's Dingle area, a notoriously tough part of the city. Stricken with rheumatic fever as a child, he was left with a permanently damaged heart, but this did not stop him voraciously consuming early rock 'n' roll records and becoming a fiery live performer. It was the movie *The Girl Can't Help It*, coupled with his redundancy from the Mersey Ferries, plus Eddie Cochran, Gene Vincent and Elvis Presley's guiding lights that finally turned tugboat-skiffle-dreamer Ron Wycherley into Billy Fury, arguably Britain's first real rock star.

Fury was seen very much as the UK's own version of Elvis Presley

When Marty Wilde's rock 'n' roll show hit Birkenhead in 1958, the unknown Wycherley took a batch of his self-penned songs over the water from Liverpool to promote himself to Wilde and his manager Larry Parnes. He had already cut a 78rpm demo in a local studio, and Wilde and Parnes convinced Wycherley to get up on stage and perform the songs himself. Invited straight onto the tour, and renamed by Parnes, Billy Fury was born. Signed to Decca, Fury's first record made the UK Top 20, and he quickly became a regular on early pop TV programmes and landed acting parts in a few TV dramas.

Paradoxically, Fury was a shy man who developed a provocative live act that got him taken offstage on occasion – eventually he had to temper his performances; however, by then Billy was hot property, and the pressures of fame were high. A bridge between 1950s rock 'n' roll and 1960s pop, Fury was a precursor to The Beatles in terms of the sheer hysteria he could whip up amongst his fans. In an era when Cliff Richard was Britain's leading rocker, Fury was seen very much as the UK's own version of Elvis Presley.

The Sound Of Fury, his first album, was released in April 1960 as a ten-inch collection. The ten tracks were all self-penned songs, some credited to Fury and some to his second pseudonym, Walter Wilberforce. Songwriters who performed their own music were uncommon: Fury's stablemate Marty Wilde was one such, but pre-Beatles it was unusual. Recorded in just two sessions *on a single day*, much of *The Sound Of Fury* was the first and only take; produced by the legendary pop-TV producer Jack Goode, and featuring Joe Brown on guitar and Andy White (who would later famously replace Ringo on 'Love Me Do') on drums. Fury's versatility was such that, like the early Elvis, he could turn his hand to rockabilly, blues and country all under a rock 'n' roll banner, with a smouldering, sexually charged vulnerability of his own.

Seen by many as one of the cornerstones of rockabilly, today the album itself inevitably sounds tinny and relatively crude in terms of production and sonics, but when listened to within the context of its creation, it is a startlingly blunt and powerful record. Fury's cohorts – the exemplary guitar work of Joe Brown and the sublime yet evocative backing vocals of the Four Jays – mean this record has track after track boasting rock 'n' roll purity: 'Turn My Back On You'; 'It's You I Need'; 'Don't Leave Me This Way' and 'Alright, Goodbye' exude a simplicity that few can match, though many have tried. The cleanliness of the guitar picking, the machine-like precision and tightness of the drum lines, the relatively

Chart History

Artist	Album Title	First Chart Week	Weeks on Chart	Highest Position
BILLY FURY	THE SOUND OF FURY	4/6/60	2	18

untreated yet still compelling vocals ... it's all there to admire. Henceforth, and by comparison, rock 'n' roll got complicated.

The album was Fury's last roll of the pure rock 'n' roll dice. Although he never sold out, and his live shows retained *a frisson* of charged-up energy, Decca led Fury more and more into ballad territory to capitalise on his commercial appeal. His best-known and most popular hit came in 1961 with 'Halfway To Paradise', a cover of US pop-star Tony Orlando's hit single, which spent almost six months in the charts, rising to Number 3 in the UK. While further single releases confirmed Billy's popularity over 1962 and 1963, it was as a live performer that he really shone. 1963's album *Billy*, and the live *We Want Billy*, confirmed his status, supported – like Elvis and The Beatles – with movies showcasing his talents.

Unlike most of his UK contemporaries, Billy survived Beatlemania and retained his popularity; however, a lucrative deal to move to Parlophone in 1965 was not reflected in record sales. By the late 1960s, ill health had begun to take its toll on Billy's work rate and the hits started to dry up, although he kept recording. A lifelong lover of animals and wildlife, Billy owned racehorses and moved to rural Wales, where he could indulge his love of nature. A part in the rocker movie *That'll Be The Day* appealed to Billy, egged on by old mate Keith Moon, who was involved in the movie himself. A rock 'n' roll revival tour followed in 1974, but damage to Fury's heart required major surgery and a further withdrawal from public life. Fury's bankruptcy in 1978 kept him busy on the cabaret circuit, and he re-recorded a number of old hits, eventually cutting a handful of tracks, which resulted in two singles that scraped the bottom end of the charts. Polydor was enthusiastic about the new material and it was seen as a welcome return, but time was not on Billy's side: he died in January 1983, aged just forty-two. He is one of Britain's early rockers, a shy yet articulate man whose reputation has improved over the years, a trend that shows no sign of abating. It is significant that in the 1960s Billy Fury had more hit singles than The Beatles.

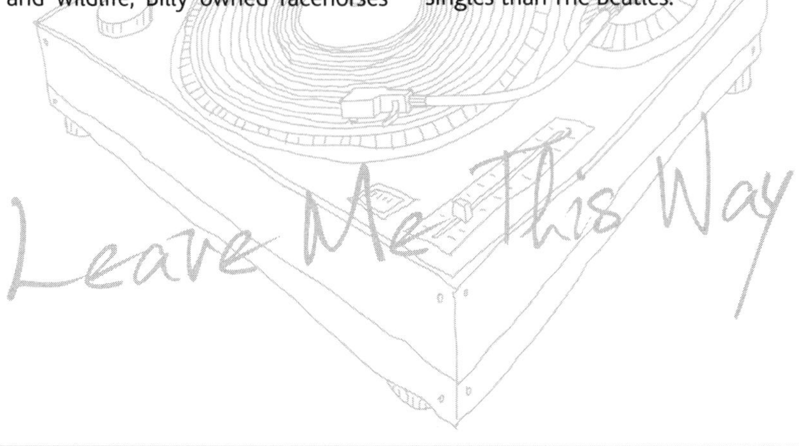

He could turn his hand to rockabilly, blues and country all under a rock 'n' roll banner

Leave Me This Way

Silver-selling ○ Gold-selling ● Platinum-selling ⊛ US No.1 ★ — Peak Position, Weeks at No.1, Weeks on Chart

Date	Title / Label	Peak Position	Weeks at No.1	Weeks on Chart
12 Nov 83	**DADA** *Warner Brothers 9239691*	93		1
1 Nov 86	**CONSTRICTOR** *MCA MCF 3341*	41		2
7 Nov 87	**RAISE YOUR FIST AND YELL** *MCA MCF 3392*	48		3
26 Aug 89	**TRASH** *Epic 4651301*	2		12
13 Jul 91	**HEY STOOPID** *Epic 4684161* ○	4		7
18 Jun 94	**THE LAST TEMPTATION** *Epic 4765949*	6		5
24 Jun 00	**BRUTAL PLANET** *Eagle EAGCD 115*	38		1
10 Mar 01	**THE DEFINITIVE ALICE COOPER** *Rhino 8122735342* ○	33		5
9 Aug 08	**ALONG CAME A SPIDER** *SPV SPV90601*	31		1

COOPER TEMPLE CLAUSE

UK, male vocal/instrumental group – Ben Gautrey, Tom Bellamy, Daniel Fisher, Didz Hammond, Jon Harper & Kieran Mahon — 7

Date	Title / Label	Peak Position	Weeks at No.1	Weeks on Chart
23 Feb 02	**SEE THIS THROUGH AND LEAVE** *Morning 19*	27		3
20 Sep 03	**KICK UP THE FIRE AND LET THE FLAMES BREAK LOOSE** *Morning 36*	5		3
3 Feb 07	**MAKE THIS YOUR OWN** *Sequel SEQCD001*	33		1

JULIAN COPE

UK, male vocalist. See Teardrop Explodes — 35

Date	Title / Label	Peak Position	Weeks at No.1	Weeks on Chart
3 Mar 84	**WORLD SHUT YOUR MOUTH** *Mercury MERL 37*	40		4
24 Nov 84	**FRIED'** *Mercury MERL 48*	87		1
14 Mar 87	**SAINT JULIAN** *Island ILPS 9861* ○	11		10
29 Oct 88	**MY NATION UNDERGROUND** *Island ILPS 9918*	42		2
16 Mar 91	**PEGGY SUICIDE** *Island ILPSD 9977*	23		7
15 Aug 92	**FLOORED GENIUS – THE BEST OF JULIAN COPE AND THE TEARDROP EXPLODES** *Island CID 8000* & THE TEARDROP EXPLODES	22		3
31 Oct 92	**JEHOVAHKILL** *Island 5140522*	20		2
16 Jul 94	**AUTOGEDDON** *Echo ECHCD 1*	16		3
9 Sep 95	**JULIAN COPE PRESENTS 20 MOTHERS** *Echo ECHCD 5*	20		2
26 Oct 96	**INTERPRETER** *Echo ECHCD 012*	39		1

ROSS COPPERMAN

US, male vocalist/guitarist — 1

Date	Title / Label	Peak Position	Weeks at No.1	Weeks on Chart
9 Jun 07	**WELCOME TO REALITY** *Phonogenic 88697055422*	59		1

CORAL

UK, male vocal/instrumental group – James Skelly, Paul Duffy, Nick Power, Bill Ryder-Jones, Ian Skelly & Lee Southall — 57

Date	Title / Label	Peak Position	Weeks at No.1	Weeks on Chart
10 Aug 02	**THE CORAL** *Deltasonic DLTCD 006* ●	5		34
9 Aug 03	**MAGIC AND MEDICINE** *Deltasonic DLTCDPS014* ●	1	1	9
7 Feb 04	**NIGHTFREAK AND THE SONS OF BECKER** *Deltasonic DLTCD018*	5		3
4 Jun 05	**THE INVISIBLE INVASION** *Deltasonic DLTCDLE036*	3		5
18 Aug 07	**ROOTS & ECHOES** *Deltasonic DLTCD069*	8		3
27 Sep 08	**SINGLES COLLECTION** *Deltasonic 88697359581*	13		3

CORDUROY

UK, male vocal/instrumental group — 1

Date	Title / Label	Peak Position	Weeks at No.1	Weeks on Chart
8 Oct 94	**OUT OF HERE** *Acid Jazz JAZIDCD 107*	73		1

CHRIS CORNELL

US, male vocalist/multi-instrumentalist (Christopher Boyle). See Audioslave, Soundgarden — 3

Date	Title / Label	Peak Position	Weeks at No.1	Weeks on Chart
2 Oct 99	**EUPHORIA MORNING** *A&M 4904222*	31		1
9 Jun 07	**CARRY ON** *Interscope 1734884*	25		2

CORNERSHOP

UK, male vocal/instrumental group — 18

Date	Title / Label	Peak Position	Weeks at No.1	Weeks on Chart
20 Sep 97	**WHEN I WAS BORN FOR THE 7TH TIME** *Wiiija WIJCD 1065* ●	17		15
13 Apr 02	**HANDCREAM FOR A GENERATION** *Wiiija WIJCD 1115*	30		3

HUGH CORNWELL

UK, male vocalist/guitarist. See Stranglers — 1

Date	Title / Label	Peak Position	Weeks at No.1	Weeks on Chart
18 Jun 88	**WOLF** *Virgin V 2420*	98		1

CORO DE MUNJES DEL MONASTERIO BENEDICTINO DE SANTO DOMINGO DE SILOS

Spain, monastic choir — 28

Date	Title / Label	Peak Position	Weeks at No.1	Weeks on Chart
5 Mar 94	**CANTO GREGORIANO** *EMI Classics CMS 5652172* ●	7		25
17 Dec 94	**CANTO NOEL** *EMI Classics CDC 5552172*	53		3

CORONA

Brazil, male producer (Francesco Bontempi) & female vocalist (Olga de Souza) — 7

Date	Title / Label	Peak Position	Weeks at No.1	Weeks on Chart
20 May 95	**THE RHYTHM OF THE NIGHT** *Eternal 0630103312*	18		7

ANDREA CORR

Ireland, female vocalist. See Corrs — 1

Date	Title / Label	Peak Position	Weeks at No.1	Weeks on Chart
7 Jul 07	**TEN FEET HIGH** *Atlantic 5144209312*	38		1

CORRIES

UK, male vocal/instrumental duo — 5

Date	Title / Label	Peak Position	Weeks at No.1	Weeks on Chart
9 May 70	**SCOTTISH LOVE SONGS** *Fontana 6306 004*	46		4
16 Sep 72	**SOUND OF PIBROCH** *Columbia SCX 6511*	39		1

CORROSION OF CONFORMITY

US, male vocal/instrumental group — 1

Date	Title / Label	Peak Position	Weeks at No.1	Weeks on Chart
14 Sep 96	**WISEBLOOD** *Columbia 4843282*	43		1

CORRS

Ireland, female/male vocal/instrumental group – Andrea Corr*, Caroline, Jim & Sharon Corr. Family quartet who honed their Celtic folk roots and developed a more contemporary sound, selling more than five million albums in the UK in the process. *Talk On Corners* was the UK's best-selling album of 1998 — 367

Date	Title / Label	Peak Position	Weeks at No.1	Weeks on Chart
2 Mar 96	**FORGIVEN, NOT FORGOTTEN** *Atlantic 7567926122* ⊛	2		113
1 Nov 97	**TALK ON CORNERS** *Atlantic 7567831062* ⊛**x9**	1	10	142
27 Nov 99	**UNPLUGGED** *Atlantic 7567809862* ⊛	7		25
29 Jul 00	**IN BLUE** *Atlantic 7567833522* ⊛**x3**	1	2	45
17 Nov 01	**THE BEST OF** *Atlantic 7567930752* ⊛	6		21
12 Jun 04	**BORROWED HEAVEN** *Atlantic 7567932432* ○	2		14
8 Oct 05	**HOME** *Atlantic 5101102932* ○	14		6
2 Dec 06	**DREAMS – THE ULTIMATE COLLECTION** *Atlantic 799525*	67		1

Top 3 Best-Selling Albums

	Title	Approximate Sales
1	TALK ON CORNERS	2,950,000
2	IN BLUE	1,030,000
3	FORGIVEN NOT FORGOTTEN	990,000

GARDAR THOR CORTES

Iceland, male vocalist — 3

Date	Title / Label	Peak Position	Weeks at No.1	Weeks on Chart
28 Apr 07	**CORTES** *Believer Music BELIEVECDA2*	27		3

COSMIC BABY

Germany, male producer — 1

Date	Title / Label	Peak Position	Weeks at No.1	Weeks on Chart
23 Apr 94	**THINKING ABOUT MYSELF** *Logic 74321196052*	60		1

ELVIS COSTELLO

UK, male vocalist/multi-instrumentalist (Declan MacManus) — 229

Date	Title / Label	Peak Position	Weeks at No.1	Weeks on Chart
6 Aug 77	**MY AIM IS TRUE** *Stiff SEEZ 3* ○	14		12
1 Apr 78	**THIS YEAR'S MODEL** *Radar RAD 3* ●	4		14
20 Jan 79	**ARMED FORCES** *Radar RAD 14* & THE ATTRACTIONS ⊛	2		28
23 Feb 80	**GET HAPPY!** *F-Beat XXLP 1* & THE ATTRACTIONS ●	2		14
31 Jan 81	**TRUST** *F-Beat XXLP 11* & THE ATTRACTIONS	9		7
31 Oct 81	**ALMOST BLUE** *F-Beat XXLP 13* & THE ATTRACTIONS ●	7		18
10 Jul 82	**IMPERIAL BEDROOM** *F-Beat XXLP 17* & THE ATTRACTIONS	6		12
6 Aug 83	**PUNCH THE CLOCK** *F-Beat XXLP 19* & THE ATTRACTIONS	3		13
7 Jul 84	**GOODBYE CRUEL WORLD** *F-Beat ZL 70317* & THE ATTRACTIONS ○	10		10
20 Apr 85	**THE BEST OF ELVIS COSTELLO – THE MAN** *Telstar STAR 2247* & THE ATTRACTIONS ●	8		25
1 Mar 86	**KING OF AMERICA** *F-Beat ZL 70496* COSTELLO SHOW ○	11		9

Silver-selling ○ · Gold-selling ● · Platinum-selling ⊛ · US No.1 ★ · Peak Position · Weeks at No.1 · Weeks on Chart

Date	Title	Peak	Wks at No.1	Wks on Chart
27 Sep 86	**BLOOD AND CHOCOLATE** *Imp XFIEND 80* & THE ATTRACTIONS ●	16		5
18 Feb 89	**SPIKE** *Warner Brothers WX 238* ●	5		16
28 Oct 89	**GIRLS GIRLS GIRLS** *Demon DFIEND 160*	67		1
25 May 91	**MIGHTY LIKE A ROSE** *Warner Brothers WX 419* ○	5		6
30 Jan 93	**THE JULIET LETTERS** *Warner Brothers 9362451802* & THE BRODSKY QUARTET	18		3
19 Mar 94	**BRUTAL YOUTH** *Warner Brothers 9362455352* & THE ATTRACTIONS ○	2		5
12 Nov 94	**THE VERY BEST OF ELVIS COSTELLO AND THE ATTRACTIONS** *Demon DPAM 13* & THE ATTRACTIONS	57		2
27 May 95	**KOJAK VARIETY** *Warner Brothers 9362459032*	21		2
12 Aug 95	**KING OF AMERICA** *Demon DPAM 11* COSTELLO SHOW	71		1
25 May 96	**ALL THIS USELESS BEAUTY** *Warner Brothers 9362461982* & THE ATTRACTIONS	28		3
10 Oct 98	**PAINTED FROM MEMORY** *Mercury 5380022* WITH BURT BACHARACH ○	32		2
14 Aug 99	**THE VERY BEST OF ELVIS COSTELLO** *Universal Music TV 5464902* ●	4		13
31 Mar 01	**FOR THE STARS** *Deutsche Grammophon 4695302* ANNE SOFIE VON OTTER MEETS ELVIS COSTELLO	67		1
27 Apr 02	**WHEN I WAS CRUEL** *Mercury 5868292* ○	17		4
27 Sep 03	**NORTH** *Deutsche Grammophon 9809656*	44		2
2 Oct 04	**THE DELIVERY MAN** *Lost Highway 9863727* & THE IMPOSTERS	73		1

PHIL COULTER

Ireland, male pianist/orchestra leader — 15

Date	Title	Peak	Wks at No.1	Wks on Chart
13 Oct 84	**SEA OF TRANQUILLITY** *K-Tel Ireland KLP 185*	46		14
18 May 85	**PHIL COULTER'S IRELAND** *K-Tel ONE 1296*	86		1

COUNTING CROWS

US, male vocal/instrumental group – Adam Duritz, Steve Bowman, Dave Bryson, Charlie Gillingham, David Immerglück, Matt Malley & Dan Vickrey — 68

Date	Title	Peak	Wks at No.1	Wks on Chart
12 Mar 94	**AUGUST AND EVERYTHING AFTER** *Geffen GED 24528* ●	16		38
26 Oct 96	**RECOVERING THE SATELLITES** *Geffen GED 24975* ● ★	4		4
25 Jul 98	**ACROSS THE WIRE – LIVE IN NEW YORK** *Geffen GED 25226*	27		4
13 Nov 99	**THIS DESERT LIFE** *Geffen 4904152* ○	19		3
20 Jul 02	**HARD CANDY** *Geffen 4933662* ●	9		11
7 Feb 04	**FILMS ABOUT GHOSTS – THE BEST OF** *Geffen 9861505*	15		5
5 Apr 08	**SATURDAY NIGHT & SUNDAY MORNINGS** *Geffen 1749847*	12		3

COURTEENERS

UK, male vocal/instrumental group – Liam Fray, Michael Campbell, Mark Cuppello & Daniel Conan Moores — 5

Date	Title	Peak	Wks at No.1	Wks on Chart
19 Apr 08	**ST JUDE** *Polydor 1763529*	4		5

TINA COUSINS

UK, female vocalist — 1

Date	Title	Peak	Wks at No.1	Wks on Chart
24 Jul 99	**KILLING TIME** *Jive 0519342*	50		1

DAVID COVERDALE

UK, male vocalist/guitarist. See Deep Purple, Whitesnake — 10

Date	Title	Peak	Wks at No.1	Wks on Chart
27 Feb 82	**NORTHWINDS** *Purple TTS 3513*	78		1
27 Mar 93	**COVERDALE PAGE** *EMI CDEMD 1041* COVERDALE PAGE ○	4		8
7 Oct 00	**INTO THE LIGHT** *EMI 5281242*	75		1

COWBOY JUNKIES

US, male/female vocal/instrumental group — 7

Date	Title	Peak	Wks at No.1	Wks on Chart
24 Mar 90	**THE CAUTION HORSES** *RCA PL 90450*	33		4
15 Feb 92	**BLACK EYED MAN** *RCA PD 90620*	21		3

CARL COX

UK, male producer — 4

Date	Title	Peak	Wks at No.1	Wks on Chart
15 Jun 96	**AT THE END OF THE CLICHÉ** *Edel 00990752COX*	23		4

PETER COX

UK, male vocalist. See Go West — 1

Date	Title	Peak	Wks at No.1	Wks on Chart
29 Nov 97	**PETER COX** *Chrysalis 4949692*	64		1

GRAHAM COXON

UK, male vocalist/guitarist. See Blur — 7

Date	Title	Peak	Wks at No.1	Wks on Chart
22 Aug 98	**THE SKY IS TOO HIGH** *Transcopic TRANCD 005*	31		2
29 May 04	**HAPPINESS IN MAGAZINES** *Transcopic 5775192* ○	19		3
25 Mar 06	**LOVE TRAVELS AT ILLEGAL SPEEDS** *Parlophone 3541342*	24		2

CRACKER

US, male vocal/instrumental group — 2

Date	Title	Peak	Wks at No.1	Wks on Chart
25 Jun 94	**KEROSENE HAT** *Virgin CDVUS 67*	44		2

CRADLE OF FILTH

UK, male vocal/instrumental group — 6

Date	Title	Peak	Wks at No.1	Wks on Chart
16 May 98	**CRUELTY AND THE BEAST** *Music For Nations CDMFN 242*	48		1
11 Nov 00	**MIDIAN** *Music For Nations CDMFN 666*	63		1
30 Jun 01	**BITTER SUITES TO SUCCUBI** *Snapper Music COF 001CD*	63		1
22 Mar 03	**DAMNATION AND A DAY** *Epic 5109632*	44		1
28 Oct 06	**THORNOGRAPHY** *Roadrunner RR81132*	46		1
8 Nov 08	**GODSPEED ON THE DEVILS THUNDER** *Roadrunner RR79232*	73		1

CRAMPS

US, male/female vocal/instrumental group — 13

Date	Title	Peak	Wks at No.1	Wks on Chart
25 Jun 83	**OFF THE BONE** *Illegal ILP 012* ○	44		4
26 Nov 83	**SMELL OF FEMALE** *Ace NED 6*	74		2
1 Mar 86	**A DATE WITH ELVIS** *Big Beat WIKA 46*	34		6
24 Feb 90	**STAY STICK!** *Ensign ENVLP 1001*	62		1

CRANBERRIES

Ireland, female/male vocal/instrumental group – Dolores O'Riordan*, Michael & Noel Hogan & Fergal Lawler — 193

Date	Title	Peak	Wks at No.1	Wks on Chart
13 Mar 93	**EVERYBODY ELSE IS DOING IT, SO WHY CAN'T WE?** *Island CID 8003* ⊛x2	1	1	86
15 Oct 94	**NO NEED TO ARGUE** *Island CID 8029* ⊛x3	2		78
11 May 96	**TO THE FAITHFUL DEPARTED** *Island CID 8048* ●	2		19
1 May 99	**BURY THE HATCHET** *Island US 5246442* ○	7		5
3 Nov 01	**WAKE UP AND SMELL THE COFFEE** *MCA 1127062*	61		1
28 Sep 02	**STARS – THE BEST OF 1992-2002** *Universal Music TV 0633862*	20		4

CRANES

UK, male/female vocal/instrumental group — 2

Date	Title	Peak	Wks at No.1	Wks on Chart
28 Sep 91	**WINGS OF JOY** *Dedicated DEDLP 003*	52		1
8 May 93	**FOREVER** *Dedicated DEDCD 009*	40		1

CRASH TEST DUMMIES

Canada, male vocal/instrumental group – Brad Roberts, Benjamin Darvill, Mitch Dorge, Ellen Reid & Dan Roberts — 23

Date	Title	Peak	Wks at No.1	Wks on Chart
14 May 94	**GOD SHUFFLED HIS FEET** *RCA 74321201522* ●	2		23

CRASS

UK, male vocal/instrumental group — 2

Date	Title	Peak	Wks at No.1	Wks on Chart
28 Aug 82	**CHRIST THE ALBUM** *Crass BOLLOX 2U2*	26		2

BEVERLEY CRAVEN

UK, female vocalist/keyboard player — 67

Date	Title	Peak	Wks at No.1	Wks on Chart
2 Mar 91	**BEVERLEY CRAVEN** *Epic 4670531* ⊛x2	3		52
9 Oct 93	**LOVE SCENES** *Epic 4745172* ●	4		13
12 Jun 99	**MIXED EMOTIONS** *Epic 4941502*	46		2

MICHAEL CRAWFORD

UK, male actor/vocalist (Michael Dumble-Smith) — 76

Date	Title	Peak	Wks at No.1	Wks on Chart
28 Nov 87	**SONGS FROM STAGE AND SCREEN** *Telstar STAR 2308* MICHAEL CRAWFORD & THE LONDON SYMPHONY ORCHESTRA ⊛	12		13
2 Dec 89	**WITH LOVE** *Telstar STAR 2340* ●	31		7
9 Nov 91	**MICHAEL CRAWFORD PERFORMS ANDREW LLOYD WEBBER** *Telstar STAR 2544* & THE ROYAL PHILHARMONIC ORCHESTRA ⊛x2	3		36
13 Nov 93	**A TOUCH OF MUSIC IN THE NIGHT** *Telstar TCD 2676* ⊛	12		11
19 Nov 94	**THE LOVE SONGS ALBUM** *Telstar TCD 2748*	64		3
21 Nov 98	**ON EAGLE'S WINGS** *Atlantic 7567830762*	65		2
25 Dec 99	**THE MOST WONDERFUL TIME OF THE YEAR** *Telstar TV TTVCD 3111*	69		1
4 Dec 04	**THE VERY BEST OF** *Virgin/EMI VTCD685*	54		3

Silver-selling ○ · Gold-selling ● · Platinum-selling ⊛ · US No.1 ★ · Peak Position · Weeks at No.1 · Weeks on Chart

RANDY CRAWFORD

US, female vocalist (Veronica Crawford) — Weeks on Chart: 158

Date	Title / Label	Peak Position	Weeks at No.1	Weeks on Chart
28 Jun 80	**NOW WE MAY BEGIN** *Warner Brothers K 56791* ○	10		16
16 May 81	**SECRET COMBINATION** *Warner Brothers K 56904* ⊛x2	2		60
12 Jun 82	**WINDSONG** *Warner Brothers K 57011* ○	7		17
22 Oct 83	**NIGHTLINE** *Warner Brothers 9239761*	37		4
13 Oct 84	**MISS RANDY CRAWFORD – THE GREATEST HITS** *K-Tel NE 1281* ●	10		17
28 Jun 86	**ABSTRACT EMOTIONS** *Warner Brothers WX 46* ○	14		10
10 Oct 87	**THE LOVE SONGS** *Telstar STAR 2299* ●	27		13
21 Oct 89	**RICH AND POOR** *Warner Brothers WX 308*	63		1
27 Mar 93	**THE VERY BEST OF RANDY CRAWFORD** *Dino DINCD 58*	8		13
12 Feb 00	**LOVES SONGS – THE VERY BEST OF RANDY CRAWFORD** *warner.esp WMMCD 002*	22		4
18 Jun 05	**THE ULTIMATE COLLECTION** *WSM 5046787972*	31		3

ROBERT CRAY BAND

US, male vocal/instrumental group — Weeks on Chart: 53

Date	Title / Label	Peak Position	Weeks at No.1	Weeks on Chart
12 Oct 85	**FALSE ACCUSATIONS** *Demon FIEND 43* ○	68		1
15 Nov 86	**STRONG PERSUADER** *Mercury MERH 97* ○	34		28
3 Sep 88	**DON'T BE AFRAID OF THE DARK** *Mercury MERH 129* ●	13		12
29 Sep 90	**MIDNIGHT STROLL** *Mercury 8466521* WITH THE MEMPHIS HORNS ○	19		7
12 Sep 92	**I WAS WARNED** *Mercury 5127212* ROBERT CRAY	29		3
16 Jan 93	**SHAME AND SIN** *Mercury 5185172*	48		1
20 May 95	**SOME RAINY MORNING** *Mercury 5269282* ROBERT CRAY	63		1

CRAZY FROG

Sweden, computer animated frog created by male production duo Daniel Malmedahl & Erik Wernquist — Weeks on Chart: 10

Date	Title / Label	Peak Position	Weeks at No.1	Weeks on Chart
6 Aug 05	**CRAZY HITS** *Gut GUSCD03* ●	5		8
24 Dec 05	**CRAZY HITS – CRAZY CHRISTMAS EDITION** *Gusto GUSCD03Y*	75		1
8 Jul 06	**MORE CRAZY HITS** *Gusto GUSCD04*	64		1

CRAZY TOWN

US, male vocal/rap/instrumental group — Weeks on Chart: 9

Date	Title / Label	Peak Position	Weeks at No.1	Weeks on Chart
21 Apr 01	**THE GIFT OF GAME** *Columbia 4952972* ○	15		9

CREAM

UK, male vocal/instrumental trio – Ginger Baker*, Jack Bruce* & Eric Clapton*. The first rock supergroup proved to be one of the most groundbreaking acts of the rock era. Their short, productive life resulted in over 35 million album sales for the progressive rock pioneers, who briefly but successfully re-united in 2005 — Weeks on Chart: 300

Date	Title / Label	Peak Position	Weeks at No.1	Weeks on Chart
24 Dec 66	**FRESH CREAM** *Reaction 593001*	6		17
18 Nov 67	**DISRAELI GEARS** *Reaction 594003*	5		42
17 Aug 68	**WHEELS OF FIRE (SINGLE: IN THE STUDIO)** *Polydor 583033*	7		13
17 Aug 68	**WHEELS OF FIRE (DOUBLE: LIVE AND STUDIO)** *Polydor 583031/2* ★	3		26
8 Feb 69	**FRESH CREAM** *Reaction 594001*	7		2
15 Mar 69	**GOODBYE** *Polydor 583053*	1	4	28
8 Nov 69	**THE BEST OF CREAM** *Polydor 583060*	6		34
2 Dec 72	**LIVE CREAM** *Polydor 2383 016*	4		15
24 Jun 72	**LIVE CREAM VOLUME 2** *Polydor 2383 119*	15		5
26 Sep 87	**THE CREAM OF ERIC CLAPTON** *Polydor ECTV 1* ERIC CLAPTON & CREAM ⊛x3	3		109
14 May 05	**I FEEL FREE – ULTIMATE CREAM** *Polydor 9871430* ●	6		7
15 Oct 05	**ROYAL ALBERT HALL 2005** *Reprise 9362494162*	61		2

CREATURES

UK, male/female vocal/instrumental group — Weeks on Chart: 9

Date	Title / Label	Peak Position	Weeks at No.1	Weeks on Chart
28 May 83	**FEAST** *Wonderland SHELP 1*	17		9

CREDIT TO THE NATION

UK, male rap group — Weeks on Chart: 3

Date	Title / Label	Peak Position	Weeks at No.1	Weeks on Chart
9 Apr 94	**TAKE DIS** *One Little Indian TPLP 44CDH*	20		3

CREED

US, male vocal/instrumental group — Weeks on Chart: 21

Date	Title / Label	Peak Position	Weeks at No.1	Weeks on Chart
3 Feb 01	**HUMAN CLAY** *Epic 4950272* ★	29		4
1 Dec 01	**WEATHERED** *Epic 5049792* ● ★	44		17

CREEDENCE CLEARWATER REVIVAL

US, male vocal/instrumental group – John Fogerty*, Doug Clifford, Stu Cook & Tom Fogerty, d. 6 Sep 1990 — Weeks on Chart: 67

Date	Title / Label	Peak Position	Weeks at No.1	Weeks on Chart
24 Jan 70	**GREEN RIVER** *Liberty LBS 83273* ★	20		6
28 Mar 70	**WILLY AND THE POOR BOYS** *Liberty LBS 83338*	10		24
2 May 70	**BAYOU COUNTRY** *Liberty LBS 83261*	62		1
12 Sep 70	**COSMO'S FACTORY** *Liberty LBS 83388* ★	1	1	15
23 Jan 71	**PENDULUM** *Liberty LBG 83400*	8		12
30 Jun 79	**GREATEST HITS** *Fantasy FT 558*	35		5
19 Oct 85	**THE CREEDENCE COLLECTION** *Impression IMDP 3*	68		2
14 Jun 08	**BEST OF** *Concord 7230870*	46		2

KID CREOLE & THE COCONUTS

US, male vocalist (August Darnell Browder) & female vocal group — Weeks on Chart: 54

Date	Title / Label	Peak Position	Weeks at No.1	Weeks on Chart
22 May 82	**TROPICAL GANGSTERS** *Ze ILPS 7016* ⊛	3		40
26 Jun 82	**FRESH FRUIT IN FOREIGN PLACES** *Ze ILPS 7014*	99		1
17 Sep 83	**DOPPELGANGER** *Island ILPS 9743*	21		6
15 Sep 84	**CRE-OLE (BEST OF KID CREOLE AND COCONUTS)** *Island IMA 13*	21		7

CRIBS

UK, male vocal/instrumental trio — Weeks on Chart: 3

Date	Title / Label	Peak Position	Weeks at No.1	Weeks on Chart
2 Jun 07	**MEN'S NEEDS WOMEN'S NEEDS WHATEVER** *Wichita WEBB126CDL*	13		3

CRICKETS

US, male vocal/instrumental group – Buddy Holly*, Jerry Allison, Sonny Curtis & Joe B. Mauldin — Weeks on Chart: 67

Date	Title / Label	Peak Position	Weeks at No.1	Weeks on Chart
19 Apr 58	**CHIRPING CRICKETS** *Coral LVA 9081*	5		1
25 Mar 61	**IN STYLE WITH THE CRICKETS** *Coral LVA 9142*	13		7
27 Oct 62	**BOBBY VEE MEETS THE CRICKETS** *Liberty LBY 1086* BOBBY VEE & THE CRICKETS	2		27
11 Mar 78	**20 GOLDEN GREATS** *EMI EMTV 8* BUDDY HOLLY & THE CRICKETS ⊛	1	3	20
20 Feb 93	**WORDS OF LOVE** *Polygram TV 5144872* BUDDY HOLLY & THE CRICKETS ●	1	1	9
28 Aug 99	**THE VERY BEST OF BUDDY HOLLY AND THE CRICKETS** *Universal Music TV 1120462* BUDDY HOLLY & THE CRICKETS	25		3

BING CROSBY

US, male vocalist/actor (Harry Crosby), d. 14 Oct 1977 (age 74) — Weeks on Chart: 45

Date	Title / Label	Peak Position	Weeks at No.1	Weeks on Chart
8 Oct 60	**JOIN BING AND SING ALONG** *Warner Brothers WM 4021*	7		11
21 Dec 74	**WHITE CHRISTMAS** *MCA MCF 2568* ○	45		3
20 Sep 75	**THAT'S WHAT LIFE IS ALL ABOUT** *United Artists UAG 29730* ○	28		6
5 Nov 77	**LIVE AT THE LONDON PALLADIUM** *K-Tel NE 951*	9		2
5 Nov 77	**THE BEST OF BING** *MCA MCF 2540*	41		7
17 Dec 77	**SEASONS** *Polydor 2442 151* ○	25		7
5 May 79	**SONGS OF A LIFETIME** *Philips 6641 923*	29		3
14 Dec 91	**CHRISTMAS WITH BING CROSBY** *Telstar STAR 2468*	66		3
23 Nov 96	**THE BEST OF BING CROSBY** *MCA MCD 11561*	59		3

DAVID CROSBY

US, male vocalist/guitarist. See Crosby, Stills, Nash & Young — Weeks on Chart: 110

Date	Title / Label	Peak Position	Weeks at No.1	Weeks on Chart
24 Apr 71	**IF ONLY I COULD REMEMBER MY NAME** *Atlantic 2401 005*	12		7
13 May 72	**GRAHAM NASH AND DAVID CROSBY** *Atlantic K 50011* GRAHAM NASH & DAVID CROSBY	13		5
23 Aug 69	**CROSBY, STILLS AND NASH** *Atlantic 588189* CROSBY, STILLS & NASH	25		5
30 May 70	**DÉJÀ VU** *Atlantic 2401 001* CROSBY, STILL, NASH & YOUNG ★	5		61
22 May 71	**FOUR-WAY STREET** *Atlantic 2956 004* CROSBY, STILL, NASH & YOUNG ★	5		12
21 Sep 74	**SO FAR** *Atlantic K 50023* CROSBY, STILL, NASH & YOUNG ★	25		6
9 Jul 77	**CSN** *Atlantic K 50369* CROSBY, STILLS & NASH ○	23		9
6 Nov 99	**LOOKING FORWARD** *Atlantic 9362474362* CROSBY, STILL, NASH & YOUNG	54		1
12 Mar 05	**GREATEST HITS** *Rhino 8122765372* CROSBY, STILLS & NASH	38		4

CROSS

UK/US, male vocal/instrumental group — Weeks on Chart: 2

Date	Title / Label	Peak Position	Weeks at No.1	Weeks on Chart
6 Feb 88	**SHOVE IT** *Virgin V 2477*	58		2

CHRISTOPHER CROSS
US, male vocalist (Christopher Geppert) — 93

Date	Title / Label	Peak	Wks at No.1	Wks on Chart
21 Feb 81	**CHRISTOPHER CROSS** *Warner Brothers K 56789* ⊛	14		77
19 Feb 83	**ANOTHER PAGE** *Warner Brothers W 3757* ●	4		16

SHERYL CROW
US, female vocalist/guitarist — 185

Date	Title / Label	Peak	Wks at No.1	Wks on Chart
12 Feb 94	**TUESDAY NIGHT MUSIC CLUB** *A&M 5401262* ⊛x2	8		55
12 Oct 96	**SHERYL CROW** *A&M 5405902* ⊛x3	5		70
3 Oct 98	**THE GLOBE SESSIONS** *A&M 5409742* ⊛	2		32
20 Apr 02	**C'MON C'MON** *A&M 4932622* ●	2		8
25 Oct 03	**THE VERY BEST OF** *A&M 9861092* ⊛	2		16
8 Oct 05	**WILDFLOWER** *A&M 9884810*	25		2
1 Mar 08	**DETOURS** *A&M 1757003*	20		2

CROWDED HOUSE
New Zealand/Australia, male vocal/instrumental group – Neil Finn*, Tim Finn*, Mark Hart, Paul Hester, d. 26 Mar 2005 (replaced by Peter Jones), & Nick Seymour — 190

Date	Title / Label	Peak	Wks at No.1	Wks on Chart
13 Jul 91	**WOODFACE** *Capitol EST 2144* ⊛x2	6		86
23 Oct 93	**TOGETHER ALONE** *Capitol CDESTU 2215* ⊛	4		32
6 Jul 96	**RECURRING DREAM – THE VERY BEST OF CROWDED HOUSE** *Capitol CDESTX 2283* ⊛x4	1	2	66
19 Feb 00	**AFTERGLOW** *Capitol 5248042*	18		2
14 Jul 07	**TIME ON EARTH** *Parlophone 3960272* ○	3		4

CROWN HEIGHTS AFFAIR
US, male vocal/instrumental group — 3

Date	Title / Label	Peak	Wks at No.1	Wks on Chart
23 Sep 78	**DREAM WORLD** *Philips 6372 754*	40		3

CRUSADERS
US, male instrumental group – Wilton Felder*, Wayne Henderson, Stix Hooper & Joe Sample — 30

Date	Title / Label	Peak	Wks at No.1	Wks on Chart
21 Jul 79	**STREET LIFE** *MCA MCF 3008*	10		16
19 Jul 80	**RHAPSODY AND BLUE** *MCA MCG 4010*	40		5
12 Sep 81	**STANDING TALL** *MCA MCF 3122*	47		5
7 Apr 84	**GHETTO BLASTER** *MCA MCF 3176*	46		4

BOBBY CRUSH
UK, male pianist — 12

Date	Title / Label	Peak	Wks at No.1	Wks on Chart
25 Nov 72	**BOBBY CRUSH** *Philips 6308 135*	15		7
18 Dec 82	**THE BOBBY CRUSH INCREDIBLE DOUBLE DECKER PARTY 101 GREAT SONGS** *Warwick WW 5126/7*	53		5

TAIO CRUZ
UK, male vocalist/producer — 15

Date	Title / Label	Peak	Wks at No.1	Wks on Chart
29 Mar 08	**DEPARTURE** *Fourth & Broadway 1761182* ●	17		15

CRYSTAL CASTLES
Canada, female/male vocal duo — 1

Date	Title / Label	Peak	Wks at No.1	Wks on Chart
10 May 08	**CRYSTAL CASTLES** *Different Recordings DIFB1200CD*	47		1

CSS
Brazil, female/male vocal/instrumental group — 2

Date	Title / Label	Peak	Wks at No.1	Wks on Chart
19 May 07	**CANSEI DE SER SEXY** *Sub Pop SPCD717*	69		1
2 Aug 08	**DONKEY** *Sire 5144289832*	32		1

CUD
UK, male vocal/instrumental group — 2

Date	Title / Label	Peak	Wks at No.1	Wks on Chart
11 Jul 92	**ASQUARIUS** *A&M 3953902*	30		1
23 Apr 94	**SHOWBIZ** *A&M 5402112*	46		1

JAMIE CULLUM
UK, male vocalist/pianist — 65

Date	Title / Label	Peak	Wks at No.1	Wks on Chart
1 Nov 03	**TWENTYSOMETHING** *UCJ 9865574* ⊛x3	3		50
13 Mar 04	**POINTLESS NOSTALGIC** *Candid CCD79782* ●	55		2
8 Oct 05	**CATCHING TALES** *UCJ 9873432* ●	4		13

CULT
UK, male vocal/instrumental group – Ian Astbury, Billy Duffy & various musicians — 87

Date	Title / Label	Peak	Wks at No.1	Wks on Chart
18 Jun 83	**THE SOUTHERN DEATH CULT** *Beggars Banquet BEGA 46*	43		3
8 Sep 84	**DREAMTIME** *Beggars Banquet BEGA 57* ○	21		8
26 Oct 85	**LOVE SCENES** *Beggars Banquet BEGA 65* ●	4		22
18 Apr 87	**ELECTRIC** *Beggars Banquet BEGA 80* ●	4		27
22 Apr 89	**SONIC TEMPLE** *Beggars Banquet BEGA 98* ●	3		11
5 Oct 91	**CEREMONY** *Beggars Banquet BEGA 122*	9		4
13 Feb 93	**PURE CULT** *Beggars Banquet BEGACD 130* ●	1	1	8
22 Oct 94	**THE CULT** *Beggars Banquet BBQCD 164*	21		2
23 Jun 01	**BEYOND GOOD AND EVIL** *Atlantic 7567834402*	69		1
13 Oct 07	**BORN INTO THIS** *Roadrunner RR79712*	72		1

CULTURE
Jamaica, male vocal/instrumental group — 1

Date	Title / Label	Peak	Wks at No.1	Wks on Chart
1 Apr 78	**TWO SEVENS CLASH** *Lightning LIP 1*	60		1

CULTURE BEAT
UK/US/Germany, male/female vocal/instrumental group — 10

Date	Title / Label	Peak	Wks at No.1	Wks on Chart
25 Sep 93	**SERENITY** *Dance Pool 4741012* ●	13		10

CULTURE CLUB
UK, male vocal/instrumental group – Boy George* (George O'Dowd), Mikey Craig, Roy Hay & Jon Moss — 163

Date	Title / Label	Peak	Wks at No.1	Wks on Chart
16 Oct 82	**KISSING TO BE CLEVER** *Virgin V 2232* ⊛	5		59
22 Oct 83	**COLOUR BY NUMBERS** *Virgin V 2285* ⊛x3	1	5	56
3 Nov 84	**WAKING UP WITH THE HOUSE ON FIRE** *Virgin V 2330* ⊛	2		13
12 Apr 86	**FROM LUXURY TO HEARTACHE** *Virgin V 2380* ○	10		6
18 Apr 87	**THIS TIME THE FIRST FOUR YEARS** *Virgin VTV 1* ●	8		10
2 Oct 93	**AT WORST...THE BEST OF BOY GEORGE & CULTURE CLUB** *Virgin VTCD 19* BOY GEORGE/CULTURE CLUB ○	24		5
21 Nov 98	**GREATEST MOMENTS** *Virgin CDV 2865* ⊛	15		13
4 Dec 99	**DON'T MIND IF I DO** *Virgin CDV 2887*	64		1

CURE
UK, male vocal/instrumental group – Robert Smith, Simon Gallup, Lol Tolhurst, Porl Thompson & Boris Williams — 215

Date	Title / Label	Peak	Wks at No.1	Wks on Chart
2 Jun 79	**THREE IMAGINARY BOYS** *Fiction FIX 001*	44		3
3 May 80	**17 SECONDS** *Fiction FIX 004*	20		10
25 Apr 81	**FAITH** *Fiction FIX 6* ○	14		8
15 May 82	**PORNOGRAPHY** *Fiction FIX D7*	8		9
3 Sep 83	**BOYS DON'T CRY** *Fiction SPELP 26* ⊛	71		7
24 Dec 83	**JAPANESE WHISPERS: SINGLES NOV 82 – NOV 83** *Fiction FIXM 8* ○	26		14
12 May 84	**THE TOP** *Fiction FIXS 9* ○	10		10
3 Nov 84	**CONCERT – THE CURE LIVE** *Fiction FIXH 10*	26		4
7 Sep 85	**THE HEAD ON THE DOOR** *Fiction FIXH 11* ●	7		13
31 May 86	**STANDING ON A BEACH – THE SINGLES** *Fiction FIXH 12* ●	4		35
6 Jun 87	**KISS ME KISS ME KISS ME** *Fiction FIXH 13* ●	6		15
13 May 89	**DISINTEGRATION** *Fiction FIXH 14* ●	3		26
17 Nov 90	**MIXED UP** *Fiction 8470991* ●	8		17
6 Apr 91	**ENTREAT** *Fiction FIXH 17*	10		5
2 May 92	**WISH** *Fiction FIXCD 20* ●	1	1	13
25 Sep 93	**SHOWBIZ** *Fiction FIXCD 25*	29		2
6 Nov 93	**PARIS** *Fiction FIXCD 26*	56		1
18 May 96	**WILD MOOD SWINGS** *Fiction FIXCD 28*	9		6
15 Nov 97	**GALORE – THE SINGLES 1987 – 1997** *Fiction FIXCD 30*	37		2
26 Feb 00	**BLOODFLOWERS** *Fiction FIXCD 31*	14		2
24 Nov 01	**GREATEST HITS** *Fiction 5894352*	33		6
10 Jul 04	**THE CURE** *I Am/Geffen 9862890* ○	8		5
8 Nov 08	**4:13 DREAM** *Suretone/Geffen 1764225*	33		2

CURIOSITY KILLED THE CAT
UK, male vocal/instrumental group – Ben Volpeliere-Pierrot, Julian Godfrey Brookhouse, Migi Drummond & Nick Thorpe — 27

Date	Title / Label	Peak	Wks at No.1	Wks on Chart
9 May 87	**KEEP YOUR DISTANCE** *Mercury CATLP 1* ⊛	1	2	24
4 Nov 89	**GETAHEAD** *Mercury 8420101* ○	29		3

CURVE
UK, male/female vocal/instrumental duo — 6

Date	Title / Label	Peak	Wks at No.1	Wks on Chart
21 Mar 92	**DOPPELGANGER** *AnXious ANXCD 77*	11		3
19 Jun 93	**RADIO SESSIONS** *AnXious ANXCD 80*	72		1
25 Sep 93	**CUCKOO** *AnXious ANXCD 81*	23		2

CURVED AIR

UK, female/male vocal/instrumental group – Sonja Kristina Linwood, Rob Martin, Francis Monkman, Florian Pilkington-Miksa & Darryl Way

Date	Title	Peak Position	Weeks at No.1	Weeks on Chart
				32
5 Dec 70	**AIR CONDITIONING** *Warner Brothers WSX 3012*	8		21
9 Oct 71	**CURVED AIR** *Warner Brothers K 46092*	11		6
13 May 72	**PHANTASMAGORIA** *Reprise K 46158*	20		5

MALACHI CUSH

UK, male vocalist

Date	Title	Peak Position	Weeks at No.1	Weeks on Chart
				4
5 Apr 03	**MALACHI** *Mercury/Universal TV 0772802*	17		4

CUTTING CREW

UK/Canada, male vocal/instrumental group

Date	Title	Peak Position	Weeks at No.1	Weeks on Chart
				6
29 Nov 86	**BROADCAST** *Siren SIRENLP 7* ○	41		6

CYPRESS HILL

US, male rap group – Louis 'B-Real' Freese, Eric 'Bobo' Correa, Lawrence 'DJ Muggs' Muggerud & Senen 'Sen Dog' Reyes

Date	Title	Peak Position	Weeks at No.1	Weeks on Chart
				68
7 Aug 93	**BLACK SUNDAY** *Columbia 4740752* ● ★	13		49
11 Nov 95	**CYPRESS HILL III (TEMPLES OF BOOM)** *Columbia 4781279* ○	11		5
24 Aug 96	**UNRELEASED AND REVAMPED** *Columbia 4852302*	29		4
17 Oct 98	**IV** *Columbia 4916046*	25		3
6 May 00	**SKULL & BONES** *Columbia 4951839*	6		5
15 Dec 01	**STONED RAIDERS** *Columbia 5041712*	71		1
3 Apr 04	**TILL DEATH DO US PART** *Columbia 5150292*	53		1

BILLY RAY CYRUS

US, male vocalist/guitarist

Date	Title	Peak Position	Weeks at No.1	Weeks on Chart
				10
29 Aug 92	**SOME GAVE ALL** *Mercury 5106352* ● ★	9		10

MILEY CYRUS

US, female vocalist (Destiny Cyrus)

Date	Title	Peak Position	Weeks at No.1	Weeks on Chart
				25
26 Apr 08	**BEST OF BOTH WORLDS CONCERT** *EMI 2079752* HANNAH MONTANA & MILEY CYRUS	29		4
13 Sep 08	**BREAKOUT** *Hollywood 8712353*	10		21

HOLGAR CZUKAY

Germany, male bass player

Date	Title	Peak Position	Weeks at No.1	Weeks on Chart
				1
2 Apr 88	**PLIGHT AND PREMONITION** *Virgin VE 11* DAVID SYLVIAN & HOLGAR CZUKAY	71		1

D

JUGGY D

UK, male vocalist (Jagwinder Dhaliwal)

Date	Title	Peak Position	Weeks at No.1	Weeks on Chart
				1
4 Sep 04	**JUGGY D** *2Point9 2POINT9100CD*	70		1

D-INFLUENCE

UK, male/female vocal/instrumental group

Date	Title	Peak Position	Weeks at No.1	Weeks on Chart
				1
25 Oct 97	**LONDON** *Echo ECHDD 27*	56		1

D-MOB

UK, male producer (Danny Poku)

Date	Title	Peak Position	Weeks at No.1	Weeks on Chart
				11
11 Nov 89	**A LITTLE BIT OF THIS, A LITTLE BIT OF THAT** *ffrr 8281591*	46		11

D:REAM

UK, male vocalist/producer (Peter Cunnah)

Date	Title	Peak Position	Weeks at No.1	Weeks on Chart
				41
30 Oct 93	**D:REAM ON VOLUME 1** *Magnet 4509933712* ⊛	5		37
30 Sep 95	**WORLD** *Magnet 0630117962* ○	5		4

D-SIDE

Ireland, male vocal group

Date	Title	Peak Position	Weeks at No.1	Weeks on Chart
				1
17 Jan 04	**STRONGER TOGETHER** *Blacklist/Edel 9866006*	62		1

D-TRAIN

US, male vocal/instrumental duo

Date	Title	Peak Position	Weeks at No.1	Weeks on Chart
				4
8 May 82	**D-TRAIN** *Epic EPC 85683*	72		4

DAFT PUNK

France, male instrumental/production duo – Thomas Bangalter & Guy-Manuel de Homem-Christo

Date	Title	Peak Position	Weeks at No.1	Weeks on Chart
				60
1 Feb 97	**HOMEWORK** *Virgin CDV 2821* ●	8		17
24 Mar 01	**DISCOVERY** *Virgin CDVX 2940* ⊛	2		37
26 Mar 05	**HUMAN AFTER ALL** *Virgin CDV2996* ○	10		4
15 Apr 06	**MUSIQUE – VOLUME I – 1993-2005** *Virgin CDVX3019*	34		2

DAISY CHAINSAW

UK, male/female vocal/instrumental group

Date	Title	Peak Position	Weeks at No.1	Weeks on Chart
				1
10 Oct 92	**ELEVENTEEN** *Deva TPLP 100CD*	62		1

DALEK I

UK, male vocal/instrumental group

Date	Title	Peak Position	Weeks at No.1	Weeks on Chart
				2
9 Aug 80	**COMPASS KUMPAS** *Backdoor OPEN 1*	54		2

DALI'S CAR

UK, male vocal/instrumental duo

Date	Title	Peak Position	Weeks at No.1	Weeks on Chart
				1
1 Dec 84	**THE WAKING HOUR** *Paradox DOXLP 1*	84		1

ROGER DALTREY

UK, male vocalist/guitarist. See Who

Date	Title	Peak Position	Weeks at No.1	Weeks on Chart
				24
26 Jul 75	**RIDE A ROCK HORSE** *Polydor 2442 135* ○	14		10
4 Jun 77	**ONE OF THE BOYS** *Polydor 2442 146*	45		1
23 Aug 80	**McVICAR (OST)** *Polydor POLD 5034*	39		11
2 Nov 85	**UNDER A RAGING MOON** *10 Records DIX 17*	52		2

GLEN DALY

UK, male vocalist

Date	Title	Peak Position	Weeks at No.1	Weeks on Chart
				2
20 Nov 71	**GLASGOW NIGHT OUT** *Pye Golden Guinea GGL 0479*	28		2

DAMAGE

UK, male vocal group

Date	Title	Peak Position	Weeks at No.1	Weeks on Chart
				22
19 Apr 97	**FOREVER** *Big Life BLRCD 31X* ○	13		12
14 Apr 01	**SINCE YOU'VE BEEN GONE** *Cooltempo 5289592* ●	16		10

DAMNED

UK, male vocal/instrumental group

Date	Title	Peak Position	Weeks at No.1	Weeks on Chart
				54
12 Mar 77	**DAMNED DAMNED DAMNED** *Stiff SEEZ 1*	36		10
17 Nov 79	**MACHINE GUN ETIQUETTE** *Chiswick CWK 3011* ○	31		5
29 Nov 80	**THE BLACK ALBUM** *Chiswick CWK 3015*	29		3
28 Nov 81	**THE BEST OF THE DAMNED** *Big Beat DAM 1*	43		12
23 Oct 82	**STRAWBERRIES** *Bronze BRON 542*	15		4
27 Jul 85	**PHANTASMAGORIA** *MCA MCF 542* ○	11		17
13 Dec 86	**ANYTHING** *MCA MCG 6015* ○	40		2
12 Dec 87	**LIGHT AT THE END OF THE TUNNEL** *MCA MCSP 312*	87		1

VIC DAMONE

US, male vocalist (Vito Farinola)

Date	Title	Peak Position	Weeks at No.1	Weeks on Chart
				8
25 Apr 81	**NOW** *RCA International INTS 5080*	28		7
2 Apr 83	**VIC DAMONE SINGS THE GREAT SONGS** *Cameo 32261*	87		1

DANA

Ireland, female vocalist (Rosemary Brown)

Date	Title	Peak Position	Weeks at No.1	Weeks on Chart
				3
27 Dec 80	**EVERYTHING IS BEAUTIFUL** *Warwick WW 5099*	43		3

EVAN DANDO
US, male vocalist/guitarist. See Lemonheads

Date	Title	Peak Position	Weeks at No.1	Weeks on Chart (total 1)
29 Mar 03	**BABY I'M BORED** *Setanta SETCD 114*	30		1

SUZANNE DANDO
UK, female exercise instructor

Date	Title	Peak Position	Weeks at No.1	Weeks on Chart (total 1)
17 Mar 84	**SHAPE UP AND DANCE WITH SUZANNE DANDO** *Lifestyle LEG 21*	87		1

DANDY WARHOLS
US, male/female vocal/instrumental group

Date	Title	Peak Position	Weeks at No.1	Weeks on Chart (total 21)
16 May 98	**COME DOWN** *Capitol 8365052*	16		8
24 Jun 00	**THIRTEEN TALES FROM URBAN BOHEMIA** *Capitol 8577872* ●	32		9
31 May 03	**WELCOME TO THE MONKEYHOUSE** *Parlophone 5901232*	20		3
24 Sep 05	**ODDITORIUM OR WARLORDS OF MARS** *Parlophone 8745902*	67		1

D'ANGELO
US, male vocalist (Michael D'Angelo)

Date	Title	Peak Position	Weeks at No.1	Weeks on Chart (total 5)
28 Oct 95	**BROWN SUGAR** *Cooltempo CTCD 46* ●	57		2
26 Feb 00	**VOODOO** *Cooltempo 5233732* ★	21		3

CHARLIE DANIELS BAND
US, male vocal/instrumental group

Date	Title	Peak Position	Weeks at No.1	Weeks on Chart (total 1)
10 Nov 79	**MILLION MILE REFLECTIONS** *Epic EPC 83446*	74		1

DANNY WILSON
UK, male vocal/instrumental group

Date	Title	Peak Position	Weeks at No.1	Weeks on Chart (total 11)
30 Apr 88	**MEET DANNY WILSON** *Virgin V 2419*	65		5
29 Jul 89	**BEEBOP MOPTOP** *Virgin V 2594*	24		5
31 Aug 91	**SWEET DANNY WILSON** *Virgin V 2669*	54		1

DANSE SOCIETY
UK, male vocal/instrumental group

Date	Title	Peak Position	Weeks at No.1	Weeks on Chart (total 4)
11 Feb 84	**HEAVEN IS WAITING** *Society 205 972*	39		4

STEVEN DANTE
UK, male vocalist (Steven Dennis)

Date	Title	Peak Position	Weeks at No.1	Weeks on Chart (total 1)
3 Sep 88	**FIND OUT** *Cooltempo CTLP 6*	87		1

TERENCE TRENT D'ARBY
US, male vocalist/multi-instrumentalist (Sananda Maitreya, b. Terence Trent Howard)

Date	Title	Peak Position	Weeks at No.1	Weeks on Chart (total 96)
25 Jul 87	**INTRODUCING THE HARDLINE ACCORDING TO TERENCE TRENT D'ARBY** *CBS 4509111* ⊛x5	1	9	67
4 Nov 89	**NEITHER FISH NOR FLESH** *CBS 4658091* ●	12		5
15 May 93	**SYMPHONY OR DAMN** *Columbia 4735612* ●	4		19
29 Apr 95	**TERENCE TRENT D'ARBY'S VIBRATOR** *Columbia 4785052*	11		5

DARE
UK, male vocal/instrumental group

Date	Title	Peak Position	Weeks at No.1	Weeks on Chart (total 1)
14 Sep 91	**BLOOD FROM STONE** *A&M 3953601*	48		1

BOBBY DARIN
US, male vocalist/multi-instrumentalist (Walden Robert Cassotto), d. 20 dec 1973 (age 37)

Date	Title	Peak Position	Weeks at No.1	Weeks on Chart (total 22)
19 Mar 60	**THIS IS DARIN** *London HA 2235*	4		8
9 Apr 60	**THAT'S ALL** *London HAE 2172*	15		1
5 Oct 85	**THE LEGEND OF BOBBY DARIN – HIS GREATEST HITS** *Stylus SMR 8504*	39		6
24 Jul 04	**BEYOND THE SEA – THE VERY BEST OF** *warner.esp WSMCD183*	26		7

DARIO G
UK, male DJ/production trio

Date	Title	Peak Position	Weeks at No.1	Weeks on Chart (total 4)
11 Jul 98	**SUNMACHINE** *Eternal 3984233782*	26		4

DARIUS
UK, male vocalist (Darius Danesh)

Date	Title	Peak Position	Weeks at No.1	Weeks on Chart (total 21)
14 Dec 02	**DIVE IN** *Mercury 0635922* ⊛	6		19
6 Nov 04	**LIVE TWICE** *Mercury 9868263*	36		2

DARKNESS
UK, male vocal/instrumental group – Justin Hawkins, Ed Graham, Dan Hawkins & Frankie Poullain

Date	Title	Peak Position	Weeks at No.1	Weeks on Chart (total 50)
19 Jul 03	**PERMISSION TO LAND** *Must Destroy 5046674522* ⊛x4	1	4	46
10 Dec 05	**ONE WAY TICKET TO HELL…AND BACK** *Atlantic 5101112182* ○	11		4

DARLING BUDS
UK, male/female vocal/instrumental group

Date	Title	Peak Position	Weeks at No.1	Weeks on Chart (total 3)
18 Feb 89	**POP SAID** *Epic 4628941*	23		3

DARTS
UK, male/female vocal group – Ian Collier, George Currie, John Dummer, Bob Fish, Den Hegarty, Hammy Howell, d. 13 Jan 1999, Rita Ray, Thump Thomson & Nigel Trubridge

Date	Title	Peak Position	Weeks at No.1	Weeks on Chart (total 57)
3 Dec 77	**DARTS** *Magnet MAG 5020* ●	9		22
3 Jun 78	**EVERYONE PLAY DARTS** *Magnet MAG 5022* ●	12		18
18 Nov 78	**AMAZING DARTS** *Magnet DLP 7981* ●	8		13
6 Oct 79	**DART ATTACK** *Magnet MAG 5030* ○	38		4

DATSUNS
New Zealand, male vocal/instrumental group

Date	Title	Peak Position	Weeks at No.1	Weeks on Chart (total 4)
19 Oct 02	**THE DATSUNS** *V2 VVR 1020962* ○	17		3
19 Jun 04	**OUTTA SIGHT OUTTA MIND** *V2 VVR 1026942*	58		1

DAUGHTRY
US, male vocal/instrumental group

Date	Title	Peak Position	Weeks at No.1	Weeks on Chart (total 3)
1 Sep 07	**DAUGHTRY** *Epic 828768886021*	13		3

CRAIG DAVID
UK, male vocalist

Date	Title	Peak Position	Weeks at No.1	Weeks on Chart (total 113)
26 Aug 00	**BORN TO DO IT** *Wildstar CDWILD 32* ⊛x6	1	2	50
23 Nov 02	**SLICKER THAN YOUR AVERAGE** *Wildstar CDWILD 42* ⊛x2	4		35
3 Sep 05	**THE STORY GOES** *Warner Brothers 2564625222*	5		19
24 Nov 07	**TRUST ME** *Warner Brothers 2564697131*	18		7
6 Dec 08	**GREATEST HITS** *Warner Brothers 825646926978* ○	48		2

F.R. DAVID
France, male vocalist (Robert Fitoussi)

Date	Title	Peak Position	Weeks at No.1	Weeks on Chart (total 6)
7 May 83	**WORDS** *Carrere CAK 145*	46		6

DAVID DEVANT & HIS SPIRIT WIFE
UK, male vocal/instrumental group

Date	Title	Peak Position	Weeks at No.1	Weeks on Chart (total 1)
5 Jul 97	**WORK, LOVELIFE, MISCELLANEOUS** *Kindness KINDCD 1*	70		1

RAY DAVIES
UK, male vocalist/guitarist. See Kinks

Date	Title	Peak Position	Weeks at No.1	Weeks on Chart (total 1)
4 Mar 06	**OTHER PEOPLE'S LIVES** *V2 VVR1035352*	36		1

CARL DAVIS & THE ROYAL LIVERPOOL PHILHARMONIC ORCHESTRA & CHOIR
US, male conductor & orchestra

Date	Title	Peak Position	Weeks at No.1	Weeks on Chart (total 4)
19 Oct 91	**PAUL McCARTNEY'S LIVERPOOL ORATORIO** *EMI Classics PAUL 1*	36		4

MILES DAVIS
US, male trumpet player/band leader, d. 28 Sep 1991 (age 65)

Date	Title	Peak Position	Weeks at No.1	Weeks on Chart (total 10)
18 Jul 70	**BITCHES BREW** *CBS 66236*	71		1
15 Jun 85	**YOU'RE UNDER ARREST** *CBS 26447*	88		1
18 Oct 86	**TUTU** *Warner Brothers 9254901*	74		2
3 Jun 89	**AMANDLA** *Warner Brothers WX 250*	49		2

Silver-selling ○ Gold-selling ● Platinum-selling ⊛ US No.1 ★ | Peak Position | Weeks at No.1 | Weeks on Chart

Date	Album	Peak Position	Weeks at No.1	Weeks on Chart
5 Oct 96	**THE VERY BEST OF MILES DAVIS** *Columbia SONYTV 17CD*	64		1
28 Apr 01	**KIND OF BLUE** *Columbia CK 64935* ●	63		2
26 Aug 06	**THE VERY BEST OF – COOL & COLLECTED** *Columbia 82876847842*	69		1

SAMMY DAVIS JR
US, male vocalist, d. 16 May 1990 (age 64). See Ratpack — **2**

Date	Album	Peak Position	Weeks at No.1	Weeks on Chart
13 Apr 63	**SAMMY DAVIS JR AT THE COCONUT GROVE** *Reprise R 6063/2*	19		1
6 Aug 05	**THE ULTIMATE COLLECTION** *WSM 8122764442*	75		1

SPENCER DAVIS GROUP
UK, male vocal/instrumental group – Spencer Davis, Muff Winwood, Steve Winwood* & Peter York — **47**

Date	Album	Peak Position	Weeks at No.1	Weeks on Chart
8 Jan 66	**THEIR FIRST LP** *Fontana TL 5242*	6		9
22 Jan 66	**THE SECOND ALBUM** *Fontana TL 5295*	3		18
10 Sep 66	**AUTUMN '66** *Fontana TL 5359*	4		20

DAWN
US, male/female vocal group — **2**

Date	Album	Peak Position	Weeks at No.1	Weeks on Chart
4 May 74	**GOLDEN RIBBONS** *Bell BELLS 236*	46		2

DAWN OF THE REPLICANTS
UK, male vocal/instrumental group — **1**

Date	Album	Peak Position	Weeks at No.1	Weeks on Chart
28 Feb 98	**ONE HEAD, TWO ARMS, TWO LEGS** *East West 0630196002*	62		1

DAY ONE
UK, male vocal/instrumental duo — **1**

Date	Album	Peak Position	Weeks at No.1	Weeks on Chart
25 Mar 00	**ORDINARY MAN** *Melankolic CDSAD 8*	70		1

DARREN DAY
UK, male vocalist — **1**

Date	Album	Peak Position	Weeks at No.1	Weeks on Chart
18 Apr 98	**DARREN DAY** *East Coast DAYCD 01*	62		1

DORIS DAY
US, female vocalist/actor (Doris Kappelhoff) — **44**

Date	Album	Peak Position	Weeks at No.1	Weeks on Chart
6 Jan 79	**20 GOLDEN GREATS** *Warwick PR 5053*	12		11
11 Nov 89	**A PORTRAIT OF DORIS DAY** *Stylus SMR 984* ●	32		9
6 Nov 93	**GREATEST HITS** *Telstar TCD 2659* ●	14		12
10 Dec 94	**THE LOVE ALBUM** *Vision VIS CD2*	64		3
20 Nov 99	**THE MAGIC OF THE MOVIES** *Columbia SONYTV 79CD*	63		1
20 Apr 02	**41 HOLLYWOOD GREATS – THE BEST OF** *Columbia 5079632*	73		1
10 Feb 07	**THE MAGIC OF DORIS DAY** *Sony BMG 88697055812*	20		7

TAYLOR DAYNE
US, female vocalist (Leslie Wundermann) — **17**

Date	Album	Peak Position	Weeks at No.1	Weeks on Chart
5 Mar 88	**TELL IT TO MY HEART** *Arista 208898*	24		17

CHRIS DE BURGH
Ireland (b. Argentina), male vocalist/guitarist (Christopher Davidson) — **286**

Date	Album	Peak Position	Weeks at No.1	Weeks on Chart
12 Sep 81	**BEST MOVES** *A&M AMLH 68532*	65		4
9 Oct 82	**THE GETAWAY** *A&M AMLH 58549*	30		16
19 May 84	**MAN ON THE LINE** *A&M AMLX 65002* ○	11		24
29 Dec 84	**THE VERY BEST OF CHRIS DE BURGH** *Telstar STAR 2248* ●	6		70
24 Aug 85	**SPANISH TRAIN AND OTHER STORIES** *A&M AMLH 68343*	78		3
7 Jun 86	**INTO THE LIGHT** *A&M AM 5121* ⊛x2	2		59
4 Oct 86	**CRUSADER** *A&M AMLH 64746*	72		1
15 Oct 88	**FLYING COLOURS** *A&M AMA 5224* ⊛	1	1	30
4 Nov 89	**FROM A SPARK TO A FLAME – THE VERY BEST OF CHRIS DE BURGH** *A&M CDBLP 100* ⊛x2	4		29
22 Sep 90	**HIGH ON EMOTION – LIVE FROM DUBLIN** *A&M 3970861* ●	15		6
9 May 92	**POWER OF TEN** *A&M 3971882* ●	3		10
28 May 94	**THIS WAY UP** *A&M 5402332* ○	5		6
18 Nov 95	**BEAUTIFUL DREAMS** *A&M 5404322* ●	33		8
11 Oct 97	**THE LOVE SONGS** *A&M 5407942* ●	8		7
2 Oct 99	**QUIET REVOLUTION** *A&M 4904462*	23		3
31 Mar 01	**THE ULTIMATE COLLECTION** *Mercury 4908992*	19		4
28 Sep 02	**TIMING IS EVERYTHING** *Mercury 4934292*	41		1
27 Mar 04	**THE ROAD TO FREEDOM** *Ferryman FERRY888*	75		1
21 Oct 06	**THE STORYMAN** *Edel 0174542ERE*	38		1
3 May 08	**NOW AND THEN** *UMTV 5307573*	12		3

DE LA SOUL
US, male vocal/production trio – Posdnuos (Kelvin Mercer), Maseo (Vincent Mason) & Trugoy the Dove (David Jude Jolicoeur) — **88**

Date	Album	Peak Position	Weeks at No.1	Weeks on Chart
25 Mar 89	**3 FEET HIGH AND RISING** *Big Life DLSLP 1* ⊛	13		56
25 May 91	**DE LA SOUL IS DEAD** *Big Life BLRLP 8*	7		11
9 Oct 93	**BUHLOONE MINDSTATE** *Big Life BLRCD 25*	37		2
13 Jul 96	**STAKES IS HIGH** *Tommy Boy TBCD 1149*	42		1
9 Oct 99	**3 FEET HIGH AND RISING** *Tommy Boy TBCD 1019*	17		2
19 Aug 00	**ART OFFICIAL INTELLIGENCE: MOSIAC THUMP** *Tommy Boy TBCD 1348*	22		4
14 Jun 03	**THE BEST OF** *Tommy Boy 8122736652* ●	17		12

WALDO DE LOS RIOS
Argentina, male composer/conductor/orchestra leader (Osvaldo Ferraro Guiterrez), d. 28 Mar 1977 (age 42) — **26**

Date	Album	Peak Position	Weeks at No.1	Weeks on Chart
1 May 71	**SYMPHONIES FOR THE SEVENTIES** *A&M AMLS 2014*	6		26

MANITAS DE PLATA
France, male guitarist (Ricardo Baliardo) — **1**

Date	Album	Peak Position	Weeks at No.1	Weeks on Chart
29 Jul 67	**FLAMENCO GUITAR** *Philips SBL 7786*	40		1

DEACON BLUE
UK, male/female vocal/instrumental group – Ricky Ross*, Graeme Kelling, d. 10 Jun 2004, Lorraine McIntosh, James Prime, Ewen Vernal & Dougie Vipond — **221**

Date	Album	Peak Position	Weeks at No.1	Weeks on Chart
6 Jun 87	**RAINTOWN** *CBS 4505491* ⊛	14		77
15 Apr 89	**WHEN THE WORLD KNOWS YOUR NAME** *CBS 4633211* ⊛x2	1	2	54
22 Sep 90	**OOH LAS VEGAS** *CBS 4672421* ●	3		8
15 Jun 91	**FELLOW HOODLUMS** *Columbia 4685501* ⊛	2		27
13 Mar 93	**WHATEVER YOU SAY, SAY NOTHING** *Columbia 4735272* ●	4		10
16 Apr 94	**OUR TOWN – THE GREATEST HITS OF DEACON BLUE** *Columbia 4766422* ⊛x2	1	2	38
23 Oct 99	**WALKING BACK HOME** *Columbia 4963802*	39		2
12 May 01	**HOMESICK** *Papillion BTFLYCD 0014*	59		1
28 Oct 06	**SINGLES** *Columbia 82876884872*	18		4

DEAD CAN DANCE
Australia, male/female vocal/instrumental duo — **3**

Date	Album	Peak Position	Weeks at No.1	Weeks on Chart
25 Sep 93	**INTO THE LABYRINTH** *4AD CAD 3013CD*	47		1
29 Jun 96	**SPIRITCHASER** *4AD CAD 6008CD*	43		2

DEAD KENNEDYS
US, male vocal/instrumental group — **8**

Date	Album	Peak Position	Weeks at No.1	Weeks on Chart
13 Sep 80	**FRESH FRUIT FOR ROTTING VEGETABLES** *Cherry Red BRED 10* ●	33		6
4 Jul 87	**GIVE ME CONVENIENCE OR GIVE ME DEATH** *Alternative Tentacles VIRUS 5* ●	84		2

DEAD OR ALIVE
UK, male vocal/instrumental group – Pete Burns, Steve Coy, Timothy Lever & Mike Percy — **22**

Date	Album	Peak Position	Weeks at No.1	Weeks on Chart
28 Apr 84	**SOPHISTICATED BOOM BOOM** *Epic EPC 25835*	29		3
25 May 85	**YOUTHQUAKE** *Epic EPC 26420* ●	9		15
14 Feb 87	**MAD, BAD AND DANGEROUS TO KNOW** *Epic 4502571*	27		4

DEAD 60'S
UK, male vocal/instrumental group — **3**

Date	Album	Peak Position	Weeks at No.1	Weeks on Chart
8 Oct 05	**THE DEAD 60'S** *Deltasonic DLTCD038*	23		3

HAZELL DEAN
UK, female vocalist — **3**

Date	Album	Peak Position	Weeks at No.1	Weeks on Chart
22 Oct 88	**ALWAYS** *EMI EMC 3546*	38		3

DEATH CAB FOR CUTIE
US, male vocal/instrumental group – Benjamin Gibbard, Nicholas Harmer, Jason McGerr & Chris Walla — **2**

Date	Album	Peak Position	Weeks at No.1	Weeks on Chart
24 May 08	**NARROW STAIRS** *Fueled By Ramen 7567899465* ★	24		2

DEATH IN VEGAS
UK, male instrumental/production duo — **16**

Date	Title	Peak	Wks at No.1	Wks on Chart
29 Mar 97	**DEAD ELVIS** *Concrete HARD 22LPCD*	52		1
25 Sep 99	**THE CONTINO SESSIONS** *Concrete HARD 41CDU* ○	19		12
28 Sep 02	**SCORPIO RISING** *Concrete HARD 53CD*	19		3

DeBARGE
US, male/female vocal group — **2**

Date	Title	Peak	Wks at No.1	Wks on Chart
25 May 85	**RHYTHM OF THE NIGHT** *Gordy ZL 72340*	94		2

DECLAN
UK, male vocalist (Declan Galbraith) — **3**

Date	Title	Peak	Wks at No.1	Wks on Chart
5 Oct 02	**DECLAN** *Liberty 5416012*	44		3

DAVE DEE, DOZY, BEAKY, MICK & TICH
UK, male vocal/instrumental group – Dave Dee, d. 9 Jan 2009 — **17**

Date	Title	Peak	Wks at No.1	Wks on Chart
2 Jul 66	**DAVE DEE, DOZY, BEAKY, MICK AND TICH** *Fontana STL 5350*	11		10
7 Jan 67	**IF MUSIC BE THE FOOD OF LOVE...PREPARE FOR INDIGESTION** *Fontana STL 5388*	27		5
20 Sep 08	**THE VERY BEST OF** *Universal TV 1782476*	24		2

KIKI DEE
UK, female vocalist (Pauline Matthews) — **11**

Date	Title	Peak	Wks at No.1	Wks on Chart
26 Mar 77	**KIKI DEE** *Rocket ROLA 3*	24		5
18 Jul 81	**PERFECT TIMING** *Ariola ARL 5050*	47		4
9 Apr 94	**THE VERY BEST OF KIKI DEE** *Rocket 5167282*	62		2

DEEE-LITE
US/Russia/Japan, female/male vocal/instrumental group — **19**

Date	Title	Peak	Wks at No.1	Wks on Chart
8 Sep 90	**WORLD CLIQUE** *Elektra EKT 77* ●	14		18
4 Jul 92	**INFINITY WITHIN** *Elektra 7559613132*	37		1

DEEJAY PUNK-ROC
US, male DJ/producer (Charles Gettis) — **1**

Date	Title	Peak	Wks at No.1	Wks on Chart
30 May 98	**CHICKENEYE** *Independiente ISOM 5CD*	47		1

DEEP BLUE SOMETHING
US, male vocal/instrumental group — **5**

Date	Title	Peak	Wks at No.1	Wks on Chart
5 Oct 96	**HOME** *Interscope IND 90002*	24		5

DEEP DISH
Iran, male/instrumental/production duo — **3**

Date	Title	Peak	Wks at No.1	Wks on Chart
18 Jul 98	**JUNK SCIENCE** *Deconstruction 74321580342*	37		2
6 Aug 05	**GEORGE IS ON** *Positiva 3313382*	54		1

DEEP FOREST
France, male instrumental/production duo — **17**

Date	Title	Peak	Wks at No.1	Wks on Chart
26 Feb 94	**DEEP FOREST** *Columbia 4741782* ●	15		11
3 Jun 95	**BOHEME** *Columbia 4786232*	12		5
31 Jan 98	**COMPARSA** *Columbia 4887252*	60		1

DEEP PURPLE
UK, male vocal/instrumental group – Ian Gillan*, Ritchie Blackmore, Roger Glover, Jon Lord & Ian Paice; members also included David Coverdale* (1973–1976) — **282**

Date	Title	Peak	Wks at No.1	Wks on Chart
24 Jan 70	**CONCERTO FOR GROUP AND ORCHESTRA** *Harvest SHVL 767*	26		4
20 Jun 70	**DEEP PURPLE IN ROCK** *Harvest SHVL 777*	4		68
18 Sep 71	**FIREBALL** *Harvest SHVL 793*	1	1	25
15 Apr 72	**MACHINE HEAD** *Purple TPSA 7504* ●	1	3	24
6 Jan 73	**MADE IN JAPAN** *Purple TPSP 351* ●	16		14
17 Feb 73	**WHO DO WE THINK WE ARE** *Purple TPSA 7508*	4		11
2 Mar 74	**BURN** *Purple TPA 3505* ●	3		21
23 Nov 74	**STORM BRINGER** *Purple TPS 3508* ○	6		12
5 Jul 75	**24 CARAT PURPLE** *Purple TPSM 2002* ○	14		17
22 Nov 75	**COME TASTE THE BAND** *Purple TPSA 7515* ○	19		4
27 Nov 76	**DEEP PURPLE MADE IN EUROPE** *Purple TPSA 7517*	12		6
21 Apr 79	**THE MARK II PURPLE SINGLES** *Purple TPS 3514*	24		6
19 Jul 80	**DEEPEST PURPLE** *Harvest EMTV 25* ●	1	1	15
13 Dec 80	**IN CONCERT** *Harvest SHDW 4121/4122*	30		8
4 Sep 82	**DEEP PURPLE LIVE IN LONDON** *Harvest SHSP 4124*	23		5
10 Nov 84	**PERFECT STRANGERS** *Polydor POLH 16* ●	5		15
29 Jun 85	**THE ANTHOLOGY** *Harvest PUR 1*	50		3
24 Jan 87	**THE HOUSE OF BLUE LIGHT** *Polydor POLH 32* ○	10		9
16 Jul 88	**NOBODY'S PERFECT** *Polydor PODV 10*	38		2
3 Nov 90	**SLAVES AND MASTERS** *RCA PL 90535*	45		2
7 Aug 93	**THE BATTLE RAGES ON...** *RCA 74321154202*	21		3
17 Feb 96	**PURPENDICULAR** *RCA 74321338022*	58		1
31 Jan 98	**MADE IN JAPAN** *EMI 8578642*	73		1
24 Oct 98	**VERY BEST OF DEEP PURPLE** *EMI 4968072*	39		2
18 Jun 05	**THE PLATINUM COLLECTION** *EMI 5785912*	39		2
5 Apr 08	**THE VERY BEST OF** *EMI 2131212*	43		2

DEEPEST BLUE
Israel/UK, male vocal/production duo — **3**

Date	Title	Peak	Wks at No.1	Wks on Chart
19 Jun 04	**LATE SEPTEMBER** *Open OPENCD3* ○	22		3

DEF LEPPARD
UK, male vocal/instrumental group – Joe Elliott, Rick Allen, Steve Clark, d. 8 Jan 1991 (replaced by Vivian Campbell), Phil Collen & Rick Savage — **200**

Date	Title	Peak	Wks at No.1	Wks on Chart
22 Mar 80	**ON THROUGH THE NIGHT** *Vertigo 9102 040*	15		8
25 Jul 81	**HIGH 'N' DRY** *Vertigo 6359 045*	26		8
12 Mar 83	**PYROMANIA** *Vertigo VERS 2* ○	18		8
29 Aug 87	**HYSTERIA** *Bludgeon Riffola HYSLP 1* ⊛x2 ★	1	1	101
11 Apr 92	**ADRENALIZE** *Bludgeon Riffola 5109782* ● ★	1	1	30
16 Oct 93	**RETRO ACTIVE** *Bludgeon Riffola 5183052*	6		5
4 Nov 95	**VAULT – THE GREATEST HITS 1980–1995** *Bludgeon Riffola 5286572* ⊛x2	3		14
25 May 96	**SLANG** *Bludgeon Riffola 5324862* ●	5		8
26 Jun 99	**EUPHORIA** *Bludgeon Riffola 5462442*	11		5
24 Aug 02	**X** *Bludgeon Riffola 0631202*	14		3
6 Nov 04	**BEST OF** *Mercury 9868512* ●	6		7
3 Jun 06	**YEAH** *Mercury 9858285*	52		1
17 May 08	**SONGS FROM THE SPARKLE LOUNGE** *Mercury 1762675*	10		2

DEFINITION OF SOUND
UK, male rap duo — **3**

Date	Title	Peak	Wks at No.1	Wks on Chart
29 Jun 91	**LOVE AND LIFE** *Circa 14*	38		3

DEFTONES
US, male vocal/instrumental group – Chino Moreno, Stephen Carpenter, Chi Cheng, Abe Cunningham & Frank Delgado — **8**

Date	Title	Peak	Wks at No.1	Wks on Chart
8 Nov 97	**AROUND THE FUR** *Maverick 9362468102* ○	56		1
1 Jul 00	**WHITE PONY** *Maverick 9362477992*	13		2
24 Mar 01	**BACK TO SCHOOL (MINI MAGGIT)** *WEA 9362480822*	35		1
31 May 03	**DEFTONES** *Maverick 9362483912*	7		3
11 Nov 06	**SATURDAY NIGHT WRIST** *Maverick 9362432392*	33		1

DEICIDE
US, male vocal/instrumental group — **1**

Date	Title	Peak	Wks at No.1	Wks on Chart
13 May 95	**ONCE UPON THE CROSS** *Roadrunner RR 89492*	66		1

DESMOND DEKKER
Jamaica, male vocalist (Desmond Dacres) — **4**

Date	Title	Peak	Wks at No.1	Wks on Chart
5 Jul 69	**THIS IS DESMOND DEKKER** *Trojan TTL 4*	27		4

DEL AMITRI
UK, male vocal/instrumental group – Justin Currie, Andy Alston, David Cummings, Iain Harvie & Brian McDermott (replaced by Ashley Soan) — **108**

Date	Title	Peak	Wks at No.1	Wks on Chart
24 Feb 90	**WAKING HOURS** *A&M AMA 9006* ⊛x2	6		44
13 Jun 92	**CHANGE EVERYTHING** *A&M 3953852* ●	2		20
11 Mar 95	**TWISTED** *A&M 5403112* ●	3		25
12 Jul 97	**SOME OTHER SUCKER'S PARADE** *A&M 5407052*	6		5
19 Sep 98	**THE BEST OF DEL AMITRI – HATFUL OF RAIN** *Mercury 5410312* ●	5		11
20 Apr 02	**CAN YOU DO ME GOOD** *Mercury 4932162*	30		3

Silver-selling ○ · Gold-selling ● · Platinum-selling ⊛ · US No.1 ★ · Peak Position · Weeks at No.1 · Weeks on Chart

DE'LACY
US, male/female vocal/instrumental group — 1

Date	Title / Label	Peak Position	Weeks at No.1	Weeks on Chart
1 Jul 95	**HIDEAWAY** *Slip 'N' Slide SLIP 023*	53		1

DELAKOTA
UK, male vocal/instrumental duo — 1

Date	Title / Label	Peak Position	Weeks at No.1	Weeks on Chart
3 Oct 98	**ONE LOVE** *Go. Beat 5578612*	58		1

DELANEY & BONNIE & FRIENDS
US, male/female vocal duo – Delaney Bramlett, d. 27 Dec 2008 (age 69), & Bonnie Bramlett — 3

Date	Title / Label	Peak Position	Weeks at No.1	Weeks on Chart
6 Jun 70	**ON TOUR WITH ERIC CLAPTON** *Atlantic 2400 013*	39		3

DELAYS
UK, male vocal/instrumental group — 7

Date	Title / Label	Peak Position	Weeks at No.1	Weeks on Chart
17 Apr 04	**FADED SEASIDE GLAMOUR** *Rough Trade RTRADDVCD114* ○	17		4
18 Mar 06	**YOU SEE COLOURS** *Rough Trade RTRADCD214*	24		2
17 May 08	**EVERYTHING'S THE RUSH** *Fiction 1758391*	26		1

DELGADOS
UK, male/female vocal/instrumental group — 3

Date	Title / Label	Peak Position	Weeks at No.1	Weeks on Chart
20 Jun 98	**PELOTON** *Chemikal Underground CHEM 024CD*	56		1
29 Apr 00	**THE GREAT EASTERN** *Chemikal Underground CHEM 040CD*	72		1
26 Oct 02	**HATE** *Mantra MNTCD 1031*	57		1

DELIRIOUS?
UK, male vocal/instrumental group — 6

Date	Title / Label	Peak Position	Weeks at No.1	Weeks on Chart
28 Jun 97	**KING OF FOOLS** *Furious? FURYCD 1*	13		3
24 Apr 99	**MEZZAMORPHIS** *Furious? FURYCD 002*	25		2
18 Aug 01	**AUDIO LESSNOVER** *Furious? FURYCD4*	58		1

DEMON
UK, male vocal/instrumental group — 5

Date	Title / Label	Peak Position	Weeks at No.1	Weeks on Chart
14 Aug 82	**THE UNEXPECTED GUEST** *Carrere CAL 139*	47		3
2 Jul 83	**THE PLAGUE** *Clay CLAYLP 6*	73		2

CHAKA DEMUS & PLIERS
Jamaica, male vocal duo – Everton Bonner & John Taylor — 30

Date	Title / Label	Peak Position	Weeks at No.1	Weeks on Chart
10 Jul 93	**TEASE ME** *Mango CIDM 1102* ⊛	1	2	30

CATHY DENNIS
UK, female vocalist — 35

Date	Title / Label	Peak Position	Weeks at No.1	Weeks on Chart
10 Aug 91	**MOVE TO THIS** *Polydor 8495031* ●	3		31
23 Jan 93	**INTO THE SKYLINE** *Polydor 5139352*	8		4

SANDY DENNY
UK, female vocalist. See Fairport Convention, Fotheringay — 2

Date	Title / Label	Peak Position	Weeks at No.1	Weeks on Chart
2 Oct 71	**THE NORTH STAR GRASSMAN AND THE RAVENS** *Island ILPS 9765*	31		2

JOHN DENVER
US, male vocalist/guitarist (Henry John Deutschendorf), d. 12 Oct 1997 (age 53) — 256

Date	Title / Label	Peak Position	Weeks at No.1	Weeks on Chart
17 Mar 73	**ROCKY MOUNTAIN HIGH** *RCA Victor SF 2308*	11		15
2 Jun 73	**POEMS, PRAYERS AND PROMISES** *RCA Victor SF 8219*	19		5
23 Jun 73	**RHYMES AND REASONS** *RCA Victor SF 8348* ○	21		5
30 Mar 74	**THE BEST OF JOHN DENVER** *RCA Victor APL1 0374* ●	7		69
7 Sep 74	**BACK HOME AGAIN** *RCA Victor APL1 0548* ● ★	3		29
22 Mar 75	**AN EVENING WITH JOHN DENVER** *RCA Victor LSA 3211/12*	31		4
11 Oct 75	**WIND SONG** *RCA Victor APL1 1183* ★	14		21
15 May 76	**LIVE IN LONDON** *RCA Victor RS 1050*	2		29
4 Sep 76	**SPIRIT** *RCA Victor APL1 1694*	9		11
19 Mar 77	**BEST OF JOHN DENVER VOLUME 2** *RCA Victor PL 42120* ●	9		9
11 Feb 78	**I WANT TO LIVE** *RCA Victor PL 12561*	25		5
21 Apr 79	**JOHN DENVER** *RCA Victor PL 13075*	68		1
28 Nov 81	**PERHAPS LOVE** *CBS 73592* PLACIDO DOMINGO & JOHN DENVER	17		21
22 Oct 83	**IT'S ABOUT TIME** *RCA RCALP 6087*	90		2
1 Dec 84	**JOHN DENVER – COLLECTION** *Telstar STAR 2253* ●	20		11
23 Aug 86	**ONE WORLD** *RCA PL 85811*	91		3
22 Mar 97	**THE ROCKY MOUNTAIN COLLECTION** *RCA 07863668372* ●	19		9
2 Oct 04	**A SONG'S BEST FRIEND – THE VERY BEST OF** *RCA 82876652742*	18		7

KARL DENVER
UK, male vocalist (Angus McKenzie), d. 21 Dec 1998 (age 67) — 27

Date	Title / Label	Peak Position	Weeks at No.1	Weeks on Chart
23 Dec 61	**WIMOWEH** *Ace Of Clubs ACL 1098*	7		27

DEPECHE MODE
UK, male vocal/instrumental group – Dave Gahan*, Vince Clarke (replaced by Alan Wilder), Andy Fletcher & Martin Gore — 197

Date	Title / Label	Peak Position	Weeks at No.1	Weeks on Chart
14 Nov 81	**SPEAK AND SPELL** *Mute STUMM 5* ●	10		33
9 Oct 82	**A BROKEN FRAME** *Mute STUMM 9* ●	8		11
3 Sep 83	**CONSTRUCTION TIME AGAIN** *Mute STUMM 13* ●	6		12
6 Oct 84	**SOME GREAT REWARD** *Mute STUMM 19* ○	5		12
26 Oct 85	**THE SINGLES 81-85** *Mute MUTEL 1* ●	6		22
29 Mar 86	**BLACK CELEBRATION** *Mute STUMM 26* ○	4		11
10 Oct 87	**MUSIC FOR THE MASSES** *Mute STUMM 47* ○	10		4
25 Mar 89	**101** *Mute STUMM 101* ○	5		8
31 Mar 90	**VIOLATOR** *Mute STUMM 64* ●	2		30
3 Apr 93	**SONGS OF FAITH AND DEVOTION** *Mute CDSTUMM 106* ● ★	1	1	16
26 Apr 97	**ULTRA** *Mute CDSTUMM 148* ●	1	1	11
10 Oct 98	**THE SINGLES 86-98** *Mute CDMUTEL 005* ●	5		6
7 Nov 98	**THE SINGLES 81-85** *Mute LCDMUTEL 1*	57		1
26 May 01	**EXCITER** *Mute CDSTUMM 190*	9		4
6 Nov 04	**REMIXES 81-04** *Mute XLCDMUTEL8*	24		2
29 Oct 05	**PLAYING THE ANGEL** *Mute LCDSTUMM260*	6		4
25 Nov 06	**THE BEST OF – VOLUME 1** *Mute LCDMUTEL15* ●	18		10

DEREK & THE DOMINOS
See Eric Clapton — 1

Date	Title / Label	Peak Position	Weeks at No.1	Weeks on Chart
24 Mar 73	**DEREK AND THE DOMINOS IN CONCERT** *RSO 2659 020*	36		1

DES'REE
UK, female vocalist (Desiree Weekes) — 27

Date	Title / Label	Peak Position	Weeks at No.1	Weeks on Chart
29 Feb 92	**MIND ADVENTURES** *Dusted Sound 4712632* ○	26		5
21 May 94	**I AIN'T MOVIN'** *Dusted Sound 4758432*	13		6
11 Jul 98	**SUPERNATURAL** *Dusted Sound 4897192*	16		16

DESTINY'S CHILD
US, female vocal group – Beyoncé Knowles*, LeToya Luckett, Latavia Roberson, Kelly Rowland* & Michelle Williams — 169

Date	Title / Label	Peak Position	Weeks at No.1	Weeks on Chart
14 Mar 98	**DESTINY'S CHILD** *Columbia 4885352*	45		4
7 Aug 99	**THE WRITING'S ON THE WALL** *Columbia 4943942* ⊛x3	10		87
12 May 01	**SURVIVOR** *Columbia 5017832* ⊛x3 ★	1	4	44
30 Mar 02	**THIS IS THE REMIX** *Columbia 5076272*	25		3
27 Nov 04	**DESTINY FULFILLED** *Columbia 5179162* ⊛	5		21
5 Nov 05	**NO 1'S** *Columbia 82876740332* ★	6		10

MARCELLA DETROIT
US, female vocalist/guitarist (Marcella Levy). See Shakespear's Sister — 5

Date	Title / Label	Peak Position	Weeks at No.1	Weeks on Chart
9 Apr 94	**JEWEL** *London 8284912* ○	15		5

DETROIT SPINNERS
US, male vocal group — 3

Date	Title / Label	Peak Position	Weeks at No.1	Weeks on Chart
14 May 77	**DETROIT SPINNERS' SMASH HITS** *Atlantic K 50363*	37		3

DEUCE
UK, male/female vocal group — 2

Date	Title / Label	Peak Position	Weeks at No.1	Weeks on Chart
9 Sep 95	**ON THE LOOSE** *London 8286642*	18		2

dEUS
Belgium, male vocal/instrumental group — 1

Date	Title / Label	Peak Position	Weeks at No.1	Weeks on Chart
3 Apr 99	**THE IDEAL CRASH** *Island CID 8082*	64		1

SIDNEY DEVINE

UK, male vocalist — **11**

Date	Title / Label	Peak Position	Weeks at No.1	Weeks on Chart
10 Apr 76	**DOUBLE DEVINE** *Philips 6625 019*	14		10
11 Dec 76	**DEVINE TIME** *Philips 6308 283*	49		1

DEVO

US, male vocal/instrumental group — **22**

Date	Title / Label	Peak Position	Weeks at No.1	Weeks on Chart
16 Sep 78	**Q: ARE WE NOT MEN? A: NO WE ARE DEVO** *Virgin V 2106*	12		7
23 Jun 79	**DUTY NOW FOR THE FUTURE** *Virgin V 2125*	49		6
24 May 80	**FREEDOM OF CHOICE** *Virgin V 2162*	47		5
5 Sep 81	**NEW TRADITIONALISTS** *Virgin V 2191*	50		4

HOWARD DEVOTO

UK, male vocalist (Howard Trafford). See Buzzcocks, Magazine — **2**

Date	Title / Label	Peak Position	Weeks at No.1	Weeks on Chart
6 Aug 83	**JERKY VERSIONS OF THE DREAM** *Virgin V 2272*	57		2

DEXYS MIDNIGHT RUNNERS

UK, male/female vocal/instrumental group – Kevin Rowland, Billy Adams, Kevin 'Al' Archer, Helen O'Hara, Seb Shelton & various musicians — **80**

Date	Title / Label	Peak Position	Weeks at No.1	Weeks on Chart
26 Jul 80	**SEARCHING FOR THE YOUNG SOUL REBELS** *Parlophone PCS 7213*	6		10
7 Aug 82	**TOO-RYE-AY** *Mercury MERS 5* KEVIN ROWLAND & DEXY'S MIDNIGHT RUNNERS ⊛x3	2		46
26 Mar 83	**GENO** *EMI EMS 1007*	79		2
21 Sep 85	**DON'T STAND ME DOWN** *Mercury MERH 56*	22		6
8 Jun 91	**THE VERY BEST OF DEXY'S MIDNIGHT RUNNERS** *Mercury 8464601*	12		15
4 Oct 03	**LET'S MAKE THIS PRECIOUS – THE BEST OF** *EMI 5926802*	75		1

JIM DIAMOND

UK, male vocalist. See PhD — **5**

Date	Title / Label	Peak Position	Weeks at No.1	Weeks on Chart
22 May 93	**JIM DIAMOND** *Polygram TV 8438472*	16		5

NEIL DIAMOND

US, male vocalist/guitarist. Celebrated singer/songwriter, who first found UK fame writing for The Monkees, has been one of the most popular live entertainers and top album sellers on both sides of the Atlantic for 40 years — **676**

Date	Title / Label	Peak Position	Weeks at No.1	Weeks on Chart
13 Mar 71	**GOLD** *Uni UNLS 116*	23		13
20 Mar 71	**TAP ROOT MANUSCRIPT** *Uni UNLS 117*	19		14
11 Dec 71	**STONES** *Uni UNLS 121*	17		21
5 Aug 72	**MOODS** *Uni UNLS 128*	7		19
17 Jan 73	**HOT AUGUST NIGHT** *Uni ULD 1*	21		20
16 Feb 74	**JONATHAN LIVINGSTONE SEAGULL (OST)** *CBS 69047*	35		1
9 Mar 74	**RAINBOW** *MCA MCF 2529*	39		5
29 Jun 74	**HIS 12 GREATEST HITS** *MCA MCF 2550*	13		78
9 Nov 74	**SERENADE** *CBS 69067*	11		14
10 Jul 76	**BEAUTIFUL NOISE** *CBS 86004*	10		26
12 Mar 77	**LOVE AT THE GREEK** *CBS 95001* ⊛	3		32
6 Aug 77	**HOT AUGUST NIGHT** *MCA MCSP 255*	60		1
17 Dec 77	**I'M GLAD YOU'RE HERE WITH ME TONIGHT** *CBS 86044*	16		11
25 Nov 78	**20 GOLDEN GREATS** *MCA EMTV 14* ⊛	2		29
6 Jan 79	**YOU DON'T BRING ME FLOWERS** *CBS 86077*	15		23
19 Jan 80	**SEPTEMBER MORN** *CBS 86096*	14		11
22 Nov 80	**THE JAZZ SINGER (OST)** *Capitol EAST 12120* ⊛	3		110
28 Feb 81	**LOVE SONGS** *MCA MCF 3092*	43		6
5 Dec 81	**THE WAY TO THE SKY** *CBS 85343*	39		13
19 Jun 82	**12 GREATEST HITS VOLUME 2** *CBS 85844*	32		8
13 Nov 82	**HEARTLIGHT** *CBS 25073*	43		10
10 Dec 83	**THE VERY BEST OF NEIL DIAMOND** *K-Tel NE 1265*	33		11
28 Jul 84	**PRIMITIVE** *CBS 86306*	7		10
24 May 86	**HEADED FOR THE FUTURE** *CBS 26952*	36		8
28 Nov 87	**HOT AUGUST NIGHT II** *CBS 4604081*	74		4
25 Feb 89	**THE BEST YEARS OF OUR LIVES** *CBS 4632011*	42		6
9 Nov 91	**LOVESCAPE** *Columbia 4688901*	36		13
4 Jul 92	**THE GREATEST HITS 1966–1992** *Columbia 4715022* ⊛	1	3	30
28 Nov 92	**THE CHRISTMAS ALBUM** *Columbia 4724102*	50		6
9 Oct 93	**UP ON THE ROOF – SONGS FROM THE BRILL BUILDING** *Columbia 4743562*	28		10
17 Feb 96	**TENNESSEE MOON (THE NASHVILLE COLLECTION)** *Columbia 4813782*	12		13
25 May 96	**THE BEST OF NEIL DIAMOND** *MCA MCD 11452*	68		1
31 Aug 96	**THE ULTIMATE COLLECTION** *Sony TV/MCA MOODCD 45*	5		20
14 Nov 98	**THE MOVIE ALBUM – AS TIME GOES BY** *Columbia 4916552*	68		2
15 Sep 01	**THREE CHORD OPERA** *Columbia 5024932*	49		1
16 Mar 02	**THE ESSENTIAL COLLECTION** *Columbia 5010662*	11		12
4 Mar 06	**12 SONGS** *Columbia SNY77508*	5		10
9 Dec 06	**THE BEST OF** *MCA MCD11452*	30		9
26 Jan 08	**THE ESSENTIAL** *Columbia/UMTV 5010662*	11		9
24 May 08	**HOME BEFORE DARK** *Columbia 88697154652* ⊛ ★	1	1	15
31 May 08	**THE BEST OF** *UMTV 9838711*	7		21

DIAMOND HEAD

UK, male vocal/instrumental group — **9**

Date	Title / Label	Peak Position	Weeks at No.1	Weeks on Chart
23 Oct 82	**BORROWED TIME** *MCA DH 1001*	24		5
24 Sep 83	**CANTERBURY** *MCA DH 1002*	32		4

DICKIES

US, male vocal/instrumental group — **19**

Date	Title / Label	Peak Position	Weeks at No.1	Weeks on Chart
17 Feb 79	**THE INCREDIBLE SHRINKING DICKIES** *A&M AMLE 64742*	18		17
24 Nov 79	**DAWN OF THE DICKIES** *A&M AMLE 68510*	60		2

BRUCE DICKINSON

UK, male vocalist/guitarist. See Iron Maiden, Samson — **16**

Date	Title / Label	Peak Position	Weeks at No.1	Weeks on Chart
19 May 90	**TATTOOED MILLIONAIRE** *EMI EMC 3574*	14		9
18 Jun 94	**BALLS TO PICASSO** *EMI CDEMX 1057*	21		3
9 Mar 96	**SKUNKWORTHS** *Raw Power RAWCD 106*	41		1
24 May 97	**ACCIDENT OF BIRTH** *Raw Power ESMCD 767*	53		1
26 Sep 98	**THE CHEMICAL WEDDING** *Air Raid AIRCD 1*	55		1
4 Jun 05	**TYRANNY OF SOULS** *Sanctuary Midline MYNCD035*	50		1

BARBARA DICKSON

UK, female vocalist/guitarist — **145**

Date	Title / Label	Peak Position	Weeks at No.1	Weeks on Chart
18 Jun 77	**MORNING COMES QUICKLY** *RSO 2394 188*	58		1
12 Apr 80	**THE BARBARA DICKSON ALBUM** *Epic EPC 84088*	7		12
16 May 81	**YOU KNOW IT'S ME** *Epic EPC 84551*	39		6
6 Feb 82	**ALL FOR A SONG** *Epic 10030* ⊛	3		38
24 Sep 83	**TELL ME IT'S NOT TRUE 'FROM THE MUSICAL BLOOD BROTHERS'** *Legacy LLM 101*	100		1
23 Jun 84	**HEARTBEATS** *Epic EPC 25706*	21		8
12 Jan 85	**THE BARBARA DICKSON SONGBOOK** *K-Tel NE 1287*	5		19
23 Nov 85	**GOLD** *K-Tel ONE 1312* ⊛	11		18
15 Nov 86	**THE VERY BEST OF BARBARA DICKSON** *Telstar STAR 2276*	78		8
29 Nov 86	**THE RIGHT MOMENT** *K-Tel ONE 1335*	39		8
6 May 89	**COMING ALIVE AGAIN** *Telstar STAR 2349*	30		7
15 Aug 92	**DON'T THINK TWICE IT'S ALL RIGHT** *Columbia MOODCD 25*	32		5
28 Nov 92	**THE BEST OF ELAINE PAIGE AND BARBARA DICKSON TOGETHER** *Telstar TCD 2632* ELAINE PAIGE & BARBARA DICKSON	22		9
5 Mar 94	**PARCEL OF ROGUES** *Castle Communications CTVCD 126*	30		3
20 Mar 04	**THE PLATINUM COLLECTION** *Sony Music TV 5161092*	35		2

BO DIDDLEY

US, male vocalist/guitarist (Ellas Bates, aka Ellas McDaniel), d. 2 Jun 2008 (age 79) — **16**

Date	Title / Label	Peak Position	Weeks at No.1	Weeks on Chart
5 Oct 63	**BO DIDDLEY** *Pye International NPL 28026*	11		8
9 Nov 63	**BO DIDDLEY IS A GUNSLINGER** *Pye NJL 33*	20		1
30 Nov 63	**BO DIDDLEY RIDES AGAIN** *Pye International NPL 28029*	19		1
15 Feb 64	**BO DIDDLEY'S BEACH PARTY** *Pye NPL 28032*	13		6

DIDO

UK, female vocalist/multi-instrumentalist (Florian Cloud de Bounevialle Armstrong) — **193**

Date	Title / Label	Peak Position	Weeks at No.1	Weeks on Chart
28 Oct 00	**NO ANGEL** *Cheeky 74321832742* ⊛x9	1	7	133
11 Oct 03	**LIFE FOR RENT** *Cheeky 82876545982* ⊛x7	1	10	54
29 Nov 08	**SAFE TRIP HOME** *Cheeky 88697162972*	2		6+

DIESEL PARK WEST

UK, male vocal/instrumental group — **3**

Date	Title / Label	Peak Position	Weeks at No.1	Weeks on Chart
11 Feb 89	**SHAKESPEARE ALABAMA** *Food FOODLP 2*	55		2
15 Feb 92	**DECENCY** *Food FOODCD 7*	57		1

DIFFORD & TILBROOK

UK, male vocal/instrumental duo. See Squeeze — **3**

Date	Title / Label	Peak Position	Weeks at No.1	Weeks on Chart
14 Jul 84	**DIFFORD AND TILBROOK** *A&M AMLX 64985*	47		3

Key: Silver-selling ○ · Gold-selling ● · Platinum-selling ⊛ · US No.1 ★ · Peak Position · Weeks at No.1 · Weeks on Chart

DIGITAL UNDERGROUND
US, male rap group

Date	Title	Label	Peak	Wks at No.1	Wks on Chart (total 2)
7 Apr 90	**SEX PACKETS**	*BCM 377LP*	59		1
30 Jun 90	**DOOWUTCHYALIKE/PACKET MAN**	*BCM 463X*	59		1

DILATED PEOPLES
US, male vocal/DJ/production group

Date	Title	Label	Peak	Wks at No.1	Wks on Chart (total 1)
2 Mar 02	**EXPANSION TEAM**	*Capitol 5314772*	55		1

RICHARD DIMBLEBY
UK, male broadcaster, d. 22 Dec 1965 (age 52)

Date	Title	Label	Peak	Wks at No.1	Wks on Chart (total 5)
4 Jun 66	**THE VOICE OF RICHARD DIMBLEBY**	*MFP 1087*	14		5

DINOSAUR JR
US, male vocalist/guitarist – Joseph Mascis

Date	Title	Label	Peak	Wks at No.1	Wks on Chart (total 8)
2 Mar 91	**GREEN MIND**	*Blanco Y Negro BYN 24*	36		2
20 Feb 93	**WHERE YOU BEEN**	*Blanco Y Negro 4509916272*	10		3
10 Sep 94	**WITHOUT A SOUND**	*Blanco Y Negro 4509969332*	24		2
12 May 07	**BEYOND**	*PIAS PILO70CD*	52		1

DIO
UK/US, male vocal/instrumental group – Ronnie James Dio, Vinny Appice, Jimmy Bain, Vivian Campbell & Claude Schnell

Date	Title	Label	Peak	Wks at No.1	Wks on Chart (total 48)
11 Jun 83	**HOLY DIVER**	*Vertigo VERS 5* ○	13		15
21 Jul 84	**THE LAST IN LINE**	*Vertigo VERL 16* ○	4		14
7 Sep 85	**SACRED HEART**	*Vertigo VERH 30*	4		6
5 Jul 86	**INTERMISSION**	*Vertigo VERB 40*	22		5
22 Aug 87	**DREAM EVIL**	*Vertigo VERH 46*	8		5
26 May 90	**LOCK UP THE WOLVES**	*Vertigo 8460331*	28		3

DION & THE BELMONTS
US, male vocal trio

Date	Title	Label	Peak	Wks at No.1	Wks on Chart (total 5)
12 Apr 80	**20 GOLDEN GREATS**	*K-Tel NE 1057*	31		5

CELINE DION
Canada, female vocalist. The multi-award winning bilingual chanteuse, who won the Eurovision Song Contest for Switzerland in 1988, joined a select group of artists when, in 2007, her record label Sony BMG announced that she had sold over 200 million records worldwide

Date	Title	Label	Peak	Wks at No.1	Wks on Chart (total 453)
5 Mar 94	**THE COLOUR OF MY LOVE**	*Epic 4747432* ⊛x5	1	7	109
16 Sep 95	**UNISON**	*Epic 4672032*	55		3
7 Oct 95	**D'EUX – THE FRENCH ALBUM**	*Epic 4802862* ●	7		9
23 Mar 96	**FALLING INTO YOU**	*Epic 4837922* ⊛x7 ★	1	1	113
9 Nov 96	**LIVE A PARIS**	*Epic 4866062*	53		1
15 Mar 97	**C'EST POUR VIVRE**	*Nectar Masters EURCD 405*	49		3
29 Nov 97	**LET'S TALK ABOUT LOVE**	*Epic 4891592* ⊛x6 ★	1	5	73
19 Sep 98	**S'IL SUFFISAIT D'AIMER**	*Epic 4918592* ●	17		4
26 Sep 98	**CELINE DION**	*Epic 4715089*	70		2
14 Nov 98	**THESE ARE SPECIAL TIMES**	*Epic 4927302* ●	20		10
27 Nov 99	**ALL THE WAY. . .A DECADE OF SONGS**	*Epic 4960942* ⊛x2 ★	1	1	57
11 Nov 00	**THE COLLECTOR'S SERIES VOLUME 1**	*Epic 5009952*	30		3
6 Apr 02	**A NEW DAY HAS COME**	*Epic 5062262* ⊛ ★	1	4	23
5 Apr 03	**ONE HEART**	*Epic 5108772* ●	4		10
26 Jun 04	**A NEW DAY – LIVE IN LAS VEGAS**	*Columbia 5152253*	22		4
23 Oct 04	**MIRACLE**	*Columbia 5187487* ●	5		5
24 Nov 07	**TAKING CHANCES**	*Columbia 88697081142* ⊛	5		15
8 Nov 08	**MY LOVE: ESSENTIAL COLLECTION**	*Sony BMG 88697411422*	5		9+

Top 3 Best-Selling Albums

	Title	Approximate Sales
1	FALLING INTO YOU	2,115,000
2	LET'S TALK ABOUT LOVE	1,995,000
3	THE COLOUR OF MY LOVE	1,850,000

DIRE STRAITS
UK, male vocal/instrumental group – Mark Knopfler*, Alan Clark, Guy Fletcher, John Illsley, David Knopfler (replaced by Hal Lindes) & Pick Withers (replaced by Terry Williams). Stadium-packing, record-shattering rock superstars who released five albums that spent over 100 weeks on the chart. *Brothers In Arms* reached No.1 in 22 countries and the band have sold more than 100 million albums worldwide

Date	Title	Label	Peak	Wks at No.1	Wks on Chart (total 1146)
22 Jul 78	**DIRE STRAITS**	*Vertigo 9102 021* ⊛x2	5		132
23 Jun 79	**COMMUNIQUE**	*Vertigo 9102 031* ⊛	5		32
25 Oct 80	**MAKING MOVIES**	*Vertigo 6359 034* ⊛x2	4		251
2 Oct 82	**LOVE OVER GOLD**	*Vertigo 6359 109* ⊛x2	1	4	200
24 Mar 84	**ALCHEMY – DIRE STRAITS LIVE**	*Vertigo VERY 11* ⊛	3		163
25 May 85	**BROTHERS IN ARMS**	*Vertigo VERH 25* ⊛x13	1	14	228
29 Oct 88	**MONEY FOR NOTHING**	*Vertigo VERH 64* ⊛x4	1	3	64
21 Sep 91	**ON EVERY STREET**	*Vertigo 5101601* ⊛x2	1	1	35
22 May 93	**ON THE NIGHT**	*Vertigo 5147662*	4		7
8 Jul 95	**LIVE AT THE BBC**	*Windsong WINCD 072X*	71		1
31 Oct 98	**SULTANS OF SWING – THE VERY BEST OF DIRE STRAITS**	*Vertigo 5586582* ●	6		23
19 Nov 05	**PRIVATE INVESTIGATIONS**	*Mercury 9873054* & MARK KNOPFLER ●	20		7
6 Sep 08	**BROTHERS IN ARMS**	*Vertigo 8244992*	59		3

DIRTY PRETTY THINGS
UK, male vocal/instrumental group – Carl Barât, Didz Hammond, Gary Powell & Anthony Rossomando

Date	Title	Label	Peak	Wks at No.1	Wks on Chart (total 12)
20 May 06	**WATERLOO TO ANYWHERE**	*Vertigo 9856134* ●	3		11
12 Jul 08	**ROMANCE AT SHORT NOTICE**	*Vertigo 1772351*	35		1

DIRTY VEGAS
UK, male production trio

Date	Title	Label	Peak	Wks at No.1	Wks on Chart (total 3)
17 Aug 02	**DIRTY VEGAS**	*Credence 5399852* ○	40		3

DISCHARGE
UK, male vocal/instrumental group

Date	Title	Label	Peak	Wks at No.1	Wks on Chart (total 5)
15 May 82	**HEAR NOTHING, SEE NOTHING, SAY NOTHING**	*Clay CLAYLP 3*	40		5

DISPOSABLE HEROES OF HIPHOPRISY
US, male rap/instrumental duo

Date	Title	Label	Peak	Wks at No.1	Wks on Chart (total 3)
16 May 92	**HYPOCRISY IS THE GREATEST LUXURY**	*Fourth & Broadway BRCD 584*	40		3

SACHA DISTEL
France, male vocalist, d. 22 Jul 2004 (age 71)

Date	Title	Label	Peak	Wks at No.1	Wks on Chart (total 14)
2 May 70	**SACHA DISTEL**	*Warner Brothers WS 3003*	21		14

DISTILLERS
Australia/US, male/female vocal/instrumental group

Date	Title	Label	Peak	Wks at No.1	Wks on Chart (total 1)
25 Oct 03	**CORAL FANG**	*Sire 9362484202*	46		1

DISTURBED
US, male vocal/instrumental group

Date	Title	Label	Peak	Wks at No.1	Wks on Chart (total 5)
5 Oct 02	**BELIEVE**	*Reprise WB 483202* ★	41		1
1 Oct 05	**TEN THOUSAND FISTS**	*Reprise 9362494572* ○ ★	59		1
14 Jun 08	**INDESTRUCTABLE**	*Reprise 9362498782* ★	20		3

DIVINE COMEDY
UK, male vocalist/guitarist (Neil Hannon)

Date	Title	Label	Peak	Wks at No.1	Wks on Chart (total 47)
11 May 96	**CASANOVA**	*Setanta SETCD 025* ●	48		9
22 Feb 97	**A SHORT ALBUM ABOUT LOVE**	*Setanta SETCD 036*	13		6
12 Sep 98	**FIN DE SIECLE**	*Setanta SETCD 057* ●	9		14
11 Sep 99	**A SECRET HISTORY – THE BEST OF DIVINE COMEDY**	*Setanta SETCDL 100* ●	3		11
24 Mar 01	**REGENERATION**	*Parlophone 5317612* ○	14		3
10 Apr 04	**ABSENT FRIENDS**	*Parlophone 5962802*	23		3
1 Jul 06	**VICTORY FOR THE COMIC MUSE**	*Parlophone 3677962*	43		1

Silver-selling ○ Gold-selling ● Platinum-selling ⊛ US No.1 ★ — Peak Position, Weeks at No.1, Weeks on Chart

DIVINE WORKS
Germany, male producer (Claus Zundel). See Sacred Spirit — Weeks on chart: 2

Date	Title	Label	Peak	Wks at No.1	Wks on Chart
16 Aug 97	DIVINE WORKS	Virgin VTCD 119	43		2

DIVINYLS
Australia, female/male vocal/instrumental duo — Weeks on chart: 1

Date	Title	Label	Peak	Wks at No.1	Wks on Chart
20 Jul 91	DIVINYLS	Virgin America VUSLP 30	59		1

DIXIE CHICKS
US, female vocal/instrumental trio — Weeks on chart: 32

Date	Title	Label	Peak	Wks at No.1	Wks on Chart
3 Jul 99	WIDE OPEN SPACES	Epic 4898422 ○	26		6
11 Sep 99	FLY	Epic 4951512 ★	38		2
22 Mar 03	HOME	Epic 5096032 ●	33		13
24 Jun 06	TAKING THE LONG WAY	Open Wide 82876807392 ● ★	10		11

ALESHA DIXON
UK, female vocalist/rapper. See Mis-Teeq — Weeks on chart: 5

Date	Title	Label	Peak	Wks at No.1	Wks on Chart
6 Dec 08	THE ALESHA SHOW	Asylum 5186510332 ●	26		5+

DJ FORMAT
UK, male DJ/producer (Matt Ford) — Weeks on chart: 1

Date	Title	Label	Peak	Wks at No.1	Wks on Chart
23 Apr 05	IF YOU CAN'T JOIN 'EM BEAT 'EM	Genuine GEN030LTDCD	73		1

DJ HYPE PRESENTS GANJA KRU
UK, male producer (Kevin Ford) — Weeks on chart: 1

Date	Title	Label	Peak	Wks at No.1	Wks on Chart
30 Aug 97	NEW FRONTIERS (EP)	Parousia 74321501072	56		1

DJ KRUSH
Japan, male producer (Hideaki Ishi) — Weeks on chart: 2

Date	Title	Label	Peak	Wks at No.1	Wks on Chart
3 Sep 94	BAD BROTHERS (RONNY JORDAN MEETS DJ KRUSH)	Island IMCD 8024	58		1
11 Nov 95	MEISO	Mo Wax MW 039CD	64		1

DJ QUICKSILVER
Turkey, male DJ/producer (Orhan Terzi) — Weeks on chart: 3

Date	Title	Label	Peak	Wks at No.1	Wks on Chart
7 Mar 98	QUICKSILVER	Positiva 4934942	26		3

DJ SAMMY
Spain, male DJ/producer (Samuel Bouriah) — Weeks on chart: 9

Date	Title	Label	Peak	Wks at No.1	Wks on Chart
22 Mar 03	HEAVEN	Data/Ministry Of Sound DATACD 01X ●	14		9

DJ SHADOW
US, male producer (Josh Davis) — Weeks on chart: 9

Date	Title	Label	Peak	Wks at No.1	Wks on Chart
28 Sep 96	ENTRODUCING...	Mo Wax MW 059CD ●	17		3
15 Jun 02	THE PRIVATE PRESS	Island CIDD 8118 ●	8		3
30 Sep 06	THE OUTSIDER	Island 1703468	24		3

DMX
US, male rapper (Earl Simmons) — Weeks on chart: 14

Date	Title	Label	Peak	Wks at No.1	Wks on Chart
3 Nov 01	THE GREAT DEPRESSION	Def Jam 5864502 ○ ★	20		3
27 Sep 03	GRAND CHAMP	Def Jam 9861021 ★	6		8
15 Aug 06	YEAR OF THE DOG AGAIN	Columbia 82876878862	22		3

DO ME BAD THINGS
UK, male/female vocal/instrumental group — Weeks on chart: 1

Date	Title	Label	Peak	Wks at No.1	Wks on Chart
23 Apr 05	YES	Must Destroy 5046775732	68		1

DOCTOR & THE MEDICS
UK, male/female vocal/instrumental group — Weeks on chart: 3

Date	Title	Label	Peak	Wks at No.1	Wks on Chart
21 Jun 86	LAUGHING AT THE PIECES	I.R.S. MIRG 1010	25		3

DR DRE
US, male rapper/producer (Andre Young). See N.W.A. — Weeks on chart: 80

Date	Title	Label	Peak	Wks at No.1	Wks on Chart
27 Nov 99	2001	Interscope 4904862 ●	4		76
9 Sep 00	THE CHRONIC	Interscope 7567922332 ○	43		4

DR. FEELGOOD
UK, male vocal/instrumental group – Lee Brilleaux, d. 7 Apr 1994, The Big Figure (John Martin), Wilko Johnson & John B. Sparks — Weeks on chart: 33

Date	Title	Label	Peak	Wks at No.1	Wks on Chart
18 Oct 75	MALPRACTICE	United Artists UAS 29880 ○	17		6
2 Oct 76	STUPIDITY	United Artists UAS 29990 ○	1	1	9
4 Jun 77	SNEAKIN' SUSPICION	United Artists UAS 30075	10		6
8 Oct 77	BE SEEING YOU	United Artists UAS 30123	55		3
7 Oct 78	PRIVATE PRACTICE	United Artists UAG 30184	41		5
2 Jun 79	AS IT HAPPENS	United Artists UAK 30239	42		4

DR. HOOK
US, male vocal/instrumental group – Dennis Locorriere, Rik Elswit, Billy Francis, Bob Henke & Ray Sawyer — Weeks on chart: 166

Date	Title	Label	Peak	Wks at No.1	Wks on Chart
26 Jun 76	A LITTLE BIT MORE	Capitol EST 23795 ●	5		42
29 Oct 77	MAKING LOVE AND MUSIC	Capitol EST 11632	39		4
27 Oct 79	PLEASURE AND PAIN	Capitol EAST 11859	47		6
17 Nov 79	SOMETIMES YOU WIN	Capitol EST 12018 ●	14		44
29 Nov 80	RISING	Mercury 6302 076 ○	44		5
6 Dec 80	DR. HOOK'S GREATEST HITS	Capitol EST 26037 ⊛	2		28
14 Nov 81	DR. HOOK LIVE IN THE UK	Capitol EST 26706	90		1
13 Jun 92	COMPLETELY HOOKED – THE BEST OF DR. HOOK	Capitol CDESTV 2 ⊛	3		19
13 Feb 99	LOVE SONGS	EMI 4979432 ●	8		8
10 Mar 07	HITS AND HISTORY	Capitol 3865022 ●	14		9

DR. JOHN
US, male vocalist/pianist (Mac Rebennack) — Weeks on chart: 3

Date	Title	Label	Peak	Wks at No.1	Wks on Chart
27 Jun 98	ANUTHA ZONE	Parlophone 4954902	33		3

KEN DODD
UK, male vocalist/comedian — Weeks on chart: 36

Date	Title	Label	Peak	Wks at No.1	Wks on Chart
25 Dec 65	TEARS OF HAPPINESS	Columbia 33SX 1793	6		12
23 Jul 66	HITS FOR NOW AND ALWAYS	Columbia SX 6060	14		11
14 Jan 67	FOR SOMEONE SPECIAL	Columbia SCX 6224	40		1
29 Nov 80	20 GOLDEN GREATS OF KEN DODD	Warwick WW 5098 ●	8		12

DODGY
UK, male vocal/instrumental group – Nigel Clark, Andy Miller & Mathew Priest — Weeks on chart: 54

Date	Title	Label	Peak	Wks at No.1	Wks on Chart
5 Jun 93	THE DODGY ALBUM	A&M 5400822	75		1
5 Nov 94	HOMEGROWN	A&M 5402822 ○	28		14
29 Jun 96	FREE PEACE SWEET	A&M 5405732 ⊛	7		38
17 Oct 98	ACE A'S + KILLER B'S	A&M 5410182	55		1

DOES IT OFFEND YOU, YEAH?
UK, male vocal/instrumental group — Weeks on chart: 1

Date	Title	Label	Peak	Wks at No.1	Wks on Chart
5 Apr 08	YOU HAVE NO IDEA WHAT YOU'RE GETTING YOURSELF INTO	Virgin CDV3045	48		1

DOG EAT DOG
US, male vocal/instrumental group — Weeks on chart: 2

Date	Title	Label	Peak	Wks at No.1	Wks on Chart
27 Jul 96	PLAY GAMES	Roadrunner RR 88762	40		2

DOGS D'AMOUR
UK, male vocal/instrumental group — Weeks on chart: 12

Date	Title	Label	Peak	Wks at No.1	Wks on Chart
22 Oct 88	IN THE DYNAMITE JET SALOON	China WOL 8	97		1
25 Mar 89	A GRAVEYARD OF EMPTY BOTTLES	China 8390741	16		4
30 Sep 89	ERROL FLYNN	China 8397001	22		3
6 Oct 90	STRAIGHT	China 8437961	32		2
7 Sep 91	DOG'S HITS AND THE BOOTLEG ALBUM	China WOL 1020	58		1
15 May 93	...MORE UNCHARTED HEIGHTS OF DISGRACE	China WOLCD 1032	30		1

Dr Dre

IN December 2008, it was announced that 50 Cent was the music world's highest-earning star of the year, with a staggering income of just over $100 million; in previous years, the white Detroit rap sensation Eminem had also been at the top of similar lists; likewise, Snoop Dogg, the laconic and towering Dogg Father of modern gangsta rap, and recent acolyte The Game – and they all share one common denominator: the production genius of Dr Dre.

His school attendance was poor but it was noted that, when he did attend, he achieved high grades

Although it is easy to become almost bored by the sheer extent of rap's omnipotence as the world's most commercially successful music genre, it is important to remember the handful of originators, the pioneers who were recording music long before it was multi-million-selling, before radio and TV supported it (at all), before the police stopped staking out its main protagonists.

Dr Dre is one such originator. Born Andrew Romelle Young in February1965, as a child he was thrust into the urban decay and precarious reality of Compton, south-central LA's violent, drug-riddled inner-city ghetto. Inevitably, Young's childhood was far from straightforward and by his mid-teens he was a regular visitor to the Eve After Dark club, where he started mingling with the underground names on the burgeoning rap circuit. Interestingly, his school attendance was poor but it was noted that, when he did attend, he achieved high grades. As a performer, he started off as Dr J – the Master of Mixology – then mutated this into using his first name abbreviated too.

Nonetheless, his eye was roving away from the schoolroom and soon he began to formulate ideas for his first group – The World Class Wreckin' Crew, whose single 'Surgery' was a massive hit on the local scene (selling 50,000 copies in Compton alone). But Dre's vision was always beyond the confines of his suffocatingly dangerous locale. After meeting Ice Cube in 1986, he began recording songs for Ruthless Records, run by erstwhile rap legend Eazy-E. But it was the next step that sent Dre stratospheric.

Dre really pierced the mainstream consciousness – or rather disturbed it – with NWA, the crew who took Public Enemy's racially charged political template and fired it up into savagely profane, angry and compelling anti-establishment pieces. NWA never backed off from controversy and their more brutal take on Public Enemy's righteous ire won fans quickly and in huge numbers. This was partly due to their refusal to gloss over the ugly reality of life on the streets of LA, their songs about street violence and the black gangster lifestyle was just day-to-day life in Compton. Instead of Chuck D's political positivity, NWA immersed themselves in the street violence and held up a mirror to modern America. It was not a pretty sight, especially to the powers that be – and their notoriety exploded with the hugely controversial anthem 'Fuck Tha Police'. Despite being tracked by the FBI, despite no radio play, their album *Straight Outta Compton* was a massive hit. Dre was now a known face in a global phenomenon.

Before NWA started splintering, Dre produced their second album, which catapulted him into a position he commands to this day – as one of the truly great super-producers. When you scan the artists he has produced, it reads like a *Who's Who* of rap's greatest names. Like Timbaland after him, part of Dre's appeal was his refusal to use obvious samples and his willingness to write genuinely stunning music – played by actual musicians – alongside the more standard sampled structures of so many of his lesser contemporaries.

But Dre was never going to be just a producer – he co-founded Death Row Records, one of rap's highest-profile labels; he swiftly became one of the key figures

Biggest-Selling Album				
Artist	Album	Week	Highest Position	Approx Sales
DR DRE	2001	27/11/99	4	985,000

in the 1990s rap boom that saw the genre storm mainstream America, whilst conversely he seemed to be rapping about darker and more dangerous themes.

In 2001, Dre released his own album called *The Chronic*, a record that will be a cornerstone of rap history for ever. The list of tracks that are considered rap classics pretty much reads just as the track-listing of the album itself, piece by piece: consider then such monumental cuts as 'Nuthin' But A "G" Thang', 'Let Me Ride' and 'F**k With Dre Day'.

Dre's instantly distinctive production style created G-funk, which became the predominant rap form of the 1990s (also known as gangsta-funk, renowned for its laconic tempos, female backing vocals, synthesised backdrops and the blending of funk sounds with distinctive sampling). Perhaps his work with Snoop Dogg – on *The Chronic* but also on the latter's own solo records – is the pinnacle of his earlier production work.

The Chronic was a massive multi-platinum smash and asserted Dre's rightful claim to being both rap's most sought-after producer and also its leading solo light. Yet, Dre has never shied away from championing potential 'rivals' to his crown and it is this laser-guided ability to spot the next rap sensation that has cemented his comprehensive contribution to the remarkable progress of the genre in the last twenty years. For example, when Death Row started to crumble, he set up Aftermath Records. After an initial period of slow progress, with the encouragement of Jimmy Iovine, CEO of Aftermath's parent label, Interscope, Dre signed a young white rapper called Eminem aka Marshall Mathers. The latter's own rap legacy is widely documented but suffice to say that taking a 'white-trash' boy and placing him in the mainstream with a truly authentic rap background broke all the rules of modern American music. Eminem is, of course, a fantastic rapper but it's Dr Dre's musical backdrops that have fuelled the project, they are instantly catchy slices of sly pop funk, with clever samples that combine unlikely sources into one whole – indisputable proof of Dr Dre's production genius. Certainly Dre's legendary work ethic fuels this creative spark to such heights – one anecdote recounts that he made an up-and-coming rap artist record a bar of vocals over 100 times to get it exactly right.

Dre's Midas Touch is exponentially wider than just Snoop and Eminem. His family tree extends further, to cover Mary J. Blige and The Game, one of the most exciting and focused artists in recent years and, perhaps most famously of all, 50 Cent. Dre's production of Fiddy's debut album, *Get Rich Or Die Tryin'* is nothing short of bewildering in its scope. In the accompanying video for opening hit single, 'In Da Club' (which launched 50 Cent onto the world), both Eminem and Dre were featured as scientists in lab coats who had seemingly 'created' this new artist. It's a simple visual analogy for much of what Dre has achieved, creating so many classic rap records, producing still more, influencing generations of performers, re-inventing the way record labels operate

Dre's instantly distinctive production style created G-funk

and, all the time, retaining an air of musical knowledge and calm dignity that is sometimes lacking in his numerous counterparts.

Dre is now involved in film production and there *still* seems no limit to what he can achieve. Sadly, in August 2008, it was reported that Dre's son, Andre Young Jnr, had passed away suddenly. Dre went into mourning and has yet to emerge with his long-awaited new concept album *Detox*. When he recovers from this terrible tragedy and releases this record (scheduled for 2009), it will surely remind the waiting world why his beacon burns so brightly across the entire landscape of rap history.

Silver-selling ○ Gold-selling ● Platinum-selling ⊛ US No.1 ★ | Peak Position · Weeks at No.1 · Weeks on Chart

DOGS DIE IN HOT CARS

UK, male/female vocal/instrumental group — Weeks on Chart: 2

Date	Title	Peak	Wks at No.1	Wks on Chart
24 Jul 04	**PLEASE DESCRIBE YOURSELF** *V2 VVR 1027142*	44		2

DOKKEN

US, male vocal/instrumental group — Weeks on Chart: 1

Date	Title	Peak	Wks at No.1	Wks on Chart
21 Nov 87	**BACK FOR THE ATTACK** *Elektra EKT 43*	96		1

THOMAS DOLBY

UK, male vocalist/multi-instrumentalist (Thomas Robertson) — Weeks on Chart: 29

Date	Title	Peak	Wks at No.1	Wks on Chart
22 May 82	**THE GOLDEN AGE OF WIRELESS** *Venice In Peril VIP 1001*	65		10
18 Feb 84	**THE FLAT EARTH** *Parlophone Odeon PCS 2400341* ○	14		14
7 May 88	**ALIENS ATE MY BUICK** *Manhattan MTL 1020*	30		3
8 Aug 92	**ASTRONAUTS AND HERETICS** *Virgin CDV 2701*	35		2

DOLLAR

UK, male/female vocal duo — Weeks on Chart: 28

Date	Title	Peak	Wks at No.1	Wks on Chart
15 Sep 79	**SHOOTING STARS** *Carrere CAL 111*	36		8
24 Apr 82	**THE VERY BEST OF DOLLAR** *Carrere CAL 3001* ○	31		9
30 Oct 82	**THE DOLLAR ALBUM** *WEA DTV 1* ○	18		11

PLACIDO DOMINGO

Spain, male vocalist — Weeks on Chart: 217

Date	Title	Peak	Wks at No.1	Wks on Chart
28 Nov 81	**PERHAPS LOVE** *CBS 73592* PLACIDO DOMINGO & JOHN DENVER ●	17		21
21 May 83	**MY LIFE FOR A SONG** *CBS 73683*	31		8
23 Mar 85	**ANDREW LLOYD WEBBER: REQUIEM** *HMV ALW 1* SARAH BRIGHTMAN, PAUL MILES-KINGSTON, WINCHESTER CATHEDRAL CHOIR & THE ENGLISH CHAMBER ORCHESTRA CONDUCTED BY LORIN MAAZEL ⊛	4		18
27 Dec 86	**PLACIDO DOMINGO COLLECTION** *Stylus SMR 625*	30		14
23 Apr 88	**GREATEST LOVE SONGS** *CBS 44701*	63		2
17 Jun 89	**THE ESSENTIAL DOMINGO** *Deutsche Grammophon PDTV 1* ●	20		8
17 Jun 89	**GOYA…A LIFE IN A SONG** *CBS 4632941*	36		4
1 Sep 90	**IN CONCERT** *Decca 4304331* LUCIANO PAVAROTTI, PLACIDO DOMINGO & JOSE CARRERAS ⊛x5	1	5	78
24 Nov 90	**BE MY LOVE…AN ALBUM OF LOVE** *EMI EMTV 54*	14		12
7 Dec 91	**THE BROADWAY I LOVE** *East West 9031755901* WITH THE LONDON SYMPHONY ORCHESTRA CONDUCTED BY EUGENE KOHN ○	45		6
13 Jun 92	**DOMINGO: ARIAS AND SPANISH SONGS** *Deutsche Grammophon 4371122* ○	47		3
8 Aug 92	**FROM THE OFFICIAL BARCELONA GAMES CEREMONY** *RCA Red Seal 9026612042* , JOSE CARRERAS & MONTSERRAT CABALLE	41		3
25 Dec 93	**CHRISTMAS IN VIENNA** *Sony Classical SK 53358* , DIANA ROSS & JOSE CARRERAS	71		2
10 Sep 94	**THE THREE TENORS IN CONCERT 1994** *Teldec 4509962002* CARRERAS DOMINGO PAVAROTTI WITH ORCHESTRA CONDUCTED BY ZUBIN MEHTA ⊛x2	1	1	26
10 Dec 94	**CHRISTMAS IN VIENNA II** *Sony Classical SK 64304* DIONNE WARWICK PLACIDO DOMINGO	60		2
29 Aug 98	**THE THREE TENORS PARIS 1998** *Decca 4605002* CARRERAS DOMINGO PAVAROTTI WITH JAMES LEVINE	14		6
28 Oct 00	**SONGS OF LOVE** *EMI CDC 5571042*	53		2
23 Dec 00	**THE THREE TENORS CHRISTMAS** *Sony Classical SK 89131* CARRERAS/DOMINGO/PAVAROTTI FEATURING MEHTA	57		2

FATS DOMINO

US, male vocalist/pianist (Antoine Domino) — Weeks on Chart: 3

Date	Title	Peak	Wks at No.1	Wks on Chart
16 May 70	**VERY BEST OF FATS DOMINO** *Liberty LBS 83331*	56		1
6 Mar 04	**THE BEST OF** *EMI 5964972*	58		2

LONNIE DONEGAN

UK, male vocalist/guitarist/banjo player (Anthony Donegan), d. 4 Nov 2002 (age 71) — Weeks on Chart: 69

Date	Title	Peak	Wks at No.1	Wks on Chart
17 Nov 56	**LONNIE DONEGAN SHOWCASE** *Pye Nixa NPT 19012*	2		22
12 Jul 58	**LONNIE** *Pye Nixa NPT 19027*	3		13
1 Sep 62	**GOLDEN AGE OF DONEGAN** *Pye Golden Guinea GGL 0135*	3		23
9 Feb 63	**GOLDEN AGE OF DONEGAN VOLUME 2** *Pye Golden Guinea GGL 0170*	15		3
25 Feb 78	**PUTTING ON THE STYLE** *Chrysalis CHR 1158*	51		3
29 Jan 00	**THE SKIFFLE SESSIONS – LIVE IN BELFAST** *Venture CDVE 945* VAN MORRISON/LONNIE DONEGAN/CHRIS BARBER	14		3
8 Mar 03	**PUTTIN' ON THE STYLE – THE GREATEST HITS** *Castle Music TVSAN002*	45		2

TANYA DONELLY

US, female vocalist/guitarist. See Belly, Throwing Muses — Weeks on Chart: 1

Date	Title	Peak	Wks at No.1	Wks on Chart
20 Sep 97	**LOVESONGS FOR UNDERDOGS** *4AD CAD 7008CD*	36		1

DONOVAN

UK, male vocalist/guitarist (Donovan Leitch) — Weeks on Chart: 76

Date	Title	Peak	Wks at No.1	Wks on Chart
5 Jun 65	**WHAT'S BIN DID AND WHAT'S BIN HID** *Pye NPL 18117*	3		16
6 Nov 65	**FAIRY TALE** *Pye NPL 18128*	20		2
8 Jul 67	**SUNSHINE SUPERMAN** *Pye NPL 18181*	25		7
14 Oct 67	**UNIVERSAL SOLDIER** *Marble Arch MAL 718*	5		18
11 May 68	**A GIFT FROM A FLOWER TO A GARDEN** *Pye NSPL 20000*	13		14
12 Sep 70	**OPEN ROAD** *Dawn DNLS 3009*	30		4
24 Mar 73	**COSMIC WHEELS** *Epic EPC 65450*	15		12
12 Aug 06	**THE BEST OF – SUNSHINE SUPERMAN** *EMI 3718282*	47		3

JASON DONOVAN

Australia, male vocalist/actor — Weeks on Chart: 139

Date	Title	Peak	Wks at No.1	Wks on Chart
13 May 89	**TEN GOOD REASONS** *PWL HF 7* ⊛x5	1	4	54
9 Jun 90	**BETWEEN THE LINES** *PWL HF 14* ⊛	2		26
31 Aug 91	**JOSEPH AND THE AMAZING TECHNICOLOUR DREAMCOAT (ORIGINAL LONDON STAGE CAST SOUNDTRACK)** *Really Useful/Polydor 5111301* ORIGINAL LONDON STAGE CAST SOUNDTRACK ⊛	1	2	38
28 Sep 91	**GREATEST HITS** *PWL HF 20*	9		17
11 Sep 93	**ALL AROUND THE WORLD** *Polydor 8477452*	27		2
22 Nov 08	**LET IT BE ME** *Decca 4781029*	28		2

DOOBIE BROTHERS

US, male vocal/instrumental group — Weeks on Chart: 33

Date	Title	Peak	Wks at No.1	Wks on Chart
30 Mar 74	**WHAT WERE ONCE VICES ARE NOW HABITS** *Warner Brothers K 56206* ○	19		10
17 May 75	**STAMPEDE** *Warner Brothers K 56094* ○	14		11
10 Apr 76	**TAKIN' IT TO THE STREETS** *Warner Brothers K 56196* ○	42		2
17 Sep 77	**LIVING ON THE FAULT LINE** *Warner Brothers K 56383*	25		5
11 Oct 80	**ONE STEP CLOSER** *Warner Brothers K 56824*	53		2
10 Jul 04	**GREATEST HITS** *WSM 8122765112*	45		3

DOOLEYS

UK, male vocal/instrumental group – Jim Dooley, Al Bogan, Anne, Frank, Helen, John & Kathy Dooley & Bob Walsh — Weeks on Chart: 27

Date	Title	Peak	Wks at No.1	Wks on Chart
30 Jun 79	**BEST OF THE DOOLEYS** *GTO GTTV 038* ●	6		21
3 Nov 79	**THE CHOSEN FEW** *GTO GTLP 040*	56		4
25 Oct 80	**FULL HOUSE** *GTO GTTV 050*	54		2

VAL DOONICAN

Ireland, male vocalist/guitarist (Michael Doonican) — Weeks on Chart: 173

Date	Title	Peak	Wks at No.1	Wks on Chart
12 Dec 64	**LUCKY 13 SHADES OF VAL DOONICAN** *Decca LK 4648*	2		27
3 Dec 66	**GENTLE SHADES OF VAL DOONICAN** *Decca LK 4831*	5		52
2 Dec 67	**VAL DOONICAN ROCKS BUT GENTLY** *Pye NSPL 18204*	1	3	23
30 Nov 68	**VAL** *Pye NSPL 18236*	6		11
14 Jun 69	**THE WORLD OF VAL DOONICAN** *Decca SPA 3*	2		31
13 Dec 69	**SOUNDS GENTLE** *Pye NSPL 18321*	22		9
19 Dec 70	**THE MAGIC OF VAL DOONICAN** *Philips 6642 003*	34		3
27 Nov 71	**THIS IS VAL DOONICAN** *Philips 6382 017*	40		1
22 Feb 75	**I LOVE COUNTRY MUSIC** *Philips 9299 261*	37		2
21 May 77	**SOME OF MY BEST FRIENDS ARE SONGS** *Philips 6641 607* ●	29		5
24 Mar 90	**SONGS FROM MY SKETCHBOOK** *Parkfield PMLP 5014* ○	33		6
11 Oct 08	**THE VERY BEST OF** *UMTV 5312558*	33		3

DOORS

US, male vocal/instrumental group – Jim Morrison, d. 3 Jul 1971, John Densmore, Robby Krieger & Ray Manzarek — Weeks on Chart: 120

Date	Title	Peak	Wks at No.1	Wks on Chart
28 Sep 68	**WAITING FOR THE SUN** *Elektra EKS7 4024* ● ★	16		10
11 Apr 70	**MORRISON HOTEL** *Elektra EKS 75007*	12		8
26 Sep 70	**ABSOLUTELY LIVE** *Elektra 2665 002*	69		1
31 Jul 71	**L.A. WOMAN** *Elektra K 42090* ●	28		4
1 Apr 72	**WEIRD SCENES INSIDE THE GOLD MINE** *Elektra K 62009*	50		1
29 Oct 83	**ALIVE, SHE CRIED** *Elektra 9602691*	36		5
4 Jul 87	**LIVE AT THE HOLLYWOOD BOWL** *Elektra EKT 40*	51		3
6 Apr 91	**THE DOORS (OST)** *Elektra EKT 85* ●	11		17
20 Apr 91	**THE BEST OF THE DOORS** *Elektra EKT 21* ○	17		18
20 Apr 91	**THE DOORS** *Elektra K 42012*	43		15
1 Jun 91	**IN CONCERT** *Elektra EKT 88* ○	24		5
21 Mar 98	**THE BEST OF THE DOORS** *Elektra K9803452*	37		8

Date	Title / Label	Peak Position	Weeks at No.1	Weeks on Chart
23 Sep 00	**THE BEST OF THE DOORS** *Elektra 1592812* ○	9		19
25 Jun 05	**THE BEST OF** *Elektra 7559625692*	71		1
7 Apr 07	**THE VERY BEST OF** *Elektra/Rhino 8122799959*	15		5

LEE DORSEY

US, male vocalist (Irving Dorsey), d. 1 Dec 1986 (age 61) — **4**

Date	Title / Label	Peak Position	Weeks at No.1	Weeks on Chart
17 Dec 66	**NEW LEE DORSEY** *Stateside SSL 10192*	34		4

DOUBLE

Switzerland, male vocal/instrumental duo — **4**

Date	Title / Label	Peak Position	Weeks at No.1	Weeks on Chart
8 Mar 86	**BLUE** *Polydor POLD 5187*	69		4

DOUBLE TROUBLE

UK, male production/instrumental duo – Michael Menson, d. 13 Feb 1997, & Laigh Guest — **1**

Date	Title / Label	Peak Position	Weeks at No.1	Weeks on Chart
4 Aug 90	**AS ONE** *Desire LULP 6*	73		1

CRAIG DOUGLAS

UK, male vocalist (Terence Perkins) — **2**

Date	Title / Label	Peak Position	Weeks at No.1	Weeks on Chart
6 Aug 60	**CRAIG DOUGLAS** *Top Rank BUY 049*	17		2

DOVES

UK, male vocal/instrumental group – Jimi Goodwin & Andy & Jez Williams — **54**

Date	Title / Label	Peak Position	Weeks at No.1	Weeks on Chart
15 Apr 00	**LOST SOULS** *Heavenly HVNLP 26CD* ⊛	16		16
11 May 02	**THE LAST BROADCAST** *Heavenly HVNLP 35CD* ●	1	2	23
11 Oct 03	**LOST SIDES** *Heavenly HVNLP 46CDX*	50		1
5 Mar 05	**SOME CITIES** *Heavenly HVNLP50CDX* ●	1	1	14

DOWN

US, male vocal/instrumental group — **2**

Date	Title / Label	Peak Position	Weeks at No.1	Weeks on Chart
30 Sep 95	**NOLA** *Atlantic 7559618302*	68		1
6 Oct 07	**OVER THE UNDER** *Roadrunner RR79562*	46		1

ROBERT DOWNEY JR

US, male vocalist/actor — **1**

Date	Title / Label	Peak Position	Weeks at No.1	Weeks on Chart
7 May 05	**THE FUTURIST** *Sony Classical SK92654*	56		1

WILL DOWNING

US, male vocalist — **28**

Date	Title / Label	Peak Position	Weeks at No.1	Weeks on Chart
26 Mar 88	**WILL DOWNING** *Fourth & Broadway BRLP 518* ●	20		23
18 Nov 89	**COME TOGETHER AS ONE** *Fourth & Broadway BRLP 538*	36		2
6 Apr 91	**A DREAM FULFILLED** *Fourth & Broadway BRLP 565*	43		3

JASON DOWNS

US, male vocalist — **1**

Date	Title / Label	Peak Position	Weeks at No.1	Weeks on Chart
28 Jul 01	**WHITE BOY WITH A FEATHER** *Pepper 9230452*	64		1

DOWNSIDE ABBEY MONKS & CHOIRBOYS

UK, male monastic group — **6**

Date	Title / Label	Peak Position	Weeks at No.1	Weeks on Chart
2 Nov 96	**THE ABBEY** *Virgin VTCD 99* ○	54		5
3 Jan 98	**GREGORIAN MOODS** *Virgin VTCD 171*	59		1

DRAGONFORCE

UK, male vocal/instrumental group — **3**

Date	Title / Label	Peak Position	Weeks at No.1	Weeks on Chart
21 Jan 06	**INHUMAN RAMPAGE** *Roadrunner RR80702* ○	70		1
6 Sep 08	**ULTRA BEATDOWN** *Roadrunner RR79372*	18		2

NICK DRAKE

UK, male vocalist, d. 25 Nov 1974 (age 26) — **2**

Date	Title / Label	Peak Position	Weeks at No.1	Weeks on Chart
5 Jun 04	**MADE TO LOVE MAGIC** *Island CID 8141*	27		2

DREAD ZEPPELIN

US, male vocal/instrumental group — **2**

Date	Title / Label	Peak Position	Weeks at No.1	Weeks on Chart
11 Aug 90	**UN-LED-ED** *I.R.S. EIRSA 1042*	71		2

DREADZONE

UK, male vocal/instrumental group — **5**

Date	Title / Label	Peak Position	Weeks at No.1	Weeks on Chart
10 Jun 95	**SECOND LIGHT** *Virgin CDV 2778*	37		4
9 Aug 97	**BIOLOGICAL RADIO** *Virgin CDV 2808*	45		1

DREAM ACADEMY

UK, male/female vocal/instrumental group — **2**

Date	Title / Label	Peak Position	Weeks at No.1	Weeks on Chart
12 Oct 85	**THE DREAM ACADEMY** *Blanco Y Negro BYN 6*	58		2

DREAM ON

UK, male vocalists — **3**

Date	Title / Label	Peak Position	Weeks at No.1	Weeks on Chart
23 Feb 08	**DREAM ON** *Bill Kenwright ANYDCD1*	43		3

DREAM THEATER

US, male vocal/instrumental group — **3**

Date	Title / Label	Peak Position	Weeks at No.1	Weeks on Chart
15 Oct 94	**AWAKE** *East West 7567901262*	65		1
18 Jun 05	**OCTAVARIUM** *Atlantic 7567837932*	72		1
16 Jun 07	**SYSTEMATIC CHAOS** *Roadrunner RR79928*	25		1

DREAM WARRIORS

Canada, male rap group — **7**

Date	Title / Label	Peak Position	Weeks at No.1	Weeks on Chart
16 Feb 91	**AND NOW THE LEGACY BEGINS** *Fourth & Broadway BRLP 560* ○	18		7

DREAMKEEPER

UK, female vocal duo — **1**

Date	Title / Label	Peak Position	Weeks at No.1	Weeks on Chart
9 Aug 97	**SPIRIT OF RELAXATION** *Flute SPIRICD 1*	71		1

DRIFTERS

US, male vocal group – members included Ben E. King*, Rudy Lewis, d. 20 May 1964, Clyde McPhatter, d. 13 Jun 1972, Johnny Moore, d. 30 Dec 1998, Bill Pinkney, d. 4 Jul 2007, & Charlie Thomas — **110**

Date	Title / Label	Peak Position	Weeks at No.1	Weeks on Chart
18 May 68	**GOLDEN HITS** *Atlantic 588103*	27		7
10 Jun 72	**GOLDEN HITS** *Atlantic K 40018*	26		8
8 Nov 75	**24 ORIGINAL HITS** *Atlantic K 60106* ⊛	2		34
13 Dec 75	**LOVE GAMES** *Bell BELLS 246* ○	51		1
18 Oct 86	**THE VERY BEST OF THE DRIFTERS** *Telstar STAR 2280* ●	24		15
14 Mar 87	**STAND BY ME (THE ULTIMATE COLLECTION)** *Atlantic WX 90* BEN E. KING & THE DRIFTERS ●	14		8
20 Oct 90	**THE VERY BEST OF BEN E. KING & THE DRIFTERS** *Telstar STAR 2373* BEN E. KING & THE DRIFTERS ●	15		16
7 Nov 98	**THE VERY BEST OF BEN E. KING & THE DRIFTERS** *warner.esp/Global TV RADCD 108* BEN E. KING & THE DRIFTERS	41		3
17 May 03	**THE DEFINITIVE** *Atlantic WSMCD137* ●	8		17
7 Oct 06	**THE VERY BEST OF** *WMTV WMTV029*	46		1

JULIE DRISCOLL, BRIAN AUGER & THE TRINITY

UK, female vocalist & male instrumental group — **13**

Date	Title / Label	Peak Position	Weeks at No.1	Weeks on Chart
8 Jun 68	**OPEN** *Marmalade 608002*	12		13

MINNIE DRIVER

UK, female actor/vocalist — **1**

Date	Title / Label	Peak Position	Weeks at No.1	Weeks on Chart
30 Oct 04	**EVERYTHING I'VE GOT IN MY POCKET** *Liberty 8742702*	44		1

DRIZA-BONE

UK/US, male/female vocal/instrumental group — **1**

Date	Title / Label	Peak Position	Weeks at No.1	Weeks on Chart
19 Nov 94	**CONSPIRACY** *Fourth & Broadway BRCD 593*	72		1

DROWNING POOL

US, male vocal/instrumental group — **2**

Date	Title / Label	Peak Position	Weeks at No.1	Weeks on Chart
16 Feb 02	**SINNER** *Epic 5040912*	70		1
1 May 04	**DESENSITIZED** *Epic 5154112*	66		1

DRU HILL
US, male vocal group

Date	Album	Peak Position	Weeks at No.1	Weeks on Chart
				7
7 Nov 98	**ENTER THE DRU** *Island Black Music 5245422* ○	42		7

DRUGSTORE
UK/US/Brazil, male/female vocal/instrumental group

Date	Album	Peak Position	Weeks at No.1	Weeks on Chart
				3
8 Apr 95	**DRUGSTORE** *Honey 8286170*	31		2
16 May 98	**WHITE MAGIC FOR LOVERS** *Roadrunner RR 87112*	45		1

DRUM CLUB
UK, male production/instrumental duo

Date	Album	Peak Position	Weeks at No.1	Weeks on Chart
				1
20 Aug 94	**DRUMS ARE DANGEROUS** *Butterfly BFLCD 10*	53		1

D12
US, male rap group – Eminem* (Marshall Mathers III), Bizarre* (Rufus Johnson), Bugz (Karnail Pitts), d. 21 May 1999 (replaced by Swift (Ondre Moore)), Kon Artis (Denaun Porter), Kuniva (Von Carlisle) & Proof (DeShaun Holton), d. 11 Apr 2006

Date	Album	Peak Position	Weeks at No.1	Weeks on Chart
				37
30 Jun 01	**DEVIL'S NIGHT** *Shady 4930792* ● ★	2		17
8 May 04	**D12 WORLD** *Interscope 9862431* ⊛	1	1	20

DUBLINERS
Ireland, male vocal/instrumental group – Ronnie Drew, d. 16 Aug 2008, Ciaran Bourke, 10 May 1988, Luke Kelly, d. 30 Jan 1984, Barney McKenna & John Sheahan

Date	Album	Peak Position	Weeks at No.1	Weeks on Chart
				92
13 May 67	**A DROP OF THE HARD STUFF** *Major Minor MMLP 3*	5		41
9 Sep 67	**BEST OF THE DUBLINERS** *Transatlantic TRA 158*	25		11
7 Oct 67	**MORE OF THE HARD STUFF** *Major Minor MMLP 5*	8		23
2 Mar 68	**DRINKIN' AND COURTIN'** *Major Minor SMLP 14*	31		3
25 Apr 87	**THE DUBLINERS 25 YEARS CELEBRATION** *Stylus SMR 731*	43		10
22 Mar 03	**SPIRIT OF THE IRISH** *Sanctuary TVSAN 003* ○	19		3
28 Oct 06	**TOO LATE TO STOP NOW – THE VERY BEST OF** *DMG TV DMGTV031*	54		1

DUBSTAR
UK, female/male vocal/instrumental group

Date	Album	Peak Position	Weeks at No.1	Weeks on Chart
				20
21 Oct 95	**DISGRACEFUL** *Food FOODCDX 13* ●	30		18
4 Oct 97	**GOODBYE** *Food FOODCD 23*	18		2

DUEL
UK, male violinists (duo)

Date	Album	Peak Position	Weeks at No.1	Weeks on Chart
				2
28 Feb 04	**DUEL** *Decca 4739992*	47		2

HILARY DUFF
US, female vocalist/actor

Date	Album	Peak Position	Weeks at No.1	Weeks on Chart
				9
15 Nov 03	**METAMORPHOSIS** *Hollywood 5046692682*	69		1
12 Nov 05	**MOST WANTED** *Angel CDANGE04* ●	31		5
7 Apr 07	**DIGNITY** *Angel CDANGEX33*	25		3

MARY DUFF
Ireland, female vocalist

Date	Album	Peak Position	Weeks at No.1	Weeks on Chart
				17
6 Apr 96	**TIMELESS** *Ritz RITZBCD 707* DANIEL O'DONNELL & MARY DUFF	13		5
1 Oct 05	**THE ULTIMATE COLLECTION** *DMG TV DMGTV019*	52		4
10 Nov 07	**TOGETHER AGAIN** *Rosette ROSCD2090* DANIEL O'DONNELL & MARY DUFF	6		8

DUFFY
UK, female vocalist (Aimee Duffy)

Date	Album	Peak Position	Weeks at No.1	Weeks on Chart
				43
15 Mar 08	**ROCKFERRY** *A&M 1756423* ⊛x4	1	5	43+

STEPHEN 'TIN TIN' DUFFY
UK, male vocalist

Date	Album	Peak Position	Weeks at No.1	Weeks on Chart
				7
20 Apr 85	**THE UPS AND DOWNS** *10 Records DIX 5*	35		7

GEORGE DUKE
US, male vocalist/keyboard player

Date	Album	Peak Position	Weeks at No.1	Weeks on Chart
				4
26 Jul 80	**BRAZILIAN LOVE AFFAIR** *Epic EPC 84311*	33		4

DUKE SPIRIT
UK, male/female vocal/instrumental group

Date	Album	Peak Position	Weeks at No.1	Weeks on Chart
				2
28 May 05	**CUTS ACROSS THE LAND** *Loog 9871475*	40		1
16 Feb 08	**NEPTUNE** *You Are Here YAHM001*	63		1

CANDY DULFER
Holland, female saxophonist

Date	Album	Peak Position	Weeks at No.1	Weeks on Chart
				11
18 Aug 90	**SAXUALITY** *RCA PL 74661* ●	27		9
13 Mar 93	**SAX-A-GO-GO** *Ariola 74321111812*	56		2

DUM DUMS
UK, male vocal/instrumental group

Date	Album	Peak Position	Weeks at No.1	Weeks on Chart
				2
30 Sep 00	**IT GOES WITHOUT SAYING** *Good Behaviour CDGOOD 4*	27		2

SIMON DUPREE & THE BIG SOUND
UK, male vocal/instrumental group

Date	Album	Peak Position	Weeks at No.1	Weeks on Chart
				1
19 Aug 67	**WITHOUT RESERVATIONS** *Parlophone PCS 7029*	39		1

DURAN DURAN
UK, male vocal/instrumental group – Simon Le Bon, Nick Rhodes & Andy, John & Roger Taylor. The Outstanding Contribution to British Music award-winners (BRITs, 2004) went from New Romantic pioneers to pop idols with their catchy melodies and stylish videos. They have sold an estimated 70 million records around the world

Date	Album	Peak Position	Weeks at No.1	Weeks on Chart
				427
27 Jun 81	**DURAN DURAN** *EMI EMC 3372* ⊛	3		118
22 May 82	**RIO** *EMI EMC 3411* ⊛	2		109
3 Dec 83	**SEVEN AND THE RAGGED TIGER** *EMI DD 1* ⊛	1	1	47
24 Nov 84	**ARENA** *Parlophone DD 2* ⊛	6		31
6 Dec 86	**NOTORIOUS** *EMI DDN 331* ●	16		16
29 Oct 88	**BIG THING** *EMI DDB 33* ○	15		5
25 Nov 89	**DECADE** *EMI DDX 10* ⊛	5		16
1 Sep 90	**LIBERTY** *Parlophone PCSD 112* ○	8		4
27 Feb 93	**DURAN DURAN (THE WEDDING ALBUM)** *Parlophone CDDB 34* ●	4		23
8 Apr 95	**THANK YOU** *Parlophone CDDDB 36*	12		3
21 Nov 98	**GREATEST** *EMI 4962392* ⊛x2	4		48
27 Mar 99	**STRANGE BEHAVIOUR** *EMI 4939722*	70		1
1 Jul 00	**POP TRASH** *Hollywood 0107512HWR*	53		1
23 Oct 04	**ASTRONAUT** *Epic 5179208* ●	3		4
1 Dec 07	**RED CARPET MASSACRE** *Epic 88697073622*	44		1

DEANNA DURBIN
Canada, female vocalist

Date	Album	Peak Position	Weeks at No.1	Weeks on Chart
				4
30 Jan 82	**THE BEST OF DEANNA DURBIN** *MCA International MCL 1634* ○	84		4

JUDITH DURHAM
Australia, female vocalist. See Seekers

Date	Album	Peak Position	Weeks at No.1	Weeks on Chart
				16
23 Apr 94	**CARNIVAL OF HITS** *EMI CDEMTV 83* JUDITH DURHAM & THE SEEKERS ●	7		14
30 Mar 96	**MONA LISAS** *EMI Premier CDJDTV 112*	46		2

IAN DURY & THE BLOCKHEADS
UK, male vocal/instrumental group – Ian Dury, Charley Charles, Mickey Gallagher, Chaz Jankel, Davey Payne, John Turnbull & Norman Watt-Roy

Date	Album	Peak Position	Weeks at No.1	Weeks on Chart
22 Oct 77	**NEW BOOTS AND PANTIES** *Stiff SEEZ 4* ⊛	5		90
2 Jun 79	**DO IT YOURSELF** *Stiff SEEZ 14* ●	2		18
6 Dec 80	**LAUGHTER** *Stiff SEEZ 30* ○	48		4
10 Oct 81	**LORD UPMINSTER** *Polydor POLD 5042*	53		4
4 Feb 84	**4,000 WEEKS HOLIDAY** *Polydor POLD 5112* IAN DURY & THE MUSIC STUDENTS	54		2
11 Jul 98	**MR. LOVE PANTS** *Ronnie Harris DUR 1*	57		2
9 Oct 99	**REASONS TO BE CHEERFUL – THE VERY BEST OF IAN DURY AND THE BLOCKHEADS** *EMI 5228882* ○	40		2
21 Apr 01	**BRAND NEW BOOTS AND PANTIES** *East Central One NEWBOOTS 2CD* BLOCKHEADS	44		3
30 Mar 02	**TEN MORE TURNIPS FROM THE TIP** *Ronnie Harris DUR 2*	60		1

DUST JUNKYS

UK, male vocal/instrumental group — Peak Position / Weeks at No.1 / 128

Date	Title	Peak Position	Weeks at No.1	Weeks on Chart
21 Mar 98	**DONE AND DUSTED** *Polydor 5570432*	35		2

BOB DYLAN

US, male vocalist/guitarist (Robert Zimmerman). Arguably the most important and influential composer of the rock 'n' roll era. Not only did Dylan stretch the boundaries of songwriting, but he helped change the public's long-accepted perception of how a singer should look, and even sound — Peak Position / Weeks at No.1 / 648

Date	Title	Peak Position	Weeks at No.1	Weeks on Chart
23 May 64	**THE FREEWHEELIN' BOB DYLAN** *CBS BPG 62193*	1	2	49
11 Jul 64	**THE TIMES THEY ARE A-CHANGIN'** *CBS BPG 62251*	4		20
21 Nov 64	**ANOTHER SIDE OF BOB DYLAN** *CBS BPG 62429*	8		19
8 May 65	**BOB DYLAN** *CBS BPG 62022*	13		6
15 May 65	**BRINGING IT ALL BACK HOME** *CBS BPG 62515*	1	1	29
9 Oct 65	**HIGHWAY 61 REVISITED** *CBS BPG 62572*	4		15
20 Aug 66	**BLONDE ON BLONDE** *CBS DDP 66012*	3		15
14 Jan 67	**GREATEST HITS** *CBS SBPG 62847*	6		82
2 Mar 68	**JOHN WESLEY HARDING** *CBS SBPG 63252*	1	13	29
17 May 69	**NASHVILLE SKYLINE** *CBS 63601*	1	4	42
11 Jul 70	**SELF PORTRAIT** *CBS 66250*	1	1	15
28 Nov 70	**NEW MORNING** *CBS 69001*	1	1	11
25 Dec 71	**MORE BOB DYLAN GREATEST HITS** *CBS 67238/9*	12		15
29 Sep 73	**PAT GARRETT & BILLY THE KID (OST)** *CBS 69042*	29		11
23 Feb 74	**PLANET WAVES** *Island ILPS 9261* ○ ★	7		8
13 Jul 74	**BEFORE THE FLOOD** *Asylum IDBD 1* ○	8		7
15 Feb 75	**BLOOD ON THE TRACKS** *CBS 69097* ● ★	4		16
26 Jul 75	**THE BASEMENT TAPES** *CBS 88147* ●	8		10
31 Jan 76	**DESIRE** *CBS 86003* ● ★	3		35
9 Oct 76	**HARD RAIN** *CBS 86016* ●	3		7
1 Jul 78	**STREET LEGAL** *CBS 86067* ⊛	2		20
26 May 79	**BOB DYLAN AT BUDOKAN** *CBS 96004* ●	4		19
8 Sep 79	**SLOW TRAIN COMING** *CBS 86095* ●	2		13
28 Jun 80	**SAVED** *CBS 86113* ○	3		8
29 Aug 81	**SHOT OF LOVE** *CBS 85178* ○	6		8
12 Nov 83	**INFIDELS** *CBS 25539* ○	9		12
15 Dec 84	**REAL LIVE** *CBS 26334*	54		2
22 Jun 85	**EMPIRE BURLESQUE** *CBS 86313*	11		6
2 Aug 86	**KNOCKED OUT LOADED** *CBS 86326*	35		5
25 Jun 88	**GREATEST HITS VOLUME 3** *CBS 4602671*	47		3
23 Apr 88	**DOWN IN THE GROOVE** *CBS 4602671*	32		3
18 Feb 89	**DYLAN AND THE DEAD** *CBS 4633811* & THE GRATEFUL DEAD	38		3
14 Oct 89	**OH MERCY** *CBS 4658001* ●	6		7
29 Sep 90	**UNDER THE RED SKY** *CBS 4671881* ○	13		3
13 Apr 91	**THE BOOTLEG SERIES VOLUMES 1-3** *Columbia 4680861*	32		5
14 Nov 92	**GOOD AS I BEEN TO YOU** *Columbia 4727102*	18		3
20 Nov 93	**WORLD GONE WRONG** *Columbia 4748572*	35		2
29 Apr 95	**UNPLUGGED** *Columbia 4783742*	10		5
14 Jun 97	**THE BEST OF BOB DYLAN** *Columbia SONYTV 28CD* ●	6		18
11 Oct 97	**TIME OUT OF MIND** *Columbia 4869362* ●	10		6
24 Oct 98	**LIVE AT THE ROYAL ALBERT HALL** *Legacy 4914852*	19		2
20 May 00	**BEST OF – VOLUME 2** *Columbia 4983619*	22		2
2 Jun 01	**THE ESSENTIAL** *Columbia STVCD 116* ⊛	9		19
22 Sep 01	**LOVE AND THEFT** *Columbia 5043642*	3		5
7 Dec 02	**LIVE 1975 – THE ROLLING THUNDER REVUE** *Columbia 5101403*	69		1
10 Apr 04	**BOOTLEG SERIES VOLUME 6** *Columbia 5123582*	33		1
17 Sep 05	**NO DIRECTION HOME (OST)** *Columbia 5203582*	21		5
9 Sep 06	**MODERN TIMES** *Columbia 82876876062* ★	3		12
13 Oct 07	**DYLAN** *Columbia 88697109542*	10		6
18 Oct 08	**TELL TALE SIGNS – THE BOOTLEG SERIES VOLUME 8** *Columbia 88697347472*	9		3

Top 10 Albums with Biggest First-Week Sales

Pos	Album Title Artist	Approx Sales
1	**BE HERE NOW** OASIS	663,000
2	**X&Y** COLDPLAY	465,000
3	**THE CIRCUS** TAKE THAT	432,000
4	**LIFE FOR RENT** DIDO	400,000
5	**SPIRIT** LEONA LEWIS	376,000
6	**INTENSIVE CARE** ROBBIE WILLIAMS	374,000
7	**WHATEVER PEOPLE SAY I AM, THAT'S WHAT I'M NOT** ARCTIC MONKEYS	364,000
8	**RATTLE AND HUM** U2	360,000
9	**BAD** MICHAEL JACKSON	350,000
10	**(WHAT'S THE STORY) MORNING GLORY?** OASIS	344,000

BIOGRAPHIES

Biographies include the nationality and category for every chart entrant.

Each entrant has at least a mini biography. The 100 acts with the most weeks on the chart (see page 290 for the top 100 chart) each have extended biographies.

Real names are included for all solo artists and, where applicable, dates of death and age of the artist at the time. "See..." links are included for soloists who also had album chart entries in other acts.

The best known line-up is listed for every group that had a Top 10 album, with the vocalist/leader mentioned first and the others following in alphabetical order. In cases where later replacements had similar success both people are named and, where applicable, the dates of death are also shown for every group/duo member listed.

Certified Awards are given by the BPI to mark unit sales to retailers. The certified awards were introduced in April 1973, based on revenue received by manufacturers. In January 1978 the qualification rules were changed and the system based on unit sales to the trade was adopted.

Silver symbol	●	=	60,000 units
Gold symbol	●	=	100,000 units
Platinum symbol	⊛	=	300,000 units

E–H

KEY TO ARTIST ENTRIES

Artist/Group Name — Artist/Group Biography — Silver-selling — Gold-selling — Platinum-selling — US No.1 ★ — Peak Position — Weeks at No.1 — Weeks on Chart

Asterisks (*) indicate group members with hits in their own right that are listed elsewhere in this book

TOM JONES

UK, male vocalist (Thomas Woodward). Perennially popular Welsh vocalist, who has a 43-year span of UK hit albums, was the No.1 UK solo singer of the 1960s on both sides of the Atlantic. The unmistakable Vegas veteran received the Outstanding Contribution award at the 2003 BRITs

Artist's Total Weeks On Chart: 530

Date	Album	Peak	Wks at No.1	Wks
5 Jun 65	**ALONG CAME JONES** *Decca LK 6693*	11		5
8 Oct 66	**FROM THE HEART** *Decca LK 4814*	23		8
8 Apr 67	**GREEN GREEN GRASS OF HOME** *Decca SKL 4855*	3		49
24 Jun 67	**LIVE AT THE TALK OF THE TOWN** *Decca SKL 4874*	6		90
30 Dec 67	**13 SMASH HITS** *Decca SKL 4909*	5		49
27 Jul 68	**DELILAH** *Decca SKL 4946*	1	2	29
21 Dec 68	**HELP YOURSELF** *Decca SKL 4982*	4		9
28 Jun 69	**THIS IS TOM JONES** *Decca SKL 5007*	2		20
15 Nov 69	**TOM JONES LIVE IN LAS VEGAS** *Decca SKL 5032*	2		45
25 Apr 70	**TOM** *Decca SKL 5045*	4		18
14 Nov 70	**I WHO HAVE NOTHING** *Decca SKL 5072*	10		10
29 May 71	**SHE'S A LADY** *Decca SKL 5089*	9		7
27 Nov 71	**LIVE AT CAESAR'S PALACE** *Decca D 1/11/2*	27		5
24 Jun 72	**CLOSE UP** *Decca SKL 5132*	17		4
23 Jun 73	**THE BODY AND SOUL OF TOM JONES** *Decca SKL 5162*	31		1
5 Jan 74	**GREATEST HITS** *Decca SKL 5176*	15		13
22 Mar 75	**20 GREATEST HITS** *Decca TJD 1/11/2* ●	1	4	21
7 Oct 78	**I'M COMING HOME** *Lotus WH 5001* ●	12		9
16 May 87	**THE GREATEST HITS** *Telstar STAR 2296*	16		12
13 May 89	**AT THIS MOMENT** *Jive TOMTV 1*	34		3
8 Jul 89	**AFTER DARK** *Stylus SMR 978*	46		4
6 Apr 91	**CARRYING A TORCH** *Dover ADD 20*	44		4
27 Jun 92	**THE COMPLETE TOM JONES** *The Hit Label 8442862* ●	8		6
26 Nov 94	**THE LEAD AND HOW TO SWING IT** *ZTT 6544924982*	55		1
14 Nov 98	**THE ULTIMATE HITS COLLECTION** *Polygram TV 8449012*	26		6
9 Oct 99	**RELOAD** *Gut GUTCD 009* ⊛x4	1	3	65
16 Nov 02	**MR JONES** *V2 VVR 1021072*	36		2
1 Mar 03	**GREATEST HITS** *Universal TV 8828632* ⊛	2		16
9 Oct 04	**TOM JONES AND JOOLS HOLLAND** *Radar RADAR004CD* & JOOLS HOLLAND ●	5		13
29 Nov 08	**24 HOURS** *S-Curve 2649852*	32		6+

Date of entry into chart

Artist collaboration or where artist's name has changed

Album Title — Label and Catalogue Number

Cross (+) indicates album is still on chart in last week of 2008

EAGLES

US, male vocal/instrumental group – Glenn Frey*, Don Henley*, Don Felder, Bernie Leadon (replaced by Joe Walsh) & Randy Meisner (replaced by Timothy B. Schmit). Legendary, high-flying West Coast rock group whose *Their Greatest Hits 1971–1975* is America's top-seller of all time at 29 million. They re-united in 1994 and are one of the 21st century's top-earning live acts

Date	Title	Peak Position	Weeks at No.1	517
27 Apr 74	**ON THE BORDER** *Asylum SYL 9016* ◯	28		9
12 Jul 75	**DESPERADO** *Asylum SYLA 8759*	39		9
12 Jul 75	**ONE OF THESE NIGHTS** *Asylum SYLL 9011* ⊛ ★	8		41
6 Mar 76	**THEIR GREATEST HITS 1971–1975** *Asylum K 53017* ⊛ ★	2		118
25 Dec 76	**HOTEL CALIFORNIA** *Asylum K 53051* ⊛x6 ★	2		74
13 Oct 79	**THE LONG RUN** *Asylum K 52181* ● ★	4		16
22 Nov 80	**LIVE** *Asylum K 62032* ●	24		13
18 May 85	**THE BEST OF THE EAGLES** *Asylum EKT 5* ⊛x4	8		74
23 Jul 94	**THE VERY BEST OF THE EAGLES** *Elektra 9548323752* ⊛	4		55
19 Nov 94	**HELL FREEZES OVER** *Geffen GED 24725* ● ★	18		21
9 Jun 01	**THE VERY BEST OF** *Elektra 7559626802* ⊛x2	3		46
1 Nov 03	**THE COMPLETE GREATEST HITS** *WSM 8122737312* ●	9		15
10 Nov 07	**LONG ROAD OUT OF EDEN** *Polydor 1749406* ★	1	1	26

EAMON

US, male vocalist (Eamon Doyle)

Date	Title	Peak Position	Weeks at No.1	9
17 Apr 04	**I DON'T WANT YOU BACK (IMPORT)** *Jive JIV583702* ●	6		9

STEVE EARLE

US, male vocalist/guitarist

Date	Title	Peak Position	Weeks at No.1	24
4 Jul 87	**EXIT O** *MCA MCF 3379*	77		3
19 Nov 88	**COPPERHEAD ROAD** *MCA MCF 3426* ◯	42		8
7 Jul 90	**THE HARD WAY** *MCA MCG 6095* & THE DUKES	22		4
19 Oct 91	**SHUT UP AND DIE LIKE AN AVIATOR** *MCA 10315* & THE DUKES	62		1
23 Mar 96	**I FEEL ALRIGHT** *Transatlantic TRACD 227*	44		3
18 Oct 97	**EL CORAZON** *Warner Brothers 9362467892*	59		1
6 Mar 99	**THE MOUNTAIN** *Grapevine GRACD 252* & THE DEL McCOURY BAND	51		1
17 Jun 00	**TRANSCENDENTAL BLUES** *Epic 4989749*	32		1
4 Sep 04	**THE REVOLUTION STARTS NOW** *Rykodisc RCD17023*	66		1
13 Oct 07	**WASHINGTON SQUARE SERENADE** *New West NW6128*	55		1

EARTH WIND & FIRE

US, male vocal/instrumental group – Philip Bailey*; members also included Larry Dunn, Ralph Johnson & Fred, Maurice & Verdine White

Date	Title	Peak Position	Weeks at No.1	171
21 Jan 78	**ALL 'N' ALL** *CBS 86051* ◯	13		23
16 Dec 78	**THE BEST OF EARTH WIND & FIRE VOLUME 1** *CBS 83284* ⊛	6		42
23 Jun 79	**I AM** *CBS 86084* ⊛	5		41
1 Nov 80	**FACES** *CBS 88498*	10		6
14 Nov 81	**RAISE** *CBS 85272* ●	14		22
19 Feb 83	**POWERLIGHT** *CBS 25120*	22		7
9 Mar 85	**THE ARTISTS VOLUME 1** *Street Sounds ARTIS 1* EARTH WIND & FIRE/JEAN CARN/ROSE ROYCE	65		4
10 May 86	**THE COLLECTION – 24 ESSENTIAL HITS** *K-Tel NE 1322* ●	5		13
28 Nov 92	**THE VERY BEST OF EARTH WIND & FIRE** *Telstar TCD 2631*	40		6
28 Sep 96	**BOOGIE WONDERLAND – THE VERY BEST OF EARTH WIND & FIRE** *Telstar TCD 2879*	29		4
7 Aug 99	**THE ULTIMATE COLLECTION** *Columbia SONYTV 66CD*	34		3

EARTHLING

UK, male vocal/instrumental duo

Date	Title	Peak Position	Weeks at No.1	1
3 Jun 95	**RADAR** *Cooltempo CTCD 44*	66		1

EAST OF EDEN

UK, male instrumental group

Date	Title	Peak Position	Weeks at No.1	2
14 Mar 70	**SNAFU** *Deram SML 1050*	29		2

EAST 17

UK, male vocal group – Brian Harvey, Terry Coldwell, John Hendy & Tony Mortimer

Date	Title	Peak Position	Weeks at No.1	105
27 Feb 93	**WALTHAMSTOW** *London 8283732* ⊛	1	1	33
29 Oct 94	**STEAM** *London 8285422* ⊛x2	3		36
25 Nov 95	**UP ALL NIGHT** *London 8286992* ⊛	7		15
16 Nov 96	**AROUND THE WORLD – THE JOURNEY SO FAR** *London 8288522* ⊛x2	3		16
28 Nov 98	**RESURRECTION** *Telstar TCD 3015* E–17 ●	43		2
12 Feb 05	**THE VERY BEST OF** *London WSMCD200*	34		3

EASTERHOUSE

UK, male vocal/instrumental group

Date	Title	Peak Position	Weeks at No.1	1
28 Jun 86	**CONTENDERS** *Rough Trade ROUGH 94*	91		1

SHEENA EASTON

UK, female vocalist (Sheena Orr)

Date	Title	Peak Position	Weeks at No.1	27
31 Jan 81	**TAKE MY TIME** *EMI EMC 3354* ●	17		9
3 Oct 81	**YOU COULD HAVE BEEN WITH ME** *EMI EMC 3378* ◯	33		6
25 Sep 82	**MADNESS, MONEY AND MUSIC** *EMI EMC 3414*	44		4
15 Oct 83	**BEST KEPT SECRET** *EMI EMC 1077951*	99		1
4 Mar 89	**THE LOVER IN ME** *MCA MCG 6036*	30		7

CLINT EASTWOOD & GENERAL SAINT

UK, male vocal duo

Date	Title	Peak Position	Weeks at No.1	3
6 Feb 82	**TWO BAD DJ** *Greensleeves GREL 24*	99		2
28 May 83	**STOP THAT TRAIN** *Greensleeves GREL 53*	98		1

EAT STATIC

UK, male production duo

Date	Title	Peak Position	Weeks at No.1	5
15 May 93	**ABDUCTION** *Planet Dog BARKCD 1*	62		1
25 Jun 94	**IMPLANT** *Planet Dog BARKCD 005*	13		3
25 Oct 97	**SCIENCE OF THE GODS** *Planet Dog BARKCD 029*	60		1

EAZY-E

US, male rapper (Eric Wright), d. 26 Mar 1995 (age 31). See N.W.A.

Date	Title	Peak Position	Weeks at No.1	1
10 Feb 96	**STR8 OFF THA STREETZ OF MUTHAPHUKKIN COMPTON** *Epic 4835762*	66		1

ECHO & THE BUNNYMEN

UK, male vocal/instrumental group – Ian McCulloch*, Pete de Freitas, Les Pattinson & Will Sergeant

Date	Title	Peak Position	Weeks at No.1	101
26 Jul 80	**CROCODILES** *Korova KODE 1* ●	17		6
6 Jan 81	**HEAVEN UP HERE** *Korova KODE 3*	10		16
12 Feb 83	**PORCUPINE** *Korova KODE 6* ●	2		17
12 May 84	**OCEAN RAIN** *Korova KODE 8* ●	4		26
23 Nov 85	**SONGS TO LEARN AND SING** *Korova KODE 13* ●	6		15
18 Jul 87	**ECHO AND THE BUNNYMEN** *WEA WX 108* ◯	4		9
21 Jun 97	**BALLYHOO – THE BEST OF ECHO AND THE BUNNYMEN** *Korova 0630191032*	59		1
26 Jul 97	**EVERGREEN** *London 8289052*	8		7
17 Apr 99	**WHAT ARE YOU GOING TO DO WITH YOUR LIFE?** *London 5560802*	21		2
26 May 01	**FLOWERS** *Cooking Vinyl COOKCD 208*	56		1
23 Sep 06	**THE VERY BEST OF – MORE SONGS TO LEARN** *Korova KODE1011*	47		1

ECHOBELLY

UK/Sweden, female/male vocal/instrumental group – Sonya Aurora Madan, Andy Henderson, Glenn Johansson, Alex Keyser & Debbie Smith

Date	Title	Peak Position	Weeks at No.1	28
3 Sep 94	**EVERYONE'S GOT ONE** *Fauve FAUV 3CD* ◯	8		3
30 Sep 95	**ON** *Fauve FAUV 6CD* ●	4		24
22 Nov 97	**LUSTRA** *Epic 4889672*	47		1

EDDIE & THE HOT RODS

UK, male vocal/instrumental group

Date	Title	Peak Position	Weeks at No.1	5
18 Dec 76	**TEENAGE DEPRESSION** *Island ILPS 9457*	43		1
3 Dec 77	**LIFE ON THE LINE** *Island ILPS 9509*	27		3
24 Mar 79	**THRILLER** *Island ILPS 9563*	50		1

DUANE EDDY

US, male guitarist

Date	Title	Peak Position	Weeks at No.1	88
6 Jun 59	**HAVE TWANGY GUITAR WILL TRAVEL** *London HAW 2160*	6		3
31 Oct 59	**ESPECIALLY FOR YOU** *London HAW 2191*	6		8
19 Mar 60	**THE TWANG'S THE THANG** *London HAW 2236*	2		25
26 Nov 60	**SONGS OF OUR HERITAGE** *London HAW 2285*	13		5
1 Apr 61	**$1,000,000.00 WORTH OF TWANG** *London HAW 2325*	5		19
9 Jun 62	**$1,000,000.00 WORTH OF TWANG VOLUME 2** *London HAW 2435*	18		1
21 Jul 62	**TWISTIN' AND TWANGIN'** *RCA RD 27264*	8		12
8 Dec 62	**TWANGY GUITAR – SILKY STRINGS** *RCA Victor RD 7510*	13		11
16 Mar 63	**DANCE WITH THE GUITAR MAN** *RCA Victor RD 7545*	14		4

Silver-selling ○ Gold-selling ● Platinum-selling ⊛ US No.1 ★ | Peak Position | Weeks at No.1 | Weeks on Chart

EDITORS

UK, male vocal/instrumental group – Tom Smith, Edward Lay, Russell Leetch & Chris Urbanowicz

Date	Title	Peak Position	Weeks at No.1	Weeks on Chart
				55
6 Aug 05	**THE BACK ROOM** *Kitchenware KWCD342* ⊛	2		30
7 Jul 07	**AN END HAS A START** *Kitchenware KWCD372* ⊛	1	1	25

DAVE EDMUNDS

UK, male vocalist/guitarist

Date	Title	Peak Position	Weeks at No.1	Weeks on Chart
				23
23 Jun 79	**REPEAT WHEN NECESSARY** *Swan Song SSK 59409* ○	39		12
18 Apr 81	**TWANGIN'** *Swan Song SSK 59411*	37		4
3 Apr 82	**DE 7** *Arista SPART 1184*	60		3
30 Apr 83	**INFORMATION** *Arista 205 348*	92		2
4 Oct 08	**THE MANY SIDES OF – THE GREATEST HITS** *Rhino/UMTV 1782360*	38		2

DENNIS EDWARDS

US, male vocalist. See Temptations

Date	Title	Peak Position	Weeks at No.1	Weeks on Chart
				1
14 Apr 84	**DON'T LOOK ANY FURTHER** *Gordy ZL 72148*	91		1

TODD EDWARDS

US, male DJ/producer

Date	Title	Peak Position	Weeks at No.1	Weeks on Chart
				1
24 Aug 96	**SAVED MY LIFE** *ffrr FX 279*	69		1

EEK-A-MOUSE

Jamaica, male vocalist (Ripton Hylton)

Date	Title	Peak Position	Weeks at No.1	Weeks on Chart
				3
14 Aug 82	**SKIDIP** *Greensleeves GREL 41*	61		3

EELS

US, male vocal/instrumental group – Mark Everett, Jonathan 'Butch' Norton & Tommy Walter

Date	Title	Peak Position	Weeks at No.1	Weeks on Chart
				47
8 Feb 97	**BEAUTIFUL FREAK** *DreamWorks DRD 50001* ●	5		27
3 Oct 98	**ELECTRO-SHOCK BLUES** *DreamWorks DRD 50052*	12		4
11 Mar 00	**DAISIES OF THE GALAXY** *DreamWorks 4502182* ○	8		5
6 Oct 01	**SOULJACKER** *DreamWorks 4503462*	12		2
14 Jun 03	**SHOOTENANNY** *DreamWorks 4504588*	35		2
7 May 05	**BLINKING LIGHTS & OTHER REVELATIONS** *Vagrant 9881785*	16		4
2 Feb 08	**MEET THE EELS** *Geffen 1746011*	26		2
2 Feb 08	**USELESS TRINKETS – B-SIDES SOUNDTRACKS** *Geffen 1746014*	69		1

EIFFEL 65

Italy, male vocal/instrumental/production trio

Date	Title	Peak Position	Weeks at No.1	Weeks on Chart
				4
4 Mar 00	**EUROPOP** *Eternal 8573814552*	12		4

EIGHTH WONDER

UK, female/male vocal/instrumental group

Date	Title	Peak Position	Weeks at No.1	Weeks on Chart
				4
23 Jul 88	**FEARLESS** *CBS 4606281*	47		4

801

UK, male vocal/instrumental group

Date	Title	Peak Position	Weeks at No.1	Weeks on Chart
				2
20 Nov 76	**801 LIVE** *Island ILPS 9444*	52		2

808 STATE

UK, male DJ/production/instrumental group – Andrew Barker, Graham Massey, Darren Partington, Martin Price & Gerald Simpson

Date	Title	Peak Position	Weeks at No.1	Weeks on Chart
				20
16 Dec 89	**NINETY** *ZTT 2* ●	57		5
16 Mar 91	**EX-EL** *ZTT 6* ●	4		10
13 Feb 93	**GORGEOUS** *ZTT 4509911002*	17		3
30 May 98	**808:88:98** *ZTT 100CD*	40		2

EIGHTIES MATCHBOX B-LINE DISASTER

UK, male vocal/instrumental group

Date	Title	Peak Position	Weeks at No.1	Weeks on Chart
				1
6 Nov 04	**THE ROYAL SOCIETY** *Universal MCD60097*	68		1

LUDOVICO EINAUDI

Italy, male pianist

Date	Title	Peak Position	Weeks at No.1	Weeks on Chart
				5
13 Sep 03	**ECHOES – THE COLLECTION** *BMG 82876550892* ○	40		4
18 Sep 04	**UNA MATTINA** *Decca 4756292*	59		1

EL PRESIDENTE

UK, male/female vocal/instrumental group

Date	Title	Peak Position	Weeks at No.1	Weeks on Chart
				1
5 Nov 05	**EL PRESIDENTE** *One 82876710712*	57		1

ELASTICA

UK, female/male vocal/instrumental group – Justine Frischmann, Annie Holland, Donna Matthews & Justin Welch

Date	Title	Peak Position	Weeks at No.1	Weeks on Chart
				27
25 Mar 95	**ELASTICA** *Deceptive BLUFF 014CD* ●	1	1	25
15 Apr 00	**THE MENACE** *Deceptive BLUFF 075CD*	24		2

ELBOW

UK, male vocal/instrumental group – Guy Garvey, Richard Jupp, Craig & Mark Potter & Pete Turner

Date	Title	Peak Position	Weeks at No.1	Weeks on Chart
				47
19 May 01	**ASLEEP IN THE BACK** *V2 VVR 1015882* ●	14		5
30 Aug 03	**CAST OF THOUSANDS** *V2 VVR 1021812*	7		4
24 Sep 05	**LEADERS OF THE FREE WORLD** *V2 VVR1032558* ○	12		3
29 Mar 08	**THE SELDOM SEEN KID** *Fiction 1748990* ⊛	5		35+

ELECTRAFIXION

UK, male vocal/instrumental group

Date	Title	Peak Position	Weeks at No.1	Weeks on Chart
				2
7 Oct 95	**BURNED** *Space Junk 00630112482*	38		2

ELECTRASY

UK, male vocal/instrumental group

Date	Title	Peak Position	Weeks at No.1	Weeks on Chart
				1
26 Sep 98	**BEAUTIFUL INSANE** *MCA MCD 60051*	48		1

ELECTRIBE 101

UK/Germany, male/female vocal/instrumental group

Date	Title	Peak Position	Weeks at No.1	Weeks on Chart
				3
20 Oct 90	**ELECTRIBAL MEMORIES** *Mercury 8429651*	26		3

ELECTRIC BOYS

Sweden, male vocal/instrumental group

Date	Title	Peak Position	Weeks at No.1	Weeks on Chart
				1
6 Jun 92	**GROOVUS MAXIMUS** *Vertigo 5122552*	61		1

ELECTRIC LIGHT ORCHESTRA

UK, male vocal/instrumental group – Jeff Lynne*, Bev Bevan, Kelly Groucutt, Richard Tandy & Roy Wood* (left 1972). The distinctive-sounding and innovative group, masterminded by the multi-talented Lynne, proved to be one of the biggest-selling UK album acts on both sides of the Atlantic in the 1970s

Date	Title	Peak Position	Weeks at No.1	Weeks on Chart
				440
12 Aug 72	**ELECTRIC LIGHT ORCHESTRA** *Harvest SHVL 797*	32		4
31 Mar 73	**ELECTRIC LIGHT ORCHESTRA II** *Harvest SHVL 806*	35		1
11 Dec 76	**A NEW WORLD RECORD** *Jet UAG 30017* ⊛	6		100
12 Nov 77	**OUT OF THE BLUE** *Jet UAR 100* ⊛	4		108
6 Jan 79	**THREE LIGHT YEARS** *Jet BX 1* ●	38		9
16 Jun 79	**DISCOVERY** *Jet LX 500* ⊛	1	5	46
1 Dec 79	**ELO'S GREATEST HITS** *Jet LX 525* ⊛	7		18
19 Jul 80	**XANADU (OST)** *Jet LX 526* OLIVIA NEWTON-JOHN/ELECTRIC LIGHT ORCHESTRA ●	2		17
8 Aug 81	**TIME** *Jet JETLP 236* ⊛	1	2	32
2 Jul 83	**SECRET MESSAGES** *Jet LX 527* ●	4		15
15 Mar 86	**BALANCE OF POWER** *Epic EPC 26467* ○	9		12
16 Dec 89	**THE GREATEST HITS** *Telstar STAR 2370* ●	23		21
1 Jun 91	**ELECTRIC LIGHT ORCHESTRA PART TWO** *Telstar STAR 2503* PART TWO	34		4
2 Jul 94	**THE VERY BEST OF THE ELECTRIC LIGHT ORCHESTRA** *Dino DINCD 90*	4		11
8 Nov 97	**LIGHT YEARS – THE VERY BEST OF ELECTRIC LIGHT ORCHESTRA** *Epic 4890392* ○	60		4
23 Jun 01	**ZOOM** *Epic 5025002*	34		2
3 Nov 01	**THE ULTIMATE COLLECTION** *Columbia STVCD 126* ●	18		6
18 Jun 05	**ALL OVER THE WORLD – THE VERY BEST OF** *Epic 5201292* ⊛	6		26
10 Mar 07	**OUT OF THE BLUE** *Epic 88697053232*	18		4

ELECTRIC SIX

US, male vocal/instrumental group – Tyler Spencer, Joe Frezza, Cory Martin, Steve Nawara & Christopher Tait — Weeks on Chart: **10**

Date	Title	Label	Peak Position	Weeks at No.1	Weeks on Chart
12 Jul 03	FIRE	*XL Recordings XLCD 169* ●	7		10

ELECTRIC SOFT PARADE

UK, male vocal/instrumental group — Weeks on Chart: **3**

Date	Title	Label	Peak Position	Weeks at No.1	Weeks on Chart
16 Feb 02	HOLES IN THE WALL	*DB DB002 CDLP*	35		2
25 Oct 03	THE AMERICAN ADVENTURE	*BMG 82876563692*	45		1

ELECTRIC WIND ENSEMBLE

UK, male instrumental group — Weeks on Chart: **9**

Date	Title	Label	Peak Position	Weeks at No.1	Weeks on Chart
18 Feb 84	HAUNTING MELODIES	*Nouveau Music NML 1007*	28		9

ELECTRONIC

UK, male vocal/instrumental duo – Bernard Sumner & Johnny Marr — Weeks on Chart: **24**

Date	Title	Label	Peak Position	Weeks at No.1	Weeks on Chart
8 Jun 91	ELECTRONIC	*Factory FACT 290* ●	2		16
20 Jul 96	RAISED THE PRESSURE	*Parlophone CDPCS 7382* ○	8		5
8 May 99	TWISTED TENDERNESS	*Parlophone 5201462*	9		3

DANNY ELFMAN

US, male composer/orchestra leader — Weeks on Chart: **6**

Date	Title	Label	Peak Position	Weeks at No.1	Weeks on Chart
19 Aug 89	BATMAN (OST)	*Warner Brothers WX 287*	45		6

DUKE ELLINGTON

US, male pianist/band leader (Edward Ellington), d. 24 May 1974 (age 75) — Weeks on Chart: **2**

Date	Title	Label	Peak Position	Weeks at No.1	Weeks on Chart
8 Apr 61	NUT CRACKER SUITE	*Philips BBL 7418*	11		2

ELLIOT MINOR

UK, male vocal/instrumental group – Alex Davies, Dan & Ed Hetherton, Ed Minton & Ali Paul — Weeks on Chart: **3**

Date	Title	Label	Peak Position	Weeks at No.1	Weeks on Chart
26 Apr 08	ELLIOT MINOR	*Warner Brothers 2564695623*	6		3

MISSY 'MISDEMEANOR' ELLIOTT

US, female rapper/producer (Melissa Elliott) — Weeks on Chart: **63**

Date	Title	Label	Peak Position	Weeks at No.1	Weeks on Chart
10 Jul 99	DA REAL WORLD	*Elektra 7559624362* ○	40		2
26 May 01	MISS E. . . SO ADDICTIVE	*Elektra 7559626432* ●	10		26
23 Nov 02	UNDER CONSTRUCTION	*Elektra 7559628132* MISSY ELLIOTT ●	23		22
6 Dec 03	THIS IS NOT A TEST	*Elektra 7559629052* MISSY ELLIOTT ●	47		4
16 Jul 05	THE COOKBOOK	*East West 7567837792* MISSY ELLIOTT	33		3
16 Sep 06	RESPECT ME	*Atlantic 7567839552* MISSY ELLIOTT ●	7		6

SOPHIE ELLIS BEXTOR

UK, female vocalist — Weeks on Chart: **49**

Date	Title	Label	Peak Position	Weeks at No.1	Weeks on Chart
15 Sep 01	READ MY LIPS	*Polydor 5891742* ⊛x2	2		44
8 Nov 03	SHOOT FROM THE HIP	*Polydor 9865834*	19		2
2 Jun 07	TRIP THE LIGHT FANTASTIC	*Fascination 1705086*	7		3

BEN ELTON

UK, male comedian — Weeks on Chart: **2**

Date	Title	Label	Peak Position	Weeks at No.1	Weeks on Chart
14 Nov 87	MOTORMOUTH	*Mercury BENLP 1*	86		2

EMBRACE

UK, male vocal/instrumental group – Danny McNamara, Mickey Dale, Steve Firth, Mike Heaton & Richard McNamara — Weeks on Chart: **81**

Date	Title	Label	Peak Position	Weeks at No.1	Weeks on Chart
20 Jun 98	THE GOOD WILL OUT	*Hut CDHUT 46* ⊛	1	1	21
8 Apr 00	DRAWN FROM MEMORY	*Hut CDHUT 60* ●	8		13
15 Sep 01	IF YOU'VE NEVER BEEN	*Hut CDHUT 68*	9		3
6 Apr 02	FIREWORKS (SINGLES 1997 – 2002)	*Hut CDHUT 74*	36		2
25 Sep 04	OUT OF NOTHING	*Independiente ISOM45CD* ⊛	1	1	30
8 Apr 06	THIS NEW DAY	*Independiente ISOM60CD* ●	1	1	12

EMERSON, LAKE & PALMER

UK, male vocal/instrumental group – Keith Emerson, Greg Lake* & Carl Palmer — Weeks on Chart: **142**

Date	Title	Label	Peak Position	Weeks at No.1	Weeks on Chart
5 Dec 70	EMERSON, LAKE AND PALMER	*Island ILPS 9132*	4		28
19 Jun 71	TARKUS	*Island ILPS 9155*	1	1	17
4 Dec 71	PICTURES AT AN EXHIBITION	*Island HELP 1* ○	3		5
8 Jul 72	TRILOGY	*Island ILPS 9186*	2		29
22 Dec 73	BRAIN SALAD SURGERY	*Manticore K 53501* ●	2		17
24 Aug 74	WELCOME BACK MY FRIENDS TO THE SHOW THAT NEVER ENDS – LADIES AND GENTLEMEN: EMERSON, LAKE AND PALMER	*Manticore K 63500*	5		5
9 Apr 77	WORKS	*Atlantic K 80009* ●	9		25
10 Dec 77	WORKS VOLUME 2	*Atlantic K 50422*	20		5
9 Dec 78	LOVE BEACH	*Atlantic K 50552* ○	48		4
14 Jun 86	EMERSON, LAKE AND POWELL	*Polydor POLD 5191* EMERSON, LAKE & POWELL	35		5
26 Jun 04	THE ULTIMATE COLLECTION	*Sanctuary TDSAN009X*	43		2

EMF

UK, male vocal/instrumental group – James Atkin, Derry Brownson, Mark Decloedt, Ian Dench & Zac Foley, d. 2 Jan 2002 — Weeks on Chart: **22**

Date	Title	Label	Peak Position	Weeks at No.1	Weeks on Chart
18 May 91	SCHUBERT DIP	*Parlophone PCS 7353* ●	3		19
10 Oct 92	STIGMA	*Parlophone CDPCSD 122*	19		2
18 Mar 95	CHA CHA CHA	*Parlophone CDPCSD 165*	30		1

EMINEM

US, male rapper/producer (Marshall Mathers III). Controversial figure, also known as Slim Shady, who racked up four consecutive transatlantic No.1s before announcing his short-lived retirement in 2005. *The Marshall Mathers LP* sold 1.76 million copies in the US in the first week to become the fastest-selling solo album of all time. See D12 — Weeks on Chart: **311**

Date	Title	Label	Peak Position	Weeks at No.1	Weeks on Chart
24 Apr 99	SLIM SHADY	*Interscope IND 90321* ⊛x2	10		114
3 Jun 00	THE MARSHALL MATHERS LP	*Interscope 4906292* ⊛x6 ★	1	2	74
8 Jun 02	THE EMINEM SHOW	*Interscope 4932922* ⊛x4 ★	1	5	71
20 Nov 04	ENCORE	*Interscope 9864884* ⊛x3 ★	1	2	35
10 Dec 05	CURTAIN CALL – THE HITS	*Interscope 9889084* ⊛x3 ★	1	5	17

Top 3 Best-Selling Albums

	Title	Approximate Sales
1	THE MARSHALL MATHERS LP	2,250,000
2	THE EMINEM SHOW	1,495,000
3	CURTAIN CALL - THE HITS	1,215,000

AN EMOTIONAL FISH

Ireland, male vocal/instrumental group — Weeks on Chart: **3**

Date	Title	Label	Peak Position	Weeks at No.1	Weeks on Chart
25 Aug 90	AN EMOTIONAL FISH	*East West WX 359*	40		3

ALEC EMPIRE

Germany, male producer — Weeks on Chart: **1**

Date	Title	Label	Peak Position	Weeks at No.1	Weeks on Chart
4 May 02	INTELLIGENCE AND SACRIFICE	*Digital Hardcore DHRCD 29*	71		1

EN VOGUE

US, female vocal group – Terry Ellis, Cindy Herron, Maxine Jones & Dawn Robinson — Weeks on Chart: **52**

Date	Title	Label	Peak Position	Weeks at No.1	Weeks on Chart
2 Jun 90	BORN TO SING	*Atlantic 7567820841* ○	23		13
23 May 92	FUNKY DIVAS	*East West America 7567921212* ●	4		29
28 Jun 97	EV3	*East West America 7559620972* ○	9		8
31 Oct 98	BEST OF EN VOGUE	*East West America 7559623222*	39		2

ENEMY

US, male vocal/instrumental group – Troy Van Leeuwen, Alan Cage (replaced by Kelli Scott) & Eddie Nappi — Weeks on Chart: **46**

Date	Title	Label	Peak Position	Weeks at No.1	Weeks on Chart
21 Jul 07	WE'LL LIVE AND DIE IN THESE TOWNS	*Warner Brothers 2564698852* ⊛	1	1	46

ENERGY ORCHARD

Ireland, male vocal/instrumental group — Weeks on Chart: **2**

Date	Title	Label	Peak Position	Weeks at No.1	Weeks on Chart
12 May 90	ENERGY ORCHARD	*MCA MCG 6083*	53		2

Silver-selling ○ Gold-selling ● Platinum-selling ⊛ US No.1 ★ Peak Position Weeks at No.1 Weeks on Chart

ENGLAND FOOTBALL WORLD CUP SQUAD

UK, male footballers/vocalists — 18

Date	Title	Peak	Wks No.1	Wks
16 May 70	**THE WORLD BEATERS SING THE WORLD BEATERS** *Pye NSPL 18337* ENGLAND FOOTBALL WORLD CUP SQUAD 1970	4		8
15 May 82	**THIS TIME** *K-Tel NE 1169* ○	37		10

ENGLISH CHAMBER ORCHESTRA

UK, male/female orchestra — 115

Date	Title	Peak	Wks No.1	Wks
7 Feb 76	**RODRIGO: CONCERTO DE ARANJUEZ** *CBS 79369* JOHN WILLIAMS WITH THE ENGLISH CHAMBER ORCHESTRA CONDUCTED BY DANIEL BARENBOIM ●	20		9
2 Apr 83	**CHANTS D'AUVERGNE VOLUME 1** *Decca SXDL 7604* KIRI TE KANAWA WITH THE ENGLISH CHAMBER ORCHESTRA	57		1
7 Oct 89	**VIVALDI: THE FOUR SEASONS** *EMI NIGE 2* NIGEL KENNEDY WITH THE ENGLISH CHAMBER ORCHESTRA ⊛x2	3		81
5 May 90	**MENDELSSOHN/BRUCH/SCHUBERT** *HMV 7496631* NIGEL KENNEDY WITH JEFFREY TATE CONDUCTING THE ENGLISH CHAMBER ORCHESTRA ●	28		15
27 Mar 99	**THE BEYONDNESS OF THINGS** *Decca 4600092*	67		1
27 Mar 99	**RETURN TO THE CENTRE OF THE EARTH** *EMI Classics CDC 5567632* RICK WAKEMAN; LONDON SYMPHONY ORCHESTRA; ENGLISH CHAMBER CHOIR; NARRATED BY PATRICK STEWART	34		2
6 Nov 99	**CLASSIC KENNEDY** *EMI Classics CDC 5568902* NIGEL KENNEDY WITH THE ENGLISH CHAMBER ORCHESTRA	51		6

ENIGMA

UK, male/female vocal/instrumental group — 3

Date	Title	Peak	Wks No.1	Wks
5 Sep 81	**AIN'T NO STOPPIN'** *Creole CRX 1*	80		3

ENIGMA

Romania/Germany, male vocal/production group – Michael Cretu & various musicians including Peter Cornelius, Sandra Cretu, David Fairstein, Jens Gad & Frank Peterson — 143

Date	Title	Peak	Wks No.1	Wks
22 Dec 90	**MCMXC A.D** *Virgin International VIR 11* ⊛x3	1	1	83
19 Feb 94	**THE CROSS OF CHANGES** *Virgin CDVIR 20* ⊛x2	1	1	35
7 Dec 96	**LE ROI EST MORT, VIVE LE ROI!** *Virgin CDVIR 60* ●	12		12
29 Jan 00	**THE SCREEN BEHIND THE MIRROR** *Virgin DGVIR 100* ●	7		6
17 Nov 01	**LOVE SENSUALITY DEVOTION – GREATEST HITS** *Virgin DGVIR 150* ○	29		4
20 Sep 03	**VOYAGEUR** *Virgin CDVIRX 211*	46		3

BRIAN ENO

UK, male producer/composer/keyboard player. See Roxy Music — 17

Date	Title	Peak	Wks No.1	Wks
9 Mar 74	**HERE COME THE WARM JETS** *Island ILPS 9268*	26		2
21 Oct 78	**MUSIC FOR FILMS** *Polydor 2310 623*	55		1
21 Feb 81	**MY LIFE IN THE BUSH OF GHOSTS** *E.G. EGLP 48* & DAVID BYRNE	29		8
8 May 82	**AMBIENT 4 ON LAND** *E.G. EGED 20*	93		1
12 Sep 92	**NERVE NET** *Opal 9362450332*	70		1
24 Sep 94	**WAH WAH** *Fontana 5228272* JAMES & BRIAN ENO	11		2
14 Oct 95	**SPINNER** *All Saints ASCD 023* & JAH WOBBLE	71		1
25 Jun 05	**ANOTHER DAY ON EARTH** *Hannibal HNCD1475*	75		1

ENTER SHIKARI

UK, male vocal/instrumental group – Rou Reynolds, Chris Batten, Liam Clewlow & Rob Rolfe — 7

Date	Title	Peak	Wks No.1	Wks
31 Mar 07	**TAKE TO THE SKIES** *Ambush Reality DVDAMBR001* ●	4		7

ENTOMBED

Sweden, male vocal/instrumental group — 1

Date	Title	Peak	Wks No.1	Wks
15 Mar 97	**TO RIDE, SHOOT STRAIGHT AND SPEAK THE TRUTH** *Threeman Recordings CDMFNX 216*	75		1

ENUFF Z'NUFF

US, male vocal/instrumental group — 1

Date	Title	Peak	Wks No.1	Wks
13 Apr 91	**STRENGTH** *Atco 7567916381*	56		1

ENYA

Ireland, female vocalist/multi-instrumentalist (Eithne Ni Bhraonáin). The world's biggest-selling 'New Age' artist has sold more than 65 million albums. In 2001, she was the best-selling female artist around the globe with album sales topping 15 million – more than Eva Cassidy, Dido, Jennifer Lopez and Kylie Minogue. See Clannad — 293

Date	Title	Peak	Wks No.1	Wks
6 Jun 87	**ENYA (OST-TV)** *BBC REB 605*	69		4
15 Oct 88	**WATERMARK** *WEA WX 199* ⊛x4	5		92
16 Nov 91	**SHEPHERD MOONS** *WEA WX 431* ⊛x4	1	1	90
28 Nov 92	**THE CELTS** *WEA 4509911672* ⊛	10		19
2 Dec 95	**THE MEMORY OF TREES** *WEA 0630128792* ⊛x2	5		24
15 Nov 97	**PAINT THE SKY WITH STARS – THE BEST OF ENYA** *WEA 3984208952* ⊛	4		28
2 Dec 00	**A DAY WITHOUT RAIN** *WEA 8573859862* ⊛	6		17
3 Dec 05	**AMARANTINE** *Warner Brothers 2564627972* ○	8		9
25 Nov 06	**AMARANTINE** *Warner Brothers 2564641402*	53		3
22 Nov 08	**AND WINTER CAME** *Warner Brothers 2564693306* ●	6		7+

E.P.M.D.

US, male rap/DJ duo — 1

Date	Title	Peak	Wks No.1	Wks
16 Feb 91	**BUSINESS AS USUAL** *Def Jam 4676971*	69		1

EQUALS

UK, male vocal/instrumental group – Eddy Grant*, Derv & Lincoln Gordon, John Hall & Pat Lloyd — 10

Date	Title	Peak	Wks No.1	Wks
18 Nov 67	**UNEQUALLED EQUALS** *President PTL 1006*	10		9
9 Mar 68	**EQUALS EXPLOSION** *President PTLS 1015*	32		1

ERASURE

UK, male vocal/instrumental/production duo – Andy Bell & Vince Clarke. Prolific synthpop pioneers and former Depeche Mode and Yazoo member Clarke's most successful project, with five consecutive No.1 debuts, 20 million albums sold and almost 25 years of hit-making to their credit — 326

Date	Title	Peak	Wks No.1	Wks
14 Jun 86	**WONDERLAND** *Mute STUMM 25*	71		7
11 Apr 87	**THE CIRCUS** *Mute STUMM 35* ⊛	6		107
30 Apr 88	**THE INNOCENTS** *Mute STUMM 55* ⊛x2	1	1	78
28 Oct 89	**WILD!** *Mute STUMM 75* ⊛x2	1	2	48
26 Oct 91	**CHORUS** *Mute STUMM 95* ⊛	1	1	25
28 Nov 92	**POP! – THE FIRST 20 HITS** *Mute CDMUTEL 2* ⊛x3	1	2	26
28 May 94	**I SAY I SAY I SAY** *Mute LCDSTUMM 115* ●	1	1	15
4 Nov 95	**ERASURE** *Mute CDSTUMM 145*	14		5
12 Apr 97	**COWBOY** *Mute CDSTUMM 155*	10		4
4 Nov 00	**LOVEBOAT** *Mute CDSTUMM 175*	45		1
8 Feb 03	**OTHER PEOPLE'S SONGS** *Mute CDSTUMM 215*	17		2
1 Nov 03	**HITS! THE VERY BEST OF ERASURE** *Mute LCDMUTEL 10* ●	15		5
5 Feb 05	**NIGHTBIRD** *Mute CDSTUMM245*	27		2
2 Jun 07	**LIGHT AT THE END OF THE WORLD** *Mute LCDSTUMM285*	29		1

DAVID ESSEX

UK, male vocalist/actor (David Cook) — 186

Date	Title	Peak	Wks No.1	Wks
24 Nov 73	**ROCK ON** *CBS 65823* ○	7		22
19 Oct 74	**DAVID ESSEX** *CBS 69088* ●	2		24
27 Sep 75	**ALL THE FUN OF THE FAIR** *CBS 69160* ●	3		20
5 Jun 76	**ON TOUR** *CBS 95000* ○	51		1
30 Oct 76	**OUT ON THE STREET** *CBS 86017* ●	31		9
8 Oct 77	**GOLD AND IVORY** *CBS 86038* ○	29		4
6 Jan 79	**THE DAVID ESSEX ALBUM** *CBS 10011* ○	29		7
31 Mar 79	**IMPERIAL WIZARD** *Mercury 6359 616*	12		9
12 Jul 80	**HOT LOVE** *Mercury 6359 017*	75		1
19 Jun 82	**STAGE-STRUCK** *Mercury MERS 4*	31		15
27 Nov 82	**THE VERY BEST OF DAVID ESSEX** *TV Records TVA 4*	37		11
15 Oct 83	**MUTINY (STUDIO CAST RECORDING)** *Mercury MERH 30* , FRANK FINLAY & VARIOUS ARTISTS	39		4
17 Dec 83	**THE WHISPER** *Mercury MERH 34*	67		6
6 Dec 86	**CENTRE STAGE** *K-Tel ONE 1333*	82		4
19 Oct 91	**HIS GREATEST HITS** *Mercury 5103081* ●	13		13
10 Apr 93	**COVER SHOT** *Polygram TV 5145632* ●	3		8
22 Oct 94	**BACK TO BACK** *Polygram TV 5237902*	33		2
9 Dec 95	**MISSING YOU** *Polygram TV 5295822* ○	26		9
17 May 97	**A NIGHT AT THE MOVIES** *Polygram TV 5376082*	14		5
13 Jun 98	**GREATEST HITS** *Polygram TV 5584842*	31		4
18 Mar 06	**GREATEST HITS** *Columbia/UMTV 82876813242* ●	7		6
27 Sep 08	**ALL THE FUN OF THE FAIR** *Sony BMG/UMTV 1784019*	23		2

GLORIA ESTEFAN
Cuba, female vocalist (Gloria Fajardo) — 252

Date	Title	Peak	Wks at No.1	Wks on Chart
19 Nov 88	**ANYTHING FOR YOU** *Epic 4631251* GLORIA ESTEFAN & MIAMI SOUND MACHINE ⊛x4	1	1	54
5 Aug 89	**CUTS BOTH WAYS** *Epic 4651451* ⊛x3	1	6	64
16 Feb 91	**INTO THE LIGHT** *Epic 4677821* ⊛	2		36
14 Nov 92	**GREATEST HITS** *Epic 4723322* ⊛x3	2		47
10 Jul 93	**MI TIERRA** *Epic 4737992*	11		11
29 Oct 94	**HOLD ME, THRILL ME, KISS ME** *Epic 4774162* ⊛	5		19
21 Oct 95	**ABRIENDO PUERTAS** *Epic 4809922*	70		1
15 Jun 96	**DESTINY** *Epic 4839322*	12		9
13 Jun 98	**GLORIA!** *Epic 4898502*	16		4
27 May 00	**ALMA CARIBENA – CARIBBEAN SOUL** *Epic 4976172*	44		1
24 Feb 01	**GREATEST HITS VOLUME 2** *Epic 5016372*	60		1
2 Dec 06	**THE VERY BEST OF** *Epic 82876890872*	40		5

ESTELLE
UK, female vocalist/rapper (Estelle Swaray) — 18

Date	Title	Peak	Wks at No.1	Wks on Chart
30 Oct 04	**THE 18TH DAY** *V2 JAD1027838*	35		2
12 Apr 08	**SHINE** *Atlantic 7567899542*	6		16

DON ESTELLE & WINDSOR DAVIES
UK, male actors/vocal duo – Don Estelle, d. 2 Aug 2003 (age 70) — 8

Date	Title	Peak	Wks at No.1	Wks on Chart
10 Jan 76	**SING LOFTY** *EMI EMC 3102* ○	10		8

ETERNAL
UK, female vocal group – Easther & Vernie Bennett, Kéllé Bryan & Louise Nurding (Louise*) — 163

Date	Title	Peak	Wks at No.1	Wks on Chart
11 Dec 93	**ALWAYS & FOREVER** *EMI CDEMD 1053* ⊛x4	2		76
11 Nov 95	**POWER OF A WOMAN** *EMI CDEMD 1090* ⊛x2	6		31
29 Mar 97	**BEFORE THE RAIN** *EMI CDEMD 1103* ⊛	3		29
1 Nov 97	**GREATEST HITS** *EMI 8217982* ⊛x3	2		27

MELISSA ETHERIDGE
US, female vocalist/guitarist — 2

Date	Title	Peak	Wks at No.1	Wks on Chart
30 Sep 89	**BRAVE AND CRAZY** *Island ILPS 9939*	63		1
9 May 92	**NEVER ENOUGH** *Island CID 9990*	56		1

EUROPE
Sweden, male vocal/instrumental group – Joey Tempest, Ian Haugland, John Levén, Mic Michaeli & John Norum (replaced by Kee Marcello) — 43

Date	Title	Peak	Wks at No.1	Wks on Chart
22 Nov 86	**THE FINAL COUNTDOWN** *Epic EPC 26808* ●	9		37
17 Sep 88	**OUT OF THIS WORLD** *Epic 4624491*	12		5
19 Oct 91	**PRISONERS IN PARADISE** *Epic 4687551*	61		1

EUROPEANS
UK, male vocal/instrumental group — 1

Date	Title	Peak	Wks at No.1	Wks on Chart
11 Feb 84	**LIVE** *A&M SCOT 1*	100		1

EURYTHMICS
UK, female/male vocal/instrumental duo – Annie Lennox* & David A. Stewart*. Innovative and distinctive act who are the most charted male/female duo in the UK. Lennox has won more BRIT awards than any other female and they received the Outstanding Contribution award at 1999 BRITs. See Tourists — 495

Date	Title	Peak	Wks at No.1	Wks on Chart
12 Feb 83	**SWEET DREAMS (ARE MADE OF THIS)** *RCA RCALP 6063* ⊛	3		60
26 Nov 83	**TOUCH** *RCA PL 70109* ⊛	1	2	48
9 Jun 84	**TOUCH DANCE** *RCA PG 70354*	31		5
24 Nov 84	**1984 (FOR THE LOVE OF BIG BROTHER) (OST)** *Virgin V 1984* ●	23		17
11 May 85	**BE YOURSELF TONIGHT** *RCA PL 70711* ⊛x2	3		80
12 Jul 86	**REVENGE** *RCA PL 71050* ⊛x2	3		52
21 Nov 87	**SAVAGE** *RCA PL 71555* ⊛	7		33
23 Sep 89	**WE TOO ARE ONE** *RCA PL 74251* ⊛x2	1	1	32
30 Mar 91	**GREATEST HITS** *RCA PL 74856* ⊛x6	1	10	123
27 Nov 93	**EURYTHMICS LIVE 1983–1989** *RCA 74321171452* ●	22		7
30 Oct 99	**PEACE** *RCA 74321695622* ●	4		20
19 Nov 05	**ULTIMATE COLLECTION** *RCA 82876748412* ⊛	5		18

EVANESCENCE
US, female/male vocal/instrumental group – Amy Lee, Will Boyd, Rocky Gray, John LeCompt & Ben Moody (replaced by Terry Balsamo) — 89

Date	Title	Peak	Wks at No.1	Wks on Chart
10 May 03	**FALLEN** *Epic 5108792* ⊛x3	1	1	74
14 Oct 06	**THE OPEN DOOR** *Wind Up 82876860822*	2		15

FAITH EVANS
US, female vocalist — 5

Date	Title	Peak	Wks at No.1	Wks on Chart
7 Nov 98	**KEEP THE FAITH** *Puff Daddy 74321614672*	69		1
28 May 05	**FIRST LADY** *EMI 4771172*	22		4

EVE
US, female rapper (Eve Jeffers) — 13

Date	Title	Peak	Wks at No.1	Wks on Chart
11 Aug 01	**SCORPION** *Interscope 4930212*	22		8
7 Sep 02	**EVE-OLUTION** *Interscope 4934722*	47		5

EVERCLEAR
US, male vocal/instrumental group — 3

Date	Title	Peak	Wks at No.1	Wks on Chart
14 Mar 98	**SO MUCH FOR THE AFTERGLOW** *Capitol 8365032*	63		1
19 Aug 00	**SONGS FROM AN AMERICAN MOVIE VOLUME 1: LEARNING HOW TO SMILE** *Capitol 5278642*	51		1
28 Apr 01	**SONGS FROM AN AMERICAN MOVIE VOLUME 2: GOOD TIME FOR A BAD ATTITUDE** *Capitol 5304192*	69		1

EVERLAST
US, male vocalist (Erik Schrody) — 1

Date	Title	Peak	Wks at No.1	Wks on Chart
13 Mar 99	**WHITEY FORD SINGS THE BLUES** *Tommy Boy TBCD 1236*	65		1

PHIL EVERLY
US, male vocalist/guitarist. See Everly Brothers — 1

Date	Title	Peak	Wks at No.1	Wks on Chart
7 May 83	**PHIL EVERLY** *Capitol EST 27670*	61		1

EVERLY BROTHERS
US, male vocal/instrumental duo – Don & Phil Everly — 130

Date	Title	Peak	Wks at No.1	Wks on Chart
2 Jul 60	**IT'S EVERLY TIME** *Warner Brothers WM 4006*	2		23
15 Oct 60	**FABULOUS STYLE OF THE EVERLY BROTHERS** *London HAA 2266*	4		11
4 Mar 61	**A DATE WITH THE EVERLY BROTHERS** *Warner Brothers WM 4028*	3		14
21 Jul 62	**INSTANT PARTY** *Warner Brothers WM 4061*	20		1
12 Sep 70	**ORIGINAL GREATEST HITS** *CBS 66255*	7		16
8 Jun 74	**THE VERY BEST OF THE EVERLY BROTHERS** *Warner Brothers K 46008*	43		1
29 Nov 75	**WALK RIGHT BACK WITH THE EVERLYS** *Warner Brothers K 56118* ⊛	10		10
9 Apr 77	**LIVING LEGENDS** *Warwick WW 5027*	12		10
18 Dec 82	**LOVE HURTS** *K-Tel NE 1197* ●	22		22
7 Jan 84	**EVERLY BROTHERS REUNION CONCERT – LIVE AT THE ROYAL ALBERT HALL** *Impression IMDP 1* ○	47		6
3 Nov 84	**THE EVERLY BROTHERS** *Mercury MERH 44*	36		4
29 May 93	**THE GOLDEN YEARS OF THE EVERLY BROTHERS – THEIR 24 GREATEST HITS** *Warner Brothers 9548319922* ○	26		5
1 Jun 02	**THE DEFINITIVE** *WSM 0927473042* ○	10		7

EVERYTHING BUT THE GIRL
UK, female/male vocal/instrumental duo – Tracey Thorn* & Ben Watt — 132

Date	Title	Peak	Wks at No.1	Wks on Chart
16 Jun 84	**EDEN** *Blanco Y Negro BYN 2* ●	14		22
27 Apr 85	**LOVE NOT MONEY** *Blanco Y Negro BYN 3* ●	10		9
6 Sep 86	**BABY THE STARS SHINE BRIGHT** *Blanco Y Negro BYN 9* ●	22		9
12 Mar 88	**IDLEWILD** *Blanco Y Negro BYN 14* ●	13		9
6 Aug 88	**IDLEWILD** *Blanco Y Negro BYN 16*	21		6
17 Feb 90	**THE LANGUAGE OF LIFE** *Blanco Y Negro BYN 21* ●	10		6
5 Oct 91	**WORLD WIDE** *Blanco Y Negro BYN 25*	29		5
22 May 93	**HOME MOVIES – THE BEST OF EVERYTHING BUT THE GIRL** *Blanco Y Negro 4509923192* ●	5		8
25 Jun 94	**AMPLIFIED HEART** *Blanco Y Negro 4509964822* ●	20		15
18 May 96	**WALKING WOUNDED** *Blanco Y Negro CDV 2803* ⊛	4		27
9 Nov 96	**THE BEST OF EVERYTHING BUT THE GIRL** *Blanco Y Negro 0630166372* ⊛	23		12
9 Oct 99	**TEMPERAMENTAL** *Blanco Y Negro CDV 2892*	16		3
2 Nov 02	**LIKE THE DESERTS MISS THE RAIN** *Virgin CDV 2966*	58		1

The Jimi Hendrix Experience:
Are You Experienced

FOUR decades after Jimi Hendrix exploded onto the scene in the late 1960s, it's difficult to understand the initial impact this unique artist must have had. Likewise, so much has been written about *Are You Experienced* that it is a challenge to be an objective observer, to treat the record with the isolated analysis it deserves. But make no mistake – if listening to his records in the 2000s can be a mind-blowing adventure, in 1967 it must have felt as if a whole new world had just been discovered.

In 1967, Britain was already drenched in the Summer of Love's psychedelia, progressive music and mind-altering substances, and it must have felt that nothing more could be done until Jimi upped the ante into the stratosphere, just like Elvis had done ten years earlier. *Everything* went into full colour when Hendrix arrived. His hair, his clothes, his music, his guitar-playing was so damn flamboyant and thrilling that it made the likes of Eric Clapton – who saw him play live early on – want to stop playing. And, remember, Clapton was the man heralded as 'God' among guitar players; Hendrix was *that* good.

Hendrix re-invented the six-string in a way that many have tried – and failed – to do since then

Hendrix had arrived in England in 1966 from America and was taken under the wing of manager, Chas Chandler, who put a band together around the prodigiously – outrageously – talented young guitar player. With Mitch Mitchell on drums and Noel Redding on bass, the group signed with Track Records (newly formed by The Who's managers Kit Lambert and Chris Stamp). The band released three classic Top 10 hit UK singles produced by Chandler: 'Hey Joe'/'Stone Free' (December 1966), 'Purple Haze'/'51st Anniversary' (March 1967), and 'The Wind Cries Mary'/'Highway Chile' (May 1967). It was during sessions for these singles that the band also recorded the debut album, which was released in May 1967. Notably, the three preceding singles were not included on this record.

Are You Experienced (there was no question mark on the sleeve artwork; in France they added one and some later versions had the mark in the track-listing) captured Hendrix at this pivotal moment in both his and the decade's pop story. The guitar-playing was *astounding*. It was acutely revolutionary and 'way, way out there, man', effectively rewriting the rulebook of what you could do with a guitar. Utilising feedback and a myriad of pioneering techniques (playing with his teeth, scratching strings, howling feedback loops, the list is endless), Hendrix re-invented the six-string in a way that many have tried – and failed – to do since then. The fact that he also managed to do this inside great songs – that perfectly captured the feeling of the time – only added to the album's genius.

Produced by Chas Chandler and engineered by Eddie Kramer, the album is a perfect document from the highpoint of the Summer of Love. In the guitar-playing and in the songs themselves, there is a revolutionary, euphoric, 'we can do anything' vibe that means this album has that rare duality of being both a perfect time-piece and yet a timeless classic. It was an international hit too, although in apartheid South Africa

Chart History

Artist	Album Title	First Chart Week	Weeks on Chart	Highest Position
THE JIMI HENDRIX EXPERIENCE	ARE YOU EXPERIENCED	27/5/67	33	2

the band's photograph was replaced with a plain sleeve and lettering. After some delay and the inclusion of the three hit singles, the album was finally repackaged for the USA – but not before Hendrix was told 'Red House' was to be removed 'because the US and Latin America doesn't like the blues'. Back in the UK, the album never made it to Number 1 as it was competing with The Beatles' *Sgt. Pepper's Lonely Hearts Club Band*, one of the few albums in history that, musically at least, could genuinely match Hendrix's own gift.

Hendrix's vocals – all too often overlooked – were key to the songs, his husky voice added sex and authority to the music. Hendrix himself hated his own singing, yet remarkably it is almost as accomplished as his guitar-playing, if not for its radical tone then certainly for its looseness and feeling.

This album is a startling melting pot, a cacophony of inspiration: Jimi Hendrix took the blues – the backbone of rock 'n' roll – and the absolute cutting-edge music of the underground hipsters and blasted them both right into the here and now; he added an outer-space infinity and a spectral otherworldliness to the acid-drenched, frizzing feedback of the guitars; he added a Bob Dylan and Beatles songwriting *nous*; and he added the purest essence of the zeitgeist. You don't need to watch any television documentaries on 1967 to understand *Are You Experienced*, you simply have to listen to the album – it is the sound of a confused, positive *and* negative world exploding from monochrome to Technicolor in one cycle of songs. Before *Are You Experienced*, modern rock was a theory; afterwards it was reality.

His husky voice added sex and authority to the music

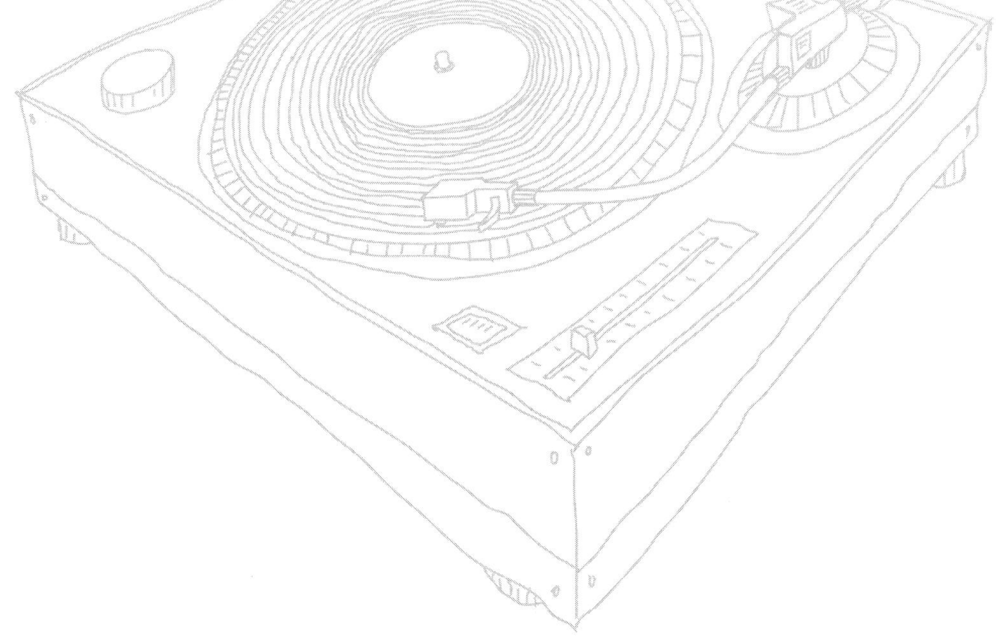

Silver-selling ○ · Gold-selling ● · Platinum-selling ⊛ · US No.1 ★ · Peak Position · Weeks at No.1 · Weeks on Chart

EXODUS

US, male vocal/instrumental group — Weeks on Chart: 1

Date	Title / Label	Peak Position	Weeks at No.1	Weeks on Chart
11 Feb 89	**FABULOUS DISASTER** *Music For Nations MFN 90*	67		1

EXPLOITED

UK, male vocal/instrumental group — Weeks on Chart: 26

Date	Title / Label	Peak Position	Weeks at No.1	Weeks on Chart
16 May 81	**PUNK'S NOT DEAD** *Secret SEC 1*	20		11
14 Nov 81	**EXPLOITED LIVE** *Superville EXPLP 2001*	52		3
19 Jun 82	**TROOPS OF TOMORROW** *Secret SEC 8*	17		12

EXPLOSIONS IN THE SKY

US, male instrumental group — Weeks on Chart: 1

Date	Title / Label	Peak Position	Weeks at No.1	Weeks on Chart
3 Mar 07	**ALL OF A SUDDEN I MISS EVERYONE** *Bella Union BELLACD135X*	58		1

EXTREME

US, male vocal/instrumental group – Gary Cherone, Pat Badger, Nuno Bettencourt & Paul Geary (replaced by Michael Mangini) — Weeks on Chart: 75

Date	Title / Label	Peak Position	Weeks at No.1	Weeks on Chart
1 Jun 91	**EXTREME II PORNAGRAFFITTI** *A&M 3953131* ⊛	12		61
26 Sep 92	**III SIDES TO EVERY STORY** *A&M 5400062* ●	2		11
11 Feb 95	**WAITING FOR THE PUNCHLINE** *A&M 5403052*	10		3

E.Y.C.

US, male vocal group — Weeks on Chart: 5

Date	Title / Label	Peak Position	Weeks at No.1	Weeks on Chart
16 Apr 94	**EXPRESS YOURSELF CLEARLY** *MCA MCD 11061*	14		5

F

ADAM F

UK, male producer (Adam Fenton) — Weeks on Chart: 3

Date	Title / Label	Peak Position	Weeks at No.1	Weeks on Chart
15 Nov 97	**COLOURS** *Positiva 8217252*	47		1
22 Sep 01	**KAOS – THE ANTI ACOUSTIC WARFARE** *Chrysalis 5342502*	44		2

F.A.B.

UK, male production group — Weeks on Chart: 3

Date	Title / Label	Peak Position	Weeks at No.1	Weeks on Chart
10 Nov 90	**POWER THEMES 90** *Telstar STAR 2430* ○	53		3

FABOLOUS

US, male rapper (John Jackson) — Weeks on Chart: 11

Date	Title / Label	Peak Position	Weeks at No.1	Weeks on Chart
2 Aug 03	**STREET DREAMS** *Elektra 7559627912*	51		10
20 Nov 04	**REAL TALK** *Atlantic 7567837542*	66		1

FACES

UK, male vocal/instrumental group – Rod Stewart*, Kenney Jones, Ronnie Lane*, d. 4 Jun 1997 (replaced by Tetsu Yamauchi), Ian McLagan & Ronnie Wood — Weeks on Chart: 62

Date	Title / Label	Peak Position	Weeks at No.1	Weeks on Chart
4 Apr 70	**FIRST STEP** *Warner Brothers WS 3000*	45		1
8 May 71	**LONG PLAYER** *Warner Brothers W 3011*	31		7
25 Dec 71	**A NOD'S AS GOOD AS A WINK...TO A BLIND HORSE** *Warner Brothers K 56006*	2		22
21 Apr 73	**OOH-LA-LA** *Warner Brothers K 56011*	1	1	13
26 Jan 74	**OVERTURE AND BEGINNERS** *Mercury 9100 001* ROD STEWART & THE FACES	3		7
21 May 77	**THE BEST OF THE FACES** *Riva RVLP 3*	24		6
7 Nov 92	**THE BEST OF ROD STEWART AND THE FACES 1971–1975** *Mercury 5141802* ROD STEWART & THE FACES	58		1
1 Nov 03	**CHANGING FACES – THE VERY BEST OF** *Universal TV 9812604* ROD STEWART & THE FACES ●	13		5

DONALD FAGEN

US, male vocalist/keyboard player. See Steely Dan — Weeks on Chart: 27

Date	Title / Label	Peak Position	Weeks at No.1	Weeks on Chart
30 Oct 82	**THE NIGHTFLY** *Warner Brothers 9236961* ⊛	44		16
5 Jun 93	**KAMAKIRIAD** *Reprise 9362452302* ●	3		9
25 Mar 06	**MORPH THE CAT** *Reprise 9362499752*	35		2

FAIRGROUND ATTRACTION

UK, female/male vocal/instrumental group – Eddi Reader*, Roy Dodds, Simon Edwards & Mark E. Nevin — Weeks on Chart: 54

Date	Title / Label	Peak Position	Weeks at No.1	Weeks on Chart
28 May 88	**THE FIRST OF A MILLION KISSES** *RCA PL 71696* ⊛x2	2		52
30 Jun 90	**AY FOND KISS** *RCA PL 74596*	55		2

FAIRPORT CONVENTION

UK, male/female vocal/instrumental group – Sandy Denny*, d. 21 Apr 1978, Ashley Hutchings, Dave Mattacks, Simon Nicol, Dave Swarbrick & Richard Thompson* — Weeks on Chart: 41

Date	Title / Label	Peak Position	Weeks at No.1	Weeks on Chart
2 Aug 69	**UNHALFBRICKING** *Island ILPS 9102*	12		8
17 Jan 70	**LIEGE AND LIEF** *Island ILPS 9115*	17		15
18 Jul 70	**FULL HOUSE** *Island ILPS 9130*	13		11
3 Jul 71	**ANGEL DELIGHT** *Island ILPS 9162*	8		5
12 Jul 75	**RISING FOR THE MOON** *Island ILPS 9313*	52		1
28 Jan 89	**RED AND GOLD** *New Routes RUE 002*	74		1

ADAM FAITH

UK, male vocalist (Terence Nelhams-Wright), d. 8 Mar 2003 (age 62) — Weeks on Chart: 46

Date	Title / Label	Peak Position	Weeks at No.1	Weeks on Chart
19 Nov 60	**ADAM** *Parlophone PMC 1128*	6		36
11 Feb 61	**BEAT GIRL (OST)** *Columbia 33SX 1225*	11		3
24 Mar 62	**ADAM FAITH** *Parlophone PMC 1162*	20		1
25 Sep 65	**FAITH ALIVE** *Parlophone PMC 1249*	19		1
19 Dec 81	**24 GOLDEN GREATS** *Warwick WW 5113*	61		3
27 Nov 93	**MIDNIGHT POSTCARDS** *Polygram TV 8213982*	43		2

FAITH BROTHERS

UK, male vocal/instrumental group — Weeks on Chart: 1

Date	Title / Label	Peak Position	Weeks at No.1	Weeks on Chart
9 Nov 85	**EVENTIDE** *Siren SIRENLP 1*	66		1

FAITH NO MORE

US, male vocal/instrumental group – Mike Patton, Mike Bordin, Roddy Bottum, Bill Gould & Jim Martin — Weeks on Chart: 74

Date	Title / Label	Peak Position	Weeks at No.1	Weeks on Chart
17 Feb 90	**THE REAL THING** *Slash 8281541* ○	30		35
16 Feb 91	**LIVE AT THE BRIXTON ACADEMY** *Slash 8282381*	20		4
20 Jun 92	**ANGEL DUST** *Slash 8283212* ○	2		25
25 Mar 95	**KING FOR A DAY, FOOL FOR A LIFETIME** *Slash 8285602* ●	5		6
21 Jun 97	**ALBUM OF THE YEAR** *Slash 8288022*	7		3
21 Nov 98	**WHO CARES A LOT? – THE GREATEST HITS** *Slash 5560522* ○	37		1

MARIANNE FAITHFULL

UK, female vocalist — Weeks on Chart: 19

Date	Title / Label	Peak Position	Weeks at No.1	Weeks on Chart
5 Jun 65	**COME MY WAY** *Decca LK 4688*	12		7
5 Jun 65	**MARIANNE FAITHFULL** *Decca LK 4689*	15		2
24 Nov 79	**BROKEN ENGLISH** *Island M1*	57		3
17 Oct 81	**DANGEROUS ACQUAINTANCES** *Island ILPS 9648*	45		4
26 Mar 83	**A CHILD'S ADVENTURE** *Island ILPS 9734*	99		1
8 Aug 87	**STRANGE WEATHER** *Island ILPS 9874*	78		2

FAITHLESS

UK, male/female vocal/instrumental/production trio – Maxi Jazz (Maxwell Frazer), Rollo Armstrong & Sister Bliss (Alayah Bentovim) — Weeks on Chart: 129

Date	Title / Label	Peak Position	Weeks at No.1	Weeks on Chart
23 Nov 96	**REVERENCE** *Cheeky CHEKLP 500* ●	26		14
3 Oct 98	**SUNDAY 8PM** *Cheeky CHEKCD 503* ●	10		7
30 Jun 01	**OUTROSPECTIVE** *Cheeky 74321862802* ●	4		22
19 Jun 04	**NO ROOTS** *Cheeky 82876618702* ●	1	1	14
28 May 05	**FOREVER FAITHLESS – THE GREATEST HITS** *Cheeky 82876684322* ⊛x3	1	1	67
9 Dec 06	**TO ALL NEW ARRIVALS** *Columbia 88697027612* ●	30		5

FALCO

Austria, male vocalist (Johann Holzel), d. 6 Feb 1988 (age 40) — Weeks on Chart: 15

Date	Title / Label	Peak Position	Weeks at No.1	Weeks on Chart
26 Apr 86	**FALCO 3** *A&M AMA 5105*	32		15

FALL

UK, male/female vocal/instrumental group – Mark E. Smith & various musicians; members also included Steve Hanley, Craig Scanlon, Brix Smith & Simon Wolstencroft — Weeks on Chart: 33

Date	Title / Label	Peak Position	Weeks at No.1	Weeks on Chart
20 Mar 82	**HEX ENDUCATION HOUR** *Kamera KAM 005*	71		3
20 Oct 84	**THE WONDERFUL AND FRIGHTENING WORLD OF...** *Beggars Banquet BEGA 58*	62		2

Date	Title / Label	Peak Position	Weeks at No.1	Weeks on Chart
5 Oct 85	**THIS NATION'S SAVING GRACE** *Beggars Banquet BEGA 67*	54		2
11 Oct 86	**BEND SINISTER** *Beggars Banquet BEGA 75*	36		3
12 Mar 88	**THE FRENZ EXPERIMENT** *Beggars Banquet BEGA 91*	19		4
12 Nov 88	**I AM KURIOUS, ORANJ** *Beggars Banquet BEGA 96*	54		2
8 Jul 89	**SEMNINAL LIVE** *Beggars Banquet BBL 102*	40		2
3 Mar 90	**EXTRICATE** *Cog Sinister 8422041*	31		3
15 Sep 90	**458489 A-SIDES** *Beggars Banquet BEGA 111*	44		2
4 May 91	**SHIFT-WORK** *Cog Sinister 8485941*	17		2
28 Mar 92	**CODE-SELFISH** *Cog Sinister 5121622*	21		1
8 May 93	**INFOTAINMENT SCAN** *Permanent PERMCD 12*	9		3
14 May 94	**MIDDLE CLASS REVOLT** *Permanent PERMCD 16*	48		1
11 Mar 95	**CEREBRAL CAUSTIC** *Permanent PERMCD 30*	67		1
22 Jun 96	**THE LIGHT USER SYNDROME** *Jet JETLP 1012*	54		1
10 May 08	**IMPERIAL WAX SOLVENT** *Sanctuary 1765729*	35		1

FALL OUT BOY

US, male vocal/instrumental group – Patrick Stump, Andy Hurley, Joe Trohman & Pete Wentz — Weeks on Chart: 65

Date	Title / Label	Peak Position	Weeks at No.1	Weeks on Chart
28 Jan 06	**FROM UNDER THE CORK TREE** *Mercury B000414002* ⊛	12		31
17 Feb 07	**INFINITY ON HIGH** *Mercury 1723786* ⊛ ★	3		32
27 Dec 08	**FOLIE A DEUX** *Mercury 1788407*	39		2+

AGNETHA FÄLTSKOG

Sweden, female vocalist. See Abba — Weeks on Chart: 21

Date	Title / Label	Peak Position	Weeks at No.1	Weeks on Chart
11 Jun 83	**WRAP YOUR ARMS AROUND ME** *Epic EPC 25505*	18		13
4 May 85	**EYES OF A WOMAN** *Epic EPC 26446*	38		3
12 Mar 88	**I STAND ALONE** *WEA WX 150*	72		1
1 May 04	**MY COLOURING BOOK** *WEA 5046731222* ○	12		4

GEORGIE FAME

UK, male vocalist/keyboard player (Clive Powell) — Weeks on Chart: 72

Date	Title / Label	Peak Position	Weeks at No.1	Weeks on Chart
17 Oct 64	**FAME AT LAST** *Columbia 33SX 1638*	15		8
14 May 66	**SWEET THINGS** *Columbia SX 6043*	6		22
15 Oct 66	**SOUND VENTURE** *Columbia SX 6076*	9		9
11 Mar 67	**HALL OF FAME** *Columbia SX 6120*	12		18
1 Jul 67	**THE TWO FACES OF FAME** *CBS DBPG 63018*	22		15

FAMILY

UK, male vocal/instrumental group – Roger Chapman, Rick Grech, d. 16 Mar 1990, John Palmer, Rob Townsend, John Weider & John Whitney — Weeks on Chart: 41

Date	Title / Label	Peak Position	Weeks at No.1	Weeks on Chart
10 Aug 68	**MUSIC IN THE DOLLS HOUSE** *Reprise RLP 6312*	35		3
22 Mar 69	**FAMILY ENTERTAINMENT** *Reprise RLP 6340*	6		3
7 Feb 70	**A SONG FOR ME** *Reprise RSLP 9001*	4		13
28 Nov 70	**ANYWAY** *Reprise RSX 9005*	7		7
20 Nov 71	**FEARLESS** *Reprise K 54003*	14		2
30 Sep 72	**BANDSTAND** *Reprise K 54006*	15		10
29 Sep 73	**IT'S ONLY A MOVIE** *Raft RA 58501*	30		3

FAMILY CAT

UK, male vocal/instrumental group — Weeks on Chart: 1

Date	Title / Label	Peak Position	Weeks at No.1	Weeks on Chart
4 Jul 92	**FURTHEST FROM THE SUN** *Dedicated DEDCD 007*	55		1

FAMILY STAND

US, female/male vocal/instrumental group — Weeks on Chart: 3

Date	Title / Label	Peak Position	Weeks at No.1	Weeks on Chart
19 May 90	**CHAIN** *Atlantic WX 349*	52		3

CHRIS FARLOWE

UK, male vocalist (John Deighton) — Weeks on Chart: 3

Date	Title / Label	Peak Position	Weeks at No.1	Weeks on Chart
2 Apr 66	**14 THINGS TO THINK ABOUT** *Immediate IMLP 005*	19		1
10 Dec 66	**THE ART OF CHRIS FARLOWE** *Immediate IMLP 006*	37		2

FARM

UK, male vocal/instrumental group – Peter Hooton, Roy Boulter, Steve Grimes, Carl Hunter, Ben Leach & Keith Mullin — Weeks on Chart: 17

Date	Title / Label	Peak Position	Weeks at No.1	Weeks on Chart
16 Mar 91	**SPARTACUS** *Produce MILKLP 1* ●	1	1	17

FARMER'S BOYS

UK, male vocal/instrumental group — Weeks on Chart: 1

Date	Title / Label	Peak Position	Weeks at No.1	Weeks on Chart
29 Oct 83	**GET OUT AND WALK** *EMI EMC 1077991*	49		1

JOHN FARNHAM

Australia (b. UK), male vocalist — Weeks on Chart: 9

Date	Title / Label	Peak Position	Weeks at No.1	Weeks on Chart
11 Jul 87	**WHISPERING JACK** *RCA PL 71224*	35		9

FASHION

UK, male vocal/instrumental group – Dave Harris, Alan Darby, Dik Davis, John Mulligan & Marlon Recchi — Weeks on Chart: 17

Date	Title / Label	Peak Position	Weeks at No.1	Weeks on Chart
3 Jul 82	**FABRIQUE** *Arista SPART 1185*	10		16
16 Jun 84	**TWILIGHT OF IDOLS** *De Stijl EPC 25909*	69		1

FASTER PUSSYCAT

US, male vocal/instrumental group — Weeks on Chart: 3

Date	Title / Label	Peak Position	Weeks at No.1	Weeks on Chart
16 Sep 89	**WAKE ME WHEN IT'S OVER** *Elektra EKT 64*	35		2
22 Aug 92	**WHIPPED!** *Elektra 7559611242*	58		1

FASTWAY

UK, male vocal/instrumental group — Weeks on Chart: 2

Date	Title / Label	Peak Position	Weeks at No.1	Weeks on Chart
30 Apr 83	**FASTWAY** *CBS 25359*	43		2

FAT BOYS

US, male rap group — Weeks on Chart: 5

Date	Title / Label	Peak Position	Weeks at No.1	Weeks on Chart
3 Oct 87	**CRUSHIN'** *Urban URBLP 3*	49		4
30 Jul 88	**COMING BACK HARD AGAIN** *Urban URBLP 13*	98		1

FAT JOE

US, male rapper (Joseph Cartagena) — Weeks on Chart: 10

Date	Title / Label	Peak Position	Weeks at No.1	Weeks on Chart
27 Apr 02	**JEALOUS ONES STILL ENVY (J.O.S.E.)** *Atlantic 7567834722* ○	19		10

FAT LADY SINGS

Ireland, male vocal/instrumental group — Weeks on Chart: 1

Date	Title / Label	Peak Position	Weeks at No.1	Weeks on Chart
18 May 91	**TWIST** *East West WX 418*	50		1

FAT LARRY'S BAND

US, male vocal/instrumental group — Weeks on Chart: 4

Date	Title / Label	Peak Position	Weeks at No.1	Weeks on Chart
9 Oct 82	**BREAKIN' OUT** *WMOT V 2229*	58		4

FATBACK BAND

US, male vocal/instrumental group — Weeks on Chart: 7

Date	Title / Label	Peak Position	Weeks at No.1	Weeks on Chart
6 Mar 76	**RAISING HELL** *Polydor 2391 203*	19		6
4 Jul 87	**FATBACK LIVE** *Start STL 12*	80		1

FATBOY SLIM

UK, male DJ/producer – Norman Cook (Quentin Cook). See Beats International, Housemartins — Weeks on Chart: 129

Date	Title / Label	Peak Position	Weeks at No.1	Weeks on Chart
28 Sep 96	**BETTER LIVING THROUGH CHEMISTRY** *Skint BRASSIC 2CD*	69		3
31 Oct 98	**YOU'VE COME A LONG WAY, BABY** *Skint BRASSIC 11CD* ⊛x3	1	4	86
18 Nov 00	**HALFWAY BETWEEN THE GUTTER AND THE STARS** *Skint BRASSIC 20CD* ⊛	8		22
16 Oct 04	**PALOOKAVILLE** *Skint BRASSIC 29CD*	14		3
1 Jul 06	**WHY TRY HARDER – THE GREATEST HITS** *Skint BRASSIC40CDL* ⊛	2		15

FATHER ABRAHAM & THE SMURFS

Holland, male vocalist (Pierre Kartner) & Smurf Village, fictional cartoon characters — Weeks on Chart: 77

Date	Title / Label	Peak Position	Weeks at No.1	Weeks on Chart
25 Nov 78	**FATHER ABRAHAM IN SMURFLAND** *Decca SMURF 1* ●	19		11
6 Jul 96	**THE SMURFS GO POP!** *EMI TV CDEMTV 121* SMURFS ⊛x2	2		33
16 Nov 96	**SMURF'S CHRISTMAS PARTY** *EMI TV CDEMTV 140* SMURFS ⊛	8		9
22 Feb 97	**THE SMURFS HITS '97 – VOLUME 1** *EMI TV CDEMTV 150* SMURFS ●	2		11
6 Sep 97	**GO POP! AGAIN** *EMI CDEMTV 155* SMURFS	15		7
18 Apr 98	**GREATEST HITS** *EMI 4941952* SMURFS	28		6

FATIMA MANSIONS

Ireland, male vocal/instrumental group — Weeks on Chart: 1

Date	Title / Label	Peak Position	Weeks at No.1	Weeks on Chart
6 Jun 92	**VALHALLA AVENUE** *Radioactive KWCD 18*	52		1

Silver-selling ○ Gold-selling ● Platinum-selling ⊛ US No.1 ★ | Peak Position | Weeks at No.1 | Weeks on Chart

NEWTON FAULKNER
UK, male vocalist/guitarist (Sam Faulkner)

		Peak	Wks at No.1	46
11 Aug 07	**HAND BUILT BY ROBOTS** *Ugly Truth 88697113062* ⊛	1	2	46

FEAR FACTORY
US, male vocal/instrumental group

		Peak	Wks at No.1	7
1 Jul 95	**DEMANUFACTURE** *Roadrunner RR 89565* ○	27		1
14 Jun 97	**REMANUFACTURE – CLONING TECHNOLOGY** *Roadrunner RR 88342*	22		1
8 Aug 98	**OBSOLETE** *Roadrunner RR 87525*	20		2
5 May 01	**DIGIMORTAL** *Roadrunner RR 85615*	24		2
1 May 04	**ARCHETYPE** *Roadrunner RR 83115*	41		1

PHIL FEARON & GALAXY
UK, male/female vocal/instrumental/production group

		Peak	Wks at No.1	9
25 Aug 84	**PHIL FEARON AND GALAXY** *Ensign ENCL 2*	8		8
14 Sep 85	**THIS KIND OF LOVE** *Ensign ENCL 4*	98		1

FEEDER
UK/Japan, male vocal/instrumental group – Grant Nicholas, Taka Hirose & Jon Lee, d. 7 Jan 2002 (replaced by Mark Richardson)

		Peak	Wks at No.1	98
31 May 97	**POLYTHENE** *Echo ECHCD 015* ○	65		1
11 Sep 99	**YESTERDAY WENT TOO SOON** *Echo ECHCD 28* ●	8		3
5 May 01	**ECHO PARK** *Echo ECHCD 34* ⊛	5		9
2 Nov 02	**COMFORT IN SOUND** *Echo ECHCD 43* ⊛	6		36
12 Feb 05	**PUSHING THE SENSES** *Echo ECHDV60* ●	2		15
27 May 06	**THE SINGLES** *Echo ECHDV69* ⊛	2		30
31 Mar 07	**PICTURE OF PERFECT YOUTH** *Echo ECHCD52*	65		1
28 Jun 08	**SILENT CRY** *Echo ECHCD79*	8		3

FEELING
UK, male vocal/instrumental group – Dan Gillespie Sells, Ciaran & Kevin Jeremiah, Richard Jones & Paul Stewart

		Peak	Wks at No.1	74
17 Jun 06	**TWELVE STOPS AND HOME** *Island/Uni-Island 9857881* ⊛	2		51
1 Mar 08	**JOIN WITH US** *Island 1761894* ●	1	1	23

FEIST
Canada, female vocalist/guitarist (Leslie Feist)

		Peak	Wks at No.1	9
5 May 07	**THE REMINDER** *Polydor 9848785*	28		9

WILTON FELDER
US, male saxophonist

		Peak	Wks at No.1	3
23 Feb 85	**SECRETS** *MCA MCF 3237 FEATURING BOBBY WOMACK & INTRODUCING ALLTRINA GRAYSON*	77		3

JOSE FELICIANO
US (b. Puerto Rico), male vocalist/guitarist

		Peak	Wks at No.1	40
2 Nov 68	**FELICIANO** *RCA Victor SF 7946*	6		36
29 Nov 69	**JOSE FELICIANO** *RCA Victor LSP 4421*	29		2
14 Feb 70	**10 TO 23** *RCA Victor SF 8044*	38		1
22 Aug 70	**FIREWORKS** *RCA Victor SF 8124*	65		1

FELIX
UK, male producer (Francis Wright)

		Peak	Wks at No.1	4
10 Apr 93	**FELIX #1** *Deconstruction 74321137002*	26		4

JULIE FELIX
US, female vocalist/guitarist

		Peak	Wks at No.1	4
10 Sep 66	**CHANGES** *Fontana TL 5368*	27		4

FERGIE
US, female vocalist (Stacy Ferguson). See Black Eyed Peas

		Peak	Wks at No.1	30
30 Sep 06	**THE DUTCHESS** *A&M 1707562*	18		30

IBRAHIM FERRER
Cuba, male vocalist/pianist

		Peak	Wks at No.1	3
5 Jun 99	**BUENA VISTA SOCIAL CLUB PRESENTS IBRAHIM FERRER** *World Circuit WCD 055*	42		3

BRYAN FERRY
UK, male vocalist. Suave and sophisticated song stylist who first came to the public's attention as leader of the critically-acclaimed Roxy Music. His span of newly-recorded UK Top 5 solo albums is in excess of 33 years. See Roxy Music

		Peak	Wks at No.1	339
3 Nov 73	**THESE FOOLISH THINGS** *Island ILPS 9249* ●	5		42
20 Jul 74	**ANOTHER TIME, ANOTHER PLACE** *Island ILPS 9284* ●	4		25
2 Oct 76	**LET'S STICK TOGETHER** *Island ILPSX 1*	19		5
5 Mar 77	**IN YOUR MIND** *Polydor 2302 055* ●	5		17
30 Sep 78	**THE BRIDE STRIPPED BARE** *Polydor POLD 5003* ○	13		5
15 Jun 85	**BOYS AND GIRLS** *E.G. EGLP 62* ⊛x3	1	2	44
26 Apr 86	**STREET LIFE – 20 GREAT HITS** *E.G. EGTV 1* & ROXY MUSIC ⊛	1	5	77
14 Nov 87	**BETE NOIRE** *Virgin V 2474* ●	9		16
19 Nov 88	**THE ULTIMATE COLLECTION** *E.G. EGTV 2* & ROXY MUSIC ⊛x3	6		35
3 Apr 93	**TAXI** *Virgin CDV 2700* ●	2		14
17 Sep 94	**MAMOUNA** *Virgin CDV 2751*	11		4
4 Nov 95	**MORE THAN THIS – THE BEST OF BRYAN FERRY AND ROXY MUSIC** *Virgin CDV 2791* & ROXY MUSIC ⊛	15		15
6 Nov 99	**AS TIME GOES BY** *Virgin CDVIR 89* ●	16		10
22 Jul 00	**SLAVE TO LOVE** *Virgin CDV 2921* ●	11		11
11 May 02	**FRANTIC** *Virgin CDVIR 167* ○	6		5
19 Jun 04	**PLATINUM COLLECTION** *Virgin BFRM1* & ROXY MUSIC ○	17		4
17 Mar 07	**DYLANESQUE** *Virgin CDV3026* ●	5		10

FFWD
UK/Germany, male instrumental group

		Peak	Wks at No.1	1
13 Aug 94	**FFWD** *Inter INTA 001CD*	48		1

LUPE FIASCO
US, male rapper (Wasalu Jaco)

		Peak	Wks at No.1	6
7 Oct 06	**FOOD & LIQUOR** *Atlantic 7567935902*	31		2
2 Feb 08	**THE COOL** *Atlantic 7567899599*	7		4

BRAD FIEDEL
US, male arranger/composer

		Peak	Wks at No.1	7
31 Aug 91	**TERMINATOR 2 (OST)** *Varese Sarabande VS 5335*	26		7

GRACIE FIELDS
UK, female vocalist (Grace Stansfield), d. 27 Sep 1979 (age 81)

		Peak	Wks at No.1	3
20 Dec 75	**THE GOLDEN YEARS** *Warwick WW 5007*	48		3

FIELDS OF THE NEPHILIM
UK, male vocal/instrumental group

		Peak	Wks at No.1	9
30 May 87	**DAWNRAZOR** *Situation Two SITU 18*	62		2
17 Sep 88	**THE NEPHILIM** *Situation Two SITU 22*	14		3
6 Oct 90	**ELIZIUM** *Beggars Banquet BEGA 115*	22		2
6 Apr 91	**EARTH INFERNO** *Beggars Banquet BEGA 120*	39		2

FIERCE
UK, female vocal group

		Peak	Wks at No.1	2
28 Aug 99	**RIGHT HERE RIGHT NOW** *Wildstar CXWILD 14*	27		2

50 CENT
US, male rapper (Curtis Jackson). See G-Unit

		Peak	Wks at No.1	130
1 Feb 03	**GET RICH OR DIE TRYIN'** *Interscope ISC 4935442* ⊛x2 ★	2		69
18 Sep 04	**50 CENT IS THE FUTURE (IMPORT)** *Street Dance SDR0166752* & G UNIT	65		1
19 Mar 05	**THE MASSACRE** *Interscope 9880667* ⊛ ★	1	1	35
19 Nov 05	**GET RICH OR DIE TRYIN' (OST)** *Interscope 9887992* & G UNIT	18		15
22 Sep 07	**CURTIS** *Interscope 1746491*	2		10

52ND STREET
UK, male/female vocal/instrumental group

		Peak	Wks at No.1	1
19 Apr 86	**CHILDREN OF THE NIGHT** *10 Records DIX 25*	71		1

FIGHTSTAR
UK, male vocal/instrumental group — 4

Date	Title	Peak	Wks at No.1	Wks
25 Mar 06	**GRAND UNIFICATION** *Island CID8165*	28		2
6 Oct 07	**ONE DAY SON THIS WILL ALL BE YOURS** *Institute INSRECCD04*	27		2

FILTER
US, male vocal/instrumental duo — 2

Date	Title	Peak	Wks at No.1	Wks
4 Sep 99	**TITLE OF RECORD** *Reprise 9362475192*	75		1
10 Aug 02	**THE AMALGAMUT** *Reprise 9362479632*	68		1

FINCH
US, male vocal/instrumental group — 1

Date	Title	Peak	Wks at No.1	Wks
18 Jun 05	**SAY HELLO TO SUNSHINE** *Geffen 9882656*	48		1

FINE YOUNG CANNIBALS
UK, male vocal/instrumental trio – Roland Gift, Andy Cox & David Steele — 107

Date	Title	Peak	Wks at No.1	Wks
21 Dec 85	**FINE YOUNG CANNIBALS** *London LONLP 16* ●	11		27
18 Feb 89	**THE RAW AND THE COOKED** *London 8280691* ⊛x3 ★	1	1	66
15 Dec 90	**FYC** *London 8282211*	61		1
23 Nov 96	**THE FINEST** *ffrr 8288552* ⊛	10		13

FINN BROTHERS
New Zealand, male vocal/instrumental duo – Neil Finn* & Tim Finn* — 7

Date	Title	Peak	Wks at No.1	Wks
28 Oct 95	**FINN** *Parlophone CDFINN 1* FINN	15		3
4 Sep 04	**EVERYONE IS HERE** *Parlophone 8647762* ○	8		4

NEIL FINN
New Zealand, male vocalist/guitarist. See Crowded House, Finn Brothers — 15

Date	Title	Peak	Wks at No.1	Wks
27 Jun 98	**TRY WHISTLING THIS** *Parlophone 4951392* ●	5		11
21 Apr 01	**ONE NIL** *Parlophone 5326962* ○	14		4

TIM FINN
New Zealand, male vocalist/guitarist. See Crowded House, Finn Brothers — 2

Date	Title	Peak	Wks at No.1	Wks
10 Jul 93	**BEFORE AND AFTER** *Capitol CDEST 2202*	29		2

FIRM
UK, male vocal/instrumental group — 8

Date	Title	Peak	Wks at No.1	Wks
2 Mar 85	**THE FIRM** *Atlantic 7812391* ★	15		5
5 Apr 86	**MEAN BUSINESS** *Atlantic WX 35*	46		3

FIRST CIRCLE
US, male vocal/instrumental group — 2

Date	Title	Peak	Wks at No.1	Wks
2 May 87	**BOY'S NIGHT OUT** *EMI America AML 3118*	70		2

FISCHER-Z
UK, male vocal/instrumental group — 1

Date	Title	Peak	Wks at No.1	Wks
23 Jun 79	**WORD SALAD** *United Artists UAG 30232*	66		1

FISH
UK, male vocalist (Derek Dick). See Marillion — 17

Date	Title	Peak	Wks at No.1	Wks
10 Feb 90	**VIGIL IN A WILDERNESS OF MIRRORS** *EMI EMD 1015* ○	5		6
9 Nov 91	**INTERNAL EXILE** *Polydor 5110491*	21		3
30 Jan 93	**SONGS FROM THE MIRROR** *Polydor 5174992*	46		2
11 Jun 94	**SUITS** *The Dick Brothers DDICK 004CD*	18		2
16 Sep 95	**YANG** *The Dick Brothers DDICK 012CD*	52		1
16 Sep 95	**YIN** *The Dick Brothers DDICK 011CD*	58		1
31 May 97	**SUNSETS ON EMPIRE** *The Dick Brothers DDICK 25CD*	42		1
1 May 99	**RAINGODS WITH ZIPPOS** *Roadrunner RR 86772*	57		1

FISHBONE
US, male vocal/instrumental group — 1

Date	Title	Peak	Wks at No.1	Wks
13 Jul 91	**THE REALITY OF MY SURROUNDINGS** *Columbia 4676151*	75		1

CONNIE FISHER
UK, female vocalist/actor — 3

Date	Title	Peak	Wks at No.1	Wks
21 Oct 06	**FAVOURITE THINGS** *Polydor 1713038*	14		3

ELLA FITZGERALD
US, female vocalist, d. 15 Jun 1996 (age 79) — 63

Date	Title	Peak	Wks at No.1	Wks
19 Jul 58	**ELLA FITZGERALD SINGS THE IRVING BERLIN SONG BOOK** *HMV CLP 1183*	5		1
11 Jun 60	**ELLA SINGS GERSHWIN** *Brunswick LA 8648*	13		3
18 Jun 60	**ELLA AT THE OPERA HOUSE** *Columbia 35X 10126*	16		1
23 Jul 60	**ELLA SINGS GERSHWIN VOLUME 5** *HMV CLP 1353*	18		2
10 May 80	**THE INCOMPARABLE ELLA** *Polydor POLTV 9*	40		7
27 Feb 88	**A PORTRAIT OF ELLA FITZGERALD** *Stylus SMR 847* ○	42		10
19 Nov 94	**ESSENTIAL ELLA** *Polygram TV 5239902* ●	35		14
23 Mar 96	**FOREVER ELLA** *Verve/Polygram TV 5293872*	19		6
15 Feb 03	**GOLD** *Verve 654842* ●	15		13
18 Sep 04	**ELLA AND LOUIS TOGETHER** *UCJ 9867768* & LOUIS ARMSTRONG	43		1
29 Oct 05	**LOVE SONGS** *UCJ 9831065*	61		1
5 May 07	**FOREVER ELLA** *UCJ 9848373*	20		4

FIVE
UK, male vocal group – Richard Breen (Abs*), Jason Brown, Sean Conlon, Ritchie Neville & Scott Robinson — 96

Date	Title	Peak	Wks at No.1	Wks
4 Jul 98	**FIVE** *RCA 74321589762* ⊛	1	1	36
20 Nov 99	**INVINCIBLE** *RCA 74321713922* ⊛x2	4		39
8 Sep 01	**KINGSIZE** *RCA 74321875972* ●	3		11
1 Dec 01	**GREATEST HITS** *RCA 74321913432* ⊛	9		10

FIVE STAR
UK, female/male vocal/instrumental group – Denise, Delroy, Doris, Lorraine & Stedman Pearson — 153

Date	Title	Peak	Wks at No.1	Wks
3 Aug 85	**LUXURY OF LIFE** *Tent PL 70735* ⊛	12		70
30 Aug 86	**SILK AND STEEL** *Tent PL 71100* ⊛x4	1	1	58
26 Sep 87	**BETWEEN THE LINES** *Tent PL 71505* ⊛	7		17
27 Aug 88	**ROCK THE WORLD** *Tent PL 71747* ○	17		5
21 Oct 89	**GREATEST HITS** *Tent PL 74080*	53		3

FIVE THIRTY
UK, male vocal/instrumental group — 1

Date	Title	Peak	Wks at No.1	Wks
31 Aug 91	**BED** *East West WX 530*	57		1

FIVEPENNY PIECE
UK, male/female vocal/instrumental group – John Meeks, Eddie Crotty, Lynda Meeks & Colin & George Radcliffe, d. Dec 2002 — 6

Date	Title	Peak	Wks at No.1	Wks
24 Mar 73	**MAKING TRACKS** *Columbia SCX 6536*	37		1
3 Jul 76	**KING COTTON** *EMI EMC 3129*	9		5

FIXX
UK, male vocal/instrumental group — 7

Date	Title	Peak	Wks at No.1	Wks
22 May 82	**SHUTTERED ROOM** *MCA FX 1001*	54		6
21 May 83	**REACH THE BEACH** *MCA FX 1002*	91		1

ROBERTA FLACK
US, female vocalist/pianist — 51

Date	Title	Peak	Wks at No.1	Wks
15 Jul 72	**FIRST TAKE** *Atlantic K 40040* ★	47		2
13 Oct 73	**KILLING ME SOFTLY** *Atlantic K 50021*	40		2
7 Jun 80	**ROBERTA FLACK AND DONNY HATHAWAY** *Atlantic K 50696* & DONNY HATHAWAY	31		7
17 Sep 83	**BORN TO LOVE** *Capitol EST 7122841* PEABO BRYSON & ROBERTA FLACK ○	15		10
31 Mar 84	**ROBERTA FLACK'S GREATEST HITS** *K-Tel NE 1269*	35		14
19 Feb 94	**SOFTLY WITH THESE SONGS – THE BEST OF ROBERTA FLACK** *Atlantic 7567824982* ⊛	7		15
22 Apr 06	**THE VERY BEST OF** *Atlantic/Rhino 8122733322*	50		1

FLAMING LIPS
US, male vocal/instrumental group – Wayne Coyne, Steven Drozd, Michael Ivins & Kliph Scurlock — 22

Date	Title	Peak	Wks at No.1	Wks
29 May 99	**THE SOFT BULLETIN** *Warner Brothers 9362473932* ●	39		2
27 Jul 02	**YOSHIMI BATTLES THE PINK ROBOTS** *Warner Brothers 9362481412* ●	13		15

Key: ○ Silver-selling · ● Gold-selling · ⊛ Platinum-selling · ★ US No.1 · Peak Position · Weeks at No.1 · Weeks on Chart

Date	Title	Label	Peak	Wks at No.1	Wks on Chart
15 Apr 06	**AT WAR WITH THE MYSTICS**	*Warner Brothers 9362499662* ●	6		5

FLASH & THE PAN
Australia, male vocal/instrumental group — Total weeks on chart: **2**

Date	Title	Label	Peak	Wks at No.1	Wks on Chart
16 Jul 83	**PAN-ORAMA**	*Easy Beat EASLP 100*	69		2

RICHARD FLEESHMAN
UK, male actor/vocalist — Total weeks on chart: **1**

Date	Title	Label	Peak	Wks at No.1	Wks on Chart
8 Dec 07	**NEON**	*UMRL 1753072*	71		1

FLEET FOXES
US, male vocal/instrumental group — Total weeks on chart: **10**

Date	Title	Label	Peak	Wks at No.1	Wks on Chart
28 Jun 08	**FLEET FOXES**	*Bella Union BELLACD167* ○	11		10

FLEETWOOD MAC
UK/US, male/female vocal/instrumental group – members included Peter Green* (left 1970), Lindsey Buckingham*, Mick Fleetwood, Danny Kirwan, Christine McVie* (Christine Perfect), John McVie, Stevie Nicks* & Jeremy Spencer. Acclaimed British blues band turned Anglo/American rock superstars. Their three million-selling *Rumours* has spent longer on the UK chart than any album and in the US it sold 19 million and was No.1 for 31 weeks. — Total weeks on chart: **908**

Date	Title	Label	Peak	Wks at No.1	Wks on Chart
2 Mar 68	**FLEETWOOD MAC**	*Blue Horizon BPG 763200*	4		37
7 Sep 68	**MR. WONDERFUL**	*Blue Horizon 763205*	10		11
30 Aug 69	**THE PIOUS BIRD OF GOOD OMEN**	*Blue Horizon 763215*	18		4
4 Oct 69	**THEN PLAY ON**	*Reprise RSLP 9000*	6		11
10 Oct 70	**KILN HOUSE**	*Reprise RSLP 9004*	39		2
19 Feb 72	**GREATEST HITS**	*CBS 69011*	36		14
6 Nov 76	**FLEETWOOD MAC**	*Reprise K 54043* ● ★	23		19
29 Jan 77	**RUMOURS**	*Warner Brothers K 56344* ⊛x10 ★	1	1	477
27 Oct 79	**TUSK**	*Warner Brothers K 66088* ⊛	1	1	26
13 Dec 80	**FLEETWOOD MAC LIVE**	*Warner Brothers K 66097* ●	31		9
10 Jul 82	**MIRAGE**	*Warner Brothers K 56592* ⊛ ★	5		39
25 Apr 87	**TANGO IN THE NIGHT**	*Warner Brothers WX 65* ⊛x8	1	5	115
14 May 88	**GREATEST HITS**	*Warner Brothers WX 221* ⊛x3	3		59
21 Apr 90	**BEHIND THE MASK**	*Warner Brothers WX 335* ⊛	1	1	21
23 Sep 95	**LIVE AT THE BBC**	*Essential EDFCD 297*	48		2
21 Oct 95	**TIME**	*Warner Brothers 9362459202*	47		1
6 Sep 97	**THE DANCE**	*Reprise 9362467022* ○ ★	15		10
26 Oct 02	**THE VERY BEST OF**	*Warner Special Markets 8122736352* ⊛x2	7		42
10 May 03	**SAY YOU WILL**	*WEA WB 48467* ●	6		8
24 Sep 05	**RUMOURS**	*Warner Bros 8122738822* ●	69		1

FLIGHT OF THE CONCHORDS
New Zealand, male comedy/vocal duo — Total weeks on chart: **2**

Date	Title	Label	Peak	Wks at No.1	Wks on Chart
24 May 08	**FLIGHT OF THE CONCHORDS**	*Sub Pop 5144281482*	32		2

BERNI FLINT
UK, male vocalist/guitarist — Total weeks on chart: **6**

Date	Title	Label	Peak	Wks at No.1	Wks on Chart
2 Jul 77	**I DON'T WANT TO PUT A HOLD ON YOU**	*EMI EMC 3184*	37		6

FLIP & FILL
UK, male production duo — Total weeks on chart: **7**

Date	Title	Label	Peak	Wks at No.1	Wks on Chart
19 Jul 03	**FLOOR FILLAS**	*All Around The World 0392192*	29		7

FLO RIDA
US, male rapper (Tramar Dillard) — Total weeks on chart: **10**

Date	Title	Label	Peak	Wks at No.1	Wks on Chart
12 Apr 08	**MAIL ON SUNDAY**	*Atlantic 7567899494* ○	29		10

FLOATERS
US, male vocal group — Total weeks on chart: **8**

Date	Title	Label	Peak	Wks at No.1	Wks on Chart
20 Aug 77	**FLOATERS**	*ABC ABCL 5229*	17		8

FLOBOTS
US, male vocal/rap/instrumental group — Total weeks on chart: **2**

Date	Title	Label	Peak	Wks at No.1	Wks on Chart
27 Sep 08	**FIGHT WITH TOOLS**	*Universal Republic 1125802*	51		2

FLOCK
UK, male vocal/instrumental group — Total weeks on chart: **2**

Date	Title	Label	Peak	Wks at No.1	Wks on Chart
2 May 70	**FLOCK**	*CBS 63733*	59		2

A FLOCK OF SEAGULLS
UK, male vocal/instrumental group — Total weeks on chart: **59**

Date	Title	Label	Peak	Wks at No.1	Wks on Chart
17 Apr 82	**A FLOCK OF SEAGULLS**	*Jive HOP 201* ○	32		44
7 May 83	**LISTEN**	*Arista HIP 4*	16		10
1 Sep 84	**THE STORY OF A YOUNG HEART**	*Jive HIP 14*	30		5

FLOWERED UP
UK, male vocal/instrumental group — Total weeks on chart: **3**

Date	Title	Label	Peak	Wks at No.1	Wks on Chart
7 Sep 91	**A LIFE WITH BRIAN**	*London 8282441*	23		3

EDDIE FLOYD
US, male vocalist — Total weeks on chart: **5**

Date	Title	Label	Peak	Wks at No.1	Wks on Chart
29 Apr 67	**KNOCK ON WOOD**	*Stax 589006*	36		5

FLUKE
UK, male production/instrumental group — Total weeks on chart: **3**

Date	Title	Label	Peak	Wks at No.1	Wks on Chart
23 Oct 93	**SIX WHEELS ON MY WAGON**	*Circa CIRCDX 27*	41		1
19 Aug 95	**OTO**	*Circa CIRCD 31*	44		1
11 Oct 97	**RISOTTO**	*Circa CIRCD 33*	45		1

A FLUX OF PINK INDIANS
UK, male vocal/instrumental group — Total weeks on chart: **2**

Date	Title	Label	Peak	Wks at No.1	Wks on Chart
5 Feb 83	**STRIVE TO SURVIVE CAUSING LEAST SUFFERING POSSIBLE**	*Spiderleg SDL 8*	79		2

FLYING LIZARDS
UK, male/female vocal/instrumental group — Total weeks on chart: **3**

Date	Title	Label	Peak	Wks at No.1	Wks on Chart
16 Feb 80	**FLYING LIZARDS**	*Virgin V 2150*	60		3

FLYING PICKETS
UK, male vocal group — Total weeks on chart: **22**

Date	Title	Label	Peak	Wks at No.1	Wks on Chart
17 Dec 83	**LIVE AT THE ALBANY EMPIRE**	*Vam AVMLP 0001* ○	48		11
9 Jun 84	**LOST BOYS**	*10 Records DIX 4* ○	11		11

FM
UK, male vocal/instrumental group — Total weeks on chart: **3**

Date	Title	Label	Peak	Wks at No.1	Wks on Chart
20 Sep 86	**INDISCREET**	*Portrait PRT 26827*	76		1
14 Oct 89	**TOUGH IT OUT**	*Epic 4655891*	34		2

FOALS
UK, male vocal/instrumental group – Yannis Philippakis, Jack Bevan, Edwin Congreave, Walter Gervers & Jimmy Smith — Total weeks on chart: **5**

Date	Title	Label	Peak	Wks at No.1	Wks on Chart
5 Apr 08	**ANTIDOTES**	*Transgressive 5144270032* ○	3		5

FOCUS
Holland, male instrumental group – Thijs van Leer, Jan Akkerman, Cyril Havermans (replaced by Bert Ruiter) & Pierre van der Linden (replaced by Colin Allen) — Total weeks on chart: **65**

Date	Title	Label	Peak	Wks at No.1	Wks on Chart
11 Nov 72	**MOVING WAVES**	*Polydor 2931 002*	2		34
4 Jul 70	**FOCUS 3**	*Polydor 2383 016*	6		15
20 Oct 73	**FOCUS AT THE RAINBOW**	*Polydor 2442 118* ○	23		5
25 May 74	**HAMBURGER CONCERTO**	*Polydor 2442 124* ○	20		5
9 Aug 75	**FOCUS**	*Polydor 2384 070*	23		6

DAN FOGELBERG
US, male vocalist/multi-instrumentalist, d. 16 Dec 2007 (age 56) — Total weeks on chart: **3**

Date	Title	Label	Peak	Wks at No.1	Wks on Chart
29 Mar 80	**PHOENIX**	*Full Moon EPC 83317*	42		3

JOHN FOGERTY
US, male vocalist/guitarist. See Creedence Clearwater Revival — **17**

Date	Title / Label	Peak	Wks at No.1	Wks
16 Feb 85	**CENTERFIELD** *Warner Brothers 9252031* ★	48		11
20 May 06	**THE LONG ROAD HOME** *Universal TV 1896892*	32		6

BEN FOLDS FIVE
US, male vocal/instrumental group — **6**

Date	Title / Label	Peak	Wks at No.1	Wks
15 Mar 97	**WHATEVER AND EVER AMEN** *Epic 4866982*	30		3
24 Jan 98	**NAKED BABY PHOTOS** *Virgin CAR 7554*	65		1
8 May 99	**THE UNAUTHORIZED BIOGRAPHY OF REINHOLD MESSNER** *Epic 4933122*	22		2

BEN FOLDS
US, male vocalist/multi-instrumentalist. See Ben Folds Five — **3**

Date	Title / Label	Peak	Wks at No.1	Wks
6 Oct 01	**ROCKIN' THE SUBURBS** *Epic 5040632*	73		1
7 May 05	**SONGS FOR SILVERMAN** *Epic 5170123*	65		1
11 Oct 08	**WAY TO NORMAL** *Epic 88697098492*	70		1

ELLEN FOLEY
US, female vocalist — **3**

Date	Title / Label	Peak	Wks at No.1	Wks
17 Nov 79	**NIGHTOUT** *Epic EPC 83718*	68		1
4 Apr 81	**SPIRIT OF ST LOUIS** *Epic EPC 84809*	57		2

JANE FONDA
US, female exercise instructor/actor — **51**

Date	Title / Label	Peak	Wks at No.1	Wks
29 Jan 83	**JANE FONDA'S WORKOUT RECORD** *CBS 88581* ●	7		47
22 Sep 84	**JANE FONDA'S WORKOUT RECORD: NEW AND IMPROVED** *CBS 88640*	60		4

WAYNE FONTANA & THE MINDBENDERS
UK, male vocalist (Glyn Ellis) & vocal/instrumental group — **1**

Date	Title / Label	Peak	Wks at No.1	Wks
20 Feb 65	**WAYNE FONTANA AND THE MINDBENDERS** *Fontana TL 5230*	18		1

FOO FIGHTERS
US, male vocal/instrumental group – Dave Grohl, William Goldsmith (replaced by Taylor Hawkins), Nate Mendel & Pat Smear (replaced by Franz Stahl; Stahl replaced by Chris Shiflett) — **176**

Date	Title / Label	Peak	Wks at No.1	Wks
8 Jul 95	**FOO FIGHTERS** *Roswell CDSET 2266* ●	3		17
24 May 97	**THE COLOUR AND THE SHAPE** *Roswell CDEST 2295* ●	3		13
13 Nov 99	**THERE IS NOTHING LEFT TO LOSE** *RCA 74321716992* ●	10		16
2 Nov 02	**ONE BY ONE** *RCA 74321973482* ⊛	1	1	47
25 Jun 05	**IN YOUR HONOR** *RCA 82876701952* ⊛x2	2		40
2 Dec 06	**SKIN AND BONES** *RCA 82876888572*	35		8
6 Oct 07	**ECHOES SILENCE PATIENCE & GRACE** *RCA 88697115162* ⊛x2	1	1	35

STEVE FORBERT
US, male vocalist — **3**

Date	Title / Label	Peak	Wks at No.1	Wks
9 Jun 79	**ALIVE ON ARRIVAL** *Epic EPC 83308*	56		1
24 Nov 79	**JACKRABBIT SLIM** *Epic EPC 83879*	54		2

CLINTON FORD
UK, male vocalist (Ian Stopford Harrison) — **4**

Date	Title / Label	Peak	Wks at No.1	Wks
26 May 62	**CLINTON FORD** *Oriole PS 40021*	16		4

LITA FORD
UK, female vocalist — **4**

Date	Title / Label	Peak	Wks at No.1	Wks
26 May 84	**DANCIN' ON THE EDGE** *Vertigo VERL 13*	96		1
23 Jun 90	**STILETTO** *RCA PL 82090*	66		1
25 Jan 92	**DANGEROUS CURVES** *RCA PD 90592*	51		2

JULIA FORDHAM
UK, female vocalist — **36**

Date	Title / Label	Peak	Wks at No.1	Wks
18 Jun 88	**JULIA FORDHAM** *Circa 4* ●	20		22
21 Oct 89	**PORCELAIN** *Circa 10* ○	13		5
2 Nov 91	**SWEPT** *Circa 18*	33		6
21 May 94	**FALLING FORWARD** *Circa CIRCD 28*	21		3

FOREIGNER
UK/US, male vocal/instrumental group – Lou Gramm, Dennis Elliott, Al Greenwood (replaced by Bob Mayo), Mick Jones, Ian McDonald, Mark Rivera & Rick Wills — **129**

Date	Title / Label	Peak	Wks at No.1	Wks
26 Aug 78	**DOUBLE VISION** *Atlantic K 50476*	32		5
25 Jul 81	**4** *Atlantic K 50796* ● ★	5		62
18 Dec 82	**RECORDS: THE BEST OF FOREIGNER** *Atlantic A 0999* ○	58		11
22 Dec 84	**AGENT PROVOCATEUR** *Atlantic 7819991* ⊛	1	3	32
19 Dec 87	**INSIDE INFORMATION** *Atlantic WX 143* ○	64		7
6 Jul 91	**UNUSUAL HEAT** *Atlantic WX 424*	56		1
2 May 92	**THE VERY BEST OF FOREIGNER** *Atlantic 7567805112* ○	19		7
12 Nov 94	**MR. MOONLIGHT** *Arista 74321232852*	59		1
18 Jun 05	**THE DEFINITIVE** *Atlantic/Rhino 8122735962* ○	33		3

49ERS
Italy, male producer (Gianfranco Bortolotti) — **5**

Date	Title / Label	Peak	Wks at No.1	Wks
10 Mar 90	**THE 49ERS** *Fourth & Broadway BRLP 547*	51		5

iFORWARD! RUSSIA
UK, male/female vocal/instrumental group — **1**

Date	Title / Label	Peak	Wks at No.1	Wks
27 May 06	**GIVE ME A WALL** *Dance To The Radio DTTR012CD*	53		1

FOSTER & ALLEN
Ireland, male vocal/instrumental duo — **237**

Date	Title / Label	Peak	Wks at No.1	Wks
14 May 83	**MAGGIE** *Ritz RITZLP 0012* ○	72		6
5 Nov 83	**I WILL LOVE YOU ALL OF MY LIFE** *Ritz RITZLP 0015*	71		6
17 Nov 84	**THE VERY BEST OF FOSTER AND ALLEN** *Ritz LPTV 1*	18		18
29 Mar 86	**AFTER ALL THESE YEARS** *Ritz RITZLP 0032*	82		2
25 Oct 86	**REMINISCING** *Stylus SMR 623* ⊛	11		15
27 Jun 87	**LOVE SONGS – THE VERY BEST OF FOSTER AND ALLEN VOLUME 2** *Ritz RITZLP 0036*	92		1
10 Oct 87	**REFLECTIONS** *Stylus SMR 739* ⊛	16		16
30 Apr 88	**REMEMBER YOU'RE MINE** *Stylus SMR 853* ●	16		15
1 Oct 88	**THE WORLDS OF FOSTER AND ALLEN** *Stylus SMR 861* ●	16		18
28 Oct 89	**THE MAGIC OF FOSTER AND ALLEN (THEIR GREATEST HITS)** *Stylus SMR 989* ●	29		12
9 Dec 89	**FOSTERS AND ALLEN'S CHRISTMAS COLLECTION** *Stylus SMR 995* ●	40		4
10 Nov 90	**SOUVENIRS** *Telstar STAR 2457* ●	15		12
8 Dec 90	**THE CHRISTMAS COLLECTION** *Telstar STAR 2459*	44		4
2 Nov 91	**MEMORIES** *Telstar STAR 2527* ●	18		11
31 Oct 92	**HEART STRINGS** *Telstar TCD 2608*	37		10
23 Oct 93	**BY REQUEST** *Telstar TCD 2670* ●	14		12
5 Nov 94	**SONGS WE LOVE TO SING** *Telstar TCD 2741*	41		9
4 Nov 95	**100 GOLDEN GREATS** *Telstar TCD 2791* ●	30		12
2 Nov 96	**SOMETHING SPECIAL – 100 GOLDEN LOVE SONGS** *Telstar TCD 2791*	46		10
26 Apr 97	**SHADES OF GREEN** *Telstar TCD 2899*	55		2
15 Nov 97	**BEST FRIENDS** *Telstar TV TTVCD 2935* ●	36		8
12 Dec 98	**GREATEST HITS** *Telstar TV TTVCD 3000*	52		4
25 Dec 99	**ONE DAY AT A TIME** *Telstar TV TTVCD 3090*	61		1
15 Nov 03	**BY SPECIAL REQUEST – THE VERY BEST OF** *DMG TV DMGTV003*	30		8
13 Nov 04	**SING THE SIXTIES** *DMG TV DMGTV012*	31		8
19 Nov 05	**SING THE NUMBER 1'S** *DMG TV DMGTV022*	30		7
18 Nov 06	**AT THE MOVIES** *DMG TV DMGTV033*	48		2
8 Dec 07	**SONGS OF LOVE AND LAUGHTER** *DMG TV DMGTV034*	50		4

FOTHERINGAY
UK, male/female vocal/instrumental group — **6**

Date	Title / Label	Peak	Wks at No.1	Wks
11 Jul 70	**FOTHERINGAY** *Island ILPS 9125*	18		6

FOUNTAINS OF WAYNE
US, male vocal/instrumental group — **1**

Date	Title / Label	Peak	Wks at No.1	Wks
7 Jun 97	**FOUNTAINS OF WAYNE** *Atlantic 7567927252*	67		1

4 HERO
UK, male instrumental duo — **7**

Date	Title / Label	Peak	Wks at No.1	Wks
25 Jul 98	**TWO PAGES** *Talkin Loud 5584652*	38		6
10 Nov 01	**CREATING PATTERNS** *Talkin Loud 5860572*	65		1

Flood/Youth

THERE was a theory in the 1970s and 1980s that, as technology advanced, producers would become more and more important. Who could expect poor, simple musicians to cope with the banks of glowering computers that were expected to be a feature of studios in the future? They would end up standing back as a man in a white coat changed everything about their music at the press of a button. It hasn't happened quite like that. Modern software programs like Pro-Tools have instead democratised production. Musicians can change everything about their music *themselves*, on a laptop at the back of their tour bus. Many bands and music lovers have therefore asked that intriguing question: what exactly is a producer for?

The answer, probably, is that it depends on the producer. In R&B and hip-hop, producers like Timbaland are indisputably artists in their own right. In the alternative rock scene, many of the most celebrated producers – such as Steve Albini – prefer to think of themselves purely as engineers, just there to capture the band's sound rather than exert excessive creative control. There are even a few, like George Martin or Nigel Godrich, who become so closely linked with the bands they're associated with (The Beatles and Radiohead respectively) that they're almost considered honorary members.

There's no such thing as 'a Flood sound'

But, despite the fact that access to pitch-control technology, and all the rest of the paraphernalia of modern music-making, is so widely available, there's still a crucial role for the old-style studio guru or 'Super Producer' in the creation of an album. Two of the most celebrated, Martin 'Youth' Glover and Mark 'Flood' Ellis, have barely stopped working since the 1980s and command respect from the likes of U2, Paul McCartney, The Killers and Depeche Mode.

Both born in 1960, they've followed very different career paths. Flood started his career as a runner at Morgan Studios in London in 1978. When he arrived, The Cure were busy bashing out their debut single in one room while Thin Lizzy were in another. One of Flood's main tasks was to make tea and, according to legend, during the recording of The Cure's debut album *Three Imaginary Boys*, he was enthusiastically diligent, while another assistant, also called Mark, was less keen. House engineer Chris Tsangarides dubbed one of the Marks 'drought' and the other 'flood'.

In 1981, Flood got a new job as an assistant engineer, working with legendary Manchester maverick and revered producer Martin Hannett on New Order's debut album *Movement*. It wasn't an auspicious start. New Order hadn't got over the death of Ian Curtis the year before and Martin was suffering from alcohol and drug problems. Production on the album was heavily criticised at the time. But Flood nonetheless found himself in demand at recording sessions of many of the most acclaimed, electronic and avant-garde acts of the early 1980s, including Soft Cell, Psychic TV and Cabaret Voltaire. His first full production credit came with Nick Cave's *From Her To Eternity* in 1984 and he'd go on to work closely with the Australian singer on five more albums.

In 1987, though, he made the leap into the mainstream, engineering U2's global breakthrough album *The Joshua Tree*. By 1993 he wasn't just engineering U2's albums, he was co-producing them, sharing the role with Brian Eno on *Zooropa*; in 1994, he side-stepped into the industrial genre and produced Nine Inch Nails' acclaimed *Pretty Hate Machine*.

Biggest-Selling Albums

Producer	Album	Artist	Week	Highest Position	Approx Sales
FLOOD	THE JOSHUA TREE	U2	21/3/87	1	2,700,000
YOUTH	URBAN HYMNS	VERVE	11/10/97	1	3,150,000

The production of such huge albums is a role that would seemingly cry out for someone with an ego large enough to play the role of father/confessor to some of the biggest names in the rock universe. One of Flood's strengths, though, seems to be a widely recognised humility. There's no such thing as 'a Flood sound'. He's appreciated by the likes of Bono and Billy Corgan of Smashing Pumpkins for helping them realise their own visions, not imposing his.

This is true of Youth as well, although perhaps to a lesser extent. He has a very strong personal aesthetic that goes back to his days as the bass player in dark, groove-orientated rock band Killing Joke – a combination of shamanistic psychedelia and post-punk rigour. Nevertheless, when co-producing on albums ranging from The Verve's *Urban Hymns* to Guns N' Roses *Chinese Democracy*, he's been recognised as a master of sonic manipulation in a wide variety of genres. His nickname came from reggae artist Big Youth and he's always been a fan of techno, acid house and trance, but he's had some of his greatest success producing indie bands like Embrace. It was Youth who encouraged The Verve to unleash their pop side with songs like 'Bitter Sweet Symphony'. He also co-wrote The Orb's hit 'Little Fluffy Clouds' and took on the doomed task of trying to make Bananarama cool in the 1990s. Perhaps more successfully he's also attempted the same feat with Paul McCartney, working with him as The Fireman on three albums of experimental psychedelia. The producer, then, may be a shaman but it helps if he is also a chameleon.

The job is, in some respects, the same now as it was when George Martin and The Beatles re-invented it in the 1960s. The technology may have changed but it's still principally about getting the best out of *people*, rather than computers. More than anything else, experienced acts like U2 need a sounding board that they can trust. They need somebody who can listen to an idea and tell them how it can be realised – or how it should be abandoned. Producers like Youth and Flood know how important they are in creating some of the most successful music of our era, but their future employment prospects decree that it's best they never mention it. The music business has always dictated that bands and musicians are the 'talent'. This exclusivity of acclaim should be open to discussion, particularly with producers like Flood and Youth in circulation. Production is partly about technology but it's predominantly about psychology.

It was Youth who encouraged The Verve to unleash their pop side

Legend: Silver-selling ○ · Gold-selling ● · Platinum-selling ⊛ · US No.1 ★ · Peak Position · Weeks at No.1 · Weeks on Chart

4 NON BLONDES
US, female/male vocal/instrumental group – Linda Perry, Christa Hillhouse, Dawn Richardson & Roger Rocha

Date	Album	Peak	Wks at No.1	Wks on Chart
				18
17 Jul 93	**BIGGER, BETTER, FASTER, MORE!** *Interscope 7567921122* ●	4		18

4 OF US
Ireland, male vocal/instrumental group

Date	Album	Peak	Wks at No.1	Wks on Chart
				1
20 Mar 93	**MAN ALIVE** *Columbia 4723262*	64		1

411
UK, female vocal group

Date	Album	Peak	Wks at No.1	Wks on Chart
				2
4 Dec 04	**BETWEEN THE SHEETS** *Sony Music 5190842* ○	46		2

FOUR PENNIES
UK, male vocal/instrumental group

Date	Album	Peak	Wks at No.1	Wks on Chart
				5
7 Nov 64	**TWO SIDES OF THE FOUR PENNIES** *Philips BL 7642*	13		5

FOUR SEASONS
US, male vocal/instrumental group – Frankie Valli, Tommy DeVito, Bob Gaudio & Nick Massi, d. 24 Dec 2000 (replaced by Joe Long)

Date	Album	Peak	Wks at No.1	Wks on Chart
				70
6 Jul 63	**SHERRY** *Stateside SL 10033*	20		1
10 Apr 71	**EDIZIOBE D'ORO** *Philips 6640 002*	11		7
20 Nov 71	**THE BIG ONES** *Philips 6336 208*	37		1
6 Mar 76	**THE FOUR SEASONS STORY** *Private Stock DAPS 1001* ○	20		8
6 Mar 76	**WHO LOVES YOU** *Warner Brothers K 56179* ●	12		17
20 Mar 76	**GREATEST HITS** *K-Tel NE 942* ⊛	4		6
21 May 88	**THE COLLECTION – THE 20 GREATEST HITS** *Telstar STAR 2320*	38		9
7 Mar 92	**THE VERY BEST OF FRANKIE VALLI AND THE FOUR SEASONS** *Polygram TV 5131192* FRANKIE VALLI & THE FOUR SEASONS ●	7		15
13 Oct 01	**THE DEFINITIVE FRANKIE VALLI & THE FOUR SEASONS** *WSM 812273552* FRANKIE VALLI & THE FOUR SEASONS ○	26		4
17 May 08	**THE VERY BEST OF – JERSEY'S BEST** *Rhino 8122799376* FRANKIE VALLI & THE FOUR SEASONS	25		2

FOUR TET
UK, male DJ/producer (Keiran Hebden)

Date	Album	Peak	Wks at No.1	Wks on Chart
				2
17 May 03	**ROUNDS** *Domino Recordings WIGCD126*	60		1
4 Jun 05	**EVERYTHING ECTSTATIC** *Domino WIGCD154*	59		1

FOUR TOPS
US, male vocal group – Levi Stubbs, d. 17 Oct 2008, Renaldo Benson, d. 1 Jul 2005, Abdul Fakir & Lawrence Payton, d. 20 Jun 1997

Date	Album	Peak	Wks at No.1	Wks on Chart
				255
19 Nov 66	**FOUR TOPS ON TOP** *Tamla Motown STML 11037*	9		23
11 Feb 67	**FOUR TOPS LIVE!** *Tamla Motown STML 11041*	4		72
25 Nov 67	**REACH OUT** *Tamla Motown STML 11056*	4		34
20 Jan 68	**FOUR TOPS GREATEST HITS** *Tamla Motown STML 11061*	1	1	67
8 Feb 69	**YESTERDAY'S DREAMS** *Tamla Motown STML 11087*	37		1
27 Jun 70	**STILL WATERS RUN DEEP** *Tamla Motown STML 11149*	29		8
29 May 71	**THE MAGNIFICENT SEVEN** *Tamla Motown STML 11179* SUPREMES & THE FOUR TOPS	6		11
27 Nov 71	**FOUR TOPS GREATEST HITS VOLUME 2** *Tamla Motown STML 11195*	25		10
10 Nov 73	**THE FOUR TOPS STORY 1964–1972** *Tamla Motown TMSP 11241/2*	35		5
13 Feb 82	**THE BEST OF THE FOUR TOPS** *K-Tel NE 1160* ●	13		13
8 Dec 90	**THEIR GREATEST HITS** *Telstar STAR 2437*	47		6
19 Sep 92	**THE SINGLES COLLECTION** *Polygram TV 5157102* ○	11		5

4-SKINS
UK, male vocal/instrumental group

Date	Album	Peak	Wks at No.1	Wks on Chart
				4
17 Apr 82	**THE GOOD, THE BAD AND THE 4-SKINS** *Secret SEC 4*	80		4

FOX
UK/US/Australia, male/female vocal/instrumental group – Noosha Fox, Herbie Armstrong, Jim Frank, Jim Gannon, Mike Lavender, Pete Solley, Gary Taylor & Kenny Young

Date	Album	Peak	Wks at No.1	Wks on Chart
				8
17 May 75	**FOX** *GTO GTLP 001* ○	7		8

SAMANTHA FOX
UK, female vocalist/model

Date	Album	Peak	Wks at No.1	Wks on Chart
				18
26 Jul 86	**TOUCH ME** *Jive HIP 39* ○	17		10
1 Aug 87	**SAMANTHA FOX** *Jive HIP 48*	22		6
18 Feb 89	**I WANNA HAVE SOME FUN** *Jive HIP 72*	46		2

FOXBORO HOT TUBS
US, male vocal/instrumental group. See Green Day

Date	Album	Peak	Wks at No.1	Wks on Chart
				1
31 May 08	**STOP DROP AND ROLL** *Warner Brothers 9362498647*	37		1

BRUCE FOXTON
UK, male vocalist/bass player. See Jam

Date	Album	Peak	Wks at No.1	Wks on Chart
				4
12 May 84	**TOUCH SENSITIVE** *Arista 206 251*	68		4

JAMIE FOXX
US, male actor/comedian/vocalist (Eric Bishop)

Date	Album	Peak	Wks at No.1	Wks on Chart
				5
6 May 06	**UNPREDICTABLE** *J 82876730492* ○	9		5

JOHN FOXX
UK, male vocalist (Dennis Leigh)

Date	Album	Peak	Wks at No.1	Wks on Chart
				17
2 Feb 80	**METAMATIC** *Metal Beat V 2146*	18		7
3 Oct 81	**THE GARDEN** *Metal Beat V 2194*	24		6
8 Oct 83	**THE GOLDEN SECTION** *Virgin V 2233*	27		3
5 Oct 85	**IN MYSTERIOUS WAYS** *Virgin V 2355*	85		1

FRAGGLES
UK/US, TV puppets

Date	Album	Peak	Wks at No.1	Wks on Chart
				4
21 Apr 84	**FRAGGLE ROCK** *RCA PL 70221*	38		4

FRAGMA
Germany, male production trio & female vocalists

Date	Album	Peak	Wks at No.1	Wks on Chart
				12
27 Jan 01	**TOCA** *Positiva 8506770* ●	19		12

RODDY FRAME
UK, male vocalist/guitarist. See Aztec Camera

Date	Album	Peak	Wks at No.1	Wks on Chart
				1
3 Oct 98	**THE NORTH STAR** *Independiente ISOM 7CD*	55		1

PETER FRAMPTON
UK, male vocalist. See Herd, Humble Pie

Date	Album	Peak	Wks at No.1	Wks on Chart
				49
22 May 76	**FRAMPTON COMES ALIVE** *A&M AMLM 63703* ● ★	6		39
18 Jun 77	**I'M IN YOU** *A&M AMLK 64039* ○	19		10

CONNIE FRANCIS
US, female vocalist (Concetta Franconero)

Date	Album	Peak	Wks at No.1	Wks on Chart
				31
26 Mar 60	**ROCK 'N' ROLL MILLION SELLERS** *MGM C 804*	12		1
11 Feb 61	**CONNIE'S GREATEST HITS** *MGM C 831*	16		3
18 Jun 77	**20 ALL TIME GREATS** *Polydor 2391 290* ●	1	2	22
24 Apr 93	**THE SINGLES COLLECTION** *Polygram TV 5191312*	12		5

FRANK & WALTERS
Ireland, male vocal/instrumental group

Date	Album	Peak	Wks at No.1	Wks on Chart
				1
7 Nov 92	**TRAINS, BOATS AND PLANES** *Setanta 8283692*	36		1

FRANKEE
US, female vocalist (Nicole Francine Aiello)

Date	Album	Peak	Wks at No.1	Wks on Chart
				2
19 Jun 04	**THE GOOD THE BAD THE UGLY** *Universal TV 9867000*	51		2

FRANKIE GOES TO HOLLYWOOD
UK, male vocal/instrumental group – Holly Johnson*, Peter Gill, Brian Nash, Mark O'Toole & Paul Rutherford

Date	Album	Peak	Wks at No.1	Wks on Chart
				95
10 Nov 84	**WELCOME TO THE PLEASUREDOME** *ZTT ZTTIQ 1* ⊛x3	1	1	66
1 Nov 86	**LIVERPOOL** *ZTT ZTTIQ 8* ●	5		13
30 Oct 93	**BANG! – GREATEST HITS OF FRANKIE GOES TO HOLLYWOOD** *ZTT 4509939122* ●	4		15
7 Oct 00	**MAXIMUM JOY** *ZTT 165CD*	54		1

ARETHA FRANKLIN
US, female vocalist/pianist — 85

Date	Title	Label	Peak	Wks at No.1	Wks on Chart
12 Aug 67	I NEVER LOVED A MAN THE WAY I LOVE YOU	*Atlantic 587066*	36		2
13 Apr 68	LADY SOUL	*Atlantic 588099*	25		18
14 Sep 68	ARETHA NOW	*Atlantic 588114*	6		11
18 Jan 86	WHO'S ZOOMIN' WHO?	*Arista 207 202* ○	49		12
24 May 86	THE FIRST LADY OF SOUL	*Stylus SMR 8506* ○	89		1
8 Nov 86	ARETHA	*Arista 208 020*	51		13
3 Jun 89	THROUGH THE STORM	*Arista 209842*	46		1
19 Mar 94	GREATEST HITS 1980–1994	*Arista 74321162022*	27		3
29 Oct 94	QUEEN OF SOUL – THE VERY BEST OF ARETHA FRANKLIN	*Atlantic 8122713962* ○	20		5
21 Nov 98	GREATEST HITS	*Global Television RADCD 110* ●	38		10
15 Jun 02	RESPECT – THE VERY BEST OF	*WSM/BMG 0927470542* ●	15		9

RODNEY FRANKLIN
US, male pianist — 2

Date	Title	Label	Peak	Wks at No.1	Wks on Chart
24 May 80	YOU'LL NEVER KNOW	*CBS 83812*	64		2

FRANZ FERDINAND
UK, male vocal/instrumental group – Alex Kapranos, Bob Hardy, Nick McCarthy & Paul Thomson — 98

Date	Title	Label	Peak	Wks at No.1	Wks on Chart
21 Feb 04	FRANZ FERDINAND	*Domino WIGCD136X* ⊛x4	3		74
15 Oct 05	YOU COULD HAVE IT SO MUCH BETTER	*Domino WIGCD161* ⊛	1	1	24

FRATELLIS
UK, male vocal/instrumental trio – Jon Fratelli (John Lawler), Barry Fratelli (Barry Wallace) & Mince Fratelli (Gordon McRory) — 73

Date	Title	Label	Peak	Wks at No.1	Wks on Chart
23 Sep 06	COSTELLO MUSIC	*Fallout 1707193* ⊛x3	2		61
21 Jun 08	HERE WE STAND	*Fallout 1772498* ●	5		12

FRAY
US, male vocal/instrumental group – Isaac Slade, Joe King, Dave Welsh & Ben Wysocki — 30

Date	Title	Label	Peak	Wks at No.1	Wks on Chart
17 Feb 07	HOW TO SAVE A LIFE	*Epic SNY939312* ⊛	4		30

FRAZIER CHORUS
UK, male/female vocal/instrumental group — 2

Date	Title	Label	Peak	Wks at No.1	Wks on Chart
20 May 89	SUE	*Virgin V 2578*	56		1
16 Mar 91	RAY	*Virgin VFC 2654*	66		1

FREAK OF NATURE
US/Denmark, male vocal/instrumental group — 1

Date	Title	Label	Peak	Wks at No.1	Wks on Chart
1 Oct 94	GATHERING OF FREAKS	*Music For Nations CDMFN 169*	66		1

FREAK POWER
UK/Canada, male vocal/instrumental group — 5

Date	Title	Label	Peak	Wks at No.1	Wks on Chart
15 Apr 95	DRIVE-THRU BOOTY	*Fourth & Broadway BRCDX 606*	11		5

FREDDIE & THE DREAMERS
UK, male vocal/instrumental group – Freddie Garrity, d. 19 May 2006, Peter Birrell, Roy Crewdson, Bernie Dwyer, d. 4 Dec 2002, & Derek Quinn — 26

Date	Title	Label	Peak	Wks at No.1	Wks on Chart
9 Nov 63	FREDDIE AND THE DREAMERS	*Columbia 33SX 1577*	5		26

FREE
UK, male vocal/instrumental group – Paul Rodgers*, John Bundrick, Andy Fraser (replaced by Tetsu Yamauchi), Simon Kirke & Paul Kossoff, d. 19 Mar 1976 — 72

Date	Title	Label	Peak	Wks at No.1	Wks on Chart
11 Jul 70	FIRE AND WATER	*Island ILPS 9120*	2		18
23 Jan 71	HIGHWAY	*Island ILPS 9138*	41		10
26 Jun 71	FREE LIVE!	*Island ILPS 9160*	4		12
17 Jun 72	FREE AT LAST	*Island ILPS 9192*	9		9
3 Feb 73	HEARTBREAKER	*Island ILPS 9217*	9		7
16 Mar 74	THE FREE STORY	*Island ISLD 4*	2		6
2 Mar 91	THE BEST OF FREE – ALL RIGHT NOW	*Island ILPTV 2* ○	9		9
30 Sep 06	CHRONICLES – THE VERY BEST OF	*Island/UMTV 9822554*	42		1

FREE THE SPIRIT
UK, male instrumental duo – Nick Magnus & Rono Tse — 42

Date	Title	Label	Peak	Wks at No.1	Wks on Chart
4 Feb 95	PAN PIPE MOODS	*Polygram TV 5271972* ⊛	2		26
4 Nov 95	PAN PIPE MOODS TWO	*Polygram TV 5293952* ●	18		11
25 May 96	PAN PIPE MOODS IN PARADISE	*Polygram TV 5319612*	26		5

FREEEZ
UK, male vocal/instrumental group — 18

Date	Title	Label	Peak	Wks at No.1	Wks on Chart
7 Feb 81	SOUTHERN FREEZ	*Beggars Banquet BEGA 22*	17		15
22 Oct 83	GONNA GET YOU	*Beggars Banquet BEGA 48*	46		3

FREEMASONS
UK, male production duo — 3

Date	Title	Label	Peak	Wks at No.1	Wks on Chart
19 Jul 08	UNMIXED	*Loaded LOADED11CD*	58		3

FREESTYLERS
UK, male vocal/instrumental group — 3

Date	Title	Label	Peak	Wks at No.1	Wks on Chart
15 Aug 98	WE ROCK HARD	*Freskanova FNTCD 004*	33		3

FREHLEY'S COMET
US, male vocal/instrumental group — 1

Date	Title	Label	Peak	Wks at No.1	Wks on Chart
18 Jun 88	SECOND SIGHTING	*Atlantic 7818621*	79		1

STEPHEN FRETWELL
UK, male vocalist/guitarist — 7

Date	Title	Label	Peak	Wks at No.1	Wks on Chart
30 Jul 05	MAGPIE	*Fiction/Polydor 9868907* ○	27		6
22 Sep 07	MAN ON THE ROOF	*Fiction/Polydor 1735396*	44		1

GLENN FREY
US, male vocalist/guitarist. See Eagles — 9

Date	Title	Label	Peak	Wks at No.1	Wks on Chart
6 Jul 85	THE ALLNIGHTER	*MCA MCF 3277*	31		9

FRIDA
Norway, female vocalist (Anni-Frid Lyngstad). See Abba — 8

Date	Title	Label	Peak	Wks at No.1	Wks on Chart
18 Sep 82	SOMETHING'S GOING ON	*Epic EPC 85966* ○	18		7
20 Oct 84	SHINE	*Epic EPC 26178*	67		1

FRIDAY HILL
UK, male vocal/rap trio. See Blazin' Squad — 1

Date	Title	Label	Peak	Wks at No.1	Wks on Chart
11 Mar 06	TIMES LIKE THESE	*Longside LONG100CD*	67		1

DEAN FRIEDMAN
US, male vocalist/keyboard player — 14

Date	Title	Label	Peak	Wks at No.1	Wks on Chart
21 Oct 78	WELL, WELL SAID THE ROCKING CHAIR	*Lifesong LSLP 6019* ●	21		14

FRIENDLY FIRES
UK, male vocal/instrumental group — 2

Date	Title	Label	Peak	Wks at No.1	Wks on Chart
13 Sep 08	FRIENDLY FIRES	*XL Recordings XLCD383*	38		2

ROBERT FRIPP
UK, male guitarist/producer. See King Crimson — 3

Date	Title	Label	Peak	Wks at No.1	Wks on Chart
12 May 79	EXPOSURE	*Polydor EGLP 101*	71		1
17 Jul 93	THE FIRST DAY	*Virgin CDVX 2712* DAVID SYLVIAN & ROBERT FRIPP	21		2

FRON MALE VOICE CHOIR
UK, male choir — 33

Date	Title	Label	Peak	Wks at No.1	Wks on Chart
2 Dec 06	VOICES OF THE VALLEY	*UCJ 4765720* ⊛	9		18
1 Dec 07	VOICES OF THE VALLEY – ENCORE	*UCJ 1740835*	11		8
22 Nov 08	VOICES OF THE VALLEY – HOME	*UCJ 1779253*	14		7+

FRONT 242
Belgium/US, male vocal/instrumental group — Weeks on Chart: **3**

Date	Title / Label	Peak Position	Weeks at No.1	Weeks on Chart
2 Feb 91	**TYRANNY FOR YOU** *RRE 011*	49		1
22 May 93	**06:21:03:11 UP EVIL** *RRE 021CD*	44		1
4 Sep 93	**05:22:09:12 OFF** *RRE 022CD*	46		1

JOHN FRUSCIANTE
US, male vocalist/guitarist. See Red Hot Chili Peppers — Weeks on Chart: **1**

Date	Title / Label	Peak Position	Weeks at No.1	Weeks on Chart
13 Mar 04	**SHADOWS COLLIDE WITH PEOPLE** *Warner Brothers 9362486602*	53		1

FUGAZI
US, male vocal/instrumental group — Weeks on Chart: **7**

Date	Title / Label	Peak Position	Weeks at No.1	Weeks on Chart
21 Sep 91	**STEADY DIET OF NOTHIMG** *Dischord 60*	63		1
19 Jun 93	**IN ON THE KILLTAKER** *Dischord DIS 70CD*	24		2
13 May 95	**RED MEDICINE** *Dischord DIS 90CD*	18		2
25 Apr 98	**END HITS** *Dischord DIS 100CD*	47		1
20 Oct 01	**THE ARGUMENT** *Dischord DIS 130CD*	63		1

FUGEES
US/Haiti, female/male vocal/rap/production trio – Lauryn Hill*, Wyclef Jean* & Pras Michel* — Weeks on Chart: **74**

Date	Title / Label	Peak Position	Weeks at No.1	Weeks on Chart
30 Mar 96	**THE SCORE** *Columbia 4935242* ⊛x4 ★	2		72
7 Dec 96	**THE BOOTLEG VERSIONS** *Columbia 4868242*	55		2

FUN BOY THREE
UK, male vocal/instrumental trio – Terry Hall*, Lynval Golding & Neville Staple. See Specials — Weeks on Chart: **40**

Date	Title / Label	Peak Position	Weeks at No.1	Weeks on Chart
20 Mar 82	**THE FUN BOY THREE** *Chrysalis CHR 1383* ●	7		20
19 Feb 83	**WAITING** *Chrysalis CHR 1417* ○	14		20

FUN DA MENTAL
UK, male rap group — Weeks on Chart: **1**

Date	Title / Label	Peak Position	Weeks at No.1	Weeks on Chart
25 Jun 94	**SEIZE THE TIME** *Nation NATCD 33*	74		1

FUN LOVIN' CRIMINALS
US, male vocal/instrumental group – Huey Morgan, Steve Borgovini (replaced by Maxwell Jayson) & Brian Leiser — Weeks on Chart: **123**

Date	Title / Label	Peak Position	Weeks at No.1	Weeks on Chart
13 Jul 96	**COME FIND YOURSELF** *Chrysalis CDCHR 6114* ⊛	7		72
5 Sep 98	**100% COLOMBIAN** *Chrysalis 4970562* ⊛	3		26
11 Dec 99	**MIMOSA** *Chrysalis 5234592* ●	37		9
10 Mar 01	**LOCO** *Chrysalis 5314712* ●	5		6
3 Aug 02	**BAG OF HITS** *Chrysalis 5399542* ●	11		6
20 Sep 03	**WELCOME TO POPPY'S** *Sanctuary SANCD 187*	20		3
3 Sep 05	**LIVIN IN THE CITY** *Sanctuary SANCD381*	57		1

FUNERAL FOR A FRIEND
UK, male vocal/instrumental group – Kris Coombs-Roberts, Gavin Burrough, Matthew Davies-Kreye, Ryan Richards & Darran Smith — Weeks on Chart: **13**

Date	Title / Label	Peak Position	Weeks at No.1	Weeks on Chart
25 Oct 03	**CASUALLY DRESSED AND DEEP IN CONVERSATION** *Infectious 2564609472* ●	12		3
25 Jun 05	**HOURS** *Atlantic 5046784442* ●	12		4
26 May 07	**TALES DON'T TELL THEMSELVES** *Atlantic 5144209952* ○	3		4
25 Oct 08	**MEMORY AND HUMANITY** *Join Us JOINUS003*	17		2

FUNKADELIC
US, male vocal/instrumental group — Weeks on Chart: **5**

Date	Title / Label	Peak Position	Weeks at No.1	Weeks on Chart
23 Dec 78	**ONE NATION UNDER A GROOVE** *Warner Brothers K 56539*	56		5

FUNKDOOBIEST
US, male rap group — Weeks on Chart: **1**

Date	Title / Label	Peak Position	Weeks at No.1	Weeks on Chart
15 Jul 95	**BROTHAS DOOBIE** *Epic 4783812*	62		1

BOB MARLEY VS FUNKSTAR DELUXE
Denmark, male producer (Martin Ottesen) — Weeks on Chart: **3**

Date	Title / Label	Peak Position	Weeks at No.1	Weeks on Chart
4 Sep 99	**THE SUN IS SHINING** *Club Tools 0066735 CLU*	40		3

FUREYS & DAVEY ARTHUR
Ireland, male vocal duo & UK, male vocalist — Weeks on Chart: **38**

Date	Title / Label	Peak Position	Weeks at No.1	Weeks on Chart
8 May 82	**WHEN YOU WERE SWEET SIXTEEN** *Ritz RITZLP 0004* ○	99		1
10 Nov 84	**GOLDEN DAYS** *K-Tel ONE 1283* ●	17		19
26 Oct 85	**AT THE END OF THE DAY** *K-Tel ONE 1310* ●	35		11
21 Nov 87	**FUREYS FINEST** *Telstar HSTAR 2311*	65		7

NELLY FURTADO
Canada, female vocalist — Weeks on Chart: **134**

Date	Title / Label	Peak Position	Weeks at No.1	Weeks on Chart
24 Mar 01	**WHOA NELLY** *DreamWorks 4502852* ⊛x2	2		47
6 Dec 03	**FOLKLORE** *DreamWorks 4505089* ●	11		14
24 Jun 06	**LOOSE** *Geffen 9853919* ⊛x2 ★	4		73

BILLY FURY
UK, male vocalist/actor (Ronald Wycherley), d. 28 Jan 1983 (age 41) — Weeks on Chart: **59**

Date	Title / Label	Peak Position	Weeks at No.1	Weeks on Chart
4 Jun 60	**THE SOUND OF FURY** *Decca LF 1329*	18		2
23 Sep 61	**HALFWAY TO PARADISE** *Ace Of Clubs ACL 1083*	5		9
11 May 63	**BILLY** *Decca LK 4533*	6		21
26 Oct 63	**WE WANT BILLY** *Decca LK 4548*	14		2
19 Feb 83	**THE BILLY FURY HIT PARADE** *Decca TAB 37*	44		15
26 Mar 83	**THE ONE AND ONLY BILLY FURY** *Polydor POLD 5069*	56		2
9 Feb 08	**HIS WONDROUS STORY** *UMTV 5305875* ●	10		8

F.U.S.E.
Canada, male DJ/producer (Richie Hawtin). See Plastik Man — Weeks on Chart: **1**

Date	Title / Label	Peak Position	Weeks at No.1	Weeks on Chart
19 Jun 93	**DIMENSION INTRUSION** *Warp WARPCD 12*	63		1

FUTURE SOUND OF LONDON
UK, male production/instrumental duo – Gary Cobain & Brian Dougans — Weeks on Chart: **10**

Date	Title / Label	Peak Position	Weeks at No.1	Weeks on Chart
18 Jul 92	**ACCELERATOR** *Jumpin' & Pumpin' CDTOT 2*	75		1
4 Jun 94	**LIFEFORMS** *Virgin CDV 2722* ○	6		5
17 Dec 94	**ISDN** *Virgin CDV 2755*	62		1
17 Jun 95	**ISDN (REMIX)** *Virgin CDVX 2755*	44		1
9 Nov 96	**DEAD CITIES** *Virgin CDV 2184*	26		2

FUTUREHEADS
UK, male vocal/instrumental group — Weeks on Chart: **14**

Date	Title / Label	Peak Position	Weeks at No.1	Weeks on Chart
19 Mar 05	**THE FUTUREHEADS** *679 5046738482* ●	11		10
10 Jun 06	**NEWS AND TRIBUTES** *679 2564633522*	12		2
7 Jun 08	**THIS IS NOT THE WORLD** *Nul NUL103CD*	17		2

G

GINA G
Australia, female vocalist (Gina Gardiner) — Weeks on Chart: **4**

Date	Title / Label	Peak Position	Weeks at No.1	Weeks on Chart
5 Apr 97	**FRESH!** *Eternal 0630178402* ○	12		4

KENNY G
US, male saxophonist (Kenny Gorelick) — Weeks on Chart: **62**

Date	Title / Label	Peak Position	Weeks at No.1	Weeks on Chart
17 Mar 84	**G FORCE** *Arista 206 168*	56		5
8 Aug 87	**DUOTONES** *Arista 207 792*	28		5
14 Apr 90	**MONTAGE** *Arista 210621*	32		7
15 May 93	**BREATHLESS** *Arista 07822186462* ●	4		27
19 Oct 96	**THE MOMENT** *Arista 07822189352* ●	19		9
13 Dec 97	**GREATEST HITS** *Arista 07822189912* ○	38		5
14 Aug 04	**SONGBIRD – THE ULTIMATE COLLECTION** *Arista 82876625622*	24		4

WARREN G
US, male rapper (Warren Griffin) — Weeks on Chart: **10**

Date	Title / Label	Peak Position	Weeks at No.1	Weeks on Chart
6 Aug 94	**REGULATE...G FUNK ERA** *RAL 5233352* ○	25		6
8 Mar 97	**TAKE A LOOK OVER YOUR SHOULDER (REALITY)** *Def Jam 5334842*	20		4

G-UNIT
US, male rap trio — 29

Date	Title	Peak	Wks at No.1	Wks on Chart
29 Nov 03	**BEG FOR MERCY** *Interscope 9861498* ●	13		11
18 Sep 04	**50 CENT IS THE FUTURE (IMPORT)** *Street Dance SDR0166752* 50 CENT & G UNIT	65		1
19 Nov 05	**GET RICH OR DIE TRYIN' (OST)** *Interscope 9887992* 50 CENT & G UNIT	18		15
12 Jul 08	**TOS** *Interscope 1769306*	39		2

PETER GABRIEL
UK, male vocalist/multi-instrumentalist. See Genesis — 215

Date	Title	Peak	Wks at No.1	Wks on Chart
12 Mar 77	**PETER GABRIEL** *Charisma CDS 4006* ●	7		19
17 Jun 78	**PETER GABRIEL** *Charisma CDS 4013*	10		8
7 Jun 80	**PETER GABRIEL** *Charisma CDC 4019* ●	1	2	18
18 Sep 82	**PETER GABRIEL** *Charisma PG 4* ●	6		16
18 Jun 83	**PETER GABRIEL PLAYS LIVE** *Charisma PGDL 1*	8		9
30 Mar 85	**BIRDY (OST)** *Charisma CAS 1167*	51		3
31 May 86	**SO** *Virgin PG 5* ⊛x3	1	2	76
17 Jun 89	**PASSION** *Virgin RWLP 1*	29		5
1 Dec 90	**SHAKING THE TREE – GOLDEN GREATS** *Virgin PGTV 6* ⊛x2	11		18
10 Oct 92	**US** *Virgin PGCD 7* ⊛	2		29
10 Sep 94	**SECRET WORLD LIVE** *Virgin PGDCD 8* ○	10		4
24 Jun 00	**OVO** *Realworld RWPG 01*	24		2
5 Oct 02	**UP** *Realworld PGCD 11* ○	11		4
15 Nov 03	**HIT** *Realworld 5952372* ●	29		4

GABRIELLE
UK, female vocalist (Louisa Gabrielle Bobb) — 181

Date	Title	Peak	Wks at No.1	Wks on Chart
30 Oct 93	**FIND YOUR WAY** *Go. Beat 8284412* ●	9		22
8 Jun 96	**GABRIELLE** *Go. Beat 8287242* ⊛	11		30
30 Oct 99	**RISE** *Go. Beat 5477682* ⊛x4	1	3	87
24 Nov 01	**DREAMS CAN COME TRUE – GREATEST HITS VOLUME 1** *Go. Beat 5893742* ⊛x4	2		28
29 May 04	**PLAY TO WIN** *Go Beat 9866530* ●	10		10
13 Oct 07	**ALWAYS** *Universal 1748902*	11		4

DAVE GAHAN
UK, male vocalist. See Depeche Mode — 3

Date	Title	Peak	Wks at No.1	Wks on Chart
14 Jun 03	**PAPER MONSTERS** *Mute CDSTUMM216*	36		2
3 Nov 07	**HOURGLASS** *Mute CDSTUMM288*	50		1

RORY GALLAGHER
Ireland, male vocalist/guitarist, d. 14 Jun 1995 (age 47). See Taste — 45

Date	Title	Peak	Wks at No.1	Wks on Chart
29 May 71	**RORY GALLAGHER** *Polydor 2383 044* ●	32		2
4 Dec 71	**DEUCE** *Polydor 2383 076* ●	39		1
20 May 72	**LIVE! IN EUROPE** *Polydor 2383 112* ●	9		15
24 Feb 73	**BLUE PRINT** *Polydor 2383 189* ●	12		7
17 Nov 73	**TATTOO** *Polydor 2383 230* ●	32		3
27 Jul 74	**IRISH TOUR '74** *Polydor 2659 031* ●	36		2
30 Oct 76	**CALLING CARD** *Chrysalis CHR 1124* ○	32		1
22 Sep 79	**TOP PRIORITY** *Chrysalis CHR 1235* ○	56		4
8 Nov 80	**STAGE STRUCK** *Chrysalis CHR 1280* ○	40		3
8 May 82	**JINX** *Chrysalis CHR 1359* ○	68		5
25 Jun 05	**BIG GUNS – THE VERY BEST OF** *Capo CAPOX705*	31		2

GALLAGHER & LYLE
UK, male vocal/instrumental duo – Benny Gallagher & Graham Lyle — 44

Date	Title	Peak	Wks at No.1	Wks on Chart
28 Feb 76	**BREAKAWAY** *A&M AMLH 68348* ●	6		35
29 Jan 77	**LOVE ON THE AIRWAYS** *A&M AMLH 64620* ○	19		9

GALLIANO
UK, male/female vocal/instrumental group – Rob Gallagher, Valerie Etienne, Ernie McKone, Crispin Robinson, Mick Talbot, Crispin Taylor & Constantine Weir — 15

Date	Title	Peak	Wks at No.1	Wks on Chart
20 Jun 92	**A JOYFUL NOISE UNTO THE CREATOR** *Talkin Loud 8480802*	28		3
11 Jun 94	**THE PLOT THICKENS** *Talkin Loud 5224522*	7		12

GALLON DRUNK
UK, male vocal/instrumental group — 1

Date	Title	Peak	Wks at No.1	Wks on Chart
13 Mar 93	**FROM THE HEART OF TOWN** *Clawfist HUNKACDL 005*	67		1

GALLOWS
UK, male/female vocal/instrumental group — 1

Date	Title	Peak	Wks at No.1	Wks on Chart
30 Jun 07	**ORCHESTRA OF WOLVES** *Warner Brothers 2564699005*	57		1

JAMES GALWAY
UK, male flautist — 102

Date	Title	Peak	Wks at No.1	Wks on Chart
27 May 78	**THE MAGIC FLUTE OF JAMES GALWAY** *RCA Red Seal LRL1 5131*	43		6
1 Jul 78	**THE MAN WITH THE GOLDEN FLUTE** *RCA Red Seal LRL1 5127*	52		3
9 Sep 78	**JAMES GALWAY PLAYS SONGS FOR ANNIE** *RCA Red Seal RL 25163* ⊛	7		40
15 Dec 79	**SONGS OF THE SEASHORE** *Solar RL 25253* ●	39		6
31 May 80	**SOMETIMES WHEN WE TOUCH** *RCA PL 25296* CLEO LAINE & JAMES GALWAY ●	15		14
18 Dec 82	**THE JAMES GALWAY COLLECTION** *Telstar STAR 2224*	41		8
8 Dec 84	**IN THE PINK** *RCA Red Seal RL 85315* & HENRY MANCINI	62		6
28 Mar 87	**JAMES GALWAY AND THE CHIEFTAINS IN IRELAND** *RCA Red Seal RL 85798* & THE CHIEFTAINS	32		5
17 Apr 93	**MASTERPIECES – THE ESSENTIAL FLUTE OF JAMES GALWAY** *RCA Victor 74321133852*	30		5
18 Feb 95	**I WILL ALWAYS LOVE YOU** *RCA Victor 74321262212*	59		2
20 Jul 96	**CLASSICAL MEDITATIONS** *RCA Victor 74321377312*	45		5
25 Sep 04	**WINGS OF SONG** *Deutsche Grammophon 4775236*	45		2

GAME
US, male rapper (Jayceon Taylor). See G-Unit — 45

Date	Title	Peak	Wks at No.1	Wks on Chart
5 Feb 05	**THE DOCUMENTARY** *Interscope 9864143* ⊛ ★	7		33
25 Nov 06	**DOCTOR'S ADVOCATE** *Geffen 1713812* ● ★	21		6
6 Sep 08	**LAX** *Geffen 1774529*	9		6

GANG OF FOUR
UK, male vocal/instrumental group — 9

Date	Title	Peak	Wks at No.1	Wks on Chart
13 Oct 79	**ENTERTAINMENT** *EMI EMC 3313*	45		3
21 Mar 81	**SOLID GOLD** *EMI EMC 3364*	52		2
29 May 82	**SONGS OF THE FREE** *EMI EMC 3412*	61		4

GANG STARR
US, male rap duo — 10

Date	Title	Peak	Wks at No.1	Wks on Chart
26 Jan 91	**STEP IN THE ARENA** *Cooltempo ZCTLP 21*	36		3
12 Mar 94	**HARD TO EARN** *Cooltempo CTCD 38*	29		3
11 Apr 98	**MOMENT OF TRUTH** *Cooltempo 8455852*	43		1
7 Aug 99	**FULL CLIP: A DECADE OF GANG STARR** *Cooltempo 5211892*	47		2
5 Jul 03	**THE OWNERZ** *Virgin CDVUS235*	74		1

GAP BAND
US, male vocal/instrumental trio — 3

Date	Title	Peak	Wks at No.1	Wks on Chart
7 Feb 87	**GAP BAND 8** *Total Experience FL 89992*	47		3

GARBAGE
UK/US, female/male vocal/instrumental group – Shirley Manson, Duke Erikson, Steve Marker & Butch Vig — 177

Date	Title	Peak	Wks at No.1	Wks on Chart
14 Oct 95	**GARBAGE** *Mushroom D 31450* ⊛x2	6		100
23 May 98	**VERSION 2.0** *Mushroom MUSH 29CD* ⊛x2	1	1	65
13 Oct 01	**BEAUTIFUL GARBAGE** *Mushroom MUSH 95CDX* ●	6		4
23 Apr 05	**BLEED LIKE ME** *A&E 5046776812*	4		5
4 Aug 07	**ABSOLUTE** *Warner Brothers 5144224892*	11		3

JAN GARBAREK
Norway, male saxophonist — 1

Date	Title	Peak	Wks at No.1	Wks on Chart
4 May 96	**VISIBLE WORLD** *ECM 5290862*	69		1

ART GARFUNKEL
US, male vocalist/guitarist. See Simon & Garfunkel — 64

Date	Title	Peak	Wks at No.1	Wks on Chart
13 Oct 73	**ANGEL CLARE** *CBS 69021* ○	14		7
1 Nov 75	**BREAKAWAY** *CBS 86002* ●	7		10
18 Mar 78	**WATER MARK** *CBS 86054* ○	25		5
21 Apr 79	**FATE FOR BREAKFAST** *CBS 86082* ●	2		20
19 Sep 81	**SCISSORS CUT** *CBS 85259*	51		3
17 Nov 84	**THE ART GARFUNKEL ALBUM** *CBS 10046* ●	12		13
14 Dec 96	**THE VERY BEST OF ART GARFUNKEL – ACROSS AMERICA** *Virgin VTCD 113* ○	35		6

Silver-selling ○ Gold-selling ● Platinum-selling ⊛ US No.1 ★ Peak Position Weeks at No.1 Weeks in Chart

Top 20 Best-Selling Download Albums of All Time

Pos	Album Title	Artist	Label
1	**VIVA LA VIDA OR DEATH AND ALL HIS FRIENDS**	COLDPLAY	PARLOPHONE
2	**BACK TO BLACK**	AMY WINEHOUSE	ISLAND
3	**ONLY BY THE NIGHT**	KINGS OF LEON	HAND ME DOWN
4	**ROCKFERRY**	DUFFY	A&M
5	**EYES OPEN**	SNOW PATROL	FICTION
6	**SPIRIT**	LEONA LEWIS	SYCO MUSIC
7	**LIFE IN CARTOON MOTION**	MIKA	CASABLANCA/ISLAND
8	**BEAUTIFUL WORLD**	TAKE THAT	POLYDOR
9	**UNDISCOVERED**	JAMES MORRISON	POLYDOR
10	**THE SCRIPT**	SCRIPT	PHONOGENIC
11	**VERSION**	MARK RONSON	COLUMBIA
12	**HAND BUILT BY ROBOTS**	NEWTON FAULKNER	UGLY TRUTH
13	**SAM'S TOWN**	KILLERS	VERTIGO
14	**SCOUTING FOR GIRLS**	SCOUTING FOR GIRLS	EPIC
15	**RAZORLIGHT**	RAZORLIGHT	VERTIGO
16	**FAVOURITE WORST NIGHTMARE**	ARCTIC MONKEYS	DOMINO RECORDINGS
17	**COSTELLO MUSIC**	FRATELLIS	FALLOUT
18	**DIG OUT YOUR SOUL**	OASIS	BIG BROTHER
19	**GOOD GIRL GONE BAD**	RIHANNA	DEF JAM
20	**DAY & AGE**	KILLERS	VERTIGO

JUDY GARLAND

US, female vocalist/actor (Frances Gumm), d. 22 Jun 1969 (age 47) — 3

Date	Title	Peak	Wks at No.1	Wks in Chart
3 Mar 62	**JUDY AT CARNEGIE HALL** *Capitol W 1569* ★	13		3

ERROLL GARNER

US, male pianist, d. 2 Jan 1977 (age 55) — 1

Date	Title	Peak	Wks at No.1	Wks in Chart
14 Jul 62	**CLOSE UP IN SWING** *Philips BBL 7579*	20		1

DAVID GARRETT

UK, male violinist (David Bongartz) — 2

Date	Title	Peak	Wks at No.1	Wks in Chart
5 Apr 08	**VIRTUOSO** *Decca 4780080*	17		2

LESLEY GARRETT

UK, female vocalist — 52

Date	Title	Peak	Wks at No.1	Wks in Chart
12 Feb 94	**THE LESLEY GARRETT ALBUM** *Telstar TCD 2709*	25		7
18 Nov 95	**SOPRANO IN RED** *Silva Classics SILKTVCD 1* ○	59		8
19 Oct 96	**SOPRANO IN HOLLYWOOD** *Silva Classics SILKTVCD 2*	53		4
18 Oct 97	**THE SOPRANO'S GREATEST HITS** *Silva Classics SILKTVCD 3* ○	53		2
22 Nov 97	**A SOPRANO INSPIRED** *Conifer Classics 75605513292* ○	48		7
14 Nov 98	**LESLEY GARRETT** *BBC 75605513382*	34		8
27 May 00	**I WILL WAIT FOR YOU** *BBC/BMG Conifer 75605513542*	28		7
24 Nov 01	**TRAVELLING LIGHT** *EMI Classics CDC 5572512*	75		1
17 Feb 07	**WHEN I FALL IN LOVE** *UCJ 1720319*	11		7
6 Dec 08	**AMAZING GRACE** *UCJ 4766493*	50		1

STEPHEN GATELY

Ireland, male vocalist. See Boyzone — 4

Date	Title	Peak	Wks at No.1	Wks in Chart
1 Jul 00	**NEW BEGINNING** *A&M 5439102*	9		4

DAVID GATES

US, male vocalist. See Bread — 32

Date	Title	Peak	Wks at No.1	Wks in Chart
31 May 75	**NEVER LET HER GO** *Elektra K 52012*	32		1
29 Jul 78	**GOODBYE GIRL** *Elektra K 52091* ○	28		3
28 Nov 87	**THE COLLECTION – THE VERY BEST OF BREAD AND DAVID GATES** *Telstar STAR 2303* BREAD & DAVID GATES	94		2
5 Jul 97	**DAVID GATES AND BREAD: ESSENTIALS** *warner.esp/Jive 9548354082* & BREAD ●	9		19
12 Oct 02	**SONGBOOK – A LIFETIME OF MUSIC** *Jive 0927491402* ●	11		7

GARETH GATES

UK, male vocalist — 23

Date	Title	Peak	Wks at No.1	Wks in Chart
9 Nov 02	**WHAT MY HEART WANTS TO SAY** *S 74321975172* ⊛x2	2		17
4 Oct 03	**GO YOUR OWN WAY** *S 82876557452*	11		4
7 Jul 07	**PICTURES OF THE OTHER SIDE** *19 1730679*	23		2

GAY DAD

UK, male/female vocal/instrumental group — 3

Date	Title	Peak	Wks at No.1	Wks in Chart
19 Jun 99	**LEISURE NOISE** *London 5561032*	14		3

MARVIN GAYE

US, male vocalist, d. 1 Apr 1984 (age 44) — 193

Date	Title	Peak	Wks at No.1	Wks in Chart
16 Mar 68	**GREATEST HITS** *Tamla Motown STML 11065*	40		1
22 Aug 70	**GREATEST HITS** *Tamla Motown STML 11153* & TAMMI TERRELL	60		4
10 Nov 73	**LET'S GET IT ON** *Tamla Motown STMA 8013*	39		1
19 Jan 74	**DIANA AND MARVIN** *Tamla Motown STMA 8015* DIANA ROSS & MARVIN GAYE ●	6		43
15 May 76	**I WANT YOU** *Tamla Motown STML 12025*	22		5
30 Oct 76	**THE BEST OF MARVIN GAYE** *Tamla Motown STML 12042*	56		1
28 Feb 81	**IN OUR LIFETIME** *Motown STML 12149*	48		4
29 Aug 81	**DIANA AND MARVIN** *Motown STMS 5001* DIANA ROSS & MARVIN GAYE	78		2
20 Nov 82	**MIDNIGHT LOVE** *CBS 85977* ●	10		16
12 Nov 83	**GREATEST HITS** *Telstar STAR 2234* ●	13		61
15 Jun 85	**DREAM OF A LIFETIME** *CBS 26239*	46		4
12 Nov 88	**LOVE SONGS** *Telstar STAR 2331* & SMOKEY ROBINSON ●	69		9
3 Nov 90	**LOVE SONGS** *Telstar STAR 2427*	39		5
9 Apr 94	**THE VERY BEST OF MARVIN GAYE** *Motown 5302922* ●	3		19
24 Jul 99	**WHAT'S GOING ON?** *Motown 5300222*	56		5
19 Feb 00	**THE LOVE SONGS** *Motown 5454702* ●	8		7
1 Sep 01	**THE VERY BEST OF MARVIN GAYE** *Motown 0143672*	15		4
25 Mar 06	**THE LOVE COLLECTION** *Universal TV 9838401*	44		2

Silver-selling ○ Gold-selling ● Platinum-selling ⊛ US No.1 ★ | Peak Position | Weeks at No.1 | Weeks on Chart

GAYE BYKERS ON ACID

UK, male vocal/instrumental group — 1

Date	Title	Peak Position	Weeks at No.1	Weeks on Chart
14 Nov 87	**DRILL YOUR OWN HOLE** *Virgin V 2478*	95		1

CRYSTAL GAYLE

US, female vocalist (Brenda Gail Webb) — 25

Date	Title	Peak Position	Weeks at No.1	Weeks on Chart
21 Jan 78	**WE MUST BELIEVE IN MAGIC** *United Artists UAG 30108* ○	15		7
23 Sep 78	**WHEN I DREAM** *United Artists UAG 30169* ○	25		8
22 Mar 80	**THE CRYSTAL GAYLE SINGLES ALBUM** *United Artists UAG 30287* ●	7		10

MICHELLE GAYLE

UK, female vocalist/actor — 13

Date	Title	Peak Position	Weeks at No.1	Weeks on Chart
22 Oct 94	**MICHELLE GAYLE** *RCA 74321234122* ●	30		10
10 May 97	**SENSATIONAL** *RCA 74321419322*	17		3

GLORIA GAYNOR

US, female vocalist (Gloria Fowles) — 17

Date	Title	Peak Position	Weeks at No.1	Weeks on Chart
8 Mar 75	**NEVER CAN SAY GOODBYE** *MGM 2315 321* ○	32		8
24 Mar 79	**LOVE TRACKS** *Polydor 2391 385*	31		7
16 Aug 86	**THE POWER OF GLORIA GAYNOR** *Stylus SMR 618*	81		2

J. GEILS BAND

US, male vocal/instrumental group — 15

Date	Title	Peak Position	Weeks at No.1	Weeks on Chart
27 Feb 82	**FREEZE-FRAME** *EMI America AML 3020* ★	12		15

BOB GELDOF

Ireland, male vocalist. See Boomtown Rats — 10

Date	Title	Peak Position	Weeks at No.1	Weeks on Chart
6 Dec 86	**DEEP IN THE HEART OF NOWHERE** *Mercury BOBLP 1* ●	79		1
4 Aug 90	**THE VEGETARIANS OF LOVE** *Mercury 8462501*	21		6
9 Jul 94	**LOUDMOUTH – THE BEST OF THE BOOMTOWN RATS AND BOB GELDOF** *Vertigo 5222832* BOOMTOWN RATS & BOB GELDOF	10		3

GENE

UK, male vocal/instrumental group – Martin Rossiter, Matt James, Steve Mason & Kevin Miles — 14

Date	Title	Peak Position	Weeks at No.1	Weeks on Chart
1 Apr 95	**OLYMPIAN** *Costermonger 5274462* ○	8		6
3 Feb 96	**TO SEE THE LIGHTS** *Costermonger GENE 002CD*	11		3
1 Mar 97	**DRAWN TO THE DEEP END** *Polydor GENEC 3*	8		3
13 Mar 99	**REVELATIONS** *Polydor GENEC 4*	25		2

GENE LOVES JEZEBEL

UK, male vocal/instrumental group — 5

Date	Title	Peak Position	Weeks at No.1	Weeks on Chart
19 Jul 86	**DISCOVER** *Beggars Banquet BEGA 73*	32		4
24 Oct 87	**HOUSE OF DOLLS** *Beggars Banquet BEGA 87*	81		1

GENERATION X

UK, male vocal/instrumental group — 9

Date	Title	Peak Position	Weeks at No.1	Weeks on Chart
8 Apr 78	**GENERATION X** *Chrysalis CHR 1169*	29		4
17 Feb 79	**VALLEY OF THE DOLLS** *Chrysalis CHR 1193*	51		5

GENESIS

UK, male vocal/instrumental group – Peter Gabriel* (replaced by Phil Collins*, left 1996), Tony Banks*, Steve Hackett* & Mike Rutherford*. In the beginning, the group that launched many successful solo artists were a pop act. In the late 70s, they were acclaimed progressive rockers, and in the 80s became one of the world's most popular rock bands — 511

Date	Title	Peak Position	Weeks at No.1	Weeks on Chart
14 Oct 72	**FOXTROT** *Charisma CAS 1058*	12		7
11 Aug 73	**GENESIS LIVE** *Charisma CLASS 1*	9		10
20 Oct 73	**SELLING ENGLAND BY THE POUND** *Charisma CAS 1074* ○	3		21
11 May 74	**NURSERY CRYME** *Charisma CAS 1052*	39		1
7 Dec 74	**THE LAMB LIES DOWN ON BROADWAY** *Charisma CGS 101* ●	10		6
28 Feb 76	**A TRICK OF THE TAIL** *Charisma CDS 4001* ●	3		39
15 Jan 77	**WIND AND WUTHERING** *Charisma CDS 4005* ●	7		22
29 Oct 77	**SECONDS OUT** *Charisma GE 2001* ●	4		17
15 Apr 78	**...AND THEN THERE WERE THREE...** *Charisma CDS 4010* ●	3		32
5 Apr 80	**DUKE** *Charisma CBR 101* ⊛x2	1	2	30
26 Sep 81	**ABACAB** *Charisma CBR 102* ●	1	2	27
12 Jun 82	**THREE SIDES LIVE** *Charisma GE 2002* ●	2		19
15 Oct 83	**GENESIS** *Charisma GENLP 1* ⊛x2	1	1	51
31 Mar 84	**NURSERY CRYME** *Charisma CHC 22*	68		1
21 Apr 84	**TRESPASS** *Charisma CHC 12*	98		1
21 Jun 86	**INVISIBLE TOUCH** *Charisma GENLP 2* ⊛x4	1	3	96
23 Nov 91	**WE CAN'T DANCE** *Virgin GENLP 3* ⊛x5	1	2	61
28 Nov 92	**LIVE – THE WAY WE WALK VOLUME 1: THE SHORTS** *Virgin GENCD 4* ⊛x2	3		18
23 Jan 93	**LIVE – THE WAY WE WALK VOLUME 2: THE LONGS** *Virgin GENCD 5* ●	1	2	9
13 Sep 97	**CALLING ALL STATIONS** *Virgin GENCD 6* ●	2		7
4 Jul 98	**ARCHIVE 1967–1975** *Virgin CDBOX 6*	35		1
6 Nov 99	**TURN IT ON AGAIN – THE HITS** *Virgin GENCD 8* ⊛	4		15
11 Dec 04	**PLATINUM COLLECTION** *Virgin GENCDX9* ⊛	21		9
16 Jun 07	**TURN IT ON AGAIN – THE HITS** *Virgin GENCDZ8*	5		7
8 Dec 07	**LIVE OVER EUROPE 2007** *Virgin GENCD10*	51		4

GENEVA

UK, male vocal/instrumental group — 2

Date	Title	Peak Position	Weeks at No.1	Weeks on Chart
21 Jun 97	**FURTHER** *Nude 7CD*	20		2

GENIUS/GZA

US, male rapper (Gary Crice). See Wu-Tang Clan — 2

Date	Title	Peak Position	Weeks at No.1	Weeks on Chart
2 Dec 95	**LIQUID SWORDS** *Geffen GED 24813*	73		1
10 Jul 99	**BENEATH THE SURFACE** *MCA MCD 11969*	56		1

JACKIE GENOVA

UK (b. Australia), female exercise instructor — 2

Date	Title	Peak Position	Weeks at No.1	Weeks on Chart
21 May 83	**WORK THAT BODY** *Island ILPS 9732*	74		2

BOBBIE GENTRY

US, female vocalist (Roberta Streeter) — 2

Date	Title	Peak Position	Weeks at No.1	Weeks on Chart
25 Oct 69	**TOUCH 'EM WITH LOVE** *Capitol EST 155*	21		1
28 Feb 70	**BOBBIE GENTRY AND GLEN CAMPBELL** *Capitol ST 2928*	50		1

LOWELL GEORGE

US, male vocalist/guitarist, d. 29 Jun 1979 (age 34). See Little Feat — 1

Date	Title	Peak Position	Weeks at No.1	Weeks on Chart
21 Apr 79	**THANKS BUT I'LL EAT IT HERE** *Warner Brothers K 56487*	71		1

ROBIN GEORGE

UK, male vocalist — 3

Date	Title	Peak Position	Weeks at No.1	Weeks on Chart
2 Mar 85	**DANGEROUS MUSIC** *Bronze BRON 554*	65		3

GEORGIA SATELLITES

US, male vocal/instrumental group — 9

Date	Title	Peak Position	Weeks at No.1	Weeks on Chart
7 Feb 87	**GEORGIA SATELLITES** *Elektra 9804961*	52		7
2 Jul 88	**OPEN ALL NIGHT** *Elektra EKT 47*	39		2

GERRY & THE PACEMAKERS

UK, male vocal/instrumental group – Gerry Marsden, Les Chadwick, Les Maguire & Freddie Marsden, d. 9 Dec 2006 — 29

Date	Title	Peak Position	Weeks at No.1	Weeks on Chart
26 Oct 63	**HOW DO YOU LIKE IT?** *Columbia 33SX 1546*	2		28
6 Feb 65	**FERRY ACROSS THE MERSEY** *Columbia 33SX 1676*	19		1

GET CAPE WEAR CAPE FLY

UK, male vocalist/guitarist (Sam Duckworth) — 4

Date	Title	Peak Position	Weeks at No.1	Weeks on Chart
30 Sep 06	**THE CHRONICLES OF A BOHEMIAN TEENAGER** *Atlantic 5101159052* ○	26		3
22 Mar 08	**SEARCHING FOR THE HOWS AND WHYS** *Atlantic 5144267102*	30		1

STAN GETZ & CHARLIE BYRD

US, male saxophonist (Stanley Gayetzsky), d. 6 Jun 1991, & guitarist, d. 30 Nov 1999 — 7

Date	Title	Peak Position	Weeks at No.1	Weeks on Chart
23 Feb 63	**JAZZ SAMBA** *Verve SULP 9013*	15		7

G4

UK, male vocal group – Jonathan Ansell*, Mike Christie, Matthew Stiff & Ben Thapa

Date	Title	Label	Peak Position	Weeks at No.1	Weeks on Chart: 26
12 Mar 05	G4	Sony Music 5197342 ⊛x2	1	1	15
10 Dec 05	G4 & FRIENDS	Sony Music 82876747382 ⊛	6		7
9 Dec 06	ACT THREE	White Rabbit 88697019892 ●	21		4

GHOSTFACE KILLAH

US, male rapper (Dennis Coles). See Wu-Tang Clan

Date	Title	Label	Peak Position	Weeks at No.1	Weeks on Chart: 2
9 Nov 96	IRONMAN	Epic 4853892	38		2

GHOSTS

UK, male vocal/instrumental group

Date	Title	Label	Peak Position	Weeks at No.1	Weeks on Chart: 2
30 Jun 07	THE WORLD IS OUTSIDE	Atlantic 5144207722	18		2

ANDY GIBB

UK, male vocalist, d. 10 Mar 1988 (age 30)

Date	Title	Label	Peak Position	Weeks at No.1	Weeks on Chart: 9
19 Aug 78	SHADOW DANCING	RSO RSS 0001 ○	15		9

BARRY GIBB

UK, male vocalist. See Bee Gees

Date	Title	Label	Peak Position	Weeks at No.1	Weeks on Chart: 2
20 Oct 84	NOW VOYAGER	Polydor POLH 14	85		2

ROBIN GIBB

UK, male vocalist. See Bee Gees

Date	Title	Label	Peak Position	Weeks at No.1	Weeks on Chart: 1
15 Feb 03	MAGNET	SPV Recordings SPV 08571472	43		1

BETH GIBBONS & RUSTIN MAN

UK, female vocalist & male producer/multi-instrumentalist (Paul Webb)

Date	Title	Label	Peak Position	Weeks at No.1	Weeks on Chart: 2
9 Nov 02	OUT OF SEASON	Go! Beat 665742	28		2

STEVE GIBBONS BAND

UK, male vocal/instrumental group

Date	Title	Label	Peak Position	Weeks at No.1	Weeks on Chart: 3
22 Oct 77	CAUGHT IN THE ACT	Polydor 2478 112	22		3

DEBBIE GIBSON

US, female vocalist/producer

Date	Title	Label	Peak Position	Weeks at No.1	Weeks on Chart: 52
30 Jan 88	OUT OF THE BLUE	Atlantic WX 139 ●	26		35
11 Feb 89	ELECTRIC YOUTH	Atlantic WX 231 ● ★	8		16
30 Mar 91	ANYTHING IS POSSIBLE	Atlantic WX 399	69		1

DON GIBSON

US, male vocalist/guitarist, d. 17 Nov 2003 (age 75)

Date	Title	Label	Peak Position	Weeks at No.1	Weeks on Chart: 10
22 Mar 80	COUNTRY NUMBER ONE	Warwick WW 5079	13		10

GIBSON BROTHERS

Martinique, male vocal/instrumental group

Date	Title	Label	Peak Position	Weeks at No.1	Weeks on Chart: 3
30 Aug 80	ON THE RIVIERA	Island ILPS 9620	50		3

BEBEL GILBERTO

Brazil, female vocalist

Date	Title	Label	Peak Position	Weeks at No.1	Weeks on Chart: 8
31 Aug 02	TANTO TEMPO	East West 0927474072 ●	49		5
19 Jun 04	BEBEL GILBERTO	East West 5046732665	49		3

JOHNNY GILL

US, male vocalist. See New Edition

Date	Title	Label	Peak Position	Weeks at No.1	Weeks on Chart: 3
19 Jun 93	PROVOCATIVE	Motown 5302062	41		3
17 Jul 76	CHILD IN TIME	Polydor 2490 136 IAN GILLAN BAND	55		1

GILLAN

UK, male vocal/instrumental group – members included Ian Gillan*, Steve Byrd, John McCoy, Bernie Tormé*, Colin Towns & Mick Underwood

Date	Title	Label	Peak Position	Weeks at No.1	Weeks on Chart
20 Oct 79	MR. UNIVERSE	Acrobat ACRO 3	11		6
16 Aug 80	GLORY ROAD	Virgin V 2171 ○	3		12
25 Apr 81	FUTURE SHOCK	Virgin VK 2196 ○	2		13
7 Nov 81	DOUBLE TROUBLE	Virgin VGD 3506	12		15
2 Oct 82	MAGIC	Virgin V 2238	17		6

IAN GILLAN

UK, male vocalist. See Black Sabbath, Deep Purple, Gillan

Date	Title	Label	Peak Position	Weeks at No.1	Weeks on Chart: 54
28 Jul 90	NAKED THUNDER	Teldec 9031718991	63		1

THEA GILMORE

UK, female vocalist/guitarist

Date	Title	Label	Peak Position	Weeks at No.1	Weeks on Chart: 2
23 Aug 03	AVALANCHE	Hungry Dog YRGNUHA 1	63		1
2 Sep 06	HARPO'S GHOST	Sanctuary SANCD394	69		1

DAVID GILMOUR

UK, male vocalist/guitarist. See Pink Floyd

Date	Title	Label	Peak Position	Weeks at No.1	Weeks on Chart: 39
10 Jun 78	DAVID GILMOUR	Harvest SHVL 817	17		9
17 Mar 84	ABOUT FACE	Harvest SHSP 2400791	21		9
18 Mar 06	ON AN ISLAND	EMI 3556952 ●	1	1	14
4 Oct 08	LIVE IN GDANSK	EMI 2354841	10		7

GORDON GILTRAP

UK, male guitarist

Date	Title	Label	Peak Position	Weeks at No.1	Weeks on Chart: 7
18 Feb 78	PERILOUS JOURNEY	Electric TRIX 4	29		7

GIN BLOSSOMS

US, male vocal/instrumental group

Date	Title	Label	Peak Position	Weeks at No.1	Weeks on Chart: 6
26 Feb 94	NEW MISERABLE EXPERIENCE	Fontana 3954032	53		4
24 Feb 96	CONGRATULATIONS, I'M SORRY	A&M 5404702	42		2

GINUWINE

US, male rapper (Elgin Lumpkin)

Date	Title	Label	Peak Position	Weeks at No.1	Weeks on Chart: 2
28 Mar 98	GINUWINE...THE BACHELOR	Epic 4895892	74		1
27 Mar 99	100% GINUWINE	Epic 4919922	42		1

GIPSY KINGS

France, male vocal/instrumental group

Date	Title	Label	Peak Position	Weeks at No.1	Weeks on Chart: 70
15 Apr 89	GIPSY KINGS	Telstar STAR 2355 ●	16		29
25 Nov 89	MOSAIQUE	Telstar STAR 2398 ●	27		13
13 Jul 91	ESTE MUNDO	Columbia 4686481 ○	19		7
6 Aug 94	GREATEST HITS	Columbia 4772422 ○	11		11
24 Jul 99	VOLARE – THE VERY BEST OF THE GIPSY KINGS	Columbia SONYTV 69CD	20		5
23 Jul 05	THE VERY BEST OF	Columbia 5202172	32		5

GIRL

UK, male vocal/instrumental group

Date	Title	Label	Peak Position	Weeks at No.1	Weeks on Chart: 6
9 Feb 80	SHEER GREED	Jet JETLP 224	33		5
23 Jan 82	WASTED YOUTH	Jet JETLP 238	92		1

GIRLS ALOUD

UK, female vocal group – Cheryl Cole (née Tweedy), Nadine Coyle, Sarah Harding, Nicola Roberts & Kimberley Walsh

Date	Title	Label	Peak Position	Weeks at No.1	Weeks on Chart: 113
7 Jun 03	SOUND OF THE UNDERGROUND	Polydor 9865315 ⊛	2		20
11 Dec 04	WHAT WILL THE NEIGHBOURS SAY	Polydor 9868948 ⊛	6		17
17 Dec 05	CHEMISTRY	Polydor 9875462 ⊛	11		10
11 Nov 06	THE SOUND OF – THE GREATEST HITS	Fascination FASC010 ⊛x2	1	1	24+
1 Dec 07	TANGLED UP	Fascination 1750580 ⊛	4		32
1 Dec 07	MIXED UP	Fascination 1753391	56		1
15 Nov 08	OUT OF CONTROL	Fascination 1790073	1	1	8+
15 Nov 08	GIRLS A LIVE	Fascination 1790107	29		1

GIRLS AT OUR BEST
UK, male/female vocal/instrumental group — 3

Date	Title / Label	Peak	Wks at No.1	Wks on Chart
7 Nov 81	**PLEASURE** *Happy Birthday RVLP 1*	60		3

GIRLSCHOOL
UK, female vocal/instrumental group – Kim McAuliffe, Denise Dufort, Kelly Johnson, Enid Williams (replaced by Gil Weston) — 23

Date	Title / Label	Peak	Wks at No.1	Wks on Chart
5 Jul 80	**DEMOLITION** *Bronze BRON 525*	28		10
25 Apr 81	**HIT 'N' RUN** *Bronze BRON 534*	5		6
12 Jun 82	**SCREAMING BLUE MURDER** *Bronze BRON 541*	27		6
12 Nov 83	**PLAY DIRTY** *Bronze BRON 548*	66		1

GLAMMA KID
UK, male vocalist/rapper (Lyael Constable) — 1

Date	Title / Label	Peak	Wks at No.1	Wks on Chart
16 Sep 00	**KIDOLOGY** *WEA 3984298572*	66		1

GLASVEGAS
UK, male/female vocal/instrumental group – James & Rab Allan, Paul Donoghue & Caroline McKay — 7

Date	Title / Label	Peak	Wks at No.1	Wks on Chart
20 Sep 08	**GLASVEGAS** *Columbia GOWOW010* ●	2		7

GARY GLITTER
UK, male vocalist (Paul Gadd) — 100

Date	Title / Label	Peak	Wks at No.1	Wks on Chart
21 Oct 72	**GLITTER** *Bell BELLS 216* ○	8		40
16 Jun 73	**TOUCH ME** *Bell BELLS 222* ○	2		33
29 Jun 74	**REMEMBER ME THIS WAY** *Bell BELLS 237*	5		14
27 Mar 76	**GARY GLITTER'S GREATEST HITS** *Bell BELLS 262*	33		5
14 Nov 92	**MANY HAPPY RETURNS – THE HITS** *EMI CDEMTV 68*	35		8

GLITTER BAND
UK, male vocal/instrumental group. See Gary Glitter — 17

Date	Title / Label	Peak	Wks at No.1	Wks on Chart
14 Sep 74	**HEY** *Bell BELLS 241* ○	13		12
3 May 75	**ROCK 'N' ROLL DUDES** *Bell BELLS 253* ○	17		4
19 Jun 76	**GREATEST HITS** *Bell BELLS 264*	52		1

GLOVE
UK, male vocal/instrumental group — 3

Date	Title / Label	Peak	Wks at No.1	Wks on Chart
17 Sep 83	**BLUE SUNSHINE** *Wonderland SHELP 2*	35		3

DANA GLOVER
US, female vocalist — 2

Date	Title / Label	Peak	Wks at No.1	Wks on Chart
17 May 03	**TESTIMONY** *DreamWorks 4504522*	43		2

GNARLS BARKLEY
US, male vocal/rap/production/instrumental duo – Danger Mouse (Brian Burton) & Cee-Lo Green (Thomas Callaway) — 38

Date	Title / Label	Peak	Wks at No.1	Wks on Chart
6 May 06	**ST ELSEWHERE** *Warner Brothers 2564632672* ⊛	1	1	35
12 Apr 08	**THE ODD COUPLE** *Warner Brothers 2564695680*	19		3

GO-BETWEENS
Australia, male/female vocal/instrumental group — 2

Date	Title / Label	Peak	Wks at No.1	Wks on Chart
13 Jun 87	**TALLULAH** *Beggars Banquet BEGA 81*	91		1
10 Sep 88	**16 LOVER'S LANE** *Beggars Banquet BEGA 95*	81		1

GO-GO'S
US, female vocal/instrumental group — 4

Date	Title / Label	Peak	Wks at No.1	Wks on Chart
21 Aug 82	**VACATION** *I.R.S. SP 70031*	75		3
18 Mar 95	**RETURN TO THE VALLEY OF THE GO-GO'S** *I.R.S. EIRSCD 1071*	52		1

THE GO! TEAM
UK, male/female vocal/instrumental group — 7

Date	Title / Label	Peak	Wks at No.1	Wks on Chart
4 Feb 06	**THUNDER LIGHTNING STRIKE** *Memphis Industries MI040CD* ●	48		5
22 Sep 07	**PROOF OF YOUTH** *Memphis Industries MI099CD*	21		2

GO WEST
UK, male vocal/instrumental duo – Peter Cox* & Richard Drummie — 119

Date	Title / Label	Peak	Wks at No.1	Wks on Chart
13 Apr 85	**GO WEST/BANGS AND CRASHES** *Chrysalis CHR 1495* ⊛x2	8		83
6 Jun 87	**DANCING ON THE COUCH** *Chrysalis CDL 1550*	19		5
14 Nov 92	**INDIAN SUMMER** *Chrysalis CDCHR 1964* ●	13		16
16 Oct 93	**ACES AND KINGS – THE BEST OF GO WEST** *Chrysalis CDCHR 6050* ●	5		15

GOATS
US, male rap group — 1

Date	Title / Label	Peak	Wks at No.1	Wks on Chart
27 Aug 94	**NO GOATS, NO GLORY** *Columbia 4769372*	58		1

GOD MACHINE
US, male vocal/instrumental group — 1

Date	Title / Label	Peak	Wks at No.1	Wks on Chart
20 Feb 93	**SCENES FROM THE SECOND STORY** *Fiction 5171562*	55		1

GODFATHERS
UK, male vocal/instrumental group — 3

Date	Title / Label	Peak	Wks at No.1	Wks on Chart
13 Feb 88	**BIRTH, SCHOOL, WORK, DEATH** *Epic 4602631*	80		2
20 May 89	**MORE SONGS ABOUT LOVE AND HATE** *Epic 4633941*	49		1

KEVIN GODLEY & LOL CRÈME
UK, male vocal/instrumental duo – Kevin Godley & Lol Crème. See 10cc — 34

Date	Title / Label	Peak	Wks at No.1	Wks on Chart
19 Nov 77	**CONSEQUENCES** *Mercury CONS 017*	52		1
9 Sep 78	**L** *Mercury 9109 611*	47		2
17 Oct 81	**ISMISM** *Polydor POLD 5043*	29		13
29 Aug 87	**CHANGING FACES – THE VERY BEST OF 10CC AND GODLEY AND CRÈME** *ProTV TGCLP 1* 10CC & GODLEY & CRÈME	4		18

GODSPEED YOU BLACK EMPEROR!
Canada, male instrumental group — 1

Date	Title / Label	Peak	Wks at No.1	Wks on Chart
21 Oct 00	**LIFT YOUR SKINNY FISTS LIKE ANTENNAS TO** *Kranky KRANK 043*	66		1

GOGOL BORDELLO
International, male/female vocal/instrumental group — 1

Date	Title / Label	Peak	Wks at No.1	Wks on Chart
21 Jul 07	**SUPER TARANTA** *Side One Dummy SD13342*	67		1

ANDREW GOLD
US, male vocalist/pianist — 7

Date	Title / Label	Peak	Wks at No.1	Wks on Chart
15 Apr 78	**ALL THIS AND HEAVEN TOO** *Asylum K 53072* ○	31		7

MURRAY GOLD
UK, male musical director/composer — 1

Date	Title / Label	Peak	Wks at No.1	Wks on Chart
17 Nov 07	**DOCTOR WHO – SERIES 3 – OST** *Silva Screen SILCD1250*	65		1

GOLDEN EARRING
Holland, male vocal/instrumental group — 4

Date	Title / Label	Peak	Wks at No.1	Wks on Chart
2 Feb 74	**MOONTAN** *Track 2406 112*	24		4

GOLDFRAPP
UK, female/male vocal/instrumental duo – Alison Goldfrapp & Will Gregory — 74

Date	Title / Label	Peak	Wks at No.1	Wks on Chart
25 Aug 01	**FELT MOUNTAIN** *Mute CDSTUMM 188* ●	57		5
10 May 03	**BLACK CHERRY** *Mute CDSTUMM196* ⊛	19		26
3 Sep 05	**SUPERNATURE** *Mute LCDSTUMM250* ⊛	2		31
8 Mar 08	**SEVENTH TREE** *Mute CDSTUMM280* ●	2		12

GOLDIE
UK, male producer (Clifford Price) — 16

Date	Title / Label	Peak	Wks at No.1	Wks on Chart
19 Aug 95	**TIMELESS** *ffrr 8286142* ●	7		12
14 Feb 98	**SATURNZ RETURN** *ffrr 8289902*	15		4

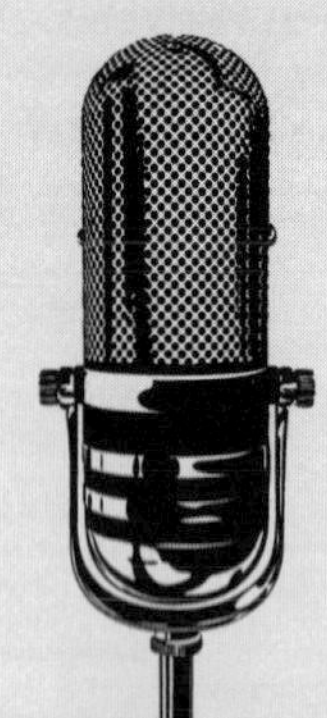

The Small Faces

Ogdens' Nut Gone Flake

BY 1968, the words 'concept' and 'album' were yet to become linked. Nonetheless, once The Beatles had released *Sgt. Pepper* the previous summer, the art of making albums would never quite be the same. Everyone duly took note, not least four East End boys known as The Small Faces, who had already enjoyed a hit or two themselves but lacked that all-important, laudable album.

Formed in 1965, they were sharply dressed, no-nonsense London boys with an attitude and a lot of energy. Unlike The Who (who would become mods), The Small Faces were mods who became a band. Although small of stature, their talent was significant.

Fronted by the ebullient, animated figure of writer/guitarist/vocalist Steve Marriott, co-writer/bassist Ronnie Lane, together with drummer Kenney Jones and Ian McLagan on keyboards, they had already firmly established themselves as a successful and respected British Top 10 singles band. But a punishing live schedule and miserly recording allowance meant they were less successful at producing the type of albums that they (particularly Marriott) really wanted to make.

London boys with an attitude and a lot of energy

It would be a change of management (to Andrew Loog-Oldham, former manager of The Rolling Stones from 1963 to 1967) and record label (Immediate) that finally gave them the opportunity to experiment and extend themselves. The subsequent *Ogdens' Nut Gone Flake* sessions were conducted over a six-month period, utilising at least four different studios, with recording overseen and produced by the legendary sound-engineer Glyn Johns. Very quickly it seems, the project became an album of two sides, each containing a diverse collection of material. If ever there were an LP with a split personality, it was this one.

Side 1 was an eclectic and bizarre amalgam of sharply penned songs, prefaced with a catchy instrumental title track. Experimentation was high and the results were a mosaic of styles, with psychedelic rock rubbing shoulders with pop, R&B and folk. Closing Side 1 was the album's only hit single, the unforgettable 'Lazy Sunday' which, although it went to Number 2 in the UK, was actually disliked by its writer Steve Marriott. He felt it was unrepresentative of the band's talent and lacked artistic authority (it was actually far better than he gave it credit for). Its success naturally proved a valuable asset for the album, and the lyric's semi-autobiographical, observational humour provided a neat bridge between Sides 1 and 2.

'Oh! What a mind-blast...' Ogdens' conceptual second side would also include an unusual and unexpected addition in the form of comedian and actor Stanley Unwin (Spike Milligan turned the band's approach down). Unwin was the inventor of his own unique gobbledegook language called *Unwinese*. His surreal Lewis Carroll nonsense verse fitted seamlessly with the collective Small Faces street-urchin character and Unwin's narrative occasionally incorporated their East End inflections, which he'd picked up during the album's production.

Unwin's entertaining links helped to create a surreal fairy-tale about Happiness Stan and a fly, who joined forces to search for the missing half of the moon. It was

Chart History

Artist	Album Title	First Chart Week	Weeks on Chart	Highest Position
THE SMALL FACES	OGDENS' NUT GONE FLAKE	15/6/68	19	1

a style (though without the gobbledegook) that *The Who Sell Out* had introduced the year before, and one that Pete Townshend would develop further with the musical *Tommy*.

It's impossible to consider this album without mention of its sleeve, which became an integral part of the project and perhaps as famous as the music. Its iconic circular tobacco-tin cover (designed by Mick Swan) made it instantly identifiable. The pop-art graphic neatly combined everyday working-class rolling tobacco with 1960s hedonism (particularly appropriate as it was Ogden's tobacco that the band used to roll their joints). Whilst trying to think up a title, the tin was there in front of them the whole time. 'We called it Nut Gone because your nut's gone if you smoke that stuff,' Kenney Jones later recalled.

Ogdens' Nut Gone Flake was evocative of its time. Although flawed in places, it captured the exuberance of happening London and combined it with off-beat humour and catchy tunes. The album provided The Small Faces with that much sought-after combination: critical and commercial success. The album may not have turned out exactly the way they'd planned and, sadly, it proved to be their swansong but ultimately the record became a landmark in all of their careers. They disbanded in January 1969, after which their creativity dispersed into Humble Pie and The Faces and continued apace to new horizons.

An eclectic and bizarre amalgam of sharply penned songs

On its release, *Ogdens' Nut Gone Flake* made Number 1, where it remained for an impressive six weeks. Now entering its forty-first year, it is possibly one of the oddest pop albums ever released.

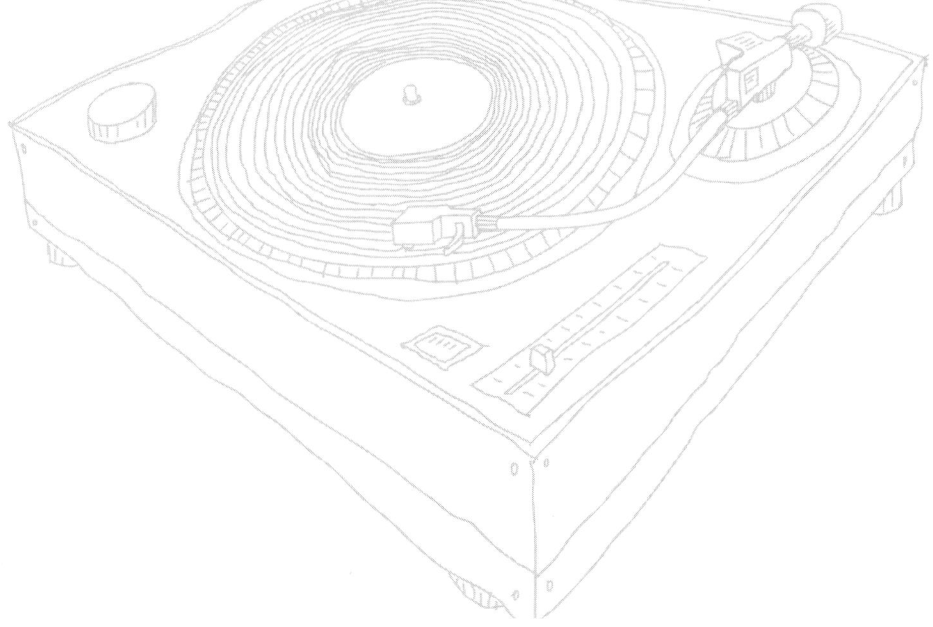

GOLDIE LOOKIN CHAIN
UK, male rap/production group – Maggot (Andrew Major), Mike Balls, Eggsy (John Routledge), Adam Hussain, Mystikal (Christopher Edge), 2Hats (Andrew David), Billy Webb & Dwain Xain Zedong

Date	Title / Label	Peak Position	Weeks at No.1	Weeks on Chart
				17
25 Sep 04	**GREATEST HITS** *Atlantic 5046748802* ●	5		14
1 Oct 05	**SAFE AS FUCK** *Atlantic 5101103042* ○	16		3

GLEN GOLDSMITH
UK, male vocalist

Date	Title / Label	Peak Position	Weeks at No.1	Weeks on Chart
				9
23 Jul 88	**WHAT YOU SEE IS WHAT YOU GET** *RCA PL 71750* ○	14		9

GOMEZ
UK, male vocal/instrumental group – Ian Ball, Paul Blackburn, Tom Gray, Ben Ottewell & Olly Peacock

Date	Title / Label	Peak Position	Weeks at No.1	Weeks on Chart
				102
25 Apr 98	**BRING IT ON** *Hut CDHUTX 49* ⊛	11		60
25 Sep 99	**LIQUID SKIN** *Hut CDHUT 54* ⊛	2		28
7 Oct 00	**ABANDONED SHOPPING TROLLEY HOTLINE** *Hut CDHUTX 64* ○	10		4
30 Mar 02	**IN OUR GUN** *Hut CDHUT 72* ○	8		7
29 May 04	**SPLIT THE DIFFERENCE** *Hut CDHUT 84*	35		2
17 Jun 06	**HOW WE OPERATE** *Independiente ISOM63CD*	69		1

JOSE GONZALEZ
Sweden, male vocalist/guitarist

Date	Title / Label	Peak Position	Weeks at No.1	Weeks on Chart
				38
14 Jan 06	**VENEER** *Peacefrog PFG066CD* ⊛	7		35
6 Oct 07	**IN OUR NATURE** *Peacefrog PFG114CD*	19		3

GOO GOO DOLLS
US, male vocal/instrumental trio

Date	Title / Label	Peak Position	Weeks at No.1	Weeks on Chart
				5
31 Jul 99	**DIZZY UP THE GIRL** *Hollywood 0102042HWR*	47		1
4 May 02	**GUTTERFLOWER** *Warner Brothers 9362483112*	56		1
6 May 06	**LET LOVE IN** *Warner Brothers 9362497482*	58		3

GOOD CHARLOTTE
US, male vocal/instrumental group – Joel & Benji Madden, Billy Martin, Paul Thomas & Chris Wilson (replaced by Dean Butterworth)

Date	Title / Label	Peak Position	Weeks at No.1	Weeks on Chart
				50
25 Jan 03	**THE YOUNG AND THE HOPELESS** *Epic 5094889* ⊛	15		39
23 Oct 04	**THE CHRONICLES OF LIFE AND DEATH** *Epic 5176859* ●	8		5
31 Mar 07	**GOOD MORNING REVIVAL** *Epic 88697069352*	13		6

GOOD SHOES
UK, male vocal/instrumental group

Date	Title / Label	Peak Position	Weeks at No.1	Weeks on Chart
				1
7 Apr 07	**THINK BEFORE YOU SPEAK** *Brille BRILCD108DLX*	55		1

GOOD THE BAD & THE QUEEN
UK/Nigeria, male vocal/instrumental group – Damon Albarn, Tony Allen, Paul Simonon & Simon Tong

Date	Title / Label	Peak Position	Weeks at No.1	Weeks on Chart
				5
3 Feb 07	**THE GOOD THE BAD & THE QUEEN** *Honest Jons 3819452* ●	2		5

GOODBYE MR. MACKENZIE
UK, male/female vocal/instrumental group

Date	Title / Label	Peak Position	Weeks at No.1	Weeks on Chart
				4
22 Apr 89	**GOOD DEEDS AND DIRTY RAGS** *Capitol EST 2089*	26		3
16 Mar 91	**HAMMER AND TONGS** *Radioactive RAR 10227*	61		1

GOODIES
UK, male comedy/vocal group

Date	Title / Label	Peak Position	Weeks at No.1	Weeks on Chart
				11
8 Nov 75	**THE NEW GOODIES LP** *Bradley's BRADL 1010*	25		11

BENNY GOODMAN
US, male clarinettist/band leader, d. 13 Jun 1986 (age 77)

Date	Title / Label	Peak Position	Weeks at No.1	Weeks on Chart
				1
3 Apr 71	**BENNY GOODMAN TODAY** *Decca DDS 3*	49		1

DELTA GOODREM
Australia, female vocalist/actor

Date	Title / Label	Peak Position	Weeks at No.1	Weeks on Chart
				43
12 Jul 03	**INNOCENT EYES** *Epic 5109512* ⊛x2	2		33
4 Dec 04	**MISTAKEN IDENTITY** *Epic 5189159* ●	25		10

RON GOODWIN & HIS ORCHESTRA
UK, male conductor, d. 8 Jan 2003 (age 77), & orchestra

Date	Title / Label	Peak Position	Weeks at No.1	Weeks on Chart
				3
2 May 70	**LEGEND OF THE GLASS MOUNTAIN** *Studio Two 220*	49		1
14 Jul 79	**BEATLES CONCERTO** *Parlophone PAS 10014* ROSTAL & SCHAEFER, RON GOODWIN & ROYAL LIVERPOOL PHILHARMONIC ORCHESTRA	61		2

GOOMBAY DANCE BAND
Germany/Montserrat, male/female vocal/instrumental group

Date	Title / Label	Peak Position	Weeks at No.1	Weeks on Chart
				9
10 Apr 82	**SEVEN TEARS** *Epic EPC 85702*	16		9

GOONS
UK, male comedy/vocal group

Date	Title / Label	Peak Position	Weeks at No.1	Weeks on Chart
				31
28 Nov 59	**BEST OF THE GOONS SHOWS** *Parlophone PMC 1108*	8		14
17 Dec 60	**BEST OF THE GOONS SHOWS VOLUME 2** *Parlophone PMC 1129*	11		6
4 Nov 72	**LAST GOON SHOW OF ALL** *BBC REB 142*	8		11

MARTIN L. GORE
UK, male vocalist/guitarist. See Depeche Mode

Date	Title / Label	Peak Position	Weeks at No.1	Weeks on Chart
				1
24 Jun 89	**COUNTERFEIT (EP)** *Mute STUMM 67*	51		1

GORILLAZ
UK/US/Japan, male/female virtual cartoon group – 2D (Stuart Pot), Murdoc (Murdoc Niccals), Noodle & Russel (Russel Hobbs); all characters created by Damon Albarn & Jamie Hewlett

Date	Title / Label	Peak Position	Weeks at No.1	Weeks on Chart
				135
7 Apr 01	**GORILLAZ** *Parlophone 5320930* ⊛x2	3		67
23 Mar 02	**G SIDES** *Parlophone 536942*	65		1
4 Jun 05	**DEMON DAYS** *Parlophone GORDEM1* ⊛x5	1	1	66
1 Dec 07	**D SIDES** *Parlophone 5105452*	63		1

GORKY'S ZYGOTIC MYNCI
UK, male/female vocal/instrumental group

Date	Title / Label	Peak Position	Weeks at No.1	Weeks on Chart
				2
19 Apr 97	**BARAFUNDLE** *Fontana 5347692*	46		1
12 Sep 98	**GORKY 5** *Fontana 5588222*	67		1

GOSSIP
US, female/male vocal/instrumental group

Date	Title / Label	Peak Position	Weeks at No.1	Weeks on Chart
				14
3 Feb 07	**STANDING IN THE WAY OF CONTROL** *Backyard BACK17CDC1* ●	22		14

GOTAN PROJECT
France/Argentina/Switzerland, male DJ/production trio

Date	Title / Label	Peak Position	Weeks at No.1	Weeks on Chart
				1
22 Apr 06	**LUNATICO** *XL Recordings XLCD195*	66		1

IRV GOTTI PRESENTS THE INC
US, male rapper/producer (Irving Lorenzo) & male/female rap/vocal group

Date	Title / Label	Peak Position	Weeks at No.1	Weeks on Chart
				3
20 Jul 02	**IRV GOTTI PRESENTS THE INC** *Murder Inc 0630332*	68		3

JAKI GRAHAM
UK, female vocalist

Date	Title / Label	Peak Position	Weeks at No.1	Weeks on Chart
				10
14 Sep 85	**HEAVEN KNOWS** *EMI JK 1*	48		5
20 Sep 86	**BREAKING AWAY** *EMI EMC 3514* ○	25		5

GRAND PRIX
UK, male vocal/instrumental group

Date	Title / Label	Peak Position	Weeks at No.1	Weeks on Chart
				2
18 Jun 83	**SAMURAI** *Chrysalis CHR 1430*	65		2

GRAND FUNK
US, male vocal/instrumental group

Date	Title / Label	Peak Position	Weeks at No.1	Weeks on Chart
				1
13 Feb 71	**GRAND FUNK LIVE** *Capitol E-STDW 1/2*	29		1

GRANDADDY
US, male vocal/instrumental group

Date	Album	Peak Position	Weeks at No.1	Weeks on Chart
				7
20 May 00	**SOPHTWARE SLUMP** *V2 VVR 1012252* ○	36		4
21 Jun 03	**SUMDAY** *V2 VVR 1022238*	22		2
27 May 06	**JUST LIKE THE FAMBLY CAT** *V2 VVR1039472*	50		1

GRANDMASTER FLASH
US, male vocalist/rapper/DJ (Joseph Saddler)

Date	Album	Peak Position	Weeks at No.1	Weeks on Chart
				20
23 Oct 82	**THE MESSAGE** *Sugar Hill SHLP 1007* GRANDMASTER FLASH & THE FURIOUS FIVE	77		3
23 Jun 84	**GREATEST MESSAGES** *Sugar Hill SHLP 5552* GRANDMASTER FLASH & THE FURIOUS FIVE	41		16
23Feb 85	**THEY SAID IT COULDN'T BE DONE** *Elektra 9603891*	95		1

GRANDMASTER MELLE MEL
US, male vocalist (Melvin Glover)

Date	Album	Peak Position	Weeks at No.1	Weeks on Chart
				5
20 Oct 84	**WORK PARTY** *Sugar Hill SHLP 5553* & THE FURIOUS FIVE	45		5

AMY GRANT
US, female vocalist/guitarist

Date	Album	Peak Position	Weeks at No.1	Weeks on Chart
				15
22 Jun 91	**HEART IN MOTION** *A&M 3953211* ●	25		15

DAVID GRANT
UK, male vocalist. See Linx

Date	Album	Peak Position	Weeks at No.1	Weeks on Chart
				7
5 Nov 83	**DAVID GRANT** *Chrysalis CHR 1448*	32		6
18 May 85	**HOPES AND DREAMS** *Chrysalis CHR 1483*	96		1

EDDY GRANT
Guyana, male vocalist/guitarist. See Equals

Date	Album	Peak Position	Weeks at No.1	Weeks on Chart
				69
30 May 81	**CAN'T GET ENOUGH** *Ice ICELP 21*	39		6
27 Nov 82	**KILLER ON THE RAMPAGE** *Ice ICELP 3023* ○	7		23
17 Nov 84	**ALL THE HITS** *K-Tel NE 1284* ●	23		10
1 Jul 89	**WALKING ON SUNSHINE (THE VERY BEST OF EDDY GRANT)** *Parlophone PCSD 108* ○	20		8
19 May 01	**THE GREATEST HITS** *East West 8573885972* ⊛	3		15
12 Jul 08	**VERY BEST OF EDDY GRANT** *Mercury/UMTV 1775167*	14		7

PETER GRANT
UK, male vocalist

Date	Album	Peak Position	Weeks at No.1	Weeks on Chart
				7
29 Apr 06	**NEW VINTAGE** *Globe 9877257*	8		6
29 Sep 07	**TRADITIONAL** *Universal TV 1730336*	29		1

GRANT LEE BUFFALO
US, male vocal/instrumental group

Date	Album	Peak Position	Weeks at No.1	Weeks on Chart
				5
10 Jul 93	**FUZZY** *Slash 8283892*	74		1
1 Oct 94	**MIGHTY JOE MOON** *Slash 8285412*	24		2
15 Jun 96	**COPPEROPOLIS** *Slash 8287602*	34		2

GRATEFUL DEAD
US, male vocal/instrumental group

Date	Album	Peak Position	Weeks at No.1	Weeks on Chart
				14
19 Sep 70	**WORKINGMAN'S DEAD** *Warner Brothers WS 1869*	69		2
20 Feb 71	**AMERICAN BEAUTY** *Warner Brothers WS 1893*	27		2
3 Aug 74	**GRATEFUL DEAD FROM THE MARS HOTEL** *Warner Brothers K 59302*	47		1
1 Nov 75	**BLUES FOR ALLAH** *United Artists UAS 29895*	45		1
4 Sep 76	**STEAL YOUR FACE** *United Artists UAS 60131/2*	42		1
20 Aug 77	**TERRAPIN STATION** *Arista SPARTY 1016*	30		1
19 Sep 87	**IN THE DARK** *Arista 208 564*	57		3
18 Feb 89	**DYLAN AND THE DEAD** *CBS 4633811* BOB DYLAN & THE GRATEFUL DEAD	38		3

GRAVEDIGGAZ
US, male rap group

Date	Album	Peak Position	Weeks at No.1	Weeks on Chart
				1
4 Oct 97	**THE PICK, THE SICKLE AND THE SHOVEL** *Gee Street GEE 1000562*	24		1

DAVID GRAY & TOMMY TYCHO
UK, male vocalist & Australia, male orchestra leader

Date	Album	Peak Position	Weeks at No.1	Weeks on Chart
				6
16 Oct 76	**ARMCHAIR MELODIES** *K-Tel NE 927*	21		6

DAVID GRAY
UK, male vocalist/guitarist

Date	Album	Peak Position	Weeks at No.1	Weeks on Chart
				245
13 May 00	**WHITE LADDER** *IHT/East West 8573829832* ⊛x9	1	2	153
12 Aug 00	**LOST SONGS 95-98** *IHT IHTCD 002*	55		1
24 Feb 01	**LOST SONGS 95-98** *East West 8573869532* ●	7		10
14 Jul 01	**THE EP'S 1992–1994** *Hut CDHUT 67*	68		1
9 Nov 02	**A NEW DAY AT MIDNIGHT** *East West 5046616582* ⊛x3	1	1	47
24 Sep 05	**LIFE IN SLOW MOTION** *Atlantic 5046797662* ⊛x2	1	2	25
24 Nov 07	**GREATEST HITS** *Atlantic 5144241642* ●	11		8

MACY GRAY
US, female vocalist (Natalie McIntyre)

Date	Album	Peak Position	Weeks at No.1	Weeks on Chart
				83
17 Jul 99	**ON HOW LIFE IS** *Epic 4944232* ⊛x4	3		67
29 Sep 01	**THE ID** *Epic 5040899* ●	1	1	8
10 May 03	**THE TROUBLE WITH BEING MYSELF** *Epic 5108102*	17		5
11 Sep 04	**THE VERY BEST OF** *Epic 5179132*	36		2
14 Apr 07	**BIG** *Geffen 1726750*	62		1

GREAT WHITE
US, male vocal/instrumental group

Date	Album	Peak Position	Weeks at No.1	Weeks on Chart
				1
9 Mar 91	**HOOKED** *Capitol EST 2138*	43		1

MARTIN GRECH
UK, male vocalist/guitarist

Date	Album	Peak Position	Weeks at No.1	Weeks on Chart
				2
3 Aug 02	**OPEN HEART ZOO** *Island CID 8119*	54		2

AL GREEN
US, male vocalist (Al Greene)

Date	Album	Peak Position	Weeks at No.1	Weeks on Chart
				31
26 Apr 75	**AL GREEN'S GREATEST HITS** *London SHU 8481* ○	18		16
1 Oct 88	**HI LIFE – THE BEST OF AL GREEN** *K-Tel NE 1420* ○	34		7
24 Oct 92	**AL** *Beechwood AGREECD 1*	41		2
16 Feb 02	**LOVE – THE ESSENTIAL** *Hi ALTV 2002*	18		6

PETER GREEN
UK, male vocalist/guitarist (Peter Greenbaum). See Fleetwood Mac

Date	Album	Peak Position	Weeks at No.1	Weeks on Chart
				19
9 Jun 79	**IN THE SKIES** *Creole PULS 101*	32		13
24 May 80	**LITTLE DREAMER** *Puk PULS 102*	34		4
24 May 97	**SPLINTER GROUP** *Artisan SARCD 101*	71		1
30 May 98	**THE ROBERT JOHNSON SONGBOOK** *Artisan SARCD 002* WITH NIGEL WATSON & THE SPLINTER GROUP	57		1

ROBSON GREEN
UK, male actor/vocalist

Date	Album	Peak Position	Weeks at No.1	Weeks on Chart
				57
25 Nov 95	**ROBSON & JEROME** *RCA 74321323902* ROBSON & JEROME ⊛x6	1	7	31
23 Nov 96	**TAKE TWO** *RCA 74321426252* ROBSON & JEROME ⊛x4	1	2	16
29 Nov 97	**HAPPY DAYS – THE BEST OF ROBSON AND JEROME** *RCA 74321542602* ROBSON & JEROME	20		6
14 Dec 02	**MOMENT IN TIME** *T2 TCD3300*	49		4

GREEN DAY
US, male vocal/instrumental trio – Billie Joe Armstrong, Tré Cool (Frank Wright III) & Mike Dirnt. See Foxboro Hot Tubs

Date	Album	Peak Position	Weeks at No.1	Weeks on Chart
				253
5 Nov 94	**DOOKIE** *Reprise 9362457952* ⊛x3	13		61
21 Oct 95	**INSOMNIAC** *Reprise 9362460462* ○	8		5
25 Oct 97	**NIMROD** *Reprise 9362467942* ○	11		11
14 Oct 00	**WARNING** *Reprise 9362480302* ●	4		14
24 Nov 01	**INTERNATIONAL SUPERHITS** *Reprise 9362481452* ⊛	15		40
13 Jul 02	**SHENANIGANS** *Reprise 9362482082*	32		3
2 Oct 04	**AMERICAN IDIOT** *Reprise 9362488502* ⊛x6 ★	1	2	104
26 Nov 05	**BULLET IN A BIBLE** *Reprise 9362494662* ⊛	6		15

GREEN JELLY
US, male vocal/instrumental group

Date	Album	Peak Position	Weeks at No.1	Weeks on Chart
				10
3 Jul 93	**CEREAL KILLER SOUNDTRACK** *Zoo 72445110382*	18		10

Silver-selling ○ · Gold-selling ● · Platinum-selling ⊛ · US No.1 ★ · Peak Position · Weeks at No.1 · Weeks on Chart

GREEN ON RED
US, male vocal/instrumental group — Weeks on Chart: 1

Date	Title	Label	Peak Position	Weeks at No.1	Weeks on Chart
26 Oct 85	**NO FREE LUNCH**	*Mercury MERM 78*	99		1

GREENSLADE
UK, male vocal/instrumental group — Weeks on Chart: 3

Date	Title	Label	Peak Position	Weeks at No.1	Weeks on Chart
14 Sep 74	**SPYGLASS GUEST**	*Warner Brothers K 56055*	34		3

CHRISTINA GREGG
UK, female exercise instructor — Weeks on Chart: 1

Date	Title	Label	Peak Position	Weeks at No.1	Weeks on Chart
27 May 78	**MUSIC 'N' MOTION**	*Warwick WW 5041*	51		1

GRID
UK, male production/instrumental duo — Weeks on Chart: 4

Date	Title	Label	Peak Position	Weeks at No.1	Weeks on Chart
1 Oct 94	**EVOLVER**	*Deconstruction 74321227182*	14		3
14 Oct 95	**MUSIC FOR DANCING**	*Deconstruction 74321276702*	67		1

ALISTAIR GRIFFIN
UK, male vocalist — Weeks on Chart: 3

Date	Title	Label	Peak Position	Weeks at No.1	Weeks on Chart
24 Jan 04	**BRING IT ON**	*Universal TV 9816116*	12		3

NANCI GRIFFITH
US, female vocalist/guitarist — Weeks on Chart: 27

Date	Title	Label	Peak Position	Weeks at No.1	Weeks on Chart
26 Mar 88	**LITTLE LOVE AFFAIRS**	*MCA MCF 3413*	78		1
23 Sep 89	**STORMS**	*MCA MCG 6066*	38		3
28 Sep 91	**LATE NIGHT GRANDE HOTEL**	*MCA 10306*	40		5
20 Mar 93	**OTHER VOICES/OTHER ROOMS**	*MCA 10796*	18		6
13 Nov 93	**THE BEST OF NANCI GRIFFITH**	*MCA MCD 10966* ○	27		4
1 Oct 94	**FLYER**	*MCA MCD 11155*	20		4
5 Apr 97	**BLUE ROSES FROM THE MOONS**	*Elektra 7559620152*	64		3
11 Aug 01	**CLOCK WITHOUT HANDS**	*Elektra 7559626602*	61		1

VITTORIO GRIGOLO
Italy, male vocalist — Weeks on Chart: 6

Date	Title	Label	Peak Position	Weeks at No.1	Weeks on Chart
25 Mar 06	**IN THE HANDS OF LOVE**	*Polydor 9874521* ●	6		6

GRIMETHORPE COLLIERY BAND
UK, male brass band — Weeks on Chart: 5

Date	Title	Label	Peak Position	Weeks at No.1	Weeks on Chart
6 Jun 98	**BRASSED OFF (OST)**	*RCA Victor 09026687572*	36		4
11 Sep 04	**THE VERY BEST OF**	*BMG 82876637222*	59		1

GRINDERMAN
Australia/UK, male vocal/instrumental group — Weeks on Chart: 2

Date	Title	Label	Peak Position	Weeks at No.1	Weeks on Chart
17 Mar 07	**GRINDERMAN**	*Mute CDSTUMM272*	23		2

JOSH GROBAN
US, male vocalist — Weeks on Chart: 26

Date	Title	Label	Peak Position	Weeks at No.1	Weeks on Chart
15 Feb 03	**JOSH GROBAN**	*Reprise 9362481542*	32		8
10 Feb 07	**AWAKE**	*Reprise 9362499991*	17		11
29 Dec 07	**NOEL**	*Reprise 9362499295* ★	58		1
24 May 08	**AWAKE – LIVE**	*Reprise 9362498871*	22		2
13 Dec 08	**A COLLECTION**	*Reprise 9362498177* ●	22		4+

GROOVE ARMADA
UK, male production/instrumental duo – Andy Cato & Tom Findlay — Weeks on Chart: 45

Date	Title	Label	Peak Position	Weeks at No.1	Weeks on Chart
5 Jun 99	**VERTIGO**	*Pepper 0530332* ●	23		18
6 May 00	**THE REMIXES**	*Pepper 9230102*	68		1
22 Sep 01	**GOODBYE COUNTRY (HELLO NIGHTCLUB)**	*Pepper 9230492* ●	5		8
16 Nov 02	**LOVEBOX**	*Pepper 9230682* ○	41		2
9 Oct 04	**THE BEST OF**	*Jive 82876652562*	6		8
19 May 07	**SOUNDBOY ROCK**	*Columbia 88697076862*	10		7
10 Nov 07	**GREATEST HITS**	*Columbia 88697185082*	65		1

GROOVERIDER
UK, male DJ/producer (Ray Bingham) — Weeks on Chart: 1

Date	Title	Label	Peak Position	Weeks at No.1	Weeks on Chart
10 Oct 98	**MYSTERIES OF FUNK**	*Higher Ground HIGH 6CD*	50		1

GROUNDHOGS
UK, male vocal/instrumental trio – Tony McPhee, Peter Cruickshank (b. India) & Ken Pustelnik — Weeks on Chart: 51

Date	Title	Label	Peak Position	Weeks at No.1	Weeks on Chart
6 Jun 70	**THANK CHRIST FOR THE BOMB**	*Liberty LBS 83295*	9		13
27 Mar 71	**SPLIT**	*Liberty LBG 83401*	5		28
18 Mar 72	**WHO WILL SAVE THE WORLD**	*United Artists UAG 29237*	8		9
13 Jul 74	**SOLID**	*WWA 004*	31		1

G.T.R.
UK, male vocal/instrumental group — Weeks on Chart: 4

Date	Title	Label	Peak Position	Weeks at No.1	Weeks on Chart
19 Jul 86	**GTR**	*Arista 207 716*	41		4

DAVID GUETTA
France, male producer — Weeks on Chart: 1

Date	Title	Label	Peak Position	Weeks at No.1	Weeks on Chart
1 Sep 07	**POP LIFE**	*Charisma 3964012*	44		1

GUILDFORD CATHEDRAL CHOIR
CONDUCTOR: BARRIE ROSE
UK, male/female choir & male conductor — Weeks on Chart: 4

Date	Title	Label	Peak Position	Weeks at No.1	Weeks on Chart
10 Dec 66	**CHRISTMAS CAROLS FROM GUILDFORD CATHEDRAL**	*MFP 1104*	24		4

GUILLEMOTS
UK/Canada/Brazil, male/female vocal/instrumental group – Fyfe Dangerfield, Aristazabal Hawkes, MC Lord Magrão & Greig Stewart — Weeks on Chart: 20

Date	Title	Label	Peak Position	Weeks at No.1	Weeks on Chart
22 Jul 06	**THROUGH THE WINDOWPANE**	*Polydor 9877824*	17		16
5 Apr 07	**RED**	*Polydor 1762524*	9		4

GUITAR CORPORATION
UK, male instrumental group — Weeks on Chart: 5

Date	Title	Label	Peak Position	Weeks at No.1	Weeks on Chart
15 Feb 92	**IMAGES**	*Quality Television QTVCD 002*	41		5

GUN
UK, male vocal/instrumental group – Mark Rankin, Dante & Guiliano Gizzi, Scott Shields & Baby Stafford — Weeks on Chart: 23

Date	Title	Label	Peak Position	Weeks at No.1	Weeks on Chart
22 Jul 89	**TAKING ON THE WORLD**	*A&M AMA 7007* ○	44		10
18 Apr 92	**GALLUS**	*A&M 3953832*	14		4
13 Aug 94	**SWAGGER**	*A&M 5402542* ○	5		7
24 May 97	**0141 632 6326**	*A&M 5407232*	32		2

GUNS N' ROSES
US, male vocal/instrumental group – Axl Rose (William Bailey); members also included Steven Adler (replaced by Matt Sorum), Gilby Clarke*, Duff McKagan, Dizzy Reed, Slash (Saul Hudson) (Slash's Snakepit*) & Izzy Stradlin'*. Controversial Los Angeles rockers who have the unique distinction of being the only band to debut at No.1 and No.2 on both sides of the Atlantic with albums released in the same week (*Use Your Illusion I* and *Use Your Illusion II*) — Weeks on Chart: 443

Date	Title	Label	Peak Position	Weeks at No.1	Weeks on Chart
1 Aug 87	**APPETITE FOR DESTRUCTION**	*Geffen WX 125* ⊛x2 ★	5		163
17 Dec 88	**G N' R THE LIES, THE SEX, THE DRUGS, THE VIOLENCE, THE SHOCKING TRUTH**	*Geffen WX 218* ●	22		41
28 Sep 91	**USE YOUR ILLUSION I**	*Geffen GEF 24415* ⊛	2		84
28 Sep 91	**USE YOUR ILLUSION II**	*Geffen GEF 24420* ⊛ ★	1	1	84
4 Dec 93	**THE SPAGHETTI INCIDENT?**	*Geffen GED 24617* ●	2		10
11 Dec 99	**LIVE – ERA '87-'93**	*Geffen 4905142*	45		2
27 Mar 04	**GREATEST HITS**	*Geffen 9862108* ⊛x3	1	3	54
6 Dec 08	**CHINESE DEMOCRACY**	*Black Frog/Geffen 1790607*	2		5+

GUNSHOT
UK, male rap group — Weeks on Chart: 1

Date	Title	Label	Peak Position	Weeks at No.1	Weeks on Chart
19 Jun 93	**PATRIOT GAMES**	*Vinyl Solution STEAM 43CD*	60		1

DAVID GUNSON
UK, male after-dinner speaker — Weeks on Chart: 2

Date	Title	Label	Peak Position	Weeks at No.1	Weeks on Chart
25 Dec 82	**WHAT GOES UP MIGHT COME DOWN**	*Big Ben BB 0012*	92		2

GURU

US, male rapper/producer (Keith Elam) — 12

Date	Title / Label	Peak	Wks No.1	Wks on Chart
29 May 93	**JAZZMATAZZ** *Cooltempo CTCD 34*	58		2
15 Jul 95	**JAZZMATAZZ VOLUME II – THE NEW REALITY** *Cooltempo CTCD 47*	12		9
14 Oct 00	**STREETSOUL** *Virgin CDVUS 178* 'S JAZZMATAZZ	74		1

GURU JOSH

UK, male producer (Paul Walden) — 2

Date	Title / Label	Peak	Wks No.1	Wks on Chart
14 Jul 90	**INFINITY** *Deconstruction PL 74701*	41		2

G.U.S. (FOOTWEAR) BAND & THE MORRISTON ORPHEUS CHOIR

UK, male instrumental group & male/female vocal group — 1

Date	Title / Label	Peak	Wks No.1	Wks on Chart
3 Oct 70	**LAND OF HOPE AND GLORY** *Columbia SCX 6406*	54		1

ARLO GUTHRIE

US, male vocalist/guitarist — 1

Date	Title / Label	Peak	Wks No.1	Wks on Chart
7 Mar 70	**ALICE'S RESTAURANT** *Reprise RSLP 6267*	44		1

GWEN GUTHRIE

US, female vocalist, d. 3 Feb 1999 (age 48) — 14

Date	Title / Label	Peak	Wks No.1	Wks on Chart
23 Aug 86	**GOOD TO GO LOVER** *Boiling Point POLD 5201*	42		14

GUTTER TWINS

US, male vocal/instrumental duo — 1

Date	Title / Label	Peak	Wks No.1	Wks on Chart
15 Mar 08	**SATURNALIA** *Sub Pop SPCD761*	54		1

GUY

US, male vocal group — 1

Date	Title / Label	Peak	Wks No.1	Wks on Chart
5 Feb 00	**III** *MCA 1121702*	55		1

BUDDY GUY

US, male vocalist/guitarist — 9

Date	Title / Label	Peak	Wks No.1	Wks on Chart
22 Jun 91	**DAMN RIGHT, I'VE GOT THE BLUES** *Silvertone ORELP 516*	43		5
13 Mar 93	**FEELS LIKE RAIN** *Silvertone ORECD 525*	36		4

A GUY CALLED GERALD

UK, male producer (Gerald Simpson) — 2

Date	Title / Label	Peak	Wks No.1	Wks on Chart
14 Apr 90	**AUTOMANIKK** *Subscape 4664821*	68		1
1 Apr 95	**BLACK SECRET TECHNOLOGY** *Juice Box JBCD 25*	64		1

GUYS 'N' DOLLS

UK, male/female vocal group — 1

Date	Title / Label	Peak	Wks No.1	Wks on Chart
31 May 75	**GUYS 'N' DOLLS** *Magnet MAG 5005*	43		1

GYM CLASS HEROES

US, male vocal/rap/instrumental group — 12

Date	Title / Label	Peak	Wks No.1	Wks on Chart
19 May 07	**AS CRUEL AS SCHOOL CHILDREN** *Decaydance/Fueled By Ramen 094512*	19		11
27 Sep 08	**THE QUILT** *Decaydance/Fueled By Ramen 7567899316*	41		1

H

H & CLAIRE

UK, male/female vocal duo. See Steps — 1

Date	Title / Label	Peak	Wks No.1	Wks on Chart
30 Nov 02	**ANOTHER YOU ANOTHER ME** *WEA 0927494622*	58		1

STEVE HACKETT

UK, male vocalist/guitarist. See GTR, Genesis — 38

Date	Title / Label	Peak	Wks No.1	Wks on Chart
1 Nov 75	**VOYAGE OF THE ACOLYTE** *Charisma CAS 1111*	26		4
6 May 78	**PLEASE DON'T TOUCH** *Charisma CDS 4012*	38		5
26 May 79	**SPECTRAL MORNINGS** *Charisma CDS 4017*	22		11
21 Jun 80	**DEFECTOR** *Charisma CDS 4018*	9		7
29 Aug 81	**CURED** *Charisma CDS 4021*	15		5
30 Apr 83	**HIGHLY STRUNG** *Charisma HACK 1*	16		3
19 Nov 83	**BAY OF KINGS** *Lamborghini LMGLP 3000*	70		1
22 Sep 84	**TILL WE HAVE FACES** *Lamborghini LMGLP 4000*	54		2

HADDAWAY

Trinidad & Tobago, male vocalist (Nester Haddaway) — 16

Date	Title / Label	Peak	Wks No.1	Wks on Chart
23 Oct 93	**HADDAWAY – THE ALBUM** *Logic 74321169222*	9		16

TONY HADLEY

UK, male vocalist. See Spandau Ballet — 6

Date	Title / Label	Peak	Wks No.1	Wks on Chart
20 Sep 97	**TONY HADLEY** *Polygram TV 5393012*	45		3
10 May 03	**TRUE BALLADS** *Universal TV 0382882*	31		3

HADOUKEN

UK, male/female vocal/instrumental/production group — 3

Date	Title / Label	Peak	Wks No.1	Wks on Chart
17 May 08	**MUSIC FOR AN ACCELERATED CULTURE** *Surface Noise 5144279342*	12		3

SAMMY HAGAR

US, male vocalist/guitarist. See Hagar Schon Aaronson Shrieve, Montrose, Van Halen

Date	Title / Label	Peak	Wks No.1	Wks on Chart
29 Sep 79	**STREET MACHINE** *Capitol EST 11983*	38		4
22 Mar 80	**LOUD AND CLEAR** *Capitol EST 25330*	12		8
7 Jun 80	**DANGER ZONE** *Capitol EST 12069*	25		3
13 Feb 82	**STANDING HAMPTON** *Geffen GEF 85456*	84		2
4 Jul 87	**SAMMY HAGAR** *Geffen WX 114*	86		2

HAGAR, SCHON, AARONSON, SHRIEVE

US, male vocal/instrumental group — 20

Date	Title / Label	Peak	Wks No.1	Wks on Chart
19 May 84	**THROUGH THE FIRE** *Geffen GEF 25893*	92		1

PAUL HAIG

UK, male vocalist — 2

Date	Title / Label	Peak	Wks No.1	Wks on Chart
22 Oct 83	**RHYTHM OF LIFE** *Crepuscule ILPS 9742*	82		2

HAIRCUT 100

UK, male vocal/instrumental group – Nick Heyward*, Blair Cunningham, Mark Fox, Graham Jones, Les Nemes & Phil Smith — 34

Date	Title / Label	Peak	Wks No.1	Wks on Chart
6 Mar 82	**PELICAN WEST** *Arista HCC 100*	2		34

HAL

Ireland, male vocal/instrumental group — 2

Date	Title / Label	Peak	Wks No.1	Wks on Chart
7 May 05	**HAL** *Rough Trade RTRADCD160*	31		2

BILL HALEY & HIS COMETS

US, male vocal/instrumental group – Haley, d. 9 Feb 1981 — 32

Date	Title / Label	Peak	Wks No.1	Wks on Chart
4 Aug 56	**ROCK AROUND THE CLOCK** *Brunswick LAT 8177*	2		18
20 Oct 56	**ROCK 'N ROLL STAGE SHOWS** *Brunswick LAT 8139*	1	1	8
16 Feb 57	**ROCK THE JOINT** *London HAF 2037*	5		1
18 May 68	**ROCK AROUND THE CLOCK** *Ace Of Clubs AH 13* BILL HALEY & HIS COMETS	34		5

HALF MAN HALF BISCUIT

UK, male vocal/instrumental group — 14

Date	Title / Label	Peak	Wks No.1	Wks on Chart
8 Feb 86	**BACK IN THE D.H.S.S.** *Probe Plus 4*	60		9
21 Feb 87	**BACK AGAIN IN THE D.H.S.S.** *Probe Plus 8*	59		5

Bill Haley

BILL Haley – or William John Clifton Haley, as he was christened – was the son of a Kentucky father and an English mother, Maude Green, who had emigrated to the US from the picturesque English Lake District. Haley started early. His parents were both musicians, and by his early teens he was playing and singing in local bands with other kids, appearing on regional radio, though his disability (he was blind in one eye) made him shy and self-conscious. His first record deal was in 1948, as one quarter of The Kings of Western Swing.

By 1949 Haley had formed The Saddlemen, the nucleus of what would become the better-known Comets. In 1951 the band covered 'Rocket 88', a hit that had been recorded by Ike Turner's Kings of Rhythm

A new music, untried and untested, but perfect for the post-war children of Uncle Sam and in Blighty too

under the name Jackie Brenston And His Delta Cats. The argument pertains that this cross-over – a white country band covering a black rhythm-and-blues hit – was the first true rock 'n' roll record (as opposed to R&B). The band followed up with 'Rock The Joint' and 'Crazy Man, Crazy', a national hit in 1953. However, it was two truly seminal tracks that they recorded in spring of 1954 that went on to define pre-Elvis, foetal rock and roll.

'Shake Rattle & Roll' was at that time a big hit on the R&B charts for Joe Turner, the mighty Kansas blues shouter who recorded for one of the great vintage labels, Chess Records. Turner's recordings had a saucy, lascivious air about them, filled with humour and barrelhouse bawdiness. When he sang the song, it *worked*. However, undeterred by the storming original, Haley stripped the lyrics down and shortened the verses, lining up the irresistible chorus and pumping it up with a stripped-down rockabilly arrangement and Joey D'Ambrosio's tenor sax. As if to endorse his confident re-arrangement, this version worked even better.

The other important track, recorded in April, made Haley a worldwide star and laid the foundations of a legend. 'Rock Around The Clock' essentially *sold* rock 'n' roll to America and then the world, a new music, untried and untested, but perfect for the post-war children of Uncle Sam and in Blighty too. It went on to sell some 25 million copies worldwide over several decades, and is one of the undisputed signposts of pop history.

The song has confused beginnings. Written by James E. Myers (aka Jimmy DeKnight) and Max C. Freedman, it was initially recorded by Sonny Dae And His Knights. Not surprisingly perhaps, at a time when musical styles were cross-pollinating and influencing each other at a frantic pace, the verse bears a striking resemblance to that of Hank Williams's 'Move It On Over', itself born of many classic early blues songs. Sonny Dae's recording has many of the hallmarks of Haley's version, the stop-starts and the downhill rush into the chorus, but there's a defining, mighty energy in Haley's version that is missing in the former. Incredibly, one of rock 'n' roll's Ten Commandments was initially a B-side to 'Thirteen Women (And Only One Man In Town)'; the song was certainly not the flop that history has remembered it to be at first, but neither was it an immediate big hit. It took the release of early teen-rebellion movie *The Blackboard Jungle*, starring Sidney Poitier and Glen Ford, to make the record a success. Played over the opening credits, it set a tone for the confrontational bent of the movie, screenings of which were often accompanied by teenage riots, scaremongering press headlines about teenagers and the evil music that was rock 'n' roll ... and so the 1950s proper was born. 'Rock Around The Clock' was a Number 1 hit in the US, Britain and

Biggest-Selling Album			Highest	
Artist	Album	Week	Position	Approx Sales
BILL HAYLEY	ROCK AROUND THE CLOCK	4/8/56	2	260,000

elsewhere – indeed, when it was re-issued in the 1960s and 1970s, it was a hit all over again each time.

'Shake Rattle & Roll' followed up the hit, and became the first rock 'n' roll record to sell one million copies. A change of personnel in the Comets introduced Rudy Pompilli on sax and Al Rex on bass, and their onstage antics as they rocked out made the Comets as visually appealing as the records they released. Though pushing thirty, partially blind and hardly rake-thin, Haley was suddenly a star, a teenage icon. Further hits ensued, most notably 'See You Later, Alligator', recorded late in 1955 and formerly a Chess hit for Bobby Charles. In 1956 the movie *Rock Around The Clock* cashed in on the new-fangled music 'fad', co-starring DJ Alan Freed, and this was swiftly followed by a second movie, *Don't Knock The Rock*. (Unfortunately, his roles in movies, including *Rock Around The Clock*, seemed to highlight his age and image in stark contrast to the youthful sexuality of Elvis and others.)There was even an air of panic exploitation among the establishment about the brevity of rock 'n' roll's expected lifespan – in early 1955, *Variety* had said, "Rock 'n' roll will be gone by June."

Albums and further singles followed, but the young audience was nothing if not fickle and soon fell for artists such as Elvis, Little Richard and Gene Vincent with a harder-burning passion, a newer flame. By the time Elvis joined the army and the whole world mourned his temporary loss, Bill Haley was thirty-three years old. He wasn't past it, but there were other things afoot. He became one of the first casualties of the rock 'n' roll fan's brutally unforgiving thirst for new sensations.

When the rock 'n' roll torch was picked up and carried by these young guns – many from the UK – Haley moved to Mexico, where he learned the language and became enormously successful with the Comets in rolling out instrumental hits and Spanish-language songs. After an attempt to revive his US career at Decca failed, he signed for a Swedish label. The re-release of 'Rock Around The Clock' in the UK in '68 gave him a break again in the US, and his *Rock Around The Country* album was well received, though not a huge seller. While live work kept Haley active, he never achieved the long-term recording career that he perhaps deserved. Of an older school than the other 1950s rockers, he nonetheless survived many of them.

Haley can probably boast more rock 'n' roll 'firsts' than any other artist

After the success of his glory years in 1955–56 dwindled, Haley drank heavily and is said to have lived out his final days riddled with paranoia, in his garage whose walls he had painted black. When he succumbed to a heart attack in 1981, aged just fifty-five, his neighbours were reported to be unaware of his musical past.

Haley can probably boast more rock 'n' roll 'firsts' than any other artist: the first rock 'n' roll hit, ('Rocket 88'); his first sessions at Decca producing 'Rock Around The Clock', arguably the first rock 'n' roll No. 1; the first to cause rock 'n' roll riots and hysteria; the first artist to introduce the form to white America; with his kiss curl and raucous live set, Haley was the first rock 'n' roll icon. Along with Chuck Berry, Bill Haley knocked down the doors for the thousands of performers who followed him. Perhaps he deserves a better mention in history.

Silver-selling ● Gold-selling ● Platinum-selling ⊛ US No.1 ★ | Peak Position | Weeks at No.1 | Weeks on Chart

DARYL HALL

US, male vocalist (Daryl Hohl). See Daryl Hall & John Oates — 9

Date	Title / Label	Peak	Wks at No.1	Wks
23 Aug 86	**THREE HEARTS IN THE HAPPY ENDING MACHINE** *RCA PL 87196*	26		5
23 Oct 93	**SOUL ALONE** *Epic 4732912*	55		4

DARYL HALL & JOHN OATES

US, male vocal/instrumental duo – Daryl Hall* & John Oates — 157

Date	Title / Label	Peak	Wks at No.1	Wks
3 Jul 76	**HALL AND OATES** *RCA Victor APL1 1144*	56		1
18 Sep 76	**BIGGER THAN BOTH OF US** *RCA Victor APL1 1467*	25		7
15 Oct 77	**BEAUTY ON A BACK STREET** *RCA Victor PL 12300*	40		2
6 Feb 82	**PRIVATE EYES** *RCA RCALP 6001* ●	8		21
23 Oct 82	**H2O** *RCA RCALP 6056* ●	24		35
29 Oct 83	**ROCK 'N' SOUL (PART ONE)** *RCA PL 84858*	16		45
27 Oct 84	**BIG BAM BOOM** *RCA PL 85309* ●	28		13
28 Sep 85	**HALL AND OATES LIVE AT THE APOLLO WITH DAVID RUFFIN AND EDDIE KENDRICK** *RCA PL 87035*	32		5
18 Jun 88	**OOH YEAH!** *RCA 208895*	52		3
27 Oct 90	**CHANGE OF SEASON** *Arista 210548*	44		2
19 Oct 91	**THE BEST OF DARYL HALL AND JOHN OATES – LOOKING BACK** *Arista PL 90388* ●	9		16
6 Oct 01	**THE ESSENTIAL COLLECTION** *RCA 74321886972*	26		2
12 Apr 03	**DO IT FOR LOVE** *Sanctuary SANCD 166*	37		2
14 Jun 08	**THE SINGLES** *Sony BMG 88697312422*	29		3

LYNDEN DAVID HALL

UK, male vocalist/guitarist, d. 14 Feb 2006 (age 31) — 4

Date	Title / Label	Peak	Wks at No.1	Wks
14 Nov 98	**MEDICINE 4 MY PAIN** *Cooltempo 4959952* ●	43		2
10 Jun 00	**THE OTHER SIDE** *Cooltempo 5261492*	36		2

TERRY HALL

UK, male vocalist. See Colourfield, Fun Boy Three, Specials — 1

Date	Title / Label	Peak	Wks at No.1	Wks
18 Oct 97	**LAUGH** *Southsea Bubble Co CDBUBBLE 3*	50		1

GERI HALLIWELL

UK, female vocalist. See Spice Girls — 59

Date	Title / Label	Peak	Wks at No.1	Wks
19 Jun 99	**SCHIZOPHONIC** *EMI 5210092* ⊛x2	4		43
26 May 01	**SCREAM IF YOU WANT TO GO FASTER** *EMI 5333692* ●	5		15
18 Jun 05	**PASSION** *Innocent CDSIN19*	41		1

HALO JAMES

UK, male vocal/instrumental group — 4

Date	Title / Label	Peak	Wks at No.1	Wks
14 Apr 90	**WITNESS** *Epic 4667611* ●	18		4

HAMBURG STUDENTS CHOIR

Germany, male choir — 6

Date	Title / Label	Peak	Wks at No.1	Wks
17 Dec 60	**HARK THE HERALD ANGELS SING** *Pye Golden Guinea GGL 0023*	11		6

GEORGE HAMILTON IV

US, male vocalist/guitarist — 11

Date	Title / Label	Peak	Wks at No.1	Wks
10 Apr 71	**CANADIAN PACIFIC** *RCA Victor SF 8062*	45		1
10 Feb 79	**REFLECTIONS** *Lotus WH 5008* ●	25		9
13 Nov 82	**SONGS FOR A WINTER'S NIGHT** *Ronco RTL 2082*	94		1

MARVIN HAMLISCH

US, male pianist — 35

Date	Title / Label	Peak	Wks at No.1	Wks
23 Mar 74	**THE STING (OST)** *MCA MCF 2537* ● ★	7		35

MC HAMMER

US, male rapper (Stanley Burrell) — 67

Date	Title / Label	Peak	Wks at No.1	Wks
28 Jul 90	**PLEASE HAMMER DON'T HURT 'EM** *Capitol EST 2120* ⊛x2 ★	8		59
6 Apr 91	**LET'S GET IT STARTED** *Capitol EST 2140*	46		2
2 Nov 91	**TOO LEGIT TO QUIT** *Capitol ESTP 26* HAMMER ●	41		6

JAN HAMMER

Czech Republic, male keyboard player — 12

Date	Title / Label	Peak	Wks at No.1	Wks
14 Nov 87	**ESCAPE FROM TV** *MCA MCF 3407* ●	34		12

ALBERT HAMMOND JR

US, male vocalist/guitarist. See Strokes — 1

Date	Title / Label	Peak	Wks at No.1	Wks
21 Oct 06	**YOURS TO KEEP** *Rough Trade RTRADCD338*	74		1

HERBIE HANCOCK

US, male vocalist/keyboard player — 24

Date	Title / Label	Peak	Wks at No.1	Wks
9 Sep 78	**SUNLIGHT** *CBS 82240*	27		6
24 Feb 79	**FEETS DON'T FAIL ME NOW** *CBS 83491*	28		8
27 Aug 83	**FUTURE SHOCK** *CBS 25540*	27		10

TONY HANCOCK

UK, male comedian, d. 25 Jun 1968 (age 44) — 51

Date	Title / Label	Peak	Wks at No.1	Wks
9 Apr 60	**THIS IS HANCOCK** *Pye NPL 10845*	2		22
12 Nov 60	**PIECES OF HANCOCK** *Pye NPL 18054*	17		2
3 Mar 62	**HANCOCK** *Pye NPL 18068*	12		23
14 Sep 63	**THIS IS HANCOCK** *Pye Golden Guinea GGL 0206*	16		4

BO HANSSON

Sweden, male multi-instrumentalist — 2

Date	Title / Label	Peak	Wks at No.1	Wks
18 Nov 72	**LORD OF THE RINGS** *Charisma CAS 1059*	34		2

HANOI ROCKS

Finland/UK, male vocal/instrumental group — 4

Date	Title / Label	Peak	Wks at No.1	Wks
11 Jun 83	**BACK TO THE MYSTERY CITY** *Lick LICLP 1*	87		1
20 Oct 84	**TWO STEPS FROM THE MOVE** *CBS 26066*	28		3

HANSON

US, male vocal/instrumental trio – Isaac, Taylor & Zac Hanson — 32

Date	Title / Label	Peak	Wks at No.1	Wks
21 Jun 97	**MIDDLE OF NOWHERE** *Mercury 5346152* ●	1	1	29
13 Jun 98	**3 CAR GARAGE – INDIE RECORDINGS 95-96** *Mercury 5583992*	39		1
13 May 00	**THIS TIME AROUND** *Mercury 5427212*	33		1
19 Feb 05	**UNDERNEATH** *Cooking Vinyl COOKCD326*	49		1

JOHN HANSON

UK (b. Canada), male vocalist, d. 3 Dec 1998 (age 76) — 12

Date	Title / Label	Peak	Wks at No.1	Wks
23 Apr 60	**THE STUDENT PRINCE** *Pye NPL 18046*	17		1
2 Sep 61	**THE STUDENT PRINCE/THE VAGABOND KING** *Pye Golden Guinea GGL 0086*	9		7
10 Dec 77	**JOHN HANSON SINGS 20 SHOWTIME GREATS** *K-Tel NE 1002*	16		4

HAPPY MONDAYS

UK, male vocal/instrumental group – Shaun Ryder, Mark 'Bez' Berry, Paul Davis, Mark Day, Paul Ryder & Gary Whelan — 63

Date	Title / Label	Peak	Wks at No.1	Wks
27 Jan 90	**BUMMED** *Factory FACT 220*	59		14
17 Nov 90	**PILLS 'N' THRILLS AND BELLYACHES** *Factory FACT 320* ⊛	4		29
12 Oct 91	**HAPPY MONDAYS – LIVE** *Factory FACT 322*	21		3
10 Oct 92	**...YES PLEASE!** *Factory FACD 420*	14		3
18 Nov 95	**LOADS – THE BEST OF THE HAPPY MONDAYS** *Factory Once 5203432*	41		2
5 Jun 99	**GREATEST HITS** *London 5561052* ●	11		9
6 Jul 02	**PILLS 'N' THRILLS AND BELLYACHES** *London 3984282512* ●	47		2
14 Jul 07	**UNCLE DYSFUNKTIONAL** *Sequel SEQCD012*	73		1

HAR MAR SUPERSTAR

US, male vocalist (Sean Tillman) — 1

Date	Title / Label	Peak	Wks at No.1	Wks
18 Sep 04	**THE HANDLER** *Record Collection 9362488102*	68		1

ED HARCOURT

UK, male vocalist/multi-instrumentalist — 2

Date	Title / Label	Peak	Wks at No.1	Wks
1 Mar 03	**FROM EVERY SPHERE** *Heavenly HVNLP 39CD*	39		1
25 Sep 04	**STRANGERS** *Heavenly HVNLP49CD*	57		1

HARD-FI

UK, male vocal/instrumental group – Richard Archer, Steve Kemp, Ross Phillips & Kai Stephens — 62

Date	Title / Label	Peak	Wks at No.1	Wks
19 Jul 05	**STARS OF CCTV** *Atlantic/Necessary 5046786912* ⊛x2	1	1	52
20 May 06	**IN OPERATION** *Necessary/Atlantic 5101138285*	62		1

Key: ○ Silver-selling · ● Gold-selling · ⊛ Platinum-selling · ★ US No.1 · Peak Position · Weeks at No.1 · Weeks on Chart

Date	Title	Peak Position	Weeks at No.1	Weeks on Chart
15 Sep 07	**ONCE UPON A TIME IN THE WEST** *Necessary/Atlantic 5144229602* ●	1	1	9

PAUL HARDCASTLE
UK, male producer/keyboard player — Weeks on Chart: 5

Date	Title	Peak Position	Weeks at No.1	Weeks on Chart
30 Nov 85	**PAUL HARDCASTLE** *Chrysalis CHR 1517* ○	53		5

HARDFLOOR
Germany, male production/instrumental duo — Weeks on Chart: 1

Date	Title	Peak Position	Weeks at No.1	Weeks on Chart
29 Jun 96	**HOME RUN** *Harthouse HHCD 19*	68		1

RONAN HARDIMAN
Ireland, male composer/ochesrta leader — Weeks on Chart: 8

Date	Title	Peak Position	Weeks at No.1	Weeks on Chart
2 Nov 96	**MICHAEL FLATLEY'S LORD OF THE DANCE** *Polygram TV 5337572* ●	37		8

MIKE HARDING
UK, male vocalist/comedian/radio presenter — Weeks on Chart: 24

Date	Title	Peak Position	Weeks at No.1	Weeks on Chart
30 Aug 75	**MRS 'ARDIN'S KID** *Rubber RUB 011*	24		6
10 Jul 76	**ONE MAN SHOW** *Philips 6625 022* ○	19		10
11 Jun 77	**OLD FOUR EYES IS BACK** *Philips 6308 290*	31		6
24 Jun 78	**CAPTAIN PARALYTIC AND THE BROWN ALE COWBOY** *Philips 6641 798*	60		2

STEVE HARLEY & COCKNEY REBEL
UK, male vocal/instrumental group – Steve Harley (Stephen Nice), John Crocker (replaced by Jim Cregan), Stuart Elliott, Paul Jeffreys, d. 21 Dec 1988 (replaced by George Ford), & Milton Reame-James (replaced by Duncan MacKay) — Weeks on Chart: 52

Date	Title	Peak Position	Weeks at No.1	Weeks on Chart
22 Jun 74	**THE PSYCHOMODO** *EMI EMC 3033* COCKNEY REBEL ●	8		20
22Mar 75	**THE BEST YEARS OF OUR LIVES** *EMI EMC 3068* ●	4		19
14 Feb 76	**TIMELESS FLIGHT** *EMI EMA 775* ○	18		6
27 Nov 76	**LOVE'S A PRIMA DONNA** *EMI EMC 3156* ○	28		3
30 Jul 77	**FACE TO FACE – A LIVE RECORDING** *EMI EMSP 320*	40		4

HARMONIUM
UK, male production/instrumental duo. See Blowing Free, Hypnosis, In Tune, Raindance, School Of Excellence — Weeks on Chart: 4

Date	Title	Peak Position	Weeks at No.1	Weeks on Chart
21 Mar 98	**SPIRIT OF TRANQUILLITY** *Global Television RADCD 79*	25		4

ROY HARPER
UK, male vocalist/guitarist — Weeks on Chart: 10

Date	Title	Peak Position	Weeks at No.1	Weeks on Chart
17 Jan 70	**FLAT, BAROQUE AND BERSERK** *Harvest SHVL 766*	20		1
9 Mar 74	**VALENTINE** *Harvest SHSP 4027*	27		1
21 Jun 75	**H.Q.** *Harvest SHSP 4046*	31		2
12 Mar 77	**BULLINAMINGVASE** *Harvest SHSP 4060*	25		2
16 Mar 85	**WHATEVER HAPPENED TO JUGULA?** *Beggars Banquet BEGA 60* WITH JIMMY PAGE	44		4

ANITA HARRIS
UK, female vocalist — Weeks on Chart: 5

Date	Title	Peak Position	Weeks at No.1	Weeks on Chart
27 Jan 68	**JUST LOVING YOU** *CBS SBPG 63182*	29		5

CALVIN HARRIS
UK, male vocalist/producer — Weeks on Chart: 10

Date	Title	Peak Position	Weeks at No.1	Weeks on Chart
30 Jun 07	**I CREATED DISCO** *Columbia FLYEYE010* ●	8		10

EMMYLOU HARRIS
US, female vocalist/guitarist — Weeks on Chart: 46

Date	Title	Peak Position	Weeks at No.1	Weeks on Chart
14 Feb 76	**ELITE HOTEL** *Reprise K 54060* ○	17		11
26 Feb 77	**LUXURY LINER** *Warner Brothers K 56344* ○	17		6
4 Feb 78	**QUARTER MOONS IN A TEN CENT TOWN** *Warner Brothers K 56433*	40		5
29 Mar 80	**HER BEST SONGS** *K-Tel NE 1058*	36		3
14 Feb 81	**EVANGELINE** *Warner Brothers K 56880*	53		4
14 Mar 87	**TRIO** *Warner Brothers 9254911* DOLLY PARTON, LINDA RONSTADT & EMMYLOU HARRIS	60		4
7 Oct 95	**WRECKING BALL** *Grapevine GRACD 102*	46		1
29 Aug 98	**SPYBOY** *Grapevine GRACD 241*	57		1
30 Sep 00	**RED DIRT GIRL** *Grapevine GRACD 103*	45		1
4 Oct 03	**STUMBLE INTO GRACE** *Nonesuch 7559798052*	52		1
6 May 06	**ALL THE ROADRUNNING** *Mercury 9877385* MARK KNOPFLER & EMMYLOU HARRIS ●	8		8
21 Jun 08	**ALL I INTENDED TO BE** *Nonesuch 7559799285*	40		1

KEITH HARRIS, ORVILLE & CUDDLES
UK, male ventriloquist vocalist & puppets — Weeks on Chart: 1

Date	Title	Peak Position	Weeks at No.1	Weeks on Chart
4 Jun 83	**AT THE END OF THE RAINBOW** *BBC REH 465*	92		1

ROLF HARRIS
Australia, male vocalist/wobble board player/TV presenter — Weeks on Chart: 1

Date	Title	Peak Position	Weeks at No.1	Weeks on Chart
1 Nov 97	**CAN YOU TELL WHAT IT IS YET?** *EMI 8218802*	70		1

GEORGE HARRISON
UK, male vocalist/guitarist, d. 29 Nov 2001 (age 58). See Beatles, Traveling Wilburys — Weeks on Chart: 82

Date	Title	Peak Position	Weeks at No.1	Weeks on Chart
26 Dec 70	**ALL THINGS MUST PASS** *Apple STCH 639*	1	8	24
7 Jul 73	**LIVING IN THE MATERIAL WORLD** *Apple PAS 10006* ★	2		12
18 Oct 75	**EXTRA TEXTURE (READ ALL ABOUT IT)** *Apple PAS 10009*	16		4
18 Dec 76	**THIRTY THREE AND A THIRD** *Dark Horse K 56319* ○	35		4
17 Mar 79	**GEORGE HARRISON** *Dark Horse K 56562*	39		5
13 Jun 81	**SOMEWHERE IN ENGLAND** *Dark Horse K 56870*	13		4
14 Nov 87	**CLOUD NINE** *Dark Horse WX 123* ●	10		23
3 Feb 01	**ALL THINGS MUST PASS** *Parlophone CDS 7466888* ★	68		2
30 Nov 02	**BRAINWASHED** *Parlophone 5803450* ●	29		4

JANE HARRISON
UK, female vocalist — Weeks on Chart: 1

Date	Title	Peak Position	Weeks at No.1	Weeks on Chart
4 Feb 89	**NEW DAY** *Stylus SMR 869*	70		1

DEBBIE HARRY
US, female vocalist. See Blondie — Weeks on Chart: 53

Date	Title	Peak Position	Weeks at No.1	Weeks on Chart
8 Aug 81	**KOO KOO** *Chrysalis CHR 1347* ○	6		7
29 Nov 86	**ROCKBIRD** *Chrysalis CHR 1540* ●	31		11
17 Dec 88	**ONCE MORE INTO THE BLEACH** *Chrysalis CJB 2* & BLONDIE	50		4
28 Oct 89	**DEF DUMB AND BLONDE** *Chrysalis CHR 1650* DEBORAH HARRY ○	12		7
16 Mar 91	**THE COMPLETE PICTURE – THE VERY BEST OF DEBORAH HARRY AND BLONDIE** *Chrysalis CHR 1817* DEBORAH HARRY & BLONDIE ●	3		22
31 Jul 93	**DEBRAVATION** *Chrysalis CDCHR 6033* DEBORAH HARRY	24		2

VICTORIA HART
UK (b. US), female vocalist — Weeks on Chart: 1

Date	Title	Peak Position	Weeks at No.1	Weeks on Chart
21 Jul 07	**WHATEVER HAPPENED TO ROMANCE** *Decca 4759354*	61		1

KEEF HARTLEY BAND
UK, male vocal/instrumental group — Weeks on Chart: 3

Date	Title	Peak Position	Weeks at No.1	Weeks on Chart
5 Sep 70	**THE TIME IS NEAR** *Deram SML 1071*	41		3

SENSATIONAL ALEX HARVEY BAND
UK, male vocal/instrumental group – Alex Harvey, d. 4 Feb 1982, Zal Cleminson, Chris Glen & Hugh & Ted McKenna — Weeks on Chart: 42

Date	Title	Peak Position	Weeks at No.1	Weeks on Chart
26 Oct 74	**THE IMPOSSIBLE DREAM** *Vertigo 6360 112* ○	16		4
10 May 75	**TOMORROW BELONGS TO ME** *Vertigo 9102 003* ○	9		10
23 Aug 75	**NEXT** *Vertigo 6360 103* ○	37		5
27 Sep 75	**SENSATIONAL ALEX HARVEY BAND LIVE** *Vertigo 6360 122* ○	14		7
10 Apr 76	**PENTHOUSE TAPES** *Vertigo 9102 007* ○	14		7
31 Jul 76	**SAHB STORIES** *Mountain TOPS 112* ○	11		9

PJ HARVEY
UK, female vocalist/guitarist (Polly Jean Harvey) — Weeks on Chart: 39

Date	Title	Peak Position	Weeks at No.1	Weeks on Chart
11 Apr 92	**DRY** *Too Pure PURECD 10* ○	11		5
8 May 93	**RID OF ME** *Island CID 8002* ○	3		4
30 Oct 93	**4-TRACK DEMOS** *Island IMCD 170*	19		2
11 Mar 95	**TO BRING YOU MY LOVE** *Island CID 8035* ○	12		6
5 Oct 96	**DANCE HALL AT LOUSE POINT** *Island CIDX 8051* JOHN PARISH & POLLY JEAN HARVEY	46		1
10 Oct 98	**IS THIS DESIRE?** *Island CID 8076*	17		2

Key: Silver-selling ○ · Gold-selling ● · Platinum-selling ⊛ · US No.1 ★ · Peak Position · Weeks at No.1 · Weeks on Chart

Date	Title / Label	Peak Position	Weeks at No.1	Weeks on Chart
4 Nov 00	**STORIES FROM THE CITY STORIES FROM THE SEA** *Island CIDX8099* ●	23		13
12 Jun 04	**UH HUH HER** *Island CIDX 8143* ○	12		3
6 Oct 07	**WHITE CHALK** *Island 1740335* ○	11		3

RICHARD HARVEY & FRIENDS
UK, male instrumental group — Weeks on Chart: **1**

Date	Title / Label	Peak Position	Weeks at No.1	Weeks on Chart
6 May 89	**EVENING FALLS** *Telstar STAR 2350*	72		1

GORDON HASKELL
UK, male vocalist/guitarist — Weeks on Chart: **11**

Date	Title / Label	Peak Position	Weeks at No.1	Weeks on Chart
19 Jan 02	**HARRY'S BAR** *East West 0927439762* ●	2		10
26 Oct 02	**SHADOWS ON THE WALL** *Flying Sparks TDBCD 068*	44		1

HATFIELD & THE NORTH
UK, male/female vocal/instrumental group — Weeks on Chart: **1**

Date	Title / Label	Peak Position	Weeks at No.1	Weeks on Chart
29 Mar 75	**ROTTERS CLUB** *Virgin V 2030*	43		1

JULIANA HATFIELD
US, female vocalist/guitarist — Weeks on Chart: **3**

Date	Title / Label	Peak Position	Weeks at No.1	Weeks on Chart
14 Aug 93	**BECOME WHAT YOU ARE** *Mammoth 4509935292* JULIANA HATFIELD THREE	44		2
8 Apr 95	**ONLY EVERYTHING** *East West 4509998862*	59		1

CHARLOTTE HATHERLEY
UK, female vocalist/guitarist. See Ash — Weeks on Chart: **1**

Date	Title / Label	Peak Position	Weeks at No.1	Weeks on Chart
28 Aug 04	**GREY WILL FADE** *Double Dragon DD2015CD*	51		1

HAVEN
UK, male vocal/instrumental group — Weeks on Chart: **3**

Date	Title / Label	Peak Position	Weeks at No.1	Weeks on Chart
16 Feb 02	**BETWEEN THE SENSES** *Radiate RDTCD 1*	26		3

CHESNEY HAWKES
UK, male vocalist — Weeks on Chart: **8**

Date	Title / Label	Peak Position	Weeks at No.1	Weeks on Chart
13 Apr 91	**BUDDY'S SONG (OST)** *Chrysalis CHR 1812* ○	18		8

SOPHIE B HAWKINS
US, female vocalist/guitarist — Weeks on Chart: **6**

Date	Title / Label	Peak Position	Weeks at No.1	Weeks on Chart
1 Aug 92	**TONGUES AND TAILS** *Columbia 4688232*	46		2
3 Sep 94	**WHALER** *Columbia 4765122*	46		4

TED HAWKINS
US, male vocalist/guitarist, d. 1 Jan 1995 (age 58) — Weeks on Chart: **1**

Date	Title / Label	Peak Position	Weeks at No.1	Weeks on Chart
18 Apr 87	**HAPPY HOUR** *Windows WOLP 2*	82		1

HAWKWIND
UK, male vocal/instrumental group – Dave Brock & various musicians; members also included Harvey Bainbridge, Robert Calvert, Simon King, Lemmy (Ian Willis/Kilmister), Huw Lloyd-Langton & Nik Turner — Weeks on Chart: **101**

Date	Title / Label	Peak Position	Weeks at No.1	Weeks on Chart
6 Nov 71	**IN SEARCH OF SPACE** *United Artists UAS 29202* ●	18		19
23 Dec 72	**DOREMI FASOL LATIDO** *United Artists UAS 29364*	14		5
2 Jun 73	**SPACE RITUAL ALIVE** *United Artists UAD 60037/8* ○	9		5
21 Sep 74	**HALL OF THE MOUNTAIN GRILL** *United Artists UAG 29672* ○	16		5
31 May 75	**WARRIOR ON THE EDGE OF TIME** *United Artists UAG 29766* ○	13		7
24 Apr 76	**ROAD HAWKS** *United Artists UAK 29919* ○	34		4
18 Sep 76	**ASTONISHING SOUNDS, AMAZING MUSIC** *Charisma CDS 4004*	33		5
9 Jul 77	**QUARK STRANGENESS AND CHARM** *Charisma CDS 4008*	30		6
21 Oct 78	**25 YEARS ON** *Charisma CD 4014* HAWKLORDS	48		3
30 Jun 79	**PXR 5** *Charisma CDS 4016*	59		5
9 Aug 80	**LIVE 1979** *Bronze BRON 527*	15		7
8 Nov 80	**LEVITATION** *Bronze BRON 530*	21		4
24 Oct 81	**SONIC ATTACK** *RCA RCALP 5004*	19		5
22 May 82	**THE CHURCH OF HAWKWIND** *RCA RCALP 9004*	26		6
23 Oct 82	**CHOOSE YOUR MASQUES** *RCA RCALP 6055*	29		5
5 Nov 83	**ZONES** *Flicknife SHARP 014*	57		2
25 Feb 84	**HAWKWIND** *Liberty SLS 1972921*	75		1
16 Nov 85	**CHRONICLE OF THE BLACK SWORD** *Flicknife SHARP 033*	65		2
14 May 88	**THE XENON CODEX** *GWR GWLP 26*	79		2
6 Oct 90	**SPACE BANDITS** *GWR GWLP 103*	70		1
23 May 92	**ELECTRIC TEPEE** *Essential ESSCD 181*	53		1
6 Nov 93	**IT IS THE BUSINESS OF THE FUTURE TO BE DANGEROUS** *Essential ESCDCD 196*	75		1

RICHARD HAWLEY
UK, male vocalist/guitarist. See Longpigs — Weeks on Chart: **11**

Date	Title / Label	Peak Position	Weeks at No.1	Weeks on Chart
17 Sep 05	**COLES CORNER** *Mute CDSTUMM251* ●	37		6
1 Sep 07	**LADY'S BRIDGE** *Mute CDSTUMM278* ○	6		5

DARREN HAYES
Australia, male vocalist. See Savage Garden — Weeks on Chart: **33**

Date	Title / Label	Peak Position	Weeks at No.1	Weeks on Chart
13 Apr 02	**SPIN** *Columbia 5053192* ⊛	2		28
25 Sep 04	**THE TENSION AND THE SPARK** *Columbia 5154312*	13		2
1 Sep 07	**THIS DELICATE THING WE'VE MADE** *Powdered Sugar POWSUGCD1*	14		3

GEMMA HAYES
Ireland, female vocalist/guitarist — Weeks on Chart: **1**

Date	Title / Label	Peak Position	Weeks at No.1	Weeks on Chart
8 Jun 02	**NIGHT ON MY SIDE** *Source CDSOUR 049*	52		1

ISAAC HAYES
US, male vocalist/multi-instrumentalist, d. 10 Aug 2008 (age 65) — Weeks on Chart: **14**

Date	Title / Label	Peak Position	Weeks at No.1	Weeks on Chart
18 Dec 71	**SHAFT** *Polydor 2659 007* ★	17		13
12 Feb 72	**BLACK MOSES** *Stax 2628 004*	38		1

HAYSI FANTAYZEE
UK, male/female vocal/production duo — Weeks on Chart: **5**

Date	Title / Label	Peak Position	Weeks at No.1	Weeks on Chart
26 Feb 83	**BATTLE HYMNS FOR CHILDREN SINGING** *Regard RGLP 6000*	53		5

JUSTIN HAYWARD
UK, male vocalist/guitarist (David Hayward). See Moody Blues — Weeks on Chart: **35**

Date	Title / Label	Peak Position	Weeks at No.1	Weeks on Chart
29 Mar 75	**BLUE JAYS** *Threshold THS 12* JUSTIN HAYWARD & JOHN LODGE ●	4		18
5 Mar 77	**SONGWRITER** *Deram SDL 15*	28		5
19 Jul 80	**NIGHT FLIGHT** *Decca TXS 138*	41		4
19 Oct 85	**MOVING MOUNTAINS** *Towerbell TOWLP 15*	78		1
28 Oct 89	**CLASSIC BLUE** *Trax MODEM 1040* WITH MIKE BATT & THE LONDON PHILHARMONIC ORCHESTRA	47		7

LEE HAZLEWOOD
US, male vocalist/producer, d. 4 Aug 2007 (age 78) — Weeks on Chart: **17**

Date	Title / Label	Peak Position	Weeks at No.1	Weeks on Chart
29 Jun 68	**NANCY AND LEE** *Reprise RSLP 6273* WITH NANCY SINATRA	17		12
25 Sep 71	**NANCY AND LEE** *Reprise K 44126* WITH NANCY SINATRA	42		1
29 Jan 72	**DID YOU EVER** *RCA Victor SF 8240* WITH NANCY SINATRA	31		4

HEADSWIM
UK, male vocal/instrumental group — Weeks on Chart: **2**

Date	Title / Label	Peak Position	Weeks at No.1	Weeks on Chart
30 May 98	**DESPITE YOURSELF** *Epic 4877262*	24		2

JEFF HEALEY BAND
Canada, male vocal/instrumental group – Healey, d. 2 Mar 2008 — Weeks on Chart: **16**

Date	Title / Label	Peak Position	Weeks at No.1	Weeks on Chart
14 Jan 89	**SEE THE LIGHT** *Arista 209441* ○	58		7
9 Jun 90	**HELL TO PAY** *Arista 210815* ○	18		6
28 Nov 92	**FEEL THIS** *Arista 74321120872*	72		1
18 Mar 95	**COVER TO COVER** *Arista 74321238882*	50		2

HEAR'SAY
UK, female/male vocal group – Danny Foster, Myleene Klass*, Kym Marsh*, Suzanne Shaw & Noel Sullivan — Weeks on Chart: **32**

Date	Title / Label	Peak Position	Weeks at No.1	Weeks on Chart
7 Apr 01	**POPSTARS** *Polydor 5498212* ⊛x3	1	2	27
15 Dec 01	**EVERYBODY** *Polydor 5895412*	24		5

HEART
US, female/male vocal/instrumental group – Ann Wilson, Mark Andes, Denny Carmassi, Howard Leese & Nancy Wilson — Weeks on Chart: **143**

Date	Title / Label	Peak Position	Weeks at No.1	Weeks on Chart
22 Jan 77	**DREAMBOAT ANNIE** *Arista ARTY 139*	36		8
23 Jul 77	**LITTLE QUEEN** *Portrait PRT 82075*	34		4

Date	Title / Label	Peak Position	Weeks at No.1	Weeks on Chart
19 Jun 82	**PRIVATE AUDITION** *Epic EPC 85792*	77		2
26 Oct 85	**HEART** *Capitol EJ 2403721* ● ★	19		43
6 Jun 87	**BAD ANIMALS** *Capitol ESTU 2032* ⊛	7		56
14 Apr 90	**BRIGADE** *Capitol ESTU 2121* ●	3		20
28 Sep 91	**ROCK THE HOUSE 'LIVE'** *Capitol ESTU 2154*	45		2
11 Dec 93	**DESIRE WALKS ON** *Capitol CDEST 2216*	32		2
19 Apr 97	**THESE DREAMS – GREATEST HITS** *Capitol CDEMC 3765* ○	33		6

HEARTBREAKERS
US, male vocal/instrumental group — 1

Date	Title / Label	Peak Position	Weeks at No.1	Weeks on Chart
5 Nov 77	**L.A.M.F.** *Track 2409 218*	55		1

TED HEATH & HIS MUSIC
UK, male band leader (George Heath), d. 18 Nov 1969 (age 67), & orchestra — 5

Date	Title / Label	Peak Position	Weeks at No.1	Weeks on Chart
21 Apr 62	**BIG BAND PERCUSSION** *Decca PFM 24004*	17		5

PAUL HEATON
UK, male vocalist/guitarist. See Beautiful South, Housemartins — 1

Date	Title / Label	Peak Position	Weeks at No.1	Weeks on Chart
19 Jul 08	**THE CROSS EYED RAMBLER** *W14 1774599*	43		1

HEATWAVE
UK/US, male vocal/instrumental group — 27

Date	Title / Label	Peak Position	Weeks at No.1	Weeks on Chart
11 Jun 77	**TOO HOT TO HANDLE** *GTO GTLP 013* ○	46		2
6 May 78	**CENTRAL HEATING** *GTO GTLP 027* ○	26		15
14 Feb 81	**CANDLES** *GTO GTLP 047*	29		9
23 Feb 91	**GANGSTERS OF THE GROOVE – THE 90'S MIX** *Telstar STAR 2434*	56		1

HEAVEN 17
UK, male vocal/instrumental trio – Glenn Gregory, Ian Craig Marsh & Martyn Ware — 128

Date	Title / Label	Peak Position	Weeks at No.1	Weeks on Chart
26 Sep 81	**PENTHOUSE AND PAVEMENT** *Virgin V 2208* ●	14		76
7 May 83	**THE LUXURY GAP** *Virgin V 2253* ⊛	4		36
6 Oct 84	**HOW MEN ARE** *B.E.F. V 2326* ○	12		11
12 Jul 86	**ENDLESS** *Virgin TCVB/CDV 2383*	70		2
29 Nov 86	**PLEASURE ONE** *Virgin V 2400*	78		1
20 Mar 93	**HIGHER AND HIGHER – THE BEST OF HEAVEN 17** *Virgin CVD 2717*	31		2

HEAVY D & THE BOYZ
Jamaica/US, male vocal/rap group — 3

Date	Title / Label	Peak Position	Weeks at No.1	Weeks on Chart
10 Aug 91	**PEACEFUL JOURNEY** *MCA 10289*	40		3

HEAVY PETTIN'
UK, male vocal/instrumental group — 4

Date	Title / Label	Peak Position	Weeks at No.1	Weeks on Chart
29 Oct 83	**LETTIN' LOOSE** *Polydor HEPLP 1*	55		2
13 Jul 85	**ROCK AIN'T DEAD** *Polydor HEPLP 2*	81		2

HED P E
UK, male vocal/rap/instrumental group — 1

Date	Title / Label	Peak Position	Weeks at No.1	Weeks on Chart
2 Sep 00	**BROKE** *Music For Nations CDFMN 262*	73		1

HELL IS FOR HEROES
UK, male vocal/instrumental group — 2

Date	Title / Label	Peak Position	Weeks at No.1	Weeks on Chart
15 Feb 03	**THE NEON HANDSHAKE** *EMI 5409232*	16		2

HELLOGOODBYE
US, male vocal/instrumental group — 3

Date	Title / Label	Peak Position	Weeks at No.1	Weeks on Chart
2 Jun 07	**ZOMBIES ALIENS VAMPIRES DINOSAURS** *Drive Thru DRVT836452PMI*	17		3

HELLOWEEN
US, male vocal/instrumental group — 9

Date	Title / Label	Peak Position	Weeks at No.1	Weeks on Chart
17 Sep 88	**KEEPER OF THE SEVEN KEYS PART 2** *Noise International NUK 117*	24		5
15 Apr 89	**LIVE IN THE UK** *EMI EMC 3558*	26		2
23 Mar 91	**PINK BUBBLES GO APE** *EMI EMC 3588*	41		2

HELMET
US, male vocal/instrumental group — 1

Date	Title / Label	Peak Position	Weeks at No.1	Weeks on Chart
2 Jul 94	**BETTY** *Interscope 6544924042*	38		1

JIMI HENDRIX EXPERIENCE
US, male vocal/instrumental group – Jimi Hendrix* (Johnny/James Hendrix), d. 18 Sep 1970, Mitch Mitchell, d. 12 Nov 2008, & Noel Redding, d. 11 May 2003

Date	Title / Label	Peak Position	Weeks at No.1	Weeks on Chart
27 May 67	**ARE YOU EXPERIENCED** *Track 612001*	2		33
16 Dec 67	**AXIS: BOLD AS LOVE** *Track 613003*	5		16
27 Apr 68	**SMASH HITS** *Track 613004*	4		25
18 May 68	**GET THAT FEELING** *London HA 8349* JIMI HENDRIX & CURTIS KNIGHT	39		2
16 Nov 68	**ELECTRIC LADYLAND** *Track 613008/9* ★	6		12

JIMI HENDRIX
US, male vocalist/guitarist (Johnny/James Hendrix), d. 18 Sep 1970 (age 27) — 283

Date	Title / Label	Peak Position	Weeks at No.1	Weeks on Chart
6 Jun 70	**BAND OF GYPSIES** *Track 2406 001*	6		30
3 Apr 71	**CRY OF LOVE** *Track 2408 101*	2		14
28 Aug 71	**EXPERIENCE** *Ember NR 5057*	9		6
20 Nov 71	**JIMI HENDRIX AT THE ISLE OF WIGHT** *Track 2302 016*	17		2
4 Dec 71	**RAINBOW FRIDGE (OST)** *Reprise K 44159*	16		8
5 Feb 72	**HENDRIX IN THE WEST** *Polydor 2302 018*	7		14
11 Nov 72	**WAR HEROES** *Polydor 2302 020*	23		3
21 Jul 73	**SOUNDTRACK RECORDINGS FROM THE FILM 'JIMI HENDRIX' (OST)** *Warner Brothers K 64017*	37		1
29 Mar 75	**JIMI HENDRIX** *Polydor 2343 080*	35		4
30 Aug 75	**CRASH LANDING** *Polydor 2310 398*	35		3
29 Nov 75	**MIDNIGHT LIGHTNING** *Polydor 2310 415*	46		1
14 Aug 82	**THE JIMI HENDRIX CONCERTS** *CBS 88592*	16		11
19 Feb 83	**THE SINGLES ALBUM** *Polydor PODV 6*	77		4
11 Mar 89	**RADIO ONE** *Castle Collectors CCSLP 212* ●	30		6
3 Nov 90	**CORNERSTONES – JIMI HENDRIX 1967–1970** *Polydor 8472311* ●	5		16
14 Nov 92	**JIMI HENDRIX – THE ULTIMATE EXPERIENCE** *Polygram TV 5172352* ●	25		26
30 Apr 94	**BLUES** *Polydor 5210372*	10		3
13 Aug 94	**WOODSTOCK** *Polydor 5233842*	32		3
10 May 97	**FIRST RAYS OF THE NEW RISING SUN** *MCA MCD 11599*	37		2
2 Aug 97	**ELECTRIC LADYLAND** *MCA MCD 11600*	47		1
13 Sep 97	**EXPERIENCE HENDRIX – THE BEST OF JIMI HENDRIX** *Telstar TV TTVCD 2930* ○	18		15
13 Jun 98	**BBC SESSIONS** *MCA MCD 11742* EXPERIENCE	42		2
23 Sep 00	**EXPERIENCE HENDRIX – THE BEST** *Universal TV 1123832* ○	10		7
20 Jul 02	**VOODOO CHILD – THE COLLECTION** *Universal TV 1703222* ●	10		13

DON HENLEY
US, male vocalist/multi-instrumentalist. See Eagles — 30

Date	Title / Label	Peak Position	Weeks at No.1	Weeks on Chart
9 Mar 85	**BUILDING THE PERFECT BEAST** *Geffen GEF 25939* ○	14		11
8 Jul 89	**THE END OF INNOCENCE** *Geffen WX 253* ●	17		16
3 Jun 00	**INSIDE JOB** *Warner Brothers 9362470832*	25		3

PAULINE HENRY
UK, female vocalist. See Chimes — 1

Date	Title / Label	Peak Position	Weeks at No.1	Weeks on Chart
19 Feb 94	**PAULINE** *Sony S2 4747442*	45		1

HEPBURN
UK, female vocal/instrumental group — 2

Date	Title / Label	Peak Position	Weeks at No.1	Weeks on Chart
11 Sep 99	**HEPBURN** *Columbia 4948352*	28		2

BAND & CHORUS OF HER MAJESTY'S GUARDS DIVISION
UK, military band — 4

Date	Title / Label	Peak Position	Weeks at No.1	Weeks on Chart
22 Nov 75	**30 SMASH HITS OF THE WAR YEARS** *Warwick WW 5006*	38		4

HERBALISER
UK, male DJ/production duo — 1

Date	Title / Label	Peak Position	Weeks at No.1	Weeks on Chart
30 Mar 02	**SOMETHING WICKED THIS WAY COMES** *Ninja Tune zencd 64*	71		1

MC5

Kick Out The Jams

DELIBERATELY included here as a partner to *Chuck Berry Is On Top*, this album failed to chart in the UK; however, follow its seismic influence through the late 1960s onwards and you will be taken on a journey that features some of this book's absolute highlights. *Kick Out The Jams* is a record that helped inspire some of the album chart's most visceral and raucous entries.

The year 1968 saw the city of Detroit in turmoil. In 1967, infamous race riots had caused chaos when a large number from the African-American community ran out of patience with prejudice seemingly endemic in American society, and their rage-filled indignation finally boiled over. Detroit was a war zone. By the end, over 1,000 people were injured and, tragically, forty-three had been killed. Socially the city was in tatters and the riot had disastrous effects economically because it led to the 'white flight' – frightened white people fleeing the city in large numbers to settle in the suburbs. Detroit was scarred.

Rock writers assumed 'kick out the jams' meant fight against the establishment

Musicians the MC5 (standing for Motor City 5) were among those that upped and left, preferring the calmer surroundings of nearby Ann Arbor on Lake Michigan. The band, consisting of singer Rob Tyner, guitarists Wayne Kramer and Fred 'Sonic' Smith, bassist Mike Davis and drummer Dennis 'Machine Gun' Thompson, had formed in the mid-1960s and gigged primarily as a covers band before settling into their art and crafting their own material.

It was amidst this turbulence and chaos that the MC5 recorded their debut album, *Kick Out The Jams*. The band and their manager, the inimitable poet and leader of the White Panthers, John Sinclair, decided to take the unusual step of making their debut album a live, full-length recording, so proud were they of their famously ferocious live show. Over the Halloween period of 1968, on both 30 and 31 October, the band played shows at Detroit's Grande Ballroom, a venue they practically called their own after becoming the house band under legendary owner Russ Gibb and opening up (and usually blowing away) all of the visiting big names, such as The Who, Cream and Led Zeppelin. The two concerts were recorded and the best version of each song was used on the final edit. Incidentally, although rock writers assumed 'kick out the jams' meant fight against the establishment, the actual meaning of the phrase was rather more prosaic. Wayne Kramer later said it was in fact a habitual heckling they used when British bands over-indulged their fret-boards and egos onstage at the Ballroom.

Friend of the band and local rabble-rouser/preacher J.C. Crawford is the first voice heard on the album – his brief monologue, inviting the listener to choose whether they are aligned with the 'problem' or the 'solution', has gone down in rock 'n' roll history and serves as the perfect introduction to the record, before the band kick in with a cover of Ted Taylor's 'Ramblin' Rose'. Following that, the band play the album's title track – their anthem and an incendiary call to arms. Widely considered to be one of the best rock ballads ever recorded, it would go on

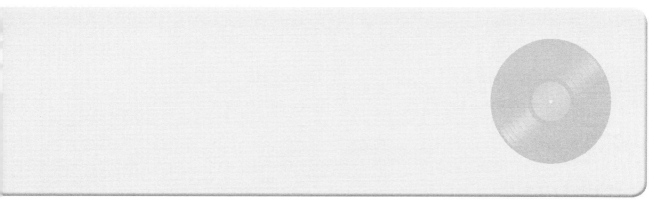

to be covered by bands like Rage Against The Machine, the Presidents Of The United States Of America and Bad Brains with Henry Rollins.

Every song on *Kick Out The Jams* is a classic, from the sex-themed 'Come Together' to the covers of The Troggs' 'I Want You Right Now', Sun Ra's 'Starship' and John Lee Hooker's 'Motor City's Burnin''. While debate raged within the MC5 camp prior to the recording, regarding whether a live album was the right avenue to take as a debut, the songs benefit from the raw, ragged feel, the loose production and the between-song banter. The decision was, without a doubt, the right one. The album was released the following year by Elektra, and met with mixed reviews, including a critical mauling in *Rolling Stone*; however, the controversy had only just begun – MC5 remain perhaps one of the most divisive bands of all. Their inclusion here – in a book of listings in which they superficially play no part – reinforces that controversial reputation.

The original choice of cover art, featuring a marijuana leaf in the middle of the American flag, was deemed too upsetting by the record-label executives and was replaced with a psychedelic collage of the band onstage (the original artwork was, as a compromise, placed inside the sleeve). Still the problems rained down. Next, hometown Detroit's Hudson's department stores refused to stock the record due to the expletives adorning the sleeve (the title track was originally called 'Kick Out The Jams, Motherf**kers!'). Again, the band buckled under pressure and the song title was shortened. Still, when Hudson's threatened to cease stocking other Elektra titles, the label started to tire of the constant trouble; as a result, the MC5's lifespan with the label was effectively over (they would release their next two albums, *Back In The USA* and *High Time* with Atlantic).

MC5 remain perhaps one of the most divisive bands of all

Over forty years later, *Kick Out The Jams* is widely considered to be one of the most important rock 'n' roll albums ever released. Along with The New York Dolls, The Stooges and The Velvet Underground, the MC5 are largely held responsible for the punk explosion that would engulf much of the 1970s (hence the term proto-punk). Even now, bands like Green Day, Rage Against The Machine, The White Stripes and anyone else that plays hard and loose cite the MC5 as a major influence.

Key: ○ Silver-selling · ● Gold-selling · ⊛ Platinum-selling · ★ US No.1 — Peak Position · Weeks at No.1 · Weeks on Chart

HERCULES AND LOVE AFFAIR

US, male/female vocal/DJ/production/instrumental group — Weeks on Chart: 2

Date	Title	Label	Peak Position	Weeks at No.1	Weeks on Chart
22 Mar 08	**HERCULES AND LOVE AFFAIR**	*DFA/EMI 2081102*	31		2

HERD

UK, male vocal/instrumental group — Weeks on Chart: 1

Date	Title	Label	Peak Position	Weeks at No.1	Weeks on Chart
24 Feb 68	**PARADISE LOST**	*Fontana STL 5458*	38		1

HERMAN'S HERMITS

UK, male vocal/instrumental group — Weeks on Chart: 14

Date	Title	Label	Peak Position	Weeks at No.1	Weeks on Chart
18 Sep 65	**HERMAN'S HERMITS**	*Columbia 33SX 1727*	16		2
25 Sep 71	**THE MOST OF HERMAN'S HERMITS**	*MFP 5216*	14		5
8 Oct 77	**GREATEST HITS**	*Columbia NE 1001*	37		4
5 Jul 08	**THE BEST OF HERMAN'S HERMITS**	*EMI CDEMTV200*	24		3

KRISTIN HERSH

US, female vocalist/guitarist. See Throwing Muses — Weeks on Chart: 5

Date	Title	Label	Peak Position	Weeks at No.1	Weeks on Chart
5 Feb 94	**HIPS AND MAKERS**	*4AD CAD 4002CD*	7		4
14 Feb 98	**STRANGE ANGELS**	*4AD CAD 8003CD*	64		1

NICK HEYWARD

UK, male vocalist/guitarist. See Haircut 100 — Weeks on Chart: 13

Date	Title	Label	Peak Position	Weeks at No.1	Weeks on Chart
29 Oct 83	**NORTH OF A MIRACLE**	*Arista NORTH 1* ●	10		13

HI-JACK

US, male vocal group — Weeks on Chart: 1

Date	Title	Label	Peak Position	Weeks at No.1	Weeks on Chart
19 Oct 91	**THE HORNS OF JERICO**	*Warner Brothers 7599263861*	54		1

HI TENSION

UK, male vocal/instrumental group — Weeks on Chart: 4

Date	Title	Label	Peak Position	Weeks at No.1	Weeks on Chart
6 Jan 79	**HI TENSION**	*Island ILPS 9564*	74		4

JOHN HIATT

US, male vocalist/guitarist — Weeks on Chart: 3

Date	Title	Label	Peak Position	Weeks at No.1	Weeks on Chart
7 Jul 90	**STOLEN MOMENTS**	*A&M 3953101*	72		1
11 Sep 93	**PERFECTLY GOOD GUITAR**	*A&M 5401302*	67		1
11 Nov 95	**WALK ON**	*Capitol CDP 8334162*	74		1

HINDA HICKS

UK, female vocalist — Weeks on Chart: 4

Date	Title	Label	Peak Position	Weeks at No.1	Weeks on Chart
29 Aug 98	**HINDA**	*Island CID 8068*	20		4

HIGH

UK, male vocal group — Weeks on Chart: 2

Date	Title	Label	Peak Position	Weeks at No.1	Weeks on Chart
17 Nov 90	**SOMEWHERE SOON**	*London 8282241*	59		2

HIGH LLAMAS

UK, male vocal/instrumental group — Weeks on Chart: 1

Date	Title	Label	Peak Position	Weeks at No.1	Weeks on Chart
6 Apr 96	**HAWAII**	*Alpaca Park CDWOOL 2*	62		1

BENNY HILL

UK, male comedian/vocalist (Alfred Hill), d. 20 Apr 1992 (age 68) — Weeks on Chart: 8

Date	Title	Label	Peak Position	Weeks at No.1	Weeks on Chart
11 Dec 71	**WORDS AND MUSIC**	*Columbia SCX 6479*	9		8

FAITH HILL

US, female vocalist (Audrey Hill) — Weeks on Chart: 29

Date	Title	Label	Peak Position	Weeks at No.1	Weeks on Chart
3 Jun 00	**BREATHE**	*Warner Brothers 2473732* ● ★	19		16
27 Oct 01	**THERE YOU'LL BE**	*Warner Brothers 9362482402* ●	6		11
9 Nov 02	**CRY**	*Warner Brothers 9362483682* ★	29		2

LAURYN HILL

US, female vocalist. See Fugees — Weeks on Chart: 74

Date	Title	Label	Peak Position	Weeks at No.1	Weeks on Chart
10 Oct 98	**THE MISEDUCATION OF LAURYN HILL**	*Ruffhouse 4898432* ⊛x2 ★	2		72
18 May 02	**MTV UNPLUGGED 2.0**	*Columbia 5080032*	40		2

VINCE HILL

UK, male vocalist — Weeks on Chart: 10

Date	Title	Label	Peak Position	Weeks at No.1	Weeks on Chart
20 May 67	**EDELWEISS**	*Columbia SCX 6141*	23		9
29 Apr 78	**THAT LOVING FEELING**	*K-Tel NE 1017*	51		1

STEVE HILLAGE

UK, male vocalist/guitarist — Weeks on Chart: 41

Date	Title	Label	Peak Position	Weeks at No.1	Weeks on Chart
3 May 75	**FISH RISING**	*Virgin V 2031*	33		3
16 Oct 76	**L**	*Virgin V 2066* ○	10		12
22 Oct 77	**MOTIVATION RADIO**	*Virgin V 2777*	28		5
29 Apr 78	**GREEN VIRGIN**	*Virgin 2098*	30		8
17 Feb 79	**LIVE HERALD**	*Virgin VGD 3502*	54		5
5 May 79	**RAINBOW DOME MUSIC**	*Virgin VR 1*	52		5
27 Oct 79	**OPEN**	*Virgin V 2135*	71		1
5 Mar 83	**FOR TO NEXT**	*Virgin V 2244*	48		2

PARIS HILTON

US, female TV personality/model/vocalist — Weeks on Chart: 1

Date	Title	Label	Peak Position	Weeks at No.1	Weeks on Chart
2 Sep 06	**PARIS**	*Warner Brothers 9362441392*	29		1

H.I.M.

Finland, male vocal/instrumental group — Weeks on Chart: 9

Date	Title	Label	Peak Position	Weeks at No.1	Weeks on Chart
26 Apr 03	**LOVE METAL**	*RCA 82876505042*	55		3
27 Mar 04	**AND LOVE SAID NO – 1997-2004**	*RCA 82876606102*	30		2
8 Oct 05	**DARK LIGHT**	*WEA 9362494362*	18		3
29 Sep 07	**VENUS DOOM**	*Sire 9362499888*	31		1

HIPSWAY

UK, male vocal/instrumental group — Weeks on Chart: 23

Date	Title	Label	Peak Position	Weeks at No.1	Weeks on Chart
19 Apr 86	**HIPSWAY**	*Mercury MERH 85*	42		23

DAVID HIRSCHFELDER

Australia, male composer/pianist — Weeks on Chart: 9

Date	Title	Label	Peak Position	Weeks at No.1	Weeks on Chart
2 Aug 97	**SHINE (OST)**	*Philips 4547102*	46		9

HIVES

Sweden, male vocal/instrumental group – Per & Niklas Almqvist, Mikael Karlsson Åström, Mattias Bernvall & Christian Grahn — Weeks on Chart: 39

Date	Title	Label	Peak Position	Weeks at No.1	Weeks on Chart
12 Jan 02	**YOUR NEW FAVOURITE BAND**	*Poptones MC5055CD* ⊛	7		30
31 Jul 04	**TYRANNOSAURUS HIVES**	*Polydor 9866991* ●	7		7
27 Oct 07	**THE BLACK AND WHITE ALBUM**	*Polydor 1747354*	29		2

ROGER HODGSON

UK, male vocalist/bass player. See Supertramp — Weeks on Chart: 4

Date	Title	Label	Peak Position	Weeks at No.1	Weeks on Chart
20 Oct 84	**IN THE EYE OF THE STORM**	*A&M AMA 5004*	70		4

GERARD HOFFNUNG

UK (b. Germany), male comedian/tuba player/cartoonist, d. 28 Sep 1959 (age 34) — Weeks on Chart: 20

Date	Title	Label	Peak Position	Weeks at No.1	Weeks on Chart
3 Sep 60	**AT THE OXFORD UNION**	*Decca LF 1330*	4		20

SUSANNA HOFFS

US, female vocalist/guitarist. See Bangles — Weeks on Chart: 2

Date	Title	Label	Peak Position	Weeks at No.1	Weeks on Chart
6 Apr 91	**WHEN YOU'RE A BOY**	*Columbia 4672021*	56		2

HOLD STEADY

US, male vocal/instrumental group — Weeks on Chart: 2

Date	Title	Label	Peak Position	Weeks at No.1	Weeks on Chart
26 Jul 08	**STAY POSITIVE**	*Rough Trade RTRADCDX450*	15		2

HOLE

US/Canada, female/male vocal/instrumental group — Weeks on Chart: 10

Date	Title	Peak Position	Weeks at No.1	Weeks on Chart
12 Oct 91	**PRETTY ON THE INSIDE** *City Slang E 04071*	59		1
23 Apr 94	**LIVE THROUGH THIS** *City Slang EFA 049352*	13		5
19 Sep 98	**CELEBRITY SKIN** *Geffen GED 25164*	11		4

BILLIE HOLIDAY

US, female vocalist (Eleanora Fagan), d. 17 Jul 1959 (age 44) — Weeks on Chart: 11

Date	Title	Peak Position	Weeks at No.1	Weeks on Chart
16 Nov 85	**THE LEGEND OF BILLIE HOLIDAY** *MCA BHTV 1* ●	60		10
6 Sep 97	**LADY DAY – THE VERY BEST OF BILLIE HOLIDAY** *Columbia MOODCD 52*	63		1

JOOLS HOLLAND

UK, male vocalist/pianist/TV presenter. See Squeeze — Weeks on Chart: 99

Date	Title	Peak Position	Weeks at No.1	Weeks on Chart
5 May 90	**WORLD OF HIS OWN** *I.R.S. EIRSA 1018*	71		1
26 Oct 96	**SEX & JAZZ & ROCK & ROLL** *Coliseum HF 51CD* & HIS R&B ORCHESTRA	38		2
25 Oct 97	**LIFT THE LID** *Coalition 3984205252* & HIS R&B ORCHESTRA	50		1
1 Dec 01	**SMALL WORLD BIG BAND** *WSM 0927426562* ⊛x2	8		37
30 Nov 02	**MORE FRIENDS – SMALL WORLD BIG BAND 2** *WSM 0927494192* ⊛	17		14
29 Nov 03	**JACK O THE GREEN – SMALL WORLD BIG BAND** *Radar RADAR001CD* & HIS R&B ORCHESTRA ●	39		9
9 Oct 04	**TOM JONES AND JOOLS HOLLAND** *Radar RADAR004CD* TOM JONES & JOOLS HOLLAND ●	5		13
19 Nov 05	**SWINGING THE BLUES DANCING THE SKA** *Radar RADAR006CD* & HIS R&B ORCHESTRA	36		8
2 Dec 06	**MOVING OUT TO THE COUNTRY** *Radar RADAR008CD* & HIS R&B ORCHESTRA	45		5
27 Oct 07	**BEST OF FRIENDS** *Rhino 5144246662* ○	9		6
29 Nov 08	**THE INFORMER** *Rhino 2564692908* & HIS R&B ORCHESTRA	48		3

HOLLIES

UK, male vocal/instrumental group – Allan Clarke, Bobby Elliott, Eric Haydock (replaced by Bernie Calvert), Tony Hicks & Graham Nash* (replaced by Terry Sylvester) — Weeks on Chart: 154

Date	Title	Peak Position	Weeks at No.1	Weeks on Chart
15 Feb 64	**STAY WITH THE HOLLIES** *Parlophone PMC 1220*	2		25
2 Oct 65	**HOLLIES** *Parlophone PMC 1261*	8		14
16 Jul 66	**WOULD YOU BELIEVE** *Parlophone PMC 7008*	16		8
17 Dec 66	**FOR CERTAIN BECAUSE** *Parlophone PCS 17011*	23		7
17 Jun 67	**EVOLUTION** *Parlophone PCS 7022*	13		10
17 Aug 68	**THE HOLLIES' GREATEST** *Parlophone PCS 7057*	1	7	27
17 May 69	**HOLLIES SING DYLAN** *Parlophone PCS 7078*	3		7
28 Nov 70	**CONFESSIONS OF THE MIND** *Parlophone PCS 7117*	30		5
16 Mar 74	**HOLLIES** *Polydor 2383 262*	38		3
19 Mar 77	**HOLLIES LIVE HITS** *Polydor 3283 428* ●	4		12
22 Jul 78	**20 GOLDEN GREATS** *EMI EMTV 11* ●	2		20
1 Oct 88	**ALL THE HITS AND MORE** *EMI EM 1301*	51		5
3 Apr 93	**THE AIR THAT I BREATHE – THE BEST OF THE HOLLIES** *EMI CDEMTV 74* ●	15		7
5 Apr 03	**GREATEST HITS** *EMI 5820122* ○	21		4

MARK HOLLIS

UK, male vocalist/multi-instrumentalist. See Talk Talk — Weeks on Chart: 1

Date	Title	Peak Position	Weeks at No.1	Weeks on Chart
14 Feb 98	**MARK HOLLIS** *Polydor 5376882*	53		1

HOLLOWAYS

UK, male vocal/instrumental group — Weeks on Chart: 1

Date	Title	Peak Position	Weeks at No.1	Weeks on Chart
11 Nov 06	**SO THIS IS GREAT BRITAIN** *TVT HOLLOLPCD1*	54		1

BUDDY HOLLY

US, male vocalist/guitarist (Charles Hardin Holley), d. 3 Feb 1959 (age 22). See Crickets — Weeks on Chart: 339

Date	Title	Peak Position	Weeks at No.1	Weeks on Chart
2 May 59	**THE BUDDY HOLLY STORY** *Coral LVA 9105*	2		156
15 Oct 60	**THE BUDDY HOLLY STORY VOLUME 2** *Coral LVA 9127*	7		14
21 Oct 61	**THAT'LL BE THE DAY** *Ace Of Hearts AH 3*	5		14
6 Apr 63	**REMINISCING** *Coral LVA 9212*	2		31
13 Jun 64	**BUDDY HOLLY SHOWCASE** *Coral LVA 9222*	3		16
26 Jun 65	**HOLLY IN THE HILLS** *Coral LVA 9227*	13		6
15 Jul 67	**BUDDY HOLLY'S GREATEST HITS** *Ace Of Hearts AH 148*	9		40
12 Apr 69	**GIANT** *MCA MUPS 371*	13		1
21 Aug 71	**BUDDY HOLLY'S GREATEST HITS** *Coral CP 8*	32		6
12 Jul 75	**BUDDY HOLLY'S GREATEST HITS** *Coral CDLM 8007*	42		3
11 Mar 78	**20 GOLDEN GREATS** *EMI EMTV 8* & THE CRICKETS ⊛	1	3	20
8 Sep 84	**BUDDY HOLLY'S GREATEST HITS** *MCA MCL 1618*	100		1
18 Feb 89	**TRUE LOVE WAYS** *Telstar STAR 2339* ●	8		11
20 Feb 93	**WORDS OF LOVE** *Polygram TV 5144872* & THE CRICKETS ●	1	1	9
7 Dec 96	**THE VERY BEST OF BUDDY HOLLY** *Dino DINCD 133* ●	24		8
28 Aug 99	**THE VERY BEST OF BUDDY HOLLY AND THE CRICKETS** *Universal Music TV 1120462* & THE CRICKETS	25		3

DAVID HOLMES

UK, male producer — Weeks on Chart: 6

Date	Title	Peak Position	Weeks at No.1	Weeks on Chart
22 Jul 95	**THIS FILM'S CRAP, LET'S SLASH THE SEATS** *Go! Discs 8286312*	51		1
13 Sep 97	**LET'S GET KILLED** *Go! Discs 5391002* ○	34		2
24 Jun 00	**BOW DOWN TO THE EXIT SIGN** *Go. Beat 5438662*	22		2
20 Sep 08	**THE HOLY PICTURES** *Mercury 1777275*	65		1

JOHN HOLT

Jamaica, male vocalist — Weeks on Chart: 2

Date	Title	Peak Position	Weeks at No.1	Weeks on Chart
1 Feb 75	**A THOUSAND VOLTS OF HOLT** *Trojan TRLS 75*	42		2

HOME

UK, male vocal/instrumental group — Weeks on Chart: 1

Date	Title	Peak Position	Weeks at No.1	Weeks on Chart
11 Nov 72	**DREAMER** *CBS 67522*	41		1

HONEYCRACK

UK, male vocal/instrumental group — Weeks on Chart: 1

Date	Title	Peak Position	Weeks at No.1	Weeks on Chart
1 Jun 96	**PROZIAC** *Epic 4842302*	34		1

HONEYDRIPPERS

UK/US, male vocal/instrumental group — Weeks on Chart: 10

Date	Title	Peak Position	Weeks at No.1	Weeks on Chart
1 Dec 84	**THE HONEYDRIPPERS VOLUME ONE** *Es Paranza 790220*	56		10

HONEYZ

UK/France, female vocal trio — Weeks on Chart: 22

Date	Title	Peak Position	Weeks at No.1	Weeks on Chart
5 Dec 98	**WONDER NO. 8** *Mercury 5588142* ●	33		22

HOOBASTANK

US, male vocal/instrumental group — Weeks on Chart: 5

Date	Title	Peak Position	Weeks at No.1	Weeks on Chart
5 Jun 04	**THE REASON** *Mercury 9862261* ○	41		5

JOHN LEE HOOKER

US, male vocalist/guitarist, d. 21 Jun 2001 (age 83) — Weeks on Chart: 31

Date	Title	Peak Position	Weeks at No.1	Weeks on Chart
4 Feb 67	**HOUSE OF THE BLUES** *Marble Arch MAL 663*	34		2
11 Nov 89	**THE HEALER** *Silvertone ORELP 508* ●	63		8
21 Sep 91	**MR. LUCKY** *Silvertone ORELP 519* ●	3		10
7 Nov 92	**BOOM BOOM** *Pointblank VPBCD 12* ●	15		4
4 Mar 95	**CHILL OUT** *Pointblank VPBCD 22*	23		5
22 Mar 97	**DON'T LOOK BACK** *Pointblank VPBCD 39*	63		2

HOOSIERS

UK/Sweden, male vocal/instrumental trio – Irwin Sparkes, Alphonso Sharland & Martin Skarendahl — Weeks on Chart: 33

Date	Title	Peak Position	Weeks at No.1	Weeks on Chart
3 Nov 07	**THE TRICK TO LIFE** *RCA 88697156912* ⊛x2	1	1	33

HOOTIE & THE BLOWFISH

US, male vocal/instrumental group – Darius Rucker, Mark Bryan, Dean Felder & Jim Sonefeld — Weeks on Chart: 30

Date	Title	Peak Position	Weeks at No.1	Weeks on Chart
18 Mar 95	**CRACKED REAR VIEW** *Atlantic 7826132* ● ★	12		11
4 May 96	**FAIRWEATHER JOHNSON** *Atlantic 7567828852* ○ ★	9		16
26 Sep 98	**MUSICAL CHAIRS** *Atlantic 7567831362*	15		3

HOPE OF THE STATES

UK, male vocal/instrumental group — Weeks on Chart: 3

Date	Title	Peak Position	Weeks at No.1	Weeks on Chart
19 Jun 04	**THE LOST RIOTS** *Sony Music 5172649*	21		2
1 Jul 06	**LEFT** *Columbia LEFTDD04*	50		1

Silver-selling ○ Gold-selling ● Platinum-selling ⊛ US No.1 ★ | Peak Position | Weeks at No.1 | Weeks on Chart

MARY HOPKIN
UK, female vocalist/guitarist

Date	Album	Peak Position	Weeks at No.1	Weeks on Chart
				9
1 Mar 69	**POSTCARD** *Apple SAPCOR 5*	3		9

JAMES HORNER
US, male composer/arranger/conductor

Date	Album	Peak Position	Weeks at No.1	Weeks on Chart
				82
23 Sep 95	**BRAVEHEART (OST)** *Decca 4482952* LONDON SYMPHONY ORCHESTRA, CONDUCTOR JAMES HORNER	27		9
31 Jan 98	**TITANIC (OST)** *Sony Classical SK 63213* ⊛x3 ★	1	3	55
12 Sep 98	**BACK TO TITANIC** *Sony Classical SK 60691* ●	10		18

BRUCE HORNSBY & THE RANGE
US, male vocal/instrumental group

Date	Album	Peak Position	Weeks at No.1	Weeks on Chart
				54
13 Sep 86	**THE WAY IT IS** *RCA PL 89901* ○	16		26
14 May 88	**SCENES FROM THE SOUTHSIDE** *RCA PL 86686* ●	18		18
30 Jun 90	**A NIGHT ON THE TOWN** *RCA PL 82041* ○	23		7
8 May 93	**HARBOR LIGHTS** *RCA 07863661142*	32		3

JANE HORROCKS
UK, female actor/vocalist

Date	Album	Peak Position	Weeks at No.1	Weeks on Chart
				1
21 Oct 00	**FURTHER ADVENTURES OF LITTLE VOICE** *Liberty 5287542*	63		1

HORRORS
UK, male vocal/instrumental group

Date	Album	Peak Position	Weeks at No.1	Weeks on Chart
				1
17 Mar 07	**STRANGE HOUSE** *Loog 1726282*	37		1

HORSE
UK, female/male vocal/instrumental group

Date	Album	Peak Position	Weeks at No.1	Weeks on Chart
				4
23 Jun 90	**THE SAME SKY** *Echo Chamber EST 2123*	44		2
13 Nov 93	**GOD'S HOME MOVIE** *Oxygen MCD 10935*	42		2

HORSLIPS
Ireland, male vocal/instrumental group

Date	Album	Peak Position	Weeks at No.1	Weeks on Chart
				3
30 Apr 77	**THE BOOK OF INVASIONS – A CELTIC SYMPHONY** *DJM DJF 20498*	39		3

HOT CHIP
UK, male vocal/instrumental group

Date	Album	Peak Position	Weeks at No.1	Weeks on Chart
				14
3 Jun 06	**THE WARNING** *EMI 3566402* ●	34		8
16 Feb 08	**MADE IN THE DARK** *EMI 5179172* ○	4		6

HOT CHOCOLATE
UK/Bahamas/Jamaica/Trinidad & Tobago, male vocal/instrumental group – Errol Brown*, Larry Ferguson, Harvey Hinsley, Ian King (replaced by Tony Connor) & Tony Wilson (replaced by Patrick Olive)

Date	Album	Peak Position	Weeks at No.1	Weeks on Chart
				153
15 Nov 75	**HOT CHOCOLATE** *RAK SRAK 516* ○	34		7
7 Aug 76	**MAN TO MAN** *RAK SRAK 522* ○	32		7
20 Nov 76	**GREATEST HITS** *RAK SRAK 524* ●	6		35
8 Apr 78	**EVERY 1'S A WINNER** *RAK SRAK 531* ○	30		8
15 Dec 79	**20 HOTTEST HITS** *RAK EMTV 22* ⊛	3		19
25 Sep 82	**MYSTERY** *RAK SRAK 549*	24		7
21 Feb 87	**THE VERY BEST OF HOT CHOCOLATE** *RAK EMTV 42* ⊛	1	1	28
20 Mar 93	**THEIR GREATEST HITS** *EMI CDEMTV 73* ⊛	1	1	42

HOT HOT HEAT
Canada, male vocal/instrumental group

Date	Album	Peak Position	Weeks at No.1	Weeks on Chart
				4
12 Apr 03	**MAKE UP THE BREAKDOWN** *B Unique 5046646202*	35		2
7 May 05	**ELEVATOR** *Sire 9362489882*	34		2

HOTHOUSE FLOWERS
Ireland, male vocal/instrumental group – Liam Ó Maonlaí, Fiachna Ó Braonáin, Dave Clarke & Peter O'Toole

Date	Album	Peak Position	Weeks at No.1	Weeks on Chart
				51
18 Jun 88	**PEOPLE** *London LONLP 58* ●	2		19
16 Jun 90	**HOME** *London 8281971* ●	5		21
20 Mar 93	**SONGS FROM THE RAIN** *London 8283502* ○	7		11

STEVEN HOUGHTON
UK, male actor/vocalist

Date	Album	Peak Position	Weeks at No.1	Weeks on Chart
				7
29 Nov 97	**STEVEN HOUGHTON** *RCA 74321542592*	21		7

HOUND DOG & THE MEGAMIXERS
UK, male producer (Chris Marshall)

Date	Album	Peak Position	Weeks at No.1	Weeks on Chart
				9
1 Dec 90	**THE GREATEST EVER JUNIOR PARTY MEGAMIX** *Pop & Arts PATLP 201*	34		9

HOURS
UK, male vocal/instrumental/DJ/production duo

Date	Album	Peak Position	Weeks at No.1	Weeks on Chart
				1
17 Feb 07	**NARCISSUS ROAD** *A&M/Polydor 1718264*	47		1

HOUSE OF LOVE
UK, male vocal/instrumental group – Guy Chadwick, Pete Evans, Chris Groothuizen & Simon Walker

Date	Album	Peak Position	Weeks at No.1	Weeks on Chart
				14
10 Mar 90	**HOUSE OF LOVE** *Fontana 8422931*	8		10
10 Nov 90	**THE HOUSE OF LOVE** *Fontana 8469781*	49		1
18 Jul 92	**BABE RAINBOW** *Fontana 5125492*	34		2
3 Jul 93	**AUDIENCE WITH THE MIND** *Fontana 5148802*	38		1

HOUSE OF PAIN
US/Latvia, male rap/DJ/production group – Everlast* (Erik Schrody), Danny Boy (Daniel O'Connor) & DJ Lethal (Leor Dimant)

Date	Album	Peak Position	Weeks at No.1	Weeks on Chart
				7
21 Nov 92	**HOUSE OF PAIN** *XL Recordings XLCD 111* ●	73		1
30 Jul 94	**SAME AS IT EVER WAS** *XL Recordings XLCD 115*	8		6

HOUSEMARTINS
UK, male vocal/instrumental group – Paul Heaton*, Norman Cook (aka Fatboy Slim*), Stan Cullimore & Dave Hemingway

Date	Album	Peak Position	Weeks at No.1	Weeks on Chart
				89
5 Jul 86	**LONDON 0 HULL 4** *Go! Discs AGOLP 7* ⊛	3		41
27 Dec 86	**THE HOUSEMARTINS' CHRISTMAS SINGLES BOX** *Go! Discs GOD 816*	84		1
3 Oct 87	**THE PEOPLE WHO GRINNED THEMSELVES TO DEATH** *Go! Discs AGOLP 9* ●	9		18
21 May 88	**NOW THAT'S WHAT I CALL QUITE GOOD** *Go! Discs AGOLP 11* ●	8		11
10 Apr 04	**THE BEST OF** *Go! Discs 9818214*	29		3
24 Nov 07	**SOUP** *Mercury 1747147* BEAUTIFUL SOUTH & THE HOUSEMARTINS	15		15

MARQUES HOUSTON
US, male vocalist

Date	Album	Peak Position	Weeks at No.1	Weeks on Chart
				1
14 Feb 04	**MH** *Elektra 7559629352* ○	73		1

WHITNEY HOUSTON
US, female vocalist. Multi-award winning superstar whose first two albums sold more than 50 million copies worldwide. The soundtrack album *The Bodyguard* sold over two million copies in the UK and 20 million in the US. Whitney's worldwide record sales exceed 150 million

Date	Album	Peak Position	Weeks at No.1	Weeks on Chart
				413
14 Dec 85	**WHITNEY HOUSTON** *Arista 206978* ⊛x4 ★	2		119
13 Jun 87	**WHITNEY** *Arista 208141* ⊛x6 ★	1	6	101
17 Nov 90	**I'M YOUR BABY TONIGHT** *Arista 211039* ⊛	4		29
4 Jan 97	**THE PREACHERS WIFE (OST)** *Arista 74321441252*	35		7
28 Nov 98	**MY LOVE IS YOUR LOVE** *Arista 07822190372* ⊛x3	4		67
27 May 00	**THE GREATEST HITS** *Arista 74321757392* ⊛x4	1	2	63
16 Feb 02	**LOVE, WHITNEY** *Arista 74321910272*	22		3
10 Nov 07	**ULTIMATE COLLECTION** *Arista 88697177012* ⊛x2	3		24

Top 3 Best-Selling Albums

	Album	Approximate Sales
1	WHITNEY	2,240,000
2	THE GREATEST HITS	1,650,000
3	WHITNEY HOUSTON	1,250,000

Key: ○ Silver-selling · ● Gold-selling · ⊛ Platinum-selling · ★ US No.1 · Peak Position · Weeks at No.1 · Weeks on Chart

STEVE HOWE

UK, male vocalist/guitarist. See Anderson Bruford Wakeman Howe, Asia, GTR, Yes

Date	Title	Peak Position	Weeks at No.1	Weeks on Chart
				6
15 Nov 75	**BEGINNINGS** *Atlantic K 50151* ○	22		4
24 Nov 79	**THE STEVE HOWE ALBUM** *Atlantic K 50621*	68		2

HUDDERSFIELD CHORAL SOCIETY

UK, male/female choir

Date	Title	Peak Position	Weeks at No.1	Weeks on Chart
				14
15 Mar 86	**THE HYMNS ALBUM** *EMI EMTV 43* ●	8		10
13 Dec 86	**THE CAROLS ALBUM** *EMI EMTV 40* ●	29		4

JENNIFER HUDSON

US, female vocalist/actor

Date	Title	Peak Position	Weeks at No.1	Weeks on Chart
				8
11 Oct 08	**JENNIFER HUDSON** *Sony BMG 88697386482*	21		8

HUE & CRY

UK, male vocal/instrumental duo – Greg & Pat Kane

Date	Title	Peak Position	Weeks at No.1	Weeks on Chart
				74
7 Nov 87	**SEDUCED AND ABANDONED** *Circa 2* ○	22		11
10 Dec 88	**REMOTE/THE BITTER SUITE** *Circa 6* ●	10		48
29 Jun 91	**STARS CRASH DOWN** *Circa 15*	10		9
29 Aug 92	**TRUTH AND LOVE** *Fidelity FIDELCD 1*	33		2
10 Apr 93	**LABOURS ON LOVE – THE BEST OF HUE AND CRY** *Circa HACCD 1*	27		4

ALAN HULL

UK, male vocalist (James Hull), d. 17 Nov 1995 (age 50). See Lindisfarne

Date	Title	Peak Position	Weeks at No.1	Weeks on Chart
				3
28 Jul 73	**PIPEDREAM** *Charisma CAS 1069*	29		3

HUMAN LEAGUE

UK, male/female vocal/instrumental group – Philip Oakey*, Joanne Catherall & Susanne Sulley; members also included Ian Burden, Jo Callis & Philip Wright

Date	Title	Peak Position	Weeks at No.1	Weeks on Chart
				263
31 May 80	**TRAVELOGUE** *Virgin V 2160* ●	16		42
22 Aug 81	**REPRODUCTION** *Virgin V 2133* ●	34		23
24 Oct 81	**DARE** *Virgin V 2192* ⊛x3	1	4	72
17 Jul 82	**LOVE AND DANCING** *Virgin OVED 6* LEAGUE UNLIMITED ORCHESTRA ⊛	3		52
19 May 84	**HYSTERIA** *Virgin V 2315* ●	3		18
20 Sep 86	**CRASH** *Virgin V 2391* ●	7		6
12 Nov 88	**GREATEST HITS** *Virgin HLTV 1* ⊛x2	3		24
29 Sep 90	**ROMANTIC?** *Virgin V 2624*	24		2
4 Feb 95	**OCTOPUS** *East West 4509987502* ●	6		12
11 Nov 95	**GREATEST HITS** *Virgin CDV 2792* ●	28		8
18 Aug 01	**SECRETS** *Papillon BTFLYCD 0019*	44		1
27 Sep 03	**THE VERY BEST OF** *Virgin HLCDX2* ○	24		3

HUMBLE PIE

UK, male vocal/instrumental group

Date	Title	Peak Position	Weeks at No.1	Weeks on Chart
				10
6 Sep 69	**AS SAFE AS YESTERDAY IS** *Immediate IMSP 025*	32		1
22 Jan 72	**ROCKING AT THE FILLMORE** *A&M AMLH 63506*	32		2
15 Apr 72	**SMOKIN'** *A&M AMLS 64342*	28		5
7 Apr 73	**EAT IT** *A&M AMLS 6004*	34		2

ENGELBERT HUMPERDINCK

UK (b. India), male vocalist (Arnold Dorsey)

Date	Title	Peak Position	Weeks at No.1	Weeks on Chart
				271
20 May 67	**RELEASE ME** *Decca SKL 4868*	6		58
25 Nov 67	**THE LAST WALTZ** *Decca SKL 4901*	3		33
3 Aug 68	**A MAN WITHOUT LOVE** *Decca SKL 4939*	3		45
1 Mar 69	**ENGELBERT** *Decca SKL 4985*	3		8
6 Dec 69	**ENGELBERT HUMPERDINCK** *Decca SKL 5030*	5		23
11 Jul 70	**WE MADE IT HAPPEN** *Decca SKL 5054*	17		11
18 Sep 71	**ANOTHER TIME, ANOTHER PLACE** *Decca SKL 5097*	48		1
26 Feb 72	**LIVE AT THE RIVIERA LAS VEGAS** *Decca TXS 105*	45		1
21 Dec 74	**ENGELBERT HUMPERDINCK – HIS GREATEST HITS** *Decca SKL 5198* ●	1	3	34
4 May 85	**GETTING SENTIMENTAL** *Telstar STAR 2254*	35		10
4 Apr 87	**THE ENGELBERT HUMPERDINCK COLLECTION** *Telstar STAR 2294*	35		9
10 Jun 95	**LOVE UNCHAINED** *EMI CDEMTV 94*	16		6
8 Apr 00	**AT HIS VERY BEST** *Universal TV 8449742* ●	5		14
20 Oct 01	**I WANT TO WAKE UP WITH YOU** *Universal TV 0149462*	42		2
20 Mar 04	**HIS GREATEST LOVE SONGS** *Universal TV 9817857* ●	4		12
26 Feb 05	**LET THERE BE LOVE** *Decca 4756606*	67		1
14 Apr 07	**GREATEST HITS AND MORE** *Universal TV 9847095*	21		3

HUNDRED REASONS

UK, male vocal/instrumental group – Colin Doran, Andy Bews, Andy Gilmour, Larry Hibbitt & Paul Townsend

Date	Title	Peak Position	Weeks at No.1	Weeks on Chart
				9
1 Jun 02	**IDEAS ABOVE OUR STATION** *Columbia 5081482*	6		7
13 Mar 04	**SHATTERPROOF IS NOT A CHALLENGE** *Columbia 5136932*	20		2

IAN HUNTER

UK, male vocalist/guitarist/keyboard player (Ian Patterson). See Mott The Hoople

Date	Title	Peak Position	Weeks at No.1	Weeks on Chart
				26
12 Apr 75	**IAN HUNTER** *CBS 80710*	21		15
29 May 76	**ALL AMERICAN ALIEN BOY** *CBS 81310*	29		4
5 May 79	**YOU'RE NEVER ALONE WITH A SCHIZOPHRENIC** *Chrysalis CHR 1214*	49		3
26 Apr 80	**WELCOME TO THE CLUB** *Chrysalis CJT 6*	61		2
29 Aug 81	**SHORT BACK 'N' SIDES** *Chrysalis CHR 1326*	79		2

HURRAH!

UK, male vocal/instrumental group

Date	Title	Peak Position	Weeks at No.1	Weeks on Chart
				1
28 Feb 87	**TELL GOD I'M HERE** *Kitchenware 208201*	71		1

HURRICANE #1

UK, male vocal/instrumental group

Date	Title	Peak Position	Weeks at No.1	Weeks on Chart
				3
27 Sep 97	**HURRICANE #1** *Creation CRECD 206*	11		2
1 May 99	**ONLY THE STRONGEST WILL SURVIVE** *Creation CRECD 237*	55		1

HUSKER DU

US, male vocal/instrumental group

Date	Title	Peak Position	Weeks at No.1	Weeks on Chart
				1
14 Feb 87	**WAREHOUSE: SONGS AND STORIES** *Warner Brothers 9255441*	72		1

HYBRID

UK, male production trio

Date	Title	Peak Position	Weeks at No.1	Weeks on Chart
				1
25 Sep 99	**WIDE ANGLE** *Distinctive DISNCD 54*	45		1

PHYLLIS HYMAN

US, female vocalist, d. 30 Jun 1995 (age 45)

Date	Title	Peak Position	Weeks at No.1	Weeks on Chart
				1
20 Sep 86	**LIVING ALL ALONE** *Philadelphia International PHIL 4001*	97		1

HYPNOSIS

UK, male production/instrumental duo. See Blowing Free, Harmonium, In Tune, Raindance, School Of Excellence

Date	Title	Peak Position	Weeks at No.1	Weeks on Chart
				16
17 Aug 96	**VOICES OF TRANQUILLITY** *Dino DINCD 123* ●	16		12
15 Mar 97	**VOICES OF TRANQUILLITY – VOLUME 2** *Dino DINCD 135*	32		4

BIOGRAPHIES

Biographies include the nationality and category for every chart entrant.

Each entrant has at least a mini biography. The 100 acts with the most weeks on the chart (see page 290 for the top 100 chart) each have extended biographies.

Real names are included for all solo artists and, where applicable, dates of death and age of the artist at the time. "See..." links are included for soloists who also had album chart entries in other acts.

The best known line-up is listed for every group that had a Top 10 album, with the vocalist/leader mentioned first and the others following in alphabetical order. In cases where later replacements had similar success both people are named and, where applicable, the dates of death are also shown for every group/duo member listed.

Certified Awards are given by the BPI to mark unit sales to retailers. The certified awards were introduced in April 1973, based on revenue received by manufacturers. In January 1978 the qualification rules were changed and the system based on unit sales to the trade was adopted.

Silver symbol	●	=	60,000 units
Gold symbol	●	=	100,000 units
Platinum symbol	⊛	=	300,000 units

I–L

KEY TO ARTIST ENTRIES

Artist/Group Name — Artist/Group Biography — Silver-selling — Gold-selling — Platinum-selling — US No.1 ★ — Peak Position — Weeks at No.1 — Weeks on Chart

Asterisks (*) indicate group members with hits in their own right that are listed elsewhere in this book

Artist's Total Weeks On Chart

TOM JONES

UK, male vocalist (Thomas Woodward). Perennially popular Welsh vocalist, who has a 43-year span of UK hit albums, was the No.1 UK solo singer of the 1960s on both sides of the Atlantic. The unmistakable Vegas veteran received the Outstanding Contribution award at the 2003 BRITs

Date	Title / Label	Peak	Wks at No.1	Wks (530)
5 Jun 65	**ALONG CAME JONES** *Decca LK 6693*	11		5
8 Oct 66	**FROM THE HEART** *Decca LK 4814*	23		8
8 Apr 67	**GREEN GREEN GRASS OF HOME** *Decca SKL 4855*	3		49
24 Jun 67	**LIVE AT THE TALK OF THE TOWN** *Decca SKL 4874*	6		90
30 Dec 67	**13 SMASH HITS** *Decca SKL 4909*	5		49
27 Jul 68	**DELILAH** *Decca SKL 4946*	1	2	29
21 Dec 68	**HELP YOURSELF** *Decca SKL 4982*	4		9
28 Jun 69	**THIS IS TOM JONES** *Decca SKL 5007*	2		20
15 Nov 69	**TOM JONES LIVE IN LAS VEGAS** *Decca SKL 5032*	2		45
25 Apr 70	**TOM** *Decca SKL 5045*	4		18
14 Nov 70	**I WHO HAVE NOTHING** *Decca SKL 5072*	10		10
29 May 71	**SHE'S A LADY** *Decca SKL 5089*	9		7
27 Nov 71	**LIVE AT CAESAR'S PALACE** *Decca D 1/11/2*	27		5
24 Jun 72	**CLOSE UP** *Decca SKL 5132*	17		4
23 Jun 73	**THE BODY AND SOUL OF TOM JONES** *Decca SKL 5162*	31		1
5 Jan 74	**GREATEST HITS** *Decca SKL 5176*	15		13
22 Mar 75	**20 GREATEST HITS** *Decca TJD 1/11/2* ●	1	4	21
7 Oct 78	**I'M COMING HOME** *Lotus WH 5001* ●	12		9
16 May 87	**THE GREATEST HITS** *Telstar STAR 2296*	16		12
13 May 89	**AT THIS MOMENT** *Jive TOMTV 1*	34		3
8 Jul 89	**AFTER DARK** *Stylus SMR 978*	46		4
6 Apr 91	**CARRYING A TORCH** *Dover ADD 20*	44		4
27 Jun 92	**THE COMPLETE TOM JONES** *The Hit Label 8442862* ●	8		6
26 Nov 94	**THE LEAD AND HOW TO SWING IT** *ZTT 6544924982*	55		1
14 Nov 98	**THE ULTIMATE HITS COLLECTION** *Polygram TV 8449012*	26		6
9 Oct 99	**RELOAD** *Gut GUTCD 009* ⊛ **x4**	1	3	65
16 Nov 02	**MR JONES** *V2 VVR 1021072*	36		2
1 Mar 03	**GREATEST HITS** *Universal TV 8828632* ⊛	2		16
9 Oct 04	**TOM JONES AND JOOLS HOLLAND** *Radar RADAR004CD* & JOOLS HOLLAND ●	5		13
29 Nov 08	**24 HOURS** *S-Curve 2649852*	32		6+

Date of entry into chart

Artist collaboration or where artist's name has changed

Album Title — Label and Catalogue Number

Cross (+) indicates album is still on chart in last week of 2008

Silver-selling ○ Gold-selling ● Platinum-selling ⊛ US No.1 ★ | Peak Position | Weeks at No.1 | Weeks on Chart

I AM KLOOT
UK, male vocal/instrumental group

Date	Title / Label	Peak Position	Weeks at No.1	Weeks on Chart (3)
27 Sep 03	**I AM KLOOT** *Echo ECHCD 46*	68		2
23 Apr 05	**GODS AND MONSTERS** *Echo ECHDV62*	74		1

I-LEVEL
UK, male vocal/instrumental group

Date	Title / Label	Peak Position	Weeks at No.1	Weeks on Chart (4)
9 Jul 83	**I-LEVEL** *Virgin V 2270*	50		4

IAN VAN DAHL
Belgium, female/male vocal/production group – Annemie Coenen, Christophe Chantzis, Peter Luts, Erik Vanspauwen & David Vervoort

Date	Title / Label	Peak Position	Weeks at No.1	Weeks on Chart (7)
8 Jun 02	**ACE** *NuLife 74321934812*	7		7

ICE CUBE
US, male rapper/producer/actor (O'Shea Jackson)

Date	Title / Label	Peak Position	Weeks at No.1	Weeks on Chart (11)
28 Jul 90	**AMERIKKA'S MOST WANTED** *Fourth & Broadway BRLP 551*	48		5
9 Mar 91	**KILL AT WILL** *Fourth & Broadway BRLM 572*	66		3
5 Dec 92	**THE PREDATOR** *Fourth & Broadway BRCD 592* ○ ★	73		1
18 Dec 93	**LETHAL INJECTION** *Fourth & Broadway BRCD 609*	52		1
1 Apr 00	**WAR & PEACE – VOLUME II** *Priority CDPTY 183*	56		1

ICE-T
US, male rapper/actor (Tracy Marrow)

Date	Title / Label	Peak Position	Weeks at No.1	Weeks on Chart (15)
21 Oct 89	**THE ICEBERG/FREEDOM OF SPEECH** *Sire WX 316*	42		2
25 May 91	**O.G. ORIGINAL GANGSTER** *Sire WX 412* ○	38		4
3 Apr 93	**HOME INVASION** *Rhyme Syndicate RSYND 1* ●	15		7
8 Jun 96	**VI: RETURN OF THE REAL** *Rhyme Syndicate RSYND 3*	26		2

ICEHOUSE
Australia, male vocal/instrumental group

Date	Title / Label	Peak Position	Weeks at No.1	Weeks on Chart (7)
5 Mar 83	**LOVE IN MOTION** *Chrysalis CHR 1390*	64		6
2 Apr 88	**MAN OF COLOURS** *Chrysalis CHR 1592*	93		1

ICICLE WORKS
UK, male vocal/instrumental group

Date	Title / Label	Peak Position	Weeks at No.1	Weeks on Chart (19)
31 Mar 84	**THE ICICLE WORKS** *Beggars Banquet BEGA 50*	24		6
28 Sep 85	**THE SMALL PRICE OF A BICYCLE** *Beggars Banquet BEGA 61*	55		3
1 Mar 86	**SEVEN SINGLES DEEP** *Beggars Banquet BEGA 71*	52		2
21 Mar 87	**IF YOU WANT TO DEFEAT YOUR ENEMY SING HIS SONG** *Beggars Banquet BEGA 78*	28		4
14 May 88	**BLIND** *Beggars Banquet IWA 2*	40		3
5 Sep 92	**THE BEST OF THE ICICLE WORKS** *Beggars Banquet BEGA 124CD*	60		1

IDLEWILD
UK, male vocal/instrumental group – Roddy Woomble, Bob Fairfoull (replaced by Gareth Russell), Rod Jones, Jeremy Mills (replaced by Allan Stewart) & Colin Newton

Date	Title / Label	Peak Position	Weeks at No.1	Weeks on Chart (18)
7 Nov 98	**HOPE IS IMPORTANT** *Food 4971322*	53		1
22 Apr 00	**100 BROKEN WINDOWS** *Food FOODCD 32* ○	15		4
27 Jul 02	**THE REMOTE PART** *Parlophone 5402432* ●	3		8
19 Mar 05	**WARNINGS/PROMISES** *Parlophone 5607752* ○	9		3
17 Mar 07	**MAKE ANOTHER WORLD** *Sequel SEQCD005*	24		2

BILLY IDOL
UK, male vocalist/guitarist (William Broad). See Generation X

Date	Title / Label	Peak Position	Weeks at No.1	Weeks on Chart (102)
8 Jun 85	**VITAL IDOL** *Chrysalis CUX 1502* ⊛	7		34
28 Sep 85	**REBEL YELL** *Chrysalis CHR 1450* ○	36		11
1 Nov 86	**WHIPLASH SMILE** *Chrysalis CDL 1514* ●	8		20
2 Jul 88	**IDOL SONGS: 11 OF THE BEST** *Chrysalis BILTVD 1* ⊛	2		25
12 May 90	**CHARMED LIFE** *Chrysalis CHR 1735* ○	15		8
10 Jul 93	**CYBERPUNK** *Chrysalis CDCHR 6000*	20		2
2 Aug 08	**THE VERY BEST OF – IDOLIZE YOURSELF** *EMI 2151402*	37		2

FRANK IFIELD
Australia (b. UK), male vocalist

Date	Title / Label	Peak Position	Weeks at No.1	Weeks on Chart (83)
16 Feb 63	**I'LL REMEMBER YOU** *Columbia 33SX 1467*	3		36
21 Sep 63	**BORN FREE** *Columbia 33SX 1462*	3		32
28 Mar 64	**BLUE SKIES** *Columbia 33SX 1588*	10		12
19 Dec 64	**GREATEST HITS** *Columbia 33SX 1633*	9		3

ENRIQUE IGLESIAS
Spain, male vocalist (Enrique Miguel Iglesias Preysler)

Date	Title / Label	Peak Position	Weeks at No.1	Weeks on Chart (120)
26 Jan 02	**ESCAPE** *Interscope 4931822* ⊛x4	1	2	71
6 Dec 03	**SEVEN** *Interscope 9861477* ●	13		13
30 Jun 07	**INSOMNIAC** *Interscope 1734820* ●	3		28
15 Nov 08	**GREATEST HITS** *Interscope 1788453*	3		8+

JULIO IGLESIAS
Spain, male vocalist (Julio Iglesias de la Cueva)

Date	Title / Label	Peak Position	Weeks at No.1	Weeks on Chart (179)
7 Nov 81	**DE NINA A MUJER** *CBS 85063*	43		5
28 Nov 81	**BEGIN THE BEGUINE** *CBS 85462* ●	5		28
16 Oct 82	**AMOR** *CBS 25103* ●	14		14
2 Jul 83	**JULIO** *CBS 10038* ●	5		17
1 Sep 84	**1100 BEL AIR PLACE** *CBS 86308* ○	14		14
19 Oct 85	**LIBRA** *CBS 26623*	61		4
3 Sep 88	**NON STOP** *CBS 4609901* ●	33		14
1 Dec 90	**STARRY NIGHT** *CBS 4672841* ●	27		20
28 May 94	**CRAZY** *Columbia 4747382* ⊛	6		37
12 Aug 95	**LA CARRETERA** *Columbia 4807042*	6		6
30 Nov 96	**TANGO** *Columbia 4866752* ○	56		3
7 Nov 98	**MY LIFE: GREATEST HITS** *Columbia 4910902* ●	18		9
22 Jul 00	**NOCHE DE CUATRO LUNAS** *Columbia 4974222*	32		3
19 Jul 03	**LOVE SONGS** *Columbia 5126042*	64		1
18 Nov 06	**ROMANTIC CLASSICS** *Columbia 88697012812*	42		4

IGLU & HARTLY
US, male vocal/instrumental group

Date	Title / Label	Peak Position	Weeks at No.1	Weeks on Chart (2)
11 Oct 08	**AND THEN BOOM** *Mercury 1778762*	36		2

IL DIVO
Switzerland/France/Spain/US, male vocal group – Urs Bühler, Sébastien Izambard, Carlos Marín & David Miller

Date	Title / Label	Peak Position	Weeks at No.1	Weeks on Chart (85)
13 Nov 04	**IL DIVO** *Syco Music 82876651952* ⊛x4	1	1	40
19 Nov 05	**ANCORA** *Syco Music 82876731062* ⊛x3 ★	1	1	25
9 Dec 06	**SIEMPRE** *Syco Music 88697015522* ⊛x2	2		11
21 Jul 07	**THE COMPLETE COLLECTION** *Syco Music 88697069432*	32		2
22 Nov 08	**THE PROMISE** *Syco Music 88697399682*	1	1	7+

IMAGINATION
UK/Jamaica, male vocal/instrumental trio – Leee John (John McGregor), Ashley Ingram & Errol Kennedy

Date	Title / Label	Peak Position	Weeks at No.1	Weeks on Chart (122)
24 Oct 81	**BODY TALK** *R&B RBLP 1001* ●	20		53
11 Sep 82	**IN THE HEAT OF THE NIGHT** *R&B RBLP 1002* ●	7		29
14 May 83	**NIGHT DUBBING** *R&B RBDUB 1* ●	9		20
12 Nov 83	**SCANDALOUS** *R&B RBLP 1004* ●	25		8
12 Aug 89	**IMAGINATION – ALL THE HITS** *Stylus SMR 985* ●	4		12

NATALIE IMBRUGLIA
Australia, female vocalist/actor

Date	Title / Label	Peak Position	Weeks at No.1	Weeks on Chart (123)
6 Dec 97	**LEFT OF THE MIDDLE** *RCA 74321571382* ⊛x3	5		87
17 Nov 01	**WHITE LILIES ISLAND** *RCA 74321891212* ●	15		15
16 Apr 05	**COUNTING DOWN THE DAYS** *Brightside 82876683712* ●	1	1	16
22 Sep 07	**GLORIOUS – THE SINGLES 97 – 07** *Brightside 88697139762* ●	5		5

IMMACULATE FOOLS
UK, male vocal/instrumental group

Date	Title / Label	Peak Position	Weeks at No.1	Weeks on Chart (2)
11 May 85	**HEARTS OF FORTUNE** *A&M AMA 5030*	65		2

IN FLAMES
Sweden, male vocal/instrumental group

Date	Title / Label	Peak Position	Weeks at No.1	Weeks on Chart (2)
18 Feb 06	**COME CLARITY** *Nuclear Blast NB1309DCD*	67		1
19 Apr 08	**A SENSE OF PURPOSE** *Nuclear Blast NB2083CD*	54		1

Silver-selling ○ · Gold-selling ● · Platinum-selling ⊛ · US No.1 ★ · Peak Position · Weeks at No.1 · Weeks on Chart

IN TUNE

UK, male instrumental duo. See Blowing Free, Harmonium, Hypnosis, Raindance, School Of Excellence — 3

Date	Title	Peak	No.1	Weeks
17 Jun 95	**ACOUSTIC MOODS** *Global Television RADCD 13*	21		3

INCANTATION

UK/Ireland/Chile, male/female instrumental group – members included Sergio Avila, Claudia Figuerora, Forbes Henderson, Tony Hinnigan, Simon Rogers, Chris Swithinbank, Mike Taylor & Mauricio Venegas — 52

Date	Title	Peak	No.1	Weeks
11 Dec 82	**CACHARPAYA (PANPIPES OF THE ANDES)** *Beggars Banquet BEGA 39* ●	9		26
17 Dec 83	**DANCE OF THE FLAMES** *Beggars Banquet BEGA 49*	61		7
28 Dec 85	**THE BEST OF INCANTATION: MUSIC FROM THE ANDES** *West Five CODA 19* ○	28		19

INCOGNITO

UK, male/female vocal/instrumental group — 19

Date	Title	Peak	No.1	Weeks
18 Apr 81	**JAZZ FUNK** *Ensign ENVY 504*	28		8
27 Jul 91	**INSIDE LIFE** *Talkin Loud 8485461*	44		2
4 Jul 92	**TRIBES, VIBES AND SCRIBES** *Talkin Loud 5123632*	41		2
6 Nov 93	**POSITIVITY** *Talkin Loud 5182602*	55		2
17 Jun 95	**100 DEGREES AND RISING** *Talkin Loud 5280002*	11		4
1 Jun 96	**REMIXED** *Talkin Loud 5323092*	56		1

INCREDIBLE STRING BAND

UK, male/female vocal/instrumental group – Robin Williamson, Mike Heron, Licorice McKechnie & Rose Simpson — 37

Date	Title	Peak	No.1	Weeks
21 Oct 67	**5,000 SPIRITS OR THE LAYERS OF THE ONION** *Elektra EUKS 257*	25		5
6 Apr 68	**THE HANGMAN'S BEAUTIFUL DAUGHTER** *Elektra EVKS7 258*	5		21
20 Jul 68	**THE INCREDIBLE STRING BAND** *Elektra EKL 254*	34		3
24 Jan 70	**CHANGING HORSES** *Elektra EKS 74057*	30		1
9 May 70	**I LOOKED UP** *Elektra 2469 002*	30		4
31 Oct 70	**U** *Elektra 2665 001*	34		2
30 Oct 71	**LIQUID ACROBAT AS REGARDS THE AIR** *Island ILPS 9172*	46		1

INCUBUS

US, male vocal/instrumental group – Brandon Boyd, Mike Einziger, Ben Kenney, Chris Kilmore & Jose Pasillas — 9

Date	Title	Peak	No.1	Weeks
3 Nov 01	**MORNING VIEW** *Epic 5040612* ●	15		4
14 Feb 04	**A CROW LEFT OF THE MURDER** *Epic 5150473*	6		4
9 Dec 06	**LIGHT GRENADES** *Epic/Immortal 82876838522* ★	52		1

INDIGO GIRLS

US, female vocal/instrumental duo — 3

Date	Title	Peak	No.1	Weeks
11 Jun 94	**SWAMP OPHELIA** *Epic 4759312*	66		1
15 Jul 95	**4.5 THE BEST OF THE INDIGO GIRLS** *Epic 4804392*	43		2

INFA RIOT

UK, male vocal/instrumental group — 4

Date	Title	Peak	No.1	Weeks
7 Aug 82	**STILL OUT OF ORDER** *Secret SEC 7*	42		4

INFERNAL

Denmark, female/male vocal/production duo — 2

Date	Title	Peak	No.1	Weeks
9 Jun 07	**FROM PARIS TO BERLIN** *Europa(Universal) EUROPA001CD*	44		2

JAMES INGRAM

US, male vocalist — 19

Date	Title	Peak	No.1	Weeks
31 Mar 84	**IT'S YOUR NIGHT** *Warner Brothers 9239701*	25		17
30 Aug 86	**NEVER FELT SO GOOD** *Qwest WX 44*	72		2

INME

UK, male vocal/instrumental group — 4

Date	Title	Peak	No.1	Weeks
8 Feb 03	**OVERGROWN EDEN** *Music For Nations CDMFN275*	15		2
2 Jul 05	**WHITE BUTTERFLY** *V2 PBCDS001NME*	56		1
22 Sep 07	**DAYDREAM ANONYMOUS** *Graphite GRAPHFAR02CD*	71		1

INNER CIRCLE

Jamaica, male vocal/instrumental group — 2

Date	Title	Peak	No.1	Weeks
29 May 93	**BAD TO THE BONE** *Magnet 9031776772*	44		2

INNER CITY

US, female/male vocal/production duo – Paris Grey & Kevin Saunderson — 39

Date	Title	Peak	No.1	Weeks
20 May 89	**PARADISE** *10 Records DIX 81* ⊛	3		30
10 Feb 90	**PARADISE REMIXED** *10 Records XID 81*	17		6
11 Jul 92	**PRAISE** *10 Records 4718862*	52		1
15 May 93	**TESTAMENT '93** *10 Records CDOVD 438*	33		2

INNOCENCE

UK, male/female vocal/instrumental group — 20

Date	Title	Peak	No.1	Weeks
10 Nov 90	**BELIEF** *Cooltempo CTLP 20* ●	24		19
31 Oct 92	**BUILD** *Cooltempo CTCD 26*	66		1

INSPIRAL CARPETS

UK, male vocal/instrumental group – Tom Hingley, Clint Boon, Craig Gill, Graham Lambert & Martyn Walsh — 37

Date	Title	Peak	No.1	Weeks
5 May 90	**LIFE** *Cow DUNG 8*	2		21
4 May 91	**THE BEAST INSIDE** *Cow DUNG 14* ○	5		6
17 Oct 92	**REVENGE OF THE GOLDFISH** *Cow DUNG 19*	17		3
19 Mar 94	**DEVIL HOPPING** *Cow LDUNG 25CD*	10		3
30 Sep 95	**THE SINGLES** *Cow CDMOOTEL 3*	17		3
31 May 03	**COOL AS** *Mute DUNG30CD*	65		1

INSPIRATIONAL CHOIR

US, male/female choir — 4

Date	Title	Peak	No.1	Weeks
18 Jan 86	**SWEET INSPIRATION** *Portrait PRT 10048*	59		4

INSPIRATIONS

UK, male keyboard player (Neil Palmer) — 35

Date	Title	Peak	No.1	Weeks
29 Apr 95	**PAN PIPE INSPIRATIONS** *Pure Music PMCD 7011*	10		10
23 Sep 95	**PAN PIPE DREAMS** *Pure Music PMCD 7016*	10		8
11 Nov 95	**PURE EMOTIONS** *Pure Music PMCD 7023*	37		4
6 Apr 96	**PAN PIPE IMAGES** *Telstar TCD 2819*	23		6
12 Oct 96	**THE VERY BEST OF THE PAN PIPES** *Telstar TCD 2845*	37		7

INTERPOL

US, male vocal/instrumental group — 8

Date	Title	Peak	No.1	Weeks
9 Oct 04	**ANTICS** *Matador OLE6162* ○	21		3
21 Jul 07	**OUR LOVE TO ADMIRE** *Capitol 3962492*	2		5

INTI ILLIMANI-GUAMARY

Chile, male vocal/panpipe group — 7

Date	Title	Peak	No.1	Weeks
17 Dec 83	**THE FLIGHT OF THE CONDOR (OST-TV)** *BBC REB 440*	62		7

INXS

Australia, male vocal/instrumental group – Michael Hutchence, d. 22 Nov 1997, Garry Beers, Andrew, Jon & Tim Farriss & Kirk Pengilly — 240

Date	Title	Peak	No.1	Weeks
8 Feb 86	**LISTEN LIKE THIEVES** *Mercury MERH 82*	48		15
28 Nov 87	**KICK** *Mercury MERH 114* ⊛x3	9		103
6 Oct 90	**X** *Mercury 8466681* ⊛	2		44
16 Nov 91	**LIVE BABY LIVE** *Mercury 5105801*	8		9
15 Aug 92	**WELCOME TO WHEREVER YOU ARE** *Mercury 5125072* ●	1	1	33
13 Nov 93	**FULL MOON, DIRTY HEARTS** *Mercury 5186382* ●	3		8
12 Nov 94	**INXS – THE GREATEST HITS** *Mercury 5262302* ⊛	3		22
19 Apr 97	**ELEGANTLY WASTED** *Mercury 5346132*	16		3
26 Oct 02	**DEFINITIVE** *Mercury 0633562*	15		3

IQ

UK, male vocal/instrumental group — 1

Date	Title	Peak	No.1	Weeks
22 Jun 85	**THE WAKE** *Sahara SAH 136*	72		1

IRON AND WINE

US, male vocalist/guitarist (Samuel Beam) — Weeks on chart: 1

Date	Title / Label	Peak	Wks at No.1	Wks on Chart
6 Oct 07	**THE SHEPHERD'S DOG** *Transgressive 2564697669*	74		1

IRON MAIDEN

UK, male vocal/instrumental group – Bruce Dickinson*, Janick Gers, Steve Harris, Nicko McBrain, Dave Murray & Adrian Smith; members also included Blaze Bayley, Clive Burr & Paul Di'Anno — Weeks on chart: 219

Date	Title / Label	Peak	Wks at No.1	Wks on Chart
26 Apr 80	**IRON MAIDEN** *EMI EMC 3330* ⊛	4		15
28 Feb 81	**KILLERS** *EMI EMC 3357* ●	12		8
10 Apr 82	**THE NUMBER OF THE BEAST** *EMI EMC 3400* ⊛	1	2	31
28 May 83	**PIECE OF MIND** *EMI EMA 800* ⊛	3		18
15 Sep 84	**POWERSLAVE** *EMI POWER 1* ●	2		13
15 Jun 85	**IRON MAIDEN** *Fame FA 4131211*	71		2
26 Oct 85	**LIVE AFTER DEATH** *EMI RIP 1* ●	2		14
11 Oct 86	**SOMEWHERE IN TIME** *EMI EMC 3512* ●	3		11
20 Jun 87	**THE NUMBER OF THE BEAST** *Fame FA 3178*	98		1
23 Apr 88	**SEVENTH SON OF A SEVENTH SON** *EMI EMD 1006* ●	1	1	18
24 Feb 90	**RUNNING/SANCTUARY** *EMI IRN 1*	10		4
3 Mar 90	**WOMEN IN UNIFORM/TWILIGHT ZONE** *EMI IRN 2*	10		3
10 Mar 90	**PURGATORY/MAIDEN JAPAN** *EMI IRN 3*	5		3
17 Mar 90	**RUN TO THE HILLS/THE NUMBER OF THE BEAST** *EMI IRN 4*	3		2
24 Mar 90	**FLIGHT OF ICARUS/THE TROOPER** *EMI IRN 5*	7		2
31 Mar 90	**2 MINUTES TO MIDNIGHT/ACES HIGH** *EMI IRN 6*	11		2
7 Apr 90	**RUNNING FREE (LIVE)/RUN TO THE HILLS (LIVE)** *EMI IRN 7*	9		2
14 Apr 90	**WASTED YEARS/STRANGER IN A STRANGE LAND** *EMI IRN 8*	9		2
21 Apr 90	**CAN I PLAY WITH MADNESS/THE EVIL THAT MEN DO** *EMI IRN 9*	10		3
28 Apr 90	**THE CLAIRVOYANT/INFINITE DREAMS (LIVE)** *EMI IRN 10*	11		2
13 Oct 90	**NO PRAYER FOR THE DYING** *EMI EMD 1017* ●	2		14
23 May 92	**FEAR OF THE DARK** *EMI CDEMD 1032* ●	1	1	5
3 Apr 93	**A REAL LIVE ONE** *EMI CDEMD 1042*	3		4
30 Oct 93	**A REAL DEAD ONE** *EMI CDEMD 1048*	12		3
20 Nov 93	**LIVE AT DONNINGTON** *EMI CDDON 1*	23		1
14 Oct 95	**THE X FACTOR** *EMI CDEMD 1087*	8		4
5 Oct 96	**THE BEST OF THE BEAST** *EMI CDEMDX 1097* ○	16		5
4 Apr 98	**VIRTUAL XI** *EMI 4939152*	16		2
10 Jun 00	**BRAVE NEW WORLD** *EMI 5266052* ●	7		4
6 Apr 02	**ROCK IN RIO** *EMI 5386430*	15		3
16 Nov 02	**EDWARD THE GREAT – THE GREATEST HITS** *EMI 05431032* ●	57		1
20 Sep 03	**DANCE OF DEATH** *EMI 5923402* ○	2		5
10 Sep 05	**DEATH ON THE ROAD** *EMI 3364372* ○	22		2
9 Sep 06	**A MATTER OF LIFE AND DEATH** *EMI 3723212* ●	4		5
30 Sep 06	**THE NUMBER OF THE BEAST** *EMI 4969180*	54		2
24 May 08	**SOMEWHERE BACK IN TIME – THE BEST OF** *EMI 2147072*	14		3

IRONIK

UK, male vocalist/rapper/DJ (Michael Laurence) — Weeks on chart: 3

Date	Title / Label	Peak	Wks at No.1	Wks on Chart
11 Oct 08	**NO POINT IN WASTING TEARS** *Asylum 2564693494*	21		3

GREGORY ISAACS

Jamaica, male vocalist — Weeks on chart: 6

Date	Title / Label	Peak	Wks at No.1	Wks on Chart
12 Sep 81	**MORE GREGORY** *Pre PREX 9*	93		1
4 Sep 82	**NIGHT NURSE** *Island ILPS 9721*	32		5

CHRIS ISAAK

US, male vocalist/guitarist — Weeks on chart: 39

Date	Title / Label	Peak	Wks at No.1	Wks on Chart
26 Jan 91	**WICKED GAME** *Reprise WX 406* ⊛	3		30
24 Apr 93	**SAN FRANCISCO DAYS** *Reprise 9362451162* ○	12		5
3 Jun 95	**FOREVER BLUE** *Reprise 9362458452*	27		3
30 Sep 06	**THE BEST OF** *Reprise 9362494182*	65		1

ISLEY BROTHERS

US, male vocal/instrumental group — Weeks on chart: 25

Date	Title / Label	Peak	Wks at No.1	Wks on Chart
14 Dec 68	**THIS OLD HEART OF MINE** *Tamla Motown STML 11034*	23		6
14 Aug 76	**HARVEST FOR THE WORLD** *Epic EPC 81268*	50		5
14 May 77	**GO FOR YOUR GUNS** *Epic EPC 86027*	46		2
24 Jun 78	**SHOWDOWN** *Epic EPC 86039*	50		1
5 Mar 88	**GREATEST HITS** *Telstar STAR 2306*	41		10
30 Jul 05	**SUMMER BREEZE – GREATEST HITS** *Epic 5204612*	69		1

IT BITES

UK, male vocal/instrumental group — Weeks on chart: 12

Date	Title / Label	Peak	Wks at No.1	Wks on Chart
6 Sep 86	**THE BIG LAD IN THE WINDMILL** *Virgin V 2378*	35		5
2 Apr 88	**ONCE AROUND THE WORLD** *Virgin V 2456*	43		3
24 Jun 89	**EAT ME IN ST LOUIS** *Virgin V 2591*	40		3
31 Aug 91	**THANK YOU AND GOODNIGHT** *Virgin VGD 24233*	59		1

IT'S A BEAUTIFUL DAY

US, male/female vocal/instrumental group — Weeks on chart: 3

Date	Title / Label	Peak	Wks at No.1	Wks on Chart
23 May 70	**IT'S A BEAUTIFUL DAY** *CBS 63722*	58		1
11 Jul 70	**MARRYING MAIDEN** *CBS 66236*	45		2

IT'S IMMATERIAL

UK, male vocal/instrumental group — Weeks on chart: 3

Date	Title / Label	Peak	Wks at No.1	Wks on Chart
27 Sep 86	**LIFE'S HARD AND THEN YOU DIE** *Siren SIRENLP 4*	62		3

BON IVER

US, male vocal/instrumental group — Weeks on chart: 3

Date	Title / Label	Peak	Wks at No.1	Wks on Chart
24 May 08	**FOR EMMA FOREVER AGO** *4AD CAD2809CD*	42		3

J

JA RULE

US, male rapper/actor (Jeffrey Atkins) — Weeks on chart: 69

Date	Title / Label	Peak	Wks at No.1	Wks on Chart
27 Oct 01	**PAIN IS LOVE** *Def Jam 5864372* ⊛ ★	3		50
30 Nov 02	**THE LAST TEMPTATION** *Def Jam 0635432* ●	14		13
15 Nov 03	**BLOOD IN MY EYE** *Def Jam 9861329*	51		2
20 Nov 04	**RULE** *Def Jam 9862918* ○	33		2
21 Jan 06	**EXODUS** *The Inc 9887328*	50		2

ALAN JACKSON

US, male vocalist/guitarist — Weeks on chart: 2

Date	Title / Label	Peak	Wks at No.1	Wks on Chart
3 Jul 04	**THE VERY BEST OF** *Arista Nashville 82876601122*	47		2

FREDDIE JACKSON

US, male vocalist — Weeks on chart: 48

Date	Title / Label	Peak	Wks at No.1	Wks on Chart
18 May 85	**ROCK ME TONIGHT** *Capitol EJ 2403161* ○	27		22
8 Nov 86	**JUST LIKE THE FIRST TIME** *Capitol EST 2023*	30		15
30 Jul 88	**DON'T LET LOVE SLIP AWAY** *Capitol EST 2067*	24		9
17 Nov 90	**DO ME AGAIN** *Capitol EST 2134*	48		2

JANET JACKSON

US, female vocalist — Weeks on chart: 272

Date	Title / Label	Peak	Wks at No.1	Wks on Chart
5 Apr 86	**CONTROL** *A&M AMA 5106* ⊛ ★	8		72
14 Nov 87	**CONTROL – THE REMIXES** *Breakout MIXLP 1* ●	20		14
30 Sep 89	**RHYTHM NATION 1814** *A&M AMA 3920* ⊛ ★	4		43
29 May 93	**JANET** *Virgin CDV 2720* ⊛x2 ★	1	2	57
14 Oct 95	**DESIGN OF A DECADE 1986 – 1996** *A&M 5404222* ⊛x2	2		21
18 Oct 97	**THE VELVET ROPE** *Virgin CDV 2860* ⊛ ★	6		43
5 May 01	**ALL FOR YOU** *Virgin CDVX 2950* ● ★	2		18
10 Apr 04	**DAMITA JO** *Virgin CDVUS 251* ○	32		2
7 Oct 06	**20 Y.O.** *Virgin CDVUS258*	63		1
8 Mar 08	**DISCIPLINE** *Mercury 1762969* ★	63		1

JERMAINE JACKSON

US, male vocalist. See Jacksons — Weeks on chart: 12

Date	Title / Label	Peak	Wks at No.1	Wks on Chart
31 May 80	**LET'S GET SERIOUS** *Motown STML 12127*	22		6
12 May 84	**DYNAMITE** *Arista 206 317*	57		6

JOE JACKSON

UK, male vocalist/pianist — Weeks on chart: 107

Date	Title / Label	Peak	Wks at No.1	Wks on Chart
17 Mar 79	**LOOK SHARP** *A&M AMLH 64743* ○	40		11
13 Oct 79	**I'M THE MAN** *A&M AMLH 64794* ●	12		16
18 Oct 80	**BEAT CRAZY** *A&M AMLH 64837*	42		3
4 Jul 81	**JUMPIN' JIVE** *A&M AMLH 68530* 'S JUMPIN' JIVE	14		14

Key: ○ Silver-selling · ● Gold-selling · ⊛ Platinum-selling · ★ US No.1 · Peak Position · Weeks at No.1 · Weeks on Chart

Date	Title / Label	Peak Position	Weeks at No.1	Weeks on Chart
3 Jul 82	**NIGHT AND DAY** *A&M AMLH 64906* ●	3		27
7 Apr 84	**BODY AND SOUL** *A&M AMLX 65000* ○	14		14
5 Apr 86	**BIG WORLD** *A&M JWA 3*	41		5
7 May 88	**LIVE 1980 – 1986** *A&M AMA 6706*	66		2
29 Apr 89	**BLAZE OF GLORY** *A&M AMA 5249*	36		3
15 Sep 90	**STEPPING OUT – THE VERY BEST OF JOE JACKSON** *A&M 3970521* ●	7		9
11 May 91	**LAUGHTER AND LUST** *Virgin America VUSLP 34*	41		2
9 Jun 07	**THE VERY BEST OF JOE JACKSON** *Universal TV 9842273*	60		1

LEON JACKSON

UK, male vocalist

Total weeks on chart: 9

Date	Title / Label	Peak Position	Weeks at No.1	Weeks on Chart
1 Nov 08	**RIGHT NOW** *Syco 88697395242*	4		9

MICHAEL JACKSON

US, male vocalist. The headline-grabbing 'King of Pop' recorded the world's biggest-selling album, *Thriller*, which has sold more than 50 million copies. *HIStory* was the fastest-selling double-album and *Dangerous* sold 10 million copies worldwide in the first month. See Jacksons

Total weeks on chart: 1028

Date	Title / Label	Peak Position	Weeks at No.1	Weeks on Chart
3 Jun 72	**GOT TO BE THERE** *Tamla Motown STML 11205*	37		5
13 Jan 73	**BEN** *Tamla Motown STML 11220* ○	17		7
29 Sep 79	**OFF THE WALL** *Epic EPC 84368* ⊛x6	5		189
4 Jul 81	**BEST OF MICHAEL JACKSON** *Motown STMR 9009* ○	11		18
18 Jul 81	**ONE DAY IN YOUR LIFE** *Motown STML 12158*	29		8
11 Dec 82	**THRILLER** *Epic EPC 85930* ⊛x11 ★	1	8	201
12 Feb 83	**E.T. THE EXTRA TERRESTRIAL** *MCA 7000*	82		2
9 Jul 83	**18 GREATEST HITS** *Telstar STAR 2232* PLUS THE JACKSON FIVE ⊛	1	3	58
3 Dec 83	**MICHAEL JACKSON 9 SINGLE PACK** *Epic MJ 1*	66		3
9 Jun 84	**FAREWELL MY SUMMER LOVE** *Motown ZL 72227* ●	9		14
15 Nov 86	**DIANA ROSS. MICHAEL JACKSON. GLADYS KNIGHT. STEVIE WONDER. THEIR VERY BEST BACK TO BACK** *PrioriTyV PTVR2* DIANA ROSS/MICHAEL JACKSON/GLADYS KNIGHT/STEVIE WONDER	21		10
12 Sep 87	**BAD** *Epic EPC 4502901* ⊛x13 ★	1	5	125
31 Oct 87	**LOVE SONGS** *Telstar STAR 2298* DIANA ROSS & MICHAEL JACKSON ⊛	12		24
26 Dec 87	**THE MICHAEL JACKSON MIX** *Stylus SMR 745* ⊛	27		25
30 Jul 88	**SOUVENIR SINGLES PACK** *Epic MJ 5*	91		1
30 Nov 91	**DANGEROUS** *Epic 4658021* ⊛x6 ★	1	1	96
29 Feb 92	**MOTOWN'S GREATEST HITS** *Motown 5300142*	53		2
15 Aug 92	**TOUR SOUVENIR PACK** *Epic MJ 4*	32		3
24 Jun 95	**HISTORY – PAST PRESENT AND FUTURE BOOK 1** *Epic 4747092* ⊛x4 ★	1	1	78
24 May 97	**BLOOD ON THE DANCE FLOOR – HISTORY IN THE MIX** *Epic 4875002* ●	1	2	16
19 Jul 97	**THE BEST OF MICHAEL JACKSON AND THE JACKSON FIVE** *Polygram TV 5308042* & THE JACKSON FIVE ●	5		12
10 Nov 01	**INVINCIBLE** *Epic 4951782* ⊛ ★	1	1	12
24 Nov 01	**GREATEST HITS – HISTORY VOLUME 1** *Epic 5018692*	15		16
29 Nov 03	**NUMBER ONES** *Epic 5138002* ⊛x4	1	1	57
4 Dec 04	**THE ULTIMATE COLLECTION** *Epic 5177433*	75		2
30 Jul 05	**THE ESSENTIAL** *Epic 5204222*	2		10
23 Feb 08	**THRILLER – 25TH ANNIVERSARY EDITION** *Epic 88697179862*	3		18
6 Sep 08	**KING OF POP** *Epic 88697356512*	3		14+
13 Sep 08	**THE MOTOWN YEARS** *Motown 5311546* & THE JACKSON FIVE	34		2

Top 3 Best-Selling Albums

	Album	Approximate Sales
1	THRILLER	3,870,000
2	BAD	3,570,000
3	DANGEROUS	2,165,000

MILLIE JACKSON

US, female vocalist

Total weeks on chart: 7

Date	Title / Label	Peak Position	Weeks at No.1	Weeks on Chart
18 Feb 84	**E.S.P.** *Sire 250382*	59		5
6 Apr 85	**LIVE AND UNCENSORED** *Important TADLP 001*	81		2

JACKSON FIVE

US, male vocal group – Michael (Michael Jackson*), Jackie, Jermaine (Jermaine Jackson*), Marlon, Randy (joined 1977) & Tito Jackson

Total weeks on chart: 164

Date	Title / Label	Peak Position	Weeks at No.1	Weeks on Chart
21 Mar 70	**DIANA ROSS PRESENTS THE JACKSON FIVE** *Tamla Motown STML 11142*	16		4
15 Aug 70	**ABC** *Tamla Motown STML 11156*	22		6
7 Oct 72	**GREATEST HITS** *Tamla Motown STML 11212* ○	26		14
18 Nov 72	**LOOKIN' THROUGH THE WINDOWS** *Tamla Motown STML 11214* ○	16		8
16 Jul 77	**THE JACKSONS** *Epic EPC 86009* JACKSONS	54		1
3 Dec 77	**GOIN' PLACES** *Epic EPC 86035* JACKSONS	45		1
5 May 79	**DESTINY** *Epic EPC 83200* JACKSONS	33		7
11 Oct 80	**TRIUMPH** *Epic EPC 86112* JACKSONS ●	13		16
12 Dec 81	**THE JACKSONS LIVE** *Epic EPC 88562* JACKSONS	53		9
9 Jul 83	**18 GREATEST HITS** *Telstar STAR 2232* MICHAEL JACKSON PLUS THE JACKSON FIVE ⊛	1	3	58
21 Jul 84	**VICTORY** *Epic EPC 86303* JACKSONS ●	3		13
1 Jul 89	**2300 JACKSON ST** *Epic 4633521* JACKSONS	39		3
19 Jul 97	**THE BEST OF MICHAEL JACKSON AND THE JACKSON FIVE** *Polygram TV 5308042* MICHAEL JACKSON & THE JACKSON FIVE ●	5		12
10 Jul 04	**THE VERY BEST OF** *Sony TV/Universal TV 5163669* JACKSONS ●	7		10
13 Sep 08	**THE MOTOWN YEARS** *Motown 5311546* MICHAEL JACKSON & THE JACKSON FIVE	34		2

JADAKISS

US, male rapper (Jason Phillips)

Total weeks on chart: 1

Date	Title / Label	Peak Position	Weeks at No.1	Weeks on Chart
3 Jul 04	**KISS OF DEATH** *Interscope 9862661* ★	65		1

JADE

US, female vocal group

Total weeks on chart: 3

Date	Title / Label	Peak Position	Weeks at No.1	Weeks on Chart
29 May 93	**JADE TO THE MAX** *Giant 74321148002*	43		3

MICK JAGGER

UK, male vocalist. See Rolling Stones

Total weeks on chart: 25

Date	Title / Label	Peak Position	Weeks at No.1	Weeks on Chart
16 Mar 85	**SHE'S THE BOSS** *CBS 86310* ○	6		11
26 Sep 87	**PRIMITIVE COOL** *CBS 4601231*	26		5
20 Feb 93	**WANDERING SPIRIT** *Atlantic 7567824362*	12		4
1 Dec 01	**GODDESS IN THE DOORWAY** *Virgin CDVUS 214* ○	44		4
13 Oct 07	**THE VERY BEST OF MICK JAGGER** *Atlantic 8122799610*	57		1

JAHEIM

US, male rapper (Jaheim Hoagland)

Total weeks on chart: 1

Date	Title / Label	Peak Position	Weeks at No.1	Weeks on Chart
7 Apr 01	**GHETTO LOVE** *WEA 9362474522*	50		1

JAIMESON

UK, male producer(Jamie Williams)

Total weeks on chart: 2

Date	Title / Label	Peak Position	Weeks at No.1	Weeks on Chart
21 Feb 04	**THINK ON YOUR FEET** *V2/J-Did JAD1021722*	42		2

JAKATTA

UK, male producer (Dave Lee)

Total weeks on chart: 4

Date	Title / Label	Peak Position	Weeks at No.1	Weeks on Chart
26 Oct 02	**VISIONS** *Rulin' RULINCD 01* ○	12		4

JAM

UK, male vocal/instrumental trio – Paul Weller*, Rick Buckler & Bruce Foxton*

Total weeks on chart: 212

Date	Title / Label	Peak Position	Weeks at No.1	Weeks on Chart
28 May 77	**IN THE CITY** *Polydor 2383 447*	20		18
26 Nov 77	**THIS IS THE MODERN WORLD** *Polydor 2383 475* ○	22		5
11 Nov 78	**ALL MOD CONS** *Polydor POLD 5008* ●	6		17
24 Nov 79	**SETTING SONS** *Polydor POLD 5028* ●	4		19
6 Dec 80	**SOUND EFFECTS** *Polydor POLD 5035* ●	2		19
20 Mar 82	**THE GIFT** *Polydor POLD 5055* ●	1	1	24
18 Dec 82	**DIG THE NEW BREED** *Polydor POLD 5075* ●	2		15
27 Aug 83	**IN THE CITY (REISSUE)** *Polydor SPELP 27*	100		1
22 Oct 83	**SNAP** *Polydor SNAP 1* ⊛	2		30
13 Jul 91	**GREATEST HITS** *Polydor 8495541* ●	2		21
18 Apr 92	**EXTRAS** *Polydor 5131772*	15		4
6 Nov 93	**LIVE JAM** *Polydor 5196672*	28		2
27 Jul 96	**THE JAM COLLECTION** *Polydor 5314932*	58		1
7 Jun 97	**DIRECTION REACTION CREATION** *Polydor 5371432*	8		4
25 Oct 97	**THE VERY BEST OF THE JAM** *Polydor 5374232*	9		10
18 May 02	**THE SOUND OF** *Polydor 5897812* ●	3		8
15 Jun 02	**AT THE BBC** *Polydor 5896902*	33		2
2 Jul 05	**COMPACT SNAP** *Polydor 8217122*	39		4
25 Feb 06	**SNAP!** *Polydor 9877182* ●	8		7
17 Jun 06	**ALL MOD CONS** *Polydor 9839238*	62		1

JAM & SPOON

Germany, male production duo & US, female vocalist (Plavka Lonich)

Total weeks on chart: 1

Date	Title / Label	Peak Position	Weeks at No.1	Weeks on Chart
19 Feb 94	**TRIPTOMATIC FAIRYTALES** *Epic 4749282*	71		1

JAMELIA
UK, female vocalist (Jamelia Davis) — Weeks on Chart: 52

Date	Title / Label	Peak	Wks No.1	Wks
8 Jul 00	**DRAMA** *Parlophone Rhythm Series 5272272*	39		3
11 Oct 03	**THANK YOU** *Parlophone 5837772* ⊛	4		43
7 Oct 06	**WALK WITH ME** *Parlophone 3735522* ●	20		5
6 Oct 07	**SUPERSTAR – THE HITS** *Parlophone 5071562*	55		1

JAMES
UK, male vocal/instrumental group – Tim Booth (Booth & The Bad Angel*), David Baynton-Power, Saul Davies, Andy Diagram, Jim Glennie, Larry Gott & Mark Hunter — Weeks on Chart: 162

Date	Title / Label	Peak	Wks No.1	Wks
2 Aug 86	**STUTTER** *Blanco Y Negro JIMLP 1*	68		2
8 Oct 88	**STRIP MINE** *Sire JIMLP 2*	90		1
16 Jun 90	**GOLD MOTHER** *Fontana 8485951* ●	2		34
29 Feb 92	**SEVEN** *Fontana 5109322* ●	2		14
9 Oct 93	**LAID** *Fontana 5149432* ○	3		16
24 Sep 94	**WAH WAH** *Fontana 5228272* & BRIAN ENO	11		2
8 Mar 97	**WHIPLASH** *Fontana 5343542* ●	9		19
4 Apr 98	**THE BEST OF JAMES** *Fontana 5368982* ⊛	1	1	53
23 Oct 99	**MILLIONAIRES** *Mercury 5467892* ●	2		11
14 Jul 01	**PLEASED TO MEET YOU** *Mercury 5861462* ○	11		3
12 May 07	**FRESH AS A DAISY – THE SINGLES** *Mercury 1731846*	12		4
19 Apr 08	**HEY MA** *Mercury 1764287*	10		3

DUNCAN JAMES
UK, male vocalist. See Blue — Weeks on Chart: 1

Date	Title / Label	Peak	Wks No.1	Wks
24 Jun 06	**FUTURE PAST** *Innocent CDSIN21*	55		1

RICK JAMES
US, male vocalist (James Johnson), d. 6 Aug 2004 (age 56) — Weeks on Chart: 2

Date	Title / Label	Peak	Wks No.1	Wks
24 Jul 82	**THROWIN' DOWN** *Motown STML 12167*	93		2

WENDY JAMES
UK, female vocalist. See Transvision Vamp — Weeks on Chart: 1

Date	Title / Label	Peak	Wks No.1	Wks
20 Mar 93	**NOW AIN'T THE TIME FOR YOUR TEARS** *MCA MCD 10800*	43		1

JAMIROQUAI
UK, male vocal/instrumental group – Jay Kay (Jason Cheetham), Derrick McKenzie and various musicians; members also included Wallis Buchanan, Nick Fyffe, Matt Johnson, Mike & Toby Smith & Stuart Zender — Weeks on Chart: 258

Date	Title / Label	Peak	Wks No.1	Wks
26 Jun 93	**EMERGENCY ON PLANET EARTH** *Sony S2 4740692* ⊛	1	3	32
29 Oct 94	**THE RETURN OF THE SPACE COWBOY** *Sony S2 4778132* ⊛	2		29
21 Sep 96	**TRAVELLING WITHOUT MOVING** *Sony S2 4839992* ⊛x3	2		74
26 Jun 99	**SYNKRONIZED** *Sony S2 4945172* ⊛	1	1	29
15 Sep 01	**A FUNK ODYSSEY** *Sony S2 5040692* ⊛x2	1	2	51
2 Jul 05	**DYNAMITE** *Sony Music 5201112* ⊛	3		17
18 Nov 06	**HIGH TIMES SINGLES 1992–2006** *Columbia 88697019962* ⊛x2	1	1	26

JAN & DEAN
US, male vocal duo – Jan Berry, d. 27 Mar 2004, & Dean Torrence — Weeks on Chart: 2

Date	Title / Label	Peak	Wks No.1	Wks
12 Jul 80	**THE JAN AND DEAN STORY** *K-Tel NE 1084*	67		2

JANE'S ADDICTION
US, male vocal/instrumental group — Weeks on Chart: 5

Date	Title / Label	Peak	Wks No.1	Wks
8 Sep 90	**RITUAL DE LO HABITUAL** *Warner Brothers WX 306* ●	37		2
2 Aug 03	**STRAYS** *Parlophone 5921980* ○	14		3

JAPAN
UK, male vocal/instrumental group – David Sylvian*, Richard Barbieri, Rob Dean, Steve Jansen & Mick Karn — Weeks on Chart: 135

Date	Title / Label	Peak	Wks No.1	Wks
9 Feb 80	**QUIET LIFE** *Ariola Hansa AHAL 8011* ●	53		8
15 Nov 80	**GENTLEMEN TAKE POLAROIDS** *Virgin V 2180* ●	45		10
26 Sep 81	**ASSEMBLAGE** *Hansa HANLP 1* ●	26		46
28 Nov 81	**TIN DRUM** *Virgin V 2209* ●	12		50
18 Jun 83	**OIL ON CANVAS** *Virgin VD 2513* ●	5		14
8 Dec 84	**EXORCISING GHOSTS** *Virgin VGD 3510* ●	45		7

JEFF JARRATT & DON REEDMAN
UK, male producers — Weeks on Chart: 8

Date	Title / Label	Peak	Wks No.1	Wks
22 Nov 80	**MASTERWORKS** *K-Tel ONE 1093* ○	39		8

JEAN-MICHEL JARRE
France, male synthesizer player/composer/producer — Weeks on Chart: 243

Date	Title / Label	Peak	Wks No.1	Wks
20 Aug 77	**OXYGENE** *Polydor 2310 555* ⊛	2		24
16 Dec 78	**EQUINOXE** *Polydor POLD 5007* ●	11		26
6 Jun 81	**MAGNETIC FIELDS** *Polydor POLS 1033* ●	6		17
15 May 82	**THE CONCERTS IN CHINA** *Polydor PODV 3* ●	6		17
12 Nov 83	**THE ESSENTIAL JEAN-MICHEL JARRE** *Polydor PROLP 3* ●	14		29
24 Nov 84	**ZOOLOOK** *Polydor POLH 15* ○	47		14
12 Apr 86	**RENDEZ-VOUS** *Polydor POLH 27*	9		38
18 Jul 87	**IN CONCERT LYONS/HOUSTON** *Polydor POLH 36* ○	18		15
8 Oct 88	**REVOLUTIONS** *Polydor POLH 45* ●	2		13
14 Oct 89	**JARRE LIVE** *Polydor 8412581* ○	16		4
23 Jun 90	**WAITING FOR COUSTEAU** *Dreyfus 8436141*	14		10
26 Oct 91	**IMAGES – THE BEST OF JEAN-MICHEL JARRE** *Dreyfus 5113061* ●	14		12
5 Jun 93	**CHRONOLOGIE** *Polydor 5193732*	11		8
28 May 94	**CHRONOLOGIE PART 6** *Polydor 5195792*	60		1
1 Mar 97	**OXYGENE 7–13** *Epic 4869842*	11		5
23 May 98	**ODYSSEY THROUGH 02** *Epic 4897642*	50		2
12 Feb 00	**METAMORPHOSES** *Epic 4960222*	37		1
2 Oct 04	**AERO** *WSM 2564618512* ●	14		7

MAURICE JARRE
France, male composer/conductor — Weeks on Chart: 106

Date	Title / Label	Peak	Wks No.1	Wks
10 Sep 66	**DOCTOR ZHIVAGO (OST)** *MGM C 8007*	3		106

AL JARREAU
US, male vocalist — Weeks on Chart: 37

Date	Title / Label	Peak	Wks No.1	Wks
5 Sep 81	**BREAKING AWAY** *Warner Brothers K 56917*	60		8
30 Apr 83	**JARREAU** *Warner International U 0070*	39		18
17 Nov 84	**HIGH CRIME** *WEA 2508071*	81		1
13 Sep 86	**L IS FOR LOVER** *WEA International 2530801*	45		10

JAVINE
UK, female vocalist (Javine Hylton) — Weeks on Chart: 1

Date	Title / Label	Peak	Wks No.1	Wks
10 Jul 04	**SURRENDER** *Innocent CDSIN15*	73		1

JAY-Z
US, male rapper (Shawn Carter) — Weeks on Chart: 45

Date	Title / Label	Peak	Wks No.1	Wks
29 Sep 01	**THE BLUEPRINT** *Roc-A-Fella/Def Jam 5863962* ● ★	30		4
30 Mar 02	**THE BEST OF BOTH WORLDS** *Jive 9223512* R KELLY & JAY-Z	37		2
30 Mar 02	**CHAPTER ONE** *Roc-A-Fella 74321920462*	65		1
30 Nov 02	**THE BLUEPRINT 2 THE GIFT & THE CURSE** *Def Jam 0633812* ● ★	23		7
29 Nov 03	**THE BLACK ALBUM** *Roc-A-Fella 9861121* ● ★	34		7
6 Nov 04	**UNFINISHED BUSINESS** *Jive 82876658682* R KELLY & JAY-Z ★	61		1
11 Dec 04	**COLLISION COURSE** *WEA 9362489662* & LINKIN PARK ⊛ ★	15		16
9 Dec 06	**KINGDOM COME** *Roc-A-Fella B000804700CD* ★	35		4
17 Nov 07	**AMERICAN GANGSTER** *Def Jam 1749989* ★	30		3

JAYHAWKS
US, male/female vocal/instrumental group — Weeks on Chart: 4

Date	Title / Label	Peak	Wks No.1	Wks
25 Feb 95	**TOMORROW THE GREEN GRASS** *American Recordings 74321236802*	41		1
3 May 97	**SOUND OF LIES** *American Recordings 4917962*	61		1
20 May 00	**SMILE** *Columbia 4979712*	60		1
19 Apr 03	**RAINY DAY MUSIC** *American Recordings 0771362*	70		1

DJ JAZZY JEFF & THE FRESH PRINCE
US, male rap/DJ duo — Weeks on Chart: 15

Date	Title / Label	Peak	Wks No.1	Wks
28 Feb 87	**ROCK THE HOUSE** *Champion CHAMP 1004*	97		1
21 May 88	**HE'S THE DJ, I'M THE RAPPER** *Jive HIP 61*	68		2
14 Sep 91	**HOMEBASE** *Jive HIP 116*	69		1
11 Dec 93	**CODE RED** *Jive CHIP 140* JAZZY JEFF & THE FRESH PRINCE	50		6
16 May 98	**GREATEST HITS** *Jive 0518482*	20		5

Key: ○ Silver-selling · ● Gold-selling · ⊛ Platinum-selling · ★ US No.1 · Peak Position · Weeks at No.1 · Weeks on Chart

WYCLEF JEAN
Haiti, male vocalist/rapper/producer. See Fugees

Date	Title	Peak Position	Weeks at No.1	Weeks on Chart: 23
5 Jul 97	**THE CARNIVAL** *Columbia 4874422*	40		6
2 Sep 00	**THE ECLEFTIC – TWO SIDES TO A BOOK** *Columbia 4979792* ●	5		15
20 Jul 02	**MASQUERADE – MESSAGE TO THE STREET** *Columbia 5078542*	30		2

JEFFERSON AIRPLANE
US/UK, female/male vocal/instrumental group

Date	Title	Peak Position	Weeks at No.1	Weeks on Chart: 34
28 Jun 69	**BLESS ITS POINTED LITTLE HEAD** *RCA SF 8019*	38		1
7 Mar 70	**VOLUNTEERS** *RCA SF 8076*	34		7
13 Feb 71	**BLOWS AGAINST THE EMPIRE** *RCA SF 8163* PAUL KANTNER & JEFFERSON AIRPLANE	12		6
2 Oct 71	**BARK** *Grunt FTR 1001*	42		1
2 Sep 72	**LONG JOHN SILVER** *Grunt FTR 1007*	30		1
31 Jul 76	**SPITFIRE** *Grunt RFL 1557* JEFFERSON STARSHIP	30		2
9 Feb 80	**FREEDOM AT POINT ZERO** *Grunt FL 13452* JEFFERSON STARSHIP	22		11
18 Jul 87	**NO PROTECTION** *Grunt 86413* STARSHIP	26		5

JELLYBEAN
US, male producer (John Benitez)

Date	Title	Peak Position	Weeks at No.1	Weeks on Chart: 35
31 Oct 87	**JUST VISITING THIS PLANET** *Chrysalis CHR 1569* ●	15		28
3 Sep 88	**ROCKS THE HOUSE!** *Chrysalis CJB 1* ○	16		7

JELLYFISH
US, male vocal/instrumental group

Date	Title	Peak Position	Weeks at No.1	Weeks on Chart: 2
22 May 93	**SPILT MILK** *Charisma CDCUS 20*	21		2

JEM
UK, female vocalist (Jem Griffiths)

Date	Title	Peak Position	Weeks at No.1	Weeks on Chart: 32
5 Mar 05	**FINALLY WOKEN** *Ato 82876655682* ⊛	6		32

KATHERINE JENKINS
UK, female vocalist

Date	Title	Peak Position	Weeks at No.1	Weeks on Chart: 78
17 Apr 04	**PREMIERE** *UCJ 9866064* ○	31		4
30 Oct 04	**SECOND NATURE** *UCJ 9868047* ⊛	16		28
12 Nov 05	**LIVING A DREAM** *UCJ 4763067* ⊛	4		12
18 Nov 06	**SERENADE** *UCJ 4765718* ⊛	5		15
1 Dec 07	**REJOICE** *UCJ 1749273*	3		9
1 Nov 08	**SACRED ARIAS** *UCJ 4766853*	5		10+

JESUS & MARY CHAIN
UK, male vocal/instrumental group – Jim Reid, Bobby Gillespie, Douglas Hart & William Reid

Date	Title	Peak Position	Weeks at No.1	Weeks on Chart: 40
30 Nov 85	**PSYCHOCANDY** *Blanco Y Negro BYN 7* ●	31		10
12 Sep 87	**DARKLANDS** *Blanco Y Negro BYN 11* ●	5		7
30 Apr 88	**BARBED WIRE KISSES** *Blanco Y Negro BYN 15* ●	9		7
21 Oct 89	**AUTOMATIC** *Blanco Y Negro BYN 20* ○	11		4
4 Apr 92	**HONEY'S DEAD** *Blanco Y Negro 9031765542*	14		5
24 Jul 93	**THE SOUND OF SPEED** *Blanco Y Negro 4509931052*	15		3
27 Aug 94	**STONED AND DETHRONED** *Blanco Y Negro 4509967172*	13		3
13 Jun 98	**MUNKI** *Creation CRECD 232*	47		1

JESUS JONES
UK, male vocal/instrumental group – Mike Edwards, Iain Baker, Jerry de Borg, Al Doughty & Gen (Simon Matthews)

Date	Title	Peak Position	Weeks at No.1	Weeks on Chart: 31
14 Oct 89	**LIQUIDIZER** *Food FOODLP 3* ○	31		3
9 Feb 91	**DOUBT** *Food FOODLP 5* ●	1	1	24
6 Feb 93	**PERVERSE** *Food FOODCD 8*	6		4

JESUS LIZARD
US, male vocal/instrumental group

Date	Title	Peak Position	Weeks at No.1	Weeks on Chart: 1
10 Sep 94	**DOWN** *Touch And Go TG 131CD*	64		1

JET
Australia, male vocal/instrumental group

Date	Title	Peak Position	Weeks at No.1	Weeks on Chart: 41
27 Sep 03	**GET BORN** *Elektra 7559628922* ⊛	14		38
14 Oct 06	**SHINE ON** *Atlantic 7567935912* ●	13		3

JETHRO TULL
UK, male vocal/instrumental group – Ian Anderson*, Martin Barre, Clive Bunker (replaced by Barriemore Barlow), Glen Cornick (replaced by Jeffrey Hammond) & John Evan

Date	Title	Peak Position	Weeks at No.1	Weeks on Chart: 236
2 Nov 68	**THIS WAS** *Island ILPS 9085*	10		22
9 Aug 69	**STAND UP** *Island ILPS 9103*	1	5	29
9 May 70	**BENEFIT** *Island ILPS 9123*	3		13
3 Apr 71	**AQUALUNG** *Island ILPS 9145*	4		21
18 Mar 72	**THICK AS A BRICK** *Chrysalis CHR 1003* ★	5		14
15 Jul 72	**LIVING IN THE PAST** *Chrysalis CJT 1*	8		11
28 Jul 73	**A PASSION PLAY** *Chrysalis CHR 1040* ○ ★	13		8
2 Nov 74	**WAR CHILD** *Chrysalis CHR 1067*	14		4
27 Sep 75	**MINSTREL OF THE GALLERY** *Chrysalis CHR 1082* ○	20		6
31 Jan 76	**M.U. THE BEST OF JETHRO TULL** *Chrysalis CHR 1078* ●	44		5
15 May 76	**TOO OLD TO ROCK 'N' ROLL TOO YOUNG TO DIE** *Chrysalis CHR 1111*	25		10
19 Feb 77	**SONGS FROM THE WOOD** *Chrysalis CHR 1132*	13		12
29 Apr 78	**HEAVY HORSES** *Chrysalis CHR 1175* ○	20		10
14 Oct 78	**LIVE BURSTING OUT** *Chrysalis CJT 4* ○	17		8
6 Oct 79	**STORM WATCH** *Chrysalis CDL 1238*	27		4
6 Sep 80	**A** *Chrysalis CDL 1301*	25		5
17 Apr 82	**BROADSWORD AND THE BEAST** *Chrysalis CDL 1380* ○	27		19
15 Sep 84	**UNDER WRAPS** *Chrysalis CDL 1461*	18		5
2 Nov 85	**ORIGINAL MASTERS** *Chrysalis JTTV 1* ○	63		3
19 Sep 87	**CREST OF A KNAVE** *Chrysalis CDL 1590* ●	19		10
9 Jul 88	**20 YEARS OF JETHRO TULL** *Chrysalis TBOX 1*	78		1
2 Sep 89	**ROCK ISLAND** *Chrysalis CHR 1708* ○	18		6
14 Sep 91	**CATFISH RISING** *Chrysalis CHNR 1886*	27		3
26 Sep 92	**A LITTLE LIGHT MUSIC** *Chrysalis CCD 1954*	34		2
16 Sep 95	**ROOTS TO BRANCHES** *Chrysalis CDCHR 6109*	20		3
29 Jun 96	**AQUALUNG** *Chrysalis CD25 AQUA1*	53		1
4 Sep 99	**J-TULL DOT COM** *Papillion BTFLYCD 0001*	44		1

JETS
UK, male vocal/instrumental group

Date	Title	Peak Position	Weeks at No.1	Weeks on Chart: 6
10 Apr 82	**100 PERCENT COTTON** *EMI EMC 3399*	30		6

JETS
US, male/female vocal/instrumental group

Date	Title	Peak Position	Weeks at No.1	Weeks on Chart: 4
11 Apr 87	**CRUSH ON YOU** *MCA MCF 3312*	57		4

JOAN JETT & THE BLACKHEARTS
US, female/male vocal/instrumental group

Date	Title	Peak Position	Weeks at No.1	Weeks on Chart: 7
8 May 82	**I LOVE ROCK 'N' ROLL** *Epic EPC 85686*	25		7

JEWEL
US, female vocalist/guitarist (Jewel Kilcher)

Date	Title	Peak Position	Weeks at No.1	Weeks on Chart: 4
28 Nov 98	**SPIRIT** *Atlantic 7567829502*	54		1
9 Mar 02	**THIS WAY** *Atlantic 7567835192*	34		3

JIMMY EAT WORLD
US, male vocal/instrumental group

Date	Title	Peak Position	Weeks at No.1	Weeks on Chart: 8
9 Feb 02	**BLEED AMERICAN** *DreamWorks 4503482*	62		4
23 Oct 04	**FUTURES** *Interscope 9864241*	22		2
27 Oct 07	**CHASE THIS LIGHT** *Interscope 1747542*	27		2

JIVE BUNNY & THE MIXMASTERS
UK, male DJ/production group – Andy & John Pickles, Les Hemstock & Ian Morgan

Date	Title	Peak Position	Weeks at No.1	Weeks on Chart: 29
9 Dec 89	**JIVE BUNNY – THE ALBUM** *Telstar STAR 2390* ⊛**x3**	2		22
8 Dec 90	**IT'S PARTY TIME** *Telstar STAR 2449* ●	23		7

JJ72
Ireland, male/female vocal/instrumental group

Date	Title	Peak Position	Weeks at No.1	Weeks on Chart: 22
9 Sep 00	**JJ72** *Lakota LAK CD0017* ●	16		20
26 Oct 02	**I TO SKY** *Lakota 5095292*	20		2

JOAN AS POLICE WOMAN
US, female vocalist/violinist/guitarist (Joan Wasser)

Date	Title	Peak Position	Weeks at No.1	Weeks on Chart: 1
21 Jun 08	**TO SURVIVE** *Reveal REVEAL42*	56		1

JOBOXERS
UK/US, male vocal/instrumental group

Date	Title	Peak Position	Weeks at No.1	Weeks on Chart
				5
24 Sep 83	**LIKE GANGBUSTERS** *RCA BOXXLP 1*	18		5

JODECI
US, male vocal group – Donald DeGrate, Jr., Dalvin DeGrate, Cedric 'K-Ci' Hailey & Joel 'Jo-Jo' Hailey (K-Ci & Jo-Jo*)

Date	Title	Peak Position	Weeks at No.1	Weeks on Chart
				8
29 Jul 95	**THE SHOW THE AFTER-PARTY THE HOTEL** *Uptown MCD 11258*	4		8

JOE
US, male vocalist (Joseph Thomas)

Date	Title	Peak Position	Weeks at No.1	Weeks on Chart
				15
12 Feb 94	**EVERYTHING** *Mercury 5188072*	53		1
9 Aug 97	**ALL THAT I AM** *Jive CHIP 183* ○	26		4
29 Apr 00	**MY NAME IS JOE** *Jive 9220352*	46		4
8 May 04	**AND THEN** *Jive 82876586402*	73		3
5 May 07	**AIN'T NOTHING LIKE ME** *Jive 88697069052*	25		3

BILLY JOEL
US, male vocalist/multi-instrumentalist. This Grammy Living Legend award recipient is one of the world's most popular live performers. In his homeland, he has 80 million certified album sales and was the first act to have five LPs pass the seven million sales mark

Date	Title	Peak Position	Weeks at No.1	Weeks on Chart
				379
25 Mar 78	**THE STRANGER** *CBS 82311* ●	25		40
25 Nov 78	**52ND STREET** *CBS 83181* ● ★	10		43
22 Mar 80	**GLASS HOUSES** *CBS 86108* ● ★	9		24
10 Oct 81	**SONGS IN THE ATTIC** *CBS 85273*	57		3
2 Oct 82	**NYLON CURTAIN** *CBS 85959*	27		8
10 Sep 83	**AN INNOCENT MAN** *CBS 25554* ⊛x3	2		95
4 Feb 84	**COLD SPRING HARBOUR** *CBS 32400*	95		1
23 Jun 84	**PIANO MAN** *CBS 32002*	98		1
20 Jul 85	**GREATEST HITS VOLUME 1 & VOLUME II** *CBS 88666* ⊛	7		39
16 Aug 86	**THE BRIDGE** *CBS 86323* ○	38		10
28 Nov 87	**KOHYEPT – LIVE IN LENINGRAD** *CBS 4604071*	92		1
4 Nov 89	**STORM FRONT** *CBS 4656581* ⊛ ★	5		25
14 Aug 93	**RIVER OF DREAMS** *Columbia 4738722* ⊛ ★	3		26
1 Nov 97	**GREATEST HITS VOLUME III** *Columbia 4882362* ○	23		4
13 Jun 98	**GREATEST HITS – VOLUMES I, II & III** *Columbia 4912742*	33		4
27 May 00	**2000 YEARS – THE MILLENNIUM CONCERT** *Columbia 4979812*	68		1
31 Mar 01	**THE ULTIMATE COLLECTION** *Columbia SONYTV98CD* ⊛	4		24
27 Nov 04	**PIANO MAN – THE VERY BEST OF** *Columbia 5190182* ⊛	9		30

SCARLETT JOHANSSON
US, female actor/vocalist

Date	Title	Peak Position	Weeks at No.1	Weeks on Chart
				1
31 May 08	**ANYWHERE I LAY ME HEAD** *Rhino 8122799258*	64		1

ELTON JOHN
UK, male vocalist/pianist (Reginald Dwight). The flamboyant entertainer has sold more albums in the UK and US than any other UK male artist. He was the first act to enter the US albums chart at No.1 and had a hit UK album every year from 1970–90

Date	Title	Peak Position	Weeks at No.1	Weeks on Chart
				1013
23 May 70	**ELTON JOHN** *DJM DJLPS 406*	5		22
16 Jan 71	**TUMBLEWEED CONNECTION** *DJM DJLPS 410*	2		20
1 May 71	**THE ELTON JOHN LIVE ALBUM 17-11-70** *DJM DJLPS 414*	20		2
20 May 72	**MADMAN ACROSS THE WATER** *DJM DJLPH 420*	41		2
3 Jun 72	**HONKY CHATEAU** *DJM DJLPH 423* ★	2		23
10 Feb 73	**DON'T SHOOT ME I'M ONLY THE PIANO PLAYER** *DJM DJLPH 427* ★	1	6	42
3 Nov 73	**GOODBYE YELLOW BRICK ROAD** *DJM DJLPO 1001* ⊛ ★	1	2	84
13 Jul 74	**CARIBOU** *DJM DJLPH 439* ● ★	1	2	18
23 Nov 74	**ELTON JOHN'S GREATEST HITS** *DJM DJLPH 442* ⊛ ★	1	11	84
7 Jun 75	**CAPTAIN FANTASTIC AND THE BROWN DIRT COWBOY** *DJM DJLPX 1* ● ★	2		24
8 Nov 75	**ROCK OF THE WESTIES** *DJM DJLPH 464* ● ★	5		12
15 May 76	**HERE AND THERE** *DJM DJLPH 473* ○	6		9
6 Nov 76	**BLUE MOVES** *Rocket ROSP 1* ●	3		15
15 Oct 77	**GREATEST HITS VOLUME 2** *DJM DJH 20520* ●	6		24
4 Nov 78	**A SINGLE MAN** *Rocket TRAIN 1* ●	8		26
20 Oct 79	**VICTIM OF LOVE** *Rocket HISPD 125*	41		3
8 Mar 80	**LADY SAMANTHA** *DJM 22085*	56		2
31 May 80	**21 AT 33** *Rocket HISPD 126*	12		13
25 Oct 80	**THE VERY BEST OF ELTON JOHN** *K-Tel NE 1094* ●	24		13
30 May 81	**THE FOX** *Rocket TRAIN 16* ○	12		12
17 Apr 82	**JUMP UP** *Rocket HISPD 127* ○	13		12
6 Nov 82	**LOVE SONGS** *TV Records TVA 3*	39		13
11 Jun 83	**TOO LOW FOR ZERO** *Rocket HISPD 24* ⊛	7		73
30 Jun 84	**BREAKING HEARTS** *Rocket HISPD 25* ●	2		23
16 Nov 85	**ICE ON FIRE** *Rocket HISPD 26* ⊛	3		23
15 Nov 86	**LEATHER JACKETS** *Rocket EJLP 1* ●	24		9
12 Sep 87	**LIVE IN AUSTRALIA** *Rocket EJBXL 1* & THE MELBOURNE SYMPHONY ORCHESTRA	43		7
16 Jul 88	**REG STRIKES BACK** *Rocket EJLP 3* ○	18		6
23 Sep 89	**SLEEPING WITH THE PAST** *Rocket 8388391* ⊛x3	1	5	42
10 Nov 90	**THE VERY BEST OF ELTON JOHN** *Rocket 8469471* ⊛x9	1	2	96
27 Jun 92	**THE ONE** *Rocket 5123602* ●	2		18
4 Dec 93	**DUETS** *Rocket 5184782* & VARIOUS ARTISTS ⊛	5		18
1 Apr 95	**MADE IN ENGLAND** *Rocket 5261852* ●	3		14
18 Nov 95	**LOVE SONGS** *Rocket 5287882* ⊛x3	4		50
11 Oct 97	**THE BIG PICTURE** *Rocket 5362662* ⊛	3		23
3 Apr 99	**ELTON JOHN AND TIM RICE'S AIDA** *Rocket 5246512* & FRIENDS	29		2
25 Nov 00	**ONE NIGHT ONLY – THE GREATEST HITS** *Mercury 5483342* ⊛	7		13
13 Oct 01	**SONGS FROM THE WEST COAST** *Rocket 5863302* ⊛x2	2		34
20 Oct 01	**GOODBYE YELLOW BRICK ROAD** *Rocket 5281592*	41		4
23 Nov 02	**THE GREATEST HITS 1970 – 2002** *Mercury 634992* ⊛x4	3		54
20 Nov 04	**PEACHTREE ROAD** *Rocket 9868762* ●	21		8
30 Sep 06	**THE CAPTAIN & THE KID** *Mercury 1705710*	6		4
7 Apr 07	**ROCKET MAN – THE DEFINITIVE HITS** *Mercury 1726850* ●	2		17

JOHNNY & THE HURRICANES
US, male instrumental group – Johnny Paris (Johnny Pocisk), d. 1 May 2006

Date	Title	Peak Position	Weeks at No.1	Weeks on Chart
				5
3 Dec 60	**STORMSVILLE** *London HAI 2269*	18		1
1 Apr 61	**BIG SOUND OF JOHNNY AND THE HURRICANES** *London HAK 2322*	14		4

JOHNNY HATES JAZZ
UK, male vocal/instrumental group – Clark Datchler, Calvin Hayes & Mike Nocito (b. Germany)

Date	Title	Peak Position	Weeks at No.1	Weeks on Chart
				39
23 Jan 88	**TURN BACK THE CLOCK** *Virgin V 2475* ⊛x2	1	1	39

ANDREAS JOHNSON
Sweden, male vocalist

Date	Title	Peak Position	Weeks at No.1	Weeks on Chart
				2
19 Feb 00	**LIEBLING** *WEA 3984269142*	46		2

HOLLY JOHNSON
UK, male vocalist (William Johnson). See Frankie Goes To Hollywood

Date	Title	Peak Position	Weeks at No.1	Weeks on Chart
				17
6 May 89	**BLAST** *MCA MCG 6042* ⊛	1	1	17

JACK JOHNSON
US, male vocalist/guitarist

Date	Title	Peak Position	Weeks at No.1	Weeks on Chart
				178
12 Mar 05	**IN BETWEEN DREAMS** *Island/Uni-Island 9880252* ⊛x4	1	1	82
11 Feb 06	**ON AND ON** *Island AA4400750122* ⊛	30		23
18 Feb 06	**CURIOUS GEORGE (OST)** *Brushfire/Island 9850967* ● ★	15		33
25 Feb 06	**BRUSHFIRE FAIRYTALES** *Universal AA4228609942* ●	36		25
16 Feb 08	**SLEEP THROUGH THE STATIC** *Brushfire/Island 1756126* ● ★	1	2	15

LINTON KWESI JOHNSON
Jamaica, male poet

Date	Title	Peak Position	Weeks at No.1	Weeks on Chart
				8
30 Jun 79	**FORCE OF VICTORY** *Island ILPS 9566*	66		1
31 May 80	**BASS CULTURE** *Island ILPS 9605*	46		5
10 Mar 84	**MAKING HISTORY** *Island ILPS 9770*	73		2

PAUL JOHNSON
UK, male vocalist

Date	Title	Peak Position	Weeks at No.1	Weeks on Chart
				3
4 Jul 87	**PAUL JOHNSON** *CBS 4506401*	63		2
16 Sep 89	**PERSONAL** *CBS 4632841*	70		1

ANDREW JOHNSTON
UK, male vocalist

Date	Title	Peak Position	Weeks at No.1	Weeks on Chart
				5
11 Oct 08	**ONE VOICE** *Syco 88697351872*	4		5

Silver-selling ○ Gold-selling ● Platinum-selling ◉ US No.1 ★ | Peak Position | Weeks at No.1 | Weeks on Chart

JAMES A JOHNSTON
US, male composer (Jim Johnston III) — 17

Date	Title	Peak	No.1	Weeks
13 Nov 99	WORLD WRESTLING FEDERATION – THE MUSIC – VOLUME 4 *Koch International 333612* ●	44		9
10 Mar 01	WORLD WRESTLING FEDERATION – THE MUSIC – VOLUME 5 *Koch KOCCD8830* ●	11		8

BRIAN JOHNSTON
UK, male cricket commentator ('Johnners'), d. 5 Jan 1994 (age 81) — 3

Date	Title	Peak	No.1	Weeks
5 Mar 94	AN EVENING WITH JOHNNERS *Listen For Pleasure LFP 7742*	46		3

JOJO
US, female vocalist (Joanne Levesque) — 29

Date	Title	Peak	No.1	Weeks
18 Sep 04	JOJO *Mercury 9867855* ●	22		17
20 Jan 07	THE HIGH ROAD *Mercury 1713769* ●	24		12

AL JOLSON
US (b. Lithuania), male vocalist/actor (Asa Yoelson), d. 23 Oct 1950 (age 64) — 11

Date	Title	Peak	No.1	Weeks
14 Mar 81	20 GOLDEN GREATS *MCA MCTV 4*	18		7
17 Dec 83	THE AL JOLSON COLLECTION *Ronco RON LP 5* ○	67		4

JON & VANGELIS
UK, male vocalist (Jon Anderson*) & Greece, male multi-instrumentalist (Evangelos Papathanassiou – Vangelis*) — 53

Date	Title	Peak	No.1	Weeks
26 Jan 80	SHORT STORIES *Polydor POLD 5030* ●	4		11
11 Jul 81	THE FRIENDS OF MR. CAIRO *Polydor POLD 5039*	17		8
23 Jan 82	THE FRIENDS OF MR. CAIRO *Polydor POLD 5053* ●	6		15
2 Jul 83	PRIVATE COLLECTION *Polydor POLH 4*	22		10
11 Aug 84	THE BEST OF JON AND VANGELIS *Polydor POLH 6*	42		9

JONAS BROTHERS
US, male vocal/instrumental trio – Kevin, Joe & Nick Jonas — 14

Date	Title	Peak	No.1	Weeks
5 Jul 08	JONAS BROTHERS *Hollywood 1773059*	9		6
11 Oct 08	A LITTLE BIT LONGER *Hollywood 8712158* ★	19		8

ALED JONES
UK, male vocalist/TV presenter — 175

Date	Title	Peak	No.1	Weeks
27 Apr 85	VOICES FROM THE HOLY LAND *BBC REC 564* ALED JONES WITH THE BBC WELSH CHORUS ◉	6		43
29 Jun 85	ALL THROUGH THE NIGHT *BBC REH 569* ALED JONES WITH THE BBC WELSH CHORUS ◉	2		44
23 Nov 85	ALED JONES WITH THE BBC WELSH CHORUS *10 Records AJ 1* ALED JONES WITH THE BBC WELSH CHORUS ●	11		10
22 Feb 86	WHERE E'ER YOU WALK *10 Records DIX 21*	36		6
12 Jul 86	PIE JESU *10 Records AJ 2* ○	25		16
29 Nov 86	AN ALBUM OF HYMNS *Telstar STAR 2272* ●	18		11
14 Mar 87	ALED (MUSIC FROM THE TV SERIES) *10 Records AJ 3* ○	52		6
5 Dec 87	THE BEST OF ALED JONES *10 Records AJ 5* ○	59		5
26 Oct 02	ALED *UCJ 0644792* ●	27		12
11 Oct 03	HIGHER *UCJ 9865579* ●	21		7
4 Dec 04	THE CHRISTMAS ALBUM *UCJ 9868649* ●	37		5
29 Oct 05	NEW HORIZONS *UCJ 4763062* ○	21		4
9 Dec 06	YOU RAISE ME UP – THE BEST OF *UCJ 4765721*	63		2
20 Oct 07	REASON TO BELIEVE *UCJ 1738932*	15		4

DONELL JONES
US, male vocalist — 5

Date	Title	Peak	No.1	Weeks
29 Jan 00	WHERE I WANNA BE *LaFace 73008260602*	47		3
22 Jun 02	LIFE GOES ON *Arista ARI 147602*	62		2

GLENN JONES
US, male vocalist — 1

Date	Title	Peak	No.1	Weeks
31 Oct 87	GLENN JONES *Jive HIP 51*	62		1

GRACE JONES
Jamaica, female vocalist (Grace Mendoza) — 81

Date	Title	Peak	No.1	Weeks
30 Aug 80	WARM LEATHERETTE *Island ILPS 9592*	45		2
23 May 81	NIGHTCLUBBING *Island ILPS 9624*	35		16
20 Nov 82	LIVING MY LIFE *Island ILPS 9722*	15		22
9 Nov 85	SLAVE TO THE RHYTHM *ZTT GRACE 1*	12		8
14 Dec 85	ISLAND LIFE *Island GJ 1* ●	4		30
29 Nov 86	INSIDE STORY *Manhattan MTL 1007* ○	61		2
15 Nov 08	HURRICANE *Wall Of Sound WOS050CD*	42		1

HOWARD JONES
UK, male vocalist/keyboard/synthesizer player (John Howard Jones) — 122

Date	Title	Peak	No.1	Weeks
17 Mar 84	HUMAN'S LIB *WEA WX 1* ◉x2	1	2	57
8 Dec 84	THE 12" ALBUM *WEA WX 14* ●	15		33
23 Mar 85	DREAM INTO ACTION *WEA WX 15* ●	2		25
25 Oct 86	ONE TO ONE *WEA WX 68* ●	10		4
1 Apr 89	CROSS THAT LINE *WEA WX 225*	64		1
5 Jun 93	THE BEST OF HOWARD JONES *East West 4509927012* ○	36		2

JACK JONES
US, male vocalist — 70

Date	Title	Peak	No.1	Weeks
29 Apr 72	A SONG FOR YOU *RCA Victor SF 8228*	9		6
3 Jun 72	BREAD WINNERS *RCA Victor SF 8280* ●	7		36
7 Apr 73	TOGETHER *RCA Victor SF 8342*	8		10
23 Feb 74	HARBOUR *RCA Victor APL1 0408*	10		5
19 Feb 77	THE FULL LIFE *RCA Victor PL 12067*	41		5
21 May 77	ALL TO YOURSELF *RCA TVL 2*	10		8

NORAH JONES
US, female vocalist/pianist — 182

Date	Title	Peak	No.1	Weeks
11 May 02	COME AWAY WITH ME *Parlophone 5386092* ◉x7 ★	1	4	136
21 Feb 04	FEELS LIKE HOME *Blue Note 5983660* ◉x3 ★	1	2	37
10 Feb 07	NOT TOO LATE *Blue Note 3878442* ★	1	1	9

QUINCY JONES
US, male producer/keyboard player — 49

Date	Title	Peak	No.1	Weeks
18 Apr 81	THE DUDE *A&M AMLK 63721* ○	19		25
20 Mar 82	THE BEST *A&M AMLH 68542*	41		4
18 Aug 84	L.A. IS MY LADY *Qwest 925145* FRANK SINATRA WITH THE QUINCY JONES ORCHESTRA	41		8
20 Jan 90	BACK ON THE BLOCK *Qwest WX 313* ●	26		12

RICKIE LEE JONES
US, female vocalist/guitarist — 39

Date	Title	Peak	No.1	Weeks
16 Jun 79	RICKY LEE JONES *Warner Brothers K 56628* ○	18		19
8 Aug 81	PIRATES *Warner Brothers K 56816* ○	37		11
2 Jul 83	GIRL AT HER VOLCANO *Warner Brothers 9238051*	51		3
13 Aug 84	THE MAGAZINE *Warner Brothers 9251171*	40		4
7 Oct 89	FLYING COWBOYS *Geffen WX 309*	50		2

TAMMY JONES
UK, female vocalist — 5

Date	Title	Peak	No.1	Weeks
12 Jul 75	LET ME TRY AGAIN *Epic EPC 80853*	38		5

TOM JONES
UK, male vocalist (Thomas Woodward). Perennially popular Welsh vocalist, who has a 43-year span of UK hit albums, was the No.1 UK solo singer of the 1960s on both sides of the Atlantic. The unmistakable Vegas veteran received the Outstanding Contribution award at the 2003 BRITs — 530

Date	Title	Peak	No.1	Weeks
5 Jun 65	ALONG CAME JONES *Decca LK 6693*	11		5
8 Oct 66	FROM THE HEART *Decca LK 4814*	23		8
8 Apr 67	GREEN GREEN GRASS OF HOME *Decca SKL 4855*	3		49
24 Jun 67	LIVE AT THE TALK OF THE TOWN *Decca SKL 4874*	6		90
30 Dec 67	13 SMASH HITS *Decca SKL 4909*	5		49
27 Jul 68	DELILAH *Decca SKL 4946*	1	2	29
21 Dec 68	HELP YOURSELF *Decca SKL 4982*	4		9
28 Jun 69	THIS IS TOM JONES *Decca SKL 5007*	2		20
15 Nov 69	TOM JONES LIVE IN LAS VEGAS *Decca SKL 5032*	2		45
25 Apr 70	TOM *Decca SKL 5045*	4		18
14 Nov 70	I WHO HAVE NOTHING *Decca SKL 5072*	10		10
29 May 71	SHE'S A LADY *Decca SKL 5089*	9		7
27 Nov 71	LIVE AT CAESAR'S PALACE *Decca D 1/11/2*	27		5
24 Jun 72	CLOSE UP *Decca SKL 5132*	17		4
23 Jun 73	THE BODY AND SOUL OF TOM JONES *Decca SKL 5162*	31		1
5 Jan 74	GREATEST HITS *Decca SKL 5176*	15		13
22 Mar 75	20 GREATEST HITS *Decca TJD 1/11/2* ●	1	4	21
7 Oct 78	I'M COMING HOME *Lotus WH 5001* ●	12		9
16 May 87	THE GREATEST HITS *Telstar STAR 2296*	16		12

Silver-selling ○ | Gold-selling ● | Platinum-selling ⊛ | US No.1 ★ | Peak Position | Weeks at No.1 | Weeks on Chart

Date	Title / Label	Peak Position	Weeks at No.1	Weeks on Chart
13 May 89	**AT THIS MOMENT** *Jive TOMTV 1*	34		3
8 Jul 89	**AFTER DARK** *Stylus SMR 978*	46		4
6 Apr 91	**CARRYING A TORCH** *Dover ADD 20*	44		4
27 Jun 92	**THE COMPLETE TOM JONES** *The Hit Label 8442862* ●	8		6
26 Nov 94	**THE LEAD AND HOW TO SWING IT** *ZTT 6544924982*	55		1
14 Nov 98	**THE ULTIMATE HITS COLLECTION** *Polygram TV 8449012*	26		6
9 Oct 99	**RELOAD** *Gut GUTCD 009* ⊛x4	1	3	65
16 Nov 02	**MR JONES** *V2 VVR 1021072*	36		2
1 Mar 03	**GREATEST HITS** *Universal TV 8828632* ⊛	2		16
9 Oct 04	**TOM JONES AND JOOLS HOLLAND** *Radar RADAR004CD* & JOOLS HOLLAND ●	5		13
29 Nov 08	**24 HOURS** *S-Curve 2649852*	32		6+

TREVOR JONES

South Africa, male composer/conductor/synthesizer player — **2**

Date	Title / Label	Peak	Wks at No.1	Wks
5 Jul 86	**LABYRINTH (OST)** *EMI America AML 3104*	38		2

JANIS JOPLIN

US, female vocalist/guitarist, d. 4 Oct 1970 (age 27) — **14**

Date	Title / Label	Peak	Wks at No.1	Wks
13 Mar 71	**PEARL** *CBS 64188* ★	20		4
22 Jul 72	**JANIS JOPLIN IN CONCERT** *CBS 67241*	30		6
29 Aug 98	**THE ULTIMATE COLLECTION** *Columbia SONYTV 52CD*	26		4

DAVID JORDAN

UK, male vocalist — **11**

Date	Title / Label	Peak	Wks at No.1	Wks
9 Feb 08	**SET THE MOOD** *Mercury 1725566* ●	13		11

MONTELL JORDAN

US, male vocalist — **3**

Date	Title / Label	Peak	Wks at No.1	Wks
24 Jun 95	**THIS IS HOW WE DO IT** *RAL 5271792*	53		2
14 Sep 96	**MORE TO TELL** *Def Jam 5331912*	66		1

RONNY JORDAN

UK, male guitarist (Ronnie Simpson) — **7**

Date	Title / Label	Peak	Wks at No.1	Wks
7 Mar 92	**THE ANTIDOTE** *Island CID 9988*	52		4
9 Oct 93	**THE QUIET REVOLUTION** *Island CID 8009*	49		2
3 Sep 94	**BAD BROTHERS** *Island IMCD 8024* MEETS DJ KRUSH	58		1

JOURNEY

US, male vocal/instrumental group – Steve Perry*, Jonathan Cain, Neal Schon, Steve Smith & Ross Valory — **31**

Date	Title / Label	Peak	Wks at No.1	Wks
20 Mar 82	**ESCAPE** *CBS 85138* ★	32		16
19 Feb 83	**FRONTIERS** *CBS 25261*	6		8
6 Aug 83	**EVOLUTION** *CBS 32342*	100		1
24 May 86	**RAISED ON RADIO** *CBS 26902*	22		5
21 Jun 08	**REVELATION** *Frontiers FRCD376*	68		1

JOURNEY SOUTH

UK, male vocal/instrumental duo – Andy & Carl Pemberton — **14**

Date	Title / Label	Peak	Wks at No.1	Wks
1 Apr 06	**JOURNEY SOUTH** *Syco Music 82876815382* ⊛	1	1	12
3 Nov 07	**HOME** *Anca ANCACD100*	43		2

JOY DIVISION

UK, male vocal/instrumental group – Ian Curtis, d. 18 May 1980, Peter Hook, Stephen Morris & Bernard Sumner — **34**

Date	Title / Label	Peak	Wks at No.1	Wks
26 Jul 80	**CLOSER** *Factory FACT 25*	6		8
30 Aug 80	**UNKNOWN PLEASURES** *Factory FACT 10*	71		1
17 Oct 81	**STILL** *Factory DFACT 40*	5		12
23 Jul 88	**1977–1980 SUBSTANCE** *Factory FAC 250* ●	7		8
1 Jul 95	**PERMANENT: JOY DIVISION 1995** *London 8286242*	16		3
7 Feb 98	**HEART AND SOUL** *London 3984290402*	70		1
5 Apr 08	**THE BEST OF** *Rhino 5144273022*	63		1

JUDAS PRIEST

UK, male vocal/instrumental group – Rob Halford, K.K. Downing, Ian Hill, Dave Holland (replaced by Scott Travis) & Glen Tipton — **81**

Date	Title / Label	Peak	Wks at No.1	Wks
14 May 77	**SIN AFTER SIN** *CBS 82008*	23		6
25 Feb 78	**STAINED CLASS** *CBS 82430*	27		5
11 Nov 78	**KILLING MACHINE** *CBS 83135*	32		9
6 Oct 79	**UNLEASHED IN THE EAST** *CBS 83852*	10		8
19 Apr 80	**BRITISH STEEL** *CBS 84160* ○	4		17
7 Mar 81	**POINT OF ENTRY** *CBS 84834* ○	14		5
17 Jul 82	**SCREAMING FOR VENGEANCE** *CBS 85941*	11		9
28 Jan 84	**DEFENDERS OF THE FAITH** *CBS 25713*	19		5
19 Apr 86	**TURBO** *CBS 26641*	33		4
13 Jun 87	**PRIEST...LIVE** *CBS 4506391*	47		2
28 May 88	**RAM IT DOWN** *CBS 4611081*	24		5
22 Sep 90	**PAINKILLER** *CBS 4672901*	26		2
8 May 93	**METAL WORKS 73-93** *Columbia 4730502*	37		1
12 Mar 05	**ANGEL OF RETRIBUTION** *Sony Music 5193003*	39		2
28 Jun 08	**NOSTRADAMUS** *Columbia 88697315572*	30		1

JUDGE DREAD

UK, male vocalist (Alex Hughes), d. 13 Mar 1998 (age 52) — **14**

Date	Title / Label	Peak	Wks at No.1	Wks
6 Dec 75	**BEDTIME STORIES** *Cactus CTLP 113*	26		12
7 Mar 81	**40 BIG ONES** *Creole BIG 1*	51		2

JUICY LUCY

UK, male vocal/instrumental group — **5**

Date	Title / Label	Peak	Wks at No.1	Wks
18 Apr 70	**JUICY LUCY** *Vertigo VO 2*	41		4
21 Nov 70	**LIE BACK AND ENJOY IT** *Vertigo 6360 014*	53		1

GARY JULES

US, male vocalist/multi-instrumentalist (Gary Jules Aguirre) — **3**

Date	Title / Label	Peak	Wks at No.1	Wks
31 Jan 04	**TRADING SNAKEOIL FOR WOLFTICKETS** *Adventure/Sanctuary SANDP 252*	12		3

JULUKA

UK/South Africa, male/female vocal/instrumental group — **3**

Date	Title / Label	Peak	Wks at No.1	Wks
23 Jul 83	**SCATTERLINGS** *Safari SHAKA 1*	50		3

JUNGLE BROTHERS

US, male rap duo — **3**

Date	Title / Label	Peak	Wks at No.1	Wks
3 Feb 90	**DONE BY THE FORCES OF NATURE** *Eternal WX 332*	41		3

JUNIOR

UK, male vocalist (Norman Giscombe) — **14**

Date	Title / Label	Peak	Wks at No.1	Wks
5 Jun 82	**JI** *Mercury MERS 3*	28		14

JUNIOR SENIOR

Denmark, male vocal/instrumental duo — **3**

Date	Title / Label	Peak	Wks at No.1	Wks
22 Mar 03	**D D DON'T DON'T STOP THE BEAT** *Mercury FROG 0262CD*	29		3

JURASSIC 5

US, male rap group — **7**

Date	Title / Label	Peak	Wks at No.1	Wks
13 Jun 98	**JURASSIC 5** *Pan PAN 015CD* ●	70		1
1 Jul 00	**QUALITY CONTROL** *Interscope 4907102*	23		3
19 Oct 02	**POWER IN NUMBERS** *Interscope 4934372*	46		2
5 Aug 06	**FEEDBACK** *Interscope 1704028*	59		1

JUST JACK

UK, male vocalist/rapper/DJ/producer (Jack Allsopp) — **16**

Date	Title / Label	Peak	Wks at No.1	Wks
10 Feb 07	**OVERTONES** *Mercury 9859723* ●	6		16

JUSTICE

France, male production/DJ/instrumental duo — **1**

Date	Title / Label	Peak	Wks at No.1	Wks
30 Jun 07	**CROSS** *Because/Ed Banger BEC5772109*	49		1

K

K-CI & JOJO

US, male vocal duo. See Jodeci — **3**

Date	Title / Label	Peak	Wks at No.1	Wks
28 Jun 97	**LOVE ALWAYS** *MCA MCD 11613*	51		2
3 Jul 99	**IT'S REAL** *MCA MCD 11975*	56		1

Led Zeppelin

IV

SOME albums fade into obscurity. Many do not stand the test of time. Released to a slavering public in November 1971, Led Zeppelin's fourth album is not one of them. In response to the mixed reviews of their previous LP, Led Zeppelin dispensed with titles and names altogether for this record, which would prove to be a watershed moment in rock-music history.

The outer sleeve contained neither title nor any information pertaining to the musicians involved. Despite staunch opposition from some of their press and publicity advisers, Zeppelin opted for anonymity. Of course, *everyone* would know who the album was by; nonetheless the band were advised this faceless approach would be catastrophic. This was partly due to the fact that Zeppelin were not a 'singles' band; not musically, but quite literally. Zeppelin's reputation was built on a solid base of touring and word of mouth – a kind of prehistoric viral marketing. The band solidly resisted releasing seven-inch 45rpm singles in the UK, instead relying on their long-players and burgeoning reputation as a live force. To release an untitled album seemed tantamount to professional suicide. Fans disagreed and the record flew out of the shops, making it a global Number 1 record.

A framed painting of an old man bent under the burden of a bundle of sticks

The controversial and now iconic album cover is simply a framed painting of an old man bent under the burden of a bundle of sticks (apparently, the picture was purchased from a junk shop in Reading, Berkshire). The picture frame is fixed to a crumbling house wall with a block of flats in the background. The now-demolished high-rise building was in Dudley, West Midlands, not far from Robert Plant's birthplace of West Bromwich.

The remaining band members are known to refer to the record as the 'fourth album', but it is also known as 'Four Symbols' by record buyers. Each band member – Jimmy Page, John Paul Jones, John Bonham and Robert Plant – are represented by self-chosen sigils (commonly mistaken for runes) on the inner sleeve. The graphic chosen by guitarist Page gave rise to another alternative title – ZoSo (rumoured to be linked to his interest in the occult and alchemy). To enforce this imagery, and perhaps enhance the mystique, the four symbols were also used as stage projections during the winter tour in support of the album. The band's label Atlantic Records was forced to distribute pictorials of the symbols for promotional use.

Clocking in at just under forty-three minutes, Led Zeppelin's *IV* contains eight tracks – four per side in the days when albums were presented as twelve-inch slices of vinyl that rotated at 33rpm on a record deck. *IV* is, of course, the one that contains 'Stairway To Heaven', the eight minutes or so of indulgent fret-work you used to be able to hear emanating from guitar shops on a Saturday afternoon, before Health and Safety sensibly put an end to spotty youths mangling its chord sequence at obscene volumes just before the football scores. However, the album is so much more than this epic '*Wayne's World*/ wedding song' that closes side one.

The opening brace of 'Black Dog' and 'Rock and Roll' are pumping, riff-laden rock tracks underpinned by the

Chart History

Artist	Album Title	First Chart Week	Weeks on Chart	Highest Position
LED ZEPPELIN	IV	27/11/71	77	1

terrifying power of John Henry Bonham's drums. Page's guitar work explodes from the speakers, both assaulting and massaging the ears of the listener. Robert Plant's unique vocal style and astonishing range meld perfectly with the music, augmented by the oft-underestimated bass of John Paul Jones.

The opening barrage is followed by 'The Battle Of Evermore' featuring Sandy Denny, late of Fairport Convention (interestingly, Ms Denny is also represented by her own symbol on the inner bag). 'Evermore' delves deeply into the realms of English Folk rock, a genre particularly favoured by both Page and Plant. The lightness of the song, highlighted by Page's mandolin work, serves as a fitting counterpoint to the opening two-track fusillade.

'Stairway ...' is up next, starting quietly before slowly building to its crunching climax, then it's on to the hard rock of 'Misty Mountain Hop' with the thumping bass of Jones up front in the mix. 'Four Sticks' is built on a hypnotic rhythm, but is perhaps the weakest track on the album, sounding almost messy in places.

The penultimate work, 'Going To California', is also a song with a light folksy feeling, reminiscent of 'Evermore', albeit with more haunting, wistful vocals. Again, a mandolin is to the fore, this time played by Jones.

Bonham is in fine form on the final track, 'When The Levee Breaks', a heavy Delta blues number re-worked from the 1929 Kansas Joe McCoy and Memphis Minnie original, complete with backwards echo, backwards harmonica and phasing between left and right. Perhaps tellingly, Bonham's drums have been endlessly sampled by hip-hop artistes including the Beastie Boys – further testament to the influence of the behemoth that was Led Zeppelin's *IV*.

Page's guitar work explodes from the speakers, both assaulting and massaging the ears of the listener

This is the package that confirmed Zeppelin, via rabid critical acclaim and colossal commercial success, as the biggest band in the world. Global sales of 40 million (and still counting) admirably back this up, confirming *IV* as one of the biggest-selling albums in music history.

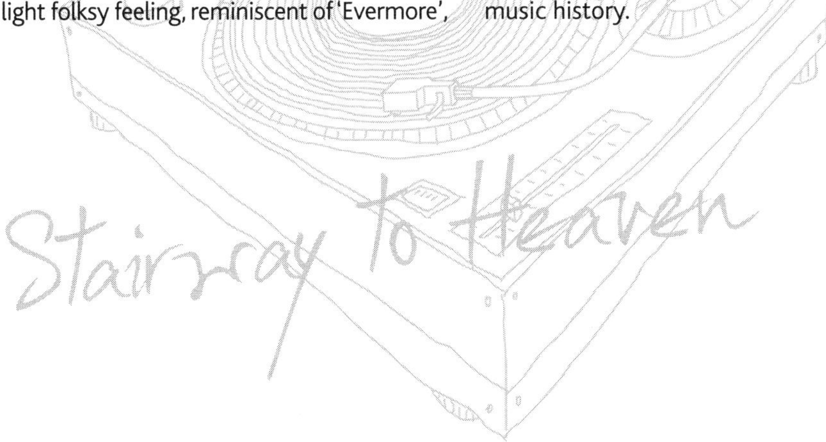

Stairway to Heaven

Silver-selling ● Gold-selling ● Platinum-selling ⊛ US No.1 ★ | Peak Position | Weeks at No.1 | Weeks on Chart

K-KLASS
UK, male/female vocal/instrumental group

Date	Title / Label	Peak Position	Weeks at No.1	Weeks on Chart
				1
4 Jun 94	**UNIVERSAL** *Deconstruction CDPCSDX 149*	73		1

KACI
US, female vocalist (Kaci Battaglia)

Date	Title / Label	Peak Position	Weeks at No.1	Weeks on Chart
				2
16 Feb 02	**PARADISE** *Curb 0927402912*	47		2

JOSHUA KADISON
US, male vocalist/pianist

Date	Title / Label	Peak Position	Weeks at No.1	Weeks on Chart
				4
27 May 95	**PAINTED DESERT SERENADE** *SBK SBKCD 22*	45		4

BERT KAEMPFERT & HIS ORCHESTRA
Germany, male band leader/composer/multi-instrumentalist (Berthold Kämpfert), d. 21 Jun 1980 (age 56) & orchestra

Date	Title / Label	Peak Position	Weeks at No.1	Weeks on Chart
				104
5 Mar 66	**BYE BYE BLUES** *Polydor LPHM 84086*	4		22
16 Apr 66	**BEST OF BERT KAEMPFERT** *Polydor LPHM 84012*	27		1
28 May 66	**A SWINGIN' SAFARI** *Polydor LPHM 46384*	20		15
30 Jul 66	**STRANGERS IN THE NIGHT** *Polydor LPHM 84053*	13		26
4 Feb 67	**RELAXING SOUND OF BERT KAEMPFERT** *Polydor 583501*	33		3
18 Feb 67	**BERT KAEMPFERT – BEST SELLER** *Polydor 583551*	25		18
29 Apr 67	**HOLD ME** *Polydor 184072*	36		5
26 Aug 67	**KAEMPFERT SPECIAL** *Polydor 236207*	24		5
19 Jun 71	**ORANGE COLOURED SKY** *Polydor 2310 091*	49		1
5 Jul 80	**SOUNDS SENSATIONAL** *Polydor POLTB 10* ● (silver)	17		8

KAISER CHIEFS
UK, male vocal/instrumental group – Ricky Wilson, Nick 'Peanut' Baines, Nick Hodgson, Simon Rix & Andrew 'Whitey' White

Date	Title / Label	Peak Position	Weeks at No.1	Weeks on Chart
				159
19 Mar 05	**EMPLOYMENT** *B Unique/Polydor BUN093CDX* ⊛x5	3		86
10 Mar 07	**YOURS TRULY ANGRY MOB** *B Unique/Polydor BUN122CDS* ⊛	1	2	63
1 Nov 08	**OFF WITH THEIR HEADS** *B Unique/Polydor BUN144CD*	2		10+

KAJAGOOGOO
UK, male vocal/instrumental group – Chris Hamill (Limahl*), Steve Askew, Nick Beggs, Stuart Croxford Neale & Jez Strode

Date	Title / Label	Peak Position	Weeks at No.1	Weeks on Chart
				23
30 Apr 83	**WHITE FEATHERS** *EMI EMC 3433* ● (silver)	5		20
2 Jun 84	**ISLANDS** *EMI KAJA 1*	35		3

NICK KAMEN
UK, male vocalist

Date	Title / Label	Peak Position	Weeks at No.1	Weeks on Chart
				7
18 Apr 87	**NICK KAMEN** *WEA WX 84*	34		7

KANE GANG
UK, male vocal/instrumental group

Date	Title / Label	Peak Position	Weeks at No.1	Weeks on Chart
				12
23 Feb 85	**THE BAD AND LOWDOWN WORLD OF THE KANE GANG** *Kitchenware KWLP 2*	21		8
8 Aug 87	**MIRACLE** *Kitchenware KWLP 7*	41		4

KANO
US, male rapper (Kane Robinson)

Date	Title / Label	Peak Position	Weeks at No.1	Weeks on Chart
				14
9 Jul 05	**HOME SWEET HOME** *679 Recordings 5046788872*	36		8
22 Sep 07	**LONDON TOWN** *679 Recordings 2564697895*	14		5
11 Oct 08	**140 GRIME ST.** *Bigger Picture BPM001*	48		1

MICK KARN
UK, male bass player (Anthony Michaelides). See Japan

Date	Title / Label	Peak Position	Weeks at No.1	Weeks on Chart
				4
20 Nov 82	**TITLES** *Virgin V 2249*	74		3
28 Feb 87	**DREAMS OF REASON PRODUCE MONSTERS** *Virgin V 2389*	89		1

KASABIAN
UK, male vocal/instrumental group – Tom Meighan, Chris Edwards, Ash Hannis (replaced by Ian Matthews), Chris Karloff (replaced by Jay Mehler) & Sergio Pizzorno

Date	Title / Label	Peak Position	Weeks at No.1	Weeks on Chart
				102
18 Sep 04	**KASABIAN** *RCA PARADISE16* ⊛x2	4		62
9 Sep 06	**EMPIRE** *Columbia PARADISE37* ⊛x2	1	1	40

KATRINA & THE WAVES
US/UK, female/male vocal/instrumental group

Date	Title / Label	Peak Position	Weeks at No.1	Weeks on Chart
				7
8 Jun 85	**KATRINA AND THE WAVES** *Capitol KTW 1*	28		6
10 May 86	**WAVES** *Capitol EST 2010*	70		1

KAVANA
UK, male vocalist (Anthony Kavanagh)

Date	Title / Label	Peak Position	Weeks at No.1	Weeks on Chart
				2
10 May 97	**KAVANA** *Nemesis CDNMS 1*	29		2

PETER KAY
UK, male comedian/vocalist

Date	Title / Label	Peak Position	Weeks at No.1	Weeks on Chart
				1
3 Dec 05	**THE BEST OF – SO FAR** *EMI Virgin VTCD768* ● (silver)	62		1

KC & THE SUNSHINE BAND
US, male vocal/instrumental group – Harry 'KC' Wayne Casey, Richard Finch, Robert Johnson, Jerome Smith, d. 28 Jul 2000, & various musicians

Date	Title / Label	Peak Position	Weeks at No.1	Weeks on Chart
				17
30 Aug 75	**KC AND THE SUNSHINE BAND** *Jay Boy JSL 9*	26		7
1 Mar 80	**GREATEST HITS** *TK TKR 83385* ● (silver)	10		6
27 Aug 83	**ALL IN A NIGHT'S WORK** *Epic EPC 85847*	46		4

KEANE
UK, male vocal/instrumental trio – Tom Chaplin, Richard Hughes & Tim Rice-Oxley

Date	Title / Label	Peak Position	Weeks at No.1	Weeks on Chart
				149
22 May 04	**HOPES AND FEARS** *Island CID 8145* ⊛x8	1	5	97
24 Jun 06	**UNDER THE IRON SEA** *Island/Uni-Island CIDX8167* ⊛x2	1	2	41
25 Oct 08	**PERFECT SYMMETRY** *Island 1784417* ● (gold)	1	1	11+

RONAN KEATING
Ireland, male vocalist. See Boyzone

Date	Title / Label	Peak Position	Weeks at No.1	Weeks on Chart
				155
12 Aug 00	**RONAN** *Polydor 5491032* ⊛x4	1	2	56
1 Jun 02	**DESTINATION** *Polydor 5897892* ⊛x2	1	1	40
29 Nov 03	**TURN IT ON** *Polydor 9865882*	21		17
23 Oct 04	**10 YEARS OF HITS** *Polydor 9868455* ⊛x3	1	1	30
17 Jun 06	**BRING YOU HOME** *Polydor 9858272* ● (gold)	3		12

KEEL
US, male vocal/instrumental group

Date	Title / Label	Peak Position	Weeks at No.1	Weeks on Chart
				2
17 May 86	**THE FINAL FRONTIER** *Vertigo VERH 33*	83		2

HOWARD KEEL
US, male vocalist/actor (Harold Leek), d. 7 Nov 2004 (age 85)

Date	Title / Label	Peak Position	Weeks at No.1	Weeks on Chart
				36
14 Apr 84	**AND I LOVE YOU SO** *Warwick WW 5137*	6		19
9 Nov 85	**REMINISCING – THE HOWARD KEEL COLLECTION** *Telstar STAR 2259* ● (gold)	20		12
26 Mar 88	**JUST FOR YOU** *Telstar STAR 2318*	51		5

KELIS
US, female vocalist/rapper (Kelis Rogers-Jones)

Date	Title / Label	Peak Position	Weeks at No.1	Weeks on Chart
				58
11 Mar 00	**KALEIDOSCOPE** *Virgin CDVUS 167* ● (gold)	43		13
17 Jan 04	**TASTY** *Virgin CDV 2978* ⊛	11		42
23 Sep 06	**KELIS WAS HERE** *Virgin CDV3020* ● (silver)	41		2
15 Mar 08	**THE HITS** *Virgin CDV3042*	71		1

LAURA MICHELLE KELLY
UK, female actor/vocalist

Date	Title / Label	Peak Position	Weeks at No.1	Weeks on Chart
				1
13 May 06	**THE STORM INSIDE** *Angel CDANGE08*	72		1

R KELLY
US, male vocalist/producer (Robert Kelly)

Date	Title / Label	Peak Position	Weeks at No.1	Weeks on Chart
				158
29 Feb 92	**BORN INTO THE 90'S** *Jive CHIP 123* R KELLY & PUBLIC ANNOUNCEMENT	67		1
27 Nov 93	**12 PLAY** *Jive CHIP 144* ● (gold)	20		44
25 Nov 95	**R KELLY** *Jive CHIP 166* ● (gold) ★	18		10
21 Nov 98	**R** *Jive 0517932* ⊛	27		26
18 Nov 00	**TP-2.COM** *Jive 9220262* ● (gold) ★	21		3
30 Mar 02	**THE BEST OF BOTH WORLDS** *Jive 9223512* & JAY-Z	37		2
1 Mar 03	**CHOCOLATE FACTORY** *Jive 9225082* ● (gold)	10		22

Date	Title	Peak Position	Weeks at No.1	Weeks on Chart
4 Oct 03	**THE R IN R&B – GREATEST HITS VOLUME 1** *Jive 82876561792* ⊛**x2**	4		34
4 Sep 04	**HAPPY PEOPLE/U SAVED ME** *BMG 82876615082*	11		8
6 Nov 04	**UNFINISHED BUSINESS** *Jive 82876658682* & JAY-Z ★	61		1
16 Jul 05	**TP 3 RELOADED** *Jive 82876710062* ○ ★	23		4
9 Jun 07	**DOUBLE UP** *Jive 88697093292* ★	10		3

FELICITY KENDAL

UK, female actor/exercise instructor — 47

Date	Title	Peak Position	Weeks at No.1	Weeks on Chart
19 Jun 82	**SHAPE UP AND DANCE WITH FELICITY KENDAL (VOLUME ONE)** *Lifestyle LEG 1* ●	29		47

KENICKIE

UK, female/male vocal/instrumental group – Lauren Laverne, Emmy-Kate Montrose, Marie du Santiago & Johnny X (Pete Gofton) — 5

Date	Title	Peak Position	Weeks at No.1	Weeks on Chart
24 May 97	**AT THE CLUB** *Emidisc ADISCCD 002*	9		3
12 Sep 98	**GET IN** *EMI 4958512*	32		2

BRIAN KENNEDY

UK, male vocalist/guitarist — 4

Date	Title	Peak Position	Weeks at No.1	Weeks on Chart
31 Mar 90	**THE GREAT WAR OF WORDS** *RCA PL 74475*	64		1
19 Oct 96	**A BETTER MAN** *RCA 74321409132* ○	19		3

NIGEL KENNEDY

UK, male violinist — 124

Date	Title	Peak Position	Weeks at No.1	Weeks on Chart
1 Mar 86	**ELGAR: VIOLIN CONCERTO** *EMI EMX 4120581* NIGEL KENNEDY WITH THE LONDON PHILHARMONIC ORCHESTRA	97		1
7 Oct 89	**VIVALDI: THE FOUR SEASONS** *EMI NIGE 2* NIGEL KENNEDY WITH THE ENGLISH CHAMBER ORCHESTRA ⊛**x2**	3		81
5 May 90	**MENDELSSOHN/BRUCH/SCHUBERT** *HMV 7496631* NIGEL KENNEDY WITH JEFFREY TATE CONDUCTING THE ENGLISH CHAMBER ORCHESTRA ●	28		15
6 Apr 91	**BRAHMS: VIOLIN CONCERTO** *EMI NIGE 3* NIGEL KENNEDY WITH THE LONDON PHILHARMONIC ORCHESTRA ●	16		12
22 Feb 92	**JUST LISTEN** *EMI Classics CDNIGE 4* NIGEL KENNEDY WITH THE LONDON PHILHARMONIC ORCHESTRA CONDUCTED BY SIMON RATTLE	56		1
21 Nov 92	**BEETHOVEN VIOLIN CONCERTO, CORIOLAN OVERTURE** *EMI Classics CDC 7545742* NIGEL KENNEDY WITH KLAUS TENNSTEDT CONDUCTING THE NORTH GERMAN RADIO SYMPHONY ORCHESTRA	40		6
29 Jun 96	**KAFKA** *EMI CDEMD 1095*	67		1
6 Nov 99	**CLASSIC KENNEDY** *EMI Classics CDC 5568902* WITH THE ENGLISH CHAMBER ORCHESTRA	51		6
2 Nov 02	**GREATEST HITS** *EMI Classics 5574112*	71		1

KENNY

UK, male vocal/instrumental group — 1

Date	Title	Peak Position	Weeks at No.1	Weeks on Chart
17 Jan 76	**THE SOUND OF SUPER K** *RAK SRAK 518*	56		1

GERARD KENNY

US, male vocalist — 4

Date	Title	Peak Position	Weeks at No.1	Weeks on Chart
21 Jul 79	**MADE IT THROUGH THE RAIN** *RCA Victor PL 25218*	19		4

KERBDOG

Ireland, male vocal/instrumental group — 1

Date	Title	Peak Position	Weeks at No.1	Weeks on Chart
12 Apr 97	**ON THE TURN** *Fontana 5329992*	64		1

NIK KERSHAW

UK, male vocalist/guitarist — 100

Date	Title	Peak Position	Weeks at No.1	Weeks on Chart
10 Mar 84	**HUMAN RACING** *MCA MCF 3197* ⊛	5		61
1 Dec 84	**THE RIDDLE** *MCA MCF 3245* ⊛	8		36
8 Nov 86	**RADIO MUSICOLA** *MCA MCG 6016* ○	47		3

KEY SESSIONS QUARTET

UK, male instrumental group — 2

Date	Title	Peak Position	Weeks at No.1	Weeks on Chart
20 Mar 04	**THE PIANO SESSIONS** *T2/Telstar TCD3387*	54		2

ALICIA KEYS

US, female vocalist/pianist (Alicia Cook) — 137

Date	Title	Peak Position	Weeks at No.1	Weeks on Chart
22 Sep 01	**SONGS IN A MINOR** *J Records 80813200022* ⊛**x3** ★	6		79
13 Dec 03	**THE DIARY OF ALICIA KEYS** *J Records 82876586202* ⊛ ★	13		36
22 Oct 05	**UNPLUGGED** *J Records 82876718082* ★	52		1
1 Dec 07	**AS I AM** *J Records 88697190512* ⊛ ★	11		21

NUSRAT FATEH ALI KHAN/MICHAEL BROOK

Pakistan, male vocalist & Canada, male producer/guitarist — 1

Date	Title	Peak Position	Weeks at No.1	Weeks on Chart
6 Apr 96	**NIGHT SONG** *Realworld CDRW 50*	65		1

CHAKA KHAN

US, female vocalist (Yvette Stevens) — 45

Date	Title	Peak Position	Weeks at No.1	Weeks on Chart
21 Apr 84	**STOMPIN' AT THE SAVOY** *Warner Brothers 9236791* RUFUS & CHAKA KHAN	64		5
20 Oct 84	**I FEEL FOR YOU** *Warner Brothers 9251621* ●	15		22
9 Aug 86	**DESTINY** *Warner Brothers WX 45*	77		2
3 Jun 89	**LIFE IS A DANCE – THE REMIX PROJECT** *Warner Brothers WX 268* ●	14		15
4 Sep 99	**BEST OF CHAKA KHAN – I'M EVERY WOMAN** *warner.esp 9362475072*	62		1

KID ROCK

US, male vocalist/rapper (Robert Ritchie) — 12

Date	Title	Peak Position	Weeks at No.1	Weeks on Chart
10 Jun 00	**THE HISTORY OF ROCK** *East West 7567833142* ○	73		1
9 Aug 08	**ROCK N ROLL JESUS** *Atlantic 7567899717* ●	4		11

KIDS FROM FAME

US, male/female vocalists/actors led by dance teacher Debbie Allen and backed by session musicians — 117

Date	Title	Peak Position	Weeks at No.1	Weeks on Chart
24 Jul 82	**THE KIDS FROM FAME** *BBC REP 447* ⊛	1	12	45
16 Oct 82	**THE KIDS FROM FAME AGAIN** *RCA RCALP 6057* ⊛	2		21
26 Feb 83	**THE KIDS FROM FAME LIVE** *RCA KIDLP 003* ○	8		28
14 May 83	**THE KIDS FROM FAME SONGS** *BBC KIDLP 004*	14		16
20 Aug 83	**THE KIDS FROM FAME SING FOR YOU** *BBC KIDLP 005*	28		7

KIDS IN GLASS HOUSES

UK, male vocal/instrumental group — 1

Date	Title	Peak Position	Weeks at No.1	Weeks on Chart
7 Jun 08	**SMART CASUAL** *Roadrunner RR79342*	29		1

KILLERS

US, male vocal/instrumental group – Brandon Flowers, Dave Keuning, Mark Stoermer & Ronnie Vannucci, Jr. — 257

Date	Title	Peak Position	Weeks at No.1	Weeks on Chart
19 Jun 04	**HOT FUSS** *Lizard King LIZARD011* ⊛**x4**	1	2	153
14 Oct 06	**SAM'S TOWN** *Vertigo 1702675* ⊛**x4**	1	3	74
24 Nov 07	**SAWDUST** *Vertigo 1753374* ⊛	7		25
6 Dec 08	**DAY & AGE** *Vertigo 1785121* ⊛**x2**	1	1	5+

KILLING JOKE

UK, male vocal/instrumental group — 35

Date	Title	Peak Position	Weeks at No.1	Weeks on Chart
25 Oct 80	**KILLING JOKE** *Polydor EGMD 545*	39		4
20 Jun 81	**WHAT'S THIS FOR** *E.G. EGMD 550*	42		4
8 May 82	**REVELATIONS** *E.G. EGMD 3*	12		6
27 Nov 82	**HA' – KILLING JOKE LIVE** *E.G. EGMDT 4*	66		2
23 Jul 83	**FIRE DANCES** *E.G. EGMD 5*	29		3
9 Mar 85	**NIGHT TIME** *E.G. EGLP 61* ○	11		9
22 Nov 86	**BRIGHTER THAN A THOUSAND SUNS** *E.G. EGLP 66*	54		1
9 Jul 88	**OUTSIDE THE GATE** *E.G. EGLP 73*	92		1
6 Aug 94	**PANDEMONIUM** *Butterfly BFLCD 9*	16		3
13 Apr 96	**DEMOCRACY** *Butterfly BFLCD 17*	71		1
9 Aug 03	**KILLING JOKE** *Zuma ZUMACD002*	43		1

KILLS

UK, male/female vocal/instrumental duo — 3

Date	Title	Peak Position	Weeks at No.1	Weeks on Chart
22 Mar 03	**KEEP ON YOUR MEAN SIDE** *Domino Recordings WIGCD 124*	47		1
5 Mar 05	**NO WOW** *Domino WIGCD149X*	56		1
22 Mar 08	**MIDNIGHT BOOM** *Domino WIGCD184*	47		1

Silver-selling ○ Gold-selling ● Platinum-selling ✪ US No.1 ★ | Peak Position | Weeks at No.1 | Weeks on Chart

KILLSWITCH ENGAGE

US, male vocal/instrumental group — 2

Date	Title / Label	Peak Position	Weeks at No.1	Weeks on Chart
22 May 04	**THE END OF HEARTACHE** *Roadrunner RR83732* ○	40		1
2 Dec 06	**AS DAYLIGHT DIES** *Roadrunner RR80582*	64		1

KIMERA WITH THE LONDON SYMPHONY ORCHESTRA

Korea, female vocalist (Kim Hong-Hee) & UK, orchestra — 4

Date	Title / Label	Peak Position	Weeks at No.1	Weeks on Chart
26 Oct 85	**HITS ON OPERA** *Stylus SMR 8505*	38		4

KING

UK/Ireland, male vocal/instrumental group – Paul King, John Hewitt, Jim Lantsbery, Mick Roberts & Anthony Wall — 32

Date	Title / Label	Peak Position	Weeks at No.1	Weeks on Chart
9 Feb 85	**STEPS IN TIME** *CBS 26095* ●	6		21
23 Nov 85	**BITTER SWEET** *CBS 86320* ●	16		11

B.B. KING

US, male vocalist/guitarist (Riley B. King) — 24

Date	Title / Label	Peak Position	Weeks at No.1	Weeks on Chart
25 Aug 79	**TAKE IT HOME** *MCA MCF 3010*	60		5
1 May 99	**HIS DEFINITIVE GREATEST HITS** *Universal TV 5473402*	24		4
24 Jun 00	**RIDING WITH THE KING** *Reprise 9362476122* & ERIC CLAPTON ●	15		15

BEN E. KING

US, male vocalist (Benjamin Nelson). See Drifters — 30

Date	Title / Label	Peak Position	Weeks at No.1	Weeks on Chart
1 Jul 67	**SPANISH HARLEM** *Atlantic 590001*	30		3
14 Mar 87	**STAND BY ME (THE ULTIMATE COLLECTION)** *Atlantic WX 90* & THE DRIFTERS ●	14		8
20 Oct 90	**THE VERY BEST OF BEN E. KING AND THE DRIFTERS** *Telstar STAR 2373* & THE DRIFTERS	15		16
7 Nov 98	**THE VERY BEST OF BEN E. KING AND THE DRIFTERS** *warner.esp/Global TV RADCD 108* & THE DRIFTERS	41		3

CAROLE KING

US, female vocalist/pianist (Carole Klein) — 108

Date	Title / Label	Peak Position	Weeks at No.1	Weeks on Chart
24 Jul 71	**TAPESTRY** *A&M AMLS 2025*	4		90
15 Jan 72	**MUSIC** *A&M AMLH 67013* ★	18		10
2 Dec 72	**RHYMES AND REASONS** *Ode 77016*	40		2
7 Feb 98	**TAPESTRY** *Epic CD 82308* ★	24		3
30 Sep 00	**NATURAL WOMAN – THE VERY BEST OF** *Columbia SONYTV 93CD*	31		3

DIANA KING

Jamaica, female vocalist — 2

Date	Title / Label	Peak Position	Weeks at No.1	Weeks on Chart
12 Aug 95	**TOUGHER THAN LOVE** *Columbia 4777562*	50		2

EVELYN KING

US, female vocalist — 9

Date	Title / Label	Peak Position	Weeks at No.1	Weeks on Chart
11 Sep 82	**GET LOOSE** *RCA RCALP 3093*	35		9

MARK KING

US, male vocalist/bass guitarist. See Level 42 — 2

Date	Title / Label	Peak Position	Weeks at No.1	Weeks on Chart
21 Jul 84	**INFLUENCES** *Polydor MKLP 1*	77		2

SOLOMON KING

US, male vocalist (Allen Levy), d. 20 Jan 2005 (age 74) — 1

Date	Title / Label	Peak Position	Weeks at No.1	Weeks on Chart
22 Jun 68	**SHE WEARS MY RING** *Columbia SCX 6250*	40		1

KING ADORA

UK, male vocal/instrumental group — 1

Date	Title / Label	Peak Position	Weeks at No.1	Weeks on Chart
2 Jun 01	**VIBRATE YOU** *Superior Quality RQS 13CD*	30		1

KING CRIMSON

UK/US, male vocal/instrumental group – Robert Fripp*; members also included Bill Bruford, Boz Burrell, Mel Collins, David Cross, Michael Giles, Gordon Haskell*, Greg Lake*, Ian McDonald, Jamie Muir, Richard Palmer-James, Peter Sinfield, Ian Wallace & John Wetton — 55

Date	Title / Label	Peak Position	Weeks at No.1	Weeks on Chart
1 Nov 69	**IN THE COURT OF THE CRIMSON KING** *Island ILPS 9111*	5		18
30 May 70	**IN THE WAKE OF POSEIDON** *Island ILPS 9127*	4		13
16 Jan 71	**LIZARD** *Island ILPS 9141*	29		2
8 Jan 72	**ISLANDS** *Island ILPS 9175*	30		1
7 Apr 73	**LARKS' TONGUES IN ASPIC** *Island ILPS 9230*	20		4
13 Apr 74	**STARLESS AND BIBLE BLACK** *Island ILPS 9275*	28		2
26 Oct 74	**RED** *Island ILPS 9308*	45		1
10 Oct 81	**DISCIPLINE** *E.G. EGLP 49*	41		4
26 Jun 82	**BEAT** *E.G. EGLP 51*	39		5
31 Mar 84	**THREE OF A PERFECT PAIR** *E.G. EGLP 55*	30		4
15 Apr 95	**THRAK** *Virgin KCCDY 1*	58		1

KING KURT

UK, male vocal/instrumental group — 5

Date	Title / Label	Peak Position	Weeks at No.1	Weeks on Chart
10 Dec 83	**OOH WALLAH WALLAH** *Stiff SEEZ 52*	99		1
8 Mar 86	**BIG COCK** *Stiff SEEZ 62*	50		4

KINGDOM COME

US, male vocal/instrumental group — 10

Date	Title / Label	Peak Position	Weeks at No.1	Weeks on Chart
26 Mar 88	**KINGDOM COME** *Polydor KCLP 1*	43		6
13 May 89	**IN YOUR FACE** *Polydor 8391921*	25		4

KINGMAKER

UK, male vocal/instrumental group — 10

Date	Title / Label	Peak Position	Weeks at No.1	Weeks on Chart
19 Oct 91	**EAT YOURSELF WHOLE** *Scorch CHR 1878*	29		3
29 May 93	**SLEEPWALKING** *Scorch CDCHR 6014*	15		7

CHOIR OF KING'S COLLEGE, CAMBRIDGE

UK, choir — 3

Date	Title / Label	Peak Position	Weeks at No.1	Weeks on Chart
11 Dec 71	**THE WORLD OF CHRISTMAS** *Argo SPAA 104*	38		3

KING'S X

US, male vocal/instrumental group — 4

Date	Title / Label	Peak Position	Weeks at No.1	Weeks on Chart
1 Jul 89	**GRETCHEN GOES TO NEBRASKA** *Megaforce WX 279*	52		1
10 Nov 90	**FAITH HOPE LOVE** *Megaforce 7567821451*	70		1
28 Mar 92	**KING'S X** *Atlantic 7567805062*	46		1
12 Feb 94	**DOGMAN** *Atlantic 7567825582*	49		1

KINGS OF CONVENIENCE

Norway, male vocal/instrumental duo — 2

Date	Title / Label	Peak Position	Weeks at No.1	Weeks on Chart
10 Feb 01	**QUIET IS THE NEW LORD** *Source SOURCD 019*	72		1
3 Jul 04	**RIOT ON AN EMPTY STREET** *Source CDSOUR 099*	49		1

KINGS OF LEON

US, male vocal/instrumental group – Caleb, Jared, Matthew & Nathan Followill — 127

Date	Title / Label	Peak Position	Weeks at No.1	Weeks on Chart
19 Jul 03	**YOUTH AND YOUNG MANHOOD** *Hand Me Down HMD27* ●	3		33
13 Nov 04	**AHA SHAKE HEARTBREAK** *Hand Me Down HMD39* ✪	3		24
14 Apr 07	**BECAUSE OF THE TIMES** *Hand Me Down 88697077412* ✪	1	2	55
12 Jul 08	**YOUTH AND YOUNG MANHOOD/AHA SHAKE HEARTBREAK** *Hand Me Down 88697003552*	67		1
4 Oct 08	**ONLY BY THE NIGHT** *Hand Me Down 88697327121* ✪x2	1	2	14+

KINGS OF SWING ORCHESTRA

Australia, orchestra — 11

Date	Title / Label	Peak Position	Weeks at No.1	Weeks on Chart
29 May 82	**SWITCHED ON SWING** *K-Tel ONE 1166*	28		11

SEAN KINGSTON

Jamaica (b. US), male vocalist/rapper (Kisean Anderson) — 8

Date	Title / Label	Peak Position	Weeks at No.1	Weeks on Chart
15 Sep 07	**SEAN KINGSTON** *Beluga Heights/Epic 88697129992*	8		8

KINKS
UK, male vocal/instrumental group – Ray Davies*, Mick Avory, Dave Davies & Pete Quaife (replaced by John Dalton) — Weeks on Chart: 150

Date	Title	Peak Position	Weeks at No.1	Weeks on Chart
17 Oct 64	**KINKS** *Pye NPL 18096*	3		25
13 Mar 65	**KINDA KINKS** *Pye NPL 18112*	3		15
4 Dec 65	**KINKS KONTROVERSY** *Pye NPL 18131*	9		12
10 Sep 66	**WELL RESPECTED KINKS** *Marble Arch MAL 612*	5		31
5 Nov 66	**FACE TO FACE** *Pye NPL 18149*	12		11
14 Oct 67	**SOMETHING ELSE BY THE KINKS** *Pye NSPL 18193*	35		2
2 Dec 67	**SUNNY AFTERNOON** *Marble Arch MAL 716*	9		11
23 Oct 71	**GOLDEN HOUR OF THE KINKS** *Pye Golden Hour GH 501*	21		4
14 Oct 78	**20 GOLDEN GREATS** *Ronco RPL 2031*	19		6
5 Nov 83	**KINKS GREATEST HITS – DEAD END STREET** *PRT KINK 1*	96		1
16 Sep 89	**THE ULTIMATE COLLECTION** *Castle Communications CTVLP 001* ●	35		7
18 Sep 93	**THE DEFINITIVE COLLECTION** *Polygram TV 5164652* ●	18		7
12 Apr 97	**THE VERY BEST OF THE KINKS** *Polygram TV 5375542*	42		3
8 Jun 02	**THE ULTIMATE COLLECTION** *Sanctuary SANDD 109* ○	32		15

KATHY KIRBY
UK, female vocalist (Kathleen O'Rourke) — Weeks on Chart: 8

Date	Title	Peak Position	Weeks at No.1	Weeks on Chart
4 Jan 64	**16 HITS FROM 'STARS AND GARTERS'** *Decca LK 5475*	11		8

DOMINIC KIRWAN
Ireland, male vocalist — Weeks on Chart: 1

Date	Title	Peak Position	Weeks at No.1	Weeks on Chart
1 Nov 97	**THE MUSIC'S BACK** *Ritz RZCD 0084*	54		1

KISS
US/Israel, male vocal/instrumental group – Gene Simmons, Paul Stanley, Peter Criss (replaced by Eric Carr) & Ace Frehley (Frehley's Comet*) (replaced by Bruce Kulick) — Weeks on Chart: 71

Date	Title	Peak Position	Weeks at No.1	Weeks on Chart
29 May 76	**DESTROYER** *Casablanca CBSP 4008*	22		5
26 Jun 76	**ALIVE!** *Casablanca CBSP 401*	49		2
17 Dec 77	**ALIVE** *Casablanca CALD 5004*	60		1
7 Jul 79	**DYNASTY** *Casablanca CALH 2051*	50		6
28 Jun 80	**UNMASKED** *Mercury 6302 032*	48		3
5 Dec 81	**THE ELDER** *Casablanca 6302 163*	51		3
26 Jun 82	**KILLERS** *Casablanca CANL 1*	42		6
6 Nov 82	**CREATURES OF THE NIGHT** *Casablanca CANL 4*	22		4
8 Oct 83	**LICK IT UP** *Casablanca VERL 9*	7		7
6 Oct 84	**ANIMALIZE** *Vertigo VERL 18*	11		4
5 Oct 85	**ASYLUM** *Vertigo VERH 32*	12		3
7 Nov 87	**CRAZY NIGHTS** *Vertigo VERH 49*	4		14
10 Dec 88	**SMASHES, THRASHES AND HITS** *Vertigo 8367591*	62		2
4 Nov 89	**HOT IN THE SHADE** *Fontana 8389131*	35		2
23 May 92	**REVENGE** *Mercury 8480372*	10		3
29 May 93	**ALIVE III** *Mercury 5148272*	24		2
23 May 96	**MTV UNPLUGGED** *Mercury 5289502*	74		1
12 Jul 97	**GREATEST HITS** *Polygram TV 5361592*	58		2
3 Oct 98	**PSYCHO-CIRCUS** *Mercury 5589922*	47		1

KISSING THE PINK
UK, male/female vocal/instrumental group — Weeks on Chart: 5

Date	Title	Peak Position	Weeks at No.1	Weeks on Chart
4 Jun 83	**NAKED** *Magnet KTPL 1001*	54		5

KITCHENS OF DISTINCTION
UK, male vocal/instrumental group — Weeks on Chart: 2

Date	Title	Peak Position	Weeks at No.1	Weeks on Chart
30 Mar 91	**STRANGE FREE WORLD** *One Little Indian TPLP 19*	45		1
15 Aug 92	**THE DEATH OF COOL** *One Little Indian TPLP 39CD*	72		1

EARTHA KITT
US, female vocalist, d. 25 Dec 2008 (age 81) — Weeks on Chart: 1

Date	Title	Peak Position	Weeks at No.1	Weeks on Chart
11 Feb 61	**REVISITED** *London HA 2296*	17		1

MYLEENE KLASS
UK, female vocalist/pianist. See Hear'Say — Weeks on Chart: 3

Date	Title	Peak Position	Weeks at No.1	Weeks on Chart
1 Nov 03	**MOVING ON** *UCJ 9865632* ○	32		3

KLAXONS
UK, male vocal/instrumental group – Jamie Reynolds, Steffan Halperin, James Righton & Simon Taylor-Davis — Weeks on Chart: 37

Date	Title	Peak Position	Weeks at No.1	Weeks on Chart
10 Feb 07	**MYTHS OF THE NEAR FUTURE** *Rinse RINSELP1* ⊛	2		37

KLEEER
US, male/female vocal/instrumental group — Weeks on Chart: 3

Date	Title	Peak Position	Weeks at No.1	Weeks on Chart
6 Jul 83	**SEEKRET** *Atlantic 7812541*	96		1
12 Oct 85	**THE ARTISTS VOLUME III** *Street Sounds ARTIS 3* WOMACK & WOMACK/THE O'JAYS/KLEEER/THE S.O.S. BAND	87		2

KLF
UK, male vocal/instrumental duo – Jimmy Cauty & Bill Drummond — Weeks on Chart: 46

Date	Title	Peak Position	Weeks at No.1	Weeks on Chart
16 Mar 91	**THE WHITE ROOM** *KLF Communications JAMSLP 6* ⊛	3		46

KNACK
US, male vocal/instrumental group — Weeks on Chart: 2

Date	Title	Peak Position	Weeks at No.1	Weeks on Chart
4 Aug 79	**GET THE KNACK** *Capitol EST 11948* ★	65		2

BEVERLEY KNIGHT
UK, female vocalist (Beverley Smith) — Weeks on Chart: 67

Date	Title	Peak Position	Weeks at No.1	Weeks on Chart
5 Sep 98	**PRODIGAL SISTA** *Parlophone Rhythm Series 4962962* ●	42		14
23 Mar 02	**WHO I AM** *Parlophone Rhythm Series 5360320* ●	7		24
10 Jul 04	**AFFIRMATION** *Parlophone 4733102* ●	11		9
1 Apr 06	**VOICE – THE BEST OF** *Parlophone 3545662* ●	9		16
19 May 07	**MUSIC CITY SOUL** *Parlophone 3886172* ○	8		4

GLADYS KNIGHT & THE PIPS
US, female/male vocal/instrumental group – Gladys Knight, William Guest, Merald 'Bubba' Knight & Edward Patten, d. 25 Feb 2005 — Weeks on Chart: 120

Date	Title	Peak Position	Weeks at No.1	Weeks on Chart
31 May 75	**I FEEL A SONG** *Buddah BDLP 4030* ○	20		15
28 Feb 76	**THE BEST OF GLADYS KNIGHT & THE PIPS** *Buddah BDLH 5013* ●	6		43
16 Jul 77	**STILL TOGETHER** *Buddah BDLH 5014*	42		3
12 Nov 77	**30 GREATEST** *K-Tel NE 1004* ⊛	3		22
4 Oct 80	**THE TOUCH OF LOVE** *K-Tel NE 1090* ○	16		6
4 Feb 84	**THE COLLECTION – 20 GREATEST HITS** *Starblend NITE 1*	43		5
15 Nov 86	**DIANA ROSS. MICHAEL JACKSON. GLADYS KNIGHT. STEVIE WONDER. THEIR VERY BEST BACK TO BACK** *PrioriTyV PTVR2* DIANA ROSS/MICHAEL JACKSON/GLADYS KNIGHT/STEVIE WONDER	21		10
27 Feb 88	**ALL OUR LOVE** *MCA MCF 3409*	80		1
28 Oct 89	**THE SINGLES ALBUM** *Polygram TV GKTV 1* ●	12		10
29 Mar 97	**THE SINGLES ALBUM** *Polygram TV 8420032*	69		2
25 Mar 06	**THE GREATEST HITS** *Columbia/UMTV 82876738812*	33		3

KNIGHTSBRIDGE STRINGS
UK, male orchestra — Weeks on Chart: 1

Date	Title	Peak Position	Weeks at No.1	Weeks on Chart
25 Jun 60	**STRING SWAY** *Top Rank BUY 017*	20		1

DAVID KNOPFLER
UK, male vocalist/guitarist. See Dire Straits — Weeks on Chart: 1

Date	Title	Peak Position	Weeks at No.1	Weeks on Chart
19 Nov 83	**RELEASE** *Peach River DAVID 1*	82		1

MARK KNOPFLER
UK, male vocalist/guitarist. See Dire Straits, Notting Hillbillies — Weeks on Chart: 83

Date	Title	Peak Position	Weeks at No.1	Weeks on Chart
16 Apr 83	**LOCAL HERO (OST)** *Vertigo VERL 4* ○	14		11
20 Oct 84	**CAL (OST)** *Vertigo VERH 17*	65		3
24 Nov 90	**NECK AND NECK** *CBS 4674351* CHET ATKINS & MARK KNOPFLER	41		11
6 Apr 96	**GOLDEN HEART** *Vertigo 5147322* ●	9		17
7 Oct 00	**SAILING TO PHILADELPHIA** *Mercury 5429812* ●	4		13
12 Oct 02	**THE RAGPICKER'S DREAM** *Mercury 0632932* ○	7		5
9 Oct 04	**SHANGRI-LA** *Mercury 9867715* ○	11		4
19 Nov 05	**PRIVATE INVESTIGATIONS** *Mercury 9873054* DIRE STRAITS & MARK KNOPFLER ●	20		7
6 May 06	**ALL THE ROADRUNNING** *Mercury 9877385* & EMMYLOU HARRIS ●	8		8
29 Sep 07	**KILL TO GET CRIMSON** *Mercury 1724908*	9		4

BEYONCE KNOWLES
US, female vocalist. See Destiny's Child — Weeks on Chart: 96

Date	Title	Peak Position	Weeks at No.1	Weeks on Chart
5 Jul 03	**DANGEROUSLY IN LOVE** *Columbia 5093952* ⊛x2 ★	1	5	52
16 Sep 06	**B'DAY** *Columbia 82876881322* ⊛ ★	3		26
5 May 07	**B'DAY** *Columbia 88697091252* ●	8		12
29 Nov 08	**I AM SASHA FIERCE** *Columbia 88697194922* ★	10		6+

Key: ○ Silver-selling · ● Gold-selling · ⊛ Platinum-selling · ★ US No.1 · Peak Position · Weeks at No.1 · Weeks on Chart

FRANKIE KNUCKLES
US, male producer — **2**

Date	Title / Label	Peak Position	Weeks at No.1	Weeks on Chart
17 Aug 91	**BEYOND THE MIX** *Virgin America VUSLP 6*	59		2

JOHN KONGOS
South Africa, male vocalist/multi-instrumentalist — **2**

Date	Title / Label	Peak Position	Weeks at No.1	Weeks on Chart
15 Jan 72	**KONGOS** *Fly HIFLY 7*	29		2

KOOKS
UK, male vocal/instrumental group – Luke Pritchard, Paul Garred, Hugh Harris & Max Rafferty (replaced by Dan Logan) — **104**

Date	Title / Label	Peak Position	Weeks at No.1	Weeks on Chart
4 Feb 06	**INSIDE IN/INSIDE OUT** *Virgin CDV3016A* ⊛x4	2		81
26 Apr 08	**KONK** *Virgin CDV3043* ●	1	1	23

KOOL & THE GANG
US, male vocal/instrumental group – James 'JT' Taylor, Robert 'Kool' Bell, Ronald Bell (Khalis Bayyan), George Brown, Robert Mickens, Claydes Charles Smith, d. 20 Jun 2006, Dennis Thomas & Ricky Westfield, d. 1985 — **116**

Date	Title / Label	Peak Position	Weeks at No.1	Weeks on Chart
21 Nov 81	**SOMETHING SPECIAL** *De-Lite DSR 001* ●	10		20
2 Oct 82	**AS ONE** *De-Lite DSR 3*	49		10
7 May 83	**TWICE AS KOOL** *Polystar PROLP 2* ●	4		23
14 Jan 84	**IN THE HEART** *De-Lite DSR 4* ○	18		23
15 Dec 84	**EMERGENCY** *De-Lite DSR 6* ○	47		25
12 Nov 88	**THE SINGLES COLLECTION** *De-Lite KGTV 1* ●	28		13
27 Oct 90	**KOOL LOVE** *Telstar STAR 2435*	50		1
26 Jun 04	**THE HITS – RELOADED** *Unique Corp/Virgin/EMI VTDCD618*	56		1

KORGIS
UK, male vocal/instrumental group — **4**

Date	Title / Label	Peak Position	Weeks at No.1	Weeks on Chart
26 Jul 80	**DUMB WAITERS** *Rialto TENOR 104*	40		4

KORN
US, male vocal/instrumental group – Jonathan Davis, Reginald 'Fieldy' Arvizu, James 'Munky' Shaffer, David Silveria & Brian 'Head' Welch — **24**

Date	Title / Label	Peak Position	Weeks at No.1	Weeks on Chart
26 Oct 96	**LIFE IS PEACHY** *Epic 4853696*	32		2
29 Aug 98	**FOLLOW THE LEADER** *Epic 4912212* ★	5		4
27 Nov 99	**ISSUES** *Epic 4963592* ★	37		1
22 Jun 02	**UNTOUCHABLES** *Epic 5017702* ●	4		9
6 Dec 03	**TAKE A LOOK IN THE MIRROR** *Epic 05133253*	53		1
16 Oct 04	**GREATEST HITS VOLUME 1** *Epic 5187923* ○	22		3
17 Dec 05	**SEE YOU ON THE OTHER SIDE** *Virgin CDVUSX274*	71		1
11 Aug 07	**UNTITLED** *Virgin 5038802*	15		3

KOSHEEN
UK, female/male vocal/production trio – Sian Evans, Darren Decoder & Markee Substance — **30**

Date	Title / Label	Peak Position	Weeks at No.1	Weeks on Chart
29 Sep 01	**RESIST** *Moksha/Arista 74321880812* ●	8		23
23 Aug 03	**KOKOPELLI** *Moksha/Arista 82876527232* ●	7		7

KRAFTWERK
Germany, male vocal/instrumental/production group – Ralf Hütter, Karl Bartos, Wolfgang Flür & Florian Schneider — **75**

Date	Title / Label	Peak Position	Weeks at No.1	Weeks on Chart
17 May 75	**AUTOBAHN** *Vertigo 6360 620* ○	4		18
20 May 78	**THE MAN-MACHINE** *Capitol EST 11728* ●	9		13
23 May 81	**COMPUTER WORLD** *EMI EMC 3370* ○	15		22
6 Feb 82	**TRANS-EUROPE EXPRESS** *Capitol EST 11603*	49		7
22 Jun 85	**AUTOBAHN** *Parlophone AUTO 1*	61		3
15 Nov 86	**ELECTRIC CAFÉ** *EMI EMD 1001*	58		2
22 Jun 91	**THE MIX** *EMI EM 1408* ○	15		6
16 Aug 03	**TOUR DE FRANCE SOUNDTRACKS** *EMI 5917082*	21		2
18 Jun 05	**MINIMUM – MAXIMUM** *EMI 5606112*	29		2

DIANA KRALL
Canada, female vocalist/pianist — **28**

Date	Title / Label	Peak Position	Weeks at No.1	Weeks on Chart
12 Jun 99	**WHEN I LOOK IN YOUR EYES** *Verve IMP 13042*	72		1
29 Sep 01	**THE LOOK OF LOVE** *Verve 5498462*	23		7
23 Nov 02	**A NIGHT IN PARIS** *Verve 0653692*	30		6
24 Apr 04	**THE GIRL IN THE OTHER ROOM** *Verve 9862063*	4		8
23 Sep 06	**FROM THIS MOMENT ON** *Verve 1705042*	29		4
29 Sep 07	**THE VERY BEST OF DIANA KRALL** *Universal 1743809*	35		2

BILLY J. KRAMER WITH THE DAKOTAS
UK, male vocal/instrumental group — **17**

Date	Title / Label	Peak Position	Weeks at No.1	Weeks on Chart
16 Nov 63	**LISTEN TO BILLY J. KRAMER** *Parlophone PMC 1209*	11		17

ALISON KRAUSS
US, female vocalist/violinist & male instrumental group — **49**

Date	Title / Label	Peak Position	Weeks at No.1	Weeks on Chart
25 Aug 01	**NEW FAVOURITE** *Rounder ROUCD 0495* & UNION STATION	72		1
14 Apr 07	**A HUNDRED MILES OR MORE: A COLLECTION** *Rounder ROUCD555*	38		4
10 Nov 07	**RAISING SAND** *Rounder 4759382* ALISON KRAUSS & ROBERT PLANT ⊛	2		44

LENNY KRAVITZ
US, male vocalist/multi-instrumentalist — **115**

Date	Title / Label	Peak Position	Weeks at No.1	Weeks on Chart
26 May 90	**LET LOVE RULE** *Virgin America VUSLP 10* ●	56		4
13 Apr 91	**MAMA SAID** *Virgin America VUSLP 31* ⊛	8		27
13 Mar 93	**ARE YOU GONNA GO MY WAY** *Virgin CDVUS 60* ⊛	1	2	47
23 Sep 95	**CIRCUS** *Virgin CDVUS 86* ●	5		4
23 May 98	**5** *Virgin CDVUS 140* ●	18		13
4 Nov 00	**GREATEST HITS** *Virgin CDVUSX 183* ⊛	12		17
10 Nov 01	**LENNY** *Virgin CDVUS 213*	55		1
29 May 04	**BAPTISM** *Virgin CDVUS 252*	74		1
16 Feb 08	**IT IS TIME FOR A LOVE REVOLUTION** *Virgin 5142772*	42		1

KREUZ
UK, male vocal group — **2**

Date	Title / Label	Peak Position	Weeks at No.1	Weeks on Chart
18 Mar 95	**KREUZ KONTROL** *Diesel DESCD 01*	48		2

KRIS KROSS
US, male rap duo — **8**

Date	Title / Label	Peak Position	Weeks at No.1	Weeks on Chart
27 Jun 92	**TOTALLY KROSSED OUT** *Columbia 4714342* ★	31		8

KRIS KRISTOFFERSON & RITA COOLIDGE
US, male vocalist/guitarist/actor & female vocalist — **4**

Date	Title / Label	Peak Position	Weeks at No.1	Weeks on Chart
6 May 78	**NATURAL ACT** *A&M AMLH 64690*	35		4

KROKUS
Switzerland/Malta, male vocal/instrumental group — **11**

Date	Title / Label	Peak Position	Weeks at No.1	Weeks on Chart
21 Feb 81	**HARDWARE** *Ariola ARL 5064*	44		4
20 Feb 82	**ONE VICE AT A TIME** *Ariola SPART 1189*	28		5
16 Apr 83	**HEADHUNTER** *Ariola 205 255*	74		2

KRS ONE
US, male rapper (Lawrence Parker) — **1**

Date	Title / Label	Peak Position	Weeks at No.1	Weeks on Chart
31 May 97	**I GOT NEXT** *Jive CHIP 179*	58		1

K7
US, male vocal/rap group — **3**

Date	Title / Label	Peak Position	Weeks at No.1	Weeks on Chart
5 Feb 94	**SWING BATTA SWING** *Big Life BLRCD 27*	27		3

KUBB
UK, male vocal/instrumental group — **9**

Date	Title / Label	Peak Position	Weeks at No.1	Weeks on Chart
26 Nov 05	**MOTHER** *Mercury 9870767* ●	26		9

KULA SHAKER
UK, male vocal/instrumental group – Crispian Mills, Alonza Bevan, Jay Darlington & Paul Winterhart — **55**

Date	Title / Label	Peak Position	Weeks at No.1	Weeks on Chart
28 Sep 96	**K** *Columbia SHAKER 1CD* ⊛x2	1	2	44
20 Mar 99	**PEASANTS, PIGS & ASTRONAUTS** *Columbia SHAKER 2CD* ●	9		10
1 Sep 07	**STRANGE FOLK** *Strangefolk SFKS001CD*	69		1

CHARLIE KUNZ
US, male pianist, d. 16 Mar 1958 (age 61) — **11**

Date	Title / Label	Peak Position	Weeks at No.1	Weeks on Chart
14 Jun 69	**THE WORLD OF CHARLIE KUNZ** *Decca SPA 15*	9		11

L

L.A. GUNS
US, male/female vocal/instrumental group — 4

Date	Title	Peak Position	Weeks at No.1	Weeks on Chart
5 Mar 88	**L.A. GUNS** *Vertigo VERH 55*	73		1
30 Sep 89	**COCKED AND LOADED** *Vertigo 8385921*	45		2
13 Jul 91	**HOLLYWOOD VAMPIRES** *Mercury 8496041*	44		1

LA'S
UK, male vocal/instrumental group — 23

Date	Title	Peak Position	Weeks at No.1	Weeks on Chart
13 Oct 90	**THE LA'S** *Go! Discs 8282021* ○	30		23

PATTI LABELLE
US, female vocalist (Patricia Holt) — 17

Date	Title	Peak Position	Weeks at No.1	Weeks on Chart
24 May 86	**WINNER IN YOU** *MCA MCF 3319* ○ ★	30		17

LACUNA COIL
Italy, male/female vocal/instrumental group — 1

Date	Title	Peak Position	Weeks at No.1	Weeks on Chart
15 Apr 06	**KARMACODE** *Century Media 776602*	47		1

LADY SOVEREIGN
UK, female rapper (Louise Harman) — 1

Date	Title	Peak Position	Weeks at No.1	Weeks on Chart
17 Feb 07	**PUBLIC WARNING** *Def Jam/Island 1705563*	58		1

LADYHAWKE
New Zealand, female vocalist/multi-instrumentalist (Phillipa Brown) — 1

Date	Title	Peak Position	Weeks at No.1	Weeks on Chart
4 Oct 08	**LADYHAWKE** *Modular MODCD098*	47		1

LADYSMITH BLACK MAMBAZO
South Africa, male vocal group formed by Joseph Shabalala — 69

Date	Title	Peak Position	Weeks at No.1	Weeks on Chart
11 Apr 87	**SHAKA ZULU** *Warner Brothers WX 94* ○	34		11
22 Nov 97	**HEAVENLY** *A&M 5407902* ●	53		16
3 Oct 98	**THE BEST OF LADYSMITH BLACK MAMBAZO – THE STAR AND WISEMAN** *Polygram TV 5652982* ⊛x3	2		34
16 Oct 99	**IN HARMONY** *Universal Music TV 1537392*	15		5
12 May 01	**THE ULTIMATE COLLECTION** *Universal Music TV 5566822*	37		3

LADYTRON
UK/Bulgaria, male/female vocal/production group — 1

Date	Title	Peak Position	Weeks at No.1	Weeks on Chart
14 Jun 08	**VELOCIFERO** *Nettwerk 307902*	75		1

CLEO LAINE
UK, female vocalist (Clementina Campbell) — 37

Date	Title	Peak Position	Weeks at No.1	Weeks on Chart
7 Jan 78	**BEST FRIENDS** *RCA Victor RS 1094* ○ CLEO LAINE & JOHN WILLIAMS	18		22
2 Dec 78	**CLEO** *Arcade ADEP 37*	68		1
31 May 80	**SOMETIMES WHEN WE TOUCH** *RCA PL 25296* CLEO LAINE & JAMES GALWAY ●	15		14

FRANKIE LAINE
US, male vocalist (Frank Lovecchio), d. 6 Feb 2007 (age 93) — 29

Date	Title	Peak Position	Weeks at No.1	Weeks on Chart
24 Jun 61	**HELL BENT FOR LEATHER** *Philips BBL 7468*	7		23
24 Sep 77	**THE VERY BEST OF FRANKIE LAINE** *Warwick PR 5032* ○	7		6

GREG LAKE
UK, male vocalist/guitarist. See Emerson, Lake & Palmer, King Crimson — 3

Date	Title	Peak Position	Weeks at No.1	Weeks on Chart
17 Oct 81	**GREG LAKE** *Chrysalis CHR 1357*	62		3

SETH LAKEMAN
UK, male vocalist/guitarist — 10

Date	Title	Peak Position	Weeks at No.1	Weeks on Chart
2 Sep 06	**FREEDOM FIELDS** *I Scream ISCD007*	32		5
12 Jul 08	**POOR MAN'S HEAVEN** *Relentless CDREL18*	8		5

LAMB
UK, male/female vocal/production duo — 2

Date	Title	Peak Position	Weeks at No.1	Weeks on Chart
29 May 99	**FEAR OF FOURS** *Fontana 5588212*	37		1
20 Oct 01	**WHAT SOUND** *Mercury 5865382*	54		1

ANNABEL LAMB
UK, female vocalist — 1

Date	Title	Peak Position	Weeks at No.1	Weeks on Chart
28 Apr 84	**THE FLAME** *A&M AMLX 68564*	84		1

LAMBCHOP
US, male/female vocal/instrumental group — 6

Date	Title	Peak Position	Weeks at No.1	Weeks on Chart
19 Feb 00	**NIXON** *City Slang 201522*	60		1
2 Mar 02	**IS A WOMAN** *City Slang 201902*	38		2
21 Feb 04	**AW C'MON/NO YOU C'MON** *City Slang 5958900*	45		2
26 Aug 06	**DAMAGED** *City Slang SLANG1041092*	43		1

LAMBRETTAS
UK, male vocal/instrumental group — 8

Date	Title	Peak Position	Weeks at No.1	Weeks on Chart
5 Jul 80	**BEAT BOYS IN THE JET AGE** *Rocket TRAIN 10*	28		8

RAY LAMONTAGNE
US, male vocalist/guitarist — 33

Date	Title	Peak Position	Weeks at No.1	Weeks on Chart
1 Jul 06	**TROUBLE** *Echo ECHCD57* ⊛	5		28
21 Oct 06	**TILL THE SUN TURNS BLACK** *RCA 2564639032*	35		3
25 Oct 08	**GOSSIP IN THE GRAIN** *14th Floor 5186510202*	23		2

CHARLIE LANDSBOROUGH
UK, male vocalist/guitarist — 29

Date	Title	Peak Position	Weeks at No.1	Weeks on Chart
12 Oct 96	**WITH YOU IN MIND** *Ritz RITZBCD 0078*	49		6
8 Nov 97	**FURTHER DOWN THE ROAD** *Ritz RZCD 0085*	42		3
10 Oct 98	**THE VERY BEST OF CHARLIE LANDSBOROUGH** *Ritz RZCD 0087*	41		2
2 Oct 99	**STILL CAN'T SAY GOODBYE** *Ritz RZCD 0092*	39		2
16 Aug 03	**SMILE** *Telstar Premiere TPECD5516*	37		6
26 Feb 05	**A PORTRAIT OF – THE ULTIMATE COLLECTION** *DMG TV DMGTV014*	23		5
22 Oct 05	**MY HEART WOULD KNOW** *Rosette ROSCD2056*	60		2
23 Sep 06	**HEART AND SOUL** *Rosette ROSCD2066*	56		2
16 Feb 08	**UNDER BLUE SKIES** *Rosette ROSCD2083*	73		1

LANDSCAPE
UK, male vocal/instrumental group — 13

Date	Title	Peak Position	Weeks at No.1	Weeks on Chart
21 Mar 81	**FROM THE TEA ROOMS OF MARS...TO THE HELLHOLES OF URANUS** *RCA RCALP 5003*	16		13

RONNIE LANE
UK, male vocal/instrumental group. See Small Faces — 4

Date	Title	Peak Position	Weeks at No.1	Weeks on Chart
17 Aug 74	**ANYMORE FOR ANYMORE** *GM GML 1013* RONNIE LANE & SLIM CHANCE	48		1
15 Oct 77	**ROUGH MIX** *Polydor 2442 147* PETE TOWNSHEND & RONNIE LANE	44		3

MARK LANEGAN
US, male vocal/instrumental group — 2

Date	Title	Peak Position	Weeks at No.1	Weeks on Chart
14 Aug 04	**BUBBLEGUM** *Beggars Banquet BBQCD237*	43		1
11 Feb 06	**BALLAD OF THE BROKEN SEAS** *V2 VVR1035822* ISOBEL CAMPBELL & MARK LANEGAN	38		1

k.d. lang
Canada, female vocalist (Katherine Dawn Lang) — 73

Date	Title	Peak Position	Weeks at No.1	Weeks on Chart
28 Mar 92	**INGENUE** *Sire 7599268402* ⊛	3		52
13 Nov 93	**EVEN COW GIRLS GET THE BLUES (OST)** *Sire 9362454332*	36		2
14 Oct 95	**ALL YOU CAN EAT** *Warner Brothers 9362460342* ○	7		5
12 Jul 97	**DRAG** *Warner Brothers 9362466232*	19		3
15 Jul 00	**INVINCIBLE SUMMER** *Warner Brothers 9362476052*	17		6
5 Jul 03	**A WONDERFUL WORLD** *Columbia 5098702* TONY BENNETT & K.D. LANG	33		3
9 Feb 08	**WATERSHED** *Nonesuch 7559799908*	35		2

Silver-selling ○ Gold-selling ● Platinum-selling ⊛ US No.1 ★ — Peak Position, Weeks at No.1, Weeks on Chart

THOMAS LANG

UK, male vocalist — 1

Date	Title	Peak Position	Weeks at No.1	Weeks on Chart
20 Feb 88	**SCALLYWAG JAZ** *Epic 4509961*	92		1

MARIO LANZA

US, male vocalist (Alfredo Cocozza), d. 7 Oct 1959 (age 38) — 68

Date	Title	Peak Position	Weeks at No.1	Weeks on Chart
11 Aug 56	**SONGS FROM THE STUDENT PRINCE AND OTHER FAMOUS MELODIES** *HMV ALP 1186*	5		1
6 Dec 58	**THE STUDENT PRINCE/THE GREAT CARUSO (OST)** *RCA RB 16113*	4		21
23 Jul 60	**THE GREAT CARUSO** *RCA RB 16112*	3		15
9 Jan 71	**THE GREATEST HITS VOLUME 1** *RCA Victor LSB 4000*	39		1
3 Sep 81	**THE LEGEND OF MARIO LANZA** *K-Tel NE 1110* ●	29		11
14 Nov 87	**A PORTRAIT OF MARIO LANZA** *Stylus SMR 741* ○	49		8
12 Mar 94	**MARIO LANZA – THE ULTIMATE COLLECTION** *RCA Victor 74321185742*	13		7
12 Jun 04	**THE DEFINITIVE COLLECTION** *BMG 82876614032*	41		4

LARD

UK, male vocal/instrumental group — 1

Date	Title	Peak Position	Weeks at No.1	Weeks on Chart
6 Oct 90	**THE LAST TEMPTATION OF REID** *Alternative Tentacles VIRUS 84*	69		1

LARRIKIN LOVE

UK, male vocal/instrumental group — 2

Date	Title	Peak Position	Weeks at No.1	Weeks on Chart
7 Oct 06	**THE FREEDOM SPARK** *Infectious 2564639052*	37		2

LASGO

Belgium, male/female vocal/production/instrumental trio — 3

Date	Title	Peak Position	Weeks at No.1	Weeks on Chart
7 Sep 02	**SOME THINGS** *Positiva 5419362*	30		3

JAMES LAST

Germany, male producer/composer/trumpeter/orchestra leader (Hans Last). Before he formed his world famous band, Last was one of his country's best-known musicians and arrangers. Despite never having a UK Top 40 single, the band can boast an amazing 64 chart albums — 446

Date	Title	Peak Position	Weeks at No.1	Weeks on Chart
15 Apr 67	**THIS IS JAMES LAST** *Polydor 104678*	6		48
22 Jul 67	**HAMMOND A-GO-GO** *Polydor 249043*	27		10
26 Aug 67	**LOVE THIS IS MY SONG** *Polydor 583553*	32		2
26 Aug 67	**NON-STOP DANCING** *Polydor 236203*	35		1
29 Jun 68	**JAMES LAST GOES POP** *Polydor 249160*	32		3
8 Feb 69	**DANCING '68 VOLUME 1** *Polydor 249216*	40		1
31 May 69	**TRUMPET A-GO-GO** *Polydor 249239*	13		1
9 Aug 69	**NON-STOP DANCING '69** *Polydor 249294*	26		1
24 Jan 70	**NON-STOP DANCING '69/2** *Polydor 249354*	27		3
23 May 70	**NON-STOP EVERGREENS** *Polydor 249370*	26		1
11 Jul 70	**CLASSICS UP TO DATE** *Polydor 249371*	44		1
11 Jul 70	**NON-STOP DANCING '70** *Polydor 237104*	67		1
24 Oct 70	**VERY BEST OF JAMES LAST** *Polydor 2371 054*	45		4
8 May 71	**NON-STOP DANCING '71** *Polydor 2371 111*	21		4
26 Jun 71	**SUMMER HAPPENING** *Polydor 2371 133*	38		1
18 Sep 71	**BEACH PARTY 2** *Polydor 2371 211*	47		1
2 Oct 71	**YESTERDAY'S MEMORIES** *Contour 2870 117*	17		14
16 Oct 71	**NON-STOP DANCING 12** *Polydor 2371 141*	30		3
19 Feb 72	**NON-STOP DANCING 13** *Polydor 2371 189*	32		2
4 Mar 72	**POLKA PARTY** *Polydor 2371 190*	22		3
29 Apr 72	**JAMES LAST IN CONCERT** *Polydor 2371 191*	13		6
24 Jun 72	**VOODOO PARTY** *Polydor 2371 235*	45		1
16 Sep 72	**CLASSICS UP TO DATE VOLUME 2** *Polydor 184061*	49		1
30 Sep 72	**LOVE MUST BE THE REASON** *Polydor 2371 281*	32		2
27 Jan 73	**THE MUSIC OF JAMES LAST** *Polydor 2683 010*	19		12
24 Feb 73	**JAMES LAST IN RUSSIA** *Polydor 2371 293*	12		9
24 Feb 73	**NON-STOP DANCING VOLUME 14** *Polydor 2371 319*	27		3
28 Jul 73	**OLE** *Polydor 2371 384* ○	24		5
1 Sep 73	**NON-STOP DANCING VOLUME 15** *Polydor 2371 376* ○	34		2
20 Apr 74	**NON-STOP DANCING VOLUME 16** *Polydor 2371 444* ○	43		2
29 Jun 74	**IN CONCERT VOLUME 2** *Polydor 2371 320* ○	49		1
23 Nov 74	**GOLDEN MEMORIES** *Polydor 2371 472* ○	39		2
26 Jul 75	**TEN YEARS NON-STOP JUBILEE** *Polydor 2660 111* ●	5		16
2 Aug 75	**VIOLINS IN LOVE** *K-Tel 1*	60		1
22 Nov 75	**MAKE THE PARTY LAST** *Polydor 2371 612* ●	3		19
8 May 76	**CLASSICS UP TO DATE VOLUME 3** *Polydor 2371 538*	54		1
6 May 78	**EAST TO WEST** *Polydor 2630 092*	49		4
14 Apr 79	**LAST THE WHOLE NIGHT LONG** *Polydor PTD 001* ⊛x2	2		45
23 Aug 80	**THE BEST FROM 150 GOLD RECORDS** *Polydor 2681 211* ●	56		3
1 Nov 80	**CLASSICS FOR DREAMING** *Polydor POLTV 11* ⊛	12		18
14 Feb 81	**ROSES FROM THE SOUTH** *Polydor 2372 051*	41		5
21 Nov 81	**HANSIMANIA** *Polydor POLTV 14* ●	18		13
28 Nov 81	**LAST FOREVER** *Polydor 2630 135* ●	88		2
5 Mar 83	**BLUEBIRD** *Polydor POLD 5072*	57		3
30 Apr 83	**NON-STOP DANCING '83 – PARTY POWER** *Polydor POLD 5094*	56		2
30 Apr 83	**THE BEST OF MY GOLD RECORDS** *Polydor PODV 7*	42		5
3 Dec 83	**THE GREATEST SONGS OF THE BEATLES** *Polydor POLD 5119* ○	52		8
24 Mar 84	**THE ROSE OF TRALEE AND OTHER IRISH FAVOURITES** *Polydor POLD 5131*	21		11
13 Oct 84	**PARADISE** *Polydor POLD 5163*	74		2
8 Dec 84	**JAMES LAST IN SCOTLAND** *Polydor POLD 5166* ●	68		9
14 Sep 85	**LEAVE THE BEST TO LAST** *Polydor PROLP 7* ⊛	11		27
18 Apr 87	**BY REQUEST** *Polydor POLH 34* ●	22		11
26 Nov 88	**DANCE DANCE DANCE** *Polydor JLTV 1* ●	38		8
14 Apr 90	**CLASSICS BY MOONLIGHT** *Polydor 8432181* ●	12		12
15 Jun 91	**POP SYMPHONIES** *Polydor 8494291* ●	10		11
9 Nov 91	**TOGETHER AT LAST** *Decca Delpine 5115251* RICHARD CLAYDERMAN & JAMES LAST ⊛	14		15
12 Sep 92	**VIVA ESPANA** *Polygram TV 5172202* ○	23		5
20 Nov 93	**JAMES LAST PLAYS ANDREW LLOYD WEBBER** *Polydor 5199102* ●	12		10
19 Nov 94	**IN HARMONY** *Polydor 5238242* RICHARD CLAYDERMAN & JAMES LAST ●	28		7
18 Nov 95	**THE VERY BEST OF JAMES LAST AND HIS ORCHESTRA** *Polydor 5295562*	36		7
28 Mar 98	**POP SYMPHONIES 2** *Polydor 5396242*	32		3
24 Apr 99	**COUNTRY ROADS** *Polydor 5474022*	18		5
3 Nov 01	**PLAYS ABBA** *Polydor 5891982*	29		4
6 Sep 03	**THE CLASSICAL COLLECTION** *UCJ 9810457*	44		3

LAST SHADOW PUPPETS

UK, male vocal/instrumental group – Alex Turner, James Ford & Miles Kane — 24

Date	Title	Peak Position	Weeks at No.1	Weeks on Chart
3 May 08	**THE AGE OF THE UNDERSTATEMENT** *Domino WIGCD208* ●	1	1	24

LATE OF THE PIER

UK, male vocal/instrumental group — 1

Date	Title	Peak Position	Weeks at No.1	Weeks on Chart
23 Aug 08	**FANTASY BLACK CHANNEL** *Parlophone 2280331*	28		1

LATIN QUARTER

UK, male/female vocal/instrumental group — 3

Date	Title	Peak Position	Weeks at No.1	Weeks on Chart
1 Mar 86	**MODERN TIMES** *Rockin' Horse RHLP 1*	91		2
6 Jun 87	**MICK AND CAROLINE** *Rockin' Horse 208 142*	96		1

CYNDI LAUPER

US, female vocalist — 93

Date	Title	Peak Position	Weeks at No.1	Weeks on Chart
18 Feb 84	**SHE'S SO UNUSUAL** *Portrait PRT 25792* ●	16		32
11 Oct 86	**TRUE COLOURS** *Portrait PRT 26948* ○	25		12
1 Jul 89	**A NIGHT TO REMEMBER** *Epic 4624991*	9		12
27 Nov 93	**HAT FULL OF STARS** *Epic 4730542*	56		1
3 Sep 94	**TWELVE DEADLY CYNS...AND THEN SOME** *Epic 4773632* ⊛x2	2		34
22 Feb 97	**SISTERS OF AVALON** *Epic 4853702*	59		1
25 Mar 06	**THE BODY ACOUSTIC** *Epic 82876804342*	55		1

LAUREL & HARDY

UK/US, male comedy/vocal duo – Stan Laurel, d. 23 Feb 1965 & Oliver Hardy, d. 7 Aug 1957 — 4

Date	Title	Peak Position	Weeks at No.1	Weeks on Chart
6 Dec 75	**THE GOLDEN AGE OF HOLLYWOOD COMEDY** *United Artists UAG 29676*	55		4

AVRIL LAVIGNE

Canada, female vocalist/guitarist — 141

Date	Title	Peak Position	Weeks at No.1	Weeks on Chart
14 Sep 02	**LET GO** *Arista 74321949312* ⊛x5	1	3	67
5 Jun 04	**UNDER MY SKIN** *Arista 82876617872* ⊛	1	1	34
28 Apr 07	**THE BEST DAMN THING** *RCA 88697094862* ⊛ ★	1	1	40

LAW

US, male vocal/instrumental duo — 1

Date	Title	Peak Position	Weeks at No.1	Weeks on Chart
6 Apr 91	**THE LAW** *Atlantic 7567821951*	61		1

Silver-selling ○ Gold-selling ● Platinum-selling ⊛ US No.1 ★ Peak Position Weeks at No.1 Weeks on Chart

JOEY LAWRENCE
US, male vocalist

Date	Album	Peak Position	Weeks at No.1	Weeks on Chart
				3
31 Jul 93	**JOEY LAWRENCE** *EMI CDEMC 3657*	39		3

SYD LAWRENCE
UK, male band leader, d. 5 May 1998 (age 73)

Date	Album	Peak Position	Weeks at No.1	Weeks on Chart
				9
8 Aug 70	**MORE MILLER AND OTHER BIG BAND MAGIC** *Philips 6642 001*	14		4
25 Dec 71	**MUSIC OF GLENN MILLER IN SUPER STEREO** *Philips 6641 017*	43		2
25 Dec 71	**SYD LAWRENCE WITH THE GLENN MILLER SOUND** *Fontana SFL 13178*	31		2
26 Feb 72	**SOMETHING OLD, SOMETHING NEW** *Philips 6308 090*	34		1

RONNIE LAWS
US, male vocalist/saxophonist

Date	Album	Peak Position	Weeks at No.1	Weeks on Chart
				1
17 Oct 81	**SOLID GROUND** *Liberty LBG 30336*	100		1

MARIA LAWSON
UK, female vocalist

Date	Album	Peak Position	Weeks at No.1	Weeks on Chart
				1
9 Sep 06	**MARIA LAWSON** *Phonogenic 88697003482*	41		1

LAYO & BUSHWACKA!
UK, male DJ/production duo

Date	Album	Peak Position	Weeks at No.1	Weeks on Chart
				1
13 Jul 02	**NIGHT WORKS** *XL Recordings XLCD 154*	61		1

DOUG LAZY
US, male rapper (Gene Finley)

Date	Album	Peak Position	Weeks at No.1	Weeks on Chart
				1
10 Mar 90	**DOUG LAZY GETTIN' CRAZY** *Atlantic 7567820661*	65		1

LCD SOUNDSYSTEM
US, male production duo

Date	Album	Peak Position	Weeks at No.1	Weeks on Chart
				7
5 Feb 05	**LCD SOUNDSYSTEM** *DFA/EMI DFAEMI2138CD* ●	20		4
24 Mar 07	**SOUND OF SILVER** *DFA/EMI DFAEMI2164CD*	28		3

KELE LE ROC
UK, female vocalist (Kelly Biggs)

Date	Album	Peak Position	Weeks at No.1	Weeks on Chart
				2
10 Apr 99	**EVERYBODY'S SOMEBODY** *Wild Card 5596662*	44		2

DAN LE SAC VS SCROOBIUS PIP
UK, male vocal/DJ/production duo

Date	Album	Peak Position	Weeks at No.1	Weeks on Chart
				1
24 May 08	**ANGLES** *Sunday Best SBESTCD24*	31		1

LEAVES
Iceland, male vocal/instrumental group

Date	Album	Peak Position	Weeks at No.1	Weeks on Chart
				1
31 Aug 02	**BREATHE** *B Unique 0927487392*	71		1

LED ZEPPELIN
UK, male vocal/instrumental group – Robert Plant*, John Bonham, d. 25 Sep 1980, John Paul Jones & Jimmy Page*. The biggest-selling hard-rock act have over 250 million album sales worldwide, including over 110 million in the US. The groundbreaking group performed a successful live comeback show in 2007

Date	Album	Peak Position	Weeks at No.1	Weeks on Chart
				535
12 Apr 69	**LED ZEPPELIN** *Atlantic 588171* ⊛**x4**	6		79
8 Nov 69	**LED ZEPPELIN 2** *Atlantic 588198* ★	1	1	138
7 Nov 70	**LED ZEPPELIN 3** *Atlantic 2401 002* ★	1	4	40
27 Nov 71	**FOUR SYMBOLS (LED ZEPPELIN 4)** *Atlantic 2401 012* ⊛**x6**	1	2	77
14 Apr 73	**HOUSE OF THE HOLY** *Atlantic K 50014* ⊛ ★	1	2	13
15 Mar 75	**PHYSICAL GRAFFITI** *Swan Song SSK 89400* ⊛**x2** ★	1	1	27
24 Apr 76	**PRESENCE** *Swan Song SSK 59402* ⊛ ★	1	1	14
6 Nov 76	**THE SONG REMAINS THE SAME (OST)** *Swan Song SSK 89402* ⊛	1	1	15
8 Sep 79	**IN THROUGH THE OUT DOOR** *Swan Song SSK 59410* ⊛ ★	1	2	16
4 Dec 82	**CODA** *Swan Song A 0051* ○	4		7
27 Oct 90	**REMASTERS** *Atlantic ZEP 1* ⊛**x2**	10		45
10 Nov 90	**LED ZEPPELIN (BOX SET)** *Atlantic 7567821441*	48		2
9 Oct 93	**LED ZEPPELIN BOXED SET II** *Atlantic 7567824772*	56		1
29 Nov 97	**BBC SESSIONS** *Atlantic 7567830612* ○	23		7
1 Apr 00	**LATTER DAYS – THE BEST OF – VOLUME 2** *Atlantic 7567832782*	40		1
1 Apr 00	**EARLY DAYS – THE BEST OF – VOLUME ONE** *Atlantic 7567832682*	55		1
8 Mar 03	**VERY BEST OF – EARLY DAYS AND LATTER DAYS** *Atlantic 7567836195* ⊛	11		23
7 Jun 03	**HOW THE WEST WAS WON** *Atlantic 7567835872* ● ★	5		7
24 Sep 05	**PHYSICAL GRAFFITI** *Swan Song 7567924425*	57		4
24 Nov 07	**MOTHERSHIP – THE BEST OF** *Atlantic 8122799613* ⊛	4		17
1 Dec 07	**THE SONG REMAINS THE SAME** *Swan Song 8122799611*	73		1

BRENDA LEE
US, female vocalist (Brenda Tarpley)

Date	Album	Peak Position	Weeks at No.1	Weeks on Chart
				64
24 Nov 62	**ALL THE WAY** *Brunswick LAT 8383*	20		2
16 Feb 63	**BRENDA – THAT'S ALL** *Brunswick LAT 8516*	13		9
13 Apr 63	**ALL ALONE AM I** *Brunswick LAT 8530*	8		20
16 Jul 66	**BYE BYE BLUES** *Brunswick LAT 8649*	21		2
1 Nov 80	**LITTLE MISS DYNAMITE – BRENDA LEE** *Warwick WW 5083* ●	15		11
7 Jan 84	**25TH ANNIVERSARY** *MCA MCLD 609*	65		4
30 Mar 85	**THE VERY BEST OF BRENDA LEE** *MCA LETV 1* ●	16		9
15 Oct 94	**THE VERY BEST OF BRENDA LEE...WITH LOVE** *Telstar TCD 2738*	20		7

PEGGY LEE
US, female vocalist (Norma Jean Egstrom), d. 22 Jan 2002 (age 81)

Date	Album	Peak Position	Weeks at No.1	Weeks on Chart
				23
4 Jun 60	**LATIN A LA LEE** *Capitol T 1290*	8		15
11 Jun 60	**BEAUTY AND THE BEAT** *Capitol T 1219* & GEORGE SHEARING	16		6
20 May 61	**BEST OF PEGGY LEE VOLUME 2** *Brunswick LAT 8355*	18		1
21 Oct 61	**BLACK COFFEE** *Ace Of Hearts AH 5*	20		1

RAYMOND LEFEVRE
France, male orchestra leader, d. 27 Jun 2008 (age 78)

Date	Album	Peak Position	Weeks at No.1	Weeks on Chart
				9
7 Oct 67	**RAYMOND LEFEVRE** *Major Minor MMLP 4*	10		7
17 Feb 68	**RAYMOND LEFEVRE VOLUME 2** *Major Minor SMLP 13*	37		2

LEFTFIELD
UK, male instrumental/production duo – Neil Barnes & Paul Daley

Date	Album	Peak Position	Weeks at No.1	Weeks on Chart
				117
11 Feb 95	**LEFTISM** *Hard Hands HANDCD 2* ⊛	3		94
2 Oct 99	**RHYTHM AND STEALTH** *Hard Hands HANDCD 4* ⊛	1	1	20
15 Oct 05	**A FINAL HIT – GREATEST HITS** *Hard Hands/Columbia 82876726082*	32		3

JOHN LEGEND
US, male vocalist/pianist (John Stephens)

Date	Album	Peak Position	Weeks at No.1	Weeks on Chart
				42
22 Jan 05	**GET LIFTED** *Columbia 05185772* ●	12		34
4 Nov 06	**ONCE AGAIN** *Columbia 82876803232* ●	10		5
1 Nov 08	**EVOLVER** *Columbia 88697387452*	21		3

TOM LEHRER
US, male comedian/vocalist

Date	Album	Peak Position	Weeks at No.1	Weeks on Chart
				26
8 Nov 58	**SONGS BY TOM LEHRER** *Decca LF 1311*	7		19
25 Jun 60	**AN EVENING WASTED WITH TOM LEHRER** *Decca LK 4332*	7		7

DENISE LEIGH & JANE GILCHRIST
UK, female vocalists

Date	Album	Peak Position	Weeks at No.1	Weeks on Chart
				2
8 Nov 03	**OPERATUNITY WINNERS** *EMI Classics 05575942* ○	60		2

LEMAR
UK, male vocalist (Lemar Obika)

Date	Album	Peak Position	Weeks at No.1	Weeks on Chart
				78
6 Dec 03	**DEDICATED** *Sony Music 5137912* ⊛	16		23
11 Dec 04	**TIME TO GROW** *Sony Music 5190822* ⊛**x2**	8		27
23 Sep 06	**THE TRUTH ABOUT LOVE** *White Rabbit 82876894642* ⊛	3		25
6 Dec 08	**THE REASON** *White Rabbit 88697339882*	41		3

LEMON JELLY
UK, male production duo

Date	Album	Peak Position	Weeks at No.1	Weeks on Chart
				9
2 Nov 02	**LOST HORIZONS** *Impotent Fury IFXLCD 160* ●	20		6
12 Feb 05	**64-'95** *XL Recordings IFXLCD182X* ○	17		3

Silver-selling ○ Gold-selling ● Platinum-selling ⊛ US No.1 ★ — Peak Position / Weeks at No.1 / Weeks on Chart

LEMONHEADS

US/Australia, male vocal/instrumental group – Evan Dando*, Nic Dalton & David Ryan

Date	Title	Peak	Wks No.1	Wks 33
1 Aug 92	**IT'S A SHAME ABOUT RAY** *Atlantic 7567824602* ●	33		16
23 Oct 93	**COME ON FEEL THE LEMONHEADS** *Atlantic 7567825372* ●	5		14
12 Oct 96	**CAR BUTTON CLOTH** *Atlantic 7567927262*	28		2
7 Oct 06	**THE LEMONHEADS** *Vagrant 9104402*	56		1

JOHN LENNON

UK, male vocalist/guitarist, d. 8 Dec 1980 (age 40). Together with Paul McCartney, he was not only a member of the most popular group of all time, the record-shattering Beatles, but he also formed the most successful songwriting partnership of the rock era. See Beatles

Date	Title	Peak	Wks No.1	Wks 355
16 Jan 71	**JOHN LENNON AND THE PLASTIC ONO BAND** *Apple PCS 7124*	8		11
30 Oct 71	**IMAGINE** *Apple PAS 10004* (WITH THE FLUX FIDDLERS) ★	1	2	101
14 Oct 72	**SOMETIME IN NEW YORK CITY** *Apple PCSP 716* JOHN AND YOKO LENNON WITH THE PLASTIC ONO BAND & ELEPHANT'S MEMORY	11		6
8 Dec 73	**MIND GAMES** *Apple PCS 7165* ●	13		12
19 Oct 74	**WALLS AND BRIDGES** *Apple PCTC 253* ○	6		10
8 Mar 75	**ROCK 'N' ROLL** *Apple PCS 7169* ●	6		28
8 Mar 75	**SHAVED FISH** *Apple PCS 7173* ●	8		29
22 Nov 80	**DOUBLE FANTASY** *Geffen K 99131* JOHN LENNON & YOKO ONO ⊛ ★	1	2	36
20 Nov 82	**THE JOHN LENNON COLLECTION** *Parlophone EMTV 37* ⊛x3	1	6	43
4 Feb 84	**MILK AND HONEY – A HEART PLAY** *Polydor POLH 5* JOHN LENNON & YOKO ONO ●	3		13
8 Mar 86	**JOHN LENNON LIVE IN NEW YORK CITY** *Parlophone PCS 7031*	55		3
22 Oct 88	**IMAGINE JOHN LENNON (OST)** *Parlophone PCSP 722* ●	64		6
8 Nov 97	**LENNON LEGEND – THE VERY BEST OF JOHN LENNON** *Parlophone 8219542* ⊛x2	4		45
14 Nov 98	**THE JOHN LENNON ANTHOLOGY** *Capitol 8306142*	62		1
26 Feb 00	**IMAGINE** *Parlophone 5248582*	51		1
15 Oct 05	**WORKING CLASS HERO – THE DEFINITIVE** *Parlophone 3400802* ●	11		10

JULIAN LENNON

UK, male vocalist

Date	Title	Peak	Wks No.1	Wks 20
3 Nov 84	**VALOTTE** *Charisma JLLP 1* ○	20		15
5 Apr 86	**THE SECRET VALUE OF DAYDREAMING** *Charisma CAS 1171*	93		1
5 Oct 91	**HELP YOURSELF** *Virgin V 2668*	42		4

ANNIE LENNOX

UK, female vocalist. See Eurythmics, Tourists

Date	Title	Peak	Wks No.1	Wks 147
18 Apr 92	**DIVA** *RCA PD 75326* ⊛x4	1	2	80
18 Mar 95	**MEDUSA** *RCA 74321257172* ⊛x2	1	1	49
21 Jun 03	**BARE** *RCA 82876524052* ●	3		14
13 Oct 07	**SONGS OF MASS DESTRUCTION** *RCA 88697152582*	7		4

DEKE LEONARD

UK, male vocalist

Date	Title	Peak	Wks No.1	Wks 1
13 Apr 74	**KAMIKAZE** *United Artists UAG 29544* DEKE LEONARD	50		1

PAUL LEONI

UK, male pan flute player

Date	Title	Peak	Wks No.1	Wks 19
24 Sep 83	**FLIGHTS OF FANCY** *Nouveau Music NML 1002* ○	17		19

KRISTIAN LEONTIOU

UK, male vocalist

Date	Title	Peak	Wks No.1	Wks 11
12 Jun 04	**SOME DAY SOON** *Polydor 9866206* ●	14		11

LES RHYTHMES DIGITALES

UK, male DJ/producer

Date	Title	Peak	Wks No.1	Wks 1
5 Jun 99	**DARKDANCER** *Wall Of Sound WALLCD 021*	53		1

LESS THAN JAKE

UK, male vocal/instrumental group

Date	Title	Peak	Wks No.1	Wks 3
31 May 03	**ANTHEM** *Sire 9362484852*	37		2
3 Jun 06	**IN WITH THE OUT CROWD** *Sire 9362499842*	55		1

LET LOOSE

UK, male vocal/instrumental group

Date	Title	Peak	Wks No.1	Wks 15
19 Nov 94	**LET LOOSE** *Mercury 5260182* ○	20		14
5 Oct 96	**ROLLERCOASTER** *Mercury 5329552*	42		1

LEVEL 42

UK, male vocal/instrumental group – Mark King*, Boon Guild, Phil Gould & Mark Lindup

Date	Title	Peak	Wks No.1	Wks 231
29 Aug 81	**LEVEL 42** *Polydor POLS 1036* ○	20		18
10 Apr 82	**THE EARLY TAPES JULY-AUGUST 1980** *Polydor POLS 1064*	46		6
18 Sep 82	**THE PURSUIT OF ACCIDENTS** *Polydor POLD 5067* ○	17		16
3 Sep 83	**STANDING IN THE LIGHT** *Polydor POLD 5110* ●	9		13
13 Oct 84	**TRUE COLOURS** *Polydor POLH 10* ○	14		8
6 Jul 85	**A PHYSICAL PRESENCE** *Polydor POLH 23*	28		5
26 Oct 85	**WORLD MACHINE** *Polydor POLH 25* ⊛x2	3		72
28 Mar 87	**RUNNING IN THE FAMILY** *Polydor POLH 42* ⊛x2	2		54
1 Oct 88	**STARING AT THE SUN** *Polydor POLH 50* ●	2		11
18 Nov 89	**LEVEL BEST** *Polydor LEVTV 1* ⊛	5		15
14 Sep 91	**GUARANTEED** *RCA PL 75005* ○	3		5
26 Mar 94	**FOREVER NOW** *RCA 74321189962*	8		3
7 Nov 98	**THE VERY BEST OF LEVEL 42** *Polydor 5593732*	41		2
24 Jun 06	**THE DEFINITIVE COLLECTION** *Polydor 9859043* ○	20		3

LEVELLERS

UK, male vocal/instrumental group – Mark Chadwick, Jeremy Cunningham, Simon Friend, Charlie Heather & Jon Sevink

Date	Title	Peak	Wks No.1	Wks 82
19 Oct 91	**LEVELLING THE LAND** *China WOL 1022* ●	14		30
4 Sep 93	**LEVELLERS** *China WOLCD 1034* ●	2		14
9 Sep 95	**ZEITGEIST** *China WOLCD 1064* ●	1	1	14
31 Aug 96	**BEST LIVE – HEADLIGHTS WHITE LINES BLACK TAR RIVERS** *China WOLCDX 1074*	13		4
6 Sep 97	**MOUTH TO MOUTH** *China 0630198562* ●	5		6
7 Nov 98	**ONE WAY OF LIFE – THE BEST OF THE LEVELLERS** *China 0521732* ●	15		11
16 Sep 00	**HELLO PIG** *China 8573843392*	28		2
23 Aug 08	**LETTERS FROM THE UNDERGROUND** *On The Fiddle OTFCX003*	24		1

LEVERT

US, male vocal group

Date	Title	Peak	Wks No.1	Wks 1
29 Aug 87	**THE BIG THROWDOWN** *Atlantic 7817731*	86		1
16 May 92	**NEED FOR NOT** *Rough Trade R 2862* LEVITATION	45		1

C.J. LEWIS

UK, male vocalist (Steven Lewis)

Date	Title	Peak	Wks No.1	Wks 2
3 Sep 94	**DOLLARS** *Black Market MCD 11131* ○	44		2

DONNA LEWIS

UK, female vocalist

Date	Title	Peak	Wks No.1	Wks 1
12 Oct 96	**NOW IN A MINUTE** *Atlantic 7567827622*	52		1

HUEY LEWIS & THE NEWS

US, male vocal/instrumental group – Huey Lewis, Mario Cipollina, Johnny Colla, Bill Gibson, Chris Hayes & Sean Hopper

Date	Title	Peak	Wks No.1	Wks 94
14 Sep 85	**SPORTS** *Chrysalis CHR 1412* ● ★	23		24
20 Sep 86	**FORE!** *Chrysalis CDL 1534* ⊛x2 ★	8		52
6 Aug 88	**SMALL WORLD** *Chrysalis CDL 1622* ●	12		8
18 May 91	**HARD AT PLAY** *Chrysalis CHR 1847*	39		2
21 Nov 92	**THE HEART OF ROCK AND ROLL – BEST OF HUEY LEWIS AND THE NEWS** *Chrysalis CDCHR 1934* ○	23		8

JENNY LEWIS

US, female vocalist

Date	Title	Peak	Wks No.1	Wks 2
4 Feb 06	**RABBIT FUR COAT** *Rough Trade RTRADCD291* WITH THE WATSON TWINS	63		1
4 Oct 08	**ACID TONGUE** *Rough Trade RTRADCD491*	55		1

JERRY LEE LEWIS

US, male vocalist/pianist

Date	Title	Peak	Wks No.1	Wks 6
2 Jun 62	**JERRY LEE LEWIS VOLUME 2** *London HA 2440*	14		6

LEONA LEWIS
UK, female vocalist

Date	Title	Peak Position	Weeks at No.1	50
24 Nov 07	**SPIRIT** *Syco 88697185262* ⊛x6 ★	1	8	50+

LINDA LEWIS
UK, female vocalist

Date	Title	Peak Position	Weeks at No.1	4
9 Aug 75	**NOT A LITTLE GIRL ANYMORE** *Arista ARTY 109*	40		4

RAMSEY LEWIS TRIO
US, male instrumental trio

Date	Title	Peak Position	Weeks at No.1	4
21 May 66	**HANG ON RAMSEY** *Chess CRL 4520*	20		4

SHAZNAY LEWIS
UK, female vocalist. See All Saints

Date	Title	Peak Position	Weeks at No.1	3
31 Jul 04	**OPEN** *London 2564617602*	22		3

LFO
UK, male instrumental group

Date	Title	Peak Position	Weeks at No.1	3
3 Aug 91	**FREQUENCIES** *Warp WARPLP 3*	42		2
10 Feb 96	**ADVANCE** *Warp WARPCD 39*	44		1

LIBERTINES
UK, male vocal/instrumental group – Pete Doherty, Carl Barât, John Hassall & Gary Powell

Date	Title	Peak Position	Weeks at No.1	30
2 Nov 02	**UP THE BRACKET** *Rough Trade RTRADECD 065* ●	35		7
11 Sep 04	**THE LIBERTINES** *Rough Trade RTRADCD 166* ⊛	1	1	21
10 Nov 07	**TIME FOR HEROES: BEST OF** *Rough Trade RTRADCD 421*	23		2

LIBERTY X
UK/Ireland, female/male vocal group – Michelle Heaton, Tony Lundon, Jessica Taylor & Kelli Young

Date	Title	Peak Position	Weeks at No.1	64
8 Jun 02	**THINKING IT OVER** *V2 VVR 1017782* ⊛x2	3		58
15 Nov 03	**BEING SOMEBODY** *V2 VVR 1023562*	12		4
22 Oct 05	**X** *EMI Virgin/Unique CDVCM1*	27		2

LIGHT OF THE WORLD
UK, male vocal/instrumental group

Date	Title	Peak Position	Weeks at No.1	1
24 Jan 81	**ROUND TRIP** *Ensign ENVY 14*	73		1

GORDON LIGHTFOOT
Canada, male vocalist/guitarist

Date	Title	Peak Position	Weeks at No.1	2
20 May 72	**DON QUIXOTE** *Reprise K 44166*	44		1
17 Aug 74	**SUNDOWN** *Reprise K 54020*	45		1

LIGHTHOUSE FAMILY
UK/Nigeria, male vocal/instrumental duo – Tunde Baiyewu (Tunde*) & Paul Tucker

Date	Title	Peak Position	Weeks at No.1	263
18 Nov 95	**OCEAN DRIVE** *Wild Card 5237872* ⊛x6	3		154
1 Nov 97	**POSTCARDS FROM HEAVEN** *Wild Card 5395162* ⊛x4	2		73
1 Dec 01	**WHATEVER GETS YOU THROUGH THE DAY** *Wild Card 5894122* ⊛	7		18
30 Nov 02	**GREATEST HITS** *Wild Card 0654482* ●	23		6
19 Apr 03	**THE VERY BEST OF** *Wild Card 0761662* ⊛	9		12

LIGHTNING SEEDS
UK, male vocal/instrumental group – Ian Broudie, Martin Campbell, Paul Hemmings & Chris Sharrock

Date	Title	Peak Position	Weeks at No.1	141
10 Feb 90	**CLOUDCUCKOOLAND** *Ghetto GHETT 3*	50		2
18 Apr 92	**SENSE** *Virgin CDV 2690* ○	53		1
17 Sep 94	**JOLLIFICATION** *Epic 4772379* ⊛	12		58
18 May 96	**PURE LIGHTNING SEEDS** *Virgin CDV 2805* ○	27		9
23 Nov 96	**DIZZY HEIGHTS** *Epic 4866402* ●	11		26
22 Nov 97	**LIKE YOU DO...THE BEST OF LIGHTNING SEEDS** *Epic 4890342* ⊛x2	5		41
4 Dec 99	**TILT** *Epic 4962632*	46		2
24 Jun 06	**THE VERY BEST OF** *Epic 82876848002*	33		2

LIGHTSPEED CHAMPION
UK (b. US), male vocalist (Devonte Hynes)

Date	Title	Peak Position	Weeks at No.1	2
2 Feb 08	**FALLING OFF THE LAVENDER BRIDGE** *Domino WIGCD186*	45		2

LIL' CHRIS
UK, male vocalist (Chris Hardman)

Date	Title	Peak Position	Weeks at No.1	3
16 Dec 06	**LIL' CHRIS** *RCA 88697019772*	54		3

LIL' JON & THE EAST SIDE BOYZ
US, male rap group

Date	Title	Peak Position	Weeks at No.1	2
28 May 05	**CRUNK JUICE** *TVT TV26942*	52		2

LIL' KIM
US, female rapper (Kimberly Jones)

Date	Title	Peak Position	Weeks at No.1	1
8 Jul 00	**THE NOTORIOUS KIM** *Atlantic 7567928402*	67		1

LIL' LOUIS
US, male producer (Marvin Burns)

Date	Title	Peak Position	Weeks at No.1	5
26 Aug 89	**FRENCH KISSES** *ffrr 8281701*	35		5

LIL' WAYNE
US, male rapper (Dwayne Carter, Jr.)

Date	Title	Peak Position	Weeks at No.1	11
21 Jun 08	**THA CARTER III** *Island 1768848* ○ ★	23		11

LIMAHL
UK, male vocalist (Chris Hamill). See Kajagoogoo

Date	Title	Peak Position	Weeks at No.1	3
1 Dec 84	**DON'T SUPPOSE** *EMI PLML 1*	63		3

ALISON LIMERICK
UK, female vocalist

Date	Title	Peak Position	Weeks at No.1	2
4 Apr 92	**AND STILL I RISE** *Arista 262365*	53		2

LIMP BIZKIT
US, male vocal/instrumental group – Fred Durst, Wes Borland, John Otto & Sam Rivers

Date	Title	Peak Position	Weeks at No.1	96
3 Jul 99	**SIGNIFICANT OTHER** *Interscope IND 90335* ● ★	10		37
9 Sep 00	**THREE DOLLAR BILL Y'ALL** *Interscope IND 90124*	50		5
28 Oct 00	**CHOCOLATE STARFISH AND THE HOT DOG FLAVOURED WATER** *Interscope 4907932* ⊛x2 ★	1	1	48
4 Oct 03	**RESULTS MAY VARY** *Interscope 9860976* ●	7		5
14 May 05	**THE UNQUESTIONABLE TRUTH – PART 1** *Polydor 9882180*	71		1

LINDISFARNE
UK, male vocal/instrumental group – Alan Hull*, d. 17 Nov 1995, Rod Clements, Simon Cowe, Jesmond Dene, Ray Jackson & Ray Laidlaw

Date	Title	Peak Position	Weeks at No.1	118
30 Oct 71	**FOG ON THE TYNE** *Charisma CAS 1050*	1	4	56
15 Jan 72	**NICELY OUT OF TUNE** *Charisma CAS 1025*	8		30
30 Sep 72	**DINGLY DELL** *Charisma CAS 1057*	5		10
11 Aug 73	**LINDISFARNE LIVE** *Charisma CLASS 2*	25		6
18 Oct 75	**FINEST HOUR** *Charisma CAS 1108*	55		1
24 Jun 78	**BACK AND FOURTH** *Mercury 9109 609* ○	22		11
9 Dec 78	**MAGIC IN THE AIR** *Mercury 6641 877*	71		1
23 Oct 82	**SLEEPLESS NIGHTS** *LMP GET 1*	59		3

LINKIN PARK
US, male vocal/instrumental group – Chester Bennington, Rob Bourdon, Brad Delson, David Farrell, Joseph Hahn & Mike Shinoda

Date	Title	Peak Position	Weeks at No.1	179
20 Jan 01	**HYBRID THEORY** *Warner Brothers 9362477552* ⊛x4	4		81
10 Aug 02	**REANIMATION** *Warner Brothers 9362483542*	3		8
5 Apr 03	**METEORA** *Warner Brothers 9362484612* ⊛ ★	1	1	33
6 Dec 03	**LIVE IN TEXAS** *Warner Brothers WB 485632* ●	47		3
11 Dec 04	**COLLISION COURSE** *WEA 9362489662* JAY-Z & LINKIN PARK ⊛ ★	15		16
26 May 07	**MINUTES TO MIDNIGHT** *Warner Brothers 9362499963* ⊛ ★	1	1	37
6 Dec 08	**ROAD TO REVOLUTION: LIVE AT MILTON KEYNES** *Warner Brothers 9362498095*	58		1

Silver-selling ○ Gold-selling ● Platinum-selling ⊛ US No.1 ★ Peak Position Weeks at No.1 Weeks on Chart

LINX
UK, male vocal/instrumental duo – David Grant* & Peter Martin — 23

Date	Title	Peak	Wks at No.1	Wks
28 Mar 81	**INTUITION** *Chrysalis CHR 1332* ○	8		19
31 Oct 81	**GO AHEAD** *Chrysalis CHR 1358*	35		4

LIONROCK
UK, male producer (Justin Robertson) — 3

Date	Title	Peak	Wks at No.1	Wks
20 Apr 96	**AN INSTINCT FOR DETECTION** *Deconstruction 74321342812*	30		2
28 Mar 98	**CITY DELIRIOUS** *Concrete HARD 32CDX*	73		1

LIQUID GOLD
UK, male/female vocal/instrumental group — 3

Date	Title	Peak	Wks at No.1	Wks
16 Aug 80	**LIQUID GOLD** *Polo POLP 101*	34		3

LISA LISA & CULT JAM WITH FULL FORCE
US, female/male vocal/instrumental group — 1

Date	Title	Peak	Wks at No.1	Wks
21 Sep 85	**LISA LISA AND CULT JAM WITH FULL FORCE** *CBS 26593*	96		1

LIT
US, male vocal/instrumental group — 1

Date	Title	Peak	Wks at No.1	Wks
10 Jul 99	**A PLACE IN THE SUN** *RCA 07863677752*	55		1

LITTLE ANGELS
UK, male vocal/instrumental group – Toby Jepson, Bruce J. Dickinson, Jim Dickinson, Michael Lee & Mark Plunkett — 15

Date	Title	Peak	Wks at No.1	Wks
2 Mar 91	**YOUNG GODS** *Polydor 8478461*	17		6
6 Feb 93	**JAM** *Polydor 5176422* ○	1	1	5
23 Apr 94	**LITTLE OF THE PAST** *Polydor 5219362*	20		2
2 Jul 94	**TOO POSH TO MOSH, TOO GOOD TO LAST?** *Essential ESSCD 213*	18		2

LITTLE FEAT
US, male vocal/instrumental group – Lowell George*, d. 29 Jun 1979, Paul Barrere, Sam Clayton, Kenny Gradney, Richie Hayward & Bill Payne — 19

Date	Title	Peak	Wks at No.1	Wks
6 Dec 75	**THE LAST RECORD ALBUM** *Warner Brothers K 56156* ○	36		3
21 May 77	**TIME LOVES A HERO** *Warner Brothers K 56349* ○	8		11
11 Mar 78	**WAITING FOR COLUMBUS** *Warner Brothers K 66075*	43		1
1 Dec 79	**DOWN ON THE FARM** *Warner Brothers K 56667*	46		3
8 Aug 81	**HOY-HOY!** *Warner Brothers K 66100*	76		1

LITTLE MAN TATE
UK, male vocal/instrumental group — 1

Date	Title	Peak	Wks at No.1	Wks
10 Feb 07	**ABOUT WHAT YOU KNOW** *V2 VVR1041728*	27		1

LITTLE STEVEN
US, male vocalist/guitarist (Steven Van Zandt). See Bruce Springsteen — 4

Date	Title	Peak	Wks at No.1	Wks
6 Nov 82	**MEN WITHOUT WOMEN** *EMI America 3027* & THE DISCIPLES OF SOUL	73		2
6 Jun 87	**FREEDOM NO COMPROMISE** *Manhattan MTL 1010*	52		2

LITTLE VILLAGE
UK/US, male vocal/instrumental group — 4

Date	Title	Peak	Wks at No.1	Wks
29 Feb 92	**LITTLE VILLAGE** *Reprise 7599267132*	23		4

LITTLE WILLIES
US, female/male vocal/instrumental group — 2

Date	Title	Peak	Wks at No.1	Wks
18 Mar 06	**THE LITTLE WILLIES** *Blue Note 3506712*	41		2

LIVE
US, male vocal/instrumental group — 9

Date	Title	Peak	Wks at No.1	Wks
15 Jul 95	**THROWING COPPER** *Radioactive RAD 10997* ○ ★	37		6
29 Mar 97	**SECRET SAMADHI** *Radioactive RAD 11590* ★	31		2
16 Oct 99	**THE DISTANCE TO HERE** *Radioactive RAD 11966*	56		1

LIVIN' JOY
US/Italy, female/male vocal/instrumental group — 2

Date	Title	Peak	Wks at No.1	Wks
16 Nov 96	**DON'T STOP MOVIN'** *Undiscovered MCD 60023*	41		2

LIVING COLOUR
US, male vocal/instrumental group — 22

Date	Title	Peak	Wks at No.1	Wks
15 Sep 90	**TIME'S UP** *Epic 4669201*	20		19
6 Mar 93	**STAIN** *Epic 4728562*	19		3

LIVING IN A BOX
UK, male vocal/instrumental group — 35

Date	Title	Peak	Wks at No.1	Wks
9 May 87	**LIVING IN A BOX** *Chrysalis CDL 1547* ●	25		19
8 Jul 89	**GATECRASHING** *Chrysalis CDL 1676* ●	21		16

LL COOL J
US, male rapper (James Todd Smith) — 44

Date	Title	Peak	Wks at No.1	Wks
15 Feb 86	**RADIO** *Def Jam DEF 26745*	71		1
13 Jun 87	**BIGGER AND DEFFER** *Def Jam 4505151*	54		19
8 Jul 89	**WALKING WITH A PANTHER** *Def Jam 4651121*	43		3
13 Oct 90	**MAMA SAID KNOCK YOU OUT** *Def Jam 4673151*	49		2
17 Apr 93	**14 SHOTS TO THE DOME** *Def Jam 4736782*	74		1
16 Nov 96	**ALL WORLD** *Def Jam 5343032*	23		8
25 Oct 97	**PHENOMENON** *Def Jam 5391862*	37		4
23 Sep 00	**THE GREATEST OF ALL TIME** *Def Jam 5429972* ★	29		2
2 Nov 02	**10** *Def Jam 0632192*	26		3
11 Sep 04	**THE DEFINITION** *Def Jam 9863650*	66		1

KELLY LLORENNA
UK, female vocalist — 2

Date	Title	Peak	Wks at No.1	Wks
7 Dec 02	**ALL CLUBBED UP – THE BEST OF KELLY LLORENNA** *Universal TV 0666082* ○	62		2

ANDREW LLOYD WEBBER
UK, male composer/producer — 58

Date	Title	Peak	Wks at No.1	Wks
11 Feb 78	**VARIATIONS** *MCA MCF 2824* ANDREW LLOYD WEBBER FEATURING JULIAN LLOYD WEBBER ⊛	2		19
23 Mar 85	**ANDREW LLOYD WEBBER: REQUIEM** *HMV ALW 1* PLACIDO DOMINGO, SARAH BRIGHTMAN, PAUL MILES-KINGSTON, WINCHESTER CATHEDRAL CHOIR & THE ENGLISH CHAMBER ORCHESTRA CONDUCTED BY LORIN MAAZEL ⊛	4		18
25 Dec 04	**PHANTOM OF THE OPERA (OST)** *Sony Classical SK93521* ●	40		7
28 Apr 07	**JOSEPH & THE AMAZING TECHNICOLOUR DREAMCOAT** *Polydor 5111302*	34		14

JULIAN LLOYD WEBBER
UK, male cellist. See Andrew Lloyd Webber — 38

Date	Title	Peak	Wks at No.1	Wks
11Feb 78	**VARIATIONS** *MCA MCF 2824* ANDREW LLOYD WEBBER FEATURING JULIAN LLOYD WEBBER ⊛	2		19
14 Sep 85	**PIECES** *Polydor PROLP 6* & THE LONDON SYMPHONY ORCHESTRA	59		5
21 Feb 87	**ELGAR CELLO CONCERTO** *Philips 4163541* JULIAN LLOYD WEBBER WITH THE ROYAL PHILHARMONIC ORCHESTRA CONDUCTED BY SIR YEHUDI MENUHIN	94		1
27 Oct 90	**LLOYD WEBBER PLAYS LLOYD WEBBER** *Philips 4322911* JULIAN LLOYD WEBBER WITH THE ROYAL PHILHARMONIC ORCHESTRA ●	15		13

LO FIDELITY ALLSTARS
UK, male vocal/instrumental group — 4

Date	Title	Peak	Wks at No.1	Wks
6 Jun 98	**HOW TO OPERATE WITH A BLOWN MIND** *Skint BRASSIC 8CD*	15		4

TONE LOC
US, male rapper (Anthony Smith) — 16

Date	Title	Peak	Wks at No.1	Wks
25 Mar 89	**LOC'ED AFTER DARK** *Delicious BRLP 526* ★	22		16

JOSEF LOCKE
Ireland, male vocalist (Joseph McLaughlin), d. 15 Oct 1999 (age 82) — 20

Date	Title	Peak	Wks at No.1	Wks
28 Jun 69	**THE WORLD OF JOSEF LOCKE TODAY** *Decca SPA 21*	29		1
21 Mar 92	**HEAR MY SONG (THE BEST OF JOSEF LOCKE)** *EMI CDGO 2034* ●	7		17
27 Jun 92	**TAKE A PAIR OF SPARKLING EYES** *EMI CDGO 2038*	41		2

JOHN LODGE
UK, male vocalist/guitarist. See Moody Blues — 20

Date	Title	Peak	No.1	Weeks
29 Mar 75	**BLUE JAYS** *Threshold THS 12* JUSTIN HAYWARD	4		18
19 Feb 77	**NATURAL AVENUE** *Decca TXS 120*	38		2

LISA LOEB & NINE STORIES
US, female/male vocal/instrumental group — 2

Date	Title	Peak	No.1	Weeks
7 Oct 95	**TAILS** *Geffen GED 24734*	39		2

NILS LOFGREN
US, male vocalist/guitarist — 30

Date	Title	Peak	No.1	Weeks
17 Apr 76	**CRY TOUGH** *A&M AMLH 64573*	8		11
26 Mar 77	**I CAME TO DANCE** *A&M AMLH 64628*	30		4
5 Nov 77	**NIGHT AFTER NIGHT** *A&M AMLH 68439*	38		2
26 Sep 81	**NIGHT FADES AWAY** *Backstreet/A&M MCF 3121*	50		3
1 May 82	**A RHYTHM ROMANCE** *A&M AMLH 68543*	100		1
6 Jul 85	**FLIP** *Towerbell TOWLP 11*	36		7
5 Apr 86	**CODE OF THE ROAD** *Towerbell TOWDLP 17*	86		1
27 Apr 91	**SILVER LINING** *Essential ESSLP 145*	61		1

JOHNNY LOGAN
Ireland, male vocalist — 1

Date	Title	Peak	No.1	Weeks
22 Aug 87	**HOLD ME NOW** *CBS 4510731*	83		1

LOLLY
UK, female vocalist (Anna Kumble) — 12

Date	Title	Peak	No.1	Weeks
2 Oct 99	**MY FIRST ALBUM** *Polydor 5479622*	21		12

LONDON BOYS
UK, male vocal duo – Eden Ephraim & Dennis Fuller, both d. 21 Sep 1996 — 29

Date	Title	Peak	No.1	Weeks
29 Jul 89	**THE TWELVE COMMANDMENTS OF DANCE** *WEA WX 278*	2		29

LONDON PHILHARMONIC CHOIR
UK, choir — 20

Date	Title	Peak	No.1	Weeks
3 Dec 60	**THE MESSIAH** *Pye Golden Guinea GGL 0062* LONDON PHILHARMONIC CHOIR WITH THE LONDON ORCHESTRA CONDUCTED BY WALTER SUSSKIND	10		7
13 Nov 76	**SOUND OF GLORY** *Arcade ADEP 25* LONDON PHILHARMONIC CHOIR WITH THE NATIONAL PHILHARMONIC ORCHESTRA CONDUCTED BY JOHN ALDISS	10		10
13 Apr 91	**PRAISE – 18 CHORAL MASTERPIECES** *Pop & Arts PATLP 301* LONDON PHILHARMONIC CHOIR WITH THE NATIONAL PHILHARMONIC ORCHESTRA CONDUCTED BY JOHN ALDISS	54		3

LONDON PHILHARMONIC ORCHESTRA
UK, orchestra — 47

Date	Title	Peak	No.1	Weeks
23 Apr 60	**RAVEL'S BOLERO** *London HAV 2189*	15		4
8 Apr 61	**VICTORY AT SEA** *Pye Golden Guinea GGL 0073*	12		1
21 May 83	**DRESSED FOR THE OCCASION** *EMI EMC 3432* CLIFF RICHARD & THE LONDON PHILHARMONIC ORCHESTRA	7		17
1 Mar 86	**ELGAR: VIOLIN CONCERTO** *EMI EMX 4120581* NIGEL KENNEDY WITH THE LONDON PHILHARMONIC ORCHESTRA	97		1
7 Mar 87	**THE MISSION (OST)** *Virgin V 2402* ENNIO MORRICONE WITH THE LONDON PHILHARMONIC ORCHESTRA	73		4
28 Oct 89	**CLASSIC BLUE** *Trax MODEM 1040* JUSTIN HAYWARD WITH MIKE BATT & THE LONDON PHILHARMONIC ORCHESTRA	47		7
6 Apr 91	**BRAHMS: VIOLIN CONCERTO** *EMI NIGE 3* NIGEL KENNEDY WITH THE LONDON PHILHARMONIC ORCHESTRA	16		12
22 Feb 92	**JUST LISTEN** *EMI Classics CDNIGE 4* NIGEL KENNEDY WITH THE LONDON PHILHARMONIC ORCHESTRA CONDUCTED BY SIMON RATTLE	56		1

LONDON SYMPHONY ORCHESTRA
UK, orchestra — 223

Date	Title	Peak	No.1	Weeks
18 Mar 72	**TOP TV THEMES** *Studio Two STWO 372*	13		7
16 Dec 72	**THE STRAUSS FAMILY (OST)** *Polydor 2659 014* CONDUCTED BY CYRIL ORNADEL	2		21
5 Jul 75	**MUSIC FROM 'EDWARD VII' (OST-TV)** *Polydor 2659 041*	52		1
18 Dec 76	**THE SNOW GOOSE** *RCA Victor RS 1088* SPIKE MILLIGAN WITH THE LONDON SYMPHONY ORCHESTRA	49		1
21 Jan 78	**STAR WARS (OST)** *20th Century BTD 541* JOHN WILLIAMS & THE LONDON SYMPHONY ORCHESTRA	21		12
8 Jul 78	**CLASSIC ROCK** *K-Tel ONE 1009*	3		39
10 Feb 79	**CLASSIC ROCK – THE SECOND MOVEMENT** *K-Tel NE 1039*	26		8
5 Jan 80	**RHAPSODY IN BLACK** *K-Tel ONE 1063*	34		5
1 Aug 81	**CLASSIC ROCK – ROCK CLASSICS** *K-Tel ONE 1123* WITH THE ROYAL CHORAL SOCIETY	5		23
27 Nov 82	**THE BEST OF CLASSIC ROCK** *K-Tel ONE 1080* WITH THE ROYAL CHORAL SOCIETY & THE ROGER SMITH CHORALE	35		11
27 Aug 83	**CLASSIC ROCK – ROCK SYMPHONIES** *K-Tel ONE 1243* WITH THE ROYAL CHORAL SOCIETY & THE ROGER SMITH CHORALE	40		9
26 Oct 85	**HITS ON OPERA** *Stylus SMR 8505* KIMERA WITH THE LONDON SYMPHONY ORCHESTRA	38		4
16 Nov 85	**THE POWER OF CLASSIC ROCK** *Portrait PRT 10049* WITH THE ROYAL CHORAL SOCIETY & THE ROGER SMITH CHORALE	13		15
14 Nov 87	**CLASSIC ROCK COUNTDOWN** *CBS MOOD 3*	32		16
18 Nov 89	**CLASSIC ROCK – THE LIVING YEARS** *CBS MOOD 9*	51		6
18 Jan 92	**WIND OF CHANGE – CLASSIC ROCK** *Columbia MOODCD 19* & THE ROYAL CHORAL SOCIETY	24		8
19 Nov 94	**THE WORKS OF RICE AND LLOYD WEBBER** *Vision VISCD 4*	55		2
23 Sep 95	**BRAVEHEART (OST)** *Decca 4482952* , CONDUCTOR JAMES HORNER	27		9
25 Oct 97	**PAUL McCARTNEY'S STANDING STONE** *EMI Classics CDC 5564842* CONDUCTED BY LAURENCE FOSTER	34		2
8 May 99	**RETURN TO THE CENTRE OF THE EARTH** *EMI Classics CDC 5567632* RICK WAKEMAN; LONDON SYMPHONY ORCHESTRA; ENGLISH CHAMBER CHOIR; NARRATED BY PATRICK STEWART	34		2
15 May 99	**STAR WARS – THE PHANTOM MENACE (OST)** *Sony Classical SK 61816* JOHN WILLIAMS & THE LONDON SYMPHONY ORCHESTRA	8		17
11 May 02	**STAR WARS EPISODE II: ATTACK OF THE CLONES (OST)** *Sony Classical SK 89965* JOHN WILLIAMS & THE LONDON SYMPHONY ORCHESTRA	15		5

LONDON WELSH MALE VOICE CHOIR
UK, male choir — 10

Date	Title	Peak	No.1	Weeks
5 Sep 81	**SONGS OF THE VALLEYS** *K-Tel NE 1117*	61		10

LONDONBEAT
UK/US, male vocal group — 6

Date	Title	Peak	No.1	Weeks
13 Oct 90	**IN THE BLOOD** *AnXious ZL 74810*	34		6

LONE JUSTICE
US, female/male vocal/instrumental group — 5

Date	Title	Peak	No.1	Weeks
6 Jul 85	**LONE JUSTICE** *Geffen GEF 26288*	49		2
8 Nov 86	**SHELTER** *Geffen WX 73*	84		3

Fastest-Selling Albums
By number of days it took to reach 1m sales

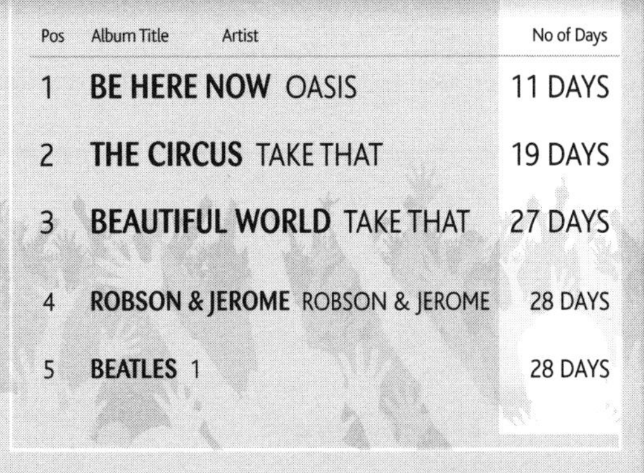

Pos	Album Title	Artist	No of Days
1	BE HERE NOW	OASIS	11 DAYS
2	THE CIRCUS	TAKE THAT	19 DAYS
3	BEAUTIFUL WORLD	TAKE THAT	27 DAYS
4	ROBSON & JEROME	ROBSON & JEROME	28 DAYS
5	BEATLES 1		28 DAYS

Silver-selling ○ Gold-selling ● Platinum-selling ⊛ US No.1 ★ — Peak Position | Weeks at No.1 | Weeks on Chart

LONE STAR
UK, male vocal/instrumental group — 7

Date	Title	Label	Peak	Wks No.1	Wks
2 Oct 76	LONE STAR	Epic EPC 81545	47		1
17 Sep 77	FIRING ON ALL SIX	CBS 82213	36		6

LONG BLONDES
UK, female/male vocal/instrumental group — 2

Date	Title	Label	Peak	Wks No.1	Wks
18 Nov 06	SOMEONE TO DRIVE YOU HOME	Rough Trade RTRADCD364	44		1
19 Apr 08	COUPLES	Rough Trade RTRADCD464	48		1

LONG RYDERS
US, male vocal/instrumental group — 1

Date	Title	Label	Peak	Wks No.1	Wks
16 Nov 85	STATE OF OUR UNION	Island ILPS 9802	66		1

LONGPIGS
UK, male vocal/instrumental group — 10

Date	Title	Label	Peak	Wks No.1	Wks
11 May 96	THE SUN IS OFTEN OUT	Mother MUMCD 9602	26		9
23 Oct 99	MOBILE HOME	Mother MUMCD 9902	33		1

JOE LONGTHORNE
UK, male vocalist — 32

Date	Title	Label	Peak	Wks No.1	Wks
3 Dec 88	THE JOE LONGTHORNE SONGBOOK	Telstar STAR 2353 ●	16		12
29 Jul 89	ESPECIALLY FOR YOU	Telstar STAR 2365	22		10
9 Dec 89	THE JOE LONGTHORNE CHRISTMAS ALBUM	Telstar STAR 2385 ●	44		4
13 Nov 93	I WISH YOU LOVE	EMI CDEMC 3662	47		4
8 Oct 94	LIVE AT THE ROYAL ALBERT HALL	Premier CDDPR 126	57		2

LONGVIEW
UK, male vocal/instrumental group — 6

Date	Title	Label	Peak	Wks No.1	Wks
2 Aug 03	MERCURY	14th Floor 5046668862 ○	29		6

LOOP
UK, male vocal/instrumental group — 2

Date	Title	Label	Peak	Wks No.1	Wks
4 Feb 89	FADE OUT	Chapter 22 CHAPLP 34	51		1
3 Feb 90	A GILDED ETERNITY	Situation Two SITU 27	39		1

LOOSE ENDS
UK, male/female vocal group — 41

Date	Title	Label	Peak	Wks No.1	Wks
21 Apr 84	A LITTLE SPICE	Virgin V 2301	46		9
20 Apr 85	SO WHERE ARE YOU?	Virgin V 2340 ○	13		13
18 Oct 86	ZAGORA	Virgin V 2384 ○	15		8
2 Jul 88	THE REAL CHUCKEEBOO	Virgin V 2528	52		4
29 Sep 90	LOOK HOW LONG	10 Records DIX 94 ○	19		5
19 Sep 92	TIGHTEN UP VOLUME 1	10 Records DIXCD 112	40		2

JENNIFER LOPEZ
US, female vocalist/actor — 150

Date	Title	Label	Peak	Wks No.1	Wks
17 Jul 99	ON THE 6	Columbia 4949302 ●	14		30
3 Feb 01	J.LO	Epic 5005502 ⊛ ★	2		48
30 Mar 02	J TO THA L-O! - THE REMIXES	Epic 5060242 ⊛ ★	4		27
7 Dec 02	THIS IS ME...THEN	Epic 5101282 ⊛	13		34
12 Mar 05	REBIRTH	Epic 5193913 ●	8		9
27 Oct 07	BRAVE	Epic 82796977542	24		2

TRINI LOPEZ
US, male vocalist (Trinidad Lopez) — 42

Date	Title	Label	Peak	Wks No.1	Wks
26 Oct 63	TRINI LOPEZ AT P.J.'S	Reprise R 6093	7		25
25 Mar 67	TRINI LOPEZ IN LONDON	Reprise RSLP 6238	6		17

JEFF LORBER
US, male vocalist/keyboard player — 2

Date	Title	Label	Peak	Wks No.1	Wks
18 May 85	STEP BY STEP	Club JABH 9	97		2

L'ORCHESTRE ELECTRONIQUE
UK, synthesizer orchestra — 1

Date	Title	Label	Peak	Wks No.1	Wks
29 Oct 83	SOUND WAVES	Nouveau Music NML 1005	75		1

LORDS OF THE UNDERGROUND
US, male rap group — 1

Date	Title	Label	Peak	Wks No.1	Wks
12 Nov 94	KEEPERS OF THE FUNK	Pendulum CDCHR 6088	68		1

LOS BRAVOS
Spain/Germany, male vocal/instrumental group — 1

Date	Title	Label	Peak	Wks No.1	Wks
8 Oct 66	BLACK IS BLACK	Decca LK 4822	29		1

LOS CAMPESINOS
UK, male/female vocal/instrumental group — 1

Date	Title	Label	Peak	Wks No.1	Wks
8 Mar 08	HOLD ON NOW YOUNGSTER	Wichita WEBB160CD	72		1

LOS LOBOS
US, male vocal/instrumental group — 24

Date	Title	Label	Peak	Wks No.1	Wks
6 Apr 85	HOW WILL THE WOLF SURVIVE?	Slash SLMP 3	77		6
7 Feb 87	BY THE LIGHT OF THE MOON	Slash SLAP 13	77		3
22 Aug 87	LA BAMBA (OST)	London LONLP 36 ● ★	24		15

LOS NINOS
UK, male instrumental group — 1

Date	Title	Label	Peak	Wks No.1	Wks
22 Jul 95	FRAGILE - MYSTICAL SOUNDS OF THE PANPIPES	Pearls DPWKF 4253	74		1

JOE LOSS & HIS ORCHESTRA
UK, male orchestra – Joe Loss, d. 6 Jun 1990 (age 80) — 10

Date	Title	Label	Peak	Wks No.1	Wks
30 Oct 71	ALL-TIME PARTY HITS	MFP 5227	24		10

LOST BOYZ
US, male rap group — 1

Date	Title	Label	Peak	Wks No.1	Wks
6 Jul 96	LEGAL DRUG MONEY	MCA UND 50310	64		1

LOSTPROPHETS
UK, male vocal/instrumental group – Ian Watkins, Mike Chiplin, Lee Gaze, Mike Lewis, Jamie Oliver & Stuart Richardson — 51

Date	Title	Label	Peak	Wks No.1	Wks
2 Mar 02	THE FAKE SOUND OF PROGRESS	Visible Noise TORMENT 005CD ●	44		8
14 Feb 04	START SOMETHING	Visible Noise TORMENT 32 ⊛	4		28
8 Jul 06	LIBERATION TRANSMISSION	Visible Noise TORMENT68CD ●	1	1	15

LOTUS EATERS
UK, male vocal/instrumental duo — 1

Date	Title	Label	Peak	Wks No.1	Wks
16 Jun 84	NO SENSE OF SIN	Sylvan 206 263	96		1

LOUISE
UK, female vocalist (Louise Redknapp, nee Nurding). See Eternal — 59

Date	Title	Label	Peak	Wks No.1	Wks
6 Jul 96	NAKED	EMI CDEMC 3748 ⊛	7		31
18 Oct 97	WOMAN IN ME	EMI 8219032 ⊛	5		19
12 Aug 00	ELBOW BEACH	1st Avenue 5276142 ○	12		4
22 Sep 01	CHANGING FACES - THE BEST OF	1st Avenue 5349672 ○	9		5

JACQUES LOUSSIER
France, male pianist — 3

Date	Title	Label	Peak	Wks No.1	Wks
30 Mar 85	JACQUES LOUSSIER - THE BEST OF PLAY BACH	Start STL 1	58		3

LOVE
US, male vocal/instrumental group — 9

Date	Title	Label	Peak	Wks No.1	Wks
24 Feb 68	FOREVER CHANGES	Elektra EKS7 4013	24		6
16 May 70	OUT HERE	Harvest SHOW 3/4	29		2
3 Mar 01	FOREVER CHANGES	Elektra 8122735372 ●	63		1

COURTNEY LOVE
US, female vocalist/guitarist (Love Michelle Harrison). See Hole — 1

Date	Title	Label	Peak	Wks No.1	Wks
21 Feb 04	AMERICA'S SWEETHEART	Virgin CDVUS 249	56		1

GEOFF LOVE & HIS ORCHESTRA
UK, orchestra – Geoff Love, d. 8 Jul 1991 (age 73). See Manuel & his Music of the Mountains — **28**

Date	Title	Peak	Wks at No.1	Wks
7 Aug 71	**BIG WAR MOVIE THEMES** *MFP 5171*	11		20
21 Aug 71	**BIG WESTERN MOVIE THEMES** *MFP 5204*	38		3
30 Oct 71	**BIG LOVE MOVIE THEMES** *MFP 5221*	28		5

MONIE LOVE
UK, female rapper (Simone Johnson) — **3**

Date	Title	Peak	Wks at No.1	Wks
20 Oct 90	**DOWN TO EARTH** *Cooltempo CTLP 14*	30		3

LOVE & MONEY
UK, male vocal/instrumental group — **2**

Date	Title	Peak	Wks at No.1	Wks
29 Oct 88	**STRANGE KIND OF LOVE** *Fontana SFLP 7*	71		1
3 Aug 91	**DOGS IN THE TRAFFIC** *Fontana 8489931*	41		1

LOVE/HATE
UK, male vocal/instrumental group — **5**

Date	Title	Peak	Wks at No.1	Wks
7 Mar 92	**WASTED IN AMERICA** *Columbia 4694532*	20		4
24 Jul 93	**LET'S RUMBLE** *RCA 74321153112*	24		1

LOVE UNLIMITED ORCHESTRA
US, orchestra — **1**

Date	Title	Peak	Wks at No.1	Wks
6 Apr 74	**RHAPSODY IN WHITE** *Pye International NSPL 28191*	50		1

LYLE LOVETT
US, male vocalist/guitarist — **2**

Date	Title	Peak	Wks at No.1	Wks
8 Oct 94	**I LOVE EVERYBODY** *MCA MCD 10808*	54		1
29 Jun 96	**THE ROAD TO ENSENADA** *MCA MCD 11409*	62		1

LENA LOVICH
US, female vocalist (Lili Premilovich) — **17**

Date	Title	Peak	Wks at No.1	Wks
17 Mar 79	**STATELESS** *Stiff SEEZ 7* LENE LOVICH	35		11
2 Feb 80	**FLEX** *Stiff SEEZ 19* LENE LOVICH	19		6

LOVIN' SPOONFUL
US, male vocal/instrumental group – John Sebastian, Steve Boone, Joe Butler & Zal Yanovsky, d. 13 Dec 2002 — **11**

Date	Title	Peak	Wks at No.1	Wks
7 May 66	**DAYDREAM** *Pye International NPL 28078*	8		11

LOW
US, male/female vocal/instrumental group — **1**

Date	Title	Peak	Wks at No.1	Wks
5 Feb 05	**THE GREAT DESTROYER** *Rough Trade RTRADCD206*	70		1

NICK LOWE
UK, male vocalist. See Rockpile — **17**

Date	Title	Peak	Wks at No.1	Wks
11 Mar 78	**THE JESUS OF COOL** *Radar RAD 1*	22		9
23 Jun 79	**LABOUR OF LUST** *Radar RAD 21*	43		6
20 Feb 82	**NICK THE KNIFE** *F-Beat XXLP 14*	99		2

LOWGOLD
UK, male vocal/instrumental group — **2**

Date	Title	Peak	Wks at No.1	Wks
24 Feb 01	**JUST BACKWARD OF SQUARE** *Nude 17CD*	33		2

L7
US, female vocal/instrumental group — **8**

Date	Title	Peak	Wks at No.1	Wks
2 May 92	**BRICKS ARE HEAVY** *Slash 8283072*	24		6
23 Jul 94	**HUNGRY FOR STINK** *Slash 8285312*	26		2

LUCK & NEAT
UK, male DJs/producers/rappers — **2**

Date	Title	Peak	Wks at No.1	Wks
8 Jun 02	**IT'S ALL GOOD** *Island CID 8117*	34		2

LUDACRIS
US, male rapper (Christopher Bridges) — **7**

Date	Title	Peak	Wks at No.1	Wks
29 Jun 02	**WORD OF MOUF** *Def Jam 5864462* ○	57		2
18 Oct 03	**CHICKEN N BEER** *Def Jam 9861137* ★	44		4
14 Oct 06	**RELEASE THERAPY** *Def Jam 1708937* ★	69		1

LULU
UK, female vocalist (Marie Lawrie) — **22**

Date	Title	Peak	Wks at No.1	Wks
25 Sep 71	**THE MOST OF LULU** *MFP 5215*	15		6
6 Mar 93	**INDEPENDENCE** *Dome DOMECD 1*	67		1
1 Jun 02	**TOGETHER** *Mercury 630212* ●	4		9
22 Nov 03	**THE GREATEST HITS** *Universal TV 9865879* ○	35		2
27 Mar 04	**BACK ON TRACK** *Mercury 9866136*	68		1
20 Aug 05	**A LITTLE SOUL IN YOUR HEART** *Globe Records 9872859*	29		3

BOB LUMAN
US, male vocalist, d. 27 Dec 1978 (age 41) — **1**

Date	Title	Peak	Wks at No.1	Wks
14 Jan 61	**LET'S THINK ABOUT LIVING** *Warner Brothers WM 4025*	18		1

LUMIDEE
US, female vocalist (Lumidee Cadino) — **3**

Date	Title	Peak	Wks at No.1	Wks
16 Aug 03	**ALMOST FAMOUS** *Universal 9860622*	70		3

LUNIZ
US, male rap duo — **3**

Date	Title	Peak	Wks at No.1	Wks
16 Mar 96	**OPERATION STACKOLA** *Virgin CDVUS 94*	41		3

LURKERS
UK, male vocal/instrumental group — **1**

Date	Title	Peak	Wks at No.1	Wks
1 Jul 78	**FULHAM FALLOUT** *Beggars Banquet BEGA 2*	57		1

LUSCIOUS JACKSON
US, female vocal/instrumental group — **1**

Date	Title	Peak	Wks at No.1	Wks
26 Apr 97	**FEVER IN FEVER OUT** *Grand Royal GR 038*	55		1

LUSH
UK, female/male vocal/instrumental group – Miki Berenyi, Christopher Acland, Emma Anderson & Phil King — **10**

Date	Title	Peak	Wks at No.1	Wks
8 Feb 92	**SPOOKY** *4AD CAD 2002CD*	7		3
25 Jun 94	**SPLIT** *4AD CAD 4011CD*	19		2
30 Mar 96	**LOVELIFE** *4AD CAD 6004CD*	8		5

VERA LYNN
UK, female vocalist (Vera Welch) — **4**

Date	Title	Peak	Wks at No.1	Wks
21 Nov 81	**20 FAMILY FAVOURITES** *EMI EMTV 28* ●	25		12
9 Sep 89	**WE'LL MEET AGAIN** *Telstar STAR 2369*	44		3
4 Aug 90	**ARMCHAIR THEATRE** *Reprise WX 347* JEFF LYNNE	24		4

PHIL LYNOTT
Ireland, male vocalist/guitarist, d. 4 Jan 1986 (age 36). See Thin Lizzy — **16**

Date	Title	Peak	Wks at No.1	Wks
26 Apr 80	**SOLO IN SOHO** *Vertigo 9102 038*	28		6
14 Nov 87	**SOLDIER OF FORTUNE – THE BEST OF PHIL LYNOTT AND THIN LIZZY** *Telstar STAR 2300* & THIN LIZZY	55		10

LYNYRD SKYNYRD
US, male vocal/instrumental group — **24**

Date	Title	Peak	Wks at No.1	Wks
3 May 75	**NUTHIN' FANCY** *MCA MCF 2700*	43		1
28 Feb 76	**GIMME BACK MY BULLETS** *MCA MCF 2744*	34		5
6 Nov 76	**ONE MORE FOR THE ROAD** *MCA MCPS 279* ○	17		4
12 Nov 77	**STREET SURVIVORS** *MCA MCG 3525*	13		4
4 Nov 78	**SKYNYRD'S FIRST AND LAST** *MCA MCG 3529*	50		1
9 Feb 80	**GOLD AND PLATINUM** *MCA MCSP 308*	49		4
18 Jun 05	**GREATEST HITS** *Universal TV 9830565*	16		5

LYTE FUNKIE ONES
US, male vocal/rap group — **1**

Date	Title	Peak	Wks at No.1	Wks
26 Feb 00	**LYTE FUNKIE ONES** *Logic 74321706832*	62		1

Long Gaps and Fast Follow ups

'What's the worst that could happen?'

AS far as marketing strategies go, Dr Pepper must have felt pretty confident when, in March 2008, they offered every American a can of their 'vegetable extract' drink if Guns N' Roses' long-delayed opus *Chinese Democracy* finally hit the shops by the close of the year. The offer extended to every American except GNR's former members Slash and Buckethead. 'We completely understand and empathise with Axl's quest for perfection – for something more than the average album,' came the official Dr Pepper statement. It was a bizarre twist in the surreal creation of an album that many thought they would never see.

For 'anticipated', perhaps read 'delayed'

So when it was announced that Axl Rose and Co. had finally confirmed a release date for what was classed by many (including GNR's own advertising campaign), as 'the most anticipated album in history', you could almost hear Dr Pepper's collective lump in the throat.

For 'anticipated', perhaps read 'delayed'.

It was way back in September 1991 that GNR had last released new material, the double-album *Use Your Illusion I* and *II*, at which point they pretty much ruled the rock world. They were called the most dangerous band on the planet, their hell-bent nihilism and fiery, unpredictable personalities combined with undeniable creative genius only reinforced the notion – courtesy of sold-out stadiums the world over – that the 1990s was going to be Guns N' Roses' decade.

However, it panned out a little differently.

Following a modestly received album of cover versions in late1993 (*The Spaghetti Incident*), GNR retreated to write and record the next studio album. Who could have foreseen what happened next?

Rumours of delays swirled around; there seemed more gossip than songs. Slash left the band, so too did other founder members, until only singer Axl Rose remained; he bought the legal rights to the band's name and continued, undeterred, with work on *Chinese Democracy*. The number of studios, producers, engineers and other contributors escalated and album release dates came and went, such that by the late 1990s, the album – and its prolonged gestation – was already the stuff of music-industry legend.

The signs of indecisiveness were there in earlier GNR work – *Use Your Illusion I* and *II* was a double-album project partly due to the difficulty Rose had in whittling down the tracks to a single piece of vinyl. Focusing specifically on one track on that record – 'November Rain' – gives yet more indications that this was not a band famed for clinical decisiveness. Some rumours suggested Axl Rose had been working on a version of this track since 1983; GNR guitarist Slash later stated that they even recorded an eighteen-minute version, before the final released album song came in at (a still-mighty) nine minutes. So GNR were

never going to win a 'Most Prolific Rock Band' award any time soon.

Then, in the autumn of 2008, after years of delay, remarkable news started to spread. Guns N' Roses had confirmed a release date for their new album. And so it came to pass, on 24 November in the UK, that *Chinese Democracy* was finally released. Online reactions were feverish, with the world's biggest-ever so-called 'Listening Party' on one social networking site (in this instance the number and speed of streaming of the album from MySpace). What this meant in plain English was that on the day of release, in any one given second, twenty-five people were listening to a track off the album. Reviews were reasonably good, sales strong and the general reception probably better than many had suspected. But it didn't change the world; it wasn't the greatest album ever made, it was just a very good one with a unique story.

It's worth dwelling on what has happened on this mortal coil in the time between Guns N' Roses' records: the Cold War has officially ended; Grunge, Britpop and Girl Power have all long since come and gone and, in some cases, even had time to re-form; eBay, Google, Yahoo, iTunes, Napster, MySpace, Facebook, YouTube et al. have gone from not existing at all to pretty much running the planet; New Labour arrived and sent the Tories into the political wilderness; Princess Diana died in a car crash; the 'Y2K bug' failed to impede the dawn of an entirely different millennium; 11 September 2001; and Barack Obama was voted in as the first non-Caucasian President of the United States. Even Axl's former cohorts have been busy with Slash flitting through various high-profile session projects before creating his own rock animal, Velvet Revolver. Which has since split up. Oh, and China is being infected by democracy...

Although *Chinese Democracy* isn't the slowest follow-up album ever made (more of that later), it seems to have solicited the most press about this delay. Why is that? Axl Rose is far from the tabloids' friend, having a famously irate relationship with the paparazzi and a less than warm position with even such lofty publications as the *New York Times* (his former manager, the legendary Merck Mercuriadis, once wrote a vehement open letter of criticism to the paper). The fact that Axl is the sole surviving member of the 1991 line-up and also legally owns the GNR name distracts from the fact that *Chinese Democracy* is his own personal triumph/folly, depending on your point of view.

Music history seems particularly harsh on Mr Rose. Axl's follow-up to 1991's *Use Your Illusion I* and *II* only took around the seventeen-year mark; compared to others, however, this is almost firing them out. The Eagles almost did the same stretch between their 1979 album, *The Long Run*, a fittingly titled precursor to a gap of fifteen years before 1994's *Hell Freezes Over*. Many Eagles observers don't even class this last record as an original release, noting that it included only four original, new songs. If you accept this qualification, then the gap until their next studio album, *Long Road Out Of Eden* (30 October 2007), is a stupendous twenty-eight years. In retrospect, maybe the most remarkable fact about this long gap is that there was ever a follow-up album at all. The 1979 effort had itself taken over two years and was followed by an acrimonious series of live shows, including one at Long Beach, California in 1980, where members of the group berated each other and shared loving inter-band moments such as the line, 'Only three more songs till I kick your ass, pal.'

That year's live album – released to fulfil contractual obligations to their record company – should surely have been a nail in the coffin of one of the greatest bands in rock history; not so ... on 30 October 2007, the Eagles released *Long Road Out Of Eden*, their first full studio album of all-new material since 1979. They might not have had the same line-up that was in place in 1979, but compared to GNR, with Axl as the only remaining member, it seems churlish to criticise. If they take the same amount of time to release their next follow-up studio album, most of the band would be about to celebrate their eightieth birthdays.

Of course, it's not always personnel tensions that stifle a band's creativity. Sometimes it's legal wrangling and back-room business. After their seismic, eponymous debut in 1989, The Stone Roses pretty much conquered the music vista in the UK, culminating in an historic gig at Spike Island in Widnes in front of nearly 30,000 fans. Unfortunately, protracted legal arguments with their record label, Silvertone, could not be quickly resolved and they were actually prevented from releasing any new studio material for five years. At the time, this seemed like an age but that was for very different reasons than the sheer number of years that had passed, for the music scene in late 1994 had changed so dramatically The Stone Roses may as well have come from a different planet. Five years? It felt as if it had been 500.

In the interim, October 1991 brought us Nirvana's *Nevermind*, held aloft by many – rightly or wrongly – as the moment when alternative music was re-invented as a lucrative form of mass commercialism. The crunching behemoth that was grunge was then usurped (on British shores at least), by the Anglophilia of Britpop, with the net-curtain twitching and ultra-realism of acts such as Blur, Pulp and Oasis, whose lead singer, the inimitable Liam Gallagher, freely admitted that Stone Roses' frontman Ian Brown was his visual and creative inspiration, even going as far as to say the Spike Island gig was a moment that had changed his life. However, such plaudits held little sway with the post-Baggy generation of Britpop kids who were more interested in lads' mags, greyhound racing and Burberry. Amazingly, The Stone Roses went from being bastions of innovation that had genuinely shaken the establishment to a band that represented a throwback, all within the space of one long-delayed album. So, although The Stone Roses

Of course, it's not always personnel tensions that stifle a band's creativity

'only' took five years to follow up with their second album, they could probably carry home the trophy for 'Most Ill-Timed Absence In Music'. By the time they returned to the melee their peculiar Mancunian slant on the world seemed almost instantly out of date. By contrast, hard-dance act The Prodigy took seven years to follow up their global smash album, *The Fat Of The Land* with the less critically revered and commercially poorer cousin *Always Outnumbered, Never Outgunned*. Fortunately, they had been such outsiders since their inception that their lengthy absence seemed to matter little to their success. As if to prove a point, in February 2009, their next album, *Invaders Must Die*, went straight in at Number 1, their fifth consecutive chart topper.

There are other factors that can lead to inordinate gaps between studio albums. The post-millennial fashion for bands re-forming and releasing new material has seen a spate of follow-up albums that span the years. Take That took eleven years to release the next in line after 1995's *Nobody Else*, but this was largely due to Robbie Williams becoming one of the world's biggest solo stars and Gary Barlow and his remaining cohorts becoming largely laughing stocks, who provided, with the respective failures of their various solo careers,

regular fodder for cutting comedians. Cue the pop world's most almighty last laugh as rumours circulated in 2005 that Take That were re-forming.

Tagged by some critics as 'the greatest comeback in British pop history', Take That have since played to several million fans in sold-out tours such as 2009's record-breaking stadium shows – which sold 700,000 tickets in six hours and seized the crown of the fastest ticket sales in British music history. The key here was not just the stunning live shows – many re-formed bands have generous live show budgets designed at reaping maximum reward from music's most lucrative sector – but perhaps of the sheer quality of the new studio material. It may have been over a decade since a record of new original songs hit the record stores from Mr Barlow and friends, but songs such as 'Patience' and 'Rule The World' quite literally saw Take That become the biggest band in Britain.

Multifarious other bands have split up only to re-form and release new material but notable examples include:

The Stooges – the 1976 album *Metallic KO* was in fact a live record so you'd have to go back to 1973 and *Raw Power* for their previous effort; fast-forward to the 2007 re-formed Stooges releasing *The Weirdness* and you have yourself a thirty-four-year gap – twice that of *Chinese Democracy* (although Iggy Pop did record some new songs with his bandmates for the 2003 solo album *Skull Ring*).

Jane's Addiction – Perry Farrell's maverick band of troubadours released three albums in as many years and redefined the alternative genre with a blast of scathing vocals and eccentric personalities, before imploding spectacularly with onstage fights and butt-naked vocals. The thirteen-year gap to their next studio album, *Strays*, was filled with solo projects, another re-formation/split and what they themselves called a 'Sexual Psycho Circus'.

After The Yardbirds mutated into Led Zeppelin in the late 1960s the former band didn't release any new material until 2003's *Birdland*, some thirty-five years later, albeit with many founding members missing, most notably Jimmy Page. Similar circumstances surround the lengthy gaps preceding new studio albums by the likes of The New York Dolls, Queen and George Harrison, to name a few.

Artists often have songs re-mixed or re-issued, sometimes without their prior knowledge and the resulting hit single can lead to a new album. Recent examples include Leo Sayer, who featured on a February 2006 re-mix of his 1977 smash song 'Thunder In My Heart'. He subsequently released a new album of material but had, in the intervening years, been recording and releasing new material regardless. So, if you extend the definition of long gaps to include bands such as these who split up and then re-formed, the Guns N' Roses delay seems almost negligible.

Spare a thought in among all the re-scheduled release dates, sacked producers and painful arguments in the wee small hours about track-listing, for that most maligned of music-business animals: the record-company accountant. It's worth pausing a moment to sympathise with the battered bank accounts of companies that have long been derided for their apparently amoral corporate greed. *Chinese Democracy* is said to have cost approximately $14 million; the video for 'November Rain' is in the Top 20 most expensive music videos ever, coming in at $1.5 million. In a climate of global economic retraction, such statistics are a graveyard for any company's balance sheet.

Fortunately, for every action there is an equal and opposite reaction. Yet the examples of artists releasing fast follow-up albums is far more sparse. It doesn't make for quite such rock'n'roll headlines if you read, 'Rock Star In Diligent Shocker' or 'Debauched Singer Delivers Album Ahead of Schedule'. Scratch beneath the surface of many rapid-fire follow-ups and you will often find disappointing sales of the previous record, embarrassed managers offering various excuses for poor songs and chart placings and then a rushed and often even more inferior new album. However, there are a few worthy and genuine examples of over-productivity in an industry that almost prides itself on tardiness. Westlife released nine albums in ten years; Sir Cliff, bless him, has released well over fifty albums in forty years; Frank Zappa wrote fifty-seven studio albums and has had more than twenty released posthumously – he regularly released three or more albums in a calendar year; artists such as Jim Reeves and Frank Sinatra are typical of the prolific nature of albums from that era, somewhat making a mockery of the post-millennial pop-star gripe of feeling like they are on an 'album-tour-album-tour treadmill'.

Perhaps one of the most unusual and inspired examples of rapid album releases comes from Sheffield-born genius Stephen Jones aka Babybird. Better known in the mainstream for his Top 3 hit 'You're Gorgeous', Jones had begun his artistic career as a member of the Dogs In Honey 'anti-theatre' group. The multi-instrumentalist then bought a rudimentary four-track home-recording machine and penned 400 songs within a startling burst of only a few months. His maverick talent was first heard with the debut album *I Was Born A Man*, and this was followed by four more extremely well received albums in nine months exactly, all on his own label (including *Bad Shave*, *Fatherhood* and *The Happiest Man Alive*).

There was no historical inspiration but, instead, as Jones revealed with great honesty later, 'Me, my friend and my manager got drunk one night and thought after two years of knock-backs, let's tick out five records on vinyl. So we did.' Self-releasing obviously allows such productivity to transform into actual releases. Another example of rapid-release artists would be Daniel Johnson (widely admired by artists such as Kurt Cobain), who released scores of records on tape. Of even greater note, perhaps, is the eccentric ambient composer Aphex Twin aka Richard James. This electronics wizard claims to compose his songs in his dreams then wake up and write out his subconscious creations instantly from start to finish. In this way, he was able to write several thousand songs, telling a shocked media that for his first two albums, *Selected Ambient Works I* and *II,* he'd actually 'lost' over 2000 tunes. Five albums in four years might not be as prolific as Babybird, but the sheer quantity of new material certainly warrants him a mention.

Babybird might be the happiest man alive, but the marketing brains at Dr Pepper probably weren't when GNR finally did release their new record. It turned out that every American could indeed get a free can of Dr Pepper, *provided* they registered online for it on the day of the record's release (effectively disqualifying 80 million Americans who are without access to the web). They'd said 'The Dr Peppers are on us' and, to be fair, they did a pretty good job, despite Axl Rose criticising the qualifying conditions. In fact, Axl admirably bought into the whole spectacle and announced that, as Buckethead had some guitar work on the new album, he would share his can with him. So that just left Slash as the only American on the planet who didn't qualify. Perhaps he could wait another seventeen years for his next chance ...

BIOGRAPHIES

Biographies include the nationality and category for every chart entrant.

Each entrant has at least a mini biography. The 100 acts with the most weeks on the chart (see page 290 for the top 100 chart) each have extended biographies.

Real names are included for all solo artists and, where applicable, dates of death and age of the artist at the time. "See..." links are included for soloists who also had album chart entries in other acts.

The best known line-up is listed for every group that had a Top 10 album, with the vocalist/leader mentioned first and the others following in alphabetical order. In cases where later replacements had similar success both people are named and, where applicable, the dates of death are also shown for every group/duo member listed.

Certified Awards are given by the BPI to mark unit sales to retailers. The certified awards were introduced in April 1973, based on revenue received by manufacturers. In January 1978 the qualification rules were changed and the system based on unit sales to the trade was adopted.

Silver symbol	●	=	60,000 units
Gold symbol	●	=	100,000 units
Platinum symbol	⊛	=	300,000 units

M–P

KEY TO ARTIST ENTRIES

Artist/Group Name — Artist/Group Biography — Silver-selling — Gold-selling — Platinum-selling — US No.1 ★ — Peak Position — Weeks at No.1 — Weeks on Chart

Asterisks (*) indicate group members with hits in their own right that are listed elsewhere in this book

TOM JONES

UK, male vocalist (Thomas Woodward). Perennially popular Welsh vocalist, who has a 43-year span of UK hit albums, was the No.1 UK solo singer of the 1960s on both sides of the Atlantic. The unmistakable Vegas veteran received the Outstanding Contribution award at the 2003 BRITs

Artist's Total Weeks On Chart: 530

Date	Album Title / Label and Catalogue Number	Peak Position	Weeks at No.1	Weeks on Chart
5 Jun 65	**ALONG CAME JONES** *Decca LK 6693*	11		5
8 Oct 66	**FROM THE HEART** *Decca LK 4814*	23		8
8 Apr 67	**GREEN GREEN GRASS OF HOME** *Decca SKL 4855*	3		49
24 Jun 67	**LIVE AT THE TALK OF THE TOWN** *Decca SKL 4874*	6		90
30 Dec 67	**13 SMASH HITS** *Decca SKL 4909*	5		49
27 Jul 68	**DELILAH** *Decca SKL 4946*	1	2	29
21 Dec 68	**HELP YOURSELF** *Decca SKL 4982*	4		9
28 Jun 69	**THIS IS TOM JONES** *Decca SKL 5007*	2		20
15 Nov 69	**TOM JONES LIVE IN LAS VEGAS** *Decca SKL 5032*	2		45
25 Apr 70	**TOM** *Decca SKL 5045*	4		18
14 Nov 70	**I WHO HAVE NOTHING** *Decca SKL 5072*	10		10
29 May 71	**SHE'S A LADY** *Decca SKL 5089*	9		7
27 Nov 71	**LIVE AT CAESAR'S PALACE** *Decca D 1/11/2*	27		5
24 Jun 72	**CLOSE UP** *Decca SKL 5132*	17		4
23 Jun 73	**THE BODY AND SOUL OF TOM JONES** *Decca SKL 5162*	31		1
5 Jan 74	**GREATEST HITS** *Decca SKL 5176*	15		13
22 Mar 75	**20 GREATEST HITS** *Decca TJD 1/11/2* ●	1	4	21
7 Oct 78	**I'M COMING HOME** *Lotus WH 5001* ●	12		9
16 May 87	**THE GREATEST HITS** *Telstar STAR 2296*	16		12
13 May 89	**AT THIS MOMENT** *Jive TOMTV 1*	34		3
8 Jul 89	**AFTER DARK** *Stylus SMR 978*	46		4
6 Apr 91	**CARRYING A TORCH** *Dover ADD 20*	44		4
27 Jun 92	**THE COMPLETE TOM JONES** *The Hit Label 8442862* ●	8		6
26 Nov 94	**THE LEAD AND HOW TO SWING IT** *ZTT 6544924982*	55		1
14 Nov 98	**THE ULTIMATE HITS COLLECTION** *Polygram TV 8449012*	26		6
9 Oct 99	**RELOAD** *Gut GUTCD 009* ⊛x4	1	3	65
16 Nov 02	**MR JONES** *V2 VVR 1021072*	36		2
1 Mar 03	**GREATEST HITS** *Universal TV 8828632* ⊛	2		16
9 Oct 04	**TOM JONES AND JOOLS HOLLAND** *Radar RADAR004CD* & JOOLS HOLLAND ●	5		13
29 Nov 08	**24 HOURS** *S-Curve 2649852*	32		6+

Date of entry into chart

Artist collaboration or where artist's name has changed

Album Title — Label and Catalogue Number

Cross (+) indicates album is still on chart in last week of 2008

M PEOPLE

UK, female/male vocal/instrumental group – Heather Small*, Paul Heard & Mike Pickering — 285

Date	Title	Peak	Wks at No.1	Wks
6 Mar 93	**NORTHERN SOUL** *Deconstruction 74321117772*	53		2
16 Oct 93	**ELEGANT SLUMMING** *Deconstruction 74321166782* ⊛x3	2		87
26 Nov 94	**BIZARRE FRUIT/BIZARRE FRUIT II** *Deconstruction 74321240812* ⊛x5	4		115
16 Sep 95	**NORTHERN SOUL** *RCA PD 75157*	26		3
25 Oct 97	**FRESCO** *M People 74321524902* ⊛x2	2		40
14 Nov 98	**THE BEST OF M PEOPLE** *M People 74321613872* ⊛x3	2		33
5 Mar 05	**ULTIMATE COLLECTION** *Sony BMG 82876669192* FEATURING HEATHER SMALL	17		5

TIMO MAAS

Germany, male DJ/producer — 3

Date	Title	Peak	Wks at No.1	Wks
16 Mar 02	**LOUD** *Perfecto PERFALB 08CD*	41		3

MAC BAND FEATURING THE McCAMPBELL BROTHERS

US, male vocal group — 3

Date	Title	Peak	Wks at No.1	Wks
20 Aug 88	**THE MAC BAND** *MCA MCC 6032*	61		3

McALMONT & BUTLER

UK, male vocal/instrumental duo – David McAlmont & Bernard Butler* — 10

Date	Title	Peak	Wks at No.1	Wks
9 Dec 95	**THE SOUND OF McALMONT AND BUTLER** *Hut CDHUT 32*	33		8
24 Aug 02	**BRING IT BACK** *Chrysalis 5399772*	18		2

FRANKIE McBRIDE

Ireland, male vocalist — 3

Date	Title	Peak	Wks at No.1	Wks
17 Feb 68	**FRANKIE McBRIDE** *Emerald SLD 28*	29		3

MACC LADS

UK, male vocal/instrumental group — 1

Date	Title	Peak	Wks at No.1	Wks
7 Oct 89	**FROM BEER TO ETERNITY** *Hectic House HHLP 12*	72		1

MACCABEES

UK, male vocal/instrumental group — 4

Date	Title	Peak	Wks at No.1	Wks
26 May 07	**COLOUR IT IN** *Fiction/Polydor 1724312*	24		3
26 Jan 08	**COLOUR IT IN – SPECIAL EDITION** *Fiction/Polydor 1756822*	55		1

JESSE McCARTNEY

US, male vocalist — 1

Date	Title	Peak	Wks at No.1	Wks
18 Feb 06	**BEAUTIFUL SOUL** *Angel CDANGE07*	53		1

PAUL McCARTNEY

UK, male vocalist (James McCartney). The most successful pop-music composer of the rock era is also one of the world's most popular live acts and the biggest-earning UK artist of all time. The multi-award-winning ex-Beatle's composition 'Yesterday' is the most recorded song ever. See Beatles — 584

Date	Title	Peak	Wks at No.1	Wks
2 May 70	**McCARTNEY** *Apple PCS 7102* ★	2		32
5 Jun 71	**RAM** *Apple PAS 10003* PAUL & LINDA McCARTNEY	1	2	24
18 Dec 71	**WINGS WILDLIFE** *Apple PCS 7142* WINGS	11		9
19 May 73	**RED ROSE SPEEDWAY** *Apple PCTC 251* & WINGS ● ★	5		16
15 Dec 73	**BAND ON THE RUN** *Apple PAS 10007* & WINGS ⊛ ★	1	7	125
21 Jun 75	**VENUS AND MARS** *Apple PCTC 254* WINGS ⊛ ★	1	2	29
17 Apr 76	**WINGS AT THE SPEED OF SOUND** *Apple PAS 10010* WINGS ● ★	2		35
15 Jan 77	**WINGS OVER AMERICA** *Parlophone PAS 720* WINGS ● ★	8		22
15 Apr 78	**LONDON TOWN** *Parlophone PAS 10012* WINGS ●	4		23
16 Dec 78	**WINGS GREATEST HITS** *Parlophone PCTC 256* WINGS ⊛	5		32
23 Jun 79	**BACK TO THE EGG** *Parlophone PCTC 257* WINGS ●	6		15
31 May 80	**McCARTNEY II** *Parlophone PCTC 258* ●	1	2	18
7 Mar 81	**THE McCARTNEY INTERVIEW** *EMI CHAT 1*	34		4
8 May 82	**TUG OF WAR** *Parlophone PCTC 259* ● ★	1	2	27
12 Nov 83	**PIPES OF PEACE** *Parlophone PCTC 1652301* ⊛	4		23
3 Nov 84	**GIVE MY REGARDS TO BROAD STREET (OST)** *Parlophone PCTC 2* ⊛	1	1	21
13 Sep 86	**PRESS TO PLAY** *Parlophone PCSD 103* ●	8		6
14 Nov 87	**ALL THE BEST!** *Parlophone PMTV 1* ⊛x3	2		21
17 Jun 89	**FLOWERS IN THE DIRT** *Parlophone PCSD 106* ⊛	1	1	20
17 Nov 90	**TRIPPING THE LIVE FANTASTIC** *Parlophone PCST 7346* ●	17		11
1 Jun 91	**UNPLUGGED – THE OFFICIAL BOOTLEG** *Parlophone PCSD 116*	7		3
12 Oct 91	**CHOBA B CCCP (THE RUSSIAN ALBUM)** *Parlophone CDPCSD 117*	63		1
13 Feb 93	**OFF THE GROUND** *Parlophone CDPCSD 125* ○	5		4
20 Nov 93	**PAUL IS LIVE** *Parlophone PDPCSD 147*	34		2
17 May 97	**FLAMING PIE** *Parlophone CDPCSD 171* ⊛	2		15
27 Mar 99	**BAND ON THE RUN** *Parlophone 4991762* & WINGS	69		1
16 Oct 99	**RUN DEVIL RUN** *Parlophone 5223512* ●	12		11
19 May 01	**WINGSPAN – HITS AND HISTORY** *Parlophone 5328762* ●	5		7
24 Nov 01	**DRIVING RAIN** *Parlophone 5355102* ○	46		1
29 Mar 03	**BACK IN THE WORLD** *Parlophone 5830052* ●	5		13
24 Sep 05	**CHAOS AND CREATION IN THE BACKYARD** *Parlophone 3379612* ●	10		3
16 Jun 07	**MEMORY ALMOST FULL** *Hearmusic 7230358*	5		10

KIRSTY MACCOLL

UK, female vocalist, d. 18 Dec 2000 (age 41) — 65

Date	Title	Peak	Wks at No.1	Wks
20 May 89	**KITE** *Virgin KMLP 1* ○	34		12
6 Jul 91	**ELECTRIC LANDLADY** *Virgin V 2663*	17		8
12 Mar 94	**TITANIC DAYS** *ZTT 4509947112*	46		2
18 Mar 95	**GALORE – THE BEST OF KIRSTY MacCOLL** *Virgin CDV 2763* ○	6		27
1 Apr 00	**TROPICAL BRAINSTORM** *V2 VVR 1009872* ○	39		9
13 Aug 05	**THE BEST OF** *Virgin CDV3008*	12		7

VAN McCOY & THE SOUL CITY SYMPHONY

US, male producer/band leader, d. 6 Jul 1979 (age 39) & orchestra — 11

Date	Title	Peak	Wks at No.1	Wks
5 Jul 75	**DISCO BABY** *Avco 9109 004*	32		11

GEORGE McCRAE

US, male vocalist — 29

Date	Title	Peak	Wks at No.1	Wks
3 Aug 74	**ROCK YOUR BABY** *Jay Boy JSL 3* ○	13		28
13 Sep 75	**GEORGE McCRAE** *Jay Boy JSL 10*	54		1

IAN McCULLOCH

UK, male vocalist. See Echo & The Bunnymen — 4

Date	Title	Peak	Wks at No.1	Wks
7 Oct 89	**CANDLELAND** *WEA WX 303*	18		3
21 Mar 92	**MYSTERIO** *East West 9031762642*	46		1

MARTINE McCUTCHEON

UK, female actor/vocalist — 36

Date	Title	Peak	Wks at No.1	Wks
18 Sep 99	**YOU, ME & US** *Innocent CDSIN 4* ⊛	2		20
25 Nov 00	**WISHING** *Innocent CDSIN 7* ●	25		14
14 Dec 02	**MUSICALITY** *Liberty 5805492* ○	55		2

AMY MacDONALD

UK, female vocalist/guitarist — 61

Date	Title	Peak	Wks at No.1	Wks
11 Aug 07	**THIS IS THE LIFE** *Vertigo 1732124* ⊛x2	1	1	61

JANE McDONALD

UK, female vocalist — 48

Date	Title	Peak	Wks at No.1	Wks
25 Jul 98	**JANE McDONALD** *Focus Music International FMCD 001* ⊛	1	3	27
17 Jun 00	**INSPIRATION** *Universal TV 1578612* ●	6		9
27 Oct 01	**LOVE AT THE MOVIES** *Universal TV 0149472*	24		3
5 Feb 05	**YOU BELONG TO ME** *DMG TV DMGTV013*	21		4
23 Aug 08	**JANE** *JMD JANEMOD1*	7		5

MICHAEL McDONALD

US, male vocalist. See Doobie Brothers — 54

Date	Title	Peak	Wks at No.1	Wks
22 Nov 86	**SWEET FREEDOM: BEST OF MICHAEL McDONALD** *Warner Brothers WX 67* ⊛	6		35
26 May 90	**TAKE IT TO HEART** *Reprise WX 285*	35		4
17 Mar 01	**THE VERY BEST OF** *Rhino 8122735302*	21		6
17 May 03	**MOTOWN** *Universal TV 9800233*	29		4
19 Feb 05	**MOTOWN AND MOTOWN II** *Mercury 9869523*	29		3
12 Apr 08	**SOUL SPEAK** *Mercury 1762413*	27		2

Key: ○ Silver-selling · ● Gold-selling · ⊛ Platinum-selling · ★ US No.1 · Peak Position · Weeks at No.1 · Weeks on Chart

MACDONALD BROTHERS
UK, male vocal duo — Weeks on Chart: 4

Date	Title / Label	Peak Position	Weeks at No.1	Weeks on Chart
14 Apr 07	**MACDONALD BROTHERS** *The Music Kitchen TMKCD064*	18		3
27 Oct 07	**THE WORLD OUTSIDE** *The Music Kitchen TMKCD067*	41		1

BRIAN McFADDEN
Ireland, male vocalist. See Westlife — Weeks on Chart: 13

Date	Title / Label	Peak Position	Weeks at No.1	Weeks on Chart
11 Dec 04	**IRISH SON** *Modest/Sony Music 5190022*	24		13

BOBBY McFERRIN
US, male vocalist — Weeks on Chart: 1

Date	Title / Label	Peak Position	Weeks at No.1	Weeks on Chart
29 Oct 88	**SIMPLE PLEASURES** *Manhattan MTL 1018*	92		1

McFLY
UK, male vocal/instrumental group – Tom Fletcher, Danny Jones, Harry Judd & Dougie Poynter — Weeks on Chart: 79

Date	Title / Label	Peak Position	Weeks at No.1	Weeks on Chart
17 Jul 04	**ROOM ON THE 3RD FLOOR** *Universal MCD60094* ⊛x2	1	1	38
10 Sep 05	**WONDERLAND** *Island MCDX60099* ⊛	1	1	17
18 Nov 06	**MOTION IN THE OCEAN** *Island 1712727* ●	6		12
17 Nov 07	**GREATEST HITS** *Island 1749098* ●	4		8
4 Oct 08	**RADIOACTIVE** *Super SUPRCD1*	8		4

KATE & ANNA McGARRIGLE
Canada, female vocal duo — Weeks on Chart: 4

Date	Title / Label	Peak Position	Weeks at No.1	Weeks on Chart
26 Feb 77	**DANCER WITH BRUISED KNEES** *Warner Brothers K 56356*	35		4

SHANE MacGOWAN & THE POPES
UK, male vocal group — Weeks on Chart: 3

Date	Title / Label	Peak Position	Weeks at No.1	Weeks on Chart
29 Oct 94	**THE SNAKE** *ZTT 4509981042*	37		2
8 Nov 97	**THE CROCK OF GOLD** *ZTT MACG 002CD*	59		1

MARY MacGREGOR
US, female vocalist — Weeks on Chart: 1

Date	Title / Label	Peak Position	Weeks at No.1	Weeks on Chart
23 Apr 77	**TORN BETWEEN TWO LOVERS** *Ariola America AAS 1504*	59		1

McGUINNESS FLINT
UK, male vocal/instrumental group. See Manfred Mann — Weeks on Chart: 10

Date	Title / Label	Peak Position	Weeks at No.1	Weeks on Chart
23 Jan 71	**McGUINNESS FLINT** *Capitol EAST 22625*	9		10

MACHINE HEAD
US, male vocal/instrumental group — Weeks on Chart: 12

Date	Title / Label	Peak Position	Weeks at No.1	Weeks on Chart
20 Aug 94	**BURN MY EYES** *Roadrunner RR 90169* ○	25		3
5 Apr 97	**THE MORE THINGS CHANGE...** *Roadrunner RR 88602*	16		3
21 Aug 99	**THE BURNING RED** *Roadrunner RR 86512*	13		2
13 Oct 01	**SUPERCHARGER** *Roadrunner 12085005*	34		1
7 Apr 07	**THE BLACKENING** *Roadrunner RR80168*	16		3

DUFF McKAGAN
US, male vocalist/bass guitarist. See Guns N' Roses — Weeks on Chart: 2

Date	Title / Label	Peak Position	Weeks at No.1	Weeks on Chart
9 Oct 93	**BELIEVE IN ME** *Geffen GED 24605*	27		2

MARIA McKEE
US, female vocalist — Weeks on Chart: 6

Date	Title / Label	Peak Position	Weeks at No.1	Weeks on Chart
24 Jun 89	**MARIA McKEE** *Geffen WX 270*	49		3
12 Jun 93	**YOU GOTTA SIN TO GET SAVED** *Geffen GED 24508*	26		3

KENNETH McKELLAR
UK, male vocalist — Weeks on Chart: 10

Date	Title / Label	Peak Position	Weeks at No.1	Weeks on Chart
28 Jun 69	**THE WORLD OF KENNETH McKELLAR** *Decca SPA 11*	27		7
31 Jan 70	**ECO DI NAPOLI** *Decca SKL 5018*	45		3

BILLY MacKENZIE
UK, male vocalist, d. 22 Jan 1997 (age 39). See Associates — Weeks on Chart: 1

Date	Title / Label	Peak Position	Weeks at No.1	Weeks on Chart
18 Oct 97	**BEYOND THE SUN** *Nude 8CD*	64		1

CRAIG McLACHLAN & CHECK 1-2
Australia, male vocal group — Weeks on Chart: 11

Date	Title / Label	Peak Position	Weeks at No.1	Weeks on Chart
21 Jul 90	**CRAIG McLACHLAN AND CHECK 1-2** *Epic 4663471*	10		11

SARAH McLACHLAN
Canada, female vocalist/guitarist — Weeks on Chart: 15

Date	Title / Label	Peak Position	Weeks at No.1	Weeks on Chart
17 Oct 98	**SURFACING** *Arista 189702*	47		2
14 Feb 04	**AFTERGLOW** *Arista 82876596712* ●	33		13

MALCOLM McLAREN
UK, male vocalist — Weeks on Chart: 41

Date	Title / Label	Peak Position	Weeks at No.1	Weeks on Chart
4 Jun 83	**DUCK ROCK** *Charisma MMLP 1* ○	18		17
26 May 84	**WOULD YA LIKE MORE SCRATCHIN'** *Charisma CLAM1* & THE WORLD FAMOUS SUPREME TEAM SHOW	44		4
29 Dec 84	**FANS** *Charisma MMDL 2*	47		8
15 Jul 89	**WALTZ DARLING** *Epic 4607361* & THE BOOTZILLA ORCHESTRA	30		11
20 Aug 94	**PARIS** *No! NOCD 101*	44		1

BITTY McLEAN
UK, male vocalist — Weeks on Chart: 11

Date	Title / Label	Peak Position	Weeks at No.1	Weeks on Chart
19 Feb 94	**JUST TO LET YOU KNOW** *Brilliant BRILCD 1* ●	19		11

DON McLEAN
US, male vocalist/guitarist — Weeks on Chart: 93

Date	Title / Label	Peak Position	Weeks at No.1	Weeks on Chart
11 Mar 72	**AMERICAN PIE** *United Artists UAS 29285* ○ ★	3		54
17 Jun 72	**TAPESTRY** *United Artists UAS 29350*	16		12
24 Nov 73	**PLAYIN' FAVOURITES** *United Artists UAG 29528*	42		2
14 Jun 80	**CHAIN LIGHTNING** *EMI International INS 3025*	19		9
27 Sep 80	**THE VERY BEST OF DON McLEAN** *United Artists UAG 30314* ●	4		12
15 Apr 00	**AMERICAN PIE – THE GREATEST HITS** *Capitol 5258472*	30		3
13 Oct 07	**THE LEGENDARY** *EMI 5067632*	71		1

JACK McMANUS
UK, male vocalist/pianist — Weeks on Chart: 2

Date	Title / Label	Peak Position	Weeks at No.1	Weeks on Chart
17 May 08	**EITHER SIDE OF MIDNIGHT** *UMRL/Polydor 1754211*	22		2

ANDY McNABB
UK, male soldier/author — Weeks on Chart: 2

Date	Title / Label	Peak Position	Weeks at No.1	Weeks on Chart
21 May 94	**BRAVO TWO ZERO** *Polygram TV 5222002*	45		2

IAN McNABB
UK, male vocalist. See Icicle Works — Weeks on Chart: 5

Date	Title / Label	Peak Position	Weeks at No.1	Weeks on Chart
30 Jan 93	**TRUTH AND BEAUTY** *This Way Up 5143782*	51		1
16 Jul 94	**HEAD LIKE A ROCK** *This Way Up 5222982*	29		2
18 May 96	**MERSEYBEAST** *This Way Up 5242152*	30		2

LUTRICIA McNEAL
US, female vocalist — Weeks on Chart: 16

Date	Title / Label	Peak Position	Weeks at No.1	Weeks on Chart
25 Jul 98	**LUTRICIA McNEAL** *Wildstar CDWILD 5X*	16		16

RITA MacNEIL
Canada, female vocalist — Weeks on Chart: 4

Date	Title / Label	Peak Position	Weeks at No.1	Weeks on Chart
24 Nov 90	**REASON TO BELIEVE** *Polydor 8471061* ○	32		4

TOM McRAE
UK, male vocalist/guitarist — Weeks on Chart: 4

Date	Title / Label	Peak Position	Weeks at No.1	Weeks on Chart
15 Feb 03	**JUST LIKE BLOOD** *DB DB006CDLP*	26		2
14 May 05	**ALL MAPS WELCOME** *BMG 82876689502*	47		1
26 May 07	**KING OF CARDS** *V2 VVR1041862*	72		1

IAN McSHANE
UK, male vocalist — Weeks on Chart: 7

Date	Title	Label	Peak	Wks at No.1	Wks on Chart
21 Nov 92	FROM BOTH SIDES NOW	Polygram TV 5176192 ○	40		7

RALPH McTELL
UK, male vocalist/guitarist (Ralph May) — Weeks on Chart: 17

Date	Title	Label	Peak	Wks at No.1	Wks on Chart
18 Nov 72	NOT TILL TOMORROW	Reprise K 44210	36		1
2 Mar 74	EASY	Reprise K 54013 ○	31		4
15 Feb 75	STREETS	Warner Brothers K 56105 ○	13		12

CHRISTINE McVIE
UK, female vocalist (Christine Perfect). See Chicken Shack, Fleetwood Mac — Weeks on Chart: 4

Date	Title	Label	Peak	Wks at No.1	Wks on Chart
11 Feb 84	CHRISTINE McVIE	Warner Brothers 9250591	58		4

DAVID McWILLIAMS
UK, male vocalist, d. 9 Jan 2002 (age 56) — Weeks on Chart: 9

Date	Title	Label	Peak	Wks at No.1	Wks on Chart
10 Jun 67	DAVID McWILLIAMS SINGS	Major Minor MMLP 2	38		2
4 Nov 67	DAVID McWILLIAMS VOLUME 2	Major Minor MMLP 10	23		6
9 Mar 68	DAVID McWILLIAMS VOLUME 3	Major Minor MMLP 11	39		1

MAD SEASON
UK, male vocal/instrumental group — Weeks on Chart: 1

Date	Title	Label	Peak	Wks at No.1	Wks on Chart
25 Mar 95	ABOVE	Columbia 4785072	41		1

MADDER ROSE
US, male/female vocal/instrumental group — Weeks on Chart: 2

Date	Title	Label	Peak	Wks at No.1	Wks on Chart
9 Apr 94	PANIC ON	Atlantic 7567825812	52		2

MADHOUSE
France/Holland, male/female production/vocal trio — Weeks on Chart: 1

Date	Title	Label	Peak	Wks at No.1	Wks on Chart
31 Aug 02	ABSOLUTELY MAD	Serious SERRCD 001	57		1

MADINA LAKE
US, male vocal/instrumental group — Weeks on Chart: 1

Date	Title	Label	Peak	Wks at No.1	Wks on Chart
7 Apr 07	FROM THEM THROUGH US TO YOU	Roadrunner RR80852	60		1

MADISON AVENUE
Australia, male producer & female vocalist — Weeks on Chart: 1

Date	Title	Label	Peak	Wks at No.1	Wks on Chart
4 Nov 00	THE POLYESTER EMBASSY	VC Recordings CDVCR 7	74		1

MADNESS
UK, male vocal/instrumental group – Suggs* (Graham McPherson), Mike Barson, Mark Bedford, Chris Foreman, Carl Smythe, Lee Thompson & Dan Woodgate. The 'Nutty Boys' helped kick-start the 2 Tone/ska music craze of the early 1980s and no group spent longer on the charts in the 80s than the popular act who officially (first) split up in 1986 — Weeks on Chart: 418

Date	Title	Label	Peak	Wks at No.1	Wks on Chart
3 Nov 79	ONE STEP BEYOND	Stiff SEEZ 17 ⊛	2		78
4 Oct 80	ABSOLUTELY	Stiff SEEZ 29 ⊛	2		46
10 Oct 81	MADNESS 7	Stiff SEEZ 39 ●	5		29
1 May 82	COMPLETE MADNESS	Stiff HIT-TV 1 ⊛	1	3	88
13 Nov 82	THE RISE AND FALL	Stiff SEEZ 46 ●	10		22
3 Mar 84	KEEP MOVING	Stiff SEEZ 53 ○	6		19
12 Oct 85	MAD NOT MAD	Zarjazz JZLP 1 ○	16		9
6 Dec 86	UTTER MADNESS	Zarjazz JZLP 2 ●	29		8
7 May 88	THE MADNESS	Virgin V 2507	65		1
7 Mar 92	DIVINE MADNESS	Virgin CDV 2692 ⊛x3	1	3	96
14 Nov 92	MADSTOCK!	Go! Discs 8283672	22		9
13 Jun 98	THE HEAVY HEAVY HITS	Virgin CDV 2862 ●	19		5
13 Nov 99	WONDERFUL	Virgin CDV 2889	17		2
2 Nov 02	OUR HOUSE – THE ORIGINAL SONGS	Virgin CDV 2965	45		2
13 Aug 05	THE DANGERMAN SESSIONS – VOLUME 1	V2 VVR1033232	11		4

MADONNA
US, female vocalist (Madonna Ciccone). The most successful female chart star of all time on both sides of the Atlantic. The trend-setting and often controversial singer/songwriter has sold an estimated 200 million LPs worldwide and released 15 consecutive Top 5 albums between 1984 and 2005 — Weeks on Chart: 1137

Date	Title	Label	Peak	Wks at No.1	Wks on Chart
11 Feb 84	MADONNA	Sire 923867 ⊛	6		123
24 Nov 84	LIKE A VIRGIN	Sire 925157 ⊛x3 ★	1	2	152
12 Jul 86	TRUE BLUE	Sire WX 54 ⊛x7 ★	1	6	85
28 Nov 87	YOU CAN DANCE	Sire WX 76 ⊛	5		16
1 Apr 89	LIKE A PRAYER	Sire WX 239 ⊛x4 ★	1	2	70
2 Jun 90	I'M BREATHLESS	Sire WX 351 ⊛	2		20
24 Nov 90	THE IMMACULATE COLLECTION	Sire WX 370 ⊛x12	1	9	242
24 Oct 92	EROTICA	Maverick 9362450312 ⊛x2	2		38
5 Nov 94	BEDTIME STORIES	Maverick 9362457672 ⊛	2		27
18 Nov 95	SOMETHING TO REMEMBER	Maverick 9362461002 ⊛x3	3		29
9 Nov 96	EVITA (OST)	Warner Brothers 9362464322 ⊛x2	1	1	36
14 Mar 98	RAY OF LIGHT	Maverick 9362468472 ⊛x5	1	2	116
30 Sep 00	MUSIC	Maverick 9362479212 ⊛x5 ★	1	2	64
24 Nov 01	GHV2	Maverick 9362480002 ⊛x2	2		24
3 May 03	AMERICAN LIFE	Maverick 9362484542 ⊛ ★	1	1	19
26 Nov 05	CONFESSIONS ON A DANCE FLOOR	Warner Brothers 9362494602 ⊛x4 ★	1	2	44
1 Jul 06	I'M GOING TO TELL YOU A SECRET	Warner Brothers 9362499902	18		3
10 Feb 07	THE CONFESSIONS TOUR	Warner Brothers 9362444892	7		4
10 May 08	HARD CANDY	Warner Brothers 9362498849 ⊛ ★	1	1	25

Top 3 Best-Selling Albums

	Album	Approximate Sales
1	THE IMMACULATE COLLECTION	3,550,000
2	TRUE BLUE	1,970,000
3	RAY OF LIGHT	1,700,000

LISA MAFFIA
UK, female vocalist. See So Solid Crew — Weeks on Chart: 1

Date	Title	Label	Peak	Wks at No.1	Wks on Chart
23 Aug 03	FIRST LADY	Independiente ISOM 39CD	44		1

MAGAZINE
UK, male vocal/instrumental group — Weeks on Chart: 24

Date	Title	Label	Peak	Wks at No.1	Wks on Chart
24 Jun 78	REAL LIFE	Virgin V 2100	29		8
14 Apr 79	SECONDHAND DAYLIGHT	Virgin V 2121	38		8
10 May 80	CORRECT USE OF SOAP	Virgin V 2156	28		4
13 Dec 80	PLAY	Virgin V 2184	69		1
27 Jun 81	MAGIC, MURDER AND THE WEATHER	Virgin V 2200	39		3

MAGIC NUMBERS
Trinidad & Tobago/UK, male/female vocal/instrumental group – Romeo & Michele Stodart & Sean & Angela Gannon — Weeks on Chart: 47

Date	Title	Label	Peak	Wks at No.1	Wks on Chart
25 Jun 05	THE MAGIC NUMBERS	Heavenly HVNLP53CD ⊛x2	7		44
18 Nov 06	THOSE THE BROKES	Heavenly HVNLP57CDX ●	11		3

MAGNA CARTA
UK, male vocal/instrumental group — Weeks on Chart: 2

Date	Title	Label	Peak	Wks at No.1	Wks on Chart
8 Aug 70	SEASONS	Vertigo 6360 003	55		2

MAGNUM
UK, male vocal/instrumental group – Bob Catley, Mickey Barker, Tony Clarkin, Wally Lowe & Mark Stanway — Weeks on Chart: 48

Date	Title	Label	Peak	Wks at No.1	Wks on Chart
16 Sep 78	KINGDOM OF MADNESS	Jet JETLP 210	58		1
19 Apr 80	MARAUDER	Jet JETLP 230	34		5
6 Mar 82	CHASE THE DRAGON	Jet JETLP 235	17		7
21 May 83	THE ELEVENTH HOUR	Jet JETLP 240	38		4
25 May 85	ON A STORYTELLER'S NIGHT	FM WKFM LP 34 ●	24		7
4 Oct 86	VIGILANTE	Polydor POLD 5198	24		5
9 Apr 88	WINGS OF HEAVEN	Polydor POLD 5221 ○	5		9
21 Jul 90	GOODNIGHT L.A.	Polydor 8435681	9		5
14 Sep 91	THE SPIRIT	Polydor 5111691	50		1
24 Oct 92	SLEEPWALKING	Music For Nations CDMFN 143	27		2
18 Jun 94	ROCK ART	EMI CDEMD 1066	57		1
7 Apr 07	PRINCESS ALICE & THE BROKEN ARROW	SPV Recordings SPV95912	70		1

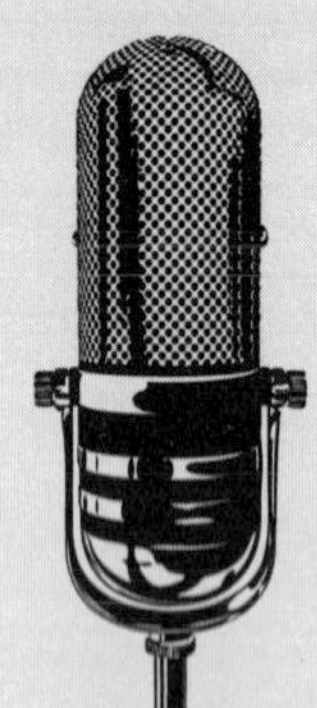

David Bowie

Diamond Dogs

OF all the great Bowie albums, one in particular stands out for its confidence, its depth and the sheer brilliance of its audacity: *Diamond Dogs*. Rarely, if ever, does this make the all-time 100 greatest albums lists (of Bowie's output, those honours usually go to *Ziggy Stardust* and *Hunky Dory*) but, despite this omission, its significance and influence run deeper than is often recognised. If you were of a certain age and disposition it was an album that opened your eyes to a whole new world of possibilities.

Released in April 1974, *Diamond Dogs* was Bowie's eighth solo album, a pivotal record, not just for Bowie but also for many younger British musicians who were about to make their own statements. Bowie's untutored, thrashed lead guitar, with its desolate feel and rough mix, fed into a new style of rock decadence which would partly mutate into punk rock itself (listen to the title track and in particular the bridge between 'Sweet Thing (Reprise)' and 'Rebel Rebel').

Violent, snaggle-toothed street urchins, mutant creatures who hid behind trees ready to hunt

The original premise was straightforward. Bowie would turn George Orwell's classic novel *Nineteen Eighty-Four* into an LP and musical. A few months before recording began, he had spent an enlightening week travelling through Russia and Eastern Europe by train. It's no wonder then that his next work would be so bleak and unforgiving.

Midway through recording, having already prepared half the material, David's management approached Orwell's estate for the appropriate licence but were flatly refused. Rather than abort the whole concept, David coolly adjusted his canvas and created his feral *Diamond Dogs*: violent, snaggle-toothed street urchins, mutant creatures who hid behind trees ready to hunt. Even though the Orwell link was duly abridged, songs like '1984' and 'We Are The Dead' captured the prophetic writer's mood as well as any other direct appreciation of his work. And Bowie had the skill to realign the ruins of the abandoned project into a complete and consistent collection.

The foreboding 'Future Legend' opens the album and quickly sets the tone. David's narrative is mixed with the hook line from 'Bewitched, Bothered, And Bewildered' (a popular show tune from the 1940 Rodgers and Hart musical *Pal Joey*). If the brilliant Guy Peellaert half-man, half-dog album cover hadn't provided a clue, the opening track left listeners in no doubt where this album would take them, telling them clearly this was 'genocide ...'

During the recording, David met the surreal Beat writer William Burroughs. The timing was perfect and the style of Bowie's lyrics began to incorporate the American's famous 'cut-up' technique to brilliant effect (whereby words and phrases are literally cut up and remixed to create new sentences). This approach became particularly evident on 'Sweet Thing/Candidate/Sweet Thing (Reprise)'. The song was packed with suggestive, allegorical imagery. Its subtle and wide-ranging references included nods to the dreaded French Revolution feminists (*les tricoteuses*, who sat by the

Chart History

Artist	Album Title	First Chart Week	Weeks on Chart	Highest Position
DAVID BOWIE	DIAMOND DOGS	8/6/74	17	1

guillotine knitting nonchalantly and pronouncing the ultimate fate of the accused); Perry Como (on the street where you live); The Beatles (let it be); and Rodgers and Hammerstein (on Broadway). Even Charlie Manson and Cassius Clay were name-checked.

The album's biggest single was a stunner and another early punk indicator: 'Rebel Rebel' was David's farewell to glam rock and to a fashion that was now dirty and torn. The main man had spoken: it was clearly time to move on.

Diamond Dogs followed a string of big-selling Bowie albums, all of which had featured the killer-team of producer Ken Scott, guitarist and creative foil Mick Ronson as well as the reliable back-up band, the Spiders From Mars, all of whom he subsequently let go at the height of their success. It was a brave move by Bowie, but necessary for his own artistic and personal development. Only pianist Mike Garson made the cut, and his contribution was once again profound.

Stripped away from his comfort zone, away from most of the people he had previously worked with, *Diamond Dogs* relied on Bowie's raw capability and aptitude, his strength as a writer, producer and performer. If he felt under great pressure to prove himself it didn't show. *Diamond Dogs* created a category of its own.

'Rebel Rebel' was David's farewell to glam rock and to a fashion that was now dirty and torn

By 1974, a David Bowie album making the UK Number 1 spot was a regular occurrence, and *Diamond Dogs* remained there for a month. In the US it became Bowie's biggest album success to date, making Number 5. This achievement helped Bowie establish a loyal market base and cemented his arrival in America. Notably, it also marked his departure from the UK, where he has never returned to live.

We Are The Dead

Silver-selling ○ Gold-selling ● Platinum-selling ⊛ US No.1 ★ — Peak Position / Weeks at No.1 / Weeks on Chart

SEAN MAGUIRE
UK, male actor/vocalist

Date	Title / Label	Peak	Wks at No.1	Wks (3)
26 Nov 94	**SEAN MAGUIRE** *Parlophone CDPCSDX 164*	75		1
15 Jun 96	**SPIRIT** *Parlophone CDPCSD 169*	43		2

MAHAVISHNU ORCHESTRA
UK/US, male instrumental group

Date	Title / Label	Peak	Wks at No.1	Wks (14)
31 Mar 73	**BIRDS OF FIRE** *CBS 65321*	20		5
28 Jul 73	**LOVE, DEVOTION, SURRENDER** *CBS 69037* CARLOS SANTANA & MAHAVISHNU JOHN McLAUGHLIN	7		9

MAI TAI
Guyana, female vocal group

Date	Title / Label	Peak	Wks at No.1	Wks (1)
6 Jul 85	**HISTORY** *Holt Melt V 2359*	91		1

MAJESTICS
UK, male/female vocal group

Date	Title / Label	Peak	Wks at No.1	Wks (4)
4 Apr 87	**TUTTI FRUTTI** *BBC REN 629*	64		4

STEPHEN MALKMUS
US, male vocalist/guitarist. See Pavement

Date	Title / Label	Peak	Wks at No.1	Wks (2)
24 Feb 01	**STEPHEN MALKMUS** *Domino WIGCD 90*	49		1
29 Mar 03	**PIG LIB** *Domino WIGCD 122X* & THE JICKS	63		1

YNGWIE J MALMSTEEN
Sweden, male guitarist

Date	Title / Label	Peak	Wks at No.1	Wks (11)
21 May 88	**ODYSSEY** *Polydor POLD 5224*	27		7
4 Nov 89	**TRIAL OF FIRE – LIVE IN LENINGRAD** *Polydor 8397261*	65		1
28 Apr 90	**ECLIPSE** *Polydor 8434611*	43		2
29 Feb 92	**FIRE AND ICE** *Elektra 7559611372*	57		1

MAMA'S BOYS
Ireland, male vocal/instrumental group

Date	Title / Label	Peak	Wks at No.1	Wks (4)
6 Apr 85	**POWER AND PASSION** *Jive HIP 24*	55		4

MAMAS & THE PAPAS
US, male/female vocal/instrumental group – John & Michelle Phillips, Mama Cass Elliott (Mama Cass*) & Denny Doherty

Date	Title / Label	Peak	Wks at No.1	Wks (75)
25 Jun 66	**IF YOU CAN BELIEVE YOUR EYES AND EARS** *RCA Victor RD 7803* ★	3		18
28 Jan 67	**CASS, JOHN, MICHELLE, DENNY** *RCA Victor SF 7639*	24		6
24 Jun 67	**MAMAS AND PAPAS DELIVER** *RCA Victor SF 7880*	4		22
26 Apr 69	**HITS OF GOLD** *Stateside S 5007* ○	7		2
18 Jun 77	**THE BEST OF THE MAMAS AND PAPAS** *Arcade ADEP 30*	6		13
28 Jan 95	**CALIFORNIA DREAMIN' – THE VERY BEST OF THE MAMAS AND THE PAPAS** *Polygram TV 5239732*	14		6
6 Sep 97	**CALIFORNIA DREAMIN' – GREATEST HITS OF THE MAMAS AND THE PAPAS** *Telstar TV TTVCD 2931*	30		4
26 Aug 06	**CALIFORNIA DREAMIN' – THE BEST OF** *Universal TV 9841715*	21		4

MAN
UK, male vocal/instrumental group

Date	Title / Label	Peak	Wks at No.1	Wks (11)
20 Oct 73	**BACK INTO THE FUTURE** *United Artists UAD 60053/4*	23		3
25 May 74	**RHINOS WINOS AND LUNATICS** *United Artists UAG 29631*	24		4
11 Oct 75	**MAXIMUM DARKNESS** *United Artists UAG 29872*	25		2
17 Apr 76	**WELSH COLLECTION** *MCA MCF 2753*	40		2

MANCHESTER BOYS CHOIR
UK, male choir

Date	Title / Label	Peak	Wks at No.1	Wks (2)
21 Dec 85	**THE NEW SOUND OF CHRISTMAS** *K-Tel ONE 1314* ○	80		2

HENRY MANCINI
US, male composer/conductor, d. 14 Jun 1994 (age 70)

Date	Title / Label	Peak	Wks at No.1	Wks (23)
16 Oct 76	**HENRY MANCINI** *Arcade ADEP 24* ●	26		8
30 Jun 84	**MAMMA** *Decca 411959* LUCIANO PAVAROTTI WITH THE HENRY MANCINI ORCHESTRA	96		1
8 Dec 84	**IN THE PINK** *RCA Red Seal RL 85315* JAMES GALWAY & HENRY MANCINI	62		6
13 Dec 86	**THE HOLLYWOOD MUSICALS** *CBS 4502581* JOHNNY MATHIS & HENRY MANCINI ○	46		8

MANFRED MANN
UK, male vocal/instrumental group – Manfred Mann, Paul Jones* (replaced by Mike D'Abo), Mike Hugg, Tom McGuinness, Dave Richmond & Mike Vickers

Date	Title / Label	Peak	Wks at No.1	Wks (104)
19 Sep 64	**FIVE FACES OF MANFRED MANN** *HMV CLP 1731*	3		24
23 Oct 65	**MANN MADE** *HMV CLP 1911*	7		11
17 Sep 66	**MANN MADE HITS** *HMV CLP 3559*	11		18
29 Oct 66	**AS IS** *Fontana TL 5377*	22		4
21 Jan 67	**SOUL OF MANN** *HMV CSD 3594*	40		1
17 Jun 78	**WATCH** *Bronze BRON 507* MANFRED MANN'S EARTH BAND	33		6
24 Mar 79	**ANGEL STATION** *Bronze BRON 516* MANFRED MANN'S EARTH BAND	30		8
15 Sep 79	**SEMI-DETACHED SUBURBAN** *EMI EMTV 19* ●	9		14
26 Feb 83	**SOMEWHERE IN AFRIKA** *Bronze BRON 543*	87		1
18 Sep 86	**THE ROARING SILENCE** *Bronze ILPS 9357* MANFRED MANN'S EARTH BAND ○	10		9
23 Jan 93	**AGES OF MANN – 22 CLASSIC HITS OF THE 60'S** *Polygram TV 5143622*	23		4
10 Sep 94	**THE VERY BEST OF MANFRED MANN'S EARTH BAND** *Arcade ARC 3100162* MANFRED MANN'S EARTH BAND	69		1
17 Jun 06	**WORLD OF MANN – THE VERY BEST OF** *Universal TV 9839162*	24		3

MANHATTAN TRANSFER
US, male/female vocal group – Tim Hauser, Laurel Masse (replaced by Cheryl Bentyne), Alan Paul & Janis Siegel

Date	Title / Label	Peak	Wks at No.1	Wks (85)
12 Mar 77	**COMING OUT** *Atlantic K 50291*	12		20
19 Mar 77	**MANHATTAN TRANSFER** *Atlantic K 50138* ●	49		7
25 Feb 78	**PASTICHE** *Atlantic K 50444* ●	10		34
11 Nov 78	**LIVE** *Atlantic K 50540* ⊛	4		17
17 Nov 79	**EXTENSIONS** *Atlantic K 50674*	63		3
18 Feb 84	**BODIES AND SOULS** *Atlantic 7801041*	53		4

MANHATTANS
US, male vocal group

Date	Title / Label	Peak	Wks at No.1	Wks (3)
14 Aug 76	**MANHATTANS** *CBS 81513*	37		3

MANIC STREET PREACHERS
UK, male vocal/instrumental group – James Dean Bradfield, Richey Edwards (presumed d. Feb 1995), Sean Moore & Nicky Wire

Date	Title / Label	Peak	Wks at No.1	Wks (215)
22 Feb 92	**GENERATION TERRORISTS** *Columbia 4710602* ●	13		17
3 Jul 93	**GOLD AGAINST THE SOUL** *Columbia 4640642* ○	8		11
10 Sep 94	**THE HOLY BIBLE** *Epic 4774219*	6		4
1 Jun 96	**EVERYTHING MUST GO** *Epic 4839302* ⊛x2	2		82
26 Sep 98	**THIS IS MY TRUTH TELL ME YOURS** *Epic 4917039* ⊛x3	1	3	60
31 Mar 01	**KNOW YOUR ENEMY** *Epic 5018802*	2		14
9 Nov 02	**FOREVER DELAYED – THE GREATEST HITS** *Epic 5095519* ⊛	4		12
26 Jul 03	**LIPSTICK TRACES – A SECRET HISTORY OF** *Epic 5123862*	11		3
13 Nov 04	**LIFEBLOOD** *Sony Music 5188852*	13		2
19 May 07	**SEND AWAY THE TIGERS** *Columbia 88697075632* ●	2		10

BARRY MANILOW
US, male vocalist/pianist (Barry Pincus). Seventy-five million albums and counting for this evergreen balladeer. His career was revived in the 00s by a series of albums featuring revivals of some of his favourite tracks from past decades, the first of which reached No.1 in the US

Date	Title / Label	Peak	Wks at No.1	Wks (366)
23 Sep 78	**EVEN NOW** *Arista SPART 1047* ○	12		28
3 Mar 79	**MANILOW MAGIC – THE BEST OF BARRY MANILOW** *Arista ARTV 2* ⊛	3		151
20 Oct 79	**ONE VOICE** *Arista SPART 1106* ●	18		7
29 Nov 80	**BARRY** *Arista DLART 2* ⊛	5		34
25 Apr 81	**GIFT SET** *Arista BOX 1*	62		1
3 Oct 81	**IF I SHOULD LOVE AGAIN** *Arista BMAN 1* ⊛	5		26
1 May 82	**BARRY LIVE IN BRITAIN** *Arista ARTV 4* ⊛ ★	1	1	23
27 Nov 82	**I WANNA DO IT WITH YOU** *Arista BMAN 2* ●	7		9
8 Oct 83	**A TOUCH MORE MAGIC** *Arista BMAN 3* ●	10		12
1 Dec 84	**2.00 A.M. PARADISE CAFÉ** *Arista 206 496* ○	28		6
16 Nov 85	**MANILOW** *RCA PL 87044* ○	40		6
20 Feb 88	**SWING STREET** *Arista 208860*	81		1
20 May 89	**SONGS TO MAKE THE WHOLE WORLD SING** *Arista 209927*	20		4
17 Mar 90	**LIVE ON BROADWAY** *Arista 303785*	19		3
30 Jun 90	**THE SONGS 1975 – 1990** *Arista 303868*	13		7

Key: ○ Silver-selling · ● Gold-selling · ⊛ Platinum-selling · ★ US No.1 · Peak Position · Weeks at No.1 · Weeks on Chart

Date	Album / Label	Peak Position	Weeks at No.1	Weeks on Chart
2 Nov 91	**SHOWSTOPPERS** *Arista 212091*	53		3
3 Apr 93	**HIDDEN TREASURES** *Arista 74321135682*	36		7
27 Nov 93	**THE PLATINUM COLLECTION – GREATEST HITS** *Arista 74321175452* ○	37		6
5 Nov 94	**SINGIN' WITH THE BIG BANDS** *Arista 07822187712*	54		2
30 Nov 96	**SUMMER OF '78** *Arista 07822188092*	66		2
21 Nov 98	**BARRY SINGS SINATRA** *Arista 07822190332*	72		2
25 May 02	**HERE AT THE MAYFLOWER** *Columbia COJ 21022*	18		3
20 Mar 04	**ULTIMATE MANILOW** *Arista 82876604552*	8		11
3 Sep 05	**ULTIMATE LIVE** *Sony BMG 82876719142*	51		1
25 Mar 06	**THE GREATEST SONGS OF THE FIFTIES** *Arista ARI77210DD* ●	12		4
9 Dec 06	**THE GREATEST SONGS OF THE SIXTIES** *Arista 88697035082* ●	70		3
29 Sep 07	**THE GREATEST SONGS OF THE SEVENTIES** *Arista 88697160742*	27		2
20 Dec 08	**MUSIC & PASSION: THE BEST OF BARRY MANILOW** *Arista 88697420842*	54		2

AIMEE MANN

US, female vocalist/guitarist **3**

Date	Album / Label	Peak Position	Weeks at No.1	Weeks on Chart
18 Sep 93	**WHATEVER** *Imago 72787210172*	39		1
11 Nov 95	**I'M WITH STUPID** *Geffen GED 24951*	51		1
14 Sep 02	**LOST IN SPACE** *V2 VVR 1020882*	72		1

ROBERTO MANN

UK, male orchestra leader **8**

Date	Album / Label	Peak Position	Weeks at No.1	Weeks on Chart
9 Dec 67	**GREAT WALTZES** *Deram SML 1010*	19		9

SHELLY MANNE

US, male percussionist, d. 29 Sep 1984 (age 64) **1**

Date	Album / Label	Peak Position	Weeks at No.1	Weeks on Chart
18 Jun 60	**MY FAIR LADY** *Vogue LAC 12100*	20		1

MANOWAR

US, male vocal/instrumental group **3**

Date	Album / Label	Peak Position	Weeks at No.1	Weeks on Chart
18 Feb 84	**HAIL TO ENGLAND** *Music For Nations MFN 19*	83		2
6 Oct 84	**SIGN OF THE HAMMER** *10 Records DIX 10*	73		1

MANSUN

UK, male vocal/instrumental group – Paul Draper, Dominic Chad, Stove King & Andie Rathbone **27**

Date	Album / Label	Peak Position	Weeks at No.1	Weeks on Chart
1 Mar 97	**ATTACK OF THE GREY LANTERN** *Parlophone CDPCS 7387* ●	1	1	19
19 Sep 98	**SIX** *Parlophone 4967232* ●	6		4
26 Aug 00	**LITTLE KIX** *Parlophone 5277822* ○	12		4

MANTOVANI & HIS ORCHESTRA

UK, male band leader (Annunzio Mantovani), d. 29 Mar 1980 (age 74), & orchestra **151**

Date	Album / Label	Peak Position	Weeks at No.1	Weeks on Chart
21 Feb 59	**CONTINENTAL ENCORES** *Decca LK 4297*	4		12
18 Feb 61	**CONCERT SPECTACULAR** *Decca LK 4377*	16		2
16 Apr 66	**MANTOVANI MAGIC** *Decca LK 7949*	3		15
15 Oct 66	**MR. MUSIC – MANTOVANI** *Decca LK 4809*	24		3
14 Jan 67	**MANTOVANI'S GOLDEN HITS** *Decca SKL 4818*	10		43
30 Sep 67	**HOLLYWOOD** *Decca SKL 4887*	37		1
14 Jun 69	**THE WORLD OF MANTOVANI** *Decca SPA 1*	6		31
4 Oct 69	**THE WORLD OF MANTOVANI VOLUME 2** *Decca SPA 36*	4		19
16 May 70	**MANTOVANI TODAY** *Decca SKL 5003*	16		8
26 Feb 72	**TO LOVERS EVERYWHERE** *Decca SKL 5112*	44		1
3 Nov 79	**20 GOLDEN GREATS** *Warwick WW 5067* ⊛	9		13
16 Mar 85	**MANTOVANI MAGIC** *Telstar STAR 2237*	52		3

MANTRONIX

US/Jamaica, male vocal/instrumental duo **17**

Date	Album / Label	Peak Position	Weeks at No.1	Weeks on Chart
29 Mar 86	**THE ALBUM** *10 Records DIX 37*	45		3
13 Dec 86	**MUSICAL MADNESS** *10 Records DIX 50*	66		3
2 Apr 88	**IN FULL EFFECT** *10 Records DIX 74*	39		3
17 Feb 90	**THIS SHOULD MOVE YA** *Capitol EST 2117* ○	18		6
30 Mar 91	**THE INCREDIBLE SOUND MACHINE** *Capitol EST 2139*	36		2

MANUEL & THE MUSIC OF THE MOUNTAINS

UK, male orchestra – leader Geoff Love*, d. 8 Jul 1991 (age 73) **38**

Date	Album / Label	Peak Position	Weeks at No.1	Weeks on Chart
10 Sep 60	**MUSIC OF THE MOUNTAINS** *Columbia 33SX 1212*	17		1
7 Aug 71	**THIS IS MANUEL** *Studio Two STWO 5*	18		19
31 Jan 76	**CARNIVAL** *Studio Two 337* ○	3		18

PHIL MANZANERA

UK, male vocalist/guitarist (Philip Targett-Adams). See Roxy Music **1**

Date	Album / Label	Peak Position	Weeks at No.1	Weeks on Chart
24 May 75	**DIAMOND HEAD** *Island ILPS 9315*	40		1

MARCY PLAYGROUND

US, male vocal/instrumental trio **1**

Date	Album / Label	Peak Position	Weeks at No.1	Weeks on Chart
9 May 98	**MARCY PLAYGROUND** *EMI 85335692*	61		1

IDA MARIA

Norway, female vocalist/guitarist (Ida Maria Sivertsen) **2**

Date	Album / Label	Peak Position	Weeks at No.1	Weeks on Chart
9 Aug 08	**FORTRESS ROUND MY HEART** *RCA 88697314862*	39		2

ROSE MARIE

Ireland, female vocalist **35**

Date	Album / Label	Peak Position	Weeks at No.1	Weeks on Chart
13 Apr 85	**ROSE MARIE SINGS JUST FOR YOU** *A.1 RMTV 1*	30		13
24 May 86	**SO LUCKY** *A.1 RMLP 2*	62		3
14 Nov 87	**SENTIMENTALLY YOURS** *Telstar STAR 2302* ●	22		11
19 Nov 88	**TOGETHER AGAIN** *Telstar STAR 2333* ●	52		7
23 Mar 96	**MEMORIES OF HOME** *Telstar TCD 2788*	51		1

MARILLION

UK, male vocal/instrumental group – Derek Dick (aka Fish*, replaced by Steve Hogarth), Brian Jelliman, Diz Minnitt, Mick Pointer & Steve Rothary **166**

Date	Album / Label	Peak Position	Weeks at No.1	Weeks on Chart
26 Mar 83	**SCRIPT FOR A JESTER'S TEAR** *EMI EMC 3429* ⊛	7		31
24 Mar 84	**FUGAZI** *EMI EMC 2400851* ●	5		20
17 Nov 84	**REAL TO REEL** *EMI JEST 1* ●	8		22
29 Jun 85	**MISPLACED CHILDHOOD** *EMI MRL 2* ⊛	1	1	41
4 Jul 87	**CLUTCHING AT STRAWS** *EMI EMD 1002* ●	2		15
23 Jul 88	**B SIDES THEMSELVES** *EMI EMS 1295*	64		6
10 Dec 88	**THE THIEVING MAGPIE** *EMI MARIL 1* ●	25		6
7 Oct 89	**SEASON'S END** *EMI EMD 1011* ●	7		4
6 Jul 91	**HOLIDAYS IN EDEN** *EMI EMD 1022*	7		7
20 Jun 92	**A SINGLES COLLECTION 1982–1992** *EMI CDEMD 1033*	27		2
19 Feb 94	**BRAVE** *EMI CDEMC 1054*	10		4
8 Jul 95	**AFRAID OF SUNLIGHT** *EMI CDEMD 1079*	16		2
6 Apr 96	**MADE AGAIN** *EMI CDEMD 1094*	37		1
3 May 97	**THIS STRANGE ENGINE** *Raw Power RAWCD 121*	27		2
3 Oct 98	**RADIATION** *Raw Power RAWCD 126*	35		1
30 Oct 99	**MARILLION.COM** *Raw Power RAWCD 144*	53		1
21 Apr 07	**SOMEWHERE ELSE** *Intact INTACTCD11*	24		1

MARILYN MANSON

US, male vocal/instrumental group – Brian Warner (aka Marilyn Manson), Steve Bier, Scott Putesky, Jeordi White & Ken Wilson **23**

Date	Album / Label	Peak Position	Weeks at No.1	Weeks on Chart
26 Oct 96	**ANTICHRIST SUPERSTAR** *Interscope IND 90086*	73		1
26 Sep 98	**MECHANICAL ANIMAL** *Interscope IND 90273* ★	8		4
27 Nov 99	**THE LAST TOUR ON EARTH** *Interscope 4905242*	61		1
25 Nov 00	**HOLY WOOD** *Nothing 4908592*	23		2
24 May 03	**THE GOLDEN AGE OF GROTESQUE** *Interscope 9800093* ● ★	4		7
9 Oct 04	**LEST WE FORGET – THE BEST OF** *Interscope 9863975* ●	4		6
16 Jun 07	**EAT ME DRINK ME** *Interscope 1736524*	8		2

MARIO

US, male vocalist (Mario Barrett) **22**

Date	Album / Label	Peak Position	Weeks at No.1	Weeks on Chart
12 Feb 05	**TURNING POINT** *J Records 82876618852* ●	8		22

MARION

UK, male vocal/instrumental group – Jamie Harding, Phil Cunningham, Anthony Grantham, Murad Mousa & Julian Phillips **2**

Date	Album / Label	Peak Position	Weeks at No.1	Weeks on Chart
17 Feb 96	**THIS WORLD AND BODY** *London 8286952*	10		2

YANNIS MARKOPOULOS

Greece, male composer/orchestra leader **8**

Date	Album / Label	Peak Position	Weeks at No.1	Weeks on Chart
26 Aug 78	**WHO PAYS THE FERRYMAN** *BBC REB 315*	22		8

MARKY MARK & THE FUNKY BUNCH

US, male/female vocal/rap/instrumental group **1**

Date	Album / Label	Peak Position	Weeks at No.1	Weeks on Chart
5 Oct 91	**MUSIC FOR THE PEOPLE** *Interscope 7567917371*	61		1

Silver-selling ○ Gold-selling ● Platinum-selling ⊛ US No.1 ★ Peak Position Weeks at No.1 Weeks on Chart

BOB MARLEY & THE WAILERS

Jamaica, male vocal/instrumental group – Bob Marley, Junior Braithwaite, Beverley Kelso, Bunny Livingston (aka Bunny Wailer), Cherry Smith & Peter Tosh. The biggest-selling, most influential and most important West Indian recording artist, who helped put reggae onto the world's music map. *Legend* has sold over 17 million copies worldwide, including 10 million in the US

Weeks on chart: 584

Date	Title	Peak Position	Weeks at No.1	Weeks on Chart
4 Oct 75	**NATTY DREAD** *Island ILPS 9281* ●	43		5
25 Jul 81	**LIVE** *Island ILPS 9376* ○	38		5
8 May 76	**RASTAMAN VIBRATION** *Island ILPS 9383* ●	15		13
11 Jun 77	**EXODUS** *Island ILPS 9498* ●	8		56
1 Apr 78	**KAYA** *Island ILPS 9517* ●	4		24
16 Dec 78	**BABYLON BY BUS** *Island ISLD 11*	40		11
13 Oct 79	**SURVIVAL** *Island ILPS 9542*	20		6
28 Jun 80	**UPRISING** *Island ILPS 9596*	6		17
20 Dec 75	**LIVE AT THE LYCEUM** *Island ILPS 9376*	68		6
28 May 83	**CONFRONTATION** *Island ILPS 9760*	5		19
19 May 84	**LEGEND – THE BEST OF BOB MARLEY AND THE WAILERS** *Island/Tuff Gong BMWX 1* ⊛x6	1	12	339
28 Jun 86	**REBEL MUSIC** *Island ILPS 9843*	54		3
3 Oct 92	**SONGS OF FREEDOM** *Tuff Gong TGCBX 1* BOB MARLEY ○	10		5
3 Jun 95	**NATURAL MYSTIC** *Tuff Gong BMWCD 2* ●	5		8
4 Sep 99	**THE SUN IS SHINING** *Club Tools 0066735 CLU* BOB MARLEY VS FUNKSTAR DELUXE	40		3
2 Jun 01	**ONE LOVE – THE VERY BEST OF** *Tuff Gong BMWCD 3* ●	5		15
7 Jul 01	**LIVELY UP YOURSELF** *Music Collection 12691* BOB MARLEY	75		1
10 Nov 01	**ONE LOVE** *Tuff Gong 5865512*	24		8
5 Jun 04	**ROOTS OF A LEGEND** *Trojan TJODX 176*	51		2
19 Nov 05	**AFRICA UNITE – THE SINGLES** *Tuff Gong BMWCDX4* ●	26		5
16 Jun 07	**EXODUS** *Tuff Gong 1734084*	44		2
10 Nov 07	**LEGEND** *Tuff Gong 5301640*	36		31

DAMIAN JR GONG MARLEY

Jamaica, male vocalist

Weeks on chart: 10

Date	Title	Peak Position	Weeks at No.1	Weeks on Chart
24 Sep 05	**WELCOME TO JAMROCK** *Universal 9885698* ●	34		10

LENE MARLIN

Norway, female vocalist (Lene Marlin Pederson)

Weeks on chart: 34

Date	Title	Peak Position	Weeks at No.1	Weeks on Chart
25 Mar 00	**PLAYING MY GAME** *Virgin CDVIR 83* ⊛	18		34

LAURA MARLING

UK, female vocalist/guitarist

Weeks on chart: 2

Date	Title	Peak Position	Weeks at No.1	Weeks on Chart
23 Feb 08	**ALAS I CANNOT SWIM** *Virgin CDVY3040*	45		2

NEVILLE MARRINER & THE ACADEMY OF ST. MARTIN IN THE FIELDS

UK, male conductor & chamber orchestra

Weeks on chart: 6

Date	Title	Peak Position	Weeks at No.1	Weeks on Chart
6 Apr 85	**AMADEUS (OST)** *London LONDP 6*	64		6

MAROON 5

US, male vocal/instrumental group – Adam Levine, Jesse Carmichael, Matt Flynn, Mickey Madden & James Valentine

Weeks on chart: 102

Date	Title	Peak Position	Weeks at No.1	Weeks on Chart
31 Jan 04	**SONGS ABOUT JANE** *J Records 82876584302* ⊛x5	1	1	73
5 Mar 05	**1 22 03 – ACOUSTIC (IMPORT)** *J Records OCTN624682*	58		1
2 Jun 07	**IT WON'T BE SOON BEFORE LONG** *A&M/Octone 1734584* ⊛ ★	1	2	28

MARS VOLTA

US, male vocal/instrumental group

Weeks on chart: 5

Date	Title	Peak Position	Weeks at No.1	Weeks on Chart
5 Jul 03	**DE-LOUSED IN THE COMATORIUM** *Universal 9860460* ○	43		1
5 Mar 05	**FRANCES THE MUTE** *Universal 2103977*	23		2
23 Sep 06	**AMPUTECHTURE** *Universal 1702802*	49		1
9 Feb 08	**BEDLAM IN GOLIATH** *Island 1758443*	42		1

BERNIE MARSDEN

UK, male vocalist/guitarist. See Whitesnake

Weeks on chart: 2

Date	Title	Peak Position	Weeks at No.1	Weeks on Chart
5 Sep 81	**LOOK AT ME NOW** *Parlophone PCF 7217*	71		2

KYM MARSH

UK, female vocalist. See Hear'Say

Weeks on chart: 3

Date	Title	Peak Position	Weeks at No.1	Weeks on Chart
2 Aug 03	**STANDING TALL** *Universal 9800035*	9		3

NATASHA MARSH

UK, female vocalist

Weeks on chart: 1

Date	Title	Peak Position	Weeks at No.1	Weeks on Chart
3 Mar 07	**AMOUR** *EMI Classics CDANGE17*	56		1

AMANDA MARSHALL

Canada, female vocalist

Weeks on chart: 2

Date	Title	Peak Position	Weeks at No.1	Weeks on Chart
3 Aug 96	**AMANDA MARSHALL** *Epic 4837912*	47		2

LENA MARTELL

UK, female vocalist (Helen Thomson)

Weeks on chart: 71

Date	Title	Peak Position	Weeks at No.1	Weeks on Chart
25 May 74	**THAT WONDERFUL SOUND OF LENA MARTELL** *Pye SPL 18427*	35		2
8 Jan 77	**THE BEST OF LENA MARTELL** *Pye NSPL 18506* ●	13		16
27 May 78	**THE LENA MARTELL COLLECTION** *Ronco RTL 2028* ●	12		19
20 Oct 79	**LENA'S MUSIC ALBUM** *Pye N 123* ⊛	5		18
19 Apr 80	**BY REQUEST** *Ronco RTL 2046* ●	9		9
29 Nov 80	**BEAUTIFUL SUNDAY** *Ronco RTL 2052* ●	23		7

MARTHA & THE MUFFINS

Canada, female/male vocal/instrumental group

Weeks on chart: 6

Date	Title	Peak Position	Weeks at No.1	Weeks on Chart
15 Mar 80	**METRO MUSIC** *Dindisc DID 1*	34		6

MARTIKA

US, female vocalist (Marta Marrera)

Weeks on chart: 52

Date	Title	Peak Position	Weeks at No.1	Weeks on Chart
16 Sep 89	**MARTIKA** *CBS 4633551* ⊛	11		37
7 Sep 91	**MARTIKA'S KITCHEN** *Columbia 4671891* ●	15		15

BILLIE RAY MARTIN

Germany, female vocalist (Birgit Dieckmann)

Weeks on chart: 2

Date	Title	Peak Position	Weeks at No.1	Weeks on Chart
3 Feb 96	**DEADLINE FOR MY MEMORIES** *Magnet 0630121802*	47		2

DEAN MARTIN

US, male vocalist (Dino Crocetti)

Weeks on chart: 64

Date	Title	Peak Position	Weeks at No.1	Weeks on Chart
13 May 61	**THIS TIME I'M SWINGING** *Capitol T 1442*	18		1
25 Feb 67	**AT EASE WITH DEAN** *Reprise RSLP 6322*	35		1
4 Nov 67	**WELCOME TO MY WORLD** *Philips DBL 001*	39		1
12 Oct 68	**DEAN MARTIN'S GREATEST HITS VOLUME I** *Reprise RSLP 6301*	40		1
22 Feb 69	**GENTLE ON MY MIND** *Reprise RSLP 6330*	9		8
22 Feb 69	**THE BEST OF DEAN MARTIN** *Capitol ST 21194*	9		1
27 Nov 71	**WHITE CHRISTMAS** *MFP 5224* NAT 'KING' COLE & DEAN MARTIN	45		1
13 Nov 76	**20 ORIGINAL DEAN MARTIN HITS** *Reprise K 54066* ●	7		11
5 Jun 99	**THE VERY BEST OF DEAN MARTIN – THE CAPITOL & REPRISE YEARS** *EMI 4967212* ⊛	5		29
26 Aug 00	**THE VERY BEST OF VOLUME 2** *Capitol 5277712*	40		2
16 Feb 02	**LOVE SONGS** *Capitol 5377482* ○	24		3
10 Jan 04	**VERY BEST OF** *EMI 5920802*	59		2
18 Sep 04	**DINO – THE ESSENTIAL DEAN MARTIN** *EMI 8665272* ○	25		3

GEORGE MARTIN

UK, male producer

Weeks on chart: 13

Date	Title	Peak Position	Weeks at No.1	Weeks on Chart
4 Apr 98	**IN MY LIFE** *Echo ECHCD 020* ●	5		13

JUAN MARTIN WITH THE ROYAL PHILHARMONIC ORCHESTRA

Spain, male guitarist

Weeks on chart: 9

Date	Title	Peak Position	Weeks at No.1	Weeks on Chart
11 Feb 84	**SERENADE** *K-Tel NE 1267*	21		9

RICKY MARTIN

Puerto Rico, male vocalist

Weeks on chart: 76

Date	Title	Peak Position	Weeks at No.1	Weeks on Chart
12 Jun 99	**RICKY MARTIN** *Columbia 4944060* ⊛ ★	2		48
18 Nov 00	**SOUND LOADED** *Columbia 4977692* ⊛	14		21
1 Dec 01	**THE BEST OF** *Columbia 5050192* ●	42		6
22 Oct 05	**LIFE** *Columbia 5205492*	40		1

WILL MARTIN

New Zealand, male vocalist/pianist

Weeks on chart: 3

Date	Title	Peak Position	Weeks at No.1	Weeks on Chart
4 Oct 08	**A NEW WORLD** *UCJ 1747031*	21		3

JOHN MARTYN
UK, male vocalist/guitarist

Date	Album	Peak Position	Weeks at No.1	Weeks on Chart 30
4 Feb 78	**ONE WORLD** *Island ILPS 9492*	54		1
1 Nov 80	**GRACE AND DANGER** *Island ILPS 9560*	54		2
26 Sep 81	**GLORIOUS FOOL** *Geffen K 99178*	25		7
4 Sep 82	**WELL KEPT SECRET** *WEA K 99255*	20		7
17 Nov 84	**SAPPHIRE** *Island ILPS 9779*	57		2
8 Mar 86	**PIECE BY PIECE** *Island ILPS 9807*	28		4
10 Oct 92	**COULDN'T LOVE YOU MORE** *Permanent PERMCD 9*	65		2
10 Aug 96	**AND** *Go! Discs 8287982*	32		3
4 Apr 98	**THE CHURCH WITH ONE BELL** *Independiente ISOM 3CD*	51		1
3 Jun 00	**GLASGOW WALKER** *Independiente ISOM 15CD*	66		1

HANK MARVIN
UK, male vocalist/guitarist (Brian Rankin). See Shadows

Date	Album	Peak Position	Weeks at No.1	Weeks on Chart 81
22 Nov 69	**HANK MARVIN** *Columbia SCX 6352*	14		2
3 Apr 71	**MARVIN, WELCH AND FARRAR** *Regal Zonophone SRZA 8502*, BRUCE WELCH & JOHN FARRAR	30		4
20 Mar 82	**WORDS AND MUSIC** *Polydor POLD 5054*	66		3
31 Oct 92	**INTO THE LIGHT** *Polydor 5171482* ●	18		10
20 Nov 93	**HEARTBEAT** *Polygram TV 5213222* ●	17		9
22 Oct 94	**THE BEST OF HANK MARVIN AND THE SHADOWS** *Polygram TV 5238212* & THE SHADOWS ●	19		11
18 Nov 95	**HANK PLAYS CLIFF** *Polygram TV 5294262* ●	33		7
23 Nov 96	**HANK PLAYS HOLLY** *Polygram TV 5337132* ●	34		7
5 Apr 97	**HANKS PLAYS LIVE** *Polygram TV 5374282*	71		1
22 Nov 97	**PLAY ANDREW LLOYD WEBBER AND TIM RICE** *Polygram TV 5394792* & THE SHADOWS ○	41		6
14 Nov 98	**VERY BEST OF HANK MARVIN AND THE SHADOWS – THE FIRST 40 YEARS** *Polygram TV 5592112* & THE SHADOWS ○	56		5
15 Apr 00	**MARVIN AT THE MOVIES** *Universal TV 1570572*	17		5
20 Apr 02	**GUITAR PLAYER** *Universal TV 0171242*	10		6
16 Jun 07	**GUITAR MAN** *Universal TV 1735754*	6		5

RICHARD MARX
US, male vocalist/multi-instrumentalist

Date	Album	Peak Position	Weeks at No.1	Weeks on Chart 42
9 Apr 88	**RICHARD MARX** *Manhattan MTL 1017*	68		2
20 May 89	**REPEAT OFFENDER** *EMI-USA MTL 1043* ● ★	8		12
16 Nov 91	**RUSH STREET** *Capitol ESTU 2158* ●	7		20
19 Feb 94	**PAID VACATION** *Capitol CDESTU 2208*	11		5
21 Feb 98	**GREATEST HITS** *Capitol 8219142*	34		3

MARXMAN
UK/Ireland, male rap/instrumental goup

Date	Album	Peak Position	Weeks at No.1	Weeks on Chart 1
3 Apr 93	**33 REVOLUTIONS PER MINUTE** *Talkin Loud 5145382*	69		1

MARY JANE GIRLS
US, female vocal group

Date	Album	Peak Position	Weeks at No.1	Weeks on Chart 9
28 May 83	**MARY JANES GIRLS** *Gordy STML 12189*	51		9

MASE
US, male rapper (Mason Betha)

Date	Album	Peak Position	Weeks at No.1	Weeks on Chart 10
24 Jan 98	**HARLEM WORLD** *Puff Daddy 78612730172* ★	53		7
24 Jul 99	**DOUBLE UP** *Puff Daddy 74321674332*	47		2
4 Sep 04	**WELCOME BACK** *Bad Boy 9863122*	68		1

JOHN MASON
UK, male violinist/conductor

Date	Album	Peak Position	Weeks at No.1	Weeks on Chart 1
27 Dec 75	**STRINGS OF SCOTLAND** *Philips 6382 108*	50		1

WILLY MASON
UK, male vocalist/guitarist

Date	Album	Peak Position	Weeks at No.1	Weeks on Chart 8
19 Feb 05	**WHERE THE HUMANS EAT** *Virgin CDV2993* ○	38		6
17 Mar 07	**IF THE OCEAN GETS ROUGH** *Radiate CDV3029*	33		2

MASSED WELSH CHOIRS
UK, male choir

Date	Album	Peak Position	Weeks at No.1	Weeks on Chart 7
9 Aug 69	**CYMANSA GANN** *BBC REC 53M*	5		7

MASSIVE ATTACK
UK, male vocal/instrumental group – Robert Del Naja, Grantley Marshall & Andrew Vowles

Date	Album	Peak Position	Weeks at No.1	Weeks on Chart 260
20 Apr 91	**BLUE LINES** *Wild Bunch WBRCD 1* ⊛x2	13		88
8 Oct 94	**PROTECTION/NO PROTECTION** *Wild Bunch WBRCD 2* ⊛	4		78
2 May 98	**MEZZANINE** *Circa WBRCDX 4* ⊛	1	2	54
22 Feb 03	**100TH WINDOW** *Virgin CDV 2967* ●	1	1	6
23 Oct 04	**DANNY THE DOG (OST)** *Virgin CDV 2988*	70		1
8 Apr 06	**COLLECTED – THE BEST OF** *Virgin CDVX3017* ⊛	2		33

MASTODON
US, male vocal/instrumental group

Date	Album	Peak Position	Weeks at No.1	Weeks on Chart 2
23 Sep 06	**BLOOD MOUNTAIN** *Reprise 9362443642*	46		2

MATCHBOX
UK, male vocal/instrumental group

Date	Album	Peak Position	Weeks at No.1	Weeks on Chart 14
2 Feb 80	**MATCHBOX** *Magnet MAG 5031*	44		5
11 Oct 80	**MIDNITE DYNAMOS** *Magnet MAG 5036* ○	23		9

MATCHBOX 20
US, male vocal/instrumental group

Date	Album	Peak Position	Weeks at No.1	Weeks on Chart 6
25 Apr 98	**YOURSELF OR SOMEONE LIKE YOU** *Atlantic 7567927212* ○	50		1
3 Jun 00	**MAD SEASON BY MATCHBOX 20** *Atlantic 7567833392* ○	31		2
8 Mar 03	**MORE THAN YOU THINK YOU ARE** *Atlantic ATL 836122*	31		2
27 Oct 07	**EXILE ON MAINSTREAM** *Atlantic 297340*	53		1

MIREILLE MATHIEU
France, female vocalist

Date	Album	Peak Position	Weeks at No.1	Weeks on Chart 1
2 Mar 68	**MIREILLE MATHIEU** *Columbia SCX 6210*	39		1

JOHNNY MATHIS
US, male vocalist

Date	Album	Peak Position	Weeks at No.1	Weeks on Chart 241
8 Nov 58	**WARM** *Fontana TBA TFL 5015*	6		2
24 Jan 59	**SWING SOFTLY** *Fontana TBA TFL 5039*	10		1
13 Feb 60	**RIDE ON A RAINBOW** *Fontana TFL 5061*	10		2
10 Dec 60	**RHYTHMS AND BALLADS OF BROADWAY** *Fontana SET 101*	6		10
17 Jun 61	**I'LL BUY YOU A STAR** *Fontana TFL 5143*	18		1
16 May 70	**RAINDROPS KEEP FALLING ON MY HEAD** *CBS 63587*	23		10
3 Apr 71	**LOVE STORY** *CBS 64334*	27		5
9 Sep 72	**FIRST TIME EVER I SAW YOUR FACE** *CBS 64930*	40		3
16 Dec 72	**MAKE IT EASY ON YOURSELF** *CBS 65161*	49		1
8 Mar 75	**I'M COMING HOME** *CBS 65690* ○	18		11
5 Apr 75	**THE HEART OF A WOMAN** *CBS 80533*	39		2
26 Jul 75	**WHEN WILL I SEE YOU AGAIN** *CBS 80738* ○	13		10
3 Jul 76	**I ONLY HAVE EYES FOR YOU** *CBS 81329* ●	14		12
19 Feb 77	**GREATEST HITS VOLUME IV** *CBS 86022*	31		5
18 Jun 77	**THE JOHNNY MATHIS COLLECTION** *CBS 10003* ⊛	1	4	40
17 Dec 77	**SWEET SURRENDER** *CBS 86036* ○	55		1
29 Apr 78	**YOU LIGHT UP MY LIFE** *CBS 86055* ●	3		19
26 Aug 78	**THAT'S WHAT FRIENDS ARE FOR** *CBS 86068* & DENIECE WILLIAMS ●	16		11
7 Apr 79	**THE BEST DAYS OF MY LIFE** *CBS 86080*	38		5
3 Nov 79	**MATHIS MAGIC** *CBS 86103* ○	59		4
8 Mar 80	**TEARS AND LAUGHTER** *CBS 10019* ●	1	2	15
12 Jul 80	**ALL FOR YOU** *CBS 86115*	20		8
19 Sep 81	**CELEBRATION** *CBS 10028* ●	9		16
15 May 82	**FRIENDS IN LOVE** *CBS 85652*	34		7
17 Sep 83	**UNFORGETTABLE: A MUSICAL TRIBUTE TO NAT KING COLE** *CBS 10042* & NATALIE COLE ●	5		16
15 Sep 84	**A SPECIAL PART OF ME** *CBS 25475*	45		3
13 Dec 86	**THE HOLLYWOOD MUSICALS** *CBS 4502581* & HENRY MANCINI ○	46		8
4 Feb 06	**THE VERY BEST OF** *Columbia 82876738722* ●	6		11
8 Mar 08	**A NIGHT TO REMEMBER** *Sony BMG 88697100382*	29		2

MATT BIANCO
UK, male vocal/instrumental group

Date	Album	Peak Position	Weeks at No.1	Weeks on Chart 67
8 Sep 84	**WHOSE SIDE ARE YOU ON** *WEA WX 7* ●	35		39
22 Mar 86	**MATT BIANCO** *WEA WX 35* ○	26		13
9 Jul 88	**INDIGO** *WEA WX 181* ●	23		13
3 Nov 90	**THE BEST OF MATT BIANCO** *East West WX 376* ○	49		2

KATHY MATTEA
US, female vocalist/guitarist

Date	Title	Peak Position	Weeks at No.1	Weeks on Chart
				2
15 Apr 95	**READY FOR THE STORM (FAVOURITE CUTS)** *Mercury 5280062*	61		1
8 Feb 97	**LOVE TRAVELS** *Mercury 5328992*	65		1

CERYS MATTHEWS
UK, female vocalist. See Catatonia

Date	Title	Peak Position	Weeks at No.1	Weeks on Chart
				6
31 May 03	**COCKAHOOP** *Blanco Y Negro 2564603062*	30		5
2 Sep 06	**NEVER SAID GOODBYE** *Rough Trade RTRADCD227*	43		1

SCOTT MATTHEWS
UK, male vocalist/guitarist

Date	Title	Peak Position	Weeks at No.1	Weeks on Chart
				2
14 Oct 06	**PASSING STRANGER** *San Remo REMOCD001*	45		2

MATTHEWS' SOUTHERN COMFORT
UK, male vocal/instrumental group

Date	Title	Peak Position	Weeks at No.1	Weeks on Chart
				4
25 Jul 70	**SECOND SPRING** *Uni UNLS 112*	52		4

MAVERICKS
US, male vocal/instrumental group – Raul Malo, Paul Deakin, Nick Kane & Robert Reynolds

Date	Title	Peak Position	Weeks at No.1	Weeks on Chart
				60
11 May 96	**MUSIC FOR ALL OCCASIONS** *MCA MCD 11344* ● (silver)	56		1
14 Mar 98	**TRAMPOLINE** *MCA Nashville UMD 80456* ⊛	10		48
4 Dec 99	**THE BEST OF THE MAVERICKS** *Mercury 1701202* ●	40		9
4 Oct 03	**MAVERICKS** *Sanctuary SANCD 192*	65		2

MAX Q
Australia, male vocal/instrumental duo

Date	Title	Peak Position	Weeks at No.1	Weeks on Chart
				1
4 Nov 89	**MAX Q** *Mercury 8389421*	69		1

MAXIMO PARK
UK, male vocal/instrumental group – Paul Smith, Tom English, Duncan Lloyd, Archis Tiku & Lukas Wooller

Date	Title	Peak Position	Weeks at No.1	Weeks on Chart
				31
28 May 05	**A CERTAIN TRIGGER** *Warp WARPCD130X* ●	15		13
14 Apr 07	**OUR EARTHLY PLEASURES** *Warp WARPCD155* ●	2		18

MAXWELL
US, male vocalist (Maxwell Menard)

Date	Title	Peak Position	Weeks at No.1	Weeks on Chart
				20
13 Apr 96	**URBAN SUITE** *Columbia 4836992* ●	39		10
26 Jul 97	**MTV UNPLUGGED (EP)** *Columbia 4882922*	45		2
4 Jul 98	**EMBRYA** *Columbia 4894202*	11		6
22 Sep 01	**NOW** *Columbia 4974542* ★	46		2

MAXX
UK/Sweden/Germany, male/female vocal/instrumental group

Date	Title	Peak Position	Weeks at No.1	Weeks on Chart
				1
23 Jul 94	**TO THE MAXXIMUM** *Pulse 8 PULSE 15CD*	66		1

BRIAN MAY
UK, male vocalist/guitarist

Date	Title	Peak Position	Weeks at No.1	Weeks on Chart
				23
12 Nov 83	**STAR FLEET PROJECT** *EMI SFLT 1078061* BRIAN MAY & FRIENDS	35		4
10 Oct 92	**BACK TO THE LIGHT** *Parlophone CDPCSD 123* ●	6		14
19 Feb 94	**LIVE AT BRIXTON ACADEMY** *Parlophone CDPCSD 150* BRIAN MAY BAND	20		3
13 Jun 98	**ANOTHER WORLD** *Parlophone 4949732*	23		2

IMELDA MAY
Ireland, female vocalist

Date	Title	Peak Position	Weeks at No.1	Weeks on Chart
				1
1 Nov 08	**LOVE TATTOO** *Blue Thumb 1790561*	58		1

SIMON MAY ORCHESTRA
UK, orchestra

Date	Title	Peak Position	Weeks at No.1	Weeks on Chart
				7
27 Sep 86	**SIMON'S WAY** *BBC REB 594*	59		7

JOHN MAYALL
UK, male vocalist/pianist

Date	Title	Peak Position	Weeks at No.1	Weeks on Chart
				3
30 Jul 66	**BLUES BREAKERS** *Decca LK 4804* JOHN MAYALL WITH ERIC CLAPTON	6		17
4 Mar 67	**A HARD ROAD** *Decca SKL 4853* JOHN MAYALL & THE BLUESBREAKERS	10		19
23 Sep 67	**CRUSADE** *Decca SKL 4890* JOHN MAYALL & THE BLUESBREAKERS	8		14
25 Nov 67	**THE BLUES ALONE** *Ace Of Clubs SCL 1243*	24		5
16 Mar 68	**THE DIARY OF A BAND VOLUME 1** *Decca SKL 4918* JOHN MAYALL & THE BLUESBREAKERS	27		9
16 Mar 68	**THE DIARY OF A BAND VOLUME 2** *Decca SKL 4919* JOHN MAYALL & THE BLUESBREAKERS	28		5
20 Jul 68	**BARE WIRES** *Decca SKL 4945* JOHN MAYALL & THE BLUESBREAKERS	3		17
18 Jan 69	**BLUES FROM LAUREL CANYON** *Decca SKL 4972*	33		3
23 Aug 69	**LOOKING BACK** *Decca SKL 5010*	14		7
15 Nov 69	**THE TURNING POINT** *Polydor 583571*	11		7
11 Apr 70	**EMPTY ROOMS** *Polydor 583580*	9		8
12 Dec 70	**U.S.A. UNION** *Polydor 2425 020*	50		1
26 Jun 71	**BACK TO THE ROOTS** *Polydor 2657 005*	31		2
17 Apr 93	**WAKE UP CALL** *Silvertone ORECD 527*	61		1

JON MAYER
US, male vocalist/guitarist

Date	Title	Peak Position	Weeks at No.1	Weeks on Chart
				3
25 Oct 03	**HEAVIER THINGS** *Columbia 5134722* JOHN MAYER	74		1
28 Oct 06	**CONTINUUM** *Columbia 88697011522* JOHN MAYER	46		2

CURTIS MAYFIELD
US, male vocalist/guitarist, d. 26 Dec 1999 (age 57)

Date	Title	Peak Position	Weeks at No.1	Weeks on Chart
				5
23 Mar 71	**CURTIS** *Buddah 2318 015*	30		1
31 Mar 73	**SUPERFLY (OST)** *Buddah 2318 065* ★	26		2
15 Feb 97	**NEW WORLD ORDER** *Warner Brothers 9362463482*	44		2

MAZE FEATURING FRANKIE BEVERLY
US, male vocal/instrumental group

Date	Title	Peak Position	Weeks at No.1	Weeks on Chart
				25
7 May 83	**WE ARE ONE** *Capitol EST 12262*	38		6
9 Mar 85	**CAN'T STOP THE LOVE** *Capitol MAZE 1*	41		12
27 Sep 86	**LIVE IN LOS ANGELES** *Capitol ESTSP 24*	70		2
16 Sep 89	**SILKY SOUL** *Warner Brothers WX 301*	43		5

MAZZY STAR
US, male/female vocal/instrumental group

Date	Title	Peak Position	Weeks at No.1	Weeks on Chart
				2
9 Oct 93	**SO TONIGHT THAT I MIGHT SEE** *Capitol CDEST 2206*	68		1
16 Nov 96	**AMONG MY SWAN** *Capitol CDEST 2288*	57		1

MC TUNES
UK, male rapper (Nicholas Lockett)

Date	Title	Peak Position	Weeks at No.1	Weeks on Chart
				3
13 Oct 90	**THE NORTH AT ITS HEIGHTS** *ZTT 3*	26		3

LEE MEAD
UK, male vocalist

Date	Title	Peak Position	Weeks at No.1	Weeks on Chart
				7
1 Dec 07	**LEE MEAD** *Fascination/Rug 1753349* ●	16		7

VAUGHN MEADER
US, male comedian, d. 29 Oct 2004 (age 68)

Date	Title	Peak Position	Weeks at No.1	Weeks on Chart
				8
29 Dec 62	**THE FIRST FAMILY** *London HAA 8048* ★	12		8

ROBERT MEADMORE
UK, male vocalist

Date	Title	Peak Position	Weeks at No.1	Weeks on Chart
				3
12 Mar 05	**AFTER A DREAM** *Dramatico DRAMCD0003*	49		3

MEAT LOAF
US, male vocalist. High energy rocker whose partnership with Jim Steinman resulted in *Bat Out Of Hell*, which has spent 474 weeks on the chart (only Fleetwood Mac's *Rumours* has a longer chart run) and sold more than two million copies in the UK

Date	Title	Peak Position	Weeks at No.1	Weeks on Chart
				816
11 Mar 78	**BAT OUT OF HELL** *Epic EPC 82419* ⊛x7	9		474
12 Sep 81	**DEAD RINGER** *Epic EPC 83645* ⊛	1	2	46
7 May 83	**MIDNIGHT AT THE LOST AND FOUND** *Epic EPC 25243* ●	7		23
10 Nov 84	**BAD ATTITUDE** *Arista 206 619* ●	8		16
26 Jan 85	**HITS OUT OF HELL** *Epic EPC 26156* ⊛	2		80
11 Oct 86	**BLIND BEFORE I STOP** *Arista 207 741* ● (silver)	28		6

Silver-selling ○ Gold-selling ● Platinum-selling ⊛ US No.1 ★ | Peak Position | Weeks at No.1 | Weeks on Chart

Date	Title	Peak Position	Weeks at No.1	Weeks on Chart
7 Nov 87	**LIVE' AT WEMBLEY** *RCA 208599*	60		2
25 Nov 89	**HEAVEN AND HELL** *Telstar STAR 2361* /BONNIE TYLER	9		12
18 Sep 93	**BAT OUT OF HELL II – BACK INTO HELL** *Virgin CDV 2710* ⊛x6 ★	1	11	59
22 Oct 94	**ALIVE IN HELL** *Pure Music PMCD 7002*	33		4
11 Nov 95	**WELCOME TO THE NEIGHBOURHOOD** *Virgin CDV 2799* ⊛	3		27
14 Nov 98	**THE VERY BEST OF MEAT LOAF** *Virgin/Sony TV CDV 2868* ⊛	14		39
3 May 03	**COULDN'T HAVE SAID IT BETTER** *Mercury 0761192* ●	4		14
30 Oct 04	**BAT OUT OF HELL – LIVE** *Mercury 9868074* ○	14		4
4 Nov 06	**BAT OUT OF HELL 3 – THE MONSTER IS LOOSE** *Mercury 1707640* ●	3		10

GLENN MEDEIROS
US, male vocalist — 2

Date	Title	Peak Position	Weeks at No.1	Weeks on Chart
8 Oct 88	**NOT ME** *London LONLP 68*	63		2

MEDIAEVAL BAEBES
UK, female vocal group — 7

Date	Title	Peak Position	Weeks at No.1	Weeks on Chart
29 Nov 97	**SALVA NOS** *Venture CDVE 935* ○	62		6
31 Oct 98	**WORLDES BLYSSE** *Venture CDVE 941*	73		1

MEGA CITY FOUR
UK, male vocal/instrumental group — 3

Date	Title	Peak Position	Weeks at No.1	Weeks on Chart
17 Jun 89	**TRANZOPHOBIA** *Decoy DYL 3*	67		1
7 Mar 92	**SEBASTAPOL ROAD** *Big Life MEGCD 1*	41		1
22 May 93	**MAGIC BULLETS** *Big Life MEGCD 3*	57		1

MEGADETH
US, male vocal/instrumental group – Dave Mustaine, Dave Ellefson, Marty Friedman & Nick Menza — 29

Date	Title	Peak Position	Weeks at No.1	Weeks on Chart
26 Mar 88	**SO FAR, SO GOOD...SO WHAT!** *Capitol EST 2053*	18		5
6 Oct 90	**RUST IN PEACE** *Capitol EST 2132* ○	8		4
18 Jul 92	**COUNTDOWN TO EXTINCTION** *Capitol CDESTU 2175* ○	5		8
25 Mar 95	**YOUTHANASIA/HIDDEN TREASURE** *Capitol CDEST 2244*	6		5
19 Jul 97	**CRYPTIC WRITINGS** *Capitol CDEST 2297*	38		1
18 Sep 99	**RISK** *Capitol 4991340*	29		2
26 May 01	**THE WORLD NEEDS A HERO** *Metal Is MISCD 006*	45		1
25 Sep 04	**THE SYSTEM HAS FAILED** *Sanctuary SANCD297*	60		1
26 May 07	**UNITED ABOMINATIONS** *Roadrunner RR80292*	23		2

ZUBIN MEHTA
India, male conductor — 28

Date	Title	Peak Position	Weeks at No.1	Weeks on Chart
10 Sep 94	**THE THREE TENORS IN CONCERT 1994** *Teldec 4509962002* CARRERAS, DOMINGO, PAVAROTTI WITH ORCHESTRA CONDUCTED BY MEHTA ⊛x2	1	1	26
23 Dec 00	**THE THREE TENORS CHRISTMAS** *Sony Classical SK 89131* CARRERAS/DOMINGO/PAVAROTTI FEATURING MEHTA	57		2

MEL & KIM
UK, female vocal duo – Mel Appleby, d. 18 Jan 1990, & Kim Appleby — 25

Date	Title	Peak Position	Weeks at No.1	Weeks on Chart
25 Apr 87	**F.L.M.** *Supreme SU 2* ⊛	3		25

MELANIE
US, female vocalist/guitarist (Melanie Safka) — 66

Date	Title	Peak Position	Weeks at No.1	Weeks on Chart
19 Sep 70	**CANDLES IN THE RAIN** *Buddah 2318 009*	5		31
16 Jan 71	**LEFTOVER WINE** *Buddah 2318 011*	22		4
29 May 71	**THE GOOD BOOK** *Buddah 2322 001*	9		9
8 Jan 72	**GATHER ME** *Buddah 2322 002*	14		14
1 Apr 72	**GARDEN IN THE CITY** *Buddah 2318 054*	19		6
7 Oct 72	**THE FOUR SIDES OF MELANIE** *Buddah 2659 013*	23		2

MELEE
US, male vocal/instrumental group — 1

Date	Title	Peak Position	Weeks at No.1	Weeks on Chart
9 Aug 08	**DEVILS & ANGELS** *Warner Brothers 9362498500* MELEE	61		1

JOHN MELLENCAMP
US, male vocalist/guitarist — 31

Date	Title	Peak Position	Weeks at No.1	Weeks on Chart
6 Nov 82	**AMERICAN FOOL** *Riva RVLP 16* JOHN COUGAR ★	37		6
3 Mar 84	**UH-HUH** *Riva RIVL 1* JOHN COUGAR MELLENCAMP	92		1
3 Oct 87	**THE LONESOME JUBILEE** *Mercury MERH 109* JOHN COUGAR MELLENCAMP	31		12
27 May 89	**BIG DADDY** *Mercury MERH 8382201* JOHN COUGAR MELLENCAMP	25		4
19 Oct 91	**WHENEVER WE WANTED** *Mercury 5101511*	39		2
18 Sep 93	**HUMAN WHEELS** *Mercury 5180882*	37		2
17 Jan 98	**THE BEST THAT I COULD DO 1978–1988** *Mercury 5367382*	25		4

KATIE MELUA
UK (b. Georgia), female vocalist/guitarist — 160

Date	Title	Peak Position	Weeks at No.1	Weeks on Chart
15 Nov 03	**CALL OFF THE SEARCH** *Dramatico DRAMCD 0002* ⊛x5	1	6	78
8 Oct 05	**PIECE BY PIECE** *Dramatico DRAMCD0007* ⊛x4	1	2	47
13 Oct 07	**PICTURES** *Dramatico DRAMCD0035* ⊛	2		26
8 Nov 08	**THE KATIE MELUA COLLECTION** *Dramatico DRAMCD0040*	15		9+

MEMBERS
UK, male vocal/instrumental group — 5

Date	Title	Peak Position	Weeks at No.1	Weeks on Chart
28 Apr 79	**AT THE CHELSEA NIGHTCLUB** *Virgin V 2120*	45		5

MEN AT WORK
Australia, male vocal/instrumental group – Colin James Hay, Greg Ham, John Rees & Jerry Speiser — 71

Date	Title	Peak Position	Weeks at No.1	Weeks on Chart
15 Jan 83	**BUSINESS AS USUAL** *Epic EPC 85669* ⊛ ★	1	5	44
30 Apr 83	**CARGO** *Epic EPC 25372* ●	8		27

MEN THEY COULDN'T HANG
UK, male vocal/instrumental group — 9

Date	Title	Peak Position	Weeks at No.1	Weeks on Chart
27 Jul 85	**NIGHT OF A THOUSAND CANDLES** *Imp FIEND 50*	91		2
8 Nov 86	**HOW GREEN IS THE VALLEY** *MCA MCF 3337*	68		2
23 Apr 88	**WAITING FOR BONAPARTE** *Magnet MAGL 5075*	41		2
6 May 89	**SILVER TOWN** *Silvertone ORELP 503*	39		2
1 Sep 90	**THE DOMINO CLUB** *Silvertone ORELP 512*	53		1

MEN WITHOUT HATS
Canada, male vocal/instrumental group — 1

Date	Title	Peak Position	Weeks at No.1	Weeks on Chart
12 Nov 83	**RHYTHM OF YOUTH** *Statik STATLP 10*	96		1

SERGIO MENDES
Brazil, male pianist/band leader — 7

Date	Title	Peak Position	Weeks at No.1	Weeks on Chart
1 Jul 06	**TIMELESS** *Concord 3123152* ●	15		7

MENSWEAR
UK, male vocal/instrumental group — 6

Date	Title	Peak Position	Weeks at No.1	Weeks on Chart
21 Oct 95	**NUISANCE** *Laurel 8286792*	11		6

IDINA MENZEL
US, female vocalist/actor — 1

Date	Title	Peak Position	Weeks at No.1	Weeks on Chart
25 Oct 08	**I STAND** *Warner Brothers 9362444232*	54		1

NATALIE MERCHANT
US, female vocalist. See 10,000 Maniacs — 3

Date	Title	Peak Position	Weeks at No.1	Weeks on Chart
1 Jul 95	**TIGERLILY** *Elektra 7559617452*	39		2
13 Jun 98	**OPHELIA** *Elektra 7559621962*	52		1

FREDDIE MERCURY
UK (b. Zanzibar), male vocalist, d. 24 Nov 1991 (age 45). See Queen — 71

Date	Title	Peak Position	Weeks at No.1	Weeks on Chart
11 May 85	**MR BAD GUY** *CBS 86312* ●	6		23
22 Oct 88	**BARCELONA** *Polydor POLH 44* & MONTSERRAT CABALLE ○	15		8
28 Nov 92	**THE FREDDIE MERCURY ALBUM** *Parlophone CDPCSD 124* ⊛x2	4		25
4 Nov 00	**SOLO** *Parlophone 5280472* ●	13		9
16 Sep 06	**THE VERY BEST OF FREDDIE MERCURY SOLO** *Parlophone 3671692* ●	6		6

MERCURY REV
US, male vocal/instrumental group — 20

Date	Title	Peak Position	Weeks at No.1	Weeks on Chart
12 Jun 93	**BOCES** *Beggars Banquet BBQCD 140*	43		1
17 Oct 98	**DESERTER'S SONG** *V2 VVR 1002772* ●	27		12
8 Sep 01	**ALL IS DREAM** *V2 VVR 1017528*	11		4
5 Feb 05	**THE SECRET MIGRATION** *V2 VVR1029238*	16		2
11 Oct 08	**SNOWFLAKE MIDNIGHT** *Cooperative Music/V2 VVR1051271*	52		1

Key: ○ Silver-selling · ● Gold-selling · ⊛ Platinum-selling · ★ US No.1 · Peak Position · Weeks at No.1 · Weeks on Chart

MERLE & ROY
UK, female/male vocal/instrumental duo — Weeks on Chart: 5

Date	Title / Label	Peak	Wks at No.1	Wks on Chart
26 Sep 87	**REQUESTS** *Myndd Mawr RMBR 8713*	74		5

MERSEYBEATS
UK, male vocal/instrumental group — Weeks on Chart: 9

Date	Title / Label	Peak	Wks at No.1	Wks on Chart
20 Jun 64	**THE MERSEYBEATS** *Fontana TL 5210*	12		9

METALLICA
US, male vocal/instrumental group – James Hetfield, Cliff Burton, d. 27 Sep 1986, Kirk Hammett & Lars Ulrich — Weeks on Chart: 144

Date	Title / Label	Peak	Wks at No.1	Wks on Chart
11 Aug 84	**RIDE THE LIGHTNING** *Music For Nations MFN 27* ●	87		2
15 Mar 86	**MASTER OF PUPPETS** *Music For Nations MFN 60* ●	41		4
17 Sep 88	**...AND JUSTICE FOR ALL** *Vertigo VERH 61* ○	4		6
19 May 90	**THE GOOD THE BAD AND THE LIVE: THE 6 1/2 YEARS ANNIVERSARY COLLECTION** *Vertigo 8754871*	56		1
24 Aug 91	**METALLICA** *Vertigo 5100221* ⊛ ★	1	1	77
11 Dec 93	**LIVE SHIT – BINGE AND PURGE** *Vertigo 5187250*	54		1
15 Jun 96	**LOAD** *Vertigo 5326182* ● ★	1	1	18
5 Oct 96	**HERO OF THE DAY** *Vertigo METCY 13*	47		1
29 Nov 97	**RELOAD** *Vertigo 5364092* ● ★	4		9
5 Dec 98	**GARAGE INC.** *Vertigo 5383512*	29		2
4 Dec 99	**S&M** *Vertigo 5487972*	33		2
14 Jun 03	**ST ANGER** *Vertigo 9865403* ● ★	3		11
20 Sep 08	**DEATH MAGNETIC** *Vertigo 1773726* ●	1	3	10

METEORS
UK, male vocal/instrumental group — Weeks on Chart: 3

Date	Title / Label	Peak	Wks at No.1	Wks on Chart
26 Feb 83	**WRECKIN' CREW** *I.D. NOSE 1*	53		3

METHOD MAN
US, male rapper (Clifford Smith). See Wu-Tang Clan — Weeks on Chart: 7

Date	Title / Label	Peak	Wks at No.1	Wks on Chart
28 Nov 98	**TICAL 2000: JUDGEMENT DAY** *Def Jam 5589202*	49		1
9 Oct 99	**BLACK OUT!** *Def Jam 5466092* & REDMAN	45		3
29 May 04	**TICAL 0 – THE PREQUEL** *Def Jam 9862641*	29		3

MEZZOFORTE
Iceland, male instrumental group — Weeks on Chart: 10

Date	Title / Label	Peak	Wks at No.1	Wks on Chart
5 Mar 83	**SURPRISE SURPRISE** *Steinar STELP 02*	23		9
2 Jul 83	**CATCHING UP WITH MEZZOFORTE** *Steinar STELP 03*	95		1

MGMT
US, male vocal/instrumental duo — Weeks on Chart: 34

Date	Title / Label	Peak	Wks at No.1	Wks on Chart
22 Mar 08	**ORACULAR SPECTACULAR** *Columbia 88697195121* ●	12		34+

MIA
UK, female vocalist/producer (Mathangi 'Maya' Arulpragasam) — Weeks on Chart: 3

Date	Title / Label	Peak	Wks at No.1	Wks on Chart
1 Sep 07	**KALA** *XL Recordings XLCD281*	39		3

GEORGE MICHAEL
UK, male vocalist. Award-winning songwriter/producer who won an Album of the Year Grammy for transatlantic chart-topper *Faith* and became the first act in UK chart history to release six Top 3 singles from one album (*Older*). See Wham! — Weeks on Chart: 360

Date	Title / Label	Peak	Wks at No.1	Wks on Chart
14 Nov 87	**FAITH** *Epic 4600001* ⊛x4 ★	1	1	77
15 Sep 90	**LISTEN WITHOUT PREJUDICE VOLUME 1** *Epic 4672951* ⊛x4	1	1	57
25 May 96	**OLDER/OLDER & UPPER** *Virgin CDVX 2802* ⊛x6	1	3	99
21 Nov 98	**LADIES & GENTLEMEN – THE BEST OF GEORGE MICHAEL** *Epic 4927052* ⊛x7	1	8	70
18 Dec 99	**SONGS FROM THE LAST CENTURY** *Virgin CDVX 2920* ⊛x2	2		17
27 Mar 04	**PATIENCE** *Aegean 5154022* ⊛x2	1	1	23
25 Nov 06	**TWENTY FIVE** *Aegean/Sony 88697009012* ⊛x2	1	1	17

Top 3 Best-Selling Albums

	Title	Approximate Sales
1	LADIES & GENTLEMEN - THE BEST OF	2,415,000
2	OLDER	1,715,000
3	LISTEN WITHOUT PREJUDICE VOL 1	1,325,000

PRAS MICHEL
US, male rapper/producer (Prakazrel Michael). See Fugees — Weeks on Chart: 3

Date	Title / Label	Peak	Wks at No.1	Wks on Chart
14 Nov 98	**GHETTO SUPERSTAR** *Columbia 4914892*	44		3

KEITH MICHELL
Australia, male actor/vocalist — Weeks on Chart: 12

Date	Title / Label	Peak	Wks at No.1	Wks on Chart
9 Feb 80	**CAPTAIN BEAKY AND HIS BAND** *Polydor 2383 462* ○	28		12

MICHELLE
UK, female vocalist (Michelle McManus) — Weeks on Chart: 7

Date	Title / Label	Peak	Wks at No.1	Wks on Chart
28 Feb 04	**THE MEANING OF LOVE** *S 82876590662* ●	3		7

BETTE MIDLER
US, female vocalist — Weeks on Chart: 56

Date	Title / Label	Peak	Wks at No.1	Wks on Chart
8 Mar 80	**THE ROSE (OST)** *Atlantic K 50681*	68		1
15 Jul 89	**BEACHES (OST)** *Atlantic 7819931* ●	21		9
13 Jul 91	**SOME PEOPLE'S LIVES** *Atlantic 7567821291* ●	5		11
15 Feb 92	**FOR THE BOYS (OST)** *Atlantic 7567823292*	75		1
30 Oct 93	**EXPERIENCE THE DIVINE – GREATEST HITS** *Atlantic 7567824972* ⊛	3		15
25 Nov 95	**BETTE OF ROSES** *Atlantic 7567828232*	55		4
1 Apr 06	**SINGS THE PEGGY LEE SONGBOOK** *Columbia 82876754582*	41		1
4 Oct 08	**THE BEST OF BETTE** *Rhino 8122798931* ●	6		14+

MIDNIGHT OIL
Australia, male vocal/instrumental group — Weeks on Chart: 21

Date	Title / Label	Peak	Wks at No.1	Wks on Chart
25 Jun 88	**DIESEL AND DUST** *CBS 4600051* ●	19		16
10 Mar 90	**BLUE SKY MINING** *CBS 4656531*	28		3
1 May 93	**EARTH AND SUN AND MOON** *Columbia 4736052*	27		2

MIDNIGHT STAR
US, male vocal/instrumental group — Weeks on Chart: 6

Date	Title / Label	Peak	Wks at No.1	Wks on Chart
2 Feb 85	**PLANETARY INVASION** *Solar MCF 3251*	85		2
5 Jul 86	**HEADLINES** *Solar MCF 3322*	42		4

MIGHTY LEMON DROPS
UK, male vocal/instrumental group — Weeks on Chart: 5

Date	Title / Label	Peak	Wks at No.1	Wks on Chart
4 Oct 86	**HAPPY HEAD** *Blue Guitar AZLP 1*	58		2
27 Feb 88	**THE WORLD WITHOUT END** *Blue Guitar AZLP 4*	34		3

MIGHTY MIGHTY BOSSTONES
US, male vocal/instrumental group — Weeks on Chart: 2

Date	Title / Label	Peak	Wks at No.1	Wks on Chart
16 May 98	**LET'S FACE IT** *Mercury 5344722*	40		2

MIGHTY MORPH'N POWER RANGERS
US, male/female vocal group (dressed as Power Rangers) — Weeks on Chart: 3

Date	Title / Label	Peak	Wks at No.1	Wks on Chart
24 Dec 94	**POWER RANGERS – THE ALBUM – A ROCK ADVENTURE** *RCA 74321252982* ○	50		3

MIKA
UK (b. Lebanon), male vocalist/keyboard player (Michael Penniman) — Weeks on Chart: 82

Date	Title / Label	Peak	Wks at No.1	Wks on Chart
17 Feb 07	**LIFE IN CARTOON MOTION** *Casablanca/Island 1717335* ⊛x5	1	1	82

MIKE & THE MECHANICS
UK, male vocal/instrumental group – Mike Rutherford*, Paul Carrack*, Adrian Lee, Peter Van Hooke & Paul Young — Weeks on Chart: 101

Date	Title / Label	Peak	Wks at No.1	Wks on Chart
15 Mar 86	**MIKE AND THE MECHANICS** *WEA WX 49*	78		3
26 Nov 88	**THE LIVING YEARS** *WEA WX 203* ●	2		19
27 Apr 91	**WORD OF MOUTH** *Virgin V 2662* ○	11		7
18 Mar 95	**BEGGAR ON A BEACH OF GOLD** *Virgin CDV 2772* ●	9		33
2 Mar 96	**THE LIVING YEARS** *Atlantic K 2560042*	67		2
16 Mar 96	**HITS** *Virgin CDV 2797* ⊛x2	3		31
12 Jun 99	**MIKE AND THE MECHANICS** *Virgin CDV 2885*	14		4
19 Jun 04	**REWIRED** *Virgin CDVX 2984*	61		1
18 Sep 04	**REWIRED/THE HITS** *Virgin CDVX 2990*	42		1

MILBURN

UK, male vocal/instrumental group — Weeks on chart: 2

Date	Title / Label	Peak Position	Weeks at No.1	Weeks on Chart
21 Oct 06	**WELL WELL WELL** *Mercury 1701767*	32		1
6 Oct 07	**THESE ARE THE FACTS** *Mercury 1741314*	51		1

JOHN MILES

UK, male vocalist/multi-instrumentalist — Weeks on chart: 25

Date	Title / Label	Peak Position	Weeks at No.1	Weeks on Chart
27 Mar 76	**REBEL** *Decca SKL 5231* ○	9		10
26 Feb 77	**STRANGER IN THE CITY** *Decca TXS 118* ○	37		3
1 Apr 78	**ZARAGON** *Decca TXS 126*	43		5
21 Apr 79	**MORE MILES PER HOUR** *Decca TXS 135*	46		5
29 Aug 81	**MILES HIGH** *EMI EMC 3374*	96		2

ROBERT MILES

Italy, male keyboard player (Robert Concina) — Weeks on chart: 51

Date	Title / Label	Peak Position	Weeks at No.1	Weeks on Chart
22 Jun 96	**DREAMLAND** *Deconstruction 74321391262* ⊛	7		48
6 Dec 97	**23AM** *Deconstruction 74321541132*	42		3

CHRISTINA MILIAN

US, female vocalist — Weeks on chart: 16

Date	Title / Label	Peak Position	Weeks at No.1	Weeks on Chart
2 Feb 02	**CHRISTINA MILIAN** *Def Soul 5867392* ○	23		11
12 Jun 04	**IT'S ABOUT TIME** *Def Jam UK 9862835* ○	21		4
20 May 06	**SO AMAZIN'** *Def Jam 9878036*	67		1

MILK INC.

Belgium, male/female production/vocal duo — Weeks on chart: 1

Date	Title / Label	Peak Position	Weeks at No.1	Weeks on Chart
5 Oct 02	**MILK INC.** *Positiva 5419532*	47		1

DOMINIC MILLER

Argentina, male guitarist — Weeks on chart: 3

Date	Title / Label	Peak Position	Weeks at No.1	Weeks on Chart
14 Jun 03	**SHAPES** *BBC Music WMSF60702*	38		3

FRANKIE MILLER

UK, male vocalist — Weeks on chart: 1

Date	Title / Label	Peak Position	Weeks at No.1	Weeks on Chart
14 Apr 79	**FALLING IN LOVE** *Chrysalis CHR 1220*	54		1

GLENN MILLER & HIS ORCHESTRA

US, male composer/band leader (Alton Glenn Miller), d. 15 Dec 1944 (age 40) & orchestra — Weeks on chart: 82

Date	Title / Label	Peak Position	Weeks at No.1	Weeks on Chart
28 Jan 61	**GLENN MILLER PLAYS SELECTIONS FROM 'THE GLENN MILLER STORY' AND OTHER HITS (OST)** *RCA 27068 0023*	10		18
5 Jul 69	**THE BEST OF GLENN MILLER** *RCA International 1002*	5		14
6 Sep 69	**NEARNESS OF YOU** *RCA International INTS 1019*	30		2
25 Apr 70	**A MEMORIAL 1944–1969** *RCA Victor GM 1*	18		17
25 Dec 71	**THE REAL GLENN MILLER AND HIS ORCHESTRA PLAY THE ORIGINAL MUSIC OF THE FILM 'THE GLENN MILLER STORY' AND OTHER HITS (OST)** *RCA International NTS 1157*	28		2
14 Feb 76	**A LEGENDARY PERFORMER** *RCA Victor DPM 2065*	41		5
14 Feb 76	**A LEGENDARY PERFORMER VOLUME 2** *RCA Victor CPL 11349*	53		2
9 Apr 77	**THE UNFORGETTABLE GLENN MILLER** *RCA Victor TVL 1*	4		8
20 Mar 93	**THE ULTIMATE GLENN MILLER** *Bluebird 74321131372*	11		6
25 Feb 95	**THE LOST RECORDINGS** *Happy Days CDHD 4012* ○	22		6
18 Oct 03	**IN THE MOOD – THE DEFINITIVE** *BMG 82876560302* GLENN MILLER	43		2

STEVE MILLER BAND

US, male vocal/instrumental group – Steve Miller, James Cook, Tim Davis, Gary Mallaber & Lonnie Turner — Weeks on chart: 51

Date	Title / Label	Peak Position	Weeks at No.1	Weeks on Chart
12 Jun 76	**FLY LIKE AN EAGLE** *Mercury 9286 177* ●	11		17
4 Jun 77	**BOOK OF DREAMS** *Mercury 9286 456* ○	12		12
19 Jun 82	**ABRACADABRA** *Mercury 6302 204* ○	10		16
7 May 83	**STEVE MILLER BAND LIVE!** *Mercury MERL 18*	79		2
6 Oct 90	**THE BEST OF 1968–1973** *Capitol EST 2133*	34		3
10 Oct 98	**GREATEST HITS** *Polygram TV 5592402*	58		1

MILLI VANILLI

Germany/France, male vocal duo – Fabrice Morvan & Rob Pilatus, d. 2 Apr 1998 — Weeks on chart: 25

Date	Title / Label	Peak Position	Weeks at No.1	Weeks on Chart
28 Oct 89	**ALL OR NOTHING/2 X 2** *Cooltempo CTLP 11* ⊛	6		25

MILLICAN & NESBITT

UK, male vocal duo – Alan Millican & Tim Nesbitt — Weeks on chart: 24

Date	Title / Label	Peak Position	Weeks at No.1	Weeks on Chart
23 Mar 74	**MILLICAN AND NESBITT** *Pye NSPL 18428* ●	3		21
4 Jan 75	**EVERYBODY KNOWS MILLICAN AND NESBITT** *Pye NSPL 18446* ●	23		3

SPIKE MILLIGAN

UK, male comedian, d. 27 Feb 2002 (age 83) — Weeks on chart: 6

Date	Title / Label	Peak Position	Weeks at No.1	Weeks on Chart
25 Nov 61	**MILLIGAN PRESERVED** *Parlophone PMC 1152*	11		4
18 Apr 64	**HOW TO WIN AN ELECTION** *Philips AL 3464* HARRY SECOMBE, PETER SELLERS & SPIKE MILLIGAN	20		1
18 Dec 76	**THE SNOW GOOSE** *RCA Victor RS 1088* WITH THE LONDON SYMPHONY ORCHESTRA	49		1

BEN MILLS

UK, male vocalist — Weeks on chart: 4

Date	Title / Label	Peak Position	Weeks at No.1	Weeks on Chart
24 Mar 07	**PICTURE OF YOU** *Modest 88697074822*	3		4

MILLTOWN BROTHERS

UK, male vocal/instrumental group — Weeks on chart: 5

Date	Title / Label	Peak Position	Weeks at No.1	Weeks on Chart
23 Mar 91	**SLINKY** *A&M 3953461*	27		5

WAYNE FONTANA & THE MINDBENDERS

UK, male vocal/instrumental group — Weeks on chart: 5

Date	Title / Label	Peak Position	Weeks at No.1	Weeks on Chart
20 Feb 65	**WAYNE FONTANA AND THE MINDBENDERS** *Fontana TL 5230*	18		1
25 Jun 66	**THE MINDBENDERS** *Fontana TL 5324* MINDBENDERS	28		4

MINDFUNK

UK, male vocal/instrumental group — Weeks on chart: 1

Date	Title / Label	Peak Position	Weeks at No.1	Weeks on Chart
15 May 93	**DROPPED** *Megaforce CDZAZ 3*	60		1

ZODIAC MINDWARP & THE LOVE REACTION

UK, male/female vocal group — Weeks on chart: 5

Date	Title / Label	Peak Position	Weeks at No.1	Weeks on Chart
5 Mar 88	**TATTOOED BEAT MESSIAH** *Mercury ZODLP 1*	20		5

MINIPOPS

UK, male/female vocal group — Weeks on chart: 12

Date	Title / Label	Peak Position	Weeks at No.1	Weeks on Chart
26 Dec 81	**MINIPOPS** *K-Tel NE 1102* ●	63		7
19 Feb 83	**WE'RE THE MINIPOPS** *K-Tel ONE 1187*	54		5

MINISTRY

US, male vocal/instrumental group — Weeks on chart: 6

Date	Title / Label	Peak Position	Weeks at No.1	Weeks on Chart
25 Jul 92	**PSALM 69** *Sire 7599267272*	33		5
10 Feb 96	**FILTH PIG** *Warner Brothers 9362458382*	43		1

LIZA MINNELLI

US, female vocalist — Weeks on chart: 27

Date	Title / Label	Peak Position	Weeks at No.1	Weeks on Chart
7 Apr 73	**LIZA WITH A 'Z'** *CBS 65212*	9		15
16 Jun 73	**THE SINGER** *CBS 65555*	45		1
21 Oct 89	**RESULTS** *Epic 4655111* ●	6		10
6 Jul 96	**GENTLY** *Angel CDQ 8354702*	58		1

DANNII MINOGUE

Australia, female vocalist — Weeks on chart: 32

Date	Title / Label	Peak Position	Weeks at No.1	Weeks on Chart
15 Jun 91	**LOVE AND KISSES** *MCA 10340* ●	8		20
16 Oct 93	**GET INTO YOU** *MCA MCD 10909*	52		1
20 Sep 97	**GIRL** *Eternal 3984205492*	57		1
29 Mar 03	**NEON NIGHTS** *London 2564600032* ●	8		7
1 Jul 06	**THE HITS AND BEYOND** *UMTV/AATW 9840363*	17		3

KYLIE MINOGUE

Australia, female vocalist. No Australian act has earned more from live shows than the chameleon-like soap star turned pop/dance diva who has remained a constant chart fixture for 20 years. In the UK, Kylie was the top-selling album by a female and the biggest-selling debut album

Date	Album	Peak Position	Weeks at No.1	Weeks on Chart
				351
16 Jul 88	**KYLIE! - THE ALBUM** *PWL HF 3* KYLIE MINOGUE ⊛x6	1	6	67
21 Oct 89	**ENJOY YOURSELF** *PWL HF 9* ⊛x4	1	1	33
24 Nov 90	**RHYTHM OF LOVE** *PWL HF 18* ●	9		22
26 Oct 91	**LET'S GO TO IT** *PWL HF 21*	15		12
5 Sep 92	**KYLIE'S GREATEST HITS** *PWL International HFCD 25* ○	1	1	10
1 Oct 94	**KYLIE MINOGUE** *Deconstruction 74321227492* ●	4		15
4 Apr 98	**KYLIE MINOGUE** *Deconstruction 74321517272*	10		4
15 Aug 98	**MIXES** *Deconstruction 74321587152*	63		1
7 Oct 00	**LIGHT YEARS** *Parlophone 5284002* ⊛	2		28
28 Oct 00	**HITS PLUS** *Deconstruction 74321785342*	41		1
13 Oct 01	**FEVER** *Parlophone 5358042* ⊛x5	1	2	70
30 Nov 02	**GREATEST HITS 87-92** *PWL 9224682* ⊛	20		11
29 Nov 03	**BODY LANGUAGE** *Parlophone 5957582* ⊛	6		18
4 Dec 04	**ULTIMATE KYLIE** *Parlophone 8753652* ⊛x2	4		28
20 Jan 07	**SHOWGIRL - HOMECOMING LIVE** *Parlophone 3853312* ○	7		4
8 Dec 07	**X** *Parlophone 5139522*	4		27

MIRAGE

UK, male production group – Kiki Billy, Nigel Wright & various musicians

Date	Album	Peak Position	Weeks at No.1	Weeks on Chart
				3
26 Dec 87	**THE BEST OF MIRAGE: JACK MIX '88** *Stylus SMR 746* ●	7		15
25 Jun 88	**JACK MIX IN FULL EFFECT** *Stylus SMR 856* ●	7		12
7 Jan 89	**ROYAL MIX '89** *Stylus SMR 871*	34		6
23 Sep 95	**CLASSIC GUITAR MOODS** *Polygram TV 5290562*	25		3

MIS-TEEQ

UK, female vocal group – Alesha Dixon*, Su-Elise Nash, Zena Playford & Sabrena Washington

Date	Album	Peak Position	Weeks at No.1	Weeks on Chart
				54
10 Nov 01	**LICKIN' ON BOTH SIDES** *Inferno/Telstar TCD 3212* ⊛	3		31
12 Apr 03	**EYE CANDY** *Telstar TCD 3304* ●	6		21
7 May 05	**GREATEST HITS** *Universal TV 9871410*	28		2

MISSION

UK, male vocal/instrumental group – Wayne Hussey, Craig Adams, Mick Brown & Simon Hinkler

Date	Album	Peak Position	Weeks at No.1	Weeks on Chart
				48
22 Nov 86	**GOD'S OWN MEDICINE** *Mercury MERH 102* ○	14		20
4 Jul 87	**THE FIRST CHAPTER** *Mercury MISH 1*	35		4
12 Mar 88	**CHILDREN** *Mercury MISH 2* ●	2		9
17 Feb 90	**CARVED IN SAND** *Mercury 8422511* ●	7		8
3 Nov 90	**GRAINS OF SAND** *Mercury 8469371*	28		2
4 Jul 92	**MASQUE** *Vertigo 5121212*	23		2
19 Feb 94	**SUM AND SUBSTANCE** *Vertigo 5184472*	49		1
25 Feb 95	**NEVERLAND** *Neverland SMEECD 001*	58		1
15 Jun 96	**BLUE** *Equator SMEECD 002*	73		1

MRS. MILLS

UK, female pianist (Gladys Mills), d. 25 Feb 1978 (age 56)

Date	Album	Peak Position	Weeks at No.1	Weeks on Chart
				13
10 Dec 66	**COME TO MY PARTY** *Parlophone PMC 7010*	17		7
28 Dec 68	**MRS. MILLS PARTY PIECES** *Parlophone PCS 7066*	32		3
13 Dec 69	**LET'S HAVE ANOTHER PARTY** *Parlophone PCS 7035*	23		2
6 Nov 71	**I'M MIGHTY GLAD** *MFP 5225*	49		1

MR. BIG

US, male vocal/instrumental group

Date	Album	Peak Position	Weeks at No.1	Weeks on Chart
				14
22 Jul 89	**MR. BIG** *Atlantic 7819901*	60		1
13 Apr 91	**LEAN INTO IT** *Atlantic 7567822091*	28		12
2 Oct 93	**BUMP AHEAD** *Atlantic 7567824952*	61		1

MR. BUNGLE

UK, male vocal/instrumental group

Date	Album	Peak Position	Weeks at No.1	Weeks on Chart
				1
21 Sep 91	**MR. BUNGLE** *London 8282671*	57		1

MR HUDSON & THE LIBRARY

UK, male vocal/instrumental group

Date	Album	Peak Position	Weeks at No.1	Weeks on Chart
				1
17 Mar 07	**A TALE OF TWO CITIES** *Mercury 1719879*	69		1

MR. MISTER

US, male vocal/instrumental group – Richard Page, Steve Farris, Steve George & Pat Mastelotto

Date	Album	Peak Position	Weeks at No.1	Weeks on Chart
				24
15 Feb 86	**WELCOME TO THE REAL WORLD** *RCA PL 89647* ● ★	6		24

MR. SCRUFF

UK, male DJ/producer (Andy Carthy)

Date	Album	Peak Position	Weeks at No.1	Weeks on Chart
				3
21 Sep 02	**TROUSER JAZZ** *Ninja Tune ZENCD65* ○	29		2
18 Oct 08	**NINJA TUNA** *Ninja Tune ZENCD143*	60		1

GEORGE MITCHELL MINSTRELS

UK, male vocal ensemble – George Mitchell, d. 27 Aug 2002 (age 85). Mitchell's non-P/C recreation of a Victorian minstrel show proved very popular on both TV and record at the start of the sixties. They had three successive No.1 albums and gave EMI their first 100,000-selling LP

Date	Album	Peak Position	Weeks at No.1	Weeks on Chart
				292
26 Nov 60	**THE BLACK AND WHITE MINSTREL SHOW** *HMV CLP 1399*	1	7	142
21 Oct 61	**ANOTHER BLACK AND WHITE MINSTREL SHOW** *HMV CLP 1460*	1	8	64
20 Oct 62	**ON STAGE WITH THE GEORGE MITCHELL MINSTRELS** *HMV CLP 1599*	1	2	26
2 Nov 63	**ON TOUR WITH THE GEORGE MITCHELL MINSTRELS** *HMV CLP 1667*	6		18
12 Dec 64	**SPOTLIGHT ON THE GEORGE MITCHELL MINST6RELS** *HMV CLP 1803*	6		7
4 Dec 65	**MAGIC OF THE MINSTRELS** *HMV CLP 1917*	9		7
26 Nov 66	**HERE COME THE MINSTRELS** *HMV CLP 3579*	11		11
16 Dec 67	**SHOWTIME** *HMV CSD 3642*	26		2
14 Dec 68	**SING THE IRVING BERLIN SONGBOOK** *Columbia SCX 6267*	33		1
19 Dec 70	**THE MAGIC OF CHRISTMAS** *Columbia SCX 6431*	32		4
19 Nov 77	**30 GOLDEN GREATS** *EMI EMTV 7* WITH THE JOE LOSS ORCHESTRA	10		10

JONI MITCHELL

Canada, female vocalist/guitarist (Roberta Anderson)

Date	Album	Peak Position	Weeks at No.1	Weeks on Chart
				122
6 Jun 70	**LADIES OF THE CANYON** *Reprise RSLP 6376*	8		25
24 Jul 71	**BLUE** *Reprise K 44128*	3		18
16 Mar 74	**COURT AND SPARK** *Asylum SYLA 8756* ●	14		11
1 Feb 75	**MILES OF AISLES** *Asylum SYSP 902*	34		4
27 Dec 75	**THE HISSING OF SUMMER LAWNS** *Asylum SYLA 8763*	14		10
11 Dec 76	**HEJIRA** *Asylum K 53053* ○	11		5
21 Jan 78	**DON JUAN'S RECKLESS DAUGHTER** *Asylum K 63003* ○	20		7
14 Jul 79	**MINGUS** *Asylum K 53091* ○	24		7
4 Oct 80	**SHADOWS AND LIGHT** *Elektra K 62030*	63		3
4 Dec 82	**WILD THINGS RUN FAST** *Geffen GEF 25102*	32		8
30 Nov 85	**DOG EAT DOG** *Geffen GEF 26455*	57		3
2 Apr 88	**CHALK FARM IN A RAIN STORM** *Geffen WX 141*	26		7
9 Mar 91	**NIGHT RIDE HOME** *Geffen GEF 24302*	25		5
5 Nov 94	**TURBULENT INDIGO** *Reprise 9362457862*	53		2
10 Oct 98	**TAMING THE TIGER** *Reprise 9362464512*	57		1
11 Mar 00	**BOTH SIDES NOW** *Reprise 9362476202*	50		2
25 Sep 04	**DREAMLAND** *WSM 8122765202*	43		2
6 Oct 07	**SHINE** *Hearmusic 7230457*	36		2

MITCHELL BROTHERS

UK, male rap duo

Date	Album	Peak Position	Weeks at No.1	Weeks on Chart
				1
3 Sep 05	**A BREATH OF FRESH ATTIRE** *The Beats 2564625892*	56		1

MN8

UK/Trinidad & Tobago, male vocal group

Date	Album	Peak Position	Weeks at No.1	Weeks on Chart
				4
27 May 95	**TO THE NEXT LEVEL** *Columbia 4802802* ○	13		4

MOBB DEEP

US, male rap group

Date	Album	Peak Position	Weeks at No.1	Weeks on Chart
				3
23 Nov 96	**HELL ON EARTH** *Loud 74321425582*	67		1
21 Aug 04	**AMERIKAZ NIGHTMARE** *Jive 82876571312*	68		1
20 May 06	**BLOOD MONEY** *Interscope 9857207*	70		1

MOBY

US, male producer/vocalist/multi-instrumentalist (Richard Hall)

Date	Album	Peak Position	Weeks at No.1	Weeks on Chart
				145
27 Jan 96	**EVERYTHING IS WRONG/MIXED & REMIXED** *Mute LCDSTUMM 130*	21		7
5 Oct 96	**ANIMAL RIGHTS** *Mute CDSTUMM 150*	38		1
29 May 99	**PLAY** *Mute CDSTUMM 172* ⊛x5	1	5	83
1 Jul 00	**I LIKE TO SCORE** *Mute CDSTUMM 168*	54		2

Date	Title / Label	Peak Position	Weeks at No.1	Weeks on Chart
4 Nov 00	**PLAY/THE B SIDES** *Mute LCDSTUMM 172*	24		3
25 May 02	**18** *Mute CDSTUMM 202* ⊛	1	1	34
26 Mar 05	**HOTEL** *Mute LCDSTUMM240*	8		6
18 Nov 06	**GO – THE VERY BEST OF** *Mute LCDMUTEL14* ●	23		7
24 May 08	**LAST NIGHT** *Mute CDSTUMM275*	28		2

MOCK TURTLES
UK, male/female vocal/instrumental group — 4

Date	Title / Label	Peak	No.1	Weeks
25 May 91	**TURTLE SOUP** *Imaginary ILLUSION 012*	54		1
27 Jul 91	**TWO SIDES** *Siren SRNLP31*	33		3

MODERN EON
UK, male vocal/instrumental group — 1

Date	Title / Label	Peak	No.1	Weeks
13 Jun 81	**FICTION TALES** *Dindisc DID 11*	65		1

MODERN ROMANCE
UK, male vocal/instrumental group — 13

Date	Title / Label	Peak	No.1	Weeks
16 Apr 83	**TRICK OF THE LIGHT** *WEA X 0127*	53		7
3 Dec 83	**PARTY TONIGHT** *Ronco RONLP 3* ●	45		6

MODERN TALKING
Germany, male vocal/instrumental duo — 3

Date	Title / Label	Peak	No.1	Weeks
11 Oct 86	**READY FOR ROMANCE** *RCA PL 71133*	76		3

MODEST MOUSE
US, male vocal/instrumental group — 6

Date	Title / Label	Peak	No.1	Weeks
31 Jul 04	**GOOD NEWS FOR PEOPLE WHO LOVE BAD NEWS** *Epic 5162722*	40		2
14 Apr 07	**WE WERE DEAD BEFORE THE SHIP EVEN SANK** *Epic 88697083992* ★	47		4

MOFFATTS
Canada, male vocal/instrumental group — 1

Date	Title / Label	Peak	No.1	Weeks
6 Mar 99	**CHAPTER 1: A NEW BEGINNING** *Chrysalis 4992072*	62		1

MOGWAI
UK, male vocal/instrumental group — 9

Date	Title / Label	Peak	No.1	Weeks
8 Nov 97	**YOUNG TEAM** *Chemikal Underground CHEM 018CD*	75		1
10 Apr 99	**COME ON, DIE YOUNG** *Chemikal Underground CHEM 033CD*	29		2
12 May 01	**ROCK ACTION** *Southpaw PAW CD1*	23		2
21 Jun 03	**HAPPY SONGS FOR HAPPY PEOPLE** *PIAS Recordings PIASX035CD*	47		2
18 Mar 06	**MR BEAST** *PIAS PIASX062CD*	31		1
4 Oct 08	**THE HAWK IS HOWLING** *Wall Of Sound WOS040CD*	35		1

MOIST
Canada, male vocal/instrumental group — 3

Date	Title / Label	Peak	No.1	Weeks
26 Aug 95	**SILVER TOWN** *Chrysalis CDCHR 6080*	49		3

MOLLY HATCHET
US, male vocal/instrumental group — 1

Date	Title / Label	Peak	No.1	Weeks
25 Jan 86	**DOUBLE TROUBLE – LIVE** *Epic EPC 88670*	94		1

MOLOKO
Ireland/UK, male/female vocal/instrumental duo – Roisin Murphy* & Mark Brydon — 30

Date	Title / Label	Peak	No.1	Weeks
5 Sep 98	**I AM NOT A DOCTOR** *Echo ECHCD 021*	64		1
22 Apr 00	**THINGS TO MAKE AND DO** *Echo ECHCD 31* ⊛	3		26
15 Mar 03	**STATUES** *Echo ECHCD 44* ●	18		3

MONACO
UK, male vocal/instrumental group — 3

Date	Title / Label	Peak	No.1	Weeks
21 Jun 97	**MUSIC FOR PLEASURE** *Polydor 5372422*	11		3

MONEY MARK
US, male vocalist/keyboard player/producer (Mark Ramos-Nishita) — 6

Date	Title / Label	Peak	No.1	Weeks
9 Sep 95	**MARK'S KEYBOARD REPAIR** *Mo Wax MW 034CD*	35		2
16 May 98	**PUSH THE BUTTON** *Mo Wax MW 090CD*	17		4

ZOOT MONEY & THE BIG ROLL BAND
UK, male vocal/instrumental group — 3

Date	Title / Label	Peak	No.1	Weeks
15 Oct 66	**ZOOT** *Columbia SCX 6075*	23		3

MONICA
US, female vocalist (Monica Arnold) — 10

Date	Title / Label	Peak	No.1	Weeks
25 Jul 98	**THE BOY IS MINE** *Arista 07822190112*	52		10

MONKEES
US, male vocal/instrumental group – Micky Dolenz, Davy Jones, Michael Nesmith & Peter Tork — 118

Date	Title / Label	Peak	No.1	Weeks
28 Jan 67	**THE MONKEES** *RCA Victor SF 7844* ★	1	7	36
15 Apr 67	**MORE OF THE MONKEES** *RCA Victor SF 7868* ★	1	2	25
8 Jul 67	**HEADQUARTERS** *RCA Victor SF 7886* ★	2		19
13 Jan 68	**PISCES, AQUARIUS, CAPRICORN & JONES LTD.** *RCA Victor SF 7912* ★	5		11
28 Nov 81	**THE MONKEES** *Arista DARTY 12*	99		1
15 Apr 89	**HEY HEY IT'S THE MONKEES – GREATEST HITS** *K-Tel NE 1432*	12		9
22 Mar 97	**HERE THEY COME: THE GREATEST HITS OF THE MONKEES** *warner.esp/Telstar 9548352182*	15		10
10 Mar 01	**THE DEFINITIVE** *warner.esp 8573866922* ●	15		7

MONKEY
UK/China, male vocal/instrumental group – Damon Albarn, Jamie Hewlett & Chen Shi-zheng — 3

Date	Title / Label	Peak	No.1	Weeks
30 Aug 08	**JOURNEY TO THE WEST** *XL Recordings XLCD388*	5		3

MONKEY MAFIA
UK, male vocal/instrumental/production group — 1

Date	Title / Label	Peak	No.1	Weeks
16 May 98	**SHOOT THE BOSS** *Heavenly HVNLP 21CD*	69		1

MONKS OF AMPLEFORTH ABBEY
UK, monastic choir — 2

Date	Title / Label	Peak	No.1	Weeks
17 Jun 95	**VISION OF PEACE** *Classic FM CFMCD 1783*	73		2

MONO
UK, male/female vocal/instrumental duo — 1

Date	Title / Label	Peak	No.1	Weeks
8 Aug 98	**FORMICA BLUES** *Echo ECHDD 017*	71		1

MONOCHROME SET
UK, male vocal/instrumental group — 4

Date	Title / Label	Peak	No.1	Weeks
3 May 80	**STRANGE BOUTIQUE** *Dindisc DID 4*	62		4

TONY MONOPOLY
UK, male vocalist — 4

Date	Title / Label	Peak	No.1	Weeks
12 Jun 76	**TONY MONOPOLY** *BUK BULP 2000*	25		4

MATT MONRO
UK, male vocalist (Terence Parsons), d. 7 Feb 1985 (age 52) — 29

Date	Title / Label	Peak	No.1	Weeks
7 Aug 65	**I HAVE DREAMED** *Parlophone PMC 1250*	20		1
17 Sep 66	**THIS IS THE LIFE** *Capitol T 2540*	25		2
26 Aug 67	**INVITATION TO THE MOVIES** *Capitol ST 2730*	30		1
15 Mar 80	**HEARTBREAKERS** *EMI EMTV 23* ●	5		11
12 Feb 05	**THE ULTIMATE** *EMI 5609392* ●	7		10
17 Feb 07	**FROM MATT WITH LOVE** *EMI 3845212*	30		4

MONSTER MAGNET
US, male vocal/instrumental group — 2

Date	Title / Label	Peak	No.1	Weeks
1 Apr 95	**DOPES TO INFINITY** *A&M 5403152*	51		1
13 Jun 98	**POWERTRIP** *A&M 5409082*	65		1

HANNAH MONTANA

US, female vocalist (Destiny Cyrus) — 4

Date	Title	Peak	Wks at No.1	Wks
26 Apr 08	**BEST OF BOTH WORLDS CONCERT** *EMI 2079752* HANNAH MONTANA & MILEY CYRUS	29		4

MONTROSE

US, male vocal/instrumental group — 1

Date	Title	Peak	Wks at No.1	Wks
15 Jun 74	**MONTROSE** *Warner Brothers K 46276*	43		1

MONTY PYTHON'S FLYING CIRCUS

UK, male comedy group — 33

Date	Title	Peak	Wks at No.1	Wks
30 Oct 71	**ANOTHER MONTY PYTHON RECORD** *Charisma CAS 1049*	26		3
27 Jan 73	**MONTY PYTHON'S PREVIOUS RECORD** *Charisma CAS 1063*	39		3
23 Feb 74	**THE MONTY PYTHON MATCHING TIE AND HANDKERCHIEF** *Charisma CAS 1080*	49		2
27 Jul 74	**MONTY PYTHON LIVE AT DRURY LANE** *Charisma CLASS 4* ○	19		8
9 Aug 75	**THE ALBUM OF THE SOUNDTRACK OF THE TRAILER OF THE FILM OF MONTY PYTHON AND THE HOLY GRAIL (OST)** *Charisma CAS 1003*	45		4
24 Nov 79	**MONTY PYTHON'S LIFE OF BRIAN (OST)** *Warner Brothers K 56751*	63		3
18 Oct 80	**MONTY PYTHON'S CONTRACTUAL OBLIGATION ALBUM** *Charisma CAS 1152*	13		8
16 Nov 91	**MONTY PYTHON SINGS** *Virgin MONT 1* MONTY PYTHON	62		2

MOODY BLUES

UK, male vocal/instrumental group – Graham Edge, Justin Hayward*, Denny Laine, John Lodge*, Michael Pinder, Ray Thomas* & Clint Warwick, d. 15 May 2004 — 335

Date	Title	Peak	Wks at No.1	Wks
27 Jan 68	**DAYS OF FUTURE PASSED** *Deram SML 707*	27		16
3 Aug 68	**IN SEARCH OF THE LOST CHORD** *Deram SML 711*	5		32
3 May 69	**ON THE THRESHOLD OF A DREAM** *Deram SML 1035*	1	2	73
6 Dec 69	**TO OUR CHILDREN'S CHILDREN'S CHILDREN** *Threshold THS 1*	2		44
15 Aug 70	**A QUESTION OF BALANCE** *Threshold THS 3*	1	7	19
7 Aug 71	**EVERY GOOD BOY DESERVES FAVOUR** *Threshold THS 5*	1	1	21
2 Dec 72	**SEVENTH SOJOURN** *Threshold THS 7* ★	5		18
16 Nov 74	**THIS IS THE MOODY BLUES** *Threshold MB 1/2* ●	14		18
24 Jun 78	**OCTAVE** *Decca TXS 129* ●	6		18
10 Nov 79	**OUT OF THIS WORLD** *K-Tel NE 1051* ●	15		10
23 May 81	**LONG DISTANCE VOYAGER** *Threshold TXS 139* ○ ★	7		19
10 Sep 83	**THE PRESENT** *Threshold TXS 140*	15		8
10 May 86	**THE OTHER SIDE OF LIFE** *Threshold POLD 5190*	24		6
25 Jun 88	**SUR LA MER** *Polydor POLH 43*	21		5
20 Jan 90	**GREATEST HITS** *Threshold 8406591*	71		1
13 Jul 91	**KEYS OF THE KINGDOM** *Threshold 8494331*	54		2
5 Oct 96	**THE VERY BEST OF THE MOODY BLUES** *Polygram TV 5358002* ●	13		15
22 Apr 00	**THE VERY BEST OF/STRANGE TIMES** *Universal TV 5358002/1535652*	19		6
11 May 02	**THE VERY BEST OF** *Universal Music TV 5833442*	27		4

IAN MOOR

UK, male vocalist — 2

Date	Title	Peak	Wks at No.1	Wks
7 Oct 00	**NATURALLY** *BMG TV 74321783862*	38		2

CHRISTY MOORE

Ireland, male vocalist — 8

Date	Title	Peak	Wks at No.1	Wks
4 May 91	**SMOKE AND STRONG WHISKEY** *Newbury CM 21*	49		3
21 Sep 91	**THE CHRISTY MOORE COLLECTION 81-91** *East West WX 434*	69		1
6 Nov 93	**KING PUCK** *Equator ATLASCD 003*	66		2
14 Sep 96	**GRAFFITI TONGUE** *Grapevine GRACD 215*	35		2

DUDLEY MOORE

UK, male comedian/vocalist/pianist, d. 27 Mar 2002 (age 66) — 58

Date	Title	Peak	Wks at No.1	Wks
4 Dec 65	**THE OTHER SIDE OF DUDLEY MOORE** *Decca LK 4732* DUDLEY MOORE TRIO	11		9
21 May 66	**ONCE MOORE WITH COOK** *Decca LK 4785* PETER COOK & DUDLEY MOORE	25		1
11 Jun 66	**GENUINE DUD** *Decca LK 4788*	13		10
18 Sep 76	**DEREK AND CLIVE LIVE** *Island ILPS 9434* PETER COOK & DUDLEY MOORE ○	12		25
24 Dec 77	**COME AGAIN** *Virgin V 2094* PETER COOK & DUDLEY MOORE ○	18		8
26 Jan 91	**ORCHESTRA!** *Decca 4308361* SIR GEORG SOLTI & DUDLEY MOORE	38		5

GARY MOORE

UK, male vocalist/guitarist. See Colosseum, Skid Row, Thin Lizzy — 104

Date	Title	Peak	Wks at No.1	Wks
3 Feb 79	**BACK ON THE STREETS** *MCA MCF 2853*	70		1
16 Oct 82	**CORRIDORS OF POWER** *Virgin V 2245*	30		6
18 Feb 84	**VICTIMS OF THE FUTURE** *10 Records DIX 2*	12		7
13 Oct 84	**WE WANT MOORE?** *10 Records GMDL 1*	32		3
14 Sep 85	**RUN FOR COVER** *10 Records DIX 16* ○	12		8
12 Jul 86	**ROCKIN' EVERY NIGHT** *10 Records XID 1*	99		1
14 Mar 87	**WILD FRONTIER** *10 Records DIX 56* ○	8		14
11 Feb 89	**AFTER THE WAR** *Virgin V 2575* ○	23		5
7 Apr 90	**STILL GOT THE BLUES** *Virgin V 2612* ⊛	13		26
21 Mar 92	**AFTER HOURS** *Virgin CDV 2684* ●	4		13
22 May 93	**BLUES ALIVE** *Virgin CDVX 2716* ●	8		5
26 Nov 94	**BALLADS AND BLUES 1982–1994** *Virgin CDV 2768* ●	33		6
10 Jun 95	**BLUES FOR GREENEY** *Virgin CDV 2784*	14		5
7 Jun 97	**DARK DAYS IN PARADISE** *Virgin CDV 2826*	43		2
31 Oct 98	**OUT IN THE FIELDS – THE VERY BEST OF GARY MOORE** *Virgin CDVX 2871*	54		1
24 Mar 01	**BACK TO THE BLUES** *Sanctuary SANCD 072*	53		1

MANDY MOORE

US, female vocalist — 1

Date	Title	Peak	Wks at No.1	Wks
20 May 00	**I WANNA BE WITH YOU** *Epic 4982769*	52		1

M.O.P.

US, male rap duo — 3

Date	Title	Peak	Wks at No.1	Wks
25 Aug 01	**WARRIOZ** *Epic 4982772*	40		3

PATRICK MORAZ

Switzerland, male keyboard player — 8

Date	Title	Peak	Wks at No.1	Wks
10 Apr 76	**PATRICK MORAZ** *Charisma CDS 4002*	28		7
23 Jul 77	**OUT IN THE SUN** *Charisma CDS 4007*	44		1

MORCHEEBA

UK, male/female vocal/instrumental group – Skye Edwards & Paul & Ross Godfrey — 114

Date	Title	Peak	Wks at No.1	Wks
12 Apr 97	**WHO CAN YOU TRUST?** *Indochina ZEN 009CD* ○	57		3
28 Mar 98	**BIG CALM** *Indochina ZEN 017CDX* ⊛	18		71
22 Jul 00	**FRAGMENTS OF FREEDOM** *East West 8573840272* ●	6		14
13 Jul 02	**CHARANGO** *East West 0927469632* ●	7		8
12 Jul 03	**PARTS OF THE PROCESS** *East West 5046658702* ●	6		13
21 May 05	**THE ANTIDOTE** *Echo ECHCD65*	17		4
16 Feb 08	**DIVE DEEP** *Echo ECHCD77*	59		1

MORDRED

UK, male vocal/instrumental group — 1

Date	Title	Peak	Wks at No.1	Wks
16 Feb 91	**IN THIS LIFE** *Noise International NO 1591*	70		1

ALANIS MORISSETTE

Canada, female vocalist/guitarist — 222

Date	Title	Peak	Wks at No.1	Wks
26 Aug 95	**JAGGED LITTLE PILL** *Maverick 9362459012* ⊛x10 ★	1	11	172
14 Nov 98	**SUPPOSED FORMER INFATUATION JUNKIE** *Maverick 9362470942* ⊛ ★	3		21
4 Dec 99	**MTV UNPLUGGED** *Maverick 9362475892* ●	56		5
16 Mar 02	**UNDER RUG SWEPT** *Maverick 9362482722* ● ★	2		10
29 May 04	**SO CALLED CHAOS** *Maverick 9362487732* ○	8		4
6 Aug 05	**JAGGED LITTLE PILL – ACOUSTIC** *Maverick 9362493452*	12		6
26 Nov 05	**THE COLLECTION** *Maverick 9362494902*	44		2
14 Jun 08	**FLAVORS OF ENTANGLEMENT** *Maverick 9362498636*	15		2

MORNING RUNNER

UK, male vocal/instrumental group — 2

Date	Title	Peak	Wks at No.1	Wks
18 Mar 06	**WILDERNESS IS PARADISE NOW** *Parlophone 3560972*	25		2

ENNIO MORRICONE

Italy, male composer/conductor — 37

Date	Title	Peak	Wks at No.1	Wks
12 Oct 68	**THE GOOD, THE BAD AND THE UGLY (OST)** *United Artists SULP 1197*	2		18
5 Mar 77	**MOSES (OST)** *Pye 28503*	43		2
2 May 81	**THIS IS ENNIO MORRICONE** *EMI THIS 33*	23		5
9 May 81	**CHI MAI** *BBC REH 414*	29		6

Date	Title	Peak Position	Weeks at No.1	Weeks on Chart
7 Mar 87	**THE MISSION (OST)** *Virgin V 2402* WITH THE LONDON PHILHARMONIC ORCHESTRA ●	73		4
30 Sep 00	**THE VERY BEST OF** *Virgin CDV 2929*	48		1
10 Apr 04	**MOVIE MASTERPIECES** *BMG 82876596932*	69		1

JAMES MORRISON

UK, male vocalist/guitarist

Date	Title	Peak Position	Weeks at No.1	82
12 Aug 06	**UNDISCOVERED** *Polydor 9878240* ⊛x3	1	2	69
11 Oct 08	**SONGS FOR YOU, TRUTHS FOR ME** *Polydor 1779250* ●	3		13+

MARK MORRISON

UK, male vocalist (Abdul Rahman)

Date	Title	Peak Position	Weeks at No.1	39
4 May 96	**RETURN OF THE MACK** *WEA 0630145862* ●	4		38
27 Sep 97	**ONLY GOD CAN JUDGE ME** *WEA 0630195392*	50		1

VAN MORRISON

Ireland, male vocalist/guitarist. Critically acclaimed, album-orientated Rock and Roll Hall of Famer who was awarded an OBE in 1996. *Astral Weeks*, arguably his finest work, amazingly failed to chart in 1968 – or anytime since. See Them

Date	Title	Peak Position	Weeks at No.1	312
18 Apr 70	**MOONDANCE** *Warner Brothers WS 1835*	32		2
13 Feb 71	**VAN MORRISON, HIS BAND AND THE STREET CHOIR** *Warner Brothers WS 1884*	18		6
11 Aug 73	**HARD NOSE THE HIGHWAY** *Warner Brothers K 46242*	22		3
16 Nov 74	**VEEDON FLEECE** *Warner Brothers K 56068* ○	41		1
7 May 77	**A PERIOD OF TRANSITION** *Warner Brothers K 56322*	23		5
21 Oct 78	**WAVELENGTH** *Warner Brothers K 56526* ○	27		6
8 Sep 79	**INTO THE MUSIC** *Vertigo 9120 852* ○	21		9
20 Sep 80	**COMMON ONE** *Mercury 6302 021*	53		3
27 Feb 82	**BEAUTIFUL VISION** *Mercury 6302 122*	31		14
26 Mar 83	**INARTICULATE SPEECH OF THE HEART** *Mercury MERL 16*	14		8
3 Mar 84	**LIVE AT THE GRAND OPERA HOUSE BELFAST** *Mercury MERL 36*	47		4
9 Feb 85	**A SENSE OF WONDER** *Mercury MERH 54*	25		5
2 Aug 86	**NO GURU, NO METHOD, NO TEACHER** *Mercury MERH 94*	27		5
19 Sep 87	**POETIC CHAMPIONS COMPOSE** *Mercury MERH 110*	26		6
2 Jul 88	**IRISH HEARTBEAT** *Mercury MERH 124* & THE CHIEFTAINS	18		7
10 Jun 89	**AVALON SUNSET** *Polydor 8392621* ●	13		14
7 Apr 90	**THE BEST OF VAN MORRISON** *Polydor 8419701* ●	4		87
20 Oct 90	**ENLIGHTENMENT** *Polydor 8471001* ●	5		14
21 Sep 91	**HYMNS TO THE SILENCE** *Polydor 8490261* ○	5		6
27 Feb 93	**THE BEST OF VAN MORRISON VOLUME 2** *Polydor 5177602*	31		3
12 Jun 93	**TOO LONG IN EXILE** *Exile 5192192* ○	4		9
30 Apr 94	**A NIGHT IN SAN FRANCISCO** *Polydor 5212902*	8		5
24 Jun 95	**DAYS LIKE THIS** *Exile 5273072* ●	5		15
15 Mar 97	**THE HEALING GAME** *Exile 5371012* ○	10		7
27 Jun 98	**THE PHILOSOPHER'S STONE** *Exile 5317892*	20		3
20 Mar 99	**BACK ON TOP** *Pointblank VPBCD 50* ●	11		16
29 Jan 00	**THE SKIFFLE SESSIONS – LIVE IN BELFAST** *Venture CDVE 945* /LONNIE DONEGAN/CHRIS BARBER	14		3
7 Oct 00	**YOU WIN AGAIN** *Pointblank VPBCD 54* /LINDA GAIL LEWIS	34		2
25 May 02	**DOWN THE ROAD** *Exile 5891772* ○	6		6
1 Nov 03	**WHAT'S WRONG WITH THIS PICTURE** *Blue Note 5901672*	43		2
28 May 05	**MAGIC TIME** *Exile/Polydor 9871528*	3		7
18 Mar 06	**PAY THE DEVIL** *Exile/Polydor 9876290*	8		5
24 Feb 07	**AT THE MOVIES – SOUNDTRACK HITS** *EMI 3842242* ○	17		6
23 Jun 07	**THE BEST OF...VOLUME 3** *EMI 3789682*	23		2
3 Nov 07	**STILL ON TOP – BEST OF** *Exile 1747483*	2		11
29 Mar 08	**KEEP IT SIMPLE** *Exile 1762683*	10		5

MORRISSEY

UK, male vocalist (Steven Morrissey). See The Smiths

Date	Title	Peak Position	Weeks at No.1	90
26 Mar 88	**VIVA HATE** *HMV CSD 3787* ●	1	1	20
27 Oct 90	**BONA DRAG** *HMV CLP 3788* ○	9		4
16 Mar 91	**KILL UNCLE** *HMV CSD 3789* ○	8		4
8 Aug 92	**YOUR ARSENAL** *HMV CDCSD 3790*	4		5
22 May 93	**BEETHOVEN WAS DEAF** *HMV CDCSD 3791*	13		2
26 Mar 94	**VAUXHALL AND I** *Parlophone CDPCSD 148* ●	1	1	5
18 Feb 95	**WORLD OF MORRISSEY** *Parlophone CDPCSD 163*	15		2
9 Sep 95	**SOUTHPAW GRAMMAR** *RCA Victor 74321299532* ○	4		3
23 Aug 97	**MALADJUSTED** *Island CID 8059*	8		3
20 Sep 97	**THE BEST OF SUEDEHEAD** *EMI CDEMC 3771*	26		9
29 May 04	**YOU ARE THE QUARRY** *Attack ATKDX001* ⊛	2		18
16 Apr 05	**LIVE AT EARLS COURT** *Attack ATKDP014*	18		2
15 Apr 06	**RINGLEADER OF THE TORMENTORS** *Attack ATKDX016* ●	1	1	10
23 Feb 08	**GREATEST HITS** *Decca 4780355*	5		3

MORRISSEY MULLEN

UK, male vocal/instrumental duo – Dick Morrissey, d. 8 Nov 2000, & Jim Mullen

Date	Title	Peak Position	Weeks at No.1	11
18 Jul 81	**BADNESS** *Beggars Banquet BEGA 27*	43		5
3 Apr 82	**LIFE ON THE WIRE** *Beggars Banquet BEGA 33*	47		5
23 Apr 83	**IT'S ABOUT TIME** *Beggars Banquet BEGA 44*	95		1

MOS DEF

US, male rapper (Dante Smith)

Date	Title	Peak Position	Weeks at No.1	1
30 Oct 04	**THE NEW DANGER** *Geffen 9864634*	56		1

WENDY MOTEN

US, female vocalist

Date	Title	Peak Position	Weeks at No.1	2
19 Mar 94	**WENDY MOTEN** *EMI CDMTL 1073*	42		2

MOTHER EARTH

UK, male vocal/instrumental group

Date	Title	Peak Position	Weeks at No.1	2
5 Mar 94	**THE PEOPLE TREE** *Acid Jazz JAZIDCD 083*	45		2

MOTHERS OF INVENTION

US, male vocal/instrumental group

Date	Title	Peak Position	Weeks at No.1	12
29 Jun 68	**WE'RE ONLY IN IT FOR THE MONEY** *Verve SVLP 9199*	32		5
28 Mar 70	**BURNT WEENY SANDWICH** *Reprise RSLP 6370*	17		3
3 Oct 70	**WEASELS RIPPED MY FLESH** *Reprise RSLP 2028*	28		4

MOTLEY CRUE

US, male vocal/instrumental group – Vince Neil, Tommy Lee, Mick Mars & Nikki Sixx

Date	Title	Peak Position	Weeks at No.1	28
13 Jul 85	**THEATRE OF PAIN** *Elektra EKT 8*	36		3
30 May 87	**GIRLS, GIRLS, GIRLS** *Elektra EKT 39* ○	14		11
16 Sep 89	**DR. FEELGOOD** *Elektra EKT 59* ● ★	4		7
19 Oct 91	**DECADE OF DECADENCE '81-'91** *Elektra EKT 95*	20		3
26 Mar 94	**MOTLEY CRUE** *Elektra 7559615342*	17		2
11 Jun 05	**RED WHITE & CRUE** *Universal HIPPB0003909022*	67		2

MOTORHEAD

UK, male vocal/instrumental group – Ian 'Lemmy' Kilmister, Eddie Clarke, Phil Taylor & Larry Wallis

Date	Title	Peak Position	Weeks at No.1	105
24 Sep 77	**MOTORHEAD** *Chiswick WIK 2* ○	43		5
24 Mar 79	**OVERKILL** *Bronze BRON 515* ○	24		11
27 Oct 79	**BOMBER** *Bronze BRON 523* ○	12		13
8 Dec 79	**ON PAROLE** *United Artists LBR 1004*	65		2
8 Nov 80	**ACE OF SPADES** *Bronze BRON 531* ●	4		16
27 Jun 81	**NO SLEEP 'TIL HAMMERSMITH** *Bronze BRON 535* ●	1	1	21
17 Apr 82	**IRONFIST** *Bronze BRNA 539* ○	6		9
26 Feb 83	**WHAT'S WORDS WORTH** *Big Beat NED 2*	71		2
4 Jun 83	**ANOTHER PERFECT DAY** *Bronze BRON 546*	20		4
15 Sep 84	**NO REMORSE** *Bronze PROTV MOTOR 1* ○	14		6
9 Aug 86	**ORGASMATRON** *GWR GWLP 1*	21		4
5 Sep 87	**ROCK 'N' ROLL** *GWR GWLP 14*	34		3
15 Oct 88	**NO SLEEP AT ALL** *GWR GWR 31*	79		1
2 Feb 91	**1916** *Epic 4674811*	24		4
8 Aug 92	**MARCH OR DIE** *Epic 4717232*	60		1
9 Sep 00	**THE BEST OF MOTORHEAD** *Metal Is MISDD 002*	52		1
9 Sep 06	**KISS OF DEATH** *SPV Recordings SPV99910*	45		1
13 Sep 08	**MOTORIZER** *SPV Recordings SPV91630*	32		1

MOTORS

UK, male vocal/instrumental group

Date	Title	Peak Position	Weeks at No.1	6
15 Oct 77	**THE MOTORS** *Virgin V 2089*	46		5
3 Jun 78	**APPROVED BY THE MOTORS** *Virgin V 2101*	60		1

MOTT THE HOOPLE

UK, male vocal/instrumental group – Ian Hunter*, Dale Griffin, Mick Ralphs & Pete Watts

Date	Title	Peak Position	Weeks at No.1	32
2 May 70	**MOTT THE HOOPLE** *Island ILPS 9108*	66		1
17 Oct 70	**MAD SHADOWS** *Island ILPS 9119*	48		2
17 Apr 71	**WILD LIFE** *Island ILPS 9144*	44		2
23 Sep 72	**ALL THE YOUNG DUDES** *CBS 65184*	21		4
11 Aug 73	**MOTT** *CBS 65184* ○	7		15
13 Apr 74	**THE HOOPLE** *CBS 69062* ●	11		5

Key: ○ Silver-selling · ● Gold-selling · ⊛ Platinum-selling · ★ US No.1 · Peak Position · Weeks at No.1 · Weeks on Chart

Date	Title	Label	Peak Position	Weeks at No.1	Weeks on Chart
23 Nov 74	MOTT THE HOOPLE – LIVE	*CBS 69093*	32		2
4 Oct 75	DRIVE ON	*CBS 69154* MOTT	45		1

BOB MOULD

US, male vocalist/guitarist. See Husker Du, Sugar — 2

Date	Title	Label	Peak Position	Weeks at No.1	Weeks on Chart
11 May 96	BOB MOULD	*Creation CRECD 188*	52		1
5 Sep 98	THE LAST DOG AND PONY SHOW	*Creation CRECD 215*	58		1

MOUNTAIN

US, male vocal/instrumental group — 4

Date	Title	Label	Peak Position	Weeks at No.1	Weeks on Chart
5 Jun 71	NANTUCKET SLEIGHRIDE	*Island ILPS 9148*	43		1
8 Jul 72	THE ROAD GOES EVER ON	*Island ILPS 9199*	21		3

NANA MOUSKOURI

Greece, female vocalist/guitarist — 213

Date	Title	Label	Peak Position	Weeks at No.1	Weeks on Chart
7 Jun 69	OVER AND OVER	*Fontana S 5511*	10		105
4 Apr 70	THE EXQUISITE NANA MOUSKOURI	*Fontana STL 5536*	10		25
10 Oct 70	RECITAL '70	*Fontana 6312 003*	68		1
3 Apr 71	TURN ON THE SUN	*Fontana 6312 008*	16		15
29 Jul 72	BRITISH CONCERT	*Fontana 6651 003*	29		11
28 Apr 73	SONGS FROM HER TV SERIES	*Fontana 6312 036*	29		11
28 Sep 74	SPOTLIGHT ON NANA MOUSKOURI	*Fontana 6641 197*	38		6
10 Jul 76	PASSPORT	*Philips 9101 061* ●	3		16
22 Feb 86	ALONE	*Philips PHH 3* ○	19		10
8 Oct 88	THE MAGIC OF NANA MOUSKOURI	*Philips NMTV 1* ●	44		8
3 Mar 01	AT HER VERY BEST	*Philips 5485492*	39		5

MOVE

UK, male vocal/instrumental group — 9

Date	Title	Label	Peak Position	Weeks at No.1	Weeks on Chart
13 Apr 68	MOVE	*Regal Zonophone SLPZ 1002*	15		9

ALISON MOYET

UK, female vocalist. See Yazoo — 207

Date	Title	Label	Peak Position	Weeks at No.1	Weeks on Chart
17 Nov 84	ALF	*CBS 26229* ⊛x4	1	1	84
18 Apr 87	RAINDANCING	*CBS 4501521* ⊛x2	2		52
4 May 91	HOODOO	*Columbia 4682721* ○	11		6
2 Apr 94	ESSEX	*Columbia 4759552*	24		4
3 Jun 95	SINGLES	*Columbia 4806632* ⊛	1	1	37
22 Sep 01	THE ESSENTIAL	*Columbia STVCD 123* ○	16		4
31 Aug 02	HOMETIME	*Sanctuary SANCD 128* ○	18		9
18 Sep 04	VOICE	*Sanctuary SANCD 270* ●	7		8
27 Oct 07	THE TURN	*W14 1746275*	21		3

MS DYNAMITE

UK, female vocalist (Niomi McLean-Daley) — 44

Date	Title	Label	Peak Position	Weeks at No.1	Weeks on Chart
22 Jun 02	A LITTLE DEEPER	*Polydor 5899552* ⊛	10		42
15 Oct 05	JUDGEMENT DAYS	*Polydor 9873941*	43		2

MTUME

US, male/female instrumental group — 1

Date	Title	Label	Peak Position	Weeks at No.1	Weeks on Chart
6 Oct 84	YOU, ME AND HE	*Epic EPC 26077*	85		1

MUD

UK, male vocal/instrumental group – Les Gray, d. 21 Feb 2004, Rob Davis, Dave Mount & Ray Stiles — 58

Date	Title	Label	Peak Position	Weeks at No.1	Weeks on Chart
28 Sep 74	MUD ROCK	*RAK SRAK 508* ●	8		35
26 Jul 75	MUD ROCK VOLUME 2	*RAK SRAK 513* ●	6		12
1 Nov 75	MUD'S GREATEST HITS	*RAK STRAK 6755* ○	25		6
27 Dec 75	USE YOUR IMAGINATION	*Private Stock PVLP 1003* ○	33		5

MUDHONEY

US, male vocal/instrumental group — 5

Date	Title	Label	Peak Position	Weeks at No.1	Weeks on Chart
31 Aug 91	EVERY GOOD BOY DESERVES FUDGE	*Sub-Pop SP 18160*	34		2
17 Oct 92	PIECE OF CAKE	*Reprise 9362450902*	39		2
8 Apr 95	MY BROTHER THE COW	*Reprise 9362458402*	70		1

MULL HISTORICAL SOCIETY

UK, male vocal/instrumental group — 5

Date	Title	Label	Peak Position	Weeks at No.1	Weeks on Chart
27 Oct 01	LOSS	*Blanco Y Negro 0927413072*	43		1
15 Mar 03	US	*Blanco Y Negro 0927499562*	19		3
31 Jul 04	THIS IS HOPE	*B Unique BUN082*	58		1

GERRY MULLIGAN & BEN WEBSTER

US, male sax players – Gerry Mulligan, d. 20 Jan 96, & Ben Webster, d. 20 Sep 73 — 1

Date	Title	Label	Peak Position	Weeks at No.1	Weeks on Chart
24 Sep 60	GERRY MULLIGAN MEETS BEN WEBSTER	*HMV CLP 1373*	15		1

SHAWN MULLINS

US, male vocalist/guitarist — 1

Date	Title	Label	Peak Position	Weeks at No.1	Weeks on Chart
20 Mar 99	SOUL'S CORE	*Columbia 4930372*	60		1

SAMANTHA MUMBA

Ireland, female vocalist — 16

Date	Title	Label	Peak Position	Weeks at No.1	Weeks on Chart
11 Nov 00	GOTTA TELL YOU	*Wild Card 5492262* ●	9		16

MUMM-RA

UK, male vocal/instrumental group — 1

Date	Title	Label	Peak Position	Weeks at No.1	Weeks on Chart
9 Jun 07	THESE THINGS MOVE IN THREES	*Columbia BEXHILL19*	42		1

MUNGO JERRY

UK, male vocal/instrumental group — 14

Date	Title	Label	Peak Position	Weeks at No.1	Weeks on Chart
8 Aug 70	MUNGO JERRY	*Dawn DNLS 3008*	13		6
4 Nov 78	ELECTRONICALLY TESTED	*Dawn DNLS 3020*	14		8

MUNROS FEATURING DAVID METHREN

UK, male pipe band — 3

Date	Title	Label	Peak Position	Weeks at No.1	Weeks on Chart
27 Jun 98	THE LONE PIPER	*Virgin VTCD 185*	46		3

MUPPETS

US, male/female puppets – members included Kermit the Frog, Animal, Fozzie Bear, Gonzo the Great & Miss Piggy — 45

Date	Title	Label	Peak Position	Weeks at No.1	Weeks on Chart
11 Jun 77	THE MUPPET SHOW	*Pye NSPH 19* ●	1	1	35
25 Feb 78	THE MUPPET SHOW VOLUME 2	*Pye NSPH 21* ○	16		10

MURDERDOLLS

US, male vocal/instrumental group — 1

Date	Title	Label	Peak Position	Weeks at No.1	Weeks on Chart
31 Aug 02	BEYOND THE VALLEY OF THE MURDERDOLLS	*Roadrunner RR 84262* ○	40		1

PETER MURPHY

UK, male vocalist. See Bauhaus — 1

Date	Title	Label	Peak Position	Weeks at No.1	Weeks on Chart
26 Jul 86	SHOULD THE WORLD FAIL TO FALL APART	*Beggars Banquet BEGA 69*	82		1

ROISIN MURPHY

Ireland, female vocalist/producer — 3

Date	Title	Label	Peak Position	Weeks at No.1	Weeks on Chart
27 Oct 07	OVERPOWERED	*EMI 5070902*	20		3

ANNE MURRAY

Canada, female vocalist — 10

Date	Title	Label	Peak Position	Weeks at No.1	Weeks on Chart
3 Oct 81	THE VERY BEST OF ANNE MURRAY	*Capitol EMTV 31* ○	14		10

PAULINE MURRAY & THE INVISIBLE GIRLS

US, female/male vocal/instrumental group — 4

Date	Title	Label	Peak Position	Weeks at No.1	Weeks on Chart
11 Oct 80	PAULINE MURRAY AND THE INVISIBLE GIRLS	*Elusive 2394 227*	25		4

MUSE

UK, male vocal/instrumental group – Matt Bellamy, Dominic Howard & Chris Wolstenholme — 159

Date	Title	Label	Peak Position	Weeks at No.1	Weeks on Chart
16 Oct 99	SHOWBIZ	*Mushroom MUSH 59CD* ●	29		16
30 Jun 01	ORIGIN OF SYMMETRY	*Mushroom MUSH 93CD* ⊛	3		25
13 Jul 02	HULLABALOO	*Mushroom MUSH 105CDXX* ○	10		4

Date	Title	Peak Position	Weeks at No.1	Weeks on Chart
4 Oct 03	**ABSOLUTION** *Taste Media Ltd 5046685872* ⊛	1	1	58
15 Jul 06	**BLACK HOLES & REVELATIONS** *Helium 3/Warner Bros 2564635095* ⊛	1	2	50
29 Mar 08	**HAARP** *Helium 3/Warner Bros 2564696779* ○	2		6

MUSIC
UK, male vocal/instrumental group – Robert Harvey, Stuart Coleman, Phil Jordan & Adam Nutter — 12

Date	Title	Peak Position	Weeks at No.1	Weeks on Chart
14Sep 02	**THE MUSIC** *Hut CDHUTX 76* MUSIC ●	4		5
2 Oct 04	**WELCOME TO THE NORTH** *Virgin CDV2989* ●	8		5
28 Jun 08	**STRENGTH IN NUMBERS** *Polydor 1766122*	19		2

MUSICAL YOUTH
UK, male vocal/instrumental group — 22

Date	Title	Peak Position	Weeks at No.1	Weeks on Chart
4 Dec 82	**THE YOUTH OF TODAY** *MCA YOULP 1* ●	24		22

MUTTON BIRDS
New Zealand, male vocal/instrumental group — 1

Date	Title	Peak Position	Weeks at No.1	Weeks on Chart
12 Jul 97	**ENVY OF ANGELS** *Virgin CDVIR 55*	64		1

MY BLOODY VALENTINE
UK, male vocal/instrumental group — 2

Date	Title	Peak Position	Weeks at No.1	Weeks on Chart
23 Nov 91	**LOVELESS** *Creation CRELP 060*	24		2

MY CHEMICAL ROMANCE
US, male vocal/instrumental group – Gerard Way, Frank Iero, Matt Pelissier, Ray Toto & Mikey Way — 70

Date	Title	Peak Position	Weeks at No.1	Weeks on Chart
26 Mar 05	**THREE CHEERS FOR SWEET REVENGE** *WEA WB486152* ⊛	34		18
1 Apr 06	**LIFE ON THE MURDER SCENE** *Reprise 9362494762*	53		1
4 Nov 06	**THE BLACK PARADE** *Warner Brothers 9362444272* ⊛	2		48
12 Jul 08	**THE BLACK PARADE IS DEAD!** *Reprise 9362499038*	12		3

MY LIFE STORY
UK, male/female vocal/instrumental group — 1

Date	Title	Peak Position	Weeks at No.1	Weeks on Chart
22 Mar 97	**THE GOLDEN MILE** *Parlophone CDPCSY 7386*	36		1

MY MORNING JACKET
US, male vocal/instrumental group — 2

Date	Title	Peak Position	Weeks at No.1	Weeks on Chart
20 Sep 03	**IT STILL MOVES** *RCA 82876559252*	62		1
29 Oct 05	**Z** *RCA ATOR710672*	74		1

MY VITRIOL
UK, male/female vocal/instrumental group — 2

Date	Title	Peak Position	Weeks at No.1	Weeks on Chart
17 Mar 01	**FINELINES** *Infectious INFECT 96CDX*	24		2

BILLIE MYERS
UK, female vocalist — 9

Date	Title	Peak Position	Weeks at No.1	Weeks on Chart
2 May 98	**GROWING PAINS** *Universal UND 53100*	19		9

ALANNAH MYLES
Canada, female vocalist — 21

Date	Title	Peak Position	Weeks at No.1	Weeks on Chart
28 Apr 90	**ALANNAH MYLES** *Atlantic 7819561* ●	3		21

MYLO
UK, male producer (Myles MacInnes) — 17

Date	Title	Peak Position	Weeks at No.1	Weeks on Chart
15 Jan 05	**DESTROY ROCK N ROLL** *Breastfed BFD007CD* ●	26		17

MYSTERY JETS
UK, male vocal/instrumental group — 5

Date	Title	Peak Position	Weeks at No.1	Weeks on Chart
18 Mar 06	**MAKING DENS** *679 2564632105*	32		2
5 Apr 08	**TWENTY ONE** *679 82564696124*	42		3

N

N-DUBZ
UK, male/female vocal/rap trio — 6

Date	Title	Peak Position	Weeks at No.1	Weeks on Chart
29 Nov 08	**UNCLE B** *All Around The World 1790382* ●	11		6+

N SYNC
US, male vocal group — 32

Date	Title	Peak Position	Weeks at No.1	Weeks on Chart
17 Jul 99	**N SYNC** *Northwestside 74321681902*	30		2
1 Apr 00	**NO STRINGS ATTACHED** *Jive 9220272* ● ★	14		22
4 Aug 01	**CELEBRITY** *Jive 9222032* ● ★	12		8

N-TYCE
UK, female vocal group — 1

Date	Title	Peak Position	Weeks at No.1	Weeks on Chart
20 Jun 98	**ALL DAY EVERY DAY** *Telstar TCD 2945*	44		1

JIMMY NAIL
UK, male actor/vocalist (James Bradford) — 85

Date	Title	Peak Position	Weeks at No.1	Weeks on Chart
8 Aug 92	**GROWING UP IN PUBLIC** *East West 4509901442* ●	2		12
3 Dec 94	**CROCODILE SHOES** *East West 4509985562* ⊛x3	2		31
18 Nov 95	**BIG RIVER** *East West 0630128232* ⊛	8		15
30 Nov 96	**CROCODILE SHOES II** *East West 0630169352* ⊛	10		13
18 Oct 97	**THE NAIL FILE – THE BEST OF JIMMY NAIL** *East West 3984207392* ●	8		14

NAILBOMB
Brazil/UK, male vocal/instrumental duo — 1

Date	Title	Peak Position	Weeks at No.1	Weeks on Chart
2 Apr 94	**POINT BLANK** *Roadrunner RR 90552*	62		1

NAPALM DEATH
UK, male vocal/instrumental group — 3

Date	Title	Peak Position	Weeks at No.1	Weeks on Chart
15 Sep 90	**HARMONY CORRUPTION** *Earache MOSH 19*	67		1
30 May 92	**UTOPIA BANISHED** *Earache MOSH 53CD*	58		1
3 Feb 96	**DIATRIBES** *Earache MOSH 141CDD*	74		1

NAS
US, male rapper (Nasir Jones) — 23

Date	Title	Peak Position	Weeks at No.1	Weeks on Chart
13 Jul 96	**IT WAS WRITTEN** *Columbia 4841962* ★	38		6
17 Apr 99	**I AM...** *Columbia 4894192* ★	31		4
25 Jan 03	**GOD'S SON** *Columbia 5098115* ○	57		6
11 Dec 04	**STREETS DISCIPLE** *Columbia 5177249* ○	45		2
30 Dec 06	**HIP HOP IS DEAD** *Def Jam 1718420* ★	68		2
26 Jul 08	**NAS** *Def Jam 1779532* ★	23		3

GRAHAM NASH
UK, male vocalist/guitarist. See Crosby, Stills, Nash & Young, Hollies — 13

Date	Title	Peak Position	Weeks at No.1	Weeks on Chart
26 Jun 71	**SONGS FOR BEGINNERS** *Atlantic 2401 011*	13		8
13 May 72	**GRAHAM NASH AND DAVID CROSBY** *Atlantic K 50011* & DAVID CROSBY	13		5

JOHNNY NASH
US, male vocalist — 17

Date	Title	Peak Position	Weeks at No.1	Weeks on Chart
5 Aug 72	**I CAN SEE CLEARLY NOW** *CBS 64860*	39		6
10 Dec 77	**JOHNNY NASH COLLECTION** *Epic EPC 10008* ●	18		11

KATE NASH
UK, female vocalist/guitarist — 42

Date	Title	Peak Position	Weeks at No.1	Weeks on Chart
18 Aug 07	**MADE OF BRICKS** *Fiction/Polydor 1743143*	1	1	42+

NASH THE SLASH
Canada, male vocalist/multi-instrumentalist (Jeff Plewman) — 1

Date	Title	Peak Position	Weeks at No.1	Weeks on Chart
21 Feb 81	**CHILDREN OF THE NIGHT** *Dindisc DID 9*	61		1

Madness

One Step Beyond

ALTHOUGH their string of classic pop hit singles is most associated with the early 1980s, Madness had in fact formed in 1976, at the tail end of the London pub-rock scene and just before punk took over. With a whiff of Ian Dury And The Blockheads' music hall and a big dollop of ska, Madness made their mark on the London pub circuit long before being swept into the mainstream by the Two Tone explosion spearheaded by Coventry band The Specials in 1979.

Before 'Baggy Trousers', before 'Embarrassment' and before 'House of Fun' had soundtracked the nation's playgrounds and youth clubs, Madness was a distinctly underground, kitchen-sink drama of a band. Like others in the Two Tone scene, Madness dipped into an eclectic melting pot of influences, combining elements of Caribbean, mento and calypso with American jazz and rhythm and blues, as did so many other ska bands. Madness's 1979 debut single, 'The Prince' (released by the titular Two Tone label, brainchild of The Specials' Jerry Dammers) had catapulted the band into the Top 20. The single was a tribute to the band's hero Prince Buster and set the stall with its infectious beat and good-time bonhomie.

Madness dipped into an eclectic melting pot of influences . . .

They set themselves apart from their contemporaries, however, with their debut album, *One Step Beyond*, which captures Madness at their ska-infused best with a series of songs celebrating everyday normality, like a dose of acne on the face of a pre-1980s pop that was too-cutesy-clean and mundane. 'Land Of Hope And Glory', for example, was written by saxophonist Lee Thompson about his real-life experience in Borstal after being convicted of theft as a teenager. There were also the occasional moments of pop melancholia that the band were so adept at later in their career – their minor-key melodies captured a delinquent sombreness, the tears of a clown. That they did all this and encouraged a multi-racial musical blend was both laudable and crucial in the confused and bitter times of post-punk fallout.

Not content with just releasing classic records, Madness's sharp post-skinhead look of Crombies, Sta-prest and Dr Martens boots reinvented street style too. For the next year, Two Tone's huge success – the ultimate punky reggae party – would see Madness (now signed to Stiff Records, the home of pub rock) and The Specials becoming two of the biggest bands in the country.

One Step Beyond captured the band so early in their recording career that the cover photo – with the band caught in full-on 'nutty walk' flow – didn't even feature chief rabble-rouser Chas Smash. The record captured the quintessential good-time Madness that had been packing the pubs just before they broke big with their bouncing celebratory music. This was their defining document and an album that set the template for all the ska and ska-punk bands that came in their wake for the next three decades. *One Step Beyond* was a huge Number 2 hit and stayed in the British charts for seventy-eight weeks.

Too often, British pop has been terrified of letting its hair down, for fear of not being taken seriously. Somehow, Madness were always able to release stunning music that was taken extremely seriously, yet was accompanied by comedic, slapstick videos that

Chart History Artist	Album Title	First Chart Week	Weeks on Chart	Highest Position
MADNESS	ONE STEP BEYOND	3/11/79	78	2

entertained greatly but never diminished the band's credibility. Few have been able to achieve the same precarious balancing act.

Madness went on to eclipse The Specials in terms of record sales and were very much the sound of the UK in the early 1980s, the first choice sound of the council estates, of football lads looking for good times in a recession, the soundtrack to cheap lager, love-bites and endless grey days living in the UK.

Later on, Madness would cross this early ska sound with Kinks-style English musical-hall melancholia and Beatles mid-1960s pop and muzak with even greater success. But it is *One Step Beyond* that set their stall out so brilliantly from the beginning. The influence of this album can be felt across later UK pop, with its echoes in the Madchester explosion, the Mockney knees-up of Blur and a whole generation of 1990s musicians who were pulled in by the band's innate skill at combining infectious pop with an acute depth of emotion. With *One Step Beyond*, Madness made the mundane magical.

Accompanied by comedic, slapstick videos that entertained greatly but never diminished the band's credibility

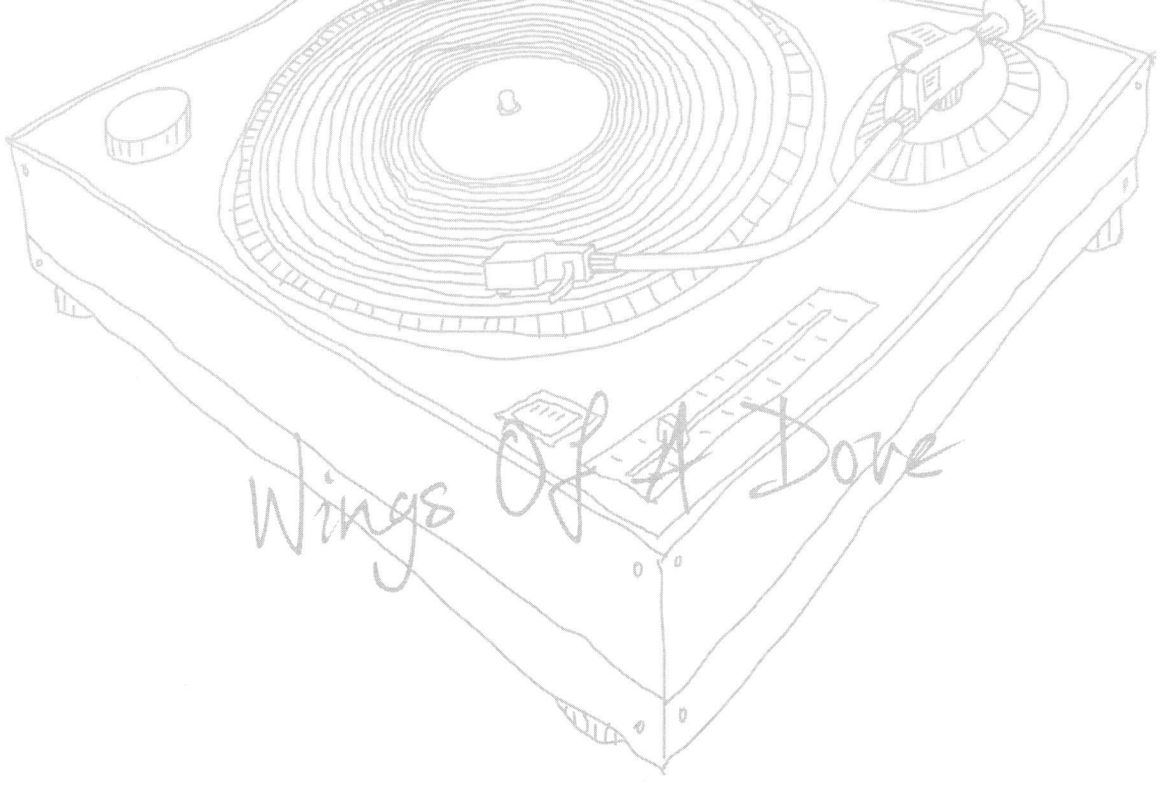

NATASHA
UK, female vocalist (Natasha England)

Date	Title / Label	Peak	Wks No.1	Wks on Chart (3)
9 Oct 82	**CAPTURED** *Towerbell TOWLP 2*	53		3

ULTRA NATE
US, female vocalist (Ultra Nate Wyche)

Date	Title / Label	Peak	Wks No.1	Wks on Chart (4)
9 May 98	**SITUATION: CRITICAL** *AM:PM 5408242*	17		4

NATIONAL
US, male vocal/instrumental group

Date	Title / Label	Peak	Wks No.1	Wks on Chart (1)
2 Jun 07	**BOXER** *Beggars Banquet BBQCD252*	57		1

NATIONAL BRASS BAND
UK, brass band

Date	Title / Label	Peak	Wks No.1	Wks on Chart (10)
10 May 80	**GOLDEN MEMORIES** *K-Tel ONE 1075* ○	15		10

NATTY
UK, male vocalist/guitarist

Date	Title / Label	Peak	Wks No.1	Wks on Chart (2)
16 Aug 08	**MAN LIKE I** *Atlantic 5144285982*	21		2

NAUGHTY BY NATURE
US, male rap group

Date	Title / Label	Peak	Wks No.1	Wks on Chart (5)
6 Mar 93	**19 NAUGHTY III** *Big Life BLRCD 23*	40		2
27 May 95	**POVERTY'S PARADISE** *Big Life BLRCD 28*	20		3

NAZARETH
UK, male vocal/instrumental group – Dan McCafferty, Pete Agnew, Manny Charlton, John Locke, Billy Rankin & Darrell Sweet, d. 30 Apr 1999

Date	Title / Label	Peak	Wks No.1	Wks on Chart (51)
26 May 73	**RAZAMANAZ** *Mooncrest CREST 1*	11		25
24 Nov 73	**LOUD 'N' PROUD** *Mooncrest CREST 4*	10		7
18 May 74	**RAMPANT** *Mooncrest CREST 15*	13		3
13 Dec 75	**GREATEST HITS** *Mooncrest TOPS 108* ○	54		1
3 Feb 79	**NO MEAN CITY** *Mooncrest TOPS 123*	34		9
28 Feb 81	**THE FOOL CIRCLE** *NEMS NEWL 6019*	60		3
3 Oct 81	**NAZARETH LIVE** *NEMS NELD 102*	78		3

NE-YO
US, male rapper (Shaffer Smith)

Date	Title / Label	Peak	Wks No.1	Wks on Chart (45)
11 Mar 06	**IN MY OWN WORDS** *Mercury 9852886* ● ★	14		21
12 May 07	**BECAUSE OF YOU** *Def Jam 1732691* ○ ★	6		9
27 Sep 08	**YEAR OF THE GENTLEMAN** *Def Jam 1774984* ⊛	2		151+

NEARLY GOD
UK, male/female vocal/instrumental group. See Tricky

Date	Title / Label	Peak	Wks No.1	Wks on Chart (4)
4 May 96	**NEARLY GOD – POEMS** *Durban Poison DPCD 1001*	10		4

NED'S ATOMIC DUSTBIN
UK, male vocal/instrumental group – Jonn Penney, Matt Cheslin, Alex Griffin, Gareth Pring & Dan Warton

Date	Title / Label	Peak	Wks No.1	Wks on Chart (8)
9 Feb 91	**BITE** *Rough Trade Germany RTD 14011831*	72		1
13 Apr 91	**GOD FODDER** *Furtive 4681121* ○	4		5
31 Oct 92	**ARE YOU NORMAL?** *Furtive 4726332*	13		2

VINCE NEIL
US, male vocalist (Vince Wharton). See Motley Crue

Date	Title / Label	Peak	Wks No.1	Wks on Chart (1)
8 May 93	**EXPOSED** *Warner Brothers 9362452602*	44		1

NELLY
US, male rapper (Cornell Haynes)

Date	Title / Label	Peak	Wks No.1	Wks on Chart (103)
3 Feb 01	**COUNTRY GRAMMAR** *Universal 1578572* ● ★	14		31
13 Jul 02	**NELLYVILLE** *Universal 0186902* ⊛x2 ★	2		38
25 Sep 04	**SUIT** *Universal 9863936* ⊛ ★	8		21
25 Sep 04	**SWEAT** *Universal 9863935* ●	11		4
28 May 05	**SWEAT & SUIT** *Universal 9882176*	41		7
27 Sep 08	**BRASS KNUCKLES** *Island 1768847*	20		2

BILL NELSON
UK, male vocalist/guitarist. See Be Bop Deluxe

Date	Title / Label	Peak	Wks No.1	Wks on Chart (21)
24 Feb 79	**SOUND ON SOUND** *Harvest SHSP 4095* BILL NELSON'S RED NOISE	33		5
23 May 81	**QUIT DREAMING AND GET ON THE BEAM** *Mercury 6359 055* BILL NELSON	7		6
3 Jul 82	**THE LOVE THAT WHIRLS (DIARY OF A THINKING HEART)** *Mercury WHIRL 3* BILL NELSON	28		4
14 May 83	**CHIMERA** *Mercury MERB 19* BILL NELSON	30		5
3 May 86	**GETTING THE HOLY GHOST ACROSS** *Portrait PRT 26602* BILL NELSON	91		1

PHYLLIS NELSON
US, female vocalist, d. 12 Jan 1998 (age 47)

Date	Title / Label	Peak	Wks No.1	Wks on Chart (10)
20 Apr 85	**MOVE CLOSER** *Carrere CAL 203*	29		10

SHARA NELSON
UK, female vocalist. See Massive Attack

Date	Title / Label	Peak	Wks No.1	Wks on Chart (11)
2 Oct 93	**WHAT SILENCE KNOWS** *Cooltempo CTCD 35* ●	22		9
7 Oct 95	**FRIENDLY FIRE** *Cooltempo CTCD 48*	44		2

WILLIE NELSON
US, male vocalist

Date	Title / Label	Peak	Wks No.1	Wks on Chart (8)
17 May 08	**LEGEND: THE BEST OF WILLIE NELSON** *Sony BMG 88697271642*	16		8

NENA
Germany, female/male vocal/instrumental group

Date	Title / Label	Peak	Wks No.1	Wks on Chart (5)
24 Mar 84	**NENA** *Epic EPC 25925*	31		5

NEON NEON
UK, male vocal/instrumental/production duo

Date	Title / Label	Peak	Wks No.1	Wks on Chart (1)
29 Mar 08	**STAINLESS STYLE** *Lex LEX067CD*	67		1

N*E*R*D
US, male vocal/production trio – Pharrell Williams (Pharrell*), Shae Haley & Chad Hugo

Date	Title / Label	Peak	Wks No.1	Wks on Chart (38)
17 Aug 02	**IN SEARCH OF** *Virgin CDVUSX 216* ●	28		18
3 Apr 04	**FLY OR DIE** *Virgin CDVUS 250* ●	4		16
21 Jun 08	**SEEING SOUNDS** *Interscope 1774995*	20		4

ROBBIE NEVIL
US, male vocalist

Date	Title / Label	Peak	Wks No.1	Wks on Chart (1)
13 Jun 87	**C'EST LA VIE** *Manhattan MTL 1006*	93		1

NEVILLE BROTHERS
US, male vocal/instrumental group

Date	Title / Label	Peak	Wks No.1	Wks on Chart (3)
18 Aug 90	**BROTHER'S KEEPER** *A&M 3953121*	35		3

NEW EDITION
US, male vocal group

Date	Title / Label	Peak	Wks No.1	Wks on Chart (3)
14 Sep 96	**HOME AGAIN** *MCA MCD 11480* ★	22		3

NEW FAST AUTOMATIC DAFFODILS
UK, male vocal/instrumental group

Date	Title / Label	Peak	Wks No.1	Wks on Chart (2)
17 Nov 90	**PIGEON HOLE** *Play It Again Sam BIAS 185*	49		1
24 Oct 92	**BODY EXIT MIND** *Play It Again Sam BIAS 205CD*	57		1

NEW FOUND GLORY
US, male vocal/instrumental group – Jordan Pundik, Cyrus Bolooki, Chad Gilbert, Ian Grushka & Steve Klein

Date	Title / Label	Peak	Wks No.1	Wks on Chart (10)
29 Jun 02	**STICKS AND STONES** *MCA 1129722*	10		8
29 May 04	**CATALYST** *Geffenr 9862440*	27		2

NEW KIDS ON THE BLOCK

US, male vocal group – Jon Knight, Jordan Knight, Joey McIntyre, Donny Wahlberg & Danny Wood — **108**

Date	Title	Peak	Wks No.1	Wks
9 Dec 89	**HANGIN' TOUGH** *CBS 4608741* ⊛x2 ★	2		41
30 Jun 90	**STEP BY STEP** *CBS 4666861* ⊛ ★	1	1	31
3 Nov 90	**NEW KIDS ON THE BLOCK** *CBS 4675041* ●	6		13
15 Dec 90	**MERRY, MERRY CHRISTMAS** *CBS 4659071* ●	13		5
2 Mar 91	**NO MORE GAMES/THE REMIX ALBUM** *Columbia 4674941*	15		11
21 Dec 91	**H.I.T.S.** *Columbia 4694381*	50		4
12 Mar 94	**FACE THE MUSIC** *Columbia 4743592* NKOTB	36		1
20 Sep 08	**THE BLOCK** *Interscope 1783568*	16		2

NEW MODEL ARMY

UK, male vocal/instrumental group — **21**

Date	Title	Peak	Wks No.1	Wks
12 May 84	**VENGEANCE** *Abstract ABT 008*	73		5
25 May 85	**NO REST FOR THE WICKED** *EMI NMAL 1*	22		3
11 Oct 86	**THE GHOST OF CAIN** *EMI EMC 3516*	45		3
18 Feb 89	**THUNDER AND CONSOLATION** *EMI EMC 3552*	20		3
6 Oct 90	**IMPURITY** *EMI EMC 3581*	23		2
22 Jun 91	**RAW MELODY MAN** *EMI EMC 3595*	43		2
10 Apr 93	**THE LOVE OF HOPELESS CAUSES** *Epic 4735622*	22		2
25 Apr 98	**STRANGE BROTHERHOOD** *Eagle EAGCD 021*	72		1

NEW MUSIK

UK, male vocal/instrumental group — **11**

Date	Title	Peak	Wks No.1	Wks
17 May 80	**FROM A TO B** *GTO GTLP 041*	35		9
14 Mar 81	**ANYWHERE** *GTO GTLP 044*	68		2

NEW ORDER

UK, male vocal/instrumental group – Bernard Sumner, Gillian Gilbert, Peter Hook & Stephen Morris — **158**

Date	Title	Peak	Wks No.1	Wks
28 Nov 81	**MOVEMENT** *Factory FACT 50*	30		10
14 May 83	**POWER, CORRUPTION AND LIES** *Factory FACT 75*	4		29
25 May 85	**LOW-LIFE** *Factory FACT 100*	7		10
11 Oct 86	**BROTHERHOOD** *Factory FACT 150*	9		5
29 Aug 87	**SUBSTANCE** *Factory FACT 200* ⊛	3		37
11 Feb 89	**TECHNIQUE** *Factory FACT 275* ●	1	1	14
22 Feb 92	**BBC RADIO 1 LIVE IN CONCERT** *Windsong International WINCD 011* ○	33		2
15 May 93	**REPUBLIC** *London 8284132* ●	1	1	19
17 Jul 93	**SUBSTANCE** *London 5200082*	32		2
3 Dec 94	**? (THE BEST OF NEW ORDER)/? (THE REST OF NEW ORDER)** *Centredate Co 8285802* ⊛	4		17
8 Sep 01	**GET READY** *London 8573896212* ●	6		4
9 Apr 05	**WAITING FOR THE SIRENS' CALL** *London 2564622022*	5		4
15 Oct 05	**SINGLES** *London 2564626902*	14		5

NEW POWER GENERATION

US, male vocal/instrumental group — **5**

Date	Title	Peak	Wks No.1	Wks
8 Apr 95	**EXODUS** *NPG 0061032*	11		3
11 Jul 98	**NEWPOWER SOUL** *NPG 74321605982*	38		2

NEW RADICALS

US, male vocalist (Gregg Alexander) — **14**

Date	Title	Peak	Wks No.1	Wks
17 Apr 99	**MAYBE YOU'VE BEEN BRAINWASHED TOO** *MCA MCD 11858* ●	10		14

NEW SEEKERS

UK/Australia/Germany, female/male vocal group – Peter Doyle, d. 22 Oct 2001, Eve Graham, Marty Kristian, Paul Layton & Lyn Paul — **49**

Date	Title	Peak	Wks No.1	Wks
5 Feb 72	**NEW COLOURS** *Polydor 2383 066*	40		4
1 Apr 72	**WE'D LIKE TO TEACH THE WORLD TO SING** *Polydor 2883 103*	2		25
12 Aug 72	**NEVER ENDING SONG OF LOVE** *Polydor 2383 126*	35		4
14 Oct 72	**CIRCLES** *Polydor 2442 102*	23		5
21 Apr 73	**NOW** *Polydor 2383 195*	47		2
30 Mar 74	**TOGETHER** *Polydor 2383 264* ○	12		9

NEW WORLD THEATRE ORCHESTRA

UK, orchestra — **1**

Date	Title	Peak	Wks No.1	Wks
24 Dec 60	**LET'S DANCE TO THE HITS OF THE 30'S AND 40'S** *Pye Golden Guinea GGL 0026*	16		2

NEW YOUNG PONY CLUB

UK, female/male vocal/instrumental group — **1**

Date	Title	Peak	Wks No.1	Wks
21 Jul 07	**FANTASTIC PLAYROOM** *Island/Modular MODCD64*	54		1

NEWCLEUS

US, male rap/instrumental group — **2**

Date	Title	Peak	Wks No.1	Wks
25 Aug 84	**JAM ON REVENGE** *Sunnyview SVLP 6600*	84		2

BOB NEWHART

US, male comedian — **37**

Date	Title	Peak	Wks No.1	Wks
1 Oct 60	**THE BUTTON-DOWN MIND OF BOB NEWHART** *Warner Brothers WM 4010* ★	2		37

ANTHONY NEWLEY

UK, male actor/vocalist, d. 14 Apr 1999 (age 67) — **24**

Date	Title	Peak	Wks No.1	Wks
14 May 60	**LOVE IS A NOW AND THEN THING** *Decca LK 4343*	19		2
8 Jul 61	**TONY** *Decca LK 4406*	5		12
28 Sep 63	**FOOL BRITANNIA** *Ember CEL 902* , PETER SELLERS, JOAN COLLINS	10		10

RANDY NEWMAN

US, male vocalist/pianist — **1**

Date	Title	Peak	Wks No.1	Wks
16 Aug 08	**HARPS AND ANGELS** *Nonesuch 7559799893*	46		1

JOANNA NEWSOM

US, female vocalist/harp player — **1**

Date	Title	Peak	Wks No.1	Wks
18 Nov 06	**YS** *Drag City DC303CD*	41		1

OLIVIA NEWTON-JOHN

Australia (b. UK), female vocalist — **133**

Date	Title	Peak	Wks No.1	Wks
2 Mar 74	**MUSIC MAKES MY DAY** *Pye NSPL 28186*	37		3
29 Jun 74	**LONG LIVE LOVE** *EMI EMC 3028*	40		2
26 Apr 75	**HAVE YOU NEVER BEEN MELLOW** *EMI EMC 3069*	37		2
29 May 76	**COME ON OVER** *EMI EMC 3124*	49		4
27 Aug 77	**MAKING A GOOD THING BETTER** *EMI EMC 3192*	60		1
21 Jan 78	**GREATEST HITS** *EMI EMA 785* ●	19		9
9 Dec 78	**TOTALLY HOT** *EMI EMA 789* ●	30		9
19 Jul 80	**XANADU (OST)** *Jet LX 526* /ELECTRIC LIGHT ORCHESTRA ●	2		17
31 Oct 81	**PHYSICAL** *EMI EMC 3386* ●	11		22
23 Oct 82	**GREATEST HITS** *EMI EMTV 36* ⊛	8		38
8 Mar 86	**SOUL KISS** *Mercury MERH 77*	66		3
25 Jul 92	**BACK TO BASICS – THE ESSENTIAL COLLECTION 1971–1992** *Mercury 5126412*	12		6
4 Feb 95	**GAIA (ONE WOMAN'S JOURNEY)** *D-Sharp DSHLCD 7017*	33		4
30 Oct 04	**THE DEFINITIVE COLLECTION** *Universal TV 05842792* ●	11		11
23 Apr 05	**INDIGO – WOMEN OF SONG** *Universal TV 9870906*	27		2

NICE

UK, male vocal/instrumental group – Keith Emerson, Brian Davison & Lee Jackson — **38**

Date	Title	Peak	Wks No.1	Wks
13 Sep 69	**NICE** *Immediate IMSP 026*	3		6
27 Jun 70	**FIVE BRIDGES** *Charisma CAS 1014*	2		21
17 Apr 71	**ELEGY** *Charisma CAS 1030*	5		11

PAUL NICHOLAS

UK, male actor/vocalist, d. 14 Apr 1999 (age 67) — **8**

Date	Title	Peak	Wks No.1	Wks
29 Nov 86	**JUST GOOD FRIENDS** *K-Tel ONE 1334* ○	30		8

NICKELBACK

Canada, male vocal/instrumental group – Chad Kroeger, Mike Kroeger, Ryan Peake & Ryan Vikedal — **137**

Date	Title	Peak	Wks No.1	Wks
19 Jan 02	**SILVER SIDE UP** *Roadrunner 12084852* ⊛x3	1	2	74
4 Oct 03	**THE LONG ROAD** *Roadrunner RR84005* ⊛	5		12
15 Oct 05	**ALL THE RIGHT REASONS** *Roadrunner RR83002* ⊛x2	2		45
29 Nov 08	**DARK HORSE** *Roadrunner RR80282*	4		6+

Silver-selling ○ Gold-selling ● Platinum-selling ⊛ US No.1 ★ — Peak Position / Weeks at No.1 / Weeks on Chart

STEVIE NICKS
US, female vocalist/guitarist. See Fleetwood Mac — 82

Date	Title	Peak Position	Weeks at No.1	Weeks on Chart
8 Aug 81	**BELLA DONNA** *WEA K 99169* ★	11		16
2 Jul 83	**THE WILD HEART** *WEA International 2500711* ○	28		19
14 Dec 85	**ROCK A LITTLE** *Modern PCS 7300* ●	30		22
10 Jun 89	**THE OTHER SIDE OF THE MIRROR** *EMI EMD 1008* ●	3		14
14 Sep 91	**TIMESPACE – THE BEST OF STEVIE NICKS** *EMI EMD 3595* ●	15		6
4 Jun 94	**STREET ANGEL** *EMI CDEMC 3671*	16		3
12 May 01	**TROUBLE IN SHANGRI-LA** *Reprise 9362473722*	43		2

HECTOR NICOL
UK, male comedian — 1

Date	Title	Peak Position	Weeks at No.1	Weeks on Chart
28 Apr 84	**BRAVO JULIET** *Klub KLP 42*	92		1

NICOLE
Germany, female vocalist (Nicole Hohloch) — 2

Date	Title	Peak Position	Weeks at No.1	Weeks on Chart
2 Oct 82	**A LITTLE PEACE** *CBS 85011*	85		2

NICOLETTE
UK, female vocalist. See Massive Attack — 2

Date	Title	Peak Position	Weeks at No.1	Weeks on Chart
10 Aug 96	**LET NO ONE LIVE RENT FREE IN YOUR HEAD** *Talkin Loud 5326342*	36		2

NIGHTCRAWLERS
UK, male/female vocal/production group — 5

Date	Title	Peak Position	Weeks at No.1	Weeks on Chart
30 Sep 95	**LET'S PUSH IT** *Final Vinyl 74321309702*	14		5

NIGHTMARES ON WAX
UK, male vocalist/producer (George Evelyn) — 4

Date	Title	Peak Position	Weeks at No.1	Weeks on Chart
24 Apr 99	**CAR BOOT SOUL** *Warp WARPCD 061* ○	71		2
14 Sep 02	**MIND ELEVATION** *Warp WARPCD 95*	47		2

NIGHTWISH
Finland, male/female vocal/instrumental group — 2

Date	Title	Peak Position	Weeks at No.1	Weeks on Chart
13 Oct 07	**DARK PASSION PLAY** *Nuclear Blast NB1923CD*	25		2

NILSSON
US, male vocalist (Harry Nilsson), d. 15 Jan 1994 (age 52) — 43

Date	Title	Peak Position	Weeks at No.1	Weeks on Chart
29 Jan 72	**THE POINT (OST-TV)** *RCA Victor SF 8166*	46		1
5 Feb 72	**NILSSON SCHMILSSON** *RCA Victor SF 8242*	4		22
19 Aug 72	**SON OF SCHMILSSON** *RCA Victor SF 8297*	41		1
28 Jul 73	**A LITTLE TOUCH OF SCHMILSSON IN THE NIGHT** *RCA Victor SF 8371*	20		19

NINA & FREDERIK
Denmark, female/male vocal duo – Baroness Nina & Baron Frederik von Pallandt, d. 15 May 1994 — 6

Date	Title	Peak Position	Weeks at No.1	Weeks on Chart
13 Feb 60	**NINA AND FREDERIK** *Pye NPT 19023*	9		2
29 Apr 61	**NINA AND FREDERIK** *Columbia COL 1314*	11		4

9 BELOW ZERO
UK, male vocal/instrumental group — 12

Date	Title	Peak Position	Weeks at No.1	Weeks on Chart
14 Mar 81	**DON'T POINT YOUR FINGER** *A&M AMLH 68521*	56		6
20 Mar 82	**THIRD DEGREE** *A&M AMLH 68537*	38		6

NINE BLACK ALPS
UK, male vocal/instrumental group — 4

Date	Title	Peak Position	Weeks at No.1	Weeks on Chart
25 Jun 05	**EVERYTHING IS** *Island CID8158*	51		3
10 Nov 07	**LOVE/HATE** *Island 1740807*	69		1

NINE INCH NAILS
US, male vocalist/multi-instrumentalist (Trent Reznor) & various musicians — 23

Date	Title	Peak Position	Weeks at No.1	Weeks on Chart
12 Oct 91	**PRETTY HATE MACHINE** *TVT ILPS 9973* ○	67		1
17 Oct 92	**BROKEN** *Interscope IMCD 8004*	18		3
19 Mar 94	**THE DOWNWARD SPIRAL** *Island CID 8012* ○	9		4
9 Oct 99	**THE FRAGILE** *Island CIDD 8091* ★	10		4
16 Mar 02	**AND ALL THAT COULD HAVE BEEN – LIVE** *Nothing CIDD 8113*	54		1
14 May 05	**WITH TEETH** *Island CID8155* ○ ★	3		4
28 Apr 07	**YEAR ZERO** *Interscope 1732422*	6		4
19 Apr 08	**GHOSTS I-IV** *Null Corporation HALO26CD*	60		1
9 Aug 08	**SLIP** *Null Corporation HALO27CD*	25		1

999
UK, male vocal/instrumental group — 1

Date	Title	Peak Position	Weeks at No.1	Weeks on Chart
25 Mar 78	**999** *United Artists UAG 30199*	53		1

911
UK, male vocal trio – Lee Brennan, Jimmy Constable & Simon Dawbarn — 26

Date	Title	Peak Position	Weeks at No.1	Weeks on Chart
8 Mar 97	**THE JOURNEY** *Virgin CDV 2820* ●	13		17
18 Jul 98	**MOVING ON** *Virgin CDV 2852* ○	10		4
6 Feb 99	**THERE IT IS** *Virgin CDV 2873* ○	8		4
6 Nov 99	**THE GREATEST HITS AND A LITTLE MORE...** *Virgin CDV 2899*	40		1

NIRVANA
US, male vocal/instrumental trio – Kurt Cobain, d. 5 Apr 1994, Dave Grohl & Krist Novoselic. Seattle grunge pioneers who enjoyed chart-topping albums before and after the death of their ill-fated frontman. The genre-defining *Nevermind* brought alternative rock into the mainstream and has sold more than 10 million copies in the US alone — 331

Date	Title	Peak Position	Weeks at No.1	Weeks on Chart
5 Oct 91	**NEVERMIND** *DGC 24425* ⊛x2 ★	7		198
7 Mar 92	**BLEACH** *Tupelo TUPCD 6*	33		7
26 Dec 92	**INCESTICIDE** *Geffen GED 24504* ●	14		11
25 Sep 93	**IN UTERO** *Geffen GED 24536* ● ★	1	1	43
12 Nov 94	**UNPLUGGED IN NEW YORK** *Geffen GED 24727* ⊛ ★	1	1	40
12 Oct 96	**FROM THE MUDDY BANKS OF THE WISHKAH** *Geffen GED 25105* ★	4		6
9 Nov 02	**NIRVANA** *Geffen 4935232* ⊛	3		23
4 Dec 04	**WITH THE LIGHTS OUT** *Geffen 9864838*	56		2
12 Nov 05	**SLIVER – THE BEST OF THE BOX** *Geffen 9886718*	56		1

NO DOUBT
US, female/male vocal/instrumental group – Gwen Stefani*, Tom Dumont, Tony Kanai & Adrian Young — 81

Date	Title	Peak Position	Weeks at No.1	Weeks on Chart
18 Jan 97	**TRAGIC KINGDOM** *Interscope IND 90003* ⊛ ★	3		44
22 Apr 00	**RETURN OF SATURN** *Interscope 4906382*	31		2
16 Feb 02	**ROCK STEADY** *Interscope 4931582* ○	43		6
13 Dec 03	**THE SINGLES 1992 – 2003** *Interscope 9861382* ⊛	5		29

NO MERCY
US, male vocal/instrumental group — 4

Date	Title	Peak Position	Weeks at No.1	Weeks on Chart
7 Jun 97	**MY PROMISE** *Arista 74321466902*	17		4

NOAH & THE WHALE
UK, male vocal/instrumental group – Charlie Fink, Doug Fink, Tom Hobden & Matt Owens — 9

Date	Title	Peak Position	Weeks at No.1	Weeks on Chart
23 Aug 08	**PEACEFUL THE WORLD LAYS ME DOWN** *Vertigo 1768177* ○	5		9

NOFX
US, male vocal/instrumental group — 4

Date	Title	Peak Position	Weeks at No.1	Weeks on Chart
10 Feb 96	**HEAVY PETTING ZOO** *Epitaph 864572*	60		1
10 Jun 00	**PUMP UP THE VALUUM** *Epitaph 65842*	50		1
23 Mar 02	**SPLIT SERIES – VOLUME 3** *BYO 079CD* RANCID/NOFX	75		1
17 May 03	**WAR ON ERRORISM** *Fat Wreck FAT657CD*	48		1

NOISETTES
UK, male/female vocal/instrumental group — 1

Date	Title	Peak Position	Weeks at No.1	Weeks on Chart
17 Feb 07	**WHAT'S THE TIME MR WOLF** *Vertigo 9841570*	75		1

NOLAN SISTERS
Ireland, female vocal group – Anne, Bernadette, Denise & Maureen Nolan — 84

Date	Title	Peak Position	Weeks at No.1	Weeks on Chart
29 Jul 78	**20 GIANT HITS** *Target TGS 502* ●	3		12
19 Jan 80	**NOLANS** *Epic 83892* NOLANS ●	15		13

Silver-selling ○ | Gold-selling ● | Platinum-selling ⊛ | US No.1 ★ | Peak Position | Weeks at No.1 | Weeks on Chart

Date	Title / Label	Peak	Wks at No.1	Wks on Chart
25 Oct 80	**MAKING WAVES** *Epic EPC 10023* NOLANS ●	11		33
27 Mar 82	**PORTRAIT** *Epic EPC 10033* NOLANS ●	7		10
20 Nov 82	**ALTOGETHER** *Epic EPC 10037* NOLANS ○	52		8
17 Nov 84	**GIRLS JUST WANNA HAVE FUN** *Towerbell TOWLP 10* NOLANS ○	39		8

NOMAD
UK, male/female vocal/instrumental duo — 2

Date	Title / Label	Peak	Wks at No.1	Wks on Chart
22 Jun 96	**CHANGING CABINS** *Rumour RULCD 100*	48		2

NOREAGA
US, male rapper (Victor Santiago) — 1

Date	Title / Label	Peak	Wks at No.1	Wks on Chart
25 Jul 98	**N.O.R.E.** *Penalty Recordings PENCD 3077*	72		1

NORTHERN UPROAR
UK, male vocal/instrumental group — 2

Date	Title / Label	Peak	Wks at No.1	Wks on Chart
11 May 96	**NORTHERN UPROAR** *Heavenly HVNLP 012CD*	22		2

NORTHSIDE
UK, male vocal/instrumental group — 3

Date	Title / Label	Peak	Wks at No.1	Wks on Chart
29 Jun 91	**CHICKEN RHYTHMS** *Factory FACT 310*	19		3

NOT THE NINE O'CLOCK NEWS CAST
UK/New Zealand, male/female vocalists/comedians – Rowan Atkinson, Griff Rhys Jones, Mel Smith & Pamela Stephenson — 51

Date	Title / Label	Peak	Wks at No.1	Wks on Chart
8 Nov 80	**NOT THE NINE O'CLOCK NEWS** *BBC REB 400* ⊛	5		23
17 Oct 81	**NOT THE NINE O'CLOCK NEWS – HEDGEHOG SANDWICH** *BBC REB 421* ●	5		24
23 Oct 82	**THE MEMORY KINDA LINGERS** *BBC REF 453*	63		4

NOTORIOUS B.I.G.
US, male rapper (Christopher Wallace), d. 9 Mar 1997 (age 24) — 28

Date	Title / Label	Peak	Wks at No.1	Wks on Chart
5 Apr 97	**LIFE AFTER DEATH** *Puff Daddy 78612730112* ★	23		16
18 Dec 99	**BORN AGAIN** *Puff Daddy 74321717182* ★	70		1
7 Jan 06	**DUETS – THE FINAL CHAPTER** *Bad Boy 7567838852* ●	13		11

NOTTING HILLBILLIES
UK, male vocal/instrumental group – Mark Knopfler*, Brendan Croker, Guy Fletcher & Steve Phillips — 14

Date	Title / Label	Peak	Wks at No.1	Wks on Chart
17 Mar 90	**MISSING...PRESUMED HAVING A GOOD TIME** *Vertigo 8426711* ●	2		14

HEATHER NOVA
Bermuda, female vocalist — 2

Date	Title / Label	Peak	Wks at No.1	Wks on Chart
8 Apr 95	**OYSTER** *Butterfly BFLCD 12*	72		1
20 Jun 98	**SIREN** *V2 VVR 1001872*	55		1

NU SHOOZ
US, male/female vocal duo — 8

Date	Title / Label	Peak	Wks at No.1	Wks on Chart
14 Jun 86	**POOLSIDE** *Atlantic WX 60*	32		8

NUCLEAR ASSAULT
US, male vocal/instrumental group — 1

Date	Title / Label	Peak	Wks at No.1	Wks on Chart
7 Oct 89	**HANDLE WITH CARE** *Under One Flag FLAG 35*	60		1

NUCLEUS
UK, male instrumental group — 1

Date	Title / Label	Peak	Wks at No.1	Wks on Chart
11 Jul 70	**ELASTIC ROCK** *Vertigo 6360 006*	46		1

TED NUGENT
US, male vocalist/guitarist — 14

Date	Title / Label	Peak	Wks at No.1	Wks on Chart
4 Sep 76	**TED NUGENT** *Epic EPC 81268*	56		1
30 Oct 76	**FREE FOR ALL** *Epic EPC 81397*	33		2
2 Jul 77	**CAT SCRATCH FEVER** *Epic EPC 82010*	28		5
11 Mar 78	**DOUBLE LIVE GONZO!** *Epic EPC 88282*	47		2
14 Jun 80	**SCREAM DREAM** *Epic EPC 86111*	37		3
25 Apr 81	**INTENSITIES (IN 10 CITIES)** *Epic EPC 84917*	75		1

GARY NUMAN
UK, male vocalist/synthesizer player (Gary Webb) — 146

Date	Title / Label	Peak	Wks at No.1	Wks on Chart
9 Jun 79	**REPLICAS** *Beggars Banquet BEGA 7* TUBEWAY ARMY ●	1	1	31
25 Aug 79	**TUBEWAY ARMY** *Beggars Banquet BEGA 5* TUBEWAY ARMY	14		10
22 Sep 79	**THE PLEASURE PRINCIPLE** *Beggars Banquet BEGA 10* ●	1	2	21
13 Sep 80	**TELEKON** *Beggars Banquet BEGA 19* ●	1	1	11
2 May 81	**LIVING ORNAMENTS 1979–1980** *Beggars Banquet BOX 1*	2		4
2 May 81	**LIVING ORNAMENTS 1980** *Beggars Banquet BEGA 25*	39		3
2 May 81	**LIVING ORNAMENTS 1979** *Beggars Banquet BEGA 24*	47		3
12 Sep 81	**DANCE** *Beggars Banquet BEGA 28*	3		8
18 Sep 82	**I, ASSASSIN** *Beggars Banquet BEGA 40*	8		6
27 Nov 82	**NEW MAN NUMAN – THE BEST OF GARY NUMAN** *TV Records TVA 7*	45		7
24 Sep 83	**WARRIORS** *Beggars Banquet BEGA 47*	12		6
6 Oct 84	**THE PLAN 1978** *Beggars Banquet BEGA 55*	29		4
24 Nov 84	**BERSERKER** *Numa 1001*	45		3
13 Apr 85	**WHITE NOISE – LIVE** *Numa NUMAD 1002*	29		5
28 Sep 85	**THE FURY** *Numa 1003*	24		5
8 Nov 86	**STRANGE CHARM** *Numa 1005*	59		2
3 Oct 87	**EXHIBITION** *Beggars Banquet BEGA 88*	43		3
8 Oct 88	**METAL RHYTHM** *Illegal ILP 035*	48		2
8 Jul 89	**AUTOMATIC** *Polydor 8395201* SHARPE & NUMAN	59		1
28 Oct 89	**SKIN MECHANIC** *I.R.S. EIRSA 1019*	55		1
30 Mar 91	**OUTLAND** *I.R.S. EIRSA 1039*	39		1
22 Aug 92	**MACHINE + SOUL** *Numa NUMACD 1009*	42		1
2 Oct 93	**BEST OF GARY NUMAN 1978-83** *Beggars Banquet BEGA 150CD*	70		1
30 Mar 96	**THE PREMIER HITS** *Polygram TV 5311492* GARY NUMAN/TUBEWAY ARMY	21		3
1 Nov 97	**EXILE** *Eagle EAGCD 008*	48		1
21 Oct 00	**PURE** *Eagle EAGCD 078*	58		1
1 Jun 02	**EXPOSURE – THE BEST OF 1977 – 2002** *Jagged Halo JHCD2*	44		1
25 Mar 06	**JAGGED** *Cooking Vinyl MORTALCD001*	59		1

PAOLO NUTINI
UK, male vocalist/guitarist — 74

Date	Title / Label	Peak	Wks at No.1	Wks on Chart
29 Jul 06	**THESE STREETS** *Atlantic 5101150172* ⊛x3	3		74

NUYORICAN SOUL
US, male DJ/production group — 2

Date	Title / Label	Peak	Wks at No.1	Wks on Chart
1 Mar 97	**NUYORICAN SOUL** *Talkin Loud 5344512*	25		2

N.W.A.
US, male rap group – Dr. Dre* (Andre Young), Easy-E* (Eric Wright), d. 26 Mar 1995, Ice Cube* (O'Shea Jackson), M.C. Ren (Lorenzo Patterson) & Yella (Antoine Carraby) — 12

Date	Title / Label	Peak	Wks at No.1	Wks on Chart
30 Sep 89	**STRAIGHT OUTTA COMPTON** *Fourth & Broadway BRLP 534* ○	41		4
15 Jun 91	**EFIL4ZAGGIN** *Fourth & Broadway BRLP 562* ★	25		2
31 Aug 96	**GREATEST HITS** *Priority CDPTY 126*	56		1
5 Jul 03	**STRAIGHT OUTTA COMPTON** *Priority 5379362* ●	35		5

MICHAEL NYMAN
UK, male pianist — 15

Date	Title / Label	Peak	Wks at No.1	Wks on Chart
12 Feb 94	**THE PIANO (OST)** *Venture CDVE 919* ●	31		15

O

O-TOWN
US, male vocal group – Ashley Parker Angel, Erik-Michael Estrada, Dan Miller, Trevor Penick & Jacob Underwood — 5

Date	Title / Label	Peak	Wks at No.1	Wks on Chart
18 Aug 01	**O-TOWN** *J Records 80813200002*	7		5

PAUL OAKENFOLD
UK, male DJ/producer — 13

Date	Title / Label	Peak	Wks at No.1	Wks on Chart
6 Jul 02	**BUNKKA** *Perfecto PERFALB 09CD* PAUL OAKENFOLD ○	25		12
17 Jun 06	**A LIVELY MIND** *Perfecto PERCD003*	57		1

PHILIP OAKEY & GIORGIO MORODER

US, male vocalist/keyboard player & Italy, male producer/synthesizer player. See Human League — 5

Date	Title	Peak Position	Weeks at No.1	Weeks on Chart
10 Aug 85	**PHILIP OAKEY AND GIORGIO MORODER** *Virgin V 2351*	52		5

OASIS

UK, male vocal/instrumental group – Noel & Liam Gallagher, Paul Arthurs, Tony McCarroll (replaced by Tony White) & Paul McGuigan. Outspoken rock band who put the swagger into Britpop. Their first five studio albums sold over one million copies and *Be Here Now* is the fastest-selling album in UK chart history, shifting 356,000 copies on day one, 695,761 in a week and a million in 11 days — 622

Date	Title	Peak Position	Weeks at No.1	Weeks on Chart
28 Apr 84	**OASIS** *WEA WX 3*	23		14
10 Sep 94	**DEFINITELY MAYBE** *Creation CRECD 169* ⊛x7	1	1	177
14 Oct 95	**(WHAT'S THE STORY) MORNING GLORY?** *Creation CRECD 189* ⊛x14	1	10	145
16 Nov 96	**DEFINITELY MAYBE SINGLES BOX – SILVER** *Creation CREDM 002*	23		3
16 Nov 96	**(WHAT'S THE STORY) MORNING GLORY? SINGLES BOX – GOLD** *Creation CREEMG 002*	24		3
30 Aug 97	**BE HERE NOW** *Creation CRECD 219* ⊛x6	1	5	36
14 Nov 98	**THE MASTERPLAN** *Creation CRECD 241* ⊛	2		28
11 Mar 00	**STANDING ON THE SHOULDER OF GIANTS** *Big Brother RKIDCD 002* ⊛x2	1	1	29
17 Jun 00	**(WHAT'S THE STORY) MORNING GLORY?** *Big Brother RKIDCD 008*	36		26
25 Nov 00	**FAMILIAR TO MILLIONS** *Big Brother RKIDCD 005* ⊛	5		10
13 Jul 02	**HEATHEN CHEMISTRY** *Big Brother RKIDCD 25* ⊛x3	1	1	44
18 Sep 04	**DEFINITELY MAYBE** *Big Brother CRECD 169*	45		10
11 Jun 05	**DON'T BELIEVE THE TRUTH** *Big Brother RKIDCD30* ⊛x3	1	1	41
2 Dec 06	**STOP THE CLOCKS** *Big Brother RKIDCD36X* ⊛x4	2		58
18 Oct 08	**DIG OUT YOUR SOUL** *Big Brother RKIDCD51X* ⊛	1	1	12+

Top 3 Best-Selling Albums

		Approximate Sales
1	WHAT'S THE STORY MORNING GLORY	4,400,000
2	BE HERE NOW	1,825,000
3	DEFINITELY MAYBE	1,820,000

CONOR OBERST

US, male vocalist/guitarist. See Bright Eyes — 1

Date	Title	Peak Position	Weeks at No.1	Weeks on Chart
16 Aug 08	**CONOR OBERST** *Wichita WEBB175CDL*	37		1

OBITUARY

US, male vocal/instrumental group — 2

Date	Title	Peak Position	Weeks at No.1	Weeks on Chart
18 Apr 92	**THE END COMPLETE** *Roadrunner RC 920121*	52		1
17 Sep 94	**WORLD DEMISE** *Roadrunner RR 89955*	65		1

BILLY OCEAN

Trinidad & Tobago, male vocalist — 147

Date	Title	Peak Position	Weeks at No.1	Weeks on Chart
24 Nov 84	**SUDDENLY** *Jive JIP 12* ●	9		59
17 May 86	**LOVE ZONE** *Jive HIP 35* ●	2		32
19 Mar 88	**TEAR DOWN THESE WALLS** *Jive HIP 57* ●	3		13
28 Oct 89	**GREATEST HITS** *Jive BOTV 1* ⊛	4		17
16 Aug 97	**LOVE IS FOR EVER** *Jive BOCD 2* ●	7		21
15 Feb 03	**LET'S GET BACK TOGETHER – THE LOVE SONGS** *Jive 9225232*	69		1
19 Jun 04	**ULTIMATE COLLECTION** *Jive 82876614022*	28		4

OCEAN COLOUR SCENE

UK, male vocal/instrumental group – Steve Cradock, Simon Fowler, Oscar Harrison & Damon Minchella — 154

Date	Title	Peak Position	Weeks at No.1	Weeks on Chart
20 Apr 96	**MOSELEY SHOALS** *MCA MCD 60008* ⊛x3	2		73
21 Sep 96	**OCEAN COLOUR SCENE** *Fontana 5122692*	54		2
15 Mar 97	**B-SIDES, SEASIDES & FREERIDES** *MCA MCD 60034* ●	4		14
27 Sep 97	**MARCHIN' ALREADY** *MCA MCD 60053* ⊛	1	1	37
25 Sep 99	**ONE FROM THE MODERN** *Island CID 8090* ●	4		11
21 Apr 01	**MECHANICAL WONDER** *Island CID 8104* ○	7		4
17 Nov 01	**SONGS FROM THE FRONT ROW – THE BEST OF** *Island CIDD 8111* ●	16		4
19 Jul 03	**NORTH ATLANTIC DRIFT** *Sanctuary SANCD160* ○	14		3
13 Sep 03	**ANTHOLOGY** *Island 9807210*	75		1
2 Apr 05	**A HYPERACTIVE WORKOUT FOR THE FLYING SQUAD** *Sanctuary SANCD332*	30		3
20 May 06	**LIVE ACOUSTIC AT THE JAM HOUSE** *Moseley Shoals OCSCD2*	73		1
12 May 07	**ON THE LEYLINE** *Moseley Shoals OCSCD5*	37		1

OCEANIA

New Zealand, male/female vocal/instrumental group — 1

Date	Title	Peak Position	Weeks at No.1	Weeks on Chart
23 Oct 99	**OCEANIA** *Point Music 5367752*	70		1

OCEANIC

UK, male production duo — 2

Date	Title	Peak Position	Weeks at No.1	Weeks on Chart
4 Jul 92	**THAT ALBUM BY OCEANIC** *Dead Dead Good 4509900832*	49		2

DES O'CONNOR

UK, male comedian/vocalist — 47

Date	Title	Peak Position	Weeks at No.1	Weeks on Chart
7 Dec 68	**I PRETEND** *Columbia SCX 6295*	8		10
5 Dec 70	**WITH LOVE** *Columbia SCX 6417*	40		4
2 Dec 72	**SING A FAVOURITE SONG** *Pye NSPL 18390*	25		6
2 Feb 80	**JUST FOR YOU** *Warwick WW 5071*	17		7
13 Oct 84	**DES O'CONNOR NOW** *Telstar STAR 2245* ●	24		14
5 Dec 92	**PORTRAIT** *Columbia 4727302* ○	63		4
17 Nov 01	**A TRIBUTE TO THE CROONERS** *Decca 4704702*	51		2

HAZEL O'CONNOR

UK, female vocalist — 45

Date	Title	Peak Position	Weeks at No.1	Weeks on Chart
9 Aug 80	**BREAKING GLASS (OST)** *A&M AMLH 64820* ●	5		38
12 Sep 81	**COVER PLUS** *Albion ALB 108*	32		7

SINEAD O'CONNOR

Ireland, female vocalist — 90

Date	Title	Peak Position	Weeks at No.1	Weeks on Chart
23 Jan 88	**THE LION AND THE COBRA** *Ensign CHEN 7* ●	27		20
24 Mar 90	**I DO NOT WANT WHAT I HAVEN'T GOT** *Ensign CHEN 14* ⊛x2 ★	1	1	51
26 Sep 92	**AM I NOT YOUR GIRL?** *Ensign CCD 1952* ●	6		6
24 Sep 94	**UNIVERSAL MOTHER** *Ensign CDCHEN 34* ●	19		8
22 Nov 97	**SO FAR...THE BEST OF SINEAD O'CONNOR** *Chrysalis 8215812* ○	28		3
24 Jun 00	**FAITH AND COURAGE** *Atlantic 7567833372*	61		1
19 Oct 02	**SEAN-NOS-NUA** *R&M Entertainment RAMCD 001*	52		1

DANIEL O'DONNELL

Ireland, male vocalist — 235

Date	Title	Peak Position	Weeks at No.1	Weeks on Chart
15 Oct 88	**FROM THE HEART** *Telstar STAR 2327* ●	56		12
28 Oct 89	**THOUGHTS OF HOME** *Telstar STAR 2372*	43		10
21 Apr 90	**FAVOURITES** *Ritz RITZLP 052*	61		3
17 Nov 90	**THE LAST WALTZ** *Ritz RITZALP 058*	46		7
9 Nov 91	**THE VERY BEST OF DANIEL O'DONNELL** *Ritz RITZBLD 700*	34		14
21 Nov 92	**FOLLOW YOUR DREAM** *Ritz RITZBCD 701*	17		9
6 Nov 93	**A DATE WITH DANIEL – LIVE** *Ritz RITZBCD 702*	21		10
22 Oct 94	**ESPECIALLY FOR YOU** *Ritz RITZBCD 703*	14		11
3 Dec 94	**CHRISTMAS WITH DANIEL** *Ritz RITZBCD 704*	34		5
11 Nov 95	**THE CLASSIC COLLECTION** *Ritz RITZBCD 705*	34		9
6 Apr 96	**TIMELESS** *Ritz RITZBCD 707* & MARY DUFF	13		5
20 Jul 96	**THE DANIEL O'DONNELL IRISH COLLECTION** *Ritz RITZCD 0080*	35		3
26 Oct 96	**SONGS OF INSPIRATION** *Ritz RITZBCD 709*	11		16
8 Nov 97	**I BELIEVE** *Ritz RZBCD 710*	11		11
31 Oct 98	**LOVE SONGS** *Ritz RZBCD 715*	9		10
2 Oct 99	**GREATEST HITS** *Ritz RZBCD 716*	10		8
28 Oct 00	**FAITH & INSPIRATION** *Ritz RZBCD 717*	4		10
1 Dec 01	**LIVE LAUGH LOVE** *Rosette ROSCD 2002*	27		5
2 Nov 02	**YESTERDAY'S MEMORIES** *Rosette ROSCD 2020*	19		3
22 Mar 03	**DANIEL IN BLUE JEANS** *DMG TV DMGTV001*	3		10
25 Oct 03	**AT THE END OF THE DAY** *Rosette ROSCD 2040*	11		6
20 Mar 04	**THE JUKEBOX YEARS** *DMG TV DMGTV005*	3		8
23 Oct 04	**WELCOME TO MY WORLD** *Rosette ROSCD2050*	6		10
1 Oct 05	**TEENAGE DREAMS** *Rosette ROSCD2060*	10		6
4 Feb 06	**FROM DANIEL WITH LOVE** *DMG TV DMGTV027*	5		10
14 Oct 06	**UNTIL THE NEXT TIME** *Rosette ROSCD2080*	10		7
10 Nov 07	**TOGETHER AGAIN** *Rosette ROSCD2090* & MARY DUFF	6		8
8 Nov 08	**COUNTRY BOY** *DMG TV DMGTV035*	6		9+

RYAN & RACHEL O'DONNELL
Ireland, male/female vocal/instrumental duo

Date	Album	⬆	✪	17
16 Mar 02	**THE CELTIC CHILLOUT ALBUM** *Decadance DECTV 001*	17		4
30 Nov 02	**THE CELTIC CHILLOUT ALBUM** *Decadance DECTV 007*	37		10
22 Mar 03	**THE CELTIC CHILLOUT ALBUM 2** *Decadance DECTV 009*	37		3

ODYSSEY
US, male/female vocal trio

Date	Album	⬆	✪	32
16 Aug 80	**HANG TOGETHER** *RCA PL 13526*	38		3
4 Jul 81	**I'VE GOT THE MELODY** *RCA RCALP 5028*	29		7
3 Jul 82	**HAPPY TOGETHER** *RCA RCALP 6036*	21		9
20 Nov 82	**THE MAGIC TOUCH OF ODYSSEY** *Telstar STAR 2223*	69		5
26 Sep 87	**THE GREATEST HITS** *Stylus SMR 735* ○	26		8

ESTHER & ABI OFARIM
Israel, female/male vocal duo – Esther Zaled & Abraham Reichstadt

Date	Album	⬆	✪	24
24 Feb 68	**2 IN 3** *Philips SBL 7825*	6		20
12 Jul 69	**OFARIM CONCERT – LIVE '69** *Philips XL 4*	29		4

OFFSPRING
US, male vocal/instrumental group – Brian Holland, Greg Kriesal, Kevin Wasserman & Ron Welty

Date	Album	⬆	✪	114
4 Mar 95	**SMASH** *Epitaph E 864322*	21		34
15 Feb 97	**IXNAY ON THE HOMBRE** *Epitaph 64872*	17		3
28 Nov 98	**AMERICANA** *Columbia 4916562* ⊛	10		44
25 Nov 00	**CONSPIRACY OF ONE** *Columbia 4984819* ●	12		18
13 Dec 03	**SPLINTER** *Columbia 5122013*	27		7
16 Jul 05	**GREATEST HITS** *Columbia 5187463*	14		7
28 Jun 08	**RISE AND FALL RAGE AND GRACE** *Columbia 88697029082*	39		1

MARY O'HARA
UK, female vocalist/harp player

Date	Album	⬆	✪	12
8 Apr 78	**MARY O'HARA AT THE ROYAL FESTIVAL HALL** *Chrysalis CHR 1159* ○	37		3
1 Dec 79	**TRANQUILLITY** *Warwick WW 5072* ⊛	12		9

THE O'JAYS
US, male vocal/instrumental group

Date	Album	⬆	✪	2
12 Oct 85	**THE ARTISTS VOLUME III** *Street Sounds ARTIS 3* WOMACK & WOMACK/THE O'JAYS/KLEEER/THE S.O.S. BAND	87		2

MIKE OLDFIELD
UK, male producer/multi-instrumentalist. Virgin Records' first hit artist spent five years on the chart with his 1973 debut album *Tubular Bells*, which took 15 months to reach No.1. The long-awaited *Tubular Bells 2* took just seven days to reach the top in 1992

Date	Album	⬆	✪	559
14 Jul 73	**TUBULAR BELLS** *Virgin V 2001* ⊛x7	1	1	278
14 Sep 74	**HERGEST RIDGE** *Virgin V 2013* ●	1	3	17
8 Feb 75	**THE ORCHESTRAL TUBULAR BELLS** *Virgin V 2026* WITH THE ROYAL PHILHARMONIC ORCHESTRA ○	17		7
15 Nov 75	**OMMADAWN** *Virgin V 2043* ●	4		23
20 Nov 76	**BOXED** *Virgin V BOX 1* ●	22		13
9 Dec 78	**INCANTATIONS** *Virgin VDT 101* ⊛	14		17
11 Aug 79	**EXPOSED** *Virgin VD 2511* ○	16		9
8 Dec 79	**PLATINUM** *Virgin V 2141* ●	24		9
8 Nov 80	**QE 2** *Virgin V 2181* ●	27		12
27 Mar 82	**FIVE MILES OUT** *Virgin V 2222* ●	7		27
4 Jun 83	**CRISES** *Virgin V 2262* ●	6		29
7 Jul 84	**DISCOVERY** *Virgin V 2308* ●	15		16
15 Dec 84	**THE KILLING FIELDS (OST)** *Virgin V 2328* ○	97		1
2 Nov 85	**THE COMPLETE MIKE OLDFIELD** *Virgin MOC 1* ●	36		17
10 Oct 87	**ISLANDS** *Virgin V 2466* ●	29		5
22 Jul 89	**EARTH MOVING** *Virgin V 2610*	30		5
9 Jun 90	**AMAROK** *Virgin V 2640*	49		2
12 Sep 92	**TUBULAR BELLS II** *WEA 4509906182* ⊛x2	1	2	30
25 Sep 93	**ELEMENTS – THE BEST OF MIKE OLDFIELD** *Virgin VTCD 18* ●	5		10
3 Dec 94	**THE SONGS OF DISTANT EARTH** *WEA 4509985812* ●	24		6
7 Sep 96	**VOYAGER** *WEA 0630158962* ○	12		5
12 Sep 98	**TUBULAR BELLS III** *WEA 3984243492* ●	4		7
5 Jun 99	**GUITARS** *WEA 3984274012*	40		2
16 Jun 01	**THE BEST OF TUBULAR BELLS** *Virgin CDV 2936*	60		2
7 Jun 03	**TUBULAR BELLS 2003** *WEA 2564602042*	51		1
25 Mar 06	**THE PLATINUM COLLECTION** *Virgin MIKECDX17*	36		3
29 Mar 08	**MUSIC OF THE SPHERES** *UCJ 4766206*	9		6

OLIVE
UK, female/male vocal/instrumental group

Date	Album	⬆	✪	3
31 May 97	**EXTRA VIRGIN** *RCA 74321486872*	15		3

OMAR
UK, male vocalist (Omar Hammer)

Date	Album	⬆	✪	14
14 Jul 90	**THERE'S NOTHING LIKE THIS** *Kongo Dance KDLP 2*	54		4
27 Jul 91	**THERE'S NOTHING LIKE THIS** *Talkin Loud 5100211*	19		6
24 Oct 92	**MUSIC MAKES MY DAY** *Talkin Loud 5124012*	37		2
2 Jul 94	**FOR PLEASURE** *RCA 74321208532*	50		1
16 Aug 97	**THIS IS NOT A LOVE SONG** *RCA 74321496262*	50		1

OMARION
US, male vocalist (Omarion Grandberry)

Date	Album	⬆	✪	4
10 Mar 07	**21** *Epic 88697049082*	24		4

JO O'MEARA
UK, female vocalist. See S Club 7

Date	Album	⬆	✪	2
15 Oct 05	**RELENTLESS** *Sanctuary SANCD402*	48		2

OMNI TRIO
UK, male producer (Rob Haigh)

Date	Album	⬆	✪	2
11 Feb 95	**THE DEEPEST CUT – VOLUME 1** *Morning Shadow ASHADOW 1CD*	60		1
24 Aug 96	**THE HAUNTED SCIENCE** *Morning Shadow ASHADOW 6CD*	43		1

ONE DOVE
UK, male/female vocal/instrumental group

Date	Album	⬆	✪	2
25 Sep 93	**MORNING DOVE WHITE** *London 8283522*	30		2

ONE GIANT LEAP
UK, male production duo

Date	Album	⬆	✪	3
27 Apr 02	**ONE GIANT LEAP** *Palm Pictures PALMCD 2077*	51		3

101 STRINGS
Germany, orchestra

Date	Album	⬆	✪	35
26 Sep 59	**GYPSY CAMPFIRES** *Pye Golden Guinea GGL 0009*	9		7
26 Mar 60	**THE SOUL OF SPAIN** *Pye Golden Guinea GGL 0017*	17		1
16 Apr 60	**GRAND CANYON SUITE** *Pye Golden Guinea GGL 0048*	10		1
27 Aug 60	**DOWN DRURY LANE TO MEMORY LANE** *Pye Golden Guinea GGL 0061*	1	5	21
15 Oct 83	**MORNING NOON AND NIGHT** *Ronco RTL 2094*	32		5

ONE MINUTE SILENCE
UK, male vocal/rap/instrumental group

Date	Album	⬆	✪	1
22 Apr 00	**BUY NOW... SAVED LATER** *V2 VVR 1012362*	61		1

ONE NIGHT ONLY
UK, male vocal/instrumental group – George Craig, Sam Ford, Mark Hayton, Daniel Parkin & Jack Sails

Date	Album	⬆	✪	12
23 Feb 08	**STARTED A FIRE** *Vertigo 1751839* ●	10		12

ONE WORLD
UK, male vocal/instrumental group

Date	Album	⬆	✪	3
9 Jun 90	**ONE WORLD ONE VOICE** *Virgin V 2632*	27		3

ONEREPUBLIC
US, male vocal/instrumental group – Ryan Tedder, Drew Brown, Zach Filkins, Eddie Fisher & Brent Kutzle

Date	Album	⬆	✪	18
22 Mar 08	**DREAMING OUT LOUD** *Interscope 1754743*	2		18

ALEXANDER O'NEAL
US, male vocalist

Date	Album	⬆	✪	170
1 Jun 85	**ALEXANDER O'NEAL** *Tabu TBU 26485* ●	19		18
8 Aug 87	**HEARSAY/ALL MIXED UP** *Tabu 4509361* ⊛x3	4		103
17 Dec 88	**MY GIFT TO YOU** *Tabu 4631521*	53		3

Silver-selling ○ Gold-selling ● Platinum-selling ⊛ US No.1 ★ — Peak Position / Weeks at No.1 / Weeks on Chart

Date	Title	Peak Position	Weeks at No.1	Weeks on Chart
2 Feb 91	**ALL TRUE MAN** *Tabu 4658821* ●	2		16
30 May 92	**THIS THING CALLED LOVE – THE GREATEST HITS OF ALEXANDER O'NEAL** *Tabu 4717142* ●	4		18
20 Feb 93	**LOVE MAKES NO SENSE** *Tabu 5495022*	14		4
4 Sep 04	**GREATEST HITS** *EMI 5785022* ●	12		6
16 Feb 08	**ALEX LOVES...** *EMI 5179582*	49		2

ONLY MEN ALOUD!

UK, male choristers — 5

Date	Title	Peak Position	Weeks at No.1	Weeks on Chart
6 Dec 08	**ONLY MEN ALOUD!** *UCJ 1789189*	16		5+

ONLY ONES

UK, male vocal/instrumental group — 8

Date	Title	Peak Position	Weeks at No.1	Weeks on Chart
3 Jun 78	**THE ONLY ONES** *CBS 82830*	56		1
31 Mar 79	**EVEN SERPENT'S SHINE** *CBS 83451*	42		2
3 May 80	**BABY'S GOT A GUN** *CBS 84089*	37		5

YOKO ONO

Japan, female vocalist. See John Lennon — 57

Date	Title	Peak Position	Weeks at No.1	Weeks on Chart
14 Oct 72	**SOMETIME IN NEW YORK CITY** *Apple PCSP 716* JOHN AND YOKO LENNON WITH THE PLASTIC ONO BAND & ELEPHANT'S MEMORY	11		6
22 Nov 80	**DOUBLE FANTASY** *Geffen K 99131* JOHN LENNON & YOKO ONO ⊛ ★	1	2	36
20 Jun 81	**SEASON OF GLASS** *Geffen K 99164*	47		2
4 Feb 84	**MILK AND HONEY – A HEART PLAY** *Polydor POLH 5* JOHN LENNON & YOKO ONO ●	3		13

ONSLAUGHT

UK, male vocal/instrumental group — 2

Date	Title	Peak Position	Weeks at No.1	Weeks on Chart
20 May 89	**IN SEARCH OF SANITY** *London 8281421*	46		2

ONYX

US, male rap group — 3

Date	Title	Peak Position	Weeks at No.1	Weeks on Chart
4 Sep 93	**BACDAFUCUP** *Columbia 4729802*	59		3

OPEN

UK, male vocal/instrumental group — 1

Date	Title	Peak Position	Weeks at No.1	Weeks on Chart
17 Jul 04	**THE SILENT HOURS** *Loog 9866160*	72		1

OPERABABES

UK, female vocal duo — 6

Date	Title	Peak Position	Weeks at No.1	Weeks on Chart
8 Jun 02	**BEYOND IMAGINATION** *Sony Classical SK89916*	24		6

OPETH

Sweden, male/vocal instrumental group — 2

Date	Title	Peak Position	Weeks at No.1	Weeks on Chart
10 Sep 05	**GHOST REVERIES** *Roadrunner RR81232*	62		1
14 Jun 08	**WATERSHED** *Roadrunner RR79622*	34		1

OPM

US, male vocal/instrumental group – Brian Holland, Greg Kriesal, Kevin Wasserman & Ron Welty — 8

Date	Title	Peak Position	Weeks at No.1	Weeks on Chart
21 Jul 01	**MENACE TO SOBRIETY** *Atlantic 7567929772* ○	31		8

ORANGE JUICE

UK, male vocal/instrumental group — 18

Date	Title	Peak Position	Weeks at No.1	Weeks on Chart
6 Mar 82	**YOU CAN'T HIDE YOUR LOVE FOREVER** *Polydor POLS 1057*	21		6
20 Nov 82	**RIP IT UP** *Polydor POLS 1076*	39		8
10 Mar 84	**TEXAS FEVER** *Polydor OJMLP 1*	34		4

ORB

UK, male production/instrumental duo – Dr. Alex Patterson & Kris Weston — 28

Date	Title	Peak Position	Weeks at No.1	Weeks on Chart
27 Apr 91	**THE ORB'S ADVENTURES BEYOND THE ULTRAWORLD** *Big Life BLRDLP 5*	29		5
18 Jul 92	**U.F. ORB** *Big Life BLRCD 18*	1	1	9
4 Dec 93	**LIVE 93** *Island CIDD 8022* ○	23		2
25 Jun 94	**POMME FRITZ** *Inter-Modo ORBCD 1*	6		4
1 Apr 95	**ORBVS TERRERVM** *Island CIDX 8037*	20		3
8 Mar 97	**ORBLIVION** *Island CID 8055*	19		3
17 Oct 98	**U.F. OFF – THE BEST OF ORB** *Island CID 8078*	38		2

ROY ORBISON

US, male vocalist, d. 6 Dec 1988 (age 52) — 254

Date	Title	Peak Position	Weeks at No.1	Weeks on Chart
8 Jun 63	**LONELY AND BLUE** *London HAU 2342*	15		8
29 Jun 63	**CRYING** *London HAU 2437*	17		3
30 Nov 63	**IN DREAMS** *London HAU 8108*	6		58
25 Jul 64	**THE EXCITING SOUNDS OF ROY ORBISON** *Ember NR 5013*	17		2
5 Dec 64	**OH PRETTY WOMAN** *London HAU 8207*	4		16
25 Sep 65	**THERE IS ONLY ONE ROY ORBISON** *London HAU 8252*	10		12
26 Feb 66	**THE ORBISON WAY** *London HAU 8279*	11		10
24 Sep 66	**THE CLASSIC ROY ORBISON** *London HAU 8297*	12		8
22 Jul 67	**ORBISONGS** *Monument SMO 5004*	40		1
30 Sep 67	**ROY ORBISON'S GREATEST HITS** *Monument SMO 5007*	40		1
27 Jan 73	**ALL-TIME GREATEST HITS** *Monument MNT 67290*	39		3
29 Nov 75	**THE BEST OF ROY ORBISON** *Arcade ADEP 19* ●	1	1	20
18 Jul 81	**GOLDEN DAYS** *Monument MNT 10026*	63		1
4 Jul 87	**IN DREAMS: THE GREATEST HITS** *Virgin VGD 3514* ○	86		2
29 Oct 88	**THE LEGENDARY ROY ORBISON** *Telstar STAR 2330* ⊛x2	1	3	38
11 Feb 89	**MYSTERY GIRL** *Virgin V 2576* ⊛	2		23
25 Nov 89	**A BLACK AND WHITE NIGHT** *Virgin V 2601*	51		3
3 Nov 90	**BALLADS – 22 CLASSIC LOVE SONGS** *Telstar STAR 2441*	38		10
28 Nov 92	**KING OF HEARTS** *Virgin America CDVUS 58*	23		4
16 Nov 96	**THE VERY BEST OF ROY ORBISON** *Virgin CDV 2804* ●	18		11
10 Feb 01	**LOVE SONGS** *Virgin VTDCD 360* ●	4		10
14 Aug 04	**THE PLATINUM COLLECTION** *Virgin/EMI VTDCDX 632* ○	16		5
28 Oct 06	**THE VERY BEST OF** *Monument 82876812762*	20		5

WILLIAM ORBIT

UK, male producer (William Wainwright) — 14

Date	Title	Peak Position	Weeks at No.1	Weeks on Chart
29 Jan 00	**PIECES IN A MODERN STYLE** *WEA 3984289572* ●	2		14

ORBITAL

UK, male instrumental duo – Paul & Phil Hartnoll — 37

Date	Title	Peak Position	Weeks at No.1	Weeks on Chart
12 Oct 91	**ORBITAL** *ffrr 8282481*	71		1
5 Jun 93	**ORBITAL** *Internal TRUCD 2*	28		2
19 Mar 94	**PEEL SESSIONS** *Internal LIECD 12*	32		2
20 Aug 94	**SNIVILISATION** *Internal Dance TRUCD 5*	4		4
11 May 96	**IN SIDES** *Internal 8287632* ●	5		12
25 Jan 97	**SATAN LIVE** *Internal LIARX 37*	48		1
17 Apr 99	**THE MIDDLE OF NOWHERE** *ffrr 5560762* ○	4		7
12 May 01	**THE ALTOGETHER** *ffrr 8573877822* ○	11		4
15 Jun 02	**WORK 1989 – 2002** *London 0927461902*	36		3
3 Jul 04	**BLUE ALBUM** *Orbital Music ORBITALCD001*	44		1

ORCHESTRAL MANOEUVRES IN THE DARK

UK, male vocal/instrumental group – Andrew McCluskey, Martin Cooper, Malcolm Holmes & Paul Humphreys — 226

Date	Title	Peak Position	Weeks at No.1	Weeks on Chart
1 Mar 80	**ORCHESTRAL MANOEUVRES IN THE DARK** *Dindisc DID 2* ○	27		29
1 Nov 80	**ORGANISATION** *Dindisc DID 6* ●	6		25
14 Nov 81	**ARCHITECTURE AND MORALITY** *Dindisc DID 12* ⊛	3		39
12 Mar 83	**DAZZLE SHIPS** *Telegraph V 2261* ●	5		13
12 May 84	**JUNK CULTURE** *Virgin V 2310* ●	9		27
29 Jun 85	**CRUSH** *Virgin V 2349* ○	13		12
11 Oct 86	**THE PACIFIC AGE** *Virgin V 2398* ○	15		7
12 Mar 88	**THE BEST OF O.M.D.** *Virgin OMD 1* ⊛x3	2		33
18 May 91	**SUGAR TAX** *Virgin V 2648* ⊛	3		29
26 Jun 93	**LIBERATOR** *Virgin CDV 2715*	14		6
14 Sep 96	**UNIVERSAL** *Virgin CDV 2807*	24		2
10 Oct 98	**THE OMD SINGLES** *Virgin CDV 2859* ○	16		4

ORCHESTRE NATIONAL DE LA RADIO DIFFUSION FRANCAISE, CONDUCTED BY SIR THOMAS BEECHAM

France, orchestra & UK, male conductor, d. 8 Mar 1961 — 2

Date	Title	Peak Position	Weeks at No.1	Weeks on Chart
26 Mar 60	**CARMEN** *HMV ALP 1762/4*	18		2

ORDINARY BOYS

UK, male vocal/instrumental group — 2

Date	Title	Peak Position	Weeks at No.1	Weeks on Chart
17 Jul 04	**OVER THE COUNTER CULTURE** *B Unique 5046745432* ○	19		4
2 Jul 05	**BRASSBOUND** *B Unique 5046791952* ●	11		9
4 Nov 06	**HOW TO GET EVERYTHING YOU EVER WANTED IN TEN EASY STEPS** *B Unique/Polydor BUN114*	15		9

DOLORES O'RIORDAN
Ireland, female vocalist/guitarist. See Cranberries

Date	Title	Peak Position	Weeks at No.1	2
19 May 07	**ARE YOU LISTENING** *Sequel SEQCD007*	28		2

STACIE ORRICO
US, female vocalist

Date	Title	Peak Position	Weeks at No.1	20
4 Oct 03	**STACIE ORRICO** *Virgin CDVUS 238* ●	37		19
9 Sep 06	**BEAUTIFUL AWAKENING** *Virgin CDVUS283*	64		1

ORSON
US, male vocal/instrumental group – Jason Pebworth, George Astasio, Chris Cano, Johnny Lonely & Kevin Roentgen

Date	Title	Peak Position	Weeks at No.1	26
10 Jun 06	**BRIGHT IDEA** *Mercury 9877384* ⊛	1	1	24
3 Nov 07	**CULTURE VULTURES** *Mercury 1746461*	25		2

BETH ORTON
UK, female vocalist/guitarist

Date	Title	Peak Position	Weeks at No.1	21
26 Oct 96	**TRAILER PARK** *Heavenly HVNLP 17CD*	68		3
27 Mar 99	**CENTRAL RESERVATION** *Heavenly HVNLP 22CD*	17		8
10 Aug 02	**DAYBREAKER** *Heavenly HVNLP 37CD* ○	8		5
4 Oct 03	**PASS IN TIME – THE DEFINITIVE COLLECTION** *Heavenly HVNLP 45CD*	45		2
25 Feb 06	**COMFORT OF STRANGERS** *EMI 3534012*	24		3

JEFFREY OSBORNE
US, male vocalist

Date	Title	Peak Position	Weeks at No.1	10
5 May 84	**STAY WITH ME TONIGHT** *A&M AMLX 64940*	56		7
13 Oct 84	**DON'T STOP** *A&M AMA 5017*	59		3

JOAN OSBORNE
US, female vocalist/guitarist

Date	Title	Peak Position	Weeks at No.1	18
9 Mar 96	**RELISH** *Blues Gorilla 5266922* ●	5		18

KELLY OSBOURNE
UK, female vocalist

Date	Title	Peak Position	Weeks at No.1	3
22 Feb 03	**SHUT UP** *Epic 5094782*	31		2
4 Jun 05	**SLEEPING IN THE NOTHING** *Sanctuary SANCD338*	57		1

OZZY OSBOURNE
UK, male vocalist (John Osbourne). See Black Sabbath

Date	Title	Peak Position	Weeks at No.1	72
20 Sep 80	**OZZY OSBOURNE'S BLIZZARD OF OZ** *Jet JETLP 234* OZZY OSBOURNE'S BLIZZARD OF OZ ○	7		8
7 Nov 81	**DIARY OF A MADMAN** *Jet JETLP 237*	14		12
27 Nov 82	**TALK OF THE DEVIL** *Jet JETDP 401* ○	21		6
10 Dec 83	**BARK AT THE MOON** *Epic EPC 25739* ○	24		7
22 Feb 86	**THE ULTIMATE SIN** *Epic EPC 26404* ○	8		10
23 May 87	**TRIBUTE** *Epic 4504751*	13		6
22 Oct 88	**NO REST FOR THE WICKED** *Epic 4625811*	23		4
17 Mar 90	**JUST SAY OZZY (LIVE)** *Epic 4659401*	69		1
19 Oct 91	**NO MORE TEARS** *Epic 4678591*	17		3
4 Nov 95	**OZZMOSIS** *Epic 4810222*	22		3
15 Nov 97	**THE OZZMAN COMETH – THE BEST OF OZZY OSBOURNE** *Epic 4872602*	68		1
27 Oct 01	**DOWN TO EARTH** *Epic 4984742*	19		3
15 Mar 03	**THE ESSENTIAL** *Epic 5108402*	21		3
10 Dec 05	**UNDER COVER** *Epic 82876743162*	67		1
2 Jun 07	**BLACK RAIN** *Epic 88697101892*	8		4

OSIBISA
Ghana/Nigeria, male vocal/instrumental group

Date	Title	Peak Position	Weeks at No.1	17
22 May 71	**OSIBISA** *MCA MDKS 8001*	11		10
5 Feb 72	**WOYAYA** *MCA MDKS 8005*	11		7

DONNY OSMOND
US, male vocalist. See Osmonds

Date	Title	Peak Position	Weeks at No.1	126
23 Sep 72	**PORTRAIT OF DONNY** *MGM 2315 108*	5		43
16 Dec 72	**TOO YOUNG** *MGM 2315 113*	7		24
26 May 73	**ALONE TOGETHER** *MGM 2315 210* ●	6		19
15 Dec 73	**A TIME FOR US** *MGM 2315 273* ●	4		13
8 Feb 75	**DONNY** *MGM 2315 314* ○	16		4
2 Oct 76	**DISCOTRAIN** *Polydor 2391 226*	59		1
21 Apr 01	**THIS IS THE MOMENT** *Decca Broadway 1587772*	10		3
7 Dec 02	**SOMEWHERE IN TIME** *Decca 0665302* ⊛	12		10
27 Nov 04	**WHAT I MEANT TO SAY** *Decca 9863139*	26		3
17 Mar 07	**LOVE SONGS OF THE 70S** *Decca 1725560* ●	7		4
8 Mar 08	**FROM DONNY WITH LOVE** *Decca 1760974*	8		2

DONNY & MARIE OSMOND
US, male/female vocal duo

Date	Title	Peak Position	Weeks at No.1	19
2 Nov 74	**I'M LEAVING IT ALL UP TO YOU** *MGM 2315 307* ○	13		15
26 Jul 75	**MAKE THE WORLD GO AWAY** *MGM 2315 343*	30		3
5 Jun 76	**DEEP PURPLE** *Polydor 2391 220*	48		1

LITTLE JIMMY OSMOND
US, male vocalist

Date	Title	Peak Position	Weeks at No.1	12
17 Feb 73	**KILLER JOE** *MGM 2315 157*	20		12

MARIE OSMOND
US, female vocalist (Olive Osmond)

Date	Title	Peak Position	Weeks at No.1	1
9 Feb 74	**PAPER ROSES** *MGM 2315 262*	46		1

OSMONDS
US, male vocal group – Alan, Donny, Jay, Merrill & Wayne Osmond

Date	Title	Peak Position	Weeks at No.1	123
18 Nov 72	**OSMONDS LIVE** *MGM 2315 117*	13		22
16 Dec 72	**CRAZY HORSES** *MGM 2315 123*	9		19
25 Aug 73	**THE PLAN** *MGM 2315 251* ●	6		25
17 Aug 74	**OUR BEST TO YOU** *MGM 2315 300* ●	5		20
7 Dec 74	**LOVE ME FOR A REASON** *MGM 2315 312* ○	13		9
14 Jun 75	**I'M STILL GONNA NEED YOU** *MGM 2315 342* ○	19		7
10 Jan 76	**AROUND THE WORLD – LIVE IN CONCERT** *MGM 2659 044* ○	41		1
20 Apr 96	**THE VERY BEST OF THE OSMONDS** *Polydor 5270722*	17		5
12 Jul 03	**ULTIMATE COLLECTION** *Universal TV 9808355*	4		11
31 May 08	**THE VERY BEST OF** *UMTV 9808355* ⊛	11		4

GILBERT O'SULLIVAN
Ireland, male vocalist/pianist

Date	Title	Peak Position	Weeks at No.1	200
25 Sep 71	**GILBERT O'SULLIVAN HIMSELF** *MAM 501*	5		82
18 Nov 72	**BACK TO FRONT** *MAM 502*	1	1	64
6 Oct 73	**I'M A WRITER NOT A FIGHTER** *MAM 505* ●	2		25
26 Oct 74	**STRANGER IN MY OWN BACK YARD** *MAM MAMS 506* ○	9		8
18 Dec 76	**GREATEST HITS** *MAM MAMA 2003* ○	13		11
12 Sep 81	**20 GOLDEN GREATS** *K-Tel NE 1133*	98		1
11 May 91	**NOTHING BUT THE BEST** *Castle Communications CTVLP 107*	50		4
27 Mar 04	**THE BERRY VEST OF** *EMI 5986722* ○	20		5

OTHERS
UK, male vocal/instrumental group

Date	Title	Peak Position	Weeks at No.1	1
12 Feb 05	**THE OTHERS** *Mercury/Poptones 2103607*	51		1

JOHN OTWAY & WILD WILLY BARRETT
UK, male vocal/instrumental duo

Date	Title	Peak Position	Weeks at No.1	1
1 Jul 78	**DEEP AND MEANINGLESS** *Polydor 2382 501*	44		1

OUI 3
UK/US/Switzerland, male/female rap/instrumental group

Date	Title	Peak Position	Weeks at No.1	3
7 Aug 93	**OUI LOVE YOU** *MCA MCD 10833*	39		3

OUTHERE BROTHERS
US, male rap/vocal duo

Date	Title	Peak Position	Weeks at No.1	9
27 May 95	**1 POLISH 2 BISCUITS AND A FISH SANDWICH** *Eternal 0630105852*	56		5
30 Dec 95	**PARTY ALBUM** *Eternal 0630127812*	41		4

OUTKAST
US, male rap/vocal duo – 'André 3000' Benjamin & Antwan 'Big Boi' Patton

Date	Title	Peak Position	Weeks at No.1	74
20 Jan 01	**STANKONIA** *Arista 73008260722*	10		15
11 Oct 03	**SPEAKERBOXXX/THE LOVE BELOW** *Arista 82876529052* ⊛x2 ★	8		56
2 Sep 06	**IDLEWILD** *LaFace 82876757912*	16		3

Top 100 Studio Albums of All Time

Based on UK Sales

Pos	Album Title / Artist	Approx Sales
1	**SGT. PEPPER'S LONELY HEARTS CLUB BAND** BEATLES	4,900,000
2	**WHAT'S THE STORY MORNING GLORY** OASIS	4,400,000
3	**BROTHERS IN ARMS** DIRE STRAITS	4,050,000
4	**THE DARK SIDE OF THE MOON** PINK FLOYD	3,940,000
5	**THRILLER** MICHAEL JACKSON	3,870,000
6	**BAD** MICHAEL JACKSON	3,570,000
7	**STARS** SIMPLY RED	3,400,000
8	**COME ON OVER** SHANIA TWAIN	3,360,000
9	**RUMOURS** FLEETWOOD MAC	3,240,000
10	**BACK TO BEDLAM** JAMES BLUNT	3,170,000
11	**URBAN HYMNS** VERVE	3,160,000
12	**BRIDGE OVER TROUBLED WATER** SIMON & GARFUNKEL	3,050,000
13	**NO ANGEL** DIDO	3,040,000
14	**TALK ON CORNERS** CORRS	2,950,000
15	**BAT OUT OF HELL** MEAT LOAF	2,940,000
16	**SPICE** SPICE GIRLS	2,930,000
17	**BACK TO BLACK** AMY WINEHOUSE	2,910,000
18	**WHITE LADDER** DAVID GRAY	2,900,000
19	**LIFE FOR RENT** DIDO	2,850,000
20	**BUT SERIOUSLY** PHIL COLLINS	2,740,000
21	**SCISSOR SISTERS** SCISSOR SISTERS	2,700,000
22	**A RUSH OF BLOOD TO THE HEAD** COLDPLAY	2,690,000
23	**HOPES AND FEARS** KEANE	2,685,000
24	**THE JOSHUA TREE** U2	2,680,000
25	**THE MAN WHO** TRAVIS	2,670,000
26	**SPIRIT** LEONA LEWIS	2,660,000
27	**TUBULAR BELLS** MIKE OLDFIELD	2,630,000
28	**JAGGED LITTLE PILL** ALANIS MORISSETTE	2,600,000

Pos	Album Title / Artist	Approx Sales
29	**I'VE BEEN EXPECTING YOU** ROBBIE WILLIAMS	2,560,000
30	**X&Y** COLDPLAY	2,540,000
31	**WAR OF THE WORLDS** JEFF WAYNE'S MUSICAL VERSION	2,540,000
32	**BEAUTIFUL WORLD** TAKE THAT	2,535,000
33	**COME AWAY WITH ME** NORAH JONES	2,440,000
34	**TRACY CHAPMAN** TRACY CHAPMAN	2,435,000
35	**PARACHUTES** COLDPLAY	2,435,000
36	**TANGO IN THE NIGHT** FLEETWOOD MAC	2,360,000
37	**ROBSON & JEROME** ROBSON & JEROME	2,335,000
38	**AUTOMATIC FOR THE PEOPLE** REM	2,300,000
39	**THE MARSHALL MATHERS LP** EMINEM	2,250,000
40	**WHITNEY** WHITNEY HOUSTON	2,240,000
41	**GRACELAND** PAUL SIMON	2,240,000
42	**SWING WHEN YOU'RE WINNING** ROBBIE WILLIAMS	2,235,000
43	**EYES OPEN** SNOW PATROL	2,210,000
44	**SING WHEN YOU'RE WINNING** ROBBIE WILLIAMS	2,190,000
45	**DANGEROUS** MICHAEL JACKSON	2,165,000
46	**FALLING INTO YOU** CELINE DION	2,115,000
47	**KYLIE – THE ALBUM** KYLIE MINOGUE	2,100,000
48	**LIFE THRU A LENS** ROBBIE WILLIAMS	2,080,000
49	**APPETITE FOR DESTRUCTION** GUNS N' ROSES	2,070,000
50	**ESCAPOLOGY** ROBBIE WILLIAMS	2,050,000
51	**LET'S TALK ABOUT LOVE** CELINE DION	1,995,000
52	**EMPLOYMENT** KAISER CHIEFS	1,990,000
53	**TRUE BLUE** MADONNA	1,970,000
54	**ABBEY ROAD** BEATLES	1,965,000
55	**BY THE WAY** RED HOT CHILI PEPPERS	1,950,000
56	**NO JACKET REQUIRED** PHIL COLLINS	1,940,000
57	**STRIPPED** CHRISTINA AGUILERA	1,935,000
58	**AMERICAN IDIOT** GREEN DAY	1,930,000
59	**SONGS ABOUT JANE** MAROON 5	1,930,000
60	**A NEW FLAME** SIMPLY RED	1,925,000
61	**NEVERMIND** NIRVANA	1,910,000
62	**JUSTIFIED** JUSTIN TIMBERLAKE	1,900,000
63	**CAN'T SLOW DOWN** LIONEL RICHIE	1,895,000
64	**CALL OFF THE SEARCH** KATIE MELUA	1,860,000
65	**HOT FUSS** KILLERS	1,850,000
66	**THE COLOUR OF MY LOVE** CELINE DION	1,850,000

Pos	Album Title Artist	Approx Sales
67	**PLAY** MOBY	1,845,000
68	**BORN TO DO IT** CRAIG DAVID	1,825,000
69	**BE HERE NOW** OASIS	1,820,000
70	**DEFINITELY MAYBE** OASIS	1,820,000
71	**OUT OF TIME** REM	1,810,000
72	**BAT OUT OF HELL II** MEAT LOAF	1,780,000
73	**MISSUNDAZTOOD** PINK	1,770,000
74	**JUST ENOUGH EDUCATION TO PERFORM** STEREOPHONICS	1,760,000
75	**LET GO** AVRIL LAVIGNE	1,750,000
76	**PARALLEL LINES** BLONDIE	1,740,000
77	**PERFORMANCE AND COCKTAILS** STEREOPHONICS	1,735,000
78	**INTRODUCING THE HARDLINE ACCORDING TO…** TERENCE TRENT D'ARBY	1,730,000
79	**FOUR SYMBOLS** LED ZEPPELIN	1,720,000
80	**SONGBIRD** EVA CASSIDY	1,715,000
81	**OLDER** GEORGE MICHAEL	1,715,000
82	**RAY OF LIGHT** MADONNA	1,700,000
83	**FRIDAY'S CHILD** WILL YOUNG	1,695,000
84	**IN CONCERT** CARRERAS/DOMINGO/PAVAROTTI	1,690,000
85	**FEVER** KYLIE MINOGUE	1,690,000
86	**DEMON DAYS** GORILLAZ	1,685,000
87	**ROCKFERRY** DUFFY	1,685,000
88	**10 GOOD REASONS** JASON DONOVAN	1,680,000
89	**COAST TO COAST** WESTLIFE	1,680,000
90	**FINAL STRAW** SNOW PATROL	1,660,000
91	**ARRIVAL** ABBA	1,655,000
92	**WHITE ON BLONDE** TEXAS	1,645,000
93	**OCEAN DRIVE** LIGHTHOUSE FAMILY	1,635,000
94	**LIKE A VIRGIN** MADONNA	1,630,000
95	**EYE TO THE TELESCOPE** KT TUNSTALL	1,625,000
96	**GOTTA GET THRU THIS** DANIEL BEDINGFIELD	1,625,000
97	**MUSIC** MADONNA	1,615,000
98	**INTENSIVE CARE** ROBBIE WILLIAMS	1,610,000
99	**BORN IN THE USA** BRUCE SPRINGSTEEN	1,595,000
100	**HOTEL CALIFORNIA** EAGLES	1,590,000

OVERLORD X

UK, male rapper (Benjamin Balogun)

Date	Title	Peak	Wks at No.1	1
4 Feb 89	**WEAPON IS MY LYRIC** *Mango Street ILPS 9924*	68		1

MARK OWEN

UK, male vocalist. See Take That

Date	Title	Peak	Wks at No.1	12
14 Dec 96	**GREEN MAN** *RCA 74321435142* ●	33		11
15 Nov 03	**IN YOUR OWN TIME** *Universal MCD 60092*	59		1

OXIDE & NEUTRINO

UK, male production/rap duo

Date	Title	Peak	Wks at No.1	22
6 May 00	**BOUND 4 DA RELOAD (CASUALTY)** *East West OXIDE01T*	71		1
9 Jun 01	**EXECUTE** *East West 8573885612* ●	11		19
12 Oct 02	**2 STEPZ AHEAD** *East West 5046607562* ○	28		2

OZRIC TENTACLES

UK, male vocal/instrumental group

Date	Title	Peak	Wks at No.1	7
31 Aug 91	**STRANGEITUDE** *Dovetail DOVELP 3*	70		1
1 May 93	**JURASSIC SHIFT** *Dovetail DOVELP 6*	11		4
9 Jul 94	**ARBORESCENCE** *Dovetail DOVELP 7*	18		2

P

PADDINGTONS

UK, male vocal/instrumental group

Date	Title	Peak	Wks at No.1	1
12 Nov 05	**FIRST COMES FIRST** *Mercury 9873476*	65		1

JIMMY PAGE

UK, male guitarist. See Coverdale Page, Led Zeppelin, Yardbirds

Date	Title	Peak	Wks at No.1	17
27 Feb 82	**DEATHWISH II (OST)** *Swan Song SSK 59415*	40		4
16 Mar 85	**WHATEVER HAPPENED TO JUGULA?** *Beggars Banquet BEGA 60* ROY HARPER & JIMMY PAGE	44		4
2 Jul 88	**OUTRIDER** *Geffen WX 155*	27		6
19 Nov 94	**NO QUARTER – JIMMY PAGE AND ROBERT PLANT UNLEDDED** *Fontana 5263622* & ROBERT PLANT ●	7		13
2 May 98	**WALKING INTO CLARKSDALE** *Mercury 5583242* & ROBERT PLANT	3		6
22 Jul 00	**LIVE AT THE GREEK** *SPV Recordings SPV 09172022* & THE BLACK CROWES	39		4

ELAINE PAIGE

UK, female vocalist/actor (Elaine Bickerstaff)

Date	Title	Peak	Wks at No.1	160
1 May 82	**ELAINE PAIGE** *WEA K 58385* ○	56		6
5 Nov 83	**STAGES** *K-Tel NE 1262* ⊛x2	2		48
20 Oct 84	**CINEMA** *K-Tel NE 1282* ⊛	12		25
16 Nov 85	**LOVE HURTS** *WEA WX 28* ⊛	8		20
29 Nov 86	**CHRISTMAS** *WEA WX 80* ●	27		6
5 Dec 87	**MEMORIES – THE BEST OF ELAINE PAIGE** *Telstar STAR 2313* ⊛	14		15
19 Nov 88	**THE QUEEN ALBUM** *Siren SRNLP 22* ●	51		8
27 Apr 91	**LOVE CAN DO THAT** *RCA PL 74932*	36		4
28 Nov 92	**THE BEST OF ELAINE PAIGE AND BARBARA DICKSON TOGETHER** *Telstar TCD 2632* & BARBARA DICKSON	22		9
10 Apr 93	**ROMANCE AND THE STAGE** *RCA 74321136152*	71		1
19 Nov 94	**PIAF** *WEA 4509946412* ○	46		3
1 Jul 95	**ENCORE** *WEA 0630104762*	20		6
28 Nov 98	**ON REFLECTION – THE VERY BEST OF ELAINE PAIGE** *Telstar TV/WEA TTVCD 2999*	60		4
5 Jun 04	**CENTRE STAGE** *WSM WSMCD171*	35		4
4 Nov 06	**ESSENTIAL MUSICALS** *UMTV/W14 1709789*	46		1

JENNIFER PAIGE

US, female vocalist

Date	Title	Peak	Wks at No.1	1
31 Oct 98	**JENNIFER PAIGE** *E.A.R. 0039842ERE*	67		1

Silver-selling ◌ Gold-selling ● Platinum-selling ⊛ US No.1 ★ | Peak Position | Weeks at No.1 | Weeks on Chart

PALE FOUNTAINS
UK, male vocal/instrumental group — 3

Date	Title	Label	Peak	Wks at No.1	Wks on Chart
10 Mar 84	PACIFIC STREET	Virgin V 2274	85		2
16 Feb 85	FROM ACROSS THE KITCHEN TABLE	Virgin V 2333	94		1

PALE SAINTS
UK, male/female vocal/instrumental group — 3

Date	Title	Label	Peak	Wks at No.1	Wks on Chart
24 Feb 90	THE COMFORTS OF MADNESS	4AD CAD 0002	40		2
4 Apr 92	IN RIBBONS	4AD CAD 2004CD	61		1

PALLAS
UK, male vocal/instrumental group — 4

Date	Title	Label	Peak	Wks at No.1	Wks on Chart
25 Feb 84	SENTINEL	Harvest SHSP 2400121	41		3
22 Feb 86	THE WEDGE	Harvest SHVL 850	70		1

NERINA PALLOT
UK, female vocalist/guitarist — 16

Date	Title	Label	Peak	Wks at No.1	Wks on Chart
6 May 06	FIRES	Idaho 5101132862 ●	21		16

ROBERT PALMER
UK, male vocalist (Alan Palmer). See Power Station — 166

Date	Title	Label	Peak	Wks at No.1	Wks on Chart
6 Nov 76	SOME PEOPLE CAN DO WHAT THEY LIKE	Island ILPS 9420	46		1
14 Jul 79	SECRETS	Island ILPS 9544	54		4
6 Sep 80	CLUES	Island ILPS 9595	31		8
3 Apr 82	MAYBE IT'S LIVE	Island ILPS 9665	32		6
23 Apr 83	PRIDE	Island ILPS 9720	37		9
16 Nov 85	RIPTIDE	Island ILPS 9801 ●	5		37
9 Jul 88	HEAVY NOVA	EMI EMD 1007 ●	17		25
11 Nov 89	ADDICTIONS VOLUME 1	Island ILPS 9944 ⊛	7		17
17 Nov 90	DON'T EXPLAIN	EMI EMDX 1018 ●	9		20
4 Apr 92	ADDICTIONS VOLUME 2	Island CIDTV 4 ◌	12		7
31 Oct 92	RIDIN' HIGH	EMI CDEMD 1038	32		3
24 Sep 94	HONEY	EMI CDEMD 1069	25		4
28 Oct 95	THE VERY BEST OF ROBERT PALMER	EMI CDEMD 1088 ⊛	4		21
16 Nov 02	AT HIS VERY BEST	Universal TV 697812	38		4

PANIC! AT THE DISCO
US, male vocal/instrumental group – Brendon Urie, Ryan Ross, Spencer Smith & Jon Walker — 30

Date	Title	Label	Peak	Wks at No.1	Wks on Chart
25 Feb 06	A FEVER YOU CAN'T SWEAT OUT	Decaydance/Fueled By Ramen FBR077CD ◌	17		25
5 Apr 08	PRETTY ODD	Decaydance/Fueled By Ramen 7567899507 PANIC AT THE DISCO ◌	2		5

PANTERA
US, male vocal/instrumental group – Phil Anselmo, Darrell & Paul Abbott & Rex Brown — 10

Date	Title	Label	Peak	Wks at No.1	Wks on Chart
7 Mar 92	VULGAR DISPLAYS OF POWER	Atco 7567917582 ●	64		1
2 Apr 94	FAR BEYOND DRIVEN	Atco 7567923752 ● ★	3		4
18 May 96	THE GREAT SOUTHERN TRENDKILL	East West 7556199082	17		3
30 Aug 97	OFFICIAL LIVE – 101 PROOF	East West 7559620682	54		1
8 Apr 00	REINVENTING THE STEEL	Elektra 7559624512 ●	33		1

PAPA ROACH
US, male vocal/instrumental group – Coby Dick, Dave Buckner, Tobin Esperance & Jerry Horton — 46

Date	Title	Label	Peak	Wks at No.1	Wks on Chart
13 Jan 01	INFEST	DreamWorks 4502232 ●	9		36
29 Jun 02	LOVE HATE TRAGEDY	DreamWorks 4503672 ●	4		7
11 Sep 04	GETTING AWAY WITH MURDER	Geffen 9863643	30		2
23 Sep 06	THE PARAMOUR SESSIONS	Geffen 1706231	61		1

VANESSA PARADIS
France, female vocalist — 2

Date	Title	Label	Peak	Wks at No.1	Wks on Chart
7 Nov 92	VANESSA PARADIS	Remark 5139542	45		2

PARADISE LOST
UK, male vocal/instrumental group — 6

Date	Title	Label	Peak	Wks at No.1	Wks on Chart
24 Jun 95	DRACONIAN TIMES	Music For Nations CDMFNX 184	16		3
26 Jul 97	ONE SECOND	Music For Nations CDMFNX 222	31		2
19 Jun 99	HOST	EMI 5205672	61		1

PARAMORE
US, female/male vocal/instrumental group — 21

Date	Title	Label	Peak	Wks at No.1	Wks on Chart
7 Jul 07	RIOT	Fueled By Ramen ATL1596122PMI ●	24		21

MICA PARIS
UK, female vocalist (Michelle Wallen) — 40

Date	Title	Label	Peak	Wks at No.1	Wks on Chart
3 Sep 88	SO GOOD	Fourth & Broadway BRLP 525 ⊛	6		32
27 Oct 90	CONTRIBUTION	Fourth & Broadway BRLP 558 ◌	26		3
26 Jun 93	WHISPER A PRAYER	Fourth & Broadway BRCD 591	20		4
22 Aug 98	BLACK ANGEL	Cooltempo 4958132	59		1

PARIS ANGELS
UK, male/female vocal/instrumental group — 2

Date	Title	Label	Peak	Wks at No.1	Wks on Chart
17 Aug 91	SUNDEW	Virgin V 2667	37		2

JOHN PARISH & POLLY JEAN HARVEY
UK, male producer/multi-instrumentalist & female vocalist. See PJ Harvey — 1

Date	Title	Label	Peak	Wks at No.1	Wks on Chart
5 Oct 96	DANCE HALL AT LOUSE POINT	Island CIDX 8051	46		1

GRAHAM PARKER & THE RUMOUR
UK, male vocal/instrumental group — 35

Date	Title	Label	Peak	Wks at No.1	Wks on Chart
27 Nov 76	HEAT TREATMENT	Vertigo 6360 137	52		2
12 Nov 77	STICK TO ME	Vertigo 9102 017	19		4
27 May 78	PARKERILLA	Vertigo 6641 797	14		5
7 Apr 79	SQUEEZING OUT SPARKS	Vertigo 9102 030	18		8
7 Jun 80	THE UP ESCALATOR	Stiff SEEZ 23	11		10
27 Mar 82	ANOTHER GREY AREA	RCA RCALP 6029 GRAHAM PARKER	40		6

RAY PARKER JR
US, male vocalist/guitarist — 7

Date	Title	Label	Peak	Wks at No.1	Wks on Chart
10 Oct 87	AFTER DARK	Geffen WX 122	40		7

ALEX PARKS
UK, female vocalist — 17

Date	Title	Label	Peak	Wks at No.1	Wks on Chart
6 Dec 03	INTRODUCTION	Polydor 9866005 ⊛	5		15
5 Nov 05	HONESTY	Polydor 9873924	24		2

JOHN PARR
UK, male vocalist — 2

Date	Title	Label	Peak	Wks at No.1	Wks on Chart
2 Nov 85	JOHN PARR	London LONLP 12	60		2

ALAN PARSONS PROJECT
UK, male vocal/instrumental group — 38

Date	Title	Label	Peak	Wks at No.1	Wks on Chart
28 Aug 76	TALES OF MYSTERY AND IMAGINATION	Charisma CDS 4003 ◌	56		1
13 Aug 77	I ROBOT	Arista SPARTY 1016 ◌	30		1
10 Jun 78	PYRAMID	Arista SPART 1054	49		4
29 Sep 79	EVE	Arista SPARTY 1100	74		1
15 Nov 80	THE TURN OF A FRIENDLY CARD	Arista DLART 1	38		4
29 May 82	EYE IN THE SKY	Arista 204 666 ◌	27		11
26 Nov 83	THE BEST OF THE ALAN PARSONS PROJECT	Arista APP 1	99		1
3 Mar 84	AMMONIA AVENUE	Arista 206 100	24		8
23 Feb 85	VULTURE CULTURE	Arista 206 577	40		5
14 Feb 87	GAUDI	Arista 208 084	66		2

PARTISANS
UK, male vocal/instrumental group — 1

Date	Title	Label	Peak	Wks at No.1	Wks on Chart
19 Feb 83	THE PARTISANS	No Future PUNK 4	94		1

DOLLY PARTON
US, female vocalist/guitarist — 78

Date	Title	Label	Peak	Wks at No.1	Wks on Chart
25 Nov 78	BOTH SIDES OF DOLLY PARTON	Lotus WH 5006 ●	24		12
7 Sep 85	GREATEST HITS	RCA PL 84422	74		1
14 Mar 87	TRIO	Warner Brothers 9254911 LINDA RONSTADT & EMMYLOU HARRIS	60		4
22 Oct 94	THE GREATEST HITS	Telstar TCD 2739	65		2
8 Nov 97	A LIFE IN MUSIC – ULTIMATE COLLECTION	RCA 74321443632	38		3

Key: ○ Silver-selling · ● Gold-selling · ⊛ Platinum-selling · ★ US No.1 · Peak Position · Weeks at No.1 · Weeks on Chart

Date	Title / Label	Peak Position	Weeks at No.1	Weeks on Chart
26 Sep 98	**HUNGRY AGAIN** *MCA Nashville UMD 80522*	41		3
24 Feb 01	**LITTLE SPARROW** *Sanctuary SANCD 074* ○	30		6
3 Mar 01	**GOLD – THE HITS COLLECTION** *RCA 74321840202*	23		5
20 Jul 02	**HALOS AND HORNS** *Sanctuary SANCD 126*	37		5
2 Aug 03	**ULTIMATE** *RCA 82876542012*	17		6
4 Mar 06	**THOSE WERE THE DAYS** *EMI 3501422*	35		3
17 Mar 07	**THE VERY BEST OF** *Sony BMG 88697060742*	8		23
21 Jun 08	**BACKWOODS BARBIE** *Dolly 1774178*	35		5

ALAN PARTRIDGE

UK, male comedian (Steve Coogan) — **3**

Date	Title / Label	Peak Position	Weeks at No.1	Weeks on Chart
18 Mar 95	**KNOWING ME, KNOWING YOU 3** *BBC Canned Laughter ZBBC 1671CD*	41		3

PARTRIDGE FAMILY

US, male/female actors/vocal/instrumental group — **15**

Date	Title / Label	Peak Position	Weeks at No.1	Weeks on Chart
8 Jan 72	**UP TO DATE** *Bell SBLL 143*	46		2
22 Apr 72	**THE PARTRIDGE FAMILY SOUND MAGAZINE** *Bell BELLS 206*	14		7
30 Sep 72	**SHOPPING BAG** *Bell BELLS 212*	28		3
9 Dec 72	**CHRISTMAS CARD** *Bell BELLS 214*	45		1
25 Nov 06	**COULD IT BE FOREVER – THE GREATEST HITS** *Sony BMG 88697020582* DAVID CASSIDY & THE PARTRIDGE FAMILY	52		2

PASADENAS

UK, male vocal/instrumental group – John Banfield, Jeff Brown, David & Michael Milliner & Hammish Seelochan — **32**

Date	Title / Label	Peak Position	Weeks at No.1	Weeks on Chart
22 Oct 88	**TO WHOM IT MAY CONCERN** *CBS 4628771* ⊛	3		21
7 Mar 92	**YOURS SINCERELY** *Columbia 4712642* ○	6		11

PASSENGERS

Ireland/UK/Italy, male vocal/instrumental group — **5**

Date	Title / Label	Peak Position	Weeks at No.1	Weeks on Chart
18 Nov 95	**ORIGINAL SOUNDTRACKS 1** *Island CID 8043* ●	12		5

PASSIONS

UK, male/female vocal/instrumental group — **1**

Date	Title / Label	Peak Position	Weeks at No.1	Weeks on Chart
3 Oct 81	**THIRTY THOUSAND FEET OVER CHINA** *Polydor POLS 1041*	92		1

SEAN PAUL

Jamaica, male vocalist (Sean Paul Henriques) — **59**

Date	Title / Label	Peak Position	Weeks at No.1	Weeks on Chart
10 May 03	**DUTTY ROCK** *Atlantic 7567836202* ⊛x2	2		45
8 Oct 05	**THE TRINITY** *VP/Atlantic 7567837882* ●	11		14

LUCIANO PAVAROTTI

Italy, male vocalist, d. 6 Sep 2007 (age 71). Legendary tenor who helped popularise classical music in the late 20th century. He enjoyed mainstream success with José Carreras and Placido Domingo, 'Nessun Dorma' and two volumes of Essential hits. *In Concert* remains the world's best-selling classical album — **309**

Date	Title / Label	Peak Position	Weeks at No.1	Weeks on Chart
15 May 82	**PAVAROTTI'S GREATEST HITS** *Decca D 2362* ●	95		1
30 Jun 84	**MAMMA** *Decca 411959* WITH THE HENRY MANCINI ORCHESTRA	96		1
9 Aug 86	**THE PAVAROTTI COLLECTION** *Stylus SMR 8617* ⊛	12		34
16 Jul 88	**THE NEW PAVAROTTI COLLECTION LIVE!** *Stylus SMR 857*	63		8
17 Mar 90	**THE ESSENTIAL PAVAROTTI** *Decca 4302101* ⊛x3	1	4	72
1 Sep 90	**IN CONCERT** *Decca 4304331* , PLACIDO DOMINGO & JOSE CARRERAS ⊛x5	1	5	78
20 Jul 91	**ESSENTIAL PAVAROTTI II** *Decca 4304701* ⊛	1	2	28
15 Feb 92	**PAVAROTTI IN HYDE PARK** *Decca 4363202* ○	19		7
4 Sep 93	**TI AMO – PUCCINI'S GREATEST LOVE SONGS** *Decca 4250992*	23		4
12 Feb 94	**MY HEART'S DELIGHT** *Decca 4432602* WITH THE ROYAL PHILHARMONIC ORCHESTRA	44		4
10 Sep 94	**THE THREE TENORS IN CONCERT 1994** *Teldec 4509962002* CARRERAS DOMINGO PAVAROTTI WITH ORCHESTRA CONDUCTED BY ZUBIN MEHTA ⊛x2	1	1	26
30 Mar 96	**TOGETHER FOR THE CHILDREN OF BOSNIA** *Decca 4521002*	11		6
14 Dec 96	**PAVAROTTI AND FRIENDS FOR WAR CHILD** *Decca 4529002* & FRIENDS	45		4
25 Oct 97	**THE ULTIMATE COLLECTION** *Decca 4580002*	39		5
29 Aug 98	**THE THREE TENORS PARIS 1998** *Decca 4605002* CARRERAS DOMINGO PAVAROTTI WITH JAMES LEVINE	14		6
19 Jun 99	**LOVE SONGS** *Decca 4664002*	26		6
23 Dec 00	**THE THREE TENORS CHRISTMAS** *Sony Classical SK 89131* CARRERAS/DOMINGO/PAVAROTTI FEATURING MEHTA	57		2
21 Jul 01	**AMORE – THE LOVE ALBUM** *Decca 4701302*	41		2
15 Nov 03	**TI ADORO** *Decca 4754602*	21		4
22 Sep 07	**THE ULTIMATE COLLECTION** *UCJ 9842723*	8		9
16 Feb 08	**LOVE SONGS** *Decca 4766419*	52		2

PAVEMENT

US, male vocal/instrumental group — **13**

Date	Title / Label	Peak Position	Weeks at No.1	Weeks on Chart
25 Apr 92	**SLANTED AND ENCHANTED** *Big Cat ABB 34CD*	72		1
3 Apr 93	**WESTING (BY MUSKET AND SEXTANT)** *Big Cat ABBCD 40*	30		2
26 Feb 94	**CROOKED RAIN CROOKED RAIN** *Big Cat ABB 56CD*	15		3
22 Apr 95	**WOWEE ZOWEE** *Big Cat ABB 84CD*	18		2
22 Feb 97	**BRIGHTEN THE CORNERS** *Domino WIGCD 031*	27		2
19 Jun 99	**TERROR TWILIGHT** *Domino WIGCD 066*	19		3

TOM PAXTON

US, male vocalist/guitarist — **11**

Date	Title / Label	Peak Position	Weeks at No.1	Weeks on Chart
13 Jun 70	**NO. 6** *Elektra 2469 003*	23		5
27 Mar 71	**THE COMPLEAT TOM PAXTON** *Elektra EKD 2003*	18		5
1 Jul 72	**PEACE WILL COME** *Elektra K 44182*	47		1

CANDIE PAYNE

UK, female vocalist — **1**

Date	Title / Label	Peak Position	Weeks at No.1	Weeks on Chart
2 Jun 07	**I WISH I COULD HAVE LOVED YOU MORE** *Deltasonic DLTCD062*	56		1

PEARL JAM

US, male vocal/instrumental group – Eddie Vedder, Jeff Ament, Stone Gossard, Jack Irons, Dave Krusen (replaced by Dave Abbruzzese) & Mike McCready — **124**

Date	Title / Label	Peak Position	Weeks at No.1	Weeks on Chart
7 Mar 92	**TEN** *Epic 4688842* ●	18		65
23 Oct 93	**VS** *Epic 4745492* ● ★	2		24
3 Dec 94	**VITALOGY** *Epic 4778611* ● ★	4		11
7 Sep 96	**NO CODE** *Epic 4844482* ★	3		5
14 Feb 98	**YIELD** *Epic 4893652* ○	7		7
5 Dec 98	**LIVE – ON TWO LEGS** *Epic 4928592*	68		1
27 May 00	**BINAURAL** *Epic 4945902*	5		4
23 Nov 02	**RIOT ACT** *Epic 5100002*	34		2
11 Dec 04	**REARVIEW MIRROR – GREATEST HITS '91-'03** *Epic 5191132*	58		1
13 May 06	**PEARL JAM** *J 82876714672*	5		4

DAVID PEASTON

US, male vocalist — **1**

Date	Title / Label	Peak Position	Weeks at No.1	Weeks on Chart
26 Aug 89	**INTRODUCING...DAVID PEASTON** *Geffen 9242281*	66		1

PEBBLES

US, female vocalist (Perri McKissack) — **4**

Date	Title / Label	Peak Position	Weeks at No.1	Weeks on Chart
14 May 88	**PEBBLES** *MCA MCF 3418*	56		4

PEDDLERS

UK, male vocal/instrumental group — **16**

Date	Title / Label	Peak Position	Weeks at No.1	Weeks on Chart
16 Mar 68	**FREE WHEELERS** *CBS SBPG 63183*	27		13
7 Feb 70	**BIRTHDAY** *CBS 63682*	16		3

KEVIN PEEK

UK, male guitarist. See Sky — **8**

Date	Title / Label	Peak Position	Weeks at No.1	Weeks on Chart
21 Mar 81	**AWAKENING** *Ariola ARL 5065*	52		2
13 Oct 84	**BEYOND THE PLANETS** *Telstar STAR 2244* & RICK WAKEMAN FEATURING JEFF WAYNE NARRATION PATRICK ALLEN	64		6

MARTI PELLOW

UK, male vocalist. See Wet Wet Wet — **18**

Date	Title / Label	Peak Position	Weeks at No.1	Weeks on Chart
7 Jul 01	**SMILE** *Mercury 5860032* ●	7		7
30 Nov 02	**SINGS THE HITS OF WET WET WET & SMILE** *Universal TV 0632902* ●	34		8
29 Nov 03	**BETWEEN THE COVERS** *Universal TV 9812067*	66		1
14 Oct 06	**MOONLIGHT OVER MEMPHIS** *DMG TV DMGTV032*	27		2

Silver-selling ○ Gold-selling ● Platinum-selling ⊛ US No.1 ★ | Peak Position | Weeks at No.1 | Weeks on Chart

JACK PENATE
UK, male vocalist/guitarist — Weeks on Chart: 5

Date	Title	Label	Peak	Wks No.1	Wks
20 Oct 07	**MATINEE**	*XL Recordings XLCD289* ●	7		5

TEDDY PENDERGRASS
US, male vocalist — Weeks on Chart: 15

Date	Title	Label	Peak	Wks No.1	Wks
13 Jul 85	**THE ARTISTS VOLUME 2** LUTHER VANDROSS/TEDDY PENDERGRASS/CHANGE/ATLANTIC STARR	*Street Sounds ARTIS 2*	45		4
21 May 88	**JOY**	*Elektra 9607751*	45		8
20 Mar 04	**SATISFACTION GUARANTEED: THE VERY BEST**	*WSM WSMCD166*	26		3

PENDULUM
Australia, male DJ/production group – Rob Swire, Peredur ap Gwynedd, Paul Harding, Paul Kodish, Gareth McGrillen & Ben Mount — Weeks on Chart: 48

Date	Title	Label	Peak	Wks No.1	Wks
6 Aug 05	**HOLD YOUR COLOUR**	*Breakbeat Kaos BBK002CD*	35		26
24 May 08	**IN SILICO**	*Warner Brothers 82564695661* ●	2		22

PENETRATION
UK, male/female vocal/instrumental group — Weeks on Chart: 8

Date	Title	Label	Peak	Wks No.1	Wks
28 Oct 78	**MOVING TARGETS**	*Virgin V2109*	22		4
6 Oct 79	**COMING UP FOR AIR**	*Virgin V2131*	36		4

PENGUIN CAFÉ ORCHESTRA
UK, male vocal/instrumental group — Weeks on Chart: 5

Date	Title	Label	Peak	Wks No.1	Wks
4 Apr 87	**SIGNS OF LIFE**	*Edition E.G. EGED 50*	49		5

CE CE PENISTON
US, female vocalist (Cecilia Peniston) — Weeks on Chart: 21

Date	Title	Label	Peak	Wks No.1	Wks
8 Feb 92	**FINALLY**	*A&M 3971822* ○	10		19
5 Feb 94	**THOUGHT 'YA KNEW**	*A&M 5402012*	31		2

DAWN PENN
Jamaica, female vocalist (Dawn Pickering) — Weeks on Chart: 2

Date	Title	Label	Peak	Wks No.1	Wks
9 Jul 94	**NO, NO, NO**	*Big Beat 7567923652*	51		2

PENTANGLE
UK, male/female vocal/instrumental group – Jacqui McShee, Terry Cox, Bert Jansch, John Renbourn & Danny Thompson — Weeks on Chart: 39

Date	Title	Label	Peak	Wks No.1	Wks
15 Jun 68	**THE PENTANGLE**	*Transatlantic TRA 162*	21		9
1 Nov 69	**BASKET OF LIGHT**	*Transatlantic TRA 205*	5		28
12 Dec 70	**CRUEL SISTER**	*Transatlantic TRA 228*	51		2

PEPSI & SHIRLIE
UK, female vocal duo — Weeks on Chart: 2

Date	Title	Label	Peak	Wks No.1	Wks
7 Nov 87	**ALL RIGHT NOW**	*Polydor POLH 38*	69		2

A PERFECT CIRCLE
UK, male vocal/instrumental group — Weeks on Chart: 3

Date	Title	Label	Peak	Wks No.1	Wks
3 Jun 00	**MER DE NOMS**	*Virgin CDVUS 173*	55		1
27 Sep 03	**THIRTEENTH STEP**	*Virgin CDVUS 247*	37		2

CARL PERKINS
US, male vocalist — Weeks on Chart: 3

Date	Title	Label	Peak	Wks No.1	Wks
15 Apr 78	**OL' BLUE SUEDES IS BACK**	*Jet UATV 30146*	38		3

KATY PERRY
US, female vocalist/guitarist (Katheryn Hudson) — Weeks on Chart: 14

Date	Title	Label	Peak	Wks No.1	Wks
4 Oct 08	**ONE OF THE BOYS**	*Virgin CAP042492* ●	11		14+

LEE 'SCRATCH' PERRY
Jamaica, male producer/vocalist (Rainford Perry) — Weeks on Chart: 1

Date	Title	Label	Peak	Wks No.1	Wks
26 Jul 97	**ARKOLOGY**	*Island Jamaica CRNCD 6*	49		1

STEVE PERRY
US, male vocalist. See Journey — Weeks on Chart: 3

Date	Title	Label	Peak	Wks No.1	Wks
14 Jul 84	**STREET TALK**	*CBS 25967*	59		2
27 Aug 94	**FOR THE LOVE OF STRANGE MEDICINE**	*Columbia 4771962*	64		1

PESHAY
UK, male DJ/producer (Paul Pesce) — Weeks on Chart: 1

Date	Title	Label	Peak	Wks No.1	Wks
31 Jul 99	**MILES FROM HOME**	*Island Blue PFA 1CD*	63		1

PESTALOZZI CHILDREN'S CHOIR
International, male/female vocal ensemble — Weeks on Chart: 2

Date	Title	Label	Peak	Wks No.1	Wks
26 Dec 81	**SONGS OF JOY**	*K-Tel NE 1140* ●	65		2

PET SHOP BOYS
UK, male vocal/instrumental duo – Neil Tennant & Chris Lowe. Pioneering pop/dance favourites who became synonymous with groundbreaking videos and one-word album titles. Seven of their 16 hit albums have been certified platinum for UK sales of more than 300,000 — Weeks on Chart: 357

Date	Title	Label	Peak	Wks No.1	Wks
5 Apr 86	**PLEASE**	*Parlophone PSB 1* ⊛	3		82
29 Nov 86	**DISCO**	*EMI PRG 1001* ⊛	15		72
19 Sep 87	**PET SHOP BOYS, ACTUALLY**	*Parlophone PCSD 104* ⊛x3	2		59
22 Oct 88	**INTROSPECTIVE**	*Parlophone PCS 7325* ⊛x2	2		39
3 Nov 90	**BEHAVIOUR**	*Parlophone PCSD 113* ⊛	2		14
16 Nov 91	**DISCOGRAPHY**	*Parlophone PMTV 3* ⊛	3		30
9 Oct 93	**VERY**	*Parlophone CDPCSD 143* ⊛	1	1	22
24 Sep 94	**DISCO 2**	*Parlophone CDPCSD 159*	6		4
19 Aug 95	**ALTERNATIVE**	*Parlophone CDPCSD 166* ○	2		5
14 Sep 96	**BILINGUAL**	*Parlophone CDPCSD 170* ●	4		8
23 Oct 99	**NIGHTLIFE**	*Parlophone 5218572* ●	7		3
13 Apr 02	**RELEASE**	*Parlophone 5385982* ○	7		4
15 Feb 03	**DISCO 3**	*Parlophone 5821402*	36		1
6 Dec 03	**POPART – THE HITS**	*Parlophone 5950932* ●	30		9
3 Jun 06	**FUNDAMENTAL**	*Parlophone 3628602* ○	5		4
4 Nov 06	**CONCRETE**	*Parlophone 3774602*	61		1

PETE & THE PIRATES
UK, male vocal/instrumental group — Weeks on Chart: 1

Date	Title	Label	Peak	Wks No.1	Wks
1 Mar 08	**LITTLE DEATH**	*Stolen SR011*	71		1

PETER BJORN & JOHN
Sweden, male vocal/instrumental/production trio — Weeks on Chart: 1

Date	Title	Label	Peak	Wks No.1	Wks
13 Oct 07	**WRITER'S BLOCK**	*Wichita WEBB108CD*	68		1

PETER & GORDON
UK, male vocal/instrumental duo — Weeks on Chart: 1

Date	Title	Label	Peak	Wks No.1	Wks
20 Jun 64	**PETER AND GORDON**	*Columbia 33SX 1630*	18		1

PETER, PAUL & MARY
US, male/female vocal trio — Weeks on Chart: 26

Date	Title	Label	Peak	Wks No.1	Wks
4 Jan 64	**PETER PAUL AND MARY**	*Warner Brothers WM 4064* ★	18		1
21 Mar 64	**IN THE WIND**	*Warner Brothers WM 8142* ★	11		19
13 Feb 65	**IN CONCERT VOLUME 1**	*Warner Brothers WM 8158*	20		2
5 Sep 70	**TEN YEARS TOGETHER**	*Warner Brothers WS 2552*	60		4

PETERS & LEE
UK, male/female vocal/instrumental duo – Lenny Peters, d. 10 Oct 1992, & Dianne Lee — Weeks on Chart: 166

Date	Title	Label	Peak	Wks No.1	Wks
30 Jun 73	**WE CAN MAKE IT**	*Philips 6308 165* ●	1	2	55
22 Dec 73	**BY YOUR SIDE**	*Philips 6308 192* ●	9		48
21 Sep 74	**RAINBOW**	*Philips 6308 208* ●	6		27
4 Oct 75	**FAVOURITES**	*Philips 9109 205* ●	2		32
18 Dec 76	**INVITATION**	*Philips 9101 027* ○	44		4

TOM PETTY & THE HEARTBREAKERS
US, male vocal/instrumental group – Tom Petty, Ron Blair (replaced by Howie Epstein, d. Feb 2003), Mike Campbell, Stan Lynch & Benmont Tench. See Traveling Wilburys — Weeks on Chart: 107

Date	Title	Label	Peak	Wks No.1	Wks
4 Jun 77	**TOM PETTY AND THE HEARTBREAKERS**	*Shelter ISA 5014*	24		12
1 Jul 78	**YOU'RE GONNA GET IT**	*Island ISA 5017*	34		5

Key: ○ Silver-selling · ● Gold-selling · ⊛ Platinum-selling · ★ US No.1 · Peak Position · Weeks at No.1 · Weeks on Chart

Date	Title / Label	Peak Position	Weeks at No.1	Weeks on Chart
17 Nov 79	**DAMN THE TORPEDOES** *MCA MCF 3044*	57		4
23 May 81	**HARD PROMISES** *MCA MCF 3098*	32		5
20 Nov 82	**LONG AFTER DARK** *MCA MCF 3155*	45		4
20 Apr 85	**SOUTHERN ACCENTS** *MCA MCF 3260*	23		6
2 May 87	**LET ME UP (I'VE HAD ENOUGH)** *MCA MCG 6014*	59		2
8 Jul 89	**FULL MOON FEVER** *MCA MCG 6034* TOM PETTY ●	8		16
20 Jul 91	**INTO THE GREAT WIDE OPEN** *MCA 10317* ●	3		18
13 Nov 93	**GREATEST HITS** *MCA MCD 10964* ●	10		20
12 Nov 94	**WILDFLOWERS** *Warner Brothers 9362457592*	36		2
24 Aug 96	**SHE'S THE ONE (OST)** *Warner Brothers 9362462852*	37		2
1 May 99	**ECHO** *Warner Brothers 9362472942*	43		2
16 Jun 01	**ANTHOLOGY – THROUGH THE YEARS** *MCA 1701772* ○	14		6
5 Aug 06	**HIGHWAY COMPANION** *American Recordings 9362442852* TOM PETTY	56		1
14 Jun 08	**GREATEST HITS** *Geffen 1774395*	37		2

MADELEINE PEYROUX
US, female vocalist — 19

Date	Title / Label	Peak Position	Weeks at No.1	Weeks on Chart
19 Mar 05	**CARELESS LOVE** *Rounder 9823583* ●	7		18
11 Nov 06	**HALF THE PERFECT WORLD** *Rounder/UCJ 1703279*	12		9

PHARCYDE
US, male rap group — 2

Date	Title / Label	Peak Position	Weeks at No.1	Weeks on Chart
21 Aug 93	**BIZARRE RIDE II THE PHARCYDE** *Atlantic 7567922222*	58		1
13 Apr 96	**LABCABINCALIFORNIA** *Delicious Vinyl/Go. Beat 8287332*	46		1

P.H.D.
UK, male vocal/instrumental duo — 8

Date	Title / Label	Peak Position	Weeks at No.1	Weeks on Chart
1 May 82	**P.H.D.** *WEA K 99150*	33		8

BARRINGTON PHELOUNG
Australia, male conductor — 55

Date	Title / Label	Peak Position	Weeks at No.1	Weeks on Chart
2 Mar 91	**INSPECTOR MORSE – ORIGINAL MUSIC FROM THE TV SERIES** *Virgin VTLP 2* ⊛	4		30
7 Mar 92	**INSPECTOR MORSE VOLUME 2 – MUSIC FROM THE TV SERIES** *Virgin Television VTCD 14* ○	18		12
16 Jan 93	**INSPECTOR MORSE VOLUME 3** *Virgin VTCD 16* ○	20		11
25 Nov 00	**THE MAGIC OF INSPECTOR MORSE** *Virgin VTDCD 353*	62		2

PHENOMENA
UK, male vocal/instrumental group — 2

Date	Title / Label	Peak Position	Weeks at No.1	Weeks on Chart
6 Jul 85	**PHENOMENA** *Bronze PM 1*	63		2

ARLENE PHILLIPS
UK, female dancer/exercise instructor — 25

Date	Title / Label	Peak Position	Weeks at No.1	Weeks on Chart
28 Aug 82	**KEEP IN SHAPE SYSTEM WITH ARLENE PHILLIPS** *Supershape SUP 01* ●	41		24
18 Feb 84	**KEEP IN SHAPE VOLUME 2** *Supershape SUP 2*	100		1

PHOTEK
UK, male producer (Rupert Parkes) — 9

Date	Title / Label	Peak Position	Weeks at No.1	Weeks on Chart
15 Jun 96	**THE HIDDEN CAMERA** *Science QEDCD 1*	39		1
27 Sep 97	**MODUS OPERANDI** *Science CDQED 1*	30		2
26 Sep 98	**FORM & FUNCTION** *Science CDQED 2*	61		1
21 Jun 80	**THE PHOTOS** *CBS PHOTO 5* PHOTOS	4		9

EDITH PIAF
France, female vocalist (Edith Gassion), d. 11 Oct 1963 (age 47) — 5

Date	Title / Label	Peak Position	Weeks at No.1	Weeks on Chart
26 Sep 87	**HEART AND SOUL** *Stylus SMR 736*	58		5

PIGBAG
UK, male instrumental group — 14

Date	Title / Label	Peak Position	Weeks at No.1	Weeks on Chart
13 Mar 82	**DR. HECKLE AND MR. JIVE** *Y Records Y 17*	18		14

PIGEON DETECTIVES
UK, male vocal/instrumental group – Matt Bowman, Dave Best, Oliver Main, Jimmi Naylor & Ryan Wilson — 57

Date	Title / Label	Peak Position	Weeks at No.1	Weeks on Chart
9 Jun 07	**WAIT FOR ME** *Dance To The Radio DTTR030CD* ⊛	3		41
7 Jun 08	**EMERGENCY** *Dance To The Radio DTTR044* ●	5		16

PILOT
UK, male vocal/instrumental group — 1

Date	Title / Label	Peak Position	Weeks at No.1	Weeks on Chart
31 May 75	**SECOND FLIGHT** *EMI EMC 3075*	48		1

COURTNEY PINE
UK, male saxophonist — 13

Date	Title / Label	Peak Position	Weeks at No.1	Weeks on Chart
25 Oct 86	**JOURNEY TO THE URGE WITHIN** *Island ILPS 9846* ○	39		11
6 Feb 88	**DESTINY'S SONGS AND THE IMAGE OF PURSUANCE** *Anitlles AN 8275*	54		2

P!NK
US, female vocalist (Alecia Moore) — 233

Date	Title / Label	Peak Position	Weeks at No.1	Weeks on Chart
27 May 00	**CAN'T TAKE ME HOME** *LaFace 73008260622* ⊛	13		41
9 Feb 02	**M!SSUNDAZTOOD** *Arista 07822147182* ⊛x5	2		73
22 Nov 03	**TRY THIS** *Arista 82876571852* ⊛	3		24
15 Apr 06	**I'M NOT DEAD** *LaFace 82876803342* ⊛x3	3		86
8 Nov 08	**FUNHOUSE** *LaFace 88697406922*	1	1	9+

Top 3 Best-Selling Albums

		Approximate Sales
1	MISSUNDAZTOOD	1,770,000
2	I'M NOT DEAD	1,245,000
3	FUNHOUSE	590,000

PINK FAIRIES
UK, male vocal/instrumental group — 1

Date	Title / Label	Peak Position	Weeks at No.1	Weeks on Chart
29 Jul 72	**WHAT A BUNCH OF SWEETIES** *Polydor 2383 132*	48		1

PINK FLOYD
UK, male vocal/instrumental group – Syd Barrett, d. 7 Jul 2006 (replaced by David Gilmour*), Nick Mason, Roger Waters* & Rick Wright, d. 15 Sep 2008. In the US, the revered rock band's *The Dark Side Of The Moon* has spent an unprecedented 32 years on the chart, and no UK album has sold more there than *The Wall*, with certified sales of 23 million — 938

Date	Title / Label	Peak Position	Weeks at No.1	Weeks on Chart
19 Aug 67	**THE PIPER AT THE GATES OF DAWN** *EMI SCX 6157*	6		14
13 Jul 68	**SAUCERFUL OF SECRETS** *Columbia SCX 6258*	9		11
28 Jun 69	**MORE (OST)** *Columbia SCX 6346*	9		5
15 Nov 69	**UMMAGUMMA** *Harvest SHDW 1/2*	5		21
24 Oct 70	**ATOM HEART MOTHER** *Harvest SHVL 781*	1	1	23
7 Aug 71	**RELICS** *Starline SRS 5071*	32		6
20 Nov 71	**MEDDLE** *Harvest SHVL 795*	3		82
17 Jun 72	**OBSCURED BY CLOUDS (OST)** *Harvest SHSP 4020* ○	6		14
31 Mar 73	**THE DARK SIDE OF THE MOON** *Harvest SHVL 804* ⊛x9 ★	2		351
19 Jan 74	**A NICE PAIR** *Harvest SHDW 403* ●	21		20
27 Sep 75	**WISH YOU WERE HERE** *Harvest SHVL 814* ● ★	1	1	89
19 Feb 77	**ANIMALS** *Harvest SHVL 815* ●	2		33
8 Dec 79	**THE WALL** *Harvest SHDW 411* ⊛	3		51
5 Dec 81	**A COLLECTION OF GREAT DANCE SONGS** *Harvest SHVL 822* ●	37		10
2 Apr 83	**THE FINAL CUT** *Harvest SHPF 1983* ●	1	2	25
19 Sep 87	**A MOMENTARY LAPSE OF REASON** *EMI EMD 1003* ●	3		34
3 Dec 88	**DELICATE SOUND OF THUNDER** *EMI EQ 5009* ●	11		12
9 Apr 94	**THE DIVISION BELL** *EMI CDEMD 1055* ⊛x2 ★	1	4	51
10 Jun 95	**PULSE** *EMI CDEMD 1078* ⊛x2 ★	1	2	24
9 Mar 96	**RELICS** *EMI CDEMD 7082*	48		2
16 Aug 97	**THE PIPER AT THE GATES OF DAWN** *EMI CDEMD 1073*	44		2
8 Apr 00	**IS THERE ANYBODY OUT THERE? – LIVE** *EMI 5240752* ○	15		5
17 Nov 01	**ECHOES – THE BEST OF PINK FLOYD** *EMI 5361112* ⊛x2	2		23
20 Apr 02	**THE WALL** *EMI CDEMD 1071* ★	64		6
12 Apr 03	**THE DARK SIDE OF THE MOON** *EMI CDEMD 1064*	17		21
16 Jul 05	**WISH YOU WERE HERE** *EMI CDP 7460352*	65		1
15 Sep 07	**THE PIPER AT THE GATES OF DAWN** *EMI 5039192*	22		2

PINK MARTINI
US, male/female vocal/instrumental ensemble — 2

Date	Title / Label	Peak Position	Weeks at No.1	Weeks on Chart
26 May 07	**HEY EUGENE** *Wrasse WRASS193*	47		2

BILLIE PIPER
UK, female vocalist — 27

Date	Title / Label	Peak Position	Weeks at No.1	Weeks on Chart
31 Oct 98	**HONEY TO THE B** *Innocent CDSIN 1* ⊛	14		23
14 Oct 00	**WALK OF LIFE** *Innocent CDSINX 3* ○	14		4

Madonna

Like A Virgin

'TRANSIENT pop fluff' could have been Madonna's epitaph had it not been for this career-defining album, the platform from which la Ciccone launched her irresistible brand of world domination. Madonna had, of course, had some considerable success before *Like A Virgin*. Singles 'Holiday', 'Lucky Star' and the wistful 'Borderline' (which some would argue is the best of the three) had established her in the charts after early club success, and Sire/Warner clearly recognised a potential beyond the one- or two-hit-wonder status that her early releases might have predicted. A Top 10 eponymous first album cemented her potential.

However, by pop's unforgiving and ultra-youthful standards, Madonna was no spring chicken. By the time *Virgin* was a hit she was in her mid-twenties. As Blondie's Debbie Harry had managed before her, Madonna presented an image of knowing maturity with breathtaking ease while at the same time pulling off the sex-kitten persona. And, like Debbie, she retained her own cool and composure in the process. The *Like A Virgin* album sleeve – shot by Steven Meisel, who went on to shoot her for the highly controversial *Sex* book – typified this. The vulnerable upward glance, the shyly lowered forehead and retracted chin, the suspicious stare, all contrast with the passionate, unruly hair, the more-than-ample cleavage: a woman with a sophisticated message.

Madonna blended street dancer with porn star, bride with bitch, cheap with chic

The title track, its video shot around Venice, Italy, on gondolas and inside the city's majestic houses, was a joy – especially for the tourists who can be seen on the bridges of the city, watching Madonna cavorting onboard. She had already launched the song at the MTV Music Awards, dressed provocatively in a white wedding dress while ensuring that her garter belt and panties were equally visible. Released in November 1984, the 'Like A Virgin' single was a Number 1 hit in America and Top 3 in the UK. Madonna blended street dancer with porn star, bride with bitch, cheap with chic.

While a thousand pop careers have floundered on far higher budgets, the response to Madonna's visual image was astonishing. Straightaway the Madonna look was copied by girls across the globe – not only did she look great, but she gave them a look that could be easily achieved: wrapped in beads and bracelets, she taught teenage girls how to accessorise the Madonna way.

Her great success was to realise that in order to keep ahead of the game she had to *constantly* change her image. Like David Bowie before her, she managed to surprise her increasing legion of fans with changes of costume, hair or musical style at every turn. The Beatles were a different band on each of their albums, and Bowie had been a different character five times in one show; Madonna understood this dynamic perfectly, and knew exactly how to get headlines. Having seen Bowie finally achieve a level of mainstream global fame with *Let's Dance*, Madonna brought in much of the same back-room team from that album. Chic's Nile Rogers and Bernard Edwards, Tony Thompson on drums and backing singers Frank and George Sims gave the album musical clout, and Madonna shared the production credit with

Chart History Artist	Album Title	First Chart Week	Weeks on Chart	Highest Position
MADONNA	LIKE A VIRGIN	24/11/84	152	1

Rogers and Steven Bray, her co-writer on many of the tracks.

Musically, *Like A Virgin* had more hooks than was decent on most singles. It's hard not to read out the track-listing and instantly hear the iconic melodies from titles such as 'Dress You Up', 'Over And Over' and, of course, the career-defining songs such as 'Material Girl' and the album's eponymous title track. Although some critics berated her vocals as too shrill and without real substance (and most major award ceremonies, such as the Grammys, snubbed her), the passage of time reveals a selection of hooks, keyboard riffs, disco beats and controversial lyrics that make *Like A Virgin* undoubtedly one of the foundation blocks of 1980s pop.

Madonna's quasi-religious name and the reference to virginity ensured that a controversy built up around her – a swirling publicity-grabbing characteristic that she would use to great effect for most of the next two decades. By the time 'Material Girl' was released in early 1985, she surprised again, this time with a style svelte and Marilyn-esque, the sentiment perfect for the Wall Street and Thatcherite generation. 'Angel' and 'Crazy For You' followed, again hitting the top reaches of the charts. However, it was a track not originally on the album – 'Into The Groove', originally the B-side to 'Angel' – that really confirmed Madonna's place in the major league. By the summer of 1985, the movie *Desperately Seeking Susan* had established her versatility, and her appearance at Live Aid confirmed to doubters that – among the plodding and aged – here was a girl who could really perform. Quick as a flash, the album was re-released in Europe with 'Into The Groove' now included. The video, using scenes from the movie, caught the public's imagination, big time, with Madonna's armpits perhaps the true stars of the show.

The boys all fancied her and their dads kept worryingly quiet

Teenage girls across the globe fell for her again and again. Shy girls found a route to confidence; ballsy ones found a soulmate. The boys all fancied her and their dads kept worryingly quiet. Madonna was now on every bedroom wall, magazine and music show. By the time of her next album, *True Blue*, she would hit pay dirt on a global scale. But *Like A Virgin* is the record that made Madonna a mega-star and, after twenty years, it is an album that remains hard to resist.

Like A Virgin

Silver-selling · Gold-selling · Platinum-selling · US No.1 ★ · Peak Position · Weeks at No.1 · Weeks on Chart

PIPETTES
UK, female vocal trio — Weeks on Chart: 1

Date	Album	Peak Position	Weeks at No.1	Weeks on Chart
29 Jul 06	**WE ARE THE PIPETTES** *Memphis Industries MI072CD*	41		1

PIRANHAS
UK, male vocal/instrumental group — Weeks on Chart: 3

Date	Album	Peak Position	Weeks at No.1	Weeks on Chart
20 Sep 80	**PIRANHAS** *Sire SRK 6098*	69		3

PIRATES
UK, male vocal/instrumental group — Weeks on Chart: 3

Date	Album	Peak Position	Weeks at No.1	Weeks on Chart
19 Nov 77	**OUT OF THEIR SKULLS** *Warner Brothers K 56411*	57		3

PITCHSHIFTER
UK, male vocal/instrumental group — Weeks on Chart: 2

Date	Album	Peak Position	Weeks at No.1	Weeks on Chart
3 Jun 00	**DEVIANT** *MCA 1122542*	35		1
11 May 02	**PSI** *Mayan MYNCD 004*	54		1

GENE PITNEY
US, male vocalist, d. 5 Apr 2006 (age 66) — Weeks on Chart: 75

Date	Album	Peak Position	Weeks at No.1	Weeks on Chart
11 Apr 64	**BLUE GENE** *United Artists ULP 1061*	7		11
6 Feb 65	**GENE PITNEY'S BIG SIXTEEN** *Stateside SL 10118*	12		6
20 Mar 65	**I'M GONNA BE STRONG** *Stateside SL 10120*	15		2
20 Nov 65	**LOOKIN' THRU THE EYES OF LOVE** *Stateside SL 10148*	15		5
17 Sep 66	**NOBODY NEEDS YOUR LOVE** *Stateside SL 10183*	13		17
4 Mar 67	**YOUNG WARM AND WONDERFUL** *Stateside SSL 10194*	39		1
22 Apr 67	**GENE PITNEY'S BIG SIXTEEN** *Stateside SSL 10199*	40		1
20 Sep 69	**BEST OF GENE PITNEY** *Stateside SSL 10286*	8		9
2 Oct 76	**HIS 20 GREATEST HITS** *Arcade ADEP 22*	6		14
20 Oct 90	**BACKSTAGE – THE GREATEST HITS AND MORE** *Polydor 8471191*	17		7
22 Sep 01	**THE ULTIMATE COLLECTION** *Sequel NEECD 380*	40		2

PIXIES
US, male/female vocal/instrumental group – Frank Black*, Kim Deal, David Lovering & Joey Santiago — Weeks on Chart: 34

Date	Album	Peak Position	Weeks at No.1	Weeks on Chart
29 Apr 89	**DOOLITTLE** *4AD CAD 905*	8		9
25 Aug 90	**BOSSANOVA** *4AD CAD 0010*	3		8
5 Oct 91	**TROMPE LE MONDE** *4AD CAD 1014*	7		5
18 Oct 97	**DEATH TO THE PIXIES** *4AD DAD 7011CD*	28		3
18 Oct 97	**DEATH TO THE PIXIES – DELUXE EDITION** *4AD DADD 7011CD*	20		2
18 Jul 98	**PIXIES AT THE BBC** *4AD GAD 8013CD*	45		1
17 Mar 01	**THE COMPLETE B-SIDES** *4AD GAD 2103CD*	53		1
15 May 04	**BEST OF – WAVE OF MUTILATION** *4AD CAD 2406CD*	16		5

PLACEBO
Belgium/Sweden/UK, male vocal/instrumental group – Brian Molko, Stefan Olsdal & Robert Schultzberg (replaced by Steve Hewitt) — Weeks on Chart: 56

Date	Album	Peak Position	Weeks at No.1	Weeks on Chart
29 Jun 96	**PLACEBO** *Elevator Music CDFLOORX 002*	5		13
24 Oct 98	**WITHOUT YOU I'M NOTHING** *Hut CDFLOOR 8*	7		17
21 Oct 00	**BLACK MARKET MUSIC** *Hut CDFLORXX 13*	6		5
5 Apr 03	**SLEEPING WITH GHOSTS** *Hut CDFLOOR 17*	11		10
4 Oct 03	**SLEEPING WITH GHOSTS** *Hut CDFLOORX 17*	50		1
6 Nov 04	**ONCE MORE WITH FEELING – SINGLES 1996-2004** *Virgin CDFLOORX23*	8		6
25 Mar 06	**MEDS** *Virgin CDFLOORX26*	7		4

PLAIN WHITE T'S
US, male vocal/instrumental group – Tom Higgenson, De'Mar Hamilton, Tim Lopez, Mike Retondo & Dave Tirio — Weeks on Chart: 10

Date	Album	Peak Position	Weeks at No.1	Weeks on Chart
15 Sep 07	**EVERY SECOND COUNTS** *Hollywood/Angel CDANGE46*	3		10

PLAN B
UK, male rapper/DJ (Ben Drew) — Weeks on Chart: 3

Date	Album	Peak Position	Weeks at No.1	Weeks on Chart
8 Jul 06	**WHO NEEDS ACTIONS WHEN YOU GOT WORDS** *679 5101149792*	30		3

PLANETS
UK, male/female instrumental group — Weeks on Chart: 13

Date	Album	Peak Position	Weeks at No.1	Weeks on Chart
2 Mar 02	**CLASSICAL GRAFFITI** *EMI/Dramatico CD5573162*	34		13

ROBERT PLANT
UK, male vocalist. See Honeydrippers, Led Zeppelin — Weeks on Chart: 133

Date	Album	Peak Position	Weeks at No.1	Weeks on Chart
10 Jul 82	**PICTURES AT ELEVEN** *Swan Song SSK 59418*	2		15
23 Jul 83	**THE PRINCIPLE OF MOMENTS** *Atlantic 7901011*	7		14
1 Jun 85	**SHAKEN 'N' STIRRED** *Es Paranza 7902651*	19		4
12 Mar 88	**NOW AND ZEN** *Es Paranza WX 149*	10		7
31 Mar 90	**MANIC NIRVANA** *Es Paranza WX 339*	15		9
5 Jun 93	**FATE OF NATIONS** *Es Paranza 5148672*	6		8
19 Nov 94	**NO QUARTER – JIMMY PAGE AND ROBERT PLANT UNLEDDED** *Fontana 5263622* JIMMY PAGE & ROBERT PLANT	7		13
2 May 98	**WALKING INTO CLARKSDALE** *Mercury 5583242* JIMMY PAGE & ROBERT PLANT	3		6
6 Jul 02	**DREAMLAND** *Mercury 5869632*	20		3
15 Nov 03	**SIXTY SIX TO TIMBUKTU** *Mercury 9813199*	27		3
14 May 05	**MIGHTY REARRANGER** *Sanctuary SANCD356* & STRANGE SENSATION	4		7
10 Nov 07	**RAISING SAND** *Rounder 4759382* & ALISON KRAUSS	2		44

PLASMATICS
US, female/male vocal/instrumental group — Weeks on Chart: 3

Date	Album	Peak Position	Weeks at No.1	Weeks on Chart
11 Oct 80	**NEW HOPE FOR THE WRETCHED** *Stiff SEEZ 24*	55		3

PLASTIK MAN
Canada, male DJ/producer (Richie Hawtin). See F.U.S.E — Weeks on Chart: 1

Date	Album	Peak Position	Weeks at No.1	Weeks on Chart
19 Nov 94	**MUSIK** *Novamute NOMU 37CD*	58		1

PLATTERS
US, male/female vocal group – Tony Williams, David Lynch, Herb Reed, Paul Robi & Zola Taylor — Weeks on Chart: 22

Date	Album	Peak Position	Weeks at No.1	Weeks on Chart
8 Apr 78	**20 CLASSIC HITS** *Mercury 9100 049*	8		13
10 May 08	**THE VERY BEST OF** *Universal TV UMTV7944*	8		9

PLAYERS ASSOCIATION
US, male vocal/instrumental group — Weeks on Chart: 4

Date	Album	Peak Position	Weeks at No.1	Weeks on Chart
17 Mar 79	**TURN THE MUSIC UP** *Vanguard VSD 79421*	54		4

PLAYN JAYN
UK, male vocal/instrumental group — Weeks on Chart: 1

Date	Album	Peak Position	Weeks at No.1	Weeks on Chart
1 Sep 84	**FRIDAY THE 13TH (AT THE MARQUEE CLUB)** *A&M JAYN 13*	93		1

PLUS 44
US, male vocal/instrumental group — Weeks on Chart: 1

Date	Album	Peak Position	Weeks at No.1	Weeks on Chart
25 Nov 06	**WHEN YOUR HEART STOPS BEATING** *Interscope 1712627*	50		1

PM DAWN
US, rap duo – Attrell & Jarrett Cordes — Weeks on Chart: 17

Date	Album	Peak Position	Weeks at No.1	Weeks on Chart
14 Sep 91	**OF THE HEART, OF THE SOUL AND THE CROSS – THE UTOPIAN EXPERIENCE** *Gee Street GEEA 7*	8		12
3 Apr 93	**THE BLISS ALBUM...? (VIBRATIONS OF LOVE AND ANGER AND THE PONDERANCE OF LIFE AND EXISTENCE)** *Gee Street GEED 9*	9		5

P.O.D.
US, male vocal/instrumental group — Weeks on Chart: 6

Date	Album	Peak Position	Weeks at No.1	Weeks on Chart
19 Jan 02	**SATELLITE** *Atlantic 7567834752*	16		6

POGUES
UK, male vocal/instrumental group – Shane MacGowan*, James Fearnley, Jem Finer, Caitlin O'Riordan & Andrew Rankin — Weeks on Chart: 92

Date	Album	Peak Position	Weeks at No.1	Weeks on Chart
3 Nov 84	**RED ROSES FOR ME** *Stiff SEEZ 55*	89		1
17 Aug 85	**RUM, SODOMY AND THE LASH** *Stiff SEEZ 58*	13		14
30 Jan 88	**IF I SHOULD FALL FROM GRACE WITH GOD** *Stiff NYR 1*	3		16
29 Jul 89	**PEACE AND LOVE** *Pogue Mahone WX 247*	5		8
13 Oct 90	**HELL'S DITCH** *Pogue Mahone WX 366*	12		5
12 Oct 91	**THE BEST OF THE POGUES** *PM WX 430*	11		17
11 Sep 93	**WAITING FOR HERB** *PM 4509934632*	20		3
17 Mar 01	**THE VERY BEST OF** *warner.esp 8573874592*	18		22
19 Mar 05	**THE ULTIMATE COLLECTION** *WSM 2564622542*	15		6

Silver-selling ○ · Gold-selling ● · Platinum-selling ⊛ · US No.1 ★ · Peak Position · Weeks at No.1 · Weeks on Chart

POINT BREAK
UK, male vocal group — 3

Date	Title	Peak Position	Weeks at No.1	Weeks on Chart
19 Aug 00	**APOCADELIC** *Eternal 8573828882*	21		3

POINTER SISTERS
US, female vocal group – Anita, Bonnie, June, d. 11 Apr 2006, & Ruth Pointer — 88

Date	Title	Peak Position	Weeks at No.1	Weeks on Chart
29 Aug 81	**BLACK AND WHITE** *Planet K 52300*	21		13
5 May 84	**BREAK OUT** *Planet PL 84705* ●	9		58
27 Jul 85	**CONTACT** *Planet PL 85457*	34		7
29 Jul 89	**JUMP – THE BEST OF THE POINTER SISTERS** *RCA PL 90319* ●	11		10

POISON
US, male vocal/instrumental group – Bret Michaels, Bobby Dall, C.C. DeVille (replaced by Richie Kotzen) & Rikki Rockett — 37

Date	Title	Peak Position	Weeks at No.1	Weeks on Chart
21 May 88	**OPEN UP AND SAY...AAH!** *Capitol EST 2059* ●	18		21
21 Jul 90	**FLESH AND BLOOD** *Capitol EST 2126* ●	3		11
14 Dec 91	**SWALLOW THIS LIVE** *Capitol ESTU 2159*	52		2
6 Mar 93	**NATIVE TONGUE** *Capitol CDESTU 2190*	20		3

POLECATS
UK, male vocal/instrumental group — 2

Date	Title	Peak Position	Weeks at No.1	Weeks on Chart
4 Jul 81	**POLECATS** *Vertigo 6359 057*	28		2

POLICE
UK/US, male vocal/instrumental trio – Sting* (Gordon Sumner), Stewart Copeland & Andy Summers. This internationally-acclaimed act were one of the top album sellers of the 1980s. The multi-award-winners had five successive albums enter at No.1. Their 2008 re-union resulted in one of the world's top-earning tours of all time — 424

Date	Title	Peak Position	Weeks at No.1	Weeks on Chart
21 Apr 79	**OUTLANDOS D'AMOUR** *A&M AMLH 68502* ⊛	6		96
13 Oct 79	**REGGATTA DE BLANC** *A&M AMLH 64792* ⊛	1	4	74
11 Oct 80	**ZENYATTA MONDATTA** *A&M AMLH 64831* ⊛	1	4	31
10 Oct 81	**GHOST IN THE MACHINE** *A&M AMLK 63730* ⊛	1	3	27
25 Jun 83	**SYNCHRONICITY** *A&M AMLX 63735* ⊛ ★	1	2	48
8 Nov 86	**EVERY BREATH YOU TAKE – THE SINGLES** *A&M EVERY 1* ⊛x4	1	2	55
10 Oct 92	**GREATEST HITS** *A&M 5400302* ●	10		21
10 Jun 95	**LIVE!** *A&M 5402222*	25		3
22 Nov 97	**THE VERY BEST OF STING AND THE POLICE** *A&M 5404282* STING & THE POLICE ⊛	1	2	50
23 Jun 07	**THE POLICE** *A&M/Polydor 1736144* ●	3		19

SU POLLARD
UK, female actor/vocalist — 3

Date	Title	Peak Position	Weeks at No.1	Weeks on Chart
22 Nov 86	**SU** *K-Tel NE 1327* ○	86		3

POLYPHONIC SPREE
US, male/female vocal/instrumental ensemble — 2

Date	Title	Peak Position	Weeks at No.1	Weeks on Chart
12 Jul 03	**THE BEGINNING STAGES OF** *679 Recordings 5046609182* ○	70		1
24 Jul 04	**TOGETHER WE'RE HEAVY** *Good POLYCD1*	61		1

IGGY POP
US, male vocalist (James Jewel Osterburg) — 27

Date	Title	Peak Position	Weeks at No.1	Weeks on Chart
9 Apr 77	**THE IDIOT** *RCA Victor PL 12275*	30		3
4 Jun 77	**RAW POWER** *Embassy 31464* & THE STOOGES	44		2
1 Oct 77	**LUST FOR LIFE** *RCA Victor PL 12488*	28		5
19 May 79	**NEW VALUES** *Arista SPART 1092*	60		4
16 Feb 80	**SOLDIER** *Arista SPART 1117*	62		2
11 Oct 86	**BLAH BLAH BLAH** *A&M AMA 5145*	43		7
2 Jul 88	**INSTINCT** *A&M AMA 5198*	61		1
21 Jul 90	**BRICK BY BRICK** *Virgin America VUSLP 19*	50		2
25 Sep 93	**AMERICAN CAESAR** *Virgin CDVUS 64*	43		1

POP WILL EAT ITSELF
UK, male vocal/instrumental group — 14

Date	Title	Peak Position	Weeks at No.1	Weeks on Chart
13 May 89	**THIS IS THE DAY...THIS IS THE HOUR...THIS IS THIS?** *RCA PL 74141*	24		2
3 Nov 90	**CURE FOR SANITY** *RCA PL 74828*	33		3
19 Sep 92	**THE LOOKS OR THE LIFESTYLE** *RCA 74321102650*	15		3
6 Mar 93	**WEIRD'S BAR AND GRILLS** *RCA 74321133432*	44		1
6 Nov 93	**16 DIFFERENT FLAVOURS OF HELL** *RCA 74321153172*	73		1
1 Oct 94	**DOS DEDOS MIS AMIGOS** *Infectious INFECT 10CDX*	11		2
18 Mar 95	**TWO FINGERS MY FRIENDS?** *Infectious INFECT 10CDRX*	25		2

POPE JOHN PAUL II
Poland, male pontiff (Karol Jozef Wojtyla), d. 2 Apr 2005 (age 84) — 8

Date	Title	Peak Position	Weeks at No.1	Weeks on Chart
3 Jul 82	**JOHN PAUL II – THE PILGRIM POPE** *BBC REB 445*	71		4
10 Dec 94	**THE ROSARY** *Pure Music PMCD 7009* /FATHER COLM KILCOYNE	50		4

PORCUPINE TREE
UK, male vocal/instrumental group — 1

Date	Title	Peak Position	Weeks at No.1	Weeks on Chart
28 Apr 07	**FEAR OF A BLANK PLANET** *Roadrunner RR80115*	31		1

PORNO FOR PYROS
US, male vocal/instrumental group — 5

Date	Title	Peak Position	Weeks at No.1	Weeks on Chart
8 May 93	**PORNO FOR PYROS** *Warner Brothers 9362452282*	13		3
8 Jun 96	**GOOD GOD'S URGE** *Warner Brothers 9362460522*	40		2

PORTISHEAD
UK, female/male vocal/instrumental trio – Beth Gibbons*, Geoff Barrow & Adrian Utley — 105

Date	Title	Peak Position	Weeks at No.1	Weeks on Chart
3 Sep 94	**DUMMY** *Go. Beat 8285222* ⊛x2	2		75
11 Oct 97	**PORTISHEAD** *Go. Beat 5391892* ●	2		22
14 Nov 98	**PNYC** *Go. Beat 5594242*	40		2
10 May 08	**THIRD** *Island 1764013* ●	2		6

SANDY POSEY
US, female vocalist — 1

Date	Title	Peak Position	Weeks at No.1	Weeks on Chart
11 Mar 67	**BORN A WOMAN** *MGM MGMCS 8035*	39		1

PAUL POTTS
UK, male vocalist — 15

Date	Title	Peak Position	Weeks at No.1	Weeks on Chart
28 Jul 07	**ONE CHANCE** *Syco Music 88697138682* ⊛	1	3	10
8 Dec 07	**ONE CHANCE – CHRISTMAS EDITION** *Syco Music 88697189862*	19		5

FRANK POURCEL
France, male orchestra leader, d. 12 Nov 2000 (age 87) — 7

Date	Title	Peak Position	Weeks at No.1	Weeks on Chart
20 Nov 71	**THIS IS POURCEL** *Studio Two STWO 7*	8		7

COZY POWELL
UK, male drummer, d. 5 Apr 1998 (age 50) — 8

Date	Title	Peak Position	Weeks at No.1	Weeks on Chart
26 Jan 80	**OVER THE TOP** *Ariola ARL 5038*	34		3
19 Sep 81	**TILT** *Polydor POLD 5047*	58		4
28 May 83	**OCTOPUSS** *Polydor POLD 5093*	86		1

PETER POWELL
UK, male DJ/exercise instructor — 13

Date	Title	Peak Position	Weeks at No.1	Weeks on Chart
20 Mar 82	**KEEP FIT AND DANCE** *K-Tel NE 1167* ●	9		13

POWER STATION
UK/US, male vocal/instrumental group — 23

Date	Title	Peak Position	Weeks at No.1	Weeks on Chart
6 Apr 85	**THE POWER STATION** *Parlophone POST 1* ●	12		23

DANIEL POWTER
Canada, male vocalist/pianist — 22

Date	Title	Peak Position	Weeks at No.1	Weeks on Chart
20 Aug 05	**DANIEL POWTER** *Warner Brothers 9362493322*	5		21
27 Sep 08	**UNDER THE RADAR** *Warner Brothers 9362498211*	43		1

PRAYING MANTIS
UK, male vocal/instrumental group — 2

Date	Title	Peak Position	Weeks at No.1	Weeks on Chart
11 Apr 81	**TIME TELLS NO LIES** *Arista SPART 1153*	60		2

Silver-selling ○ Gold-selling ● Platinum-selling ⊛ US No.1 ★ | Peak Position | Weeks at No.1 | Weeks on Chart

PREFAB SPROUT

UK, male vocal/instrumental group – Paddy McAloon, Martin McAloon, Mick Salmon (replaced by Neil Conti) & Wendy Smith — 106

Date	Title	Peak Position	Weeks at No.1	Weeks on Chart
17 Mar 84	**SWOON** *Kitchenware KWLP 1*	22		7
22 Jun 85	**STEVE McQUEEN** *Kitchenware KWLP 3* ●	21		35
26 Mar 88	**FROM LANGLEY PARK TO MEMPHIS** *Kitchenware KWLP 9* ●	5		24
1 Jul 89	**PROTEST SONGS** *Kitchenware KWLP 4* ○	18		4
8 Sep 90	**JORDAN: THE COMEBACK** *Kitchenware KWLP 14* ●	7		17
11 Jul 92	**A LIFE OF SURPRISES – THE BEST OF PREFAB SPROUT** *Kitchenware 4718862* ●	3		13
17 May 97	**ANDROMEDA HEIGHTS** *Kitchenware KWCD 30*	7		5
30 Jun 01	**THE GUNMAN AND OTHER STORIES** *Liberty 5326132*	60		1

PRESIDENTS OF THE UNITED STATES OF AMERICA

US, male vocal/instrumental group — 31

Date	Title	Peak Position	Weeks at No.1	Weeks on Chart
13 Jan 96	**THE PRESIDENTS OF THE UNITED STATES OF AMERICA** *Columbia 4810392* ●	14		29
16 Nov 96	**II** *Columbia 4850922*	36		2

ELVIS PRESLEY

US, male vocalist/actor. 'The King' of rock 'n' roll has sold more records, had more hits and collected more awards around the globe than any other artist. The most imitated and influential entertainer of all time has a 46-year chart span of No.1 albums — 1333

Date	Title	Peak Position	Weeks at No.1	Weeks on Chart
3 Nov 56	**ROCK 'N' ROLL** *HMV CLP 1093*	1	1	16
4 May 57	**ROCK 'N' ROLL NO.2** *HMV CLP 1105*	3		3
31 Aug 57	**LOVING YOU (OST)** *RCA RD 24001*	1	3	25
26 Oct 57	**BEST OF ELVIS** *HMV DLP 1159*	3		7
30 Nov 57	**ELVIS'S CHRISTMAS ALBUM** *RCA RD 27052* ★	2		6
13 Sep 58	**KING CREOLE (OST)** *RCA RD 27088*	1	7	22
11 Oct 58	**ELVIS' GOLDEN RECORDS** *RCA RB 16069*	2		48
8 Aug 59	**A DATE WITH ELVIS** *RCA RD 27128*	4		15
18 Jun 60	**ELVIS' GOLDEN RECORDS VOLUME 2** *RCA RD 27159*	4		20
23 Jul 60	**ELVIS IS BACK!** *RCA RD 27171*	1	1	27
10 Dec 60	**G.I. BLUES (OST)** *RCA RD 27192* ★	1	22	55
20 May 61	**HIS HAND IN MINE** *RCA RD 27211*	3		25
4 Nov 61	**SOMETHING FOR EVERYBODY** *RCA RD 27224* ★	2		18
9 Dec 61	**BLUE HAWAII (OST)** *RCA RD 27238*	1	18	65
7 Jul 62	**POT LUCK** *RCA RD 27265*	1	6	25
8 Dec 62	**ROCK 'N' ROLL NO. 2** *RCA Victor RD 7528*	3		17
26 Jan 63	**GIRLS! GIRLS! GIRLS! (OST)** *RCA Victor RD 7534*	2		21
11 May 63	**IT HAPPENED AT THE WORLD'S FAIR (OST)** *RCA Victor RD 7565*	4		21
28 Dec 63	**FUN IN ACAPULCO (OST)** *RCA Victor RD 7609*	9		14
11 Apr 64	**ELVIS' GOLDEN RECORDS VOLUME 3** *RCA Victor RD 7630*	6		13
4 Jul 64	**KISSIN' COUSINS (OST)** *RCA Victor RD 7645*	5		17
9 Jan 65	**ROUSTABOUT (OST)** *RCA Victor RD 7678* ★	12		4
1 May 65	**GIRL HAPPY (OST)** *RCA Victor RD 7714*	7		18
25 Sep 65	**FLAMING STAR AND SUMMER KISSES** *RCA Victor RD 7723*	11		4
4 Dec 65	**ELVIS FOR EVERYONE** *RCA Victor RD 7782*	8		8
15 Jan 66	**HAREM HOLIDAY (OST)** *RCA Victor RD 7767*	11		5
30 Apr 66	**FRANKIE AND JOHNNY (OST)** *RCA Victor RD 7793*	11		5
6 Aug 66	**PARADISE HAWAIIAN STYLE (OST)** *RCA Victor RD 7810*	7		9
26 Nov 66	**CALIFORNIA HOLIDAY (OST)** *RCA Victor RD 7820*	17		6
8 Apr 67	**HOW GREAT THOU ART** *RCA Victor SF 7867*	11		14
2 Sep 67	**DOUBLE TROUBLE (OST)** *RCA Victor SF 7892*	34		1
20 Apr 68	**CLAMBAKE (OST)** *RCA Victor SD 7917*	39		1
3 May 69	**ELVIS – NBC TV SPECIAL (OST-TV)** *RCA Victor RD 8011*	2		26
5 Jul 69	**ELVIS' SINGS FLAMING STAR** *RCA International INTS 1012*	2		14
23 Aug 69	**FROM ELVIS IN MEMPHIS** *RCA Victor SF 8029*	1	1	13
28 Feb 70	**PORTRAIT IN MUSIC** *RCA Victor 558*	36		1
14 Mar 70	**FROM MEMPHIS TO VEGAS – FROM VEGAS TO MEMPHIS** *RCA Victor SF 8080/1*	3		15
4 Apr 70	**ELVIS' GOLDEN RECORDS VOLUME 1** *RCA SF 8129*	21		12
1 Aug 70	**ON STAGE FEBRUARY 1970** *RCA Victor SF 8128*	2		18
12 Dec 70	**WORLDWIDE 50 GOLD AWARD HITS VOLUME 1 – A TOUCH OF GOLD** *RCA Victor LPM 6401*	49		2
30 Jan 71	**THAT'S THE WAY IT IS (OST)** *RCA Victor SF 8162*	12		35
10 Apr 71	**I'M 10,000 YEARS OLD – ELVIS COUNTRY** *RCA Victor SF 8172*	6		9
24 Jul 71	**LOVE LETTERS FROM ELVIS** *RCA Victor SF 8202*	7		5
7 Aug 71	**C'MON EVERYBODY** *RCA International INTS 1286*	5		21
7 Aug 71	**YOU'LL NEVER WALK ALONE** *RCA Camden CDM 1088*	20		4
25 Sep 71	**ALMOST IN LOVE** *RCA International INTS 1206*	38		2
4 Dec 71	**ELVIS CHRISTMAS ALBUM** *RCA International INTS 1126* ★	7		5
18 Dec 71	**I GOT LUCKY** *RCA International INTS 1322*	26		3
27 May 72	**ELVIS NOW** *RCA Victor SF 8266*	12		8
3 Jun 72	**ROCK 'N' ROLL** *RCA Victor SF 8233*	34		4
3 Jun 72	**ELVIS FOR EVERYONE** *RCA Victor SF 8232*	48		1
15 Jul 72	**ELVIS AS RECORDED AT MADISON SQUARE GARDEN** *RCA Victor SF 8296*	3		20
12 Aug 72	**HE TOUCHED ME** *RCA Victor SF 8275*	38		3
24 Feb 73	**ALOHA FROM HAWAII VIA SATELLITE (OST-TV)** *RCA Victor DPS 2040* ★	11		10
15 Sep 73	**ELVIS** *RCA Victor SF 8378* ★	16		4
2 Mar 74	**ELVIS – A LEGENDARY PERFORMER VOLUME 1** *RCA Victor CPLI 0341*	20		3
25 May 74	**GOOD TIMES** *RCA Victor APLI 0475*	42		1
7 Sep 74	**ELVIS LIVE ON STAGE IN MEMPHIS** *RCA Victor APLI 0606*	44		1
22 Feb 75	**PROMISED LAND** *RCA Victor APLI 0873*	21		4
14 Jun 75	**TODAY** *RCA Victor RS 1011*	48		3
5 Jul 75	**ELVIS'S 40 GREATEST HITS** *Arcade ADEP 12* ⊛	1	1	38
6 Sep 75	**THE ELVIS PRESLEY SUN COLLECTION** *RCA Starcall HY 1001*	16		13
19 Jun 76	**FROM ELVIS PRESLEY BOULEVARD, MEMPHIS, TENNESSEE** *RCA Victor RS 1060*	29		5
19 Feb 77	**ELVIS IN DEMAND** *RCA Victor PL 42003*	12		12
27 Aug 77	**MOODY BLUE** *RCA Victor PL 12428*	3		15
3 Sep 77	**WELCOME TO MY WORLD** *RCA Victor PL 12274*	7		9
3 Sep 77	**G.I. BLUES (OST)** *RCA SF 5078*	14		10
10 Sep 77	**BLUE HAWAII (OST)** *RCA SF 8145* ★	26		6
10 Sep 77	**ELVIS' GOLDEN RECORDS VOLUME 2** *RCA SF 8151*	27		4
10 Sep 77	**HITS OF THE 70'S** *RCA Victor LPLI 7527*	30		4
10 Sep 77	**ELVIS' GOLDEN RECORDS VOLUME 3** *RCA SF 7630*	49		2
10 Sep 77	**PICTURES OF ELVIS** *RCA Starcall HY 1023*	52		1
8 Oct 77	**THE SUN YEARS** *Charly SUN 1001*	31		2
15 Oct 77	**LOVING YOU** *RCA Victor PL 42358* ★	24		3
19 Nov 77	**ELVIS IN CONCERT (OST-TV)** *RCA Victor PL 02578*	13		11
22 Apr 78	**HE WALKS BESIDE ME** *RCA Victor PL 12772*	37		1
3 Jun 78	**THE '56 SESSIONS VOLUME 1** *RCA Victor PL 42101*	47		4
2 Sep 78	**TV SPECIAL** *RCA Victor PL 42370*	50		2
11 Nov 78	**ELVIS'S 40 GREATEST HITS** *RCA Victor PL 42691*	40		14
3 Feb 79	**A LEGENDARY PERFORMER VOLUME 3** *RCA Victor PL 13082*	43		4
5 May 79	**OUR MEMORIES OF ELVIS** *RCA Victor PL 13279*	72		1
24 Nov 79	**LOVE SONGS** *K-Tel NE 1062* ⊛	4		13
21 Jun 80	**ELVIS PRESLEY SINGS LEIBER AND STOLLER** *RCA International INTS 5031*	32		5
23 Aug 80	**ELVIS AARON PRESLEY** *RCA ELVIS 25*	21		4
23 Aug 80	**PARADISE HAWAIIAN STYLE (OST)** *RCA International INTS 5037*	53		2
29 Nov 80	**INSPIRATION** *K-Tel NE 1101* ⊛	6		8
14 Mar 81	**GUITAR MAN** *RCA RCALP 5010*	33		5
9 May 81	**THIS IS ELVIS PRESLEY (OST)** *RCA RCALP 5029*	47		4
28 Nov 81	**THE ULTIMATE PERFORMANCE** *K-Tel NE 1141* ●	45		6
13 Feb 82	**THE SOUND OF YOUR CRY** *RCA RCALP 3060*	31		12
6 Mar 82	**ELVIS PRESLEY EP PACK** *RCA EP1*	97		1
21 Aug 82	**ROMANTIC ELVIS – 20 LOVE SONGS/ROCKIN' ELVIS – THE SIXTIES 20 GREAT TRACKS** *RCA RCALP 1000/1*	62		5
18 Dec 82	**IT WON'T SEEM LIKE CHRISTMAS WITHOUT YOU** *RCA International INTS 5235*	80		1
30 Apr 83	**JAILHOUSE ROCK/LOVE IN LAS VEGAS** *RCA RCALP 9020*	40		2
20 Aug 83	**I WAS THE ONE** *RCA RCALP 3105*	83		1
3 Dec 83	**A LEGENDARY PERFORMER VOLUME 4** *RCA PL 84848*	91		1
7 Apr 84	**I CAN HELP** *RCA PL 89287*	71		3
21 Jul 84	**THE FIRST LIVE RECORDINGS** *RCA International PG 89387*	69		2
26 Jan 85	**20 GREATEST HITS VOLUME 2** *RCA International NL 89168*	98		1
25 May 85	**RECONSIDER BABY** *RCA PL 85418*	92		1
12 Oct 85	**ELVIS PRESLEY – BALLADS: 18 CLASSIC LOVE SONGS** *Telstar STAR 2264* ●	23		17
29 Aug 87	**PRESLEY – THE ALL TIME GREATEST HITS** *RCA PL 90100* ●	4		34
28 Jan 89	**STEREO '57 (ESSENTIAL ELVIS VOLUME 2)** *RCA PL 90250*	60		2
21 Jul 90	**HITS LIKE NEVER BEFORE (ESSENTIAL ELVIS VOLUME 3)** *RCA PL 90486*	71		1
1 Sep 90	**THE GREAT PERFORMANCES** *RCA PL 82227*	62		1
24 Aug 91	**COLLECTORS GOLD** *RCA PL 90574*	57		1
22 Feb 92	**FROM THE HEART – HIS GREATEST LOVE SONGS** *RCA PD 90642* ●	4		18
10 Sep 94	**THE ESSENTIAL COLLECTION** *RCA 74321228712* ⊛	6		25
11 May 96	**ELVIS 56** *RCA 07863668562*	42		3
7 Jun 97	**ALWAYS ON MY MIND – ULTIMATE LOVE SONGS** *RCA 74321489842* ⊛	3		33
28 Feb 98	**BLUE SUEDE SHOES** *RCA 74321556282*	39		4
2 Dec 00	**THE 50 GREATEST HITS** *RCA 74321811022* ⊛x2	8		25
31 Mar 01	**THE LIVE GREATEST HITS** *RCA 74321847082*	50		3
24 Nov 01	**THE 50 GREATEST LOVE SONGS** *RCA 74321900752*	21		9
5 Oct 02	**ELV1S: 30 #1 HITS** *RCA 07863680792* ⊛x2 ★	1	2	52
18 Oct 03	**2ND TO NONE** *RCA 82876570852*	4		12
6 Dec 03	**CHRISTMAS PEACE** *RCA 82876574892*	41		10
12 Feb 05	**LOVE ELVIS** *RCA 82876674482*	8		9
28 May 05	**ELVIS BY THE PRESLEYS** *Sony BMG TV 82876678832*	13		5
19 Nov 05	**HITSTORY** *RCA 82876739352* ●	31		19
25 Aug 07	**THE KING** *RCA 88697118042*	1	1	10

LISA MARIE PRESLEY
US, female vocalist — 1

Date	Title	Peak Position	Weeks at No.1	Weeks on Chart
26 Jul 03	**TO WHOM IT MAY CONCERN** *Capitol 5905220*	52		1

PRETENDERS
US/UK, female/male vocal/instrumental group – Chrissie Hynde, Martin Chambers, Pete Farndon, d. 14 Apr 1983 (replaced by Malcolm Foster) & James 'Honeyman' Scott, d. 16 Jun 1982 (replaced by Robbie McIntosh) — 171

Date	Title	Peak Position	Weeks at No.1	Weeks on Chart
19 Jan 80	**PRETENDERS** *Real RAL 3* ●	1	4	35
15 Aug 81	**PRETENDERS II** *Real SRK 3572* ○	7		27
21 Jan 84	**LEARNING TO CRAWL** *Real WX 2* ●	11		16
1 Nov 86	**GET CLOSE** *Real WX 64* ●	6		28
7 Nov 87	**THE SINGLES** *Real WX 135* ⊛x3	6		32
26 May 90	**PACKED!** *WEA WX 346* ○	19		5
21 May 94	**LAST OF THE INDEPENDENTS** *WEA 4509958222* ●	8		13
28 Oct 95	**THE ISLE OF VIEW** *WEA 0630120592* ○	23		4
29 May 99	**VIVA EL AMOR** *WEA 3984271522*	32		2
30 Sep 00	**GREATEST HITS** *warner.esp 8573846072* ●	21		8
31 May 03	**LOOSE SCREW** *Eagle EAGCD256*	55		1

PRETTY THINGS
UK, male vocal/instrumental group – Phil May, Brian Pendleton, Viv Prince (replaced by Skip Alan), John Stax & Dick Taylor — 13

Date	Title	Peak Position	Weeks at No.1	Weeks on Chart
27 Mar 65	**PRETTY THINGS** *Fontana TL 5239*	6		10
27 Jun 70	**PARACHUTE** *Harvest SHVL 774*	43		3

ALAN PRICE
UK, male vocalist/pianist. See Animals — 10

Date	Title	Peak Position	Weeks at No.1	Weeks on Chart
8 Jun 74	**BETWEEN TODAY AND YESTERDAY** *Warner Brothers K 56032* ○	9		10

CHARLEY PRIDE
US, male vocalist — 17

Date	Title	Peak Position	Weeks at No.1	Weeks on Chart
10 Apr 71	**CHARLEY PRIDE SPECIAL** *RCA Victor SF 8171*	29		1
28 May 77	**SHE'S JUST AN OLD LOVE TURNED MEMORY** *RCA Victor PL 12261*	34		2
3 Jun 78	**SOMEONE LOVES YOU HONEY** *RCA Victor PL 12478*	48		2
26 Jan 80	**GOLDEN COLLECTION** *K-Tel NE 1056* ●	6		12

MAXI PRIEST
UK, male vocalist (Max Elliott) — 35

Date	Title	Peak Position	Weeks at No.1	Weeks on Chart
6 Dec 86	**INTENTIONS** *10 Records DIX 32*	96		1
5 Dec 87	**MAXI** *10 Records DIX 64* ●	25		15
14 Jul 90	**BONAFIDE** *10 Records DIX 92* ●	11		13
9 Nov 91	**THE BEST OF ME** *10 Records DIX 111* ●	23		5
14 Nov 92	**FE REAL** *10 Records DIXCD 113*	60		1

PRIESTS
UK, male priests — 5

Date	Title	Peak Position	Weeks at No.1	Weeks on Chart
6 Dec 08	**THE PRIESTS** *Epic 88697339692* ●	5		5+

PRIMAL SCREAM
UK, male vocal/instrumental group – Bobby Gillespie, Andrew Innes, Gary 'Mani' Mounfield & various musicians — 91

Date	Title	Peak Position	Weeks at No.1	Weeks on Chart
17 Oct 87	**SONIC FLOWER GROOVE** *Elevation ELV 2*	62		1
5 Oct 91	**SCREAMADELICA** *Creation CRELP 076* ●	8		30
9 Apr 94	**GIVE OUT, BUT DON'T GIVE UP** *Creation CRECD 146* ●	2		18
19 Jul 97	**VANISHING POINT** *Creation CRECD 178* ●	2		10
8 Nov 97	**ECHO DEK** *Creation CRECD 224*	43		1
12 Feb 00	**EXTERMINATOR** *Creation CRECD 239* ●	3		10
17 Aug 02	**EVIL HEAT** *Columbia 5089232*	9		3
15 Nov 03	**DIRTY HITS** *Columbia 5136039*	25		3
17 Jun 06	**RIOT CITY BLUES** *Columbia 8287683165* ●	5		12
2 Aug 08	**BEAUTIFUL FUTURE** *B Unique 5144292372*	9		3

PRIMITIVES
UK/Australia, male/female vocal/instrumental group – Tracy Tracy (Tracy Cattell), Paul Court, Steve Dullaghan (replaced by Andy Hobson) & Pete Tweedie (replaced by Tig Williams) — 13

Date	Title	Peak Position	Weeks at No.1	Weeks on Chart
9 Apr 88	**LOVELY** *Lazy PL 71688* ●	6		10
2 Sep 89	**LAZY 86-88** *Lazy 15*	73		1
28 Oct 89	**PURE** *RCA PL 74252*	33		2

PRIMUS
UK, male vocal/instrumental group — 1

Date	Title	Peak Position	Weeks at No.1	Weeks on Chart
8 May 93	**PORK SODA** *Interscope 7567922572*	56		1

PRINCE
US, male vocalist/producer/multi-instrumentalist (Prince Rogers Nelson). Innovative and often controversial musician who is one of the most popular live acts of all time. In 2004, the multi-monikered one offered *Musicology* with tickets to his tour of the same name and the chart-ineligible *Planet Earth* (2007) was given away free with a Sunday newspaper — 473

Date	Title	Peak Position	Weeks at No.1	Weeks on Chart
21 Jul 84	**PURPLE RAIN (OST)** *Warner Brothers 9251101* PRINCE & THE REVOLUTION ⊛x2 ★	7		91
8 Sep 84	**1999** *Warner Brothers 9237201* ⊛	30		21
4 May 85	**AROUND THE WORLD IN A DAY** *Warner Brothers 9252861* ● ★	5		20
12 Apr 86	**PARADE – MUSIC FROM 'UNDER THE CHERRY MOON' (OST)** *Warner Brothers WX 39* ⊛	4		26
11 Apr 87	**SIGN 'O' THE TIMES** *Paisley Park WX 88* ⊛	4		32
21 May 88	**LOVESEXY** *Paisley Park WX 164* ⊛	1	1	32
1 Jul 89	**BATMAN (OST)** *Warner Brothers WX 281* ⊛ ★	1	1	20
1 Sep 90	**GRAFFITI BRIDGE** *Paisley Park WX 361* ●	1	1	8
24 Aug 91	**GETT OFF** *Paisley Park 9401382* PRINCE & THE NEW POWER GENERATION	33		3
12 Oct 91	**DIAMONDS AND PEARLS** *Paisley Park WX 432* PRINCE & THE NEW POWER GENERATION ⊛x3	2		57
17 Oct 92	**SYMBOLS** *Paisley Park 9362450372* PRINCE & THE NEW POWER GENERATION ⊛	1	1	21
25 Sep 93	**THE HITS 1** *Paisley Park 9362454312* ⊛	5		27
25 Sep 93	**THE HITS 2** *Paisley Park 9362454352* ⊛	5		28
25 Sep 93	**THE HITS/THE B-SIDES** *Paisley Park 9362454402* ○	4		14
27 Aug 94	**COME** *Warner Brothers 9362457002* ●	1	1	8
3 Dec 94	**THE BLACK ALBUM** *Warner Brothers 9362457932*	36		3
7 Oct 95	**THE GOLD EXPERIENCE** *Warner Brothers 9362459992* ●	4		5
20 Jul 96	**CHAOS AND DISORDER** *Warner Brothers 9362463172*	14		4
30 Nov 96	**EMANCIPATION** *NPG CDEMD 1102*	18		6
4 Sep 99	**THE VAULT…OLD FRIENDS 4 SALE** *Warner Brothers 9362475222*	47		1
11 Aug 01	**THE VERY BEST OF PRINCE** *Warner Brothers 8122742722* ⊛	2		24
1 May 04	**MUSICOLOGY** *Columbia/NPG 5171659* ●	3		6
1 Apr 06	**3121** *Universal 9852072* ★	9		4
2 Sep 06	**ULTIMATE** *Warner Brothers 8122733812* ●	6		12

PRINCE CHARLES & THE CITY BEAT BAND
US, male vocal/instrumental group — 1

Date	Title	Peak Position	Weeks at No.1	Weeks on Chart
30 Apr 83	**STONE KILLERS** *Virgin V 2271*	84		1

PRINCESS
UK, female vocalist (Desiree Heslop) — 14

Date	Title	Peak Position	Weeks at No.1	Weeks on Chart
17 May 86	**PRINCESS** *Supreme SU1* ○	15		14

PRIORY OF THE RESURRECTION
UK, choir — 1

Date	Title	Peak Position	Weeks at No.1	Weeks on Chart
31 Mar 01	**ETERNAL LIGHT – MUSIC OF INNER PEACE** *Deutsche Grammophon 4710902*	68		1

PROBOT
UK, male vocal/instrumental group — 2

Date	Title	Peak Position	Weeks at No.1	Weeks on Chart
28 Feb 04	**PROBOT** *Southern Lord STHL302*	34		2

P.J. PROBY
US, male vocalist (James Smith) — 3

Date	Title	Peak Position	Weeks at No.1	Weeks on Chart
27 Feb 65	**I'M P.J. PROBY** *Liberty LBY 1235*	16		3

PROCLAIMERS
UK, male vocal/instrumental duo – Charlie & Craig Reid — 77

Date	Title	Peak Position	Weeks at No.1	Weeks on Chart
9 May 87	**THIS IS THE STORY** *Chrysalis CHR 1602* ●	43		21
24 Sep 88	**SUNSHINE ON LEITH** *Chrysalis CHR 1668* ⊛	6		27
19 Mar 94	**HIT THE HIGHWAY** *Chrysalis CDCHR 6066* ○	8		6
9 Jun 01	**PERSEVERE** *Persevere PERSRECCD 04*	61		1
25 May 02	**THE BEST OF** *Chrysalis 5396822* ●	5		14
27 Sep 03	**BORN INNOCENT** *Persevere PERSRECCD 09*	70		2
20 Aug 05	**RESTLESS SOUL** *Persevere PERSRECCD10*	74		1
15 Sep 07	**LIFE WITH YOU** *W14 1740870*	13		5

Key: ○ Silver-selling · ● Gold-selling · ⊛ Platinum-selling · ★ US No.1 · Peak Position · Weeks at No.1 · Weeks on Chart

PROCOL HARUM
UK, male vocal/instrumental group — **11**

Date	Title / Label	Peak Position	Weeks at No.1	Weeks on Chart
19 Jul 69	**A SALTY DOG** *Regal Zonophone SLRZ 1009*	27		2
27 Jun 70	**HOME** *Regal Zonophone SLRZ 1014*	49		1
3 Jul 71	**BROKEN BARRICADES** *Island ILPS 9158*	42		1
6 May 72	**A WHITER SHADE OF PALE/A SALTY DOG** *Fly Double Back TOOFA 7/8*	26		4
6 May 72	**PROCOL HARUM LIVE IN CONCERT WITH THE EDMONTON SYMPHONY ORCHESTRA** *Chrysalis CHR 1004*	48		1
30 Aug 75	**PROCOL'S NINTH** *Chrysalis CHR 1080*	41		2

PRODIGY
UK, male vocal/instrumental group – Keith Flint, Liam Howlett, Keith Palmer & Leeroy Thornhill — **217**

Date	Title / Label	Peak Position	Weeks at No.1	Weeks on Chart
10 Oct 92	**EXPERIENCE** *XL Recordings XLCD 110* ⊛	12		31
16 Jul 94	**MUSIC FOR THE JILTED GENERATION** *XL Recordings XLCD 114* ⊛	1	1	98
12 Jul 97	**THE FAT OF THE LAND** *XL Recordings XLCD 121* ⊛x3 ★	1	6	60
4 Sep 04	**ALWAYS OUTNUMBERED NEVER OUTGUNNED** *XL Recordings XLCD 183* ●	1	1	6
29 Oct 05	**THEIR LAW – THE SINGLES 1990-2005** *XL Recordings XLCD190* ⊛x2	1	1	22

PROJECT D
UK, male instrumental duo — **18**

Date	Title / Label	Peak Position	Weeks at No.1	Weeks on Chart
17 Feb 90	**THE SYNTHESIZER ALBUM** *Telstar STAR 2371*	13		11
29 Sep 90	**SYNTHESIZER 2** *Telstar STAR 2428*	25		7

PRONG
UK, male vocal/instrumental group — **1**

Date	Title / Label	Peak Position	Weeks at No.1	Weeks on Chart
12 Feb 94	**CLEANSING** *Epic 4747962*	71		1

PROPAGANDA
Germany, male/female vocal/instrumental group — **16**

Date	Title / Label	Peak Position	Weeks at No.1	Weeks on Chart
13 Jul 85	**SECRET WISH** *ZTT ZTTIQ 3*	16		12
23 Nov 85	**WISHFUL THINKING** *ZTT ZTTIQ 20*	82		2
9 Jun 90	**1234** *Virgin V 2625*	46		2

PROPELLERHEADS
UK, male production/instrumental duo – Alex Gifford & Will White — **13**

Date	Title / Label	Peak Position	Weeks at No.1	Weeks on Chart
7 Feb 98	**DECKSANDRUMSANDROCKANDROLL** *Wall Of Sound WALLCD 015* ●	6		13

DOROTHY PROVINE
US, female actor/vocalist — **49**

Date	Title / Label	Peak Position	Weeks at No.1	Weeks on Chart
2 Dec 61	**THE ROARING TWENTIES – SONGS FROM THE TV SERIES** *Warner Brothers WM 4035*	3		42
10 Feb 62	**VAMP OF THE ROARING TWENTIES** *Warner Brothers WM 4053*	9		7

PSYCHEDELIC FURS
UK, male vocal/instrumental group — **39**

Date	Title / Label	Peak Position	Weeks at No.1	Weeks on Chart
15 Mar 80	**PSYCHEDELIC FURS** *CBS 84084*	18		6
23 May 81	**TALK TALK TALK** *CBS 84892*	30		9
2 Oct 82	**FOREVER NOW** *CBS 85909*	20		6
19 May 84	**MIRROR MOVES** *CBS 25950*	15		9
14 Feb 87	**MIDNIGHT TO MIDNIGHT** *CBS 4502561* ○	12		5
13 Aug 88	**ALL OF THIS AND NOTHING** *CBS 4611101*	67		2
18 Nov 89	**BOOK OF DAYS** *CBS 4659821*	74		1
13 Jul 91	**WORLD OUTSIDE** *East West WX 422*	68		1

PUBLIC ENEMY
US, male rap group – Chuck D (Carlton Ridenhour), Flavor Flav (William Drayton), Professor Griff (William Griffin) & Terminator X (Norman Rogers) — **40**

Date	Title / Label	Peak Position	Weeks at No.1	Weeks on Chart
30 Jul 88	**IT TAKES A NATION OF MILLIONS TO HOLD US BACK** *Def Jam 4624151* ○	8		9
28 Apr 90	**FEAR OF A BLACK PLANET** *Def Jam 4662811* ●	4		10
19 Oct 91	**APOCALYPSE 91...THE ENEMY STRIKES BLACK** *Def Jam 4687511* ○	8		7
3 Oct 92	**GREATEST MISSES** *Def Jam 4720312*	14		3
3 Sep 94	**MUSE SICK-N-HOUR MESS AGE** *Def Jam 5233622*	12		3
16 May 98	**HE GOT GAME (OST)** *Def Jam 5581302*	50		4
31 Jul 99	**THERE'S A POISON GOIN' ON...** *PIAS Recordings PIASXCD 004*	55		1
13 Aug 05	**POWER TO THE PEOPLE AND THE BEATS** *Def Jam/UMTV 9861661*	39		3

PUBLIC IMAGE LTD
UK, male vocal/instrumental group — **51**

Date	Title / Label	Peak Position	Weeks at No.1	Weeks on Chart
23 Dec 78	**PUBLIC IMAGE** *Virgin V 2114* ○	22		11
8 Dec 79	**METAL BOX** *Virgin METAL 1*	18		8
8 Mar 80	**SECOND EDITION OF PIL** *Virgin VD 2512*	46		2
22 Nov 80	**PARIS AU PRINTEMPS (PARIS IN THE SPRING)** *Virgin V 2183*	61		2
18 Apr 81	**FLOWERS OF ROMANCE** *Virgin V 2189*	11		5
8 Oct 83	**PIL LIVE IN TOKYO** *Virgin VGD 3508*	28		6
21 Jul 84	**THIS IS WHAT YOU WANT...THIS IS WHAT YOU GET** *Virgin V 2309*	56		2
15 Feb 86	**ALBUM/CASSETTE** *Virgin V 2366*	14		6
26 Sep 87	**HAPPY?** *Virgin V 2455*	40		2
10 Jun 89	**9** *Virgin V 2588*	36		2
10 Nov 90	**THE GREATEST HITS, SO FAR** *Virgin V 2644*	20		3
7 Mar 92	**THAT WHAT IS NOT** *Virgin CDV 2681*	46		2

GARY PUCKETT & THE UNION GAP
US, male vocal/instrumental group — **4**

Date	Title / Label	Peak Position	Weeks at No.1	Weeks on Chart
29 Jun 68	**UNION GAP** *CBS 63342*	24		4

PUDDLE OF MUDD
US, male vocal/instrumental group — **36**

Date	Title / Label	Peak Position	Weeks at No.1	Weeks on Chart
2 Feb 02	**COME CLEAN** *Interscope 4930742* ⊛	12		36

PUFF DADDY
US, male rapper (Sean Combs) — **50**

Date	Title / Label	Peak Position	Weeks at No.1	Weeks on Chart
2 Aug 97	**NO WAY OUT** *Puff Daddy 78612730122* ● ★	8		13
4 Sep 99	**FOREVER** *Puff Daddy 74321689052* ●	9		6
8 Jun 02	**WE INVENTED THE REMIX** *Puff Daddy 74321945402* P DIDDY & THE BAD BOY FAMILY ● ★	17		12
28 Oct 06	**PRESS PLAY** *Bad Boy 7567935752* P DIDDY ●	11		19

PULP
UK, male vocal/instrumental group – Jarvis Cocker*, Nicholas Banks, Candida Doyle, Steve Mackey & Russell Senior (replaced by Mark Webber) — **138**

Date	Title / Label	Peak Position	Weeks at No.1	Weeks on Chart
30 Apr 94	**HIS 'N' HERS** *Island CID 8025* ●	9		43
11 Nov 95	**DIFFERENT CLASS** *Island CID 8041* ⊛x4	1	1	64
23 Mar 96	**COUNTDOWN 1992–1983** *Nectar Masters NTMCDD 521*	10		6
11 Apr 98	**THIS IS HARDCORE** *Island CID 8066* ●	1	1	21
3 Nov 01	**WE LOVE LIFE** *Island CID 8110* ○	6		3
30 Nov 02	**HITS** *Island CID 8126*	71		1

PUPPINI SISTERS
UK, female vocal group — **7**

Date	Title / Label	Peak Position	Weeks at No.1	Weeks on Chart
15 Aug 06	**BETCHA BOTTOM DOLLAR** *UCJ 9857592*	17		6
13 Oct 07	**THE RISE AND FALL OF RUBY WOO** *UCJ 1743243*	73		1

PURESSENCE
UK, male vocal/instrumental group — **2**

Date	Title / Label	Peak Position	Weeks at No.1	Weeks on Chart
29 Aug 98	**ONLY FOREVER** *Island CID 8064*	36		2

PUSSYCAT DOLLS
US, female vocal group – Nicole Scherzinger, Carmit Bachar, Ashley Roberts, Jessica Sutta, Melody Thornton & Kimberly Wyatt — **87**

Date	Title / Label	Peak Position	Weeks at No.1	Weeks on Chart
24 Sep 05	**PCD** *A&M 9885657* ⊛x3	7		73
4 Oct 08	**DOLL DOMINATION** *Interscope 1784995* ●	4		14+

A History of the UK Album Chart

28 July 1956 — The first ever album chart is launched in the UK by magazine *Record Mirror*. The Chart consists of only **5** positions

The First ever No.1 is 'Songs For Swingin' Lovers' by Frank Sinatra

8 November 1958 — *Melody Maker* launches a **top 10** album chart, which becomes the basis for the Official Album Chart for the next 16 months

12 March 1960 — *Record Retailer* magazine creates its own album chart. This is the precursor of the current album chart. Initially a **top 10** it is expanded to a **top 20** two weeks after launch

14 April 1966 — Chart becomes a **top 30**

8 December 1966 — Chart is lengthened to a **top 40**

16 January 1971 — Chart length is increased again to become a **top 50**

18 March 1972 — *Music Week* becomes the new name for *Record Retailer*

5 July 1975 — Chart becomes a **top 60**

2 December 1978 — The Chart is expanded again to a **top 75**

8 August 1981 — The album chart becomes a **top 100**

14 January 1989 — Artist and compilation albums (ie Various Artist and Soundtracks) are separated out to create two album charts. Details of both charts are listed within this book

The artist album chart becomes a **top 75** and the compilation album chart becomes a **top 20**. These chart lengths remain to this day

December 2008 — **No.1 in the final album chart of 2008 is 'The Circus' by Take That**

BIOGRAPHIES

Biographies include the nationality and category for every chart entrant.

Each entrant has at least a mini biography. The 100 acts with the most weeks on the chart (see page 290 for the top 100 chart) each have extended biographies.

Real names are included for all solo artists and, where applicable, dates of death and age of the artist at the time. "See..." links are included for soloists who also had album chart entries in other acts.

The best known line-up is listed for every group that had a Top 10 album, with the vocalist/leader mentioned first and the others following in alphabetical order. In cases where later replacements had similar success both people are named and, where applicable, the dates of death are also shown for every group/duo member listed.

Certified Awards are given by the BPI to mark unit sales to retailers. The certified awards were introduced in April 1973, based on revenue received by manufacturers. In January 1978 the qualification rules were changed and the system based on unit sales to the trade was adopted.

Silver symbol	●	=	60,000 units
Gold symbol	●	=	100,000 units
Platinum symbol	⊛	=	300,000 units

Q–T

KEY TO ARTIST ENTRIES

Artist/Group Name — Artist/Group Biography — Silver-selling ● — Gold-selling ● — Platinum-selling ⊛ — US No.1 ★ — Peak Position — Weeks at No.1 — Weeks on Chart

Asterisks (*) indicate group members with hits in their own right that are listed elsewhere in this book

TOM JONES

UK, male vocalist (Thomas Woodward). Perennially popular Welsh vocalist, who has a 43-year span of UK hit albums, was the No.1 UK solo singer of the 1960s on both sides of the Atlantic. The unmistakable Vegas veteran received the Outstanding Contribution award at the 2003 BRITs

Artist's Total Weeks On Chart: 530

Date	Album Title / Label and Catalogue Number	Peak Position	Weeks at No.1	Weeks on Chart
5 Jun 65	**ALONG CAME JONES** *Decca LK 6693*	11		5
8 Oct 66	**FROM THE HEART** *Decca LK 4814*	23		8
8 Apr 67	**GREEN GREEN GRASS OF HOME** *Decca SKL 4855*	3		49
24 Jun 67	**LIVE AT THE TALK OF THE TOWN** *Decca SKL 4874*	6		90
30 Dec 67	**13 SMASH HITS** *Decca SKL 4909*	5		49
27 Jul 68	**DELILAH** *Decca SKL 4946*	1	2	29
21 Dec 68	**HELP YOURSELF** *Decca SKL 4982*	4		9
28 Jun 69	**THIS IS TOM JONES** *Decca SKL 5007*	2		20
15 Nov 69	**TOM JONES LIVE IN LAS VEGAS** *Decca SKL 5032*	2		45
25 Apr 70	**TOM** *Decca SKL 5045*	4		18
14 Nov 70	**I WHO HAVE NOTHING** *Decca SKL 5072*	10		10
29 May 71	**SHE'S A LADY** *Decca SKL 5089*	9		7
27 Nov 71	**LIVE AT CAESAR'S PALACE** *Decca D 1/11/2*	27		5
24 Jun 72	**CLOSE UP** *Decca SKL 5132*	17		4
23 Jun 73	**THE BODY AND SOUL OF TOM JONES** *Decca SKL 5162*	31		1
5 Jan 74	**GREATEST HITS** *Decca SKL 5176*	15		13
22 Mar 75	**20 GREATEST HITS** *Decca TJD 1/11/2* ●	1	4	21
7 Oct 78	**I'M COMING HOME** *Lotus WH 5001* ●	12		9
16 May 87	**THE GREATEST HITS** *Telstar STAR 2296*	16		12
13 May 89	**AT THIS MOMENT** *Jive TOMTV 1*	34		3
8 Jul 89	**AFTER DARK** *Stylus SMR 978*	46		4
6 Apr 91	**CARRYING A TORCH** *Dover ADD 20*	44		4
27 Jun 92	**THE COMPLETE TOM JONES** *The Hit Label 8442862* ●	8		6
26 Nov 94	**THE LEAD AND HOW TO SWING IT** *ZTT 6544924982*	55		1
14 Nov 98	**THE ULTIMATE HITS COLLECTION** *Polygram TV 8449012*	26		6
9 Oct 99	**RELOAD** *Gut GUTCD 009* ⊛ **x4**	1	3	65
16 Nov 02	**MR JONES** *V2 VVR 1021072*	36		2
1 Mar 03	**GREATEST HITS** *Universal TV 8828632* ⊛	2		16
9 Oct 04	**TOM JONES AND JOOLS HOLLAND** *Radar RADAR004CD* & JOOLS HOLLAND ●	5		13
29 Nov 08	**24 HOURS** *S-Curve 2649852*	32		6+

Date of entry into chart

Artist collaboration or where artist's name has changed

Album Title — Label and Catalogue Number

Cross (+) indicates album is still on chart in last week of 2008

Key: ○ Silver-selling · ● Gold-selling · ⊛ Platinum-selling · ★ US No.1 · Peak Position · Weeks at No.1 · Weeks on Chart

Q-TIPS
UK, male vocal/instrumental group — Weeks on Chart: **1**

Date	Album / Label	Peak Position	Weeks at No.1	Weeks on Chart
30 Aug 80	**Q-TIPS** *Chrysalis CHR 1255*	50		1

QFX
UK, male/female vocal/instrumental/production group — Weeks on Chart: **1**

Date	Album / Label	Peak Position	Weeks at No.1	Weeks on Chart
8 Mar 97	**ALIEN CHILD** *Epidemic EPICD 9*	62		1

SUZI QUATRO
US, female vocalist/guitarist (Suzy Quatrocchio) — Weeks on Chart: **13**

Date	Album / Label	Peak Position	Weeks at No.1	Weeks on Chart
13 Oct 73	**SUZI QUATRO** *RAK SRAK 505* ○	32		4
26 Apr 80	**SUZI QUATRO'S GREATEST HITS** *RAK EMTV 24* ●	4		9

FINLEY QUAYE
UK, male vocalist/guitarist — Weeks on Chart: **59**

Date	Album / Label	Peak Position	Weeks at No.1	Weeks on Chart
4 Oct 97	**MAVERICK A STRIKE** *Epic 4887582* ⊛	3		56
14 Oct 00	**VANGUARD** *Epic 4997102*	35		2
11 Oct 03	**MUCH MORE THAN LOVE** *Sony Music 05125492*	56		1

QUEEN
UK, male vocal/instrumental group – Freddie Mercury*, d. 24 Nov 1991, John Deacon, Brian May* & Roger Taylor*. No act has spent longer on the UK albums chart than this legendary rock group, whose *Greatest Hits* is the biggest-selling album of all time in the UK, and in total their Hits collections have sold over 25 million worldwide. They received the Outstanding Contribution award at the 1992 BRITs — Weeks on Chart: **1423**

Date	Album / Label	Peak Position	Weeks at No.1	Weeks on Chart
23 Mar 74	**QUEEN 2** *EMI EMA 767* ●	5		29
30 Mar 74	**QUEEN** *EMI EMC 3006* ●	24		18
23 Nov 74	**SHEER HEART ATTACK** *EMI EMC 3061* ⊛	2		46
13 Dec 75	**A NIGHT AT THE OPERA** *EMI EMTC 103* ⊛	1	4	50
25 Dec 76	**A DAY AT THE RACES** *EMI EMTC 103* ●	1	1	24
12 Nov 77	**NEWS OF THE WORLD** *EMI EMA 784* ●	4		20
25 Nov 78	**JAZZ** *EMI EMA 788* ●	2		27
7 Jul 79	**LIVE KILLERS** *EMI EMSP 330* ●	3		27
12 Jul 80	**THE GAME** *EMI EMA 795* ● ★	1	2	18
20 Dec 80	**FLASH GORDON (ORIGINAL FILM SOUNDTRACK)** *EMI EMC 3351* ●	10		15
7 Nov 81	**QUEEN'S GREATEST HITS** *Parlophone EMYV 30* ⊛x11	1	4	475
15 May 82	**HOT SPACE** *EMI EMA 797* ●	4		19
10 Mar 84	**THE WORKS** *EMI EMC 240014* ⊛	2		93
14 Jun 86	**A KIND OF MAGIC** *EMI EU 3509* ⊛x2	1	1	63
13 Dec 86	**LIVE MAGIC** *EMI EMC 3519* ⊛	3		43
3 Jun 89	**THE MIRACLE** *Parlophone PCSD 107* ⊛	1	1	32
16 Dec 89	**QUEEN AT THE BEEB** *Band Of Joy BOJLP 001*	67		1
16 Feb 91	**INNUENDO** *Parlophone PCSD 115* ⊛	1	2	37
9 Nov 91	**GREATEST HITS II** *Parlophone PMTV 2* ⊛x8	1	5	110
6 Jun 92	**LIVE AT WEMBLEY** *Parlophone CDPCSP 725* ●	2		15
19 Nov 94	**GREATEST HITS I & II** *Parlophone CDPCSD 161*	37		7
18 Nov 95	**MADE IN HEAVEN** *Parlophone CDPCSD 167* ⊛x4	1	1	28
15 Nov 97	**QUEEN ROCKS** *Parlophone 8230912* ⊛	7		12
20 Nov 99	**GREATEST HITS III** *Parlophone 5238942* ⊛	5		19
25 Nov 00	**GREATEST HITS I II & III** *Parlophone 5298832* ⊛x3	2		155
21 Jun 03	**LIVE AT WEMBLEY '86** *Parlophone 5904402*	38		3
6 Nov 04	**ON FIRE – LIVE AT THE BOWL** *Parlophone 8632112* ●	20		4
30 Apr 05	**LIVE AT WEMBLEY STADIUM '86** *Parlophone 5910922*	24		20
1 Oct 05	**RETURN OF THE CHAMPIONS** *Parlophone 3369792* & PAUL RODGERS ○	12		4
10 Nov 07	**QUEEN ROCK MONTREAL** *Parlophone 5040472*	20		3
27 Sep 08	**THE COSMOS ROCKS** *Parlophone 2161432* & PAUL RODGERS	5		6

Top 3 Best-Selling Albums

	Album	Approximate Sales
1	GREATEST HITS	5,650,000
2	GREATEST HITS II	3,740,000
3	GREATEST HITS I, II & III	1,675,000

QUEENS OF THE STONE AGE
US, male vocal/instrumental group – Josh Homme, Joey Castillo, Nick Oliveri & Troy Van Leeuwen — Weeks on Chart: **37**

Date	Album / Label	Peak Position	Weeks at No.1	Weeks on Chart
2 Sep 00	**RATED R** *Interscope 4906832* ○	54		3
7 Sep 02	**SONGS FOR THE DEAF** *Interscope 4934440* ●	4		22
2 Apr 05	**LULLABIES TO PARALYZE** *Interscope 9880313* ●	4		8
23 Jun 07	**ERA VULGARIS** *Interscope 1736526*	7		4

QUEENSRYCHE
US, male vocal/instrumental group — Weeks on Chart: **12**

Date	Album / Label	Peak Position	Weeks at No.1	Weeks on Chart
29 Sep 84	**THE WARNING** *EMI America EJ 2402201*	100		1
26 Jul 86	**RAGE FOR ORDER** *EMI America AML 3105*	66		1
4 Jun 88	**OPERATION MINDCRIME** *Manhattan MTL 1023*	58		3
22 Sep 90	**EMPIRE** *EMI-USA MTL 1058* ○	13		3
22 Oct 94	**PROMISED LAND** *EMI CDMTL 1081*	13		3
29 Mar 97	**HEAR IN THE NOW FRONTIER** *EMI CDEMC 3764*	46		1

QUIET RIOT
US, male vocal/instrumental group — Weeks on Chart: **1**

Date	Album / Label	Peak Position	Weeks at No.1	Weeks on Chart
4 Aug 84	**CONDITION CRITICAL** *Epic EPC 26075*	71		1

RAY QUINN
UK, male vocalist — Weeks on Chart: **8**

Date	Album / Label	Peak Position	Weeks at No.1	Weeks on Chart
24 Mar 07	**DOING IT MY WAY** *Syco Music 88697068192*	1	1	8

SINEAD QUINN
UK, female vocalist — Weeks on Chart: **2**

Date	Album / Label	Peak Position	Weeks at No.1	Weeks on Chart
26 Jul 03	**READY TO RUN** *Fontana 9865367*	48		2

QUINTESSENCE
UK/Australia, male vocal/instrumental group — Weeks on Chart: **6**

Date	Album / Label	Peak Position	Weeks at No.1	Weeks on Chart
27 Jun 70	**QUINTESSENCE** *Island ILPS 9128*	22		4
3 Apr 71	**DIVE DEEP** *Island ILPS 9143*	43		1
27 May 72	**SELF** *RCA Victor SF 8273*	50		1

QUIREBOYS
UK, male vocal/instrumental group – Jonathan 'Spike' Grey, Gus Bailey, Nick Connel, Chris Johnstone & Nigel Mogg — Weeks on Chart: **17**

Date	Album / Label	Peak Position	Weeks at No.1	Weeks on Chart
10 Feb 90	**A BIT OF WHAT YOU FANCY** *Parlophone PCS 7335* ●	2		15
27 Mar 93	**BITTER SWEET AND TWISTED** *Parlophone CSPCSD 120*	31		2

R

RACING CARS
UK, male vocal/instrumental group — Weeks on Chart: **6**

Date	Album / Label	Peak Position	Weeks at No.1	Weeks on Chart
19 Feb 77	**DOWNTOWN MIDNIGHT** *Chrysalis CHR 1099*	39		6

RACONTEURS
US, male vocal/instrumental group – Jack White, Brendan Benson*, Patrick Keeler & Jack Lawrence — Weeks on Chart: **31**

Date	Album / Label	Peak Position	Weeks at No.1	Weeks on Chart
27 May 06	**BROKEN BOY SOLDIERS** *XL Recordings XLCD196* ●	2		19
5 Apr 08	**CONSOLERS OF THE LONELY** *XL Recordings XLCD359* ●	8		12

RADIOHEAD
UK, male vocal/instrumental group – Thom Yorke, Colin & Jonny Greenwood, Ed O'Brien & Phil Selway. Distinctive, innovative and critically-acclaimed Oxford band who conquered the world. *Kid A* was the first US No.1 album by a UK act in the 21st century and *In Rainbows* was offered as a "pay what you like" digital download before its physical release — Weeks on Chart: **388**

Date	Album / Label	Peak Position	Weeks at No.1	Weeks on Chart
6 Mar 93	**PABLO HONEY** *Parlophone CDPCS 7360* ⊛	22		82
25 Mar 95	**THE BENDS** *Parlophone CDPCS 7372* ⊛x3	4		160
28 Jun 97	**OK COMPUTER** *Parlophone CDNODATA 02* ⊛x3	1	2	77
14 Oct 00	**KID A** *Parlophone CDKIDA 1* ⊛ ★	1	2	15
16 Jun 01	**AMNESIAC** *Parlophone CDSFHEIT 45101* ●	1	1	12
24 Nov 01	**I MIGHT BE WRONG** *Parlophone CDFEIT 45104*	23		2
21 Jun 03	**HAIL TO THE THIEF** *Parlophone 5848082* ⊛	1	1	14
22 May 04	**COM LAG 2+2=5** *Parlophone TOCP 66280*	37		1
12 Jan 08	**IN RAINBOWS** *XL Recordings XLCD324* ● ★	1	1	16
14 Jun 08	**BEST OF** *Parlophone 2121071* ●	4		9

Silver-selling ○ Gold-selling ● Platinum-selling ⊛ US No.1 ★ — Peak Position · Weeks at No.1 · Weeks on Chart

CORINNE BAILEY RAE

UK, female vocalist — Weeks on Chart: 47

Date	Title / Label	Peak Position	Weeks at No.1	Weeks on Chart
11 Mar 06	**CORINNE BAILEY RAE** *Good Groove/EMI 3541172* ⊛x2	1	2	46
24 Feb 07	**CORINNE BAILEY RAE** *EMI 3860812*	69		1

RAE & CHRISTIAN

UK, male production duo — Weeks on Chart: 1

Date	Title / Label	Peak Position	Weeks at No.1	Weeks on Chart
10 Mar 01	**SLEEPWALKING** *IK7 K7 096CD*	57		1

GERRY RAFFERTY

UK, male vocalist/pianist. See Stealers Wheel — Weeks on Chart: 99

Date	Title / Label	Peak Position	Weeks at No.1	Weeks on Chart
25 Feb 78	**CITY TO CITY** *United Artists UAS 30104* ● ★	6		37
2 Jun 79	**NIGHT OWL** *United Artists UAK 30238* ●	9		24
26 Apr 80	**SNAKES AND LADDERS** *United Artists UAK 30298* ○	15		9
25 Sep 82	**SLEEPWALKING** *Liberty LBG 30352*	39		4
21 May 88	**NORTH AND SOUTH** *London LONLP 55*	43		4
13 Feb 93	**A WING AND A PRAYER** *A&M 5174952*	73		1
28 Oct 95	**ONE MORE DREAM – THE VERY BEST OF GERRY RAFFERTY** *Polygram TV 5292792* ●	17		20

RAGE AGAINST THE MACHINE

US, male vocal/instrumental group – Zack de la Rocha, Tim Commerford, Tom Morello & Brad Wilk — Weeks on Chart: 54

Date	Title / Label	Peak Position	Weeks at No.1	Weeks on Chart
13 Feb 93	**RAGE AGAINST THE MACHINE** *Epic 4722242* ●	17		44
27 Apr 96	**EVIL EMPIRE** *Epic 4810262* ○ ★	4		7
13 Nov 99	**THE BATTLE OF LOS ANGELES** *Epic 4919932* ★	23		2
9 Dec 00	**RENEGADES** *Epic 4999219*	71		1

RAGGA TWINS

UK, male vocal duo — Weeks on Chart: 5

Date	Title / Label	Peak Position	Weeks at No.1	Weeks on Chart
1 Jun 91	**REGGAE OWES ME MONEY** *Shut Up And Dance SUADLP 2*	26		5

RAGHAV

Canada, male vocalist (Raghav Mathur) — Weeks on Chart: 2

Date	Title / Label	Peak Position	Weeks at No.1	Weeks on Chart
18 Sep 04	**STORYTELLER** *V2 ARV1028642*	36		2

RAGING SPEEDHORN

UK, male vocal/instrumental group — Weeks on Chart: 1

Date	Title / Label	Peak Position	Weeks at No.1	Weeks on Chart
17 Aug 02	**WE WILL BE DEAD TOMORROW** *ZTT RSH 002CD*	63		1

RAH BAND

UK, male/female vocal/instrumental group — Weeks on Chart: 6

Date	Title / Label	Peak Position	Weeks at No.1	Weeks on Chart
6 Apr 85	**MYSTERY** *RCA PL 70640*	60		6

RAHMAN/ORIGINAL SOUND RECORDING

India, male composer/producer/instrumentalist (Allah Rakkha Rahman) — Weeks on Chart: 1

Date	Title / Label	Peak Position	Weeks at No.1	Weeks on Chart
29 Jun 02	**RAHMAN: BOMBAY DREAMS** *Sony Classical 5084352*	61		1

RAILWAY CHILDREN

UK, male vocal/instrumental group — Weeks on Chart: 3

Date	Title / Label	Peak Position	Weeks at No.1	Weeks on Chart
21 May 88	**RECURRENCE** *Virgin V 2525*	96		1
16 Mar 91	**NATIVE PLACE** *Virgin V 2627*	59		2

RAIN PARADE

US, male vocal/instrumental group — Weeks on Chart: 1

Date	Title / Label	Peak Position	Weeks at No.1	Weeks on Chart
29 Jun 85	**BEYOND THE SUNSET** *Island IMA 17*	78		1

RAIN TREE CROW

UK, male vocal/instrumental group — Weeks on Chart: 3

Date	Title / Label	Peak Position	Weeks at No.1	Weeks on Chart
20 Apr 91	**RAIN TREE CROW** *Virgin V 2659*	24		3

RAINBOW

UK, male vocal/instrumental group – Ritchie Blackmore; members also included Graham Bonnet, Tony Carey, Ronnie James Dio, Roger Glover, Cozy Powell, d. 5 Apr 1998, & Joe Lynn Turner — Weeks on Chart: 163

Date	Title / Label	Peak Position	Weeks at No.1	Weeks on Chart
13 Sep 75	**RITCHIE BLACKMORE'S RAINBOW** *Oyster OYA 2001* RITCHIE BLACKMORE'S RAINBOW ○	11		6
5 Jun 76	**RAINBOW RISING** *Polydor 2490 137* RITCHIE BLACKMORE'S RAINBOW ○	11		33
30 Jul 77	**ON STAGE** *Polydor 2657 016* ○	7		10
6 May 78	**LONG LIVE ROCK 'N' ROLL** *Polydor POLD 5002* ○	7		12
18 Aug 79	**DOWN TO EARTH** *Polydor POLD 5023* ●	6		37
21 Feb 81	**DIFFICULT TO CURE** *Polydor POLD 5036* ●	3		22
8 Aug 81	**RITCHIE BLACKMORE'S RAINBOW** *Polydor 2940 141* RITCHIE BLACKMORE'S RAINBOW	91		2
21 Nov 81	**BEST OF RAINBOW** *Polydor POLDV 2* ●	14		17
24 Apr 82	**STRAIGHT BETWEEN THE EYES** *Polydor POLD 5056* ○	5		14
17 Sep 83	**BENT OUT OF SHAPE** *Polydor POLD 5116*	11		6
8 Mar 86	**FINYL VINYL** *Polydor PODV 8*	31		4

RAINDANCE

UK, male production/instrumental duo. See Blowing Free, Harmonium, Hypnosis, In Tune, School Of Excellence — Weeks on Chart: 7

Date	Title / Label	Peak Position	Weeks at No.1	Weeks on Chart
27 Apr 96	**RAINDANCE** *Polygram TV 5298622* ○	15		7

BONNIE RAITT

US, female vocalist/guitarist — Weeks on Chart: 17

Date	Title / Label	Peak Position	Weeks at No.1	Weeks on Chart
28 Apr 90	**NICK OF TIME** *Capitol EST 2095* ★	51		5
6 Jul 91	**LUCK OF THE DRAW** *Capitol EST 2145*	38		3
16 Apr 94	**LONGING IN THEIR HEARTS** *Capitol CDEST 2227* ★	26		5
25 Nov 95	**ROAD TESTED** *Capitol CDEST 2274*	69		1
18 Apr 98	**FUNDAMENTAL** *Capitol 8563972*	52		1
24 May 03	**THE BEST OF BONNIE RAITT 1989-2003** *Capitol 5821132*	37		2

RAKES

UK, male vocal/instrumental group — Weeks on Chart: 3

Date	Title / Label	Peak Position	Weeks at No.1	Weeks on Chart
27 Aug 05	**CAPTURE RELEASE** *V2 VVR1032762*	32		2
31 Mar 07	**TEN NEW MESSAGES** *V2 VVR1041852*	38		1

RAKIM

US, male rapper (William Griffin Jr.). See Erik B & Rakim — Weeks on Chart: 1

Date	Title / Label	Peak Position	Weeks at No.1	Weeks on Chart
22 Nov 97	**18TH LETTER** *Universal UD2 53111*	72		1

KAREN RAMIREZ

US, female vocalist (Karen Ramelize) — Weeks on Chart: 2

Date	Title / Label	Peak Position	Weeks at No.1	Weeks on Chart
1 Aug 98	**DISTANT DREAMS** *Manifesto 5369462*	45		2

RAMMSTEIN

Germany, male/female vocal/instrumental group — Weeks on Chart: 2

Date	Title / Label	Peak Position	Weeks at No.1	Weeks on Chart
9 Oct 04	**REISE REISE** *Universal 9868150*	37		1
12 Nov 05	**ROSENROT** *Universal 9874589*	29		1

RAMONES

US, male vocal/instrumental group — Weeks on Chart: 30

Date	Title / Label	Peak Position	Weeks at No.1	Weeks on Chart
23 Apr 77	**LEAVE HOME** *Philips 9103 254*	45		1
24 Dec 77	**ROCKET TO RUSSIA** *Sire 9103 255*	60		2
7 Oct 78	**ROAD TO RUIN** *Sire SRK 6063*	32		2
16 Jun 79	**IT'S ALIVE** *Sire SRK 26074*	27		8
19 Jan 80	**END OF THE CENTURY** *Sire SRK 6077*	14		8
26 Jan 85	**TOO TOUGH TO DIE** *Beggars Banquet BEGA 59*	63		3
31 May 86	**ANIMAL BOY** *Beggars Banquet BEGA 70*	38		2
10 Oct 87	**HALFWAY TO SANITY** *Beggars Banquet BEGA 89*	78		1
19 Aug 89	**BRAIN DRAIN** *Chrysalis CHR 1725*	75		1
8 Jul 95	**IADIOS AMIGOS!** *Chrysalis CDCHR 6104*	62		1
9 Jun 01	**HEY HO LET'S GO! – ANTHOLOGY** *Rhino 8122758172* ○	74		1

RANCID

US, male vocal/instrumental group — Weeks on Chart: 7

Date	Title / Label	Peak Position	Weeks at No.1	Weeks on Chart
2 Sep 95	**...AND OUT COME THE WOLVES** *Epitaph 864442*	55		1
4 Jul 98	**LIFE WON'T WAIT** *Epitaph 64972*	32		2
5 Aug 00	**RANCID** *Hellcat 04272*	68		1
23 Mar 02	**SPLIT SERIES – VOLUME 3** *BYO 079CD* /NOFX	75		1

Date	Title	Peak	No.1	Wks
6 Sep 03	**INDESTRUCTIBLE** *WEA 9362485392*	29		2

SHABBA RANKS
Jamaica, male vocalist (Rexton Gordon) — 10

Date	Title	Peak	No.1	Wks
22 Jun 91	**AS RAW AS EVER** *Epic 4681021*	51		2
22 Aug 92	**ROUGH AND READY VOL 1** *Epic 4714422*	71		2
24 Apr 93	**X-TRA NAKED** *Epic 4723332*	38		6

RAPTURE
US, male vocal/instrumental group — 4

Date	Title	Peak	No.1	Wks
20 Sep 03	**ECHOES** *DFA/Output/Vertigo 9865447*	32		3
30 Sep 06	**PIECES OF THE PEOPLE WE LOVE** *Vertigo 1706604*	40		1

DIZZEE RASCAL
UK, male rapper (Dylan Mills) — 39

Date	Title	Peak	No.1	Wks
2 Aug 03	**BOY IN DA CORNER** *XL Recordings XLCD170* ●	23		15
18 Sep 04	**SHOWTIME** *XL Recordings XLCD181* ●	8		11
16 Jun 07	**MATHS & ENGLISH** *XL Recordings XLCD273* ●	7		13

RASCAL FLATTS
US, male vocal/instrumental group — 1

Date	Title	Peak	No.1	Wks
16 Feb 08	**RASCAL FLATTS** *Lyric Street CASCD2013*	64		1

RASMUS
Finland, male vocal/instrumental group – Lauri Yionen, Aki Markus Hakala, Eero Aleksi Heinonen & Pauli Antero Rantasalmi — 24

Date	Title	Peak	No.1	Wks
3 Apr 04	**DEAD LETTERS** *Motor 9806934* ●	10		23
24 Sep 05	**HIDE FROM THE SUN** *Universal 9873692*	65		1

ROLAND RAT SUPERSTAR
UK, male rodent rapper — 3

Date	Title	Peak	No.1	Wks
15 Dec 84	**THE CASSETTE OF THE ALBUM** *Rodent RATL 1001*	67		3

RATPACK
UK, male instrumental/production duo — 1

Date	Title	Peak	No.1	Wks
27 Nov 04	**BOYS NIGHT OUT** *Capitol 5708902*	70		1

RATT
US, male vocal/instrumental group — 5

Date	Title	Peak	No.1	Wks
13 Jul 85	**INVASION OF YOUR PRIVACY** *Atlantic 7812571*	50		2
25 Oct 86	**DANCING UNDERCOVER** *Atlantic 7816831*	51		1
12 Nov 88	**REACH FOR THE SKY** *Atlantic 7819291*	82		1
8 Sep 90	**DETONATOR** *Atlantic 7567821271*	55		1

MARK RATTRAY
UK, male vocalist — 8

Date	Title	Peak	No.1	Wks
8 Dec 90	**MARK RATTRAY PERFORMS THE SONGS OF THE MUSICALS** *Telstar STAR 2458*	46		7
10 Oct 92	**THE MAGIC OF THE MUSICALS** *Quality Television QTV 013* MARTI WEBB & MARK RATTRAY	55		1

RAVEN
UK, male vocal/instrumental group — 3

Date	Title	Peak	No.1	Wks
17 Oct 81	**ROCK UNTIL YOU DROP** *Neat 001*	63		3

RAVEONETTES
Denmark, male/female vocal/instrumental group — 2

Date	Title	Peak	No.1	Wks
6 Sep 03	**CHAIN GANG OF LOVE** *Columbia 5123782*	43		1
6 Aug 05	**PRETTY IN BLACK** *Columbia 5194269*	71		1

JOHNNIE RAY
US, male vocalist — 1

Date	Title	Peak	No.1	Wks
31 May 08	**JUST WALKIN' IN THE RAIN – VERY BEST OF** *Sony BMG 88697312092*	67		1

RAZORLIGHT
UK/Sweden, male vocal/instrumental group – Johnny Borrell, Bjorn Agren, Carl Dalemo & Christian Smith-Pancorvo (replaced by Andy Burrows) — 140

Date	Title	Peak	No.1	Wks
10 Jul 04	**UP ALL NIGHT** *Vertigo 9866944* ⊛**x4**	3		70
29 Jul 06	**RAZORLIGHT** *Vertigo 1701089* ⊛**x4**	1	2	63
15 Nov 08	**SLIPWAY FIRES** *Vertigo 1785801*	4		7

CHRIS REA
UK, male vocalist/guitarist. Popular singer/songwriter and consistent hit-maker who waited nearly a decade for his first top 10 success. The Middlesbrough native has sold more than 30 million records worldwide — 364

Date	Title	Peak	No.1	Wks
28 Apr 79	**DELTICS** *Magnet MAG 5028*	54		3
12 Apr 80	**TENNIS** *Magnet MAG 5032*	60		1
3 Apr 82	**CHRIS REA** *Magnet MAGL 5040*	52		4
18 Jun 83	**WATER SIGN** *Magnet MAGL 5048*	64		2
21 Apr 84	**WIRED TO THE MOON** *Magnet MAGL 5057*	35		7
25 May 85	**SHAMROCK DIARIES** *Magnet MAGL 5062* ○	15		14
26 Apr 86	**ON THE BEACH** *Magnet MAGL 5069* ⊛	11		37
26 Sep 87	**DANCING WITH STRANGERS** *Magnet MAGL 5071* ⊛	2		46
13 Aug 88	**ON THE BEACH** *Magnet WX 191*	37		10
29 Oct 88	**THE BEST OF CHRIS REA – NEW LIGHT THROUGH OLD WINDOWS** *WEA WX 200* ⊛**x3**	5		51
11 Nov 89	**THE ROAD TO HELL** *WEA WX 317* ⊛**x6**	1	1	76
9 Mar 91	**AUBERGE** *WEA 9031735801* ⊛**x2**	1	3	37
14 Nov 92	**GOD'S GREAT BANANA SKIN** *East West 4509909952* ⊛	4		15
13 Nov 93	**ESPRESSO LOGIC** *East West 4509943112* ●	8		10
5 Nov 94	**THE BEST OF CHRIS REA** *East West 4509980402* ⊛	3		18
23 Nov 96	**LA PASSION (OST)** *East West 0630166952* ○	43		4
31 Jan 98	**THE BLUE CAFÉ** *East West 3984216882* ○	10		7
20 Nov 99	**THE ROAD TO HELL – PART 2** *East West 8573803992* ○	54		1
14 Oct 00	**KING OF THE BEACH** *East West 8573850172*	26		3
1 Dec 01	**THE VERY BEST OF** *East West 0927421282* ●	69		1
28 Sep 02	**DANCING DOWN THE STONEY ROAD** *Jazzee Blue JBLUECD 01X* ○	14		7
3 Apr 04	**THE BLUE JUKEBOX** *Jazzee Blue JBLUECD08X*	27		3
13 Aug 05	**HEARTBEATS – GREATEST HITS** *warner.esp 5046754542* ○	24		5
28 Oct 06	**THE ROAD TO HELL & BACK** *Polydor 1704477*	34		2

EDDI READER
UK, female vocalist. See Fairground Attraction — 19

Date	Title	Peak	No.1	Wks
7 Mar 92	**MIRMAMA** *RCA PD 75156*	34		2
2 Jul 94	**EDDI READER** *Blanco Y Negro 4509961772* ●	4		12
20 Jul 96	**CANDYFLOSS AND MEDICINE** *Blanco Y Negro 0630151202*	24		5
23 May 98	**ANGELS & ELECTRICITY** *Blanco Y Negro 3984228162*	49		2

REAL McCOY
Germany/US, male/female vocal/instrumental trio – Lisa Cork, Olaf Jeglitza & Vanessa Mason — 5

Date	Title	Peak	No.1	Wks
20 May 95	**ANOTHER NIGHT – U.S. ALBUM** *Logic 74321280972*	6		5

REAL PEOPLE
UK, male vocal/instrumental group — 1

Date	Title	Peak	No.1	Wks
18 May 91	**THE REAL PEOPLE** *Columbia 4680841*	59		1

REAL THING
UK, male vocal group — 17

Date	Title	Peak	No.1	Wks
6 Nov 76	**REAL THING** *Pye NSPL 18507* ○	34		3
7 Apr 79	**CAN YOU FEEL THE FORCE** *Pye NSPH 18601*	73		1
10 May 80	**20 GREATEST HITS** *K-Tel NE 1073*	56		2
12 Jul 86	**THE BEST OF THE REAL THING** *West Five NRT 1* ○	24		11

REBEL MC
UK, male rapper (Mike West) — 11

Date	Title	Peak	No.1	Wks
28 Apr 90	**REBEL MUSIC** *Desire LUVLP 5*	18		7
13 Jul 91	**BLACK MEANING GOOD** *Desire LUVLP 12*	23		4

IVAN REBROFF
Germany, male vocalist (Hans Rippert) — 4

Date	Title	Peak	No.1	Wks
16 Jun 90	**THE VERY BEST OF IVAN REBROFF** *BBC REB 778*	57		4

RED BOX

UK, male vocal/instrumental duo — Weeks on chart: 4

Date	Album	Peak	Wks at No.1	Wks
6 Dec 86	**THE CIRCLE AND THE SQUARE** *Sire WX 79*	73		4

RED HOT CHILI PEPPERS

US, male vocal/instrumental group – Anthony Kiedis, Michael 'Flea' Balzary, John Frusciante*, Dave Navarro & Chad Smith. Rock/funk group awarded a star on the Hollywood Walk of Fame in 2008 whose three concerts at Hyde Park in 2004 sold 258,000 tickets and took £9,115,282 – the highest-grossing UK concert at a single venue — Weeks on chart: 411

Date	Album	Peak	Wks at No.1	Wks
12 Oct 91	**BLOOD SUGAR SEX MAGIK** *Warner Brothers WX441* ⊛	25		86
17 Oct 92	**WHAT HITS!?** *EMI USA CDMTL 1071* ●	23		4
19 Nov 94	**OUT IN LA** *EMI CDMTL 1082*	61		1
23 Sep 95	**ONE HOT MINUTE** *Warner Brothers 9362457332* ●	2		11
19 Jun 99	**CALIFORNICATION** *Warner Brothers 9362473862* ⊛x3	5		130
20 Jul 02	**BY THE WAY** *Warner Brothers 9362481402* ⊛x5	1	5	77
29 Nov 03	**GREATEST HITS** *Warner Brothers 9362485962* ⊛x3	4		54
7 Aug 04	**LIVE IN HYDE PARK** *Warner Brothers 9362488632* ●	1	2	9
20 May 06	**STADIUM ARCADIUM** *Warner Brothers 9362499962* ⊛x2 ★	1	3	39

Top 3 Best-Selling Albums

	Album	Approximate Sales
1	BY THE WAY	1,950,000
2	GREATEST HITS	1,190,000
3	CALIFORNICATION	1,140,000

RED HOUSE PAINTERS

US, male vocal/instrumental group — Weeks on chart: 2

Date	Album	Peak	Wks at No.1	Wks
5 Jun 93	**RED HOUSE PAINTERS** *4AD DAD 3008CD*	63		1
30 Oct 93	**RED HOUSE PAINTERS** *4AD CAD 3016CD*	68		1

RED SNAPPER

UK, male vocal/instrumental group — Weeks on chart: 2

Date	Album	Peak	Wks at No.1	Wks
21 Sep 96	**PRINCE BLIMEY** *Warp WARPCD 45*	60		1
10 Oct 98	**MAKING BONES** *Warp WARPCD 056*	59		1

SHARON REDD

US, female vocalist, d. 1 May 1992 (age 46) — Weeks on chart: 5

Date	Album	Peak	Wks at No.1	Wks
23 Oct 82	**REDD HOTT** *Prelude PRL 25056*	59		5

OTIS REDDING

US, male vocalist, d. 10 Dec 1967 (age 26) — Weeks on chart: 235

Date	Album	Peak	Wks at No.1	Wks
19 Feb 66	**OTIS BLUE: OTIS REDDING SINGS SOUL** *Atlantic ATL 5041*	6		21
23 Apr 66	**THE GREAT OTIS REDDING SINGS SOUL BALLADS** *Atlantic ATL 5029*	30		1
23 Jul 66	**THE SOUL ALBUM** *Atlantic 587011*	22		9
21 Jan 67	**OTIS BLUE: OTIS REDDING SINGS SOUL** *Atlantic 587036* ○	7		54
21 Jan 67	**COMPLETE AND UNBELIEVABLE...THE OTIS REDDING DICTIONARY OF SOUL** *Atlantic 588050*	23		16
29 Apr 67	**PAIN IN MY HEART** *Atlantic 587042*	28		9
1 Jul 67	**KING AND QUEEN** *Atlantic 589007* & CARLA THOMAS	18		17
10 Feb 68	**THE HISTORY OF OTIS REDDING** *Volt S 418*	2		43
30 Mar 68	**OTIS REDDING IN EUROPE** *Stax 589016*	14		16
1 Jun 68	**DOCK OF THE BAY** *Stax 231001*	1	1	15
12 Oct 68	**IMMORTAL OTIS REDDING** *Atlantic 588113*	19		8
11 Sep 93	**DOCK OF THE BAY – THE DEFINITIVE COLLECTION** *Atlantic 9548317092* ⊛x2	44		18
11 Nov 00	**THE VERY BEST OF** *Atco 9548380872* ●	26		8

HELEN REDDY

Australia, female vocalist — Weeks on chart: 27

Date	Album	Peak	Wks at No.1	Wks
8 Feb 75	**FREE AND EASY** *Capitol EST 11348* ○	17		9
14 Feb 76	**THE BEST OF HELEN REDDY** *Capitol EST 11467* ●	5		18

REDHEAD KINGPIN & THE F.B.I.

US, male rapper & rap group — Weeks on chart: 3

Date	Album	Peak	Wks at No.1	Wks
9 Sep 89	**A SHADE OF RED** *10 Records DIX 85*	35		3

REDMAN

US, male rapper (Reggie Noble) — Weeks on chart: 7

Date	Album	Peak	Wks at No.1	Wks
9 Oct 99	**BLACK OUT!** *Def Jam 5466092* METHOD MAN & REDMAN	45		3
9 Jun 01	**MALPRACTICE** *Def Jam 5483812*	57		4

REDSKINS

UK, male vocal/instrumental trio — Weeks on chart: 4

Date	Album	Peak	Wks at No.1	Wks
22 Mar 86	**NEITHER WASHINGTON NOR MOSCOW...** *Decca FLP 1*	31		4

ALEX REECE

UK, male DJ/producer — Weeks on chart: 5

Date	Album	Peak	Wks at No.1	Wks
17 Aug 96	**SO FAR** *Fourth & Broadway BRCD 621*	19		5

DAN REED NETWORK

US, male vocal/instrumental group — Weeks on chart: 6

Date	Album	Peak	Wks at No.1	Wks
4 Nov 89	**SLAM** *Mercury 8388681*	66		2
27 Jul 91	**THE HEAT** *Mercury 8488551*	15		4

LOU REED

US, male vocalist (Lou Firbank). See Velvet Underground — Weeks on chart: 98

Date	Album	Peak	Wks at No.1	Wks
21 Apr 73	**TRANSFORMER** *RCA Victor LSP 4807*	13		25
20 Oct 73	**BERLIN** *RCA Victor RS 1002* ○	7		5
16 Mar 74	**ROCK 'N' ROLL ANIMAL** *RCA Victor APL1 0472*	26		1
14 Feb 76	**CONEY ISLAND BABY** *RCA Victor RS 1035*	52		1
3 Jul 82	**TRANSFORMER** *RCA International INTS 5061*	91		2
9 Jun 84	**NEW SENSATIONS** *RCA PL 84998*	92		1
24 May 86	**MISTRIAL** *RCA PL 87190*	69		1
28 Jan 89	**NEW YORK** *Sire WX 246* ●	14		22
7 Oct 89	**RETRO** *RCA PL 90389* ○	29		5
5 May 90	**SONGS FOR DRELLA** *Sire WX 345* & JOHN CALE	22		5
25 Jan 92	**MAGIC AND LOSS** *Sire 7599266622*	6		6
28 Oct 95	**THE BEST OF LOU REED AND THE VELVET UNDERGROUND** *Global Television RADCD 21* & THE VELVET UNDERGROUND	56		4
2 Mar 96	**SET THE TWILIGHT REELING** *Warner Brothers 9362461592*	26		2
7 Feb 98	**TRANSFORMER** *RCA 74321601812*	16		12
15 Apr 00	**ECSTASY** *Reprise 9362474252*	54		1
24 May 03	**NYC MAN** *BMG 74321984012*	31		3
7 Aug 04	**NYC MAN – GREATEST HITS** *BMG 82876631122*	43		2

REEF

UK, male vocal/instrumental group – Gary Stringer, Jack Bessant, Dominic Greensmith, Kenwyn House & Benmont Tench — Weeks on chart: 55

Date	Album	Peak	Wks at No.1	Wks
1 Jul 95	**REPLENISH** *Sony S2 4806982* ○	9		11
8 Feb 97	**GLOW** *Sony S2 4869402* ●	1	1	32
1 May 99	**RIDES** *Sony S2 4928822*	3		7
2 Sep 00	**GETAWAY** *Sony S2 4988912*	15		4
8 Feb 03	**TOGETHER – THE BEST OF** *Sony S2 5094352*	52		1

REEL 2 REAL FEATURING THE MAD STUNTMAN

US, male vocal/production duo – Erick Morillo & Mark Quashie — Weeks on chart: 8

Date	Album	Peak	Wks at No.1	Wks
22 Oct 94	**MOVE IT!** *Positiva CDTIVA 1003* ●	8		8

CONNOR REEVES

UK, male vocalist — Weeks on chart: 8

Date	Album	Peak	Wks at No.1	Wks
6 Dec 97	**EARTHBOUND** *Wildstar CDWILD 3* ○	25		8

JIM REEVES

US, male vocalist, d. 31 Jul 1964 (age 39). The velvet-voiced country music balladeer who achieved most of his UK albums chart success after he was tragically killed in a plane crash. Shortly after his death, "Gentleman Jim" had a record eight albums simultaneously in the Top 20 — Weeks on chart: 412

Date	Album	Peak	Wks at No.1	Wks
28 Mar 64	**GOOD 'N' COUNTRY** *RCA Camden CDN 5114*	10		35
9 May 64	**GENTLEMAN JIM** *RCA Victor RD 7541*	3		23
15 Aug 64	**A TOUCH OF VELVET** *RCA Victor RD 7521*	8		9
15 Aug 64	**INTERNATIONAL JIM REEVES** *RCA Victor RD 7577*	11		17
22 Aug 64	**HE'LL HAVE TO GO** *RCA Victor RD 27176*	16		4
29 Aug 64	**GOD BE WITH YOU** *RCA Victor RD 27193*	10		10
29 Aug 64	**THE INTIMATE JIM REEVES** *RCA Victor RD 7636*	12		4
5 Sep 64	**MOONLIGHT AND ROSES** *RCA Victor RD 7639*	2		52

Date	Title / Label	Peak Position	Weeks at No.1	Weeks on Chart
19 Sep 64	**COUNTRY SIDE OF JIM REEVES** *RCA Camden CDN 5100*	12		5
26 Sep 64	**WE THANK THEE** *RCA Victor RD 7637*	17		3
28 Nov 64	**TWELVE SONGS OF CHRISTMAS** *RCA Victor RD 7663*	4		17
30 Jan 65	**THE BEST OF JIM REEVES** *RCA Victor RDC 7666*	3		47
10 Apr 65	**HAVE I TOLD YOU LATELY THAT I LOVE YOU** *RCA Camden CDN 5122*	12		5
22 May 65	**THE JIM REEVES WAY** *RCA Victor RD 7694*	16		4
5 Nov 66	**DISTANT DRUMS** *RCA Victor RD 7814*	2		34
18 Jan 69	**A TOUCH OF SADNESS** *RCA Victor RD 7978*	15		5
5 Jul 69	**ACCORDING TO MY HEART** *RCA International INTS 1013*	1	4	14
23 Aug 69	**JIM REEVES AND SOME FRIENDS** *RCA Victor SF 8022*	24		4
29 Nov 69	**ON STAGE** *RCA Victor SF 8047*	13		4
26 Dec 70	**MY CATHEDRAL** *RCA Victor SF 8146*	48		2
3 Jul 71	**JIM REEVES WRITES YOU A RECORD** *RCA Victor SF 8176*	47		2
7 Aug 71	**JIM REEVES' GOLDEN RECORDS** *RCA International INTS 1070*	9		21
14 Aug 71	**THE INTIMATE JIM REEVES** *RCA International INTS 1256*	8		15
21 Aug 71	**GIRLS I HAVE KNOWN** *RCA International INTS 1140*	35		5
27 Nov 71	**TWELVE SONGS OF CHRISTMAS** *RCA International INTS 1188*	3		6
27 Nov 71	**A TOUCH OF VELVET** *RCA International INTS 1089*	49		2
15 Apr 72	**MY FRIEND** *RCA Victor SF 8258*	32		5
20 Sep 75	**40 GOLDEN GREATS** *Arcade ADEP 16* ⊛	1	3	25
6 Sep 80	**COUNTRY GENTLEMAN** *K-Tel NE 1088*	53		4
8 Aug 92	**THE DEFINITIVE JIM REEVES** *Arcade ARC 94982*	9		10
28 Sep 96	**THE ULTIMATE COLLECTION** *RCA Victor 74321410872* ○	17		6
5 Jul 03	**GENTLEMAN JIM – DEFINITIVE COLLECTION** *RCA 82876530372*	21		10
3 Jul 04	**GENTLEMAN JIM – MEMORIES ARE MADE OF THIS** *RCA 82876627842*	35		3

VIC REEVES

UK, male comedian/vocalist (Jim Moir)

Date	Title / Label	Peak Position	Weeks at No.1	Weeks on Chart: 9
16 Nov 91	**I WILL CURE YOU** *Sense SIGN 111* VIC REEVES ○	16		9

NEIL REID

UK, male vocalist

Date	Title / Label	Peak Position	Weeks at No.1	Weeks on Chart: 18
5 Feb 72	**NEIL REID** *Decca SKL 5122*	1	3	16
2 Sep 72	**SMILE** *Decca SKL 5136*	47		2

R.E.M.

US, male vocal/instrumental group – Michael Stipe, Bill Berry, Peter Buck & Mike Mills. Award-winning Georgia quartet with a political conscience, once dubbed "America's Best Rock Band" by *Rolling Stone* magazine, who have released a string of critically-acclaimed albums and packed stadiums worldwide

Date	Title / Label	Peak Position	Weeks at No.1	Weeks on Chart: 623
28 Apr 84	**RECKONING** *I.R.S. A 7045*	91		2
29 Jun 85	**FABLES OF THE RECONSTRUCTION** *I.R.S. MIRF 1003*	35		4
6 Sep 86	**LIFE'S RICH PAGEANT** *I.R.S. MIRG 1014*	43		4
16 May 87	**DEAD LETTER OFFICE** *I.R.S. SP 70054*	60		2
26 Sep 87	**DOCUMENT** *I.R.S. MIRG 1025*	28		5
29 Oct 88	**EPONYMOUS** *I.R.S. MIRG 1038*	69		3
19 Nov 88	**GREEN** *Warner Brothers WX 234* ⊛	27		22
23 Mar 91	**OUT OF TIME** *Warner Brothers WX 404* ⊛x5	1	1	183
10 Oct 92	**THE BEST OF R.E.M.** *I.R.S. MIRH 1* ●	7		28
10 Oct 92	**AUTOMATIC FOR THE PEOPLE** *Warner Brothers 9362450552* ⊛x6	1	4	179
8 Oct 94	**MONSTER** *Warner Brothers 9362457632* ⊛x3 ★	1	2	56
21 Sep 96	**NEW ADVENTURES IN HI-FI** *Warner Brothers 9362463212* ⊛	1	1	20
7 Nov 98	**UP** *Warner Brothers 9362471122* ⊛	2		29
26 May 01	**REVEAL** *Warner Brothers 9362479462* ⊛	1	2	15
8 Nov 03	**IN TIME – THE BEST OF – 1988-2003** *Warner Brothers 9362483812* ⊛x5	1	1	52
8 Nov 03	**IN TIME – THE BEST OF – 1988-2003 LIMITED EDITION** *Warner Brothers 9362486022*	36		1
16 Oct 04	**AROUND THE SUN** *Warner Brothers 9362489112* ●	1	1	7
23 Sep 06	**AND I FEEL FINE – BEST OF THE IRS YEARS** *Capitol 3699412*	70		1
27 Oct 07	**LIVE** *Warner Brothers 9362499253*	12		3
12 Apr 08	**ACCELERATE** *Warner Brothers 9362498741* ○	1	1	7

Top 3 Best-Selling Albums

		Approximate Sales
1	AUTOMATIC FOR THE PEOPLE	2,300,000
2	OUT OF TIME	1,810,000
3	IN TIME - THE BEST OF - 1988-2003	1,600,000

REMBRANDTS

US, male vocal/instrumental duo

Date	Title / Label	Peak Position	Weeks at No.1	Weeks on Chart: 5
23 Sep 95	**LP** *East West America 7559617522*	14		5

RENAISSANCE

UK, male/female vocal/instrumental group

Date	Title / Label	Peak Position	Weeks at No.1	Weeks on Chart: 10
21 Feb 70	**RENAISSANCE** *Island ILPS 9114*	60		1
19 Aug 78	**A SONG FOR ALL SEASONS** *Warner Brothers K 56460* ○	35		8
2 Jun 79	**AZUR D'OR** *Warner Brothers K 56633*	73		1

RENATO

UK/Italy, female/male vocal duo

Date	Title / Label	Peak Position	Weeks at No.1	Weeks on Chart: 14
25 Dec 82	**SAVE YOUR LOVE** *Lifestyle LEG 9*	26		14

RENEGADE SOUNDWAVE

UK, male vocal/instrumental group

Date	Title / Label	Peak Position	Weeks at No.1	Weeks on Chart: 1
24 Mar 90	**SOUNDCLASH** *Mute STUMM 63*	74		1

REO SPEEDWAGON

US, male vocal/instrumental group – Kevin Cronin, Neil Doughty, Alan Gratzer, Bruce Hall & Gary Richrath

Date	Title / Label	Peak Position	Weeks at No.1	Weeks on Chart: 36
25 Apr 81	**HI INFIDELITY** *Epic EPC 84700* ○ ★	6		29
17 Jul 82	**GOOD TROUBLE** *Epic EPC 85789*	29		7

REPUBLICA

UK/Nigeria, female/male vocal/instrumental group – Samantha 'Saffron' Sprackling, Dave Barbarossa, Tim Dorney, Johnny Male & Andy Todd

Date	Title / Label	Peak Position	Weeks at No.1	Weeks on Chart: 38
15 Mar 97	**REPUBLICA** *Deconstruction 74321410522* ●	4		36
17 Oct 98	**SPEED BALLADS** *Deconstruction 74321610462*	37		2

REVEREND & THE MAKERS

UK, male/female vocal/instrumental group – Jon 'The Reverend' McClure, Ed Cosens, Stuart Doughty, Tom Jarvis, Laura Manuel, Joe Moskow & Richy Westley

Date	Title / Label	Peak Position	Weeks at No.1	Weeks on Chart: 10
29 Sep 07	**THE STATE OF THINGS** *Wall Of Sound WOS015CD* ●	5		10

REVOLTING COCKS

UK, male vocal/instrumental group

Date	Title / Label	Peak Position	Weeks at No.1	Weeks on Chart: 1
2 Oct 93	**LINGER FICKEN' GOOD** *Devotion CDDVN 22*	39		1

REZILLOS

UK, male/female vocal/instrumental group

Date	Title / Label	Peak Position	Weeks at No.1	Weeks on Chart: 15
5 Aug 78	**CAN'T STAND THE REZILLOS** *Sire K 56530* ○	16		10
28 Apr 79	**MISSION ACCOMPLISHED BUT THE BEAT GOES ON** *Sire SRK 6069*	30		5

RHYDIAN

UK, male vocalist (Rhydian Roberts)

Date	Title / Label	Peak Position	Weeks at No.1	Weeks on Chart: 5
6 Dec 08	**RHYDIAN** *Syco 88697418512*	3		5+

BUSTA RHYMES

US, male rapper (Trevor Smith)

Date	Title / Label	Peak Position	Weeks at No.1	Weeks on Chart: 29
30 Mar 96	**THE COMING** *Elektra 7559617422*	48		4
4 Oct 97	**WHEN DISASTER STRIKES** *Elektra 7559622602*	34		5
16 Jan 99	**EXTINCTION LEVEL EVENT/FINAL WORLD FRONT** *Elektra 7559622112*	54		7
1 Jul 00	**ANARCHY** *Elektra 7559625172*	38		1
29 Sep 01	**TURN IT UP – THE VERY BEST OF** *Elektra 8122735802* ○	44		3
23 Mar 02	**GENESIS** *J Records 80813200092*	58		1
24 Jun 06	**THE BIG BANG** *Interscope 9878436* ○ ★	19		8

GRUFF RHYS

UK, male vocalist/guitarist. See Super Furry Animals

Date	Title / Label	Peak Position	Weeks at No.1	Weeks on Chart: 1
20 Jan 07	**CANDYLION** *Rough Trade RTRADCD371*	50		1

RIALTO

UK, male vocal/instrumental group

Date	Title / Label	Peak Position	Weeks at No.1	Weeks on Chart: 3
25 Jul 98	**RIALTO** *China 0630197452*	21		3

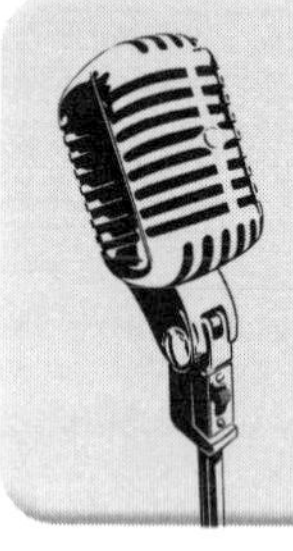

Otis Redding

'(Sittin' On) The Dock Of The Bay' is one of the greatest pop songs ever recorded. It is an undeniable classic, a gold standard that will be played for all time. It also includes an entire verse which is whistled by the singer Otis Redding. Why? Because the Georgia-born R&B pioneer felt the song was unfinished and wanted to come back to the recording a few days later once he'd completed the lyrics.

Otis never came back to record that new verse because just three days later he was killed in a plane crash in Madison, Wisconsin. His body was recovered from the bed of a lake and with that, the music world was prematurely robbed of one of its key voices. Redding's plane seated seven, so the eight-person entourage took it in turns to be the lone person to catch a commercial flight; on this night, Otis was one of the seven – only one, Ben Cauley, survived the impact.

Despite his career being so abruptly and tragically cut short (he was only twenty-six), Redding's influence at the time of his death was already massive. In the months preceding the plane crash, he had toppled Elvis as 'Best Singer in the World' from a poll in *Melody Maker*. His albums, *Otis Redding Sings Soul* and *Soul Ballads* had both enjoyed UK chart success as well as American acclaim, and his future seemed as bright as any contemporary soul artist.

Otis effortlessly combined the traditions of gospel and R&B into a fire-breathing, funky, soul music

Born in September 1941, Otis's family did not enjoy the wealth he later accumulated due to his prodigious talent. Like many of the great vocalists, Otis sang gospel regularly, in his case at the Vineville Baptist Church, in his hometown of Macon. As one of six children, money was always short and he left school early to bring in cash from singing – his voice was an electric combination of the authenticity of the blues and a shatteringly soulful tone. At first he competed in local talent competitions, but after winning the $5 prize fifteen times, he was banned from competing. Instead, he turned to professional bands, with this first role being alongside The Upsetters (previously a backing band for fellow Macon native Little Richard, who was hailed by Otis as a massive personal influence).

Otis effortlessly combined the traditions of gospel and R&B into a fire-breathing, funky, soul music, a spectacular hybrid that was testament to his extraordinary passion for music and a talent that was a gift from the gods. Long before the accolades and smash hits, Redding had learned his craft touring the deep South, starting off as a bus driver for Johnny Jenkins before eventually progressing to his own headline band, Otis and the Shooters. Even this early on, if you listen to songs like 'She's All Right' or 'Shout Bamalama', there are signs of his impending stardom.

In one of those twists of circumstance that music often throws up, Otis found himself with some spare studio time one day while working with Jenkins and took advantage of the opportunity by singing 'These Arms Of Mine', which he'd written himself – this became his first hit record. The mid-1960s saw his career start to gain momentum, whether it was singing originals (he wrote far more than most realise) or revamped covers, such as his startling rendition of 'Try A Little Tenderness'. He would go on to release over thirty singles and ten original studio albums; in September 1966 the influential British TV show *Ready Steady Go* even broadcast their own dedicated Otis show. Notably, Aretha Franklin's signature tune 'Respect' was actually first released by Otis, 'The Big O', as he was known due to his grand stature. He came up with his most famous song, '(Sittin' On) The Dock Of The Bay', during a week-long stay on a houseboat in Sausalito.

Chart History

Artist	Best-Selling Album	Week	Highest Position	Approx Sales
OTIS	OTIS BLUE: OTIS REDDING SINGS SOUL	19/2/66	1	325,000

Otis Redding's actual album sales and chart success is relatively modest: *Dock of the Bay* being his only Number 1, posthumously too. Many of the releases made after his death are evidence of his prolific recording activity in the months leading up to his demise – most of his work was recorded at Stax in Memphis. But his impact goes way beyond the charts. Even the word 'soul' owed a debt to Otis, whose ability to appeal to all audiences had taken a previously marginalised form and thrust it very firmly into the mainstream.

Europe and Britain loved Otis and in 1967 he'd famously headlined the Stax Revue tour which was received with wild accolades across the Continent. It wasn't just as an R&B pioneer that Otis revelled – at the time, he was immediately revered by the likes of The Rolling Stones, whose own Keith Richards was a huge fan. And you can hear Otis in the intonation of numerous Jagger moments. The perfect example of Otis's wide-ranging appeal is his blistering performance in front of 30,000 at the 1967 Monterey Pop Festival, where he delivered one of the most impassioned vocal performances ever captured on film.

Otis had a fierce humanitarian streak too – he had a white manager at a time when this was unheard of and championed his racially mixed band; he provided scholarships for local kids and even held barbeques at his house for impoverished children in his hometown when he was back from his gruelling touring schedules.

His own soul lives on in the endless samples, radio and television snippets and cover versions of his watershed work. He has been awarded Grammys, songwriters' and singers' Hall of Fame induction, countless tributes and even his own commemorative US stamp. Christina Aguilera, Pearl Jam, The Black Crowes and Kanye West are just a small number of the artists who have covered his songs. The inevitable retrospective albums always do well, but even all these striking statistics fail to explain his true seismic significance in the genesis of modern urban music and, indeed, modern music itself. Along with the likes of Sam Cooke, James Brown, Jackie Wilson and Little Richard, Otis Redding shaped R&B and his albums are the benchmark for any R&B artist since.

His own soul lives on in the endless samples, radio and television snippets and cover versions

What might he have achieved had his life not been tragically snuffed out? His entire recording career only spanned six years, yet his influence and shadow is cast in every corner of the decades that followed his death. He was buried at the Big O Ranch, a sprawling 450-acre estate, and his sons offer perhaps his most fitting and poignant legacy, with both Dexter and Otis III being highly respected music producers and songwriters.

Silver-selling ○ Gold-selling ● Platinum-selling ⊛ US No.1 ★ | Peak Position | Weeks at No.1 | Weeks on Chart

DAMIEN RICE
Ireland, male vocalist/guitarist — 111

Date	Title	Peak	Wks No.1	Wks
2 Aug 03	**O** *DRM/14th Floor DRM002CD* ⊛x3	8		97
18 Nov 06	**9** *Heffa/14th Floor 2564640422* ●	4		14

CHARLIE RICH
US, male vocalist/pianist, d. 25 Jul 1995 (age 62) — 28

Date	Title	Peak	Wks No.1	Wks
23 Mar 74	**BEHIND CLOSED DOORS** *Epic 65716* ●	4		26
13 Jul 74	**VERY SPECIAL LOVE SONGS** *Epic 80031*	34		2

RICHIE RICH
UK, male DJ/producer (Richard Morgan) — 1

Date	Title	Peak	Wks No.1	Wks
22 Jul 89	**I CAN MAKE YOU DANCE** *Gee Street GEEA 3*	65		1

TONY RICH PROJECT
US, male vocalist (Antonio Jeffries) — 10

Date	Title	Peak	Wks No.1	Wks
25 May 96	**WORDS** *LaFace 73008260222*	27		10

RICH KIDS
UK, male vocal/instrumental group — 1

Date	Title	Peak	Wks No.1	Wks
7 Oct 78	**GHOST OF PRINCES IN TOWERS** *EMI EMC 3263*	51		1

CLIFF RICHARD
UK, male vocalist (Harry Webb). The most successful British chart act of all time, whose span of hits exceeds 50 years. Sir Cliff's 38 Top 10 albums is a record for a British act and he had more Top 10 albums in the 80s than any other artist — 841

Date	Title	Peak	Wks No.1	Wks
18 Apr 59	**CLIFF** *Columbia 33SX 1147* CLIFF RICHARD & THE DRIFTERS	4		31
14 Nov 59	**CLIFF SINGS** *Columbia 33SX 1192* CLIFF RICHARD & THE SHADOWS	2		36
15 Oct 60	**ME AND MY SHADOWS** *Columbia 33SX 1261* CLIFF RICHARD & THE SHADOWS	2		33
22 Apr 61	**LISTEN TO CLIFF** *Columbia 33SX 1320* CLIFF RICHARD & THE SHADOWS	2		28
21 Oct 61	**21 TODAY** *Columbia 33SX 1368* CLIFF RICHARD & THE SHADOWS	1	1	16
23 Dec 61	**THE YOUNG ONES (OST)** *Columbia 33SX 1384* CLIFF RICHARD & THE SHADOWS	1	6	42
29 Sep 62	**32 MINUTES AND 17 SECONDS** *Columbia 33SX 1431* CLIFF RICHARD & THE SHADOWS	3		21
26 Jan 63	**SUMMER HOLIDAY (OST)** *Columbia 33SX 1472* CLIFF RICHARD & THE SHADOWS	1	14	36
13 Jul 63	**CLIFF'S HIT ALBUM** *Columbia 33SX 1512* CLIFF RICHARD & THE SHADOWS	2		19
28 Sep 63	**WHEN IN SPAIN** *Columbia 33SX 1541* CLIFF RICHARD & THE SHADOWS	8		10
11 Jul 64	**WONDERFUL LIFE (OST)** *Columbia 33SX 1628* CLIFF RICHARD & THE SHADOWS	2		23
9 Jan 65	**ALADDIN AND HIS WONDERFUL LAMP** *Columbia 33SX 1676* CLIFF RICHARD & THE SHADOWS	13		5
17 Apr 65	**CLIFF RICHARD** *Columbia 33SX 1709*	9		5
14 Aug 65	**MORE HITS BY CLIFF** *Columbia 33SX 1737* CLIFF RICHARD & THE SHADOWS	20		1
8 Jan 66	**LOVE IS FOREVER** *Columbia 33SX 1769* CLIFF RICHARD & THE SHADOWS	19		1
21 May 66	**KINDA LATIN** *Columbia SX 6039*	9		12
17 Dec 66	**FINDERS KEEPERS (OST)** *Columbia SX 6079*	6		18
7 Jan 67	**CINDERELLA** *Columbia 33SX 6103*	30		6
15 Apr 67	**DON'T STOP ME NOW...** *Columbia SCX 6133*	23		9
11 Nov 67	**GOOD NEWS** *Columbia SCX 6167*	37		1
1 Jan 68	**CLIFF IN JAPAN** *Columbia SCX 6244*	29		2
16 Nov 68	**ESTABLISHED 1958** *Columbia SCX 6282* CLIFF RICHARD & THE SHADOWS	30		4
12 Jul 69	**THE BEST OF CLIFF** *Columbia SCX 6343* CLIFF RICHARD & THE SHADOWS	5		17
27 Sep 69	**SINCERELY** *Columbia SCX 6357*	24		3
12 Dec 70	**TRACKS 'N' GROOVES** *Columbia SCX 6435*	37		2
23 Dec 72	**THE BEST OF CLIFF VOLUME 2** *Columbia SCX 6519* CLIFF RICHARD & THE SHADOWS	49		2
19 Jan 74	**TAKE ME HIGH (OST)** *EMI EMC 3016*	41		4
29 May 76	**I'M NEARLY FAMOUS** *EMI EMC 3122* ●	5		21
26 Mar 77	**EVERY FACE TELLS A STORY** *EMI EMC 3172*	8		10
22 Oct 77	**40 GOLDEN GREATS** *EMI EMTV 6* ⊛	1	1	19
4 Mar 78	**SMALL CORNERS** *EMI EMC 3219*	33		5
21 Oct 78	**GREEN LIGHT** *EMI EMC 3231*	25		3
17 Feb 79	**THANK YOU VERY MUCH – REUNION CONCERT AT THE LONDON PALLADIUM** *EMI EMTV 15* CLIFF RICHARD & THE SHADOWS ●	5		12
15 Sep 79	**ROCK 'N' ROLL JUVENILE** *EMI EMC 3307* ●	3		22
13 Sep 80	**I'M NO HERO** *EMI EMA 796* ●	4		12
4 Jul 81	**LOVE SONGS** *EMI EMTV 27* ⊛	1	5	43
26 Sep 81	**WIRED FOR SOUND** *EMI EMC 3377* ⊛	4		25
4 Sep 82	**NOW YOU SEE ME...NOW YOU DON'T** *EMI EMC 3415* ●	4		14
21 May 83	**DRESSED FOR THE OCCASION** *EMI EMC 3432* CLIFF RICHARD & THE LONDON PHILHARMONIC ORCHESTRA ○	7		17
15 Oct 83	**SILVER** *EMI EMC 1077871* ●	7		24
14 Jul 84	**20 ORIGINAL GREATS** *EMI CRS 1*	43		6
1 Dec 84	**THE ROCK CONNECTION** *EMI CLIF 2* ○	43		5
26 Sep 87	**ALWAYS GUARANTEED** *EMI EMD 1004* ⊛	5		25
19 Nov 88	**PRIVATE COLLECTION 1979–1988** *EMI CRTV 30* ⊛x4	1	2	26
11 Nov 89	**STRONGER** *EMI EMD 1012* ⊛	7		21
17 Nov 90	**FROM A DISTANCE...THE EVENT** *EMI CRTV 31* ⊛x2	3		15
30 Nov 91	**TOGETHER WITH CLIFF RICHARD** *EMI EMD 1028* ⊛	10		7
1 May 93	**CLIFF RICHARD – THE ALBUM** *EMI CDEMD 1043* ●	1	1	15
15 Oct 94	**THE HIT LIST** *EMI CDEMTV 84* ⊛	3		21
11 Nov 95	**SONGS FROM 'HEATHCLIFF'** *EMI CDEMD 1091* ●	15		9
24 Aug 96	**CLIFF AT THE MOVIES – 1959–1974** *EMI CDEMD 1096*	17		3
2 Aug 97	**THE ROCK 'N' ROLL YEARS** *EMI CDEMD 1109*	32		3
31 Oct 98	**REAL AS I WANNA BE** *EMI 4974062*	10		9
21 Oct 00	**THE WHOLE STORY – HIS GREATEST HITS** *EMI 5293222* ⊛	6		13
17 Nov 01	**WANTED** *Papillon WANTED 1* ●	11		8
29 Nov 03	**CLIFF AT CHRISTMAS** *EMI 5934982* ⊛	9		8
6 Nov 04	**SOMETHING'S GOIN' ON** *Decca/UCJ 4756408* ●	7		4
26 Nov 05	**THE PLATINUM COLLECTION** *EMI 3338032* ●	51		6
18 Nov 06	**TWO'S COMPANY – THE DUETS** *EMI 3770722* ●	8		8
24 Nov 07	**LOVE – THE ALBUM** *EMI 5093702* ○	13		7
15 Nov 08	**THE 50TH ANNIVERSARY ALBUM** *EMI 2423892*	11		8+

KEITH RICHARDS
UK, male vocalist/guitarist. See Rolling Stones — 4

Date	Title	Peak	Wks No.1	Wks
15 Oct 88	**TALK IS CHEAP** *Virgin V 2554*	37		3
31 Oct 92	**MAIN OFFENDER** *Virgin America CDVUS 59*	45		1

LIONEL RICHIE
US, male vocalist/pianist. After 12 years as lead singer of The Commodores, Richie became one of the top album acts of the 1980s and one of the most successful US composers ever. *Can't Slow Down*, Grammy Album of the Year in 1984, sold 10 million in the US. See Commodores — 488

Date	Title	Peak	Wks No.1	Wks
27 Nov 82	**LIONEL RICHIE** *Motown STMA 8037* ⊛	9		86
29 Oct 83	**CAN'T SLOW DOWN** *Motown STMA 8041* ⊛x3 ★	1	3	154
23 Aug 86	**DANCING ON THE CEILING** *Motown ZL 72412* ⊛x2 ★	2		53
6 Jun 92	**BACK TO FRONT** *Motown 5300182* ⊛x4	1	6	81
20 Apr 96	**LOUDER THAN WORDS** *Mercury 5322412* ○	11		5
31 Jan 98	**TRULY – THE LOVE SONGS** *Motown 5308432* ⊛	5		21
11 Jul 98	**TIME** *Mercury 5585182*	31		3
28 Oct 00	**RENAISSANCE** *Mercury 5482222* ⊛	6		24
7 Dec 02	**ENCORE** *Mercury 0633482* ●	8		10
22 Nov 03	**THE DEFINITIVE COLLECTION** *Universal TV 9861394* /COMMODORES ⊛	10		33
20 Mar 04	**JUST FOR YOU** *Mercury 9861710* ●	5		8
23 Sep 06	**COMING HOME** *Def Jam 1706602* ○	15		10

JONATHAN RICHMAN & THE MODERN LOVERS
US, male vocal/instrumental group — 3

Date	Title	Peak	Wks No.1	Wks
27 Aug 77	**ROCK 'N' ROLL WITH THE MODERN LOVERS** *Beserkeley BSERK 9*	50		3

RICHMOND STRINGS WITH THE MIKE SAMMES SINGERS
UK, orchestra & male/female vocal group – Mike Sammes, d. 19 May 2001 (age 83) — 7

Date	Title	Peak	Wks No.1	Wks
17 Jan 76	**MUSIC OF AMERICA** *Ronco TRD 2016*	18		7

ADAM RICKITT
UK, male actor/vocalist — 1

Date	Title	Peak	Wks No.1	Wks
30 Oct 99	**GOOD TIMES** *Polydor 5431422*	41		1

FRANK RICOTTI ALL STARS
UK, male instrumental group — 8

Date	Title	Peak	Wks No.1	Wks
26 Jun 93	**THE BEIDERBECKE COLLECTION** *Dormouse DM 20CD*	89		2
24 Dec 88	**THE BEIDERBECKE COLLECTION** *Dormouse DM 20CD* ○	14		5
14 Jan 89	**THE BEIDERBECKE COLLECTION** *Dormouse DM 20CD*	73		1

NELSON RIDDLE ORCHESTRA
US, male orchestra – Nelson Riddle, d. 6 Oct 1985 (age 64) — 42

Date	Title	Peak Position	Weeks at No.1	Weeks on Chart
15 Dec 62	**LET'S FACE THE MUSIC** *Columbia 33SX 1454* SHIRLEY BASSEY WITH THE NELSON RIDDLE ORCHESTRA ●	12		7
26 Oct 85	**BLUE SKIES** *London KTKT 1* KIRI TE KANAWA WITH NELSON RIDDLE & HIS ORCHESTRA ●	40		29
28 Jan 84	**WHAT'S NEW** *Asylum 9602601* LINDA RONSTADT WITH THE NELSON RIDDLE ORCHESTRA	31		5
19 Jan 85	**LUSH LIFE** *Asylum 9603871* LINDA RONSTADT WITH THE NELSON RIDDLE ORCHESTRA	100		1

RIDE
UK, male vocal/instrumental group – Mark Gardner, Andy Bell, Laurence Colbert & Stephen Queralt — 16

Date	Title	Peak Position	Weeks at No.1	Weeks on Chart
27 Oct 90	**NOWHERE** *Creation CRELP 074* ○	11		5
21 Mar 92	**GOING BLANK AGAIN** *Creation CRECD 124* ○	5		5
2 Jul 94	**CARNIVAL OF LIGHT** *Creation CRECD 147*	5		4
23 Mar 96	**TARANTULA** *Creation CRECD 180*	21		2

ANDRE RIEU
Holland, male composer/conductor/violinist — 2

Date	Title	Peak Position	Weeks at No.1	Weeks on Chart
22 Apr 00	**CELEBRATION!** *Philips 5430692*	51		2

RIFLES
UK, male vocal/instrumental group — 1

Date	Title	Peak Position	Weeks at No.1	Weeks on Chart
29 Jul 06	**NO LOVE LOST** *Red Ink 82876859722*	68		1

RIGHT SAID FRED
UK, male vocal/instrumental group – Fred & Richard Fairbrass & Rob Manzoli — 53

Date	Title	Peak Position	Weeks at No.1	Weeks on Chart
28 Mar 92	**UP** *Tug SNOGCD 1* ⊛x2	1	1	49
13 Nov 93	**SEX AND TRAVEL** *Tug SNOGCD 2*	35		4

RIGHTEOUS BROTHERS
US, male vocal duo – Bobby Hatfield, d. 5 Nov 2003, & Bill Medley — 20

Date	Title	Peak Position	Weeks at No.1	Weeks on Chart
1 Dec 90	**THE VERY BEST OF THE RIGHTEOUS BROTHERS: UNCHAINED MELODY** *Verve 8472481* ⊛	11		17
25 Mar 06	**GOLD – GREATEST HITS** *Polydor 9853558*	24		3

RIHANNA
Barbados, female vocalist (Robyn Rihanna Fenty) — 115

Date	Title	Peak Position	Weeks at No.1	Weeks on Chart
10 Sep 05	**MUSIC OF THE SUN** *Def Jam 9885146* ●	35		3
6 May 06	**A GIRL LIKE ME** *Def Jam 9878575* ⊛	5		30+
16 Jun 07	**GOOD GIRL GONE BAD** *Def Jam 1736599* ⊛x4	1	1	82+

RILO KILEY
US, female/male vocal/instrumental group — 1

Date	Title	Peak Position	Weeks at No.1	Weeks on Chart
1 Sep 07	**UNDER THE BLACKLIGHT** *Warner Brothers 9362499565*	34		1

LEANN RIMES
US, female vocalist (Margaret LeAnn Rimes) — 65

Date	Title	Peak Position	Weeks at No.1	Weeks on Chart
6 Jun 98	**SITTIN' ON TOP OF THE WORLD** *Curb 5560682* ●	11		22
14 Apr 01	**I NEED YOU** *Curb 8573876382* ●	7		15
26 Oct 02	**TWISTED ANGEL** *Curb 5046611562* ○	14		3
14 Feb 04	**THE BEST OF** *Curb 5046714812* ⊛	2		20
17 Jun 06	**WHATEVER WE WANNA** *Curb/London 2564634142*	15		3
20 Oct 07	**FAMILY** *Curb 5144244752*	31		2

RIP RIG & PANIC
UK/US, male/female vocal/instrumental group — 3

Date	Title	Peak Position	Weeks at No.1	Weeks on Chart
26 Jun 82	**I AM COLD** *Virgin V 2228*	67		3

MINNIE RIPERTON
US, female vocalist, d. 12 Jul 1979 (age 31) — 3

Date	Title	Peak Position	Weeks at No.1	Weeks on Chart
17 May 75	**PERFECT ANGEL** *Epic EPC 80426*	33		3

ANGELA RIPPON
UK, female TV presenter/exercise instructor — 26

Date	Title	Peak Position	Weeks at No.1	Weeks on Chart
17 Apr 82	**SHAPE UP AND DANCE FEATURING ANGELA RIPPON (VOLUME II)** *Lifestyle LEG 2* ●	8		26

RISE AGAINST
US, male vocal/instrumental group — 1

Date	Title	Peak Position	Weeks at No.1	Weeks on Chart
18 Oct 08	**APPEAL TO REASON** *Geffen 1784353*	68		1

RIVER CITY PEOPLE
UK, male/female vocal/instrumental group — 10

Date	Title	Peak Position	Weeks at No.1	Weeks on Chart
25 Aug 90	**SAY SOMETHING GOOD** *EMI EMCX 3561*	23		9
2 Nov 91	**THIS IS THE WORLD** *EMI EMC 3611*	56		1

RIVER DETECTIVES
UK, male vocal/instrumental duo — 1

Date	Title	Peak Position	Weeks at No.1	Weeks on Chart
23 Sep 89	**SATURDAY NIGHT SUNDAY MORNING** *WEA WX 2955*	51		1

DAVID ROACH
UK, male vocalist/saxophonist — 1

Date	Title	Peak Position	Weeks at No.1	Weeks on Chart
14 Apr 84	**I LOVE SAX** *Nouveau Music NML 1006*	73		1

ROACHFORD
UK, male/female vocal/instrumental group — 56

Date	Title	Peak Position	Weeks at No.1	Weeks on Chart
23 Jul 88	**ROACHFORD** *CBS 4606301* ○	11		27
18 May 91	**GET READY!** *Columbia 4681361*	20		5
16 Apr 94	**PERMANENT SHADE OF BLUE** *Columbia 4758429* ●	25		21
25 Oct 97	**FEEL** *Columbia 4885262*	19		3

ROADRUNNER UNITED
International, male vocalists/guitarists/drummers — 2

Date	Title	Peak Position	Weeks at No.1	Weeks on Chart
22 Oct 05	**ROADRUNNER UNITED – ALL-STAR SESSIONS** *Roadrunner RR81578*	45		2

MARTY ROBBINS
US, male vocalist/guitarist, d. 8 Dec 1982 (age 57) — 15

Date	Title	Peak Position	Weeks at No.1	Weeks on Chart
13 Aug 60	**GUNFIGHTER BALLADS AND TRAIL SONGS** *Fontana TFL 5063*	20		1
10 Feb 79	**MARTY ROBBINS COLLECTION** *Lotus WH 5009* ○	5		14

JULIET ROBERTS
UK, female vocalist — 1

Date	Title	Peak Position	Weeks at No.1	Weeks on Chart
2 Apr 94	**NATURAL THING** *Cooltempo CTCD 39*	65		1

PADDY ROBERTS
South Africa, male vocalist (John Roberts), d. 24 Aug 1975 (age 65) — 6

Date	Title	Peak Position	Weeks at No.1	Weeks on Chart
26 Sep 59	**STRICTLY FOR GROWN UPS** *Decca LF 1322*	8		5
17 Sep 60	**PADDY ROBERTS TRIES AGAIN** *Decca LK 4358*	16		1

B.A. ROBERTSON
UK, male vocalist (Brian Alexander Robertson) — 10

Date	Title	Peak Position	Weeks at No.1	Weeks on Chart
29 Mar 80	**INITIAL SUCCESS** *Asylum K 52216*	32		8
4 Apr 81	**BULLY FOR YOU** *Asylum K 52275*	61		2

ROBBIE ROBERTSON
Canada, male vocalist/guitarist. See Band — 16

Date	Title	Peak Position	Weeks at No.1	Weeks on Chart
14 Nov 87	**ROBBIE ROBERTSON** *Geffen WX 133* ●	23		14
12 Oct 91	**STORYVILLE** *Geffen GEF 24303*	30		2

SMOKEY ROBINSON
US, male vocalist (William Robinson). See Miracles — 23

Date	Title	Peak Position	Weeks at No.1	Weeks on Chart
20 Jun 81	**BEING WITH YOU** *Motown STML 12151*	17		10
12 Nov 88	**LOVE SONGS** *Telstar STAR 2331* MARVIN GAYE & SMOKEY ROBINSON	69		9
14 Nov 92	**THE GREATEST HITS** *Polygram TV 5301212* & THE MIRACLES ○	65		2

Silver-selling ● Gold-selling ● Platinum-selling ⊛ US No.1 ★ | Peak Position | Weeks at No.1 | Weeks on Chart

Date	Title	Peak Position	Weeks at No.1	Weeks on Chart
11 Nov 06	**THE DEFINITIVE COLLECTION & TIMELESS** *Universal TV 9844194*	39		2

TOM ROBINSON BAND
UK, male vocal/instrumental group – Tom Robinson, Mark Ambler, Danny Kustow & Brian Taylor — 23

Date	Title	Peak Position	Weeks at No.1	Weeks on Chart
3 Jun 78	**POWER IN THE DARKNESS** *EMI EMC 3226* ●	4		12
24 Mar 79	**TRB2** *EMI EMC 3296*	18		6
29 Sep 84	**HOPE AND GLORY** *Castaway ZL 70483* TOM ROBINSON	21		5

ROBYN
Sweden, female vocalist (Robyn Carlsson) — 22

Date	Title	Peak Position	Weeks at No.1	Weeks on Chart
25 Aug 07	**ROBYN** *Konichiwa 1744780* ●	13		22

PETE ROCK & C.L. SMOOTH
US, male DJ/rap duo — 1

Date	Title	Peak Position	Weeks at No.1	Weeks on Chart
19 Nov 94	**THE MAIN INGREDIENT** *Elektra 7559616612*	69		1

ROCK GODDESS
UK, female vocal/instrumental group — 3

Date	Title	Peak Position	Weeks at No.1	Weeks on Chart
12 Mar 83	**ROCK GODDESS** *A&M AMLH 68554*	65		2
29 Oct 83	**HELL HATH NO FURY** *A&M AMLX 68560*	84		1

ROCKET FROM THE CRYPT
US, male vocal/instrumental group — 4

Date	Title	Peak Position	Weeks at No.1	Weeks on Chart
3 Feb 96	**SCREAM, DRACULA, SCREAM!** *Elemental ELM 34CD*	41		3
18 Jul 98	**RFTC** *Elemental ELM 50CD*	63		1

ROCKIN' BERRIES
UK, male vocal/instrumental group — 1

Date	Title	Peak Position	Weeks at No.1	Weeks on Chart
19 Jun 65	**IN TOWN** *Pye NPL 38013*	15		1

ROCKPILE
UK, male vocal/instrumental group — 5

Date	Title	Peak Position	Weeks at No.1	Weeks on Chart
18 Oct 80	**SECONDS OF PLEASURE** *F-Beat XXLP 7*	34		5

ROCKSTEADY CREW
US, male/female vocal group — 1

Date	Title	Peak Position	Weeks at No.1	Weeks on Chart
16 Jun 84	**READY FOR BATTLE** *Charisma RSC LP1*	73		1

ROCKWELL
US, male vocalist (Kennedy Gordy) — 5

Date	Title	Peak Position	Weeks at No.1	Weeks on Chart
25 Feb 84	**SOMEBODY'S WATCHING ME** *Motown ZL 72147*	52		5

CLODAGH RODGERS
Ireland, female vocalist — 1

Date	Title	Peak Position	Weeks at No.1	Weeks on Chart
13 Sep 69	**CLODAGH RODGERS** *RCA Victor SF 8033*	27		1

PAUL RODGERS
UK, male vocalist. See Bad Company, Firm, Free, Law — 21

Date	Title	Peak Position	Weeks at No.1	Weeks on Chart
3 Jul 93	**MUDDY WATER BLUES – A TRIBUTE TO MUDDY WATERS** *London 8284242*	9		7
15 Feb 97	**NOW** *SPV Recordings SPV 08544662*	30		4
1 Oct 05	**RETURN OF THE CHAMPIONS** *Parlophone 3369792* QUEEN & PAUL RODGERS ●	12		4
27 Sep 08	**THE COSMOS ROCKS** *Parlophone 2161432* QUEEN & PAUL RODGERS	5		6

RODRIGO Y GABRIELA
Mexico, male/female guitarists — 2

Date	Title	Peak Position	Weeks at No.1	Weeks on Chart
1 Sep 07	**RODRIGO Y GABRIELA** *Ruby Works RWXCD37* ●	53		2

RODS
UK, male vocal/instrumental group — 4

Date	Title	Peak Position	Weeks at No.1	Weeks on Chart
24 Jul 82	**WILD DOGS** *Arista SPART 1196*	75		4

KENNY ROGERS
US, male vocalist — 113

Date	Title	Peak Position	Weeks at No.1	Weeks on Chart
18 Jun 77	**KENNY ROGERS** *United Artists UAS 30046*	14		7
6 Oct 79	**THE KENNY ROGERS SINGLES ALBUM** *United Artists UAK 30263* ●	12		22
9 Feb 80	**KENNY** *United Artists UAG 30273* ●	7		10
31 Jan 81	**LADY** *Liberty LBG 30334*	40		5
1 Oct 83	**EYES THAT SEE IN THE DARK** *RCA RCALP 6088*	53		19
27 Oct 84	**WHAT ABOUT ME?** *RCA PL 85043*	97		1
27 Jul 85	**THE KENNY ROGERS STORY** *Liberty EMTV 39* ⊛	4		29
25 Sep 93	**DAYTIME FRIENDS – THE VERY BEST OF KENNY ROGERS** *EMI CDEMTV 79* ●	16		5
22 Nov 97	**LOVE SONGS** *Virgin KENNYCD 1* ●	27		7
29 May 99	**ALL THE HITS & ALL NEW LOVE SONGS** *EMI 5207782*	14		6
16 Feb 08	**LOVE SONGS** *Capitol 5175272*	47		2

ROGUE TRADERS
Australia, female/male vocal/instrumental group — 1

Date	Title	Peak Position	Weeks at No.1	Weeks on Chart
5 Aug 06	**HERE COME THE DRUMS** *Ariola 82876735272*	46		1

ROLL DEEP
UK, male rap collective — 4

Date	Title	Peak Position	Weeks at No.1	Weeks on Chart
18 Jun 05	**IN AT THE DEEP END** *Relentless CDRELX07* ●	50		4

ROLLING STONES
UK, male vocal/instrumental group – Mick Jagger*, Brian Jones, Keith Richards*, Mick Taylor, Charlie Watts, Ron Wood & Bill Wyman*. No act has ever earned more money from touring than the world's No.1 rock group. They have amassed more Top 10 albums in the UK and US and more gold- and platinum-selling LPs than any other group — 833

Date	Title	Peak Position	Weeks at No.1	Weeks on Chart
25 Apr 64	**THE ROLLING STONES** *Decca LK 4605*	1	12	51
23 Jan 65	**ROLLING STONES NUMBER 2** *Decca LK 4661*	1	10	37
2 Oct 65	**OUT OF OUR HEADS** *Decca LK 4733* ★	2		24
23 Apr 66	**AFTERMATH** *Decca LK 4786*	1	8	28
12 Nov 66	**BIG HITS (HIGH TIDE AND GREEN GRASS)** *Decca TXS 101*	4		43
28 Jan 67	**BETWEEN THE BUTTONS** *Decca SKL 4852*	3		22
23 Dec 67	**THEIR SATANIC MAJESTIES REQUEST** *Decca TXS 103*	3		13
21 Dec 68	**BEGGARS BANQUET** *Decca SKL 4955*	3		12
27 Sep 69	**THROUGH THE PAST DARKLY (BIG HITS VOLUME 2)** *Decca SKL 5019*	2		37
20 Dec 69	**LET IT BLEED** *Decca SKL 5025* ⊛	1	1	29
19 Sep 70	**GET YER YA-YA'S OUT!' – THE ROLLING STONES IN CONCERT** *Decca SKL 5065*	1	2	15
27 Mar 71	**STONE AGE** *Decca SKL 5084*	4		8
8 May 71	**STICKY FINGERS** *Rolling Stones COC 59100* ★	1	5	25
18 Sep 71	**GIMME SHELTER** *Decca SKL 5101*	19		5
11 Mar 72	**MILESTONES** *Decca SKL 5098*	14		8
10 Jun 72	**EXILE ON MAIN STREET** *Rolling Stones COC 69100* ★	1	1	16
11 Nov 72	**ROCK 'N' ROLLING STONES** *Decca SKL 5149*	41		1
22 Sep 73	**GOAT'S HEAD SOUP** *Rolling Stones COC 59101* ● ★	1	2	14
2 Nov 74	**IT'S ONLY ROCK 'N' ROLL** *Rolling Stones COC 59103* ● ★	2		9
28 Jun 75	**MADE IN THE SHADE** *Rolling Stones COC 59104*	14		12
28 Jun 75	**METAMORPHOSIS** *Decca SKL 5212*	45		1
29 Nov 75	**ROLLED GOLD – THE VERY BEST OF THE ROLLING STONES** *Decca ROST 1/2* ●	7		50
8 May 76	**BLACK AND BLUE** *Rolling Stones COC 59106* ● ★	2		14
8 Oct 77	**LOVE YOU LIVE** *Rolling Stones COC 89101* ●	3		8
5 Nov 77	**GET STONED** *Arcade ADEP 32*	8		15
24 Jun 78	**SOME GIRLS** *Rolling Stones CUN 39108* ● ★	2		25
5 Jul 80	**EMOTIONAL RESCUE** *Rolling Stones CUN 39111* ● ★	1	2	18
12 Sep 81	**TATTOO YOU** *Rolling Stones CUNS 39114* ● ★	2		29
12 Jun 82	**STILL LIFE (AMERICAN CONCERTS 1981)** *Rolling Stones CUN 39115* ●	4		18
31 Jul 82	**IN CONCERT** *Decca 6640 037*	94		3
11 Dec 82	**STORY OF THE STONES** *K-Tel NE 1201* ●	24		12
19 Nov 83	**UNDERCOVER** *Rolling Stones CUN 1654361* ●	3		18
7 Jul 84	**REWIND 1971–1984 (THE BEST OF THE ROLLING STONES)** *Rolling Stones 4501991*	23		18
5 Apr 86	**DIRTY WORK** *Rolling Stones CUN 86321* ●	4		10
23 Sep 89	**STEEL WHEELS** *Rolling Stones 4657521* ●	2		18
7 Jul 90	**HOT ROCKS – THE GREATEST HITS 1964–1971** *London 8201401* ⊛x2	3		24
20 Apr 91	**FLASHPOINT** *Rolling Stones 4681351* ●	6		7
4 Dec 93	**JUMP BACK – THE BEST OF THE ROLLING STONES 1971-93** *Virgin CDV 2726* ⊛x2	16		28
2 Jul 94	**STICKY FINGERS** *Virgin CDVX 2730*	74		1
23 Jul 94	**VOODOO LOUNGE** *Virgin CDV 2750* ●	1	1	24
25 Nov 95	**STRIPPED** *Virgin CDV 2801* ●	9		11

Key: ○ Silver-selling · ● Gold-selling · ⊛ Platinum-selling · ★ US No.1 · Peak Position · Weeks at No.1 · Weeks on Chart

Date	Title	Peak	Wks at No.1	Wks on Chart
11 Oct 97	**BRIDGES TO BABYLON** *Virgin CDV 2840* ●	6		6
14 Nov 98	**NO SECURITY** *Virgin CDV 2880*	67		1
12 Oct 02	**FORTY LICKS** *Virgin Decca CDVDX 2964* ⊛x3	2		45
13 Nov 04	**LIVE LICKS** *Virgin CDVDX3000* ○	38		4
17 Sep 05	**A BIGGER BANG** *Virgin CDV3012* ●	2		4
24 Nov 07	**ROLLED GOLD +** *Decca 5303281*	26		7
19 Apr 08	**SHINE A LIGHT (OST)** *Polydor 1764747*	2		5

ROLLINS BAND

UK, male vocal/instrumental group — 2

Date	Title	Peak	Wks at No.1	Wks on Chart
23 Apr 94	**WEIGHT** *Imago 72787210342* ROLLINS BAND	22		2

ROMAN HOLLIDAY

UK, male vocal/instrumental group — 3

Date	Title	Peak	Wks at No.1	Wks on Chart
22 Oct 83	**COOKIN' ON THE ROOF** *Jive HIP 9*	31		3

ROMEO

UK, male rapper (Marvin Dawkins). See So Solid Crew — 2

Date	Title	Peak	Wks at No.1	Wks on Chart
23 Nov 02	**SOLID LOVE** *Relentless RELEN 006CD* ○	46		2

RONDO VENEZIANO

Italy, male/female orchestra — 33

Date	Title	Peak	Wks at No.1	Wks on Chart
5 Nov 83	**VENICE IN PERIL** *Ferroway RON 1* ●	39		13
10 Nov 84	**THE GENIUS OF VENICE** *Ferroway RON 2*	60		13
9 Jul 88	**VENICE IN PERIL** *Fanfare RON 1*	34		7

MARK RONSON

UK, male DJ/producer — 67

Date	Title	Peak	Wks at No.1	Wks on Chart
28 Apr 07	**VERSION** *Columbia 88697080032* ⊛x2	2		65
28 Apr 07	**HERE COMES THE FUZZ** *Elektra 7559628392* ○	70		2

MICK RONSON

UK, male vocalist/guitarist, d. 29 Apr 1993 (age 46). See Mott The Hoople — 10

Date	Title	Peak	Wks at No.1	Wks on Chart
16 Mar 74	**SLAUGHTER ON TENTH AVENUE** *RCA Victor APLI 0353*	9		7
8 Mar 75	**PLAY DON'T WORRY** *RCA Victor APLI 0681*	29		3

LINDA RONSTADT

US, female vocalist/guitarist — 46

Date	Title	Peak	Wks at No.1	Wks on Chart
4 Sep 76	**HASTEN DOWN THE WIND** *Asylum K 53045* ○	32		8
25 Dec 76	**GREATEST HITS** *Asylum K 53055*	37		9
1 Oct 77	**SIMPLE DREAMS** *Asylum K 53065* ★	15		5
14 Oct 78	**LIVING IN THE USA** *Asylum K 53085* ○ ★	39		2
8 Mar 80	**MAD LOVE** *Asylum K 52210*	65		1
28 Jan 84	**WHAT'S NEW** *Asylum 9602601* WITH THE NELSON RIDDLE ORCHESTRA	31		5
19 Jan 85	**LUSH LIFE** *Asylum 9603871* WITH THE NELSON RIDDLE ORCHESTRA	100		1
14 Mar 87	**TRIO** *Warner Brothers 9254911* DOLLY PARTON, LINDA RONSTADT & EMMYLOU HARRIS	60		4
11 Nov 89	**CRY LIKE A RAINSTORM – HOWL LIKE THE WIND** *Elektra EKT 76* FEATURING AARON NEVILLE ●	43		8
11 Oct 03	**THE VERY BEST OF** *Elektra 8122736052*	46		3

ROOSTER

UK, male vocal/instrumental group – Nick Atkinson, Dave Neale, Luke Potashnick & Ben Smyth — 15

Date	Title	Peak	Wks at No.1	Wks on Chart
5 Feb 05	**ROOSTER** *Brightside 82876676352* ●	3		15

ROOTJOOSE

UK, male vocal/instrumental group — 1

Date	Title	Peak	Wks at No.1	Wks on Chart
18 Oct 97	**RHUBARB** *Rage RAGECD 6*	58		1

ROOTS

US, male rap/production group — 1

Date	Title	Peak	Wks at No.1	Wks on Chart
24 Jul 04	**THE TIPPING POINT** *Geffen 9863067*	71		1

ROOTS MANUVA

UK, male rapper (Rodney Hylton Smith) — 9

Date	Title	Peak	Wks at No.1	Wks on Chart
25 Aug 01	**RUN COME SAVE ME** *Big Dada BDCD 032* ●	33		3
20 Jul 02	**DUB COME SAVE ME** *Big Dada BDCD 040*	75		1
12 Feb 05	**AWFULLY DEEP** *Big Dada BDCD072X*	24		3
13 Sep 08	**SLIME & REASON** *Big Dada BD123*	22		2

ROSE ROYCE

US, female/male vocal/instrumental group – Gwen Dickey, Kenji Brown, Ken Copeland, Fred Dunn, Henry Garner, Lequient Jobe, Mike Moore, Victor Nix & Terrai Santiel — 66

Date	Title	Peak	Wks at No.1	Wks on Chart
22 Oct 77	**IN FULL BLOOM** *Whitfield K 56394* ●	18		13
30 Sep 78	**STRIKES AGAIN** *Whitfield K 56257* ●	7		11
22 Sep 79	**RAINBOW CONNECTION IV** *Whitfield K 56714*	72		2
1 Mar 80	**ROSE ROYCE GREATEST HITS** *Whitfield RRTV 1* ⊛	1	2	34
13 Oct 84	**MUSIC MAGIC** *Streetwave MKL 2*	69		2
9 Mar 85	**THE ARTISTS VOLUME 1** *Street Sounds ARTIS 1* EARTH WIND & FIRE/JEAN CARN/ROSE ROYCE	65		4

ROSE TATTOO

Australia, male vocal/instrumental group — 4

Date	Title	Peak	Wks at No.1	Wks on Chart
26 Sep 81	**ASSAULT AND BATTERY** *Carrere CAL 127*	40		4

ANDREA ROSS

US, female vocalist — 2

Date	Title	Peak	Wks at No.1	Wks on Chart
17 Mar 07	**MOON RIVER** *UCJ 1701161*	42		2

DIANA ROSS

US, female vocalist (Diane Earle). After fronting the most successful female group of the 1960s, The Supremes, Diana has continued to chart regularly as a solo artist and has amassed more hit albums in the UK than any other American female. See Supremes — 770

Date	Title	Peak	Wks at No.1	Wks on Chart
20 Jan 68	**DIANA ROSS AND THE SUPREMES GREATEST HITS** *Tamla Motown STML 11063* DIANA ROSS & THE SUPREMES ★	1	3	60
30 Mar 68	**LIVE' AT LONDON'S TALK OF THE TOWN** *Tamla Motown STML 11070* DIANA ROSS & THE SUPREMES	6		18
20 Jul 68	**REFLECTIONS** *Tamla Motown STML 11073* DIANA ROSS & THE SUPREMES	30		2
25 Jan 69	**DIANA ROSS AND THE SUPREMES JOIN THE TEMPTATIONS** *Tamla Motown STML 11096* DIANA ROSS & THE SUPREMES & THE TEMPTATIONS	1	4	15
1 Feb 69	**LOVE CHILD** *Tamla Motown STML 11095* DIANA ROSS & THE SUPREMES	8		6
28 Jun 69	**THE ORIGINAL SOUNDTRACK FROM TCB (OST-TV)** *Tamla Motown STML 11110* DIANA ROSS & THE SUPREMES & THE TEMPTATIONS ★	11		12
14 Feb 70	**TOGETHER** *Tamla Motown STML 11122* DIANA ROSS & THE SUPREMES & THE TEMPTATIONS	28		4
14 Feb 70	**CREAM OF THE CROP** *Tamla Motown STML 11137* DIANA ROSS & THE SUPREMES	34		4
23 May 70	**GREATEST HITS VOLUME II** *Tamla Motown STML 11146*	29		4
24 Oct 70	**DIANA ROSS** *Tamla Motown STML 11159*	14		5
19 Jun 71	**EVERYTHING IS EVERYTHING** *Tamla Motown STML 11178*	31		3
9 Oct 71	**DIANA (OST-TV)** *Tamla Motown STMA 8001*	43		1
9 Oct 71	**I'M STILL WAITING** *Tamla Motown STML 11193* ○	10		11
11 Nov 72	**GREATEST HITS** *Tamla Motown STMA 8006* ●	34		10
1 Sep 73	**TOUCH ME IN THE MORNING** *Tamla Motown STML 11239* ●	7		35
27 Oct 73	**LADY SINGS THE BLUES (OST)** *Tamla Motown TMSP 1131* ● ★	50		1
19 Jan 74	**DIANA AND MARVIN** *Tamla Motown STMA 8015* DIANA ROSS & MARVIN GAYE ●	6		43
2 Mar 74	**LAST TIME I SAW HIM** *Tamla Motown STML 11255*	41		1
8 Jun 74	**DIANA ROSS LIVE AT CAESAR'S PALACE** *Tamla Motown STML 11248*	21		8
27 Mar 76	**DIANA ROSS** *Tamla Motown STML 12022* ●	4		26
7 Aug 76	**GREATEST HITS 2** *Tamla Motown STML 12036* ●	2		29
19 Mar 77	**AN EVENING WITH DIANA ROSS** *Motown TMSP 6005* ○	52		1
17 Sep 77	**DIANA ROSS AND THE SUPREMES 20 GOLDEN GREATS** *Motown EMTV 5*	1	7	34
4 Aug 79	**THE BOSS** *Motown STML 12118*	52		2
17 Nov 79	**20 GOLDEN GREATS** *Motown EMTV 21* ⊛	2		29
21 Jun 80	**DIANA** *Motown STMA 8033* ●	12		32
28 Mar 81	**TO LOVE AGAIN** *Motown STML 12152*	26		10
29 Aug 81	**DIANA AND MARVIN** *Motown STMS 5001* DIANA ROSS & MARVIN GAYE	78		2
7 Nov 81	**WHY DO FOOLS FALL IN LOVE** *Capitol EST 26733* ●	17		24
21 Nov 81	**ALL THE GREAT HITS** *Motown STMA 8036* ⊛	21		31

Silver-selling ○ Gold-selling ● Platinum-selling ⊛ US No.1 ★

Date	Title	Peak Position	Weeks at No.1	Weeks on Chart
13 Feb 82	**DIANA'S DUETS** *Motown STML 12163* ○	43		6
23 Oct 82	**SILK ELECTRIC** *Capitol EAST 27313* ○	33		12
4 Dec 82	**LOVE SONGS** *K-Tel NE 1200* ⊛	5		17
16 Jul 83	**ROSS** *Capitol EST 1867051*	44		5
24 Dec 83	**PORTRAIT** *Telstar STAR 2238* ●	8		31
6 Oct 84	**SWEPT AWAY** *Capitol ROSS 1*	40		5
28 Sep 85	**EATEN ALIVE** *Capitol ROSS 2*	11		19
15 Nov 86	**DIANA ROSS. MICHAEL JACKSON. GLADYS KNIGHT. STEVIE WONDER. THEIR VERY BEST BACK TO BACK** *PrioriTyV PTVR2* DIANA ROSS/MICHAEL JACKSON/GLADYS KNIGHT/ STEVIE WONDER	21		10
30 May 87	**RED HOT RHYTHM 'N' BLUES** *EMI EMC 3532*	47		4
31 Oct 87	**LOVE SONGS** *Telstar STAR 2298* DIANA ROSS & MICHAEL JACKSON ⊛	12		24
21 Jan 89	**LOVE SUPREME** *Motown ZL 72701* DIANA ROSS & THE SUPREMES ○	10		9
27 May 89	**WORKIN' OVERTIME** *EMI EMD 1009* ○	23		4
25 Nov 89	**GREATEST HITS LIVE** *EMI EMDC 1001* ●	34		6
14 Dec 91	**THE FORCE BEHIND THE POWER** *EMI EMD 1023* ⊛	11		31
29 Feb 92	**MOTOWN'S GREATEST HITS** *Motown 5300132*	20		11
24 Apr 93	**LIVE, STOLEN MOMENTS – THE LADY SINGS THE BLUES** *EMI CDEMD 1044*	45		2
30 Oct 93	**ONE WOMAN – THE ULTIMATE COLLECTION** *EMI CDONE 1* ⊛x4	1	2	67
25 Dec 93	**CHRISTMAS IN VIENNA** *Sony Classical SK 53358* PLACIDO DOMINGO, DIANA ROSS & JOSE CARRERAS	71		2
23 Apr 94	**DIANA EXTENDED – THE REMIXES** *EMI CDDREX 1*	58		1
26 Nov 94	**A VERY SPECIAL SEASON** *EMI CDEMD 1075* ●	37		6
16 Sep 95	**TAKE ME HIGHER** *EMI CDEMD 1085*	10		3
23 Nov 96	**VOICE OF LOVE** *EMI CDEMD 1100*	42		7
31 Oct 98	**40 GOLDEN MOTOWN GREATS** *Motown 5309612* DIANA ROSS & THE SUPREMES	35		4
20 Nov 99	**EVERY DAY IS A NEW DAY** *EMI 5214762*	71		1
17 Nov 01	**LOVE AND LIFE – THE VERY BEST OF** *EMI/Universal TV 5358622* ●	28		7
29 May 04	**THE NO 1'S** *Motown 9818019* DIANA ROSS & THE SUPREMES ●	15		12
14 Oct 06	**I LOVE YOU** *Angel CDANGE12*	60		1

RICKY ROSS

UK, male vocalist/guitarist. See Deacon Blue — Weeks on Chart: **1**

Date	Title	Peak Position	Weeks at No.1	Weeks on Chart
15 Jun 96	**WHAT YOU ARE** *Epic 4839982*	36		1

ROSTAL & SCHAEFER

UK, male instrumental duo — Weeks on Chart: **2**

Date	Title	Peak Position	Weeks at No.1	Weeks on Chart
14 Jul 79	**BEATLES CONCERTO** *Parlophone PAS 10014* WITH RON GOODWIN & ROYAL LIVERPOOL PHILHARMONIC ORCHESTRA	61		2

DAVID LEE ROTH

US, male vocalist. See Van Halen — Weeks on Chart: **32**

Date	Title	Peak Position	Weeks at No.1	Weeks on Chart
2 Mar 85	**CRAZY FROM THE HEAT** *Warner Brothers 9252221*	91		2
19 Jul 86	**EAT 'EM AND SMILE** *Warner Brothers WX 56* ●	28		9
6 Feb 88	**SKYSCRAPER** *Warner Brothers 9256711* ○	11		12
26 Jan 91	**A LITTLE AIN'T ENOUGH** *Warner Brothers WX 403* ○	4		7
19 Mar 94	**YOUR FILTHY LITTLE MOUTH** *Reprise 9362453912*	28		2

ULI JON ROTH & ELECTRIC SUN

Germany, male vocal/instrumental group — Weeks on Chart: **2**

Date	Title	Peak Position	Weeks at No.1	Weeks on Chart
23 Feb 85	**BEYOND THE ASTRAL SKIES** *EMI ROTH 1*	64		2

JOSH ROUSE

US, male vocalist/guitarist — Weeks on Chart: **1**

Date	Title	Peak Position	Weeks at No.1	Weeks on Chart
26 Feb 05	**NASHVILLE** *Rykodisc RCD10679*	66		1

DEMIS ROUSSOS

Greece, male vocalist/multi-instrumentalist — Weeks on Chart: **147**

Date	Title	Peak Position	Weeks at No.1	Weeks on Chart
22 Jun 74	**FOREVER AND EVER** *Philips 6325 021* ⊛	2		68
19 Apr 75	**SOUVENIRS** *Philips 6325 201* ●	25		18
24 Apr 76	**HAPPY TO BE** *Philips 9101 027* ●	4		34
3 Jul 76	**MY ONLY FASCINATION** *Philips 6325 094* ●	39		6
16 Apr 77	**THE MAGIC OF DEMIS ROUSSOS** *Philips 9101 131* ○	29		6
28 Oct 78	**LIFE AND LOVE** *Philips 9199 873* ○	36		11
16 Mar 02	**FOREVER AND EVER – DEFINITIVE COLLECTION** *Philips 5867702*	17		4

KELLY ROWLAND

US, female vocalist (Kelendria Rowland). See Destiny's Child — Weeks on Chart: **31**

Date	Title	Peak Position	Weeks at No.1	Weeks on Chart
15 Feb 03	**SIMPLY DEEP** *Columbia 5096042* ⊛	1	1	26
7 Jul 07	**MS KELLY** *Columbia 88697110292*	37		2
24 May 08	**MS KELLY – DELUXE EDITION** *Columbia 88697288112*	23		3

BETH ROWLEY

UK (b. Peru), female vocalist — Weeks on Chart: **7**

Date	Title	Peak Position	Weeks at No.1	Weeks on Chart
31 May 08	**LITTLE DREAMER** *Blue Thumb 1754713*	6		7

ROXETTE

Sweden, female/male vocal/instrumental duo – Marie Fredriksson & Per Gessle — Weeks on Chart: **164**

Date	Title	Peak Position	Weeks at No.1	Weeks on Chart
17 Jun 89	**LOOK SHARP!** *EMI EMC 3557* ⊛	4		53
13 Apr 91	**JOYRIDE** *EMI EMD 1019* ⊛x2	2		48
12 Sep 92	**TOURISM** *EMI CDEMD 1036* ●	2		17
23 Apr 94	**CRASH BOOM BANG** *EMI CDEMD 1056* ●	3		16
4 Nov 95	**DON'T BORE US, GET TO THE CHORUS! – GREATEST HITS** *EMI CDXEMTV 98* ⊛	5		20
10 Apr 99	**HAVE A NICE DAY** *EMI 4994612*	28		3
15 Feb 03	**THE BALLAD HITS** *Capitol 5427982* ○	11		4
28 Oct 06	**ROXETTE HITS** *Capitol 3679782*	22		3

ROXY MUSIC

UK, male vocal/instrumental group – Bryan Ferry*; members also included Brian Eno*, Eddie Jobson, Andy Mackay, Phil Manzanera*, Graham Simpson & Paul Thompson. This innovative art rock ensemble, which introduced the world to Ferry and Eno, influenced countless punk, new wave and electronic groups and, more recently, the likes of Pulp, Suede and Radiohead — Weeks on Chart: **430**

Date	Title	Peak Position	Weeks at No.1	Weeks on Chart
29 Jul 72	**ROXY MUSIC** *Island ILPS 9200* ●	10		16
7 Apr 73	**FOR YOUR PLEASURE** *Island ILPS 9232* ●	4		27
1 Dec 73	**STRANDED** *Island ILPS 9252* ●	1	1	17
30 Nov 74	**COUNTRY LIFE** *Island ILPS 9303* ●	3		10
8 Nov 75	**SIREN** *Island ILPS 9344* ●	4		17
31 Jul 76	**VIVA! ROXY MUSIC** *Island ILPS 9400* ○	6		12
19 Nov 77	**GREATEST HITS** *Polydor 2302 073* ●	20		11
24 Mar 79	**MANIFESTO** *Polydor POLH 001* ●	7		34
31 May 80	**FLESH AND BLOOD** *Polydor POLH 002* ⊛	1	4	60
5 Jun 82	**AVALON** *Polydor EGLP 50* ⊛	1	3	57
19 Mar 83	**MUSIQUE/THE HIGH ROAD** *E.G. EGMLP 1*	26		7
12 Nov 83	**ROXY MUSIC – THE ATLANTIC YEARS (1973–1980)** *E.G. EGLP 54* ●	23		25
26 Apr 86	**STREET LIFE – 20 GREAT HITS** *E.G. EGTV 1* BRYAN FERRY & ROXY MUSIC ⊛	1	5	77
19 Nov 88	**THE ULTIMATE COLLECTION** *E.G. EGTV 2* BRYAN FERRY & ROXY MUSIC ⊛x3	6		35
4 Nov 95	**MORE THAN THIS – THE BEST OF BRYAN FERRY AND ROXY MUSIC** *Virgin CDV 2791* BRYAN FERRY & ROXY MUSIC ⊛	15		15
23 Jun 01	**BEST OF** *Virgin CDV 2939* ●	12		6
19 Jun 04	**PLATINUM COLLECTION** *Virgin BFRM1* BRYAN FERRY & ROXY MUSIC ○	17		4

ROYAL PHILHARMONIC ORCHESTRA

UK, orchestra — Weeks on Chart: **235**

Date	Title	Peak Position	Weeks at No.1	Weeks on Chart
8 Feb 75	**THE ORCHESTRAL TUBULAR BELLS** *Virgin V 2026* MIKE OLDFIELD WITH THE ROYAL PHILHARMONIC ORCHESTRA ○	17		7
8 Jan 77	**CLASSICAL GOLD** *Ronco RTD 42020* ●	24		13
23 Dec 78	**CLASSIC GOLD VOLUME 2** *Ronco RTD 42032*	31		4
19 Sep 81	**HOOKED ON CLASSICS** *K-Tel ONE 1146* LOUIS CLARK CONDUCTING THE ROYAL PHILHARMONIC ORCHESTRA ⊛	4		43
31 Jul 82	**CAN'T STOP THE CLASSICS – HOOKED ON CLASSICS 2** *K-Tel ONE 1173* LOUIS CLARK CONDUCTING THE ROYAL PHILHARMONIC ORCHESTRA ●	13		26
9 Apr 83	**JOURNEY THROUGH THE CLASSICS – HOOKED ON CLASSICS 3** *K-Tel ONE 1266* LOUIS CLARK CONDUCTING THE ROYAL PHILHARMONIC ORCHESTRA	19		15
8 Oct 83	**LOVE CLASSICS** *Nouveau Music NML 1003* ROYAL PHILHARMONIC ORCHESTRA CONDUCTED BY NICK PORTLOCK ○	30		9
10 Dec 83	**THE BEST OF HOOKED ON CLASSICS** *K-Tel ONE 1266* ROYAL PHILHARMONIC ORCHESTRA CONDUCTED BY LOUIS CLARK ○	51		6
11 Feb 84	**SERENADE** *K-Tel NE 1267* JUAN MARTIN WITH THE ROYAL PHILHARMONIC ORCHESTRA	21		9
26 May 84	**AS TIME GOES BY** *Telstar STAR 2240* ROYAL PHILHARMONIC ORCHESTRA CONDUCTED BY HARRY RABINOVITZ	95		2
23 Nov 85	**THE CLASSIC TOUCH** *Decca SKL 5343* RICHARD CLAYDERMAN WITH THE ROYAL PHILHARMONIC ORCHESTRA	17		18
21 Feb 87	**ELGAR CELLO CONCERTO** *Philips 4163541* JULIAN LLOYD WEBBER WITH THE ROYAL PHILHARMONIC ORCHESTRA CONDUCTED BY SIR YEHUDI MENUHIN	94		1
26 Nov 88	**RHYTHM AND CLASSICS** *Telstar STAR 2344* LOUIS CLARK CONDUCTING THE ROYAL PHILHARMONIC ORCHESTRA	96		1

Date	Title / Label / Artist	Peak Position	Weeks at No.1	Weeks on Chart
21 Apr 90	**OPERA EXTRAVAGANZA** *Epic MOOD 12* THE ROYAL PHILHARMONIC ORCHESTRA, CHORUS ROYAL OPERA HOUSE, THE LONDON SYMPHONY ORCHESTRA, CONDUCTOR LUIS COBOS	72		1
29 Sep 90	**MUSIC FOR THE LAST NIGHT OF THE PROMS** *Cirrus TVLP 501* SIR CHARLES GROVES CONDUCTING THE ROYAL PHILHARMONIC ORCHESTRA & CHORUS WITH SARAH WALKER (SOPRANO)	39		4
27 Oct 90	**LLOYD WEBBER PLAYS LLOYD WEBBER** *Philips 4322911* JULIAN LLOYD WEBBER WITH THE ROYAL PHILHARMONIC ORCHESTRA	15		13
24 Nov 90	**MY CLASSIC COLLECTION** *Decca 8282281* RICHARD CLAYDERMAN WITH THE ROYAL PHILHARMONIC ORCHESTRA	29		7
5 Oct 91	**SERIOUSLY ORCHESTRA** *Virgin RPOLP 1* LOUIS CLARK CONDUCTING THE ROYAL PHILHARMONIC ORCHESTRA	31		6
9 Nov 91	**MICHAEL CRAWFORD PERFORMS ANDREW LLOYD WEBBER** *Telstar STAR 2544* MICHAEL CRAWFORD & THE ROYAL PHILHARMONIC ORCHESTRA ⊛x2	3		36
14 Nov 92	**THE VERY BEST OF RICHARD CLAYDERMAN** *Decca Delpine 8283362* RICHARD CLAYDERMAN WITH THE ROYAL PHILHARMONIC ORCHESTRA	47		5
12 Feb 94	**MY HEART'S DELIGHT** *Decca 4432602* LUCIANO PAVAROTTI WITH THE ROYAL PHILHARMONIC ORCHESTRA	44		4
30 Jul 94	**BIG SCREEN CLASSICS** *Quality Television GIGSCD 1*	49		2
13 Apr 96	**AMAZING** *Carlton Premiere 3036000282* ELKIE BROOKS WITH THE ROYAL PHILHARMONIC ORCHESTRA	49		2
26 Jun 04	**SYMPHONIC ROCK** *Virgin/EMI VTDCD620* ROYAL PHILHARMONIC ORCHESTRA	42		1

ROYAL SCOTS DRAGOON GUARDS

UK, military band — 13

Date	Title / Label	Peak Position	Weeks at No.1	Weeks on Chart
8 Dec 07	**SPIRIT OF THE GLEN** *UCJ 1747159*	13		9
13 Dec 08	**SPIRIT OF THE GLEN – JOURNEY** *UCJ 1779258*	29		4+

ROYKSOPP

Norway, male production duo – Svein Berge & Torbjorn Brundtland — 48

Date	Title / Label	Peak Position	Weeks at No.1	Weeks on Chart
24 Aug 02	**MELODY AM** *Wall Of Sound WALLCD 027*	9		41
16 Jul 05	**THE UNDERSTANDING** *Wall Of Sound WALLCD035X*	13		7

ROYWORLD

UK, male vocal/instrumental group — 1

Date	Title / Label	Peak Position	Weeks at No.1	Weeks on Chart
14 Jun 08	**MAN IN THE MACHINE** *Virgin CDV3041*	52		1

ROZALLA

Zimbabwe, female vocalist (Rozalla Miller) — 4

Date	Title / Label	Peak Position	Weeks at No.1	Weeks on Chart
4 Apr 92	**EVERYBODY'S FREE** *Pulse 8 PULSECD 3*	20		4

RUBETTES

UK, male vocal/instrumental group — 1

Date	Title / Label	Peak Position	Weeks at No.1	Weeks on Chart
10 May 75	**WE CAN DO IT** *Start ETAT 001*	41		1

JIMMY RUFFIN

US, male vocalist — 10

Date	Title / Label	Peak Position	Weeks at No.1	Weeks on Chart
13 May 67	**THE JIMMY RUFFIN WAY** *Tamla Motown STML 11048*	32		6
1 Jun 74	**GREATEST HITS** *Tamla Motown STML 11259*	41		4

RUFUS

US, female/male vocal/instrumental group — 7

Date	Title / Label	Peak Position	Weeks at No.1	Weeks on Chart
12 Apr 75	**RUFUSIZED** *ABC ABCL 5063*	48		2
21 Apr 84	**STOMPIN' AT THE SAVOY** *Warner Brothers 9236791* & CHAKA KHAN	64		5

RUMBLE STRIPS

UK, male vocal/instrumental group — 1

Date	Title / Label	Peak Position	Weeks at No.1	Weeks on Chart
29 Sep 07	**GIRLS AND WEATHER** *Fallout 1736448*	70		1

RUN D.M.C.

US, male rap group — 44

Date	Title / Label	Peak Position	Weeks at No.1	Weeks on Chart
26 Jul 86	**RAISING HELL** *Profile LONLP 21*	41		26
4 Jun 88	**TOUGHER THAN LEATHER** *Profile LONLP 38*	13		5
15 May 93	**DOWN WITH THE KING** *Profile FILECD 440*	44		2
6 Jun 98	**TOGETHER FOREVER – GREATEST HITS 1983–1998** *Profile FILECD 474*	31		3

Date	Title / Label	Peak Position	Weeks at No.1	Weeks on Chart
26 Apr 03	**GREATEST HITS** *Arista 74321980602*	15		8

TODD RUNDGREN

US, male vocalist/guitarist. See Utopia — 9

Date	Title / Label	Peak Position	Weeks at No.1	Weeks on Chart
29 Jan 77	**RA** *Bearsville K 55514*	27		6
6 May 78	**HERMIT OF MINK HOLLOW** *Bearsville K 55521*	42		3

BIC RUNGA

New Zealand, female vocalist/guitarist (Briolette Kah Bic Runga) — 2

Date	Title / Label	Peak Position	Weeks at No.1	Weeks on Chart
3 Apr 04	**BEAUTIFUL COLLISION** *Epic 5127279*	55		2

RUNRIG

UK, male vocal/instrumental group – Donnie Munro, Iain Bayne, Bruce Guthro, Malcolm Jones, Calum MacDonald, Rory MacDonald & Peter Wishart — 51

Date	Title / Label	Peak Position	Weeks at No.1	Weeks on Chart
26 Nov 88	**ONCE IN A LIFETIME** *Chrysalis CHR 1695*	61		2
7 Oct 89	**SEARCHLIGHT** *Chrysalis CHR 1713*	11		4
22 Jun 91	**THE BIG WHEEL** *Chrysalis CHR 1858*	4		15
27 Mar 93	**AMAZING THINGS** *Chrysalis CDCHR 2000*	2		6
26 Nov 94	**TRANSMITTING LIVE** *Chrysalis CDCHR 6090*	41		3
20 May 95	**THE CUTTER AND THE CLAN** *Chrysalis CCD 1669*	45		2
18 Nov 95	**MARA** *Chrysalis CDCHR 6111*	24		4
19 Oct 96	**LONG DISTANCE – THE BEST OF RUNRIG** *Chrysalis CDCHR 6116*	13		10
23 May 98	**THE GAELIC COLLECTION 1973–1995** *Ridge RR 009*	71		1
13 Mar 99	**IN SEARCH OF ANGELS** *Ridge RR 010*	29		2
26 May 01	**THE STAMPING GROUND** *Ridge RR 16*	64		1
26 May 07	**EVERYTHING YOU SEE** *Ridge RR044*	61		1

KATE RUSBY

UK, female vocalist/guitarist — 4

Date	Title / Label	Peak Position	Weeks at No.1	Weeks on Chart
9 Jun 01	**LITTLE LIGHTS** *Pure PRCD 07*	75		1
17 Sep 05	**GIRL WHO COULDN'T FLY** *Pure PRCD17*	45		1
15 Sep 07	**AWKWARD ANNIE** *Pure PRCD23*	32		2

RUSH

Canada, male vocal/instrumental group – Geddy Lee, Alex Lifeson & Neal Peart — 104

Date	Title / Label	Peak Position	Weeks at No.1	Weeks on Chart
8 Oct 77	**FAREWELL TO KINGS** *Mercury 9100 042*	22		4
25 Nov 78	**HEMISPHERES** *Mercury 9100 059*	14		6
26 Jan 80	**PERMANENT WAVES** *Mercury 9100 071*	3		16
21 Feb 81	**MOVING PICTURES** *Mercury 6337 160*	3		11
7 Nov 81	**EXIT STAGE LEFT** *Mercury 6619 053*	6		14
18 Sep 82	**SIGNALS** *Mercury 6337 243*	3		9
28 Apr 84	**GRACE UNDER PRESSURE** *Vertigo VERH 12*	5		12
9 Nov 85	**POWER WINDOWS** *Vertigo VERH 31*	9		4
21 Nov 87	**HOLD YOUR FIRE** *Vertigo VERH 47*	10		4
28 Jan 89	**A SHOW OF HANDS** *Vertigo 8363461*	12		4
9 Dec 89	**PRESTO** *Atlantic WX 327*	27		2
13 Oct 90	**CHRONICLES** *Vertigo CBTV 1*	42		2
14 Sep 91	**ROLL THE BONES** *Atlantic WX 436*	10		4
30 Oct 93	**COUNTERPARTS** *Atlantic 7567825282*	14		3
21 Sep 96	**TEST FOR ECHO** *Atlantic 7567829252*	25		3
25 May 02	**VAPOR TRAILS** *Atlantic 7567835312*	38		2
17 Jul 04	**FEEDBACK** *Atlantic 7567837282*	68		1
12 May 07	**SNAKES & ARROWS** *Atlantic 7567899868*	13		3

JENNIFER RUSH

US, female vocalist (Heidi Stern) — 43

Date	Title / Label	Peak Position	Weeks at No.1	Weeks on Chart
16 Nov 85	**JENNIFER RUSH** *CBS 26488*	7		35
3 May 86	**MOVIN'** *CBS 26710*	32		5
18 Apr 87	**HEART OVER MIND** *CBS 4504701*	48		3

PATRICE RUSHEN

US, female vocalist — 17

Date	Title / Label	Peak Position	Weeks at No.1	Weeks on Chart
1 May 82	**STRAIGHT FROM THE HEART** *Elektra K 52352*	24		14
16 Jun 84	**NOW** *Elektra 960360*	73		3

BRENDA RUSSELL

US, female vocalist/keyboard player (Brenda Gordon) — 4

Date	Title / Label	Peak Position	Weeks at No.1	Weeks on Chart
23 Apr 88	**GET HERE** *A&M AMA 5178*	77		4

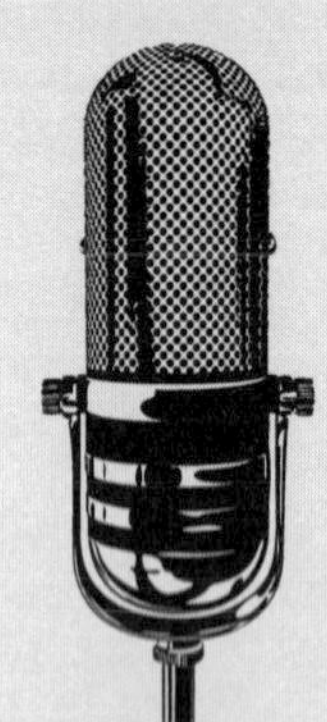

Public Enemy

It Takes A Nation Of Millions To Hold Us Back

FEW albums have had as much cultural impact as Public Enemy's June 1988, Number 8 hit, *It Takes A Nation Of Millions To Hold Us Back*. The rap crew based in Long Island took that emerging underground genre and created a template that was to be used time and time again, whilst simultaneously bridging the gap to an initially hostile rock world with an album that combined the dynamics of both forms into a wholly new and complete super-hybrid.

With this album – still hard to believe it was only their second effort – Public Enemy took their edgy street politics and placed them into the mainstream with an articulate, powerful record that combined the force of rock with a dense wall of samples and break beats – courtesy of their very own Bomb Squad – that made a very brutal sonic point. The material that emerged was breathtaking, especially when combined with the articulate rapping of former furniture-delivery man Chuck D, and the deceptively compelling clowning-around of his sidekick, Flavor Flav.

An avalanche of noise that almost sounds like the background cacophony of the city

Peel back the multiple layers on this album and you can see that the team's innovative producers, The Bomb Squad, had certainly done their homework: their kaleidoscope of samples included Funkadelic, James Brown (whose 'Funky Drummer' loop dominated the album's grooves), Rufus Thomas, Bobby Byrd, Isaac Hayes, The Temptations and Slayer. They even dropped a nod to their fellow rap pioneers Run DMC and, with acidic self-reference, themselves. It was a potent chemical stew of licks meshed together in the primitive days of sampling when the rules were not set, at a time when the concept of sampling itself was still controversial. Yet Public Enemy's brilliantly incisive choices were imaginative and innovative and showed that, with sharp and focused creativity, this approach could be used to generate an entirely new sound. Listen now to The Bomb Squad's work and you're lost in an avalanche of noise that almost sounds like the background cacophony of the city – a ghetto blaster on constant full volume. *It Takes A Nation Of Millions* ... is nothing if not an urban record.

And *every* song was an anthem. Any record kicking off with 'Bring The Noise' and 'Don't Believe The Hype' is going to be a winner. They were two of the most anthemic cuts of the time, sending shivers down the spines of the media the band so readily berated, and a brace of stand-up tunes that still wake you up to this day, combining the pure street funk of the 1970s with a Marshall amp spirit of punk rock and hardcore, all backdropped by a metallic love of noise.

The Bomb Squad's loops (especially the feedback loop twisted into one of the most unlikely hooks in the history of pop) provided a huge sound that enveloped the listener, drawing them into their world, where they might sit silently, waiting for Chuck D to lay down the law. One of the great modern vocalists, Chuck D has a rich voice that makes him sound as if he were a speechmaker from the pulpit of the pop apocalypse, his baritone monologuing effortlessly yet compulsively making a stand, like so few records have ever done. He

Chart History

Artist / Album Title	First Chart Week	Weeks on Chart	Highest Position
PUBLIC ENEMY IT TAKES A NATION OF MILLIONS TO HOLD US BACK	30/7/88	9	8

was smart and he instinctively knew how to forge a direct sense of communication with the record-buyer. This combination made Public Enemy one of the most potent musical melting pots of the late 1980s. Their songs were *monsters*. The album didn't let up there. 'Louder Than Bombs', 'Night Of the Living Baseheads' continued the rampage ...

Public Enemy were one-part pop group and one-part political organisation, with an inspiring message that was not only ostensibly touting black power but also a positive, affirmative manifesto for everyone, black or white. Onstage, this was particularly effective – whereas many rap bands were fairly weak in the live area, particularly in the formative days, Public Enemy had the dynamics of a rock band with frontman Chuck D's stunningly physical delivery, ably assisted by Flavor Flav's freaky outfits making them more like a prime-time arena band. Background dancers dressed in full paramilitary regalia gave the show a guerrilla-chic look and Terminator X dropping the records onto the turntable simply looked thrilling.

How could a group relying on samples have such a huge sound? Not only were Public Enemy using the funkiest of loops and squeezing the full sonic force out of them, they were also heavy, with a huge bass that saw them storm into the apparently unsuited rock-festival circuit and dominate like no other rap group has ever done, before or since.

Public Enemy were one-part pop group and one-part political organisation

And it was in back in 1988 with this album that they first worked it out. Year Zero. *It Takes A Nation Of Millions ... is* one of the greatest albums ever released in terms of the scale of imagination, the sound, direction and vision.

A work of pure genius.

Don't Believe The Hype

LEON RUSSELL
US, male vocalist/multi-instrumentalist (Claude Russell Bridges)

Date	Title	Peak	Wks at No.1	Wks on Chart
				1
3 Jul 71	**LEON RUSSELL AND THE SHELTER PEOPLE** *A&M AMLS 65003*	29		1

MIKE RUTHERFORD
UK, male vocalist/guitarist. See Genesis, Mike & The Mechanics

Date	Title	Peak	Wks at No.1	Wks on Chart
				11
23 Feb 80	**SMALLCREEP'S DAY** *Charisma CAS 1149*	13		7
18 Sep 82	**ACTING VERY STRANGE** *WEA K 99249*	23		4

RUTLES
UK, male actor/vocal/instrumental group

Date	Title	Peak	Wks at No.1	Wks on Chart
				11
15 Apr 78	**THE RUTLES** *Warner Brothers K 56459* ○	12		11

RUTS
UK, male vocal/instrumental group

Date	Title	Peak	Wks at No.1	Wks on Chart
				10
13 Oct 79	**THE CRACK** *Virgin V 2132*	16		6
18 Oct 80	**GRIN AND BEAR IT** *Virgin V 2188* D.C.	28		4

JOHN RUTTER
UK, male producer/conductor

Date	Title	Peak	Wks at No.1	Wks on Chart
				1
2 Nov 02	**THE COLLECTION** *UCJ 4726222*	75		1

LEE RYAN
UK, male vocalist. See Blue

Date	Title	Peak	Wks at No.1	Wks on Chart
				8
13 Aug 05	**LEE RYAN** *Brightside 82876719152*	6		8

RYANDAN
Canada, male vocal duo – Dan & Ryan Kowarsky

Date	Title	Peak	Wks at No.1	Wks on Chart
				3
6 Oct 07	**RYANDAN** *UCJ 1733741*	7		3

RZA
US, male producer/rapper (Robert Diggs). See Gravediggaz, Wu-Tang Clan

Date	Title	Peak	Wks at No.1	Wks on Chart
				1
28 Nov 98	**BOBBY DIGITAL IN STEREO** *Gee Street GEE 1003802*	70		1

ROBIN S
US, female vocalist (Robin Stone)

Date	Title	Peak	Wks at No.1	Wks on Chart
				3
4 Sep 93	**SHOW ME LOVE** *Champion CHAMPCD 1028*	34		3

S

S CLUB JUNIORS
UK, male/female vocal group – Jay Asforis, Daisy Evans, Calvin Goldspink, Stacey McClean, Aaron Renfree, Hannah Richings, Frankie Sandford & Rochelle Wiseman

Date	Title	Peak	Wks at No.1	Wks on Chart
				17
2 Nov 02	**TOGETHER** *Polydor 0652502* ⊛	5		13
25 Oct 03	**SUNDOWN** *Polydor 9865703* S CLUB 8	13		4

S CLUB 7
UK, female/male vocal/actor group – Jo O'Meara*, Tina Barrett, Paul Cattermole, John Lee, Bradley McIntosh, Hannah Spearritt & Rachel Stevens*

Date	Title	Peak	Wks at No.1	Wks on Chart
				149
16 Oct 99	**S CLUB** *Polydor 5431032* ⊛x2	2		46
24 Jun 00	**7** *Polydor 5438572* ⊛x4	1	1	61
8 Dec 01	**SUNSHINE** *Polydor 5894092* ⊛x2	3		24
7 Dec 02	**SEEING DOUBLE** *Polydor 0654962* S CLUB	17		5
14 Jun 03	**BEST – THE GREATEST HITS OF** *Polydor 9807374* S CLUB ●	2		13

S-EXPRESS
UK, male/female vocal/instrumental group – Mark Moore, Mark D, Pascal Gabriel, Billie Ray Martin*, Jocasta & Michellé

Date	Title	Peak	Wks at No.1	Wks on Chart
				9
1 Apr 89	**ORIGINAL SOUNDTRACK** *Rhythm King LEFTLP 8* ●	5		9

SABRES OF PARADISE
UK, male production group

Date	Title	Peak	Wks at No.1	Wks on Chart
				3
23 Oct 93	**SABRESONIC** *Warp WARPCD 16*	29		2
10 Dec 94	**HAUNTED DANCEHALL** *Warp WARPCD 26*	57		1

SACRED SPIRIT
Germany, male producer (Claus Zundel). See Divine Works

Date	Title	Peak	Wks at No.1	Wks on Chart
				30
1 Apr 95	**CHANTS AND DANCES OF THE NATIVE AMERICAN INDIAN** *Virgin CDV 2753* ⊛	9		27
26 Apr 97	**VOLUME 2 – CULTURE CLASH** *Virgin CDV 2827* ○	24		3

SAD CAFÉ
UK, male vocal/instrumental group – Paul Young, d. 17 Jul 2000, Tony Cresswell, Vic Emerson, Mike Hehir, Lenni, Ashley Mulford, John Stimpson & Ian Wilson

Date	Title	Peak	Wks at No.1	Wks on Chart
				36
1 Oct 77	**FANX TA RA** *RCA Victor PL 25101*	56		1
29 Apr 78	**MISPLACED IDEALS** *RCA Victor PL 25133*	50		1
29 Sep 79	**FACADES** *RCA PL 25249* ●	8		23
25 Oct 80	**SAD CAFÉ** *RCA SADLP 4* ○	46		5
21 Mar 81	**LIVE** *RCA SADLP 5*	37		4
24 Oct 81	**OLE** *Polydor POLD 5045*	72		2

SADE
Nigeria, female/male vocalist (Helen Folasade Adu)

Date	Title	Peak	Wks at No.1	Wks on Chart
				213
28 Jul 84	**DIAMOND LIFE** *Epic EPC 26044* ⊛x4	2		99
16 Nov 85	**PROMISE** *Epic EPC 86318* ⊛x2 ★	1	2	31
14 May 88	**STRONGER THAN PRIDE** *Epic 4604971* ⊛	3		17
7 Nov 92	**LOVE DELUXE** *Epic 4726262* ●	10		27
12 Nov 94	**THE BEST OF SADE** *Epic 4777932* ⊛	6		16
25 Nov 00	**LOVERS ROCK** *Epic 5007662* ●	18		21
2 Mar 02	**LOVERS LIVE** *Epic 5061252*	51		2

ALESSANDRO SAFINA
Italy, male vocalist

Date	Title	Peak	Wks at No.1	Wks on Chart
				2
30 Mar 02	**SAFINA** *Mercury 0167432*	27		2

BALLY SAGOO
UK (b. India), male DJ/producer/instrumentalist

Date	Title	Peak	Wks at No.1	Wks on Chart
				1
9 Nov 96	**RISING FROM THE EAST** *Higher Ground 4850162*	63		1

SAILOR
UK, male vocal/instrumental group

Date	Title	Peak	Wks at No.1	Wks on Chart
				8
7 Feb 76	**TROUBLE** *Epic EPC 69192* ○	45		8

SAINT ETIENNE
UK, female/male vocal/instrumental trio – Sarah Cracknell, Bob Stanley & Peter Wiggs

Date	Title	Peak	Wks at No.1	Wks on Chart
				32
26 Oct 91	**FOXBASE ALPHA** *Heavenly HVNLP 1*	34		3
6 Mar 93	**SO TOUGH** *Heavenly HVNLP 6CD*	7		7
12 Mar 94	**TIGER BAY** *Heavenly HVNLP 8CD*	8		4
25 Nov 95	**TOO YOUNG TO DIE – THE SINGLES** *Heavenly HVNLP 10CD* ○	17		9
27 Jan 96	**RESERECTION** *Virgin DINSD 150* DAHO	50		1
19 Oct 96	**CASINO CLASSICS** *Heavenly HVNLP 16CDL*	34		2
16 May 98	**GOOD HUMOUR** *Creation CRECD 225*	18		3
3 Jun 00	**SOUND OF WATER** *Mantra MNTCD 1018*	33		1
19 Oct 02	**FINISTERRE** *Mantra MNTCD 1033*	55		1
25 Jun 05	**TALES FROM TURNPIKE HOUSE** *Sanctuary SANDD271*	72		1

ST. GERMAIN
France, male producer (Ludovic Navarre)

Date	Title	Peak	Wks at No.1	Wks on Chart
				1
20 May 00	**TOURIST** *Blue Note 5262012* ●	73		1

ST. PAUL'S BOYS' CHOIR
UK, male choir

Date	Title	Peak	Wks at No.1	Wks on Chart
				8
29 Nov 80	**REJOICE** *K-Tel NE 1064*	36		8

BUFFY SAINTE-MARIE
Canada, female vocalist/guitarist (Beverly Sainte-Marie)

Date	Title	Peak Position	Weeks at No.1	Weeks on Chart
				2
21 Mar 92	**COINCIDENCE (AND LIKELY STORIES)** *Ensign CCD 1920*	39		2

RYUICHI SAKAMOTO
Japan, male keyboard player.

Date	Title	Peak Position	Weeks at No.1	Weeks on Chart
				9
3 Sep 83	**MERRY CHRISTMAS MR LAWRENCE (OST)** *Virgin V 2276* ○	36		9

SALAD
UK/Holland, male/female vocal/instrumental group

Date	Title	Peak Position	Weeks at No.1	Weeks on Chart
				2
27 May 95	**DRINK ME** *Island Red CIRDX 1002*	16		2

SALT-N-PEPA
US/Jamaica, female rappers – Cheryl 'Salt' James & Sandra 'Pepa' Denton

Date	Title	Peak Position	Weeks at No.1	Weeks on Chart
				57
6 Aug 88	**A SALT WITH A DEADLY PEPA** *London FFRLP 3* ●	19		27
12 May 90	**BLACKS' MAGIC** *ffrr 8281641*	70		1
6 Jul 91	**A BLITZ OF SALT-N-PEPA HITS (THE HITS REMIXED)** *ffrr 8282491*	70		2
19 Oct 91	**THE GREATEST HITS** *ffrr 8282911* ⊛	6		20
25 Apr 92	**RAPPED IN REMIXES** *ffrr 8282972*	37		2
23 Apr 94	**VERY NECESSARY** *ffrr 8284542*	36		5

SALVATION ARMY
UK, brass band

Date	Title	Peak Position	Weeks at No.1	Weeks on Chart
				10
24 Dec 77	**BY REQUEST** *Warwick WW 5038*	16		5
6 Dec 08	**TOGETHER** *UCJ 1782154*	20		5+

SAM & DAVE
US, male vocal duo – Sam Moore & Dave Prater, d. 9 Apr 1998

Date	Title	Peak Position	Weeks at No.1	Weeks on Chart
				20
21 Jan 67	**HOLD ON I'M COMIN'** *Atlantic 588045*	35		7
22 Apr 67	**DOUBLE DYNAMITE** *Stax 589003*	28		5
23 Mar 68	**SOUL MEN** *Stax 589015*	32		8

RICHIE SAMBORA
US, male vocalist/guitarist. See Bon Jovi

Date	Title	Peak Position	Weeks at No.1	Weeks on Chart
				5
14 Sep 91	**STRANGER IN THIS TOWN** *Mercury 8488951*	20		3
14 Mar 98	**UNDISCOVERED SOUL** *Mercury 5369722*	24		2

SAME DIFFERENCE
UK, male/female vocal duo

Date	Title	Peak Position	Weeks at No.1	Weeks on Chart
				4
13 Dec 08	**POP** *Syco Music 88697414682*	22		4+

SAMSON
UK, male vocal/instrumental group

Date	Title	Peak Position	Weeks at No.1	Weeks on Chart
				6
26 Jul 80	**HEAD ON** *Gem GEMLP 108*	34		6

DAVID SANBORN
US, male saxophonist

Date	Title	Peak Position	Weeks at No.1	Weeks on Chart
				1
14 Mar 87	**A CHANGE OF HEART** *Warner Brothers 9254791*	86		1

ROGER SANCHEZ
US, male producer

Date	Title	Peak Position	Weeks at No.1	Weeks on Chart
				2
11 Aug 01	**FIRST CONTACT** *Defected SMAN 01CD*	34		2

SANTA/ELVES/CHILDREN'S CHOIR
North Pole, male vocalist (Father Christmas)

Date	Title	Peak Position	Weeks at No.1	Weeks on Chart
				2
10 Dec 05	**SANTA SINGS** *Brightspark 82876755312*	49		2

SANTANA
US, male vocal/instrumental group – Carlos Santana; members also included David Brown, Alex Ligertwood, Leon Patillo, Gregg Rolie, Neal Schon, Michael Shrieve & Greg Walker. Enduring rock superstars who hit a career peak with *Supernatural*, their first US No.1 for 28 years. It won eight Grammys in 2000 (including Album of the Year) and has sold more than 25 million copies worldwide

Date	Title	Peak Position	Weeks at No.1	Weeks on Chart
				303
2 May 70	**SANTANA** *CBS 63815*	26		11
28 Nov 70	**ABRAXAS** *CBS 64807* ● ★	7		52
13 Nov 71	**SANTANA III** *CBS 69015* ★	6		14
26 Aug 72	**CARLOS SANTANA AND BUDDY MILES LIVE** *CBS 65142* CARLOS SANTANA & BUDDY MILES	29		4
25 Nov 72	**CARAVANSERAI** *CBS 65299*	6		11
28 Jul 73	**LOVE, DEVOTION, SURRENDER** *CBS 69037* CARLOS SANTANA & MAHAVISHNU JOHN McLAUGHLIN	7		9
8 Dec 73	**WELCOME** *CBS 69040* ○	8		6
21 Sep 74	**GREATEST HITS** *CBS 69081* ●	14		15
2 Nov 74	**ILLUMINATIONS** *CBS 69063* CARLOS SANTANA & ALICE COLTRANE	40		1
30 Nov 74	**BORBOLETTA** *CBS 69084* ○	18		5
10 Apr 76	**AMIGOS** *CBS 86005* ○	21		9
8 Jan 77	**FESTIVAL** *CBS 86020* ○	27		3
5 Nov 77	**MOONFLOWER** *CBS 88272* ●	7		27
11 Nov 78	**INNER SECRETS** *CBS 86075* ●	17		16
24 Mar 79	**ONENESS – SILVER DREAMS GOLDEN REALITY** *CBS 86037* CARLOS SANTANA	55		4
27 Oct 79	**MARATHON** *CBS 86098* ○	28		5
20 Sep 80	**THE SWING OF DELIGHT** *CBS 22075* CARLOS SANTANA	65		2
18 Apr 81	**ZEBOP!** *CBS 84946*	33		4
14 Aug 82	**SHANGO** *CBS 85914*	35		7
30 Apr 83	**HAVANA MOON** *CBS 25350* CARLOS SANTANA	84		3
23 Mar 85	**BEYOND APPEARANCES** *CBS 86307*	58		3
15 Nov 86	**VIVA! SANTANA – THE VERY BEST** *K-Tel NE 1338* ●	50		8
14 Jul 90	**SPIRITS DANCING IN THE FLESH** *CBS 4669131*	68		1
15 Aug 98	**THE ULTIMATE COLLECTION** *Columbia SONYTV 47CD* ●	12		26
4 Sep 99	**SUPERNATURAL** *Arista 07822190802* ⊛x2 ★	1	2	47
2 Nov 02	**SHAMAN** *Arista 74321959382* ● ★	15		5
12 Nov 05	**ALL THAT I AM** *Arista 82876696202*	36		2
3 Nov 07	**ULTIMATE SANTANA** *Arista 88697155022*	16		3

SANTOGOLD
US, female vocalist/producer (Santi White)

Date	Title	Peak Position	Weeks at No.1	Weeks on Chart
				2
24 May 08	**SANTOGOLD** *Atlantic 5144283082*	26		2

PETER SARSTEDT
UK, male vocalist

Date	Title	Peak Position	Weeks at No.1	Weeks on Chart
				4
15 Mar 69	**PETER SARSTEDT** *United Artists SULP 1219*	8		4

SASH!
Germany, male DJ/production group – Sascha Lappessen, Ralf Kappmeier & Thomas Ludke & various vocalists

Date	Title	Peak Position	Weeks at No.1	Weeks on Chart
				75
19 Jul 97	**IT'S MY LIFE – THE ALBUM** *Multiply MULTYCD 1* ⊛	6		38
5 Sep 98	**LIFE GOES ON** *Multiply MULTYCD 2* ●	5		19
29 Apr 00	**TRILENIUM** *Multiply MULTY CD7*	13		5
11 Nov 00	**ENCORE UNE FOIS – THE GREATEST HITS** *Multiply MULTY CD10*	33		3
1 Nov 08	**THE BEST OF** *Hard2Beat H2BCD02*	9		10+

SASHA
UK, male producer (Alexander Coe)

Date	Title	Peak Position	Weeks at No.1	Weeks on Chart
				9
12 Mar 94	**THE QAT COLLECTION** *Deconstruction 74321191962*	55		2
17 Jul 99	**XPANDER (EP)** *Deconstruction 74321681992*	18		3
17 Aug 02	**AIRDRAWN DAGGER** *Arista 74321947862*	18		3
26 Jun 04	**INVOLVER** *Global Underground GUSA001CDX*	61		1

JOE SATRIANI
US, male guitarist

Date	Title	Peak Position	Weeks at No.1	Weeks on Chart
				14
15 Aug 92	**THE EXTREMIST** *Epic 4716722*	13		6
6 Nov 93	**TIME MACHINE** *Epic 4745152*	32		2
14 Oct 95	**JOE SATRIANI** *Epic 4811022*	21		3
14 Mar 98	**CRYSTAL PLANET** *Epic 4894732*	32		2
12 Apr 08	**PROFESSOR SATCHAFUNKILUS AND THE MUSTERION OF ROCK** *Epic 88697212622*	75		1

Silver-selling ○ Gold-selling ● Platinum-selling ⊛ US No.1 ★ | Peak Position | Weeks at No.1 | Weeks on Chart

SATURDAYS
UK/Ireland, female vocal group — Weeks on Chart: 4

Date	Title / Label	Peak Position	Weeks at No.1	Weeks on Chart
8 Nov 08	**CHASING LIGHTS** *Fascination 1785979*	11		4

CHANTAY SAVAGE
US, female vocalist — Weeks on Chart: 1

Date	Title / Label	Peak Position	Weeks at No.1	Weeks on Chart
25 May 96	**I WILL SURVIVE (DOIN' IT MY WAY)** *RCA 74321381622*	66		1

SAVAGE GARDEN
Australia, male vocal/instrumental duo – Darren Hayes* & Daniel Jones — Weeks on Chart: 138

Date	Title / Label	Peak Position	Weeks at No.1	Weeks on Chart
14 Mar 98	**SAVAGE GARDEN** *Columbia 4871612* ⊛x2	2		68
20 Nov 99	**AFFIRMATION** *Columbia 4949352* ⊛x3	7		64
26 Nov 05	**TRULY MADLY COMPLETELY – THE BEST OF** *Columbia 82876739412* ●	25		6

TELLY SAVALAS
US, male actor/vocalist (Aristottle Savalas), d. 22 Jan 1994 (age 70) — Weeks on Chart: 10

Date	Title / Label	Peak Position	Weeks at No.1	Weeks on Chart
22 Mar 75	**TELLY** *MCA MCF 2699* ○	12		10

JACK SAVORETTI
UK, male vocalist/guitarist — Weeks on Chart: 1

Date	Title / Label	Peak Position	Weeks at No.1	Weeks on Chart
17 Mar 07	**BETWEEN THE MINDS** *Mercury 1719879*	70		1

SAVOY BROWN
UK, male vocal/instrumental group — Weeks on Chart: 1

Date	Title / Label	Peak Position	Weeks at No.1	Weeks on Chart
28 Nov 70	**LOOKIN' IN** *Decca SKL 5066*	50		1

SAW DOCTORS
Ireland, male vocal/instrumental group – Davy Carton & Leo Moran; members also included John Burke, Pearse Doherty, Kevin Duffy, John Donnelly, Tony Lambert & Anthony Thislethwaite — Weeks on Chart: 12

Date	Title / Label	Peak Position	Weeks at No.1	Weeks on Chart
8 Jun 91	**IF THIS IS ROCK AND ROLL, I WANT MY OLD JOB BACK** *Solid ROCK 7*	69		2
31 Oct 92	**ALL THE WAY FROM TUAM** *Solid 4509911462*	33		2
24 Feb 96	**SAME OUL' TOWN** *Shamtown SAWDOC 004CD* ●	6		5
24 Oct 98	**SONGS FROM SUN STREET** *Shamtown SAWDOC 006CD*	24		2
13 Oct 01	**VILLIANS** *Shamtown SAWDOC 008CD*	58		1

NITIN SAWHNEY
UK, male producer/multi-instrumentalist — Weeks on Chart: 6

Date	Title / Label	Peak Position	Weeks at No.1	Weeks on Chart
25 Sep 99	**BEYOND SKIN** *Outcaste CASTE 9CD*	44		2
30 Jun 01	**PROPHESY** *V2 VVR 1015912* ○	40		1
26 Jul 03	**HUMAN** *V2 VVR 1021852*	54		1
14 May 05	**PHILTRE** *V2 VVR1031272*	69		1
25 Oct 08	**LONDON UNDERSOUND** *Cooking Vinyl POSITIVIDCD1*	68		1

SAXON
UK, male vocal/instrumental group – Peter 'Biff' Byford, Pete Gill (replaced by Nigel Glockler), Steve Lawson, Graham Oliver & Paul Quinn — Weeks on Chart: 97

Date	Title / Label	Peak Position	Weeks at No.1	Weeks on Chart
12 Apr 80	**WHEELS OF STEEL** *Carrere CAL 115* ●	5		29
15 Nov 80	**STRONG ARM OF THE LAW** *Carrere CAL 120* ●	11		13
3 Oct 81	**DENIM AND LEATHER** *Carrere CAL 128* ○	9		11
22 May 82	**THE EAGLE HAS LANDED** *Carrere CAL 157* ○	5		19
26 Mar 83	**POWER AND THE GLORY** *Carrere CAL 147*	15		9
11 Feb 84	**CRUSADER** *Carrere CAL 200*	18		7
14 Sep 85	**INNOCENCE IS NO EXCUSE** *Parlophone SAXON 2*	36		4
27 Sep 86	**ROCK THE NATIONS** *EMI EMC 3515*	34		3
9 Apr 88	**DESTINY** *EMI EMC 3543*	49		2

LEO SAYER
UK, male vocalist — Weeks on Chart: 248

Date	Title / Label	Peak Position	Weeks at No.1	Weeks on Chart
5 Jan 74	**SILVER BIRD** *Chrysalis CHR 1050* ○	2		22
26 Oct 74	**JUST A BOY** *Chrysalis CHR 1068* ○	4		14
20 Sep 75	**ANOTHER YEAR** *Chrysalis CHR 1087* ○	8		9
27 Nov 76	**ENDLESS FLIGHT** *Chrysalis CHR 1125* ⊛	4		66
22 Oct 77	**THUNDER IN MY HEART** *Chrysalis CDL 1154* ●	8		16
2 Sep 78	**LEO SAYER** *Chrysalis CDL 1198* ●	15		25
31 Mar 79	**THE VERY BEST OF LEO SAYER** *Chrysalis CDL 1222* ⊛	1	3	37
13 Oct 79	**HERE** *Chrysalis CDL 1240* ●	44		4
23 Aug 80	**LIVING IN A FANTASY** *Chrysalis CDL 1297* ○	15		9
8 May 82	**WORLD RADIO** *Chrysalis CDL 1345*	30		12
12 Nov 83	**HAVE YOU EVER BEEN IN LOVE** *Chrysalis LEOTV 1* ●	15		18
6 Mar 93	**ALL THE BEST** *Chrysalis CDCHR 1980*	26		4
20 Feb 99	**THE DEFINITIVE HITS COLLECTION** *Polygram TV 5471152*	35		2
18 Feb 06	**ENDLESS JOURNEY – THE ESSENTIAL** *DMG TV DMGTV010*	43		6
18 Mar 06	**AT HIS VERY BEST** *Universal TV 9837818*	30		4

ALEXEI SAYLE
UK, male comedian/vocalist — Weeks on Chart: 5

Date	Title / Label	Peak Position	Weeks at No.1	Weeks on Chart
17 Mar 84	**THE FISH PEOPLE TAPES** *Island IMA 9*	62		5

BOZ SCAGGS
US, male vocalist (Willam Royce Scaggs) — Weeks on Chart: 29

Date	Title / Label	Peak Position	Weeks at No.1	Weeks on Chart
12 Mar 77	**SILK DEGREES** *CBS 81193* ○	37		24
17 Dec 77	**DOWN TWO, THEN LEFT** *CBS 86036*	55		1
3 May 80	**MIDDLE MAN** *CBS 86094*	52		4

SCARLET
UK, female vocal/instrumental duo — Weeks on Chart: 2

Date	Title / Label	Peak Position	Weeks at No.1	Weeks on Chart
11 Mar 95	**NAKED** *WEA 4509976432*	59		2

SCARS
UK, male vocal/instrumental group — Weeks on Chart: 3

Date	Title / Label	Peak Position	Weeks at No.1	Weeks on Chart
18 Apr 81	**AUTHOR! AUTHOR!** *Pre PREX 5*	67		3

SCARS ON BROADWAY
US, male vocal/instrumental group — Weeks on Chart: 1

Date	Title / Label	Peak Position	Weeks at No.1	Weeks on Chart
9 Aug 08	**SCARS ON BROADWAY** *Interscope 1778247*	41		1

MICHAEL SCHENKER GROUP
Germany/UK, male vocal/instrumental group – Michael Schenker; members also included Gary Barden, Graham Bonnet* & Robin McAuley — Weeks on Chart: 44

Date	Title / Label	Peak Position	Weeks at No.1	Weeks on Chart
6 Sep 80	**MICHAEL SCHENKER GROUP** *Chrysalis CHR 1302*	8		8
19 Sep 81	**MSG** *Chrysalis CHR 1336*	14		8
13 Mar 82	**ONE NIGHT AT BUDOKAN** *Chrysalis CTY 1375* ○	5		11
23 Oct 82	**ASSAULT ATTACK** *Chrysalis CHR 1393*	19		5
10 Sep 83	**BUILT TO DESTROY** *Chrysalis CHR 1441*	23		5
23 Jun 84	**ROCK WILL NEVER DIE** *Chrysalis CUX 1470*	24		5
24 Oct 87	**PERFECT TIMING** *EMI EMC 3539* MSG	65		2

SCISSOR SISTERS
US, male/female vocal/instrumental group – Jake Shears (Jason Sellards), Paddy Boom (Paddy Seacor, b. Singapore), Babydaddy (Scott Hoffman), Ana Matronic (Ana Lynch) & Del Marquis (Derek Gruen) — Weeks on Chart: 163

Date	Title / Label	Peak Position	Weeks at No.1	Weeks on Chart
14 Feb 04	**SCISSOR SISTERS** *Polydor 9866058* ⊛x7	1	4	113
30 Sep 06	**TA-DAH** *Polydor 1705087* ⊛x4	1	1	50

SCHOOL OF EXCELLENCE
UK, male production/instrumental duo. See Blowing Free, Harmonium, Hypnosis, In Tune & Raindance — Weeks on Chart: 2

Date	Title / Label	Peak Position	Weeks at No.1	Weeks on Chart
28 Oct 95	**PIANO MOODS** *Dino DINCD 114*	47		2

SCOOCH
UK, male/female vocal group — Weeks on Chart: 2

Date	Title / Label	Peak Position	Weeks at No.1	Weeks on Chart
19 Aug 00	**FOUR SURE** *Accolade 5278190*	41		2

SCOOTER
UK/Germany, male vocal/instrumental trio – H.P. Baxxter, Ferris Bueller (replaced by Axel Coon) & Rick J. Jordan — Weeks on Chart: 43

Date	Title / Label	Peak Position	Weeks at No.1	Weeks on Chart
13 Apr 96	**OUR HAPPY HARDCORE** *Club Tools 0062282 CLU*	24		5
10 Aug 02	**PUSH THE BEAT FOR THIS JAM – THE SINGLES** *Sheffield Tunes 0141172STU* ●	6		14
26 Apr 03	**THE STADIUM TECHNO EXPERIENCE** *Sheffield Tunes STU00147112CD* ○	20		4
17 May 08	**JUMPING ALL OVER THE WORLD** *AATW/UMTV 1772192* ⊛	1	1	20

SCORPIONS
Germany, male vocal/instrumental group

Date	Title	Peak Position	Weeks at No.1	Weeks on Chart (56)
21 Apr 79	**LOVE DRIVE** *Harvest SHSP 4097*	36		11
3 May 80	**ANIMAL MAGNETISM** *Harvest SHSP 4113*	23		6
10 Apr 82	**BLACKOUT** *Harvest SHVL 823*	11		11
24 Mar 84	**LOVE AT FIRST STING** *Harvest ATAK 69*	17		6
29 Jun 85	**WORLD WIDE LIVE** *Harvest SCORP 1*	18		8
14 May 88	**SAVAGE AMUSEMENT** *Harvest SHSP 4125*	18		6
17 Nov 90	**CRAZY WORLD** *Vertigo 8469081* ○	27		7
25 Sep 93	**FACE THE HEAT** *Mercury 5182802*	51		1

SCOTLAND FOOTBALL WORLD CUP SQUAD 1974
UK, male football squad vocalists

Date	Title	Peak Position	Weeks at No.1	Weeks on Chart (9)
25 May 74	**EASY EASY** *Polydor 2383 282*	3		9

BAND OF THE SCOTS GUARDS
UK, military band

Date	Title	Peak Position	Weeks at No.1	Weeks on Chart (2)
28 Jun 69	**BAND OF THE SCOTS GUARDS** *Fontana SFXL 54*	25		2

JACK SCOTT
Canada, male vocalist (Jack Scafone, Jr.)

Date	Title	Peak Position	Weeks at No.1	Weeks on Chart (12)
7 May 60	**I REMEMBER HANK WILLIAMS** *Top Rank BUY 034*	7		11
3 Sep 60	**WHAT IN THE WORLD'S COME OVER YOU** *Top Rank BUY 024*	11		1

JAMIE SCOTT & THE TOWN
UK, male vocalist/guitarist

Date	Title	Peak Position	Weeks at No.1	Weeks on Chart (2)
15 Sep 07	**PARK BENCH THEORIES** *Polydor 1730552*	24		2

JILL SCOTT
US, female vocalist

Date	Title	Peak Position	Weeks at No.1	Weeks on Chart (7)
29 Jul 00	**WHO IS JILL SCOTT – WORDS AND SOUNDS VOLUME 1** *Epic 4986252* ●	69		4
11 Sep 04	**BEAUTIFULLY HUMAN – WORDS AND SOUNDS VOLUME 2** *Epic 5176522*	27		3

MIKE SCOTT
UK, male vocalist/guitarist. See Waterboys

Date	Title	Peak Position	Weeks at No.1	Weeks on Chart (4)
30 Sep 95	**BRING 'EM ALL IN** *Chrysalis CDCHR 6108*	23		2
11 Oct 97	**STILL BURNING** *Chrysalis CDCHR 6122*	34		2

SCOUTING FOR GIRLS
UK, male vocal/instrumental trio – Roy Stride, Greg Churchouse & Peter Ellard

Date	Title	Peak Position	Weeks at No.1	Weeks on Chart (65)
29 Sep 07	**SCOUTING FOR GIRLS** *Epic 88697155192* ⊛x2	1	2	65+

SCREAMING BLUE MESSIAHS
US/UK, male vocal/instrumental group

Date	Title	Peak Position	Weeks at No.1	Weeks on Chart (1)
17 May 86	**GUN-SHY** *WEA WX 41*	90		1

SCREAMING TREES
US, male vocal/instrumental group

Date	Title	Peak Position	Weeks at No.1	Weeks on Chart (4)
20 Jul 96	**DUST** *Epic 4839802*	32		4

SCREEN II
UK, male vocal/instrumental group

Date	Title	Peak Position	Weeks at No.1	Weeks on Chart (1)
9 Apr 94	**LET THE RECORD SPIN** *Cleveland City CLE 13015*	36		1

THE SCRIPT
Ireland, male vocal/instrumental trio – Danny O'Donoghue, Glen Power & Mark Sheehan

Date	Title	Peak Position	Weeks at No.1	Weeks on Chart (20)
23 Aug 08	**THE SCRIPT** *Phonogenic 88697361942* ⊛	1	2	20+

SCRITTI POLITTI
UK, male vocal/instrumental group – Green Gartside, David Gamson, Niall Jinks, Fred Maher & Tom Morley

Date	Title	Peak Position	Weeks at No.1	Weeks on Chart (39)
11 Sep 82	**SONGS TO REMEMBER** *Rough Trade ROUGH 20*	12		7
22 Jun 85	**CUPID AND PSYCHE 85** *Virgin V 2350* ●	5		19
18 Jun 88	**PROVISION** *Virgin V 2515* ●	8		11
7 Aug 99	**ANOMIE & BONHOMIE** *Virgin CDV 2884*	33		2

SEAHORSES
UK, male vocal/instrumental group – Chris Helme, Stuart Fletcher, John Squire* & Andy Watts

Date	Title	Peak Position	Weeks at No.1	Weeks on Chart (38)
7 Jun 97	**DO IT YOURSELF** *Geffen GED 25134* ⊛	2		38

SEAL
UK, male vocalist (Sealhenry Samuel)

Date	Title	Peak Position	Weeks at No.1	Weeks on Chart (153)
1 Jun 91	**SEAL** *ZTT 9* ⊛x2	1	3	65
4 Jun 94	**SEAL II** *ZTT 4509962562* ⊛x2	1	2	64
28 Nov 98	**HUMAN BEING** *Warner Brothers 9362468282* ○	44		2
27 Sep 03	**IV** *Warner Brothers 9362485412*	4		6
20 Nov 04	**BEST 1991-2004** *Warner Brothers 9362489582* ●	27		7
24 Nov 07	**SYSTEM** *Warner Brothers 9362499309*	37		2
22 Nov 08	**SOUL** *Warner Brothers 9362498246* ○	17		7+

JAY SEAN
UK, male vocalist (Kamaljit Jhooti)

Date	Title	Peak Position	Weeks at No.1	Weeks on Chart (6)
20 Nov 04	**ME AGAINST MYSELF** *Relentless CDREL05* ○	29		2
24 May 08	**MY OWN WAY** *2 Point 9/Jayded JAY2P9CD1*	6		4

SEARCHERS
UK, male vocal/instrumental group – Tony Jackson, d. 18 Aug 2003 (replaced by Frank Allen), Chris Curtis, d. 28 Feb 2005, John McNally & Mike Pender

Date	Title	Peak Position	Weeks at No.1	Weeks on Chart (93)
10 Aug 63	**MEET THE SEARCHERS** *Pye NPL 18086*	2		44
16 Nov 63	**SUGAR AND SPICE** *Pye NPL 18089*	5		21
30 May 64	**IT'S THE SEARCHERS** *Pye NPL 18092*	4		17
27 Mar 65	**SOUNDS LIKE THE SEARCHERS** *Pye NPL 18111*	8		5
24 May 08	**THE VERY BEST OF** *UMTV 5308616*	11		6

SEASICK STEVE
US, male vocalist/guitarist (Steve Wold)

Date	Title	Peak Position	Weeks at No.1	Weeks on Chart (20)
19 Jan 08	**DOG HOUSE MUSIC** *Bronzerat BR04* ●	47		12
11 Oct 08	**I STARTED OUT WITH NOTHIN' AND STILL GOT MOST OF IT LEFT** *Warner Brothers 2564694111* ○	9		8

SEBADOH
US, male vocal/instrumental group

Date	Title	Peak Position	Weeks at No.1	Weeks on Chart (5)
8 May 93	**BUBBLE AND SCRAPE** *Domino WIGCD 4*	63		1
3 Sep 94	**BAKESALE** *Domino WIGCD 11*	40		2
31 Aug 96	**HARMACY** *Domino WIGCD 26*	38		1
6 Mar 99	**THE SEBADOH** *Domino WIGCD 057*	45		1

JON SECADA
Cuba, male vocalist (Juan Secada)

Date	Title	Peak Position	Weeks at No.1	Weeks on Chart (16)
5 Sep 92	**JON SECADA** *SBK SBKCD 19* ●	20		11
4 Jun 94	**HEART, SOUL AND VOICE** *SBK SBKCD 29*	17		5
31 Mar 62	**SACRED SONGS** *Philips RBL 7501* HARRY SECOMBE	16		1

HARRY SECOMBE
UK, male vocalist/comedian, d. 12 Apr 2001 (age 79)

Date	Title	Peak Position	Weeks at No.1	Weeks on Chart (62)
18 Apr 64	**HOW TO WIN AN ELECTION** *Philips AL 3464* HARRY SECOMBE, PETER SELLERS & SPIKE MILLIGAN	20		1
22 Apr 67	**SECOMBE'S PERSONAL CHOICE** *Philips BETS 707*	6		13
7 Aug 71	**IF I RULED THE WORLD** *Contour 6870 501*	17		20
16 Dec 78	**20 SONGS OF JOY** *Warwick WW 5052*	8		12
5 Dec 81	**GOLDEN MEMORIES** *Warwick WW 5107* HARRY SECOMBE & MOIRA ANDERSON	46		5
13 Dec 86	**HIGHWAY OF LIFE** *Telstar STAR 2289*	45		5
30 Nov 91	**YOURS SINCERELY** *Philips 5107321* ○	46		5

Silver-selling · Gold-selling · Platinum-selling · US No.1 ★ · Peak Position · Weeks at No.1 · Weeks on Chart

SECOND IMAGE

UK, male vocal/instrumental group

Date	Title	Peak Position	Weeks at No.1	Weeks on Chart
				1
30 Mar 85	**STRANGE REFLECTIONS** *MCA MCF 3255*	100		1

SECRET AFFAIR

UK, male vocal/instrumental group

Date	Title	Peak Position	Weeks at No.1	Weeks on Chart
				15
1 Dec 79	**GLORY BOYS** *I-Spy 1*	41		8
20 Sep 80	**BEHIND CLOSED DOORS** *I-Spy 2*	48		4
13 Mar 82	**BUSINESS AS USUAL** *I-Spy 3*	84		3

SECRET MACHINES

US, male vocal/instrumental trio

Date	Title	Peak Position	Weeks at No.1	Weeks on Chart
				1
15 Apr 06	**TEN SILVER DROPS** *Reprise 9362499872*	43		1

NEIL SEDAKA

US, male vocalist/pianist

Date	Title	Peak Position	Weeks at No.1	Weeks on Chart
				85
1 Sep 73	**THE TRA-LA DAYS ARE OVER** *MGM 2315 248*	13		10
22 Jun 74	**LAUGHTER IN THE RAIN** *Polydor 2383 265*	17		10
23 Nov 74	**LIVE AT THE ROYAL FESTIVAL HALL** *Polydor 2383 299*	48		1
1 Mar 75	**OVERNIGHT SUCCESS** *Polydor 2442 131*	31		6
10 Jul 76	**LAUGHTER AND TEARS – THE BEST OF NEIL SEDAKA TODAY** *Polydor 2383 399*	2		25
2 Nov 91	**TIMELESS – THE VERY BEST OF NEIL SEDAKA** *Polydor 5114421*	10		16
4 Nov 95	**CLASSICALLY SEDAKA** *Vision VISCD 5*	23		9
19 Jun 99	**THE VERY BEST OF NEIL SEDAKA** *Universal Music TV 5646452*	33		3
1 Apr 06	**THE VERY BEST OF – THE SHOW GOES ON** *Universal TV 9837951*	20		5

SEEKERS

Australia, female/male vocal/instrumental group – Judith Durham*, Athol Guy, Keith Potger & Bruce Woodley

Date	Title	Peak Position	Weeks at No.1	Weeks on Chart
				283
3 Jul 65	**A WORLD OF OUR OWN** *Columbia 33SX 1722*	5		36
3 Jul 65	**THE SEEKERS** *Decca LK 4694*	16		1
19 Nov 66	**COME THE DAY** *Columbia SX 6093*	3		67
25 Nov 67	**SEEKERS – SEEN IN GREEN** *Columbia SCX 6193*	15		10
14 Sep 68	**LIVE AT THE TALK OF THE TOWN** *Columbia SCX 6278*	2		30
16 Nov 68	**THE BEST OF THE SEEKERS** *Columbia SCX 6268*	1	6	125
23 Apr 94	**CARNIVAL OF HITS** *EMI CDEMTV 83* JUDITH DURHAM & THE SEEKERS	7		14

BOB SEGER & THE SILVER BULLET BAND

US, male vocal/instrumental group – Bob Seger (Robert Seger), Drew Abbott, Chris Campbell, Charlie Martin, Alto Reed & Robyn Robbins

Date	Title	Peak Position	Weeks at No.1	Weeks on Chart
				52
3 Jun 78	**STRANGER IN TOWN** *Capitol EAST 11698*	31		6
15 Mar 80	**AGAINST THE WIND** *Capitol EAST 12041* ★	26		6
26 Sep 81	**NINE TONIGHT** *Capitol ESTSP 23*	24		10
8 Jan 83	**THE DISTANCE** *Capitol EST 12254*	45		10
26 Apr 86	**LIKE A ROCK** *Capitol EST 2011*	35		6
21 Sep 91	**THE FIRE INSIDE** *Capitol EST 2149*	54		2
18 Feb 95	**GREATEST HITS** *Capitol CDEST 2241*	6		12

SELECTER

UK, male/female vocal/instrumental group – Pauline Black; members also included Megan Amanor, Charley Anderson, Charley Bembridge, Desmond Brown, Neol Davies & Arthur Hendrickson

Date	Title	Peak Position	Weeks at No.1	Weeks on Chart
				17
23 Feb 80	**TOO MUCH PRESSURE** *2-Tone CDL TT 5002*	5		13
7 Mar 81	**CELEBRATE THE BULLET** *Chrysalis CHR 1306*	41		4

PETER SELLERS

UK, male comedian/vocalist (Richard Sellers), d. 24 Jul 1980 (age 54)

Date	Title	Peak Position	Weeks at No.1	Weeks on Chart
				113
14 Feb 59	**THE BEST OF SELLERS** *Parlophone PMD 1069*	3		47
12 Dec 59	**SONGS FOR SWINGING SELLERS** *Parlophone PMC 1111*	3		37
3 Dec 60	**PETER AND SOPHIA** *Parlophone PMC 1131* & SOPHIA LOREN	5		18
28 Sep 63	**FOOL BRITANNIA** *Ember CEL 902* ANTHONY NEWLEY, PETER SELLERS, JOAN COLLINS	10		10
18 Apr 64	**HOW TO WIN AN ELECTION** *Philips AL 3464* HARRY SECOMBE, PETER SELLERS & SPIKE MILLIGAN	20		1

SEMISONIC

US, male vocal/instrumental group

Date	Title	Peak Position	Weeks at No.1	Weeks on Chart
				41
24 Jul 99	**FEELING STRANGELY FINE** *MCA MCD 11733*	16		37
17 Mar 01	**ALL ABOUT CHEMISTRY** *MCA 1125012*	13		4

SENSELESS THINGS

UK, male vocal/instrumental group

Date	Title	Peak Position	Weeks at No.1	Weeks on Chart
				2
26 Oct 91	**THE FIRST OF TOO MANY** *Epic 4691571*	66		1
13 Mar 93	**EMPIRE OF THE SENSELESS** *Epic 4735252*	37		1

SENSER

UK, male/female vocal/instrumental group – Heitham Al-Sayed, James Barrett, Andy Clinton, Paul Haggerty, Kerstin Haigh, Nick Michaelson & John Morgan

Date	Title	Peak Position	Weeks at No.1	Weeks on Chart
				6
7 May 94	**STACKED UP** *Ultimate TOPPCD 008*	4		5
2 May 98	**ASYLUM** *Ultimate TOPPCD 064*	73		1

SEPULTURA

Brazil, male vocal/instrumental group – Max Cavalera, Igor Cavalera, Andreas Kisser & Paulo Jr. (Paulo Junior)

Date	Title	Peak Position	Weeks at No.1	Weeks on Chart
				12
6 Apr 91	**ARISE** *Roadracer RO 93281*	40		2
23 Oct 93	**CHAOS A.D.** *Roadrunner RR 90002*	11		4
9 Mar 96	**ROOTS** *Roadrunner RR 89002*	4		5
17 Oct 98	**AGAINST** *Roadrunner RR 87002*	40		1

ERIC SERRA

France, male guitarist

Date	Title	Peak Position	Weeks at No.1	Weeks on Chart
				2
28 Jun 97	**THE FIFTH ELEMENT (OST)** *Virgin CDVIR 63*	58		2

TAJA SEVELLE

US, female vocalist

Date	Title	Peak Position	Weeks at No.1	Weeks on Chart
				4
26 Mar 88	**TAJA SEVELLE** *Paisley Park WX 165*	48		4

SEX PISTOLS

UK, male vocal/instrumental group – Johnny Rotten (John Lydon), Paul Cook, Steve Jones, Glen Matlock (replaced by Sid Vicious (John Ritchie/Beverley))

Date	Title	Peak Position	Weeks at No.1	Weeks on Chart
				125
12 Nov 77	**NEVER MIND THE BOLLOCKS, HERE'S THE SEX PISTOLS** *Virgin V 2086/SPUNK 1*	1	2	56
10 Mar 79	**THE GREAT ROCK 'N' ROLL SWINDLE (OST)** *Virgin VD 2410*	7		33
11 Aug 79	**SOME PRODUCT – CARRI ON SEX PISTOLS** *Virgin VR 2*	6		10
16 Feb 80	**FLOGGING A DEAD HORSE** *Virgin V 2142*	23		6
7 Jun 80	**THE GREAT ROCK 'N' ROLL SWINDLE (OST)** *Virgin V 2168*	16		11
17 Oct 92	**KISS THIS** *Virgin CDV 2702*	10		4
10 Aug 96	**FILTHY LUCRE LIVE** *Virgin CDVUS 116*	26		2
15 Jun 02	**JUBILEE** *Virgin CDV 2961*	29		3

DANNY SEWARD

UK, male actor/vocalist

Date	Title	Peak Position	Weeks at No.1	Weeks on Chart
				1
30 Jul 05	**WHERE MY HEART IS** *Liberty VTCD722*	56		1

SHACK

UK, male vocal/instrumental group

Date	Title	Peak Position	Weeks at No.1	Weeks on Chart
				4
3 Jul 99	**H.M.S. FABLE** *London 5561132*	25		2
23 Aug 03	**HERE'S TOM WITH THE WEATHER** *North Country NCCD 002*	55		1
27 May 06	**THE CORNER OF MILES AND GIL** *Sour Mash JDNCCD006X*	55		1

SHADES OF RHYTHM

UK, male production/instrumental group

Date	Title	Peak Position	Weeks at No.1	Weeks on Chart
				3
17 Aug 91	**SHADES** *ZTT 8*	51		3

SHADOWS

UK, male vocal/instrumental group – Hank Marvin* & Bruce Welch; members also included Brian Bennett, John Farrar, Jet Harris, Brian Locking, Tony Meehan & John Rostill, d. 26 Nov 1973. The most successful instrumental act of all time started out as Cliff Richard's backing band. Britain's most influential and most imitated act before The Beatles

Date	Title	Peak Position	Weeks at No.1	Weeks on Chart
				833
18 Apr 59	**CLIFF** *Columbia 33SX 1147* CLIFF RICHARD & THE DRIFTERS	4		31
14 Nov 59	**CLIFF SINGS** *Columbia 33SX 1192* CLIFF RICHARD & THE SHADOWS	2		36
15 Oct 60	**ME AND MY SHADOWS** *Columbia 33SX 1261* CLIFF RICHARD & THE SHADOWS	2		33
22 Apr 61	**LISTEN TO CLIFF** *Columbia 33SX 1320* CLIFF RICHARD & THE SHADOWS	2		28
16 Sep 61	**THE SHADOWS** *Columbia 33SX 1374*	1	5	57

Silver-selling ○ · Gold-selling ● · Platinum-selling ⊛ · US No.1 ★ · Peak Position · Weeks at No.1 · Weeks on Chart

Date	Title / Label	Peak Position	Weeks at No.1	Weeks on Chart
21 Oct 61	**I'M 21 TODAY** *Columbia 33SX 1368* CLIFF RICHARD & THE SHADOWS	1	1	16
23 Dec 61	**THE YOUNG ONES (OST)** *Columbia 33SX 1384* CLIFF RICHARD & THE SHADOWS	1	6	42
29 Sep 62	**32 MINUTES AND 17 SECONDS** *Columbia 33SX 1431* CLIFF RICHARD & THE SHADOWS	3		21
13 Oct 62	**OUT OF THE SHADOWS** *Columbia 33SWX 1458*	1	7	38
26 Jan 63	**SUMMER HOLIDAY (OST)** *Columbia 33SX 1472* CLIFF RICHARD & THE SHADOWS	1	14	36
22 Jun 63	**THE SHADOWS' GREATEST HITS** *Columbia 33SX 1522*	2		56
13 Jul 63	**CLIFF'S HIT ALBUM** *Columbia 33SX 1512* CLIFF RICHARD & THE SHADOWS	2		19
28 Sep 63	**WHEN IN SPAIN** *Columbia 33SX 1541* CLIFF RICHARD & THE SHADOWS	8		10
9 May 64	**DANCE WITH THE SHADOWS** *Columbia 33SX 1619*	2		27
11 Jul 64	**WONDERFUL LIFE (OST)** *Columbia 33SX 1628* CLIFF RICHARD & THE SHADOWS	2		23
9 Jan 65	**ALADDIN AND HIS WONDERFUL LAMP** *Columbia 33SX 1676* CLIFF RICHARD & THE SHADOWS	13		5
17 Jul 65	**THE SOUND OF THE SHADOWS** *Columbia 33SX 1736*	4		17
14 Aug 65	**MORE HITS BY CLIFF** *Columbia 33SX 1737* CLIFF RICHARD & THE SHADOWS	20		1
8 Jan 66	**LOVE IS FOREVER** *Columbia 33SX 1769* CLIFF RICHARD & THE SHADOWS	19		1
21 May 66	**SHADOW MUSIC** *Columbia SX 6041*	5		17
15 Jul 67	**JIGSAW** *Columbia SCX 6148*	8		16
16 Nov 68	**ESTABLISHED 1958** *Columbia SCX 6282* CLIFF RICHARD & THE SHADOWS	30		4
12 Jul 69	**THE BEST OF CLIFF** *Columbia SCX 6343* CLIFF RICHARD & THE SHADOWS	5		17
24 Oct 70	**SHADES OF ROCK** *Columbia SCX 6420*	30		4
23 Dec 72	**THE BEST OF CLIFF VOLUME 2** *Columbia SCX 6519* CLIFF RICHARD & THE SHADOWS	49		2
13 Apr 74	**ROCKIN' WITH CURLY LEADS** *EMI EMA 762*	45		1
11 May 74	**THE SHADOWS' GREATEST HITS** *Columbia SCX 1522*	48		6
29 Mar 75	**SPECS APPEAL** *EMI EMC 3066*	30		5
12 Feb 77	**SHADOWS 20 GOLDEN GREATS** *EMI EMTV 3* ⊛	1	6	43
17 Feb 79	**THANK YOU VERY MUCH – REUNION CONCERT AT THE LONDON PALLADIUM** *EMI EMTV 15* CLIFF RICHARD & THE SHADOWS ●	5		12
15 Sep 79	**STRING OF HITS** *EMI EMC 3310* ⊛	1	3	43
26 Jul 80	**ANOTHER STRING OF HITS** *EMI EMC 3339* ○	16		8
13 Sep 80	**CHANGE OF ADDRESS** *Polydor 2442 179* ○	17		6
19 Sep 81	**HITS RIGHT UP YOUR STREET** *Polydor POLD 5046* ○	15		16
25 Sep 82	**LIFE IN THE JUNGLE/LIVE AT ABBEY ROAD** *Polydor SHADS 1*	24		6
22 Oct 83	**XXV** *Polydor POLD 5120*	34		6
17 Nov 84	**GUARDIAN ANGEL** *Polydor POLD 5169*	98		1
24 May 86	**MOONLIGHT SHADOWS** *Polydor PROLP 8* ●	6		19
24 Oct 87	**SIMPLY SHADOWS** *Polydor SHAD 1* ⊛	11		17
20 May 89	**STEPPIN' TO THE SHADOWS** *Polydor SHAD 30* ●	11		9
16 Dec 89	**AT THEIR VERY BEST** *Polydor 8415201* ●	12		9
13 Oct 90	**REFLECTION** *Roll Over 8471201* ⊛	5		15
16 Nov 91	**THEMES AND DREAMS** *Polydor 5113741* ●	21		11
15 May 93	**SHADOWS IN THE NIGHT – 16 CLASSIC TRACKS** *Polygram TV 8437982*	22		4
22 Oct 94	**THE BEST OF HANK MARVIN AND THE SHADOWS** *Polygram TV 5238212* HANK MARVIN & THE SHADOWS	19		11
22 Nov 97	**PLAY ANDREW LLOYD WEBBER AND TIM RICE** *Polygram TV 5394792* HANK MARVIN & THE SHADOWS	41		6
14 Nov 98	**VERY BEST OF HANK MARVIN AND THE SHADOWS – THE FIRST 40 YEARS** *Polygram TV 5592112* HANK MARVIN & THE SHADOWS	56		5
12 Aug 00	**50 GOLDEN GREATS** *EMI 5275862*	35		3
8 May 04	**LIFE STORY** *Universal TV 9817819* ●	7		10
27 Aug 05	**PLATINUM COLLECTION** *EMI 3349382* ○	30		4

SHAGGY

Jamaica, male vocalist (Orville Burrell) — 64

Date	Title / Label	Peak Position	Weeks at No.1	Weeks on Chart
24 Jul 93	**PURE PLEASURE** *Greensleeves GRELCD 184*	67		1
14 Oct 95	**BOOMBASTIC** *Virgin CDV 2782* ○	37		6
17 Feb 01	**HOT SHOT** *MCA 1122932* ⊛x3 ★	1	1	47
16 Feb 02	**MR LOVER LOVER – THE BEST OF – PART 1** *Virgin VTCD 429* ○	20		5
16 Nov 02	**LUCKY DAY** *MCA 1131192*	54		2
6 Sep 08	**BEST OF – THE BOOMBASTIC COLLECTION** *Geffen 5310674*	22		3

SHAKATAK

UK, female/male vocal/instrumental group – Jill Saward, George Anderson, Roger Odell, Bill Sharpe (Sharpe & Numan*), Keith Winter & Nigel Wright — 73

Date	Title / Label	Peak Position	Weeks at No.1	Weeks on Chart
30 Jan 82	**DRIVIN' HARD** *Polydor POLS 1030* ○	35		17
15 May 82	**NIGHT BIRDS** *Polydor POLS 1059* ●	4		28
27 Nov 82	**INVITATIONS** *Polydor POLD 5068* ●	30		11
22 Oct 83	**OUT OF THIS WORLD** *Polydor POLD 5115*	30		4
25 Aug 84	**DOWN ON THE STREET** *Polydor POLD 5148*	17		9
23 Feb 85	**LIVE!** *Polydor POLH 21*	82		3
22 Oct 88	**THE COOLEST CUTS** *K-Tel NE 1422*	73		1

SHAKESPEAR'S SISTER

UK/US, female vocal/instrumental duo – Marcella Detroit* (Marcella Levy) & Siobhan Fahey — 63

Date	Title / Label	Peak Position	Weeks at No.1	Weeks on Chart
2 Sep 89	**SACRED HEART** *London 8281311* ●	9		8
29 Feb 92	**HORMONALLY YOURS** *London 8282262* ⊛x2	3		55

SHAKIN' PYRAMIDS

UK, male vocal/instrumental group — 4

Date	Title / Label	Peak Position	Weeks at No.1	Weeks on Chart
4 Apr 81	**SKIN 'EM UP** *Cuba Libra V 2199*	48		4

SHAKIRA

Colombia, female vocalist (Shakira Isabel Mebarak Ripoll) — 71

Date	Title / Label	Peak Position	Weeks at No.1	Weeks on Chart
23 Mar 02	**LAUNDRY SERVICE** *Epic SNY 639002 (Import)* ⊛x2	2		47
18 Mar 06	**ORAL FIXATION VOLUME 2** *Epic SNY977082* ⊛	12		24

SHALAMAR

US, male/female vocal trio – Jeffrey Daniel, Howard Hewitt & Jody Watley* — 121

Date	Title / Label	Peak Position	Weeks at No.1	Weeks on Chart
27 Mar 82	**FRIENDS** *Solar K 52345* ⊛	6		72
11 Sep 82	**GREATEST HITS** *Solar SOLA 3001*	71		5
30 Jul 83	**THE LOOK** *Solar 960239* ●	7		20
12 Apr 86	**THE GREATEST HITS** *Stylus SMR 8615* ●	5		24

SHAM 69

UK, male vocal/instrumental group – Jimmy Pursey, Mark Cain (replaced by Rick Goldstein), Albie Maskell (replaced by Dave Treganna) & Dave Parsons — 27

Date	Title / Label	Peak Position	Weeks at No.1	Weeks on Chart
11 Mar 78	**TELL US THE TRUTH** *Polydor 2383 491*	25		8
2 Dec 78	**THAT'S LIFE** *Polydor POLD 5010* ○	27		11
29 Sep 79	**THE ADVENTURES OF THE HERSHAM BOYS** *Polydor POLD 5025* ○	8		8

SHAMEN

UK, male vocal/instrumental duo – Colin Angus & Richard West — 54

Date	Title / Label	Peak Position	Weeks at No.1	Weeks on Chart
3 Nov 90	**EN-TACT** *One Little Indian TPLP 22*	31		10
28 Sep 91	**PROGENY** *One Little Indian TPLP 32*	23		2
26 Sep 92	**BOSS DRUM/DIFFERENT DRUM** *One Little Indian TPLP 42CD* ⊛	3		35
20 Nov 93	**ON AIR – BBC SESSIONS** *Band Of Joy BOJCD 006*	61		1
4 Nov 95	**AXIS MUTATIS** *One Little Indian TPLP 52CDL*	27		2
2 May 98	**THE SHAMEN COLLECTION** *One Little Indian TPLP 72CDE*	26		4

SHAMPOO

UK, female duo — 2

Date	Title / Label	Peak Position	Weeks at No.1	Weeks on Chart
5 Nov 94	**WE ARE SHAMPOO** *Food FOODCD 12*	45		2

JIMMY SHAND & HIS BAND

UK, male/female instrumental group – Jimmy Shand, d. 23 Dec 2000 (age 92) — 2

Date	Title / Label	Peak Position	Weeks at No.1	Weeks on Chart
24 Dec 83	**FIFTY YEARS ON WITH JIMMY SHAND** *Ross WGR 062*	97		2

SHANICE

US, female vocalist (Shanice Wilson) — 4

Date	Title / Label	Peak Position	Weeks at No.1	Weeks on Chart
21 Mar 92	**INNER CHILD** *Motown 5300082*	21		4

SHANNON

US, female vocalist (Brenda Shannon Greene) — 12

Date	Title / Label	Peak Position	Weeks at No.1	Weeks on Chart
10 Mar 84	**LET THE MUSIC PLAY** *Club JABL 1*	52		12

DEL SHANNON

US, male vocalist (Charles Westover), d. 8 Feb 1990 (age 55) — 23

Date	Title / Label	Peak Position	Weeks at No.1	Weeks on Chart
11 May 63	**HATS OFF TO LARRY** *London HAX 8071*	9		17
2 Nov 63	**LITTLE TOWN FLIRT** *London HAX 8091*	15		6

Silver-selling ○ Gold-selling ● Platinum-selling ⊛ US No.1 ★ Peak Position Weeks at No.1 Weeks on Chart

HELEN SHAPIRO
UK, female vocalist — 25

Date	Title	Peak Position	Weeks at No.1	Weeks on Chart
10 Mar 62	**TOPS WITH ME** *Columbia 33SX 1397*	2		25

FEARGAL SHARKEY
UK, male vocalist. See Undertones — 24

Date	Title	Peak Position	Weeks at No.1	Weeks on Chart
23 Nov 85	**FEARGAL SHARKEY** *Virgin V 2360* ●	12		20
20 Apr 91	**SONGS FROM THE MARDI GRAS** *Virgin V 2642*	27		4

SHARPE & NUMAN
UK, male vocal/instrumental duo — 1

Date	Title	Peak Position	Weeks at No.1	Weeks on Chart
8 Jul 89	**AUTOMATIC** *Polydor 8395201*	59		1

SANDIE SHAW
UK, female vocalist (Sandra Goodrich) — 15

Date	Title	Peak Position	Weeks at No.1	Weeks on Chart
6 Mar 65	**SANDIE** *Pye NPL 18110*	3		13
19 Nov 94	**NOTHING LESS THAN BRILLIANT** *Virgin VTCD 34*	64		1
12 Mar 05	**THE VERY BEST OF** *EMI 8661102*	60		1

GEORGE SHEARING
US (b. UK), male pianist — 13

Date	Title	Peak Position	Weeks at No.1	Weeks on Chart
11 Jun 60	**BEAUTY AND THE BEAT** *Capitol T 1219* PEGGY LEE & GEORGE SHEARING	16		6
20 Oct 62	**NAT 'KING' COLE SINGS AND THE GEORGE SHEARING QUARTET PLAYS** *Capitol W 1675* NAT 'KING' COLE/GEORGE SHEARING QUARTET	8		7

SHED SEVEN
UK, male vocal/instrumental group – Rick Witter, Paul Banks, Tim Gladwin & Alan Leach — 46

Date	Title	Peak Position	Weeks at No.1	Weeks on Chart
17 Sep 94	**CHANGE GIVER** *Polydor 5236152*	16		2
13 Apr 96	**A MAXIMUM HIGH** *Polydor 5310392* ●	8		26
13 Jun 98	**LET IT RIDE** *Polydor 5573592*	9		7
12 Jun 99	**GOING FOR GOLD – THE GREATEST HITS** *Polydor 5474422* ○	7		10
19 May 01	**TRUTH BE TOLD** *Artful ARTFULCD 38*	42		1

SHEEP ON DRUGS
UK, male/vocal instrumental duo — 1

Date	Title	Peak Position	Weeks at No.1	Weeks on Chart
10 Apr 93	**GREATEST HITS** *Transglobal CID 8006*	55		1

PETE SHELLEY
UK, male vocalist. See Buzzcocks — 4

Date	Title	Peak Position	Weeks at No.1	Weeks on Chart
2 Jul 83	**XL – 1** *Genetic XL 1*	42		4

VONDA SHEPARD
US, female vocalist/pianist/actor — 49

Date	Title	Peak Position	Weeks at No.1	Weeks on Chart
17 Oct 98	**SONGS FROM 'ALLY McBEAL' (OST-TV)** *Epic 4911242* ⊛	3		34
12 Jun 99	**BY 7.30** *Epic 4945792*	39		2
20 Nov 99	**HEART & SOUL – NEW SONGS FROM ALLY McBEAL (OST-TV)** *Epic 4950912* ●	9		13

SHERRICK
US, male vocalist (Lamotte Smith), d. 22 Jan 1999 (age 41) — 6

Date	Title	Peak Position	Weeks at No.1	Weeks on Chart
29 Aug 87	**SHERRICK** *Warner Brothers WX 118*	27		6

BRENDAN SHINE
Ireland, male vocalist — 29

Date	Title	Peak Position	Weeks at No.1	Weeks on Chart
12 Nov 83	**THE BRENDAN SHINE COLLECTION** *Play PLAYTV 1* ○	51		12
3 Nov 84	**WITH LOVE** *Play PLAYTV 2*	74		4
16 Nov 85	**MEMORIES** *Play PLAYTV 3*	81		7
18 Nov 89	**MAGIC MOMENTS** *Stylus SMR 991* ○	62		6

SHINING
UK, male vocal/instrumental group — 1

Date	Title	Peak Position	Weeks at No.1	Weeks on Chart
28 Sep 02	**TRUE SKIES** *Zuma Recordings ZUMACD 001*	73		1

SHINS
UK, male vocal/instrumental group — 2

Date	Title	Peak Position	Weeks at No.1	Weeks on Chart
10 Feb 07	**WINCING THE NIGHT AWAY** *Transgressive 5101194515*	16		2

SHIREHORSES
UK, male vocal/instrumental group — 8

Date	Title	Peak Position	Weeks at No.1	Weeks on Chart
15 Nov 97	**THE WORST ALBUM IN THE WORLD EVER…EVER!** *East West 3984208512* ○	22		4
26 May 01	**OUR KID EH** *Columbia 5030492*	20		4

MICHELLE SHOCKED
US, female vocalist/guitarist (Karen Michelle Johnston) — 24

Date	Title	Peak Position	Weeks at No.1	Weeks on Chart
10 Sep 88	**SHORT SHARP SHOCKED** *Cooking Vinyl CVLP 1* ●	33		19
18 Nov 89	**CAPTAIN SWING** *Cooking Vinyl 8388781*	31		3
11 Apr 92	**ARKANSAS TRAVELER** *London 5121892*	46		2

SHOP ASSISTANTS
UK, male/female vocal/instrumental group — 1

Date	Title	Peak Position	Weeks at No.1	Weeks on Chart
29 Nov 86	**WILL ANYTHING HAPPEN** *Blue Guitar AZLP 2*	100		1

HOWARD SHORE
US, male conductor/producer — 34

Date	Title	Peak Position	Weeks at No.1	Weeks on Chart
5 Jan 02	**THE LORD OF THE RINGS – OST** *Reprise 9362481102* ○	10		14
11 Jan 03	**LORD OF THE RINGS – THE TWO TOWERS (OST)** *Reprise 9362484212* ●	28		9
27 Dec 03	**LORD OF THE RINGS – RETURN OF THE KING (OST)** *Reprise 9362486092* ●	34		11

SHOWADDYWADDY
UK, male vocal/instrumental group – Dave Bartram, Buddy Gask, Malcolm Allured, Romeo Challenger, Rod Deas, Russ Field, Al James & Trevor Oakes — 131

Date	Title	Peak Position	Weeks at No.1	Weeks on Chart
7 Dec 74	**SHOWADDYWADDY** *Bell BELLS 248*	9		19
12 Jul 75	**STEP TWO** *Bell BELLS 256* ○	7		17
29 May 76	**TROCADERO** *Bell SYBEL 8003* ○	41		3
25 Dec 76	**GREATEST HITS** *Arista ARTY 145* ⊛	4		26
3 Dec 77	**RED STAR** *Arista SPARTY 1023* ●	20		10
9 Dec 78	**GREATEST HITS (1976–1978)** *Arista ARTV 1* ⊛	1	2	17
10 Nov 79	**CREPES AND DRAPES** *Arista ARTV 3* ●	8		14
20 Dec 80	**BRIGHT LIGHTS** *Arista SPART 1142* ○	33		8
7 Nov 81	**THE VERY BEST OF SHOWADDYWADDY** *Arista SPART 1178* ●	33		11
5 Dec 87	**THE BEST STEPS TO HEAVEN** *Tiger SHTV 1*	90		1
27 Nov 04	**HEY ROCK 'N' ROLL – THE VERY BEST OF** *DMG TV DMGTV011*	56		5

SHRIEKBACK
UK, male vocal/instrumental group — 1

Date	Title	Peak Position	Weeks at No.1	Weeks on Chart
11 Aug 84	**JAM SCIENCE** *Arista 206 416*	85		1

SHUT UP & DANCE
UK, male vocal/production duo — 2

Date	Title	Peak Position	Weeks at No.1	Weeks on Chart
27 Jun 92	**DEATH IS NOT THE END** *Shut Up And Dance SUADCD 005*	38		2

SHY
UK, male vocal/instrumental group — 2

Date	Title	Peak Position	Weeks at No.1	Weeks on Chart
11 Apr 87	**EXCESS ALL AREAS** *RCA PL 71221*	74		2

LABI SIFFRE
UK, male vocalist/guitarist — 2

Date	Title	Peak Position	Weeks at No.1	Weeks on Chart
24 Jul 71	**SINGER AND THE SONG** *Pye NSPL 28147*	47		1
14 Oct 72	**CRYING, LAUGHING, LOVING, LYING** *Pye NSPL 28163*	46		1

SIGUE SIGUE SPUTNIK
UK, male vocal/instrumental group – Martin Degville, Tony James, Chris Kavanagh, Ray Mayhew, Neil Whitmore & Yana YaYa (Jane Farrimond) — 7

Date	Title	Peak Position	Weeks at No.1	Weeks on Chart
9 Aug 86	**FLAUNT IT** *Parlophone PCS 7305*	10		6
15 Apr 89	**DRESS FOR EXCESS** *Parlophone PCS 7328*	53		1

Silver-selling ○ Gold-selling ● Platinum-selling ⊛ US No.1 ★ | Peak Position | Weeks at No.1 | Weeks on Chart

SIGUR ROS

Iceland, male vocal/instrumental group – Jón Thor Birgisson, Orri Páll Dýrason, Georg Hólm & Kjartan Sveinsson — Weeks on Chart: 20

Date	Title	Peak	Wks at No.1	Wks on Chart
26 Aug 00	**AGAETIS BYRJUN** *Fat Cat FATCD 11*	52		1
9 Nov 02	**( )** *Fat Cat FATCD 22*	49		1
24 Sep 05	**TAKK** *EMI 3384622* ●	16		11
17 Nov 07	**HVARF/HEIM** *EMI 5025662* ○	23		2
5 Jul 08	**MEO SUO I EYRUM VIO SPILUM ENDALAUST** *EMI 2287282*	5		5

SILENCERS

UK, male vocal/instrumental group — 3

Date	Title	Peak	Wks at No.1	Wks on Chart
23 Mar 91	**DANCE TO THE HOLY MAN** *RCA PL 74924*	39		2
5 Jun 93	**SECONDS OF PLEASURE** *RCA 74321141132*	52		1

LUCIE SILVAS

UK, female vocalist/pianist (Lucie Silverman) — 32

Date	Title	Peak	Wks at No.1	Wks on Chart
23 Oct 04	**BREATHE IN** *Mercury 9867025* ⊛	11		31
24 Mar 07	**THE SAME SIDE** *Mercury 1707300*	62		1

SILVER BULLET

UK, male rapper (Richard Brown) — 2

Date	Title	Peak	Wks at No.1	Wks on Chart
4 May 91	**BRING DOWN THE WALLS NO LIMIT SQUAD RETURNS** *Parlophone PCS 7350*	38		2

SILVER CONVENTION

Germany/US, female vocal group — 3

Date	Title	Peak	Wks at No.1	Wks on Chart
25 Jun 77	**SILVER CONVENTION: GREATEST HITS** *Magnet MAG 6001*	34		3

SILVER SUN

UK, male vocal/instrumental group — 2

Date	Title	Peak	Wks at No.1	Wks on Chart
24 May 97	**SILVER SUN** *Polydor 5372082*	30		1
17 Oct 98	**NEO WAVE** *Polydor 5590852*	74		1

SILVERCHAIR

Australia, male vocal/instrumental group — 5

Date	Title	Peak	Wks at No.1	Wks on Chart
23 Sep 95	**FROGSTOMP** *Murmur 4803402*	49		1
15 Feb 97	**FREAK SHOW** *Murmur 4871032*	38		2
27 Mar 99	**NEON BALLROOM** *Murmur 4933092*	29		2

SILVERFISH

US, male vocal/instrumental group — 1

Date	Title	Peak	Wks at No.1	Wks on Chart
27 Jun 92	**ORGAN FAN** *Creation CRECD 118*	65		1

SIMIAN MOBILE DISCO

UK, male DJ/production duo — 1

Date	Title	Peak	Wks at No.1	Wks on Chart
30 Jun 07	**ATTACK DECAY SUSTAIN RELEASE** *Wichita WEBB144CDL*	59		1

CARLY SIMON

US, female vocalist/guitarist — 74

Date	Title	Peak	Wks at No.1	Wks on Chart
20 Jan 73	**NO SECRETS** *Elektra K 42127* ★	3		26
16 Mar 74	**HOT CAKES** *Elektra K 52005*	19		9
9 May 87	**COMING AROUND AGAIN** *Arista 208 140* ○	25		20
3 Sep 88	**GREATEST HITS LIVE** *Arista 209 196*	49		6
20 Mar 99	**NOBODY DOES IT BETTER – THE VERY BEST OF CARLY SIMON** *warner.esp/Global TV RADCD 103*	22		6
12 Jun 04	**REFLECTIONS – GREATEST HITS** *Elektra/Rhino 8122789702*	25		7

PAUL SIMON

US, male vocalist/guitarist. New Jersey singer/songwriter who brought world music into the mainstream with his Grammy-winning *Graceland* album. He has twice been inducted into the Rock and Roll Hall of Fame – in 1990 (Simon & Garfunkel) and 2001 (solo). See Simon & Garfunkel — 300

Date	Title	Peak	Wks at No.1	Wks on Chart
26 Feb 72	**PAUL SIMON** *CBS 69007*	1	1	26
2 Jun 73	**THERE GOES RHYMIN' SIMON** *CBS 69035* ●	4		22
1 Nov 75	**STILL CRAZY AFTER ALL THESE YEARS** *CBS 86001* ● ★	6		31
3 Dec 77	**GREATEST HITS, ETC.** *CBS 10007* ●	6		15
30 Aug 80	**ONE-TRICK PONY (OST)** *Warner Brothers K 56846* ○	17		12
12 Nov 83	**HEARTS AND BONES** *Warner Brothers 9239421*	34		8
13 Sep 86	**GRACELAND** *Warner Brothers WX 52* ⊛x5	1	8	115
24 Jan 87	**GREATEST HITS, ETC.** *CBS 4501661*	73		2
5 Nov 88	**NEGOTIATIONS AND LOVE SONGS 1971–1986** *Warner Brothers WX 223* ⊛	17		15
27 Oct 90	**THE RHYTHM OF THE SAINTS** *Warner Brothers WX 340* ⊛x2	1	2	28
23 Nov 91	**PAUL SIMON'S CONCERT IN THE PARK – AUGUST 15TH 1991** *Warner Brothers WX 448*	60		1
27 May 00	**GREATEST HITS/SHINING LIKE A NATIONAL GUITAR** *Warner Brothers 9362477212* ●	6		12
14 Oct 00	**YOU'RE THE ONE** *Warner Brothers 9362478442* ○	20		4
17 Jun 06	**SURPRISE** *Warner Brothers 9362499822*	4		5
14 Jun 08	**THE ESSENTIAL PAUL SIMON** *Warner Brothers 9362499697*	12		4

SIMON & GARFUNKEL

US, male vocal/instrumental duo – Paul Simon* & Art Garfunkel*. The most successful album duo of all time. *Bridge Over Troubled Water* was named Top Album of All Time at the BRIT Awards and their *Greatest Hits* has sold over 14 million in the US alone — 1128

Date	Title	Peak	Wks at No.1	Wks on Chart
16 Apr 66	**SOUNDS OF SILENCE** *CBS 62690*	13		104
3 Aug 68	**BOOKENDS** *CBS 63101* ★	1	7	77
31 Aug 68	**PARSLEY, SAGE, ROSEMARY AND THYME** *CBS 62860*	13		66
26 Oct 68	**THE GRADUATE (OST)** *CBS 70042* ★	3		71
9 Nov 68	**WEDNESDAY MORNING 3 A.M.** *CBS 63370*	24		6
21 Feb 70	**BRIDGE OVER TROUBLED WATER** *CBS 63699* ⊛ ★	1	25	307
22 Jul 72	**GREATEST HITS** *CBS 69003* ⊛	2		283
4 Apr 81	**SOUNDS OF SILENCE** *CBS 32020* ●	68		1
21 Nov 81	**THE SIMON AND GARFUNKEL COLLECTION** *CBS 10029* ⊛x3	4		80
20 Mar 82	**THE CONCERT IN CENTRAL PARK** *Geffen GEF 96008* ●	6		43
30 Nov 91	**THE DEFINITIVE SIMON AND GARFUNKEL** *Columbia MOODCD 21* ⊛	8		57
5 Feb 00	**TALES FROM NEW YORK – THE VERY BEST OF SIMON & GARFUNKEL** *Columbia SONYTV 81CD*	8		12
6 Dec 03	**THE ESSENTIAL** *Columbia 5134702* ●	25		13
11 Dec 04	**OLD FRIENDS – LIVE ON STAGE** *Columbia 5191732*	61		2
8 Dec 07	**THE COLLECTION** *Sony BMG 88697134662*	47		6

NINA SIMONE

US, female vocalist/pianist (Eunice Waymon), d. 21 Apr 2003 (age 70) — 63

Date	Title	Peak	Wks at No.1	Wks on Chart
24 Jul 65	**I PUT A SPELL ON YOU** *Philips BL 7671*	18		3
15 Feb 69	**NUFF SAID** *RCA Victor SF 7979*	11		1
14 Nov 87	**MY BABY JUST CARES FOR ME** *Charly CR 30217* ●	56		8
16 Jul 94	**FEELING GOOD – THE VERY BEST OF NINA SIMONE** *Polygram TV 5226692* ○	9		8
7 Feb 98	**BLUE FOR YOU – THE VERY BEST OF NINA SIMONE** *Global Television RADCD 84* ●	12		10
21 Jun 03	**GOLD** *UCJ 9808087*	27		3
13 May 06	**THE VERY BEST OF** *RCA 82876805532* ⊛	6		30

SIMPLE MINDS

UK, male vocal/instrumental group – Jim Kerr, Charles Burchill, Mel Gaynor, John Giblin & Michael MacNeil. The most successful Scottish band of the 80s, the decade they achieved four No.1 debuts and spent more than 250 weeks on the chart. Their worldwide sales have topped 30 million — 356

Date	Title	Peak	Wks at No.1	Wks on Chart
5 May 79	**LIFE IN A DAY** *Zoom ZULP 1*	30		6
27 Sep 80	**EMPIRES AND DANCE** *Arista SPART 1140*	41		3
12 Sep 81	**SONS AND FASCINATIONS/SISTERS FEELINGS CALL** *Arista V 2207* ●	11		7
27 Feb 82	**CELEBRATION** *Virgin SPART 1183*	45		7
25 Sep 82	**NEW GOLD DREAM (81,82,83,84)** *Arista V 2230* ⊛	3		52
18 Feb 84	**SPARKLE IN THE RAIN** *Virgin V 2300* ⊛	1	1	57
2 Nov 85	**ONCE UPON A TIME** *Virgin V 2364* ⊛x3	1	1	83
6 Jun 87	**LIVE IN THE CITY OF LIGHT** *Virgin V SMDL 1* ⊛x2	1	1	26
13 May 89	**STREET FIGHTING YEARS** *Virgin MINDS 1* ⊛x2	1	1	28
20 Apr 91	**REAL LIFE** *Virgin V 2660* ⊛	2		25
24 Oct 92	**GLITTERING PRIZE 81/92** *Virgin SMTVD 1* ⊛x3	1	3	39
11 Feb 95	**GOOD NEWS FROM THE NEXT WORLD** *Virgin CDV 2760* ●	2		14
28 Mar 98	**NEAPOLIS** *Chrysalis 4937122*	19		3
17 Nov 01	**THE BEST OF SIMPLE MINDS** *Virgin CDVD 2953* ●	34		4
24 Sep 05	**BLACK & WHITE 050505** *Sanctuary SANCD390*	37		2

SIMPLE PLAN

US, male vocal/instrumental group — 2

Date	Title	Peak	Wks at No.1	Wks on Chart
1 Mar 08	**SIMPLE PLAN** *Lava 7567899565*	31		2

Silver-selling ○ Gold-selling ● Platinum-selling ⊛ US No.1 ★ Peak Position Weeks at No.1 Weeks on Chart

SIMPLY RED

UK, male vocal/instrumental group – Mick Hucknall (Hucknall*); members also included Tony Bowers, Chris Joyce, Tim Kellett, Ian Kirkham, Fritz McIntyre & Sylvan Richardson. Stylish, internationally popular outfit who have graced the Top 10 for almost 25 years. At the height of their fame, the melodic *Stars* was the UK's best-selling album in both 1991 and 1992

Date	Title	Peak	Wks No.1	637
26 Oct 85	**PICTURE BOOK** *Elektra EKT 27* ⊛x5	2		130
21 Mar 87	**MEN AND WOMEN** *WEA WX 85* ⊛x3	2		60
25 Feb 89	**A NEW FLAME** *WEA WX 242* ⊛x7	1	7	84
12 Oct 91	**STARS** *East West WX 427* ⊛x12	1	12	134
21 Oct 95	**LIFE** *East West 0630120692* ⊛x5	1	3	47
24 Feb 96	**A NEW FLAME** *East West 2446892*	28		6
24 Feb 96	**PICTURE BOOK** *East West 9031769932*	33		5
2 Mar 96	**MEN AND WOMEN** *East West 2420712*	50		3
19 Oct 96	**GREATEST HITS** *East West 0630165522* ⊛x6	1	2	52
30 May 98	**BLUE** *East West 3984230972* ⊛x2	1	2	26
13 Nov 99	**LOVE AND THE RUSSIAN WINTER** *East West 8573803592* ⊛	6		17
25 Nov 00	**IT'S ONLY LOVE** *East West 8573855372* ●	27		6
5 Apr 03	**HOME** *Simply Red.com SRA 001CD* ⊛x2	2		35
29 Oct 05	**SIMPLIFIED** *Simplyred.com SRA002CD* ●	3		9
24 Mar 07	**STAY** *Simplyred.com SRA003CD* ●	4		13
8 Mar 08	**STARS: SPECIAL EDITION** *Rhino 5144262732*	31		2
31 May 08	**TRIBUTE TO BOBBY** *Simplyred.com SRA004CDX* HUCKNALL	18		2
29 Nov 08	**GREATEST HITS 25** *Simplyred.com SRA006CD*	9		6+

Top 3 Best-Selling Albums

		Approximate Sales
1	STARS	3,400,000
2	A NEW FLAME	1,925,000
3	GREATEST HITS	1,610,000

ASHLEE SIMPSON

US, female vocalist/actor

Date	Title	Peak	Wks No.1	12
16 Oct 04	**AUTOBIOGRAPHY** *Geffen 9863256* ● ★	31		9
18 Feb 06	**I AM ME** *Geffen 9886590*	50		2
7 Jun 08	**BITTERSWEET WORLD** *Geffen 1767879*	57		1

JESSICA SIMPSON

US, female vocalist/actor

Date	Title	Peak	Wks No.1	8
6 May 00	**SWEET KISSES** *Columbia 4949332*	36		2
1 May 04	**IN THIS SKIN** *Columbia SNY865602*	36		5
24 Feb 07	**A PUBLIC AFFAIR** *Epic 88697059592*	65		1

SIMPSONS

US, male/female cartoon vocal group – Bart, Homer, Lisa, Maggie & Marge Simpson

Date	Title	Peak	Wks No.1	32
2 Feb 91	**THE SIMPSONS SING THE BLUES** *Geffen 7599243081* ●	6		30
12 Sep 98	**THE SIMPSONS – SONGS IN THE KEY OF SPRINGFIELD** *Rhino 8122759852* ○	18		2

JOYCE SIMS

US, female vocalist

Date	Title	Peak	Wks No.1	25
9 Jan 88	**COME INTO MY LIFE** *London LONLP 47* ●	5		24
16 Sep 89	**ALL ABOUT LOVE** *ffrr 8281291*	64		1

KYM SIMS

US, female vocalist

Date	Title	Peak	Wks No.1	2
18 Apr 92	**TOO BLIND TO SEE IT** *Atco 7567921042*	39		2

FRANK SINATRA

US, male vocalist/actor, d. 14 May 1998 (age 82). The legendary song stylist had the first ever UK No.1 album with *Songs For Swingin' Lovers*. No solo artist can match the 33 US Top 10 albums amassed by the man often called 'the greatest singer of the 20th century'

Date	Title	Peak	Wks No.1	926
28 Jul 56	**SONGS FOR SWINGIN' LOVERS** *Capitol LCT 6106*	1	3	35
16 Feb 57	**THIS IS SINATRA!** *Capitol LCT 6123*	1	4	13
25 May 57	**CLOSE TO YOU** *Capitol LCT 6130*	2		9
20 Jul 57	**FRANKIE** *Philips BBL 7168*	3		7
7 Sep 57	**A SWINGIN' AFFAIR!** *Capitol LCT 6135*	1	7	18
1 Mar 58	**WHERE ARE YOU?** *Capitol LCT 6152*	3		5
21 Jun 58	**THIS IS SINATRA (VOLUME 2)** *Capitol LCT 6155*	3		12
13 Sep 58	**COME FLY WITH ME** *Capitol LCT 6154* ★	2		26
29 Nov 58	**FRANK SINATRA STORY** *Fontana TFL 5030*	8		1
13 Dec 58	**FRANK SINATRA SINGS FOR ONLY THE LONELY** *Capitol LCT 6168* ★	5		13
16 May 59	**COME DANCE WITH ME!** *Capitol LCT 6179* WITH BILLY MAY & HIS ORCHESTRA	2		30
22 Aug 59	**LOOK TO YOUR HEART** *Capitol LCT 6181*	5		8
11 Jun 60	**COME BACK TO SORRENTO** *Fontana TFL 5082*	6		9
29 Oct 60	**SWING EASY** *Capitol W 587*	5		17
21 Jan 61	**NICE 'N EASY** *Capitol W 1417* ★	4		28
15 Jul 61	**SINATRA SOUVENIR** *Fontana TFL 5138*	18		1
19 Aug 61	**WHEN YOUR LOVER HAS GONE** *Encore ENC 101*	6		10
23 Sep 61	**SINATRA'S SWINGING SESSION!!! AND MORE** *Capitol W 1491*	6		8
28 Oct 61	**SINATRA SWINGS** *Reprise R 1002*	8		8
25 Nov 61	**SINATRA PLUS** *Fontana SET 303*	7		9
16 Dec 61	**RING-A-DING-DING** *Reprise R 1001*	8		9
17 Feb 62	**COME SWING WITH ME** *Capitol W 1594*	13		4
7 Apr 62	**I REMEMBER TOMMY…** *Reprise R 1003*	10		12
9 Jun 62	**SINATRA AND STRINGS** *Reprise R 1004*	6		20
27 Oct 62	**GREAT SONGS FROM GREAT BRITAIN** *Reprise R 1006*	12		9
29 Dec 62	**SINATRA WITH SWINGING BRASS** *Reprise R 1005*	14		11
23 Feb 63	**SINATRA-BASIE** *Reprise R 1008* & COUNT BASIE	2		23
27 Jul 63	**CONCERT SINATRA** *Reprise R 1009*	8		18
5 Oct 63	**SINATRA'S SINATRA** *Reprise R 1010*	9		24
19 Sep 64	**IT MIGHT AS WELL BE SWING** *Reprise R 1012* & COUNT BASIE & HIS ORCHESTRA	17		4
20 Mar 65	**SOFTLY AS I LEAVE YOU** *Reprise R 1013*	20		1
22 Jan 66	**A MAN AND HIS MUSIC** *Reprise R 1016*	9		19
21 May 66	**MOONLIGHT SINATRA** *Reprise R 1018*	18		8
2 Jul 66	**STRANGERS IN THE NIGHT** *Reprise R 1017* ★	4		18
1 Oct 66	**IN CONCERT: SINATRA AT 'THE SANDS'** *Reprise RLP 1019*	7		18
3 Dec 66	**FRANK SINATRA SINGS SONGS FOR PLEASURE** *MFP 1120*	26		2
25 Feb 67	**THAT'S LIFE** *Reprise RSLP 1020*	22		12
7 Oct 67	**FRANK SINATRA** *Reprise RSLP 1022*	28		5
19 Oct 68	**GREATEST HITS** *Reprise RSLP 1025*	8		38
7 Dec 68	**BEST OF FRANK SINATRA** *Capitol ST 21140*	17		10
7 Jun 69	**MY WAY** *Reprise RSLP 1029*	2		59
4 Oct 69	**A MAN ALONE – THE WORDS AND MUSIC OF ROD McKUEN** *Reprise RSLP 1030*	18		7
9 May 70	**WATERTOWN** *Reprise RSLP 1031*	14		9
12 Dec 70	**GREATEST HITS VOLUME 2** *Reprise RSLP 1032*	6		40
5 Jun 71	**SINATRA AND COMPANY** *Reprise RSLP 1033*	9		9
27 Nov 71	**FRANK SINATRA SINGS RODGERS AND HART** *Starline SRS 5083*	35		1
8 Jan 72	**GREATEST HITS VOLUME 2** *Reprise K 44018*	29		3
8 Jan 72	**MY WAY** *Reprise K 44015*	35		1
1 Dec 73	**OL' BLUE EYES IS BACK** *Warner Brothers K 44249* ●	12		13
17 Aug 74	**SOME NICE THINGS I'VE MISSED** *Reprise K 54020* ○	35		3
15 Feb 75	**SINATRA – THE MAIN EVENT LIVE (OST-TV)** *Reprise K 54031* ○	30		2
14 Jun 75	**THE BEST OF OL' BLUE EYES** *Reprise K 54042* ○	30		3
19 Mar 77	**PORTRAIT OF SINATRA** *Reprise K 64039* ⊛	1	2	18
13 May 78	**20 GOLDEN GREATS** *Capitol EMTV 10* ●	4		11
18 Aug 84	**L.A. IS MY LADY** *Qwest 925145* WITH THE QUINCY JONES ORCHESTRA	41		8
22 Mar 86	**NEW YORK, NEW YORK (GREATEST HITS)** *Warner Brothers WX 32* ⊛	13		12
4 Oct 86	**THE FRANK SINATRA COLLECTION** *Capitol EMTV 41*	40		5
6 Nov 93	**DUETS** *Capitol CDEST 2218* ⊛	5		14
26 Nov 94	**DUETS II** *Capitol CDEST 2245*	29		6
11 Mar 95	**THIS IS FRANK SINATRA 1953–1957** *MFP CDDL 1275*	56		1
2 Dec 95	**SINATRA 80TH – ALL THE BEST** *Capitol CDESTD 2*	49		5
16 Aug 97	**MY WAY – THE BEST OF FRANK SINATRA** *Reprise 9362467122* ⊛x5	7		136
30 May 98	**SONGS FOR SWINGING LOVERS** *Capitol CDP 7465702*	63		2
24 Jun 00	**CLASSIC SINATRA** *Capitol 5235022* ●	10		7
9 Feb 02	**A FINE ROMANCE – THE LOVE SONGS OF** *Reprise 8122735892* ●	6		9
28 Aug 04	**THE PLATINUM COLLECTION** *Capitol 8647602* ○	11		4
25 Mar 06	**DUETS & DUETS II** *Capitol 3533372*	65		1
24 May 08	**NOTHING BUT THE BEST** *Rhino 8122799345*	10		5

NANCY SINATRA

US, female vocalist

Date	Title	Peak	Wks No.1	33
16 Apr 66	**BOOTS** *Reprise R 6202*	12		9
18 Jun 66	**HOW DOES THAT GRAB YOU** *Reprise R 6207*	17		3
29 Jun 68	**NANCY AND LEE** *Reprise RSLP 6273* & LEE HAZLEWOOD	17		12
10 Oct 70	**NANCY'S GREATEST HITS** *Reprise RSLP 6409*	39		3
25 Sep 71	**NANCY AND LEE** *Reprise K 44126* & LEE HAZLEWOOD	42		1
29 Jan 72	**DID YOU EVER** *RCA Victor SF 8240* & LEE HAZLEWOOD	31		4
25 Mar 06	**THE ESSENTIAL** *Liberty 3562332*	73		1

TALVIN SINGH

UK, male producer/composer/multi-instrumentalist — Weeks in Chart: 5

Date	Title / Label	Peak Position	Weeks at No.1	Weeks in Chart
18 Sep 99	**OK** *Island CID 8075*	41		4
7 Apr 01	**HA** *Island CID 8103*	57		1

SINITTA

UK, female vocalist (Sinitta Malone) — Weeks in Chart: 23

Date	Title / Label	Peak Position	Weeks at No.1	Weeks in Chart
26 Dec 87	**SINITTA!** *Fanfare BOYLP 1*	34		19
9 Dec 89	**WICKED** *Fanfare FARE 2*	52		4

SIOUXSIE & THE BANSHEES

UK, male/female vocal/instrumental group – Susan 'Siouxsie' Ballion, Peter 'Budgie' Clark, Steve Severin & various musicians — Weeks in Chart: 120

Date	Title / Label	Peak Position	Weeks at No.1	Weeks in Chart
2 Dec 78	**THE SCREAM** *Polydor POLD 5009*	12		11
22 Sep 79	**JOIN HANDS** *Polydor POLD 5024*	13		5
16 Aug 80	**KALEIDOSCOPE** *Polydor 2442 177*	5		6
27 Jun 81	**JU JU** *Polydor POLS 1034*	7		17
12 Dec 81	**ONCE UPON A TIME – THE SINGLES** *Polydor POLS 1056*	21		26
13 Nov 82	**A KISS IN THE DREAMHOUSE** *Polydor POLD 5064*	11		11
3 Dec 83	**NOCTURNE** *Wonderland SHAH 1*	29		10
16 Jun 84	**HYENA** *Wonderland SHELP 2*	15		6
26 Apr 86	**TINDERBOX** *Wonderland SHELP 3*	13		6
14 Mar 87	**THROUGH THE LOOKING GLASS** *Wonderland SHELP 4*	15		8
17 Sep 88	**PEEPSHOW** *Wonderland SHELP 5*	20		5
22 Jun 91	**SUPERSTITION** *Wonderland 8477311*	25		4
17 Oct 92	**TWICE UPON A TIME – THE SINGLES** *Wonderland 5171602*	26		2
28 Jan 95	**THE RAPTURE** *Wonderland 5237252*	33		2
22 Sep 07	**MANTARAY** *W14 1739955* SIOUXSIE	39		1

SISQO

US, male vocalist (Mark Andrews). See Dru Hill — Weeks in Chart: 41

Date	Title / Label	Peak Position	Weeks at No.1	Weeks in Chart
26 Feb 00	**UNLEASH THE DRAGON** *Def Soul 5469392*	15		36
4 Aug 01	**RETURN OF DRAGON** *Def Soul 5864182*	22		5

SISSEL

Norway, female vocalist — Weeks in Chart: 1

Date	Title / Label	Peak Position	Weeks at No.1	Weeks in Chart
20 May 95	**DEEP WITHIN MY SOUL** *Mercury 5267752*	58		1

SISTER SLEDGE

US, female vocal group – Debbie, Joni, Kathy & Kim Sledge — Weeks in Chart: 58

Date	Title / Label	Peak Position	Weeks at No.1	Weeks in Chart
12 May 79	**WE ARE FAMILY** *Atlantic K 50587*	7		39
22 Jun 85	**WHEN THE BOYS MEET THE GIRLS** *Atlantic 7812551*	19		11
5 Dec 87	**FREAK OUT** *Telstar STAR 2319* CHIC & SISTER SLEDGE	72		3
20 Feb 93	**THE VERY BEST OF SISTER SLEDGE 1973–1993** *Atlantic 9548318132*	19		5

SISTERHOOD

UK, male vocal/instrumental group — Weeks in Chart: 1

Date	Title / Label	Peak Position	Weeks at No.1	Weeks in Chart
26 Jul 86	**GIFT** *Merciful Release SIS 020*	90		1

SISTERS OF MERCY

UK/US, male/female vocal/instrumental group – Andrew Eldritch; members also included Wayne Hussey, Tony James, Gary Marx & Patricia Morrison — Weeks in Chart: 42

Date	Title / Label	Peak Position	Weeks at No.1	Weeks in Chart
23 Mar 85	**FIRST AND LAST AND ALWAYS** *Merciful Release MR 337L*	14		8
28 Nov 87	**FLOODLAND** *Merciful Release MR 441L*	9		20
3 Nov 90	**VISION THING** *Merciful Release MR 449L*	11		4
9 May 92	**SOME GIRLS WANDER BY MISTAKE** *Merciful Release 9031764762*	5		5
4 Sep 93	**GREATEST HITS VOLUME 1** *Merciful Release 4509935792*	14		5

SIX BY SEVEN

UK, male vocal/instrumental group — Weeks in Chart: 1

Date	Title / Label	Peak Position	Weeks at No.1	Weeks in Chart
23 Mar 02	**THE WAY I FEEL TODAY** *Mantra MNTCD 1027*	69		1

SIXPENCE NONE THE RICHER

US, male/female vocal/instrumental group — Weeks in Chart: 3

Date	Title / Label	Peak Position	Weeks at No.1	Weeks in Chart
26 Jun 99	**SIXPENCE NONE THE RICHER** *Elektra 7559624202*	27		3

Top 20 Albums by Weeks at No.1

Pos	Album Title Artist	Weeks at No.1
1	**PLEASE PLEASE ME** BEATLES	30
2	**SGT PEPPER'S LONELY HEARTS CLUB BAND** BEATLES	27
3	**BRIDGE OVER TROUBLED WATER** SIMON & GARFUNKEL	25
4	**G.I. BLUES (OST)** ELVIS PRESLEY	22
5	**WITH THE BEATLES** BEATLES	21
6	**A HARD DAY'S NIGHT** BEATLES	21
7	**BLUE HAWAII (OST)** ELVIS PRESLEY	18
8	**ABBEY ROAD** BEATLES	17
9	**THE SINGLES 1969–1973** CARPENTERS	17
10	**... BUT SERIOUSLY** PHIL COLLINS	15
11	**SPICE** SPICE GIRLS	15
12	**BROTHERS IN ARMS** DIRE STRAITS	14
13	**SUMMER HOLIDAY (OST)** CLIFF RICHARD & THE SHADOWS	14
14	**JOHN WESLEY HARDING** BOB DYLAN	13
15	**KINGS OF THE WILD FRONTIER** ADAM & THE ANTS	12
16	**THE KIDS FROM FAME** KIDS FROM FAME	12
17	**LEGEND – THE BEST OF BOB MARLEY AND THE WAILERS** BOB MARLEY & THE WAILERS	12
18	**THE ROLLING STONES** ROLLING STONES	12
19	**STARS** SIMPLY RED	12
20	**URBAN HYMNS** VERVE	12

60FT DOLLS
UK, male vocal/instrumental group — **2**

Date	Title / Label	Peak	Wks No.1	Wks
8 Jun 96	**THE BIG 3** *Indolent DOLLSCD 004*	36		2

RONI SIZE / REPRAZENT
UK, male producer (Ryan Williams) & male/female vocal/instrumental group – Bahamadia (Antonia Reid), DJ Die (Daniel Kausman), Krust (Keith Thompson), MC Dynamite (Dominic Smith), Onallee (Tracey Bowen) & Suv (Paul Southey) — **39**

Date	Title / Label	Peak	Wks No.1	Wks
5 Jul 97	**NEW FORMS** *Talkin Loud 5349342*	8		34
21 Oct 00	**IN THE MODE** *Talkin Loud 5480762*	15		4
2 Nov 02	**TOUCHING DOWN** *Full Cycle FCYCDLP 010* RONI SIZE	72		1

PETER SKELLERN
UK, male vocalist/keyboard player — **31**

Date	Title / Label	Peak	Wks No.1	Wks
9 Sep 78	**SKELLERN** *Mercury 9109 701*	48		3
8 Dec 79	**ASTAIRE** *Mercury 9102 702*	23		20
4 Dec 82	**A STRING OF PEARLS** *Mercury MERL 10*	67		5
1 Apr 95	**STARDUST MEMORIES** *WEA 4509981322*	50		3

SKID ROW
US, male vocal/instrumental group – Sebastian Bach, Rob Affuso, Rachel Bolan, Scott Hill & Dave Sabo — **31**

Date	Title / Label	Peak	Wks No.1	Wks
10 Oct 70	**SKID** *CBS 63965*	30		3
2 Sep 89	**SKID ROW** *Atlantic 7819361*	30		16
22 Jun 91	**SLAVE TO THE GRIND** *Atlantic WX 423* ★	5		9
8 Apr 95	**SUBHUMAN RACE** *Atlantic 7567827302*	8		3

SKIDS
UK, male vocal/instrumental group – Richard Jobson, Stuart Adamson, Mike Baillie, Tom Kellichan & Bill Simpson (replaced by Russell Webb) — **21**

Date	Title / Label	Peak	Wks No.1	Wks
17 Mar 79	**SCARED TO DANCE** *Virgin V 2116*	19		10
27 Oct 79	**DAYS IN EUROPA** *Virgin V 2138*	32		5
27 Sep 80	**THE ABSOLUTE GAME** *Virgin V 2174*	9		5
8 Jun 02	**THE GREATEST HITS OF BIG COUNTRY AND THE SKIDS – THE BEST OF STUART ADAMSON** *Universal TV 5869892* BIG COUNTRY & THE SKIDS	71		1

SKIN
UK/Germany, male vocal/instrumental group – Neville MacDonald, Dicki Fliszar, Myke Gray & Andy Robbins — **7**

Date	Title / Label	Peak	Wks No.1	Wks
14 May 94	**SKIN** *Parlophone CDPCSD 151*	9		3
6 Apr 96	**LUCKY** *Parlophone CDPCSD 168*	38		1
13 Sep 97	**EXPERIENCE ELECTRIC** *Recall SRECD 705*	72		1
14 Jun 03	**FLESHWOUNDS** *EMI 5841592*	43		2

SKINNYMAN
UK, male rapper (Alex Holland) — **1**

Date	Title / Label	Peak	Wks No.1	Wks
21 Aug 04	**COUNCIL ESTATE OF THE MIND** *Lowlife LOW36CD*	65		1

SKUNK ANANSIE
UK, female/male vocal/instrumental group – Deborah Dyer (Skin*), Martin Kent, Cass Lewis & Mark Richardson — **101**

Date	Title / Label	Peak	Wks No.1	Wks
30 Sep 95	**PARANOID & SUNBURNT** *One Little Indian TPLP 55CD*	8		32
19 Oct 96	**STOOSH** *One Little Indian TPLP 85CDL*	9		55
3 Apr 99	**POST ORGASMIC CHILL** *Virgin CDV 2881*	16		14

SKY
UK/Australia, male instrumental group – John Williams*, Herbie Flowers, Tristan Fry, Francis Monkman & Kevin Peek* — **202**

Date	Title / Label	Peak	Wks No.1	Wks
2 Jun 79	**SKY** *Ariola ARLH 5022*	9		56
26 Apr 80	**SKY 2** *Ariola Hansa ADSKY 2*	1	2	53
28 Mar 81	**SKY 3** *Ariola ASKY 3*	3		23
3 Apr 82	**SKY 4 – FORTHCOMING** *Ariola ASKY 4*	7		22
22 Jan 83	**SKY FIVE LIVE** *Ariola 302 171*	14		14
3 Dec 83	**CADMIUM** *Ariola 205 885*	44		10
12 May 84	**MASTERPIECES – THE VERY BEST OF SKY** *Telstar STAR 2241*	15		18
13 Apr 85	**THE GREAT BALLOON RACE** *Epic EPC 26419*	63		6

SKYY
US, male vocal/instrumental group — **1**

Date	Title / Label	Peak	Wks No.1	Wks
21 Jun 86	**FROM THE LEFT SIDE** *Capitol EST 2014*	85		1

SLADE
UK, male vocal/instrumental group – Noddy Holder, Dave Hill, Jimmy Lea & Don Powell — **216**

Date	Title / Label	Peak	Wks No.1	Wks
8 Apr 72	**SLADE ALIVE!** *Polydor 2383 101*	2		58
9 Dec 72	**SLAYED?** *Polydor 2383 163*	1	3	34
6 Oct 73	**SLADEST** *Polydor 2442 119*	1	4	24
23 Feb 74	**OLD NEW BORROWED AND BLUE** *Polydor 2383 261*	1	1	16
14 Dec 74	**SLADE IN FLAME (OST)** *Polydor 2442 126*	6		18
27 Mar 76	**NOBODY'S FOOL** *Polydor 2383 377*	14		4
22 Nov 80	**SLADE SMASHES** *Polydor POLTV 13*	21		15
21 Mar 81	**WE'LL BRING THE HOUSE DOWN** *Cheapskate SKATE 1*	25		4
28 Nov 81	**TILL DEAF US DO PART** *RCA RCALP 6021*	68		2
18 Dec 82	**SLADE ON STAGE** *RCA RCALP 3107*	58		3
24 Dec 83	**THE AMAZING KAMIKAZE SYNDROME** *RCA PL 70116*	49		13
9 Jun 84	**SLADE'S GREATZ** *Polydor SLAD 1*	89		1
6 Apr 85	**ROGUES GALLERY** *RCA PL 70604*	60		2
30 Nov 85	**CRACKERS' – THE SLADE CHRISTMAS PARTY ALBUM** *Telstar STAR 2271*	34		7
9 May 87	**YOU BOYZ MAKE BIG NOIZE** *RCA PL 71260*	98		1
23 Nov 91	**WALL OF HITS** *Polydor 5116121*	34		5
25 Jan 97	**GREATEST HITS – FEEL THE NOIZE** *Polydor 5371052*	19		5
10 Dec 05	**THE VERY BEST OF** *Polydor/Universal TV 9800715*	39		4

SLASH'S SNAKEPIT
US, male vocal/instrumental group — **4**

Date	Title / Label	Peak	Wks No.1	Wks
25 Feb 95	**IT'S FIVE O'CLOCK SOMEWHERE** *Geffen GED 24730*	15		4

SLAUGHTER
US, male vocal/instrumental group — **1**

Date	Title / Label	Peak	Wks No.1	Wks
23 May 92	**THE WILD LIFE** *Chrysalis CCD 1911*	64		1

SLAYER
US, male vocal/instrumental group — **23**

Date	Title / Label	Peak	Wks No.1	Wks
2 May 87	**REIGN IN BLOOD** *London LONLP 34*	47		3
23 Jul 88	**SOUTH OF HEAVEN** *London LONLP 63*	25		4
6 Oct 90	**SEASONS IN THE ABYSS** *Def American 8468711*	18		3
2 Nov 91	**DECADE OF AGGRESSION – LIVE** *Def American 5106051*	29		2
15 Oct 94	**DIVINE INTERVENTION** *American Recordings 74321236772*	15		4
1 Jun 96	**UNDISPUTED ATTITUDE** *American Recordings 74321357592*	31		2
20 Jun 98	**DIABOLUS IN MUSICA** *American Recordings 4913022*	27		2
22 Sep 01	**GOD HATES US ALL** *Mercury 5863312*	31		1
2 Sep 06	**CHRIST ILLUSION** *American Recordings WB44422*	23		2

PERCY SLEDGE
US, male vocalist — **4**

Date	Title / Label	Peak	Wks No.1	Wks
14 Mar 87	**WHEN A MAN LOVES A WOMAN (THE ULTIMATE COLLECTION)** *Atlantic WX 89*	36		4

SLEEPER
UK/Somalia, female/male vocal/instrumental group – Louise Wener, Andy Maclure, Kenadiid Osman & Jon Stewart — **48**

Date	Title / Label	Peak	Wks No.1	Wks
25 Feb 95	**SMART** *Indolent SLEEPCD 007*	5		11
18 May 96	**THE IT GIRL** *Indolent SLEEPCD 012*	5		34
25 Oct 97	**PLEASED TO MEET YOU** *Indolent SLEEPCD 016*	7		3

SLEEPY JACKSON
Australia, male vocal/instrumental trio — **1**

Date	Title / Label	Peak	Wks No.1	Wks
26 Jul 03	**LOVERS** *Virgin CDVIR 208*	69		1

SLEIGHRIDERS
UK, male vocal/instrumental group — **1**

Date	Title / Label	Peak	Wks No.1	Wks
17 Dec 83	**A VERY MERRY DISCO** *Warwick WW 5136*	100		1

GRACE SLICK
US, female vocalist (Grace Wing). See Jefferson Airplane — **6**

Date	Title / Label	Peak	Wks No.1	Wks
31 May 80	**DREAMS** *RCA PL 13544*	28		6

SLIK
UK, male vocal/instrumental group

Date	Title	Peak Position	Weeks at No.1	Weeks on Chart: 1
12 Jun 76	**SLIK** *Bell SYBEL 8004*	58		1

SLIPKNOT
US, male vocal/instrumental group – Corey Taylor, Shawn Crahan, Chris Fehn, Paul Gray, Craig Jones, Joey Jordison, Jim Root, Mick Thomson & Sid Wilson

Date	Title	Peak Position	Weeks at No.1	Weeks on Chart: 25
10 Jul 99	**SLIPKNOT** *Roadrunner RR 86555* ⊛	37		5
8 Sep 01	**IOWA** *Roadrunner 12085642* ●	1	1	7
5 Jun 04	**VOLUME 3 (THE SUBLIMINAL VERSES)** *Roadrunner RR 83888* ●	5		5
12 Nov 05	**9.0 LIVE** *Roadrunner RR81152*	53		1
6 Sep 08	**ALL HOPE IS GONE** *Roadrunner RR79382* ● ★	2		7

SLITS
UK, female vocal/instrumental group

Date	Title	Peak Position	Weeks at No.1	Weeks on Chart: 5
22 Sep 79	**CUT** *Island ILPS 9573*	30		5

SLOWDIVE
UK, male/female vocal/instrumental group

Date	Title	Peak Position	Weeks at No.1	Weeks on Chart: 3
14 Sep 91	**JUST FOR A DAY** *Creation CRELP 094*	32		2
12 Jun 93	**SOUVLAKI** *Creation CRECD 139*	51		1

SLY & THE FAMILY STONE
US, male/female vocal/instrumental group

Date	Title	Peak Position	Weeks at No.1	Weeks on Chart: 2
5 Feb 72	**THERE'S A RIOT GOIN' ON** *Epic EPC 64613* ★	31		2

SLY & ROBBIE
Jamaica, male vocal/instrumental duo

Date	Title	Peak Position	Weeks at No.1	Weeks on Chart: 5
9 May 87	**RHYTHM KILLERS** *Fourth & Broadway BRLP 512*	35		5

HEATHER SMALL
UK, female vocalist. See M People

Date	Title	Peak Position	Weeks at No.1	Weeks on Chart: 10
10 Jun 00	**PROUD** *Arista 74321765482*	12		4
5 Mar 05	**ULTIMATE COLLECTION** *Sony BMG 82876669192* M PEOPLE FEATURING HEATHER SMALL	17		5
5 Aug 06	**CLOSE TO A MIRACLE** *Private & Confidential PNCCD101*	57		1

SMALL FACES
UK, male vocal/instrumental group – Steve Marriott, d. 20 Apr 1991, Kenney Jones, Ronnie Lane, d. 4 Jun 1997, & Ian McLagan

Date	Title	Peak Position	Weeks at No.1	Weeks on Chart: 71
14 May 66	**SMALL FACES** *Decca LK 4790*	3		25
17 Jun 67	**FROM THE BEGINNING** *Decca LK 4879*	17		5
1 Jul 67	**SMALL FACES** *Immediate IMSP 008*	21		17
15 Jun 68	**OGDEN'S NUT GONE FLAKE** *Immediate IMLP 012*	1	6	19
11 May 96	**THE DECCA ANTHOLOGY 1965–1967** *Decca 8445832*	66		1
7 Jun 03	**ULTIMATE COLLECTION** *Sanctuary TDSAN004* ○	24		4

S*M*A*S*H
UK, male vocal/instrumental group

Date	Title	Peak Position	Weeks at No.1	Weeks on Chart: 4
2 Apr 94	**S*M*A*S*H** *Hi-Rise Recordings FLATMCD 2*	28		3
17 Sep 94	**SELF ABUSED** *Hi-Rise Recordings FLATCD 6*	59		1

SMASHING PUMPKINS
US, male/female vocal/instrumental group – Billy Corgan, Jimmy Chamberlain, Melissa Auf Der Maur (Auf Der Maur*), James Iha & D'Arcy Wretzky

Date	Title	Peak Position	Weeks at No.1	Weeks on Chart: 74
31 Jul 93	**SIAMESE DREAM** *Hut CDHUT 11* ●	4		15
4 Nov 95	**MELLON COLLIE AND THE INFINITE SADNESS** *Virgin CDHUTD 30* ⊛ ★	4		37
13 Jun 98	**ADORE** *Hut CDHUTX 51* ●	5		12
11 Mar 00	**MACHINA/THE MACHINES OF GOD** *Hut CDHUT 59* ○	7		4
1 Dec 01	**ROTTEN APPLES – THE GREATEST HITS** *Hut HUTD 70* ○	28		3
21 Jul 07	**ZETGEIST** *Reprise 9362499780*	4		3

BRYAN SMITH & HIS HAPPY PIANO
UK, male pianist

Date	Title	Peak Position	Weeks at No.1	Weeks on Chart: 1
19 Sep 81	**PLAY IT AGAIN** *Deram DS 047*	97		1

ELLIOTT SMITH
US, male vocalist/guitarist (Steven Smith), d. 21 Oct 2003 (age34)

Date	Title	Peak Position	Weeks at No.1	Weeks on Chart: 4
29 Apr 00	**FIGURE 8** *DreamWorks 4502252*	37		2
30 Oct 04	**FROM A BASEMENT ON THE HILL** *Domino WIGCD147*	41		1
19 May 07	**NEW MOON** *Domino WIGCD198*	39		1

JIMMY SMITH
US, male organist, d. 8 Feb 2005 (age 79)

Date	Title	Peak Position	Weeks at No.1	Weeks on Chart: 3
18 Jun 66	**GOT MY MOJO WORKING** *Verve VLP 912*	19		3

KEELY SMITH
US, female vocalist (Dorothy Smith)

Date	Title	Peak Position	Weeks at No.1	Weeks on Chart: 9
16 Jan 65	**LENNON-McCARTNEY SONGBOOK** *Reprise R 6142*	12		9

O.C. SMITH
US, male vocalist (Ocie Smith), d. 23 Nov 2001 (age 69)

Date	Title	Peak Position	Weeks at No.1	Weeks on Chart: 1
17 Aug 68	**HICKORY HOLLER REVISITED** *CBS 63362*	40		1

PATTI SMITH GROUP
US, female/male vocal/instrumental group

Date	Title	Peak Position	Weeks at No.1	Weeks on Chart: 25
1 Apr 78	**EASTER** *Arista SPART 1043* ○	16		14
19 May 79	**WAVE** *Arista SPART 1086*	41		6
16 Jul 88	**DREAM OF LIFE** *Arista 209172* PATTI SMITH	70		1
13 Jul 96	**GONE AGAIN** *Arista 07822187472* PATTI SMITH	44		2
8 May 04	**TRAMPIN'** *Columbia 5152159* PATTI SMITH	70		1
28 Apr 07	**TWELVE** *Columbia 82876872512* PATTI SMITH	63		1

STEVEN SMITH AND FATHER
UK, male vocal/instrumental duo

Date	Title	Peak Position	Weeks at No.1	Weeks on Chart: 3
13 May 72	**STEVEN SMITH AND FATHER AND 16 GREAT SONGS** *Decca SKL 5128*	17		3

WILL SMITH
US, male actor/rapper. See Jazzy Jeff & Fresh Prince

Date	Title	Peak Position	Weeks at No.1	Weeks on Chart: 95
6 Dec 97	**BIG WILLIE STYLE** *Columbia 4886622* ⊛x2	9		70
27 Nov 99	**WILLENNIUM** *Columbia 4949392* ⊛	10		15
24 Aug 02	**BORN TO REIGN** *Columbia 5079552*	24		2
9 Apr 05	**LOST AND FOUND** *Interscope 9880929* ○	15		8

SMITH & JONES
UK, male comedy duo

Date	Title	Peak Position	Weeks at No.1	Weeks on Chart: 8
15 Nov 86	**SCRATCH AND SNIFF** *10 Records DIX 51*	62		8

SMITHS
UK, male vocal/instrumental group – Morrissey* (Stephen Morrissey), Mike Joyce, Johnny Marr & Andy Rourke

Date	Title	Peak Position	Weeks at No.1	Weeks on Chart: 219
3 Mar 84	**THE SMITHS** *Rough Trade ROUGH 61* ●	2		33
24 Nov 84	**HATFUL OF HOLLOW** *Rough Trade ROUGH 76* ⊛	7		46
23 Feb 85	**MEAT IS MURDER** *Rough Trade ROUGH 81* ●	1	1	13
28 Jun 86	**THE QUEEN IS DEAD** *Rough Trade ROUGH 96* ●	2		22
7 Mar 87	**THE WORLD WON'T LISTEN** *Rough Trade ROUGH 101* ●	2		15
30 May 87	**LOUDER THAN BOMBS** *Rough Trade ROUGH 255* ●	38		5
10 Oct 87	**STRANGEWAYS, HERE WE COME** *Rough Trade ROUGH 106* ●	2		17
17 Sep 88	**RANK** *Rough Trade ROUGH 126* ●	2		7
29 Aug 92	**BEST...1** *WEA 4509903272* ●	1	1	9
14 Nov 92	**BEST...2** *WEA 4509904062* ●	29		5
4 Mar 95	**SINGLES** *WEA 4509990902* ⊛	5		13
4 Mar 95	**HATFUL OF HOLLOW** *WEA 4509918932*	26		3
4 Mar 95	**THE QUEEN IS DEAD** *WEA 4509918962*	30		4
4 Mar 95	**STRANGEWAYS, HERE WE COME** *WEA 4509918992*	38		4
4 Mar 95	**MEAT IS MURDER** *WEA 4509918952*	39		2
4 Mar 95	**THE SMITHS** *WEA 4509918922*	42		4
4 Mar 95	**THE WORLD WON'T LISTEN** *WEA 4509918982*	52		2
14 Oct 00	**LOUDER THAN BOMBS** *WEA 4509938332*	52		2
16 Jun 01	**THE VERY BEST OF** *WEA 8573889482* ●	30		9
22 Nov 08	**THE SOUND OF THE SMITHS DELUXE EDITION** *Rhino 2564693709* ○	21		4

The Smiths

The Queen Is Dead

WHEN the Smiths released their third album, *The Queen Is Dead*, in June 1986, British rock was in one of its periodic creative lows. The by-now flabby New Romantic bands had been storming America and MTV with their excessive and pompous videos, because seeing rotund men in frilly shirts sipping champagne on yachts was still thrilling the average perma-tanned 1980s male.

The Smiths, however, were the antithesis to this. They had burst onto the scene in 1984 and somehow managed to combine the classic British pop of the primetime 1960s bands like The Rolling Stones with frontman Morrissey's beloved New York Dolls, generously mixed up with the passion and beauty of the girl groups. This was flavoured with a million hipster references and licks from the endless guitar canyon of super-cool guitar gunslinger Johnny Marr and, of course, the idiosyncratic and quite special lyrics and vocal delivery of their outspoken singer. Morrissey was forever armed to the teeth with a wit polished in his Stretford bedroom, sitting next to a James Dean cardboard cut-out for company.

He was busy planting bombs in an otherwise banal zeitgeist

The Smiths were born out of punk and post-punk yet in 1986 they defined it. This was a band whose members had grown up through punk: there was Morrissey lurking at the back corner of the classic Sex Pistols gig at the Lesser Free Trade Hall in 1976 and hanging around the fringes of the thriving Mancunian post-punk scene; here was Johnny Marr running round town a couple of years later telling everyone he was going to get to the top. No one believed him at the time but they must have noticed that singular zeal in his eyes and the fact that he was always carrying his guitar around learning every lick off every cool record from rock 'n' roll to cutting-edge electro. Marr was on a one-man mission to soak up every aspect of pop culture. This man was a combustible, walking rock'n'roll encyclopaedia. The Smiths turned that post-punk thinking into pure pop – they had a post-punk *knowing* but with a classic feel. Marr's guitar-playing was astonishingly accomplished, the melodies were the perfect combination with Morrissey's great crooning voice. Morrissey also had a keen sense of humour and a dark honesty that rubbed up against the rank conservatism of the times.

All these unique collisions of personal chemistry and individual talent culminated in *The Queen Is Dead*, which is the band's masterpiece; the album is, effectively, classic guitar-driven British beat translated through post-punk sounds, even though The Smiths themselves apparently prefer their final effort, *Strangeways Here We Come*. But even the title, The Queen Is Dead, was taking no prisoners – was it Morrissey messing around with the public perception of his sexuality, in direct contrast to the macho strut preferred by so many old-school singers? At the time he was claiming to be celibate – the ultimate rebellion – and the pundits were kept busy guessing: Was Morrissey gay? Did he have sex, at all, ever? Like a modern Oscar Wilde, he was busy planting bombs in an otherwise banal zeitgeist.

He never seemed to run out of lyrical ideas to go with Marr's inexhaustible supply of new riffs. While the

Artist	Album Title	First Chart Week	Weeks on Chart	Highest Position
THE SMITHS	THE QUEEN IS DEAD	28/6/86	22	2

guitar man turned up with the chassis for the new songs, Morrissey added the vocal body – it was a spectacular team and one that defined a decade.

The album's lead-off single was 'Bigmouth Strikes Again' a swaggering neo-Stones rush that announced the upcoming album in no uncertain terms; aligned to the hilarious and possibly autobiographical title, the single surprisingly stalled at twenty-six in the charts perhaps because the band were struggling to get much radio play from the BBC. Despite this, *The Queen Is Dead* went on to pull off a spectacular coup: to become as loved by the football hooligans who were flocking to Smiths gigs as by the bespectacled students walking through the halls of their universities – it's even Tory toff David Cameron's favourite record, proving that no matter how great the lyrics are, most people seem to ignore them.

The Queen Is Dead was the band's tour de force and they were there for every detail from co-producing it with Stephen Street to the album cover, which was designed by Morrissey, featuring Alain Delon – every note, image and lyric is perfect. This is a band at the height of their powers. This album – and the rest of The Smiths' canon – has made the band one of the classic British pop groups up there with The Beatles and The Stones.

Loved by the football hooligans who were flocking to Smiths gigs

Silver-selling ○ Gold-selling ● Platinum-selling ⊛ US No.1 ★ | Peak Position | Weeks at No.1 | Weeks on Chart

SMOKIE
UK, male vocal/instrumental group

Date	Title	Peak Position	Weeks at No.1	Weeks on Chart
				44
1 Nov 75	**SMOKIE/CHANGING ALL THE TIME** *RAK SRAK 517* SMOKIE ○	18		5
30 Apr 77	**GREATEST HITS** *RAK SRAK 526* SMOKIE ○	6		22
4 Nov 78	**THE MONTREUX ALBUM** *RAK SRAK 6757* SMOKIE ○	52		2
11 Oct 80	**SMOKIE'S HITS** *RAK SRAK 540* SMOKIE ●	23		13
17 Mar 01	**UNCOVERED – THE VERY BEST OF SMOKIE** *Universal TV 0138172* SMOKIE	63		2

SNAP!
Germany/US, male/female production/vocal/instrumental group – Luca Anzilotti & Michael Münzing; members also included Thea Austin, Turbo B (Durron Butler), Penny Ford, Niki Haris & Jackie Harris

Date	Title	Peak Position	Weeks at No.1	Weeks on Chart
				56
26 May 90	**WORLD POWER** *Arista 210682* ●	10		39
8 Aug 92	**THE MADMAN'S RETURN** *Logic 262552* ●	8		15
15 Oct 94	**WELCOME TO TOMORROW** *Arista 74321223842*	69		1
7 Sep 96	**SNAP! ATTACK – THE BEST OF SNAP!/SNAP! ATTACK – THE REMIXES** *Arista 74321384862*	47		1

SNEAKER PIMPS
UK, male/female vocal/instrumental group

Date	Title	Peak Position	Weeks at No.1	Weeks on Chart
				7
31 Aug 96	**BECOMING X** *Clean Up CUP 020CD* ●	27		7

DAVID SNEDDON
UK, male vocalist

Date	Title	Peak Position	Weeks at No.1	Weeks on Chart
				5
10 May 03	**SEVEN YEARS – TEN WEEKS** *Fontana 9800063* ●	5		5

SNOOP DOGG
US, male rapper (Calvin Broadus)

Date	Title	Peak Position	Weeks at No.1	Weeks on Chart
				95
11 Dec 93	**DOGGYSTYLE** *Death Row 654492279* SNOOP DOGGY DOGG ● ★	38		27
23 Nov 96	**THA DOGGFATHER** *Interscope INTD 90038* SNOOP DOGGY DOGG ★	15		11
15 Aug 98	**DA GAMES IS TO BE SOLD, NOT TO BE TOLD** *Priority CDPTYX 153* SNOOP DOGGY DOGG ★	28		3
5 Jun 99	**TOP DOGG** *Priority CDPTY 171*	48		1
5 May 01	**THA LAST MEAL** *Priority CDPTY 199* ●	62		2
10 May 03	**PAID THA COST TO BE THA BOSS** *Priority 5391572* ●	64		6
4 Dec 04	**R&G – THE MASTERPIECE** *Geffen 9864841* ⊛	12		39
15 Oct 05	**THE BEST OF** *Capitol 3339572*	50		2
9 Dec 06	**THA BLUE CARPET TREATMENT** *Geffen B0008023CD*	47		2
12 Apr 08	**EGO TRIPPIN'** *Geffen 1764227*	23		2

SNOW
Canada, male rapper (Darrin O'Brien)

Date	Title	Peak Position	Weeks at No.1	Weeks on Chart
				4
17 Apr 93	**12 INCHES OF SNOW** *East West America 7567922072*	41		4

MARK SNOW
US, male keyboard player

Date	Title	Peak Position	Weeks at No.1	Weeks on Chart
				2
12 Oct 96	**TRUTH AND THE LIGHT: MUSIC FROM THE X-FILES** *Warner Brothers 9362462492* ○	42		2

SNOW PATROL
UK, male vocal/instrumental group – Gary Lightbody, Nathan Connelly, Jonny Quinn, Tom Simpson & Paul Wilson

Date	Title	Peak Position	Weeks at No.1	Weeks on Chart
				224
14 Feb 04	**FINAL STRAW** *Fiction 9865408* ⊛x5	3		106
13 May 06	**EYES OPEN** *Fiction/Polydor 9853361* ⊛x7	1	2	109
8 Nov 08	**A HUNDRED MILLION SUNS** *Fiction/Polydor 1785255* ⊛	2		9+

SO SOLID CREW
UK, male/female rap/production group – members included Asher D (Ashley Walters), Lisa Maffia*, Harvey (Michael Harvey, Jr.), Oxide & Neutrino* (Mark Oseitutu & Alex Rivers) & Romeo* (Marvin Dawkins)

Date	Title	Peak Position	Weeks at No.1	Weeks on Chart
				21
1 Dec 01	**THEY DON'T KNOW** *Independiente ISOM 27CD* ⊛	6		20
11 Oct 03	**2ND VERSE** *Independiente ISOM 35CD*	70		1

SOFT CELL
UK, male vocal/instrumental duo – Marc Almond* & David Ball

Date	Title	Peak Position	Weeks at No.1	Weeks on Chart
				103
12 Dec 81	**NON-STOP EROTIC CABARET** *Some Bizzare BZLP 2* ⊛	5		46
26 Jun 82	**NON-STOP ECSTATIC DANCING** *Some Bizzare BZX 1012* ●	6		18
22 Jan 83	**THE ART OF FALLING APART** *Some Bizzare BIZL 3* ●	5		10
31 Mar 84	**THIS LAST NIGHT IN SODOM** *Some Bizzare BIZL 6*	12		5
20 Dec 86	**THE SINGLES ALBUM** *Some Bizzare BZLP 3*	58		9
1 Jun 91	**MEMORABILIA – THE SINGLES** *Mercury 8485121* & MARC ALMOND	8		13
13 Apr 02	**THE VERY BEST OF** *Universal TV 5868342*	37		2

SOFT MACHINE
UK, male vocal/instrumental group

Date	Title	Peak Position	Weeks at No.1	Weeks on Chart
				8
4 Apr 70	**THIRD** *CBS 66246*	18		6
3 Apr 71	**FOURTH** *CBS 64280*	32		2

SOLID SENDERS
UK, male vocal/instrumental group

Date	Title	Peak Position	Weeks at No.1	Weeks on Chart
				3
23 Sep 78	**SOLID SENDERS** *Virgin V 2105*	42		3

DIANE SOLOMON
UK, female vocalist

Date	Title	Peak Position	Weeks at No.1	Weeks on Chart
				9
9 Aug 75	**TAKE TWO** *Philips 6308 236*	26		6

SIR GEORG SOLTI
UK (b. Hungary), male orchestra leader, d. 5 Sep 1997 (age 84)

Date	Title	Peak Position	Weeks at No.1	Weeks on Chart
				5
26 Jan 91	**ORCHESTRA!** *Decca 4308361* SIR GEORG SOLTI & DUDLEY MOORE	38		5

JIMMY SOMERVILLE
UK, male vocalist. See Bronski Beat, Communards

Date	Title	Peak Position	Weeks at No.1	Weeks on Chart
				46
9 Dec 89	**READ MY LIPS** *London 8281661* ●	29		14
24 Nov 90	**THE SINGLES COLLECTION 1984/1990** *London 8282261*	4		26
24 Jun 95	**DARE TO LOVE** *London 8285402*	38		2
22 Sep 01	**THE VERY BEST OF JIMMY SOMERVILLE BRONSKI BEAT AND THE COMMUNARDS** *London 0927412582* BRONSKI BEAT & THE COMMUNARDS	29		4

SON OF DORK
UK, male vocal/instrumental group

Date	Title	Peak Position	Weeks at No.1	Weeks on Chart
				2
3 Dec 05	**WELCOME TO LOSERVILLE** *Mercury 9875452* ●	35		2

STEPHEN SONDHEIM
US, male composer/lyricist

Date	Title	Peak Position	Weeks at No.1	Weeks on Chart
				5
2 Feb 08	**SWEENEY TODD – THE DEMON BARBER OF FLEET STREET** *Nonesuch 7559799580*	38		5

SONIA
UK, female vocalist (Sonia Evans)

Date	Title	Peak Position	Weeks at No.1	Weeks on Chart
				14
5 May 90	**EVERYBODY KNOWS** *Chrysalis CHR 1734* ●	7		10
19 Oct 91	**SONIA** *IQ ZL 751675*	33		2
29 May 93	**BETTER THE DEVIL YOU KNOW** *Arista 74321149802*	32		2

SONIC BOOM
UK, male vocal/instrumental group

Date	Title	Peak Position	Weeks at No.1	Weeks on Chart
				1
17 Mar 90	**SPECTRUM** *Silvertone ORELP 56*	65		1

SONIC YOUTH
US, male/female vocal/instrumental group – Thurston Moore, Kim Gordon, Lee Ranaldo & Steve Shelley

Date	Title	Peak Position	Weeks at No.1	Weeks on Chart
				15
29 Oct 88	**DAYDREAM NATION** *Blast First BFFP 34*	99		1
4 Feb 89	**THE WHITEY ALBUM** *Blast First BFFP 28* CICCONE YOUTH	63		1
7 Jul 90	**GOO'** *DGC 7599242971*	32		2
4 May 91	**THE DIRTY BOOTS EP – PLUS 5 LIVE TRACKS** *DGC 21634*	69		1
1 Aug 92	**DIRTY** *DGC DGCD 24485*	6		5
21 May 94	**EXPERIMENTAL JET SET, TRASH AND NO STAR** *Geffen GED 24632*	10		2
14 Oct 95	**WASHING MACHINE** *Geffen GED 24825*	39		1
23 May 98	**A THOUSAND LEAVES** *Geffen GED 25203*	38		1
17 Jun 06	**RATHER RIPPED** *Geffen 9878304*	64		1

Peak Position · Weeks at No.1 · Weeks on Chart

SONIQUE
UK, female vocalist (Sonia Clarke)

Date	Title / Label	Peak Position	Weeks at No.1	Weeks on Chart
				37
24 Jun 00	**HEAR MY CRY** *Universal 1592302* ⊛	6		37

SONNY & CHER
US, male/female vocal duo – Sonny Bono, d. 5 Jan 1998, & Cher* (Cherilyn LaPierre)

Date	Title / Label	Peak Position	Weeks at No.1	Weeks on Chart
				20
16 Oct 65	**LOOK AT US** *Atlantic ATL 5036*	7		13
14 May 66	**THE WONDROUS WORLD OF SONNY AND CHER** *Atlantic 587006*	15		7

SONS & DAUGHTERS
UK, male/female vocal/instrumental group

Date	Title / Label	Peak Position	Weeks at No.1	Weeks on Chart
				2
18 Jun 05	**THE REPULSION BOX** *Domino WIGCD155*	70		1
9 Feb 08	**THIS GIFT** *Domino WIGCD197*	66		1

S.O.S. BAND
US, male vocal/instrumental group

Date	Title / Label	Peak Position	Weeks at No.1	Weeks on Chart
				21
1 Sep 84	**JUST THE WAY YOU LIKE IT** *Tabu TBU 26058*	29		10
12 Oct 85	**THE ARTISTS VOLUME III** *Street Sounds ARTIS 3* WOMACK & WOMACK/THE O'JAYS/KLEEER/THE S.O.S. BAND	87		2
17 May 86	**SANDS OF TIME** *Tabu TBU 26863*	15		9

DAVID SOUL
US, male vocalist (David Solberg)

Date	Title / Label	Peak Position	Weeks at No.1	Weeks on Chart
				51
27 Nov 76	**DAVID SOUL** *Private Stock PVLP 1012* ●	2		28
17 Sep 77	**PLAYING TO AN AUDIENCE OF ONE** *Private Stock PVLP 1026* ●	8		23

SOUL ASYLUM
US, male vocal/instrumental group

Date	Title / Label	Peak Position	Weeks at No.1	Weeks on Chart
				29
31 Jul 93	**GRAVE DANCERS UNION** *Columbia 4722532* ●	27		25
1 Jul 95	**LET YOUR DIM LIGHT SHINE** *Columbia 4803202*	22		4

SOUL II SOUL
UK, male/female vocal/instrumental group – Jazzie B (Beresford Romeo) & Nellee Hooper; members also included Philip Harvey, Simon Law, Doreen Waddell, Caron Wheeler & Rose Windross

Date	Title / Label	Peak Position	Weeks at No.1	Weeks on Chart
				108
22 Apr 89	**CLUB CLASSICS VOLUME ONE** *10 Records DIX 82* ⊛	1	1	60
2 Jun 90	**VOLUME II (A NEW DECADE)** *10 Records DIX 90* ⊛	1	3	20
25 Apr 92	**VOLUME III JUST RIGHT** *10 Records DIXCD 100* ●	3		11
27 Nov 93	**VOLUME IV THE CLASSIC SINGLES 88-93** *Virgin CDV 2724* ⊛	10		13
12 Aug 95	**VOLUME V – BELIEVE** *Virgin CDV 2739*	13		4

SOULFLY
Brazil/US, male vocal/instrumental group

Date	Title / Label	Peak Position	Weeks at No.1	Weeks on Chart
				5
2 May 98	**SOULFLY** *Roadrunner RR 87482* ○	16		2
7 Oct 00	**PRIMITIVE** *Roadrunner RR 85655*	45		1
6 Jul 02	**3** *Roadrunner RR 84555*	61		1
9 Aug 08	**CONQUER** *Roadrunner RR79422*	64		1

SOULWAX
Belgium, male vocal/instrumental duo

Date	Title / Label	Peak Position	Weeks at No.1	Weeks on Chart
				1
4 Sep 04	**ANY MINUTE NOW** *PIAS PIASB060CD*	53		1

SOUNDGARDEN
US, male vocal/instrumental group – Chris Cornell* (Christopher Boyle), Matt Cameron, Ben Shepherd & Kim Thayil

Date	Title / Label	Peak Position	Weeks at No.1	Weeks on Chart
				32
25 Apr 92	**BADMOTORFINGER** *A&M 3953742*	39		2
19 Mar 94	**SUPERUNKNOWN** *A&M 5402152* ● ★	4		24
1 Jun 96	**DOWN ON THE UPSIDE** *A&M 5405582*	7		6

SOUNDS OF BLACKNESS
US, male/female vocal group

Date	Title / Label	Peak Position	Weeks at No.1	Weeks on Chart
				6
30 Apr 94	**AFRICA TO AMERICA: THE JOURNEY OF THE DRUM** *A&M 5490092*	28		6

SOUNDS ORCHESTRAL
UK, male orchestra

Date	Title / Label	Peak Position	Weeks at No.1	Weeks on Chart
				1
12 Jun 65	**CAST YOUR FATE TO THE WIND** *Piccadilly NPL 38041*	17		1

SOUP DRAGONS
UK, male vocal/instrumental group – Sean Dickinson, Sushil Dade, Jim McCulloch & Paul Quinn

Date	Title / Label	Peak Position	Weeks at No.1	Weeks on Chart
				17
7 May 88	**THIS IS OUR ART** *Siren WX 169*	60		1
5 May 90	**LOVEGOD** *Raw TV Products SOUPLP 2* ○	7		15
16 May 92	**HOTWIRED** *Big Life BLRCD 15*	74		1

SOUTH BANK ORCHESTRA
UK, orchestra

Date	Title / Label	Peak Position	Weeks at No.1	Weeks on Chart
				6
2 Dec 78	**LILLIE (OST-TV)** *Sounds MOR 516* SOUTH BANK ORCHESTRA CONDUCTED BY JOSEPH MOROVITZ & LAURIE HOLLOWAY	47		6

SPACE
France, male instrumental group

Date	Title / Label	Peak Position	Weeks at No.1	Weeks on Chart
				9
17 Sep 77	**MAGIC FLY** *Pye International NSPL 28232* ○	11		9

SPACE
UK, male vocal/instrumental group – Tommy Scott, Francis Griffiths, James Murphy & Andrew Parle

Date	Title / Label	Peak Position	Weeks at No.1	Weeks on Chart
				67
28 Sep 96	**SPIDERS** *Gut GUTCD 1* ⊛	5		42
21 Mar 98	**TIN PLANET** *Gut GUTCD 005* ●	3		25

SPACEHOG
UK, male vocal/instrumental group

Date	Title / Label	Peak Position	Weeks at No.1	Weeks on Chart
				2
15 Feb 97	**RESIDENT ALIEN** *Siren 7559618342*	40		2

SPACEMEN 3
UK, male instrumental group

Date	Title / Label	Peak Position	Weeks at No.1	Weeks on Chart
				1
9 Mar 91	**RECURRING** *Fire FIRELP 23*	46		1

SPANDAU BALLET
UK, male vocal/instrumental group – Tony Hadley*, John Keeble, Gary & Martin Kemp & Martin Norman

Date	Title / Label	Peak Position	Weeks at No.1	Weeks on Chart
				274
14 Mar 81	**JOURNEY TO GLORY** *Reformation CHR 1331* ●	5		29
20 Mar 82	**DIAMOND** *Reformation CDL 1353* ●	15		18
12 Mar 83	**TRUE** *Reformation CDL 1403* ⊛	1	1	90
7 Jul 84	**PARADE** *Reformation CDL 1473* ⊛	2		39
16 Nov 85	**THE SINGLES COLLECTION** *Chrysalis SBTV 1* ⊛x2	3		50
29 Nov 86	**THROUGH THE BARRICADES** *Reformation 4502591* ⊛	7		19
30 Sep 89	**HEART LIKE A SKY** *CBS 4633181*	31		3
28 Sep 91	**THE BEST OF SPANDAU BALLET** *Chrysalis CHR 1894*	44		3
16 Sep 00	**GOLD – THE BEST OF** *Chrysalis 5267002* ⊛	7		20
28 Apr 01	**THE BEST OF** *Chrysalis CCD 1894*	56		3

SPARKLE
US, female vocalist (Stephanie Edwards)

Date	Title / Label	Peak Position	Weeks at No.1	Weeks on Chart
				1
1 Aug 98	**SPARKLE** *Jive 0521462*	57		1

SPARKLEHORSE
US, male vocal/instrumental group

Date	Title / Label	Peak Position	Weeks at No.1	Weeks on Chart
				5
18 May 96	**VIVADIXIESUBMARINETRANSMISSIONPLOT** *Capitol CDEST 2280*	58		1
1 Aug 98	**GOOD MORNING SPIDER** *Parlophone 4960142*	30		2
23 Jun 01	**IT'S A WONDERFUL LIFE** *Capitol 5334272*	49		1
7 Oct 06	**DREAMT FOR LIGHT YEARS IN THE BELLY OF A MOUNTAIN** *Capitol 3709462*	60		1

SPARKS
US/UK, male vocal/instrumental group – Ron & Russell Mael, Norman Diamond, d. 10 Sep 2004, Adrian Fisher, d 31 Mar 2000, & Martin Gordon

Date	Title / Label	Peak Position	Weeks at No.1	Weeks on Chart
				44
1 Jun 74	**KIMONO MY HOUSE** *Island ILPS 9272* ●	4		24
23 Nov 74	**PROPAGANDA** *Island ILPS 9312* ○	9		13
18 Oct 75	**INDISCREET** *Island ILPS 9345*	18		4

Legend: Silver-selling ○ · Gold-selling ● · Platinum-selling ⊛ · US No.1 ★ · Peak Position · Weeks at No.1 · Weeks on Chart

Date	Title	Label	Peak Position	Weeks at No.1	Weeks on Chart
8 Sep 79	NUMBER ONE IN HEAVEN	Virgin V 2115	73		1
18 Feb 06	HELLO YOUNG LOVERS	Gut GUTCD53	66		1
31 May 08	EXOTIC CREATURES OF THE DEEP	Lil Beethoven LBRCD111	54		1

JORDIN SPARKS
US, female vocalist — 14

Date	Title	Label	Peak Position	Weeks at No.1	Weeks on Chart
19 Jul 08	JORDIN SPARKS	RCA 88697296602 ○	17		14

SAM SPARRO
Australia, male vocalist/producer (Sam Falson) — 15

Date	Title	Label	Peak Position	Weeks at No.1	Weeks on Chart
10 May 08	SAM SPARRO	Island 1769065 ●	4		15

SPEAR OF DESTINY
UK, male vocal/instrumental group — 35

Date	Title	Label	Peak Position	Weeks at No.1	Weeks on Chart
23 Apr 83	GRAPES OF WRATH	Epic EPC 25318	62		2
28 Apr 84	ONE EYED JACKS	Burning Rome EPC 25836	22		7
7 Sep 85	WORLD SERVICE	Burning Rome EPC 26514	11		7
2 May 87	OUTLAND	Virgin DIX 59 ○	16		13
16 May 87	S.O.D. THE EPIC YEARS	Epic 4508721	53		3
22 Oct 88	THE PRICE YOU PAY	Virgin V 2549	37		3

SPEARHEAD
UK, male vocal/instrumental group — 1

Date	Title	Label	Peak Position	Weeks at No.1	Weeks on Chart
29 Mar 97	CHOCOLATE SUPA HIGHWAY	Capitol CDEST 2293	68		1

BILLIE JO SPEARS
US, female vocalist — 28

Date	Title	Label	Peak Position	Weeks at No.1	Weeks on Chart
11 Sep 76	WHAT I'VE GOT IN MIND	United Artists UAS 29955 ○	47		2
19 May 79	THE BILLIE JO SPEARS SINGLES ALBUM	United Artists UAK 30231 ○	7		17
21 Nov 81	COUNTRY GIRL	Warwick WW 5109 ●	17		9

BRITNEY SPEARS
US, female vocalist — 267

Date	Title	Label	Peak Position	Weeks at No.1	Weeks on Chart
20 Mar 99	...BABY ONE MORE TIME	Jive 0522172 ⊛x3 ★	2		88
27 May 00	OOPS! I DID IT AGAIN	Jive 9220392 ⊛x3 ★	2		45
17 Nov 01	BRITNEY	Jive 9222532 ⊛ ★	4		36
29 Nov 03	IN THE ZONE	Jive 82876576442 ⊛ ★	13		43
20 Nov 04	GREATEST HITS – MY PREROGATIVE	Jive 82876666162	2		23
10 Nov 07	BLACKOUT	Jive 88697190732 ●	2		28
13 Dec 08	CIRCUS	Jive 88697406982 ★	4		4+

SPECIALS
UK, male vocal/instrumental group – Jerry Dammers, John Bradbury, Horace Gentleman (Stephen Panter), Lynval Golding (b. Jamaica), Terry Hall*, Roddy Radiation (Roderick Byers) & Neville Staple (b. Jamaica) — 85

Date	Title	Label	Peak Position	Weeks at No.1	Weeks on Chart
3 Nov 79	SPECIALS	2-Tone CDL TT 5001 ●	4		45
4 Oct 80	MORE SPECIALS	2-Tone CHR TT 5003 ●	5		19
23 Jun 84	SPECIALS	Chrysalis CCD 5001	22		3
7 Sep 91	IN THE STUDIO	2-Tone CHR TT 5008 SPECIAL AKA	34		6
7 Jul 01	THE SPECIALS SINGLES	2-Tone CHR TT 5010 ●	10		9
12 Apr 08	THE BEST OF	Chrysalis CHRTV20082	28		3

PHIL SPECTOR
US, male producer — 29

Date	Title	Label	Peak Position	Weeks at No.1	Weeks on Chart
23 Dec 72	PHIL SPECTOR'S CHRISTMAS ALBUM	Apple SAPCOR 24	21		3
15 Oct 77	PHIL SPECTOR'S ECHOES OF THE 60'S	Phil Spector International 2307 013 ○	21		10
25 Dec 82	PHIL SPECTOR'S CHRISTMAS ALBUM	Phil Spector International 2307 005	96		2
10 Dec 83	PHIL SPECTOR'S GREATEST HITS/PHIL SPECTOR'S CHRISTMAS ALBUM	Impression PSLP 1/2 ●	19		8
12 Dec 87	PHIL SPECTOR'S CHRISTMAS ALBUM	Chrysalis CDL 1625 ●	69		6

SPEEDWAY
UK, male/female vocal/instrumental duo — 1

Date	Title	Label	Peak Position	Weeks at No.1	Weeks on Chart
6 Mar 04	SAVE YOURSELF	Innocent CDSIN12	42		1

SPEEDY J
Holland, male producer (Jochem Paap) — 1

Date	Title	Label	Peak Position	Weeks at No.1	Weeks on Chart
10 Jul 93	GINGER	Warp WARPCD 14	68		1

REGINA SPEKTOR
US (b. Russia), female vocalist/pianist — 7

Date	Title	Label	Peak Position	Weeks at No.1	Weeks on Chart
22 Jul 06	BEGIN TO HOPE	Sire 9362443152	53		7

NICKY SPENCE
UK, male vocalist — 1

Date	Title	Label	Peak Position	Weeks at No.1	Weeks on Chart
27 Jan 07	MY FIRST LOVE	UCJ 4765717	69		1

JON SPENCER BLUES EXPLOSION
US, male vocal/instrumental group — 2

Date	Title	Label	Peak Position	Weeks at No.1	Weeks on Chart
12 Oct 96	NOW I GOT WORRY	Mute CDSTUMM 132	50		1
31 Oct 98	ACME	Mute CDSTUMM 154	72		1

SPICE GIRLS
UK, female vocal group – Victoria Beckham* (née Adams), Melanie B* (Melanie Brown), Emma Bunton*, Melanie C* (Melanie Chisholm) & Geri Halliwell* — 147

Date	Title	Label	Peak Position	Weeks at No.1	Weeks on Chart
16 Nov 96	SPICE	Virgin CDV 2812 ⊛x10	1	15	72
15 Nov 97	SPICEWORLD	Virgin CDV 2850 ⊛x5	1	3	55
18 Nov 00	FOREVER	Virgin CDVX 2928 ⊛	2		8
24 Nov 07	GREATEST HITS	Virgin SPICECD1 ⊛	2		12

SPIDER
UK, male vocal/instrumental group — 2

Date	Title	Label	Peak Position	Weeks at No.1	Weeks on Chart
23 Oct 82	ROCK 'N' ROLL GYPSIES	RCA RCALP 3101	75		1
7 Apr 84	ROUGH JUSTICE	A&M AMLX 68563	96		1

SPIN DOCTORS
US, male vocal/instrumental group – Christopher Barron, Aaron Comess, Eric Schenkman (replaced by Anthony Krizan) & Mark White — 57

Date	Title	Label	Peak Position	Weeks at No.1	Weeks on Chart
20 Mar 93	POCKET FULL OF KRYPTONITE	Epic 4682502 ⊛	2		48
9 Jul 94	TURN IT UPSIDE DOWN	Epic 4768862	3		9

SPINAL TAP
UK/US, male vocal/instrumental group — 2

Date	Title	Label	Peak Position	Weeks at No.1	Weeks on Chart
11 Apr 92	BREAK LIKE THE WIND	MCA MCAD 10514	51		2

SPINNERS
UK, male vocal/instrumental group — 24

Date	Title	Label	Peak Position	Weeks at No.1	Weeks on Chart
5 Sep 70	THE SPINNERS ARE IN TOWN	Fontana 6309 014	40		5
7 Aug 71	SPINNERS LIVE PERFORMANCE	Contour 6870 502	14		12
13 Nov 71	THE SWINGING CITY	Philips 6382 002	20		3
8 Apr 72	LOVE IS TEASING	Columbia SCX 6493	33		4

SPIRIT
US, male vocal/instrumental group — 3

Date	Title	Label	Peak Position	Weeks at No.1	Weeks on Chart
13 Mar 71	TWELVE DREAMS OF DR SARDONICUS	Epic EPC 64191	29		1
18 Apr 81	POTATO LAND	Beggars Banquet BEGA 23	40		2

SPIRITUALIZED
UK, male/female vocal/instrumental group – Jason Pierce, Sean Cook, Willie Curruthers, John Mattock, Kate Radley & Mark Refoy — 29

Date	Title	Label	Peak Position	Weeks at No.1	Weeks on Chart
11 Apr 92	LAZER GUIDED MELODIES	Dedicated DEDCD 004	27		2
18 Feb 95	PURE PHASE	Dedicated DEDCD 017S ELECTRIC MAINLINE	20		2
28 Jun 97	LADIES & GENTLEMEN WE ARE FLOATING IN SPACE	Dedicated DEDCD 034 ●	4		15
7 Nov 98	LIVE AT THE ROYAL ALBERT HALL	Deconstruction 74321622852	38		1
29 Sep 01	LET IT COME DOWN	Spaceman OPM 001CD	3		4
20 Sep 03	AMAZING GRACE	Spaceman/Sanctuary SANCD 214X	25		3
7 Jun 08	SONGS IN A&E	Sanctuary 1765583	15		2

SHARLEEN SPITERI
UK, female vocalist. See Texas — Weeks on Chart: 16

Date	Title / Label	Peak Position	Weeks at No.1	Weeks on Chart
26 Jul 08	**MELODY** *Mercury 1769263* ●	3		16

SPITTING IMAGE
UK, male/female puppets — Weeks on Chart: 3

Date	Title / Label	Peak Position	Weeks at No.1	Weeks on Chart
18 Oct 86	**SPIT IN YOUR EAR** *Virgin V 2403*	55		3

SPLIT ENZ
New Zealand, male/female vocal/instrumental group — Weeks on Chart: 9

Date	Title / Label	Peak Position	Weeks at No.1	Weeks on Chart
30 Aug 80	**TRUE COLOURS** *A&M AMLH 64822*	42		8
8 May 82	**TIME AND TIDE** *A&M AMLH 64894*	71		1

SPOOKS
US, male/female vocal/rap group — Weeks on Chart: 12

Date	Title / Label	Peak Position	Weeks at No.1	Weeks on Chart
17 Feb 01	**S.I.O.S.O.S. VOLUME 1** *Epic 4982612* ○	25		12

SPOTNICKS
Sweden, male instrumental group — Weeks on Chart: 1

Date	Title / Label	Peak Position	Weeks at No.1	Weeks on Chart
9 Feb 63	**OUT-A-SPACE** *Oriole PS 40036*	20		1

DUSTY SPRINGFIELD
UK, female vocalist (Mary O'Brien), d. 2 Mar 1999 (age 59) — Weeks on Chart: 140

Date	Title / Label	Peak Position	Weeks at No.1	Weeks on Chart
25 Apr 64	**A GIRL CALLED DUSTY** *Philips BL 7594*	6		23
23 Oct 65	**EVERYTHING'S COMING UP DUSTY** *Philips RBL 1002*	6		12
22 Oct 66	**GOLDEN HITS** *Philips BL 7737*	2		36
11 Nov 67	**WHERE AM I GOING?** *Philips SBL 7820*	40		1
21 Dec 68	**DUSTY…DEFINITELY** *Philips SBL 7864*	30		6
2 May 70	**FROM DUSTY…WITH LOVE** *Philips SBL 7927*	35		2
4 Mar 78	**IT BEGINS AGAIN** *Mercury 9109 607*	41		2
30 Jan 88	**DUSTY – THE SILVER COLLECTION** *Phonogram DUSTV 1* ●	14		10
7 Jul 90	**REPUTATION** *Parlophone PCSD 111* ○	18		6
14 May 94	**GOIN' BACK – THE VERY BEST OF DUSTY SPRINGFIELD 1962–1994** *Philips 8487892* ●	5		11
8 Jul 95	**A VERY FINE LOVE** *Columbia 4785082*	43		1
7 Nov 98	**THE BEST OF DUSTY SPRINGFIELD** *Mercury/Polygram TV 5383452* ●	19		24
13 Mar 04	**THE LOOK OF LOVE** *Universal TV 9816495* ○	25		4
24 Jun 06	**AT HER VERY BEST** *Mercury 9840305*	31		2

RICK SPRINGFIELD
Australia, male actor/vocalist/guitarist (Richard Springthorpe) — Weeks on Chart: 8

Date	Title / Label	Peak Position	Weeks at No.1	Weeks on Chart
11 Feb 84	**LIVING IN OZ** *RCA PL 84660*	41		4
25 May 85	**TAO** *RCA PL 85370*	68		3
26 Mar 88	**ROCK OF LIFE** *RCA PL 86620*	80		1

BRUCE SPRINGSTEEN
US, male vocalist/guitarist. No act can match the record-breaking 10 shows 'The Boss' performed at New Jersey's Giants Stadium in 2003 which grossed $37.8 million. He recorded the biggest-selling box set of all time, *Live 1975-85*, and has collected 18 Grammy awards, including three for *The Rising* in 2002 — Weeks on Chart: 574

Date	Title / Label	Peak Position	Weeks at No.1	Weeks on Chart
1 Nov 75	**BORN TO RUN** *CBS 69170* ⊛	17		50
17 Jun 78	**DARKNESS ON THE EDGE OF TOWN** *CBS 86061* ●	16		40
25 Oct 80	**THE RIVER** *CBS 88510* ⊛ ★	2		88
2 Oct 82	**NEBRASKA** *CBS 25100* ○	3		19
16 Jun 84	**BORN IN THE U.S.A.** *CBS 86304* ⊛x3 ★	1	5	129
15 Jun 85	**GREETINGS FROM ASBURY PARK** *CBS 32210* ○	41		10
15 Jun 85	**THE WILD, THE INNOCENT AND THE E. STREET SHUFFLE** *CBS 32363* ○	33		12
22 Nov 86	**LIVE 1975–1985** *CBS 4502271* & THE E. STREET BAND ● ★	4		9
17 Oct 87	**TUNNEL OF LOVE** *CBS 4602701* ⊛ ★	1	1	33
4 Apr 92	**HUMAN TOUCH** *Columbia 4714232* ●	1	1	17
4 Apr 92	**LUCKY TOWN** *Columbia 4714242* ●	2		11
24 Apr 93	**IN CONCERT – MTV UNPLUGGED** *Columbia 4738602* ●	4		7
11 Mar 95	**GREATEST HITS** *Columbia 4785552* ⊛x2 ★	1	2	56
25 Nov 95	**THE GHOST OF TOM JOAD** *Columbia 4816502* ●	16		14
21 Nov 98	**TRACKS** *Columbia 4926052*	50		1
24 Apr 99	**18 TRACKS** *Columbia 4942002*	23		7
14 Apr 01	**LIVE IN NEW YORK CITY** *Columbia 5000002* & THE E. STREET BAND ○	12		6
10 Aug 02	**THE RISING** *Columbia 5080009* ● ★	1	1	16
22 Nov 03	**THE ESSENTIAL** *Columbia 5137009*	28		2
22 Nov 03	**THE ESSENTIAL** *Columbia 5137002*	32		9
7 May 05	**DEVILS & DUST** *Columbia 5200002* ●	1	1	8
26 Nov 05	**BORN TO RUN – 30TH ANNIVERSARY EDITION** *Columbia 82876755892*	63		1
11 Mar 06	**HAMMERSMITH ODEON LONDON '75** *Columbia 82876779952* & THE E. STREET BAND	33		1
6 May 06	**WE SHALL OVERCOME – THE SEEGER SESSIONS** *Columbia 82876830742*	3		10
16 Jun 07	**LIVE IN DUBLIN** *Columbia 88697108762* & SESSIONS	21		2
13 Oct 07	**MAGIC** *Columbia 88697170602* ★	1	2	16

(SPUNGE)
UK, male vocal/instrumental group — Weeks on Chart: 1

Date	Title / Label	Peak Position	Weeks at No.1	Weeks on Chart
7 Sep 02	**THE STORY SO FAR** *B Unique 0927487452*	48		1

SPYRO GYRA
US, male instrumental group — Weeks on Chart: 22

Date	Title / Label	Peak Position	Weeks at No.1	Weeks on Chart
14 Jul 79	**MORNING DANCE** *Infinity INS 2003* ○	11		16
23 Feb 80	**CATCHING THE SUN** *MCA MCG 4009*	31		6

SQUEEZE
UK, male vocal/instrumental group – Chris Difford & Glenn Tilbrook (Difford & Tilbrook*); members also included Paul Gunn (replaced by Gilson Lavis), Jools Holland* (replaced by Paul Carrack*) & Henry Kakoulli (replaced by John Bentley) — Weeks on Chart: 134

Date	Title / Label	Peak Position	Weeks at No.1	Weeks on Chart
28 Apr 79	**COOL FOR CATS** *A&M AMLH 68503* ○	45		11
16 Feb 80	**ARGY BARGY** *A&M AMLH 64802*	32		15
23 May 81	**EAST SIDE STORY** *A&M AMLH 64854* ○	19		26
15 May 82	**SWEETS FROM A STRANGER** *A&M AMLH 64899*	20		7
6 Nov 82	**SINGLES – 45'S AND UNDER** *A&M AMLH 68552* ⊛	3		29
7 Sep 85	**COSI FAN TUTTI FRUTTI** *A&M AMA 5085*	31		7
19 Sep 87	**BABYLON AND ON** *A&M AMA 5161* ○	14		8
23 Sep 89	**FRANK** *A&M AMA 5278*	58		1
7 Apr 90	**A ROUND AND A BOUT** *I.R.S. DFCLP 1*	50		1
7 Sep 91	**PLAY** *Reprise WX 428*	41		1
23 May 92	**GREATEST HITS** *A&M 3971812* ●	6		13
25 Sep 93	**SOME FANTASTIC PLACE** *A&M 5401402*	26		4
25 Nov 95	**RIDICULOUS** *A&M 5404402*	50		1
22 Jun 02	**THE BIG SQUEEZE – THE VERY BEST OF** *Universal TV 4932532* ●	8		6
12 May 07	**ESSENTIAL** *Universal TV 9846252*	25		4

CHRIS SQUIRE
UK, male vocalist/bass guitarist. See Yes — Weeks on Chart: 7

Date	Title / Label	Peak Position	Weeks at No.1	Weeks on Chart
6 Dec 75	**FISH OUT OF WATER** *Atlantic K 50203* ○	25		7

JOHN SQUIRE
UK, male vocalist/guitarist. See Seahorses, Stone Roses — Weeks on Chart: 2

Date	Title / Label	Peak Position	Weeks at No.1	Weeks on Chart
28 Sep 02	**TIME CHANGES EVERYTHING** *North Country NCCDS 001*	17		2

STAIND
US, male vocal/instrumental group – Aaron Lewis, Johnny April, Mike Mushok & Jon Wysocki — Weeks on Chart: 30

Date	Title / Label	Peak Position	Weeks at No.1	Weeks on Chart
1 Sep 01	**BREAK THE CYCLE** *Elektra 7559626642* ⊛ ★	1	1	26
31 May 03	**14 SHADES OF GREY** *Elektra 7559628822* ★	16		3
20 Sep 08	**THE ILLUSION OF PROGRESS** *Roadrunner RR79022*	73		1

STANDS
UK, male vocal/instrumental group — Weeks on Chart: 3

Date	Title / Label	Peak Position	Weeks at No.1	Weeks on Chart
6 Mar 04	**ALL YEARS LEAVING** *Echo ECHCD50*	28		2
6 Aug 05	**HORSE FABULOUS** *Echo ECHCD64*	62		1

LISA STANSFIELD
UK, female vocalist — Weeks on Chart: 126

Date	Title / Label	Peak Position	Weeks at No.1	Weeks on Chart
2 Dec 89	**AFFECTION** *Arista 210379* ⊛x3	2		31
23 Nov 91	**REAL LOVE** *Arista 212300* ⊛x2	3		51
20 Nov 93	**SO NATURAL** *Arista 74321172312* ●	6		14
5 Apr 97	**LISA STANSFIELD** *Arista 74321458512*	2		18
7 Jul 01	**FACE UP** *Arista 74321863462*	38		2
15 Feb 03	**BIOGRAPHY – THE GREATEST HITS** *Arista 82876502222*	3		9
9 Oct 04	**THE MOMENT** *ZTT ZTT192CD*	57		1

Phil Spector

WHEN the death of American actress Lana Clarkson hit the headlines in February 2003, it was not because of her own celebrity but because the man accused of her murder was one of America's foremost cultural icons – Phil Spector – a man behind more truly great hit records than almost any other living American. While the high-profile case eventually ended in mistrial (with a re-trial looking likely at the time of writing), the television footage of the accused reminded the world of a man largely lost from the headlines, whose eccentric career established him as perhaps the first celebrity record producer. Seeing him sitting in court with a shock of white hair, it was easy to forget that here was a genuine living legend, a man who was so revered that for decades his name on a record label was a guarantee of its quality. Speaking musically, make no mistake, Phil Spector's work stands alongside some of the very best pop music anyone has created.

Phil Spector is best known for the so-called 'Wall Of Sound'

Born on Boxing Day 1939, Harvey Philip Spector was born in the Bronx but was raised in Los Angeles. The grandson of a Russian immigrant (Spektor), Spector was proficient on a number of instruments at an early age, then began writing songs at high school and playing in jazz bands around LA by his mid-teens – school years were not easy for him and he was bullied. His first group, The Teddy Bears, released their debut single and had a huge hit on both sides of the Atlantic with 'To Know Him Is To Love Him' in 1958, the title paraphrasing the inscription on the gravestone of Spector's father, who had killed himself when the boy was nine. The band appeared on the classic US TV programme *American Bandstand*, but wrangling over royalties stalled the Teddy Bears' career and they failed to capitalise on their success. Spector enrolled at UCLA, and worked as a court stenographer for a while, but inevitably returned to the music business.

Work with Lee Hazlewood and Lester Sill initially failed to produce anything significant, but Spector's interest now clearly lay in production rather than performance. Despatched to New York by Sill and Hazlewood, Spector renewed an early acquaintance with Mike Stoller and Jerry Leiber, writers of some of rock 'n' roll's greatest hits, and was installed as a staff producer at the newly instituted Dune Records. By 1960 he had scored a major hit as the co-writer, with Leiber, of Ben E. King's 'Spanish Harlem', and rapidly became a valuable asset in the business. He played on 'On Broadway' for The Drifters, and was involved in a string of hits for various artists, including Gene Pitney, The Paris Sisters and Curtis Lee. By 1961, in partnership with Lester Sill, he founded Philles Records, recording The Crystals' 'There's No Other (Like My Baby)', and a string of other hits.

However, more than any specific record, Phil Spector is best known for the so-called 'Wall Of Sound', the perfect description for his trademark production style. Overdubbed, multi-instrumental arrangements would include several drummers and percussionists building a vast, megalithic rhythm section, a bank of guitars and pianos, echo-chamber grandeur, and an orchestral approach to instrumentation that defined a broad landscape of early 1960s pop. By the end of 1962, Spector had acquired Sill's shares in Philles Records, and with a glittering array of session musicians including Glen Campbell, Hal Blaine, Sonny Bono and Leon Russell, began an unprecedented and as yet little-rivalled assault on the charts. Alongside The Crystals' classics 'Da Doo Ron Ron' and 'Then He Kissed Me', hits by Darlene Love, Bob B. Soxx and The Blue Jeans, 1963's classic Christmas album and more, Spector produced The Ronettes' timeless 'Be My Baby' and 'Baby I Love You'. Ike and Tina Turner's 'River Deep, Mountain High' and 'You've Lost That Loving

Biggest-Selling Album					
Producer	Album	Artist	Week	Highest Position	Approx Sales
PHIL SPECTOR	LET IT BE	BEATLES	23/5/70	1	900,000

Feeling' by The Righteous Brothers still bear the hallmark of their producer and still sing out brightly nearly a half century after their release.

By 1968, Spector was married to Ronette vocalist Veronica 'Ronnie' Bennett, with whom his relationship was famously, and increasingly, dysfunctional. The onslaught of The Beatles and Rolling Stones in the US market threatened Spector's singles-chart hegemony. New business ventures never recaptured the spirit of his greatest work – he launched Annette Records and Phil Spector Records – and for much of the late 1960s Spector was seen as a reclusive fringe figure, even appearing as a drug dealer in *Easy Rider.*

Although they may have stolen his crown, The Beatles were always fans of Spector's work, and of The Ronettes in particular. In 1969 he was brought in by Beatles manager Allen Klein and John Lennon to tidy up the ragged recordings that became *Let It Be.* Spector called the experience 'hostile', but his lush string arrangements – while not adored by hardcore Beatle collectors who knew the original demos – made the album a hugely successful and commercial swansong. Spector was back on form with Lennon's own *Plastic Ono Band, Imagine* and *Some Time In New York City,* while eternal Ronnie Spector fan George Harrison's own solo debut *All Things Must Pass* was another later Spector highlight of the early 1970s. Lennon's *Rock 'n' Roll* album was the result of drinking and recording sessions with Spector during Lennon's LA 'lost weekend', an endearing collection of standards – although the pair then fell out amidst stories of missing tapes and blazing studio rows.

Spector was divorced from Ronnie in 1974 and then worked with Leonard Cohen's *Death Of A Ladies' Man* (1977) – a lascivious shambles of an album, loved by many, loathed by more, which brought Cohen, Dylan and Allen Ginsberg together on vinyl. The blend of Cohen's reflective songwriting and Spector's supercharged-Wagner-esque production was a shock to established Cohen fans. Spector ended the decade with The Ramones' *End Of The Century* (1980), a glorious valediction to punk that provided the band with an enduring hit in The Ronette's own 'Be My Baby'.

Spector's supercharged-Wagner-esque production was a shock to established Cohen fans

Spector has long been described in the media as a 'recluse'. Whatever motivates him nowadays – a production project for Celine Dion was stalled in the 1990s, yet retrospective awards befall him on a regular basis – he is responsible for some of the most glorious pop music you could wish to hear. Although his UK career as a solo artist is limited to compilation-style albums this should not detract from his genius. Though his body of work may be equalled, it is hard to see where his best productions have been bettered. If he is remembered for anything in a hundred years time – and he surely will be – it will be for the work of others that he presented so beautifully.

Silver-selling · Gold-selling · Platinum-selling · US No.1 ★ · Peak Position · Weeks at No.1 · Weeks on Chart

ALVIN STARDUST
UK, male vocalist (Bernard Jewry) — 17

Date	Title	Label	Peak Position	Weeks at No.1	Weeks on Chart
16 Mar 74	THE UNTOUCHABLE	Magnet MAG 5001	4		12
21 Dec 74	ALVIN STARDUST	Magnet MAG 5004	37		3
4 Oct 75	ROCK WITH ALVIN	Magnet MAG 5007	52		2

ED STARINK
US, male synthesizer player — 11

Date	Title	Label	Peak Position	Weeks at No.1	Weeks on Chart
27 Oct 90	SYNTHESIZER GREATEST	Arcade ARC 938101	22		5
9 Jan 93	SYNTHESIZER GOLD	Arcade ARC 3100012	29		6

FREDDIE STARR
UK, male comedian/vocalist (Fred Smith) — 16

Date	Title	Label	Peak Position	Weeks at No.1	Weeks on Chart
18 Nov 89	AFTER THE LAUGHTER	Dover ADD 10	10		9
17 Nov 90	THE WANDERER	Dover ADD 17	33		7

KAY STARR
US, female vocalist (Katherine Starks) — 1

Date	Title	Label	Peak Position	Weeks at No.1	Weeks on Chart
26 Mar 60	MOVIN'!	Capitol 1254	16		1

RINGO STARR
UK, male drummer/vocalist (Richard Starkey). See Beatles — 30

Date	Title	Label	Peak Position	Weeks at No.1	Weeks on Chart
18 Apr 70	SENTIMENTAL JOURNEY	Apple PCS 7101	7		6
8 Dec 73	RINGO	Apple PCTC 252	7		20
7 Dec 74	GOODNIGHT VIENNA	Apple PMC 7168	30		2
8 Sep 07	PHOTOGRAPH – THE VERY BEST OF	Capitol 3938272	26		2

STARSAILOR
UK, male vocal/instrumental group – James Walsh, Ben Byrne, James Stelfox & Barry Westhead — 59

Date	Title	Label	Peak Position	Weeks at No.1	Weeks on Chart
20 Oct 01	LOVE IS HERE	Chrysalis 5353502	2		41
27 Sep 03	SILENCE IS EASY	EMI 5900072	2		13
29 Oct 05	ON THE OUTSIDE	EMI 3437222	13		5

STARSOUND
Holland, male producer (Jaap Eggermont) & male/female session singers — 28

Date	Title	Label	Peak Position	Weeks at No.1	Weeks on Chart
16 May 81	STARS ON 45	CBS 86132	1	5	21
19 Sep 81	STARS ON 45 VOLUME 2	CBS 85181	18		6
3 Apr 82	STARS MEDLEY	CBS 85651	94		1

STARTRAX
UK, male/female vocal group — 7

Date	Title	Label	Peak Position	Weeks at No.1	Weeks on Chart
1 Aug 81	STARTRAX CLUB DISCO	Picksy KSYA 1001	26		7

STATE OF THE HEART
UK, male vocal/instrumental group — 9

Date	Title	Label	Peak Position	Weeks at No.1	Weeks on Chart
16 Mar 96	PURE SAX	Virgin VTCD 78	18		7
12 Oct 96	SAX AT THE MOVIES	Virgin VTCD 98	62		2

STATIC-X
US, male vocal/instrumental group — 2

Date	Title	Label	Peak Position	Weeks at No.1	Weeks on Chart
23 Jun 01	MACHINE	Warner Brothers 9362479482	56		2

CANDI STATON
US, female vocalist (Canzata Staton) — 3

Date	Title	Label	Peak Position	Weeks at No.1	Weeks on Chart
24 Jul 76	YOUNG HEARTS RUN FREE	Warner Brothers K 56259	34		3

STATUS QUO
UK, male vocal/instrumental group – Francis Rossi; members also included Andy Bown, John Coghlan, John Edwards, Alan Lancaster & Rick Parfitt. No group has had more chart singles than the three-chord boogie band that has remained at the top for over 40 years, with only The Beatles and The Stones amassing more Top 20 albums — 480

Date	Title	Label	Peak Position	Weeks at No.1	Weeks on Chart
20 Jan 73	PILEDRIVER	Vertigo 6360 082	5		37
9 Jun 73	THE BEST OF STATUS QUO	Pye NSPL 18402	32		7
6 Oct 73	HELLO	Vertigo 6360 098	1	1	28
18 May 74	QUO	Vertigo 9102 001	2		16
1 Mar 75	ON THE LEVEL	Vertigo 9102 002	1	2	27
8 Mar 75	DOWN THE DUSTPIPE	Pye Golden Hour CH 604	20		6
20 Mar 76	BLUE FOR YOU	Vertigo 9102 006	1	3	30
12 Mar 77	STATUS QUO – LIVE	Vertigo 6641 580	3		14
26 Nov 77	ROCKIN' ALL OVER THE WORLD	Vertigo 9102 014	5		15
11 Nov 78	IF YOU CAN'T STAND THE HEAT	Vertigo 9102 027	3		14
20 Oct 79	WHATEVER YOU WANT	Vertigo 9102 037	3		14
22 Mar 80	12 GOLD BARS	Vertigo QUO TV 1	3		48
25 Oct 80	JUST SUPPOSIN'	Vertigo 6302 057	4		18
28 Mar 81	NEVER TOO LATE	Vertigo 6302 104	2		13
10 Oct 81	FRESH QUOTA	PRT DOW 2	74		1
24 Apr 82	1982	Vertigo 6302 169	1	1	20
13 Nov 82	FROM THE MAKERS OF...	Vertigo PROLP 1	4		18
3 Dec 83	BACK TO BACK	Vertigo VERH 10	9		22
4 Aug 84	STATUS QUO LIVE AT THE N.E.C.	Vertigo 8189 471	83		3
1 Dec 84	12 GOLD BARS VOLUME TWO – (AND ONE)	Vertigo QUO TV 2	12		18
6 Sep 86	IN THE ARMY NOW	Vertigo VERH 36	7		23
18 Jun 88	AIN'T COMPLAINING	Vertigo VERH 58	12		5
2 Dec 89	PERFECT REMEDY	Vertigo 8420981	49		2
20 Oct 90	ROCKING ALL OVER THE YEARS	Vertigo 8467971 (x2)	2		25
5 Oct 91	ROCK 'TIL YOU DROP	Vertigo 5103411	10		7
14 Nov 92	LIVE ALIVE QUO	Polydor 5173672	37		1
3 Sep 94	THIRSTY WORK	Polydor 5236072	13		3
17 Feb 96	DON'T STOP – THE 30TH ANNIVERSARY ALBUM	Polygram TV 5310352	2		11
25 Oct 97	WHATEVER YOU WANT – THE VERY BEST OF STATUS QUO	Mercury TV 5535072	13		6
10 Apr 99	UNDER THE INFLUENCE	Eagle EAGCD 076	26		2
29 Apr 00	FAMOUS IN THE LAST CENTURY	Universal TV 1578142	19		5
5 Oct 02	HEAVY TRAFFIC	Universal TV 0187902	15		3
29 Nov 03	RIFFS	Universal TV 9813909	44		2
2 Oct 04	XS ALL AREAS – THE GREATEST HITS	Universal TV 9824883	16		3
25 Jun 05	NOW AND THEN	Crimson 3 CRIMBX55	49		1
1 Oct 05	THE PARTY AIN'T OVER YET	Sanctuary SANCD389	18		2
29 Sep 07	IN SEARCH OF THE FOURTH CHORD	Fourth Chord QUOCD001	15		2
15 Nov 08	PICTURES – 40 YEARS OF HITS	Universal TV 5313056	8		8+

STEEL PULSE
UK, male vocal/instrumental group – David Hinds, Selwyn Brown, Basil Gabbidon, Fonso Martin, Ronnie McQueen, Steve Nesbitt & Michael Riley — 18

Date	Title	Label	Peak Position	Weeks at No.1	Weeks on Chart
5 Aug 78	HANDSWORTH REVOLUTION	Island ILPS 9502	9		12
14 Jul 79	TRIBUTE TO MARTYRS	Island ILPS 9568	42		6

TOMMY STEELE
UK, male vocalist (Tommy Hicks) — 34

Date	Title	Label	Peak Position	Weeks at No.1	Weeks on Chart
27 Apr 57	TOMMY STEELE STAGE SHOW	Decca LF 1287	5		1
8 Jun 57	THE TOMMY STEELE STORY	Decca LF 1288	1	4	21
12 Apr 58	THE DUKE WORE JEANS (OST)	Decca LF 1308	1	3	12

STEELEYE SPAN
UK, male/female vocal/instrumental group – Maddy Prior, Tim Hart, Bob Johnson, Rick Kemp, Peter Knight & Nigel Pegrum — 48

Date	Title	Label	Peak Position	Weeks at No.1	Weeks on Chart
10 Apr 71	PLEASE TO SEE THE KING	B&C CAS 1029	45		2
14 Oct 72	BELOW THE SALT	Chrysalis CHR 1008	43		1
28 Apr 73	PARCEL OF ROGUES	Chrysalis CHR 1046	26		5
23 Mar 74	NOW WE ARE SIX	Chrysalis CHR 1053	13		13
15 Feb 75	COMMONER'S CROWN	Chrysalis CHR 1071	21		4
25 Oct 75	ALL AROUND MY HAT	Chrysalis CHR 1091	7		20
16 Oct 76	ROCKET COTTAGE	Chrysalis CHR 1123	41		3

STEELY DAN
US, male vocal/instrumental group – Walter Becker, Donald Fagen* & various session musicians — 92

Date	Title	Label	Peak Position	Weeks at No.1	Weeks on Chart
30 Mar 74	PRETZEL LOGIC	Probe SPBA 6282	37		2
3 May 75	KATY LIED	ABC ABCL 5094	13		6
20 Sep 75	CAN'T BUY A THRILL	ABC ABCL 5024	38		1
22 May 76	ROYAL SCAM	ABC ABCL 5161	11		13
8 Oct 77	AJA	ABC ABCL 5225	5		10
2 Dec 78	GREATEST HITS	ABC BLD 616	41		18
29 Nov 80	GAUCHO	MCA MCF 3090	27		12
3 Jul 82	GOLDEN HITS	MCA MCF 3145	44		6
26 Oct 85	REELIN' IN THE YEARS – THE VERY BEST OF STEELY DAN	MCA DANTV 1	43		5
10 Oct 87	DO IT AGAIN – THE VERY BEST OF STEELY DAN	Telstar STAR 2297	64		4

Date	Title / Label	Peak	Wks at No.1	Wks on Chart
20 Nov 93	**REMASTERED – THE BEST OF STEELY DAN** *MCA MCD 10967*	42		5
28 Oct 95	**ALIVE IN AMERICA** *Giant 74321286912*	62		1
11 Mar 00	**TWO AGAINST NATURE** *Giant 74321621902*	11		5
21 Jun 03	**EVERYTHING MUST GO** *Reprise 9362484902*	21		3
28 May 05	**SHOWBIZ KIDS – THE STEELY DAN STORY** *UMTV/MCA 9811741*	53		1

WOUT STEENHUIS

Holland, male guitarist, d. 12 Oct 1996 — 7

Date	Title / Label	Peak	Wks at No.1	Wks on Chart
21 Nov 81	**HAWAIIAN PARADISE/CHRISTMAS** *Warwick WW 5106*	28		7

GWEN STEFANI

US, female vocalist. See No Doubt — 90

Date	Title / Label	Peak	Wks at No.1	Wks on Chart
4 Dec 04	**LOVE ANGEL MUSIC BABY** *Interscope 2103177* ⊛x3	4		54
16 Dec 06	**THE SWEET ESCAPE** *Interscope 1717390* ●	14		36

JIM STEINMAN

US, male producer/composer/lyricist — 25

Date	Title / Label	Peak	Wks at No.1	Wks on Chart
9 May 81	**BAD FOR GOOD** *Epic EPC 84361* ○	7		25

MARTIN STEPHENSON & THE DAINTEES

UK, male vocal/instrumental group — 11

Date	Title / Label	Peak	Wks at No.1	Wks on Chart
17 May 86	**BOAT TO BOLIVIA** *Kitchenware KWLP 5*	85		3
16 Apr 88	**GLADSOME, HUMOUR AND BLUE** *Kitchenware KWLP 8*	39		4
19 May 90	**SALUTATION ROAD** *Kitchenware 8281981*	35		3
25 Jul 92	**THE BOY'S HEART** *Kitchenware 8283242*	68		1

STEPPENWOLF

US/Canada, male vocal/instrumental group — 20

Date	Title / Label	Peak	Wks at No.1	Wks on Chart
28 Feb 70	**MONSTER** *Stateside SSL 5021*	43		4
25 Apr 70	**STEPPENWOLF** *Stateside SSL 5020*	59		2
4 Jul 70	**STEPPENWOLF LIVE** *Stateside SSL 5029*	16		14

STEPS

UK, female/male vocal group – Lee Latchford-Evans, Claire Richards (H & Claire*), Lisa Scott-Lee, Faye Tozer & Ian 'H' Watkins (H & Claire*) — 172

Date	Title / Label	Peak	Wks at No.1	Wks on Chart
26 Sep 98	**STEP ONE** *Jive 0519112* ⊛x5	2		62
6 Nov 99	**STEPTACULAR** *Ebul 0519442* ⊛x4	1	4	62
11 Nov 00	**BUZZ** *Ebul 9201172* ⊛x2	4		26
27 Oct 01	**GOLD – THE GREATEST HITS** *Ebul/Jive 9201412* ⊛x4	1	3	21
7 Dec 02	**THE LAST DANCE** *Jive 9201522*	57		1

Top 3 Best-Selling Albums

		Approximate Sales
1	STEP ONE	1,400,000
2	STEPTACULAR	1,290,000
3	GOLD - THE GREATEST HITS	1,100,000

STEREO MC'S

UK/Kenya, male/female vocal/rap group – Cath Coffey, Rob Birch, Nick Hallam & Owen Rossiter — 55

Date	Title / Label	Peak	Wks at No.1	Wks on Chart
17 Oct 92	**CONNECTED** *Fourth & Broadway BRCD 589* ⊛	2		52
9 Jun 01	**DEEP DOWN AND DIRTY** *Island CID 8106* ○	17		3

STEREOLAB

UK/France/Australia, male/female vocal/instrumental group — 11

Date	Title / Label	Peak	Wks at No.1	Wks on Chart
18 Sep 93	**TRANSIENT RANDOM-NOISE BURSTS** *Duophonic Ultra High Frequency DUHFCD 02*	62		1
20 Aug 94	**MARS AUDIAC QUINTET** *Duophonic Ultra High Frequency DUHFCD 05X*	16		3
29 Apr 95	**MUSIC FOR AMORPHOUS BODY STUDY CENTRE** *Duophonic Ultra High Frequency DUHFCD 08*	59		1
16 Sep 95	**REFRIED ECTOPLASM (SWITCHED ON – VOLUME 2)** *Duophonic Ultra High Frequency DUHFCD 09*	30		2
30 Mar 96	**EMPEROR TOMATO KETCHUP** *Duophonic Ultra High Frequency DUHFCD 11*	27		2
4 Oct 97	**DOTS AND LOOPS** *Duophonic Ultra High Frequency DUHFCD 017*	19		2

STEREOPHONICS

UK, male vocal/instrumental group – Kelly Jones, Stuart Cable, Richard Jones & Javier Weyler. Distinctive Welsh band who squeezed five hit singles from each of their first two albums. They amassed five consecutive No.1 studio albums, the first two of which were among the top five best-selling UK albums of the year — 406

Date	Title / Label	Peak	Wks at No.1	Wks on Chart
6 Sep 97	**WORD GETS AROUND** *V2 VVR 1000438* ⊛x2	6		118
20 Mar 99	**PERFORMANCE AND COCKTAILS** *V2 VVR 1004492* ⊛x5	1	1	101
21 Apr 01	**JUST ENOUGH EDUCATION TO PERFORM** *V2 VVR 1015838* ⊛x5	1	5	87
14 Jun 03	**YOU GOTTA GO THERE TO COME BACK** *V2 VVR1021902* ⊛x2	1	1	43
26 Mar 05	**LANGUAGE SEX VIOLENCE OTHER?** *V2 VVR1031058* ⊛	1	1	34
15 Apr 06	**LIVE FROM DAKOTA** *V2 VVR1038098*	13		4
27 Oct 07	**PULL THE PIN** *V2 VVRV1048561*	1	1	12
22 Nov 08	**A DECADE IN THE SUN – BEST OF** *V2 1780699*	2		7+

CAT STEVENS

UK, male vocalist/guitarist (Steven Georgiou/Yusuf Islam) — 290

Date	Title / Label	Peak	Wks at No.1	Wks on Chart
25 Mar 67	**MATTHEW AND SON** *Deram SML 1004*	7		16
11 Jul 70	**MONA BONE JAKON** *Island ILPS 9118*	63		4
28 Nov 70	**TEA FOR THE TILLERMAN** *Island ILPS 9135*	20		39
2 Oct 71	**TEASER AND THE FIRECAT** *Island ILPS 9154* ●	3		93
7 Oct 72	**CATCH BULL AT FOUR** *Island ILPS 9206* ★	2		27
21 Jul 73	**FOREIGNER** *Island ILPS 9240* ●	3		10
6 Apr 74	**BUDDAH AND THE CHOCOLATE BOX** *Island ILPS 9274* ●	3		15
19 Jul 75	**GREATEST HITS** *Island ILPS 9310* ●	2		24
14 May 77	**IZITSO** *Island ILPS 9451* ○	18		15
3 Feb 90	**THE VERY BEST OF CAT STEVENS** *Island CATV 1* ●	4		16
27 Nov 99	**REMEMBER CAT STEVENS – THE ULTIMATE COLLECTION** *Island CID 8079* ●	31		6
25 Oct 03	**THE VERY BEST OF CAT STEVENS** *Universal TV 9811208* ⊛	6		18
25 Nov 06	**ANOTHER CUP** *Polydor 1708478* YUSUF ●	20		7

RACHEL STEVENS

UK, female vocalist. See S Club 7 — 17

Date	Title / Label	Peak	Wks at No.1	Wks on Chart
11 Oct 03	**FUNKY DORY** *19 9865702* ●	9		15
29 Oct 05	**COME AND GET IT** *Polydor 9874712*	28		2

RAY STEVENS

US, male vocalist (Ray Ragsdale) — 8

Date	Title / Label	Peak	Wks at No.1	Wks on Chart
26 Sep 70	**EVERYTHING IS BEAUTIFUL** *CBS 64074*	62		1
13 Sep 75	**MISTY** *Janus 9109 401*	23		7

SHAKIN' STEVENS

UK, male vocalist (Michael Barratt) — 168

Date	Title / Label	Peak	Wks at No.1	Wks on Chart
15 Mar 80	**TAKE ONE!** *Epic EPC 83978*	62		2
4 Apr 81	**THIS OLE HOUSE** *Epic EPC 84985* ●	2		28
8 Aug 81	**SHAKIN' STEVENS** *Hallmark SHM 3065* ●	34		5
19 Sep 81	**SHAKY** *Epic EPC 10027* ⊛	1	1	28
9 Oct 82	**GIVE ME YOUR HEART TONIGHT** *Epic EPC 10035* ⊛	3		18
26 Nov 83	**THE BOP WON'T STOP** *Epic EPC 86301* ●	21		27
17 Nov 84	**SHAKIN' STEVENS GREATEST HITS** *Epic EPC 10047* ⊛	8		22
16 Nov 85	**LIPSTICK POWDER AND PAINT** *Epic EPC 26646* ●	37		9
31 Oct 87	**LET'S BOOGIE** *Epic 4601261*	59		7
19 Nov 88	**A WHOLE LOTTA SHAKY** *Epic MOOD 5*	42		8
20 Oct 90	**THERE'S TWO KINDS OF MUSIC: ROCK 'N' ROLL!** *Telstar STAR 2454*	65		2
31 Oct 92	**THE EPIC YEARS** *Epic 4724222* SHAKY	57		2
23 Apr 05	**THE COLLECTION** *Epic 5198823* ●	4		10

AL STEWART

UK, male vocalist/guitarist — 20

Date	Title / Label	Peak	Wks at No.1	Wks on Chart
11 Apr 70	**ZERO SHE FLIES** *CBS 63848*	40		4
5 Feb 77	**YEAR OF THE CAT** *RCA Victor RS 1082* ●	38		7
21 Oct 78	**TIME PASSAGES** *RCA Victor PL 25173* ○	39		1
6 Sep 80	**24 CARAT** *RCA PL 25306*	55		6
9 Jun 84	**RUSSIANS AND AMERICANS** *RCA PL 70307*	83		2

ANDY STEWART

UK, male vocalist, d. 11 Oct 1993 (age 59) — 2

Date	Title / Label	Peak	Wks at No.1	Wks on Chart
3 Feb 62	**ANDY STEWART** *Top Rank 35116*	13		2

Key: ○ Silver-selling · ● Gold-selling · ⊛ Platinum-selling · ★ US No.1 · Peak Position · Weeks at No.1 · Weeks on Chart

DAVID A STEWART

UK, male guitarist/producer. See Eurythmics, Tourists

Date	Title	Peak Position	Weeks at No.1	Weeks on Chart
				2
7 Apr 90	**LILY WAS HERE (OST)** *AnXious ZL 74233*	35		5
15 Sep 90	**DAVE STEWART AND THE SPIRITUAL COWBOYS** *RCA OB 74710* DAVE STEWART & THE SPIRITUAL COWBOYS	38		2

JERMAINE STEWART

US, male vocalist, d. 17 Mar 1997 (age 39)

Date	Title	Peak Position	Weeks at No.1	Weeks on Chart
				12
4 Oct 86	**FRANTIC ROMANTIC** *10 Records DIX 26*	49		4
5 Mar 88	**SAY IT AGAIN** *Sire SRNLP 14*	32		8

ROD STEWART

UK, male vocalist. The perennially popular gravel-voiced rock superstar is one of the biggest-selling UK album acts ever in the US, with 16 Top 10 singles and 10 Top 5 LPs and has a 33-year span of chart-topping US albums. See Faces

Date	Title	Peak Position	Weeks at No.1	Weeks on Chart
				983
3 Oct 70	**GASOLINE ALLEY** *Vertigo 6360 500*	62		1
24 Jul 71	**EVERY PICTURE TELLS A STORY** *Mercury 6338 063* ★	1	6	81
5 Aug 72	**NEVER A DULL MOMENT** *Philips 6499 153*	1	2	36
25 Aug 73	**SING IT AGAIN ROD** *Mercury 6499 484* ●	1	3	30
26 Jan 74	**OVERTURE AND BEGINNERS** *Mercury 9100 001* & THE FACES	3		7
19 Oct 74	**SMILER** *Mercury 9104 011* ●	1	2	20
30 Aug 75	**ATLANTIC CROSSING** *Warner Brothers K 56151* ⊛	1	7	88
3 Jul 76	**A NIGHT ON THE TOWN** *Riva RVLP 1* ⊛	1	2	47
16 Jul 77	**THE BEST OF ROD STEWART** *Mercury 6643 030* ●	18		22
19 Nov 77	**FOOT LOOSE AND FANCY FREE** *Riva RVLP 5* ⊛	3		26
21 Jan 78	**ATLANTIC CROSSING** *Riva RVLP 4*	60		1
9 Dec 78	**BLONDES HAVE MORE FUN** *Riva RVLP 8* ⊛ ★	3		31
10 Nov 79	**ROD STEWART – GREATEST HITS VOL. 1** *Riva ROD TV 1* ⊛	1	5	74
22 Nov 80	**FOOLISH BEHAVIOUR** *Riva RVLP 11* ⊛	4		13
14 Nov 81	**TONIGHT I'M YOURS** *Riva RVLP 14* ●	8		21
13 Nov 82	**ABSOLUTELY LIVE** *Riva RVLP 17*	35		5
18 Jun 83	**BODY WISHES** *Warner Brothers 9238771* ●	5		27
23 Jun 84	**CAMOUFLAGE** *Warner Brothers 9250951* ○	8		17
5 Jul 86	**EVERY BEAT OF MY HEART** *Warner Brothers WX 53* ●	5		17
4 Jun 88	**OUT OF ORDER** *Warner Brothers WX 152* ●	11		8
25 Nov 89	**THE BEST OF ROD STEWART** *Warner Brothers WX 314* ⊛x5	3		131
6 Apr 91	**VAGABOND HEART** *Warner Brothers WX 408* ⊛	2		27
7 Nov 92	**THE BEST OF ROD STEWART AND THE FACES 1971–1975** *Mercury 5141802* & THE FACES	58		1
6 Mar 93	**ROD STEWART: LEAD VOCALIST** *Warner Brothers 9362452582* ●	3		9
5 Jun 93	**UNPLUGGED...AND SEATED** *Warner Brothers 9362452892* ⊛	2		27
10 Jun 95	**A SPANNER IN THE WORKS** *Warner Brothers 9362458672* ●	4		12
16 Nov 96	**IF WE FALL IN LOVE TONIGHT** *Warner Brothers 9362464672* ⊛	8		30
13 Jun 98	**WHEN WE WERE THE NEW BOYS** *Atlantic 9362467922* ●	2		11
7 Apr 01	**HUMAN** *Atlantic ATL 83411* ●	9		8
24 Nov 01	**THE STORY SO FAR – THE VERY BEST OF** *Warner Brothers 8122735812* ⊛	7		60
9 Nov 02	**IT HAD TO BE YOU – THE GREAT AMERICAN SONGBOOK** *J Records 74321968672* ⊛	8		18
1 Nov 03	**AS TIME GOES BY – THE GREAT AMERICAN SONGBOOK VOLUME 2** *J Records 82876574842* ⊛	4		17
1 Nov 03	**CHANGING FACES – THE VERY BEST OF** *Universal TV 9812604* & THE FACES ●	13		5
30 Oct 04	**STARDUST – THE GREAT AMERICAN SONGBOOK VOLUME III** *J Records 82876659282* ⊛ ★	3		17
12 Nov 05	**THANKS FOR THE MEMORY – THE GREAT AMERICAN SONGBOOK IV** *J Records 82876751902* ⊛	3		9
4 Nov 06	**STILL THE SAME...GREAT ROCK CLASSICS OF OUR TIME** *J 88697022042* ●	4		10
23 Jun 07	**THE SEVENTIES COLLECTION** *Mercury/Universal TV 9848077*	20		2
14 Jul 07	**THE COMPLETE AMERICAN SONGBOOK 1-4** *J 88697124632*	13		11
29 Nov 08	**SOME GUYS HAVE ALL THE LUCK** *Warner Brothers 8122798823*	19		6+

STIFF LITTLE FINGERS

UK, male vocal/instrumental group – Jake Burns, Henry Cluney, Brian Falloon & Ali McMordie

Date	Title	Peak Position	Weeks at No.1	Weeks on Chart
				57
3 Mar 79	**INFLAMMABLE MATERIAL** *Rough Trade ROUGH 1* ●	14		19
15 Mar 80	**NOBODY'S HEROES** *Chrysalis CHR 1270* ○	8		10
20 Sep 80	**HANX** *Chrysalis CHR 1300* ○	9		5
25 Apr 81	**GO FOR IT** *Chrysalis CHX 1339*	14		8
2 Oct 82	**NOW THEN...** *Chrysalis CHR 1400*	24		6
12 Feb 83	**ALL THE BEST** *Chrysalis CTY 1414* ○	19		9

CURTIS STIGERS

US, male vocalist/saxophonist

Date	Title	Peak Position	Weeks at No.1	Weeks on Chart
				53
29 Feb 92	**CURTIS STIGERS** *Arista 261953* ⊛x2	7		50
1 Jul 95	**TIME WAS** *Arista 74321282792*	34		2

Date	Title	Peak Position	Weeks at No.1	Weeks on Chart
29 Apr 06	**THE COLLECTION** *Concord 9878526*	50		1

STILLS

Canada, male vocal/instrumental group

Date	Title	Peak Position	Weeks at No.1	Weeks on Chart
				1
6 Mar 04	**LOGIC WILL BREAK YOUR HEART** *679 Recordings/Vice 7567836742*	66		1

STEPHEN STILLS

US, male vocalist/guitarist. See Crosby, Stills, Nash & Young

Date	Title	Peak Position	Weeks at No.1	Weeks on Chart
				27
19 Dec 70	**STEPHEN STILLS** *Atlantic 2401 004*	8		9
14 Aug 71	**STEPHEN STILLS 2** *Atlantic 2401 013*	22		3
20 May 72	**MANASSAS** *Atlantic K 60021* ' MANASSAS	30		5
19 May 73	**DOWN THE ROAD** *Atlantic K 40440* ' MANASSAS	33		2
26 Jul 75	**STILLS** *CBS 69146*	31		1
29 May 76	**ILLEGAL STILLS** *CBS 81330*	54		2
9 Oct 76	**LONG MAY YOU RUN** *Reprise K 54081* STILLS-YOUNG BAND ○	12		5

STILTSKIN

UK, male vocal/instrumental group

Date	Title	Peak Position	Weeks at No.1	Weeks on Chart
				4
29 Oct 94	**THE MIND'S EYE** *White Water WWD 1*	17		4

STING

UK, male vocalist/bass guitarist (Gordon Sumner). The ex-Police man has amassed eight No.1 albums, two as a solo artist, and sold in excess of 100 million records. *The Very Best Of Sting And The Police*, updated with three new tracks, reached No.1 more than four years after the original album's release. See Police

Date	Title	Peak Position	Weeks at No.1	Weeks on Chart
				391
29 Jun 85	**THE DREAM OF BLUE TURTLES** *A&M DREAM 1* ⊛x2	3		64
28 Jun 86	**BRING ON THE NIGHT** *A&M BRING 1* ○	16		12
24 Oct 87	**NOTHING LIKE THE SUN** *A&M AMA 6402* ⊛	1	1	47
2 Feb 91	**THE SOUL CAGES** *A&M 3964051* ●	1	1	16
13 Mar 93	**TEN SUMMONER'S TALES** *A&M 5400752* ⊛x2	2		60
19 Nov 94	**FIELDS OF GOLD – THE BEST OF STING 1984–1994** *A&M 5403072* ⊛x3	2		41
16 Mar 96	**MERCURY FALLING** *A&M 5404862* ⊛	4		27
22 Nov 97	**THE VERY BEST OF STING AND THE POLICE** *A&M 5404282* & THE POLICE ⊛	1	2	50
9 Oct 99	**BRAND NEW DAY** *A&M 4904512* ⊛	5		44
17 Nov 01	**ALL THIS TIME** *A&M 4931802* ●	3		15
4 Oct 03	**SACRED LOVE** *A&M 9860619* ●	3		11
21 Oct 06	**SONGS FROM THE LABYRINTH** *Deutsche Grammophon 1703139*	24		4

ANGIE STONE

US, female vocalist

Date	Title	Peak Position	Weeks at No.1	Weeks on Chart
				4
11 Mar 00	**BLACK DIAMOND** *Arista 74321727752*	62		3
10 Jul 04	**STONE LOVE** *J 82876597922*	56		1

JOSS STONE

UK, female vocalist (Jocelyn Stoker)

Date	Title	Peak Position	Weeks at No.1	Weeks on Chart
				120
17 Jan 04	**THE SOUL SESSIONS** *Relentless CDREL2* ⊛x3	4		70
9 Oct 04	**MIND BODY & SOUL** *Relentless/Virgin CDREL04* ⊛x3	1	1	46
24 Mar 07	**INTRODUCING** *Relentless/Virgin CDRELX13*	12		4

STONE GODS

UK, male vocal/instrumental group

Date	Title	Peak Position	Weeks at No.1	Weeks on Chart
				1
19 Jul 08	**SILVER SPOONS & BROKEN BONES** *Stone Gods SG0004*	67		1

STONE ROSES

UK, male vocal/instrumental group – Ian Brown*, Andy Couzens, Gary 'Mani' Mounfield, John Squire* & Alan 'Reni' Wren (replaced by Robbie Maddix)

Date	Title	Peak Position	Weeks at No.1	Weeks on Chart
				167
13 May 89	**THE STONE ROSES** *Silvertone ORELP 502* ⊛	9		95
1 Aug 92	**TURNS INTO STONE** *Silvertone ORECD 521*	32		3
17 Dec 94	**SECOND COMING** *Geffen GED 24503* ⊛	4		28
27 May 95	**THE COMPLETE STONE ROSES** *Silvertone ORECD 535* ⊛	4		25
7 Dec 96	**GARAGE FLOWER** *Silvertone GARAGECD 1*	58		1
16 Oct 99	**STONE ROSES – 10TH ANNIVERSARY EDITION** *Silvertone 0591242*	26		3
11 Nov 00	**THE REMIXES** *Silvertone 9260152* ○	41		2
16 Nov 02	**THE VERY BEST OF** *Silvertone 9260382* ●	19		10

STONE SOUR
US, male vocal/instrumental group — 3

Date	Title / Label	Peak	Wks at No.1	Wks
7 Sep 02	**STONE SOUR** *Roadrunner RR 84252* ○	41		1
15 Aug 06	**COME WHAT (EVER) MAY** *Roadrunner RR80732* ○	27		2

STONE TEMPLE PILOTS
US, male vocal/instrumental group – Scott Weiland, Dean & Robert DeLeo & Eric Kretz — 19

Date	Title / Label	Peak	Wks at No.1	Wks
4 Sep 93	**CORE** *Atlantic 7567824182* ○	27		8
18 Jun 94	**PURPLE** *Atlantic 7567826072* ○ ★	10		9
6 Apr 96	**TINY MUSIC...MUSIC FROM THE VATICAN GIFT SHOP** *Atlantic 7567828712*	31		2

STONE THE CROWS
UK, male/female vocal/instrumental group — 3

Date	Title / Label	Peak	Wks at No.1	Wks
7 Oct 72	**CONTINUOUS PERFORMANCE** *Polydor 2391 043*	33		3

IZZY STRADLIN' & THE JU JU HOUNDS
US, male vocalist/guitarist (Jeffrey Isbell). See Guns N' Roses — 1

Date	Title / Label	Peak	Wks at No.1	Wks
24 Oct 92	**IZZY STRADLIN' AND THE JU JU HOUNDS** *Geffen GED 24490*	52		1

STRANGELOVE
UK, male vocal/instrumental group — 3

Date	Title / Label	Peak	Wks at No.1	Wks
13 Aug 94	**TIME FOR THE REST OF YOUR LIFE** *Food FOODCD 11*	69		1
29 Jun 96	**LOVE AND OTHER DEMONS** *Food FOODCD 15*	44		1
18 Oct 97	**STRANGELOVE** *Food FOODCD 24*	67		1

STRANGLERS
UK, male vocal/instrumental group – Hugh Cornwell; members also included Jet Black, Jean-Jacques Burnel, John Ellis, Dave Greenfield, Paul Roberts & Baz Warne — 225

Date	Title / Label	Peak	Wks at No.1	Wks
30 Apr 77	**STRANGLERS IV (RATTUS NORVEGICUS)** *United Artists UAG 30045* ⊛	4		34
8 Oct 77	**NO MORE HEROES** *United Artists UAG 30200* ●	2		19
3 Jun 78	**BLACK AND WHITE** *United Artists UAK 30222* ●	2		18
10 Mar 79	**LIVE (X CERT)** *United Artists UAG 30224* ○	7		10
6 Oct 79	**THE RAVEN** *United Artists UAG 30262* ●	4		8
21 Feb 81	**THEMENINBLACK** *Liberty LBG 30313*	8		5
21 Nov 81	**L.A. FOLIE** *Liberty LBG 30342*	11		18
25 Sep 82	**THE COLLECTION 1977–1982** *Liberty LBS 30353* ○	12		16
22 Jan 83	**FELINE** *Epic EPC 25237* ○	4		11
17 Nov 84	**AURAL SCULPTURE** *Epic EPC 26220* ○	14		10
20 Sep 86	**OFF THE BEATEN TRACK** *Liberty LBG 5001*	80		2
8 Nov 86	**DREAMTIME** *Epic EPC 26648* ○	16		6
20 Feb 88	**ALL LIVE AND ALL OF THE NIGHT** *Epic 4652591* ●	12		6
18 Feb 89	**THE SINGLES – THE UA YEARS** *EMI EM 1314*	57		2
17 Mar 90	**10** *Epic 4664831* ○	15		4
1 Dec 90	**GREATEST HITS 1977–1990** *Epic 4675411* ⊛	4		47
19 Sep 92	**STRANGLERS IN THE NIGHT** *Psycho WOLCD 1030*	33		1
27 May 95	**ABOUT TIME** *When! WENCD 001*	31		1
8 Feb 97	**WRITTEN IN RED** *When! WENCD 009*	52		1
22 Jun 02	**PEACHES – THE VERY BEST OF** *EMI 5402022* ○	21		3
28 Feb 04	**NORFOLK COAST** *Liberty 5969512*	70		1
24 Jun 06	**THE VERY BEST OF** *EMI/Epic 82876862092*	28		2

STRAWBERRY SWITCHBLADE
UK, female vocal duo — 4

Date	Title / Label	Peak	Wks at No.1	Wks
13 Apr 85	**STRAWBERRY SWITCHBLADE** *Korova KODE 11*	25		4

STRAWBS
UK, male vocal/instrumental group – Dave Cousins; members also included Sandy Denny*, John Ford, Tony Hooper, Richard Hudson, Sonja Kristina, Dave Lambert, Rick Wakeman* & Blue Weaver (Derek Weaver) — 31

Date	Title / Label	Peak	Wks at No.1	Wks
21 Nov 70	**JUST A COLLECTION OF ANTIQUES AND CURIOS** *A&M AMLS 994*	27		2
17 Jul 71	**FROM THE WITCHWOOD** *A&M AMLH 64304*	39		2
26 Feb 72	**GRAVE NEW WORLD** *A&M AMLH 68078*	11		12
24 Feb 73	**BUSTING AT THE SEAMS** *A&M AMLH 68144*	2		12
27 Apr 74	**HERO AND HEROINE** *A&M AMLH 63607*	35		3

STRAY CATS
US, male vocal/instrumental group – Brian Setzer, Lee Rocker (Leon Drucher) & Slim Jim Phantom (Jim McDonnell) — 32

Date	Title / Label	Peak	Wks at No.1	Wks
28 Feb 81	**STRAY CATS** *Arista STRAY 1* ●	6		22
21 Nov 81	**GONNA BALL** *Arista STRAY 2* ○	48		4
3 Sep 83	**RANT 'N' RAVE WITH THE STRAY CATS** *Arista STRAY 3*	51		5
8 Apr 89	**BLAST OFF** *EMI MTL 1040*	58		1

STREETS
UK, rapper/producer (Mike Skinner) — 115

Date	Title / Label	Peak	Wks at No.1	Wks
6 Apr 02	**ORIGINAL PIRATE MATERIAL** *Locked On/679 Recordings 0927435682* ⊛	10		57
22 May 04	**A GRAND DON'T COME FOR FREE** *Locked On/679 Recordings 2564615342* ⊛x3	1	2	42
22 Apr 06	**THE HARDEST WAY TO MAKE AN EASY LIVING** *Locked On/679 Recordings 2564632302* ●	1	1	11
27 Sep 08	**EVERYTHING IS BORROWED** *679 Recordings 2564693760* ○	7		4
27 Sep 08	**A GRAND DON'T COME FOR FREE/ORIGINAL PIRATE MATERIAL** *Rhino 2564694597*	68		1

STREETWALKERS
UK, male vocal/instrumental group — 6

Date	Title / Label	Peak	Wks at No.1	Wks
12 Jun 76	**RED CARD** *Vertigo 9102 010*	16		6

BARBRA STREISAND
US, female vocalist. Brooklyn-born balladeer who has amassed more gold albums than any other female artist. This award-winning singer/actress scored three transatlantic chart-toppers in three years and has an impressive 25-year span of UK No.1 albums — 578

Date	Title / Label	Peak	Wks at No.1	Wks
22 Jan 66	**MY NAME IS BARBRA, TWO** *CBS BPG 62603*	6		22
30 Apr 66	**FUNNY GIRL** *Capitol W 2059*	19		3
10 May 69	**FUNNY GIRL (OST)** *CBS 70044*	11		22
14 Mar 70	**HELLO DOLLY! (OST)** *EMI Stateside SSL 10292*	45		2
4 Apr 70	**BARBRA STREISAND'S GREATEST HITS** *CBS 63921*	44		2
17 Apr 71	**STONEY END** *CBS 64269*	28		2
15 Jun 74	**THE WAY WE WERE** *CBS 69057* ○ ★	49		1
9 Apr 77	**A STAR IS BORN (OST)** *CBS 86021* ⊛ ★	1	2	54
23 Jul 77	**STREISAND SUPERMAN** *CBS 86030*	32		9
15 Jul 78	**SONGBIRD** *CBS 86060* ○	50		2
17 Mar 79	**BARBRA STREISAND GREATEST HITS VOLUME 2** *CBS 10012* ⊛ ★	1	4	30
17 Nov 79	**WET** *CBS 86104* ●	25		13
11 Oct 80	**GUILTY** *CBS 86122* ⊛ ★	1	2	82
16 Jan 82	**LOVE SONGS** *CBS 10031* ⊛	1	9	129
19 Nov 83	**YENTL (OST)** *CBS 86302* ●	21		35
27 Oct 84	**EMOTION** *CBS 86309* ●	15		12
18 Jan 86	**THE BROADWAY ALBUM** *CBS 86322* ● ★	3		16
30 May 87	**ONE VOICE** *CBS 4508901* ○	27		7
3 Dec 88	**TILL I LOVED YOU** *CBS 4629431* ●	29		13
25 Nov 89	**A COLLECTION – GREATEST HITS...AND MORE** *CBS 4658451* ●	22		23
10 Jul 93	**BACK TO BROADWAY** *Columbia 4738802* ● ★	4		17
29 Oct 94	**BARBRA – THE CONCERT** *Columbia 4775992*	63		1
22 Nov 97	**HIGHER GROUND** *Columbia 4885322* ● ★	12		12
2 Oct 99	**A LOVE LIKE OURS** *Columbia 4949342*	12		9
30 Sep 00	**TIMELESS – LIVE IN CONCERT** *Columbia 4974352*	54		1
9 Mar 02	**THE ESSENTIAL** *Columbia 5062572* ⊛	1	1	29
30 Nov 02	**DUETS** *Columbia 5098129* ●	30		6
8 Nov 03	**THE MOVIE ALBUM** *Columbia 5134213*	25		3
1 Oct 05	**GUILTY TOO** *Columbia 82876732612* ⊛	3		17
21 Jul 07	**LIVE IN CONCERT 2006** *Columbia SNY7019222*	25		4

STRICTLY COME DANCING BAND
UK, male/female vocal/instrumental ensemble — 5

Date	Title / Label	Peak	Wks at No.1	Wks
1 Nov 08	**STRICTLY COME DANCING** *Universal TV 1784446*	48		5

STRINGS FOR PLEASURE
UK, orchestra — 1

Date	Title / Label	Peak	Wks at No.1	Wks
4 Dec 71	**THE BEST OF BACHARACH** *MFP 1334*	49		1

STROKES
US, male vocal/instrumental group – Julian Casablancas, Nikolai Fraiture, Albert Hammond Jr.*, Fab Moretti & Nick Valensi — 69

Date	Title / Label	Peak	Wks at No.1	Wks
8 Sep 01	**IS THIS IT** *Rough Trade RTRADECD 030* ⊛	2		40
1 Nov 03	**ROOM ON FIRE** *Rough Trade RTRADECD 130* ⊛	2		20
14 Jan 06	**FIRST IMPRESSIONS OF EARTH** *Rough Trade RTRADCDX330* ●	1	1	9

Silver-selling ○ Gold-selling ● Platinum-selling ⊛ US No.1 ★ | Peak Position | Weeks at No.1 | Weeks on Chart

JOE STRUMMER

UK (b. Turkey), male vocalist (John Mellor), d. 23 Dec 2002 (age 50). See Clash

Date	Title	Peak Position	Weeks at No.1	Weeks on Chart
				4
14 Oct 89	**EARTHQUAKE WEATHER** *Epic 4653471*	58		1
30 Oct 99	**ROCK ART AND THE X-RAY STYLE** *Mercury 5466542* & THE MESCALEROS	71		1
28 Jul 01	**GLOBAL A GO GO** *Hellcat 04402* & THE MESCALEROS	68		1
1 Nov 03	**STREETCORE** *Hellcat 04542* & THE MESCALEROS	50		1

AMY STUDT

UK, female vocalist

Date	Title	Peak Position	Weeks at No.1	Weeks on Chart
				11
12 Jul 03	**FALSE SMILES** *Polydor 9801074* ●	18		11

STYLE COUNCIL

UK, male/female vocal/instrumental group – Paul Weller*, Dee C. Lee, Mick Talbot & Steve White

Date	Title	Peak Position	Weeks at No.1	Weeks on Chart
				100
24 Mar 84	**CAFÉ BLEU** *Polydor TSCLP 1* ●	2		38
8 Jun 85	**OUR FAVOURITE SHOP** *Polydor TSCLP 2* ●	1	1	22
17 May 86	**HOME AND ABROAD** *Polydor TSCLP 3* ○	8		8
14 Feb 87	**THE COST OF LOVING** *Polydor TSCLP 4* ●	2		7
2 Jul 88	**CONFESSIONS OF A POP GROUP** *Polydor TSCMC 5* ○	15		3
18 Mar 89	**THE SINGULAR ADVENTURES OF THE STYLE COUNCIL GREATEST HITS VOLUME 1** *Polydor TSCTV 1* ●	3		15
10 Jul 93	**HERE'S SOME THAT GOT AWAY** *Polydor 5193722*	39		1
2 Mar 96	**THE STYLE COUNCIL COLLECTION** *Polydor 5294832*	60		1
2 Sep 00	**GREATEST HITS** *Polydor 5579002*	28		5

DARREN STYLES

UK, male producer (Darren Mew)

Date	Title	Peak Position	Weeks at No.1	Weeks on Chart
				11
28 Jun 08	**SKYDIVIN'** *AATW 1774381* ●	4		11

STYLISTICS

US, male vocal group – Russell Thompkins Jr., James Dunn, Airrion Love, Herbie Murrell & James Smith

Date	Title	Peak Position	Weeks at No.1	Weeks on Chart
				151
24 Aug 74	**ROCKIN' ROLL BABY** *Avco 6466 012* ○	42		3
21 Sep 74	**LET'S PUT IT ALL TOGETHER** *Avco 6466 013* ○	26		14
1 Mar 75	**FROM THE MOUNTAIN** *Avco 9109 002* ○	36		1
5 Apr 75	**THE BEST OF THE STYLISTICS** *Avco 9109 003* ⊛	1	9	63
5 Jul 75	**THANK YOU BABY** *Avco 9109 005* ●	5		23
6 Dec 75	**YOU ARE BEAUTIFUL** *Avco 9109 006* ○	26		9
12 Jun 76	**FABULOUS** *H&L 9109 008* ○	21		5
18 Sep 76	**BEST OF THE STYLISTICS VOLUME 2** *H&L 9109 010* ●	1	1	21
17 Oct 92	**THE GREATEST HITS OF THE STYLISTICS** *Mercury 5129852*	34		3
3 Nov 07	**THE VERY BEST OF** *UMTV 5303961*	30		9

STYX

US, male vocal/instrumental group – Dennis DeYoung, Chuck Panozzo, John Panozzo, d. 16 Jul 1996, Tommy Shaw & James Young

Date	Title	Peak Position	Weeks at No.1	Weeks on Chart
				24
3 Nov 79	**CORNERSTONE** *A&M AMLK 63711*	36		8
24 Jan 81	**PARADISE THEATER** *A&M AMLH 63719* ○ ★	8		8
12 Mar 83	**KILROY WAS HERE** *A&M AMLX 63734*	67		6
5 May 84	**CAUGHT IN THE ACT** *A&M AMLM 66704*	44		2

SUBWAYS

UK, male/female vocal/instrumental group

Date	Title	Peak Position	Weeks at No.1	Weeks on Chart
				10
16 Jul 05	**YOUNG FOR ETERNITY** *WEA 2564624842* ●	32		8
12 Jul 08	**ALL OR NOTHING** *Infectious 2564695248*	17		2

SUEDE

UK, male vocal/instrumental group – Brett Anderson*, Bernard Butler* (replaced by Richard Oakes), Neil Codling, Simon Gilbert & Mat Osman

Date	Title	Peak Position	Weeks at No.1	Weeks on Chart
				105
10 Apr 93	**SUEDE** *Nude 1CD* ●	1	1	22
22 Oct 94	**DOG MAN STAR** *Nude 4778112* ●	3		16
14 Sep 96	**COMING UP** *Nude 6CD* ⊛	1	1	44
18 Oct 97	**SCI-FI LULLABIES** *Nude 9CD*	9		3
15 May 99	**HEAD MUSIC** *Nude 14CD* ●	1	1	16
12 Oct 02	**A NEW MORNING** *Epic 5089569*	24		2
1 Nov 03	**SINGLES** *Sony Music 5136042*	31		2

SUGABABES

UK, female vocal group – Keisha Buchanan, Mutya Buena (replaced by Amelle Berrabah) & Siobhan Donaghy (replaced by Heidi Range)

Date	Title	Peak Position	Weeks at No.1	Weeks on Chart
				195
23 Dec 00	**ONE TOUCH** *London 8573861072* ●	26		15
7 Sep 02	**ANGELS WITH DIRTY FACES** *Island CID 8122* ⊛x3	2		40
8 Nov 03	**THREE** *Island CID 8137* ⊛x2	3		39
22 Oct 05	**TALLER IN MORE WAYS** *Island CID8162* ⊛x3	1	1	34
25 Nov 06	**OVERLOADED – THE SINGLES COLLECTION** *Island 1709334* ⊛	3		25
20 Oct 07	**CHANGE** *Island 1747641* ⊛	1	1	36
1 Nov 08	**CATFIGHTS AND SPOTLIGHTS** *Island 1787209* ●	8		6

SUGAR

US, male vocal/instrumental group – Bob Mould*, David Barbe & Malcolm Travis

Date	Title	Peak Position	Weeks at No.1	Weeks on Chart
				19
19 Sep 92	**COPPER BLUE** *Creation CRECD 129* ○	10		11
17 Apr 93	**BEASTER** *Creation CRECD 153*	3		5
17 Sep 94	**FILE UNDER EASY LISTENING** *Creation CRECD 172*	7		3

SUGAR RAY

US, male vocal/instrumental group

Date	Title	Peak Position	Weeks at No.1	Weeks on Chart
				1
19 Jun 99	**0.62430555556** *Atlantic 7567831512*	60		1

SUGARCUBES

Iceland, male/female vocal/instrumental group

Date	Title	Peak Position	Weeks at No.1	Weeks on Chart
				14
7 May 88	**LIFE'S TOO GOOD** *One Little Indian TPLP 5*	14		6
14 Oct 89	**HERE TODAY, TOMORROW NEXT WEEK!** *One Little Indian TPLP 15*	15		3
22 Feb 92	**STICK AROUND FOR JOY** *One Little Indian TPLP 30CD*	16		4
17 Oct 92	**IT'S IT** *One Little Indian TPLP 40CD*	47		1

SUGGS

UK, male vocalist (Graham McPherson). See Madness

Date	Title	Peak Position	Weeks at No.1	Weeks on Chart
				5
28 Oct 95	**THE LONE RANGER** *WEA 0630124782* ○	14		5

SUICIDAL TENDENCIES

US, male vocal/instrumental group

Date	Title	Peak Position	Weeks at No.1	Weeks on Chart
				2
9 May 87	**JOIN THE ARMY** *Virgin V 2424*	81		1
21 Jul 90	**LIGHTS...CAMERA...REVOLUTION** *Epic 4665691*	59		1

SULTANS OF PING F.C.

Ireland, male vocal/instrumental group

Date	Title	Peak Position	Weeks at No.1	Weeks on Chart
				3
13 Feb 93	**CASUAL SEX IN THE CINEPLEX** *Rhythm King 4724952*	26		2
5 Mar 94	**TEENAGE DRUG** *Epic 4747162* SULTANS OF PING	57		1

SUM 41

Canada, male vocal/instrumental group – Deryck Whibley, Dave Baksh, Steve Jocz & Jason McCaslin

Date	Title	Peak Position	Weeks at No.1	Weeks on Chart
				51
11 Aug 01	**ALL KILLER NO FILLER** *Island 5486622* ⊛	7		43
7 Dec 02	**DOES THIS LOOK INFECTED** *Mercury 0635590* ○	39		6
23 Oct 04	**CHUCK** *Mercury 9864426*	59		1
4 Aug 07	**UNDERCLASS HERO** *Mercury 1741781*	46		1

DONNA SUMMER

US, female vocalist (Ladonna Gaines)

Date	Title	Peak Position	Weeks at No.1	Weeks on Chart
				204
31 Jan 76	**LOVE TO LOVE YOU BABY** *GTO GTLP 008* ●	16		9
22 May 76	**A LOVE TRILOGY** *GTO GTLP 010* ●	41		10
25 Jun 77	**I REMEMBER YESTERDAY** *GTO GTLP 025* ●	3		23
26 Nov 77	**ONCE UPON A TIME** *Casablanca CALD 5003* ●	24		13
7 Jan 78	**GREATEST HITS** *GTO GTLP 028* ●	4		18
21 Oct 78	**LIVE AND MORE** *Casablanca CALD 5006* ● ★	16		16
2 Jun 79	**BAD GIRLS** *Casablanca CALD 5007* ○ ★	23		23
10 Nov 79	**ON THE RADIO – GREATEST HITS VOLUME 1 & 2** *Casablanca CALD 5008* ● ★	24		22
1 Nov 80	**THE WANDERER** *Geffen K 99124*	55		2
31 Jul 82	**DONNA SUMMER** *Warner Brothers K 99163*	13		16
16 Jul 83	**SHE WORKS HARD FOR THE MONEY** *Mercury MERL 21*	28		5
15 Sep 84	**CATS WITHOUT CLAWS** *Warner Brothers 250806*	69		2
25 Mar 89	**ANOTHER PLACE AND TIME** *Warner Brothers WX 219* ●	17		28
24 Nov 90	**THE BEST OF DONNA SUMMER** *Warner Brothers WX 397* ●	24		9
26 Nov 94	**ENDLESS SUMMER – GREATEST HITS** *Mercury 5262172*	37		2
26 Jun 04	**THE JOURNEY – THE VERY BEST OF** *Mercury 9862858* ●	6		6

SUNDAYS

UK, female/male vocal/instrumental group – Harriet Wheeler, Paul Brindley, David Gavurin & Patrick Hannan — 15

Date	Title / Label	Peak Position	Weeks at No.1	Weeks on Chart
27 Jan 90	**READING WRITING AND ARITHMETIC** *Rough Trade ROUGH 148* ○	4		8
31 Oct 92	**BLIND** *Parlophone CDPCSD 121*	15		3
4 Oct 97	**STATIC & SILENCE** *Parlophone CDEST 2300* ○	10		4

SUNSCREEM

UK, male vocal/instrumental group — 6

Date	Title / Label	Peak Position	Weeks at No.1	Weeks on Chart
13 Feb 93	**O3** *Sony S2 4722182*	33		5
30 Mar 96	**CHANGE OR DIE** *Sony S2 4813132*	53		1

SUNSHINE UNDERGROUND

UK, male vocal/instrumental group — 1

Date	Title / Label	Peak Position	Weeks at No.1	Weeks on Chart
9 Sep 06	**RAISE THE ALARM** *City Rockers CITYROCK10CD*	66		1

SUPER FURRY ANIMALS

UK, male vocal/instrumental group – Gruff Rhys*, Huw Bunford, Cian Ciaran, Dafydd Ieuan & Guto Pryce — 38

Date	Title / Label	Peak Position	Weeks at No.1	Weeks on Chart
1 Jun 96	**FUZZY LOGIC** *Creation CRECD 190*	23		6
6 Sep 97	**RADIATOR** *Creation CRECD 214*	8		3
5 Dec 98	**OUT SPACED** *Creation CRECD 229*	44		1
26 Jun 99	**GUERRILLA** *Creation CRECD 242*	10		9
27 May 00	**MWNG** *Placid Casual PLC 03CD*	11		2
4 Aug 01	**RINGS AROUND THE WORLD** *Epic 5024132* ●	3		7
2 Aug 03	**PHANTOM POWER** *Epic 5123759* ○	4		4
16 Oct 04	**SONGBOOK – THE SINGLES VOLUME 1** *Epic 5176719*	18		2
3 Sep 05	**LOVE KRAFT** *Epic 5205016*	19		2
8 Sep 07	**HEY VENUS** *Rough Trade RTRADCD346*	11		2

SUPERGRASS

UK, male vocal/instrumental group – Gaz Coombes, Bob Coombes, Danny Goffey & Mick Quinn — 111

Date	Title / Label	Peak Position	Weeks at No.1	Weeks on Chart
27 May 95	**I SHOULD COCO** *Parlophone CDPCS 7373* ⊛	1	3	36
3 May 97	**IN IT FOR THE MONEY** *Parlophone CDPCS 7388* ⊛	2		25
2 Oct 99	**SUPERGRASS** *Parlophone 5220562* ⊛	3		25
12 Oct 02	**LIFE ON OTHER PLANETS** *Parlophone 5418002* ●	9		6
19 Jun 04	**SUPERGRASS IS 10 – THE BEST OF 94-04** *Parlophone 5708602* ●	4		13
27 Aug 05	**ROAD TO ROUEN** *Parlophone 3333342* ○	9		4
5 Apr 08	**DIAMOND HOO HA** *Parlophone 5197341*	19		2

SUPERNATURALS

UK, male vocal/instrumental group — 7

Date	Title / Label	Peak Position	Weeks at No.1	Weeks on Chart
17 May 97	**IT DOESN'T MATTER ANYMORE** *Food FOODCD 21*	9		4
22 Aug 98	**A TUNE A DAY** *Food 4995762*	21		3

SUPERTRAMP

US/UK, male vocal/instrumental group – Roger Hodgson*, Rick Davies, John Helliwell, Bob Siebenberg & Dougie Thomson — 196

Date	Title / Label	Peak Position	Weeks at No.1	Weeks on Chart
23 Nov 74	**CRIME OF THE CENTURY** *A&M AMLS 68258* ●	4		22
6 Dec 75	**CRISIS? WHAT CRISIS?** *A&M AMLH 68347*	20		15
23 Apr 77	**EVEN IN THE QUIETEST MOMENTS...** *A&M AMLK 64634* ○	12		22
31 Mar 79	**BREAKFAST IN AMERICA** *A&M AMLK 63708* ⊛ ★	3		53
4 Oct 80	**PARIS** *A&M AMLM 66702* ●	7		17
6 Nov 82	**...FAMOUS LAST WORDS...'** *A&M AMLK 63732* ●	6		16
25 May 85	**BROTHER WHERE YOU BOUND** *A&M AMA 5014*	20		5
18 Oct 86	**THE AUTOBIOGRAPHY OF SUPERTRAMP** *A&M TRAMP 1* ⊛	9		19
31 Oct 87	**FREE AS A BIRD** *A&M AMA 5181*	93		1
15 Aug 92	**THE VERY BEST OF SUPERTRAMP** *A&M TRACD 1992*	24		4
3 May 97	**SOME THINGS NEVER CHANGE** *EMI CDCHR 6121*	74		1
27 Sep 97	**THE VERY BEST OF SUPERTRAMP** *Polygram TV 3970912* ●	8		6
5 Nov 05	**RETROSPECTACLE** *A&M 9886928* ⊛	9		15

SUPREMES

US, female vocal trio – Diana Ross*, Florence Ballard, d. 22 Feb 1976, & Mary Wilson — 246

Date	Title / Label	Peak Position	Weeks at No.1	Weeks on Chart
5 Dec 64	**MEET THE SUPREMES** *Stateside SL 10109*	8		6
17 Dec 66	**SUPREMES A GO-GO** *Tamla Motown STML 11039* ★	15		21
13 May 67	**THE SUPREMES SING MOTOWN** *Tamla Motown STML 11047*	15		16
30 Sep 67	**THE SUPREMES SING RODGERS AND HART** *Tamla Motown STML 11054*	25		7
20 Jan 68	**DIANA ROSS AND THE SUPREMES GREATEST HITS** *Tamla Motown STML 11063* DIANA ROSS & THE SUPREMES ★	1	3	60
30 Mar 68	**LIVE' AT LONDON'S TALK OF THE TOWN** *Tamla Motown STML 11070* DIANA ROSS & THE SUPREMES	6		18
20 Jul 68	**REFLECTIONS** *Tamla Motown STML 11073* DIANA ROSS & THE SUPREMES	30		2
25 Jan 69	**DIANA ROSS AND THE SUPREMES JOIN THE TEMPTATIONS** *Tamla Motown STML 11096* DIANA ROSS & THE SUPREMES & THE TEMPTATIONS	1	4	15
1 Feb 69	**LOVE CHILD** *Tamla Motown STML 11095* DIANA ROSS & THE SUPREMES	8		6
28 Jun 69	**THE ORIGINAL SOUNDTRACK FROM TCB (OST-TV)** *Tamla Motown STML 11110* DIANA ROSS & THE SUPREMES & THE TEMPTATIONS ★	11		12
14 Feb 70	**TOGETHER** *Tamla Motown STML 11122* DIANA ROSS & THE SUPREMES & THE TEMPTATIONS	28		4
14 Feb 70	**CREAM OF THE CROP** *Tamla Motown STML 11137* DIANA ROSS & THE SUPREMES	34		4
23 May 70	**GREATEST HITS VOLUME II** *Tamla Motown STML 11146* DIANA ROSS & THE SUPREMES	29		4
29 May 71	**THE MAGNIFICENT SEVEN** *Tamla Motown STML 11179* & THE FOUR TOPS	6		11
25 Sep 71	**TOUCH** *Tamla Motown STML 11189*	40		1
17 Sep 77	**DIANA ROSS AND THE SUPREMES 20 GOLDEN GREATS** *Motown EMTV 5* DIANA ROSS & THE SUPREMES	1	7	34
21 Jan 89	**LOVE SUPREME** *Motown ZL 72701* DIANA ROSS & THE SUPREMES ○	10		9
31 Oct 98	**40 GOLDEN MOTOWN GREATS** *Motown 5309612* DIANA ROSS & THE SUPREMES	35		4
29 May 04	**THE NO 1'S** *Motown 9818019* DIANA ROSS & THE SUPREMES	15		12

SURVIVOR

US, male vocal/instrumental group — 10

Date	Title / Label	Peak Position	Weeks at No.1	Weeks on Chart
21 Aug 82	**EYE OF THE TIGER** *Scotti Brothers SCT 85845*	12		10

SUTHERLAND BROTHERS & QUIVER

UK, male vocal/instrumental group — 11

Date	Title / Label	Peak Position	Weeks at No.1	Weeks on Chart
15 May 76	**REACH FOR THE SKY** *CBS 69191* ○	26		8
9 Oct 76	**SLIPSTREAM** *CBS 81593* ○	49		3

SWANS WAY

UK, male/female vocal/instrumental group — 1

Date	Title / Label	Peak Position	Weeks at No.1	Weeks on Chart
3 Nov 84	**THE FUGITIVE KIND** *Balgier SWAN 1*	88		1

SWAY

UK, male rapper (Derek Safo) — 2

Date	Title / Label	Peak Position	Weeks at No.1	Weeks on Chart
18 Feb 06	**THIS IS MY DEMO** *All City ACM1005LTD*	45		1
18 Oct 08	**THE SIGNATURE LP** *Dcypha Productions DCY011CD*	51		1

KEITH SWEAT

US, male vocalist — 32

Date	Title / Label	Peak Position	Weeks at No.1	Weeks on Chart
29 Oct 88	**MAKE IT LAST FOREVER** *Elektra 9607631* ○	41		21
23 Jun 90	**I'LL GIVE ALL MY LOVE TO YOU** *Vintertainment EKT 60*	47		4
9 Jul 94	**GET UP ON IT** *Elektra 7559615502*	20		4
29 Jun 96	**KEITH SWEAT** *Elektra 7559617072*	36		2
3 Oct 98	**STILL IN THE GAME** *Elektra 7559622622*	62		1

CLAIRE SWEENEY

UK, female actor/vocalist — 3

Date	Title / Label	Peak Position	Weeks at No.1	Weeks on Chart
27 Jul 02	**CLAIRE** *T2 TCD 3254*	15		3

SWEET

UK, male vocal/instrumental group — 15

Date	Title / Label	Peak Position	Weeks at No.1	Weeks on Chart
18 May 74	**SWEET FANNY ADAMS** *RCA Victor LPI 5038* ●	27		2
22 Sep 84	**SWEET SIXTEEN – IT'S IT'S...SWEET HITS** *Anagram GRAM 16*	49		6
20 Jan 96	**BALLROOM HITZ – THE VERY BEST OF SWEET** *Polygram TV 5350012*	15		6
29 Jan 05	**THE VERY BEST OF** *BMG 82876668172*	72		1

SWERVEDRIVER

UK, male vocal/instrumental group — 2

Date	Title / Label	Peak Position	Weeks at No.1	Weeks on Chart
12 Oct 91	**RAISE** *Creation CRELP 093*	44		1
9 Oct 93	**MEZCAL HEAD** *Creation CCRE 143*	55		1

Silver-selling ○ Gold-selling ● Platinum-selling ⊛ US No.1 ★ Peak Position Weeks at No.1 Weeks on Chart

SWING OUT SISTER
UK, female/male vocal/instrumental group – Corinne Drewery, Andy Connell & Martin Jackson

Date	Title	Peak	Wks No.1	36
23 May 87	**IT'S BETTER TO TRAVEL** *Mercury OUTLP 1* ⊛	1	2	21
20 May 89	**KALEIDOSCOPE WORLD** *Fontana 8382931* ●	9		11
16 May 92	**GET IN TOUCH WITH YOURSELF** *Fontana 5122412*	27		4

SWINGLE SINGERS
US/France, male/female vocal group

Date	Title	Peak	Wks No.1	18
1 Feb 64	**JAZZ SEBASTIAN BACH** *Philips BL 7572*	13		18

SWITCHES
UK, male vocal/instrumental group

Date	Title	Peak	Wks No.1	1
5 May 07	**HEART TUNED TO DEAD** *Atlantic 505144200782*	64		1

SWV
US, female vocal group

Date	Title	Peak	Wks No.1	27
17 Jul 93	**IT'S ABOUT TIME** *RCA 7863660742*	17		17
4 May 96	**NEW BEGINNING** *RCA 07863664872*	26		5
16 Aug 97	**RELEASE SOME TENSION** *RCA 74321496162*	19		5

SYBIL
US, female vocalist (Sybil Lynch)

Date	Title	Peak	Wks No.1	12
5 Sep 87	**LET YOURSELF GO** *Champion CHAMP 1009*	92		1
24 Feb 90	**WALK ON BY** *PWL HF 10*	21		5
12 Jun 93	**GOOD 'N' READY** *PWL International HFCD 28*	13		6

SYLVESTER
US, male vocalist (Sylvester James), d. 16 Dec 1988 (age 41)

Date	Title	Peak	Wks No.1	3
23 Jun 79	**MIGHTY REAL** *Fantasy FTA 3009*	62		3

DAVID SYLVIAN
UK, male vocalist (David Batt). See Japan

Date	Title	Peak	Wks No.1	27
7 Jul 84	**BRILLIANT TREES** *Virgin V 2290* ●	4		14
13 Sep 86	**GONE TO EARTH** *Virgin VDL 1* ○	24		5
7 Nov 87	**SECRETS OF THE BEEHIVE** *Virgin V 2471*	37		2
2 Apr 88	**PLIGHT AND PREMONITION** *Virgin VE 11* & HOLGAR CZUKAY	71		1
17 Jul 93	**THE FIRST DAY** *Virgin CDVX 2712* & ROBERT FRIPP	21		2
10 Apr 99	**DEAD BEES ON A CAKE** *Virgin CDV 2876*	31		2
21 Oct 00	**EVERYTHING & NOTHING** *Virgin CDVDX 2897*	57		1

SYMPHONIQUE
UK, male keyboard player (David Cozens). See Project D

Date	Title	Peak	Wks No.1	4
1 Apr 95	**MOODS SYMPHONIQUE 95** *Vision VISCD 10*	21		4

SYMPOSIUM
UK, male vocal/instrumental group

Date	Title	Peak	Wks No.1	3
8 Nov 97	**ONE DAY AT A TIME** *Infectious INFECT 49CD*	29		2
30 May 98	**ON THE OUTSIDE** *Infectious INFECT 056CD*	32		1

SYNTHPHONIC VARIATIONS
UK, male instrumental group

Date	Title	Peak	Wks No.1	1
1 Nov 86	**SEASONS** *CBS 4501491*	84		1

SYSTEM OF A DOWN
US, male vocal/instrumental group – Serj Tankian*, John Dolmayan, Daron Malakian & Shavo Odadjian

Date	Title	Peak	Wks No.1	41
8 Sep 01	**TOXICITY** *Columbia 5015346* ● ★	13		27
7 Dec 02	**STEAL THIS ALBUM** *American Recordings 5102489*	56		1
28 May 05	**MEZMERIZE** *American/Columbia 5190002* ★	2		8
3 Dec 05	**HYPNOTIZE** *American/Columbia 82876726122* ★	11		5

SYSTEM 7
UK/France, male/female instrumental duo

Date	Title	Peak	Wks No.1	3
20 Jun 92	**ALTITUDE** *10 Records TENG 403*	75		1
20 Mar 93	**777** *Wau BFLCD 1*	30		2

T

JAMIE T
UK, male vocalist/guitarist (Jamie Treays)

Date	Title	Peak	Wks No.1	13
10 Feb 07	**PANIC PREVENTION** *Virgin CDVX3023* ●	4		13

T. REX
UK, male vocal/instrumental group – Marc Bolan*, d. 16 Sep 1977, Steve Currie, d. 28 Apr 1981, Mickey Finn, d. 11 Jan 2003, Bill Legend & Steve Peregrine Took, d. 27 Oct 1980

Date	Title	Peak	Wks No.1	237
13 Jul 68	**MY PEOPLE WERE FAIR AND HAD SKY IN THEIR HAIR BUT NOW THEY'RE CONTENT TO WEAR STARS ON THEIR BROWS** *Regal Zonophone SLRZ 1003* TYRANNOSAURUS REX	15		9
7 Jun 69	**UNICORN** *Regal Zonophone S 1007* TYRANNOSAURUS REX	12		3
14 Mar 70	**A BEARD OF STARS** *Regal Zonophone SLRZ 1013* TYRANNOSAURUS REX	21		6
16 Jan 71	**T. REX** *Fly HIFLY 2*	7		25
27 Mar 71	**THE BEST OF T. REX** *Flyback TON 2*	21		8
9 Oct 71	**ELECTRIC WARRIOR** *Fly HIFLY 6*	1	8	44
29 Apr 72	**PROPHETS, SEERS AND SAGES THE ANGELS OF THE AGES/MY PEOPLE WERE FAIR AND HAD SKY IN THEIR HAIR BUT NOW THEY'RE CONTENT TO WEAR STARS ON THEIR BROWS** *Fly Double Back TOOFA 3/4* TYRANNOSAURUS REX	1	1	12
20 May 72	**BOLAN BOOGIE** *Fly HIFLY 8*	1	3	19
5 Aug 72	**THE SLIDER** *EMI BLN 5001*	4		18
9 Dec 72	**A BEARD OF STARS/UNICORN** *Cube TOOFA 9/10*	44		2
31 Mar 73	**TANX** *EMI BLN 5002*	4		12
10 Nov 73	**GREAT HITS** *EMI BLN 5003*	32		3
16 Mar 74	**ZINC ALLOY AND THE HIDDEN RIDERS OF TOMORROW** *EMI BLNA 7751* MARC BOLAN & T. REX	12		3
21 Feb 76	**FUTURISTIC DRAGON** *EMI BLN 5004*	50		1
9 Apr 77	**DANDY IN THE UNDERWORLD** *EMI BLN 5005*	26		3
30 Jun 79	**SOLID GOLD** *EMI NUT 5*	51		3
12 Sep 81	**T. REX IN CONCERT** *Marc ABOLAN 1*	35		6
7 Nov 81	**YOU SCARE ME TO DEATH** *Cherry Red ERED 20* MARC BOLAN	88		1
24 Sep 83	**DANCE IN THE MIDNIGHT** *Marc On Wax MARCL 501* MARC BOLAN	83		3
4 May 85	**BEST OF THE 20TH CENTURY BOY** *K-Tel NE 1297* MARC BOLAN & T. REX ●	5		21
28 Sep 91	**THE ULTIMATE COLLECTION** *Telstar TCD 2539* MARC BOLAN & T. REX ●	4		16
7 Oct 95	**THE ESSENTIAL COLLECTION** *Polygram TV 5259612* MARC BOLAN & T. REX	24		6
28 Sep 02	**THE ESSENTIAL COLLECTION** *Universal TV 4934882* MARC BOLAN & T. REX	18		8
22 Sep 07	**GREATEST HITS** *Universal TV 5303043* MARC BOLAN & T. REX ○	15		5

TAKE THAT
UK, male vocal group – Gary Barlow*, Howard Donald, Jason Orange, Mark Owen* & Robbie Williams* (left 1995). Boy band comeback kings who sold nine million albums before their headline-making split in 1996. Since 2006, *Beautiful World* has sold 2.5 million copies in the UK and *The Circus* became the second best-seller of 2008 in just four weeks

Date	Title	Peak	Wks No.1	411
5 Sep 92	**TAKE THAT AND PARTY** *RCA 74321109* ⊛**x2**	2		73
23 Oct 93	**EVERYTHING CHANGES** *RCA 74321169262* ⊛**x4**	1	2	78
13 May 95	**NOBODY ELSE** *RCA 74321279092* ⊛**x2**	1	2	33
26 Aug 95	**NOBODY ELSE (US VERSION)** *Arista 07822188002*	26		4
6 Apr 96	**GREATEST HITS** *RCA 74321355582* ⊛**x3**	1	4	40
26 Nov 05	**NEVER FORGET – THE ULTIMATE COLLECTION** *RCA 82876748522* ⊛**x3**	2		95+
9 Dec 06	**BEAUTIFUL WORLD** *Polydor 1715551* ⊛**x8**	1	8	84+
13 Dec 08	**THE CIRCUS** *Polydor 1787444* ⊛**x5**	1	4	4+

Top 3 Best-Selling Albums

		Approximate Sales
1	BEAUTIFUL WORLD	2,535,000
2	NEVER FORGET - THE ULTIMATE COLLECTION	1,710,000
3	THE CIRCUS	1,450,000

TAKING BACK SUNDAY
US, male vocal/instrumental group — Weeks on Chart: 7

Date	Title	Label	Peak Position	Weeks at No.1	Weeks on Chart
7 Aug 04	**WHERE YOU WANT TO BE**	*Victory VR228CD*	71		1
6 May 06	**LOUDER NOW**	*Warner Brothers 9362494242*	18		6

CONNIE TALBOT
UK, female vocalist — Weeks on Chart: 4

Date	Title	Label	Peak Position	Weeks at No.1	Weeks on Chart
8 Dec 07	**OVER THE RAINBOW**	*Pebble Beach CONNIECD001*	35		4

TALK TALK
UK, male vocal/instrumental group – Mark Hollis*, Simon Bremner, Lee Harris & Paul Webb — Weeks on Chart: 86

Date	Title	Label	Peak Position	Weeks at No.1	Weeks on Chart
24 Jul 82	**THE PARTY'S OVER**	*EMI EMC 3413*	21		25
25 Feb 84	**IT'S MY LIFE**	*EMI EMC 2400021*	35		8
1 Mar 86	**THE COLOUR OF SPRING**	*EMI EMC 3506*	8		21
24 Sep 88	**SPIRIT OF EDEN**	*Parlophone PCSD 105*	19		5
9 Jun 90	**THE VERY BEST OF TALK TALK – NATURAL HISTORY**	*Parlophone PCSD 109*	3		21
6 Apr 91	**HISTORY REVISITED – THE REMIXES**	*Parlophone PCS 7349*	35		2
28 Sep 91	**LAUGHING STOCK**	*Verve 8477171*	26		2
8 Feb 97	**THE VERY BEST OF TALK TALK**	*EMI CDEMC 3763*	54		2

TALKING HEADS
US/UK, male/female vocal/instrumental group – David Byrne*, Chris Frantz, Jerry Harrison & Tina Weymouth — Weeks on Chart: 237

Date	Title	Label	Peak Position	Weeks at No.1	Weeks on Chart
25 Feb 78	**TALKING HEADS '77**	*Sire 9103 328*	60		1
29 Jul 78	**MORE SONGS ABOUT BUILDINGS AND FOOD**	*Sire K 56531*	21		3
15 Sep 79	**FEAR OF MUSIC**	*Sire SRK 6076*	33		5
1 Nov 80	**REMAIN IN LIGHT**	*Sire SRK 6095*	21		17
10 Apr 82	**THE NAME OF THIS BAND IS TALKING HEADS**	*Sire SRK 23590*	22		5
18 Jun 83	**SPEAKING IN TONGUES**	*Sire K 9238831*	21		12
27 Oct 84	**STOP MAKING SENSE**	*EMI TAH 1*	37		81
29 Jun 85	**LITTLE CREATURES**	*EMI TAH 2*	10		65
27 Sep 86	**TRUE STORIES**	*EMI EU 3511*	7		9
26 Mar 88	**NAKED**	*EMI EMD 1005*	3		15
24 Oct 92	**ONCE IN A LIFETIME – THE BEST OF TALKING HEADS/SAND IN THE VASELINE**	*EMI CDEQ 5010*	7		16
18 Sep 99	**STOP MAKING SENSE**	*EMI 5224532*	24		4
30 Oct 04	**THE BEST OF**	*Rhino 8122764882*	30		4

TANGERINE DREAM
Germany, male instrumental group — Weeks on Chart: 77

Date	Title	Label	Peak Position	Weeks at No.1	Weeks on Chart
20 Apr 74	**PHAEDRA**	*Virgin V 2010*	15		15
5 Apr 75	**RUBYCON**	*Virgin V 2025*	12		14
20 Dec 75	**RICOCHET**	*Virgin V 2044*	40		2
13 Nov 76	**STRATOSFEAR**	*Virgin V 2068*	39		4
23 Jul 77	**SORCERER (OST)**	*MCA MCF 2806*	25		7
19 Nov 77	**ENCORE**	*Virgin VD 2506*	55		1
1 Apr 78	**CYCLONE**	*Virgin V 2097*	37		4
17 Feb 79	**FORCE MAJEURE**	*Virgin V 2111*	26		7
7 Jun 80	**TANGRAM**	*Virgin V 2147*	36		5
18 Apr 81	**THIEF (OST)**	*Virgin V 2198*	43		3
19 Sep 81	**EXIT**	*Virgin V 2212*	43		5
10 Apr 82	**WHITE EAGLE**	*Virgin V 2226*	57		5
5 Nov 83	**HYPERBOREA**	*Virgin V 2292*	45		2
10 Nov 84	**POLAND**	*Jive Electro HIP 22*	90		1
26 Jul 86	**UNDERWATER SUNLIGHT**	*Jive Electro HIP 40*	97		1
27 Jun 87	**TYGER**	*Jive HIP 47*	88		1

TANK
UK, male vocal/instrumental group — Weeks on Chart: 5

Date	Title	Label	Peak Position	Weeks at No.1	Weeks on Chart
13 Mar 82	**FILTH HOUNDS OF HADES**	*Kamaflage KAMLP 1*	33		5

SERJ TANKIAN
Lebanon, male vocalist/multi-instrumentalist. See System Of A Down — Weeks on Chart: 3

Date	Title	Label	Peak Position	Weeks at No.1	Weeks on Chart
3 Nov 07	**ELECT THE DEAD**	*Reprise 9362499282*	26		3

BILL TARMEY
UK, male actor/vocalist (Bill Piddington) — Weeks on Chart: 25

Date	Title	Label	Peak Position	Weeks at No.1	Weeks on Chart
27 Nov 93	**A GIFT OF LOVE**	*EMI CDEMC 3665*	15		14
5 Nov 94	**TIME FOR LOVE**	*EMI CDEMTV 85*	28		9
18 May 96	**AFTER HOURS**	*EMI Premier PRMTVCD 2*	61		2

TASTE
Ireland, male vocal/instrumental group — Weeks on Chart: 16

Date	Title	Label	Peak Position	Weeks at No.1	Weeks on Chart
7 Feb 70	**ON THE BOARDS**	*Polydor 583083*	18		11
6 Mar 71	**LIVE TASTE**	*Polydor 2310 082*	14		4
9 Sep 72	**TASTE – LIVE AT THE ISLE OF WIGHT**	*Polydor 2383 120*	41		1

t.A.T.u.
Russia, female vocal duo — Weeks on Chart: 15

Date	Title	Label	Peak Position	Weeks at No.1	Weeks on Chart
25 Jan 03	**200 KHM IN THE WRONG LANE**	*Interscope 0674562*	20		15

TAVARES
US, male vocal group — Weeks on Chart: 15

Date	Title	Label	Peak Position	Weeks at No.1	Weeks on Chart
21 Aug 76	**SKY HIGH**	*Capitol Soul EST 11533*	22		13
1 Apr 78	**THE BEST OF TAVARES**	*Capitol EST 11701*	39		2

ANDY TAYLOR
UK, male vocalist/guitarist. See Duran Duran — Weeks on Chart: 1

Date	Title	Label	Peak Position	Weeks at No.1	Weeks on Chart
30 May 87	**THUNDER**	*MCA MCG 6018*	61		1

BECKY TAYLOR
UK, female vocalist — Weeks on Chart: 1

Date	Title	Label	Peak Position	Weeks at No.1	Weeks on Chart
23 Jun 01	**A DREAM COME TRUE**	*EMI Classics CDC 5571422*	67		1

JAMES TAYLOR
US, male vocalist/guitarist — Weeks on Chart: 124

Date	Title	Label	Peak Position	Weeks at No.1	Weeks on Chart
21 Nov 70	**SWEET BABY JAMES**	*Warner Brothers ES 1843*	6		53
29 May 71	**MUD SLIDE SLIM AND THE BLUE HORIZON**	*Warner Brothers WS 2561*	4		41
8 Jan 72	**SWEET BABY JAMES**	*Warner Brothers K 46043*	34		6
18 Mar 72	**MUD SLIDE SLIM AND THE BLUE HORIZON**	*Warner Brothers K 46085*	49		1
9 Dec 72	**ONE MAN DOG**	*Warner Brothers K 46185*	27		5
4 Apr 87	**CLASSIC SONGS**	*CBS/WEA JTV 1*	53		5
21 Jun 97	**HOURGLASS**	*Columbia 4877482*	46		1
24 Aug 02	**OCTOBER ROAD**	*Columbia 5032929*	39		3
13 Sep 03	**YOU'VE GOT A FRIEND – THE BEST OF**	*Warner Brothers 8122738372*	4		9

JAMES TAYLOR QUARTET
UK, male instrumental trio — Weeks on Chart: 5

Date	Title	Label	Peak Position	Weeks at No.1	Weeks on Chart
1 May 93	**SUPERNATURAL FEELING**	*Big Life BLRCD 21*	36		3
29 Oct 94	**EXTENDED PLAY**	*Acid Jazz JAZID 110CD*	70		1
11 Mar 95	**IN THE HAND OF THE INEVITABLE**	*Acid Jazz JAZID CD115*	63		1

ROGER TAYLOR
UK, male vocalist/drummer. See Queen — Weeks on Chart: 11

Date	Title	Label	Peak Position	Weeks at No.1	Weeks on Chart
18 Apr 81	**FUN IN SPACE**	*EMI EMC 3369*	18		5
7 Jul 84	**STRANGE FRONTIER**	*EMI RTA 1*	30		4
17 Sep 94	**HAPPINESS?**	*Parlophone CDPCSD 157*	22		1
10 Oct 98	**ELECTRIC FIRE**	*Parlophone 4967242*	53		1

KIRI TE KANAWA
New Zealand, female vocalist — Weeks on Chart: 53

Date	Title	Label	Peak Position	Weeks at No.1	Weeks on Chart
2 Apr 83	**CHANTS D'AUVERGNE VOLUME 1**	*Decca SXDL 7604* KIRI TE KANAWA WITH THE ENGLISH CHAMBER ORCHESTRA	57		1
26 Oct 85	**BLUE SKIES**	*London KTKT 1* KIRI TE KANAWA WITH NELSON RIDDLE & HIS ORCHESTRA	40		29
13 Dec 86	**CHRISTMAS WITH KIRI**	*Decca PROLP 12*	47		4
17 Dec 88	**KIRI**	*K-Tel NE 1424*	70		3
29 Feb 92	**THE ESSENTIAL KIRI**	*Decca 4362862*	23		10
23 May 92	**KIRI SIDETRACKS – THE JAZZ ALBUM**	*Philips 4340922*	73		1
9 Apr 94	**KIRI!**	*Polygram TV 4436002*	16		4
10 Nov 01	**KIRI**	*EMI Classics CDC 5572312*	73		1

CLARE TEAL
UK, female vocalist — Weeks on Chart: 3

Date	Title	Label	Peak Position	Weeks at No.1	Weeks on Chart
30 Oct 04	**DON'T TALK**	*Columbia 5186702*	20		3

TEARDROP EXPLODES

UK, male vocal/instrumental group

Date	Title	Peak Position	Weeks at No.1	Weeks on Chart (45)
18 Oct 80	**KILIMANJARO** *Mercury 6359 035* ○	24		35
5 Dec 81	**WILDER** *Mercury 6359 056* ○	29		6
14 Apr 90	**EVERYBODY WANTS TO SHAG...THE TEARDROP EXPLODES** *Fontana 8424391*	72		1
15 Aug 92	**FLOORED GENIUS – THE BEST OF JULIAN COPE AND THE TEARDROP EXPLODES** *Island CID 8000* JULIAN COPE & THE TEARDROP EXPLODES	22		3

TEARS

UK, male vocal/instrumental duo. See Suede

Date	Title	Peak Position	Weeks at No.1	Weeks on Chart (2)
18 Jun 05	**HERE COME THE TEARS** *Independiente ISOM49CD*	15		2

TEARS FOR FEARS

UK, male vocal/instrumental duo – Roland Orzabal & Curt Smith

Date	Title	Peak Position	Weeks at No.1	Weeks on Chart (223)
19 Mar 83	**THE HURTING** *Mercury MERS 17* ⊛	1	1	65
9 Mar 85	**SONGS FROM THE BIG CHAIR** *Mercury MERH 58* ⊛x3 ★	2		82
7 Oct 89	**THE SEEDS OF LOVE** *Fontana 8387301* ⊛	1	1	30
14 Mar 92	**TEARS ROLL DOWN (GREATEST HITS 1982–1992)** *Fontana 5109392* ⊛x2	2		37
19 Jun 93	**ELEMENTAL** *Mercury 5148752* ○	5		7
28 Oct 95	**RAOUL AND THE KINGS OF SPAIN** *Epic 4809822*	41		1
19 Mar 05	**EVERYBODY LOVES A HAPPY ENDING** *Gut GUTCD37*	45		1

TEATRO

UK/US, male vocal group

Date	Title	Peak Position	Weeks at No.1	Weeks on Chart (4)
8 Dec 07	**TEATRO** *Sony BMG 88697194312* ●	43		4

TECHNOTRONIC

Belgium, male producer (Jo Bogaert, aka Thomas De Quincey); members also included Felly (Felly Kilingi, b. Zaire), MC Eric (Eric Martin, b. UK) & Ya Kid K (Manuela Barbara Kamosi Moaso Djogi, b. Democratic Republic of Congo)

Date	Title	Peak Position	Weeks at No.1	Weeks on Chart (62)
6 Jan 90	**PUMP UP THE JAM** *Swanyard SYRLP 1* ⊛	2		44
3 Nov 90	**TRIP ON THIS – REMIXES** *Telstar STAR 2461* & HI TEK 3 ●	7		14
15 Jun 91	**BODY TO BODY** *ARS 4683421*	27		4

TEENAGE FANCLUB

UK, male vocal/instrumental group – Norman Blake, Gerard Love, Raymond McGinley & Brendan O'Hare (replaced by Paul Quinn)

Date	Title	Peak Position	Weeks at No.1	Weeks on Chart (25)
7 Sep 91	**THE KING** *Creation CRELP 096*	53		2
16 Nov 91	**BANDWAGONESQUE** *Creation CRELP 106*	22		7
16 Oct 93	**THIRTEEN** *Creation CRECD 144*	14		3
10 Jun 95	**GRAND PRIX** *Creation CRECD 173*	7		4
2 Aug 97	**SONGS FROM NORTHERN BRITAIN** *Creation CRECD 196*	3		5
4 Nov 00	**HOWDY** *Columbia 5006222*	33		2
8 Feb 03	**4766 SECONDS: A SHORTCUT TO TEENAGE FANCLUB** *Poolside POOLS 3CDX*	47		1
21 May 05	**MAN-MADE** *Pema PEMA002CD*	34		1

TELETUBBIES

Teletubbyland/UK, male/female alien vocal group

Date	Title	Peak Position	Weeks at No.1	Weeks on Chart (4)
4 Apr 98	**THE ALBUM** *BBC Worldwide Music WMXU 00142*	31		4

TELEVISION

US, male vocal/instrumental group – Tom Verlaine*, Billy Ficca, Richard Lloyd & Fred Smith

Date	Title	Peak Position	Weeks at No.1	Weeks on Chart (17)
26 Mar 77	**MARQUEE MOON** *Elektra K 52046* ●	28		13
29 Apr 78	**ADVENTURE** *Elektra K 52072*	7		4

TEMPERANCE SEVEN

UK, male vocal/instrumental group – Paul MacDowell, Colin Bowles, Alan Swainston Cooper, John R.T. Davies, Martin Fry, John Grieves-Watson, Phillip Harrison, Cephas Howard & Brian Innes

Date	Title	Peak Position	Weeks at No.1	Weeks on Chart
13 May 61	**TEMPERANCE SEVEN PLUS ONE** *Argo RG 11*	19		1
25 Nov 61	**TEMPERANCE SEVEN 1961** *Parlophone PMC 1152*	8		9

TEMPLE CHURCH CHOIR

UK, male choir

Date	Title	Peak Position	Weeks at No.1	Weeks on Chart (13)
16 Dec 61	**CHRISTMAS CAROLS** *HMV CLP 1309*	8		3

TEMPTATIONS

US, male vocal/instrumental group – members included Dennis Edwards, Melvin Franklin, d. 23 Feb 1995, Eddie Kendricks, d. 5 Oct 1992, David Ruffin, d. 1 Jun 1991, Richard Street, Otis Williams & Paul Williams, d. 17 Aug 1973

Date	Title	Peak Position	Weeks at No.1	Weeks on Chart (142)
24 Dec 66	**GETTING READY** *Tamla Motown STML 11035*	40		2
11 Feb 67	**TEMPTATIONS GREATEST HITS** *Tamla Motown STML 11042*	17		40
22 Jul 67	**THE TEMPTATIONS LIVE!** *Tamla Motown STML 11053*	20		4
18 Nov 67	**TEMPTATIONS WITH A LOT OF SOUL** *Tamla Motown STML 11057*	19		18
25 Jan 69	**DIANA ROSS AND THE SUPREMES JOIN THE TEMPTATIONS** *Tamla Motown STML 11096* DIANA ROSS & THE SUPREMES & THE TEMPTATIONS	1	4	15
28 Jun 69	**THE ORIGINAL SOUNDTRACK FROM TCB (OST-TV)** *Tamla Motown STML 11110* DIANA ROSS & THE SUPREMES & THE TEMPTATIONS ★	11		12
20 Sep 69	**CLOUD NINE** *Tamla Motown STML 11109*	32		1
14 Feb 70	**TOGETHER** *Tamla Motown STML 11122* DIANA ROSS & THE SUPREMES & THE TEMPTATIONS	28		4
14 Feb 70	**PUZZLE PEOPLE** *Tamla Motown STML 11133*	20		4
11 Jul 70	**PSYCHEDELIC SHACK** *Tamla Motown STML 11147*	56		1
26 Dec 70	**GREATEST HITS VOLUME 2** *Tamla Motown STML 11170*	28		5
29 Apr 72	**SOLID ROCK** *Tamla Motown STML 11202*	34		2
20 Jan 73	**ALL DIRECTIONS** *Tamla Motown STML 11218*	19		7
7 Jul 73	**MASTERPIECE** *Tamla Motown STML 11229*	28		3
8 Dec 84	**TRULY FOR YOU** *Motown ZL 72342*	75		5
11 Apr 92	**MOTOWN'S GREATEST HITS** *Motown 5300152*	8		9
27 Jan 01	**AT THEIR VERY BEST** *Universal TV 135782*	28		5
22 Mar 08	**CLASSIC SOUL HITS** *UMTV 5306688*	8		5

10 C.C.

UK, male vocal/instrumental group – Lol Crème, Kevin Godley (Godley & Crème*), Graham Gouldman & Eric Stewart

Date	Title	Peak Position	Weeks at No.1	Weeks on Chart (221)
1 Sep 73	**10 C.C.** *UK UKAL 1005* ○	36		5
15 Jun 74	**SHEET MUSIC** *UK UKAL 1007* ●	9		24
22 Mar 75	**THE ORIGINAL SOUNDTRACK** *Mercury 9102 500* ●	4		40
7 Jun 75	**100CC: GREATEST HITS OF 10 C.C.** *Decca UKAL 1012* ●	9		18
31 Jan 76	**HOW DARE YOU?** *Mercury 9102 501* ●	5		31
14 May 77	**DECEPTIVE BENDS** *Mercury 9102 502* ●	3		21
10 Dec 77	**LIVE AND LET LIVE** *Mercury 6641 698* ●	14		15
23 Sep 78	**BLOODY TOURISTS** *Mercury 9102 503* ●	3		15
6 Oct 79	**GREATEST HITS 1972–1978** *Mercury 9102 504* ●	5		21
5 Apr 80	**LOOK HEAR?** *Mercury 9102 505*	35		5
15 Oct 83	**WINDOW IN THE JUNGLE** *Mercury MERL 28*	70		2
29 Aug 87	**CHANGING FACES – THE VERY BEST OF 10CC AND GODLEY AND CRÈME** *ProTV TGCLP 1* 10CC & GODLEY & CRÈME ●	4		18
5 Apr 97	**THE VERY BEST OF 10CC** *Mercury TV 5346122*	37		4
18 Nov 06	**GREATEST HITS AND MORE** *Universal TV 9844414*	42		2

TEN CITY

US, male vocal/instrumental group

Date	Title	Peak Position	Weeks at No.1	Weeks on Chart (12)
18 Feb 89	**FOUNDATION** *Atlantic WX 249* ○	22		12

TEN POLE TUDOR

UK, male vocal/instrumental group

Date	Title	Peak Position	Weeks at No.1	Weeks on Chart (8)
9 May 81	**EDDIE, OLD BOB, DICK & GARRY** *Stiff SEEZ 31*	44		8

TEN SHARP

Holland, male vocal/instrumental duo

Date	Title	Peak Position	Weeks at No.1	Weeks on Chart (2)
9 May 92	**UNDER THE WATER-LINE** *Columbia 4690702*	46		2

10,000 MANIACS

US, female/male vocal/instrumental group

Date	Title	Peak Position	Weeks at No.1	Weeks on Chart (12)
27 May 89	**BLIND MAN'S ZOO** *Elektra EKT 57* ○	18		8
10 Oct 92	**OUR TIME IN EDEN** *Elektra 7559613852*	33		2
6 Nov 93	**UNPLUGGED...AND SEATED** *Elektra 7559615692*	40		2

TEN YEARS AFTER

UK, male vocal/instrumental group – Alvin Lee, Chick Churchill, Ric Lee & Leo Lyons

Date	Title / Label	Peak Position	Weeks at No.1	Weeks on Chart
				70
21 Sep 68	**UNDEAD** *Deram SML 1023*	26		7
22 Feb 69	**STONEDHENGE** *Deram SML 1029*	6		5
4 Oct 69	**SSSSH** *Deram SML 1052*	4		18
2 May 70	**CRICKLEWOOD GREEN** *Deram SML 1065*	4		27
9 Jan 71	**WATT** *Deram SML 1078*	5		9
13 Nov 71	**A SPACE IN TIME** *Chrysalis CHR 1001*	36		1
7 Oct 72	**ROCK & ROLL MUSIC TO THE WORLD** *Chrysalis CHR 1009*	27		1
28 Jul 73	**RECORDED LIVE** *Chrysalis CHR 1049*	36		2

TENACIOUS D

US, male vocal/instrumental duo – Jack Black & Kyle Gass

Date	Title / Label	Peak Position	Weeks at No.1	Weeks on Chart
				41
13 Jul 02	**TENACIOUS D** *Epic 5077352* ●	38		35
25 Nov 06	**THE PICK OF DESTINY** *Epic 82796948912*	10		6

BRYN TERFEL

UK, male vocalist

Date	Title / Label	Peak Position	Weeks at No.1	Weeks on Chart
				39
16 Nov 96	**SOMETHING WONDERFUL** *Deutsche Grammophon 4491632*	72		1
28 Oct 00	**WE'LL KEEP A WELCOME** *Deutsche Grammophon 4635932* ○	33		10
3 Nov 01	**SOME ENCHANTED EVENING** *Deutsche Grammophon 4714252*	49		2
8 Nov 03	**BRYN** *Deutsche Grammophon 4747032* ⊛	6		11
22 Oct 05	**SIMPLE GIFTS** *Deutsche Grammophon 4775919* ●	10		11
23 Sep 06	**TUTTO MOZART** *Deutsche Grammophon 4775886*	59		1
27 Sep 08	**FIRST LOVE: SONGS FROM THE BRITISH ISLES** *Deutsche Grammophon 4777865*	16		3

TERRAPLANE

UK, male vocal/instrumental group

Date	Title / Label	Peak Position	Weeks at No.1	Weeks on Chart
				1
25 Jan 86	**BLACK AND WHITE** *Epic EPC 26439*	74		1

TAMMI TERRELL

US, female vocalist (Tammy Montgomery), d. 16 Mar 1970 (age 24)

Date	Title / Label	Peak Position	Weeks at No.1	Weeks on Chart
				4
22 Aug 70	**GREATEST HITS** *Tamla Motown STML 11153* MARVIN GAYE & TAMMI TERRELL	60		4

TERRORVISION

UK, male vocal/instrumental group – Tony Wright, Leigh Marklew, David Shuttleworth & Mark Yates

Date	Title / Label	Peak Position	Weeks at No.1	Weeks on Chart
				41
15 May 93	**FORMALDEHYDE** *Total Vegas VEGASCD 1*	75		1
30 Apr 94	**HOW TO MAKE FRIENDS AND INFLUENCE PEOPLE** *Total Vegas VEGASCD 2* ●	18		25
23 Mar 96	**REGULAR URBAN SURVIVORS** *Total Vegas VEGASCD 3* ●	8		12
17 Oct 98	**SHAVING PEACHES** *Total Vegas 4996082*	34		2
17 Feb 01	**GOOD TO GO** *Papillion BTFLYCD 0011*	48		1

TODD TERRY

US, male producer

Date	Title / Label	Peak Position	Weeks at No.1	Weeks on Chart
				1
5 Aug 95	**THE MINISTRY OF SOUND PRESENTS A DAY IN THE LIFE OF TODD TERRY** *Sound Of Ministry SOMCD 2*	73		1

TESLA

US, male vocal/instrumental group

Date	Title / Label	Peak Position	Weeks at No.1	Weeks on Chart
				6
11 Feb 89	**THE GREAT RADIO CONTROVERSY** *Geffen WX 244*	34		2
2 Mar 91	**FIVE MAN ACOUSTICAL JAM** *Geffen 9243111*	59		1
21 Sep 91	**PSYCHOTIC SUPPER** *Geffen GEF 24424*	44		2
3 Sep 94	**BUST A NUT** *Geffen GED 24713*	51		1

TEST ICICLES

UK, male vocal/instrumental group

Date	Title / Label	Peak Position	Weeks at No.1	Weeks on Chart
				1
12 Nov 05	**FOR SCREENING PURPOSES ONLY** *Domino WIGCD163*	69		1

TESTAMENT

US, male vocal/instrumental group

Date	Title / Label	Peak Position	Weeks at No.1	Weeks on Chart
				6
28 May 88	**THE NEW ORDER** *Megaforce 7818491*	81		1
19 Aug 89	**PRACTICE WHAT YOU PREACH** *Atlantic WX 297*	40		2
6 Oct 90	**SOULS OF BLACK** *Megaforce 7567821431*	35		2
30 May 92	**THE RITUAL** *Atlantic 7567823922*	48		1

TEXAS

UK, female/male vocal/instrumental group – Sharleen Spiteri*, Eddie Campbell, Richard Hynd & Ally McErlaine

Date	Title / Label	Peak Position	Weeks at No.1	Weeks on Chart
				255
25 Mar 89	**SOUTHSIDE** *Mercury 8381711* ●	3		30
5 Oct 91	**MOTHERS HEAVEN** *Mercury 8485781*	32		4
13 Nov 93	**RICKS ROAD** *Vertigo 5182522* ○	18		2
15 Feb 97	**WHITE ON BLONDE** *Mercury 5343152* ⊛x6	1	2	102
22 May 99	**THE HUSH** *Mercury 5389722* ⊛x3	1	1	47
4 Nov 00	**THE GREATEST HITS** *Mercury 5482622* ⊛x6	1	2	56
1 Nov 03	**CAREFUL WHAT YOU WISH FOR** *Mercury 9865712*	5		4
19 Nov 05	**RED BOOK** *Mercury 9874219* ●	16		10

THA DOGG POUND

US, male rap group

Date	Title / Label	Peak Position	Weeks at No.1	Weeks on Chart
				2
11 Nov 95	**DOGG FOOD** *Death Row 5241772* ★	66		2

THAT PETROL EMOTION

UK/US, male vocal/instrumental group

Date	Title / Label	Peak Position	Weeks at No.1	Weeks on Chart
				8
10 May 86	**MANIC POP THRILL** *Demon FIEND 70*	84		2
23 May 87	**BABBLE** *Polydor TPE LP 1*	30		3
24 Sep 88	**END OF MILLENNIUM PSYCHOSIS BLUES** *Virgin V 2550*	53		2
21 Apr 90	**CHEMICRAZY** *Virgin V 2618*	62		1

THE THE

UK, male vocalist/multi-instrumentalist (Matt Johnson) & various musicians

Date	Title / Label	Peak Position	Weeks at No.1	Weeks on Chart
				53
29 Oct 83	**SOUL MINING** *Epic EPC 25525*	27		5
29 Nov 86	**INFECTED** *Some Bizzare EPC 26770* ●	14		30
27 May 89	**MIND BOMB** *Epic 4633191*	4		9
6 Feb 93	**DUSK** *Epic 4724682*	2		4
19 Jun 93	**BURNING BLUE SOUL** *4AD HAD 113CD*	65		1
25 Feb 95	**HANKY PANKY** *Epic 4781392*	28		2
11 Mar 00	**NAKEDSELF** *Nothing 4905102*	45		1
1 Jun 02	**45 RPM – THE SINGLES OF THE THE** *Epic 5044699*	60		1

THEATRE OF HATE

UK, male vocal/instrumental group

Date	Title / Label	Peak Position	Weeks at No.1	Weeks on Chart
				9
13 Mar 82	**WESTWORLD** *Burning Rome TOH 1*	17		6
18 Aug 84	**REVOLUTION** *Burning Rome TOH 2*	67		3

THEAUDIENCE

UK, male/female vocal/instrumental group

Date	Title / Label	Peak Position	Weeks at No.1	Weeks on Chart
				2
29 Aug 98	**THEAUDIENCE** *Ellefre 5587712*	22		2

THEN JERICO

UK, male vocal/instrumental group – Mark Shaw, Keith Airey, Rob Downes, Jasper Stainthorpe, Scott Taylor & Steve Wren

Date	Title / Label	Peak Position	Weeks at No.1	Weeks on Chart
				24
3 Oct 87	**FIRST (THE SOUND OF MUSIC)** *London LONLP 26*	35		7
4 Mar 89	**THE BIG AREA** *London 8281221*	4		17

THERAPY?

UK/Ireland, male vocal/instrumental group – Andy Cairns, Fyfe Ewing, Graham Hopkins, Martin McCarrick & Michael McKeegan

Date	Title / Label	Peak Position	Weeks at No.1	Weeks on Chart
				24
8 Feb 92	**PLEASURE DEATH** *Wiiija WIJ 11*	52		1
14 Nov 92	**NURSE** *A&M 5400442*	38		3
19 Feb 94	**TROUBLEGUM** *A&M 5401962* ●	5		11
24 Jun 95	**INFERNAL LOVE** *A&M 5403792* ○	9		7
11 Apr 98	**SEMI-DETACHED** *A&M 5408912*	21		1
30 Oct 99	**SUICIDE PACT – YOU FIRST** *Ark 21 1539722*	61		1

THESE ANIMAL MEN

UK, male vocal/instrumental group

Date	Title / Label	Peak Position	Weeks at No.1	Weeks on Chart
				4
2 Jul 94	**TOO SUSSED?** *Hi-Rise Recordings FLATMCD 4*	39		2
8 Oct 94	**(COME ON, JOIN) THE HIGH SOCIETY** *Hi-Rise Recordings FLATCD 8*	62		1
25 Mar 95	**TAXI FOR THESE ANIMAL MEN** *Hi-Rise Recordings FLATMCD 14*	64		1

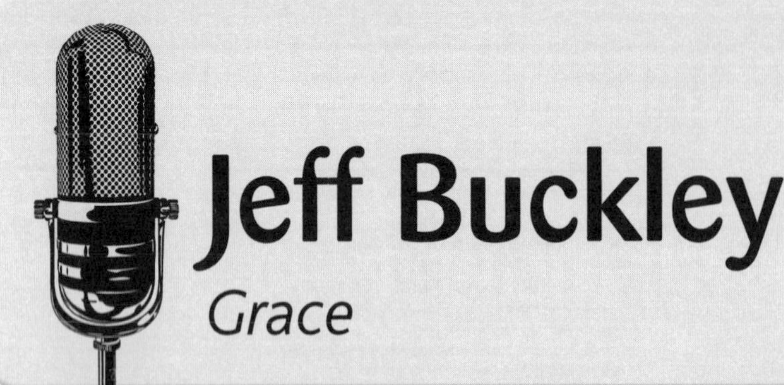

Jeff Buckley

Grace

ON 29 May 1997, Jeff Buckley strode fully clothed into the Wolf River near the studio where he was about to record the follow-up to his cornerstone album *Grace*. He was apparently in an upbeat mood, singing 'Whole Lotta Love' by Led Zeppelin as he splashed through the water. At that point, although he'd received some enthusiastic reviews for *Grace,* most critics had put it into the 'promising' pile. A small cult following had been waiting eagerly for the second album, which was to be called *My Sweetheart The Drunk*. That, surely, was to be the record where his extraordinary talent would finally be captured at its peak. Sadly, we'll never know. He didn't come back from his spontaneous dip in the Wolf River, he got caught up in the currents and accidentally drowned at the age of thirty. All that we have of the putative second album is some demos, posthumously released as *Sketches For My Sweetheart The Drunk*.

It is the definitive flawed masterpiece

Grace, then, has been reassessed. Tragically it still can't be seen as exponentially promising but it is the definitive flawed masterpiece. Its impact goes well beyond even the two million copies sold since Buckley's premature death. In short, for many, *Grace* changed the musical climate: Radiohead's Thom Yorke famously delivered the vocal take for 'Fake Plastic Trees' immediately after coming home from a Jeff Buckley concert; Muse's Matt Bellamy has built a career on a similar basis of hyperbolic vocals allied to sky-scraping rock; Rufus Wainwright is one of many who has tried to wear the mantle of the 'male diva'. Talented as they all are, though, none of them can sing quite like Jeff Buckley.

Most of the two million people who bought *Grace* probably came to it via his extraordinary version of Leonard Cohen's 'Hallelujah' (initially the record only sold very modestly, despite reasonable critical acclaim; in late 2008 Buckley's own version of the track re-entered at Number 3 in the UK charts after the winner of that year's *X Factor*, Alexandra Burke, released her own cover as her triumphant debut single). It's a song that's unrepresentative of the rest of the album because Buckley, for once in a complicated life, chose to keep things simple and use an arrangement created by ex-Velvet Underground man John Cale (the album was co-produced with Andy Wallace, who'd previously worked on Nirvana's caustic *Nevermind*). It stripped the original fifteen verses down to six and tiptoed through them with nothing but sparse guitar. In such a setting, the swooping virtuosity of Buckley's vocal is set off like a diamond resting on a velvet cloth. It may have appeared as a soundtrack on everything from news reports to slow-motion montages of England losing football matches on penalties, but Buckley's 'Hallelujah' still sounds startling.

Jeff Buckley had been criticised for being a vocal diva and dubbed 'the male Mariah Carey' for the way he occasionally allows the sheer, show-off joy of his vocal range to run away with a song. Perhaps his time at the Musicians Institute – which he claimed was a 'waste' – had infected him after all. The title track of this album, for example, finishes with an orgasmic wail that seems to have little or nothing to do with the subtle twists and

Chart History

Artist	Album Title	First Chart Week	Weeks on Chart	Highest Position
JEFF BUCKLEY	GRACE	27/8/94	3+	42

turns and beautiful guitar lines of the rest of the tune. But this ignores the fact that, extraordinarily, he didn't even consider himself a singer at the start of his career. He played guitar in reggae and metal bands and sang backing vocals.

Perhaps he was conscious of avoiding comparisons with his father. Tim Buckley was a singer who also used his voice as if it were an instrument with unusual jazz and folk stylings that he let wander freely through a song. He was the definitive child of the 1960s but left his wife and child before succumbing to a drugs overdose in 1975. Jeff later said he was eight years old when he met his father for the one and only time. At times on *Grace*, Jeff seems to be defiantly trying to channel the Led Zeppelin wail of Robert Plant, rather than give in to his own genetic inheritance. But, of the original songs on the album, it's perhaps the vocals that sound most like his father's best moments that are the most successful. This is anything but a negative observation.

There are songs like 'Lover, You Should've Come Over' or the beautiful final track 'Dream Brother', in which he warns a friend not to abandon his newborn baby (surely in reference to the way that he was himself left). Jeff made peace with his father at a memorial service in 1991, when he sang 'I Didn't Ask To Be Your Mountain', a track that Buckley Snr wrote for him and his mother. It's doubly tragic, then, that he followed in his father's footsteps and died so young himself.

It's doubly tragic, then, that he followed in his father's footsteps

Hauntingly 'Dream Brother' – and *Grace* as an album – finishes with Buckley singing about being asleep on the sand with the 'ocean washing over'. It's the kind of thing that can only add to the Buckley myth; however, that legend at times does him a disservice because of the quantity and varied quality of some of the demos and unfinished songs that have been released posthumously. Sad as it is, the only place to hear Jeff Buckley's music as he intended it to be heard is on his first and only studio album, *Grace*. Listen, and wonder what might have been.

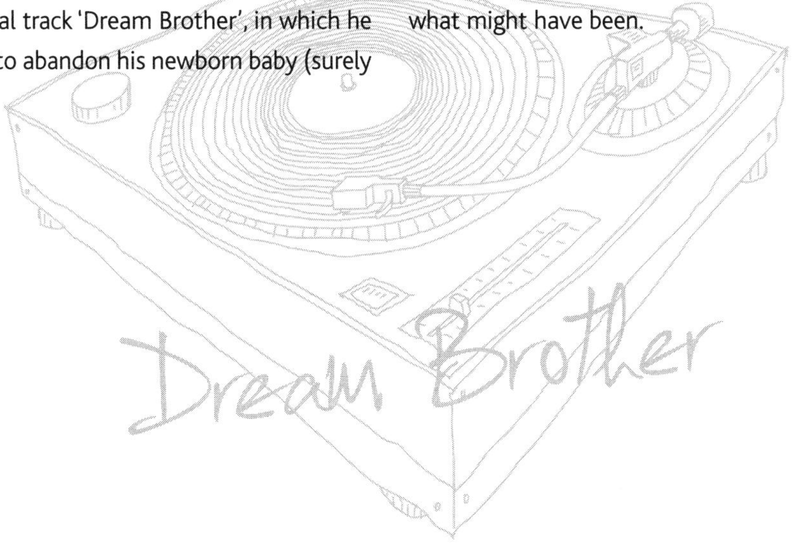

Dream Brother

Silver-selling ○ · Gold-selling ● · Platinum-selling ⊛ · US No.1 ★ · Peak Position · Weeks at No.1 · Weeks on Chart

THEY MIGHT BE GIANTS
US, male vocal/instrumental duo

12

Date	Title / Label	Peak Position	Weeks at No.1	Weeks on Chart
7 Apr 90	**FLOOD** *Elektra EKT 68* ●	14		12

THIEVERY CORPORATION
US, male DJ/production duo

1

Date	Title / Label	Peak Position	Weeks at No.1	Weeks on Chart
5 Mar 05	**THE COSMIC GAME** *ESL ESL081*	74		1

ROBIN THICKE
US, male vocalist

3

Date	Title / Label	Peak Position	Weeks at No.1	Weeks on Chart
14 Jul 07	**THE EVOLUTION OF ROBIN THICKE** *Interscope 1735710*	30		3

THIN LIZZY
Ireland/UK, male vocal/instrumental group – Phil Lynott*, d. 4 Jan 1986; members also included Brian Downey, Scott Gorham, Gary Moore*, Brian Robertson, Midge Ure* & Snowy White*

263

Date	Title / Label	Peak Position	Weeks at No.1	Weeks on Chart
27 Sep 75	**FIGHTING** *Vertigo 6360 121*	60		1
10 Apr 76	**JAILBREAK** *Vertigo 9102 008* ●	10		50
6 Nov 76	**JOHNNY THE FOX** *Vertigo 9102 012* ●	11		24
1 Oct 77	**BAD REPUTATION** *Vertigo 9102 016* ●	4		9
17 Jun 78	**LIVE AND DANGEROUS** *Vertigo 6641 807* ⊛	2		62
5 May 79	**BLACK ROSE (A ROCK LEGEND)** *Vertigo 9102 032* ●	2		21
18 Oct 80	**CHINATOWN** *Vertigo 6359 030* ○	7		7
11 Apr 81	**THE ADVENTURES OF THIN LIZZY** *Vertigo LIZTV 1*	6		13
5 Dec 81	**RENEGADE** *Vertigo 6359 083*	38		8
12 Mar 83	**THUNDER AND LIGHTNING** *Vertigo VERL 3* ○	4		11
26 Nov 83	**LIFE – LIVE** *Vertigo VERD 6*	29		6
14 Nov 87	**SOLDIER OF FORTUNE – THE BEST OF PHIL LYNOTT AND THIN LIZZY** *Telstar STAR 2300* PHIL LYNOTT & THIN LIZZY ●	55		10
16 Feb 91	**DEDICATION – THE VERY BEST OF THIN LIZZY** *Vertigo 8481921*	8		17
13 Jan 96	**WILD ONE – THE VERY BEST OF THIN LIZZY** *Vertigo 5281132* ○	18		11
19 Jun 04	**GREATEST HITS** *Universal TV 9821111* ●	3		13

3RD BASS
US, male rap group

1

Date	Title / Label	Peak Position	Weeks at No.1	Weeks on Chart
20 Jul 91	**DERELICTS OF DIALECT** *Def Jam 4683171*	46		1

THIRD EAR BAND
UK, male instrumental group

2

Date	Title / Label	Peak Position	Weeks at No.1	Weeks on Chart
27 Jun 70	**AIR, EARTH, FIRE, WATER** *Harvest SHVL 773*	49		2

THIRD WORLD
Jamaica, male vocal/instrumental group

18

Date	Title / Label	Peak Position	Weeks at No.1	Weeks on Chart
21 Oct 78	**JOURNEY TO ADDIS** *Island ILPS 9554*	30		6
11 Jul 81	**ROCKS THE WORLD** *CBS 85027*	37		9
15 May 82	**YOU'VE GOT THE POWER** *CBS 85563*	87		3

THIRTEEN SENSES
UK, male vocal/instrumental group

4

Date	Title / Label	Peak Position	Weeks at No.1	Weeks on Chart
9 Oct 04	**THE INVITATION** *Vertigo 9866910* ○	14		4

30 SECONDS TO MARS
US, male vocal/instrumental group

16

Date	Title / Label	Peak Position	Weeks at No.1	Weeks on Chart
10 Mar 07	**A BEAUTIFUL LIE** *Virgin VOID23* ●	38		16

36 CRAZYFISTS
US, male vocal/instrumental group

1

Date	Title / Label	Peak Position	Weeks at No.1	Weeks on Chart
24 Jun 06	**REST INSIDE THE FLAMES** *Roadrunner RR80792*	71		1

THIS MORTAL COIL
UK, male/female vocal/instrumental group

10

Date	Title / Label	Peak Position	Weeks at No.1	Weeks on Chart
20 Oct 84	**IT'LL END IN TEARS** *4AD CAD 411*	38		4
11 Oct 86	**FILIGREE AND SHADOW** *4AD DAD 609*	53		3
4 May 91	**BLOOD** *4AD DAD 1005*	28		3

SANDI THOM
UK, female vocalist/guitarist

25

Date	Title / Label	Peak Position	Weeks at No.1	Weeks on Chart
17 Jun 06	**SMILE IT CONFUSES PEOPLE** *RCA 82876843432* ⊛	1	1	23
7 Jun 08	**THE PINK & THE LILY** *RCA 88697299402*	25		2

KENNY THOMAS
UK, male vocalist

28

Date	Title / Label	Peak Position	Weeks at No.1	Weeks on Chart
26 Oct 91	**VOICES** *Cooltempo CTLP 24* ⊛	3		23
25 Sep 93	**WAIT FOR ME** *Cooltempo CTVD 36* ●	10		5

LILLO THOMAS
US, male vocalist

7

Date	Title / Label	Peak Position	Weeks at No.1	Weeks on Chart
2 May 87	**LILLO** *Capitol EST 2031*	43		7

RAY THOMAS
UK, male vocalist/guitarist. See Moody Blues

3

Date	Title / Label	Peak Position	Weeks at No.1	Weeks on Chart
26 Jul 75	**FROM MIGHTY OAKS** *Threshold THS 16*	23		3

ROB THOMAS
US, male vocalist. See Matchbox 20

4

Date	Title / Label	Peak Position	Weeks at No.1	Weeks on Chart
11 Jun 05	**SOMETHING TO BE** *Atlantic ATL83723DD* ○	11		4

RICHARD THOMPSON
UK, male vocalist/guitarist. See Fairport Convention

18

Date	Title / Label	Peak Position	Weeks at No.1	Weeks on Chart
27 Apr 85	**ACROSS A CROWDED ROOM** *Polydor POLD 5175*	80		2
18 Oct 86	**DARING ADVENTURES** *Polydor POLD 5202*	92		1
29 Oct 88	**AMNESIA** *Capitol EST 2075*	89		1
25 May 91	**RUMOUR AND SIGH** *Capitol EST 2142*	32		3
29 Jan 94	**MIRROR BLUE** *Capitol CDEST 2207*	23		3
20 Apr 96	**YOU? ME? US?** *Capitol CDEST 2282*	32		2
24 May 97	**INDUSTRY** *Parlophone CDPCS 7383* RICHARD & DANNY THOMPSON	69		1
4 Sep 99	**MOCK TUDOR** *Capitol 4988602*	28		2
15 Feb 03	**THE OLD KIT BAG** *Cooking Vinyl COOKCD251*	52		1
20 Aug 05	**FRONT PARLOUR BALLADS** *Cooking Vinyl COOKCD325*	54		1
9 Jun 07	**SWEET WARRIOR** *Proper PRPCD032*	39		1

TEDDY THOMPSON
UK, male vocalist/guitarist

3

Date	Title / Label	Peak Position	Weeks at No.1	Weeks on Chart
6 Sep 08	**A PIECE OF WHAT YOU NEED** *Blue Thumb/UCJ 1779769*	10		3

THOMPSON TWINS
UK/New Zealand, male/female vocal/instrumental trio – Tom Bailey, Alannah Currie & Joe Leeway

128

Date	Title / Label	Peak Position	Weeks at No.1	Weeks on Chart
13 Mar 82	**SET** *Tee TELP 2*	48		3
26 Feb 83	**QUICK STEP & SIDE KICK** *Arista 204 924* ⊛	2		56
25 Feb 84	**INTO THE GAP** *Arista 205 971* ⊛x2	1	3	51
28 Sep 85	**HERE'S TO FUTURE DAYS** *Arista 207 164* ●	5		9
2 May 87	**CLOSE TO THE BONE** *Arista 208 143*	90		1
10 Mar 90	**THOMPSON TWINS – THE GREATEST HITS** *Stylus SMR 92* ○	23		8

TRACEY THORN
UK, female vocalist. See Everything But The Girl

2

Date	Title / Label	Peak Position	Weeks at No.1	Weeks on Chart
17 Mar 07	**OUT OF THE WOODS** *Virgin CDVX3030*	38		2

THORNS
US, male vocal/instrumental trio

1

Date	Title / Label	Peak Position	Weeks at No.1	Weeks on Chart
14 Jun 03	**THE THORNS** *Columbia 5113732*	68		1

GEORGE THOROGOOD & THE DESTROYERS
US, male vocal/instrumental group

1

Date	Title / Label	Peak Position	Weeks at No.1	Weeks on Chart
2 Dec 78	**GEORGE THOROGOOD AND THE DESTROYERS** *Sonet SNTF 781*	67		1

THOUSAND YARD STARE
UK, male vocal/instrumental group

2

Date	Title / Label	Peak Position	Weeks at No.1	Weeks on Chart
7 Mar 92	**HANDS ON** *Polydor 5130012*	38		2

Silver-selling · Gold-selling · Platinum-selling · US No.1 ★ · Peak Position · Weeks at No.1 · Weeks on Chart

3 COLOURS RED
UK, male vocal/instrumental group — Weeks on Chart: 4

Date	Title / Label	Peak	Wks No.1	Wks
24 May 97	**PURE** *Creation CRECD 208*	16		2
20 Feb 99	**REVOLT** *Creation CRECD 227*	17		2

THREE DEGREES
US, female vocal group – Sheila Ferguson, Valerie Holiday & Fayette Pinkney — 91

Date	Title / Label	Peak	Wks No.1	Wks
10 Aug 74	**THREE DEGREES** *Philadelphia International 65858* ●	12		22
17 May 75	**TAKE GOOD CARE OF YOURSELF** *Philadelphia International PIR 69137* ●	6		16
24 Feb 79	**NEW DIMENSIONS** *Ariola ARLH 5012* ●	34		13
3 Mar 79	**A COLLECTION OF THEIR 20 GREATEST HITS** *Epic EPC 10013* ●	8		18
15 Dec 79	**3D** *Ariola 3D 1*	61		7
27 Sep 80	**GOLD** *Ariola 3D 2* ●	9		15

3LW
US, female vocal group — 1

Date	Title / Label	Peak	Wks No.1	Wks
16 Jun 01	**3LW** *Epic 4989142*	75		1

3T
US, male vocal group — 15

Date	Title / Label	Peak	Wks No.1	Wks
24 Feb 96	**BROTHERHOOD** *Epic 4816942* ●	11		15

THRILLS
Ireland, male vocal/instrumental group – Conor Deasy, Ben Carrigan, Kevin Horan, Padraic McMahon & Daniel Ryan — 30

Date	Title / Label	Peak	Wks No.1	Wks
12 Jul 03	**SO MUCH FOR THE CITY** *Virgin CDV2974* ⊛	3		25
25 Sep 04	**LET'S BOTTLE BOHEMIA** *Virgin CDV2986* ●	9		4
4 Aug 07	**TEENAGER** *Virgin CDVX3037*	48		1

THROWING MUSES
US, female/male vocal/instrumental group – Kristin Hersh*, Tanya Donelly*, Fred Abong, Elaine Adamedes, Bernard Georges, Leslie Langston & David Narcizo — 14

Date	Title / Label	Peak	Wks No.1	Wks
4 Feb 89	**HUNKPAPA** *4AD CAD 901*	59		1
2 Mar 91	**THE REAL RAMONA** *4AD CAD 1002*	26		4
22 Aug 92	**RED HEAVEN** *4AD CAD 2013CD*	13		3
28 Nov 92	**THE CURSE** *4AD TAD 2019CD*	74		1
28 Jan 95	**UNIVERSITY** *4AD CADD 5002CD*	10		3
31 Aug 96	**LIMBO** *4AD CAD 6014CD*	36		1
29 Mar 03	**THROWING MUSES** *4AD CAD 2301CD*	75		1

THUNDER
UK, male vocal/instrumental group – Danny Bowes, Gary James, Mark Lockhurst, Ben Matthews & Luke Morley — 42

Date	Title / Label	Peak	Wks No.1	Wks
17 Mar 90	**BACK STREET SYMPHONY** *EMI EMC 3570* ●	21		16
5 Sep 92	**LAUGHING ON JUDGEMENT DAY** *EMI CDEMD 1035* ●	2		10
4 Feb 95	**BEHIND CLOSED DOORS** *EMI CDEMD 1076*	5		5
7 Oct 95	**BEST OF THUNDER – THE FINEST HOUR (AND A BIT)** *EMI CDEMD 1086*	22		3
15 Feb 97	**THE THRILL OF IT ALL** *Raw Power RAWCD 115*	14		3
28 Feb 98	**LIVE** *Eagle EDGCD 016*	35		1
27 Mar 99	**GIVING THE GAME AWAY** *Eagle EAGCD 046*	49		1
5 Mar 05	**THE MAGNIFICENT SEVENTH** *STC STC20051*	70		1
11 Nov 06	**ROBERT JOHNSON'S TOMBSTONE** *STC STC20063*	56		1
15 Nov 08	**BANG** *STC STC20083*	62		1

THURSDAY
US, male vocal/instrumental group — 2

Date	Title / Label	Peak	Wks No.1	Wks
27 Sep 03	**WAR ALL THE TIME** *Island 9860874*	62		2

T.I.
US, male rapper (Clifford Harris) — 5

Date	Title / Label	Peak	Wks No.1	Wks
11 Oct 08	**THE PAPER TRAIL** *Atlantic 7567898198* ★	49		5

TIESTO
Holland, male DJ/producer (Tijs Verwest) — 7

Date	Title / Label	Peak	Wks No.1	Wks
29 May 04	**JUST BE** *Nebula NEBCD9010*	54		2
28 Apr 07	**ELEMENTS OF LIFE** *Nebula NEBCD9015*	14		5

TIFFANY
US, female vocalist (Tiffany Darwish) — 27

Date	Title / Label	Peak	Wks No.1	Wks
27 Feb 88	**TIFFANY** *MCA MCF 3415* ● ★	5		21
17 Dec 88	**HOLD AN OLD FRIEND'S HAND** *MCA MCF 3437* ●	56		6

TIGERTAILZ
US, male vocal/instrumental group — 2

Date	Title / Label	Peak	Wks No.1	Wks
7 Apr 90	**BEZERK** *Music For Nations MFN 96*	36		2

TIGHT FIT
UK, male/female vocal trio — 6

Date	Title / Label	Peak	Wks No.1	Wks
26 Sep 81	**BACK TO THE SIXTIES** *Jive HIP 1*	38		4
4 Sep 82	**TIGHT FIT** *Jive HIP 2*	87		2

TIK & TOK
UK, male vocal duo — 2

Date	Title / Label	Peak	Wks No.1	Wks
4 Aug 84	**INTOLERANCE** *Survival SUR LP 008*	89		2

TANITA TIKARAM
UK, female vocalist/guitarist — 62

Date	Title / Label	Peak	Wks No.1	Wks
24 Sep 88	**ANCIENT HEART** *WEA WX 210* ⊛x2	3		49
10 Feb 90	**THE SWEET KEEPER** *East West WX 330* ●	3		7
16 Feb 91	**EVERYBODY'S ANGEL** *East West WX 401*	19		4
25 Feb 95	**LOVERS IN THE CITY** *East West 4509988042*	75		1
19 Sep 98	**THE CAPPUCCINO SONGS** *Mother MUMCD 9801*	69		1

TIMBALAND
US, male rapper/producer (Tim Mosley) — 65

Date	Title / Label	Peak	Wks No.1	Wks
14 Apr 07	**TIMBALAND PRESENTS SHOCK VALUE** *Interscope 1726606*	2		65

JUSTIN TIMBERLAKE
US, male vocalist. See N Sync — 148

Date	Title / Label	Peak	Wks No.1	Wks
16 Nov 02	**JUSTIFIED** *Jive 9224772* ⊛x5	1	7	84
23 Sep 06	**FUTURESEX/LOVESOUNDS** *Jive 82876870682* ⊛x2 ★	1	1	64

TIMBUK 3
US, male/female vocal/instrumental duo — 4

Date	Title / Label	Peak	Wks No.1	Wks
14 Feb 87	**GREETINGS FROM TIMBUK 3** *I.R.S. MIRF 1015*	51		4

TIME
US, male vocal/instrumental group — 1

Date	Title / Label	Peak	Wks No.1	Wks
28 Jul 90	**PANDEMONIUM** *Paisley Park WX 336*	66		1

TIME FREQUENCY
UK, male/female vocal/instrumental/production group — 4

Date	Title / Label	Peak	Wks No.1	Wks
18 Jun 94	**DOMINATOR** *Internal Affairs KGBD 500*	23		4

TIN MACHINE
UK/US, male vocal/instrumental group – Davie Bowie*, Reeves Gabrels, Hunt Sales & Tony Sales — 12

Date	Title / Label	Peak	Wks No.1	Wks
3 Jun 89	**TIN MACHINE** *EMI USA MTLS 1044* ●	3		9
14 Sep 91	**TIN MACHINE II** *London 8282721*	23		3

TIN TIN OUT
UK, male instrumental/production duo — 1

Date	Title / Label	Peak	Wks No.1	Wks
5 Oct 96	**ADVENTURES IN TIN TIN OUT LAND** *VC Recordings VCRLPX 1*	65		1

TINDERSTICKS
UK, male vocal/instrumental group — 9

Date	Title / Label	Peak	Wks No.1	Wks
23 Oct 93	**TINDERSTICKS** *This Way Up 5183062*	56		1
15 Apr 95	**THE SECOND TINDERSTICKS ALBUM** *This Way Up 5263032*	13		3
28 Oct 95	**LIVE AT THE BLOOMSBURY THEATRE 12.3.95** *This Way Up 5285972*	32		1
21 Jun 97	**CURTAINS** *This Way Up 5243442*	37		2
18 Sep 99	**SIMPLE PLEASURE** *Island CID 8085*	36		1
2 Jun 01	**CAN OUR LOVE** *RTM BBQCD 222X*	47		1

Silver-selling ○ Gold-selling ● Platinum-selling ⊛ US No.1 ★ | Peak Position | Weeks at No.1 | Weeks on Chart

TING TINGS
UK, female/male vocal/instrumental duo – Katie White & Jules de Martino — Weeks on Chart: 28

Date	Title	Peak	Wks at No.1	Wks on Chart
31 May 08	**WE STARTED NOTHING** *Columbia 88697313342* ⊛	1	1	28+

TINY DANCERS
UK, male vocal/instrumental group — Weeks on Chart: 1

Date	Title	Peak	Wks at No.1	Wks on Chart
23 Jun 07	**FREE SCHOOL MILK** *Parlophone 3941602*	64		1

TLC
US, female vocal group – Lisa 'Left Eye' Lopes, d. 25 Apr 2002, Rozonda 'Chilli' Thomas & Tionne 'T-Boz' Watkins — Weeks on Chart: 98

Date	Title	Peak	Wks at No.1	Wks on Chart
20 May 95	**CRAZYSEXYCOOL** *LaFace 73008260092* ⊛	4		39
6 Mar 99	**FANMAIL** *LaFace 73008260552* ⊛ ★	7		57
23 Nov 02	**3D** *Arista 74321981502*	45		1
1 Sep 07	**THE VERY BEST OF – CRAZY SEXY HITS** *Sony BMG 88697119302*	57		1

TOM TOM CLUB
US, female/male vocal/instrumental group — Weeks on Chart: 1

Date	Title	Peak	Wks at No.1	Wks on Chart
24 Oct 81	**TOM TOM CLUB** *Island ILPS 9686*	78		1

TOMITA
Japan, male synthesizer player (Isao Tomita) — Weeks on Chart: 33

Date	Title	Peak	Wks at No.1	Wks on Chart
7 Jun 75	**SNOWFLAKES ARE DANCING** *RCA Red Seal ARL 10488* ●	17		20
16 Aug 75	**PICTURES AT AN EXHIBITION** *RCA Red Seal ARL 10838*	42		5
7 May 77	**HOLST: THE PLANETS** *RCA Red Seal RL 11919*	41		6
9 Feb 80	**TOMITA'S GREATEST HITS** *RCA Red Seal RL 43076*	66		2

TONGUE 'N' CHEEK
UK, male/female vocal/instrumental group

Date	Title	Peak	Wks at No.1	Wks on Chart
22 Sep 90	**THIS IS TONGUE 'N' CHEEK** *Syncopate SYLP 6006*	45		3

TONY! TONI! TONE!
US, male vocal group — Weeks on Chart: 4

Date	Title	Peak	Wks at No.1	Wks on Chart
2 Oct 93	**SONS OF SOUL** *Polydor 5149332*	66		1

TOOL
US, male vocal/instrumental group – Maynard James Keenan, Danny Carey, Justin Chancellor & Adam Jones — Weeks on Chart: 7

Date	Title	Peak	Wks at No.1	Wks on Chart
26 May 01	**LATERALUS** *Tool Dissectional 9210132* ○ ★	16		3
13 May 06	**10,000 DAYS** *Tool Dissectional 82876819912*	4		4

MARTINA TOPLEY BIRD
UK, female vocalist/guitarist — Weeks on Chart: 1

Date	Title	Peak	Wks at No.1	Wks on Chart
26 Jul 03	**QUIXOTIC** *Independiente ISOM34CD*	70		1

TOPLOADER
UK, male vocal/instrumental group – Joseph Washbourn, Julian Deane, Rob Green, Dan Hipgrave & Matt Knight — Weeks on Chart: 66

Date	Title	Peak	Wks at No.1	Wks on Chart
3 Jun 00	**ONKA'S BIG MOKA** *Sony S2 4947802* ⊛x3	5		61
31 Aug 02	**MAGIC HOTEL** *Sony S2 5084712*	3		5

TOPOL
Israel, male vocalist/actor (Chaim Topol) — Weeks on Chart: 1

Date	Title	Peak	Wks at No.1	Wks on Chart
11 May 85	**TOPOL'S ISRAEL** *BBC REH 529*	80		1

BERNIE TORME
Ireland, male vocalist/guitarist. See Gillan — Weeks on Chart: 3

Date	Title	Peak	Wks at No.1	Wks on Chart
3 Jul 82	**TURN OUT THE LIGHTS** *Kamaflage KAMLP 2*	50		3

MEL TORME
US, male vocalist, d. 5 Jun 1999 (age 73) — Weeks on Chart: 8

Date	Title	Peak	Wks at No.1	Wks on Chart
28 Jul 56	**MEL TORME AT 'THE CRESCENDO'** *Vogue Coral LVA 9004*	3		4
18 Aug 56	**MEL TORME WITH THE MARTY PAICH DEK-TETTE** *London Jazz LTZ N 15009*	3		4

PETER TOSH
Jamaica, male vocalist (Winston McIntosh), d. 11 Sep 1987 (age 42). See Bob Marley & The Wailers — Weeks on Chart: 1

Date	Title	Peak	Wks at No.1	Wks on Chart
25 Sep 76	**LEGALIZE IT** *Virgin V 2061*	54		1

TOTAL CONTRAST
UK, male vocal/instrumental duo — Weeks on Chart: 3

Date	Title	Peak	Wks at No.1	Wks on Chart
8 Mar 86	**TOTAL CONTRAST** *London LONLP 15*	66		3

TOTO
US, male vocal/instrumental group – Bobby Kimball; members also included David Hungate, Steve Lukather, David Paich, Jeff Porcaro, d. 5 Aug 1992, Mike Porcaro & Steve Porcaro — Weeks on Chart: 39

Date	Title	Peak	Wks at No.1	Wks on Chart
31 Mar 79	**TOTO** *CBS 83148*	37		5
26 Feb 83	**TOTO IV** *CBS 85529* ●	4		30
17 Nov 84	**ISOLATION** *CBS 86305*	67		2
20 Sep 86	**FAHRENHEIT** *CBS 57091*	99		1
9 Apr 88	**THE SEVENTH ONE** *CBS 4604651*	73		1

ALI FARKA TOURE
Mali, male vocalist/guitarist — Weeks on Chart: 5

Date	Title	Peak	Wks at No.1	Wks on Chart
9 Apr 94	**TALKING TIMBUKTU** *World Circuit WCD 040* ALI FARKA TOURE & RY COODER	44		3
29 Jul 06	**SAVANE** *World Circuit WCD075*	34		2

TOURISTS
UK, male/female vocal/instrumental group. See Eurythmics — Weeks on Chart: 18

Date	Title	Peak	Wks at No.1	Wks on Chart
14 Jul 79	**THE TOURISTS** *Logo GO 1018*	72		1
3 Nov 79	**REALITY EFFECT** *Logo GO 1019* ○	23		16
22 Nov 80	**LUMINOUS BASEMENT** *RCA Red Seal RCALP 5001*	75		1

PETE TOWNSHEND
UK, male vocalist. See Who — Weeks on Chart: 28

Date	Title	Peak	Wks at No.1	Wks on Chart
21 Oct 72	**WHO CAME FIRST** *Track 2408 201*	30		2
15 Oct 77	**ROUGH MIX** *Polydor 2442 147* & RONNIE LANE	44		3
3 May 80	**EMPTY GLASS** *Atco K 50699* ○	11		14
3 Jul 82	**ALL THE BEST COWBOYS HAVE CHINESE EYES** *Atco K 50889*	32		8
30 Nov 85	**WHITE CITY A NOVEL** *Atco 2523921*	70		1

TOY DOLLS
UK, male vocal/instrumental group — Weeks on Chart: 1

Date	Title	Peak	Wks at No.1	Wks on Chart
25 May 85	**A FAR OUT DISC** *Volume VOLP 2*	71		1

TOYAH
UK, female vocalist (Toyah Willcox) — Weeks on Chart: 97

Date	Title	Peak	Wks at No.1	Wks on Chart
14 Jun 80	**THE BLUE MEANING** *Safari IEYA 666*	40		4
17 Jan 81	**TOYAH! TOYAH! TOYAH!** *Safari LIVE 2* ○	22		14
30 May 81	**ANTHEM** *Safari VOOR 1* ●	2		46
19 Jun 82	**THE CHANGELING** *Safari VOOR 9* ○	6		12
13 Nov 82	**WARRIOR ROCK – TOYAH ON TOUR** *Safari TNT 1*	20		6
5 Nov 83	**LOVE IS THE LAW** *Safari VOOR 10*	28		7
25 Feb 84	**TOYAH! TOYAH! TOYAH!** *K-Tel NE 1268*	43		4
3 Aug 85	**MINX** *Portrait PRT 26415*	24		4

T'PAU
UK, female/male vocal/instrumental group – Carol Decker, Tim Burgess, Michael Chetwood, Paul Jackson, Ronnie Rogers & Taj Wyzgowski (replaced by Dean Howard) — Weeks on Chart: 85

Date	Title	Peak	Wks at No.1	Wks on Chart
26 Sep 87	**BRIDGE OF SPIES** *Siren SIRENLP 8* ⊛x4	1	1	59

Date	Title	Peak Position	Weeks at No.1	Weeks on Chart
5 Nov 88	**RAGE** *Siren SRNLP 20* ⊛	4		17
22 Jun 91	**THE PROMISE** *Siren SRNLP 32* ○	10		7
27 Feb 93	**HEART AND SOUL – THE VERY BEST OF T'PAU** *Virgin TPAUD 1*	35		2

TQ

US, male rapper (Terrance Quaites) — 9

Date	Title	Peak Position	Weeks at No.1	Weeks on Chart
8 May 99	**THEY NEVER SAW ME COMING** *Epic 4914032*	27		7
20 May 00	**THE SECOND COMING** *Epic 4977602*	32		2

IAN TRACEY WITH THE LIVERPOOL CATHEDRALS' CHOIRS

UK, male conductor & male/female choir — 3

Date	Title	Peak Position	Weeks at No.1	Weeks on Chart
21 Mar 92	**YOUR FAVOURITE HYMNS** *Virgin Classics 7912092*	62		3

TRACIE

UK, female vocalist (Tracie Young) — 2

Date	Title	Peak Position	Weeks at No.1	Weeks on Chart
30 Jun 84	**FAR FROM THE HURTING KIND** *Respond RRL 502*	64		2

TRAFFIC

UK, male vocal/instrumental group – Steve Winwood*, Jim Capaldi, d. 26 Jan 2005, Dave Mason & Chris Wood, d. 12 Jul 1983 — 41

Date	Title	Peak Position	Weeks at No.1	Weeks on Chart
30 Dec 67	**MR. FANTASY** *Island ILP 9061*	8		16
26 Oct 68	**TRAFFIC** *Island ILPS 9081*	9		8
8 Aug 70	**JOHN BARLEYCORN MUST DIE** *Island ILPS 9116*	11		9
24 Nov 73	**TRAFFIC – ON THE ROAD** *Island ISLD 2*	40		3
28 Sep 74	**WHEN THE EAGLE FLIES** *Island ILPS 9273*	31		1
21 May 94	**FAR FROM HOME** *Virgin CDV 2727*	29		4

TRAIN

US, male vocal/instrumental group – Patrick Monahan, Charlie Colin, Rob Hotchkiss, Jimmy Stafford & Scott Underwood — 9

Date	Title	Peak Position	Weeks at No.1	Weeks on Chart
18 Aug 01	**DROPS OF JUPITER** *Columbia 5023069* ●	8		9

TRANSGLOBAL UNDERGROUND

UK, male/female vocal/instrumental group — 3

Date	Title	Peak Position	Weeks at No.1	Weeks on Chart
30 Oct 93	**DREAM OF 100 NATIONS** *Nation NR 021CD*	45		1
29 Oct 94	**INTERNATIONAL TIMES** *Nation NATCD 38*	40		1
25 May 96	**PSYCHIC KARAOKE** *Nation NRCD 1067*	62		1

TRANSPLANTS

US, male vocal/instrumental group — 1

Date	Title	Peak Position	Weeks at No.1	Weeks on Chart
2 Jul 05	**HAUNTED CITIES** *Atlantic 7567941042*	72		1

TRANSVISION VAMP

UK, female/male vocal/instrumental group – Wendy James*, Tex Axile, Pol Burton, Dave Parsons & Nick Christian Sayer — 58

Date	Title	Peak Position	Weeks at No.1	Weeks on Chart
15 Oct 88	**POP ART** *MCA MCF 3421* ●	4		32
8 Jul 89	**VELVETEEN** *MCA MCG 6050* ⊛	1	1	26

TRASH CAN SINATRAS

UK, male vocal/instrumental group — 2

Date	Title	Peak Position	Weeks at No.1	Weeks on Chart
7 Jul 90	**CAKE** *Go! Discs 8282011*	74		1
15 May 93	**I'VE SEEN EVERYTHING** *Go! Discs 8284082*	50		1

TRAVELING WILBURYS

US/UK, male vocal/instrumental group – Bob Dylan*, George Harrison*, d. 29 Nov 2001, Jeff Lynne*, Roy Orbison*, d. 12 Jun 1988 & Tom Petty* — 61

Date	Title	Peak Position	Weeks at No.1	Weeks on Chart
5 Nov 88	**THE TRAVELING WILBURYS VOLUME 1** *Wilbury WX 224* TRAVELING WILBURYS ⊛	16		35
10 Nov 90	**THE TRAVELING WILBURYS VOLUME 3** *Wilbury WX 384* ●	14		9
23 Jun 07	**COLLECTION** *Rhino 8122799824* ⊛	1	1	17

PAT TRAVERS

Canada, male guitarist — 3

Date	Title	Peak Position	Weeks at No.1	Weeks on Chart
2 Apr 77	**MAKIN' MAGIC** *Polydor 2383 436*	40		3

TRAVIS

UK, male vocal/instrumental group – Fran Healy, Andrew Dunlop, Douglas Payne & Neil Primrose — 208

Date	Title	Peak Position	Weeks at No.1	Weeks on Chart
20 Sep 97	**GOOD FEELING** *Independiente ISOM 1CD* ●	9		16
5 Jun 99	**THE MAN WHO** *Independiente ISOM 9CDX* ⊛x9	1	9	102
23 Jun 01	**THE INVISIBLE BAND** *Independiente ISOM 25CD* ⊛x4	1	4	54
25 Oct 03	**12 MEMORIES** *Independiente ISOM 40CD* ⊛	3		11
13 Nov 04	**SINGLES** *Independiente ISOM 46CD* ⊛	4		15
19 May 07	**THE BOY WITH NO NAME** *Independiente ISOM67CD* ●	4		8
11 Oct 08	**ODE TO J SMITH** *Red Telephone Box PHONE004*	20		2

Top 3 Best-Selling Albums

		Approximate Sales
1	THE MAN WHO	2,670,000
2	THE INVISIBLE BAND	1,220,000
3	SINGLES	520,000

RANDY TRAVIS

US, male vocalist/guitarist — 2

Date	Title	Peak Position	Weeks at No.1	Weeks on Chart
6 Aug 88	**OLD 8 X 10** *Warner Brothers WX 162*	64		2

JOHN TRAVOLTA

US, male vocalist/actor — 6

Date	Title	Peak Position	Weeks at No.1	Weeks on Chart
23 Dec 78	**SANDY** *Midsong POLD 5014* ●	40		6

TREMELOES

UK, male vocal/instrumental group — 7

Date	Title	Peak Position	Weeks at No.1	Weeks on Chart
3 Jun 67	**HERE COMES THE TREMELOES** *CBS SBPG 63017*	15		7

RALPH TRESVANT

US, male vocalist. See New Edition — 3

Date	Title	Peak Position	Weeks at No.1	Weeks on Chart
23 Feb 91	**RALPH TRESVANT** *MCA MCG 6120*	37		3

A TRIBE CALLED QUEST

US, male rap group — 9

Date	Title	Peak Position	Weeks at No.1	Weeks on Chart
19 May 90	**PEOPLE'S INSTINCTIVE TRAVELS...** *Jive HIP 96*	54		2
12 Oct 91	**THE LOW END THEORY** *Jive HIP 117*	58		1
27 Nov 93	**MIDNIGHT MARAUDERS** *Jive CHIP 143*	70		1
10 Aug 96	**BEATS, RHYMES AND LIFE** *Jive CHIP 170* ★	28		4
10 Oct 98	**THE LOVE MOVEMENT** *Jive 0521032*	38		1

OBIE TRICE

US, male rapper — 9

Date	Title	Peak Position	Weeks at No.1	Weeks on Chart
11 Oct 03	**CHEERS** *Interscope 9860986*	11		8
2 Sep 06	**SECOND ROUND'S ON ME** *Interscope 9857229*	46		1

TRICKY

UK, male vocalist/multi-instrumentalist (Adrian Thaws). See Nearly God — 44

Date	Title	Peak Position	Weeks at No.1	Weeks on Chart
4 Mar 95	**MAXINQUAYE** *Fourth & Broadway BRCD 610* ●	3		35
23 Nov 96	**PRE-MILLENNIUM TENSION** *Fourth & Broadway BRCDX 623*	30		2
6 Jun 98	**ANGELS WITH DIRTY FACES** *Island CID 8071*	23		2
28 Aug 99	**JUXTAPOSE** *Island CID 8087* WITH DJ MUGGS & GREASE	22		2
14 Jul 01	**BLOWBACK** *Anti/Epitaph 65962*	34		2
19 Jul 08	**KNOWLE WEST BOY** *Domino WIGCD195*	63		1

TRIFFIDS

Australia, male vocal/instrumental group — 1

Date	Title	Peak Position	Weeks at No.1	Weeks on Chart
22 Apr 89	**THE BLACK SWAN** *Island ILPS 9928*	63		1

Pete Townshend

IN the standard, approved, history of rock music, there's a strict hierarchy. It goes: The Beatles, then The Rolling Stones, and then everybody else, jostling for position behind. At the head of that scrum, though, you'll usually find The Who. They're an awful lot of people's second, third or fourth favourite band. Unlike The Beatles, you'll struggle to find anybody who'll say – even to be controversial – that they don't like them.

Even this status doesn't do justice to a band, and particularly a man – their chief songwriter Pete Townshend – who has quite possibly done as much to shape rock music as any other figure. His list of firsts is considerable. He was arguably the first songwriter to introduce synthesisers to rock music; he was one of the first to use controlled blasts of feedback as part of his sound; he invented the rock opera; he was the first guitarist to brutally smash his guitar at the end of every show. Since the 1960s, many of these achievements have become staples, even clichés, of rock 'n' roll, but at the time they were revolutionary.

Even the guitar-pulverising was in part a publicity stunt

Ironically, considering he helped invent the concept of the generation gap, he didn't come from a strict family background. His family was almost bohemian by the standards of the early 1950s. Both parents were musicians. His dad, Cliff Townshend, was a professional saxophonist and his mother, Betty, a singer. At the age of six, when their marriage was struggling, he was sent away for about a year to live with his grandmother. He later said that, in his memory, this would be one of the murkiest parts of his life and a period that understandably cast a dark shadow. At the age of twelve, when he was practising with school friend John Entwistle, his grandmother came into the room and told him to stop making a racket. In a rage he flung the amplifier at her and, as she shut the glass door, it went right through it. This was one side of what would later be The Who's unique selling point – sheer, unfettered anger at the older generation. The other side, the thoughtful, intellectual profile, came out in 1961 when he enrolled at Ealing Art College and when he and Entwhistle formed their first band, The Confederates.

The group was a trad jazz band with Pete on banjo but, under the influence of the skiffle boom and then The Beatles, they formed a rock 'n' roll band called The Detours with a welder called Roger Daltrey on vocals. At this point another major influence on Townshend's life was coming into play: Mod. The Mods were working-class kids who wore smart suits, rode scooters and were famous for their running battles with motorbike-riding rockers. Daltrey, Townshend, Entwistle and new drummer Keith Moon even attempted to cash in on the phenomenon with the name The High Numbers and a Mod song 'Zoot Suit'.

At this point, like so many 1960s bands, they were happy to do what they thought the times required. Even when they became The Who, on their debut album *My Generation*, there was a calculated attempt to give the kids what they wanted. Townshend admitted later that even the classic 'My Generation' single was written to order after a conversation in which he was asked to 'make a statement'. He wrote the song in one night.

Even the guitar-pulverising was in part a publicity stunt. Townshend accidentally broke a guitar during a gig at a pub in Harrow. Annoyed at the laughter of the crowd he pretended that he'd done it on purpose. Towards the end of the tour, this had already become part of the band's mythology and they were approached by a *Daily Mail* photographer promising that they'd get a page in the newspaper if they did it again. Despite worries about the expensive guitars, Townshend readily complied, although in that instance the promised publicity never materialised.

Biggest-Selling Album

Album	Artist	Week	Highest Position	Approx Sales
WHO'S NEXT	WHO	11/9/71	1	325,000

But he was too clever to carry on playing the 2-D rebel. By 1968 he was already working on his rock opera *Tommy*. This was the moment when rock was growing up and many people, not least the punks a few years later, thought that it was losing touch with its youthful energy. But Townshend has always been more than just a pop star. *Tommy* was an album (and later a film) that delved right into his own psyche. The protagonist, a deaf, dumb and blind kid abused by relatives was an attempt to deal with some of his own demons.

And, if anyone thought they'd gone soft, songs like the blistering 'Pinball Wizard' and the shows The Who played throughout the 1970s were a stunning riposte. 1970's *Live At Leeds* is still widely considered the best live album of all time , their 1976 performance at Charlton Athletic FC was the loudest gig in history (Townshend is partially deaf due to the tinnitus induced by such massive decibels) and Pete's second rock opera, *Quadrophenia*, became a cult classic. But the rock lifestyle was taking a major toll on the whole band. Not only did Townshend suffer serious hearing damage, in 1978, drummer Keith Moon died after an overdose of sedatives he had been prescribed to help deal with his drinking problem.

This ended The Who's domination as one of Britain's greatest rock bands. They released two more studio albums then broke up in 1983, only reforming for major events such as Live Aid; nevertheless, the comeback tours were highly successful and Townshend was still active as a writer, solo performer and charity worker. He has written over 100 songs for his solo work and is, despite his legendary status on the guitar, a superb singer and keyboardist. He is also a published author and has a voracious literary brain.

He has written over 100 songs for his solo work and is, despite his legendary status on the guitar, a superb singer and keyboardist

His worst period came in 2002 with the death of his childhood friend John Entwistle and then, in 2003, his entanglement in a controversy regarding website research for his autobiography which resulted in police very clearly stating there was no inappropriate activity on his part whatsoever. More recently, he has been at the very forefront of cutting-edge internet technology and how it is used to create music, even hosting a complex website that can compose music based around people's personalities. Pete Townshend's compelling need to push the boundaries, it seems, is burning as brightly as ever. Long may it continue.

Silver-selling ○ Gold-selling ● Platinum-selling ⊛ US No.1 ★ | Peak Position | Weeks at No.1 | Weeks on Chart

TRINITI
Ireland, female vocal trio — Weeks on Chart: 5

Date	Title / Label	Peak	Wks at No.1	Wks on Chart
1 Jul 06	**TRINITI** *UCJ 9877250*	28		5

TRIUMPH
Canada, male vocal/instrumental group — Weeks on Chart: 8

Date	Title / Label	Peak	Wks at No.1	Wks on Chart
10 May 80	**PROGRESSIONS OF POWER** *RCA PL 13524*	61		5
3 Oct 81	**ALLIED FORCES** *RCA RCALP 6002*	64		3

TRIVIUM
US, male vocal/instrumental group – Matt Heafy, Corey Beaulieu, Paolo Gregoletto & Travis Smith — Weeks on Chart: 6

Date	Title / Label	Peak	Wks at No.1	Wks on Chart
21 Oct 06	**THE CRUSADE** *Roadrunner RR80592*	7		4
11 Oct 08	**SHOGUN** *Roadrunner RR79852*	17		2

TROGGS
UK, male vocal/instrumental group – Reg Presley, Ronnie Bond, d. 13 Nov 1992, Chris Britton & Pete Staples — Weeks on Chart: 35

Date	Title / Label	Peak	Wks at No.1	Wks on Chart
30 Jul 66	**FROM NOWHERE...THE TROGGS** *Fontana TL 5355*	6		16
25 Feb 67	**TROGGLODYNAMITE** *Page One POL 001*	10		11
5 Aug 67	**THE BEST OF THE TROGGS** *Page One FOR 001*	24		5
16 Jul 94	**GREATEST HITS** *Polygram TV 5227392*	27		3

TROUBADOURS DU ROI BAUDOUIN
Zaire, male/female vocal group — Weeks on Chart: 1

Date	Title / Label	Peak	Wks at No.1	Wks on Chart
22 May 76	**MISSA LUBA** *Philips SBL 7592*	59		1

TROUBLE FUNK
US, male vocal/instrumental group — Weeks on Chart: 4

Date	Title / Label	Peak	Wks at No.1	Wks on Chart
8 Nov 86	**SAY WHAT!** *Fourth & Broadway DCLP 101*	75		2
5 Sep 87	**TROUBLE OVER HERE, TROUBLE OVER THERE** *Fourth & Broadway BRLP 513*	54		2

ROBIN TROWER
UK, male vocalist/guitarist. See Procol Harum — Weeks on Chart: 16

Date	Title / Label	Peak	Wks at No.1	Wks on Chart
1 Mar 75	**FOR EARTH BELOW** *Chrysalis CHR 1073*	26		4
13 Mar 76	**ROBIN TROWER LIVE** *Chrysalis CHR 1089*	15		6
30 Oct 76	**LONG MISTY DAYS** *Chrysalis CHR 1107*	31		1
29 Oct 77	**IN CITY DREAMS** *Chrysalis CHR 1148*	58		1
16 Feb 80	**VICTIMS OF THE FURY** *Chrysalis CHR 1215*	61		4

TRUTH HURTS
US, female vocalist (Shari Watson) — Weeks on Chart: 4

Date	Title / Label	Peak	Wks at No.1	Wks on Chart
24 Aug 02	**TRUTHFULLY SPEAKING** *Interscope 4933312*	61		4

TUBES
US, male vocal/instrumental group — Weeks on Chart: 7

Date	Title / Label	Peak	Wks at No.1	Wks on Chart
4 Mar 78	**WHAT DO YOU WANT FROM LIFE** *A&M AMS 68460*	38		1
2 Jun 79	**REMOTE CONTROL** *A&M AMLH 64751*	40		5
4 Jun 83	**OUTSIDE INSIDE** *Capitol EST 12260*	77		1

TUNDE
Nigeria, male vocalist (Tunde Baiyewu). See Lighthouse Family — Weeks on Chart: 2

Date	Title / Label	Peak	Wks at No.1	Wks on Chart
30 Oct 04	**TUNDE** *RCA 82876652262*	32		2

KT TUNSTALL
UK, female vocalist/guitarist (Kate Tunstall) — Weeks on Chart: 116

Date	Title / Label	Peak	Wks at No.1	Wks on Chart
29 Jan 05	**EYE TO THE TELESCOPE** *Relentless CDREL06* ⊛x5	3		94
14 Oct 06	**ACOUSTIC EXTRAVAGANZA** *Relentless CDRELX08*	32		2
22 Sep 07	**DRASTIC FANTASTIC** *Relentless CDREL15*	3		20

TURIN BRAKES
UK, male vocal/instrumental duo – Gale 'Magpie' Paridjanian & Olly Knights — Weeks on Chart: 34

Date	Title / Label	Peak	Wks at No.1	Wks on Chart
17 Mar 01	**THE OPTIMIST** *Source SOURCD 023* ●	27		18
15 Mar 03	**ETHER SONG** *Source CDSOUR 054* ●	4		11
11 Jun 05	**JACKINABOX** *Source CDSOURX110* ○	9		4
29 Sep 07	**DARK ON FIRE** *Source CDSOURX128*	36		1

IKE & TINA TURNER
US, male/female vocal/instrumental duo – Ike Turner, d. 12 Dec 2007 — Weeks on Chart: 1

Date	Title / Label	Peak	Wks at No.1	Wks on Chart
1 Oct 66	**RIVER DEEP – MOUNTAIN HIGH** *London HAU 8298*	27		1

RUBY TURNER
UK, female vocalist — Weeks on Chart: 19

Date	Title / Label	Peak	Wks at No.1	Wks on Chart
18 Oct 86	**WOMEN HOLD UP HALF THE SKY** *Jive HIP 36* ○	47		11
8 Oct 88	**THE MOTOWN SONG BOOK** *Jive HIP 58* ○	22		6
17 Feb 90	**PARADISE** *Jive HIP 89*	74		2

TINA TURNER
US, female vocalist (Anna Mae Bullock). The veteran Nutbush native went from soul superstar to rock royalty with *Private Dancer*, which sold over 15 million copies worldwide. The popular live performer took home four Grammys in 1985. See Ike & Tina Turner — Weeks on Chart: 536

Date	Title / Label	Peak	Wks at No.1	Wks on Chart
30 Jun 84	**PRIVATE DANCER** *Capitol TINA 1* ⊛x3	2		147
20 Sep 86	**BREAK EVERY RULE** *Capitol EST 2018* ⊛	2		49
2 Apr 88	**LIVE IN EUROPE** *Capitol ESTD 1* ●	8		13
30 Sep 89	**FOREIGN AFFAIR** *Capitol ESTU 2103* ⊛x5	1	1	78
12 Oct 91	**SIMPLY THE BEST** *Capitol ESTV 1* ⊛x8	2		141
19 Jun 93	**WHAT'S LOVE GOT TO DO WITH IT (OST)** *Parlophone CDPCSD 128* ⊛	1	1	33
13 Apr 96	**WILDEST DREAMS** *Parlophone CDEST 2279* ⊛x2	4		41
13 Nov 99	**TWENTY FOUR SEVEN** *Parlophone 5231802* ⊛	9		19
13 Nov 04	**ALL THE BEST** *Parlophone 8667172* ⊛	6		15

TURTLES
US, male vocal/instrumental group — Weeks on Chart: 9

Date	Title / Label	Peak	Wks at No.1	Wks on Chart
22 Jul 67	**HAPPY TOGETHER** *London HAU 8330*	18		9

TV ON THE RADIO
US, male vocal/instrumental group — Weeks on Chart: 3

Date	Title / Label	Peak	Wks at No.1	Wks on Chart
4 Oct 08	**DEAR SCIENCE** *4AD CAD2821CD*	33		3

SHANIA TWAIN
Canada, female vocalist (Eileen Edwards) — Weeks on Chart: 227

Date	Title / Label	Peak	Wks at No.1	Wks on Chart
21 Mar 98	**COME ON OVER** *Mercury 1700812* ⊛x10	1	11	138
18 Mar 00	**THE WOMAN IN ME** *Mercury 5228862* ⊛	7		25
15 Jul 00	**WILD & WICKED** *RWP RWPCD1123*	62		2
30 Nov 02	**UP** *Mercury 1703442* ⊛x2 ★	4		45
20 Nov 04	**GREATEST HITS** *Mercury 9863604* ⊛x2	6		17

TWANG
UK, male vocal/instrumental group – Phil Etheridge, Matty Clinton, Stuart Hartland, Martin Saunders & Jon Watkin — Weeks on Chart: 11

Date	Title / Label	Peak	Wks at No.1	Wks on Chart
16 Jun 07	**LOVE IT WHEN I FEEL LIKE THIS** *B Unique/Polydor BUN127CDS* ●	3		11

TWEENIES
UK, male/female puppet vocalists — Weeks on Chart: 9

Date	Title / Label	Peak	Wks at No.1	Wks on Chart
25 Nov 00	**FRIENDS FOREVER** *BBC Music/Polydor WMSF 60362* ○	56		4
1 Dec 01	**THE CHRISTMAS ALBUM** *BBC Music WMSF 60482*	34		5

TWEET
US, female vocalist (Charlene Keys) — Weeks on Chart: 5

Date	Title / Label	Peak	Wks at No.1	Wks on Chart
25 May 02	**SOUTHERN HUMMINGBIRD** *Elektra 7559627462*	15		5

TWELFTH NIGHT
UK, male vocal/instrumental group — Weeks on Chart: 2

Date	Title / Label	Peak	Wks at No.1	Wks on Chart
27 Oct 84	**ART AND ILLUSION** *Music For Nations MFN 36*	83		2

TWENTY 4 SEVEN FEATURING CAPTAIN HOLLYWOOD

UK, male vocal group

Date	Title	Peak Position	Weeks at No.1	Weeks on Chart (total 2)
19 Jan 91	**STREET MOVES** *BCM 3124*	69		2

22-20S

UK, male vocal/instrumental group

Date	Title	Peak Position	Weeks at No.1	Weeks on Chart (total 1)
2 Oct 04	**22-20S** *Heavenly HVNLP51CD*	40		1

TWIGGY

UK, female vocalist/model (Leslie Hornby)

Date	Title	Peak Position	Weeks at No.1	Weeks on Chart (total 11)
21 Aug 76	**TWIGGY** *Mercury 9102 600* (Silver)	33		8
30 Apr 77	**PLEASE GET MY NAME RIGHT** *Mercury 9102 601*	35		3

TWISTA

US, male rapper (Carl Mitchell)

Date	Title	Peak Position	Weeks at No.1	Weeks on Chart (total 22)
28 Feb 04	**KAMIKAZE** *Atlantic 7567835982* (Gold) ★	19		22

TWISTED SISTER

US, male vocal/instrumental group

Date	Title	Peak Position	Weeks at No.1	Weeks on Chart (total 20)
25 Sep 82	**UNDER THE BLADE** *Secret SECX 9*	70		3
7 May 83	**YOU CAN'T STOP ROCK 'N' ROLL** *Atlantic A 0074*	14		9
16 Jun 84	**STAY HUNGRY** *Atlantic 7801561*	34		5
14 Dec 85	**COME OUT AND PLAY** *Atlantic 7812751*	95		1
25 Jul 87	**LOVE IS FOR SUCKERS** *Atlantic WX 120*	57		2

2 IN A ROOM

US, male vocal duo

Date	Title	Peak Position	Weeks at No.1	Weeks on Chart (total 1)
2 Mar 91	**WIGGLE IT** *SBK SBKLP 11*	73		1

2PAC

US, male rapper (Tupac Shakur), d. 13 Sep 1996 (age 25)

Date	Title	Peak Position	Weeks at No.1	Weeks on Chart (total 80)
9 Mar 96	**ALL EYEZ ON ME** *Death Row 5242492* (Silver) ★	32		7
16 Nov 96	**THE DOM KILLUMINATI – THE SEVEN DAY THEORY** *Death Row IND 90039* MAKAVELI ★	53		1
6 Dec 97	**R U STILL DOWN? (REMEMBER ME)** *Jive CHIP 195*	44		1
8 Aug 98	**IN HIS OWN WORDS** *Eagle EAGCD 050*	65		1
12 Dec 98	**GREATEST HITS** *Jive 0522662* (Platinum)	17		35
8 Jan 00	**STILL I RISE** *Interscope 4904132* & OUTLAWZ	75		1
21 Apr 01	**UNTIL THE END OF TIME** *Interscope 4908402* (Silver) ★	33		17
14 Dec 02	**BETTER DAYZ** *Interscope 4970702*	68		1
22 Nov 03	**RESURRECTION (OST)** *Interscope 9861159*	62		1
28 Aug 04	**LIVE** *Koch 2357462*	67		1
25 Dec 04	**LOYAL TO THE GAME** *Interscope 2103291* (Gold)	20		13
12 Feb 05	**READY 2 DIE (IMPORT)** *Street Dance SDR0166882*	70		1

2 UNLIMITED

Belgium, male producers – Jean-Paul de Coster & Phil Wilde, & Holland, male/female vocal duo – Ray Slijngaard & Anita Doth

Date	Title	Peak Position	Weeks at No.1	Weeks on Chart (total 38)
7 Mar 92	**GET READY** *PWL Continental HFCD 23*	37		3
22 May 93	**NO LIMITS** *PWL Continental HFCD 27*	1	1	21
18 Jun 94	**REAL THINGS** *PWL Continental HFCD 38* (Gold)	1	1	9
11 Nov 95	**HITS UNLIMITED** *PWL Continental HF 47CD*	27		5

TYGERS OF PAN TANG

UK, male vocal/instrumental group

Date	Title	Peak Position	Weeks at No.1	Weeks on Chart (total 20)
30 Aug 80	**WILD CAT** *MCA MCF 3075*	18		5
18 Apr 81	**SPELLBOUND** *MCA MCF 3104*	33		4
21 Nov 81	**CRAZY NIGHTS** *MCA MCF 3123*	51		3
28 Aug 82	**THE CAGE** *MCA MCF 3150*	13		8

BONNIE TYLER

UK, female vocalist (Gaynor Hopkins)

Date	Title	Peak Position	Weeks at No.1	Weeks on Chart (total 94)
16 Apr 83	**FASTER THAN THE SPEED OF NIGHT** *CBS 25304* (Silver)	1	1	45
17 May 86	**SECRET DREAMS AND FORBIDDEN FIRE** *CBS 86319*	24		12
29 Nov 86	**THE GREATEST HITS** *Telstar STAR 2291*	24		17
21 May 88	**HIDE YOUR HEART** *CBS 4601251*	78		1
25 Nov 89	**HEAVEN AND HELL** *Telstar STAR 2361* MEAT LOAF/BONNIE TYLER	9		12
14 Jul 01	**THE GREATEST HITS** *Sanctuary/Sony TV SANCD 082* (Silver)	18		4
24 Mar 07	**FROM THE HEART – GREATEST HITS** *Sony BMG 88697071982*	31		3

TYPE O NEGATIVE

US, male vocal/instrumental group

Date	Title	Peak Position	Weeks at No.1	Weeks on Chart (total 2)
14 Sep 96	**OCTOBER RUST** *Roadrunner RR 88742*	26		1
2 Oct 99	**WORLD COMING DOWN** *Roadrunner RR 86602*	49		1

JUDIE TZUKE

UK, female vocalist

Date	Title	Peak Position	Weeks at No.1	Weeks on Chart (total 61)
4 Aug 79	**WELCOME TO THE CRUISE** *Rocket TRAIN 7* (Gold)	14		17
10 May 80	**SPORTS CAR** *Rocket TRAIN 9* (Gold)	7		11
16 May 81	**I AM PHOENIX** *Rocket TRAIN 15*	17		10
17 Apr 82	**SHOOT THE MOON** *Chrysalis CDL 1382*	19		10
30 Oct 82	**ROAD NOISE – THE OFFICIAL BOOTLEG** *Chrysalis CTY 1405*	39		4
1 Oct 83	**RITMO** *Chrysalis CDL 1442*	26		5
15 Jun 85	**THE CAT IS OUT** *Legacy LLP 102*	35		3
29 Apr 89	**TURNING STONES** *Polydor 8390871*	57		1

BIOGRAPHIES

Biographies include the nationality and category for every chart entrant.

Each entrant has at least a mini biography. The 100 acts with the most weeks on the chart (see page 290 for the top 100 chart) each have extended biographies.

Real names are included for all solo artists and, where applicable, dates of death and age of the artist at the time. "See…" links are included for soloists who also had album chart entries in other acts.

The best known line-up is listed for every group that had a Top 10 album, with the vocalist/leader mentioned first and the others following in alphabetical order. In cases where later replacements had similar success both people are named and, where applicable, the dates of death are also shown for every group/duo member listed.

Certified Awards are given by the BPI to mark unit sales to retailers. The certified awards were introduced in April 1973, based on revenue received by manufacturers. In January 1978 the qualification rules were changed and the system based on unit sales to the trade was adopted.

Silver symbol	●	=	60,000 units
Gold symbol	●	=	100,000 units
Platinum symbol	⊛	=	300,000 units

U–X

KEY TO ARTIST ENTRIES

Artist/Group Name — Artist/Group Biography — Silver-selling — Gold-selling — Platinum-selling — US No.1 ★ — Peak Position — Weeks at No.1 — Weeks on Chart

Asterisks (*) indicate group members with hits in their own right that are listed elsewhere in this book

TOM JONES
UK, male vocalist (Thomas Woodward). Perennially popular Welsh vocalist, who has a 43-year span of UK hit albums, was the No.1 UK solo singer of the 1960s on both sides of the Atlantic. The unmistakable Vegas veteran received the Outstanding Contribution award at the 2003 BRITs

Artist's Total Weeks On Chart: 530

Date	Album Title / Label and Catalogue Number	Peak Position	Weeks at No.1	Weeks on Chart
5 Jun 65	**ALONG CAME JONES** *Decca LK 6693*	11		5
8 Oct 66	**FROM THE HEART** *Decca LK 4814*	23		8
8 Apr 67	**GREEN GREEN GRASS OF HOME** *Decca SKL 4855*	3		49
24 Jun 67	**LIVE AT THE TALK OF THE TOWN** *Decca SKL 4874*	6		90
30 Dec 67	**13 SMASH HITS** *Decca SKL 4909*	5		49
27 Jul 68	**DELILAH** *Decca SKL 4946*	1	2	29
21 Dec 68	**HELP YOURSELF** *Decca SKL 4982*	4		9
28 Jun 69	**THIS IS TOM JONES** *Decca SKL 5007*	2		20
15 Nov 69	**TOM JONES LIVE IN LAS VEGAS** *Decca SKL 5032*	2		45
25 Apr 70	**TOM** *Decca SKL 5045*	4		18
14 Nov 70	**I WHO HAVE NOTHING** *Decca SKL 5072*	10		10
29 May 71	**SHE'S A LADY** *Decca SKL 5089*	9		7
27 Nov 71	**LIVE AT CAESAR'S PALACE** *Decca D 1/11/2*	27		5
24 Jun 72	**CLOSE UP** *Decca SKL 5132*	17		4
23 Jun 73	**THE BODY AND SOUL OF TOM JONES** *Decca SKL 5162*	31		1
5 Jan 74	**GREATEST HITS** *Decca SKL 5176*	15		13
22 Mar 75	**20 GREATEST HITS** *Decca TJD 1/11/2* ●	1	4	21
7 Oct 78	**I'M COMING HOME** *Lotus WH 5001* ●	12		9
16 May 87	**THE GREATEST HITS** *Telstar STAR 2296*	16		12
13 May 89	**AT THIS MOMENT** *Jive TOMTV 1*	34		3
8 Jul 89	**AFTER DARK** *Stylus SMR 978*	46		4
6 Apr 91	**CARRYING A TORCH** *Dover ADD 20*	44		4
27 Jun 92	**THE COMPLETE TOM JONES** *The Hit Label 8442862* ●	8		6
26 Nov 94	**THE LEAD AND HOW TO SWING IT** *ZTT 6544924982*	55		1
14 Nov 98	**THE ULTIMATE HITS COLLECTION** *Polygram TV 8449012*	26		6
9 Oct 99	**RELOAD** *Gut GUTCD 009* ⊛**x4**	1	3	65
16 Nov 02	**MR JONES** *V2 VVR 1021072*	36		2
1 Mar 03	**GREATEST HITS** *Universal TV 8828632* ⊛	2		16
9 Oct 04	**TOM JONES AND JOOLS HOLLAND** *Radar RADAR004CD* & JOOLS HOLLAND ●	5		13
29 Nov 08	**24 HOURS** *S-Curve 2649852*	32		6+

Date of entry into chart

Artist collaboration or where artist's name has changed

Album Title

Label and Catalogue Number

Cross (+) indicates album is still on chart in last week of 2008

UB40

UK, male vocal/instrumental group – Ali Campbell*, James Brown, Robin Campbell, Earl Falconer, Norman Hassan, Brian Travers, Mickey Virtue & Terence Wilson. Reggae-infused Birmingham collective who brought the genre to a new transatlantic audience. They have sold an estimated 70 million records during a career which has spawned 24 Top 50 albums

Date	Title	Peak Position	Weeks at No.1	Weeks on Chart
				623
6 Sep 80	**SIGNING OFF** *Graduate GRAD LP2* ⊛	2		71
6 Jun 81	**PRESENT ARMS** *DEP International LPDEP 1* ⊛	2		38
10 Oct 81	**PRESENT ARMS IN DUB** *DEP International LPDEP 2*	38		7
28 Aug 82	**THE SINGLES ALBUM** *Graduate GRADLSP 3*	17		8
9 Oct 82	**UB 44** *DEP International LPDEP 3* ●	4		8
26 Feb 83	**UB40 LIVE** *DEP International LPDEP 4*	44		5
24 Sep 83	**LABOUR OF LOVE** *DEP International LPDEP 5* ⊛ **x2**	1	1	76
20 Oct 84	**GEFFERY MORGAN...** *DEP International DEP 6* ○	3		14
14 Sep 85	**BAGGARIDDIM** *DEP International LPDEP 10* ●	14		23
9 Aug 86	**RAT IN THE KITCHEN** *DEP International LPDEP 11* ●	8		20
7 Nov 87	**THE BEST OF UB40 – VOLUME ONE** *DEP International UBTV 1* ⊛**x6**	3		133
23 Jul 88	**UB40** *DEP International LPDEP 13* ●	12		12
9 Dec 89	**LABOUR OF LOVE II** *DEP International LPDEP 14* ⊛**x3**	3		69
24 Jul 93	**PROMISES AND LIES** *DEP International DEPCD 15* ⊛**x2**	1	7	37
12 Nov 94	**LABOUR OF LOVE – VOLUMES I AND II** *DEP International DEPDD 1* ●	5		15
11 Nov 95	**THE BEST OF UB40 – VOLUME TWO** *DEP International DUBTV 2* ⊛	12		11
12 Jul 97	**GUNS IN THE GHETTO** *DEP International CADEP 16* ○	7		9
24 Oct 98	**LABOUR OF LOVE III** *DEP International DEPCD 18* ●	8		12
4 Nov 00	**THE VERY BEST OF – 1980-2000** *Virgin DUBTVX 3* ⊛	7		23
3 Nov 01	**COVER UP** *Virgin DEPCD 19*	29		2
14 Jun 03	**LABOUR OF LOVE – VOLUMES I, II & III** *Virgin 5847242* ●	7		17
15 Nov 03	**HOMEGROWN** *DEP International DEPCD 22*	49		2
25 Jun 05	**WHO YOU FIGHTING FOR** *DEP International DEPCD23*	20		5
26 Nov 05	**THE BEST OF VOLUMES 1 & 2** *DEP International DEPDDX2* ●	47		6

UFO

UK/Germany, male vocal/instrumental group – Phil Mogg, Andy Parker, Paul Raymond, Michael Schenker* (replaced by Paul Chapman) & Pete Way

Date	Title	Peak Position	Weeks at No.1	Weeks on Chart
				48
4 Jun 77	**LIGHTS OUT** *Chrysalis CHR 1127*	54		2
15 Jul 78	**OBSESSION** *Chrysalis CHR 1182*	26		7
10 Feb 79	**STRANGERS IN THE NIGHT** *Chrysalis CJT 5* ○	8		11
19 Jan 80	**NO PLACE TO RUN** *Chrysalis CDL 1239* ○	11		7
24 Jan 81	**THE WILD THE WILLING AND THE INNOCENT** *Chrysalis CHR 1307*	19		5
20 Feb 82	**MECHANIX** *Chrysalis CHR 1360*	8		6
12 Feb 83	**MAKING CONTACT** *Chrysalis CHR 1402*	32		4
3 Sep 83	**HEADSTONE – THE BEST OF UFO** *Chrysalis CTY 1437*	39		4
16 Nov 85	**MISDEMEANOUR** *Chrysalis CHR 1518*	74		2

UGLY KID JOE

US, male vocal/instrumental group – Whitfield Crane, Cordell Crockett, Mark Davis, Klaus Eichstadt & Dave Fortman

Date	Title	Peak Position	Weeks at No.1	Weeks on Chart
				42
13 Jun 92	**AS UGLY AS THEY WANNA BE** *Mercury 8688232*	9		13
12 Sep 92	**AMERICA'S LEAST WANTED** *Vertigo 5125712*	11		24
17 Jun 95	**MENACE TO SOBRIETY** *Mercury 5282622*	25		5

U.K.

UK, male vocal/instrumental group

Date	Title	Peak Position	Weeks at No.1	Weeks on Chart
				3
27 May 78	**U.K.** *Polydor 2302 080*	43		3

U.K. SUBS

UK, male vocal/instrumental group – Charlie Harper, Pete Davies, Nicky Garratt & Paul Slack

Date	Title	Peak Position	Weeks at No.1	Weeks on Chart
				26
13 Oct 79	**ANOTHER KIND OF BLUES** *Gem GEMLP 100*	21		6
19 Apr 80	**BRAND NEW AGE** *Gem GEMLP 106*	18		9
27 Sep 80	**CRASH COURSE** *Gem GEMLP 111*	8		6
21 Feb 81	**DIMINISHED RESPONSIBILITY** *Gem GEMLP 112*	18		5

TRACEY ULLMAN

US (b. UK), female vocalist/comedian/actor

Date	Title	Peak Position	Weeks at No.1	Weeks on Chart
				22
3 Dec 83	**YOU BREAK MY HEART IN 17 PLACES** *Stiff SEEZ 51* ○	14		20
8 Dec 84	**YOU CAUGHT ME OUT** *Stiff SEEZ 56*	92		2

ULTIMATE KAOS

UK, male vocal group

Date	Title	Peak Position	Weeks at No.1	Weeks on Chart
				1
29 Apr 95	**ULTIMATE KAOS** *Wild Card 5274442*	51		1

ULTRA

UK, male vocal/instrumental group

Date	Title	Peak Position	Weeks at No.1	Weeks on Chart
				2
6 Feb 99	**ULTRA** *East West 3984222452*	37		2

ULTRA-SONIC

UK, male instrumental/production duo

Date	Title	Peak Position	Weeks at No.1	Weeks on Chart
				1
11 Nov 95	**GLOBALTEKNO** *Clubscene DCSR 007*	58		1

ULTRA VIVID SCENE

UK, male vocalist (Kurt Ralske)

Date	Title	Peak Position	Weeks at No.1	Weeks on Chart
				1
19 May 90	**JOY 1967–1990** *4AD CAD 005*	58		1

ULTRABEAT

UK, male vocal/DJ/production group – Mike Di Scala, Chris Henry, Ian Redman & Rebecca Rudd

Date	Title	Peak Position	Weeks at No.1	Weeks on Chart
				6
22 Sep 07	**THE ALBUM** *All Around The World GLOBECD46*	8		6

ULTRAMARINE

UK, male instrumental duo

Date	Title	Peak Position	Weeks at No.1	Weeks on Chart
				1
4 Sep 93	**UNITED KINGDOMS** *Blanco Y Negro 4509934252*	49		1

ULTRASOUND

UK, male/female vocal/instrumental group

Date	Title	Peak Position	Weeks at No.1	Weeks on Chart
				1
1 May 99	**EVERYTHING PICTURE** *Nude 12CD*	23		1

ULTRAVOX

UK, male vocal/instrumental group – Midge Ure*, Warren Cann, Chris Cross & Billy Currie

Date	Title	Peak Position	Weeks at No.1	Weeks on Chart
				233
19 Jul 80	**VIENNA** *Chrysalis CHR 1296* ⊛	3		72
19 Sep 81	**RAGE IN EDEN** *Chrysalis CDL 1338* ●	4		23
23 Oct 82	**QUARTET** *Chrysalis CDL 1394* ●	6		30
22 Oct 83	**MONUMENT – THE SOUNDTRACK** *Chrysalis CUX 1452* ●	9		15
14 Apr 84	**LAMENT** *Chrysalis CDL 1459* ●	8		26
10 Nov 84	**THE COLLECTION** *Chrysalis UTV 1* ⊛**x3**	2		53
25 Oct 86	**U-VOX** *Chrysalis CDL 1545* ●	9		6
6 Mar 93	**IF I WAS: THE VERY BEST OF MIDGE URE AND ULTRAVOX** *Chrysalis CDCHR 1987* MIDGE URE/ULTRAVOX ○	10		6
10 Nov 01	**THE VERY BEST OF** *EMI 5358112* MIDGE URE & ULTRAVOX	45		2

UNBELIEVABLE TRUTH

UK, male vocal/instrumental group

Date	Title	Peak Position	Weeks at No.1	Weeks on Chart
				2
23 May 98	**ALMOST HERE** *Virgin CDVX 2849*	21		2

UNCLE KRACKER

US, male vocalist (Matt Shafer)

Date	Title	Peak Position	Weeks at No.1	Weeks on Chart
				3
22 Sep 01	**DOUBLE WIDE** *Atlantic 7567832792*	40		3

UNDERCOVER

UK, male vocal/instrumental group

Date	Title	Peak Position	Weeks at No.1	Weeks on Chart
				9
5 Dec 92	**CHECK OUT THE GROOVE** *PWL International HFCD 26*	26		9

UNDERTONES

UK, male vocal/instrumental group – Feargal Sharkey*, Michael Bradley, Billy Doherty, Damien O'Neill & John O'Neill

Date	Title	Peak Position	Weeks at No.1	Weeks on Chart
				52
19 May 79	**THE UNDERTONES** *Sire SRK 6071*	13		21
26 Apr 80	**HYPNOTISED** *Sire SRK 6088*	6		10
16 May 81	**POSITIVE TOUCH** *Ardeck ARD 103*	17		6
19 Mar 83	**THE SIN OF PRIDE** *Ardeck ARD 104*	43		5
10 Dec 83	**ALL WRAPPED UP** *Ardeck ARD 1654281/3*	67		4
14 Jun 86	**CHER O'BOWLIES – PICK OF THE UNDERTONES** *Ardeck EMS 1172* FEATURING FEARGAL SHARKEY	96		1
25 Sep 93	**THE BEST OF THE UNDERTONES – TEENAGE KICKS** *Castle Communications CTVCD 121*	45		3
13 Sep 03	**TEENAGE KICKS – THE BEST OF** *Sanctuary TVSAN005*	35		2

Silver-selling ○ Gold-selling ● Platinum-selling ⊛ US No.1 ★ — Peak Position · Weeks at No.1 · Weeks on Chart

UNDERWORLD
UK, male vocal/instrumental group – Karl Hyde, Darren Emerson & Rick Smith **55**

Date	Title	Peak	Wks at No.1	Wks on Chart
5 Feb 94	**DUBNOBASSWITHMYHEADMAN** *Junior Boy's Own JBOCD 1* ●	12		4
23 Mar 96	**SECOND TOUGHEST IN THE INFANTS** *Junior Boy's Own JBOCD 4* ●	9		28
13 Mar 99	**BEAUCOUP FISH** *JBO 1005438* ●	3		12
16 Sep 00	**EVERYTHING EVERYTHING** *JBO 1012548*	22		3
28 Sep 02	**A HUNDRED DAYS OFF** *JBO 1020102*	16		3
5 Oct 02	**DUBNOBASSWITHMYHEADMAN** *JBO 1001992*	53		2
15 Nov 03	**1992 – 2002** *JBO 1024698*	43		2
27 Oct 07	**OBLIVION WITH BELLS** *Underworld Live UWR000173*	45		1

UNION
UK/Holland, male instrumental group & rugby team vocalists **6**

Date	Title	Peak	Wks at No.1	Wks on Chart
26 Oct 91	**WORLD IN UNION** *Columbia 4690471*	17		6

UNKLE
US/UK, male DJ/production duo – Josh Davis & James Lavelle **14**

Date	Title	Peak	Wks at No.1	Wks on Chart
21 Jan 95	**THE TIME HAS COME (EP)** *Mo Wax MW028P*	73		1
5 Sep 98	**PSYENCE FICTION** *Mo Wax MW085CD* ●	4		9
4 Oct 03	**NEVER, NEVER, LAND** *Mo Wax MWU 001CDX*	24		2
14 Jul 07	**WAR STORIES** *Surrender All SURR005CDXX*	58		1
19 Jul 08	**END TITLES – STORIES FOR FILM** *All Surrender SURR009CD*	70		1

UNTOUCHABLES
US, male vocal/instrumental group **7**

Date	Title	Peak	Wks at No.1	Wks on Chart
13 Jul 85	**WILD CHILD** *Stiff SEEZ 57*	51		7

UPPER ROOM
UK, male vocal/instrumental group **1**

Date	Title	Peak	Wks at No.1	Wks on Chart
10 Jun 06	**OTHER PEOPLE'S PROBLEMS** *Columbia 82876857302*	50		1

DAWN UPSHAW
US, female vocalist **18**

Date	Title	Peak	Wks at No.1	Wks on Chart
23 Jan 93	**GORECKI: SYMPHONY NO. 3** *Elektra Nonsuch 755979822* DAWN UPSHAW (SOPRANO)/THE LONDON SINFONIETTA/ DAVID ZINMAN (CONDUCTOR) ●	6		18

KEITH URBAN
Australia (b. New Zealand), male vocalist/guitarist **4**

Date	Title	Peak	Wks at No.1	Wks on Chart
11 Jun 05	**DAYS GO BY** *Capitol 4775812*	40		3
25 Nov 06	**LOVE PAIN & THE WHOLE CRAZY THING** *Capitol 3811410*	73		1

URBAN COOKIE COLLECTIVE
UK, male/female vocal/instrumental group **2**

Date	Title	Peak	Wks at No.1	Wks on Chart
26 Mar 94	**HIGH ON A HAPPY VIBE** *Pulse 8 PULSE 13CD*	28		2

URBAN SPECIES
UK, male vocal/instrumental group **2**

Date	Title	Peak	Wks at No.1	Wks on Chart
7 May 94	**LISTEN** *Talkin Loud 5186482*	43		2

MIDGE URE
UK, male vocalist. See Rich Kids, Slik, Ultravox & Visage **28**

Date	Title	Peak	Wks at No.1	Wks on Chart
19 Oct 85	**THE GIFT** *Chrysalis CHR 1508* ●	2		15
10 Sep 88	**ANSWERS TO NOTHING** *Chrysalis CHR 1649*	30		3
28 Sep 91	**PURE** *Arista 211922*	36		2
6 Mar 93	**IF I WAS: THE VERY BEST OF MIDGE URE AND ULTRAVOX** *Chrysalis CDCHR 1987* /ULTRAVOX ○	10		6
10 Nov 01	**THE VERY BEST OF** *EMI 5358112* & ULTRAVOX	45		2

URIAH HEEP
UK, male vocal/instrumental group – David Byron, d. 28 Feb 1985, Keith Baker, Mick Box, Ken Hensley, Gary Thain, d. 19 Mar 1976 **51**

Date	Title	Peak	Wks at No.1	Wks on Chart
13 Nov 71	**LOOK AT YOURSELF** *Island ILPS 9169*	39		1
10 Jun 72	**DEMONS AND WIZARDS** *Bronze ILPS 9193*	20		11
2 Dec 72	**THE MAGICIAN'S BIRTHDAY** *Bronze ILPS 9213*	28		3
19 May 73	**URIAH HEEP LIVE** *Island ISLD 1* ○	23		8
29 Sep 73	**SWEET FREEDOM** *Island ILPS 9245* ○	18		3
29 Jun 74	**WONDERWORLD** *Bronze ILPS 9280* ○	23		3
5 Jul 75	**RETURN TO FANTASY** *Bronze ILPS 9335* ○	7		6
12 Jun 76	**HIGH AND MIGHTY** *Island ILPS 9384*	55		1
22 Mar 80	**CONQUEST** *Bronze BRON 524*	37		3
17 Apr 82	**ABOMINOG** *Bronze BRON 538*	34		6
18 Jun 83	**HEAD FIRST** *Bronze BRON 545*	46		4
6 Apr 85	**EQUATOR** *Portrait PRT 26414*	79		2

URUSEI YATSURA
UK, male/female vocal/instrumental group **1**

Date	Title	Peak	Wks at No.1	Wks on Chart
14 Mar 98	**SLAIN BY** *CHE 3984222212*	64		1

USA FOR AFRICA
US, male/female vocal ensemble **5**

Date	Title	Peak	Wks at No.1	Wks on Chart
25 May 85	**WE ARE THE WORLD** *CBS USAID F1*	31		5

USED
US, male vocal/instrumental group **1**

Date	Title	Peak	Wks at No.1	Wks on Chart
2 Jun 07	**LIES FOR THE LIARS** *Reprise 9362433092*	39		1

USHER
US, male vocalist (Usher Raymond) **144**

Date	Title	Peak	Wks at No.1	Wks on Chart
17 Jan 98	**MY WAY** *LaFace 73008260432* ●	16		18
21 Jul 01	**8701** *LaFace 74321874712* ⊛	1	1	47
3 Apr 04	**CONFESSIONS** *Arista 82876609902* ⊛x4 ★	1	1	66
7 Jun 08	**HERE I STAND** *LaFace 88697233882* ● ★	1	1	13

US3
UK, male vocal/instrumental/production trio **6**

Date	Title	Peak	Wks at No.1	Wks on Chart
31 Jul 93	**HAND ON THE TORCH/JAZZ MIXES** *Blue Note CDEST 2195*	40		6

UTAH SAINTS
UK, male instrumental/production duo – Tim Garbutt & Jez Willis **15**

Date	Title	Peak	Wks at No.1	Wks on Chart
5 Jun 93	**UTAH SAINTS** *ffrr 8283792* ○	10		15

U.T.F.O.
US, male rap group **1**

Date	Title	Peak	Wks at No.1	Wks on Chart
16 Mar 85	**ROXANNE ROXANNE (6 TRACK VERSION)** *Streetwave XKHAN 506*	72		1

UTOPIA
UK, male vocal/instrumental group **3**

Date	Title	Peak	Wks at No.1	Wks on Chart
1 Oct 77	**OOPS! SORRY WRONG PLANET** *Bearsville K 53517*	59		1
16 Feb 80	**ADVENTURES IN UTOPIA** *Island ILPS 9602*	57		2

U2
Ireland/UK, male vocal/instrumental group – Paul 'Bono' Hewson, Adam Clayton, David 'The Edge' Evans & Larry Mullen Jr. The most successful band of the past 25 years have sold more than 120 million albums, won 22 Grammys and collected six BRITs for Best International Group. The first act to sell one million copies of an album on CD (*The Joshua Tree*) **1189**

Date	Title	Peak	Wks at No.1	Wks on Chart
29 Aug 81	**BOY** *Island ILPS 9646* ●	52		31
24 Oct 81	**OCTOBER** *Island ILPS 9680* ⊛	11		42
12 Mar 83	**WAR** *Island ILPS 9733* ⊛x2	1	1	147
3 Dec 83	**U2 LIVE 'UNDER A BLOOD RED SKY'** *Island IMA 3* ⊛x3	2		203
13 Oct 84	**THE UNFORGETTABLE FIRE** *Island U 25* ⊛x2	1	2	130
27 Jul 85	**WIDE AWAKE IN AMERICA** *Island 902791A* ○	11		16
21 Mar 87	**THE JOSHUA TREE** *Island U 26* ⊛x5 ★	1	2	163
20 Feb 88	**THE JOSHUA TREE SINGLES** *Island U2 PK 1*	100		1
22 Oct 88	**RATTLE AND HUM** *Island U2 7* ⊛x4 ★	1	1	61
30 Nov 91	**ACHTUNG BABY** *Island U 28* ⊛x4 ★	2		87
17 Jul 93	**ZOOROPA** *Island CIDU 29* ⊛ ★	1	1	31
15 Mar 97	**POP** *Island CIDU 210* ⊛ ★	1	1	35
14 Nov 98	**THE BEST OF 1980–1990 & B SIDES** *Island CIDDU 211* ⊛	1	1	12
21 Nov 98	**THE BEST OF 1980–1990** *Island CIDU 211* ⊛x5	4		75
11 Nov 00	**ALL THAT YOU CAN'T LEAVE BEHIND** *Island CIDU 212* ⊛x3	1	1	62
16 Nov 02	**THE BEST OF 1990-2000 & B-SIDES** *Island CIDTU 213* ⊛x2	2		21
23 Nov 02	**THE BEST OF 1990 – 2000** *Island CIDU 213*	37		14
4 Dec 04	**HOW TO DISMANTLE AN ATOMIC BOMB** *Island CIDXU214* ⊛x4 ★	1	3	38

Date	Album	Peak	Wks No.1	Wks
2 Dec 06	**U218 SINGLES** *Mercury 1713593* ⊛x2	4		17
15 Dec 07	**THE JOSHUA TREE DELUXE** *Mercury 1744939*	51		3

Top 3 Best-Selling Albums

		Approximate Sales
1	THE JOSHUA TREE	2,680,000
2	THE BEST OF 1980-1990	1,470,000
3	RATTLE AND HUM	1,430,000

V

STEVE VAI
US, male guitarist — 20

Date	Album	Peak	Wks No.1	Wks
2 Jun 90	**PASSION AND WARFARE** *Food For Thought GRUB 17* ○	8		10
7 Aug 93	**SEX AND RELIGION** *Relativity 4729472*	17		6
15 Apr 95	**ALIEN LOVE SECRETS** *Relativity 4785862*	39		2
28 Sep 96	**FIRE GARDEN** *Epic 4850622*	41		2

HOLLY VALANCE
Australia, female vocalist (Holly Vukadinovic) — 12

Date	Album	Peak	Wks No.1	Wks
26 Oct 02	**FOOTPRINTS** *London 0927493722* ●	9		11
22 Nov 03	**STATE OF MIND** *London 5046701625*	60		1

BOBBY VALENTINO
US, male vocalist (Bobby Wilson) — 8

Date	Album	Peak	Wks No.1	Wks
7 May 05	**DISTURBING THA PEACE PRESENTS** *Def Jam 9880210* ●	34		8

VAMPIRE WEEKEND
US, male vocal/instrumental group — 27

Date	Album	Peak	Wks No.1	Wks
9 Feb 08	**VAMPIRE WEEKEND** *XL Recordings XLCD318* ●	15		27

VAN DE GRAAF GENERATOR
UK, male vocal/instrumental group — 2

Date	Album	Peak	Wks No.1	Wks
25 Apr 70	**THE LEAST WE CAN DO IS WAVE TO EACH OTHER** *Charisma CAS 1007*	47		2

PAUL VAN DYK
Germany, male DJ/producer — 4

Date	Album	Peak	Wks No.1	Wks
17 Jun 00	**OUT THERE & BACK** *Deviant DVNT 37DCD*	12		3
8 Sep 07	**IN BETWEEN** *Postiva 5043201*	63		1

VAN HALEN
US/Holland, male vocal/instrumental group – David Lee Roth*, Sammy Hagar*, Michael Anthony, Alex Van Halen & Eddie Van Halen — 111

Date	Album	Peak	Wks No.1	Wks
27 May 78	**VAN HALEN** *Warner Brothers K 56470* ●	34		11
14 Apr 79	**VAN HALEN II** *Warner Brothers K 56616*	23		7
5 Apr 80	**WOMEN AND CHILDREN FIRST** *Warner Brothers K 56793*	15		7
23 May 81	**FAIR WARNING** *Warner Brothers K 56899*	49		4
1 May 82	**DIVER DOWN** *Warner Brothers K 57003*	36		5
4 Feb 84	**1984** *Warner Brothers 9239851* ●	15		24
5 Apr 86	**5150** *Warner Brothers WS 5150* ○ ★	16		18
4 Jun 88	**OU812** *Warner Brothers WX 177* ○ ★	16		12
29 Jun 91	**FOR UNLAWFUL CARNAL KNOWLEDGE** *Warner Brothers WX 420* ★	12		5
6 Mar 93	**LIVE: RIGHT HERE, RIGHT NOW** *Warner Brothers 9362451982*	24		4
4 Feb 95	**BALANCE** *Warner Brothers 9362457602* ★	8		3
9 Nov 96	**THE BEST OF VAN HALEN – VOLUME 1** *Warner Brothers 9362464742* ★	45		1
28 Mar 98	**VAN HALEN 3** *Warner Brothers 9362466622*	43		1
31 Jul 04	**THE BEST OF BOTH WORLDS** *Warner Brothers 8122765152*	15		9

ARMAND VAN HELDEN
US, male DJ/producer — 9

Date	Album	Peak	Wks No.1	Wks
10 Apr 99	**2 FUTURE 4 U** *ffrr 5560902* ○	22		6
10 Jun 00	**KILLING PURITANS** *ffrr 8573833192*	38		1
4 Oct 08	**YOU DON'T KNOW ME – THE BEST OF** *Rhino/UMTV 5312525*	41		2

DENISE VAN OUTEN
UK, female actor/vocalist — 2

Date	Album	Peak	Wks No.1	Wks
26 Apr 03	**TELL ME ON A SUNDAY** *Really Useful 0761742*	34		2

LUTHER VANDROSS
US, male vocalist, d. 1 July 2005 (age 54). Respected soul legend who amassed 10 successive platinum albums Stateside. He won eight Grammy awards and garnered four 1995 nominations for Songs, his No.1 album of cover versions. See Change — 309

Date	Album	Peak	Wks No.1	Wks
21 Jan 84	**BUSY BODY** *Epic EPC 25608*	42		8
6 Apr 85	**THE NIGHT I FELL IN LOVE** *Epic EPC 26387*	19		10
13 Jul 85	**THE ARTISTS VOLUME 2** *Street Sounds ARTIS 2* /TEDDY PENDERGRASS/CHANGE/ATLANTIC STARR	45		4
1 Nov 86	**GIVE ME THE REASON** *Epic 4501341* ⊛x2	3		99
21 Feb 87	**NEVER TOO MUCH** *Epic EPC 32807*	41		30
4 Jul 87	**FOREVER, FOR ALWAYS, FOR LOVE** *Epic EPC 25013* ⊛	23		16
16 Apr 88	**BUSY BODY** *Epic 4601831*	78		4
29 Oct 88	**ANY LOVE** *Epic 4629081* ●	3		22
11 Nov 89	**BEST OF LUTHER VANDROSS – BEST OF LOVE** *Epic 4658011*	14		13
25 May 91	**POWER OF LOVE** *Epic 4680121* ○	9		9
12 Jun 93	**NEVER LET ME GO** *Epic 4735982*	11		5
1 Oct 94	**SONGS** *Epic 4766562* ⊛	1	1	28
28 Oct 95	**GREATEST HITS 1981–1995** *Epic 4811002* ●	12		14
19 Oct 96	**YOUR SECRET LOVE** *Epic 6638382* ○	14		4
11 Oct 97	**ONE NIGHT WITH YOU – THE BEST OF LOVE** *Epic 4888882*	56		2
22 Aug 98	**I KNOW** *EMI 8460892*	42		1
16 Feb 02	**THE ESSENTIAL LUTHER VANDROSS** *Epic 5050252*	72		2
5 Jul 03	**DANCE WITH MY FATHER** *J Records 82876540732* ○	41		15
23 Aug 03	**THE ESSENTIAL LUTHER VANDROSS** *Epic 5133532*	18		7
21 Oct 06	**THE ULTIMATE LUTHER VANDROSS** *J 88697016102* ●	10		16

VANESSA-MAE
Singapore, female vocalist/violinist (Vanessa-Mae Vanakorn Nicholson) — 34

Date	Album	Peak	Wks No.1	Wks
25 Feb 95	**THE VIOLIN PLAYER** *EMI CDC 5550892* ●	11		21
2 Nov 96	**CLASSICAL ALBUM 1** *EMI Premier CDC 5553952*	47		2
8 Nov 97	**STORM** *EMI 8218002* ○	27		5
7 Feb 98	**CHINA GIRL – THE CLASSICAL ALBUM 2** *EMI Classics CDC 5564832*	56		3
26 May 01	**SUBJECT TO CHANGE** *EMI 5331002*	58		2
30 Oct 04	**CHOREOGRAPHY** *Sony Classical SK90895*	66		1

VANGELIS
Greece, male keyboard/synthesizer player (Evangelos Papathanassiou). See Jon & Vangelis — 164

Date	Album	Peak	Wks No.1	Wks
10 Jan 76	**HEAVEN AND HELL** *RCA Victor RS 1025*	31		7
9 Oct 76	**ALBEDO 0.39** *RCA Victor RS 1080*	18		6
18 Apr 81	**CHARIOTS OF FIRE (OST)** *Polydor POLS 1026* ⊛ ★	5		97
5 May 84	**CHARIOTS OF FIRE (OST)** *Polydor POLD 5160*	39		9
13 Oct 84	**SOIL FESTIVITIES** *Polydor POLH 11*	55		4
30 Mar 85	**MASK** *Polydor POLH 19*	69		2
22 Jul 89	**THEMES** *Polydor VGTV 1* ●	11		13
24 Oct 92	**1492 – THE CONQUEST OF PARADISE (OST)** *East West 4509910142* ●	33		6
18 Jun 94	**BLADERUNNER (OST)** *East West 4509965742* ●	20		6
2 Mar 96	**VOICES** *East West 0630127862*	58		1
20 Apr 96	**PORTRAIT (SO LONG AGO, SO CLEAR)** *Polydor 5311542*	14		6
8 Nov 03	**ODYSSEY – THE DEFINITIVE COLLECTION** *Universal TV 9813149* ●	20		7

VANILLA FUDGE
US, male vocal/instrumental group — 3

Date	Album	Peak	Wks No.1	Wks
4 Nov 67	**VANILLA FUDGE** *Atlantic 588086*	31		3

VANILLA ICE
US, male rapper (Robert Van Winkle) — 23

Date	Album	Peak	Wks No.1	Wks
15 Dec 90	**TO THE EXTREME** *SBK SBKLP 9* ⊛ ★	4		20
6 Jul 91	**EXTREMELY LIVE** *SBK SBKLP 12*	35		3

VAPORS
UK, male vocal/instrumental group — 6

Date	Album	Peak	Wks No.1	Wks
7 Jun 80	**NEW CLEAR DAYS** *United Artists UAG 30300*	44		6

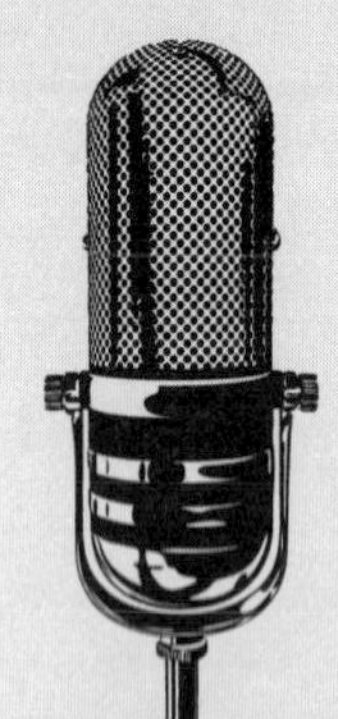

Paul Weller

Stanley Road

THE Jam ensured that, like him or loathe him, Paul Weller's reputation would endure. While follow-up act The Style Council's retro-smooth mediocrity undermined it somewhat, they too had a string of successful singles and albums. By the end of the 1980s, in terms of his current output however, Paul Weller was adrift. 1992's *Paul Weller* was a reassuring if inconsistent, soul-tinged solo debut. *Wild Wood* (1994) allowed Weller's true lone voice to be heard for the first time – a subtle blend of influences from Traffic and Neil Young to Nick Drake.

However, the commercial success of *Wild Wood* left Weller in an awkward spot. Fêted by the substantial crop of new Britpop sensations as one of their key influences, Weller's Jam recordings were being rediscovered by a new generation of younger listeners. The demise of his marriage to Dee C. Lee and a year and a half touring *Wild Wood* meant that by the time Weller came down he had a tempestuous life to calm – plus a batch of songs that had grown organically out of the experience. Thus *Stanley Road*.

As he edged towards his fortieth year, he was duly re-christened 'The Modfather'

The album was an instant classic, from Peter Blake's beautifully English cover art (the famous designer was behind The Beatles' legendary *Sgt. Pepper's Lonely Hearts Club Band* artwork), the Traffic/Cream edge of opener 'Changing Man', to the sublime and romantic 'You Do Something To Me'. Weller's version of Dr John's 'Walk On Gilded Splinters' nods more to Steve Marriott than to the Dr himself. Guests included Noel Gallagher, in part responsible for Weller's 'revival', and Steve Winwood, keyboard legend and a huge influence on Weller's own vocal style. The record took its title from the street where Weller was brought up, in a Victorian council house in working-class Woking (with his scaffolder/bricklayer father and cleaner mother). The house had no central heating, no running hot water and an outside toilet.

Fast-forward over two decades and the same Paul Weller was about to use one of the most prestigious and plush recording studios in the world. The album was recorded 'the old-fashioned way', as Weller and band decamped to the Manor Studios in Oxfordshire, where other typically English classics tinged with whimsy – *Tubular Bells*, *Never Mind The Bollocks* to name but two – were recorded. The spontaneity of the mainly live sessions rings out on every track. What Weller manages to do perfectly is recreate a tradition without slipping into pastiche, and make it his own. Notably on 'Woodcutter's Son', he distils the Memphis soul that informed bands like Traffic and Humble Pie, and pours it back into his own Englishness. The result is redolent of both traditions whilst retaining Weller's own voice. There's a whiff of The Band on 'Pink On White Walls', and of gospel in 'Wings Of Speed', yet it is undeniably Paul Weller. It's a neat trick that enchanted die-hard fans and sceptics alike.

The album established Weller as the responsible adult looking over the careers of the generation of British bands he had influenced. Ever more stylish as he edged towards his fortieth year, he was duly re-

Chart History

Artist	Album Title	First Chart Week	Weeks on Chart	Highest Position
PAUL WELLER	STANLEY ROAD	27/5/95	87	1

christened 'The Modfather'. However, Weller was not simply dragged out of mothballs because he fitted the moment. *Stanley Road* confirmed what *Wild Wood* had hinted at: its author was one of the finest songwriters of his era, and there were precious few who could claim their current material had as much influence in 1995 as it had in 1978.

After *Stanley Road*, Weller went on to release some nine more albums by the end of 2008, with new material tapped from the same sap-rich wood as *Stanley Road*, interspersed with live albums. Ten years after its original release, the album was commemorated with a special edition, including nineteen previously unreleased demos, alternative versions and new material. Where once he had been the 'spokesman for a generation', *Stanley Road* firmly, and finally, established Paul Weller as a spokesman for himself.

Its author was one of the finest songwriters of his era

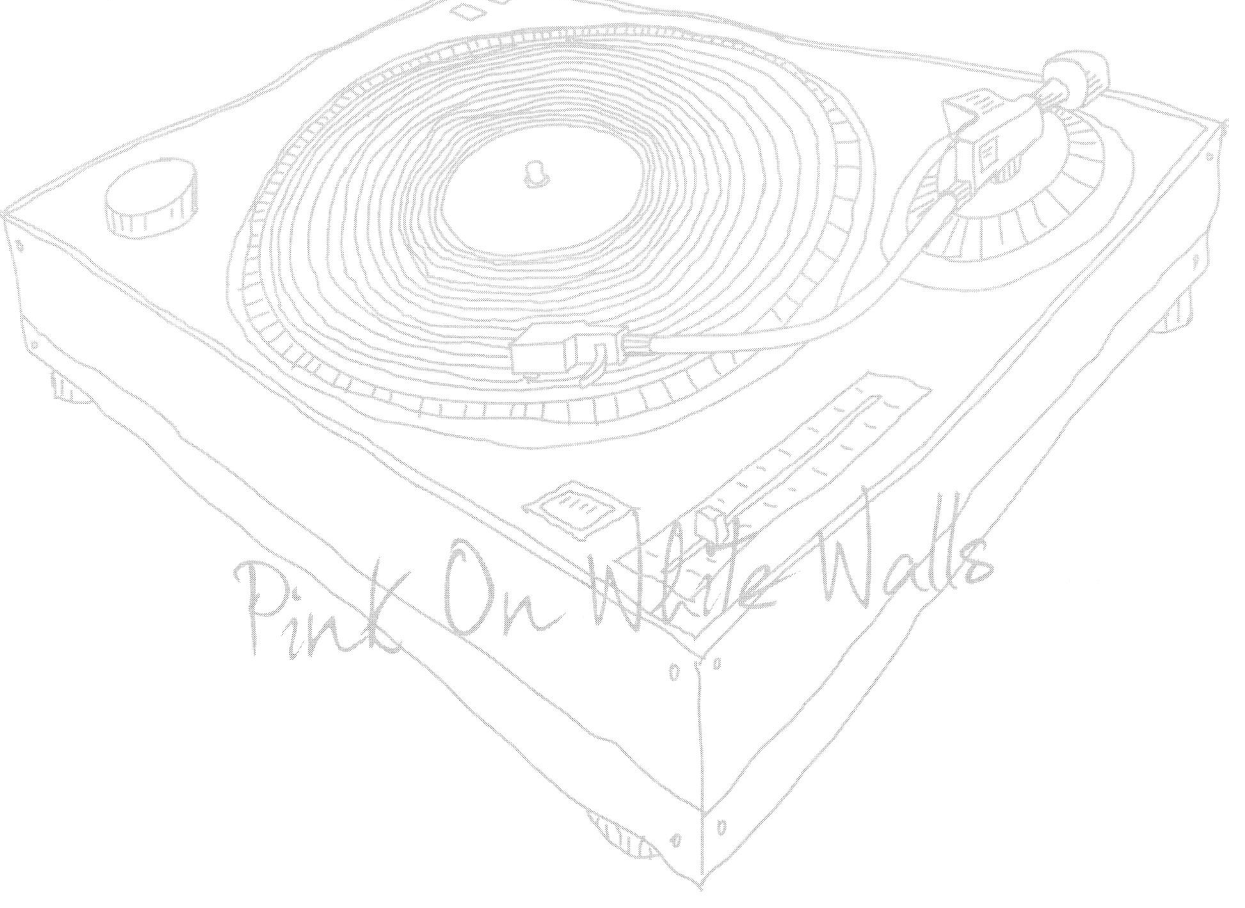

Silver-selling ○ Gold-selling ● Platinum-selling ⊛ US No.1 ★ | Peak Position | Weeks at No.1 | Weeks on Chart

VARDIS
UK, male vocal/instrumental group — Peak Position / Weeks at No.1 / Weeks on Chart: 1

Date	Title	Peak Position	Weeks at No.1	Weeks on Chart
1 Nov 80	**100 MPH** *Logo MOGO 4012*	52		1

FRANKIE VAUGHAN
UK, male vocalist (Frank Abelson), d. 17 Sep 1999 (age 71) — 20

Date	Title	Peak Position	Weeks at No.1	Weeks on Chart
5 Sep 59	**FRANKIE VAUGHAN AT THE LONDON PALLADIUM** *Philips BDL 7330*	6		2
4 Nov 67	**FRANKIE VAUGHAN SONGBOOK** *Philips DBL 001*	40		1
25 Nov 67	**THERE MUST BE A WAY** *Columbia SCX 6200*	22		8
12 Nov 77	**100 GOLDEN GREATS** *Ronco RTDX 2021* ●	24		9

SARAH VAUGHAN
US, female vocalist, d. 3 Apr 1990 (age 66) — 1

Date	Title	Peak Position	Weeks at No.1	Weeks on Chart
26 Mar 60	**NO COUNT – SARAH** *Mercury MMC 14021*	19		1

STEVIE RAY VAUGHAN & DOUBLE TROUBLE
US, male vocal/instrumental group – Stevie Ray Vaughan, d. 27 Aug 1990 (age 35) — 1

Date	Title	Peak Position	Weeks at No.1	Weeks on Chart
15 Jul 89	**IN STEP** *Epic 4633951*	63		1

VAUGHAN BROTHERS
US, male vocal/instrumental group — 1

Date	Title	Peak Position	Weeks at No.1	Weeks on Chart
20 Oct 90	**FAMILY STYLE** *Epic 4670141*	63		1

BOBBY VEE
US, male vocalist (Robert Velline) — 80

Date	Title	Peak Position	Weeks at No.1	Weeks on Chart
24 Feb 62	**TAKE GOOD CARE OF MY BABY** *London HAG 2428*	7		8
31 Mar 62	**HITS OF THE ROCKIN' 50'S** *London HAG 2406*	20		1
27 Oct 62	**BOBBY VEE MEETS THE CRICKETS** *Liberty LBY 1086* & THE CRICKETS	2		27
12 Jan 63	**A BOBBY VEE RECORDING SESSION** *Liberty LBY 1084*	10		11
20 Apr 63	**BOBBY VEE'S GOLDEN GREATS** *Liberty LBY 1112*	10		14
5 Oct 63	**THE NIGHT HAS A THOUSAND EYES** *Liberty LIB 1139*	15		2
19 Apr 80	**THE BOBBY VEE SINGLES ALBUM** *United Artists UAG 30253* ●	5		10
24 May 08	**THE VERY BEST OF** *EMI 2132292* ○	18		7

SUZANNE VEGA
US, female vocalist/guitarist — 132

Date	Title	Peak Position	Weeks at No.1	Weeks on Chart
19 Oct 85	**SUZANNE VEGA** *A&M AMA 5072* ⊛	11		71
9 May 87	**SOLITUDE STANDING** *A&M SUZLP 2* ⊛	2		39
28 Apr 90	**DAYS OF OPEN HAND** *A&M 3952931* ●	7		7
19 Sep 92	**99.9 F** *A&M 5400122* ○	20		4
8 Mar 97	**NINE OBJECTS OF DESIRE** *A&M 5405832*	43		3
31 Oct 98	**TRIED AND TRUE – THE BEST OF SUZANNE VEGA** *A&M 5409452*	46		3
19 Jul 03	**RETROSPECTIVE – THE BEST OF** *Universal TV 9808884*	27		5

TOM VEK
UK, male vocalist/guitarist — 1

Date	Title	Peak Position	Weeks at No.1	Weeks on Chart
16 Apr 05	**WE HAVE SOUND** *Go Beat/Polydor 9870389*	73		1

ROSIE VELA
US, female vocalist — 11

Date	Title	Peak Position	Weeks at No.1	Weeks on Chart
31 Jan 87	**ZAZU** *A&M AMA 5016* ○	20		11

VELVET REVOLVER
US, male vocal/instrumental group – Scott Weiland, Saul 'Slash' Hudson, Dave Kushner, Michael 'Duff' McKagan & Matt Sorum — 21

Date	Title	Peak Position	Weeks at No.1	Weeks on Chart
19 Jun 04	**CONTRABAND** *RCA 82876628352* ★	11		16
14 Jul 07	**LIBERTAD** *RCA 88697109682*	6		5

VELVET UNDERGROUND
US, male/female vocal/instrumental group — 11

Date	Title	Peak Position	Weeks at No.1	Weeks on Chart
23 Feb 85	**V.U.** *Polydor POLD 5167*	47		4
13 Nov 93	**LIVE MCMXCIII** *Sire 9362454642*	70		1
28 Oct 95	**THE BEST OF LOU REED AND THE VELVET UNDERGROUND** *Global Television RADCD 212* LOU REED & THE VELVET UNDERGROUND	56		4
6 Jul 02	**VELVET UNDERGROUND AND NICO** *Polydor 823902* VELVET UNDERGROUND AND NICO	59		2

VENGABOYS
Holland, male DJ/producers – Dennis Van Den Driesschen & Wessel Van Diepen, & Holland/Trinidad/Brazil, male/female vocal/dance group – Yorick Bakker, Roy Den Burger, Robin Pors, Kim Sassabone & Denise Post-Van Rijswijk — 77

Date	Title	Peak Position	Weeks at No.1	Weeks on Chart
3 Apr 99	**THE PARTY ALBUM!** *Positiva 4993472* ⊛x2	6		49
25 Mar 00	**THE PLATINUM ALBUM** *Positiva 5259530* ●	9		28

VENOM
UK, male vocal/instrumental group — 2

Date	Title	Peak Position	Weeks at No.1	Weeks on Chart
21 Apr 84	**AT WAR WITH SATAN** *Neat 1015*	64		1
13 Apr 85	**POSSESSED** *Neat 1024*	99		1

ANTHONY VENTURA ORCHESTRA
Switzerland, orchestra — 4

Date	Title	Peak Position	Weeks at No.1	Weeks on Chart
20 Jan 79	**DREAM MUSIC** *Lotus WH 5007*	44		4

TOM VERLAINE
US, male vocalist. See Television — 1

Date	Title	Peak Position	Weeks at No.1	Weeks on Chart
14 Mar 87	**FLASH LIGHT** *Fontana SFLP 1*	99		1

VERUCA SALT
US, male/female vocal/instrumental group — 2

Date	Title	Peak Position	Weeks at No.1	Weeks on Chart
15 Oct 94	**AMERICAN THIGHS** *Hi-Rise Recordings FLATCD 9*	47		2

VERVE
UK, male vocal/instrumental group – Richard Ashcroft*, Simon Jones, Nick McCabe & Peter Salisbury — 161

Date	Title	Peak Position	Weeks at No.1	Weeks on Chart
3 Jul 93	**A STORM IN HEAVEN** *Hut CDHUT 10*	27		2
15 Jul 95	**A NORTHERN SOUL** *Hut DGHUT 27* ●	13		11
11 Oct 97	**URBAN HYMNS** *Hut CDHUT 45* ⊛x8	1	12	124
13 Nov 04	**THIS IS MUSIC – THE SINGLES 92-98** *Virgin CDV2991* ●	15		13
6 Sep 08	**FORTH** *Parlophone 2355841*	1	1	11

VEX RED
UK, male vocal/instrumental group — 1

Date	Title	Peak Position	Weeks at No.1	Weeks on Chart
16 Mar 02	**START WITH A STRONG AND PERSISTENT** *Virgin CDVUS 215*	48		1

VIBRATORS
UK, male vocal/instrumental group — 7

Date	Title	Peak Position	Weeks at No.1	Weeks on Chart
25 Jun 77	**PURE MANIA** *Epic EPC 82907*	49		5
29 Apr 78	**V2** *Epic EPC 82495*	33		2

VICE SQUAD
UK, male/female vocal/instrumental group — 10

Date	Title	Peak Position	Weeks at No.1	Weeks on Chart
24 Oct 81	**NO CAUSE FOR CONCERN** *Zonophone ZEM 103*	32		5
22 May 82	**STAND STRONG STAND PROUD** *Riot City ZEM 104*	47		5

SID VICIOUS
UK, male vocalist (John Ritchie/Beverley), d. 2 Feb 1979 (age 21). See Sex Pistols — 8

Date	Title	Peak Position	Weeks at No.1	Weeks on Chart
15 Dec 79	**SID SINGS** *Virgin V 2144* ○	30		8

VIENNA PHILHARMONIC ORCHESTRA
Austria, orchestra — 15

Date	Title	Peak Position	Weeks at No.1	Weeks on Chart
22 Jan 72	**SPARTACUS** *Decca SXL 6000* VIENNA PHILHARMONIC ORCHESTRA CONDUCTED BY ARAM KHACHATURIAN	16		15

VIENNA SYMPHONY ORCHESTRA
Austria, orchestra — 4

Date	Title	Peak Position	Weeks at No.1	Weeks on Chart
4 Apr 87	**SYMPHONIC ROCK WITH THE VIENNA SYMPHONY ORCHESTRA** *Stylus SMR 730*	43		4

VIEW
UK, male vocal/instrumental group – Kyle Falconer, StevenMorrison, Pete Reilly & Kieren Webster — 20

Date	Title	Peak	Wks at No.1	Wks on Chart
3 Feb 07	**HATS OFF TO THE BUSKERS** *1965 OLIVELCD018*	1	1	20

VILLAGE PEOPLE
US, male vocal group – Alexander Briley, David Hodo, GlennHughes, d. 4 Mar 2001, Randy Jones, Felipe Rose & Victor Willis (replaced by Ray Simpson) — 37

Date	Title	Peak	Wks at No.1	Wks on Chart
27 Jan 79	**CRUISIN'** *Mercury 9109 614*	24		9
12 May 79	**GO WEST** *Mercury 9109 621*	14		19
16 Aug 80	**CAN'T STOP THE MUSIC (OST)** *Mercury 6399 051*	9		8
18 Dec 93	**THE BEST OF THE VILLAGE PEOPLE** *Bell 74321178312*	72		1

GENE VINCENT
US, male vocalist (Vincent Eugene Craddock), d. 12 Sep 1970 (age 36) — 2

Date	Title	Peak	Wks at No.1	Wks on Chart
16 Jul 60	**CRAZY TIMES** *Capitol T 1342*	12		2

VINNIE VINCENT
US, male vocalist/guitarist (Vincent Cusano). See Kiss — 2

Date	Title	Peak	Wks at No.1	Wks on Chart
28 May 88	**ALL SYSTEMS GO** *Chrysalis CHR 1626*	51		2

VINES
Australia, male vocal/instrumental group – Craig Nicholls, Ryan Griffiths, Patrick Matthews & David Olliffe (replaced by Hamish Rosser) — 10

Date	Title	Peak	Wks at No.1	Wks on Chart
20 Jul 02	**HIGHLY EVOLVED** *Heavenly HVNLP 36CD*	3		7
3 Apr 04	**WINNING DAYS** *Heavenly HVNLP 48CD*	29		2
15 Apr 06	**VISION VALLEY** *Heavenly HVNLP56CD*	71		1

BOBBY VINTON
US, male vocalist (Stanley Vinton) — 2

Date	Title	Peak	Wks at No.1	Wks on Chart
17 Nov 90	**BLUE VELVET** *Epic 4675701*	67		2

VIOLENT FEMMES
US, male/female vocal/instrumental group — 1

Date	Title	Peak	Wks at No.1	Wks on Chart
1 Mar 86	**THE BLIND LEADING THE NAKED** *Slash SLAP 10*	81		1

VIOLINSKI
UK, male instrumental group — 1

Date	Title	Peak	Wks at No.1	Wks on Chart
26 May 79	**NO CAUSE FOR ALARM** *Jet JETLU 219*	49		1

VISAGE
UK, male vocal/instrumental group – Steve Strange, Billy Currie, Rusty Egan, Dave Formula, John McGeoch & Midge Ure* — 58

Date	Title	Peak	Wks at No.1	Wks on Chart
24 Jan 81	**VISAGE** *Polydor 2490 157*	13		29
3 Apr 82	**THE ANVIL** *Polydor POLD 5050*	6		16
19 Nov 83	**FADE TO GREY – THE SINGLES COLLECTION** *Polydor POLD 5117*	38		11
3 Nov 84	**BEAT BOY** *Polydor POLH 12*	79		2

VIXEN
US, female vocal/instrumental group — 5

Date	Title	Peak	Wks at No.1	Wks on Chart
8 Oct 88	**VIXEN** *Manhattan MTL 1028*	66		1
18 Aug 90	**REV IT UP** *EMI USA MTL 1054*	20		4

VOICE OF THE BEEHIVE
US/UK, male/female vocal/instrumental group — 26

Date	Title	Peak	Wks at No.1	Wks on Chart
2 Jul 88	**LET IT BEE** *London LONLP 57*	13		13
24 Aug 91	**HONEY LINGERS** *London 8282591*	17		13

VON BONDIES
US, male vocal/instrumental group — 2

Date	Title	Peak	Wks at No.1	Wks on Chart
21 Feb 04	**PAWN SHOPPE HEART** *Sire 9362485492*	36		2

HERBERT VON KARAJAN
Austria, male conductor, d. 16 Jul 1989 (age 81) — 40

Date	Title	Peak	Wks at No.1	Wks on Chart
26 Sep 70	**BEETHOVEN TRIPLE CONCERTO** *HMV ASD 2582* BERLIN PHILHARMONIC ORCHESTRA CONDUCTED BY HERBERT VON KARAJAN – SOLOIST DAVID OISTRAKH (VIOLIN), MSTISLAV ROSTROPOVICH (CELLO), SVIATOSLAU RICHTER (PIANO)	51		2
16 Apr 88	**THE ESSENTIAL KARAJAN** *Deutsche Grammophon HVKTV 1*	51		5
3 Aug 91	**HOLST: THE PLANETS** *Deutsche Grammophon 4352891* HERBERT VON KARAJAN CONDUCTING THE BERLIN PHILHARMONIC ORCHESTRA	52		2
7 Oct 95	**KARAJAN: ADAGIO** *Deutsche Grammophon 4452822* HERBERT VON KARAJAN CONDUCTING THE BERLIN PHILHARMONIC ORCHESTRA	30		8
13 Apr 96	**ADAGIO 2** *Deutsche Grammophon 4495152* HERBERT VON KARAJAN CONDUCTING THE BERLIN PHILHARMONIC ORCHESTRA	63		1

ANNE SOFIE VON OTTER MEETS ELVIS COSTELLO
Sweden, female vocalist & UK, male vocalist/guitarist (Declan MacManus) — 1

Date	Title	Peak	Wks at No.1	Wks on Chart
31 Mar 01	**FOR THE STARS** *Deutsche Grammophon 4695302*	67		1

VOW WOW
Japan/US, male vocal/instrumental group — 1

Date	Title	Peak	Wks at No.1	Wks on Chart
18 Mar 89	**HELTER SKELTER** *Arista 209691*	75		1

VOYAGE
UK/France, vocal/instrumental group — 1

Date	Title	Peak	Wks at No.1	Wks on Chart
9 Sep 78	**VOYAGE** *GTO GTLP 030*	59		1

W

WAH!
UK, male vocal/instrumental group — 11

Date	Title	Peak	Wks at No.1	Wks on Chart
18 Jul 81	**NAH=POO-THE ART OF BLUFF** *Eternal CLASSIC 1*	33		5
4 Aug 84	**A WORD TO THE WISE GUY** *Beggars Banquet BEGA 54* MIGHTY WAH!	28		6

MARTHA WAINWRIGHT
Canada, female vocalist/guitarist — 4

Date	Title	Peak	Wks at No.1	Wks on Chart
16 Apr 05	**MARTHA WAINWRIGHT** *Drowned In Sound DISO011*	63		1
24 May 08	**I KNOW YOU'RE MARRIED BUT I'VE GOT FEELINGS TOO** *Drowned In Sound DISO039*	29		3

RUFUS WAINWRIGHT
Canada, male vocalist/guitarist — 8

Date	Title	Peak	Wks at No.1	Wks on Chart
19 Mar 05	**WANT TWO** *DreamWorks 9880444*	21		3
26 May 07	**RELEASE THE STARS** *Geffen 1733588*	2		5

JOHN WAITE
UK, male vocalist — 3

Date	Title	Peak	Wks at No.1	Wks on Chart
10 Nov 84	**NO BREAKS** *EMI America WAIT 1*	64		3

TOM WAITS
US, male vocalist/multi-instrumentalist — 32

Date	Title	Peak	Wks at No.1	Wks on Chart
8 Oct 83	**SWORDFISHTROMBONE** *Island ILPS 9762*	62		3
19 Oct 85	**RAIN DOGS** *Island ILPS 9803*	29		5
5 Sep 87	**FRANK'S WILD YEARS** *Island ITW 3*	20		5
8 Oct 88	**BIG TIME** *Island ITW 4*	84		1
19 Sep 92	**BONE MACHINE** *Island CID 9993*	26		3
20 Nov 93	**THE BLACK RIDER** *Island CID 8021*	47		2
27 Jun 98	**BEAUTIFUL MALADIES 1983–1993: THE ISLAND YEARS** *Island 5245192*	63		1
1 May 99	**MULE VARIATIONS** *Epitaph 65472*	9		5
18 May 02	**ALICE** *Anti 66322*	20		2
18 May 02	**BLOOD MONEY** *Anti 66292*	21		2
16 Oct 04	**REAL GONE** *Anti 66782*	16		2
2 Dec 06	**ORPHANS: BRAWLERS, BAWLERS & BASTARDS** *Anti 66772*	49		1

Top 100 Artists by Weeks on Chart

Pos	Artist	Weeks on Chart
1	**QUEEN**	**1423**
2	**ELVIS PRESLEY**	**1333**
3	**BEATLES**	**1316**
4	U2	1189
5	DIRE STRAITS	1146
6	MADONNA	1137
7	SIMON & GARFUNKEL	1128
8	MICHAEL JACKSON	1028
9	DAVID BOWIE	1026
10	ELTON JOHN	1013
11	ROD STEWART	983
12	ABBA	957
13	PINK FLOYD	938
14	FRANK SINATRA	926
15	FLEETWOOD MAC	908
16	PHIL COLLINS	879
17	CLIFF RICHARD	841
18	ROLLING STONES	833
19	SHADOWS	826
20	MEAT LOAF	816
21	DIANA ROSS	770
22	NEIL DIAMOND	677
23	BOB DYLAN	648
24	SIMPLY RED	637
25	R.E.M.	623
26	UB40	623
27	OASIS	622
28	CARPENTERS	620
29	BEACH BOYS	587
30	PAUL McCARTNEY	584
31	BOB MARLEY & THE WAILERS	584
32	ERIC CLAPTON	577
33	BARBRA STREISAND	577
34	BRUCE SPRINGSTEEN	574
35	MIKE OLDFIELD	559
36	TINA TURNER	536
37	LED ZEPPELIN	535
38	TOM JONES	530
39	EAGLES	517
40	GENESIS	511
41	EURYTHMICS	495
42	ROBBIE WILLIAMS	491
43	LIONEL RICHIE	488
44	STATUS QUO	480
45	PRINCE	473
46	BON JOVI	465
47	ANDY WILLIAMS	456
48	CELINE DION	453
49	JAMES LAST	446
50	GUNS N' ROSES	443
51	ELECTRIC LIGHT ORCHESTRA	440
52	ROXY MUSIC	430
53	DURAN DURAN	427
54	POLICE	424
55	BEE GEES	422
56	BRYAN ADAMS	420
57	MADNESS	418
58	WHITNEY HOUSTON	413
59	JIM REEVES	412
60	RED HOT CHILI PEPPERS	411
61	TAKE THAT	411
62	STEREOPHONICS	406
63	STEVIE WONDER	400
64	MARIAH CAREY	392
65	STING	391
66	RADIOHEAD	388
67	BILLY JOEL	379
68	CORRS	367
69	BARRY MANILOW	366

70	CHRIS REA	364
71	JOHNNY CASH	360
72	COLDPLAY	360
73	GEORGE MICHAEL	360
74	BLONDIE	358
75	PET SHOP BOYS	357
76	SIMPLE MINDS	356
77	JOHN LENNON	355
78	KYLIE MINOGUE	351
79	BRYAN FERRY	339
80	BUDDY HOLLY	339
81	MOODY BLUES	335
82	NIRVANA	331
83	ERASURE	326
84	HERB ALPERT	322
85	BEAUTIFUL SOUTH	312
86	VAN MORRISON	312
87	BLUR	311
88	EMINEM	311
89	CHER	310
90	LUCIANO PAVAROTTI	309
91	LUTHER VANDROSS	309
92	SHIRLEY BASSEY	307
93	GEORGE BENSON	303
94	SANTANA	303
95	CREAM	300
96	PAUL SIMON	300
97	KATE BUSH	299
98	ENYA	293
99	JEFF WAYNE	293
100	GEORGE MITCHELL MINSTRELS	292

RICK WAKEMAN

UK, male keyboard player. See Anderson Bruford Wakeman Howe, Strawbs, Yes — 131

Date	Title	Peak	Wks at No.1	Wks
24 Feb 73	**THE SIX WIVES OF HENRY VIII** *A&M AMLH 64361*	7		22
18 May 74	**JOURNEY TO THE CENTRE OF THE EARTH** *A&M AMLH 63621* WITH THE LONDON SYMPHONY ORCHESTRA ●	1	1	30
12 Apr 75	**THE MYTHS AND LEGENDS OF KING ARTHUR AND THE KNIGHTS OF THE ROUND TABLE** *A&M AMLH 64515* WITH THE ENGLISH CHAMBER CHOIR AND ORCHESTRA ●	2		28
24 Apr 76	**NO EARTHLY CONNECTION** *A&M AMLK 64583*	9		9
12 Feb 77	**WHITE ROCK** *A&M AMLH 64614* ●	14		9
3 Dec 77	**CRIMINAL RECORD** *A&M AMLK 64660*	25		5
2 Jun 79	**RHAPSODIES** *A&M AMLX 68508*	25		10
27 Jun 81	**1984** *Charisma CDS 4022*	24		9
13 Oct 84	**BEYOND THE PLANETS** *Telstar STAR 2244* KEVIN PEEK & RICK WAKEMAN FEATURING JEFF WAYNE NARRATION PATRICK ALLEN	64		6
16 May 87	**THE GOSPELS** *Stylus SMR 729*	94		1
27 Mar 99	**RETURN TO THE CENTRE OF THE EARTH** *EMI Classics CDC 5567632* ; LONDON SYMPHONY ORCHESTRA; ENGLISH CHAMBER CHOIR; NARRATED BY PATRICK STEWART	34		2

NARADA MICHAEL WARDEN

US, male vocalist/producer — 5

Date	Title	Peak	Wks at No.1	Wks
14 May 88	**DIVINE EMOTION** *Atlantic WX 172* NARADA	60		5

WALKER BROTHERS

US, male vocal/instrumental trio – Scott Walker* (Scott Engel), Gary Walker (Gary Leeds) & John Walker (John Maus) — 112

Date	Title	Peak	Wks at No.1	Wks
18 Dec 65	**TAKE IT EASY** *Philips BL 7691*	3		36
3 Sep 66	**PORTRAIT** *Philips SBL 7732*	3		23
18 Mar 67	**IMAGES** *Philips SBL 7770*	6		15
16 Sep 67	**WALKER BROTHERS' STORY** *Philips DBL 002*	9		19
21 Feb 76	**NO REGRETS** *GTO GTLP 007*	49		3
25 Jan 92	**NO REGRETS – THE BEST OF SCOTT WALKER AND THE WALKER BROTHERS** *Fontana 5108312* SCOTT WALKER & THE WALKER BROTHERS ●	4		12
15 Jul 00	**NO REGRETS – THE BEST OF 1965–1976** *Universal TV 5108312* SCOTT WALKER & THE WALKER BROTHERS	55		1
13 May 06	**THE BEST OF – THE SUN AIN'T GONNA SHINE** *Universal TV 9839598* SCOTT WALKER & THE WALKER BROTHERS	24		3

SCOTT WALKER

US, male vocalist (Noel Scott Engel). See Walker Brothers — 62

Date	Title	Peak	Wks at No.1	Wks
16 Sep 67	**SCOTT** *Philips SBL 7816*	3		17
20 Apr 68	**SCOTT 2** *Philips SBL 7840*	1	1	18
5 Apr 69	**SCOTT 3** *Philips S 7882*	3		4
5 Jul 69	**SONGS FROM HIS TV SERIES** *Philips SBL 7900*	7		3
31 Mar 84	**CLIMATE HUNTER** *Virgin V 2303*	60		2
25 Jan 92	**NO REGRETS – THE BEST OF SCOTT WALKER AND THE WALKER BROTHERS** *Fontana 5108312* SCOTT WALKER & THE WALKER BROTHERS ●	4		12
20 May 95	**TILT** *Fontana 5268592*	27		1
15 Jul 00	**NO REGRETS – THE BEST OF 1965–1976** *Universal TV 5108312* SCOTT WALKER & THE WALKER BROTHERS	55		1
13 May 06	**THE BEST OF – THE SUN AIN'T GONNA SHINE** *Universal TV 9839598* SCOTT WALKER & THE WALKER BROTHERS	24		3
20 May 06	**THE DRIFT** *4AD CAD2603CD*	51		1

WALKMEN

US, male vocal/instrumental group — 1

Date	Title	Peak	Wks at No.1	Wks
8 May 04	**BOWS AND ARROWS** *WEA 9362486802*	62		1

WALLFLOWERS

US, male vocal/instrumental group — 2

Date	Title	Peak	Wks at No.1	Wks
21 Jun 97	**BRINGING DOWN THE HORSE** *Interscope IND 90055*	58		2

BOB WALLIS & HIS STORYVILLE JAZZMEN

UK, male vocal/instrumental group – Bob Wallis, d. 10 Jan 1991 (age 56) — 1

Date	Title	Peak	Wks at No.1	Wks
11 Jun 60	**EVERYBODY LOVES SATURDAY NIGHT** *Top Rank BUY 023*	20		1

Silver-selling ○ Gold-selling ● Platinum-selling ⊛ US No.1 ★ | Peak Position | Weeks at No.1 | Weeks on Chart

JOE WALSH
US, male vocalist/guitarist. See Eagles — 14

Date	Title	Peak Position	Weeks at No.1	Weeks on Chart
17 Apr 76	**YOU CAN'T ARGUE WITH A SICK MIND** *Anchor ABCL 5156*	28		3
10 Jun 78	**BUT SERIOUSLY FOLKS...** *Asylum K 53081* ○	16		17

KATE WALSH
UK, female vocalist/pianist — 1

Date	Title	Peak Position	Weeks at No.1	Weeks on Chart
13 Oct 07	**TIM'S HOUSE** *Mercury 1736468*	75		1

WANG CHUNG
UK, male vocal/instrumental group — 5

Date	Title	Peak Position	Weeks at No.1	Weeks on Chart
21 Apr 84	**POINTS ON THE CURVE** *Geffen GEF 25589*	34		5

WANNADIES
Sweden, male/female vocal/instrumental group — 4

Date	Title	Peak Position	Weeks at No.1	Weeks on Chart
17 May 97	**BAGSY ME** *Indolent 74321429822*	37		3
18 Mar 00	**YEAH** *Indolent 74321687022*	73		1

STEPHEN WARBECK
UK, male conductor/producer — 5

Date	Title	Peak Position	Weeks at No.1	Weeks on Chart
19 May 01	**CAPTAIN CORELLI'S MANDOLIN (OST)** *Decca 4676782*	30		5

CLIFFORD T. WARD
UK, male vocalist/keyboard player, d. 18 Dec 2001 (age 57) — 5

Date	Title	Peak Position	Weeks at No.1	Weeks on Chart
21 Jul 73	**HOME THOUGHTS** *Charisma CAS 1066*	40		3
16 Feb 74	**MANTLE PIECES** *Charisma CAS 1077*	42		2

MICHAEL WARD
UK, male vocalist — 3

Date	Title	Peak Position	Weeks at No.1	Weeks on Chart
5 Jan 74	**INTRODUCING MICHAEL WARD** *Philips 6308 189*	26		3

SHAYNE WARD
UK, male vocalist — 35

Date	Title	Peak Position	Weeks at No.1	Weeks on Chart
29 Apr 06	**SHAYNE WARD** *Syco Music 82876829802* ⊛	1	1	22
8 Dec 07	**BREATHLESS** *Syco Music 88697188402*	2		13

WARLOCK
Germany, male/female vocal/instrumental group — 2

Date	Title	Peak Position	Weeks at No.1	Weeks on Chart
14 Nov 87	**TRIUMPH AND AGONY** *Vertigo VERH 50*	54		2

WARM JETS
UK/Canada, male vocal/instrumental group — 1

Date	Title	Peak Position	Weeks at No.1	Weeks on Chart
7 Mar 98	**FUTURE SIGNS** *Island 5243542*	40		1

JENNIFER WARNES
US, female vocalist — 12

Date	Title	Peak Position	Weeks at No.1	Weeks on Chart
18 Jul 87	**FAMOUS BLUE RAINCOAT – SONGS OF LEONARD COHEN** *RCA PL 90048* ○	33		12

WARRANT
US, male vocal/instrumental group — 1

Date	Title	Peak Position	Weeks at No.1	Weeks on Chart
19 Sep 92	**DOG EAT DOG** *Columbia 4720332*	74		1

DIONNE WARWICK
US, female vocalist — 159

Date	Title	Peak Position	Weeks at No.1	Weeks on Chart
23 May 64	**PRESENTING DIONNE WARWICK** *Pye NPL 28037*	14		10
7 May 66	**BEST OF DIONNE WARWICK** *Pye NPL 28078*	8		11
4 Feb 67	**HERE WHERE THERE IS LOVE** *Pye NPL 28096*	39		2
18 May 68	**VALLEY OF THE DOLLS** *Pye NSPL 28114*	10		13
23 May 70	**GREATEST HITS VOLUME 1** *Wand WNS 1*	31		26
6 Jun 70	**GREATEST HITS VOLUME 2** *Wand WNS 2*	28		14
30 Oct 82	**HEARTBREAKER** *Arista 204 974* ⊛	3		33
21 May 83	**THE DIONNE WARWICK COLLECTION** *Arista DIONE 1* ●	11		17
29 Oct 83	**SO AMAZING** *Arista 205 755*	60		3
23 Feb 85	**WITHOUT YOUR LOVE** *Arista 206 571*	86		2
6 Jan 90	**LOVE SONGS** *Arista 410441* ●	6		13
10 Dec 94	**CHRISTMAS IN VIENNA II** *Sony Classical SK 64304* PLACIDO DOMINGO	60		2
14 Dec 96	**THE ESSENTIAL COLLECTION** *Global Television RADCD 48*	58		4
3 Aug 02	**HEARTBREAKER – THE VERY BEST OF** *WSM/BMG WSMCD 101* ○	32		4
27 May 06	**WALK ON BY – THE VERY BEST OF** *Sony BMG/WMTV WMTV012*	72		1
16 Feb 08	**THE LOVE COLLECTION** *Rhino/Sony BMG 88697250142*	27		4

WAS (NOT WAS)
US, male vocal/instrumental duo — 15

Date	Title	Peak Position	Weeks at No.1	Weeks on Chart
9 Apr 88	**WHAT UP DOG?** *Fontana SFLP 4*	47		6
21 Jul 90	**ARE YOU OK?** *Fontana 8463511*	35		6
13 Jun 92	**HELLO DAD I'M IN JAIL** *Fontana 5124642*	61		3

GENO WASHINGTON
US, male vocalist — 51

Date	Title	Peak Position	Weeks at No.1	Weeks on Chart
10 Dec 66	**HAND CLAPPIN' – FOOT STOMPIN' – FUNKY BUTT – LIVE!** *Piccadilly NPL 38026*	5		38
23 Sep 67	**HIPSTERS, FLIPSTERS, AND FINGER POPPIN' DADDIES** *Piccadilly NSPL 38032*	8		13

GROVER WASHINGTON JR.
US, male saxophonist, d. 17 Dec 1999 (age 56) — 10

Date	Title	Peak Position	Weeks at No.1	Weeks on Chart
9 May 81	**WINELIGHT** *Elektra K 52262* ○	34		9
19 Dec 81	**COME MORNING** *Elektra K 52337*	98		1

W.A.S.P.
US, male vocal/instrumental group – Blackie Lawless; members also included Chris Holmes, Randy Piper, Steve Riley & Johnny Rod — 24

Date	Title	Peak Position	Weeks at No.1	Weeks on Chart
8 Sep 84	**W.A.S.P.** *Capitol EJ 2401951*	51		2
9 Nov 85	**THE LAST COMMAND** *Capitol WASP 2*	48		1
8 Nov 86	**INSIDE THE ELECTRIC CIRCUS** *Capitol EST 2025*	53		3
26 Sep 87	**LIVE IN THE RAW** *Capitol EST 2040*	23		4
15 Apr 89	**THE HEADLESS CHILDREN** *Capitol EST 2087* ○	8		10
20 Jun 92	**THE CRIMSON IDOL** *Parlophone CDPCSD 118*	21		2
6 Nov 93	**FIRST BLOOD...LAST CUTS** *Capitol CDESTFG 2217*	69		1
1 Jul 95	**STILL NOT BLACK ENOUGH** *Raw Power RAWCD 103*	52		1

WATERBOYS
UK, male vocal/instrumental group – Mike Scott*, Anthony Thistlethwaite, Karl Wallinger, Steve Wickham & Kevin Wilkinson — 73

Date	Title	Peak Position	Weeks at No.1	Weeks on Chart
16 Jun 84	**A PAGAN PLACE** *Ensign ENCL 3*	100		1
28 Sep 85	**THIS IS THE SEA** *Ensign ENCL 5* ○	37		17
29 Oct 88	**FISHERMAN'S BLUES** *Ensign CHEN 5* ●	13		19
22 Sep 90	**ROOM TO ROAM** *Ensign CHEN 16* ○	5		6
11 May 91	**BEST OF THE WATERBOYS '81-'91** *Ensign CHEN 19* ●	2		16
5 Jun 93	**DREAM HARDER** *Geffen GED 24476* ○	5		10
7 Oct 00	**A ROCK IN THE WEARY LAND** *RCA 74321783052*	47		1
21 Jul 01	**THIS IS THE SEA** *Ensign CCD 1543*	57		1
21 Jun 03	**UNIVERSAL HALL** *Puck PUCK1*	74		1
14 Apr 07	**BOOK OF LIGHTNING** *W14 1721309*	51		1

WATERFRONT
UK, male vocal/instrumental duo — 3

Date	Title	Peak Position	Weeks at No.1	Weeks on Chart
12 Aug 89	**WATERFRONT** *Polydor 8379701* WATERFRONT	45		3

ROGER WATERS
UK, male vocalist/bass guitarist. See Pink Floyd — 25

Date	Title	Peak Position	Weeks at No.1	Weeks on Chart
12 May 84	**THE PROS AND CONS OF HITCH-HIKING** *Harvest SHVL 240105*	13		11
27 Jun 87	**RADIO K.A.O.S.** *EMI KAOS 1*	25		7
22 Sep 90	**THE WALL – LIVE IN BERLIN** *Mercury 8466111* & VARIOUS ARTISTS	27		3
19 Sep 92	**AMUSED TO DEATH** *Columbia 4687612* ○	8		4

ADAM WATKISS
UK, male vocalist — 3

Date	Title	Peak Position	Weeks at No.1	Weeks on Chart
15 Dec 01	**THIS IS THE MOMENT** *UMTV/Decca 0166082* ○	65		3

JODY WATLEY
US, female vocalist. See Shalamar — 4

Date	Title	Peak Position	Weeks at No.1	Weeks on Chart
5 Sep 87	**JODY WATLEY** *MCA MCG 6024*	62		2
27 May 89	**LARGER THAN LIFE** *MCA MCG 6044*	39		2

RUSSELL WATSON
UK, male vocalist — 109

Date	Title	Peak Position	Weeks at No.1	Weeks on Chart
7 Oct 00	**THE VOICE** *Decca 4672512* ⊛x2	5		36
10 Nov 01	**ENCORE** *Decca 4703002* ⊛x2	6		21
30 Nov 02	**REPRISE** *Decca 4731002* ⊛	13		8
6 Nov 04	**AMORE MUSICA** *Decca 4756294* ●	10		9
25 Mar 06	**THE VOICE – THE ULTIMATE COLLECTION** *Decca 4757672* ●	2		13
17 Mar 07	**THAT'S LIFE** *Decca 4758157* ●	4		9
8 Dec 07	**OUTSIDE IN** *Decca 4780126*	14		7
29 Nov 08	**PEOPLE GET READY** *Decca 4781362*	20		6+

WAX
UK, male vocal/instrumental duo — 3

Date	Title	Peak Position	Weeks at No.1	Weeks on Chart
12 Sep 87	**AMERICAN ENGLISH** *RCA PL 71430*	59		3

ANTHONY WAY
UK, male vocalist — 19

Date	Title	Peak Position	Weeks at No.1	Weeks on Chart
8 Apr 95	**THE CHOIR – MUSIC FROM THE TV SERIES** *Decca 4481652* ANTHONY WAY & STANISLAS SYREWICZ ●	3		12
9 Dec 95	**THE CHOIRBOY** *Permanent PERMCD 41* ○	61		3
14 Dec 96	**THE CHOIRBOY'S CHRISTMAS** *Decca 4550502*	59		3
15 Mar 97	**WINGS OF A DOVE** *Decca 4556452*	69		1

WAY OUT WEST
UK, male instrumental/production duo — 2

Date	Title	Peak Position	Weeks at No.1	Weeks on Chart
13 Sep 97	**WAY OUT WEST** *Deconstruction 74321501952*	42		1
1 Sep 01	**INTENSIFY** *Distinctive Breaks DISNCD 76*	61		1

JEFF WAYNE
US, male producer/keyboard player. Multi-talented New Yorker who first found fame producing a string of David Essex hits. *The War Of The Worlds*, which has spent over five years on the chart, amazingly made a Top 5 return 27 years after its first visit there — 293

Date	Title	Peak Position	Weeks at No.1	Weeks on Chart
1 Jul 78	**JEFF WAYNE'S MUSICAL VERSION OF THE WAR OF THE WORLDS** *CBS 96000* ⊛x5	5		235
13 Oct 84	**BEYOND THE PLANETS** *Telstar STAR 2244* KEVIN PEEK & RICK WAKEMAN FEATURING JEFF WAYNE NARRATION PATRICK ALLEN	64		6
3 Oct 92	**SPARTACUS** *Columbia 4720302*	36		2
6 Jul 96	**JEFF WAYNE'S MUSICAL VERSION OF THE WAR OF THE WORLDS** *Columbia CDX 96000*	23		21
19 Oct 96	**HIGHLIGHTS FROM JEFF WAYNE'S MUSICAL VERSION OF THE WAR OF THE WORLDS** *Columbia 32356*	64		2
22 Apr 00	**JEFF WAYNE'S MUSICAL VERSION OF THE WAR OF THE WORLDS – ULLADUBULLA – THE REMIX ALBUM** *Columbia SONYTV 74CD*	64		1
25 Jun 05	**THE WAR OF THE WORLDS** *Columbia CDZ 96000*	5		26

WAYSTED
UK, male vocal/instrumental group — 5

Date	Title	Peak Position	Weeks at No.1	Weeks on Chart
8 Oct 83	**VICES** *Chrysalis CHR 1438*	78		3
22 Sep 84	**WAYSTED** *Music For Nations MFN 31*	73		2

WE ARE SCIENTISTS
UK, male vocal/instrumental trio — 17

Date	Title	Peak Position	Weeks at No.1	Weeks on Chart
29 Oct 05	**WITH LOVE AND SQUALOR** *Virgin CDVUS270* ●	43		14
29 Mar 08	**BRAIN THRUST MASTERY** *Virgin CDV3048*	11		3

WEATHER PROPHETS
UK, male vocal/instrumental group — 2

Date	Title	Peak Position	Weeks at No.1	Weeks on Chart
9 May 87	**MAYFLOWER** *Elevation ELV 1*	67		2

WEATHER REPORT
US, male instrumental group — 12

Date	Title	Peak Position	Weeks at No.1	Weeks on Chart
23 Apr 77	**HEAVY WEATHER** *CBS 81775*	43		6
11 Nov 78	**MR. GONE** *CBS 82775*	47		3
27 Feb 82	**WEATHER REPORT** *CBS 85326*	88		2
24 Mar 84	**DOMINO THEORY** *CBS 25839*	54		1

MARTI WEBB
UK, female vocalist — 33

Date	Title	Peak Position	Weeks at No.1	Weeks on Chart
16 Feb 80	**TELL ME ON A SUNDAY** *Polydor POLD 5031* ●	2		23
28 Sep 85	**ENCORE** *Starblend BLEND 1*	55		4
6 Dec 86	**ALWAYS THERE** *BBC REB 619*	65		5
10 Oct 92	**THE MAGIC OF THE MUSICALS** *Quality Television QTV 013* & MARK RATTRAY	55		1

SIMON WEBBE
UK, male vocalist. See Blue — 35

Date	Title	Peak Position	Weeks at No.1	Weeks on Chart
26 Nov 05	**SANCTUARY** *Innocent CDSIN20* ⊛x2	7		25
25 Nov 06	**GRACE** *Innocent CDANGE14* ●	11		10

WEDDING PRESENT
UK, male vocal/instrumental group — 22

Date	Title	Peak Position	Weeks at No.1	Weeks on Chart
24 Oct 87	**GEORGE BEST** *Reception LEEDS 001*	47		2
23 Jul 88	**TOMMY** *Reception LEEDS 2*	42		3
29 Apr 89	**UKRAINSKI VISTUIP V JOHNA PEELA** *RCA PL 74104*	22		3
4 Nov 89	**BIZZARO** *RCA PL 74302*	22		3
8 Jun 91	**SEA MONSTERS** *RCA PL 75012*	13		3
20 Jun 92	**HIT PARADE 1** *RCA PD 75343*	22		2
16 Jan 93	**HIT PARADE 2** *RCA 74321127752*	19		2
24 Sep 94	**WATUSI** *Island CID 8014*	47		1
3 Feb 96	**MINI** *Cooking Vinyl COOKCD 094*	40		1
21 Sep 96	**SATURNALIA** *Cooking Vinyl COOKCD 099*	36		1
26 Feb 05	**TAKE FOUNTAIN** *Scopitones TONECD020*	68		1

WEE PAPA GIRL RAPPERS
UK, female rap/vocal duo — 3

Date	Title	Peak Position	Weeks at No.1	Weeks on Chart
5 Nov 88	**THE BEAT, THE RHYME AND THE NOISE** *Jive HIP 67*	39		3

BERT WEEDON
UK, male guitarist — 26

Date	Title	Peak Position	Weeks at No.1	Weeks on Chart
16 Jul 60	**KING SIZE GUITAR** *Top Rank BUY 026*	18		1
23 Oct 76	**22 GOLDEN GUITAR GREATS** *Warwick WW 5019* ●	1	1	25

WEEZER
US, male vocal/instrumental group — 24

Date	Title	Peak Position	Weeks at No.1	Weeks on Chart
4 Mar 95	**WEEZER** *Geffen GED 24629*	23		11
12 Oct 96	**PINKERTON** *Geffen GED 25007*	43		1
26 May 01	**THE GREEN ALBUM** *Geffen 4930612*	31		4
25 May 02	**MALADROIT** *Geffen 4933252*	16		3
21 May 05	**MAKE BELIEVE** *Geffen 9882166*	11		3
28 Jun 08	**WEEZER** *Geffen 1774493*	21		2

GILLIAN WELCH
UK, female vocalist/guitarist — 1

Date	Title	Peak Position	Weeks at No.1	Weeks on Chart
14 Jun 03	**SOUL JOURNEY** *WEA 5046668682*	65		1
12 Sep 92	**PAUL WELLER** *Go! Discs 8283432* PAUL WELLER	8		7

PAUL WELLER
UK, male vocalist (John Weller). See Jam, Style Council — 278

Date	Title	Peak Position	Weeks at No.1	Weeks on Chart
18 Sep 93	**WILD WOOD** *Go! Discs 8284352* ⊛	2		51
24 Sep 94	**LIVE WOOD** *Go! Discs 8285612*	13		5
27 May 95	**STANLEY ROAD** *Go! Discs 8286192* ⊛x4	1	1	87
5 Jul 97	**HEAVY SOUL** *Island CID 8058* ●	2		13
21 Nov 98	**MODERN CLASSICS – THE GREATEST HITS** *Island CID 8080* ⊛	7		23
22 Apr 00	**HELIOCENTRIC** *Island CID 8093* ●	2		8
20 Oct 01	**DAYS OF SPEED** *Independiente ISOM 26CD* ⊛	3		16
28 Sep 02	**ILLUMINATION** *Independiente ISOM 33CDL* ●	1	1	7
6 Sep 03	**FLY ON THE WALL – B SIDES & RARITIES** *Island 0635272*	22		3
25 Sep 04	**STUDIO 150** *V2 VVR1026908* ●	2		13
11 Jun 05	**STANLEY ROAD** *Island 9828401*	51		1
22 Oct 05	**AS IS NOW** *V2 VVR1033208* ●	4		9
24 Jun 06	**CATCH-FLAME** *V2 VVR1039398*	17		2
18 Nov 06	**HIT PARADE** *Island/Polydor 9842615* ⊛	7		17
14 Jun 08	**22 DREAMS** *Island 1765657* ●	1	1	14
15 Nov 08	**PAUL WELLER AT THE BBC** *Island 5311906*	32		2

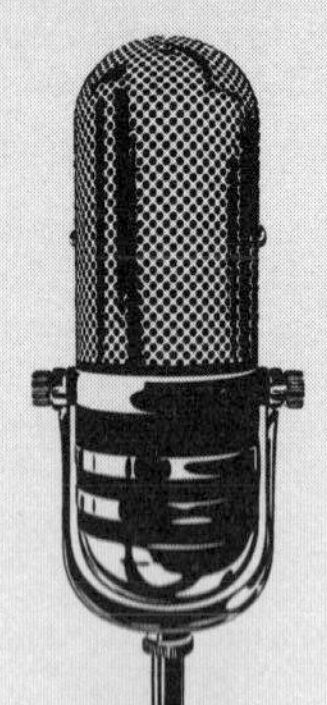

My Chemical Romance

The Black Parade

SOME would tag MCR – *wrongly* – as emo, that most maligned and slandered of recent subcultures (the name refers to the 'emotional' nature of their lyrics and imagery). According to the *Daily Mail*, Gerard Way and his 'gothic' band of equally morose and negative cohorts do little other than espouse suicide and berate themselves; all of which is, not surprisingly, nonsense.

During the shelf-life of the band's more linear yet still-blistering second album *Three Cheers For Sweet Revenge* (itself a sonic leap from the debut *I Brought You My Bullets, You Brought Me Your Love*), Way had battled against heavy drinking, an escalating rock-star lifestyle and, worst of all, the loss of his beloved grandmother after a prolonged and harrowing battle against cancer. So when mysterious Internet banners started appearing in early 2006 saying 'Welcome To The Black Parade', the rumour mill swirled into action. Fast approaching was the moment when MCR leapfrogged over the heads of all their contemporaries into the upper echelons of global stadium rock ... how did they do this? By releasing a sprawling, despairing yet uplifting masterpiece called *The Black Parade*.

The album's central concept revolves around 'The Patient', whose life is ebbing away

Looking at the sleeve notes before listening to a single tune, it is clear that the band had obviously observed the DNA of success – the most recent 'alternative rock' band to break out of the genre and go truly global was Green Day, whose own producer Rob Cavallo was also at the helm of *The Black Parade*. Green Day's 2004 album *American Idiot* – for many the best punk 'concept' album ever (for others a contradiction in terms) was a similarly lengthy and complex conceptual predecessor.

The Black Parade genesis had come during a disjointed and emotionally fractious recording period spent staying at a supposedly haunted house during which time Way's brother and bassist Mikey began treatment for depression; this uncertainty was fitting – after all, *The Black Parade* had started life with the working title *The Rise And Fall Of My Chemical Romance*. So, where next for Way and Co?

The signs of a great third album were there the instant the jarring video for MCR's opening single was played: 'Welcome To The Black Parade' saw Way's famous black hair replaced by a tight, blond French crop, the band were trussed up in militaristic uniforms, surrounded by ghastly, pallid dying cancer patients and guitarist Ray Toro spiralled into a guitar solo seemingly plucked out of the 'fave solos' book of Queen's Brian May (Way openly cited Queen, Pink Floyd and Bowie's 1970s material as a direct influence on the record). It was glorious.

The album's central concept revolves around 'The Patient', whose life is ebbing away and leaves him reflective and morose. The titular Black Parade is in fact a metaphor for the arrival of death, a snaking alternative to the Grim Reaper. Despite the hefty themes, at no point does the album become self-indulgent; only ever, self-affirming. Some might say it's ironic that an alternative band only pierced the mainstream on a global scale by reverting back to the establishment sound of the protracted 1970s rock scene; others

Chart History

Artist	Album Title	First Chart Week	Weeks on Chart	Highest Position
MY CHEMICAL ROMANCE	THE BLACK PARADE	4/11/06	48	2

highlight this album as a definitive exercise in both the creative power of knowing music history and a band's place in the contemporary axiom. *The Black Parade* debuted at Number 2 on the Albums Chart, behind Robbie Williams's *Rudebox*. It was an international hit record with high chart positions globally; in the UK, it is currently double-platinum. For Way & Co., things would never be the same again.

The album's second classic track is the next single, 'Famous Last Words', in whose video Way is his usual emotional tornado while drummer Bob Bryar actually suffered third-degree burns from on-set fires – who says no band suffers for their art these days? By the release of 'Teenagers' with its odd vaudeville video and Status Quo-esque guitars and melody, there was a sense that the band should be moving on; when Way's younger brother Mikey temporarily left the band to spend more time with his new wife, this sense increased. Despite these setbacks, the corresponding 138-date world tour was rabidly performed, as MCR's alter-ego band The Black Parade walked through the album in highly theatrical style, only to be followed by a second half of the gig with the 'return' of My Chemical Romance.

Gerard Way has the ultra-rare ability to emit a profound empathy with his audience; many performers tell us they understand our problems, our fears, our aspirations, but how many do we actually believe? Reciprocally, his own personal tragedy that provided a dark metaphorical catalyst for this album is a loss that we feel as if he were one of our own friends.

He is arguably the definitive post-millennial rock band frontman. His startling looks, piercing eyes and mop of rich dark hair, are the stuff of poster-boy legend, but he neatly balances this with an almost intangible air of 'normality'; however, make no mistake, he is anything but 'ordinary'. He will sing with such raw emotion you fear his vocal chords are about to be rendered useless permanently, and when he plunges into the heart of a track such as former single 'I'm Not Okay', and finishes the song writhing on the floor, you ask yourself, *How can he give any more to a song?*

Many performers tell us they understand our problems, our fears, our aspirations

Regardless of *Daily Mail* headlines, the appeal of MCR is actually *precisely* because they don't offer such a fatalist, pointless manifesto. Way and his band celebrate survival against the odds, they champion those feeling betrayed by society, mistreated by life and shunned by Lady Luck. Even when their words touch on the morbid or flirt with misery, there is redemption and hope, as Way demonstrates by singing that he is not scared to 'keep on living' in the inspirational 'Famous Last Words'.

With *The Black Parade*, My Chemical Romance reminded the music-loving world of one very important thing: never ignore the underdog.

Silver-selling ○ Gold-selling ● Platinum-selling ⊛ US No.1 ★ | Peak Position | Weeks at No.1 | Weeks on Chart

WENDY & LISA
US, female vocal duo — Peak Position / Weeks at No.1 / Weeks on Chart: 7

Date	Title / Label	Peak	Wks at No.1	Wks on Chart
10 Oct 87	**WENDY AND LISA** *Virgin V 2444*	84		2
18 Mar 89	**FRUIT AT THE BOTTOM** *Virgin V 2580*	45		2
4 Aug 90	**EROICA** *Virgin V 2633*	33		3

KANYE WEST
US, male rapper/producer — 119

Date	Title / Label	Peak	Wks at No.1	Wks on Chart
28 Feb 04	**THE COLLEGE DROPOUT** *Roc-A-Fella 9861739* ⊛x2	12		39
10 Sep 05	**LATE REGISTRATION** *Roc-A-Fella 9885282* ⊛x2 ★	2		41
13 May 06	**LATE ORCHESTRATION** *Roc-A-Fella 9878399*	59		1
22 Sep 07	**GRADUATION** *Roc-A-Fella 1745502* ⊛ ★	1	1	33
6 Dec 08	**808S & HEARTBREAKS** *Def Jam 1791341* ● ★	11		5+

HAYLEY WESTENRA
New Zealand, female vocalist — 50

Date	Title / Label	Peak	Wks at No.1	Wks on Chart
27 Sep 03	**PURE** *Decca 4753302* ⊛x2	7		24
25 Dec 04	**PURE** *Decca 4756538*	60		2
8 Oct 05	**ODYSSEY** *Decca 4757157* ●	10		17
10 Mar 07	**TREASURE** *Decca 4758522*	9		4
8 Nov 08	**RIVER OF DREAMS: VERY BEST OF** *Decca 4781075*	24		3

WESTLIFE
Ireland, male vocal group – Nicky Byrne, Kian Egan, Shane Filan, Mark Feehily & Bryan McFadden* (left 2004) — 271

Date	Title / Label	Peak	Wks at No.1	Wks on Chart
13 Nov 99	**WESTLIFE** *RCA 74321713212* ⊛x4	2		69
18 Nov 00	**COAST TO COAST** *RCA 74321808312* ⊛x6	1	1	28
24 Nov 01	**WORLD OF OUR OWN** *RCA 74321903082* ⊛x4	1	1	35
23 Nov 02	**UNBREAKABLE – THE GREATEST HITS VOLUME 1** *S 74321975902* ⊛x4	1	1	51
6 Dec 03	**TURNAROUND** *S 82876557412* ⊛x2	1	1	21
20 Nov 04	**ALLOW US TO BE FRANK** *S 82876651052* ⊛x2	3		12
12 Nov 05	**FACE TO FACE** *S 82876745382* ⊛x4	1	1	23
2 Dec 06	**THE LOVE ALBUM** *S 88697019822* ⊛x3	1	1	12
17 Nov 07	**BACK HOME** *S 88697176702* ⊛	1	1	20

WESTMINSTER ABBEY CHOIR/ CONDUCTOR: MARTIN NEARY
UK, male/female choir

Date	Title / Label	Peak	Wks at No.1	Wks on Chart
20 Sep 97	**JOHN TAVERNER: INNOCENCE** *Sony Classical SK 66613*	34		4
12 Sep 98	**PERFECT PEACE** *Sony Classical SONYTV 49CDS*	58		3

WESTWORLD
UK/US, male/female vocal/instrumental group — 2

Date	Title / Label	Peak	Wks at No.1	Wks on Chart
5 Sep 87	**WHERE THE ACTION IS** *RCA PL 71429*	49		2

WET WET WET
UK, male vocal/instrumental group – Marti Pellow* (Mark McLoughlin), Graeme Clark, Tom Cunningham & Neil Mitchell — 290

Date	Title / Label	Peak	Wks at No.1	Wks on Chart
3 Oct 87	**POPPED IN SOULED OUT** *Precious Organisation JWWWL 1* ⊛x5	1	1	72
19 Nov 88	**THE MEMPHIS SESSIONS** *Precious Organisation JWWWL 2* ⊛	3		13
11 Nov 89	**HOLDING BACK THE RIVER** *Precious Organisation 8420111* ⊛x2	2		26
8 Feb 92	**HIGH ON THE HAPPY SIDE** *Precious Organisation 5104272* ⊛	1	2	25
29 May 93	**LIVE AT THE ROYAL ALBERT HALL** *Precious Organisation 5147742* WITH THE WREN ORCHESTRA	10		4
20 Nov 93	**END OF PART ONE (THEIR GREATEST HITS)** *Precious Organisation 5184772* ⊛x4	1	5	67
22 Apr 95	**PICTURE THIS** *Precious Organisation 5268512* ⊛x3	1	3	45
12 Apr 97	**10** *Precious Organisation 5363192* ⊛	2		26
20 Nov 04	**THE GREATEST HITS** *Mercury 9868751* ⊛	13		10
24 Nov 07	**TIMELESS** *Dry DRY1*	41		2

WE'VE GOT A FUZZBOX & WE'RE GONNA USE IT
UK, female vocal/instrumental group – Maggie Dunne, Jo Dunne, Tina O'Neill & Vickie Perks — 6

Date	Title / Label	Peak	Wks at No.1	Wks on Chart
26 Aug 89	**BIG BANG** *WEA WX 282* ○	5		6

WHALE
Sweden, male/female vocal/instrumental group — 2

Date	Title / Label	Peak	Wks at No.1	Wks on Chart
12 Aug 95	**WE CARE** *Hut DGHUT 25*	42		2

WHAM!
UK, male vocal duo – George Michael* & Andrew Ridgeley — 259

Date	Title / Label	Peak	Wks at No.1	Wks on Chart
9 Jul 83	**FANTASTIC!** *Inner Vision IVL 25328* ⊛x3	1	2	116
18 Nov 84	**MAKE IT BIG** *Epic EPC 86311* ⊛x4 ★	1	2	72
19 Jul 86	**THE FINAL** *Epic EPC 88681* ⊛	2		47
6 Dec 97	**THE BEST OF WHAM!...IF YOU WERE THERE** *Epic 4890202* ⊛x2	4		24

WHEATUS
US, male vocal/instrumental group – Brendan Brown, Peter Brown, Phil A. Jimenez & Rich Liegey — 30

Date	Title / Label	Peak	Wks at No.1	Wks on Chart
3 Mar 01	**WHEATUS** *Columbia 4996052* ●	7		30

CARON WHEELER
UK, female vocalist. See Soul II Soul — 5

Date	Title / Label	Peak	Wks at No.1	Wks on Chart
13 Oct 90	**UK BLAK** *RCA PL 74751* ○	14		5

BILL WHELAN
Ireland, male keyboard player/arranger — 38

Date	Title / Label	Peak	Wks at No.1	Wks on Chart
25 Mar 95	**MUSIC FROM RIVERDANCE – THE SHOW** *Celtic Heartbeat 75678061112* ⊛	31		38

WHIGFIELD
Denmark, female vocalist (Sannie Carlson) — 7

Date	Title / Label	Peak	Wks at No.1	Wks on Chart
1 Jul 95	**WHIGFIELD** *Systematic 8286512* ○	13		7

THE WHIP
UK, male vocal/instrumental group — 1

Date	Title / Label	Peak	Wks at No.1	Wks on Chart
5 Apr 08	**X MARKS DESTINATION** *Southern Fried ECB143CD*	75		1

WHISPERS
US, male vocal group — 9

Date	Title / Label	Peak	Wks at No.1	Wks on Chart
14 Mar 81	**IMAGINATION** *Solar SOLA 7*	42		5
6 Jun 87	**JUST GETS BETTER WITH TIME** *Solar MCF 3381*	63		4

ALAN WHITE
UK, male drummer. See Yes — 4

Date	Title / Label	Peak	Wks at No.1	Wks on Chart
13 Mar 76	**RAMSHACKLED** *Atlantic K 50217*	41		4

BARRY WHITE
US, male vocalist/producer, d. 4 July 2003 (age 58). See Love Unlimited Orchestra — 247

Date	Title / Label	Peak	Wks at No.1	Wks on Chart
9 Mar 74	**STONE GON'** *Pye NSPL 28186* ●	18		17
2 Nov 74	**CAN'T GET ENOUGH** *20th Century BT 444* ● ★	4		34
26 Apr 75	**JUST ANOTHER WAY TO SAY I LOVE YOU** *20th Century BT 466* ○	12		15
22 Nov 75	**GREATEST HITS** *20th Century BTH 8000* ●	18		12
21 Feb 76	**LET THE MUSIC PLAY** *20th Century BT 502* ○	22		14
9 Apr 77	**BARRY WHITE'S GREATEST HITS VOLUME 2** *20th Century BTH 8001*	17		7
10 Feb 79	**THE MAN** *20th Century BT 571*	46		4
21 Dec 85	**HEART AND SOUL** *K-Tel NE 1316* ○	34		10
17 Oct 87	**THE RIGHT NIGHT AND BARRY WHITE** *Breakout AMA 5154*	74		6
2 Jul 88	**THE COLLECTION** *Mercury BWTV 1/Universal Music TV 8347902* ⊛x5	5		119
11 Feb 95	**THE ICON IS LOVE** *A&M 5402802*	44		3
15 Feb 03	**LOVE SONGS** *Universal TV 0686422*	21		3
19 Nov 05	**WHITE GOLD** *Universal TV 9834692*	37		3

KARYN WHITE
US, female vocalist — 30

Date	Title / Label	Peak	Wks at No.1	Wks on Chart
11 Mar 89	**KARYN WHITE** *Warner Brothers WX 235* ●	20		27
21 Sep 91	**RITUAL OF LOVE** *Warner Brothers WX 411*	31		3

KEISHA WHITE
UK, female vocalist — 1

Date	Title / Label	Peak	Wks at No.1	Wks on Chart
15 Jul 06	**OUT OF MY HANDS** *Korova KODE1006*	55		1

Silver-selling · Gold-selling · Platinum-selling · US No.1 · Peak Position · Weeks at No.1 · Weeks on Chart

SNOWY WHITE

UK, male vocalist/guitarist. See Thin Lizzy — **5**

Date	Title	Peak	Wks No.1	Wks
11 Feb 84	**WHITE FLAMES** *Towerbell TOWLP 3*	21		4
9 Feb 85	**SNOWY WHITE** *Towerbell TOWLP 8*	88		1

TONY JOE WHITE

US, male vocalist/guitarist — **1**

Date	Title	Peak	Wks No.1	Wks
27 Dec 69	**TONY JOE** *CBS 63800*	63		1

WHITE LION

US, male vocal/instrumental group — **3**

Date	Title	Peak	Wks No.1	Wks
1 Jul 89	**BIG GAME** *Atlantic WX 277*	47		1
20 Apr 91	**MANE ATTRACTION** *Atlantic WX 415*	31		2

WHITE STRIPES

US, male/female vocal/instrumental duo – Jack & Meg White — **105**

Date	Title	Peak	Wks No.1	Wks
18 Aug 01	**WHITE BLOOD CELLS** *Sympathy For The Record Industry SFTRI 660CD*	55		17
12 Apr 03	**ELEPHANT** *XL Recordings XLCD 162* x2	1	2	46
18 Jun 05	**GET BEHIND ME SATAN** *XL Recordings XLCD191*	3		27
30 Jun 07	**ICKY THUMP** *XL Recordings XLCD271*	1	1	15

WHITE ZOMBIE

US, male vocal/instrumental group — **6**

Date	Title	Peak	Wks No.1	Wks
27 May 95	**ASTRO CREEP 2000 – SONGS OF LOVE, DESTRUCTION AND OTHER SYNTHETIC DELUSIONS OF THE ELECTRIC HEAD** *Geffen GED 24806*	25		6

WHITEOUT

UK, male vocal/instrumental group — **1**

Date	Title	Peak	Wks No.1	Wks
1 Jul 95	**BITE IT** *Silvertone ORECD 536*	71		1

WHITESNAKE

UK/US, male vocal/instrumental group – David Coverdale*; members also included Warren Di Martini, Aynsley Dunbar, Jon Lord, Ian Paice, Cozy Powell*, Rudy Sarzo, Steve Vai* & Adrian Vandenberg — **167**

Date	Title	Peak	Wks No.1	Wks
18 Nov 78	**TROUBLE** *EMI International INS 3022*	50		2
13 Oct 79	**LOVE HUNTER** *United Artists UAG 30264*	29		7
7 Jun 80	**READY AND WILLING** *United Artists UAG 30302*	6		15
8 Nov 80	**LIVE AT THE HEART OF THE CITY** *United Artists SNAKE 1*	5		15
18 Apr 81	**COME AN' GET IT** *Liberty LBG 30327*	2		23
27 Nov 82	**SAINTS 'N' SINNERS** *Liberty LBG 30354*	9		9
11 Feb 84	**SLIDE IT IN** *Liberty LBG 2400001*	9		7
11 Apr 87	**WHITESNAKE 1987** *EMI EMC 3528*	8		57
25 Nov 89	**SLIP OF THE TONGUE** *EMI EMD 1013*	10		10
16 Jul 94	**GREATEST HITS** *EMI CDEMD 1065*	4		12
21 Jun 97	**RESTLESS HEART** *EMI CDEMD 1104* DAVID COVERDALE & WHITESNAKE	34		2
5 Apr 03	**THE BEST OF WHITESNAKE** *EMI 5812452*	44		3
3 May 08	**GOOD TO BE BAD** *SPV Recordings SPV981302CD*	7		3
21 Jun 08	**30TH ANNIVERSARY COLLECTION** *EMI 2126612*	38		2

SLIM WHITMAN

US, male vocalist/guitarist (Otis Whitman Jr.) — **61**

Date	Title	Peak	Wks No.1	Wks
14 Dec 74	**HAPPY ANNIVERSARY** *United Artists UAS 29670*	44		2
31 Jan 76	**THE VERY BEST OF SLIM WHITMAN** *United Artists UAS 29898*	1	6	17
15 Jan 77	**RED RIVER VALLEY** *United Artists UAS 29993*	1	4	14
15 Oct 77	**HOME ON THE RANGE** *United Artists UATV 30102*	2		13
13 Jan 79	**GHOST RIDERS IN THE SKY** *United Artists UATV 30202*	27		6
22 Dec 79	**SLIM WHITMAN'S 20 GREATEST LOVE SONGS** *United Artists UAG 30270*	18		7
27 Sep 97	**THE VERY BEST OF SLIM WHITMAN – 50TH ANNIVERSARY COLLECTION** *United Artists CDEMC 3772*	54		2

ROGER WHITTAKER

Kenya, male vocalist/whistler/guitarist — **116**

Date	Title	Peak	Wks No.1	Wks
27 Jun 70	**I DON'T BELIEVE IN IF ANYMORE** *Columbia SCX 6404*	23		1
3 Apr 71	**NEW WORLD IN THE MORNING** *Columbia SCX 6456*	45		2
6 Sep 75	**THE VERY BEST OF ROGER WHITTAKER** *Columbia SCX 6560*	5		42
15 May 76	**THE SECOND ALBUM OF THE VERY BEST OF ROGER WHITTAKER** *EMI EMC 3117*	27		7
9 Dec 78	**ROGER WHITTAKER SINGS THE HITS** *Columbia SCX 6601*	52		5
4 Aug 79	**20 ALL TIME GREATS** *Polydor POLTV 8*	24		9
7 Feb 81	**THE ROGER WHITTAKER ALBUM** *K-Tel NE 1105*	18		14
27 Dec 86	**THE SKYE BOAT SONG AND OTHER GREAT SONGS OF OUR ISLANDS** *Tembo TMB 113*	89		1
23 May 87	**HIS FINEST COLLECTION** *Tembo RWTV 1*	15		19
23 Sep 89	**HOME LOVIN' MAN** *Tembo RWTV 2*	20		10
11 May 96	**A PERFECT DAY – HIS GREATEST HITS AND MORE** *RCA 74321371562*	74		1
7 Feb 04	**NOW AND THEN – GREATEST HITS 1964 – 2004** *BMG 82876588332*	21		5

THE WHO

UK, male vocal/instrumental group – Roger Daltrey*, John Entwistle, d. 27 Jun 2002, Keith Moon, d. 7 Sep 1978 (replaced by Kenney Jones) & Pete Townshend* — **262**

Date	Title	Peak	Wks No.1	Wks
25 Dec 65	**THE WHO SINGS MY GENERATION** *Brunswick LAT 8616*	5		11
17 Dec 66	**A QUICK ONE** *Reaction 593002*	4		17
13 Jan 68	**THE WHO SELL-OUT** *Track 613002*	13		11
7 Jun 69	**TOMMY** *Track 613013/4*	2		9
4 Jul 70	**LIVE AT LEEDS** *Track 2406 001*	3		21
11 Sep 71	**WHO'S NEXT** *Track 2408 102*	1	1	13
18 Dec 71	**MEATY, BEATY, BIG AND BOUNCY** *Track 2406 006*	9		8
17 Nov 73	**QUADROPHENIA** *Track 2647 013*	2		13
26 Oct 74	**ODDS AND SODS** *Track 2406 116*	10		4
23 Aug 75	**TOMMY (OST)** *Track 2657 007*	30		2
18 Oct 75	**THE WHO BY NUMBERS** *Polydor 2490 129*	7		6
9 Oct 76	**THE STORY OF THE WHO** *Polydor 2683 069*	2		18
9 Dec 78	**WHO ARE YOU** *Polydor WHOD 5004*	6		9
30 Jun 79	**THE KIDS ARE ALRIGHT (OST)** *Polydor 2675 174*	26		13
6 Oct 79	**QUADROPHENIA (OST)** *Polydor 2625 037*	23		16
25 Oct 80	**MY GENERATION** *Virgin V 2179*	20		7
28 Mar 81	**FACE DANCES** *Polydor WHOD 5037*	2		9
11 Sep 82	**IT'S HARD** *Polydor WHOD 5066*	11		6
17 Nov 84	**WHO'S LAST** *MCA WHO 1*	48		4
12 Oct 85	**THE WHO COLLECTION** *Impression IMDP 4*	44		6
19 Mar 88	**WHO'S BETTER, WHO'S BEST** *Polydor WTV 1*	10		11
19 Nov 88	**THE WHO COLLECTION** *Stylus SMR 570*	71		4
24 Mar 90	**JOIN TOGETHER** *Virgin VDT 102*	59		1
16 Jul 94	**30 YEARS OF MAXIMUM R&B** *Polydor 5217512*	48		1
4 Mar 95	**LIVE AT LEEDS** *Polydor 5271692*	59		1
6 Jul 96	**QUADROPHENIA** *Polydor 5319712*	47		2
24 Aug 96	**MY GENERATION – THE VERY BEST OF THE WHO** *Polydor 5331502*	11		6
26 Feb 00	**BBC SESSIONS** *BBC Music/Polydor 5477272*	24		2
21 Sep 02	**MY GENERATION** *MCA 1129262*	47		1
2 Nov 02	**THE ULTIMATE COLLECTION** *Polydor 0653002*	17		6
12 Jul 03	**LIVE AT THE ROYAL ALBERT HALL** *SPV Recordings SPV09374882*	72		1
15 May 04	**THEN AND NOW** *Polydor 9866577*	5		20
11 Nov 06	**ENDLESSWIRE** *Polydor 1709519*	9		3

JANE WIEDLIN

US, female vocalist. See Go-Go's — **3**

Date	Title	Peak	Wks No.1	Wks
24 Sep 88	**FUR** *Manhattan MTL 1029*	48		3

WILCO

US, male vocal/instrumental group — **8**

Date	Title	Peak	Wks No.1	Wks
11 Jul 98	**MERMAID AVENUE** *Elektra 7559622042* BILLY BRAGG & WILCO	34		2
20 Mar 99	**SUMMERTEETH** *Reprise 9362472822*	38		2
10 Jun 00	**MERMAID AVENUE – VOLUME 2** *Elektra 7559625222* BILLY BRAGG & WILCO	61		1
4 May 02	**YANKEE HOTEL FOXTROT** *Nonesuch 7559796692*	40		1
3 Apr 04	**A GHOST IS BORN** *Nonesuch 7559798092*	50		1
26 May 07	**SKY BLUE SKY** *Nonesuch 7559799819*	39		1

WILD HORSES

UK, male vocal/instrumental group — **4**

Date	Title	Peak	Wks No.1	Wks
26 Apr 80	**WILD HORSES** *EMI EMC 3324*	38		4

EUGENE WILDE

US, male vocalist (Ron Broomfield) — **4**

Date	Title	Peak	Wks No.1	Wks
8 Dec 84	**EUGENE WILDE** *Fourth & Broadway BRLP 502*	67		4

Silver-selling · Gold-selling · Platinum-selling · US No.1 · Peak Position · Weeks at No.1 · Weeks on Chart

KIM WILDE

UK, female vocalist (Kim Smith) — 88

Date	Title	Peak Position	Weeks at No.1	Weeks on Chart
11 Jul 81	**KIM WILDE** *RAK SRAK 544*	3		14
22 May 82	**SELECT** *RAK SRAK 548*	19		11
26 Nov 83	**CATCH AS CATCH CAN** *RAK SRAK 165408*	90		1
17 Nov 84	**TEASES AND DARES** *MCA MCF 3250*	66		2
18 May 85	**THE VERY BEST OF KIM WILDE** *RAK WILDE 1*	78		4
15 Nov 86	**ANOTHER STEP** *MCA MCF 3339*	73		5
25 Jun 88	**CLOSE** *MCA MCG 6030*	8		38
26 May 90	**LOVE MOVES** *MCA MCG 6088*	37		3
30 May 92	**LOVE IS** *MCA MCAD 10625*	21		3
25 Sep 93	**THE SINGLES COLLECTION 1981–1993** *MCA MCD 10921*	11		7

MARTY WILDE

UK, male vocalist (Reg Smith) — 6

Date	Title	Peak Position	Weeks at No.1	Weeks on Chart
17 Mar 07	**THE GREATEST HITS – BORN TO ROCK & ROLL** *Universal TV 9847088*	19		6

WILDHEARTS

UK, male vocal/instrumental group – David 'Ginger' Walls, Ritch Battersby, Danny McCormack & Jef Streatfield — 10

Date	Title	Peak Position	Weeks at No.1	Weeks on Chart
11 Sep 93	**EARTH VS THE WILDHEARTS** *East West 4509932012*	46		1
3 Jun 95	**P.H.U.Q.** *East West 0630104372*	6		4
1 Jun 96	**FISHING FOR LUCKIES** *East West 0630148559*	16		2
8 Nov 97	**ENDLESS, NAMELESS** *Mushroom MUSH 13CD*	41		1
6 Sep 03	**THE WILDHEARTS MUST BE DESTROYED** *Gut GUTCD25*	54		1
5 May 07	**THE WILDHEARTS** *Round/Snapper ROUND0102*	55		1

WILEY

UK, male rapper/producer (Richard Cowie) — 2

Date	Title	Peak Position	Weeks at No.1	Weeks on Chart
8 May 04	**TREDDIN' ON THIN ICE** *XL Recordings XLCD 178*	45		1
16 Jun 07	**PLAYTIME IS OVER** *Big Dada BDCD104*	71		1

COLM WILKINSON

Ireland, male vocalist — 6

Date	Title	Peak Position	Weeks at No.1	Weeks on Chart
10 Jun 89	**STAGE HEROES** *RCA BL 74105*	27		6

WILL.I.AM

US, male vocalist/rapper/producer/multi-instrumentalist (William Adams, Jr.) — 4

Date	Title	Peak Position	Weeks at No.1	Weeks on Chart
17 May 08	**SONGS ABOUT GIRLS** *Interscope 1747675*	68		4

ALYSON WILLIAMS

US, female vocalist — 21

Date	Title	Peak Position	Weeks at No.1	Weeks on Chart
25 Mar 89	**RAW** *Def Jam 4632931*	29		21

ANDY WILLIAMS

US, male vocalist. Easy-on-the-ear balladeer and top-rated 1960s TV show host who first tasted success in his family group The Williams Brothers in the mid–1940s. In the US, Andy has earned 17 gold albums — 456

Date	Title	Peak Position	Weeks at No.1	Weeks on Chart
26 Jun 65	**ALMOST THERE** *CBS BPG 62533*	4		46
7 Aug 65	**CAN'T GET USED TO LOSING YOU** *CBS BPG 62146*	16		1
19 Mar 66	**MAY EACH DAY** *CBS BPG 62658*	11		6
30 Apr 66	**GREAT SONGS FROM MY FAIR LADY** *CBS BPG 62430*	30		1
23 Jul 66	**SHADOW OF YOUR SMILE** *CBS 62633*	24		4
29 Jul 67	**BORN FREE** *CBS SBPG 63027*	22		11
11 May 68	**LOVE ANDY** *CBS 63167*	1	1	22
6 Jul 68	**HONEY** *CBS 63311*	4		17
26 Jul 69	**HAPPY HEART** *CBS 63614*	22		9
26 Sep 70	**GET TOGETHER WITH ANDY WILLIAMS** *CBS 63800*	13		12
24 Jan 70	**ANDY WILLIAMS' SOUND OF MUSIC** *CBS 66214*	22		10
11 Apr 70	**ANDY WILLIAMS GREATEST HITS** *CBS 63920*	1	5	116
20 Jun 70	**CAN'T HELP FALLING IN LOVE** *CBS 64067*	7		48
5 Dec 70	**ANDY WILLIAMS SHOW** *CBS 64127*	10		6
27 Mar 71	**HOME LOVING MAN** *CBS 64286*	1	2	26
31 Jul 71	**LOVE STORY** *CBS 64467*	11		11
29 Apr 72	**THE IMPOSSIBLE DREAM** *CBS 67236*	26		3
29 Jul 72	**LOVE THEME FROM 'THE GODFATHER'** *CBS 64869*	11		16
19 Dec 72	**GREATEST HITS VOLUME 2** *CBS 65151*	23		10
22 Dec 73	**SOLITAIRE** *CBS 65638*	3		26
15 Jun 74	**THE WAY WE WERE** *CBS 80152*	7		11
11 Oct 75	**THE OTHER SIDE OF ME** *CBS 69152*	60		1
28 Jan 78	**REFLECTIONS** *CBS 10006*	2		17
27 Oct 84	**GREATEST LOVE CLASSICS** *EMI ANDY 1*	22		10
7 Nov 92	**THE BEST OF ANDY WILLIAMS** *Dino DINCD 50*	51		3
10 Apr 99	**IN THE LOUNGE WITH…ANDY WILLIAMS** *Columbia 4945082*	39		3
19 Feb 00	**THE VERY BEST OF ANDY WILLIAMS** *Columbia SONYTV 78CD*	27		7
6 Jul 02	**THE ESSENTIAL ANDY WILLIAMS** *Columbia 5084142*	32		2
9 Jul 05	**MUSIC TO WATCH GIRLS BY – THE VERY BEST** *Columbia 5203422*	50		1

DENIECE WILLIAMS

US, female vocalist (Deniece Chandler) — 23

Date	Title	Peak Position	Weeks at No.1	Weeks on Chart
21 May 77	**THIS IS NIECEY** *CBS 81869*	31		12
26 Aug 78	**THAT'S WHAT FRIENDS ARE FOR** *CBS 86068* JOHNNY MATHIS & DENIECE WILLIAMS	16		11

DON WILLIAMS

US, male vocalist/guitarist — 143

Date	Title	Peak Position	Weeks at No.1	Weeks on Chart
10 Jul 76	**GREATEST HITS VOLUME 1** *ABC ABCL 5147*	29		15
19 Feb 77	**VISIONS** *ABC ABCL 5200*	13		20
15 Oct 77	**COUNTRY BOY** *ABC ABCL 5233*	27		5
5 Aug 78	**IMAGES** *K-Tel NE 1033*	2		38
5 Aug 78	**YOU'RE MY BEST FRIEND** *ABC ABCD 5127*	58		1
4 Nov 78	**EXPRESSIONS** *ABC ABCL 5253*	28		8
22 Sep 79	**NEW HORIZONS** *K-Tel NE 1048*	29		12
15 Dec 79	**PORTRAIT** *MCA MCS 3045*	58		4
6 Sep 80	**I BELIEVE IN YOU** *MCA MCF 3077*	36		5
18 Jul 81	**ESPECIALLY FOR YOU** *MCA MCF 3114*	33		7
17 Apr 82	**LISTEN TO THE RADIO** *MCA MCF 3135*	69		3
23 Apr 83	**YELLOW MOON** *MCA MCF 3159*	52		1
15 Oct 83	**LOVE STORIES** *K-Tel NE 1252*	22		13
26 May 84	**CAFÉ CAROLINA** *MCA MCF 3225*	65		4
22 Apr 06	**THE DEFINITIVE DON WILLIAMS: HIS GREATEST HITS** *Universal TV 9839056*	26		7

IRIS WILLIAMS

UK, female vocalist — 4

Date	Title	Peak Position	Weeks at No.1	Weeks on Chart
22 Dec 79	**HE WAS BEAUTIFUL** *Columbia SCX 6627*	69		4

JOHN WILLIAMS

Australia, male guitarist. See Sky — 65

Date	Title	Peak Position	Weeks at No.1	Weeks on Chart
3 Oct 70	**PLAYS SPANISH MUSIC** *CBS 72860*	46		1
7 Feb 76	**RODRIGO: CONCERTO DE ARANJUEZ** *CBS 79369* WITH THE ENGLISH CHAMBER ORCHESTRA CONDUCTED BY DANIEL BARENBOIM	20		9
7 Jan 78	**BEST FRIENDS** *RCA Victor RS 1094* CLEO LAINE & JOHN WILLIAMS	18		22
17 Jun 78	**TRAVELLING** *Cube HIFLY 27*	23		5
30 Jun 79	**BRIDGES** *Lotus WH 5015*	5		22
4 Aug 79	**CAVATINA** *Cube HIFLY 32*	64		3
26 Oct 96	**JOHN WILLIAMS PLAYS THE MOVIES** *Sony Classical S2K 62784*	54		3

JOHN WILLIAMS

US, male orchestra leader — 75

Date	Title	Peak Position	Weeks at No.1	Weeks on Chart
31 Jan 76	**JAWS (OST)** *MCA MCF 2716*	55		1
21 Jan 78	**STAR WARS (OST)** *20th Century BTD 541* & THE LONDON SYMPHONY ORCHESTRA	21		12
29 Apr 78	**CLOSE ENCOUNTERS OF THE THIRD KIND (OST)** *Arista DLART 2001*	40		6
25 Dec 82	**E.T. – THE EXTRATERRESTRIAL (OST)** *MCA MCF 3160*	47		10
25 Jun 83	**RETURN OF THE JEDI (OST)** *RSO RSD 5023*	85		5
31 Jul 93	**JURASSIC PARK (OST)** *MCA MCD 10859*	42		5
2 Apr 94	**SCHINDLER'S LIST (OST)** *MCA MCD 10969*	59		2
15 May 99	**STAR WARS – THE PHANTOM MENACE (OST)** *Sony Classical SK 61816* & THE LONDON SYMPHONY ORCHESTRA	8		17
10 Nov 01	**HARRY POTTER (OST)** *Atlantic 7567930865*	19		7
11 May 02	**STAR WARS EPISODE II: ATTACK OF THE CLONES (OST)** *Sony Classical SK89965* & THE LONDON SYMPHONY ORCHESTRA	15		5
14 May 05	**STAR WARS EPISODE III – REVENGE OF THE SITH** *Sony Classical SK94220*	16		5

KATHRYN WILLIAMS

UK, female vocalist/guitarist — 3

Date	Title	Peak Position	Weeks at No.1	Weeks on Chart
15 Sep 01	**LITTLE BLACK NUMBERS** *East West 8573899242*	70		1
12 Oct 02	**OLD LOW LIGHT** *East West 0927475522*	56		2

LUCINDA WILLIAMS
US, female vocalist/guitarist — 5

Date	Title	Label	Peak	Wks No.1	Wks
16 Jun 01	ESSENCE	Lost Highway 1701972	63		1
19 Apr 03	WORLD WITHOUT TEARS	Lost Highway 1703552	48		1
3 Mar 07	WEST	Lost Highway 9858348	30		2
25 Oct 08	LITTLE HONEY	Lost Highway 1785915	51		1

PHARRELL WILLIAMS
US, male vocalist/producer — 7

Date	Title	Label	Peak	Wks No.1	Wks
5 Aug 06	IN MY MIND	Virgin 3461542 ○	7		7

ROBBIE WILLIAMS
UK, male vocalist. The former Take That member has won more BRIT awards than any other act (11 plus 4 with Take That). He is the first solo artist to reach No.1 with his first five albums and has recorded six of the 100 best-selling albums in UK chart history. See Take That — 491

Date	Title	Label	Peak	Wks No.1	Wks
11 Oct 97	LIFE THRU A LENS	Chrysalis CDCHR 6127 ⊛x8	1	2	123
7 Nov 98	I'VE BEEN EXPECTING YOU	Chrysalis 4978372 ⊛x10	1	3	98
9 Sep 00	SING WHEN YOU'RE WINNING	Chrysalis 5293942 ⊛x8	1	3	62
1 Dec 01	SWING WHEN YOU'RE WINNING	Chrysalis 5368262 ⊛x7	1	7	43
30 Nov 02	ESCAPOLOGY	EMI 5439942 ⊛x6	1	7	50
11 Oct 03	LIVE AT KNEBWORTH	Chrysalis 5946372 ⊛x2	2		21
30 Oct 04	GREATEST HITS	Chrysalis 8668192 ⊛x6	1	4	62
5 Nov 05	INTENSIVE CARE	Chrysalis 3437062 ⊛x5	1	1	20
4 Nov 06	RUDEBOX	Chrysalis 3770442 ⊛x2	1	1	12

VANESSA WILLIAMS
US, female vocalist — 4

Date	Title	Label	Peak	Wks No.1	Wks
25 Apr 92	THE COMFORT ZONE	Polydor 5112672	24		4

WENDY O. WILLIAMS
US, female vocalist, d. 6 Apr 1998 (age 48) — 1

Date	Title	Label	Peak	Wks No.1	Wks
30 Jun 84	W.O.W.	Music For Nations MFN 24	100		1

ANN WILLIAMSON
UK, female vocalist — 13

Date	Title	Label	Peak	Wks No.1	Wks
15 Feb 86	PRECIOUS MEMORIES	Emerald ERTV 1	16		9
6 Feb 88	COUNT YOUR BLESSINGS	Emerald Gem ERTV 2	58		4

SONNY BOY WILLIAMSON
US, male vocalist (Rice Miller), d. 25 May 1965 (age 65) — 1

Date	Title	Label	Peak	Wks No.1	Wks
20 Jun 64	DOWN AND OUT BLUES	Pye NPL 28036	20		1

BRUCE WILLIS
US, male actor/vocalist — 28

Date	Title	Label	Peak	Wks No.1	Wks
18 Apr 87	THE RETURN OF BRUNO	Motown ZL 72571 ●	4		28

MATT WILLIS
UK, male vocalist. See Busted — 1

Date	Title	Label	Peak	Wks No.1	Wks
2 Dec 06	DON'T LET IT GO TO WASTE	Mercury 9859977	66		1

BRIAN WILSON
US, male vocalist/multi-instrumentalist. See Beach Boys — 9

Date	Title	Label	Peak	Wks No.1	Wks
16 Sep 95	I JUST WASN'T MADE FOR THESE TIMES	MCA MCD 11270	59		1
27 Jun 98	IMAGINATION	Giant 74321573032	30		2
3 Jul 04	GETTIN' IN OVER MY HEAD	Rhino 8122764712	53		1
9 Oct 04	SMILE	East West 7559798462 ●	7		4
13 Sep 08	THAT LUCKY OLD SUN	EMI/Capitol 2348282	37		1

DENNIS WILSON
US, male vocalist/drummer, d. 28 Dec 1983 (age 39). See Beach Boys — 2

Date	Title	Label	Peak	Wks No.1	Wks
28 Jun 08	PACIFIC OCEAN BLUE	Epic 88697079162	16		2

GRETCHEN WILSON
US, female vocalist/guitarist — 1

Date	Title	Label	Peak	Wks No.1	Wks
11 Sep 04	HERE FOR THE PARTY	Epic 5174312	60		1

MARI WILSON
UK, female vocalist — 9

Date	Title	Label	Peak	Wks No.1	Wks
26 Feb 83	SHOWPEOPLE	Compact Organistion COMP 2	24		9

WILSON PHILLIPS
US, female vocal trio – Chynna Phillips & Carrie & Wendy Wilson — 38

Date	Title	Label	Peak	Wks No.1	Wks
30 Jun 90	WILSON PHILLIPS	SBK SBKLP 5 ⊛	7		32
13 Jun 92	SHADOWS AND LIGHT	SBK SBKCD 18 ○	6		6

WIN
UK, male vocal/instrumental group — 1

Date	Title	Label	Peak	Wks No.1	Wks
4 Apr 87	UH! TEARS BABY (A TRASH ICON)	Swampland LONLP 31	51		1

MARIO WINANS
US, male vocalist — 20

Date	Title	Label	Peak	Wks No.1	Wks
1 May 04	HURT NO MORE	Bad Boy 9862494 ⊛	3		20

WINDJAMMER
US, male vocal/instrumental group — 1

Date	Title	Label	Peak	Wks No.1	Wks
25 Aug 84	WINDJAMMER II	MCA MCF 3231	82		1

BARBARA WINDSOR
UK, female actor/vocalist — 2

Date	Title	Label	Peak	Wks No.1	Wks
3 Apr 99	YOU'VE GOT A FRIEND	Telstar TV TTVCD 3034	45		2

AMY WINEHOUSE
UK, female vocalist — 242

Date	Title	Label	Peak	Wks No.1	Wks
1 Nov 03	FRANK	Island 9812918 ⊛x2	13		110
11 Nov 06	BACK TO BLACK	Island 1713041 ⊛x6	1	3	79+
17 Nov 07	BACK TO BLACK – THE DELUXE EDITION	Island 1749097 ⊛x2	1	1	53

JOSH WINK
US, male producer (Joshua Winkelman) — 1

Date	Title	Label	Peak	Wks No.1	Wks
21 Sep 96	LEFT ABOVE THE CLOUDS	XL Recordings XLCD 119	43		1

JOHNNY WINTER
US, male vocalist/guitarist — 12

Date	Title	Label	Peak	Wks No.1	Wks
16 May 70	SECOND WINTER	CBS 66321	59		2
31 Oct 70	JOHNNY WINTER AND...	CBS 64117	29		4
15 May 71	JOHNNY WINTER AND...LIVE	CBS 64289	20		6

RUBY WINTERS
US, female vocalist — 17

Date	Title	Label	Peak	Wks No.1	Wks
10 Jun 78	RUBY WINTERS	Creole CRLP 512	27		7
23 Jun 79	SONGBIRD	K-Tel NE 1045 ○	31		10

STEVE WINWOOD
UK, male vocalist/multi-instrumentalist. See Blind Faith, Spencer Davis Group, Traffic — 123

Date	Title	Label	Peak	Wks No.1	Wks
9 Jul 77	STEVE WINWOOD	Island ILPS 9494	12		9
10 Jan 81	ARC OF A DIVER	Island ILPS 9576 ○	13		20
14 Aug 82	TALKING BACK TO THE NIGHT	Island ILPS 9777 ●	6		13
12 Jul 86	BACK IN THE HIGH LIFE	Island ILPS 9844 ●	8		42
7 Nov 87	CHRONICLES	Island SSW 1 ●	12		17
2 Jul 88	ROLL WITH IT	Virgin V 2532 ● ★	4		16
17 Nov 90	REFUGEES OF THE HEART	Virgin V 2650	26		3
14 Jun 97	JUNCTION SEVEN	Virgin CDV 2832	32		2
17 May 08	NINE LIVES	Columbia 88697222502	31		1

WIRE
UK, male vocal/instrumental group — 3

Date	Title	Label	Peak	Wks No.1	Wks
7 Oct 78	CHAIRS MISSING	Harvest SHSP 4093	48		1
13 Oct 79	154	Harvest SHSP 4105	39		1
9 May 87	THE IDEAL COPY	Mute STUMM 42	87		1

Stevie Wonder

HAD you not heard any of Stevie Wonder's back catalogue other than 1984's global Number 1 single 'I Just Called To Say I Love You', you could be forgiven for thinking that this rather unconventional-looking pop star was probably going to be just a flash in the Middle of the Road pan. Of course, by the time he was sitting at the top of most countries' singles charts, his songs and albums had already established him as one of the great songwriters and composers.

Even among Wonder fans, Motown's biggest-ever-selling single, 'I Just Called ...' is not widely regarded as his creative pinnacle – culled from a stunning array of albums, his pioneering music is heavily sampled and acutely influential and he is rightly regarded as one of the prime movers in progressing soul and R&B as a genre.

His effortless melodic creativity has sprawled into so many genres of music it sometimes disguises the moments of pure genius

Blinded by too much oxygen in an incubator shortly after his birth, Wonder would also lose his sense of smell at the age of twenty-three after a serious car crash in 1973 left him in a coma for four days. It is widely believed that, in the absence of certain primary senses, the body will accentuate the remaining senses to accommodate any shortcomings. Whether his sensitised hearing fuelled Wonder's innate musicality is open to debate, but what is true is that as a child prodigy he was a multi-instrumentalist at seven, a songwriter at eight and signed to Motown as Little Stevie Wonder aged only ten. His flop debut single 'I Call It Pretty Music But The Old People Call It The Blues' had then-session drummer Marvin Gaye in the studio. This was a young man, it seemed, who appeared to go hand in hand with the term 'historically important'.

Paradoxically to the critics' disdain over his more cheesy 1980s singles, Wonder has received nothing but gushing critical acclaim for his early-1970s body of work, including the seminal albums *Talking Book* (Number 16, complete with its title in braille on the album cover) and *Songs in the Key of Life* (Number 2) – both produced during a stunning five-year purple patch which saw him create five masterful albums. *Innervisions* from this period (a Number 8 album) won him a clutch of Grammys and is still revered.

Without doubt one of the key figures in modern music, Stevie Wonder's catalogue is a breathtaking ride through a myriad of styles. Like Paul McCartney, his effortless melodic creativity has sprawled into so many genres of music it sometimes disguises the moments of pure genius that make him stand out from the crowd, such as the sublime, sticky superfunk of 'Superstition' and the stunning 'Masterblaster' or the pop royalty that is 'Signed, Sealed, Delivered I'm Yours', moments which showcase Stevie Wonder's effortless talent for creating subtly funky masterpieces and then turning them into pop staples.

After this 1970s peak Wonder stopped recording for three years – maybe the sheer scale of songwriting achievement and the five sprawling albums in five years had burned him out, maybe he felt there was nothing left to be said and that it was time to take a break. What he had achieved was incredible – five albums that set a blueprint for pop music in the next three decades as well as a complex and intelligent set of pop songs on a par with anything recorded by any other major artist.

On his return to the studio, Wonder reaped the

Biggest-Selling Album				
Artist	Album	Week	Highest Position	Approx Sales
STEVIE WONDER	HOTTER THAN JULY	8/11/80	2	820,000

commercial rewards of this successful period. If his 1970s had been one of artistic endeavour and critical acclaim, the 1980s would see him become one of the biggest-selling artists in the world. Initially his return was low-key with the poorly received soundtrack album *Secret Life Of Plants*, but it wasn't long before the sheer force of his talent scored more victories. Even some of his bubblegum moments have a depth: the radio-friendly 'Happy Birthday', taken from the Number 2 album *Hotter Than July*, is admittedly an adept piece of saccharine pop creativity; this was actually part of a long-term campaign by Wonder for the recognition of Martin Luther King's birthday as a national holiday in the USA.

Many critics point to the duet with Paul McCartney, 'Ebony And Ivory' as a creative low, but this is harsh. Since then, it is fair to say his work has not captured the artistic heights of his golden era but, across his six decades of life, few can lay claim to such an influential and impressive canon. As recently as November 2008, 'Signed, Sealed, Delivered ...' was being used regularly during President Obama's campaign for the Presidency. He is also a prolific songwriter for other artists, and co-wrote 'The Tears Of A Clown' with Smokey Robinson when he was a staff writer for Motown – a member of that label crucial to its financial success. At the time of writing, there are rumours that Wonder is back in the studio working on two separate projects – *The Gospel Inspired By Lula*, which will deal with the various spiritual and cultural crises facing the world, and *Through The Eyes Of Wonder,* an album Wonder has described as a performance piece, reflecting his experience as a blind man.

'Signed, Sealed, Delivered ...' was being used regularly during President Obama's campaign for the Presidency

Here is a man who can make the hippest and funkiest of tracks as well as pure pop ballads that sit for ever in the mainstream; his social conscience and his understanding of the innate power of the pop song makes him one of the all-time greats.

Silver-selling · Gold-selling · Platinum-selling · US No.1 ★ · Peak Position · Weeks at No.1 · Weeks on Chart

WISHBONE ASH
UK, male vocal/instrumental group – Andy Powell, Martin Turner, Ted Turner (replaced by Laurie Wisefield) & Steve Upton — 76

Date	Title	Peak Position	Weeks at No.1	Weeks on Chart
23 Jan 71	**WISHBONE ASH** *MCA MKPS 2014*	29		3
9 Oct 71	**PILGRIMAGE** *MCA MDKS 8004*	14		9
20 May 72	**ARGUS** *MCA MDKS 8006*	3		20
26 May 73	**WISHBONE FOUR** *MCA MDKS 8011*	12		10
30 Nov 74	**THERE'S THE RUB** *MCA MCF 2585*	16		5
3 Apr 76	**LOCKED IN** *MCA MCF 2750*	36		2
27 Nov 76	**NEW ENGLAND** *MCA MCG 3523*	22		3
29 Oct 77	**FRONT PAGE NEWS** *MCA MCG 3524*	31		4
28 Oct 78	**NO SMOKE WITHOUT FIRE** *MCA MCG 3528*	43		3
2 Feb 80	**JUST TESTING** *MCA MCF 3052*	41		4
1 Nov 80	**LIVE DATES II** *MCA MCG 4012*	40		3
25 Apr 81	**NUMBER THE BRAVE** *MCA MCF 3103*	61		5
16 Oct 82	**TWIN BARRELS BURNING** *AVM ASH 1*	22		5

BILL WITHERS
US, male vocalist/guitarist — 12

Date	Title	Peak Position	Weeks at No.1	Weeks on Chart
11 Feb 78	**MENAGERIE** *CBS 82265*	27		5
15 Jun 85	**WATCHING YOU, WATCHING ME** *CBS 26200*	60		1
17 Sep 88	**GREATEST HITS** *CBS 32343*	90		4
5 Aug 06	**LOVELY DAY – THE VERY BEST OF** *Columbia 82876845522*	35		2

WITHIN TEMPTATION
Holland, female/male vocal/instrumental group — 2

Date	Title	Peak Position	Weeks at No.1	Weeks on Chart
24 Mar 07	**THE HEART OF EVERYTHING** *Roadrunner RR80032*	38		2

WITNESS
UK, male vocal/instrumental group — 2

Date	Title	Peak Position	Weeks at No.1	Weeks on Chart
24 Jul 99	**BEFORE THE CALM** *Island CID 8084*	59		1
4 Aug 01	**UNDER A SUN** *Island CID 8107*	62		1

WIZZARD
UK, male vocal/instrumental group — 11

Date	Title	Peak Position	Weeks at No.1	Weeks on Chart
19 May 73	**WIZZARD BREW** *Harvest SHSP 4025*	29		7
17 Aug 74	**INTRODUCING EDDY AND THE FALCONS** *Warner Brothers K 52029*	19		4

ANDREW WK
US, male vocalist/multi-instrumentalist (Andrew Wilkes-Krier) — 1

Date	Title	Peak Position	Weeks at No.1	Weeks on Chart
24 Nov 01	**I GET WET** *Mercury 5865882*	71		1

JAH WOBBLE'S INVADERS OF THE HEART
UK, male vocalist/multi-instrumentalist (John Wardle) — 6

Date	Title	Peak Position	Weeks at No.1	Weeks on Chart
28 May 94	**TAKE ME TO GOD** *Island CID 8017*	13		5
14 Oct 95	**SPINNER** *All Saints ASCD 023* BRIAN ENO & JAH WOBBLE	71		1

PATRICK WOLF
Ireland, male vocalist/multi-instrumentalist (Patrick Apps) — 1

Date	Title	Peak Position	Weeks at No.1	Weeks on Chart
10 Mar 07	**THE MAGIC POSITION** *A&M/Polydor 1704886*	46		1

WOLFGANG PRESS
UK, male vocal/instrumental duo — 1

Date	Title	Peak Position	Weeks at No.1	Weeks on Chart
4 Feb 95	**FUNKY LITTLE DEMONS** *4AD CADD 4016CD*	75		1

WOLFMOTHER
Australia, male vocal/instrumental trio — 16

Date	Title	Peak Position	Weeks at No.1	Weeks on Chart
6 May 06	**WOLFMOTHER** *Modular 9877684*	25		16

WOLFSBANE
UK, male vocal/instrumental group — 3

Date	Title	Peak Position	Weeks at No.1	Weeks on Chart
5 Aug 89	**LIVE FAST, DIE FAST** *Def American 8384861*	48		1
20 Oct 90	**ALL HELL'S BREAKING LOOSE DOWN AT LITTLE KATHY WILSON'S PLACE!** *Def American 8469671*	48		1
19 Oct 91	**DOWN FALL THE GOOD GUYS** *Def American 5104131*	53		1

BOBBY WOMACK
US, male vocalist/guitarist — 15

Date	Title	Peak Position	Weeks at No.1	Weeks on Chart
28 Apr 84	**THE POET II** *Motown ZL 72205*	31		8
28 Sep 85	**SO MANY RIVERS** *MCA MCF 3282*	28		7

WOMACK & WOMACK
US, male/female vocal duo – Cecil & Linda Womack — 54

Date	Title	Peak Position	Weeks at No.1	Weeks on Chart
21 Apr 84	**LOVE WARS** *Elektra 960293*	45		13
22 Jun 85	**RADIO M.U.S.C. MAN** *Elektra EKT 6*	56		2
12 Oct 85	**THE ARTISTS VOLUME III** *Street Sounds ARTIS 3* /THE O'JAYS/KLEEER/THE S.O.S. BAND	87		2
27 Aug 88	**CONSCIENCE** *Fourth & Broadway BRLP 519*	4		37

WOMBATS
UK/Norway, male vocal/instrumental group — 37

Date	Title	Peak Position	Weeks at No.1	Weeks on Chart
17 Nov 07	**A GUIDE TO LOVE, LOSS & DESPERATION** *14TH Floor 5144233372*	11		37

WOMBLES
Wimbledon Common (UK), male/female puppet vocalists — 58

Date	Title	Peak Position	Weeks at No.1	Weeks on Chart
2 Mar 74	**WOMBLING SONGS** *CBS 65803*	19		17
13 Jul 74	**REMEMBER YOU'RE A WOMBLE** *CBS 80191*	18		31
21 Dec 74	**KEEP ON WOMBLING** *CBS 80526*	17		6
8 Jan 77	**20 WOMBLING GREATS** *Warwick PR 5022*	29		1
18 Apr 98	**THE BEST WOMBLES ALBUM SO FAR – VOLUME 1** *Columbia 4895622*	26		3

STEVIE WONDER
US, male vocalist/pianist (Steveland Judkins). In 1963, the multi-talented 13 year old became the youngest artist to top the US albums chart. After a slower start in the UK, he has become one of the most successful and well-respected singer/songwriters of all time — 400

Date	Title	Peak Position	Weeks at No.1	Weeks on Chart
7 Sep 68	**STEVIE WONDER'S GREATEST HITS** *Tamla Motown STML 11075*	25		10
13 Dec 69	**MY CHERIE AMOUR** *Tamla Motown STML 11128*	17		2
12 Feb 72	**GREATEST HITS VOLUME 2** *Tamla Motown STML 11196*	30		4
3 Feb 73	**TALKING BOOK** *Tamla Motown STMA 8007*	16		48
1 Sep 73	**INNERVISIONS** *Tamla Motown STMA 8011*	8		55
17 Aug 74	**FULFILLINGNESS' FIRST FINALE** *Tamla Motown STMA 8019* ★	5		16
16 Oct 76	**SONGS IN THE KEY OF LIFE** *Tamla Motown TMSP 6002* ★	2		54
10 Nov 79	**JOURNEY THROUGH THE SECRET LIFE OF PLANTS** *Motown TMSP 6009*	8		15
8 Nov 80	**HOTTER THAN JULY** *Motown STMA 8035*	2		55
22 May 82	**ORIGINAL MUSIQUARIUM 1** *Motown TMSP 6012*	8		17
22 Sep 84	**WOMAN IN RED (OST)** *Motown ZL 72285* & FEATURING DIONNE WARWICK	2		19
24 Nov 84	**LOVE SONGS – 16 CLASSIC HITS** *Telstar STAR 2251*	20		10
28 Sep 85	**IN SQUARE CIRCLE** *Motown ZL 72005*	5		16
15 Nov 86	**DIANA ROSS. MICHAEL JACKSON. GLADYS KNIGHT. STEVIE WONDER. THEIR VERY BEST BACK TO BACK** *PrioriTyV PTVR2* DIANA ROSS/MICHAEL JACKSON/GLADYS KNIGHT/STEVIE WONDER	21		10
28 Nov 87	**CHARACTERS** *RCA ZL 72001*	33		4
8 Jun 91	**JUNGLE FEVER (OST)** *Motown ZL 71750*	56		1
25 Mar 95	**CONVERSATION PEACE** *Motown 5302382*	8		4
23 Nov 96	**SONG REVIEW – A GREATEST HITS COLLECTION** *Motown 5307572*	19		12
9 Nov 02	**THE DEFINITIVE COLLECTION** *Universal TV 0665022*	11		40
29 Oct 05	**A TIME 2 LOVE** *Motown 9882094*	24		3
20 Oct 07	**NUMBER 1'S** *Motown 1747320*	23		5

WAYNE WONDER
Jamaica, male vocalist (VonWayne Charles) — 7

Date	Title	Peak Position	Weeks at No.1	Weeks on Chart
28 Jun 03	**NO HOLDING BACK** *Atlantic/VP 7567836282*	40		7

WONDER STUFF
UK, male vocal/instrumental group – Miles Hunt, Martin Bell, Paul Clifford, Martin Gilks, Rob Jones, d. 30 Jul 1993, & Malcolm Treece — 48

Date	Title	Peak Position	Weeks at No.1	Weeks on Chart
27 Aug 88	**THE EIGHT LEGGED GROOVE MACHINE** *Polydor GONLP 1*	18		7
14 Oct 89	**HUP** *Polydor 8411871*	5		8
8 Jun 91	**NEVER LOVED ELVIS** *Polydor 8472521*	3		23
16 Oct 93	**CONSTRUCTION FOR THE MODERN IDIOT** *Polydor 5198942*	4		5
8 Oct 94	**IF THE BEATLES HAD READ HUNTER...THE SINGLES** *Polydor 5213972*	8		4
29 Jul 95	**LIVE IN MANCHESTER** *Windsong WINCD 074X*	74		1

ROY WOOD

UK, male vocalist/multi-instrumentalist (Ulysses Adrian Wood). See Electric Light Orchestra, Move, Wizzard — 14

Date	Title	Label	Peak	Wks at No.1	Wks on Chart
18 Aug 73	BOULDERS	Harvest SHVL 803	15		8
24 Jul 82	THE SINGLES	Speed 1000	37		6

WOODENTOPS

UK, male vocal/instrumental group — 6

Date	Title	Label	Peak	Wks at No.1	Wks on Chart
12 Jul 86	GIANT	Rough Trade ROUGH 87	35		4
5 Mar 88	WOODEN FOOT COPS ON THE HIGHWAY	Rough Trade ROUGH 127	48		2

EDWARD WOODWARD

UK, male actor/vocalist — 12

Date	Title	Label	Peak	Wks at No.1	Wks on Chart
6 Jun 70	THIS MAN ALONE	DJM DJLPS 405	53		2
19 Aug 72	THE EDWARD WOODWARD ALBUM	Jam JAL 103	20		10

WOOLPACKERS

UK, male/female actors/vocal group — 13

Date	Title	Label	Peak	Wks at No.1	Wks on Chart
14 Dec 96	EMMERDANCE	RCA 74321444052	26		10
29 Nov 97	THE GREATEST LINE DANCING PARTY ALBUM	RCA 74321512272	48		3

WORKING WEEK

UK, male/female vocal/instrumental group — 10

Date	Title	Label	Peak	Wks at No.1	Wks on Chart
6 Apr 85	WORKING NIGHTS	Virgin V 2343	23		9
27 Sep 86	COMPANEROS	Virgin V 2397	72		1

WORLD OF TWIST

UK, male/female vocal/instrumental group — 1

Date	Title	Label	Peak	Wks at No.1	Wks on Chart
9 Nov 91	QUALITY STREET	Circa 17	50		1

WORLD PARTY

UK/Ireland, male vocalist/keyboard player (Karl Wallinger). See Waterboys — 25

Date	Title	Label	Peak	Wks at No.1	Wks on Chart
21 Mar 87	PRIVATE REVOLUTION	Chrysalis CHEN 4	56		4
19 May 90	GOODBYE JUMBO	Ensign CHEN 10	36		10
8 May 93	BANG!	Ensign CDCHEN 33	2		8
28 Jun 97	EGYPTOLOGY	Chrysalis CDCHR 6124	34		2
2 Sep 00	DUMBING UP	Papillion BTFLYCD 0006	64		1

WRECKLESS ERIC

UK, male vocalist (Eric Goulden) — 5

Date	Title	Label	Peak	Wks at No.1	Wks on Chart
1 Apr 78	WRECKLESS ERIC	Stiff SEEZ 6	46		1
8 Mar 80	BIG SMASH	Stiff SEEZ 21	30		4

RICK WRIGHT

UK, male vocalist/keyboard player, d. 15 Sep 2008 (age 65). See Pink Floyd — 1

Date	Title	Label	Peak	Wks at No.1	Wks on Chart
19 Oct 96	BROKEN CHINA	EMI CDEMD 1098	61		1

WU-TANG CLAN

US, male rap/instrumental group – Genius/GZA* (Gary Crice), Ghostface Killah* (Dennis Coles), Inspectah Deck (Jason Hunter), Masta Killa (Elgin Turner), Method Man* (Clifford Smith), Ol' Dirty Bastard (Russell Jones), d. 13 Nov 2004, Raekwon (Corey Woods) & U-God (Lamont Hawkins) — 23

Date	Title	Label	Peak	Wks at No.1	Wks on Chart
14 Jun 97	WU-TANG FOREVER	Loud 74321457682 ★	1	1	10
2 Dec 00	THE W	Epic 4995762	19		13

KLAUS WUNDERLICH

Germany, male organist, d. 28 Oct 1997 (age 66) — 19

Date	Title	Label	Peak	Wks at No.1	Wks on Chart
30 Aug 75	THE HIT WORLD OF KLAUS WUNDERLICH	Decca SPA 434	27		8
20 May 78	THE UNIQUE KLAUS WUNDERLICH SOUND	Decca DBC 5/5	28		4
26 May 79	THE FANTASTIC SOUND OF KLAUS WUNDERLICH	Lotus LH 5013	43		5
17 Mar 84	ON THE SUNNY SIDE OF THE STREET	Polydor POLD 5133	81		2

WURZELS

UK, male vocal/instrumental group — 29

Date	Title	Label	Peak	Wks at No.1	Wks on Chart
11 Mar 67	ADGE CUTLER AND THE WURZELS	Columbia SX 6126	38		4
3 Jul 76	COMBINE HARVESTER	One Up OU 2138	15		20
2 Apr 77	GOLDEN DELICIOUS	EMI NTS 122	32		5

WWF SUPERSTARS

US/UK, male wrestlers/vocalists — 5

Date	Title	Label	Peak	Wks at No.1	Wks on Chart
17 Apr 93	WRESTLEMANIA – THE ALBUM	Arista 74321138062	10		5

BILL WYMAN

UK, male vocalist/bass guitarist (Willam Perks). See Rolling Stones — 8

Date	Title	Label	Peak	Wks at No.1	Wks on Chart
8 Jun 74	MONKEY GRIP	Rolling Stones COC 59102	39		1
10 Apr 82	BILL WYMAN	A&M AMLH 68540	55		6
27 May 00	GROOVIN	Papillion BTFLYCD 003 'S RHYTHM KINGS	52		1

TAMMY WYNETTE

US, female vocalist (Virginia Wynette Pugh), d. 6 Apr 1998 (age 55) — 48

Date	Title	Label	Peak	Wks at No.1	Wks on Chart
17 May 75	THE BEST OF TAMMY WYNETTE	Epic EPC 63578	4		23
21 Jun 75	STAND BY YOUR MAN	Epic EPC 69141	13		7
17 Dec 77	20 COUNTRY CLASSICS	CBS PR 5040	3		11
6 Jun 87	ANNIVERSARY – 20 YEARS OF HITS	Epic 4503931	45		5
19 Apr 08	STAND BY YOUR MAN – THE BEST OF	Sony BMG 88697251272	23		2

X

RICHARD X

UK, male producer (Richard Phillips) — 2

Date	Title	Label	Peak	Wks at No.1	Wks on Chart
6 Sep 03	RICHARD X PRESENTS HIS X-FACTOR VOLUME 1	Virgin CDRICH1	31		2

X MAL DEUTSCHLAND

UK/Germany, male/female vocal/instrumental group — 1

Date	Title	Label	Peak	Wks at No.1	Wks on Chart
7 Jul 84	TOCSIN	4AD CAD 407	86		1

X-PRESS 2

UK, male production/instrumental group — 3

Date	Title	Label	Peak	Wks at No.1	Wks on Chart
4 May 02	MUZIKIZUM	Skint BRASSIC 23CD	15		3

X-RAY SPEX

UK, male/female vocal/instrumental group — 14

Date	Title	Label	Peak	Wks at No.1	Wks on Chart
9 Dec 78	GERM FREE ADOLESCENTS	EMI International INS 3023	30		14

XTC

UK/Malta, male vocal/instrumental group – Andy Partridge, Terry Chambers, Dave Gregory & Colin Moulding — 51

Date	Title	Label	Peak	Wks at No.1	Wks on Chart
11 Feb 78	WHITE MUSIC	Virgin V 2095	38		4
28 Oct 78	GO 2	Virgin V 2108	21		3
1 Sep 79	DRUMS AND WIRES	Virgin V 2129	34		7
20 Sep 80	BLACK SEA	Virgin V 2173	16		7
20 Feb 82	ENGLISH SETTLEMENT	Virgin V 2223	5		11
13 Nov 82	WAXWORKS – SOME SINGLES (1977–1982)	Virgin V 2251	54		3
10 Sep 83	MUMMER	Virgin V 2264	51		4
27 Oct 84	THE BIG EXPRESS	Virgin V 2325	38		2
8 Nov 86	SKYLARKING	Virgin V 2399	90		1
11 Mar 89	ORANGES AND LEMONS	Virgin V 2581	28		3
9 May 92	NONSUCH	Virgin CDV 2699	28		2
28 Sep 96	FOSSIL FUEL – THE XTC SINGLES COLLECTION 1977–1992	Virgin CDVDX 2811	33		2
6 Mar 99	APPLE VENUS – VOLUME 1	Cooking Vinyl COOKCD 172	42		1
3 Jun 00	APPLE VENUS – VOLUME 2	Cooking Vinyl COOKCD 194 /WASP STAR	40		1

XZIBIT

US, male rapper (Alvin Joiner) — 13

Date	Title	Label	Peak	Wks at No.1	Wks on Chart
10 Feb 01	RESTLESS	Epic 4989132	27		11
12 Oct 02	MAN VS MACHINE	Epic 5047539	43		2

BIOGRAPHIES

Biographies include the nationality and category for every chart entrant.

Each entrant has at least a mini biography. The 100 acts with the most weeks on the chart (see page 290 for the top 100 chart) each have extended biographies.

Real names are included for all solo artists and, where applicable, dates of death and age of the artist at the time. "See..." links are included for soloists who also had album chart entries in other acts.

The best known line-up is listed for every group that had a Top 10 album, with the vocalist/leader mentioned first and the others following in alphabetical order. In cases where later replacements had similar success both people are named and, where applicable, the dates of death are also shown for every group/duo member listed.

Certified Awards are given by the BPI to mark unit sales to retailers. The certified awards were introduced in April 1973, based on revenue received by manufacturers. In January 1978 the qualification rules were changed and the system based on unit sales to the trade was adopted.

Silver symbol	●	=	60,000 units
Gold symbol	●	=	100,000 units
Platinum symbol	⊛	=	300,000 units

Y–Z

KEY TO ARTIST ENTRIES

Artist/Group Name — Artist/Group Biography — Silver-selling — Gold-selling — Platinum-selling — US No.1 — Peak Position — Weeks at No.1 — Weeks on Chart

Asterisks (*) indicate group members with hits in their own right that are listed elsewhere in this book

TOM JONES

UK, male vocalist (Thomas Woodward). Perennially popular Welsh vocalist, who has a 43-year span of UK hit albums, was the No.1 UK solo singer of the 1960s on both sides of the Atlantic. The unmistakable Vegas veteran received the Outstanding Contribution award at the 2003 BRITs

Artist's Total Weeks On Chart: 530

Date	Album	Peak	Wks at No.1	Wks on Chart
5 Jun 65	**ALONG CAME JONES** *Decca LK 6693*	11		5
8 Oct 66	**FROM THE HEART** *Decca LK 4814*	23		8
8 Apr 67	**GREEN GREEN GRASS OF HOME** *Decca SKL 4855*	3		49
24 Jun 67	**LIVE AT THE TALK OF THE TOWN** *Decca SKL 4874*	6		90
30 Dec 67	**13 SMASH HITS** *Decca SKL 4909*	5		49
27 Jul 68	**DELILAH** *Decca SKL 4946*	1	2	29
21 Dec 68	**HELP YOURSELF** *Decca SKL 4982*	4		9
28 Jun 69	**THIS IS TOM JONES** *Decca SKL 5007*	2		20
15 Nov 69	**TOM JONES LIVE IN LAS VEGAS** *Decca SKL 5032*	2		45
25 Apr 70	**TOM** *Decca SKL 5045*	4		18
14 Nov 70	**I WHO HAVE NOTHING** *Decca SKL 5072*	10		10
29 May 71	**SHE'S A LADY** *Decca SKL 5089*	9		7
27 Nov 71	**LIVE AT CAESAR'S PALACE** *Decca D 1/11/2*	27		5
24 Jun 72	**CLOSE UP** *Decca SKL 5132*	17		4
23 Jun 73	**THE BODY AND SOUL OF TOM JONES** *Decca SKL 5162*	31		1
5 Jan 74	**GREATEST HITS** *Decca SKL 5176*	15		13
22 Mar 75	**20 GREATEST HITS** *Decca TJD 1/11/2* ●	1	4	21
7 Oct 78	**I'M COMING HOME** *Lotus WH 5001* ●	12		9
16 May 87	**THE GREATEST HITS** *Telstar STAR 2296*	16		12
13 May 89	**AT THIS MOMENT** *Jive TOMTV 1*	34		3
8 Jul 89	**AFTER DARK** *Stylus SMR 978*	46		4
6 Apr 91	**CARRYING A TORCH** *Dover ADD 20*	44		4
27 Jun 92	**THE COMPLETE TOM JONES** *The Hit Label 8442862* ●	8		6
26 Nov 94	**THE LEAD AND HOW TO SWING IT** *ZTT 6544924982*	55		1
14 Nov 98	**THE ULTIMATE HITS COLLECTION** *Polygram TV 8449012*	26		6
9 Oct 99	**RELOAD** *Gut GUTCD 009* ⊛ **x4**	1	3	65
16 Nov 02	**MR JONES** *V2 VVR 1021072*	36		2
1 Mar 03	**GREATEST HITS** *Universal TV 8828632* ⊛	2		16
9 Oct 04	**TOM JONES AND JOOLS HOLLAND** *Radar RADAR004CD* & JOOLS HOLLAND ●	5		13
29 Nov 08	**24 HOURS** *S-Curve 2649852*	32		6+

Date of entry into chart

Artist collaboration or where artist's name has changed

Album Title — Label and Catalogue Number

Cross (+) indicates album is still on chart in last week of 2008

Y & T
US, male vocal/instrumental group — Weeks on Chart: 15

Date	Title	Label / Notes	Peak	Wks at No.1	Wks on Chart
11 Sep 82	BLACK TIGER	A&M AMLH 64910	53		8
10 Sep 83	MEAN STREAK	A&M AMLX 64960	35		4
18 Aug 84	IN ROCK WE TRUST	A&M AMLX 65007	33		3

YANNI
Greece, male keyboard player (Yanni Chryssolmalis) — Weeks on Chart: 2

Date	Title	Label / Notes	Peak	Wks at No.1	Wks on Chart
4 Apr 98	TRIBUTE	Virgin CDVUS 135	40		2

YARDBIRDS
UK, male vocal/instrumental group — Weeks on Chart: 8

Date	Title	Label / Notes	Peak	Wks at No.1	Wks on Chart
23 Jul 66	YARDBIRDS	Columbia SX 6063	20		8

TONY YAYO
US, male rapper (Marvin Bernard). See G-Unit — Weeks on Chart: 2

Date	Title	Label / Notes	Peak	Wks at No.1	Wks on Chart
17 Sep 05	THOUGHTS OF A PREDICATE FELON	Interscope 9882806	41		2

YAZOO
UK, female/male vocal/instrumental duo – Alison Moyet* & Vince Clarke — Weeks on Chart: 32

Date	Title	Label / Notes	Peak	Wks at No.1	Wks on Chart
4 Sep 82	UPSTAIRS AT ERIC'S	Mute STUMM 7 ⊛	2		63
16 Jul 83	YOU AND ME BOTH	Mute STUMM 12 ●	1	2	20
18 Sep 99	ONLY YAZOO – THE BEST OF YAZOO	Mute CDMUTEL 6	22		3
26 Nov 88	WANTED/WANTED – THE REMIXES	Big Life YAZZLP 1 YAZZ ⊛x2	3		32

YEAH YEAH YEAHS
US, male/female vocal/instrumental trio – Karen O (Karen Orzolek), Brian Chase & Nick Zinner — Weeks on Chart: 13

Date	Title	Label / Notes	Peak	Wks at No.1	Wks on Chart
10 May 03	FEVER TO TELL	Dress Up 0760612 ○	13		6
8 Apr 06	SHOW YOUR BONES	Fiction 9877235	7		7

TRISHA YEARWOOD
US, female vocalist — Weeks on Chart: 2

Date	Title	Label / Notes	Peak	Wks at No.1	Wks on Chart
25 Jul 98	WHERE YOUR ROAD LEADS	MCA Nashville UMD 80513	36		2

YELLO
Switzerland, male vocal/instrumental duo — Weeks on Chart: 15

Date	Title	Label / Notes	Peak	Wks at No.1	Wks on Chart
21 May 83	YOU GOTTA SAY YES TO ANOTHER EXCESS	Stiff SEEZ 48	65		2
6 Apr 85	STELLA	Elektra EKT 1	92		1
4 Jul 87	ONE SECOND	Mercury MERH 100	48		3
10 Dec 88	FLAG	Mercury 8367781 ○	56		7
29 Jun 91	BABY	Mercury 8487911	37		2

YELLOWCARD
US, male vocal/instrumental group — Weeks on Chart: 1

Date	Title	Label / Notes	Peak	Wks at No.1	Wks on Chart
4 Feb 06	LIGHTS AND SOUNDS	Capitol 3541442	59		1

BRYN YEMM
UK, male vocalist — Weeks on Chart: 14

Date	Title	Label / Notes	Peak	Wks at No.1	Wks on Chart
9 Jun 84	HOW DO I LOVE THEE	Lifestyle LEG 17	57		2
7 Jul 84	HOW GREAT THOU ART	Lifestyle LEG 15	67		8
22 Dec 84	THE BRYN YEMM CHRISTMAS COLLECTION	Bay 104	95		2
26 Oct 85	MY TRIBUTE – BRYN YEMM INSPIRATIONAL ALBUM	Word WSTR 9665 & THE GWENT CHORALE	85		2

YES
UK, male vocal/instrumental group – Jon Anderson*; members also included Peter Banks, Bill Bruford*, Geoff Downes, Trevor Horn, Steve Howe*, Tony Kaye, Patrick Moraz*, Chris Squire*, Rick Wakeman* & Alan White — Weeks on Chart: 226

Date	Title	Label / Notes	Peak	Wks at No.1	Wks on Chart
1 Aug 70	TIME AND A WORD	Atlantic 2400 006	45		3
27 Feb 71	THE YES ALBUM	Atlantic 2400 101	4		34
4 Dec 71	FRAGILE	Atlantic 2409 019 ⊛	7		17
23 Sep 72	CLOSE TO THE EDGE	Atlantic K 50012 ⊛	4		13
26 May 73	YESSONGS	Atlantic K 60045	7		13
22 Dec 73	TALES FROM TOPOGRAPHIC OCEANS	Atlantic K 80001 ●	1	2	15
21 Dec 74	RELAYER	Atlantic K 50096	4		11
29 Mar 75	YESTERDAYS	Atlantic K 50048	27		7
30 Jul 77	GOING FOR THE ONE	Atlantic K 50379 ●	1	2	28
7 Oct 78	TORMATO	Atlantic K 50518 ●	8		11
30 Aug 80	DRAMA	Atlantic K 50736 ○	2		8
10 Jan 81	YESSHOWS	Atlantic K 60142 ○	22		9
26 Nov 83	90125	Atco 790125 ●	16		28
29 Mar 86	9012 LIVE: THE SOLOS	Atco 790 4741	44		3
10 Oct 87	BIG GENERATOR	Atco WEX 70	17		5
11 May 91	UNION	Arista 211558	7		6
2 Apr 94	TALK	London 8284892	20		4
9 Nov 96	KEYS TO ASCENSION	Essential EDFCD 417	48		1
15 Nov 97	KEYS TO ASCENSION 2	Essential EDFCD 457	62		1
2 Oct 99	THE LADDER	Eagle EAGCD 088	36		1
22 Sep 01	MAGNIFICATION	Eagle EAGCD 189	71		1
9 Aug 03	THE ULTIMATE YES – 35TH ANNIVERSARY	WSM 8122737022 ○	10		7

DWIGHT YOAKAM
US, male vocalist/guitarist — Weeks on Chart: 4

Date	Title	Label / Notes	Peak	Wks at No.1	Wks on Chart
9 May 87	HILLBILLY DELUXE	Reprise WX 106	51		3
13 Aug 88	BUENAS NOCHES FROM A LONELY ROOM	Reprise WX 193	87		1

THOM YORKE
UK, male vocalist/guitarist. See Radiohead — Weeks on Chart: 9

Date	Title	Label / Notes	Peak	Wks at No.1	Wks on Chart
22 Jul 06	THE ERASER	XL XLCD200	3		9

YOU ME AT SIX
UK, male vocal/instrumental group — Weeks on Chart: 1

Date	Title	Label / Notes	Peak	Wks at No.1	Wks on Chart
18 Oct 08	TAKE OFF YOUR COLOURS	Slam Dunk SLAMD005	25		1

FARON YOUNG
US, male vocalist, d. 10 Dec 1996 (age 64) — Weeks on Chart: 5

Date	Title	Label / Notes	Peak	Wks at No.1	Wks on Chart
28 Oct 72	IT'S FOUR IN THE MORNING	Mercury 6338 095	27		5

NEIL YOUNG
Canada, male vocalist/guitarist. See Crosby, Stills, Nash & Young — Weeks on Chart: 283

Date	Title	Label / Notes	Peak	Wks at No.1	Wks on Chart
31 Oct 70	AFTER THE GOLDRUSH	Reprise RSLP 6383 ⊛x2	7		68
4 Mar 72	HARVEST	Reprise K 54005 ⊛x2 ★	1	1	35
27 Oct 73	TIME FADES AWAY	Warner Brothers K 54010	20		2
10 Aug 74	ON THE BEACH	Reprise K 54014 ○	42		2
5 Jul 75	TONIGHT'S THE NIGHT	Reprise K 54040	48		1
27 Dec 75	ZUMA	Reprise K 54057 & CRAZY HORSE ○	44		2
9 Oct 76	LONG MAY YOU RUN	Reprise K 54081 STILLS-YOUNG BAND	12		5
9 Jul 77	AMERICAN STARS 'N' BARS	Reprise K 54088 ○	17		8
17 Dec 77	DECADE	Reprise K 64037 ○	46		5
28 Oct 78	COMES A TIME	Reprise K 54099 ●	42		3
14 Jul 79	RUST NEVER SLEEPS	Reprise K 54105 & CRAZY HORSE ○	13		13
1 Dec 79	LIVE RUST	Reprise K 64041 & CRAZY HORSE ●	55		3
15 Nov 80	HAWKS AND DOVES	Reprise K 54109	34		3
14 Nov 81	RE-AC-TOR	Reprise K 54116 & CRAZY HORSE	69		3
5 Feb 83	TRANS	Geffen GEF 25019	29		5
3 Sep 83	EVERYBODY'S ROCKIN'	Geffen GEF 25590 & THE SHOCKING PINKS	50		3
14 Sep 85	OLD WAYS	Geffen GEF 26377	39		3
2 Aug 86	LANDING ON WATER	Geffen 9241091	52		2
4 Jul 87	LIFE	Geffen WX 109 & CRAZY HORSE	71		1
30 Apr 88	THIS NOTE'S FOR YOU	WEA WX 168 & THE BLUE NOTES	56		3
21 Oct 89	FREEDOM	Reprise WX 257	17		5
22 Sep 90	RAGGED GLORY	Reprise WX 374 & CRAZY HORSE ○	15		5
2 Nov 91	WELD	Reprise 7599266711 & CRAZY HORSE ○	20		3
14 Nov 92	HARVEST MOON	Reprise 9362450572 ●	9		18
23 Jan 93	LUCKY THIRTEEN	Geffen GED 24452	69		1
26 Jun 93	UNPLUGGED	Reprise 9362453102 ●	4		13
27 Aug 94	SLEEPS WITH ANGELS	Reprise 9362457492 & CRAZY HORSE ●	2		7
8 Jul 95	MIRROR BALL	Reprise 9362459342 ○	4		9
6 Jul 96	BROKEN ARROW	Reprise 9362462912 & CRAZY HORSE	17		5
28 Jun 97	YEAR OF THE HORSE	Reprise 9362466522 & CRAZY HORSE	36		2
6 May 00	SILVER AND GOLD	Reprise 9362473052	10		4
20 Apr 02	ARE YOU PASSIONATE	Reprise 9362481112	24		3
27 Jul 02	DECADE	Reprise 7599272332 ●	15		13
26 Jul 03	ON THE BEACH	Reprise 9362484972	42		1
30 Aug 03	GREENDALE	Reprise 9362485432 & CRAZY HORSE	24		3
27 Nov 04	GREATEST HITS	Reprise 9362489352 ●	45		8
8 Oct 05	PRAIRIE WIND	Reprise 9362495932 ○	22		4
27 May 06	LIVING WITH WAR	Reprise 9362443352	14		4
31 Mar 07	LIVE AT MASSEY HALL 1971	Reprise 9362433282	30		1
3 Nov 07	CHROME DREAMS II	Reprise 9362499062	14		3
20 Dec 08	SUGAR MOUNTAIN – LIVE AT CANTERBURY HOUSE 1968	Reprise 9362498398	72		1

Thom Yorke

WHEN Thom Yorke was just eight years old, he told his teacher that he was going to be a rock star. Predictably she laughed her head off and said, 'Of course you are, dear.' Apparently he was furious but, having had a moment of epiphany listening to Queen's Brian May, he wasn't to be dissuaded. From that age, he was absolutely certain of what he wanted to do with his life.

Now, looking back, the forty-year-old Thom Yorke is one of the world's least likely rock stars – as the lead singer of Radiohead, he is the frontman in a band that repeatedly defy convention and are only predictable in the scale of each new commercial success. In fact, of all the great rock stars of the last thirty years, there are few who seem to have enjoyed it less and lived to tell the tale than Thom Yorke, whose strangely compelling yet unusual features and mercurial thoughts make him one of rock music's most enigmatic personalities.

'Creep' became a huge hit in Israel before crossing over to become a kind of anti-star anthem in America

Part of his initial motivation seems to have been due to the classic frustration of wanting the world to pay him some respect. Born in Northamptonshire on 7 October 1968, he was a victim of bullying from an early age. A paralysed eye meant he had numerous operations before he was eight years old and at school he was nicknamed 'salamander' for the way his eye seemed to droop, but he learned to relish the unwanted attention. He dressed differently to everybody else and acted differently, flaunting his creativity and his own sense of restless dissatisfaction with the world.

When he was sixteen he formed a band with schoolmates Colin Greenwood and Ed O'Brien. When they were joined by older pupil Phil Selway and Colin's younger brother Jonny they became On A Friday. They would constantly record demo tapes but rarely played live because Thom was never certain they were any good. He even brought in a three-piece brass section to augment their sound.

But, when he was nineteen, Thom went to art college in Exeter and joined another band – Headless Chickens. Here he found a new freedom and gained confidence. They recorded a song, 'I Don't Want To Go To Woodstock', as part of a split-EP for local label Hometown Atrocities. They played to large crowds. Already Thom had started writing songs like 'High And Dry' and, crucially, 'Creep', which soon became world-famous.

When he graduated from university, On A Friday were pretty much ready to go. They were signed by EMI within a matter of months and changed their name to Radiohead in the process. Initially they struggled: their debut album *Pablo Honey* was a real effort to record and didn't live up to their promise. Their one undeniably arresting song, 'Creep', flopped on its initial release in the UK and the press spurned them because they were on a major label. It seemed as if their time in the spotlight would be over before it had started.

But then 'Creep' became a huge hit in Israel before crossing over to become a kind of anti-star anthem in America. It changed everything. They'd planned to go back into the studio straight away after *Pablo Honey* to record a follow-up but instead they toured 'Creep' for two years, and the hit song became a poisoned chalice. It nearly broke them. The recording of their second album *The Bends* saw Thom become massively frustrated with Radiohead – he thought they'd blown it. But instead *The Bends* re-invented them as one of

Biggest-Selling Album			Highest	
Artist	Album	Week	Position	Approx Sales
THOM YORKE	OK COMPUTER	28/6/97	1	1,400,000

Britain's most creative, interesting bands. With their next album, *OK Computer*, they had an audience eager to see what they'd do next. They didn't disappoint. *OK Computer* was hailed as the best album of the year and then, in many polls since, as the best album ever.

At that point, Thom was offered everything he'd ever wanted. He was offered the chance to become the new Bono, the biggest rock star in the world. He turned it down. He turned his back on rock 'n' roll and, with the next album, *Kid A*, insisted that Radiohead move away from the safety net of their familiar instruments. The next two years were to be even harder than what had come before but, with *Kid A* and *Amnesiac*, Radiohead did manage to win over their fanbase and establish themselves as the world's most innovative major rock band. *Kid A* went to Number 1 (likewise in America) and the live shows that followed proved that new songs like 'The National Anthem' were every bit as powerful as their predecessors.

Despite this, the struggle wasn't over. In 2003, Radiohead couldn't face another protracted recording session like the one they'd just had. They resolved to go to LA and bash out an album as quickly as possible. The result, *Hail To The Thief*, contained songs as good as anything they'd done before but lacked the essential feel of the previous albums. Thom felt they'd done things too quickly, and wished he could go back to complete it properly. Disillusioned, he went away and produced a solo album called *The Eraser*, full of songs he didn't think needed a band at all.

He wasn't sure he could see what the point of Radiohead was anymore, and felt that, overall, it restricted them creatively. In the meantime, he'd become much more involved with his charity work for Friends Of The Earth. The issue of climate change seemed vastly more important than writing more songs about his own emotional state. When he went back into the studio with Jonny, Ed, Colin and Phil, it was hard to see what they could produce that they hadn't done before. But, gradually, things came together and their next album, *In Rainbows*, was hailed as a magnificent fresh start (as well as innovative commercially, as it was initially released on the Internet for download at a price the listener wanted to pay). Thom had proved that it is possible to make music without compromising, but apparently only at a tremendous cost. Every time Radiohead go into the studio they seem to have to re-invent themselves or completely fall apart. It's a gruelling process that must make Thom wonder why, as a little boy, he was ever so keen to be a 'rock star'. But the results are undeniably worth it.

The issue of climate change seemed vastly more important than writing more songs about his own emotional state

Neil Young

NEIL Young remains one of rock's most enduring figures, who – alongside fellow Canadians Joni Mitchell and Leonard Cohen – helped define the folk and folk-rock movements of the mid- to late-1960s. A generation later his influence is felt across many genres, and the man once christened 'the godfather of Grunge' shows little sign of slowing down.

After his parents divorced, Young settled in Winnipeg with his mother, and started a string of high-school bands which culminated in The Squires, local hit makers with an early instrumental single ('The Sultan') in 1963. The Squires gigged around to no avail, failing to get a major record deal (although early encounters with Stephen Stills and Joni Mitchell lit a spark that was later to be re-ignited in California). After The Squires, Young joined up with The Mynah Birds, Rick James's outfit already signed to Motown and with a Canadian album under their belt. But Young's failure to progress with Motown drove him south and it was in Los Angeles in 1966 that he and Stills formed Buffalo Springfield, his first step on the road to international recognition.

His solo work moved into darker waters and more challenging musical forms

With guitarists Young, Stills and Ritchie Furay, Mynah Birds bassist Bruce Palmer and Dewey Martin on drums, their first album *Buffalo Springfield,* caused little excitement and did not trouble the UK charts. The single 'For What It's Worth' was a Top 10 hit in America however, and was quickly established as a 1960s classic anthem (although their UK profile was very modest). After two more albums, Stephen Stills had joined David Crosby (The Byrds) and Graham Nash (The Hollies) to form Crosby, Stills and Nash. Buffalo Springfield was in tatters. Young's maturing songwriting skills and delicate, vulnerable vocal style led naturally to a solo career, and in 1968 his self-titled first solo album was released by Reprise to mixed reviews. 1969's *Everybody Knows This Nowhere* teamed Young up with former Psyrcles Daniel Whitten, Ralph Molina and Billy Talbot, and the band Crazy Horse was born.

In 1970 Young toured with and formally joined Crosby, Stills and Nash. CSN&Y – supergroup *extraordinaire* – defined the Woodstock generation. Their album (*Déjà Vu*, a Top 5 hit) remains beloved of baby-boomers and advertising execs the world over, with the quartet working together (albeit on a pretty unstable basis) right up to the present.

After The Gold Rush (1970) was Young's third solo outing, and it also remains one of the era's most important releases. The album remains a document of early-1970s disenchantment rather than the last whiff of 1960s optimism it might have been. By the time the live album *4 Way Street* was released in 1971 (also a Number 5), CSN&Y were on a long-term hiatus. Young's next solo album, *Harvest*, and its single release 'Heart Of Gold', again justified his position in the vanguard of 1970s singer-songwriters. Alongside Carole King's *Tapestry* and Joni Mitchell's *Blue*, it is a peerless collection of tracks, augmented by the individual members of CS&N, Linda Ronstadt and James Taylor.

To an extent, *Harvest*'s success instinctively pushed Young away from the limelight. His solo work moved into darker waters and more challenging musical forms. 1973's fugitive live album *Time Fades Away* documented both the hard-drinking tour earlier that year and Young's response to the death of Danny Whitten. It also reflected Young's increasingly disintegrating

Biggest-Selling Album			Highest	
Artist	Album	Week	Position	Approx Sales
NEIL YOUNG	HARVEST	4/3/72	1	900,000

marriage. *Time Fades Away* remains unreleased on CD, the only exception to the rest of Young's other official releases, and is considered by many die-hard fans as *the* lost classic album. Recorded after the 1973 tour, but withheld until 1975, *Tonight's The Night* was a further bleak response to Whitten's death and that of roadie Bruce Berry, both victims to heroin. The failure of his record company to release the album on schedule (it was seen as a commercially inappropriate follow-up to *Harvest)* meant that Young's equally bleak collection *On The Beach (*1974) was the next release. For many years this album was withheld from a CD release too, and it holds a dear place in the hearts of many long-term fans. Young was in a dark place.

Throughout the rest of the 1970s and the 1980s, Young's stock remained high and his output variable. He was often experimental, frequently challenging the expectations of the *Harvest* generation. The Stills-Young band – and their 1976 album *Long May You Run* – was a short-lived collaboration and tour that kept Neil in working contact with his former bandmate. Remarried, and with two sons suffering from cerebral palsy, he co-founded a school for children suffering from the condition, organising all-star concerts that both funded the school's foundation and have helped maintain it ever since. 1983's *Trans* reflected, in its distorted, unintelligible vocals, the communication problems that cerebral-palsy sufferers have to deal with.

Appearances with CS&N at Live Aid and elsewhere re-ignited old flames, and new studio albums from the band appeared in 1988 and 1999. While a new generation of rockers picked up on the guitar-drive of his new songs, 'Rockin' In The Free World' caught the mood as the 1980s came to a close, proving that more than twenty years after the demise of Buffalo Springfield, Neil Young still had something to say. 1989's *The Bridge* tribute album – the first of several in Young's honour – testified to the fact that, while he may be ageing, there was still plenty enough of the angry or the wistful in the middle-aged Canadian to appeal to a new audience. In the early 1990s, grunge took him to its heart – indeed Kurt Cobain's own note of suicide included a nod to

With two sons suffering from cerebral palsy, he co-founded a school for children suffering from the condition

Neil's song, 'Hey, Hey, My, My (Into The Black)' with its reference to burning out rather than fading away. 1992's *Harvest Moon* squared the circle for the old guard too, a beautifully romantic and gentle nod back to 1973.

Neither burning out nor fading away, while CSN&Y shack up occasionally and take their still-faultless harmonies out on the road, Young's legacy is far from complete. While he still rages against the machine politically, he can also still cut a neat swathe through many contemporary songwriters and performers less than a half his age. There's not much sign of compromise in Neil Young, and history will reflect that to his eternal credit. Gifted with a talent that he could have sat back on complacently, he has always looked for the new. A child of the 1960s, a chronicler of the 1970s, an 1980s innovator and a 1990s legend, Young's real legacy will be the veracity of his material, the sense of genuine care and commitment throughout a lifetime of writing and performing. A sports journalist's son, he has written with the wary eye of a reporter always half-turned to some other horizon. And he has one of the most beautiful voices on record.

PAUL YOUNG

UK, male vocalist. See Q-Tips

Date	Title	Peak Position	Weeks at No.1	Weeks on Chart (232)
30 Jul 83	**NO PARLEZ** *CBS 25521* ⊛x3	1	5	119
6 Apr 85	**THE SECRET OF ASSOCIATION** *CBS 26234* ⊛x2	1	1	49
1 Nov 86	**BETWEEN TWO FIRES** *CBS 4501501* ⊛	4		17
16 Jun 90	**OTHER VOICES** *CBS 4669171* ●	4		11
14 Sep 91	**FROM TIME TO TIME – THE SINGLES COLLECTION** *Columbia 4688251* ⊛x3	1	1	27
23 Oct 93	**THE CROSSING** *Columbia 4739282*	27		2
26 Nov 94	**REFLECTIONS** *Vision VISCD 1*	64		2
31 May 97	**PAUL YOUNG** *East West 0630186192*	39		2
21 Jun 03	**THE ESSENTIAL** *Sony Music 5122992*	27		3

WILL YOUNG

UK, male vocalist

Date	Title	Peak Position	Weeks at No.1	Weeks on Chart (123)
19 Oct 02	**FROM NOW ON** *S 74321969592* ⊛x2	1	2	25
13 Dec 03	**FRIDAY'S CHILD** *S 82876557462* ⊛x4	1	2	46
3 Dec 05	**KEEP ON** *Sony BMG 82876749552* ⊛x3	2		39
11 Oct 08	**LET IT GO** *19/RCA 88697344442* ●	2		13+

YOUNG BUCK

US, male rapper (David Brown). See G-Unit

Date	Title	Peak Position	Weeks at No.1	Weeks on Chart (3)
4 Sep 04	**STRAIGHT OUTTA CASHVILLE** *Interscope 9863495*	22		3

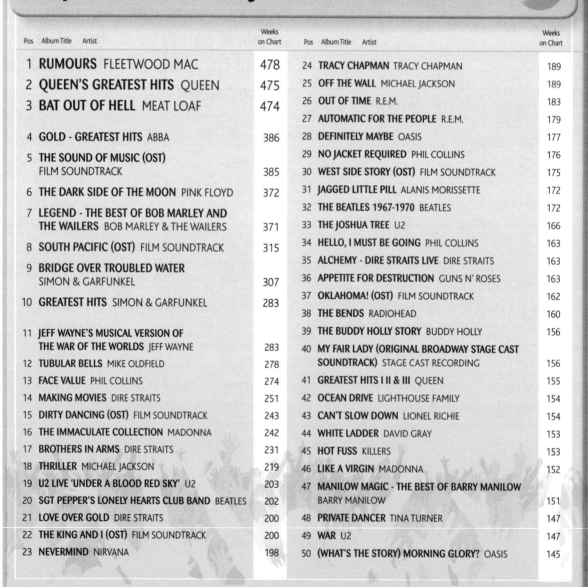

Top 50 Albums by Weeks on Chart

Pos	Album Title	Artist	Weeks on Chart
1	**RUMOURS**	FLEETWOOD MAC	478
2	**QUEEN'S GREATEST HITS**	QUEEN	475
3	**BAT OUT OF HELL**	MEAT LOAF	474
4	**GOLD - GREATEST HITS**	ABBA	386
5	**THE SOUND OF MUSIC (OST)**	FILM SOUNDTRACK	385
6	**THE DARK SIDE OF THE MOON**	PINK FLOYD	372
7	**LEGEND - THE BEST OF BOB MARLEY AND THE WAILERS**	BOB MARLEY & THE WAILERS	371
8	**SOUTH PACIFIC (OST)**	FILM SOUNDTRACK	315
9	**BRIDGE OVER TROUBLED WATER**	SIMON & GARFUNKEL	307
10	**GREATEST HITS**	SIMON & GARFUNKEL	283
11	**JEFF WAYNE'S MUSICAL VERSION OF THE WAR OF THE WORLDS**	JEFF WAYNE	283
12	**TUBULAR BELLS**	MIKE OLDFIELD	278
13	**FACE VALUE**	PHIL COLLINS	274
14	**MAKING MOVIES**	DIRE STRAITS	251
15	**DIRTY DANCING (OST)**	FILM SOUNDTRACK	243
16	**THE IMMACULATE COLLECTION**	MADONNA	242
17	**BROTHERS IN ARMS**	DIRE STRAITS	231
18	**THRILLER**	MICHAEL JACKSON	219
19	**U2 LIVE 'UNDER A BLOOD RED SKY'**	U2	203
20	**SGT PEPPER'S LONELY HEARTS CLUB BAND**	BEATLES	202
21	**LOVE OVER GOLD**	DIRE STRAITS	200
22	**THE KING AND I (OST)**	FILM SOUNDTRACK	200
23	**NEVERMIND**	NIRVANA	198
24	**TRACY CHAPMAN**	TRACY CHAPMAN	189
25	**OFF THE WALL**	MICHAEL JACKSON	189
26	**OUT OF TIME**	R.E.M.	183
27	**AUTOMATIC FOR THE PEOPLE**	R.E.M.	179
28	**DEFINITELY MAYBE**	OASIS	177
29	**NO JACKET REQUIRED**	PHIL COLLINS	176
30	**WEST SIDE STORY (OST)**	FILM SOUNDTRACK	175
31	**JAGGED LITTLE PILL**	ALANIS MORISSETTE	172
32	**THE BEATLES 1967-1970**	BEATLES	172
33	**THE JOSHUA TREE**	U2	166
34	**HELLO, I MUST BE GOING**	PHIL COLLINS	163
35	**ALCHEMY - DIRE STRAITS LIVE**	DIRE STRAITS	163
36	**APPETITE FOR DESTRUCTION**	GUNS N' ROSES	163
37	**OKLAHOMA! (OST)**	FILM SOUNDTRACK	162
38	**THE BENDS**	RADIOHEAD	160
39	**THE BUDDY HOLLY STORY**	BUDDY HOLLY	156
40	**MY FAIR LADY (ORIGINAL BROADWAY STAGE CAST SOUNDTRACK)**	STAGE CAST RECORDING	156
41	**GREATEST HITS I II & III**	QUEEN	155
42	**OCEAN DRIVE**	LIGHTHOUSE FAMILY	154
43	**CAN'T SLOW DOWN**	LIONEL RICHIE	154
44	**WHITE LADDER**	DAVID GRAY	153
45	**HOT FUSS**	KILLERS	153
46	**LIKE A VIRGIN**	MADONNA	152
47	**MANILOW MAGIC - THE BEST OF BARRY MANILOW**	BARRY MANILOW	151
48	**PRIVATE DANCER**	TINA TURNER	147
49	**WAR**	U2	147
50	**(WHAT'S THE STORY) MORNING GLORY?**	OASIS	145

YOUNG DISCIPLES
UK/US, male/female vocal/instrumental group — Weeks on chart: 5

Date	Title	Peak Position	Weeks at No.1	Weeks on Chart
31 Aug 91	**ROAD TO FREEDOM** *Talkin Loud 5100971* ○	21		5

YOUNG GODS
Switzerland, male vocal/instrumental group — Weeks on chart: 1

Date	Title	Peak Position	Weeks at No.1	Weeks on Chart
15 Feb 92	**T.V. SKY** *Play It Again Sam PIAS 201CD*	54		1

YOUNG HEART ATTACK
US, male/female vocal/instrumental group — Weeks on chart: 1

Date	Title	Peak Position	Weeks at No.1	Weeks on Chart
24 Apr 04	**MOUTHFUL OF LOVE** *XL Recordings XLCD173*	71		1

YOUNG KNIVES
UK, male vocal/instrumental trio — Weeks on chart: 5

Date	Title	Peak Position	Weeks at No.1	Weeks on Chart
2 Sep 06	**VOICES OF ANIMALS & MEN** *Transgressive 2564638482*	21		3
22 Mar 08	**SUPERABUNDANCE** *Transgressive TRANS070CD*	28		2

SYDNEY YOUNGBLOOD
UK, male vocalist (Sydney Ford) — Weeks on chart: 17

Date	Title	Peak Position	Weeks at No.1	Weeks on Chart
28 Oct 89	**FEELING FREE** *Circa 9* ●	23		17

Z

GHEORGHE ZAMFIR
Romania, male panpipes player — Weeks on chart: 1

Date	Title	Peak Position	Weeks at No.1	Weeks on Chart
20 Sep 08	**SPIRIT OF THE ANDES** *UCJ 5311851*	31		1

FRANK ZAPPA
US, male vocalist/multi-instrumentalist, d. 4 Dec 1993 (age 52). See Mothers Of Invention — Weeks on chart: 57

Date	Title	Peak Position	Weeks at No.1	Weeks on Chart
28 Feb 70	**HOT RATS** *Reprise RSLP 6356*	9		27
19 Dec 70	**CHUNGA'S REVENGE** *Reprise RSLP 2030*	43		1
6 May 78	**ZAPPA IN NEW YORK** *Discreet K 69204*	55		1
10 Mar 79	**SHEIK YERBOUTI** *CBS 88339*	32		7
13 Oct 79	**JOE'S GARAGE ACT I** *CBS 86101*	62		3
19 Jan 80	**JOE'S GARAGE ACTS II & III** *CBS 88475*	75		1
16 May 81	**TINSEL TOWN REBELLION** *CBS 88516*	55		4
24 Oct 81	**YOU ARE WHAT YOU IS** *CBS 88560*	51		2
19 Jun 82	**SHIP ARRIVING TOO LATE TO SAVE A DROWNING WITCH** *CBS 85804*	61		4
18 Jun 83	**THE MAN FROM UTOPIA** *CBS 25251*	87		1
27 Oct 84	**THEM OR US** *EMI FZD 1*	53		2
30 Apr 88	**GUITAR** *Zappa ZAPPA 6*	82		2
2 Sep 95	**STRICTLY COMMERCIAL – THE BEST OF FRANK ZAPPA** *Rykodisc RCD 40600*	45		2

LENA ZAVARONI
UK, female vocalist, d. 1 Oct 1999 (age 35) — Weeks on chart: 5

Date	Title	Peak Position	Weeks at No.1	Weeks on Chart
23 Mar 74	**MA** *Philips 6308 201*	8		5

ZERO 7
UK, male production duo – Henry Binns & Sam Hardaker — Weeks on chart: 67

Date	Title	Peak Position	Weeks at No.1	Weeks on Chart
5 May 01	**SIMPLE THINGS** *Ultimate Dilemma UDRCD 016* ●	28		43
13 Mar 04	**WHEN IT FALLS** *Ultimate Dilemma 5046709875* ●	3		18
3 Jun 06	**THE GARDEN** *Atlantic 5101128575* ●	4		6

WARREN ZEVON
US, male vocalist/keyboard player, d. 7 Sep 2003 (age 56) — Weeks on chart: 2

Date	Title	Peak Position	Weeks at No.1	Weeks on Chart
27 Sep 03	**THE WIND** *Rykodisc RCD 17001*	57		2

ZHANE
US, female vocal duo — Weeks on chart: 1

Date	Title	Peak Position	Weeks at No.1	Weeks on Chart
10 May 97	**SATURDAY NIGHT** *Motown 5307512*	52		1

HANS ZIMMER
Germany, male producer/keyboard player — Weeks on chart: 28

Date	Title	Peak Position	Weeks at No.1	Weeks on Chart
27 May 00	**GLADIATOR – OST** *Decca 46709422* HANS ZIMMER & LISA GERRARD	17		16
3 Mar 01	**HANNIBAL (OST)** *Decca 4676962*	74		2
16 Jun 01	**PEARL HARBOR (OST)** *Hollywood 9362481132* GREENAWAY/ZIMMER ○	50		2
17 Sep 05	**GLADIATOR – OST** *Decca 4765223* HANS ZIMMER & LISA GERRARD	44		2
27 May 06	**THE DA VINCI CODE (OST)** *Decca 9854041*	48		2
22 Jul 06	**PIRATES OF THE CARIBBEAN – DEAD MAN'S CHEST (OST)** *Walt Disney 3680162*	68		1
9 Jun 07	**PIRATES OF THE CARIBBEAN – AT WORLD'S END (OST)** *Walt Disney 3957032*	58		1
9 Aug 08	**THE DARK KNIGHT (OST)** *Warner Brothers 9362498600* HANS ZIMMER & NEWTON HOWARD	67		2

ZION TRAIN
UK, male/female vocal/instrumental group — Weeks on chart: 1

Date	Title	Peak Position	Weeks at No.1	Weeks on Chart
13 Jul 96	**GROW TOGETHER** *China WOLCD 1071*	56		1

ZOE
UK, female vocalist (Zoe Pollock) — Weeks on chart: 1

Date	Title	Peak Position	Weeks at No.1	Weeks on Chart
7 Dec 91	**SCARLET, RED AND BLUE** *M&G 5114431*	67		1

ROB ZOMBIE
US, male vocalist (Robert Cummings). See White Zombie — Weeks on chart: 2

Date	Title	Peak Position	Weeks at No.1	Weeks on Chart
5 Sep 98	**HELLBILLY DELUXE** *Geffen GED 25212*	37		2

ZOMBIES
UK, male vocal/instrumental group — Weeks on chart: 1

Date	Title	Peak Position	Weeks at No.1	Weeks on Chart
7 Jun 08	**THE ZOMBIES AND BEYOND** *UMTV 1773931*	43		1

ZUCCHERO
Italy, male vocalist/guitarist (Adelmo Fornaciari) — Weeks on chart: 4

Date	Title	Peak Position	Weeks at No.1	Weeks on Chart
18 May 91	**ZUCCHERO** *London EVERY 1*	29		4

ZUTONS
UK, male/female vocal/instrumental group – David McCabe, Boyan Chowdhury, Abi Harding, Paul Molloy, Sean Payne & Russell Pritchard — Weeks on chart: 71

Date	Title	Peak Position	Weeks at No.1	Weeks on Chart
1 May 04	**WHO KILLED THE ZUTONS?** *Deltasonic DLTCD019* ⊛	6		36
29 Apr 06	**TIRED OF HANGING AROUND** *Deltasonic DLTCD040* ⊛	2		30
14 Jun 08	**YOU CAN DO ANYTHING** *Deltasonic DLTCD078*	6		5

ZWAN
US, male vocal/instrumental group — Weeks on chart: 2

Date	Title	Peak Position	Weeks at No.1	Weeks on Chart
22 Feb 03	**MARY STAR OF THE SEA** *Reprise WB 484252*	33		2

ZZ TOP
US, male vocal/instrumental group – Billy Gibbons, Frank Beard & Dusty Hill — Weeks on chart: 211

Date	Title	Peak Position	Weeks at No.1	Weeks on Chart
12 Jul 75	**FANDANGO!** *London SHU 8482*	60		1
8 Aug 81	**EL LOCO** *Warner Brothers K 56929*	88		2
30 Apr 83	**ELIMINATOR** *Warner Brothers W 3774* ⊛x4	3		137
9 Nov 85	**AFTERBURNER** *Warner Brothers WX 27* ⊛	2		40
27 Oct 90	**RECYCLER** *Warner Brothers WX 390* ○	8		7
25 Apr 92	**GREATEST HITS** *Warner Brothers 7599268462* ●	5		17
5 Feb 94	**ANTENNA** *RCA 74321152602*	3		5
21 Sep 96	**RHYTHMEEN** *RCA 74321394662*	32		2

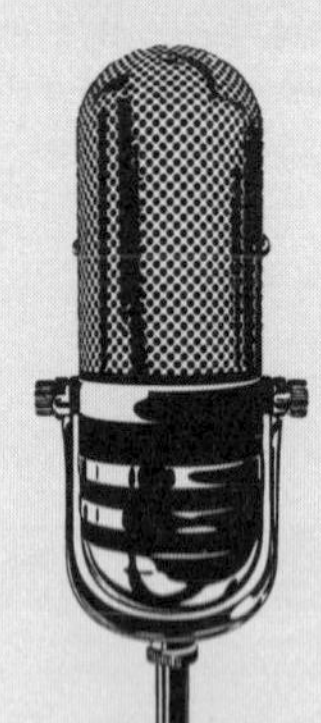

The Streets

A Grand Don't Come For Free

AFTER crawling out of the nascent UK garage scene, Mike Skinner, aka The Streets, had released one of the new millennium's finest debut albums, *Original Pirate Material*, in 2002. A critics' favourite and a strong seller, some observers expressed genuine doubt that the street-savvy Skinner would have the artistic range to top what was a mightily impressive debut.

How wrong could they have been?

His follow-up album, *A Grand Don't Come For Free*, totally overshadowed its predecessor. Two years in the making, Skinner put the finishing touches to the album in March 2004. The record's coherent whole belied a more mundane genesis – most of the album was recorded in his new house, a converted south London pub (unlike the debut, which he'd recorded at his mother's). He'd 'upgraded' from his bedroom-recording approach, however, instead using the spare bedroom for this second album.

Mike Skinner, child of garage, urbane mastermind

Three weeks before the album's release, Skinner unleashed his opening volley, the first single, 'Fit But You Know It'. Barely a sniff of garage in sight. This was The Sex Pistols doing garage. The fast-food scenario, the spoken-word ultra-high in the mix, the soulful chorus, the devastating eye for detail and the numerous characters pitching into the scene were classic Skinner. Yet somehow it felt like a progression – more sophisticated. Of course, it helped the forthcoming album's campaign no end that the song was perfect for radio, that the summer was coming and the foreign holiday that Skinner was talking about was already being booked by millions in sweaty anticipation. 'Fit But You Know It' perfectly primed the UK for his album.

Mike Skinner, child of garage, urbane mastermind. The new record? A concept album – what a phrase. Long hair. Gatefold sleeves, loon pants, sequined blusher, 128-track mixing desks, album budgets that read like phone numbers, prog rock, the mighty Rick Wakeman, Yes, Pink Floyd, etc. Yet, despite the fears, *A Grand Don't Come For Free* is one of the defining moments in British music history.

From the very first line it worked. Trumpeting fanfares and Mike's doleful voice pile into a word-heavy lyric within seconds of 'It Was Supposed To Be So Easy'. The central story/concept is simple: Skinner is taking a DVD back, getting some cash and sorting out his savings, before having tea with his mum. Simple stuff. Only then he discovers that the thousand pounds he left on his telly has vanished ...

The story – a genuine whodunnit – is told with all of Skinner's usual flair: his acute observations are still there: who hasn't sworn at their mobile phone in exactly the same way Mike does in this opening song? The soundtrack is overwhelmingly accomplished and achingly gritty, with a simple electronic drumbeat, signature stabbing keyboard notes, snippets of garage or house songs – a true maelstrom; not surprisingly, the lyrics are pure genius, with a narrative that develops effortlessly as soon as Skinner's heroine/villainess Simone is introduced (as early as the second song). Despite being a concept piece, the album is peppered with individual classics such as 'Blinded By The Lights'

Chart History

Artist	Album Title	First Chart Week	Weeks on Chart	Highest Position
THE STREETS	A GRAND DON'T COME FOR FREE	22/5/04	42	1

or the brilliantly composed comic masterpiece 'Get Out Of My House'. The radio-friendly, heard-in-Burtons-and-Asda masterpiece and Number 1 single, 'Dry Your Eyes, Mate' has a crushing intimacy. This album highlight was actually the culmination of years of creative gestation, but now became the moment when Skinner's underground life evaporated for ever as the mainstream gatecrashed his party. On first hearing the plot twist of *A Grand Don't Come For Free*, you shiver. It is *that* good.

With the album's stunning musicality, acute literacy and cinematically incredible final scene, the record set a benchmark for all future records that fall under the 'concept' banner. The critics were frenzied in their appreciation of Skinner's lofty achievement: there were obvious comparisons with Ken Loach, Alan Bennett, Alan Parker, Sean O'Casey, Francis Bacon – it was even lauded as 'the Shakespeare for the text generation'. In the *Guardian*, a renowned University College London literature professor wrote 1,800 words dissecting Skinner's lyrics and showing their genealogy to past-life literary greats, the main thrust being that Mr Mike was the new Dostoevsky. He also mentioned Samuel Pepys.

Skinner's underground life evaporated for ever as the mainstream gatecrashed his party

It is a rare event when a follow-up to a critically lauded record so easily outperforms its vaunted predecessor. Yet it was deserved. This concept piece concerned with the urban decay festering around the life of one particular anti-hero and his mundane yet epic personal battles is an album like no other. Two further stunning (yet commercially relatively modest) albums have reinforced the notion that Skinner is a modern-day poet of sublime talent, but it might just be that *A Grand Don't Come For Free* will be his epitaph.

And where was his £1,000? You'll have to buy the album to find out...

Compilation Albums

KEY TO COMPILATION ALBUM ENTRIES

Album Name / Catalogue Number / Silver-selling / Gold-selling / Platinum-selling / US No.1 / Peak Position / Weeks at No.1 / Weeks on Chart

Date	Album Name / Catalogue Number	Peak Position	Weeks at No.1	Weeks on Chart
7 Sep 02	**CHILLED JAZZ** *Verve 0692092*	14		1
21 Dec 02	**THE JAZZ ALBUM 2003** *Verve 0680672*	13		2
26 Apr 03	**DIVAS OF JAZZ** *Verve 0394222*	12		3

Compilation Category / Record Label / Labels Total Weeks at No.1 / Labels Total Weeks On Chart

VARIOUS ARTISTS (VIRGIN) — 5 — 530

Date	Album Name / Catalogue Number	Peak Position	Weeks at No.1	Weeks on Chart
25 Jul 92	**THE GREATEST DANCE ALBUM IN THE WORLD!** *Virgin Television VTCD 13* (Gold)	2		12
31 Oct 92	**NEW ROMANTIC CLASSICS** *Virgin Television VTCD 15* (Silver)	7		5
17 Jul 93	**THE BEST DANCE ALBUM IN THE WORLD...EVER!** *Virgin Television VTDCD 17* (Platinum) x2	1	4	19
23 Oct 93	**THE SINGER AND THE SONG** *Virgin Television VTDCD 21* (Gold)	5		6
20 Nov 93	**THE BEST DANCE ALBUM IN THE WORLD...EVER! 2** *Virgin Television VTDCD 22* (Platinum)	3		12
4 Dec 93	**THE BEST CHRISTMAS ALBUM IN THE WORLD...EVER!** *Virgin Television VTDCD 23* (Platinum) x3	2		10
29 Jan 94	**SWEET SOUL HARMONIES** *Virgin Television VTCD 20* (Gold)	1	1	9
26 Feb 94	**DANCE TO THE MAX** *Virgin Television VTCD 24* (Gold)	2		10
12 Mar 94	**RAP TO THE MAX** *Virgin Television VTCD 25* (Silver)	10		4
30 Apr 94	**IN THE AIR TONIGHT** *Virgin Television VTDCD 26* (Silver)	8		10
7 May 94	**PURE MOODS** *Virgin Television VTCD 28* (Platinum) x2	1	2	31
28 May 94	**DANCE TO THE MAX 2** *Virgin Television VTCD 29* (Gold)	4		8
4 Jun 94	**THE BEST REGGAE ALBUM IN THE WORLD...EVER!** *Virgin Television VTCD 27* (Platinum)	4		10

Cross (+) indicates album is still on chart in last week of 2008

Certified Awards are given by the BPI to mark unit sales to retailers. The certified awards were introduced in April 1973, based on revenue received by manufacturers. In January 1978 the qualification rules were changed and the system based on unit sales to the trade was adopted.

Silver symbol = 60,000 units
Gold symbol = 100,000 units
Platinum symbol = 300,000 units

Compilation Albums

Now That's The Greatest Hot Hits And Top Of The Best Compilation Album In The Universe

'I banged on the jukebox, but it was useless, it had no good records on, not even something weak, like *The Best Punk Album In The World, Ever! Volume 1*...'

'What If Punk Never Happened?', The King Blues, 2008

TECHNOLOGY is a brutal emperor. Let's for a moment compare the jukebox with the MP3 player. The former was once a cultural magnet, no self-respecting 1950s diner or bar was without one, and they became a social hub, a meeting place for a gaggle of heady teenagers and twenty-somethings to crowd around, to listen, chat, flirt, and just hang out. Fast-forward half a century and you have an MP3 player the same size as the cigarette packets those quiffed and newly consumerist 1950s kids would carry. Inside this digital box of tricks, there might be 25,000 songs. And inside the menu of the MP3, there is a little bonus function that, for many, was certain to herald the end of the physical compilation album: playlists. But all is not what it would seem ...

The genesis of compilations can, one might argue, be traced back to some time before the end of the nineteenth century. In 1889, two inventors by the name of Louis Glass and William S. Arnold took a refurbished Edison cylinder phonograph, ripped much of the machinery out and bolted on a coin-slot mechanism. They successfully won a pitch in the Palais Royale Saloon in San Francisco and duly set up their machine, offering a handful of the phonograph recordings of the day (largely simple instrumental or spoken-word audio recordings). At that early stage, a customer could then put a single coin in the Nickel-in-a-Slot machine and listen through one of four tubes. This might sound peculiar, but in the first six months of service, this machine collected $1,000 in nickels. Within a decade, such coin-slot machines were highly popular, largely due to the increasing number of songs they could play, and did some very lucrative business.

While the coin-slot's parent machine, the phonograph, evolved throughout the twentieth century from a piece of primitive technology to an iconic and universal must-have item (via a number of format incarnations), the coin slot veered off towards a less glamorous future. Not known as a jukebox until the 1930s, the manufacturers preferred them to be called Automatic Coin-Operated Phonographs – even the great Farney Wurlitzer, whose surname christened the most famous brand of jukebox, viewed the term as 'degrading' (his company did not use the word jukebox until 1972, after

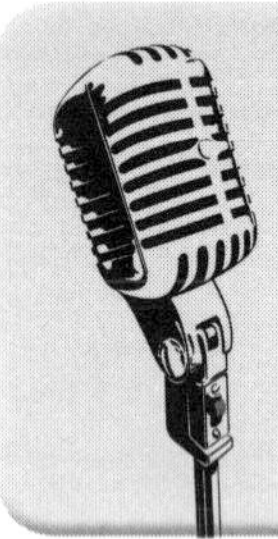

he had died). Historians argue over the origins of the slang name, suggesting it either comes from an African word 'joot', meaning 'to dance', or possibly 'jook', meaning 'disorderly and wicked'. Despite its latterday association with early rock 'n' roll – a medium rapidly adopted by white-youth culture, despite its deep origins in the blues and formative black music – the jukeboxes of the 1930s were actually one of the rare places for black recording artists to get exposure, given that radio and mainstream venues were largely for 'white' music. Regardless of the origins of its name, the jukebox was hugely popular, particularly in American culture, with over two million sold to date. Now, in the twenty-first century, the jukebox in a pub is largely decorative, often replaced by a quiz machine and a Performing Rights Society licence playing tunes through a house stereo. The digital jukebox can carry thousands of songs, but its role has been largely reduced to a time-piece, with its incumbent collectors and rare auctions.

The jukeboxes of the 1930s were actually one of the rare places for black recording artists to get exposure

However, what the jukebox and the MP3 player have in common is the ability to play *multiple records by multiple artists*. They allow music lovers to access a wider variety of music than was usual before their inception. Both appeal to the voracious appetite that many people have for more and more music. Okay, so one is the size of a small fridge and the other a cigarette packet, but the premiss remains: both offer *variety*.

Before the 1960s, the vast majority of records were by a single artist, with an occasional duet or collaboration, but essentially only one artist's name appeared on the sleeve. Music historians argue over the very first compilation album and there are certainly several that could vie for the title. Saying that, in at least one sense, the compilation album existed long before the renowned and more famous 1970s vinyl versions (such as *Nuggets* – more of which later); after the Second World War many artists enjoyed success selling collections of 78s and 45s, in essence their 'Greatest Hits'. They may not have been on the same piece of vinyl, but they were still compilations of songs, albeit spread across numerous records. Using a multi-loading record player, a fan could even stack several singles by the same artist and listen to their 'Greatest Hits' one after another, albeit manually. When the soundtrack of *South Pacific* was released on one disc in America, its hefty sales reflected the fact that the ability to hear all the music on one piece of vinyl was a seminal moment in the history of the LP.

Initially, back in the 1950s and 1960s, albums with more than one artist tended to be 'samplers' for a record label's roster. In the late 1960s, these qualified for one of the lower-priced charts that existed at the time and featured some fascinating compilations (as well as many MOR – Middle Of the Road – issues), although predominantly samplers, such as CBS's *Rock Machine I Love You*, Island's *Nice Enough To Eat* and *Trojan's Tighten Up Vol. 2*. There were also, of course, compilations in the form of 'Greatest Hits' or 'Best Of' records. However, in terms of 'compilations', these single-artist collections don't really interest and fascinate, and would perhaps be better termed as 'retrospectives'.

Like their modern-day counterparts, early compilation albums featured many tie-ins with popular TV shows, films and musicals of the day – *South Pacific* is the aforementioned obvious example – but over the years, movie soundtrack albums (from *Saturday Night Fever* to *Gangsta's Paradise* to *8 Mile* and on), TV tie-ins (take your pick, just look what *Soldier, Soldier* did for Robson & Jerome) and stage spin-offs (from West End shows and many others besides), have always sold very heavily.

One different compilation of note from this early period is *What's New In Capitol Stereo*, an album designed to showcase the capabilities of the new stereo sound system on the market. Similarly, one of the earliest charity compilations was the 1965 *Stars Charity Fantasia* on the Save The Children label (including a litany of hits by Dusty Springfield, The Walker Brothers, Val Doonican, Ken Dodd and Cliff Richard).

A starting point for the modern compilation album might be the historically influential – and now highly collectible – *Nuggets: Original Artyfacts from the First Psychedelic Era, 1965–1968*, first released in 1972 by Elektra. This was a watershed because it wasn't a blatant sampler, it wasn't a tie-in to a film or similar, but instead was a compilation album with its own identity, its own artistic value and integrity. The idea was initially the fancy of the record label's founder, Jac Holzman, ably assisted by none other than Lenny Kaye, erstwhile author, revered producer and long-time guitarist with Patti Smith.

The sleeve notes were written by Kaye and include what many see as one of the first uses of the words 'punk rock'. This is fitting, because *Nuggets* is a collection of psychedelic rock, garage rock and some pop music, including bands such as The 13th Floor Elevators, The Electric Prunes, The Blues Magoos, The Castaways and The Barabarians. While Stooges and MC5 fans have long since hailed their idols as precursors to the 1976–77 explosion of punk, those with a fine-tuned knowledge would also throw up *Nuggets* as an influence on that most incendiary of genres. Despite many people thinking *Nuggets* is but a treasure trove of the obscure, nearly 40 per cent of those featured on the album enjoyed American chart success.

The record has since been re-issued many times, in many formats, with expanded track-listings, various sleeves, and has, in effect, become a mini-collectors' market all of its own – even leading Rhino Records to release their own *Nuggets* series of albums, including *Nuggets II: Original Artyfacts from the British Empire and Beyond, 1964–1969*, *Hallucinations: Psychedelic Pop Nuggets from the WEA Vaults* and *Children of Nuggets: Original Artyfacts From The Second Psychedelic Era, 1976–1995*. It was thirty-four years before a single CD version of the original track-listing and sleeve notes was made available, also by Rhino. Notable successors to the *Nuggets* compilation crown include *Pebbles*, the *Back From the Grave* series and *Rubble*, which saw multiple releases across multiple genres. In 2003, the original *Nuggets* album was listed at Number 196 on *Rolling Stone* magazine's list of the 500 greatest albums (above *Murmur* by REM and *Highway To Hell* by AC/DC). An original copy of *Nuggets* in pristine condition can now command a hefty premium price tag.

One of the earliest charity compilations was the 1965 *Stars Charity Fantasia* on the Save The Children label

An obvious rival for the first authentic compilation album crown is Motown's *Chartbusters*, which likewise spawned its own large series of subsequent albums – many of which peppered the upper reaches of the UK album charts in the early 1970s. The original concept behind this record was as an introduction to artists on the famous label – although the first four incarnations

of this franchise had only abstract artwork on the sleeve, as mainstream music and radio was still shamefully not supporting black artists with any vigour or equality.

By distinct contrast, compilation albums originating from the UK were often banal and cheesy. In the early 1970s, no faux-leather settee and Axminster-carpeted semi was complete without a number of the compilations of 'Various Artist' songs. They were not original chart versions, but instead were performed by uncredited, 'unknown' session musicians, who recorded 'the hits of the day' in versions that often bore either (a) no resemblance at all to the original or were (b) so similar as to be almost indistinguishable. Typically, the recording 'stars' would be a conglomerate of renowned session musicians; however, several high-profile recording artists, including Elton John and David Bowie, have since revealed they cut their teeth working on these budget albums.

The TOTP albums saw ninety-two volumes between 1968 and 1985

For a brief period in the early 1970s, these albums sold enormous quantities. Today they seem like an odd throwback, a car-boot ten-pence novelty, but due to their (on/off) inclusion in the charts at the time, these records often vied with big-name artists for the top spot. By 1971, commercially huge albums of original hits were being released and attracting vast sales – *Hot Hits 6*, for example, with a woman on the front sleeve in a bikini and cricket pads. Naturally.

Quality control was sometimes almost completely absent. Various other labels made this dubious marketplace their forte, however, including Embassy (part of Woolworths), Arcade and Ronco. The songs were often listed with the damning qualifying sentence on the album sleeve, 'Originally Made Famous By ...'

The early-to-mid-1970s was undoubtedly the golden era of this genre of compilation album. During this period, chart regulations frequently shifted in response to the 'Budget', 'Mid Price' and 'Full Price' releases that at times swamped the album charts with far from impressive records; when compilations were eligible for charting, they did so high up the table and in massive quantities. Part of the appeal was undoubtedly the cheap price, but also this form of music was immensely popular in pubs, clubs and, above all, in the home. For a time in the 1970s these albums were genuinely popular. Though the cyclical nature of music fashion dictates that this is no longer the case, the former 'cover versions' labels didn't take long to see the potential in releasing compilations of original material too and, when they did, their success was even greater.

Perhaps 1972 could be regarded as the most impressive of compilation years. Back in August of the previous year, eligibility rules regarding lower-priced albums were removed, flooding the charts with cheap compilations, mostly priced at seventy-seven pence (two pence less than one song now costs on iTunes); this decision was then reversed and a flurry of rules, releases and changes put the role and chart life of the compilation in flux. Nonetheless, the year ended with compilations as the top two best-selling albums – *20 Dynamic Hits* and *20 All-Time Hits of the 50s*, both on the legendary K-Tel label. That record company, which specialised in compilations, also had the ninth-best-selling album of the year with *25 Rockin' And Rollin' Greats* – beating by one place Don McLean's *American Pie* and only slightly behind Simon & Garfunkel's *Bridge Over Troubled Water*.

One of the most successful compilation series during this period was undoubtedly the one branded by

Top of the Pops – a very successful franchise spin-off from the legendary television show, which in November 1971 topped the UK album charts with *Volume 20*. The TOTP albums saw ninety-two volumes between 1968 and 1985 and perhaps made the bikini the essential item of clothing for any self-respecting, disrespectful compilation sleeve.

These *Top of the Pops* albums are the natural predecessor to the Big Daddy of the 'Various Artist' compilation genre: *Now That's What I Call Music*. First released on vinyl in 1983, the NOW franchise is the single most successful compilation album series. Before NOW, such 'Various Artist' records tended to be single albums but the ante was upped with Volume 1 of this franchise offering thirty songs (in the current climate, the norm is for at least forty songs).

The initial germ of the idea is reported to have come from Ashley Abram of Box Records, a consultant who was working on new projects for record labels. NOW legend suggests he took the elongated album title of his famous idea from a Danish advert for pork, which was accompanied by a pig listening to a whistling cockerel – this in turn became NOW's mascot for the first five albums. The transient exclamation mark was initially placed after the word 'Now', but then moved to after the word 'Music' for *Volume 20*, no doubt in an effort to please the grammatically minded music lover.

NOW was a simple concept – thirty tracks from the biggest artists of the day, regardless of what record label they were on. Vinyl technicians will point out that releasing a double album allowed far better sound quality for the tracks, as the old single-vinyl format was erring towards being too compact for the best reproduction of the limited technology across this many songs. The simplicity of the idea, combined with the brilliant packaging and expansive track-listing made NOW an immediate and massive commercial hit.

Volume 1 – released on 10 December 1983 – hit the album top spot and a staggering seventy-one volumes have done the same since. If you include the other NOW titles, which include *Now That's What I Call Christmas* and *Now That's What I Call Dance*, the total rises to ninety-one albums. A major factor in the series' immediate success was the breadth of the artists on the vinyl. Previously, various artist compilations had typically only been able to muster a limited number of songs, as they did not work with all the popular artists of the day. NOW has become such a commercial behemoth because from day one they offered *all* the biggest hits of the day. All killer, no filler, as they say. Thus, the first album was flagged up as containing '11 Number 1 Hits!', which was unprecedented in the genre at that time.

Since its inception, the NOW series has sold 75 million copies

The seemingly limitless potential for compilation albums is perhaps typified by the NOW series. At the time of writing, *NOW Volume 71* has been released, and to celebrate the twenty-fifth anniversary, the original album has been re-released on CD and is available for download. The sales statistics are staggering: since its inception, the NOW series has sold 75 million copies. With international sales and spin-offs, that figure is closer to 100 million units; *Volume 44* is in the Top 50 best-selling UK albums ever with nearly 2.5 million copies sold, and the first-week sales of *Volume 69* make it in the Top 10 of the biggest opening-week sales figures ever.

The series also became an international phenomenon. Most overseas editions mimic the UK original closely,

except, obviously, for the inclusion of tracks from local artists – to date, there have been NOW compilations in countries including Argentina, Indonesia, Malaysia, Taiwan, Hong Kong, Australia, Canada, China, Czech Republic, Denmark, Egypt, Finland, France, Greece, Hungary, Israel, Italy, Japan, Mexico, New Zealand, Poland, Portugal, Spain, United States, South Africa, South America and Turkey. A few foreign licencees give the brand a new twist with name changes such as Greece's *Now These Are the Hits Today* and the Czech Republic's *Now Hity*. Perhaps best of all is *Now That's What I Call Arabia*.

Back in the UK, NOW is a fully fledged super-brand. Inevitably, spin-offs from the core idea followed quickly after the huge success of the first few albums: there were initially multi-format releases, followed by long-form videos, then latterly DVDs; the NOW banner was then applied to themed concepts such as NOW Dance and NOW Christmas; this was taken another step further with the release of year-specific NOW records, then NOW Decades albums; there have been Millennium editions and tie-ins with *Smash Hits* magazine (the imaginatively monickered *Now Smash Hits*); ringtones and downloads from the official site came next, a *Now That's What I Call*

The Best & The Worst

It's worth pausing in the story a moment to highlight some of the very finest/worst examples of the compilation genre: the drinking A&R man's dream, *Singalong Pub Songs*; the blatant marketing idea, *Hello Children ... Everywhere*; the peculiar, *User:MoonThing/ Sandbox*; the tenuous, *Girls and Guitars*; the obscure, *Themes and Dreams*; the honest, *The World's Worst Record Show* (in conjunction with Kenny Everett; thank you, K-Tel); the gender exploiter, *Natural Woman/Woman To Woman/I Am Woman* plus *Let's Hear It For The Girls/ The Boys Are Back In Town, Ladykillaz, Boyz Of Swing*; the petrol-head sale, *Drivetime/Open Top Cars, Girls in T-shirt, F1 Rock*; the obscure instrumental, *Strings of Scotland/ Electronic Organs Today*; the lovers' selection, *Seduction, Modern Love, Tempted, The Look of Love*; the hobbyist, *Ultimate Line Dancing*; the largely incomprehensible, *Blame Presents Logical Progression*; the record for fads, *Rock 'n' Roller Disco*; the laughable, *Chart Encounters of the Hit Kind*; the abrupt, *Shut Up And Dance/Fuck Off And Die*; the sporty, *The Magic of Torvill and Dean*; the international, *20 Italian Love Songs*; and the suggestive, *Twelve Inches of Pleasure*. Likewise the compilation genre has evoked some fantastic names, such as: *Punk And Disorderly*; *Rockabilly Psychobillies and the Garage Disease*; *Allez! Ola! Ole!* and, perhaps weirdest of all – with restraining orders at the ready – *Music To Watch Girls By*.

A particular favourite to highlight is Scala & Kolacny Brothers, which consists of a Belgian schoolgirls' choir collaborating with a classically trained pianist, Steven Kolacny, to release compilation albums of cover versions. Nothing unusual in that, you say, until you check out the highlights of their (best-selling) back-catalogue: 'Smells Like Teen Spirit' by Nirvana; 'Muscle Museum' by Muse; 'Under The Bridge', that being Red Hot Chili Peppers' ode to heroin addiction; 'I Touch Myself', the Divinyls paean to masturbation; and Sinéad O' Connor's 'Daddy, I'm Fine' complete with lyrical references to 'f**king every man in sight'.

A Music Quiz DVD and a karaoke DVD; there are even NOW fan sites. Conversely, despite the concept having become such an iconic brand, the original vinyl is still widely available and, at best, *Volume 1* will command maybe £50–100 if in mint condition. That said, urban myth tells the story of the harder-to-find *Volume 5* being sold for £875 at a Brighton record fair in the late 1990s (now that's what I call expensive). There are rival brands – *Hits*, *Best Album In The World Ever!* etc. – but none truly threatens the king. With three titles a year on average, the series is, at the time of writing, up to NOW 71 and shows no signs of slowing down.

One reason why 'various artists' compilations are so beloved of a record label is that they offer them an opportunity to earn money from low-earning back-catalogues. They will license say, a Robbie Williams track that already earns them a huge amount, but will bundle a deal also licensing tracks by lesser-known artists. This is why you often buy a compilation CD and find that twenty out of the forty tracks are by artists you haven't heard of or wish you didn't know.

The banner of 'compilation' also inevitably leads to some fairly tenuous connections being made between otherwise utterly incongruous artists. There are some obvious themes which make commercial sense and appeal to the fair-weather music buyer: Christmas time, Valentine's Day, Mother's Day, love songs, and so on. Scratch a little further down the record store's stock list and you will find a few more tentative connections: Father's Day driving songs, Big Band versions of pop songs, pop versions of Big Band songs; the *Number One* series of compilation albums probably best epitomises this approach to compilations with records such as *Number One Sci-Fi Album*; and finally it's the turn of the plain weird such as *EarthRise – The Rainforest Album* and *Themes Orchestral Plays Elvis*. That's before you delve into the mind-numbing banality of pan pipe ...

Likewise, you have the obvious genre collections: rock, dance, jazz, etc; every musical genre has been plundered, punk being perhaps the best example. The compilation of various artists' songs allows the more creative record-company archivist to have a lot of fun. Thus, over the years, there have been some truly bizarre compilation albums.

One reason why 'various artists' compilations are so beloved of a record label is that they offer them an opportunity to earn money from low-earning back-catalogues

Of course, compilation albums don't just get to the music listener through record sales. Over the years, this form of album has proved immensely popular for all manner of non-retail uses. There's the compilations that are shrink-wrapped to magazine covers, the super-producer albums of collaborations, record-label samplers given out en masse to the media, private firms handing out free compilation CDs to customers in their stores and mobile-phone companies shelling out CDs. Its commercial use is endless.

Throughout much of the 1990s, brands and large companies, magazines, newspapers and various other commercial entities looking to tap into the consumerist appeal of music issued thousands of compilations (both free and for retail). Among the dross and tenuously linked brand albums, there are a few gems – the fortieth anniversary of Dr Martens boots was celebrated in 2000 by the release of a boxed set of

forty tracks by artists who all proudly wear the iconic eight-hole boot. Thus you have a genuine musical and sartorial heritage that spans artists as diverse as Desmond Dekker to Red Hot Chili Peppers on one compilation – with the collection wrapped in genuine Dr Martens cherry-red leather. By contrast, we have 1989's *All Because The Lady Loves ...* in conjunction with Cadbury's Milk Tray chocolates.

One obviously worthy and occasionally brilliant form of compilation is the charity album. By virtue of the fact that an overriding humanitarian homogeneity is bringing a diverse array of artists together, there can be some quite stunning results. The *War Child* benefit CD has enjoyed continued support from the likes of a diverse array of artists: Gorillaz and George Michael; Bloc Party and U2; Frank Black and Brian Eno; and so on. This seemingly incongruous mix somehow works and, as a result, the series has evolved into a genuinely worthy musical collection.

The Beatles struggled to sell many copies of their 1966 album, *A Collection Of Beatles Oldies*

Tribute compilations can also throw up some really rather splendid albums. There is the more usual 'tribute' album on which other artists record cover versions of a single artist's back-catalogue, with great examples including *Beyond The Wildwood* (a tribute to Syd Barrett) and *The Art Of Shredding: A Tribute To Dime* (a posthumous nod to metal legend Dimebag Darrell). And let's not forget *The String Quartet Tribute To Guns N' Roses*.

Some 'compilations' take this further and, rather than just feature one artist, they feature one *track* – in dance hall and reggae music, a variety of different artists performing over the same instrumental rhythm is a massively popular format.

Perhaps one of the most poignant and fitting spin-offs is *A Tribute*, recorded in John Peel's memory. As probably the single most influential DJ in British music history, Peel had championed new acts and emerging/breaking bands for decades. After his premature and tragic death in 2004 aged only sixty-five, the hundreds of bands he had helped clamoured to pay their respects. The result was a double album, a veritable *Who's Who* of both alternative and rock-music legends, including artists such as The Clash, The Undertones, Joy Division, Pink Floyd, David Bowie and The Doors – overall a fine testament to his legacy.

Coming back to the concept of a 'Greatest Hits' or 'Best Of' compilation album – so beloved of the supermarket record shelf – the idea is actually nothing new, with artists such as Perry Como, Johnny Mathis, Elvis, Cliff, etc., all releasing exactly such records many decades before. However, sales in the last twenty years far outstrip many of those from those earlier decades as the concept took years to gain a place in the record-buying public's psyche. Even The Beatles struggled to sell many copies of their 1966 album *A Collection Of Beatles Oldies*, which sold so poorly it only hit Number 7 and spent a miserly three weeks in the Top 10.

Clever marketing tricks such as bonus songs and online extra content do little to make these retrospectives any more than a simple re-packaging exercise, and a very lucrative one too; likewise 'B-sides and Rarities' (the songs that didn't make the album or were recorded before a band was any good), 'Live' (we're due to fulfil another album this year but unless we just tape a concert that we're playing anyway, we are going to be in breach of our contract) and 'In Session' (we get songs recorded free, played on radio for free and now get to sell the session) and, of course, the premium Box Sets ...

Although critics might scoff, the public love compilation records. In fact, by 1989, sales of these albums were excluded from the main album chart for fear of them, quite literally, taking over. It's not just the public (and therefore by definition the profitable record labels) who love *Greatest Hits* packages. The musicians do too. For an artist's *Best Of* compilation, they might typically earn about £1.50 per CD sold – that's 15 pence per track per copy sold on a ten-track album and that usually requires no extra work other than a meeting about track-listing and artwork; if they only have one track on a 'Various Artists compilation', that figure is a lot less (but we'll come to that in a moment).

One notable and fascinating aspect of the evolution of compilation albums is how the physical sales of many of these titles have enjoyed a revival since the onset of the download age, in direct contrast to the sales of physical albums of original material. In the same way that the exponential rise in the popularity of downloads was driven by price and convenience, then so too has been the resilience of physical compilation sales. This is in spite of the fact that download now offers the listener the opportunity to create their own 'playlists' or compilations. Many observers felt that the comprehensive availability of music online would be the final death knell for compilations. Not so.

They are available in supermarkets as well as record stores and offer great value for money – even when compared to the margin-crunching cheapness of downloads. If you pick up a double compilation CD for £12.99 with forty tracks on it, the corresponding downloads, based around 79 pence per track, would set you back £31.60. Moreover, to download forty separate songs from iTunes is far from fast and convenient. So, we have entered the Indian Summer/New Dawn of the compilation album. In December 2008, when the best-selling albums of the year were compiled, the OCC's statistics revealed that three of the Top 10 sellers were Various Artists' compilations. It's a no-brainer. So the compilation album will be with us for some time yet, it seems.

So, with all these compilation albums flying off shelves in supermarkets across the land, the observer might be prone to think the 'Various Artists' featured on them are making the fabled 'money for nothing'.

Think again.

Let's take the average forty-track compilation album, selling at retail for £14.99. Let's call it *Now That's The Greatest Hot Hits And Top of The Best Compilation Album In The Universe Ever*. The record begins life in a marketing meeting. The record label releasing the idea then approaches all the other labels whose artists they wish to include on the CD. It's a quick process – a boiler-plate template licence is emailed across, approval of the artist is sought (or should be), and the subsequent agreement and digital MP3 files are sent. The compilation is then

Many observers felt that the comprehensive availability of music online would be the final death knell for compilations. Not so.

mastered and very economic artwork is designed – no budgets for flying a five-piece rock band to some far-flung destination to capture the essence of their life's work/new album and create a modern masterpiece. Just some clever typesetting and fairly loud artwork. With

Top 40 Artist Compilation Albums of All Time

Based on UK Sales

Pos	Album Title	Artist	Approx Sales
1	**GREATEST HITS**	QUEEN	5,650,000
2	**GOLD – GREATEST HITS**	ABBA	4,475,000
3	**GREATEST HITS II**	QUEEN	3,740,000
4	**THE IMMACULATE COLLECTION**	MADONNA	3,550,000
5	**1**	BEATLES	2,800,000
6	**LEGEND**	BOB MARLEY & THE WAILERS	2,775,000
7	**GREATEST HITS**	ABBA	2,600,000
8	**LADIES & GENTLEMEN – THE BEST OF**	GEORGE MICHAEL	2,415,000
9	**THE VERY BEST OF**	ELTON JOHN	2,135,000
10	**SIMPLY THE BEST**	TINA TURNER	2,130,000
11	**GREATEST HITS**	ROBBIE WILLIAMS	2,110,000
12	**CROSS ROAD – THE BEST OF**	BON JOVI	2,080,000
13	**GREATEST HITS**	EURYTHMICS	2,060,000
14	**GREATEST HITS**	SIMON & GARFUNKEL	1,960,000
15	**BACK TO FRONT**	LIONEL RICHIE	1,925,000
16	**THE GREATEST HITS**	TEXAS	1,880,000
17	**CARRY ON UP THE CHARTS – THE BEST OF**	BEAUTIFUL SOUTH	1,835,000
18	**BY REQUEST**	BOYZONE	1,800,000
19	**MY WAY – THE BEST OF**	FRANK SINATRA	1,760,000
20	**NEVER FORGET – THE ULTIMATE COLLECTION**	TAKE THAT	1,710,000
21	**THE BEST OF**	ROD STEWART	1,680,000
22	**GREATEST HITS I, II & III**	QUEEN	1,675,000
23	**THE GREATEST HITS**	WHITNEY HOUSTON	1,650,000
24	**UNBREAKABLE – THE GREATEST HITS – VOL 1**	WESTLIFE	1,645,000
25	**GREATEST HITS**	SIMPLY RED	1,610,000
26	**IN TIME – THE BEST OF – 1988-2003**	REM	1,600,000
27	**NUMBER ONES**	MICHAEL JACKSON	1,595,000
28	**HITS**	PHIL COLLINS	1,590,000
29	**THE SINGLES 1969-1973**	CARPENTERS	1,560,000
30	**ELV1S – 30 NUMBER 1 HITS**	ELVIS PRESLEY	1,520,000
31	**HISTORY – PAST PRESENT AND FUTURE BOOK 1**	MICHAEL JACKSON	1,510,000
32	**THE BEST OF 1980-1990**	U2	1,470,000
33	**MONEY FOR NOTHING**	DIRE STRAITS	1,465,000
34	**GREATEST HITS 1970-2002**	ELTON JOHN	1,440,000
35	**THE STORY SO FAR – THE VERY BEST OF**	ROD STEWART	1,390,000
36	**THE COLLECTION**	BARRY WHITE	1,380,000
37	**DREAMS CAN COME TRUE – GREATEST HITS**	GABRIELLE	1,370,000
38	**LOVE SONGS**	BARBRA STREISAND	1,365,000
39	**RECURRING DREAM – THE VERY BEST OF**	CROWDED HOUSE	1,335,000
40	**ALL THE WAY – A DECADE OF SONG**	CELINE DION	1,300,000

the artwork complete and the master ready, the CDs are pressed – costing approximately £1.15 in total to manufacture per CD. No expensive videos, no tours to support, no riders to buy and no doctor's bills for 'nervous exhaustion' to cover.

The £14.99 out of your wallet goes first to the supermarket, who take a margin, then they pass the remainder on to the distributor, who also takes his lunch money. He then pays what is called the 'dealer price' to the record label overseeing the album, typically here about £8. That is then shared out to all the other record labels who licensed their various individual songs. Then, finally, these labels pay the artists ...

So, how much does the artist get?

Well, if you are a record label, rub your hands, if you are an artist, dining out on your £1.50 per *Greatest Hits* album sold, look away now ...

A standard-UK release compilation-album licence will usually only earn the artist between *2p and 4p, per track, per copy sold.* If the song is being used on a compilation overseas, that can fall considerably. It is not uncommon for compilations in Eastern Europe and even Ireland to pay as little as 1p per song, per copy sold, to the artist.

It gets worse. That one pence has twenty per cent deducted for the artist's management, leaving just 0.8 of one penny. Then, the music-loving Inland Revenue will take forty per cent (if the artist is a high earner), leaving 0.48 of one penny. Then, considering the fact that many musical acts are not solo artists, let's assume this example is for a five-piece rock band. That leaves 0.096 of one pence per musician, paid per track for each copy sold of *Now That's The Greatest Hot Hits And Top Of The Best Compilation Album In The Universe Ever*.

That's less than a *tenth* of a penny.

The record company meanwhile? Well, the coins just keep flooding through the slot, nickel after nickel after nickel after nickel ...

ANONYMOUS COVER VERSIONS

Date	Title / Label	Peak Position	Weeks at No.1	Weeks on Chart
29 Feb 64	**BEATLEMANIA** *Top Six TSL 1*	19		2
7 Aug 71	**HOT HITS 6** *MFP 5214*	1	1	7
7 Aug 71	**TOP OF THE POPS VOLUME 18** *Hallmark SHM 745*	1	3	12
7 Aug 71	**TOP OF THE POPS VOLUME 17** *Hallmark SHM 740*	16		3
7 Aug 71	**MILLION SELLER HITS** *MFP 5203*	46		2
7 Aug 71	**HOT HITS 5** *MFP 5208*	48		1
21 Aug 71	**SMASH HITS SUPREMES STYLE** *MFP 5184*	36		3
2 Oct 71	**TOP OF THE POPS VOLUME 19** *Hallmark SHM 750*	3		9
23 Oct 71	**HOT HITS 7** *MFP 5236*	3		9
6 Nov 71	**SMASH HITS COUNTRY STYLE** *MFP 5228*	38		1
13 Nov 71	**TOP OF THE POPS VOLUME 20** *Hallmark SHM 755*	1	1	8
27 Nov 71	**NON STOP 20 VOLUME 4** *Plexium PXMS 1006*	35		2
4 Dec 71	**SMASH HITS '71** *MFP 5229*	21		3
11 Dec 71	**HOT HITS 8** *MFP 5243*	2		4
27 Sep 75	**40 SINGALONG PUB SONGS** *K-Tel NE 509*	21		7
6 Nov 76	**FORTY MANIA** *Ronco RDT 2018*	21		6

FILM SOUNDTRACK

Date	Title / Label	Peak Position	Weeks at No.1	Weeks on Chart
28 Jul 56	**CAROUSEL (OST)** *Capitol LCT 6105*	1	6	40
28 Jul 56	**OKLAHOMA! (OST)** *Capitol LCT 6100* ★	1	3	162
22 Sep 56	**THE KING AND I (OST)** *Capitol LCT 6108* ★	1	48	200
18 Jan 58	**PAL JOEY (OST)** *Capitol LCT 6148*	1	11	23
3 May 58	**SOUTH PACIFIC (OST)** *RCA RB 16065* ★	1	115	313
31 Jan 59	**GIGI (OST)** *MGM C 770* ★	2		88
10 Oct 59	**PORGY AND BESS (OST)** *Philips ABL 3282*	7		5
23 Jan 60	**THE FIVE PENNIES (OST)** *London HAU 2189*	2		15
7 May 60	**CAN CAN (OST)** *Capitol W 1301*	2		31
5 Nov 60	**BEN HUR (OST)** *MGM C 802*	15		3
21 Jan 61	**NEVER ON SUNDAY (OST)** *London HAT 2309*	17		1
18 Feb 61	**SONG WITHOUT END (OST)** *Pye Golden Guinea GGL 30169*	9		10
29 Apr 61	**SEVEN BRIDES FOR SEVEN BROTHERS (OST)** *MGM C 853*	6		22
3 Jun 61	**EXODUS (OST)** *RCA RD 27210* ★	17		1
11 Nov 61	**GLENN MILLER STORY (OST)** *Ace Of Hearts AH 12*	12		7
24 Mar 62	**WEST SIDE STORY (OST)** *Philips BBL 7530*	1	13	175
28 Apr 62	**IT'S TRAD MAN (OST)** *Columbia 33SX 1412*	3		21
22 Sep 62	**THE MUSIC MAN (OST)** *Warner Brothers WB 4066* ★	14		9
3 Nov 62	**PORGY AND BESS (OST)** *CBS APG 60002*	14		7
15 Jun 63	**JUST FOR FUN (OST)** *Decca LK 4525*	20		2
31 Oct 64	**MY FAIR LADY (OST)** *CBS BPG 72237*	9		51
16 Jan 65	**MARY POPPINS (OST)** *HMV CLP 1794* ★	2		82
10 Apr 65	**THE SOUND OF MUSIC (OST)** *RCA Victor RB 6616* ⊛ ★	1	70	381
29 Jul 67	**A MAN AND A WOMAN (OST)** *United Artists SULP 1155*	31		11
28 Oct 67	**THOROUGHLY MODERN MILLIE (OST)** *Brunswick STA 8685*	9		19
9 Mar 68	**THE JUNGLE BOOK (OST)** *Disney ST 3948* ●	5		51
21 Sep 68	**STAR! (OST)** *Stateside SSL 10233*	36		1
23 Nov 68	**OLIVER! (OST)** *RCA Victor SB 6777*	4		107
23 Nov 68	**CAMELOT (OST)** *Warner Brothers WS 1712*	37		1
8 Feb 69	**CHITTY CHITTY BANG BANG (OST)** *United Artists SULP 1200*	10		4
14 Jun 69	**2001 – A SPACE ODYSSEY (OST)** *MGM CS 8078*	3		67
20 Dec 69	**EASY RIDER (OST)** *Stateside SSL 5018*	2		67
24 Jan 70	**THE JUNGLE BOOK (OST)** *Disney BVS 4041*	25		26
7 Feb 70	**PAINT YOUR WAGON (OST)** *Paramount SPFL 257*	2		102
18 Jul 70	**WOODSTOCK (OST)** *Atlantic 2662 001* ★	35		19
24 Apr 71	**LOVE STORY (OST)** *Paramount SPFL 267*	10		33
12 Feb 72	**CLOCKWORK ORANGE (OST)** *Warner Brothers K 46127*	4		46
8 Apr 72	**FIDDLER ON THE ROOF (OST)** *United Artists UAD 60011/2*	26		2
13 May 72	**2001 – A SPACE ODYSSEY (OST)** *MGM 2315 034*	20		2
25 Nov 72	**SOUTH PACIFIC (OST)** *RCA Victor SB 2011*	25		2
31 Mar 73	**CABARET (OST)** *Probe SPB 1052*	13		22
14 Apr 73	**LOST HORIZON (OST)** *Bell SYBEL 8000*	36		3
22 Sep 73	**JESUS CHRIST SUPERSTAR (OST)** *MCA MDKS 8012/3* ★	23		18
27 Apr 74	**AMERICAN GRAFFITI (OST)** *MCA MCSP 253* ○	37		1
8 Jun 74	**A TOUCH OF CLASS (OST)** *Philips 6612 040* ○	32		1
5 Oct 74	**SUNSHINE (OST)** *MCA MCF 2566*	47		3
5 Apr 75	**TOMMY (OST)** *Polydor 2657 014* ●	21		9
27 Nov 76	**ALL THIS AND WORLD WAR II (OST)** *Riva RVLP 2* ●	23		7
2 Jul 77	**THE BEST OF CAR WASH** *MCA MCF 2799*	59		1
11 Mar 78	**SATURDAY NIGHT FEVER (OST)** *RSO 2658 123* ⊛ ★	1	18	65
22 Apr 78	**THE STUD (OST)** *Ronco RTD 2029* ●	2		19
6 May 78	**THE LAST WALTZ (OST)** *Warner Brothers K 66076*	39		4
20 May 78	**THANK GOD IT'S FRIDAY (OST)** *Casablanca TGIF 100* ○	40		5
27 May 78	**FM (OST)** *MCA MCSP 284* ○	37		7
8 Jul 78	**GREASE (OST)** *RSO RSD 2001* ⊛ ★	1	13	47
12 Aug 78	**SGT. PEPPER'S LONELY HEARTS CLUB BAND (OST)** *A&M AMLZ 66600* ○	38		2
7 Oct 78	**CONVOY (OST)** *Capitol EST 24590*	52		1
31 Mar 79	**LEMON POPSICLE (OST)** *Warwick WW 5050*	42		6
9 Jun 79	**THAT SUMMER (OST)** *Arista SPART 1088*	36		8
30 Jun 79	**THE WORLD IS FULL OF MARRIED MEN (OST)** *Ronco RTD 2038*	25		9
14 Jul 79	**THE WARRIORS (OST)** *A&M AMLH 64761*	53		7
9 Feb 80	**SUNBURN (OST)** *Warwick RTL 2044*	45		7
16 Feb 80	**GOING STEADY (OST)** *Warwick WW 5078*	25		10
8 Mar 80	**THE WANDERERS (OST)** *Gem GEMLP 103*	48		7
6 Sep 80	**FAME (OST)** *RSO 2479 253* ●	1	2	25
14 Feb 81	**DANCE CRAZE (OST)** *2-Tone CHRTT 5004* ●	5		15
17 Jul 82	**THE SOUND OF MUSIC (OST)** *RCA International 5134*	98		1
4 Sep 82	**ROCKY III (OST)** *Liberty LBG 30351*	42		7
4 Sep 82	**ANNIE (OST)** *CBS 70219*	83		2
11 Sep 82	**BRIMSTONE AND TREACLE (OST)** *A&M AMLH 64915*	67		3
12 Feb 83	**AN OFFICER AND A GENTLEMAN (OST)** *Island ISTA 3*	40		14
2 Jul 83	**FLASHDANCE (OST)** *Casablanca CANH 5* ★	9		30
1 Oct 83	**STAYING ALIVE (OST)** *RSO RSBG 3* ○	14		8
21 Apr 84	**FOOTLOOSE (OST)** *CBS 70246* ● ★	7		25
21 Apr 84	**AGAINST ALL ODDS (OST)** *Virgin V 2313*	29		10
16 Jun 84	**BREAKDANCE (OST)** *Polydor POLD 5147* ●	6		29
7 Jul 84	**BEAT STREET (OST)** *Atlantic 7801541*	30		13
18 Aug 84	**ELECTRIC DREAMS (OST)** *Virgin V 2318* ○	46		7
29 Sep 84	**GHOSTBUSTERS (OST)** *Arista 206 559* ●	24		25
12 Jan 85	**BREAKDANCE 2 – ELECTRIC BOOGALOO (OST)** *Polydor POLD 5168*	34		20
16 Feb 85	**BEVERLY HILLS COP (OST)** *MCA MCF 3253* ● ★	24		32
11 Jan 86	**BACK TO THE FUTURE (OST)** *MCA MCF 3285*	66		8
1 Feb 86	**ROCKY IV (OST)** *Scotti Brothers SCT 70272* ●	3		22
1 Feb 86	**MISTRAL'S DAUGHTER (OST-TV)** *Carrere CAL 221*	53		3
5 Apr 86	**ABSOLUTE BEGINNERS (OST)** *Virgin V 2386* ●	19		9
11 Oct 86	**TOP GUN (OST)** *CBS 70296* ⊛x2 ★	4		47
11 Apr 87	**THE BLUES BROTHERS (OST)** *Atlantic K 50715* ⊛x2	59		26
2 May 87	**PLATOON (OST)** *WEA WX 95* ●	90		2
18 Jul 87	**BEVERLY HILLS COP II (OST)** *MCA MCF 3383*	71		5
1 Aug 87	**WHO'S THAT GIRL (OST)** *Sire WX 102* ⊛	4		25
3 Oct 87	**FULL METAL JACKET (OST)** *Warner Brothers 9256131* ○	60		4
31 Oct 87	**DIRTY DANCING (OST)** *RCA BL 86408* ⊛x5 ★	4		63
16 Jan 88	**FLASHDANCE (OST)** *Mercury PRICE 111* ●	93		2
20 Feb 88	**CRY FREEDOM (OST)** *MCA MCG 6029*	73		2
14 May 88	**MORE DIRTY DANCING (OST)** *RCA BL 86965*	3		27
24 Sep 88	**BUSTER (OST)** *Virgin V 2544*	6		16
22 Oct 88	**GOOD MORNING VIETNAM (OST)** *A&M AMA 3913* ●	50		9
14 Jan 89	**DIRTY DANCING (OST)** *RCA BL 86408* ⊛x5 ★	1	2	167
14 Jan 89	**BUSTER (OST)** *Virgin V 2544* ⊛x3	2		36
21 Jan 89	**THE BLUES BROTHERS (OST)** *Atlantic K 50715* ⊛x2	4		80
21 Jan 89	**GOOD MORNING VIETNAM (OST)** *A&M AMA 3913* ●	7		29
28 Jan 89	**THE LOST BOYS (OST)** *Atlantic 7817671* ⊛	1	1	61
4 Feb 89	**COCKTAIL (OST)** *Elektra EKT 54* ●	2		15
4 Feb 89	**MORE DIRTY DANCING (OST)** *RCA BL 86965* ⊛	14		17
18 Mar 89	**SCANDAL (OST)** *Parlophone PCS 7331*	13		3
22 Apr 89	**TOP GUN (OST)** *CBS 70296* ⊛x2	4		35
15 Jul 89	**LICENCE TO KILL (OST)** *MCA MCG 6051*	17		2
22 Jul 89	**GHOSTBUSTERS II (OST)** *MCA MCG 6051*	15		4
10 Mar 90	**THE DELINQUENTS (OST)** *PWL HF 11*	16		1
26 May 90	**PRETTY WOMAN (OST)** *EMI USA MTL 1052* ⊛x2	2		72
23 Jun 90	**TEENAGE MUTANT NINJA TURTLES (OST)** *SBK SBKLP 6* ●	6		18
11 Aug 90	**DAYS OF THUNDER (OST)** *Epic 4671591* ●	4		15
27 Oct 90	**GHOST (OST)** *MILAN A 620*	15		4
2 Feb 91	**ROCKY V (OST)** *Capitol EST 2137*	9		9
2 Mar 91	**GREASE (OST)** *Polydor 8179981*	8		21
23 Mar 91	**THE GODFATHER PART III (OST)** *Columbia 4678131*	19		1
27 Apr 91	**NEW JACK CITY (OST)** *Giant 7559244091*	16		5
1 Jun 91	**MERMAIDS (OST)** *Epic 4678741* ○	6		15
27 Jul 91	**ROBIN HOOD: PRINCE OF THIEVES (OST)** *Polydor 5110502* ○	3		14
18 Jan 92	**BILL AND TED'S BOGUS JOURNEY (OST)** *Interscope 7567917252*	3		8
29 Feb 92	**MY GIRL (OST)** *Epic 4692134*	13		7
30 May 92	**WAYNE'S WORLD (OST)** *Reprise 7599258052* ● ★	5		11
19 Sep 92	**MO' MONEY (OST)** *Perspective 3610042*	16		1
14 Nov 92	**BOOMERANG (OST)** *LaFace 73008260062*	17		2
28 Nov 92	**THE BODYGUARD (OST)** *Arista 07822186992* ⊛x7 ★	1	11	80
30 Jan 93	**SISTER ACT (OST)** *Hollywood HWDCD 9*	14		4
13 Feb 93	**BRAM STOKER'S DRACULA (OST)** *Columbia 4727462*	10		6
20 Mar 93	**RESERVOIR DOGS (OST)** *MCA MCD 10793*	16		3
5 Jun 93	**INDECENT PROPOSAL (OST)** *MCA MCD 10863*	13		3
24 Jul 93	**THE LAST ACTION HERO (OST)** *Columbia 4739902*	16		6
18 Sep 93	**SLIVER** *Virgin CDVMMX 11*	20		1
16 Oct 93	**SLEEPLESS IN SEATTLE (OST)** *Epic 4735942* ○ ★	10		6
16 Oct 93	**JUDGEMENT NIGHT (OST)** *Epic 4741832*	16		3
8 Jan 94	**ALADDIN (OST)** *Pickwick DSTCD 470*	11		5
5 Mar 94	**WAYNE'S WORLD 2 (OST)** *Warner Brothers WB 45485*	17		1
12 Mar 94	**PHILADELPHIA (OST)** *Epic 4749982* ●	5		14
7 May 94	**ABOVE THE RIM (OST)** *Interscope 6544923592*	18		1
28 May 94	**FOUR WEDDINGS AND A FUNERAL (OST)** *Vertigo 5167512* ⊛	5		21
25 Jun 94	**THE CROW (OST)** *Atlantic 7567825192* ● ★	13		5
6 Aug 94	**THE FLINTSTONES (OST)** *MCA MCD 11045* ○	18		1

Key: ○ Silver-selling · ● Gold-selling · ⊛ Platinum-selling · ★ US No.1

Date	Title / Label	Peak Position	Weeks at No.1	Weeks in Chart
22 Oct 94	**THE LION KING (OST)** *Mercury 5226902* ○ ★	4		20
22 Oct 94	**FORREST GUMP (OST)** *Epic 4769412* ●	5		13
5 Nov 94	**PULP FICTION (OST)** *MCA MCD 11103* ●	5		56
11 Mar 95	**NATURAL BORN KILLERS (OST)** *Interscope 6544924602* ○	10		6
8 Jul 95	**BAD BOYS (OST)** *Work 4804532*	19		1
29 Jul 95	**BATMAN FOREVER (OST)** *Atlantic 7567827592*	11		4
3 Feb 96	**WAITING TO EXHALE (OST)** *Arista 07822187962* ★	8		5
3 Feb 96	**DANGEROUS MINDS (OST)** *MCA MCD 11228* ★	13		2
2 Mar 96	**TRAINSPOTTING (OST)** *EMI Premier CDEMC 3739* ⊛x3	2		66
20 Jul 96	**MISSION: IMPOSSIBLE (OST)** *Mother MUMCD 9603*	18		1
19 Oct 96	**THE NUTTY PROFESSOR (OST)** *Def Jam 5319112*	20		1
29 Mar 97	**SPACE JAM (OST)** *Atlantic 7567829792* ●	5		10
5 Apr 97	**ROMEO + JULIET (OST)** *Premier Soundtracks PRMDCD 28* ⊛	3		24
3 May 97	**THE SAINT (OST)** *Virgin CDVUD 126*	15		1
2 Aug 97	**MEN IN BLACK – THE ALBUM (OST)** *Columbia 4881222* ● ★	5		13
9 Aug 97	**SPAWN – THE ALBUM (OST)** *Epic 4881182*	18		1
13 Sep 97	**THE FULL MONTY (OST)** *RCA Victor 09026689042* ⊛x3	1	3	43
27 Sep 97	**TRAINSPOTTING #2 (OST)** *Premier Soundtracks PRMDCD 36* ○	11		5
31 Jan 98	**BOOGIE NIGHTS (OST)** *Premier Soundtracks 8556312*	19		1
18 Apr 98	**JACKIE BROWN (OST)** *Maverick 9362468412* ○	11		7
27 Jun 98	**THE WEDDING SINGER (OST)** *Maverick 9362468402* ○	15		4
4 Jul 98	**CITY OF ANGELS (OST)** *Reprise 9362468672* ● ★	18		3
18 Jul 98	**GREASE (OST)** *Polydor 0440412*	2		16
25 Jul 98	**GODZILLA – THE ALBUM (OST)** *Epic 4896102*	13		4
12 Sep 98	**LOCK, STOCK & TWO SMOKING BARRELS (OST)** *Island CID 8077* ●	7		23
26 Sep 98	**ARMAGEDDON (OST)** *Columbia 4913842* ★	19		2
5 Jun 99	**NOTTING HILL (OST)** *Island 5462072* ⊛	4		19
19 Jun 99	**HUMAN TRAFFIC (OST)** *London 5561092* ○	14		3
26 Jun 99	**THE MATRIX (OST)** *Maverick 9362474192* ●	16		5
17 Jul 99	**AUSTIN POWERS – THE SPY WHO SHAGGED ME (OST)** *Maverick 9362473842* ●	6		11
11 Sep 99	**SOUTH PARK: BIGGER, LONGER & UNCUT (OST)** *Atlantic 7567831992* ○	9		5
2 Oct 99	**MANUMISSION – THE MOVIE (OST)** *Telstar TV TTVCD 3066*	17		1
4 Mar 00	**THE BEACH (OST)** *London 4344310792* ●	1	3	8
25 Mar 00	**THE MILLION DOLLAR HOTEL (OST)** *Island CID 8094*	13		1
8 Apr 00	**POKEMON – THE FIRST MOVIE (OST)** *Atlantic 7567832612* ●	8		5
29 Apr 00	**KEVIN AND PERRY – GO LARGE (OST)** *Virgin/EMI VTDCDX 298* ●	4		7
1 Jul 00	**MISSION IMPOSSIBLE 2 (OST)** *Hollywood 0110302 HWR* ○	12		8
16 Sep 00	**SNATCH (OST)** *Universal 5249992*	11		3
21 Oct 00	**BILLY ELLIOT (OST)** *Polydor 5493602*	10		4
4 Nov 00	**COYOTE UGLY (OST)** *Curb/London 8573852542* ○	16		3
14 Apr 01	**SAVE THE LAST DANCE (OST)** *Hollywood 025422 HWR* ●	5		8
28 Apr 01	**BRIDGET JONES'S DIARY (OST)** *Mercury 5487962* ⊛x3	1	7	30
21 Jul 01	**TOMB RAIDER (OST)** *Elektra 7559626652*	13		2
15 Sep 01	**MOULIN ROUGE (OST)** *Interscope 4905072*	2		12
29 Sep 01	**THE FAST AND THE FURIOUS** *Def Jam 5865062*	20		2
27 Oct 01	**AMERICAN PIE 2 (OST)** *Universal 0163482* ○	17		2
10 Nov 01	**BRIDGET JONES'S DIARY 2 (OST)** *Mercury 5865982* ●	8		2
26 Jan 02	**O BROTHER WHERE ART THOU (OST)** *Mercury 1700692* ○ ★	20		1
16 Mar 02	**MOULIN ROUGE – COLLECTORS EDITION** *Interscope 4932592*	9		7
30 Mar 02	**ALI G INDAHOUSE – DA SOUNDTRACK** *Island CID 8115* ●	5		7
20 Apr 02	**24 HOUR PARTY PEOPLE (OST)** *London 0927449302*	15		2
1 Jun 02	**SPIDER-MAN (OST)** *Columbia 5075476*	14		6
10 Aug 02	**AUSTIN POWERS IN GOLDMEMBER (OST)** *Maverick 9362483492*	14		2
9 Nov 02	**8 MILE** *Interscope 4935322* ● ★	1	2	27
25 Jan 03	**CHICAGO** *Epic 5105322* ●	4		12
17 May 03	**THE MATRIX RELOADED** *Maverick 9362484112* ●	2		8
19 Jul 03	**CHARLIE'S ANGELS – FULL THROTTLE** *Columbia 5123062*	12		2
18 Oct 03	**BAD BOYS II** *Bad Boy 750327* ★	17		1
25 Oct 03	**KILL BILL VOLUME 1** *Maverick 9362485882* ●	6		11
29 Nov 03	**LOVE ACTUALLY** *Island 9814032* ●	2		23
27 Mar 04	**ULTIMATE DIRTY DANCING** *RCA 82876555252* ⊛x2	1	2	42
1 May 04	**KILL BILL VOLUME 2** *Maverick 9362486762* ○	13		4
10 Jul 04	**SHREK 2 (OST)** *DreamWorks/Polydor 9862698*	8		7
31 Jul 04	**SPIDER-MAN 2 (OST)** *Columbia 5173679*	17		1
6 Nov 04	**SHARK TALE (OST)** *DreamWorks 9863845*	18		1
20 Nov 04	**BRIDGET JONES – THE EDGE OF REASON (OST)** *Island CID8150* ⊛x2	3		20
15 Jan 05	**THE SOUND OF MUSIC (OST)** *RCA 82876668272*	16		3
1 Oct 05	**SATURDAY NIGHT FEVER** *Polydor 8253892*	19		2
18 Feb 06	**WALK THE LINE (OST)** *Sony BMG 82876762322*	8		7
17 Feb 07	**DREAMGIRLS** *Columbia 88697041032* ★	17		3
28 Jul 07	**HAIRSPRAY** *Decca Pop 4759348*	4		12
3 Nov 07	**DIRTY DANCING** *Sony BMG 88697087622*	5		13
23 Feb 08	**JUNO (OST)** *Rhino 8122799377* ○ ★	7		5
7 Jun 08	**SEX AND THE CITY** *UCJ 4780652*	6		5
19 Jul 08	**MAMMA MIA** *Polydor 1774183* ★	1	10	21
1 Nov 08	**HIGH SCHOOL MUSICAL 3 – SENIOR YEAR** *Walt Disney 2369782*	1	3	6

Top 5 Film Soundtracks of All Time

Pos	Album Title	Approx Sales
1	DIRTY DANCING	3,600,000
2	THE SOUND OF MUSIC	2,485,000
3	GREASE	2,480,000
4	THE BODYGUARD	2,220,000
5	SATURDAY NIGHT FEVER	2,170,000

MISCELLANEOUS

Date	Title / Label	Peak Position	Weeks at No.1	Weeks in Chart
12 Sep 70	**EDINBURGH MILITARY TATTOO 1970** *Waverley SZLP 2121*	34		4
18 Sep 71	**EDINBURGH MILITARY TATTOO 1971** *Waverley SZLP 2128*	44		1
11 Dec 71	**ELECTRONIC ORGANS TODAY** *Ad-Rhythm ADBS 1*	48		1
28 Dec 91	**TRIVIAL PURSUIT – THE MUSIC MASTER GAME** *Telstar STAC 2550*	20		1
22 Jul 00	**HAPPY AND GLORIOUS** *Decca 4671002*	20		1

ORIGINAL CAST RECORDINGS

Date	Title / Label	Peak Position	Weeks at No.1	Weeks in Chart
4 Aug 01	**MY FAIR LADY** *First Night CASTCD 83*	73		1
19 May 07	**HIGH SCHOOL MUSICAL – THE CONCERT** *Walt Disney 3933232*	45		2
12 Jul 08	**MAMMA MIA** *Polydor 9866307*	12		22

ORIGINAL SOUNDTRACK

Date	Title / Label	Peak Position	Weeks at No.1	Weeks in Chart
25 Aug 56	**THE EDDY DUCHIN STORY** *Brunswick LAT 8119* ★	3		4
22 Dec 56	**HIGH SOCIETY (OST)** *Capitol LCT 6116*	2		26
8 Feb 58	**PYJAMA GAME** *Philips BBL 7197*	3		9

ROYAL COMPILATION ALBUM

Date	Title / Label	Peak Position	Weeks at No.1	Weeks in Chart
8 Dec 73	**MUSIC FOR A ROYAL WEDDING (ROYAL COMPILATION ALBUM)** *BBC REW 163*	7		6
1 Aug 81	**ROYAL ROMANCE (ROYAL COMPILATION ALBUM)** *Windsor WIN001*	84		1
8 Aug 81	**THE OFFICIAL BBC ALBUM OF THE ROYAL WEDDING (ROYAL COMPILATION ALBUM)** *BBC REP 413* ●	1	2	11
9 Aug 86	**ROYAL WEDDING (ROYAL COMPILATION ALBUM)** *BBC REP 596*	55		1
27 Sep 97	**DIANA PRINCESS OF WALES 1961–1997 – FUNERAL SERVICE (ROYAL COMPILATION ALBUM)** *BBC Worldwide Classics 4498002*	3		5
13 Dec 97	**DIANA PRINCESS OF WALES – TRIBUTE (ROYAL COMPILATION ALBUM)** *Diana Memorial Fund WR 1001052*	1	4	10

STAGE CAST RECORDING

Date	Title / Label	Peak Position	Weeks at No.1	Weeks in Chart
4 Aug 56	**SALAD DAYS (ORIGINAL LONDON STAGE CAST RECORDING)** *Oriole MG 20004*	5		2
10 May 58	**MY FAIR LADY (ORIGINAL BROADWAY STAGE CAST SOUNDTRACK)** *Philips RBL 1000* ★	1	19	155
24 Jan 59	**WEST SIDE STORY (ORIGINAL BROADWAY STAGE CAST SOUNDTRACK)** *Philips BBL 7277* ★	3		27

Date	Title / Label	Peak Position	Weeks at No.1	Weeks in Chart
26 Mar 60	FINGS AIN'T WOT THEY USED TO BE (ORIGINAL LONDON STAGE CAST SOUNDTRACK) *Decca LK 4346*	5		11
26 Mar 60	AT THE DROP OF A HAT (ORIGINAL LONDON STAGE CAST SOUNDTRACK) *Parlophone PMC 1033*	9		1
2 Apr 60	FLOWER DRUM SONG (ORIGINAL BROADWAY STAGE CAST SOUNDTRACK) *Philips ABL 3302* ★	2		27
7 May 60	FOLLOW THAT GIRL (ORIGINAL LONDON STAGE CAST SOUNDTRACK) *HMV CLP 1366*	5		9
21 May 60	MOST HAPPY FELLA (ORIGINAL BROADWAY STAGE CAST SOUNDTRACK) *Philips BBL 7374*	6		13
21 May 60	MAKE ME AN OFFER (ORIGINAL LONDON STAGE CAST SOUNDTRACK) *HMV CLP 1333*	18		1
28 May 60	FLOWER DRUM SONG (ORIGINAL LONDON STAGE CAST SOUNDTRACK) *HMV CLP 1359*	10		3
25 Jun 60	SHOWBOAT (ORIGINAL STUDIO CAST RECORDING) *HMV CLP 1310*	12		1
9 Jul 60	MOST HAPPY FELLA (ORIGINAL LONDON STAGE CAST SOUNDTRACK) *HMV CLP 1365*	19		1
30 Jul 60	WEST SIDE STORY (ORIGINAL BROADWAY STAGE CAST SOUNDTRACK) *Philips SBBL 504*	14		1
10 Sep 60	OLIVER! (ORIGINAL LONDON STAGE CAST SOUNDTRACK) *Decca LK 4359*	4		91
11 Mar 61	KING KONG (ORIGINAL SOUTH AFRICAN STAGE CAST SOUNDTRACK) *Decca LK 4392*	12		8
6 May 61	MUSIC MAN (ORIGINAL LONDON STAGE CAST SOUNDTRACK) *HMV CLP 1444*	8		13
24 Jun 61	THE SOUND OF MUSIC (ORIGINAL BROADWAY STAGE CAST SOUNDTRACK) *Philips ABL 3370*	4		19
22 Jul 61	BEYOND THE FRINGE (ORIGINAL LONDON STAGE CAST SOUNDTRACK) *Parlophone PMC 1145*	13		17
22 Jul 61	BYE BYE BIRDIE (ORIGINAL LONDON STAGE CAST SOUNDTRACK) *Philips ABL 3385*	17		3
29 Jul 61	THE SOUND OF MUSIC (ORIGINAL LONDON STAGE CAST SOUNDTRACK) *HMV CLP 1453*	4		68
9 Sep 61	STOP THE WORLD – I WANT TO GET OFF (ORIGINAL LONDON STAGE CAST SOUNDTRACK) *Decca LK 4408*	8		14
14 Jul 62	BLITZ (ORIGINAL LONDON STAGE CAST SOUNDTRACK) *HMV CLP 1569*	7		21
18 May 63	HALF A SIXPENCE (ORIGINAL LONDON STAGE CAST SOUNDTRACK) *Decca LK 4521*	20		2
3 Aug 63	PICKWICK (ORIGINAL LONDON STAGE CAST SOUNDTRACK) *Philips AL 3431*	12		10
4 Jan 64	MY FAIR LADY (ORIGINAL BROADWAY STAGE CAST SOUNDTRACK) *CBS BPG 68001*	19		1
22 Feb 64	AT THE DROP OF ANOTHER HAT (ORIGINAL LONDON STAGE CAST SOUNDTRACK) *Parlophone PMC 1216*	12		11
3 Oct 64	CAMELOT (ORIGINAL BROADWAY STAGE CAST SOUNDTRACK) *CBS APG 60001* ★	10		12
16 Jan 65	CAMELOT (ORIGINAL LONDON STAGE CAST SOUNDTRACK) *HMV CLP 1756*	19		1
11 Mar 67	FIDDLER ON THE ROOF (ORIGINAL LONDON STAGE CAST SOUNDTRACK) *CBS SBPG 70030*	4		50
28 Dec 68	HAIR (ORIGINAL LONDON STAGE CAST SOUNDTRACK) *Polydor 583043*	3		94
30 Aug 69	THE WORLD OF OLIVER (ORIGINAL LONDON STAGE CAST SOUNDTRACK) *Decca SPA 30*	23		4
6 Sep 69	HAIR (ORIGINAL BROADWAY STAGE CAST SOUNDTRACK) *RCA SF 7959* ★	29		3
8 Jan 72	JESUS CHRIST SUPERSTAR (ORIGINAL STUDIO CAST RECORDING) *MCA MKPS 2011/2* ●	6		20
19 Feb 72	GODSPELL (ORIGINAL LONDON STAGE CAST SOUNDTRACK) *Arista BELLS 203*	25		17
22 Jan 77	EVITA (ORIGINAL STUDIO CAST RECORDING) *MCA MCX 503* ⊛	4		35
17 Jun 78	WHITE MANSIONS (ORIGINAL STUDIO CAST RECORDING) *A&M AMLX 64691*	51		3
18 Nov 78	EVITA (ORIGINAL LONDON STAGE CAST SOUNDTRACK) *MCA MCF 3257* ⊛	24		18
1 Aug 81	CATS (ORIGINAL LONDON STAGE CAST SOUNDTRACK) *Polydor CATX 001* ○	6		26
6 Nov 82	MACK AND MABEL (ORIGINAL BROADWAY STAGE CAST SOUNDTRACK) *MCA MCL 1728* ○	38		7
4 Aug 84	STARLIGHT EXPRESS (ORIGINAL LONDON STAGE CAST SOUNDTRACK) *Starlight LNER 1* ○	21		9
10 Nov 84	CHESS (ORIGINAL STUDIO CAST RECORDING) *RCA PL 70500* ●	10		16
18 May 85	WEST SIDE STORY (ORIGINAL STUDIO CAST RECORDING) *Deutsche Grammophon 41525* ⊛x2	11		32
2 Nov 85	CHESS PIECES (ORIGINAL STUDIO CAST RECORDING) *Telstar STAR 2274*	87		3
15 Feb 86	LES MISERABLES (ORIGINAL LONDON STAGE CAST SOUNDTRACK) *First Night ENCORE 1*	72		4
10 May 86	HIGHLIGHTS FROM WEST SIDE STORY (ORIGINAL STUDIO CAST RECORDING) *Deutsche Grammophon 45963*	72		6
17 May 86	DAVE CLARK'S TIME THE ALBUM (ORIGINAL STUDIO CAST RECORDING) *EMI AMPH 1*	21		6
11 Oct 86	SOUTH PACIFIC (ORIGINAL STUDIO CAST RECORDING) *CBS SM 42205* ⊛ ★	5		24
21 Feb 87	THE PHANTOM OF THE OPERA (ORIGINAL LONDON STAGE CAST SOUNDTRACK) *Really Useful PODV 3* ⊛x3	1	3	141
13 Jun 87	MATADOR (ORIGINAL STUDIO CAST RECORDING) *Epic VIVA 1*	26		5
21 Nov 87	MY FAIR LADY (ORIGINAL STUDIO CAST RECORDING) *Decca MFL 1* ●	41		12
16 Sep 89	ASPECTS OF LOVE (ORIGINAL LONDON STAGE CAST SOUNDTRACK) *Really Useful/Polydor 8411261* ⊛	1	1	29
24 Feb 90	MISS SAIGON (ORIGINAL LONDON STAGE CAST SOUNDTRACK) *Geffen WX 329* ●	4		11
29 Jun 91	FIVE GUYS NAMED MOE (ORIGINAL LONDON STAGE CAST SOUNDTRACK) *First Night CAST 23*	59		1
10 Oct 92	THE KING AND I (ORIGINAL STUDIO CAST RECORDING) *Philips 4380072*	57		2
10 Apr 93	LEONARD BERNSTEIN'S WEST SIDE STORY (ORIGINAL STUDIO CAST RECORDING) *IMG IMGCD 1801*	33		3
10 Apr 93	THE NEW STARLIGHT EXPRESS (ORIGINAL LONDON STAGE CAST SOUNDTRACK) *Really Useful/Polydor 5190412*	42		2
11 Sep 93	SUNSET BOULEVARD (ORIGINAL LONDON STAGE CAST SOUNDTRACK) *Really Useful/Polydor 5197672*	11		4
2 Oct 93	GREASE (ORIGINAL LONDON STAGE CAST SOUNDTRACK) *Epic 4746322*	20		3
1 Apr 95	OLIVER! (1994 LONDON CAST) (ORIGINAL LONDON STAGE CAST SOUNDTRACK) *First Night CASTCD 47*	36		3
11 May 96	LES MISERABLES – 10TH ANNIVERSARY CONCERT (ORIGINAL LONDON STAGE CAST SOUNDTRACK) *First Night ENCORECD 8*	32		7
16 Nov 96	MARTIN GUERRE (ORIGINAL LONDON STAGE CAST SOUNDTRACK) *First Night CASTCD 70*	58		1
14 Dec 96	HEATHCLIFF LIVE (THE SHOW) (ORIGINAL LONDON STAGE CAST SOUNDTRACK) *EMI CDEMDEUK 1099*	41		4
27 Jun 98	CHICAGO – THE MUSICAL (ORIGINAL LONDON STAGE CAST SOUNDTRACK) *RCA Victor 09026631552*	61		1
22 Aug 98	SATURDAY NIGHT FEVER (ORIGINAL LONDON STAGE CAST SOUNDTRACK) *Polydor 5579322*	17		6
13 Nov 99	MAMMA MIA! (ORIGINAL LONDON STAGE CAST SOUNDTRACK) *Polydor 5431152*	56		2
8 Apr 00	THE ARISTOCATS – READ ALONG (ORIGINAL CAST RECORDING) *Walt Disney WD 713914*	60		1

TELEVISION AND RADIO COMPILATION

Date	Title / Label	Peak Position	Weeks at No.1	Weeks in Chart
13 Dec 58	JACK GOOD'S 'OH BOY' (TELEVISION COMPILATION) *Parlophone PMC 1072*	9		14
4 Mar 61	HUCKLEBERRY HOUND (TELEVISION SOUNDTRACK) *Pye Golden Guinea GGL 004*	10		12
2 Mar 63	THAT WAS THE WEEK THAT WAS (TELEVISION SOUNDTRACK) *Parlophone PMC 1197*	11		9
28 Mar 64	STARS FROM STARS AND GARTERS (TELEVISION COMPILATION) *Pye Golden Guinea GGL 0252*	17		2
4 Nov 72	THE BBC 1922–1972 (TV AND RADIO EXTRACTS) *BBC 50*	16		7
6 Dec 75	SUPERSONIC (TELEVISION COMPILATION) *Stallion SSM 001*	21		6
10 Apr 76	ROCK FOLLIES (TELEVISION SOUNDTRACK) *Island ILPS 9362* ●	1	3	15
11 Mar 78	FONZIE'S FAVOURITES (TELEVISION COMPILATION) *Warwick WW 5037*	8		16
8 Apr 78	PENNIES FROM HEAVEN (TELEVISION SOUNDTRACK) *World Records SH 266* ●	10		17
1 Jul 78	MORE PENNIES FROM HEAVEN (TELEVISION SOUNDTRACK) *World Records SH 267*	31		4
9 Dec 78	STARS ON SUNDAY BY REQUEST (TELEVISION COMPILATION) *Curzon Sounds CSL 0081*	65		3
15 Dec 79	FAWLTY TOWERS (TELEVISION SOUNDTRACK) *BBC REB 377* ○	25		10
7 Feb 81	FAWLTY TOWERS VOLUME 2 (TV ORIGINAL CAST) *BBC REB 405*	26		7
14 Feb 81	THE HITCHHIKERS GUIDE TO THE GALAXY VOLUME 2 (TELEVISION SOUNDTRACK) *Original ORA 54* ○	47		4
1 Aug 81	THE MUSIC OF THE COSMOS (TELEVISION SOUNDTRACK) *RCA RCALP 5032*	43		10
21 Nov 81	BRIDESHEAD REVISITED (OST – TV – CONDUCTED BY GEOFFREY BURGON) *Chrysalis CDL 1367* ○	50		12
23 Oct 82	ON THE AIR – 60 YEARS OF BBC THEME MUSIC (TV & RADIO COMPILATION) *BBC REF 454*	85		3
26 Nov 83	REILLY ACE OF THEMES (TELEVISION SOUNDTRACK) *Red Bus BUSLP 1004*	54		6
4 Feb 84	ORIGINAL MUSIC FROM AUF WIEDERSEHEN PET (TELEVISION SOUNDTRACK) *Towerbell AUF 1*	21		6
18 Feb 84	THE TUBE (TELEVISION COMPILATION) *K-Tel NE 1261*	30		6

Silver-selling ○ Gold-selling ● Platinum-selling ⊛ US No.1 ★

Date	Title	Peak Position	Weeks at No.1	Weeks on Chart
8 Sep 84	**SONG AND DANCE (TELEVISION SOUNDTRACK)** *RCA BL 70480*	46		4
18 May 85	**VICTORY IN EUROPE – BROADCASTS AND REPORTS FROM BBC CORRESPONDENTS (RADIO SOUNDTRACK)** *BBC REC 562*	61		1
28 Sep 85	**THE TV HITS ALBUM (TELEVISION COMPILATION)** *Towerbell TVLP 3* ○	26		13
26 Oct 85	**MUSIC FROM THE TELEVISION SERIES 'MIAMI VICE' (TELEVISION SOUNDTRACK)** *BBC REMV 584* ●	11		9
16 Nov 85	**THE EASTENDERS SING-ALONG ALBUM (TELEVISION COMPILATION)** *BBC REB 586* ●	33		10
23 Nov 85	**TELLYHITS – 16 TOP TV THEMES (TELEVISION COMPILATION)** *Stylus/BBC BBSR 508* ●	34		6
15 Feb 86	**JONATHAN KING'S ENTERTAINMENT FROM THE U.S.A. (TELEVISION COMPILATION)** *Stylus SMR 6812* ●	6		11
12 Apr 86	**THE TV HITS ALBUM TWO – 16 ORIGINAL HIT-TV THEMES (TELEVISION COMPILATION)** *Towerbell TVLP 10* ○	19		7
5 Jul 86	**TELLYHITS 2 – 16 TOP TV THEMES (TELEVISION COMPILATION)** *Stylus/BBC BBSR 616*	68		2
18 Oct 86	**THE VERY BEST OF ENTERTAINMENT FROM THE U.S.A. VOLUME 2 (TELEVISION COMPILATION)** *PrioriTyV UPTVR 1*	44		4
6 Dec 86	**MUSIC FROM THE BBC-TV SERIES 'THE SINGING DETECTIVE' (TELEVISION SOUNDTRACK)** *BBC REN 608* ●	10		24
27 Jun 87	**THE ROCK 'N' ROLL YEARS 1964–1967 (TELEVISION COMPILATION)** *BBC REN 633*	71		2
27 Jun 87	**THE ROCK 'N' ROLL YEARS 1968–1971 (TELEVISION COMPILATION)** *BBC REN 634*	77		1
27 Jun 87	**THE ROCK 'N' ROLL YEARS 1956–1959 (TELEVISION COMPILATION)** *BBC REN 631*	80		2
27 Jun 87	**THE ROCK 'N' ROLL YEARS 1960–1963 (TELEVISION COMPILATION)** *BBC REN 632*	84		1
3 Oct 87	**MOONLIGHTING "THE TV SOUNDTRACK ALBUM" (TELEVISION SOUNDTRACK)** *MCA MCF 3386*	50		6
17 Oct 87	**MIAMI VICE 2 (TELEVISION SOUNDTRACK)** *MCA MCG 6019*	71		4
28 Nov 87	**THE CHART SHOW – DANCE HITS 1987 (TELEVISION COMPILATION)** *Chrysalis ADD 1* ○	39		6
26 Mar 88	**THE CHART SHOW – ROCK THE NATION (TELEVISION COMPILATION)** *Dover ADD 2* ●	16		8
1 Oct 88	**MOONLIGHTING 2 (TELEVISION SOUNDTRACK)** *WEA WX 202* ●	5		9
1 Oct 88	**MIAMI VICE III (TELEVISION SOUNDTRACK)** *MCA MCG 6033*	95		1
20 May 89	**THE CHART SHOW – ROCK THE NATION 2 (TELEVISION COMPILATION)** *Dover ADD 4* ○	8		4
3 Jun 89	**THE CHART SHOW – DANCE MASTERS (TELEVISION COMPILATION)** *Dover ADD 7* ○	4		7
23 Sep 89	**TV TUNES (TELEVISION COMPILATION)** *K-Tel NE 1446*	17		3
17 Feb 90	**PENNIES FROM HEAVEN (TELEVISION SOUNDTRACK)** *BBC REF 768*	8		13
21 Sep 91	**THE OLD GREY WHISTLE TEST – THE BEST OF THE TEST (TELEVISION COMPILATION)** *Windsong International OGWTLP 1*	13		3
18 Jul 92	**DOCTOR WHO – THE EVIL OF THE DALEKS (RADIO SOUNDTRACK)** *BBC ZBBC 1303*	72		1
28 Nov 92	**GLADIATORS (TELEVISION SOUNDTRACK)** *Polygram TV 5158772* ●	11		10
30 Jan 93	**THE BEST OF THE CLASSICAL BITS (TELEVISION COMPILATION)** *Philips 4381662*	7		10
13 Feb 93	**HEAD OVER HEELS (TELEVISION SOUNDTRACK)** *Telstar TCD 2510*	3		9
13 Mar 93	**LIPSTICK ON YOUR COLLAR – 28 ORIGINAL HITS OF THE 50S (TELEVISION SOUNDTRACK)** *Polygram TV 5160862* ●	2		13
17 Apr 93	**THE CHART SHOW – THE ULTIMATE ROCK ALBUM (TELEVISION COMPILATION)** *The Hit Label AHLCD 9* ●	4		11
7 Aug 93	**THE BIG BREAKFAST ALBUM (TELEVISION COMPILATION)** *Arcade ARC 3100082*	8		5
14 Aug 93	**DOCTOR WHO – THE POWER OF THE DALEKS (TELEVISION SOUNDTRACK)** *BBC ZBBC 1433*	71		1
18 Sep 93	**DOCTOR WHO – THE PARADISE OF DEATH (RADIO SOUNDTRACK)** *BBC ZBBC 1494*	48		1
2 Oct 93	**THE CHART SHOW – ULTIMATE ROCK 2 (TELEVISION COMPILATION)** *The Hit Label AHLCD 13* ○	10		3
23 Oct 93	**TALES FROM THE CITY (TELEVISION COMPILATION)** *Polygram TV 5165152*	17		2
20 Nov 93	**RETURN OF THE GLADIATORS (TELEVISION COMPILATION)** *Polygram TV 5165172*	20		1
4 Jun 94	**TOP GEAR (TELEVISION COMPILATION)** *Epic MOODCD 33* ●	3		13
16 Jul 94	**CHART SHOW – ULTIMATE BLUES ALBUM (TELEVISION COMPILATION)** *The Hit Label AHLCD 19*	13		3
22 Oct 94	**DR. HILARY JONES CLASSIC RELAXATION (TELEVISION COMPILATION)** *Polygram TV 4458112*	13		2
20 May 95	**THE CHART SHOW PRESENTS THE CHART MACHINE (TELEVISION COMPILATION)** *Polygram TV 5250392*	18		2
24 Jun 95	**TOP GEAR CLASSICS – TURBO CLASSICS (TELEVISION COMPILATION)** *Deutsche Grammophon 4479412*	17		1
5 Aug 95	**THE CHART SHOW DANCE ALBUM (TELEVISION COMPILATION)** *Polygram TV 5257682* ○	6		3
18 Nov 95	**THE CORONATION STREET ALBUM (TELEVISION COMPILATION)** *EMI Premier CDCOROTV 1*	20		1
9 Mar 96	**TOP GEAR 3 (TELEVISION COMPILATION)** *Columbia SONYTV 12CD*	11		4
17 Aug 96	**INDEPENDENCE DAY UK (RADIO SOUNDTRACK)** *Speaking Volumes 5329634*	66		2
9 Nov 96	**TOP GEAR – ON THE ROAD AGAIN (TELEVISION COMPILATION)** *EMI TV CDEMTVD 132* ○	12		3
2 Aug 97	**AFTER THE BREAK (TELEVISION COMPILATION)** *Columbia SONYTV 30CD*	17		1
13 Sep 97	**IBIZA UNCOVERED (TELEVISION COMPILATION)** *Virgin/EMI VTDCD 168* ⊛	1	4	10
8 Nov 97	**READY STEADY GO! – NUMBER ONE SIXTIES ALBUM (TELEVISION COMPILATION)** *Polygram TV 5539342* ●	10		2
21 Mar 98	**READY STEADY GO! – SIXTIES MOTOWN SOUND (TELEVISION COMPILATION)** *Polygram TV 5308652* ●	5		5
22 Aug 98	**IBIZA UNCOVERED 2 (TELEVISION COMPILATION)** *Virgin/EMI VTDCD 202*	2		9
26 Sep 98	**TOP GEAR ANTHEMS (TELEVISION COMPILATION)** *Virgin/EMI VTDCD 192* ○	6		6
3 Oct 98	**STARSKY AND HUTCH PRESENTS (TELEVISION COMPILATION)** *Virgin/EMI VTDCDX 205*	13		2
5 Dec 98	**CHEF AID – THE SOUTH PARK ALBUM (TELEVISION SOUNDTRACK)** *Columbia 4917002* ⊛	2		14
3 Apr 99	**LIVE & KICKING – VIEWERS CHOICE PART 1 (TELEVISION COMPILATION)** *Virgin/EMI VTCD 244*	12		3
17 Apr 99	**QUEER AS FOLK – THE WHOLE THING SORTED (TELEVISION SOUNDTRACK)** *Almighty ALMYCD 28*	2		9
12 Jun 99	**SONGS FROM DAWSON'S CREEK (TELEVISION SOUNDTRACK)** *Columbia 4943692* ●	3		11
28 Aug 99	**MTV IBIZA 99 (TELEVISION COMPILATION)** *Columbia SONYTV 72CD*	10		3
2 Oct 99	**IBIZA UNCOVERED – THE RETURN (TELEVISION COMPILATION)** *Virgin/EMI VTDCD 255* ●	2		7
23 Oct 99	**SEX, CHIPS & ROCK 'N' ROLL (TELEVISION SOUNDTRACK)** *Virgin/EMI VTDCD 264*	12		1
20 Nov 99	**BUFFY THE VAMPIRE SLAYER – THE ALBUM (TELEVISION SOUNDTRACK)** *Columbia 4966332* ●	7		2
27 Nov 99	**MUSIC OF THE MILLENNIUM (TELEVISION COMPILATION)** *Universal/Virgin/EMI 5453002* ⊛x2	2		16
26 Feb 00	**QUEER AS FOLK 2 (TELEVISION SOUNDTRACK)** *Channel 4 Music C4M 00012*	5		5
11 Mar 00	**THE GRIMLEYS – ORIGINAL TV SOUNDTRACK** *Global TV RADCD 157*	17		1
26 Aug 00	**BIG BROTHER OST (TELEVISION SOUNDTRACK)** *Channel 4 Music C4M 00062*	17		3
28 Oct 00	**SONGS FROM DAWSON'S CREEK – VOL 2 (TELEVISION SOUNDTRACK)** *Columbia 5009242*	5		3
30 Dec 00	**MORE COLD FEET – OST (TELEVISION SOUNDTRACK)** *BMG TV Projects 74321789612*	18		1
26 May 01	**TRIGGER HAPPY TV – SERIES 2** *Channel 4 Music C4M 00122*	15		2
8 Dec 01	**COLD FEET (OST)** *Universal TV 5859132* ●	13		8
15 Mar 03	**THE VERY BEST OF COLD FEET** *Universal TV 0688202* ⊛	1	2	10
1 Nov 03	**BUFFY THE VAMPIRE SLAYER** *Virgin/EMI VTCD 587*	12		2
13 Mar 04	**SEX AND THE CITY** *Sony Music TV STVCD 172* ●	6		8
22 May 04	**THE OC** *Warner Brothers 9362487672*	14		2
30 Sep 06	**HIGH SCHOOL MUSICAL** *Walt Disney 3654622* ⊛x3 ★	1	3	87
18 Nov 06	**LAZY TOWN – THE ALBUM** *Gut Active GACD10*	8		4
25 Nov 06	**THE VERY BEST OF HEARTBEAT – THE ALBUM** *EMI Virgin VTDCD828* ●	14		6
6 Jan 07	**HANNAH MONTANA** *Walt Disney DSN616202* ● ★	8		18
3 Mar 07	**LIFE ON MARS** *EMI TV/Sony BMG 88697065872*	11		11
21 Jul 07	**HANNAH MONTANA 2/MEET MILEY CYRUS** *Walt Disney 5014632* ● ★	8		6
25 Aug 07	**HIGH SCHOOL MUSICAL 2** *Walt Disney 5027642* ⊛ ★	1	7	39
27 Oct 07	**LAZY TOWN – THE NEW ALBUM** *Gut GTVCD18*	12		2
29 Mar 08	**ASHES TO ASHES** *Sony BMG 88697290762*	2		8
20 Sep 08	**CAMP ROCK** *Walt Disney 2265402*	3		11

VARIOUS ARTISTS (2 TONE)

Date	Title	Peak Position	Weeks at No.1	Weeks on Chart
26 Nov 83	**THIS ARE TWO TONE** *2-Tone CHRTT 5007*	51		9
5 Aug 89	**THE 2 TONE STORY** *2-Tone CHRTT 5009*	16		5
23 Oct 93	**THE BEST OF 2 TONE** *2-Tone CDCHRTT 5012*	10		4

VARIOUS ARTISTS (4 AD)

Date	Title	Peak Position	Weeks at No.1	Weeks on Chart
11 Jul 87	**LONELY IS AN EYESORE** *4AD CAD 703*	53		2

VARIOUS ARTISTS (4 BEAT)

Date	Title	Peak Position	Weeks at No.1	Weeks on Chart
20 Jan 96	**UNITED – VOLUME 3** *4 Beat FBRCD 334*	11		2
25 May 96	**UNITED DANCE – VOLUME FOUR** *4 Beat FBRCD 335*	17		1
9 Nov 96	**UNITED – VOLUME 5** *4 Beat FBRCD 336*	20		1
26 Apr 97	**UNITED – VOLUME 6** *4 Beat FBRCD 337*	10		3

VARIOUS ARTISTS (A&M)

Date	Title	Peak Position	Weeks at No.1	Weeks on Chart
2 May 87	**PRINCE'S TRUST TENTH ANNIVERSARY BIRTHDAY PARTY** *A&M AMA 3906*	76		3
22 Aug 87	**THE PRINCE'S TRUST CONCERT 1987** *A&M PTA 1987*	44		3
5 Dec 87	**SPECIAL OLYMPICS – A VERY SPECIAL CHRISTMAS** *A&M AMA 3911* ●	40		5
23 Dec 89	**SPECIAL OLYMPICS – A VERY SPECIAL CHRISTMAS** *A&M AMA 3911*	19		1
29 Sep 90	**SLAMMIN'** *A&M SLAMM 1* ●	1	1	6
20 Apr 91	**RAGE – MAKE SOME NOISE** *A&M AMTV 1*	12		3
29 Jun 91	**WINGS OF LOVE** *A&M 8455062* ●	1	5	21
4 Nov 95	**THE HACIENDA – PLAY BY 01/96** *A&M 5404452*	18		1

VARIOUS ARTISTS (ABKO)

Date	Title	Peak Position	Weeks at No.1	Weeks on Chart
26 Oct 96	**THE ROLLING STONES ROCK AND ROLL CIRCUS** *ABKCO 12682*	12		1

VARIOUS ARTISTS (ABSTRACT)

Date	Title	Peak Position	Weeks at No.1	Weeks on Chart
27 Mar 82	**PUNK AND DISORDERLY** *Abstract AABT 100*	48		8

VARIOUS ARTISTS (ACE OF HEARTS)

Date	Title	Peak Position	Weeks at No.1	Weeks on Chart
16 May 64	**OUT CAME THE BLUES** *Ace Of Hearts AH 72*	19		1

VARIOUS ARTISTS (ACID JAZZ)

Date	Title	Peak Position	Weeks at No.1	Weeks on Chart
29 May 93	**BEST OF ACID JAZZ VOLUME 2** *Acid Jazz JAZIDCD 66*	16		1

VARIOUS ARTISTS (ALL AROUND THE WORLD)

Date	Title	Peak Position	Weeks at No.1	Weeks on Chart
22 Aug 98	**ROCK THE DANCEFLOOR** *All Around The World GLOBECD 9*	9		2
3 Apr 99	**ROCK THE DANCEFLOOR 2** *All Around The World GLOBECD 11*	7		1
30 Jun 01	**ROCK THE DANCEFLOOR VOLUME 5** *All Around The World GLOBECD 21*	19		1
21 Jun 03	**ROCK THE DANCEFLOOR 8** *All Around The World GLOBECD 43*	17		1
3 Jun 06	**ULTIMATE NRG** *All Around The World GLOBECD49*	3		5

VARIOUS ARTISTS (ALTERNATIVE TENTACLES)

Date	Title	Peak Position	Weeks at No.1	Weeks on Chart
9 May 92	**VIRUS 100 – ALTERNATIVE TENTACLES** *Alternative Tentacles 100CD*	15		1

VARIOUS ARTISTS (ANAGRAM)

Date	Title	Peak Position	Weeks at No.1	Weeks on Chart
4 Sep 82	**PUNK AND DISORDERLY (FURTHER CHARGES)** *Anagram GRAM 001*	91		2

VARIOUS ARTISTS (APACE)

Date	Title	Peak Position	Weeks at No.1	Weeks on Chart
8 Mar 08	**JUST FOR MUM** *Apace Music PCOLLCD26*	20		1
21 Jun 08	**JUST FOR DAD** *Apace Music PCOLLCD28*	18		1

VARIOUS ARTISTS (APPLE)

Date	Title	Peak Position	Weeks at No.1	Weeks on Chart
22 Jan 72	**CONCERT FOR BANGLADESH (RECORDED LIVE)** *Apple STCX 3385*	1	1	13

VARIOUS ARTISTS (ARCADE)

Date	Title	Peak Position	Weeks at No.1	Weeks on Chart
29 Jul 72	**20 FANTASTIC HITS** *Arcade 2891 001*	1	6	24
25 Nov 72	**20 FANTASTIC HITS VOLUME 2** *Arcade 2891 002*	2		14
7 Apr 73	**40 FANTASTIC HITS FROM THE 50'S AND 60'S** *Arcade ADEP 3/4*	2		15
26 May 73	**20 FANTASTIC HITS VOLUME 3** *Arcade ADEP 5*	3		8
15 Nov 75	**DISCO HITS '75** *Arcade ADEP 18*	5		11
26 Mar 77	**ROCK ON** *Arcade ADEP 27*	16		10
4 Jun 77	**RULE BRITANNIA** *Arcade ADEP 29*	56		1
23 Feb 80	**FIRST LOVE** *Arcade ADEP 41*	58		2
12 Jan 91	**POP CLASSICS – 28 CLASSIC TRACKS** *Arcade ARC 944421*	19		2
30 Mar 91	**SOFT METAL BALLADS** *Arcade ARC 933501*	5		10
8 Jun 91	**IT STARTED WITH A KISS** *Arcade ARC 910301*	9		8
13 Jul 91	**THE HEAT IS ON** *Arcade ARC 925401*	4		9
31 Aug 91	**DANCE CLASSICS VOLUME 2** *Arcade ARC 925511*	7		5
31 Aug 91	**DANCE CLASSICS VOLUME 1** *Arcade ARC 925501*	8		4
21 Sep 91	**GROOVY GHETTO** *Arcade ARC 925601*	1	2	6
2 Nov 91	**GROOVY GHETTO – ALL THE RAGE** *Arcade ARC 925701*	15		2
14 Dec 91	**CHRISTMAS LOVE SONGS** *Arcade ARC 948201*	11		6
29 Feb 92	**GROOVY GHETTO 2** *Arcade ARC 948102*	8		4
4 Apr 92	**THE ESSENTIAL CHILL** *Arcade 948902*	16		2
18 Jul 92	**ONE LOVE – THE VERY BEST OF REGGAE** *Arcade ARC 94961*	7		6
13 Feb 93	**ROCK ROMANCE** *Arcade 3011132*	9		5
7 May 94	**WOW! – LET THE MUSIC LIFT YOU UP** *Arcade ARC 3100112*	13		3
13 Aug 94	**COMMITTED TO SOUL** *Arcade ARC 3100142*	11		7

VARIOUS ARTISTS (ARIOLA)

Date	Title	Peak Position	Weeks at No.1	Weeks on Chart
8 Oct 88	**BROTHERS IN RHYTHM** *Ariola 303374*	35		5
11 Feb 89	**RARE 3** *Ariola 209498*	15		2

VARIOUS ARTISTS (ARISTA)

Date	Title	Peak Position	Weeks at No.1	Weeks on Chart
3 Nov 79	**MODS MAYDAY 79** *Arista FOUR 1*	75		1
30 Aug 03	**THE NEPTUNES PRESENTS CLONES** *Arista 82876533862* ● ★	2		8

VARIOUS ARTISTS (ATLANTIC)

Date	Title	Peak Position	Weeks at No.1	Weeks on Chart
2 Apr 66	**SOLID GOLD SOUL** *Atlantic ATL 5048*	12		27
5 Nov 66	**MIDNIGHT SOUL** *Atlantic 587 021*	22		19
14 Jun 69	**THIS IS SOUL** *Atlantic 643 301*	16		15
25 Mar 72	**THE NEW AGE OF ATLANTIC** *Atlantic K 20024*	25		1
22 Jun 74	**ATLANTIC BLACK GOLD** *Atlantic K 40550*	23		7
3 Apr 76	**BY INVITATION ONLY** *Atlantic K 60112* ○	17		6
11 Apr 81	**CONCERTS FOR THE PEOPLE OF KAMPUCHEA** *Atlantic K 60153*	39		2
2 Feb 85	**THIS IS SOUL** *Atlantic SOUL 1*	78		7
6 Jun 87	**ATLANTIC SOUL CLASSICS** *Atlantic WX 105* ⊛	9		23
18 Jun 88	**ATLANTIC SOUL BALLADS** *Atlantic WX 98*	84		2
3 Sep 05	**GOOD TIMES – THE VERY BEST OF (CHIC & SISTER SLEDGE)** *Atlantic/WSM 8122732332*	16		1
29 Mar 08	**STEP UP 2 – THE STREETS** *Atlantic 7567899545* ●	6		14

VARIOUS ARTISTS (AZULI)

Date	Title	Peak Position	Weeks at No.1	Weeks on Chart
19 Feb 00	**BLACKMARKET PRESENTS 2 STEP** *Azuli A2CD 004*	17		1
15 Jun 02	**ANOTHER LATE NIGHT – GROOVE ARMADA** *Azuli ALNCD 05*	20		1

VARIOUS ARTISTS (B UNIQUE)

Date	Title	Peak Position	Weeks at No.1	Weeks on Chart
26 Oct 02	**NME IN ASSOCIATION WITH WAR CHILD PRESENTS 1 LOVE** *B Unique 0927493712* ○	2		3

VARIOUS ARTISTS (BBC)

Date	Title	Peak Position	Weeks at No.1	Weeks on Chart
4 Jan 75	**BBC TV'S BEST OF TOP OF THE POPS** *Super Beeb BELP 001*	21		5
22 Oct 77	**10 YEARS OF HITS – RADIO ONE** *Super Beeb DBEDP 002* ○	39		3
8 Oct 88	**ONES ON 1** *BBC REF 693* ●	10		7
17 Jun 89	**RAY MOORE – A PERSONAL CHOICE** *BBC STAR 2352*	7		4
14 Oct 00	**BBC COUNTRY HITS** *BBC 74321789652*	20		1

VARIOUS ARTISTS (BEECHWOOD)

Date	Title	Peak Position	Weeks at No.1	Weeks on Chart
11 May 91	**THE BEST OF INDIE TOP 20** *Beechwood Music BOTT 1*	10		3
9 Mar 96	**THIS IS ...SWING** *Beechwood Music BEBOXCD 1*	20		1
13 Jul 96	**THIS IS ...HOUSE** *Beechwood Music BEBOXCD 4*	18		1
12 Jul 97	**THIS IS ...CLUB NATION** *Beechwood Music BEBOXCD 13*	19		1
11 Oct 97	**THIS IS ...IBIZA** *Beechwood Music BEBOXCD 14*	13		3
31 Jan 98	**THIS IS ...SPEED GARAGE** *Beechwood Music BEBOXCD 17*	10		3
21 Mar 98	**THIS IS ...CLUB NATION 2** *Beechwood Music BEBOXCD 18*	19		1
26 Sep 98	**THIS IS ...IBIZA 98** *Beechwood Music BEBOXCD 22*	16		2
30 Jan 99	**THIS IS ...R&B** *Beechwood Music BEBOXCD 25*	14		2
5 Jun 99	**THIS IS ...IBIZA 2000** *Beechwood Music BEBOXCD 28*	17		1
17 Jul 99	**THIS IS ...TRANCE** *Beechwood Music BEBOXCD 30*	19		1
5 Feb 00	**THIS IS...TRANCELIFE** *Beechwood Music BEBOXCD 35*	19		1
19 Feb 00	**SLINKY – TECH-NIQUE** *Beechwood Music SLINKYCD 002*	10		2
1 Jul 00	**SLINKY FACTOR 3** *Beechwood Music SLINKYCD 03L*	20		1

Key: ○ Silver-selling ● Gold-selling ⊛ Platinum-selling ★ US No.1 — Peak Position / Weeks at No.1 / Weeks on Chart

VARIOUS ARTISTS (BEGGARS BANQUET)

Date	Title / Label	Peak Position	Weeks at No.1	Weeks on Chart
21 Nov 81	**SLIP STREAM** *Beggars Banquet BEGA 31*	72		3
15 May 82	**SEX SWEAT AND BLOOD** *Beggars Banquet BEGA 34*	88		1
11 Sep 82	**THE BEST OF BRITISH JAZZ FUNK VOLUME 2** *Beggars Banquet BEGA 41*	44		4

VARIOUS ARTISTS (BEYOND)

Date	Title / Label	Peak Position	Weeks at No.1	Weeks on Chart
6 Mar 93	**AMBIENT DUB VOLUME 2 – EARTH JUICE** *Beyond RABDCD 3*	20		1

VARIOUS ARTISTS (BIG BEAT)

Date	Title / Label	Peak Position	Weeks at No.1	Weeks on Chart
21 Jul 84	**ROCKABILLY PSYCHOS AND THE GARAGE DISEASE** *Big Beat WIK 18*	88		3

VARIOUS ARTISTS (BLACK HOLE)

Date	Title / Label	Peak Position	Weeks at No.1	Weeks on Chart
6 May 06	**TIESTO – IN SEARCH OF SUNRISE** *Black Hole SONGBIRDCD09*	12		1
29 Sep 07	**TIESTO – IN SEARCH OF SUNRISE 6 – IBIZA** *Black Hole SONGBIRDCD10*	12		2
28 Jun 08	**TIESTO – IN SEARCH OF SUNRISE 7 – ASIA** *Black Hole SONGBIRDCD11*	14		1

VARIOUS ARTISTS (BMG)

Date	Title / Label	Peak Position	Weeks at No.1	Weeks on Chart
14 Oct 00	**CD UK** *UMTV/Sony TV/Global 74321792852*	7		4
28 Oct 00	**STREET VIBES 6** *Sony TV/BMG TV 74321792512*	6		4
25 Nov 00	**HEARTBEAT – 10TH ANNIVERSARY ALBUM** *BMG TV Projects 74321789632*	17		2
30 Dec 00	**MOTOWN MANIA** *BMGTV/UMTV MCD 60075*	9		2
3 Feb 01	**CD:UK – MORE WICKED HITS** *UMTV/Sony TV/Global 74321826692*	9		3
31 Mar 01	**MUSIC – THE DEFINITIVE HITS COLLECTION** *BMG/Sony/Telstar/WSM MUSICCD 1*	4		5
23 Jun 01	**MUSIC – THE DEFINITIVE HITS COLLECTION 2** *BMG/Sony/Telstar/WSM MUSICCD 2*	7		3
8 Sep 01	**STREET VIBES 8** *BMG/Sony/Telstar 74321879472*	4		6
29 Sep 01	**HITS 50** *BMG/Sony/Telstar/WSM HUTSCD 501*	1	2	6
15 Dec 01	**CHRISTMAS HITS** *BMG/Sony/Telstar/WSM HITSCDX 01*	4		12
15 Dec 01	**HITS 51** *BMG/Sony/Telstar/WSM HITSCD 511*	10		6
19 Jan 02	**THE RHYTHMS OF A NATION** *BMG TV Projects 74321910092*	20		1
6 Apr 02	**HITS 52** *BMG/Sony/Telstar/WSM HITSCD 521*	2		9
25 May 02	**URBAN VIBES** *BMG TV Projects 74321941932*	13		2
10 Aug 02	**HITS 53** *BMG/Sony/Telstar/WSM HITSCD 531*	2		11
2 Nov 02	**HITS 54** *BMG/Sony/Telstar/WSM HITSCD 541* ○	1	2	4
30 Nov 02	**HUGE HITS 2003** *BMG/Sony/Telstar/WSM HITSCD 2003* ⊛	4		10
15 Feb 03	**LATE NIGHT LOVE** *Sony TV/BMG TV 82876503442*	8		2
1 Mar 03	**BRIT AWARDS ALBUM** *BMG 82876504062*	5		4
12 Apr 03	**HITS 55** *BMG/Sony/Telstar/WSM HITSCD 551*	1	2	9
26 Jul 03	**HITS 56** *BMG/Sony/Telstar HITSCD561* ●	1	1	6
2 Aug 03	**DAVE PEARCE DANCE ANTHEMS – SUMMER 2003** *BMG/MOS/Telstar INSPCD31* ○	6		4
6 Sep 03	**SK8ER ROCK** *BMG/Telstar TV/UMTV 82876552512*	8		6
1 Nov 03	**HUGE HITS 2004 – THE VERY BEST OF HITS** *BMG/Sony/Telstar/WSM 82876573442*	3		4
13 Dec 03	**HITS 57** *BMG/Sony/Telstar/WSM 82876573832*	5		6
14 Feb 04	**BEAUTIFUL** *BMG TV Projects 82876591692*	1	1	4
28 Feb 04	**THE BRIT AWARDS ALBUM 2004** *BMG 82876590892*	1	1	3
13 Mar 04	**HIT 40 UK** *BMG/Sony/Telstar/WSM 5046720232* ○	1	1	5
20 Mar 04	**NATURAL WOMAN** *BMG TV/Sony TV 82876606672*	5		4
17 Apr 04	**FOX KIDS PARTY HITS** *BMG TV/Jive 82876608142*	15		2
12 Jun 04	**HITS 58** *BMG/Sony/Telstar/WSM 5046738352*	1	1	8
19 Jun 04	**WE LOVE MAMBO** *BMG TV Projects 82876622552*	11		5
26 Jun 04	**CRUISE CONTROL** *BMG TV/UMTV 82876624302*	19		1
3 Jul 04	**ESSENTIAL R&B – THE VERY BEST OF R&B** *BMG TV Projects 82876622562*	1	2	13
3 Jul 04	**MISS INDEPENDENT** *BMG TV Projects 82876622612*	11		4
17 Jul 04	**KINGS OF ROCK 'N' ROLL** *BMG/EMI Virgin/UMTV 82876624312*	11		2
4 Sep 04	**SK8ER ROCK** *BMG TV/UMTV 82876637262*	15		2
18 Sep 04	**ESSENTIAL R & B THE LOVE COLLECTION** *BMG TV Projects 82876642462*	3		5
25 Sep 04	**CLUB CLASS** *BMG TV 82876642452*	11		2
9 Oct 04	**NEVER FORGET – THE VERY BEST OF THE 90'S** *BMG TV 82876649812*	15		1
16 Oct 04	**ULTIMATE FAME** *BMG 82876652712*	8		2
30 Oct 04	**ULTIMATE GIRLS NIGHT IN** *Sony TV/BMG TV 0828766526523*	11		1
6 Nov 04	**BEAUTIFUL – NEW COLLECTION AUTUMN 2004** *BMG TV 82876658552*	8		2
13 Nov 04	**THE WORLD'S GREATEST** *BMG/Sony/WSM 82876658592*	4		3
20 Nov 04	**ESSENTIAL R&B – WINTER 2004** *Sony TV/BMG TV 82876649802*	8		7
4 Dec 04	**CHRISTMAS HITS** *Warner/BMG TV/Sony TV 82876650602*	3		14
15 Jan 05	**WORK IT** *BMG 82876667142*	6		3
15 Jan 05	**INFINITY** *BMG 82876667122*	18		1
29 Jan 05	**FUNK SOUL ANTHEMS** *Sony TV/BMG TV 82876676192*	15		1

VARIOUS ARTISTS (BREAK DOWN)

Date	Title / Label	Peak Position	Weeks at No.1	Weeks on Chart
17 Sep 94	**DRUM AND BASS SELECTION 2** *Break Down BDRCD 003*	14		3
13 Jul 96	**MAX POWER – MAX BASS** *Break Down BDRCD 15*	13		3

VARIOUS ARTISTS (BREAKBEAT KAOS)

Date	Title / Label	Peak Position	Weeks at No.1	Weeks on Chart
25 Oct 08	**BREAKBEAT KAOS PRESENTS STADIUM DRUM AND BASS** *Breakbeat Kaos BBK005CD*	12		2

VARIOUS ARTISTS (BREAKOUT)

Date	Title / Label	Peak Position	Weeks at No.1	Weeks on Chart
3 Sep 88	**HOUSE HALLUCINATIONS (PUMP UP LONDON VOLUME 1)** *Breakout HOSA 9002*	90		2

VARIOUS ARTISTS (BRUNSWICK)

Date	Title / Label	Peak Position	Weeks at No.1	Weeks on Chart
5 Oct 02	**ANGEL BEACH** *Brunswick CDORB 1*	15		1
7 Aug 04	**ANGEL BEACH THE 3RD WAY** *Orb Recordings ORBCD6*	9		3

VARIOUS ARTISTS (BUSINESS)

Date	Title / Label	Peak Position	Weeks at No.1	Weeks on Chart
16 Jun 90	**LOVERS FOR LOVERS VOLUME 3** *Business WBRLP 903*	18		1

VARIOUS ARTISTS (CACTUS)

Date	Title / Label	Peak Position	Weeks at No.1	Weeks on Chart
31 Jan 76	**REGGAE CHARTBUSTERS 75** *Cactus CTLP 114*	53		1

VARIOUS ARTISTS (CAPITOL)

Date	Title / Label	Peak Position	Weeks at No.1	Weeks on Chart
18 Feb 89	**CAPITOL CLASSICS VOLUME 1** *Capitol EMS 1316*	16		2
13 Nov 99	**THE BEST OF BOND...JAMES BOND** *Capitol 5232942* ●	6		11
8 Dec 01	**THE BEST OF THE RAT PACK** *Capitol 5364522* ⊛	2		7
30 Nov 02	**THE BEST OF BOND JAMES BOND** *Capitol 5405542* ●	15		5
14 Dec 02	**CHRISTMAS WITH THE RAT PACK** *Capitol 5422102* ●	15		3

VARIOUS ARTISTS (CASTLE COMMUNICATIONS)

Date	Title / Label	Peak Position	Weeks at No.1	Weeks on Chart
7 Jul 90	**THE ULTIMATE 60S COLLECTION** *Castle Communications CTVLP 305* ●	4		11
12 Jan 91	**THE ULTIMATE BLUES COLLECTION** *Castle Communications CTVLP 206*	14		6
8 Aug 92	**JAZZ ON A SUMMER'S DAY** *Castle Communications CTVCD 108*	4		8
10 Oct 92	**BLOCKBUSTER – THE SENSATIONAL 70S** *Castle Communications CTVCD 209*	6		6
5 Jun 93	**ONE ORIGINAL STEP BEYOND** *Castle Communications CTVCD 115*	7		5
3 Jul 93	**MONSTER HITS OF DANCE** *Castle Communications CTVCD 220*	13		3
30 Oct 93	**GOING UNDERGROUND** *Castle Communications CTVCD 123*	18		2

VARIOUS ARTISTS (CBS)

Date	Title / Label	Peak Position	Weeks at No.1	Weeks on Chart
20 May 67	**THRILL TO THE SENSATIONAL SOUND OF SUPER STEREO** *CBS PR 5*	20		30
28 Jun 69	**ROCK MACHINE I LOVE YOU** *CBS SPR 26*	15		5
28 Jun 69	**THE ROCK MACHINE TURNS YOU ON** *CBS SPR 22*	18		7
20 May 72	**THE MUSIC PEOPLE** *CBS 66315*	10		9
21 Oct 78	**SATIN CITY** *CBS 10010* ●	10		11
2 Jun 79	**THIS IS IT** *CBS 10014* ○	6		12
19 Apr 80	**FIRST LADIES OF COUNTRY** *CBS 10018* ○	37		6
21 Jun 80	**KILLER WATTS** *CBS KW1*	27		6
4 Apr 81	**BITTER SUITE** *CBS 22082*	55		3
16 Oct 82	**REFLECTIONS** *CBS 10034* ⊛	4		92
22 Oct 83	**IMAGINATIONS** *CBS 10044* ●	15		21
1 Dec 84	**THE HITS ALBUM** *CBS/WEA HITS 1* ⊛x3	1	7	36
13 Apr 85	**THE HITS ALBUM 2** *CBS/WEA HITS 2* ⊛x2	1	6	21
20 Apr 85	**CLUB CLASSICS VOLUME 2** *CBS VAULT 2*	90		2
7 Dec 85	**HITS 3** *CBS/WEA HITS 3* ⊛x2	2		21
29 Mar 86	**HITS 4** *CBS/WEA/RCA/Ariola HITS 4* ⊛	1	4	21
22 Nov 86	**HITS 5** *CBS/WEA/RCA/Ariola HITS 5* ⊛x3	1	2	25
14 Mar 87	**MOVE CLOSER** *CBS MOOD 1* ⊛	4		19
27 Jun 87	**THE HOLIDAY ALBUM** *CBS MOOD 2* ●	13		9
25 Jul 87	**HITS 6** *CBS/WEA/BMG HITS 6* ⊛x3	1	1	19
5 Dec 87	**HITS 7** *CBS/WEA/RCA/Ariola HITS 7* ⊛x3	2		17

Key: ★ US No.1 · ⊛ Platinum-selling · ● Gold-selling · ○ Silver-selling · Peak Position · Weeks at No.1 · Weeks on Chart

Date	Title / Label	Peak Position	Weeks at No.1	Weeks on Chart
30 Apr 88	**NITE FLITE** *CBS MOOD 4* ⊛	1	4	26
30 Jul 88	**HITS 8** *CBS/WEA/BMG HITS 8* ⊛	2		13
17 Dec 88	**THE HITS ALBUM 9** *CBS/WEA/BMG HITS 9*	5		4
14 Jan 89	**THE HITS ALBUM 9** *CBS/WEA/BMG HITS 9*	4		7
4 Mar 89	**CHEEK TO CHEEK** *CBS MOOD 6* ⊛	2		32
13 May 89	**NITE FLITE 2** *CBS MOOD 8*	1	2	26
3 Jun 89	**THE HITS ALBUM 10** *CBS/WEA/BMG HITS 10* ⊛	1	6	13
2 Dec 89	**MONSTER HITS** *CBS/WEA/BMG HITS 11* ⊛x2	2		14
30 Dec 89	**LAMBADA** *CBS 4660551*	15		6
24 Mar 90	**JUST THE TWO OF US** *CBS MOOD 11* ⊛x2	1	2	37
9 Jun 90	**NITE FLITE 3 – BEING WITH YOU** *CBS MOOD 14* ●	3		11
11 Aug 90	**SNAP! IT UP – MONSTER HITS 2** *CBS/WEA/BMG HITS 12*	2		10
29 Dec 90	**THE HIT PACK: THE BEST OF CHART MUSIC** *CBS/WEA/BMG COMPC 1*	2		8
10 Aug 91	**THE HITS ALBUM 15** *CBS/WEA/BMG HITS 15*	1	2	9

VARIOUS ARTISTS (CHAMPAGNE)

Date	Title / Label	Peak Position	Weeks at No.1	Weeks on Chart
4 Apr 81	**RE-MIXTURE** *Champagne CHAMP 1*	32		5

VARIOUS ARTISTS (CHAMPION)

Date	Title / Label	Peak Position	Weeks at No.1	Weeks on Chart
8 Nov 86	**ULTIMATE TRAX VOLUME 1** *Champion CHAMP 1003*	66		2
7 Mar 87	**ULTIMATE TRAX VOLUME 2** *Champion CHAMP 1005*	50		2
18 Jul 87	**ULTIMATE TRAX 3 – BATTLE OF THE DJS** *Champion CHAMP 1008*	69		2

VARIOUS ARTISTS (CHARM)

Date	Title / Label	Peak Position	Weeks at No.1	Weeks on Chart
21 Apr 90	**PURE LOVERS VOLUME 1** *Charm CLP 101*	14		4
22 Sep 90	**PURE LOVERS VOLUME 2** *Charm CLP 102*	12		3
6 Apr 91	**PURE LOVERS VOLUME 3** *Charm CLP 103*	16		2
2 Nov 91	**PURE LOVERS VOLUME 4** *Charm CLP 104*	19		1
25 Jul 92	**JUST RAGGA** *Charm CDCD 4*	17		1
29 Aug 92	**PURE LOVERS VOLUME 5** *Charm CCDJS 105*	13		3
27 Feb 93	**JUST RAGGA VOLUME III** *Charm CRCD 16*	19		1
1 May 93	**PURE LOVERS VOLUME 6** *Charm CCDJS 106*	17		1

VARIOUS ARTISTS (CHRYSALIS)

Date	Title / Label	Peak Position	Weeks at No.1	Weeks on Chart
25 May 85	**OUT NOW! 28 HOT HITS** *Chrysalis/MCA OUTV 1* ⊛	2		16
26 Oct 85	**OUT NOW!! 2 – 28 HOT HITS** *Chrysalis/MCA OUTV 2* ⊛	3		12
3 Nov 90	**RED, HOT AND BLUE** *Chrysalis CHR 1799* ○	6		3
13 Nov 93	**SMASH HITS '93 – 40 TOP CHARTIN' GROOVES** *Chrysalis CDCHR 6058* ●	4		10

VARIOUS ARTISTS (CLASSIC FM)

Date	Title / Label	Peak Position	Weeks at No.1	Weeks on Chart
20 Apr 96	**HALL OF FAME** *Classic FM CFMCD 7*	13		4
16 Oct 99	**RELAX...** *Classic FM CFMCD 30* ●	11		7
6 May 00	**HALL OF FAME 2000** *Classic FM CFMCD 31* ●	10		8
4 Nov 00	**RELAX MORE** *Classic FM CFMCD 32* ●	7		8
14 Apr 01	**THE SOUND OF CLASSIC FM** *Classic FM CFMMC 33* ○	16		3
27 Oct 01	**TIME TO RELAX** *Classic FM CFMCD 34* ●	9		6
6 Apr 02	**CLASSIC FM HALL OF FAME – GOLD** *Classic FM CFMCD 36*	14		6
2 Nov 02	**CLASSIC FM – SMOOTH CLASSICS** *Classic FM CFMCD 37* ●	9		7
1 Nov 03	**SMOOTH CLASSICS – DO NOT DISTURB** *Classic FM CFMCD 38*	10		4
24 Apr 04	**HALL OF FAME – THE GREAT COMPOSERS** *Classic FM CFMCD 40*	15		2
20 Nov 04	**CLASSIC FM – RELAX & ESCAPE** *Classic FM CFMCD41*	14		2
26 Mar 05	**CLASSIC FM – MUSIC FOR BABIES 2005** *Classic FM CFMCD43*	13		6
29 Oct 05	**RELAXING CLASSIC FM** *Classic FM CFMCD44*	12		3
3 Jun 06	**CLASSIC FM AT THE MOVIES** *Classic FM CFMCD46* ●	8		5
11 Nov 06	**CLASSIC FM – MOST WANTED** *Classic FM CFMCD50*	13		2
26 May 07	**CLASSIC FM AT THE MOVIES – THE SEQUEL** *Classic FM CFMCD54*	5		6
8 Nov 08	**CLASSIC FM – SMOOTH CLASSICS – ULTIMATE COLLECTION** *Classic FM CFMD4*	13		2

VARIOUS ARTISTS (CLUB)

Date	Title / Label	Peak Position	Weeks at No.1	Weeks on Chart
3 Sep 83	**COME WITH CLUB (CLUB TRACKS VOLUME 2)** *Club CLUBL 002*	55		2

VARIOUS ARTISTS (CMC)

Date	Title / Label	Peak Position	Weeks at No.1	Weeks on Chart
20 May 06	**EUROVISION SONG CONTEST ATHENS 2006** *CMC 3653692*	17		1
26 May 07	**EUROVISION SONG CONTEST – HELSINKI 2007** *CMC 3945482*	16		1

VARIOUS ARTISTS (COLUMBIA)

Date	Title / Label	Peak Position	Weeks at No.1	Weeks on Chart
2 Feb 91	**THINKING OF YOU...** *Columbia MOOD 15* ●	1	2	23
2 Feb 91	**THE FISH AND THE TREE AND THE BIRD AND THE BELL** *Columbia 4678801*	9		3
30 Mar 91	**EVERYBODY DANCE NOW** *Columbia 4680501*	12		3
20 Apr 91	**FREE SPIRIT – 17 CLASSIC ROCK BALLADS** *Columbia MOODS 16* ●	4		23
20 Apr 91	**YOU'RE THE INSPIRATION – 16 ROMANTIC LOVE SONGS** *Columbia MOOD 17*	10		5
10 Aug 91	**SIMPLY...LOVE** *Columbia MOOD 17* ●	3		10
17 Aug 91	**THE SOUND OF THE SUBURBS** *Columbia MOOD 18* ●	1	3	25
29 Feb 92	**THE SOUND OF THE CITY** *Columbia MOODCD 22*	11		5
27 Jun 92	**HEARTBEAT (MUSIC FROM THE TV SERIES)** *Columbia 4719002* ●	1	4	14
27 Jun 92	**HARD FAX** *Columbia SETVCD 1*	3		6
4 Jul 92	**THE BOYS ARE BACK IN TOWN** *Columbia MOODCD 23*	11		6
3 Oct 92	**SOMETHING IN THE AIR** *Columbia SETVCD 2*	10		5
31 Oct 92	**THE ULTIMATE COUNTRY COLLECTION** *Columbia MOODCD 26* ⊛	1	2	23
21 Nov 92	**HARD FAX 2 – TWICE THE VICE!** *Columbia SETVCD 3*	6		2
29 May 93	**ORIGINALS** *Columbia MOODCD 29* ⊛	1	1	23
21 Aug 93	**AFTER DARK** *Columbia SETVCD 5*	8		4
15 Jan 94	**TRUE LOVE WAYS** *Columbia MOODCD 28*	14		2
12 Feb 94	**SECRET LOVERS** *Columbia SETVCD 4*	8		4
19 Mar 94	**ORIGINALS 2** *Columbia MOODCD 31* ●	4		10
23 Jul 94	**SOUL SEARCHING** *Columbia MOODCD 34* ●	6		5
28 Jan 95	**THE BEST OF HEARTBEAT** *Columbia MOODCD 37* ●	1	1	16
4 Mar 95	**THE AWARDS 1995** *Columbia MOODCD 39*	10		2
27 May 95	**TOP GEAR 2** *Columbia MOODCD 41* ●	4		6
10 Jun 95	**TOP OF THE POPS 1** *Columbia MOODCD 1* ●	1	2	6
1 Jul 95	**MUNDO LATINO** *Columbia SONYTV 2CD*	3		5
8 Jul 95	**PURE ATTRACTION** *Columbia SONYTV 1CD*	5		3
16 Sep 95	**HEAVEN AND HELL** *Columbia 4736662*	12		4
30 Sep 95	**HEARTBEAT – FOREVER YOURS** *Columbia SONYTV 8CD* ⊛	1	6	17
2 Dec 95	**TOP OF THE POPS 2** *Columbia SONYTV 9CD* ●	14		7
17 Feb 96	**BRIT AWARDS '96** *Columbia SONYTV 10CD*	6		4
15 Jun 96	**RAP FLAVAS** *Columbia SONYTV 15CD*	6		3
28 Sep 96	**TOP OF THE POPS – THE CUTTING EDGE** *Columbia SONYTV 19CD*	10		3
2 Nov 96	**THE ALL TIME GREATEST LOVE SONGS...** *Columbia SONYTV 21CD*	4		17
2 Nov 96	**TAKE A BREAK** *Columbia SONYTV 20CD*	10		2
22 Feb 97	**THE '97 BRIT AWARDS** *Columbia SONYTV 23CD*	2		6
29 Mar 97	**THE ALL TIME GREATEST COUNTRY SONGS** *Columbia SONYTV 24CD*	5		6
17 May 97	**WHAT A FEELING** *Columbia SONYTV 26CD* ●	4		12
31 May 97	**BOYS** *Columbia SONYTV 27CD*	15		2
18 Oct 97	**IT'S A SIXTIES NIGHT** *Columbia SONYTV 32CD*	12		3
1 Nov 97	**THE ALL TIME GREATEST LOVE SONGS...VOLUME II** *Columbia SONYTV 34CD*	4		14
7 Feb 98	**THE BRIT AWARDS 1998** *Columbia SONYTV 36CD*	11		5
7 Mar 98	**FANTASTIC 80'S!** *Columbia SONYTV 37CD* ●	1	1	13
21 Mar 98	**OH! WHAT A NIGHT** *Columbia SONYTV 38CD* ●	4		9
28 Mar 98	**PERFECT DAY** *Columbia SONYTV 42CD*	7		6
23 May 98	**FANTASTIC 80'S! 2** *Columbia SONYTV 45CD*	4		7
27 Jun 98	**ALLEZ! OLA! OLE!** *Columbia SONYTV 46CD*	8		3
25 Jul 98	**SUMMER DANCE '98** *Columbia SONYTV 50CD*	12		3
8 Aug 98	**ANOTHER PERFECT DAY** *Columbia SONYTV 51CD*	13		2
29 Aug 98	**FANTASTIC DANCE!** *Columbia MOODCD 58*	14		2
3 Oct 98	**FANTASTIC 70'S!** *Columbia SONYTV 54CD*	8		4
14 Nov 98	**FANTASTIC 80'S! 3** *Columbia SONYTV 57CD*	11		2
28 Nov 98	**THE ALL TIME GREATEST LOVE SONGS OF THE 60'S, 70'S, 80'S & 90'S VOLUME III** *Columbia SONYTV 56CD* ⊛	6		14
13 Feb 99	**THE 1999 BRIT AWARDS** *Columbia SONYTV 61CD* ●	3		7
27 Feb 99	**THIS IS NOIZE** *Columbia SONYTV 60CD*	17		1
20 Mar 99	**ESPECIALLY FOR YOU** *Columbia SONYTV 62CD*	1	1	2
8 May 99	**THE NEW SOUL ALBUM** *Columbia SONYTV 63CD*	9		4
5 Jun 99	**MUSIC TO WATCH GIRLS BY** *Columbia SONYTV 67CD* ⊛	2		27
10 Jul 99	**THE ALL TIME GREATEST POP ALBUM** *Columbia SONYTV 68CD*	12		3
4 Sep 99	**VIVA! LATINO** *Columbia SONYTV 73CD*	11		4
20 Nov 99	**MORE MUSIC TO WATCH GIRLS BY** *Columbia SONYTV 75CD*	10		4
4 Mar 00	**THE 2000 BRIT AWARDS** *Columbia SONYTV 83CD*	3		3
8 Apr 00	**FOR YOU – 20 SONGS ESPECIALLY FOR YOU** *Columbia SONYTV 84CD*	4		4
29 Apr 00	**TV 2000** *Columbia SONYTV 82CD*	16		2
24 Jun 00	**CIGARETTES AND ALCOHOL** *Columbia SONYTV 87CD* ●	7		10
1 Jul 00	**IBIZA – THE STORY SO FAR** *Columbia SONYTV 86CD*	17		1
29 Jul 00	**SUMMER BREEZE** *Columbia SONYTV 89CD*	14		1
29 Jul 00	**CAFÉ MAMBO – THE REAL SOUND OF IBIZA** *Columbia SONYTV 90CD*	19		1
2 Sep 00	**FANTASTIC 80'S – GO FOR IT** *Columbia SONYTV 92CD* ●	10		3
18 Nov 00	**JAMIE OLIVER'S COOKIN' – MUSIC TO COOK BY** *Columbia SONYTV 95CD* ○	14		1

Silver-selling ● Gold-selling ● Platinum-selling ⊛ US No.1 ★ — Peak Position, Weeks at No.1, Weeks on Chart

Date	Title / Label	Peak Position	Weeks at No.1	Weeks on Chart
20 Jan 01	**R&B MASTERS** *Columbia STVCD 102* ●	4		5
24 Feb 01	**BRIT AWARDS 2001 – ALBUM OF THE YEAR** *Columbia STVCD 105*	15		7
3 Mar 01	**CORROSION** *Columbia STVCD 103*	17		1
28 Apr 01	**ALL TIME GREATEST MOVIE SONGS 2001** *Columbia STVCD 113*	18		1
5 May 01	**MUSIC TO WATCH GIRLS BY VOLUME 3** *Columbia SONYTV 96CD* ●	20		1
9 Jun 01	**LET THE MUSIC PLAY – 80'S GROOVE** *Columbia STVCD 108*	18		1
23 Jun 01	**MUSIC TO WATCH MOVIES BY** *Columbia STVCD 114*	18		1
7 Jul 01	**INDEPENDENT WOMAN** *Columbia STVCD 117* ●	7		5
14 Jul 01	**R&B MASTERS 2** *Columbia STVCD 118*	12		2
11 Aug 01	**THE CLASSIC CHILLOUT ALBUM** *Columbia STVCD 115* ⊛x2	1	1	19
15 Sep 01	**CIGARETTES AND ALCOHOL VOLUME 2** *Columbia STVCD 122*	10		4
3 Nov 01	**SCHOOL DISCO.COM** *Columbia 5048792* ●	9		3
8 Dec 01	**THE CLASSIC CHILLOUT ALBUM 2** *Columbia STVCD 129* ●	13		6
16 Feb 02	**R&B LOVESONGS** *Columbia STVCD 135*	9		3
23 Feb 02	**SCHOOL DISCO.COM – SPRING TERM** *Columbia 5062972* ●	1	2	8
23 Feb 02	**BRIT AWARDS 2002 – ALBUM OF THE YEAR** *Columbia STVCD 134* ●	7		3
20 Apr 02	**WWF – FORCEABLE ENTRY** *Columbia 5079182*	6		3
4 May 02	**ALTERNATIVE EIGHTIES** *Columbia STVCD 141*	5		5
8 Jun 02	**CIGARETTES AND ALCOHOL – SATURDAY NIGHT** *Columbia STVCD 143*	15		1
29 Jun 02	**CLUB TROPICANA** *Columbia STVCD 145*	11		4
13 Jul 02	**SCHOOL DISCO.COM – SUMMER HOLIDAY** *Columbia 5084632*	2		6
13 Jul 02	**ALTERNATIVE 60'S** *Columbia STVCD 144*	18		1
3 Aug 02	**THE NEW CLASSIC CHILLOUT ALBUM** *Columbia STVCD 148* ●	5		7
21 Sep 02	**ALTERNATIVE 90S** *Columbia STVCD 150*	14		1
19 Oct 02	**BAD GIRLS** *Columbia STVCD 152*	15		1
26 Oct 02	**GET THE PARTY STARTED** *Columbia STVCD 156*	10		2
26 Jul 03	**THE VERY BEST OF THE FANTASTIC 80'S** *Columbia STVCD166* ●	7		5
24 Jan 04	**WWE ORIGINALS** *Columbia 5151163*	11		1
3 Jun 06	**WWE – WRECKLESS INTENT** *Columbia 82876825592*	16		1

VARIOUS ARTISTS (CONCEPT)

Date	Title / Label	Peak Position	Weeks at No.1	Weeks on Chart
12 Mar 94	**RAP ATTACK** *Concept MOODCD 32* ●	9		7

VARIOUS ARTISTS (CONCRETE)

Date	Title / Label	Peak Position	Weeks at No.1	Weeks on Chart
10 Feb 96	**BRIT HOP AND AMYL HOUSE** *Concrete HARD 10LPCD*	16		1

VARIOUS ARTISTS (CONIFER)

Date	Title / Label	Peak Position	Weeks at No.1	Weeks on Chart
21 Nov 98	**ONLY CLASSICAL ALBUM YOU'LL EVER NEED** *Conifer 75605513322* ●	17		1

VARIOUS ARTISTS (CONNOISSEUR COLLECTION)

Date	Title / Label	Peak Position	Weeks at No.1	Weeks on Chart
25 Jul 92	**32 ONES ON ONE – RADIO 1'S 25TH ANNIVERSARY** *Connoisseur Collection ONECD 32*	8		10
3 Jul 93	**ROAD SHOW HITS (21 YEARS OF RADIO 1 FM ROAD SHOW)** *Connoisseur Collection RSHCD 20*	18		2

VARIOUS ARTISTS (COOKIE JAR)

Date	Title / Label	Peak Position	Weeks at No.1	Weeks on Chart
14 Dec 91	**STEAMIN' – HARDCORE '92** *Cookie Jar JARTV 1* ●	3		8
21 Mar 92	**TECHNOSTATE** *Cookie Jar JARCD 2* ●	2		9
23 May 92	**THE RAVE GENER8TOR** *Cookie Jar JARCD 3* ●	1	2	8
5 Sep 92	**THE RAVE GENER8TOR 2** *Cookie Jar JARCD 4* ●	2		7
28 Nov 92	**RAVE 92** *Cookie Jar JARCD 5* ●	3		11
27 Mar 93	**UNDERGROUND VOLUME 1** *Cookie Jar JARCD 6*	6		5
7 Aug 93	**JAMMIN'** *Cookie Jar JARCD 7* ●	7		5
11 Sep 93	**FULL ON DANCE** *Cookie Jar JARCD 8*	12		2
6 Nov 93	**SOUL BEAT** *Cookie Jar JARCD 9*	8		2
27 Nov 93	**FULL ON DANCE '93** *Cookie Jar JARCD 10* ●	3		9

VARIOUS ARTISTS (COOLTEMPO)

Date	Title / Label	Peak Position	Weeks at No.1	Weeks on Chart
1 Aug 87	**FIERCE** *Cooltempo CTLP 4*	37		6
1 Jul 89	**THIS IS GARAGE** *Cooltempo CTLP 12*	18		2

VARIOUS ARTISTS (COWBOY6)

Date	Title / Label	Peak Position	Weeks at No.1	Weeks on Chart
8 May 93	**COWBOY COMPILATION – THE ALBUM VOLUME 1** *Cowboy RODEOCD 1*	18		1

VARIOUS ARTISTS (CREOLE)

Date	Title / Label	Peak Position	Weeks at No.1	Weeks on Chart
24 Aug 85	**20 HOLIDAY HITS** *Creole CTV 1* ●	48		6

VARIOUS ARTISTS (DANCE POOL)

Date	Title / Label	Peak Position	Weeks at No.1	Weeks on Chart
25 Sep 99	**IBIZA – THE CLOSING PARTY** *Dance Pool DP2 CD*	19		2

VARIOUS ARTISTS (DEBUT)

Date	Title / Label	Peak Position	Weeks at No.1	Weeks on Chart
27 Jun 92	**JUNGLE TEKNO VOLUME 1** *Debut CDTOT 5*	18		1

VARIOUS ARTISTS (DECADANCE)

Date	Title / Label	Peak Position	Weeks at No.1	Weeks on Chart
20 Apr 02	**PURE CLASSICAL CHILLOUT** *Decadance DECTV 002*	9		4
20 Jul 02	**PURE GLOBAL CHILLOUT** *Decadance DECTV 003*	10		4
9 Nov 02	**THE CELTIC CHILLOUT ALBUM** *Decadance DEDCTV 007*	8		3
16 Nov 02	**CLASSICAL CHILLOUT GOLD** *Decadance DECTV 005*	9		12
8 Feb 03	**THE CLASSICAL LOVE ALBUM** *Decadance DECTV 008*	10		4
31 May 03	**PIANO MOODS** *Decadance DECTV 010*	6		4
12 Jul 03	**THE VERY BEST OF LATIN JAZZ** *Decadance DECTV 011*	15		2
11 Oct 03	**THE ULTIMATE OLK SKOOL ALBUM** *Decadance DECSIX 011*	16		1
18 Oct 03	**GUITAR MOODS** *Decadance DECTV 017*	7		3
25 Oct 03	**THE VERY BEST OF COUNTRY GOLD** *Decadance DECTV 012*	6		4
15 Nov 03	**THE VERY BEST OF CLASSICAL CHILLOUT GOLD** *Decadance DECTV013*	13		3
7 Feb 04	**ROCK 'N' ROLL LOVE SONGS** *Decadance DECTV018*	9		3
6 Mar 04	**ELECTRIC MOODS** *Decadance DECTV020*	9		2
24 Jul 04	**THE ULTIMATE NORTHERN SOUL ALBUM** *Decadance DECTV022*	7		3
16 Oct 04	**THE SOUL BOX** *Decadance DECTV023*	12		2
13 Nov 04	**CLASSICAL CHILLOUT – PLATINUM** *Decadance DECTV025*	18		1
20 Nov 04	**CELTIC CHILLOUT – THE VERY BEST OF** *Decadance DECTV026*	20		1
19 Mar 05	**THE NO 1 HARD HOUSE ALBUM** *Decadance DECESS2*	19		1
25 Jun 05	**THE NO 1 SUMMER DANCE ALBUM** *Decadance DECESS4*	16		3
20 Aug 05	**THE NO 1 FUNKY HOUSE ALBUM** *Decadance DECESS3*	18		1
22 Apr 06	**THE NO 1 EUPHORIC DANCE ALBUM** *Decadance DECESS8*	8		9
29 Apr 06	**THE NO 1 DANCE HITS ALBUM** *Decadance DECESS7*	13		11
24 Jun 06	**THE NO 1 TRANCE CLASSICS ALBUM** *Decadance DECESS9*	17		4
22 Jul 06	**THE NO 1 FUNKY HOUSE ALBUM 2** *Decadance DECESS10*	13		4
30 Sep 06	**THE NO 1 HARDCORE ALBUM** *Decadance DECESS12*	7		3
7 Oct 06	**THE NO 1 SUMMER DANCE ALBUM – VOLUME 2** *Decadance DECESS11*	16		1
14 Oct 06	**THE NO 1 DANCE CLASSICS ALBUM** *Decadance DECESS13*	18		2
13 Jan 07	**THE NO 1 R & B CLASSICS ALBUM** *Decadance DECESS15*	20		1
14 Apr 07	**THE NO 1 CLUB ANTHEMS ALBUM** *Decadance DECESS18*	16		4

VARIOUS ARTISTS (DECCA)

Date	Title / Label	Peak Position	Weeks at No.1	Weeks on Chart
8 Feb 64	**READY STEADY GO** *Decca LK 4577*	20		1
28 Jun 69	**THE WORLD OF BLUES POWER** *Decca SPA 14*	24		6
5 Jul 69	**THE WORLD OF BRASS BANDS** *Decca SPA 20*	13		11
6 Sep 69	**THE WORLD OF HITS VOLUME 2** *Decca SPA 35*	7		5
20 Sep 69	**THE WORLD OF PROGRESSIVE MUSIC (WOWIE ZOWIE)** *Decca SPA 34*	17		2
20 Sep 69	**THE WORLD OF PHASE 4 STEREO** *Decca SPA 32*	29		2
7 Aug 71	**THE WORLD OF YOUR 100 BEST TUNES** *Decca SPA 112*	10		22
9 Oct 71	**THE WORLD OF YOUR 100 BEST TUNES VOLUME 2** *Decca SPA 155*	9		13
27 Sep 75	**THE WORLD OF YOUR 100 BEST TUNES VOLUME 10** *Decca SPA 400*	41		4
13 Dec 75	**THE TOP 25 FROM YOUR 100 BEST TUNES** *Decca HBT 1112*	21		5
1 Jun 91	**THE ESSENTIAL MOZART** *Decca 4333231* ●	1	2	23
16 Nov 91	**ESSENTIAL OPERA** *Decca 4338221* ⊛	2		28
26 Sep 92	**ESSENTIAL BALLET** *Decca 4366582*	9		4
12 Jun 93	**CLASSIC COMMERCIALS** *Decca 4406382* ●	8		6
6 Nov 93	**ESSENTIAL OPERA 2** *Decca 4409472* ●	17		2
6 Jun 98	**THE GREATEST CLASSICAL STARS ON EARTH** *Decca 4603902*	13		4
2 Sep 00	**CALM** *Decca 4673512*	14		2
10 Nov 01	**THE ULTIMATE MOVIE ALBUM** *Decca 5857122*	16		1
24 Nov 01	**CLASSICS 2002** *Decca 4721092* ⊛	2		7
30 Mar 02	**VOICES** *Decca 4722562*	6		3
24 Aug 02	**CLASSIC ADS** *Decca 04724162*	12		4
30 Nov 02	**CLASSICS 2003** *Decca 4726812* ●	17		3
1 Mar 03	**THE VERY BEST OF RELAXING CLASSICS** *Decca 4738672* ●	4		9
29 Mar 03	**TIMELESS** *Decca 0391862*	8		3
9 Aug 03	**GEORGE GERSHWIN – THE BEST OF** *Decca 9809662*	19		1
18 Oct 03	**WORLD IN UNION 2003** *Decca 4761240*	10		3

VARIOUS ARTISTS (DECONSTRUCTION)

Date	Title	Label	Peak Position	Weeks at No.1	Weeks on Chart
14 Oct 89	ITALIA – DANCE MUSIC FROM ITALY	*Deconstruction 64289*	4		6
27 Feb 93	FULL ON – A YEAR IN THE LIFE OF HOUSE	*Deconstruction 74321128032*	18		2
6 May 95	CREAM LIVE	*Deconstruction 74321272192*	3		17
26 Aug 95	DECONSTRUCTION CLASSICS – A HISTORY OF DANCE MUSIC	*Deconstruction 74321299002*	17		1
11 Nov 95	CREAM ANTHEMS	*Deconstruction 74321328162*	2		3
6 Jul 96	CREAM LIVE – TWO	*Deconstruction 74321391252*	3		5
29 Mar 97	CREAM SEPERATES – THE COLLECTION	*Deconstruction 74321463782*	16		1
15 Nov 97	CREAM ANTHEMS '97	*Deconstruction 74321529622*	11		2

VARIOUS ARTISTS (DEF JAM)

Date	Title	Label	Peak Position	Weeks at No.1	Weeks on Chart
8 Aug 87	KICK IT – THE DEF JAM SAMPLER VOLUME 1	*Def Jam KICKIT 1*	19		7
7 Apr 01	WESTWOOD	*Def Jam UK 5643732*	7		5
12 Jan 02	WESTWOOD 2	*Def Jam 5866192*	19		1
28 Sep 02	WESTWOOD 3	*Def Jam 0696762*	2		7
10 Apr 04	WESTWOOD – THE JUMP OFF	*Def Jam 9817185*	2		8
11 Sep 04	WESTWOOD – THE TAKEOVER	*Def Jam 9820449*	2		5
13 Nov 04	WESTWOOD – THE BIG DAWG	*Def Jam 9824925*	3		6
26 Mar 05	WESTWOOD – THE INVASION	*Def Jam 9828102*	2		7
6 Aug 05	WESTWOOD – HEAT	*Def Jam 9830948*	3		6
19 Nov 05	WESTWOOD X	*Def Jam 9834315*	4		8
27 May 06	WESTWOOD – RIDE WITH THE BIG DAWG	*Def Jam 9840062*	6		3
14 Oct 06	WESTWOOD – THE GREATEST – CLASSIC JOINTZ	*Def Jam 9842970*	6		5

VARIOUS ARTISTS (DEF SOUL)

Date	Title	Label	Peak Position	Weeks at No.1	Weeks on Chart
3 Feb 01	THE LICK – PRESENTED BY TREVOR NELSON	*Def Soul 5201682*	3		3

VARIOUS ARTISTS (DEFECTED)

Date	Title	Label	Peak Position	Weeks at No.1	Weeks on Chart
25 Mar 00	SESSIONS TEN – SUBLIMINAL SESSIONS	*Defected DEFSESS 1*	18		1
6 Nov 04	MOST RATED	*Defected RATED01CD*	14		1
10 Mar 07	DEFECTED IN THE HOUSE – MIAMI 07	*In The House ITH19CD*	19		1
29 Mar 08	PURE FUNKY HOUSE	*Defected WMTV075*	11		3

VARIOUS ARTISTS (DEMON)

Date	Title	Label	Peak Position	Weeks at No.1	Weeks on Chart
26 Mar 05	BALAMORY – STRIKE UP THE BAND	*Demon DMGCD004*	20		1

VARIOUS ARTISTS (DERAM)

Date	Title	Label	Peak Position	Weeks at No.1	Weeks on Chart
30 May 81	STRENGTH THROUGH OI!	*Deram SKIN 1*	51		5

VARIOUS ARTISTS (DEUTSCHE GRAMMOPHON)

Date	Title	Label	Peak Position	Weeks at No.1	Weeks on Chart
13 Oct 90	ESSENTIAL CLASSICS	*Deutsche Grammophon 4315411*	6		9
28 Mar 92	LIVING CLASSICS	*Deutsche Grammophon 4356432*	7		5
11 May 02	MOZART GOLD – THE ESSENTIAL COLLECTION	*Deutsche Grammophon 472342*	17		2
10 May 03	CLASSICAL GOLD	*Deutsche Grammophon 4745412*	16		1

VARIOUS ARTISTS (DINO)

Date	Title	Label	Peak Position	Weeks at No.1	Weeks on Chart
2 Dec 89	THAT LOVING FEELING	*Dino DINTV 5*	3		14
3 Mar 90	THAT LOVING FEELING VOLUME 2	*Dino DINTV 7*	5		26
23 Jun 90	LEATHER AND LACE	*Dino DINTV 9*	3		8
11 Aug 90	THE SUMMER OF LOVE	*Dino DINTV 10*	9		9
6 Oct 90	THAT LOVING FEELING VOLUME 3	*Dino DINTV 11*	1	3	31
10 Nov 90	LEATHER AND LACE – THE SECOND CHAPTER	*Dino DINTV 12*	14		4
24 Nov 90	ROCK 'N' ROLL LOVE SONGS	*Dino DINTV 13*	4		29
29 Dec 90	BACHARACH AND DAVID – THEY WRITE THE SONGS	*Dino DINTV 13*	16		3
9 Feb 91	TRACKS OF MY TEARS (SMOKEY ROBINSON – WRITER AND PERFORMER)	*Dino DINTV 17*	6		8
30 Mar 91	HARDCORE UPROAR	*Dino DINTV 20*	2		9
6 Apr 91	THAT LOVING FEELING VOLUME 4	*Dino DINTV 19*	3		14
1 Jun 91	LOVE SUPREME	*Dino DINTV 19*	4		5
15 Jun 91	THE RHYTHM DIVINE	*Dino DINTV 22*	1	1	15
13 Jul 91	HARDCORE DANCEFLOOR	*Dino DINTV 24*	2		10
27 Jul 91	CHIC AND ROSE ROYCE – THEIR GREATEST HITS SIDE BY SIDE	*Dino DINTV 23*	8		6
3 Aug 91	LA FREEWAY	*Dino DINTV 25*	6		7
12 Oct 91	WE WILL ROCK YOU	*Dino DINTV 26*	3		6
19 Oct 91	THAT LOVING FEELING VOLUME 5	*Dino DINTV 28*	2		15
2 Nov 91	HARDCORE ECSTASY	*Dino DINTV 29*	1	4	16
2 Nov 91	THE RHYTHM DIVINE VOLUME 2	*Dino DINTV 27*	6		5
23 Nov 91	MORE ROCK 'N' ROLL LOVE SONGS	*Dino DINTV 30*	6		23
7 Dec 91	PARTY MIX	*Dino DINTV 32*	8		9
28 Dec 91	ESSENTIAL HARDCORE	*Dino DINTV 33*	1	1	10
14 Mar 92	HEAVENLY HARDCORE	*Dino DINCD 35*	2		9
28 Mar 92	BREAKING HEARTS	*Dino DINCD 34*	3		10
18 Apr 92	COLD SWEAT	*Dino DINCD 36*	2		7
2 May 92	HEARTLANDS	*Dino DINCD 37*	4		11
20 Jun 92	LET'S TALK ABOUT LOVE	*Dino DINCD 39*	3		4
11 Jul 92	PRECIOUS	*Dino DINCD 38*	11		2
18 Jul 92	MIDNIGHT CRUISING	*Dino DINCD 37*	10		6
1 Aug 92	UNDER SPANISH SKIES	*Dino DINCD 41*	5		7
22 Aug 92	THE ORIGINALS!	*Dino DINCD 43*	8		6
29 Aug 92	TRANCE DANCE	*Dino DINCD 45*	7		5
19 Sep 92	SIXTIES BEAT	*Dino DINCD 42*	1	1	13
17 Oct 92	ENERGY RUSH	*Dino DINCD 53*	1	2	6
24 Oct 92	THE GREATEST VOICES	*Dino DINCD 44*	5		6
14 Nov 92	SWING HITS	*Dino DINCD 46*	19		1
28 Nov 92	ROCK 'N' ROLL IS HERE TO STAY	*Dino DINCD 48*	14		5
5 Dec 92	STOMPIN' PARTY	*Dino DINCD 52*	10		7
12 Dec 92	ENERGY RUSH II	*Dino DINCD 55*	7		7
12 Dec 92	MEMORIES ARE MADE OF THIS	*Dino DINCD 47*	8		12
30 Jan 93	ENERGY RUSH LEVEL 3	*Dino DINCD 57*	3		6
13 Feb 93	BLUES BROTHER SOUL SISTER	*Dino DINCD 56*	1	1	38
10 Apr 93	ENERGY RUSH PRESENTS DANCE HITS 93	*Dino DINCD 59*	1	3	12
5 Jun 93	ENERGY RUSH PHASE 4	*Dino DINCD 65*	2		6
10 Jul 93	HEART FULL OF SOUL	*Dino DINCD 63*	9		8
17 Jul 93	BLUES BROTHER SOUL SISTER VOLUME 2	*Dino DINCD 61*	8		8
24 Jul 93	ENERGY RUSH DANCE HITS 93 (2ND DIMENSION)	*Dino DINCD 62*	2		8
4 Sep 93	THAT LOVING FEELING VOLUME VI	*Dino DINCD 64*	3		12
11 Sep 93	ENERGY RUSH FACTOR 5	*Dino DINCD 66*	3		5
18 Sep 93	RAVE GENERATION	*Dino DINCD 68*	2		7
25 Sep 93	MORE THAN UNPLUGGED	*Dino DINCD 69*	11		3
16 Oct 93	ENERGY RUSH PRESENTS DANCE HITS OF THE YEAR	*Dino DINCD 70*	3		13
16 Oct 93	PLANET ROCK	*Dino DINCD 67*	8		2
23 Oct 93	FUTURESHOCK – 20 FURIOUS DANCE TUNES	*Dino DINCD 71*	4		4
23 Oct 93	COUNTRY WOMEN	*Dino DINCD 72*	11		3
27 Nov 93	AS TIME GOES BY	*Dino DINCD 77*	14		5
4 Dec 93	THE VERY BEST OF THAT LOVING FEELING	*Dino DINCD 78*	2		21
4 Dec 93	ENERGY RUSH – SAFE SIX	*Dino DINCD 74*	5		7
4 Dec 93	KEEP ON DANCING	*Dino DINCD 80*	14		6
25 Dec 93	LOVE IN THE SIXTIES	*Dino DINCD 81*	11		9
29 Jan 94	RAVE GENERATION 2	*Dino DINCD 75*	5		3
19 Feb 94	SOUL MATE	*Dino DINCD 82*	6		3
12 Mar 94	ENERGY RUSH – EURO DANCE HITS 94	*Dino DINCD 76*	5		4
2 Apr 94	ENERGY RUSH 7	*Dino DINCD 79*	2		5
9 Apr 94	IT'S ELECTRIC	*Dino DINCD 73*	2		12
7 May 94	BLUES BROTHER SOUL SISTER VOLUME 3	*Dino DINCD 85*	5		12
28 May 94	ENERGY RUSH – XTERMIN8	*Dino DINCD 84*	1	1	8
4 Jun 94	WONDERFUL WORLD	*Dino DINCD 89*	8		6
23 Jul 94	THE BEST OF ROCK 'N' ROLL LOVE SONGS	*Dino DINCD 91*	9		5
30 Jul 94	START – THE BEST OF BRITISH	*Dino DINCD 92*	13		3
6 Aug 94	ENERGY RUSH DANCE HITS 94	*Dino DINCD 95*	3		8
13 Aug 94	THAT LOVING FEELING VOLUME VII	*Dino DINCD 83*	4		10
3 Sep 94	DANCE MASSIVE	*Dino DINCD 94*	3		8
17 Sep 94	WHEN A MAN LOVES A WOMAN	*Dino DINCD 88*	7		6
10 Dec 94	ROCK ANTHEMS	*Dino DINCD 101*	3		17
17 Dec 94	DANCE MASSIVE 2	*Dino DINCD 103*	8		6
7 Jan 95	THE ULTIMATE JUNGLE COLLECTION	*Dino DINCD 105*	17		2
11 Feb 95	ENERGY RUSH K9	*Dino DINCD 102*	3		4
11 Mar 95	PURE SWING	*Dino DINCD 97*	2		9
8 Apr 95	DRIVE TIME	*Dino DINCD 96*	5		8
27 May 95	SKA MANIA	*Dino DINCD 86*	4		5
10 Jun 95	DANCE MASSIVE 95	*Dino DINCD 87*	2		5
10 Jun 95	PURE SWING TWO	*Dino DINCD 98*	4		5
24 Jun 95	REGGAE MASSIVE	*Dino DINCD 93*	19		1
15 Jul 95	RAVE ANTHEMS	*Dino DINCD 104*	7		5
22 Jul 95	DRIVE TIME 2	*Dino DINCD 99*	4		7
19 Aug 95	THE AMERICAN DINER	*Dino DINCD 107*	7		5
2 Sep 95	PURE SWING III	*Dino DINCD 109*	3		8
21 Oct 95	THE GREATEST DANCE ALBUM OF ALL TIME	*Dino DINCD 108*	7		4
28 Oct 95	SPIRITUALLY IBIZA	*Dino DINCD 111*	17		1
18 Nov 95	PURE SWING IV	*Dino DINCD 116*	1	1	7
25 Nov 95	THE VERY BEST OF BLUES BROTHER SOUL SISTER	*Dino DINCD 115*	11		7
9 Dec 95	THE GREATEST SOUL ALBUM OF ALL TIME	*Dino DINCD 113*	16		4
6 Jan 96	DRIVETIME 3	*Dino DINCD 119*	4		6
6 Jan 96	PURE SWING 5	*Dino DINCD 117*	6		5

Silver-selling ○ Gold-selling ● Platinum-selling ⊛ US No.1 ★ Peak Position Weeks at No.1 Weeks on Chart

Date	Title / Label	Peak Position	Weeks at No.1	Weeks on Chart
30 Mar 96	**EIGHTIES SOUL WEEKENDER** *Dino DINCD 122*	7		7
13 Apr 96	**PURE SWING 96** *Dino DINCD 120*	9		3
11 May 96	**ROCK ANTHEMS – VOLUME 2** *Dino DINCD 110*	10		4
22 Jun 96	**PURE JAZZ MOODS – COOL JAZZ FOR A SUMMERS DAY** *Dino DINCD 126*	9		3
31 Aug 96	**DRIVE TIME 4** *Dino DINCD 128*	8		3
7 Sep 96	**THE VERY BEST OF CAJUN – 40 HOT CAJUN CLASSICS** *Dino DINCD 127*	16		3
17 May 97	**THE VERY BEST OF BRASS** *Dino DINCD 139*	18		1

VARIOUS ARTISTS (DISCO DEMAND)

Date	Title / Label	Peak Position	Weeks at No.1	Weeks on Chart
15 Mar 75	**SOLID SOUL SENSATIONS** *Disco Demand DDLP 5001*	30		1

VARIOUS ARTISTS (DISCO MIX CLUB)

Date	Title / Label	Peak Position	Weeks at No.1	Weeks on Chart
18 Mar 00	**GROOVE ARMADA – BACK TO MINE** *DMC BACKCD 4*	16		1
28 Oct 00	**FAITHLESS – BACK TO MINE** *DMC BACKCD 5*	19		1

VARIOUS ARTISTS (DJ INTERNATIONAL)

Date	Title / Label	Peak Position	Weeks at No.1	Weeks on Chart
20 Sep 86	**THE HOUSE SOUND OF CHICAGO** *DJ International LONLP 22*	52		12
18 Apr 87	**THE HOUSE SOUND OF CHICAGO VOLUME 2** *DJ International LONLP 32*	38		7
31 Oct 87	**JACKMASTER VOLUME 1** *DJ International JACKLP 501*	36		4
13 Feb 88	**JACKMASTER VOLUME 2** *DJ International JACKLP 502*	38		3

VARIOUS ARTISTS (DMG TV)

Date	Title / Label	Peak Position	Weeks at No.1	Weeks on Chart
26 Apr 03	**LET'S GROOVE** *DMG TV/Sony TV DMGTV002E*	4		6
17 Apr 04	**FANTASTIC NO 1'S OF THE SEVENTIES** *DMG TV DSTV002*	9		4
31 Jul 04	**DANCEHALL 4-PLAY** *DMG TV DMGTV008*	20		1
7 May 05	**SONGS THAT WON THE WAR** *DMG TV DMGTV017*	7		3
25 Mar 06	**SONGS THAT WARM THE HEART** *DMG TV DMGTV026*	16		2
15 Apr 06	**THE NO 1 SLEEPOVER ALBUM** *DMG TV DMGTV028*	16		1
15 Apr 06	**RADIO DAYS – CELEBRATING THE GOLDEN ERA** *DMG TV DMGTV029*	17		1
16 Aug 08	**100 HITS – 80S** *DMG TV DMG100003*	19		1

VARIOUS ARTISTS (DOVER)

Date	Title / Label	Peak Position	Weeks at No.1	Weeks on Chart
29 Oct 88	**SMASH HITS PARTY '88** *Dover ADD 5* ⊛	6		11
14 Jan 89	**SMASH HITS PARTY '88** *Dover ADD 5* ⊛	12		5
4 Mar 89	**AND ALL BECAUSE THE LADY LOVES...** *Dover ADD 6* ●	2		10
28 Oct 89	**SMASH HITS PARTY '89 – 30 SMASH HITS** *Dover ADD 8* ⊛	1	3	14
10 Feb 90	**ALL BY MYSELF** *Dover ADD 12* ●	2		15
14 Jul 90	**SMASH HITS – RAVE!** *Dover ADD 14* ●	1	2	10
22 Sep 90	**JUST SEVENTEEN – GET KICKIN'** *Dover ADD 16* ●	2		6
3 Nov 90	**SMASH HITS 1990** *Dover ADD 18* ⊛	2		14
24 Nov 90	**A TON OF HITS – THE BEST OF STOCK AITKEN WATERMAN** *Dover ADD 19*	7		8
20 Apr 91	**RED HOT METAL – 18 ROCK CLASSICS** *Dover ADD 21*	4		6
25 May 91	**SMASH HITS – MASSIVE!** *Dover ADD 24*	1	2	9
8 Jun 91	**ALL BY MYSELF VOLUME 2** *Dover ADD 23*	13		5
14 Sep 91	**MOMENTS IN SOUL** *Dover ADD 25* ○	2		7
26 Oct 91	**SMASH HITS 1991** *Dover ADD 28* ⊛	3		16
16 May 92	**THE GREATEST MOMENTS IN SOUL** *Dover CCD 33*	4		7
12 Dec 92	**SMASH HITS '92 – 40 BIG HITS! SORTED!** *Dover ADDCD 35* ●	5		8

VARIOUS ARTISTS (DREAMSCAPE)

Date	Title / Label	Peak Position	Weeks at No.1	Weeks on Chart
17 Jun 95	**RADIO DREAMSCAPE – VOLUME 1** *Dreamscape DREAMCD 01*	20		1

VARIOUS ARTISTS (EARTH)

Date	Title / Label	Peak Position	Weeks at No.1	Weeks on Chart
16 Nov 96	**LTJ BUKEM PRESENTS EARTH – VOLUME 1** *Earth EARTHCD 001*	19		1

VARIOUS ARTISTS (EAST WEST)

Date	Title / Label	Peak Position	Weeks at No.1	Weeks on Chart
12 Oct 91	**I'M YOUR FAN – THE SONGS OF LEONARD COHEN** *East West WX 444*	16		2
26 Jun 93	**DISCO INFERNO** *East West 9548319632* ○	17		1
18 May 02	**HEARTLESS CREW PRESENTS CRISP BISCUIT** *East West 0927460172*	10		2
22 Jun 02	**DRIVIN' WITH JOHNNIE WALKER** *East West 0927473132* ○	10		2

VARIOUS ARTISTS (ECHO)

Date	Title / Label	Peak Position	Weeks at No.1	Weeks on Chart
2 Mar 02	**ACOUSTIC** *Echo/V2 Music ECV21*	4		4
22 Jun 02	**ACOUSTIC 2** *Echo/V2 Music ECV22*	14		2
24 Jan 04	**BEST OF ACOUSTIC** *Echo/V2 Music ECV24* ●	2		11
28 Aug 04	**ACOUSTIC 04** *Echo/V2 Music ECV25*	15		1

VARIOUS ARTISTS (ELEVATE)

Date	Title / Label	Peak Position	Weeks at No.1	Weeks on Chart
11 Apr 92	**RAVE 2 – STRICTLY HARDCORE** *Elevate ELVCD 02*	11		3
8 Aug 92	**RAVING MAD** *Elevate CDELV 01*	17		2
27 Feb 93	**THE WIND DOWN ZONE** *Elevate CDELV 04*	17		3

VARIOUS ARTISTS (ELF)

Date	Title / Label	Peak Position	Weeks at No.1	Weeks on Chart
13 Jun 92	**EARTHRISE – THE RAINFOREST ALBUM** *Elf 5154192* ●	1	1	6

VARIOUS ARTISTS (EMI)

Date	Title / Label	Peak Position	Weeks at No.1	Weeks on Chart
21 Jun 69	**IMPACT** *EMI STWO 2*	15		14
2 Jun 73	**PURE GOLD** *EMI EMK 251*	1	3	11
18 Nov 78	**DON'T WALK – BOOGIE** *EMI EMTV 13* ⊛	1	3	23
21 Apr 79	**COUNTRY LIFE** *EMI EMTV 16* ●	2		14
2 Jun 79	**KNUCKLE SANDWICH** *EMI EMYV 18*	19		6
15 Dec 79	**ALL ABOARD** *EMI EMTX 101* ●	13		8
23 Feb 80	**METAL FOR MUTHAS** *EMI EMC 3318*	16		7
14 Jun 80	**METAL FOR MUTHAS VOLUME 2** *EMI EMC 3337*	58		1
13 Mar 82	**20 WITH A BULLET** *EMI EMTV 32* ●	11		8
10 Dec 83	**NOW, THAT'S WHAT I CALL MUSIC** *EMI/Virgin NOW 1* ⊛x3	1	5	50
7 Apr 84	**NOW, THAT'S WHAT I CALL MUSIC II** *EMI/Virgin NOW 2* ⊛x2	1	5	38
26 May 84	**THEN CAME ROCK 'N' ROLL** *EMI THEN 1* ●	5		15
11 Aug 84	**NOW, THAT'S WHAT I CALL MUSIC III** *EMI/Virgin NOW 3* ⊛x2	1	8	30
8 Dec 84	**NOW, THAT'S WHAT I CALL MUSIC 4** *EMI/Virgin NOW 4* ⊛	2		43
1 Jun 85	**NOW DANCE – THE 12" MIXES** *EMI/Virgin NOD 1* ●	3		14
13 Jul 85	**KERRANG! KOMPILATION – 24 ROCK MASTERS** *EMI/Virgin KER 1*	84		2
17 Aug 85	**NOW, THAT'S WHAT I CALL MUSIC 5** *EMI/Virgin NOW 5* ⊛x2	1	5	21
30 Nov 85	**NOW – THE CHRISTMAS ALBUM** *EMI/Virgin NOX 1* ⊛x4	1	2	22
7 Dec 85	**NOW, THAT'S WHAT I CALL MUSIC 6** *EMI/Virgin NOW 6* ⊛x4	1	4	40
19 Jul 86	**NOW – THE SUMMER ALBUM – 30 SUMMER HITS** *EMI/Virgin SUMMER 1* ⊛	7		9
23 Aug 86	**NOW, THAT'S WHAT I CALL MUSIC 7** *EMI/Virgin NOW 7* ⊛x2	1	5	21
8 Nov 86	**NOW DANCE '86** *EMI/Virgin NOD 2* ●	2		13
29 Nov 86	**NOW, THAT'S WHAT I CALL MUSIC '86** *EMI/Virgin/Polygram CDNOW 86*	65		4
6 Dec 86	**NOW, THAT'S WHAT I CALL MUSIC 8** *EMI/Virgin/Polygram NOW 8* ⊛x4	1	6	23
4 Apr 87	**NOW, THAT'S WHAT I CALL MUSIC 9** *EMI/Virgin/Polygram NOW 9* ⊛x2	1	5	26
3 Oct 87	**NOW! SMASH HITS** *EMI/Virgin/Polygram NOSH 1*	5		10
5 Dec 87	**NOW THAT'S WHAT I CALL MUSIC 10** *EMI/Virgin/Polygram NOW 10* ⊛x4	1	6	21
5 Mar 88	**UNFORGETTABLE** *EMI EMTV 44* ⊛	5		21
2 Apr 88	**NOW THAT'S WHAT I CALL MUSIC 11** *EMI/Virgin/Polygram NOW 11* ⊛x2	1	3	17
23 Jul 88	**NOW THAT'S WHAT I CALL MUSIC 12** *EMI/Virgin/Polygram NOW 12* ⊛x2	1	5	17
22 Oct 88	**THE CLASSIC EXPERIENCE** *EMI EMTVD 45* ⊛	27		12
3 Dec 88	**NOW THAT'S WHAT I CALL MUSIC 13** *EMI/Virgin/Polygram NOW 13* ⊛x4	1	4	6
3 Dec 88	**HELLO CHILDREN...EVERYWHERE** *EMI EM 1307* ●	59		5
14 Jan 89	**NOW THAT'S WHAT I CALL MUSIC 13** *EMI/Virgin/Polygram NOW 13* ⊛x4	1	1	15
14 Jan 89	**THE CLASSIC EXPERIENCE** *EMI EMTVD 45* ⊛	12		58
28 Jan 89	**UNFORGETTABLE** *EMI EMTV 44*	18		1
18 Mar 89	**UNFORGETTABLE 2** *EMI EMTV 46* ●	1	1	15
1 Apr 89	**NOW THAT'S WHAT I CALL MUSIC 14** *EMI/Virgin/Polygram NOW 14* ⊛x2	1	7	18
15 Jul 89	**NOW DANCE '89 – THE 12" MIXES** *EMI/Virgin/Polygram NOD 3* ●	1	6	14
26 Aug 89	**NOW THAT'S WHAT I CALL MUSIC 15** *EMI/Virgin/Polygram NOW 15* ⊛	1	5	13
30 Sep 89	**IS THIS LOVE** *EMI EMTV 47* ●	2		10
18 Nov 89	**THE 80'S ALBUM – THE ALBUM OF THE DECADE** *EMI EMTVD 48*	1	1	12
2 Dec 89	**NOW THAT'S WHAT I CALL MUSIC 16** *EMI/Virgin/Polygram NOW 15* ⊛x3	1	7	15
9 Dec 89	**IT'S CHRISTMAS** *EMI EMTV 49* ⊛	2		16
10 Mar 90	**NOW DANCE 901 – 20 SMASH DANCE HITS – THE 12" MIXES** *EMI/Virgin/Polygram NOD 4* ⊛	1	4	14
5 May 90	**NOW THAT'S WHAT I CALL MUSIC 17** *EMI/Virgin/Polygram NOW 17* ⊛	1	5	15

Date	Title	Label / Cat. No.	Award	Peak Position	Weeks at No.1	Weeks on Chart
26 May 90	**CLASSIC EXPERIENCE II**	*EMI EMTVD 50*	Gold	1	4	32
28 Jul 90	**NOW DANCE 902**	*EMI/Virgin/Polygram NOD 5*	Platinum	1	3	13
4 Aug 90	**THE WILD ONE**	*EMI EMTV 52*		8		7
20 Oct 90	**MISSING YOU – AN ALBUM OF LOVE**	*EMI EMTV 53*	Platinum	1	3	18
10 Nov 90	**NOW DANCE 903 – THE 12" MIXES**	*EMI/Virgin/Polygram NOD 6*	Gold	1	2	9
17 Nov 90	**TRULY UNFORGETTABLE**	*EMI EMTVD 55*	Gold	6		9
1 Dec 90	**NOW! THAT'S WHAT I CALL MUSIC 18**	*EMI/Virgin/Polygram NOW 18*	Platinum x3	1	5	18
1 Dec 90	**THE BEST FROM THE MGM MUSICALS**	*EMI EMTV 56*	Gold	12		4
16 Feb 91	**MISSING YOU 2 – AN ALBUM OF LOVE**	*EMI EMTV 57*	Gold	2		11
23 Feb 91	**AWESOME!! – 20 MASSIVE HITS**	*EMI/Virgin/Polygram EMTV 58*	Platinum	1	3	12
6 Apr 91	**NOW! THAT'S WHAT I CALL MUSIC 19**	*EMI/Virgin/Polygram NOW 19*	Platinum	1	5	16
11 May 91	**CLASSIC EXPERIENCE III**	*EMI EMTVD 59*	Gold	3		14
5 Oct 91	**NOW DANCE 91**	*EMI/Virgin/Polygram NOD 7*	Gold	1	3	9
26 Oct 91	**SEXUAL HEALING**	*EMI EMTV 60*	Gold	7		6
2 Nov 91	**AWESOME! 2**	*EMI/Virgin/Polygram EVP 1*	Gold	2		11
30 Nov 91	**NOW THAT'S WHAT I CALL MUSIC! 20**	*EMI/Virgin/Polygram NOW 20*	Platinum x3	1	7	18
30 Nov 91	**A CLASSICAL CHRISTMAS**	*EMI EMTV 62*	Gold	14		7
25 Jan 92	**THE ULTIMATE RAVE**	*EMI/Virgin/Polygram CDEVP 2*	Gold	1	4	15
22 Feb 92	**TENDER LOVE – 17 ROMANTIC LOVE SONGS**	*EMI CDEMTV 64*		2		11
22 Feb 92	**THE CLASSIC ROMANCE**	*EMI CDEMTV 63*	Silver	5		7
25 Apr 92	**NOW THAT'S WHAT I CALL MUSIC! 21**	*EMI/Virgin/Polygram CDNOW 21*	Platinum	1	5	13
8 Aug 92	**NOW THAT'S WHAT I CALL MUSIC! 22**	*EMI/Virgin/Polygram CDNOW 22*	Platinum	1	8	14
22 Aug 92	**MAXIMUM RAVE**	*EMI CDEMTV 65*	Gold	2		9
12 Sep 92	**THE BEST OF JAMES BOND – 30TH ANNIVERSARY COLLECTION**	*EMI CDBOND 007*	Gold	2		11
17 Oct 92	**WICKED!**	*EMI CDEMTV 66*		2		5
31 Oct 92	**SMASHIE AND NICEY PRESENT LET'S ROCK!**	*EMI CDEMTV 67*		8		4
14 Nov 92	**NOW DANCE 92**	*EMI/Virgin/Polygram CDNOD 8*	Gold	3		11
21 Nov 92	**IT'S CHRISTMAS TIME**	*EMI CDEMTV 69*	Platinum	3		15
28 Nov 92	**NOW THAT'S WHAT I CALL MUSIC! 23**	*EMI/Virgin/Polygram CDNOW 23*	Platinum x3	1	5	18
5 Dec 92	**FOREVER**	*EMI CDEMTV 70*		17		2
30 Jan 93	**THE MEGA RAVE**	*EMI/Virgin/Polygram CDEVP 3*		2		8
20 Feb 93	**SOUL MOODS**	*EMI CDEMTV 71*	Gold	4		8
13 Mar 93	**MEGA DANCE – THE POWER ZONE**	*EMI/Virgin/Polygram CDEVP 4*	Gold	2		8
27 Mar 93	**CLASSIC EXPERIENCE IV**	*EMI CDEMTVD 72*		9		6
10 Apr 93	**LOADED**	*EMI/Virgin/Polygram CDEVP 5*	Silver	6		6
17 Apr 93	**MEGA DANCE 2 – THE ENERGY ZONE**	*EMI/Virgin/Polygram CDEVP 6*	Silver	3		6
8 May 93	**NOW THAT'S WHAT I CALL MUSIC! 24**	*EMI/Virgin/Polygram CDNOW 24*	Platinum	1	6	13
26 Jun 93	**NOW DANCE 93**	*EMI/Virgin/Polygram CDNOD 9*		1	2	9
3 Jul 93	**INNA DANCEHALL STYLE**	*EMI CDEMTV 76*		11		4
14 Aug 93	**NOW THAT'S WHAT I CALL MUSIC! 25**	*EMI/Virgin/Polygram CDNOW 25*	Platinum	1	5	10
4 Sep 93	**NOW THAT'S WHAT I CALL MUSIC! 1983**	*EMI/Virgin/Polygram CDNOW 1983*	Silver	10		5
4 Sep 93	**NOW THAT'S WHAT I CALL MUSIC! 1984**	*EMI/Virgin/Polygram CDNOW 1984*	Silver	13		4
4 Sep 93	**NOW THAT'S WHAT I CALL MUSIC! 1985**	*EMI/Virgin/Polygram CDNOW 1985*	Silver	15		4
4 Sep 93	**NOW THAT'S WHAT I CALL MUSIC! 1986**	*EMI/Virgin/Polygram CDNOW 1986*		16		2
4 Sep 93	**NOW THAT'S WHAT I CALL MUSIC! 1987**	*EMI/Virgin/Polygram CDNOW 1987*		17		2
18 Sep 93	**BACK TO THE 70'S**	*EMI CDEMTV 77*		8		6
25 Sep 93	**NOW THAT'S WHAT I CALL MUSIC! 1992**	*EMI/Virgin/Polygram CDNOW 1992*		14		2
25 Sep 93	**NOW THAT'S WHAT I CALL MUSIC! 1988**	*EMI/Virgin/Polygram CDNOW 1988*		20		1
9 Oct 93	**NOW THAT'S WHAT I CALL MUSIC! 1993**	*EMI/Virgin/Polygram CDNOW 1993*	Gold	1	1	8
30 Oct 93	**NOW DANCE – THE BEST OF '93**	*EMI/Virgin/Polygram CDNOD 10*	Gold	1	1	6
6 Nov 93	**LET'S GO DISCO**	*EMI CDEMTV 78*		12		3
27 Nov 93	**NOW THAT'S WHAT I CALL MUSIC! 26**	*EMI/Virgin/Polygram CDNOW 26*	Platinum x3	1	8	15
27 Nov 93	**IT TAKES TWO – LOVE'S GREATEST DUETS**	*EMI CDEMTV 80*	Silver	17		1
29 Jan 94	**NOW DANCE 94 VOLUME 1**	*EMI/Virgin/Polygram CDNOD 11*	Gold	1	2	7
26 Feb 94	**THE BRIT AWARDS**	*EMI CDAWARD 1*		6		3
19 Mar 94	**NOW! THAT'S WHAT I CALL LOVE**	*EMI/Virgin/Polygram CDEVP 7*		6		6
19 Mar 94	**NOW DANCE 94 VOLUME 2**	*EMI/Virgin/Polygram CDNOD 12*		8		5
9 Apr 94	**NOW THAT'S WHAT I CALL MUSIC! 27**	*EMI/Virgin/Polygram CDNOW 27*	Platinum	1	4	15
25 Jun 94	**TRANQUILLITY**	*EMI CDC 5552432*		14		5
2 Jul 94	**NOW DANCE – SUMMER 94**	*EMI/Virgin/Polygram CDNOD 13*		1	2	8
13 Aug 94	**NOW THAT'S WHAT I CALL MUSIC! 28**	*EMI/Virgin/Polygram CDNOW 28*	Platinum x2	1	5	13
8 Oct 94	**CLUB TOGETHER**	*EMI CDEMC 3692*		10		4
15 Oct 94	**NOW THAT'S WHAT I CALL MUSIC! 1994**	*EMI/Virgin/Polygram CDNOW 1994*	Platinum	1	4	8
29 Oct 94	**MISSING YOU**	*EMI CDEMTVD 86*		8		5
26 Nov 94	**NOW THAT'S WHAT I CALL MUSIC! 29**	*EMI/Virgin/Polygram CDNOW 29*	Platinum x5	1	9	13
26 Nov 94	**THE BEST COUNTRY ALBUM IN THE WORLD...EVER!**	*EMI CDEMTVD 93*	Platinum	4		12
10 Dec 94	**NOW DANCE – THE BEST OF 94**	*EMI/Virgin/Polygram CDNOD 14*	Gold	4		9
10 Dec 94	**THAT'S CHRISTMAS**	*EMI CDEMTV 88*	Gold	10		4
11 Mar 95	**UNLACED**	*EMI CDEMTV 90*	Silver	8		4
1 Apr 95	**NOW DANCE 95**	*EMI/Virgin/Polygram CDNOD 15*	Gold	3		6
22 Apr 95	**NOW THAT'S WHAT I CALL MUSIC! 30**	*EMI/Virgin/Polygram CDNOW 30*	Platinum x2	1	4	12
29 Apr 95	**CLUB TOGETHER 2**	*EMI CDEMC 3704*		9		4
15 Jul 95	**THE BEST CLASSICAL ALBUM IN THE WORLD...EVER!**	*EMI CDEMTVD 93*	Gold	6		6
22 Jul 95	**MOST EXCELLENT DANCE**	*EMI CDMXD 1*		8		4
29 Jul 95	**NOW DANCE SUMMER 95**	*EMI/Virgin/Polygram CDNOD 16*		3		5
29 Jul 95	**DEDICATED TO PLEASURE**	*EMI CDEMTV 91*		18		3
12 Aug 95	**NOW THAT'S WHAT I CALL MUSIC! 31**	*EMI/Virgin/Polygram CDNOW 31*	Platinum x2	1	4	12
23 Sep 95	**TECHNO NIGHTS AMBIENT DAWN**	*EMI CDEMTV 97*		16		3
14 Oct 95	**NOW THAT'S WHAT I CALL MUSIC! 1995**	*EMI/Virgin/Polygram CDNOW 1995*	Platinum	2		6
28 Oct 95	**THAT'S ROCK 'N' ROLL**	*EMI CDEMTVD 100*	Gold	12		2
4 Nov 95	**THAT'S COUNTRY**	*EMI CDEMTV 103*	Gold	11		6
11 Nov 95	**THE GREATEST PARTY ALBUM UNDER THE SUN!**	*EMI TV CDEMTVD 107*		1	1	7
25 Nov 95	**NOW THAT'S WHAT I CALL MUSIC! 32**	*EMI/Virgin/Polygram CDNOW 32*	Platinum x4	1	9	15
16 Dec 95	**THAT'S CHRISTMAS**	*EMI TV CDEMTVD 105*		15		2
2 Mar 96	**THE GREATEST DANCE ALBUM UNDER THE SUN!**	*EMI TV CDEMTVD 115*		8		4
9 Mar 96	**THE BEST OF THE NINETIES...SO FAR**	*EMI TV CDEMTVD 116*	Silver	9		5
16 Mar 96	**BABY LOVE**	*EMI TV CDEMTV 117*		11		2
30 Mar 96	**NOW THAT'S WHAT I CALL MUSIC! 33**	*EMI/Virgin/Polygram CDNOW 33*	Platinum x2	1	5	13
11 May 96	**MIX'O'MATIC**	*EMI TV CDEMTVD 123*	Silver	8		3
18 May 96	**LOST PROPERTY**	*EMI TV CDEMTVD 122*		12		2
1 Jun 96	**COMMON GROUND**	*EMI Premier PRMTVCD 1*		17		2
8 Jun 96	**CLUB TOGETHER 3**	*EMI TV CDEMTVD 124*		7		3
15 Jun 96	**LOVERMAN**	*EMI TV CDEMTVD 125*		17		2
20 Jul 96	**BIG MIX 96**	*EMI TV/warner.esp CDEMTVD 129*	Gold	1	4	8
24 Aug 96	**NOW THAT'S WHAT I CALL MUSIC! 34**	*EMI/Virgin/Polygram CDNOW 34*	Platinum x3	1	7	15
28 Sep 96	**BIG MIX '96 – VOLUME 2**	*EMI TV/warner.esp CDEMTVD 131*		7		4
9 Nov 96	**EASY MOODS**	*EMI TV CDEMTVD 137*		15		1
30 Nov 96	**NOW THAT'S WHAT I CALL MUSIC! 35**	*EMI/Virgin/Polygram CDNOW 35*	Platinum x5	1	7	18
30 Nov 96	**GREATEST NON-STOP PARTY UNDER THE SUN**	*EMI TV CDEMTVD 149*	Gold	13		4
7 Dec 96	**LOVE AT THE MOVIES...THE ALBUM**	*EMI TV/Sony TV CDEMTVD 144*	Gold	16		3
28 Dec 96	**THE DOG'S...!**	*EMI TV CDEMTVD 143*	Silver	20		2
5 Apr 97	**NOW THAT'S WHAT I CALL MUSIC! 36**	*EMI/Virgin/Polygram CDNOW 36*	Platinum x2	1	3	16
26 Jul 97	**NOW THAT'S WHAT I CALL MUSIC! 37**	*EMI/Virgin/Polygram CDNOW 37*	Platinum x2	1	4	16
1 Nov 97	**NOW DANCE 97**	*EMI/Virgin CDNOD 17*	Platinum	1	1	6
29 Nov 97	**NOW THAT'S WHAT I CALL MUSIC! 38**	*EMI/Virgin/Polygram CDNOW 38*		1	4	17
18 Apr 98	**NOW THAT'S WHAT I CALL MUSIC! 39**	*EMI/Virgin/Polygram CDNOW 39*		1	8	17
25 Apr 98	**TWENTIETH CENTURY BLUES**	*EMI 4946312*		14		1
16 May 98	**A SONG FOR EUROTRASH**	*EMI 4950622*		19		1
15 Aug 98	**NOW THAT'S WHAT I CALL MUSIC! 40**	*EMI/Virgin/Polygram CDNOW 40*	Platinum x3	1	4	14
7 Nov 98	**NOW DANCE 98**	*EMI/Virgin CDNOD 18*	Gold	3		5
5 Dec 98	**NOW THAT'S WHAT I CALL MUSIC! 41**	*EMI/Virgin/Polygram CDNOW 41*	Platinum x5	1	7	18
10 Apr 99	**NOW THAT'S WHAT I CALL MUSIC! 42**	*EMI/Virgin/Universal Music TV CDNOW 42*	Platinum x3	1	7	16
31 Jul 99	**NOW THAT'S WHAT I CALL MUSIC! 43**	*EMI/Virgin/Universal Music TV CDNOW 43*	Platinum x3	1	4	15
30 Oct 99	**NOW DANCE 2000**	*EMI/Virgin VTDCD 267*	Platinum	1	1	8
4 Dec 99	**NOW THAT'S WHAT I CALL MUSIC! 44**	*EMI/Virgin/Universal Music TV CDNOW 44*	Platinum x7	1	8	18

Silver-selling ○ · Gold-selling ● · Platinum-selling ⊛ · US No.1 ★

Date	Title / Label	Peak Position	Weeks at No.1	Weeks on Chart
29 Apr 00	**NOW THAT'S WHAT I CALL MUSIC! 45** *EMI/Virgin/Universal CDNOW 45* ⊛x3	1	6	15
5 Aug 00	**NOW THAT'S WHAT I CALL MUSIC! 46** *EMI/Virgin/Universal CDNOW 46* ⊛x3	1	4	16
18 Nov 00	**Q AWARDS: THE ALBUM** *EMI/Virgin/Universal VTDCDX 330* ●	6		4
2 Dec 00	**NOW THAT'S WHAT I CALL MUSIC! 47** *EMI/Virgin/Universal CDNOW 47* ⊛x6	1	7	18
2 Dec 00	**THE CLASSICAL ALBUM 2001** *EMI/Virgin/Universal CLCD 2* ●	4		10
9 Dec 00	**NOW THE CHRISTMAS ALBUM** *EMI/Virgin/Universal CDNOX 2* ⊛	2		8
20 Jan 01	**THE GREATEST NO 1 SINGLES** *EMI/Virgin/Universal VTDCD 357* ●	2		6
21 Apr 01	**NOW THAT'S WHAT I CALL MUSIC! 48** *EMI/Virgin/Universal CDNOW 48* ⊛x3	1	3	15
9 Jun 01	**SMASH HITS SUMMER 2001** *EMI/Virgin/Universal VTDCD 373* ●	2		7
11 Aug 01	**NOW THAT'S WHAT I CALL MUSIC! 49** *EMI/Virgin/Universal CDNOW 49* ⊛x3	1	6	14
17 Nov 01	**THE BEST AIR GUITAR ALBUM IN THE WORLD…EVER!** *EMI/Virgin/Universal VTDCD 416* ⊛	2		14
1 Dec 01	**NOW THAT'S WHAT I CALL MUSIC! 50** *EMI/Virgin/Universal CDNOW 50* ⊛x6	1	7	14
22 Dec 01	**SMASH HITS 2002** *EMI/Virgin/Universal VTDCD 398* ●	5		8
6 Apr 02	**NOW THAT'S WHAT I CALL MUSIC! 51** *EMI/Virgin/Universal CDNOW 51* ⊛x3	1	3	17
3 Aug 02	**NOW THAT'S WHAT I CALL MUSIC! 52** *EMI/Virgin/Universal CDNOW 52* ⊛x3	1	4	14
14 Sep 02	**SMASH HITS – LET'S PARTY** *EMI/Virgin/Universal VTDCD 503* ⊛	1	5	10
23 Nov 02	**50 YEARS OF THE GREATEST HIT SINGLES** *EMI/Virgin/Universal VTDCDX 491* ⊛	5		11
30 Nov 02	**NOW THAT'S WHAT I CALL MUSIC! 53** *EMI/Virgin/Universal CDNOW 53* ⊛x4	1	7	15
30 Nov 02	**THE BEST AIR GUITAR ALBUM IN THE WORLD 2** *EMI/Virgin/Universal VTDCD 488* ⊛x2	3		11
11 Jan 03	**SMASH HITS 2003** *EMI/Virgin/Universal VTDCD 492*	20		1
22 Feb 03	**I LUV SMASH HITS** *EMI/Virgin/Universal VTDCD 511* ●	2		5
26 Apr 03	**NOW THAT'S WHAT I CALL MUSIC! 54** *EMI/Virgin/Universal CDNOW 54* ⊛x2	1	7	14
2 Aug 03	**NOW THAT'S WHAT I CALL MUSIC! 55** *EMI/Virgin/Universal CDNOW 55* ⊛x2	1	4	15
9 Aug 03	**ONE STEP BEYOND** *EMI Virgin/Sanctuary VTDCDX546* ○	9		3
30 Aug 03	**NEW WOMAN – THE NEW COLLECTION 2003** *EMI/BMG/Telstar VTDCD576* ●	3		8
11 Oct 03	**NOW DECADES** *EMI/Virgin/Universal VTDCD 580* ⊛	1	3	17
1 Nov 03	**SMASH HITS – LET'S PARTY ON** *EMI/Virgin/Universal VTDCD 581* ○	8		2
29 Nov 03	**NOW THAT'S WHAT I CALL MUSIC! 56** *EMI/Virgin/Universal CDNOW 56* ⊛x5	1	7	15
6 Dec 03	**THE BEST AIR GUITAR ALBUM EVER III** *EMI/Virgin/Universal VTDCD 557* ●	14		9
13 Dec 03	**I LOVE CHRISTMAS** *EMI/Virgin/Universal VTDCDX 560*	15		3
21 Feb 04	**I LUV SMASH HITS 2004** *EMI/Virgin/Universal VTDCD 563*	7		3
27 Mar 04	**BEST OF R&B** *EMI/Sony TV VTDCD 604* ●	3		12
17 Apr 04	**NOW THAT'S WHAT I CALL MUSIC! 57** *EMI/Virgin/Universal CDNOW 57* ⊛x3	1	7	17
19 Jun 04	**ENGLAND – THE ALBUM** *EMI TV/Sony TV VTCD 621* ●	2		3
26 Jun 04	**CAPITAL GOLD JAZZ LEGENDS** *Virgin/EMI/UCJ VTDCD 615*	10		1
7 Aug 04	**NOW THAT'S WHAT I CALL MUSIC! 58** *EMI/Virgin/Universal CDNOW 58* ⊛x3	1	6	15
21 Aug 04	**THE BEST OF R&B – SUMMER SELECTION** *EMI/Virgin/BMG TV/ VTDCD 636* ○	2		8
9 Oct 04	**NOW YEARS** *EMI/Virgin/Universal VTDCD 672* ●	1	2	7
27 Nov 04	**NOW THAT'S WHAT I CALL MUSIC! 59** *EMI/Virgin/Universal CDNOW59* ⊛x4	1	5	14
4 Dec 04	**CAPITAL GOLD GUITAR LEGENDS** *EMI/Virgin/Universal VTDCD653* ●	8		6
4 Dec 04	**THE BEST NO 1 SINGLES IN THE WORLD EVER** *EMI/Virgin/Universal VTDCD643* ●	14		6
11 Dec 04	**THE BEST CHRISTMAS ALBUM IN THE WORLD** *EMI/Virgin/Universal VTDCD648* ⊛	5		7
8 Jan 05	**BEST BANDS 2005** *EMI TV/Sony TV VTDCD639* ●	3		10
5 Mar 05	**NEW WOMAN – SPRING COLLECTION** *EMI Virgin/Sony BMG TV VTDCD703* ●	3		4
2 Apr 05	**NOW THAT'S WHAT I CALL MUSIC! 60** *EMI/Virgin/Universal CDNOW60* ⊛x3	1	5	18
9 Apr 05	**REAL EIGHTIES – HITS PLUS EXTENDED MIXES** *EMI/Virgin/Universal VTDCD709* ○	8		4
9 Jul 05	**12 INCH 80'S VOLUME 2** *EMI Virgin/Family 9829762*	16		3
30 Jul 05	**THE BEST BBQ ALBUM EVER** *EMI/Virgin/Universal VTDCD732* ○	5		5
6 Aug 05	**NOW THAT'S WHAT I CALL MUSIC! 61** *EMI/Virgin/Universal CDNOW61* ⊛x3	1	7	16
3 Sep 05	**NEW WOMAN – THE NEW COLLECTION 2005** *EMI Virgin/Sony BMG TV VTDCD741*	4		5
15 Oct 05	**HOUSEWORK SONGS** *EMI Virgin VTDCD750* ⊛	3		28
22 Oct 05	**THE ALBUM 6** *EMI Virgin VTDCD755* ○	5		4
5 Nov 05	**R&B PARTY** *EMI Virgin VTDCD751*	18		1
19 Nov 05	**THE VERY BEST OF POWER BALLADS** *EMI Virgin VTDCD756* ●	10		61
19 Nov 05	**SCHOOL REUNION – THE PARTY** *EMI Virgin VTDCD757*	15		2
26 Nov 05	**CAPITAL GOLD – PLATINUM LEGENDS** *EMI Virgin VTDCD766*	20		1
3 Dec 05	**NOW THAT'S WHAT I CALL MUSIC! 62** *EMI/Virgin/Universal CDNOW62* ⊛x4	1	6	17
10 Dec 05	**NOW XMAS** *EMI/Virgin/Universal VTCD767* ●	8		3
10 Dec 05	**THE BEST OF THE BEST AIR GUITAR ALBUMS** *EMI/Virgin/Universal VTDCD759* ●	15		5
17 Dec 05	**THE BEST CLUB ANTHEMS CLASSICS** *EMI Virgin VTDCD764* ●	3		15
17 Dec 05	**I LOVE SIXTIES** *EMI Virgin VTDCD769* ●	19		1
28 Jan 06	**SOAPSTAR SUPERSTAR – THE ALBUM** *EMI Virgin VTCD778*	5		1
28 Jan 06	**I LOVE MUSICALS** *EMI Virgin VTDCD779*	12		1
4 Feb 06	**GODSKITCHEN – ANTHEMS** *EMI Virgin VTDCD777*	7		7
4 Feb 06	**BIG SOFTIES – 41 SENSITIVE SOUL CLASSICS** *EMI Virgin/Sony BMG TV VTDCD736*	8		4
11 Feb 06	**THE VERY BEST OF LOVE LEGENDS** *EMI Virgin VTDCD780* ○	4		4
11 Feb 06	**SUNDAY MORNING SONGS** *EMI Virgin VTDCD787*	18		1
18 Mar 06	**RELAXING SONGS** *EMI Virgin VTCD792*	16		1
25 Mar 06	**NEW WOMAN – HITS FROM THE CHICK FLICKS** *EMI Virgin VTDCD783* ●	3		5
25 Mar 06	**BRINGING ON BACK THE GOOD TIMES** *EMI Virgin VTDCD789*	10		3
8 Apr 06	**THE HACIENDA CLASSICS** *EMI Virgin/WMTV VTDCD790* ○	4		7
15 Apr 06	**CLUB FEVER 2006** *EMI Virgin VTDCD793*	4		3
22 Apr 06	**NOW THAT'S WHAT I CALL MUSIC! 63** *EMI/Virgin/Universal CDNOW63*	1	5	14
6 May 06	**HOUSEWORK SONGS II** *EMI Virgin VTDCD796* ○	3		6
27 May 06	**BACK IN THE DAY** *EMI Virgin VTDCD797*	7		4
3 Jun 06	**THE BANDS 06** *EMI Virgin VTDCD675* ○	7		3
10 Jun 06	**ENGLAND – THE ALBUM** *EMI TV/Sony TV VTCD803*	1	1	5
17 Jun 06	**DIY SONGS** *EMI Virgin VTDCD801*	4		3
8 Jul 06	**FEELGOOD SONGS** *EMI Virgin VTDCD812* ○	9		8
8 Jul 06	**PLAYSCHOOL POP** *EMI Virgin VTDCDX799*	13		3
15 Jul 06	**IN THE MIX – IBIZA CLASSICS** *EMI Virgin VTDCD811*	6		3
29 Jul 06	**THE ACOUSTIC ALBUM** *EMI/Virgin/Universal VTDCD813*	5		4
5 Aug 06	**NOW THAT'S WHAT I CALL MUSIC! 64** *EMI/Virgin/UMTV CDNOW64* ⊛x2	1	5	17
5 Aug 06	**GODSKITCHEN – GLOBAL GATHERING 2006** *EMI Virgin VTDCD805*	8		3
19 Aug 06	**THE BEST CLUB ANTHEMS 2006** *EMI Virgin/Sony BMG TV VTDCD848*	5		5
26 Aug 06	**LET'S HEAR IT FOR THE GIRLS** *EMI Virgin VTDCD844*	6		5
16 Sep 06	**DRIVING SONGS** *EMI Virgin VTDCD785*	9		3
23 Sep 06	**CAPITAL GOLD – FIFTIES LEGENDS** *EMI Virgin/Sony BMG TV VTDCD851*	9		3
30 Sep 06	**CLASSIC TRANCE ANTHEMS** *EMI Virgin VTDCD852*	12		2
28 Oct 06	**NOW DANCE 2007** *EMI Virgin/Ministry Of Sound VTDCD817* ●	3		4
28 Oct 06	**THE VERY BEST OF BACK TO THE MOVIES** *EMI TV/Sony TV VTDCD820*	8		3
4 Nov 06	**BBC RADIO 2 PRESENTS THE PLAYLIST** *EMI Virgin VTDCD800*	14		1
11 Nov 06	**NOW THAT'S WHAT I CALL NO 1'S** *EMI/Virgin/Universal VTDCD818* ○	5		7
18 Nov 06	**THE BEST COUNTRY ALBUM EVER** *EMI/Virgin/Universal VTDCD834* ●	10		5
18 Nov 06	**THE ULTIMATE BANDS – THE CLASSIC ANTHEMS** *EMI Virgin VTDCD822*	13		1
2 Dec 06	**NOW THAT'S WHAT I CALL MUSIC! 65** *EMI/Virgin/Universal CDNOW65* ⊛x3	1	5	18
2 Dec 06	**NOW THAT'S WHAT I CALL XMAS** *EMI/Virgin/Universal VTDCD836* ●	5		6
9 Dec 06	**MONSTERS OF ROCK** *EMI Virgin VTDCD824* ●	14		5
17 Feb 07	**UNFORGETTABLE LOVESONGS** *EMI Virgin VTDCD859*	9		2
24 Feb 07	**MASHED** *EMI Virgin VTCD858*	14		3
10 Mar 07	**101 80S HITS** *EMI Virgin VTDCDX865* ●	1	1	12
17 Mar 07	**HEARTBEAT – LOVESONGS** *EMI Virgin VTDCD863* ○	5		3
17 Mar 07	**NEW WOMAN – THE CLASSICS** *EMI Virgin VTDCD864*	11		3
24 Mar 07	**I LOVE MUM** *EMI Virgin VTCD862*	4		1
7 Apr 07	**HEARTBEAT – 50 GROOVY TRACKS FROM THE 60S** *EMI Gold 3891062*	20		1
14 Apr 07	**NOW THAT'S WHAT I CALL MUSIC 66** *EMI/Virgin/Universal CDNOW66* ⊛x3	1	6	17
5 May 07	**IN THE MIX – RAVE REVIVAL** *EMI Virgin VTDCD867*	8		2
12 May 07	**101 SIXTIES HITS** *EMI Virgin VTDCDX866*	4		3
2 Jun 07	**TOP GEAR ANTHEMS** *EMI Virgin VTDCD869* ●	1	1	9
16 Jun 07	**1977 – THE SPIRIT OF PUNK** *EMI TV/Sony BMG VTDCD870*	7		3
16 Jun 07	**101 JUKEBOX CLASSICS** *EMI Virgin VTDCDX871* ○	9		3
7 Jul 07	**HEARTBEAT SUMMER** *EMI TV VTDCD872* ○	5		3
14 Jul 07	**MYLEENE'S MUSIC FOR ROMANCE** *EMI Classics 3956032*	9		3
21 Jul 07	**101 CLUB ANTHEMS** *EMI TV VTDCDX875* ●	3		9
4 Aug 07	**NOW THAT'S WHAT I CALL MUSIC 67** *EMI/Virgin/Universal CDNOW67* ⊛x2	1	3	16

Date	Title / Label	Peak Position	Weeks at No.1	Weeks on Chart
4 Aug 07	THE SATURDAY SESSIONS – THE DERMOT O'LEARY SHOW *EMI Virgin VTDCD873*	11		3
1 Sep 07	101 70S HITS *EMI/Virgin VTDCDX894*	6		8
1 Sep 07	THE CAVERN: THE MOST FAMOUS CLUB IN THE WORLD *EMI 5074532*	8		3
8 Sep 07	CLUB ANTHEMS 2007 *EMI/Virgin VTDCD892*	7		3
6 Oct 07	THE SONGS *EMI/Virgin VTDCD896*	7		4
20 Oct 07	HEAD FULL OF ROCK *EMI VTDCD876*	16		1
27 Oct 07	NOW DANCE 2008 *EMI Virgin VTDCD878*	4		3
27 Oct 07	CLASSICAL 2008 *EMI Virgin VTDCD897*	10		2
3 Nov 07	SIXTIES POWER BALLADS *EMI Virgin VTDCD893*	10		3
10 Nov 07	NOW THAT'S WHAT I CALL THE 80'S *EMI Virgin VTDCD877*	6		3
17 Nov 07	101 NUMBER 1'S *EMI Virgin VTDCDX884*	8		3
24 Nov 07	TOP GEAR SERIOUSLY COOL DRIVING MUSIC *EMI Virgin VTDCD882*	9		14
24 Nov 07	101 COUNTRY HITS *EMI Virgin VTDCDX881*	18		1
1 Dec 07	NOW THAT'S WHAT I CALL MUSIC 68 *EMI/Virgin/Universal CDNOW68* x4	1	7	19
1 Dec 07	JACKIE: THE ALBUM *EMI Virgin VTDCDX883*	3		21
8 Dec 07	NOW THAT'S WHAT I CALL XMAS *EMI/Virgin/Universal VTDCD836*	7		5
8 Dec 07	101 CHRISTMAS SONGS *EMI Virgin VTDCDX890*	15		4
8 Dec 07	HEARTBEAT NUMBER 1'S *EMI Virgin VTDCD880*	19		1
16 Feb 08	101 LOVE SONGS *EMI Virgin VTDCDX901*	2		3
1 Mar 08	MYLEENE'S MUSIC FOR MOTHERS *EMI Classics 5044142*	14		2
8 Mar 08	MUM'S FAVOURITE SONGS *EMI Virgin VTDCD904*	6		2
8 Mar 08	TOP OF THE POP'S – THE 80'S *EMI Virgin VTDCD903*	8		4
22 Mar 08	NME CLASSICS *EMI Virgin VTDCD900*	8		3
22 Mar 08	MORNING HAS BROKEN *EMI Classics 2083632*	17		1
29 Mar 08	NOW THAT'S WHAT I CALL MUSIC 69 *EMI/Virgin/Universal CDNOW69* x3	1	3	19
26 Apr 08	101 DRIVING SONGS *EMI Virgin VTDCDX905*	5		15
10 May 08	101 TRANCE ANTHEMS *EMI Virgin VTDCDX902*	6		4
24 May 08	101 CLASSICAL HITS *EMI Virgin VTDCDX906*	13		1
7 Jun 08	EUROVISION SONG CONTEST – BELGRADE 2008 *EMI 2169972*	20		1
14 Jun 08	TOP GEAR ANTHEMS 2008 *EMI Virgin VTDCD910*	2		5
14 Jun 08	DAD ROCKS *EMI Virgin VTDCD720*	3		3
14 Jun 08	101 ROCK 'N' ROLL HITS *EMI Virgin VTDCDX913*	11		3
5 Jul 08	TV AD SONGS *EMI Virgin VTDCD914*	18		1
12 Jul 08	JIVE BUNNY'S SUMMER PARTY 2008 *EMI Virgin VTDCD911*	9		3
19 Jul 08	101 SUMMER SONGS *EMI Virgn VTDCDX915*	12		4
2 Aug 08	NOW THAT'S WHAT I CALL MUSIC 70 *EMI/Virgin/Universal CDNOW70*	1	3	17
23 Aug 08	101 90S HITS *EMI Virgin VTDCDX916*	7		6
23 Aug 08	STORY SONGS *EMI Virgin VTDCD917*	16		1
27 Sep 08	THE GIRLS *EMI Virgin VTDCD942*	5		8
4 Oct 08	THE MIX TAPES – ALTERNATIVE MUSIC FROM THE LATE 70S AND 80S *EMI Virgin VTDCD923*	15		1
11 Oct 08	101 FIFTIES SONGS *EMI Virgin VTDCDX925*	8		3
11 Oct 08	SEVENTIES POWER BALLADS *EMI Virgin VTDCD921*	11		2
1 Nov 08	THE WEEKEND STARTS HERE – ORIGINAL *EMI Virgin VTDCD922*	13		1
8 Nov 08	NOW THAT'S WHAT I CALL MUSIC: 25 YEARS *EMI Virgin CDNOWX25*	3		5
8 Nov 08	THE BEST OF BOND JAMES BOND *EMI 5405542*	9		3
22 Nov 08	101 POWER BALLADS *EMI Virgin VTDCDX944*	9		3
22 Nov 08	GRANGE HILL – THE ALBUM *EMI Virgin VTDCD940*	13		1
29 Nov 08	NOW THAT'S WHAT I CALL MUSIC 71 *EMI/Virgin/Universal CDNOW71*	1	2	2
29 Nov 08	JACKIE: THE ALBUM – VOLUME 2 *EMI Virgin VTDCD926*	9		2

VARIOUS ARTISTS (EMPORIO)

Date	Title / Label	Peak Position	Weeks at No.1	Weeks on Chart
16 Jun 01	PAVAROTTI/DOMINGO/CARRERAS *Emporio EMTBX 320*	14		1

VARIOUS ARTISTS (EPIC)

Date	Title / Label	Peak Position	Weeks at No.1	Weeks on Chart
2 Jul 83	DANCE MIX – DANCE HITS VOLUME 1 *Epic EPC 25564*	85		2
24 Sep 83	DANCE MIX – DANCE HITS VOLUME 2 *Epic DM 2*	51		3
3 Mar 84	DANCE MIX – DANCE HITS VOLUME 3 *Epic DM 3*	70		1
3 Mar 84	ELECTRO SHOCK VOLTAGE ONE *Epic VOLT 1*	73		1
16 Jun 84	AMERICAN HEARTBEAT *Epic EPC 10045*	4		22
16 Jun 84	DANCE MIX – DANCE HITS VOLUME 4 *Epic DM 4*	99		1
8 Mar 86	HITS FOR LOVERS *Epic EPC 10050*	2		14
9 Nov 91	MELLOW MADNESS *Epic MOOD 20*	14		2
18 Jul 92	RED HOT + DANCE *Epic 4718212*	6		5
29 Aug 92	ROMANCING THE SCREEN *Epic 4719012*	5		11
6 Sep 97	MIX HEAVEN '97 *Epic SONYTV 31CD*	19		1
17 Oct 98	VH1 DIVAS LIVE *Epic SONYTV 55CD*	3		4
5 May 01	ALLY McBEAL – FOR ONCE IN MY LIFE *Epic 5005772*	10		2

VARIOUS ARTISTS (ERATO)

Date	Title / Label	Peak Position	Weeks at No.1	Weeks on Chart
11 Jul 92	THE ULTIMATE OPERA COLLECTION *Erato 2292457972*	14		5

VARIOUS ARTISTS (ESSENTIAL RECORDINGS)

Date	Title / Label	Peak Position	Weeks at No.1	Weeks on Chart
6 May 00	ESSENTIAL SELECTION SPRING 2000 *Essential Recordings 8573828142*	8		4
9 Sep 00	ESSENTIAL SELECTION IBIZA 2000 *Essential Recordings 8573847842*	11		3

VARIOUS ARTISTS (EXPANSION)

Date	Title / Label	Peak Position	Weeks at No.1	Weeks on Chart
24 Apr 93	WINNER'S CIRCLE *Expansion CDEXP 2*	20		1

VARIOUS ARTISTS (FAME)

Date	Title / Label	Peak Position	Weeks at No.1	Weeks on Chart
8 Dec 84	THE CHRISTMAS CAROL COLLECTION *Fame WHS 413000*	75		3

VARIOUS ARTISTS (FAMILY)

Date	Title / Label	Peak Position	Weeks at No.1	Weeks on Chart
6 Oct 07	12 INCH 80S GROOVE *Family 5303387*	2		4

VARIOUS ARTISTS (FAMILY RECORDINGS)

Date	Title / Label	Peak Position	Weeks at No.1	Weeks on Chart
19 Mar 05	12 INCH 80'S *Family Recordings 9826602*	5		6
13 Aug 05	NAUGHTY BUT NICE *Family 9826988*	19		1
11 Mar 06	12 INCH 80S DANCE *Family 9832726*	4		6
9 Feb 08	12 INCH 80S LOVE *Family Recordings 5306279*	9		3

VARIOUS ARTISTS (FANFARE)

Date	Title / Label	Peak Position	Weeks at No.1	Weeks on Chart
12 Nov 88	THE HIT FACTORY VOLUME 2 *Fanfare/PWL HF 4*	16		9
14 Jan 89	THE HIT FACTORY VOLUME 2 *Fanfare/PWL HF 4*	13		3
15 Jul 89	THE HIT FACTORY VOLUME 3 *Fanfare/PWL HF 8*	3		10
23 Sep 89	JUST SEVENTEEN – HEARTBEATS *Fanfare FARE 1*	3		6

VARIOUS ARTISTS (FANTAZIA)

Date	Title / Label	Peak Position	Weeks at No.1	Weeks on Chart
5 Dec 92	FANTAZIA – THE FIRST TASTE *Fantazia FANTA 001*	13		5
24 Jul 93	FANTAZIA – TWICE AS NICE *Fantazia FANTA 002CD*	17		3
25 Jun 94	FANTAZIA III – MADE IN HEAVEN *Fantazia FANTA 005CD*	16		2
29 Apr 95	THE HOUSE COLLECTION – VOLUME 2 *Fantazia FHC 002CD*	6		6
30 Sep 95	THE HOUSE COLLECTION – VOLUME 3 *Fantazia FHC 3DL*	4		7
17 Feb 96	THE HOUSE COLLECTION – CLUB CLASSICS *Fantazia FHCC 1CDL*	3		10
29 Jun 96	FANTAZIA PRESENT THE HOUSE COLLECTION 4 *Fantazia FHC 4CDL*	2		9
14 Sep 96	THE HOUSE COLLECTION CLUB CLASSICS – 2 *Fantazia FHCCC 2CDL*	4		8
8 Mar 97	THE HOUSE COLLECTION – VOLUME 5 *Fantazia FHC 5CD*	3		7
7 Jun 97	CLUB CLASSICS – VOLUME 3 *Fantazia FHCCC 3CD*	4		6
27 Sep 97	THE HOUSE COLLECTION 6 – PAUL OAKENFOLD/PAUL COSFORD *Fantazia FHC 6CD*	10		3
21 Feb 98	FANTAZIA – BRITISH ANTHEMS *Fantazia FBA 1CD*	2		5

VARIOUS ARTISTS (FEVERPITCH)

Date	Title / Label	Peak Position	Weeks at No.1	Weeks on Chart
16 Sep 95	TRADE *Feverpitch FVRCD 1001*	14		2
20 Apr 96	TRADE – VOLUME TWO *Feverpitch FVRCD 2*	11		3
9 Nov 96	TRADE – VOLUME THREE *Feverpitch FVRCD 3*	19		1
12 Apr 97	TRADE – VOLUME FOUR *Feverpitch FVRCD 5*	15		2

VARIOUS ARTISTS (FFRR)

Date	Title / Label	Peak Position	Weeks at No.1	Weeks on Chart
30 Jan 88	THE HOUSE SOUND OF CHICAGO VOLUME 3 *ffrr FFRLP 1*	40		4
27 Aug 88	THE HOUSE SOUND OF LONDON VOLUME 4 *ffrr FFRDP 4*	70		7
1 Oct 88	BALEARIC BEATS VOLUME 1 *ffrr FFRLP 5*	58		2
20 Jan 96	ESSENTIAL MIX – TONG COX SASHA OAKENFOLD *ffrr 8287042*	12		3
20 Apr 96	LTJ BUKEM PRESENTS LOGICAL PROGRESSION *ffrr 8287472*	14		1
11 May 96	ESSENTIAL MIX 2 – TONG, MACKINTOSH… *ffrr 5354312*	6		3
10 Aug 96	METALHEADZ – PLATINUM BREAKZ *ffrr 8287832*	12		2
7 Sep 96	ESSENTIAL MIX 3 – TONG, SEAMAN, JULES ETC *ffrr 5358292*	12		3
15 Nov 97	PETE TONG ESSENTIAL SELECTION – WINTER 97 *ffrr 5550932*	10		2
18 Apr 98	PETE TONG ESSENTIAL SELECTION *ffrr 5557862*	4		7

Silver-selling ○ Gold-selling ● Platinum-selling ⊛ US No.1 ★

Date	Title	Label / Cat. No.	Peak Position	Weeks at No.1	Weeks on Chart
8 Aug 98	CARL COX – NON STOP 98/01	*ffrr 5560302* ○	8		5
29 Aug 98	PETE TONG ESSENTIAL SELECTION – SUMMER 1998 (3 CD)	*ffrr 5560422*	2		7
29 Aug 98	PETE TONG ESSENTIAL SELECTION – SUMMER 1998	*ffrr 5560422* ●	4		9
5 Dec 98	ESSENTIAL SELECTION '98 – PETE TONG/PAUL OAKENFOLD	*ffrr 5659642* ●	11		6
9 Jan 99	ESSENTIAL SELECTION '98 – PETE TONG/PAUL OAKENFOLD	*ffrr 5659642*	13		5
20 Mar 99	PETE TONG – ESSENTIAL SELECTION – SPRING 1999	*ffrr 5560842*	3		6
20 Mar 99	PETE TONG – ESSENTIAL SELECTION – SPRING 1999	*ffrr 5560882*	13		3
31 Jul 99	PETE TONG ESSENTIAL SELECTION – IBIZA 99	*ffrr 3984290822* ●	7		3
31 Jul 99	PETE TONG ESSENTIAL SELECTION – IBIZA 99	*ffrr 3984290832* ●	11		5
30 Oct 99	CARL COX – NON STOP 2000	*ffrr 8573804212*	13		2
13 Nov 99	ESSENTIAL MILLENNIUM – PETE TONG FATBOY SLIM PAUL OAKENFOLD	*ffrr 8573806292* ●	10		3

VARIOUS ARTISTS (FIRM)

Date	Title	Label / Cat. No.	Peak Position	Weeks at No.1	Weeks on Chart
11 Jan 97	WORLD DANCE – THE DRUM + BASS EXPERIENCE	*Firm FIRMCD 10*	10		4

VARIOUS ARTISTS (FOURTH & BROADWAY)

Date	Title	Label / Cat. No.	Peak Position	Weeks at No.1	Weeks on Chart
7 Mar 92	THE REBIRTH OF COOL, TOO	*Fourth & Broadway BRCD 582*	13		2
15 May 93	THE REBIRTH OF COOL III	*Fourth & Broadway BRCD 590*	9		4

VARIOUS ARTISTS (FREESTYLE)

Date	Title	Label / Cat. No.	Peak Position	Weeks at No.1	Weeks on Chart
3 Oct 98	BROTHER'S GONNA WORK IT OUT	*Freestyle XDUSTCDX 101*	7		3

VARIOUS ARTISTS (FRESH)

Date	Title	Label / Cat. No.	Peak Position	Weeks at No.1	Weeks on Chart
3 Jun 95	FRESHEN UP VOLUME 1	*Fresh FRSHCD 1*	20		1

VARIOUS ARTISTS (GATECRASHER)

Date	Title	Label / Cat. No.	Peak Position	Weeks at No.1	Weeks on Chart
20 Oct 01	GATECRASHER DIGITAL	*Gatecrasher Music GATECD 1* ○	6		4
2 Feb 02	GATECRASHER EXPERIENCE	*Gatecrasher GATECD 2*	2		3
4 May 02	GATECRASHER DIGITAL TRANCE	*Gatecrasher GATECD 3*	8		2

VARIOUS ARTISTS (GLOBAL TELEVISION)

Date	Title	Label / Cat. No.	Peak Position	Weeks at No.1	Weeks on Chart
17 Dec 94	SOUNDS OF THE SEVENTIES	*Global Television RADCD 01* ●	11		5
17 Dec 94	HITS, HITS AND MORE DANCE HITS	*Global Television RADCD 02*	13		4
21 Jan 95	SOFT REGGAE	*Global Television RADCD 04* ●	2		7
18 Feb 95	NEW SOUL REBELS	*Global Television RADCD 05*	6		6
25 Feb 95	ON A DANCE TIP	*Global Television RADCD 07*	1	3	9
4 Mar 95	GIRLS AND GUITARS	*Global Television RADCD 06*	8		4
15 Apr 95	FIFTY NUMBER ONES OF THE '60S	*Global Television RADCD 08* ●	8		4
22 Apr 95	CLUB CLASS	*Global Television RADCD 10* ○	4		5
22 Apr 95	INTO THE EIGHTIES	*Global Television RADCD 09* ○	5		5
20 May 95	ON A DANCE TIP 2	*Global Television RADCD 12* ●	1	3	7
17 Jun 95	DANCE BUZZ	*Global Television RADCD 17* ●	3		4
1 Jul 95	CHARTBUSTERS	*Global Television RADCD 15*	2		6
1 Jul 95	GREAT SEX	*Global Television RADCD 16*	13		2
15 Jul 95	THEMES AND DREAMS	*Global Television RADCD 11*	11		2
29 Jul 95	NATURAL WOMAN	*Global Television RADCD 14*	7		8
12 Aug 95	SUMMER DANCE PARTY	*Global Television RADCD 18*	2		5
26 Aug 95	HITZ BLITZ	*Global Television RADCD 20*	2		5
23 Sep 95	DANCE TIP 3	*Global Television RADCD 20*	2		6
30 Sep 95	DRIVING ROCK	*Global Television RADCD 03*	9		6
28 Oct 95	NIGHTFEVER	*Global Television RADCD 24*	7		5
18 Nov 95	DANCE TIP ' 95	*Global Television RADCD 27* ⊛	3		12
23 Dec 95	HITS 96	*Global Television RADCD 30* ⊛	1	5	14
17 Feb 96	VYBIN' – YOUNG SOUL REBELS	*Global Television RADCD 19* ○	9		4
2 Mar 96	DANCE TIP 4	*warner.esp TV/Global TV RADCD 26*	7		3
6 Apr 96	COUNTRY GOLD	*Global Television RADCD 25*	12		3
27 Apr 96	UNTITLED	*Global Television RADCD 32* ○	6		4
4 May 96	VYBIN' 3 – NEW SOUL REBELS	*Global Television RADCD 33* ●	2		5
11 May 96	DANCE MIX UK	*Global Television RADCD 37* ○	6		4
18 May 96	NEW HITS 96	*Global TV/Warner TV RADCD 36* ⊛	1	9	16
25 May 96	NATURAL WOMAN – VOLUME 2	*Global Television RADCD 28* ○	10		3
15 Jun 96	THE BEST OF ACID JAZZ	*Global Television RADCD 35*	5		5
13 Jul 96	NO GREATER LOVE	*Global Television RADCD 34*	4		6
20 Jul 96	SHADES OF SOUL	*Global Television RADCD 40*	15		1
27 Jul 96	VYBIN' 4	*Global Television RADCD 38*	7		5
3 Aug 96	UNTITLED 2	*Global Television RADCD 39*	6		6
17 Aug 96	THE ULTIMATE LINE DANCING ALBUM	*Global Television RADCD 41* ○	9		6
14 Sep 96	DANCE MIX 2	*Global Television RADCD 42*	10		4
19 Oct 96	HEARTBEAT – NUMBER 1 LOVE SONGS OF THE '60S	*Global Television RADCD 46* ⊛	2		21
16 Nov 96	THE BEST OF VYBIN'	*Sony TV/Global TV RADCD 45*	12		2
16 Nov 96	UNTITLED 3	*Global Television RADCD 44*	20		1
30 Nov 96	THE ULTIMATE PARTY ANIMAL	*Global Television RADCD 47* ●	4		10
21 Dec 96	DANCE TIP 2000	*warner.esp/Global TV RADCD 50*	7		7
8 Feb 97	THE ULTIMATE LINE DANCING ALBUM	*Global Television RADCD 41*	7		8
15 Feb 97	BEST OF ACID JAZZ VOLUME 2	*Global TV/Polygram TV RADCD 52*	13		4
15 Mar 97	GIRL POWER	*Global Television RADCD 56* ●	9		5
5 Apr 97	THE OLD SKOOL	*Polygram TV/Global TV RADCD 59* ○	6		7
19 Apr 97	KLUBHOPPIN'	*Global Television RADCD 60* ○	6		4
26 Apr 97	NEW HITS 1997	*Global Television RADCD 67* ●	1	4	11
24 May 97	CHARTBUSTERS	*Global Television RADCD 65*	4		6
31 May 97	MODROPHENIA	*Global Television RADCD 62*	14		3
28 Jun 97	THE ULTIMATE SUMMER PARTY ANIMAL	*Global Television RADCD 63*	2		8
26 Jul 97	THE OLD SKOOL REUNION	*Polygram TV/Global TV RADCD 69*	12		2
16 Aug 97	FRESH HITS 1997	*warner.esp/Global TV/Sony TV RADCD 70*	1	3	12
30 Aug 97	DRIVE ON	*Global Television RADCD 55*	10		3
6 Sep 97	THE BEST DANCE ALBUM OF THE YEAR	*Global Television RADCD 61*	6		5
20 Sep 97	PURE REGGAE	*Global Television RADCD 71*	12		3
18 Oct 97	SPEED GARAGE ANTHEMS	*Global Television RADCD 78* ○	5		4
1 Nov 97	HUGE HITS 1997	*warner.esp/Global TV/Sony TV RADCD 75* ⊛	1	1	7
1 Nov 97	HEARTBEAT – LOVE ME TENDER	*Global Television RADCD 72* ●	6		5
22 Nov 97	A PERFECT LOVE	*warner.esp/Global TV RADCD 80* ⊛	4		15
20 Dec 97	BIG HITS	*warner.esp/Global TV/Sony TV RADCD 88*	4		7
27 Dec 97	FUNKY DIVAS	*Global Television RADCD 77* ●	3		13
17 Jan 98	THE EIGHTIES MIX	*Global Television RADCD 85* ●	1	2	7
17 Jan 98	SHADES OF SOUL	*Global Television RADCD 66*	9		3
31 Jan 98	ONE WORLD	*Global Television RADCD 74* ○	8		3
21 Feb 98	DROP DEAD GORGEOUS	*Global Television RADCD 73* ●	4		7
21 Feb 98	SPEED GARAGE ANTHEMS – VOLUME 2	*Global Television RADCD 83* ○	5		8
4 Apr 98	CLUB CULTURE EXPOSED!	*Global Television RADCD 93* ○	5		4
18 Apr 98	URBAN RHYMES	*Global TV/Polygram TV RADCD 89* ○	5		5
23 May 98	THE BEST DANCE ALBUM OF THE YEAR	*Global Television RADCD 97*	13		3
30 May 98	DROP DEAD GORGEOUS 2	*Global Television RADCD 94*	10		3
1 Aug 98	SPEED GARAGE ANTHEMS IN IBIZA	*Global Television RADCD 98X* ○	7		4
8 Aug 98	HEART FULL OF SOUL	*warner.esp/Global TV RADCD 99* ●	8		3
22 Aug 98	STREET VIBES	*warner.esp/Global TV/Sony Music TV RADCD 95*	6		7
24 Oct 98	THE FEMALE TOUCH	*warner.esp/Global TV RADCD 107* ●	2		5
21 Nov 98	A PERFECT LOVE II	*warner.esp/Global TV RADCD 105* ●	9		3
28 Nov 98	HEARTBEAT – THE 60'S GOLD COLLECTION	*Global Television RADCD 90*	7		12
5 Dec 98	FUNKY DIVAS 2	*Global Television RADCD 106* ●	16		8
16 Jan 99	STREET VIBES 2	*warner.esp/Global TV/Sony Music TV RADCD 116*	5		4
13 Feb 99	THE GREATEST ROCK 'N' ROLL LOVE SONGS	*Global Television RADCD 115*	6		4
6 Mar 99	DISCO HOUSE	*Global Television RADCD 120* ○	7		2
3 Apr 99	NEW HITS 99	*warner.esp/Global TV/Sony TV RADCD 121* ⊛	1	1	12
10 Apr 99	THE FEMALE TOUCH 2	*warner.esp/Global TV RADCD 117* ○	9		7
1 May 99	HEART FULL OF SOUL – 2	*warner.esp/Global TV RADCD 122*	12		4
15 May 99	THE VERY BEST OF LATIN JAZZ – 2	*Global Television RADCD 118*	15		3
12 Jun 99	FAT DANCE HITS	*Global Television RADCD 125* ●	5		5
12 Jun 99	STREET VIBES 3	*warner.esp/Global TV/Sony Music TV RADCD 124* ○	6		5
26 Jun 99	MIDSUMMER CLASSICS	*Global Television RADCD 127*	20		2
3 Jul 99	FRESH HITS 99	*warner.esp/Global Music TV/Sony Music TV RADCD 126*	1	3	9
17 Jul 99	UNDER LATIN SKIES	*Global Television RADCD 130*	14		2
24 Jul 99	IBIZA 99 – THE YEAR OF TRANCE	*Global Television RADCD 128*	2		5
31 Jul 99	SALSA FEVER!	*Global Television RADCD 133*	12		4
28 Aug 99	IBIZA DEL MAR	*Global Television RADCD 137*	11		2
4 Sep 99	BIG HITS 99	*warner.esp/Global TV/Sony TV RADCD 134*	1	2	11
11 Sep 99	SPEED GARAGE ANTHEMS 99	*Global Television RADCD 142*	13		3
2 Oct 99	FAT POP HITS	*Global Television RADCD 135*	6		5
9 Oct 99	ROCK THE WORLD	*Global Television RADCD 138*	9		4
9 Oct 99	IBIZA 99 – THE YEAR OF TRANCE – VOLUME TWO	*Global Television RADCD 150*	11		2

Date	Title / Label	Peak Position	Weeks at No.1	Weeks on Chart
23 Oct 99	**AYIA NAPA – CLUBBERS PARADISE** *Global Television RADCD 151*	14		2
6 Nov 99	**HUGE HITS 99** *warner.esp/Global TV/Sony TV RADCD 147*	1	4	13
20 Nov 99	**FUNK SOUL BROTHER – THE BEST OF DANCE SOUL & SWING** *Global Television RADCD 136*	19		1
20 Nov 99	**THE BIGGEST CLUB ALBUM OF THE YEAR** *Global Television RADCD 148*	20		1
18 Dec 99	**HITS 2000** *warner.esp/Global TV/Sony TV RADCD 154*	2		12
18 Dec 99	**RADIO 2 – SONGS OF THE CENTURY** *Global TV RADCD 119*	9		8
15 Jan 00	**FUNKY DIVAS 3** *Global Television RADCD 141*	18		3
15 Jan 00	**DISCO FEVER** *Global Television RADCD 131*	19		1
18 Mar 00	**STREET VIBES 4** *warner.esp/Global TV/Sony TV RADCD 146*	4		6
29 Apr 00	**A PERFECT LOVE III** *warner.esp/Universal TV/Global TV RADCD 149X*	6		6
13 May 00	**SOUNDTRACK TO THE WEEKEND** *Global TV RADCD 162*	8		4
3 Jun 00	**CRUISIN' – THE BEST OF DRIVETIME** *Global TV RADCD 160*	5		3
17 Jun 00	**ALL YOU NEED IS LOVE** *Global Television RADCD 163*	18		1
24 Jun 00	**STREET VIBES 5** *Sony TV/Global TV RADCD 161*	2		8
8 Jul 00	**HEADRUSH** *Global Television RADCD 166*	10		5
29 Jul 00	**TRASHED IN IBIZA** *Global TV RADCD 169*	16		2

VARIOUS ARTISTS (GLOBAL UNDERGROUND)

Date	Title / Label	Peak Position	Weeks at No.1	Weeks on Chart
25 Apr 98	**JOHN DIGWEED SYDNEY** *Global Underground GU 006CD*	16		1
6 Jun 98	**PAUL OAKENFOLD – NEW YORK** *Global Underground GU 007CDX*	12		3
21 Nov 98	**SASHA – SAN FRANCISCO** *Global Underground GU 009CD*	18		1
27 Feb 99	**DANNY TENEAGLIA LIVE IN ATHENS** *Global Underground GU 010CDX*	16		1
19 Jun 99	**NICK WARREN – BUDAPEST** *Global Underground GU 011CD*	20		1
2 Oct 99	**SASHA – IBIZA** *Global Underground GU 013CDX*	12		2
22 Apr 00	**PROTOTYPE3 – SEB FONTAINE** *Global Underground PRO 003CD*	19		1
27 May 00	**URUGUAY – DARREN EMERSON** *Global Underground GUO 015CDX*	20		1
10 Mar 01	**JOHN DIGWEED – LOS ANGELES** *Global Underground GUO 19CDX*	14		1
12 Oct 02	**JAMES LAVELLE – BARCELONA 023** *Global Underground GU 023CDX*	18		1
27 May 06	**GU 10** *Global Underground GUXCDX*	10		3
19 May 07	**GUMIXED** *Global Underground GUMIX1CDX*	18		1
20 Sep 08	**SASHA – INVOL2VER** *Global Underground GUSA002CDX*	19		1

VARIOUS ARTISTS (GO! DISCS)

Date	Title / Label	Peak Position	Weeks at No.1	Weeks on Chart
16 Sep 95	**HELP – WAR CHILD** *Go! Discs 8286822*	1	2	7

VARIOUS ARTISTS (GODSKITCHEN)

Date	Title / Label	Peak Position	Weeks at No.1	Weeks on Chart
25 Jan 03	**GODSKITCHEN DIRECT** *Godskitchen GKCD 001*	9		2
9 Aug 03	**GODSKITCHEN – WORLDWIDE** *Godskitchen GKCD002*	18		1

VARIOUS ARTISTS (GOOD LOOKING)

Date	Title / Label	Peak Position	Weeks at No.1	Weeks on Chart
10 May 97	**BLAME PRESENT LOGICAL PROGRESSION LEVEL 2** *Good Looking GLRCD 002X*	12		2
11 Oct 97	**LTJ BUKEM PRESENTS EARTH – VOLUME TWO** *Good Looking EARTHCD 002*	18		1
16 May 98	**INTENSE PRESENTS LOGICAL PROGRESSION LEVEL 3** *Good Looking GLRCD 003*	18		1

VARIOUS ARTISTS (GTO)

Date	Title / Label	Peak Position	Weeks at No.1	Weeks on Chart
16 Aug 75	**NEVER TOO YOUNG TO ROCK** *GTO GTLP 004*	30		5

VARIOUS ARTISTS (GTV)

Date	Title / Label	Peak Position	Weeks at No.1	Weeks on Chart
20 May 06	**FOOTBALL CRAZY – HEAR THE SONGS** *GTV GTVCD02*	5		8
2 Sep 06	**THE PACHA EXPERIENCE** *GTV GTVCD04*	3		7
3 Feb 07	**HARDCORE ADRENALINE** *GTV GTVCD09*	2		3
21 Apr 07	**WE LOVE GREASE** *GTV GTVCD12*	15		2
30 Jun 07	**CLUB NIGHTS – LIVE IT** *GTV GTVCD11*	9		2
7 Jul 07	**THE BEST PUB ALBUM** *GTV GTVCD03*	14		2
21 Jul 07	**HARDCORE ADRENALINE 2** *GTV GTVCD14*	6		3
18 Aug 07	**GALAXY DANCE ANTHEMS** *GTV GTVCD15*	10		2
15 Sep 07	**THE PACHA EXPERIENCE 2** *GTV GTVCD13*	10		3
6 Oct 07	**TRUE HARDCORE – IT'S A WAY OF LIFE** *GTV GTVCD17*	6		4
5 Jul 08	**TRUE HARDCORE 2** *Gut GTVCD21*	10		2

VARIOUS ARTISTS (GUERILLA)

Date	Title / Label	Peak Position	Weeks at No.1	Weeks on Chart
17 Apr 93	**DUB HOUSE DISCO 2000** *Guerilla GRCD 7*	18		1

VARIOUS ARTISTS (GUT)

Date	Title / Label	Peak Position	Weeks at No.1	Weeks on Chart
26 Jun 04	**COME ON ENGLAND** *Gut GUTCD30*	17		1
4 Feb 06	**CLUB NIGHTS – SOUNDTRACK TO THE WEEKEND** *Gut GTVCD01*	3		3
7 Oct 06	**MILKSHAKE – THE ALBUM** *Gut GTVCD07*	15		1

VARIOUS ARTISTS (HAPPY DAYS)

Date	Title / Label	Peak Position	Weeks at No.1	Weeks on Chart
13 May 95	**YOU MUST REMEMBER THIS…** *Happy Days CDHD 2656*	16		1

VARIOUS ARTISTS (HARD2BEAT)

Date	Title / Label	Peak Position	Weeks at No.1	Weeks on Chart
3 May 08	**HARD2BEAT – CLUB ANTHEMS 2008** *Hard2Beat H2BCD03*	8		3
2 Aug 08	**PUT YOUR HANDS UP 4** *Hard2Beat HANDUPCD4*	4		5
11 Oct 08	**CLASSIC BIG TUNES** *Hard2Beat H2BCD05*	2		7

VARIOUS ARTISTS (HARVEST)

Date	Title / Label	Peak Position	Weeks at No.1	Weeks on Chart
16 Jul 77	**THE ROXY LONDON WC2 (JAN–APR 77)** *Harvest SHSP 4069*	24		5
26 May 79	**A MONUMENT TO BRITISH ROCK** *Harvest EMTV 17*	13		12

VARIOUS ARTISTS (HEART & SOUL)

Date	Title / Label	Peak Position	Weeks at No.1	Weeks on Chart
19 Aug 89	**HEART AND SOUL** *Heart & Soul HASTV 1*	2		12
17 Feb 90	**BODY AND SOUL – HEART AND SOUL II** *Heart & Soul 8407761*	2		14
4 Aug 90	**HEART AND SOUL III – HEART FULL OF SOUL** *Heart & Soul 8450091*	4		9
16 Feb 91	**SOUL REFLECTION** *Heart & Soul 8453341*	2		12

VARIOUS ARTISTS (HEAVEN MUSIC)

Date	Title / Label	Peak Position	Weeks at No.1	Weeks on Chart
5 Apr 97	**HARDCORE HEAVEN – VOLUME ONE** *Heaven Music HMLCD 101*	12		4
9 Aug 97	**HARDCORE HEAVEN – VOLUME 2** *Heaven Music HMLCD 102*	13		2
14 Feb 98	**HARDCORE HEAVEN – VOLUME 3** *Heaven Music HMLCD 103*	12		2
8 Aug 98	**HARDCORE HEAVEN – VOLUME 4** *Heaven Music HMLCD 104*	17		1
13 Feb 99	**HARDCORE HEAVEN – VOLUME 5** *Heaven Music HMLCD 105*	17		4

VARIOUS ARTISTS (HEAVENLY)

Date	Title / Label	Peak Position	Weeks at No.1	Weeks on Chart
25 May 96	**LIVE AT THE SOCIAL – VOLUME 1** *Heavenly HVNLP 13CD*	19		1

VARIOUS ARTISTS (HED KANDI)

Date	Title / Label	Peak Position	Weeks at No.1	Weeks on Chart
27 Sep 03	**DISCO KANDI 05.03** *Hed Kandi HEDK 034*	17		1
13 Mar 04	**DISCO HEAVEN 01.04** *Hed Kandi HEDK037*	18		1
1 May 04	**TWISTED DISCO 02.04** *Hed Kandi HEDK 038*	16		3
11 Sep 04	**HED KANDI SUMMER 2004** *Jazz FM HEDK041*	5		5
16 Oct 04	**DISCO KANDI 05.04** *Hed Kandi HEDK043*	19		1
26 Feb 05	**DISCO HEAVEN** *Hed Kandi HEDK046*	18		2
9 Apr 05	**TWISTED DISCO 0205** *Hed Kandi HEDK047*	18		2
11 Jun 05	**BACK TO LOVE 0305** *Hed Kandi HEDK048*	20		1
13 Aug 05	**BEACH HOUSE 04 05** *Hed Kandi HEDK049*	17		1
17 Sep 05	**HED KANDI THE MIX 50** *Hed Kandi HEDK050*	5		5
6 May 06	**HED KANDI – DISCO HEAVEN** *Hed Kandi HEDK058*	7		3
19 Aug 06	**HED KANDI – THE MIX SUMMER 2006** *Hed Kandi HEDK061*	2		9
4 Nov 06	**DISCO KANDI** *Hed Kandi HEDK063*	15		2
2 Dec 06	**HED KANDI CLASSICS** *Hed Kandi HEDK064*	12		1
7 Apr 07	**HED KANDI – DISCO KANDI – THE MIX** *Hed Kandi HEDK067*	3		5
7 Apr 07	**RHYTHMS DEL MUNDO – CUBA** *Universal TV 1709595*	5		4
25 Aug 07	**HED KANDI – THE MIX – SUMMER 2007** *Hed Kandi HEDK070*	3		6
29 Sep 07	**HED KANDI – BACK TO LOVE** *Hed Kandi HEDK071*	20		1
27 Oct 07	**HED KANDI – DISCO HEAVEN** *Hed Kandi HEDK072*	18		1
1 Dec 07	**HED KANDI – THE MIX 2008** *Hed Kandi HEDK074*	9		2
5 Apr 08	**HED KANDI – BACK TO LOVE: THE MIX** *Hed Kandi HEDK077*	6		3
17 May 08	**HED KANDI – WORLD SERIES LIVE – SAN FRANCISCO** *Hed Kandi HEDK078*	17		1
12 Jul 08	**HED KANDI – THE MIX – SUMMER 2008** *Hed Kandi HEDK074*	7		5
9 Aug 08	**HED KANDI – BEACH HOUSE** *Hed Kandi HEDK081*	17		1
20 Sep 08	**HED KANDI WORLD SERIES – IBIZA** *Hed Kandi HEDK083*	9		3
1 Nov 08	**HED KANDI – DISCO HEAVEN** *Hed Kandi HEDK084*	19		1
29 Nov 08	**HED KANDI – THE MIX 2009** *Hed Kandi HEDK085*	14		2

VARIOUS ARTISTS (HI-LIFE)

Date	Title / Label	Peak Position	Weeks at No.1	Weeks on Chart
2 Nov 96	**THE SUMMER OF NINETY SIX – UP YER RONSON** *Hi-Life/Polydor 5332422*	17		1

Silver-selling · Gold-selling · Platinum-selling · US No.1 ★ · Peak Position · Weeks at No.1 · Weeks on Chart

VARIOUS ARTISTS (HIGHER GROUND)

Date	Title / Label	Peak Position	Weeks at No.1	Weeks on Chart
12 Apr 97	**GROOVERIDER PRESENTS THE PROTOTYPE YEARS** *Higher Ground 4872192*	19		1

VARIOUS ARTISTS (HIT LABEL)

Date	Title / Label	Peak Position	Weeks at No.1	Weeks on Chart
27 Jun 92	**Q THE BLUES** *The Hit Label AHLCD 1*	6		5
22 Aug 92	**SMASH HITS – PARTY ON!** *The Hit Label CCD 34*	9		5
17 Oct 92	**BEST OF CAPITAL GOLD – 24 CARAT CLASSIC HITS** *The Hit Label AHLCD 2*	20		1
28 Nov 92	**BIG! DANCE HITS OF 92** *The Hit Label AHLCD 4*	11		7
5 Dec 92	**REMEMBER WHEN SINGERS COULD SING** *The Hit Label AHLCD 3*	16		2
10 Apr 93	**Q RHYTHM AND BLUES** *The Hit Label AHLCD 7*	14		4
8 May 93	**THE LEGENDARY JOE BLOGGS ALBUM** *The Hit Label AHLCD 10*	3		8
31 Jul 93	**GET IT ON – GREATEST HITS OF THE 70'S** *The Hit Label AHLCD 12*	12		5
30 Oct 93	**THE LEGENDARY JOE BLOGGS ALBUM 2** *The Hit Label AHLCD 13*	15		2
13 Nov 93	**IT MUST BE LOVE** *The Hit Label AHLCD 17*	11		4
5 Mar 94	**THE BOYZ WHO SOULED THE WORLD** *The Hit Label AHLCD 18*	9		4
21 May 94	**Q COUNTRY** *The Hit Label AHLCD 16*	20		1
18 Jun 94	**KERRANG! THE ALBUM** *The Hit Label AHLCD 21*	12		5
27 Aug 94	**THE ULTIMATE GOLD COLLECTION** *The Hit Label AHLCD 22*	12		4
4 Feb 95	**ULTIMATE LOVE** *The Hit Label AHLCD 24*	13		4
18 Feb 95	**FEEL LIKE MAKING LOVE** *The Hit Label AHLCD 25*	17		2
8 Jul 95	**REGGAE GROOVE** *The Hit Label ULTCD 020*	12		1

VARIOUS ARTISTS (HMV)

Date	Title / Label	Peak Position	Weeks at No.1	Weeks on Chart
10 Mar 62	**GREAT MOTION PICTURE THEMES** *HMV CLP 1508*	19		1

VARIOUS ARTISTS (IGNITION)

Date	Title / Label	Peak Position	Weeks at No.1	Weeks on Chart
13 Nov 99	**FIRE & SKILL – THE SONGS OF THE JAM** *Ignition IGNCD 3*	12		1

VARIOUS ARTISTS (IMMEDIATE)

Date	Title / Label	Peak Position	Weeks at No.1	Weeks on Chart
11 May 68	**BLUES ANYTIME** *Immediate IMLP 014*	40		1

VARIOUS ARTISTS (IMP CLASSICS)

Date	Title / Label	Peak Position	Weeks at No.1	Weeks on Chart
11 Apr 92	**DISCOVER THE CLASSICS VOLUME 2** *IMP Classics/Pickwick CDBOXD 22*	12		3
11 Apr 92	**DISCOVER THE CLASSICS VOLUME 1** *IMP Classics/Pickwick CDBOXD 21*	15		3

VARIOUS ARTISTS (IMPRESSION)

Date	Title / Label	Peak Position	Weeks at No.1	Weeks on Chart
16 Oct 82	**BEST FRIENDS** *Impression LP IMP 1*	28		21
3 Sep 83	**SUNNY AFTERNOON** *Impression LP IMP 2*	13		8
26 Nov 83	**PRECIOUS MOMENTS** *Impression LP IMP 3*	77		5
7 Apr 84	**ALWAYS AND FOREVER – THE COLLECTION** *Impression LP IMP 4*	24		12
21 Jul 84	**WIPEOUT – 20 INSTRUMENTAL GREATS** *Impression LP IMP 5*	37		3
28 Jul 84	**SUNNY AFTERNOON VOLUME TWO** *Impression LP IMP 7*	90		1
22 Dec 84	**FRIENDS AGAIN** *Impression LP IMP 8*	91		1

VARIOUS ARTISTS (IN THE HOUSE)

Date	Title / Label	Peak Position	Weeks at No.1	Weeks on Chart
25 Mar 06	**DEFECTED IN THE HOUSE – MIAMI 06** *In The House ITH16CD*	20		1

VARIOUS ARTISTS (INCREDIBLE)

Date	Title / Label	Peak Position	Weeks at No.1	Weeks on Chart
31 Oct 98	**GATECRASHER** *INCredible INC 2CDX*	7		2
6 Mar 99	**NORTHERN EXPOSURE – SASHA + JOHN DIGWEED** *INCredible INC 4CD*	6		2
20 Mar 99	**INCREDIBLE SOUND OF TREVOR NELSON** *INCredible INC 3CD*	14		3
10 Apr 99	**GATECRASHER RED** *INCredible INC 5CD*	4		8
8 May 99	**GOLDIE – INCREDIBLE SOUND OF DRUM 'N' BASS** *INCredible INC 6CD*	16		2
7 Aug 99	**GATECRASHER WET** *INCredible INC 8CD*	3		6
20 Nov 99	**GATECRASHER DISCO-TECH** *INCredible INC 11CD*	6		3
29 Apr 00	**TREVOR NELSON'S RHYTHM NATION** *INCredible INC 15CD*	9		4
8 Jul 00	**COMMUNICATE – SASHA & DIGWEED** *INCredible INC 14CDX*	13		2
12 Aug 00	**GATECRASHER – GLOBAL SOUND SYSTEM** *INCredible INC 12CD*	3		4
19 Aug 00	**INCREDIBLE SOUND OF THE DREEM TEEM** *INCredible INC 18CD*	14		2
9 Dec 00	**GATECRASHER – NATIONAL ANTHEMS** *INCredible INC 22CDX*	13		2
7 Apr 01	**GATECRASHER DISCOTECH GENERATION** *INCredible 5020749*	10		2
15 Sep 01	**GARAGE NATION** *INCredible 5040712*	11		4
29 Sep 01	**GODS KITCHEN – THE TRUE SOUND OF A CLUBBING SUMMER** *INCredible 5044892*	17		1
26 Jan 02	**GODSKITCHEN JOURNEYS** *INCredible 5053252*	5		3
30 Mar 02	**GODSKITCHEN – LIFE** *INCredible 5076212*	13		2
11 May 02	**GARAGE NATION 02** *INCredible 5053242*	9		2
24 Aug 02	**GODSKITCHEN – SUMMER TRANCE** *INCredible 5089442*	15		1

VARIOUS ARTISTS (INDEPENDIENTE)

Date	Title / Label	Peak Position	Weeks at No.1	Weeks on Chart
8 Oct 05	**HELP – A DAY IN THE LIFE** *Warchild/Independiente ISOM59CD*	4		3

VARIOUS ARTISTS (INSPIRED)

Date	Title / Label	Peak Position	Weeks at No.1	Weeks on Chart
12 Feb 00	**LOVED UP** *Inspired INSPCD 1*	8		4
27 May 00	**ULTIMATE AYIA NAPA** *Inspired INSPCD 2*	7		3
7 Oct 00	**ULTIMATE IBIZA** *Inspired INSPCD 3*	14		3
3 Feb 01	**FEELS SO GOOD** *Inspired INSPCD 5*	13		2
9 Jun 01	**DANCESTAR 2001** *Inspired INSPCD 9*	12		3
21 Jul 01	**DREAMSTATES** *Inspired INSPCD 8*	18		1
25 Aug 01	**LOVIN' IT** *INCredible/Inspired INSPCD 12*	3		9
22 Sep 01	**BIG CLUB HITS** *Inspired INSPCD 13*	5		3
3 Nov 01	**RAVE NATION** *Inspired INSPCD 16*	16		2
22 Dec 01	**LOVIN' IT 2** *INCredible/Inspired INSPCD 15*	11		7
2 Mar 02	**CLUB HITS 2002** *INCredible/Inspired INSPCD 17*	5		3
5 Oct 02	**TUNE IN-CHILL OUT** *Inspired INSPCD 23*	17		3
26 Oct 02	**ORIGINAL HARDCORE** *Inspired INSPCD 24*	7		3
8 Feb 03	**CLUB HITS 2003** *Inspired/Sony TV INSPCD 25*	12		2
8 Mar 03	**ORIGINAL HARDCORE – THE BATTLE** *Inspired INSPCD 26*	19		1
7 Feb 04	**ORIGINAL HARDCORE – THE NU BREED** *Inspired INSPCD34*	19		1
28 Feb 04	**ANTHEMS OF TRANCE** *Inspired/UMTV INSPCD35*	3		3
6 Mar 04	**DAVE PEARCE DANCE ANTHEMS SPRING 2004** *Inspired/BMG TV INSPCD033*	3		2
13 Mar 04	**JAZZ CAFÉ – THE SOUL MIX** *Inspired/UCJ INSPCD37*	9		1
10 Apr 04	**ANTHEMS OF HOUSE** *Inspired/UMTV INSPCD 36*	8		3
8 May 04	**ANTHEMS OF OLD SKOOL** *Inspired INSPCD 38*	7		5
21 Aug 04	**ANTHEMS OF IBIZA** *Inspired/UMTV INSPCD41*	16		1
4 Sep 04	**THE VERY BEST OF DRIVETIME** *Inspired INSPCD44*	8		2
23 Oct 04	**PURE GROOVES – 80'S SLOWJAMS** *Inspired/UMTV INSPCD 43*	12		1
12 Mar 05	**JUST THE WAY YOU ARE** *Inspired INSPCD46*	15		1
23 Jul 05	**ANGEL BEACH – THE FOURTH WAVE** *Inspired INSPCD48*	15		1
26 Jul 08	**SUMMER HOLIDAY DANCE PARTY** *Inspired NSPCD49*	12		2

VARIOUS ARTISTS (ISLAND)

Date	Title / Label	Peak Position	Weeks at No.1	Weeks on Chart
26 Aug 67	**CLUB SKA '67** *Island ILP 956*	37		19
14 Jun 69	**YOU CAN ALL JOIN IN** *Island IWPS 2*	18		10
5 Jan 80	**THE SECRET POLICEMAN'S BALL** *Island ILPS 9601*	33		6
29 Mar 80	**CLUB SKA '67** *Island IRSP 4*	53		6
16 Jun 84	**CREW CUTS** *Island IMA 11*	71		4
27 Oct 84	**CREW CUTS – LESSON 2** *Island IMA 14*	95		2
18 Jul 87	**THE ISLAND STORY** *Island ISL 25*	9		10
3 Nov 90	**HAPPY DAZE...VOLUME 1** *Island ILPTV 1*	7		4
6 Apr 91	**HAPPY DAZE VOLUME 2** *Island ILPTV 3*	17		2
30 Oct 93	**REGGAE 93** *Island CIDTV 7*	5		6
27 Aug 94	**PURE REGGAE – VOLUME 1** *Island CIDTV 8*	10		5

VARIOUS ARTISTS (JACK TRAX)

Date	Title / Label	Peak Position	Weeks at No.1	Weeks on Chart
18 Jul 87	**JACK TRAX – THE FIRST ALBUM** *Jack Trax JTRAX 1*	83		2
3 Oct 87	**JACK TRAX – THE SECOND ALBUM** *Jack Trax JTRAX 2*	61		2
5 Mar 88	**JACK TRAX – THE THIRD ALBUM** *Jack Trax JTRAX 4*	49		4

VARIOUS ARTISTS (JDJ)

Date	Title / Label	Peak Position	Weeks at No.1	Weeks on Chart
30 Mar 96	**DANCE WARS – JUDGE JULES VS. JOHN KELLY** *JDJ JDJCD 10*	11		2

VARIOUS ARTISTS (JETSTAR)

Date	Title	Label	Peak Position	Weeks at No.1	Weeks on Chart
30 Mar 85	REGGAE HITS VOLUME 1	*Jetstar JETLP 1001*	32		11
26 Oct 85	REGGAE HITS VOLUME 2	*Jetstar JETLP 1002*	86		2
4 Jun 88	REGGAE HITS VOLUME 4	*Jetstar JETLP 1004*	56		7
17 Dec 88	REGGAE HITS VOLUME 5	*Jetstar JETLP 1005*	96		1
5 Aug 89	REGGAE HITS VOLUME 6	*Jetstar JETLP 1006*	13		6
23 Dec 89	REGGAE HITS VOLUME 7	*Jetstar JETLP 1007*	13		6
30 Jun 90	REGGAE HITS VOLUME 8	*Jetstar JETLP 1008*	7		5
20 Jul 91	REGGAE HITS VOLUME 10	*Jetstar JETLP 1010*	6		7
18 Apr 92	REGGAE HITS VOLUME 12	*Jetstar JECD 1012*	5		6
28 Aug 93	REGGAE HITS VOLUME 14	*Jetstar JECD 1014*	13		1
3 Sep 94	JUNGLE HITS VOLUME 1	*Jetstar STRCD 1*	9		8

VARIOUS ARTISTS (JIVE)

Date	Title	Label	Peak Position	Weeks at No.1	Weeks on Chart
26 Mar 88	THE WORD VOLUME 2	*Jive HOP 220*	70		2

VARIOUS ARTISTS (JUMPIN' & PUMPIN')

Date	Title	Label	Peak Position	Weeks at No.1	Weeks on Chart
18 Jan 92	NOISE	*Jumpin' & Pumpin' CDTOT 3*	20		1
16 May 92	NOISE 2	*Jumpin' & Pumpin' CDTOT 4*	11		3

VARIOUS ARTISTS (JUNIOR BOY'S OWN)

Date	Title	Label	Peak Position	Weeks at No.1	Weeks on Chart
13 Aug 94	JUNIOR BOY'S OWN COLLECTION	*Junior Boy's Own JBOCD 2*	20		1

VARIOUS ARTISTS (K-TEL)

Date	Title	Label	Peak Position	Weeks at No.1	Weeks on Chart
10 Jun 72	20 DYNAMIC HITS	*K-Tel TE 292*	1	8	28
7 Oct 72	20 ALL TIME GREATS OF THE 50'S	*K-Tel NE 490*	1	11	22
25 Nov 72	25 DYNAMIC HITS VOLUME 2	*K-Tel TE 291*	2		12
2 Dec 72	25 ROCKIN' AND ROLLIN' GREATS	*K-Tel NE 493*	1	3	18
31 Mar 73	20 FLASHBACK GREATS OF THE SIXTIES	*K-Tel NE 494*	1	2	11
21 Apr 73	BELIEVE IN MUSIC	*K-Tel TE 294*	2		8
8 Nov 75	GOOFY GREATS	*K-Tel NE 707*	19		7
13 Dec 75	40 SUPER GREATS	*K-Tel NE 708*	9		8
31 Jan 76	MUSIC EXPRESS	*K-Tel TE 702*	3		10
10 Apr 76	JUKE BOX JIVE	*K-Tel NE 709*	3		13
17 Apr 76	GREAT ITALIAN LOVE SONGS	*K-Tel NE 303*	17		14
15 May 76	HIT MACHINE	*K-Tel TE 713*	4		10
5 Jun 76	EUROVISION FAVOURITES	*K-Tel NE 712*	44		1
2 Oct 76	SUMMER CRUISING	*K-Tel NE 918*	30		1
16 Oct 76	SOUL MOTION	*K-Tel NE 930*	1	2	14
16 Oct 76	COUNTRY COMFORT	*K-Tel NE 294*	8		12
4 Dec 76	DISCO ROCKET	*K-Tel NE 948*	3		14
11 Dec 76	44 SUPERSTARS	*K-Tel NE 939*	14		10
12 Feb 77	HEARTBREAKERS	*K-Tel NE 954*	2		18
19 Feb 77	DANCE TO THE MUSIC	*K-Tel NE 957*	5		9
7 May 77	HIT ACTION	*K-Tel NE 993*	15		9
29 Oct 77	SOUL CITY	*K-Tel NE 1003*	12		7
12 Nov 77	FEELINGS	*K-Tel NE 1006*	3		24
26 Nov 77	DISCO FEVER	*K-Tel NE 1014*	1	6	20
21 Jan 78	40 NUMBER ONE HITS	*K-Tel NE 1008*	15		7
4 Mar 78	DISCO STARS	*K-Tel NE 1022*	6		8
10 Jun 78	DISCO DOUBLE	*K-Tel NE 1024*	10		6
8 Jul 78	ROCK RULES	*K-Tel RL 001*	12		11
8 Jul 78	THE WORLD'S WORST RECORD SHOW	*Yuk/K-Tel NE 1023*	47		2
19 Aug 78	STAR PARTY	*K-Tel NE 1034*	4		9
4 Nov 78	EMOTIONS	*K-Tel NE 1035*	2		17
25 Nov 78	MIDNIGHT HUSTLE	*K-Tel NE 1037*	2		13
20 Jan 79	ACTION REPLAY	*K-Tel NE 1040*	1	1	14
7 Apr 79	DISCO INFERNO	*K-Tel NE 1043*	11		9
5 May 79	HI ENERGY	*K-Tel NE 1044*	17		7
22 Sep 79	HOT TRACKS	*K-Tel NE 1049*	31		8
24 Nov 79	NIGHT MOVES	*K-Tel NE 1065*	10		10
24 Nov 79	TOGETHER	*K-Tel NE 1053*	35		8
12 Jan 80	VIDEO STARS	*K-Tel NE 1066*	5		10
26 Jan 80	THE SUMMIT	*K-Tel NE 1067*	17		5
29 Mar 80	STAR TRACKS	*K-Tel NE 1070*	6		8
26 Apr 80	GOOD MORNING AMERICA	*K-Tel NE 1072*	15		12
17 May 80	MAGIC REGGAE	*K-Tel NE 1074*	9		17
17 May 80	HAPPY DAYS	*K-Tel NE 1076*	32		6
14 Jun 80	HOT WAX	*K-Tel NE 1082*	3		10
27 Sep 80	MOUNTING EXCITEMENT	*K-Tel NE 1091*	2		8
11 Oct 80	THE LOVE ALBUM	*K-Tel NE 1062*	6		16
25 Oct 80	AXE ATTACK	*K-Tel NE 1100*	15		14
15 Nov 80	CHART EXPLOSION	*K-Tel NE 1103*	6		17
27 Dec 80	NIGHTLIFE	*K-Tel NE 1107*	25		10
14 Feb 81	HIT MACHINE	*K-Tel NE 1113*	17		6
21 Mar 81	RHYTHM 'N' REGGAE	*K-Tel NE 1115*	42		4
25 Apr 81	CHARTBUSTERS 81	*K-Tel NE 1118*	3		9
2 May 81	AXE ATTACK 2	*K-Tel NE 1120*	31		6
23 May 81	THEMES	*K-Tel NE 1122*	6		15
29 Aug 81	CALIFORNIA DREAMING	*K-Tel NE 1126*	27		11
19 Sep 81	DANCE DANCE DANCE	*K-Tel NE 1143*	29		5
3 Oct 81	THE PLATINUM ALBUM	*K-Tel NE 1134*	32		11
10 Oct 81	LOVE IS…	*K-Tel NE 1129*	10		15
21 Nov 81	CHART HITS '81	*K-Tel NE 1142*	1	1	17
9 Jan 82	MODERN DANCE	*K-Tel NE 1156*	6		10
6 Feb 82	DREAMING	*K-Tel NE 1159*	2		12
6 Mar 82	ACTION TRAX	*K-Tel NE 1162*	2		12
1 May 82	MIDNIGHT HOUR	*K-Tel NE 1157*	98		1
3 Jul 82	TURBO TRAX	*K-Tel NE 1176*	17		7
4 Sep 82	THE NO. 1 SOUNDS OF THE SEVENTIES	*K-Tel NE 1172*	83		1
11 Sep 82	CHARTBEAT/CHARTHEAT	*K-Tel NE 1180*	2		14
30 Oct 82	THE LOVE SONGS ALBUM	*K-Tel NE 1179*	28		8
6 Nov 82	CHART HITS '82	*K-Tel NE 1195*	11		17
6 Nov 82	DISCO DANCER	*K-Tel NE 1190*	26		8
18 Dec 82	STREETSCENE	*K-Tel NE 1183*	42		6
15 Jan 83	VISIONS	*K-Tel ONE 1199*	5		21
12 Feb 83	HEAVY	*K-Tel NE 1023*	46		12
5 Mar 83	HOTLINE	*K-Tel NE 1027*	3		9
11 Jun 83	CHART STARS	*K-Tel NE 1225*	7		9
20 Aug 83	COOL HEAT	*K-Tel NE 1231*	79		3
10 Sep 83	HEADLINE HITS	*K-Tel NE 1253*	5		6
8 Oct 83	THE TWO OF US	*K-Tel NE 1222*	3		16
8 Oct 83	IMAGES	*K-Tel ONE 1254*	33		6
12 Nov 83	CHART HITS '83 VOLUME 1 AND 2	*K-Tel NE 1256*	6		11
24 Mar 84	NIGHT MOVES	*K-Tel NE 1255*	15		11
26 May 84	HUNGRY FOR HITS	*K-Tel NE 1272*	4		11
23 Jun 84	THE THEMES ALBUM	*K-Tel NE 1257*	43		3
28 Jul 84	BREAKDANCE, YOU CAN DO IT!	*K-Tel ONE 1276*	18		12
22 Sep 84	ALL BY MYSELF	*K-Tel NE 1273*	7		16
1 Dec 84	HOOKED ON NUMBER ONES – 100 NON-STOP HITS	*K-Tel ONE 1285*	25		15
2 Feb 85	FOUR STAR COUNTRY	*K-Tel NE 1278*	52		6
2 Mar 85	MODERN LOVE – 24 LOVE SONGS FOR TODAY	*K-Tel NE 1286*	13		7
5 Oct 85	EXPRESSIONS – 24 BEAUTIFUL BALLADS	*K-Tel NE 1307*	11		8
9 Nov 85	ROCK ANTHEMS	*K-Tel NE 1309*	10		11
9 Nov 85	OVATION – THE BEST OF ANDREW LLOYD WEBBER	*K-Tel ONE 1311*	34		12
22 Mar 86	MASTERS OF METAL	*K-Tel NE 1295*	38		4
12 Apr 86	HEART TO HEART – 24 LOVE SONG DUETS	*K-Tel NE 1318*	8		15
19 Apr 86	ROCK ANTHEMS – VOLUME 2	*K-Tel NE 1319*	43		9
5 Jul 86	RAP IT UP – RAP'S GREATEST HITS	*K-Tel NE 1324*	50		4
19 Jul 86	DRIVE TIME USA – 22 SUMMER CRUISING GREATS	*K-Tel NE 1321*	20		8
18 Oct 86	DANCE HITS '86	*K-Tel NE 1344*	35		7
1 Nov 86	TOGETHER	*K-Tel NE 1345*	20		10
7 Feb 87	IMPRESSIONS – 15 INSTRUMENTAL IMAGES	*K-Tel NE 1346*	15		14
21 Mar 87	RHYTHM OF THE NIGHT	*K-Tel NE 1348*	36		7
21 Mar 87	HITS REVIVAL	*K-Tel Holland KTLP 2351*	63		1
13 Jun 87	FRIENDS AND LOVERS	*K-Tel NE 1352*	10		10
27 Jun 87	HITS REVIVAL	*K-Tel NE 1363*	10		9
17 Oct 87	TRUE LOVE	*K-Tel NE 1359*	38		5
31 Oct 87	FROM MOTOWN WITH LOVE	*K-Tel NE 1381*	9		21
14 Nov 87	ALWAYS	*K-Tel NE 1377*	65		4
19 Dec 87	WOW WHAT A PARTY	*K-Tel NE 1388*	97		2
5 Mar 88	HORIZONS	*K-Tel NE 1360*	13		10
30 Apr 88	HITS REVIVAL 2: REPLAY	*K-Tel NE 1405*	45		3
14 May 88	TSOP – THE SOUND OF PHILADELPHIA	*K-Tel NE 1406*	26		9
11 Jun 88	THE HITS OF HOUSE ARE HERE	*K-Tel NE 1419*	12		12
15 Oct 88	MOTOWN IN MOTION	*K-Tel NE 1410*	28		13
15 Oct 88	THE RETURN OF SUPERBAD	*K-Tel NE 1421*	83		4
5 Nov 88	THE LOVERS	*K-Tel NE 1426*	50		5
26 Nov 88	RAPPIN' UP THE HOUSE	*K-Tel NE 1428*	43		7
14 Jan 89	RAPPIN' UP THE HOUSE	*K-Tel NE 1428*	19		1
4 Feb 89	FROM MOTOWN WITH LOVE	*K-Tel NE 1381*	6		7
25 Mar 89	HIP HOUSE – THE DEEPEST BEATS IN TOWN	*K-Tel NE 1430*	10		5
29 Jul 89	GLAM SLAM	*K-Tel NE 1434*	5		8
23 Sep 89	LOVE HOUSE	*K-Tel NE 1446*	5		7
30 Sep 89	ETERNAL LOVE	*K-Tel NE 1447*	5		7
21 Oct 89	RAP ATTACK	*K-Tel NE 1450*	6		7
25 Nov 89	SEDUCTION	*K-Tel NE 1451*	15		4
10 Mar 90	CAN U FEEL IT? – THE CHAMPION LEGEND	*K-Tel ONE 1452*	12		3
21 Apr 90	HOOKED ON COUNTRY	*K-Tel NE 1459*	6		12

VARIOUS ARTISTS (KASINO)

Date	Title	Label	Peak Position	Weeks at No.1	Weeks on Chart
16 Feb 85	STARGAZERS	*Kasino KTV 1*	69		3

Silver-selling ● Gold-selling ● Platinum-selling ⊛ US No.1 ★ | Peak Position | Weeks at No.1 | Weeks on Chart

VARIOUS ARTISTS (KNIGHT)

Date	Title / Label	Peak Position	Weeks at No.1	Weeks on Chart
18 May 91	**SOUTHERN KNIGHTS** *Knight KTVLP 1*	13		2

VARIOUS ARTISTS (KOCH)

Date	Title / Label	Peak Position	Weeks at No.1	Weeks on Chart
22 Apr 00	**POKEMON – 2 B A MASTER** *Koch 333622* [silver]	20		1

VARIOUS ARTISTS (LEGENDS IN)

Date	Title / Label	Peak Position	Weeks at No.1	Weeks on Chart
22 Dec 90	**CHRISTMAS GREATEST HITS** *Legends In LELP 501*	16		1

VARIOUS ARTISTS (LIBERTY)

Date	Title / Label	Peak Position	Weeks at No.1	Weeks on Chart
27 Mar 82	**JAMES BOND'S GREATEST HITS** *Liberty EMTV 007* [gold]	4		13

VARIOUS ARTISTS (LIFE AID ARMENIA)

Date	Title / Label	Peak Position	Weeks at No.1	Weeks on Chart
21 Apr 90	**THE EARTHQUAKE ALBUM...ROCK AID ARMENIA** *Life Aid Armenia AIDLP 001* [gold]	3		10

VARIOUS ARTISTS (LIMBO)

Date	Title / Label	Peak Position	Weeks at No.1	Weeks on Chart
18 May 96	**THE TUNNEL MIXES** *Limbo LIMB 56CD*	17		1

VARIOUS ARTISTS (LONDON)

Date	Title / Label	Peak Position	Weeks at No.1	Weeks on Chart
10 Jun 89	**FFRR – SILVER ON BLACK** *London 8281551*	8		5
11 Nov 89	**DANCE DECADE – DANCE HITS OF THE 80'S** *London DDTV 1* [gold]	8		7
16 Jun 90	**THE NORTHERN BEAT** *London 8409681* [silver]	4		8
7 Jul 90	**MASSIVE 4** *London 8282101*	20		2
8 Feb 92	**ONLY FOR THE HEADSTRONG** *London 8283032*	10		1
20 Jun 92	**ONLY FOR THE HEADSTRONG II** *London 8283162*	18		1
15 Jul 00	**G-A-Y** *London 9548387682*	18		1
26 Aug 00	**ARTFUL DODGER PRESENTS REWIND** *London 8573844602* [silver]	6		4
3 May 03	**HOPE** *London 5046658462* [silver]	6		2

VARIOUS ARTISTS (LOOSE END)

Date	Title / Label	Peak Position	Weeks at No.1	Weeks on Chart
11 Aug 84	**CHUNKS OF FUNK** *Loose End CHUNK 1*	46		5

VARIOUS ARTISTS (LOTUS)

Date	Title / Label	Peak Position	Weeks at No.1	Weeks on Chart
28 Oct 78	**ECSTASY** *Lotus WH 5003*	24		6

VARIOUS ARTISTS (MANGO)

Date	Title / Label	Peak Position	Weeks at No.1	Weeks on Chart
3 Jul 93	**ON A REGGAE TIP** *Mango CIDTV 5* [gold]	3		9

VARIOUS ARTISTS (MANIFESTO)

Date	Title / Label	Peak Position	Weeks at No.1	Weeks on Chart
23 Aug 97	**CAFÉ DEL MAR IBIZA – VOLUMEN CUATRO** *Manifesto 5539072*	18		1
25 Jul 98	**CAFÉ DEL MAR IBIZA – VOLUMEN CINCO** *Manifesto 5652282*	16		2
21 Aug 99	**CAFÉ DEL MAR IBIZA – VOLUMEN SEIS** *Manifesto 5648612*	15		2
8 Jul 00	**CAFÉ DEL MAR – VOLUMEN SIETE** *Manifesto 5249122*	14		3
30 Jun 01	**CAFE DEL MAR VOLUMEN OCHO** *Manifesto 5860592* [silver]	12		3

VARIOUS ARTISTS (MARBLE ARCH)

Date	Title / Label	Peak Position	Weeks at No.1	Weeks on Chart
10 Feb 68	**STARS OF '68** *Marble Arch MAL 762*	23		3

VARIOUS ARTISTS (MARQUEE)

Date	Title / Label	Peak Position	Weeks at No.1	Weeks on Chart
4 May 91	**MARQUEE METAL** *Marquee 8454171* [silver]	5		6

VARIOUS ARTISTS (MASSIVE MUSIC)

Date	Title / Label	Peak Position	Weeks at No.1	Weeks on Chart
25 Apr 98	**101% SPEED GARAGE VOLUME 2** *Massive Music MMCCD 011*	16		2
17 Apr 99	**101% SPEED GARAGE ANTHEMS** *Massive Music MMCCD 012*	14		5

VARIOUS ARTISTS (MASTERCUTS)

Date	Title / Label	Peak Position	Weeks at No.1	Weeks on Chart
28 Sep 91	**CLASSIC MELLOW MASTERCUTS VOLUME 1** *Mastercuts CUTSLP 3*	18		2
21 Mar 92	**NEW JACK SWING MASTERCUTS VOLUME 1** *Mastercuts CUTSCD 5*	8		5
16 May 92	**CLASSIC FUNK MASTERCUTS VOLUME 1** *Mastercuts CUTSCD 6*	14		3
4 Jul 92	**CLASSIC JAZZ-FUNK MASTERCUTS VOLUME 3** *Mastercuts CUTSCD 7*	18		1
15 Aug 92	**CLASSIC MELLOW MASTERCUTS VOLUME 2** *Mastercuts CUTSCD 8*	12		3
6 Mar 93	**CLASSIC SALSOUL MASTERCUTS VOLUME 1** *Mastercuts CUTSCD 10*	16		3
24 Apr 93	**CLASSIC RARE GROOVE MASTERCUTS VOLUME 1** *Mastercuts CUTSCD 11*	14		3
22 May 93	**CLASSIC P-FUNK MASTERCUTS VOLUME 1** *Mastercuts CUTSCD 12*	16		1
22 Jan 94	**CLASSIC JAZZ-FUNK MASTERCUTS VOLUME 4** *Mastercuts CUTSCD 16*	19		2
26 Mar 94	**NEW JACK SWING VOLUME 3** *Mastercuts CUTSCD 18*	18		1
14 May 94	**CLASSIC ELECTRO MASTERCUTS VOLUME 1** *Mastercuts CUTSCD 19*	18		1
18 Jun 94	**CLASSIC HOUSE MASTERCUTS VOLUME 1** *Mastercuts CUTSCD 20*	11		2

VARIOUS ARTISTS (MASTERSOUND)

Date	Title / Label	Peak Position	Weeks at No.1	Weeks on Chart
28 Mar 87	**HEART OF SOUL VOLUME 1** *Mastersound MASL 001*	96		1

VARIOUS ARTISTS (MASTERWORKS)

Date	Title / Label	Peak Position	Weeks at No.1	Weeks on Chart
5 Dec 92	**TAKE 2: OPERA FAVOURITES/ORCHESTRAL CLASSICS** *Masterworks S2K 48226*	18		3

VARIOUS ARTISTS (MAWSON & WARSHAM)

Date	Title / Label	Peak Position	Weeks at No.1	Weeks on Chart
16 Mar 91	**PETER HETHERINGTON: SONGS FROM THE HEART** *Mawson And Warsham PHMC 2*	10		3

VARIOUS ARTISTS (MCA)

Date	Title / Label	Peak Position	Weeks at No.1	Weeks on Chart
24 May 80	**PRECIOUS METAL** *MCA MCF 3069*	60		2
23 Apr 94	**RHYTHM COUNTRY AND BLUES** *MCA MCD 10965*	19		2
27 May 95	**MORE BUMP 'N' GRIND** *MCA MCD 11286*	9		3
2 Nov 96	**THE TARANTINO COLLECTION** *MCA MCD 80325*	18		1

VARIOUS ARTISTS (MCI)

Date	Title / Label	Peak Position	Weeks at No.1	Weeks on Chart
4 Mar 95	**BORN TO BE WILD** *MCI Music MUSCD 001*	20		1

VARIOUS ARTISTS (MERCURY)

Date	Title / Label	Peak Position	Weeks at No.1	Weeks on Chart
2 Jul 83	**WIRED FOR CLUBS (CLUB TRACKS VOLUME 1)** *Mercury CLUBL 1001*	58		4
26 Nov 83	**FORMULA 30** *Mercury PROLP 4* [gold]	6		17
14 Jun 86	**BEAT RUNS WILD** *Mercury WILD 1*	70		2
1 Nov 86	**FORMULA THIRTY – 2** *Mercury PROLP 9* [gold]	80		3
26 Oct 91	**TWO ROOMS – CELEBRATING THE SONGS OF ELTON JOHN AND BERNIE TAUPIN** *Mercury 8457491* [platinum]	1	1	21
21 Dec 02	**FAME ACADEMY** *Mercury 0636132* [platinum]	2		7
27 Sep 03	**BEST OF CAFÉ DEL MAR** *Mercury 9811381*	9		4
3 Jul 04	**DISCOMANIA** *Mercury 9821319* [silver]	7		2

VARIOUS ARTISTS (METROPOLE MUSIC)

Date	Title / Label	Peak Position	Weeks at No.1	Weeks on Chart
25 May 96	**DANNY RAMPLING – LOVE GROOVE DANCE PARTY** *Metropole Music LGCD 1*	10		3
8 Feb 97	**DANNY RAMPLING – LOVE GROOVE DANCE PARTY** *Metropole Music LGCD 2*	17		2
7 Jun 97	**DANNY RAMPLING/LOVE GROOVE PARTY 5 & 6** *Metropole Music LGCD 3*	12		2

VARIOUS ARTISTS (MFP)

Date	Title / Label	Peak Position	Weeks at No.1	Weeks on Chart
4 Dec 71	**BREAKTHROUGH** *MFP 1334*	49		1

VARIOUS ARTISTS (MINISTRY OF SOUND)

Date	Title / Label	Peak Position	Weeks at No.1	Weeks on Chart
11 Sep 93	**MINISTRY OF SOUND: THE SESSIONS VOLUME 1** *Ministry Of Sound MINSTCD 1*	16		2
30 Apr 94	**MINISTRY OF SOUND – THE SESSIONS VOLUME 2** *Ministry Of Sound MINSTCD 002*	6		5
22 Oct 94	**MINISTRY OF SOUND – THE SESSIONS VOLUME 3** *Ministry Of Sound MINSTCD 003*	8		3

Silver-selling ○ Gold-selling ● Platinum-selling ⊛ US No.1 ★

Date	Title / Label	Peak Position	Weeks at No.1	Weeks on Chart
1 Apr 95	**THE FUTURE SOUND OF NEW YORK** *Ministry Of Sound SOMCD 1*	19		1
6 May 95	**MINISTRY OF SOUND – THE SESSIONS 4** *Ministry Of Sound MINCDB 4*	9		5
30 Sep 95	**MINISTRY OF SOUND SESSIONS – VOLUME 5** *Ministry Of Sound MINCD 5*	15		5
25 Nov 95	**THE ANNUAL** *Ministry Of Sound ANNCD 95*	13		6
16 Mar 96	**MINISTRY OF SOUND SESSION SIX – FRANKIE KNUCKLES** *Ministry Of Sound MINCD 6*	8		4
13 Apr 96	**DANCE NATION** *Ministry Of Sound DNCD 96* ○	5		6
20 Jul 96	**MINISTRY OF SOUND – DANCE NATION 2** *Ministry Of Sound DNCD 962*	4		8
21 Sep 96	**ONE HALF OF A WHOLE DECADE – 5 YEARS** *Ministry Of Sound MOS 5CD*	9		6
12 Oct 96	**NORTHERN EXPOSURE – SASHA & JOHN DIGWEED** *Ministry Of Sound NECD 1*	7		4
23 Nov 96	**THE ANNUAL II – PETE TONG & BOY GEORGE** *Ministry Of Sound ANNCD 96* ⊛x2	1	5	24
1 Mar 97	**SESSIONS SEVEN** *Ministry Of Sound MINCD 7*	4		4
29 Mar 97	**DANCE NATION 3 – PETE TONG & JUDGE JULES** *Ministry Of Sound DNCD 3* ●	1	1	10
21 Jun 97	**MINISTRY OF SOUND CLASSICS MIXED BY JUDGE JULES** *Ministry Of Sound CLACD 1*	12		3
26 Jul 97	**SESSION EIGHT – TODD TERRY** *Ministry Of Sound MINCD 8*	11		3
13 Sep 97	**DANCE NATION 4 – PETE TONG/BOY GEORGE** *Ministry Of Sound DNCD 4* ●	2		8
27 Sep 97	**NORTHERN EXPOSURE 2 – SASHA & DIGWEED** *Ministry Of Sound NECD 2*	15		2
15 Nov 97	**THE ANNUAL III – PETE TONG & BOY GEORGE** *Ministry Of Sound ANNCD 97* ⊛	1	2	15
14 Mar 98	**SESSIONS NINE – ERICK MORILLO** *Ministry Of Sound MINCD 9*	17		1
28 Mar 98	**PETE TONG/BOY GEORGE – DANCE NATION 5** *Ministry Of Sound DNCD 5*	2		9
4 Jul 98	**CLUBBER'S GUIDE TO…IBIZA – JULES/TONG** *Ministry Of Sound MOSCD 1*	2		9
5 Sep 98	**THE IBIZA ANNUAL** *Ministry Of Sound MOSCD 2* ●	1	1	9
14 Nov 98	**THE ANNUAL IV – JUDGE JULES & BOY GEORGE** *Ministry Of Sound ANNCD 98* ⊛	1	2	15
30 Jan 99	**CLUBBER'S GUIDE TO…NINETY NINE** *Ministry Of Sound MOSCD 3*	1	2	7
27 Mar 99	**DANCE NATION 6 – TALL PAUL & BRANDON BLOCK** *Ministry Of Sound DNCD 6*	1	1	11
15 May 99	**GALAXY WEEKEND: MIXED BY BOY GEORGE & ALLISTER WHITEHEAD** *Ministry Of Sound GALCD 1*	6		4
29 May 99	**TRANCE NATION: MIXED BY SYSTEM F** *Ministry Of Sound TNCD 1*	1	3	9
19 Jun 99	**CLUBBER'S GUIDE TO IBIZA – SUMMER '99** *Ministry Of Sound MOSCD 4* ○	1	2	10
7 Aug 99	**CLUBBER'S GUIDE TO …TRANCE: MIXED BY ATB** *Ministry Of Sound MOSCD 5* ●	4		5
28 Aug 99	**THE IBIZA ANNUAL: MIXED BY JUDGE JULES + TALL PAUL** *Ministry Of Sound MOSCD 6* ●	1	1	8
9 Oct 99	**TRANCE NATION 2: MIXED BY FERRY CORSTEN** *Ministry Of Sound TNCD 2* ●	1	1	6
30 Oct 99	**GALAXY MIX – BOY GEORGE** *Ministry Of Sound GAL CD2*	8		3
13 Nov 99	**THE ANNUAL – MILLENNIUM EDITION** *Ministry Of Sound ANNCD 99* ⊛	2		15
29 Jan 00	**CLUBBER'S GUIDE TO…2000** *Ministry Of Sound MOSCD 7* ●	1	2	8
26 Feb 00	**REWIND – THE SOUND OF UK GARAGE** *Ministry Of Sound MOSCD 8*	1	1	7
8 Apr 00	**DANCE NATION – TALL PAUL/BRANDON BLOCK** *Ministry Of Sound DNCD 7* ●	1	1	5
13 May 00	**TRANCE NATION 3** *Ministry Of Sound TNCD 3*	2		6
27 May 00	**GALAXY HIT MIX** *Ministry Of Sound GALCD 3*	14		2
10 Jun 00	**CLUBBER'S GUIDE TO IBIZA – SUMMER 2000** *Ministry Of Sound MOSCD 9*	1	1	7
15 Jul 00	**HEADLINERS – TALL PAUL** *Ministry Of Sound MINCD 11*	20		1
22 Jul 00	**AYIA NAPA THE ALBUM – SHANKS & BIGFOOT** *Ministry Of Sound MOSCD 10*	5		7
2 Sep 00	**THE IBIZA ANNUAL – SUMMER 2000** *Ministry Of Sound MOSCD 11L* ⊛	1	3	10
7 Oct 00	**TRANCE NATION 4** *Ministry Of Sound TNCD 4*	1	4	7
11 Nov 00	**THE ANNUAL 2000 – JUDGE JULES/TALL PAUL** *Ministry Of Sound ANNCD 2KL* ⊛	1	2	12
2 Dec 00	**UK GARAGE – THE ALBUM** *Ministry Of Sound MOSCD 12* ●	9		7
20 Jan 01	**CLUBBERS GUIDE TO 2001** *Ministry Of Sound MOSCD 13*	1	2	5
17 Feb 01	**THE CHILL OUT SESSION** *Ministry Of Sound MOSCD 15* ⊛	1	6	18
24 Feb 01	**REAL GARAGE – MIXED LIVE BY MASTERSTEPZ** *Ministry Of Sound MOSCD 16*	6		5
3 Mar 01	**HARD ENERGY** *Ministry Of Sound MOSCD 14*	10		3
7 Apr 01	**THE ANNUAL – SPRING 2001** *Ministry Of Sound MOSCD 17*	1	2	9
12 May 01	**TRANCE NATION 5** *Ministry Of Sound TNCD 5*	4		5
9 Jun 01	**CLUBBERS GUIDE TO IBIZA – SUMMER 2001** *Ministry Of Sound MOSCD 18*	4		5
16 Jun 01	**AYIA NAPA – THE ALBUM 2001** *Ministry Of Sound MOSCD 19*	9		3
23 Jun 01	**THE CHILLOUT SESSION 2** *Ministry Of Sound MOSCD 20* ⊛	2		11
1 Sep 01	**IBIZA ANNUAL** *Ministry Of Sound MOSCD 21*	3		5
8 Sep 01	**IBIZA CHILLOUT SESSION** *Ministry Of Sound MOSCD 22*	12		3
6 Oct 01	**CLUB NATION** *Ministry Of Sound MOSCD 28*	4		4
13 Oct 01	**BACK TO THE OLD SKOOL** *Ministry Of Sound MOSCD 23* ●	2		8
17 Nov 01	**THE ANNUAL 2002** *Ministry Of Sound ANCD 2K1* ●	1	1	12
1 Dec 01	**BACK TO THE OLD SKOOL 2** *Ministry Of Sound MOSCD 29*	11		2
19 Jan 02	**CLUBBERS GUIDE TO 2002** *Ministry Of Sound MOSCD 27* ●	1	3	6
16 Feb 02	**ADDICTED TO BASS** *Ministry Of Sound MOSCD 36*	5		4
16 Feb 02	**THE KARMA COLLECTION** *Ministry Of Sound MOSCD 30*	7		6
9 Mar 02	**BACK TO THE OLD SKOOL – HIP HOP** *Ministry Of Sound MOSCD 32*	7		3
23 Mar 02	**TRANCE NATION** *Ministry Of Sound MOSCD 34*	2		5
30 Mar 02	**BACK TO THE OLD SKOOL – DRUM & BASS** *Ministry Of Sound MOSCD 38*	20		1
6 Apr 02	**SPRING ANNUAL 2002** *Ministry Of Sound MOSCD 35*	3		6
27 Apr 02	**CLUB NATION – MIAMI 2002** *Ministry Of Sound MOSCD 44*	7		2
4 May 02	**THE CHILLOUT SESSION – IBIZA 2002** *Ministry Of Sound MOSCD 40*	4		5
18 May 02	**BACK TO THE OLD SKOOL – IBIZA** *Ministry Of Sound MOSCD 40*	6		4
25 May 02	**21ST CENTURY DISCO** *Ministry Of Sound MOSCD 31*	3		4
8 Jun 02	**CLUBBERS GUIDE TO IBIZA 2002** *Ministry Of Sound MOSCD 42*	1	1	6
29 Jun 02	**ADDICTED TO TRANCE** *Ministry Of Sound MOSCD 49*	3		4
27 Jul 02	**CLUB NATION IBIZA** *Ministry Of Sound MOSCD 47*	9		3
24 Aug 02	**SORTED** *Ministry Of Sound MOSCD 46*	19		1
31 Aug 02	**THE ANNUAL IBIZA 2002** *Ministry Of Sound MOSCD 50*	4		6
28 Sep 02	**DANCE NATION ANTHEMS** *Ministry Of Sound MOSCD 52*	3		7
19 Oct 02	**TRANCE CLASSICS** *Ministry Of Sound MOSCD 54*	9		2
16 Nov 02	**THE ANNUAL 2003** *Ministry Of Sound ANCD 2K2*	1	1	11
30 Nov 02	**THE CHILLOUT SESSION 2003** *Ministry Of Sound MOSCD 56*	20		1
7 Dec 02	**TRANCE NATION 2003** *Ministry Of Sound MOSCD 55*	18		1
18 Jan 03	**CLUBBERS GUIDE 2003** *Ministry Of Sound MOSCD 58*	1	1	8
8 Feb 03	**THE KARMA COLLECTION 2003** *Ministry Of Sound MOSCD 59*	17		2
15 Mar 03	**TRANCE NATION – FUTURE** *Ministry Of Sound MOSCD 61*	3		4
5 Apr 03	**LATE NIGHT SESSIONS** *Ministry Of Sound MOSCD 64*	9		3
12 Apr 03	**THE ANNUAL SPRING 2003** *Ministry Of Sound MOSCD 63*	3		6
26 Apr 03	**BACK TO THE OLD SKOOL CLUB CLASSICS** *Ministry Of Sound MOSCD 62*	2		10
17 May 03	**TRANCE NATION DEEPER** *Ministry Of Sound MOSCD 66*	8		4
31 May 03	**CHILLOUT SESSION – SUMMER COLLECTION 2003** *Ministry Of Sound MOSCD 65*	10		3
28 Jun 03	**CLUBBERS GUIDE TO SUMMER 2003** *Ministry Of Sound MOSCD 67*	2		7
12 Jul 03	**BACK TO THE OLD SKOOL – IBIZA ANTHEMS** *Ministry Of Sound MOSCD 70*	4		3
2 Aug 03	**ELECTROTECH** *Ministry Of Sound MOSCD 69*	17		1
16 Aug 03	**ON THE BEACH** *Ministry Of Sound MOSCD 71*	16		2
6 Sep 03	**THE ANNUAL SUMMER 2003** *Ministry Of Sound MOSCD 73*	5		5
20 Sep 03	**SMOOVE PRESENTS STREET BEATS** *Ministry Of Sound MOSCD 72*	16		1
27 Sep 03	**THE CHILLOUT SESSION – IBIZA SUNSETS** *Ministry Of Sound MOSCD 68*	11		3
11 Oct 03	**TRANCE NATION HARDER** *Ministry Of Sound MOSCD 75*	4		4
25 Oct 03	**HOUSE CLASSICS** *Ministry Of Sound MOSCD 76*	10		2
15 Nov 03	**THE ANNUAL 2004** *Ministry Of Sound ANCD2K3*	2		13
29 Nov 03	**TRANCE NATION ANTHEMS – JUDGE JULES** *Ministry Of Sound MOSCD 78*	16		1
17 Jan 04	**CLUBBERS GUIDE – 2004** *Ministry Of Sound MOSCD 80*	1	3	5
28 Feb 04	**FUNK SOUL CLASSICS** *Ministry Of Sound MOSCD 84*	2		7
20 Mar 04	**TRANCE NATION ELECTRIC – JUDGE JULE** *Ministry Of Sound MOSCD 81*	13		2
17 Apr 04	**THE SOUND OF SMOOVE** *Ministry Of Sound/UMTV MOSCD86*	19		1
8 May 04	**ANNUAL SPRING 2004** *Ministry Of Sound MOSCD 87*	6		5
5 Jun 04	**ACID JAZZ CLASSICS** *Ministry Of Sound MOSCD 91*	12		1
12 Jun 04	**REWIND GARAGE CLASSICS** *Ministry Of Sound MOSCD 93*	8		2
26 Jun 04	**DISCO CLASSICS** *Ministry Of Sound/UMTV MOSCD 81*	9		3
3 Jul 04	**FRANTIC EUPHORIA** *Ministry Of Sound EUPCD1*	4		5
10 Jul 04	**CLUBBERS GUIDE SUMMER '04** *Ministry Of Sound MOSCD 90*	2		4
7 Aug 04	**HARD HOUSE CLASSICS** *Ministry Of Sound MOSCD 88*	7		4
4 Sep 04	**THE ANNUAL SUMMER 2004** *Ministry Of Sound MOSCD 95*	4		4
11 Sep 04	**INFINITE EUPHORIA – FERRY CORSTEN** *Ministry Of Sound EUPCD3*	9		2
25 Sep 04	**CLUB CLASSICS** *Ministry Of Sound MOSCD 83*	5		3
2 Oct 04	**BIG TUNES** *Ministry Of Sound MOSCD 94*	1	2	7
16 Oct 04	**EXTREME EUPHORIA** *Ministry Of Sound EUPCD4*	16		1
13 Nov 04	**THE ANNUAL 2005** *Ministry Of Sound ANCD2K4*	2		16
27 Nov 04	**VERY BEST OF TRIED AND TESTED EUPHORIA** *Ministry Of Sound EUPCD5*	15		2

Silver-selling · Gold-selling · Platinum-selling · US No.1 ★ · Peak Position · Weeks at No.1 · Weeks on Chart

Date	Title / Label	Peak Position	Weeks at No.1	Weeks on Chart
15 Jan 05	**CLUBBERS GUIDE 05** *Ministry Of Sound MOSCD100*	2		7
19 Feb 05	**THE VERY BEST OF EUPHORIC FUNKY HOUSE** *Ministry Of Sound BRKCD1*	3		7
5 Mar 05	**THE MASH UP MIX – CUT UP BOYS** *Ministry Of Sound MOSCD98*	2		5
19 Mar 05	**BEYOND EUPHORIA – MIXED BY DT8 PROJECT** *Ministry Of Sound EUPCD7*	11		2
9 Apr 05	**BIG TUNES 2 – LIVING FOR THE WEEKEND** *Ministry Of Sound MOSCD101*	4		7
30 Apr 05	**MAXIMUM BASS** *Ministry Of Sound MOSCD103*	3		5
4 Jun 05	**FUNKY HOUSE SESSIONS** *Ministry Of Sound MOSCD107*	5		5
18 Jun 05	**CLUBBERS GUIDE SUMMER 2005** *Ministry Of Sound MOSCD108*	2		6
2 Jul 05	**TIDY EUPHORIA** *Ministry Of Sound EUPCD8*	10		2
9 Jul 05	**GATECRASHER CLASSICS** *Ministry Of Sound GCCD01*	1	3	11
6 Aug 05	**JUDGEMENT EUPHORIA** *Ministry Of Sound EUPCD9*	12		3
20 Aug 05	**IBIZA ANNUAL 2005** *Ministry Of Sound MOSCD109*	3		5
17 Sep 05	**BIG TUNES 3 – LIVING FOR THE WEEKEND** *Ministry Of Sound MOSCD105*	3		4
8 Oct 05	**THE VERY BEST OF BACK TO THE OLD SKOOL** *Ministry Of Sound MOSCD111*	10		5
12 Nov 05	**THE ANNUAL 2006** *Ministry Of Sound ANCD2K5*	2		13
19 Nov 05	**GATECRASHER CLASSICS 2** *Ministry Of Sound GCCD02*	6		6
3 Dec 05	**VERY BEST OF UPLIFTING HOUSE EUPHORIA** *EMI Virgin/Ministry Of Sound EUPCD11*	20		1
7 Jan 06	**HELTER SKELTER PRESENTS HARDCORE CLASSICS** *Ministry Of Sound HELTCD01*	2		8
14 Jan 06	**CLUBBERS GUIDE 2006** *Ministry Of Sound MOSCD112*	1	4	8
28 Jan 06	**DRUM & BASS ARENA – THE CLASSICS** *Ministry Of Sound DABA01*	9		2
11 Feb 06	**THE VERY BEST OF EUPHORIC DANCE** *Ministry Of Sound BRKCD2*	2		6
11 Feb 06	**THE CHILLOUT SESSION** *Ministry Of Sound MOSCD116*	15		1
11 Mar 06	**THE MASH UP MIX 2006** *Ministry Of Sound MOSCD115*	1	1	6
8 Apr 06	**DANCE NATION** *Ministry Of Sound MOSCD118*	3		8
22 Apr 06	**MAXIMUM BASS 2 – THE NEXT LEVEL** *Ministry Of Sound MOSCD120*	4		5
13 May 06	**FUNKY HOUSE SESSIONS 06** *Ministry Of Sound MOSCD119*	2		8
3 Jun 06	**CLASSIC EUPHORIA** *Ministry Of Sound EUPCD14*	2		11
24 Jun 06	**CLUBBERS GUIDE SUMMER 2006** *Ministry Of Sound MOSCD122*	1	1	7
1 Jul 06	**HELTER SKELTER UNITED IN HARDCORE** *Ministry Of Sound HELTCD02*	6		4
8 Jul 06	**GATECRASHER FOREVER** *Ministry Of Sound GCCD3*	6		1
5 Aug 06	**CREAM SUMMER 2006** *Ministry Of Sound CREAMCD1*	3		5
12 Aug 06	**LASHED EUPHORIA** *Ministry Of Sound EUPCD16*	5		3
19 Aug 06	**BIG TUNES X-RATED** *Ministry Of Sound MOSCD125*	3		5
9 Sep 06	**IBIZA ANNUAL 2006** *Ministry Of Sound MOSCD127*	2		7
23 Sep 06	**DAVE PEARCE – DANCE ANTHEMS – CLASSICS** *Ministry Of Sound MOSCD131*	4		8
21 Oct 06	**FANTAZIA CLUB CLASSICS** *Ministry Of Sound FANTCD1*	7		2
28 Oct 06	**HARDCORE EUPHORIA** *Ministry Of Sound EUPCD19*	9		3
11 Nov 06	**THE ANNUAL 2007** *Ministry Of Sound ANCD2K6*	2		13
18 Nov 06	**CLASSIC EUPHORIA – LEVEL 2** *Ministry Of Sound EUPCD17*	11		3
16 Dec 06	**PUT YOUR HANDS UP** *Ministry Of Sound HANDCD1*	9		10
6 Jan 07	**HELTER SKELTER V RAINDANCE HARDCORE 2007** *Ministry Of Sound HELTCD03*	5		5
13 Jan 07	**CLUBBERS GUIDE 2007** *Ministry Of Sound MOSCD132*	3		6
10 Feb 07	**THE VERY BEST OF EUPHORIC DANCE** *Ministry Of Sound BRKCD3*	2		5
10 Feb 07	**ELECTRO HOUSE SESSIONS** *Ministry Of Sound MOSCD134*	3		5
24 Feb 07	**DANCE ENERGY** *Ministry Of Sound ENERGY1*	6		3
3 Mar 07	**THE MASH UP MIX 2007** *Ministry Of Sound MOSCD135*	2		7
17 Mar 07	**DAVE PEARCE – DANCE ANTHEMS 2007** *Ministry Of Sound MOSCD137*	4		10
17 Mar 07	**KISS PRESENTS BOOTY HOUSE** *Ministry Of Sound KISSED1*	6		5
14 Apr 07	**PUT YOUR HANDS UP 2** *Ministry Of Sound HANDUPCD2*	2		8
5 May 07	**FUNKY HOUSE SESSIONS 07** *Ministry Of Sound MOSCD138*	2		6
26 May 07	**DANCEMIX – SUMMER ANTHEMS** *Ministry Of Sound DMIXCD01*	8		4
2 Jun 07	**MAXIMUM BASS 2007** *Ministry Of Sound MOSCD140*	5		3
9 Jun 07	**RETURN TO IBIZA – EUPHORIA** *Ministry Of Sound EUPCD20*	5		6
16 Jun 07	**CLUBBERS GUIDE SUMMER 2007** *Ministry Of Sound MOSCD142*	3		7
14 Jul 07	**HARD ENERGY – YOUR XXXTREME NIGHT OUT** *Ministry Of Sound ENERGY2*	3		3
21 Jul 07	**CLASSIC TRANCE NATION** *Ministry Of Sound MOSCD145*	2		13
28 Jul 07	**HARDCORE 2007 – THE NEW GENERATION** *Ministry Of Sound HELTCD04*	7		3
4 Aug 07	**CREAM SUMMER 2007** *Ministry Of Sound CREAMCD3*	8		4
11 Aug 07	**THE RIDE** *Ministry Of Sound MOSCD146*	3		7
8 Sep 07	**IBIZA ANNUAL 2007** *Ministry Of Sound MOSCD147*	2		7
15 Sep 07	**GATECRASHER IMMORTAL** *Ministry Of Sound GCCD05*	2		7
13 Oct 07	**DAVE PEARCE DANCE ANTHEMS** *Ministry Of Sound MOSCD152*	3		5
3 Nov 07	**DRUM & BASS ARENA** *Ministry Of Sound DABA02*	11		3
10 Nov 07	**THE ANNUAL 2008** *Ministry Of Sound ANCD2K7*	2		13
1 Dec 07	**MINISTRY OF SOUND ANTHEMS 1991–2008** *Ministry Of Sound MOSCD154*	1	1	31
8 Dec 07	**PUT YOUR HANDS UP! 3** *Ministry Of Sound HANDUPCD3*	16		1
12 Jan 08	**RAVE NATION – THE ANTHEMS** *Ministry Of Sound HELTCD05*	7		3
19 Jan 08	**CLUBBERS GUIDE 2008** *Ministry Of Sound MOSCD155*	3		5
26 Jan 08	**BIG TUNES 2008** *Ministry Of Sound H2BCD01*	1	3	8
2 Feb 08	**THE RUSH** *Ministry Of Sound MOSCD158*	8		2
1 Mar 08	**THE VERY BEST OF EUPHORIC DANCE BREAKDOWN** *Ministry Of Sound BRKCD4*	1	2	10
8 Mar 08	**THE SOUND OF BASSLINE** *Ministry Of Sound MOSCD164*	2		9
15 Mar 08	**THE MASH UP MIX 2008** *Ministry Of Sound MOSCD159*	3		6
12 Apr 08	**MINISTRY OF SOUND PRESENTS GARAGE CLASSICS** *Ministry Of Sound MOSCD161*	3		8
19 Apr 08	**DAVE PEARCE TRANCE ANTHEMS 2008** *Ministry Of Sound MOSCD163*	3		12
10 May 08	**CREAM – 15 YEARS** *Ministry Of Sound CREAMCD4*	3		7
31 May 08	**CHILLED 1991–2008** *Ministry Of Sound MOSCD165*	1	5	15
14 Jun 08	**CLUBBERS GUIDE – SUMMER 2008** *Ministry Of Sound MOSCD169*	3		5
12 Jul 08	**INNOVATION – THE ALBUM** *Ministry Of Sound MOSCD166*	17		1
9 Aug 08	**GARAGE CLASSICS VOLUME 2 – SUMMER EDITION** *Ministry Of Sound MOSCD170*	3		4
16 Aug 08	**THE VERY BEST OF EUPHORIC DANCE BREAKDOWN – SUMMER 2008** *Ministry Of Sound BRKCD5*	4		5
23 Aug 08	**RENAISSANCE ANTHEMS** *Ministry Of Sound 01REN*	15		1
30 Aug 08	**THE MASH UP MIX – OLD SKOOL** *Ministry Of Sound MOSCD174*	3		8
6 Sep 08	**CREAMFIELDS – 10 YEARS – THE ALBUM** *Ministry Of Sound CREAMCD5*	4		4
13 Sep 08	**IBIZA ANNUAL 2008** *Ministry Of Sound MOSCD176*	3		5
8 Nov 08	**THE ANNUAL 2009** *Ministry Of Sound ANCD2K8*	4		5
29 Nov 08	**ANTHEMS 2 – 1991–2009** *Ministry Of Sound MOSCD178*	6		2
6 Dec 08	**HARDCORE – THE CLASSICS – 1994–2009** *Ministry Of Sound MOSCD180*	18		1

VARIOUS ARTISTS (MIRACLE)

Date	Title / Label	Peak Position	Weeks at No.1	Weeks on Chart
4 Feb 95	**LOVE ETERNAL** *Miracle MIRCD 0001*	5		4

VARIOUS ARTISTS (MISS MONEYPENNY'S)

Date	Title / Label	Peak Position	Weeks at No.1	Weeks on Chart
22 Mar 97	**GLAMOROUS ONE** *Miss Moneypenny's MPENNYCD 1*	12		1

VARIOUS ARTISTS (MORE PROTEIN)

Date	Title / Label	Peak Position	Weeks at No.1	Weeks on Chart
1 Feb 92	**CLOSET CLASSICS VOLUME 1 – MORE PROTEIN SAMPLER** *More Protein CMMD 1*	20		1

VARIOUS ARTISTS (MOTOWN)

Date	Title / Label	Peak Position	Weeks at No.1	Weeks on Chart
3 Apr 65	**A COLLECTION OF TAMLA MOTOWN HITS** *Tamla Motown TML 11001*	16		4
4 Mar 67	**16 ORIGINAL BIG HITS – VOLUME 4** *Tamla Motown TML 11043*	33		3
17 Jun 67	**TAMLA MOTOWN HITS VOLUME 5** *Tamla Motown TML 11050*	11		40
21 Oct 67	**BRITISH MOTOWN CHARTBUSTERS** *Tamla Motown TML 11055*	2		54
10 Feb 68	**MOTOWN MEMORIES** *Tamla Motown TML 11064*	21		13
24 Aug 68	**TAMLA MOTOWN HITS VOLUME 6** *Tamla Motown STML 11074*	32		2
30 Nov 68	**BRITISH MOTOWN CHARTBUSTERS VOLUME 2** *Tamla Motown STML 11082*	8		11
25 Oct 69	**MOTOWN CHARTBUSTERS VOLUME 3** *Tamla Motown STML 11121*	1	1	93
21 Feb 70	**COLLECTION OF BIG HITS VOLUME 8** *Tamla Motown STML 11130*	56		1
24 Oct 70	**MOTOWN CHARTBUSTERS VOLUME 4** *Tamla Motown STML 11162*	1	1	40
13 Mar 71	**MOTOWN CHARTBUSTERS VOLUME 5** *Tamla Motown STML 11181*	1	3	36
23 Oct 71	**MOTOWN CHARTBUSTERS VOLUME 6** *Tamla Motown STML 11191*	2		36
26 Feb 72	**MOTOWN MEMORIES** *Tamla Motown STML 11200*	22		4
18 Mar 72	**MOTOWN STORY** *Tamla Motown TMSP 1130*	21		8
25 Nov 72	**MOTOWN CHARTBUSTERS VOLUME 7** *Tamla Motown STML 11215*	9		16
3 Nov 73	**MOTOWN CHARTBUSTERS VOLUME 8** *Tamla Motown STML 11246*	9		15
26 Oct 74	**MOTOWN CHARTBUSTERS VOLUME 9** *Tamla Motown STML 11270*	14		15
1 Nov 75	**MOTOWN GOLD** *Tamla Motown STML 12003*	8		35
5 Nov 77	**MOTOWN GOLD VOLUME 2** *Motown STML 12070*	28		4
7 Oct 78	**BIG WHEELS OF MOTOWN** *Motown EMTV 12*	2		18
2 Feb 80	**THE LAST DANCE** *Motown EMTV 20*	1	2	23
2 Aug 80	**THE 20TH ANNIVERSARY ALBUM** *Motown TMSP 6010*	53		2
21 May 88	**MOTOWN DANCE PARTY** *Motown ZC 72700*	3		18
19 May 90	**MOTOWN DANCE PARTY 2** *Motown ZL 72703*	10		7
6 Oct 90	**SOUL DECADE: THE SIXTIES** *Motown ZL 74816*	3		10
24 Oct 92	**MOTOWN'S GREATEST LOVE SONGS** *Motown 5300062*	5		5

Date	Title / Label	Peak Position	Weeks at No.1	Weeks on Chart
12 Nov 94	MOTOWN – THE ULTIMATE HITS COLLECTION *Motown 5304652* ●	6		13
4 Nov 95	MOTOWN – THE HITS COLLECTION – VOLUME 2 *Motown 5306042*	19		1
12 Sep 98	MOTOWN 40 FOREVER *Motown 5308492*	15		2
25 Mar 06	TO MUM LOVE MOTOWN *Motown 9837640*	2		4

VARIOUS ARTISTS (MOUNTAIN)

Date	Title / Label	Peak Position	Weeks at No.1	Weeks on Chart
3 Jul 76	GOLDEN FIDDLE AWARDS 1976 *Mountain TOPC 5002*	45		2

VARIOUS ARTISTS (MUSIC UNITES)

Date	Title / Label	Peak Position	Weeks at No.1	Weeks on Chart
12 Mar 94	JOURNEYS BY DJ VOLUME 4 *Music Unites JDJCD 4*	19		1

VARIOUS ARTISTS (NEEDLE)

Date	Title / Label	Peak Position	Weeks at No.1	Weeks on Chart
4 Jul 87	DANCE MANIA VOLUME 1 *Needle DAMA 1*	46		4
20 Feb 88	MAD ON HOUSE VOLUME 1 *Needle MADD 1*	81		2
14 May 88	HOUSE HITS *Needle HOHI 88*	25		8

VARIOUS ARTISTS (NEMS)

Date	Title / Label	Peak Position	Weeks at No.1	Weeks on Chart
12 Dec 81	LIVE AND HEAVY *NEMS NEL 6020*	100		2

VARIOUS ARTISTS (NETWORK)

Date	Title / Label	Peak Position	Weeks at No.1	Weeks on Chart
20 Jan 96	RENAISSANCE – MIX COLLECTION – PART 2 *Network RENMIX 2CD*	16		2
13 Apr 96	BACK TO BASICS – CUT THE CRAP *Network B2BCD 1*	20		1

VARIOUS ARTISTS (NEW STATE)

Date	Title / Label	Peak Position	Weeks at No.1	Weeks on Chart
26 May 07	GODSKITCHEN – ELECTRIC *New State NEWCD9011*	14		1
4 Aug 07	GODSKITCHEN – GLOBAL GATHERING *New State NEWCD9016*	14		3
3 Nov 07	PAUL OAKENFOLD – GREATEST HITS AND REMIXES *New State NEWCDX9020*	13		1
12 Jan 08	GODSKITCHEN – TRANCE ANTHEMS *New State NEWCD9023*	19		1
5 Jul 08	CREAM IBIZA *New State NEWCD9028*	15		2

VARIOUS ARTISTS (NICE)

Date	Title / Label	Peak Position	Weeks at No.1	Weeks on Chart
14 Sep 96	TRIBUTE TO THE SMALL FACES – LONG AGOS/WORLDS APART *Nice NYCE 1CD*	20		1

VARIOUS ARTISTS (NME)

Date	Title / Label	Peak Position	Weeks at No.1	Weeks on Chart
9 Apr 88	SERGEANT PEPPER KNEW MY FATHER *NME/Island PELP 100*	37		8

VARIOUS ARTISTS (NONSUCH)

Date	Title / Label	Peak Position	Weeks at No.1	Weeks on Chart
9 Sep 06	FANTASTIC 80'S EXTENDED *Nonsuch 88697001632*	11		1

VARIOUS ARTISTS (NOUVEAU MUSIC)

Date	Title / Label	Peak Position	Weeks at No.1	Weeks on Chart
24 Sep 83	CLASSIC THEMES *Nouveau Music NML 1001*	61		2
2 Jun 84	ESSENTIAL DISCO AND DANCE *Nouveau Music NML 1010*	96		1
30 Mar 85	DREAM MELODIES *Nouveau Music NML 1013*	91		1

VARIOUS ARTISTS (NPG)

Date	Title / Label	Peak Position	Weeks at No.1	Weeks on Chart
20 Aug 94	1-800 NEW FUNK *NPG BR 7110062*	15		1

VARIOUS ARTISTS (NUMA)

Date	Title / Label	Peak Position	Weeks at No.1	Weeks on Chart
22 Mar 86	NUMA RECORDS YEAR 1 *Numa NUMA 1004*	94		1

VARIOUS ARTISTS (OLD GOLD)

Date	Title / Label	Peak Position	Weeks at No.1	Weeks on Chart
7 Apr 90	LET'S DANCE – SOUND OF THE SIXTIES PART 1 *Old Gold OG 1702*	18		1

VARIOUS ARTISTS (ORB RECORDINGS)

Date	Title / Label	Peak Position	Weeks at No.1	Weeks on Chart
26 Jul 03	ANGEL BEACH – THE SECOND WAVE *Orb Recordings CDORB4*	16		2

VARIOUS ARTISTS (ORIOLE)

Date	Title / Label	Peak Position	Weeks at No.1	Weeks on Chart
24 Aug 63	THE MERSEY BEAT VOLUME 1 *Oriole PS 40047*	17		5

VARIOUS ARTISTS (PARKFIELD)

Date	Title / Label	Peak Position	Weeks at No.1	Weeks on Chart
28 Jul 90	NOTHING COMPARES TO THIS *Parkfield PMLP 5020*	13		2

VARIOUS ARTISTS (PARLOPHONE)

Date	Title / Label	Peak Position	Weeks at No.1	Weeks on Chart
22 Jun 91	IT'S COOL *Parlophone PCSTV 1* ●	3		7
4 Jul 92	DANCE ENERGY 4 – FEEL THE RHYTHM *Parlophone CDPMTV 4* ●	6		4
3 Sep 94	60'S SOUL 90'S SOUL *Parlophone CDPCSTV 4*	6		5
20 Oct 07	DISCO 4 – REMIXED BY THE PET SHOP BOYS *Parlophone 5060462*	15		1
3 Nov 07	SOULWAX – MOST OF THE REMIXES WE'VE MADE *Parlophone 5092472*	16		1

VARIOUS ARTISTS (PERFECTO)

Date	Title / Label	Peak Position	Weeks at No.1	Weeks on Chart
1 Aug 92	HARDCORE DJS...TAKE CONTROL *Perfecto 74321101812*	15		4
9 Nov 96	PERFECTO FLUORO:OAKENFOLD *Perfecto 0630166942*	18		1
4 Nov 00	PERFECTO PRESENTS PAUL OAKENFOLD – TRAVELLING *Perfecto PERFALB 02CD*	12		2
19 May 01	TIMO MAAS – CONNECTED *Perfecto PERFALB 04CD*	20		1
25 Aug 01	IBIZA – PAUL OAKENFOLD *Perfecto PERFALB 05CD*	13		1

VARIOUS ARTISTS (PHILIPS)

Date	Title / Label	Peak Position	Weeks at No.1	Weeks on Chart
9 Mar 63	ALL STAR FESTIVAL *Philips DL 99500*	4		19
2 Jun 73	20 ORIGINAL CHART HITS *Philips TV 1*	9		11
2 Jun 73	NICE 'N' EASY *Philips 6441 076* ●	36		1
6 Aug 77	NEW WAVE *Philips 5300 902*	11		12
3 Nov 01	UTOPIA – CHILLED CLASSICS *Philips 4720642*	10		3

VARIOUS ARTISTS (PICKWICK)

Date	Title / Label	Peak Position	Weeks at No.1	Weeks on Chart
20 Nov 93	THE VERY BEST OF DISNEY *Pickwick DISCD 471*	4		12
5 Nov 94	THE LION KING SING-ALONG *Pickwick/Disney DSMCD 477* ●	16		3
19 Nov 94	THE VERY BEST OF DISNEY 2 *Pickwick/Disney DISCD 480*	9		4

VARIOUS ARTISTS (POLYDOR)

Date	Title / Label	Peak Position	Weeks at No.1	Weeks on Chart
10 Dec 66	STEREO MUSICALE SHOWCASE *Polydor 104450*	26		2
9 Oct 71	THE A-Z OF EASY LISTENING *Polydor 2661 005*	24		4
24 Feb 79	20 OF ANOTHER KIND *Polydor POLS 1006*	45		3
19 May 79	BOOGIE BUS *Polydor 9198 174*	23		11
3 May 80	CHAMPAGNE AND ROSES *Polydor ROSTV 1*	7		14
30 Aug 80	I AM WOMAN *Polydor WOMTV 1* ●	11		13
11 Oct 80	COUNTRY ROUND UP *Polydor KOWTV 1*	64		3
18 Oct 80	MONSTERS OF ROCK *Polydor 2488 810*	16		5
6 Dec 80	THE HITMAKERS *Polydor HOPTV 1* ●	45		10
4 Apr 81	ROLL ON *Polydor REDTV 1* ●	3		13
17 Oct 81	MONSTER TRACKS *Polydor HOTTV 2* ●	20		8
1 Nov 86	SIMON BATES – OUR TUNE *Polydor PROLP 10* ●	58		5
12 Nov 88	ANDREW LLOYD WEBBER – THE PREMIER COLLECTION *Polydor ALWTV 1* ⊛x3	3		9
14 Jan 89	ANDREW LLOYD WEBBER – THE PREMIER COLLECTION *Polydor ALWTV 1*	1	1	55
4 Feb 89	THE MARQUEE – 30 LEGENDARY YEARS *Polydor MOTV 1* ⊛	1	4	21
31 Mar 90	SKINBEAT – THE FIRST TOUCH *Polydor SKINL 101*	6		8
18 Aug 90	KNEBWORTH – THE ALBUM *Polydor 843912* ●	1	2	10
13 Jul 91	PURPLE RAINBOWS *Polydor/EMI 8455341* ●	1	1	13
5 Oct 91	ABSOLUTION – ROCK THE ALTERNATIVE WAY *Polydor 8457471* ●	6		5
20 Nov 99	ABBAMANIA *Polydor/Universal Music TV 5433592* ⊛x2	2		14
8 Dec 01	ANDREW LLOYD WEBBER – GOLD *Polydor 5894922* ●	5		7
6 Sep 03	FAME ACADEMY – BEE GEES SPECIAL *Polydor 9865586*	17		1
18 Oct 03	FAME ACADEMY – THE FINALISTS *Polydor 9865835* ●	2		4
1 Nov 03	GREASEMANIA *Polydor/S 9865823*	1	1	3
26 Nov 05	ANDREW LLOYD WEBBER – DIVAS *Polydor 9875388*	10		2

VARIOUS ARTISTS (POLYGRAM)

Date	Title / Label	Peak Position	Weeks at No.1	Weeks on Chart
22 Feb 92	THE AWARDS 1992 *Polygram TV 5152072* ●	1	2	9
21 Mar 92	SOUL EMOTION *Polygram TV 5151882*	1	3	10
2 May 92	COUNTRY MOODS *Polygram TV 5152992* ●	2		10
30 May 92	BEATS RHYMES AND BASSLINES – THE BEST OF RAP *Polygram TV 5153842*	7		3

Silver-selling · Gold-selling · Platinum-selling ⊛ · US No.1 ★ · Peak Position · Weeks at No.1 · Weeks on Chart

Date	Title / Label	Peak Position	Weeks at No.1	Weeks on Chart
6 Jun 92	**POWER CUTS – ROCK'S GREATEST HITS** *Polygram TV 5154152*	5		9
20 Jun 92	**MODERN LOVE** *Polygram TV 5155182*	1	1	20
18 Jul 92	**DANCING ON SUNSHINE** *Polygram TV/Virgin 5155192*	4		11
1 Aug 92	**BLAME IT ON THE BOOGIE** *Polygram TV 5155172*	5		8
5 Sep 92	**READING – THE INDIE ALBUM** *Polygram TV 5156482*	5		5
20 Feb 93	**THE AWARDS 1993** *Polygram TV 5160752*	3		7
27 Mar 93	**COUNTRY ROADS** *Polygram TV 5161002*	3		10
17 Apr 93	**MEGA-LO-MANIA** *Polygram TV 5158132*	8		6
24 Apr 93	**UNDER THE COVERS** *Polygram TV 5160742*	11		5
8 May 93	**MIDNIGHT MOODS – THE LIGHTER SIDE OF JAZZ** *Polygram TV 5158162*	3		8
5 Jun 93	**WOMAN TO WOMAN** *Polygram TV 5161632*	5		10
19 Jun 93	**THE GIFT OF SONG** *Polygram TV 5160582*	7		4
26 Jun 93	**SOUL INSPIRATION** *Polygram TV 5162262*	4		7
3 Jul 93	**THE BLUES EXPERIENCE** *Polygram TV 5162282*	7		6
24 Jul 93	**TEMPTED** *Polygram TV 5163052*	10		4
14 Aug 93	**LEADERS OF THE PACK** *Polygram TV 5163762*	9		9
14 Aug 93	**ALL NIGHT LONG** *Polygram TV 5163752*	15		3
4 Sep 93	**PROGRESSION** *Polygram TV 5163982*	9		3
2 Oct 93	**ROUND MIDNIGHT** *Polygram TV 5164712*	16		2
9 Oct 93	**DISCO DIVAS** *Polygram TV 5164802*	4		5
22 Jan 94	**THE SOUND OF KISS 100FM** *Polygram TV 5164862*	1	1	4
19 Feb 94	**THE MOVIES' GREATEST LOVE SONGS** *Polygram TV 5166512*	4		6
19 Feb 94	**DANCE DIVAS** *Polygram TV 5166522*	11		3
5 Mar 94	**FACE THE MUSIC – TORVILL AND DEAN** *Polygram TV 8450652*	8		3
12 Mar 94	**SOUL DEVOTION** *Polygram TV 5166242* ⊛	1	4	14
19 Mar 94	**I KNOW THEM SO WELL – TIM RICE** *Polygram TV 5166502*	2		7
9 Apr 94	**WOMAN 2 WOMAN TWO** *Polygram TV 5163302*	9		4
23 Apr 94	**ACOUSTIC MOODS** *Polygram TV 5166592*	4		8
7 May 94	**DANCE ZONE – LEVEL ONE** *Polygram TV 5167142*	1	4	8
21 May 94	**REMEMBER THEN – 30 DOO-WOP GREATS** *Polygram TV 5167922*	10		3
25 Jun 94	**THE ULTIMATE EIGHTIES** *Polygram TV 5168312*	2		9
2 Jul 94	**ROCK THERAPY** *Polygram TV 5168612*	9		6
16 Jul 94	**DANCE ZONE – LEVEL TWO** *Polygram TV 5169122*	1	2	6
23 Jul 94	**POWER AND SOUL** *Polygram TV 5168962*	5		10
27 Aug 94	**GROOVIN'** *Polygram TV 5169682*	2		7
10 Sep 94	**SATIN THE STEEL – WOMEN IN ROCK** *Polygram TV 5169712*	3		7
17 Sep 94	**SOUL NIGHTS** *Polygram TV 5250052*	3		6
1 Oct 94	**SENSES** *Polygram TV 5166272*	5		5
8 Oct 94	**DANCE ZONE – LEVEL THREE** *Polygram TV 5250732*	1	1	6
15 Oct 94	**AFTER MIDNIGHT** *Polygram TV 5168712*	17		1
29 Oct 94	**THE ULTIMATE 80'S BALLADS** *Polygram TV 5251132*	5		3
12 Nov 94	**DANCE ZONE '94** *Polygram TV 5251302*	2		12
11 Feb 95	**ENDLESS LOVE** *Polygram TV 5253412*	3		6
25 Feb 95	**ELECTRIC DREAMS** *Polygram TV 5254352*	3		8
11 Mar 95	**THE ESSENTIAL GROOVE** *Polygram TV 5254382*	11		3
25 Mar 95	**DANCE ZONE LEVEL FOUR** *Polygram TV 5169442* ⊛	1	2	8
25 Mar 95	**EMERALD ROCK** *Polygram TV 5169612*	14		3
1 Apr 95	**TOGETHER** *Polygram TV 5254612*	2		5
8 Apr 95	**EVERY SONG TELLS A STORY** *Polygram TV 5251702*	17		1
15 Apr 95	**ROCKS OFF** *Polygram TV 5254872*	4		5
6 May 95	**LET'S HEAR IT FOR THE GIRLS** *Polygram TV 5165522*	8		5
13 May 95	**SHINE: 20 BRILLIANT INDIE HITS** *Polygram TV 5255672*	4		5
20 May 95	**SILK AND STEEL** *Polygram TV 5255692*	3		6
3 Jun 95	**TEENAGE KICKS** *Polygram TV 5253382*	8		3
10 Jun 95	**WORLD IN UNION – ANTHEMS** *Polygram TV 5278072*	8		4
24 Jun 95	**DANCE ZONE LEVEL FIVE** *Polygram TV 5256332*	1	3	10
1 Jul 95	**SUNNY AFTERNOONS** *Polygram TV 5256002*	6		3
15 Jul 95	**THE NUMBER ONE CLASSIC SOUL ALBUM** *Polygram TV 5256562*	5		7
22 Jul 95	**THE NUMBER ONE REGGAE ALBUM** *Polygram TV 5256392*	14		2
19 Aug 95	**ACOUSTIC FREEWAY** *Polygram TV 5257352*	7		4
26 Aug 95	**THE NUMBER ONE 70'S ROCK ALBUM** *Polygram TV 5257172*	3		5
26 Aug 95	**SUMMERTIME SOUL** *Polygram TV 5258002*	5		4
2 Sep 95	**DANCE ZONE LEVEL SIX** *Polygram TV 5258602*	1	1	7
2 Sep 95	**SHINE TOO** *Polygram TV 5258582*	4		5
23 Sep 95	**ACOUSTIC ROCK** *Polygram TV 5258962*	7		5
14 Oct 95	**KISS IN IBIZA '95** *Polygram TV 5259112*	3		5
4 Nov 95	**THE NUMBER ONE MOVIES ALBUM** *Polygram TV 5259622* ⊛	2		12
11 Nov 95	**DANCE ZONE '95** *Polygram TV 5350452*	8		4
11 Nov 95	**THE NUMBER ONE ALL TIME ROCK ALBUM** *Polygram TV 5350542*	16		2
18 Nov 95	**SHINE 3** *Polygram TV 5259652*	13		6
9 Dec 95	**THE NUMBER ONE CHRISTMAS ALBUM** *Polygram TV 5259782* ⊛x2	4		13
3 Feb 96	**SISTERS OF SWING** *Polygram TV 5352252*	1	1	10
10 Feb 96	**SOFT ROCK** *Polygram TV 5352482*	3		6
10 Feb 96	**PASS THE VIBES** *Polygram TV 5352212*	4		3
10 Feb 96	**THE LOOK OF LOVE** *Polygram TV 5351902*	6		7
10 Feb 96	**CLASSIC MOODS** *Polygram TV 4522492*	7		8
17 Feb 96	**THE NUMBER ONE LOVE ALBUM** *Polygram TV 5352622*	1	1	6
2 Mar 96	**FREEWAY** *Polygram TV 5259192*	17		1
9 Mar 96	**SHINE 2** *Polygram TV 5353212*	3		6
9 Mar 96	**AMBIENT MOODS** *Polygram TV 5259522*	7		5
23 Mar 96	**THE BEST OF WOMAN TO WOMAN** *Polygram TV 5353572*	3		5
6 Apr 96	**CLUB MIX 96** *Polygram TV 5354122*	2		7
27 Apr 96	**GO WITH THE FLOW – ESSENTIAL ACID JAZZ** *Polygram TV 5352412*	9		2
4 May 96	**DANCE ZONE LEVEL SEVEN** *Polygram TV 5354272*	1	1	5
11 May 96	**BOYZ OF SWING** *Polygram TV 5354232*	1	1	5
1 Jun 96	**LADYKILLERS** *Polygram TV 5355362*	3		4
1 Jun 96	**SISTERS OF SWING 2** *Polygram TV 5354752*	4		3
8 Jun 96	**FUNKMASTER MIX** *Polygram TV 5355762*	16		2
15 Jun 96	**TRUEBRIT** *Polygram TV 5354792*	7		4
22 Jun 96	**MIX ZONE** *Polygram TV 5355822*	2		5
29 Jun 96	**SUMMER VYBES** *Polygram TV 5356442*	8		3
6 Jul 96	**HORIZONS – 12 DREAMHOUSE ANTHEMS** *Polygram TV 8287932*	17		1
13 Jul 96	**KISS MIX '96** *Polygram TV 5357012*	5		3
20 Jul 96	**SHINE 5** *Polygram TV 5356892*	2		9
27 Jul 96	**THE NUMBER ONE EIGHTIES ALBUM** *Polygram TV 5356832*	10		4
27 Jul 96	**THE NUMBER ONE SUMMER ALBUM** *Polygram TV 5356312*	12		3
3 Aug 96	**CLUB MIX 96 – VOLUME 2** *Polygram TV 5357652*	2		8
17 Aug 96	**THE NUMBER ONE COUNTRY ALBUM** *Polygram TV 5357222*	16		2
7 Sep 96	**PURE DANCE '96** *Polygram TV 5357892*	5		4
7 Sep 96	**THE SAX ALBUM** *Polygram TV 5358052*	6		4
14 Sep 96	**BOYZ OF SWING II** *Polygram TV 5357552*	6		5
21 Sep 96	**DANCE ZONE LEVEL EIGHT** *Polygram TV 5359032*	4		6
5 Oct 96	**SHINE 6** *Polygram TV 5359202*	2		5
12 Oct 96	**THE NUMBER ONE ACOUSTIC ROCK ALBUM** *Polygram TV 5358142*	6		4
19 Oct 96	**KISS IN IBIZA '96** *Polygram TV 5359672*	1	4	8
2 Nov 96	**THE NUMBER ONE RAP ALBUM** *Polygram TV 5358112*	12		1
16 Nov 96	**THE NUMBER ONE ROCK BALLADS ALBUM** *Polygram TV 5359412*	18		2
7 Dec 96	**SHINE 7** *Polygram TV 5530512*	13		7
14 Dec 96	**HITS ZONE '97** *Polygram TV 5531872*	11		5
21 Dec 96	**CLUB MIX 97** *Polygram TV 5532012*	7		8
18 Jan 97	**THE NUMBER ONE MOTOWN ALBUM** *Polygram TV 5307642*	2		15
1 Feb 97	**WIRED** *Polygram TV 5532572*	2		6
8 Feb 97	**CRUSH** *Polygram TV 5532952*	5		5
15 Feb 97	**AMOUR – THE ULTIMATE LOVE COLLECTION** *Polygram TV 5533322*	3		5
1 Mar 97	**CLUB MIX 97 – VOLUME 2** *Polygram TV 5533642*	1	2	6
22 Mar 97	**DRUM & BASS MIX 97** *Polygram TV 5533952*	11		2
29 Mar 97	**THE NUMBER ONE SCI-FI ALBUM** *Polygram TV 5533602*	13		4
5 Apr 97	**THE NUMBER ONE SKA ALBUM** *Polygram TV 5534192*	9		5
19 Apr 97	**KISS ANTHEMS** *Polygram TV 5534792*	2		7
3 May 97	**SHINE 8** *Polygram TV 5534522*	6		5
10 May 97	**SISTERS OF SWING III** *Polygram TV/Global TV 5534652*	7		4
17 May 97	**FUSED** *Polygram TV 5534822*	14		2
24 May 97	**TRACKSPOTTING** *Polygram TV 5534302*	12		4
31 May 97	**DANCE ZONE LEVEL NINE** *Polygram TV 5377162*	7		3
7 Jun 97	**LADYKILLERS 2** *Polygram TV 5533812*	15		2
21 Jun 97	**MIXED EMOTIONS** *Polygram TV 5536842*	6		5
28 Jun 97	**CLUB MIX 97 – VOLUME 3** *Polygram TV 5536912*	4		5
5 Jul 97	**KISS 100FM – SMOOTH GROOVES** *Polygram TV 5333412*	3		8
12 Jul 97	**SUGAR HITS!** *Polygram TV 5536982*	9		3
2 Aug 97	**THE FIRST SUMMER OF LOVE** *Polygram TV/Sony TV 5538622*	6		7
9 Aug 97	**KISS MIX '97** *Polygram TV 5538402*	3		6
23 Aug 97	**PETE TONG ESSENTIAL SELECTION – SUMMER 97** *Polygram TV 5538862*	4		5
30 Aug 97	**HITS ZONE SUMMER '97** *Polygram TV 5538262*	8		4
30 Aug 97	**DANGER ZONE** *Polygram TV 5538702*	15		2
6 Sep 97	**THE NUMBER ONE DRIVE ALBUM** *Polygram TV 5539402*	14		2
13 Sep 97	**SHINE 9** *Polygram TV 5539752*	7		4
20 Sep 97	**THE NUMBER ONE JAZZ ALBUM** *Polygram TV 5539372*	13		3
27 Sep 97	**KISS IN IBIZA '97** *Polygram TV 5550352*	1	1	7
4 Oct 97	**THE NUMBER ONE LINE DANCING ALBUM** *Polygram TV 5538582*	10		4
11 Oct 97	**THE NUMBER ONE ROCK 'N' ROLL ALBUM** *Polygram TV 5550172*	20		1
18 Oct 97	**PURE DANCE '97** *Polygram TV 5550842*	9		3
1 Nov 97	**THE NUMBER ONE SEVENTIES ALBUM** *Polygram TV 5550542*	13		2
8 Nov 97	**HEART & SOUL** *Polygram TV 5550632*	17		1
15 Nov 97	**HITS ZONE – THE BEST OF '97** *Polygram TV 5550702*	18		1
29 Nov 97	**KISS ANTHEMS '97 – 2** *Polygram TV 5550902*	6		7
17 Jan 98	**SHINE – BEST OF 97** *Polygram TV 5550732*	20		1
7 Feb 98	**ULTIMATE CLUB MIX** *Polygram TV 5550962*	1	1	7
14 Feb 98	**LOVE – 39 ALL TIME LOVE CLASSICS** *Polygram TV 5550602*	1	1	4
21 Feb 98	**PURE ROCK BALLADS** *Polygram TV 5555892*	10		4
28 Feb 98	**KISS SMOOTH GROOVES '98** *Polygram TV 5555742*	2		7
28 Mar 98	**INTO THE BLUE** *Polygram TV 5556652*	10		3
4 Apr 98	**ULTIMATE DISCO MIX** *Polygram TV 5556622*	15		2
11 Apr 98	**UNDISPUTED** *Polygram TV 5556952*	6		3
25 Apr 98	**FRIDAY NIGHT FEVER** *Polygram TV 5557332*	6		4

Silver-selling ○ Gold-selling ● Platinum-selling ⊛ US No.1 ★ — Peak Position, Weeks at No.1, Weeks on Chart

Date	Title / Label	Peak Position	Weeks at No.1	Weeks on Chart
2 May 98	**CONNECTED** *Polygram TV T21CD 1000*	18		1
9 May 98	**KISS GARAGE** *Polygram TV 5558872* ●	3		7
16 May 98	**TOP OF THE POPS 1998 – VOLUME 1** *Polygram TV 5557132* ●	2		7
30 May 98	**DAVE PEARCE PRESENTS DANCE ANTHEMS** *Polygram TV 5559602* ○	4		7
13 Jun 98	**MASSIVE DANCE: 98 – VOLUME 2** *warner.esp/Polygram TV/Global TV 5650632* ●	2		6
27 Jun 98	**THE ULTIMATE SUMMER PARTY ALBUM** *Polygram TV 5650502* ○	7		3
4 Jul 98	**MIXED EMOTIONS II** *Polygram TV 5650342* ●	3		8
11 Jul 98	**SISTERS OF SWING 98** *Polygram TV 5650762* ○	5		5
25 Jul 98	**KISS MIX '98** *Polygram TV 5652312* ●	4		4
1 Aug 98	**THE SUMMER OF LOVE GOES ON – SIXTIES** *Polygram TV/Sony TV 5651312*	16		1
8 Aug 98	**RELAX! THE ULTIMATE 80'S MIX** *Polygram TV 5652852* ●	4		11
15 Aug 98	**ULTIMATE CLUB MIX 2** *Polygram TV 5652922* ○	5		5
29 Aug 98	**SHINE 10** *Polygram TV 5650472* ○	10		3
5 Sep 98	**COOL GROOVES** *Polygram TV 5651622*	12		3
12 Sep 98	**POWER & SOUL** *Polygram TV 5654422* ○	5		5
19 Sep 98	**KISS IN IBIZA '98** *Polygram TV 5654102* ●	2		7
26 Sep 98	**TOP OF THE POPS 1998 – VOLUME 2** *Polygram TV/BBC Music 5654362* ●	3		6
17 Oct 98	**DAVE PEARCE PRESENTS DANCE ANTHEMS VOLUME 2** *Polygram TV 5592622*	5		3
24 Oct 98	**MOBO 1998 – MUSIC OF BLACK ORIGIN** *Polygram TV 5656592*	13		2
31 Oct 98	**THE BEST OF DRIVE TIME** *Polygram TV 5654672*	12		1
7 Nov 98	**SOUL** *Polygram TV 5654332* ○	10		3
7 Nov 98	**ULTIMATE CLUB MIX – 98** *Polygram TV 5592782*	13		1
21 Nov 98	**WOMAN** *Polygram TV/Sony TV 5654392* ⊛	5		17
28 Nov 98	**KISS ANTHEMS '98** *Polygram TV 5592652* ●	8		9
28 Nov 98	**TOP OF THE POPS – BEST OF 1998** *Polygram TV 5592752*	11		2
12 Dec 98	**MUSIC OF THE NIGHT** *Polygram TV 5654962* ⊛	5		20
12 Dec 98	**MASSIVE DANCE: 99** *warner.esp/Polygram TV/Global TV 5655352* ●	5		9
12 Dec 98	**THE ULTIMATE CHRISTMAS COLLECTION** *Polygram TV 5654582* ⊛	11		7
9 Jan 99	**PARTY** *Polygram TV 5654492* ●	19		1
6 Feb 99	**KISS SMOOTH GROOVES '99** *Polygram TV 5654452* ●	3		6
6 Feb 99	**RELAX! THE ULTIMATE 80'S MIX – VOLUME 2** *Polygram TV 5640882* ○	8		3
13 Feb 99	**LOVE SONGS** *Polygram TV/warner.esp 5641122* ⊛	1	1	12
27 Feb 99	**KISS HOUSE NATION** *Polygram TV 5471862* ●	1	2	9
3 Apr 99	**MASSIVE DANCE: 99 – VOLUME TWO** *warner.esp/Universal Music TV/Global TV 5643102*	3		5

VARIOUS ARTISTS (PORTRAIT)

Date	Title / Label	Peak Position	Weeks at No.1	Weeks on Chart
16 Aug 86	**THE HEAT IS ON – 16 TRACKS** *Portrait PRT 10051* ○	9		12
16 Aug 86	**SUMMER DAYS, BOOGIE NIGHTS – 16 TRACKS** *Portrait PRT 10052*	40		6

VARIOUS ARTISTS (POSITIVA)

Date	Title / Label	Peak Position	Weeks at No.1	Weeks on Chart
2 Apr 94	**PHASE ONE** *Positiva CDTIVA 1002*	15		1
26 Apr 97	**ACCESS ALL AREAS** *Positiva CDTIVA 1015*	11		3
24 May 03	**A DECADE OF DANCE** *Positiva 5834792*	11		2
3 May 08	**POSITIVA – ESSENTIAL CLUB ANTHEMS** *Positiva 2069422*	14		1

VARIOUS ARTISTS (PRIORITY)

Date	Title / Label	Peak Position	Weeks at No.1	Weeks on Chart
15 Apr 00	**WWF AGGRESSION** *Priority CDPTY 194* ○	13		8

VARIOUS ARTISTS (PROTO)

Date	Title / Label	Peak Position	Weeks at No.1	Weeks on Chart
26 Nov 83	**TWELVE INCHES OF PLEASURE** *Proto 1*	100		1

VARIOUS ARTISTS (PUMP)

Date	Title / Label	Peak Position	Weeks at No.1	Weeks on Chart
20 Jul 96	**EIGHTIES SOUL WEEKENDER 2** *Pump DINCD 124*	11		4
7 Dec 96	**THE VERY BEST OF PURE SWING** *Pump DINCD 100* ●	17		3
8 Feb 97	**SLOW JAMS** *Pump DINCD 129*	10		3
10 May 97	**EIGHTIES SOUL WEEKENDER 3** *Pump DINCD 138*	15		2

VARIOUS ARTISTS (PURE MUSIC)

Date	Title / Label	Peak Position	Weeks at No.1	Weeks on Chart
22 Oct 94	**THE LADY SINGS THE BLUES** *Pure Music PMCD 7001*	9		4
5 Nov 94	**THE GREATEST NUMBER ONES OF THE EIGHTIES** *Pure Music PMCD 7003*	11		4
11 Feb 95	**DANCE MANIA 95 – VOLUME 1** *Pure Music PMCD 7008* ●	1	2	11
8 Apr 95	**DANCE MANIA 95 – VOLUME 2** *Pure Music PMCD 7010*	1	2	9
15 Jul 95	**DANCE MANIA 95 – VOLUME 3** *Pure Music PMCD 7013* ●	1	3	7
30 Sep 95	**DANCE MANIA 95 – VOLUME 4** *Pure Music PMCD 7015*	7		4
11 Nov 95	**THE BEST OF DANCE MANIA 95** *Pure Music PMCD 7025* ●	5		11

VARIOUS ARTISTS (PURE SILK)

Date	Title / Label	Peak Position	Weeks at No.1	Weeks on Chart
6 Nov 99	**PURE SILK – A NEW DIMENSION** *Pure Silk PURESCD 2* ○	15		2
26 Feb 00	**PURE SILK – THE THIRD DIMENSION** *Pure Silk PURESCD 3*	12		3
1 Jul 00	**PURE SILK IN AYIA NAPA** *Pure Silk PSRANCD 1*	8		6
11 Nov 00	**GARAGE VIBES** *Pure Silk VIBECD 1*	20		1
9 Jun 01	**PURE SILK IN AYIA NAPA 2** *Pure Silk PSRANCD 2*	20		1

VARIOUS ARTISTS (PYE)

Date	Title / Label	Peak Position	Weeks at No.1	Weeks on Chart
9 May 59	**CURTAIN UP** *Pye Nixa BRTH 0059*	4		13
23 Jun 62	**HONEY HIT PARADE** *Pye Golden Guinea GGL 0129*	13		7
1 Dec 62	**ALL THE HITS BY ALL THE STARS** *Pye Golden Guinea GGL 0162*	19		2
7 Sep 63	**HITSVILLE** *Pye Golden Guinea GGL 0202*	11		6
14 Sep 63	**THE BEST OF RADIO LUXEMBOURG** *Pye Golden Guinea GGL 0208*	14		2
23 Nov 63	**HITSVILLE VOLUME 2** *Pye Golden Guinea GGL 0233*	20		1
4 Jan 64	**THE BLUES VOLUME 1** *Pye NPL 28030*	15		3
22 Feb 64	**FOLK FESTIVAL OF THE BLUES (LIVE RECORDING)** *Pye NPL 28033*	16		4
30 May 64	**THE BLUES VOLUME 2** *Pye NPL 28035*	16		3
16 Oct 71	**PYE CHARTBUSTERS** *Pye PCB 15000*	36		1
18 Dec 71	**PYE CHARTBUSTERS VOLUME 2** *Pye PCB 15001*	29		3

VARIOUS ARTISTS (QUALITY PRICE MUSIC)

Date	Title / Label	Peak Position	Weeks at No.1	Weeks on Chart
4 Nov 95	**CLUB IBIZA** *Quality Price Music QPMCD 1* ●	15		1
30 Mar 96	**CLUB IBIZA SILVER EDITION** *Quality Price Music QPMXCD 1*	19		1
19 Oct 96	**CLUB IBIZA – VOLUME 2** *Quality Price Music QPMCD 6*	19		1

VARIOUS ARTISTS (QUALITY TELEVISION)

Date	Title / Label	Peak Position	Weeks at No.1	Weeks on Chart
15 Feb 92	**HIT THE DECKS VOLUME 1 – BATTLE OF THE DJS** *Quality Television QTVCD 003*	3		7
4 Apr 92	**ALL WOMAN** *Quality Television QTVCD 004*	1	2	15
2 May 92	**TEMPTATION** *Quality Television QTVCD 005*	3		8
6 Jun 92	**THE SOUND OF SKA** *Quality Television QTVCD 007*	4		6
20 Jun 92	**TO HAVE AND TO HOLD – THE WEDDING ALBUM** *Quality Television QTVCD 006*	7		4
4 Jul 92	**HIT THE DECKS VOLUME 2 – BATTLE OF THE DJS** *Quality Television QTVCD 008*	3		6
11 Jul 92	**CELEBRATION – THE BEST OF REGGAE – 25 YEARS OF TROJAN** *Quality Television QTVCD 0101*	5		8
18 Jul 92	**DANGER ZONE VOLUME 1** *Quality Television QTVCD 009*	16		3
12 Sep 92	**THREE STEPS TO HEAVEN – ROCK 'N' ROLL LEGENDS** *Quality Television QTVCD 011*	6		5
10 Oct 92	**ALL WOMAN 2** *Quality Television QTVCD 012*	1	1	7
7 Nov 92	**HIT THE DECKS VOLUME III** *Quality Television QTVCD 017*	3		4
7 Nov 92	**THE POWER OF LOVE** *Quality Television QTVCD 015*	4		7
21 Nov 92	**RARE GROOVE – DYNAMIC DISCO HITS** *Quality Television QTVCD 016*	7		14
16 Jan 93	**ALL WOMAN – THE COMPLETE WOMAN** *Quality Television QTVCD 019*	19		1
30 Jan 93	**THE NASHVILLE DREAM** *Quality Television QTVCD 014*	10		3
8 May 93	**GLAM MANIA** *Quality Television MANIACD 1*	10		4
19 Mar 94	**ALL WOMAN 3** *Quality Television ALLWOCD 3*	2		11
3 Dec 94	**ALL WOMAN 4** *Quality Television ALLWOCD 4*	18		4
7 Oct 95	**THE BEST OF ALL WOMAN** *Quality Television BOWOCD 001*	6		13

VARIOUS ARTISTS (R&S)

Date	Title / Label	Peak Position	Weeks at No.1	Weeks on Chart
16 Nov 91	**R&S RECORDS – ORDER TO DANCE** *R&S RSLP 1*	18		1
24 Sep 94	**IN ORDER TO DANCE 5** *R&S RS 94003CDXX*	16		1

VARIOUS ARTISTS (RCA)

Date	Title / Label	Peak Position	Weeks at No.1	Weeks on Chart
28 May 83	**GET ON UP** *RCA BSLP 5001*	35		5
5 Sep 87	**RARE** *RCA NL 90010*	80		1
23 Apr 88	**RARE 2** *RCA PL 71681*	88		1
13 May 89	**DIRTY DANCING – LIVE IN CONCERT** *RCA BL 90336*	19		2
24 Jun 89	**RAINBOW WARRIORS** *RCA PL 74065*	2		10
13 Feb 93	**CELTIC HEART** *RCA 74321131662* ○	6		10
1 Jul 95	**PRIDE – THE VERY BEST OF SCOTLAND** *RCA 74321284372*	13		4
1 Jun 96	**THE BEAUTIFUL GAME – EUFA EURO '96** *RCA 74321382082* ○	10		6
11 Apr 98	**EVERY WOMAN** *RCA 74321573352*	19		1

Silver-selling ○ Gold-selling ● Platinum-selling ⊛ US No.1 ★ — Peak Position, Weeks at No.1, Weeks on Chart

VARIOUS ARTISTS (REACHIN')

Date	Title	Peak Position	Weeks at No.1	Weeks on Chart
9 Nov 91	**RAVE** *Reachin' REMULP 01*	18		2

VARIOUS ARTISTS (REACT)

Date	Title	Peak Position	Weeks at No.1	Weeks on Chart
22 Jun 91	**REACTIVATE VOLUME 1 – THE BELGIAN TECHNO ANTHEMS** *React REACTLP 1*	13		4
5 Oct 91	**REACTIVATE VOLUME 2 – PHASERS ON FULL** *React REACTLP 2*	9		4
16 May 92	**REACTIVATE VOLUME 4 – TECHNOVATION** *React REACTCD 6*	16		2
5 Sep 92	**REACTIVATE VOLUME 5 – PURE TRANCE AND TECHNO** *React REACTCD 10*	18		2
4 Jun 94	**FRESKA!** *React REACTCD 39*	20		1
24 Sep 94	**HOUSE NATION 1** *React REACTCD 48*	20		1
3 Jun 95	**REACTIVATE 10** *React REACTCDX 060*	14		1
12 Aug 95	**CAFÉ DEL MAR IBIZA – VOLUMEN DOS** *React REACTCDL 062*	17		1
10 Aug 96	**CAFÉ DEL MAR IBIZA – VOLUMEN TRES** *React REACTCD 084*	16		1
26 Oct 96	**REACTIVATE 11 – STINGER BEAT AND TECHNO RAYS** *React REACTCDX 088*	14		1
2 Nov 96	**LAURENT GARNIER – LABORATOIRE MIX** *React REACTCD 87*	16		1
10 May 97	**BONKERS 2** *React REACTCD 101*	10		3
21 Jun 97	**REACTIVATE 12** *React REACTCDX 102*	17		2
1 Nov 97	**BONKERS 3 – JOURNEY INTO MADNESS** *React REACTCD 115* ○	9		3
30 May 98	**BONKERS 4 – WORLD FRENZY** *React REACTCD 122*	8		4
7 Nov 98	**BONKERS 5 – ANARCHY IN THE UNIVERSE** *React REACTCD 141*	12		2
1 May 99	**BONKERS 6 (WHEEL CRAZY)** *React REACTCD 150*	10		4
16 Oct 99	**BONKERS 7 – MILLENNIUM MADNESS** *React REACTCD 167*	18		1
16 Oct 99	**TWICE AS NICE IN AYIA NAPA – DJ SPOONY** *React REACTCD 164*	18		3
17 May 03	**BONKERS X** *React REACTCD 231*	18		1
24 Apr 04	**BONKERS 12** *React REACTCD 246*	7		4

VARIOUS ARTISTS (REALLY USEFUL)

Date	Title	Peak Position	Weeks at No.1	Weeks on Chart
28 Nov 92	**THE PREMIERE COLLECTION – ENCORE (ANDREW LLOYD WEBBER)** *Really Useful/Polydor 5173362* ⊛	2		11
5 Nov 94	**THE VERY BEST OF ANDREW LLOYD WEBBER** *Really Useful/Polydor 5238602* ⊛**x2**	3		18
31 Oct 98	**SONGS FROM WHISTLE DOWN THE WIND** *Really Useful/Polydor 5594412* ●	3		4
18 Oct 08	**ANDREW LLOYD WEBBER – 60** *Really Useful/Polydor 5305517*	4		4

VARIOUS ARTISTS (RECORD SHACK)

Date	Title	Peak Position	Weeks at No.1	Weeks on Chart
8 Sep 84	**RECORD SHACK PRESENTS – VOLUME ONE** *Record Shack RSTV 1*	41		4

VARIOUS ARTISTS (REINFORCED RIVET)

Date	Title	Peak Position	Weeks at No.1	Weeks on Chart
29 May 93	**INFORCERS 3** *Reinforced RIVET 1242CD*	18		1

VARIOUS ARTISTS (RELENTLESS)

Date	Title	Peak Position	Weeks at No.1	Weeks on Chart
26 Jan 02	**SO SOLID CREW – FUCK IT** *Relentless REL 004CD*	3		4
9 Mar 02	**OLD SKOOL JUNGLE** *Relentless RELEN 005CD*	11		3
27 Jul 02	**OLD SKOOL REGGAE** *Relentless RELEN 008CD*	16		2
15 Jan 05	**GARAGE ANTHEMS 2005** *Relentless VTDCD689*	15		2

VARIOUS ARTISTS (RENAISSANCE)

Date	Title	Peak Position	Weeks at No.1	Weeks on Chart
9 Jul 05	**RENAISSANCE – THE CLASSICS** *Renaissance 82876705392*	2		13

VARIOUS ARTISTS (RENAISSANCE MUSIC)

Date	Title	Peak Position	Weeks at No.1	Weeks on Chart
18 Oct 97	**RENAISSANCE WORLDWIDE LONDON** *Renaissance Music RENWW 1CD*	16		2
1 Apr 00	**RENAISSANCE – AWAKENING – DAVE SEAMAN** *Renaissance Music RENCD 1*	18		1
19 Aug 00	**RENAISSANCE IBIZA – MIXED BY DEEP DISH** *Renaissance Records REN 2CD*	20		1
17 Mar 01	**PROGRESSION VOLUME 1** *Renaissance Music REN 3CD*	17		1
28 Jul 01	**RENAISSANCE IBIZA 2001** *Renaissance REN 5CD*	2		5
1 Jul 06	**RENAISSANCE – THE CLASSICS PART 2** *Renaissance 82876851082*	2		8

VARIOUS ARTISTS (REPRISE)

Date	Title	Peak Position	Weeks at No.1	Weeks on Chart
22 Nov 03	**LIVE & SWINGING – THE ULTIMATE RAT PACK** *Reprise 8122737362*	14		3

VARIOUS ARTISTS (RESIST)

Date	Title	Peak Position	Weeks at No.1	Weeks on Chart
14 Aug 04	**DRUM & BASS ARENA – FABIO & GROOVERIDER** *Resist RESISTCD1*	20		1
6 Nov 04	**BONKERS 13 – HARDCORE HORROR SHOW** *Resist RESISTCD9*	13		2
11 Jun 05	**BONKERS 14 HARDCORE STRIKES BACK** *Resist RESISTCD49*	12		2
10 Sep 05	**SLAMMIN' VINYL PRESENTS HARDCORE HEAVEN 2** *Resist RESISTCD52*	15		2
22 Apr 06	**HARDCORE HEAVEN 3** *Resist RESISTCD66*	7		6
22 Jul 06	**BONKERS 16** *Resist RESISTCD69*	15		2
14 Oct 06	**HARDCORE HEAVEN 4** *Resist RESISTCD80*	8		2
27 Jan 07	**BEST OF BONKERS** *Resist RESISTCD82*	9		2
14 Apr 07	**DRUM & BASS ARENA – ANDY C/GROOVERIDER** *Resist RESISTCD87*	14		3
10 Nov 07	**BONKERS 17 REBOOTED** *Resist RESISTD110*	18		1

VARIOUS ARTISTS (RESPOND)

Date	Title	Peak Position	Weeks at No.1	Weeks on Chart
15 Oct 83	**RESPOND PACKAGE – LOVE THE REASON** *Respond RRL 501*	50		3

VARIOUS ARTISTS (RHYTHM KING)

Date	Title	Peak Position	Weeks at No.1	Weeks on Chart
6 Jun 87	**CHICAGO JACKBEAT VOLUME 2** *Rhythm King LEFTLP 2*	67		2

VARIOUS ARTISTS (RITZ)

Date	Title	Peak Position	Weeks at No.1	Weeks on Chart
18 Jun 83	**TEARDROPS** *Ritz RITZSP 399*	37		6

VARIOUS ARTISTS (RONCO)

Date	Title	Peak Position	Weeks at No.1	Weeks on Chart
21 Oct 72	**20 STAR TRACKS** *Ronco PP 2001*	2		13
23 Jun 73	**THAT'LL BE THE DAY** *Ronco MR 2002/3*	1	7	8
8 Nov 75	**BLAZING BULLETS** *Ronco RTI 2012*	17		8
6 Dec 75	**GREATEST HITS OF WALT DISNEY** *Ronco RTD 2013* ●	11		12
6 Dec 75	**A CHRISTMAS GIFT** *Ronco P 12430*	39		5
24 Jan 76	**STAR TRACKIN' 76** *Ronco RTL 2014*	9		5
8 Jan 77	**CLASSICAL GOLD** *Ronco RTD 42020* ⊛	24		12
16 Jul 77	**SUPERGROUPS** *Ronco RTL 2023*	57		1
26 Nov 77	**BLACK JOY** *Ronco RTL 2025* ●	26		13
18 Mar 78	**BOOGIE NIGHTS** *Ronco RTL 2027* ●	5		7
18 Nov 78	**BOOGIE FEVER** *Ronco RTL 2034* ●	15		11
9 Jun 79	**ROCK LEGENDS** *Ronco RTL 2037*	54		3
3 Nov 79	**ROCK 'N' ROLLER DISCO** *Ronco RTL 2040* ⊛	3		11
8 Dec 79	**PEACE IN THE VALLEY** *Ronco RTL 2043* ⊛	6		18
22 Dec 79	**MILITARY GOLD** *Ronco RTD 42042*	62		3
25 Oct 80	**STREET LEVEL** *Ronco RTL 2048*	29		5
8 Nov 80	**COUNTRY LEGENDS** *Ronco RTL 2050* ●	9		12
15 Nov 80	**RADIOACTIVE** *Ronco RTL 2049* ●	13		9
29 Nov 80	**SPACE INVADERS** *Ronco RTL 2051* ●	47		3
6 Dec 80	**THE LEGENDARY BIG BANDS** *Ronco RTL 2047* ●	24		6
9 May 81	**DISCO DAZE AND DISCO NITES** *Ronco RTL 2057 A/B* ●	1	1	23
19 Sep 81	**SUPER HITS 1 & 2** *Ronco RTL 2058 A/B* ⊛	2		17
24 Oct 81	**COUNTRY SUNRISE/COUNTRY SUNSET** *Ronco RTL 2057 A/B* ●	27		11
14 Nov 81	**ROCK HOUSE** *Ronco RTL 2061* ●	44		9
12 Dec 81	**MISTY MORNINGS** *Ronco RTL 2066*	44		5
12 Dec 81	**MEMORIES ARE MADE OF THIS** *Ronco RTL 2062*	84		4
19 Dec 81	**WE ARE MOST AMUSED (THE BEST OF BRITISH COMEDY)** *Ronco/Charisma RTD 2067* ●	30		9
26 Dec 81	**HITS, HITS, HITS** *Ronco RTL 2063* ⊛	2		10
24 Apr 82	**DISCO UK AND DISCO USA** *Ronco RTL 2073* ●	7		10
15 May 82	**CHARTBUSTERS 82** *Ronco RTL 2074* ●	3		10
3 Jul 82	**OVERLOAD** *Ronco RTL 2079*	10		8
28 Aug 82	**SOUL DAZE/SOUL NITES** *Ronco RTL 2080* ○	25		10
11 Sep 82	**BREAKOUT** *Ronco RTL 2081* ●	4		8
30 Oct 82	**MUSIC FOR THE SEASONS** *Ronco RTL 2075* ●	41		10
27 Nov 82	**CHART WARS** *Ronco RTL 2086* ●	30		7
27 Nov 82	**THE GREAT COUNTRY MUSIC SHOW** *Ronco RTD 2083* ○	38		7
18 Dec 82	**THE BEST OF THE COMPOSERS: BEETHOVEN/STRAUSS/TCHAIKOVSKY/MOZART** *Ronco RTL 2084* ●	49		10
25 Dec 82	**RAIDERS OF THE POP CHARTS** *Ronco RTL 2088* ⊛	1	2	17
19 Mar 83	**CHART RUNNERS** *Ronco RTL 2090* ●	4		13
21 May 83	**CHART ENCOUNTERS OF THE HIT KIND** *Ronco RTL 2091* ●	5		10
18 Jun 83	**LOVERS ONLY** *Ronco RTL 2093* ●	12		13
16 Jul 83	**HITS ON FIRE** *Ronco RTL 2095* ●	11		10
17 Sep 83	**THE HIT SQUAD – CHART TRACKING** *Ronco RON LP 1*	4		9
17 Sep 83	**THE HIT SQUAD – NIGHT CLUBBING** *Ronco RON LP 2*	28		7

Key: Silver-selling ○ · Gold-selling ● · Platinum-selling ⊛ · US No.1 ★ · Peak Position · Weeks at No.1 · Weeks on Chart

Date	Title / Label	Peak Position	Weeks at No.1	Weeks on Chart
12 Nov 83	**THE HIT SQUAD – HITS OF '83** *Ronco RON LP 4* ●	12		11
17 Dec 83	**GREEN VELVET** *Ronco RON LP 6* ●	6		17
7 Jan 84	**CHART TREK VOLUMES 1 AND 2** *Ronco RON LP 8*	20		9
21 Jan 84	**SOMETIMES WHEN WE TOUCH** *Ronco RON LP 9*	8		14
24 Mar 84	**BABY LOVE** *Ronco RON LP 11*	47		6
7 Apr 84	**DREAMS AND THEMES** *Ronco RON LP 10*	75		2

VARIOUS ARTISTS (ROUGH TRADE)

Date	Title / Label	Peak Position	Weeks at No.1	Weeks on Chart
14 Aug 82	**SOWETO** *Rough Trade ROUGH 37*	66		3

VARIOUS ARTISTS (RUMOUR)

Date	Title / Label	Peak Position	Weeks at No.1	Weeks on Chart
16 Sep 89	**WAREHOUSE RAVES** *Rumour RUMLD 101*	15		4
31 Mar 90	**WAREHOUSE RAVES 3** *Rumour RUMLD 103*	12		5
29 Sep 90	**WAREHOUSE RAVES 4** *Rumour RUMLD 104*	13		3
11 May 91	**WAREHOUSE RAVES 5** *Rumour RUMLD 105*	18		1
20 Jul 91	**BREAKS, BASS AND BLEEPS 2** *Rumour RAID 504*	20		1
21 Mar 92	**WAREHOUSE RAVES 6** *Rumour CDRUMD 106*	16		2
18 Apr 92	**BREAKS, BASS AND BLEEPS 4** *Rumour CDRAID 507*	20		1
27 Jun 92	**MOVIN' ON** *Rumour RULCD 300*	20		1
29 Aug 92	**WAREHOUSE RAVES 7** *Rumour CDRUMD 107*	20		1
26 Sep 92	**TRANCE** *Rumour CDRAID 508*	18		1
24 Oct 92	**MOVIN' ON 2** *Rumour RULCD 301*	15		2

VARIOUS ARTISTS (S)

Date	Title / Label	Peak Position	Weeks at No.1	Weeks on Chart
20 Dec 03	**THE IDOLS – THE XMAS FACTOR** *S 82876581592*	2		3

VARIOUS ARTISTS (S RECORDS)

Date	Title / Label	Peak Position	Weeks at No.1	Weeks on Chart
20 Apr 02	**POP IDOL – THE BIG BAND ALBUM** *S 74321932412* ⊛x2	1	4	10

VARIOUS ARTISTS (SANCTUARY)

Date	Title / Label	Peak Position	Weeks at No.1	Weeks on Chart
8 Feb 03	**REGGAE LOVE SONGS: 50 JAMAICAN LOVERS CLASSICS** *Sanctuary TDSAN 001* ●	2		6
17 Apr 04	**THE ESSENTIAL ACOUSTIC ALBUM** *Sanctuary/BMG TV TDSAN010*	12		3
9 Oct 04	**THE SIXTIES ALBUM** *Sanctuary TLSAN011* ○	9		4
22 Jan 05	**THE SEVENTIES ALBUM** *Sanctuary TLSAN013*	9		2
16 Apr 05	**TEENAGE KICKS** *EMI Virgin/Sanctuary TDSAN015* ●	2		13
3 Sep 05	**SHAKE RATTLE & ROLL** *Sanctuary/UMTV TDSAN019*	13		2
19 Nov 05	**GOING UNDERGROUND – TEENAGE KICKS 2** *EMI Virgin/Sanctuary TV/UMTV TDSAN021*	19		1
20 Jan 07	**100 HUGE HITS OF THE 60S & 70S** *Sanctuary TV TVSAN022*	2		5
10 Feb 07	**I'M IN THE MOOD FOR LOVE** *Sanctuary TV TVSAN023*	7		3
14 Jul 07	**100 HUGE HITS OF REGGAE** *Sanctuary TV TVSAN026*	5		5

VARIOUS ARTISTS (SATELLITE)

Date	Title / Label	Peak Position	Weeks at No.1	Weeks on Chart
19 Jul 97	**TUFF JAM PRESENTS UNDERGROUND FREQUENCIES – 1** *Satellite 74321494672*	20		1
23 May 98	**TUFF JAM PRESENTS UNDERGROUND FREQUENCIES – 2** *Satellite 74321564462*	14		2

VARIOUS ARTISTS (SCF)

Date	Title / Label	Peak Position	Weeks at No.1	Weeks on Chart
10 Sep 66	**STARS CHARITY FANTASIA SAVE THE CHILDREN FUND** *SCF PL 145*	6		16

VARIOUS ARTISTS (SECRET)

Date	Title / Label	Peak Position	Weeks at No.1	Weeks on Chart
31 Oct 81	**CARRY ON OI!** *Secret SEC 2*	60		4
25 Sep 82	**OI! OI! THAT'S YER LOT** *Secret SEC 5*	54		4

VARIOUS ARTISTS (SERIOUS)

Date	Title / Label	Peak Position	Weeks at No.1	Weeks on Chart
7 Jun 86	**UPFRONT 1 – 14 DANCE TRACKS** *Serious UPFT 1*	17		10
23 Aug 86	**UPFRONT 2 – 14 DANCE TRACKS** *Serious UPFT 2*	27		6
1 Nov 86	**UPFRONT 3** *Serious UPFT 3*	37		5
31 Jan 87	**UPFRONT 4** *Serious UPFT 4*	21		5
28 Mar 87	**UPFRONT 5** *Serious UPFT 5*	21		6
28 Mar 87	**SERIOUS HIP-HOP 2** *Serious SHOP 2*	95		1
23 May 87	**UPFRONT 6** *Serious UPFT 6*	22		6
4 Jul 87	**THE BEST OF HOUSE VOLUME 1** *Serious BEHO 1*	55		12
15 Aug 87	**UPFRONT 7** *Serious UPFT 7*	31		4
12 Sep 87	**BEST OF HOUSE VOLUME 2** *Serious BEHO 2*	30		7
17 Oct 87	**UPFRONT 8** *Serious UPFT 8*	22		6
17 Oct 87	**HIP-HOP '87** *Serious HHOP 87*	81		1
14 Nov 87	**BEST OF HOUSE VOLUME 3** *Serious BEHO 3*	61		3
12 Dec 87	**BEST OF HOUSE MEGAMIX** *Serious BOIT 1*	77		4
19 Dec 87	**UPFRONT 9** *Serious UPFT 9*	92		1
20 Feb 88	**DANCE MANIA VOLUME 2** *Serious DAMA 2*	59		2
12 Mar 88	**BEST OF HOUSE VOLUME 4** *Serious BEHO 4*	27		8
9 Apr 88	**UPFRONT 10** *Serious UPFT 10*	45		5
14 May 88	**BEST OF HOUSE MEGAMIX VOLUME 2** *Serious BOIT 2*	73		2
29 Oct 88	**ACID TRAX MAGAMIX VOLUME 1** *Serious DUIX 1*	93		1
18 Feb 89	**UPFRONT 89** *Serious UPFT 89*	15		1
21 Sep 02	**JUDGE JULES PRESENTS TRIED AND TESTED** *Serious 0690572*	18		2

VARIOUS ARTISTS (SHUT UP AND DANCE)

Date	Title / Label	Peak Position	Weeks at No.1	Weeks on Chart
22 Feb 92	**SHUT UP AND DANCE** *Shut Up And Dance SUADCOMPCD 001*	20		1

VARIOUS ARTISTS (SIX6)

Date	Title / Label	Peak Position	Weeks at No.1	Weeks on Chart
1 Oct 94	**RENAISSANCE** *SIX6 REMNIX 1CD* ○	9		5
6 Jul 96	**RENAISSANCE THE MIX COLLECTION – PART 3** *SIX6 RENMIXCD 3*	12		3

VARIOUS ARTISTS (SLINKY MUSIC)

Date	Title / Label	Peak Position	Weeks at No.1	Weeks on Chart
17 Feb 01	**SLINKY PRESENTS SUPERCLUB DJ'S – GUY ORNADEL** *Slinky Music SLINKYCD 005*	17		1

VARIOUS ARTISTS (SOLAR)

Date	Title / Label	Peak Position	Weeks at No.1	Weeks on Chart
30 May 87	**THE SOLAR SYSTEM** *Solar MCG 3338*	70		1

VARIOUS ARTISTS (SOLID STATE)

Date	Title / Label	Peak Position	Weeks at No.1	Weeks on Chart
8 Feb 97	**HIP HOP DON'T STOP – 20 CLASSIC HIP HOP SUPERJAMS** *Solid State SOLIDSCD 6*	16		1
29 Mar 97	**HOUSE OF HANDBAG – NUOVO DISCO COLLECTION** *Solid State SOLIDSCD 7*	17		2

VARIOUS ARTISTS (SOME BIZZARE)

Date	Title / Label	Peak Position	Weeks at No.1	Weeks on Chart
14 Mar 81	**THE Some Bizzare ALBUM** *Some Bizzare BZLP 1*	58		1

VARIOUS ARTISTS (SONY)

Date	Title / Label	Peak Position	Weeks at No.1	Weeks on Chart
25 Nov 95	**THIS YEAR'S LOVE IS FOREVER** *Sony TV/Global TV MOODCD 42* ⊛	4		11
13 Apr 96	**IT TAKES TWO** *Sony TV/Global TV MOODCD 43*	6		6
13 Jul 96	**MUNDO AFRIKA** *Polygram TV/Sony TV MOODCD 44*	17		1
31 Aug 96	**FRESH HITS 96** *warner.esp/Global TV/Sony TV MOODCD 46* ⊛	2		10
9 Nov 96	**HUGE HITS 1996** *warner.esp/Global TV/Sony TV MOODCD 50* ⊛	1	2	12
30 Nov 96	**THIS YEAR'S LOVE (WILL LAST FOREVER) XXX** *Sony TV/Global TV MOODCD 48* ●	12		7
21 Dec 96	**HITS 97** *warner.esp/Global TV/Sony TV MOODCD 49* ⊛	2		13
1 Feb 97	**ABSOLUTE GOLD** *Sony TV SONYTV 22CD*	3		5
8 Nov 97	**THE ALL TIME GREATEST ROCK SONGS** *Sony TV/warner.esp MOODCD 53* ●	7		4
4 Apr 98	**NEW HITS 98** *warner.esp/Global TV/Sony TV MOODCD 57* ⊛	1	2	12
18 Apr 98	**LOVE TRAIN – THE SOUND OF PHILADELPHIA** *Sony TV/MCI MOODCD 56*	18		1
4 Jul 98	**FRESH HITS 98** *warner.esp/Global TV/Sony TV MOODCD 59* ⊛	1	6	17
19 Sep 98	**BIG HITS 98** *warner.esp/Global TV/Sony TV MOODCD 60*	1	5	9
7 Nov 98	**HUGE HITS 1998** *warner.esp/Global TV/Sony TV MOODCD 62* ⊛	1	2	11
7 Nov 98	**THE ALL TIME GREATEST MOVIE SONGS** *Sony TV/Polygram TV MOODCD 61* ●	3		8
19 Dec 98	**HITS 99** *warner.esp/Global TV/Sony TV MOODCD 64* ⊛x2	2		14
26 Jun 99	**THE CELTIC COLLECTION** *warner.esp/Columbia MOODCD 65*	14		3
13 Nov 99	**THE ALL TIME GREATEST MOVIE SONGS – VOLUME TWO** *Sony TV/Universal Music TV MOODCD 67*	7		4
27 Nov 99	**THE ALL TIME GREATEST LOVE SONGS – VOLUME 4** *Sony TV/Universal Music TV MOODCD 68* ⊛	9		8
24 Jun 00	**AMERICAN DREAM** *Sony TV/warner.esp MOODCD 69*	17		1
2 Dec 00	**THE ALL TIME GREATEST LOVE SONGS** *Sony TV/Universal TV MOODCD 71* ⊛	20		1
13 Oct 01	**MOBO 2001 – THE ALBUM** *BMG/Sony/Telstar MOODCD 72*	13		3
6 Apr 02	**THE CLASSIC SCORE** *Sony TV/Decca MOODCD 73*	11		2
10 May 03	**NU SOUL** *Sony Music STVCD 161*	8		4
14 Jun 03	**ALWAYS & FOREVER** *Sony Music STVCD 163* ●	4		8

Silver-selling ○ Gold-selling ● Platinum-selling ⊛ US No.1 ★ | Peak Position | Weeks at No.1 | Weeks on Chart

Date	Title / Label	Peak Position	Weeks at No.1	Weeks on Chart
20 Sep 03	**LET'S GROOVE AGAIN** *Sony Music STVCD 168*	8		3
27 Sep 03	**HOT CITY NIGHTS** *Sony Music STVCD 167*	2		5
18 Oct 03	**THE VERY BEST OF ALL WOMAN** *Sony/BMG/Telstar MOODCD77*	4		4
25 Oct 03	**ALWAYS & FOREVER II** *Sony Music TV STVCD 170*	8		2
14 Feb 04	**MY HEART WILL GO ON** *Sony Music TV STVCD 173*	4		4
20 Mar 04	**FIRST LADIES OF COUNTRY** *Sony TV/Universal TV MOODCD 81*	14		3
3 Apr 04	**SOUL MAN** *Sony Music TV STVCD 177*	10		2
5 Jun 04	**MORE THAN A FEELING** *Sony Music TV STVCD 183* ●	2		7
12 Jun 04	**BACK TO THE 80S** *Sony Music TV STVCD 184* ○	7		3
19 Jun 04	**HEROES** *Sony Music TV STVCD 182* ○	11		2
3 Jul 04	**ULTIMATE ACOUSTIC** *Sony TV/EMI TV MOODCD82* ●	3		9
28 Aug 04	**SLEEPOVER** *Sony Music TV STVCD 188*	16		1
25 Sep 04	**ROCK CHICKS** *Sony TV/Universal TV MOODCD 87*	3		7
2 Oct 04	**HITS 59** *Sony/BMG/WSM MOODCD 85*	2		6
2 Oct 04	**THE ALL TIME GREATEST LOVE SONGS** *Sony TV/Universal TV MOODCD 86*	4		5
16 Oct 04	**ULTIMATE FEELGOOD ANTHEMS** *Sony Music TV STVCD191*	11		2
30 Oct 04	**NATURAL WOMAN – THE AUTUMN COLLECTION** *Sony TV/BMG TV MOODCD88*	19		1
27 Nov 04	**HITS 60** *BMG/Sony/WSM MOODCD90*	5		5
15 Jan 05	**R&B ANTHEMS 2005** *Sony TV/BMG TV STVCD194*	1	5	12
5 Feb 05	**SOFT ROCK ANTHEMS** *Sony BMG TV/UMTV MOODCD91*	2		4

VARIOUS ARTISTS (SONY BMG)

Date	Title / Label	Peak Position	Weeks at No.1	Weeks on Chart
12 Feb 05	**BRITS 25** *Sony BMG TV 82876676642*	2		5
12 Feb 05	**THIS LOVE** *Sony BMG TV 82876676652*	4		4
12 Feb 05	**EVERLASTING LOVE** *Sony BMG TV STVCD195*	10		3
19 Feb 05	**STREET BEATZ** *Sony BMG TV 82876676662*	9		4
17 Nov 07	**DIVAS** *Sony BMG 88697199752*	7		3
24 Nov 07	**NEVER FORGET** *Sony BMG 88697202602*	15		1
8 Dec 07	**CHRISTMAS HITS – 80 FESTIVE FAVOURITES** *Sony BMG 88697202612*	9		6
5 Jan 08	**R&B YEARBOOK 2007** *Sony BMG 88697202552*	16		2
2 Feb 08	**THE POWER OF LOVE** *Sony BMG 88697223112*	3		6
2 Feb 08	**RAW – GREATEST HITS – THE MUSIC** *Sony BMG 88697225912*	9		4
9 Feb 08	**R&B LOVESONGS 2008** *Sony BMG 88697228542*	5		6
16 Feb 08	**WITH LOVE** *Sony BMG 88697268452*	8		3
16 Feb 08	**LOVE & AFFECTION** *Sony BMG 88697268462*	12		2
12 Apr 08	**THE EDGE OF THE EIGHTIES** *Sony BMG 88697293402*	6		8
19 Apr 08	**AMERICAN HEARTBEAT** *Sony BMG 88697291912*	9		3
10 May 08	**NITE FLITE** *Sony BMG 88697310902*	9		3
24 May 08	**ULTIMATE EUROVISION PARTY** *Sony BMG 88697315552*	9		3
7 Jun 08	**GIRLS IN THE CITY** *Sony BMG 88697313372*	13		1
21 Jun 08	**CIGARETTES AND ALCOHOL – 40 ANTHEMS FROM NOW AND THEN** *Sony BMG 88697317582*	7		3
28 Jun 08	**TAKE MY BREATH AWAY – ULTIMATE MOVIE HITS** *Sony BMG 88697326382* ⊛x2	8		3
28 Jun 08	**INSOMNIA** *Sony BMG 88697311132*	13		2
19 Jul 08	**ULTIMATE STREETDANCE** *Sony BMG 88697345272*	3		6
19 Jul 08	**70'S DINNER PARTY** *Sony BMG 88697325362*	13		2
26 Jul 08	**ULTIMATE DISCO PARTY** *Sony BMG 88697343792*	10		2
9 Aug 08	**ULTIMATE HOLIDAY PARTY** *Sony BMG 88697324412*	9		4
16 Aug 08	**CHILLED R&B** *Sony BMG 88697359072*	4		8
30 Aug 08	**ESSENTIAL R&B – HIT SELECTION** *Sony BMG 88697365662*	4		10
13 Sep 08	**SINGER** *Sony BMG 88697369992*	10		5
4 Oct 08	**THE EDGE OF THE SEVENTIES** *Sony BMG 88697372412*	9		2
11 Oct 08	**GIRLS NIGHT IN** *Sony BMG 88697216142*	13		3
1 Nov 08	**RADIO I'S LIVE LOUNGE – VOLUME 3** *Sony BMG TV 88697391402*	2		6
8 Nov 08	**Q – THE ALBUM 2008** *Sony BMG 88697405112*	15		1
29 Nov 08	**R&B YEARBOOK 2008** *Sony BMG 88697418452*	10		2

VARIOUS ARTISTS (SONY/BMG)

Date	Title / Label	Peak Position	Weeks at No.1	Weeks on Chart
5 Mar 05	**WORLD'S BEST MUM** *Sony BMG TV 82876682152*	2		3
5 Mar 05	**THE WAY WE WERE** *Sony BMG TV 82876682492*	4		4
19 Mar 05	**ESSENTIAL R&B – SPRING 2005** *Sony BMG TV/UMTV 82876686052*	1	1	9
2 Apr 05	**RED HOT HITS** *Sony BMG TV 82876686632*	19		1
7 May 05	**ROCK GODZ** *Sony BMG TV/UMTV 82876691482*	9		1
7 May 05	**THE KINGS & QUEENS OF COUNTRY** *BMG TV Projects 82876686072*	12		1
14 May 05	**SLOW JAMZ** *Sony BMG TV 82876691492*	4		6
28 May 05	**LEATHER & LACE** *Sony BMG TV 82876695362*	9		3
28 May 05	**REVOLUTIONS** *Sony BMG TV/UMTV 8287665982*	10		2
4 Jun 05	**WE LOVE LIFE** *Sony BMG 82876703992*	13		1
11 Jun 05	**ULTIMATE ACOUSTIC SONGBOOK** *EMI TV/Sony TV 82876704792*	18		1
25 Jun 05	**WORLD'S BEST DAD** *Sony BMG 82876705322*	6		1
2 Jul 05	**ULTIMATE 70'S POP** *Sony BMG 82876704802*	7		3
9 Jul 05	**SMOOTH SUMMER SOUL** *Sony BMG 82876705332*	13		2
16 Jul 05	**ESSENTIAL R&B – SUMMER 2005** *Sony BMG TV/UMTV 82876707682*	4		7
30 Jul 05	**R&B DANCE MIX** *Sony BMG TV 82876713782*	4		6
30 Jul 05	**ELECTRIC 80'S** *Sony BMG TV 82876705382*	11		2
13 Aug 05	**POP ROCKS** *Sony BMG TV 82876712792*	10		4
3 Sep 05	**PLAY TIME – THE COMPLETE FUN PACKAGE** *Sony BMG 82876705402*	10		3
17 Sep 05	**EVEN MORE THAN A FEELING** *Sony BMG TV 82876722962*	15		1
24 Sep 05	**POWER & PASSION** *Sony BMG TV 82876731882*	13		2
24 Sep 05	**THE RELAXING ALBUM** *Sony BMG TV 82876719922*	18		1
15 Oct 05	**STUDENT DAZE** *Sony BMG 82876729322*	17		1
22 Oct 05	**ESSENTIAL WOMAN** *Sony BMG TV 82876688722*	13		2
29 Oct 05	**HUGE CLUB TUNES** *Sony BMG 82876694152*	13		2
12 Nov 05	**SWINGING SIXTIES** *Sony BMG 82876748392*	16		1
19 Nov 05	**STOCK/AITKEN/WATERMAN – GOLD** *Sony BMG 82876730982*	12		2
3 Dec 05	**THE R&B YEARBOOK** *Sony BMG TV/UMTV 82876762652*	4		9
14 Jan 06	**WORK IT 06** *Sony BMG 82876767422*	17		2
28 Jan 06	**R&B CLUBMIX** *Sony BMG TV/UMTV 82876782632*	2		8
11 Feb 06	**BEAUTIFUL LOVESONGS** *Sony BMG 82876774422*	2		5
18 Feb 06	**SIMON BATES – THE VERY BEST OF OUR TUNE** *Sony BMG 82876791852*	6		2
25 Feb 06	**BRIT AWARDS 2006 – THE MUSIC EVENT** *Sony BMG TV 82876779642*	1	1	5
25 Mar 06	**WORLD'S BEST MUM** *Sony BMG TV 82876810572*	1	1	3
25 Mar 06	**MAGICAL MEMORIES FOR MUM** *Sony BMG TV 82876748712*	7		3
22 Apr 06	**IT'S POP TIME** *Sony BMG TV/UMTV 82876831452*	4		6
24 Jun 06	**WORLD'S BEST DAD** *Sony BMG TV 82876855392*	2		2
24 Jun 06	**NEW WAVE HEROES** *Sony BMG 82876851032*	15		1
1 Jul 06	**R&B CLASSICS** *Sony BMG TV/UMTV 82876855382*	3		10
8 Jul 06	**BEYOND THE SEA** *Sony BMG TV 82876855372*	3		6
15 Jul 06	**R&B SUMMERTIME** *Sony BMG TV 82876855402*	6		5
2 Sep 06	**KEEP ON MOVIN'** *EMI TV/Sony TV 88697001672*	11		2
7 Oct 06	**ESSENTIAL R&B – AUTUMN 2006** *Sony BMG TV/UMTV 82876895122*	4		7
21 Oct 06	**THE COLLECTION AUTUMN 2006** *EMI Virgin/Sony BMG TV 88697012762*	6		2
28 Oct 06	**RADIO 1'S LIVE LOUNGE** *Sony BMG TV 82876833092* ⊛x2	1	7	30
2 Dec 06	**THE R&B YEARBOOK 2006** *Sony BMG TV/UMTV 88697032662*	14		7
27 Jan 07	**SOAPSTAR SUPERSTAR 2007** *Sony BMG 88697047292*	8		2
10 Feb 07	**R&B LOVESONGS 2007** *Sony BMG TV/UMTV 88697055802*	2		6
10 Feb 07	**MY LOVE** *Sony BMG 88697055792*	4		3
17 Mar 07	**WORLD'S BEST MUM 2007** *Sony BMG 88697074852*	2		3
28 Apr 07	**70S HEART THROBS** *Sony BMG/UMTV 88697090902*	6		1
12 May 07	**JUST GREAT SONGS** *EMI TV/Sony BMG 88697097712*	2		25
23 Jun 07	**WORLD'S BEST DAD 2007** *Sony BMG 88697109512*	7		1
30 Jun 07	**HEADLINERS** *Sony BMG TV 88697116772*	16		1
7 Jul 07	**HERE COMES SUMMER** *Sony BMG 88697116832*	17		1
14 Jul 07	**ESSENTIAL R&B – SUMMER 2007** *Sony BMG 88697116782*	4		5
21 Jul 07	**GET DOWN** *Ministry/Sony BMG 88697122712*	16		1
18 Aug 07	**R&B ANTHEMS** *Sony BMG 88697143462*	5		9
1 Sep 07	**CLASSICAL VOICES** *Sony BMG 88697164442*	17		1
27 Oct 07	**POP HITS!** *Sony BMG 88697194842*	9		2
3 Nov 07	**RADIO 1'S LIVE LOUNGE – VOLUME 2** *Sony BMG 88697164462*	1	2	15
10 Nov 07	**JUST GREAT SONGS 2** *Sony BMG 88697199642*	13		2

VARIOUS ARTISTS (SONY CLASSICAL)

Date	Title / Label	Peak Position	Weeks at No.1	Weeks on Chart
20 May 00	**ALAN TITCHMARSH – IN A COUNTRY GARDEN** *Sony Classical SONYTV 85CD*	20		1

VARIOUS ARTISTS (SOUND DIMENSION)

Date	Title / Label	Peak Position	Weeks at No.1	Weeks on Chart
5 Aug 95	**A RETROSPECTIVE OF HOUSE '91–'95 – VOLUME 1** *Sound Dimension SDIMCD 3* ○	10		10
13 Jan 96	**A RETROSPECTIVE OF HOUSE '91–'95 – VOLUME 2** *Sound Dimension SDIMCD 4* ○	15		3
1 Jun 96	**A RETROSPECTIVE OF HOUSE '91–'96 – VOLUME 3: JAY/KELLY/ANDERSON** *Sound Dimension SDIMCD 5*	9		2
7 Sep 96	**A RETROSPECTIVE OF HOUSE '91–'96 – VOLUME 4** *Sound Dimension SDIMCD 6*	7		5
1 Feb 97	**AN INTROSPECTIVE OF HOUSE: 1ST DIMENSION** *Sound Dimension SDIMCD 7* ○	18		2
14 Jun 97	**AN INTROSPECTIVE OF HOUSE: 2ND DIMENSION** *Sound Dimension SDIMCD 8*	9		4
13 Sep 97	**AN INTROSPECTIVE OF HOUSE: 3RD DIMENSION** *Sound Dimension SDIMCD 9*	14		2

VARIOUS ARTISTS (SOUTHERN FRIED)

Date	Title / Label	Peak Position	Weeks at No.1	Weeks on Chart
9 Mar 02	**FATBOY SLIM – LIVE ON BIRGHTON BEACH** *Southern Fried ECB 26CD*	19		1
19 Oct 02	**BIG BEACH BOUTIQUE II** *Southern Fried ECB 34CDX*	11		2

Silver-selling ○ · Gold-selling ● · Platinum-selling ⊛ · US No.1 ★ · Peak Position · Weeks at No.1 · Weeks on Chart

VARIOUS ARTISTS (SPRINGTIME)

Date	Title / Label	Peak Position	Weeks at No.1	Weeks on Chart
12 Dec 81	**THE SECRET POLICEMAN'S OTHER BALL** *Springtime HAHA 6003*	69		4
20 Mar 82	**THE SECRET POLICEMAN'S OTHER BALL (THE MUSIC)** *Springtime HAHA 6004*	29		5

VARIOUS ARTISTS (STARBLEND)

Date	Title / Label	Peak Position	Weeks at No.1	Weeks on Chart
12 Nov 83	**IN TOUCH** *Starblend STD 9*	89		2
23 Jun 84	**BROKEN DREAMS** *Starblend SLTD 1*	48		7
27 Apr 85	**12 X 12 MEGA MIXES** *Starblend INCH 1*	77		2
3 Aug 85	**AMERICAN DREAMS** *Starblend SLTD 12*	43		8
21 Dec 85	**CHRISTMAS AT THE COUNTRY STORE** *Starblend NOEL 1*	94		1
12 Jul 86	**DISCOVER COUNTRY/DISCOVER NEW COUNTRY** *Starblend DNC 1*	60		3
16 Aug 86	**HEARTBREAKERS – 18 CLASSICAL LOVE HITS** *Starblend BLEND 3*	38		8
20 Sep 86	**ABSOLUTE ROCK 'N' ROLL** *Starblend SLTD 15*	88		1

VARIOUS ARTISTS (START)

Date	Title / Label	Peak Position	Weeks at No.1	Weeks on Chart
15 Apr 89	**THE SONGS OF BOB DYLAN** *START STDL 20*	13		5

VARIOUS ARTISTS (STAX)

Date	Title / Label	Peak Position	Weeks at No.1	Weeks on Chart
8 Apr 67	**HIT THE ROAD STAX** *Stax 589005*	10		16
9 Jun 07	**SWEET SOUL MUSIC – THE BEST OF** *Stax 1736322*	20		1

VARIOUS ARTISTS (STIFF)

Date	Title / Label	Peak Position	Weeks at No.1	Weeks on Chart
11 Mar 78	**STIFF'S LIVE STIFFS** *Stiff GET 1*	28		7

VARIOUS ARTISTS (STOIC)

Date	Title / Label	Peak Position	Weeks at No.1	Weeks on Chart
16 Jun 84	**EMERALD CLASSICS** *Stoic SRTV 1*	35		14

VARIOUS ARTISTS (STREET SOUNDS)

Date	Title / Label	Peak Position	Weeks at No.1	Weeks on Chart
23 Oct 82	**STREETNOISE VOLUME 1** *Streetwave STR 32234*	51		4
19 Feb 83	**STREET SOUNDS EDITION 2** *Street Sounds STSND 002*	35		6
23 Apr 83	**STREET SOUNDS EDITION 3** *Street Sounds STSND 003*	21		5
25 Jun 83	**STREET SOUNDS EDITION 4** *Street Sounds STSND 004*	14		8
13 Aug 83	**STREET SOUNDS EDITION 5** *Street Sounds STSND 005*	16		8
8 Oct 83	**STREET SOUNDS EDITION 6** *Street Sounds STSND 006*	23		5
22 Oct 83	**STREET SOUNDS ELECTRO 1** *Street Sounds ELCST 1*	18		8
17 Dec 83	**STREET SOUNDS EDITION 7** *Street Sounds STSND 007*	48		4
7 Jan 84	**STREET SOUNDS ELECTRO 2** *Street Sounds ELCST 2*	49		7
3 Mar 84	**STREET SOUNDS HI-ENERGY NO 1** *Street Sounds HINRG 16*	71		1
10 Mar 84	**STREET SOUNDS EDITION 8** *Street Sounds STSND 008*	22		7
10 Mar 84	**STREET SOUNDS CRUCIAL ELECTRO** *Street Sounds ELCST 999*	24		10
7 Apr 84	**STREET SOUNDS ELECTRO 3** *Street Sounds ELCST 3*	25		9
12 May 84	**STREET SOUNDS EDITION 9** *Street Sounds STSND 009*	22		5
9 Jun 84	**STREET SOUNDS ELECTRO 4** *Street Sounds ELCST 4*	25		9
30 Jun 84	**STREET SOUNDS UK ELECTRO** *Street Sounds ELCST 1984*	60		4
21 Jul 84	**LET THE MUSIC SCRATCH** *Street Sounds MKL 1*	91		3
11 Aug 84	**STREET SOUNDS CRUCIAL ELECTRO 2** *Street Sounds ELCST 100*	35		6
18 Aug 84	**STREET SOUNDS EDITION 10** *Street Sounds STSND 010*	24		6
6 Oct 84	**STREET SOUNDS ELECTRO 5** *Street Sounds ELCST 5*	17		6
10 Nov 84	**STREET SOUNDS EDITION 11** *Street Sounds STSND 011*	48		4
9 Mar 85	**STREET SOUNDS ELECTRO 6** *Street Sounds ELCST 6*	24		10
18 May 85	**STREET SOUNDS ELECTRO 7** *Street Sounds ELCST 7*	12		7
18 May 85	**STREET SOUNDS EDITION 12** *Street Sounds STSND 012*	23		4
13 Jul 85	**STREET SOUNDS ELECTRO 8** *Street Sounds ELCST 8*	23		5
17 Aug 85	**STREET SOUNDS EDITION 13** *Street Sounds STSND 013*	19		9
17 Aug 85	**STREET SOUNDS N.Y. VS L.A. BEATS** *Street Sounds ELCST 1001*	65		4
5 Oct 85	**STREET SOUNDS ELECTRO 9** *Street Sounds ELCST 9*	18		6
16 Nov 85	**STREET SOUNDS EDITION 14** *Street Sounds STSND 014*	43		3
21 Dec 85	**STREET SOUNDS EDITION 15** *Street Sounds STSND 015*	58		8
21 Dec 85	**STREET SOUNDS ELECTRO 10** *Street Sounds ELCST 10*	72		6
29 Mar 86	**STREET SOUNDS HIP-HOP ELECTRO 11** *Street Sounds ELCST 11*	19		5
5 Apr 86	**STREET SOUNDS EDITION 16** *Street Sounds STSND 016*	17		7
21 Jun 86	**JAZZ JUICE 2** *Street Sounds SOUND 4*	96		1
28 Jun 86	**STREET SOUNDS HIP-HOP ELECTRO 12** *Street Sounds ELCST 12*	28		4
19 Jul 86	**STREET SOUNDS EDITION 17** *Street Sounds STSND 017*	35		5
6 Sep 86	**STREET SOUNDS HIP-HOP ELECTRO 13** *Street Sounds ELCST 13*	23		5
11 Oct 86	**STREET SOUNDS EDITION 18** *Street Sounds STSND 018*	20		5
11 Oct 86	**STREET SOUNDS HIP-HOP ELECTRO 14** *Street Sounds ELCST 14*	40		3
11 Oct 86	**JAZZ JUICE 3** *Street Sounds SOUND 5*	88		1
15 Nov 86	**STREET SOUNDS HIP-HOP ELECTRO 15** *Street Sounds ELCST 15*	46		2
6 Dec 86	**STREET SOUNDS EDITION 19** *Street Sounds STSND 019*	61		3
24 Jan 87	**STREET SOUNDS CRUCIAL ELECTRO 3** *Street Sounds ELCST 1002*	41		3
7 Feb 87	**STREET SOUNDS ANTHEMS – VOLUME 1** *Street Sounds MUSIC 5*	61		3
14 Feb 87	**STREET SOUNDS EDITION 20** *Street Sounds STSND 020*	25		4
13 Jun 87	**STREET SOUNDS HIP-HOP ELECTRO 16** *Street Sounds ELCST 16*	40		3
4 Jul 87	**STREET SOUNDS DANCE MUSIC '87** *Street Sounds STSND 871*	40		5
15 Aug 87	**STREET SOUNDS HIP-HOP 17** *Street Sounds ELCST 17*	38		3
15 Aug 87	**JAZZ JUICE 5** *Street Sounds SOUND 8*	97		1
12 Sep 87	**STREET SOUNDS 87 VOLUME 2** *Street Sounds STSND 872*	47		3
12 Sep 87	**BEST OF WEST COAST HIP HOP** *Street Sounds MACA 1*	80		2
24 Oct 87	**STREET SOUNDS HIP-HOP 18** *Street Sounds ELCST 18*	67		1
19 Mar 88	**STREET SOUNDS HIP-HOP 20** *Street Sounds ELCST 20*	39		4
19 Mar 88	**STREET SOUNDS 88–1** *Street Sounds STSND 881*	73		2
4 Jun 88	**STREET SOUNDS HIP-HOP 21** *Street Sounds ELCST 21*	87		1

VARIOUS ARTISTS (STRICTLY UNDERGROUND)

Date	Title / Label	Peak Position	Weeks at No.1	Weeks on Chart
19 Sep 92	**ILLEGAL RAVE** *Strictly Underground STHCCD 1*	20		1

VARIOUS ARTISTS (STUDIO TWO)

Date	Title / Label	Peak Position	Weeks at No.1	Weeks on Chart
21 Oct 67	**BREAKTHROUGH** *Studio Two STWO 1*	2		19
4 Sep 71	**TOTAL SOUND** *Studio Two STWO 4*	39		4
30 Oct 71	**STUDIO TWO CLASSICS** *Studio Two STWO 6*	16		4

VARIOUS ARTISTS (STYLUS)

Date	Title / Label	Peak Position	Weeks at No.1	Weeks on Chart
3 Aug 85	**THE MAGIC OF TORVILL AND DEAN** *Stylus SMR 8502* ●	35		9
17 Aug 85	**NIGHT BEAT** *Stylus SMR 8501* ○	15		8
24 Aug 85	**DISCO BEACH PARTY** *Stylus SMR 8503* ○	29		10
14 Dec 85	**VELVET WATERS** *Stylus SMR 8507* ○	54		4
28 Dec 85	**CHOICES OF THE HEART** *Stylus SMR 8511*	87		2
8 Mar 86	**NIGHT BEAT II** *Stylus SMR 8613* ○	7		9
17 May 86	**LET'S HEAR IT FOR THE GIRLS** *Stylus SMR 8614* ○	17		10
1 Nov 86	**BLACK MAGIC** *Stylus SMR 619*	26		9
8 Nov 86	**HIT MIX '86** *Stylus SMR 624* ●	10		14
22 Nov 86	**CLASSICS BY CANDLELIGHT** *Stylus SMR 620*	74		4
14 Mar 87	**BANDS OF GOLD – THE SWINGING SIXTIES** *Stylus SMR 726*	48		6
21 Mar 87	**BANDS OF GOLD – THE SENSATIONAL SEVENTIES** *Stylus SMR 727*	75		4
28 Mar 87	**BANDS OF GOLD – THE ELECTRIC EIGHTIES** *Stylus SMR 728*	82		1
11 Jul 87	**SIXTIES MIX – 60 SEQUENCED HITS FROM THE SIXTIES** *Stylus SMR 733* ⊛	3		44
24 Oct 87	**THE HIT FACTORY: THE BEST OF STOCK AITKEN WATERMAN** *Stylus SMR 740* ●	18		17
21 Nov 87	**HIT MIX – HITS OF THE YEAR** *Stylus SMR 744* ○	29		11
2 Apr 88	**HIP HOP AND RAPPING IN THE HOUSE** *Stylus SMR 852*	5		13
7 May 88	**SIXTIES MIX 2** *Stylus SMR 855* ●	14		20
4 Jun 88	**BACK ON THE ROAD** *Stylus SMR 854*	29		11
30 Jul 88	**THE GREATEST EVER ROCK 'N' ROLL MIX** *Stylus SMR 858* ⊛	8		15
3 Sep 88	**RAP TRAX** *Stylus SMR 859* ●	3		13
1 Oct 88	**RARE GROOVE MIX – 70 SMASH HITS OF THE 70'S** *Stylus SMR 863* ●	20		10
22 Oct 88	**SOFT METAL** *Stylus SMR 862* ⊛	7		12
26 Nov 88	**HIT MIX '88** *Stylus SMR 865*	48		7
17 Dec 88	**THE GREATEST HITS OF HOUSE** *Stylus SMR 867*	26		4
14 Jan 89	**THE GREATEST HITS OF HOUSE** *Stylus SMR 867* ●	5		9
14 Jan 89	**SOFT METAL** *Stylus SMR 862*	7		27
14 Jan 89	**HIT MIX '88** *Stylus SMR 865* ●	15		2
18 Feb 89	**BEAT THIS – 20 HITS OF RHYTHM KING** *Stylus SMR 973*	9		8
11 Mar 89	**NEW ROOTS** *Stylus SMR 972*	18		1
25 Mar 89	**HIP HOUSE** *Stylus SMR 974* ●	3		8
22 Apr 89	**THE SINGER AND THE SONG** *Stylus SMR 975* ○	5		11
27 May 89	**PRECIOUS METAL** *Stylus SMR 976* ⊛	2		29
24 Jun 89	**DON'T STOP THE MUSIC** *Stylus SMR 977* ○	7		6
15 Jul 89	**HOT SUMMER NIGHTS** *Stylus SMR 980* ●	4		11
19 Aug 89	**SUNSHINE MIX** *Stylus SMR 986* ○	9		7
26 Aug 89	**THE GREATEST EVER ROCK 'N' ROLL MIX** *Stylus SMR 858*	5		9
2 Sep 89	**MIDNIGHT LOVE** *Stylus SMR 981*	7		6
16 Sep 89	**LEGENDS AND HEROES** *Stylus SMR 987* ○	6		10

Silver-selling ○ Gold-selling ● Platinum-selling ⊛ US No.1 ★ | Peak Position | Weeks at No.1 | Weeks on Chart

Date	Title / Label	Peak Position	Weeks at No.1	Weeks on Chart
21 Oct 89	**THE RIGHT STUFF – REMIX '89** *Stylus SMR 990* ●	2		11
25 Nov 89	**JUKE BOX JIVE – ROCK 'N' ROLL GREATS** *Stylus SMR 993* ●	13		8
30 Dec 89	**WARE'S THE HOUSE?** *Stylus SMR 997* ●	2		10
13 Jan 90	**PURE SOFT METAL** *Stylus SMR 996* ⊛	1	5	23
10 Mar 90	**THE RIGHT STUFF 2 – NOTHING BUT A HOUSE PARTY** *Stylus SMR 998* ●	2		15
26 May 90	**SIXTIES MIX 3** *Stylus SMR 021*	4		9
20 Oct 90	**MOMENTS IN SOUL** *Stylus SMR 023*	9		2

VARIOUS ARTISTS (SUNDISSENTIAL)

Date	Title / Label	Peak Position	Weeks at No.1	Weeks on Chart
27 Apr 02	**SUNDISSENTIAL – HARDER FASTER** *Sundissential SUNDICD 302*	16		1

VARIOUS ARTISTS (SUPREME UNDERGROUND)

Date	Title / Label	Peak Position	Weeks at No.1	Weeks on Chart
8 Mar 97	**HARDCORE EXPLOSION '97** *Supreme Underground SUMCD 116*	20		1

VARIOUS ARTISTS (SYCO MUSIC)

Date	Title / Label	Peak Position	Weeks at No.1	Weeks on Chart
17 Jun 06	**VOICES FROM THE FIFA WORLD CUP** *Syco Music 82876834232*	16		1

VARIOUS ARTISTS (TALKIN' LOUD)

Date	Title / Label	Peak Position	Weeks at No.1	Weeks on Chart
30 Jan 93	**TALKIN LOUD TWO** *Talkin' Loud 5159362*	6		3

VARIOUS ARTISTS (TELDEC)

Date	Title / Label	Peak Position	Weeks at No.1	Weeks on Chart
21 Nov 92	**SENSUAL CLASSICS** *Teldec 4509900552* ○	19		2

VARIOUS ARTISTS (TELSTAR)

Date	Title / Label	Peak Position	Weeks at No.1	Weeks on Chart
16 Oct 82	**CHART ATTACK** *Telstar STAR 2221* ●	7		6
6 Nov 82	**MIDNIGHT IN MOTOWN** *Telstar STAR 2222* ●	34		16
18 Dec 82	**DIRECT HITS** *Telstar STAR 2226*	89		1
8 Jan 83	**DANCIN' – 20 ORIGINAL MOTOWN MOVERS** *Telstar STAR 2225*	97		1
5 Feb 83	**INSTRUMENTAL MAGIC** *Telstar STAR 2227*	68		5
30 Apr 83	**20 GREAT ITALIAN LOVE SONGS** *Telstar STAR 2230*	28		6
4 Jun 83	**IN THE GROOVE – THE 12 INCH DISCO PARTY** *Telstar STAR 2228*	20		12
12 Nov 83	**ROOTS REGGAE 'N' REGGAE ROCK** *Telstar STAR 2233*	34		6
19 Nov 83	**SUPERCHART '83** *Telstar STAR 2236*	22		9
4 Feb 84	**THE VERY BEST OF MOTOWN LOVE SONGS** *Telstar STAR 2239* ●	10		22
26 May 84	**DON'T STOP DANCING** *Telstar STAR 2242*	11		12
13 Oct 84	**HITS, HITS, HITS – 18 SMASH ORIGINALS** *Telstar STAR 2243* ●	6		9
8 Dec 84	**LOVE SONGS – 16 CLASSIC LOVE SONGS** *Telstar STAR 2246* ●	20		12
15 Dec 84	**GREEN VELVET** *Telstar STAR 2252*	10		10
7 Sep 85	**OPEN TOP CARS AND GIRLS IN T'SHIRTS** *Telstar STAR 2257*	13		9
16 Nov 85	**THE GREATEST HITS OF 1985** *Telstar STAR 2269* ⊛	1	1	17
16 Nov 85	**THE LOVE ALBUM – 16 CLASSIC LOVE SONGS** *Telstar STAR 2268* ⊛	7		18
30 Nov 85	**THE PRINCE'S TRUST COLLECTION** *Telstar STAR 2275* ●	64		5
7 Dec 85	**PERFORMANCE – THE VERY BEST OF TIM RICE AND ANDREW LLOYD WEBBER** *Telstar STAR 2262* ●	33		7
7 Dec 85	**MORE GREEN VELVET** *Telstar STAR 2267*	42		5
18 Oct 86	**THE CHART** *Telstar STAR 2278* ●	6		12
1 Nov 86	**ROCK LEGENDS** *Telstar STAR 2290*	54		7
8 Nov 86	**THE GREATEST HITS OF 1986** *Telstar STAR 2286* ●	8		13
8 Nov 86	**LOVERS** *Telstar STAR 2279* ●	14		16
22 Nov 86	**SIXTIES MANIA** *Telstar STAR 2287* ●	19		22
6 Dec 86	**MOTOWN CHARTBUSTERS** *Telstar STAR 2283* ●	25		12
28 Mar 87	**THE DANCE CHART** *Telstar STAR 2285*	23		8
3 Oct 87	**TRACKS OF MY TEARS** *Telstar STAR 2295* ●	27		7
21 Nov 87	**THE GREATEST HITS OF 1987** *Telstar STAR 2309* ●	12		11
28 Nov 87	**DANCE MIX '87** *Telstar STAR 2314* ●	39		10
28 Nov 87	**ALWAYS AND FOREVER THE LOVE ALBUM** *Telstar STAR 2301* ●	41		10
28 Nov 87	**SIXTIES PARTY MEGAMIX ALBUM** *Telstar STAR 2307* ●	46		7
26 Dec 87	**LIFE IN THE FAST LANE** *Telstar STAR 2315* ●	10		12
26 Dec 87	**THE GREATEST LOVE** *Telstar STAR 2316* ⊛x2	11		40
1 Oct 88	**...AND THE BEST GOES ON** *Telstar STAR 2338* ●	12		8
5 Nov 88	**THE HEART AND SOUL OF ROCK AND ROLL** *Telstar STAR 2351*	60		6
12 Nov 88	**THE LOVE ALBUM '88** *Telstar STAR 2332* ○	51		9
19 Nov 88	**THE GREATEST HITS OF 1988** *Telstar STAR 2334* ●	11		8
19 Nov 88	**BEST OF HOUSE '88** *Telstar STAR 2347*	33		8
19 Nov 88	**INSTRUMENTAL GREATS** *Telstar STAR 2341*	79		5
3 Dec 88	**BACK TO THE SIXTIES** *Telstar STAR 2348* ●	47		6
3 Dec 88	**HYPERACTIVE** *Telstar STAR 2328* ●	78		4
17 Dec 88	**MORNING HAS BROKEN** *Telstar STAR 2337*	88		2
31 Dec 88	**THE GREATEST LOVE 2** *Telstar STAR 2352* ●	37		2
14 Jan 89	**THE GREATEST LOVE 2** *Telstar STAR 2352* ●	3		23
14 Jan 89	**THE GREATEST LOVE** *Telstar STAR 2316* ⊛x2	7		31
14 Jan 89	**THE GREATEST HITS OF 1988** *Telstar STAR 2334*	8		8
14 Jan 89	**BEST OF HOUSE '88** *Telstar STAR 2347*	11		5
14 Jan 89	**BACK TO THE SIXTIES** *Telstar STAR 2348*	14		4
14 Jan 89	**LOVE SONGS** *Telstar STAR 2298* ⊛	18		2
25 Feb 89	**THE BRITS – THE AWARDS 1989** *Telstar STAR 2346* ●	1	1	8
4 Mar 89	**DEEP HEAT – 26 HOTTEST HOUSE HITS** *Telstar STAR 2345* ●	1	1	15
22 Apr 89	**DEEP HEAT – THE SECOND BURN** *Telstar STAR 2356* ●	2		13
15 Jul 89	**PROTECT THE INNOCENT** *Telstar STAR 2363*	9		9
15 Jul 89	**RHYTHM OF THE SUN** *Telstar STAR 2362*	12		4
22 Jul 89	**DEEP HEAT 3 – THE THIRD DEGREE** *Telstar STAR 2364* ●	2		13
22 Jul 89	**THIS IS SKA** *Telstar STAR 2366*	6		10
23 Sep 89	**DEEP HEAT 4 – PLAY WITH FIRE** *Telstar STAR 2388* ●	1	5	11
14 Oct 89	**MOTOWN HEARTBREAKERS** *Telstar STAR 2343* ●	4		10
11 Nov 89	**THE GREATEST LOVE 3** *Telstar STAR 2384* ●	4		18
18 Nov 89	**NUMBER ONES OF THE EIGHTIES** *Telstar STAR 2382* ⊛	2		19
18 Nov 89	**THE GREATEST HITS OF 1989** *Telstar STAR 2389* ●	4		11
25 Nov 89	**DEEP HEAT 1989 – FIGHT THE FLAME** *Telstar STAR 2380* ⊛	4		17
25 Nov 89	**HEAVEN AND HELL** *Telstar STAR 2361* ●	9		12
9 Dec 89	**SOFT ROCK** *Telstar STAR 2397* ●	15		5
3 Feb 90	**DEEP HEAT 5 – FEED THE FEVER – 32 HOTTEST CLUB HITS** *Telstar STAR 2411* ●	1	2	11
3 Feb 90	**NEW TRADITIONS** *Telstar STAR 2399*	13		4
10 Feb 90	**MILESTONES – 20 ROCK OPERAS** *Telstar STAR 2379*	6		11
24 Feb 90	**THE AWARDS 1990** *Telstar STAR 2368* ●	3		10
17 Mar 90	**PRODUCT 2378** *Telstar STAR 2378*	16		3
31 Mar 90	**DEEP HEAT 6 – THE SIXTH SENSE** *Telstar STAR 2412* ●	1	2	14
12 May 90	**GET ON THIS! – 30 DANCE HITS VOLUME 1** *Telstar STAR 2420* ●	2		12
19 May 90	**A NIGHT AT THE OPERA** *Telstar STAR 2414* ●	2		12
7 Jul 90	**DEEP HEAT 7 – SEVENTH HEAVEN** *Telstar STAR 2422* ●	1	1	9
18 Aug 90	**MEGABASS** *Telstar STAR 2425* ●	1	4	12
25 Aug 90	**GET ON THIS!!! 2** *Telstar STAR 2424*	3		9
25 Aug 90	**MOLTEN METAL** *Telstar STAR 2429*	13		5
15 Sep 90	**COUNTRY'S GREATEST HITS** *Telstar STAR 2433*	9		7
27 Oct 90	**DEEP HEAT 8 – THE HAND OF FATE** *Telstar STAR 2447* ●	3		5
27 Oct 90	**THE GREATEST LOVE 4** *Telstar STAR 2400* ●	4		19
27 Oct 90	**THE FINAL COUNTDOWN – THE VERY BEST OF SOFT METAL** *Telstar STAR 2431* ●	9		6
3 Nov 90	**RAVE** *Telstar STAR 2453*	10		4
17 Nov 90	**THE GREATEST HITS OF 1990** *Telstar STAR 2439* ●	4		14
24 Nov 90	**DEEP HEAT 90** *Telstar STAR 2438* ⊛	3		12
24 Nov 90	**THE MOTOWN COLLECTION** *Telstar STAR 2375* ●	8		12
1 Dec 90	**60 NUMBER ONES OF THE SIXTIES** *Telstar STAR 2432* ●	7		11
8 Dec 90	**THE VERY BEST OF GREATEST LOVE** *Telstar STAR 2443* ●	5		17
8 Dec 90	**MEGABASS 2** *Telstar STAR 2448* ●	6		8
26 Jan 91	**DEEP HEAT 9 – NINTH LIFE – KISS THE BLISS** *Telstar STAR 2470* ●	1	2	7
16 Feb 91	**THE BRITS 1991 – THE MAGIC OF BRITISH MUSIC** *Telstar STAR 2481* ●	7		6
23 Feb 91	**UNCHAINED MELODIES** *Telstar STAR 2480* ●	1	3	20
23 Mar 91	**DON'T STOP...DOOWOP!** *Telstar STAR 2485*	15		4
30 Mar 91	**THIN ICE – THE FIRST STEP** *Telstar STAR 2500* ●	2		9
13 Apr 91	**AFTER THE DANCE** *Telstar STAR 2501*	16		3
11 May 91	**MASSIVE HITS** *Telstar STAR 2505*	2		6
18 May 91	**UNCHAINED MELODIES – II** *Telstar STAR 2515*	3		8
1 Jun 91	**DEEP HEAT 10 – THE AWAKENING** *Telstar STAR 2490*	2		7
8 Jun 91	**MEGABASS 3** *Telstar STAR 2483*	3		8
22 Jun 91	**FAST FORWARD** *Telstar STAR 2502*	4		8
3 Aug 91	**THIN ICE 2 – THE SECOND SHIVER** *Telstar STAR 2535*	1	1	9
14 Sep 91	**Q – THE ALBUM VOLUME 1** *Telstar STAR 2522*	10		4
28 Sep 91	**MAKE YOU SWEAT** *Telstar STAR 2542*	4		6
12 Oct 91	**BORN TO BE WILD** *Telstar STAR 2524*	8		5
19 Oct 91	**IN LOVE – GREATEST LOVE 5** *Telstar STAR 2510* ●	5		11
2 Nov 91	**BURNING HEARTS** *Telstar STAR 2492*	7		10
9 Nov 91	**THE BEST OF DANCE '91** *Telstar STAR 2537* ⊛	2		15
16 Nov 91	**THE GREATEST HITS OF 1991** *Telstar STAR 2536* ●	4		13
23 Nov 91	**LOVE AT THE MOVIES** *Telstar STAR 2545* ●	6		14
23 Nov 91	**PUNK AND DISORDERLY – NEW WAVE 1976-1981** *Telstar STAR 2520*	18		2
30 Nov 91	**CLASSICAL MASTERS** *Telstar STAR 2549* ●	13		15
7 Dec 91	**LEGENDS OF SOUL – A WHOLE STACK OF SOUL** *Telstar STAR 2489*	15		10
21 Dec 91	**DEEP HEAT 11 – SPIRIT OF ECSTASY** *Telstar STAR 2555* ●	3		8
15 Feb 92	**KAOS THEORY** *Telstar STAR 2562*	2		7
15 Feb 92	**ALL THE BEST – LOVE DUETS VOLUME 1** *Telstar STAR 2557*	5		6
29 Feb 92	**GOLD – 18 EPIC SPORTING ANTHEMS** *Telstar TCD 2563*	15		3
7 Mar 92	**THE ULTIMATE HARDCORE** *Telstar TCD 2561*	1	2	10
11 Apr 92	**CLUB FOR HEROES** *Telstar TCD 2566*	3		10
2 May 92	**KAOS THEORY 2** *Telstar STAR 2583*	2		8
2 May 92	**INDIE HITS** *Telstar TCD 2578*	13		3
9 May 92	**FLIGHT OF THE CONDOR** *Telstar TCD 2576*	11		6
23 May 92	**GARAGE CITY** *Telstar TCD 2584*	8		5
6 Jun 92	**RAVING WE'RE RAVING** *Telstar TCD 2567*	2		6

Date	Album	Peak Position	Weeks at No. 1	Weeks on Chart
18 Jul 92	**KT3 – KAOS THEORY 3** *Telstar TCD 2593*	1	2	8
1 Aug 92	**THE DIVAS OF DANCE** *Telstar TCD 2592*	9		4
8 Aug 92	**RAVE ALERT** *Telstar TCD 2594*	2		10
19 Sep 92	**BLUE EYED SOUL** *Telstar TCD 2591*	4		6
10 Oct 92	**KAOS THEORY 4** *Telstar TCD 2605*	2		5
17 Oct 92	**RAVE NATION** *Telstar TCD 2607*	2		6
17 Oct 92	**MORE THAN LOVE** *Telstar TCD 2606*	4		9
7 Nov 92	**THE BEST OF DANCE '92** *Telstar TCD 2610*	1	2	17
14 Nov 92	**THE GREATEST HITS OF 1992** *Telstar TCD 2611*	4		16
14 Nov 92	**CLASSIC LOVE** *Telstar TCD 2620*	4		15
21 Nov 92	**ROCK N ROLL HEARTBEATS** *Telstar TCD 2628*	13		1
21 Nov 92	**MY GENERATION** *Telstar TCD 2609*	16		1
28 Nov 92	**THE GREATEST HITS OF DANCE** *Telstar TCD 2616*	5		11
19 Dec 92	**SONIC SYSTEM** *Telstar TCD 2624*	17		3
23 Jan 93	**MOVIE HITS** *Telstar TCD 2615*	19		2
20 Feb 93	**HITS 93 VOLUME 1** *Telstar TCD 2641*	1	3	15
27 Feb 93	**COUNTRY LOVE** *Telstar TCD 2645*	5		15
10 Apr 93	**DEEP HEAT 93 VOLUME 1** *Telstar TCD 2651*	2		7
29 May 93	**HITS 93 VOLUME 2** *Telstar TCD 2661*	2		8
12 Jun 93	**THE PIG ATTRACTION FEATURING PINKY AND PERKY** *Telstar TCD 2668*	19		2
26 Jun 93	**100% DANCE** *Telstar TCD 2667*	1	1	15
3 Jul 93	**RAGGA HEAT REGGAE BEAT** *Telstar TCD 2666*	4		14
17 Jul 93	**FRESH DANCE 93** *Telstar TCD 2665*	4		7
14 Aug 93	**HITS 93 VOLUME 3** *Telstar TCD 2681*	2		9
18 Sep 93	**DANCE ADRENALIN** *Telstar TCD 2688*	1	2	7
2 Oct 93	**100% DANCE VOLUME 2** *Telstar TCD 2681*	1	4	9
9 Oct 93	**LOVE IS RHYTHM** *Telstar TCD 2683*	5		5
9 Oct 93	**COUNTRY LOVE 2** *Telstar TCD 2682*	11		4
6 Nov 93	**THE BEST OF DANCE '93** *Telstar TCD 2662*	1	3	14
13 Nov 93	**THE GREATEST HITS OF 1993** *Telstar TCD 2663*	4		13
20 Nov 93	**HITS 93 VOLUME 4** *Telstar CDHITS 934*	2		9
20 Nov 93	**THE ALL TIME GREATEST HITS OF DANCE** *Telstar TCD 2679*	11		7
20 Nov 93	**THE GREATEST LOVE 6 – WITH LOVE FROM THE STARS** *Telstar TCD 2686*	16		8
11 Dec 93	**100% REGGAE** *Telstar TCD 2659*	2		17
11 Dec 93	**100% DANCE VOLUME 3** *Telstar TCD 2705*	7		9
18 Dec 93	**A HEART OF GOLD** *Telstar TCD 2692*	9		4
8 Jan 94	**NO 1'S OF DANCE** *Telstar TCD 2701*	16		3
19 Feb 94	**DANCE HITS '94 – VOLUME 1** *Telstar TCD 2693*	1	3	10
19 Feb 94	**LOVE OVER GOLD** *Telstar TCD 2684*	2		6
12 Mar 94	**100% RAP** *Telstar TCD 2694*	3		10
19 Mar 94	**HITS 94 VOLUME 1** *Telstar/BMG CDHITS 941*	3		7
9 Apr 94	**LOVE ON FILM** *Telstar TCD 2545*	17		2
16 Apr 94	**MOVIE HITS** *Telstar TCD 2615*	20		1
23 Apr 94	**100% DANCE VOLUME 4** *Telstar TCD 2714*	2		7
30 Apr 94	**100% REGGAE VOLUME 2** *Telstar TCD 2716*	4		14
7 May 94	**AWESOME DANCE** *Telstar TCD 2721*	2		7
11 Jun 94	**DANCE HITS '94 VOLUME 2** *Telstar TCD 2720*	1	1	8
2 Jul 94	**JAZZ MOODS** *Telstar TCD 2722*	3		8
23 Jul 94	**IT'S THE ULTIMATE DANCE ALBUM** *Telstar TCD 2725*	1	2	11
23 Jul 94	**100% SUMMER** *Telstar TCD 2730*	4		7
6 Aug 94	**100% REGGAE VOLUME 3** *Telstar TCD 2724*	6		7
24 Sep 94	**100% HITS** *Telstar TCD 2726*	2		8
8 Oct 94	**100% ACID JAZZ** *Telstar TCD 2733*	5		14
15 Oct 94	**THE ULTIMATE HITS ALBUM** *Telstar/BMG CDHITS 942*	11		2
29 Oct 94	**JUNGLE MANIA 94** *Telstar TCD 2735*	7		6
29 Oct 94	**ULTIMATE REGGAE PARTY ALBUM!** *Telstar TCD 2731*	14		2
29 Oct 94	**JAZZ MOODS 2** *Telstar TCD 2740*	18		1
5 Nov 94	**100% PURE LOVE** *Telstar TCD 2737*	7		7
5 Nov 94	**THE BEST OF DANCE '94** *Telstar TCD 2743*	10		5
12 Nov 94	**THE GREATEST HITS OF 1994** *Telstar TCD 2744*	9		5
3 Dec 94	**SMASH HITS '94** *Telstar TCD 2750*	9		7
10 Dec 94	**100% CHRISTMAS** *Telstar TCD 2754*	9		6
24 Dec 94	**JUNGLE MANIA 2** *Telstar TCD 2756*	5		8
7 Jan 95	**THE GREATEST LOVE EVER** *Telstar TCD 2747*	6		5
7 Jan 95	**THE BEST OF 100% DANCE** *Telstar TCD 2752*	11		3
14 Jan 95	**100% CLASSICS** *Telstar TCD 2757*	8		6
28 Jan 95	**THE GREATEST HITS OF THE 90'S – PART 1** *Telstar TCD 2749*	19		2
18 Feb 95	**100% HOUSE CLASSICS – VOLUME 1** *Telstar TCD 2759*	16		4
18 Mar 95	**SMASH HITS '95 – VOLUME 1** *Telstar TCD 2764*	1	1	7
25 Mar 95	**JUNGLE MANIA 3** *Telstar TCD 2762*	5		6
6 May 95	**WARNING! DANCE BOOM** *Telstar TCD 2763*	2		6
17 Jun 95	**100% ACID JAZZ – VOLUME 2** *Telstar TCD 2767*	14		4
24 Jun 95	**SMASH HITS '95 – VOLUME 2** *Telstar TCD 2768*	4		5
8 Jul 95	**100% SUMMER '95** *Telstar TCD 2777*	7		2
5 Aug 95	**CLUB ZONE** *Telstar TCD 2779*	4		5
5 Aug 95	**100% SUMMER JAZZ** *Telstar TCD 2781*	11		4
2 Sep 95	**WARNING! DANCE BOOM 2** *Telstar TCD 2783*	7		4
2 Sep 95	**100% CARNIVAL!** *Telstar TCD 2782*	16		2
7 Oct 95	**CLUB ZONE 2** *Telstar TCD 2787*	10		3
4 Nov 95	**BEST SWING '95** *Telstar TCD 2789*	10		3
18 Nov 95	**THE GREATEST HITS OF 1995** *Telstar TCD 2792*	8		9
6 Jan 96	**BEST SWING 96** *Telstar TCD 2805*	2		7
20 Jan 96	**100% CLASSICS – VOLUME 2** *Telstar TCD 2800*	20		1
17 Feb 96	**OUR FRIENDS ELECTRIC** *Telstar TCD 2814*	8		5
24 Feb 96	**THE GREATEST 90S DANCE HITS** *Telstar TCD 2807*	16		2
9 Mar 96	**BEST SWING 96 – VOLUME 2** *Telstar TCD 2820*	6		5
23 Mar 96	**100% PURE GROOVE** *Telstar TCD 2818*	4		8
13 Apr 96	**LOVE OVER GOLD 2** *Telstar TCD 2803*	19		1
20 Apr 96	**TECHNOHEDZ – 20 FIRESTARTIN' TECHNO ANTHEMS** *Telstar TCD 2823*	12		3
27 Apr 96	**LOVE II SWING** *Telstar TCD 2817*	10		3
25 May 96	**SWING MIX 96** *Telstar TCD 2831*	3		6
8 Jun 96	**MASSIVE DANCE MIX 96** *Telstar TCD 2830*	9		4
8 Jun 96	**100% PURE GROOVE 2** *Telstar TCD 2840*	12		3
29 Jun 96	**MOVIE KILLERS** *Telstar TCD 2836*	4		16
29 Jun 96	**CAFÉ LATINO** *Telstar TCD 2841*	18		1
6 Jul 96	**100% SUMMER MIX 96** *Telstar TCD 2843*	7		9
13 Jul 96	**BEST SWING '96 – VOLUME 3** *Telstar TCD 2837*	20		1
20 Jul 96	**FI ROCK** *Telstar TCD 2835*	20		1
21 Sep 96	**100% DANCE HITS 96** *Telstar TCD 2826*	11		3
28 Sep 96	**MAD FOR IT** *Telstar TCD 2868*	12		3
5 Oct 96	**100% DRUM & BASS** *Telstar TCD 2847*	11		4
9 Nov 96	**THE MOTHER OF ALL SWING ALBUMS** *Telstar TCD 2877*	9		4
9 Nov 96	**THE BEST OF DANCE '96** *Telstar TCD 2871*	13		3
16 Nov 96	**THE GREATEST HITS OF 1996 – THE STORY OF THE YEAR** *Telstar TCD 2873*	4		9
18 Jan 97	**THE GREATEST CLASSICAL MOVIE ALBUM** *Telstar TCD 2880*	15		3
22 Feb 97	**THE MOTHER OF ALL SWING MIX ALBUMS** *Telstar TCD 2890*	7		5
8 Mar 97	**ONCE IN A LIFETIME** *Telstar TCD 2889*	13		3
10 May 97	**SOUL SURVIVORS – 40 NORTHERN SOUL ANTHEMS** *Telstar TCD 2869*	10		7
17 May 97	**CLUB CUTS 97** *Telstar TCD 2898*	5		7
14 Jun 97	**CLUBLAND** *Telstar TV TCD 2912*	3		7
21 Jun 97	**SIXTIES SUMMER MIX** *Telstar TV TCD 2908*	5		10
5 Jul 97	**A DECADE OF IBIZA – 1987–1997** *Telstar TV TCD 2902*	5		10
19 Jul 97	**CLUB CUTS 97 – VOLUME 2** *Telstar TV TTVCD 2916*	2		7
26 Jul 97	**100% SUMMER MIX 97** *Telstar TV TTVCD 2906*	8		6
2 Aug 97	**THE MOTHER OF ALL SWING II** *Telstar TV TTVCD 2896*	11		5
16 Aug 97	**PURE HITS '97** *Telstar TV TTVCD 2914*	13		2
30 Aug 97	**THE GREATEST DANCE ALBUM EVER MADE** *Telstar TV TTVCD 2918*	5		5
20 Sep 97	**MOONDANCE – THE ALBUM** *Telstar TV TTVCD 2919*	16		4
27 Sep 97	**CLUBLAND – VOLUME 2** *Telstar TV TTVCD 2928*	6		4
11 Oct 97	**CLUB CUTS 97 – VOLUME 3** *Telstar TV TTVCD 2933*	5		4
8 Nov 97	**THE BEST OF DANCE '97** *Telstar TV TTVCD 2929*	6		4
15 Nov 97	**THE GREATEST HITS OF 1997** *Telstar TV TTVCD 2938*	2		12
21 Feb 98	**MOVIE LOVERS** *Telstar TCD 2876*	17		1
7 Mar 98	**CLUBLIFE** *Telstar TV TTVCD 2946*	3		5
7 Mar 98	**POWER OF A WOMAN** *Telstar/warner.esp TTVCD 2950*	13		4
21 Mar 98	**THE BOX HITS 98** *Telstar TV TTVCD 2951*	2		5
4 Apr 98	**NON-STOP DANCE ANTHEMS** *Telstar TV TTVCD 2958*	5		6
2 May 98	**CLUB HITS 98** *Telstar TV TTVCD 2953*	2		7
23 May 98	**FANTAZIA – BRITISH ANTHEMS – SUMMERTIME** *Telstar TV FBA 2CD*	3		6
23 May 98	**STREET JAMS** *Telstar TV/Polygram TV TTVCD 2963*	14		3
13 Jun 98	**THE BOX HITS 98 – VOLUME 2** *Telstar TV TTVCD 2974*	1	3	6
20 Jun 98	**SMILE JAMAICA** *Telstar TV TTVCD 2976*	20		2
27 Jun 98	**BEST OF 100% PURE GROOVES** *Telstar TV TTVCD 2957*	13		2
4 Jul 98	**NON STOP HITS** *Telstar TV TTVCD 2962*	4		5
11 Jul 98	**IBIZA ANTHEMS** *Telstar TV TTVCD 2965*	5		7
18 Jul 98	**100% SUMMER MIX 98** *Telstar TV TTVCD 2968*	13		4
15 Aug 98	**SIXTIES SUMMER MIX 2** *Telstar TV TTVCD 2972*	19		1
22 Aug 98	**CLUBLIFE 2** *Telstar TV TTVCD 2960*	13		2
29 Aug 98	**ULTIMATE COUNTRY: 40 COUNTRY GREATS** *Telstar TV TTVCD 2986*	8		9
5 Sep 98	**NON STOP HITS – VOLUME 2** *Telstar TV TTVCD 2993*	19		1
19 Sep 98	**SOUL SURVIVORS 2** *Telstar TV TTVCD 2992*	17		2
10 Oct 98	**SUNDANCE – CHAPTER ONE** *Telstar TV TTVCD 2989*	9		3
17 Oct 98	**BOX HITS 98 – VOLUME 3** *Telstar TV TTVCD 2988*	2		4
31 Oct 98	**CARWASH** *Telstar TV TTVCD 2998*	15		1
7 Nov 98	**THE BEST OF DANCE '98** *Telstar TV TTVCD 3001*	9		2
14 Nov 98	**THE GREATEST HITS OF 1998** *Telstar TV TTVCD 3002*	3		12
5 Dec 98	**CHRIS TARRANT PRESENTS ULTIMATE PARTY MEGAMIX** *Telstar TV TTVCD 3009*	17		1
9 Jan 99	**THE BOX R&B HITS ALBUM** *Telstar TV TTVCD 3008*	6		6
30 Jan 99	**THE GREATEST LOVE** *Telstar TV TTVCD 3006*	14		2
6 Feb 99	**EUPHORIA** *Telstar TV TTVCD 3007*	1	2	17
13 Mar 99	**BORN TO BE WILD** *Telstar TV TTVCD 3012*	15		1
3 Apr 99	**THE CHILLOUT ALBUM** *Telstar TV TTVCD 3037*	4		10
10 Apr 99	**ESSENTIAL SOUNDTRACKS** *Telstar TV TTVCD 3038*	4		10
10 Apr 99	**BEST DANCE 99** *Telstar TV TTVCD 3036*	10		5
24 Apr 99	**FUNKY HOUSE** *Telstar TV TTVCD 3050*	9		3
29 May 99	**DEEPER – EUPHORIA II: MIXED BY RED JERRY** *Telstar TV TTVCD 3064*	2		6

Date	Title / Label	Peak Position	Weeks at No.1	Weeks on Chart
5 Jun 99	**NATIONAL ANTHEMS 99** *Telstar TV TTVCD 3051*	3		5
3 Jul 99	**IBIZA ANTHEMS 2** *Telstar TV TTVCD 3054*	7		4
10 Jul 99	**CHRIS TARRANT'S ULTIMATE SUMMER PARTY** *Telstar TV TTVCD 3067*	15		2
24 Jul 99	**ADRENALIN** *Telstar TV TTVCD 3075*	10		3
31 Jul 99	**THE CHILL OUT ALBUM – 2** *Telstar TV TTVCD 3076*	14		4
14 Aug 99	**SUMMER DANCE ANTHEMS 99** *Telstar TV TTVCD 3077*	10		3
4 Sep 99	**NATIONAL ANTHEMS 99 – VOLUME 2** *Telstar TV TTVCD 3081*	11		2
11 Sep 99	**IBIZA EUPHORIA** *Telstar TV TTVCD 3078*	5		5
9 Oct 99	**CLUB HITS 99** *Telstar TV TTVCD 3079*	16		1
6 Nov 99	**THE GREATEST HITS OF THE NINETIES** *Telstar TV TTVCD 3084*	19		1
13 Nov 99	**THE GREATEST HITS OF 1999 – THE STORY SO FAR** *Telstar TV TTVCD 3087*	8		3
25 Dec 99	**EUPHORIA – LEVEL 3** *Telstar TV TTVCD 3095*	5		12
15 Jan 00	**BREAKDOWN** *Telstar TV TTVCD 3098*	4		11
12 Feb 00	**AYIA NAPA – FANTASY ISLAND** *Telstar TV TTVCD 3115*	1	1	6
18 Mar 00	**GARAGE ANTHEMS** *Telstar TV TTVCD 3120*	8		6
8 Apr 00	**SWITCHED ON** *Telstar TV TTVCD 3086*	13		4
15 Apr 00	**ESSENTIAL SOUNDTRACKS** *Telstar TV TTVCD 3121*	8		3
29 Apr 00	**PURE EUPHORIA – LEVEL 4** *Telstar TV TTVCD 3118*	3		6
27 May 00	**BIG TUNES 2000** *Telstar TV TTVCD 3110*	9		6
10 Jun 00	**CHILLED EUPHORIA** *Telstar TV TTVCD 3127*	4		7
10 Jun 00	**GARAGE NATION** *Telstar TV TTVCD 3125*	10		3
24 Jun 00	**LOVE ON A SUMMER'S DAY** *Telstar TV TTVCD 3126*	14		2
19 Aug 00	**IBIZA EUPHORIA – ALEX GOLD/AGNELLI & NELSON** *Telstar TV TTVCD 3134*	4		5
2 Sep 00	**BREAKDOWN – VERY BEST OF EUPHORIC DANCE** *Telstar TV TTVCD 3133*	4		7
2 Sep 00	**PURE R&B** *Telstar TV TTVCD 3138*	7		8
30 Sep 00	**THE COOL SOUND OF THE 70S** *Telstar TV TTVCD 3148*	9		4
7 Oct 00	**LOVE 2 DANCE** *Telstar TV TTVCD 3140*	18		1
25 Nov 00	**PURE R&B 2** *Telstar TV/BMG TV TTVCD 3153*	11		3
2 Dec 00	**TRANCENDENTAL EUPHORIA** *Telstar TV/BMG TV TTVCD 3155*	6		8
2 Dec 00	**DISNEY'S GREATEST HITS** *Telstar TV/BMG TV TTVCD 3151*	19		1
16 Dec 00	**HARD HOUSE EUPHORIA** *Telstar TV/BMG TV TTVCD 3152*	10		7
23 Dec 00	**THE RECORD OF THE YEAR 2000** *Telstar TV TTVCD 3154*	16		3
23 Dec 00	**ULTIMATE SIXTIES COLLECTION** *Telstar TV TTVCD 3156*	19		1
27 Jan 01	**DEEP & CHILLED EUPHORIA** *Telstar TV/BMG TV TTVCD 3164*	5		4
3 Feb 01	**BREAKDOWN – VERY BEST OF EUPHORIC DANCE** *Telstar/BMG TTVCD 3158*	1	2	3
17 Feb 01	**LOVE UNLIMITED – THE SOULFUL SOUND OF LOVE** *Telstar TV/BMG TV TTVCD 3167*	9		2
17 Feb 01	**THE DREEM TEEM IN SESSION** *Telstar/4 Liberty LIBTCD 008*	12		1
24 Mar 01	**THE ULTIMATE SOUL COLLECTION** *Telstar TV/BMG TV TTVCD 3168*	10		3
31 Mar 01	**THE VERY BEST EUPHORIC CHILLOUT MIXES** *Telstar TV/BMG TV TTVCD 3175*	10		5
31 Mar 01	**AYIA NAPA – RETURN TO FANTASY ISLAND** *Telstar TV/BMG TV TTVCD 3157*	18		2
14 Apr 01	**TRUE EUPHORIA** *Telstar TV/BMG TV TTVCD 3176*	3		6
28 Apr 01	**STREET VIBES 7** *Telstar TV/BMG TV 74321854882*	7		6
9 Jun 01	**PURE R&B 3** *Telstar TV/BMG TV TTVCD 3188*	8		4
9 Jun 01	**ESSENTIAL TRACKS** *Telstar TV/BMG TV TTVCD 3182*	15		2
30 Jun 01	**FUNKY DIVAS – THE VERY BEST IN SOUL DANCE AND R&B** *Telstar TV/BMG TV TTVCD 3193*	5		8
7 Jul 01	**PURE HIP HOP** *BMG/Sony/Telstar TTVCD 3191*	9		3
4 Aug 01	**BEST OF EUPHORIC DANCE – BREAKDOWN IBIZA** *Telstar TV/BMG TTVCD 3195*	2		4
25 Aug 01	**CHILLED OUT EUPHORIA** *Telstar TV/BMG TTVCD 3189*	8		2
15 Sep 01	**IBIZA EUPHORIA – DAVE PEARCE** *Telstar/BMG TTVCD 3199*	3		6
3 Nov 01	**HARD HOUSE EUPHORIA – TIDY BOYS VS LISA** *Telstar TV/BMG TTVCD 3177*	12		2
9 Feb 02	**SONGS FROM THE CHILLOUT LOUNGE** *Telstar TV/BMG TTVCD 3230*	20		1
16 Feb 02	**ELECTRO BREAKDANCE – THE REAL OLD SCHOOL REVIVAL** *Telstar TV/BMG TTVCD 3240*	4		4
2 Mar 02	**PURE GROOVE – THE VERY BEST 80'S SOUL FUNK GROOVES** *Telstar TV/BMG TTVCD 3238*	3		6
2 Mar 02	**WHITE LABEL EUPHORIA – JOHN OO FLEMING** *Telstar TV/BMG TTVCD 3241*	6		4
9 Mar 02	**THE VERY BEST OF ALL WOMAN** *Telstar TV/BMG TTVCD 3242*	2		5
30 Mar 02	**RUDE BOY REVIVAL** *Telstar TV/BMG TTVCD 3247*	4		6
13 Apr 02	**ELECTRIC – THE VERY BEST OF ELECTRONIC, NEW WAVE & SYNTH** *Telstar TV/BMG TTVCD 3246*	5		6
4 May 02	**ABSOLUTE EUPHORIA – DAVE PEARCE** *Telstar TV/BMG TTVCD 3251*	3		5
25 May 02	**THE VERY BEST POP ALBUM** *Telstar TV/BMG TTVCD 3260*	18		1
22 Jun 02	**VERY BEST OF EUPHORIC DANCE BREAKDOWN** *Telstar TV/BMG TTVCD 3262*	4		5
6 Jul 02	**EXTREME EUPHORIA – LISA LASHES** *Telstar TV/BMG TTVCD 3265*	5		3
3 Aug 02	**SUMMER COUNTRY – 41 CLASSIC COUNTRY HITS FOR A MODERN WORLD** *Telstar/BMG TTVCD 3273*	16		3
17 Aug 02	**THE VERY BEST OF PURE R&B – THE SUMMER** *Telstar TV/BMG TTVCD 3244*	1	1	12
24 Aug 02	**SONGS TO MAKE YOU FEEL GOOD – – 41 UPLIFTING CLASSICS** *Telstar TV/BMG TTVCD 3270*	5		9
31 Aug 02	**IBIZA EUPHORIA – MIXED BY DAVE PEARCE** *Telstar TV/BMG TTVCD 3274*	10		3
28 Sep 02	**FUNKY DIVAS – THE AUTUMN COLLECTION** *Telstar TV/BMG TTVCD 3290*	4		6
5 Oct 02	**PURE GROOVE – THE CLASSICS** *Telstar TV/BMG TTVCD 3256*	7		4
2 Nov 02	**VERY BEST EUPHORIC OLD SKOOL BREAKDOWN** *Telstar TV/BMG TTVCD 3282*	4		4
9 Nov 02	**CHOOSE 80'S DANCE** *Telstar TV/BMG TTVCD 3272*	12		2
23 Nov 02	**THE VERY BEST OF EUPHORIA – MATT DAREY** *Telstar TV/BMG TTVCD 3297*	3		5
7 Dec 02	**THE VERY BEST OF PURE R&B – THE WINTER** *Telstar TV/BMG TTVCD 3303*	11		10
1 Feb 03	**DEEPER SHADES OF EUPHORIA** *Telstar TV/BMG TTVCD 3285*	6		3
8 Feb 03	**VERY BEST OF DAVE PEARCE DANCE ANTHEMS** *Telstar TV/BMG TTVCD 3318*	4		7
8 Feb 03	**THE FUNKIN' 80S** *Telstar TV/BMG TTVCD 3301*	11		3
8 Mar 03	**THE VERY BEST EUPHORIC HOUSE BREAKDOWN** *Telstar TV/BMG TTVCD 3307*	2		6
29 Mar 03	**THE VERY BEST OF ALL WOMAN 2003** *Telstar TV/BMG TTVCD 3299*	3		6
12 Apr 03	**THE VERY BEST OF PURE R&B – SUMMER 2003** *Telstar TV/BMG TTVCD 3325*	2		10
19 Apr 03	**WHITE LABEL EUPHORIA – LEVEL 2** *Telstar TV/BMG TTVCD 3327*	12		3
17 May 03	**ELECTRIC – LEVEL 2** *Telstar TV/BMG TTVCD 3329*	5		6
17 May 03	**THE VERY BEST OF PURE HIP HOP** *Telstar TV/BMG TTVCD 3328*	14		4
14 Jun 03	**THE VERY BEST OF DRIVE TIME** *Telstar TV/BMG TTVCD 3336*	3		8
14 Jun 03	**DARK SIDE OF THE 80'S** *Telstar TV/BMG TTVCD 3322*	4		5
21 Jun 03	**ROCKABILLY REVIVAL** *Telstar TV/BMG TTVCD 3341*	10		2
28 Jun 03	**LATIN LEGENDS** *Telstar TV/BMG TTVCD 3271*	12		2
5 Jul 03	**VERY BEST OF EUPHORIC DANCE BREAKDOWN** *Telstar TV/BMG TTVCD 3344*	8		3
19 Jul 03	**EXTREME EUPHORIA – LISA LASHES** *Telstar TV/BMG TTVCD 3346*	6		3
2 Aug 03	**THE VERY BEST OF STREET VIBES** *Telstar TV/BMG TTVCD3330*	4		5
30 Aug 03	**ALL TIME CLASSIC SOUL HEARTBREAKERS** *Telstar TV/BMG TTVCD 3352*	10		3
13 Sep 03	**BOMBAY MIX** *Telstar TV/BMG TTVCD 3354*	12		4
27 Sep 03	**THE VERY BEST OF PURE DANCEHALL** *Telstar TV/BMG TTVCD 3353*	8		4
8 Nov 03	**THE VERY BEST OF PURE R&B – WINTER 2003** *Telstar TV/BMG TTVCD 3362*	3		9
8 Nov 03	**100% PURE OLD SKOOL CLUB CLASSICS** *Telstar TV/BMG TTVCD 3361*	9		3
22 Nov 03	**EUPHORIA** *Telstar TV/BMG TTVCD 3365*	14		1
7 Feb 04	**BLING** *Telstar TV/BMG TTVCD 3381*	2		7
21 Feb 04	**LOVE SONGS TO MAKE YOU FEEL GOOD** *Telstar TV/BMG TTVCD 3382*	10		1
21 Feb 04	**VERY BEST OF EUPHORIC DISCO BREAKDOWN** *Telstar TV/BMG TTVCD 3379*	17		1
27 Mar 04	**LOVELY DAY** *Telstar TV/EMI TV TTVCD 3384*	16		1
10 Apr 04	**LOVE BITES & SCHOOL NITES** *Telstar TV/BMG TTVCD 3385*	9		2
12 Jun 04	**CRASH INDIE ANTHEMS 1982–2004** *Telstar TV/BMG TTVCD 3389*	19		1

VARIOUS ARTISTS (TOMMY BOY)

Date	Title / Label	Peak Position	Weeks at No.1	Weeks on Chart
6 Apr 85	**TOMMY BOY GREATEST BEATS** *Tommy Boy ILPS 9825*	44		6

VARIOUS ARTISTS (TOPAZ)

Date	Title / Label	Peak Position	Weeks at No.1	Weeks on Chart
22 May 76	**A TOUCH OF COUNTRY** *Topaz TOC\R 1976*	7		7
3 Jul 76	**A TOUCH OF CLASS** *Topaz TOC 1976*	57		1

VARIOUS ARTISTS (TOUCHDOWN)

Date	Title / Label	Peak Position	Weeks at No.1	Weeks on Chart
13 Mar 93	**D-FROST – 20 GLOBAL DANCE WARNINGS** *Touchdown CTVCD 114*	8		4

VARIOUS ARTISTS (TOWERBELL)

Date	Title / Label	Peak Position	Weeks at No.1	Weeks on Chart
8 Feb 86	**THE DANCE HITS ALBUM** *Towerbell TVLP 8*	10		11
15 Mar 86	**THE CINEMA HITS ALBUM** *Towerbell TVLP 9*	44		9
17 May 86	**SISTERS ARE DOIN' IT** *Towerbell TVLP 11*	27		9
7 Jun 86	**TWO'S COMPANY** *Towerbell TVLP 12*	51		5
28 Jun 86	**DANCE HITS II** *Towerbell TVLP 13*	25		8

Date	Title / Label	Peak Position	Weeks at No.1	Weeks on Chart
2 Aug 86	THE ORIGINALS: 32 ALL-TIME CLASSIC GREATS *Towerbell TBDLP 14*	15		9
9 Aug 86	YOU'VE GOT TO LAUGH *Towerbell TVLP 15*	51		3

VARIOUS ARTISTS (TRAX)

Date	Title / Label	Peak Position	Weeks at No.1	Weeks on Chart
17 Dec 88	NOEL – CHRISTMAS SONGS AND CAROLS *Trax TRXLP 701*	89		2
22 Jul 89	DREAMS OF IRELAND *Trax MODEM 1035*	19		1
17 Feb 90	ROCK OF AMERICA *Trax MODEM 1036* ●	7		6
19 May 90	FREEDOM TO PARTY – FIRST LEGAL RAVE *Trax MODEM 1048* ●	4		10
28 Jul 90	SUMMER CHART PARTY *Trax BWTX 1*	9		6
3 Nov 90	FREEDOM 2 – THE ULTIMATE RAVE *Trax BWTX 4*	16		2
17 Nov 90	KARAOKE PARTY *Trax BETX 5*	20		1
16 Mar 91	KARAOKE PARTY II *Trax TXTV 1*	7		9

VARIOUS ARTISTS (TROJAN)

Date	Title / Label	Peak Position	Weeks at No.1	Weeks on Chart
27 Feb 71	REGGAE CHARTBUSTERS VOLUME 2 *Trojan TBL 147*	29		1
7 Aug 71	TIGHTEN UP VOLUME 4 *Trojan TBL 163*	20		7
21 Aug 71	CLUB REGGAE *Trojan TBL 159*	25		4
16 Jun 84	20 REGGAE CLASSICS *Trojan TRLS 222*	89		1
3 Aug 02	YOUNG GIFTED & BLACK *Trojan TJDDD 006* ●	6		6
7 Aug 04	YOUNG GIFTED & BLACK 2 *Trojan TJODD184* ○	12		2
5 Feb 05	REGGAE LOVE SONGS *Trojan TLSAN014* ○	4		4

VARIOUS ARTISTS (TV RECORDS)

Date	Title / Label	Peak Position	Weeks at No.1	Weeks on Chart
2 Oct 82	MODERN HEROES *TV Records TVA 1*	24		7
9 Oct 82	ENDLESS LOVE *TV Records TV 2*	26		8
6 Nov 82	FLASH TRACKS *TV Records PTVL 1*	19		7
25 Dec 82	PARTY FEVER/DISCO MANIA *TV Records TVA 5*	71		3

VARIOUS ARTISTS (TVD)

Date	Title / Label	Peak Position	Weeks at No.1	Weeks on Chart
9 May 98	OFF YER NUT!! *TVD Entertainment/Life On Mars TVDCD 1*	12		3

VARIOUS ARTISTS (TVT)

Date	Title / Label	Peak Position	Weeks at No.1	Weeks on Chart
8 Apr 06	CRUNK HITS *TVT TVTCD10*	16		2

VARIOUS ARTISTS (ULTRASOUND)

Date	Title / Label	Peak Position	Weeks at No.1	Weeks on Chart
15 Jul 95	THE HOUSE OF HANDBAG *Ultrasound USCD 3*	13		3
4 Nov 95	THE HOUSE OF HANDBAG – AUTUMN/WINTER COLLECTION *Ultrasound USCD 4*	16		2

VARIOUS ARTISTS (UNION SQUARE)

Date	Title / Label	Peak Position	Weeks at No.1	Weeks on Chart
21 Jun 08	GREATEST EVER DAD – THE DEFINITIVE *Union Square GTSTCD023*	17		1

VARIOUS ARTISTS (UNITED DANCE)

Date	Title / Label	Peak Position	Weeks at No.1	Weeks on Chart
18 Jan 97	THE ANTHEMS '92–'97 *United Dance UNCD 003*	8		3
12 Jul 97	UNITED DANCE PRESENTS ANTHEMS 2 – '88–'92 *United Dance UMCD 004*	17		2

VARIOUS ARTISTS (UNIVERSAL)

Date	Title / Label	Peak Position	Weeks at No.1	Weeks on Chart
17 Oct 98	THE HEART OF THE 80S AND 90S *Universal MCD 60061*	9		3
20 Mar 99	THE LOVE SONGS OF BURT BACHARACH *Universal Music TV 5642652*	5		3
27 Mar 99	BLUES BROTHER SOUL SISTER CLASSICS *Universal Music TV 5641832*	8		3
8 May 99	KISS CLUBLIFE *Universal Music TV 5474662* ●	2		7
22 May 99	TOP OF THE POPS '99 – VOLUME ONE *BBC/Universal Music TV 5644592* ●	2		6
29 May 99	DANCING IN THE STREET *Universal Music TV 5495092*	13		2
12 Jun 99	THE SOUND OF MAGIC *Universal Music TV 5644792* ○	10		5
19 Jun 99	SIXTIES SUMMER LOVE *Universal Music TV 5642712*	16		2
26 Jun 99	KISS SMOOTH GROOVES – SUMMER '99 *Universal Music TV 5645422* ●	7		4
10 Jul 99	THE BOX – DANCE HITS *Universal Music TV 5645482* ●	2		4
17 Jul 99	COUNTRY *Sony TV/Universal Music TV 5644822* ●	8		8
24 Jul 99	DAVE PEARCE PRESENTS 40 CLASSIC DANCE ANTHEMS *Universal Music TV 5471962* ○	5		6
31 Jul 99	AFRODISIAC *Universal Music TV 5648502*	14		3
21 Aug 99	CLUB MIX 99 *Universal Music TV 5648922* ●	3		7
4 Sep 99	SISTERS OF SWING 99 *Universal Music TV 5649302*	9		3
18 Sep 99	KISS IBIZA '99 *Universal Music TV 1537512* ●	1	3	8
25 Sep 99	TOP OF THE POPS '99 – VOLUME TWO *Universal Music TV 5450692* ⊛	1	1	8
2 Oct 99	THE SOUND OF MAGIC LOVE *Universal Music TV 5648842*	5		5
16 Oct 99	LAND OF MY FATHERS *Universal Music TV 4665674* ○	1	1	6
16 Oct 99	MOBO 1999 *Universal Music TV 5451432*	10		2
23 Oct 99	DAVE PEARCE PRESENTS 40 CLASSIC DANCE ANTHEMS 2 *Universal Music TV 1539732*	7		3
6 Nov 99	THE 90'S *Universal Music TV 5453532*	20		1
13 Nov 99	WOMAN 2 *Universal Music/Sony TV/Global TV 5451402* ⊛	4		19
13 Nov 99	THE BOX DANCE HITS – VOLUME 2 *Universal Music TV 1537792*	5		3
20 Nov 99	THE NUMBER ONE DANCE PARTY ALBUM *Universal Music TV 5550572* ⊛	17		2
27 Nov 99	KISS CLUBLIFE 2000 *Universal Music TV 5649422* ●	6		11
11 Dec 99	MASSIVE DANCE HITS 2000 *warner.esp/Global TV/Universal Music TV 1570942* ●	11		10
15 Jan 00	CELEBRATION 2000 *Universal TV 5450662*	14		1
5 Feb 00	CLUBMIX 2000 *Universal TV 5411542* ●	2		6
12 Feb 00	THE LOVE SONGS ALBUM *warner.esp/Universal TV/Global TV 5412002* ⊛	1	1	7
4 Mar 00	TOP OF THE POPS 2000 VOLUME 1 *Universal TV 5411972* ●	3		6
11 Mar 00	CLUB 2K *Universal TV 5413302* ●	2		6
1 Apr 00	KISS UK GARAGE – MIXED BY KARL BROWN *Universal TV 5414782* ○	3		4
1 Apr 00	THAT OLE DEVIL CALLED LOVE *Universal TV 5456062*	5		4
15 Apr 00	RELOADED *Universal TV 5415512* ●	3		7
15 Apr 00	BOX DANCE HITS 2000 *Universal TV 5414592* ○	5		2
29 Apr 00	THE CLASSICAL ALBUM *Universal/Virgin/EMI 4671402*	6		7
29 Apr 00	TOP OF THE POPS 2 *Universal TV 5412742*	15		2
6 May 00	KISS HOUSE NATION 2000 *Universal TV 1576052* ●	2		7
20 May 00	DAVE PEARCE PRESENTS 40 CLASSIC ANTHEMS – 3 *Universal TV 5418122* ○	7		4
3 Jun 00	KISS SMOOTH GROOVES 2000 *Universal TV 5246682*	3		5
10 Jun 00	DJ LUCK & MC NEAT PRESENTS *Universal TV 5246852*	6		3
10 Jun 00	THE SOUND OF MAGIC VOLUME 2 *Universal TV 5414092* ○	9		2
17 Jun 00	TOP OF THE POPS 2000 VOLUME 2 *Universal TV 5246972* ●	1	1	11
24 Jun 00	CLUB MIX IBIZA 2000 *Universal TV 5246822* ⊛	1	3	11
24 Jun 00	EURO 2000 – THE OFFICIAL ALBUM *Universal TV 1590902*	15		1
22 Jul 00	KISS CLUBLIFE SUMMER 2000 *Universal TV 5601122* ●	1	1	7
29 Jul 00	RESPECT *warner.esp/Universal TV 5248624*	15		3
5 Aug 00	LATIN FEVER *Sony TV/Universal TV 5601282* ●	3		9
12 Aug 00	CLUB 2K VOL. 2 *Universal TV/Ministry Of Sound 5601982* ●	7		3
12 Aug 00	THE REAL SOUND OF AYIA NAPA *Universal TV 5601092*	11		3
19 Aug 00	SUMMERTIME *Universal TV 5601932*	15		2
9 Sep 00	THE BOX *Universal TV 5602472*	12		2
23 Sep 00	KISS IBIZA 2000 *Universal TV 5603662* ●	1	2	7
23 Sep 00	HOT POP *Universal TV 5601322*	11		2
30 Sep 00	THE LATE NIGHT MIX *Universal TV 5606232*	15		2
14 Oct 00	MOBO 2000 *Universal TV 5606662* ○	3		5
21 Oct 00	CLUBMIX 2000 VOLUME 2 *Universal TV 5605872* ●	1	1	5
28 Oct 00	THE HIT FACTORY *Universal TV 5606692* ●	3		5
4 Nov 00	KISS GARAGE PRESENT DJ LUCK & MC NEAT *Universal TV 5605992* ●	3		4
11 Nov 00	TOP OF THE POPS 2000 – VOL 3 *Universal TV 5605652* ●	4		4
11 Nov 00	STEVE WRIGHT'S SUNDAY LOVE SONGS *Universal TV 5602902* ⊛	6		13
18 Nov 00	KISS HOUSE NATION 2001 *Universal TV 5605932*	8		2
18 Nov 00	WOMAN 3 *Sony TV/Universal TV 5603632*	10		2
2 Dec 00	MUSIC OF THE MILLENNIUM VOL. 2 *EMI/Virgin/Universal 5602302* ○	8		9
9 Dec 00	MASSIVE DANCE 2001 *BMG/M.O.S/UMTV/Warners 5201102*	20		3
3 Feb 01	RELOADED 2 *Universal TV 5602332* ●	2		7
3 Feb 01	TOP OF THE POPS 2 – 70'S ROCK *Universal TV 5606262*	10		2
10 Feb 01	PASSION *warner.esp/Universal TV/Global TV 5207042* ●	8		2
24 Feb 01	CLUB MIX 2001 *Universal TV 5209312* ●	4		8
3 Mar 01	TOP OF THE POPS 2001 – VOL 1 *Universal TV 5209862* ○	4		4
10 Mar 01	THE NATURAL BLUES ALBUM *Universal TV 5209392*	11		3
17 Mar 01	KISS SMOOTH GROOVES 2001 *Universal TV 5208542* ●	2		6
24 Mar 01	MAGIC *Universal TV 5608982*	11		3
31 Mar 01	CLUBBED *Universal TV 5561892*	6		4
7 Apr 01	MTV SELECT *Universal TV 5563142*	6		3
14 Apr 01	DJ LUCK & MC NEAT PRESENTS – II *Universal TV 5563182* ●	4		8
21 Apr 01	KISS CLUBLIFE 2001 *Universal TV 5561922*	12		2
5 May 01	DISCO FEVER *Universal TV 5564082* ●	4		7
26 May 01	SUNSET IBIZA *Universal TV 5566692* ○	7		4
2 Jun 01	PURE & SIMPLE *Universal TV 5561222* ○	7		3
23 Jun 01	RELOADED 3 *Universal TV 5567342* ○	9		4
23 Jun 01	R&B SELECTOR *Universal TV 5565202* ○	11		3
23 Jun 01	DANNY RAMPLING – LOVE GROOVE DANCE PARTY *Universal TV 5605902*	15		2
7 Jul 01	PARTY IN THE PARK *Universal TV 5850002* ●	2		5
7 Jul 01	MTV DANCE *Universal TV 5567252*	18		1

Silver-selling ○ · Gold-selling ● · Platinum-selling ⊛ · US No.1 ★

Date	Title	Label	Cert	Peak Position	Weeks at No.1	Weeks on Chart
14 Jul 01	TOP OF THE POPS – SUMMER 2001	*Universal TV 5566662*	●	4		4
14 Jul 01	KERRANG – THE ALBUM	*WSM/Universal TV 564882*	○	9		5
4 Aug 01	CLUBBED – VOLUME 2 – MIXED BY JUDGE JULES	*Universal TV 5568732*		8		3
11 Aug 01	CLUBMIX IBIZA	*UMTV/Ministry Of Sound 5853332*	●	2		8
11 Aug 01	KISS SMOOTH GROOVES SUMMER 2001	*Universal TV 5851162*	●	7		4
11 Aug 01	ATOMIC 80'S	*Universal TV 5851622*		11		4
1 Sep 01	DISCO FEVER – VOLUME 2	*Universal TV 5855102*		9		2
8 Sep 01	CLOSE TO YOU	*Universal TV 5853742*	●	5		7
8 Sep 01	MTV HITS	*Universal TV 5853922*		15		2
29 Sep 01	KISS IN IBIZA 2001	*Universal TV 5855182*	○	6		4
29 Sep 01	GOD'S KITCHEN	*Universal TV 5044892*		17		1
6 Oct 01	DJ LUCK & MC NEAT PRESENT VOLUME 3	*Universal TV 5854302*	○	7		4
13 Oct 01	URBAN CHILL	*Universal TV 5855872*		15		2
27 Oct 01	URBAN KISS	*Universal TV 5854722*	●	5		3
3 Nov 01	TOP OF THE POPS – AUTUMN 2001	*Universal TV 5858752*	●	8		3
17 Nov 01	PUMP UP THE VOLUME	*Universal TV 5841642*		11		2
17 Nov 01	ALL TOGETHER NOW	*Universal TV 5855712*	●	11		5
17 Nov 01	FEMALE	*Sony TV/Universal TV 5857662*		14		1
24 Nov 01	KERRANG! 2 – THE ALBUM	*WSM/Universal TV 5857632*	●	8		9
24 Nov 01	STEVE WRIGHT'S SUNDAY LOVE SONGS VOLUME 2	*Universal TV 5856482*	○	12		3
1 Dec 01	MOTOWN GOLD	*Universal TV 0163012*	⊛	7		10
1 Dec 01	R&B HITS	*Universal TV 5855902*		16		1
29 Dec 01	KISS HITLIST 2002	*EMI/Virgin/Universal 5841812*	●	4		7
12 Jan 02	THE LICK – TREVOR NELSON	*Universal TV 5855042*	○	4		5
2 Feb 02	RELOADED 4	*Universal TV 5840892*	○	4		4
2 Feb 02	CLUBBED 2002 – MIXED BY JUDGE JULES	*Universal TV 5843552*		7		2
9 Feb 02	CLUB MIX 2002	*Universal TV 5859562*	●	1	1	5
9 Feb 02	LOVE	*Universal TV 5845252*	●	3		4
23 Feb 02	KISS SMOOTH GROOVES 2002	*Universal TV 5844942*		10		3
9 Mar 02	RAPPERS DELIGHT	*Universal TV 5847272*		18		1
16 Mar 02	SUPERCHARGED	*UMTV/WSM 5848582*	●	1	2	9
16 Mar 02	TOGETHER	*Universal TV 5858922*		20		1
23 Mar 02	GIRLS SAY	*Universal TV 5849012*	○	7		4
30 Mar 02	MURDER ON THE DANCEFLOOR	*Universal TV 5849672*	○	7		3
30 Mar 02	TEMPTATIONS/FOUR TOPS: AT THEIR BEST	*Universal 5830142*		18		1
13 Apr 02	NEW JACK SWING	*Universal TV 5749912*		10		2
27 Apr 02	SUPA FUNKY	*Universal TV 5832352*		6		4
11 May 02	SIMPLY ACOUSTIC	*Sony TV/Universal TV 5848622*	○	5		6
18 May 02	KERRANG! 3 – THE ALBUM	*Universal TV 5845062*	○	4		5
25 May 02	KISSTORY	*Universal TV 5831082*	●	1	1	5
25 May 02	TOP OF THE POPS SPRING 2002	*Universal TV 5832322*	○	4		4
8 Jun 02	BEAUTIFUL GAME	*Universal TV 5848192*		16		1
8 Jun 02	TEENAGE KICKS	*Universal TV 5832642*		20		1
22 Jun 02	THE VERY BEST OF MTV UNPLUGGED	*WSM/Universal TV 5835452*	●	1	1	12
22 Jun 02	URBAN KISS 2002	*Universal TV 5830412*	●	3		6
22 Jun 02	EMOTIONS	*Universal TV 5832812*		13		2
6 Jul 02	CLUBLAND	*Universal TV/Serious 5836012*	⊛	1	3	12
13 Jul 02	PARTY IN THE PARK 2002	*Universal TV 5837632*	○	4		3
27 Jul 02	CLUBMIX IBIZA 2002	*Universal TV/Serious 5834602*		2		5
27 Jul 02	SEXY CRAZY COOL	*Universal TV 5847282*		5		4
17 Aug 02	ROCK MONSTERS	*Universal TV 5834142*		9		4
31 Aug 02	KISS HITLIST SUMMER 2002	*UMTV/Serious 690162*		2		5
14 Sep 02	KISSTORY IBIZA CLASSIC	*Universal TV 0694552*		13		2
21 Sep 02	WHILE MY GUITAR GENTLY WEEPS	*Universal TV 583442*	⊛	3		20
21 Sep 02	KERRANG! 4 – THE ALBUM	*Sony TV/Universal TV 691442*	○	4		6
28 Sep 02	LOUNGIN'	*UMTV/Serious 5832732*		18		1
12 Oct 02	SERIOUS CLUB HITS	*UMTV/Serious 5834802*		17		1
9 Nov 02	A WOMAN'S TOUCH	*Universal TV 0693582*		10		2
16 Nov 02	TOP OF THE POPS 2003	*Universal TV 695822*		14		2
23 Nov 02	CLUBLAND II – THE RIDE OF YOUR LIFE	*UMTV/AATW 0680632*	⊛	1	1	12
23 Nov 02	STEVE WRIGHT'S SUNDAY LOVE SONGS	*Universal TV 699232*	●	13		6
8 Feb 03	FRIENDS REUNITED	*Universal TV 0696342*	●	8		8
15 Feb 03	LOVE – ETERNAL LOVESONGS	*Universal TV 0686682*	●	1	2	6
22 Feb 03	THE LICK – BEST OF	*Universal TV 0685402*		12		4
1 Mar 03	CLUB MIX 2003	*Universal TV 0687152*	●	1	1	6
15 Mar 03	Q THE ALBUM	*EMI/Virgin/Universal 0685042*		8		3
22 Mar 03	SMOOTH JAZZ 2	*UCJ 0694612*		8		3
29 Mar 03	TOP OF THE POPS SPRING 2003	*EMI/Virgin/Universal 0689752*		6		3
5 Apr 03	HEARTBEAT LOVE SONGS	*Universal TV 0685512*	○	10		2
12 Apr 03	PURE DRUM & BASS	*Universal TV 0689202*		16		2
26 Apr 03	CLUBLAND X-TREME	*UMTV/AATW 0392142*	●	2		10
10 May 03	URBAN KISS 2003	*Universal TV 391452*		6		3
24 May 03	KISS PRESENTS HIP HOP CLASSICS	*Universal TV 9800273*	●	2		9
7 Jun 03	THE VERY BEST OF CHILLED CLASSICS	*UCJ 0690452*		18		1
14 Jun 03	THE QUIET STORM	*Universal TV 9800257*	○	2		7
28 Jun 03	60'S SOUL MIX	*Universal TV 9808144*		3		6
28 Jun 03	MAGIC – SUMMER FEELING 2003	*Universal TV 9807671*		10		4
5 Jul 03	CLUBLAND III	*UMTV/AATW 9800267*		1	3	15
5 Jul 03	KERRANG! – HIGH VOLTAGE	*UMTV/WSMS 0396382*		17		1
12 Jul 03	KISS HITLIST SUMMER 2003	*Universal TV 0396432*		8		3
2 Aug 03	THE PIANO AND THE SONG	*Universal TV 9800254*		10		5
9 Aug 03	COUNTRY LOVE	*Universal TV 9806791*		4		7
9 Aug 03	FEELIN' GOOD	*UCJ 9809935*		17		2
16 Aug 03	RIDE DA RIDDIMS	*Universal TV 9809706*		3		8
16 Aug 03	FRIENDS REUNITED – THE 90'S	*Universal TV 9808782*		18		1
23 Aug 03	CAPITAL GOLD REGGAE CLASSICS	*Universal TV 9808537*		5		4
23 Aug 03	WHAT A FEELING	*Universal TV 9809318*		15		1
30 Aug 03	KISS PRESENTS R&B COLLABORATIONS	*Universal TV/Sony TV 0391412*		1	3	9
6 Sep 03	ANTHEM CLASSICS FROM CLUBLAND	*UMTV/AATW 9811029*		7		3
6 Sep 03	TOP OF THE POPS SUMMER 2003	*Universal/EMI/Virgin 9810528*		11		3
6 Sep 03	XXX HIP HOP	*Universal TV 9865595*		12		3
13 Sep 03	KISSTORY URBAN CLASSICS	*Universal TV 9811370*		7		4
27 Sep 03	CLUBMIX SUMMER 2003	*UMTV/AATW 9811192*		1	2	7
4 Oct 03	MOBO PRESENTS URBAN BEATS 2003	*Universal TV 9811773*		5		4
11 Oct 03	THE MICHEAL PARKINSON COLLECTION	*UCJ 9811787*		9		3
18 Oct 03	URBAN FUSION	*Universal TV 9811174*		15		1
25 Oct 03	70'S SOUL MIX	*Universal TV 9811527*		13		1
8 Nov 03	WHILE MY GUITAR GENTLY WEEPS II	*Universal TV 9807760*		10		3
15 Nov 03	WESTWOOD – PLATINUM EDITION	*Def Jam/Universal Music TV 9813338*	●	1	1	7
15 Nov 03	POP PARTY	*EMI/Virgin/Universal 9812645*	⊛	2		22
22 Nov 03	CLUBLAND 4	*UMTV/AATW 9813598*	⊛	1	1	18
29 Nov 03	THE NUMBER ONE CLASSICAL ALBUM 2004	*UCJ 4761390*	⊛	4		10
29 Nov 03	KISS PRESENTS HOT JOINTS	*Universal TV 9813698*		7		11
29 Nov 03	CAPITAL GOLD MOTOWN CLASSICS	*Universal TV 9810954*		17		6
7 Feb 04	KISS SMOOTH R&B	*Sony TV/Universal TV 9815795*	●	1	1	7
14 Feb 04	CLUBMIX 2004	*UMTV/AATW 9816475*	●	1	2	8
14 Feb 04	STEVE WRIGHT'S CHOCOLATES AND CHAMPAGNE	*Universal TV 9816480*	●	2		6
13 Mar 04	LEADERS OF THE PACK – 60'S GIRLS	*Universal TV 9811326*	●	5		6
20 Mar 04	FLOORFILLERS	*UMTV/AATW 9817728*	●	1	1	12
20 Mar 04	RIDE DA RIDDIMS 2	*Universal TV 9815623*		7		4
3 Apr 04	KISS PRESENTS LAYDEEZ WITH ATTITUDE	*Universal TV 9818595*		13		2
17 Apr 04	POP PRINCESSES	*Universal TV 9817531*	⊛	3		16
17 Apr 04	60'S SOUL MIX 2	*Universal TV 9818833*		14		2
1 May 04	CLUBLAND X-TREME 2	*UMTV/AATW 9819336*	●	2		7
22 May 04	KISS PRESENTS THE HIP HOP COLLECTION	*Universal TV 9819774*		2		8
22 May 04	CAPITAL GOLD – JUST GREAT SONGS	*Universal TV 9819149*		4		4
5 Jun 04	IN THE MOOD FOR THE BLUES	*Universal TV 9820180*		15		1
12 Jun 04	THIS IS THE MODERN WORLD	*Universal TV 9819443*		9		3
12 Jun 04	THE NO 1 OPERA ALBUM	*UCJ 4762004*		11		1
19 Jun 04	PURPLE RAINBOWS	*EMI/Universal TV 9821194*	○	10		3
19 Jun 04	NEW BREED	*Universal TV 9820091*		18		1
26 Jun 04	JUST FOR YOU	*Universal TV 9820026*		13		2
10 Jul 04	MTV BASE PRESENTS BEATS RHYMES AND LIFE	*Universal TV 9820204*		12		2
17 Jul 04	RUSH HOUR	*Universal TV 9819867*	●	2		10
17 Jul 04	SONGBIRD	*UCJ 9818395*		7		8
24 Jul 04	CLUBLAND 5	*UMTV/AATW 9822063*	⊛	1	2	9
31 Jul 04	KISS PRESENTS R&B CLASSICS	*Universal TV 9818361*		6		4
21 Aug 04	REWIND	*EMI/Universal TV 9822979*		7		3
21 Aug 04	THE DEFINITIVE ELECTRO & HIP HOP	*Universal TV 9816849*		19		1
28 Aug 04	THE NUMBER ONE SWING ALBUM 2004	*UCJ/EMI Virgin 98210277*		9		5
4 Sep 04	PURE ACOUSTIC	*Sony TV/Universal TV 9823090*		20		1
18 Sep 04	CLUBMIX SUMMER 2004	*UMTV/AATW 9823913*		7		4
2 Oct 04	KISS JAMS	*Universal/EMI/Virgin 9822709*		6		5
2 Oct 04	BOY CRAZY	*UMTV/BMG TV 9823353*		10		3
9 Oct 04	FLOORFILLERS 2	*UMTV/AATW 9824681*		3		5
9 Oct 04	MTV UNPLUGGED 3 – THE VERY BEST OF	*UMTV/WSM 9823971*		14		1
16 Oct 04	DANCE DECADES	*Universal TV 9823885*		15		2
23 Oct 04	LET'S GO GIRLS	*Universal TV 9817858*	○	3		4
30 Oct 04	ULTIMATE R&B	*BMG TV/UMTV 9822576*		6		4
6 Nov 04	POP PARTY 2	*BMG/EMI Virgin/UMTV 9823966*	⊛ x2	1	1	25
20 Nov 04	CLUBLAND 6	*UMTV/AATW 9825829*	●	2		17
27 Nov 04	THE CLASSICAL ALBUM 2005	*UCJ 4762995*	⊛	6		6
27 Nov 04	KISS PRESENTS HOT JOINTS 2	*Universal TV 9826139*		17		7
4 Dec 04	THE NUMBER ONE MUSICALS ALBUM	*Universal TV 9824290*		9		6
11 Dec 04	CAPITAL GOLD SOUL CLASSICS	*Universal TV 9826141*		18		2
18 Dec 04	BARBIE GIRLS	*Universal TV 9826294*		7		6
15 Jan 05	RUSH HOUR 2	*Universal TV 9825763*	●	3		5

Silver-selling ● Gold-selling ● Platinum-selling ⊛ US No.1 ★

Date	Title / Label	Peak Position	Weeks at No.1	Weeks on Chart
12 Feb 05	**LOVE SONGS – THE ULTIMATE LOVE COLLECTION** *Universal TV 9827269* ●	1	1	4
12 Feb 05	**BE MY LOVE** *Sony BMG TV/UCJ 4767197*	19		1
26 Feb 05	**CLUBMIX 2005** *Universal TV 9826732* ●	1	2	8
26 Feb 05	**NUMBER 1'S** *EMI/Virgin/Universal 9828099*	7		2
12 Mar 05	**MOVIE'S GREATEST LOVE SONGS** *Universal TV 9827988*	11		2
2 Apr 05	**FLOORFILLERS 3** *UMTV/AATW 9828258*	2		11
2 Apr 05	**POP PRINCESSES 2** *Sony BMG TV/UMTV 9828036* ●	6		10
9 Apr 05	**KISS PRESENTS THE R&B COLLECTION** *Universal TV 9827851*	3		7
7 May 05	**INDIE ANTHEMS** *Universal TV 9826954*	6		3
14 May 05	**CLUBLAND X-TREME HARDCORE** *UMTV/AATW 9829696*	1	1	7
14 May 05	**POP JR** *Universal TV 9829857* ⊛	2		27
28 May 05	**MASSIVE R&B** *Sony BMG TV/UMTV 9829349* ●	1	2	10
28 May 05	**THE WEEKEND** *Universal TV 9829092*	4		7
28 May 05	**THE SONGS OF PRAISE ALBUM** *UCJ 9827973*	15		1
4 Jun 05	**PARTY CAPITAL – SUMMER MIX** *Universal TV 9829771*	16		1
11 Jun 05	**WHILE MY GUITAR GENTLY WEEPS III** *Universal TV 9826930*	5		4
18 Jun 05	**DRIVING ROCK** *Sony BMG TV/UMTV 9829087*	8		2
2 Jul 05	**THE NEW INDIE – ALIVE & AMPLIFIED** *Universal TV 9830962*	11		1
9 Jul 05	**CLUBLAND 7** *UMTV/AATW 9831161*	1	1	10
9 Jul 05	**BARBIE SUMMER HITS** *Universal TV 9830853*	17		2
23 Jul 05	**KISS PRESENTS HIP HOP CLASSICS** *Universal TV 9829352*	6		3
23 Jul 05	**THE LATINO MIX** *Sony BMG TV/UMTV 9831516*	7		6
3 Sep 05	**RUSH HOUR 3** *Universal TV 9832617*	5		4
10 Sep 05	**SUPER CHARGED** *Universal TV 9832184*	5		4
17 Sep 05	**DANCE PARTY** *Sony BMG TV/UMTV 9830432* ●	1	2	18
17 Sep 05	**MASSIVE R&B – VOLUME 2** *Sony BMG TV/UMTV 9832520*	2		9
24 Sep 05	**FLOORFILLERS 4** *Universal TV 9833058*	4		5
1 Oct 05	**URBAN HEAT** *Universal TV 9832393*	15		2
8 Oct 05	**DEATH ROW PRESENTS A HIP HOP HISTORY** *Universal TV 9874208*	14		4
15 Oct 05	**THE ULTIMATE MOODS AL BUM** *Universal TV 9833957*	12		3
5 Nov 05	**POP PARTY 3** *Sony BMG TV/UMTV 9834305* ●	1	2	19
5 Nov 05	**ESSENTIAL R&B – WINTER 2005** *Sony BMG TV/UMTV 9834804*	2		5
12 Nov 05	**DANCING IN THE STREETS** *Universal TV 9834392*	8		2
12 Nov 05	**TOKYO PROJECT PRESENTS THE COLLECTION** *Universal TV 9834311*	19		1
19 Nov 05	**CLUBLAND 8** *UMTV/AATW 9834546*	2		11
19 Nov 05	**STEVE WRIGHT'S ALL NEW SUNDAY LOVE SONGS** *UMTV/WSM 9834295*	14		3
26 Nov 05	**THE NUMBER ONE CLASSICAL ALBUM 2006** *Sony BMG TV/UCJ 9834883*	3		9
3 Dec 05	**BARBIE GIRLS 2** *Universal TV 9834298*	12		4
10 Dec 05	**NME PRESENTS THE ESSENTIAL BANDS** *EMI/Virgin/Universal 9835761*	5		20
24 Dec 05	**VINTAGE CHEESE** *Universal TV 9829693*	16		1
24 Dec 05	**A CLASSIC CHRISTMAS** *UCJ 4768815*	20		1
7 Jan 06	**MASSIVE DANCE** *UMTV/AATW 9836212*	15		4
7 Jan 06	**THE ULTIMATE PARTY ANIMAL** *Universal TV 9835994*	20		1
4 Feb 06	**THE NUMBER ONE MOZART ALBUM** *UCJ 4769224*	14		2
11 Feb 06	**R&B LOVESONGS** *Sony BMG TV/UMTV 9837262*	1	3	14
18 Feb 06	**THE LOVE SONGS ALBUM** *Universal TV 9836627*	6		2
25 Feb 06	**CLUBMIX 2006** *UMTV/AATW 9837394*	2		8
25 Feb 06	**POP JR 2** *Universal TV 9836764*	5		6
18 Mar 06	**CLUBLAND XTREME HARDCORE 2** *UMTV/AATW 9837866*	1	2	11
25 Mar 06	**YOU RAISE ME UP** *UCJ 9838469*	3		5
25 Mar 06	**NO 1 MUM** *Universal TV 9838555*	6		2
1 Apr 06	**FLOORFILLERS – CLUB CLASSICS** *UMTV/AATW 9838431*	1	2	38
8 Apr 06	**MASSIVE R&B – SPRING COLLECTION 2006** *Sony BMG TV/UMTV 9838361*	2		10
8 Apr 06	**POP PRINCESSES 3** *Sony BMG TV/UMTV 9838378*	6		5
22 Apr 06	**THE WEEKEND VOLUME 2** *UMTV/WMTV 9839407*	5		4
6 May 06	**THE OPERA ALBUM 2006** *UCJ 4769833*	5		4
20 May 06	**80S MOVIE HITS** *UMTV/WMTV 9838867*	4		5
27 May 06	**BIG CLUB HITS** *Universal TV 9839537*	1	3	7
17 Jun 06	**ESSENTIAL R&B – SUMMER 2006** *Sony BMG TV/UMTV 9840755*	4		11
17 Jun 06	**SOCCER AM PRESENTS THE MUSIC** *Universal TV 9840567*	13		2
1 Jul 06	**THE WEDDING DISCO** *Universal TV 9840503*	14		2
8 Jul 06	**CLUBLAND 9** *UMTV/AATW 9841267*	1	4	15
15 Jul 06	**SUMMER HOLIDAY HITS** *Universal TV 9841320*	6		4
5 Aug 06	**BACK 2 HOUSE** *Universal TV 9800781*	7		2
12 Aug 06	**THE SOUND OF THE PIRATES** *Universal TV 9841615*	7		2
26 Aug 06	**SUMMER CLUB HITS** *UMTV/AATW 9842226*	4		5
26 Aug 06	**URBAN WEEKEND** *Universal TV 9839468*	4		8
16 Sep 06	**DANCE MANIA** *UMTV/AATW 9842852* ⊛	1	3	11
23 Sep 06	**THE ANTHEMS** *Universal TV 9842770*	2		17
23 Sep 06	**FUNKY HOUSE '06** *UMTV/AATW 9842849*	8		2
23 Sep 06	**EVERY CLASSICAL TUNE YOU'LL EVER WANT** *UCJ 4428656*	10		3
30 Sep 06	**INTERSCOPE RECORDS PRESENTS CLUB BANGERS** *Interscope/UMTV 9843508*	9		1
14 Oct 06	**ESSENTIAL DANCE HITS – PETE TONG** *Mercury/Universal TV 9843086*	9		2
21 Oct 06	**TWICE AS NICE – THE ULTIMATE URBAN** *Universal TV 9843913*	8		2
28 Oct 06	**R&B DIVAS** *Sony BMG TV/UMTV 9842918*	4		4
28 Oct 06	**MOTOWN – THE ULTIMATE COLLECTION** *Universal TV 9844147*	7		5
4 Nov 06	**POP PARTY 4** *Sony BMG TV/UMTV 9843824*	1	1	14
18 Nov 06	**CLUBLAND 10** *UMTV/AATW 9844765*	1	1	12
18 Nov 06	**ULTIMATE BOY BANDS** *Universal TV 9839568*	6		13
25 Nov 06	**NME PRESENTS THE ESSENTIAL BANDS** *Universal TV 9844459*	3		15
25 Nov 06	**THE CLASSICAL ALBUM 2007** *Sony BMG TV/UCJ 4428882*	9		7
25 Nov 06	**MASSIVE R&B 4** *Sony BMG TV/UMTV 9844759*	10		2
9 Dec 06	**CLUBMIX 2007** *UMTV/AATW 9844994*	6		9
9 Dec 06	**MY CBEEBIES ALBUM** *UMTV/BBC Music 1717959*	18		2
16 Dec 06	**EMINEM PRESENTS THE RE-UP** *Interscope 1717391* ●	3		8
16 Dec 06	**ESSENTIAL SONGS** *Universal TV 9844991*	9		12
23 Dec 06	**CLUBLAND X-TREME HARDCORE 3** *UMTV/AATW 1720197*	11		6
20 Jan 07	**ULTIMATE NRG 2** *UMTV/AATW 9845943*	5		4
27 Jan 07	**12 INCH 80'S POP** *Universal TV 9845362*	4		4
10 Feb 07	**ONE LOVE** *Universal TV 9846548*	1	2	7
10 Feb 07	**THE NO 1 TCHAIKOVSKY ALBUM** *UCJ 4429000*	18		1
17 Feb 07	**BRITS HITS – THE ALBUM OF THE YEAR** *Universal TV 9846049*	1	2	8
17 Feb 07	**R&B CLUBMIX** *Sony BMG TV/UMTV 9846555*	5		5
24 Feb 07	**CLUB 2K7** *UMTV/AATW 9846751*	4		3
10 Mar 07	**HIP HOP CLASSICS** *Universal TV 9847360*	2		12
17 Mar 07	**TO MUM WITH LOVE** *Universal TV 9847544*	1	1	3
17 Mar 07	**ULTIMATE GIRL GROUPS** *Universal TV 9847328*	7		4
17 Mar 07	**YOU'RE BEAUTIFUL – 40 INSPIRING SONGS** *UCJ 9800857*	8		3
24 Mar 07	**FLOORFILLERS ANTHEMS** *UMTV/AATW 9847836*	1	2	15
24 Mar 07	**CELTIC DREAMS** *UCJ 9847031*	14		2
7 Apr 07	**PLAY IT LOUD** *Universal TV 9848405*	2		14
28 Apr 07	**ESSENTIAL SONGS – SPRING COLLECTION** *Universal TV 9848700*	3		6
12 May 07	**POP HITS – CLASS OF 2007** *EMI TV/UMTV 9849127*	4		5
12 May 07	**BIG NIGHT OUT** *Universal TV 9848654*	5		4
12 May 07	**THE NUMBER ONE OPERA ALBUM 2007** *UCJ 4429418*	17		1
26 May 07	**MASSIVE R&B – SPRING COLLECTION 2007** *Universal TV 9849590*	1	2	11
26 May 07	**THE BEST DISCO IN TOWN** *Universal TV 9849586*	3		9
9 Jun 07	**90S ANTHEMS** *Universal TV 5300215*	9		3
16 Jun 07	**OVER THE RAINBOW** *UCJ 9849972*	1	1	5
16 Jun 07	**DAD'S ANTHEMS** *UCJ 9849607*	9		2
23 Jun 07	**NME PRESENTS THE ESSENTIAL BANDS – FESTIVAL** *Universal TV 9849883*	3		4
23 Jun 07	**CLASSIC SCHOOL OF ROCK** *Universal TV 5300455*	15		1
30 Jun 07	**CLUBLAND 11** *UMTV/AATW 5300654*	1	3	9
7 Jul 07	**TWICE AS NICE – URBAN ANTHEMS** *Universal TV 5300942*	2		3
7 Jul 07	**THE VERY BEST OF LATIN JAZZ** *UCJ 5300366*	10		4
21 Jul 07	**R&B LOVE COLLECTION** *Universal TV 5301507*	1	2	14
28 Jul 07	**MY SONGS** *Universal TV 5301517*	3		26
4 Aug 07	**CLUB 80'S** *Sony BMG TV/UMTV 9849006*	4		13
11 Aug 07	**DANCE MANIA 2 – THE ULTIMATE CLUB PARTY** *UMTV/AATW 5301501*	4		5
18 Aug 07	**BIG SUMMER TUNES** *Universal TV 600753021927*	14		3
1 Sep 07	**7 INCH HEROES – THE ORIGINAL 45S** *UMTV 5302421*	14		2
15 Sep 07	**THE ANTHEMS 07** *UMTV 5302966*	5		6
22 Sep 07	**CLASSIC FM – AS HEARD ON TV** *UCJ 4429969*	9		4
22 Sep 07	**WORLD IN UNION – RUGBY WORLD CUP 2007** *UCJ 4800087*	10		2
13 Oct 07	**RADIO 1 ESTABLISHED 1967** *UMTV 5302508*	1	3	18
20 Oct 07	**MASSIVE R&B – WINTER 2007** *UMTV 5303523*	3		5
20 Oct 07	**WOMAN – THE COLLECTION 2007** *UMTV 5302513*	6		3
3 Nov 07	**POP PARTY VOLUME 5** *UMTV 5303632*	1	1	17
10 Nov 07	**CLASSIC FM – RELAX** *UCJ 4800249*	15		3
17 Nov 07	**CLUBLAND 12** *UMTV/AATW 5304593*	1	1	11
17 Nov 07	**DREAMBOATS AND PETTICOATS** *UCJ 5304248*	2		32
24 Nov 07	**R&B COLLABORATIONS** *Universal 5304989*	10		2
24 Nov 07	**CLUBMIX CLASSICS** *UMTV 5304953*	14		1
24 Nov 07	**MOTOWN GOLD 70S** *Universal 5304235*	17		2
1 Dec 07	**ULTIMATE LOVE COLLECTION** *UMTV 5305013*	14		1
1 Dec 07	**ESSENTIAL NME BANDS** *Universal 5304269*	19		1
8 Dec 07	**R&B – THE COLLECTION 2007** *UMTV 5303761*	7		9
8 Dec 07	**THE NUMBER ONE CLASSICAL ALBUM 2008** *UCJ 4800357*	10		8
15 Dec 07	**CLUBLAND X-TREME HARDCORE 4** *UMTV/AATW 1755809*	7		6
22 Dec 07	**BRATZ GIRLZ** *UMTV/Sony BMG 5305238*	19		2
19 Jan 08	**DANCEMIX 2008** *AATW/UMTV 5305118*	17		2
2 Feb 08	**SONGBIRD 2008** *UCJ 5301165*	6		2
16 Feb 08	**REAL LOVE** *UMTV 8823859*	1	1	2
16 Feb 08	**ULTIMATE NRG 3** *AATW/UMTV 5306330*	1	1	9
16 Feb 08	**LOVE – THE ULTIMATE COLLECTION** *UMTV 5305013*	15		2
23 Feb 08	**BRIT HITS – THE ALBUM OF THE YEAR** *UMTV 5306392*	2		5

Silver-selling ○ · Gold-selling ● · Platinum-selling ⊛ · US No.1 ★ · Peak Position · Weeks at No.1 · Weeks on Chart

Date	Title	Peak Position	Weeks at No.1	Weeks on Chart
1 Mar 08	**YOU RAISE ME UP 2008** *UCJ 5306436*	1	1	4
1 Mar 08	**JUST FOR YOU** *UMTV 5306255*	7		3
1 Mar 08	**CLASSIC FM – MOVIES – THE ULTIMATE COLLECTION** *UCJ 4800680*	12		2
22 Mar 08	**FLOORFILLERS 08** *UMTV 5307136*	1	1	7
22 Mar 08	**MASSIVE R&B SPRING COLLECTION 2008** *UMTV 5306569*	3		9
12 Apr 08	**CLUBLAND CLASSIX – THE ALBUM OF YOUR LIFE** *AATW/UMTV 5307568* ⊛	1	6	19
19 Apr 08	**DANCE PARTY 2** *UMTV 5307224*	7		5
26 Apr 08	**ADDICTED 2 BASSLINE** *AATW/UMTV 5307724* ●	4		9
26 Apr 08	**ESSENTIAL ALBUM** *UMTV 5308069*	11		4
24 May 08	**HERE AND NOW – THE VERY BEST OF THE 80S** *UMTV 5308642*	6		3
31 May 08	**R&B COLLECTION** *UMTV 5308610* ●	2		9
31 May 08	**NEW CLASSIX 2008** *UCJ 5308909*	13		2
14 Jun 08	**DAD'S JUKEBOX** *UMTV 5309453*	4		3
14 Jun 08	**DREAMBOATS AND PETTICOATS PRESENT FOOT TAPPERS** *UCJ 5307592*	6		4
14 Jun 08	**DAD'S ANTHEMS 2008** *UCJ 1772169*	10		2
5 Jul 08	**CLUBLAND 13** *AATW/UMTV 5309758* ●	1	1	11
5 Jul 08	**THE VERY BEST OF SMOOTH JAZZ** *UCJ 5306483*	11		3
12 Jul 08	**R&B LOVE COLLECTION 2008** *UMTV 5309749* ●	2		6
12 Jul 08	**MASSIVE REGGAE** *UMTV 5309986*	3		13
19 Jul 08	**CONNECTED 90'S 12 INCH MIXES** *UMTV 5309765*	11		3
26 Jul 08	**SUNSET TO SUNRISE** *UMTV 5310317*	8		4
9 Aug 08	**MASSIVE WEEKEND** *UMTV 5309461*	5		4
16 Aug 08	**HARDCORE TIL I DIE** *AATW/UMTV 1781171*	3		7
16 Aug 08	**R&B CLASSICS COLLECTION** *UMTV 5311284*	7		5
6 Sep 08	**LIVING FOR THE WEEKEND** *UMTV 5311235*	9		4
13 Sep 08	**THE VERY BEST OF WHILE MY GUITAR GENTLY WEEPS** *UMTV 5309421*	6		8
13 Sep 08	**POP JR TV SONGS** *UMTV 1784373*	17		2
27 Sep 08	**FLOORFILLERS CLUBMIX** *AATW/UMTV 5312200*	2		8
18 Oct 08	**MASSIVE R&B – WINTER 2008** *UMTV 5312775*	1	2	7
8 Nov 08	**POP PARTY 6** *UMTV 5313011* ●	3		5
15 Nov 08	**DREAMBOATS & PETTICOATS 2** *UCJ 5313760* ●	2		4
15 Nov 08	**HIP HOP CLASSICS** *UMTV 5312895*	16		1
22 Nov 08	**CLUBLAND 14** *UMTV/AATW 5314055* ●	1	1	3
29 Nov 08	**TOP GEAR – SUB ZERO DRIVING ANTHEMS** *UMTV 5314031*	13		2
6 Dec 08	**THE CLASSICAL ALBUM 2009** *UCJ 4801711*	19		1

VARIOUS ARTISTS (UNIVERSAL CLASSICS)

Date	Title	Peak Position	Weeks at No.1	Weeks on Chart
6 Jul 02	**THE VERY BEST OF SMOOTH JAZZ** *Universal Classics & Jazz 5834902*	7		20

VARIOUS ARTISTS (UNIVERSE)

Date	Title	Peak Position	Weeks at No.1	Weeks on Chart
15 May 93	**UNIVERSE – WORLD TECHNO TRIBE** *Universe VERSECD 1*	13		2
10 Jun 95	**UNIVERSE PRESENTS THE TRIBAL GATHERING** *Universe 8284522*	19		1
19 Oct 96	**TRIBAL GATHERING '96** *Universe UNV001CD*	15		2

VARIOUS ARTISTS (URBAN)

Date	Title	Peak Position	Weeks at No.1	Weeks on Chart
14 Nov 87	**URBAN CLASSICS** *Urban URBLP 4*	96		1
24 Sep 88	**URBAN ACID** *Urban URBLP 15*	51		8
8 Oct 88	**ACID JAZZ AND OTHER ILLICIT GROOVES** *Urban URBLP 16*	86		3

VARIOUS ARTISTS (V2)

Date	Title	Peak Position	Weeks at No.1	Weeks on Chart
24 May 97	**LOADED LOCK IN** *V2 WR 1000222*	20		1
14 Jun 97	**YOU'LL NEVER WALK ALONE** *V2 WR 1000342*	18		1
23 Oct 04	**THE VERY BEST OF SCHOOLDISCO.COM** *V2TV V2TV1029382*	5		5
18 Dec 04	**ULTIMATE DANCE CRAZE** *V2TV V2TV1030352*	7		4
5 Mar 05	**THE MELODY LINGERS ON** *V2TV V2TV1031392*	5		4
30 Apr 05	**ULTIMATE BALLROOM DANCE CRAZE** *V2TV V2TV1032142*	15		1
18 Jun 05	**SUITED & BOOTED** *V2TV/EMI Virgin V2TV1033702*	4		7
6 Aug 05	**SUMMER HOLIDAY DANCE CRAZE** *V2TV V2TV1034662*	5		8
13 Aug 05	**CLUBBIN'** *V2TV V2TV1033742*	13		2
17 Sep 05	**MY FIRST ALBUM** *V2TV V2TV1034682*	6		12
15 Oct 05	**HANDBAG** *V2TV V2TV1034672*	19		1
10 Dec 05	**MY FIRST CHRISTMAS ALBUM** *V2TV V2TV1035902*	13		2
4 Feb 06	**ULTIMATE R&B DANCE CRZE** *V2TV V2TV1036542*	19		1
29 Jul 06	**MY FIRST NURSERY RHYMES** *V2TV V2TV1041702*	19		2

VARIOUS ARTISTS (V2 TV)

Date	Title	Peak Position	Weeks at No.1	Weeks on Chart
28 Aug 04	**RAVIN'** *V2TV V2TV1028942*	8		6

VARIOUS ARTISTS (VERTIGO)

Date	Title	Peak Position	Weeks at No.1	Weeks on Chart
21 Jun 86	**HEAR 'N' AID** *Vertigo VERH 35*	50		2
27 Aug 88	**HOT CITY NIGHTS** *Vertigo PROVTV 15* ⊛	1	1	14
4 Nov 89	**ROCK CITY NIGHT** *Vertigo RCNTV 1* ●	3		14
28 Sep 91	**THE POWER AND THE GLORY** *Vertigo 5103601* ●	2		9

VARIOUS ARTISTS (VERVE)

Date	Title	Peak Position	Weeks at No.1	Weeks on Chart
7 Sep 02	**CHILLED JAZZ** *Verve 0692092*	14		1
21 Dec 02	**THE JAZZ ALBUM 2003** *Verve 0680672*	13		2
26 Apr 03	**DIVAS OF JAZZ** *Verve 0394222*	12		3

VARIOUS ARTISTS (VIRGIN)

Date	Title	Peak Position	Weeks at No.1	Weeks on Chart
22 Nov 80	**CASH COWS** *Virgin MILK 1*	49		1
17 Apr 82	**MUSIC OF QUALITY AND DISTINCTION (VOLUME 1)** *Virgin V 2219*	25		6
1 Jun 85	**MASSIVE – AN ALBUM OF REGGAE HITS** *Virgin V 2346*	61		3
19 Jan 91	**DANCE ENERGY** *Virgin Television VTDLP 3*	20		2
1 Jun 91	**DANCE ENERGY 2** *Virgin Television VTLP 4*	6		5
19 Oct 91	**MOODS** *Virgin Television VTLP 5* ⊛x2	2		22
30 Nov 91	**DANCE ENERGY 3** *Virgin Television VTLP 6* ○	10		6
29 Feb 92	**THREE MINUTE HEROES** *Virgin Television VTCD 9*	4		10
16 May 92	**MOODS 2** *Virgin Television VTCD 12* ●	3		8
25 Jul 92	**THE GREATEST DANCE ALBUM IN THE WORLD!** *Virgin Television VTCD 13* ●	2		12
31 Oct 92	**NEW ROMANTIC CLASSICS** *Virgin Television VTCD 15* ○	7		5
17 Jul 93	**THE BEST DANCE ALBUM IN THE WORLD…EVER!** *Virgin Television VTDCD 17* ⊛x2	1	4	19
23 Oct 93	**THE SINGER AND THE SONG** *Virgin Television VTDCD 21* ●	5		6
20 Nov 93	**THE BEST DANCE ALBUM IN THE WORLD…EVER! 2** *Virgin Television VTDCD 22* ⊛	3		12
4 Dec 93	**THE BEST CHRISTMAS ALBUM IN THE WORLD…EVER!** *Virgin Television VTDCD 23* ⊛x3	2		10
29 Jan 94	**SWEET SOUL HARMONIES** *Virgin Television VTCD 20* ●	1	1	9
26 Feb 94	**DANCE TO THE MAX** *Virgin Television VTCD 24* ●	2		10
12 Mar 94	**RAP TO THE MAX** *Virgin Television VTCD 25* ○	10		4
30 Apr 94	**IN THE AIR TONIGHT** *Virgin Television VTDCD 26* ○	8		10
7 May 94	**PURE MOODS** *Virgin Television VTCD 28* ⊛x2	1	2	31
28 May 94	**DANCE TO THE MAX 2** *Virgin Television VTCD 29* ●	4		8
4 Jun 94	**THE BEST REGGAE ALBUM IN THE WORLD…EVER!** *Virgin Television VTCD 27* ⊛	4		10
9 Jul 94	**SUPERFUNK** *Virgin Television VTDCD 30* ○	8		5
30 Jul 94	**THE BEST DANCE ALBUM IN THE WORLD…EVER! 3** *Virgin Television VTDCD 32* ●	2		11
20 Aug 94	**SWEET SOUL HARMONIES 2** *Virgin Television VTCD 31* ○	10		2
3 Sep 94	**THE BEST ROCK ALBUM IN THE WORLD…EVER!** *Virgin Television VTDCD 35* ⊛x3	1	3	24
3 Sep 94	**DANCE TO THE MAX 3** *Virgin Television VTCD 33*	12		3
29 Oct 94	**THE BEST ROCK 'N' ROLL ALBUM IN THE WORLD…EVER!** *Virgin Television VTDCD 37* ⊛	2		10
19 Nov 94	**THE LOVE ALBUM** *Virgin Television VTDCD 38* ⊛x3	1	1	23
19 Nov 94	**THE BEST DANCE ALBUM IN THE WORLD…EVER! 4** *Virgin Television VTDCD 40* ●	5		4
4 Feb 95	**THE BEST PUNK ALBUM IN THE WORLD…EVER!** *Virgin Television VTDCD 42* ●	1	1	13
18 Feb 95	**DANCE '95** *Virgin Television VTCD 43* ○	8		5
4 Mar 95	**THE BEST FUNK ALBUM IN THE WORLD…EVER!** *Virgin Television VTDCD 44* ○	11		3
25 Mar 95	**CELTIC MOODS** *Virgin Television VTCD 45* ○	8		2
15 Apr 95	**THE BEST ROCK ALBUM IN THE WORLD…EVER! II** *Virgin Television VTDCD 47* ●	3		8
6 May 95	**STREET SOUL** *Virgin Television VTDCD 41* ●	2		9
10 Jun 95	**DANCE HEAT '95** *Virgin Television VTCD 50* ○	8		3
17 Jun 95	**CELTIC MOODS 2** *Virgin Television VTCD 52*	6		5
15 Jul 95	**THE BEST DANCE ALBUM IN THE WORLD…EVER! 5** *Virgin Television VTCD 55* ●	4		7
15 Jul 95	**THE BLUES ALBUM** *Virgin Television VTDCD 54* ○	8		3
22 Jul 95	**THE BEST SUMMER ALBUM IN THE WORLD…EVER!** *Virgin Television VTCD 57*	1	1	11
29 Jul 95	**SUMMER SWING** *Virgin Television VTDCD 53*	18		1
19 Aug 95	**SERVE CHILLED** *Virgin Television VTCD 56*	16		1
2 Sep 95	**THE BEST ROCK BALLADS ALBUM IN THE WORLD…EVER!** *Virgin Television VTDCD 60* ⊛x2	2		23
2 Sep 95	**THIS IS CULT FICTION** *Virgin Television VTCD 59* ●	9		4
16 Sep 95	**THE BEST. . .ALBUM IN THE WORLD…EVER!** *Virgin Television VTCD 58* ⊛	2		8
21 Oct 95	**THE BEST DANCE ALBUM IN THE WORLD…95!** *Virgin Television VTCD 67* ●	3		4
11 Nov 95	**THE BEST 80'S ALBUM IN THE WORLD…EVER!** *Virgin Television VTCD 68* ●	7		4

○ Silver-selling ● Gold-selling ⊛ Platinum-selling ★ US No.1

Date	Title / Label	Peak Position	Weeks at No.1	Weeks on Chart
18 Nov 95	**THE LOVE ALBUM II** *Virgin Television VTCD 69* ⊛x2	2		16
18 Nov 95	**INSTRUMENTAL MOODS** *Virgin Television VTCD 65* ●	14		5
25 Nov 95	**THE BEST PARTY...EVER!** *Virgin Television VTCD 71* ●	5		8
2 Dec 95	**THE BEST SIXTIES ALBUM IN THE WORLD...EVER!** *Virgin Television VTCD 66* ⊛x2	2		17
10 Feb 96	**THE BEST...ALBUM IN THE WORLD...EVER! 2** *Virgin VTDCD 76* ⊛x2	1	2	12
24 Feb 96	**IN THE MIX 96** *Virgin VTDCD 77* ●	1	4	12
23 Mar 96	**THE BEST RAP ALBUM IN THE WORLD...EVER!** *Virgin VTDCD 75* ●	2		10
13 Apr 96	**THE BEST PUNK ALBUM IN THE WORLD...EVER! 2** *Virgin VTDCD 79* ○	16		2
27 Apr 96	**THE BEST...ALBUM IN THE WORLD...EVER! 3** *Virgin VTDCD 84* ●	2		7
18 May 96	**SHARPE – OVER THE HILLS & FAR AWAY** *Virgin VTCD 81*	14		3
25 May 96	**IN THE MIX 96 – 2** *Virgin VTDCD 85* ●	2		14
1 Jun 96	**THE BEST ROCK ANTHEMS ALBUM IN THE WORLD...EVER!** *Virgin VTDCD 83* ●	8		4
15 Jun 96	**THE BEST SWING ALBUM IN THE WORLD...EVER!** *Virgin VTDCD 86* ●	3		10
15 Jun 96	**SPIRITS OF NATURE** *Virgin VTCD 87* ○	5		5
29 Jun 96	**THE BEST FOOTIE ANTHEMS IN THE WORLD...EVER!** *Virgin VTCD 94* ●	5		5
29 Jun 96	**THE BIG HIT MIX** *Virgin VTCD 96*	16		2
27 Jul 96	**IN THE MIX – 90'S HITS** *Virgin VTDCD 89* ●	3		6
17 Aug 96	**THE BEST DANCE ALBUM IN THE WORLD...EVER! 6** *Virgin VTDCD 91* ⊛	1	1	13
17 Aug 96	**THE BEST JAZZ ALBUM IN THE WORLD...EVER!** *Virgin VTDCD 93* ●	8		5
17 Aug 96	**EVENING SESSION – PRIORITY TUNES** *Virgin VTDCD 93*	11		4
21 Sep 96	**THIS IS THE RETURN OF CULT FICTION** *Virgin VTCD 112*	15		3
28 Sep 96	**THE BEST OF MASTERCUTS** *Virgin VTDCD 101*	11		3
12 Oct 96	**IN THE MIX 96 – 3** *Virgin VTDCD 97* ●	1	1	6
12 Oct 96	**WIPEOUT 2097: THE SOUNDTRACK** *Virgin CDV 2815*	16		1
26 Oct 96	**THE BEST...ALBUM IN THE WORLD...EVER! 4** *Virgin VTDCD 96*	2		6
9 Nov 96	**THE BEST OPERA ALBUM IN THE WORLD...EVER!** *Virgin VTDCD 100* ●	10		10
9 Nov 96	**THE BEST IRISH ALBUM IN THE WORLD...EVER!** *Virgin VTDCD 102* ●	11		9
16 Nov 96	**THE LOVE ALBUM III** *Virgin VTDCD 104* ⊛	2		13
23 Nov 96	**THE BEST SIXTIES ALBUM IN THE WORLD...EVER! II** *Virgin VTDCD 106* ⊛x2	2		15
23 Nov 96	**THE BEST MIX ALBUM IN THE WORLD...EVER!** *Virgin VTDCD 108*	9		3
30 Nov 96	**THE BEST CHRISTMAS ALBUM IN THE WORLD...EVER!** *Virgin VTDCD 103* ⊛x3	2		19
14 Dec 96	**SMASH HITS MIX '97** *Virgin VTDCD 110* ●	8		7
8 Feb 97	**IN THE MIX 97** *Virgin VTDCD 116* ●	1	1	11
15 Feb 97	**THE SOUL ALBUM** *Virgin VTDCD 115* ●	1	1	11
22 Mar 97	**THE BEST...ALBUM IN THE WORLD...EVER! 5** *Virgin/EMI VTDCD 120* ●	1	1	7
29 Mar 97	**GORGEOUS** *Virgin VTDCD 121* ●	2		7
26 Apr 97	**IN THE MIX 97 – 2** *Virgin/EMI VTDCD 132* ●	2		7
17 May 97	**SPICE GIRLS PRESENT THE BEST GIRL POWER ALBUM IN THE WORLD...EVER!** *Virgin/EMI VTDCD 123* ●	2		9
24 May 97	**BIG MIX '97** *Warner/Virgin/EMI VTDCD 130* ●	1	2	7
24 May 97	**ELECTRONICA (FULL-ON BIG BEATS)** *Virgin/EMI VTDCD 131* ●	11		3
7 Jun 97	**SMASH HITS – SUMMER '97** *Virgin/EMI VTDCD 144* ●	1	1	8
14 Jun 97	**THE BEST CLUB ANTHEMS IN THE WORLD...EVER!** *Virgin/EMI VTDCD 124* ●	1	4	9
21 Jun 97	**THE BEST SCOTTISH ALBUM IN THE WORLD...EVER!** *Virgin/EMI VTDCD 137* ●	9		6
5 Jul 97	**THE BEST SUMMER ALBUM IN THE WORLD...EVER!** *Virgin/EMI VTDCD 140* ●	3		9
12 Jul 97	**THE BEST DISCO ALBUM IN THE WORLD** *Virgin/EMI VTDCD 143* ●	1	2	15
19 Jul 97	**THE BEST...ALBUM IN THE WORLD...EVER! 6** *Virgin/EMI VTDCD 136* ●	8		4
2 Aug 97	**IN THE MIX 97 – 3** *Virgin/EMI VTDCD 135* ●	2		6
16 Aug 97	**THE BEST DANCE ALBUM IN THE WORLD...EVER! 7** *Virgin/EMI VTDCD 138* ●	2		11
16 Aug 97	**THE BEST LATINO CARNIVAL IN THE WORLD...EVER!** *Virgin/EMI VTDCD 152* ●	5		6
30 Aug 97	**CAFÉ MAMBO** *Virgin/EMI VTDCD 150*	17		2
6 Sep 97	**MORE! GIRLS' NIGHT OUT** *Virgin/EMI VTDCD 149* ○	10		3
20 Sep 97	**CLUB HITS 97/98: SOUNDTRACK TO A SEASON** *Virgin/EMI VTDCD 167* ○	5		7
11 Oct 97	**BIG MIX '97 – VOLUME 2** *Virgin/EMI/warner.esp VTDCD 172* ●	1	1	5
25 Oct 97	**THE BEST...ANTHEMS...EVER!** *Virgin/EMI VTDCD 154*	1	1	10
8 Nov 97	**THE MOST RELAXING CLASSICAL ALBUM IN THE WORLD...EVER!** *Virgin/EMI VTDCD 155* ⊛	10		16
15 Nov 97	**THE LOVE ALBUM IV** *Virgin/EMI VTDCD 156* ⊛	11		9
22 Nov 97	**THE BEST SIXTIES ALBUM IN THE WORLD...EVER! III** *Virgin/EMI VTDCD 160* ⊛	3		12
22 Nov 97	**THE BEST SEVENTIES ALBUM IN THE WORLD...EVER!** *Virgin/EMI VTDCD 157* ●	13		9
22 Nov 97	**NEW PURE MOODS** *Virgin/EMI VTDCD 158* ●	16		3
29 Nov 97	**THE BEST ROCK BALLADS ALBUM IN THE WORLD...EVER! II** *Virgin/EMI VTDCD 159* ●	7		11
6 Dec 97	**THE BEST CLUB ANTHEMS IN THE WORLD...EVER! 2** *Virgin/EMI VTDCD 169* ●	6		11
6 Dec 97	**THE BEST PARTY IN THE WORLD...EVER!** *Virgin/EMI VTDCD 161* ●	7		6
13 Dec 97	**SMASH HITS '98** *Virgin/EMI VTDCD 164* ●	9		7
10 Jan 98	**MAXIMUM SPEED** *Virgin/EMI VTDCD 173* ○	3		6
7 Feb 98	**THE SOUL ALBUM II** *Virgin/EMI VTDCD 165* ●	3		8
14 Feb 98	**IN THE MIX 98** *Virgin/EMI VTDCD 174* ●	1	1	7
7 Mar 98	**CARIBBEAN UNCOVERED** *Virgin/EMI VTDCD 175* ○	10		5
21 Mar 98	**SUPERWOMAN** *Virgin/EMI VTDCD 179* ●	2		7
4 Apr 98	**CLUB NATION** *Virgin/EMI VTDCD 180* ●	3		6
18 Apr 98	**THE BEST...ANTHEMS...EVER! 2** *Virgin/EMI VTDCD 183* ●	3		10
25 Apr 98	**THE BEST HIP HOP ANTHEMZ IN THE WORLD...EVER!** *Virgin/EMI VTDCD 184* ○	6		5
2 May 98	**R.I.P. PRESENTS THE REAL SOUND OF UNDERGROUND** *Virgin/EMI VTDCDX 178*	18		2
16 May 98	**THE BEST CLUB ANTHEMS IN THE WORLD...EVER! III** *Virgin/EMI VTDCD 187* ●	3		6
30 May 98	**SMASH HITS – SUMMER '98** *Virgin/EMI VTDCD 186* ●	2		6
30 May 98	**THE BEST DISCO ALBUM IN THE WORLD...EVER! 2** *Virgin/EMI VTDCD 191* ●	7		5
27 Jun 98	**THE BEST SIXTIES SUMMER ALBUM IN THE WORLD...EVER!** *Virgin/EMI VTDCD 200* ●	2		11
27 Jun 98	**ALL NEW – THE BEST FOOTIE ANTHEMS IN THE WORLD...EVER!** *Virgin/EMI VTCD 193* ⊛	6		3
4 Jul 98	**IN THE MIX 98 – 2** *Virgin/EMI VTDCD 195* ●	6		4
11 Jul 98	**THE BEST SUMMER PARTY ALBUM IN THE WORLD...EVER!** *Virgin/EMI VTDCD 194* ●	6		6
18 Jul 98	**THE BEST ALBUM...IN THE WORLD...EVER! 7** *Virgin/EMI VTDCD 204*	11		3
25 Jul 98	**THE BEST DANCE ALBUM IN THE WORLD...EVER! 8** *Virgin/EMI VSCDT 196* ●	2		9
15 Aug 98	**THE BEST RAVE ANTHEMS IN THE WORLD...EVER!** *Virgin/EMI VTDCD 203*	11		3
5 Sep 98	**WORLD MOODS** *Virgin/EMI VTDCD 201*	17		2
24 Oct 98	**IN THE MIX IBIZA** *Virgin/EMI VTDCD 228* ●	1	1	4
31 Oct 98	**THE BEST CHART HITS ALBUM IN THE WORLD...EVER!** *Virgin/EMI VTDCD 225* ●	1	1	5
7 Nov 98	**CLUB NATION 2** *Virgin/EMI VTCDC 227*	8		2
7 Nov 98	**THE MOST RELAXING CLASSICAL ALBUM IN THE WORLD...EVER! II** *Virgin/EMI VTDCD 207* ●	12		9
14 Nov 98	**THE VERY BEST OF THE LOVE ALBUM** *Virgin/EMI VTDCD 213* ⊛	3		18
14 Nov 98	**THE BEST COUNTRY BALLADS IN THE WORLD...EVER!** *Virgin/EMI VTDCD 211* ●	14		3
14 Nov 98	**THE BEST...ANTHEMS...EVER! 3** *Virgin/EMI VTDCD 210* ○	19		1
21 Nov 98	**THE BEST ROCK ANTHEMS...EVER!** *Virgin/EMI VTDCD 215* ●	10		2
21 Nov 98	**THE BEST SIXTIES ALBUM IN THE WORLD...EVER! IV** *Virgin/EMI VTDCD 216* ●	11		7
28 Nov 98	**CREAM ANTHEMS MIXED BY TALL PAUL AND SEB FONTAINE** *Virgin/EMI VTDCDX 229* ○	15		1
28 Nov 98	**BIGGEST 80'S HITS IN THE WORLD...EVER!** *Virgin/EMI VTDCD 218* ●	16		2
26 Dec 98	**SMASH HITS '99!** *Virgin/EMI VTDCD 223*	10		4
23 Jan 99	**THE BEST CLUB ANTHEMS 99 IN THE WORLD...EVER!** *Virgin/EMI VTDCD 221* ●	1	1	11
13 Feb 99	**THE BEST SIXTIES LOVE ALBUM...EVER!** *Virgin/EMI VTDCD 235* ●	2		6
27 Feb 99	**THE BEST CHART HITS IN THE WORLD...EVER! 99** *Virgin/EMI VTDCD 238*	5		4
6 Mar 99	**DISCO: 1999** *Virgin/EMI VTDCD 239*	13		2
13 Mar 99	**IN THE MIX 2000** *Virgin/EMI VTDCD 240* ○	3		4
13 Mar 99	**THE '80S LOVE ALBUM** *Virgin/EMI VTDCD 241* ○	6		4
27 Mar 99	**RESIDENT – 2 YEARS OF OAKENFOLD AT CREAM** *Virgin/EMI VTDCD 237* ○	2		6
10 Apr 99	**MAXIMUM SPEED 99** *Virgin/EMI VTDCD 242*	13		4
8 May 99	**THE BEST HOUSE ANTHEMS...EVER!** *Virgin/EMI VTDCD 245* ○	5		4
15 May 99	**TRANCEFORMER** *Virgin/EMI VTDCDX 256* ○	3		5
29 May 99	**21ST CENTURY ROCK** *Virgin/EMI VTDCD 247*	9		3
5 Jun 99	**SMASH HITS – SUMMER '99** *Virgin/EMI VTDCD 246* ○	3		5
12 Jun 99	**CREAM IBIZA – ARRIVALS** *Virgin/EMI VTDCD 249* ●	2		7
10 Jul 99	**THE BEST TRANCE ANTHEMS...EVER!** *Virgin/EMI VTDCD 261* ○	7		4
24 Jul 99	**THE BEST DANCE ALBUM IN THE WORLD...EVER! 9** *Virgin/EMI VTDCD 251* ●	1	1	9
7 Aug 99	**THE BEST IBIZA ANTHEMS...EVER!** *Virgin/EMI VTDCDX 254* ⊛	2		11
28 Aug 99	**NEW WOMAN** *Virgin/EMI VTDCD 248* ●	14		4
4 Sep 99	**CLUB ANTHEMS 99** *Virgin/EMI VTDCD 281* ○	4		4

Date	Title / Label	Award	Peak Position	Weeks at No.1	Weeks on Chart
18 Sep 99	**CREAM IBIZA – DEPARTURES** *Virgin/EMI VTDCDX 266*		13		2
18 Sep 99	**THE VERY BEST OF CLASSICAL EXPERIENCE** *Virgin/EMI VTDCD 252*		18		1
25 Sep 99	**TRANCEMIX 99 – A SPRITUA; JOURNEY THROUGH TIME AND SPACE** *Virgin/EMI VTDCDX 282*		8		3
16 Oct 99	**THE CHILLOUT MIX** *Virgin/EMI VTDCDX 283*		7		4
23 Oct 99	**THE BEST PEPSI CHART ALBUM IN THE WORLD…EVER!** *Virgin/EMI VTDCD 268*	Silver	2		4
6 Nov 99	**THE BEST CLASSICAL ALBUM OF THE MILLENNIUM…EVER!** *Virgin/EMI VTDCDX 269*	Gold	10		3
20 Nov 99	**THE BEST LOVESONGS…EVER!** *Virgin/EMI VTDCDX 274*	Gold	11		14
27 Nov 99	**CREAM ANTHEMS 2000** *Virgin/EMI VTDCD 272*	Platinum	2		13
27 Nov 99	**THE SIXTIES** *Virgin/EMI VTDCDX 270*	Gold	16		2
4 Dec 99	**THE BEST… AND FRIENDS ALBUM IN THE WORLD…EVER!** *Virgin/EMI VTDCD 286*	Gold	8		12
4 Dec 99	**THE BEST MILLENNIUM PARTY…EVER!** *Virgin/EMI VTDCD 278*	Gold	11		5
11 Dec 99	**THE BEST CLUB ANTHEMS 2000…EVER!** *Virgin/EMI VTDCD 271*	Gold	8		10
11 Dec 99	**THE BEST MUSICALS ALBUM IN THE WORLD…EVER!** *Virgin/EMI VTDCD 277*	Gold	12		7
25 Dec 99	**SMASH HITS 2000** *Virgin/EMI VTDCD 279*	Gold	8		7
26 Feb 00	**BEST DANCE ALBUM IN THE WORLD EVER! 2000** *Virgin/EMI VTDCD 291*	Gold	4		5
18 Mar 00	**BEST PEPSI CHART ALBUM. . .EVER! 2000** *Virgin/EMI VTDCD 300*	Gold	7		4
18 Mar 00	**IN THE MIX 2000** *Virgin/EMI VTDCD 290*	Silver	11		3
18 Mar 00	**NUKLEUZ PRESENTS HARDHOUSE ANTHEMS** *Virgin/EMI VTDCDX 293*		14		3
25 Mar 00	**UNDERGROUND EXPLOSION – THE REAL GARAGE MIX** *Virgin/EMI VTDCDX 299*		10		4
1 Apr 00	**NEW WOMAN 2000** *Virgin/EMI VTDCD 289*	Gold	1	1	7
1 Apr 00	**MELTDOWN 2000 – BEST NEW TRANCE** *Virgin VTDCDX 301*	Silver	6		4
15 Apr 00	**BEST JAZZ ALBUM IN THE WORLD…EVER! VOLUME 2** *Virgin VTDCD 294*	Silver	11		3
22 Apr 00	**GIRLS 2K** *Virgin/EMI VTDCD 303*	Silver	1	1	5
29 Apr 00	**CREAM LIVE** *Virgin VTDCDX 304*	Silver	2		8
13 May 00	**THE BEST TV ADS…EVER!** *Virgin/EMI VTCDX 306*	Silver	10		4
3 Jun 00	**THE BEST CLUB ANTHEMS…EVER! 2K** *Virgin/EMI VTDCD 297*	Gold	2		7
17 Jun 00	**THE BEST SUMMER HOLIDAY EVER** *Virgin/EMI VTDCD 307*		6		9
17 Jun 00	**BEST FOOTIE ANTHEMS EVER** *Virgin/EMI VTDCD 310*		7		3
17 Jun 00	**THE BEST EASY ALBUM EVER** *Virgin/EMI VTDCD 296*	Silver	12		4
24 Jun 00	**THE BEST PUB JUKEBOX IN THE WORLD EVER** *Virgin/EMI VTDCD 308*	Gold	9		8
1 Jul 00	**CREAM IBIZA ARRIVALS** *Virgin/EMI VTDCDX 311*	Silver	4		5
1 Jul 00	**NUKLEUZ PRESENTS HARDHOUSE ANTHEMS VOL.2** *Virgin/EMI VTDCD 314*		16		2
22 Jul 00	**SMASH HITS SUMMER 2000** *Virgin/EMI VTDCD 315*		3		7
29 Jul 00	**CREAM RESIDENT – SEB FONTAINE** *Virgin/EMI VTDCDX 318*		18		2
12 Aug 00	**BEST IBIZA ANTHEMS EVER 2K** *Virgin/EMI VTDCDX 321*	Gold	2		8
19 Aug 00	**NEW WOMAN SUMMER 2000** *Virgin/EMI VTDCD 322*	Gold	5		5
2 Sep 00	**BEST DANCE ALBUM IN THE WORLD EVER – 10** *Virgin/EMI VTDCD 317*	Gold	3		6
9 Sep 00	**CREAMFIELDS** *Virgin/EMI VTDCDX 351*	Silver	5		4
9 Sep 00	**THE BEST PROMS ALBUM IN THE WORLD EVER!** *Virgin/EMI VTDCD 232*		19		3
23 Sep 00	**IBIZA UNCOVERED II** *Virgin/EMI VTDCD 324*	Silver	5		6
30 Sep 00	**THE BEST GARAGE ANTHEMS EVER** *Virgin/EMI VTDCD 325*	Silver	8		5
30 Sep 00	**YOUNG GUNS GO FOR IT** *Virgin/EMI VTDCD 346*	Silver	10		4
7 Oct 00	**PEPSI CHART 2001** *Virgin/EMI VTDCD 331*	Gold	2		8
7 Oct 00	**NUKLEUS PTS – HARDHOUSE ANTHEMS 3** *Virgin/EMI VTCDX 354*		13		4
4 Nov 00	**NOW DANCE 2001** *Virgin/EMI VTDCD 349*	Platinum	1	1	13
18 Nov 00	**DECADES – STORY OF THE 60'S/70'S/80'S** *Virgin/EMI VTDCDX 337*	Silver	13		2
25 Nov 00	**CREAM ANTHEMS 2001** *Virgin/EMI VTDCDX 338*	Platinum	1	1	12
25 Nov 00	**THE NEW LOVE ALBUM** *Virgin/EMI VTDCDX 339*	Platinum	7		13
25 Nov 00	**THE BEST AND FRIENDS ALBUM IN THE WORLD** *Virgin/EMI VTDCDX 333*	Silver	20		1
9 Dec 00	**THE BEST CHRISTMAS ALBUM IN THE WORLD EVER** *Virgin/EMI VTDCD 347*	Platinum	4		17
9 Dec 00	**THE BEST CLUB ANTHEMS 2001 EVER** *Virgin/EMI VTDCD 342*	Gold	14		6
16 Dec 00	**SMASH HITS 2001** *Virgin/EMI VTDCD 345*	Gold	20		7
6 Jan 01	**THE BEST PARTY IN TOWN EVER** *Virgin/EMI VTDCD 341*	Gold	19		1
27 Jan 01	**NUKLEUZ PRESENTS BIG ROOM DJS** *Virgin/EMI VTDCDX 358*		6		3
17 Feb 01	**DANCE MASTERS** *Virgin/EMI VTDCD 359*		4		5
17 Feb 01	**I LOVE 80'S** *Virgin/EMI VTDCD 361*		5		10
24 Feb 01	**A FRENCH AFFAIR** *Virgin/EMI VTDCD 356*		19		1
3 Mar 01	**THE NEW PEPSI CHART ALBUM** *Virgin/EMI VTDCD 362*	Gold	2		7
3 Mar 01	**NUKLEUZ PRESENTS HARDHOUSE ANTHEMS 2001** *Virgin/EMI VTDCDX 364*		13		2
24 Mar 01	**NEW WOMAN 2001** *Virgin/EMI VTDCD 365*	Gold	1	1	8
31 Mar 01	**NOW DANCE 2001 PART 2** *Virgin/EMI VTDCD 368*	Gold	2		6
14 Apr 01	**CREAM LIVE** *Virgin/EMI VTDCDX 369*		5		8
28 Apr 01	**THE ALBUM** *Virgin/EMI VTDCD 380*	Platinum	3		11
12 May 01	**THE BEST HARD HOUSE EVER** *Virgin/EMI VTDCD 370*		10		3
19 May 01	**THE BEST NORTHERN SOUL ALL-NIGHTER EVER** *Virgin/EMI VTDCD 377*		17		2
26 May 01	**CLUBBED OUT** *Virgin/EMI VTDCDX 381*		5		4
2 Jun 01	**I LOVE 70'S** *Virgin/EMI VTDCD 372*		9		3
9 Jun 01	**I LOVE IBIZA** *Virgin/EMI VTDCD 374*	Silver	10		3
23 Jun 01	**CAPITAL GOLD LEGENDS** *Virgin/EMI VTDCD 382*	Platinum	1	7	20
7 Jul 01	**THE BEST SUMMER HOLIDAY 2001 EVER** *Virgin/EMI VTDCD 390*	Gold	2		8
14 Jul 01	**THE CHILLOUT** *Virgin/EMI VTDCD 388*		19		1
21 Jul 01	**BEST DANCE ALBUM IN THE WORLD EVER 11** *Virgin/EMI VTDCD 386*	Silver	4		4
28 Jul 01	**UNBELIEVABLE** *Virgin/EMI VTDCD 389*	Silver	3		6
28 Jul 01	**UNCOVERED** *Virgin/EMI VTDCD 384*		10		2
18 Aug 01	**THE BEST IBIZA ANTHEMS EVER 2001** *Virgin/EMI VTDCD 391*	Silver	5		4
1 Sep 01	**CREAM IBIZA** *Virgin/EMI VTDCX 376*		7		3
1 Sep 01	**THE BEST CARNIVAL ALBUM EVER** *Virgin/EMI VTDCD 411*		11		2
22 Sep 01	**CLASSICAL CHILLOUT** *Virgin/EMI VTDCD 408*	Platinum	4		19
6 Oct 01	**I LOVE 90S** *Virgin/EMI VTDCD 410*		11		3
13 Oct 01	**IT'S A GIRL THING** *Virgin/EMI VTDCD 385*	Gold	4		5
20 Oct 01	**PEPSI CHART 2002** *Virgin/EMI VTDCD 414*	Platinum	1	2	7
20 Oct 01	**Q ANTHEMS** *Universal/Virgin/EMI VTDCD 409*		10		2
27 Oct 01	**MIXMAG PRESENTS BIG TUNES** *Virgin/EMI VTDCD 412*		12		1
3 Nov 01	**NOW DANCE 2002** *Virgin/EMI VTDCD 393*	Gold	1	3	5
17 Nov 01	**CAPITAL GOLD LEGENDS II** *Virgin/EMI VTDCD 418*	Platinum	2		13
17 Nov 01	**THE OPERA ALBUM 2002** *Virgin/EMI VTDCD 417*	Gold	7		6
24 Nov 01	**NEW WOMAN – LOVE SONGS** *Virgin/EMI VTDCD 419*	Gold	14		2
24 Nov 01	**CREAM ANTHEMS 2002** *Virgin/EMI VTDCDX 400*		18		1
8 Dec 01	**PURE CHILLOUT** *Virgin/EMI VTDCD 420*	Gold	10		11
15 Dec 01	**I LOVE 2 PARTY** *Virgin/EMI VTDCD 421*	Gold	2		6
12 Jan 02	**THE ALBUM 2** *Virgin/EMI VTDCD 394*	Gold	20		1
9 Feb 02	**BEST CLUB ANTHEMS 2002** *Virgin/EMI VTDCD 401*	Silver	1	1	5
16 Feb 02	**THE LOVE ALBUM CLASSICS** *Virgin/EMI VTDCDX 435*	Gold	2		3
16 Feb 02	**CLASSICAL CHILLOUT 2** *Virgin/EMI VTDCD 437*	Silver	10		3
23 Feb 02	**NEW PEPSI CHART 2002** *Virgin/EMI VTDCD 348*	Silver	2		5
9 Mar 02	**UNBELIEVABLE TOO** *Virgin/EMI VTDCD 436*		20		1
16 Mar 02	**NEW WOMAN 2002** *Virgin/EMI VTDCD 438*	Gold	1	1	3
16 Mar 02	**NOW DANCE 2002 PART 2** *Virgin/EMI VTDCD 439*	Gold	3		6
23 Mar 02	**PURE CELTIC CHILLOUT** *Virgin/EMI VTDCD 443*		11		1
30 Mar 02	**CAPITAL GOLD LEGENDS III** *Virgin/EMI VTDCD 440*	Gold	2		6
13 Apr 02	**LADY SINGS THE BLUES** *Virgin/EMI VTDCD 426*		8		6
20 Apr 02	**CREAM ANTHEMS SPRING 2002** *Virgin/EMI VTDCDX 442*		3		6
4 May 02	**ELECTRIC DREAMS** *Virgin/EMI VTDCD 447*		7		4
11 May 02	**THE ALBUM 3** *Virgin/EMI VTDCD 441*	Silver	3		4
18 May 02	**FUTURE TRANCE** *Virgin/EMI VTDCDX 453*		3		5
1 Jun 02	**BEST UNOFFICIAL FOOTIE ANTHEMS EVER!** *Virgin/EMI VTCDX 310*		3		5
8 Jun 02	**PUNK – THE JUBILEE** *Virgin/EMI VTDCD 452*		12		3
15 Jun 02	**BEST OF BRITISH** *Virgin/EMI VTDCD 302*		2		6
22 Jun 02	**CAPITAL GOLD ROCK LEGENDS** *Virgin/EMI VTDCD 458*	Gold	1	1	6
29 Jun 02	**CREAM BEACH 2002** *Virgin/EMI VTDCDX 464*		8		2
6 Jul 02	**PARTY AT THE PALACE** *Universal TV/Virgin/EMI VTCDX 463*		6		3
13 Jul 02	**THE BEST DANCE ALBUM EVER 2002** *Universal TV/Virgin/EMI VTDCD 476*		3		6
20 Jul 02	**THE BEST SIXTIES SUMMER PARTY EVER** *Universal TV/Virgin/EMI VTDCD 471*		6		5
27 Jul 02	**I LOVE SUMMER** *Universal TV/Virgin/EMI VTDCD 469*		7		2
3 Aug 02	**THE BEST CLUB ANTHEMS SUMMER 2002** *Universal TV/Virgin/EMI VTDCD 467*	Gold	3		6
24 Aug 02	**TRANCE MASTERS** *Virgin/EMI VTDCD 495*	Gold	4		5
24 Aug 02	**FUTURE CHILL** *Virgin/EMI VTDCDX 472*		18		1
31 Aug 02	**HOLIDAY HITS – NON STOP EURO POP** *Virgin/EMI VTDCD 494*	Silver	8		3
14 Sep 02	**THE ALBUM 4** *Virgin/EMI VTDCD 481*	Gold	3		6
21 Sep 02	**FUTURE TRANCE IBIZA** *Virgin/EMI VTDCDX 507*		17		1
5 Oct 02	**RETRO DANCE MASTERS** *Virgin/EMI VTDCD 506*		10		2
12 Oct 02	**NEW WOMAN – THE AUTUMN COLLECTION** *Virgin/EMI VTDCD 475*	Silver	1	1	6
26 Oct 02	**NOW DANCE 2003** *Virgin/EMI VTDCD 479*	Gold	1	1	5
26 Oct 02	**LADY SINGS THE BLUES – NIGHT & DAY** *Virgin/EMI VTDCD 499*		11		2
9 Nov 02	**COUNTRY LEGENDS** *Virgin/EMI VTDCD 480*	Platinum	2		13
9 Nov 02	**PEPSI CHART 2003** *Virgin/EMI VTDCD 478*	Gold	5		3
16 Nov 02	**CAPITAL GOLD SIXTIES LEGENDS** *Virgin/EMI VTDCD 485*	Platinum	8		9
16 Nov 02	**THE BEST BANDS EVER** *Virgin/EMI VTDCD 508*	Gold	9		3
16 Nov 02	**CLASSICAL LEGENDS** *Virgin/EMI VTDCD 489*	Silver	18		1
7 Dec 02	**CAPITAL GOLD EIGHTIES LEGENDS** *Virgin/EMI VTDCD 496*	Gold	11		7
28 Dec 02	**I LOVE 2 PARTY 2003** *Virgin/EMI VTDCD 483*	Gold	11		3
4 Jan 03	**BEST CLUB ANTHEMS 2003** *Virgin/EMI VTDCD 498*	Gold	17		1
8 Feb 03	**I LOVE U** *Virgin/EMI VTDCDX 493*	Gold	2		4
15 Feb 03	**THE BEST ONE HIT WONDERS IN THE WORLD** *Virgin/EMI VTDCD 497*	Silver	11		5

Silver-selling · Gold-selling · Platinum-selling · US No.1 · Peak Position · Weeks at No.1 · Weeks on Chart

Date	Title / Label	Peak Position	Weeks at No.1	Weeks on Chart
8 Mar 03	**SCOTLAND ROCKS** *Virgin/EMI VTDCD 516*	20		1
15 Mar 03	**LIVE FOREVER – THE BEST OF BRITPOP** *Virgin/EMI VTDCD 512*	7		3
22 Mar 03	**FUTURE TRANCE 2003** *Virgin VTDCD 518*	11		2
29 Mar 03	**SUPER 70'S** *Virgin/EMI VTDCD 513*	5		9
29 Mar 03	**CAPITAL GOLD SOUL LEGENDS** *Virgin/EMI VTDCD 517*	6		4
5 Apr 03	**NEW WOMAN 2003** *Virgin/EMI VTDCD 514*	2		5
12 Apr 03	**NOW DANCE 2003 PART 2** *Virgin/EMI VTDCD 515*	5		5
19 Apr 03	**THE X LIST** *Virgin/EMI VTDCD 520*	9		2
19 Apr 03	**THE VERY BEST OF CLASSICAL CHILLOUT** *Virgin/EMI VTDCD 524*	15		1
26 Apr 03	**CAPITAL GOLD BRITISH LEGENDS** *Virgin /EMI VTDCD 519*	7		5
10 May 03	**SMASH HITS – THE REUNION** *Virgin/EMI VTDCD 523*	4		5
24 May 03	**CLASSICAL HEARTBREAKERS** *Virgin/EMI VTDCD 522*	19		2
31 May 03	**UP ALL NIGHT** *Virgin/EMI/Universal VTDCD 529*	5		3
14 Jun 03	**POWER BALLADS** *Virgin/EMI VTDCD 413* ⊛x3	1	3	37
14 Jun 03	**SMASH HITS CHART SUMMER 2003** *Virgin/EMI/Universal VTDCD 530*	5		5
14 Jun 03	**COOL SUMMER JAZZ** *Virgin/EMI VTDCD 531*	15		2
21 Jun 03	**THE BEST PROG ROCK ALBUM IN THE WORLD** *Virgin/EMI VTDCD 533*	9		2
5 Jul 03	**THE BEST SUMMER HOLIDAY EVER** *Virgin/EMI VTDCD 534*	5		5
26 Jul 03	**THE RETURN OF THE SUPER 70'S** *Virgin/EMI VTDCD 567*	5		6
2 Aug 03	**BEST PANPIPES ALBUM IN THE WORLD…EVER!** *Virgin/EMI VTDCD 545*	13		2
9 Aug 03	**GOOD VIBES** *Virgin/EMI VTDCD 565*	14		3
16 Aug 03	**THE BEST DANCE ALBUM IN THE WORLD EVER** *Virgin/EMI VTDCD 536*	3		4
30 Aug 03	**THE BEST SMOOTH JAZZ EVER** *Virgin/EMI VTDCDX 570*	20		1
6 Sep 03	**THE ULTIMATE RELAXATION ALBUM** *Virgin/EMI VTDCDX 577*	16		3
20 Sep 03	**BITTERSWEET LOVESONGS** *Virgin/EMI VTDCD 574*	6		4
11 Oct 03	**LAS VEGAS LEGENDS** *Virgin/EMI VTDCD 582*	7		4
8 Nov 03	**NOW DANCE 2004** *Virgin/EMI VTDCD 539*	1	1	3
8 Nov 03	**BEST BANDS EVER 2004** *Virgin/EMI VTDCD 538*	13		1
15 Nov 03	**CAPITAL GOLD – LOVE LEGENDS** *Virgin/EMI VTDCD 553* ⊛	5		7
15 Nov 03	**SUPER 60'S** *Virgin/EMI VTDCD 547*	16		1
22 Nov 03	**SCHOOL REUNION – THE 80'S** *Virgin/EMI VTDCD 544* ⊛	4		12
22 Nov 03	**CAPITAL GOLD – ROCK 'N' ROLL LEGENDS** *Virgin/EMI VTDCD 554*	15		3
22 Nov 03	**COUNTRY BALLADS** *Virgin/EMI VTDCD 556*	17		2
10 Jan 04	**THE VERY BEST CLUB ANTHEMS EVER** *Virgin/EMI VTDCDX 569*	17		3
14 Feb 04	**LOVE IS – THE ALBUM** *Virgin/EMJI VTDCDX 596*	2		3
6 Mar 04	**BEST HEAVY METAL ALBUM IN THE WORLD EVER** *Virgin/EMI VTDCD 598*	4		5
20 Mar 04	**THE VERY BEST OF NEW WOMAN** *Virgin/EMI VTDCD 599*	1	1	8
20 Mar 04	**MEMORIES ARE MADE OF THIS** *Virgin/EMI VTDCD 602*	2		7
27 Mar 04	**PEACE – PURE CLASSICAL CALM** *Virgin/EMI VTDCD 600*	20		1
3 Apr 04	**NOW DANCE** *Virgin/EMI VTDCD 607*	4		4
10 Apr 04	**BEST WORSHIP SONGS EVER** *Virgin/EMI VTDCD 593*	8		7
1 May 04	**BACK TO THE MOVIES – HITS FROM THE FLIX** *Virgin/EMI VTDCD 611*	5		9
8 May 04	**LATE NIGHT MOODS** *Virgin/EMI VTDCD 609*	8		3
22 May 04	**TRANCE MASTERS** *Virgin/EMI VTDCDX612*	9		3
29 May 04	**SUMMER IN THE SIXTIES** *Virgin/EMI VTDCD 613*	9		2
5 Jun 04	**SUPER 70'S ROCK** *Virgin/EMI VTDCD 614*	10		2
19 Jun 04	**BIGGER, BETTER POWER BALLADS** *Virgin/EMI VTDCD 619* ⊛	1	2	20
10 Jul 04	**SUPER 70'S SUMMER** *Virgin/EMI VTDCD 617*	14		2
24 Jul 04	**INSTRUMENTAL MEMORIES ARE MADE OF THIS** *Virgin/EMI VTDCD 629*	15		1
31 Jul 04	**BEST SUMMER EVER 2004** *Virgin/EMI VTDCD 622*	4		3
7 Aug 04	**GODSKITCHEN** *Virgin/EMI VTDCD 625*	15		2
14 Aug 04	**THE BEST CLUB ANTHEMS 2004** *Virgin/EMI VTDCD 635*	3		5
14 Aug 04	**NEW WOMAN – NEW COLLECTION 2004** *BMG TV/EMI Virgin VTDCD 634*	4		8
4 Sep 04	**SHAPESHIFTERS PRESENTS HOUSE GROOVES** *Virgin/EMI VTDCD 627*	13		1
18 Sep 04	**SAD SONGS** *Virgin/EMI VTDCD 669* ⊛	1	1	12
18 Sep 04	**BEST DANCE CLASSICS** *Virgin/EMI VTDCD 671*	11		2
25 Sep 04	**WE'LL MEET AGAIN** *Virgin/EMI VTDCD 670*	16		1
16 Oct 04	**URBAN LICKS** *Virgin/EMI VTDCD 679*	7		3
23 Oct 04	**THE BEST PUB JUKEBOX EVER** *Virgin/EMI VTDCD 652*	9		2
30 Oct 04	**NOW DANCE 2005** *Virgin/EMI VTDCD 640*	3		3
6 Nov 04	**CAPITAL GOLD – THE VERY BEST OF LEGENDS** *Virgin/EMI VTDCD 650*	5		4
13 Nov 04	**ACOUSTIC SONGBOOK** *Virgin/EMI VTDCD673*	16		1
20 Nov 04	**THE BEST OF R&B – HIT SELECTION** *Virgin/EMI VTDCD 658*	6		12
20 Nov 04	**SCHOOL REUNION – THE DISCO** *Virgin/EMI VTDCD 657*	9		4
27 Nov 04	**POWER BALLADS III** *Virgin/EMI VTDCD684*	7		14
11 Dec 04	**THE BEST SIXTIES PARTY…EVER** *Virgin/EMI VTDCD645*	11		8
1 Jan 05	**THE BEST CLUB ANTHEMS 2005** *Virgin/EMI VTDCD662*	7		2
5 Feb 05	**JUNGLE DRUM & BASS ANTHEMS** *Virgin/EMI VTDCD595*	12		1
12 Feb 05	**SCHOOL REUNION – THE SMOOCHIES** *Virgin/EMI VTDCD699*	2		3
12 Feb 05	**LOVE SONGS** *Virgin/EMI VTDCD698*	6		3
5 Mar 05	**I LOVE MUM** *Virgin/EMI VTCD702*	1	1	4
5 Mar 05	**MEMORIES ARE MADE OF THIS – PART 2** *Virgin/EMI VTDCD701*	8		3
19 Mar 05	**CLUB FEVER** *Virgin/EMI VTDCD706*	2		6
26 Mar 05	**THE ALBUM 5** *Virgin/EMI VTDCD707*	2		10
26 Mar 05	**MORE BEST WORSHIP SONGS EVER** *Virgin/EMI VTDCD704*	11		3
9 Apr 05	**FRESH AND FUNKY HOUSE ANTHEMS** *Virgin/EMI VTDCD711*	20		1
16 Apr 05	**GODSKITCHEN – CLASSICS** *Virgin/EMI VTDCD708*	4		12
30 Apr 05	**HAPPY SONGS** *Virgin/EMI VTDCD712* ⊛	1	2	16
7 May 05	**VE DAY – THE ALBUM** *Virgin/EMI VTDCD713*	6		3
14 May 05	**MAX SPEED** *Virgin/EMI VTDCD715*	8		2
14 May 05	**HIT ME BABY ONE MORE TIME** *Virgin/EMI VTCD716*	16		2
21 May 05	**BEST ALBUM TRACKS EVER** *Virgin/EMI VTDCD714*	9		2
21 May 05	**STRICTLY DANCE FEVER** *Virgin/EMI VTDCD717*	18		1
4 Jun 05	**DRIVING ROCK BALLADS** *Virgin/EMI VTDCD719*	1	1	9
11 Jun 05	**DAD ROCKS** *Virgin/EMI VTDCD720*	1	3	11
18 Jun 05	**I LOVE DAD** *Virgin/EMI VTCD723*	3		4
25 Jun 05	**THE MOST RELAXING CLASSICAL ALBUM IN THE WORLD** *Virgin/EMI VTDCD724*	17		1
2 Jul 05	**THE BANDS 05 – II** *Virgin/EMI VTDCD729*	2		7
9 Jul 05	**NOVELTY NO 1'S** *Virgin/EMI VTCD730*	6		4
16 Jul 05	**BASS IN YA FACE** *Virgin/EMI VTDCD725*	11		2
16 Jul 05	**CAPITAL GOLD SUMMER LEGENDS** *Virgin/EMI VTDCD731*	17		1
23 Jul 05	**IN THE MIX – REVIVAL** *Virgin/EMI VTDCD727*	3		8
6 Aug 05	**GODSKITCHEN – GLOBAL GATHERING** *Virgin/EMI VTDCD728*	11		3
27 Aug 05	**THE BEST CLUB ANTHEMS 05** *Virgin/EMI VTDCD737*	4		3
3 Sep 05	**RAVEOLOGY** *Virgin/EMI VTDCD738*	20		1
17 Sep 05	**BREAK UP SONGS** *Virgin/EMI VTDCD746*	8		4
24 Sep 05	**GOLDEN OLDIES** *Virgin/EMI VTDCD749*	3		5
8 Oct 05	**THE VERY BEST OF NOW DANCE** *Virgin/EMI VTDCD753*	2		9

VARIOUS ARTISTS (VISION)

Date	Title / Label	Peak Position	Weeks at No.1	Weeks on Chart
4 Mar 95	**FLARED HITS AND PLATFORM SOUL** *Vision VISCD 7*	13		5
13 May 95	**DANCE NATION '95** *Vision VISCD 11*	6		5
10 Jun 95	**LOVE WITH A REGGAE RHYTHM** *Vision VISCD 13*	18		2
9 Sep 95	**THE BEST DANCE ALBUM OF THE YEAR!** *Vision VISCD 15*	5		6

VARIOUS ARTISTS (VITAL SOUNDS)

Date	Title / Label	Peak Position	Weeks at No.1	Weeks on Chart
4 Jul 92	**RED HOT AND WHITE LABELS** *Vital Sounds CDVIT 1*	17		2
26 Sep 92	**RED HOT AND WHITE 2** *Vital Sounds CDVIT 2*	13		2
29 May 93	**STRICTLY RAGGA** *Vital Sounds CDVIT 3*	12		2

VARIOUS ARTISTS (VOLUME)

Date	Title / Label	Peak Position	Weeks at No.1	Weeks on Chart
1 May 93	**VOLUME SIX** *Volume 6VCD 6*	19		1
2 Oct 93	**TRANCE EUROPE EXPRESS** *Volume TEEXCD 1*	14		3
11 Jun 94	**TRANCE EUROPE EXPRESS 2** *Volume TEEXCD 2*	17		2

VARIOUS ARTISTS (WALT DISNEY)

Date	Title / Label	Peak Position	Weeks at No.1	Weeks on Chart
22 Nov 97	**DISNEY'S HIT SINGLES & MORE!** *Walt Disney WD 115632*	9		4
28 Nov 98	**THE DISNEY EXPERIENCE** *Walt Disney WD 608202*	12		4
6 Apr 02	**THE MAGIC OF DISNEY – 20 SUPERSTAR HITS** *Walt Disney 0927452545*	15		2
27 Nov 04	**ULTIMATE DISNEY** *Walt Disney WSMCD195*	8		10
24 Sep 05	**ULTIMATE DISNEY PRINCESS** *Walt Disney WSMCD229*	5		9
26 Nov 05	**DISNEY'S GREATEST HITS** *Walt Disney VTDCD760*	14		8
22 Jul 06	**DRIVING WITH DISNEY** *Walt Disney VTDCD806*	20		1
30 Sep 06	**ULTIMATE DISNEY PRINCESS** *Walt Disney VTDCD810*	20		1
7 Apr 07	**THE VERY BEST OF DISNEY CHANNEL** *Walt Disney VTDCDX861*	6		4

VARIOUS ARTISTS (WARNER BROTHERS)

Date	Title / Label	Peak Position	Weeks at No.1	Weeks on Chart
25 Mar 78	**HOPE AND ANCHOR FRONT ROW FESTIVAL** *Warner Brothers K 66077*	28		3
21 Jul 79	**THE BEST DISCO ALBUM IN THE WORLD** *Warner Brothers K 58062* ⊛	1	6	17
14 May 83	**THE LAUGHTER AND TEARS COLLECTION** *WEA LTC 1*	19		16
4 Aug 90	**NOBODY'S CHILD – ROMANIAN ANGEL APPEAL** *Warner Brothers WX 353*	18		3
15 Aug 92	**BARCELONA GOLD** *Warner Brothers 9362450462*	15		2
18 Feb 95	**THE ULTIMATE SOUL COLLECTION – 45 SOUL CLASSICS** *Warner Music 9548333402*	4		9
5 Aug 95	**DISCO INFERNO** *Warner Music UK 9548319632*	16		1
28 Oct 95	**THE ULTIMATE SOUL COLLECTION – VOLUME 2** *Warner Music 9548338402*	11		2
6 Apr 96	**SONGS IN THE KEY OF X** *Warner Brothers 9362460792*	8		4

Silver-selling ○ Gold-selling ● Platinum-selling ⊛ US No.1 ★

Date	Title / Label	Award	Peak Position	Weeks at No.1	Weeks on Chart
6 Apr 96	**TWELVE** *warner.esp TV/Global TV 0630146802*		10		5
8 Jun 96	**VIVA! EUROPOP** *warner.esp TV/Global TV 0630152072*	○	4		5
2 Nov 96	**DISCO MIX 96** *warner.esp 9548348072*	●	7		4
15 Feb 97	**SIMPLY THE BEST LOVE SONGS** *warner.esp 9548351122*	●	2		6
5 Apr 97	**SIMPLY THE BEST CLASSIC SOUL** *warner.esp 9548352042*	○	7		6
7 Jun 97	**SUMMER GROOVE** *warner.esp 9548353822*		14		2
1 Nov 97	**ALL MY LOVE** *Polygram TV/warner.esp 9548359482*	●	7		4
13 Dec 97	**MASSIVE DANCE: 98** *warner.esp/Polygram TV/Global TV 5553432*	●	8		9
14 Feb 98	**SIMPLY THE BEST LOVE SONGS 2** *warner.esp 9548362252*	●	2		6
7 Mar 98	**A LITTLE BLUES IN YOUR SOUL** *warner.esp/Global TV 9548362232*	○	5		4
28 Mar 98	**SIMPLY THE BEST DISCO** *warner.esp 9548354282*	○	9		3
16 May 98	**CLUBBIN'** *warner.esp 9548364262*	○	6		5
11 Jul 98	**LIVE 4 EVER** *Sony TV/warner.esp 9548364372*		11		3
15 Aug 98	**CLUB CLASS** *warner.esp 3984245692*		9		2
22 Aug 98	**TOTALLY WICKED** *warner.esp/Global TV/Sony Music TV 3984246352*	●	4		6
31 Oct 98	**SIMPLY THE BEST CLASSICAL ANTHEMS** *warner.esp 3984255442*	○	14		2
14 Nov 98	**SIMPLY THE BEST RADIO HITS** *warner.esp 9548369352*	○	17		2
6 Feb 99	**TOTALLY WICKED TOO!** *warner.esp/Global TV/Sony Music TV 9548372542*	○	7		2
10 Apr 99	**CLUBZONE – DANCING IN THE CITY** *warner.esp/Radio City/3 Beat 3984270952*		20		1
19 Jun 99	**MUSIC FOR LIFE** *warner.esp 9548376472*		17		1
10 Jul 99	**CLUB IBIZA** *warner.esp 3984288992*	●	4		5
4 Sep 99	**DANCEMIX.UK.V1** *warner.esp 3984294752*		13		3
25 Sep 99	**THIS YEAR IN IBIZA** *warner.esp 8573800372*		5		5
25 Sep 99	**CRAZY LITTLE THING CALLED LOVE** *warner.esp/Global TV 9548379382*		17		1
2 Oct 99	**THE DEFINITIVE SOUND OF ATLANTIC SOUL** *warner.esp 7567805959*		18		1
12 Feb 00	**PURE GARAGE** *warner.esp WMMCD 001*	●	2		15
4 Mar 00	**DANCE HITS 2000** *warner.esp/Global TV/Sony TV WMMCD 003*	●	4		5
25 Mar 00	**NEW HITS 2000** *warner.esp/Global TV/Sony TV WMMCD 004*	⊛	1	2	8
13 May 00	**TWICE AS NICE – SEXY & STYLISH** *warner.esp WMMCD 005*	●	5		7
15 Jul 00	**FRESH HITS – VOLUME 1** *warner.esp/Global TV/Sony TV WMMCD 008*	●	1	2	7
15 Jul 00	**PURE GARAGE II** *warner.esp WMMCD 007*	○	2		11
2 Sep 00	**SPACE** *warner.esp WMMCD 010*	○	8		3
9 Sep 00	**CHILLED IBIZA** *warner.esp WMMCD 011*	●	3		26
16 Sep 00	**FRESH HITS – VOL 2** *warner.esp WMMCD 012*	○	2		7
23 Sep 00	**TWICE AS NICE – SUMMER OF LOVE** *warner.esp WMMCD 013*	○	6		7
30 Sep 00	**HARD HOUSE NATION** *warner.esp WMMCD 014*	●	4		8
4 Nov 00	**HUGE HITS 2000** *Warner/BMG TV/Sony TV WSMCD 015*		2		5
25 Nov 00	**PURE GARAGE III** *warner.esp WSMCD 016*	○	2		10
25 Nov 00	**60 NUMBER ONE'S OF THE 60'S** *warner.esp WSMCD 017*	●	13		2
9 Dec 00	**THE CLUBBER'S BIBLE** *warner.esp WSMCD 022*	●	11		6
16 Dec 00	**HITS 2001** *BMG/Sony/Telstar/WSM WSMCD 019*	⊛	3		9
16 Dec 00	**HARD HOUSE NATION – 2** *warner.esp WSMCD 023*	●	11		6
17 Mar 01	**PURE GARAGE IV** *warner.esp WSMCD 030*	●	3		6
17 Mar 01	**HARD HOUSE VOL.3** *warner.esp WSMCD 031*	○	7		3
28 Apr 01	**TWICE AS NICE – SEXY AND STYLISH** *warner.esp WSMCD 034*		11		4
5 May 01	**ESSENTIAL SELECTION PRESENTS THE CLUBBER'S BIBLE II THE SECOND COMING** *warner.esp WSMCD 035*	○	6		5
12 May 01	**FUNKOLOGY – ONE NATION UNDER A GROOVE** *warner.esp WSMCD 033*		14		4
19 May 01	**THE LOOK OF LOVE – THE BEST OF BURT BACHARACH** *WSM/Universal TV 9547396245*	⊛	4		17
16 Jun 01	**FRANTIC** *warner.esp WSMCD 039*		17		3
30 Jun 01	**URBAN RENEWAL – SONGS OF PHIL COLLINS** *WEA 8573876372*		16		1
7 Jul 01	**THE ARTFUL DODGER PRESENTS REWIND 2001** *WSM WSMCD 038*	○	12		4
14 Jul 01	**PURE HIP HOP – EXPLICIT BEATS** *WSM/Universal TV WSMCD 041*		10		3
28 Jul 01	**DANCE PARADE IBIZA** *WSM/Universal WSMCD 042*		14		2
4 Aug 01	**THE GREATEST 80'S SOUL WEEKENDER** *WSM WSMCD 043*	●	9		8
4 Aug 01	**SIMPLY THE BEST REGGAE ALBUM** *WSM WSMCD 044*	○	12		3
18 Aug 01	**MTV IBIZA 2001** *WSM WSMCD 049*		18		2
1 Sep 01	**PURE FLAVA** *WSM/Universal TV WSMCD 047*		10		4
8 Sep 01	**CHILLED IBIZA II** *WSM WSMCD 045*	●	5		6
27 Oct 01	**TEENDREEM** *WSM WSMCD 053*		19		1
10 Nov 01	**PURE GARAGE V** *WSM WSMCD 046*	○	7		2
24 Nov 01	**HARD DANCE ANTHEMS** *WSM WSMCD 055*	○	19		2
8 Dec 01	**ESSENTIAL SELECTION – CLUBBERS BIBLE** *WSM WSMCD 052*		17		1
12 Jan 02	**JUNGLE MASSIVE** *WSM WSMCD 060*		3		7
19 Jan 02	**TWICE AS NICE – ESSENTIAL GROOVES** *WSM WSMCD 059*		9		4
9 Feb 02	**LOVE SO STRONG** *WSM WSMCD 051*	●	1	1	6
16 Feb 02	**CLUBBED UP** *WSM WSMCD 069*	○	12		3
2 Mar 02	**OCEAN'S ELEVEN** *Warner Brothers 9362481122*	●	15		1
16 Mar 02	**PURE GENIUS** *WSM 0927450012*	○	7		3
16 Mar 02	**SOUL BROTHERS** *WSM WSMCD 065*	○	9		3
23 Mar 02	**FRANTIC 2002** *WSM WSMCD 066*		15		2
23 Mar 02	**JUNGLE MASSIVE – 21ST CENTURY BREAKBEAT** *warner.esp WSMCD 070*		17		1
20 Apr 02	**INSTANT KARMA** *WSM WSMCD 064*		14		4
18 May 02	**BLUES AND SOUL MASTERS** *WSM WSMCD 074*		14		3
1 Jun 02	**THE BEST SUMMER ALBUM 2002** *Sony TV/WSM WSMCD 084*	●	1	1	7
1 Jun 02	**CHILLED IBIZA III** *Warner Dance WSMCD 078*	○	12		3
8 Jun 02	**JUMPERS 4 GOALPOSTS** *WSM WSMCD 081*	●	4		7
8 Jun 02	**TWICE AS NICE PRESENTS URBAN FLAVAS** *Warner Dance WSMCD 079*	○	5		5
15 Jun 02	**THE ULTIMATE CHICK FLICK SOUNDTRACK** *WSM/Universal TV WSMCD 071*	●	4		21
6 Jul 02	**CREWS CONTROL** *Warner Dance WSMCD 077*		17		1
13 Jul 02	**BACK IN THE DAY** *Warner Dance WSMCD 090*		15		2
27 Jul 02	**BOOM SELECTION** *Sony TV/Warner Dance WSMCD 089*	●	3		6
3 Aug 02	**HANDS TO HEAVEN** *Warner Dance WSMCD 082*		9		3
24 Aug 02	**THE ULTIMATE HEN NIGHT PARTY ALBUM** *WSM WSMCD 103*	○	8		4
14 Sep 02	**GET UR FREAK ON** *Warner Dance WSMCD 062*	○	8		4
14 Sep 02	**THE PAN PIPE CHILLOUT ALBUM** *warner.esp WSMCD 106*		16		3
28 Sep 02	**IBIZA HITMIX 2002** *Warner Dance WSMCD 073*		12		2
12 Oct 02	**TWICE AS NICE PRESENTS MOBO 2002** *Warner Dance WSMCD 110*	●	3		5
2 Nov 02	**PURE GENIUS VOLUME 2** *WSM WSMCD 115*		12		1
9 Nov 02	**PURE TRANCE** *Warner Dance WSMCD 087*		11		1
23 Nov 02	**ALL TIME CLASSIC TEARJERKERS** *WSM WSMCD 116*	⊛	2		19
23 Nov 02	**PLATINUM SOUL LEGENDS – 1960–1975** *WSM WSMCD 100*	●	14		5
21 Dec 02	**PURE GARAGE PLATINUM – THE VERY BEST OF** *Warner Dance WSMCD 120*	●	4		9
11 Jan 03	**BASS BREAKS & BEATS 2003** *Warner Dance WSMCD 121*	○	5		5
11 Jan 03	**PARTY ANIMAL** *WSM WSMCD 114*	○	13		1
1 Feb 03	**URBAN EXPLOSION** *INCredible/Warner Dance WSMCD 123*		5		6
8 Feb 03	**THE POWER OF LOVE** *Sony TV/WSM WSMCD 127*	●	4		4
8 Mar 03	**THE VERY BEST OF MTV UNPLUGGED 2** *UMTV/WSM 5046623832*	●	1	2	11
15 Mar 03	**STRANGE AND BEAUTIFUL** *WSM WSMCD 122*		11		2
22 Mar 03	**CHICK FLICKS – THE SEQUEL** *UMTV/WSM WSMCD 126*	●	4		4
22 Mar 03	**SHAMROCKS AND SHENANIGANS** *WSM WSMCD 129*		10		2
5 Apr 03	**SONGBIRDS** *WSM WSMCD 119*	○	4		3
12 Apr 03	**TWICE AS NICE PRESENTS URBAN FLAVAS 2003** *Urban Explosion/WSM WSMCD 124*		8		5
19 Apr 03	**THE ULTIMATE SMOOCHY ALBUM** *WSM WSMCD 130*		7		2
17 May 03	**REPRESS – 80'S CLUB CLASSICS** *Warner Dance WSMCD 136*		10		3
24 May 03	**IBIZA – THE HISTORY OF HOUSE** *Warner Dance WSMCD 075*	●	3		5
31 May 03	**THE BEST SUMMER ALBUM 2003** *WSM/Sony WSMCD 133*	○	11		2
7 Jun 03	**ALL TIME CLASSIC ROCK N ROLL TEARJERKERS** *WSM WSMCD 128*	●	5		7
14 Jun 03	**PURE URBAN ESSENTIALS** *Warner Dance/Sony TV WSMCD 132*	●	3		13
26 Jul 03	**IBIZA – THE HISTORY OF CHILLOUT** *Warner Dance WSMCD143*	○	3		6
26 Jul 03	**SKATE TO HELL** *WSM WSMCD 139*		20		1
9 Aug 03	**IBIZA – THE HISTORY OF HARD DANCE** *Warner Dance WSMCD144*	○	6		4
30 Aug 03	**RE-PRESS – THE 70'S SOUL REVIVAL** *Warner Dance WSMCD146*		12		3
13 Sep 03	**SWING CLASSICS** *Warner Dance WSMCD149*	○	9		4
25 Oct 03	**HAIRBRUSH DIVAS** *WSM WSMCD 152*	●	3		6
8 Nov 03	**R&B LOVE** *Warner Dance/Sony TV WSMCD 148*	⊛	2		19
15 Nov 03	**ALL TIME CLASSIC COUNTRY TEARJERKERS** *WSM WSMCD 145*		18		1
6 Dec 03	**THE ULTIMATE CHICK FLICK LOVE SONGS** *UMTV/WSM WSMCD 154*	⊛	5		13
6 Dec 03	**THE ULTIMATE CHEESE PARTY** *WSM WSMCD 153*	●	12		3
13 Dec 03	**PURE URBAN ESSENTIALS 2** *Sony TV/Warner Dance WSMCD 150*	●	4		10
10 Jan 04	**PURE GARAGE PRESENTS FOUR TO THE FLOOR** *Warner Dance WSMCD 159*		12		3
31 Jan 04	**DRUM & BASS ARENA** *Warner Dance WSMCD 160*	○	3		6
20 Mar 04	**HAIRBRUSH DIVAS 2** *WSM WSMCD 164*	○	8		4
24 Apr 04	**SUPERBAD** *Warner Dance WSMCD 165*		10		3
1 May 04	**THE ULTIMATE FUNK PARTY** *WSM WSMCD 175*		8		3
15 May 04	**URBAN MUSIC FESTIVAL** *Warner Dance WSMCD 167*		8		4
29 May 04	**LOVE HURTS** *warner.esp WSMCD172*		4		7
12 Jun 04	**CHILLED IBIZA GOLD** *Warner Dance WSMCD 178*		13		4
19 Jun 04	**IBIZA – THE HISTORY OF TRANCE** *Warner Dance WSMCD 169*	○	7		6
24 Jul 04	**CREAM CLASSICS** *Warner Dance WSMCD 177*		2		12
24 Jul 04	**HIP HOP LOVE** *Warner Dance/Sony TV WSMCD181*		5		6
28 Aug 04	**SUMMER RIDDIMS 2004** *Warner Dance WSMCD185*		10		3
4 Sep 04	**PEACE & LOVE – THE WOODSTOCK GENERATION** *WSM WSMCD 168*		6		3
11 Sep 04	**PURE BLING** *Warner Dance WSMCD 179*		8		3
30 Oct 04	**R&B LOVE 2** *Sony TV/Warner Dance WSMCD188*	●	4		4
6 Nov 04	**PERFECT LOVE** *WSM WSMCD187*		15		1
13 Nov 04	**CREAM CLASSICS – VOLUME 2** *Warner Dance WSMCD189*	●	5		3

Date	Title / Label	Peak Position	Weeks at No.1	Weeks on Chart
13 Nov 04	**THE HISTORY OF HIP HOP** *warner.esp WSMCD085*	13		2
20 Nov 04	**ULTIMATE ALL TIME CLASSIC TEARJERKERS** *WSM WSMCD192*	17		1
4 Dec 04	**CHICK FLICK DIARIES** *UMTV/WSM WSMCD190*	19		1
8 Jan 05	**TWICE AS NICE – URBAN CLUB CLASSICS** *warner.esp WSMCD199*	7		6
12 Feb 05	**THAT LOVING FEELING** *WSM WSMCD202*	7		3
19 Mar 05	**HARDCORE NATION** *WSM WSMCD208*	6		8
26 Mar 05	**80'S SOUL WEEKENDER** *WSM WSMCD207*	11		2
2 Apr 05	**HEADBANGER'S BIBLE** *WSM WSMCD196*	9		5
16 Apr 05	**THE VERY BEST OF ALL WOMAN – PLATINUM** *WSM WSMCD203*	9		4
30 Apr 05	**VERY BEST OF BLUES BROTHER SOUL SISTER** *WSM WSMCD210*	9		3
28 May 05	**PURE GARAGE PRESENTS THE MAIN ROOM SESSIONS** *Warner Dance WSMCD212*	8		4
28 May 05	**THE LOVERS GUIDE TO REGGAE** *WSM WSMCD214*	14		2
4 Jun 05	**CREAM IBIZA CLASSICS** *Warner Dance WSMCD186*	7		6
2 Jul 05	**HAIRBRUSH DIVAS PRESENTS SING-A-LONG SUMMER** *WSM WSMCD211*	1	1	6
16 Jul 05	**SOUL LOVE** *warner.esp WSMCD219*	15		2
13 Aug 05	**FESTIVAL** *UMTV/WSM WSMCD220*	2		10
27 Aug 05	**DRUM & BASS ESSENTIALS** *Warner Dance WSMCD218*	8		6
27 Aug 05	**THE VERY BEST OF (ARETHA FRANKLIN & OTIS REDDING)** *WSM 5101102322*	10		2
10 Sep 05	**ELECTRIC** *Warner Dance WSMCD223*	18		1
1 Oct 05	**A LIFETIME OF ROMANCE** *Sony BMG TV/WSM WSMCD228*	12		2
8 Oct 05	**ACOUSTIC LOVE** *WSM WSMCD227*	1	2	8
8 Oct 05	**DRIVETIME** *UMTV/WSM WSMCD215*	17		1
15 Oct 05	**ALL WOMAN – THE PLATINUM COLLECTION** *warner.esp WSMCD203X*	6		5
15 Oct 05	**HARDCORE NATION 2** *Warner Dance WSMCD221*	8		5
29 Oct 05	**JOHN PEEL – A TRIBUTE** *warner.esp WSMCD226*	5		3
26 Nov 05	**URBAN DANCE EXPLOSION** *Warner Dance WSMCD225*	18		1
10 Dec 05	**MAGIC – THE ALBUM** *WSM WSMCD231*	11		15
7 Jan 06	**TWICE AS NICE – WEEKENDER** *Warner Dance WSMCD233*	4		7
18 Feb 06	**ULTIMATE TEARJERKERS** *WMTV WSMCD238*	20		1
25 Mar 06	**FOR MY MUM** *WMTV WMTV002*	8		2
15 Apr 06	**HIP HOP – THE EVOLUTION** *WMTV WMTV006*	7		5
27 May 06	**MAGIC SUMMER** *WMTV WMTV011*	9		3
17 Jun 06	**BEZ'S MADCHESTER ANTHEMS** *V2TV/WMTV WMTV013*	8		4
17 Jun 06	**JUMPERS 4 GOALPOSTS** *WMTV WMTV016*	17		1
8 Jul 06	**SUMMER HITS '06** *Sony BMG/WMTV WMTV007*	12		1
22 Jul 06	**MANUMISSION – IBIZA CLASSICS COLLECTION** *WMTV WMTV019*	13		2
12 Aug 06	**FESTIVAL 06** *WMTV WMTV005*	3		6
19 Aug 06	**ACOUSTIC LOVE 2** *WMTV WMTV010*	6		4
19 Aug 06	**HARDCORE NATION 3** *WMTV WMTV018*	8		4
2 Sep 06	**NUMBER 1 DANCE ANTHEMS** *WMTV WMTV022*	6		4
16 Sep 06	**ORIGINAL GARAGE ANTHEMS** *WMTV WMTV024*	8		4
14 Oct 06	**40 MOST BEAUTIFUL ARIAS** *WMTV WMTV032*	12		2
14 Oct 06	**BREAKTHROUGH BREAST CANCER PRESENTS LADIES** *WMTV WMTV026*	14		1
21 Oct 06	**JOHN PEEL – RIGHT TIME WRONG SPEED** *WMTV WMTV023*	10		3
17 Feb 07	**THE SOUND OF LOVE** *WMTV WMTV043*	11		2
3 Mar 07	**HARDCORE NATION CLASSICS** *WMTV WMTV039*	18		1
10 Mar 07	**MELLOW MAGIC** *WMTV WMTV046*	5		6
24 Mar 07	**ME TIME** *WMTV WMTV047*	17		1
14 Apr 07	**THE SOUND OF THE 70S** *WMTV WMTV052*	17		1
2 Jun 07	**CALIFORNIA DREAMING** *WMTV WMTV045*	8		2
2 Jun 07	**HAIRBRUSH DIVA'S PARTY** *warner.esp WSMCD232*	18		1
9 Jun 07	**R&B LOVE CLASSICS** *WMTV WMTV056*	3		5
18 Aug 07	**FESTIVAL 07** *UMTV/WMTV WMTV058*	15		2
1 Sep 07	**MAGIC – THE ALBUM 2007** *Warner Brothers WMTV059*	5		5
1 Sep 07	**PURE URBAN ESSENTIALS** *Warner Brothers WMTV060*	11		2
27 Oct 07	**SIMPLY THE BEST** *Rhino WMTV063*	16		1
3 Nov 07	**100 R&B CLASSICS** *Rhino WMTV062*	7		3
10 Nov 07	**90 CLUB HITS FROM THE 90'S** *Rhino WMTV061*	20		1
15 Dec 07	**PURE GARAGE – REWIND – BACK TO THE OLD SKOOL** *Warner Brothers WMTV067*	8		12
9 Feb 08	**LATER LIVE WITH JOOLS HOLLAND** *Warner Brothers WMTV051*	4		3
22 Mar 08	**ALED JONES PRESENTS GOOD MORNING SUNDAY** *Warner Brothers WMTV071*	12		2
26 Apr 08	**KISS PRESENTS THE MIXTAPE** *Warner Brothers WMTV068*	9		7
17 May 08	**SMASH HITS – THE 80S** *Warner Brothers WMTV072*	5		5
28 Jun 08	**PURE URBAN ESSENTIALS SUMMER 2008** *Warner Brothers WMTV076*	2		6
12 Jul 08	**PURE GARAGE PRESENTS PURE BASSLINE** *Warner Brothers WMTV078*	6		5
9 Aug 08	**100 R&B CLASSICS – THE ANTHEMS** *Warner Brothers WMTV079*	4		10
30 Aug 08	**OAKENFOLD ANTHEMS** *Warner Brothers WMTV080*	9		3
4 Oct 08	**KERRANG – THE ALBUM 08** *Warner Brothers WMTV082*	5		6
11 Oct 08	**THE R&B MIXTAPE** *Warner Brothers WMTV083*	10		3
15 Nov 08	**MICHAEL PARKINSON MY LIFE IN MUSIC** *Reprise 2564693506*	9		3
22 Nov 08	**LAST CHOIR STANDING** *Warner Brothers WMTV092*	10		2

VARIOUS ARTISTS (WARP)

Date	Title / Label	Peak Position	Weeks at No.1	Weeks on Chart
11 Jun 94	**ARTIFICIAL INTELLIGENCE** *Warp WARPLTDCD 23*	16		2

VARIOUS ARTISTS (WARWICK)

Date	Title / Label	Peak Position	Weeks at No.1	Weeks on Chart
29 Nov 75	**ALL-TIME PARTY HITS** *Warwick WW 5001*	21		8
17 Apr 76	**INSTRUMENTAL GOLD** *Warwick WW 5012*	3		24
29 May 76	**HAMILTON'S HOT SHOTS** *Warwick WW 5014*	15		5
8 Jan 77	**SONGS OF PRAISE** *Warwick WW 5020*	31		2
29 Jan 77	**HIT SCENE** *Warwick PR 5023*	19		5
4 Feb 78	**COUNTRY GIRL MEETS COUNTRY BOY** *Warwick PR 5039*	43		3
25 Nov 78	**LOVE SONGS – 16 CLASSIC LOVE SONGS** *Warwick WW 5046*	47		7
2 Dec 78	**BLACK VELVET** *Warwick WW 5047*	72		3
7 Apr 79	**COUNTRY PORTRAITS** *Warwick WW 5057*	14		10
10 Nov 79	**20 SMASH DISCO HITS (THE BITCH)** *Warwick WW 5061*	42		5
16 Feb 80	**COUNTRY GUITAR** *Warwick WW 5070*	46		3
14 Nov 81	**DISCO EROTICA** *Warwick WW 5108*	35		8
10 Apr 82	**PS I LOVE YOU** *Warwick WW 5121*	68		3
6 Nov 82	**HITS OF THE SCREAMING 60'S** *Warwick WW 5124*	24		10
22 Dec 84	**MERRY CHRISTMAS TO YOU** *Warwick WW 5141*	64		2

VARIOUS ARTISTS (WEST FIVE)

Date	Title / Label	Peak Position	Weeks at No.1	Weeks on Chart
18 Oct 86	**THE POWER OF LOVE** *West Five WEF 4*	33		7

VARIOUS ARTISTS (WESTMOOR)

Date	Title / Label	Peak Position	Weeks at No.1	Weeks on Chart
24 Mar 90	**EMERALD CLASSICS VOLUMES I AND II** *Westmoor WMTV 1*	14		2

VARIOUS ARTISTS (WESTWAY DANCE)

Date	Title / Label	Peak Position	Weeks at No.1	Weeks on Chart
18 Jul 98	**ELEMENTS – SEB FONTAINE/TONY DE VIT** *Westway Dance 3984238682*	15		3

VARIOUS ARTISTS (WHITE ISLAND)

Date	Title / Label	Peak Position	Weeks at No.1	Weeks on Chart
14 Oct 00	**MTV IBIZA 2000 – THE PARTY** *White Island MTVRCD 001*	14		3

VARIOUS ARTISTS (WONDERLAND)

Date	Title / Label	Peak Position	Weeks at No.1	Weeks on Chart
21 Oct 06	**KISS DOES FUNKY HOUSE** *Wonderland/Polydor WONDERCD01*	18		1

VARIOUS ARTISTS (WORLDS END)

Date	Title / Label	Peak Position	Weeks at No.1	Weeks on Chart
26 Sep 92	**VOLUME FOUR** *Worlds End V 4CD*	17		1

VARIOUS ARTISTS (WORLDWIDE ULTIMATUM)

Date	Title / Label	Peak Position	Weeks at No.1	Weeks on Chart
15 Mar 97	**CARL COX – FACT 2** *Worldwide Ultimatum 0091022*	13		2

VARIOUS ARTISTS (XL RECORDINGS)

Date	Title / Label	Peak Position	Weeks at No.1	Weeks on Chart
14 Sep 91	**XL RECORDINGS – THE SECOND CHAPTER** *XL Recordings XLLP 108*	5		9
25 Apr 92	**THE THIRD CHAPTER** *XL Recordings XLCD 109*	6		8
6 Mar 99	**PRODIGY PRESENTS THE DIRTCHAMBER SESSIONS 1** *XL Recordings XLCD 128*	3		3

VARIOUS ARTISTS (ZOMBA)

Date	Title / Label	Peak Position	Weeks at No.1	Weeks on Chart
24 Oct 87	**THE WORD** *Zomba HOP 217*	86		1

VARIOUS ARTISTS (ZTT)

Date	Title / Label	Peak Position	Weeks at No.1	Weeks on Chart
19 Oct 85	**IQ 6: ZANG TUMB TUM SAMPLED** *ZTT IQ 6*	40		3

Every No.1 Compilation Album from 1989–2008

Includes the date of the first week at No.1 and the number of weeks at No.1

In 1989, various artist and cast/ film soundtrack albums were separated out from the album chart. Below are all the No.1 albums from the (separate) compilation album chart from that time.

Chart Date	Album Title Artist	Artist Weeks at No.1
14/1/89	**NOW THAT'S WHAT I CALL MUSIC 13** VARIOUS ARTISTS (EMI)	1
21/1/89	**ANDREW LLOYD WEBBER – THE PREMIER COLLECTION** VARIOUS ARTISTS (POLYDOR)	1
4/2/89	**THE MARQUEE – 30 LEGENDARY YEARS** VARIOUS ARTISTS (POLYDOR)	4
4/3/89	**THE BRITS – THE AWARDS 1989** VARIOUS ARTISTS (TELSTAR)	1
11/3/89	**ANDREW LLOYD WEBBER – THE PREMIER COLLECTION** VARIOUS ARTISTS (POLYDOR)	1
18/3/89	**DEEP HEAT – 26 HOTTEST HOUSE HITS** VARIOUS ARTISTS (TELSTAR)	1
25/3/89	**UNFORGETTABLE 2** VARIOUS ARTISTS (EMI)	1
1/4/89	**NOW THAT'S WHAT I CALL MUSIC 14** VARIOUS ARTISTS (EMI)	7
20/5/89	**NITE FLITE 2** VARIOUS ARTISTS (CBS)	2
3/6/89	**THE HITS ALBUM 10** VARIOUS ARTISTS (CBS)	6
15/7/89	**NOW DANCE '89 – THE 12" MIXES** VARIOUS ARTISTS (EMI)	6
26/8/89	**NOW THAT'S WHAT I CALL MUSIC 15** VARIOUS ARTISTS (EMI)	5
30/9/89	**DEEP HEAT 4 – PLAY WITH FIRE** VARIOUS ARTISTS (TELSTAR)	5
4/11/89	**SMASH HITS PARTY '89 – 30 SMASH HITS** VARIOUS ARTISTS (DOVER)	3
25/11/89	**THE 80'S ALBUM – THE ALBUM OF THE DECADE** VARIOUS ARTISTS (EMI)	1
2/12/89	**NOW THAT'S WHAT I CALL MUSIC 16** VARIOUS ARTISTS (EMI)	7
20/1/90	**PURE SOFT METAL** VARIOUS ARTISTS (STYLUS)	2
3/2/90	**DEEP HEAT 5 – FEED THE FEVER – 32 HOTTEST CLUB HITS** VARIOUS ARTISTS (TELSTAR)	2
17/2/90	**PURE SOFT METAL** VARIOUS ARTISTS (STYLUS)	3
10/3/90	**NOW DANCE 901 – 20 SMASH DANCE HITS – THE 12" MIXES** VARIOUS ARTISTS (EMI)	4
7/4/90	**DEEP HEAT 6 – THE SIXTH SENSE** VARIOUS ARTISTS (TELSTAR)	2
21/4/90	**JUST THE TWO OF US** VARIOUS ARTISTS (CBS)	2
5/5/90	**NOW THAT'S WHAT I CALL MUSIC 17** VARIOUS ARTISTS (EMI)	5
9/6/90	**CLASSIC EXPERIENCE II** VARIOUS ARTISTS (EMI)	4
7/7/90	**DEEP HEAT 7 – SEVENTH HEAVEN** VARIOUS ARTISTS (TELSTAR)	1
14/7/90	**SMASH HITS – RAVE!** VARIOUS ARTISTS (DOVER)	2
28/7/90	**NOW DANCE 902** VARIOUS ARTISTS (EMI)	3
18/8/90	**KNEBWORTH – THE ALBUM** VARIOUS ARTISTS (POLYDOR)	2
1/9/90	**MEGABASS** VARIOUS ARTISTS (TELSTAR)	4
29/9/90	**SLAMMIN'** VARIOUS ARTISTS (A&M)	1
6/10/90	**THAT LOVING FEELING VOLUME 3** VARIOUS ARTISTS (DINO)	3
27/10/90	**MISSING YOU – AN ALBUM OF LOVE** VARIOUS ARTISTS (EMI)	3
17/11/90	**NOW DANCE 903 – THE 12" MIXES** VARIOUS ARTISTS (EMI)	2
1/12/90	**NOW! THAT'S WHAT I CALL MUSIC 18** VARIOUS ARTISTS (EMI)	5
19/1/91	**DIRTY DANCING (OST)** FILM SOUNDTRACK	2
2/2/91	**DEEP HEAT 9 – NINTH LIFE – KISS THE BLISS** VARIOUS ARTISTS (TELSTAR)	2
16/2/91	**THE LOST BOYS (OST)** FILM SOUNDTRACK	1
23/2/91	**AWESOME!! – 20 MASSIVE HITS** VARIOUS ARTISTS (EMI)	3
16/3/91	**UNCHAINED MELODIES** VARIOUS ARTISTS (TELSTAR)	3
6/4/91	**NOW! THAT'S WHAT I CALL MUSIC 19** VARIOUS ARTISTS (EMI)	5
11/5/91	**THINKING OF YOU ...** VARIOUS ARTISTS (COLUMBIA)	2
25/5/91	**SMASH HITS – MASSIVE!** VARIOUS ARTISTS (DOVER)	2
8/6/91	**THE ESSENTIAL MOZART** VARIOUS ARTISTS (DECCA)	1
15/6/91	**THE RHYTHM DIVINE** VARIOUS ARTISTS (DINO)	1
22/6/91	**THE ESSENTIAL MOZART** VARIOUS ARTISTS (DECCA)	1
29/6/91	**WINGS OF LOVE** VARIOUS ARTISTS (A&M)	5
3/8/91	**THIN ICE 2 – THE SECOND SHIVER** VARIOUS ARTISTS (TELSTAR)	1
10/8/91	**PURPLE RAINBOWS** VARIOUS ARTISTS (POLYDOR)	1
17/8/91	**THE HITS ALBUM 15** VARIOUS ARTISTS (CBS)	2
31/8/91	**THE SOUND OF THE SUBURBS** VARIOUS ARTISTS (COLUMBIA)	3
21/9/91	**GROOVY GHETTO** VARIOUS ARTISTS (ARCADE)	2
5/10/91	**NOW DANCE 91** VARIOUS ARTISTS (EMI)	3
26/10/91	**TWO ROOMS – CELEBRATING THE SONGS OF ELTON JOHN AND BERNIE TAUPIN** VARIOUS ARTISTS (MERCURY)	1
2/11/91	**HARDCORE ECSTASY** VARIOUS ARTISTS (DINO)	4
30/11/91	**NOW THAT'S WHAT I CALL MUSIC! 20** VARIOUS ARTISTS (EMI)	7
18/1/92	**ESSENTIAL HARDCORE** VARIOUS ARTISTS (DINO)	1
25/1/92	**THE ULTIMATE RAVE** VARIOUS ARTISTS (EMI)	4
22/2/92	**THE AWARDS 1992** VARIOUS ARTISTS (POLYGRAM)	2

Chart Date	Album Title Artist	Artist Weeks at No.1
7/3/92	**THE ULTIMATE HARDCORE** VARIOUS ARTISTS (TELSTAR)	2
21/3/92	**SOUL EMOTION** VARIOUS ARTISTS (POLYGRAM)	3
11/4/92	**ALL WOMAN** VARIOUS ARTISTS (QUALITY TELEVISION)	2
25/4/92	**NOW THAT'S WHAT I CALL MUSIC! 21** VARIOUS ARTISTS (EMI)	5
30/5/92	**THE RAVE GENER8TOR** VARIOUS ARTISTS (COOKIE JAR)	2
13/6/92	**EARTHRISE – THE RAINFOREST ALBUM** VARIOUS ARTISTS (ELF)	1
20/6/92	**MODERN LOVE** VARIOUS ARTISTS (POLYGRAM)	1
27/6/92	**HEARTBEAT (MUSIC FROM THE TV SERIES)** VARIOUS ARTISTS (COLUMBIA)	4
25/7/92	**KT3 – KAOS THEORY 3** VARIOUS ARTISTS (TELSTAR)	2
8/8/92	**NOW THAT'S WHAT I CALL MUSIC! 22** VARIOUS ARTISTS (EMI)	8
3/10/92	**SIXTIES BEAT** VARIOUS ARTISTS (DINO)	1
10/10/92	**ALL WOMAN 2** VARIOUS ARTISTS (QUALITY TELEVISION)	1
17/10/92	**ENERGY RUSH** VARIOUS ARTISTS (DINO)	2
31/10/92	**THE ULTIMATE COUNTRY COLLECTION** VARIOUS ARTISTS (COLUMBIA)	1
7/11/92	**THE BEST OF DANCE '92** VARIOUS ARTISTS (TELSTAR)	1
14/11/92	**THE ULTIMATE COUNTRY COLLECTION** VARIOUS ARTISTS (COLUMBIA)	1
21/11/92	**THE BEST OF DANCE '92** VARIOUS ARTISTS (TELSTAR)	1
28/11/92	**NOW THAT'S WHAT I CALL MUSIC! 23** VARIOUS ARTISTS (EMI)	5
2/1/93	**THE BODYGUARD (OST)** FILM SOUNDTRACK	8
27/2/93	**HITS 93 VOLUME 1** VARIOUS ARTISTS (TELSTAR)	3
20/3/93	**THE BODYGUARD (OST)** FILM SOUNDTRACK	2
3/4/93	**BLUES BROTHER SOUL SISTER** VARIOUS ARTISTS (DINO)	1
10/4/93	**ENERGY RUSH PRESENTS DANCE HITS 93** VARIOUS ARTISTS (DINO)	3
1/5/93	**THE BODYGUARD (OST)** FILM SOUNDTRACK	1
8/5/93	**NOW THAT'S WHAT I CALL MUSIC! 24** VARIOUS ARTISTS (EMI)	6
19/6/93	**ORIGINALS** VARIOUS ARTISTS (COLUMBIA)	1
26/6/93	**NOW DANCE 93** VARIOUS ARTISTS (EMI)	2
10/7/93	**100% DANCE** VARIOUS ARTISTS (TELSTAR)	1
17/7/93	**THE BEST DANCE ALBUM IN THE WORLD ... EVER!** VARIOUS ARTISTS (VIRGIN)	4
14/8/93	**NOW THAT'S WHAT I CALL MUSIC! 25** VARIOUS ARTISTS (EMI)	5
18/9/93	**DANCE ADRENALIN** VARIOUS ARTISTS (TELSTAR)	2
2/10/93	**100% DANCE VOLUME 2** VARIOUS ARTISTS (TELSTAR)	2
16/10/93	**NOW THAT'S WHAT I CALL MUSIC! 1993** VARIOUS ARTISTS (EMI)	1
23/10/93	**100% DANCE VOLUME 2** VARIOUS ARTISTS (TELSTAR)	2
6/11/93	**NOW DANCE – THE BEST OF '93** VARIOUS ARTISTS (EMI)	1
13/11/93	**THE BEST OF DANCE '93** VARIOUS ARTISTS (TELSTAR)	3
27/11/93	**NOW THAT'S WHAT I CALL MUSIC! 26** VARIOUS ARTISTS (EMI)	8
22/1/94	**THE SOUND OF KISS 100FM** VARIOUS ARTISTS (POLYGRAM)	1
29/1/94	**NOW DANCE 94 VOLUME 1** VARIOUS ARTISTS (EMI)	2
12/2/94	**SWEET SOUL HARMONIES** VARIOUS ARTISTS (VIRGIN)	1
19/2/94	**DANCE HITS '94 – VOLUME 1** VARIOUS ARTISTS (TELSTAR)	3
12/3/94	**SOUL DEVOTION** VARIOUS ARTISTS (POLYGRAM)	4
9/4/94	**NOW THAT'S WHAT I CALL MUSIC! 27** VARIOUS ARTISTS (EMI)	4
7/5/94	**DANCE ZONE – LEVEL ONE** VARIOUS ARTISTS (POLYGRAM)	4
4/6/94	**ENERGY RUSH – XTERMIN8** VARIOUS ARTISTS (DINO)	1
11/6/94	**DANCE HITS '94 VOLUME 2** VARIOUS ARTISTS (TELSTAR)	1
18/6/94	**PURE MOODS** VARIOUS ARTISTS (VIRGIN)	2
2/7/94	**NOW DANCE – SUMMER 94** VARIOUS ARTISTS (EMI)	2
16/7/94	**DANCE ZONE – LEVEL TWO** VARIOUS ARTISTS (POLYGRAM)	2
30/7/94	**IT'S THE ULTIMATE DANCE ALBUM** VARIOUS ARTISTS (TELSTAR)	2
13/8/94	**NOW THAT'S WHAT I CALL MUSIC! 28** VARIOUS ARTISTS (EMI)	5
17/9/94	**THE BEST ROCK ALBUM IN THE WORLD ... EVER!** VARIOUS ARTISTS (VIRGIN)	3
8/10/94	**DANCE ZONE – LEVEL THREE** VARIOUS ARTISTS (POLYGRAM)	1
15/10/94	**NOW THAT'S WHAT I CALL MUSIC! 1994** VARIOUS ARTISTS (EMI)	4
12/11/94	**THE BEST ROCK ALBUM IN THE WORLD ... EVER!** VARIOUS ARTISTS (VIRGIN)	1
19/11/94	**THE LOVE ALBUM** VARIOUS ARTISTS (VIRGIN)	1
26/11/94	**NOW THAT'S WHAT I CALL MUSIC! 29** VARIOUS ARTISTS (EMI)	9
28/1/95	**THE BEST OF HEARTBEAT** VARIOUS ARTISTS (COLUMBIA)	1
4/2/95	**THE BEST PUNK ALBUM IN THE WORLD ... EVER!** VARIOUS ARTISTS (VIRGIN)	1
11/2/95	**DANCE MANIA 95 – VOLUME 1** VARIOUS ARTISTS (PURE MUSIC)	2
25/2/95	**ON A DANCE TIP** VARIOUS ARTISTS (GLOBAL TELEVISION)	3
18/3/95	**SMASH HITS '95 – VOLUME 1** VARIOUS ARTISTS (TELSTAR)	1
25/3/95	**DANCE ZONE LEVEL FOUR** VARIOUS ARTISTS (POLYGRAM)	2
8/4/95	**DANCE MANIA 95 – VOLUME 2** VARIOUS ARTISTS (PURE MUSIC)	2
22/4/95	**NOW THAT'S WHAT I CALL MUSIC! 30** VARIOUS ARTISTS (EMI)	4
20/5/95	**ON A DANCE TIP 2** VARIOUS ARTISTS (GLOBAL TELEVISION)	3
10/6/95	**TOP OF THE POPS 1** VARIOUS ARTISTS (COLUMBIA)	2
24/6/95	**DANCE ZONE LEVEL FIVE** VARIOUS ARTISTS (POLYGRAM)	3
15/7/95	**DANCE MANIA 95 – VOLUME 3** VARIOUS ARTISTS (PURE MUSIC)	3
5/8/95	**THE BEST SUMMER ALBUM IN THE WORLD ... EVER!** VARIOUS ARTISTS (VIRGIN)	1
12/8/95	**NOW THAT'S WHAT I CALL MUSIC! 31** VARIOUS ARTISTS (EMI)	4
9/9/95	**DANCE ZONE LEVEL SIX** VARIOUS ARTISTS (POLYGRAM)	1
16/9/95	**HELP- WAR CHILD** VARIOUS ARTISTS (GO! DISCS)	2
30/9/95	**HEARTBEAT – FOREVER YOURS** VARIOUS ARTISTS (COLUMBIA)	6
11/11/95	**THE GREATEST PARTY ALBUM UNDER THE SUN!** VARIOUS ARTISTS (EMI)	1

Chart Date	Album Title Artist	Artist Weeks at No.1
18/11/95	**PURE SWING IV** VARIOUS ARTISTS (DINO)	1
25/11/95	**NOW THAT'S WHAT I CALL MUSIC! 32** VARIOUS ARTISTS (EMI)	6
23/12/95	**HITS 96** VARIOUS ARTISTS (GLOBAL TELEVISION)	5
3/2/96	**SISTERS OF SWING** VARIOUS ARTISTS (POLYGRAM)	1
10/2/96	**THE BEST. . .ALBUM IN THE WORLD ... EVER! 2** VARIOUS ARTISTS (VIRGIN)	2
24/2/96	**THE NUMBER ONE LOVE ALBUM** VARIOUS ARTISTS (POLYGRAM)	1
2/3/96	**IN THE MIX 96** VARIOUS ARTISTS (VIRGIN)	4
30/3/96	**NOW THAT'S WHAT I CALL MUSIC! 33** VARIOUS ARTISTS (EMI)	5
4/5/96	**DANCE ZONE LEVEL SEVEN** VARIOUS ARTISTS (POLYGRAM)	1
11/5/96	**BOYZ OF SWING** VARIOUS ARTISTS (POLYGRAM)	1
18/5/96	**NEW HITS 96** VARIOUS ARTISTS (GLOBAL TELEVISION)	9
20/7/96	**BIG MIX 96** VARIOUS ARTISTS (EMI)	4
17/8/96	**THE BEST DANCE ALBUM IN THE WORLD ... EVER! 6** VARIOUS ARTISTS (VIRGIN)	1
24/8/96	**NOW THAT'S WHAT I CALL MUSIC! 34** VARIOUS ARTISTS (EMI)	7
12/10/96	**IN THE MIX 96 – 3** VARIOUS ARTISTS (VIRGIN)	1
19/10/96	**KISS IN IBIZA '96** VARIOUS ARTISTS (POLYGRAM)	4
16/11/96	**HUGE HITS 1996** VARIOUS ARTISTS (SONY)	2
30/11/96	**NOW THAT'S WHAT I CALL MUSIC! 35** VARIOUS ARTISTS (EMI)	7
18/1/97	**THE ANNUAL II – PETE TONG & BOY GEORGE** VARIOUS ARTISTS (MINISTRY OF SOUND)	4
15/2/97	**IN THE MIX 97** VARIOUS ARTISTS (VIRGIN)	1
22/2/97	**THE ANNUAL II – PETE TONG & BOY GEORGE** VARIOUS ARTISTS (MINISTRY OF SOUND)	1
1/3/97	**CLUB MIX 97 – VOLUME 2** VARIOUS ARTISTS (POLYGRAM)	2
15/3/97	**THE SOUL ALBUM** VARIOUS ARTISTS (VIRGIN)	1
22/3/97	**THE BEST. . .ALBUM IN THE WORLD ... EVER! 5** VARIOUS ARTISTS (VIRGIN)	1
29/3/97	**DANCE NATION 3 – PETE TONG & JUDGE JULES** VARIOUS ARTISTS (MINISTRY OF SOUND)	1
5/4/97	**NOW THAT'S WHAT I CALL MUSIC! 36** VARIOUS ARTISTS (EMI)	3
26/4/97	**NEW HITS 1997** VARIOUS ARTISTS (GLOBAL TELEVISION)	4
24/5/97	**BIG MIX '97** VARIOUS ARTISTS (VIRGIN)	2
7/6/97	**SMASH HITS – SUMMER '97** VARIOUS ARTISTS (VIRGIN)	1
14/6/97	**THE BEST CLUB ANTHEMS IN THE WORLD ... EVER!** VARIOUS ARTISTS (VIRGIN)	4
12/7/97	**THE BEST DISCO ALBUM IN THE WORLD** VARIOUS ARTISTS (VIRGIN)	2
26/7/97	**NOW THAT'S WHAT I CALL MUSIC! 37** VARIOUS ARTISTS (EMI)	4
23/8/97	**FRESH HITS 1997** VARIOUS ARTISTS (GLOBAL TELEVISION)	3
13/9/97	**IBIZA UNCOVERED (TELEVISION COMPILATION)** TELEVISION AND RADIO COMPILATION	3
4/10/97	**KISS IN IBIZA '97** VARIOUS ARTISTS (POLYGRAM)	1
11/10/97	**IBIZA UNCOVERED (TELEVISION COMPILATION)** TELEVISION AND RADIO COMPILATION	1
18/10/97	**BIG MIX '97 – VOLUME 2** VARIOUS ARTISTS (VIRGIN)	1
25/10/97	**THE BEST ... ANTHEMS ... EVER!** VARIOUS ARTISTS (VIRGIN)	1
1/11/97	**NOW DANCE 97** VARIOUS ARTISTS (EMI)	1
8/11/97	**HUGE HITS 1997** VARIOUS ARTISTS (GLOBAL TELEVISION)	1
15/11/97	**THE ANNUAL III – PETE TONG & BOY GEORGE** VARIOUS ARTISTS (MINISTRY OF SOUND)	2
29/11/97	**NOW THAT'S WHAT I CALL MUSIC! 38** VARIOUS ARTISTS (EMI)	2
13/12/97	**DIANA PRINCESS OF WALES – TRIBUTE (ROYAL COMPILATION ALBUM)** ROYAL COMPILATION ALBUM	4
10/1/98	**NOW THAT'S WHAT I CALL MUSIC! 38** VARIOUS ARTISTS (EMI)	2
24/1/98	**THE EIGHTIES MIX** VARIOUS ARTISTS (GLOBAL TELEVISION)	2
7/2/98	**ULTIMATE CLUB MIX** VARIOUS ARTISTS (POLYGRAM)	1
14/2/98	**IN THE MIX 98** VARIOUS ARTISTS (VIRGIN)	1
21/2/98	**LOVE – 39 ALL TIME LOVE CLASSICS** VARIOUS ARTISTS (POLYGRAM)	1
28/2/98	**IN THE MIX 98** VARIOUS ARTISTS (VIRGIN)	1
7/3/98	**FANTASTIC 80'S!** VARIOUS ARTISTS (COLUMBIA)	1
14/3/98	**THE FULL MONTY (OST)** FILM SOUNDTRACK	3
4/4/98	**NEW HITS 98** VARIOUS ARTISTS (SONY)	2
18/4/98	**NOW THAT'S WHAT I CALL MUSIC! 39** VARIOUS ARTISTS (EMI)	8
13/6/98	**THE BOX HITS 98 – VOLUME 2** VARIOUS ARTISTS (TELSTAR)	3
4/7/98	**FRESH HITS 98** VARIOUS ARTISTS (SONY)	6
15/8/98	**NOW THAT'S WHAT I CALL MUSIC! 40** VARIOUS ARTISTS (EMI)	4
12/9/98	**THE IBIZA ANNUAL** VARIOUS ARTISTS (MINISTRY OF SOUND)	1
19/9/98	**BIG HITS 98** VARIOUS ARTISTS (SONY)	5
24/10/98	**IN THE MIX IBIZA** VARIOUS ARTISTS (VIRGIN)	1
31/10/98	**THE BEST CHART HITS ALBUM IN THE WORLD ... EVER!** VARIOUS ARTISTS (VIRGIN)	1
7/11/98	**HUGE HITS 1998** VARIOUS ARTISTS (SONY)	1
14/11/98	**THE ANNUAL IV – JUDGE JULES & BOY GEORGE** VARIOUS ARTISTS (MINISTRY OF SOUND)	2
28/11/98	**HUGE HITS 1998** VARIOUS ARTISTS (SONY)	1
5/12/98	**NOW THAT'S WHAT I CALL MUSIC! 41** VARIOUS ARTISTS (EMI)	7
23/1/99	**THE BEST CLUB ANTHEMS 99 IN THE WORLD ... EVER!** VARIOUS ARTISTS (VIRGIN)	1
30/1/99	**CLUBBER'S GUIDE TO ... NINETY NINE** VARIOUS ARTISTS (MINISTRY OF SOUND)	2
13/2/99	**EUPHORIA** VARIOUS ARTISTS (TELSTAR)	1
20/2/99	**LOVE SONGS** VARIOUS ARTISTS (POLYGRAM)	1
27/2/99	**EUPHORIA** VARIOUS ARTISTS (TELSTAR)	1
6/3/99	**KISS HOUSE NATION** VARIOUS ARTISTS (POLYGRAM)	2
20/3/99	**ESPECIALLY FOR YOU** VARIOUS ARTISTS (COLUMBIA)	1
27/3/99	**DANCE NATION 6 – TALL PAUL & BRANDON BLOCK** VARIOUS ARTISTS (MINISTRY OF SOUND)	1
3/4/99	**NEW HITS 99** VARIOUS ARTISTS (GLOBAL TELEVISION)	1
10/4/99	**NOW THAT'S WHAT I CALL MUSIC! 42** VARIOUS ARTISTS (EMI)	7

Chart Date	Album Title Artist	Artist Weeks at No.1
29/5/99	**TRANCE NATION: MIXED BY SYSTEM F** VARIOUS ARTISTS (MINISTRY OF SOUND)	3
19/6/99	**CLUBBER'S GUIDE TO IBIZA – SUMMER '99** VARIOUS ARTISTS (MINISTRY OF SOUND)	2
3/7/99	**FRESH HITS 99** VARIOUS ARTISTS (GLOBAL TELEVISION)	3
24/7/99	**THE BEST DANCE ALBUM IN THE WORLD ... EVER! 9** VARIOUS ARTISTS (VIRGIN)	1
31/7/99	**NOW THAT'S WHAT I CALL MUSIC! 43** VARIOUS ARTISTS (EMI)	4
28/8/99	**THE IBIZA ANNUAL: MIXED BY JUDGE JULES + TALL PAUL** VARIOUS ARTISTS (MINISTRY OF SOUND)	1
4/9/99	**BIG HITS 99** VARIOUS ARTISTS (GLOBAL TELEVISION)	2
18/9/99	**KISS IBIZA '99** VARIOUS ARTISTS (UNIVERSAL)	3
9/10/99	**TOP OF THE POPS '99 – VOLUME TWO** VARIOUS ARTISTS (UNIVERSAL)	1
16/10/99	**TRANCE NATION 2: MIXED BY FERRY CORSTEN** VARIOUS ARTISTS (MINISTRY OF SOUND)	1
23/10/99	**LAND OF MY FATHERS** VARIOUS ARTISTS (UNIVERSAL)	1
30/10/99	**NOW DANCE 2000** VARIOUS ARTISTS (EMI)	1
6/11/99	**HUGE HITS 99** VARIOUS ARTISTS (GLOBAL TELEVISION)	4
4/12/99	**NOW THAT'S WHAT I CALL MUSIC! 44** VARIOUS ARTISTS (EMI)	8
29/1/00	**CLUBBER'S GUIDE TO ... 2000** VARIOUS ARTISTS (MINISTRY OF SOUND)	2
12/2/00	**AYIA NAPA – FANTASY ISLAND** VARIOUS ARTISTS (TELSTAR)	1
19/2/00	**THE LOVE SONGS ALBUM** VARIOUS ARTISTS (UNIVERSAL)	1
26/2/00	**REWIND – THE SOUND OF UK GARAGE** VARIOUS ARTISTS (MINISTRY OF SOUND)	1
4/3/00	**THE BEACH (OST)** FILM SOUNDTRACK	3
25/3/00	**NEW HITS 2000** VARIOUS ARTISTS (WARNER BROTHERS)	2
8/4/00	**NEW WOMAN 2000** VARIOUS ARTISTS (VIRGIN)	1
15/4/00	**DANCE NATION – TALL PAUL/BRANDON BLOCK** VARIOUS ARTISTS (MINISTRY OF SOUND)	1
22/4/00	**GIRLS 2K** VARIOUS ARTISTS (VIRGIN)	1
29/4/00	**NOW THAT'S WHAT I CALL MUSIC! 45** VARIOUS ARTISTS (EMI)	6
10/6/00	**CLUBBER'S GUIDE TO IBIZA -SUMMER 2000** VARIOUS ARTISTS (MINISTRY OF SOUND)	1
17/6/00	**TOP OF THE POPS 2000 VOLUME 2** VARIOUS ARTISTS (UNIVERSAL)	1
24/6/00	**CLUB MIX IBIZA 2000** VARIOUS ARTISTS (UNIVERSAL)	3
15/7/00	**FRESH HITS – VOLUME 1** VARIOUS ARTISTS (WARNER BROTHERS)	2
29/7/00	**KISS CLUBLIFE SUMMER 2000** VARIOUS ARTISTS (UNIVERSAL)	1
5/8/00	**NOW THAT'S WHAT I CALL MUSIC! 46** VARIOUS ARTISTS (EMI)	4
2/9/00	**THE IBIZA ANNUAL – SUMMER 2000** VARIOUS ARTISTS (MINISTRY OF SOUND)	3
23/9/00	**KISS IBIZA 2000** VARIOUS ARTISTS (UNIVERSAL)	2
7/10/00	**TRANCE NATION 4** VARIOUS ARTISTS (MINISTRY OF SOUND)	3
28/10/00	**CLUBMIX 2000 VOLUME 2** VARIOUS ARTISTS (UNIVERSAL)	1
4/11/00	**NOW DANCE 2001** VARIOUS ARTISTS (VIRGIN)	1
11/11/00	**THE ANNUAL 2000 – JUDGE JULES/TALL PAUL** VARIOUS ARTISTS (MINISTRY OF SOUND)	2
25/11/00	**CREAM ANTHEMS 2001** VARIOUS ARTISTS (VIRGIN)	1
2/12/00	**NOW THAT'S WHAT I CALL MUSIC! 47** VARIOUS ARTISTS (EMI)	7
20/1/01	**CLUBBERS GUIDE TO 2001** VARIOUS ARTISTS (MINISTRY OF SOUND)	2
3/2/01	**BREAKDOWN – VERY BEST OF EUPHORIC DANCE** VARIOUS ARTISTS (TELSTAR)	2
17/2/01	**THE CHILL OUT SESSION** VARIOUS ARTISTS (MINISTRY OF SOUND)	6
31/3/01	**NEW WOMAN 2001** VARIOUS ARTISTS (VIRGIN)	1
7/4/01	**THE ANNUAL – SPRING 2001** VARIOUS ARTISTS (MINISTRY OF SOUND)	2
21/4/01	**NOW THAT'S WHAT I CALL MUSIC! 48** VARIOUS ARTISTS (EMI)	3
12/5/01	**BRIDGET JONES'S DIARY (OST)** FILM SOUNDTRACK	7
23/6/01	**CAPITAL GOLD LEGENDS** VARIOUS ARTISTS (VIRGIN)	7
11/8/01	**NOW THAT'S WHAT I CALL MUSIC! 49** VARIOUS ARTISTS (EMI)	6
29/9/01	**HITS 50** VARIOUS ARTISTS (BMG)	2
13/10/01	**THE CLASSIC CHILLOUT ALBUM** VARIOUS ARTISTS (COLUMBIA)	1
20/10/01	**PEPSI CHART 2002** VARIOUS ARTISTS (VIRGIN)	2
3/11/01	**NOW DANCE 2002** VARIOUS ARTISTS (VIRGIN)	3
24/11/01	**THE ANNUAL 2002** VARIOUS ARTISTS (MINISTRY OF SOUND)	1
1/12/01	**NOW THAT'S WHAT I CALL MUSIC! 50** VARIOUS ARTISTS (EMI)	7
19/1/02	**CLUBBERS GUIDE TO 2002** VARIOUS ARTISTS (MINISTRY OF SOUND)	3
9/2/02	**BEST CLUB ANTHEMS 2002** VARIOUS ARTISTS (VIRGIN)	1
16/2/02	**CLUB MIX 2002** VARIOUS ARTISTS (UNIVERSAL)	1
23/2/02	**LOVE SO STRONG** VARIOUS ARTISTS (WARNER BROTHERS)	1
2/3/02	**SCHOOL DISCO.COM – SPRING TERM** VARIOUS ARTISTS (COLUMBIA)	2
16/3/02	**NEW WOMAN 2002** VARIOUS ARTISTS (VIRGIN)	1
23/3/02	**SUPERCHARGED** VARIOUS ARTISTS (UNIVERSAL)	2
6/4/02	**NOW THAT'S WHAT I CALL MUSIC! 51** VARIOUS ARTISTS (EMI)	2
20/4/02	**POP IDOL – THE BIG BAND ALBUM** VARIOUS ARTISTS (S RECORDS)	4
18/5/02	**NOW THAT'S WHAT I CALL MUSIC! 51** VARIOUS ARTISTS (EMI)	1
25/5/02	**KISSTORY** VARIOUS ARTISTS (UNIVERSAL)	1
1/6/02	**THE BEST SUMMER ALBUM 2002** VARIOUS ARTISTS (WARNER BROTHERS)	1
8/6/02	**CLUBBERS GUIDE TO IBIZA 2002** VARIOUS ARTISTS (MINISTRY OF SOUND)	1
22/6/02	**CAPITAL GOLD ROCK LEGENDS** VARIOUS ARTISTS (VIRGIN)	1
29/6/02	**THE VERY BEST OF MTV UNPLUGGED** VARIOUS ARTISTS (UNIVERSAL)	1
6/7/02	**CLUBLAND** VARIOUS ARTISTS (UNIVERSAL)	4
3/8/02	**NOW THAT'S WHAT I CALL MUSIC! 52** VARIOUS ARTISTS (EMI)	5

Chart Date	Album Title Artist	Artist Weeks at No.1
7/9/02	**THE VERY BEST OF PURE R&B – THE SUMMER** VARIOUS ARTISTS (TELSTAR)	1
14/9/02	**SMASH HITS – LET'S PARTY** VARIOUS ARTISTS (EMI)	5
19/10/02	**NEW WOMAN – THE AUTUMN COLLECTION** VARIOUS ARTISTS (VIRGIN)	1
26/10/02	**NOW DANCE 2003** VARIOUS ARTISTS (VIRGIN)	1
2/11/02	**HITS 54** VARIOUS ARTISTS (BMG)	2
16/11/02	**THE ANNUAL 2003** VARIOUS ARTISTS (MINISTRY OF SOUND)	1
23/11/02	**CLUBLAND II – THE RIDE OF YOUR LIFE** VARIOUS ARTISTS (UNIVERSAL)	1
30/11/02	**NOW THAT'S WHAT I CALL MUSIC! 53** VARIOUS ARTISTS (EMI)	7
18/1/03	**CLUBBERS GUIDE 2003** VARIOUS ARTISTS (MINISTRY OF SOUND)	1
25/1/03	**8 MILE (OST)** FILM SOUNDTRACK	3
15/2/03	**LOVE – ETERNAL LOVESONGS** VARIOUS ARTISTS (UNIVERSAL)	2
1/3/03	**CLUB MIX 2003** VARIOUS ARTISTS (UNIVERSAL)	1
8/3/03	**THE VERY BEST OF MTV UNPLUGGED 2** VARIOUS ARTISTS (WARNER BROTHERS)	2
22/3/03	**THE VERY BEST OF COLD FEET** TELEVISION AND RADIO COMPILATION	3
12/4/03	**HITS 55** VARIOUS ARTISTS (BMG)	2
26/4/03	**NOW THAT'S WHAT I CALL MUSIC! 54** VARIOUS ARTISTS (EMI)	7
14/6/03	**POWER BALLADS** VARIOUS ARTISTS (VIRGIN)	3
5/7/03	**CLUBLAND III** VARIOUS ARTISTS (UNIVERSAL)	3
26/7/03	**HITS 56** VARIOUS ARTISTS (BMG)	1
2/8/03	**NOW THAT'S WHAT I CALL MUSIC! 55** VARIOUS ARTISTS (EMI)	5
6/9/03	**KISS PRESENTS R&B COLLABORATIONS** VARIOUS ARTISTS (UNIVERSAL)	3
27/9/03	**CLUBMIX SUMMER 2003** VARIOUS ARTISTS (UNIVERSAL)	2
11/10/03	**NOW DECADES** VARIOUS ARTISTS (EMI)	3
1/11/03	**GREASEMANIA** VARIOUS ARTISTS (POLYDOR)	1
8/11/03	**NOW DANCE 2004** VARIOUS ARTISTS (VIRGIN)	1
15/11/03	**WESTWOOD – PLATINUM EDITION** VARIOUS ARTISTS (UNIVERSAL)	1
22/11/03	**CLUBLAND 4** VARIOUS ARTISTS (UNIVERSAL)	1
29/11/03	**NOW THAT'S WHAT I CALL MUSIC! 56** VARIOUS ARTISTS (EMI)	7
18/1/04	**CLUBBERS GUIDE – 2004** VARIOUS ARTISTS (MINISTRY OF SOUND)	3
7/2/04	**KISS SMOOTH R&B** VARIOUS ARTISTS (UNIVERSAL)	1
14/2/04	**CLUBMIX 2004** VARIOUS ARTISTS (UNIVERSAL)	1
21/2/04	**BEAUTIFUL** VARIOUS ARTISTS (BMG)	1
28/2/04	**THE BRIT AWARDS ALBUM 2004** VARIOUS ARTISTS (BMG)	1
6/3/04	**CLUBMIX 2004** VARIOUS ARTISTS (UNIVERSAL)	1
13/3/04	**HIT 40 UK** VARIOUS ARTISTS (BMG)	1
20/3/04	**FLOORFILLERS** VARIOUS ARTISTS (UNIVERSAL)	1
27/3/04	**THE VERY BEST OF NEW WOMAN** VARIOUS ARTISTS (VIRGIN)	1
3/4/04	**ULTIMATE DIRTY DANCING** FILM SOUNDTRACK	2
17/4/04	**NOW THAT'S WHAT I CALL MUSIC! 57** VARIOUS ARTISTS (EMI)	7
12/6/04	**HITS 58** VARIOUS ARTISTS (BMG)	1
19/6/04	**BIGGER, BETTER POWER BALLADS** VARIOUS ARTISTS (VIRGIN)	2
3/7/04	**ESSENTIAL R&B – THE VERY BEST OF R&B** VARIOUS ARTISTS (BMG)	2
24/7/04	**CLUBLAND 5** VARIOUS ARTISTS (UNIVERSAL)	2
7/8/04	**NOW THAT'S WHAT I CALL MUSIC! 58** VARIOUS ARTISTS (EMI)	7
18/9/04	**SAD SONGS** VARIOUS ARTISTS (VIRGIN)	1
2/10/04	**BIG TUNES** VARIOUS ARTISTS (MINISTRY OF SOUND)	1
9/10/04	**NOW YEARS** VARIOUS ARTISTS (EMI)	2
23/10/04	**BIG TUNES** VARIOUS ARTISTS (MINISTRY OF SOUND)	2
6/11/04	**POP PARTY 2** VARIOUS ARTISTS (UNIVERSAL)	3
27/11/04	**NOW THAT'S WHAT I CALL MUSIC! 59** VARIOUS ARTISTS (EMI)	7
15/1/05	**R&B ANTHEMS 2005** VARIOUS ARTISTS (SONY)	5
12/2/05	**LOVE SONGS – THE ULTIMATE LOVE COLLECTION** VARIOUS ARTISTS (UNIVERSAL)	1
26/2/05	**CLUBMIX 2005** VARIOUS ARTISTS (UNIVERSAL)	2
5/3/05	**I LOVE MUM** VARIOUS ARTISTS (VIRGIN)	1
19/3/05	**ESSENTIAL R&B – SPRING 2005** VARIOUS ARTISTS (SONY/BMG)	2
2/4/05	**NOW THAT'S WHAT I CALL MUSIC! 60** VARIOUS ARTISTS (EMI)	5
30/4/05	**HAPPY SONGS** VARIOUS ARTISTS (VIRGIN)	1
14/5/05	**CLUBLAND X-TREME HARDCORE** VARIOUS ARTISTS (UNIVERSAL)	1
21/5/05	**HAPPY SONGS** VARIOUS ARTISTS (VIRGIN)	1
28/5/05	**MASSIVE R&B** VARIOUS ARTISTS (UNIVERSAL)	2
4/6/05	**DRIVING ROCK BALLADS** VARIOUS ARTISTS (VIRGIN)	1
11/6/05	**DAD ROCKS** VARIOUS ARTISTS (VIRGIN)	2
2/7/05	**HAIRBRUSH DIVAS PRESENTS SING-A-LONG SUMMER** VARIOUS ARTISTS (WARNER BROTHERS)	1
9/7/05	**CLUBLAND 7** VARIOUS ARTISTS (UNIVERSAL)	1
9/7/05	**GATECRASHER CLASSICS** VARIOUS ARTISTS (MINISTRY OF SOUND)	3
6/8/05	**NOW THAT'S WHAT I CALL MUSIC! 61** VARIOUS ARTISTS (EMI)	7
17/9/05	**DANCE PARTY** VARIOUS ARTISTS (UNIVERSAL)	2
8/10/05	**ACOUSTIC LOVE** VARIOUS ARTISTS (WARNER BROTHERS)	4
5/11/05	**POP PARTY 3** VARIOUS ARTISTS (UNIVERSAL)	4
3/12/05	**NOW THAT'S WHAT I CALL MUSIC! 62** VARIOUS ARTISTS (EMI)	6
14/1/06	**CLUBBERS GUIDE 2006** VARIOUS ARTISTS (MINISTRY OF SOUND)	4
11/2/06	**R&B LOVESONGS** VARIOUS ARTISTS (UNIVERSAL)	3
25/2/06	**BRIT AWARDS 2006 – THE MUSIC EVENT** VARIOUS ARTISTS (SONY/BMG)	1
11/3/06	**THE MASH UP MIX 2006** VARIOUS ARTISTS (MINISTRY OF SOUND)	1
18/3/06	**CLUBLAND XTREME HARDCORE 2** VARIOUS ARTISTS (UNIVERSAL)	2
25/3/06	**WORLD'S BEST MUM** VARIOUS ARTISTS (SONY/BMG)	1
1/4/06	**FLOORFILLERS – CLUB CLASSICS** VARIOUS ARTISTS (UNIVERSAL)	2

Chart Date	Album Title Artist	Artist Weeks at No.1
22/4/06	**NOW THAT'S WHAT I CALL MUSIC! 63** VARIOUS ARTISTS (EMI)	5
27/5/06	**BIG CLUB HITS** VARIOUS ARTISTS (UNIVERSAL)	3
10/6/06	**ENGLAND – THE ALBUM** VARIOUS ARTISTS (EMI)	1
17/6/05	**DAD ROCKS** VARIOUS ARTISTS (VIRGIN)	1
24/6/06	**CLUBBERS GUIDE SUMMER 2006** VARIOUS ARTISTS (MINISTRY OF SOUND)	1
8/7/06	**CLUBLAND 9** VARIOUS ARTISTS (UNIVERSAL)	4
5/8/06	**NOW THAT'S WHAT I CALL MUSIC! 64** VARIOUS ARTISTS (EMI)	5
16/9/06	**DANCE MANIA** VARIOUS ARTISTS (UNIVERSAL)	4
30/9/06	**HIGH SCHOOL MUSICAL** VARIOUS ARTISTS (WALT DISNEY)	3
28/10/06	**RADIO 1'S LIVE LOUNGE** VARIOUS ARTISTS (SONY/BMG)	1
4/11/06	**HIGH SCHOOL MUSICAL** VARIOUS ARTISTS (WALT DISNEY)	1
11/11/06	**RADIO 1'S LIVE LOUNGE** VARIOUS ARTISTS (SONY/BMG)	1
18/11/06	**CLUBLAND 10** VARIOUS ARTISTS (UNIVERSAL)	1
25/11/06	**POP PARTY 4** VARIOUS ARTISTS (UNIVERSAL)	1
13/1/07	**RADIO 1'S LIVE LOUNGE** VARIOUS ARTISTS (SONY/BMG)	5
17/2/07	**ONE LOVE** VARIOUS ARTISTS (UNIVERSAL)	2
3/3/07	**BRITS HITS – THE ALBUM OF THE YEAR** VARIOUS ARTISTS (UNIVERSAL)	2
17/3/07	**101 80S HITS** VARIOUS ARTISTS (EMI)	1
24/3/07	**TO MUM WITH LOVE** VARIOUS ARTISTS (UNIVERSAL)	1
31/3/07	**FLOORFILLERS ANTHEMS** VARIOUS ARTISTS (UNIVERSAL)	2
14/4/07	**NOW THAT'S WHAT I CALL MUSIC 66** VARIOUS ARTISTS (EMI)	6
26/5/07	**MASSIVE R&B – SPRING COLLECTION 2007** VARIOUS ARTISTS (UNIVERSAL)	3
16/6/07	**OVER THE RAINBOW** VARIOUS ARTISTS (UNIVERSAL)	1
23/6/07	**TOP GEAR ANTHEMS** VARIOUS ARTISTS (EMI)	1
30/6/07	**CLUBLAND 11** VARIOUS ARTISTS (UNIVERSAL)	3
21/7/07	**R&B LOVE COLLECTION** VARIOUS ARTISTS (UNIVERSAL)	2
4/8/07	**NOW THAT'S WHAT I CALL MUSIC 67** VARIOUS ARTISTS (EMI)	3
25/8/07	**HIGH SCHOOL MUSICAL 2** TELEVISION AND RADIO COMPILATION	7
13/10/07	**RADIO 1 ESTABLISHED 1967** VARIOUS ARTISTS (UNIVERSAL)	3
3/11/07	**RADIO 1'S LIVE LOUNGE – VOLUME 2** VARIOUS ARTISTS (SONY/BMG)	2
17/11/07	**CLUBLAND 12** VARIOUS ARTISTS (UNIVERSAL)	1
24/11/07	**POP PARTY VOLUME 5** VARIOUS ARTISTS (UNIVERSAL)	1
1/12/07	**NOW THAT'S WHAT I CALL MUSIC 68** VARIOUS ARTISTS (EMI)	7
19/1/08	**MINISTRY OF SOUND ANTHEMS 1991-2008** VARIOUS ARTISTS (MINISTRY OF SOUND)	1
26/1/08	**BIG TUNES 2008** VARIOUS ARTISTS (MINISTRY OF SOUND)	3
16/2/08	**ULTIMATE NRG 3** VARIOUS ARTISTS (UNIVERSAL)	1
23/2/08	**REAL LOVE** VARIOUS ARTISTS (UNIVERSAL)	1
1/3/08	**THE VERY BEST OF EUPHORIC DANCE BREAKDOWN** VARIOUS ARTISTS (MINISTRY OF SOUND)	1
8/3/08	**YOU RAISE ME UP 2008** VARIOUS ARTISTS (UNIVERSAL)	1
15/3/08	**THE VERY BEST OF EUPHORIC DANCE BREAKDOWN** VARIOUS ARTISTS (MINISTRY OF SOUND)	1
22/3/08	**FLOORFILLERS 08** VARIOUS ARTISTS (UNIVERSAL)	1
29/3/08	**NOW THAT'S WHAT I CALL MUSIC 69** VARIOUS ARTISTS (EMI)	3
19/4/08	**CLUBLAND CLASSIX – THE ALBUM OF YOUR LIFE** VARIOUS ARTISTS (UNIVERSAL)	6
31/5/08	**CHILLED 1991-2008** VARIOUS ARTISTS (MINISTRY OF SOUND)	5
5/7/08	**CLUBLAND 13** VARIOUS ARTISTS (UNIVERSAL)	2
19/7/08	**MAMMA MIA** FILM SOUNDTRACK	2
2/8/08	**NOW THAT'S WHAT I CALL MUSIC 70** VARIOUS ARTISTS (EMI)	3
23/8/08	**MAMMA MIA** FILM SOUNDTRACK	8
18/10/08	**MASSIVE R&B – WINTER 2008** VARIOUS ARTISTS (UNIVERSAL)	2
1/11/08	**HIGH SCHOOL MUSICAL 3 – SENIOR YEAR** VARIOUS ARTISTS (WALT DISNEY)	3
22/11/08	**CLUBLAND 14** VARIOUS ARTISTS (UNIVERSAL)	1
29/11/08	**NOW THAT'S WHAT I CALL MUSIC 71** VARIOUS ARTISTS (EMI)	6

Album Index

KEY TO INDEX ENTRIES

Album Title | Artist/Group | Peak Position | Year of Release

Album Title / Artist/Group	Peak Position	Year of Release
ABBA ABBA	13	1976
ABBAMANIA VARIOUS ARTISTS (POLYDOR)	2	1999
THE ABBEY DOWNSIDE ABBEY MONKS & CHOIRBOYS	54	1996
ABBEY ROAD BEATLES	1	1969
ABC JACKSON FIVE	22	1970
ABDUCTION EAT STATIC	62	1993
ABOMINOG URIAH HEEP	34	1982
ABOUT A BOY – OST BADLY DRAWN BOY	6	2002
ABOUT FACE DAVID GILMOUR	21	1984
ABOUT TIME STRANGLERS	31	1995
ABOUT TIME 2 CLOCK	56	1997
ABOUT WHAT YOU KNOW LITTLE MAN TATE	27	2007
ABOVE MAD SEASON	41	1995
ABOVE THE RIM FILM SOUNDTRACK	18	1994

Title / Artist	Peak Position	Year of Release
( ) SIGUR ROS	49	2002

A

Title / Artist	Peak Position	Year of Release
A JETHRO TULL	25	1980
THE A LIST A1	14	2000
A LITTLE BIT LONGER JONAS BROTHERS	19	2008
AALIYAH AALIYAH	5	2001
AARON CARTER AARON CARTER	12	1998
ABACAB GENESIS	1	1981
ABANDONED SHOPPING TROLLEY HOTLINE GOMEZ	10	2000
ABATTOIR BLUES/THE LYRE OF ORPHEUS NICK CAVE & THE BAD SEEDS	11	2004
ABBA ABBA	13	1976
ABBAMANIA VARIOUS ARTISTS (POLYDOR)	2	1999
THE ABBEY DOWNSIDE ABBEY MONKS & CHOIRBOYS	54	1996
ABBEY ROAD BEATLES	1	1969
ABC JACKSON FIVE	22	1970
ABDUCTION EAT STATIC	62	1993
ABOMINOG URIAH HEEP	34	1982
ABOUT A BOY – OST BADLY DRAWN BOY	6	2002
ABOUT FACE DAVID GILMOUR	21	1984
ABOUT TIME STRANGLERS	31	1995
ABOUT TIME 2 CLOCK	56	1997
ABOUT WHAT YOU KNOW LITTLE MAN TATE	27	2007
ABOVE MAD SEASON	41	1995
ABOVE THE RIM FILM SOUNDTRACK	18	1994
ABRACADABRA STEVE MILLER BAND	10	1982
ABRACADABRA ABC	50	1991
ABRAXAS SANTANA	7	1970
ABRIENDO PUERTAS GLORIA ESTEFAN	70	1995
ABSENT FRIENDS DIVINE COMEDY	23	2004
ABSOLUTE GARBAGE	11	2007
ABSOLUTE ABBA ABBA	70	1988
ABSOLUTE BEGINNERS FILM SOUNDTRACK	19	1986
ABSOLUTE EUPHORIA – DAVE PEARCE VARIOUS ARTISTS (TELSTAR)	3	2002
THE ABSOLUTE GAME SKIDS	9	1980
ABSOLUTE GOLD VARIOUS ARTISTS (SONY)	3	1997
ABSOLUTE ROCK 'N' ROLL VARIOUS ARTISTS (STARBLEND)	88	1986
ABSOLUTELY MADNESS	2	1980
ABSOLUTELY ABC	7	1990
ABSOLUTELY LIVE DOORS	69	1970
ABSOLUTELY LIVE ROD STEWART	35	1982
ABSOLUTELY MAD MADHOUSE	57	2002
ABSOLUTION MUSE	1	2003
ABSOLUTION – ROCK THE ALTERNATIVE WAY VARIOUS ARTISTS (POLYDOR)	6	1991
ABSTRACT EMOTIONS RANDY CRAWFORD	14	1986
ABSTRACT THEORY ABS	29	2003
AC/DC LIVE AC/DC	5	1992
ACCELERATE R.E.M.	1	2008
ACCELERATOR FUTURE SOUND OF LONDON	75	1992
ACCESS ALL AREAS VARIOUS ARTISTS (POSITIVA)	11	1997
ACCIDENT OF BIRTH BRUCE DICKINSON	53	1997
ACCORDING TO MY HEART JIM REEVES	1	1969
ACE IAN VAN DAHL	7	2002
ACE A'S + KILLER B'S DODGY	55	1998
ACE OF SPADES MOTORHEAD	4	1980
ACES AND KINGS – THE BEST OF GO WEST GO WEST	5	1993
ACHTUNG BABY U2	2	1991
ACID JAZZ AND OTHER ILLICIT GROOVES VARIOUS ARTISTS (URBAN)	86	1988
ACID JAZZ CLASSICS VARIOUS ARTISTS (MINISTRY OF SOUND)	12	2004
ACID TONGUE JENNY LEWIS	55	2008
ACID TRAX MAGAMIX VOLUME 1 VARIOUS ARTISTS (SERIOUS)	93	1988
ACKER MR ACKER BILK	17	1961
ACKER BILK'S OMNIBUS MR ACKER BILK	14	1960
ACME JON SPENCER BLUES EXPLOSION	72	1998
ACOUSTIC VARIOUS ARTISTS (ECHO)	4	2002
THE ACOUSTIC ALBUM VARIOUS ARTISTS (EMI)	5	2006
ACOUSTIC EXTRAVAGANZA KT TUNSTALL	32	2006
ACOUSTIC FREEWAY VARIOUS ARTISTS (POLYGRAM)	7	1995
ACOUSTIC LOVE VARIOUS ARTISTS (WARNER BROTHERS)	1	2005
ACOUSTIC LOVE 2 VARIOUS ARTISTS (WARNER BROTHERS)	6	2006
ACOUSTIC MOODS VARIOUS ARTISTS (POLYGRAM)	4	1994
ACOUSTIC MOODS IN TUNE	21	1995
ACOUSTIC 04 VARIOUS ARTISTS (ECHO)	15	2004
ACOUSTIC ROCK VARIOUS ARTISTS (POLYGRAM)	7	1995
ACOUSTIC SONGBOOK VARIOUS ARTISTS (VIRGIN)	16	2004
ACOUSTIC SOUL INDIA ARIE	55	2001
ACOUSTIC 2 VARIOUS ARTISTS (ECHO)	14	2002
ACROSS A CROWDED ROOM RICHARD THOMPSON	80	1985
ACROSS THE WIRE – LIVE IN NEW YORK COUNTING CROWS	27	1998
ACT THREE G4	21	2006
ACTING VERY STRANGE MIKE RUTHERFORD	23	1982
ACTION REPLAY VARIOUS ARTISTS (K-TEL)	1	1979
ACTION TRAX VARIOUS ARTISTS (K-TEL)	2	1982
ADAGIO 2 HERBERT VON KARAJAN CONDUCTING THE BERLIN PHILHARMONIC ORCHESTRA	63	1996
ADAM ADAM FAITH	6	1960
ADAM AND EVE CATHERINE WHEEL	53	1998
ADAM FAITH ADAM FAITH	20	1962
ADDICTED TO BASS VARIOUS ARTISTS (MINISTRY OF SOUND)	5	2002
ADDICTED TO TRANCE VARIOUS ARTISTS (MINISTRY OF SOUND)	3	2002
ADDICTED 2 BASSLINE VARIOUS ARTISTS (UNIVERSAL)	4	2008
ADDICTIONS VOLUME 1 ROBERT PALMER	7	1989
ADDICTIONS VOLUME 2 ROBERT PALMER	12	1992
ADEVA ADEVA	6	1989
ADGE CUTLER AND THE WURZELS WURZELS	38	1967
ADIEMUS II – CANTATA MUNDI ADIEMUS	15	1997
ADIEMUS III – DANCES OF TIME ADIEMUS	58	1998
ADORE SMASHING PUMPKINS	5	1998
ADRENALIN VARIOUS ARTISTS (TELSTAR)	10	1999
ADRENALIZE DEF LEPPARD	1	1992
ADVANCE LFO	44	1996
ADVENTURE TELEVISION	7	1978
ADVENTURES IN TIN TIN OUT LAND TIN TIN OUT	65	1996
ADVENTURES IN UTOPIA UTOPIA	57	1980
THE ADVENTURES OF THE HERSHAM BOYS SHAM 69	8	1979
THE ADVENTURES OF THIN LIZZY THIN LIZZY	6	1981
AERIAL KATE BUSH	3	2005
AERO JEAN-MICHEL JARRE	14	2004
AFFECTION LISA STANSFIELD	2	1989
AFFIRMATION SAVAGE GARDEN	7	1999
AFFIRMATION BEVERLEY KNIGHT	11	2004
AFRAID OF SUNLIGHT MARILLION	16	1995
AFRICA TO AMERICA: THE JOURNEY OF THE DRUM SOUNDS OF BLACKNESS	28	1994
AFRICA UNITE – THE SINGLES BOB MARLEY & THE WAILERS	26	2005
AFRODISIAC VARIOUS ARTISTS (UNIVERSAL)	14	1999
AFRODISIAC BRANDY	32	2004
AFTER A DREAM ROBERT MEADMORE	49	2005
AFTER ALL THESE YEARS FOSTER & ALLEN	82	1986
AFTER DARK RAY PARKER JR	40	1987
AFTER DARK TOM JONES	46	1989
AFTER DARK VARIOUS ARTISTS (COLUMBIA)	8	1993
AFTER HOURS GARY MOORE	4	1992
AFTER HOURS BILL TARMEY	61	1996
AFTER MIDNIGHT VARIOUS ARTISTS (POLYGRAM)	17	1994
AFTER MURDER PARK AUTEURS	53	1996
AFTER THE BREAK (TELEVISION COMPILATION) TELEVISION AND RADIO COMPILATION	17	1997
AFTER THE DANCE VARIOUS ARTISTS (TELSTAR)	16	1991
AFTER THE GOLDRUSH NEIL YOUNG	7	1970
AFTER THE LAUGHTER FREDDIE STARR	10	1989
AFTER THE WAR GARY MOORE	23	1989
AFTERBURNER ZZ TOP	2	1985
AFTERGLOW CROWDED HOUSE	18	2000
AFTERGLOW SARAH McLACHLAN	33	2004
AFTERMATH ROLLING STONES	1	1966
AGAETIS BYRJUN SIGUR ROS	52	2000
AGAINST SEPULTURA	40	1998
AGAINST ALL ODDS FILM SOUNDTRACK	29	1984
AGAINST PERFECTION ADORABLE	70	1993
AGAINST THE WIND BOB SEGER & THE SILVER BULLET BAND	26	1980
AGE AIN'T NOTHING BUT A NUMBER AALIYAH	23	1994
THE AGE OF CONSENT BRONSKI BEAT	4	1984
THE AGE OF PLASTIC BUGGLES	27	1980
THE AGE OF THE UNDERSTATEMENT LAST SHADOW PUPPETS	1	2008
AGENT PROVOCATEUR FOREIGNER	1	1984
AGENTS OF FORTUNE BLUE OYSTER CULT	26	1976
AGES OF MANN – 22 CLASSIC HITS OF THE 60'S MANFRED MANN	23	1993
AGNUS DEI CHOIR OF NEW COLLEGE OXFORD/EDWARD HIGGINBOTTOM	49	1996
AGNUS DEI II CHOIR OF NEW COLLEGE OXFORD/EDWARD HIGGINBOTTOM	57	1998
AGONY & IRONY ALKALINE TRIO	52	2008
AHA SHAKE HEARTBREAK KINGS OF LEON	3	2004
AHEAD RINGS OUT BLODWYN PIG	9	1969
AIN'T COMPLAINING STATUS QUO	12	1988
AIN'T NO STOPPIN' ENIGMA	80	1981
AIN'T NOTHING LIKE ME JOE	25	2007
AIR CONDITIONING CURVED AIR	8	1970
THE AIR THAT I BREATHE – THE BEST OF THE HOLLIES HOLLIES	15	1993
AIR, EARTH, FIRE, WATER THIRD EAR BAND	49	1970
AIRDRAWN DAGGER SASHA	18	2002
AJA STEELY DAN	5	1977
AL AL GREEN	41	1992
AL GREEN'S GREATEST HITS AL GREEN	18	1975
THE AL JOLSON COLLECTION AL JOLSON	67	1983
ALADDIN FILM SOUNDTRACK	11	1994
ALADDIN AND HIS WONDERFUL LAMP CLIFF RICHARD & THE SHADOWS	13	1965
ALADDIN SANE DAVID BOWIE	1	1973
ALAN TITCHMARSH – IN A COUNTRY GARDEN VARIOUS ARTISTS (SONY CLASSICAL)	20	2000
ALANNAH MYLES ALANNAH MYLES	3	1990
ALAS I CANNOT SWIM LAURA MARLING	45	2008
ALBEDO 0.39 VANGELIS	18	1976
THE ALBUM ABBA	1	1978
THE ALBUM MANTRONIX	45	1986
THE ALBUM TELETUBBIES	31	1998
THE ALBUM BOB THE BUILDER	4	2001

Title / Artist	Peak Position	Year of Release
THE ALBUM VARIOUS ARTISTS (VIRGIN)	3	2001
THE ALBUM ULTRABEAT	8	2007
THE ALBUM 2 VARIOUS ARTISTS (VIRGIN)	20	2002
THE ALBUM 3 VARIOUS ARTISTS (VIRGIN)	3	2002
THE ALBUM 4 VARIOUS ARTISTS (VIRGIN)	3	2002
THE ALBUM 5 VARIOUS ARTISTS (VIRGIN)	2	2005
THE ALBUM 6 VARIOUS ARTISTS (EMI)	5	2005
THE ALBUM OF THE SOUNDTRACK OF THE TRAILER OF THE FILM OF MONTY PYTHON AND THE HOLY GRAIL (OST) MONTY PYTHON'S FLYING CIRCUS	45	1975
ALBUM OF THE YEAR FAITH NO MORE	7	1997
ALBUM/CASSETTE PUBLIC IMAGE LTD	14	1986
ALCHEMY – DIRE STRAITS LIVE DIRE STRAITS	3	1984
ALED ALED JONES	27	2002
ALED JONES PRESENTS GOOD MORNING SUNDAY VARIOUS ARTISTS (WARNER BROTHERS)	12	2008
ALED JONES WITH THE BBC WELSH CHORUS ALED JONES WITH THE BBC WELSH CHORUS	11	1985
ALED (MUSIC FROM THE TV SERIES) ALED JONES	52	1987
THE ALESHA SHOW ALESHA DIXON	26	2008
ALEX LOVES... ALEXANDER O'NEAL	49	2008
ALEXANDER O'NEAL ALEXANDER O'NEAL	19	1985
ALF ALISON MOYET	1	1984
ALI G INDAHOUSE – DA SOUNDTRACK FILM SOUNDTRACK	5	2002
ALICE TOM WAITS	20	2002
ALICE COOPER GOES TO HELL ALICE COOPER	23	1976
ALICE IN CHAINS ALICE IN CHAINS	37	1995
ALICE'S RESTAURANT ARLO GUTHRIE	44	1970
ALIEN CHILD QFX	62	1997
ALIEN LOVE SECRETS STEVE VAI	39	1995
ALIENS ATE MY BUICK THOMAS DOLBY	30	1988
ALISHA RULES THE WORLD ALISHA'S ATTIC	14	1996
ALIVE KISS	60	1977
ALIVE III KISS	24	1993
ALIVE IN AMERICA STEELY DAN	62	1995
ALIVE IN HELL MEAT LOAF	33	1994
ALIVE ON ARRIVAL STEVE FORBERT	56	1979
ALIVE! KISS	49	1976
ALIVE, SHE CRIED DOORS	36	1983
ALL ABOARD VARIOUS ARTISTS (EMI)	13	1979
ALL ABOUT CHEMISTRY SEMISONIC	13	2001
ALL ABOUT EVE ALL ABOUT EVE	7	1988
ALL ABOUT LOVE JOYCE SIMS	64	1989
ALL ALONE AM I BRENDA LEE	8	1963
ALL AMERICAN ALIEN BOY IAN HUNTER	29	1976
ALL ANGELS ALL ANGELS	9	2006
ALL AROUND MY HAT STEELEYE SPAN	7	1975
ALL AROUND THE WORLD JASON DONOVAN	27	1993
ALL BY MYSELF VARIOUS ARTISTS (K-TEL)	7	1984
ALL BY MYSELF REGINA BELLE	53	1987
ALL BY MYSELF VARIOUS ARTISTS (DOVER)	2	1990
ALL BY MYSELF VOLUME 2 VARIOUS ARTISTS (DOVER)	13	1991
ALL CHANGE CAST	7	1995
ALL CLUBBED UP – THE BEST OF KELLY LLORENNA KELLY LLORENNA	62	2002
ALL DAY EVERY DAY N-TYCE	44	1998
ALL DIRECTIONS TEMPTATIONS	19	1973
ALL EYEZ ON ME 2PAC	32	1996
ALL FOR A SONG BARBARA DICKSON	3	1982
ALL FOR YOU JOHNNY MATHIS	20	1980
ALL FOR YOU JANET JACKSON	2	2001
ALL-4-ONE ALL-4-ONE	25	1994
ALL HELL'S BREAKING LOOSE DOWN AT LITTLE KATHY WILSON'S PLACE! WOLFSBANE	48	1990
ALL HITS ALL SAINTS	18	2001
ALL HOPE IS GONE SLIPKNOT	2	2008
ALL I INTENDED TO BE EMMYLOU HARRIS	40	2008
ALL I REALLY WANT TO DO CHER	7	1965
ALL IN A NIGHT'S WORK KC & THE SUNSHINE BAND	46	1983
ALL IN THE MIND KENNY 'DOPE' PRESENTS THE BUCKETHEADS	74	1996
ALL IN THE NAME OF LOVE ATLANTIC STARR	48	1987
ALL IS DREAM MERCURY REV	11	2001
ALL KILLER NO FILLER SUM 41	7	2001
ALL LIVE AND ALL OF THE NIGHT STRANGLERS	12	1988
ALL MAPS WELCOME TOM McRAE	47	2005
ALL MOD CONS JAM	6	1978
ALL MY LOVE VARIOUS ARTISTS (WARNER BROTHERS)	7	1997
ALL 'N' ALL EARTH WIND & FIRE	13	1978
ALL NEW – THE BEST FOOTIE ANTHEMS IN THE WORLD...EVER! VARIOUS ARTISTS (VIRGIN)	6	1998
ALL NIGHT LONG VARIOUS ARTISTS (POLYGRAM)	15	1993
ALL OF A SUDDEN I MISS EVERYONE EXPLOSIONS IN THE SKY	58	2007
ALL OF THIS AND NOTHING PSYCHEDELIC FURS	67	1988
ALL OR NOTHING SUBWAYS	17	2008
ALL OR NOTHING/2 X 2 MILLI VANILLI	6	1989
ALL OUR LOVE GLADYS KNIGHT & THE PIPS	80	1988
ALL OVER THE PLACE BANGLES	86	1985
ALL OVER THE WORLD – THE VERY BEST OF ELECTRIC LIGHT ORCHESTRA	6	2005
ALL RIGHT NOW PEPSI & SHIRLIE	69	1987
ALL RISE BLUE	1	2001
ALL SAINTS ALL SAINTS	2	1997
ALL STAR FESTIVAL VARIOUS ARTISTS (PHILIPS)	4	1963
ALL SYSTEMS GO VINNIE VINCENT	51	1988
ALL THAT I AM JOE	26	1997
ALL THAT I AM SANTANA	36	2005
ALL THAT JAZZ BREATHE	22	1988
ALL THAT MATTERS MICHAEL BOLTON	20	1997
ALL THAT YOU CAN'T LEAVE BEHIND U2	1	2000
ALL THE BEST STIFF LITTLE FINGERS	19	1983
ALL THE BEST LEO SAYER	26	1993
ALL THE BEST TINA TURNER	6	2004
ALL THE BEST COWBOYS HAVE CHINESE EYES PETE TOWNSHEND	32	1982
ALL THE BEST – LOVE DUETS VOLUME 1 VARIOUS ARTISTS (TELSTAR)	5	1992
ALL THE BEST! PAUL McCARTNEY	2	1987
ALL THE FUN OF THE FAIR DAVID ESSEX	3	1975
ALL THE FUN OF THE FAIR DAVID ESSEX	23	2008
ALL THE GREAT HITS DIANA ROSS	21	1981
ALL THE HITS EDDY GRANT	23	1984
ALL THE HITS & ALL NEW LOVE SONGS KENNY ROGERS	14	1999
ALL THE HITS AND MORE HOLLIES	51	1988
ALL THE HITS BY ALL THE STARS VARIOUS ARTISTS (PYE)	19	1962
ALL THE LOST SOULS JAMES BLUNT	1	2007
ALL THE RIGHT REASONS NICKELBACK	2	2005
ALL THE ROADRUNNING MARK KNOPFLER & EMMYLOU HARRIS	8	2006
ALL THE WAY BRENDA LEE	20	1962
ALL THE WAY FROM TUAM SAW DOCTORS	33	1992
ALL THE WAY. . .A DECADE OF SONGS CELINE DION	1	1999
ALL THE YOUNG DUDES MOTT THE HOOPLE	21	1972
ALL THINGS MUST PASS GEORGE HARRISON	1	1970
ALL THIS AND HEAVEN TOO ANDREW GOLD	31	1978
ALL THIS AND WORLD WAR II FILM SOUNDTRACK	23	1976
ALL THIS TIME STING	3	2001
ALL THIS USELESS BEAUTY ELVIS COSTELLO & THE ATTRACTIONS	28	1996
ALL THROUGH THE NIGHT ALED JONES WITH THE BBC WELSH CHORUS	2	1985
ALL TIME CLASSIC COUNTRY TEARJERKERS VARIOUS ARTISTS (WARNER BROTHERS)	18	2003
ALL TIME CLASSIC ROCK N ROLL TEARJERKERS VARIOUS ARTISTS (WARNER BROTHERS)	5	2003
ALL TIME CLASSIC SOUL HEARTBREAKERS VARIOUS ARTISTS (TELSTAR)	10	2003
ALL TIME CLASSIC TEARJERKERS VARIOUS ARTISTS (WARNER BROTHERS)	2	2002
THE ALL TIME GREATEST COUNTRY SONGS VARIOUS ARTISTS (COLUMBIA)	5	1997
ALL-TIME GREATEST HITS ROY ORBISON	39	1973
THE ALL TIME GREATEST HITS OF DANCE VARIOUS ARTISTS (TELSTAR)	11	1993
THE ALL TIME GREATEST LOVE SONGS VARIOUS ARTISTS (SONY)	4	2000
THE ALL TIME GREATEST LOVE SONGS OF THE 60'S, 70'S, 80'S & 90'S VOLUME III VARIOUS ARTISTS (COLUMBIA)	6	1998
THE ALL TIME GREATEST LOVE SONGS – VOLUME 4 VARIOUS ARTISTS (SONY)	9	1999
THE ALL TIME GREATEST LOVE SONGS... VARIOUS ARTISTS (COLUMBIA)	4	1996
THE ALL TIME GREATEST LOVE SONGS... VOLUME II VARIOUS ARTISTS (COLUMBIA)	4	1997
THE ALL TIME GREATEST MOVIE SONGS VARIOUS ARTISTS (SONY)	3	1998
ALL TIME GREATEST MOVIE SONGS 2001 VARIOUS ARTISTS (COLUMBIA)	18	2001
THE ALL TIME GREATEST MOVIE SONGS – VOLUME TWO VARIOUS ARTISTS (SONY)	7	1999
THE ALL TIME GREATEST POP ALBUM VARIOUS ARTISTS (COLUMBIA)	12	1999
THE ALL TIME GREATEST ROCK SONGS VARIOUS ARTISTS (SONY)	7	1997
ALL-TIME PARTY HITS VARIOUS ARTISTS (WARWICK)	21	1975
ALL TO YOURSELF JACK JONES	10	1977
ALL TOGETHER NOW ARGENT	13	1972
ALL TOGETHER NOW VARIOUS ARTISTS (UNIVERSAL)	11	2001
ALL TRUE MAN ALEXANDER O'NEAL	2	1991
ALL WOMAN VARIOUS ARTISTS (QUALITY TELEVISION)	1	1992
ALL WOMAN 2 VARIOUS ARTISTS (QUALITY TELEVISION)	1	1992
ALL WOMAN 4 VARIOUS ARTISTS (QUALITY TELEVISION)	18	1994
ALL WOMAN – THE COMPLETE WOMAN VARIOUS ARTISTS (QUALITY TELEVISION)	19	1993
ALL WOMAN – THE PLATINUM COLLECTION VARIOUS ARTISTS (WARNER BROTHERS)	6	2005
ALL WOMAN 3 VARIOUS ARTISTS (QUALITY TELEVISION)	2	1994
ALL WORLD LL COOL J	23	1996
ALL WRAPPED UP UNDERTONES	67	1983
ALL YEARS LEAVING STANDS	28	2004
ALL YOU CAN EAT k.d. lang	7	1995
ALL YOU NEED IS LOVE VARIOUS ARTISTS (GLOBAL TELEVISION)	18	2000
THE ALL-AMERICAN REJECTS ALL-AMERICAN REJECTS	50	2003
ALLEZ! OLA! OLE! VARIOUS ARTISTS (COLUMBIA)	8	1998
ALLIED FORCES TRIUMPH	64	1981
THE ALLNIGHTER GLENN FREY	31	1985
ALLOW US TO BE FRANK WESTLIFE	3	2004
ALLSTARS ALLSTARS	43	2002

Title / Artist	Peak Position	Year of Release
ALLY MCBEAL – FOR ONCE IN MY LIFE VARIOUS ARTISTS (EPIC)	10	2001
ALMA CARIBENA – CARIBBEAN SOUL GLORIA ESTEFAN	44	2000
ALMOST BLUE ELVIS COSTELLO & THE ATTRACTIONS	7	1981
ALMOST FAMOUS LUMIDEE	70	2003
ALMOST HERE UNBELIEVABLE TRUTH	21	1998
ALMOST IN LOVE ELVIS PRESLEY	38	1971
ALMOST THERE ANDY WILLIAMS	4	1965
ALOHA FROM HAWAII VIA SATELLITE ELVIS PRESLEY	11	1973
ALONE NANA MOUSKOURI	19	1986
ALONE TOGETHER DONNY OSMOND	6	1973
ALONE WITH EVERYBODY RICHARD ASHCROFT	1	2000
ALONG CAME A SPIDER ALICE COOPER	31	2008
ALONG CAME JONES TOM JONES	11	1965
ALPHA ASIA	5	1983
ALPHABET CITY ABC	7	1987
ALRIGHT, STILL LILY ALLEN	2	2006
ALTERNATIVE PET SHOP BOYS	2	1995
ALTERNATIVE 60'S VARIOUS ARTISTS (COLUMBIA)	18	2002
ALTERNATIVE 90S VARIOUS ARTISTS (COLUMBIA)	14	2002
ALTERNATIVE EIGHTIES VARIOUS ARTISTS (COLUMBIA)	5	2002
THE ALTERNATIVE TO LOVE BRENDAN BENSON	70	2005
ALTITUDE SYSTEM 7	75	1992
ALTITUDE ALT	67	1995
ALTOGETHER NOLANS	52	1982
THE ALTOGETHER ORBITAL	11	2001
ALVIN AND THE CHIPMUNKS (OST) ALVIN & THE CHIPMUNKS	61	2008
ALVIN STARDUST ALVIN STARDUST	37	1974
ALWAYS VARIOUS ARTISTS (K-TEL)	65	1987
ALWAYS HAZELL DEAN	38	1988
ALWAYS MICHAEL BALL	3	1993
ALWAYS GABRIELLE	11	2007
ALWAYS & FOREVER ETERNAL	2	1993
ALWAYS & FOREVER VARIOUS ARTISTS (SONY)	4	2003
ALWAYS & FOREVER II VARIOUS ARTISTS (SONY)	8	2003
ALWAYS AND FOREVER – THE COLLECTION VARIOUS ARTISTS (IMPRESSION)	24	1984
ALWAYS AND FOREVER THE LOVE ALBUM VARIOUS ARTISTS (TELSTAR)	41	1987
ALWAYS GUARANTEED CLIFF RICHARD	5	1987
ALWAYS ON MY MIND – ULTIMATE LOVE SONGS ELVIS PRESLEY	3	1997
ALWAYS OUTNUMBERED NEVER OUTGUNNED PRODIGY	1	2004
ALWAYS THERE MARTI WEBB	65	1986
AM I NOT YOUR GIRL? SINEAD O'CONNOR	6	1992
AMADEUS (OST) NEVILLE MARRINER & THE ACADEMY OF ST. MARTIN IN THE FIELDS	64	1985
THE AMALGAMUT FILTER	68	2002
AMANDA MARSHALL AMANDA MARSHALL	47	1996
AMANDLA MILES DAVIS	49	1989
AMARANTINE ENYA	8	2005
AMAROK MIKE OLDFIELD	49	1990
AMAZING ELKIE BROOKS WITH THE ROYAL PHILHARMONIC ORCHESTRA	49	1996
AMAZING DARTS DARTS	8	1978
AMAZING GRACE JUDY COLLINS	34	1985
AMAZING GRACE SPIRITUALIZED	25	2003
AMAZING GRACE LESLEY GARRETT	50	2008
THE AMAZING KAMIKAZE SYNDROME SLADE	49	1983
AMAZING THINGS RUNRIG	2	1993
AMAZULU AMAZULU	97	1986
AMBIENT 4 ON LAND BRIAN ENO	55	1982
AMBIENT DUB VOLUME 2 – EARTH JUICE VARIOUS ARTISTS (BEYOND)	20	1993
AMBIENT MOODS VARIOUS ARTISTS (POLYGRAM)	7	1996
AMERICA HERB ALPERT & THE TIJUANA BRASS	45	1971
AMERICA AMERICA	14	1972
THE AMERICAN ADVENTURE ELECTRIC SOFT PARADE	45	2003
AMERICAN BEAUTY GRATEFUL DEAD	27	1971
AMERICAN CAESAR IGGY POP	43	1993
THE AMERICAN DINER VARIOUS ARTISTS (DINO)	7	1995
AMERICAN DOLL POSSE TORI AMOS	50	2007
AMERICAN DREAM VARIOUS ARTISTS (SONY)	17	2000
AMERICAN DREAMS VARIOUS ARTISTS (STARBLEND)	43	1985
AMERICAN ENGLISH WAX	59	1987
AMERICAN FOOL JOHN COUGAR	37	1982
AMERICAN GANGSTER JAY-Z	30	2007
AMERICAN GRAFFITI FILM SOUNDTRACK	37	1974
AMERICAN HEARTBEAT VARIOUS ARTISTS (EPIC)	4	1984
AMERICAN HEARTBEAT VARIOUS ARTISTS (SONY BMG)	9	2008
AMERICAN IDIOT GREEN DAY	1	2004
AMERICAN LIFE MADONNA	1	2003
AMERICAN PIE DON McLEAN	3	1972
AMERICAN PIE – THE GREATEST HITS DON McLEAN	30	2000
AMERICAN PIE 2 FILM SOUNDTRACK	17	2001
AMERICAN RECORDINGS TV – THE MAN COMES AROUND JOHNNY CASH	40	2004
AMERICAN STARS 'N' BARS NEIL YOUNG	17	1977
AMERICAN THIGHS VERUCA SALT	47	1994
AMERICAN TUNE EVA CASSIDY	1	2003
AMERICAN V – A HUNDRED HIGHWAYS JOHNNY CASH	9	2006
AMERICANA OFFSPRING	10	1998
AMERICA'S LEAST WANTED UGLY KID JOE	11	1992
AMERICA'S SWEETHEART COURTNEY LOVE	56	2004
AMERIKAZ NIGHTMARE MOBB DEEP	68	2004
AMERIKKA'S MOST WANTED ICE CUBE	48	1990
AMIGOS SANTANA	21	1976
AMIGOS PARA SIEMPRE (FRIENDS FOR LIFE) JOSE CARRERAS & SARAH BRIGHTMAN	53	1992
AMMONIA AVENUE ALAN PARSONS PROJECT	24	1984
AMNESIA RICHARD THOMPSON	89	1988
AMNESIAC RADIOHEAD	1	2001
AMONG MY SWAN MAZZY STAR	57	1996
AMONG THE LIVING ANTHRAX	18	1987
AMOR JULIO IGLESIAS	14	1982
AMORE ANDREA BOCELLI	4	2006
AMORE MUSICA RUSSELL WATSON	10	2004
AMORE – THE LOVE ALBUM LUCIANO PAVAROTTI	41	2001
AMORICA BLACK CROWES	8	1994
AMOUR NATASHA MARSH	56	2007
AMOUR – THE ULTIMATE LOVE COLLECTION VARIOUS ARTISTS (POLYGRAM)	3	1997
AMPLIFIED HEART EVERYTHING BUT THE GIRL	20	1994
AMPUTECHTURE MARS VOLTA	49	2006
AMUSED TO DEATH ROGER WATERS	8	1992
AN ALBUM OF HYMNS ALED JONES	18	1986
AN EMOTIONAL FISH AN EMOTIONAL FISH	40	1990
AN END HAS A START EDITORS	1	2007
AN EVENING WASTED WITH TOM LEHRER TOM LEHRER	7	1960
AN EVENING WITH DIANA ROSS DIANA ROSS	52	1977
AN EVENING WITH JOHN DENVER JOHN DENVER	31	1975
AN EVENING WITH JOHNNERS BRIAN JOHNSTON	46	1994
AN INNOCENT MAN BILLY JOEL	2	1983
AN INSTINCT FOR DETECTION LIONROCK	30	1996
AN INTROSPECTIVE OF HOUSE: 1ST DIMENSION VARIOUS ARTISTS (SOUND DIMENSION)	18	1997
AN INTROSPECTIVE OF HOUSE: 2ND DIMENSION VARIOUS ARTISTS (SOUND DIMENSION)	9	1997
AN INTROSPECTIVE OF HOUSE: 3RD DIMENSION VARIOUS ARTISTS (SOUND DIMENSION)	14	1997
AN OFFICER AND A GENTLEMAN FILM SOUNDTRACK	40	1983
ANALOGUE A-HA	24	2006
THE ANALOGUE THEATRE C.J. BOLLAND	43	1996
ANAM CLANNAD	14	1990
ANARCHY CHUMBAWAMBA	29	1994
ANARCHY BUSTA RHYMES	38	2000
ANASTACIA ANASTACIA	1	2004
ANCIENT HEART TANITA TIKARAM	3	1988
ANCORA IL DIVO	1	2005
AND JOHN MARTYN	32	1996
AND ALL BECAUSE THE LADY LOVES... VARIOUS ARTISTS (DOVER)	2	1989
AND ALL THAT COULD HAVE BEEN – LIVE NINE INCH NAILS	54	2002
AND I FEEL FINE – BEST OF THE IRS YEARS R.E.M.	70	2006
AND I LOVE YOU SO SHIRLEY BASSEY	24	1972
AND I LOVE YOU SO PERRY COMO	1	1973
AND I LOVE YOU SO HOWARD KEEL	6	1984
...AND JUSTICE FOR ALL METALLICA	4	1988
AND LOVE SAID NO – 1997-2004 H.I.M.	30	2004
AND NOW THE LEGACY BEGINS DREAM WARRIORS	18	1991
...AND OUT COME THE WOLVES RANCID	55	1995
AND SO IT GOES BLAKE	14	2008
AND STILL I RISE ALISON LIMERICK	53	1992
...AND THE BEST GOES ON VARIOUS ARTISTS (TELSTAR)	12	1988
AND THEN JOE	73	2004
AND THEN BOOM IGLU & HARTLY	36	2008
...AND THEN THERE WERE THREE... GENESIS	3	1978
AND WINTER CAME ENYA	6	2008
ANDERSON BRUFORD WAKEMAN HOWE ANDERSON BRUFORD WAKEMAN HOWE	14	1989
ANDREA ANDREA BOCELLI	19	2004
ANDREW LLOYD WEBBER – DIVAS VARIOUS ARTISTS (POLYDOR)	10	2005
ANDREW LLOYD WEBBER – GOLD VARIOUS ARTISTS (POLYDOR)	5	2001
ANDREW LLOYD WEBBER – 60 VARIOUS ARTISTS (REALLY USEFUL)	4	2008
ANDREW LLOYD WEBBER – THE PREMIER COLLECTION VARIOUS ARTISTS (POLYDOR)	1	1988
ANDREW LLOYD WEBBER: REQUIEM PLACIDO DOMINGO, SARAH BRIGHTMAN, PAUL MILES-KINGSTON, WINCHESTER CATHEDRAL CHOIR & THE ENGLISH CHAMBER ORCHESTRA CONDUCTED BY LORIN MAAZEL	4	1985
ANDROMEDA HEIGHTS PREFAB SPROUT	7	1997
ANDY STEWART ANDY STEWART	13	1962
ANDY WILLIAMS GREATEST HITS ANDY WILLIAMS	1	1970
ANDY WILLIAMS SHOW ANDY WILLIAMS	10	1970
ANDY WILLIAMS' SOUND OF MUSIC ANDY WILLIAMS	22	1970
ANGEL BEACH VARIOUS ARTISTS (BRUNSWICK)	15	2002

Title / Artist	Peak Position	Year of Release
ANGEL BEACH – THE FOURTH WAVE VARIOUS ARTISTS (INSPIRED)	15	2005
ANGEL BEACH – THE SECOND WAVE VARIOUS ARTISTS (ORB RECORDINGS)	16	2003
ANGEL BEACH THE 3RD WAY VARIOUS ARTISTS (BRUNSWICK)	9	2004
ANGEL CLARE ART GARFUNKEL	14	1973
ANGEL DELIGHT FAIRPORT CONVENTION	8	1971
ANGEL DUST FAITH NO MORE	2	1992
ANGEL OF RETRIBUTION JUDAS PRIEST	39	2005
ANGEL STATION MANFRED MANN'S EARTH BAND	30	1979
ANGELIC UPSTARTS ANGELIC UPSTARTS	27	1981
ANGELIS ANGELIS	2	2006
ANGELS & ELECTRICITY EDDI READER	49	1998
ANGELS WITH DIRTY FACES TRICKY	23	1998
ANGELS WITH DIRTY FACES SUGABABES	2	2002
ANGLES DAN LE SAC VS SCROOBIUS PIP	31	2008
ANIMAL BOY RAMONES	38	1986
ANIMAL MAGIC BLOW MONKEYS	21	1986
ANIMAL MAGNETISM SCORPIONS	23	1980
ANIMAL RIGHTS MOBY	38	1996
ANIMAL TRACKS ANIMALS	6	1965
ANIMALISMS ANIMALS	4	1966
ANIMALIZE KISS	11	1984
THE ANIMALS ANIMALS	6	1964
ANIMALS PINK FLOYD	2	1977
ANIMATION JON ANDERSON	43	1982
ANNIE FILM SOUNDTRACK	83	1982
ANNIVERSARY – 20 YEARS OF HITS TAMMY WYNETTE	45	1987
THE ANNUAL VARIOUS ARTISTS (MINISTRY OF SOUND)	13	1995
THE ANNUAL 2000 – JUDGE JULES/TALL PAUL VARIOUS ARTISTS (MINISTRY OF SOUND)	1	2000
THE ANNUAL 2002 VARIOUS ARTISTS (MINISTRY OF SOUND)	1	2001
THE ANNUAL 2003 VARIOUS ARTISTS (MINISTRY OF SOUND)	1	2002
THE ANNUAL 2004 VARIOUS ARTISTS (MINISTRY OF SOUND)	2	2003
THE ANNUAL 2005 VARIOUS ARTISTS (MINISTRY OF SOUND)	2	2004
THE ANNUAL 2006 VARIOUS ARTISTS (MINISTRY OF SOUND)	2	2005
THE ANNUAL 2007 VARIOUS ARTISTS (MINISTRY OF SOUND)	2	2006
THE ANNUAL 2008 VARIOUS ARTISTS (MINISTRY OF SOUND)	2	2007
THE ANNUAL 2009 VARIOUS ARTISTS (MINISTRY OF SOUND)	4	2008
THE ANNUAL IBIZA 2002 VARIOUS ARTISTS (MINISTRY OF SOUND)	4	2002
THE ANNUAL II – PETE TONG & BOY GEORGE VARIOUS ARTISTS (MINISTRY OF SOUND)	1	1996
THE ANNUAL III – PETE TONG & BOY GEORGE VARIOUS ARTISTS (MINISTRY OF SOUND)	1	1997
THE ANNUAL IV – JUDGE JULES & BOY GEORGE VARIOUS ARTISTS (MINISTRY OF SOUND)	1	1998
THE ANNUAL – MILLENNIUM EDITION VARIOUS ARTISTS (MINISTRY OF SOUND)	2	1999
THE ANNUAL – SPRING 2001 VARIOUS ARTISTS (MINISTRY OF SOUND)	1	2001
THE ANNUAL SPRING 2003 VARIOUS ARTISTS (MINISTRY OF SOUND)	3	2003
ANNUAL SPRING 2004 VARIOUS ARTISTS (MINISTRY OF SOUND)	6	2004
THE ANNUAL SUMMER 2003 VARIOUS ARTISTS (MINISTRY OF SOUND)	5	2003
THE ANNUAL SUMMER 2004 VARIOUS ARTISTS (MINISTRY OF SOUND)	4	2004
ANOMIE & BONHOMIE SCRITTI POLITTI	33	1999
ANOTHER BLACK AND WHITE MINSTREL SHOW GEORGE MITCHELL MINSTRELS	1	1961
ANOTHER CUP YUSUF	20	2006
ANOTHER DAY ON EARTH BRIAN ENO	93	2005
ANOTHER GREY AREA GRAHAM PARKER	40	1982
ANOTHER KIND OF BLUES U.K. SUBS	21	1979
ANOTHER LATE NIGHT – GROOVE ARMADA VARIOUS ARTISTS (AZULI)	20	2002
ANOTHER LEVEL BLACKstreet	26	1996
ANOTHER LEVEL ANOTHER LEVEL	13	1998
ANOTHER MONTY PYTHON RECORD MONTY PYTHON'S FLYING CIRCUS	26	1971
ANOTHER MUSIC IN A DIFFERENT KITCHEN BUZZCOCKS	15	1978
ANOTHER NIGHT – U.S. ALBUM REAL McCOY	6	1995
ANOTHER PAGE CHRISTOPHER CROSS	4	1983
ANOTHER PERFECT DAY MOTORHEAD	20	1983
ANOTHER PERFECT DAY VARIOUS ARTISTS (COLUMBIA)	13	1998
ANOTHER PLACE AND TIME DONNA SUMMER	17	1989
ANOTHER SIDE JOHN BARROWMAN	22	2007
ANOTHER SIDE OF BOB DYLAN BOB DYLAN	8	1964
ANOTHER STEP KIM WILDE	73	1986
ANOTHER STRING OF HITS SHADOWS	16	1980
ANOTHER TICKET ERIC CLAPTON	18	1981
ANOTHER TIME, ANOTHER PLACE ENGELBERT HUMPERDINCK	48	1971
ANOTHER TIME, ANOTHER PLACE BRYAN FERRY	4	1974
ANOTHER WORLD BRIAN MAY	23	1998
ANOTHER YEAR LEO SAYER	8	1975
ANOTHER YOU ANOTHER ME H & CLAIRE	58	2002
ANSWERS TO NOTHING MIDGE URE	30	1988
ANTENNA ZZ TOP	3	1994
ANTENNA CAVE IN	67	2003
ANTHEM TOYAH	2	1981
ANTHEM BLACK UHURU	90	1984
ANTHEM LESS THAN JAKE	37	2003
ANTHEM CLASSICS FROM CLUBLAND VARIOUS ARTISTS (UNIVERSAL)	7	2003
THE ANTHEMS VARIOUS ARTISTS (UNIVERSAL)	2	2006
THE ANTHEMS 07 VARIOUS ARTISTS (UNIVERSAL)	5	2007
THE ANTHEMS '92-'97 VARIOUS ARTISTS (UNITED DANCE)	8	1997
ANTHEMS OF HOUSE VARIOUS ARTISTS (INSPIRED)	8	2004
ANTHEMS OF IBIZA VARIOUS ARTISTS (INSPIRED)	16	2004
ANTHEMS OF OLD SKOOL VARIOUS ARTISTS (INSPIRED)	7	2004
ANTHEMS OF TRANCE VARIOUS ARTISTS (INSPIRED)	3	2004
ANTHEMS 2 – 1991-2009 VARIOUS ARTISTS (MINISTRY OF SOUND)	6	2008
THE ANTHOLOGY DEEP PURPLE	50	1985
ANTHOLOGY ALIEN ANT FARM	11	2001
ANTHOLOGY OCEAN COLOUR SCENE	75	2003
ANTHOLOGY BRYAN ADAMS	30	2005
ANTHOLOGY 1 BEATLES	2	1995
ANTHOLOGY – THE SOUNDS OF SCIENCE BEASTIE BOYS	36	1999
ANTHOLOGY 3 BEATLES	4	1996
ANTHOLOGY – THROUGH THE YEARS TOM PETTY & HEARTBREAKERS	14	2001
ANTHOLOGY 2 BEATLES	1	1996
ANTICHRIST SUPERSTAR MARILYN MANSON	73	1996
ANTICS INTERPOL	21	2004
THE ANTIDOTE RONNY JORDAN	52	1992
THE ANTIDOTE MORCHEEBA	17	2005
ANTIDOTES FOALS	3	2008
ANTMUSIC – THE VERY BEST OF ADAM ANT ADAM ANT	6	1993
ANUTHA ZONE DR. JOHN	33	1998
THE ANVIL VISAGE	6	1982
ANY LOVE LUTHER VANDROSS	3	1988
ANY MINUTE NOW SOULWAX	53	2004
ANYMORE FOR ANYMORE RONNIE LANE & SLIM CHANCE	48	1974
ANYTHING DAMNED	40	1986
ANYTHING FOR YOU GLORIA ESTEFAN & MIAMI MUSIC MACHINE	1	1988
ANYTHING IS POSSIBLE DEBBIE GIBSON	69	1991
ANYTIME ANYWHERE RITA COOLIDGE	6	1977
ANYWAY FAMILY	7	1970
ANYWAYYAWANNA BEATMASTERS	30	1989
ANYWHERE NEW MUSIK	68	1981
ANYWHERE I LAY ME HEAD SCARLETT JOHANSSON	64	2008
APOCADELIC POINT BREAK	21	2000
APOCALYPSE 91…THE ENEMY STRIKES BLACK PUBLIC ENEMY	8	1991
APPEAL TO REASON RISE AGAINST	68	2008
APPETITE FOR DESTRUCTION GUNS N' ROSES	5	1987
APPLE VENUS – VOLUME 1 XTC	42	1999
APPLE VENUS – VOLUME 2 XTC/WASP STAR	40	2000
APPOLONIA/FEEL THE DROP B M EX	17	1993
APPROVED BY THE MOTORS MOTORS	60	1978
APRIL MOON SAM BROWN	38	1990
AQUALUNG JETHRO TULL	4	1971
AQUALUNG AQUALUNG	15	2002
AQUARIUM AQUA	6	1997
AQUARIUS AQUA	24	2000
ARBORESCENCE OZRIC TENTACLES	18	1994
ARC OF A DIVER STEVE WINWOOD	13	1981
ARCHETYPE FEAR FACTORY	41	2004
ARCHITECTURE AND MORALITY ORCHESTRAL MANOEUVRES IN THE DARK	3	1981
ARCHIVE 1967-1975 GENESIS	35	1998
ARCHIVE ONE DAVE CLARKE	36	1996
ARE YOU EXPERIENCED JIMI HENDRIX EXPERIENCE	2	1967
ARE YOU GONNA GO MY WAY LENNY KRAVITZ	1	1993
ARE YOU LISTENING DOLORES O'RIORDAN	28	2007
ARE YOU NORMAL? NED'S ATOMIC DUSTBIN	13	1992
ARE YOU OK? WAS (NOT WAS)	35	1990
ARE YOU PASSIONATE NEIL YOUNG	24	2002
ARE YOU READY? BUCKS FIZZ	10	1982
ARENA DURAN DURAN	6	1984
ARETHA ARETHA FRANKLIN	51	1986
ARETHA NOW ARETHA FRANKLIN	6	1968
THE ARGUMENT FUGAZI	63	2001
ARGUS WISHBONE ASH	3	1972
ARGY BARGY SQUEEZE	32	1980
ARIA – THE OPERA ALBUM ANDREA BOCELLI	33	1998
ARISE SEPULTURA	40	1991
THE ARISTOCATS – READ ALONG (ORIGINAL CAST RECORDING) STAGE CAST RECORDING	60	2000
ARKANSAS TRAVELER MICHELLE SHOCKED	46	1992
ARKOLOGY LEE 'SCRATCH' PERRY	49	1997
ARMAGEDDON FILM SOUNDTRACK	19	1998
ARMCHAIR MELODIES DAVID GRAY & TOMMY TYCHO	21	1976
ARMCHAIR THEATRE JEFF LYNNE	24	1990
ARMED FORCES ELVIS COSTELLO & THE ATTRACTIONS	2	1979
AROUND THE FUR DEFTONES	56	1997
AROUND THE NEXT DREAM BBM	9	1994

Title / Artist	Peak Position	Year of Release
AROUND THE SUN R.E.M.	1	2004
AROUND THE WORLD IN A DAY PRINCE	5	1985
AROUND THE WORLD – LIVE IN CONCERT OSMONDS	41	1976
AROUND THE WORLD – THE JOURNEY SO FAR EAST 17	3	1996
ARRIVAL ABBA	1	1976
ART AND ILLUSION TWELFTH NIGHT	83	1984
THE ART GARFUNKEL ALBUM ART GARFUNKEL	12	1984
THE ART OF CHRIS FARLOWE CHRIS FARLOWE	37	1966
THE ART OF FALLING APART SOFT CELL	5	1983
THE ART OF WAR BONE THUGS-N-HARMONY	42	1997
ART OFFICIAL INTELLIGENCE: MOSIAC THUMP DE LA SOUL	22	2000
ARTFUL DODGER PRESENTS REWIND VARIOUS ARTISTS (LONDON)	6	2000
THE ARTFUL DODGER PRESENTS REWIND 2001 VARIOUS ARTISTS (WARNER BROTHERS)	12	2001
ARTIFICIAL INTELLIGENCE VARIOUS ARTISTS (WARP)	16	1994
THE ARTISTS VOLUME 1 EARTH WIND & FIRE/ JEAN CARN/ROSE ROYCE	65	1985
THE ARTISTS VOLUME 2 LUTHER VANDROSS/ TEDDY PENDERGRASS/CHANGE/ATLANTIC STARR	45	1985
THE ARTISTS VOLUME III WOMACK & WOMACK/THE O'JAYS/KLEEER/THE S.O.S. BAND	87	1985
AS CRUEL AS SCHOOL CHILDREN GYM CLASS HEROES	19	2007
AS DAYLIGHT DIES KILLSWITCH ENGAGE	64	2006
AS I AM ALICIA KEYS	11	2007
AS IF TO NOTHING CRAIG ARMSTRONG	61	2002
AS IS MANFRED MANN	22	1966
AS IS NOW PAUL WELLER	4	2005
AS IT HAPPENS DR. FEELGOOD	42	1979
AS ONE KOOL & THE GANG	49	1982
AS ONE DOUBLE TROUBLE	73	1990
AS RAW AS EVER SHABBA RANKS	51	1991
AS SAFE AS YESTERDAY IS HUMBLE PIE	32	1969
AS THE BAND TURNS ATLANTIC STARR	64	1985
AS TIME GOES BY ROYAL PHILHARMONIC ORCHESTRA CONDUCTED BY HARRY RABINOVITZ	95	1984
AS TIME GOES BY VARIOUS ARTISTS (DINO)	14	1993
AS TIME GOES BY BRYAN FERRY	16	1999
AS TIME GOES BY – THE GREAT AMERICAN SONGBOOK VOLUME 2 ROD STEWART	4	2003
AS UGLY AS THEY WANNA BE UGLY KID JOE	9	1992
ASHANTI ASHANTI	3	2002
ASHES TO ASHES TELEVISION AND RADIO COMPILATION	2	2008
ASIA ASIA	11	1982
ASK A WOMAN WHO KNOWS NATALIE COLE	63	2002
ASLEEP IN THE BACK ELBOW	14	2001
ASPECTS OF LOVE STAGE CAST RECORDING	1	1989
ASQUARIUS CUD	30	1992
ASSAULT AND BATTERY ROSE TATTOO	40	1981
ASSAULT ATTACK MICHAEL SCHENKER GROUP	19	1982
ASSEMBLAGE JAPAN	26	1981
ASTAIRE PETER SKELLERN	23	1979
ASTONISHING SOUNDS, AMAZING MUSIC HAWKWIND	33	1976
ASTRA ASIA	68	1985
ASTRO CREEP 2000 – SONGS OF LOVE, DESTRUCTION AND OTHER SYNTHETIC DELUSIONS OF THE ELECTRIC HEAD WHITE ZOMBIE	25	1995
ASTRONAUT DURAN DURAN	3	2004
ASTRONAUTS AND HERETICS THOMAS DOLBY	35	1992
ASTRONOMY FOR DOGS ALIENS	46	2007
ASYLUM KISS	12	1985
ASYLUM SENSER	73	1998
AT CARNEGIE HALL BUENA VISTA SOCIAL CLUB	55	2008
AT EASE WITH DEAN DEAN MARTIN	35	1967
AT HER VERY BEST NANA MOUSKOURI	39	2001
AT HER VERY BEST DUSTY SPRINGFIELD	31	2006
AT HER VERY BEST JULIE ANDREWS	70	2006
AT HIS VERY BEST ENGELBERT HUMPERDINCK	5	2000
AT HIS VERY BEST ROBERT PALMER	38	2002
AT HIS VERY BEST LOUIS ARMSTRONG	75	2003
AT HIS VERY BEST LEO SAYER	30	2006
AT SAN QUENTIN JOHNNY CASH	20	2007
AT THE BBC JAM	33	2002
AT THE CHELSEA NIGHTCLUB MEMBERS	45	1979
AT THE CLUB KENICKIE	9	1997
AT THE CRESCENDO LOUIS ARMSTRONG	4	1956
AT THE DROP OF A HAT STAGE CAST RECORDING	9	1960
AT THE DROP OF ANOTHER HAT STAGE CAST RECORDING	12	1964
AT THE END OF THE CLICHÉ CARL COX	23	1996
AT THE END OF THE DAY FUREYS & DAVEY ARTHUR	35	1985
AT THE END OF THE DAY DANIEL O'DONNELL	11	2003
AT THE END OF THE RAINBOW KEITH HARRIS, ORVILLE & CUDDLES	92	1983
AT THE MOVIES FOSTER & ALLEN	48	2006
AT THE MOVIES – SOUNDTRACK HITS VAN MORRISON	17	2007
AT THE OXFORD UNION GERARD HOFFNUNG	4	1960
AT THEIR VERY BEST SHADOWS	12	1989
AT THEIR VERY BEST TEMPTATIONS	28	2001
AT THIS MOMENT TOM JONES	34	1989
AT THIS TIME BURT BACHARACH	60	2005
AT WAR WITH SATAN VENOM	64	1984
AT WAR WITH THE MYSTICS FLAMING LIPS	6	2006
AT WORST...THE BEST OF BOY GEORGE & CULTURE CLUB BOY GEORGE/CULTURE CLUB	24	1993
ATLANTIC BLACK GOLD VARIOUS ARTISTS (ATLANTIC)	23	1974
ATLANTIC BRIDGE BILLY CONNOLLY	20	1976
ATLANTIC CROSSING ROD STEWART	1	1975
ATLANTIC REALM CLANNAD	41	1989
ATLANTIC SOUL BALLADS VARIOUS ARTISTS (ATLANTIC)	84	1988
ATLANTIC SOUL CLASSICS VARIOUS ARTISTS (ATLANTIC)	9	1987
ATOM HEART MOTHER PINK FLOYD	1	1970
ATOMIC 80'S VARIOUS ARTISTS (UNIVERSAL)	11	2001
ATOMIC ROOSTER ATOMIC ROOSTER	49	1970
ATOMIC/ATOMIX – THE VERY BEST OF BLONDIE BLONDIE	12	1998
ATTACK AND RELEASE BLACK KEYS	34	2008
ATTACK DECAY SUSTAIN RELEASE SIMIAN MOBILE DISCO	59	2007
ATTACK OF THE GREY LANTERN MANSUN	1	1997
ATTACK OF THE KILLER B'S ANTHRAX	13	1991
AUBERGE CHRIS REA	1	1991
AUDIENCE WITH THE MIND HOUSE OF LOVE	38	1993
AUDIO LESSNOVER DELIRIOUS?	58	2001
AUDIOSLAVE AUDIOSLAVE	19	2002
AUDIOWEB AUDIOWEB	70	1996
AUF DER MAUR AUF DER MAUR	31	2004
AUGUST ERIC CLAPTON	3	1986
AUGUST AND EVERYTHING AFTER COUNTING CROWS	16	1994
AURAL SCULPTURE STRANGLERS	14	1984
AUSTIN POWERS IN GOLDMEMBER FILM SOUNDTRACK	14	2002
AUSTIN POWERS – THE SPY WHO SHAGGED ME FILM SOUNDTRACK	6	1999
AUTHOR! AUTHOR! SCARS	67	1981
AUTOAMERICAN BLONDIE	3	1980
AUTOBAHN KRAFTWERK	4	1975
AUTOBIOGRAPHY ASHLEE SIMPSON	31	2004
THE AUTOBIOGRAPHY OF SUPERTRAMP SUPERTRAMP	9	1986
AUTOGEDDON JULIAN COPE	16	1994
AUTOMANIKK A GUY CALLED GERALD	68	1990
AUTOMATIC JESUS & MARY CHAIN	11	1989
AUTOMATIC SHARPE & NUMAN	59	1989
AUTOMATIC FOR THE PEOPLE R.E.M.	1	1992
AUTUMN '66 SPENCER DAVIS GROUP	4	1966
AVALANCHE THEA GILMORE	63	2003
AVALON ROXY MUSIC	1	1982
AVALON SUNSET VAN MORRISON	13	1989
AVENGED SEVENFOLD AVENGED SEVENFOLD	24	2007
AVERAGE WHITE BAND AVERAGE WHITE BAND	6	1975
AW C'MON/NO YOU C'MON LAMBCHOP	45	2004
AWAKE DREAM THEATER	65	1994
AWAKE JOSH GROBAN	17	2007
AWAKE – LIVE JOSH GROBAN	22	2008
AWAKE AND BREATHE B*WITCHED	5	1999
AWAKENING KEVIN PEEK	52	1981
THE AWARDS 1990 VARIOUS ARTISTS (TELSTAR)	3	1990
THE AWARDS 1992 VARIOUS ARTISTS (POLYGRAM)	1	1992
THE AWARDS 1993 VARIOUS ARTISTS (POLYGRAM)	3	1993
THE AWARDS 1995 VARIOUS ARTISTS (COLUMBIA)	10	1995
AWESOME DANCE VARIOUS ARTISTS (TELSTAR)	2	1994
AWESOME! 2 VARIOUS ARTISTS (EMI)	2	1991
AWESOME!! – 20 MASSIVE HITS VARIOUS ARTISTS (EMI)	1	1991
AWFULLY DEEP ROOTS MANUVA	24	2005
AWKWARD ANNIE KATE RUSBY	32	2007
AXE ATTACK VARIOUS ARTISTS (K-TEL)	15	1980
AXE ATTACK 2 VARIOUS ARTISTS (K-TEL)	31	1981
AXIS MUTATIS SHAMEN	27	1995
AXIS: BOLD AS LOVE JIMI HENDRIX EXPERIENCE	5	1967
AY FOND KISS FAIRGROUND ATTRACTION	55	1990
AYIA NAPA – CLUBBERS PARADISE VARIOUS ARTISTS (GLOBAL TELEVISION)	14	1999
AYIA NAPA – FANTASY ISLAND VARIOUS ARTISTS (TELSTAR)	1	2000
AYIA NAPA – RETURN TO FANTASY ISLAND VARIOUS ARTISTS (TELSTAR)	18	2001
AYIA NAPA – THE ALBUM 2001 VARIOUS ARTISTS (MINISTRY OF SOUND)	9	2001
AYIA NAPA THE ALBUM – SHANKS & BIGFOOT VARIOUS ARTISTS (MINISTRY OF SOUND)	5	2000
THE A-Z OF EASY LISTENING VARIOUS ARTISTS (POLYDOR)	24	1971
AZNAVOUR SINGS AZNAVOUR VOLUME 3 CHARLES AZNAVOUR	23	1974
AZUR D'OR RENAISSANCE	73	1979

B

Title / Artist	Peak Position	Year of Release
B FOR BROTHERHOOD BROTHERHOOD OF MAN	18	1978
B-SIDES AND RARITIES BOYZONE	34	2008
B SIDES THEMSELVES MARILLION	64	1988
B*WITCHED B*WITCHED	3	1998
THE B-52'S B-52'S	22	1979
BABBLE THAT PETROL EMOTION	30	1987
BABE RAINBOW HOUSE OF LOVE	34	1992
BABY YELLO	37	1991
BABY 81 BLACK REBEL MOTORCYCLE CLUB	15	2007
BABY ANIMALS BABY ANIMALS	70	1992
BABY I'M A-WANT YOU BREAD	9	1972
BABY I'M BORED EVAN DANDO	30	2003
BABY LOVE VARIOUS ARTISTS (RONCO)	47	1984
BABY LOVE VARIOUS ARTISTS (EMI)	11	1996
...BABY ONE MORE TIME BRITNEY SPEARS	2	1999
BABY THE STARS SHINE BRIGHT EVERYTHING BUT THE GIRL	22	1986
BABYLON AND ON SQUEEZE	14	1987
BABYLON BY BUS BOB MARLEY & THE WAILERS	40	1978
BABY'S GOT A GUN ONLY ONES	37	1980
BACCARA BACCARA	26	1978
BACDAFUCUP ONYX	59	1993
BACHARACH AND DAVID – THEY WRITE THE SONGS VARIOUS ARTISTS (DINO)	16	1990
THE BACHELORS AND 16 GREAT SONGS BACHELORS	2	1964
BACHELORS' GIRLS BACHELORS	24	1966
BACK AGAIN IN THE D.H.S.S. HALF MAN HALF BISCUIT	59	1987
BACK AGAIN...NO MATTER WHAT BOYZONE	4	2008
BACK AND FOURTH LINDISFARNE	22	1978
BACK FOR THE ATTACK DOKKEN	96	1987
BACK HOME ERIC CLAPTON	19	2005
BACK HOME WESTLIFE	1	2007
BACK HOME AGAIN JOHN DENVER	3	1974
BACK IN BLACK AC/DC	1	1980
BACK IN THE D.H.S.S. HALF MAN HALF BISCUIT	60	1986
BACK IN THE DAY VARIOUS ARTISTS (WARNER BROTHERS)	15	2002
BACK IN THE DAY VARIOUS ARTISTS (EMI)	7	2006
BACK IN THE HIGH LIFE STEVE WINWOOD	8	1986
BACK IN THE WORLD PAUL McCARTNEY	5	2003
BACK INTO THE FUTURE MAN	23	1973
BACK ON THE BLOCK QUINCY JONES	26	1990
BACK ON THE ROAD VARIOUS ARTISTS (STYLUS)	29	1988
BACK ON THE STREETS GARY MOORE	70	1979
BACK ON TOP VAN MORRISON	11	1999
BACK ON TRACK LULU	68	2004
THE BACK ROOM EDITORS	2	2005
BACK STREET SYMPHONY THUNDER	21	1990
BACK TO BACHARACH MICHAEL BALL	20	2007
BACK TO BACK STATUS QUO	9	1983
BACK TO BACK DAVID ESSEX	33	1994
BACK TO BASICS BILLY BRAGG	37	1987
BACK TO BASICS CHRISTINA AGUILERA	1	2006
BACK TO BASICS – CUT THE CRAP VARIOUS ARTISTS (NETWORK)	20	1996
BACK TO BASICS – THE ESSENTIAL COLLECTION 1971-1992 OLIVIA NEWTON-JOHN	12	1992
BACK TO BEDLAM JAMES BLUNT	1	2005
BACK TO BLACK AMY WINEHOUSE	1	2006
BACK TO BLACK – THE DELUXE EDITION AMY WINEHOUSE	1	2007
BACK TO BROADWAY BARBRA STREISAND	4	1993
BACK TO FRONT GILBERT O'SULLIVAN	1	1972
BACK TO FRONT LIONEL RICHIE	1	1992
BACK TO LOVE 0305 VARIOUS ARTISTS (HED KANDI)	20	2005
BACK TO SCHOOL (MINI MAGGIT) DEFTONES	35	2001
BACK TO THE 70'S VARIOUS ARTISTS (EMI)	8	1993
BACK TO THE 80S VARIOUS ARTISTS (SONY)	7	2004
BACK TO THE BLUES GARY MOORE	53	2001
BACK TO THE EGG WINGS	6	1979
BACK TO THE FUTURE FILM SOUNDTRACK	66	1986
BACK TO THE LIGHT BRIAN MAY	6	1992
BACK TO THE MOVIES – HITS FROM THE FLIX VARIOUS ARTISTS (VIRGIN)	5	2004
BACK TO THE MYSTERY CITY HANOI ROCKS	87	1983
BACK TO THE OLD SKOOL VARIOUS ARTISTS (MINISTRY OF SOUND)	2	2001
BACK TO THE OLD SKOOL 2 VARIOUS ARTISTS (MINISTRY OF SOUND)	11	2001
BACK TO THE OLD SKOOL CLUB CLASSICS VARIOUS ARTISTS (MINISTRY OF SOUND)	2	2003
BACK TO THE OLD SKOOL – DRUM & BASS VARIOUS ARTISTS (MINISTRY OF SOUND)	20	2002
BACK TO THE OLD SKOOL – HIP HOP VARIOUS ARTISTS (MINISTRY OF SOUND)	7	2002
BACK TO THE OLD SKOOL – IBIZA VARIOUS ARTISTS (MINISTRY OF SOUND)	6	2002
BACK TO THE OLD SKOOL – IBIZA ANTHEMS VARIOUS ARTISTS (MINISTRY OF SOUND)	4	2003
BACK TO THE ROOTS JOHN MAYALL	31	1971
BACK TO THE SIXTIES TIGHT FIT	38	1981
BACK TO THE SIXTIES VARIOUS ARTISTS (TELSTAR)	14	1988
BACK TO TITANIC JAMES HORNER	10	1998
BACK 2 HOUSE VARIOUS ARTISTS (UNIVERSAL)	7	2006
BACKBEAT BACKBEAT	39	1994
BACKLASH BAD ENGLISH	64	1991
BACKLESS ERIC CLAPTON	18	1978
BACKSTAGE – THE GREATEST HITS AND MORE GENE PITNEY	17	1990
BACKSTREET BOYS BACKSTREET BOYS	12	1996
BACKSTREET'S BACK BACKSTREET BOYS	2	1997
BACKTRACKIN' ERIC CLAPTON	29	1984
BACKWOODS BARBIE DOLLY PARTON	35	2008
BAD MICHAEL JACKSON	1	1987
THE BAD AND LOWDOWN WORLD OF THE KANE GANG KANE GANG	21	1985
BAD ANIMALS HEART	7	1987
BAD ATTITUDE MEAT LOAF	8	1984
BAD BOYS FILM SOUNDTRACK	19	1995
BAD BOYS II FILM SOUNDTRACK	17	2003
BAD BOYS INC. BAD BOYS INC.	13	1994
BAD BROTHERS RONNY JORDAN MEETS DJ KRUSH	58	1994
BAD COMPANY BAD COMPANY	3	1974
BAD ENGLISH BAD ENGLISH	74	1989
BAD FOR GOOD JIM STEINMAN	7	1981
BAD GIRLS DONNA SUMMER	23	1979
BAD GIRLS VARIOUS ARTISTS (COLUMBIA)	15	2002
BAD NEWS BAD NEWS	69	1987
BAD REPUTATION THIN LIZZY	4	1977
BAD TO THE BONE INNER CIRCLE	44	1993
BAD VIBES LLOYD COLE	38	1993
BADLANDS BADLANDS	39	1989
BADMOTORFINGER SOUNDGARDEN	39	1992
BADNESS MORRISSEY MULLEN	43	1981
BADUIZM ERYKAH BADU	17	1997
BAG OF HITS FUN LOVIN' CRIMINALS	11	2002
BAGGARIDDIM UB40	14	1985
BAGSY ME WANNADIES	37	1997
BAKER-GURVITZ ARMY BAKER-GURVITZ ARMY	22	1975
BAKESALE SEBADOH	40	1994
BALAMORY – STRIKE UP THE BAND VARIOUS ARTISTS (DEMON)	20	2005
BALANCE VAN HALEN	8	1995
BALANCE OF POWER ELECTRIC LIGHT ORCHESTRA	9	1986
BALEARIC BEATS VOLUME 1 VARIOUS ARTISTS (FFRR)	58	1988
THE BALLAD HITS ROXETTE	11	2003
BALLAD OF EASY RIDER BYRDS	41	1970
BALLAD OF THE BROKEN SEAS ISOBEL CAMPBELL & MARK LANEGAN	38	2006
THE BALLADS MARIAH CAREY	17	2008
BALLADS – 22 CLASSIC LOVE SONGS ROY ORBISON	38	1990
BALLADS AND BLUES 1982-1994 GARY MOORE	33	1994
BALLADS – THE LOVE SONG COLLECTION BOYZONE	6	2003
BALLBREAKER AC/DC	6	1995
BALLROOM HITZ – THE VERY BEST OF SWEET SWEET	15	1996
BALLS TO PICASSO BRUCE DICKINSON	21	1994
BALLYHOO – THE BEST OF ECHO AND THE BUNNYMEN ECHO & THE BUNNYMEN	59	1997
BANANARAMA BANANARAMA	16	1984
BANBA CLANNAD	5	1993
THE BAND BAND	25	1970
THE BAND BAND	41	1997
BAND OF GYPSIES JIMI HENDRIX	6	1970
BAND ON THE RUN PAUL McCARTNEY & WINGS	1	1973
BANDOLIER BUDGIE	36	1975
THE BANDS 05 – II VARIOUS ARTISTS (VIRGIN)	2	2005
THE BANDS 06 VARIOUS ARTISTS (EMI)	7	2006
BANDS OF GOLD – THE ELECTRIC EIGHTIES VARIOUS ARTISTS (STYLUS)	82	1987
BANDS OF GOLD – THE SENSATIONAL SEVENTIES VARIOUS ARTISTS (STYLUS)	75	1987
BANDS OF GOLD – THE SWINGING SIXTIES VARIOUS ARTISTS (STYLUS)	48	1987
BANDSTAND FAMILY	15	1972
BANDWAGONESQUE TEENAGE FANCLUB	22	1991
BANG THUNDER	62	2008
BANG! WORLD PARTY	2	1993
BANG! – GREATEST HITS OF FRANKIE GOES TO HOLLYWOOD FRANKIE GOES TO HOLLYWOOD	4	1993
BAPTISM LENNY KRAVITZ	74	2004
BARAFUNDLE GORKY'S ZYGOTIC MYNCI	46	1997
THE BARBARA DICKSON ALBUM BARBARA DICKSON	7	1980
THE BARBARA DICKSON SONGBOOK BARBARA DICKSON	5	1985
BARBED WIRE KISSES JESUS & MARY CHAIN	9	1988
BARBIE GIRLS VARIOUS ARTISTS (UNIVERSAL)	7	2004
BARBIE GIRLS 2 VARIOUS ARTISTS (UNIVERSAL)	12	2005
BARBIE SUMMER HITS VARIOUS ARTISTS (UNIVERSAL)	17	2005
BARBRA STREISAND GREATEST HITS VOLUME 2 BARBRA STREISAND	1	1979
BARBRA STREISAND'S GREATEST HITS BARBRA STREISAND	44	1970
BARBRA – THE CONCERT BARBRA STREISAND	63	1994
BARCELONA FREDDIE MERCURY & MONTSERRAT CABALLE	15	1988
BARCELONA GOLD VARIOUS ARTISTS (WARNER BROTHERS)	15	1992

Title / Artist	Peak Position	Year of Release
BARCLAY JAMES HARVEST LIVE BARCLAY JAMES HARVEST	40	1974
BARCLAY JAMES HARVEST XII BARCLAY JAMES HARVEST	31	1978
BARE ANNIE LENNOX	3	2003
BARE WIRES JOHN MAYALL & THE BLUESBREAKERS	3	1968
BARK JEFFERSON AIRPLANE	42	1971
BARK AT THE MOON OZZY OSBOURNE	24	1983
BARRY BARRY MANILOW	5	1980
BARRY LIVE IN BRITAIN BARRY MANILOW	1	1982
BARRY SINGS SINATRA BARRY MANILOW	72	1998
BARRY WHITE'S GREATEST HITS VOLUME 2 BARRY WHITE	17	1977
THE BASEMENT TAPES BOB DYLAN	8	1975
BASKET OF LIGHT PENTANGLE	5	1969
BASS BREAKS & BEATS 2003 VARIOUS ARTISTS (WARNER BROTHERS)	5	2003
BASS CULTURE LINTON KWESI JOHNSON	46	1980
BASS IN YA FACE VARIOUS ARTISTS (VIRGIN)	11	2005
BAT OUT OF HELL MEAT LOAF	9	1978
BAT OUT OF HELL II – BACK INTO HELL MEAT LOAF	1	1993
BAT OUT OF HELL – LIVE MEAT LOAF	14	2004
BAT OUT OF HELL 3 – THE MONSTER IS LOOSE MEAT LOAF	3	2006
BATMAN DANNY ELFMAN	45	1989
BATMAN (OST) PRINCE	1	1989
BATMAN FOREVER FILM SOUNDTRACK	11	1995
BATTERIES NOT INCLUDED AFTER THE FIRE	82	1982
BATTLE HYMNS FOR CHILDREN SINGING HAYSI FANTAYZEE	53	1983
THE BATTLE OF LOS ANGELES RAGE AGAINST THE MACHINE	23	1999
THE BATTLE RAGES ON... DEEP PURPLE	21	1993
BAY OF KINGS STEVE HACKETT	70	1983
BAYOU COUNTRY CREEDENCE CLEARWATER REVIVAL	62	1970
THE BBC 1922-1972 (TV AND RADIO EXTRACTS) TELEVISION AND RADIO COMPILATION	16	1972
BBC COUNTRY HITS VARIOUS ARTISTS (BBC)	20	2000
BBC RADIO 1 LIVE IN CONCERT NEW ORDER	33	1992
BBC RADIO 2 PRESENTS THE PLAYLIST VARIOUS ARTISTS (EMI)	14	2006
BBC SESSIONS LED ZEPPELIN	23	1997
BBC SESSIONS JIMI HENDRIX EXPERIENCE	42	1998
BBC SESSIONS WHO	24	2000
BBC TV'S BEST OF TOP OF THE POPS VARIOUS ARTISTS (BBC)	21	1975
B'DAY BEYONCE KNOWLES	3	2006
BE COMMON	38	2005
BE HERE NOW OASIS	1	1997
BE MY LOVE VARIOUS ARTISTS (UNIVERSAL)	19	2005
BE MY LOVE...AN ALBUM OF LOVE PLACIDO DOMINGO	14	1990
BE NOT NOBODY VANESSA CARLTON	7	2002
BE SEEING YOU DR. FEELGOOD	55	1977
BE YOUR OWN PET BE YOUR OWN PET	47	2006
BE YOURSELF TONIGHT EURYTHMICS	3	1985
THE BEACH FILM SOUNDTRACK	1	2000
THE BEACH BOYS BEACH BOYS	60	1985
THE BEACH BOYS LOVE YOU BEACH BOYS	28	1977
BEACH BOYS PARTY BEACH BOYS	3	1966
BEACH BOYS TODAY BEACH BOYS	6	1966
BEACH HOUSE 04 05 VARIOUS ARTISTS (HED KANDI)	17	2005
BEACH PARTY 2 JAMES LAST	47	1971
BEACHES BETTE MIDLER	21	1989
A BEARD OF STARS TYRANNOSAURUS REX	21	1970
A BEARD OF STARS/UNICORN T. REX	44	1972
THE BEAST INSIDE INSPIRAL CARPETS	5	1991
BEASTER SUGAR	3	1993
BEAT KING CRIMSON	39	1982
BEAT BOY VISAGE	79	1984
BEAT BOYS IN THE JET AGE LAMBRETTAS	28	1980
BEAT CRAZY JOE JACKSON	42	1980
BEAT GIRL ADAM FAITH	11	1961
BEAT OF THE BRASS HERB ALPERT & THE TIJUANA BRASS	4	1968
BEAT RUNS WILD VARIOUS ARTISTS (MERCURY)	70	1986
BEAT STREET FILM SOUNDTRACK	30	1984
BEAT THE CARROTT JASPER CARROTT	13	1981
BEAT THIS – 20 HITS OF RHYTHM KING VARIOUS ARTISTS (STYLUS)	9	1989
THE BEAT, THE RHYME AND THE NOISE WEE PAPA GIRL RAPPERS	39	1988
BEATLEMANIA ANONYMOUS COVER VERSIONS	19	1964
THE BEATLES (WHITE ALBUM) BEATLES	1	1968
THE BEATLES 1962-1966 BEATLES	3	1973
THE BEATLES 1967-1970 BEATLES	2	1973
THE BEATLES AT THE HOLLYWOOD BOWL BEATLES	1	1977
BEATLES BALLADS BEATLES	17	1980
BEATLES CONCERTO ROSTAL & SCHAEFER	61	1979
BEATLES FOR SALE BEATLES	1	1964
THE BEATLES TAPES BEATLES	45	1976
BEATS RHYMES AND BASSLINES – THE BEST OF RAP VARIOUS ARTISTS (POLYGRAM)	7	1992
BEATS, RHYMES AND LIFE A TRIBE CALLED QUEST	28	1996
BEATSONGS BLUE AEROPLANES	33	1991
BEAUCOUP FISH UNDERWORLD	3	1999
BEAUTIFUL VARIOUS ARTISTS (BMG)	1	2004
BEAUTIFUL AWAKENING STACIE ORRICO	64	2006
BEAUTIFUL COLLISION BIC RUNGA	55	2004
BEAUTIFUL DREAMS CHRIS DE BURGH	33	1995
BEAUTIFUL FREAK EELS	5	1997
BEAUTIFUL FUTURE PRIMAL SCREAM	9	2008
BEAUTIFUL GAME VARIOUS ARTISTS (UNIVERSAL)	16	2002
THE BEAUTIFUL GAME – EUFA EURO '96 VARIOUS ARTISTS (RCA)	10	1996
BEAUTIFUL GARBAGE GARBAGE	6	2001
BEAUTIFUL INSANE ELECTRASY	48	1998
BEAUTIFUL INTENTIONS MELANIE C	24	2005
A BEAUTIFUL LIE 30 SECONDS TO MARS	38	2007
BEAUTIFUL LOVESONGS VARIOUS ARTISTS (SONY/BMG)	2	2006
BEAUTIFUL MALADIES 1983-1993: THE ISLAND YEARS TOM WAITS	63	1998
BEAUTIFUL – NEW COLLECTION AUTUMN 2004 VARIOUS ARTISTS (BMG)	8	2004
BEAUTIFUL NOISE NEIL DIAMOND	10	1976
BEAUTIFUL SOUL JESSE McCARTNEY	53	2006
BEAUTIFUL SUNDAY LENA MARTELL	23	1980
BEAUTIFUL – THE REMIX ALBUM BLONDIE	25	1995
BEAUTIFUL VISION VAN MORRISON	31	1982
BEAUTIFUL WASTELAND CAPERCAILLIE	55	1997
BEAUTIFUL WORLD TAKE THAT	1	2006
BEAUTIFULLY HUMAN – WORDS AND SOUNDS VOLUME 2 JILL SCOTT	27	2004
BEAUTY AND THE BEAT PEGGY LEE & GEORGE SHEARING	16	1960
BEAUTY ON A BACK STREET DARYL HALL & JOHN OATES	40	1977
BEAUTY STAB ABC	12	1983
BEBEL GILBERTO BEBEL GILBERTO	49	2004
BECAUSE I LOVE IT AMERIE	17	2007
BECAUSE OF THE TIMES KINGS OF LEON	1	2007
BECAUSE OF YOU NE-YO	6	2007
BECOME WHAT YOU ARE JULIANA HATFIELD THREE	44	1993
BECOMING X SNEAKER PIMPS	27	1996
BED FIVE THIRTY	57	1991
BEDLAM IN GOLIATH MARS VOLTA	42	2008
BEDTIME STORIES JUDGE DREAD	26	1975
BEDTIME STORIES MADONNA	2	1994
BEE GEE FIRST BEE GEES	8	1967
BEE GEES GREATEST BEE GEES	6	1979
BEEBOP MOPTOP DANNY WILSON	24	1989
THE BEEKEEPER TORI AMOS	24	2005
BEETHOVEN TRIPLE CONCERTO BERLIN PHILHARMONIC ORCHESTRA CONDUCTED BY HERBERT VON KARAJAN – SOLOIST DAVID OISTRAKH (VIOLIN), MSTISLAV ROSTROPOVICH (CELLO), SVIATOSLAU RICHTER (PIANO)	51	1970
BEETHOVEN VIOLIN CONCERTO, CORIOLAN OVERTURE NIGEL KENNEDY WITH KLAUS TENNSTEDT CONDUCTING THE NORTH GERMAN RADIO SYMPHONY ORCHESTRA	40	1992
BEETHOVEN WAS DEAF MORRISSEY	13	1993
BEFORE AND AFTER TIM FINN	29	1993
BEFORE THE CALM WITNESS	59	1999
BEFORE THE FLOOD BOB DYLAN	8	1974
BEFORE THE RAIN ETERNAL	3	1997
BEG FOR MERCY G-UNIT	13	2003
BEGGAR ON A BEACH OF GOLD MIKE & THE MECHANICS	9	1995
BEGGARS BANQUET ROLLING STONES	3	1968
BEGIN THE BEGUINE JULIO IGLESIAS	5	1981
BEGIN TO HOPE REGINA SPEKTOR	53	2006
THE BEGINNING STAGES OF POLYPHONIC SPREE	70	2003
BEGINNINGS STEVE HOWE	22	1975
BEGINNINGS – GREATEST HITS AND NEW SONGS CILLA BLACK	68	2003
BEHAVIOUR PET SHOP BOYS	2	1990
BEHIND CLOSED DOORS CHARLIE RICH	4	1974
BEHIND CLOSED DOORS SECRET AFFAIR	48	1980
BEHIND CLOSED DOORS THUNDER	5	1995
BEHIND THE MASK FLEETWOOD MAC	1	1990
BEHIND THE SUN ERIC CLAPTON	8	1985
BEHIND THE SUN CHICANE	10	2000
THE BEIDERBECKE COLLECTION FRANK RICOTTI ALL STARS	14	1988
BEING SOMEBODY LIBERTY X	12	2003
BEING WITH YOU SMOKEY ROBINSON	17	1981
BELIEF INNOCENCE	24	1990
BELIEVE CHER	7	1998
BELIEVE DISTURBED	41	2002
BELIEVE IN ME DUFF McKAGAN	27	1993
BELIEVE IN MUSIC VARIOUS ARTISTS (K-TEL)	2	1973
BELIEVE YOU ME BLANCMANGE	54	1985
BELLA DONNA STEVIE NICKS	11	1981
BELLAMY BROTHERS BELLAMY BROTHERS	21	1976
THE BELLE STARS BELLE STARS	15	1983
BELOW THE SALT STEELEYE SPAN	43	1972
BEN MICHAEL JACKSON	17	1973
BEN HUR FILM SOUNDTRACK	15	1960
BEND SINISTER FALL	36	1986
THE BENDS RADIOHEAD	4	1995
BENEATH THE SURFACE GENIUS/GZA	56	1999
BENEFIT JETHRO TULL	3	1970
BENNY GOODMAN TODAY BENNY GOODMAN	49	1971
BENT OUT OF SHAPE RAINBOW	11	1983
BENTLEY RHYTHM ACE BENTLEY RHYTHM ACE	13	1997
BERLIN LOU REED	7	1973
BERNSTEIN IN BERLIN – BEETHOVEN SYMPHONY NO. 9 LEONARD BERNSTEIN	54	1990
THE BERRY VEST OF GILBERT O'SULLIVAN	20	2004
BERSERKER GARY NUMAN	45	1984
BERT KAEMPFERT – BEST SELLER BERT KAEMPFERT & HIS ORCHESTRA	25	1967

Title / Artist	Peak Position	Year of Release
THE BEST QUINCY JONES	41	1982
THE BEST . . .ALBUM IN THE WORLD...EVER! 4 VARIOUS ARTISTS (VIRGIN)	2	1996
BEST 1991-2004 SEAL	27	2004
THE BEST 80'S ALBUM IN THE WORLD... EVER! VARIOUS ARTISTS (VIRGIN)	7	1995
THE BEST AIR GUITAR ALBUM EVER III VARIOUS ARTISTS (EMI)	14	2003
THE BEST AIR GUITAR ALBUM IN THE WORLD 2 VARIOUS ARTISTS (EMI)	3	2002
THE BEST AIR GUITAR ALBUM IN THE WORLD...EVER! VARIOUS ARTISTS (EMI)	2	2001
BEST ALBUM TRACKS EVER VARIOUS ARTISTS (VIRGIN)	9	2005
THE BEST ALBUM...IN THE WORLD...EVER! 7 VARIOUS ARTISTS (VIRGIN)	11	1998
THE BEST AND FRIENDS ALBUM IN THE WORLD VARIOUS ARTISTS (VIRGIN)	20	2000
BEST BANDS 2005 VARIOUS ARTISTS (EMI)	3	2005
THE BEST BANDS EVER VARIOUS ARTISTS (VIRGIN)	9	2002
BEST BANDS EVER 2004 VARIOUS ARTISTS (VIRGIN)	13	2003
THE BEST BBQ ALBUM EVER VARIOUS ARTISTS (EMI)	5	2005
THE BEST CARNIVAL ALBUM EVER VARIOUS ARTISTS (VIRGIN)	11	2001
THE BEST CHART HITS ALBUM IN THE WORLD...EVER! VARIOUS ARTISTS (VIRGIN)	1	1998
THE BEST CHART HITS IN THE WORLD... EVER! 99 VARIOUS ARTISTS (VIRGIN)	5	1999
THE BEST CHRISTMAS ALBUM IN THE WORLD VARIOUS ARTISTS (EMI)	5	2004
THE BEST CHRISTMAS ALBUM IN THE WORLD EVER VARIOUS ARTISTS (VIRGIN)	4	2000
THE BEST CHRISTMAS ALBUM IN THE WORLD...EVER! VARIOUS ARTISTS (VIRGIN)	2	1993
THE BEST CLASSICAL ALBUM IN THE WORLD...EVER! VARIOUS ARTISTS (EMI)	6	1995
THE BEST CLASSICAL ALBUM OF THE MILLENNIUM...EVER! VARIOUS ARTISTS (VIRGIN)	10	1999
THE BEST CLUB ANTHEMS 05 VARIOUS ARTISTS (VIRGIN)	4	2005
THE BEST CLUB ANTHEMS 2000...EVER! VARIOUS ARTISTS (VIRGIN)	8	1999
THE BEST CLUB ANTHEMS 2001 EVER VARIOUS ARTISTS (VIRGIN)	14	2000
BEST CLUB ANTHEMS 2002 VARIOUS ARTISTS (VIRGIN)	1	2002
BEST CLUB ANTHEMS 2003 VARIOUS ARTISTS (VIRGIN)	17	2003
THE BEST CLUB ANTHEMS 2004 VARIOUS ARTISTS (VIRGIN)	3	2004
THE BEST CLUB ANTHEMS 2005 VARIOUS ARTISTS (VIRGIN)	7	2005
THE BEST CLUB ANTHEMS 2006 VARIOUS ARTISTS (EMI)	5	2006
THE BEST CLUB ANTHEMS 99 IN THE WORLD...EVER! VARIOUS ARTISTS (VIRGIN)	1	1999
THE BEST CLUB ANTHEMS CLASSICS VARIOUS ARTISTS (EMI)	3	2005
THE BEST CLUB ANTHEMS IN THE WORLD... EVER! VARIOUS ARTISTS (VIRGIN)	1	1997
THE BEST CLUB ANTHEMS IN THE WORLD... EVER! 2 VARIOUS ARTISTS (VIRGIN)	6	1997
THE BEST CLUB ANTHEMS IN THE WORLD... EVER! III VARIOUS ARTISTS (VIRGIN)	3	1998
THE BEST CLUB ANTHEMS SUMMER 2002 VARIOUS ARTISTS (VIRGIN)	3	2002
THE BEST CLUB ANTHEMS...EVER! 2K VARIOUS ARTISTS (VIRGIN)	2	2000
THE BEST COUNTRY ALBUM EVER VARIOUS ARTISTS (EMI)	10	2006
THE BEST COUNTRY ALBUM IN THE WORLD...EVER! VARIOUS ARTISTS (EMI)	4	1994
THE BEST COUNTRY BALLADS IN THE WORLD...EVER! VARIOUS ARTISTS (VIRGIN)	14	1998
THE BEST DAMN THING AVRIL LAVIGNE	1	2007
BEST DANCE 99 VARIOUS ARTISTS (TELSTAR)	10	1999
THE BEST DANCE ALBUM EVER 2002 VARIOUS ARTISTS (VIRGIN)	3	2002
THE BEST DANCE ALBUM IN THE WORLD EVER VARIOUS ARTISTS (VIRGIN)	3	2003
BEST DANCE ALBUM IN THE WORLD EVER – 10 VARIOUS ARTISTS (VIRGIN)	3	2000
BEST DANCE ALBUM IN THE WORLD EVER 11 VARIOUS ARTISTS (VIRGIN)	4	2001
BEST DANCE ALBUM IN THE WORLD EVER! 2000 VARIOUS ARTISTS (VIRGIN)	4	2000
THE BEST DANCE ALBUM IN THE WORLD...95! VARIOUS ARTISTS (VIRGIN)	3	1995
THE BEST DANCE ALBUM IN THE WORLD... EVER! VARIOUS ARTISTS (VIRGIN)	1	1993
THE BEST DANCE ALBUM IN THE WORLD... EVER! 2 VARIOUS ARTISTS (VIRGIN)	3	1993
THE BEST DANCE ALBUM IN THE WORLD... EVER! 3 VARIOUS ARTISTS (VIRGIN)	2	1994
THE BEST DANCE ALBUM IN THE WORLD... EVER! 4 VARIOUS ARTISTS (VIRGIN)	5	1994
THE BEST DANCE ALBUM IN THE WORLD... EVER! 5 VARIOUS ARTISTS (VIRGIN)	4	1995
THE BEST DANCE ALBUM IN THE WORLD... EVER! 6 VARIOUS ARTISTS (VIRGIN)	1	1996
THE BEST DANCE ALBUM IN THE WORLD... EVER! 7 VARIOUS ARTISTS (VIRGIN)	2	1997
THE BEST DANCE ALBUM IN THE WORLD... EVER! 8 VARIOUS ARTISTS (VIRGIN)	2	1998
THE BEST DANCE ALBUM IN THE WORLD... EVER! 9 VARIOUS ARTISTS (VIRGIN)	1	1999
THE BEST DANCE ALBUM OF THE YEAR VARIOUS ARTISTS (GLOBAL TELEVISION)	6	1997
THE BEST DANCE ALBUM OF THE YEAR! VARIOUS ARTISTS (VISION)	5	1995
BEST DANCE CLASSICS VARIOUS ARTISTS (VIRGIN)	11	2004
THE BEST DAYS OF MY LIFE JOHNNY MATHIS	38	1979
THE BEST DISCO ALBUM IN THE WORLD VARIOUS ARTISTS (WARNER BROTHERS)	1	1979
THE BEST DISCO ALBUM IN THE WORLD VARIOUS ARTISTS (VIRGIN)	1	1997
THE BEST DISCO ALBUM IN THE WORLD... EVER! 2 VARIOUS ARTISTS (VIRGIN)	7	1998
THE BEST DISCO IN TOWN VARIOUS ARTISTS (UNIVERSAL)	3	2007
THE BEST EASY ALBUM EVER VARIOUS ARTISTS (VIRGIN)	12	2000
BEST FOOTIE ANTHEMS EVER VARIOUS ARTISTS (VIRGIN)	7	2000
THE BEST FOOTIE ANTHEMS IN THE WORLD...EVER! VARIOUS ARTISTS (VIRGIN)	5	1996
BEST FRIENDS VARIOUS ARTISTS (IMPRESSION)	28	1982
BEST FRIENDS FOSTER & ALLEN	36	1997
THE BEST FROM 150 GOLD RECORDS JAMES LAST	56	1980
THE BEST FROM THE MGM MUSICALS VARIOUS ARTISTS (EMI)	12	1990
THE BEST FUNK ALBUM IN THE WORLD... EVER! VARIOUS ARTISTS (VIRGIN)	11	1995
THE BEST GARAGE ANTHEMS EVER VARIOUS ARTISTS (VIRGIN)	8	2000
THE BEST HARD HOUSE EVER VARIOUS ARTISTS (VIRGIN)	10	2001
BEST HEAVY METAL ALBUM IN THE WORLD EVER VARIOUS ARTISTS (VIRGIN)	4	2004
THE BEST HIP HOP ANTHEMZ IN THE WORLD...EVER! VARIOUS ARTISTS (VIRGIN)	6	1998
THE BEST HOUSE ANTHEMS...EVER! VARIOUS ARTISTS (VIRGIN)	5	1999
THE BEST IBIZA ANTHEMS EVER 2001 VARIOUS ARTISTS (VIRGIN)	5	2001
BEST IBIZA ANTHEMS EVER 2K VARIOUS ARTISTS (VIRGIN)	2	2000
THE BEST IBIZA ANTHEMS...EVER! VARIOUS ARTISTS (VIRGIN)	2	1999
THE BEST IRISH ALBUM IN THE WORLD... EVER! VARIOUS ARTISTS (VIRGIN)	11	1996
THE BEST JAZZ ALBUM IN THE WORLD... EVER! VARIOUS ARTISTS (VIRGIN)	8	1996
BEST JAZZ ALBUM IN THE WORLD...EVER! VOLUME 2 VARIOUS ARTISTS (VIRGIN)	11	2000
BEST KEPT SECRET SHEENA EASTON	99	1983
THE BEST LATINO CARNIVAL IN THE WORLD...EVER! VARIOUS ARTISTS (VIRGIN)	5	1997
BEST LIVE – HEADLIGHTS WHITE LINES BLACK TAR RIVERS LEVELLERS	13	1996
THE BEST LOVESONGS...EVER! VARIOUS ARTISTS (VIRGIN)	11	1999
THE BEST MILLENNIUM PARTY...EVER! VARIOUS ARTISTS (VIRGIN)	11	1999
THE BEST MIX ALBUM IN THE WORLD... EVER! VARIOUS ARTISTS (VIRGIN)	9	1996
BEST MOVES CHRIS DE BURGH	65	1981
THE BEST MUSICALS ALBUM IN THE WORLD...EVER! VARIOUS ARTISTS (VIRGIN)	12	1999
THE BEST NO 1 SINGLES IN THE WORLD EVER VARIOUS ARTISTS (EMI)	14	2004
THE BEST NORTHERN SOUL ALL-NIGHTER EVER VARIOUS ARTISTS (VIRGIN)	17	2001
BEST OF ROXY MUSIC	12	2001
THE BEST OF CORRS	6	2001
THE BEST OF RICKY MARTIN	42	2001
THE BEST OF SPANDAU BALLET	56	2001
THE BEST OF PROCLAIMERS	5	2002
THE BEST OF DE LA SOUL	17	2003
BEST OF BOOMTOWN RATS	43	2004
BEST OF DEF LEPPARD	6	2004
THE BEST OF FATS DOMINO	58	2004
THE BEST OF GROOVE ARMADA	6	2004
THE BEST OF HOUSEMARTINS	29	2004
THE BEST OF LEANN RIMES	2	2004
THE BEST OF TALKING HEADS	30	2004
THE BEST OF BRANDY	24	2005
THE BEST OF DOORS	71	2005
THE BEST OF KIRSTY MacCOLL	12	2005
THE BEST OF SNOOP DOGG	50	2005
THE BEST OF CHRIS ISAAK	65	2006
THE BEST OF NEIL DIAMOND	30	2006
BEST OF CARDIGANS	32	2008
BEST OF CREEDENCE CLEARWATER REVIVAL	46	2008
BEST OF RADIOHEAD	4	2008
THE BEST OF JOY DIVISION	63	2008
THE BEST OF NEIL DIAMOND	8	2008
THE BEST OF SASH!	9	2008
THE BEST OF SPECIALS	28	2008
THE BEST OF – THE SUN AIN'T GONNA SHINE SCOTT WALKER & THE WALKER BROTHERS	24	2006

Title / Artist	Peak Position	Year of Release
THE BEST OF 10 YEARS – 32 SUPERHITS BONEY M	35	1986
THE BEST OF 100% DANCE VARIOUS ARTISTS (TELSTAR)	11	1995
BEST OF 100% PURE GROOVES VARIOUS ARTISTS (TELSTAR)	13	1998
THE BEST OF 1968-1973 STEVE MILLER BAND	34	1990
THE BEST OF 1969/1974 DAVID BOWIE	13	1998
THE BEST OF 1974/1979 DAVID BOWIE	39	1998
THE BEST OF – 1980/1987 DAVID BOWIE	34	2007
THE BEST OF 1980-1990 U2	4	1998
THE BEST OF 1980-1990 & B SIDES U2	1	1998
THE BEST OF 1990 – 2000 U2	37	2002
THE BEST OF 1990-2000 & B-SIDES U2	2	2002
BEST OF 1996-2008 CHICANE	16	2008
THE BEST OF 2 TONE VARIOUS ARTISTS (2 TONE)	10	1993
THE BEST OF ACID JAZZ VARIOUS ARTISTS (GLOBAL TELEVISION)	5	1996
BEST OF ACID JAZZ VOLUME 2 VARIOUS ARTISTS (ACID JAZZ)	16	1993
BEST OF ACID JAZZ VOLUME 2 VARIOUS ARTISTS (GLOBAL TELEVISION)	13	1997
BEST OF ACOUSTIC VARIOUS ARTISTS (ECHO)	2	2004
THE BEST OF ALED JONES ALED JONES	59	1987
THE BEST OF ALL WOMAN VARIOUS ARTISTS (QUALITY TELEVISION)	6	1995
THE BEST OF ANDY WILLIAMS ANDY WILLIAMS	51	1992
THE BEST OF ART OF NOISE ART OF NOISE	55	1988
THE BEST OF AZTEC CAMERA AZTEC CAMERA	36	1999
THE BEST OF BACHARACH STRINGS FOR PLEASURE	49	1971
BEST OF BALL, BARBER AND BILK KENNY BALL, CHRIS BARBER & ACKER BILK	1	1962
BEST OF BARBER AND BILK VOLUME 1 CHRIS BARBER & ACKER BILK	4	1961
BEST OF BARBER AND BILK VOLUME 2 CHRIS BARBER & ACKER BILK	8	1961
THE BEST OF BELINDA VOLUME 1 BELINDA CARLISLE	1	1992
BEST OF BERT KAEMPFERT BERT KAEMPFERT & HIS ORCHESTRA	27	1966
THE BEST OF BETTE BETTE MIDLER	6	2008
THE BEST OF BING BING CROSBY	41	1977
THE BEST OF BING CROSBY BING CROSBY	59	1996
THE BEST OF BLACK SABBATH BLACK SABBATH	24	2000
THE BEST OF BLONDIE BLONDIE	4	1981
BEST OF BLUE BLUE	6	2004
THE BEST OF BOB DYLAN BOB DYLAN	6	1997
THE BEST OF BOND...JAMES BOND VARIOUS ARTISTS (CAPITOL)	6	1999
THE BEST OF BOND JAMES BOND VARIOUS ARTISTS (CAPITOL)	15	2002
THE BEST OF BOND JAMES BOND VARIOUS ARTISTS (EMI)	9	2008
BEST OF BONKERS VARIOUS ARTISTS (RESIST)	9	2007
THE BEST OF BONNIE RAITT 1989-2003 BONNIE RAITT	37	2003
THE BEST OF BOTH WORLDS R KELLY & JAY-Z	37	2002
THE BEST OF BOTH WORLDS VAN HALEN	15	2004
BEST OF BOTH WORLDS CONCERT HANNAH MONTANA & MILEY CYRUS	29	2008
BEST OF BOWIE DAVID BOWIE	11	2002
THE BEST OF BREAD BREAD	7	1972
THE BEST OF BREAD VOLUME 2 BREAD	48	1974
BEST OF BRITISH VARIOUS ARTISTS (VIRGIN)	2	2002
THE BEST OF BRITISH JAZZ FUNK VOLUME 2 VARIOUS ARTISTS (BEGGARS BANQUET)	44	1982
BEST OF CAFÉ DEL MAR VARIOUS ARTISTS (MERCURY)	9	2003
BEST OF CAPITAL GOLD – 24 CARAT CLASSIC HITS VARIOUS ARTISTS (HIT LABEL)	20	1992
THE BEST OF CAR WASH FILM SOUNDTRACK	59	1977
BEST OF CHAKA KHAN – I'M EVERY WOMAN CHAKA KHAN	62	1999
BEST OF CHIC CHIC	30	1979
BEST OF CHRIS BARBER CHRIS BARBER	17	1960
THE BEST OF CHRIS REA CHRIS REA	3	1994
THE BEST OF CHRIS REA – NEW LIGHT THROUGH OLD WINDOWS CHRIS REA	5	1988
THE BEST OF CILLA BLACK CILLA BLACK	21	1968
THE BEST OF CLASSIC ROCK LONDON SYMPHONY ORCHESTRA WITH THE ROYAL CHORAL SOCIETY & THE ROGER SMITH CHORALE	35	1982
THE BEST OF CLIFF CLIFF RICHARD & THE SHADOWS	5	1969
THE BEST OF CLIFF VOLUME 2 CLIFF RICHARD & THE SHADOWS	49	1972
THE BEST OF CREAM CREAM	6	1969
THE BEST OF DANCE '91 VARIOUS ARTISTS (TELSTAR)	2	1991
THE BEST OF DANCE '92 VARIOUS ARTISTS (TELSTAR)	1	1992
THE BEST OF DANCE '93 VARIOUS ARTISTS (TELSTAR)	1	1993
THE BEST OF DANCE '94 VARIOUS ARTISTS (TELSTAR)	10	1994
THE BEST OF DANCE '96 VARIOUS ARTISTS (TELSTAR)	13	1996
THE BEST OF DANCE '97 VARIOUS ARTISTS (TELSTAR)	6	1997
THE BEST OF DANCE '98 VARIOUS ARTISTS (TELSTAR)	9	1998
THE BEST OF DANCE MANIA 95 VARIOUS ARTISTS (PURE MUSIC)	5	1995
THE BEST OF DARYL HALL AND JOHN OATES – LOOKING BACK DARYL HALL & JOHN OATES	9	1991
THE BEST OF DEAN MARTIN DEAN MARTIN	9	1969
THE BEST OF DEANNA DURBIN DEANNA DURBIN	84	1982
THE BEST OF DEL AMITRI – HATFUL OF RAIN DEL AMITRI	5	1998
BEST OF DIONNE WARWICK DIONNE WARWICK	8	1966
THE BEST OF DONNA SUMMER DONNA SUMMER	24	1990
THE BEST OF DRIVE TIME VARIOUS ARTISTS (POLYGRAM)	12	1998
THE BEST OF DUSTY SPRINGFIELD DUSTY SPRINGFIELD	19	1998
THE BEST OF EARTH WIND & FIRE VOLUME 1 EARTH WIND & FIRE	6	1978
THE BEST OF ELAINE PAIGE AND BARBARA DICKSON TOGETHER ELAINE PAIGE & BARBARA DICKSON	22	1992
BEST OF ELVIS ELVIS PRESLEY	3	1957
THE BEST OF ELVIS COSTELLO – THE MAN ELVIS COSTELLO & THE ATTRACTIONS	8	1985
BEST OF EN VOGUE EN VOGUE	39	1998
BEST OF EUPHORIC DANCE – BREAKDOWN IBIZA VARIOUS ARTISTS (TELSTAR)	2	2001
THE BEST OF EVERYTHING BUT THE GIRL EVERYTHING BUT THE GIRL	23	1996
BEST OF FRANK SINATRA FRANK SINATRA	17	1968
THE BEST OF FREE – ALL RIGHT NOW FREE	9	1991
BEST FRIENDS CLEO LAINE & JOHN WILLIAMS	18	1978
BEST OF FRIENDS JOOLS HOLLAND	9	2007
BEST OF GARY NUMAN 1978-83 GARY NUMAN	70	1993
BEST OF GENE PITNEY GENE PITNEY	8	1969
THE BEST OF GLADYS KNIGHT & THE PIPS GLADYS KNIGHT & THE PIPS	6	1976
THE BEST OF GLENN MILLER GLENN MILLER & HIS ORCHESTRA	5	1969
THE BEST OF HANK MARVIN AND THE SHADOWS HANK MARVIN & THE SHADOWS	19	1994
THE BEST OF HEARTBEAT VARIOUS ARTISTS (COLUMBIA)	1	1995
THE BEST OF HELEN REDDY HELEN REDDY	5	1976
THE BEST OF HERMAN'S HERMITS HERMAN'S HERMITS	24	2008
THE BEST OF HOOKED ON CLASSICS ROYAL PHILHARMONIC ORCHESTRA CONDUCTED BY LOUIS CLARK	51	1983
BEST OF HOUSE '88 VARIOUS ARTISTS (TELSTAR)	11	1988
BEST OF HOUSE MEGAMIX VARIOUS ARTISTS (SERIOUS)	77	1987
BEST OF HOUSE MEGAMIX VOLUME 2 VARIOUS ARTISTS (SERIOUS)	73	1988
THE BEST OF HOUSE VOLUME 1 VARIOUS ARTISTS (SERIOUS)	55	1987
BEST OF HOUSE VOLUME 2 VARIOUS ARTISTS (SERIOUS)	30	1987
BEST OF HOUSE VOLUME 3 VARIOUS ARTISTS (SERIOUS)	61	1987
BEST OF HOUSE VOLUME 4 VARIOUS ARTISTS (SERIOUS)	27	1988
THE BEST OF HOWARD JONES HOWARD JONES	36	1993
THE BEST OF – IN A LIFETIME CLANNAD	23	2003
THE BEST OF INCANTATION: MUSIC FROM THE ANDES INCANTATION	28	1985
THE BEST OF INDIE TOP 20 VARIOUS ARTISTS (BEECHWOOD)	10	1991
THE BEST OF JAMES JAMES	1	1998
THE BEST OF JAMES BOND – 30TH ANNIVERSARY COLLECTION VARIOUS ARTISTS (EMI)	2	1992
THE BEST OF JAMES BROWN – THE GODFATHER OF SOUL JAMES BROWN	17	1987
THE BEST OF JASPER CARROTT JASPER CARROTT	38	1978
THE BEST OF JIM REEVES JIM REEVES	3	1965
THE BEST OF JOHN DENVER JOHN DENVER	7	1974
BEST OF JOHN DENVER VOLUME 2 JOHN DENVER	9	1977
THE BEST OF JOHNNY CASH JOHNNY CASH	48	1976
THE BEST OF JON AND VANGELIS JON & VANGELIS	42	1984
THE BEST OF LADYSMITH BLACK MAMBAZO – THE STAR AND WISEMAN LADYSMITH BLACK MAMBAZO	2	1998
THE BEST OF LENA MARTELL LENA MARTELL	13	1977
THE BEST OF LOU REED AND THE VELVET UNDERGROUND LOU REED & THE VELVET UNDERGROUND	56	1995
BEST OF LUTHER VANDROSS – BEST OF LOVE LUTHER VANDROSS	14	1989
THE BEST OF M PEOPLE M PEOPLE	2	1998
THE BEST OF MARVIN GAYE MARVIN GAYE	56	1976
THE BEST OF MASTERCUTS VARIOUS ARTISTS (VIRGIN)	11	1996
THE BEST OF MATT BIANCO MATT BIANCO	49	1990
THE BEST OF ME MAXI PRIEST	23	1991
THE BEST OF ME BRYAN ADAMS	12	1999
THE BEST OF MICHAEL BALL MICHAEL BALL	25	1994
BEST OF MICHAEL JACKSON MICHAEL JACKSON	11	1981

Title / Artist	Peak Position	Year of Release
THE BEST OF MICHAEL JACKSON AND THE JACKSON FIVE MICHAEL JACKSON & THE JACKSON FIVE	5	1997
THE BEST OF MIRAGE: JACK MIX '88 MIRAGE	7	1987
THE BEST OF MOTORHEAD MOTORHEAD	52	2000
THE BEST OF MY GOLD RECORDS JAMES LAST	42	1983
THE BEST OF NANCI GRIFFITH NANCI GRIFFITH	27	1993
THE BEST OF NAT 'KING' COLE NAT 'KING' COLE	5	1968
THE BEST OF NAT 'KING' COLE VOLUME 2 NAT 'KING' COLE	39	1970
THE BEST OF NEIL DIAMOND NEIL DIAMOND	68	1996
? (THE BEST OF NEW ORDER)/? (THE REST OF NEW ORDER) NEW ORDER	4	1994
THE BEST OF NICK CAVE & THE BAD SEEDS NICK CAVE & THE BAD SEEDS	11	1998
THE BEST OF O.M.D. ORCHESTRAL MANOEUVRES IN THE DARK	2	1988
THE BEST OF OL' BLUE EYES FRANK SINATRA	30	1975
BEST OF PEGGY LEE VOLUME 2 PEGGY LEE	18	1961
BEST OF R&B VARIOUS ARTISTS (EMI)	3	2004
THE BEST OF R&B – HIT SELECTION VARIOUS ARTISTS (VIRGIN)	6	2004
THE BEST OF R&B – SUMMER SELECTION VARIOUS ARTISTS (EMI)	2	2004
THE BEST OF R.E.M. R.E.M.	7	1992
THE BEST OF RADIO LUXEMBOURG VARIOUS ARTISTS (PYE)	14	1963
BEST OF RAINBOW RAINBOW	14	1981
THE BEST OF RICHARD CLAYDERMAN RICHARD CLAYDERMAN	73	1997
THE BEST OF ROCK 'N' ROLL LOVE SONGS VARIOUS ARTISTS (DINO)	9	1994
THE BEST OF ROD STEWART ROD STEWART	3	1977
THE BEST OF ROD STEWART AND THE FACES 1971-1975 ROD STEWART & THE FACES	58	1992
THE BEST OF ROY ORBISON ROY ORBISON	1	1975
THE BEST OF SADE SADE	6	1994
THE BEST OF SELLERS PETER SELLERS	3	1959
THE BEST OF SHIRLEY BASSEY SHIRLEY BASSEY	27	1992
THE BEST OF SIMPLE MINDS SIMPLE MINDS	34	2001
THE BEST OF – SO FAR PETER KAY	62	2005
THE BEST OF SPANDAU BALLET SPANDAU BALLET	44	1991
THE BEST OF STATUS QUO STATUS QUO	32	1973
THE BEST OF SUEDEHEAD MORRISSEY	26	1997
THE BEST OF – SUNSHINE SUPERMAN DONOVAN	47	2006
THE BEST OF T. REX T. REX	21	1971
THE BEST OF TAMMY WYNETTE TAMMY WYNETTE	4	1975
THE BEST OF TAVARES TAVARES	39	1978
BEST OF THE 20TH CENTURY BOY MARC BOLAN & T. REX	5	1985
THE BEST OF THE ALAN PARSONS PROJECT ALAN PARSONS PROJECT	99	1983
THE BEST OF THE B-52'S – DANCE THIS MESS AROUND B-52'S	36	1990
BEST OF THE BEACH BOYS BEACH BOYS	2	1966
THE BEST OF THE BEACH BOYS BEACH BOYS	25	1995
BEST OF THE BEACH BOYS VOLUME 2 BEACH BOYS	3	1967
BEST OF THE BEACH BOYS VOLUME 3 BEACH BOYS	8	1968
THE BEST OF THE BEAST IRON MAIDEN	16	1996
BEST OF THE BEE GEES BEE GEES	7	1969
THE BEST OF THE BEST AIR GUITAR ALBUMS VARIOUS ARTISTS (EMI)	15	2005
BEST OF – THE BOOMBASTIC COLLECTION SHAGGY	22	2008
THE BEST OF THE CHRISTIANS CHRISTIANS	22	1993
THE BEST OF THE CLASSICAL BITS (TELEVISION COMPILATION) TELEVISION AND RADIO COMPILATION	7	1993
THE BEST OF THE COMPOSERS: BEETHOVEN/STRAUSS/TCHAIKOVSKY/MOZART VARIOUS ARTISTS (RONCO)	49	1982
THE BEST OF THE DAMNED DAMNED	43	1981
BEST OF THE DOOLEYS DOOLEYS	6	1979
THE BEST OF THE DOORS DOORS	9	1991
THE BEST OF THE DOORS DOORS	17	1991
BEST OF THE DUBLINERS DUBLINERS	25	1967
THE BEST OF THE EAGLES EAGLES	8	1985
THE BEST OF THE FACES FACES	24	1977
THE BEST OF THE FOUR TOPS FOUR TOPS	13	1982
BEST OF THE GOONS SHOWS GOONS	8	1959
BEST OF THE GOONS SHOWS VOLUME 2 GOONS	11	1960
THE BEST OF THE ICICLE WORKS ICICLE WORKS	60	1992
THE BEST OF THE MAMAS AND PAPAS MAMAS & THE PAPAS	6	1977
THE BEST OF THE MAVERICKS MAVERICKS	40	1999
THE BEST OF THE NINETIES...SO FAR VARIOUS ARTISTS (EMI)	9	1996
THE BEST OF THE POGUES POGUES	11	1991
THE BEST OF THE RAT PACK VARIOUS ARTISTS (CAPITOL)	2	2001
THE BEST OF THE REAL THING REAL THING	24	1986
THE BEST OF THE SEEKERS SEEKERS	1	1968
THE BEST OF THE STYLISTICS STYLISTICS	1	1975
BEST OF THE STYLISTICS VOLUME 2 STYLISTICS	1	1976
THE BEST OF THE TROGGS TROGGS	24	1967
THE BEST OF THE UNDERTONES – TEENAGE KICKS UNDERTONES	45	1993
THE BEST OF THE VILLAGE PEOPLE VILLAGE PEOPLE	72	1993
BEST OF THE WATERBOYS '81-'91 WATERBOYS	2	1991
BEST OF THUNDER – THE FINEST HOUR (AND A BIT) THUNDER	22	1995
THE BEST OF TONY CHRISTIE TONY CHRISTIE	28	1976
THE BEST OF TUBULAR BELLS MIKE OLDFIELD	60	2001
THE BEST OF UB40 – VOLUME ONE UB40	3	1987
THE BEST OF UB40 – VOLUME TWO UB40	12	1995
THE BEST OF VAN HALEN – VOLUME 1 VAN HALEN	45	1996
THE BEST OF VAN MORRISON VAN MORRISON	4	1990
THE BEST OF VAN MORRISON VOLUME 2 VAN MORRISON	31	1993
THE BEST OF – VOLUME 1 DEPECHE MODE	18	2006
BEST OF – VOLUME 2 BOB DYLAN	22	2000
THE BEST OF VOLUMES 1 & 2 UB40	47	2005
THE BEST OF VYBIN' VARIOUS ARTISTS (GLOBAL TELEVISION)	12	1996
BEST OF – WAVE OF MUTILATION PIXIES	16	2004
BEST OF WEST COAST HIP HOP VARIOUS ARTISTS (STREET SOUNDS)	80	1987
THE BEST OF WHAM!...IF YOU WERE THERE WHAM!	4	1997
THE BEST OF WHITESNAKE WHITESNAKE	44	2003
THE BEST OF WOMAN TO WOMAN VARIOUS ARTISTS (POLYGRAM)	3	1996
THE BEST OF...VOLUME 3 VAN MORRISON	23	2007
THE BEST ONE HIT WONDERS IN THE WORLD VARIOUS ARTISTS (VIRGIN)	11	2003
THE BEST OPERA ALBUM IN THE WORLD... EVER! VARIOUS ARTISTS (VIRGIN)	10	1996
BEST PANPIPES ALBUM IN THE WORLD... EVER! VARIOUS ARTISTS (VIRGIN)	13	2003
THE BEST PARTY IN THE WORLD...EVER! VARIOUS ARTISTS (VIRGIN)	7	1997
THE BEST PARTY IN TOWN EVER VARIOUS ARTISTS (VIRGIN)	19	2001
THE BEST PARTY...EVER! VARIOUS ARTISTS (VIRGIN)	5	1995
THE BEST PEPSI CHART ALBUM IN THE WORLD...EVER! VARIOUS ARTISTS (VIRGIN)	2	1999
BEST PEPSI CHART ALBUM. . .EVER! 2000 VARIOUS ARTISTS (VIRGIN)	7	2000
THE BEST PROG ROCK ALBUM IN THE WORLD VARIOUS ARTISTS (VIRGIN)	9	2003
THE BEST PROMS ALBUM IN THE WORLD EVER! VARIOUS ARTISTS (VIRGIN)	19	2000
THE BEST PUB ALBUM VARIOUS ARTISTS (GTV)	14	2007
THE BEST PUB JUKEBOX EVER VARIOUS ARTISTS (VIRGIN)	9	2004
THE BEST PUB JUKEBOX IN THE WORLD EVER VARIOUS ARTISTS (VIRGIN)	9	2000
THE BEST PUNK ALBUM IN THE WORLD... EVER! VARIOUS ARTISTS (VIRGIN)	1	1995
THE BEST PUNK ALBUM IN THE WORLD... EVER! 2 VARIOUS ARTISTS (VIRGIN)	16	1996
THE BEST RAP ALBUM IN THE WORLD... EVER! VARIOUS ARTISTS (VIRGIN)	2	1996
THE BEST RAVE ANTHEMS IN THE WORLD... EVER! VARIOUS ARTISTS (VIRGIN)	11	1998
THE BEST REGGAE ALBUM IN THE WORLD... EVER! VARIOUS ARTISTS (VIRGIN)	4	1994
THE BEST ROCK ALBUM IN THE WORLD... EVER! VARIOUS ARTISTS (VIRGIN)	1	1994
THE BEST ROCK ALBUM IN THE WORLD... EVER! II VARIOUS ARTISTS (VIRGIN)	3	1995
THE BEST ROCK ANTHEMS ALBUM IN THE WORLD...EVER! VARIOUS ARTISTS (VIRGIN)	8	1996
THE BEST ROCK ANTHEMS...EVER! VARIOUS ARTISTS (VIRGIN)	10	1998
THE BEST ROCK BALLADS ALBUM IN THE WORLD...EVER! VARIOUS ARTISTS (VIRGIN)	2	1995
THE BEST ROCK BALLADS ALBUM IN THE WORLD...EVER! II VARIOUS ARTISTS (VIRGIN)	7	1997
THE BEST ROCK 'N' ROLL ALBUM IN THE WORLD...EVER! VARIOUS ARTISTS (VIRGIN)	2	1994
THE BEST SCOTTISH ALBUM IN THE WORLD...EVER! VARIOUS ARTISTS (VIRGIN)	9	1997
THE BEST SEVENTIES ALBUM IN THE WORLD...EVER! VARIOUS ARTISTS (VIRGIN)	13	1997
BEST SHOTS PAT BENATAR	6	1987
THE BEST SIXTIES ALBUM IN THE WORLD... EVER! VARIOUS ARTISTS (VIRGIN)	2	1995
THE BEST SIXTIES ALBUM IN THE WORLD... EVER! II VARIOUS ARTISTS (VIRGIN)	2	1996
THE BEST SIXTIES ALBUM IN THE WORLD... EVER! III VARIOUS ARTISTS (VIRGIN)	3	1997
THE BEST SIXTIES ALBUM IN THE WORLD... EVER! IV VARIOUS ARTISTS (VIRGIN)	11	1998
THE BEST SIXTIES LOVE ALBUM...EVER! VARIOUS ARTISTS (VIRGIN)	2	1999
THE BEST SIXTIES PARTY...EVER VARIOUS ARTISTS (VIRGIN)	11	2004
THE BEST SIXTIES SUMMER ALBUM IN THE WORLD...EVER! VARIOUS ARTISTS (VIRGIN)	2	1998

Title / Artist	Peak Position	Year of Release
THE BEST SIXTIES SUMMER PARTY EVER VARIOUS ARTISTS (VIRGIN)	6	2002
THE BEST SMOOTH JAZZ EVER VARIOUS ARTISTS (VIRGIN)	20	2003
THE BEST STEPS TO HEAVEN SHOWADDYWADDY	90	1987
THE BEST SUMMER ALBUM 2002 VARIOUS ARTISTS (WARNER BROTHERS)	1	2002
THE BEST SUMMER ALBUM 2003 VARIOUS ARTISTS (WARNER BROTHERS)	11	2003
THE BEST SUMMER ALBUM IN THE WORLD...EVER! VARIOUS ARTISTS (VIRGIN)	1	1995
BEST SUMMER EVER 2004 VARIOUS ARTISTS (VIRGIN)	4	2004
THE BEST SUMMER HOLIDAY 2001 EVER VARIOUS ARTISTS (VIRGIN)	2	2001
THE BEST SUMMER HOLIDAY EVER VARIOUS ARTISTS (VIRGIN)	5	2000
THE BEST SUMMER PARTY ALBUM IN THE WORLD...EVER! VARIOUS ARTISTS (VIRGIN)	6	1998
BEST SWING '95 VARIOUS ARTISTS (TELSTAR)	10	1995
BEST SWING 96 VARIOUS ARTISTS (TELSTAR)	2	1996
BEST SWING 96 – VOLUME 2 VARIOUS ARTISTS (TELSTAR)	6	1996
BEST SWING '96 – VOLUME 3 VARIOUS ARTISTS (TELSTAR)	20	1996
THE BEST SWING ALBUM IN THE WORLD... EVER! VARIOUS ARTISTS (VIRGIN)	3	1996
THE BEST THAT I COULD DO 1978-1988 JOHN MELLENCAMP	25	1998
BEST – THE GREATEST HITS OF S CLUB	2	2003
THE BEST TRANCE ANTHEMS...EVER! VARIOUS ARTISTS (VIRGIN)	7	1999
THE BEST TV ADS...EVER! VARIOUS ARTISTS (VIRGIN)	10	2000
BEST UNOFFICIAL FOOTIE ANTHEMS EVER! VARIOUS ARTISTS (VIRGIN)	3	2002
THE BEST WOMBLES ALBUM SO FAR – VOLUME 1 WOMBLES	26	1998
BEST WORSHIP SONGS EVER VARIOUS ARTISTS (VIRGIN)	8	2004
THE BEST YEARS OF OUR LIVES STEVE HARLEY & COCKNEY REBEL	4	1975
THE BEST YEARS OF OUR LIVES NEIL DIAMOND	42	1989
THE BEST. . .ALBUM IN THE WORLD...EVER! VARIOUS ARTISTS (VIRGIN)	2	1995
THE BEST. . .ALBUM IN THE WORLD...EVER! 2 VARIOUS ARTISTS (VIRGIN)	1	1996
THE BEST. . .ALBUM IN THE WORLD...EVER! 3 VARIOUS ARTISTS (VIRGIN)	2	1996
THE BEST. . .ALBUM IN THE WORLD...EVER! 5 VARIOUS ARTISTS (VIRGIN)	1	1997
THE BEST. . .ALBUM IN THE WORLD...EVER! 6 VARIOUS ARTISTS (VIRGIN)	8	1997
THE BEST... AND FRIENDS ALBUM IN THE WORLD...EVER! VARIOUS ARTISTS (VIRGIN)	8	1999
BEST...1 SMITHS	1	1992
BEST...2 SMITHS	29	1992
THE BEST...ANTHEMS...EVER! VARIOUS ARTISTS (VIRGIN)	1	1997
THE BEST...ANTHEMS...EVER! 2 VARIOUS ARTISTS (VIRGIN)	3	1998
THE BEST...ANTHEMS...EVER! 3 VARIOUS ARTISTS (VIRGIN)	19	1998
THE BETA BAND BETA BAND	18	1999
BETA MALE FAIRYTALES BEN'S BROTHER	14	2007
BETCHA BOTTOM DOLLAR PUPPINI SISTERS	17	2006
BETE NOIRE BRYAN FERRY	9	1987
BETTE OF ROSES BETTE MIDLER	55	1995
BETTER DAYZ 2PAC	68	2002
BETTER LIVING THROUGH CHEMISTRY FATBOY SLIM	69	1996
A BETTER MAN BRIAN KENNEDY	19	1996
BETTER THE DEVIL YOU KNOW SONIA	32	1993
BETTY HELMET	38	1994
BETWEEN 10TH AND 11TH CHARLATANS	21	1992
BETWEEN THE BUTTONS ROLLING STONES	3	1967
BETWEEN THE COVERS MARTI PELLOW	66	2003
BETWEEN THE LINES FIVE STAR	7	1987
BETWEEN THE LINES JASON DONOVAN	2	1990
BETWEEN THE MINDS JACK SAVORETTI	70	2007
BETWEEN THE SENSES HAVEN	26	2002
BETWEEN THE SHEETS 411	46	2004
BETWEEN TODAY AND YESTERDAY ALAN PRICE	9	1974
BETWEEN TWO FIRES PAUL YOUNG	4	1986
BEVERLEY CRAVEN BEVERLEY CRAVEN	3	1991
BEVERLY HILLS COP FILM SOUNDTRACK	24	1985
BEVERLY HILLS COP II FILM SOUNDTRACK	71	1987
BEYOND DINOSAUR JR	52	2007
BEYOND APPEARANCES SANTANA	58	1985
BEYOND EUPHORIA – MIXED BY DT8 PROJECT VARIOUS ARTISTS (MINISTRY OF SOUND)	11	2005
BEYOND GOOD AND EVIL CULT	69	2001
BEYOND IMAGINATION OPERABABES	24	2002
BEYOND SKIN NITIN SAWHNEY	44	1999
BEYOND THE ASTRAL SKIES ULI JON ROTH & ELECTRIC SUN	64	1985
BEYOND THE FRINGE STAGE CAST RECORDING	13	1961
BEYOND THE MIX FRANKIE KNUCKLES	59	1991
BEYOND THE NEIGHBOURHOOD ATHLETE	5	2007
BEYOND THE PLANETS KEVIN PEEK & RICK WAKEMAN FEATURING JEFF WAYNE NARRATION PATRICK ALLEN	64	1984
BEYOND THE SEA VARIOUS ARTISTS (SONY/BMG)	3	2006
BEYOND THE SEA – THE VERY BEST OF BOBBY DARIN	26	2004
BEYOND THE SUN BILLY MacKENZIE	64	1997
BEYOND THE SUNSET RAIN PARADE	78	1985
BEYOND THE VALLEY OF THE MURDERDOLLS MURDERDOLLS	40	2002
THE BEYONDNESS OF THINGS ENGLISH CHAMBER ORCHESTRA CONDUCTED BY JOHN BARRY	67	1999
BEZERK TIGERTAILZ	36	1990
BEZ'S MADCHESTER ANTHEMS VARIOUS ARTISTS (WARNER BROTHERS)	8	2006
THE BIBLE BIBLE	67	1989
BIG MACY GRAY	62	2007
THE BIG 3 60FT DOLLS	36	1996
THE BIG AREA THEN JERICO	4	1989
BIG BAM BOOM DARYL HALL & JOHN OATES	28	1984
BIG BAND PERCUSSION TED HEATH & HIS MUSIC	17	1962
BIG BANG WE'VE GOT A FUZZBOX & WE'RE GONNA USE IT	5	1989
THE BIG BANG BUSTA RHYMES	19	2006
BIG BEACH BOUTIQUE II VARIOUS ARTISTS (SOUTHERN FRIED)	11	2002
THE BIG BREAKFAST ALBUM (TELEVISION COMPILATION) TELEVISION AND RADIO COMPILATION	8	1993
BIG BROTHER OST (TELEVISION SOUNDTRACK) TELEVISION AND RADIO COMPILATION	17	2000
BIG CALM MORCHEEBA	18	1998
BIG CLUB HITS VARIOUS ARTISTS (INSPIRED)	5	2001
BIG CLUB HITS VARIOUS ARTISTS (UNIVERSAL)	1	2006
BIG COCK KING KURT	50	1986
BIG DADDY JOHN COUGAR MELLENCAMP	25	1989
THE BIG EXPRESS XTC	38	1984
BIG GAME WHITE LION	47	1989
BIG GENERATOR YES	17	1987
BIG GUNS – THE VERY BEST OF RORY GALLAGHER	31	2005
THE BIG HIT MIX VARIOUS ARTISTS (VIRGIN)	16	1996
BIG HITS VARIOUS ARTISTS (GLOBAL TELEVISION)	4	1997
BIG HITS (HIGH TIDE AND GREEN GRASS) ROLLING STONES	4	1966
BIG HITS 98 VARIOUS ARTISTS (SONY)	1	1998
BIG HITS 99 VARIOUS ARTISTS (GLOBAL TELEVISION)	1	1999
THE BIG LAD IN THE WINDMILL IT BITES	35	1986
BIG LOVE ALI CAMPBELL	6	1995
BIG LOVE MOVIE THEMES GEOFF LOVE & HIS ORCHESTRA	28	1971
BIG MIX 96 VARIOUS ARTISTS (EMI)	1	1996
BIG MIX '96 – VOLUME 2 VARIOUS ARTISTS (EMI)	7	1996
BIG MIX '97 VARIOUS ARTISTS (VIRGIN)	1	1997
BIG MIX '97 – VOLUME 2 VARIOUS ARTISTS (VIRGIN)	1	1997
BIG NIGHT OUT VARIOUS ARTISTS (UNIVERSAL)	5	2007
THE BIG ONES FOUR SEASONS	37	1971
BIG ONES AEROSMITH	7	1994
THE BIG PICTURE ELTON JOHN	3	1997
(BIG RED LETTER DAY) BUFFALO TOM	17	1993
BIG RIVER JIMMY NAIL	8	1995
BIG SCIENCE LAURIE ANDERSON	29	1982
BIG SCREEN CLASSICS ROYAL PHILHARMONIC ORCHESTRA	49	1994
BIG SMASH WRECKLESS ERIC	30	1980
BIG SOFTIES – 41 SENSITIVE SOUL CLASSICS VARIOUS ARTISTS (EMI)	8	2006
BIG SOUND OF JOHNNY AND THE HURRICANES JOHNNY & THE HURRICANES	14	1961
BIG SPENDER SHIRLEY BASSEY	27	1971
THE BIG SQUEEZE – THE VERY BEST OF SQUEEZE	8	2002
BIG SUMMER TUNES VARIOUS ARTISTS (UNIVERSAL)	14	2007
BIG THING DURANDURAN	15	1988
THE BIG THROWDOWN LEVERT	86	1987
BIG TIME TOM WAITS	84	1988
BIG TUNES VARIOUS ARTISTS (MINISTRY OF SOUND)	1	2004
BIG TUNES 2 – LIVING FOR THE WEEKEND VARIOUS ARTISTS (MINISTRY OF SOUND)	4	2005
BIG TUNES 2000 VARIOUS ARTISTS (TELSTAR)	9	2000
BIG TUNES 2008 VARIOUS ARTISTS (MINISTRY OF SOUND)	1	2008
BIG TUNES 3 – LIVING FOR THE WEEKEND VARIOUS ARTISTS (MINISTRY OF SOUND)	3	2005
BIG TUNES X-RATED VARIOUS ARTISTS (MINISTRY OF SOUND)	3	2006
BIG WAR MOVIE THEMES GEOFF LOVE & HIS ORCHESTRA	11	1971
BIG WESTERN MOVIE THEMES GEOFF LOVE & HIS ORCHESTRA	38	1971
THE BIG WHEEL RUNRIG	4	1991
BIG WHEELS OF MOTOWN VARIOUS ARTISTS (MOTOWN)	2	1978
BIG WILLIE STYLE WILL SMITH	9	1997
BIG WORLD JOE JACKSON	41	1986
BIG! DANCE HITS OF 92 VARIOUS ARTISTS (HIT LABEL)	11	1992
BIGGER AND DEFFER LL COOL J	54	1987
A BIGGER BANG ROLLING STONES	2	2005

Title	Artist	Peak Position	Year of Release
BIGGER THAN BOTH OF US	DARYL HALL & JOHN OATES	25	1976
BIGGER, BETTER POWER BALLADS	VARIOUS ARTISTS (VIRGIN)	1	2004
BIGGER, BETTER, FASTER, MORE!	4 NON BLONDES	4	1993
BIGGEST 80'S HITS IN THE WORLD...EVER!	VARIOUS ARTISTS (VIRGIN)	16	1998
THE BIGGEST CLUB ALBUM OF THE YEAR	VARIOUS ARTISTS (GLOBAL TELEVISION)	20	1999
BILINGUAL	PET SHOP BOYS	4	1996
BILL AND TED'S BOGUS JOURNEY	FILM SOUNDTRACK	3	1992
BILL WYMAN	BILL WYMAN	55	1982
THE BILLIE JO SPEARS SINGLES ALBUM	BILLIE JO SPEARS	7	1979
BILLION DOLLAR BABIES	ALICE COOPER	1	1973
BILLY	BILLY FURY	6	1963
BILLY AND ALBERT	BILLY CONNOLLY	81	1987
BILLY ELLIOT	FILM SOUNDTRACK	10	2000
THE BILLY FURY HIT PARADE	BILLY FURY	44	1983
BILLY TALENT II	BILLY TALENT	46	2006
BINAURAL	PEARL JAM	5	2000
BIOGRAPHY – THE GREATEST HITS	LISA STANSFIELD	3	2003
BIOLOGICAL RADIO	DREADZONE	45	1997
BIRDLAND	BIRDLAND	44	1991
BIRDS OF FIRE	MAHAVISHNU ORCHESTRA	20	1973
BIRDY (OST)	PETER GABRIEL	51	1985
BIRTH, SCHOOL, WORK, DEATH	GODFATHERS	80	1988
BIRTHDAY	PEDDLERS	16	1970
A BIT OF WHAT YOU FANCY	QUIREBOYS	2	1990
BITCHES BREW	MILES DAVIS	71	1970
BITE	ALTERED IMAGES	16	1983
BITE	NED'S ATOMIC DUSTBIN	72	1991
BITE IT	WHITEOUT	71	1995
BITTER SUITE	VARIOUS ARTISTS (CBS)	55	1981
BITTER SUITES TO SUCCUBI	CRADLE OF FILTH	63	2001
BITTER SWEET	KING	16	1985
BITTER SWEET AND TWISTED	QUIREBOYS	31	1993
BITTERSWEET	BLU CANTRELL	20	2003
BITTERSWEET LOVESONGS	VARIOUS ARTISTS (VIRGIN)	6	2003
BITTERSWEET WORLD	ASHLEE SIMPSON	57	2008
BIZARRE FRUIT/BIZARRE FRUIT II	M PEOPLE	4	1994
BIZARRE RIDE II THE PHARCYDE	PHARCYDE	58	1993
BIZZARO	WEDDING PRESENT	22	1989
BLACK	BLACK	42	1991
THE BLACK ALBUM	DAMNED	29	1980
THE BLACK ALBUM	PRINCE	36	1994
THE BLACK ALBUM	JAY-Z	34	2003
BLACK AND BLUE	ROLLING STONES	2	1976
BLACK AND BLUE	BACKSTREET BOYS	13	2000
BLACK AND WHITE	STRANGLERS	2	1978
BLACK AND WHITE	POINTER SISTERS	21	1981
BLACK AND WHITE	TERRAPLANE	74	1986
BLACK & WHITE 050505	SIMPLE MINDS	37	2005
THE BLACK AND WHITE ALBUM	HIVES	29	2007
THE BLACK AND WHITE MINSTREL SHOW	GEORGE MITCHELL MINSTRELS	1	1960
A BLACK AND WHITE NIGHT	ROY ORBISON	51	1989
BLACK ANGEL	MICA PARIS	59	1998
BLACK CELEBRATION	DEPECHE MODE	4	1986
BLACK CHERRY	GOLDFRAPP	19	2003
BLACK COFFEE	PEGGY LEE	20	1961
BLACK DIAMOND	ANGIE STONE	62	2000
BLACK EYED MAN	COWBOY JUNKIES	21	1992
BLACK HOLES & REVELATIONS	MUSE	1	2006
BLACK ICE	AC/DC	1	2008
BLACK IS BLACK	LOS BRAVOS	29	1966
BLACK JOY	VARIOUS ARTISTS (RONCO)	26	1977
BLACK LOVE	AFGHAN WHIGS	41	1996
BLACK MAGIC	VARIOUS ARTISTS (STYLUS)	26	1986
THE BLACK MAN'S BURDON	ERIC BURDON & WAR	25	1971
BLACK MARKET MUSIC	PLACEBO	6	2000
BLACK MEANING GOOD	REBEL MC	23	1991
BLACK MOSES	ISAAC HAYES	38	1972
BLACK OUT!	METHOD MAN & REDMAN	45	1999
THE BLACK PARADE	MY CHEMICAL ROMANCE	2	2006
THE BLACK PARADE IS DEAD!	MY CHEMICAL ROMANCE	12	2008
BLACK RAIN	OZZY OSBOURNE	8	2007
BLACK REBEL MOTORCYCLE CLUB	BLACK REBEL MOTORCYCLE CLUB	25	2002
THE BLACK RIDER	TOM WAITS	47	1993
BLACK ROSE (A ROCK LEGEND)	THIN LIZZY	2	1979
BLACK SABBATH	BLACK SABBATH	8	1970
BLACK SABBATH LIVE AT LAST	BLACK SABBATH	5	1980
BLACK SABBATH VOLUME 4	BLACK SABBATH	8	1972
BLACK SEA	XTC	16	1980
BLACK SECRET TECHNOLOGY	A GUY CALLED GERALD	64	1995
BLACK SUNDAY	CYPRESS HILL	13	1993
THE BLACK SWAN	TRIFFIDS	63	1989
BLACK TIE WHITE NOISE	DAVID BOWIE	1	1993
BLACK TIGER	Y & T	53	1982
BLACK UHURU	BLACK UHURU	81	1981
BLACK VELVET	VARIOUS ARTISTS (WARWICK)	72	1978
BLACKBIRD	ALTER BRIDGE	37	2007
THE BLACKENING	MACHINE HEAD	16	2007
BLACKMARKET PRESENTS 2 STEP	VARIOUS ARTISTS (AZULI)	17	2000
BLACKOUT	SCORPIONS	11	1982
BLACKOUT	BRITNEY SPEARS	2	2007
BLACKS' MAGIC	SALT-N-PEPA	70	1990
BLACKSTREET	BLACKstreet	35	1994
BLADERUNNER (OST)	VANGELIS	20	1994
BLAH BLAH BLAH	IGGY POP	43	1986
BLAKE	BLAKE	18	2007
BLAM!	BROTHERS JOHNSON	48	1978
BLAME IT ON THE BOOGIE	VARIOUS ARTISTS (POLYGRAM)	5	1992
BLAME PRESENT LOGICAL PROGRESSION LEVEL 2	VARIOUS ARTISTS (GOOD LOOKING)	12	1997
BLAST	HOLLY JOHNSON	1	1989
BLAST OFF	STRAY CATS	58	1989
BLAZE OF GLORY	JOE JACKSON	36	1989
BLAZE OF GLORY/YOUNG GUNS II (OST)	JON BON JOVI	2	1990
BLAZING BULLETS	VARIOUS ARTISTS (RONCO)	17	1975
BLEACH	NIRVANA	33	1992
BLEED AMERICAN	JIMMY EAT WORLD	62	2002
BLEED LIKE ME	GARBAGE	4	2005
BLESS ITS POINTED LITTLE HEAD	JEFFERSON AIRPLANE	38	1969
BLESS THIS HOUSE – 20 SONGS OF JOY	HARRY SECOMBE	8	1978
BLESSED BURDEN	CARLEEN ANDERSON	51	1998
BLIND	ICICLE WORKS	40	1988
BLIND	SUNDAYS	15	1992
BLIND BEFORE I STOP	MEAT LOAF	28	1986
BLIND DOG AT ST. DUNSTAN'S	CARAVAN	53	1976
BLIND FAITH	BLIND FAITH	1	1969
THE BLIND LEADING THE NAKED	VIOLENT FEMMES	81	1986
BLIND MAN'S ZOO	10,000 MANIACS	18	1989
BLIND MELON	BLIND MELON	53	1994
THE BLINDING EP	BABYSHAMBLES	62	2006
BLING	VARIOUS ARTISTS (TELSTAR)	2	2004
BLINK 182	BLINK 182	22	2003
BLINKING LIGHTS & OTHER REVELATIONS	EELS	16	2005
THE BLISS ALBUM...? (VIBRATIONS OF LOVE AND ANGER AND THE PONDERANCE OF LIFE AND EXISTENCE)	PM DAWN	9	1993
BLISSED OUT	BELOVED	38	1990
BLITZ	STAGE CAST RECORDING	7	1962
A BLITZ OF SALT-N-PEPA HITS (THE HITS REMIXED)	SALT-N-PEPA	70	1991
THE BLOCK	NEW KIDS ON THE BLOCK	16	2008
BLOCKBUSTER – THE SENSATIONAL 70S	VARIOUS ARTISTS (CASTLE COMMUNICATIONS)	6	1992
BLOKE ON BLOKE	BILLY BRAGG	72	1997
BLONDE ON BLONDE	BOB DYLAN	3	1966
BLONDES HAVE MORE FUN	ROD STEWART	3	1978
BLONDIE	BLONDIE	75	1979
BLOOD	THIS MORTAL COIL	28	1991
BLOOD AND CHOCOLATE	ELVIS COSTELLO & THE ATTRACTIONS	16	1986
BLOOD FROM STONE	DARE	48	1991
BLOOD IN MY EYE	JA RULE	51	2003
BLOOD MONEY	TOM WAITS	21	2002
BLOOD MONEY	MOBB DEEP	70	2006
BLOOD MOUNTAIN	MASTODON	46	2006
BLOOD ON THE FLOOR – HISTORY IN THE MIX	MICHAEL JACKSON	1	1997
BLOOD ON THE TRACKS	BOB DYLAN	4	1975
BLOOD SUGAR SEX MAGIK	RED HOT CHILI PEPPERS	25	1991
BLOOD SWEAT AND TEARS	BLOOD, SWEAT & TEARS	15	1969
BLOOD SWEAT AND TEARS 3	BLOOD, SWEAT & TEARS	14	1970
BLOOD, FIRE AND LIVE	ALMIGHTY	62	1990
BLOODDRUNK	CHILDREN OF BODOM	44	2008
BLOODFLOWERS	CURE	14	2000
BLOODY TOURISTS	10 C.C.	3	1978
BLOW UP YOUR VIDEO	AC/DC	2	1988
BLOWBACK	TRICKY	34	2001
BLOWS AGAINST THE EMPIRE	PAUL KANTNER & JEFFERSON AIRPLANE	12	1971
BLUE	JONI MITCHELL	3	1971
BLUE	DOUBLE	69	1986
BLUE	MISSION	73	1996
BLUE	SIMPLY RED	1	1998
BLUE ALBUM	ORBITAL	44	2004
BLUE BELL KNOLL	COCTEAU TWINS	15	1988
THE BLUE CAFÉ	CHRIS REA	10	1998
BLUE EYED SOUL	VARIOUS ARTISTS (TELSTAR)	4	1992
BLUE FOR YOU	STATUS QUO	1	1976
BLUE FOR YOU – THE VERY BEST OF NINA SIMONE	NINA SIMONE	12	1998
BLUE GENE	GENE PITNEY	7	1964
BLUE HAWAII (OST)	ELVIS PRESLEY	1	1961
BLUE IS THE COLOUR	BEAUTIFUL SOUTH	1	1996
BLUE JAYS	JUSTIN HAYWARD & JOHN LODGE	4	1975
THE BLUE JUKEBOX	CHRIS REA	27	2004
BLUE LIGHT, RED LIGHT	HARRY CONNICK JR.	16	1991
BLUE LINES	MASSIVE ATTACK	13	1991
THE BLUE MEANING	TOYAH	40	1980
BLUE MOVES	ELTON JOHN	3	1976
BLUE MURDER	BLUE MURDER	45	1989
BLUE PRINT	RORY GALLAGHER	12	1973
BLUE ROSES FROM THE MOONS	NANCI GRIFFITH	64	1997
BLUE SKIES	FRANK IFIELD	10	1964
BLUE SKIES	KIRI TE KANAWA WITH NELSON RIDDLE & HIS ORCHESTRA	40	1985
BLUE SKY MINING	MIDNIGHT OIL	28	1990
BLUE SUEDE SHOES	ELVIS PRESLEY	39	1998
BLUE SUNSHINE	GLOVE	35	1983

Title / Artist	Peak Position	Year of Release
BLUE VELVET BOBBY VINTON	67	1990
BLUE VIEWS PAUL CARRACK	55	1996
THE BLUEBELLS – THE SINGLES COLLECTION BLUEBELLS	27	1993
BLUEBIRD JAMES LAST	57	1983
THE BLUEPRINT JAY-Z	30	2001
THE BLUEPRINT 2 THE GIFT & THE CURSE JAY-Z	23	2002
BLUES JIMI HENDRIX	10	1994
BLUES ERIC CLAPTON	52	1999
THE BLUES ALBUM VARIOUS ARTISTS (VIRGIN)	8	1995
BLUES ALIVE GARY MOORE	8	1993
THE BLUES ALONE JOHN MAYALL	24	1967
BLUES AND SOUL MASTERS VARIOUS ARTISTS (WARNER BROTHERS)	14	2002
BLUES ANYTIME VARIOUS ARTISTS (IMMEDIATE)	40	1968
BLUES BREAKERS JOHN MAYALL WITH ERIC CLAPTON	6	1966
BLUES BROTHER SOUL SISTER VARIOUS ARTISTS (DINO)	1	1993
BLUES BROTHER SOUL SISTER CLASSICS VARIOUS ARTISTS (UNIVERSAL)	8	1999
BLUES BROTHER SOUL SISTER VOLUME 2 VARIOUS ARTISTS (DINO)	8	1993
BLUES BROTHER SOUL SISTER VOLUME 3 VARIOUS ARTISTS (DINO)	5	1994
THE BLUES BROTHERS FILM SOUNDTRACK	4	1987
THE BLUES EXPERIENCE VARIOUS ARTISTS (POLYGRAM)	7	1993
BLUES FOR ALLAH GRATEFUL DEAD	45	1975
BLUES FOR GREENEY GARY MOORE	14	1995
BLUES FROM LAUREL CANYON JOHN MAYALL	33	1969
THE BLUES VOLUME 1 VARIOUS ARTISTS (PYE)	15	1964
THE BLUES VOLUME 2 VARIOUS ARTISTS (PYE)	16	1964
BLUR BLUR	1	1997
BLUR: BEST OF BLUR	3	2000
BLURRING THE EDGES MEREDITH BROOKS	5	1997
BO DIDDLEY BO DIDDLEY	11	1963
BO DIDDLEY IS A GUNSLINGER BO DIDDLEY	20	1963
BO DIDDLEY RIDES AGAINS BO DIDDLEY	19	1963
BO DIDDLEY'S BEACH PARTY BO DIDDLEY	13	1964
BOAT TO BOLIVIA MARTIN STEPHENSON & THE DAINTEES	85	1986
THE BOATMAN'S CALL NICK CAVE & THE BAD SEEDS	22	1997
BOB DYLAN BOB DYLAN	13	1965
BOB DYLAN AT BUDOKAN BOB DYLAN	4	1979
BOB MOULD BOB MOULD	52	1996
BOBBIE GENTRY AND GLEN CAMPBELL BOBBIE GENTRY & GLEN CAMPBELL	50	1970
BOBBY BOBBY BROWN	11	1992
BOBBY CRUSH BOBBY CRUSH	15	1972
THE BOBBY CRUSH INCREDIBLE DOUBLE DECKER PARTY 101 GREAT SONGS BOBBY CRUSH	53	1982
BOBBY DIGITAL IN STEREO RZA	70	1998
BOBBY VEE MEETS THE CRICKETS BOBBY VEE & THE CRICKETS	2	1962
A BOBBY VEE RECORDING SESSION BOBBY VEE	10	1963
THE BOBBY VEE SINGLES ALBUM BOBBY VEE	5	1980
BOBBY VEE'S GOLDEN GREATS BOBBY VEE	10	1963
BOCES MERCURY REV	43	1993
BODIES AND SOULS MANHATTAN TRANSFER	53	1984
THE BODY ACOUSTIC CYNDI LAUPER	55	2006
BODY AND SOUL JOE JACKSON	14	1984
BODY AND SOUL – HEART AND SOUL II VARIOUS ARTISTS (HEART & SOUL)	2	1990
THE BODY AND SOUL OF TOM JONES TOM JONES	31	1973
BODY EXIT MIND NEW FAST AUTOMATIC DAFFODILS	57	1992
BODY LANGUAGE KYLIE MINOGUE	6	2003
BODY TALK IMAGINATION	20	1981
BODY TO BODY TECHNOTRONIC	27	1991
BODY WISHES ROD STEWART	5	1983
THE BODYGUARD FILM SOUNDTRACK	1	1992
BOHEME DEEP FOREST	12	1995
BOING! AIRHEAD	29	1992
BOLAN BOOGIE T. REX	1	1972
BOLTON SWINGS SINATRA MICHAEL BOLTON	54	2006
BOMBAY MIX VARIOUS ARTISTS (TELSTAR)	12	2003
BOMBER MOTORHEAD	12	1979
BON JOVI BON JOVI	71	1984
BONA DRAG MORRISSEY	9	1990
BONAFIDE MAXI PRIEST	11	1990
BONE MACHINE TOM WAITS	26	1992
BONKERS 12 VARIOUS ARTISTS (REACT)	7	2004
BONKERS 13 – HARDCORE HORROR SHOW VARIOUS ARTISTS (RESIST)	13	2004
BONKERS 14 HARDCORE STRIKES BACK VARIOUS ARTISTS (RESIST)	12	2005
BONKERS 16 VARIOUS ARTISTS (RESIST)	15	2006
BONKERS 17 REBOOTED VARIOUS ARTISTS (RESIST)	18	2007
BONKERS 2 VARIOUS ARTISTS (REACT)	10	1997
BONKERS 3 – JOURNEY INTO MADNESS VARIOUS ARTISTS (REACT)	9	1997
BONKERS 4 – WORLD FRENZY VARIOUS ARTISTS (REACT)	8	1998
BONKERS 5 – ANARCHY IN THE UNIVERSE VARIOUS ARTISTS (REACT)	12	1998
BONKERS 6 (WHEEL CRAZY) VARIOUS ARTISTS (REACT)	10	1999
BONKERS 7 – MILLENNIUM MADNESS VARIOUS ARTISTS (REACT)	18	1999
BONKERS X VARIOUS ARTISTS (REACT)	18	2003
BOOGIE 2NITE BOOTY LUV	11	2007
BOOGIE BUS VARIOUS ARTISTS (POLYDOR)	23	1979
BOOGIE FEVER VARIOUS ARTISTS (RONCO)	15	1978
BOOGIE NIGHTS VARIOUS ARTISTS (RONCO)	5	1978
BOOGIE NIGHTS FILM SOUNDTRACK	19	1998
BOOGIE WITH CANNED HEAT CANNED HEAT	5	1968
BOOGIE WONDERLAND – THE VERY BEST OF EARTH WIND & FIRE EARTH WIND & FIRE	29	1996
BOOK OF DAYS PSYCHEDELIC FURS	74	1989
BOOK OF DREAMS STEVE MILLER BAND	12	1977
THE BOOK OF INVASIONS – A CELTIC SYMPHONY HORSLIPS	39	1977
BOOK OF LIGHTNING WATERBOYS	51	2007
BOOKBINDER'S KID ELKIE BROOKS	57	1988
BOOKENDS SIMON & GARFUNKEL	1	1968
BOOM BOOM JOHN LEE HOOKER	15	1992
BOOM SELECTION VARIOUS ARTISTS (WARNER BROTHERS)	3	2002
BOOMANIA BETTY BOO	4	1990
BOOMBASTIC SHAGGY	37	1995
BOOMERANG FILM SOUNDTRACK	17	1992
BOOMTOWN RATS BOOMTOWN RATS	18	1977
BOOTH AND THE BAD ANGEL BOOTH & THE BAD ANGEL	35	1996
BOOTLEG SERIES VOLUME 6 BOB DYLAN	33	2004
THE BOOTLEG SERIES VOLUMES 1-3 BOB DYLAN	32	1991
THE BOOTLEG VERSIONS FUGEES	55	1996
BOOTS NANCY SINATRA	12	1966
BOP TILL YOU DROP RY COODER	36	1979
THE BOP WON'T STOP SHAKIN' STEVENS	21	1983
BORBOLETTA SANTANA	18	1974
BORDER LINE RY COODER	35	1980
BORN CHINA BLACK	27	1995
BORN BOND	16	2000
BORN A WOMAN SANDY POSEY	39	1967
BORN AGAIN BLACK SABBATH	4	1983
BORN AGAIN NOTORIOUS B.I.G.	70	1999
BORN DEAD BODY COUNT	15	1994
BORN FREE FRANK IFIELD	3	1963
BORN FREE ANDY WILLIAMS	22	1967
BORN IN THE U.S.A. BRUCE SPRINGSTEEN	1	1984
BORN IN THE UK BADLY DRAWN BOY	17	2006
BORN INNOCENT PROCLAIMERS	70	2003
BORN INTO THE 90'S R KELLY & PUBLIC ANNOUNCEMENT	67	1992
BORN INTO THIS CULT	72	2007
BORN THIS WAY! COOKIE CREW	24	1989
BORN TO BE WILD VARIOUS ARTISTS (TELSTAR)	8	1991
BORN TO BE WILD VARIOUS ARTISTS (MCI)	20	1995
BORN TO DO IT CRAIG DAVID	1	2000
BORN TO LOVE PEABO BRYSON & ROBERTA FLACK	15	1983
BORN TO REIGN WILL SMITH	24	2002
BORN TO RUN BRUCE SPRINGSTEEN	17	1975
BORN TO RUN -30TH ANNIVERSARY EDITION BRUCE SPRINGSTEEN	63	2005
BORN TO SING EN VOGUE	23	1990
BORROWED HEAVEN CORRS	2	2004
BORROWED TIME DIAMOND HEAD	24	1982
THE BOSS DIANA ROSS	52	1979
BOSS DRUM/DIFFERENT DRUM SHAMEN	3	1992
BOSSANOVA PIXIES	3	1990
BOSTON BOSTON	11	1977
BOSTON BOSTON	58	1981
BOTH SIDES NOW JONI MITCHELL	50	2000
BOTH SIDES OF DOLLY PARTON DOLLY PARTON	24	1978
BOTH SIDES OF THE STORY PHIL COLLINS	1	1993
BOULDERS ROY WOOD	15	1973
BOUNCE BON JOVI	2	2002
BOUNCING OFF THE SATELLITES B-52'S	74	1987
BOUND 4 DA RELOAD (CASUALTY) OXIDE & NEUTRINO	71	2000
BOW DOWN TO THE EXIT SIGN DAVID HOLMES	22	2000
BOWIE AT THE BEEB DAVID BOWIE	7	2000
BOWS AND ARROWS WALKMEN	62	2004
THE BOX VARIOUS ARTISTS (UNIVERSAL)	12	2000
BOX CAR RACER BOX CAR RACER	27	2002
THE BOX – DANCE HITS VARIOUS ARTISTS (UNIVERSAL)	2	1999
BOX DANCE HITS 2000 VARIOUS ARTISTS (UNIVERSAL)	5	2000
THE BOX DANCE HITS – VOLUME 2 VARIOUS ARTISTS (UNIVERSAL)	5	1999
THE BOX HITS 98 VARIOUS ARTISTS (TELSTAR)	2	1998
THE BOX HITS 98 – VOLUME 2 VARIOUS ARTISTS (TELSTAR)	1	1998
BOX HITS 98 – VOLUME 3 VARIOUS ARTISTS (TELSTAR)	2	1998
BOX OF SECRETS BLOOD RED SHOES	47	2008
THE BOX R&B HITS ALBUM VARIOUS ARTISTS (TELSTAR)	6	1999
BOXED MIKE OLDFIELD	22	1976
BOXER NATIONAL	57	2007
BOY U2	52	1981
BOY CRAZY VARIOUS ARTISTS (UNIVERSAL)	10	2004
BOY IN DA CORNER DIZZEE RASCAL	23	2003
THE BOY IS MINE MONICA	52	1998
THE BOY WITH NO NAME TRAVIS	4	2007
THE BOY WITH THE ARAB STRAP BELLE & SEBASTIAN	12	1998
THE BOY WITH THE X-RAY EYES BABYLON ZOO	6	1996

Album / Artist	Peak Position	Year of Release
THE BOYS BOYS	50	1977
BOYS VARIOUS ARTISTS (COLUMBIA)	15	1997
BOYS AND GIRLS BRYAN FERRY	1	1985
THE BOYS ARE BACK IN TOWN VARIOUS ARTISTS (COLUMBIA)	11	1992
BOYS DON'T CRY CURE	71	1983
BOYS FOR PELE TORI AMOS	2	1996
THE BOY'S HEART MARTIN STEPHENSON & THE DAINTEES	68	1992
BOYS NIGHT OUT RATPACK	70	2004
BOY'S NIGHT OUT FIRST CIRCLE	70	1987
BOYZ OF SWING VARIOUS ARTISTS (POLYGRAM)	1	1996
BOYZ OF SWING II VARIOUS ARTISTS (POLYGRAM)	6	1996
THE BOYZ WHO SOULED THE WORLD VARIOUS ARTISTS (HIT LABEL)	9	1994
BPM...THE VERY BEST OF THE BEAT BEAT	13	1996
BRAHMS: VIOLIN CONCERTO NIGEL KENNEDY WITH THE LONDON PHILHARMONIC ORCHESTRA	16	1991
BRAIN DRAIN RAMONES	75	1989
BRAIN SALAD SURGERY EMERSON, LAKE & PALMER	2	1973
BRAIN THRUST MASTERY WE ARE SCIENTISTS	11	2008
BRAINWASHED GEORGE HARRISON	29	2002
BRAM STOKER'S DRACULA FILM SOUNDTRACK	10	1993
BRAND NEW AGE U.K. SUBS	18	1980
BRAND NEW BOOTS AND PANTIES BLOCKHEADS	44	2001
BRAND NEW DAY STING	5	1999
BRAND NEW HEAVIES BRAND NEW HEAVIES	25	1992
THE BRASS ARE COMIN' HERB ALPERT & THE TIJUANA BRASS	40	1970
BRASS CONSTRUCTION BRASS CONSTRUCTION	9	1976
BRASS KNUCKLES NELLY	20	2008
BRASSBOUND ORDINARY BOYS	11	2005
BRASSED OFF (OST) GRIMETHORPE COLLIERY BAND	36	1998
BRATZ GIRLZ VARIOUS ARTISTS (UNIVERSAL)	19	2007
BRATZ GIRLZ 2 VARIOUS ARTISTS (UNIVERSAL)	20	2008
BRATZ ROCK ANGELZ BRATZ ROCK ANGELZ	42	2005
BRAVE MARILLION	10	1994
BRAVE JENNIFER LOPEZ	24	2007
BRAVE AND CRAZY MELISSA ETHERIDGE	63	1989
BRAVE NEW WORLD IRON MAIDEN	7	2000
BRAVEHEART (OST) LONDON SYMPHONY ORCHESTRA, CONDUCTOR JAMES HORNER	27	1995
THE BRAVERY BRAVERY	5	2005
BRAVO JULIET HECTOR NICOL	92	1984
BRAVO TWO ZERO ANDY McNABB	45	1994
BRAZILIAN LOVE AFFAIR GEORGE DUKE	33	1980
BREAD WINNERS JACK JONES	7	1972
BREAK EVERY RULE TINA TURNER	2	1986
BREAK LIKE THE WIND SPINAL TAP	51	1992
BREAK MACHINE BREAK MACHINE	17	1984
BREAK OUT POINTER SISTERS	9	1984
BREAK THE CYCLE STAIND	1	2001
BREAK UP SONGS VARIOUS ARTISTS (VIRGIN)	8	2005
BREAKAWAY ART GARFUNKEL	7	1975
BREAKAWAY GALLAGHER & LYLE	6	1976
BREAKAWAY KELLY CLARKSON	3	2005
BREAKBEAT KAOS PRESENTS STADIUM DRUM AND BASS VARIOUS ARTISTS (BREAKBEAT KAOS)	12	2008
BREAKDANCE FILM SOUNDTRACK	6	1984
BREAKDANCE 2 – ELECTRIC BOOGALOO FILM SOUNDTRACK	34	1985
BREAKDANCE, YOU CAN DO IT! VARIOUS ARTISTS (K-TEL)	18	1984
BREAKDOWN VARIOUS ARTISTS (TELSTAR)	4	2000
BREAKDOWN – VERY BEST OF EUPHORIC DANCE VARIOUS ARTISTS (TELSTAR)	1	2000
BREAKFAST IN AMERICA SUPERTRAMP	3	1979
BREAKIN' OUT FAT LARRY'S BAND	58	1982
BREAKING AWAY AL JARREAU	60	1981
BREAKING AWAY JAKI GRAHAM	25	1986
BREAKING GLASS (OST) HAZEL O'CONNOR	5	1980
BREAKING HEARTS ELTON JOHN	2	1984
BREAKING HEARTS VARIOUS ARTISTS (DINO)	3	1992
BREAKING POINT CENTRAL LINE	64	1982
BREAKOUT VARIOUS ARTISTS (RONCO)	4	1982
BREAKOUT MILEY CYRUS	10	2008
BREAKS, BASS AND BLEEPS 2 VARIOUS ARTISTS (RUMOUR)	20	1991
BREAKS, BASS AND BLEEPS 4 VARIOUS ARTISTS (RUMOUR)	20	1992
BREAKTHROUGH VARIOUS ARTISTS (STUDIO TWO)	2	1967
BREAKTHROUGH VARIOUS ARTISTS (MFP)	49	1971
THE BREAKTHROUGH MARY J. BLIGE	22	2005
BREAKTHROUGH BREAST CANCER PRESENTS LADIES VARIOUS ARTISTS (WARNER BROTHERS)	14	2006
A BREATH OF FRESH ATTIRE MITCHELL BROTHERS	56	2005
BREATHE FAITH HILL	19	2000
BREATHE LEAVES	71	2002
BREATHE IN LUCIE SILVAS	11	2004
BREATHLESS CAMEL	26	1978
BREATHLESS KENNY G	4	1993
BREATHLESS SHAYNE WARD	2	2007
BRENDA – THAT'S ALL BRENDA LEE	13	1963
THE BRENDAN SHINE COLLECTION BRENDAN SHINE	51	1983
BRETT ANDERSON BRETT ANDERSON	54	2007
BREWING UP WITH BILLY BRAGG BILLY BRAGG	16	1984
BRICK BY BRICK IGGY POP	50	1990
BRICKS ARE HEAVY L7	24	1992
THE BRIDE STRIPPED BARE BRYAN FERRY	13	1978
BRIDESHEAD REVISITED (OST – TV – CONDUCTED BY GEOFFREY BURGON) TELEVISION AND RADIO COMPILATION	50	1981
THE BRIDGE BILLY JOEL	38	1986
THE BRIDGE ACE OF BASE	66	1995
BRIDGE OF SPIES T'PAU	1	1987
BRIDGE OVER TROUBLED WATER RAY CONNIFF	30	1970
BRIDGE OVER TROUBLED WATER SIMON & GARFUNKEL	1	1970
BRIDGES JOHN WILLIAMS	5	1979
BRIDGES TO BABYLON ROLLING STONES	6	1997
BRIDGET JONES – THE EDGE OF REASON FILM SOUNDTRACK	3	2004
BRIDGET JONES'S DIARY FILM SOUNDTRACK	1	2001
BRIDGET JONES'S DIARY 2 FILM SOUNDTRACK	8	2001
BRIGADE HEART	3	1990
BRIGHT IDEA ORSON	1	2006
BRIGHT LIGHTS SHOWADDYWADDY	33	1980
BRIGHTEN THE CORNERS PAVEMENT	27	1997
BRIGHTER THAN A THOUSAND SUNS KILLING JOKE	54	1986
BRILLIANT TREES DAVID SYLVIAN	4	1984
BRIMSTONE AND TREACLE FILM SOUNDTRACK	67	1982
BRING DOWN THE WALLS NO LIMIT SQUAD RETURNS SILVER BULLET	38	1991
BRING 'EM ALL IN MIKE SCOTT	23	1995
BRING IT BACK McALMONT & BUTLER	18	2002
BRING IT ON GOMEZ	11	1998
BRING IT ON ALISTAIR GRIFFIN	12	2004
BRING ON THE NIGHT STING	16	1986
BRING YOU HOME RONAN KEATING	3	2006
BRINGING DOWN THE HORSE WALLFLOWERS	58	1997
BRINGING IT ALL BACK HOME BOB DYLAN	1	1965
BRINGING ON BACK THE GOOD TIMES VARIOUS ARTISTS (EMI)	10	2006
THE BRIT AWARDS VARIOUS ARTISTS (EMI)	6	1994
THE BRIT AWARDS 1998 VARIOUS ARTISTS (COLUMBIA)	11	1998
BRIT AWARDS 2001 – ALBUM OF THE YEAR VARIOUS ARTISTS (COLUMBIA)	15	2001
BRIT AWARDS 2002 – ALBUM OF THE YEAR VARIOUS ARTISTS (COLUMBIA)	7	2002
BRIT AWARDS 2006 – THE MUSIC EVENT VARIOUS ARTISTS (SONY/BMG)	1	2006
BRIT AWARDS '96 VARIOUS ARTISTS (COLUMBIA)	6	1996
BRIT AWARDS ALBUM VARIOUS ARTISTS (BMG)	5	2003
THE BRIT AWARDS ALBUM 2004 VARIOUS ARTISTS (BMG)	1	2004
BRIT HITS – THE ALBUM OF THE YEAR VARIOUS ARTISTS (UNIVERSAL)	2	2008
BRIT HOP AND AMYL HOUSE VARIOUS ARTISTS (CONCRETE)	16	1996
BRITISH CONCERT NANA MOUSKOURI	29	1972
BRITISH MOTOWN CHARTBUSTERS VARIOUS ARTISTS (MOTOWN)	2	1967
BRITISH MOTOWN CHARTBUSTERS VOLUME 2 VARIOUS ARTISTS (MOTOWN)	8	1968
BRITISH STEEL JUDAS PRIEST	4	1980
BRITNEY BRITNEY SPEARS	4	2001
THE BRITS 1991 – THE MAGIC OF BRITISH MUSIC VARIOUS ARTISTS (TELSTAR)	7	1991
BRITS 25 VARIOUS ARTISTS (SONY BMG)	2	2005
BRITS HITS – THE ALBUM OF THE YEAR VARIOUS ARTISTS (UNIVERSAL)	1	2007
THE BRITS – THE AWARDS 1989 VARIOUS ARTISTS (TELSTAR)	1	1989
BROADCAST CUTTING CREW	41	1986
BROADSWORD AND THE BEAST JETHRO TULL	27	1982
THE BROADWAY ALBUM BARBRA STREISAND	3	1986
THE BROADWAY I LOVE PLACIDO DOMINGO WITH THE LONDON SYMPHONY ORCHESTRA CONDUCTED BY EUGENE KOHN	45	1991
BROKE HED P E	73	2000
BROKEN NINE INCH NAILS	18	1992
BROKEN ARROW NEIL YOUNG & CRAZY HORSE	17	1996
BROKEN BARRICADES PROCOL HARUM	42	1971
BROKEN BOY SOLDIERS RACONTEURS	2	2006
BROKEN CHINA RICK WRIGHT	61	1996
BROKEN DREAMS VARIOUS ARTISTS (STARBLEND)	48	1984
BROKEN ENGLISH MARIANNE FAITHFULL	57	1979
A BROKEN FRAME DEPECHE MODE	8	1982
BROTHAS DOOBIE FUNKDOOBIEST	62	1995
BROTHER SISTER BRAND NEW HEAVIES	4	1994
BROTHER WHERE YOU BOUND SUPERTRAMP	20	1985
BROTHERHOOD NEW ORDER	9	1986
BROTHERHOOD 3T	11	1996
BROTHERHOOD CHEMICAL BROTHERS	11	2008
BROTHERHOOD OF MAN BROTHERHOOD OF MAN	6	1978
BROTHERHOOD OF MAN SING 20 NUMBER ONE HITS BROTHERHOOD OF MAN	14	1980
BROTHERS AND SISTERS ALLMAN BROTHERS BAND	42	1973
BROTHER'S GONNA WORK IT OUT VARIOUS ARTISTS (FREESTYLE)	7	1998

Title / Artist	Peak Position	Year of Release
BROTHERS IN ARMS DIRE STRAITS	1	1985
BROTHERS IN RHYTHM VARIOUS ARTISTS (ARIOLA)	35	1988
BROTHER'S KEEPER NEVILLE BROTHERS	35	1990
BROWN SUGAR D'ANGELO	57	1995
BRUSHFIRE FAIRYTALES JACK JOHNSON	36	2006
BRUTAL PLANET ALICE COOPER	38	2000
BRUTAL YOUTH ELVIS COSTELLO & THE ATTRACTIONS	2	1994
BRYN BRYN TERFEL	6	2003
THE BRYN YEMM CHRISTMAS COLLECTION BRYN YEMM	95	1984
B-SIDES AND RARITIES NICE CAVE & THE BAD SEEDS	74	2005
B-SIDES, SEASIDES & FREERIDES OCEAN COLOUR SCENE	4	1997
BUBBLE AND SCRAPE SEBADOH	63	1993
BUBBLEGUM MARK LANEGAN	43	2004
BUCKS FIZZ BUCKS FIZZ	14	1981
BUDDAH AND THE CHOCOLATE BOX CAT STEVENS	3	1974
BUDDY HOLLY SHOWCASE BUDDY HOLLY	3	1964
THE BUDDY HOLLY STORY BUDDY HOLLY	2	1959
THE BUDDY HOLLY STORY VOLUME 2 BUDDY HOLLY	7	1960
BUDDY'S SONG CHESNEY HAWKES	18	1991
BUENA VISTA SOCIAL CLUB RY COODER	44	1997
BUENA VISTA SOCIAL CLUB PRESENTS IBRAHIM FERRER IBRAHIM FERRER	42	1999
BUENAS NOCHES FROM A LONELY ROOM DWIGHT YOAKAM	87	1988
THE BUFFALO SKINNERS BIG COUNTRY	25	1993
BUFFY THE VAMPIRE SLAYER TELEVISION AND RADIO COMPILATION	12	2003
BUFFY THE VAMPIRE SLAYER – THE ALBUM (TELEVISION SOUNDTRACK) TELEVISION AND RADIO COMPILATION	7	1999
BUHLOONE MINDSTATE DE LA SOUL	37	1993
BUILD INNOCENCE	66	1992
BUILDING THE PERFECT BEAST DON HENLEY	14	1985
BUILT TO DESTROY MICHAEL SCHENKER GROUP	23	1983
BULLET FROM A GUN DEREK B	11	1988
BULLET IN A BIBLE GREEN DAY	6	2005
BULLINAMINGVASE ROY HARPER	25	1977
BULLY FOR YOU B.A. ROBERTSON	61	1981
BUMMED HAPPY MONDAYS	59	1990
BUMP AHEAD MR. BIG	61	1993
BUNKKA PAUL OAKENFOLD	25	2002
BURN DEEP PURPLE	3	1974
BURN MY EYES MACHINE HEAD	25	1994
BURNED ELECTRAFIXION	38	1995
BURNIN' SKY BAD COMPANY	17	1977
BURNING BLUE SOUL THE THE	65	1993
BURNING FROM THE INSIDE BAUHAUS	13	1983
BURNING HEARTS VARIOUS ARTISTS (TELSTAR)	7	1991
THE BURNING RED MACHINE HEAD	13	1999
BURNT WEENY SANDWICH MOTHERS OF INVENTION	17	1970
BURY THE HATCHET CRANBERRIES	7	1999
BUSINESS AS USUAL SECRET AFFAIR	84	1982
BUSINESS AS USUAL MEN AT WORK	1	1983
BUSINESS AS USUAL E.P.M.D.	69	1991
BUSINESS OF PUNISHMENT CONSOLIDATED	53	1994
BUST A NUT TESLA	51	1994
BUSTED BUSTED	2	2002
BUSTER FILM SOUNDTRACK	2	1988
BUSTING AT THE SEAMS STRAWBS	2	1973
BUSY BODY LUTHER VANDROSS	42	1984
. . .BUT SERIOUSLY PHIL COLLINS	1	1989
BUT SERIOUSLY FOLKS... JOE WALSH	16	1978
BUTTERFLY MARIAH CAREY	2	1997
THE BUTTON-DOWN MIND OF BOB NEWHART BOB NEWHART	2	1960
BUY NOW. . . SAVED LATER ONE MINUTE SILENCE	61	2000
BUZZ STEPS	4	2000
BY 7.30 VONDA SHEPARD	39	1999
BY ALL MEANS BY ALL MEANS	80	1988
BY ALL MEANS NECESSARY BOOGIE DOWN PRODUCTIONS	38	1988
BY INVITATION ONLY VARIOUS ARTISTS (ATLANTIC)	17	1976
BY REQUEST SALVATION ARMY	16	1977
BY REQUEST LENA MARTELL	9	1980
BY REQUEST JAMES LAST	22	1987
BY REQUEST FOSTER & ALLEN	14	1993
BY REQUEST BOYZONE	1	1999
BY SPECIAL REQUEST – THE VERY BEST OF FOSTER & ALLEN	30	2003
BY THE LIGHT OF THE MOON LOS LOBOS	77	1987
BY THE WAY RED HOT CHILI PEPPERS	1	2002
BY YOUR SIDE PETERS & LEE	9	1973
BY YOUR SIDE BLACK CROWES	34	1999
BYE BYE BIRDIE STAGE CAST RECORDING	17	1961
BYE BYE BLUES BERT KAEMPFERT & HIS ORCHESTRA	4	1966
BYE BYE BLUES BRENDA LEE	21	1966
BYRDS BYRDS	31	1973

C

Title / Artist	Peak Position	Year of Release
CABARET FILM SOUNDTRACK	13	1973
CACHARPAYA (PANPIPES OF THE ANDES) INCANTATION	9	1982
CADMIUM SKY	44	1983
CAFÉ BLEU STYLE COUNCIL	2	1984
CAFÉ CAROLINA DON WILLIAMS	65	1984
CAFÉ DEL MAR IBIZA – VOLUMEN CINCO VARIOUS ARTISTS (MANIFESTO)	16	1998
CAFÉ DEL MAR IBIZA – VOLUMEN CUATRO VARIOUS ARTISTS (MANIFESTO)	18	1997
CAFÉ DEL MAR IBIZA – VOLUMEN DOS VARIOUS ARTISTS (REACT)	17	1995
CAFÉ DEL MAR IBIZA – VOLUMEN SEIS VARIOUS ARTISTS (MANIFESTO)	15	1999
CAFÉ DEL MAR IBIZA – VOLUMEN TRES VARIOUS ARTISTS (REACT)	16	1996
CAFE DEL MAR VOLUMEN OCHO VARIOUS ARTISTS (MANIFESTO)	12	2001
CAFÉ DEL MAR – VOLUMEN SIETE VARIOUS ARTISTS (MANIFESTO)	14	2000
CAFÉ LATINO VARIOUS ARTISTS (TELSTAR)	18	1996
CAFÉ MAMBO VARIOUS ARTISTS (VIRGIN)	17	1997
CAFÉ MAMBO – THE REAL SOUND OF IBIZA VARIOUS ARTISTS (COLUMBIA)	19	2000
THE CAGE TYGERS OF PAN TANG	13	1982
CAGE THE ELEPHANT CAGE THE ELEPHANT	38	2008
CAHOOTS BAND	41	1971
CAKE TRASH CAN SINATRAS	74	1990
CAL (OST) MARK KNOPFLER	65	1984
CALIFORNIA DREAMIN' – GREATEST HITS OF THE MAMAS AND THE PAPAS MAMAS & THE PAPAS	30	1997
CALIFORNIA DREAMIN' – THE BEST OF MAMAS & THE PAPAS	21	2006
CALIFORNIA DREAMIN' – THE VERY BEST OF THE MAMAS AND THE PAPAS MAMAS & THE PAPAS	14	1995
CALIFORNIA DREAMING VARIOUS ARTISTS (K-TEL)	27	1981
CALIFORNIA DREAMING VARIOUS ARTISTS (WARNER BROTHERS)	8	2007
CALIFORNIA HOLIDAY ELVIS PRESLEY	17	1966
CALIFORNICATION RED HOT CHILI PEPPERS	5	1999
CALL ME IRRESPONSIBLE MICHAEL BUBLE	2	2007
CALL OFF THE SEARCH KATIE MELUA	1	2003
CALLING ALL STATIONS GENESIS	2	1997
CALLING CARD RORY GALLAGHER	32	1976
CALM VARIOUS ARTISTS (DECCA)	14	2000
CAMELOT STAGE CAST RECORDING	10	1964
CAMELOT FILM SOUNDTRACK	37	1968
CAMINO PALMERO CALLING	12	2002
CAMOUFLAGE ROD STEWART	8	1984
CAMP ROCK VARIOUS ARTISTS (WALT DISNEY)	4	2008
THE CAMPFIRE HEADPHASE BOARDS OF CANADA	41	2005
CAN CAN FILM SOUNDTRACK	2	1960
CAN I PLAY WITH MADNESS/THE EVIL THAT MEN DO IRON MAIDEN	10	1990
CAN OUR LOVE TINDERSTICKS	47	2001
CAN U FEEL IT? – THE CHAMPION LEGEND VARIOUS ARTISTS (K-TEL)	12	1990
CAN YOU DO ME GOOD DEL AMITRI	30	2002
CAN YOU FEEL THE FORCE REAL THING	73	1979
CAN YOU TELL WHAT IT IS YET? ROLF HARRIS	70	1997
CANADIAN PACIFIC GEORGE HAMILTON IV	45	1971
CANDLELAND IAN McCULLOCH	18	1989
CANDLES HEATWAVE	29	1981
CANDLES IN THE RAIN MELANIE	5	1970
CANDYFLOSS AND MEDICINE EDDI READER	24	1996
CANDYLION GRUFF RHYS	50	2007
CANDY-O CARS	30	1979
CAN-I-BUS CANIBUS	43	1998
CANNED HEAT '70 CONCERT CANNED HEAT	15	1970
CANNED HEAT COOKBOOK CANNED HEAT	8	1970
CANSEI DE SER SEXY CSS	69	2007
CAN'T BE WITH YOU TONIGHT JUDY BOUCHER	95	1987
CAN'T BUY A THRILL STEELY DAN	38	1975
CAN'T GET ENOUGH BARRY WHITE	4	1974
CAN'T GET ENOUGH EDDY GRANT	39	1981
CAN'T GET USED TO LOSING YOU ANDY WILLIAMS	16	1965
CAN'T HELP FALLING IN LOVE ANDY WILLIAMS	7	1970
CAN'T SLOW DOWN LIONEL RICHIE	1	1983
CAN'T STAND THE REZILLOS REZILLOS	16	1978
CAN'T STOP THE CLASSICS – HOOKED ON CLASSICS 2 LOUIS CLARK CONDUCTING THE ROYAL PHILHARMONIC ORCHESTRA	13	1982
CAN'T STOP THE LOVE MAZE FEATURING FRANKIE BEVERLY	41	1985
CAN'T STOP THE MUSIC (OST) VILLAGE PEOPLE	9	1980
CAN'T TAKE ME HOME P!NK	13	2000
CANTERBURY DIAMOND HEAD	32	1983
CANTO GREGORIANO CORO DE MUNJES DEL MONASTERIO BENEDICTINO DE SANTO DOMINGO DE SILOS	7	1994
CANTO NOEL CORO DE MUNJES DEL MONASTERIO BENEDICTINO DE SANTO DOMINGO DE SILOS	53	1994
CAPERCAILLIE CAPERCAILLIE	61	1994
CAPITAL GOLD BRITISH LEGENDS VARIOUS ARTISTS (VIRGIN)	7	2003
CAPITAL GOLD EIGHTIES LEGENDS VARIOUS ARTISTS (VIRGIN)	11	2002
CAPITAL GOLD – FIFTIES LEGENDS VARIOUS ARTISTS (EMI)	9	2006
CAPITAL GOLD GUITAR LEGENDS VARIOUS ARTISTS (EMI)	8	2004

Title / Artist	Peak Position	Year of Release
CAPITAL GOLD JAZZ LEGENDS VARIOUS ARTISTS (EMI)	10	2004
CAPITAL GOLD – JUST GREAT SONGS VARIOUS ARTISTS (UNIVERSAL)	4	2004
CAPITAL GOLD LEGENDS VARIOUS ARTISTS (VIRGIN)	1	2001
CAPITAL GOLD LEGENDS II VARIOUS ARTISTS (VIRGIN)	2	2001
CAPITAL GOLD LEGENDS III VARIOUS ARTISTS (VIRGIN)	2	2002
CAPITAL GOLD – LOVE LEGENDS VARIOUS ARTISTS (VIRGIN)	5	2003
CAPITAL GOLD MOTOWN CLASSICS VARIOUS ARTISTS (UNIVERSAL)	17	2003
CAPITAL GOLD – PLATINUM LEGENDS VARIOUS ARTISTS (EMI)	20	2005
CAPITAL GOLD REGGAE CLASSICS VARIOUS ARTISTS (UNIVERSAL)	5	2003
CAPITAL GOLD ROCK LEGENDS VARIOUS ARTISTS (VIRGIN)	1	2002
CAPITAL GOLD – ROCK 'N' ROLL LEGENDS VARIOUS ARTISTS (VIRGIN)	15	2003
CAPITAL GOLD SIXTIES LEGENDS VARIOUS ARTISTS (VIRGIN)	8	2002
CAPITAL GOLD SOUL CLASSICS VARIOUS ARTISTS (UNIVERSAL)	18	2004
CAPITAL GOLD SOUL LEGENDS VARIOUS ARTISTS (VIRGIN)	6	2003
CAPITAL GOLD SUMMER LEGENDS VARIOUS ARTISTS (VIRGIN)	17	2005
CAPITAL GOLD – THE VERY BEST OF LEGENDS VARIOUS ARTISTS (VIRGIN)	5	2004
CAPITOL CLASSICS VOLUME 1 VARIOUS ARTISTS (CAPITOL)	16	1989
THE CAPPUCCINO SONGS TANITA TIKARAM	69	1998
THE CAPTAIN & THE KID ELTON JOHN	6	2006
CAPTAIN BEAKY AND HIS BAND KEITH MICHELL	28	1980
CAPTAIN CORELLI'S MANDOLIN (OST) STEPHEN WARBECK	30	2001
CAPTAIN FANTASTIC AND THE BROWN DIRT COWBOY ELTON JOHN	2	1975
CAPTAIN PARALYTIC AND THE BROWN ALE COWBOY MIKE HARDING	60	1978
CAPTAIN SWING MICHELLE SHOCKED	31	1989
CAPTURE RELEASE RAKES	32	2005
CAPTURED NATASHA	53	1982
CAR BOOT SOUL NIGHTMARES ON WAX	71	1999
CAR BUTTON CLOTH LEMONHEADS	28	1996
CARAVANSERAI SANTANA	6	1972
CARDINOLOGY RYAN ADAMS & THE CARDINALS	41	2008
CAREFUL WHAT YOU WISH FOR TEXAS	5	2003
CARELESS LOVE MADELEINE PEYROUX	7	2005
CARGO MEN AT WORK	8	1983
CARIBBEAN GUITAR CHET ATKINS	17	1963
CARIBBEAN UNCOVERED VARIOUS ARTISTS (VIRGIN)	10	1998
CARIBOU ELTON JOHN	1	1974
CARL AND THE PASSIONS/SO TOUGH BEACH BOYS	25	1972
CARL COX – FACT 2 VARIOUS ARTISTS (WORLDWIDE ULTIMATUM)	13	1997
CARL COX – NON STOP 2000 VARIOUS ARTISTS (FFRR)	13	1999
CARL COX – NON STOP 98/01 VARIOUS ARTISTS (FFRR)	8	1998
CARLOS SANTANA AND BUDDY MILES LIVE CARLOS SANTANA & BUDDY MILES	29	1972
CARMEL 6-TRACK (EP) CARMEL	94	1983
CARMEN ORCHESTRE NATIONAL DE LA RADIO DIFFUSION FRANCAISE, CONDUCTED BY SIR THOMAS BEECHAM	18	1960
CARNIVAL MANUEL & THE MUSIC OF THE MOUNTAINS	3	1976
THE CARNIVAL WYCLEF JEAN	40	1997
CARNIVAL OF HITS JUDITH DURHAM & THE SEEKERS	7	1994
CARNIVAL OF LIGHT RIDE	5	1994
CAROLS CHOIRBOYS	61	2007
THE CAROLS ALBUM HUDDERSFIELD CHORAL SOCIETY	29	1986
CAROUSEL FILM SOUNDTRACK	1	1956
THE CARPENTERS CARPENTERS	12	1971
THE CARPENTERS COLLECTION RICHARD CLAYDERMAN	65	1995
CARRIED TO DUST CALEXICO	55	2008
CARROTT IN NOTTS JASPER CARROTT	56	1976
CARROTT'S LIB JASPER CARROTT	80	1982
CARRY ON CHRIS CORNELL	25	2007
CARRY ON OI! VARIOUS ARTISTS (SECRET)	60	1981
CARRY ON UP THE CHARTS – THE BEST OF THE BEAUTIFUL SOUTH BEAUTIFUL SOUTH	1	1994
CARRYING A TORCH TOM JONES	44	1991
CARS CARS	29	1978
THE CARS GREATEST HITS CARS	27	1985
CARVED IN SAND MISSION	7	1990
CARWASH VARIOUS ARTISTS (TELSTAR)	15	1998
CASANOVA DIVINE COMEDY	48	1996
CASH COWS VARIOUS ARTISTS (VIRGIN)	49	1980
CA$HFLOW CA$HFLOW	33	1986
CASHMERE CASHMERE	63	1985
CASINO CLASSICS SAINT ETIENNE	34	1996
CASINO ROYALE BURT BACHARACH	35	1967
CASS, JOHN, MICHELLE, DENNY MAMAS & THE PAPAS	24	1967
CASSADAGA BRIGHT EYES	13	2007
THE CASSETTE OF THE ALBUM ROLAND RAT SUPERSTAR	67	1984
CASSIDY LIVE DAVID CASSIDY	9	1974
CASSIE CASSIE	33	2006
CAST OF THOUSANDS ELBOW	7	2003
CAST YOUR FATE TO THE WIND SOUNDS ORCHESTRAL	17	1965
CASUAL SEX IN THE CINEPLEX SULTANS OF PING F.C.	26	1993
CASUALLY DRESSED AND DEEP IN CONVERSATION FUNERAL FOR A FRIEND	12	2003
THE CAT IS OUT JUDIE TZUKE	35	1985
CAT SCRATCH FEVER TED NUGENT	28	1977
CATALYST NEW FOUND GLORY	27	2004
CATCH AS CATCH CAN KIM WILDE	90	1983
CATCH BULL AT FOUR CAT STEVENS	2	1972
CATCH US IF YOU CAN DAVE CLARK FIVE	8	1965
CATCH-FLAME PAUL WELLER	17	2006
CATCHING TALES JAMIE CULLUM	4	2005
CATCHING THE SUN SPYRO GYRA	31	1980
CATCHING UP WITH MEZZOFORTE MEZZOFORTE	95	1983
CATFIGHTS AND SPOTLIGHTS SUGABABES	8	2008
CATFISH RISING JETHRO TULL	27	1991
CATS STAGE CAST RECORDING	6	1981
CATS WITHOUT CLAWS DONNA SUMMER	69	1984
CAUGHT IN THE ACT STEVE GIBBONS BAND	22	1977
CAUGHT IN THE ACT STYX	44	1984
CAUGHT IN THE ACT MICHAEL BUBLE	25	2006
THE CAUTION HORSES COWBOY JUNKIES	33	1990
CAVATINA JOHN WILLIAMS	64	1979
THE CAVERN: THE MOST FAMOUS CLUB IN THE WORLD VARIOUS ARTISTS (EMI)	8	2007
C.C.S. C.C.S.	23	1972
CD UK VARIOUS ARTISTS (BMG)	7	2000
CD:UK – MORE WICKED HITS VARIOUS ARTISTS (BMG)	9	2001
CELEBRATE THE BULLET SELECTER	41	1981
CELEBRATION JOHNNY MATHIS	9	1981
CELEBRATION SIMPLE MINDS	45	1982
CELEBRATION 2000 VARIOUS ARTISTS (UNIVERSAL)	14	2000
CELEBRATION – THE BEST OF REGGAE – 25 YEARS OF TROJAN VARIOUS ARTISTS (QUALITY TELEVISION)	5	1992
CELEBRATION! ANDRE RIEU	51	2000
CELEBRITY N SYNC	12	2001
CELEBRITY SKIN HOLE	11	1998
CELINE DION CELINE DION	70	1998
THE CELTIC CHILLOUT ALBUM RYAN & RACHEL O'DONNELL	17	2002
THE CELTIC CHILLOUT ALBUM VARIOUS ARTISTS (DECADANCE)	8	2002
THE CELTIC CHILLOUT ALBUM 2 RYAN & RACHEL O'DONNELL	37	2003
CELTIC CHILLOUT – THE VERY BEST OF VARIOUS ARTISTS (DECADANCE)	20	2004
THE CELTIC COLLECTION VARIOUS ARTISTS (SONY)	14	1999
CELTIC DREAMS CELTIC SPIRIT	62	1998
CELTIC DREAMS VARIOUS ARTISTS (UNIVERSAL)	14	2007
CELTIC HEART VARIOUS ARTISTS (RCA)	6	1993
CELTIC MOODS VARIOUS ARTISTS (VIRGIN)	8	1995
CELTIC MOODS 2 VARIOUS ARTISTS (VIRGIN)	6	1995
CELTIC THEMES – THE VERY BEST OF CLANNAD	20	2008
THE CELTS ENYA	10	1992
CENTERFIELD JOHN FOGERTY	48	1985
CENTRAL HEATING HEATWAVE	26	1978
CENTRAL RESERVATION BETH ORTON	17	1999
CENTRE STAGE DAVID ESSEX	82	1986
CENTRE STAGE MICHAEL BALL	11	2001
CENTRE STAGE ELAINE PAIGE	35	2004
CEREAL KILLER SOUNDTRACK GREEN JELLY	18	1993
CEREBRAL CAUSTIC FALL	67	1995
CEREMONY CULT	9	1991
A CERTAIN TRIGGER MAXIMO PARK	15	2005
C'EST CHIC CHIC	2	1979
C'EST LA VIE ROBBIE NEVIL	93	1987
C'EST POUR VIVRE CELINE DION	49	1997
CHA CHA CHA EMF	30	1995
CHAIN FAMILY STAND	52	1990
CHAIN GANG OF LOVE RAVEONETTES	43	2003
CHAIN LIGHTNING DON McLEAN	19	1980
CHAIRMAN OF THE BOARD COUNT BASIE	17	1960
CHAIRS MISSING WIRE	48	1978
CHALK FARM IN A RAIN STORM JONI MITCHELL	26	1988
CHAMBER MUSIC COAL CHAMBER	21	1999
CHAMPAGNE AND ROSES VARIOUS ARTISTS (POLYDOR)	7	1980
CHANGE ALARM	13	1989
CHANGE SUGABABES	1	2007
CHANGE EVERYTHING DEL AMITRI	2	1992
CHANGE GIVER SHED SEVEN	16	1994
CHANGE OF ADDRESS SHADOWS	17	1980
CHANGE OF HEART CHANGE	34	1984
A CHANGE OF HEART DAVID SANBORN	86	1987
CHANGE OF SEASON DARYL HALL & JOHN OATES	44	1990
CHANGE OR DIE SUNSCREEM	53	1996
THE CHANGELING TOYAH	6	1982
CHANGES JULIE FELIX	27	1966
CHANGESBOWIE DAVID BOWIE	1	1990
CHANGESONEBOWIE DAVID BOWIE	2	1976
CHANGESTWOBOWIE DAVID BOWIE	24	1981
CHANGING ALL THE TIME SMOKIE	18	1975
CHANGING CABINS NOMAD	48	1996
CHANGING FACES BROS	18	1991
CHANGING FACES – THE BEST OF LOUISE	9	2001

Title / Artist	Peak Position	Year of Release
CHANGING FACES – THE VERY BEST OF ROD STEWART & THE FACES	13	2003
CHANGING FACES – THE VERY BEST OF 10CC AND GODLEY AND CRÈME 10CC & GODLEY & CRÈME	4	1987
CHANGING HORSES INCREDIBLE STRING BAND	30	1970
CHANT – MUSIC FOR PARADISE CISTERCIAN MONKS OF STIFT HEILIGENKR	7	2008
CHANTS AND DANCES OF THE NATIVE AMERICAN INDIAN SACRED SPIRIT	9	1995
CHANTS D'AUVERGNE VOLUME 1 KIRI TE KANAWA WITH THE ENGLISH CHAMBER ORCHESTRA	57	1983
CHAOS A.D. SEPULTURA	11	1993
CHAOS AND CREATION IN THE BACKYARD PAUL McCARTNEY	10	2005
CHAOS AND DISORDER PRINCE	14	1996
CHAPTER 1: A NEW BEGINNING MOFFATTS	62	1999
CHAPTER II ASHANTI	5	2003
CHAPTER ONE JAY-Z	65	2002
CHARACTERS STEVIE WONDER	33	1987
CHARANGO MORCHEEBA	7	2002
CHARIOTS OF FIRE (OST) VANGELIS	5	1981
THE CHARLATANS CHARLATANS	1	1995
CHARLEY PRIDE SPECIAL CHARLEY PRIDE	29	1971
CHARLIE'S ANGELS – FULL THROTTLE FILM SOUNDTRACK	12	2003
CHARLOTTE CHURCH CHARLOTTE CHURCH	8	1999
CHARMBRACELET MARIAH CAREY	52	2002
CHARMED LIFE BILLY IDOL	15	1990
THE CHART VARIOUS ARTISTS (TELSTAR)	6	1986
CHART ATTACK VARIOUS ARTISTS (TELSTAR)	7	1982
CHART ENCOUNTERS OF THE HIT KIND VARIOUS ARTISTS (RONCO)	5	1983
CHART EXPLOSION VARIOUS ARTISTS (K-TEL)	6	1980
CHART HITS '81 VARIOUS ARTISTS (K-TEL)	1	1981
CHART HITS '82 VARIOUS ARTISTS (K-TEL)	11	1982
CHART HITS '83 VOLUME 1 AND 2 VARIOUS ARTISTS (K-TEL)	6	1983
CHART RUNNERS VARIOUS ARTISTS (RONCO)	4	1983
THE CHART SHOW DANCE ALBUM (TELEVISION COMPILATION) TELEVISION AND RADIO COMPILATION	6	1995
THE CHART SHOW – DANCE HITS 1987 (TELEVISION COMPILATION) TELEVISION AND RADIO COMPILATION	39	1987
THE CHART SHOW – DANCE MASTERS (TELEVISION COMPILATION) TELEVISION AND RADIO COMPILATION	4	1989
THE CHART SHOW PRESENTS THE CHART MACHINE (TELEVISION COMPILATION) TELEVISION AND RADIO COMPILATION	18	1995
THE CHART SHOW – ROCK THE NATION (TELEVISION COMPILATION) TELEVISION AND RADIO COMPILATION	16	1988
THE CHART SHOW – ROCK THE NATION 2 (TELEVISION COMPILATION) TELEVISION AND RADIO COMPILATION	8	1989
THE CHART SHOW – THE ULTIMATE ROCK ALBUM (TELEVISION COMPILATION) TELEVISION AND RADIO COMPILATION	4	1993
CHART SHOW – ULTIMATE BLUES ALBUM (TELEVISION COMPILATION) TELEVISION AND RADIO COMPILATION	13	1994
THE CHART SHOW – ULTIMATE ROCK 2 (TELEVISION COMPILATION) TELEVISION AND RADIO COMPILATION	10	1993
CHART STARS VARIOUS ARTISTS (K-TEL)	7	1983
CHART TREK VOLUMES 1 AND 2 VARIOUS ARTISTS (RONCO)	20	1984
CHART WARS VARIOUS ARTISTS (RONCO)	30	1982
CHARTBEAT/CHARTHEAT VARIOUS ARTISTS (K-TEL)	2	1982
CHARTBUSTERS VARIOUS ARTISTS (GLOBAL TELEVISION)	2	1995
CHARTBUSTERS 81 VARIOUS ARTISTS (K-TEL)	3	1981
CHARTBUSTERS 82 VARIOUS ARTISTS (RONCO)	3	1982
CHAS AND DAVE'S CHRISTMAS CAROL ALBUM CHAS & DAVE	37	1986
CHAS AND DAVE'S CHRISTMAS JAMBOREE BAG CHAS & DAVE	25	1981
CHAS AND DAVE'S GREATEST HITS CHAS & DAVE	16	1984
CHAS AND DAVE'S KNEES UP – JAMBOREE BAG NUMBER 2 CHAS & DAVE	7	1983
CHASE THE DRAGON MAGNUM	17	1982
CHASE THIS LIGHT JIMMY EAT WORLD	27	2007
CHASING LIGHTS SATURDAYS	11	2008
CHAVEZ RAVINE RY COODER	35	2005
CHEAP TRICK AT BUDOKAN CHEAP TRICK	29	1979
CHEAPNESS AND BEAUTY BOY GEORGE	44	1995
CHECK OUT THE GROOVE UNDERCOVER	26	1992
CHEEK TO CHEEK VARIOUS ARTISTS (CBS)	2	1989
CHEERS OBIE TRICE	11	2003
THE CHEETAH GIRLS 2 CHEETAH GIRLS	59	2007
CHEF AID -THE SOUTH PARK ALBUM (TELEVISION SOUNDTRACK) TELEVISION AND RADIO COMPILATION	2	1998
THE CHEMICAL WEDDING BRUCE DICKINSON	55	1998
CHEMICRAZY THAT PETROL EMOTION	62	1990
CHEMISTRY GIRLS ALOUD	11	2005
CHER CHER	26	1988
CHER O'BOWLIES – PICK OF THE UNDERTONES UNDERTONES FEATURING FEARGAL SHARKEY	96	1986
CHERISH DAVID CASSIDY	2	1972
CHERISHED MEMORIES EDDIE COCHRAN	15	1963
CHER'S GREATEST HITS: 1965-1992 CHER	1	1992
CHESS (ORIGINAL STUDIO CAST RECORDING) STAGE CAST RECORDING	10	1984
CHESS PIECES (ORIGINAL STUDIO CAST RECORDING) STAGE CAST RECORDING	87	1985
CHET ATKINS WORKSHOP CHET ATKINS	19	1961
CHEWING THE FAT BLUE RONDO A LA TURK	80	1982
CHI MAI ENNIO MORRICONE	29	1981
CHIC AND ROSE ROYCE – THEIR GREATEST HITS SIDE BY SIDE VARIOUS ARTISTS (DINO)	8	1991
CHICAGO CHICAGO	6	1970
CHICAGO FILM SOUNDTRACK	4	2003
CHICAGO 16 CHICAGO	44	1982
CHICAGO 17 CHICAGO	24	1984
CHICAGO 3 CHICAGO	9	1971
CHICAGO 5 CHICAGO	24	1972
CHICAGO JACKBEAT VOLUME 2 VARIOUS ARTISTS (RHYTHM KING)	67	1987
THE CHICAGO STORY – COMPLETE GREATEST CHICAGO	11	2002
CHICAGO – THE MUSICAL STAGE CAST RECORDING	61	1998
CHICAGO TRANSIT AUTHORITY CHICAGO TRANSIT AUTHORITY	9	1969
CHICAGO X CHICAGO	21	1976
CHICK FLICK DIARIES VARIOUS ARTISTS (WARNER BROTHERS)	19	2004
CHICK FLICKS – THE SEQUEL VARIOUS ARTISTS (WARNER BROTHERS)	4	2003
CHICKEN N BEER LUDACRIS	44	2003
CHICKEN RHYTHMS NORTHSIDE	19	1991
CHICKENEYE DEEJAY PUNK-ROC	47	1998
CHILD IN TIME IAN GILLAN BAND	55	1976
CHILD IS THE FATHER TO THE MAN BLOOD, SWEAT & TEARS	40	1968
CHILDREN MISSION	2	1988
CHILDREN OF THE NIGHT NASH THE SLASH	61	1981
CHILDREN OF THE NIGHT 52ND STREET	71	1986
A CHILD'S ADVENTURE MARIANNE FAITHFULL	99	1983
CHILL OUT BLACK UHURU	38	1982
CHILL OUT JOHN LEE HOOKER	23	1995
THE CHILL OUT ALBUM – 2 VARIOUS ARTISTS (TELSTAR)	14	1999
THE CHILL OUT SESSION VARIOUS ARTISTS (MINISTRY OF SOUND)	1	2001
CHILLED 1991-2008 VARIOUS ARTISTS (MINISTRY OF SOUND)	1	2008
CHILLED EUPHORIA VARIOUS ARTISTS (TELSTAR)	4	2000
CHILLED IBIZA VARIOUS ARTISTS (WARNER BROTHERS)	3	2000
CHILLED IBIZA GOLD VARIOUS ARTISTS (WARNER BROTHERS)	13	2004
CHILLED IBIZA II VARIOUS ARTISTS (WARNER BROTHERS)	5	2001
CHILLED IBIZA III VARIOUS ARTISTS (WARNER BROTHERS)	12	2002
CHILLED JAZZ VARIOUS ARTISTS (VERVE)	14	2002
CHILLED OUT EUPHORIA VARIOUS ARTISTS (TELSTAR)	8	2001
CHILLED R&B VARIOUS ARTISTS (SONY BMG)	5	2008
THE CHILLOUT VARIOUS ARTISTS (VIRGIN)	19	2001
THE CHILLOUT ALBUM VARIOUS ARTISTS (TELSTAR)	4	1999
THE CHILLOUT MIX VARIOUS ARTISTS (VIRGIN)	7	1999
THE CHILLOUT SESSION VARIOUS ARTISTS (MINISTRY OF SOUND)	15	2006
THE CHILLOUT SESSION 2 VARIOUS ARTISTS (MINISTRY OF SOUND)	2	2001
THE CHILLOUT SESSION 2003 VARIOUS ARTISTS (MINISTRY OF SOUND)	20	2002
THE CHILLOUT SESSION – IBIZA 2002 VARIOUS ARTISTS (MINISTRY OF SOUND)	4	2002
THE CHILLOUT SESSION – IBIZA SUNSETS VARIOUS ARTISTS (MINISTRY OF SOUND)	11	2003
CHILLOUT SESSION – SUMMER COLLECTION 2003 VARIOUS ARTISTS (MINISTRY OF SOUND)	10	2003
CHIMAIRA CHIMAIRA	62	2005
CHIMERA BILL NELSON	30	1983
THE CHIMES CHIMES	17	1990
CHINA CRISIS COLLECTION – THE VERY BEST OF CHINA CRISIS CHINA CRISIS	32	1990
CHINA GIRL – THE CLASSICAL ALBUM 2 VANESSA-MAE	56	1998
CHINATOWN THIN LIZZY	7	1980
CHINESE DEMOCRACY GUNS N' ROSES	2	2008
CHINESE WALL PHILIP BAILEY	29	1985
CHIRPING CRICKETS CRICKETS	5	1958
CHITTY CHITTY BANG BANG FILM SOUNDTRACK	10	1969
CHOBA B CCCP (THE RUSSIAN ALBUM) PAUL McCARTNEY	63	1991
CHOCOLATE FACTORY R KELLY	10	2003
CHOCOLATE STARFISH AND THE HOT DOG FLAVOURED WATER LIMP BIZKIT	1	2000
CHOCOLATE SUPA HIGHWAY SPEARHEAD	68	1997
CHOICES OF THE HEART VARIOUS ARTISTS (STYLUS)	87	1985
CHOICES – THE SINGLES COLLECTION BLOW MONKEYS	5	1989
THE CHOIR – MUSIC FROM THE TV SERIES ANTHONY WAY & STANISLAS SYREWICZ	3	1995
THE CHOIRBOY ANTHONY WAY	61	1995

Title / Artist	Peak Position	Year of Release
THE CHOIRBOYS CHOIRBOYS	25	2005
THE CHOIRBOY'S CHRISTMAS ANTHONY WAY	59	1996
CHOKE BEAUTIFUL SOUTH	2	1990
CHOOSE 80'S DANCE VARIOUS ARTISTS (TELSTAR)	12	2002
CHOOSE YOUR MASQUES HAWKWIND	29	1982
CHOREOGRAPHY VANESSA-MAE	66	2004
CHORUS ERASURE	1	1991
THE CHOSEN FEW DOOLEYS	56	1979
CHRIS BARBER BAND BOX NO. 2 CHRIS BARBER	17	1960
CHRIS BROWN CHRIS BROWN	29	2006
CHRIS REA CHRIS REA	52	1982
CHRIS TARRANT PRESENTS ULTIMATE PARTY MEGAMIX VARIOUS ARTISTS (TELSTAR)	17	1998
CHRIS TARRANT'S ULTIMATE SUMMER PARTY VARIOUS ARTISTS (TELSTAR)	15	1999
CHRIST ILLUSION SLAYER	23	2006
CHRIST THE ALBUM CRASS	26	1982
THE CHRISTIANS CHRISTIANS	2	1987
CHRISTINA AGUILERA CHRISTINA AGUILERA	14	1999
CHRISTINA MILIAN CHRISTINA MILIAN	23	2002
CHRISTINE MCVIE CHRISTINE McVIE	58	1984
CHRISTMAS ELAINE PAIGE	27	1986
THE CHRISTMAS ALBUM NEIL DIAMOND	50	1992
THE CHRISTMAS ALBUM TWEENIES	34	2001
THE CHRISTMAS ALBUM ALED JONES	37	2004
CHRISTMAS AT THE COUNTRY STORE VARIOUS ARTISTS (STARBLEND)	94	1985
CHRISTMAS CARD PARTRIDGE FAMILY	45	1972
THE CHRISTMAS CAROL COLLECTION VARIOUS ARTISTS (FAME)	75	1984
CHRISTMAS CAROLS TEMPLE CHURCH CHOIR	8	1961
CHRISTMAS CAROLS FROM GUILDFORD CATHEDRAL GUILDFORD CATHEDRAL CHOIR CONDUCTOR: BARRY ROSE	24	1966
THE CHRISTMAS COLLECTION FOSTER & ALLEN	44	1990
A CHRISTMAS GIFT VARIOUS ARTISTS (RONCO)	39	1975
CHRISTMAS GREATEST HITS VARIOUS ARTISTS (LEGENDS IN)	16	1990
CHRISTMAS HITS VARIOUS ARTISTS (BMG)	3	2001
CHRISTMAS HITS – 80 FESTIVE FAVOURITES VARIOUS ARTISTS (SONY BMG)	9	2007
CHRISTMAS IN VIENNA PLACIDO DOMINGO, DIANA ROSS & JOSE CARRERAS	71	1993
CHRISTMAS IN VIENNA II DIONNE WARWICK PLACIDO DOMINGO	60	1994
CHRISTMAS LOVE SONGS VARIOUS ARTISTS (ARCADE)	11	1991
CHRISTMAS PEACE ELVIS PRESLEY	41	2003
CHRISTMAS WITH BING CROSBY BING CROSBY	66	1991
CHRISTMAS WITH DANIEL DANIEL O'DONNELL	34	1994
CHRISTMAS WITH KIRI KIRI TE KANAWA	47	1986
CHRISTMAS WITH NAT 'KING' COLE NAT 'KING' COLE	25	1988
CHRISTMAS WITH THE RAT PACK VARIOUS ARTISTS (CAPITOL)	15	2002
CHRISTOPHER CROSS CHRISTOPHER CROSS	14	1981
THE CHRISTY MOORE COLLECTION 81-91 CHRISTY MOORE	69	1991
CHROME CATHERINE WHEEL	58	1993
CHROME DREAMS II NEIL YOUNG	14	2007
THE CHRONIC DR. DRE	43	2000
CHRONIC GENERATION CHRON GEN	53	1982
CHRONICLE OF THE BLACK SWORD HAWKWIND	65	1985
CHRONICLES STEVE WINWOOD	12	1987
CHRONICLES RUSH	42	1990
THE CHRONICLES OF A BOHEMIAN TEENAGER GET CAPE WEAR CAPE FLY	26	2006
THE CHRONICLES OF LIFE AND DEATH GOOD CHARLOTTE	8	2004
CHRONICLES – THE VERY BEST OF FREE	42	2006
CHRONOLOGIE JEAN-MICHEL JARRE	11	1993
CHRONOLOGIE PART 6 JEAN-MICHEL JARRE	60	1994
CHUCK SUM 41	59	2004
CHUCK BERRY CHUCK BERRY	12	1963
CHUCK BERRY ON STAGE CHUCK BERRY	6	1963
CHUNGA'S REVENGE FRANK ZAPPA	43	1970
CHUNKS OF FUNK VARIOUS ARTISTS (LOOSE END)	46	1984
THE CHURCH OF HAWKWIND HAWKWIND	26	1982
THE CHURCH WITH ONE BELL JOHN MARTYN	51	1998
CHYNA DOLL FOXY BROWN	51	1999
CIELI DE TOSCANA ANDREA BOCELLI	3	2001
CIGARETTES AND ALCOHOL VARIOUS ARTISTS (COLUMBIA)	7	2000
CIGARETTES AND ALCOHOL – 40 ANTHEMS FROM NOW AND THEN VARIOUS ARTISTS (SONY BMG)	7	2008
CIGARETTES AND ALCOHOL – SATURDAY NIGHT VARIOUS ARTISTS (COLUMBIA)	15	2002
CIGARETTES AND ALCOHOL VOLUME 2 VARIOUS ARTISTS (COLUMBIA)	10	2001
CILLA CILLA BLACK	5	1965
CILLA SINGS A RAINBOW CILLA BLACK	4	1966
CINDERELLA CLIFF RICHARD	30	1967
CINEMA ELAINE PAIGE	12	1984
THE CINEMA HITS ALBUM VARIOUS ARTISTS (TOWERBELL)	44	1986
THE CIRCLE AND THE SQUARE RED BOX	73	1986
CIRCLE OF ONE OLETA ADAMS	1	1990
CIRCLES NEW SEEKERS	23	1972
THE CIRCUS ERASURE	6	1987
CIRCUS LENNY KRAVITZ	5	1995
CIRCUS MARY BLACK	16	1995
CIRCUS TAKE THAT	1	2008
CIRCUS BRITNEY SPEARS	4	2008
CITY BABY ATTACKED BY RATS CHARGED GBH	17	1982
CITY DELIRIOUS LIONROCK	73	1998
CITY OF ANGELS FILM SOUNDTRACK	18	1998
CITY OF EVIL AVENGED SEVENFOLD	63	2005
CITY TO CITY GERRY RAFFERTY	6	1978
CIVILIAN BOY KILL BOY	16	2006
A CIVILISED MAN JOE COCKER	100	1984
CLAIRE CLAIRE SWEENEY	15	2002
THE CLAIRVOYANT/INFINITE DREAMS (LIVE) IRON MAIDEN	11	1990
CLAMBAKE ELVIS PRESLEY	39	1968
CLAP YOUR HANDS SAY YEAH CLAP YOUR HANDS SAY YEAH	26	2006
CLAPTON CHRONICLES – THE BEST OF ERIC CLAPTON ERIC CLAPTON	6	1999
THE CLASH CLASH	12	1977
CLASSIC ADS VARIOUS ARTISTS (DECCA)	12	2002
CLASSIC BIG TUNES VARIOUS ARTISTS (HARD2BEAT)	2	2008
CLASSIC BLUE JUSTIN HAYWARD WITH MIKE BATT & THE LONDON PHILHARMONIC ORCHESTRA	47	1989
THE CLASSIC CHILLOUT ALBUM VARIOUS ARTISTS (COLUMBIA)	1	2001
THE CLASSIC CHILLOUT ALBUM 2 VARIOUS ARTISTS (COLUMBIA)	13	2001
A CLASSIC CHRISTMAS VARIOUS ARTISTS (UNIVERSAL)	20	2005
THE CLASSIC COLLECTION DANIEL O'DONNELL	34	1995
CLASSIC COMMERCIALS VARIOUS ARTISTS (DECCA)	8	1993
CLASSIC ELECTRO MASTERCUTS VOLUME 1 VARIOUS ARTISTS (MASTERCUTS)	18	1994
CLASSIC EUPHORIA VARIOUS ARTISTS (MINISTRY OF SOUND)	2	2006
CLASSIC EUPHORIA – LEVEL 2 VARIOUS ARTISTS (MINISTRY OF SOUND)	11	2006
THE CLASSIC EXPERIENCE VARIOUS ARTISTS (EMI)	12	1988
CLASSIC EXPERIENCE II VARIOUS ARTISTS (EMI)	1	1990
CLASSIC EXPERIENCE III VARIOUS ARTISTS (EMI)	3	1991
CLASSIC EXPERIENCE IV VARIOUS ARTISTS (EMI)	9	1993
CLASSIC FM – SONGS WITHOUT WORDS CITY OF PRAGUE PHILHARMONIC ORCHESTRA	21	2008
CLASSIC FM – AS HEARD ON TV VARIOUS ARTISTS (UNIVERSAL)	9	2007
CLASSIC FM AT THE MOVIES VARIOUS ARTISTS (CLASSIC FM)	8	2006
CLASSIC FM AT THE MOVIES – THE SEQUEL VARIOUS ARTISTS (CLASSIC FM)	5	2007
CLASSIC FM HALL OF FAME – GOLD VARIOUS ARTISTS (CLASSIC FM)	14	2002
CLASSIC FM – MOST WANTED VARIOUS ARTISTS (CLASSIC FM)	13	2006
CLASSIC FM – MOVIES – THE ULTIMATE COLLECTION VARIOUS ARTISTS (UNIVERSAL)	12	2008
CLASSIC FM – MUSIC FOR BABIES 2005 VARIOUS ARTISTS (CLASSIC FM)	13	2005
CLASSIC FM – RELAX VARIOUS ARTISTS (UNIVERSAL)	15	2007
CLASSIC FM – RELAX & ESCAPE VARIOUS ARTISTS (CLASSIC FM)	14	2004
CLASSIC FM – SMOOTH CLASSICS VARIOUS ARTISTS (CLASSIC FM)	9	2002
CLASSIC FM – SMOOTH CLASSICS – ULTIMATE COLLECTION VARIOUS ARTISTS (CLASSIC FM)	13	2008
CLASSIC FUNK MASTERCUTS VOLUME 1 VARIOUS ARTISTS (MASTERCUTS)	14	1992
CLASSIC GOLD VOLUME 2 ROYAL PHILHARMONIC ORCHESTRA	31	1978
CLASSIC GUITAR MOODS MIRAGE	25	1995
CLASSIC HOUSE MASTERCUTS VOLUME 1 VARIOUS ARTISTS (MASTERCUTS)	11	1994
CLASSIC JAZZ-FUNK MASTERCUTS VOLUME 3 VARIOUS ARTISTS (MASTERCUTS)	18	1992
CLASSIC JAZZ-FUNK MASTERCUTS VOLUME 4 VARIOUS ARTISTS (MASTERCUTS)	19	1994
CLASSIC KENNEDY NIGEL KENNEDY WITH THE ENGLISH CHAMBER ORCHESTRA	51	1999
CLASSIC LOVE VARIOUS ARTISTS (TELSTAR)	4	1992
CLASSIC MELLOW MASTERCUTS VOLUME 1 VARIOUS ARTISTS (MASTERCUTS)	18	1991
CLASSIC MELLOW MASTERCUTS VOLUME 2 VARIOUS ARTISTS (MASTERCUTS)	12	1992
CLASSIC MOODS VARIOUS ARTISTS (POLYGRAM)	7	1996
CLASSIC P-FUNK MASTERCUTS VOLUME 1 VARIOUS ARTISTS (MASTERCUTS)	16	1993
CLASSIC RARE GROOVE MASTERCUTS VOLUME 1 VARIOUS ARTISTS (MASTERCUTS)	14	1993
CLASSIC ROCK LONDON SYMPHONY ORCHESTRA	3	1978
CLASSIC ROCK COUNTDOWN LONDON SYMPHONY ORCHESTRA	32	1987

Title / Artist	Peak Position	Year of Release
CLASSIC ROCK – ROCK CLASSICS LONDON SYMPHONY ORCHESTRA WITH THE ROYAL CHORAL SOCIETY	5	1981
CLASSIC ROCK – ROCK SYMPHONIES LONDON SYMPHONY ORCHESTRA WITH THE ROYAL CHORAL SOCIETY & THE ROGER SMITH CHORALE	40	1983
CLASSIC ROCK – THE LIVING YEARS LONDON SYMPHONY ORCHESTRA	51	1989
CLASSIC ROCK – THE SECOND MOVEMENT LONDON SYMPHONY ORCHESTRA	26	1979
THE CLASSIC ROMANCE VARIOUS ARTISTS (EMI)	5	1992
THE CLASSIC ROY ORBISON ROY ORBISON	12	1966
CLASSIC SALSOUL MASTERCUTS VOLUME 1 VARIOUS ARTISTS (MASTERCUTS)	16	1993
CLASSIC SCHOOL OF ROCK VARIOUS ARTISTS (UNIVERSAL)	15	2007
THE CLASSIC SCORE VARIOUS ARTISTS (SONY)	11	2002
CLASSIC SINATRA FRANK SINATRA	10	2000
CLASSIC SONGS JAMES TAYLOR	53	1987
CLASSIC SONGS MY WAY PAUL ANKA	13	2007
CLASSIC SOUL HITS TEMPTATIONS	8	2008
CLASSIC THEMES VARIOUS ARTISTS (NOUVEAU MUSIC)	61	1983
THE CLASSIC TOUCH RICHARD CLAYDERMAN WITH THE ROYAL PHILHARMONIC ORCHESTRA	17	1985
CLASSIC TRANCE ANTHEMS VARIOUS ARTISTS (EMI)	12	2006
CLASSIC TRANCE NATION VARIOUS ARTISTS (MINISTRY OF SOUND)	2	2007
CLASSICAL 2008 VARIOUS ARTISTS (EMI)	10	2007
THE CLASSICAL ALBUM VARIOUS ARTISTS (UNIVERSAL)	6	2000
CLASSICAL ALBUM 1 VANESSA-MAE	47	1996
THE CLASSICAL ALBUM 2001 VARIOUS ARTISTS (EMI)	4	2000
THE CLASSICAL ALBUM 2005 VARIOUS ARTISTS (UNIVERSAL)	6	2004
THE CLASSICAL ALBUM 2007 VARIOUS ARTISTS (UNIVERSAL)	9	2006
THE CLASSICAL ALBUM 2009 VARIOUS ARTISTS (UNIVERSAL)	19	2008
CLASSICAL CHILLOUT VARIOUS ARTISTS (VIRGIN)	4	2001
CLASSICAL CHILLOUT 2 VARIOUS ARTISTS (VIRGIN)	10	2002
CLASSICAL CHILLOUT GOLD VARIOUS ARTISTS (DECADANCE)	9	2002
CLASSICAL CHILLOUT – PLATINUM VARIOUS ARTISTS (DECADANCE)	18	2004
A CLASSICAL CHRISTMAS VARIOUS ARTISTS (EMI)	14	1991
THE CLASSICAL COLLECTION JAMES LAST	44	2003
CLASSICAL GOLD ROYAL PHILHARMONIC ORCHESTRA	24	1977
CLASSICAL GOLD VARIOUS ARTISTS (RONCO)	24	1977
CLASSICAL GOLD VARIOUS ARTISTS (DEUTSCHE GRAMMOPHON)	16	2003
CLASSICAL GRAFFITI PLANETS	34	2002
CLASSICAL HEARTBREAKERS VARIOUS ARTISTS (VIRGIN)	19	2003
CLASSICAL LEGENDS VARIOUS ARTISTS (VIRGIN)	18	2002
THE CLASSICAL LOVE ALBUM VARIOUS ARTISTS (DECADANCE)	10	2003
CLASSICAL MASTERS VARIOUS ARTISTS (TELSTAR)	13	1991
CLASSICAL MEDITATIONS JAMES GALWAY	45	1996
CLASSICAL VOICES VARIOUS ARTISTS (SONY/BMG)	17	2007
CLASSICALLY SEDAKA NEIL SEDAKA	23	1995
CLASSICS APHEX TWIN	24	1995
CLASSICS 2002 VARIOUS ARTISTS (DECCA)	2	2001
CLASSICS 2003 VARIOUS ARTISTS (DECCA)	17	2002
CLASSICS BY CANDLELIGHT VARIOUS ARTISTS (STYLUS)	74	1986
CLASSICS BY MOONLIGHT JAMES LAST	12	1990
CLASSICS FOR DREAMING JAMES LAST	12	1980
CLASSICS – THE BEST OF SARAH BRIGHTMAN	38	2006
CLASSICS UP TO DATE JAMES LAST	44	1970
CLASSICS UP TO DATE VOLUME 2 JAMES LAST	49	1972
CLASSICS UP TO DATE VOLUME 3 JAMES LAST	54	1976
CLASSIFIED BOND	32	2004
CLEANSING PRONG	71	1994
CLEAR BOMB THE BASS	22	1995
CLEO CLEO LAINE	68	1978
CLIFF CLIFF RICHARD & THE DRIFTERS	4	1959
CLIFF AT CHRISTMAS CLIFF RICHARD	9	2003
CLIFF AT THE MOVIES – 1959-1974 CLIFF RICHARD	17	1996
CLIFF IN JAPAN CLIFF RICHARD	29	1968
CLIFF RICHARD CLIFF RICHARD	9	1965
CLIFF RICHARD – THE ALBUM CLIFF RICHARD	1	1993
CLIFF SINGS CLIFF RICHARD & THE SHADOWS	2	1959
CLIFF'S HIT ALBUM CLIFF RICHARD & THE SHADOWS	2	1963
CLIMATE HUNTER SCOTT WALKER	60	1984
CLINTON FORD CLINTON FORD	16	1962
CLOCK WITHOUT HANDS NANCI GRIFFITH	61	2001
CLOCKWORK ORANGE FILM SOUNDTRACK	4	1972
CLODAGH RODGERS CLODAGH RODGERS	27	1969
CLOSE KIM WILDE	8	1988
CLOSE ENCOUNTERS OF THE THIRD KIND (OST) JOHN WILLIAMS	40	1978
CLOSE TO A MIRACLE HEATHER SMALL	57	2006
CLOSE TO THE BONE THOMPSON TWINS	90	1987
CLOSE TO THE EDGE YES	4	1972
CLOSE TO YOU FRANK SINATRA	2	1957
CLOSE TO YOU CARPENTERS	23	1971
CLOSE TO YOU VARIOUS ARTISTS (UNIVERSAL)	5	2001
CLOSE UP TOM JONES	17	1972
CLOSE UP IN SWING ERROLL GARNER	20	1962
CLOSER JOY DIVISION	6	1980
CLOSET CLASSICS VOLUME 1 – MORE PROTEIN SAMPLER VARIOUS ARTISTS (MORE PROTEIN)	20	1992
CLOUD NINE TEMPTATIONS	32	1969
CLOUD NINE GEORGE HARRISON	10	1987
CLOUDCUCKOOLAND LIGHTNING SEEDS	50	1990
CLUB 2K VARIOUS ARTISTS (UNIVERSAL)	2	2000
CLUB 2K VOL. 2 VARIOUS ARTISTS (UNIVERSAL)	7	2000
CLUB 2K7 VARIOUS ARTISTS (UNIVERSAL)	4	2007
CLUB 80'S VARIOUS ARTISTS (UNIVERSAL)	4	2007
CLUB ANTHEMS 2007 VARIOUS ARTISTS (EMI)	7	2007
CLUB ANTHEMS 99 VARIOUS ARTISTS (VIRGIN)	4	1999
CLUB CLASS VARIOUS ARTISTS (GLOBAL TELEVISION)	4	1995
CLUB CLASS VARIOUS ARTISTS (WARNER BROTHERS)	9	1998
CLUB CLASS VARIOUS ARTISTS (BMG)	11	2004
CLUB CLASSICS VARIOUS ARTISTS (MINISTRY OF SOUND)	5	2004
CLUB CLASSICS VOLUME 2 VARIOUS ARTISTS (CBS)	90	1985
CLUB CLASSICS – VOLUME 3 VARIOUS ARTISTS (FANTAZIA)	4	1997
CLUB CLASSICS VOLUME ONE SOUL II SOUL	1	1989
CLUB CULTURE EXPOSED! VARIOUS ARTISTS (GLOBAL TELEVISION)	5	1998
CLUB CUTS 97 VARIOUS ARTISTS (TELSTAR)	5	1997
CLUB CUTS 97 – VOLUME 2 VARIOUS ARTISTS (TELSTAR)	2	1997
CLUB CUTS 97 – VOLUME 3 VARIOUS ARTISTS (TELSTAR)	5	1997
CLUB FEVER VARIOUS ARTISTS (VIRGIN)	2	2005
CLUB FEVER 2006 VARIOUS ARTISTS (EMI)	4	2006
CLUB FOR HEROES VARIOUS ARTISTS (TELSTAR)	3	1992
CLUB HITS 2002 VARIOUS ARTISTS (INSPIRED)	5	2002
CLUB HITS 2003 VARIOUS ARTISTS (INSPIRED)	12	2003
CLUB HITS 97/98: SOUNDTRACK TO A SEASON VARIOUS ARTISTS (VIRGIN)	5	1997
CLUB HITS 98 VARIOUS ARTISTS (TELSTAR)	2	1998
CLUB HITS 99 VARIOUS ARTISTS (TELSTAR)	16	1999
CLUB IBIZA VARIOUS ARTISTS (QUALITY PRICE MUSIC)	15	1995
CLUB IBIZA VARIOUS ARTISTS (WARNER BROTHERS)	4	1999
CLUB IBIZA SILVER EDITION VARIOUS ARTISTS (QUALITY PRICE MUSIC)	19	1996
CLUB IBIZA – VOLUME 2 VARIOUS ARTISTS (QUALITY PRICE MUSIC)	19	1996
CLUB MIX 2001 VARIOUS ARTISTS (UNIVERSAL)	4	2001
CLUB MIX 2002 VARIOUS ARTISTS (UNIVERSAL)	1	2002
CLUB MIX 2003 VARIOUS ARTISTS (UNIVERSAL)	1	2003
CLUB MIX 96 VARIOUS ARTISTS (POLYGRAM)	2	1996
CLUB MIX 96 – VOLUME 2 VARIOUS ARTISTS (POLYGRAM)	2	1996
CLUB MIX 97 VARIOUS ARTISTS (POLYGRAM)	7	1996
CLUB MIX 97 – VOLUME 2 VARIOUS ARTISTS (POLYGRAM)	1	1997
CLUB MIX 97 – VOLUME 3 VARIOUS ARTISTS (POLYGRAM)	4	1997
CLUB MIX 99 VARIOUS ARTISTS (UNIVERSAL)	3	1999
CLUB MIX IBIZA 2000 VARIOUS ARTISTS (UNIVERSAL)	1	2000
CLUB NATION VARIOUS ARTISTS (VIRGIN)	3	1998
CLUB NATION VARIOUS ARTISTS (MINISTRY OF SOUND)	4	2001
CLUB NATION 2 VARIOUS ARTISTS (VIRGIN)	8	1998
CLUB NATION IBIZA VARIOUS ARTISTS (MINISTRY OF SOUND)	9	2002
CLUB NATION – MIAMI 2002 VARIOUS ARTISTS (MINISTRY OF SOUND)	7	2002
CLUB NIGHTS – LIVE IT VARIOUS ARTISTS (GTV)	9	2007
CLUB NIGHTS – SOUNDTRACK TO THE WEEKEND VARIOUS ARTISTS (GUT)	3	2006
CLUB REGGAE VARIOUS ARTISTS (TROJAN)	25	1971
CLUB SKA '67 VARIOUS ARTISTS (ISLAND)	37	1967
CLUB TOGETHER VARIOUS ARTISTS (EMI)	10	1994
CLUB TOGETHER 2 VARIOUS ARTISTS (EMI)	9	1995
CLUB TOGETHER 3 VARIOUS ARTISTS (EMI)	7	1996
CLUB TROPICANA VARIOUS ARTISTS (COLUMBIA)	11	2002
CLUB ZONE VARIOUS ARTISTS (TELSTAR)	4	1995
CLUB ZONE 2 VARIOUS ARTISTS (TELSTAR)	10	1995
CLUBBED VARIOUS ARTISTS (UNIVERSAL)	6	2001
CLUBBED 2002 – MIXED BY JUDGE JULES VARIOUS ARTISTS (UNIVERSAL)	7	2002
CLUBBED OUT VARIOUS ARTISTS (VIRGIN)	5	2001
CLUBBED UP VARIOUS ARTISTS (WARNER BROTHERS)	12	2002

Title / Artist	Peak Position	Year of Release
CLUBBED – VOLUME 2 – MIXED BY JUDGE JULES VARIOUS ARTISTS (UNIVERSAL)	8	2001
THE CLUBBER'S BIBLE VARIOUS ARTISTS (WARNER BROTHERS)	11	2000
CLUBBERS GUIDE 05 VARIOUS ARTISTS (MINISTRY OF SOUND)	2	2005
CLUBBERS GUIDE 2003 VARIOUS ARTISTS (MINISTRY OF SOUND)	1	2003
CLUBBERS GUIDE – 2004 VARIOUS ARTISTS (MINISTRY OF SOUND)	1	2004
CLUBBERS GUIDE 2006 VARIOUS ARTISTS (MINISTRY OF SOUND)	1	2006
CLUBBERS GUIDE 2007 VARIOUS ARTISTS (MINISTRY OF SOUND)	3	2007
CLUBBERS GUIDE 2008 VARIOUS ARTISTS (MINISTRY OF SOUND)	3	2008
CLUBBERS GUIDE SUMMER '04 VARIOUS ARTISTS (MINISTRY OF SOUND)	2	2004
CLUBBERS GUIDE SUMMER 2005 VARIOUS ARTISTS (MINISTRY OF SOUND)	2	2005
CLUBBERS GUIDE SUMMER 2006 VARIOUS ARTISTS (MINISTRY OF SOUND)	1	2006
CLUBBERS GUIDE SUMMER 2007 VARIOUS ARTISTS (MINISTRY OF SOUND)	3	2007
CLUBBERS GUIDE – SUMMER 2008 VARIOUS ARTISTS (MINISTRY OF SOUND)	3	2008
CLUBBER'S GUIDE TO …TRANCE: MIXED BY ATB VARIOUS ARTISTS (MINISTRY OF SOUND)	4	1999
CLUBBERS GUIDE TO 2001 VARIOUS ARTISTS (MINISTRY OF SOUND)	1	2001
CLUBBERS GUIDE TO 2002 VARIOUS ARTISTS (MINISTRY OF SOUND)	1	2002
CLUBBERS GUIDE TO IBIZA 2002 VARIOUS ARTISTS (MINISTRY OF SOUND)	1	2002
CLUBBER'S GUIDE TO IBIZA -SUMMER 2000 VARIOUS ARTISTS (MINISTRY OF SOUND)	1	2000
CLUBBERS GUIDE TO IBIZA – SUMMER 2001 VARIOUS ARTISTS (MINISTRY OF SOUND)	4	2001
CLUBBER'S GUIDE TO IBIZA – SUMMER '99 VARIOUS ARTISTS (MINISTRY OF SOUND)	1	1999
CLUBBERS GUIDE TO SUMMER 2003 VARIOUS ARTISTS (MINISTRY OF SOUND)	2	2003
CLUBBER'S GUIDE TO…2000 VARIOUS ARTISTS (MINISTRY OF SOUND)	1	2000
CLUBBER'S GUIDE TO…IBIZA – JULES/TONG VARIOUS ARTISTS (MINISTRY OF SOUND)	2	1998
CLUBBER'S GUIDE TO…NINETY NINE VARIOUS ARTISTS (MINISTRY OF SOUND)	1	1999
CLUBBIN' VARIOUS ARTISTS (WARNER BROTHERS)	6	1998
CLUBBIN' VARIOUS ARTISTS (V2)	13	2005
CLUBLAND VARIOUS ARTISTS (TELSTAR)	3	1997
CLUBLAND VARIOUS ARTISTS (UNIVERSAL)	1	2002
CLUBLAND 10 VARIOUS ARTISTS (UNIVERSAL)	1	2006
CLUBLAND 11 VARIOUS ARTISTS (UNIVERSAL)	1	2007
CLUBLAND 12 VARIOUS ARTISTS (UNIVERSAL)	1	2007
CLUBLAND 13 VARIOUS ARTISTS (UNIVERSAL)	1	2008
CLUBLAND 14 VARIOUS ARTISTS (UNIVERSAL)	1	2008
CLUBLAND 4 VARIOUS ARTISTS (UNIVERSAL)	1	2003
CLUBLAND 5 VARIOUS ARTISTS (UNIVERSAL)	1	2004
CLUBLAND 6 VARIOUS ARTISTS (UNIVERSAL)	2	2004
CLUBLAND 7 VARIOUS ARTISTS (UNIVERSAL)	1	2005
CLUBLAND 8 VARIOUS ARTISTS (UNIVERSAL)	2	2005
CLUBLAND 9 VARIOUS ARTISTS (UNIVERSAL)	1	2006
CLUBLAND CLASSIX VARIOUS ARTISTS (UNIVERSAL)	1	2008
CLUBLAND II – THE RIDE OF YOUR LIFE VARIOUS ARTISTS (UNIVERSAL)	1	2002
CLUBLAND III VARIOUS ARTISTS (UNIVERSAL)	1	2003
CLUBLAND – VOLUME 2 VARIOUS ARTISTS (TELSTAR)	6	1997
CLUBLAND X-TREME VARIOUS ARTISTS (UNIVERSAL)	2	2003
CLUBLAND X-TREME 2 VARIOUS ARTISTS (UNIVERSAL)	2	2004
CLUBLAND X-TREME HARDCORE VARIOUS ARTISTS (UNIVERSAL)	1	2005
CLUBLAND XTREME HARDCORE 2 VARIOUS ARTISTS (UNIVERSAL)	1	2006
CLUBLAND X-TREME HARDCORE 3 VARIOUS ARTISTS (UNIVERSAL)	11	2006
CLUBLAND X-TREME HARDCORE 4 VARIOUS ARTISTS (UNIVERSAL)	7	2007
CLUBLAND X-TREME HARDCORE 5 VARIOUS ARTISTS (UNIVERSAL)	15	2008
CLUBLIFE VARIOUS ARTISTS (TELSTAR)	3	1998
CLUBLIFE 2 VARIOUS ARTISTS (TELSTAR)	13	1998
CLUBMIX 2000 VARIOUS ARTISTS (UNIVERSAL)	2	2000
CLUBMIX 2000 VOLUME 2 VARIOUS ARTISTS (UNIVERSAL)	1	2000
CLUBMIX 2004 VARIOUS ARTISTS (UNIVERSAL)	1	2004
CLUBMIX 2005 VARIOUS ARTISTS (UNIVERSAL)	1	2005
CLUBMIX 2006 VARIOUS ARTISTS (UNIVERSAL)	2	2006
CLUBMIX 2007 VARIOUS ARTISTS (UNIVERSAL)	6	2006
CLUBMIX CLASSICS VARIOUS ARTISTS (UNIVERSAL)	14	2007
CLUBMIX IBIZA VARIOUS ARTISTS (UNIVERSAL)	2	2001
CLUBMIX IBIZA 2002 VARIOUS ARTISTS (UNIVERSAL)	2	2002
CLUBMIX SUMMER 2003 VARIOUS ARTISTS (UNIVERSAL)	1	2003
CLUBMIX SUMMER 2004 VARIOUS ARTISTS (UNIVERSAL)	7	2004
CLUBZONE – DANCING IN THE CITY VARIOUS ARTISTS (WARNER BROTHERS)	20	1999
CLUES ROBERT PALMER	31	1980
CLUTCHING AT STRAWS MARILLION	2	1987
C.M.B. COLOR ME BADD	3	1991
C'MON C'MON SHERYL CROW	2	2002
C'MON EVERYBODY ELVIS PRESLEY	5	1971
C'MON EVERYBODY EDDIE COCHRAN	53	1988
C'MON KIDS BOO RADLEYS	20	1996
COAST TO COAST WESTLIFE	1	2000
COCKAHOOP CERYS MATTHEWS	30	2003
COCKED AND LOADED L.A. GUNS	45	1989
COCKTAIL FILM SOUNDTRACK	2	1989
COCO COLBIE CAILLAT	44	2007
CODA LED ZEPPELIN	4	1982
CODE OF THE ROAD NILS LOFGREN	86	1986
CODE RED JAZZY JEFF & THE FRESH PRINCE	50	1993
CODE-SELFISH FALL	21	1992
COHEN LIVE LEONARD COHEN	35	1994
COINCIDENCE (AND LIKELY STORIES) BUFFY SAINTE-MARIE	39	1992
COLD FEET TELEVISION AND RADIO COMPILATION	13	2001
COLD ROSES RYAN ADAMS & THE CARDINALS	20	2005
COLD SPRING HARBOUR BILLY JOEL	95	1984
COLD SWEAT VARIOUS ARTISTS (DINO)	2	1992
COLES CORNER RICHARD HAWLEY	37	2005
COLLABORATION GEORGE BENSON & EARL KLUGH	47	1987
COLLECTED – THE BEST OF MASSIVE ATTACK	2	2006
THE COLLECTION ULTRAVOX	2	1984
THE COLLECTION BARRY WHITE	5	1988
COLLECTION RAY CHARLES	36	1990
THE COLLECTION LLOYD COLE	24	1999
COLLECTION TRACY CHAPMAN	3	2001
THE COLLECTION JOHN RUTTER	75	2002
THE COLLECTION ALANIS MORISSETTE	44	2005
THE COLLECTION SHAKIN' STEVENS	4	2005
THE COLLECTION CURTIS STIGERS	50	2006
COLLECTION TRAVELING WILBURYS	1	2007
THE COLLECTION SIMON & GARFUNKEL	47	2007
A COLLECTION JOSH GROBAN	22	2008
THE COLLECTION 1977-1982 STRANGLERS	12	1982
THE COLLECTION – 20 GREATEST HITS GLADYS KNIGHT & THE PIPS	43	1984
THE COLLECTION – 24 ESSENTIAL HITS EARTH WIND & FIRE	5	1986
THE COLLECTION AUTUMN 2006 VARIOUS ARTISTS (SONY/BMG)	6	2008
A COLLECTION – GREATEST HITS…AND MORE BARBRA STREISAND	22	1989
A COLLECTION OF BEATLES OLDIES BEATLES	7	1966
COLLECTION OF BIG HITS VOLUME 8 VARIOUS ARTISTS (MOTOWN)	56	1970
A COLLECTION OF GREAT DANCE SONGS PINK FLOYD	37	1981
A COLLECTION OF TAMLA MOTOWN HITS VARIOUS ARTISTS (MOTOWN)	16	1965
A COLLECTION OF THEIR 20 GREATEST HITS THREE DEGREES	8	1979
THE COLLECTION – THE 20 GREATEST HITS FOUR SEASONS	38	1988
THE COLLECTION – THE VERY BEST OF BREAD AND DAVID GATES BREAD & DAVID GATES	84	1987
COLLECTORS GOLD ELVIS PRESLEY	57	1991
THE COLLECTOR'S SERIES VOLUME 1 CELINE DION	30	2000
THE COLLEGE DROPOUT KANYE WEST	12	2004
COLLISION COURSE JAY-Z & LINKIN PARK	15	2004
COLOSSEUM COLOSSEUM	15	1969
COLOSSEUM LIVE COLOSSEUM	17	1971
COLOUR CHRISTIANS	1	1990
THE COLOUR AND THE SHAPE FOO FIGHTERS	3	1997
COLOUR BY NUMBERS CULTURE CLUB	1	1983
COLOUR IT IN MACCABEES	24	2007
COLOUR IT IN – SPECIAL EDITION MACCABEES	55	2008
COLOUR MY WORLD PETULA CLARK	16	1967
THE COLOUR OF MY LOVE CELINE DION	1	1994
THE COLOUR OF SPRING TALK TALK	8	1986
COLOURBOX COLOURBOX	67	1985
THE COLOURFUL LIFE CAJUN DANCE PARTY	49	2008
COLOURS ADAM F	47	1997
COM LAG 2+2=5 RADIOHEAD	37	2004
COMBAT ROCK CLASH	2	1982
COMBINE HARVESTER WURZELS	15	1976
COME PRINCE	1	1994
COME AGAIN PETER COOK & DUDLEY MOORE	18	1977
COME AN' GET IT WHITESNAKE	2	1981
COME AND GET IT RACHEL STEVENS	28	2005
COME AWAY WITH ME NORAH JONES	1	2002
COME BACK TO SORRENTO FRANK SINATRA	6	1960
COME CLARITY IN FLAMES	67	2006
COME CLEAN PUDDLE OF MUDD	12	2002
COME DANCE WITH ME! FRANK SINATRA WITH BILLY MAY & HIS ORCHESTRA	2	1959
COME DOWN DANDY WARHOLS	16	1998
COME FIND YOURSELF FUN LOVIN' CRIMINALS	7	1996

Title / Artist	Peak Position	Year of Release
COME FLY WITH ME FRANK SINATRA	2	1958
COME FLY WITH ME MICHAEL BUBLE	52	2004
COME INTO MY LIFE JOYCE SIMS	5	1988
COME MORNING GROVER WASHINGTON JR.	98	1981
COME MY WAY MARIANNE FAITHFULL	12	1965
COME ON ENGLAND VARIOUS ARTISTS (GUT)	17	2004
COME ON FEEL THE LEMONHEADS LEMONHEADS	5	1993
COME ON OVER OLIVIA NEWTON-JOHN	49	1976
COME ON OVER SHANIA TWAIN	1	1998
COME ON, DIE YOUNG MOGWAI	29	1999
(COME ON, JOIN) THE HIGH SOCIETY THESE ANIMAL MEN	62	1994
COME OUT AND PLAY TWISTED SISTER	95	1985
COME SWING WITH ME FRANK SINATRA	13	1962
COME TASTE THE BAND DEEP PURPLE	19	1975
COME THE DAY SEEKERS	3	1966
COME TO MY PARTY MRS. MILLS	17	1966
COME TOGETHER AS ONE WILL DOWNING	36	1989
COME WHAT (EVER) MAY STONE SOUR	27	2006
COME WITH CLUB (CLUB TRACKS VOLUME 2) VARIOUS ARTISTS (CLUB)	55	1983
COME WITH US CHEMICAL BROTHERS	1	2002
COMEDY BLACK	32	1988
COMES A TIME NEIL YOUNG	42	1978
COMFORT IN SOUND FEEDER	6	2002
COMFORT OF STRANGERS BETH ORTON	24	2006
THE COMFORT ZONE VANESSA WILLIAMS	24	1992
COMFORTER COMPULSION	59	1994
THE COMFORTS OF MADNESS PALE SAINTS	40	1990
COMIC RELIEF PRESENTS UTTERLY UTTERLY LIVE! COMIC RELIEF	10	1986
COMIN' ATCHA! CLEOPATRA	20	1998
THE COMING BUSTA RHYMES	48	1996
COMING ALIVE AGAIN BARBARA DICKSON	30	1989
COMING AROUND AGAIN CARLY SIMON	25	1987
COMING BACK HARD AGAIN FAT BOYS	98	1988
COMING HOME LIONEL RICHIE	15	2006
COMING IN FOR THE KILL CLIMIE FISHER	35	1989
COMING OUT MANHATTAN TRANSFER	12	1977
COMING UP SUEDE	1	1996
COMING UP FOR AIR PENETRATION	36	1979
COMME SI DE RIEN N'ETAIT CARLA BRUNI	58	2008
THE COMMITMENTS COMMITMENTS	4	1991
THE COMMITMENTS VOLUME 2 COMMITMENTS	13	1992
COMMITTED TO SOUL VARIOUS ARTISTS (ARCADE)	11	1994
COMMODORES LIVE! COMMODORES	60	1978
COMMON GROUND VARIOUS ARTISTS (EMI)	17	1996
COMMON ONE VAN MORRISON	53	1980
COMMONER'S CROWN STEELEYE SPAN	21	1975
COMMUNARDS COMMUNARDS	7	1986
COMMUNICATE – SASHA & DIGWEED VARIOUS ARTISTS (INCREDIBLE)	13	2000
COMMUNIQUE DIRE STRAITS	5	1979
COMMUNITY MUSIC ASIAN DUB FOUNDATION	20	2000
COMO'S GOLDEN RECORDS PERRY COMO	4	1959
COMPACT SNAP JAM	39	2005
COMPANEROS WORKING WEEK	72	1986
COMPARSA DEEP FOREST	60	1998
COMPASS KUMPAS DALEK I	54	1980
THE COMPLEAT TOM PAXTON TOM PAXTON	18	1971
THE COMPLETE AMERICAN SONGBOOK 1-4 ROD STEWART	13	2007
COMPLETE AND UNBELIEVABLE...THE OTIS REDDING DICTIONARY OF SOUL OTIS REDDING	23	1967
THE COMPLETE B-SIDES PIXIES	53	2001
COMPLETE CLAPTON ERIC CLAPTON	2	2007
THE COMPLETE COLLECTION IL DIVO	32	2007
THE COMPLETE GLEN CAMPBELL GLEN CAMPBELL	47	1989
THE COMPLETE GREATEST HITS EAGLES	9	2003
COMPLETE MADNESS MADNESS	1	1982
THE COMPLETE MIKE OLDFIELD MIKE OLDFIELD	36	1985
THE COMPLETE PICTURE – THE VERY BEST OF DEBORAH HARRY AND BLONDIE DEBORAH HARRY & BLONDIE	3	1991
THE COMPLETE STONE ROSES STONE ROSES	4	1995
THE COMPLETE TOM JONES TOM JONES	8	1992
COMPLETELY HOOKED – THE BEST OF DR. HOOK DR. HOOK	3	1992
COMPOSITIONS ANITA BAKER	7	1990
COMPUTER WORLD KRAFTWERK	15	1981
CONCERT FOR BANGLADESH (RECORDED LIVE) VARIOUS ARTISTS (APPLE)	1	1972
A CONCERT FOR THE PEOPLE (BERLIN) BARCLAY JAMES HARVEST	15	1982
THE CONCERT IN CENTRAL PARK SIMON & GARFUNKEL	6	1982
CONCERT SINATRA FRANK SINATRA	8	1963
CONCERT SPECTACULAR MANTOVANI & HIS ORCHESTRA	16	1961
CONCERT – THE CURE LIVE CURE	26	1984
CONCERTO FOR GROUP AND ORCHESTRA DEEP PURPLE	26	1970
CONCERTS FOR THE PEOPLE OF KAMPUCHEA VARIOUS ARTISTS (ATLANTIC)	39	1981
THE CONCERTS IN CHINA JEAN-MICHEL JARRE	6	1982
CONCRETE PET SHOP BOYS	61	2006
CONCRETE ROSE ASHANTI	25	2005
CONDITION CRITICAL QUIET RIOT	71	1984
CONEY ISLAND BABY LOU REED	52	1976
CONFESSIONS USHER	1	2004
CONFESSIONS OF A POP GROUP STYLE COUNCIL	15	1988
CONFESSIONS OF THE MIND HOLLIES	30	1970
CONFESSIONS ON A DANCE FLOOR MADONNA	1	2005
THE CONFESSIONS TOUR MADONNA	7	2007
CONFRONTATION BOB MARLEY & THE WAILERS	5	1983
CONGRATULATIONS, I'M SORRY GIN BLOSSOMS	42	1996
CONNECTED STEREO MC'S	2	1992
CONNECTED VARIOUS ARTISTS (POLYGRAM)	18	1998
CONNECTED 90'S 12 INCH MIXES VARIOUS ARTISTS (UNIVERSAL)	11	2008
CONNIE'S GREATEST HITS CONNIE FRANCIS	16	1961
CONOR OBERST CONOR OBERST	37	2008
CONQUER SOULFLY	64	2008
CONQUEST URIAH HEEP	37	1980
CONSCIENCE WOMACK & WOMACK	4	1988
CONSCIENCE BELOVED	2	1993
CONSEQUENCES KEVIN GODLEY & LOL CRÈME	52	1977
CONSOLERS OF THE LONELY RACONTEURS	8	2008
CONSPIRACY DRIZA-BONE	72	1994
CONSPIRACY OF ONE OFFSPRING	12	2000
CONSTRICTOR ALICE COOPER	41	1986
CONSTRUCTION FOR THE MODERN IDIOT WONDER STUFF	4	1993
CONSTRUCTION TIME AGAIN DEPECHE MODE	6	1983
CONTACT POINTER SISTERS	34	1985
CONTENDERS EASTERHOUSE	91	1986
CONTINENTAL ENCORES MANTOVANI & HIS ORCHESTRA	4	1959
THE CONTINO SESSIONS DEATH IN VEGAS	19	1999
CONTINUOUS PERFORMANCE STONE THE CROWS	33	1972
CONTINUUM JOHN MAYER	46	2006
CONTRABAND VELVET REVOLVER	11	2004
CONTRIBUTION MICA PARIS	26	1990
CONTROL JANET JACKSON	8	1986
CONTROL – THE REMIXES JANET JACKSON	20	1987
CONVERSATION PEACE STEVIE WONDER	8	1995
CONVICTION AIDEN	45	2007
CONVOY FILM SOUNDTRACK	52	1978
THE COOKBOOK MISSY ELLIOTT	33	2005
COOKIN' ON THE ROOF ROMAN HOLLIDAY	31	1983
THE COOL LUPE FIASCO	7	2008
COOL AS INSPIRAL CARPETS	65	2003
COOL FOR CATS SQUEEZE	45	1979
COOL GROOVES VARIOUS ARTISTS (POLYGRAM)	12	1998
COOL HEAT VARIOUS ARTISTS (K-TEL)	79	1983
THE COOL SOUND OF THE 70S VARIOUS ARTISTS (TELSTAR)	9	2000
COOL SUMMER JAZZ VARIOUS ARTISTS (VIRGIN)	15	2003
COOL SUMMER REGGAE ASWAD	54	2002
THE COOLEST CUTS SHAKATAK	73	1988
COOLEYHIGHHARMONY BOYZ II MEN	7	1992
COP YER WHACK OF THIS BILLY CONNOLLY	10	1975
COPPER BLUE SUGAR	10	1992
COPPERHEAD ROAD STEVE EARLE	42	1988
COPPEROPOLIS GRANT LEE BUFFALO	34	1996
THE CORAL CORAL	5	2002
CORAL FANG DISTILLERS	46	2003
CORE STONE TEMPLE PILOTS	27	1993
CORINNE BAILEY RAE CORINNE BAILEY RAE	1	2006
THE CORNER OF MILES AND GIL SHACK	55	2006
CORNERSTONE STYX	36	1979
CORNERSTONES – JIMI HENDRIX 1967-1970 JIMI HENDRIX	5	1990
THE CORONATION STREET ALBUM (TELEVISION COMPILATION) TELEVISION AND RADIO COMPILATION	20	1995
CORRECT USE OF SOAP MAGAZINE	28	1980
CORRIDORS OF POWER GARY MOORE	30	1982
CORROSION VARIOUS ARTISTS (COLUMBIA)	17	2001
CORTES GARDAR THOR CORTES	27	2007
COSA NOSTRA BECK – OLA JEFF BECK	39	1969
COSI FAN TUTTI FRUTTI SQUEEZE	31	1985
COSMIC CARROTT JASPER CARROTT	66	1987
THE COSMIC GAME THIEVERY CORPORATION	74	2005
COSMIC THING B-52'S	8	1989
COSMIC WHEELS DONOVAN	15	1973
COSMO'S FACTORY CREEDENCE CLEARWATER REVIVAL	1	1970
THE COSMOS ROCKS QUEEN & PAUL RODGERS	5	2008
THE COST OF LOVING STYLE COUNCIL	2	1987
COSTELLO MUSIC FRATELLIS	2	2006
COULD IT BE FOREVER – THE GREATEST HITS DAVID CASSIDY & THE PARTRIDGE FAMILY	52	2006
COULDN'T HAVE SAID IT BETTER MEAT LOAF	4	2003
COULDN'T LOVE YOU MORE JOHN MARTYN	65	1992
COUNCIL ESTATE OF THE MIND SKINNYMAN	65	2004
COUNT THREE AND PRAY BERLIN	32	1987
COUNT YOUR BLESSINGS ANN WILLIAMSON	58	1988
COUNTDOWN 1992-1983 PULP	10	1996
COUNTDOWN TO EXTINCTION MEGADETH	5	1992
COUNTERFEIT (EP) MARTIN L. GORE	51	1989
COUNTERPARTS RUSH	14	1993
COUNTING DOWN THE DAYS NATALIE IMBRUGLIA	1	2005
COUNTRY VARIOUS ARTISTS (UNIVERSAL)	8	1999
COUNTRY BALLADS VARIOUS ARTISTS (VIRGIN)	17	2003
COUNTRY BOY DON WILLIAMS	27	1977

Title / Artist	Peak Position	Year of Release
COUNTRY BOY DANIEL O'DONNELL	6	2008
COUNTRY COMFORT VARIOUS ARTISTS (K-TEL)	8	1976
COUNTRY GENTLEMAN JIM REEVES	53	1980
COUNTRY GIRL BILLIE JO SPEARS	17	1981
COUNTRY GIRL MEETS COUNTRY BOY VARIOUS ARTISTS (WARWICK)	43	1978
COUNTRY GOLD VARIOUS ARTISTS (GLOBAL TELEVISION)	12	1996
COUNTRY GRAMMAR NELLY	14	2001
COUNTRY GUITAR VARIOUS ARTISTS (WARWICK)	46	1980
COUNTRY LEGENDS VARIOUS ARTISTS (RONCO)	9	1980
COUNTRY LEGENDS VARIOUS ARTISTS (VIRGIN)	2	2002
COUNTRY LIFE ROXY	3	1974
COUNTRY LIFE VARIOUS ARTISTS (EMI)	2	1979
COUNTRY LOVE VARIOUS ARTISTS (TELSTAR)	5	1993
COUNTRY LOVE VARIOUS ARTISTS (UNIVERSAL)	4	2003
COUNTRY LOVE 2 VARIOUS ARTISTS (TELSTAR)	11	1993
COUNTRY MOODS VARIOUS ARTISTS (POLYGRAM)	2	1992
COUNTRY NUMBER ONE DON GIBSON	13	1980
COUNTRY PORTRAITS VARIOUS ARTISTS (WARWICK)	14	1979
COUNTRY ROADS VARIOUS ARTISTS (POLYGRAM)	3	1993
COUNTRY ROADS JAMES LAST	18	1999
COUNTRY ROUND UP VARIOUS ARTISTS (POLYDOR)	64	1980
COUNTRY SIDE OF JIM REEVES JIM REEVES	12	1964
COUNTRY SUNRISE/COUNTRY SUNSET VARIOUS ARTISTS (RONCO)	27	1981
COUNTRY WOMEN VARIOUS ARTISTS (DINO)	11	1993
COUNTRY'S GREATEST HITS VARIOUS ARTISTS (TELSTAR)	9	1990
COUPLES LONG BLONDES	48	2008
COURT AND SPARK JONI MITCHELL	14	1974
THE COVENANT, THE SWORD AND THE ARM OF THE LAW CABARET VOLTAIRE	57	1985
COVER GIRL SHAWN COLVIN	67	1994
COVER PLUS HAZEL O'CONNOR	32	1981
COVER SHOT DAVID ESSEX	3	1993
COVER TO COVER JEFF HEALEY BAND	50	1995
COVER UP UB40	29	2001
COVERDALE PAGE COVERDALE PAGE	4	1993
COWBOY ERASURE	10	1997
COWBOY COMPILATION – THE ALBUM VOLUME 1 VARIOUS ARTISTS (COWBOY6)	18	1993
COYOTE UGLY FILM SOUNDTRACK	16	2000
THE CRACK RUTS	16	1979
THE CRACKDOWN CABARET VOLTAIRE	31	1983
CRACKED REAR VIEW HOOTIE & THE BLOWFISH	12	1995
CRACKERS' – THE SLADE CHRISTMAS PARTY ALBUM SLADE	34	1985
CRAIG DOUGLAS CRAIG DOUGLAS	17	1960
CRAIG MCLACHLAN AND CHECK 1-2 CRAIG McLACHLAN & CHECK 1-2	10	1990
CRANK ALMIGHTY	15	1994
CRASH HUMAN LEAGUE	7	1986
CRASH BOOM BANG ROXETTE	3	1994
CRASH COURSE U.K. SUBS	8	1980
CRASH INDIE ANTHEMS 1982-2004 VARIOUS ARTISTS (TELSTAR)	19	2004
CRASH LANDING JIMI HENDRIX	35	1975
CRAZY JULIO IGLESIAS	6	1994
CRAZY FROM THE HEAT DAVID LEE ROTH	91	1985
CRAZY HITS CRAZY FROG	5	2005
CRAZY HITS – CRAZY CHRISTMAS EDITION CRAZY FROG	75	2005
CRAZY HORSES OSMONDS	9	1972
CRAZY ITCH RADIO BASEMENT JAXX	16	2006
CRAZY LITTLE THING CALLED LOVE VARIOUS ARTISTS (WARNER BROTHERS)	17	1999
CRAZY NIGHTS TYGERS OF PAN TANG	51	1981
CRAZY NIGHTS KISS	4	1987
CRAZY TIMES GENE VINCENT	12	1960
CRAZY WORLD SCORPIONS	27	1990
THE CRAZY WORLD OF ARTHUR BROWN CRAZY WORLD OF ARTHUR BROWN	2	1968
CRAZYSEXYCOOL TLC	4	1995
CREAM – 15 YEARS VARIOUS ARTISTS (MINISTRY OF SOUND)	3	2008
CREAM ANTHEMS VARIOUS ARTISTS (DECONSTRUCTION)	2	1995
CREAM ANTHEMS 2000 VARIOUS ARTISTS (VIRGIN)	2	1999
CREAM ANTHEMS 2001 VARIOUS ARTISTS (VIRGIN)	1	2000
CREAM ANTHEMS 2002 VARIOUS ARTISTS (VIRGIN)	18	2001
CREAM ANTHEMS '97 VARIOUS ARTISTS (DECONSTRUCTION)	11	1997
CREAM ANTHEMS MIXED BY TALL PAUL AND SEB FONTAINE VARIOUS ARTISTS (VIRGIN)	15	1998
CREAM ANTHEMS SPRING 2002 VARIOUS ARTISTS (VIRGIN)	3	2002
CREAM BEACH 2002 VARIOUS ARTISTS (VIRGIN)	8	2002
CREAM CLASSICS VARIOUS ARTISTS (WARNER BROTHERS)	2	2004
CREAM CLASSICS – VOLUME 2 VARIOUS ARTISTS (WARNER BROTHERS)	5	2004
CREAM IBIZA VARIOUS ARTISTS (VIRGIN)	7	2001
CREAM IBIZA VARIOUS ARTISTS (NEW STATE)	15	2008
CREAM IBIZA – ARRIVALS VARIOUS ARTISTS (VIRGIN)	2	1999
CREAM IBIZA ARRIVALS VARIOUS ARTISTS (VIRGIN)	4	2000
CREAM IBIZA CLASSICS VARIOUS ARTISTS (WARNER BROTHERS)	7	2005
CREAM IBIZA – DEPARTURES VARIOUS ARTISTS (VIRGIN)	13	1999
CREAM LIVE VARIOUS ARTISTS (DECONSTRUCTION)	3	1995
CREAM LIVE VARIOUS ARTISTS (VIRGIN)	2	2000
CREAM LIVE – TWO VARIOUS ARTISTS (DECONSTRUCTION)	3	1996
THE CREAM OF ERIC CLAPTON ERIC CLAPTON & CREAM	3	1987
CREAM OF THE CROP DIANA ROSS & THE SUPREMES	34	1970
CREAM RESIDENT – SEB FONTAINE VARIOUS ARTISTS (VIRGIN)	18	2000
CREAM SEPERATES – THE COLLECTION VARIOUS ARTISTS (DECONSTRUCTION)	16	1997
CREAM SUMMER 2006 VARIOUS ARTISTS (MINISTRY OF SOUND)	3	2006
CREAM SUMMER 2007 VARIOUS ARTISTS (MINISTRY OF SOUND)	8	2007
CREAMFIELDS VARIOUS ARTISTS (VIRGIN)	5	2000
CREAMFIELDS – 10 YEARS – THE ALBUM VARIOUS ARTISTS (MINISTRY OF SOUND)	4	2008
CREATING PATTERNS 4 HERO	65	2001
CREATURES OF THE NIGHT KISS	22	1982
THE CREEDENCE COLLECTION CREEDENCE CLEARWATER REVIVAL	68	1985
CRE-OLE (BEST OF KID CREOLE AND COCONUTS) KID CREOLE & THE COCONUTS	21	1984
CREPES AND DRAPES SHOWADDYWADDY	8	1979
CREST OF A KNAVE JETHRO TULL	19	1987
CREW CUTS VARIOUS ARTISTS (ISLAND)	71	1984
CREW CUTS – LESSON 2 VARIOUS ARTISTS (ISLAND)	95	1984
CREWS CONTROL VARIOUS ARTISTS (WARNER BROTHERS)	17	2002
CRICKLEWOOD GREEN TEN YEARS AFTER	4	1970
CRIME OF THE CENTURY SUPERTRAMP	4	1974
CRIMINAL RECORD RICK WAKEMAN	25	1977
CRIMSON ALKALINE TRIO	34	2005
THE CRIMSON IDOL W.A.S.P.	21	1992
CRIPPLE CROW DEVENDRA BANHART	69	2005
CRISES MIKE OLDFIELD	6	1983
CRISIS ALEXISONFIRE	72	2006
CRISIS? WHAT CRISIS? SUPERTRAMP	20	1975
THE CROCK OF GOLD SHANE MacGOWAN & THE POPES	59	1997
CROCODILE SHOES JIMMY NAIL	2	1994
CROCODILE SHOES II JIMMY NAIL	10	1996
CROCODILES ECHO & THE BUNNYMEN	17	1980
CROOKED RAIN CROOKED RAIN PAVEMENT	15	1994
CROSBY, STILLS AND NASH CROSBY, STILLS & NASH	25	1969
CROSS JUSTICE	49	2007
THE CROSS EYED RAMBLER PAUL HEATON	43	2008
THE CROSS OF CHANGES ENIGMA	1	1994
CROSS PURPOSES BLACK SABBATH	41	1994
CROSS ROAD – THE BEST OF BON JOVI BON JOVI	1	1994
CROSS THAT LINE HOWARD JONES	64	1989
THE CROSSING BIG COUNTRY	3	1983
THE CROSSING PAUL YOUNG	27	1993
CROSSING THE RED SEA WITH THE ADVERTS ADVERTS	38	1978
CROSSROADS TRACY CHAPMAN	1	1989
THE CROW FILM SOUNDTRACK	13	1994
A CROW LEFT OF THE MURDER INCUBUS	6	2004
CRUEL SISTER PENTANGLE	51	1970
CRUELTY AND THE BEAST CRADLE OF FILTH	48	1998
CRUISE CONTROL VARIOUS ARTISTS (BMG)	19	2004
CRUISIN' VILLAGE PEOPLE	24	1979
CRUISIN' – THE BEST OF DRIVETIME VARIOUS ARTISTS (GLOBAL TELEVISION)	5	2000
CRUNK HITS VARIOUS ARTISTS (TVT)	16	2006
CRUNK JUICE LIL' JON & THE EAST SIDE BOYZ	52	2005
CRUSADE JOHN MAYALL & THE BLUESBREAKERS	8	1967
THE CRUSADE TRIVIUM	7	2006
CRUSADER SAXON	18	1984
CRUSADER CHRIS DE BURGH	72	1986
CRUSH ORCHESTRAL MANOEUVRES IN THE DARK	13	1985
CRUSH VARIOUS ARTISTS (POLYGRAM)	5	1997
CRUSH BON JOVI	1	2000
CRUSH ON YOU JETS	57	1987
CRUSHIN' FAT BOYS	49	1987
CRY FAITH HILL	29	2002
CRY FREEDOM FILM SOUNDTRACK	73	1988
CRY LIKE A RAINSTORM – HOWL LIKE THE WIND LINDA RONSTADT FEATURING AARON NEVILLE	43	1989
CRY OF LOVE JIMI HENDRIX	2	1971
CRY TOUGH NILS LOFGREN	8	1976
CRYING ROY ORBISON	17	1963
CRYING, LAUGHING, LOVING, LYING LABI SIFFRE	46	1972
CRYPTIC WRITINGS MEGADETH	38	1997
CRYSTAL CASTLES CRYSTAL CASTLES	47	2008
THE CRYSTAL GAYLE SINGLES ALBUM CRYSTAL GAYLE	7	1980
CRYSTAL PLANET JOE SATRIANI	32	1998
CSN CROSBY, STILLS & NASH	23	1977
CUCKOO CURVE	23	1993

Title / Artist	Peak Position	Year of Release
CUCUMBER CASTLE BEE GEES	57	1970
THE CULT CULT	21	1994
THE CULT OF ANT & DEC ANT & DEC	15	1997
THE CULT OF RAY FRANK BLACK	39	1996
CULTOSAURUS ERECTUS BLUE OYSTER CULT	12	1980
CULTURA BREED 77	61	2004
CULTURE VULTURES ORSON	25	2007
CUNNING STUNTS CARAVAN	50	1975
CUPID AND PSYCHE 85 SCRITTI POLITTI	5	1985
THE CURE CURE	8	2004
CURE FOR SANITY POP WILL EAT ITSELF	33	1990
CURED STEVE HACKETT	15	1981
A CURIOUS FEELING TONY BANKS	21	1979
CURIOUS GEORGE (OST) JACK JOHNSON	15	2006
THE CURSE THROWING MUSES	74	1992
THE CURSE OF BLONDIE BLONDIE	36	2003
CURTAIN CALL – THE HITS EMINEM	1	2005
CURTAIN UP VARIOUS ARTISTS (PYE)	4	1959
CURTAINS TINDERSTICKS	37	1997
CURTIS CURTIS MAYFIELD	30	1971
CURTIS 50 CENT	2	2007
CURTIS STIGERS CURTIS STIGERS	7	1992
CURVED AIR CURVED AIR	11	1971
CUT SLITS	30	1979
CUT THE CAKE AVERAGE WHITE BAND	28	1975
CUT THE CRAP CLASH	16	1985
CUTS ACROSS THE LAND DUKE SPIRIT	40	2005
CUTS BOTH WAYS GLORIA ESTEFAN	1	1989
CUTS LIKE A KNIFE BRYAN ADAMS	21	1986
THE CUTTER AND THE CLAN RUNRIG	45	1995
CUTTIN' HERBIE B BOYS	90	1984
CYBERPUNK BILLY IDOL	20	1993
CYCLONE TANGERINE DREAM	37	1978
CYMANFA GANU MASSED WELSH CHOIRS	5	1969
CYPRESS HILL III (TEMPLES OF BOOM) CYPRESS HILL	11	1995

D

Title / Artist	Peak Position	Year of Release
D D DON'T DON'T STOP THE BEAT JUNIOR SENIOR	29	2003
D SIDES GORILLAZ	63	2007
D12 WORLD D12	1	2004
DA GAMES IS TO BE SOLD, NOT TO BE TOLD SNOOP DOGGY DOGG	28	1998
DA REAL WORLD MISSY 'MISDEMEANOR' ELLIOTT	40	1999
THE DA VINCI CODE (OST) HANS ZIMMER	48	2006
DAD ROCKS VARIOUS ARTISTS (VIRGIN)	1	2005
DAD ROCKS VARIOUS ARTISTS (EMI)	3	2008
DADA ALICE COOPER	93	1983
DAD'S ANTHEMS VARIOUS ARTISTS (UNIVERSAL)	9	2007
DAD'S ANTHEMS 2008 VARIOUS ARTISTS (UNIVERSAL)	10	2008
DAD'S JUKEBOX VARIOUS ARTISTS (UNIVERSAL)	4	2008
DAISIES OF THE GALAXY EELS	8	2000
DAMAGED LAMBCHOP	43	2006
DAMITA JO JANET JACKSON	32	2004
DAMN RIGHT, I'VE GOT THE BLUES BUDDY GUY	43	1991
DAMN THE TORPEDOES TOM PETTY & HEARTBREAKERS	57	1979
DAMNATION AND A DAY CRADLE OF FILTH	44	2003
DAMNED DAMNED DAMNED DAMNED	36	1977
DANCE GARY NUMAN	3	1981
THE DANCE FLEETWOOD MAC	15	1997
DANCE '95 VARIOUS ARTISTS (VIRGIN)	8	1995
DANCE ADRENALIN VARIOUS ARTISTS (TELSTAR)	1	1993
DANCE BUZZ VARIOUS ARTISTS (GLOBAL TELEVISION)	3	1995
THE DANCE CHART VARIOUS ARTISTS (TELSTAR)	23	1987
DANCE CLASSICS VOLUME 1 VARIOUS ARTISTS (ARCADE)	8	1991
DANCE CLASSICS VOLUME 2 VARIOUS ARTISTS (ARCADE)	7	1991
DANCE CRAZE FILM SOUNDTRACK	5	1981
DANCE DANCE DANCE VARIOUS ARTISTS (K-TEL)	29	1981
DANCE DANCE DANCE JAMES LAST	38	1988
DANCE DECADE – DANCE HITS OF THE 80'S VARIOUS ARTISTS (LONDON)	8	1989
DANCE DECADES VARIOUS ARTISTS (UNIVERSAL)	15	2004
DANCE DIVAS VARIOUS ARTISTS (POLYGRAM)	11	1994
DANCE ENERGY VARIOUS ARTISTS (VIRGIN)	20	1991
DANCE ENERGY VARIOUS ARTISTS (MINISTRY OF SOUND)	6	2007
DANCE ENERGY 2 VARIOUS ARTISTS (VIRGIN)	6	1991
DANCE ENERGY 3 VARIOUS ARTISTS (VIRGIN)	10	1991
DANCE ENERGY 4 – FEEL THE RHYTHM VARIOUS ARTISTS (PARLOPHONE)	6	1992
DANCE HALL AT LOUSE POINT JOHN PARISH & POLLY JEAN HARVEY	46	1996
DANCE HEAT '95 VARIOUS ARTISTS (VIRGIN)	8	1995
DANCE HITS 2000 VARIOUS ARTISTS (WARNER BROTHERS)	4	2000
DANCE HITS '86 VARIOUS ARTISTS (K-TEL)	35	1986
DANCE HITS '94 – VOLUME 1 VARIOUS ARTISTS (TELSTAR)	1	1994
DANCE HITS '94 VOLUME 2 VARIOUS ARTISTS (TELSTAR)	1	1994
THE DANCE HITS ALBUM VARIOUS ARTISTS (TOWERBELL)	10	1986
DANCE HITS II VARIOUS ARTISTS (TOWERBELL)	25	1986
DANCE IN THE MIDNIGHT MARC BOLAN	83	1983
DANCE INTO THE LIGHT PHIL COLLINS	4	1996
DANCE MANIA VARIOUS ARTISTS (UNIVERSAL)	1	2006
DANCE MANIA 2 – THE ULTIMATE CLUB PARTY VARIOUS ARTISTS (UNIVERSAL)	4	2007
DANCE MANIA 95 – VOLUME 1 VARIOUS ARTISTS (PURE MUSIC)	1	1995
DANCE MANIA 95 – VOLUME 2 VARIOUS ARTISTS (PURE MUSIC)	1	1995
DANCE MANIA 95 – VOLUME 3 VARIOUS ARTISTS (PURE MUSIC)	1	1995
DANCE MANIA 95 – VOLUME 4 VARIOUS ARTISTS (PURE MUSIC)	7	1995
DANCE MANIA VOLUME 1 VARIOUS ARTISTS (NEEDLE)	46	1987
DANCE MANIA VOLUME 2 VARIOUS ARTISTS (SERIOUS)	59	1988
DANCE MASSIVE VARIOUS ARTISTS (DINO)	3	1994
DANCE MASSIVE 2 VARIOUS ARTISTS (DINO)	8	1994
DANCE MASSIVE 95 VARIOUS ARTISTS (DINO)	2	1995
DANCE MASTERS VARIOUS ARTISTS (VIRGIN)	4	2001
DANCE MIX 2 VARIOUS ARTISTS (GLOBAL TELEVISION)	10	1996
DANCE MIX '87 VARIOUS ARTISTS (TELSTAR)	39	1987
DANCE MIX – DANCE HITS VOLUME 1 VARIOUS ARTISTS (EPIC)	85	1983
DANCE MIX – DANCE HITS VOLUME 2 VARIOUS ARTISTS (EPIC)	51	1983
DANCE MIX – DANCE HITS VOLUME 3 VARIOUS ARTISTS (EPIC)	70	1984
DANCE MIX – DANCE HITS VOLUME 4 VARIOUS ARTISTS (EPIC)	99	1984
DANCE MIX UK VARIOUS ARTISTS (GLOBAL TELEVISION)	6	1996
DANCE NATION VARIOUS ARTISTS (MINISTRY OF SOUND)	3	1996
DANCE NATION 3 – PETE TONG & JUDGE JULES VARIOUS ARTISTS (MINISTRY OF SOUND)	1	1997
DANCE NATION 4 – PETE TONG/BOY GEORGE VARIOUS ARTISTS (MINISTRY OF SOUND)	2	1997
DANCE NATION 6 – TALL PAUL & BRANDON BLOCK VARIOUS ARTISTS (MINISTRY OF SOUND)	1	1999
DANCE NATION '95 VARIOUS ARTISTS (VISION)	6	1995
DANCE NATION ANTHEMS VARIOUS ARTISTS (MINISTRY OF SOUND)	3	2002
DANCE NATION – TALL PAUL/BRANDON BLOCK VARIOUS ARTISTS (MINISTRY OF SOUND)	1	2000
DANCE OF DEATH IRON MAIDEN	2	2003
DANCE OF THE FLAMES INCANTATION	61	1983
DANCE PARADE IBIZA VARIOUS ARTISTS (WARNER BROTHERS)	14	2001
DANCE PARTY VARIOUS ARTISTS (UNIVERSAL)	1	2005
DANCE PARTY 2 VARIOUS ARTISTS (UNIVERSAL)	7	2008
DANCE TIP ' 95 VARIOUS ARTISTS (GLOBAL TELEVISION)	3	1995
DANCE TIP 2000 VARIOUS ARTISTS (GLOBAL TELEVISION)	7	1996
DANCE TIP 3 VARIOUS ARTISTS (GLOBAL TELEVISION)	2	1995
DANCE TIP 4 VARIOUS ARTISTS (GLOBAL TELEVISION)	7	1996
DANCE TO THE HOLY MAN SILENCERS	39	1991
DANCE TO THE MAX VARIOUS ARTISTS (VIRGIN)	2	1994
DANCE TO THE MAX 2 VARIOUS ARTISTS (VIRGIN)	4	1994
DANCE TO THE MAX 3 VARIOUS ARTISTS (VIRGIN)	12	1994
DANCE TO THE MUSIC VARIOUS ARTISTS (K-TEL)	5	1977
DANCE WARS – JUDGE JULES VS. JOHN KELLY VARIOUS ARTISTS (JDJ)	11	1996
DANCE WITH MY FATHER LUTHER VANDROSS	41	2003
DANCE WITH THE GUITAR MAN DUANE EDDY	14	1963
DANCE WITH THE SHADOWS SHADOWS	2	1964
DANCE ZONE '94 VARIOUS ARTISTS (POLYGRAM)	2	1994
DANCE ZONE '95 VARIOUS ARTISTS (POLYGRAM)	8	1995
DANCE ZONE LEVEL EIGHT VARIOUS ARTISTS (POLYGRAM)	4	1996
DANCE ZONE LEVEL FIVE VARIOUS ARTISTS (POLYGRAM)	1	1995
DANCE ZONE LEVEL FOUR VARIOUS ARTISTS (POLYGRAM)	1	1995
DANCE ZONE LEVEL NINE VARIOUS ARTISTS (POLYGRAM)	7	1997
DANCE ZONE – LEVEL ONE VARIOUS ARTISTS (POLYGRAM)	1	1994
DANCE ZONE LEVEL SEVEN VARIOUS ARTISTS (POLYGRAM)	1	1996
DANCE ZONE LEVEL SIX VARIOUS ARTISTS (POLYGRAM)	1	1995
DANCE ZONE – LEVEL THREE VARIOUS ARTISTS (POLYGRAM)	1	1994
DANCE ZONE – LEVEL TWO VARIOUS ARTISTS (POLYGRAM)	1	1994
DANCE...YA KNOW IT! BOBBY BROWN	26	1989

Title / Artist	Peak Position	Year of Release
DANCEHALL 4-PLAY VARIOUS ARTISTS (DMG TV)	20	2004
DANCEMIX 2008 VARIOUS ARTISTS (UNIVERSAL)	17	2008
DANCEMIX – SUMMER ANTHEMS VARIOUS ARTISTS (MINISTRY OF SOUND)	8	2007
DANCEMIX.UK.V1 VARIOUS ARTISTS (WARNER BROTHERS)	13	1999
DANCER WITH BRUISED KNEES KATE & ANNA McGARRIGLE	35	1977
DANCES WITH WOLVES (FILM SOUNDTRACK) JOHN BARRY	45	1991
DANCESTAR 2001 VARIOUS ARTISTS (INSPIRED)	12	2001
DANCIN' – 20 ORIGINAL MOTOWN MOVERS VARIOUS ARTISTS (TELSTAR)	97	1983
DANCIN' IN THE KEY OF LIFE STEVE ARRINGTON	41	1985
DANCIN' ON THE EDGE LITA FORD	96	1984
DANCING '68 VOLUME 1 JAMES LAST	40	1969
DANCING DOWN THE STONEY ROAD CHRIS REA	14	2002
DANCING IN THE STREET VARIOUS ARTISTS (UNIVERSAL)	13	1999
DANCING IN THE STREETS VARIOUS ARTISTS (UNIVERSAL)	8	2005
DANCING ON SUNSHINE VARIOUS ARTISTS (POLYGRAM)	4	1992
DANCING ON THE CEILING LIONEL RICHIE	2	1986
DANCING ON THE COUCH GO WEST	19	1987
DANCING UNDERCOVER RATT	51	1986
DANCING WITH STRANGERS CHRIS REA	2	1987
DANDY IN THE UNDERWORLD T. REX	26	1977
DANGER ZONE SAMMY HAGAR	25	1980
DANGER ZONE VARIOUS ARTISTS (POLYGRAM)	15	1997
DANGER ZONE VOLUME 1 VARIOUS ARTISTS (QUALITY TELEVISION)	16	1992
THE DANGERMAN SESSIONS – VOLUME 1 MADNESS	11	2005
DANGEROUS MICHAEL JACKSON	1	1991
DANGEROUS ACQUAINTANCES MARIANNE FAITHFULL	45	1981
DANGEROUS CURVES LITA FORD	51	1992
DANGEROUS MINDS FILM SOUNDTRACK	13	1996
DANGEROUS MUSIC ROBIN GEORGE	65	1985
DANGEROUSLY IN LOVE BEYONCE KNOWLES	1	2003
DANIEL IN BLUE JEANS DANIEL O'DONNELL	3	2003
THE DANIEL O'DONNELL IRISH COLLECTION DANIEL O'DONNELL	35	1996
DANIEL POWTER DANIEL POWTER	5	2005
DANNY RAMPLING – LOVE GROOVE DANCE PARTY VARIOUS ARTISTS (METROPOLE MUSIC)	10	1996
DANNY RAMPLING – LOVE GROOVE DANCE PARTY VARIOUS ARTISTS (UNIVERSAL)	15	2001
DANNY RAMPLING/LOVE GROOVE PARTY 5 & 6 VARIOUS ARTISTS (METROPOLE MUSIC)	12	1997
DANNY TENEAGLIA LIVE IN ATHENS VARIOUS ARTISTS (GLOBAL UNDERGROUND)	16	1999
DANNY THE DOG (OST) MASSIVE ATTACK	70	2004
DARE HUMAN LEAGUE	1	1981
DARE TO LOVE JIMMY SOMERVILLE	38	1995
DARING ADVENTURES RICHARD THOMPSON	92	1986
DARK DAYS COAL CHAMBER	43	2002
DARK DAYS IN PARADISE GARY MOORE	43	1997
DARK HORSE NICKELBACK	4	2008
THE DARK KNIGHT (OST) HANS ZIMMER & NEWTON HOWARD	67	2008
DARK LIGHT H.I.M.	18	2005
DARK ON FIRE TURIN BRAKES	36	2007
DARK PASSION PLAY NIGHTWISH	25	2007
DARK SIDE OF THE 80'S VARIOUS ARTISTS (TELSTAR)	4	2003
THE DARK SIDE OF THE MOON PINK FLOYD	2	1973
DARKDANCER LES RHYTHMES DIGITALES	53	1999
DARKLANDS JESUS & MARY CHAIN	5	1987
DARKNESS ON THE EDGE OF TOWN BRUCE SPRINGSTEEN	16	1978
DARREN DAY DARREN DAY	62	1998
DART ATTACK DARTS	38	1979
DARTS DARTS	9	1977
A DATE WITH DANIEL – LIVE DANIEL O'DONNELL	21	1993
A DATE WITH ELVIS ELVIS PRESLEY	4	1959
A DATE WITH ELVIS CRAMPS	34	1986
A DATE WITH THE EVERLY BROTHERS EVERLY BROTHERS	3	1961
THE DATSUNS DATSUNS	17	2002
DAUGHTER OF TIME COLOSSEUM	23	1970
DAUGHTRY DAUGHTRY	13	2007
DAVE CLARK'S TIME THE ALBUM (ORIGINAL STUDIO CAST RECORDING) STAGE CAST RECORDING	21	1986
DAVE DEE, DOZY, BEAKY, MICK AND TICH DAVE DEE, DOZY, BEAKY, MICK & TICH	11	1966
DAVE PEARCE DANCE ANTHEMS VARIOUS ARTISTS (MINISTRY OF SOUND)	3	2007
DAVE PEARCE – DANCE ANTHEMS 2007 VARIOUS ARTISTS (MINISTRY OF SOUND)	4	2007
DAVE PEARCE – DANCE ANTHEMS – CLASSICS VARIOUS ARTISTS (MINISTRY OF SOUND)	4	2006
DAVE PEARCE DANCE ANTHEMS SPRING 2004 VARIOUS ARTISTS (INSPIRED)	3	2004
DAVE PEARCE DANCE ANTHEMS – SUMMER 2003 VARIOUS ARTISTS (BMG)	6	2003
DAVE PEARCE PRESENTS 40 CLASSIC ANTHEMS – 3 VARIOUS ARTISTS (UNIVERSAL)	7	2000
DAVE PEARCE PRESENTS 40 CLASSIC DANCE ANTHEMS VARIOUS ARTISTS (UNIVERSAL)	5	1999
DAVE PEARCE PRESENTS 40 CLASSIC DANCE ANTHEMS 2 VARIOUS ARTISTS (UNIVERSAL)	7	1999
DAVE PEARCE PRESENTS DANCE ANTHEMS VARIOUS ARTISTS (POLYGRAM)	4	1998
DAVE PEARCE PRESENTS DANCE ANTHEMS VOLUME 2 VARIOUS ARTISTS (POLYGRAM)	5	1998
DAVE PEARCE TRANCE ANTHEMS 2008 VARIOUS ARTISTS (MINISTRY OF SOUND)	3	2008
DAVE STEWART AND THE SPIRITUAL COWBOYS DAVE STEWART & THE SPIRITUAL COWBOYS	38	1990
DAVID BYRNE DAVID BYRNE	44	1994
DAVID ESSEX DAVID ESSEX	2	1974
THE DAVID ESSEX ALBUM DAVID ESSEX	29	1979
DAVID GATES AND BREAD: ESSENTIALS DAVID GATES & BREAD	9	1997
DAVID GILMOUR DAVID GILMOUR	17	1978
DAVID GRANT DAVID GRANT	32	1983
DAVID LIVE DAVID BOWIE	2	1974
DAVID MCWILLIAMS SINGS DAVID McWILLIAMS	38	1967
DAVID MCWILLIAMS VOLUME 2 DAVID McWILLIAMS	23	1967
DAVID MCWILLIAMS VOLUME 3 DAVID McWILLIAMS	39	1968
DAVID SOUL DAVID SOUL	2	1976
DAWN OF THE DICKIES DICKIES	60	1979
DAWNRAZOR FIELDS OF THE NEPHILIM	62	1987
THE DAY BABYFACE	34	1996
DAY & AGE KILLERS	1	2008
A DAY AT THE RACES QUEEN	1	1976
A DAY IN THE LIFE ERIC BENET	67	1999
A DAY WITHOUT RAIN ENYA	6	2000
DAYBREAKER BETH ORTON	8	2002
DAYDREAM LOVIN' SPOONFUL	8	1966
DAYDREAM MARIAH CAREY	1	1995
DAYDREAM ANONYMOUS INME	71	2007
DAYDREAM NATION SONIC YOUTH	99	1988
DAYS GO BY KEITH URBAN	40	2005
DAYS IN EUROPA SKIDS	32	1979
DAYS LIKE THIS VAN MORRISON	5	1995
DAYS OF FUTURE PASSED MOODY BLUES	27	1968
DAYS OF OPEN HAND SUZANNE VEGA	7	1990
DAYS OF SPEED PAUL WELLER	3	2001
DAYS OF THUNDER FILM SOUNDTRACK	4	1990
DAYTIME FRIENDS – THE VERY BEST OF KENNY ROGERS KENNY ROGERS	16	1993
DAZZLE SHIPS ORCHESTRAL MANOEUVRES IN THE DARK	5	1983
DE 7 DAVE EDMUNDS	60	1982
DE LA SOUL IS DEAD DE LA SOUL	7	1991
DE NINA A MUJER JULIO IGLESIAS	43	1981
THE DEAD 60'S DEAD 60'S	23	2005
DEAD BEES ON A CAKE DAVID SYLVIAN	31	1999
DEAD CITIES FUTURE SOUND OF LONDON	26	1996
DEAD ELVIS DEATH IN VEGAS	52	1997
DEAD LETTER OFFICE R.E.M.	60	1987
DEAD LETTERS RASMUS	10	2004
DEAD RINGER MEAT LOAF	1	1981
DEADLINE FOR MY MEMORIES BILLIE RAY MARTIN	47	1996
DEAN MARTIN'S GREATEST HITS VOLUME I DEAN MARTIN	40	1968
DEAR CATASTROPHE WAITRESS BELLE & SEBASTIAN	21	2003
DEAR HEATHER LEONARD COHEN	34	2004
DEAR PERRY PERRY COMO	6	1958
DEAR SCIENCE TV ON THE RADIO	33	2008
DEATH IS NOT THE END SHUT UP & DANCE	38	1992
DEATH MAGNETIC METALLICA	1	2008
DEATH OF A LADIES MAN LEONARD COHEN	35	1977
THE DEATH OF COOL KITCHENS OF DISTINCTION	72	1992
DEATH ON THE ROAD IRON MAIDEN	22	2005
DEATH ROW PRESENTS A HIP HOP HISTORY VARIOUS ARTISTS (UNIVERSAL)	14	2005
DEATH TO THE PIXIES PIXIES	28	1997
DEATH TO THE PIXIES – DELUXE EDITION PIXIES	20	1997
DEATH WALKS BEHIND YOU ATOMIC ROOSTER	12	1971
DEATHWISH II (OST) JIMMY PAGE	40	1982
DEBRAVATION DEBORAH HARRY	24	1993
DEBUT BJORK	3	1993
DECADE NEIL YOUNG	15	1977
DECADE DURAN DURAN	5	1989
A DECADE IN THE SUN – BEST OF STEREOPHONICS	2	2008
DECADE OF AGGRESSION – LIVE SLAYER	29	1991
A DECADE OF DANCE VARIOUS ARTISTS (POSITIVA)	11	2003
DECADE OF DECADENCE '81-'91 MOTLEY CRUE	20	1991
A DECADE OF IBIZA – 1987-1997 VARIOUS ARTISTS (TELSTAR)	5	1997
DECADES – STORY OF THE 60'S/70'S/80'S VARIOUS ARTISTS (VIRGIN)	13	2000
THE DECCA ANTHOLOGY 1965-1967 SMALL FACES	66	1996
DECEMBERUNDERGROUND AFI	16	2006
DECENCY DIESEL PARK WEST	57	1992
DECEPTION COLOUR FIELD	95	1987
DECEPTIVE BENDS 10 C.C.	3	1977
DECKSANDRUMSANDROCKANDROLL PROPELLERHEADS	6	1998

Title / Artist	Peak Position	Year of Release
DECLAN DECLAN	44	2002
DECLARATION ALARM	6	1984
THE DECLINE OF BRITISH SEA POWER BRITISH SEA POWER	54	2003
DECONSTRUCTION CLASSICS – A HISTORY OF DANCE MUSIC VARIOUS ARTISTS (DECONSTRUCTION)	17	1995
DEDICATED LEMAR	16	2003
DEDICATED TO PLEASURE VARIOUS ARTISTS (EMI)	18	1995
DEDICATION BAY CITY ROLLERS	4	1976
DEDICATION GARY U.S. BONDS	43	1981
DEDICATION – THE VERY BEST OF THIN LIZZY THIN LIZZY	8	1991
DEEP & CHILLED EUPHORIA VARIOUS ARTISTS (TELSTAR)	5	2001
DEEP AND MEANINGLESS JOHN OTWAY & WILD WILLY BARRETT	44	1978
DEEP DOWN AND DIRTY STEREO MC'S	17	2001
DEEP FOREST DEEP FOREST	15	1994
DEEP HEAT 10 – THE AWAKENING VARIOUS ARTISTS (TELSTAR)	2	1991
DEEP HEAT 11 – SPIRIT OF ECSTASY VARIOUS ARTISTS (TELSTAR)	3	1991
DEEP HEAT 1989 – FIGHT THE FLAME VARIOUS ARTISTS (TELSTAR)	4	1989
DEEP HEAT – 26 HOTTEST HOUSE HITS VARIOUS ARTISTS (TELSTAR)	1	1989
DEEP HEAT 3 – THE THIRD DEGREE VARIOUS ARTISTS (TELSTAR)	2	1989
DEEP HEAT 4 – PLAY WITH FIRE VARIOUS ARTISTS (TELSTAR)	1	1989
DEEP HEAT 5 – FEED THE FEVER – 32 HOTTEST CLUB HITS VARIOUS ARTISTS (TELSTAR)	1	1990
DEEP HEAT 6 – THE SIXTH SENSE VARIOUS ARTISTS (TELSTAR)	1	1990
DEEP HEAT 7 – SEVENTH HEAVEN VARIOUS ARTISTS (TELSTAR)	1	1990
DEEP HEAT 8 – THE HAND OF FATE VARIOUS ARTISTS (TELSTAR)	3	1990
DEEP HEAT 9 – NINTH LIFE – KISS THE BLISS VARIOUS ARTISTS (TELSTAR)	1	1991
DEEP HEAT 90 VARIOUS ARTISTS (TELSTAR)	3	1990
DEEP HEAT 93 VOLUME 1 VARIOUS ARTISTS (TELSTAR)	2	1993
DEEP HEAT – THE SECOND BURN VARIOUS ARTISTS (TELSTAR)	2	1989
DEEP IN THE HEART OF NOWHERE BOB GELDOF	79	1986
DEEP PURPLE DONNY & MARIE OSMOND	48	1976
DEEP PURPLE IN ROCK DEEP PURPLE	4	1970
DEEP PURPLE LIVE DEEP PURPLE	12	1976
DEEP PURPLE LIVE IN LONDON DEEP PURPLE	23	1982
DEEP SEA SKIVING BANANARAMA	7	1983
DEEP WITHIN MY SOUL SISSEL	58	1995
DEEPER – EUPHORIA II: MIXED BY RED JERRY VARIOUS ARTISTS (TELSTAR)	2	1999
DEEPER SHADES OF EUPHORIA VARIOUS ARTISTS (TELSTAR)	6	2003
THE DEEPEST CUT – VOLUME 1 OMNI TRIO	60	1995
DEEPEST PURPLE DEEP PURPLE	1	1980
DEF DUMB AND BLONDE DEBORAH HARRY	12	1989
DEFECTED IN THE HOUSE – MIAMI 06 VARIOUS ARTISTS (IN THE HOUSE)	20	2006
DEFECTED IN THE HOUSE – MIAMI 07 VARIOUS ARTISTS (DEFECTED)	19	2007
DEFECTOR STEVE HACKETT	9	1980
DEFENDERS OF THE FAITH JUDAS PRIEST	19	1984
DEFINITELY MAYBE OASIS	1	1994
THE DEFINITION LL COOL J	66	2004
THE DEFINITIVE MONKEES	15	2001
THE DEFINITIVE RAY CHARLES	13	2001

Title / Artist	Peak Position	Year of Release
DEFINITIVE INXS	15	2002
THE DEFINITIVE EVERLY BROTHERS	10	2002
THE DEFINITIVE DRIFTERS	8	2003
THE DEFINITIVE FOREIGNER	33	2005
THE DEFINITIVE ALICE COOPER ALICE COOPER	33	2001
THE DEFINITIVE COLLECTION KINKS	18	1993
THE DEFINITIVE COLLECTION ABBA	17	2001
THE DEFINITIVE COLLECTION STEVIE WONDER	11	2002
THE DEFINITIVE COLLECTION LIONEL RICHIE/ COMMODORES	10	2003
THE DEFINITIVE COLLECTION BLUES BROTHERS	64	2004
THE DEFINITIVE COLLECTION MARIO LANZA	41	2004
THE DEFINITIVE COLLECTION OLIVIA NEWTON-JOHN	11	2004
DEFINITIVE COLLECTION TONY CHRISTIE	1	2005
THE DEFINITIVE COLLECTION LEVEL 42	20	2006
THE DEFINITIVE COLLECTION & TIMELESS SMOKEY ROBINSON	39	2006
THE DEFINITIVE DON WILLIAMS: HIS GREATEST HITS DON WILLIAMS	26	2006
THE DEFINITIVE ELECTRO & HIP HOP VARIOUS ARTISTS (UNIVERSAL)	19	2004
THE DEFINITIVE FRANKIE VALLI & THE FOUR SEASONS FRANKIE VALLI & THE FOUR SEASONS	26	2001
THE DEFINITIVE HITS COLLECTION LEO SAYER	35	1999
THE DEFINITIVE JIM REEVES JIM REEVES	9	1992
THE DEFINITIVE PATSY CLINE 1932-1963 PATSY CLINE	11	1992
THE DEFINITIVE SIMON AND GARFUNKEL SIMON & GARFUNKEL	8	1991
THE DEFINITIVE SINGLES COLLECTION A-HA	14	2005
THE DEFINITIVE SOUND OF ATLANTIC SOUL VARIOUS ARTISTS (WARNER BROTHERS)	18	1999
DEFTONES DEFTONES	7	2003
DEHUMANIZER BLACK SABBATH	28	1992
DÉJÀ VU CROSBY, STILL, NASH & YOUNG	5	1970
DÉJÀ VU A.B.'S	80	1984
DELICATE SOUND OF THUNDER PINK FLOYD	11	1988
DELILAH TOM JONES	1	1968
THE DELINQUENTS FILM SOUNDTRACK	16	1990
DELIVER US FROM EVIL BUDGIE	62	1982
DELIVERANCE BABY D	5	1996
THE DELIVERY MAN ELVIS COSTELLO & THE IMPOSTERS	73	2004
DE-LOUSED IN THE COMATORIUM MARS VOLTA	43	2003
DELTICS CHRIS REA	54	1979
DEMANUFACTURE FEAR FACTORY	27	1995
DEMOCRACY KILLING JOKE	71	1996
DEMOLITION GIRLSCHOOL	28	1980
DEMOLITION RYAN ADAMS	22	2002
DEMON DAYS GORILLAZ	1	2005
DEMONS AND WIZARDS URIAH HEEP	20	1972
DENIM AND LEATHER SAXON	9	1981
DEPARTURE TAIO CRUZ	17	2008
DEREK AND CLIVE LIVE PETER COOK & DUDLEY MOORE	12	1976
DEREK AND THE DOMINOS IN CONCERT DEREK & THE DOMINOS	36	1973
DERELICTS OF DIALECT 3RD BASS	46	1991
DES O'CONNOR NOW DES O'CONNOR	24	1984
DESENSITIZED DROWNING POOL	66	2004
DESERTER'S SONG MERCURY REV	27	1998
DESIGN OF A DECADE 1986 – 1996 JANET JACKSON	2	1995
DESIRE BOB DYLAN	3	1976
DESIRE WALKS ON HEART	32	1993
DESIRELESS EAGLE-EYE CHERRY	3	1998

Title / Artist	Peak Position	Year of Release
DESOLATION ANGELS BAD COMPANY	10	1979
DESPERADO EAGLES	39	1975
DESPITE YOURSELF HEADSWIM	24	1998
DESTINATION RONAN KEATING	1	2002
DESTINATION ANYWHERE JON BON JOVI	2	1997
DESTINY JACKSONS	33	1979
DESTINY CHAKA KHAN	77	1986
DESTINY SAXON	49	1988
DESTINY GLORIA ESTEFAN	12	1996
DESTINY FULFILLED DESTINY'S CHILD	5	2004
DESTINY'S CHILD DESTINY'S CHILD	45	1998
DESTINY'S SONGS AND THE IMAGE OF PURSUANCE COURTNEY PINE	54	1988
DESTROY ROCK N ROLL MYLO	26	2005
DESTROYER KISS	22	1976
DETONATOR RATT	55	1990
DETOURS SHERYL CROW	20	2008
DETROIT SPINNERS' SMASH HITS DETROIT SPINNERS	37	1977
DEUCE RORY GALLAGHER	39	1971
D'EUX – THE FRENCH ALBUM CELINE DION	7	1995
DEVIANT PITCHSHIFTER	35	2000
DEVIL HOPPING INSPIRAL CARPETS	10	1994
THE DEVIL IN SISTER GEORGE BOY GEORGE/ JESUS LOVES YOU/CULTURE CLUB	26	1994
DEVILS & DUST BRUCE SPRINGSTEEN	1	2005
DEVILS & ANGELS MELEE	61	2008
DEVIL'S NIGHT D12	2	2001
DEVINE TIME SIDNEY DEVINE	49	1976
D-FROST – 20 GLOBAL DANCE WARNINGS VARIOUS ARTISTS (TOUCHDOWN)	8	1993
DIABOLUS IN MUSICA SLAYER	27	1998
DIAMOND SPANDAU BALLET	15	1982
DIAMOND DOGS DAVID BOWIE	1	1974
DIAMOND HEAD PHIL MANZANERA	40	1975
DIAMOND HOO HA SUPERGRASS	19	2008
DIAMOND LIFE SADE	2	1984
DIAMONDS AND PEARLS PRINCE & THE NEW POWER GENERATION	2	1991
DIANA (OST-TV) DIANA ROSS	43	1971
DIANA DIANA ROSS	12	1980
DIANA AND MARVIN DIANA ROSS & MARVIN GAYE	6	1974
DIANA EXTENDED – THE REMIXES DIANA ROSS	58	1994
DIANA PRINCESS OF WALES 1961-1997 – FUNERAL SERVICE (ROYAL COMPILATION ALBUM) ROYAL COMPILATION ALBUM	3	1997
DIANA PRINCESS OF WALES – TRIBUTE (ROYAL COMPILATION ALBUM) ROYAL COMPILATION ALBUM	1	1997
DIANA ROSS DIANA ROSS	14	1970
DIANA ROSS DIANA ROSS	4	1976
DIANA ROSS AND THE SUPREMES 20 GOLDEN GREATS DIANA ROSS & THE SUPREMES	1	1977
DIANA ROSS AND THE SUPREMES GREATEST HITS DIANA ROSS & THE SUPREMES	1	1968
DIANA ROSS AND THE SUPREMES JOIN THE TEMPTATIONS DIANA ROSS & THE SUPREMES & THE TEMPTATIONS	1	1969
DIANA ROSS LIVE AT CAESAR'S PALACE DIANA ROSS	21	1974
DIANA ROSS PRESENTS THE JACKSON FIVE JACKSON FIVE	16	1970
DIANA ROSS. MICHAEL JACKSON. GLADYS KNIGHT. STEVIE WONDER. THEIR VERY BEST BACK TO BACK DIANA ROSS/ MICHAEL JACKSON/GLADYS KNIGHT/ STEVIE WONDER	21	1986
DIANA'S DUETS DIANA ROSS	43	1982
THE DIARY OF A BAND VOLUME 1 JOHN MAYALL & THE BLUESBREAKERS	27	1968

Title / Artist	Peak Position	Year of Release
THE DIARY OF A BAND VOLUME 2 JOHN MAYALL & THE BLUESBREAKERS	28	1968
DIARY OF A HOLLOW HORSE CHINA CRISIS	58	1989
DIARY OF A MADMAN OZZY OSBOURNE	14	1981
THE DIARY OF ALICIA KEYS ALICIA KEYS	13	2003
DIATRIBES NAPALM DEATH	74	1996
DID YOU EVER NANCY SINATRA & LEE HAZLEWOOD	31	1972
DIESEL AND DUST MIDNIGHT OIL	19	1988
A DIFFERENT BEAT BOYZONE	1	1996
DIFFERENT CLASS PULP	1	1995
A DIFFERENT KIND OF TENSION BUZZCOCKS	26	1979
DIFFERENT LIGHT BANGLES	3	1986
DIFFICULT SHAPES AND PASSIVE RHYTHMS SOME PEOPLE THINK IT'S FUN TO ENTERTAIN CHINA CRISIS	21	1982
DIFFICULT TO CURE RAINBOW	3	1981
DIFFORD AND TILBROOK DIFFORD & TILBROOK	47	1984
DIG OUT YOUR SOUL OASIS	1	2008
DIG THE NEW BREED JAM	2	1982
DIG YOUR OWN HOLE CHEMICAL BROTHERS	1	1997
DIG!!! LAZARUS DIG!!! NICE CAVE & THE BAD SEEDS	4	2008
DIGIMORTAL FEAR FACTORY	24	2001
DIGITAL ASH IN A DIGITAL URN BRIGHT EYES	43	2005
DIGNITY HILARY DUFF	25	2007
DIMENSION INTRUSION F.U.S.E.	63	1993
DIMINISHED RESPONSIBILITY U.K. SUBS	18	1981
DINGLY DELL LINDISFARNE	5	1972
DINO – THE ESSENTIAL DEAN MARTIN DEAN MARTIN	25	2004
THE DIONNE WARWICK COLLECTION DIONNE WARWICK	11	1983
DIRE STRAITS DIRE STRAITS	5	1978
DIRECT HITS VARIOUS ARTISTS (TELSTAR)	89	1982
DIRECTION REACTION CREATION JAM	8	1997
DIRK WEARS WHITE SOX ADAM & THE ANTS	16	1981
DIRT ALICE IN CHAINS	42	1992
DIRTY SONIC YOUTH	6	1992
THE DIRTY BOOTS EP – PLUS 5 LIVE TRACKS SONIC YOUTH	69	1991
DIRTY DANCING FILM SOUNDTRACK	1	1987
DIRTY DANCING – LIVE IN CONCERT VARIOUS ARTISTS (RCA)	19	1989
DIRTY HITS PRIMAL SCREAM	25	2003
DIRTY VEGAS DIRTY VEGAS	40	2002
DIRTY WORK ROLLING STONES	4	1986
DISCIPLINE KING CRIMSON	41	1981
DISCIPLINE JANET JACKSON	63	2008
DISCO PET SHOP BOYS	15	1986
DISCO 2 PET SHOP BOYS	6	1994
DISCO 3 PET SHOP BOYS	36	2003
DISCO 4 – REMIXED BY THE PET SHOP BOYS VARIOUS ARTISTS (PARLOPHONE)	15	2007
DISCO BABY VAN McCOY & THE SOUL CITY SYMPHONY	32	1975
DISCO BEACH PARTY VARIOUS ARTISTS (STYLUS)	29	1985
DISCO CLASSICS VARIOUS ARTISTS (MINISTRY OF SOUND)	9	2004
DISCO DANCER VARIOUS ARTISTS (K-TEL)	26	1982
DISCO DAZE AND DISCO NITES VARIOUS ARTISTS (RONCO)	1	1981
DISCO DIVAS VARIOUS ARTISTS (POLYGRAM)	4	1993
DISCO DOUBLE VARIOUS ARTISTS (K-TEL)	10	1978
DISCO EROTICA VARIOUS ARTISTS (WARWICK)	35	1981
DISCO FEVER VARIOUS ARTISTS (K-TEL)	1	1977
DISCO FEVER VARIOUS ARTISTS (GLOBAL TELEVISION)	19	2000
DISCO FEVER VARIOUS ARTISTS (UNIVERSAL)	4	2001
DISCO FEVER – VOLUME 2 VARIOUS ARTISTS (UNIVERSAL)	9	2001
DISCO HEAVEN VARIOUS ARTISTS (HED KANDI)	18	2005
DISCO HEAVEN 01.04 VARIOUS ARTISTS (HED KANDI)	18	2004
DISCO HITS '75 VARIOUS ARTISTS (ARCADE)	5	1975
DISCO HOUSE VARIOUS ARTISTS (GLOBAL TELEVISION)	7	1999
DISCO INFERNO VARIOUS ARTISTS (K-TEL)	11	1979
DISCO INFERNO VARIOUS ARTISTS (EAST WEST)	17	1993
DISCO INFERNO VARIOUS ARTISTS (WARNER BROTHERS)	16	1995
DISCO KANDI VARIOUS ARTISTS (HED KANDI)	15	2006
DISCO KANDI 05.03 VARIOUS ARTISTS (HED KANDI)	17	2003
DISCO KANDI 05.04 VARIOUS ARTISTS (HED KANDI)	19	2004
DISCO MIX 96 VARIOUS ARTISTS (WARNER BROTHERS)	7	1996
DISCO ROCKET VARIOUS ARTISTS (K-TEL)	3	1976
DISCO STARS VARIOUS ARTISTS (K-TEL)	6	1978
DISCO UK AND DISCO USA VARIOUS ARTISTS (RONCO)	7	1982
DISCO: 1999 VARIOUS ARTISTS (VIRGIN)	13	1999
DISCOGRAPHY PET SHOP BOYS	3	1991
DISCOMANIA VARIOUS ARTISTS (MERCURY)	7	2004
DISCOTRAIN DONNY OSMOND	59	1976
DISCOVER GENE LOVES JEZEBEL	32	1986
DISCOVER COUNTRY/DISCOVER NEW COUNTRY VARIOUS ARTISTS (STARBLEND)	60	1986
DISCOVER THE CLASSICS VOLUME 1 VARIOUS ARTISTS (IMP CLASSICS)	15	1992
DISCOVER THE CLASSICS VOLUME 2 VARIOUS ARTISTS (IMP CLASSICS)	12	1992
DISCOVERY ELECTRIC LIGHT ORCHESTRA	1	1979
DISCOVERY MIKE OLDFIELD	15	1984
DISCOVERY DAFT PUNK	2	2001
DISGRACEFUL DUBSTAR	30	1995
DISINTEGRATION CURE	3	1989
THE DISNEY EXPERIENCE VARIOUS ARTISTS (WALT DISNEY)	12	1998
DISNEY'S GREATEST HITS VARIOUS ARTISTS (TELSTAR)	19	2000
DISNEY'S GREATEST HITS VARIOUS ARTISTS (WALT DISNEY)	14	2005
DISNEY'S HIT SINGLES & MORE! VARIOUS ARTISTS (WALT DISNEY)	9	1997
DISRAELI GEARS CREAM	5	1967
THE DISTANCE BOB SEGER & THE SILVER BULLET BAND	45	1983
THE DISTANCE TO HERE LIVE	56	1999
DISTANT DREAMS KAREN RAMIREZ	45	1998
DISTANT DRUMS JIM REEVES	2	1966
DISTANT THUNDER ASWAD	10	1988
DISTURBING THA PEACE PRESENTS BOBBY VALENTINO	34	2005
DIVA ANNIE LENNOX	1	1992
DIVA – THE ULTIMATE COLLECTION MARIA CALLAS	61	1996
DIVAS VARIOUS ARTISTS (SONY BMG)	7	2007
THE DIVAS OF DANCE VARIOUS ARTISTS (TELSTAR)	9	1992
DIVAS OF JAZZ VARIOUS ARTISTS (VERVE)	12	2003
DIVE DEEP QUINTESSENCE	43	1971
DIVE DEEP MORCHEEBA	59	2008
DIVE IN DARIUS	6	2002
DIVER DOWN VAN HALEN	36	1982
DIVINE EMOTION NARADA	60	1988
DIVINE INTERVENTION SLAYER	15	1994
DIVINE MADNESS MADNESS	1	1992
DIVINE WORKS DIVINE WORKS	43	1997
DIVINYLS DIVINYLS	59	1991
THE DIVISION BELL PINK FLOYD	1	1994
DIY SONGS VARIOUS ARTISTS (EMI)	4	2006
DIZZY HEIGHTS LIGHTNING SEEDS	11	1996
DIZZY UP THE GIRL GOO GOO DOLLS	47	1999
DJ LUCK & MC NEAT PRESENT VOLUME 3 VARIOUS ARTISTS (UNIVERSAL)	7	2001
DJ LUCK & MC NEAT PRESENTS VARIOUS ARTISTS (UNIVERSAL)	6	2000
DJ LUCK & MC NEAT PRESENTS – II VARIOUS ARTISTS (UNIVERSAL)	4	2001
DO A RUNNER ATHLETICO SPIZZ 80	27	1980
DO IT AGAIN – THE VERY BEST OF STEELY DAN STEELY DAN	64	1987
DO IT FOR LOVE DARYL HALL & JOHN OATES	37	2003
DO IT YOURSELF IAN DURY & THE BLOCKHEADS	2	1979
DO IT YOURSELF SEAHORSES	2	1997
DO ME AGAIN FREDDIE JACKSON	48	1990
DO YOU LIKE ROCK MUSIC BRITISH SEA POWER	10	2008
DOCK OF THE BAY OTIS REDDING	1	1968
DOCK OF THE BAY – THE DEFINITIVE COLLECTION OTIS REDDING	44	1993
DOCTOR ADAMSKI'S MUSICAL PHARMACY ADAMSKI	8	1990
DOCTOR WHO – SERIES 3 – OST MURRAY GOLD	65	2007
DOCTOR WHO – THE EVIL OF THE DALEKS (RADIO SOUNDTRACK) DOCTOR WHO	72	1992
DOCTOR WHO – THE PARADISE OF DEATH (RADIO SOUNDTRACK) DOCTOR WHO	48	1993
DOCTOR WHO – THE POWER OF THE DALEKS (TELEVISION SOUNDTRACK) DOCTOR WHO	71	1993
DOCTOR ZHIVAGO (OST) MAURICE JARRE	3	1966
DOCTOR'S ADVOCATE THE GAME	21	2006
DOCUMENT R.E.M.	28	1987
THE DOCUMENTARY THE GAME	7	2005
THE DODGY ALBUM DODGY	75	1993
DOES THIS LOOK INFECTED SUM 41	39	2002
DOG EAT DOG JONI MITCHELL	57	1985
DOG EAT DOG WARRANT	74	1992
DOG HOUSE MUSIC SEASICK STEVE	47	2008
DOG MAN STAR SUEDE	3	1994
DOGG FOOD THA DOGG POUND	66	1995
DOGGYSTYLE SNOOP DOGGY DOGG	38	1993
DOGMAN KING'S X	49	1994
DOG'S HITS AND THE BOOTLEG ALBUM DOGS D'AMOUR	58	1991
DOGS IN THE TRAFFIC LOVE & MONEY	41	1991
THE DOG'S...! VARIOUS ARTISTS (EMI)	20	1996
DOING IT MY WAY RAY QUINN	1	2007
DOL DOMINATION PUSSYCAT DOLLS	4	2008
DOLL REVOLUTION BANGLES	62	2003
THE DOLLAR ALBUM DOLLAR	18	1982
DOLLARS C.J. LEWIS	44	1994
THE DOM KILLUMINATI – THE SEVEN DAY THEORY MAKAVELI	53	1996
DOMINATOR TIME FREQUENCY	23	1994
DOMINGO: ARIAS AND SPANISH SONGS PLACIDO DOMINGO	47	1992
THE DOMINO CLUB MEN THEY COULDN'T HANG	53	1990
DOMINO THEORY WEATHER REPORT	54	1984
DON JUAN'S RECKLESS DAUGHTER JONI MITCHELL	20	1978
DON QUIXOTE GORDON LIGHTFOOT	44	1972
DONE AND DUSTED DUST JUNKYS	35	1998
DONE BY THE FORCES OF NATURE JUNGLE BROTHERS	41	1990
DONKEY CSS	32	2008
DONNA SUMMER DONNA SUMMER	13	1982

Title / Artist	Peak Position	Year of Release
DONNY DONNY OSMOND	16	1975
DON'T ASK TINA ARENA	11	1995
DON'T BE AFRAID OF THE DARK ROBERT CRAY BAND	13	1988
DON'T BE CRUEL BOBBY BROWN	3	1989
DON'T BELIEVE THE TRUTH OASIS	1	2005
DON'T BORE US, GET TO THE CHORUS! – GREATEST HITS ROXETTE	5	1995
DON'T EXPLAIN ROBERT PALMER	9	1990
DON'T GET WEIRD ON ME BABE LLOYD COLE	21	1991
DON'T LET IT GO TO WASTE MATT WILLIS	66	2006
DON'T LET LOVE SLIP AWAY FREDDIE JACKSON	24	1988
DON'T LOOK ANY FURTHER DENNIS EDWARDS	91	1984
DON'T LOOK BACK BOSTON	9	1978
DON'T LOOK BACK JOHN LEE HOOKER	63	1997
DON'T MIND IF I DO CULTURE CLUB	64	1999
DON'T POINT YOUR FINGER 9 BELOW ZERO	56	1981
DON'T SHOOT ME I'M ONLY THE PIANO PLAYER ELTON JOHN	1	1973
DON'T STAND ME DOWN DEXYS MIDNIGHT RUNNERS	22	1985
DON'T STOP JEFFREY OSBORNE	59	1984
DON'T STOP DANCING VARIOUS ARTISTS (TELSTAR)	11	1984
DON'T STOP ME NOW... CLIFF RICHARD	23	1967
DON'T STOP MOVIN' LIVIN' JOY	41	1996
DON'T STOP – THE 30TH ANNIVERSARY ALBUM STATUS QUO	2	1996
DON'T STOP THE MUSIC VARIOUS ARTISTS (STYLUS)	7	1989
DON'T STOP...DOOWOP! VARIOUS ARTISTS (TELSTAR)	15	1991
DON'T SUPPOSE LIMAHL	63	1984
DON'T SWEAT THE TECHNIQUE ERIC B & RAKIM	73	1992
DON'T TALK CLARE TEAL	20	2004
DON'T THINK TWICE IT'S ALL RIGHT BARBARA DICKSON	32	1992
DON'T TRY THIS AT HOME BILLY BRAGG	8	1991
DON'T WALK – BOOGIE VARIOUS ARTISTS (EMI)	1	1978
DOOKIE GREEN DAY	13	1994
DOOLITTLE PIXIES	8	1989
DOOR TO DOOR CARS	72	1987
THE DOORS DOORS	11	1991
DOOWUTCHYALIKE/PACKET MAN DIGITAL UNDERGROUND	59	1990
DOPES TO INFINITY MONSTER MAGNET	51	1995
DOPPELGANGER KID CREOLE & THE COCONUTS	21	1983
DOPPELGANGER CURVE	11	1992
DOREMI FASOL LATIDO HAWKWIND	14	1972
DOS DEDOS MIS AMIGOS POP WILL EAT ITSELF	11	1994
DOTS AND LOOPS STEREOLAB	19	1997
DOUBLE BARREL DAVE & ANSIL COLLINS	41	1971
DOUBLE DEVINE SIDNEY DEVINE	14	1976
DOUBLE DYNAMITE SAM & DAVE	28	1967
DOUBLE FANTASY JOHN LENNON & YOKO ONO	1	1980
DOUBLE LIVE GARTH BROOKS	57	1998
DOUBLE LIVE GONZO! TED NUGENT	47	1978
DOUBLE TROUBLE ELVIS PRESLEY	34	1967
DOUBLE TROUBLE GILLAN	12	1981
DOUBLE TROUBLE – LIVE MOLLY HATCHET	94	1986
DOUBLE UP MASE	47	1999
DOUBLE UP R KELLY	10	2007
DOUBLE VISION FOREIGNER	32	1978
DOUBLE WIDE UNCLE KRACKER	40	2001
DOUBT JESUS JONES	1	1991
DOUG LAZY GETTIN' CRAZY DOUG LAZY	65	1990
DOUGHNUT IN GRANNY'S GREENHOUSE BONZO DOG DOO-DAH BAND	40	1969
DOWN JESUS LIZARD	64	1994
DOWN AND OUT BLUES SONNY BOY WILLIAMSON	20	1964
DOWN DRURY LANE TO MEMORY LANE 101 STRINGS	1	1960
DOWN FALL THE GOOD GUYS WOLFSBANE	53	1991
DOWN IN ALBION BABYSHAMBLES	10	2005
DOWN IN THE GROOVE BOB DYLAN	32	1988
DOWN MEXICO WAY HERB ALPERT & THE TIJUANA BRASS	64	1970
DOWN ON THE FARM LITTLE FEAT	46	1979
DOWN ON THE STREET SHAKATAK	17	1984
DOWN ON THE UPSIDE SOUNDGARDEN	7	1996
DOWN THE DUSTPIPE STATUS QUO	20	1975
DOWN THE ROAD STEPHEN STILLS' MANASSAS	33	1973
DOWN THE ROAD VAN MORRISON	6	2002
DOWN TO EARTH RAINBOW	6	1979
DOWN TO EARTH MONIE LOVE	30	1990
DOWN TO EARTH OZZY OSBOURNE	19	2001
DOWN TWO, THEN LEFT BOZ SCAGGS	55	1977
DOWN WITH THE KING RUN D.M.C.	44	1993
DOWNTOWN MIDNIGHT RACING CARS	39	1977
THE DOWNWARD SPIRAL NINE INCH NAILS	9	1994
DR. BYRD AND MR HYDE BYRDS	15	1969
DR. FEELGOOD MOTLEY CRUE	4	1989
DR. HECKLE AND MR. JIVE PIGBAG	18	1982
DR. HILARY JONES CLASSIC RELAXATION (TELEVISION COMPILATION) TELEVISION AND RADIO COMPILATION	13	1994
DR. HOOK LIVE IN THE UK DR. HOOK	90	1981
DR. HOOK'S GREATEST HITS DR. HOOK	2	1980
DRACONIAN TIMES PARADISE LOST	16	1995
DRAG k.d. lang	19	1997
DRAMA YES	2	1980
DRAMA JAMELIA	39	2000
DRASTIC FANTASTIC KT TUNSTALL	3	2007
DRASTIC PLASTIC BE-BOP DELUXE	22	1978
DRAWN FROM MEMORY EMBRACE	8	2000
DRAWN TO THE DEEP END GENE	8	1997
DREAM A DREAM CHARLOTTE CHURCH	30	2000
THE DREAM ACADEMY DREAM ACADEMY	58	1985
A DREAM COME TRUE BECKY TAYLOR	67	2001
DREAM EVIL DIO	8	1987
A DREAM FULFILLED WILL DOWNING	43	1991
DREAM HARDER WATERBOYS	5	1993
DREAM INTO ACTION HOWARD JONES	2	1985
DREAM MELODIES VARIOUS ARTISTS (NOUVEAU MUSIC)	91	1985
DREAM MUSIC ANTHONY VENTURA ORCHESTRA	44	1979
DREAM OF 100 NATIONS TRANSGLOBAL UNDERGROUND	45	1993
DREAM OF A LIFETIME MARVIN GAYE	46	1985
THE DREAM OF BLUE TURTLES STING	3	1985
DREAM OF LIFE PATTI SMITH	70	1988
DREAM ON DREAM ON	43	2008
DREAM ON VOLUME 1 D:REAM	5	1993
DREAM POLICE CHEAP TRICK	41	1979
DREAM WORLD CROWN HEIGHTS AFFAIR	40	1978
DREAMBOAT ANNIE HEART	36	1977
DREAMBOATS & PETTICOATS 2 VARIOUS ARTISTS (UNIVERSAL)	2	2008
DREAMBOATS AND PETTICOATS VARIOUS ARTISTS (UNIVERSAL)	2	2007
DREAMBOATS AND PETTICOATS PRESENT FOOT TAPPERS VARIOUS ARTISTS (UNIVERSAL)	6	2008
DREAMGIRLS FILM SOUNDTRACK	17	2007
DREAMING VARIOUS ARTISTS (K-TEL)	2	1982
THE DREAMING KATE BUSH	3	1982
DREAMING OUT LOUD ONEREPUBLIC	2	2008
DREAMING... PATSY CLINE	55	1991
DREAMLAND BLACK BOX	14	1990
DREAMLAND AZTEC CAMERA	21	1993
DREAMLAND ROBERT MILES	7	1996
DREAMLAND ROBERT PLANT	20	2002
DREAMLAND JONI MITCHELL	43	2004
DREAMS GRACE SLICK	28	1980
DREAMS AND THEMES VARIOUS ARTISTS (RONCO)	75	1984
DREAMS ARE NUTHIN' MORE THAN WISHES DAVID CASSIDY	1	1973
DREAMS CAN COME TRUE – GREATEST HITS VOLUME 1 GABRIELLE	2	2001
DREAMS OF IRELAND VARIOUS ARTISTS (TRAX)	19	1989
DREAMS OF REASON PRODUCE MONSTERS MICK KARN	89	1987
DREAMS – THE ULTIMATE COLLECTION CORRS	67	2006
DREAMSTATES VARIOUS ARTISTS (INSPIRED)	18	2001
DREAMT FOR LIGHT YEARS IN THE BELLY OF A MOUNTAIN SPARKLEHORSE	60	2006
DREAMTIME CULT	21	1984
DREAMTIME STRANGLERS	16	1986
THE DREEM TEEM IN SESSION VARIOUS ARTISTS (TELSTAR)	12	2001
DRESS FOR EXCESS SIGUE SIGUE SPUTNIK	53	1989
DRESSED FOR THE OCCASION CLIFF RICHARD & THE LONDON PHILHARMONIC ORCHESTRA	7	1983
THE DRIFT SCOTT WALKER	51	2006
DRILL YOUR OWN HOLE GAYE BYKERS ON ACID	95	1987
DRINK ME SALAD	16	1995
DRINKIN' AND COURTIN' DUBLINERS	31	1968
DRINKING GASOLINE CABARET VOLTAIRE	71	1985
DRIVE ON MOTT	45	1975
DRIVE ON VARIOUS ARTISTS (GLOBAL TELEVISION)	10	1997
DRIVE TIME VARIOUS ARTISTS (DINO)	5	1995
DRIVE TIME 2 VARIOUS ARTISTS (DINO)	4	1995
DRIVE TIME 4 VARIOUS ARTISTS (DINO)	8	1996
DRIVE TIME USA – 22 SUMMER CRUISING GREATS VARIOUS ARTISTS (K-TEL)	20	1986
DRIVE-THRU BOOTY FREAK POWER	11	1995
DRIVETIME VARIOUS ARTISTS (WARNER BROTHERS)	17	2005
DRIVETIME 3 VARIOUS ARTISTS (DINO)	4	1996
DRIVIN' HARD SHAKATAK	35	1982
DRIVIN' WITH JOHNNIE WALKER VARIOUS ARTISTS (EAST WEST)	10	2002
DRIVIN' YOU WILD CLIFF BENNETT & THE REBEL ROUSERS	25	1966
DRIVING RAIN PAUL McCARTNEY	46	2001
DRIVING ROCK VARIOUS ARTISTS (GLOBAL TELEVISION)	9	1995
DRIVING ROCK VARIOUS ARTISTS (UNIVERSAL)	8	2005
DRIVING ROCK BALLADS VARIOUS ARTISTS (VIRGIN)	1	2005
DRIVING SONGS VARIOUS ARTISTS (EMI)	9	2006
DRIVING WITH DISNEY VARIOUS ARTISTS (WALT DISNEY)	20	2006
DROP DEAD GORGEOUS VARIOUS ARTISTS (GLOBAL TELEVISION)	4	1998
DROP DEAD GORGEOUS 2 VARIOUS ARTISTS (GLOBAL TELEVISION)	10	1998
A DROP OF THE HARD STUFF DUBLINERS	5	1967
DROPPED MINDFUNK	60	1993
DROPS OF JUPITER TRAIN	8	2001
DRUGSTORE DRUGSTORE	31	1995

Title / Artist	Peak Position	Year of Release
DRUKQS APHEX TWIN	22	2001
DRUM & BASS ARENA VARIOUS ARTISTS (WARNER BROTHERS)	3	2004
DRUM & BASS ARENA VARIOUS ARTISTS (MINISTRY OF SOUND)	11	2007
DRUM & BASS ARENA – ANDY C/ GROOVERIDER VARIOUS ARTISTS (RESIST)	14	2007
DRUM & BASS ARENA – FABIO & GROOVERIDER VARIOUS ARTISTS (RESIST)	20	2004
DRUM & BASS ARENA – THE CLASSICS VARIOUS ARTISTS (MINISTRY OF SOUND)	9	2006
DRUM & BASS ESSENTIALS VARIOUS ARTISTS (WARNER BROTHERS)	8	2005
DRUM & BASS MIX 97 VARIOUS ARTISTS (POLYGRAM)	11	1997
DRUM AND BASS SELECTION 2 VARIOUS ARTISTS (BREAK DOWN)	14	1994
THE DRUM IS EVERYTHING CARMEL	19	1984
DRUMS AND WIRES XTC	34	1979
DRUMS ARE DANGEROUS DRUM CLUB	53	1994
DRUNK ENOUGH TO DANCE BOWLING FOR SOUP	14	2002
DRY PJ HARVEY	11	1992
D-TRAIN D-TRAIN	72	1982
DUB COME SAVE ME ROOTS MANUVA	75	2002
DUB HOUSE DISCO 2000 VARIOUS ARTISTS (GUERILLA)	18	1993
THE DUBLINERS 25 YEARS CELEBRATION DUBLINERS	43	1987
DUBNOBASSWITHMYHEADMAN UNDERWORLD	12	1994
DUCK ROCK MALCOLM McLAREN	18	1983
THE DUDE QUINCY JONES	19	1981
DUEL DUEL	47	2004
DUETS ELTON JOHN & VARIOUS ARTISTS	5	1993
DUETS FRANK SINATRA	5	1993
DUETS BARBRA STREISAND	30	2002
DUETS & ARIAS ROBERTO ALAGNA/ANGELA GHEORGIU	42	1996
DUETS & DUETS II FRANK SINATRA	65	2006
DUETS – AN AMERICAN CLASSIC TONY BENNETT	15	2006
DUETS II FRANK SINATRA	29	1994
DUETS – THE FINAL CHAPTER NOTORIOUS B.I.G.	13	2006
DUKE GENESIS	1	1980
THE DUKE WORE JEANS (OST) TOMMY STEELE	1	1958
DUMB WAITERS KORGIS	40	1980
DUMBING UP WORLD PARTY	64	2000
DUMMY PORTISHEAD	2	1994
DUOPHONIC CHARLES & EDDIE	19	1992
DUOTONES KENNY G	28	1987
DURAN DURAN DURAN DURAN	3	1981
DURAN DURAN (THE WEDDING ALBUM) DURAN DURAN	4	1993
DUSK THE THE	2	1993
DUSKY SAPPHO EP CARLEEN ANDERSON	38	1993
DUST SCREAMING TREES	32	1996
DUSTY – THE SILVER COLLECTION DUSTY SPRINGFIELD	14	1988
DUSTY...DEFINITELY DUSTY SPRINGFIELD	30	1968
THE DUTCHESS FERGIE	18	2006
DUTTY ROCK SEAN PAUL	2	2003
DUTY NOW FOR THE FUTURE DEVO	49	1979
DYLAN BOB DYLAN	10	2007
DYLAN AND THE DEAD BOB DYLAN & THE GRATEFUL DEAD	38	1989
DYLANESQUE BRYAN FERRY	5	2007
DYNAMITE JERMAINE JACKSON	57	1984
DYNAMITE JAMIROQUAI	3	2005
DYNASTY KISS	50	1979

E

Title / Artist	Peak Position	Year of Release
E.1999 ETERNAL BONE THUGS-N-HARMONY	39	1996
E.C. WAS HERE ERIC CLAPTON	14	1975
E.S.P. MILLIE JACKSON	59	1984
E.S.P. BEE GEES	5	1987
E.T. THE EXTRA TERRESTRIAL MICHAEL JACKSON	82	1983
E.T. – THE EXTRATERRESTRIAL (OST) JOHN WILLIAMS	47	1982
E=MC2 MARIAH CAREY	3	2008
THE EAGLE HAS LANDED SAXON	5	1982
EARLY DAYS – THE BEST OF – VOLUME ONE LED ZEPPELIN	55	2000
THE EARLY TAPES JULY-AUGUST 1980 LEVEL 42	46	1982
EARTH AND SUN AND MOON MIDNIGHT OIL	27	1993
EARTH INFERNO FIELDS OF THE NEPHILIM	39	1991
EARTH MOVING MIKE OLDFIELD	30	1989
EARTH VS THE WILDHEARTS WILDHEARTS	46	1993
EARTHBOUND CONNOR REEVES	25	1997
EARTHLING DAVID BOWIE	6	1997
THE EARTHQUAKE ALBUM...ROCK AID ARMENIA VARIOUS ARTISTS (LIFE AID ARMENIA)	3	1990
EARTHQUAKE WEATHER JOE STRUMMER	58	1989
EARTHRISE – THE RAINFOREST ALBUM VARIOUS ARTISTS (ELF)	1	1992
EAST OF THE SUN, WEST OF THE MOON A-HA	12	1990
EAST SIDE STORY SQUEEZE	19	1981
EAST TO WEST JAMES LAST	49	1978
THE EASTENDERS SING-ALONG ALBUM (TELEVISION COMPILATION) TELEVISION AND RADIO COMPILATION	33	1985
EASTER PATTI SMITH GROUP	16	1978
EASY RALPH McTELL	31	1974
EASY EASY SCOTLAND FOOTBALL WORLD CUP SQUAD 1974	3	1974
EASY MOODS VARIOUS ARTISTS (EMI)	15	1996
EASY PIECES LLOYD COLE & THE COMMOTIONS	5	1985
EASY RIDER FILM SOUNDTRACK	2	1969
EASY TIGER RYAN ADAMS	18	2007
EAT 'EM AND SMILE DAVID LEE ROTH	28	1986
EAT IT HUMBLE PIE	34	1973
EAT ME DRINK ME MARILYN MANSON	8	2007
EAT ME IN ST LOUIS IT BITES	40	1989
EAT TO THE BEAT BLONDIE	1	1979
EAT YOURSELF WHOLE KINGMAKER	29	1991
EATEN ALIVE DIANA ROSS	11	1985
ECHO TOM PETTY & HEARTBREAKERS	43	1999
ECHO AND THE BUNNYMEN ECHO & THE BUNNYMEN	4	1987
ECHO DEK PRIMAL SCREAM	43	1997
ECHO PARK FEEDER	5	2001
ECHOES RAPTURE	32	2003
ECHOES OF GOLD ADRIAN BRETT	19	1979
ECHOES SILENCE PATIENCE & GRACE FOO FIGHTERS	1	2007
ECHOES – THE BEST OF PINK FLOYD PINK FLOYD	2	2001
ECHOES – THE COLLECTION LUDOVICO EINAUDI	40	2003
ECLECTIC BIG COUNTRY	41	1996
THE ECLEFTIC – TWO SIDES TO A BOOK WYCLEF JEAN	5	2000
ECLIPSE YNGWIE J MALMSTEEN	43	1990
ECO DI NAPOLI KENNETH McKELLAR	45	1970
ECSTASY VARIOUS ARTISTS (LOTUS)	24	1978

Title / Artist	Peak Position	Year of Release
ECSTASY LOU REED	54	2000
EDDI READER EDDI READER	4	1994
THE EDDIE COCHRAN MEMORIAL ALBUM EDDIE COCHRAN	9	1960
THE EDDIE COCHRAN SINGLES ALBUM EDDIE COCHRAN	39	1979
EDDIE, OLD BOB, DICK & GARRY TEN POLE TUDOR	44	1981
THE EDDY DUCHIN STORY ORIGINAL SOUNDTRACK	3	1956
EDELWEISS VINCE HILL	23	1967
EDEN EVERYTHING BUT THE GIRL	14	1984
THE EDGAR BROUGHTON BAND EDGAR BROUGHTON BAND	28	1971
THE EDGE OF THE EIGHTIES VARIOUS ARTISTS (SONY BMG)	6	2008
EDINBURGH MILITARY TATTOO 1970 MISCELLANEOUS	34	1970
EDINBURGH MILITARY TATTOO 1971 MISCELLANEOUS	44	1971
EDIZIOBE D'ORO FOUR SEASONS	11	1971
EDUTAINMENT BOOGIE DOWN PRODUCTIONS	52	1990
EDWARD THE GREAT – THE GREATEST HITS IRON MAIDEN	57	2002
THE EDWARD WOODWARD ALBUM EDWARD WOODWARD	20	1972
EFIL4ZAGGIN N.W.A.	25	1991
EGO TRIPPIN' SNOOP DOGG	23	2008
EGO WAR AUDIO BULLYS	19	2003
EGYPTOLOGY WORLD PARTY	34	1997
808S & HEARTBREAKS KANYE WEST	11	2008
THE EIGHT LEGGED GROOVE MACHINE WONDER STUFF	18	1988
8 MILE FILM SOUNDTRACK	1	2002
808:88:98 808 STATE	40	1998
801 LIVE 801	52	1976
8701 USHER	1	2001
18 MOBY	1	2002
18 GREATEST HITS MICHAEL JACKSON PLUS THE JACKSON FIVE	1	1983
18 HITS ABBA	17	2007
18 TIL I DIE BRYAN ADAMS	1	1996
18 TRACKS BRUCE SPRINGSTEEN	23	1999
THE 18TH DAY ESTELLE	35	2004
18TH LETTER RAKIM	72	1997
THE 80'S ALBUM – THE ALBUM OF THE DECADE VARIOUS ARTISTS (EMI)	1	1989
THE '80S LOVE ALBUM VARIOUS ARTISTS (VIRGIN)	6	1999
THE EIGHTIES MIX VARIOUS ARTISTS (GLOBAL TELEVISION)	1	1998
80S MOVIE HITS VARIOUS ARTISTS (UNIVERSAL)	4	2006
EIGHTIES SOUL WEEKENDER VARIOUS ARTISTS (DINO)	7	1996
80'S SOUL WEEKENDER VARIOUS ARTISTS (WARNER BROTHERS)	11	2005
EIGHTIES SOUL WEEKENDER 2 VARIOUS ARTISTS (PUMP)	11	1996
EIGHTIES SOUL WEEKENDER 3 VARIOUS ARTISTS (PUMP)	15	1997
80 F AFTER THE FIRE	69	1980
EITHER SIDE OF MIDNIGHT JACK McMANUS	22	2008
EL CORAZON STEVE EARLE	59	1997
EL LOCO ZZ TOP	88	1981
EL PRESIDENTE EL PRESIDENTE	57	2005
ELAINE PAIGE ELAINE PAIGE	56	1982
ELASTIC ROCK NUCLEUS	46	1970
ELASTICA ELASTICA	1	1995
ELBOW BEACH LOUISE	12	2000
THE ELDER KISS	51	1981
ELECT THE DEAD SERJ TANKIAN	26	2007

Title / Artist	Peak Position	Year of Release
ELECTRIBAL MEMORIES ELECTRIBE 101	26	1990
ELECTRIC CULT	4	1987
ELECTRIC VARIOUS ARTISTS (WARNER BROTHERS)	18	2005
ELECTRIC 80'S VARIOUS ARTISTS (SONY/BMG)	11	2005
ELECTRIC CAFÉ KRAFTWERK	58	1986
ELECTRIC DREAMS FILM SOUNDTRACK	46	1984
ELECTRIC DREAMS VARIOUS ARTISTS (POLYGRAM)	3	1995
ELECTRIC DREAMS VARIOUS ARTISTS (VIRGIN)	7	2002
ELECTRIC FIRE ROGER TAYLOR	53	1998
ELECTRIC FOLKLORE LIVE ALARM	62	1988
ELECTRIC LADYLAND JIMI HENDRIX EXPERIENCE	6	1968
ELECTRIC LADYLAND JIMI HENDRIX	47	1997
ELECTRIC LANDLADY KIRSTY MacCOLL	17	1991
ELECTRIC – LEVEL 2 VARIOUS ARTISTS (TELSTAR)	5	2003
ELECTRIC LIGHT ORCHESTRA ELECTRIC LIGHT ORCHESTRA	32	1972
ELECTRIC LIGHT ORCHESTRA II ELECTRIC LIGHT ORCHESTRA	35	1973
ELECTRIC LIGHT ORCHESTRA PART TWO ELECTRIC LIGHT ORCHESTRA PART TWO	34	1991
ELECTRIC MOODS VARIOUS ARTISTS (DECADANCE)	9	2004
ELECTRIC TEPEE HAWKWIND	53	1992
ELECTRIC – THE VERY BEST OF ELECTRONIC, NEW WAVE & SYNTH VARIOUS ARTISTS (TELSTAR)	5	2002
ELECTRIC WARRIOR T. REX	1	1971
ELECTRIC YOUTH DEBBIE GIBSON	8	1989
ELECTRO BREAKDANCE – THE REAL OLD SCHOOL REVIVAL VARIOUS ARTISTS (TELSTAR)	4	2002
ELECTRO GLIDE IN BLUE APOLLO FOUR FORTY	62	1997
ELECTRO HOUSE SESSIONS VARIOUS ARTISTS (MINISTRY OF SOUND)	3	2007
ELECTRO SHOCK VOLTAGE ONE VARIOUS ARTISTS (EPIC)	73	1984
ELECTRONIC ELECTRONIC	2	1991
ELECTRONIC ORGANS TODAY MISCELLANEOUS	48	1971
ELECTRONICA (FULL-ON BIG BEATS) VARIOUS ARTISTS (VIRGIN)	11	1997
ELECTRONICALLY TESTED MUNGO JERRY	14	1978
ELECTRO-SHOCK BLUES EELS	12	1998
ELECTROTECH VARIOUS ARTISTS (MINISTRY OF SOUND)	17	2003
ELEGANT SLUMMING M PEOPLE	2	1993
ELEGANTLY WASTED INXS	16	1997
ELEGY NICE	5	1971
ELEMENTAL TEARS FOR FEARS	5	1993
ELEMENTALZ BROTHERHOOD	50	1996
ELEMENTS OF LIFE TIESTO	14	2007
ELEMENTS – SEB FONTAINE/TONY DE VIT VARIOUS ARTISTS (WESTWAY DANCE)	15	1998
ELEMENTS – THE BEST OF MIKE OLDFIELD MIKE OLDFIELD	5	1993
ELEPHANT WHITE STRIPES	1	2003
ELEPHUNK BLACK EYED PEAS	3	2003
ELEVATOR HOT HOT HEAT	34	2005
11 BRYAN ADAMS	6	2008
1100 BEL AIR PLACE JULIO IGLESIAS	14	1984
ELEVENTEEN DAISY CHAINSAW	62	1992
THE ELEVENTH HOUR MAGNUM	38	1983
ELGAR CELLO CONCERTO JULIAN LLOYD WEBBER WITH THE ROYAL PHILHARMONIC ORCHESTRA CONDUCTED BY SIR YEHUDI MENUHIN	94	1987
ELGAR/PAYNE SYMPHONY NO. 3 BBC SYMPHONY ORCHESTRA CONDUCTED BY ANDREW DAVIS	44	1998
ELGAR: VIOLIN CONCERTO NIGEL KENNEDY WITH THE LONDON PHILHARMONIC ORCHESTRA	97	1986
ELIMINATOR ZZ TOP	3	1983
ELITE HOTEL EMMYLOU HARRIS	17	1976
ELITE SYNCOPATIONS CHRIS BARBER	18	1960
ELIZIUM FIELDS OF THE NEPHILIM	22	1990
ELLA AND LOUIS TOGETHER ELLA FITZGERALD & LOUIS ARMSTRONG	43	2004
ELLA AT THE OPERA HOUSE ELLA FITZGERALD	16	1960
ELLA FITZGERALD SINGS THE IRVING BERLIN SONG BOOK ELLA FITZGERALD	5	1958
ELLA SINGS GERSHWIN ELLA FITZGERALD	13	1960
ELLA SINGS GERSHWIN VOLUME 5 ELLA FITZGERALD	18	1960
ELLIOT MINOR ELLIOT MINOR	6	2008
ELO'S GREATEST HITS ELECTRIC LIGHT ORCHESTRA	7	1979
ELTON JOHN ELTON JOHN	5	1970
ELTON JOHN AND TIM RICE'S AIDA ELTON JOHN & FRIENDS	29	1999
THE ELTON JOHN LIVE ALBUM 17-11-70 ELTON JOHN	20	1971
ELTON JOHN'S GREATEST HITS ELTON JOHN	1	1974
ELV1S: 30 #1 HITS ELVIS PRESLEY	1	2002
ELVIS ELVIS PRESLEY	16	1973
ELVIS 56 ELVIS PRESLEY	42	1996
ELVIS – A LEGENDARY PERFORMER VOLUME 1 ELVIS PRESLEY	20	1974
ELVIS AARON PRESLEY ELVIS PRESLEY	21	1980
ELVIS AS RECORDED AT MADISON SQUARE GARDEN ELVIS PRESLEY	3	1972
ELVIS BY THE PRESLEYS ELVIS PRESLEY	13	2005
ELVIS CHRISTMAS ALBUM ELVIS PRESLEY	7	1971
ELVIS FOR EVERYONE ELVIS PRESLEY	8	1965
ELVIS' GOLDEN RECORDS ELVIS PRESLEY	2	1958
ELVIS' GOLDEN RECORDS VOLUME 1 ELVIS PRESLEY	21	1970
ELVIS' GOLDEN RECORDS VOLUME 2 ELVIS PRESLEY	4	1960
ELVIS' GOLDEN RECORDS VOLUME 3 ELVIS PRESLEY	6	1964
ELVIS IN CONCERT ELVIS PRESLEY	13	1977
ELVIS IN DEMAND ELVIS PRESLEY	12	1977
ELVIS IS BACK! ELVIS PRESLEY	1	1960
ELVIS LIVE ON STAGE IN MEMPHIS ELVIS PRESLEY	44	1974
ELVIS – NBC TV SPECIAL ELVIS PRESLEY	2	1969
ELVIS NOW ELVIS PRESLEY	12	1972
ELVIS PRESLEY – BALLADS: 18 CLASSIC LOVE SONGS ELVIS PRESLEY	23	1985
ELVIS PRESLEY EP PACK ELVIS PRESLEY	97	1982
ELVIS PRESLEY SINGS LEIBER AND STOLLER ELVIS PRESLEY	32	1980
THE ELVIS PRESLEY SUN COLLECTION ELVIS PRESLEY	16	1975
ELVIS' SINGS FLAMING STAR ELVIS PRESLEY	2	1969
ELVIS'S 40 GREATEST HITS ELVIS PRESLEY	1	1975
ELVIS'S CHRISTMAS ALBUM ELVIS PRESLEY	2	1957
EMANCIPATION PRINCE	18	1996
THE EMANCIPATION OF MIMI MARIAH CAREY	7	2005
EMBRYA MAXWELL	11	1998
EMERALD CLASSICS VARIOUS ARTISTS (STOIC)	35	1984
EMERALD CLASSICS VOLUMES I AND II VARIOUS ARTISTS (WESTMOOR)	14	1990
EMERALD ROCK VARIOUS ARTISTS (POLYGRAM)	14	1995
EMERGENCY KOOL & THE GANG	47	1984
EMERGENCY PIGEON DETECTIVES	7	2008
EMERGENCY ON PLANET EARTH JAMIROQUAI	1	1993
EMERSON, LAKE AND PALMER EMERSON, LAKE & PALMER	4	1970
EMERSON, LAKE AND POWELL EMERSON, LAKE & POWELL	35	1986
EMINEM PRESENTS THE RE-UP VARIOUS ARTISTS (UNIVERSAL)	3	2006
THE EMINEM SHOW EMINEM	1	2002
EMMERDANCE WOOLPACKERS	26	1996
EMOTION BARBRA STREISAND	15	1984
THE EMOTIONAL HOOLIGAN GARY CLAIL ON-U SOUND SYSTEM	35	1991
EMOTIONAL RESCUE ROLLING STONES	1	1980
EMOTIONS VARIOUS ARTISTS (K-TEL)	2	1978
EMOTIONS MARIAH CAREY	4	1991
EMOTIONS VARIOUS ARTISTS (UNIVERSAL)	13	2002
EMPEROR TOMATO KETCHUP STEREOLAB	27	1996
EMPIRE QUEENSRYCHE	13	1990
EMPIRE KASABIAN	1	2006
EMPIRE BURLESQUE BOB DYLAN	11	1985
EMPIRE OF THE SENSELESS SENSELESS THINGS	37	1993
EMPIRES AND DANCE SIMPLE MINDS	41	1980
EMPLOYMENT KAISER CHIEFS	3	2005
EMPTY GLASS PETE TOWNSHEND	11	1980
EMPTY ROOMS JOHN MAYALL	9	1970
ENCHANTED MARC ALMOND	52	1990
ENCHANTMENT CHARLOTTE CHURCH	24	2001
ENCORE TANGERINE DREAM	55	1977
ENCORE MARTI WEBB	55	1985
ENCORE ELAINE PAIGE	20	1995
ENCORE RUSSELL WATSON	6	2001
ENCORE LIONEL RICHIE	8	2002
ENCORE EMINEM	1	2004
ENCORE UNE FOIS – THE GREATEST HITS SASH!	33	2000
THE END COMPLETE OBITUARY	52	1992
END HITS FUGAZI	47	1998
THE END OF HEARTACHE KILLSWITCH ENGAGE	40	2004
THE END OF INNOCENCE DON HENLEY	17	1989
END OF MILLENNIUM PSYCHOSIS BLUES THAT PETROL EMOTION	53	1988
END OF PART ONE (THEIR GREATEST HITS) WET WET WET	1	1993
END OF THE CENTURY RAMONES	14	1980
END TITLES – STORIES FOR FILM UNKLE	70	2008
ENDLESS HEAVEN 17	70	1986
ENDLESS FLIGHT LEO SAYER	4	1976
ENDLESS HARMONY SOUNDTRACK BEACH BOYS	56	1998
ENDLESS JOURNEY – THE ESSENTIAL LEO SAYER	43	2006
ENDLESS LOVE VARIOUS ARTISTS (TV RECORDS)	26	1982
ENDLESS LOVE VARIOUS ARTISTS (POLYGRAM)	3	1995
ENDLESS SUMMER – GREATEST HITS DONNA SUMMER	37	1994
ENDLESS, NAMELESS WILDHEARTS	41	1997
ENDLESSWIRE WHO	9	2006
ENEMA OF THE STATE BLINK 182	15	2000
ENERGIQUE BIZARRE INC	41	1992
ENERGY ORCHARD ENERGY ORCHARD	53	1990
ENERGY RUSH VARIOUS ARTISTS (DINO)	1	1992
ENERGY RUSH 7 VARIOUS ARTISTS (DINO)	2	1994
ENERGY RUSH DANCE HITS 93 (2ND DIMENSION) VARIOUS ARTISTS (DINO)	2	1993
ENERGY RUSH DANCE HITS 94 VARIOUS ARTISTS (DINO)	3	1994

Title / Artist	Peak Position	Year of Release
ENERGY RUSH – EURO DANCE HITS 94 VARIOUS ARTISTS (DINO)	5	1994
ENERGY RUSH FACTOR 5 VARIOUS ARTISTS (DINO)	3	1993
ENERGY RUSH II VARIOUS ARTISTS (DINO)	7	1992
ENERGY RUSH K9 VARIOUS ARTISTS (DINO)	3	1995
ENERGY RUSH LEVEL 3 VARIOUS ARTISTS (DINO)	3	1993
ENERGY RUSH PHASE 4 VARIOUS ARTISTS (DINO)	2	1993
ENERGY RUSH PRESENTS DANCE HITS 93 VARIOUS ARTISTS (DINO)	1	1993
ENERGY RUSH PRESENTS DANCE HITS OF THE YEAR VARIOUS ARTISTS (DINO)	3	1993
ENERGY RUSH – SAFE SIX VARIOUS ARTISTS (DINO)	5	1993
ENERGY RUSH – XTERMIN8 VARIOUS ARTISTS (DINO)	1	1994
ENGELBERT ENGELBERT HUMPERDINCK	3	1969
ENGELBERT HUMPERDINCK ENGELBERT HUMPERDINCK	5	1969
THE ENGELBERT HUMPERDINCK COLLECTION ENGELBERT HUMPERDINCK	35	1987
ENGELBERT HUMPERDINCK – HIS GREATEST HITS ENGELBERT HUMPERDINCK	1	1974
ENGLAND HALF ENGLISH BILLY BRAGG & THE BLOKES	51	2002
ENGLAND – THE ALBUM VARIOUS ARTISTS (EMI)	1	2004
ENGLISH SETTLEMENT XTC	5	1982
ENJOY YOURSELF KYLIE MINOGUE	1	1989
ENLIGHTENMENT VAN MORRISON	5	1990
EN-TACT SHAMEN	31	1990
ENTER THE DRU DRU HILL	42	1998
ENTERTAINMENT GANG OF FOUR	45	1979
ENTREAT CURE	10	1991
ENTRODUCING… DJ SHADOW	17	1996
ENVY OF ANGELS MUTTON BIRDS	64	1997
ENYA (OST-TV) ENYA	69	1987
THE EPIC YEARS SHAKY	57	1992
EPONYMOUS R.E.M.	69	1988
THE EP'S 1992-1994 DAVID GRAY	68	2001
EQUALLY CURSED AND BLESSED CATATONIA	1	1999
EQUALS EXPLOSION EQUALS	32	1968
EQUATOR URIAH HEEP	79	1985
EQUINOXE JEAN-MICHEL JARRE	11	1978
ERA VULGARIS QUEENS OF THE STONE AGE	7	2007
THE ERASER THOM YORKE	3	2006
ERASURE ERASURE	14	1995
ERIC BURDON DECLARES WAR ERIC BURDON & WAR	50	1970
ERIC CARMEN ERIC CARMEN	58	1976
ERIC CLAPTON ERIC CLAPTON	17	1970
EROICA WENDY & LISA	33	1990
EROTICA MADONNA	2	1992
ERROL FLYNN DOGS D'AMOUR	22	1989
ESCAPE JOURNEY	32	1982
ESCAPE ENRIQUE IGLESIAS	1	2002
ESCAPE FROM TV JAN HAMMER	34	1987
ESCAPOLOGY ROBBIE WILLIAMS	1	2002
ESCM BT	35	1997
ESPECIALLY FOR YOU DUANE EDDY	6	1959
ESPECIALLY FOR YOU DON WILLIAMS	33	1981
ESPECIALLY FOR YOU JOE LONGTHORNE	22	1989
ESPECIALLY FOR YOU DANIEL O'DONNELL	14	1994
ESPECIALLY FOR YOU VARIOUS ARTISTS (COLUMBIA)	1	1999
ESPRESSO LOGIC CHRIS REA	8	1993
ESSENCE LUCINDA WILLIAMS	63	2001
THE ESSENTIAL ALISON MOYET	16	2001
THE ESSENTIAL BOB DYLAN	9	2001
THE ESSENTIAL BARBRA STREISAND	1	2002
THE ESSENTIAL BRUCE SPRINGSTEEN	28	2003
THE ESSENTIAL LEONARD COHEN	70	2003
THE ESSENTIAL OZZY OSBOURNE	21	2003
THE ESSENTIAL PAUL YOUNG	27	2003
THE ESSENTIAL SIMON & GARFUNKEL	25	2003
THE ESSENTIAL MICHAEL JACKSON	2	2005
THE ESSENTIAL NANCY SINATRA	73	2006
ESSENTIAL SQUEEZE	25	2007
ESSENTIAL LEONARD COHEN	57	2008
THE ESSENTIAL NEIL DIAMOND	11	2008
THE ESSENTIAL ACOUSTIC ALBUM VARIOUS ARTISTS (SANCTUARY)	12	2004
ESSENTIAL ALBUM VARIOUS ARTISTS (UNIVERSAL)	11	2008
THE ESSENTIAL ANDY WILLIAMS ANDY WILLIAMS	32	2002
ESSENTIAL BALLET VARIOUS ARTISTS (DECCA)	9	1992
THE ESSENTIAL CHILL VARIOUS ARTISTS (ARCADE)	16	1992
THE ESSENTIAL CLASH CLASH	18	2003
ESSENTIAL CLASSICS VARIOUS ARTISTS (DEUTSCHE GRAMMOPHON)	6	1990
THE ESSENTIAL COLLECTION ELVIS PRESLEY	6	1994
THE ESSENTIAL COLLECTION MARC BOLAN & T. REX	18	1995
THE ESSENTIAL COLLECTION DIONNE WARWICK	58	1996
THE ESSENTIAL COLLECTION DARYL HALL & JOHN OATES	26	2001
THE ESSENTIAL COLLECTION NEIL DIAMOND	11	2002
ESSENTIAL DANCE HITS – PETE TONG VARIOUS ARTISTS (UNIVERSAL)	9	2006
ESSENTIAL DISCO AND DANCE VARIOUS ARTISTS (NOUVEAU MUSIC)	96	1984
THE ESSENTIAL DOMINGO PLACIDO DOMINGO	20	1989
ESSENTIAL ELLA ELLA FITZGERALD	35	1994
THE ESSENTIAL GROOVE VARIOUS ARTISTS (POLYGRAM)	11	1995
ESSENTIAL HARDCORE VARIOUS ARTISTS (DINO)	1	1991
THE ESSENTIAL JEAN-MICHEL JARRE JEAN-MICHEL JARRE	14	1983
THE ESSENTIAL JOSE CARRERAS JOSE CARRERAS	24	1991
THE ESSENTIAL KARAJAN HERBERT VON KARAJAN	51	1988
THE ESSENTIAL KIRI KIRI TE KANAWA	23	1992
THE ESSENTIAL LUTHER VANDROSS LUTHER VANDROSS	18	2002
ESSENTIAL MILLENNIUM – PETE TONG FATBOY SLIM PAUL OAKENFOLD VARIOUS ARTISTS (FFRR)	10	1999
ESSENTIAL MIX 2 – TONG, MACKINTOSH… VARIOUS ARTISTS (FFRR)	6	1996
ESSENTIAL MIX 3 – TONG, SEAMAN, JULES ETC VARIOUS ARTISTS (FFRR)	12	1996
ESSENTIAL MIX – TONG COX SASHA OAKENFOLD VARIOUS ARTISTS (FFRR)	12	1996
THE ESSENTIAL MOZART VARIOUS ARTISTS (DECCA)	1	1991
ESSENTIAL MUSICALS ELAINE PAIGE	46	2006
ESSENTIAL NME BANDS VARIOUS ARTISTS (UNIVERSAL)	19	2007
ESSENTIAL OPERA VARIOUS ARTISTS (DECCA)	2	1991
ESSENTIAL OPERA 2 VARIOUS ARTISTS (DECCA)	17	1993
THE ESSENTIAL PAUL SIMON PAUL SIMON	12	2008
THE ESSENTIAL PAVAROTTI LUCIANO PAVAROTTI	1	1990
ESSENTIAL PAVAROTTI II LUCIANO PAVAROTTI	1	1991
THE ESSENTIAL PERRY COMO PERRY COMO	54	2003
ESSENTIAL R & B THE LOVE COLLECTION VARIOUS ARTISTS (BMG)	3	2004
ESSENTIAL R&B – AUTUMN 2006 VARIOUS ARTISTS (SONY/BMG)	4	2006
ESSENTIAL R&B – HIT SELECTION VARIOUS ARTISTS (SONY BMG)	4	2008
ESSENTIAL R&B – SPRING 2005 VARIOUS ARTISTS (SONY/BMG)	1	2005
ESSENTIAL R&B – SUMMER 2005 VARIOUS ARTISTS (SONY/BMG)	4	2005
ESSENTIAL R&B – SUMMER 2006 VARIOUS ARTISTS (UNIVERSAL)	4	2006
ESSENTIAL R&B – SUMMER 2007 VARIOUS ARTISTS (SONY/BMG)	4	2007
ESSENTIAL R&B – THE VERY BEST OF R&B VARIOUS ARTISTS (BMG)	1	2004
ESSENTIAL R&B – WINTER 2004 VARIOUS ARTISTS (BMG)	8	2004
ESSENTIAL R&B – WINTER 2005 VARIOUS ARTISTS (UNIVERSAL)	2	2005
ESSENTIAL SELECTION '98 – PETE TONG/ PAUL OAKENFOLD VARIOUS ARTISTS (FFRR)	11	1998
ESSENTIAL SELECTION – CLUBBERS BIBLE VARIOUS ARTISTS (WARNER BROTHERS)	17	2001
ESSENTIAL SELECTION IBIZA 2000 VARIOUS ARTISTS (ESSENTIAL RECORDINGS)	11	2000
ESSENTIAL SELECTION PRESENTS THE CLUBBER'S BIBLE II THE SECOND COMING VARIOUS ARTISTS (WARNER BROTHERS)	6	2001
ESSENTIAL SELECTION SPRING 2000 VARIOUS ARTISTS (ESSENTIAL RECORDINGS)	8	2000
ESSENTIAL SONGS VARIOUS ARTISTS (UNIVERSAL)	9	2006
ESSENTIAL SONGS – SPRING COLLECTION VARIOUS ARTISTS (UNIVERSAL)	3	2007
ESSENTIAL SOUNDTRACKS VARIOUS ARTISTS (TELSTAR)	4	1999
THE ESSENTIAL TONY BENNETT TONY BENNETT	49	1998
ESSENTIAL TRACKS VARIOUS ARTISTS (TELSTAR)	15	2001
ESSENTIAL WOMAN VARIOUS ARTISTS (SONY/BMG)	13	2005
ESSENTIALS – THE VERY BEST OF GEORGE BENSON GEORGE BENSON	8	1998
ESSEX ALISON MOYET	24	1994
ESTABLISHED 1958 CLIFF RICHARD & THE SHADOWS	30	1968
ESTE MUNDO GIPSY KINGS	19	1991
ETERNAL FLAME – THE BEST OF THE BANGLES BANGLES	15	2001
THE ETERNAL IDOL BLACK SABBATH	66	1987
ETERNAL LIGHT – MUSIC OF INNER PEACE PRIORY OF THE RESURRECTION	68	2001
ETERNAL LOVE VARIOUS ARTISTS (K-TEL)	5	1989
ETHER SONG TURIN BRAKES	4	2003
EUGENE WILDE EUGENE WILDE	67	1984
EUPHORIA DEF LEPPARD	11	1999
EUPHORIA VARIOUS ARTISTS (TELSTAR)	1	1999
EUPHORIA – LEVEL 3 VARIOUS ARTISTS (TELSTAR)	5	1999
EUPHORIA MORNING CHRIS CORNELL	31	1999
EUREKA BIBLE	71	1988
EURO 2000 – THE OFFICIAL ALBUM VARIOUS ARTISTS (UNIVERSAL)	15	2000
EUROMAN COMETH JEAN-JACQUES BURNEL	40	1979
EUROPOP EIFFEL 65	12	2000
EUROVISION FAVOURITES VARIOUS ARTISTS (K-TEL)	44	1976

Title / Artist	Peak Position	Year of Release
EUROVISION SONG CONTEST – BELGRADE 2008 VARIOUS ARTISTS (EMI)	20	2008
EUROVISION SONG CONTEST ATHENS 2006 VARIOUS ARTISTS (CMC)	17	2006
EUROVISION SONG CONTEST – HELSINKI 2007 VARIOUS ARTISTS (CMC)	16	2007
EURYTHMICS LIVE 1983-1989 EURYTHMICS	22	1993
EV3 EN VOGUE	9	1997
EVANGELINE EMMYLOU HARRIS	53	1981
EVE ALAN PARSONS PROJECT	74	1979
EVEN COW GIRLS GET THE BLUES (OST) k.d. lang	36	1993
EVEN IN THE QUIETEST MOMENTS... SUPERTRAMP	12	1977
EVEN MORE THAN A FEELING VARIOUS ARTISTS (SONY/BMG)	15	2005
EVEN NOW BARRY MANILOW	12	1978
EVEN SERPENT'S SHINE ONLY ONES	42	1979
EVENING FALLS RICHARD HARVEY & FRIENDS	72	1989
EVENING SESSION – PRIORITY TUNES VARIOUS ARTISTS (VIRGIN)	11	1996
EVENTIDE FAITH BROTHERS	66	1985
EVE-OLUTION EVE	47	2002
EVERGREEN MR ACKER BILK	17	1978
EVERGREEN ECHO & THE BUNNYMEN	8	1997
EVERLASTING NATALIE COLE	62	1988
EVERLASTING LOVE VARIOUS ARTISTS (SONY BMG)	10	2005
THE EVERLY BROTHERS EVERLY BROTHERS	36	1984
EVERLY BROTHERS REUNION CONCERT – LIVE AT THE ROYAL ALBERT HALL EVERLY BROTHERS	47	1984
EVERY 1'S A WINNER HOT CHOCOLATE	30	1978
EVERY BEAT OF MY HEART ROD STEWART	5	1986
EVERY BREATH YOU TAKE – THE SINGLES POLICE	1	1986
EVERY CLASSICAL TUNE YOU'LL EVER WANT VARIOUS ARTISTS (UNIVERSAL)	10	2006
EVERY DAY CINEMATIC ORCHESTRA	54	2002
EVERY DAY IS A NEW DAY DIANA ROSS	71	1999
EVERY FACE TELLS A STORY CLIFF RICHARD	8	1977
EVERY GOOD BOY DESERVES FAVOUR MOODY BLUES	1	1971
EVERY GOOD BOY DESERVES FUDGE MUDHONEY	34	1991
EVERY HOME SHOULD HAVE ONE PATTI AUSTIN	99	1981
EVERY PICTURE TELLS A STORY ROD STEWART	1	1971
EVERY SECOND COUNTS PLAIN WHITE T'S	3	2007
EVERY SONG TELLS A STORY VARIOUS ARTISTS (POLYGRAM)	17	1995
EVERY TIME WE TOUCH CASCADA	2	2007
EVERY WOMAN VARIOUS ARTISTS (RCA)	19	1998
EVERYBODY HEAR'SAY	24	2001
EVERYBODY DANCE NOW VARIOUS ARTISTS (COLUMBIA)	12	1991
EVERYBODY ELSE IS DOING IT, SO WHY CAN'T WE? CRANBERRIES	1	1993
EVERYBODY HERTZ AIR	67	2002
EVERYBODY KNOWS SONIA	7	1990
EVERYBODY KNOWS MILLICAN AND NESBITT MILLICAN & NESBITT	23	1975
EVERYBODY LOVES A HAPPY ENDING TEARS FOR FEARS	45	2005
EVERYBODY LOVES A NUT JOHNNY CASH	28	1966
EVERYBODY LOVES SATURDAY NIGHT BOB WALLIS & HIS STORYVILLE JAZZMEN	20	1960
EVERYBODY WANTS TO SHAG...THE TEARDROP EXPLODES TEARDROP EXPLODES	72	1990
EVERYBODY'S ANGEL TANITA TIKARAM	19	1991
EVERYBODY'S FREE ROZALLA	20	1992

Title / Artist	Peak Position	Year of Release
EVERYBODY'S ROCKIN' NEIL YOUNG & THE SHOCKING PINKS	50	1983
EVERYBODY'S SOMEBODY KELE LE ROC	44	1999
EVERYONE IS HERE FINN BROTHERS	8	2004
EVERYONE PLAY DARTS DARTS	12	1978
EVERYONE'S GOT ONE ECHOBELLY	8	1994
EVERYTHING BANGLES	5	1988
EVERYTHING CLIMIE FISHER	14	1988
EVERYTHING JOE	53	1994
EVERYTHING & NOTHING DAVID SYLVIAN	57	2000
EVERYTHING CHANGES TAKE THAT	1	1993
EVERYTHING ECTSTATIC FOUR TET	59	2005
EVERYTHING EVERYTHING UNDERWORLD	22	2000
EVERYTHING IS NINE BLACK ALPS	51	2005
EVERYTHING IS BEAUTIFUL RAY STEVENS	62	1970
EVERYTHING IS BEAUTIFUL DANA	43	1980
EVERYTHING IS BORROWED STREETS	7	2008
EVERYTHING IS EVERYTHING DIANA ROSS	31	1971
EVERYTHING IS WRONG/MIXED & REMIXED MOBY	21	1996
EVERYTHING I'VE GOT IN MY POCKET MINNIE DRIVER	44	2004
EVERYTHING MUST GO MANIC STREET PREACHERS	2	1996
EVERYTHING MUST GO STEELY DAN	21	2003
EVERYTHING PICTURE ULTRASOUND	23	1999
EVERYTHING YOU SEE RUNRIG	61	2007
EVERYTHING'S ALRIGHT FOREVER BOO RADLEYS	55	1992
EVERYTHING'S COMING UP DUSTY DUSTY SPRINGFIELD	6	1965
EVERYTHING'S EVENTUAL APPLETON	9	2003
EVERYTHING'S THE RUSH DELAYS	26	2008
EVIL EMPIRE RAGE AGAINST THE MACHINE	4	1996
EVIL HEAT PRIMAL SCREAM	9	2002
EVITA STAGE CAST RECORDING	24	1978
EVITA (OST) MADONNA	1	1996
EVITA (ORIGINAL STUDIO CAST RECORDING) STAGE CAST RECORDING	4	1977
EVOLUTION HOLLIES	13	1967
EVOLUTION JOURNEY	100	1983
EVOLUTION OLETA ADAMS	10	1993
EVOLUTION BOYZ II MEN	12	1997
EVOLUTION CIARA	17	2007
THE EVOLUTION OF ROBIN THICKE ROBIN THICKE	30	2007
EVOLVER GRID	14	1994
EVOLVER JOHN LEGEND	21	2008
EXCESS ALL AREAS SHY	74	1987
EXCITER DEPECHE MODE	9	2001
THE EXCITING SOUNDS OF ROY ORBISON ROY ORBISON	17	1964
EXCLUSIVE CHRIS BROWN	3	2007
EXECUTE OXIDE & NEUTRINO	11	2001
EX-EL 808 STATE	4	1991
EXHIBITION GARY NUMAN	43	1987
EXILE GARY NUMAN	48	1997
EXILE ON MAIN STREET ROLLING STONES	1	1972
EXILE ON MAINSTREAM MATCHBOX 20	53	2007
EXIT TANGERINE DREAM	43	1981
EXIT O STEVE EARLE	77	1987
EXIT PLANET DUST CHEMICAL BROTHERS	9	1995
EXIT STAGE LEFT RUSH	6	1981
EXODUS FILM SOUNDTRACK	17	1961
EXODUS BOB MARLEY & THE WAILERS	8	1977
EXODUS NEW POWER GENERATION	11	1995
EXODUS JA RULE	50	2006
EXORCISING GHOSTS JAPAN	45	1984
EXOTIC CREATURES OF THE DEEP SPARKS	54	2008
EXPANSION TEAM DILATED PEOPLES	55	2002
EXPECTING TO FLY BLUETONES	1	1996
EXPERIENCE JIMI HENDRIX	9	1971
EXPERIENCE PRODIGY	12	1992

Title / Artist	Peak Position	Year of Release
EXPERIENCE ELECTRIC SKIN	72	1997
EXPERIENCE HENDRIX – THE BEST JIMI HENDRIX	10	2000
EXPERIENCE HENDRIX – THE BEST OF JIMI HENDRIX JIMI HENDRIX	18	1997
EXPERIENCE THE DIVINE – GREATEST HITS BETTE MIDLER	3	1993
EXPERIMENTAL JET SET, TRASH AND NO STAR SONIC YOUTH	10	1994
EXPLOITED LIVE EXPLOITED	52	1981
EXPLOSIVE COMPANY AMEN CORNER	19	1969
THE EXPLOSIVE FREDDY CANNON FREDDY CANNON	1	1960
EXPOSED MIKE OLDFIELD	16	1979
EXPOSED VINCE NEIL	44	1993
EXPOSURE ROBERT FRIPP	71	1979
EXPOSURE – THE BEST OF 1977 – 2002 GARY NUMAN	44	2002
EXPRESS YOURSELF CLEARLY E.Y.C.	14	1994
EXPRESSIONS DON WILLIAMS	28	1978
EXPRESSIONS – 24 BEAUTIFUL BALLADS VARIOUS ARTISTS (K-TEL)	11	1985
THE EXQUISITE NANA MOUSKOURI NANA MOUSKOURI	10	1970
EXTENDED PLAY JAMES TAYLOR QUARTET	70	1994
EXTENSIONS MANHATTAN TRANSFER	63	1979
EXTERMINATOR PRIMAL SCREAM	3	2000
EXTINCTION LEVEL EVENT/FINAL WORLD FRONT BUSTA RHYMES	54	1999
EXTRA TEXTURE (READ ALL ABOUT IT) GEORGE HARRISON	16	1975
EXTRA VIRGIN OLIVE	15	1997
EXTRAS JAM	15	1992
EXTRATERRESTRIAL LIVE BLUE OYSTER CULT	39	1982
EXTREME EUPHORIA VARIOUS ARTISTS (MINISTRY OF SOUND)	16	2004
EXTREME EUPHORIA – LISA LASHES VARIOUS ARTISTS (TELSTAR)	5	2002
EXTREME II PORNAGRAFFITTI EXTREME	12	1991
EXTREMELY LIVE VANILLA ICE	35	1991
THE EXTREMIST JOE SATRIANI	13	1992
EXTRICATE FALL	31	1990
EYE CANDY MIS-TEEQ	6	2003
EYE IN THE SKY ALAN PARSONS PROJECT	27	1982
EYE OF THE HURRICANE ALARM	23	1987
EYE OF THE TIGER SURVIVOR	12	1982
EYE TO THE TELESCOPE KT TUNSTALL	3	2005
EYES OF A WOMAN AGNETHA FALTSKOG	38	1985
EYES OPEN SNOW PATROL	1	2006
EYES THAT SEE IN THE DARK KENNY ROGERS	53	1983

F

Title / Artist	Peak Position	Year of Release
F.L.M. MEL & KIM	3	1987
FABLES OF THE RECONSTRUCTION R.E.M.	35	1985
FABRIQUE FASHION	10	1982
FABULOUS STYLISTICS	21	1976
FABULOUS DISASTER EXODUS	67	1989
FABULOUS SHIRLEY BASSEY SHIRLEY BASSEY	12	1961
THE FABULOUS SHIRLEY BASSEY SHIRLEY BASSEY	48	1971
FABULOUS STYLE OF THE EVERLY BROTHERS EVERLY BROTHERS	4	1960
FACADES SAD CAFÉ	8	1979
FACE DANCES WHO	2	1981
FACE THE HEAT SCORPIONS	51	1993
FACE THE MUSIC NKOTB	36	1994
FACE THE MUSIC – TORVILL AND DEAN VARIOUS ARTISTS (POLYGRAM)	8	1994
FACE TO FACE KINKS	12	1966

Title / Artist	Peak Position	Year of Release
FACE TO FACE BARCLAY JAMES HARVEST	65	1987
FACE TO FACE WESTLIFE	1	2005
FACE TO FACE – A LIVE RECORDING STEVE HARLEY & COCKNEY REBEL	40	1977
FACE UP LISA STANSFIELD	38	2001
FACE VALUE PHIL COLLINS	1	1981
FACES EARTH WIND & FIRE	10	1980
THE FACTS OF LIFE BLACK BOX RECORDER	37	2000
FADE OUT LOOP	51	1989
FADE TO GREY – THE SINGLES COLLECTION VISAGE	38	1983
FADED SEASIDE GLAMOUR DELAYS	17	2004
FAHRENHEIT TOTO	99	1986
FAIR WARNING VAN HALEN	49	1981
FAIRWEATHER JOHNSON HOOTIE & THE BLOWFISH	9	1996
FAIRY TALE DONOVAN	20	1965
FAITH CURE	14	1981
FAITH GEORGE MICHAEL	1	1987
FAITH & INSPIRATION DANIEL O'DONNELL	4	2000
FAITH ALIVE ADAM FAITH	19	1965
FAITH AND COURAGE SINEAD O'CONNOR	61	2000
FAITH HOPE LOVE KING'S X	70	1990
FAITHLESS – BACK TO MINE VARIOUS ARTISTS (DISCO MIX CLUB)	19	2000
THE FAKE SOUND OF PROGRESS LOSTPROPHETS	44	2002
FALCO 3 FALCO	32	1986
FALLEN EVANESCENCE	1	2003
THE FALLING CARMEL	88	1986
FALLING FORWARD JULIA FORDHAM	21	1994
FALLING IN LOVE FRANKIE MILLER	54	1979
FALLING INTO YOU CELINE DION	1	1996
FALLING OFF THE LAVENDER BRIDGE LIGHTSPEED CHAMPION	45	2008
FALSE ACCUSATIONS ROBERT CRAY BAND	68	1985
FALSE SMILES AMY STUDT	18	2003
FAME FILM SOUNDTRACK	1	1980
FAME ACADEMY VARIOUS ARTISTS (MERCURY)	2	2002
FAME ACADEMY – BEE GEES SPECIAL VARIOUS ARTISTS (POLYDOR)	17	2003
FAME ACADEMY – THE FINALISTS VARIOUS ARTISTS (POLYDOR)	2	2003
FAME AND FASHION (BOWIE'S ALL TIME GREATEST HITS) DAVID BOWIE	40	1984
FAME AT LAST GEORGIE FAME	15	1964
FAMILIAR TO MILLIONS OASIS	5	2000
FAMILY LEANN RIMES	31	2007
FAMILY ENTERTAINMENT FAMILY	6	1969
FAMILY FAVOURITES RUSS CONWAY	3	1959
FAMILY STYLE VAUGHAN BROTHERS	63	1990
FAMOUS BLUE RAINCOAT – SONGS OF LEONARD COHEN JENNIFER WARNES	33	1987
FAMOUS IN THE LAST CENTURY STATUS QUO	19	2000
...FAMOUS LAST WORDS...' SUPERTRAMP	6	1982
FANDANGO! ZZ TOP	60	1975
FANMAIL TLC	7	1999
FANS MALCOLM McLAREN	47	1984
FANTASTIC 70'S! VARIOUS ARTISTS (COLUMBIA)	8	1998
FANTASTIC 80'S EXTENDED VARIOUS ARTISTS (NONSUCH)	11	2006
FANTASTIC 80'S – GO FOR IT VARIOUS ARTISTS (COLUMBIA)	10	2000
FANTASTIC 80'S! VARIOUS ARTISTS (COLUMBIA)	1	1998
FANTASTIC 80'S! 2 VARIOUS ARTISTS (COLUMBIA)	4	1998
FANTASTIC 80'S! 3 VARIOUS ARTISTS (COLUMBIA)	11	1998
FANTASTIC DANCE! VARIOUS ARTISTS (COLUMBIA)	14	1998
FANTASTIC NO 1'S OF THE SEVENTIES VARIOUS ARTISTS (DMG TV)	9	2004
FANTASTIC PLAYROOM NEW YOUNG PONY CLUB	54	2007
THE FANTASTIC SOUND OF KLAUS WUNDERLICH KLAUS WUNDERLICH	43	1979
FANTASTIC STAR MARC ALMOND	54	1996
FANTASTIC! WHAM!	1	1983
FANTASY BLACK CHANNEL LATE OF THE PIER	28	2008
FANTAZIA – BRITISH ANTHEMS VARIOUS ARTISTS (FANTAZIA)	2	1998
FANTAZIA – BRITISH ANTHEMS – SUMMERTIME VARIOUS ARTISTS (TELSTAR)	3	1998
FANTAZIA CLUB CLASSICS VARIOUS ARTISTS (MINISTRY OF SOUND)	7	2008
FANTAZIA III – MADE IN HEAVEN VARIOUS ARTISTS (FANTAZIA)	16	1994
FANTAZIA PRESENT THE HOUSE COLLECTION 4 VARIOUS ARTISTS (FANTAZIA)	2	1996
FANTAZIA – THE FIRST TASTE VARIOUS ARTISTS (FANTAZIA)	13	1992
FANTAZIA – TWICE AS NICE VARIOUS ARTISTS (FANTAZIA)	17	1993
FANX TA RA SAD CAFÉ	56	1977
FAR BEYOND DRIVEN PANTERA	3	1994
FAR FROM HOME TRAFFIC	29	1994
FAR FROM THE HURTING KIND TRACIE	64	1984
FAR FROM THE MADDENING CROWDS CHICANE	49	1997
A FAR OUT DISC TOY DOLLS	71	1985
FAREWELL ANGELINA JOAN BAEZ	5	1965
FAREWELL MY SUMMER LOVE MICHAEL JACKSON	9	1984
FAREWELL TO KINGS RUSH	22	1977
FASHION NUGGET CAKE	53	1997
THE FAST AND THE FURIOUS FILM SOUNDTRACK	20	2001
FAST FORWARD VARIOUS ARTISTS (TELSTAR)	4	1991
FASTER THAN THE SPEED OF NIGHT BONNIE TYLER	1	1983
FASTWAY FASTWAY	43	1983
FAT DANCE HITS VARIOUS ARTISTS (GLOBAL TELEVISION)	5	1999
THE FAT OF THE LAND PRODIGY	1	1997
FAT OUT OF HELL ROY 'CHUBBY' BROWN	67	1996
FAT POP HITS VARIOUS ARTISTS (GLOBAL TELEVISION)	6	1999
FATBACK LIVE FATBACK BAND	80	1987
FATBOY SLIM – LIVE ON BIRGHTON BEACH VARIOUS ARTISTS (SOUTHERN FRIED)	19	2002
FATE FOR BREAKFAST ART GARFUNKEL	2	1979
FATE OF NATIONS ROBERT PLANT	6	1993
FATHER ABRAHAM IN SMURFLAND FATHER ABRAHAM & THE SMURFS	19	1978
FAVOURITE THINGS CONNIE FISHER	14	2006
FAVOURITE WORST NIGHTMARE ARCTIC MONKEYS	1	2007
FAVOURITES PETERS & LEE	2	1975
FAVOURITES DANIEL O'DONNELL	61	1990
FAWLTY TOWERS FAWLTY TOWERS	25	1979
FAWLTY TOWERS VOLUME 2 (TV ORIGINAL CAST) FAWLTY TOWERS	26	1981
FE REAL MAXI PRIEST	60	1992
FEAR OF A BLACK PLANET PUBLIC ENEMY	4	1990
FEAR OF A BLANK PLANET PORCUPINE TREE	31	2007
FEAR OF FOURS LAMB	37	1999
FEAR OF MUSIC TALKING HEADS	33	1979
FEAR OF THE DARK IRON MAIDEN	1	1992
FEARGAL SHARKEY FEARGAL SHARKEY	12	1985
FEARLESS FAMILY	14	1971
FEARLESS EIGHTH WONDER	47	1988
FEAST CREATURES	17	1983
FEAST OF WIRE CALEXICO	71	2003
FEATHER AND STONE TOM BAXTER	65	2004
FEEDBACK RUSH	68	2004
FEEDBACK JURASSIC 5	59	2006
FEEL ROACHFORD	19	1997
FEEL LIKE MAKING LOVE VARIOUS ARTISTS (HIT LABEL)	17	1995
FEEL THIS JEFF HEALEY BAND	72	1992
FEELGOOD SONGS VARIOUS ARTISTS (EMI)	9	2006
FEELIN' GOOD VARIOUS ARTISTS (UNIVERSAL)	17	2003
FEELING FREE SYDNEY YOUNGBLOOD	23	1989
FEELING GOOD – THE VERY BEST OF NINA SIMONE NINA SIMONE	9	1994
FEELING STRANGELY FINE SEMISONIC	16	1999
FEELINGS VARIOUS ARTISTS (K-TEL)	3	1977
FEELS LIKE HOME NORAH JONES	1	2004
FEELS LIKE RAIN BUDDY GUY	36	1993
FEELS SO GOOD VARIOUS ARTISTS (INSPIRED)	13	2001
FEELS SO GOOD ATOMIC KITTEN	1	2002
FEETS DON'T FAIL ME NOW HERBIE HANCOCK	28	1979
FELICIANO JOSE FELICIANO	6	1968
FELINE STRANGLERS	4	1983
FELIX #1 FELIX	26	1993
FELLOW HOODLUMS DEACON BLUE	2	1991
FELT MOUNTAIN GOLDFRAPP	57	2001
FEMALE VARIOUS ARTISTS (UNIVERSAL)	14	2001
THE FEMALE TOUCH VARIOUS ARTISTS (GLOBAL TELEVISION)	2	1998
THE FEMALE TOUCH 2 VARIOUS ARTISTS (GLOBAL TELEVISION)	9	1999
FERMENT CATHERINE WHEEL	36	1992
FERRY ACROSS THE MERSEY GERRY & THE PACEMAKERS	19	1965
FESTIVAL SANTANA	27	1977
FESTIVAL VARIOUS ARTISTS (WARNER BROTHERS)	2	2005
FESTIVAL 06 VARIOUS ARTISTS (WARNER BROTHERS)	3	2006
FESTIVAL 07 VARIOUS ARTISTS (WARNER BROTHERS)	15	2007
FEVER KYLIE MINOGUE	1	2001
FEVER IN FEVER OUT LUSCIOUS JACKSON	55	1997
FEVER TO TELL YEAH YEAH YEAHS	13	2003
A FEVER YOU CAN'T SWEAT OUT PANIC! AT THE DISCO	17	2006
FFRR – SILVER ON BLACK VARIOUS ARTISTS (LONDON)	8	1989
FFWD FFWD	48	1994
FI ROCK VARIOUS ARTISTS (TELSTAR)	20	1996
FICTION COMSAT ANGELS	94	1982
FICTION TALES MODERN EON	65	1981
FIDDLER ON THE ROOF STAGE CAST RECORDING	4	1967
FIDDLER ON THE ROOF FILM SOUNDTRACK	26	1972
FIELDS OF GOLD – THE BEST OF STING 1984-1994 STING	2	1994
FIERCE VARIOUS ARTISTS (COOLTEMPO)	37	1987
15 BIG ONES BEACH BOYS	31	1976
5TH DIMENSION BYRDS	27	1966
THE FIFTH ELEMENT (OST) ERIC SERRA	58	1997
THE 50TH ANNIVERSARY ALBUM CLIFF RICHARD	11	2008
50 CENT IS THE FUTURE (IMPORT) 50 CENT & G UNIT	65	2004
50 GOLDEN GREATS SHADOWS	35	2000
THE 50 GREATEST HITS ELVIS PRESLEY	8	2000
THE 50 GREATEST LOVE SONGS ELVIS PRESLEY	21	2001

Title / Artist	Peak Position	Year of Release
FIFTY NUMBER ONES OF THE '60S VARIOUS ARTISTS (GLOBAL TELEVISION)	8	1995
5150 VAN HALEN	16	1986
52ND STREET BILLY JOEL	10	1978
THE '56 SESSIONS VOLUME 1 ELVIS PRESLEY	47	1978
50 YEARS OF THE GREATEST HIT SINGLES VARIOUS ARTISTS (EMI)	5	2002
FIFTY YEARS ON WITH JIMMY SHAND JIMMY SHAND & HIS BAND	97	1983
FIGHT WITH TOOLS FLOBOTS	52	2008
FIGHTING THIN LIZZY	60	1975
FIGURE 8 ELLIOTT SMITH	37	2000
FILE UNDER EASY LISTENING SUGAR	7	1994
FILIGREE AND SHADOW THIS MORTAL COIL	53	1986
FILMS ABOUT GHOSTS – THE BEST OF COUNTING CROWS	15	2004
FILTH HOUNDS OF HADES TANK	33	1982
FILTH PIG MINISTRY	43	1996
FILTHY LUCRE LIVE SEX PISTOLS	26	1996
FIN DE SIECLE DIVINE COMEDY	9	1998
THE FINAL WHAM!	2	1986
THE FINAL COUNTDOWN EUROPE	9	1986
THE FINAL COUNTDOWN – THE VERY BEST OF SOFT METAL VARIOUS ARTISTS (TELSTAR)	9	1990
THE FINAL CUT PINK FLOYD	1	1983
THE FINAL FRONTIER KEEL	83	1986
A FINAL HIT – GREATEST HITS LEFTFIELD	32	2005
FINAL STRAW SNOW PATROL	3	2004
FINALLY CE CE PENISTON	10	1992
FINALLY BLACKstreet	27	1999
FINALLY WOKEN JEM	6	2005
FIND OUT STEVEN DANTE	87	1988
FIND YOUR WAY GABRIELLE	9	1993
FINDERS KEEPERS CLIFF RICHARD	6	1966
FINDING FOREVER COMMON	35	2007
THE FINE ART OF SURFACING BOOMTOWN RATS	7	1979
A FINE ROMANCE – THE LOVE SONGS OF FRANK SINATRA	6	2002
FINE YOUNG CANNIBALS FINE YOUNG CANNIBALS	11	1985
FINELINES MY VITRIOL	24	2001
THE FINEST FINE YOUNG CANNIBALS	10	1996
FINEST HOUR LINDISFARNE	55	1975
FINGS AIN'T WOT THEY USED TO BE STAGE CAST RECORDING	5	1960
FINISTERRE SAINT ETIENNE	55	2002
FINN FINN	15	1995
FINYL VINYL RAINBOW	31	1986
FIRE ELECTRIC SIX	7	2003
FIRE & SKILL – THE SONGS OF THE JAM VARIOUS ARTISTS (IGNITION)	12	1999
FIRE AND ICE YNGWIE J MALMSTEEN	57	1992
FIRE AND WATER FREE	2	1970
FIRE AND WATER DAVE GREENFIELD & JEAN-JACQUES BURNEL	94	1983
FIRE DANCES KILLING JOKE	29	1983
FIRE GARDEN STEVE VAI	41	1996
THE FIRE INSIDE BOB SEGER & THE SILVER BULLET BAND	54	1991
FIRE OF UNKNOWN ORIGIN BLUE OYSTER CULT	29	1981
FIREBALL DEEP PURPLE	1	1971
FIRES NERINA PALLOT	21	2006
FIREWORKS JOSE FELICIANO	65	1970
FIREWORKS (SINGLES 1997 – 2002) EMBRACE	36	2002
FIRING ON ALL SIX LONE STAR	36	1977
THE FIRM FIRM	15	1985
FIRST AND LAST AND ALWAYS SISTERS OF MERCY	14	1985
FIRST BAND ON THE MOON CARDIGANS	18	1996
FIRST BLOOD...LAST CUTS W.A.S.P.	69	1993
THE FIRST BORN IS DEAD NICK CAVE & THE BAD SEEDS	53	1985
THE FIRST CHAPTER MISSION	35	1987
FIRST COMES FIRST PADDINGTONS	65	2005
FIRST CONTACT ROGER SANCHEZ	34	2001
THE FIRST DAY DAVID SYLVIAN & ROBERT FRIPP	21	1993
THE FIRST FAMILY VAUGHN MEADER	12	1962
FIRST IMPRESSIONS OF EARTH STROKES	1	2006
FIRST LADIES OF COUNTRY VARIOUS ARTISTS (CBS)	37	1980
FIRST LADIES OF COUNTRY VARIOUS ARTISTS (SONY)	14	2004
FIRST LADY LISA MAFFIA	44	2003
FIRST LADY FAITH EVANS	22	2005
THE FIRST LADY OF SOUL ARETHA FRANKLIN	89	1986
THE FIRST LIVE RECORDINGS ELVIS PRESLEY	69	1984
FIRST LOVE VARIOUS ARTISTS (ARCADE)	58	1980
FIRST LOVE MICHAEL BALL	4	1996
FIRST LOVE: SONGS FROM THE BRITISH ISLES BRYN TERFEL	16	2008
THE FIRST OF A MILLION KISSES FAIRGROUND ATTRACTION	2	1988
THE FIRST OF TOO MANY SENSELESS THINGS	66	1991
FIRST RAYS OF THE NEW RISING SUN JIMI HENDRIX	37	1997
FIRST STEP FACES	45	1970
THE FIRST SUMMER OF LOVE VARIOUS ARTISTS (POLYGRAM)	6	1997
FIRST TAKE ROBERTA FLACK	47	1972
FIRST TEN YEARS JOAN BAEZ	41	1971
FIRST (THE SOUND OF MUSIC) THEN JERICO	35	1987
FIRST TIME EVER I SAW YOUR FACE JOHNNY MATHIS	40	1972
THE FISH AND THE TREE AND THE BIRD AND THE BELL VARIOUS ARTISTS (COLUMBIA)	9	1991
FISH OUT OF WATER CHRIS SQUIRE	25	1975
THE FISH PEOPLE TAPES ALEXEI SAYLE	62	1984
FISH RISING STEVE HILLAGE	33	1975
FISHERMAN'S BLUES WATERBOYS	13	1988
FISHING FOR LUCKIES WILDHEARTS	16	1996
5 J.J. CALE	40	1979
5 LENNY KRAVITZ	18	1998
FIVE FIVE	1	1998
FIVE BRIDGES NICE	2	1970
FIVE FACES OF MANFRED MANN MANFRED MANN	3	1964
FIVE GUYS NAMED MOE STAGE CAST RECORDING	59	1991
FIVE MAN ACOUSTICAL JAM TESLA	59	1991
FIVE MILES OUT MIKE OLDFIELD	7	1982
THE FIVE PENNIES FILM SOUNDTRACK	2	1960
5,000 SPIRITS OR THE LAYERS OF THE ONION INCREDIBLE STRING BAND	25	1967
FLAG YELLO	56	1988
THE FLAME ANNABEL LAMB	84	1984
FLAMENCO GUITAR MANITAS DE PLATA	40	1967
FLAMING PIE PAUL McCARTNEY	2	1997
FLAMING STAR AND SUMMER KISSES ELVIS PRESLEY	11	1965
FLARED HITS AND PLATFORM SOUL VARIOUS ARTISTS (VISION)	13	1995
FLASH JEFF BECK	83	1985
FLASH GORDON (ORIGINAL FILM SOUNDTRACK) QUEEN	10	1980
FLASH LIGHT TOM VERLAINE	99	1987
FLASH TRACKS VARIOUS ARTISTS (TV RECORDS)	19	1982
FLASHDANCE FILM SOUNDTRACK	9	1983
FLASHPOINT ROLLING STONES	6	1991
THE FLAT EARTH THOMAS DOLBY	14	1984
FLAT, BAROQUE AND BERSERK ROY HARPER	20	1970
FLAUNT IT SIGUE SIGUE SPUTNIK	10	1986
FLAUNT THE IMPERFECTION CHINA CRISIS	9	1985
FLAVORS OF ENTANGLEMENT ALANIS MORISSETTE	15	2008
FLEET FOXES FLEET FOXES	11	2008
FLEETWOOD MAC FLEETWOOD MAC	4	1968
FLEETWOOD MAC LIVE FLEETWOOD MAC	31	1980
FLESH AND BLOOD ROXY	1	1980
FLESH AND BLOOD POISON	3	1990
FLESHWOUNDS SKIN	43	2003
FLEX LENE LOVICH	19	1980
FLICK OF THE SWITCH AC/DC	4	1983
FLIGHT OF ICARUS/THE TROOPER IRON MAIDEN	7	1990
FLIGHT OF THE CONCHORDS FLIGHT OF THE CONCHORDS	32	2008
THE FLIGHT OF THE CONDOR INTI ILLIMANI-GUAMARY	62	1983
FLIGHT OF THE CONDOR VARIOUS ARTISTS (TELSTAR)	11	1992
FLIGHTS OF FANCY PAUL LEONI	17	1983
THE FLINTSTONES FILM SOUNDTRACK	18	1994
FLIP NILS LOFGREN	36	1985
FLOATERS FLOATERS	17	1977
FLOCK FLOCK	59	1970
A FLOCK OF SEAGULLS A FLOCK OF SEAGULLS	32	1982
FLOGGING A DEAD HORSE SEX PISTOLS	23	1980
FLOOD THEY MIGHT BE GIANTS	14	1990
FLOODLAND SISTERS OF MERCY	9	1987
FLOOR FILLAS FLIP & FILL	29	2003
FLOORED GENIUS – THE BEST OF JULIAN COPE AND THE TEARDROP EXPLODES JULIAN COPE & THE TEARDROP EXPLODES	22	1992
FLOORFILLERS VARIOUS ARTISTS (UNIVERSAL)	1	2004
FLOORFILLERS 08 VARIOUS ARTISTS (UNIVERSAL)	1	2008
FLOORFILLERS 2 VARIOUS ARTISTS (UNIVERSAL)	3	2004
FLOORFILLERS 3 VARIOUS ARTISTS (UNIVERSAL)	2	2005
FLOORFILLERS 4 VARIOUS ARTISTS (UNIVERSAL)	4	2005
FLOORFILLERS ANTHEMS VARIOUS ARTISTS (UNIVERSAL)	1	2007
FLOORFILLERS – CLUB CLASSICS VARIOUS ARTISTS (UNIVERSAL)	1	2006
FLOORFILLERS CLUBMIX VARIOUS ARTISTS (UNIVERSAL)	2	2008
FLORAL DANCE BRIGHOUSE & RASTRICK BRASS BAND	10	1978
FLOWER DRUM SONG STAGE CAST RECORDING	2	1960
FLOWERS ACE OF BASE	15	1998
FLOWERS ECHO & THE BUNNYMEN	56	2001
FLOWERS IN THE DIRT PAUL McCARTNEY	1	1989
FLOWERS OF ROMANCE PUBLIC IMAGE LTD	11	1981
FLUSH THE FASHION ALICE COOPER	56	1980
FLY DIXIE CHICKS	38	1999
FLY LIKE AN EAGLE STEVE MILLER BAND	11	1976
FLY ON THE WALL AC/DC	7	1985
FLY ON THE WALL – B SIDES & RARITIES PAUL WELLER	22	2003
FLY OR DIE N*E*R*D	4	2004
FLYER NANCI GRIFFITH	20	1994
THE FLYING CLUB CUP BEIRUT	69	2007
FLYING COLOURS CHRIS DE BURGH	1	1988
FLYING COWBOYS RICKIE LEE JONES	50	1989
FLYING LIZARDS FLYING LIZARDS	60	1980
FM FILM SOUNDTRACK	37	1978
FOCUS FOCUS	23	1975
FOCUS 3 FOCUS	6	1972

Title / Artist	Peak Position	Year of Release
FOCUS AT THE RAINBOW FOCUS	23	1973
FOG ON THE TYNE LINDISFARNE	1	1971
FOLD YOUR HANDS CHILD YOU WALK LIKE A PEASANT BELLE & SEBASTIAN	10	2000
FOLIE A DEUX FALL OUT BOY	39	2008
FOLK FESTIVAL OF THE BLUES (LIVE RECORDING) VARIOUS ARTISTS (PYE)	16	1964
FOLKLORE NELLY FURTADO	11	2003
FOLKLORE & SUPERSTITION BLACK STONE CHERRY	23	2008
FOLLOW THAT GIRL STAGE CAST RECORDING	5	1960
FOLLOW THE LEADER ERIC B & RAKIM	25	1988
FOLLOW THE LEADER KORN	5	1998
FOLLOW YOUR DREAM DANIEL O'DONNELL	17	1992
FONTANELLE BABES IN TOYLAND	24	1992
FONZIE'S FAVOURITES (TELEVISION COMPILATION) TELEVISION AND RADIO COMPILATION	8	1978
FOO FIGHTERS FOO FIGHTERS	3	1995
FOOD & LIQUOR LUPE FIASCO	31	2006
FOOL BRITANNIA ANTHONY NEWLEY, PETER SELLERS, JOAN COLLINS	10	1963
THE FOOL CIRCLE NAZARETH	60	1981
FOOLISH BEHAVIOUR ROD STEWART	4	1980
FOOT LOOSE AND FANCY FREE ROD STEWART	3	1977
FOOTBALL CRAZY – HEAR THE SONGS VARIOUS ARTISTS (GTV)	5	2006
FOOTLOOSE FILM SOUNDTRACK	7	1984
FOOTPRINTS HOLLY VALANCE	9	2002
FOR CERTAIN BECAUSE HOLLIES	23	1966
FOR EARTH BELOW ROBIN TROWER	26	1975
FOR EMMA FOREVER AGO BON IVER	42	2008
FOR MY MUM VARIOUS ARTISTS (WARNER BROTHERS)	8	2006
FOR ONCE IN MY LIFE TONY BENNETT	29	1968
FOR PLEASURE OMAR	50	1994
FOR SCREENING PURPOSES ONLY TEST ICICLES	69	2005
FOR SOMEONE SPECIAL KEN DODD	40	1967
FOR THE BOYS BETTE MIDLER	75	1992
FOR THE GOOD TIMES PERRY COMO	41	1983
FOR THE LOVE OF STRANGE MEDICINE STEVE PERRY	64	1994
FOR THE STARS ANNE SOFIE VON OTTER MEETS ELVIS COSTELLO	67	2001
FOR THOSE ABOUT TO ROCK WE SALUTE YOU AC/DC	3	1981
FOR TO NEXT STEVE HILLAGE	48	1983
FOR TWISTERS ONLY CHUBBY CHECKER	17	1962
FOR UNLAWFUL CARNAL KNOWLEDGE VAN HALEN	12	1991
FOR YOU – 20 SONGS ESPECIALLY FOR YOU VARIOUS ARTISTS (COLUMBIA)	4	2000
FOR YOUR EARS ONLY BENTLEY RHYTHM ACE	48	2000
FOR YOUR PLEASURE ROXY	4	1973
FORBIDDEN BLACK SABBATH	71	1995
THE FORCE BEHIND THE POWER DIANA ROSS	11	1991
FORCE MAJEURE TANGERINE DREAM	26	1979
FORCE OF VICTORY LINTON KWESI JOHNSON	66	1979
FORE! HUEY LEWIS & THE NEWS	8	1986
FOREIGN AFFAIR TINA TURNER	1	1989
FOREIGNER CAT STEVENS	3	1973
FOREVER VARIOUS ARTISTS (EMI)	17	1992
FOREVER CRANES	40	1993
FOREVER DAMAGE	13	1997
FOREVER PUFF DADDY	9	1999
FOREVER SPICE GIRLS	2	2000
FOREVER JONATHAN ANSELL	32	2008
FOREVER AND EVER DEMIS ROUSSOS	2	1974
FOREVER AND EVER – DEFINITIVE COLLECTION DEMIS ROUSSOS	17	2002
FOREVER BEGINS TONIGHT PATRIZIO BUANNE	15	2006
FOREVER BLUE CHRIS ISAAK	27	1995
FOREVER CHANGES LOVE	24	1968
FOREVER DELAYED – THE GREATEST HITS MANIC STREET PREACHERS	4	2002
FOREVER ELLA ELLA FITZGERALD	19	1996
FOREVER FAITHLESS – THE GREATEST HITS FAITHLESS	1	2005
FOREVER FOR NOW HARRY CONNICK JR.	32	1993
FOREVER NOW PSYCHEDELIC FURS	20	1982
FOREVER NOW LEVEL 42	8	1994
FOREVER – THE SINGLES CHARLATANS	38	2006
FOREVER YOUR GIRL PAULA ABDUL	3	1989
FOREVER, FOR ALWAYS, FOR LOVE LUTHER VANDROSS	23	1987
FORGING AHEAD BAD MANNERS	78	1982
FORGIVEN, NOT FORGOTTEN CORRS	2	1996
FORM & FUNCTION PHOTEK	61	1998
FORMALDEHYDE TERRORVISION	75	1993
FORMICA BLUES MONO	71	1998
FORMULA 30 VARIOUS ARTISTS (MERCURY)	6	1983
FORMULA THIRTY – 2 VARIOUS ARTISTS (MERCURY)	80	1986
FORREST GUMP FILM SOUNDTRACK	5	1994
FORTH VERVE	1	2008
FORTRESS ROUND MY HEART IDA MARIA	39	2008
40 BIG ONES JUDGE DREAD	51	1981
40 FANTASTIC HITS FROM THE 50'S AND 60'S VARIOUS ARTISTS (ARCADE)	2	1973
FORTY FINGERS FRESHLY PACKED CHICKEN SHACK	12	1968
45 RPM – THE SINGLES OF THE THE THE THE	60	2002
44 SUPERSTARS VARIOUS ARTISTS (K-TEL)	14	1976
40 GOLDEN GREATS JIM REEVES	1	1975
40 GOLDEN GREATS CLIFF RICHARD	1	1977
40 GOLDEN MOTOWN GREATS DIANA ROSS & THE SUPREMES	35	1998
40 GREATEST HERB ALPERT & THE TIJUANA BRASS	45	1977
40 GREATEST HITS PERRY COMO	1	1975
FORTY LICKS ROLLING STONES	2	2002
FORTY MANIA ANONYMOUS COVER VERSIONS	21	1976
40 MOST BEAUTIFUL ARIAS VARIOUS ARTISTS (WARNER BROTHERS)	12	2006
THE 49ERS 49ERS	51	1990
40 NUMBER ONE HITS VARIOUS ARTISTS (K-TEL)	15	1978
41 HOLLYWOOD GREATS – THE BEST OF DORIS DAY	73	2002
40 SINGALONG PUB SONGS ANONYMOUS COVER VERSIONS	21	1975
40 SUPER GREATS VARIOUS ARTISTS (K-TEL)	9	1975
FOSSIL FUEL – THE XTC SINGLES COLLECTION 1977-1992 XTC	33	1996
FOSTERS AND ALLEN'S CHRISTMAS COLLECTION FOSTER & ALLEN	40	1989
FOTHERINGAY FOTHERINGAY	18	1970
FOUNDATION TEN CITY	22	1989
FOUNTAINS OF WAYNE FOUNTAINS OF WAYNE	67	1997
4 FOREIGNER	5	1981
458489 A-SIDES FALL	44	1990
4.5 THE BEST OF THE INDIGO GIRLS INDIGO GIRLS	43	1995
THE FOUR SEASONS STORY FOUR SEASONS	20	1976
THE FOUR SIDES OF MELANIE MELANIE	23	1972
461 OCEAN BOULEVARD ERIC CLAPTON	3	1974
FOUR STAR COUNTRY VARIOUS ARTISTS (K-TEL)	52	1985
FOUR SURE SCOOCH	41	2000
FOUR SYMBOLS (LED ZEPPELIN 4) LED ZEPPELIN	1	1971
4:13 DREAM CURE	33	2008
4766 SECONDS: A SHORTCUT TO TEENAGE FANCLUB TEENAGE FANCLUB	47	2003
4,000 WEEKS HOLIDAY IAN DURY & THE MUSIC STUDENTS	54	1984
FOUR TOPS GREATEST HITS FOUR TOPS	1	1968
FOUR TOPS GREATEST HITS VOLUME 2 FOUR TOPS	25	1971
FOUR TOPS LIVE! FOUR TOPS	4	1967
FOUR TOPS ON TOP FOUR TOPS	9	1966
THE FOUR TOPS STORY 1964-1972 FOUR TOPS	35	1973
4-TRACK DEMOS PJ HARVEY	19	1993
FOUR WEDDINGS AND A FUNERAL FILM SOUNDTRACK	5	1994
FOUR-CALENDAR CAFÉ COCTEAU TWINS	13	1993
14:59 SUGAR RAY	60	1999
1492 – THE CONQUEST OF PARADISE (OST) VANGELIS	33	1992
14 SHADES OF GREY STAIND	16	2003
14 SHOTS TO THE DOME LL COOL J	74	1993
14 THINGS TO THINK ABOUT CHRIS FARLOWE	19	1966
FOURTH SOFT MACHINE	32	1971
FOUR-WAY STREET CROSBY, STILL, NASH & YOUNG	5	1971
FOX FOX	7	1975
THE FOX ELTON JOHN	12	1981
FOX KIDS PARTY HITS VARIOUS ARTISTS (BMG)	15	2004
FOXBASE ALPHA SAINT ETIENNE	34	1991
FOXTROT GENESIS	12	1972
FRACTURED LIFE AIR TRAFFIC	42	2007
FRAGGLE ROCK FRAGGLES	38	1984
FRAGILE YES	7	1971
THE FRAGILE NINE INCH NAILS	10	1999
FRAGILE – MYSTICAL SOUNDS OF THE PANPIPES LOS NINOS	74	1995
FRAGMENTS OF FREEDOM MORCHEEBA	6	2000
FRAMPTON COMES ALIVE PETER FRAMPTON	6	1976
FRANCES THE MUTE MARS VOLTA	23	2005
FRANK SQUEEZE	58	1989
FRANK AMY WINEHOUSE	13	2003
FRANK BLACK FRANK BLACK	9	1993
FRANK BLACK AND THE CATHOLICS FRANK BLACK	61	1998
FRANK SINATRA FRANK SINATRA	28	1967
THE FRANK SINATRA COLLECTION FRANK SINATRA	40	1986
FRANK SINATRA SINGS FOR ONLY THE LONELY FRANK SINATRA	5	1958
FRANK SINATRA SINGS RODGERS AND HART FRANK SINATRA	35	1971
FRANK SINATRA SINGS SONGS FOR PLEASURE FRANK SINATRA	26	1966
FRANK SINATRA STORY FRANK SINATRA	8	1958
FRANKIE FRANK SINATRA	3	1957
FRANKIE AND JOHNNY ELVIS PRESLEY	11	1966
FRANKIE MCBRIDE FRANKIE McBRIDE	29	1968
FRANKIE VAUGHAN AT THE LONDON PALLADIUM FRANKIE VAUGHAN	6	1959
FRANKIE VAUGHAN SONGBOOK FRANKIE VAUGHAN	40	1967
FRANK'S WILD YEARS TOM WAITS	20	1987
FRANTIC VARIOUS ARTISTS (WARNER BROTHERS)	17	2001
FRANTIC BRYAN FERRY	6	2002

Title / Artist	Peak Position	Year of Release
FRANTIC 2002 VARIOUS ARTISTS (WARNER BROTHERS)	15	2002
FRANTIC EUPHORIA VARIOUS ARTISTS (MINISTRY OF SOUND)	4	2004
FRANTIC ROMANTIC JERMAINE STEWART	49	1986
FRANZ FERDINAND FRANZ FERDINAND	3	2004
FREAK OF NATURE ANASTACIA	4	2001
FREAK OUT CHIC & SISTER SLEDGE	72	1987
FREAK SHOW SILVERCHAIR	38	1997
FREDDIE AND THE DREAMERS FREDDIE & THE DREAMERS	5	1963
THE FREDDIE MERCURY ALBUM FREDDIE MERCURY	4	1992
FREE RICK ASTLEY	9	1991
FREE ALL ANGELS ASH	1	2001
FREE AND EASY HELEN REDDY	17	1975
FREE AS A BIRD SUPERTRAMP	93	1987
FREE AT LAST FREE	9	1972
FREE FOR ALL TED NUGENT	33	1976
FREE LIVE! FREE	4	1971
FREE ME EMMA BUNTON	7	2004
FREE PEACE SWEET DODGY	7	1996
FREE SCHOOL MILK TINY DANCERS	64	2007
FREE SPIRIT – 17 CLASSIC ROCK BALLADS VARIOUS ARTISTS (COLUMBIA)	4	1991
THE FREE STORY FREE	2	1974
FREE THE BEES BEES	26	2004
FREE WHEELERS PEDDLERS	27	1968
FREEDOM NEIL YOUNG	17	1989
FREEDOM AKON	31	2008
FREEDOM 2 – THE ULTIMATE RAVE VARIOUS ARTISTS (TRAX)	16	1990
FREEDOM AT POINT ZERO JEFFERSON STARSHIP	22	1980
FREEDOM FIELDS SETH LAKEMAN	32	2006
FREEDOM NO COMPROMISE LITTLE STEVEN	52	1987
FREEDOM OF CHOICE DEVO	47	1980
THE FREEDOM SPARK LARRIKIN LOVE	37	2006
FREEDOM TO PARTY – FIRST LEGAL RAVE VARIOUS ARTISTS (TRAX)	4	1990
FREEWAY VARIOUS ARTISTS (POLYGRAM)	17	1996
THE FREEWHEELIN' BOB DYLAN BOB DYLAN	1	1964
FREEZE-FRAME J. GEILS BAND	12	1982
A FRENCH AFFAIR VARIOUS ARTISTS (VIRGIN)	19	2001
FRENCH KISSES LIL' LOUIS	35	1989
THE FRENZ EXPERIMENT FALL	19	1988
FREQUENCIES LFO	42	1991
FRESCO M PEOPLE	2	1997
FRESH AND FUNKY HOUSE ANTHEMS VARIOUS ARTISTS (VIRGIN)	20	2005
FRESH AS A DAISY – THE SINGLES JAMES	12	2007
FRESH CREAM CREAM	6	1966
FRESH DANCE 93 VARIOUS ARTISTS (TELSTAR)	4	1993
FRESH FRUIT FOR ROTTING VEGETABLES DEAD KENNEDYS	33	1980
FRESH FRUIT IN FOREIGN PLACES KID CREOLE & THE COCONUTS	99	1982
FRESH HITS 1997 VARIOUS ARTISTS (GLOBAL TELEVISION)	1	1997
FRESH HITS 96 VARIOUS ARTISTS (SONY)	2	1996
FRESH HITS 98 VARIOUS ARTISTS (SONY)	1	1998
FRESH HITS 99 VARIOUS ARTISTS (GLOBAL TELEVISION)	1	1999
FRESH HITS – VOL 2 VARIOUS ARTISTS (WARNER BROTHERS)	2	2000
FRESH HITS – VOLUME 1 VARIOUS ARTISTS (WARNER BROTHERS)	1	2000
FRESH HORSES GARTH BROOKS	22	1995
FRESH QUOTA STATUS QUO	74	1981
FRESH! GINA G	12	1997
FRESHEN UP VOLUME 1 VARIOUS ARTISTS (FRESH)	20	1995
FRESKA! VARIOUS ARTISTS (REACT)	20	1994
FRIDAY NIGHT FEVER VARIOUS ARTISTS (POLYGRAM)	6	1998
FRIDAY THE 13TH (AT THE MARQUEE CLUB) PLAYN JAYN	93	1984
FRIDAY'S CHILD WILL YOUNG	1	2003
FRIED' JULIAN COPE	87	1984
FRIEND OR FOE ADAM ANT	5	1982
FRIENDLY FIRE SHARA NELSON	44	1995
FRIENDLY FIRES FRIENDLY FIRES	38	2008
FRIENDS BEACH BOYS	13	1968
FRIENDS SHALAMAR	6	1982
FRIENDS AGAIN VARIOUS ARTISTS (IMPRESSION)	91	1984
FRIENDS AND LOVERS VARIOUS ARTISTS (K-TEL)	10	1987
FRIENDS AND LOVERS BERNARD BUTLER	43	1999
FRIENDS FOREVER TWEENIES	56	2000
FRIENDS IN LOVE JOHNNY MATHIS	34	1982
THE FRIENDS OF MR. CAIRO JON & VANGELIS	6	1981
FRIENDS REUNITED VARIOUS ARTISTS (UNIVERSAL)	8	2003
FRIENDS REUNITED – THE 90'S VARIOUS ARTISTS (UNIVERSAL)	18	2003
FROGSTOMP SILVERCHAIR	49	1995
FROM A BASEMENT ON THE HILL ELLIOTT SMITH	41	2004
FROM A DISTANCE...THE EVENT CLIFF RICHARD	3	1990
FROM A SPARK TO A FLAME – THE VERY BEST OF CHRIS DE BURGH CHRIS DE BURGH	4	1989
FROM A TO B NEW MUSIK	35	1980
FROM ACROSS THE KITCHEN TABLE PALE FOUNTAINS	94	1985
FROM BEER TO ETERNITY MACC LADS	72	1989
FROM BOTH SIDES NOW IAN McSHANE	40	1992
FROM DANIEL WITH LOVE DANIEL O'DONNELL	5	2006
FROM DONNY WITH LOVE DONNY OSMOND	8	2008
FROM DUSTY...WITH LOVE DUSTY SPRINGFIELD	35	1970
FROM ELVIS IN MEMPHIS ELVIS PRESLEY	1	1969
FROM ELVIS PRESLEY BOULEVARD, MEMPHIS, TENNESSEE ELVIS PRESLEY	29	1976
FROM EVERY SPHERE ED HARCOURT	39	2003
FROM HER TO ETERNITY NICK CAVE FEATURING THE BAD SEEDS	40	1984
FROM HERE TO ETERNITY CLASH	13	1999
FROM LANGLEY PARK TO MEMPHIS PREFAB SPROUT	5	1988
FROM LUXURY TO HEARTACHE CULTURE CLUB	10	1986
FROM MATT WITH LOVE MATT MONRO	30	2007
FROM MEMPHIS TO VEGAS – FROM VEGAS TO MEMPHIS ELVIS PRESLEY	3	1970
FROM MIGHTY OAKS RAY THOMAS	23	1975
FROM MOTOWN WITH LOVE VARIOUS ARTISTS (K-TEL)	6	1987
FROM NOW ON WILL YOUNG	1	2002
FROM NOWHERE...THE TROGGS TROGGS	6	1966
FROM PARIS TO BERLIN INFERNAL	44	2007
FROM SEA TO SHINING SEA JOHNNY CASH	40	1968
FROM THE BEGINNING SMALL FACES	17	1967
FROM THE BOTTOM UP BROWNSTONE	18	1995
FROM THE CHOIRGIRL HOTEL TORI AMOS	6	1998
FROM THE CRADLE ERIC CLAPTON	1	1994
FROM THE HEART TOM JONES	23	1966
FROM THE HEART DANIEL O'DONNELL	56	1988
FROM THE HEART – GREATEST HITS BONNIE TYLER	31	2007
FROM THE HEART – HIS GREATEST LOVE SONGS ELVIS PRESLEY	4	1992
FROM THE HEART OF TOWN GALLON DRUNK	67	1993
FROM THE INSIDE ALICE COOPER	68	1978
FROM THE LEFT SIDE SKYY	85	1986
FROM THE MAKERS OF... STATUS QUO	4	1982
FROM THE MOUNTAIN STYLISTICS	36	1975
FROM THE MUDDY BANKS OF THE WISHKAH NIRVANA	4	1996
FROM THE OFFICIAL BARCELONA GAMES CEREMONY PLACIDO DOMINGO, JOSE CARRERAS & MONTSERRAT CABALLE	41	1992
FROM THE TEA ROOMS OF MARS...TO THE HELLHOLES OF URANUS LANDSCAPE	16	1981
FROM THE WITCHWOOD STRAWBS	39	1971
FROM THEM THROUGH US TO YOU MADINA LAKE	60	2007
FROM THIS MOMENT ON DIANA KRALL	29	2006
FROM TIME TO TIME – THE SINGLES COLLECTION PAUL YOUNG	1	1991
FROM UNDER THE CORK TREE FALL OUT BOY	12	2006
FRONT PAGE NEWS WISHBONE ASH	31	1977
FRONT PARLOUR BALLADS RICHARD THOMPSON	54	2005
FRONTIERS JOURNEY	6	1983
FRUIT AT THE BOTTOM WENDY & LISA	45	1989
FSOL PRESENTS AMORPHOUS ANDROGYNOUS: THE ISNESS AMORPHOUS ANDROGYNOUS	68	2002
FUGAZI MARILLION	5	1984
THE FUGITIVE TONY BANKS	50	1983
THE FUGITIVE KIND SWANS WAY	88	1984
FULFILLINGNESS' FIRST FINALE STEVIE WONDER	5	1974
FULHAM FALLOUT LURKERS	57	1978
FULL CIRCLE BOYZ II MEN	56	2002
FULL CLIP: A DECADE OF GANG STARR GANG STARR	47	1999
FULL HOUSE FAIRPORT CONVENTION	13	1970
FULL HOUSE DOOLEYS	54	1980
THE FULL LIFE JACK JONES	41	1977
FULL METAL JACKET FILM SOUNDTRACK	60	1987
THE FULL MONTY FILM SOUNDTRACK	1	1997
FULL MOON BRANDY	9	2002
FULL MOON FEVER TOM PETTY	8	1989
FULL MOON, DIRTY HEARTS INXS	3	1993
FULL ON – A YEAR IN THE LIFE OF HOUSE VARIOUS ARTISTS (DECONSTRUCTION)	18	1993
FULL ON DANCE VARIOUS ARTISTS (COOKIE JAR)	12	1993
FULL ON DANCE '93 VARIOUS ARTISTS (COOKIE JAR)	3	1993
FULL ON...MASK HYSTERIA ALTERN 8	11	1992
FULLY QUALIFIED SURVIVOR MICHAEL CHAPMAN	45	1970
THE FUN BOY THREE FUN BOY THREE	7	1982
FUN IN ACAPULCO (OST) ELVIS PRESLEY	9	1963
FUN IN SPACE ROGER TAYLOR	18	1981
FUNDAMENTAL BONNIE RAITT	52	1998
FUNDAMENTAL PET SHOP BOYS	5	2006
FUNERAL ARCADE FIRE	33	2005
FUNHOUSE P!NK	1	2008
A FUNK ODYSSEY JAMIROQUAI	1	2001
FUNK SOUL ANTHEMS VARIOUS ARTISTS (BMG)	15	2005
FUNK SOUL BROTHER – THE BEST OF DANCE SOUL & SWING VARIOUS ARTISTS (GLOBAL TELEVISION)	19	1999
FUNK SOUL CLASSICS VARIOUS ARTISTS (MINISTRY OF SOUND)	2	2004
THE FUNKIN' 80S VARIOUS ARTISTS (TELSTAR)	11	2003

Title / Artist	Peak Position	Year of Release
FUNKMASTER MIX VARIOUS ARTISTS (POLYGRAM)	16	1996
FUNKOLOGY – ONE NATION UNDER A GROOVE VARIOUS ARTISTS (WARNER BROTHERS)	14	2001
FUNKY DIVAS EN VOGUE	4	1992
FUNKY DIVAS VARIOUS ARTISTS (GLOBAL TELEVISION)	3	1997
FUNKY DIVAS 2 VARIOUS ARTISTS (GLOBAL TELEVISION)	16	1998
FUNKY DIVAS 3 VARIOUS ARTISTS (GLOBAL TELEVISION)	18	2000
FUNKY DIVAS – THE AUTUMN COLLECTION VARIOUS ARTISTS (TELSTAR)	4	2002
FUNKY DIVAS – THE VERY BEST IN SOUL DANCE AND R&B VARIOUS ARTISTS (TELSTAR)	5	2001
FUNKY DORY RACHEL STEVENS	9	2003
FUNKY HOUSE VARIOUS ARTISTS (TELSTAR)	9	1999
FUNKY HOUSE '06 VARIOUS ARTISTS (UNIVERSAL)	8	2006
FUNKY HOUSE SESSIONS VARIOUS ARTISTS (MINISTRY OF SOUND)	5	2005
FUNKY HOUSE SESSIONS 06 VARIOUS ARTISTS (MINISTRY OF SOUND)	2	2006
FUNKY HOUSE SESSIONS 07 VARIOUS ARTISTS (MINISTRY OF SOUND)	2	2007
FUNKY LITTLE DEMONS WOLFGANG PRESS	75	1995
FUNNY GIRL BARBRA STREISAND	19	1966
FUNNY GIRL BARBRA STREISAND	11	1969
FUNPLEX B-52'S	73	2008
FUR JANE WIEDLIN	48	1988
FUR AND GOLD BAT FOR LASHES	48	2007
FUREYS FINEST FUREYS & DAVEY ARTHUR	65	1987
FURTHER GENEVA	20	1997
FURTHER ADVENTURES OF LITTLE VOICE JANE HORROCKS	63	2000
FURTHER DOWN THE ROAD CHARLIE LANDSBOROUGH	42	1997
FURTHEST FROM THE SUN FAMILY CAT	55	1992
THE FURY GARY NUMAN	24	1985
FUSED VARIOUS ARTISTS (POLYGRAM)	14	1997
THE FUTURE LEONARD COHEN	36	1992
FUTURE BLUES CANNED HEAT	27	1970
FUTURE CHILL VARIOUS ARTISTS (VIRGIN)	18	2002
FUTURE PAST DUNCAN JAMES	55	2006
FUTURE SHOCK GILLAN	2	1981
FUTURE SHOCK HERBIE HANCOCK	27	1983
FUTURE SIGNS WARM JETS	40	1998
THE FUTURE SOUND OF NEW YORK VARIOUS ARTISTS (MINISTRY OF SOUND)	19	1995
FUTURE TRANCE VARIOUS ARTISTS (VIRGIN)	3	2002
FUTURE TRANCE 2003 VARIOUS ARTISTS (VIRGIN)	11	2003
FUTURE TRANCE IBIZA VARIOUS ARTISTS (VIRGIN)	17	2002
THE FUTUREHEADS FUTUREHEADS	11	2005
FUTURES JIMMY EAT WORLD	22	2004
FUTURESEX/LOVESOUNDS JUSTIN TIMBERLAKE	1	2006
FUTURESHOCK – 20 FURIOUS DANCE TUNES VARIOUS ARTISTS (DINO)	4	1993
THE FUTURIST ROBERT DOWNEY JR	56	2005
FUTURISTIC DRAGON T. REX	50	1976
FUZZY GRANT LEE BUFFALO	74	1993
FUZZY LOGIC SUPER FURRY ANIMALS	23	1996
FYC FINE YOUNG CANNIBALS	61	1990

G

Title / Artist	Peak Position	Year of Release
G FORCE KENNY G	56	1984
G N' R THE LIES, THE SEX, THE DRUGS, THE VIOLENCE, THE SHOCKING TRUTH GUNS N' ROSES	22	1988
G SIDES GORILLAZ	65	2002
G.I. BLUES (OST) ELVIS PRESLEY	1	1960
G4 G4	1	2005
G4 & FRIENDS G4	6	2005
GABRIELLE GABRIELLE	11	1996
THE GAELIC COLLECTION 1973-1995 RUNRIG	71	1998
GAIA (ONE WOMAN'S JOURNEY) OLIVIA NEWTON-JOHN	33	1995
GALAXY DANCE ANTHEMS VARIOUS ARTISTS (GTV)	10	2007
GALAXY HIT MIX VARIOUS ARTISTS (MINISTRY OF SOUND)	14	2000
GALAXY MIX – BOY GEORGE VARIOUS ARTISTS (MINISTRY OF SOUND)	8	1999
GALAXY WEEKEND: MIXED BY BOY GEORGE & ALLISTER WHITEHEAD VARIOUS ARTISTS (MINISTRY OF SOUND)	6	1999
GALLUS GUN	14	1992
GALORE – THE BEST OF KIRSTY MACCOLL KIRSTY MacCOLL	6	1995
GALORE – THE SINGLES 1987 – 1997 CURE	37	1997
THE GAME QUEEN	1	1980
GAMES B.B.E.	60	1998
GANGSTA'S PARADISE COOLIO	18	1995
GANGSTERS OF THE GROOVE – THE 90'S MIX HEATWAVE	56	1991
GAP BAND 8 GAP BAND	47	1987
GARAGE ANTHEMS VARIOUS ARTISTS (TELSTAR)	8	2000
GARAGE ANTHEMS 2005 VARIOUS ARTISTS (RELENTLESS)	15	2005
GARAGE CITY VARIOUS ARTISTS (TELSTAR)	8	1992
GARAGE CLASSICS VOLUME 2 – SUMMER EDITION VARIOUS ARTISTS (MINISTRY OF SOUND)	3	2008
GARAGE FLOWER STONE ROSES	58	1996
GARAGE INC. METALLICA	29	1998
GARAGE NATION VARIOUS ARTISTS (TELSTAR)	10	2000
GARAGE NATION VARIOUS ARTISTS (INCREDIBLE)	11	2001
GARAGE NATION 02 VARIOUS ARTISTS (INCREDIBLE)	9	2002
GARAGE VIBES VARIOUS ARTISTS (PURE SILK)	20	2000
GARBAGE GARBAGE	6	1995
THE GARDEN JOHN FOXX	24	1981
THE GARDEN ZERO 7	4	2006
GARDEN IN THE CITY MELANIE	19	1972
GARY GLITTER'S GREATEST HITS GARY GLITTER	33	1976
GASOLINE ALLEY ROD STEWART	62	1970
GATECRASHER VARIOUS ARTISTS (INCREDIBLE)	7	1998
GATECRASHER CLASSICS VARIOUS ARTISTS (MINISTRY OF SOUND)	1	2005
GATECRASHER CLASSICS 2 VARIOUS ARTISTS (MINISTRY OF SOUND)	6	2005
GATECRASHER DIGITAL VARIOUS ARTISTS (GATECRASHER)	6	2001
GATECRASHER DIGITAL TRANCE VARIOUS ARTISTS (GATECRASHER)	8	2002
GATECRASHER DISCO-TECH VARIOUS ARTISTS (INCREDIBLE)	6	1999
GATECRASHER DISCOTECH GENERATION VARIOUS ARTISTS (INCREDIBLE)	10	2001
GATECRASHER EXPERIENCE VARIOUS ARTISTS (GATECRASHER)	2	2002
GATECRASHER FOREVER VARIOUS ARTISTS (MINISTRY OF SOUND)	6	2006
GATECRASHER – GLOBAL SOUND SYSTEM VARIOUS ARTISTS (INCREDIBLE)	3	2000
GATECRASHER IMMORTAL VARIOUS ARTISTS (MINISTRY OF SOUND)	2	2007
GATECRASHER – NATIONAL ANTHEMS VARIOUS ARTISTS (INCREDIBLE)	13	2000
GATECRASHER RED VARIOUS ARTISTS (INCREDIBLE)	4	1999
GATECRASHER WET VARIOUS ARTISTS (INCREDIBLE)	3	1999
GATECRASHING LIVING IN A BOX	21	1989
GATHER ME MELANIE	14	1972
GATHERING OF FREAKS FREAK OF NATURE	66	1994
GAUCHO STEELY DAN	27	1980
GAUDI ALAN PARSONS PROJECT	66	1987
G-A-Y VARIOUS ARTISTS (LONDON)	18	2000
GAZE BEAUTIFUL SOUTH	14	2003
GEFFERY MORGAN... UB40	3	1984
GENE PITNEY'S BIG SIXTEEN GENE PITNEY	12	1965
GENE PITNEY'S BIG SIXTEEN VOLUME 3 GENE PITNEY	40	1967
GENERATION AUDIO BULLYS	33	2005
GENERATION TERRORISTS MANIC STREET PREACHERS	13	1992
GENERATION X GENERATION X	29	1978
GENESIS GENESIS	1	1983
GENESIS BUSTA RHYMES	58	2002
GENESIS LIVE GENESIS	9	1973
GENIUS LOVES COMPANY RAY CHARLES	18	2004
THE GENIUS OF VENICE RONDO VENEZIANO	60	1984
GENO DEXYS MIDNIGHT RUNNERS	79	1983
GENTLE ON MY MIND DEAN MARTIN	9	1969
GENTLE SHADES OF VAL DOONICAN VAL DOONICAN	5	1966
GENTLEMAN JIM JIM REEVES	3	1964
GENTLEMAN JIM – DEFINITIVE COLLECTION JIM REEVES	21	2003
GENTLEMAN JIM – MEMORIES ARE MADE OF THIS JIM REEVES	35	2004
GENTLEMEN AFGHAN WHIGS	58	1993
GENTLEMEN TAKE POLAROIDS JAPAN	45	1980
GENTLY LIZA MINNELLI	58	1996
GENUINE DUD DUDLEY MOORE TRIO	13	1966
GEOGADDI BOARDS OF CANADA	21	2002
THE GEORGE BENSON COLLECTION GEORGE BENSON	19	1981
GEORGE BEST WEDDING PRESENT	47	1987
GEORGE GERSHWIN – THE BEST OF VARIOUS ARTISTS (DECCA)	19	2003
GEORGE HARRISON GEORGE HARRISON	39	1979
GEORGE IS ON DEEP DISH	54	2005
GEORGE MCCRAE GEORGE McCRAE	54	1975
GEORGE THOROGOOD AND THE DESTROYERS GEORGE THOROGOOD & THE DESTROYERS	67	1978
GEORGIA SATELLITES GEORGIA SATELLITES	52	1987
GERM FREE ADOLESCENTS X-RAY SPEX	30	1978
GERRY MULLIGAN MEETS BEN WEBSTER GERRY MULLIGAN & BEN WEBSTER	15	1960
GET A GRIP AEROSMITH	2	1993
GET BEHIND ME SATAN WHITE STRIPES	3	2005
GET BORN JET	14	2003
GET CARTER (OST) ROY BUDD	68	1998
GET CLOSE PRETENDERS	6	1986
GET DOWN VARIOUS ARTISTS (SONY/BMG)	16	2007
GET EVEN BROTHER BEYOND	9	1988

Title / Artist	Peak Position	Year of Release
GET HAPPY! ELVIS COSTELLO & THE ATTRACTIONS	2	1980
GET HERE BRENDA RUSSELL	77	1988
GET IN KENICKIE	32	1998
GET IN TOUCH WITH YOURSELF SWING OUT SISTER	27	1992
GET INTO YOU DANNII MINOGUE	52	1993
GET IT ON – GREATEST HITS OF THE 70'S VARIOUS ARTISTS (HIT LABEL)	12	1993
GET LIFTED JOHN LEGEND	12	2005
GET LOOSE EVELYN KING	35	1982
GET NERVOUS PAT BENATAR	73	1982
GET ON THIS! – 30 DANCE HITS VOLUME 1 VARIOUS ARTISTS (TELSTAR)	2	1990
GET ON THIS!!! 2 VARIOUS ARTISTS (TELSTAR)	3	1990
GET ON UP VARIOUS ARTISTS (RCA)	35	1983
GET OUT AND WALK FARMER'S BOYS	49	1983
GET READY 2 UNLIMITED	37	1992
GET READY NEW ORDER	6	2001
GET READY! ROACHFORD	20	1991
GET RHYTHM RY COODER	75	1987
GET RICH OR DIE TRYIN' 50 CENT	2	2003
GET RICH OR DIE TRYIN' 50 CENT & G UNIT	18	2005
GET RIGHT INTAE HIM BILLY CONNOLLY	6	1975
GET STONED ROLLING STONES	8	1977
GET THAT FEELING JIMI HENDRIX & CURTIS KNIGHT	39	1968
GET THE KNACK KNACK	65	1979
GET THE PARTY STARTED VARIOUS ARTISTS (COLUMBIA)	10	2002
GET THE PARTY STARTED SHIRLEY BASSEY	6	2007
GET TOGETHER WITH ANDY WILLIAMS ANDY WILLIAMS	13	1969
GET UP ON IT KEITH SWEAT	20	1994
GET UR FREAK ON VARIOUS ARTISTS (WARNER BROTHERS)	8	2002
GET YER YA-YA'S OUT!' – THE ROLLING STONES IN CONCERT ROLLING STONES	1	1970
GETAHEAD CURIOSITY KILLED THE CAT	29	1989
THE GETAWAY CHRIS DE BURGH	30	1982
GETAWAY REEF	15	2000
GETT OFF PRINCE & THE NEW POWER GENERATION	33	1991
GETTIN' HIGH ON YOUR OWN SUPPLY APOLLO FOUR FORTY	20	1999
GETTIN' IN OVER MY HEAD BRIAN WILSON	53	2004
GETTING AWAY WITH MURDER PAPA ROACH	30	2004
GETTING READY TEMPTATIONS	40	1966
GETTING SENTIMENTAL ENGELBERT HUMPERDINCK	35	1985
GETTING THE HOLY GHOST ACROSS BILL NELSON	91	1986
GETTING TO THIS BLODWYN PIG	8	1970
GHETTO BLASTER CRUSADERS	46	1984
GHETTO LOVE JAHEIM	50	2001
GHETTO MUSIC: THE BLUEPRINT OF HIP HOP BOOGIE DOWN PRODUCTIONS	32	1989
GHETTO SUPERSTAR PRAS MICHEL	44	1998
GHOST FILM SOUNDTRACK	15	1990
GHOST IN THE MACHINE POLICE	1	1981
A GHOST IS BORN WILCO	50	2004
GHOST OF A DOG EDIE BRICKELL & THE NEW BOHEMIANS	63	1990
THE GHOST OF CAIN NEW MODEL ARMY	45	1986
GHOST OF PRINCES IN TOWERS RICH KIDS	51	1978
THE GHOST OF TOM JOAD BRUCE SPRINGSTEEN	16	1995
GHOST REVERIES OPETH	62	2005
GHOST RIDERS IN THE SKY SLIM WHITMAN	27	1979
GHOSTBUSTERS FILM SOUNDTRACK	24	1984
GHOSTBUSTERS II FILM SOUNDTRACK	15	1989
GHOSTS I-IV NINE INCH NAILS	60	2008
GHV2 MADONNA	2	2001
GIANT BUDDY HOLLY	13	1969
GIANT WOODENTOPS	35	1986
GIANT STEPS BOO RADLEYS	17	1993
THE GIFT JAM	1	1982
THE GIFT MIDGE URE	2	1985
GIFT SISTERHOOD	90	1986
A GIFT FROM A FLOWER TO A GARDEN DONOVAN	13	1968
THE GIFT OF GAME CRAZY TOWN	15	2001
A GIFT OF LOVE BILL TARMEY	15	1993
GIFT OF SCREWS LINDSEY BUCKINGHAM	59	2008
THE GIFT OF SONG VARIOUS ARTISTS (POLYGRAM)	7	1993
GIFT SET BARRY MANILOW	62	1981
GIGI FILM SOUNDTRACK	2	1959
GILBERT O'SULLIVAN HIMSELF GILBERT O'SULLIVAN	5	1971
A GILDED ETERNITY LOOP	39	1990
GIMME BACK MY BULLETS LYNYRD SKYNYRD	34	1976
GIMME SHELTER ROLLING STONES	19	1971
GINGER SPEEDY J	68	1993
GINGER BAKER'S AIR FORCE GINGER BAKER'S AIR FORCE	37	1970
GINUWINE...THE BACHELOR GINUWINE	74	1998
GIPSY KINGS GIPSY KINGS	16	1989
GIRL DANNII MINOGUE	57	1997
GIRL AT HER VOLCANO RICKIE LEE JONES	51	1983
A GIRL CALLED DUSTY DUSTY SPRINGFIELD	6	1964
GIRL HAPPY ELVIS PRESLEY	8	1965
THE GIRL IN THE OTHER ROOM DIANA KRALL	4	2004
A GIRL LIKE ME EMMA BUNTON	4	2001
A GIRL LIKE ME RIHANNA	5	2006
GIRL POWER VARIOUS ARTISTS (GLOBAL TELEVISION)	9	1997
GIRL WHO COULDN'T FLY KATE RUSBY	45	2005
THE GIRLS VARIOUS ARTISTS (EMI)	5	2008
GIRLS 2K VARIOUS ARTISTS (VIRGIN)	1	2000
GIRLS A LIVE GIRLS ALOUD	29	2008
GIRLS AND GUITARS VARIOUS ARTISTS (GLOBAL TELEVISION)	8	1995
GIRLS AND WEATHER RUMBLE STRIPS	70	2007
GIRLS GIRLS GIRLS ELVIS COSTELLO	67	1989
GIRLS I HAVE KNOWN JIM REEVES	35	1971
GIRLS IN THE CITY VARIOUS ARTISTS (SONY BMG)	13	2008
GIRLS JUST WANNA HAVE FUN NOLANS	39	1984
GIRLS NIGHT IN VARIOUS ARTISTS (SONY BMG)	13	2008
GIRLS SAY VARIOUS ARTISTS (UNIVERSAL)	7	2002
GIRLS! GIRLS! GIRLS! ELVIS PRESLEY	2	1963
GIRLS, GIRLS, GIRLS MOTLEY CRUE	14	1987
GIVE 'EM ENOUGH ROPE CLASH	2	1978
GIVE ME A WALL iFORWARD! RUSSIA	53	2006
GIVE ME CONVENIENCE OR GIVE ME DEATH DEAD KENNEDYS	84	1987
GIVE ME THE NIGHT GEORGE BENSON	3	1980
GIVE ME THE REASON LUTHER VANDROSS	3	1986
GIVE ME YOUR HEART TONIGHT SHAKIN' STEVENS	3	1982
GIVE MY REGARDS TO BROAD STREET (OST) PAUL McCARTNEY	1	1984
GIVE OUT, BUT DON'T GIVE UP PRIMAL SCREAM	2	1994
GIVING THE GAME AWAY THUNDER	49	1999
GIVING YOU THE BEST THAT I GOT ANITA BAKER	9	1988
GLAD ALL OVER AGAIN DAVE CLARK FIVE	28	1993
GLADIATOR – OST HANS ZIMMER & LISA GERRARD	17	2000
GLADIATORS (TELEVISION SOUNDTRACK) TELEVISION AND RADIO COMPILATION	11	1992
GLADSOME, HUMOUR AND BLUE MARTIN STEPHENSON & THE DAINTEES	39	1988
GLAM MANIA VARIOUS ARTISTS (QUALITY TELEVISION)	10	1993
GLAM SLAM VARIOUS ARTISTS (K-TEL)	5	1989
GLAMOROUS ONE VARIOUS ARTISTS (MISS MONEYPENNY'S)	12	1997
GLASGOW NIGHT OUT GLEN DALY	28	1971
GLASGOW WALKER JOHN MARTYN	66	2000
GLASS HOUSES BILLY JOEL	9	1980
GLASVEGAS GLASVEGAS	2	2008
THE GLEN CAMPBELL ALBUM GLEN CAMPBELL	16	1970
GLEN CAMPBELL LIVE GLEN CAMPBELL	16	1970
GLEN CAMPBELL'S GREATEST HITS GLEN CAMPBELL	8	1971
GLENN JONES GLENN JONES	62	1987
GLENN MILLER PLAYS SELECTIONS FROM 'THE GLENN MILLER STORY' AND OTHER HITS (OST) GLENN MILLER & HIS ORCHESTRA	10	1961
GLENN MILLER STORY FILM SOUNDTRACK	12	1961
GLITTER GARY GLITTER	8	1972
GLITTER MARIAH CAREY	10	2001
GLITTERING PRIZE 81/92 SIMPLE MINDS	1	1992
GLOBAL A GO GO JOE STRUMMER & THE MESCALEROS	68	2001
GLOBALTEKNO ULTRA-SONIC	58	1995
THE GLOBE BIG AUDIO DYNAMITE II	63	1991
THE GLOBE SESSIONS SHERYL CROW	2	1998
GLORIA! GLORIA ESTEFAN	16	1998
GLORIOUS FOOL JOHN MARTYN	25	1981
GLORIOUS – THE SINGLES 97 – 07 NATALIE IMBRUGLIA	5	2007
GLORY BOYS SECRET AFFAIR	41	1979
THE GLORY OF GERSHWIN LARRY ADLER	2	1994
GLORY ROAD GILLAN	3	1980
GLOW REEF	1	1997
GO 2 XTC	21	1978
GO AHEAD LINX	35	1981
GO FOR IT STIFF LITTLE FINGERS	14	1981
GO FOR YOUR GUNS ISLEY BROTHERS	46	1977
GO POP! AGAIN SMURFS	15	1997
GO – THE VERY BEST OF MOBY	23	2006
GO WEST VILLAGE PEOPLE	14	1979
GO WEST/BANGS AND CRASHES GO WEST	8	1985
GO WITH THE FLOW – ESSENTIAL ACID JAZZ VARIOUS ARTISTS (POLYGRAM)	9	1996
GO YOUR OWN WAY GARETH GATES	11	2003
GOAT'S HEAD SOUP ROLLING STONES	1	1973
GOD BE WITH YOU JIM REEVES	10	1964
GOD FODDER NED'S ATOMIC DUSTBIN	4	1991
GOD HATES US ALL SLAYER	31	2001
GOD SHUFFLED HIS FEET CRASH TEST DUMMIES	2	1994
GODDESS IN THE DOORWAY MICK JAGGER	44	2001
THE GODFATHER PART III FILM SOUNDTRACK	19	1991
THE GODFATHER – THE VERY BEST OF JAMES BROWN	30	2002
GODS AND MONSTERS I AM KLOOT	74	2005
GOD'S GREAT BANANA SKIN CHRIS REA	4	1992
GOD'S HOME MOVIE HORSE	42	1993
GOD'S KITCHEN VARIOUS ARTISTS (UNIVERSAL)	17	2001
GODS KITCHEN – THE TRUE SOUND OF A CLUBBING SUMMER VARIOUS ARTISTS (INCREDIBLE)	17	2001
GOD'S OWN MEDICINE MISSION	14	1986
GOD'S SON NAS	57	2003
GODSKITCHEN VARIOUS ARTISTS (VIRGIN)	15	2004
GODSKITCHEN – ANTHEMS VARIOUS ARTISTS (EMI)	7	2006

Title / Artist	Peak Position	Year of Release
GODSKITCHEN – CLASSICS VARIOUS ARTISTS (VIRGIN)	4	2005
GODSKITCHEN DIRECT VARIOUS ARTISTS (GODSKITCHEN)	9	2003
GODSKITCHEN – ELECTRIC VARIOUS ARTISTS (NEW STATE)	14	2007
GODSKITCHEN – GLOBAL GATHERING VARIOUS ARTISTS (VIRGIN)	11	2005
GODSKITCHEN – GLOBAL GATHERING VARIOUS ARTISTS (NEW STATE)	14	2007
GODSKITCHEN – GLOBAL GATHERING 2006 VARIOUS ARTISTS (EMI)	8	2006
GODSKITCHEN JOURNEYS VARIOUS ARTISTS (INCREDIBLE)	5	2002
GODSKITCHEN – LIFE VARIOUS ARTISTS (INCREDIBLE)	13	2002
GODSKITCHEN – SUMMER TRANCE VARIOUS ARTISTS (INCREDIBLE)	15	2002
GODSKITCHEN – TRANCE ANTHEMS VARIOUS ARTISTS (NEW STATE)	19	2008
GODSKITCHEN – WORLDWIDE VARIOUS ARTISTS (GODSKITCHEN)	18	2003
GODSPEED ON THE DEVILS THUNDER CRADLE OF FILTH	73	2008
GODSPELL STAGE CAST RECORDING	25	1972
GODZILLA – THE ALBUM FILM SOUNDTRACK	13	1998
GOIN' BACK – THE VERY BEST OF DUSTY SPRINGFIELD 1962-1994 DUSTY SPRINGFIELD	5	1994
GOIN' PLACES JACKSONS	45	1977
GOING BLANK AGAIN RIDE	5	1992
GOING FOR GOLD – THE GREATEST HITS SHED SEVEN	7	1999
GOING FOR THE ONE YES	1	1977
GOING PLACES HERB ALPERT & THE TIJUANA BRASS	4	1966
GOING STEADY FILM SOUNDTRACK	25	1980
GOING UNDERGROUND VARIOUS ARTISTS (CASTLE COMMUNICATIONS)	18	1993
GOING UNDERGROUND – TEENAGE KICKS 2 VARIOUS ARTISTS (SANCTUARY)	19	2005
GOLD NEIL DIAMOND	23	1971
GOLD THREE DEGREES	9	1980
GOLD BARBARA DICKSON	11	1985
GOLD RYAN ADAMS	20	2001
GOLD ELLA FITZGERALD	15	2003
GOLD NINA SIMONE	27	2003
GOLD – 18 EPIC SPORTING ANTHEMS VARIOUS ARTISTS (TELSTAR)	15	1992
GOLD AGAINST THE SOUL MANIC STREET PREACHERS	8	1993
GOLD AND IVORY DAVID ESSEX	29	1977
GOLD AND PLATINUM LYNYRD SKYNYRD	49	1980
THE GOLD EXPERIENCE PRINCE	4	1995
GOLD – GREATEST HITS ABBA	1	1992
GOLD – GREATEST HITS CARPENTERS	4	2000
GOLD – GREATEST HITS PERRY COMO	55	2001
GOLD – GREATEST HITS RIGHTEOUS BROTHERS	24	2006
GOLD MOTHER JAMES	2	1990
GOLD ON SILVER BEVERLEY-PHILLIPS ORCHESTRA	22	1976
GOLD PLATED CLIMAX BLUES BAND	56	1976
GOLD – THE BEST OF SPANDAU BALLET	7	2000
GOLD – THE GREATEST HITS STEPS	1	2001
GOLD – THE HITS COLLECTION DOLLY PARTON	23	2001
GOLDDIGGAS HEADNODDERS & PHOLK SONGS BEAUTIFUL SOUTH	11	2004
GOLDEN AGE OF DONEGAN LONNIE DONEGAN	3	1962
GOLDEN AGE OF DONEGAN VOLUME 2 LONNIE DONEGAN	15	1963
THE GOLDEN AGE OF GROTESQUE MARILYN MANSON	4	2003
THE GOLDEN AGE OF HOLLYWOOD COMEDY LAUREL & HARDY	55	1975
THE GOLDEN AGE OF WIRELESS THOMAS DOLBY	65	1982
GOLDEN ALL TIME HITS BACHELORS	19	1967
GOLDEN COLLECTION CHARLEY PRIDE	6	1980
GOLDEN DAYS ROY ORBISON	63	1981
GOLDEN DAYS FUREYS & DAVEY ARTHUR	17	1984
GOLDEN DELICIOUS WURZELS	32	1977
GOLDEN FIDDLE AWARDS 1976 VARIOUS ARTISTS (MOUNTAIN)	45	1976
GOLDEN GREATS IAN BROWN	14	1999
GOLDEN HEART MARK KNOPFLER	9	1996
GOLDEN HITS DUSTY SPRINGFIELD	2	1966
GOLDEN HITS DRIFTERS	26	1968
GOLDEN HITS STEELY DAN	44	1982
GOLDEN HITS OF SHIRLEY BASSEY SHIRLEY BASSEY	28	1968
GOLDEN HOUR OF THE KINKS KINKS	21	1971
GOLDEN MELODIES NATIONAL BRASS BAND	15	1980
GOLDEN MEMORIES JAMES LAST	39	1974
GOLDEN MEMORIES HARRY SECOMBE & MOIRA ANDERSON	46	1981
THE GOLDEN MILE MY LIFE STORY	36	1997
GOLDEN OLDIES VARIOUS ARTISTS (VIRGIN)	3	2005
GOLDEN RIBBONS DAWN	46	1974
THE GOLDEN SECTION JOHN FOXX	27	1983
GOLDEN STATE BUSH	53	2001
GOLDEN TREASURY OF BILK MR ACKER BILK	11	1961
THE GOLDEN YEARS GRACIE FIELDS	48	1975
GOLDEN YEARS DAVID BOWIE	33	1983
THE GOLDEN YEARS OF THE EVERLY BROTHERS – THEIR 24 GREATEST HITS EVERLY BROTHERS	26	1993
GOLDIE – INCREDIBLE SOUND OF DRUM 'N' BASS VARIOUS ARTISTS (INCREDIBLE)	16	1999
GONE AGAIN PATTI SMITH	44	1996
GONE TO EARTH BARCLAY JAMES HARVEST	30	1977
GONE TO EARTH DAVID SYLVIAN	24	1986
GONNA BALL STRAY CATS	48	1981
GONNA GET YOU FREEEZ	46	1983
GONNA MAKE YOU SWEAT C&C MUSIC FACTORY	8	1991
GOO' SONIC YOUTH	32	1990
GOOD AS I BEEN TO YOU BOB DYLAN	18	1992
THE GOOD BOOK MELANIE	9	1971
GOOD DEEDS AND DIRTY RAGS GOODBYE MR. MACKENZIE	26	1989
GOOD FEELING TRAVIS	9	1997
GOOD GIRL GONE BAD RIHANNA	1	2007
GOOD GOD'S URGE PORNO FOR PYROS	40	1996
GOOD HUMOUR SAINT ETIENNE	18	1998
GOOD MORNING AMERICA VARIOUS ARTISTS (K-TEL)	15	1980
GOOD MORNING REVIVAL GOOD CHARLOTTE	13	2007
GOOD MORNING SPIDER SPARKLEHORSE	30	1998
GOOD MORNING VIETNAM FILM SOUNDTRACK	7	1988
GOOD MOURNING ALKALINE TRIO	32	2003
GOOD 'N' COUNTRY JIM REEVES	10	1964
GOOD 'N' READY SYBIL	13	1993
GOOD NEWS CLIFF RICHARD	37	1967
GOOD NEWS FOR PEOPLE WHO LOVE BAD NEWS MODEST MOUSE	40	2004
GOOD NEWS FROM THE NEXT WORLD SIMPLE MINDS	2	1995
THE GOOD SON NICK CAVE & THE BAD SEEDS	47	1990
GOOD STUFF B-52'S	8	1992
THE GOOD THE BAD & THE QUEEN THE GOOD THE BAD & THE QUEEN	2	2007
THE GOOD THE BAD AND THE LIVE: THE 6 1/2 YEARS ANNIVERSARY COLLECTION METALLICA	56	1990
THE GOOD THE BAD THE UGLY FRANKEE	51	2004
GOOD TIMES ELVIS PRESLEY	42	1974
GOOD TIMES ADAM RICKITT	41	1999
GOOD TIMES – THE VERY BEST OF (CHIC & SISTER SLEDGE) VARIOUS ARTISTS (ATLANTIC)	16	2005
GOOD TO BE BACK NATALIE COLE	10	1989
GOOD TO BE BAD WHITESNAKE	7	2008
GOOD TO GO TERRORVISION	48	2001
GOOD TO GO LOVER GWEN GUTHRIE	42	1986
GOOD TROUBLE REO SPEEDWAGON	29	1982
GOOD VIBES VARIOUS ARTISTS (VIRGIN)	14	2003
THE GOOD WILL OUT EMBRACE	1	1998
GOOD, BAD BUT BEAUTIFUL SHIRLEY BASSEY	13	1975
THE GOOD, THE BAD AND THE 4-SKINS 4-SKINS	80	1982
THE GOOD, THE BAD AND THE UGLY ENNIO MORRICONE	2	1968
GOODBYE CREAM	1	1969
GOODBYE DUBSTAR	18	1997
GOODBYE COUNTRY (HELLO NIGHTCLUB) GROOVE ARMADA	5	2001
GOODBYE CRUEL WORLD ELVIS COSTELLO & THE ATTRACTIONS	10	1984
GOODBYE GIRL DAVID GATES	28	1978
GOODBYE JUMBO WORLD PARTY	36	1990
GOODBYE YELLOW BRICK ROAD ELTON JOHN	1	1973
GOODIES CIARA	26	2005
GOODNIGHT L.A. MAGNUM	9	1990
GOODNIGHT VIENNA RINGO STARR	30	1974
GOOFY GREATS VARIOUS ARTISTS (K-TEL)	19	1975
GOOSEFAIR CHINA DRUM	53	1996
GORECKI: SYMPHONY NO. 3 DAWN UPSHAW (SOPRANO)/THE LONDON SINFONIETTA/DAVID ZINMAN (CONDUCTOR)	6	1993
GORGEOUS 808 STATE	17	1993
GORGEOUS VARIOUS ARTISTS (VIRGIN)	2	1997
GORGEOUS GEORGE EDWYN COLLINS	8	1995
GORILLAZ GORILLAZ	3	2001
GORKY 5 GORKY'S ZYGOTIC MYNCI	67	1998
GOSH IT'S BAD MANNERS BAD MANNERS	18	1981
THE GOSPELS RICK WAKEMAN	94	1987
GOSSIP IN THE GRAIN RAY LAMONTAGNE	23	2008
GOT MY MOJO WORKING JIMMY SMITH	19	1966
GOT TO BE THERE MICHAEL JACKSON	37	1972
GOTTA GET THRU THIS DANIEL BEDINGFIELD	2	2002
GOTTA TELL YOU SAMANTHA MUMBA	9	2000
GOYA…A LIFE IN A SONG PLACIDO DOMINGO	36	1989
GRACE JEFF BUCKLEY	42	1994
GRACE SIMON WEBBE	11	2006
GRACE AND DANGER JOHN MARTYN	54	1980
GRACE UNDER PRESSURE RUSH	5	1984
GRACELAND PAUL SIMON	1	1986
THE GRADUATE (OST) SIMON & GARFUNKEL	3	1968
GRADUATION KANYE WEST	1	2007
GRAFFITI BRIDGE PRINCE	1	1990
GRAFFITI TONGUE CHRISTY MOORE	35	1996
GRAHAM NASH AND DAVID CROSBY GRAHAM NASH & DAVID CROSBY	13	1972
GRAINS OF SAND MISSION	28	1990
GRAN TURISMO CARDIGANS	8	1998
GRAND CANYON SUITE 101 STRINGS	10	1960
GRAND CHAMP DMX	6	2003
A GRAND DON'T COME FOR FREE STREETS	1	2004
GRAND FUNK LIVE GRAND FUNK	29	1971

Title / Artist	Peak Position	Year of Release
GRAND PRIX TEENAGE FANCLUB	7	1995
GRAND UNIFICATION FIGHTSTAR	28	2006
GRANGE HILL – THE ALBUM VARIOUS ARTISTS (EMI)	13	2008
GRAPES OF WRATH SPEAR OF DESTINY	62	1983
GRASSHOPPER J.J. CALE	36	1982
GRATEFUL DEAD FROM THE MARS HOTEL GRATEFUL DEAD	47	1974
GRAVE DANCERS UNION SOUL ASYLUM	27	1993
GRAVE NEW WORLD STRAWBS	11	1972
A GRAVEYARD OF EMPTY BOTTLES DOGS D'AMOUR	16	1989
GRAVITY JAMES BROWN	85	1986
GREASE FILM SOUNDTRACK	1	1978
GREASE STAGE CAST RECORDING	20	1993
GREASEMANIA VARIOUS ARTISTS (POLYDOR)	1	2003
THE GREAT BALLOON RACE SKY	63	1985
THE GREAT BURRITO EXTORTION CASE BOWLING FOR SOUP	43	2007
THE GREAT CARUSO MARIO LANZA	3	1960
THE GREAT COUNTRY MUSIC SHOW VARIOUS ARTISTS (RONCO)	38	1982
THE GREAT DEPRESSION DMX	20	2001
THE GREAT DESTROYER LOW	70	2005
THE GREAT EASTERN DELGADOS	72	2000
THE GREAT ESCAPE BLUR	1	1995
GREAT EXPECTATIONS TASMIN ARCHER	8	1992
GREAT HITS T. REX	32	1973
GREAT ITALIAN LOVE SONGS VARIOUS ARTISTS (K-TEL)	17	1976
GREAT MOTION PICTURE THEMES VARIOUS ARTISTS (HMV)	19	1962
THE GREAT OTIS REDDING SINGS SOUL BALLADS OTIS REDDING	30	1966
THE GREAT PERFORMANCES ELVIS PRESLEY	62	1990
THE GREAT RADIO CONTROVERSY TESLA	34	1989
THE GREAT ROCK 'N' ROLL SWINDLE (OST) SEX PISTOLS	7	1979
GREAT SEX VARIOUS ARTISTS (GLOBAL TELEVISION)	13	1995
GREAT SONGS FROM GREAT BRITAIN FRANK SINATRA	12	1962
GREAT SONGS FROM MY FAIR LADY ANDY WILLIAMS	30	1966
THE GREAT SOUTHERN TRENDKILL PANTERA	17	1996
GREAT WALTZES ROBERTO MANN	19	1967
THE GREAT WAR OF WORDS BRIAN KENNEDY	64	1990
THE GREAT WESTERN JAMES DEAN BRADFIELD	22	2006
GREATEST DURAN DURAN	4	1998
THE GREATEST IAN BROWN	5	2005
THE GREATEST CAT POWER	45	2006
GREATEST BEE GEES	35	2007
THE GREATEST 80'S SOUL WEEKENDER VARIOUS ARTISTS (WARNER BROTHERS)	9	2001
THE GREATEST 90S DANCE HITS VARIOUS ARTISTS (TELSTAR)	16	1996
THE GREATEST CLASSICAL MOVIE ALBUM VARIOUS ARTISTS (TELSTAR)	15	1997
THE GREATEST CLASSICAL STARS ON EARTH VARIOUS ARTISTS (DECCA)	13	1998
THE GREATEST DANCE ALBUM EVER MADE VARIOUS ARTISTS (TELSTAR)	5	1997
THE GREATEST DANCE ALBUM IN THE WORLD! VARIOUS ARTISTS (VIRGIN)	2	1992
THE GREATEST DANCE ALBUM OF ALL TIME VARIOUS ARTISTS (DINO)	7	1995
THE GREATEST DANCE ALBUM UNDER THE SUN! VARIOUS ARTISTS (EMI)	8	1996
GREATEST EVER DAD – THE DEFINITIVE VARIOUS ARTISTS (UNION SQUARE)	17	2008
THE GREATEST EVER JUNIOR PARTY MEGAMIX HOUND DOG & THE MEGAMIXERS	34	1990
THE GREATEST EVER ROCK 'N' ROLL MIX VARIOUS ARTISTS (STYLUS)	5	1988
GREATEST HITS RAY CHARLES	16	1963
GREATEST HITS FRANK IFIELD	9	1964
GREATEST HITS BOB DYLAN	6	1967
GREATEST HITS FRANK SINATRA	8	1968
GREATEST HITS MARVIN GAYE	13	1968
GREATEST HITS BEACH BOYS	5	1970
GREATEST HITS HERB ALPERT & THE TIJUANA BRASS	8	1970
GREATEST HITS MARVIN GAYE & TAMMI TERRELL	60	1970
GREATEST HITS DIANA ROSS	34	1972
GREATEST HITS FLEETWOOD MAC	3	1972
GREATEST HITS JACKSON FIVE	26	1972
GREATEST HITS SIMON & GARFUNKEL	2	1972
GREATEST HITS JIMMY RUFFIN	41	1974
GREATEST HITS SANTANA	14	1974
GREATEST HITS TOM JONES	2	1974
GREATEST HITS BARRY WHITE	18	1975
GREATEST HITS CAT STEVENS	2	1975
GREATEST HITS NAZARETH	54	1975
GREATEST HITS ABBA	1	1976
GREATEST HITS FOUR SEASONS	4	1976
GREATEST HITS GILBERT O'SULLIVAN	13	1976
GREATEST HITS GLITTER BAND	52	1976
GREATEST HITS HOT CHOCOLATE	6	1976
GREATEST HITS LINDA RONSTADT	37	1976
GREATEST HITS SHOWADDYWADDY	4	1976
GREATEST HITS ROXY	20	1977
GREATEST HITS SMOKIE	6	1977
GREATEST HITS COMMODORES	19	1978
GREATEST HITS DONNA SUMMER	4	1978
GREATEST HITS OLIVIA NEWTON-JOHN	8	1978
GREATEST HITS STEELY DAN	41	1978
GREATEST HITS CREEDENCE CLEARWATER REVIVAL	35	1979
GREATEST HITS KC & THE SUNSHINE BAND	10	1980
GREATEST HITS SHALAMAR	71	1982
GREATEST HITS BUCKS FIZZ	25	1983
GREATEST HITS DOLLY PARTON	74	1985
THE GREATEST HITS BONNIE TYLER	24	1986
THE GREATEST HITS SHALAMAR	5	1986
THE GREATEST HITS ODYSSEY	26	1987
THE GREATEST HITS TOM JONES	16	1987
GREATEST HITS BILL WITHERS	90	1988
GREATEST HITS HUMAN LEAGUE	3	1988
GREATEST HITS ISLEY BROTHERS	41	1988
GREATEST HITS LEONARD COHEN	99	1988
GREATEST HITS BILLY OCEAN	4	1989
GREATEST HITS FIVE STAR	53	1989
THE GREATEST HITS ELECTRIC LIGHT ORCHESTRA	23	1989
GREATEST HITS BANGLES	4	1990
GREATEST HITS MOODY BLUES	71	1990
GREATEST HITS EURYTHMICS	1	1991
GREATEST HITS JAM	2	1991
GREATEST HITS JASON DONOVAN	9	1991
THE GREATEST HITS SALT-N-PEPA	6	1991
GREATEST HITS GLORIA ESTEFAN	2	1992
GREATEST HITS POLICE	10	1992
GREATEST HITS SQUEEZE	6	1992
GREATEST HITS ZZ TOP	5	1992
THE GREATEST HITS SMOKEY ROBINSON & THE MIRACLES	65	1992
GREATEST HITS DORIS DAY	14	1993
GREATEST HITS SHEEP ON DRUGS	55	1993
GREATEST HITS TOM PETTY & HEARTBREAKERS	10	1993
THE GREATEST HITS BONEY M	14	1993
GREATEST HITS GIPSY KINGS	11	1994
GREATEST HITS TROGGS	27	1994
GREATEST HITS WHITESNAKE	4	1994
THE GREATEST HITS DOLLY PARTON	65	1994
GREATEST HITS ASWAD	20	1995
GREATEST HITS BOB SEGER & THE SILVER BULLET BAND	6	1995
GREATEST HITS BRUCE SPRINGSTEEN	1	1995
GREATEST HITS N.W.A.	56	1996
GREATEST HITS SIMPLY RED	1	1996
GREATEST HITS TAKE THAT	1	1996
GREATEST HITS ETERNAL	2	1997
GREATEST HITS KENNY G	38	1997
GREATEST HITS KISS	58	1997
GREATEST HITS 2PAC	17	1998
GREATEST HITS ARETHA FRANKLIN	38	1998
GREATEST HITS BEACH BOYS	28	1998
GREATEST HITS DAVID ESSEX	7	1998
GREATEST HITS DJ JAZZY JEFF & THE FRESH PRINCE	20	1998
GREATEST HITS FOSTER & ALLEN	52	1998
GREATEST HITS RICHARD MARX	34	1998
GREATEST HITS SMURFS	28	1998
GREATEST HITS STEVE MILLER BAND	58	1998
GREATEST HITS DANIEL O'DONNELL	10	1999
GREATEST HITS HAPPY MONDAYS	11	1999
GREATEST HITS JOE COCKER	24	1999
THE GREATEST HITS CHER	7	1999
GREATEST HITS LENNY KRAVITZ	12	2000
GREATEST HITS PRETENDERS	21	2000
GREATEST HITS STYLE COUNCIL	28	2000
THE GREATEST HITS TEXAS	1	2000
THE GREATEST HITS WHITNEY HOUSTON	1	2000
GREATEST HITS CURE	33	2001
GREATEST HITS FIVE	9	2001
GREATEST HITS MARIAH CAREY	7	2001
THE GREATEST HITS BONEY M	66	2001
THE GREATEST HITS BONNIE TYLER	18	2001
THE GREATEST HITS EDDY GRANT	3	2001
GREATEST HITS BJORK	53	2002
GREATEST HITS BLONDIE	38	2002
GREATEST HITS CATATONIA	24	2002
GREATEST HITS LIGHTHOUSE FAMILY	23	2002
GREATEST HITS NIGEL KENNEDY	71	2002
GREATEST HITS RICK ASTLEY	16	2002
GREATEST HITS HOLLIES	21	2003
GREATEST HITS RED HOT CHILI PEPPERS	4	2003
GREATEST HITS RUN D.M.C.	15	2003
THE GREATEST HITS LULU	35	2003
GREATEST HITS ALEXANDER O'NEAL	12	2004
GREATEST HITS DOOBIE BROTHERS	45	2004
GREATEST HITS GOLDIE LOOKIN CHAIN	5	2004
GREATEST HITS GUNS N' ROSES	1	2004
GREATEST HITS NEIL YOUNG	45	2004
GREATEST HITS ROBBIE WILLIAMS	1	2004
GREATEST HITS SHANIA TWAIN	6	2004
GREATEST HITS THIN LIZZY	3	2004
THE GREATEST HITS ATOMIC KITTEN	5	2004
THE GREATEST HITS WET WET WET	13	2004
GREATEST HITS BLINK 182	6	2005
GREATEST HITS BLONDIE	48	2005
GREATEST HITS CROSBY, STILLS & NASH	38	2005
GREATEST HITS LYNYRD SKYNYRD	16	2005
GREATEST HITS MIS-TEEQ	28	2005
GREATEST HITS OFFSPRING	14	2005
THE GREATEST HITS GLADYS KNIGHT & THE PIPS	33	2006
GREATEST HITS DAVID GRAY	11	2007
GREATEST HITS GROOVE ARMADA	65	2007
GREATEST HITS MARC BOLAN & T. REX	15	2007
GREATEST HITS McFLY	4	2007
GREATEST HITS SPICE GIRLS	2	2007
GREATEST HITS ENRIQUE IGLESIAS	3	2008

Title / Artist	Peak Position	Year of Release
GREATEST HITS MORRISSEY	5	2008
GREATEST HITS TOM PETTY & HEARTBREAKERS	37	2008
GREATEST HITS CRAIG DAVID	48	2008
THE GREATEST HITS & MORE MORE MORE BANANARAMA	61	2007
GREATEST HITS (1976-1978) SHOWADDYWADDY	1	1978
THE GREATEST HITS 1966-1992 NEIL DIAMOND	1	1992
THE GREATEST HITS 1970 – 2002 ELTON JOHN	3	2002
GREATEST HITS 1972-1978 10 C.C.	5	1979
GREATEST HITS 1977-1990 STRANGLERS	4	1990
GREATEST HITS 1980-1994 ARETHA FRANKLIN	27	1994
GREATEST HITS 1981-1995 LUTHER VANDROSS	12	1995
GREATEST HITS 1985-1995 MICHAEL BOLTON	2	1995
GREATEST HITS 2 DIANA ROSS	2	1976
GREATEST HITS 25 SIMPLY RED	9	2008
GREATEST HITS 87-92 KYLIE MINOGUE	20	2002
THE GREATEST HITS AND A LITTLE MORE... 911	40	1999
GREATEST HITS AND MORE 10 C.C.	42	2006
GREATEST HITS AND MORE ENGELBERT HUMPERDINCK	21	2007
THE GREATEST HITS – BORN TO ROCK & ROLL MARTY WILDE	19	2007
GREATEST HITS – CHAPTER ONE BACKSTREET BOYS	5	2001
THE GREATEST HITS COLLECTION BANANARAMA	3	1988
GREATEST HITS – FEEL THE NOIZE SLADE	19	1997
GREATEST HITS – HISTORY VOLUME 1 MICHAEL JACKSON	15	2001
GREATEST HITS I & II QUEEN	37	1994
GREATEST HITS I II & III QUEEN	2	2000
GREATEST HITS II QUEEN	1	1991
GREATEST HITS III QUEEN	5	1999
GREATEST HITS LIVE CARLY SIMON	49	1988
GREATEST HITS LIVE DIANA ROSS	34	1989
GREATEST HITS – MY PREROGATIVE BRITNEY SPEARS	2	2004
THE GREATEST HITS OF 1985 VARIOUS ARTISTS (TELSTAR)	1	1985
THE GREATEST HITS OF 1986 VARIOUS ARTISTS (TELSTAR)	8	1986
THE GREATEST HITS OF 1987 VARIOUS ARTISTS (TELSTAR)	12	1987
THE GREATEST HITS OF 1988 VARIOUS ARTISTS (TELSTAR)	8	1988
THE GREATEST HITS OF 1989 VARIOUS ARTISTS (TELSTAR)	4	1989
THE GREATEST HITS OF 1990 VARIOUS ARTISTS (TELSTAR)	4	1990
THE GREATEST HITS OF 1991 VARIOUS ARTISTS (TELSTAR)	4	1991
THE GREATEST HITS OF 1992 VARIOUS ARTISTS (TELSTAR)	4	1992
THE GREATEST HITS OF 1993 VARIOUS ARTISTS (TELSTAR)	4	1993
THE GREATEST HITS OF 1994 VARIOUS ARTISTS (TELSTAR)	9	1994
THE GREATEST HITS OF 1995 VARIOUS ARTISTS (TELSTAR)	8	1995
THE GREATEST HITS OF 1996 – THE STORY OF THE YEAR VARIOUS ARTISTS (TELSTAR)	4	1996
THE GREATEST HITS OF 1997 VARIOUS ARTISTS (TELSTAR)	2	1997
THE GREATEST HITS OF 1998 VARIOUS ARTISTS (TELSTAR)	3	1998

Title / Artist	Peak Position	Year of Release
THE GREATEST HITS OF 1999 – THE STORY SO FAR VARIOUS ARTISTS (TELSTAR)	8	1999
THE GREATEST HITS OF BIG COUNTRY AND THE SKIDS – THE BEST OF STUART ADAMSON BIG COUNTRY & THE SKIDS	71	2002
THE GREATEST HITS OF DANCE VARIOUS ARTISTS (TELSTAR)	5	1992
THE GREATEST HITS OF HOUSE VARIOUS ARTISTS (STYLUS)	5	1988
THE GREATEST HITS OF THE 90'S – PART 1 VARIOUS ARTISTS (TELSTAR)	19	1995
THE GREATEST HITS OF THE NINETIES VARIOUS ARTISTS (TELSTAR)	19	1999
THE GREATEST HITS OF THE STYLISTICS STYLISTICS	34	1992
GREATEST HITS OF WALT DISNEY VARIOUS ARTISTS (RONCO)	11	1975
GREATEST HITS VOLUME 1 JOHNNY CASH	23	1969
GREATEST HITS VOLUME 1 DON WILLIAMS	29	1976
GREATEST HITS VOLUME 1 COCKNEY REJECTS	22	1980
GREATEST HITS VOLUME 1 SISTERS OF MERCY	14	1993
GREATEST HITS VOLUME 1 KORN	22	2004
GREATEST HITS VOLUME 1 DIONNE WARWICK	31	1970
GREATEST HITS VOLUME 1 & VOLUME II BILLY JOEL	7	1985
GREATEST HITS VOLUME 2 RAY CHARLES	24	1968
GREATEST HITS VOLUME 2 DIONNE WARWICK	28	1970
GREATEST HITS VOLUME 2 FRANK SINATRA	6	1970
GREATEST HITS VOLUME 2 TEMPTATIONS	28	1970
GREATEST HITS VOLUME 2 ANDY WILLIAMS	23	1972
GREATEST HITS VOLUME 2 STEVIE WONDER	30	1972
GREATEST HITS VOLUME 2 ELTON JOHN	6	1977
GREATEST HITS VOLUME 2 ABBA	1	1979
GREATEST HITS VOLUME 2 COCKNEY REJECTS	23	1980
GREATEST HITS VOLUME 2 GLORIA ESTEFAN	60	2001
GREATEST HITS VOLUME 3 BOB DYLAN	47	1988
GREATEST HITS VOLUME 3 (LIVE AND LOUD) COCKNEY REJECTS	27	1981
GREATEST HITS VOLUME II DIANA ROSS & THE SUPREMES	29	1970
GREATEST HITS VOLUME III BILLY JOEL	23	1997
GREATEST HITS VOLUME IV JOHNNY MATHIS	31	1977
GREATEST HITS – VOLUMES I, II & III BILLY JOEL	33	1998
GREATEST HITS, ETC. PAUL SIMON	6	1977
THE GREATEST HITS, SO FAR PUBLIC IMAGE LTD	20	1990
GREATEST HITS/SHINING LIKE A NATIONAL GUITAR PAUL SIMON	6	2000
THE GREATEST LINE DANCING PARTY ALBUM WOOLPACKERS	48	1997
THE GREATEST LOVE VARIOUS ARTISTS (TELSTAR)	7	1987
THE GREATEST LOVE 2 VARIOUS ARTISTS (TELSTAR)	3	1988
THE GREATEST LOVE 3 VARIOUS ARTISTS (TELSTAR)	4	1989
THE GREATEST LOVE 4 VARIOUS ARTISTS (TELSTAR)	4	1990
THE GREATEST LOVE 6 – WITH LOVE FROM THE STARS VARIOUS ARTISTS (TELSTAR)	16	1993
GREATEST LOVE CLASSICS ANDY WILLIAMS	22	1984
THE GREATEST LOVE EVER VARIOUS ARTISTS (TELSTAR)	6	1995
GREATEST LOVE SONGS PLACIDO DOMINGO	63	1988
GREATEST MESSAGES GRANDMASTER FLASH & THE FURIOUS FIVE	41	1984
GREATEST MISSES PUBLIC ENEMY	14	1992

Title / Artist	Peak Position	Year of Release
GREATEST MOMENTS CULTURE CLUB	15	1998
THE GREATEST MOMENTS IN SOUL VARIOUS ARTISTS (DOVER)	4	1992
THE GREATEST NO 1 SINGLES VARIOUS ARTISTS (EMI)	2	2001
GREATEST NON-STOP PARTY UNDER THE SUN VARIOUS ARTISTS (EMI)	13	1996
THE GREATEST NUMBER ONES OF THE EIGHTIES VARIOUS ARTISTS (PURE MUSIC)	11	1994
THE GREATEST OF ALL TIME LL COOL J	29	2000
THE GREATEST PARTY ALBUM UNDER THE SUN! VARIOUS ARTISTS (EMI)	1	1995
GREATEST REMIXES VOLUME I C&C MUSIC FACTORY	45	1992
THE GREATEST ROCK 'N' ROLL LOVE SONGS VARIOUS ARTISTS (GLOBAL TELEVISION)	6	1999
THE GREATEST SONGS OF THE BEATLES JAMES LAST	52	1983
THE GREATEST SONGS OF THE FIFTIES BARRY MANILOW	12	2006
THE GREATEST SONGS OF THE SEVENTIES BARRY MANILOW	27	2007
THE GREATEST SONGS OF THE SIXTIES BARRY MANILOW	70	2006
THE GREATEST SOUL ALBUM OF ALL TIME VARIOUS ARTISTS (DINO)	16	1995
THE GREATEST STORY EVER TOLD BALAAM & THE ANGEL	67	1986
THE GREATEST VOICES VARIOUS ARTISTS (DINO)	5	1992
GREEN R.E.M.	27	1988
THE GREEN ALBUM WEEZER	31	2001
GREEN GREEN GRASS OF HOME TOM JONES	3	1967
GREEN LIGHT CLIFF RICHARD	25	1978
GREEN MAN MARK OWEN	33	1996
GREEN MIND DINOSAUR JR	36	1991
GREEN ONIONS BOOKER T & THE M.G.s	11	1964
GREEN RIVER CREEDENCE CLEARWATER REVIVAL	20	1970
GREEN VELVET VARIOUS ARTISTS (RONCO)	6	1983
GREEN VELVET VARIOUS ARTISTS (TELSTAR)	10	1984
GREEN VIRGIN STEVE HILLAGE	30	1978
GREENDALE NEIL YOUNG & CRAZY HORSE	24	2003
GREETINGS FROM ASBURY PARK BRUCE SPRINGSTEEN	41	1985
GREETINGS FROM TIMBUK 3 TIMBUK 3	51	1987
GREG LAKE GREG LAKE	62	1981
GREGORIAN MOODS DOWNSIDE ABBEY MONKS & CHOIRBOYS	59	1998
GREIG AND SCHUMANN PIANO CONCERTOS STEPHEN BISHOP	34	1972
GRETCHEN GOES TO NEBRASKA KING'S X	52	1989
GREY WILL FADE CHARLOTTE HATHERLEY	51	2004
THE GRIMLEYS – ORIGINAL TV SOUNDTRACK TELEVISION AND RADIO COMPILATION	17	2000
GRIN AND BEAR IT RUTS D.C.	28	1980
GRINDERMAN GRINDERMAN	23	2007
GROOVE ARMADA – BACK TO MINE VARIOUS ARTISTS (DISCO MIX CLUB)	16	2000
GROOVERIDER PRESENTS THE PROTOTYPE YEARS VARIOUS ARTISTS (HIGHER GROUND)	19	1997
GROOVIN BILL WYMAN'S RHYTHM KINGS	52	2000
GROOVIN' VARIOUS ARTISTS (POLYGRAM)	2	1994
GROOVUS MAXIMUS ELECTRIC BOYS	61	1992
GROOVY GHETTO VARIOUS ARTISTS (ARCADE)	1	1991
GROOVY GHETTO 2 VARIOUS ARTISTS (ARCADE)	8	1992
GROOVY GHETTO – ALL THE RAGE VARIOUS ARTISTS (ARCADE)	15	1991
GROW TOGETHER ZION TRAIN	56	1996

Title / Artist	Peak Position	Year of Release
GROWING PAINS BILLIE MYERS	19	1998
GROWING PAINS MARY J. BLIGE	6	2008
GROWING UP IN PUBLIC JIMMY NAIL	2	1992
GRRR! IT'S BETTY BOO BETTY BOO	62	1992
GTR G.T.R.	41	1986
GU 10 VARIOUS ARTISTS (GLOBAL UNDERGROUND)	10	2006
GUARANTEED LEVEL 42	3	1991
GUARDIAN ANGEL SHADOWS	98	1984
GUERO BECK	15	2005
GUERRILLA SUPER FURRY ANIMALS	10	1999
A GUIDE TO LOVE, LOSS & DESPERATION WOMBATS	11	2007
GUILTY BARBRA STREISAND	1	1980
GUILTY BLUE	1	2003
GUILTY TOO BARBRA STREISAND	3	2005
GUITAR FRANK ZAPPA	82	1988
GUITAR MAN ELVIS PRESLEY	33	1981
GUITAR MAN HANK MARVIN	6	2007
GUITAR MOODS VARIOUS ARTISTS (DECADANCE)	7	2003
GUITAR PLAYER HANK MARVIN	10	2002
GUITARS MIKE OLDFIELD	40	1999
GUMIXED VARIOUS ARTISTS (GLOBAL UNDERGROUND)	18	2007
GUNFIGHTER BALLADS AND TRAIL SONGS MARTY ROBBINS	20	1960
THE GUNMAN AND OTHER STORIES PREFAB SPROUT	60	2001
GUNS IN THE GHETTO UB40	7	1997
GUN-SHY SCREAMING BLUE MESSIAHS	90	1986
GUTTERFLOWER GOO GOO DOLLS	56	2002
GUYS 'N' DOLLS GUYS 'N' DOLLS	43	1975
GYPSY CAMPFIRES 101 STRINGS	9	1959

H

Title / Artist	Peak Position	Year of Release
H.I.T.S. NEW KIDS ON THE BLOCK	50	1991
H.M.S. FABLE SHACK	25	1999
H.Q. ROY HARPER	31	1975
H2O DARYL HALL & JOHN OATES	24	1982
HA TALVIN SINGH	57	2001
HA' – KILLING JOKE LIVE KILLING JOKE	66	1982
HAARP MUSE	2	2008
THE HACIENDA CLASSICS VARIOUS ARTISTS (EMI)	4	2006
THE HACIENDA – PLAY BY 01/96 VARIOUS ARTISTS (A&M)	18	1995
HADDAWAY – THE ALBUM HADDAWAY	9	1993
HAIL TO ENGLAND MANOWAR	83	1984
HAIL TO THE THIEF RADIOHEAD	1	2003
HAIR STAGE CAST RECORDING	3	1968
HAIRBRUSH DIVAS VARIOUS ARTISTS (WARNER BROTHERS)	3	2003
HAIRBRUSH DIVAS 2 VARIOUS ARTISTS (WARNER BROTHERS)	8	2004
HAIRBRUSH DIVA'S PARTY VARIOUS ARTISTS (WARNER BROTHERS)	18	2007
HAIRBRUSH DIVAS PRESENTS SING-A-LONG SUMMER VARIOUS ARTISTS (WARNER BROTHERS)	1	2005
HAIRSPRAY FILM SOUNDTRACK	4	2007
HAL HAL	31	2005
HALF A SIXPENCE STAGE CAST RECORDING	20	1963
HALF THE PERFECT WORLD MADELEINE PEYROUX	12	2006
HALFWAY BETWEEN THE GUTTER AND THE STARS FATBOY SLIM	8	2000
HALFWAY TO PARADISE BILLY FURY	5	1961
HALFWAY TO SANITY RAMONES	78	1987
HALL AND OATES DARYL HALL & JOHN OATES	56	1976
HALL AND OATES LIVE AT THE APOLLO WITH DAVID RUFFIN AND EDDIE KENDRICK DARYL HALL & JOHN OATES	32	1985
HALL OF FAME GEORGIE FAME	12	1967
HALL OF FAME VARIOUS ARTISTS (CLASSIC FM)	13	1996
HALL OF FAME 2000 VARIOUS ARTISTS (CLASSIC FM)	10	2000
HALL OF FAME – THE GREAT COMPOSERS VARIOUS ARTISTS (CLASSIC FM)	15	2004
HALL OF THE MOUNTAIN GRILL HAWKWIND	16	1974
HALOS AND HORNS DOLLY PARTON	37	2002
HAMBURGER CONCERTO FOCUS	20	1974
HAMILTON'S HOT SHOTS VARIOUS ARTISTS (WARWICK)	15	1976
HAMMER AND TONGS GOODBYE MR. MACKENZIE	61	1991
HAMMERSMITH ODEON LONDON '75 BRUCE SPRINGSTEEN & THE E. STREET BAND	33	2006
HAMMOND A-GO-GO JAMES LAST	27	1967
HANCOCK TONY HANCOCK	12	1962
HAND BUILT BY ROBOTS NEWTON FAULKNER	1	2007
HAND CLAPPIN' – FOOT STOMPIN' – FUNKY BUTT – LIVE! GENO WASHINGTON	5	1966
HAND CUT BUCKS FIZZ	17	1983
HAND ON THE TORCH/JAZZ MIXES US3	40	1993
HANDBAG VARIOUS ARTISTS (V2)	19	2005
HANDCREAM FOR A GENERATION CORNERSHOP	30	2002
HANDLE WITH CARE NUCLEAR ASSAULT	60	1989
THE HANDLER HAR MAR SUPERSTAR	68	2004
HANDS ON THOUSAND YARD STARE	38	1992
HANDS TO HEAVEN VARIOUS ARTISTS (WARNER BROTHERS)	9	2002
HANDSWORTH REVOLUTION STEEL PULSE	9	1978
HANG ON IN THERE BABY JOHNNY BRISTOL	12	1974
HANG ON RAMSEY RAMSEY LEWIS TRIO	20	1966
HANG TOGETHER ODYSSEY	38	1980
HANGIN' TOUGH NEW KIDS ON THE BLOCK	2	1989
THE HANGMAN'S BEAUTIFUL DAUGHTER INCREDIBLE STRING BAND	5	1968
HANGOVER YOU DON'T DESERVE BOWLING FOR SOUP	64	2004
HANK MARVIN HANK MARVIN	14	1969
HANK PLAYS CLIFF HANK MARVIN	33	1995
HANK PLAYS HOLLY HANK MARVIN	34	1996
HANKS PLAYS LIVE HANK MARVIN	71	1997
HANKY PANKY THE THE	28	1995
HANNAH MONTANA TELEVISION AND RADIO COMPILATION	8	2007
HANNAH MONTANA 2/MEET MILEY CYRUS TELEVISION AND RADIO COMPILATION	8	2007
HANNI CAP CIRCUS BIZARRE	43	2005
HANNIBAL (OST) HANS ZIMMER	74	2001
HANSIMANIA JAMES LAST	18	1981
HANX STIFF LITTLE FINGERS	9	1980
HAPPINESS BELOVED	14	1990
HAPPINESS IN MAGAZINES GRAHAM COXON	19	2004
HAPPINESS? ROGER TAYLOR	22	1994
HAPPY AND GLORIOUS MISCELLANEOUS	20	2000
HAPPY ANNIVERSARY SLIM WHITMAN	44	1974
HAPPY BIRTHDAY ALTERED IMAGES	26	1981
HAPPY DAYS VARIOUS ARTISTS (K-TEL)	32	1980
HAPPY DAYS – THE BEST OF ROBSON AND JEROME ROBSON & JEROME	20	1997
HAPPY DAZE VOLUME 2 VARIOUS ARTISTS (ISLAND)	17	1991
HAPPY DAZE...VOLUME 1 VARIOUS ARTISTS (ISLAND)	7	1990
HAPPY FAMILIES BLANCMANGE	30	1982
HAPPY HEAD MIGHTY LEMON DROPS	58	1986
HAPPY HEART ANDY WILLIAMS	22	1969
HAPPY HOUR TED HAWKINS	82	1987
HAPPY IN HELL CHRISTIANS	18	1992
HAPPY MONDAYS – LIVE HAPPY MONDAYS	21	1991
HAPPY NATION ACE OF BASE	1	1993
HAPPY PEOPLE/U SAVED ME R KELLY	11	2004
HAPPY SONGS VARIOUS ARTISTS (VIRGIN)	1	2005
HAPPY SONGS FOR HAPPY PEOPLE MOGWAI	47	2003
HAPPY TO BE DEMIS ROUSSOS	4	1976
HAPPY TOGETHER TURTLES	18	1967
HAPPY TOGETHER ODYSSEY	21	1982
HAPPY? PUBLIC IMAGE LTD	40	1987
HARBOR LIGHTS BRUCE HORNSBY & THE RANGE	32	1993
HARBOUR JACK JONES	10	1974
HARD AT PLAY HUEY LEWIS & THE NEWS	39	1991
HARD CANDY COUNTING CROWS	9	2002
HARD CANDY MADONNA	1	2008
HARD DANCE ANTHEMS VARIOUS ARTISTS (WARNER BROTHERS)	19	2001
A HARD DAY'S NIGHT BEATLES	1	1964
HARD ENERGY VARIOUS ARTISTS (MINISTRY OF SOUND)	10	2001
HARD ENERGY – YOUR XXXTREME NIGHT OUT VARIOUS ARTISTS (MINISTRY OF SOUND)	3	2007
HARD FAX VARIOUS ARTISTS (COLUMBIA)	3	1992
HARD FAX 2 – TWICE THE VICE! VARIOUS ARTISTS (COLUMBIA)	6	1992
HARD HOUSE CLASSICS VARIOUS ARTISTS (MINISTRY OF SOUND)	7	2004
HARD HOUSE EUPHORIA VARIOUS ARTISTS (TELSTAR)	10	2000
HARD HOUSE EUPHORIA – TIDY BOYS VS LISA VARIOUS ARTISTS (TELSTAR)	12	2001
HARD HOUSE NATION VARIOUS ARTISTS (WARNER BROTHERS)	4	2000
HARD HOUSE NATION – 2 VARIOUS ARTISTS (WARNER BROTHERS)	11	2000
HARD HOUSE VOL.3 VARIOUS ARTISTS (WARNER BROTHERS)	7	2001
HARD NOSE THE HIGHWAY VAN MORRISON	22	1973
HARD PROMISES TOM PETTY & HEARTBREAKERS	32	1981
HARD RAIN BOB DYLAN	3	1976
A HARD ROAD JOHN MAYALL & THE BLUESBREAKERS	10	1967
HARD TO EARN GANG STARR	29	1994
THE HARD WAY STEVE EARLE & THE DUKES	22	1990
HARD2BEAT – CLUB ANTHEMS 2008 VARIOUS ARTISTS (HARD2BEAT)	8	2008
HARDCORE 2007 – THE NEW GENERATION VARIOUS ARTISTS (MINISTRY OF SOUND)	7	2007
HARDCORE ADRENALINE VARIOUS ARTISTS (GTV)	2	2007
HARDCORE ADRENALINE 2 VARIOUS ARTISTS (GTV)	6	2007
HARDCORE DANCEFLOOR VARIOUS ARTISTS (DINO)	2	1991
HARDCORE DJS...TAKE CONTROL VARIOUS ARTISTS (PERFECTO)	15	1992
HARDCORE ECSTASY VARIOUS ARTISTS (DINO)	1	1991
HARDCORE EUPHORIA VARIOUS ARTISTS (MINISTRY OF SOUND)	9	2006
HARDCORE EXPLOSION '97 VARIOUS ARTISTS (SUPREME UNDERGROUND)	20	1997
HARDCORE HEAVEN 3 VARIOUS ARTISTS (RESIST)	7	2006

Title / Artist	Peak Position	Year of Release
HARDCORE HEAVEN 4 VARIOUS ARTISTS (RESIST)	8	2006
HARDCORE HEAVEN – VOLUME 2 VARIOUS ARTISTS (HEAVEN MUSIC)	13	1997
HARDCORE HEAVEN – VOLUME 3 VARIOUS ARTISTS (HEAVEN MUSIC)	12	1998
HARDCORE HEAVEN – VOLUME 4 VARIOUS ARTISTS (HEAVEN MUSIC)	17	1998
HARDCORE HEAVEN – VOLUME 5 VARIOUS ARTISTS (HEAVEN MUSIC)	17	1999
HARDCORE HEAVEN – VOLUME ONE VARIOUS ARTISTS (HEAVEN MUSIC)	12	1997
HARDCORE NATION VARIOUS ARTISTS (WARNER BROTHERS)	6	2005
HARDCORE NATION 2 VARIOUS ARTISTS (WARNER BROTHERS)	8	2005
HARDCORE NATION 3 VARIOUS ARTISTS (WARNER BROTHERS)	8	2006
HARDCORE NATION CLASSICS VARIOUS ARTISTS (WARNER BROTHERS)	18	2007
HARDCORE – THE CLASSICS – 1994-2009 VARIOUS ARTISTS (MINISTRY OF SOUND)	18	2008
HARDCORE TIL I DIE VARIOUS ARTISTS (UNIVERSAL)	3	2008
HARDCORE UPROAR VARIOUS ARTISTS (DINO)	2	1991
HARDER…FASTER APRIL WINE	34	1980
THE HARDEST WAY TO MAKE AN EASY LIVING STREETS	1	2006
HARDWARE KROKUS	44	1981
HAREM HOLIDAY ELVIS PRESLEY	11	1966
HARK THE HERALD ANGELS SING HAMBURG STUDENTS CHOIR	11	1960
HARLEM WORLD MASE	53	1998
HARMACY SEBADOH	38	1996
HARMONY CORRUPTION NAPALM DEATH	67	1990
HARPO'S GHOST THEA GILMORE	69	2006
HARPS AND ANGELS RANDY NEWMAN	46	2008
HARRY POTTER (OST) JOHN WILLIAMS	19	2001
HARRY'S BAR GORDON HASKELL	2	2002
HARVEST NEIL YOUNG	1	1972
HARVEST FOR THE WORLD ISLEY BROTHERS	50	1976
HARVEST MOON NEIL YOUNG	9	1992
HASTEN DOWN THE WIND LINDA RONSTADT	32	1976
HAT FULL OF STARS CYNDI LAUPER	56	1993
HAT TRICK AMERICA	41	1973
HATE DELGADOS	57	2002
HATFUL OF HOLLOW SMITHS	7	1984
HATS BLUE NILE	12	1989
HATS OFF TO LARRY DEL SHANNON	9	1963
HATS OFF TO THE BUSKERS THE VIEW	1	2007
HAUNTED CITIES TRANSPLANTS	72	2005
HAUNTED DANCEHALL SABRES OF PARADISE	57	1994
THE HAUNTED SCIENCE OMNI TRIO	43	1996
HAUNTING MELODIES ELECTRIC WINDENSEMBLE	28	1984
HAVANA MOON CARLOS SANTANA	84	1983
HAVE A GOOD FOREVER… COOL NOTES	66	1985
HAVE A LITTLE FAITH JOE COCKER	9	1994
HAVE A NICE DAY ROXETTE	28	1999
HAVE A NICE DAY BON JOVI	2	2005
HAVE I TOLD YOU LATELY THAT I LOVE YOU JIM REEVES	12	1965
HAVE TWANGY GUITAR WILL TRAVEL DUANE EDDY	6	1959
HAVE YOU EVER BEEN IN LOVE LEO SAYER	15	1983
HAVE YOU FED THE FISH? BADLY DRAWN BOY	10	2002
HAVE YOU NEVER BEEN MELLOW OLIVIA NEWTON-JOHN	37	1975
HAWAII HIGH LLAMAS	62	1996
HAWAIIAN PARADISE/CHRISTMAS WOUT STEENHUIS	28	1981
THE HAWK IS HOWLING MOGWAI	35	2008
HAWKS AND DOVES NEIL YOUNG	34	1980
HAWKWIND HAWKWIND	75	1984
HE GOT GAME (OST) PUBLIC ENEMY	50	1998
HE TOUCHED ME ELVIS PRESLEY	38	1972
HE WALKS BESIDE ME ELVIS PRESLEY	37	1978
HE WAS BEAUTIFUL IRIS WILLIAMS	69	1979
HEAD FIRST URIAH HEEP	46	1983
HEAD FULL OF ROCK VARIOUS ARTISTS (EMI)	16	2007
HEAD LIKE A ROCK IAN McNABB	29	1994
HEAD MUSIC SUEDE	1	1999
HEAD ON SAMSON	34	1980
THE HEAD ON THE DOOR CURE	7	1985
HEAD OVER HEELS COCTEAU TWINS	51	1983
HEAD OVER HEELS PAULA ABDUL	61	1995
HEAD OVER HEELS (TELEVISION SOUNDTRACK) TELEVISION AND RADIO COMPILATION	3	1993
HEADBANGER'S BIBLE VARIOUS ARTISTS (WARNER BROTHERS)	9	2005
HEADED FOR THE FUTURE NEIL DIAMOND	36	1986
HEADHUNTER KROKUS	74	1983
THE HEADLESS CHILDREN W.A.S.P.	8	1989
HEADLESS CROSS BLACK SABBATH	31	1989
HEADLINE HITS VARIOUS ARTISTS (K-TEL)	5	1983
HEADLINERS VARIOUS ARTISTS (SONY/BMG)	16	2007
HEADLINERS – TALL PAUL VARIOUS ARTISTS (MINISTRY OF SOUND)	20	2000
HEADLINES MIDNIGHT STAR	42	1986
HEADLINES AND DEADLINES – THE HITS OF A-HA A-HA	12	1991
HEADQUARTERS MONKEES	2	1967
HEADRUSH VARIOUS ARTISTS (GLOBAL TELEVISION)	10	2000
HEADSTONE – THE BEST OF UFO UFO	39	1983
THE HEALER JOHN LEE HOOKER	63	1989
THE HEALING GAME VAN MORRISON	10	1997
HEAR IN THE NOW FRONTIER QUEENSRYCHE	46	1997
HEAR MY CRY SONIQUE	6	2000
HEAR MY SONG (THE BEST OF JOSEF LOCKE) JOSEF LOCKE	7	1992
HEAR 'N' AID VARIOUS ARTISTS (VERTIGO)	50	1986
HEAR NOTHING, SEE NOTHING, SAY NOTHING DISCHARGE	40	1982
HEARSAY/ALL MIXED UP ALEXANDER O'NEAL	4	1987
HEART HEART	19	1985
HEART & SOUL VARIOUS ARTISTS (POLYGRAM)	17	1997
HEART & SOUL STEVE BROOKSTEIN	1	2005
HEART & SOUL – NEW SONGS FROM ALLY MCBEAL VONDA SHEPARD	9	1999
HEART AND SOUL BARRY WHITE	34	1985
HEART AND SOUL EDITH PIAF	58	1987
HEART AND SOUL VARIOUS ARTISTS (HEART & SOUL)	2	1989
HEART AND SOUL JOY DIVISION	70	1998
HEART AND SOUL CHARLIE LANDSBOROUGH	56	2006
HEART AND SOUL III – HEART FULL OF SOUL VARIOUS ARTISTS (HEART & SOUL)	4	1990
THE HEART AND SOUL OF ROCK AND ROLL VARIOUS ARTISTS (TELSTAR)	60	1988
HEART AND SOUL – THE VERY BEST OF T'PAU T'PAU	35	1993
HEART FULL OF SOUL VARIOUS ARTISTS (DINO)	9	1993
HEART FULL OF SOUL VARIOUS ARTISTS (GLOBAL TELEVISION)	8	1998
HEART FULL OF SOUL – 2 VARIOUS ARTISTS (GLOBAL TELEVISION)	12	1999
HEART IN MOTION AMY GRANT	25	1991
HEART LIKE A SKY SPANDAU BALLET	31	1989
HEART 'N' SOUL TINA CHARLES	35	1977
THE HEART OF A WOMAN JOHNNY MATHIS	39	1975
THE HEART OF CHICAGO CHICAGO	6	1989
THE HEART OF CHICAGO – 1967-1997 CHICAGO	21	1999
THE HEART OF EVERYTHING WITHIN TEMPTATION	38	2007
A HEART OF GOLD VARIOUS ARTISTS (TELSTAR)	9	1993
THE HEART OF ROCK AND ROLL – BEST OF HUEY LEWIS AND THE NEWS HUEY LEWIS & THE NEWS	23	1992
HEART OF SOUL VOLUME 1 VARIOUS ARTISTS (MASTERSOUND)	96	1987
HEART OF STONE CHER	7	1989
THE HEART OF THE 80S AND 90S VARIOUS ARTISTS (UNIVERSAL)	9	1998
HEART OVER MIND JENNIFER RUSH	48	1987
HEART STRINGS FOSTER & ALLEN	37	1992
HEART TO HEART – 20 HOT HITS RAY CHARLES	29	1980
HEART TO HEART – 24 LOVE SONG DUETS VARIOUS ARTISTS (K-TEL)	8	1986
HEART TUNED TO DEAD SWITCHES	64	2007
HEART, SOUL AND VOICE JON SECADA	17	1994
HEARTBEAT HANK MARVIN	17	1993
HEARTBEAT (MUSIC FROM THE TV SERIES) VARIOUS ARTISTS (COLUMBIA)	1	1992
HEARTBEAT – 10TH ANNIVERSARY ALBUM VARIOUS ARTISTS (BMG)	17	2000
HEARTBEAT – 50 GROOVY TRACKS FROM THE 60S VARIOUS ARTISTS (EMI)	20	2007
HEARTBEAT CITY CARS	25	1984
HEARTBEAT – FOREVER YOURS VARIOUS ARTISTS (COLUMBIA)	1	1995
HEARTBEAT – LOVE ME TENDER VARIOUS ARTISTS (GLOBAL TELEVISION)	6	1997
HEARTBEAT LOVE SONGS VARIOUS ARTISTS (UNIVERSAL)	10	2003
HEARTBEAT – LOVESONGS VARIOUS ARTISTS (EMI)	5	2007
HEARTBEAT – NUMBER 1 LOVE SONGS OF THE '60S VARIOUS ARTISTS (GLOBAL TELEVISION)	2	1996
HEARTBEAT NUMBER 1'S VARIOUS ARTISTS (EMI)	19	2007
HEARTBEAT SUMMER VARIOUS ARTISTS (EMI)	5	2007
HEARTBEAT – THE 60'S GOLD COLLECTION VARIOUS ARTISTS (GLOBAL TELEVISION)	7	1998
HEARTBEATS BARBARA DICKSON	21	1984
HEARTBEATS – GREATEST HITS CHRIS REA	24	2005
HEARTBREAK STATION CINDERELLA	36	1990
HEARTBREAKER FREE	9	1973
HEARTBREAKER DIONNE WARWICK	3	1982
HEARTBREAKER – THE VERY BEST OF DIONNE WARWICK	32	2002
HEARTBREAKERS VARIOUS ARTISTS (K-TEL)	2	1977
HEARTBREAKERS MATT MONRO	5	1980
HEARTBREAKERS – 18 CLASSICAL LOVE HITS VARIOUS ARTISTS (STARBLEND)	38	1986
HEARTLANDS VARIOUS ARTISTS (DINO)	4	1992
HEARTLESS CREW PRESENTS CRISP BISCUIT VARIOUS ARTISTS (EAST WEST)	10	2002
HEARTLIGHT NEIL DIAMOND	43	1982
HEARTS AND BONES PAUL SIMON	34	1983
HEARTS AND FLOWERS JOAN ARMATRADING	29	1990
HEARTS OF FORTUNE IMMACULATE FOOLS	65	1985
HEARTWORK CARCASS	67	1993
THE HEAT DAN REED NETWORK	15	1991
THE HEAT TONI BRAXTON	3	2000
THE HEAT IS ON VARIOUS ARTISTS (ARCADE)	4	1991
THE HEAT IS ON – 16 TRACKS VARIOUS ARTISTS (PORTRAIT)	9	1986
HEAT TREATMENT GRAHAM PARKER & THE RUMOUR	52	1976

Title	Peak Position	Year of Release
HEATHCLIFF LIVE (THE SHOW) STAGE CAST RECORDING	41	1996
HEATHEN DAVID BOWIE	5	2002
HEATHEN CHEMISTRY OASIS	1	2002
HEAVEN DJ SAMMY	14	2003
HEAVEN AND HELL VANGELIS	31	1976
HEAVEN AND HELL BLACK SABBATH	9	1980
HEAVEN AND HELL MEAT LOAF/BONNIE TYLER	9	1989
HEAVEN AND HELL VARIOUS ARTISTS (TELSTAR)	9	1989
HEAVEN AND HELL VARIOUS ARTISTS (COLUMBIA)	12	1995
HEAVEN IS WAITING DANSE SOCIETY	39	1984
HEAVEN KNOWS JAKI GRAHAM	48	1985
HEAVEN ON EARTH BELINDA CARLISLE	4	1988
HEAVEN OR LAS VEGAS COCTEAU TWINS	7	1990
HEAVEN UP HERE ECHO & THE BUNNYMEN	10	1981
HEAVENLY LADYSMITH BLACK MAMBAZO	53	1997
HEAVENLY HARDCORE VARIOUS ARTISTS (DINO)	2	1992
HEAVIER THINGS JOHN MAYER	74	2003
HEAVY VARIOUS ARTISTS (K-TEL)	46	1983
THE HEAVY HEAVY HITS MADNESS	19	1998
HEAVY HORSES JETHRO TULL	20	1978
HEAVY NOVA ROBERT PALMER	17	1988
HEAVY PETTING ZOO NOFX	60	1996
HEAVY RHYME EXPERIENCE VOLUME 1 BRAND NEW HEAVIES	38	1992
HEAVY ROTATION ANASTACIA	17	2008
HEAVY SOUL PAUL WELLER	2	1997
HEAVY TRAFFIC STATUS QUO	15	2002
HEAVY WEATHER WEATHER REPORT	43	1977
HED KANDI – BACK TO LOVE VARIOUS ARTISTS (HED KANDI)	6	2007
HED KANDI – BEACH HOUSE VARIOUS ARTISTS (HED KANDI)	17	2008
HED KANDI CLASSICS VARIOUS ARTISTS (HED KANDI)	12	2006
HED KANDI – DISCO HEAVEN VARIOUS ARTISTS (HED KANDI)	7	2006
HED KANDI – DISCO HEAVEN VARIOUS ARTISTS (HED KANDI)	19	2008
HED KANDI – DISCO KANDI – THE MIX VARIOUS ARTISTS (HED KANDI)	3	2007
HED KANDI SUMMER 2004 VARIOUS ARTISTS (HED KANDI)	5	2004
HED KANDI – THE MIX 2008 VARIOUS ARTISTS (HED KANDI)	9	2007
HED KANDI – THE MIX 2009 VARIOUS ARTISTS (HED KANDI)	14	2008
HED KANDI THE MIX 50 VARIOUS ARTISTS (HED KANDI)	5	2005
HED KANDI – THE MIX SUMMER 2006 VARIOUS ARTISTS (HED KANDI)	2	2006
HED KANDI – THE MIX – SUMMER 2007 VARIOUS ARTISTS (HED KANDI)	3	2007
HED KANDI – THE MIX – SUMMER 2008 VARIOUS ARTISTS (HED KANDI)	7	2008
HED KANDI WORLD SERIES – IBIZA VARIOUS ARTISTS (HED KANDI)	9	2008
HED KANDI – WORLD SERIES LIVE – SAN FRANCISCO VARIOUS ARTISTS (HED KANDI)	17	2008
THE HEIGHT OF BAD MANNERS BAD MANNERS	23	1983
HEJIRA JONI MITCHELL	11	1976
HELIOCENTRIC PAUL WELLER	2	2000
HELL BENT FOR LEATHER FRANKIE LAINE	7	1961
HELL FREEZES OVER EAGLES	18	1994
HELL HATH NO FURY ROCK GODDESS	84	1983
HE'LL HAVE TO GO JIM REEVES	16	1964
HELL ON EARTH MOBB DEEP	67	1996
HELL TO PAY JEFF HEALEY BAND	18	1990
HELLBILLY DELUXE ROB ZOMBIE	37	1998
HELLO STATUS QUO	1	1973
HELLO CHILDREN…EVERYWHERE VARIOUS ARTISTS (EMI)	59	1988
HELLO DAD I'M IN JAIL WAS (NOT WAS)	61	1992
HELLO DOLLY LOUIS ARMSTRONG	11	1964
HELLO DOLLY! BARBRA STREISAND	45	1970
HELLO I'M JOHNNY CASH JOHNNY CASH	6	1970
HELLO NASTY BEASTIE BOYS	1	1998
HELLO PIG LEVELLERS	28	2000
HELLO YOUNG LOVERS SPARKS	66	2006
HELLO, I MUST BE GOING PHIL COLLINS	2	1982
HELL'S DITCH POGUES	12	1990
HELP – A DAY IN THE LIFE VARIOUS ARTISTS (INDEPENDIENTE)	4	2005
HELP- WAR CHILD VARIOUS ARTISTS (GO! DISCS)	1	1995
HELP YOURSELF TOM JONES	4	1968
HELP YOURSELF JULIAN LENNON	42	1991
HELP! BEATLES	1	1965
HELTER SKELTER VOW WOW	75	1989
HELTER SKELTER PRESENTS HARDCORE CLASSICS VARIOUS ARTISTS (MINISTRY OF SOUND)	2	2006
HELTER SKELTER UNITED IN HARDCORE VARIOUS ARTISTS (MINISTRY OF SOUND)	6	2006
HELTER SKELTER V RAINDANCE HARDCORE 2007 VARIOUS ARTISTS (MINISTRY OF SOUND)	5	2007
HEMISPHERES RUSH	14	1978
HENDRIX IN THE WEST JIMI HENDRIX	7	1972
HENRY MANCINI 40 GREATEST HENRY MANCINI	26	1976
HENRY'S DREAM NICK CAVE & THE BAD SEEDS	29	1992
HEPBURN HEPBURN	28	1999
HER BEST SONGS EMMYLOU HARRIS	36	1980
HERCULES AND LOVE AFFAIR HERCULES AND LOVE AFFAIR	31	2008
HERE LEO SAYER	44	1979
HERE AND NOW – THE VERY BEST OF THE 80S VARIOUS ARTISTS (UNIVERSAL)	6	2008
HERE AND THERE ELTON JOHN	6	1976
HERE AT THE MAYFLOWER BARRY MANILOW	18	2002
HERE COME THE DRUMS ROGUE TRADERS	46	2006
HERE COME THE MINSTRELS GEORGE MITCHELL MINSTRELS	11	1966
HERE COME THE TEARS TEARS	15	2005
HERE COME THE WARM JETS BRIAN ENO	75	1974
HERE COMES SUMMER VARIOUS ARTISTS (SONY/BMG)	17	2007
HERE COMES THE FUZZ MARK RONSON	70	2007
HERE COMES THE TREMELOES TREMELOES	15	1967
HERE FOR THE PARTY GRETCHEN WILSON	60	2004
HERE I STAND USHER	1	2008
HERE THEY COME: THE GREATEST HITS OF THE MONKEES MONKEES	15	1997
HERE TODAY, TOMORROW NEXT WEEK! SUGARCUBES	15	1989
HERE WE COME A1	20	1999
HERE WE STAND FRATELLIS	5	2008
HERE WHERE THERE IS LOVE DIONNE WARWICK	39	1967
HERE'S SOME THAT GOT AWAY STYLE COUNCIL	39	1993
HERE'S TO FUTURE DAYS THOMPSON TWINS	5	1985
HERE'S TOM WITH THE WEATHER SHACK	55	2003
HERGEST RIDGE MIKE OLDFIELD	1	1974
HERMAN'S HERMITS HERMAN'S HERMITS	16	1965
HERMIT OF MINK HOLLOW TODD RUNDGREN	42	1978
HERO AND HEROINE STRAWBS	35	1974
HERO OF THE DAY METALLICA	47	1996
HEROES DAVID BOWIE	3	1977
HEROES COMMODORES	50	1980
HEROES VARIOUS ARTISTS (SONY)	11	2004
HEROES TO ZEROS BETA BAND	18	2004
HE'S THE DJ, I'M THE RAPPER DJ JAZZY JEFF & THE FRESH PRINCE	68	1988
HEX ENDUCATION HOUR FALL	71	1982
HEY GLITTER BAND	13	1974
HEY EUGENE PINK MARTINI	47	2007
HEY HEY IT'S THE MONKEES – GREATEST HITS MONKEES	12	1989
HEY HO LET'S GO! – ANTHOLOGY RAMONES	74	2001
HEY MA JAMES	10	2008
HEY ROCK 'N' ROLL – THE VERY BEST OF SHOWADDYWADDY	56	2004
HEY STOOPID ALICE COOPER	4	1991
HEY VENUS SUPER FURRY ANIMALS	11	2007
HI ENERGY VARIOUS ARTISTS (K-TEL)	17	1979
HI INFIDELITY REO SPEEDWAGON	6	1981
HI LIFE – THE BEST OF AL GREEN AL GREEN	34	1988
HI TENSION HI TENSION	74	1979
HICKORY HOLLER REVISITED O.C. SMITH	40	1968
THE HIDDEN CAMERA PHOTEK	39	1996
HIDDEN TREASURES BARRY MANILOW	36	1993
HIDE FROM THE SUN RASMUS	65	2005
HIDE YOUR HEART BONNIE TYLER	78	1988
HIDEAWAY DE'LACY	53	1995
HI-FI COMPANION ALBUM RAY CONNIFF	3	1960
HI-FI SERIOUS A	18	2002
HIGH BLUE NILE	10	2004
HIGH AND MIGHTY URIAH HEEP	55	1976
HIGH CIVILIZATION BEE GEES	24	1991
HIGH CRIME AL JARREAU	81	1984
HIGH LAND HARD RAIN AZTEC CAMERA	22	1983
HIGH 'N' DRY DEF LEPPARD	26	1981
HIGH ON A HAPPY VIBE URBAN COOKIE COLLECTIVE	28	1994
HIGH ON EMOTION – LIVE FROM DUBLIN CHRIS DE BURGH	15	1990
HIGH ON THE HAPPY SIDE WET WET WET	1	1992
HIGH PRIORITY CHERRELLE	17	1986
THE HIGH ROAD JOJO	24	2007
HIGH SCHOOL MUSICAL VARIOUS ARTISTS (WALT DISNEY)	1	2006
HIGH SCHOOL MUSICAL 2 TELEVISION AND RADIO COMPILATION	1	2007
HIGH SCHOOL MUSICAL 3 – SENIOR YEAR VARIOUS ARTISTS (WALT DISNEY)	1	2008
HIGH SCHOOL MUSICAL – THE CONCERT ORIGINAL CAST RECORDING	45	2007
HIGH SOCIETY ORIGINAL SOUNDTRACK	2	1956
HIGH TIMES SINGLES 1992-2006 JAMIROQUAI	1	2006
HIGHER ALED JONES	21	2003
HIGHER AND HIGHER – THE BEST OF HEAVEN 17 HEAVEN 17	31	1993
HIGHER GROUND BARBRA STREISAND	12	1997
THE HIGHER THEY CLIMB DAVID CASSIDY	22	1975
HIGHLIGHTS FROM JEFF WAYNE'S MUSICAL VERSION OF THE WAR OF THE WORLDS JEFF WAYNE	64	1996
HIGHLIGHTS FROM LAST NIGHT AT THE PROMS '82 BBC SYMPHONY ORCHESTRA, SINGS & SYMPHONY CHORUS CONDUCTED BY JAMES LOUGHRAN	69	1982
HIGHLIGHTS FROM WEST SIDE STORY (ORIGINAL STUDIO CAST RECORDING) STAGE CAST RECORDING	72	1986
HIGHLY EVOLVED VINES	3	2002
HIGHLY STRUNG STEVE HACKETT	16	1983
HIGHWAY FREE	41	1971
HIGHWAY 61 REVISITED BOB DYLAN	4	1965

Title / Artist	Peak Position	Year of Release
HIGHWAY COMPANION TOM PETTY	56	2006
HIGHWAY OF LIFE HARRY SECOMBE	45	1986
HIGHWAY SONG – BLACKFOOT LIVE BLACKFOOT	14	1982
HIGHWAY TO HELL AC/DC	8	1979
HILLBILLY DELUXE DWIGHT YOAKAM	51	1987
HINDA HINDA HICKS	20	1998
154 WIRE	39	1979
HINTERLAND AIM	47	2002
HIP HOP AND RAPPING IN THE HOUSE VARIOUS ARTISTS (STYLUS)	5	1988
HIP HOP CLASSICS VARIOUS ARTISTS (UNIVERSAL)	2	2007
HIP HOP CLASSICS VARIOUS ARTISTS (UNIVERSAL)	16	2008
HIP HOP DON'T STOP – 20 CLASSIC HIP HOP SUPERJAMS VARIOUS ARTISTS (SOLID STATE)	16	1997
HIP HOP IS DEAD NAS	68	2006
HIP HOP LOVE VARIOUS ARTISTS (WARNER BROTHERS)	5	2004
HIP HOP – THE EVOLUTION VARIOUS ARTISTS (WARNER BROTHERS)	7	2006
HIP HOUSE VARIOUS ARTISTS (STYLUS)	3	1989
HIP HOUSE – THE DEEPEST BEATS IN TOWN VARIOUS ARTISTS (K-TEL)	10	1989
HIP-HOP '87 VARIOUS ARTISTS (SERIOUS)	81	1987
HIPS AND MAKERS KRISTIN HERSH	7	1994
HIPSTERS, FLIPSTERS, AND FINGER POPPIN' DADDIES GENO WASHINGTON	8	1967
HIPSWAY HIPSWAY	42	1986
HIS 12 GREATEST HITS NEIL DIAMOND	13	1974
HIS 20 GREATEST HITS GENE PITNEY	6	1976
HIS DEFINITIVE GREATEST HITS B.B. KING	24	1999
HIS FINEST COLLECTION ROGER WHITTAKER	15	1987
HIS GREATEST HITS DAVID ESSEX	13	1991
HIS GREATEST LOVE SONGS CHARLES AZNAVOUR	73	1980
HIS GREATEST LOVE SONGS ENGELBERT HUMPERDINCK	4	2004
HIS HAND IN MINE ELVIS PRESLEY	3	1961
HIS LATEST AND GREATEST CHUCK BERRY	8	1964
HIS 'N' HERS PULP	9	1994
HIS ORCHESTRA, HIS CHORUS, HIS SINGERS, HIS SOUND RAY CONNIFF	1	1969
HIS WONDROUS STORY BILLY FURY	10	2008
THE HISSING OF SUMMER LAWNS JONI MITCHELL	14	1975
HISTORY MAI TAI	91	1985
HISTORY – AMERICA'S GREATEST HITS AMERICA	60	1976
HISTORY OF ERIC CLAPTON ERIC CLAPTON	20	1972
THE HISTORY OF HIP HOP VARIOUS ARTISTS (WARNER BROTHERS)	13	2004
THE HISTORY OF OTIS REDDING OTIS REDDING	2	1968
THE HISTORY OF ROCK KID ROCK	73	2000
THE HISTORY OF THE BONZOS BONZO DOG DOO-DAH BAND	41	1974
HISTORY OF THE BYRDS BYRDS	47	1973
HISTORY – PAST PRESENT AND FUTURE BOOK 1 MICHAEL JACKSON	1	1995
HISTORY REVISITED – THE REMIXES TALK TALK	35	1991
HIT PETER GABRIEL	29	2003
HIT 40 UK VARIOUS ARTISTS (BMG)	1	2004
HIT ACTION VARIOUS ARTISTS (K-TEL)	15	1977
THE HIT FACTORY VARIOUS ARTISTS (UNIVERSAL)	3	2000
THE HIT FACTORY VOLUME 2 VARIOUS ARTISTS (FANFARE)	13	1988
THE HIT FACTORY VOLUME 3 VARIOUS ARTISTS (FANFARE)	3	1989
THE HIT FACTORY: THE BEST OF STOCK AITKEN WATERMAN VARIOUS ARTISTS (STYLUS)	18	1987
THE HIT LIST CLIFF RICHARD	3	1994
HIT MACHINE VARIOUS ARTISTS (K-TEL)	4	1976
HIT MAKER – BURT BACHARACH BURT BACHARACH	3	1965
HIT ME BABY ONE MORE TIME VARIOUS ARTISTS (VIRGIN)	16	2005
HIT MIX '86 VARIOUS ARTISTS (STYLUS)	10	1986
HIT MIX '88 VARIOUS ARTISTS (STYLUS)	15	1988
HIT MIX – HITS OF THE YEAR VARIOUS ARTISTS (STYLUS)	29	1987
HIT 'N' RUN GIRLSCHOOL	5	1981
THE HIT PACK: THE BEST OF CHART MUSIC VARIOUS ARTISTS (CBS)	2	1990
HIT PARADE PETULA CLARK	18	1967
HIT PARADE PAUL WELLER	7	2006
HIT PARADE 1 WEDDING PRESENT	22	1992
HIT PARADE 2 WEDDING PRESENT	19	1993
HIT SCENE VARIOUS ARTISTS (WARWICK)	19	1977
THE HIT SQUAD – CHART TRACKING VARIOUS ARTISTS (RONCO)	4	1983
THE HIT SQUAD – HITS OF '83 VARIOUS ARTISTS (RONCO)	12	1983
THE HIT SQUAD – NIGHT CLUBBING VARIOUS ARTISTS (RONCO)	28	1983
HIT THE DECKS VOLUME 1 – BATTLE OF THE DJS VARIOUS ARTISTS (QUALITY TELEVISION)	3	1992
HIT THE DECKS VOLUME 2 – BATTLE OF THE DJS VARIOUS ARTISTS (QUALITY TELEVISION)	3	1992
HIT THE DECKS VOLUME III VARIOUS ARTISTS (QUALITY TELEVISION)	3	1992
HIT THE HIGHWAY PROCLAIMERS	8	1994
HIT THE ROAD STAX VARIOUS ARTISTS (STAX)	10	1967
THE HIT WORLD OF KLAUS WUNDERLICH KLAUS WUNDERLICH	27	1975
THE HITCHHIKERS GUIDE TO THE GALAXY VOLUME 2 (TELEVISION SOUNDTRACK) TELEVISION AND RADIO COMPILATION	47	1981
THE HITMAKERS VARIOUS ARTISTS (POLYDOR)	45	1980
THE HITS GARTH BROOKS	11	1994
HITS MIKE & THE MECHANICS	3	1996
HITS PHIL COLLINS	1	1998
HITS PULP	71	2002
THE HITS DAVE CLARK FIVE	15	2008
THE HITS KELIS	71	2008
THE HITS 1 PRINCE	5	1993
THE HITS 2 PRINCE	5	1993
HITS 2000 VARIOUS ARTISTS (GLOBAL TELEVISION)	2	1999
HITS 2001 VARIOUS ARTISTS (WARNER BROTHERS)	3	2000
HITS 3 VARIOUS ARTISTS (CBS)	2	1985
HITS 4 VARIOUS ARTISTS (CBS)	1	1986
HITS 5 VARIOUS ARTISTS (CBS)	1	1986
HITS 50 VARIOUS ARTISTS (BMG)	1	2001
HITS 51 VARIOUS ARTISTS (BMG)	10	2001
HITS 52 VARIOUS ARTISTS (BMG)	2	2002
HITS 53 VARIOUS ARTISTS (BMG)	2	2002
HITS 54 VARIOUS ARTISTS (BMG)	1	2002
HITS 55 VARIOUS ARTISTS (BMG)	1	2003
HITS 56 VARIOUS ARTISTS (BMG)	1	2003
HITS 57 VARIOUS ARTISTS (BMG)	5	2003
HITS 58 VARIOUS ARTISTS (BMG)	1	2004
HITS 59 VARIOUS ARTISTS (SONY)	2	2004
HITS 6 VARIOUS ARTISTS (CBS)	1	1987
HITS 60 VARIOUS ARTISTS (SONY)	5	2004
HITS 7 VARIOUS ARTISTS (CBS)	2	1987
HITS 8 VARIOUS ARTISTS (CBS)	2	1988
HITS 93 VOLUME 1 VARIOUS ARTISTS (TELSTAR)	1	1993
HITS 93 VOLUME 2 VARIOUS ARTISTS (TELSTAR)	2	1993
HITS 93 VOLUME 3 VARIOUS ARTISTS (TELSTAR)	2	1993
HITS 93 VOLUME 4 VARIOUS ARTISTS (TELSTAR)	2	1993
HITS 94 VOLUME 1 VARIOUS ARTISTS (TELSTAR)	3	1994
HITS 96 VARIOUS ARTISTS (GLOBAL TELEVISION)	1	1995
HITS 97 VARIOUS ARTISTS (SONY)	2	1996
HITS 99 VARIOUS ARTISTS (SONY)	2	1998
THE HITS ALBUM VARIOUS ARTISTS (CBS)	1	1984
THE HITS ALBUM 10 VARIOUS ARTISTS (CBS)	1	1989
THE HITS ALBUM 15 VARIOUS ARTISTS (CBS)	1	1991
THE HITS ALBUM 2 VARIOUS ARTISTS (CBS)	1	1985
THE HITS ALBUM 9 VARIOUS ARTISTS (CBS)	4	1988
THE HITS AND BEYOND DANNII MINOGUE	17	2006
HITS AND HISTORY DR. HOOK	14	2007
HITS FOR LOVERS VARIOUS ARTISTS (EPIC)	2	1986
HITS FOR NOW AND ALWAYS KEN DODD	14	1966
HITS LIKE NEVER BEFORE (ESSENTIAL ELVIS VOLUME 3) ELVIS PRESLEY	71	1990
HITS OF GOLD MAMAS & THE PAPAS	7	1969
THE HITS OF HOUSE ARE HERE VARIOUS ARTISTS (K-TEL)	12	1988
HITS OF THE 70'S ELVIS PRESLEY	30	1977
HITS OF THE ROCKIN' 50'S BOBBY VEE	20	1962
HITS OF THE SCREAMING 60'S VARIOUS ARTISTS (WARWICK)	24	1982
HITS OF THE SIXTIES BACHELORS	12	1966
HITS ON FIRE VARIOUS ARTISTS (RONCO)	11	1983
HITS ON OPERA KIMERA WITH THE LONDON SYMPHONY ORCHESTRA	38	1985
HITS OUT OF HELL MEAT LOAF	2	1985
HITS PLUS KYLIE MINOGUE	41	2000
THE HITS – RELOADED KOOL & THE GANG	56	2004
HITS REVIVAL VARIOUS ARTISTS (K-TEL)	10	1987
HITS REVIVAL 2: REPLAY VARIOUS ARTISTS (K-TEL)	45	1988
HITS RIGHT UP YOUR STREET SHADOWS	15	1981
THE HITS/THE B-SIDES PRINCE	4	1993
HITS UNLIMITED 2 UNLIMITED	27	1995
HITS ZONE '97 VARIOUS ARTISTS (POLYGRAM)	11	1996
HITS ZONE SUMMER '97 VARIOUS ARTISTS (POLYGRAM)	8	1997
HITS ZONE – THE BEST OF '97 VARIOUS ARTISTS (POLYGRAM)	18	1997
HITS! THE VERY BEST OF ERASURE ERASURE	15	2003
HITS, HITS AND MORE DANCE HITS VARIOUS ARTISTS (GLOBAL TELEVISION)	13	1994
HITS, HITS, HITS VARIOUS ARTISTS (RONCO)	2	1981
HITS, HITS, HITS – 18 SMASH ORIGINALS VARIOUS ARTISTS (TELSTAR)	6	1984
HITSTORY ELVIS PRESLEY	31	2005
HITSVILLE VARIOUS ARTISTS (PYE)	11	1963
HITSVILLE VOLUME 2 VARIOUS ARTISTS (PYE)	20	1963
HITZ BLITZ VARIOUS ARTISTS (GLOBAL TELEVISION)	2	1995
HOLD AN OLD FRIEND'S HAND TIFFANY	56	1988
HOLD ME BERT KAEMPFERT & HIS ORCHESTRA	36	1967
HOLD ME LAURA BRANIGAN	64	1985
HOLD ME IN YOUR ARMS RICK ASTLEY	8	1988
HOLD ME NOW JOHNNY LOGAN	83	1987
HOLD ME, THRILL ME, KISS ME GLORIA ESTEFAN	5	1994
HOLD ON I'M COMIN' SAM & DAVE	35	1967
HOLD ON NOW YOUNGSTER LOS CAMPESINOS	72	2008

Title / Artist	Peak Position	Year of Release
HOLD OUT JACKSON BROWNE	44	1980
HOLD YOUR COLOUR PENDULUM	35	2005
HOLD YOUR FIRE RUSH	10	1987
HOLDING BACK THE RIVER WET WET WET	2	1989
HOLES IN THE WALL ELECTRIC SOFT PARADE	35	2002
THE HOLIDAY ALBUM VARIOUS ARTISTS (CBS)	13	1987
HOLIDAY HITS – NON STOP EURO POP VARIOUS ARTISTS (VIRGIN)	8	2002
HOLIDAYS IN EDEN MARILLION	7	1991
HOLLAND BEACH BOYS	20	1973
HOLLIES HOLLIES	8	1965
THE HOLLIES' GREATEST HOLLIES	1	1968
HOLLIES LIVE HITS HOLLIES	4	1977
HOLLIES SING DYLAN HOLLIES	3	1969
HOLLY IN THE HILLS BUDDY HOLLY	13	1965
HOLLYWOOD MANTOVANI & HIS ORCHESTRA	37	1967
HOLLYWOOD AND BROADWAY RICHARD CLAYDERMAN	28	1986
HOLLYWOOD GOLDEN CLASSICS JOSE CARRERAS	47	1991
THE HOLLYWOOD MUSICALS JOHNNY MATHIS & HENRY MANCINI	46	1986
HOLLYWOOD VAMPIRES L.A. GUNS	44	1991
HOLST: THE PLANETS TOMITA	41	1977
HOLST: THE PLANETS HERBERT VON KARAJAN CONDUCTING THE BERLIN PHILHARMONIC ORCHESTRA	52	1991
THE HOLY BIBLE MANIC STREET PREACHERS	6	1994
HOLY DIVER DIO	13	1983
THE HOLY GROUND MARY BLACK	58	1993
THE HOLY PICTURES DAVID HOLMES	65	2008
HOLY WOOD MARILYN MANSON	23	2000
HOME PROCOL HARUM	49	1970
HOME HOME	46	1972
HOME HOTHOUSE FLOWERS	5	1990
HOME DEEP BLUE SOMETHING	24	1996
HOME DIXIE CHICKS	33	2003
HOME SIMPLY RED	2	2003
HOME CORRS	14	2005
HOME JOURNEY SOUTH	43	2007
HOME AGAIN NEW EDITION	22	1996
HOME AND ABROAD STYLE COUNCIL	8	1986
HOME BEFORE DARK NEIL DIAMOND	1	2008
HOME INVASION ICE-T	15	1993
HOME LOVIN' MAN ROGER WHITTAKER	20	1989
HOME LOVING MAN ANDY WILLIAMS	1	1971
HOME MOVIES – THE BEST OF EVERYTHING BUT THE GIRL EVERYTHING BUT THE GIRL	5	1993
HOME ON THE RANGE SLIM WHITMAN	2	1977
HOME RUN HARDFLOOR	68	1996
HOME SWEET HOME KANO	36	2005
HOME THOUGHTS CLIFFORD T. WARD	40	1973
HOMEBASE DJ JAZZY JEFF & THE FRESH PRINCE	69	1991
HOMEBREW NENEH CHERRY	27	1992
HOMECOMING AMERICA	21	1972
HOMEGROWN DODGY	28	1994
HOMEGROWN UB40	49	2003
HOMESICK DEACON BLUE	59	2001
HOMETIME ALISON MOYET	18	2002
HOMEWORK DAFT PUNK	8	1997
HOMOGENIC BJORK	4	1997
HONESTY ALEX PARKS	24	2005
HONEY ANDY WILLIAMS	4	1968
HONEY ROBERT PALMER	25	1994
HONEY HIT PARADE VARIOUS ARTISTS (PYE)	13	1962
HONEY LINGERS VOICE OF THE BEEHIVE	17	1991
HONEY TO THE B BILLIE PIPER	14	1998
THE HONEYDRIPPERS VOLUME ONE HONEYDRIPPERS	56	1984
HONEY'S DEAD JESUS & MARY CHAIN	14	1992
HONKIN' ON BOBO AEROSMITH	28	2004
HONKY CHATEAU ELTON JOHN	2	1972
HOODOO ALISON MOYET	11	1991
HOOKED GREAT WHITE	43	1991
HOOKED ON CLASSICS LOUIS CLARK CONDUCTING THE ROYAL PHILHARMONIC ORCHESTRA	4	1981
HOOKED ON COUNTRY VARIOUS ARTISTS (K-TEL)	6	1990
HOOKED ON NUMBER ONES – 100 NON-STOP HITS VARIOUS ARTISTS (K-TEL)	25	1984
THE HOOPLE MOTT THE HOOPLE	11	1974
HOORAY FOR BOOBIES BLOODHOUND GANG	37	2000
HOPE VARIOUS ARTISTS (LONDON)	6	2003
HOPE AND ANCHOR FRONT ROW FESTIVAL VARIOUS ARTISTS (WARNER BROTHERS)	28	1978
HOPE AND GLORY TOM ROBINSON	21	1984
HOPE IS IMPORTANT IDLEWILD	53	1998
HOPES AND DREAMS DAVID GRANT	96	1985
HOPES AND FEARS KEANE	1	2004
HORACE BROWN HORACE BROWN	48	1996
HORIZON CARPENTERS	1	1975
HORIZONS VARIOUS ARTISTS (K-TEL)	13	1988
HORIZONS – 12 DREAMHOUSE ANTHEMS VARIOUS ARTISTS (POLYGRAM)	17	1996
HORIZONTAL BEE GEES	16	1968
HORMONALLY YOURS SHAKESPEARS SISTER	3	1992
THE HORNS OF JERICO HI-JACK	54	1991
HORSE FABULOUS STANDS	62	2005
HOST PARADISE LOST	61	1999
HOT MELANIE B	28	2000
HOT AUGUST NIGHT NEIL DIAMOND	21	1974
HOT AUGUST NIGHT II NEIL DIAMOND	74	1987
HOT CAKES CARLY SIMON	19	1974
HOT CHOCOLATE HOT CHOCOLATE	34	1975
HOT CITY NIGHTS VARIOUS ARTISTS (VERTIGO)	1	1988
HOT CITY NIGHTS VARIOUS ARTISTS (SONY)	2	2003
HOT FUSS KILLERS	1	2004
HOT HITS 5 ANONYMOUS COVER VERSIONS	48	1971
HOT HITS 6 ANONYMOUS COVER VERSIONS	1	1971
HOT HITS 7 ANONYMOUS COVER VERSIONS	3	1971
HOT HITS 8 ANONYMOUS COVER VERSIONS	2	1971
HOT IN THE SHADE KISS	35	1989
HOT LOVE DAVID ESSEX	75	1980
HOT POP VARIOUS ARTISTS (UNIVERSAL)	11	2000
HOT RAIL CALEXICO	57	2000
HOT RATS FRANK ZAPPA	9	1970
HOT ROCKS – THE GREATEST HITS 1964-1971 ROLLING STONES	3	1990
HOT SHOT SHAGGY	1	2001
HOT SHOTS II BETA BAND	13	2001
HOT SPACE QUEEN	4	1982
HOT SUMMER NIGHTS VARIOUS ARTISTS (STYLUS)	4	1989
HOT TRACKS VARIOUS ARTISTS (K-TEL)	31	1979
HOT WAX VARIOUS ARTISTS (K-TEL)	3	1980
HOTEL MOBY	8	2005
HOTEL CALIFORNIA EAGLES	2	1976
HOTEL PAPER MICHELLE BRANCH	35	2003
HOTLINE VARIOUS ARTISTS (K-TEL)	3	1983
HOTTER THAN JULY STEVIE WONDER	2	1980
HOTWIRED SOUP DRAGONS	74	1992
HOUNDS OF LOVE KATE BUSH	1	1985
THE HOUR OF BEWILDERBEAST BADLY DRAWN BOY	13	2000
HOURGLASS JAMES TAYLOR	46	1997
HOURGLASS DAVE GAHAN	50	2007
HOURS FUNERAL FOR A FRIEND	12	2005
HOURS... DAVID BOWIE	5	1999
HOUSE CLASSICS VARIOUS ARTISTS (MINISTRY OF SOUND)	10	2003
THE HOUSE COLLECTION -VOLUME 2 VARIOUS ARTISTS (FANTAZIA)	6	1995
THE HOUSE COLLECTION -VOLUME 3 VARIOUS ARTISTS (FANTAZIA)	4	1995
THE HOUSE COLLECTION 6 – PAUL OAKENFOLD/PAUL COSFORD VARIOUS ARTISTS (FANTAZIA)	10	1997
THE HOUSE COLLECTION – CLUB CLASSICS VARIOUS ARTISTS (FANTAZIA)	3	1996
THE HOUSE COLLECTION CLUB CLASSICS – 2 VARIOUS ARTISTS (FANTAZIA)	4	1996
THE HOUSE COLLECTION – VOLUME 5 VARIOUS ARTISTS (FANTAZIA)	3	1997
HOUSE HALLUCINATIONS (PUMP UP LONDON VOLUME 1) VARIOUS ARTISTS (BREAKOUT)	90	1988
HOUSE HITS VARIOUS ARTISTS (NEEDLE)	25	1988
HOUSE NATION 1 VARIOUS ARTISTS (REACT)	20	1994
THE HOUSE OF BLUE LIGHT DEEP PURPLE	10	1987
HOUSE OF DOLLS GENE LOVES JEZEBEL	81	1987
THE HOUSE OF HANDBAG VARIOUS ARTISTS (ULTRASOUND)	13	1995
THE HOUSE OF HANDBAG – AUTUMN/WINTER COLLECTION VARIOUS ARTISTS (ULTRASOUND)	16	1995
HOUSE OF HANDBAG – NUOVO DISCO COLLECTION VARIOUS ARTISTS (SOLID STATE)	17	1997
HOUSE OF LOVE HOUSE OF LOVE	8	1990
THE HOUSE OF LOVE HOUSE OF LOVE	49	1990
HOUSE OF PAIN HOUSE OF PAIN	73	1992
HOUSE OF THE BLUES JOHN LEE HOOKER	34	1967
HOUSE OF THE HOLY LED ZEPPELIN	1	1973
THE HOUSE SOUND OF CHICAGO VARIOUS ARTISTS (DJ INTERNATIONAL)	52	1986
THE HOUSE SOUND OF CHICAGO VOLUME 2 VARIOUS ARTISTS (DJ INTERNATIONAL)	38	1987
THE HOUSE SOUND OF CHICAGO VOLUME 3 VARIOUS ARTISTS (FFRR)	40	1988
THE HOUSE SOUND OF LONDON VOLUME 4 VARIOUS ARTISTS (FFRR)	70	1988
THE HOUSE WE BUILT ALISHA'S ATTIC	55	2001
THE HOUSEMARTINS' CHRISTMAS SINGLES BOX HOUSEMARTINS	84	1986
HOUSEWORK SONGS VARIOUS ARTISTS (EMI)	3	2005
HOUSEWORK SONGS II VARIOUS ARTISTS (EMI)	3	2006
HOW 'BOUT US CHAMPAIGN	38	1981
HOW DARE YOU? 10 C.C.	5	1976
HOW DO I LOVE THEE BRYN YEMM	57	1984
HOW DO YOU LIKE IT? GERRY & THE PACEMAKERS	2	1963
HOW DOES THAT GRAB YOU NANCY SINATRA	17	1966
HOW GREAT THOU ART ELVIS PRESLEY	11	1967
HOW GREAT THOU ART BRYN YEMM	67	1984
HOW GREEN IS THE VALLEY MEN THEY COULDN'T HANG	68	1986
HOW MEN ARE HEAVEN 17	12	1984
HOW THE WEST WAS WON LED ZEPPELIN	5	2003
HOW TO BE A ZILLIONAIRE ABC	28	1985
HOW TO DISMANTLE AN ATOMIC BOMB U2	1	2004
HOW TO GET EVERYTHING YOU EVER WANTED IN TEN EASY STEPS ORDINARY BOYS	15	2006
HOW TO MAKE FRIENDS AND INFLUENCE PEOPLE TERRORVISION	18	1994
HOW TO OPERATE WITH A BLOWN MIND LO FIDELITY ALLSTARS	15	1998
HOW TO SAVE A LIFE FRAY	4	2007
HOW TO WIN AN ELECTION HARRY SECOMBE, PETER SELLERS & SPIKE MILLIGAN	20	1964
HOW WE OPERATE GOMEZ	69	2006

Title / Artist	Peak Position	Year of Release
HOW WILL THE WOLF SURVIVE? LOS LOBOS	77	1985
HOWDY TEENAGE FANCLUB	33	2000
HOWL BLACK REBEL MOTORCYCLE CLUB	14	2005
HOY-HOY! LITTLE FEAT	76	1981
HUCKLEBERRY HOUND (TELEVISION SOUNDTRACK) TELEVISION AND RADIO COMPILATION	10	1961
HUGE CLUB TUNES VARIOUS ARTISTS (SONY/BMG)	13	2005
HUGE HITS 1996 VARIOUS ARTISTS (SONY)	1	1996
HUGE HITS 1997 VARIOUS ARTISTS (GLOBAL TELEVISION)	1	1997
HUGE HITS 1998 VARIOUS ARTISTS (SONY)	1	1998
HUGE HITS 2000 VARIOUS ARTISTS (WARNER BROTHERS)	2	2000
HUGE HITS 2003 VARIOUS ARTISTS (BMG)	4	2002
HUGE HITS 2004 – THE VERY BEST OF HITS VARIOUS ARTISTS (BMG)	3	2003
HUGE HITS 99 VARIOUS ARTISTS (GLOBAL TELEVISION)	1	1999
HUGGIN' AN' A KISSIN' BOMBALURINA FEATURING TIMMY MALLETT	55	1990
HULLABALOO MUSE	10	2002
HUMAN ROD STEWART	9	2001
HUMAN NITIN SAWHNEY	54	2003
HUMAN AFTER ALL DAFT PUNK	10	2005
HUMAN BEING SEAL	44	1998
HUMAN CLAY CREED	29	2001
HUMAN CONDITIONS RICHARD ASHCROFT	3	2002
HUMAN RACING NIK KERSHAW	5	1984
HUMAN TOUCH BRUCE SPRINGSTEEN	1	1992
HUMAN TRAFFIC FILM SOUNDTRACK	14	1999
HUMAN WHEELS JOHN MELLENCAMP	37	1993
HUMAN'S LIB HOWARD JONES	1	1984
101 DEPECHE MODE	5	1989
101 70S HITS VARIOUS ARTISTS (EMI)	6	2007
101 80S HITS VARIOUS ARTISTS (EMI)	1	2007
101 CHRISTMAS SONGS VARIOUS ARTISTS (EMI)	15	2007
101 CHRISTMAS SONGS VARIOUS ARTISTS (EMI)	20	2008
101 CLUB ANTHEMS VARIOUS ARTISTS (EMI)	3	2007
101 COUNTRY HITS VARIOUS ARTISTS (EMI)	18	2007
101 DAMNATIONS CARTER – THE UNSTOPPABLE SEX MACHINE	29	1991
101 DRIVING SONGS VARIOUS ARTISTS (EMI)	6	2008
101 FIFTIES SONGS VARIOUS ARTISTS (EMI)	8	2008
101 JUKEBOX CLASSICS VARIOUS ARTISTS (EMI)	9	2007
101 LOVE SONGS VARIOUS ARTISTS (EMI)	2	2008
101 90S HITS VARIOUS ARTISTS (EMI)	7	2008
101 NUMBER 1'S VARIOUS ARTISTS (EMI)	8	2007
101% SPEED GARAGE ANTHEMS VARIOUS ARTISTS (MASSIVE MUSIC)	14	1999
101% SPEED GARAGE VOLUME 2 VARIOUS ARTISTS (MASSIVE MUSIC)	16	1998
101 POWER BALLADS VARIOUS ARTISTS (EMI)	9	2008
101 ROCK 'N' ROLL HITS VARIOUS ARTISTS (EMI)	11	2008
101 SIXTIES HITS VARIOUS ARTISTS (EMI)	4	2007
101 SUMMER SONGS VARIOUS ARTISTS (EMI)	12	2008
100 BROKEN WINDOWS IDLEWILD	15	2000
A HUNDRED DAYS OFF UNDERWORLD	16	2002
100 DEGREES AND RISING INCOGNITO	11	1995
100 GOLDEN GREATS MAX BYGRAVES	3	1976
100 GOLDEN GREATS FRANKIE VAUGHAN	24	1977
100 GOLDEN GREATS FOSTER & ALLEN	30	1995
100 HUGE HITS OF REGGAE VARIOUS ARTISTS (SANCTUARY)	5	2007
100 HUGE HITS OF THE 60S & 70S VARIOUS ARTISTS (SANCTUARY)	2	2007
A HUNDRED MILES OR MORE: A COLLECTION ALISON KRAUSS	38	2007
100 MPH VARDIS	52	1980
A HUNDRED MILLION SUNS SNOW PATROL	2	2008
100% ACID JAZZ VARIOUS ARTISTS (TELSTAR)	5	1994
100% ACID JAZZ – VOLUME 2 VARIOUS ARTISTS (TELSTAR)	14	1995
100% CARNIVAL! VARIOUS ARTISTS (TELSTAR)	16	1995
100% CHRISTMAS VARIOUS ARTISTS (TELSTAR)	9	1994
100% CLASSICS VARIOUS ARTISTS (TELSTAR)	8	1995
100% CLASSICS – VOLUME 2 VARIOUS ARTISTS (TELSTAR)	20	1996
100% COLOMBIAN FUN LOVIN' CRIMINALS	3	1998
100% DANCE VARIOUS ARTISTS (TELSTAR)	1	1993
100% DANCE HITS 96 VARIOUS ARTISTS (TELSTAR)	11	1996
100% DANCE VOLUME 2 VARIOUS ARTISTS (TELSTAR)	1	1993
100% DANCE VOLUME 3 VARIOUS ARTISTS (TELSTAR)	7	1993
100% DANCE VOLUME 4 VARIOUS ARTISTS (TELSTAR)	2	1994
100% DRUM & BASS VARIOUS ARTISTS (TELSTAR)	11	1996
100% GINUWINE GINUWINE	42	1999
100% HITS VARIOUS ARTISTS (TELSTAR)	2	1994
100% HOUSE CLASSICS – VOLUME 1 VARIOUS ARTISTS (TELSTAR)	16	1995
100% PURE GROOVE VARIOUS ARTISTS (TELSTAR)	4	1996
100% PURE GROOVE 2 VARIOUS ARTISTS (TELSTAR)	12	1996
100% PURE LOVE VARIOUS ARTISTS (TELSTAR)	7	1994
100% PURE OLD SKOOL CLUB CLASSICS VARIOUS ARTISTS (TELSTAR)	9	2003
100% RAP VARIOUS ARTISTS (TELSTAR)	3	1994
100% REGGAE VARIOUS ARTISTS (TELSTAR)	2	1993
100% REGGAE VOLUME 2 VARIOUS ARTISTS (TELSTAR)	4	1994
100% REGGAE VOLUME 3 VARIOUS ARTISTS (TELSTAR)	6	1994
100% SUMMER VARIOUS ARTISTS (TELSTAR)	4	1994
100% SUMMER '95 VARIOUS ARTISTS (TELSTAR)	7	1995
100% SUMMER JAZZ VARIOUS ARTISTS (TELSTAR)	11	1995
100% SUMMER MIX 96 VARIOUS ARTISTS (TELSTAR)	7	1996
100% SUMMER MIX 97 VARIOUS ARTISTS (TELSTAR)	8	1997
100% SUMMER MIX 98 VARIOUS ARTISTS (TELSTAR)	13	1998
100 PERCENT COTTON JETS	30	1982
100 R&B CLASSICS VARIOUS ARTISTS (WARNER BROTHERS)	7	2007
HUNDREDS AND THOUSANDS BRONSKI BEAT	24	1985
100TH WINDOW MASSIVE ATTACK	1	2003
THE HUNGER MICHAEL BOLTON	44	1990
THE HUNGER FOR MORE LLOYD BANKS	15	2004
HUNGRY AGAIN DOLLY PARTON	41	1998
HUNGRY FOR HITS VARIOUS ARTISTS (K-TEL)	4	1984
HUNGRY FOR STINK L7	26	1994
HUNKPAPA THROWING MUSES	59	1989
HUNKY DORY DAVID BOWIE	3	1972
THE HUNTER BLONDIE	9	1982
HUNTING HIGH AND LOW A-HA	2	1985
HUP WONDER STUFF	5	1989
HURRICANE GRACE JONES	42	2008
HURRICANE #1 HURRICANE #1	11	1997
HURT NO MORE MARIO WINANS	3	2004
THE HURTING TEARS FOR FEARS	1	1983
THE HUSH TEXAS	1	1999
HVARF/HEIM SIGUR ROS	23	2007
HYBRID THEORY LINKIN PARK	4	2001
HYENA SIOUXSIE & THE BANSHEES	15	1984
HYMN FOR MY SOUL JOE COCKER	9	2007
THE HYMNS ALBUM HUDDERSFIELD CHORAL SOCIETY	8	1986
HYMNS TO THE SILENCE VAN MORRISON	5	1991
HYMNS WE HAVE LOVED PAT BOONE	12	1960
HYMNS WE LOVE PAT BOONE	14	1960
HYPERACTIVE VARIOUS ARTISTS (TELSTAR)	78	1988
A HYPERACTIVE WORKOUT FOR THE FLYING SQUAD OCEAN COLOUR SCENE	30	2005
HYPERBOREA TANGERINE DREAM	45	1983
HYPNOTISED UNDERTONES	6	1980
HYPNOTIZE SYSTEM OF A DOWN	11	2005
HYPOCRISY IS THE GREATEST LUXURY DISPOSABLE HEROES OF HIPHOPRISY	40	1992
HYSTERIA HUMAN LEAGUE	3	1984
HYSTERIA DEF LEPPARD	1	1987

Title / Artist	Peak Position	Year of Release
I AIN'T MOVIN' DES'REE	13	1994
I AM EARTH WIND & FIRE	5	1979
I AM A BIRD NOW ANTONY & THE JOHNSONS	16	2005
I AM COLD RIP RIG & PANIC	67	1982
I AM KLOOT I AM KLOOT	68	2003
I AM KURIOUS, ORANJ FALL	54	1988
I AM ME ASHLEE SIMPSON	50	2006
I AM NOT A DOCTOR MOLOKO	64	1998
I AM PHOENIX JUDIE TZUKE	17	1981
I AM SASHA FIERCE BEYONCE KNOWLES	8	2008
I AM WHAT I AM SHIRLEY BASSEY	25	1984
I AM WOMAN VARIOUS ARTISTS (POLYDOR)	11	1980
I AM... NAS	31	1999
I BELIEVE DANIEL O'DONNELL	11	1997
I BELIEVE TIM BURGESS	38	2003
I BELIEVE IN YOU DON WILLIAMS	36	1980
I BELIEVE – THE VERY BEST OF BACHELORS	7	2008
I CAME TO DANCE NILS LOFGREN	30	1977
I CAN HELP ELVIS PRESLEY	71	1984
I CAN MAKE YOU DANCE RICHIE RICH	65	1989
I CAN SEE CLEARLY NOW JOHNNY NASH	39	1972
I CAN SEE YOUR HOUSE FROM HERE CAMEL	45	1979
I CAPRICORN SHIRLEY BASSEY	13	1972
I CARE 4 U AALIYAH	4	2003
...I CARE BECAUSE YOU DO APHEX TWIN	24	1995
I COULDN'T LIVE WITHOUT YOUR LOVE PETULA CLARK	11	1966
I CREATED DISCO CALVIN HARRIS	8	2007
I DID WHAT I DID FOR MARIA TONY CHRISTIE	37	1971
I DO NOT WANT WHAT I HAVEN'T GOT SINEAD O'CONNOR	1	1990
I DON'T BELIEVE IN IF ANYMORE ROGER WHITTAKER	23	1970
I DON'T WANT TO PUT A HOLD ON YOU BERNI FLINT	37	1977
I DON'T WANT YOU BACK (IMPORT) EAMON	6	2004
I FEEL A SONG GLADYS KNIGHT & THE PIPS	20	1975
I FEEL ALRIGHT STEVE EARLE	44	1996
I FEEL FOR YOU CHAKA KHAN	15	1984
I FEEL FREE – ULTIMATE CREAM CREAM	6	2005
I FEEL NO FRET AVERAGE WHITE BAND	15	1979
I GET WET ANDREW WK	71	2001
I GOT LUCKY ELVIS PRESLEY	26	1971
I GOT NEXT KRS ONE	58	1997

Title / Artist	Peak Position	Year of Release
I HAVE DREAMED MATT MONRO	20	1965
I HEAR TALK BUCKS FIZZ	66	1984
I JUST WASN'T MADE FOR THESE TIMES BRIAN WILSON	59	1995
I KNOW LUTHER VANDROSS	42	1998
I KNOW COS I WAS THERE MAX BOYCE	6	1978
I KNOW THEM SO WELL – TIM RICE VARIOUS ARTISTS (POLYGRAM)	2	1994
I KNOW YOU'RE MARRIED BUT I'VE GOT FEELINGS TOO MARTHA WAINWRIGHT	29	2008
I LEFT MY HEART IN SAN FRANCISCO TONY BENNETT	13	1965
I-LEVEL I-LEVEL	50	1983
I LIKE TO SCORE MOBY	54	2000
I LOOKED UP INCREDIBLE STRING BAND	30	1970
I LOVE 2 PARTY VARIOUS ARTISTS (VIRGIN)	2	2001
I LOVE 2 PARTY 2003 VARIOUS ARTISTS (VIRGIN)	11	2002
I LOVE 70'S VARIOUS ARTISTS (VIRGIN)	9	2001
I LOVE 80'S VARIOUS ARTISTS (VIRGIN)	5	2001
I LOVE 90S VARIOUS ARTISTS (VIRGIN)	11	2001
I LOVE A PARTY RUSS ABBOT	12	1985
I LOVE CHRISTMAS VARIOUS ARTISTS (EMI)	15	2003
I LOVE COUNTRY MUSIC VAL DOONICAN	37	1975
I LOVE DAD VARIOUS ARTISTS (VIRGIN)	3	2005
I LOVE EVERYBODY LYLE LOVETT	54	1994
I LOVE IBIZA VARIOUS ARTISTS (VIRGIN)	10	2001
I LOVE MUM VARIOUS ARTISTS (VIRGIN)	1	2005
I LOVE MUM VARIOUS ARTISTS (EMI)	4	2007
I LOVE MUSICALS VARIOUS ARTISTS (EMI)	12	2006
I LOVE ROCK 'N' ROLL JOAN JETT & THE BLACKHEARTS	25	1982
I LOVE SAX DAVID ROACH	73	1984
I LOVE SIXTIES VARIOUS ARTISTS (EMI)	19	2005
I LOVE SUMMER VARIOUS ARTISTS (VIRGIN)	7	2002
I LOVE U VARIOUS ARTISTS (VIRGIN)	2	2003
I LOVE YOU DIANA ROSS	60	2006
I LUV SMASH HITS VARIOUS ARTISTS (EMI)	2	2003
I LUV SMASH HITS 2004 VARIOUS ARTISTS (EMI)	7	2004
I MIGHT BE WRONG RADIOHEAD	23	2001
I NEED YOU LEANN RIMES	7	2001
I NEVER LOVED A MAN THE WAY I LOVE YOU ARETHA FRANKLIN	36	1967
I ONLY HAVE EYES FOR YOU JOHNNY MATHIS	14	1976
I PRETEND DES O'CONNOR	8	1968
I PUT A SPELL ON YOU NINA SIMONE	18	1965
I REMEMBER HANK WILLIAMS JACK SCOTT	7	1960
I REMEMBER TOMMY... FRANK SINATRA	10	1962
I REMEMBER YESTERDAY DONNA SUMMER	3	1977
I ROBOT ALAN PARSONS PROJECT	30	1977
I SAY I SAY I SAY ERASURE	1	1994
I SHOULD COCO SUPERGRASS	1	1995
I STAND IDINA MENZEL	54	2008
I STAND ALONE AGNETHA FALTSKOG	72	1988
I STARTED OUT WITH NOTHIN' AND STILL GOT MOST OF IT LEFT SEASICK STEVE	9	2008
I TO SKY JJ72	20	2002
I WANNA BE WITH YOU MANDY MOORE	52	2000
I WANNA DO IT WITH YOU BARRY MANILOW	7	1982
I WANNA HAVE SOME FUN SAMANTHA FOX	46	1989
I WANT CANDY BOW WOW WOW	26	1982
I WANT TO LIVE JOHN DENVER	25	1978
I WANT TO WAKE UP WITH YOU ENGELBERT HUMPERDINCK	42	2001
I WANT YOU MARVIN GAYE	22	1976
I WAS THE ONE ELVIS PRESLEY	83	1983
I WAS WARNED ROBERT CRAY	29	1992
I WHO HAVE NOTHING TOM JONES	10	1970
I WILL ALWAYS LOVE YOU JAMES GALWAY	59	1995
I WILL CURE YOU VIC REEVES	16	1991
I WILL LOVE YOU ALL OF MY LIFE FOSTER & ALLEN	71	1983
I WILL SURVIVE (DOIN' IT MY WAY) CHANTAY SAVAGE	66	1996
I WILL WAIT FOR YOU LESLEY GARRETT	28	2000
I WISH I COULD HAVE LOVED YOU MORE CANDIE PAYNE	56	2007
I WISH YOU LOVE JOE LONGTHORNE	47	1993
I, ASSASSIN GARY NUMAN	8	1982
_ADIOS AMIGOS! RAMONES	62	1995
IAN HUNTER IAN HUNTER	21	1975
IBIZA 99 – THE YEAR OF TRANCE VARIOUS ARTISTS (GLOBAL TELEVISION)	2	1999
IBIZA 99 – THE YEAR OF TRANCE – VOLUME TWO VARIOUS ARTISTS (GLOBAL TELEVISION)	11	1999
THE IBIZA ANNUAL VARIOUS ARTISTS (MINISTRY OF SOUND)	1	1998
IBIZA ANNUAL VARIOUS ARTISTS (MINISTRY OF SOUND)	3	2001
IBIZA ANNUAL 2005 VARIOUS ARTISTS (MINISTRY OF SOUND)	3	2005
IBIZA ANNUAL 2006 VARIOUS ARTISTS (MINISTRY OF SOUND)	2	2006
IBIZA ANNUAL 2007 VARIOUS ARTISTS (MINISTRY OF SOUND)	2	2007
IBIZA ANNUAL 2008 VARIOUS ARTISTS (MINISTRY OF SOUND)	3	2008
THE IBIZA ANNUAL – SUMMER 2000 VARIOUS ARTISTS (MINISTRY OF SOUND)	1	2000
THE IBIZA ANNUAL: MIXED BY JUDGE JULES + TALL PAUL VARIOUS ARTISTS (MINISTRY OF SOUND)	1	1999
IBIZA ANTHEMS VARIOUS ARTISTS (TELSTAR)	5	1998
IBIZA ANTHEMS 2 VARIOUS ARTISTS (TELSTAR)	7	1999
IBIZA CHILLOUT SESSION VARIOUS ARTISTS (MINISTRY OF SOUND)	12	2001
IBIZA DEL MAR VARIOUS ARTISTS (GLOBAL TELEVISION)	11	1999
IBIZA EUPHORIA VARIOUS ARTISTS (TELSTAR)	5	1999
IBIZA EUPHORIA – ALEX GOLD/AGNELLI & NELSON VARIOUS ARTISTS (TELSTAR)	4	2000
IBIZA EUPHORIA – DAVE PEARCE VARIOUS ARTISTS (TELSTAR)	3	2001
IBIZA EUPHORIA – MIXED BY DAVE PEARCE VARIOUS ARTISTS (TELSTAR)	10	2002
IBIZA HITMIX 2002 VARIOUS ARTISTS (WARNER BROTHERS)	12	2002
IBIZA – PAUL OAKENFOLD VARIOUS ARTISTS (PERFECTO)	13	2001
IBIZA – THE CLOSING PARTY VARIOUS ARTISTS (DANCE POOL)	19	1999
IBIZA – THE HISTORY OF CHILLOUT VARIOUS ARTISTS (WARNER BROTHERS)	3	2003
IBIZA – THE HISTORY OF HARD DANCE VARIOUS ARTISTS (WARNER BROTHERS)	6	2003
IBIZA – THE HISTORY OF HOUSE VARIOUS ARTISTS (WARNER BROTHERS)	3	2003
IBIZA – THE HISTORY OF TRANCE VARIOUS ARTISTS (WARNER BROTHERS)	7	2004
IBIZA – THE STORY SO FAR VARIOUS ARTISTS (COLUMBIA)	17	2000
IBIZA UNCOVERED (TELEVISION COMPILATION) TELEVISION AND RADIO COMPILATION	1	1997
IBIZA UNCOVERED 2 (TELEVISION COMPILATION) TELEVISION AND RADIO COMPILATION	2	1998
IBIZA UNCOVERED II VARIOUS ARTISTS (VIRGIN)	5	2000
IBIZA UNCOVERED – THE RETURN (TELEVISION COMPILATION) TELEVISION AND RADIO COMPILATION	2	1999
ICE CREAM FOR CROW CAPTAIN BEEFHEART & HIS MAGIC BAND	90	1982
ICE ON FIRE ELTON JOHN	3	1985
THE ICEBERG/FREEDOM OF SPEECH ICE-T	42	1989
THE ICICLE WORKS ICICLE WORKS	24	1984
ICKY THUMP WHITE STRIPES	1	2007
THE ICON IS LOVE BARRY WHITE	44	1995
THE ID MACY GRAY	1	2001
I'D LIKE TO TEACH THE WORLD TO SING RAY CONNIFF	17	1972
IDEA BEE GEES	4	1968
THE IDEAL COPY WIRE	87	1987
THE IDEAL CRASH dEUS	64	1999
IDEAS ABOVE OUR STATION HUNDRED REASONS	6	2002
THE IDIOT IGGY POP	30	1977
IDLEWILD EVERYTHING BUT THE GIRL	13	1988
IDLEWILD OUTKAST	16	2006
IDOL SONGS: 11 OF THE BEST BILLY IDOL	2	1988
THE IDOLS – THE XMAS FACTOR VARIOUS ARTISTS (S)	2	2003
I-EMPIRE ANGELS & AIRWAVES	29	2007
IF I RULED THE WORLD HARRY SECOMBE	17	1971
IF I SHOULD FALL FROM GRACE WITH GOD POGUES	3	1988
IF I SHOULD LOVE AGAIN BARRY MANILOW	5	1981
IF I WAS: THE VERY BEST OF MIDGE URE AND ULTRAVOX MIDGE URE/ULTRAVOX	10	1993
IF MUSIC BE THE FOOD OF LOVE...PREPARE FOR INDIGESTION DAVE DEE, DOZY, BEAKY, MICK & TICH	27	1967
IF ONLY I COULD REMEMBER MY NAME DAVID CROSBY	12	1971
IF THE BEATLES HAD READ HUNTER...THE SINGLES WONDER STUFF	8	1994
IF THE OCEAN GETS ROUGH WILLY MASON	33	2007
IF THIS IS ROCK AND ROLL, I WANT MY OLD JOB BACK SAW DOCTORS	69	1991
IF WE FALL IN LOVE TONIGHT ROD STEWART	8	1996
IF YOU CAN BELIEVE YOUR EYES AND EARS MAMAS & THE PAPAS	3	1966
IF YOU CAN'T JOIN 'EM BEAT 'EM DJ FORMAT	73	2005
IF YOU CAN'T STAND THE HEAT STATUS QUO	3	1978
IF YOU HAPPY WITH YOU NEED DO NOTHING ALFIE	62	2001
IF YOU WANT BLOOD YOU'VE GOT IT AC/DC	13	1978
IF YOU WANT TO DEFEAT YOUR ENEMY SING HIS SONG ICICLE WORKS	28	1987
IF YOU'VE NEVER BEEN EMBRACE	9	2001
IL DIVO IL DIVO	1	2004
I'LL BUY YOU A STAR JOHNNY MATHIS	18	1961
ILL COMMUNICATION BEASTIE BOYS	10	1994
I'LL GIVE ALL MY LOVE TO YOU KEITH SWEAT	47	1990
I'LL REMEMBER YOU FRANK IFIELD	3	1963
ILLEGAL RAVE VARIOUS ARTISTS (STRICTLY UNDERGROUND)	20	1992
ILLEGAL STILLS STEPHEN STILLS	54	1976
ILLUMINA ALISHA'S ATTIC	15	1998
ILLUMINATION PAUL WELLER	1	2002
ILLUMINATIONS CARLOS SANTANA & ALICE COLTRANE	40	1974
THE ILLUSION OF PROGRESS STAIND	73	2008
I'M 10,000 YEARS OLD – ELVIS COUNTRY ELVIS PRESLEY	6	1971
I'M 21 TODAY CLIFF RICHARD & THE SHADOWS	1	1961
I'M A WRITER NOT A FIGHTER GILBERT O'SULLIVAN	2	1973
I'M ALIVE JACKSON BROWNE	35	1993
I'M BREATHLESS MADONNA	2	1990

Title / Artist	Peak Position	Year of Release
I'M COMING HOME JOHNNY MATHIS	18	1975
I'M COMING HOME TOM JONES	12	1978
I'M GLAD YOU'RE HERE WITH ME TONIGHT NEIL DIAMOND	16	1977
I'M GOING TO TELL YOU A SECRET MADONNA	18	2006
I'M GONNA BE STRONG GENE PITNEY	15	1965
I'M IN THE MOOD FOR LOVE VARIOUS ARTISTS (SANCTUARY)	7	2007
I'M IN YOU PETER FRAMPTON	19	1977
I'M LEAVING IT ALL UP TO YOU DONNY & MARIE OSMOND	13	1974
I'M MIGHTY GLAD MRS. MILLS	49	1971
I'M NEARLY FAMOUS CLIFF RICHARD	5	1976
I'M NO HERO CLIFF RICHARD	4	1980
I'M NOT DEAD P!NK	3	2006
I'M NOT FOLLOWING YOU EDWYN COLLINS	55	1997
I'M P.J. PROBY P.J. PROBY	16	1965
I'M REAL JAMES BROWN	27	1988
I'M STILL GONNA NEED YOU OSMONDS	19	1975
I'M STILL WAITING DIANA ROSS	10	1971
I'M THE MAN JOE JACKSON	12	1979
I'M WIDE AWAKE IT'S MORNING BRIGHT EYES	23	2005
I'M WITH STUPID AIMEE MANN	51	1995
I'M YOUR BABY TONIGHT WHITNEY HOUSTON	4	1990
I'M YOUR FAN – THE SONGS OF LEONARD COHEN VARIOUS ARTISTS (EAST WEST)	16	1991
I'M YOUR MAN LEONARD COHEN	48	1988
IMA BT	45	1995
IMAGES WALKER BROTHERS	6	1967
IMAGES DON WILLIAMS	2	1978
IMAGES VARIOUS ARTISTS (K-TEL)	33	1983
IMAGES GUITAR CORPORATION	41	1992
IMAGES – THE BEST OF JEAN-MICHEL JARRE JEAN-MICHEL JARRE	14	1991
IMAGINATION WHISPERS	42	1981
IMAGINATION BRIAN WILSON	30	1998
IMAGINATION – ALL THE HITS IMAGINATION	4	1989
IMAGINATIONS VARIOUS ARTISTS (CBS)	15	1983
IMAGINE JOHN LENNON WITH THE PLASTIC ONO BAND (WITH THE FLUX FIDDLERS)	1	1971
IMAGINE JOHN LENNON	51	2000
IMAGINE EVA CASSIDY	1	2002
IMAGINE JOHN LENNON (OST) JOHN LENNON	64	1988
THE IMMACULATE COLLECTION MADONNA	1	1990
IMMORTAL OTIS REDDING OTIS REDDING	19	1968
IMPACT VARIOUS ARTISTS (EMI)	15	1969
IMPERIAL BEDROOM ELVIS COSTELLO & THE ATTRACTIONS	6	1982
IMPERIAL WAX SOLVENT FALL	35	2008
IMPERIAL WIZARD DAVID ESSEX	12	1979
IMPLANT EAT STATIC	13	1994
THE IMPOSSIBLE DREAM ANDY WILLIAMS	26	1972
THE IMPOSSIBLE DREAM SENSATIONAL ALEX HARVEY BAND	16	1974
THE IMPOSSIBLE DREAM ANDY ABRAHAM	2	2006
IMPRESSIONS – 15 INSTRUMENTAL IMAGES VARIOUS ARTISTS (K-TEL)	15	1987
IMPURITY NEW MODEL ARMY	23	1990
IN AT THE DEEP END ROLL DEEP	50	2005
IN BETWEEN PAUL VAN DYK	63	2007
IN BETWEEN DREAMS JACK JOHNSON	1	2005
IN BLUE CORRS	1	2000
IN CITY DREAMS ROBIN TROWER	58	1977
IN CONCERT DEEP PURPLE	30	1980
IN CONCERT ROLLING STONES	94	1982
IN CONCERT LUCIANO PAVAROTTI, PLACIDO DOMINGO & JOSE CARRERAS	1	1990
IN CONCERT DOORS	24	1991
IN CONCERT LYONS/HOUSTON JEAN-MICHEL JARRE	18	1987
IN CONCERT – MTV UNPLUGGED BRUCE SPRINGSTEEN	4	1993
IN CONCERT VOLUME 1 PETER, PAUL & MARY	20	1965
IN CONCERT VOLUME 2 JAMES LAST	49	1974
IN CONCERT: SINATRA AT 'THE SANDS' FRANK SINATRA	7	1966
IN DEEP ARGENT	49	1973
IN DREAMS ROY ORBISON	6	1963
IN DREAMS BRENDA COCHRANE	55	1991
IN DREAMS: THE GREATEST HITS ROY ORBISON	86	1987
IN FLIGHT GEORGE BENSON	19	1977
IN FOR THE KILL BUDGIE	29	1974
IN FULL BLOOM ROSE ROYCE	18	1977
IN FULL EFFECT MANTRONIX	39	1988
IN HARMONY RICHARD CLAYDERMAN & JAMES LAST	28	1994
IN HARMONY LADYSMITH BLACK MAMBAZO	15	1999
IN HEARING OF ATOMIC ROOSTER ATOMIC ROOSTER	18	1971
IN HIS GREATEST HITS FROM OPERATTAS AND MUSICALS MARIO LANZA	39	1971
IN HIS OWN WORDS 2PAC	65	1998
IN IT FOR THE MONEY SUPERGRASS	2	1997
IN LOVE – GREATEST LOVE 5 VARIOUS ARTISTS (TELSTAR)	5	1991
IN MY LIFE GEORGE MARTIN	5	1998
IN MY MIND PHARRELL WILLIAMS	7	2006
IN MY OWN WORDS NE-YO	14	2006
IN MYSTERIOUS WAYS JOHN FOXX	85	1985
IN NO SENSE/NONSENSE ART OF NOISE	55	1987
IN ON THE KILLTAKER FUGAZI	24	1993
IN OPERATION HARD-FI	62	2006
IN ORDER TO DANCE 5 VARIOUS ARTISTS (R&S)	16	1994
IN OUR GUN GOMEZ	8	2002
IN OUR LIFETIME MARVIN GAYE	48	1981
IN OUR NATURE JOSE GONZALEZ	19	2007
IN PIECES GARTH BROOKS	2	1994
IN RAINBOWS RADIOHEAD	1	2008
IN RIBBONS PALE SAINTS	61	1992
IN ROCK WE TRUST Y & T	33	1984
IN SEARCH OF N*E*R*D	28	2002
IN SEARCH OF ANGELS RUNRIG	29	1999
IN SEARCH OF SANITY ONSLAUGHT	46	1989
IN SEARCH OF SPACE HAWKWIND	18	1971
IN SEARCH OF THE FOURTH CHORD STATUS QUO	15	2007
IN SEARCH OF THE LOST CHORD MOODY BLUES	5	1968
IN SIDES ORBITAL	5	1996
IN SILICO PENDULUM	2	2008
THE IN SOUND FROM WAY OUT! BEASTIE BOYS	45	1996
IN SQUARE CIRCLE STEVIE WONDER	5	1985
IN STEP STEVIE RAY VAUGHAN & DOUBLE TROUBLE	63	1989
IN STEREO BOMFUNK MCs	33	2000
IN STYLE WITH THE CRICKETS CRICKETS	13	1961
IN THE AIR TONIGHT VARIOUS ARTISTS (VIRGIN)	8	1994
IN THE ARMY NOW STATUS QUO	7	1986
IN THE BEGINNING BLAZIN' SQUAD	33	2002
IN THE BLOOD LONDONBEAT	34	1990
IN THE CITY JAM	20	1977
IN THE CITY (REISSUE) JAM	100	1983
IN THE COURT OF THE CRIMSON KING KING CRIMSON	5	1969
IN THE DARK GRATEFUL DEAD	57	1987
IN THE DYNAMITE JET SALOON DOGS D'AMOUR	97	1988
IN THE EYE OF THE STORM ROGER HODGSON	70	1984
IN THE FLAT FIELD BAUHAUS	72	1980
IN THE FUTURE BLACK MOUNTAIN	72	2008
IN THE GROOVE – THE 12 INCH DISCO PARTY VARIOUS ARTISTS (TELSTAR)	20	1983
IN THE HAND OF THE INEVITABLE JAMES TAYLOR QUARTET	63	1995
IN THE HANDS OF LOVE VITTORIO GRIGOLO	6	2006
IN THE HEART KOOL & THE GANG	18	1984
IN THE HEAT OF THE NIGHT IMAGINATION	7	1982
IN THE HEAT OF THE NIGHT PAT BENATAR	98	1985
IN THE LOUNGE WITH...ANDY WILLIAMS ANDY WILLIAMS	39	1999
IN THE MIX 2000 VARIOUS ARTISTS (VIRGIN)	3	1999
IN THE MIX – 90'S HITS VARIOUS ARTISTS (VIRGIN)	3	1996
IN THE MIX 96 VARIOUS ARTISTS (VIRGIN)	1	1996
IN THE MIX 96 – 2 VARIOUS ARTISTS (VIRGIN)	2	1996
IN THE MIX 96 – 3 VARIOUS ARTISTS (VIRGIN)	1	1996
IN THE MIX 97 VARIOUS ARTISTS (VIRGIN)	1	1997
IN THE MIX 97 – 2 VARIOUS ARTISTS (VIRGIN)	2	1997
IN THE MIX 97 – 3 VARIOUS ARTISTS (VIRGIN)	2	1997
IN THE MIX 98 VARIOUS ARTISTS (VIRGIN)	1	1998
IN THE MIX 98 – 2 VARIOUS ARTISTS (VIRGIN)	6	1998
IN THE MIX IBIZA VARIOUS ARTISTS (VIRGIN)	1	1998
IN THE MIX – IBIZA CLASSICS VARIOUS ARTISTS (EMI)	6	2006
IN THE MIX – RAVE REVIVAL VARIOUS ARTISTS (EMI)	8	2007
IN THE MIX – REVIVAL VARIOUS ARTISTS (VIRGIN)	3	2005
IN THE MODE RONI SIZE / REPRAZENT	15	2000
IN THE MOOD FOR THE BLUES VARIOUS ARTISTS (UNIVERSAL)	15	2004
IN THE MOOD – THE DEFINITIVE GLENN MILLER	43	2003
IN THE PINK JAMES GALWAY & HENRY MANCINI	62	1984
IN THE POCKET COMMODORES	69	1981
IN THE SKIES PETER GREEN	32	1979
IN THE STUDIO SPECIAL AKA	34	1991
IN THE WAKE OF POSEIDON KING CRIMSON	4	1970
IN THE WIND PETER, PAUL & MARY	11	1964
IN THE ZONE BRITNEY SPEARS	13	2003
IN THIS LIFE MORDRED	70	1991
IN THIS SKIN JESSICA SIMPSON	36	2004
IN THROUGH THE OUT DOOR LED ZEPPELIN	1	1979
IN TIME – THE BEST OF – 1988-2003 R.E.M.	1	2003
IN TIME – THE BEST OF – 1988-2003 LIMITED EDITION R.E.M.	36	2003
IN TOUCH VARIOUS ARTISTS (STARBLEND)	89	1983
IN TOWN ROCKIN' BERRIES	15	1965
IN UTERO NIRVANA	1	1993
IN VISIBLE SILENCE ART OF NOISE	18	1986
IN WITH THE OUT CROWD LESS THAN JAKE	55	2006
IN YOUR EYES GEORGE BENSON	3	1983
IN YOUR FACE KINGDOM COME	25	1989
IN YOUR HONOR FOO FIGHTERS	2	2005
IN YOUR MIND BRYAN FERRY	5	1977
IN YOUR OWN TIME MARK OWEN	59	2003
INARTICULATE SPEECH OF THE HEART VAN MORRISON	14	1983
INCANTATIONS MIKE OLDFIELD	14	1978
INCANTO ANDREA BOCELLI	12	2008
INCESTICIDE NIRVANA	14	1992
THE INCOMPARABLE ELLA ELLA FITZGERALD	40	1980
THE INCREDIBLE PLAN MAX BOYCE	9	1976
THE INCREDIBLE SHRINKING DICKIES DICKIES	18	1979

Title / Artist	Peak Position	Year of Release
THE INCREDIBLE SOUND MACHINE MANTRONIX	36	1991
INCREDIBLE SOUND OF THE DREEM TEEM VARIOUS ARTISTS (INCREDIBLE)	14	2000
INCREDIBLE SOUND OF TREVOR NELSON VARIOUS ARTISTS (INCREDIBLE)	14	1999
THE INCREDIBLE STRING BAND INCREDIBLE STRING BAND	34	1968
INDECENT PROPOSAL FILM SOUNDTRACK	13	1993
INDEPENDENCE LULU	67	1993
INDEPENDENCE DAY DAVID ARNOLD	71	1996
INDEPENDENCE DAY UK (RADIO SOUNDTRACK) TELEVISION AND RADIO COMPILATION	66	1996
INDEPENDENT WOMAN VARIOUS ARTISTS (COLUMBIA)	7	2001
INDEPENDENT WORM SALOON BUTTHOLE SURFERS	73	1993
INDESTRUCTABLE DISTURBED	20	2008
INDESTRUCTIBLE RANCID	29	2003
INDIAN SUMMER GO WEST	13	1992
INDIE ANTHEMS VARIOUS ARTISTS (UNIVERSAL)	6	2005
INDIE HITS VARIOUS ARTISTS (TELSTAR)	13	1992
INDIGO MATT BIANCO	23	1988
INDIGO – WOMEN OF SONG OLIVIA NEWTON-JOHN	27	2005
INDISCREET SPARKS	18	1975
INDISCREET FM	76	1986
INDUSTRY RICHARD & DANNY THOMPSON	69	1997
INFECTED THE THE	14	1986
INFERNAL LOVE THERAPY?	9	1995
INFEST PAPA ROACH	9	2001
INFIDELS BOB DYLAN	9	1983
INFINITE EUPHORIA – FERRY CORSTEN VARIOUS ARTISTS (MINISTRY OF SOUND)	9	2004
INFINITY GURU JOSH	41	1990
INFINITY VARIOUS ARTISTS (BMG)	18	2005
INFINITY LAND BIFFY CLYRO	47	2004
INFINITY ON HIGH FALL OUT BOY	3	2007
INFINITY WITHIN DEEE-LITE	37	1992
INFLAMMABLE MATERIAL STIFF LITTLE FINGERS	14	1979
INFLUENCES MARK KING	77	1984
INFORCERS 3 VARIOUS ARTISTS (REINFORCED RIVET)	18	1993
INFORMATION DAVE EDMUNDS	92	1983
THE INFORMER JOOLS HOLLAND & HIS R&B ORCHESTRA	48	2008
INFOTAINMENT SCAN FALL	9	1993
INGENUE k.d. lang	3	1992
INHUMAN RAMPAGE DRAGONFORCE	70	2006
INITIAL SUCCESS B.A. ROBERTSON	32	1980
INNA DANCEHALL STYLE VARIOUS ARTISTS (EMI)	11	1993
INNER CHILD SHANICE	21	1992
INNER SECRETS SANTANA	17	1978
INNERVISIONS STEVIE WONDER	8	1973
INNOCENCE IS NO EXCUSE SAXON	36	1985
INNOCENT EYES DELTA GOODREM	2	2003
THE INNOCENTS ERASURE	1	1988
INNOVATION – THE ALBUM VARIOUS ARTISTS (MINISTRY OF SOUND)	17	2008
INNUENDO QUEEN	1	1991
INSIDE IN/INSIDE OUT KOOKS	2	2006
INSIDE INFORMATION FOREIGNER	64	1987
INSIDE JOB DON HENLEY	25	2000
INSIDE LIFE INCOGNITO	44	1991
INSIDE SHELLEY BERMAN SHELLEY BERMAN	12	1960
INSIDE STORY GRACE JONES	61	1986
INSIDE THE ELECTRIC CIRCUS W.A.S.P.	53	1986
INSOMNIA VARIOUS ARTISTS (SONY BMG)	13	2008
INSOMNIAC GREEN DAY	8	1995
INSOMNIAC ENRIQUE IGLESIAS	3	2007
INSOMNIATIC ALY & AJ	72	2007
INSPECTOR MORSE – ORIGINAL MUSIC FROM THE TV SERIES BARRINGTON PHELOUNG	4	1991
INSPECTOR MORSE VOLUME 2 – MUSIC FROM THE TV SERIES BARRINGTON PHELOUNG	18	1992
INSPECTOR MORSE VOLUME 3 BARRINGTON PHELOUNG	20	1993
INSPIRATION ELVIS PRESLEY	6	1980
INSPIRATION JANE McDONALD	6	2000
INSPIRATIONS ELKIE BROOKS	58	1989
INSTANT KARMA VARIOUS ARTISTS (WARNER BROTHERS)	14	2002
INSTANT PARTY EVERLY BROTHERS	20	1962
INSTINCT IGGY POP	61	1988
INSTRUMENTAL GOLD VARIOUS ARTISTS (WARWICK)	3	1976
INSTRUMENTAL GREATS VARIOUS ARTISTS (TELSTAR)	79	1988
INSTRUMENTAL MAGIC VARIOUS ARTISTS (TELSTAR)	68	1983
INSTRUMENTAL MEMORIES ARE MADE OF THIS VARIOUS ARTISTS (VIRGIN)	15	2004
INSTRUMENTAL MOODS VARIOUS ARTISTS (VIRGIN)	14	1995
INTELLIGENCE AND SACRIFICE ALEC EMPIRE	71	2002
INTENSE PRESENTS LOGICAL PROGRESSION LEVEL 3 VARIOUS ARTISTS (GOOD LOOKING)	18	1998
INTENSIFY WAY OUT WEST	61	2001
INTENSITIES (IN 10 CITIES) TED NUGENT	75	1981
INTENSIVE CARE ROBBIE WILLIAMS	1	2005
INTENTIONS MAXI PRIEST	96	1986
INTERGALACTIC SONIC 7'S ASH	3	2002
INTERMISSION DIO	22	1986
INTERNAL EXILE FISH	21	1991
INTERNATIONAL JIM REEVES JIM REEVES	11	1964
INTERNATIONAL SUPERHITS GREEN DAY	15	2001
INTERNATIONAL TIMES TRANSGLOBAL UNDERGROUND	40	1994
INTERNATIONAL VELVET CATATONIA	1	1998
THE INTERNATIONALE BILLY BRAGG	34	1990
INTERPRETATIONS CARPENTERS	29	1994
INTERPRETER JULIAN COPE	39	1996
INTERSCOPE RECORDS PRESENTS CLUB BANGERS VARIOUS ARTISTS (UNIVERSAL)	9	2006
INTIMACY BLOC PARTY	8	2008
THE INTIMATE JIM REEVES JIM REEVES	8	1964
INTO PARADISE ALL ANGELS	44	2007
INTO THE BLUE VARIOUS ARTISTS (POLYGRAM)	10	1998
INTO THE DRAGON BOMB THE BASS	18	1988
INTO THE EIGHTIES VARIOUS ARTISTS (GLOBAL TELEVISION)	5	1995
INTO THE FIRE BRYAN ADAMS	10	1987
INTO THE GAP THOMPSON TWINS	1	1984
INTO THE GREAT WIDE OPEN TOM PETTY & HEARTBREAKERS	3	1991
INTO THE LABYRINTH DEAD CAN DANCE	47	1993
INTO THE LIGHT CHRIS DE BURGH	2	1986
INTO THE LIGHT GLORIA ESTEFAN	2	1991
INTO THE LIGHT HANK MARVIN	18	1992
INTO THE LIGHT DAVID COVERDALE	75	2000
INTO THE MUSIC VAN MORRISON	21	1979
INTO THE SKYLINE CATHY DENNIS	8	1993
INTOLERANCE TIK & TOK	89	1984
INTRODUCING JOSS STONE	12	2007
INTRODUCING EDDY AND THE FALCONS WIZZARD	19	1974
INTRODUCING MICHAEL WARD MICHAEL WARD	26	1974
INTRODUCING RICHARD CLAYDERMAN RICHARD CLAYDERMAN	2	1982
INTRODUCING THE HARDLINE ACCORDING TO TERENCE TRENT D'ARBY TERENCE TRENT D'ARBY	1	1987
INTRODUCING...DAVID PEASTON DAVID PEASTON	66	1989
INTRODUCTION ALEX PARKS	5	2003
INTROSPECTIVE PET SHOP BOYS	2	1988
INTUITION LINX	8	1981
INVASION OF YOUR PRIVACY RATT	50	1985
INVINCIBLE FIVE	4	1999
INVINCIBLE MICHAEL JACKSON	1	2001
INVINCIBLE SUMMER k.d. lang	17	2000
THE INVISIBLE BAND TRAVIS	1	2001
THE INVISIBLE INVASION CORAL	3	2005
INVISIBLE TOUCH GENESIS	1	1986
INVITATION PETERS & LEE	44	1976
THE INVITATION THIRTEEN SENSES	14	2004
INVITATION TO THE MOVIES MATT MONRO	30	1967
INVITATIONS SHAKATAK	30	1982
INVOLVER SASHA	61	2004
INXS – THE GREATEST HITS INXS	3	1994
IOWA SLIPKNOT	1	2001
IQ 6: ZANG TUMB TUM SAMPLED VARIOUS ARTISTS (ZTT)	40	1985
IRISH HEARTBEAT VAN MORRISON & THE CHIEFTAINS	18	1988
IRISH SON BRIAN McFADDEN	24	2004
IRISH TOUR '74 RORY GALLAGHER	36	1974
IRON MAIDEN IRON MAIDEN	4	1980
IRONFIST MOTORHEAD	6	1982
IRONMAN GHOSTFACE KILLAH	38	1996
IRREPLACEABLE GEORGE BENSON	58	2004
IRV GOTTI PRESENTS THE INC IRV GOTTI PRESENTS THE INC	68	2002
IS A WOMAN LAMBCHOP	38	2002
IS THERE ANYBODY OUT THERE? – LIVE PINK FLOYD	15	2000
IS THERE ANYTHING ABOUT BRAND X	93	1982
IS THIS DESIRE? PJ HARVEY	17	1998
IS THIS IT STROKES	2	2001
IS THIS LOVE VARIOUS ARTISTS (EMI)	2	1989
ISDN FUTURE SOUND OF LONDON	62	1994
ISDN (REMIX) FUTURE SOUND OF LONDON	44	1995
ISLAND LIFE GRACE JONES	4	1985
THE ISLAND STORY VARIOUS ARTISTS (ISLAND)	9	1987
ISLANDS KING CRIMSON	30	1972
ISLANDS KAJAGOOGOO	35	1984
ISLANDS MIKE OLDFIELD	29	1987
THE ISLE OF VIEW PRETENDERS	23	1995
ISMISM KEVIN GODLEY & LOL CRÈME	29	1981
ISN'T IT GRAND BOYS CLANCY BROTHERS & TOMMY MAKEM	22	1966
ISOLATION TOTO	67	1984
ISSUES KORN	37	1999
IT BEGINS AGAIN DUSTY SPRINGFIELD	41	1978
IT DOESN'T MATTER ANYMORE SUPERNATURALS	9	1997
THE IT GIRL SLEEPER	5	1996
IT GOES WITHOUT SAYING DUM DUMS	27	2000
IT HAD TO BE YOU – THE GREAT AMERICAN SONGBOOK ROD STEWART	8	2002
IT HAPPENED AT THE WORLD'S FAIR (OST) ELVIS PRESLEY	4	1963
IT IS THE BUSINESS OF THE FUTURE TO BE DANGEROUS HAWKWIND	75	1993
IT IS TIME FOR A LOVE REVOLUTION LENNY KRAVITZ	42	2008
IT MIGHT AS WELL BE SWING FRANK SINATRA & COUNT BASIE & HIS ORCHESTRA	17	1964

Title / Artist	Peak Position	Year of Release
IT MUST BE HIM VIKKI CARR	12	1967
IT MUST BE LOVE VARIOUS ARTISTS (HIT LABEL)	11	1993
IT STARTED WITH A KISS VARIOUS ARTISTS (ARCADE)	9	1991
IT STILL MOVES MY MORNING JACKET	62	2003
IT TAKES A NATION OF MILLIONS TO HOLD US BACK PUBLIC ENEMY	8	1988
IT TAKES A THIEF COOLIO	67	1994
IT TAKES TWO VARIOUS ARTISTS (SONY)	6	1996
IT TAKES TWO – LOVE'S GREATEST DUETS VARIOUS ARTISTS (EMI)	17	1993
IT WAS WRITTEN NAS	38	1996
IT WON'T BE SOON BEFORE LONG MAROON 5	1	2007
IT WON'T SEEM LIKE CHRISTMAS WITHOUT YOU ELVIS PRESLEY	80	1982
ITALIA – DANCE MUSIC FROM ITALY VARIOUS ARTISTS (DECONSTRUCTION)	4	1989
THE ITALIAN PATRIZIO BUANNE	10	2005
ITCHY FEET JOHNNY CASH	36	1978
ITCHY FEET BLUES BAND	60	1981
IT'LL END IN TEARS THIS MORTAL COIL	38	1984
IT'S A BEAUTIFUL DAY IT'S A BEAUTIFUL DAY	58	1970
IT'S A BIG DADDY THING BIG DADDY	37	1989
IT'S A GAME BAY CITY ROLLERS	18	1977
IT'S A GIRL THING VARIOUS ARTISTS (VIRGIN)	4	2001
IT'S A MAN'S WORLD CHER	10	1995
IT'S A SHAME ABOUT RAY LEMONHEADS	33	1992
IT'S A SIXTIES NIGHT VARIOUS ARTISTS (COLUMBIA)	12	1997
IT'S A WONDERFUL LIFE SPARKLEHORSE	49	2001
IT'S ABOUT TIME JOHN DENVER	90	1983
IT'S ABOUT TIME MORRISSEY MULLEN	95	1983
IT'S ABOUT TIME SWV	17	1993
IT'S ABOUT TIME CHRISTINA MILIAN	21	2004
IT'S ALIVE RAMONES	27	1979
IT'S ALL ABOUT THE STRAGGLERS ARTFUL DODGER	18	2000
IT'S ALL GOOD LUCK & NEAT	34	2002
IT'S BETTER TO TRAVEL SWING OUT SISTER	1	1987
IT'S CHRISTMAS VARIOUS ARTISTS (EMI)	2	1989
IT'S CHRISTMAS TIME VARIOUS ARTISTS (EMI)	3	1992
IT'S COOL VARIOUS ARTISTS (PARLOPHONE)	3	1991
IT'S ELECTRIC VARIOUS ARTISTS (DINO)	2	1994
IT'S EVERLY TIME EVERLY BROTHERS	2	1960
IT'S FIVE O'CLOCK SOMEWHERE SLASH'S SNAKEPIT	15	1995
IT'S FOUR IN THE MORNING FARON YOUNG	27	1972
IT'S GREAT WHEN YOU'RE STRAIGHT…YEAH BLACK GRAPE	1	1995
IT'S HARD WHO	11	1982
IT'S IMPOSSIBLE PERRY COMO	13	1971
IT'S IT SUGARCUBES	47	1992
IT'S MAGIC SHIRLEY BASSEY	32	1971
IT'S MY LIFE TALK TALK	35	1984
IT'S MY LIFE – THE ALBUM SASH!	6	1997
IT'S ONLY A MOVIE FAMILY	30	1973
IT'S ONLY LOVE SIMPLY RED	27	2000
IT'S ONLY ROCK 'N' ROLL ROLLING STONES	2	1974
IT'S PARTY TIME JIVE BUNNY & THE MIXMASTERS	23	1990
IT'S POP TIME VARIOUS ARTISTS (SONY/BMG)	4	2006
IT'S REAL K-CI & JOJO	56	1999
IT'S THE SEARCHERS SEARCHERS	4	1964
IT'S THE TALK OF THE TOWN RAY CONNIFF	15	1960
IT'S THE ULTIMATE DANCE ALBUM VARIOUS ARTISTS (TELSTAR)	1	1994
IT'S TIME MICHAEL BUBLE	4	2005
IT'S TIME… CLOCK	27	1995
IT'S TRAD MAN FILM SOUNDTRACK	3	1962
IT'S YOUR NIGHT JAMES INGRAM	25	1984
IV CYPRESS HILL	25	1998
IV SEAL	4	2003
I'VE BEEN EXPECTING YOU ROBBIE WILLIAMS	1	1998
I'VE GOT A SONG FOR YOU SHIRLEY BASSEY	26	1966
I'VE GOT THE MELODY ODYSSEY	29	1981
I'VE NEVER BEEN TO ME CHARLENE	43	1982
I'VE SEEN EVERYTHING TRASH CAN SINATRAS	50	1993
IXNAY ON THE HOMBRE OFFSPRING	17	1997
IZITSO CAT STEVENS	18	1977
IZZY STRADLIN' AND THE JU JU HOUNDS IZZY STRADLIN' & THE JU JU HOUNDS	52	1992

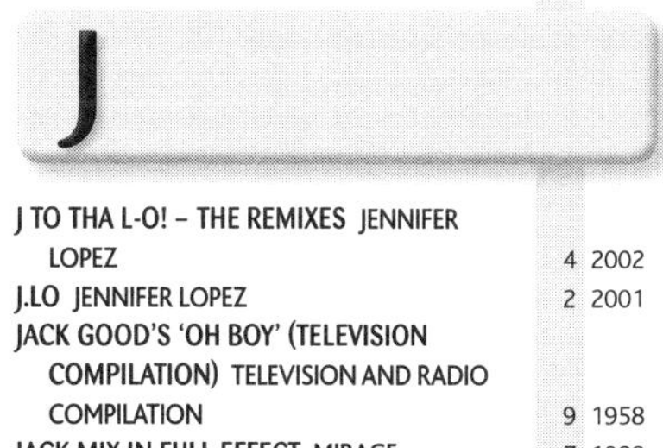

Title / Artist	Peak Position	Year of Release
J TO THA L-O! – THE REMIXES JENNIFER LOPEZ	4	2002
J.LO JENNIFER LOPEZ	2	2001
JACK GOOD'S 'OH BOY' (TELEVISION COMPILATION) TELEVISION AND RADIO COMPILATION	9	1958
JACK MIX IN FULL EFFECT MIRAGE	7	1988
JACK O THE GREEN – SMALL WORLD BIG BAND JOOLS HOLLAND & HIS R&B ORCHESTRA	39	2003
JACK RABBIT SLIM STEVE FORBERT	54	1979
JACK TRAX – THE FIRST ALBUM VARIOUS ARTISTS (JACK TRAX)	83	1987
JACK TRAX – THE SECOND ALBUM VARIOUS ARTISTS (JACK TRAX)	61	1987
JACK TRAX – THE THIRD ALBUM VARIOUS ARTISTS (JACK TRAX)	49	1988
JACKIE BROWN FILM SOUNDTRACK	11	1998
JACKIE: THE ALBUM VARIOUS ARTISTS (EMI)	3	2007
JACKIE: THE ALBUM – VOLUME 2 VARIOUS ARTISTS (EMI)	9	2008
JACKINABOX TURIN BRAKES	9	2005
JACKMASTER VOLUME 1 VARIOUS ARTISTS (DJ INTERNATIONAL)	36	1987
JACKMASTER VOLUME 2 VARIOUS ARTISTS (DJ INTERNATIONAL)	38	1988
JACKPOT CHINGY	73	2004
THE JACKSONS JACKSONS	54	1977
THE JACKSONS LIVE JACKSONS	53	1981
JACKSONVILLE CITY LIGHTS RYAN ADAMS & THE CARDINALS	59	2005
JACQUES LOUSSIER – THE BEST OF PLAY BACH JACQUES LOUSSIER	58	1985
JADE TO THE MAX JADE	43	1993
JAGGED GARY NUMAN	59	2006
JAGGED LITTLE PILL ALANIS MORISSETTE	1	1995
JAGGED LITTLE PILL – ACOUSTIC ALANIS MORISSETTE	12	2005
JAILBREAK THIN LIZZY	10	1976
JAILHOUSE ROCK/LOVE IN LAS VEGAS ELVIS PRESLEY	40	1983
JAM LITTLE ANGELS	1	1993
THE JAM COLLECTION JAM	58	1996
JAM ON REVENGE NEWCLEUS	84	1984
JAM SCIENCE SHRIEKBACK	85	1984
JAMBOREE BAG NUMBER 3 CHAS & DAVE	15	1985
JAMES BOND 007 – A VIEW TO A KILL (OST) JOHN BARRY	81	1985
JAMES BOND 007 – GOLDFINGER (OST) JOHN BARRY	14	1964
JAMES BOND 007 – THE LIVING DAYLIGHTS (OST) JOHN BARRY	57	1987
JAMES BOND'S GREATEST HITS VARIOUS ARTISTS (LIBERTY)	4	1982
JAMES GALWAY AND THE CHIEFTAINS IN IRELAND JAMES GALWAY & THE CHIEFTAINS	32	1987
THE JAMES GALWAY COLLECTION JAMES GALWAY	41	1982
JAMES GALWAY PLAYS SONGS FOR ANNIE JAMES GALWAY	7	1978
JAMES LAST GOES POP JAMES LAST	32	1968
JAMES LAST IN CONCERT JAMES LAST	13	1972
JAMES LAST IN RUSSIA JAMES LAST	12	1973
JAMES LAST IN SCOTLAND JAMES LAST	68	1984
JAMES LAST PLAYS ANDREW LLOYD WEBBER JAMES LAST	12	1993
JAMES LAVELLE – BARCELONA 023 VARIOUS ARTISTS (GLOBAL UNDERGROUND)	18	2002
JAMIE OLIVER'S COOKIN' – MUSIC TO COOK BY VARIOUS ARTISTS (COLUMBIA)	14	2000
JAMMIN' VARIOUS ARTISTS (COOKIE JAR)	7	1993
THE JAN AND DEAN STORY JAN & DEAN	67	1980
JANE JANE McDONALD	7	2008
JANE FONDA'S WORKOUT RECORD JANE FONDA	7	1983
JANE FONDA'S WORKOUT RECORD: NEW AND IMPROVED JANE FONDA	60	1984
JANE MCDONALD JANE McDONALD	1	1998
JANET JANET JACKSON	1	1993
JANIS JOPLIN IN CONCERT JANIS JOPLIN	30	1972
JAPANESE WHISPERS: SINGLES NOV 82 – NOV 83 CURE	26	1983
JAR OF FLIES/SAP ALICE IN CHAINS	4	1994
JARRE LIVE JEAN-MICHEL JARRE	16	1989
JARREAU AL JARREAU	39	1983
JARVIS JARVIS COCKER	37	2006
JAWS (OST) JOHN WILLIAMS	55	1976
JAZZ QUEEN	2	1978
THE JAZZ ALBUM 2003 VARIOUS ARTISTS (VERVE)	13	2002
JAZZ CAFÉ – THE SOUL MIX VARIOUS ARTISTS (INSPIRED)	9	2004
JAZZ CLASSICS LOUIS ARMSTRONG	20	1961
JAZZ FUNK INCOGNITO	28	1981
JAZZ JUICE 2 VARIOUS ARTISTS (STREET SOUNDS)	96	1986
JAZZ JUICE 3 VARIOUS ARTISTS (STREET SOUNDS)	88	1986
JAZZ JUICE 5 VARIOUS ARTISTS (STREET SOUNDS)	97	1987
JAZZ MOODS VARIOUS ARTISTS (TELSTAR)	3	1994
JAZZ MOODS 2 VARIOUS ARTISTS (TELSTAR)	18	1994
JAZZ ON A SUMMER'S DAY VARIOUS ARTISTS (CASTLE COMMUNICATIONS)	4	1992
JAZZ SAMBA STAN GETZ & CHARLIE BYRD	15	1963
JAZZ SEBASTIAN BACH SWINGLE SINGERS	13	1964
THE JAZZ SINGER (OST) NEIL DIAMOND	3	1980
JAZZMATAZZ GURU	58	1993
JAZZMATAZZ VOLUME II – THE NEW REALITY GURU	12	1995
JEALOUS ONES STILL ENVY (J.O.S.E.) FAT JOE	19	2002
JEFF BECK, TIM BOGERT & CARMINE APPICE JEFF BECK, TIM BOGERT & CARMINE APPICE	28	1973
JEFF WAYNE'S AL VERSION OF THE WAR OF THE WORLDS JEFF WAYNE	5	1978
JEFF WAYNE'S MUSICAL VERSION OF THE WAR OF THE WORLDS JEFF WAYNE	23	1996
JEFF WAYNE'S MUSICAL VERSION OF THE WAR OF THE WORLDS – ULLADUBULLA – THE REMIX ALBUM JEFF WAYNE	64	2000
JEHOVAHKILL JULIAN COPE	20	1992
JENNIFER HUDSON JENNIFER HUDSON	21	2008
JENNIFER PAIGE JENNIFER PAIGE	67	1998
JENNIFER RUSH JENNIFER RUSH	7	1985
JERKY VERSIONS OF THE DREAM HOWARD DEVOTO	57	1983

Title / Artist	Peak Position	Year of Release
JERRY LEE LEWIS VOLUME 2 JERRY LEE LEWIS	14	1962
JESTA GIGGLE BARRON KNIGHTS	45	1980
JESUS CHRIST SUPERSTAR FILM SOUNDTRACK	23	1973
JESUS CHRIST SUPERSTAR (ORIGINAL STUDIO CAST RECORDING) STAGE CAST RECORDING	6	1972
THE JESUS OF COOL NICK LOWE	22	1978
JEWEL MARCELLA DETROIT	15	1994
JI JUNIOR	28	1982
JIGSAW SHADOWS	8	1967
JIM DIAMOND JIM DIAMOND	16	1993
JIM REEVES AND SOME FRIENDS JIM REEVES	24	1969
JIM REEVES' GOLDEN RECORDS JIM REEVES	9	1971
THE JIM REEVES WAY JIM REEVES	16	1965
JIM REEVES WRITES YOU A RECORD JIM REEVES	47	1971
JIMI HENDRIX JIMI HENDRIX	35	1975
JIMI HENDRIX AT THE ISLE OF WIGHT JIMI HENDRIX	17	1971
THE JIMI HENDRIX CONCERTS JIMI HENDRIX	16	1982
JIMI HENDRIX – THE ULTIMATE EXPERIENCE JIMI HENDRIX	25	1992
THE JIMMY RUFFIN WAY JIMMY RUFFIN	32	1967
JINX RORY GALLAGHER	68	1982
JIVE BUNNY – THE ALBUM JIVE BUNNY & THE MIXMASTERS	2	1989
JIVE BUNNY'S SUMMER PARTY 2008 VARIOUS ARTISTS (EMI)	9	2008
JJ72 JJ72	16	2000
JOAN ARMATRADING JOAN ARMATRADING	12	1976
JOAN BAEZ JOAN BAEZ	9	1965
JOAN BAEZ IN CONCERT VOLUME 2 JOAN BAEZ	8	1964
JOAN BAEZ NO. 5 JOAN BAEZ	3	1965
JOAN BAEZ ON VANGUARD JOAN BAEZ	15	1969
JOB LOT CHAS & DAVE	59	1983
JODY WATLEY JODY WATLEY	62	1987
JOE BROWN – LIVE JOE BROWN	14	1963
JOE BUDDEN JOE BUDDEN	55	2003
JOE COCKER/WITH A LITTLE HELP FROM MY FRIENDS JOE COCKER	29	1972
THE JOE LONGTHORNE CHRISTMAS ALBUM JOE LONGTHORNE	44	1989
THE JOE LONGTHORNE SONGBOOK JOE LONGTHORNE	16	1988
JOE SATRIANI JOE SATRIANI	21	1995
JOE'S GARAGE ACT I FRANK ZAPPA	62	1979
JOE'S GARAGE ACTS II & III FRANK ZAPPA	75	1980
JOEY LAWRENCE JOEY LAWRENCE	39	1993
JOHN BARLEYCORN MUST DIE TRAFFIC	11	1970
JOHN DENVER JOHN DENVER	68	1979
JOHN DENVER – COLLECTION JOHN DENVER	20	1984
JOHN DIGWEED – LOS ANGELES VARIOUS ARTISTS (GLOBAL UNDERGROUND)	14	2001
JOHN DIGWEED SYDNEY VARIOUS ARTISTS (GLOBAL UNDERGROUND)	16	1998
JOHN HANSON SINGS 20 SHOWTIME GREATS JOHN HANSON	16	1977
JOHN LENNON AND THE PLASTIC ONO BAND JOHN LENNON WITH THE PLASTIC ONO BAND	8	1971
THE JOHN LENNON ANTHOLOGY JOHN LENNON	62	1998
THE JOHN LENNON COLLECTION JOHN LENNON	1	1982
JOHN LENNON LIVE IN NEW YORK CITY JOHN LENNON	55	1986
JOHN PARR JOHN PARR	60	1985
JOHN PAUL II – THE PILGRIM POPE POPE JOHN PAUL II	71	1982
JOHN PEEL – A TRIBUTE VARIOUS ARTISTS (WARNER BROTHERS)	5	2005
JOHN PEEL – RIGHT TIME WRONG SPEED VARIOUS ARTISTS (WARNER BROTHERS)	10	2008
JOHN TAVERNER: INNOCENCE WESTMINSTER ABBEY CHOIR/CONDUCTOR: MARTIN NEARY	34	1997
JOHN WESLEY HARDING BOB DYLAN	1	1968
JOHN WILLIAMS PLAYS THE MOVIES JOHN WILLIAMS	54	1996
JOHNNY CASH JOHNNY CASH	43	1971
JOHNNY CASH AT FOLSOM PRISON JOHNNY CASH	8	1968
JOHNNY CASH AT SAN QUENTIN JOHNNY CASH	2	1969
THE JOHNNY CASH SHOW JOHNNY CASH	18	1970
THE JOHNNY MATHIS COLLECTION JOHNNY MATHIS	1	1977
JOHNNY NASH COLLECTION JOHNNY NASH	18	1977
JOHNNY THE FOX THIN LIZZY	11	1976
JOHNNY WINTER AND... JOHNNY WINTER	29	1970
JOHNNY WINTER AND...LIVE JOHNNY WINTER	20	1971
JOIN BING AND SING ALONG BING CROSBY	7	1960
JOIN HANDS SIOUXSIE & THE BANSHEES	13	1979
JOIN THE ARMY SUICIDAL TENDENCIES	81	1987
JOIN TOGETHER WHO	59	1990
JOIN WITH US THE FEELING	1	2008
JOJO JOJO	22	2004
JOLLIFICATION LIGHTNING SEEDS	12	1994
JON SECADA JON SECADA	20	1992
JONAS BROTHERS JONAS BROTHERS	9	2008
JONATHAN BUTLER JONATHAN BUTLER	12	1987
JONATHAN KING'S ENTERTAINMENT FROM THE U.S.A. (TELEVISION COMPILATION) TELEVISION AND RADIO COMPILATION	6	1986
JONATHAN LIVINGSTONE SEAGULL (OST) NEIL DIAMOND	35	1974
JORDAN: THE COMEBACK PREFAB SPROUT	7	1990
JORDIN SPARKS JORDIN SPARKS	17	2008
JOSE CARRERAS COLLECTION JOSE CARRERAS	90	1988
JOSE CARRERAS SINGS ANDREW LLOYD WEBBER JOSE CARRERAS	42	1989
JOSE FELICIANO JOSE FELICIANO	29	1969
JOSEPH & THE AMAZING TECHNICOLOUR DREAMCOAT ANDREW LLOYD WEBBER	34	2007
JOSEPH AND THE AMAZING TECHNICOLOUR DREAMCOAT JASON DONOVAN/ORIGINAL LONDON STAGE CAST SOUNDTRACK	1	1991
JOSH GROBAN JOSH GROBAN	32	2003
THE JOSHUA TREE U2	1	1987
THE JOSHUA TREE DELUXE U2	51	2007
THE JOSHUA TREE SINGLES U2	100	1988
THE JOURNEY 911	13	1997
JOURNEY INWARDS LTJ BUKEM	40	2000
JOURNEY SOUTH JOURNEY SOUTH	1	2006
JOURNEY THROUGH THE CLASSICS – HOOKED ON CLASSICS 3 LOUIS CLARK CONDUCTING THE ROYAL PHILHARMONIC ORCHESTRA	19	1983
JOURNEY THROUGH THE SECRET LIFE OF PLANTS STEVIE WONDER	8	1979
JOURNEY TO ADDIS THIRD WORLD	30	1978
JOURNEY TO GLORY SPANDAU BALLET	5	1981
JOURNEY TO THE CENTRE OF THE EARTH RICK WAKEMAN WITH THE LONDON SYMPHONY ORCHESTRA	1	1974
JOURNEY TO THE URGE WITHIN COURTNEY PINE	39	1986
JOURNEY TO THE WEST MONKEY	5	2008
THE JOURNEY – THE VERY BEST OF DONNA SUMMER	6	2004
JOURNEYMAN ERIC CLAPTON	2	1989
JOURNEYS BY DJ VOLUME 4 VARIOUS ARTISTS (MUSIC UNITES)	19	1994
JOY TEDDY PENDERGRASS	45	1988
JOY 1967-1990 ULTRA VIVID SCENE	58	1990
A JOYFUL NOISE UNTO THE CREATOR GALLIANO	28	1992
JOYRIDE ROXETTE	2	1991
J-TULL DOT COM JETHRO TULL	44	1999
JU JU SIOUXSIE & THE BANSHEES	7	1981
JUBILEE SEX PISTOLS	29	2002
JUDGE JULES PRESENTS TRIED AND TESTED VARIOUS ARTISTS (SERIOUS)	18	2002
JUDGEMENT DAYS MS DYNAMITE	43	2005
JUDGEMENT EUPHORIA VARIOUS ARTISTS (MINISTRY OF SOUND)	12	2005
JUDGEMENT NIGHT FILM SOUNDTRACK	16	1993
JUDITH JUDY COLLINS	7	1975
JUDY AT CARNEGIE HALL JUDY GARLAND	13	1962
JUGGY D JUGGY D	70	2004
JUICY LUCY JUICY LUCY	41	1970
JUKE BOX JIVE VARIOUS ARTISTS (K-TEL)	3	1976
JUKE BOX JIVE – ROCK 'N' ROLL GREATS VARIOUS ARTISTS (STYLUS)	13	1989
JUKEBOX CAT POWER	32	2008
THE JUKEBOX YEARS DANIEL O'DONNELL	3	2004
JULIA FORDHAM JULIA FORDHAM	20	1988
JULIAN COPE PRESENTS 20 MOTHERS JULIAN COPE	20	1995
THE JULIET LETTERS ELVIS COSTELLO & THE BRODSKY QUARTET	18	1993
JULIO JULIO IGLESIAS	5	1983
JUMP BACK – THE BEST OF THE ROLLING STONES 1971-93 ROLLING STONES	16	1993
JUMP – THE BEST OF THE POINTER SISTERS POINTER SISTERS	11	1989
JUMP UP ELTON JOHN	13	1982
JUMPERS 4 GOALPOSTS VARIOUS ARTISTS (WARNER BROTHERS)	4	2002
JUMPIN' JIVE JOE JACKSON'S JUMPIN' JIVE	14	1981
JUMPING ALL OVER THE WORLD SCOOTER	1	2008
JUNCTION SEVEN STEVE WINWOOD	32	1997
THE JUNGLE BOOK FILM SOUNDTRACK	5	1968
JUNGLE DRUM & BASS ANTHEMS VARIOUS ARTISTS (VIRGIN)	12	2005
JUNGLE FEVER (OST) STEVIE WONDER	56	1991
JUNGLE HITS VOLUME 1 VARIOUS ARTISTS (JETSTAR)	9	1994
JUNGLE MANIA 2 VARIOUS ARTISTS (TELSTAR)	5	1994
JUNGLE MANIA 3 VARIOUS ARTISTS (TELSTAR)	5	1995
JUNGLE MANIA 94 VARIOUS ARTISTS (TELSTAR)	7	1994
JUNGLE MASSIVE VARIOUS ARTISTS (WARNER BROTHERS)	3	2002
JUNGLE MASSIVE – 21ST CENTURY BREAKBEAT VARIOUS ARTISTS (WARNER BROTHERS)	17	2002
JUNGLE TEKNO VOLUME 1 VARIOUS ARTISTS (DEBUT)	18	1992
JUNIOR BOY'S OWN COLLECTION VARIOUS ARTISTS (JUNIOR BOY'S OWN)	20	1994
JUNK CULTURE ORCHESTRAL MANOEUVRES IN THE DARK	9	1984
JUNK SCIENCE DEEP DISH	37	1998
JUNKYARD BIRTHDAY PARTY	73	1982
JUNO FILM SOUNDTRACK	7	2008
JURASSIC 5 JURASSIC 5	70	1998
JURASSIC PARK (OST) JOHN WILLIAMS	42	1993
JURASSIC SHIFT OZRIC TENTACLES	11	1993
JUST A BOY LEO SAYER	4	1974
JUST A COLLECTION OF ANTIQUES AND CURIOS STRAWBS	27	1970
JUST ADD LIFE ALMIGHTY	34	1996

Title / Artist	Peak Position	Year of Release
JUST ANOTHER WAY TO SAY I LOVE YOU BARRY WHITE	12	1975
JUST BACKWARD OF SQUARE LOWGOLD	33	2001
JUST BE TIESTO	54	2004
JUST CAN'T STOP IT BEAT	3	1980
JUST ENOUGH EDUCATION TO PERFORM STEREOPHONICS	1	2001
JUST FOR A DAY SLOWDIVE	32	1991
JUST FOR DAD VARIOUS ARTISTS (APACE)	18	2008
JUST FOR FUN FILM SOUNDTRACK	20	1963
JUST FOR MUM VARIOUS ARTISTS (APACE)	20	2008
JUST FOR YOU DES O'CONNOR	17	1980
JUST FOR YOU HOWARD KEEL	51	1988
JUST FOR YOU LIONEL RICHIE	5	2004
JUST FOR YOU VARIOUS ARTISTS (UNIVERSAL)	7	2004
JUST GETS BETTER WITH TIME WHISPERS	63	1987
JUST GOOD FRIENDS PAUL NICHOLAS	30	1986
JUST GREAT SONGS VARIOUS ARTISTS (SONY/BMG)	2	2007
JUST GREAT SONGS 2 VARIOUS ARTISTS (SONY/BMG)	13	2007
JUST LIKE BLOOD TOM McRAE	26	2003
JUST LIKE THE FAMBLY CAT GRANDADDY	50	2006
JUST LIKE THE FIRST TIME FREDDIE JACKSON	30	1986
JUST LISTEN NIGEL KENNEDY WITH THE LONDON PHILHARMONIC ORCHESTRA CONDUCTED BY SIMON RATTLE	56	1992
JUST LOVING YOU ANITA HARRIS	29	1968
JUST ONE NIGHT ERIC CLAPTON	3	1980
JUST PUSH PLAY AEROSMITH	7	2001
JUST RAGGA VARIOUS ARTISTS (CHARM)	17	1992
JUST RAGGA VOLUME III VARIOUS ARTISTS (CHARM)	19	1993
JUST SAY OZZY (LIVE) OZZY OSBOURNE	69	1990
JUST SEVENTEEN – GET KICKIN' VARIOUS ARTISTS (DOVER)	2	1990
JUST SEVENTEEN – HEARTBEATS VARIOUS ARTISTS (FANFARE)	3	1989
JUST SUPPOSIN' STATUS QUO	4	1980
JUST TESTING WISHBONE ASH	41	1980
JUST THE TWO OF US VARIOUS ARTISTS (CBS)	1	1990
JUST THE WAY YOU ARE VARIOUS ARTISTS (INSPIRED)	15	2005
JUST THE WAY YOU LIKE IT S.O.S. BAND	29	1984
JUST TO LET YOU KNOW BITTY McLEAN	19	1994
JUST VISITING THIS PLANET JELLYBEAN	15	1987
JUST WALKIN' IN THE RAIN – VERY BEST OF JOHNNIE RAY	67	2008
JUSTIFIED JUSTIN TIMBERLAKE	1	2002
JUXTAPOSE TRICKY WITH DJ MUGGS & GREASE	22	1999

K

Title / Artist	Peak Position	Year of Release
K KULA SHAKER	1	1996
KAEMPFERT SPECIAL BERT KAEMPFERT & HIS ORCHESTRA	24	1967
KAFKA NIGEL KENNEDY	67	1996
KAIZOKU-BAN ACCEPT	91	1986
KALA MIA	39	2007
KALEIDOSCOPE SIOUXSIE & THE BANSHEES	5	1980
KALEIDOSCOPE KELIS	43	2000
KALEIDOSCOPE WORLD SWING OUT SISTER	9	1989
KAMAKIRIAD DONALD FAGEN	3	1993
KAMIKAZE DEKE LEONARD	50	1974
KAMIKAZE TWISTA	19	2004
KAOS – THE ANTI ACOUSTIC WARFARE ADAM F	44	2001
KAOS THEORY VARIOUS ARTISTS (TELSTAR)	2	1992
KAOS THEORY 2 VARIOUS ARTISTS (TELSTAR)	2	1992
KAOS THEORY 4 VARIOUS ARTISTS (TELSTAR)	2	1992
KARAJAN: ADAGIO HERBERT VON KARAJAN CONDUCTING THE BERLIN PHILHARMONIC ORCHESTRA	30	1995
KARAOKE PARTY VARIOUS ARTISTS (TRAX)	20	1990
KARAOKE PARTY II VARIOUS ARTISTS (TRAX)	7	1991
THE KARMA COLLECTION VARIOUS ARTISTS (MINISTRY OF SOUND)	7	2002
THE KARMA COLLECTION 2003 VARIOUS ARTISTS (MINISTRY OF SOUND)	17	2003
KARMACODE LACUNA COIL	47	2006
KARYN WHITE KARYN WHITE	20	1989
KASABIAN KASABIAN	4	2004
THE KATIE MELUA COLLECTION KATIE MELUA	15	2008
KATRINA AND THE WAVES KATRINA & THE WAVES	28	1985
KATY LIED STEELY DAN	13	1975
KAVANA KAVANA	29	1997
KAYA BOB MARLEY & THE WAILERS	4	1978
KC AND THE SUNSHINE BAND KC & THE SUNSHINE BAND	26	1975
KEEP FIT AND DANCE PETER POWELL	9	1982
KEEP IN SHAPE SYSTEM WITH ARLENE PHILLIPS ARLENE PHILLIPS	41	1982
KEEP IN SHAPE VOLUME 2 ARLENE PHILLIPS	100	1984
KEEP IT SIMPLE VAN MORRISON	10	2008
KEEP MOVING MADNESS	6	1984
KEEP ON WILL YOUNG	2	2005
KEEP ON DANCING VARIOUS ARTISTS (DINO)	14	1993
KEEP ON MOVIN' VARIOUS ARTISTS (SONY/BMG)	11	2006
KEEP ON WOMBLING WOMBLES	17	1974
KEEP ON YOUR MEAN SIDE KILLS	47	2003
KEEP THE FAITH BON JOVI	1	1992
KEEP THE FAITH FAITH EVANS	69	1998
KEEP THE MUSIC PLAYING SHIRLEY BASSEY	25	1991
KEEP YOUR DISTANCE CURIOSITY KILLED THE CAT	1	1987
KEEP YOUR EYE ON ME HERB ALPERT	79	1987
KEEPER OF THE SEVEN KEYS PART 2 HELLOWEEN	24	1988
KEEPERS OF THE FUNK LORDS OF THE UNDERGROUND	68	1994
KEEPING THE SUMMER ALIVE BEACH BOYS	54	1980
KEEPS GETTING BETTER – A DECADE OF HITS CHRISTINA AGUILERA	10	2008
KEITH SWEAT KEITH SWEAT	36	1996
KELIS WAS HERE KELIS	41	2006
KENNY KENNY ROGERS	7	1980
KENNY BALL'S GOLDEN HITS KENNY BALL	4	1963
KENNY ROGERS KENNY ROGERS	14	1977
THE KENNY ROGERS SINGLES ALBUM KENNY ROGERS	12	1979
THE KENNY ROGERS STORY KENNY ROGERS	4	1985
KEROSENE HAT CRACKER	44	1994
KERRANG – THE ALBUM VARIOUS ARTISTS (UNIVERSAL)	9	2001
KERRANG! 2 – THE ALBUM VARIOUS ARTISTS (UNIVERSAL)	8	2001
KERRANG! 3 – THE ALBUM VARIOUS ARTISTS (UNIVERSAL)	4	2002
KERRANG! 4 – THE ALBUM VARIOUS ARTISTS (UNIVERSAL)	4	2002
KERRANG! – HIGH VOLTAGE VARIOUS ARTISTS (UNIVERSAL)	17	2003
KERRANG! KOMPILATION – 24 ROCK MASTERS VARIOUS ARTISTS (EMI)	84	1985
KERRANG! THE ALBUM VARIOUS ARTISTS (HIT LABEL)	12	1994
KEVIN AND PERRY – GO LARGE FILM SOUNDTRACK	4	2000
THE KEY JOAN ARMATRADING	10	1983
KEYS OF THE KINGDOM MOODY BLUES	54	1991
KEYS TO ASCENSION YES	48	1996
KEYS TO ASCENSION 2 YES	62	1997
KEYS TO THE WORLD RICHARD ASHCROFT	2	2006
KICK INXS	9	1987
THE KICK INSIDE KATE BUSH	3	1978
KICK IT – THE DEF JAM SAMPLER VOLUME 1 VARIOUS ARTISTS (DEF JAM)	19	1987
KICK UP THE FIRE AND LET THE FLAMES BREAK LOOSE COOPER TEMPLE CLAUSE	5	2003
KICKING AGAINST THE PRICKS NICK CAVE & THE BAD SEEDS	89	1986
KID A RADIOHEAD	1	2000
KIDOLOGY GLAMMA KID	66	2000
THE KIDS ARE ALRIGHT (OST) WHO	26	1979
THE KIDS FROM FAME KIDS FROM FAME	1	1982
THE KIDS FROM FAME AGAIN KIDS FROM FAME	2	1982
THE KIDS FROM FAME LIVE KIDS FROM FAME	8	1983
THE KIDS FROM FAME SING FOR YOU KIDS FROM FAME	28	1983
THE KIDS FROM FAME SONGS KIDS FROM FAME	14	1983
KIKI DEE KIKI DEE	24	1977
KILIMANJARO TEARDROP EXPLODES	24	1980
KILL AT WILL ICE CUBE	66	1991
KILL BILL VOLUME 1 FILM SOUNDTRACK	6	2003
KILL BILL VOLUME 2 FILM SOUNDTRACK	13	2004
KILL TO GET CRIMSON MARK KNOPFLER	9	2007
KILL UNCLE MORRISSEY	8	1991
KILLER ALICE COOPER	27	1972
KILLER JOE LITTLE JIMMY OSMOND	20	1973
KILLER ON THE RAMPAGE EDDY GRANT	7	1982
KILLER WATTS VARIOUS ARTISTS (CBS)	27	1980
KILLERS IRON MAIDEN	12	1981
KILLERS KISS	42	1982
THE KILLING FIELDS (OST) MIKE OLDFIELD	97	1984
KILLING JOKE KILLING JOKE	39	1980
KILLING MACHINE JUDAS PRIEST	32	1978
KILLING ME SOFTLY ROBERTA FLACK	40	1973
KILLING PURITANS ARMAND VAN HELDEN	38	2000
KILLING TIME TINA COUSINS	50	1999
KILN HOUSE FLEETWOOD MAC	39	1970
KILROY WAS HERE STYX	67	1983
KIM APPLEBY KIM APPLEBY	23	1990
KIM WILDE KIM WILDE	3	1981
KIMONO MY HOUSE SPARKS	4	1974
KIND OF BLUE MILES DAVIS	63	2001
A KIND OF HUSH CARPENTERS	3	1976
A KIND OF MAGIC QUEEN	1	1986
KINDA KINKS KINKS	3	1965
KINDA LATIN CLIFF RICHARD	9	1966
THE KING TEENAGE FANCLUB	53	1991
KING BELLY	6	1995
THE KING ELVIS PRESLEY	1	2007
THE KING AND I FILM SOUNDTRACK	1	1956
THE KING AND I (ORIGINAL STUDIO CAST RECORDING) STAGE CAST RECORDING	57	1992
KING AND QUEEN OTIS REDDING & CARLA THOMAS	18	1967
KING COTTON FIVEPENNY PIECE	9	1976
KING CREOLE (OST) ELVIS PRESLEY	1	1958
KING FOR A DAY, FOOL FOR A LIFETIME FAITH NO MORE	5	1995
KING KONG (ORIGINAL SOUTH AFRICAN STAGE CAST SOUNDTRACK) STAGE CAST RECORDING	12	1961
KING OF AMERICA COSTELLO SHOW	11	1986
KING OF CARDS TOM McRAE	72	2007
KING OF FOOLS DELIRIOUS?	13	1997
KING OF HEARTS ROY ORBISON	23	1992
KING OF POP MICHAEL JACKSON	3	2008
KING OF STAGE BOBBY BROWN	40	1989
KING OF THE BEACH CHRIS REA	26	2000

Title / Artist	Peak Position	Year of Release
KING OF THE ROAD BOXCAR WILLIE	5	1980
KING PUCK CHRISTY MOORE	66	1993
KING SIZE GUITAR BERT WEEDON	18	1960
KINGDOM COME KINGDOM COME	43	1988
KINGDOM COME JAY-Z	35	2006
KINGDOM OF MADNESS MAGNUM	58	1978
THE KINGS & QUEENS OF COUNTRY VARIOUS ARTISTS (SONY/BMG)	12	2005
KINGS OF ROCK 'N' ROLL VARIOUS ARTISTS (BMG)	11	2004
KINGS OF THE WILD FRONTIER ADAM & THE ANTS	1	1980
KING'S X KING'S X	46	1992
KINGSIZE BOO RADLEYS	62	1998
KINGSIZE FIVE	3	2001
KINKS KINKS	3	1964
KINKS GREATEST HITS – DEAD END STREET KINKS	96	1983
KINKS KONTROVERSY KINKS	9	1965
KIRI KIRI TE KANAWA	70	1988
KIRI SIDETRACKS – THE JAZZ ALBUM KIRI TE KANAWA	73	1992
KIRI! KIRI TE KANAWA	16	1994
KISH KASH BASEMENT JAXX	17	2003
KISS 100FM – SMOOTH GROOVES VARIOUS ARTISTS (POLYGRAM)	3	1997
KISS ANTHEMS VARIOUS ARTISTS (POLYGRAM)	2	1997
KISS ANTHEMS '97 – 2 VARIOUS ARTISTS (POLYGRAM)	6	1997
KISS ANTHEMS '98 VARIOUS ARTISTS (POLYGRAM)	8	1998
KISS CLUBLIFE VARIOUS ARTISTS (UNIVERSAL)	2	1999
KISS CLUBLIFE 2000 VARIOUS ARTISTS (UNIVERSAL)	6	1999
KISS CLUBLIFE 2001 VARIOUS ARTISTS (UNIVERSAL)	12	2001
KISS CLUBLIFE SUMMER 2000 VARIOUS ARTISTS (UNIVERSAL)	1	2000
KISS DOES FUNKY HOUSE VARIOUS ARTISTS (WONDERLAND)	18	2008
KISS GARAGE VARIOUS ARTISTS (POLYGRAM)	3	1998
KISS GARAGE PRESENT DJ LUCK & MC NEAT VARIOUS ARTISTS (UNIVERSAL)	3	2000
KISS HITLIST 2002 VARIOUS ARTISTS (UNIVERSAL)	4	2001
KISS HITLIST SUMMER 2002 VARIOUS ARTISTS (UNIVERSAL)	2	2002
KISS HITLIST SUMMER 2003 VARIOUS ARTISTS (UNIVERSAL)	8	2003
KISS HOUSE NATION VARIOUS ARTISTS (POLYGRAM)	1	1999
KISS HOUSE NATION 2000 VARIOUS ARTISTS (UNIVERSAL)	2	2000
KISS HOUSE NATION 2001 VARIOUS ARTISTS (UNIVERSAL)	8	2000
KISS IBIZA 2000 VARIOUS ARTISTS (UNIVERSAL)	1	2000
KISS IBIZA '99 VARIOUS ARTISTS (UNIVERSAL)	1	1999
KISS IN IBIZA 2001 VARIOUS ARTISTS (UNIVERSAL)	6	2001
KISS IN IBIZA '95 VARIOUS ARTISTS (POLYGRAM)	3	1995
KISS IN IBIZA '96 VARIOUS ARTISTS (POLYGRAM)	1	1996
KISS IN IBIZA '97 VARIOUS ARTISTS (POLYGRAM)	1	1997
KISS IN IBIZA '98 VARIOUS ARTISTS (POLYGRAM)	2	1998
A KISS IN THE DREAMHOUSE SIOUXSIE & THE BANSHEES	11	1982
KISS JAMS VARIOUS ARTISTS (UNIVERSAL)	6	2004
KISS ME KISS ME KISS ME CURE	6	1987
KISS MIX '96 VARIOUS ARTISTS (POLYGRAM)	5	1996
KISS MIX '97 VARIOUS ARTISTS (POLYGRAM)	3	1997
KISS MIX '98 VARIOUS ARTISTS (POLYGRAM)	4	1998
KISS OF DEATH JADAKISS	65	2004
KISS OF DEATH MOTORHEAD	45	2006
KISS PRESENTS BOOTY HOUSE VARIOUS ARTISTS (MINISTRY OF SOUND)	6	2007
KISS PRESENTS HIP HOP CLASSICS VARIOUS ARTISTS (UNIVERSAL)	2	2003
KISS PRESENTS HOT JOINTS VARIOUS ARTISTS (UNIVERSAL)	7	2003
KISS PRESENTS HOT JOINTS 2 VARIOUS ARTISTS (UNIVERSAL)	17	2004
KISS PRESENTS LAYDEEZ WITH ATTITUDE VARIOUS ARTISTS (UNIVERSAL)	13	2004
KISS PRESENTS R&B CLASSICS VARIOUS ARTISTS (UNIVERSAL)	6	2004
KISS PRESENTS R&B COLLABORATIONS VARIOUS ARTISTS (UNIVERSAL)	1	2003
KISS PRESENTS THE HIP HOP COLLECTION VARIOUS ARTISTS (UNIVERSAL)	2	2004
KISS PRESENTS THE MIXTAPE VARIOUS ARTISTS (WARNER BROTHERS)	9	2008
KISS PRESENTS THE R&B COLLECTION VARIOUS ARTISTS (UNIVERSAL)	3	2005
KISS SMOOTH GROOVES 2000 VARIOUS ARTISTS (UNIVERSAL)	3	2000
KISS SMOOTH GROOVES 2001 VARIOUS ARTISTS (UNIVERSAL)	2	2001
KISS SMOOTH GROOVES 2002 VARIOUS ARTISTS (UNIVERSAL)	10	2002
KISS SMOOTH GROOVES '98 VARIOUS ARTISTS (POLYGRAM)	2	1998
KISS SMOOTH GROOVES '99 VARIOUS ARTISTS (POLYGRAM)	3	1999
KISS SMOOTH GROOVES SUMMER 2001 VARIOUS ARTISTS (UNIVERSAL)	7	2001
KISS SMOOTH GROOVES – SUMMER '99 VARIOUS ARTISTS (UNIVERSAL)	7	1999
KISS SMOOTH R&B VARIOUS ARTISTS (UNIVERSAL)	1	2004
KISS THE LIPS OF LIFE BRILLIANT	83	1986
KISS THE SKY TATYANA ALI	41	1999
KISS THIS SEX PISTOLS	10	1992
KISS UK GARAGE – MIXED BY KARL BROWN VARIOUS ARTISTS (UNIVERSAL)	3	2000
KISSIN' COUSINS (OST) ELVIS PRESLEY	5	1964
KISSING TO BE CLEVER CULTURE CLUB	5	1982
KISSTORY VARIOUS ARTISTS (UNIVERSAL)	1	2002
KISSTORY IBIZA CLASSIC VARIOUS ARTISTS (UNIVERSAL)	13	2002
KISSTORY URBAN CLASSICS VARIOUS ARTISTS (UNIVERSAL)	7	2003
KITE KIRSTY MacCOLL	34	1989
KLUBHOPPIN' VARIOUS ARTISTS (GLOBAL TELEVISION)	6	1997
KNEBWORTH – THE ALBUM VARIOUS ARTISTS (POLYDOR)	1	1990
KNIFE AZTEC CAMERA	14	1984
KNOCK ON WOOD EDDIE FLOYD	36	1967
KNOCKED OUT LOADED BOB DYLAN	35	1986
KNOW YOUR ENEMY MANIC STREET PREACHERS	2	2001
KNOWING ME, KNOWING YOU 3 ALAN PARTRIDGE	41	1995
KNOWLE WEST BOY TRICKY	63	2008
KNUCKLE SANDWICH VARIOUS ARTISTS (EMI)	19	1979
KOHYEPT – LIVE IN LENINGRAD BILLY JOEL	92	1987
KOJAK VARIETY ELVIS COSTELLO	21	1995
KOKOPELLI KOSHEEN	7	2003
KONGOS JOHN KONGOS	29	1972
KONK KOOKS	1	2008
KONVICTED AKON	16	2006
KOO KOO DEBBIE HARRY	6	1981
KOOL LOVE KOOL & THE GANG	50	1990
KOOL-AID BIG AUDIO DYNAMITE II	55	1990
KREUZ KONTROL KREUZ	48	1995
KT3 – KAOS THEORY 3 VARIOUS ARTISTS (TELSTAR)	1	1992
KYLIE MINOGUE KYLIE MINOGUE	4	1994
KYLIE! – THE ALBUM KYLIE MINOGUE	1	1988
KYLIE'S GREATEST HITS KYLIE MINOGUE	1	1992

L

Title / Artist	Peak Position	Year of Release
L STEVE HILLAGE	10	1976
L KEVIN GODLEY & LOL CRÈME	47	1978
L IS FOR LOVER AL JARREAU	45	1986
L.A. FOLIE STRANGLERS	11	1981
L.A. GUNS L.A. GUNS	73	1988
L.A. IS MY LADY FRANK SINATRA WITH THE QUINCY JONES ORCHESTRA	41	1984
L.A. WOMAN DOORS	28	1971
L.A.M.F. HEARTBREAKERS	55	1977
LA (LIGHT ALBUM) BEACH BOYS	32	1979
LA BAMBA (OST) LOS LOBOS	24	1987
LA CARRETERA JULIO IGLESIAS	6	1995
LA FREEWAY VARIOUS ARTISTS (DINO)	6	1991
LA LUNA SARAH BRIGHTMAN	37	2001
LA PASSION CHRIS REA	43	1996
LA RADIOLINA MANU CHAO	41	2007
LA VERITE CLASSIX NOUVEAUX	44	1982
LABCABINCALIFORNIA PHARCYDE	46	1996
LABOUR OF LOVE UB40	1	1983
LABOUR OF LOVE II UB40	3	1989
LABOUR OF LOVE III UB40	8	1998
LABOUR OF LOVE – VOLUMES I AND II UB40	5	1994
LABOUR OF LOVE – VOLUMES I, II & III UB40	7	2003
LABOUR OF LUST NICK LOWE	43	1979
LABOURS ON LOVE – THE BEST OF HUE AND CRY HUE & CRY	27	1993
LABYRINTH (OST) TREVOR JONES	38	1986
LACE AND WHISKY ALICE COOPER	33	1977
THE LADDER YES	36	1999
LADIES & GENTLEMEN – THE BEST OF GEORGE MICHAEL GEORGE MICHAEL	1	1998
LADIES & GENTLEMEN WE ARE FLOATING IN SPACE SPIRITUALIZED	4	1997
LADIES NIGHT ATOMIC KITTEN	5	2003
LADIES OF THE CANYON JONI MITCHELL	8	1970
LADY KENNY ROGERS	40	1981
LADY DAY – THE VERY BEST OF BILLIE HOLIDAY BILLIE HOLIDAY	63	1997
LADY SAMANTHA ELTON JOHN	56	1980
LADY SINGS THE BLUES DIANA ROSS	50	1973
THE LADY SINGS THE BLUES VARIOUS ARTISTS (PURE MUSIC)	9	1994
LADY SINGS THE BLUES VARIOUS ARTISTS (VIRGIN)	8	2002
LADY SINGS THE BLUES – NIGHT & DAY VARIOUS ARTISTS (VIRGIN)	11	2002
LADY SOUL ARETHA FRANKLIN	25	1968
LADYHAWKE LADYHAWKE	47	2008
LADYKILLERS VARIOUS ARTISTS (POLYGRAM)	3	1996
LADYKILLERS 2 VARIOUS ARTISTS (POLYGRAM)	15	1997
LADY'S BRIDGE RICHARD HAWLEY	6	2007
LAID JAMES	3	1993
THE LAMB LIES DOWN ON BROADWAY GENESIS	10	1974
LAMBADA VARIOUS ARTISTS (CBS)	15	1989
LAMENT ULTRAVOX	8	1984

Title / Artist	Peak Position	Year of Release
LAND COMSAT ANGELS	91	1983
LAND OF HOPE AND GLORY G.U.S. (FOOTWEAR) BAND & THE MORRISTON ORPHEUS CHOIR	54	1970
LAND OF MY FATHERS VARIOUS ARTISTS (UNIVERSAL)	1	1999
LANDING ON WATER NEIL YOUNG	52	1986
LANDMARKS CLANNAD	34	1998
THE LANGUAGE OF LIFE EVERYTHING BUT THE GIRL	10	1990
LANGUAGE SEX VIOLENCE OTHER? STEREOPHONICS	1	2005
LARGER THAN LIFE JODY WATLEY	39	1989
LARKS' TONGUES IN ASPIC KING CRIMSON	20	1973
THE LA'S LA'S	30	1990
LAS VEGAS LEGENDS VARIOUS ARTISTS (VIRGIN)	7	2003
LASER LOVE AFTER THE FIRE	57	1979
LASHED EUPHORIA VARIOUS ARTISTS (MINISTRY OF SOUND)	5	2006
THE LAST ACTION HERO FILM SOUNDTRACK	16	1993
THE LAST BROADCAST DOVES	1	2002
THE LAST CALL ANTI-PASTI	31	1981
LAST CHOIR STANDING VARIOUS ARTISTS (WARNER BROTHERS)	10	2008
THE LAST COMMAND W.A.S.P.	48	1985
THE LAST DANCE VARIOUS ARTISTS (MOTOWN)	1	1980
THE LAST DANCE STEPS	57	2002
THE LAST DOG AND PONY SHOW BOB MOULD	58	1998
LAST FOREVER JAMES LAST	88	1981
LAST GOON SHOW OF ALL GOONS	8	1972
THE LAST IN LINE DIO	4	1984
LAST NIGHT MOBY	28	2008
LAST NIGHT AT THE PROMS COLIN DAVIS CONDUCTING THE BBC SYMPHONY ORCHESTRA, SINGERS & CHORUS	36	1969
LAST OF THE INDEPENDENTS PRETENDERS	8	1994
THE LAST RECORD ALBUM LITTLE FEAT	36	1975
LAST SPLASH BREEDERS	5	1993
THE LAST TEMPTATION ALICE COOPER	6	1994
THE LAST TEMPTATION JA RULE	14	2002
THE LAST TEMPTATION OF REID LARD	69	1990
LAST THE WHOLE NIGHT LONG JAMES LAST	2	1979
LAST TIME I SAW HIM DIANA ROSS	41	1974
THE LAST TOUR ON EARTH MARILYN MANSON	61	1999
LAST TRAIN TO LHASA BANCO DE GAIA	31	1995
THE LAST WALTZ ENGELBERT HUMPERDINCK	3	1967
THE LAST WALTZ FILM SOUNDTRACK	39	1978
THE LAST WALTZ DANIEL O'DONNELL	46	1990
LATE NIGHT GRANDE HOTEL NANCI GRIFFITH	40	1991
LATE NIGHT LOVE VARIOUS ARTISTS (BMG)	8	2003
THE LATE NIGHT MIX VARIOUS ARTISTS (UNIVERSAL)	15	2000
LATE NIGHT MOODS VARIOUS ARTISTS (VIRGIN)	8	2004
LATE NIGHT SAX AFTER DARK	18	1996
LATE NIGHT SESSIONS VARIOUS ARTISTS (MINISTRY OF SOUND)	9	2003
LATE ORCHESTRATION KANYE WEST	59	2006
LATE REGISTRATION KANYE WEST	2	2005
LATE SEPTEMBER DEEPEST BLUE	22	2004
LATER LIVE WITH JOOLS HOLLAND VARIOUS ARTISTS (WARNER BROTHERS)	4	2008
LATERALUS TOOL	16	2001
LATIN A LA LEE PEGGY LEE	8	1960
LATIN FEVER VARIOUS ARTISTS (UNIVERSAL)	3	2000
LATIN LEGENDS VARIOUS ARTISTS (TELSTAR)	12	2003
THE LATINO MIX VARIOUS ARTISTS (UNIVERSAL)	7	2005
LATTER DAYS – THE BEST OF – VOLUME 2 LED ZEPPELIN	40	2000
LAUGH TERRY HALL	50	1997
LAUGHING AT THE PIECES DOCTOR & THE MEDICS	25	1986
LAUGHING ON JUDGEMENT DAY THUNDER	2	1992
LAUGHING STOCK TALK TALK	26	1991
LAUGHTER IAN DURY & THE BLOCKHEADS	48	1980
LAUGHTER AND LUST JOE JACKSON	41	1991
THE LAUGHTER AND TEARS COLLECTION VARIOUS ARTISTS (WARNER BROTHERS)	19	1983
LAUGHTER AND TEARS – THE BEST OF NEIL SEDAKA TODAY NEIL SEDAKA	2	1976
LAUGHTER IN THE RAIN NEIL SEDAKA	17	1974
LAUNDRY SERVICE SHAKIRA	2	2002
LAURENT GARNIER – LABORATOIRE MIX VARIOUS ARTISTS (REACT)	16	1996
THE LAW LAW	61	1991
LAWYERS IN LOVE JACKSON BROWNE	37	1983
LAX THE GAME	9	2008
LAZER GUIDED MELODIES SPIRITUALIZED	27	1992
LAZY 86-88 PRIMITIVES	73	1989
LAZY TOWN – THE ALBUM TELEVISION AND RADIO COMPILATION	8	2006
LAZY TOWN – THE NEW ALBUM TELEVISION AND RADIO COMPILATION	12	2007
LCD SOUNDSYSTEM LCD SOUNDSYSTEM	20	2005
LE ROI EST MORT, VIVE LE ROI! ENIGMA	12	1996
THE LEAD AND HOW TO SWING IT TOM JONES	55	1994
LEAD SAILS PAPER ANCHOR ATREYU	61	2007
LEADERS OF THE FREE WORLD ELBOW	12	2005
LEADERS OF THE PACK VARIOUS ARTISTS (POLYGRAM)	9	1993
LEADERS OF THE PACK – 60'S GIRLS VARIOUS ARTISTS (UNIVERSAL)	5	2004
LEAN INTO IT MR. BIG	28	1991
LEARNING TO CRAWL PRETENDERS	11	1984
THE LEAST WE CAN DO IS WAVE TO EACH OTHER VAN DE GRAAF GENERATOR	47	1970
LEATHER & LACE VARIOUS ARTISTS (SONY/BMG)	9	2005
LEATHER AND LACE VARIOUS ARTISTS (DINO)	3	1990
LEATHER AND LACE – THE SECOND CHAPTER VARIOUS ARTISTS (DINO)	14	1990
LEATHER JACKETS ELTON JOHN	24	1986
LEAVE HOME RAMONES	45	1977
LEAVE THE BEST TO LAST JAMES LAST	11	1985
LED ZEPPELIN LED ZEPPELIN	6	1969
LED ZEPPELIN (BOX SET) LED ZEPPELIN	48	1990
LED ZEPPELIN 2 LED ZEPPELIN	1	1969
LED ZEPPELIN 3 LED ZEPPELIN	1	1970
LED ZEPPELIN BOXED SET II LED ZEPPELIN	56	1993
LEE MEAD LEE MEAD	16	2007
LEE RYAN LEE RYAN	6	2005
LEFT HOPE OF THE STATES	50	2006
LEFT ABOVE THE CLOUDS JOSH WINK	43	1996
LEFT OF THE MIDDLE NATALIE IMBRUGLIA	5	1997
LEFTISM LEFTFIELD	3	1995
LEFTOVER WINE MELANIE	22	1971
LEGACY – THE GREATEST HITS COLLECTION BOYZ II MEN	2	2002
LEGAL DRUG MONEY LOST BOYZ	64	1996
LEGALIZE IT PETER TOSH	54	1976
LEGEND BOB MARLEY & THE WAILERS	39	2007
THE LEGEND – THE ESSENTIAL COLLECTION JOE COCKER	4	1992
LEGEND (MUSIC FROM ROBIN OF SHERWOOD) CLANNAD	15	1984
THE LEGEND OF BILLIE HOLIDAY BILLIE HOLIDAY	60	1985
THE LEGEND OF BOBBY DARIN – HIS GREATEST HITS BOBBY DARIN	39	1985
THE LEGEND OF MARIO LANZA MARIO LANZA	29	1981
LEGEND OF THE GLASS MOUNTAIN RON GOODWIN & HIS ORCHESTRA	49	1970
LEGEND – THE BEST OF BOB MARLEY AND THE WAILERS BOB MARLEY & THE WAILERS	1	1984
LEGEND: THE BEST OF WILLIE NELSON WILLIE NELSON	16	2008
THE LEGENDARY DON McLEAN	71	2007
THE LEGENDARY BIG BANDS VARIOUS ARTISTS (RONCO)	24	1980
THE LEGENDARY JOE BLOGGS ALBUM VARIOUS ARTISTS (HIT LABEL)	3	1993
THE LEGENDARY JOE BLOGGS ALBUM 2 VARIOUS ARTISTS (HIT LABEL)	15	1993
A LEGENDARY PERFORMER GLENN MILLER & HIS ORCHESTRA	41	1976
A LEGENDARY PERFORMER VOLUME 2 GLENN MILLER & HIS ORCHESTRA	53	1976
A LEGENDARY PERFORMER VOLUME 3 ELVIS PRESLEY	43	1979
A LEGENDARY PERFORMER VOLUME 4 ELVIS PRESLEY	91	1983
THE LEGENDARY ROY ORBISON ROY ORBISON	1	1988
LEGENDS AND HEROES VARIOUS ARTISTS (STYLUS)	6	1989
LEGENDS OF SOUL – A WHOLE STACK OF SOUL VARIOUS ARTISTS (TELSTAR)	15	1991
LEISURE BLUR	7	1991
LEISURE NOISE GAY DAD	14	1999
LEMON POPSICLE FILM SOUNDTRACK	42	1979
THE LEMONHEADS LEMONHEADS	56	2006
THE LENA MARTELL COLLECTION LENA MARTELL	12	1978
LENA'S MUSIC ALBUM LENA MARTELL	5	1979
LENNON LEGEND – THE VERY BEST OF JOHN LENNON JOHN LENNON	4	1997
LENNON-McCARTNEY SONGBOOK KEELY SMITH	12	1965
LENNY LENNY KRAVITZ	55	2001
LEO SAYER LEO SAYER	15	1978
LEON RUSSELL AND THE SHELTER PEOPLE LEON RUSSELL	29	1971
LEONARD BERNSTEIN'S WEST SIDE STORY (ORIGINAL STUDIO CAST RECORDING) STAGE CAST RECORDING	33	1993
LES MISERABLES STAGE CAST RECORDING	72	1986
LES MISERABLES – 10TH ANNIVERSARY CONCERT STAGE CAST RECORDING	32	1996
LESLEY GARRETT LESLEY GARRETT	34	1998
THE LESLEY GARRETT ALBUM LESLEY GARRETT	25	1994
LESSONS TO BE LEARNED GABRIELLA CILMI	8	2008
LEST WE FORGET – THE BEST OF MARILYN MANSON	4	2004
LET GO AVRIL LAVIGNE	1	2002
LET IT BE BEATLES	1	1970
LET IT BE ME JASON DONOVAN	28	2008
LET IT BE – NAKED BEATLES	7	2003
LET IT BEE VOICE OF THE BEEHIVE	13	1988
LET IT BLEED ROLLING STONES	1	1969
LET IT COME DOWN SPIRITUALIZED	3	2001
LET IT GO WILL YOUNG	2	2008
LET IT RAIN TRACY CHAPMAN	36	2002
LET IT RIDE SHED SEVEN	9	1998
LET LOOSE LET LOOSE	20	1994
LET LOVE IN NICK CAVE & THE BAD SEEDS	12	1994
LET LOVE IN GOO GOO DOLLS	58	2006
LET LOVE RULE LENNY KRAVITZ	56	1990
LET ME COME OVER BUFFALO TOM	49	1992
LET ME TRY AGAIN TAMMY JONES	38	1975

Title / Artist	Peak Position	Year of Release
LET ME UP (I'VE HAD ENOUGH) TOM PETTY & HEARTBREAKERS	59	1987
LET NO ONE LIVE RENT FREE IN YOUR HEAD NICOLETTE	36	1996
LET THE MUSIC PLAY BARRY WHITE	22	1976
LET THE MUSIC PLAY SHANNON	52	1984
LET THE MUSIC PLAY – 80'S GROOVE VARIOUS ARTISTS (COLUMBIA)	18	2001
LET THE MUSIC SCRATCH VARIOUS ARTISTS (STREET SOUNDS)	91	1984
LET THE RECORD SPIN SCREEN II	36	1994
LET THE RHYTHM HIT 'EM ERIC B & RAKIM	58	1990
LET THEM EAT BINGO BEATS INTERNATIONAL	17	1990
LET THERE BE LOVE ENGELBERT HUMPERDINCK	67	2005
LET THERE BE ROCK AC/DC	17	1977
LET US PLAY! COLDCUT	33	1997
LET YOUR DIM LIGHT SHINE SOUL ASYLUM	22	1995
LET YOURSELF GO SYBIL	92	1987
LETHAL INJECTION ICE CUBE	52	1993
LET'S BOOGIE SHAKIN' STEVENS	59	1987
LET'S BOTTLE BOHEMIA THRILLS	9	2004
LET'S DANCE DAVID BOWIE	1	1983
LET'S DANCE – SOUND OF THE SIXTIES PART 1 VARIOUS ARTISTS (OLD GOLD)	18	1990
LET'S DANCE TO THE HITS OF THE 30'S AND 40'S NEW WORLD THEATRE ORCHESTRA	16	1960
LET'S FACE IT MIGHTY MIGHTY BOSSTONES	40	1998
LET'S FACE THE MUSIC SHIRLEY BASSEY WITH THE NELSON RIDDLE ORCHESTRA	12	1962
LET'S GET BACK TOGETHER – THE LOVE SONGS BILLY OCEAN	69	2003
LET'S GET IT ON MARVIN GAYE	39	1973
LET'S GET IT STARTED MC HAMMER	46	1991
LET'S GET KILLED DAVID HOLMES	34	1997
LET'S GET SERIOUS JERMAINE JACKSON	22	1980
LET'S GO DISCO VARIOUS ARTISTS (EMI)	12	1993
LET'S GO GIRLS VARIOUS ARTISTS (UNIVERSAL)	3	2004
LET'S GO ROUND AGAIN – THE BEST OF AWB AVERAGE WHITE BAND	38	1994
LET'S GO TO IT KYLIE MINOGUE	15	1991
LET'S GROOVE VARIOUS ARTISTS (DMG TV)	4	2003
LET'S GROOVE AGAIN VARIOUS ARTISTS (SONY)	8	2003
LET'S HAVE ANOTHER PARTY MRS. MILLS	23	1969
LET'S HEAR IT FOR THE GIRLS VARIOUS ARTISTS (STYLUS)	17	1986
LET'S HEAR IT FOR THE GIRLS VARIOUS ARTISTS (POLYGRAM)	8	1995
LET'S HEAR IT FOR THE GIRLS VARIOUS ARTISTS (EMI)	6	2006
LET'S MAKE THIS PRECIOUS – THE BEST OF DEXYS MIDNIGHT RUNNERS	75	2003
LET'S PUSH IT NIGHTCRAWLERS	14	1995
LET'S PUT IT ALL TOGETHER STYLISTICS	26	1974
LET'S RUMBLE LOVE/HATE	24	1993
LET'S STICK TOGETHER BRYAN FERRY	19	1976
LET'S TALK ABOUT LOVE VARIOUS ARTISTS (DINO)	3	1992
LET'S TALK ABOUT LOVE CELINE DION	1	1997
LET'S THINK ABOUT LIVING BOB LUMAN	18	1961
LETTERS FROM THE UNDERGROUND LEVELLERS	24	2008
LETTIN' LOOSE HEAVY PETTIN'	55	1983
THE LETTING GO BONNIE PRINCE BILLY	70	2006
LEVEL 42 LEVEL 42	20	1981
LEVEL BEST LEVEL 42	5	1989
LEVELLERS LEVELLERS	2	1993
LEVELLING THE LAND LEVELLERS	14	1991
LEVITATION HAWKWIND	21	1980
THE LEXICON OF LOVE ABC	1	1982
LIBERATION TRANSMISSION LOSTPROPHETS	1	2006
LIBERATOR ORCHESTRAL MANOEUVRES IN THE DARK	14	1993
LIBERTAD VELVET REVOLVER	6	2007
THE LIBERTINES LIBERTINES	1	2004
LIBERTY DURAN DURAN	8	1990
LIBRA JULIO IGLESIAS	61	1985
LICENCE TO KILL FILM SOUNDTRACK	17	1989
LICENSE TO ILL BEASTIE BOYS	7	1987
THE LICK – BEST OF VARIOUS ARTISTS (UNIVERSAL)	12	2003
LICK IT UP KISS	7	1983
LICK MY DECALS OFF BABY CAPTAIN BEEFHEART & HIS MAGIC BAND	20	1971
THE LICK – PRESENTED BY TREVOR NELSON VARIOUS ARTISTS (DEF SOUL)	3	2001
THE LICK – TREVOR NELSON VARIOUS ARTISTS (UNIVERSAL)	4	2002
LICKIN' ON BOTH SIDES MIS-TEEQ	3	2001
LIE BACK AND ENJOY IT JUICY LUCY	53	1970
LIEBLING ANDREAS JOHNSON	46	2000
LIEGE AND LIEF FAIRPORT CONVENTION	17	1970
LIES FOR THE LIARS USED	39	2007
LIFE NEIL YOUNG & CRAZY HORSE	71	1987
LIFE INSPIRAL CARPETS	2	1990
LIFE CARDIGANS	51	1995
LIFE SIMPLY RED	1	1995
LIFE RICKY MARTIN	40	2005
LIFE AFTER DEATH NOTORIOUS B.I.G.	23	1997
LIFE & LOVE – HIS 20 GREATEST SONGS DEMIS ROUSSOS	36	1978
LIFE FOR RENT DIDO	1	2003
LIFE GOES ON SASH!	5	1998
LIFE GOES ON DONELL JONES	62	2002
LIFE IN A DAY SIMPLE MINDS	30	1979
LIFE IN CARTOON MOTION MIKA	1	2007
LIFE IN MONO EMMA BUNTON	65	2006
A LIFE IN MUSIC – ULTIMATE COLLECTION DOLLY PARTON	38	1997
LIFE IN SLOW MOTION DAVID GRAY	1	2005
LIFE IN THE FAST LANE VARIOUS ARTISTS (TELSTAR)	10	1987
LIFE IN THE JUNGLE/LIVE AT ABBEY ROAD SHADOWS	24	1982
LIFE IS A DANCE – THE REMIX PROJECT CHAKA KHAN	14	1989
LIFE IS PEACHY KORN	32	1996
LIFE – LIVE THIN LIZZY	29	1983
LIFE MODEL BLUE AEROPLANES	59	1994
A LIFE OF SURPRISES – THE BEST OF PREFAB SPROUT PREFAB SPROUT	3	1992
LIFE ON MARS TELEVISION AND RADIO COMPILATION	11	2007
LIFE ON OTHER PLANETS SUPERGRASS	9	2002
LIFE ON THE LINE EDDIE & THE HOT RODS	27	1977
LIFE ON THE MURDER SCENE MY CHEMICAL ROMANCE	53	2006
LIFE ON THE WIRE MORRISSEY MULLEN	47	1982
THE LIFE PURSUIT BELLE & SEBASTIAN	8	2006
LIFE STORY SHADOWS	7	2004
LIFE THRU A LENS ROBBIE WILLIAMS	1	1997
A LIFE WITH BRIAN FLOWERED UP	23	1991
LIFE WITH YOU PROCLAIMERS	13	2007
LIFE WON'T WAIT RANCID	32	1998
LIFEBLOOD MANIC STREET PREACHERS	13	2004
LIFEFORMS FUTURE SOUND OF LONDON	6	1994
LIFELINES A-HA	67	2002
LIFE'S A RIOT WITH SPY VS SPY BILLY BRAGG	30	1984
LIFE'S HARD AND THEN YOU DIE IT'S IMMATERIAL	62	1986
LIFE'S RICH PAGEANT R.E.M.	43	1986
LIFE'S TOO GOOD SUGARCUBES	14	1988
A LIFETIME OF ROMANCE VARIOUS ARTISTS (WARNER BROTHERS)	12	2005
LIFT THE LID JOOLS HOLLAND & HIS R&B ORCHESTRA	50	1997
LIFT YOUR SKINNY FISTS LIKE ANTENNAS TO GODSPEED YOU BLACK EMPEROR!	66	2000
LIGHT AT THE END OF THE TUNNEL DAMNED	87	1987
LIGHT AT THE END OF THE WORLD ERASURE	29	2007
LIGHT GRENADES INCUBUS	52	2006
LIGHT UP THE NIGHT BROTHERS JOHNSON	22	1980
THE LIGHT USER SYNDROME FALL	54	1996
LIGHT YEARS KYLIE MINOGUE	2	2000
LIGHT YEARS – THE VERY BEST OF ELECTRIC LIGHT ORCHESTRA ELECTRIC LIGHT ORCHESTRA	60	1997
LIGHTS AND SOUNDS YELLOWCARD	59	2006
LIGHTS OUT UFO	54	1977
LIGHTS...CAMERA...REVOLUTION SUICIDAL TENDENCIES	59	1990
LIKE A PRAYER MADONNA	1	1989
LIKE A ROCK BOB SEGER & THE SILVER BULLET BAND	35	1986
LIKE A VIRGIN MADONNA	1	1984
LIKE GANGBUSTERS JOBOXERS	18	1983
LIKE THE DESERTS MISS THE RAIN EVERYTHING BUT THE GIRL	58	2002
LIKE YOU DO...THE BEST OF LIGHTNING SEEDS LIGHTNING SEEDS	5	1997
LIL' CHRIS LIL' CHRIS	54	2006
LILAC TIME JUNE BRONHILL & THOMAS ROUND	17	1960
LILLIE SOUTH BANK ORCHESTRA CONDUCTED BY JOSEPH MOROVITZ & LAURIE HOLLOWAY	47	1978
LILLO LILLO THOMAS	43	1987
LILY WAS HERE DAVID A STEWART	35	1990
LIMBO THROWING MUSES	36	1996
LINDISFARNE LIVE LINDISFARNE	25	1973
LINDY'S PARTY BOLSHOI	100	1987
LINE UP GRAHAM BONNET	62	1981
LINGALONGAMAX MAX BYGRAVES	39	1978
LINGER FICKEN' GOOD REVOLTING COCKS	39	1993
THE LION AND THE COBRA SINEAD O'CONNOR	27	1988
THE LION KING FILM SOUNDTRACK	4	1994
THE LION KING SING-ALONG VARIOUS ARTISTS (PICKWICK)	16	1994
LIONEL RICHIE LIONEL RICHIE	9	1982
LIONHEART KATE BUSH	6	1978
LIONS BLACK CROWES	37	2001
LIPSTICK ON YOUR COLLAR – 28 ORIGINAL HITS OF THE 50S (TELEVISION SOUNDTRACK) TELEVISION AND RADIO COMPILATION	2	1993
LIPSTICK POWDER AND PAINT SHAKIN' STEVENS	37	1985
LIPSTICK TRACES – A SECRET HISTORY OF MANIC STREET PREACHERS	11	2003
LIQUID ACROBAT AS REGARDS THE AIR INCREDIBLE STRING BAND	46	1971
LIQUID GOLD LIQUID GOLD	34	1980
LIQUID SKIN GOMEZ	2	1999
LIQUID SWORDS GENIUS/GZA	73	1995
LIQUIDIZER JESUS JONES	31	1989
LISA LISA AND CULT JAM WITH FULL FORCE LISA LISA & CULT JAM WITH FULL FORCE	96	1985
LISA STANSFIELD LISA STANSFIELD	2	1997
LISTEN A FLOCK OF SEAGULLS	16	1983
LISTEN URBAN SPECIES	43	1994
LISTEN LIKE THIEVES INXS	48	1986
LISTEN TO BILLY J. KRAMER BILLY J. KRAMER WITH THE DAKOTAS	11	1963
LISTEN TO CLIFF CLIFF RICHARD & THE SHADOWS	2	1961

Title / Artist	Peak Position	Year of Release
LISTEN TO THE RADIO DON WILLIAMS	69	1982
LISTEN WITHOUT PREJUDICE VOLUME 1 GEORGE MICHAEL	1	1990
A LITTLE AIN'T ENOUGH DAVID LEE ROTH	4	1991
A LITTLE BIT MORE DR. HOOK	5	1976
A LITTLE BIT OF MAMBO LOU BEGA	50	1999
A LITTLE BIT OF THIS, A LITTLE BIT OF THAT D-MOB	46	1989
LITTLE BLACK NUMBERS KATHRYN WILLIAMS	70	2001
A LITTLE BLUES IN YOUR SOUL VARIOUS ARTISTS (WARNER BROTHERS)	5	1998
LITTLE CREATURES TALKING HEADS	10	1985
LITTLE DEATH PETE & THE PIRATES	71	2008
A LITTLE DEEPER MS DYNAMITE	10	2002
LITTLE DREAMER PETER GREEN	34	1980
LITTLE DREAMER BETH ROWLEY	6	2008
LITTLE EARTHQUAKES TORI AMOS	14	1992
LITTLE HONEY LUCINDA WILLIAMS	51	2008
LITTLE KIX MANSUN	12	2000
A LITTLE LIGHT MUSIC JETHRO TULL	34	1992
LITTLE LIGHTS KATE RUSBY	75	2001
LITTLE LOVE AFFAIRS NANCI GRIFFITH	78	1988
LITTLE MISS DYNAMITE – BRENDA LEE BRENDA LEE	15	1980
A LITTLE NIGHT MUSIC RICHARD CLAYDERMAN	52	1988
LITTLE OF THE PAST LITTLE ANGELS	20	1994
A LITTLE PEACE NICOLE	85	1982
LITTLE QUEEN HEART	34	1977
A LITTLE SOUL IN YOUR HEART LULU	29	2005
A LITTLE SOUTH OF SANITY AEROSMITH	36	1998
LITTLE SPARROW DOLLY PARTON	30	2001
A LITTLE SPICE LOOSE ENDS	46	1984
A LITTLE TOUCH OF SCHMILSSON IN THE NIGHT NILSSON	20	1973
LITTLE TOWN FLIRT DEL SHANNON	15	1963
LITTLE VILLAGE LITTLE VILLAGE	23	1992
LITTLE VOICE SARA BAREILLES	9	2008
THE LITTLE WILLIES LITTLE WILLIES	41	2006
LIVE BOB MARLEY & THE WAILERS	38	1975
LIVE MANHATTAN TRANSFER	4	1978
LIVE EAGLES	24	1980
LIVE SAD CAFÉ	37	1981
LIVE EUROPEANS	100	1984
LIVE THUNDER	35	1998
LIVE 2PAC	67	2004
LIVE R.E.M.	12	2007
LIVE AVENGED SEVENFOLD	42	2008
LIVE & KICKING – VIEWERS CHOICE PART 1 (TELEVISION COMPILATION) TELEVISION AND RADIO COMPILATION	12	1999
LIVE & SWINGING – THE ULTIMATE RAT PACK VARIOUS ARTISTS (REPRISE)	14	2003
LIVE (X CERT) STRANGLERS	7	1979
LIVE 1975 – THE ROLLING THUNDER REVUE BOB DYLAN	69	2002
LIVE 1979 HAWKWIND	15	1980
LIVE 1980 – 1986 JOE JACKSON	66	1988
LIVE 2003 COLDPLAY	73	2008
LIVE 4 EVER VARIOUS ARTISTS (WARNER BROTHERS)	11	1998
LIVE 93 ORB	23	1993
LIVE A PARIS CELINE DION	53	1996
LIVE – A TICKET FOR EVERYONE BUSTED	11	2004
LIVE ACOUSTIC AT THE JAM HOUSE OCEAN COLOUR SCENE	73	2006
LIVE AFTER DEATH IRON MAIDEN	2	1985
LIVE ALIVE QUO STATUS QUO	37	1992
LIVE AND DANGEROUS THIN LIZZY	2	1978
LIVE AND DIRECT ASWAD	57	1983
LIVE AND HEAVY VARIOUS ARTISTS (NEMS)	100	1981
LIVE AND LEARN ELKIE BROOKS	34	1979
LIVE AND LET LIVE 10 C.C.	14	1977
LIVE AND MORE DONNA SUMMER	16	1978
LIVE AND UNCENSORED MILLIE JACKSON	81	1985
LIVE AT BRIXTON ACADEMY BRIAN MAY BAND	20	1994
LIVE AT CAESAR'S PALACE TOM JONES	27	1971
LIVE AT DONNINGTON IRON MAIDEN	23	1993
LIVE AT EARLS COURT MORRISSEY	18	2005
LIVE AT KNEBWORTH ROBBIE WILLIAMS	2	2003
LIVE AT LEEDS WHO	3	1970
LIVE' AT LONDON'S TALK OF THE TOWN DIANA ROSS & THE SUPREMES	6	1968
LIVE AT MASSEY HALL 1971 NEIL YOUNG	30	2007
LIVE AT SHEA STADIUM CLASH	31	2008
LIVE AT THE ALBANY EMPIRE FLYING PICKETS	48	1983
LIVE AT THE BBC BEATLES	1	1994
LIVE AT THE BBC DIRE STRAITS	71	1995
LIVE AT THE BBC FLEETWOOD MAC	48	1995
LIVE AT THE BLOOMSBURY THEATRE 12.3.95 TINDERSTICKS	32	1995
LIVE AT THE BRIXTON ACADEMY FAITH NO MORE	20	1991
LIVE AT THE GRAND OPERA HOUSE BELFAST VAN MORRISON	47	1984
LIVE AT THE GREEK JIMMY PAGE & THE BLACK CROWES	39	2000
LIVE AT THE HEART OF THE CITY WHITESNAKE	5	1980
LIVE AT THE HOLLYWOOD BOWL DOORS	51	1987
LIVE AT THE LONDON PALLADIUM BING CROSBY	9	1977
LIVE AT THE LYCEUM BOB MARLEY & THE WAILERS	68	1981
LIVE AT THE PALLADIUM CARPENTERS	28	1977
LIVE AT THE RIVIERA LAS VEGAS ENGELBERT HUMPERDINCK	45	1972
LIVE AT THE ROYAL ALBERT HALL WET WET WET WITH THE WREN ORCHESTRA	10	1993
LIVE AT THE ROYAL ALBERT HALL JOE LONGTHORNE	57	1994
LIVE AT THE ROYAL ALBERT HALL BOB DYLAN	19	1998
LIVE AT THE ROYAL ALBERT HALL SPIRITUALIZED	38	1998
LIVE AT THE ROYAL ALBERT HALL WHO	72	2003
LIVE AT THE ROYAL FESTIVAL HALL NEIL SEDAKA	48	1974
LIVE AT THE SOCIAL – VOLUME 1 VARIOUS ARTISTS (HEAVENLY)	19	1996
LIVE AT THE TALK OF THE TOWN TOM JONES	6	1967
LIVE AT THE TALK OF THE TOWN SEEKERS	2	1968
LIVE AT THE TALK OF THE TOWN SHIRLEY BASSEY	38	1970
LIVE AT TREORCHY MAX BOYCE	21	1975
LIVE AT WEMBLEY QUEEN	2	1992
LIVE' AT WEMBLEY MEAT LOAF	60	1987
LIVE AT WEMBLEY '86 QUEEN	38	2003
LIVE AT WEMBLEY STADIUM '86 QUEEN	24	2005
LIVE BABY LIVE INXS	8	1991
LIVE BURSTING OUT JETHRO TULL	17	1978
LIVE CREAM CREAM	4	1970
LIVE CREAM VOLUME 2 CREAM	15	1972
LIVE DATES II WISHBONE ASH	40	1980
LIVE – ERA '87-'93 GUNS N' ROSES	45	1999
LIVE EVIL BLACK SABBATH	13	1983
LIVE FAST, DIE FAST WOLFSBANE	48	1989
LIVE FOREVER – THE BEST OF BRITPOP VARIOUS ARTISTS (VIRGIN)	7	2003
LIVE FROM DAKOTA STEREOPHONICS	13	2006
LIVE FROM EARTH PAT BENATAR	60	1983
LIVE – FROM NOWHERE IN PARTICULAR JOE BONAMASSA	45	2008
THE LIVE GREATEST HITS ELVIS PRESLEY	50	2001
LIVE HERALD STEVE HILLAGE	54	1979
LIVE IN AUSTRALIA ELTON JOHN & THE MELBOURNE SYMPHONY ORCHESTRA	43	1987
LIVE IN BELFAST ROWAN ATKINSON	44	1981
LIVE IN CONCERT 2006 BARBRA STREISAND	25	2007
LIVE IN DUBLIN BRUCE SPRINGSTEEN & SESSIONS	21	2007
LIVE IN EUROPE TINA TURNER	8	1988
LIVE IN GDANSK DAVID GILMOUR	10	2008
LIVE IN HYDE PARK RED HOT CHILI PEPPERS	1	2004
LIVE IN LONDON JOHN DENVER	2	1976
LIVE IN LOS ANGELES MAZE FEATURING FRANKIE BEVERLY	70	1986
LIVE IN MANCHESTER WONDER STUFF	74	1995
LIVE IN NEW YORK CITY BRUCE SPRINGSTEEN & THE E. STREET BAND	12	2001
LIVE IN TEXAS LINKIN PARK	47	2003
LIVE IN THE CITY OF LIGHT SIMPLE MINDS	1	1987
LIVE IN THE RAW W.A.S.P.	23	1987
LIVE IN THE UK HELLOWEEN	26	1989
LIVE IN YUGOSLAVIA ANTI-NOWHERE LEAGUE	88	1983
LIVE IT LIKE YOU LOVE IT CHARLATANS	40	2002
LIVE JAM JAM	28	1993
LIVE KILLERS QUEEN	3	1979
LIVE LAUGH LOVE DANIEL O'DONNELL	27	2001
LIVE LICKS ROLLING STONES	38	2004
LIVE MAGIC QUEEN	3	1986
LIVE MCMXCIII VELVET UNDERGROUND	70	1993
LIVE ON BROADWAY BARRY MANILOW	19	1990
LIVE – ON TWO LEGS PEARL JAM	68	1998
LIVE ONE NIGHT ONLY BEE GEES	4	1998
LIVE OVER EUROPE 2007 GENESIS	51	2007
LIVE RUST NEIL YOUNG & CRAZY HORSE	55	1979
LIVE SANTA MONICA '72 DAVID BOWIE	61	2008
LIVE SEEDS NICK CAVE & THE BAD SEEDS	67	1993
LIVE SHIT – BINGE AND PURGE METALLICA	54	1993
LIVE TASTE TASTE	14	1971
LIVE – THE WAY WE WALK VOLUME 1: THE SHORTS GENESIS	3	1992
LIVE – THE WAY WE WALK VOLUME 2: THE LONGS GENESIS	1	1993
LIVE THROUGH THIS HOLE	13	1994
LIVE TWICE DARIUS	36	2004
LIVE WOOD PAUL WELLER	13	1994
LIVE YOUR LIFE BE FREE BELINDA CARLISLE	7	1991
LIVE! SHAKATAK	82	1985
LIVE! POLICE	25	1995
LIVE! IN EUROPE RORY GALLAGHER	9	1972
LIVE! IN THE AIR AGE BE-BOP DELUXE	10	1977
LIVE! LIVE! LIVE! BRYAN ADAMS	17	1994
LIVE, STOLEN MOMENTS – THE LADY SINGS THE BLUES DIANA ROSS	45	1993
LIVE/1975-1985 BRUCE SPRINGSTEEN & THE E. STREET BAND	4	1986
LIVE: RIGHT HERE, RIGHT NOW VAN HALEN	24	1993
LIVEANDIRECT ADAMSKI	47	1989
A LIVELY MIND PAUL OAKENFOLD	57	2006
LIVELY UP YOURSELF BOB MARLEY	75	2001
LIVERPOOL FRANKIE GOES TO HOLLYWOOD	5	1986
LIVES IN THE BALANCE JACKSON BROWNE	36	1986
LIVIN IN THE CITY FUN LOVIN' CRIMINALS	57	2005
LIVING A DREAM KATHERINE JENKINS	4	2005
LIVING ALL ALONE PHYLLIS HYMAN	97	1986
LIVING CLASSICS VARIOUS ARTISTS (DEUTSCHE GRAMMOPHON)	7	1992
LIVING EYES BEE GEES	73	1981
LIVING FOR THE WEEKEND VARIOUS ARTISTS (UNIVERSAL)	9	2008
LIVING IN A BOX LIVING IN A BOX	25	1987
LIVING IN A FANTASY LEO SAYER	15	1980
LIVING IN OZ RICK SPRINGFIELD	41	1984
LIVING IN THE MATERIAL WORLD GEORGE HARRISON	2	1973

Title / Artist	Peak Position	Year of Release
LIVING IN THE PAST JETHRO TULL	8	1972
LIVING IN THE PRESENT FUTURE EAGLE-EYE CHERRY	12	2000
LIVING IN THE USA LINDA RONSTADT	39	1978
LIVING INSIDE YOUR LOVE GEORGE BENSON	24	1979
LIVING LEGENDS EVERLY BROTHERS	12	1977
LIVING MY LIFE GRACE JONES	15	1982
LIVING ON THE FAULT LINE DOOBIE BROTHERS	25	1977
LIVING ORNAMENTS 1979 GARY NUMAN	47	1981
LIVING ORNAMENTS 1979-1980 GARY NUMAN	2	1981
LIVING ORNAMENTS 1980 GARY NUMAN	39	1981
LIVING PROOF CHER	46	2001
LIVING WITH WAR NEIL YOUNG	14	2006
THE LIVING YEARS MIKE & THE MECHANICS	2	1988
LIZA WITH A 'Z' LIZA MINNELLI	9	1973
LIZARD KING CRIMSON	29	1971
LLOYD COLE LLOYD COLE	11	1990
LLOYD WEBBER PLAYS LLOYD WEBBER JULIAN LLOYD WEBBER WITH THE ROYAL PHILHARMONIC ORCHESTRA	15	1990
LOAD METALLICA	1	1996
LOADED VARIOUS ARTISTS (EMI)	6	1993
LOADED LOCK IN VARIOUS ARTISTS (V2)	20	1997
LOADS – THE BEST OF THE HAPPY MONDAYS HAPPY MONDAYS	41	1995
LOCAL HERO (OST) MARK KNOPFLER	14	1983
LOC'ED AFTER DARK TONE LOC	22	1989
LOCK UP THE WOLVES DIO	28	1990
LOCK, STOCK & TWO SMOKING BARRELS FILM SOUNDTRACK	7	1998
LOCKED IN WISHBONE ASH	36	1976
LOCO FUN LOVIN' CRIMINALS	5	2001
LODGER DAVID BOWIE	4	1979
LOGIC WILL BREAK YOUR HEART STILLS	66	2004
LONDON D-INFLUENCE	56	1997
LONDON 0 HULL 4 HOUSEMARTINS	3	1986
LONDON CALLING CLASH	9	1979
LONDON CALLING – 25TH ANNIVERSARY CLASH	26	2004
LONDON TOWN WINGS	4	1978
LONDON TOWN KANO	14	2007
LONDON UNDERSOUND NITIN SAWHNEY	68	2008
LONDON WARSAW NEW YORK BASIA	68	1990
LONE JUSTICE LONE JUSTICE	49	1985
THE LONE PIPER MUNROS FEATURING DAVID METHREN	46	1998
THE LONE RANGER SUGGS	14	1995
LONE STAR LONE STAR	47	1976
LONELY AND BLUE ROY ORBISON	15	1963
LONELY IS AN EYESORE VARIOUS ARTISTS (4 AD)	53	1987
THE LONESOME JUBILEE JOHN COUGAR MELLENCAMP	31	1987
LONG AFTER DARK TOM PETTY & HEARTBREAKERS	45	1982
THE LONG BLACK VEIL CHIEFTAINS	17	1995
LONG COLD WINTER CINDERELLA	30	1988
LONG DISTANCE – THE BEST OF RUNRIG RUNRIG	13	1996
LONG DISTANCE VOYAGER MOODY BLUES	7	1981
LONG GONE BEFORE DAYLIGHT CARDIGANS	47	2003
LONG JOHN SILVER JEFFERSON AIRPLANE	30	1972
LONG LIVE LOVE OLIVIA NEWTON-JOHN	40	1974
LONG LIVE ROCK 'N' ROLL RAINBOW	7	1978
LONG MAY YOU RUN STILLS-YOUNG BAND	12	1976
LONG MISTY DAYS ROBIN TROWER	31	1976
LONG PLAYER FACES	31	1971
THE LONG ROAD NICKELBACK	5	2003
THE LONG ROAD BACK PETER ANDRE	44	2004
THE LONG ROAD HOME JOHN FOGERTY	32	2006
LONG ROAD OUT OF EDEN EAGLES	1	2007
THE LONG RUN EAGLES	4	1979
LONGING IN THEIR HEARTS BONNIE RAITT	26	1994
LONNIE LONNIE DONEGAN	3	1958
LONNIE DONEGAN SHOWCASE LONNIE DONEGAN	2	1956
THE LOOK SHALAMAR	7	1983
LOOK BETH NIELSEN CHAPMAN	63	2004
LOOK AT ME NOW BERNIE MARSDEN	71	1981
LOOK AT US SONNY & CHER	7	1965
LOOK AT YOURSELF URIAH HEEP	39	1971
LOOK HEAR? 10 C.C.	35	1980
LOOK HOW LONG LOOSE ENDS	19	1990
LOOK INTO THE EYEBALL DAVID BYRNE	58	2001
THE LOOK OF LOVE VARIOUS ARTISTS (POLYGRAM)	6	1996
THE LOOK OF LOVE DIANA KRALL	23	2001
THE LOOK OF LOVE DUSTY SPRINGFIELD	25	2004
THE LOOK OF LOVE – THE BEST OF BURT BACHARACH VARIOUS ARTISTS (WARNER BROTHERS)	4	2001
LOOK OF LOVE – THE VERY BEST OF ABC ABC	69	2001
LOOK SHARP JOE JACKSON	40	1979
LOOK SHARP! ROXETTE	4	1989
LOOK TO YOUR HEART FRANK SINATRA	5	1959
LOOKIN' IN SAVOY BROWN	50	1970
LOOKIN' THROUGH THE WINDOWS JACKSON FIVE	16	1972
LOOKIN' THRU THE EYES OF LOVE GENE PITNEY	15	1965
LOOKING BACK JOHN MAYALL	14	1969
LOOKING EAST JACKSON BROWNE	47	1996
LOOKING FORWARD CROSBY, STILL, NASH & YOUNG	54	1999
THE LOOKS OR THE LIFESTYLE POP WILL EAT ITSELF	15	1992
LOONEE TUNES BAD MANNERS	36	1980
LOOSE NELLY FURTADO	4	2006
LOOSE SCREW PRETENDERS	55	2003
LORD OF THE RINGS BO HANSSON	34	1972
THE LORD OF THE RINGS – OST HOWARD SHORE	10	2002
LORD OF THE RINGS – RETURN OF THE KING (OST) HOWARD SHORE	34	2003
LORD OF THE RINGS – THE TWO TOWERS (OST) HOWARD SHORE	28	2003
LORD UPMINSTER IAN DURY & THE BLOCKHEADS	53	1981
LORE CLANNAD	14	1996
LOSS MULL HISTORICAL SOCIETY	43	2001
LOST AND FOUND WILL SMITH	15	2005
LOST BOYS FLYING PICKETS	11	1984
THE LOST BOYS FILM SOUNDTRACK	1	1989
LOST HIGHWAY BON JOVI	2	2007
LOST HORIZON FILM SOUNDTRACK	36	1973
LOST HORIZONS LEMON JELLY	20	2002
LOST IN SPACE AIMEE MANN	72	2002
LOST PROPERTY VARIOUS ARTISTS (EMI)	12	1996
THE LOST RECORDINGS GLENN MILLER & HIS ORCHESTRA	22	1995
THE LOST RIOTS HOPE OF THE STATES	21	2004
LOST SIDES DOVES	50	2003
LOST SONGS 95-98 DAVID GRAY	7	2000
LOST SOULS DOVES	16	2000
LOST WITHOUT YOUR LOVE BREAD	17	1977
LOUD TIMO MAAS	41	2002
LOUD AND CLEAR SAMMY HAGAR	12	1980
LOUD 'N' PROUD NAZARETH	10	1973
LOUDER NOW TAKING BACK SUNDAY	18	2006
LOUDER THAN BOMBS SMITHS	38	1987
LOUDER THAN WORDS LIONEL RICHIE	11	1996
LOUDMOUTH – THE BEST OF THE BOOMTOWN RATS & BOB GELDOF BOOMTOWN RATS & BOB GELDOF	10	1994
LOUNGIN' VARIOUS ARTISTS (UNIVERSAL)	18	2002
LOVE AZTEC CAMERA	10	1987
LOVE VARIOUS ARTISTS (UNIVERSAL)	3	2002
LOVE BEATLES	3	2006
LOVE & AFFECTION VARIOUS ARTISTS (SONY BMG)	12	2008
LOVE & LIFE MARY J. BLIGE	8	2003
LOVE 2 DANCE VARIOUS ARTISTS (TELSTAR)	18	2000
LOVE – 39 ALL TIME LOVE CLASSICS VARIOUS ARTISTS (POLYGRAM)	1	1998
LOVE ACTUALLY FILM SOUNDTRACK	2	2003
THE LOVE ALBUM VARIOUS ARTISTS (K-TEL)	6	1980
THE LOVE ALBUM DORIS DAY	64	1994
THE LOVE ALBUM VARIOUS ARTISTS (VIRGIN)	1	1994
THE LOVE ALBUM WESTLIFE	1	2006
THE LOVE ALBUM – 16 CLASSIC LOVE SONGS VARIOUS ARTISTS (TELSTAR)	7	1985
THE LOVE ALBUM '88 VARIOUS ARTISTS (TELSTAR)	51	1988
THE LOVE ALBUM CLASSICS VARIOUS ARTISTS (VIRGIN)	2	2002
THE LOVE ALBUM II VARIOUS ARTISTS (VIRGIN)	2	1995
THE LOVE ALBUM III VARIOUS ARTISTS (VIRGIN)	2	1996
THE LOVE ALBUM IV VARIOUS ARTISTS (VIRGIN)	11	1997
LOVE ALWAYS K-CI & JOJO	51	1997
LOVE AND AFFECTION – CLASSICS (1975-83) JOAN ARMATRADING	24	2004
LOVE AND DANCING LEAGUE UNLIMITED ORCHESTRA	3	1982
LOVE AND KISSES DANNII MINOGUE	8	1991
LOVE AND KISSES FROM BROTHERHOOD OF MAN	20	1976
LOVE AND LIFE DEFINITION OF SOUND	38	1991
LOVE AND LIFE – THE VERY BEST OF DIANA ROSS	28	2001
LOVE AND OTHER DEMONS STRANGELOVE	44	1996
LOVE AND THE RUSSIAN WINTER SIMPLY RED	6	1999
LOVE AND THEFT BOB DYLAN	3	2001
LOVE ANDY ANDY WILLIAMS	1	1968
LOVE ANGEL MUSIC BABY GWEN STEFANI	4	2004
LOVE AT FIRST STING SCORPIONS	17	1984
LOVE AT THE GREEK NEIL DIAMOND	3	1977
LOVE AT THE MOVIES VARIOUS ARTISTS (TELSTAR)	6	1991
LOVE AT THE MOVIES JANE McDONALD	24	2001
LOVE AT THE MOVIES...THE ALBUM VARIOUS ARTISTS (EMI)	16	1996
LOVE BEACH EMERSON, LAKE & PALMER	48	1978
LOVE BITES BUZZCOCKS	13	1978
LOVE BITES & SCHOOL NITES VARIOUS ARTISTS (TELSTAR)	9	2004
LOVE BYRD DONALD BYRD	70	1981
LOVE CAN DO THAT ELAINE PAIGE	36	1991
LOVE CHANGES EVERYTHING – THE ESSENTIAL MICHAEL BALL	21	2004
LOVE CHILD DIANA ROSS & THE SUPREMES	8	1969
LOVE CLASSICS ROYAL PHILHARMONIC ORCHESTRA CONDUCTED BY NICK PORTLOCK	30	1983
THE LOVE COLLECTION MARVIN GAYE	44	2006
THE LOVE COLLECTION DIONNE WARWICK	27	2008
LOVE DELUXE SADE	10	1992
LOVE DRIVE SCORPIONS	36	1979
LOVE ELVIS ELVIS PRESLEY	8	2005
LOVE ETERNAL VARIOUS ARTISTS (MIRACLE)	5	1995
LOVE – ETERNAL LOVESONGS VARIOUS ARTISTS (UNIVERSAL)	1	2003

Title / Artist	Peak Position	Year of Release
LOVE FOR SALE BONEY M	60	1977
LOVE GAMES DRIFTERS	51	1975
LOVE HAS FOUND ITS WAY DENNIS BROWN	72	1982
LOVE HATE TRAGEDY PAPA ROACH	4	2002
LOVE HOUSE VARIOUS ARTISTS (K-TEL)	5	1989
LOVE HUNTER WHITESNAKE	29	1979
LOVE HURTS EVERLY BROTHERS	22	1982
LOVE HURTS ELAINE PAIGE	8	1985
LOVE HURTS CHER	1	1991
LOVE HURTS VARIOUS ARTISTS (WARNER BROTHERS)	4	2004
LOVE II SWING VARIOUS ARTISTS (TELSTAR)	10	1996
LOVE IN MOTION ICEHOUSE	64	1983
LOVE IN THE SIXTIES VARIOUS ARTISTS (DINO)	11	1993
LOVE IS KIM WILDE	21	1992
LOVE IS A NOW AND THEN THING ANTHONY NEWLEY	19	1960
LOVE IS FOR EVER BILLY OCEAN	7	1997
LOVE IS FOR SUCKERS TWISTED SISTER	57	1987
LOVE IS FOREVER CLIFF RICHARD & THE SHADOWS	19	1966
LOVE IS HELL RYAN ADAMS	68	2004
LOVE IS HELL PART 1 RYAN ADAMS	62	2003
LOVE IS HERE STARSAILOR	2	2001
LOVE IS RHYTHM VARIOUS ARTISTS (TELSTAR)	5	1993
LOVE IS TEASING SPINNERS	33	1972
LOVE IS – THE ALBUM VARIOUS ARTISTS (VIRGIN)	2	2004
LOVE IS THE LAW TOYAH	28	1983
LOVE IS THE THING NAT 'KING' COLE	1	1957
LOVE IS... VARIOUS ARTISTS (K-TEL)	10	1981
LOVE IT TO DEATH ALICE COOPER	28	1972
LOVE IT WHEN I FEEL LIKE THIS TWANG	3	2007
THE LOVE JUNK STORE ALICE BAND	55	2002
LOVE KRAFT SUPER FURRY ANIMALS	19	2005
LOVE LETTERS FROM ELVIS ELVIS PRESLEY	7	1971
A LOVE LIKE OURS BARBRA STREISAND	12	1999
LOVE MAKES NO SENSE ALEXANDER O'NEAL	14	1993
LOVE ME AGAIN RITA COOLIDGE	51	1978
LOVE ME FOR A REASON OSMONDS	13	1974
LOVE ME RIGHT ANGEL CITY	44	2005
LOVE ME TENDER JULIE ANDREWS	63	1983
LOVE METAL H.I.M.	55	2003
THE LOVE MOVEMENT A TRIBE CALLED QUEST	38	1998
LOVE MOVES KIM WILDE	37	1990
LOVE MUST BE THE REASON JAMES LAST	32	1972
LOVE NOT MONEY EVERYTHING BUT THE GIRL	10	1985
THE LOVE OF HOPELESS CAUSES NEW MODEL ARMY	22	1993
LOVE ON A SUMMER'S DAY VARIOUS ARTISTS (TELSTAR)	14	2000
LOVE ON FILM VARIOUS ARTISTS (TELSTAR)	17	1994
LOVE ON THE AIRWAYS GALLAGHER & LYLE	19	1977
LOVE OVER GOLD DIRE STRAITS	1	1982
LOVE OVER GOLD VARIOUS ARTISTS (TELSTAR)	2	1994
LOVE OVER GOLD 2 VARIOUS ARTISTS (TELSTAR)	19	1996
LOVE PAIN & THE WHOLE CRAZY THING KEITH URBAN	73	2006
LOVE SCENES CULT	4	1985
LOVE SCENES BEVERLEY CRAVEN	4	1993
LOVE SENSUALITY DEVOTION – GREATEST HITS ENIGMA	29	2001
LOVE SO STRONG VARIOUS ARTISTS (WARNER BROTHERS)	1	2002
LOVE SONGS BEATLES	7	1977
LOVE SONGS ELVIS PRESLEY	4	1979
LOVE SONGS CLIFF RICHARD	1	1981
LOVE SONGS NEIL DIAMOND	43	1981

Title / Artist	Peak Position	Year of Release
LOVE SONGS BARBRA STREISAND	1	1982
LOVE SONGS CHICAGO	42	1982
LOVE SONGS COMMODORES	5	1982
LOVE SONGS DIANA ROSS	5	1982
LOVE SONGS ELTON JOHN	4	1982
LOVE SONGS SHIRLEY BASSEY	48	1982
THE LOVE SONGS GEORGE BENSON	1	1985
LOVE SONGS DIANA ROSS & MICHAEL JACKSON	12	1987
THE LOVE SONGS RANDY CRAWFORD	27	1987
LOVE SONGS MARVIN GAYE & SMOKEY ROBINSON	69	1988
LOVE SONGS VARIOUS ARTISTS (TELSTAR)	18	1989
LOVE SONGS DIONNE WARWICK	6	1990
LOVE SONGS MARVIN GAYE	39	1990
LOVE SONGS CARPENTERS	47	1997
LOVE SONGS KENNY ROGERS	27	1997
THE LOVE SONGS CHRIS DE BURGH	8	1997
LOVE SONGS ABBA	51	1998
LOVE SONGS DANIEL O'DONNELL	9	1998
LOVE SONGS DR. HOOK	8	1999
LOVE SONGS LUCIANO PAVAROTTI	26	1999
LOVE SONGS VARIOUS ARTISTS (POLYGRAM)	1	1999
THE LOVE SONGS MARVIN GAYE	8	2000
LOVE SONGS ROY ORBISON	4	2001
LOVE SONGS DEAN MARTIN	24	2002
LOVE SONGS BARRY WHITE	21	2003
LOVE SONGS JULIO IGLESIAS	64	2003
LOVE SONGS NAT 'KING' COLE	20	2003
LOVE SONGS PHIL COLLINS	7	2004
LOVE SONGS BEE GEES	51	2005
LOVE SONGS ELLA FITZGERALD	61	2005
LOVE SONGS VARIOUS ARTISTS (VIRGIN)	6	2005
LOVE SONGS – 16 CLASSIC HITS STEVIE WONDER	20	1984
LOVE SONGS – 16 CLASSIC LOVE SONGS VARIOUS ARTISTS (WARWICK)	47	1978
LOVE SONGS – 16 CLASSIC LOVE SONGS VARIOUS ARTISTS (TELSTAR)	20	1984
THE LOVE SONGS ALBUM VARIOUS ARTISTS (K-TEL)	28	1982
THE LOVE SONGS ALBUM MICHAEL CRAWFORD	64	1994
THE LOVE SONGS ALBUM VARIOUS ARTISTS (UNIVERSAL)	1	2000
THE LOVE SONGS OF ANDREW LLOYD WEBBER RICHARD CLAYDERMAN	18	1989
THE LOVE SONGS OF BURT BACHARACH VARIOUS ARTISTS (UNIVERSAL)	5	1999
LOVE SONGS OF THE 70S DONNY OSMOND	7	2007
LOVE SONGS – THE ULTIMATE LOVE COLLECTION VARIOUS ARTISTS (UNIVERSAL)	1	2005
LOVE SONGS – THE VERY BEST OF FOSTER AND ALLEN VOLUME 2 FOSTER & ALLEN	92	1987
LOVE SONGS TO MAKE YOU FEEL GOOD VARIOUS ARTISTS (TELSTAR)	10	2004
LOVE STORIES DON WILLIAMS	22	1983
LOVE STORY ANDY WILLIAMS	11	1971
LOVE STORY FILM SOUNDTRACK	10	1971
LOVE STORY JOHNNY MATHIS	27	1971
LOVE STORY RAY CONNIFF	34	1971
LOVE STORY LLOYD COLE	27	1995
A LOVE STORY MICHAEL BALL	41	2003
LOVE SUPREME DIANA ROSS & THE SUPREMES	10	1989
LOVE SUPREME VARIOUS ARTISTS (DINO)	4	1991
LOVE TATTOO IMELDA MAY	58	2008
THE LOVE THAT WHIRLS (DIARY OF A THINKING HEART) BILL NELSON	28	1982
LOVE – THE ALBUM CLIFF RICHARD	13	2007
LOVE – THE ESSENTIAL AL GREEN	18	2002

Title / Artist	Peak Position	Year of Release
LOVE – THE ULTIMATE COLLECTION VARIOUS ARTISTS (UNIVERSAL)	15	2008
LOVE THEME FROM 'THE GODFATHER' ANDY WILLIAMS	11	1972
LOVE THIS IS MY SONG JAMES LAST	32	1967
LOVE TO LOVE YOU BABY DONNA SUMMER	16	1976
LOVE TRACKS GLORIA GAYNOR	31	1979
LOVE TRAIN – THE SOUND OF PHILADELPHIA VARIOUS ARTISTS (SONY)	18	1998
LOVE TRAVELS KATHY MATTEA	65	1997
LOVE TRAVELS AT ILLEGAL SPEEDS GRAHAM COXON	24	2006
A LOVE TRILOGY DONNA SUMMER	41	1976
LOVE UNCHAINED ENGELBERT HUMPERDINCK	16	1995
LOVE UNLIMITED – THE SOULFUL SOUND OF LOVE VARIOUS ARTISTS (TELSTAR)	9	2001
LOVE WARS WOMACK & WOMACK	45	1984
LOVE WITH A REGGAE RHYTHM VARIOUS ARTISTS (VISION)	18	1995
LOVE YOU LIVE ROLLING STONES	3	1977
LOVE YOU TILL TUESDAY DAVID BOWIE	53	1984
LOVE ZONE BILLY OCEAN	2	1986
LOVE, DEVOTION, SURRENDER CARLOS SANTANA & MAHAVISHNU JOHN McLAUGHLIN	7	1973
LOVE, LIFE AND FEELINGS SHIRLEY BASSEY	13	1976
LOVE, WHITNEY WHITNEY HOUSTON	22	2002
LOVE/HATE NINE BLACK ALPS	69	2007
LOVEBOAT ERASURE	45	2000
LOVEBOX GROOVE ARMADA	41	2002
LOVED UP VARIOUS ARTISTS (INSPIRED)	8	2000
LOVEGOD SOUP DRAGONS	7	1990
LOVELESS MY BLOODY VALENTINE	24	1991
LOVELIFE LUSH	8	1996
LOVELINES CARPENTERS	73	1990
LOVELY PRIMITIVES	6	1988
LOVELY DAY VARIOUS ARTISTS (TELSTAR)	16	2004
LOVELY DAY – THE VERY BEST OF BILL WITHERS	35	2006
THE LOVER IN ME SHEENA EASTON	30	1989
LOVERMAN VARIOUS ARTISTS (EMI)	17	1996
LOVERS VARIOUS ARTISTS (TELSTAR)	14	1986
THE LOVERS VARIOUS ARTISTS (K-TEL)	50	1988
LOVERS SLEEPY JACKSON	69	2003
LOVERS FOR LOVERS VOLUME 3 VARIOUS ARTISTS (BUSINESS)	18	1990
THE LOVERS GUIDE TO REGGAE VARIOUS ARTISTS (WARNER BROTHERS)	14	2005
LOVERS IN THE CITY TANITA TIKARAM	75	1995
LOVERS LIVE SADE	51	2002
LOVERS ONLY VARIOUS ARTISTS (RONCO)	12	1983
LOVERS ROCK SADE	18	2000
LOVE'S A PRIMA DONNA STEVE HARLEY & COCKNEY REBEL	28	1976
LOVES SONGS – THE VERY BEST OF RANDY CRAWFORD RANDY CRAWFORD	22	2000
LOVESCAPE NEIL DIAMOND	36	1991
LOVESEXY PRINCE	1	1988
LOVESONGS FOR UNDERDOGS TANYA DONELLY	36	1997
LOVIN' IT VARIOUS ARTISTS (INSPIRED)	3	2001
LOVIN' IT 2 VARIOUS ARTISTS (INSPIRED)	11	2001
LOVING YOU (OST) ELVIS PRESLEY	1	1957
LOW DAVID BOWIE	2	1977
THE LOW END THEORY A TRIBE CALLED QUEST	58	1991
LOW-LIFE NEW ORDER	7	1985
LOYAL TO THE GAME 2PAC	20	2004
LOYALTY TO LOYALTY COLD WAR KIDS	68	2008
LP REMBRANDTS	14	1995
LTJ BUKEM PRESENTS EARTH – VOLUME 1 VARIOUS ARTISTS (EARTH)	19	1996

	Peak Position	Year of Release
LTJ BUKEM PRESENTS EARTH – VOLUME TWO VARIOUS ARTISTS (GOOD LOOKING)	18	1997
LTJ BUKEM PRESENTS LOGICAL PROGRESSION VARIOUS ARTISTS (FFRR)	14	1996
LUCK OF THE DRAW BONNIE RAITT	38	1991
LUCKY SKIN	38	1996
LUCKY 13 SHADES OF VAL DOONICAN VAL DOONICAN	2	1964
LUCKY DAY SHAGGY	54	2002
LUCKY THIRTEEN NEIL YOUNG	69	1993
LUCKY TOWN BRUCE SPRINGSTEEN	2	1992
LULLABIES TO PARALYZE QUEENS OF THE STONE AGE	4	2005
LUMINOUS BASEMENT TOURISTS	75	1980
LUNATICO GOTAN PROJECT	66	2006
LUSH LIFE LINDA RONSTADT WITH THE NELSON RIDDLE ORCHESTRA	100	1985
LUST FOR LIFE IGGY POP	28	1977
LUSTRA ECHOBELLY	47	1997
LUTRICIA MCNEAL LUTRICIA McNEAL	16	1998
LUXEMBOURG BLUETONES	49	2003
THE LUXURY GAP HEAVEN 17	4	1983
LUXURY LINER EMMYLOU HARRIS	17	1977
LUXURY OF LIFE FIVE STAR	12	1985
LYTE FUNKIE ONES LYTE FUNKIE ONES	62	2000

M

	Peak Position	Year of Release
M!SSUNDAZTOOD P!NK	2	2002
M.U. THE BEST OF JETHRO TULL JETHRO TULL	44	1976
MA LENA ZAVARONI	8	1974
MA FLEUR CINEMATIC ORCHESTRA	44	2007
THE MAC BAND MAC BAND FEATURING THE McCAMPBELL BROTHERS	61	1988
MACALLA CLANNAD	33	1985
MACDONALD BROTHERS MACDONALD BROTHERS	18	2007
MACHINA/THE MACHINES OF GOD SMASHING PUMPKINS	7	2000
MACHINE STATIC-X	56	2001
MACHINE + SOUL GARY NUMAN	42	1992
MACHINE GUN ETIQUETTE DAMNED	31	1979
MACHINE HEAD DEEP PURPLE	1	1972
MACHISMO CAMEO	86	1988
MACK AND MABEL STAGE CAST RECORDING	38	1982
MAD DOGS AND ENGLISHMEN JOE COCKER	16	1970
MAD FOR IT VARIOUS ARTISTS (TELSTAR)	12	1996
MAD LOVE LINDA RONSTADT	65	1980
MAD NOT MAD MADNESS	16	1985
MAD ON HOUSE VOLUME 1 VARIOUS ARTISTS (NEEDLE)	81	1988
MAD SEASON BY MATCHBOX 20 MATCHBOX 20	31	2000
MAD SHADOWS MOTT THE HOOPLE	48	1970
MAD, BAD AND DANGEROUS TO KNOW DEAD OR ALIVE	27	1987
MADCAP LAUGHS SYD BARRETT	40	1970
MADE AGAIN MARILLION	37	1996
MADE IN AMERICA CARPENTERS	12	1981
MADE IN ENGLAND ELTON JOHN	3	1995
MADE IN HEAVEN QUEEN	1	1995
MADE IN JAPAN DEEP PURPLE	16	1973
MADE IN THE DARK HOT CHIP	4	2008
MADE IN THE SHADE ROLLING STONES	14	1975
MADE IT THROUGH THE RAIN GERARD KENNY	19	1979
MADE OF BRICKS KATE NASH	1	2007
MADE TO LOVE MAGIC NICK DRAKE	27	2004
MADMAN ACROSS THE WATER ELTON JOHN	41	1972
THE MADMAN'S RETURN SNAP!	8	1992
THE MADNESS MADNESS	65	1988
MADNESS 7 MADNESS	5	1981
MADNESS, MONEY AND MUSIC SHEENA EASTON	44	1982
MADONNA MADONNA	6	1984
MADSTOCK! MADNESS	22	1992
THE MAGAZINE RICKIE LEE JONES	40	1984
MAGGIE FOSTER & ALLEN	72	1983
MAGIC GILLAN	17	1982
MAGIC VARIOUS ARTISTS (UNIVERSAL)	11	2001
MAGIC BRUCE SPRINGSTEEN	1	2007
MAGIC AND LOSS LOU REED	6	1992
MAGIC AND MEDICINE CORAL	1	2003
MAGIC BULLETS MEGA CITY FOUR	57	1993
THE MAGIC FLUTE OF JAMES GALWAY JAMES GALWAY	43	1978
MAGIC FLY SPACE	11	1977
MAGIC HOTEL TOPLOADER	3	2002
MAGIC HOUR CAST	6	1999
MAGIC IN THE AIR LINDISFARNE	71	1978
THE MAGIC IS YOU SHIRLEY BASSEY	40	1979
MAGIC MOMENTS BRENDAN SHINE	62	1989
THE MAGIC NUMBERS MAGIC NUMBERS	7	2005
THE MAGIC OF BONEY M BONEY M	1	1980
THE MAGIC OF BONEY M BONEY M	48	2006
THE MAGIC OF CHRISTMAS GEORGE MITCHELL MINSTRELS	32	1970
THE MAGIC OF DEMIS ROUSSOS DEMIS ROUSSOS	29	1977
THE MAGIC OF DISNEY – 20 SUPERSTAR HITS VARIOUS ARTISTS (WALT DISNEY)	15	2002
THE MAGIC OF DORIS DAY DORIS DAY	20	2007
THE MAGIC OF FOSTER AND ALLEN (THEIR GREATEST HITS) FOSTER & ALLEN	29	1989
THE MAGIC OF INSPECTOR MORSE BARRINGTON PHELOUNG	62	2000
THE MAGIC OF NANA MOUSKOURI NANA MOUSKOURI	44	1988
MAGIC OF THE MINSTRELS GEORGE MITCHELL MINSTRELS	9	1965
THE MAGIC OF THE MOVIES DORIS DAY	63	1999
THE MAGIC OF THE MUSICALS MARTI WEBB & MARK RATTRAY	55	1992
THE MAGIC OF TORVILL AND DEAN VARIOUS ARTISTS (STYLUS)	35	1985
THE MAGIC OF VAL DOONICAN VAL DOONICAN	34	1970
THE MAGIC POSITION PATRICK WOLF	46	2007
MAGIC REGGAE VARIOUS ARTISTS (K-TEL)	9	1980
MAGIC SUMMER VARIOUS ARTISTS (WARNER BROTHERS)	9	2006
MAGIC – SUMMER FEELING 2003 VARIOUS ARTISTS (UNIVERSAL)	10	2003
MAGIC – THE ALBUM VARIOUS ARTISTS (WARNER BROTHERS)	11	2005
MAGIC – THE ALBUM 2007 VARIOUS ARTISTS (WARNER BROTHERS)	5	2007
MAGIC TIME VAN MORRISON	3	2005
THE MAGIC TOUCH OF ODYSSEY ODYSSEY	69	1982
MAGIC, MURDER AND THE WEATHER MAGAZINE	39	1981
MAGICAL MEMORIES FOR MUM VARIOUS ARTISTS (SONY/BMG)	7	2006
MAGICAL MYSTERY TOUR (IMPORT) BEATLES	31	1968
MAGICAL RING CLANNAD	26	1983
MAGICAL RING CLANNAD	91	1984
THE MAGICIAN'S BIRTHDAY URIAH HEEP	28	1972
MAGNET ROBIN GIBB	43	2003
MAGNETIC FIELDS JEAN-MICHEL JARRE	6	1981
MAGNIFICATION YES	71	2001
THE MAGNIFICENT SEVEN SUPREMES & THE FOUR TOPS	6	1971
THE MAGNIFICENT SEVENTH THUNDER	70	2005
MAGPIE STEPHEN FRETWELL	27	2005
MAIL ON SUNDAY FLO-RIDA	29	2008
THE MAIN INGREDIENT PETE ROCK & C.L. SMOOTH	69	1994
MAIN OFFENDER KEITH RICHARDS	45	1992
MAINSTREAM LLOYD COLE & THE COMMOTIONS	9	1987
MAIRE MAIRE BRENNAN	53	1992
MAKE ANOTHER WORLD IDLEWILD	24	2007
MAKE BELIEVE WEEZER	11	2005
MAKE IT BIG WHAM!	1	1984
MAKE IT EASY ON YOURSELF JOHNNY MATHIS	49	1972
MAKE IT GOOD A1	15	2002
MAKE IT LAST FOREVER KEITH SWEAT	41	1988
MAKE ME AN OFFER STAGE CAST RECORDING	18	1960
MAKE THE PARTY LAST JAMES LAST	3	1975
MAKE THE WORLD GO AWAY DONNY & MARIE OSMOND	30	1975
MAKE THIS YOUR OWN COOPER TEMPLE CLAUSE	33	2007
MAKE UP THE BREAKDOWN HOT HOT HEAT	35	2003
MAKE YOU SWEAT VARIOUS ARTISTS (TELSTAR)	4	1991
MAKE YOUR MOVE CAPTAIN & TENNILLE	33	1980
MAKIN' MAGIC PAT TRAVERS	40	1977
MAKING A GOOD THING BETTER OLIVIA NEWTON-JOHN	60	1977
MAKING BONES RED SNAPPER	59	1998
MAKING CONTACT UFO	32	1983
MAKING DENS MYSTERY JETS	32	2006
MAKING HISTORY LINTON KWESI JOHNSON	73	1984
MAKING LOVE AND MUSIC DR. HOOK	39	1977
MAKING MOVIES DIRE STRAITS	4	1980
MAKING TRACKS FIVEPENNY PIECE	37	1973
MAKING WAVES NOLANS	11	1980
MALACHI MALACHI CUSH	17	2003
MALADJUSTED MORRISSEY	8	1997
MALADROIT WEEZER	16	2002
MALPRACTICE DR. FEELGOOD	17	1975
MALPRACTICE REDMAN	57	2001
MAMA SAID LENNY KRAVITZ	8	1991
MAMA SAID KNOCK YOU OUT LL COOL J	49	1990
MAMAS AND PAPAS DELIVER MAMAS & THE PAPAS	4	1967
MAMBO SINUENDO RY COODER & MANUEL GALBAM	40	2003
MAMMA LUCIANO PAVAROTTI WITH THE HENRY MANCINI ORCHESTRA	96	1984
MAMMA MIA FILM SOUNDTRACK	1	2008
MAMMA MIA ORIGINAL CAST RECORDING	12	2008
MAMOUNA BRYAN FERRY	11	1994
THE MAN BARRY WHITE	46	1979
MAN NENEH CHERRY	16	1996
MAN ALIVE 4 OF US	64	1993
A MAN ALONE – THE WORDS AND MUSIC OF ROD MCKUEN FRANK SINATRA	18	1969
A MAN AND HIS MUSIC FRANK SINATRA	9	1966
THE MAN AND HIS MUSIC SAM COOKE	8	1986
A MAN AND A WOMAN FILM SOUNDTRACK	31	1967
THE MAN FROM UTOPIA FRANK ZAPPA	87	1983
MAN IN BLACK JOHNNY CASH	18	1971
THE MAN IN BLACK – DEFINITIVE COLLECTION JOHNNY CASH	15	1994
MAN IN BLACK – THE VERY BEST OF JOHNNY CASH	39	2002
MAN IN THE MACHINE ROYWORLD	52	2008
MAN LIKE I NATTY	21	2008
MAN OF COLOURS ICEHOUSE	93	1988
MAN ON THE LINE CHRIS DE BURGH	11	1984
MAN ON THE ROOF STEPHEN FRETWELL	44	2007
MAN TO MAN HOT CHOCOLATE	32	1976

Title / Artist	Peak Position	Year of Release
MAN VS MACHINE XZIBIT	43	2002
THE MAN WHO TRAVIS	1	1999
THE MAN WHO SOLD THE WORLD DAVID BOWIE	26	1972
THE MAN WITH THE GOLDEN FLUTE JAMES GALWAY	52	1978
A MAN WITHOUT LOVE ENGELBERT HUMPERDINCK	3	1968
MANASSAS STEPHEN STILLS' MANASSAS	30	1972
MANE ATTRACTION WHITE LION	31	1991
MANGE TOUT BLANCMANGE	8	1984
MANHATTAN TRANSFER MANHATTAN TRANSFER	49	1977
MANHATTANS MANHATTANS	37	1976
MANIC NIRVANA ROBERT PLANT	15	1990
MANIC POP THRILL THAT PETROL EMOTION	84	1986
MANIFESTO ROXY	7	1979
MANILOW BARRY MANILOW	40	1985
MANILOW MAGIC – THE BEST OF BARRY MANILOW BARRY MANILOW	3	1979
THE MAN-MACHINE KRAFTWERK	9	1978
MAN-MADE TEENAGE FANCLUB	34	2005
MANN MADE MANFRED MANN	7	1965
MANN MADE HITS MANFRED MANN	11	1966
MANNERS AND PHYSIQUE ADAM ANT	19	1990
MANTARAY SIOUXSIE	39	2007
MANTLE PIECES CLIFFORD T. WARD	42	1974
THE MANTOVANI GOLDEN COLLECTION MANTOVANI & HIS ORCHESTRA	9	1979
MANTOVANI MAGIC MANTOVANI & HIS ORCHESTRA	3	1966
MANTOVANI TODAY MANTOVANI & HIS ORCHESTRA	16	1970
MANTOVANI'S GOLDEN HITS MANTOVANI & HIS ORCHESTRA	10	1967
MANUMISSION – IBIZA CLASSICS COLLECTION VARIOUS ARTISTS (WARNER BROTHERS)	13	2006
MANUMISSION – THE MOVIE FILM SOUNDTRACK	17	1999
MANY HAPPY RETURNS – THE HITS GARY GLITTER	35	1992
THE MANY SIDES OF – THE GREATEST HITS DAVE EDMUNDS	38	2008
MARA RUNRIG	24	1995
MARATHON SANTANA	28	1979
MARAUDER MAGNUM	34	1980
MARAUDER BLACKFOOT	38	1981
MARC COHN MARC COHN	27	1991
MARCH OR DIE MOTORHEAD	60	1992
MARCHIN' ALREADY OCEAN COLOUR SCENE	1	1997
MARCY PLAYGROUND MARCY PLAYGROUND	61	1998
THE MARIA CALLAS COLLECTION MARIA CALLAS	50	1987
MARIA LAWSON MARIA LAWSON	41	2006
MARIA MCKEE MARIA McKEE	49	1989
MARIAH CAREY MARIAH CAREY	6	1990
MARIANNE FAITHFULL MARIANNE FAITHFULL	15	1965
MARILLION.COM MARILLION	53	1999
MARIO LANZA – THE ULTIMATE COLLECTION MARIO LANZA	13	1994
MARK HOLLIS MARK HOLLIS	53	1998
THE MARK II PURPLE SINGLES DEEP PURPLE	24	1979
MARK RATTRAY PERFORMS THE SONGS OF THE MUSICALS MARK RATTRAY	46	1990
THE MARK TOM & TRAVIS SHOW BLINK 182	69	2000
MARK'S KEYBOARD REPAIR MONEY MARK	35	1995
MAROON BARENAKED LADIES	64	2000
THE MARQUEE – 30 LEGENDARY YEARS VARIOUS ARTISTS (POLYDOR)	1	1989
MARQUEE METAL VARIOUS ARTISTS (MARQUEE)	5	1991
MARQUEE MOON TELEVISION	28	1977
MARRYING MAIDEN IT'S A BEAUTIFUL DAY	45	1970
MARS AUDIAC QUINTET STEREOLAB	16	1994
THE MARSHALL MATHERS LP EMINEM	1	2000
MARTHA WAINWRIGHT MARTHA WAINWRIGHT	63	2005
MARTIKA MARTIKA	11	1989
MARTIKA'S KITCHEN MARTIKA	15	1991
MARTIN GUERRE STAGE CAST RECORDING	58	1996
MARTY ROBBINS COLLECTION MARTY ROBBINS	5	1979
THE MARTYR MANTRAS JESUS LOVES YOU	60	1991
MARVIN AT THE MOVIES HANK MARVIN	17	2000
MARVIN, WELCH AND FARRAR HANK MARVIN, BRUCE WELCH & JOHN FARRAR	30	1971
MARY MARY J. BLIGE	5	1999
MARY JANES GIRLS MARY JANE GIRLS	51	1983
MARY O'HARA AT THE ROYAL FESTIVAL HALL MARY O'HARA	37	1978
MARY POPPINS FILM SOUNDTRACK	2	1965
MARY STAR OF THE SEA ZWAN	33	2003
THE MASH UP MIX 2006 VARIOUS ARTISTS (MINISTRY OF SOUND)	1	2006
THE MASH UP MIX 2007 VARIOUS ARTISTS (MINISTRY OF SOUND)	2	2007
THE MASH UP MIX 2008 VARIOUS ARTISTS (MINISTRY OF SOUND)	3	2008
THE MASH UP MIX – CUT UP BOYS VARIOUS ARTISTS (MINISTRY OF SOUND)	2	2005
THE MASH UP MIX – OLD SKOOL VARIOUS ARTISTS (MINISTRY OF SOUND)	3	2008
MASHED VARIOUS ARTISTS (EMI)	14	2007
MASK BAUHAUS	30	1981
MASK VANGELIS	69	1985
MASQUE MISSION	23	1992
MASQUERADE – MESSAGE TO THE STREET WYCLEF JEAN	30	2002
THE MASSACRE 50 CENT	1	2005
MASSIVE 4 VARIOUS ARTISTS (LONDON)	20	1990
MASSIVE – AN ALBUM OF REGGAE HITS VARIOUS ARTISTS (VIRGIN)	61	1985
MASSIVE DANCE VARIOUS ARTISTS (UNIVERSAL)	15	2006
MASSIVE DANCE 2001 VARIOUS ARTISTS (UNIVERSAL)	20	2000
MASSIVE DANCE HITS 2000 VARIOUS ARTISTS (UNIVERSAL)	11	1999
MASSIVE DANCE MIX 96 VARIOUS ARTISTS (TELSTAR)	9	1996
MASSIVE DANCE: 98 VARIOUS ARTISTS (WARNER BROTHERS)	8	1997
MASSIVE DANCE: 98 – VOLUME 2 VARIOUS ARTISTS (POLYGRAM)	2	1998
MASSIVE DANCE: 99 VARIOUS ARTISTS (POLYGRAM)	5	1998
MASSIVE DANCE: 99 – VOLUME TWO VARIOUS ARTISTS (POLYGRAM)	3	1999
MASSIVE HITS VARIOUS ARTISTS (TELSTAR)	2	1991
MASSIVE R&B VARIOUS ARTISTS (UNIVERSAL)	1	2005
MASSIVE R&B 4 VARIOUS ARTISTS (UNIVERSAL)	10	2006
MASSIVE R&B – SPRING COLLECTION 2006 VARIOUS ARTISTS (UNIVERSAL)	2	2006
MASSIVE R&B – SPRING COLLECTION 2007 VARIOUS ARTISTS (UNIVERSAL)	1	2007
MASSIVE R&B SPRING COLLECTION 2008 VARIOUS ARTISTS (UNIVERSAL)	3	2008
MASSIVE R&B – VOLUME 2 VARIOUS ARTISTS (UNIVERSAL)	2	2005
MASSIVE R&B – WINTER 2007 VARIOUS ARTISTS (UNIVERSAL)	3	2007
MASSIVE R&B – WINTER 2008 VARIOUS ARTISTS (UNIVERSAL)	1	2008
MASSIVE REGGAE VARIOUS ARTISTS (UNIVERSAL)	3	2008
MASSIVE WEEKEND VARIOUS ARTISTS (UNIVERSAL)	5	2008
MASTER AND EVERYONE BONNIE PRINCE BILLY	48	2003
MASTER OF PUPPETS METALLICA	41	1986
MASTER OF REALITY BLACK SABBATH	5	1971
MASTERPIECE TEMPTATIONS	28	1973
MASTERPIECES – THE ESSENTIAL FLUTE OF JAMES GALWAY JAMES GALWAY	30	1993
MASTERPIECES – THE VERY BEST OF SKY SKY	15	1984
THE MASTERPLAN OASIS	2	1998
MASTERS OF METAL VARIOUS ARTISTS (K-TEL)	38	1986
MASTERWORKS JEFF JARRATT & DON REEDMAN	39	1980
MATA LEAO BIOHAZARD	72	1996
MATACHIN BELLOWHEAD	73	2008
MATADOR (ORIGINAL STUDIO CAST RECORDING) STAGE CAST RECORDING	26	1987
MATCHBOX MATCHBOX	44	1980
MATHIS MAGIC JOHNNY MATHIS	59	1979
MATHS & ENGLISH DIZZEE RASCAL	7	2007
MATINEE JACK PENATE	7	2007
THE MATRIX FILM SOUNDTRACK	16	1999
THE MATRIX RELOADED FILM SOUNDTRACK	2	2003
MATT BIANCO MATT BIANCO	26	1986
A MATTER OF LIFE AND DEATH IRON MAIDEN	4	2006
MATTERS OF THE HEART TRACY CHAPMAN	19	1992
MATTHEW AND SON CAT STEVENS	7	1967
MAVERICK A STRIKE FINLEY QUAYE	3	1997
MAVERICKS MAVERICKS	65	2003
MAX POWER – MAX BASS VARIOUS ARTISTS (BREAK DOWN)	13	1996
MAX Q MAX Q	69	1989
MAX SPEED VARIOUS ARTISTS (VIRGIN)	8	2005
MAXI MAXI PRIEST	25	1987
MAXIMUM BASS VARIOUS ARTISTS (MINISTRY OF SOUND)	3	2005
MAXIMUM BASS 2 – THE NEXT LEVEL VARIOUS ARTISTS (MINISTRY OF SOUND)	4	2006
MAXIMUM BASS 2007 VARIOUS ARTISTS (MINISTRY OF SOUND)	5	2007
MAXIMUM DARKNESS MAN	25	1975
A MAXIMUM HIGH SHED SEVEN	8	1996
MAXIMUM JOY FRANKIE GOES TO HOLLYWOOD	54	2000
MAXIMUM RAVE VARIOUS ARTISTS (EMI)	2	1992
MAXIMUM SECURITY ALIEN SEX FIEND	100	1985
MAXIMUM SPEED VARIOUS ARTISTS (VIRGIN)	3	1998
MAXIMUM SPEED 99 VARIOUS ARTISTS (VIRGIN)	13	1999
MAXINQUAYE TRICKY	3	1995
MAXWELL'S URBAN HANG SUITE MAXWELL	39	1996
MAY EACH DAY ANDY WILLIAMS	11	1966
MAYA BANCO DE GAIA	34	1994
MAYBE IT'S LIVE ROBERT PALMER	32	1982
MAYBE YOU SHOULD DRIVE BARENAKED LADIES	57	1994
MAYBE YOU'VE BEEN BRAINWASHED TOO NEW RADICALS	10	1999
MAYFLOWER WEATHER PROPHETS	67	1987
MCCARTNEY PAUL McCARTNEY	2	1970
MCCARTNEY II PAUL McCARTNEY	1	1980
THE MCCARTNEY INTERVIEW PAUL McCARTNEY	34	1981
MCGUINNESS FLINT McGUINNESS FLINT	9	1971
MCLEMORE AVENUE BOOKER T & THE M.G.s	70	1970
MCMXC A.D ENIGMA	1	1990
MCVICAR (OST) ROGER DALTREY	39	1980

Title / Artist	Peak Position	Year of Release
ME AGAINST MYSELF JAY SEAN	29	2004
ME AND BILLY WILLIAMS MAX BOYCE	37	1980
ME AND MR JOHNSON ERIC CLAPTON	10	2004
ME AND MY SHADOWS CLIFF RICHARD & THE SHADOWS	2	1960
ME MYSELF I JOAN ARMATRADING	5	1980
ME TIME VARIOUS ARTISTS (WARNER BROTHERS)	17	2007
MEAN BUSINESS FIRM	46	1986
MEAN STREAK Y & T	35	1983
THE MEANING OF LOVE MICHELLE	3	2004
MEAT IS MURDER SMITHS	1	1985
MEATY, BEATY, BIG AND BOUNCY WHO	9	1971
MECHANICAL ANIMAL MARILYN MANSON	8	1998
MECHANICAL WONDER OCEAN COLOUR SCENE	7	2001
MECHANIX UFO	8	1982
MEDDLE PINK FLOYD	3	1971
MEDICINE 4 MY PAIN LYNDEN DAVID HALL	43	1998
MEDS PLACEBO	7	2006
MEDULLA BJORK	9	2004
MEDUSA ANNIE LENNOX	1	1995
MEET DANNY WILSON DANNY WILSON	65	1988
MEET GLEN CAMPBELL GLEN CAMPBELL	54	2008
MEET THE BELLRAYS BELLRAYS	73	2002
MEET THE EELS EELS	26	2008
MEET THE SEARCHERS SEARCHERS	2	1963
MEET THE SUPREMES SUPREMES	8	1964
MEGA DANCE 2 – THE ENERGY ZONE VARIOUS ARTISTS (EMI)	3	1993
MEGA DANCE – THE POWER ZONE VARIOUS ARTISTS (EMI)	2	1993
THE MEGA RAVE VARIOUS ARTISTS (EMI)	2	1993
MEGABASS VARIOUS ARTISTS (TELSTAR)	1	1990
MEGABASS 2 VARIOUS ARTISTS (TELSTAR)	6	1990
MEGABASS 3 VARIOUS ARTISTS (TELSTAR)	3	1991
MEGA-LO-MANIA VARIOUS ARTISTS (POLYGRAM)	8	1993
MEGATOP PHOENIX BIG AUDIO DYNAMITE	26	1989
MEISO DJ KRUSH	64	1995
MEL TORME AT 'THE CRESCENDO' MEL TORME	3	1956
MEL TORME WITH THE MARTY PAICH DEK-TETTE MEL TORME	3	1956
MELLON COLLIE AND THE INFINITE SADNESS SMASHING PUMPKINS	4	1995
MELLOW GOLD BECK	41	1994
MELLOW MADNESS VARIOUS ARTISTS (EPIC)	14	1991
MELLOW MAGIC VARIOUS ARTISTS (WARNER BROTHERS)	5	2007
MELODY SHARLEEN SPITERI	3	2008
MELODY AM ROYKSOPP	9	2002
THE MELODY LINGERS ON VARIOUS ARTISTS (V2)	5	2005
MELTDOWN ASH	5	2004
MELTDOWN 2000 – BEST NEW TRANCE VARIOUS ARTISTS (VIRGIN)	6	2000
MELTING POT CHARLATANS	4	1998
MEMORABILIA – THE SINGLES SOFT CELL & MARC ALMOND	8	1991
A MEMORIAL 1944-1969 GLENN MILLER & HIS ORCHESTRA	18	1970
MEMORIAL BEACH A-HA	17	1993
MEMORIES BRENDAN SHINE	81	1985
MEMORIES FOSTER & ALLEN	18	1991
MEMORIES ARE MADE OF HITS PERRY COMO	14	1975
MEMORIES ARE MADE OF THIS RAY CONNIFF	14	1961
MEMORIES ARE MADE OF THIS VARIOUS ARTISTS (RONCO)	84	1981
MEMORIES ARE MADE OF THIS VARIOUS ARTISTS (DINO)	8	1992
MEMORIES ARE MADE OF THIS VARIOUS ARTISTS (VIRGIN)	2	2004
MEMORIES ARE MADE OF THIS – PART 2 VARIOUS ARTISTS (VIRGIN)	8	2005
MEMORIES OF HOME ROSE MARIE	51	1996
MEMORIES – THE BEST OF ELAINE PAIGE ELAINE PAIGE	14	1987
MEMORY ALMOST FULL PAUL McCARTNEY	5	2007
MEMORY AND HUMANITY FUNERAL FOR A FRIEND	17	2008
THE MEMORY KINDA LINGERS NOT THE NINE O'CLOCK NEWS CAST	63	1982
THE MEMORY OF TREES ENYA	5	1995
THE MEMPHIS SESSIONS WET WET WET	3	1988
MEN AND WOMEN SIMPLY RED	2	1987
MEN IN BLACK – THE ALBUM FILM SOUNDTRACK	5	1997
MEN WITHOUT WOMEN LITTLE STEVEN & THE DISCIPLES OF SOUL	73	1982
THE MENACE ELASTICA	24	2000
MENACE TO SOBRIETY UGLY KID JOE	25	1995
MENACE TO SOBRIETY OPM	31	2001
MENAGERIE BILL WITHERS	27	1978
MENDELSSOHN/BRUCH/SCHUBERT NIGEL KENNEDY WITH JEFFREY TATE CONDUCTING THE ENGLISH CHAMBER ORCHESTRA	28	1990
MEN'S NEEDS WOMEN'S NEEDS WHATEVER CRIBS	13	2007
MEO SUO I EYRUM VIO SPILUM ENDALAUST SIGUR ROS	5	2008
MER DE NOMS A PERFECT CIRCLE	55	2000
MERCURY AMERICAN MUSIC CLUB	41	1993
MERCURY LONGVIEW	29	2003
MERCURY FALLING STING	4	1996
MERMAID AVENUE BILLY BRAGG & WILCO	34	1998
MERMAID AVENUE – VOLUME 2 BILLY BRAGG & WILCO	61	2000
MERMAIDS FILM SOUNDTRACK	6	1991
MERRY CHRISTMAS MARIAH CAREY	32	1994
MERRY CHRISTMAS MR LAWRENCE (OST) RYUICHI SAKAMOTO	36	1983
MERRY CHRISTMAS TO YOU VARIOUS ARTISTS (WARWICK)	64	1984
MERRY, MERRY CHRISTMAS NEW KIDS ON THE BLOCK	13	1990
THE MERSEY BEAT VOLUME 1 VARIOUS ARTISTS (ORIOLE)	17	1963
MERSEYBEAST IAN McNABB	30	1996
THE MERSEYBEATS MERSEYBEATS	12	1964
MESOPOTAMIA B-52'S	18	1982
THE MESSAGE GRANDMASTER FLASH & THE FURIOUS FIVE	77	1982
THE MESSIAH LONDON PHILHARMONIC CHOIR WITH THE LONDON ORCHESTRA CONDUCTED BY WALTER SUSSKIND	10	1960
METAL BOX PUBLIC IMAGE LTD	18	1979
METAL FOR MUTHAS VARIOUS ARTISTS (EMI)	16	1980
METAL FOR MUTHAS VOLUME 2 VARIOUS ARTISTS (EMI)	58	1980
METAL HEART ACCEPT	50	1985
METAL RHYTHM GARY NUMAN	48	1988
METAL WORKS 73-93 JUDAS PRIEST	37	1993
METALHEADZ – PLATINUM BREAKZ VARIOUS ARTISTS (FFRR)	12	1996
METALLICA METALLICA	1	1991
METAMATIC JOHN FOXX	18	1980
METAMORPHOSES JEAN-MICHEL JARRE	37	2000
METAMORPHOSIS ROLLING STONES	45	1975
METAMORPHOSIS HILARY DUFF	69	2003
METEORA LINKIN PARK	1	2003
METRO MUSIC MARTHA & THE MUFFINS	34	1980
MEZCAL HEAD SWERVEDRIVER	55	1993
MEZMERIZE SYSTEM OF A DOWN	2	2005
MEZZAMORPHIS DELIRIOUS?	25	1999
MEZZANINE MASSIVE ATTACK	1	1998
MH MARQUES HOUSTON	73	2004
MI TIERRA GLORIA ESTEFAN	11	1993
MIAMI VICE 2 (TELEVISION SOUNDTRACK) TELEVISION AND RADIO COMPILATION	71	1987
MIAMI VICE III (TELEVISION SOUNDTRACK) TELEVISION AND RADIO COMPILATION	95	1988
MIAOW BEAUTIFUL SOUTH	6	1994
MICHAEL BALL MICHAEL BALL	1	1992
MICHAEL BUBLE MICHAEL BUBLE	6	2003
MICHAEL CRAWFORD PERFORMS ANDREW LLOYD WEBBER MICHAEL CRAWFORD & THE ROYAL PHILHARMONIC ORCHESTRA	3	1991
MICHAEL FLATLEY'S LORD OF THE DANCE RONAN HARDIMAN	37	1996
MICHAEL JACKSON 9 SINGLE PACK MICHAEL JACKSON	66	1983
THE MICHAEL JACKSON MIX MICHAEL JACKSON	27	1987
MICHAEL PARKINSON MY LIFE IN MUSIC VARIOUS ARTISTS (WARNER BROTHERS)	9	2008
MICHAEL SCHENKER GROUP MICHAEL SCHENKER GROUP	8	1980
THE MICHEAL PARKINSON COLLECTION VARIOUS ARTISTS (UNIVERSAL)	9	2003
MICHELLE GAYLE MICHELLE GAYLE	30	1994
MICK AND CAROLINE LATIN QUARTER	96	1987
MICRO-PHONIES CABARET VOLTAIRE	69	1984
MIDDLE CLASS REVOLT FALL	48	1994
MIDDLE MAN BOZ SCAGGS	52	1980
MIDDLE OF NOWHERE HANSON	1	1997
THE MIDDLE OF NOWHERE ORBITAL	4	1999
MIDIAN CRADLE OF FILTH	63	2000
MIDNIGHT AT THE LOST AND FOUND MEAT LOAF	7	1983
MIDNIGHT BOOM KILLS	47	2008
MIDNIGHT CRUISING VARIOUS ARTISTS (DINO)	10	1992
MIDNIGHT HOUR VARIOUS ARTISTS (K-TEL)	98	1982
MIDNIGHT HUSTLE VARIOUS ARTISTS (K-TEL)	2	1978
MIDNIGHT IN MOTOWN VARIOUS ARTISTS (TELSTAR)	34	1982
MIDNIGHT LIGHTNING JIMI HENDRIX	46	1975
MIDNIGHT LOVE MARVIN GAYE	10	1982
MIDNIGHT LOVE VARIOUS ARTISTS (STYLUS)	7	1989
MIDNIGHT MAGIC COMMODORES	15	1979
MIDNIGHT MARAUDERS A TRIBE CALLED QUEST	70	1993
MIDNIGHT MOODS – THE LIGHTER SIDE OF JAZZ VARIOUS ARTISTS (POLYGRAM)	3	1993
MIDNIGHT MOODS – THE LOVE COLLECTION GEORGE BENSON	25	1991
MIDNIGHT POSTCARDS ADAM FAITH	43	1993
MIDNIGHT SOUL VARIOUS ARTISTS (ATLANTIC)	22	1966
MIDNIGHT STROLL ROBERT CRAY BAND WITH THE MEMPHIS HORNS	19	1990
MIDNIGHT TO MIDNIGHT PSYCHEDELIC FURS	12	1987
MIDNITE DYNAMOS MATCHBOX	23	1980
MIDNITE VULTURES BECK	19	1999
MIDSUMMER CLASSICS VARIOUS ARTISTS (GLOBAL TELEVISION)	20	1999
MIGHTY JOE MOON GRANT LEE BUFFALO	24	1994
MIGHTY LIKE A ROSE ELVIS COSTELLO	5	1991
MIGHTY REAL SYLVESTER	62	1979
MIGHTY REARRANGER ROBERT PLANT & STRANGE SENSATION	4	2005
MIKE AND THE MECHANICS MIKE & THE MECHANICS	14	1986
MILES FROM HOME PESHAY	63	1999
MILES HIGH JOHN MILES	96	1981

Title / Artist	Peak Position	Year of Release
MILES OF AISLES JONI MITCHELL	34	1975
MILESTONES ROLLING STONES	14	1972
MILESTONES – 20 ROCK OPERAS VARIOUS ARTISTS (TELSTAR)	6	1990
MILITARY GOLD VARIOUS ARTISTS (RONCO)	62	1979
MILK & KISSES COCTEAU TWINS	17	1996
MILK AND HONEY – A HEART PLAY JOHN LENNON & YOKO ONO	3	1984
MILK INC. MILK INC.	47	2002
MILKSHAKE – THE ALBUM VARIOUS ARTISTS (GUT)	15	2006
MILLENNIUM BACKSTREET BOYS	2	1999
MILLICAN AND NESBITT MILLICAN & NESBITT	3	1974
MILLIGAN PRESERVED SPIKE MILLIGAN	11	1961
THE MILLION DOLLAR HOTEL FILM SOUNDTRACK	13	2000
$1,000,000.00 WORTH OF TWANG DUANE EDDY	5	1961
$1,000,000.00 WORTH OF TWANG VOLUME 2 DUANE EDDY	18	1962
MILLION MILE REFLECTIONS CHARLIE DANIELS BAND	74	1979
MILLION SELLER HITS ANONYMOUS COVER VERSIONS	46	1971
MILLIONAIRES JAMES	2	1999
MIMOSA FUN LOVIN' CRIMINALS	37	1999
MIND ADVENTURES DES'REE	26	1992
MIND AND SOUL COLLABORATORS BACK TO THE PLANET	32	1993
MIND BODY & SOUL JOSS STONE	1	2004
MIND BOMB THE THE	4	1989
MIND ELEVATION NIGHTMARES ON WAX	47	2002
MIND GAMES JOHN LENNON	13	1973
THE MINDBENDERS MINDBENDERS	28	1966
THE MIND'S EYE STILTSKIN	17	1994
MINGUS JONI MITCHELL	24	1979
MINI WEDDING PRESENT	40	1996
MINIMUM – MAXIMUM KRAFTWERK	29	2005
MINIPOPS MINIPOPS	63	1981
MINISTRY OF SOUND ANTHEMS 1991-2008 VARIOUS ARTISTS (MINISTRY OF SOUND)	1	2007
MINISTRY OF SOUND CLASSICS MIXED BY JUDGE JULES VARIOUS ARTISTS (MINISTRY OF SOUND)	12	1997
MINISTRY OF SOUND – DANCE NATION 2 VARIOUS ARTISTS (MINISTRY OF SOUND)	4	1996
THE MINISTRY OF SOUND PRESENTS A DAY IN THE LIFE OF TODD TERRY TODD TERRY	73	1995
MINISTRY OF SOUND PRESENTS GARAGE CLASSICS VARIOUS ARTISTS (MINISTRY OF SOUND)	3	2008
MINISTRY OF SOUND SESSION SIX – FRANKIE KNUCKLES VARIOUS ARTISTS (MINISTRY OF SOUND)	8	1996
MINISTRY OF SOUND SESSIONS – VOLUME 5 VARIOUS ARTISTS (MINISTRY OF SOUND)	15	1995
MINISTRY OF SOUND – THE SESSIONS 4 VARIOUS ARTISTS (MINISTRY OF SOUND)	9	1995
MINISTRY OF SOUND – THE SESSIONS VOLUME 2 VARIOUS ARTISTS (MINISTRY OF SOUND)	6	1994
MINISTRY OF SOUND – THE SESSIONS VOLUME 3 VARIOUS ARTISTS (MINISTRY OF SOUND)	8	1994
MINISTRY OF SOUND: THE SESSIONS VOLUME 1 VARIOUS ARTISTS (MINISTRY OF SOUND)	16	1993
MINOR EARTH MAJOR SKY A-HA	27	2000
MINSTREL OF THE GALLERY JETHRO TULL	20	1975
MINUTES ELKIE BROOKS	35	1984
MINUTES TO MIDNIGHT LINKIN PARK	1	2007
MINX TOYAH	24	1985
MIRACLE KANE GANG	41	1987
THE MIRACLE QUEEN	1	1989
MIRACLE CELINE DION	5	2004
MIRAGE FLEETWOOD MAC	5	1982
MIREILLE MATHIEU MIREILLE MATHIEU	39	1968
MIRMAMA EDDI READER	34	1992
MIRROR BALL NEIL YOUNG	4	1995
MIRROR BLUE RICHARD THOMPSON	23	1994
MIRROR MAN CAPTAIN BEEFHEART & HIS MAGIC BAND	49	1971
MIRROR MOVES PSYCHEDELIC FURS	15	1984
MIRRORED BATTLES	70	2007
MIRRORS BLUE OYSTER CULT	46	1979
MISDEMEANOUR UFO	74	1985
THE MISEDUCATION OF LAURYN HILL LAURYN HILL	2	1998
MISPLACED CHILDHOOD MARILLION	1	1985
MISPLACED IDEALS SAD CAFÉ	50	1978
MISS E. . . SO ADDICTIVE MISSY 'MISDEMEANOR' ELLIOTT	10	2001
MISS INDEPENDENT VARIOUS ARTISTS (BMG)	11	2004
MISS RANDY CRAWFORD – THE GREATEST HITS RANDY CRAWFORD	10	1984
MISS SAIGON STAGE CAST RECORDING	4	1990
MISSA LUBA TROUBADOURS DU ROI BAUDOUIN	59	1976
MISSING YOU VARIOUS ARTISTS (EMI)	8	1994
MISSING YOU DAVID ESSEX	26	1995
MISSING YOU 2 – AN ALBUM OF LOVE VARIOUS ARTISTS (EMI)	2	1991
MISSING YOU – AN ALBUM OF LOVE VARIOUS ARTISTS (EMI)	1	1990
MISSING...PRESUMED HAVING A GOOD TIME NOTTING HILLBILLIES	2	1990
THE MISSION (OST) ENNIO MORRICONE WITH THE LONDON PHILHARMONIC ORCHESTRA	73	1987
MISSION ACCOMPLISHED BUT THE BEAT GOES ON REZILLOS	30	1979
MISSION IMPOSSIBLE 2 FILM SOUNDTRACK	12	2000
MISSION: IMPOSSIBLE FILM SOUNDTRACK	18	1996
MRS 'ARDIN'S KID MIKE HARDING	24	1975
MRS. MILLS PARTY PIECES MRS. MILLS	32	1968
MISTAKEN IDENTITY KIM CARNES	26	1981
MISTAKEN IDENTITY DELTA GOODREM	25	2004
MR BEAST MOGWAI	31	2006
MR. BIG MR. BIG	60	1989
MR. BUNGLE MR. BUNGLE	57	1991
MR. FANTASY TRAFFIC	8	1967
MR. GONE WEATHER REPORT	47	1978
MISTER HEARTBREAK LAURIE ANDERSON	93	1984
MR JONES TOM JONES	36	2002
MR LOVE & JUSTICE BILLY BRAGG	33	2008
MR. LOVE PANTS IAN DURY & THE BLOCKHEADS	57	1998
MR LOVER LOVER – THE BEST OF – PART 1 SHAGGY	20	2002
MR. LUCKY JOHN LEE HOOKER	3	1991
MR. MOONLIGHT FOREIGNER	59	1994
MR. MUSIC – MANTOVANI MANTOVANI & HIS ORCHESTRA	24	1966
MR. TAMBOURINE MAN BYRDS	7	1965
MR. UNIVERSE GILLAN	11	1979
MR. WONDERFUL FLEETWOOD MAC	10	1968
MISTRAL'S DAUGHTER FILM SOUNDTRACK	53	1986
MISTRIAL LOU REED	69	1986
MISTY RAY STEVENS	23	1975
MISTY MORNINGS VARIOUS ARTISTS (RONCO)	44	1981
THE MIX KRAFTWERK	15	1991
MIX HEAVEN '97 VARIOUS ARTISTS (EPIC)	19	1997
MIX ZONE VARIOUS ARTISTS (POLYGRAM)	2	1996
MIXED EMOTIONS VARIOUS ARTISTS (POLYGRAM)	6	1997
MIXED EMOTIONS BEVERLEY CRAVEN	46	1999
MIXED EMOTIONS II VARIOUS ARTISTS (POLYGRAM)	3	1998
MIXED UP CURE	8	1990
MIXED UP GIRLS ALOUD	56	2007
MIXES KYLIE MINOGUE	63	1998
MIXMAG PRESENTS BIG TUNES VARIOUS ARTISTS (VIRGIN)	12	2001
MIX'O'MATIC VARIOUS ARTISTS (EMI)	8	1996
MO' MONEY FILM SOUNDTRACK	16	1992
MOB RULES BLACK SABBATH	12	1981
MOBILE HOME LONGPIGS	33	1999
MOBO 1998 – MUSIC OF BLACK ORIGIN VARIOUS ARTISTS (POLYGRAM)	13	1998
MOBO 1999 VARIOUS ARTISTS (UNIVERSAL)	10	1999
MOBO 2000 VARIOUS ARTISTS (UNIVERSAL)	3	2000
MOBO 2001 – THE ALBUM VARIOUS ARTISTS (SONY)	13	2001
MOBO PRESENTS URBAN BEATS 2003 VARIOUS ARTISTS (UNIVERSAL)	5	2003
MOCK TUDOR RICHARD THOMPSON	28	1999
MODERN CLASSICS – THE GREATEST HITS PAUL WELLER	7	1998
MODERN DANCE VARIOUS ARTISTS (K-TEL)	6	1982
MODERN GUILT BECK	9	2008
MODERN HEROES VARIOUS ARTISTS (TV RECORDS)	24	1982
MODERN LIFE IS RUBBISH BLUR	15	1993
MODERN LOVE VARIOUS ARTISTS (POLYGRAM)	1	1992
MODERN LOVE – 24 LOVE SONGS FOR TODAY VARIOUS ARTISTS (K-TEL)	13	1985
MODERN MUSIC BE-BOP DELUXE	12	1976
MODERN SOUNDS IN COUNTRY AND WESTERN RAY CHARLES	6	1962
MODERN TIMES LATIN QUARTER	91	1986
MODERN TIMES BOB DYLAN	3	2006
MODROPHENIA VARIOUS ARTISTS (GLOBAL TELEVISION)	14	1997
MODS MAYDAY 79 VARIOUS ARTISTS (ARISTA)	75	1979
MODUS OPERANDI PHOTEK	30	1997
MOLTEN METAL VARIOUS ARTISTS (TELSTAR)	13	1990
THE MOMENT KENNY G	19	1996
THE MOMENT LISA STANSFIELD	57	2004
MOMENT IN TIME ROBSON GREEN	49	2002
MOMENT OF TRUTH GANG STARR	43	1998
A MOMENTARY LAPSE OF REASON PINK FLOYD	3	1987
MOMENTS IN SOUL VARIOUS ARTISTS (STYLUS)	9	1990
MOMENTS IN SOUL VARIOUS ARTISTS (DOVER)	2	1991
MONA BONE JAKON CAT STEVENS	63	1970
MONA LISAS JUDITH DURHAM	46	1996
MONDO BONGO BOOMTOWN RATS	6	1981
MONEY & CIGARETTES ERIC CLAPTON	13	1983
MONEY FOR NOTHING DIRE STRAITS	1	1988
THE MONKEES MONKEES	1	1967
MONKEY BUSINESS BLACK EYED PEAS	4	2005
MONKEY GRIP BILL WYMAN	39	1974
MONKEY KONG A	62	1999
MONSTER STEPPENWOLF	43	1970
MONSTER R.E.M.	1	1994
MONSTER HITS VARIOUS ARTISTS (CBS)	2	1989
MONSTER HITS OF DANCE VARIOUS ARTISTS (CASTLE COMMUNICATIONS)	13	1993
MONSTER TRACKS VARIOUS ARTISTS (POLYDOR)	20	1981
MONSTERS OF ROCK VARIOUS ARTISTS (POLYDOR)	16	1980

Title / Artist	Peak Position	Year of Release
MONSTERS OF ROCK VARIOUS ARTISTS (EMI)	14	2006
MONTAGE KENNY G	32	1990
THE MONTREUX ALBUM SMOKIE	52	1978
MONTROSE MONTROSE	43	1974
MONTY PYTHON LIVE AT DRURY LANE MONTY PYTHON'S FLYING CIRCUS	19	1974
THE MONTY PYTHON MATCHING TIE AND HANDKERCHIEF MONTY PYTHON'S FLYING CIRCUS	49	1974
MONTY PYTHON SINGS MONTY PYTHON	62	1991
MONTY PYTHON'S CONTRACTUAL OBLIGATION ALBUM MONTY PYTHON'S FLYING CIRCUS	13	1980
MONTY PYTHON'S LIFE OF BRIAN (OST) MONTY PYTHON'S FLYING CIRCUS	63	1979
MONTY PYTHON'S PREVIOUS RECORD MONTY PYTHON'S FLYING CIRCUS	39	1973
MONUMENT – THE SOUNDTRACK ULTRAVOX	9	1983
A MONUMENT TO BRITISH ROCK VARIOUS ARTISTS (HARVEST)	13	1979
MOODS NEIL DIAMOND	7	1972
MOODS VARIOUS ARTISTS (VIRGIN)	2	1991
MOODS 2 VARIOUS ARTISTS (VIRGIN)	3	1992
MOODS SYMPHONIQUE 95 SYMPHONIQUE	21	1995
MOODY BLUE ELVIS PRESLEY	3	1977
THE MOON AND THE MELODIES HAROLD BUDD, ELIZABETH FRASER, ROBIN GUTHRIE & SIMON RAYMONDE	46	1986
MOON MADNESS CAMEL	15	1976
MOON RIVER ANDREA ROSS	42	2007
MOON SAFARI AIR	6	1998
MOONDANCE VAN MORRISON	32	1970
MOONDANCE – THE ALBUM VARIOUS ARTISTS (TELSTAR)	16	1997
MOONFLOWER SANTANA	7	1977
MOONLIGHT AND ROSES JIM REEVES	2	1964
MOONLIGHT OVER MEMPHIS MARTI PELLOW	27	2006
MOONLIGHT SHADOWS SHADOWS	6	1986
MOONLIGHT SINATRA FRANK SINATRA	18	1966
MOONLIGHTING "THE TV SOUNDTRACK ALBUM" (TELEVISION SOUNDTRACK) TELEVISION AND RADIO COMPILATION	50	1987
MOONLIGHTING 2 (TELEVISION SOUNDTRACK) TELEVISION AND RADIO COMPILATION	5	1988
MOONTAN GOLDEN EARRING	24	1974
MORE (OST) PINK FLOYD	9	1969
MORE ABBA GOLD ABBA	63	2008
MORE ABBA GOLD – MORE ABBA HITS ABBA	13	1993
MORE BEST WORSHIP SONGS EVER VARIOUS ARTISTS (VIRGIN)	11	2005
MORE BOB DYLAN GREATEST HITS BOB DYLAN	12	1971
MORE BUMP 'N' GRIND VARIOUS ARTISTS (MCA)	9	1995
MORE CHUCK BERRY CHUCK BERRY	9	1963
MORE COLD FEET – OST (TELEVISION SOUNDTRACK) TELEVISION AND RADIO COMPILATION	18	2000
MORE CRAZY HITS CRAZY FROG	64	2006
MORE DIRTY DANCING FILM SOUNDTRACK	3	1988
MORE FRIENDS – SMALL WORLD BIG BAND 2 JOOLS HOLLAND	17	2002
MORE GREAT SONG HITS FROM THE BACHELORS BACHELORS	15	1965
MORE GREEN VELVET VARIOUS ARTISTS (TELSTAR)	42	1985
MORE GREGORY GREGORY ISAACS	93	1981
MORE HITS BY CLIFF CLIFF RICHARD & THE SHADOWS	20	1965
MORE JUNK WILFRED BRAMBELL & HARRY H. CORBETT	19	1964
MORE MILES PER HOUR JOHN MILES	46	1979
MORE MILLER AND OTHER BIG BAND MAGIC SYD LAWRENCE	14	1970
MORE MINSTREL MELODIES BIG BEN BANJO BAND	20	1960
MORE MUSIC TO WATCH GIRLS BY VARIOUS ARTISTS (COLUMBIA)	10	1999
MORE OF THE HARD STUFF DUBLINERS	8	1967
MORE OF THE MONKEES MONKEES	1	1967
MORE PENNIES FROM HEAVEN (TELEVISION SOUNDTRACK) TELEVISION AND RADIO COMPILATION	31	1978
MORE ROCK 'N' ROLL LOVE SONGS VARIOUS ARTISTS (DINO)	6	1991
MORE SONGS ABOUT BUILDINGS AND FOOD TALKING HEADS	21	1978
MORE SONGS ABOUT LOVE AND HATE GODFATHERS	49	1989
MORE SPECIALS SPECIALS	5	1980
MORE THAN A FEELING VARIOUS ARTISTS (SONY)	2	2004
MORE THAN ALOT CHASE & STATUS	49	2008
MORE THAN FRIENDS JONATHAN BUTLER	29	1989
MORE THAN LOVE VARIOUS ARTISTS (TELSTAR)	4	1992
MORE THAN THIS – THE BEST OF BRYAN FERRY AND ROXY MUSIC BRYAN FERRY & ROXY MUSIC	15	1995
MORE THAN UNPLUGGED VARIOUS ARTISTS (DINO)	11	1993
MORE THAN YOU THINK YOU ARE MATCHBOX 20	31	2003
THE MORE THINGS CHANGE... MACHINE HEAD	16	1997
MORE TO TELL MONTELL JORDAN	66	1996
...MORE UNCHARTED HEIGHTS OF DISGRACE DOGS D'AMOUR	30	1993
MORE! GIRLS' NIGHT OUT VARIOUS ARTISTS (VIRGIN)	10	1997
MORNING COMES QUICKLY BARBARA DICKSON	58	1977
MORNING DANCE SPYRO GYRA	11	1979
MORNING DOVE WHITE ONE DOVE	30	1993
MORNING HAS BROKEN VARIOUS ARTISTS (TELSTAR)	88	1988
MORNING HAS BROKEN VARIOUS ARTISTS (EMI)	17	2008
MORNING NOON AND NIGHT 101 STRINGS	32	1983
MORNING VIEW INCUBUS	15	2001
MOROCCAN ROLL BRAND X	37	1977
MORPH THE CAT DONALD FAGEN	35	2006
MORRISON HOTEL DOORS	12	1970
MOSAIQUE GIPSY KINGS	27	1989
MOSE ALIVE MOSE ALLISON	30	1966
MOSELEY SHOALS OCEAN COLOUR SCENE	2	1996
MOSES (OST) ENNIO MORRICONE	43	1977
MOST EXCELLENT DANCE VARIOUS ARTISTS (EMI)	8	1995
MOST HAPPY FELLA STAGE CAST RECORDING	6	1960
THE MOST OF HERMAN'S HERMITS HERMAN'S HERMITS	14	1971
THE MOST OF LULU LULU	15	1971
MOST OF THE ANIMALS ANIMALS	4	1966
MOST OF THE ANIMALS ANIMALS	18	1971
MOST RATED VARIOUS ARTISTS (DEFECTED)	14	2004
THE MOST RELAXING CLASSICAL ALBUM IN THE WORLD VARIOUS ARTISTS (VIRGIN)	17	2005
THE MOST RELAXING CLASSICAL ALBUM IN THE WORLD...EVER! VARIOUS ARTISTS (VIRGIN)	10	1997
THE MOST RELAXING CLASSICAL ALBUM IN THE WORLD...EVER! II VARIOUS ARTISTS (VIRGIN)	12	1998
MOST WANTED HILARY DUFF	31	2005
THE MOST WONDERFUL TIME OF THE YEAR MICHAEL CRAWFORD	69	1999
MOTHER KUBB	26	2005
MOTHER FIST AND HER FIVE DAUGHTERS MARC ALMOND & THE WILLING SINNERS	41	1987
MOTHER NATURE CALLS CAST	3	1997
THE MOTHER OF ALL SWING ALBUMS VARIOUS ARTISTS (TELSTAR)	9	1996
THE MOTHER OF ALL SWING II VARIOUS ARTISTS (TELSTAR)	11	1997
THE MOTHER OF ALL SWING MIX ALBUMS VARIOUS ARTISTS (TELSTAR)	7	1997
MOTHERS HEAVEN TEXAS	32	1991
MOTHERSHIP – THE BEST OF LED ZEPPELIN	4	2007
MOTION IN THE OCEAN McFLY	6	2006
MOTIVATION RADIO STEVE HILLAGE	28	1977
MOTLEY CRUE MOTLEY CRUE	17	1994
MOTORHEAD MOTORHEAD	43	1977
MOTORIZER MOTORHEAD	32	2008
MOTORMOUTH BEN ELTON	86	1987
THE MOTORS MOTORS	46	1977
MOTORVATIN' CHUCK BERRY	7	1977
MOTOWN MICHAEL McDONALD	29	2003
MOTOWN 40 FOREVER VARIOUS ARTISTS (MOTOWN)	15	1998
MOTOWN AND MOTOWN II MICHAEL McDONALD	29	2005
MOTOWN CHARTBUSTERS VARIOUS ARTISTS (TELSTAR)	25	1986
MOTOWN CHARTBUSTERS VOLUME 3 VARIOUS ARTISTS (MOTOWN)	1	1969
MOTOWN CHARTBUSTERS VOLUME 4 VARIOUS ARTISTS (MOTOWN)	1	1970
MOTOWN CHARTBUSTERS VOLUME 5 VARIOUS ARTISTS (MOTOWN)	1	1971
MOTOWN CHARTBUSTERS VOLUME 6 VARIOUS ARTISTS (MOTOWN)	2	1971
MOTOWN CHARTBUSTERS VOLUME 7 VARIOUS ARTISTS (MOTOWN)	9	1972
MOTOWN CHARTBUSTERS VOLUME 8 VARIOUS ARTISTS (MOTOWN)	9	1973
MOTOWN CHARTBUSTERS VOLUME 9 VARIOUS ARTISTS (MOTOWN)	14	1974
THE MOTOWN COLLECTION VARIOUS ARTISTS (TELSTAR)	8	1990
MOTOWN DANCE PARTY VARIOUS ARTISTS (MOTOWN)	3	1988
MOTOWN DANCE PARTY 2 VARIOUS ARTISTS (MOTOWN)	10	1990
MOTOWN 50 VARIOUS ARTISTS (UNIVERSAL)	6	2008
MOTOWN GOLD VARIOUS ARTISTS (MOTOWN)	8	1975
MOTOWN GOLD VARIOUS ARTISTS (UNIVERSAL)	7	2001
MOTOWN GOLD 70S VARIOUS ARTISTS (UNIVERSAL)	17	2007
MOTOWN GOLD VOLUME 2 VARIOUS ARTISTS (MOTOWN)	28	1977
MOTOWN HEARTBREAKERS VARIOUS ARTISTS (TELSTAR)	4	1989
MOTOWN IN MOTION VARIOUS ARTISTS (K-TEL)	28	1988
MOTOWN MANIA VARIOUS ARTISTS (BMG)	9	2000
MOTOWN MEMORIES VARIOUS ARTISTS (MOTOWN)	21	1968
THE MOTOWN SONG BOOK RUBY TURNER	22	1988
MOTOWN STORY VARIOUS ARTISTS (MOTOWN)	21	1972

Title / Artist	Peak Position	Year of Release
MOTOWN – THE HITS COLLECTION – VOLUME 2 VARIOUS ARTISTS (MOTOWN)	19	1995
MOTOWN – THE ULTIMATE COLLECTION VARIOUS ARTISTS (UNIVERSAL)	7	2006
MOTOWN – THE ULTIMATE HITS COLLECTION VARIOUS ARTISTS (MOTOWN)	6	1994
THE MOTOWN YEARS MICHAEL JACKSON & THE JACKSON FIVE	34	2008
MOTOWN: HITSVILLE USA BOYZ II MEN	8	2007
MOTOWN'S GREATEST HITS DIANA ROSS	20	1992
MOTOWN'S GREATEST HITS MICHAEL JACKSON	53	1992
MOTOWN'S GREATEST HITS TEMPTATIONS	8	1992
MOTOWN'S GREATEST LOVE SONGS VARIOUS ARTISTS (MOTOWN)	5	1992
MOTT MOTT THE HOOPLE	7	1973
MOTT THE HOOPLE MOTT THE HOOPLE	66	1970
MOTT THE HOOPLE – LIVE MOTT THE HOOPLE	32	1974
MOULIN ROUGE FILM SOUNDTRACK	2	2001
MOULIN ROUGE – COLLECTORS EDITION FILM SOUNDTRACK	9	2002
THE MOUNTAIN STEVE EARLE & THE DEL McCOURY BAND	51	1999
MOUNTAIN BATTLES BREEDERS	46	2008
MOUNTING EXCITEMENT VARIOUS ARTISTS (K-TEL)	2	1980
MOUTH TO MOUTH LEVELLERS	5	1997
MOUTHFUL OF LOVE YOUNG HEART ATTACK	71	2004
MOVE MOVE	15	1968
MOVE ALONG ALL-AMERICAN REJECTS	45	2006
MOVE CLOSER PHYLLIS NELSON	29	1985
MOVE CLOSER VARIOUS ARTISTS (CBS)	4	1987
MOVE IT! REEL 2 REAL FEATURING THE MAD STUNTMAN	8	1994
MOVE TO THIS CATHY DENNIS	3	1991
MOVE YOUR SKIN AND WHY NOT	24	1990
MOVEMENT NEW ORDER	30	1981
THE MOVIE ALBUM BARBRA STREISAND	25	2003
THE MOVIE ALBUM – AS TIME GOES BY NEIL DIAMOND	68	1998
MOVIE HITS VARIOUS ARTISTS (TELSTAR)	19	1993
MOVIE KILLERS VARIOUS ARTISTS (TELSTAR)	4	1996
MOVIE LOVERS VARIOUS ARTISTS (TELSTAR)	17	1998
MOVIE MASTERPIECES ENNIO MORRICONE	69	2004
THE MOVIES MICHAEL BALL	13	1998
MOVIE'S GREATEST LOVE SONGS VARIOUS ARTISTS (UNIVERSAL)	11	2005
THE MOVIES' GREATEST LOVE SONGS VARIOUS ARTISTS (POLYGRAM)	4	1994
MOVIN' KAY STARR	16	1960
MOVIN' JENNIFER RUSH	32	1986
MOVIN MELODIES ATB	32	2000
MOVIN' ON VARIOUS ARTISTS (RUMOUR)	20	1992
MOVIN' ON 2 VARIOUS ARTISTS (RUMOUR)	15	1992
MOVING MOUNTAINS JUSTIN HAYWARD	78	1985
MOVING ON OLETA ADAMS	59	1995
MOVING ON 911	10	1998
MOVING ON MYLEENE KLASS	32	2003
MOVING OUT TO THE COUNTRY JOOLS HOLLAND & HIS R&B ORCHESTRA	45	2006
MOVING PICTURES RUSH	3	1981
MOVING TARGETS PENETRATION	22	1978
MOVING WAVES FOCUS	2	1972
MOZART GOLD – THE ESSENTIAL COLLECTION VARIOUS ARTISTS (DEUTSCHE GRAMMOPHON)	17	2002
MR BAD GUY FREDDIE MERCURY	6	1985
MS KELLY KELLY ROWLAND	37	2007
MS KELLY – DELUXE EDITION KELLY ROWLAND	23	2008
MSG MICHAEL SCHENKER GROUP	14	1981
MTV BASE PRESENTS BEATS RHYMES AND LIFE VARIOUS ARTISTS (UNIVERSAL)	12	2004
MTV DANCE VARIOUS ARTISTS (UNIVERSAL)	18	2001
MTV HITS VARIOUS ARTISTS (UNIVERSAL)	15	2001
MTV IBIZA 2000 – THE PARTY VARIOUS ARTISTS (WHITE ISLAND)	14	2000
MTV IBIZA 2001 VARIOUS ARTISTS (WARNER BROTHERS)	18	2001
MTV IBIZA 99 (TELEVISION COMPILATION) TELEVISION AND RADIO COMPILATION	10	1999
MTV SELECT VARIOUS ARTISTS (UNIVERSAL)	6	2001
MTV UNPLUGGED ALICE IN CHAINS	20	1996
MTV UNPLUGGED KISS	74	1996
MTV UNPLUGGED ALANIS MORISSETTE	56	1999
MTV UNPLUGGED (EP) MARIAH CAREY	3	1992
MTV UNPLUGGED (EP) MAXWELL	45	1997
MTV UNPLUGGED 2.0 LAURYN HILL	40	2002
MTV UNPLUGGED 3 – THE VERY BEST OF VARIOUS ARTISTS (UNIVERSAL)	14	2004
MUCH LOVE SHOLA AMA	6	1997
MUCH MORE THAN LOVE FINLEY QUAYE	56	2003
MUD ROCK MUD	8	1974
MUD ROCK VOLUME 2 MUD	6	1975
MUD SLIDE SLIM AND THE BLUE HORIZON JAMES TAYLOR	4	1971
MUDDY WATER BLUES – A TRIBUTE TO MUDDY WATERS PAUL RODGERS	9	1993
MUD'S GREATEST HITS MUD	25	1975
MULE VARIATIONS TOM WAITS	9	1999
MUMMER XTC	51	1983
MUM'S FAVOURITE SONGS VARIOUS ARTISTS (EMI)	6	2008
MUNDO AFRIKA VARIOUS ARTISTS (SONY)	17	1996
MUNDO LATINO VARIOUS ARTISTS (COLUMBIA)	3	1995
MUNGO JERRY MUNGO JERRY	13	1970
MUNKI JESUS & MARY CHAIN	47	1998
THE MUPPET SHOW MUPPETS	1	1977
THE MUPPET SHOW VOLUME 2 MUPPETS	16	1978
MURDER BALLADS NICK CAVE & THE BAD SEEDS	8	1996
MURDER ON THE DANCEFLOOR VARIOUS ARTISTS (UNIVERSAL)	7	2002
MUSCLE OF LOVE ALICE COOPER	34	1974
MUSE SICK-N-HOUR MESS AGE PUBLIC ENEMY	12	1994
MUSIC CAROLE KING	18	1972
MUSIC MADONNA	1	2000
THE MUSIC MUSIC	4	2002
MUSIC MICHAEL BALL	11	2005
MUSIC & PASSION: THE BEST OF BARRY MANILOW	54	2008
MUSIC BOX MARIAH CAREY	1	1993
MUSIC CITY SOUL BEVERLEY KNIGHT	8	2007
MUSIC EXPRESS VARIOUS ARTISTS (K-TEL)	3	1976
MUSIC FOR A ROYAL WEDDING (ROYAL COMPILATION ALBUM) ROYAL COMPILATION ALBUM	7	1973
MUSIC FOR ALL OCCASIONS MAVERICKS	56	1996
MUSIC FOR AMORPHOUS BODY STUDY CENTRE STEREOLAB	59	1995
MUSIC FOR AN ACCELERATED CULTURE HADOUKEN	12	2008
MUSIC FOR DANCING GRID	67	1995
MUSIC FOR FILMS BRIAN ENO	26	1978
MUSIC FOR LIFE VARIOUS ARTISTS (WARNER BROTHERS)	17	1999
MUSIC FOR PLEASURE MONACO	11	1997
MUSIC FOR THE JILTED GENERATION PRODIGY	1	1994
MUSIC FOR THE LAST NIGHT OF THE PROMS SIR CHARLES GROVES CONDUCTING THE ROYAL PHILHARMONIC ORCHESTRA & CHORUS WITH SARAH WALKER (SOPRANO)	39	1990
MUSIC FOR THE MASSES DEPECHE MODE	10	1987
MUSIC FOR THE PEOPLE MARKY MARK & THE FUNKY BUNCH	61	1991
MUSIC FOR THE SEASONS VARIOUS ARTISTS (RONCO)	41	1982
MUSIC FROM 'EDWARD VII' LONDON SYMPHONY ORCHESTRA	52	1975
MUSIC FROM RIVERDANCE – THE SHOW BILL WHELAN	31	1995
MUSIC FROM THE BBC-TV SERIES 'THE SINGING DETECTIVE' (TELEVISION SOUNDTRACK) TELEVISION AND RADIO COMPILATION	10	1986
MUSIC FROM THE TELEVISION SERIES 'MIAMI VICE' (TELEVISION SOUNDTRACK) TELEVISION AND RADIO COMPILATION	11	1985
MUSIC FROM 'TWIN PEAKS' ANGELO BADALAMENTI	27	1990
MUSIC IN THE DOLLS HOUSE FAMILY	35	1968
MUSIC MAGIC ROSE ROYCE	69	1984
MUSIC MAKES MY DAY OLIVIA NEWTON-JOHN	37	1974
MUSIC MAKES MY DAY OLIVIA NEWTON-JOHN	37	1974
MUSIC MAKES MY DAY OMAR	37	1992
MUSIC MAN STAGE CAST RECORDING	8	1961
THE MUSIC MAN FILM SOUNDTRACK	14	1962
MUSIC MUSIC MUSIC JOHN BARROWMAN	35	2008
MUSIC 'N' MOTION CHRISTINA GREGG	51	1978
MUSIC OF AMERICA RICHMOND STRINGS WITH THE MIKE SAMMES SINGERS	18	1976
THE MUSIC OF THE COSMOS (TELEVISION SOUNDTRACK) TELEVISION AND RADIO COMPILATION	43	1981
MUSIC OF GLENN MILLER IN SUPER STEREO SYD LAWRENCE	43	1971
THE OF MUSIC JAMES LAST JAMES LAST	19	1973
THE MUSIC OF JAMES LAST JAMES LAST	19	1973
THE MUSIC OF LOVE RICHARD CLAYDERMAN	28	1984
MUSIC OF QUALITY AND DISTINCTION (VOLUME 1) VARIOUS ARTISTS (VIRGIN)	25	1982
THE MUSIC OF RICHARD CLAYDERMAN RICHARD CLAYDERMAN	21	1983
MUSIC OF THE MILLENNIUM (TELEVISION COMPILATION) TELEVISION AND RADIO COMPILATION	2	1999
MUSIC OF THE MILLENNIUM VOL. 2 VARIOUS ARTISTS (UNIVERSAL)	8	2000
MUSIC OF THE MOUNTAINS MANUEL & THE MUSIC OF THE MOUNTAINS	17	1960
MUSIC OF THE NIGHT VARIOUS ARTISTS (POLYGRAM)	5	1998
MUSIC OF THE SPHERES IAN BROWN	3	2001
MUSIC OF THE SPHERES MIKE OLDFIELD	9	2008
MUSIC OF THE SUN RIHANNA	35	2005
THE MUSIC PEOPLE VARIOUS ARTISTS (CBS)	10	1972
MUSIC – THE DEFINITIVE HITS COLLECTION VARIOUS ARTISTS (BMG)	4	2001
MUSIC – THE DEFINITIVE HITS COLLECTION 2 VARIOUS ARTISTS (BMG)	7	2001
MUSIC TO WATCH GIRLS BY VARIOUS ARTISTS (COLUMBIA)	2	1999
MUSIC TO WATCH GIRLS BY – THE VERY BEST ANDY WILLIAMS	50	2005
MUSIC TO WATCH GIRLS BY VOLUME 3 VARIOUS ARTISTS (COLUMBIA)	20	2001
MUSIC TO WATCH MOVIES BY VARIOUS ARTISTS (COLUMBIA)	18	2001
MUSICAL CHAIRS HOOTIE & THE BLOWFISH	15	1998

Album / Artist	Peak Position	Year of Release
MUSICAL MADNESS MANTRONIX	66	1986
MUSICALITY MARTINE McCUTCHEON	55	2002
THE MUSICALS MICHAEL BALL	20	1996
MUSICOLOGY PRINCE	3	2004
THE MUSIC'S BACK DOMINIC KIRWAN	54	1997
MUSIK PLASTIK MAN	58	1994
MUSIQUE – VOLUME I – 1993-2005 DAFT PUNK	34	2006
MUSIQUE/THE HIGH ROAD ROXY MUSIC	26	1983
MUST I PAINT YOU A PICTURE BILLY BRAGG	49	2003
MUSTN'T GRUMBLE CHAS & DAVE	35	1982
MUTATIONS BECK	24	1998
MUTINY (STUDIO CAST RECORDING) DAVID ESSEX, FRANK FINLAY & VARIOUS ARTISTS	39	1983
MUZIKIZUM X-PRESS 2	15	2002
MWNG SUPER FURRY ANIMALS	11	2000
MY AIM IS TRUE ELVIS COSTELLO	14	1977
MY BABY JUST CARES FOR ME NINA SIMONE	56	1987
MY BROTHER THE COW MUDHONEY	70	1995
MY CATHEDRAL JIM REEVES	48	1970
MY CBEEBIES ALBUM VARIOUS ARTISTS (UNIVERSAL)	18	2006
MY CHERIE AMOUR STEVIE WONDER	17	1969
MY CLASSIC COLLECTION RICHARD CLAYDERMAN WITH THE ROYAL PHILHARMONIC ORCHESTRA	29	1990
MY COLOURING BOOK AGNETHA FALTSKOG	12	2004
MY CONCERTO FOR YOU RUSS CONWAY	5	1960
MY DECEMBER KELLY CLARKSON	2	2007
MY FAIR LADY STAGE CAST RECORDING	1	1958
MY FAIR LADY SHELLY MANNE	20	1960
MY FAIR LADY FILM SOUNDTRACK	9	1964
MY FAIR LADY ORIGINAL CAST RECORDING	73	2001
MY FAIR LADY (ORIGINAL STUDIO CAST RECORDING) STAGE CAST RECORDING	41	1987
MY FIRST ALBUM LOLLY	21	1999
MY FIRST ALBUM VARIOUS ARTISTS (V2)	6	2005
MY FIRST CHRISTMAS ALBUM VARIOUS ARTISTS (V2)	13	2005
MY FIRST LOVE NICKY SPENCE	69	2007
MY FIRST NURSERY RHYMES VARIOUS ARTISTS (V2)	19	2006
MY FRIEND JIM REEVES	32	1972
MY GENERATION WHO	20	1980
MY GENERATION VARIOUS ARTISTS (TELSTAR)	16	1992
MY GENERATION – THE VERY BEST OF THE WHO WHO	11	1996
MY GIFT TO YOU ALEXANDER O'NEAL	53	1988
MY GIRL FILM SOUNDTRACK	13	1992
MY HEART WILL GO ON VARIOUS ARTISTS (SONY)	4	2004
MY HEART WOULD KNOW CHARLIE LANDSBOROUGH	60	2005
MY HEART'S DELIGHT LUCIANO PAVAROTTI WITH THE ROYAL PHILHARMONIC ORCHESTRA	44	1994
MY HITS AND LOVE SONGS GLEN CAMPBELL	50	1999
MY LIFE MARY J. BLIGE	59	1994
MY LIFE FOR A SONG PLACIDO DOMINGO	31	1983
MY LIFE IN THE BUSH OF GHOSTS BRIAN ENO & DAVID BYRNE	29	1981
MY LIFE: GREATEST HITS JULIO IGLESIAS	18	1998
MY LOVE VARIOUS ARTISTS (SONY/BMG)	4	2007
MY LOVE: ESSENTIAL COLLECTION CELINE DION	5	2008
MY LOVE IS YOUR LOVE WHITNEY HOUSTON	4	1998
MY NAME IS BARBRA, TWO BARBRA STREISAND	6	1966
MY NAME IS BUDDY RY COODER	41	2007
MY NAME IS JOE JOE	46	2000
MY NATION UNDERGROUND JULIAN COPE	42	1988
MY NEW ORLEANS HARRY CONNICK JR.	63	2007
MY ONLY FASCINATION DEMIS ROUSSOS	39	1976
MY OWN WAY JAY SEAN	6	2008
MY PEOPLE WERE FAIR AND HAD SKY IN THEIR HAIR BUT NOW THEY'RE CONTENT TO WEAR STARS ON THEIR BROWS TYRANNOSAURUS REX	15	1968
MY PROMISE NO MERCY	17	1997
MY SECRET PASSION – THE ARIAS MICHAEL BOLTON	25	1998
MY SONGS VARIOUS ARTISTS (UNIVERSAL)	3	2007
MY SOUL COOLIO	28	1997
MY TRIBUTE – BRYN YEMM INSPIRATIONAL ALBUM BRYN YEMM & THE GWENT CHORALE	85	1985
MY WAY FRANK SINATRA	2	1969
MY WAY USHER	16	1998
MY WAY – THE BEST OF FRANK SINATRA FRANK SINATRA	7	1997
MY WORLD BRYN CHRISTOPHER	18	2008
MYLEENE'S MUSIC FOR MOTHERS VARIOUS ARTISTS (EMI)	14	2008
MYLEENE'S MUSIC FOR ROMANCE VARIOUS ARTISTS (EMI)	9	2007
MYSTERIES OF FUNK GROOVERIDER	50	1998
MYSTERIO IAN McCULLOCH	46	1992
MYSTERY HOT CHOCOLATE	24	1982
MYSTERY RAH BAND	60	1985
MYSTERY GIRL ROY ORBISON	2	1989
MYSTERY WHITE BOY – LIVE 95-96 JEFF BUCKLEY	8	2000
THE MYTHS AND LEGENDS OF KING ARTHUR AND THE KNIGHTS OF THE ROUND TABLE RICK WAKEMAN WITH THE ENGLISH CHAMBER CHOIR AND ORCHESTRA	2	1975
MYTHS OF THE NEAR FUTURE KLAXONS	2	2007

N

Album / Artist	Peak Position	Year of Release
N SYNC N SYNC	30	1999
N.O.R.E. NOREAGA	72	1998
NAH=POO-THE ART OF BLUFF WAH!	33	1981
THE NAIL FILE – THE BEST OF JIMMY NAIL JIMMY NAIL	8	1997
NAKED KISSING THE PINK	54	1983
NAKED TALKING HEADS	3	1988
NAKED BLUE PEARL	58	1990
NAKED SCARLET	59	1995
NAKED LOUISE	7	1996
NAKED BABY PHOTOS BEN FOLDS FIVE	65	1998
THE NAKED RIDE HOME JACKSON BROWNE	53	2002
NAKED THUNDER IAN GILLAN	63	1990
NAKEDSELF THE THE	45	2000
THE NAME OF THIS BAND IS TALKING HEADS TALKING HEADS	22	1982
NANCY AND LEE NANCY SINATRA & LEE HAZLEWOOD	17	1971
NANCY'S GREATEST HITS NANCY SINATRA	39	1970
NANTUCKET SLEIGHRIDE MOUNTAIN	43	1971
NARCISSUS ROAD HOURS	47	2007
NARROW STAIRS DEATH CAB FOR CUTIE	24	2008
NAS NAS	23	2008
NASHVILLE JOSH ROUSE	66	2005
THE NASHVILLE DREAM VARIOUS ARTISTS (QUALITY TELEVISION)	10	1993
NASHVILLE SKYLINE BOB DYLAN	1	1969
NAT 'KING' COLE SINGS AND THE GEORGE SHEARING QUARTET PLAYS NAT 'KING' COLE/GEORGE SHEARING QUARTET	8	1962
NATHAN MICHAEL SHAWN WANYA BOYZ II MEN	54	2000
NATIONAL ANTHEMS 99 VARIOUS ARTISTS (TELSTAR)	3	1999
NATIONAL ANTHEMS 99 – VOLUME 2 VARIOUS ARTISTS (TELSTAR)	11	1999
NATIVE PLACE RAILWAY CHILDREN	59	1991
NATIVE TONGUE POISON	20	1993
NATTY DREAD BOB MARLEY & THE WAILERS	43	1975
NATURAL PETER ANDRE	1	1996
NATURAL ACT KRIS KRISTOFFERSON & RITA COOLIDGE	35	1978
NATURAL AVENUE JOHN LODGE	38	1977
THE NATURAL BLUES ALBUM VARIOUS ARTISTS (UNIVERSAL)	11	2001
NATURAL BORN KILLERS FILM SOUNDTRACK	10	1995
NATURAL HIGH COMMODORES	8	1978
NATURAL MYSTIC BOB MARLEY & THE WAILERS	5	1995
NATURAL THING JULIET ROBERTS	65	1994
NATURAL WOMAN VARIOUS ARTISTS (GLOBAL TELEVISION)	7	1995
NATURAL WOMAN VARIOUS ARTISTS (BMG)	5	2004
NATURAL WOMAN – THE AUTUMN COLLECTION VARIOUS ARTISTS (SONY)	19	2004
NATURAL WOMAN – THE VERY BEST OF CAROLE KING	31	2000
NATURAL WOMAN – VOLUME 2 VARIOUS ARTISTS (GLOBAL TELEVISION)	10	1996
NATURALLY IAN MOOR	38	2000
THE NATURE OF THE BEAST APRIL WINE	48	1981
NAUGHTY BUT NICE VARIOUS ARTISTS (FAMILY RECORDINGS)	19	2005
NAZARETH LIVE NAZARETH	78	1981
NB NATASHA BEDINGFIELD	9	2007
NEAPOLIS SIMPLE MINDS	19	1998
NEARLY GOD – POEMS NEARLY GOD	10	1996
NEARNESS OF YOU GLENN MILLER & HIS ORCHESTRA	30	1969
NEBRASKA BRUCE SPRINGSTEEN	3	1982
NECK AND NECK CHET ATKINS & MARK KNOPFLER	41	1990
NEED FOR NOT LEVITATION	45	1992
NEGOTIATIONS AND LOVE SONGS 1971-1986 PAUL SIMON	17	1988
NEIL REID NEIL REID	1	1972
NEITHER FISH NOR FLESH TERENCE TRENT D'ARBY	12	1989
NEITHER WASHINGTON NOR MOSCOW... REDSKINS	31	1986
NELLYVILLE NELLY	2	2002
NENA NENA	31	1984
NEO WAVE SILVER SUN	74	1998
NEON RICHARD FLEESHMAN	71	2007
NEON BALLROOM SILVERCHAIR	29	1999
NEON BIBLE ARCADE FIRE	2	2007
THE NEON HANDSHAKE HELL IS FOR HEROES	16	2003
NEON NIGHTS DANNII MINOGUE	8	2003
THE NEPHILIM FIELDS OF THE NEPHILIM	14	1988
NEPTUNE DUKE SPIRIT	63	2008
THE NEPTUNES PRESENTS CLONES VARIOUS ARTISTS (ARISTA)	2	2003
NERVE NET BRIAN ENO	70	1992
NEVER A DULL MOMENT ROD STEWART	1	1972
NEVER CAN SAY GOODBYE GLORIA GAYNOR	32	1975
NEVER ENDING SONG OF LOVE NEW SEEKERS	35	1972
NEVER ENOUGH MELISSA ETHERIDGE	56	1992
NEVER FELT SO GOOD JAMES INGRAM	72	1986
NEVER FOR EVER KATE BUSH	1	1980
NEVER FORGET VARIOUS ARTISTS (SONY BMG)	15	2007
NEVER FORGET – THE ULTIMATE COLLECTION TAKE THAT	2	2005

Title / Artist	Peak Position	Year of Release
NEVER FORGET – THE VERY BEST OF THE 90'S VARIOUS ARTISTS (BMG)	15	2004
NEVER GONE BACKSTREET BOYS	11	2005
NEVER LET HER GO DAVID GATES	32	1975
NEVER LET ME DOWN DAVID BOWIE	6	1987
NEVER LET ME GO LUTHER VANDROSS	11	1993
NEVER LOVED ELVIS WONDER STUFF	3	1991
NEVER MIND THE BOLLOCKS, HERE'S THE SEX PISTOLS SEX PISTOLS	1	1977
NEVER NEVER NEVER SHIRLEY BASSEY	10	1973
NEVER NEVERLAND ANNIHILATOR	48	1990
NEVER ON SUNDAY FILM SOUNDTRACK	17	1961
NEVER SAID GOODBYE CERYS MATTHEWS	43	2006
NEVER SAY DIE BLACK SABBATH	12	1978
NEVER S-A-Y NEVER BRANDY	19	1998
NEVER TOO LATE STATUS QUO	2	1981
NEVER TOO MUCH LUTHER VANDROSS	41	1987
NEVER TOO YOUNG TO ROCK VARIOUS ARTISTS (GTO)	30	1975
NEVER, NEVER, LAND UNKLE	24	2003
NEVERLAND MISSION	58	1995
NEVERMIND NIRVANA	7	1991
NEW ADVENTURES IN HI-FI R.E.M.	1	1996
THE NEW AGE OF ATLANTIC VARIOUS ARTISTS (ATLANTIC)	25	1972
NEW AMERYKAH PART ONE (4TH WORLD WAR) ERYKAH BADU	55	2008
NEW BEGINNING SWV	26	1996
NEW BEGINNING STEPHEN GATELY	9	2000
NEW BOOTS AND PANTIES IAN DURY & THE BLOCKHEADS	5	1977
NEW BREED VARIOUS ARTISTS (UNIVERSAL)	18	2004
THE NEW CLASSIC CHILLOUT ALBUM VARIOUS ARTISTS (COLUMBIA)	5	2002
NEW CLASSIX 2008 VARIOUS ARTISTS (UNIVERSAL)	13	2008
NEW CLEAR DAYS VAPORS	44	1980
NEW COLOURS NEW SEEKERS	40	1972
THE NEW DANGER MOS DEF	56	2004
NEW DAY JANE HARRISON	70	1989
A NEW DAY AT MIDNIGHT DAVID GRAY	1	2002
A NEW DAY HAS COME CELINE DION	1	2002
A NEW DAY – LIVE IN LAS VEGAS CELINE DION	22	2004
NEW DIMENSIONS THREE DEGREES	34	1979
NEW ENGLAND WISHBONE ASH	22	1976
NEW FAVOURITE ALISON KRAUSS & UNION STATION	72	2001
A NEW FLAME SIMPLY RED	1	1989
NEW FORMS RONI SIZE / REPRAZENT	8	1997
NEW FRONTIERS (EP) DJ HYPE PRESENTS GANJA KRU	56	1997
NEW FUNKY NATION BOO-YAA T.R.I.B.E.	74	1990
NEW GOLD DREAM (81,82,83,84) SIMPLE MINDS	3	1982
THE NEW GOODIES LP GOODIES	25	1975
NEW HITS 1997 VARIOUS ARTISTS (GLOBAL TELEVISION)	1	1997
NEW HITS 2000 VARIOUS ARTISTS (WARNER BROTHERS)	1	2000
NEW HITS 96 VARIOUS ARTISTS (GLOBAL TELEVISION)	1	1996
NEW HITS 98 VARIOUS ARTISTS (SONY)	1	1998
NEW HITS 99 VARIOUS ARTISTS (GLOBAL TELEVISION)	1	1999
NEW HOPE FOR THE WRETCHED PLASMATICS	55	1980
NEW HORIZONS DON WILLIAMS	29	1979
NEW HORIZONS ALED JONES	21	2005
THE NEW INDIE – ALIVE & AMPLIFIED VARIOUS ARTISTS (UNIVERSAL)	11	2005
NEW JACK CITY FILM SOUNDTRACK	16	1991
NEW JACK SWING VARIOUS ARTISTS (UNIVERSAL)	10	2002
NEW JACK SWING MASTERCUTS VOLUME 1 VARIOUS ARTISTS (MASTERCUTS)	8	1992
NEW JACK SWING VOLUME 3 VARIOUS ARTISTS (MASTERCUTS)	18	1994
NEW JERSEY BON JOVI	1	1988
NEW KIDS ON THE BLOCK NEW KIDS ON THE BLOCK	6	1990
NEW LEE DORSEY LEE DORSEY	34	1966
THE NEW LOVE ALBUM VARIOUS ARTISTS (VIRGIN)	7	2000
NEW MAN NUMAN – THE BEST OF GARY NUMAN GARY NUMAN	45	1982
NEW MISERABLE EXPERIENCE GIN BLOSSOMS	53	1994
NEW MOON ELLIOTT SMITH	39	2007
NEW MORNING BOB DYLAN	1	1970
A NEW MORNING SUEDE	24	2002
THE NEW ORDER TESTAMENT	81	1988
THE NEW PAVAROTTI COLLECTION LIVE! LUCIANO PAVAROTTI	63	1988
NEW PEPSI CHART 2002 VARIOUS ARTISTS (VIRGIN)	2	2002
THE NEW PEPSI CHART ALBUM VARIOUS ARTISTS (VIRGIN)	2	2001
NEW PURE MOODS VARIOUS ARTISTS (VIRGIN)	16	1997
NEW ROMANTIC CLASSICS VARIOUS ARTISTS (VIRGIN)	7	1992
NEW ROOTS VARIOUS ARTISTS (STYLUS)	18	1989
NEW SENSATIONS LOU REED	92	1984
NEW SKIN FOR THE OLD CEREMONY LEONARD COHEN	24	1974
THE NEW SOUL ALBUM VARIOUS ARTISTS (COLUMBIA)	9	1999
NEW SOUL REBELS VARIOUS ARTISTS (GLOBAL TELEVISION)	6	1995
THE NEW SOUND OF CHRISTMAS MANCHESTER BOYS CHOIR	80	1985
THE NEW STARLIGHT EXPRESS STAGE CAST RECORDING	42	1993
NEW TRADITIONALISTS DEVO	50	1981
NEW TRADITIONS VARIOUS ARTISTS (TELSTAR)	13	1990
THE NEW TRANSISTOR HEROES BIS	55	1997
NEW VALUES IGGY POP	60	1979
NEW VINTAGE PETER GRANT	8	2006
NEW WAVE VARIOUS ARTISTS (PHILIPS)	11	1977
NEW WAVE AUTEURS	35	1993
NEW WAVE HEROES VARIOUS ARTISTS (SONY/BMG)	15	2006
NEW WOMAN VARIOUS ARTISTS (VIRGIN)	14	1999
NEW WOMAN 2000 VARIOUS ARTISTS (VIRGIN)	1	2000
NEW WOMAN 2001 VARIOUS ARTISTS (VIRGIN)	1	2001
NEW WOMAN 2002 VARIOUS ARTISTS (VIRGIN)	1	2002
NEW WOMAN 2003 VARIOUS ARTISTS (VIRGIN)	2	2003
NEW WOMAN – HITS FROM THE CHICK FLICKS VARIOUS ARTISTS (EMI)	3	2006
NEW WOMAN – LOVE SONGS VARIOUS ARTISTS (VIRGIN)	14	2001
NEW WOMAN – NEW COLLECTION 2004 VARIOUS ARTISTS (VIRGIN)	4	2004
NEW WOMAN – SPRING COLLECTION VARIOUS ARTISTS (EMI)	3	2005
NEW WOMAN SUMMER 2000 VARIOUS ARTISTS (VIRGIN)	5	2000
NEW WOMAN – THE AUTUMN COLLECTION VARIOUS ARTISTS (VIRGIN)	1	2002
NEW WOMAN – THE CLASSICS VARIOUS ARTISTS (EMI)	11	2007
NEW WOMAN – THE NEW COLLECTION 2003 VARIOUS ARTISTS (EMI)	3	2003
NEW WOMAN – THE NEW COLLECTION 2005 VARIOUS ARTISTS (EMI)	4	2005
A NEW WORLD WILL MARTIN	21	2008
NEW WORLD IN THE MORNING ROGER WHITTAKER	45	1971
NEW WORLD ORDER CURTIS MAYFIELD	44	1997
A NEW WORLD RECORD ELECTRIC LIGHT ORCHESTRA	6	1976
NEW YORK LOU REED	14	1989
NEW YORK, NEW YORK (GREATEST HITS) FRANK SINATRA	13	1986
NEWPOWER SOUL NEW POWER GENERATION	38	1998
NEWS AND TRIBUTES FUTUREHEADS	12	2006
NEWS OF THE WORLD QUEEN	4	1977
NEXT SENSATIONAL ALEX HARVEY BAND	37	1975
NEXUS ANOTHER LEVEL	7	1999
NICE NICE	3	1969
NICE 'N EASY FRANK SINATRA	4	1961
NICE 'N' EASY VARIOUS ARTISTS (PHILIPS)	36	1973
A NICE PAIR PINK FLOYD	21	1974
NICELY OUT OF TUNE LINDISFARNE	8	1972
NICK BERRY NICK BERRY	28	1986
NICK KAMEN NICK KAMEN	34	1987
NICK OF TIME BONNIE RAITT	51	1990
NICK THE KNIFE NICK LOWE	99	1982
NICK WARREN – BUDAPEST VARIOUS ARTISTS (GLOBAL UNDERGROUND)	20	1999
NIGHT AFTER NIGHT NILS LOFGREN	38	1977
NIGHT AND DAY JOE JACKSON	3	1982
A NIGHT AT THE MOVIES DAVID ESSEX	14	1997
A NIGHT AT THE OPERA QUEEN	1	1975
A NIGHT AT THE OPERA VARIOUS ARTISTS (TELSTAR)	2	1990
NIGHT BEAT VARIOUS ARTISTS (STYLUS)	15	1985
NIGHT BEAT II VARIOUS ARTISTS (STYLUS)	7	1986
NIGHT BIRDS SHAKATAK	4	1982
NIGHT CALLS JOE COCKER	25	1992
NIGHT DUBBING IMAGINATION	9	1983
NIGHT FADES AWAY NILS LOFGREN	50	1981
NIGHT FLIGHT JUSTIN HAYWARD	41	1980
NIGHT FLIGHT BUDGIE	68	1981
NIGHT FLIGHT TO VENUS BONEY M	1	1978
NIGHT GALLERY BARRON KNIGHTS	15	1978
THE NIGHT HAS A THOUSAND EYES BOBBY VEE	15	1963
THE NIGHT I FELL IN LOVE LUTHER VANDROSS	19	1985
A NIGHT IN PARIS DIANA KRALL	30	2002
A NIGHT IN SAN FRANCISCO VAN MORRISON	8	1994
NIGHT MOVES VARIOUS ARTISTS (K-TEL)	10	1979
NIGHT NURSE GREGORY ISAACS	32	1982
NIGHT OF A THOUSAND CANDLES MEN THEY COULDN'T HANG	91	1985
NIGHT ON MY SIDE GEMMA HAYES	52	2002
A NIGHT ON THE TOWN ROD STEWART	1	1976
A NIGHT ON THE TOWN BRUCE HORNBY & THE RANGE	23	1990
NIGHT OUT ELLEN FOLEY	68	1979
NIGHT OWL GERRY RAFFERTY	9	1979
NIGHT PEOPLE CLASSIX NOUVEAUX	66	1981
NIGHT RIDE HOME JONI MITCHELL	25	1991
NIGHT SONG NUSRAT FATEH ALI KHAN/ MICHAEL BROOK	65	1996
NIGHT TIME KILLING JOKE	11	1985
A NIGHT TO REMEMBER CYNDI LAUPER	9	1989
A NIGHT TO REMEMBER JOHNNY MATHIS	29	2008
NIGHT WORKS LAYO & BUSHWACKA!	61	2002

Title / Artist	Peak Position	Year of Release
NIGHTBIRD ERASURE	27	2005
NIGHTCLUBBING GRACE JONES	35	1981
NIGHTFEVER VARIOUS ARTISTS (GLOBAL TELEVISION)	7	1995
THE NIGHTFLY DONALD FAGEN	44	1982
NIGHTFREAK AND THE SONS OF BECKER CORAL	5	2004
NIGHTLIFE VARIOUS ARTISTS (K-TEL)	25	1980
NIGHTLIFE PET SHOP BOYS	7	1999
NIGHTLINE RANDY CRAWFORD	37	1983
NIGHTSHIFT COMMODORES	13	1985
NILSSON SCHMILSSON NILSSON	4	1972
NIMROD GREEN DAY	11	1997
NINA AND FREDERIK NINA & FREDERIK	9	1960
9 PUBLIC IMAGE LTD	36	1989
9 DAMIEN RICE	4	2006
9.0 LIVE SLIPKNOT	53	2005
NINE LIVES AEROSMITH	4	1997
NINE LIVES STEVE WINWOOD	31	2008
999 999	53	1978
NINE OBJECTS OF DESIRE SUZANNE VEGA	43	1997
NINE TONIGHT BOB SEGER & THE SILVER BULLET BAND	24	1981
19 ADELE	1	2008
1984 RICK WAKEMAN	24	1981
1984 VAN HALEN	15	1984
1984 (FOR THE LOVE OF BIG BROTHER) (OST) EURYTHMICS	23	1984
1984-1989 LLOYD COLE & THE COMMOTIONS	14	1989
1982 STATUS QUO	1	1982
19 NAUGHTY III NAUGHTY BY NATURE	40	1993
1992 – THE LOVE ALBUM CARTER – THE UNSTOPPABLE SEX MACHINE	1	1992
1992 – 2002 UNDERWORLD	43	2003
1999 PRINCE	30	1984
1999 CASSIUS	28	1999
THE 1999 BRIT AWARDS VARIOUS ARTISTS (COLUMBIA)	3	1999
1979-1983 BAUHAUS	36	1985
1977 ASH	1	1996
1977-1980 SUBSTANCE JOY DIVISION	7	1988
1977 – THE SPIRIT OF PUNK VARIOUS ARTISTS (EMI)	7	2007
1916 MOTORHEAD	24	1991
THE 90'S VARIOUS ARTISTS (UNIVERSAL)	20	1999
90S ANTHEMS VARIOUS ARTISTS (UNIVERSAL)	9	2007
NINETY 808 STATE	57	1989
90 CLUB HITS FROM THE 90'S VARIOUS ARTISTS (WARNER BROTHERS)	20	2007
99.9 F SUZANNE VEGA	20	1992
90125 YES	16	1983
THE '97 BRIT AWARDS VARIOUS ARTISTS (COLUMBIA)	2	1997
9012 LIVE: THE SOLOS YES	44	1986
NINJA TUNA MR. SCRUFF	60	2008
NINTH HERB ALPERT & THE TIJUANA BRASS	26	1968
NIRVANA NIRVANA	3	2002
NITE FLITE VARIOUS ARTISTS (CBS)	1	1988
NITE FLITE VARIOUS ARTISTS (SONY BMG)	9	2008
NITE FLITE 2 VARIOUS ARTISTS (CBS)	1	1989
NITE FLITE 3 – BEING WITH YOU VARIOUS ARTISTS (CBS)	3	1990
NIXON LAMBCHOP	60	2000
NME CLASSICS VARIOUS ARTISTS (EMI)	8	2008
NME IN ASSOCIATION WITH WAR CHILD PRESENTS 1 LOVE VARIOUS ARTISTS (B UNIQUE)	2	2002
NME PRESENTS THE ESSENTIAL BANDS VARIOUS ARTISTS (UNIVERSAL)	3	2005
NME PRESENTS THE ESSENTIAL BANDS – FESTIVAL VARIOUS ARTISTS (UNIVERSAL)	3	2007
NO ANGEL DIDO	1	2000
NO BREAKS JOHN WAITE	64	1984
NO CAUSE FOR ALARM VIOLINSKI	49	1979
NO CAUSE FOR CONCERN VICE SQUAD	32	1981
NO CODE PEARL JAM	3	1996
NO COUNT – SARAH SARAH VAUGHAN	19	1960
NO DIRECTION HOME BOB DYLAN	21	2005
NO EARTHLY CONNECTION RICK WAKEMAN	9	1976
NO EXIT BLONDIE	3	1999
NO FREE LUNCH GREEN ON RED	99	1985
NO GOATS, NO GLORY GOATS	58	1994
NO GREATER LOVE VARIOUS ARTISTS (GLOBAL TELEVISION)	4	1996
NO GURU, NO METHOD, NO TEACHER VAN MORRISON	27	1986
NO HOLDING BACK WAYNE WONDER	40	2003
NO JACKET REQUIRED PHIL COLLINS	1	1985
NO LIMITS 2 UNLIMITED	1	1993
NO LOVE LOST RIFLES	68	2006
NO MEAN CITY NAZARETH	34	1979
NO MORE DRAMA MARY J. BLIGE	4	2001
NO MORE GAMES/THE REMIX ALBUM NEW KIDS ON THE BLOCK	15	1991
NO MORE HEROES STRANGLERS	2	1977
NO MORE SHALL WE PART NICK CAVE & THE BAD SEEDS	15	2001
NO MORE TEARS OZZY OSBOURNE	17	1991
NO MORE THE FOOL ELKIE BROOKS	5	1986
NO NEED TO ARGUE CRANBERRIES	2	1994
NO, NO, NO DAWN PENN	51	1994
NO ORDINARY WORLD JOE COCKER	63	1999
NO PARLEZ PAUL YOUNG	1	1983
NO PLACE LIKE HOME BIG COUNTRY	28	1991
NO PLACE TO RUN UFO	11	1980
NO POINT IN WASTING TEARS IRONIK	21	2008
NO PRAYER FOR THE DYING IRON MAIDEN	2	1990
NO PROMISES CARLA BRUNI	65	2007
NO PROTECTION STARSHIP	26	1987
NO QUARTER – JIMMY PAGE AND ROBERT PLANT UNLEDDED JIMMY PAGE & ROBERT PLANT	7	1994
NO REASON TO CRY ERIC CLAPTON	8	1976
NO REGRETS WALKER BROTHERS	49	1976
NO REGRETS – THE BEST OF 1965-1976 SCOTT WALKER & THE WALKER BROTHERS	55	2000
NO REGRETS – THE BEST OF SCOTT WALKER AND THE WALKER BROTHERS SCOTT WALKER & THE WALKER BROTHERS	4	1992
NO REMORSE MOTORHEAD	14	1984
NO RESERVATIONS APACHE INDIAN	36	1993
NO REST FOR THE WICKED NEW MODEL ARMY	22	1985
NO REST FOR THE WICKED OZZY OSBOURNE	23	1988
NO ROOTS FAITHLESS	1	2004
NO SECRETS CARLY SIMON	3	1973
NO SECURITY ROLLING STONES	67	1998
NO SENSE OF SIN LOTUS EATERS	96	1984
NO SLEEP AT ALL MOTORHEAD	79	1988
NO SLEEP 'TIL HAMMERSMITH MOTORHEAD	1	1981
NO SMOKE WITHOUT FIRE WISHBONE ASH	43	1978
NO STRINGS ATTACHED N SYNC	14	2000
NO WAY OUT PUFF DADDY	8	1997
NO WORLD FOR TOMORROW COHEED & CAMBRIA	41	2007
NO WOW KILLS	56	2005
NOBODY DOES IT BETTER – THE VERY BEST OF CARLY SIMON CARLY SIMON	22	1999
NOBODY ELSE TAKE THAT	1	1995
NOBODY ELSE (US VERSION) TAKE THAT	26	1995
NOBODY NEEDS YOUR LOVE GENE PITNEY	13	1966
NOBODY'S CHILD – ROMANIAN ANGEL APPEAL VARIOUS ARTISTS (WARNER BROTHERS)	18	1990
NOBODY'S FOOL SLADE	14	1976
NOBODY'S HEROES STIFF LITTLE FINGERS	8	1980
NOBODY'S PERFECT DEEP PURPLE	38	1988
NOCHE DE CUATRO LUNAS JULIO IGLESIAS	32	2000
NOCTURAMA NICK CAVE & THE BAD SEEDS	20	2003
NOCTURNE SIOUXSIE & THE BANSHEES	29	1983
A NOD'S AS GOOD AS A WINK...TO A BLIND HORSE FACES	2	1971
NOEL JOSH GROBAN	58	2007
NOEL – CHRISTMAS SONGS AND CAROLS VARIOUS ARTISTS (TRAX)	89	1988
NOISE VARIOUS ARTISTS (JUMPIN' & PUMPIN')	20	1992
NOISE 2 VARIOUS ARTISTS (JUMPIN' & PUMPIN')	11	1992
NOLA DOWN	68	1995
NOLANS NOLANS	15	1980
NON STOP JULIO IGLESIAS	33	1988
NON STOP 20 VOLUME 4 ANONYMOUS COVER VERSIONS	35	1971
NON STOP HITS VARIOUS ARTISTS (TELSTAR)	4	1998
NON STOP HITS – VOLUME 2 VARIOUS ARTISTS (TELSTAR)	19	1998
NON-STOP DANCE ANTHEMS VARIOUS ARTISTS (TELSTAR)	5	1998
NON-STOP DANCING JAMES LAST	35	1967
NON-STOP DANCING 12 JAMES LAST	30	1971
NON-STOP DANCING 13 JAMES LAST	32	1972
NON-STOP DANCING '69 JAMES LAST	26	1969
NON-STOP DANCING '69/2 JAMES LAST	27	1970
NON-STOP DANCING '70 JAMES LAST	67	1970
NON-STOP DANCING '71 JAMES LAST	21	1971
NON-STOP DANCING '83 – PARTY POWER JAMES LAST	56	1983
NON-STOP DANCING VOLUME 14 JAMES LAST	27	1973
NON-STOP DANCING VOLUME 15 JAMES LAST	34	1973
NON-STOP DANCING VOLUME 16 JAMES LAST	43	1974
NON-STOP ECSTATIC DANCING SOFT CELL	6	1982
NON-STOP EROTIC CABARET SOFT CELL	5	1981
NON-STOP EVERGREENS JAMES LAST	26	1970
NONSUCH XTC	28	1992
NORFOLK COAST STRANGLERS	70	2004
NORTH ELVIS COSTELLO	44	2003
NORTH AND SOUTH GERRY RAFFERTY	43	1988
THE NORTH AT ITS HEIGHTS MC TUNES	26	1990
NORTH ATLANTIC DRIFT OCEAN COLOUR SCENE	14	2003
NORTH OF A MIRACLE NICK HEYWARD	10	1983
THE NORTH STAR RODDY FRAME	55	1998
THE NORTH STAR GRASSMAN AND THE RAVENS SANDY DENNY	31	1971
THE NORTHERN BEAT VARIOUS ARTISTS (LONDON)	4	1990
NORTHERN EXPOSURE 2 – SASHA & DIGWEED VARIOUS ARTISTS (MINISTRY OF SOUND)	15	1997
NORTHERN EXPOSURE – SASHA & JOHN DIGWEED VARIOUS ARTISTS (MINISTRY OF SOUND)	7	1996
NORTHERN EXPOSURE – SASHA + JOHN DIGWEED VARIOUS ARTISTS (INCREDIBLE)	6	1999
NORTHERN SOUL M PEOPLE	26	1993
A NORTHERN SOUL VERVE	13	1995
NORTHERN STAR MELANIE C	4	1999
NORTHERN UPROAR NORTHERN UPROAR	22	1996
NORTHWINDS DAVID COVERDALE	78	1982
NOSTRADAMUS JUDAS PRIEST	30	2008
NOT A LITTLE GIRL ANYMORE LINDA LEWIS	40	1975

Title / Artist	Peak Position	Year of Release
NOT ACCEPTED ANYWHERE AUTOMATIC	3	2006
NOT FRAGILE BACHMAN-TURNER OVERDRIVE	12	1974
NOT ME GLENN MEDEIROS	63	1988
NOT SATISFIED ASWAD	50	1982
NOT THAT I'M BIASED MAX BOYCE	27	1979
NOT THAT KIND ANASTACIA	2	2000
NOT THE NINE O'CLOCK NEWS NOT THE NINE O'CLOCK NEWS CAST	5	1980
NOT THE NINE O'CLOCK NEWS – HEDGEHOG SANDWICH NOT THE NINE O'CLOCK NEWS CAST	5	1981
NOT TILL TOMORROW RALPH McTELL	36	1972
NOT TOO LATE NORAH JONES	1	2007
NOTHIN' BUT THE BLUE ELKIE BROOKS	58	1994
NOTHING BUT THE BEST GILBERT O'SULLIVAN	50	1991
NOTHING BUT THE BEST FRANK SINATRA	10	2008
NOTHING COMPARES TO THIS VARIOUS ARTISTS (PARKFIELD)	13	1990
NOTHING LESS THAN BRILLIANT SANDIE SHAW	64	1994
NOTHING LIKE THE SUN STING	1	1987
NOTORIOUS DURAN DURAN	16	1986
THE NOTORIOUS BYRD BROTHERS BYRDS	12	1968
THE NOTORIOUS KIM LIL' KIM	67	2000
NOTTING HILL FILM SOUNDTRACK	4	1999
NOVELTY NO 1'S VARIOUS ARTISTS (VIRGIN)	6	2005
NOW NEW SEEKERS	47	1973
NOW VIC DAMONE	28	1981
NOW PATRICE RUSHEN	73	1984
NOW PAUL RODGERS	30	1997
NOW MAXWELL	46	2001
NOW AIN'T THE TIME FOR YOUR TEARS WENDY JAMES	43	1993
NOW AND THEN CARPENTERS	2	1973
NOW AND THEN STATUS QUO	49	2005
NOW AND THEN CHRIS DE BURGH	12	2008
NOW AND THEN – GREATEST HITS 1964 – 2004 ROGER WHITTAKER	21	2004
NOW AND ZEN ROBERT PLANT	10	1988
NOW DANCE VARIOUS ARTISTS (VIRGIN)	4	2004
NOW DANCE 2000 VARIOUS ARTISTS (EMI)	1	1999
NOW DANCE 2001 VARIOUS ARTISTS (VIRGIN)	1	2000
NOW DANCE 2001 PART 2 VARIOUS ARTISTS (VIRGIN)	2	2001
NOW DANCE 2002 VARIOUS ARTISTS (VIRGIN)	1	2001
NOW DANCE 2002 PART 2 VARIOUS ARTISTS (VIRGIN)	3	2002
NOW DANCE 2003 VARIOUS ARTISTS (VIRGIN)	1	2002
NOW DANCE 2003 PART 2 VARIOUS ARTISTS (VIRGIN)	5	2003
NOW DANCE 2004 VARIOUS ARTISTS (VIRGIN)	1	2003
NOW DANCE 2005 VARIOUS ARTISTS (VIRGIN)	3	2004
NOW DANCE 2007 VARIOUS ARTISTS (EMI)	3	2006
NOW DANCE 2008 VARIOUS ARTISTS (EMI)	4	2007
NOW DANCE '86 VARIOUS ARTISTS (EMI)	2	1986
NOW DANCE '89 – THE 12" MIXES VARIOUS ARTISTS (EMI)	1	1989
NOW DANCE 901 – 20 SMASH DANCE HITS – THE 12" MIXES VARIOUS ARTISTS (EMI)	1	1990
NOW DANCE 902 VARIOUS ARTISTS (EMI)	1	1990
NOW DANCE 903 – THE 12" MIXES VARIOUS ARTISTS (EMI)	1	1990
NOW DANCE 91 VARIOUS ARTISTS (EMI)	1	1991
NOW DANCE 92 VARIOUS ARTISTS (EMI)	3	1992
NOW DANCE 93 VARIOUS ARTISTS (EMI)	1	1993
NOW DANCE 94 VOLUME 1 VARIOUS ARTISTS (EMI)	1	1994
NOW DANCE 94 VOLUME 2 VARIOUS ARTISTS (EMI)	8	1994
NOW DANCE 95 VARIOUS ARTISTS (EMI)	3	1995
NOW DANCE 97 VARIOUS ARTISTS (EMI)	1	1997
NOW DANCE 98 VARIOUS ARTISTS (EMI)	3	1998
NOW DANCE – SUMMER 94 VARIOUS ARTISTS (EMI)	1	1994
NOW DANCE SUMMER 95 VARIOUS ARTISTS (EMI)	3	1995
NOW DANCE – THE 12" MIXES VARIOUS ARTISTS (EMI)	3	1985
NOW DANCE – THE BEST OF '93 VARIOUS ARTISTS (EMI)	1	1993
NOW DANCE – THE BEST OF 94 VARIOUS ARTISTS (EMI)	4	1994
NOW DECADES VARIOUS ARTISTS (EMI)	1	2003
NOW I GOT WORRY JON SPENCER BLUES EXPLOSION	50	1996
NOW I'M A COWBOY AUTEURS	27	1994
NOW IN A MINUTE DONNA LEWIS	52	1996
NOW OR NEVER BLAZIN' SQUAD	37	2003
NOW THAT'S WHAT I CALL MUSIC 10 VARIOUS ARTISTS (EMI)	1	1987
NOW THAT'S WHAT I CALL MUSIC 11 VARIOUS ARTISTS (EMI)	1	1988
NOW THAT'S WHAT I CALL MUSIC 12 VARIOUS ARTISTS (EMI)	1	1988
NOW THAT'S WHAT I CALL MUSIC 13 VARIOUS ARTISTS (EMI)	1	1988
NOW THAT'S WHAT I CALL MUSIC 14 VARIOUS ARTISTS (EMI)	1	1989
NOW THAT'S WHAT I CALL MUSIC 15 VARIOUS ARTISTS (EMI)	1	1989
NOW THAT'S WHAT I CALL MUSIC 16 VARIOUS ARTISTS (EMI)	1	1989
NOW THAT'S WHAT I CALL MUSIC 17 VARIOUS ARTISTS (EMI)	1	1990
NOW THAT'S WHAT I CALL MUSIC! 1983 VARIOUS ARTISTS (EMI)	10	1993
NOW THAT'S WHAT I CALL MUSIC! 1984 VARIOUS ARTISTS (EMI)	13	1993
NOW THAT'S WHAT I CALL MUSIC! 1985 VARIOUS ARTISTS (EMI)	15	1993
NOW THAT'S WHAT I CALL MUSIC! 1986 VARIOUS ARTISTS (EMI)	16	1993
NOW THAT'S WHAT I CALL MUSIC! 1987 VARIOUS ARTISTS (EMI)	17	1993
NOW THAT'S WHAT I CALL MUSIC! 1988 VARIOUS ARTISTS (EMI)	20	1993
NOW THAT'S WHAT I CALL MUSIC! 1992 VARIOUS ARTISTS (EMI)	14	1993
NOW THAT'S WHAT I CALL MUSIC! 1993 VARIOUS ARTISTS (EMI)	1	1993
NOW THAT'S WHAT I CALL MUSIC! 1994 VARIOUS ARTISTS (EMI)	1	1994
NOW THAT'S WHAT I CALL MUSIC! 1995 VARIOUS ARTISTS (EMI)	2	1995
NOW THAT'S WHAT I CALL MUSIC! 20 VARIOUS ARTISTS (EMI)	1	1991
NOW THAT'S WHAT I CALL MUSIC! 21 VARIOUS ARTISTS (EMI)	1	1992
NOW THAT'S WHAT I CALL MUSIC! 22 VARIOUS ARTISTS (EMI)	1	1992
NOW THAT'S WHAT I CALL MUSIC! 23 VARIOUS ARTISTS (EMI)	1	1992
NOW THAT'S WHAT I CALL MUSIC! 24 VARIOUS ARTISTS (EMI)	1	1993
NOW THAT'S WHAT I CALL MUSIC! 25 VARIOUS ARTISTS (EMI)	1	1993
NOW THAT'S WHAT I CALL MUSIC 25 YEARS VARIOUS ARTISTS (EMI)	3	2008
NOW THAT'S WHAT I CALL MUSIC! 26 VARIOUS ARTISTS (EMI)	1	1993
NOW THAT'S WHAT I CALL MUSIC! 27 VARIOUS ARTISTS (EMI)	1	1994
NOW THAT'S WHAT I CALL MUSIC! 28 VARIOUS ARTISTS (EMI)	1	1994
NOW THAT'S WHAT I CALL MUSIC! 29 VARIOUS ARTISTS (EMI)	1	1994
NOW THAT'S WHAT I CALL MUSIC! 30 VARIOUS ARTISTS (EMI)	1	1995
NOW THAT'S WHAT I CALL MUSIC! 31 VARIOUS ARTISTS (EMI)	1	1995
NOW THAT'S WHAT I CALL MUSIC! 32 VARIOUS ARTISTS (EMI)	1	1995
NOW THAT'S WHAT I CALL MUSIC! 33 VARIOUS ARTISTS (EMI)	1	1996
NOW THAT'S WHAT I CALL MUSIC! 34 VARIOUS ARTISTS (EMI)	1	1996
NOW THAT'S WHAT I CALL MUSIC! 35 VARIOUS ARTISTS (EMI)	1	1996
NOW THAT'S WHAT I CALL MUSIC! 36 VARIOUS ARTISTS (EMI)	1	1997
NOW THAT'S WHAT I CALL MUSIC! 37 VARIOUS ARTISTS (EMI)	1	1997
NOW THAT'S WHAT I CALL MUSIC! 38 VARIOUS ARTISTS (EMI)	1	1997
NOW THAT'S WHAT I CALL MUSIC! 39 VARIOUS ARTISTS (EMI)	1	1998
NOW THAT'S WHAT I CALL MUSIC! 40 VARIOUS ARTISTS (EMI)	1	1998
NOW THAT'S WHAT I CALL MUSIC! 41 VARIOUS ARTISTS (EMI)	1	1998
NOW THAT'S WHAT I CALL MUSIC! 42 VARIOUS ARTISTS (EMI)	1	1999
NOW THAT'S WHAT I CALL MUSIC! 43 VARIOUS ARTISTS (EMI)	1	1999
NOW THAT'S WHAT I CALL MUSIC! 44 VARIOUS ARTISTS (EMI)	1	1999
NOW THAT'S WHAT I CALL MUSIC! 45 VARIOUS ARTISTS (EMI)	1	2000
NOW THAT'S WHAT I CALL MUSIC! 46 VARIOUS ARTISTS (EMI)	1	2000
NOW THAT'S WHAT I CALL MUSIC! 47 VARIOUS ARTISTS (EMI)	1	2000
NOW THAT'S WHAT I CALL MUSIC! 48 VARIOUS ARTISTS (EMI)	1	2001
NOW THAT'S WHAT I CALL MUSIC! 49 VARIOUS ARTISTS (EMI)	1	2001
NOW THAT'S WHAT I CALL MUSIC! 50 VARIOUS ARTISTS (EMI)	1	2001
NOW THAT'S WHAT I CALL MUSIC! 51 VARIOUS ARTISTS (EMI)	1	2002
NOW THAT'S WHAT I CALL MUSIC! 52 VARIOUS ARTISTS (EMI)	1	2002
NOW THAT'S WHAT I CALL MUSIC! 53 VARIOUS ARTISTS (EMI)	1	2002
NOW THAT'S WHAT I CALL MUSIC! 54 VARIOUS ARTISTS (EMI)	1	2003
NOW THAT'S WHAT I CALL MUSIC! 55 VARIOUS ARTISTS (EMI)	1	2003
NOW THAT'S WHAT I CALL MUSIC! 56 VARIOUS ARTISTS (EMI)	1	2003
NOW THAT'S WHAT I CALL MUSIC! 57 VARIOUS ARTISTS (EMI)	1	2004
NOW THAT'S WHAT I CALL MUSIC! 58 VARIOUS ARTISTS (EMI)	1	2004
NOW THAT'S WHAT I CALL MUSIC! 59 VARIOUS ARTISTS (EMI)	1	2004
NOW THAT'S WHAT I CALL MUSIC! 60 VARIOUS ARTISTS (EMI)	1	2005
NOW THAT'S WHAT I CALL MUSIC! 61 VARIOUS ARTISTS (EMI)	1	2005

Title / Artist	Peak Position	Year of Release
NOW THAT'S WHAT I CALL MUSIC! 62 VARIOUS ARTISTS (EMI)	1	2005
NOW THAT'S WHAT I CALL MUSIC! 63 VARIOUS ARTISTS (EMI)	1	2006
NOW THAT'S WHAT I CALL MUSIC! 64 VARIOUS ARTISTS (EMI)	1	2006
NOW THAT'S WHAT I CALL MUSIC! 65 VARIOUS ARTISTS (EMI)	1	2006
NOW THAT'S WHAT I CALL MUSIC 66 VARIOUS ARTISTS (EMI)	1	2007
NOW THAT'S WHAT I CALL MUSIC 67 VARIOUS ARTISTS (EMI)	1	2007
NOW THAT'S WHAT I CALL MUSIC 68 VARIOUS ARTISTS (EMI)	1	2007
NOW THAT'S WHAT I CALL MUSIC 69 VARIOUS ARTISTS (EMI)	1	2008
NOW THAT'S WHAT I CALL MUSIC 70 VARIOUS ARTISTS (EMI)	1	2008
NOW THAT'S WHAT I CALL MUSIC 71 VARIOUS ARTISTS (EMI)	1	2008
NOW THAT'S WHAT I CALL NO 1'S VARIOUS ARTISTS (EMI)	5	2006
NOW THAT'S WHAT I CALL QUITE GOOD HOUSEMARTINS	8	1988
NOW THAT'S WHAT I CALL THE 80'S VARIOUS ARTISTS (EMI)	6	2007
NOW THAT'S WHAT I CALL XMAS VARIOUS ARTISTS (EMI)	5	2006
NOW – THE CHRISTMAS ALBUM VARIOUS ARTISTS (EMI)	1	1985
NOW THE CHRISTMAS ALBUM VARIOUS ARTISTS (EMI)	2	2000
NOW – THE SUMMER ALBUM – 30 SUMMER HITS VARIOUS ARTISTS (EMI)	7	1986
NOW THEN... STIFF LITTLE FINGERS	24	1982
NOW VOYAGER BARRY GIBB	85	1984
NOW WE ARE SIX STEELEYE SPAN	13	1974
NOW WE MAY BEGIN RANDY CRAWFORD	10	1980
NOW XMAS VARIOUS ARTISTS (EMI)	8	2005
NOW YEARS VARIOUS ARTISTS (EMI)	1	2004
NOW YOU SEE ME...NOW YOU DON'T CLIFF RICHARD	4	1982
NOW YOU'RE GONE BASSHUNTER	1	2008
NOW! SMASH HITS VARIOUS ARTISTS (EMI)	5	1987
NOW! THAT'S WHAT I CALL LOVE VARIOUS ARTISTS (EMI)	6	1994
NOW! THAT'S WHAT I CALL MUSIC 18 VARIOUS ARTISTS (EMI)	1	1990
NOW! THAT'S WHAT I CALL MUSIC 19 VARIOUS ARTISTS (EMI)	1	1991
NOW, THAT'S WHAT I CALL MUSIC VARIOUS ARTISTS (EMI)	1	1983
NOW, THAT'S WHAT I CALL MUSIC 4 VARIOUS ARTISTS (EMI)	2	1984
NOW, THAT'S WHAT I CALL MUSIC 5 VARIOUS ARTISTS (EMI)	1	1985
NOW, THAT'S WHAT I CALL MUSIC 6 VARIOUS ARTISTS (EMI)	1	1985
NOW, THAT'S WHAT I CALL MUSIC 7 VARIOUS ARTISTS (EMI)	1	1986
NOW, THAT'S WHAT I CALL MUSIC 8 VARIOUS ARTISTS (EMI)	1	1986
NOW, THAT'S WHAT I CALL MUSIC '86 VARIOUS ARTISTS (EMI)	65	1986
NOW, THAT'S WHAT I CALL MUSIC 9 VARIOUS ARTISTS (EMI)	1	1987
NOW, THAT'S WHAT I CALL MUSIC II VARIOUS ARTISTS (EMI)	1	1984
NOW, THAT'S WHAT I CALL MUSIC III VARIOUS ARTISTS (EMI)	1	1984
NOWHERE RIDE	11	1990
NU FLOW BIG BROVAZ	6	2002
NU SOUL VARIOUS ARTISTS (SONY)	8	2003
NU-CLEAR SOUNDS ASH	7	1998
NUDE CAMEL	34	1981
NUFF SAID NINA SIMONE	11	1969
NUISANCE MENSWEAR	11	1995
NUKLEUS PTS – HARDHOUSE ANTHEMS 3 VARIOUS ARTISTS (VIRGIN)	13	2000
NUKLEUZ PRESENTS BIG ROOM DJS VARIOUS ARTISTS (VIRGIN)	6	2001
NUKLEUZ PRESENTS HARDHOUSE ANTHEMS VARIOUS ARTISTS (VIRGIN)	14	2000
NUKLEUZ PRESENTS HARDHOUSE ANTHEMS 2001 VARIOUS ARTISTS (VIRGIN)	13	2001
NUKLEUZ PRESENTS HARDHOUSE ANTHEMS VOL.2 VARIOUS ARTISTS (VIRGIN)	16	2000
NUMA RECORDS YEAR 1 VARIOUS ARTISTS (NUMA)	94	1986
NUMBER 1 DANCE ANTHEMS VARIOUS ARTISTS (WARNER BROTHERS)	6	2006
NUMBER 10 J.J. CALE	58	1992
NUMBER 1'S VARIOUS ARTISTS (UNIVERSAL)	7	2005
NUMBER 1'S STEVIE WONDER	23	2007
NUMBER 8 J.J. CALE	47	1983
THE NUMBER OF THE BEAST IRON MAIDEN	1	1982
THE NUMBER ONE 70'S ROCK ALBUM VARIOUS ARTISTS (POLYGRAM)	3	1995
THE NUMBER ONE ACOUSTIC ROCK ALBUM VARIOUS ARTISTS (POLYGRAM)	6	1996
THE NUMBER ONE ALL TIME ROCK ALBUM VARIOUS ARTISTS (POLYGRAM)	16	1995
THE NUMBER ONE CHRISTMAS ALBUM VARIOUS ARTISTS (POLYGRAM)	4	1995
THE NUMBER ONE CLASSIC SOUL ALBUM VARIOUS ARTISTS (POLYGRAM)	5	1995
THE NUMBER ONE CLASSICAL ALBUM 2004 VARIOUS ARTISTS (UNIVERSAL)	4	2003
THE NUMBER ONE CLASSICAL ALBUM 2006 VARIOUS ARTISTS (UNIVERSAL)	3	2005
THE NUMBER ONE CLASSICAL ALBUM 2008 VARIOUS ARTISTS (UNIVERSAL)	10	2007
THE NO 1 CLUB ANTHEMS ALBUM VARIOUS ARTISTS (DECADANCE)	16	2007
THE NUMBER ONE COUNTRY ALBUM VARIOUS ARTISTS (POLYGRAM)	16	1996
THE NO 1 DANCE CLASSICS ALBUM VARIOUS ARTISTS (DECADANCE)	18	2006
THE NO 1 DANCE HITS ALBUM VARIOUS ARTISTS (DECADANCE)	13	2006
THE NUMBER ONE DANCE PARTY ALBUM VARIOUS ARTISTS (UNIVERSAL)	17	1999
THE NUMBER ONE DRIVE ALBUM VARIOUS ARTISTS (POLYGRAM)	14	1997
THE NUMBER ONE EIGHTIES ALBUM VARIOUS ARTISTS (POLYGRAM)	10	1996
THE NO 1 EUPHORIC DANCE ALBUM VARIOUS ARTISTS (DECADANCE)	8	2006
THE NO 1 FUNKY HOUSE ALBUM VARIOUS ARTISTS (DECADANCE)	18	2005
THE NO 1 FUNKY HOUSE ALBUM 2 VARIOUS ARTISTS (DECADANCE)	13	2006
THE NO 1 HARD HOUSE ALBUM VARIOUS ARTISTS (DECADANCE)	19	2005
THE NO 1 HARDCORE ALBUM VARIOUS ARTISTS (DECADANCE)	7	2006
NUMBER ONE IN HEAVEN SPARKS	73	1979
THE NUMBER ONE JAZZ ALBUM VARIOUS ARTISTS (POLYGRAM)	13	1997
THE NUMBER ONE LINE DANCING ALBUM VARIOUS ARTISTS (POLYGRAM)	10	1997
THE NUMBER ONE LOVE ALBUM VARIOUS ARTISTS (POLYGRAM)	1	1996
THE NUMBER ONE MOTOWN ALBUM VARIOUS ARTISTS (POLYGRAM)	2	1997
THE NUMBER ONE MOVIES ALBUM VARIOUS ARTISTS (POLYGRAM)	2	1995
THE NUMBER ONE MOZART ALBUM VARIOUS ARTISTS (UNIVERSAL)	14	2006
NO 1 MUM VARIOUS ARTISTS (UNIVERSAL)	6	2006
THE NUMBER ONE MUSICALS ALBUM VARIOUS ARTISTS (UNIVERSAL)	9	2004
THE NO 1 OPERA ALBUM VARIOUS ARTISTS (UNIVERSAL)	11	2004
THE NUMBER ONE OPERA ALBUM 2007 VARIOUS ARTISTS (UNIVERSAL)	17	2007
THE NO 1 R & B CLASSICS ALBUM VARIOUS ARTISTS (DECADANCE)	20	2007
THE NUMBER ONE RAP ALBUM VARIOUS ARTISTS (POLYGRAM)	12	1996
THE NUMBER ONE REGGAE ALBUM VARIOUS ARTISTS (POLYGRAM)	14	1995
THE NUMBER ONE ROCK BALLADS ALBUM VARIOUS ARTISTS (POLYGRAM)	18	1996
THE NUMBER ONE ROCK 'N' ROLL ALBUM VARIOUS ARTISTS (POLYGRAM)	20	1997
THE NUMBER ONE SCI-FI ALBUM VARIOUS ARTISTS (POLYGRAM)	13	1997
THE NUMBER ONE SEVENTIES ALBUM VARIOUS ARTISTS (POLYGRAM)	13	1997
THE NUMBER ONE SKA ALBUM VARIOUS ARTISTS (POLYGRAM)	9	1997
THE NO 1 SLEEPOVER ALBUM VARIOUS ARTISTS (DMG TV)	16	2006
THE NO. 1 SOUNDS OF THE SEVENTIES VARIOUS ARTISTS (K-TEL)	83	1982
THE NUMBER ONE SUMMER ALBUM VARIOUS ARTISTS (POLYGRAM)	12	1996
THE NO 1 SUMMER DANCE ALBUM VARIOUS ARTISTS (DECADANCE)	16	2005
THE NO 1 SUMMER DANCE ALBUM – VOLUME 2 VARIOUS ARTISTS (DECADANCE)	16	2006
THE NUMBER ONE SWING ALBUM 2004 VARIOUS ARTISTS (UNIVERSAL)	9	2004
THE NO 1 TCHAIKOVSKY ALBUM VARIOUS ARTISTS (UNIVERSAL)	18	2007
THE NO 1 TRANCE CLASSICS ALBUM VARIOUS ARTISTS (DECADANCE)	17	2006
#1S MARIAH CAREY	10	1998
NUMBER ONES MICHAEL JACKSON	1	2003
NUMBER ONES BEE GEES	7	2004
THE NO 1'S DIANA ROSS & THE SUPREMES	15	2004
NO 1'S DESTINY'S CHILD	6	2005
NUMBER ONES ABBA	15	2006
NO 1'S OF DANCE VARIOUS ARTISTS (TELSTAR)	16	1994
NUMBER ONES OF THE EIGHTIES VARIOUS ARTISTS (TELSTAR)	2	1989
NO. 6 TOM PAXTON	23	1970
NO. 10 UPPING STREET BIG AUDIO DYNAMITE	11	1986
NUMBER THE BRAVE WISHBONE ASH	61	1981
NURSE THERAPY?	38	1992
NURSERY CRYME GENESIS	39	1974
NUT CRACKER SUITE DUKE ELLINGTON	11	1961
NUTHIN' FANCY LYNYRD SKYNYRD	43	1975
THE NUTTY PROFESSOR FILM SOUNDTRACK	20	1996
NUYORICAN SOUL NUYORICAN SOUL	25	1997
NYC MAN LOU REED	31	2003
NYC MAN – GREATEST HITS LOU REED	43	2004
NYLON CURTAIN BILLY JOEL	27	1982

O

Title / Artist	Peak Position	Year of Release
O DAMIEN RICE	8	2003
O BROTHER WHERE ART THOU FILM SOUNDTRACK	20	2002
0898: BEAUTIFUL SOUTH BEAUTIFUL SOUTH	4	1992
05:22:09:12 OFF FRONT 242	46	1993
0141 632 6326 GUN	32	1997
06:21:03:11 UP EVIL FRONT 242	44	1993
O YEAH – ULTIMATE HITS AEROSMITH	6	2002
O.G. ORIGINAL GANGSTER ICE-T	38	1991
O3 SUNSCREEM	33	1993
OAKENFOLD ANTHEMS VARIOUS ARTISTS (WARNER BROTHERS)	9	2008
OASIS OASIS	23	1984
OBLIVION WITH BELLS UNDERWORLD	45	2007
OBSCURED BY CLOUDS (OST) PINK FLOYD	6	1972
OBSESSION UFO	26	1978
OBSOLETE FEAR FACTORY	20	1998
THE OC TELEVISION AND RADIO COMPILATION	14	2004
OCEAN COLOUR SCENE OCEAN COLOUR SCENE	54	1996
OCEAN DRIVE LIGHTHOUSE FAMILY	3	1995
OCEAN RAIN ECHO & THE BUNNYMEN	4	1984
OCEANIA OCEANIA	70	1999
OCEAN'S ELEVEN VARIOUS ARTISTS (WARNER BROTHERS)	15	2002
OCEANS OF FANTASY BONEY M	1	1979
OCTAVARIUM DREAM THEATER	72	2005
OCTAVE MOODY BLUES	6	1978
OCTOBER U2	11	1981
OCTOBER ROAD JAMES TAYLOR	39	2002
OCTOBER RUST TYPE O NEGATIVE	26	1996
OCTOBERON BARCLAY JAMES HARVEST	19	1976
OCTOPUS HUMAN LEAGUE	6	1995
OCTOPUS BEES	26	2007
OCTOPUSS COZY POWELL	86	1983
THE ODD COUPLE GNARLS BARKLEY	19	2008
ODDITORIUM OR WARLORDS OF MARS DANDY WARHOLS	67	2005
ODDS AND SODS WHO	10	1974
ODE TO J SMITH TRAVIS	20	2008
O-DE-LAY BECK	17	1996
ODESSA BEE GEES	10	1969
ODYSSEY YNGWIE J MALMSTEEN	27	1988
ODYSSEY HAYLEY WESTENRA	10	2005
ODYSSEY – THE DEFINITIVE COLLECTION VANGELIS	20	2003
ODYSSEY THROUGH 02 JEAN-MICHEL JARRE	50	1998
OEDIPUS SCHMOEDIPUS BARRY ADAMSON	51	1996
OF THE HEART, OF THE SOUL AND THE CROSS – THE UTOPIAN EXPERIENCE PM DAWN	8	1991
OFARIM CONCERT – LIVE '69 ESTHER & ABI OFARIM	29	1969
OFF THE BEATEN TRACK STRANGLERS	80	1986
OFF THE BONE CRAMPS	44	1983
OFF THE GROUND PAUL McCARTNEY	5	1993
OFF THE WALL MICHAEL JACKSON	5	1979
OFF WITH THEIR HEADS KAISER CHIEFS	2	2008
OFF YER NUT!! VARIOUS ARTISTS (TVD)	12	1998
THE OFFICIAL BBC ALBUM OF THE ROYAL WEDDING (ROYAL COMPILATION ALBUM) ROYAL COMPILATION ALBUM	1	1981
OFFICIAL BOOTLEG ALBUM BLUES BAND	40	1980
OFFICIAL LIVE – 101 PROOF PANTERA	54	1997
OGDEN'S NUT GONE FLAKE SMALL FACES	1	1968
OH MERCY BOB DYLAN	6	1989
OH PRETTY WOMAN ROY ORBISON	4	1964
OH! WHAT A NIGHT VARIOUS ARTISTS (COLUMBIA)	4	1998
OI! OI! THAT'S YER LOT VARIOUS ARTISTS (SECRET)	54	1982
OIL ON CANVAS JAPAN	5	1983
OK TALVIN SINGH	41	1999
OK COMPUTER RADIOHEAD	1	1997
OK KEN? CHICKEN SHACK	9	1969
OKLAHOMA! FILM SOUNDTRACK	1	1956
OL' BLUE EYES IS BACK FRANK SINATRA	12	1973
OL' BLUE SUEDES IS BACK CARL PERKINS	38	1978
OLD 8 X 10 RANDY TRAVIS	64	1988
OLD FOUR EYES IS BACK MIKE HARDING	31	1977
OLD FRIENDS – LIVE ON STAGE SIMON & GARFUNKEL	61	2004
OLD GOLDEN THROAT JOHNNY CASH	37	1968
THE OLD GREY WHISTLE TEST – THE BEST OF THE TEST (TELEVISION COMPILATION) TELEVISION AND RADIO COMPILATION	13	1991
THE OLD KIT BAG RICHARD THOMPSON	52	2003
OLD LOW LIGHT KATHRYN WILLIAMS	56	2002
OLD NEW BORROWED AND BLUE SLADE	1	1974
THE OLD SKOOL VARIOUS ARTISTS (GLOBAL TELEVISION)	6	1997
OLD SKOOL JUNGLE VARIOUS ARTISTS (RELENTLESS)	11	2002
OLD SKOOL REGGAE VARIOUS ARTISTS (RELENTLESS)	16	2002
THE OLD SKOOL REUNION VARIOUS ARTISTS (GLOBAL TELEVISION)	12	1997
OLD WAYS NEIL YOUNG	39	1985
OLDER/OLDER & UPPER GEORGE MICHAEL	1	1996
OLE JAMES LAST	24	1973
OLE SAD CAFÉ	72	1981
OLIAS OF SUNHILLOW JON ANDERSON	8	1976
OLIVER! STAGE CAST RECORDING	4	1960
OLIVER! FILM SOUNDTRACK	4	1968
OLYMPIAN GENE	8	1995
THE OMD SINGLES ORCHESTRAL MANOEUVRES IN THE DARK	16	1998
OMMADAWN MIKE OLDFIELD	4	1975
ON ECHOBELLY	4	1995
ON A DANCE TIP VARIOUS ARTISTS (GLOBAL TELEVISION)	1	1995
ON A DANCE TIP 2 VARIOUS ARTISTS (GLOBAL TELEVISION)	1	1995
ON A DAY LIKE TODAY BRYAN ADAMS	11	1998
ON A REGGAE TIP VARIOUS ARTISTS (MANGO)	3	1993
ON A STORYTELLER'S NIGHT MAGNUM	24	1985
ON AIR – BBC SESSIONS SHAMEN	61	1993
ON AN ISLAND DAVID GILMOUR	1	2006
ON AND ON JACK JOHNSON	30	2006
ON EAGLE'S WINGS MICHAEL CRAWFORD	65	1998
ON EVERY STREET DIRE STRAITS	1	1991
ON FIRE – LIVE AT THE BOWL QUEEN	20	2004
ON HOW LIFE IS MACY GRAY	3	1999
ON PARADE BAND OF THE SCOTS GUARDS	25	1969
ON PAROLE MOTORHEAD	65	1979
ON REFLECTION – THE VERY BEST OF ELAINE PAIGE ELAINE PAIGE	60	1998
ON STAGE JIM REEVES	13	1969
ON STAGE RAINBOW	7	1977
ON STAGE FEBRUARY 1970 ELVIS PRESLEY	2	1970
ON STAGE WITH THE GEORGE MITCHELL MINSTRELS GEORGE MITCHELL MINSTRELS	1	1962
ON THE 6 JENNIFER LOPEZ	14	1999
ON THE AIR – 60 YEARS OF BBC THEME MUSIC (TV & RADIO COMPILATION) TELEVISION AND RADIO COMPILATION	85	1982
ON THE BEACH NEIL YOUNG	42	1974
ON THE BEACH CHRIS REA	11	1986
ON THE BEACH VARIOUS ARTISTS (MINISTRY OF SOUND)	16	2003
ON THE BOARDS TASTE	18	1970
ON THE BORDER EAGLES	28	1974
ON THE LEVEL STATUS QUO	1	1975
ON THE LEYLINE OCEAN COLOUR SCENE	37	2007
ON THE LINE GARY U.S. BONDS	55	1982
ON THE LOOSE DEUCE	18	1995
ON THE NIGHT DIRE STRAITS	4	1993
ON THE OUTSIDE SYMPOSIUM	32	1998
ON THE OUTSIDE STARSAILOR	13	2005
ON THE RADIO – GREATEST HITS VOLUME 1 & 2 DONNA SUMMER	24	1979
ON THE RIVIERA GIBSON BROTHERS	50	1980
ON THE SUNNY SIDE OF THE STREET KLAUS WUNDERLICH	81	1984
ON THE THRESHOLD OF A DREAM MOODY BLUES	1	1969
ON THE TURN KERBDOG	64	1997
ON THE WATERS BREAD	34	1970
ON THROUGH THE NIGHT DEF LEPPARD	15	1980
ON TOUR DAVID ESSEX	51	1976
ON TOUR WITH ERIC CLAPTON DELANEY & BONNIE & FRIENDS	39	1970
ON TOUR WITH THE GEORGE MITCHELL MINSTRELS GEORGE MITCHELL MINSTRELS	6	1963
ONCE AGAIN JOHN LEGEND	10	2006
ONCE AROUND THE WORLD IT BITES	43	1988
ONCE IN A LIFETIME RUNRIG	61	1988
ONCE IN A LIFETIME VARIOUS ARTISTS (TELSTAR)	13	1997
ONCE IN A LIFETIME – THE BEST OF TALKING HEADS/SAND IN THE VASELINE TALKING HEADS	7	1992
ONCE MOORE WITH COOK PETER COOK & DUDLEY MOORE	25	1966
ONCE MORE INTO THE BLEACH DEBBIE HARRY & BLONDIE	50	1988
ONCE MORE WITH FEELING – SINGLES 1996-2004 PLACEBO	8	2004
ONCE UPON A STAR BAY CITY ROLLERS	1	1975
ONCE UPON A TIME DONNA SUMMER	24	1977
ONCE UPON A TIME SIMPLE MINDS	1	1985
ONCE UPON A TIME IN THE WEST HARD-FI	1	2007
ONCE UPON A TIME – THE SINGLES SIOUXSIE & THE BANSHEES	21	1981
ONCE UPON THE CROSS DEICIDE	66	1995
ONE BEE GEES	29	1989
THE ONE ELTON JOHN	2	1992
1 BEATLES	1	2000
THE ONE AND ONLY BILLY FURY BILLY FURY	56	1983
ONE BY ONE FOO FIGHTERS	1	2002
ONE CAREFUL OWNER MICHAEL BALL	7	1994
ONE CHANCE PAUL POTTS	1	2007
ONE CHANCE – CHRISTMAS EDITION PAUL POTTS	19	2007
ONE DAY AT A TIME SYMPOSIUM	29	1997
ONE DAY AT A TIME FOSTER & ALLEN	61	1999
ONE DAY IN YOUR LIFE MICHAEL JACKSON	29	1981
ONE DAY SON THIS WILL ALL BE YOURS FIGHTSTAR	27	2007
1-800 NEW FUNK VARIOUS ARTISTS (NPG)	15	1994
ONE EYED JACKS SPEAR OF DESTINY	22	1984
THE ONE FOR ME MR ACKER BILK	38	1976
ONE FROM THE MODERN OCEAN COLOUR SCENE	4	1999
ONE GIANT LEAP ONE GIANT LEAP	51	2002
ONE HALF OF A WHOLE DECADE – 5 YEARS VARIOUS ARTISTS (MINISTRY OF SOUND)	9	1996
ONE HEAD, TWO ARMS, TWO LEGS DAWN OF THE REPLICANTS	62	1998
ONE HEART CELINE DION	4	2003

Title / Artist	Peak Position	Year of Release
100 R&B CLASSICS – THE ANTHEMS VARIOUS ARTISTS (WARNER BROTHERS)	4	2008
ONE HOT MINUTE RED HOT CHILI PEPPERS	2	1995
140 GRIME ST. KANO	48	2008
101 CLASSICAL HITS VARIOUS ARTISTS (EMI)	13	2008
101 TRANCE ANTHEMS VARIOUS ARTISTS (EMI)	6	2008
100CC: GREATEST HITS OF 10 C.C. 10 C.C.	9	1975
100 HITS – 80S VARIOUS ARTISTS (DMG TV)	19	2008
ONE IN A MILLION AALIYAH	33	1996
ONE LOVE DELAKOTA	58	1998
ONE LOVE BOB MARLEY & THE WAILERS	24	2001
ONE LOVE BLUE	1	2002
ONE LOVE VARIOUS ARTISTS (UNIVERSAL)	1	2007
ONE LOVE – THE VERY BEST OF BOB MARLEY & THE WAILERS	5	2001
ONE LOVE – THE VERY BEST OF REGGAE VARIOUS ARTISTS (ARCADE)	7	1992
ONE MAN DOG JAMES TAYLOR	27	1972
ONE MAN SHOW MIKE HARDING	19	1976
ONE MORE CAR ONE MORE RIDER ERIC CLAPTON	69	2002
ONE MORE DREAM – THE VERY BEST OF GERRY RAFFERTY GERRY RAFFERTY	17	1995
ONE MORE FOR THE ROAD LYNYRD SKYNYRD	17	1976
ONE NATION UNDER A GROOVE FUNKADELIC	56	1978
ONE NIGHT AT BUDOKAN MICHAEL SCHENKER GROUP	5	1982
ONE NIGHT ONLY – THE GREATEST HITS ELTON JOHN	7	2000
ONE NIGHT WITH YOU – THE BEST OF LOVE LUTHER VANDROSS	56	1997
ONE NIL NEIL FINN	14	2001
ONE OF THE BOYS ROGER DALTREY	45	1977
ONE OF THE BOYS KATY PERRY	11	2008
ONE OF THESE NIGHTS EAGLES	8	1975
ONE ON ONE CHEAP TRICK	95	1982
ONE ORIGINAL STEP BEYOND VARIOUS ARTISTS (CASTLE COMMUNICATIONS)	7	1993
ONE PIECE AT A TIME JOHNNY CASH	49	1976
ONE PLUS ONE IS ONE BADLY DRAWN BOY	9	2004
1 POLISH 2 BISCUITS AND A FISH SANDWICH OUTHERE BROTHERS	56	1995
ONE SECOND YELLO	48	1987
ONE SECOND PARADISE LOST	31	1997
ONE STEP BEYOND MADNESS	2	1979
ONE STEP BEYOND VARIOUS ARTISTS (EMI)	9	2003
ONE STEP CLOSER DOOBIE BROTHERS	53	1980
THE ONE THING MICHAEL BOLTON	4	1993
ONE TO ONE HOWARD JONES	10	1986
ONE TOUCH SUGABABES	26	2000
1 22 03 – ACOUSTIC (IMPORT) MAROON 5	58	2005
1234 PROPAGANDA	46	1990
ONE VICE AT A TIME KROKUS	28	1982
ONE VOICE BARRY MANILOW	18	1979
ONE VOICE BARBRA STREISAND	27	1987
ONE VOICE MICHAEL BALL	22	2006
ONE VOICE ANDREW JOHNSTON	4	2008
ONE WAY OF LIFE – THE BEST OF THE LEVELLERS LEVELLERS	15	1998
ONE WAY TICKET TO HELL...AND BACK DARKNESS	11	2005
ONE WILD NIGHT – LIVE 1985-2001 BON JOVI	2	2001
ONE WOMAN – THE ULTIMATE COLLECTION DIANA ROSS	1	1993
ONE WORLD JOHN MARTYN	54	1978
ONE WORLD JOHN DENVER	91	1986
ONE WORLD VARIOUS ARTISTS (GLOBAL TELEVISION)	8	1998
ONE WORLD ONE VOICE ONE WORLD	27	1990
ONENESS – SILVER DREAMS GOLDEN REALITY CARLOS SANTANA	55	1979
ONES ON 1 VARIOUS ARTISTS (BBC)	10	1988
ONE-TRICK PONY (OST) PAUL SIMON	17	1980
ONKA'S BIG MOKA TOPLOADER	5	2000
ONLY A WOMAN LIKE YOU MICHAEL BOLTON	19	2002
ONLY BY THE NIGHT KINGS OF LEON	1	2008
ONLY CLASSICAL ALBUM YOU'LL EVER NEED VARIOUS ARTISTS (CONIFER)	17	1998
ONLY EVERYTHING JULIANA HATFIELD	59	1995
ONLY FOR THE HEADSTRONG VARIOUS ARTISTS (LONDON)	10	1992
ONLY FOR THE HEADSTRONG II VARIOUS ARTISTS (LONDON)	18	1992
ONLY FOREVER PURESSENCE	36	1998
ONLY GOD CAN JUDGE ME MARK MORRISON	50	1997
ONLY HUMAN DINA CARROLL	2	1996
ONLY MEN ALOUD! ONLY MEN ALOUD!	16	2008
THE ONLY ONES ONLY ONES	56	1978
ONLY THE STRONGEST WILL SURVIVE HURRICANE #1	55	1999
ONLY YAZOO – THE BEST OF YAZOO YAZOO	22	1999
ONLY YESTERDAY – RICHARD & KAREN CARPENTER'S GREATEST HITS CARPENTERS	1	1990
ONLY YOU HARRY CONNICK JR.	6	2004
ONWARD ALFIE BOE	72	2007
OOH LAS VEGAS DEACON BLUE	3	1990
OOH WALLAH WALLAH KING KURT	99	1983
OOH YEAH! DARYL HALL & JOHN OATES	52	1988
OOH-LA-LA FACES	1	1973
OOPS! I DID IT AGAIN BRITNEY SPEARS	2	2000
OOPS! SORRY WRONG PLANET UTOPIA	59	1977
OPEN JULIE DRISCOLL, BRIAN AUGER & THE TRINITY	12	1968
OPEN STEVE HILLAGE	71	1979
OPEN SHAZNAY LEWIS	22	2004
OPEN ALL NIGHT GEORGIA SATELLITES	39	1988
THE OPEN DOOR EVANESCENCE	2	2006
OPEN HEART ZOO MARTIN GRECH	54	2002
OPEN ROAD DONOVAN	30	1970
OPEN ROAD GARY BARLOW	1	1997
OPEN SEASON BRITISH SEA POWER	13	2005
OPEN TOP CARS AND GIRLS IN T'SHIRTS VARIOUS ARTISTS (TELSTAR)	13	1985
OPEN UP AND SAY...AAH! POISON	18	1988
THE OPERA ALBUM 2002 VARIOUS ARTISTS (VIRGIN)	7	2001
THE OPERA ALBUM 2006 VARIOUS ARTISTS (UNIVERSAL)	5	2006
THE OPERA BAND AMICI FOREVER	39	2003
OPERA EXTRAVAGANZA THE ROYAL PHILHARMONIC ORCHESTRA, CHORUS ROYAL OPERA HOUSE, THE LONDON SYMPHONY ORCHESTRA, CONDUCTOR LUIS COBOS	72	1990
OPERATION MINDCRIME QUEENSRYCHE	58	1988
OPERATION STACKOLA LUNIZ	41	1996
OPERATUNITY WINNERS DENISE LEIGH & JANE GILCHRIST	60	2003
OPHELIA NATALIE MERCHANT	52	1998
THE OPTIMIST TURIN BRAKES	27	2001
ORACULAR SPECTACULAR MGMT	12	2008
ORAL FIXATION VOLUME 2 SHAKIRA	12	2006
ORANGE COLOURED SKY BERT KAEMPFERT & HIS ORCHESTRA	49	1971
ORANGES AND LEMONS XTC	28	1989
THE ORBISON WAY ROY ORBISON	11	1966
ORBISONGS ROY ORBISON	40	1967
ORBITAL ORBITAL	28	1991
ORBLIVION ORB	19	1997
THE ORB'S ADVENTURES BEYOND THE ULTRAWORLD ORB	29	1991
ORBVS TERRERVM ORB	20	1995
ORCHESTRA OF WOLVES GALLOWS	57	2007
ORCHESTRA! SIR GEORG SOLTI & DUDLEY MOORE	38	1991
ORCHESTRAL MANOEUVRES IN THE DARK ORCHESTRAL MANOEUVRES IN THE DARK	27	1980
THE ORCHESTRAL TUBULAR BELLS MIKE OLDFIELD WITH THE ROYAL PHILHARMONIC ORCHESTRA	17	1975
ORDINARY MAN DAY ONE	70	2000
ORGAN FAN SILVERFISH	65	1992
ORGANIC JOE COCKER	49	1996
ORGANISATION ORCHESTRAL MANOEUVRES IN THE DARK	6	1980
ORGASMATRON MOTORHEAD	21	1986
ORIGIN OF SYMMETRY MUSE	3	2001
ORIGINAL FLAVA BRAND NEW HEAVIES	64	1994
ORIGINAL GARAGE ANTHEMS VARIOUS ARTISTS (WARNER BROTHERS)	8	2006
ORIGINAL GREATEST HITS EVERLY BROTHERS	7	1970
ORIGINAL HARDCORE VARIOUS ARTISTS (INSPIRED)	7	2002
ORIGINAL HARDCORE – THE BATTLE VARIOUS ARTISTS (INSPIRED)	19	2003
ORIGINAL HARDCORE – THE NU BREED VARIOUS ARTISTS (INSPIRED)	19	2004
ORIGINAL MASTERS JETHRO TULL	63	1985
ORIGINAL MUSIC FROM AUF WIEDERSEHEN PET (TELEVISION SOUNDTRACK) TELEVISION AND RADIO COMPILATION	21	1984
ORIGINAL MUSIQUARIUM 1 STEVIE WONDER	8	1982
ORIGINAL PIRATE MATERIAL STREETS	10	2002
THE ORIGINAL SOUNDTRACK 10 C.C.	4	1975
ORIGINAL SOUNDTRACK S-EXPRESS	5	1989
THE ORIGINAL SOUNDTRACK FROM TCB DIANA ROSS & THE SUPREMES & THE TEMPTATIONS	11	1969
ORIGINAL SOUNDTRACKS 1 PASSENGERS	12	1995
ORIGINALS VARIOUS ARTISTS (COLUMBIA)	1	1993
ORIGINALS 2 VARIOUS ARTISTS (COLUMBIA)	4	1994
THE ORIGINALS! VARIOUS ARTISTS (DINO)	8	1992
THE ORIGINALS: 32 ALL-TIME CLASSIC GREATS VARIOUS ARTISTS (TOWERBELL)	15	1986
ORPHANS: BRAWLERS, BAWLERS & BASTARDS TOM WAITS	49	2006
OSIBISA OSIBISA	11	1971
OSMONDS LIVE OSMONDS	13	1972
THE OTHER CHET ATKINS CHET ATKINS	20	1961
THE OTHER MAN'S GRASS IS ALWAYS GREENER PETULA CLARK	37	1968
OTHER PEOPLE'S LIVES RAY DAVIES	36	2006
OTHER PEOPLE'S PROBLEMS UPPER ROOM	50	2006
OTHER PEOPLE'S SONGS ERASURE	17	2003
THE OTHER SIDE LYNDEN DAVID HALL	36	2000
THE OTHER SIDE OF DUDLEY MOORE DUDLEY MOORE	11	1965
THE OTHER SIDE OF LIFE MOODY BLUES	24	1986
THE OTHER SIDE OF ME ANDY WILLIAMS	60	1975
THE OTHER SIDE OF THE MIRROR STEVIE NICKS	3	1989
OTHER VOICES PAUL YOUNG	4	1990
OTHER VOICES/OTHER ROOMS NANCI GRIFFITH	18	1993
THE OTHERS OTHERS	51	2005
OTIS BLUE: OTIS REDDING SINGS SOUL OTIS REDDING	6	1966
OTIS REDDING IN EUROPE OTIS REDDING	14	1968
OTO FLUKE	44	1995
O-TOWN O-TOWN	7	2001
OU812 VAN HALEN	16	1988
OUI LOVE YOU OUI 3	39	1993
OUR BEST TO YOU OSMONDS	5	1974
OUR BRIGHT FUTURE TRACY CHAPMAN	75	2008

Title / Artist	Peak Position	Year of Release
OUR EARTHLY PLEASURES MAXIMO PARK	2	2007
OUR FAVOURITE SHOP STYLE COUNCIL	1	1985
OUR FRIENDS ELECTRIC VARIOUS ARTISTS (TELSTAR)	8	1996
OUR HAPPY HARDCORE SCOOTER	24	1996
OUR HOUSE – THE ORIGINAL SONGS MADNESS	45	2002
OUR KID EH SHIREHORSES	20	2001
OUR LOVE TO ADMIRE INTERPOL	2	2007
OUR MEMORIES OF ELVIS ELVIS PRESLEY	72	1979
OUR TIME IN EDEN 10,000 MANIACS	33	1992
OUR TOWN – THE GREATEST HITS OF DEACON BLUE DEACON BLUE	1	1994
OUT CAME THE BLUES VARIOUS ARTISTS (ACE OF HEARTS)	19	1964
OUT HERE LOVE	29	1970
OUT IN LA RED HOT CHILI PEPPERS	61	1994
OUT IN THE FIELDS – THE VERY BEST OF GARY MOORE GARY MOORE	54	1998
OUT IN THE SUN PATRICK MORAZ	44	1977
OUT NOW! 28 HOT HITS VARIOUS ARTISTS (CHRYSALIS)	2	1985
OUT NOW!! 2 – 28 HOT HITS VARIOUS ARTISTS (CHRYSALIS)	3	1985
OUT OF AFRICA (OST) JOHN BARRY	81	1986
OUT OF CONTROL GIRLS ALOUD	1	2008
OUT OF EXILE AUDIOSLAVE	5	2005
OUT OF HERE CORDUROY	73	1994
OUT OF MY HANDS KEISHA WHITE	55	2006
OUT OF NOTHING EMBRACE	1	2004
OUT OF ORDER ROD STEWART	11	1988
OUT OF OUR HEADS ROLLING STONES	2	1965
OUT OF SEASON BETH GIBBONS & RUSTIN MAN	28	2002
OUT OF THE BLUE ELECTRIC LIGHT ORCHESTRA	4	1977
OUT OF THE BLUE DEBBIE GIBSON	26	1988
OUT OF THE CRADLE LINDSEY BUCKINGHAM	51	1992
OUT OF THE SHADOWS SHADOWS	1	1962
OUT OF THE WOODS TRACEY THORN	38	2007
OUT OF THEIR SKULLS PIRATES	57	1977
OUT OF THIS WORLD MOODY BLUES	15	1979
OUT OF THIS WORLD SHAKATAK	30	1983
OUT OF THIS WORLD EUROPE	12	1988
OUT OF THIS WORLD APOLLO 2000	43	1996
OUT OF TIME R.E.M.	1	1991
OUT ON THE STREET DAVID ESSEX	31	1976
OUT SPACED SUPER FURRY ANIMALS	44	1998
OUT THERE & BACK PAUL VAN DYK	12	2000
OUT-A-SPACE SPOTNICKS	20	1963
OUTLAND SPEAR OF DESTINY	16	1987
OUTLAND GARY NUMAN	39	1991
OUTLANDOS D'AMOUR POLICE	6	1979
OUTRIDER JIMMY PAGE	27	1988
OUTROSPECTIVE FAITHLESS	4	2001
OUTSIDE DAVID BOWIE	8	1995
OUTSIDE IN RUSSELL WATSON	14	2007
OUTSIDE INSIDE TUBES	77	1983
OUTSIDE THE GATE KILLING JOKE	92	1988
THE OUTSIDER DJ SHADOW	24	2006
OUTTA SIGHT OUTTA MIND DATSUNS	58	2004
OVATION – THE BEST OF ANDREW LLOYD WEBBER VARIOUS ARTISTS (K-TEL)	34	1985
OVER AND OVER NANA MOUSKOURI	10	1969
OVER THE COUNTER CULTURE ORDINARY BOYS	19	2004
OVER THE RAINBOW CONNIE TALBOT	35	2007
OVER THE RAINBOW VARIOUS ARTISTS (UNIVERSAL)	1	2007
OVER THE TOP COZY POWELL	34	1980
OVER THE UNDER DOWN	46	2007
OVERGROWN EDEN INME	15	2003
OVERKILL MOTORHEAD	24	1979
OVERLOAD VARIOUS ARTISTS (RONCO)	10	1982
OVERLOADED – THE SINGLES COLLECTION SUGABABES	3	2006
OVERNIGHT SUCCESS NEIL SEDAKA	31	1975
OVERPOWERED ROISIN MURPHY	20	2007
OVERTONES JUST JACK	6	2007
OVERTURE AND BEGINNERS ROD STEWART & THE FACES	3	1974
OVO PETER GABRIEL	24	2000
THE OWNERZ GANG STARR	74	2003
OXYGENE JEAN-MICHEL JARRE	2	1977
OXYGENE 7-13 JEAN-MICHEL JARRE	11	1997
OYSTER HEATHER NOVA	72	1995
THE OZZMAN COMETH – THE BEST OF OZZY OSBOURNE OZZY OSBOURNE	68	1997
OZZMOSIS OZZY OSBOURNE	22	1995
OZZY OSBOURNE'S BLIZZARD OF OZ OZZY OSBOURNE'S BLIZZARD OF OZ	7	1980

P

Title / Artist	Peak Position	Year of Release
P.H.D. P.H.D.	33	1982
P.H.U.Q. WILDHEARTS	6	1995
PABLO HONEY RADIOHEAD	22	1993
PACER AMPS	60	1995
THE PACHA EXPERIENCE VARIOUS ARTISTS (GTV)	3	2006
THE PACHA EXPERIENCE 2 VARIOUS ARTISTS (GTV)	10	2007
THE PACIFIC AGE ORCHESTRAL MANOEUVRES IN THE DARK	15	1986
PACIFIC OCEAN BLUE DENNIS WILSON	16	2008
PACIFIC STREET PALE FOUNTAINS	85	1984
PACK UP YOUR TROUBLES RUSS CONWAY	9	1958
PACKED! PRETENDERS	19	1990
PADDY ROBERTS TRIES AGAIN PADDY ROBERTS	16	1960
A PAGAN PLACE WATERBOYS	100	1984
PAID IN FULL ERIC B & RAKIM	85	1987
PAID THA COST TO BE THA BOSS SNOOP DOGG	64	2003
PAID VACATION RICHARD MARX	11	1994
PAIN IN MY HEART OTIS REDDING	28	1967
PAIN IS LOVE JA RULE	3	2001
PAINKILLER JUDAS PRIEST	26	1990
PAINKILLER BABES IN TOYLAND	53	1993
PAINT THE SKY WITH STARS – THE BEST OF ENYA ENYA	4	1997
PAINT YOUR WAGON FILM SOUNDTRACK	2	1970
PAINTED DESERT SERENADE JOSHUA KADISON	45	1995
PAINTED FROM MEMORY ELVIS COSTELLO WITH BURT BACHARACH	32	1998
PAINTING IT RED BEAUTIFUL SOUTH	2	2000
PAL JOEY FILM SOUNDTRACK	1	1958
PALOOKAVILLE FATBOY SLIM	14	2004
THE PAN PIPE CHILLOUT ALBUM VARIOUS ARTISTS (WARNER BROTHERS)	16	2002
PAN PIPE DREAMS INSPIRATIONS	10	1995
PAN PIPE IMAGES INSPIRATIONS	23	1996
PAN PIPE INSPIRATIONS INSPIRATIONS	10	1995
PAN PIPE MOODS FREE THE SPIRIT	2	1995
PAN PIPE MOODS IN PARADISE FREE THE SPIRIT	26	1996
PAN PIPE MOODS TWO FREE THE SPIRIT	18	1995
PAN PIPES – ROMANCE OF IRELAND JOHN ANDERSON ORCHESTRA	56	1995
PANDEMONIUM TIME	66	1990
PANDEMONIUM KILLING JOKE	16	1994
PANDEMONIUM B2K	35	2003
PANIC ON MADDER ROSE	52	1994
PANIC PREVENTION JAMIE T	4	2007
PAN-ORAMA FLASH & THE PAN	69	1983
PAPA LOVES MAMBO – THE VERY BEST OF PERRY COMO	63	2004
PAPER MONSTERS DAVE GAHAN	36	2003
PAPER ROSES MARIE OSMOND	46	1974
PAPER SCISSORS STONE CATATONIA	6	2001
PAPER TIGERS CAESARS	40	2005
THE PAPER TRAIL T.I.	49	2008
PARACHUTE PRETTY THINGS	43	1970
PARACHUTES COLDPLAY	1	2000
PARADE SPANDAU BALLET	2	1984
PARADE – MUSIC FROM 'UNDER THE CHERRY MOON' (OST) PRINCE	4	1986
PARADISE JAMES LAST	74	1984
PARADISE INNER CITY	3	1989
PARADISE RUBY TURNER	74	1990
PARADISE KACI	47	2002
PARADISE HAWAIIAN STYLE (OST) ELVIS PRESLEY	7	1966
PARADISE LOST HERD	38	1968
PARADISE REMIXED INNER CITY	17	1990
PARADISE THEATER STYX	8	1981
PARALLEL LINES BLONDIE	1	1978
PARALLEL LINES BLONDIE	60	2004
THE PARAMOUR SESSIONS PAPA ROACH	61	2006
PARANOID BLACK SABBATH	1	1970
PARANOID BLACK SABBATH	54	1980
PARANOID BLACK SABBATH	63	2002
PARANOID & SUNBURNT SKUNK ANANSIE	8	1995
PARCEL OF ROGUES STEELEYE SPAN	26	1973
PARCEL OF ROGUES BARBARA DICKSON	30	1994
PARIS SUPERTRAMP	7	1980
PARIS CURE	56	1993
PARIS MALCOLM McLAREN	44	1994
PARIS PARIS HILTON	29	2006
PARIS AU PRINTEMPS (PARIS IN THE SPRING) PUBLIC IMAGE LTD	61	1980
PARK BENCH THEORIES JAMIE SCOTT & THE TOWN	24	2007
PARKERILLA GRAHAM PARKER & THE RUMOUR	14	1978
PARKLIFE BLUR	1	1994
PARSLEY, SAGE, ROSEMARY AND THYME SIMON & GARFUNKEL	13	1968
PARTIE TRAUMATIC BLACK KIDS	5	2008
THE PARTISANS PARTISANS	94	1983
THE PARTRIDGE FAMILY SOUND MAGAZINE PARTRIDGE FAMILY	14	1972
PARTS OF THE PROCESS MORCHEEBA	6	2003
PARTY VARIOUS ARTISTS (POLYGRAM)	19	1999
THE PARTY AIN'T OVER YET STATUS QUO	18	2005
PARTY ALBUM OUTHERE BROTHERS	41	1995
THE PARTY ALBUM! VENGABOYS	6	1999
PARTY ANIMAL VARIOUS ARTISTS (WARNER BROTHERS)	13	2003
PARTY AT THE PALACE VARIOUS ARTISTS (VIRGIN)	6	2002
PARTY CAPITAL – SUMMER MIX VARIOUS ARTISTS (UNIVERSAL)	16	2005
PARTY CRAZY BLACK LACE	58	1986
PARTY DOLL AND OTHER FAVOURITES MARY CHAPIN CARPENTER	65	1999
PARTY FEVER/DISCO MANIA VARIOUS ARTISTS (TV RECORDS)	71	1982
PARTY IN THE PARK VARIOUS ARTISTS (UNIVERSAL)	2	2001
PARTY IN THE PARK 2002 VARIOUS ARTISTS (UNIVERSAL)	4	2002
PARTY MIX VARIOUS ARTISTS (DINO)	8	1991
THE PARTY MIX ALBUM B-52'S	36	1981

Title / Artist	Peak Position	Year of Release
PARTY PARTY – 16 GREAT PARTY ICEBREAKERS BLACK LACE	4	1984
PARTY PARTY 2 BLACK LACE	18	1985
PARTY TIME RUSS CONWAY	7	1960
PARTY TIME CHEEKY GIRLS	14	2003
PARTY TONIGHT MODERN ROMANCE	45	1983
THE PARTY'S OVER TALK TALK	21	1982
PASS IN TIME – THE DEFINITIVE COLLECTION BETH ORTON	45	2003
PASS THE VIBES VARIOUS ARTISTS (POLYGRAM)	4	1996
PASSAGE CARPENTERS	12	1977
PASSING STRANGER SCOTT MATTHEWS	45	2006
PASSION PETER GABRIEL	29	1989
PASSION JOSE CARRERAS	21	1996
PASSION VARIOUS ARTISTS (UNIVERSAL)	8	2001
PASSION GERI HALLIWELL	41	2005
PASSION AND WARFARE STEVE VAI	8	1990
A PASSION PLAY JETHRO TULL	13	1973
PASSPORT NANA MOUSKOURI	3	1976
PAST MASTERS VOLUME 1 BEATLES	46	1988
PAST MASTERS VOLUME 2 BEATLES	49	1988
PASTICHE MANHATTAN TRANSFER	10	1978
PASTPRESENT CLANNAD	5	1989
PAT BOONE ORIGINALS PAT BOONE	16	1976
PAT GARRETT & BILLY THE KID BOB DYLAN	29	1973
PATASHNIK BIOSPHERE	50	1994
PATIENCE GEORGE MICHAEL	1	2004
PATRICK MORAZ PATRICK MORAZ	28	1976
PATRIOT GAMES GUNSHOT	60	1993
PAUL HARDCASTLE PAUL HARDCASTLE	53	1985
PAUL IS LIVE PAUL McCARTNEY	34	1993
PAUL JOHNSON PAUL JOHNSON	63	1987
PAUL MCCARTNEY'S LIVERPOOL ORATORIO CARL DAVIS & THE ROYAL LIVERPOOL PHILHARMONIC ORCHESTRA & CHOIR	36	1991
PAUL MCCARTNEY'S STANDING STONE LONDON SYMPHONY ORCHESTRA CONDUCTED BY LAURENCE FOSTER	34	1997
PAUL OAKENFOLD – GREATEST HITS AND REMIXES VARIOUS ARTISTS (NEW STATE)	13	2007
PAUL OAKENFOLD – NEW YORK VARIOUS ARTISTS (GLOBAL UNDERGROUND)	12	1998
PAUL SIMON PAUL SIMON	1	1972
PAUL SIMON'S CONCERT IN THE PARK – AUGUST 15TH 1991 PAUL SIMON	60	1991
PAUL WELLER PAUL WELLER	8	1992
PAUL WELLER AT THE BBC PAUL WELLER	32	2008
PAUL YOUNG PAUL YOUNG	39	1997
PAULINE PAULINE HENRY	45	1994
PAULINE MURRAY AND THE INVISIBLE GIRLS PAULINE MURRAY & THE INVISIBLE GIRLS	25	1980
PAUL'S BOUTIQUE BEASTIE BOYS	44	1989
PAVAROTTI AND FRIENDS FOR WAR CHILD LUCIANO PAVAROTTI & FRIENDS	45	1996
THE PAVAROTTI COLLECTION LUCIANO PAVAROTTI	12	1986
PAVAROTTI IN HYDE PARK LUCIANO PAVAROTTI	19	1992
PAVAROTTI/DOMINGO/CARRERAS VARIOUS ARTISTS (EMPORIO)	14	2001
PAVAROTTI'S GREATEST HITS LUCIANO PAVAROTTI	95	1982
PAWN SHOPPE HEART VON BONDIES	36	2004
PAWNSHOP GUITARS GILBY CLARKE	39	1994
PAY THE DEVIL VAN MORRISON	8	2006
PCD PUSSYCAT DOLLS	7	2005
PEACE EURYTHMICS	4	1999
PEACE & LOVE – THE WOODSTOCK GENERATION VARIOUS ARTISTS (WARNER BROTHERS)	6	2004
PEACE AND LOVE POGUES	5	1989
PEACE AT LAST BLUE NILE	13	1996
PEACE IN OUR TIME BIG COUNTRY	9	1988
PEACE IN THE VALLEY VARIOUS ARTISTS (RONCO)	6	1979
PEACE – PURE CLASSICAL CALM VARIOUS ARTISTS (VIRGIN)	20	2004
PEACE WILL COME TOM PAXTON	47	1972
PEACEFUL JOURNEY HEAVY D & THE BOYZ	40	1991
PEACEFUL THE WORLD LAYS ME DOWN NOAH & THE WHALE	5	2008
PEACHES – THE VERY BEST OF STRANGLERS	21	2002
PEACHTREE ROAD ELTON JOHN	21	2004
PEARL JANIS JOPLIN	20	1971
PEARL HARBOR (OST) GREENAWAY/ZIMMER	50	2001
PEARL JAM PEARL JAM	5	2006
PEARLS ELKIE BROOKS	2	1981
PEARLS II ELKIE BROOKS	5	1982
PEASANTS, PIGS & ASTRONAUTS KULA SHAKER	9	1999
PEBBLES PEBBLES	56	1988
PEEL SESSIONS ORBITAL	32	1994
PEEPSHOW SIOUXSIE & THE BANSHEES	20	1988
PEGGY SUICIDE JULIAN COPE	23	1991
PELICAN WEST HAIRCUT 100	2	1982
PELOTON DELGADOS	56	1998
PENDULUM CREEDENCE CLEARWATER REVIVAL	8	1971
PENNIES FROM HEAVEN (TELEVISION SOUNDTRACK) TELEVISION AND RADIO COMPILATION	8	1978
THE PENTANGLE PENTANGLE	21	1968
PENTHOUSE AND PAVEMENT HEAVEN 17	14	1981
PENTHOUSE TAPES SENSATIONAL ALEX HARVEY BAND	14	1976
PEOPLE HOTHOUSE FLOWERS	2	1988
PEOPLE GET READY RUSSELL WATSON	20	2008
PEOPLE MOVE ON BERNARD BUTLER	11	1998
THE PEOPLE TREE MOTHER EARTH	45	1994
THE PEOPLE WHO GRINNED THEMSELVES TO DEATH HOUSEMARTINS	9	1987
PEOPLE'S INSTINCTIVE TRAVELS... A TRIBE CALLED QUEST	54	1990
PEPSI CHART 2001 VARIOUS ARTISTS (VIRGIN)	2	2000
PEPSI CHART 2002 VARIOUS ARTISTS (VIRGIN)	1	2001
PEPSI CHART 2003 VARIOUS ARTISTS (VIRGIN)	5	2002
PERFECT ANGEL MINNIE RIPERTON	33	1975
PERFECT DAY VARIOUS ARTISTS (COLUMBIA)	7	1998
PERFECT DAY CASCADA	9	2007
A PERFECT DAY – HIS GREATEST HITS AND MORE ROGER WHITTAKER	74	1996
A PERFECT LOVE VARIOUS ARTISTS (GLOBAL TELEVISION)	4	1997
PERFECT LOVE VARIOUS ARTISTS (WARNER BROTHERS)	15	2004
A PERFECT LOVE II VARIOUS ARTISTS (GLOBAL TELEVISION)	9	1998
A PERFECT LOVE III VARIOUS ARTISTS (GLOBAL TELEVISION)	6	2000
PERFECT PEACE WESTMINSTER ABBEY CHOIR/CONDUCTOR: MARTIN NEARY	58	1998
PERFECT REMEDY STATUS QUO	49	1989
PERFECT STRANGERS DEEP PURPLE	5	1984
PERFECT SYMMETRY KEANE	1	2008
PERFECT TIMING KIKI DEE	47	1981
PERFECT TIMING MSG	65	1987
PERFECTLY GOOD GUITAR JOHN HIATT	67	1993
PERFECTO FLUORO:OAKENFOLD VARIOUS ARTISTS (PERFECTO)	18	1996
PERFECTO PRESENTS PAUL OAKENFOLD – TRAVELLING VARIOUS ARTISTS (PERFECTO)	12	2000
PERFORMANCE AND COCKTAILS STEREOPHONICS	1	1999
PERFORMANCE – THE VERY BEST OF TIM RICE AND ANDREW LLOYD WEBBER VARIOUS ARTISTS (TELSTAR)	33	1985
PERHAPS ASSOCIATES	23	1985
PERHAPS LOVE PLACIDO DOMINGO & JOHN DENVER	17	1981
PERILOUS JOURNEY GORDON GILTRAP	29	1978
A PERIOD OF TRANSITION VAN MORRISON	23	1977
PERMANENT SHADE OF BLUE ROACHFORD	25	1994
PERMANENT VACATION AEROSMITH	37	1987
PERMANENT WAVES RUSH	3	1980
PERMANENT: JOY DIVISION 1995 JOY DIVISION	16	1995
PERMISSION TO LAND DARKNESS	1	2003
PERRY PERRY COMO	26	1974
PERSEVERE PROCLAIMERS	61	2001
PERSISTENCE OF TIME ANTHRAX	13	1990
PERSONAL PAUL JOHNSON	70	1989
THE PERSUADERS JOHN BARRY	18	1972
PERVERSE JESUS JONES	6	1993
PET SHOP BOYS, ACTUALLY PET SHOP BOYS	2	1987
PET SOUNDS BEACH BOYS	2	1966
PET SOUNDS BEACH BOYS	59	1995
PETE TONG ESSENTIAL SELECTION VARIOUS ARTISTS (FFRR)	4	1998
PETE TONG ESSENTIAL SELECTION – IBIZA 99 VARIOUS ARTISTS (FFRR)	7	1999
PETE TONG – ESSENTIAL SELECTION – SPRING 1999 VARIOUS ARTISTS (FFRR)	3	1999
PETE TONG ESSENTIAL SELECTION – SUMMER 1998 VARIOUS ARTISTS (FFRR)	4	1998
PETE TONG ESSENTIAL SELECTION – SUMMER 1998 (3 CD) VARIOUS ARTISTS (FFRR)	2	1998
PETE TONG ESSENTIAL SELECTION – SUMMER 97 VARIOUS ARTISTS (POLYGRAM)	4	1997
PETE TONG ESSENTIAL SELECTION – WINTER 97 VARIOUS ARTISTS (FFRR)	10	1997
PETE TONG/BOY GEORGE – DANCE NATION 5 VARIOUS ARTISTS (MINISTRY OF SOUND)	2	1998
PETER AND GORDON PETER & GORDON	18	1964
PETER AND SOPHIA PETER SELLERS & SOPHIA LOREN	5	1960
PETER COX PETER COX	64	1997
PETER GABRIEL PETER GABRIEL	7	1977
PETER GABRIEL PETER GABRIEL	10	1978
PETER GABRIEL PETER GABRIEL	1	1980
PETER GABRIEL PETER GABRIEL	6	1982
PETER GABRIEL PLAYS LIVE PETER GABRIEL	8	1983
PETER HETHERINGTON: SONGS FROM THE HEART VARIOUS ARTISTS (MAWSON & WARSHAM)	10	1991
PETER PAUL AND MARY PETER, PAUL & MARY	18	1964
PETER SARSTEDT PETER SARSTEDT	8	1969
PHAEDRA TANGERINE DREAM	15	1974
PHANTASMAGORIA CURVED AIR	20	1972
PHANTASMAGORIA DAMNED	11	1985
THE PHANTOM OF THE OPERA STAGE CAST RECORDING	1	1987
PHANTOM OF THE OPERA ANDREW LLOYD WEBBER	40	2004
PHANTOM POWER SUPER FURRY ANIMALS	4	2003
PHASE ONE VARIOUS ARTISTS (POSITIVA)	15	1994
PHENOMENA PHENOMENA	63	1985
PHENOMENON LL COOL J	37	1997
PHIL COULTER'S IRELAND PHIL COULTER	86	1985
PHIL EVERLY PHIL EVERLY	61	1983
PHIL FEARON AND GALAXY PHIL FEARON & GALAXY	8	1984

Album / Artist	Peak Position	Year of Release
PHIL SPECTOR'S CHRISTMAS ALBUM PHIL SPECTOR	21	1972
PHIL SPECTOR'S ECHOES OF THE 60'S PHIL SPECTOR	21	1977
PHIL SPECTOR'S GREATEST HITS/PHIL SPECTOR'S CHRISTMAS ALBUM PHIL SPECTOR	19	1983
PHILADELPHIA FILM SOUNDTRACK	5	1994
PHILIP OAKEY AND GIORGIO MORODER PHILIP OAKEY & GIORGIO MORODER	52	1985
PHILOPHOBIA ARAB STRAP	37	1998
THE PHILOSOPHER'S STONE VAN MORRISON	20	1998
PHILTRE NITIN SAWHNEY	69	2005
PHOENIX DAN FOGELBERG	42	1980
PHOTOGRAPH – THE VERY BEST OF RINGO STARR	26	2007
THE PHOTOS PHOTOS	4	1980
PHYSICAL OLIVIA NEWTON-JOHN	11	1981
PHYSICAL GRAFFITI LED ZEPPELIN	1	1975
A PHYSICAL PRESENCE LEVEL 42	28	1985
PIAF ELAINE PAIGE	46	1994
THE PIANO (OST) MICHAEL NYMAN	31	1994
THE PIANO AND THE SONG VARIOUS ARTISTS (UNIVERSAL)	10	2003
PIANO MAN BILLY JOEL	98	1984
PIANO MAN – THE VERY BEST OF BILLY JOEL	9	2004
PIANO MOODS SCHOOL OF EXCELLENCE	47	1995
PIANO MOODS VARIOUS ARTISTS (DECADANCE)	6	2003
THE PIANO SESSIONS KEY SESSIONS QUARTET	54	2004
THE PICK OF BILLY CONNOLLY BILLY CONNOLLY	23	1981
THE PICK OF DESTINY TENACIOUS D	10	2006
THE PICK, THE SICKLE AND THE SHOVEL GRAVEDIGGAZ	24	1997
PICKLED EGGS & SHERBET ALL SEEING I	45	1999
PICKWICK STAGE CAST RECORDING	12	1963
PICTURE BOOK SIMPLY RED	2	1985
PICTURE OF PERFECT YOUTH FEEDER	65	2007
A PICTURE OF YOU JOE BROWN & THE BRUVVERS	3	1962
PICTURE OF YOU BEN MILLS	3	2007
PICTURE PERFECT MORNING EDIE BRICKELL	59	1994
PICTURE THIS WET WET WET	1	1995
PICTURES KATIE MELUA	2	2007
PICTURES AT AN EXHIBITION EMERSON, LAKE & PALMER	3	1971
PICTURES AT AN EXHIBITION TOMITA	42	1975
PICTURES AT ELEVEN ROBERT PLANT	2	1982
PICTURES – 40 YEARS OF HITS STATUS QUO	8	2008
PICTURES OF ELVIS ELVIS PRESLEY	52	1977
PICTURES OF THE OTHER SIDE GARETH GATES	23	2007
PIE JESU ALED JONES	25	1986
PIECE BY PIECE JOHN MARTYN	28	1986
PIECE BY PIECE KATIE MELUA	1	2005
PIECE OF CAKE MUDHONEY	39	1992
PIECE OF MIND IRON MAIDEN	3	1983
A PIECE OF WHAT YOU NEED TEDDY THOMPSON	10	2008
PIECES JULIAN LLOYD WEBBER & THE LONDON SYMPHONY ORCHESTRA	59	1985
PIECES IN A MODERN STYLE WILLIAM ORBIT	2	2000
PIECES OF A DREAM ANASTACIA	6	2005
PIECES OF HANCOCK TONY HANCOCK	17	1960
PIECES OF THE PEOPLE WE LOVE RAPTURE	40	2006
THE PIG ATTRACTION FEATURING PINKY AND PERKY VARIOUS ARTISTS (TELSTAR)	19	1993
PIG LIB STEPHEN MALKMUS & THE JICKS	63	2003
PIGEON HOLE NEW FAST AUTOMATIC DAFFODILS	49	1990
PIL LIVE IN TOKYO PUBLIC IMAGE LTD	28	1983
PILEDRIVER STATUS QUO	5	1973
PILGRIM ERIC CLAPTON	6	1998
PILGRIMAGE WISHBONE ASH	14	1971
THE PILLAGE CAPPADONNA	43	1998
PILLS 'N' THRILLS AND BELLYACHES HAPPY MONDAYS	4	1990
THE PINK & THE LILY SANDI THOM	25	2008
PINK BUBBLES GO APE HELLOWEEN	41	1991
PINKERTON WEEZER	43	1996
PINKY BLUE ALTERED IMAGES	12	1982
PIN-UPS DAVID BOWIE	1	1973
PIOUHGD BUTTHOLE SURFERS	68	1991
THE PIOUS BIRD OF GOOD OMEN FLEETWOOD MAC	18	1969
PIPEDREAM ALAN HULL	29	1973
THE PIPER AT THE GATES OF DAWN PINK FLOYD	6	1967
PIPES OF PEACE PAUL McCARTNEY	4	1983
PIRANHAS PIRANHAS	69	1980
PIRATES RICKIE LEE JONES	37	1981
PIRATES OF THE CARIBBEAN – AT WORLD'S END (OST) HANS ZIMMER	58	2007
PIRATES OF THE CARIBBEAN – DEAD MAN'S CHEST (OST) HANS ZIMMER	68	2006
PISCES, AQUARIUS, CAPRICORN & JONES LTD. MONKEES	5	1968
PIXIES AT THE BBC PIXIES	45	1998
A PLACE IN THE SUN LIT	55	1999
A PLACE IN THE WORLD MARY CHAPIN CARPENTER	36	1996
A PLACE ON EARTH – THE GREATEST HITS BELINDA CARLISLE	15	1999
PLACEBO PLACEBO	5	1996
PLACIDO DOMINGO COLLECTION PLACIDO DOMINGO	30	1986
THE PLAGUE DEMON	73	1983
THE PLAN OSMONDS	6	1973
THE PLAN 1978 TUBEWAY ARMY & GARY NUMAN	29	1984
PLANET ROCK VARIOUS ARTISTS (DINO)	8	1993
PLANET WAVES BOB DYLAN	7	1974
PLANETARY INVASION MIDNIGHT STAR	85	1985
PLASTIC LETTERS BLONDIE	10	1978
PLATINUM MIKE OLDFIELD	24	1979
THE PLATINUM ALBUM VARIOUS ARTISTS (K-TEL)	32	1981
THE PLATINUM ALBUM VENGABOYS	9	2000
PLATINUM COLLECTION BRYAN FERRY & ROXY MUSIC	17	2004
PLATINUM COLLECTION GENESIS	21	2004
THE PLATINUM COLLECTION BARBARA DICKSON	35	2004
THE PLATINUM COLLECTION FRANK SINATRA	11	2004
THE PLATINUM COLLECTION PHIL COLLINS	4	2004
THE PLATINUM COLLECTION ROY ORBISON	16	2004
PLATINUM COLLECTION SHADOWS	30	2005
THE PLATINUM COLLECTION BEACH BOYS	30	2005
THE PLATINUM COLLECTION CLIFF RICHARD	51	2005
THE PLATINUM COLLECTION DAVID BOWIE	55	2005
THE PLATINUM COLLECTION DEEP PURPLE	39	2005
THE PLATINUM COLLECTION MIKE OLDFIELD	36	2006
THE PLATINUM COLLECTION – GREATEST HITS BARRY MANILOW	37	1993
PLATINUM SOUL LEGENDS – 1960-1975 VARIOUS ARTISTS (WARNER BROTHERS)	14	2002
PLATOON FILM SOUNDTRACK	90	1987
PLAY MAGAZINE	69	1980
PLAY SQUEEZE	41	1991
PLAY MOBY	1	1999
PLAY ANDREW LLOYD WEBBER AND TIM RICE HANK MARVIN & THE SHADOWS	41	1997
PLAY DIRTY GIRLSCHOOL	66	1983
PLAY DON'T WORRY MICK RONSON	29	1975
PLAY GAMES DOG EAT DOG	40	1996
PLAY IT AGAIN BRIAN SMITH & HIS HAPPY PIANO	97	1981
PLAY IT LOUD VARIOUS ARTISTS (UNIVERSAL)	2	2007
PLAY TIME – THE COMPLETE FUN PACKAGE VARIOUS ARTISTS (SONY/BMG)	10	2005
PLAY TO WIN GABRIELLE	10	2004
PLAY/THE B SIDES MOBY	24	2000
PLAYED BODINES	94	1987
PLAYIN' FAVOURITES DON McLEAN	42	1973
PLAYING MY GAME LENE MARLIN	18	2000
PLAYING THE ANGEL DEPECHE MODE	6	2005
PLAYING TO AN AUDIENCE OF ONE DAVID SOUL	8	1977
PLAYING WITH A DIFFERENT SEX AU PAIRS	33	1981
PLAYS ABBA JAMES LAST	29	2001
PLAYS SPANISH MUSIC JOHN WILLIAMS	46	1970
PLAYS YOUR ALL-TIME PARTY HITS JOE LOSS & HIS ORCHESTRA	24	1971
PLAYSCHOOL POP VARIOUS ARTISTS (EMI)	13	2006
PLAYTIME IS OVER WILEY	71	2007
PLEASE PET SHOP BOYS	3	1986
PLEASE DESCRIBE YOURSELF DOGS DIE IN HOT CARS	44	2004
PLEASE DON'T TOUCH STEVE HACKETT	38	1978
PLEASE GET MY NAME RIGHT TWIGGY	35	1977
PLEASE HAMMER DON'T HURT 'EM MC HAMMER	8	1990
PLEASE PLEASE ME BEATLES	1	1963
PLEASE TO SEE THE KING STEELEYE SPAN	45	1971
PLEASE YOURSELF BANANARAMA	46	1993
PLEASED TO MEET YOU SLEEPER	7	1997
PLEASED TO MEET YOU JAMES	11	2001
PLEASURE GIRLS AT OUR BEST	60	1981
PLEASURE AND PAIN DR. HOOK	47	1979
PLEASURE DEATH THERAPY?	52	1992
PLEASURE ONE HEAVEN 17	78	1986
THE PLEASURE PRINCIPLE GARY NUMAN	1	1979
PLIGHT AND PREMONITION DAVID SYLVIAN & HOLGAR CZUKAY	71	1988
THE PLOT THICKENS GALLIANO	7	1994
PNYC PORTISHEAD	40	1998
POCKET FULL OF KRYPTONITE SPIN DOCTORS	2	1993
POCKET SYMPHONY AIR	22	2007
A POCKETFUL OF DREAMS BIG FUN	7	1990
POD BREEDERS	22	1990
POEMS, PRAYERS AND PROMISES JOHN DENVER	19	1973
THE POET II BOBBY WOMACK	31	1984
POETIC CHAMPIONS COMPOSE VAN MORRISON	26	1987
THE POINT NILSSON	46	1972
POINT BLANK BONFIRE	74	1989
POINT BLANK NAILBOMB	62	1994
POINT OF ENTRY JUDAS PRIEST	14	1981
POINTLESS NOSTALGIC JAMIE CULLUM	55	2004
POINTS ON THE CURVE WANG CHUNG	34	1984
POISON BELL BIV DEVOE	35	1990
THE POISON BULLET FOR MY VALENTINE	21	2005
POKEMON – 2 B A MASTER VARIOUS ARTISTS (KOCH)	20	2000
POKEMON – THE FIRST MOVIE FILM SOUNDTRACK	8	2000
POLAND TANGERINE DREAM	90	1984
POLECATS ARE GO POLECATS	28	1981
THE POLICE POLICE	3	2007
POLKA PARTY JAMES LAST	22	1972
THE POLYESTER EMBASSY MADISON AVENUE	74	2000
POLYTHENE FEEDER	65	1997

Title / Artist	Peak Position	Year of Release
POMME FRITZ ORB	6	1994
POOLSIDE NU SHOOZ	32	1986
POOR MAN'S HEAVEN SETH LAKEMAN	8	2008
POP U2	1	1997
POP SAME DIFFERENCE	22	2008
POP ART TRANSVISION VAMP	4	1988
POP CLASSICS – 28 CLASSIC TRACKS VARIOUS ARTISTS (ARCADE)	19	1991
POP HITS – CLASS OF 2007 VARIOUS ARTISTS (UNIVERSAL)	4	2007
POP HITS! VARIOUS ARTISTS (SONY/BMG)	9	2007
POP IDOL – THE BIG BAND ALBUM VARIOUS ARTISTS (S RECORDS)	1	2002
POP JR VARIOUS ARTISTS (UNIVERSAL)	2	2005
POP JR 2 VARIOUS ARTISTS (UNIVERSAL)	5	2006
POP JR TV SONGS VARIOUS ARTISTS (UNIVERSAL)	17	2008
POP LIFE BANANARAMA	42	1991
POP LIFE DAVID GUETTA	44	2007
POP PARTY VARIOUS ARTISTS (UNIVERSAL)	2	2003
POP PARTY 2 VARIOUS ARTISTS (UNIVERSAL)	1	2004
POP PARTY 3 VARIOUS ARTISTS (UNIVERSAL)	1	2005
POP PARTY 4 VARIOUS ARTISTS (UNIVERSAL)	1	2006
POP PARTY 6 VARIOUS ARTISTS (UNIVERSAL)	3	2008
POP PARTY VOLUME 5 VARIOUS ARTISTS (UNIVERSAL)	1	2007
POP PRINCESSES VARIOUS ARTISTS (UNIVERSAL)	3	2004
POP PRINCESSES 2 VARIOUS ARTISTS (UNIVERSAL)	6	2005
POP PRINCESSES 3 VARIOUS ARTISTS (UNIVERSAL)	6	2006
POP ROCKS VARIOUS ARTISTS (SONY/BMG)	10	2005
POP SAID DARLING BUDS	23	1989
POP SYMPHONIES JAMES LAST	10	1991
POP SYMPHONIES 2 JAMES LAST	32	1998
POP TRASH DURAN DURAN	53	2000
POP! – THE FIRST 20 HITS ERASURE	1	1992
POPART – THE HITS PET SHOP BOYS	30	2003
POPPED IN SOULED OUT WET WET WET	1	1987
POPSTARS HEAR'SAY	1	2001
POPULAR MUSIC FROM TV FILM & OPERA MARIA CALLAS	45	2000
PORCELAIN JULIA FORDHAM	13	1989
PORCUPINE ECHO & THE BUNNYMEN	2	1983
PORGY AND BESS FILM SOUNDTRACK	7	1959
PORK SODA PRIMUS	56	1993
PORNO FOR PYROS PORNO FOR PYROS	13	1993
PORNOGRAPHY CURE	8	1982
PORTISHEAD PORTISHEAD	2	1997
PORTRAIT WALKER BROTHERS	3	1966
PORTRAIT DON WILLIAMS	58	1979
PORTRAIT NOLANS	7	1982
PORTRAIT DIANA ROSS	8	1983
PORTRAIT DES O'CONNOR	63	1992
PORTRAIT RICK ASTLEY	26	2005
PORTRAIT (SO LONG AGO, SO CLEAR) VANGELIS	14	1996
PORTRAIT IN MUSIC ELVIS PRESLEY	36	1970
PORTRAIT IN MUSIC BURT BACHARACH	5	1971
PORTRAIT OF A LEGEND SAM COOKE	19	2003
PORTRAIT OF A LEGEND 1951-1964 SAM COOKE	26	2005
PORTRAIT OF DONNY DONNY OSMOND	5	1972
A PORTRAIT OF DORIS DAY DORIS DAY	32	1989
A PORTRAIT OF ELLA FITZGERALD ELLA FITZGERALD	42	1988
A PORTRAIT OF MARIO LANZA MARIO LANZA	49	1987
PORTRAIT OF SINATRA FRANK SINATRA	1	1977
A PORTRAIT OF – THE ULTIMATE COLLECTION CHARLIE LANDSBOROUGH	23	2005
POSITIVA – ESSENTIAL CLUB ANTHEMS VARIOUS ARTISTS (POSITIVA)	14	2008
POSITIVE REACTION CAVEMAN	43	1991
POSITIVE TOUCH UNDERTONES	17	1981
POSITIVITY INCOGNITO	55	1993
POSSESSED VENOM	99	1985
POST HISTORIC MONSTERS CARTER – THE UNSTOPPABLE SEX MACHINE	5	1993
POST ORGASMIC CHILL SKUNK ANANSIE	16	1999
POST/TELEGRAM BJORK	2	1995
POSTCARD MARY HOPKIN	3	1969
POSTCARDS FROM HEAVEN LIGHTHOUSE FAMILY	2	1997
POT LUCK ELVIS PRESLEY	1	1962
POTATO LAND SPIRIT	40	1981
POVERTY'S PARADISE NAUGHTY BY NATURE	20	1995
POWER & PASSION VARIOUS ARTISTS (SONY/BMG)	13	2005
POWER & SOUL VARIOUS ARTISTS (POLYGRAM)	5	1998
POWER AND PASSION MAMA'S BOYS	55	1985
POWER AND SOUL VARIOUS ARTISTS (POLYGRAM)	5	1994
POWER AND THE GLORY SAXON	15	1983
THE POWER AND THE GLORY VARIOUS ARTISTS (VERTIGO)	2	1991
POWER BALLADS VARIOUS ARTISTS (VIRGIN)	1	2003
POWER BALLADS III VARIOUS ARTISTS (VIRGIN)	7	2004
POWER CUTS – ROCK'S GREATEST HITS VARIOUS ARTISTS (POLYGRAM)	5	1992
POWER IN NUMBERS JURASSIC 5	46	2002
POWER IN THE DARKNESS TOM ROBINSON BAND	4	1978
POWER OF A WOMAN ETERNAL	6	1995
POWER OF A WOMAN VARIOUS ARTISTS (TELSTAR)	13	1998
THE POWER OF CLASSIC ROCK LONDON SYMPHONY ORCHESTRA WITH THE ROYAL CHORAL SOCIETY & THE ROGER SMITH CHORALE	13	1985
THE POWER OF GLORIA GAYNOR GLORIA GAYNOR	81	1986
THE POWER OF LOVE VARIOUS ARTISTS (WEST FIVE)	33	1986
POWER OF LOVE LUTHER VANDROSS	9	1991
THE POWER OF LOVE VARIOUS ARTISTS (QUALITY TELEVISION)	4	1992
THE POWER OF LOVE VARIOUS ARTISTS (WARNER BROTHERS)	4	2003
THE POWER OF LOVE VARIOUS ARTISTS (SONY BMG)	3	2008
POWER OF TEN CHRIS DE BURGH	3	1992
POWER RANGERS – THE ALBUM – A ROCK ADVENTURE MIGHTY MORPH'N POWER RANGERS	50	1994
THE POWER STATION POWER STATION	12	1985
POWER THEMES 90 F.A.B.	53	1990
POWER TO THE PEOPLE AND THE BEATS PUBLIC ENEMY	39	2005
POWER WINDOWS RUSH	9	1985
POWER, CORRUPTION AND LIES NEW ORDER	4	1983
POWERAGE AC/DC	26	1978
POWERLIGHT EARTH WIND & FIRE	22	1983
POWERSLAVE IRON MAIDEN	2	1984
POWERTRIP MONSTER MAGNET	65	1998
POWERTRIPPIN' ALMIGHTY	5	1993
PRACTICE WHAT YOU PREACH TESTAMENT	40	1989
PRAIRIE WIND NEIL YOUNG	22	2005
PRAISE INNER CITY	52	1992
PRAISE – 18 CHORAL MASTERPIECES LONDON PHILHARMONIC CHOIR WITH THE NATIONAL PHILHARMONIC ORCHESTRA CONDUCTED BY JOHN ALDISS	54	1991
THE PREACHERS WIFE (OST) WHITNEY HOUSTON	35	1997
PRECIOUS VARIOUS ARTISTS (DINO)	11	1992
PRECIOUS MEMORIES ANN WILLIAMSON	16	1986
PRECIOUS METAL VARIOUS ARTISTS (MCA)	60	1980
PRECIOUS METAL VARIOUS ARTISTS (STYLUS)	2	1989
PRECIOUS MOMENTS VARIOUS ARTISTS (IMPRESSION)	77	1983
PRECIOUS TIME PAT BENATAR	30	1981
THE PREDATOR ICE CUBE	73	1992
THE PREMIER HITS GARY NUMAN/TUBEWAY ARMY	21	1996
PREMIERE KATHERINE JENKINS	31	2004
THE PREMIERE COLLECTION – ENCORE (ANDREW LLOYD WEBBER) VARIOUS ARTISTS (REALLY USEFUL)	2	1992
PREMIERS SYMPTOMES AIR	12	1999
PRE-MILLENNIUM TENSION TRICKY	30	1996
PRESENCE LED ZEPPELIN	1	1976
THE PRESENT MOODY BLUES	15	1983
PRESENT ARMS UB40	2	1981
PRESENT ARMS IN DUB UB40	38	1981
A PRESENT FOR EVERYONE BUSTED	2	2003
PRESENTING DIONNE WARWICK DIONNE WARWICK	14	1964
THE PRESIDENTS OF THE UNITED STATES OF AMERICA PRESIDENTS OF THE UNITED STATES OF AMERICA	14	1996
PRESLEY – THE ALL TIME GREATEST HITS ELVIS PRESLEY	4	1987
PRESS PLAY P DIDDY	11	2006
PRESS TO PLAY PAUL McCARTNEY	8	1986
PRESTO RUSH	27	1989
THE PRETENDER JACKSON BROWNE	26	1976
PRETENDERS PRETENDERS	1	1980
PRETENDERS II PRETENDERS	7	1981
PRETTY HATE MACHINE NINE INCH NAILS	67	1991
PRETTY IN BLACK RAVEONETTES	71	2005
PRETTY ODD PANIC AT THE DISCO	2	2008
PRETTY ON THE INSIDE HOLE	59	1991
PRETTY THINGS PRETTY THINGS	6	1965
PRETTY WOMAN FILM SOUNDTRACK	2	1990
PRETZEL LOGIC STEELY DAN	37	1974
THE PRICE YOU PAY SPEAR OF DESTINY	37	1988
PRIDE ROBERT PALMER	37	1983
PRIDE – THE VERY BEST OF SCOTLAND VARIOUS ARTISTS (RCA)	13	1995
PRIEST...LIVE JUDAS PRIEST	47	1987
THE PRIESTS PRIESTS	5	2008
PRIMITIVE NEIL DIAMOND	7	1984
PRIMITIVE SOULFLY	45	2000
PRIMITIVE COOL MICK JAGGER	26	1987
PRINCE BLIMEY RED SNAPPER	60	1996
PRINCE CHARMING ADAM & THE ANTS	2	1981
THE PRINCE'S TRUST COLLECTION VARIOUS ARTISTS (TELSTAR)	64	1985
THE PRINCE'S TRUST CONCERT 1987 VARIOUS ARTISTS (A&M)	44	1987
PRINCE'S TRUST TENTH ANNIVERSARY BIRTHDAY PARTY VARIOUS ARTISTS (A&M)	76	1987
PRINCESS PRINCESS	15	1986
PRINCESS ALICE & THE BROKEN ARROW MAGNUM	70	2007
THE PRINCIPLE OF MOMENTS ROBERT PLANT	7	1983
PRISONERS IN PARADISE EUROPE	61	1991
PRIVATE AUDITION HEART	77	1982
PRIVATE COLLECTION JON & VANGELIS	22	1983

Title / Artist	Peak Position	Year of Release
PRIVATE COLLECTION 1979-1988 CLIFF RICHARD	1	1988
PRIVATE DANCER TINA TURNER	2	1984
PRIVATE EYES DARYL HALL & JOHN OATES	8	1982
PRIVATE INVESTIGATIONS DIRE STRAITS & MARK KNOPFLER	20	2005
PRIVATE PRACTICE DR. FEELGOOD	41	1978
THE PRIVATE PRESS DJ SHADOW	8	2002
PRIVATE REVOLUTION WORLD PARTY	56	1987
PROBOT PROBOT	34	2004
PROCOL HARUM LIVE IN CONCERT WITH THE EDMONTON SYMPHONY ORCHESTRA PROCOL HARUM	48	1972
PROCOL'S NINTH PROCOL HARUM	41	1975
PRODIGAL SISTA BEVERLEY KNIGHT	42	1998
PRODIGY PRESENTS THE DIRTCHAMBER SESSIONS 1 VARIOUS ARTISTS (XL RECORDINGS)	3	1999
PRODUCT 2378 VARIOUS ARTISTS (TELSTAR)	16	1990
PROFESSOR SATCHAFUNKILUS AND THE MUSTERION OF ROCK JOE SATRIANI	75	2008
PROGENY SHAMEN	23	1991
PROGRESSION VARIOUS ARTISTS (POLYGRAM)	9	1993
PROGRESSION VOLUME 1 VARIOUS ARTISTS (RENAISSANCE MUSIC)	17	2001
PROGRESSIONS OF POWER TRIUMPH	61	1980
PROMISE SADE	1	1985
THE PROMISE T'PAU	10	1991
THE PROMISE IL DIVO	1	2008
PROMISED LAND ELVIS PRESLEY	21	1975
PROMISED LAND QUEENSRYCHE	13	1994
PROMISES AND LIES UB40	1	1993
PROOF OF YOUTH THE GO! TEAM	21	2007
PROPAGANDA SPARKS	9	1974
PROPHESY NITIN SAWHNEY	40	2001
PROPHETS, SEERS AND SAGES THE ANGELS OF THE AGES/MY PEOPLE WERE FAIR AND HAD SKY IN THEIR HAIR BUT NOW THEY'RE CONTENT TO WEAR STARS ON THEIR BROWS TYRANNOSAURUS REX	1	1972
THE PROS AND CONS OF HITCH-HIKING ROGER WATERS	13	1984
PROSPECKT'S MARCH COLDPLAY	38	2008
PROTECT THE INNOCENT VARIOUS ARTISTS (TELSTAR)	9	1989
PROTECTION/NO PROTECTION MASSIVE ATTACK	4	1994
PROTEST SONGS PREFAB SPROUT	18	1989
PROTOTYPE3 – SEB FONTAINE VARIOUS ARTISTS (GLOBAL UNDERGROUND)	19	2000
PROUD HEATHER SMALL	12	2000
PROVISION SCRITTI POLITTI	8	1988
PROVOCATIVE JOHNNY GILL	41	1993
PROZIAC HONEYCRACK	34	1996
PS I LOVE YOU VARIOUS ARTISTS (WARWICK)	68	1982
PSALM 69 MINISTRY	33	1992
PSI PITCHSHIFTER	54	2002
PSYCHE – THE ALBUM PJ & DUNCAN	5	1994
PSYCHEDELIC FURS PSYCHEDELIC FURS	18	1980
PSYCHEDELIC SHACK TEMPTATIONS	56	1970
PSYCHIC KARAOKE TRANSGLOBAL UNDERGROUND	62	1996
PSYCHOCANDY JESUS & MARY CHAIN	31	1985
PSYCHO-CIRCUS KISS	47	1998
THE PSYCHOMODO COCKNEY REBEL	8	1974
PSYCHOTIC SUPPER TESLA	44	1991
PSYENCE FICTION UNKLE	4	1998
A PUBLIC AFFAIR JESSICA SIMPSON	65	2007
PUBLIC IMAGE PUBLIC IMAGE LTD	22	1978
PUBLIC WARNING LADY SOVEREIGN	58	2007
PULL THE PIN STEREOPHONICS	1	2007
PULP FICTION FILM SOUNDTRACK	5	1994
PULSE PINK FLOYD	1	1995
PUMP AEROSMITH	3	1989
PUMP UP THE JAM TECHNOTRONIC	2	1990
PUMP UP THE VALUUM NOFX	50	2000
PUMP UP THE VOLUME VARIOUS ARTISTS (UNIVERSAL)	11	2001
PUNCH THE CLOCK ELVIS COSTELLO & THE ATTRACTIONS	3	1983
PUNK AND DISORDERLY VARIOUS ARTISTS (ABSTRACT)	48	1982
PUNK AND DISORDERLY (FURTHER CHARGES) VARIOUS ARTISTS (ANAGRAM)	91	1982
PUNK AND DISORDERLY – NEW WAVE 1976-1981 VARIOUS ARTISTS (TELSTAR)	18	1991
PUNK – THE JUBILEE VARIOUS ARTISTS (VIRGIN)	12	2002
PUNK'S NOT DEAD EXPLOITED	20	1981
PURE PRIMITIVES	33	1989
PURE MIDGE URE	36	1991
PURE 3 COLOURS RED	16	1997
PURE GARY NUMAN	58	2000
PURE HAYLEY WESTENRA	7	2003
PURE & SIMPLE VARIOUS ARTISTS (UNIVERSAL)	7	2001
PURE ACOUSTIC VARIOUS ARTISTS (UNIVERSAL)	20	2004
PURE ATTRACTION VARIOUS ARTISTS (COLUMBIA)	5	1995
PURE BLING VARIOUS ARTISTS (WARNER BROTHERS)	8	2004
PURE CELTIC CHILLOUT VARIOUS ARTISTS (VIRGIN)	11	2002
PURE CHILLOUT VARIOUS ARTISTS (VIRGIN)	10	2001
PURE CLASSICAL CHILLOUT VARIOUS ARTISTS (DECADANCE)	9	2002
PURE CULT CULT	1	1993
PURE DANCE '96 VARIOUS ARTISTS (POLYGRAM)	5	1996
PURE DANCE '97 VARIOUS ARTISTS (POLYGRAM)	9	1997
PURE DRUM & BASS VARIOUS ARTISTS (UNIVERSAL)	16	2003
PURE EMOTIONS INSPIRATIONS	37	1995
PURE EUPHORIA – LEVEL 4 VARIOUS ARTISTS (TELSTAR)	3	2000
PURE FLAVA VARIOUS ARTISTS (WARNER BROTHERS)	10	2001
PURE FUNKY HOUSE VARIOUS ARTISTS (DEFECTED)	11	2008
PURE GARAGE VARIOUS ARTISTS (WARNER BROTHERS)	2	2000
PURE GARAGE II VARIOUS ARTISTS (WARNER BROTHERS)	2	2000
PURE GARAGE III VARIOUS ARTISTS (WARNER BROTHERS)	2	2000
PURE GARAGE IV VARIOUS ARTISTS (WARNER BROTHERS)	3	2001
PURE GARAGE PLATINUM – THE VERY BEST OF VARIOUS ARTISTS (WARNER BROTHERS)	4	2002
PURE GARAGE PRESENTS FOUR TO THE FLOOR VARIOUS ARTISTS (WARNER BROTHERS)	12	2004
PURE GARAGE PRESENTS PURE BASSLINE VARIOUS ARTISTS (WARNER BROTHERS)	6	2008
PURE GARAGE PRESENTS THE MAIN ROOM SESSIONS VARIOUS ARTISTS (WARNER BROTHERS)	8	2005
PURE GARAGE – REWIND – BACK TO THE OLD SKOOL VARIOUS ARTISTS (WARNER BROTHERS)	8	2007
PURE GARAGE V VARIOUS ARTISTS (WARNER BROTHERS)	7	2001
PURE GENIUS VARIOUS ARTISTS (WARNER BROTHERS)	7	2002
PURE GENIUS VOLUME 2 VARIOUS ARTISTS (WARNER BROTHERS)	12	2002
PURE GLOBAL CHILLOUT VARIOUS ARTISTS (DECADANCE)	10	2002
PURE GOLD VARIOUS ARTISTS (EMI)	1	1973
PURE GROOVE – THE CLASSICS VARIOUS ARTISTS (TELSTAR)	7	2002
PURE GROOVE – THE VERY BEST 80'S SOUL FUNK GROOVES VARIOUS ARTISTS (TELSTAR)	3	2002
PURE GROOVES – 80'S SLOWJAMS VARIOUS ARTISTS (INSPIRED)	12	2004
PURE HIP HOP VARIOUS ARTISTS (TELSTAR)	9	2001
PURE HIP HOP – EXPLICIT BEATS VARIOUS ARTISTS (WARNER BROTHERS)	10	2001
PURE HITS '97 VARIOUS ARTISTS (TELSTAR)	13	1997
PURE JAZZ MOODS – COOL JAZZ FOR A SUMMERS DAY VARIOUS ARTISTS (DINO)	9	1996
PURE LIGHTNING SEEDS LIGHTNING SEEDS	27	1996
PURE LOVERS VOLUME 1 VARIOUS ARTISTS (CHARM)	14	1990
PURE LOVERS VOLUME 2 VARIOUS ARTISTS (CHARM)	12	1990
PURE LOVERS VOLUME 3 VARIOUS ARTISTS (CHARM)	16	1991
PURE LOVERS VOLUME 4 VARIOUS ARTISTS (CHARM)	19	1991
PURE LOVERS VOLUME 5 VARIOUS ARTISTS (CHARM)	13	1992
PURE LOVERS VOLUME 6 VARIOUS ARTISTS (CHARM)	17	1993
PURE MANIA VIBRATORS	49	1977
PURE MOODS VARIOUS ARTISTS (VIRGIN)	1	1994
PURE PHASE SPIRITUALIZED ELECTRIC MAINLINE	20	1995
PURE PLEASURE SHAGGY	67	1993
PURE R&B VARIOUS ARTISTS (TELSTAR)	7	2000
PURE R&B 2 VARIOUS ARTISTS (TELSTAR)	11	2000
PURE R&B 3 VARIOUS ARTISTS (TELSTAR)	8	2001
PURE REGGAE VARIOUS ARTISTS (GLOBAL TELEVISION)	12	1997
PURE REGGAE- VOLUME 1 VARIOUS ARTISTS (ISLAND)	10	1994
PURE ROCK BALLADS VARIOUS ARTISTS (POLYGRAM)	10	1998
PURE SAX STATE OF THE HEART	18	1996
PURE SILK – A NEW DIMENSION VARIOUS ARTISTS (PURE SILK)	15	1999
PURE SILK IN AYIA NAPA VARIOUS ARTISTS (PURE SILK)	8	2000
PURE SILK IN AYIA NAPA 2 VARIOUS ARTISTS (PURE SILK)	20	2001
PURE SILK – THE THIRD DIMENSION VARIOUS ARTISTS (PURE SILK)	12	2000
PURE SOFT METAL VARIOUS ARTISTS (STYLUS)	1	1990
PURE SWING VARIOUS ARTISTS (DINO)	2	1995
PURE SWING 5 VARIOUS ARTISTS (DINO)	6	1996
PURE SWING 96 VARIOUS ARTISTS (DINO)	9	1996
PURE SWING III VARIOUS ARTISTS (DINO)	3	1995
PURE SWING IV VARIOUS ARTISTS (DINO)	1	1995
PURE SWING TWO VARIOUS ARTISTS (DINO)	4	1995
PURE TRANCE VARIOUS ARTISTS (WARNER BROTHERS)	11	2002
PURE URBAN ESSENTIALS VARIOUS ARTISTS (WARNER BROTHERS)	3	2003
PURE URBAN ESSENTIALS 2 VARIOUS ARTISTS (WARNER BROTHERS)	4	2003
PURE URBAN ESSENTIALS SUMMER 2008 VARIOUS ARTISTS (WARNER BROTHERS)	2	2008
PURGATORY/MAIDEN JAPAN IRON MAIDEN	5	1990

Title / Artist	Peak Position	Year of Release
PURPENDICULAR DEEP PURPLE	58	1996
PURPLE STONE TEMPLE PILOTS	10	1994
PURPLE RAIN (OST) PRINCE & THE REVOLUTION	7	1984
PURPLE RAINBOWS VARIOUS ARTISTS (POLYDOR)	1	1991
PURPLE RAINBOWS VARIOUS ARTISTS (UNIVERSAL)	10	2004
THE PURSUIT OF ACCIDENTS LEVEL 42	17	1982
PUSH BROS	2	1988
PUSH BARMAN TO OPEN OLD WOUNDS BELLE & SEBASTIAN	40	2005
PUSH THE BEAT FOR THIS JAM – THE SINGLES SCOOTER	6	2002
PUSH THE BUTTON MONEY MARK	17	1998
PUSH THE BUTTON CHEMICAL BROTHERS	1	2005
PUSHING THE SENSES FEEDER	2	2005
PUT YOUR HANDS UP VARIOUS ARTISTS (MINISTRY OF SOUND)	9	2006
PUT YOUR HANDS UP 2 VARIOUS ARTISTS (MINISTRY OF SOUND)	2	2007
PUT YOUR HANDS UP 4 VARIOUS ARTISTS (HARD2BEAT)	4	2008
PUT YOUR HANDS UP! 3 VARIOUS ARTISTS (MINISTRY OF SOUND)	16	2007
PUTTIN' ON THE STYLE – THE GREATEST HITS LONNIE DONEGAN	45	2003
PUTTING ON THE STYLE LONNIE DONEGAN	51	1978
PUZZLE BIFFY CLYRO	2	2007
PUZZLE PEOPLE TEMPTATIONS	20	1970
PXR 5 HAWKWIND	59	1979
PYE CHARTBUSTERS VARIOUS ARTISTS (PYE)	36	1971
PYE CHARTBUSTERS VOLUME 2 VARIOUS ARTISTS (PYE)	29	1971
PYJAMA GAME ORIGINAL SOUNDTRACK	3	1958
PYRAMID ALAN PARSONS PROJECT	49	1978
PYROMANIA DEF LEPPARD	18	1983

Q

Title / Artist	Peak Position	Year of Release
Q ANTHEMS VARIOUS ARTISTS (VIRGIN)	10	2001
Q AWARDS: THE ALBUM VARIOUS ARTISTS (EMI)	6	2000
Q COUNTRY VARIOUS ARTISTS (HIT LABEL)	20	1994
Q RHYTHM AND BLUES VARIOUS ARTISTS (HIT LABEL)	14	1993
Q THE ALBUM VARIOUS ARTISTS (UNIVERSAL	8	2003
Q – THE ALBUM 2008 VARIOUS ARTISTS (SONY BMG)	15	2008
Q – THE ALBUM VOLUME 1 VARIOUS ARTISTS (TELSTAR)	10	1991
Q THE BLUES VARIOUS ARTISTS (HIT LABEL)	6	1992
Q: ARE WE NOT MEN? A: NO WE ARE DEVO DEVO	12	1978
THE QAT COLLECTION SASHA	55	1994
QE 2 MIKE OLDFIELD	27	1980
Q-TIPS Q-TIPS	50	1980
QUADROPHENIA WHO	2	1973
QUALITY CONTROL JURASSIC 5	23	2000
QUALITY STREET WORLD OF TWIST	50	1991
QUANTUM OF SOLACE (OST) DAVID ARNOLD	64	2008
QUARK STRANGENESS AND CHARM HAWKWIND	30	1977
QUARTER MOONS IN A TEN CENT TOWN EMMYLOU HARRIS	40	1978
QUARTET ULTRAVOX	6	1982
QUEEN QUEEN	24	1974
QUEEN 2 QUEEN	5	1974
THE QUEEN ALBUM ELAINE PAIGE	51	1988
QUEEN AT THE BEEB QUEEN	67	1989
THE QUEEN IS DEAD SMITHS	2	1986
QUEEN OF SOUL – THE VERY BEST OF ARETHA FRANKLIN ARETHA FRANKLIN	20	1994
QUEEN ROCK MONTREAL QUEEN	20	2007
QUEEN ROCKS QUEEN	7	1997
QUEEN'S GREATEST HITS QUEEN	1	1981
QUEER AS FOLK 2 (TELEVISION SOUNDTRACK) TELEVISION AND RADIO COMPILATION	5	2000
QUEER AS FOLK – THE WHOLE THING SORTED (TELEVISION SOUNDTRACK) TELEVISION AND RADIO COMPILATION	2	1999
QUENCH BEAUTIFUL SOUTH	1	1998
A QUESTION OF BALANCE MOODY BLUES	1	1970
A QUICK ONE WHO	4	1966
QUICK STEP & SIDE KICK THOMPSON TWINS	2	1983
QUICKSILVER DJ QUICKSILVER	26	1998
QUIET IS THE NEW LORD KINGS OF CONVENIENCE	72	2001
QUIET LIFE JAPAN	53	1980
THE QUIET REVOLUTION RONNY JORDAN	49	1993
QUIET REVOLUTION CHRIS DE BURGH	23	1999
THE QUIET STORM VARIOUS ARTISTS (UNIVERSAL)	2	2003
THE QUILT GYM CLASS HEROES	41	2008
QUINTESSENCE QUINTESSENCE	22	1970
QUIT DREAMING AND GET ON THE BEAM BILL NELSON	7	1981
QUIXOTIC MARTINA TOPLEY BIRD	70	2003
QUO STATUS QUO	2	1974

R

Title / Artist	Peak Position	Year of Release
R R KELLY	27	1998
THE R IN R&B – GREATEST HITS VOLUME 1 R KELLY	4	2003
R KELLY R KELLY	18	1995
R U STILL DOWN? (REMEMBER ME) 2PAC	44	1997
R&B ANTHEMS VARIOUS ARTISTS (SONY/BMG)	5	2007
R&B ANTHEMS 2005 VARIOUS ARTISTS (SONY)	1	2005
R&B CLASSICS VARIOUS ARTISTS (SONY/BMG)	3	2006
R&B CLASSICS COLLECTION VARIOUS ARTISTS (UNIVERSAL)	7	2008
R&B CLUBMIX VARIOUS ARTISTS (SONY/BMG)	2	2006
R&B CLUBMIX VARIOUS ARTISTS (UNIVERSAL)	5	2007
R&B COLLABORATIONS VARIOUS ARTISTS (UNIVERSAL)	10	2007
R&B COLLECTION VARIOUS ARTISTS (UNIVERSAL)	2	2008
R&B DANCE MIX VARIOUS ARTISTS (SONY/BMG)	4	2005
R&B DIVAS VARIOUS ARTISTS (UNIVERSAL)	4	2006
R&B HITS VARIOUS ARTISTS (UNIVERSAL)	16	2001
R&B LOVE VARIOUS ARTISTS (WARNER BROTHERS)	2	2003
R&B LOVE 2 VARIOUS ARTISTS (WARNER BROTHERS)	4	2004
R&B LOVE CLASSICS VARIOUS ARTISTS (WARNER BROTHERS)	3	2007
R&B LOVE COLLECTION VARIOUS ARTISTS (UNIVERSAL)	1	2007
R&B LOVE COLLECTION 2008 VARIOUS ARTISTS (UNIVERSAL)	1	2008
R&B LOVESONGS VARIOUS ARTISTS (COLUMBIA)	9	2002
R&B LOVESONGS VARIOUS ARTISTS (UNIVERSAL)	1	2006
R&B LOVESONGS 2007 VARIOUS ARTISTS (SONY/BMG)	2	2007
R&B LOVESONGS 2008 VARIOUS ARTISTS (SONY BMG)	5	2008
R&B MASTERS VARIOUS ARTISTS (COLUMBIA)	4	2001
R&B MASTERS 2 VARIOUS ARTISTS (COLUMBIA)	12	2001
THE R&B MIXTAPE VARIOUS ARTISTS (WARNER BROTHERS)	10	2008
R&B PARTY VARIOUS ARTISTS (EMI)	18	2005
R&B SELECTOR VARIOUS ARTISTS (UNIVERSAL)	11	2001
R&B SUMMERTIME VARIOUS ARTISTS (SONY/BMG)	6	2006
R&B – THE COLLECTION 2007 VARIOUS ARTISTS (UNIVERSAL)	7	2007
THE R&B YEARBOOK VARIOUS ARTISTS (SONY/BMG)	4	2005
THE R&B YEARBOOK 2006 VARIOUS ARTISTS (SONY/BMG)	14	2006
R&B YEARBOOK 2007 VARIOUS ARTISTS (SONY BMG)	16	2008
R&B YEARBOOK 2008 VARIOUS ARTISTS (SONY BMG)	10	2008
R&G – THE MASTERPIECE SNOOP DOGG	12	2004
R&S RECORDS – ORDER TO DANCE VARIOUS ARTISTS (R&S)	18	1991
R.I.P. PRESENTS THE REAL SOUND OF UNDERGROUND VARIOUS ARTISTS (VIRGIN)	18	1998
RA TODD RUNDGREN	27	1977
RABBIT FUR COAT JENNY LEWIS WITH THE WATSON TWINS	63	2006
RABBITS ON AND ON JASPER CARROTT	10	1975
RADAR EARTHLING	66	1995
RADIATION MARILLION	35	1998
RADIATOR SUPER FURRY ANIMALS	8	1997
RADIO LL COOL J	71	1986
RADIO 1 ESTABLISHED 1967 VARIOUS ARTISTS (UNIVERSAL)	1	2007
RADIO 1'S LIVE LOUNGE VARIOUS ARTISTS (SONY/BMG)	1	2006
RADIO 1'S LIVE LOUNGE – VOLUME 2 VARIOUS ARTISTS (SONY/BMG)	1	2007
RADIO 2 – SONGS OF THE CENTURY VARIOUS ARTISTS (GLOBAL TELEVISION)	9	1999
RADIO DAYS – CELEBRATING THE GOLDEN ERA VARIOUS ARTISTS (DMG TV)	17	2006
RADIO DREAMSCAPE – VOLUME 1 VARIOUS ARTISTS (DREAMSCAPE)	20	1995
RADIO I'S LIVE LOUNGE – VOLUME 3 VARIOUS ARTISTS (SONY BMG)	2	2008
RADIO K.A.O.S. ROGER WATERS	25	1987
RADIO M.U.S.C. MAN WOMACK & WOMACK	56	1985
RADIO MUSICOLA NIK KERSHAW	47	1986
RADIO ONE JIMI HENDRIX	30	1989
RADIO SESSIONS CURVE	72	1993
RADIOACTIVE VARIOUS ARTISTS (RONCO)	13	1980
RADIOACTIVE McFLY	8	2008
RAFI'S REVENGE ASIAN DUB FOUNDATION	20	1998
RAGE T'PAU	4	1988
RAGE AGAINST THE MACHINE RAGE AGAINST THE MACHINE	17	1993
RAGE FOR ORDER QUEENSRYCHE	66	1986
RAGE IN EDEN ULTRAVOX	4	1981
RAGE – MAKE SOME NOISE VARIOUS ARTISTS (A&M)	12	1991
RAGGA HEAT REGGAE BEAT VARIOUS ARTISTS (TELSTAR)	4	1993
RAGGED GLORY NEIL YOUNG & CRAZY HORSE	15	1990

	Peak Position	Year of Release
THE RAGPICKER'S DREAM MARK KNOPFLER	7	2002
RAHMAN: BOMBAY DREAMS RAHMAN/ ORIGINAL SOUND RECORDING	61	2002
RAIDERS OF THE POP CHARTS VARIOUS ARTISTS (RONCO)	1	1982
RAIN DANCES CAMEL	20	1977
RAIN DOGS TOM WAITS	29	1985
RAIN TREE CROW RAIN TREE CROW	24	1991
RAINBOW NEIL DIAMOND	39	1974
RAINBOW PETERS & LEE	6	1974
RAINBOW MARIAH CAREY	8	1999
RAINBOW CONNECTION IV ROSE ROYCE	72	1979
RAINBOW DOME MUSIC STEVE HILLAGE	52	1979
RAINBOW FRIDGE (OST) JIMI HENDRIX	16	1971
RAINBOW RISING RITCHIE BLACKMORE'S RAINBOW	11	1976
RAINBOW WARRIORS VARIOUS ARTISTS (RCA)	2	1989
RAINDANCE RAINDANCE	15	1996
RAINDANCING ALISON MOYET	2	1987
RAINDROPS KEEP FALLING ON MY HEAD JOHNNY MATHIS	23	1970
RAINGODS WITH ZIPPOS FISH	57	1999
RAINTOWN DEACON BLUE	14	1987
RAINY DAY MUSIC JAYHAWKS	70	2003
THE RAINY SEASON MARC COHN	24	1993
RAISE EARTH WIND & FIRE	14	1981
RAISE SWERVEDRIVER	44	1991
RAISE THE ALARM SUNSHINE UNDERGROUND	66	2006
RAISE YOUR FIST AND YELL ALICE COOPER	48	1987
RAISED ON RADIO JOURNEY	22	1986
RAISED THE PRESSURE ELECTRONIC	8	1996
RAISING HELL FATBACK BAND	19	1976
RAISING HELL RUN D.M.C.	41	1986
RAISING SAND ROBERT PLANT & ALISON KRAUSS	2	2007
RALPH TRESVANT RALPH TRESVANT	37	1991
RAM PAUL & LINDA McCARTNEY	1	1971
RAM IT DOWN JUDAS PRIEST	24	1988
RAMPANT NAZARETH	13	1974
RAMSHACKLED ALAN WHITE	41	1976
RANCID RANCID	68	2000
RANK SMITHS	2	1988
RANT 'N' RAVE WITH THE STRAY CATS STRAY CATS	51	1983
RAOUL AND THE KINGS OF SPAIN TEARS FOR FEARS	41	1995
RAP ATTACK VARIOUS ARTISTS (K-TEL)	6	1989
RAP ATTACK VARIOUS ARTISTS (CONCEPT)	9	1994
RAP FLAVAS VARIOUS ARTISTS (COLUMBIA)	6	1996
RAP IT UP – RAP'S GREATEST HITS VARIOUS ARTISTS (K-TEL)	50	1986
RAP TO THE MAX VARIOUS ARTISTS (VIRGIN)	10	1994
RAP TRAX VARIOUS ARTISTS (STYLUS)	3	1988
RAPPED IN REMIXES SALT-N-PEPA	37	1992
RAPPERS DELIGHT VARIOUS ARTISTS (UNIVERSAL)	18	2002
RAPPIN' UP THE HOUSE VARIOUS ARTISTS (K-TEL)	19	1988
RAPTURE ANITA BAKER	13	1986
THE RAPTURE SIOUXSIE & THE BANSHEES	33	1995
RARE DAVID BOWIE	34	1983
RARE VARIOUS ARTISTS (RCA)	80	1987
RARE 2 VARIOUS ARTISTS (RCA)	88	1988
RARE 3 VARIOUS ARTISTS (ARIOLA)	15	1989
RARE GROOVE – DYNAMIC DISCO HITS VARIOUS ARTISTS (QUALITY TELEVISION)	7	1992
RARE GROOVE MIX – 70 SMASH HITS OF THE 70'S VARIOUS ARTISTS (STYLUS)	20	1988
RARITIES BEATLES	71	1979
RASCAL FLATTS RASCAL FLATTS	64	2008
RASTAMAN VIBRATION BOB MARLEY & THE WAILERS	15	1976
RAT IN THE KITCHEN UB40	8	1986
RATED R QUEENS OF THE STONE AGE	54	2000
RATHER RIPPED SONIC YOUTH	64	2006
RATTLE AND HUM U2	1	1988
RATTLESNAKES LLOYD COLE & THE COMMOTIONS	13	1984
RAVE VARIOUS ARTISTS (TELSTAR)	10	1990
RAVE VARIOUS ARTISTS (REACHIN')	18	1991
RAVE 2 – STRICTLY HARDCORE VARIOUS ARTISTS (ELEVATE)	11	1992
RAVE 92 VARIOUS ARTISTS (COOKIE JAR)	3	1992
RAVE ALERT VARIOUS ARTISTS (TELSTAR)	2	1992
RAVE ANTHEMS VARIOUS ARTISTS (DINO)	7	1995
THE RAVE GENER8TOR VARIOUS ARTISTS (COOKIE JAR)	1	1992
THE RAVE GENER8TOR 2 VARIOUS ARTISTS (COOKIE JAR)	2	1992
RAVE GENERATION VARIOUS ARTISTS (DINO)	2	1993
RAVE GENERATION 2 VARIOUS ARTISTS (DINO)	5	1994
RAVE NATION VARIOUS ARTISTS (TELSTAR)	2	1992
RAVE NATION VARIOUS ARTISTS (INSPIRED)	16	2001
RAVE NATION – THE ANTHEMS VARIOUS ARTISTS (MINISTRY OF SOUND)	7	2008
RAVEL'S BOLERO LONDON PHILHARMONIC ORCHESTRA	15	1960
THE RAVEN STRANGLERS	4	1979
RAVEOLOGY VARIOUS ARTISTS (VIRGIN)	20	2005
RAVIN' VARIOUS ARTISTS (V2 TV)	8	2004
RAVING MAD VARIOUS ARTISTS (ELEVATE)	17	1992
RAVING WE'RE RAVING VARIOUS ARTISTS (TELSTAR)	2	1992
RAW ALYSON WILLIAMS	29	1989
RAW ALARM	33	1991
THE RAW AND THE COOKED FINE YOUNG CANNIBALS	1	1989
RAW – GREATEST HITS – THE MUSIC VARIOUS ARTISTS (SONY BMG)	9	2008
RAW LIKE SUSHI NENEH CHERRY	2	1989
RAW MEAT FOR THE BALCONY BILLY CONNOLLY	57	1978
RAW MELODY MAN NEW MODEL ARMY	43	1991
RAW POWER IGGY POP & THE STOOGES	44	1977
RAY FRAZIER CHORUS	66	1991
RAY (OST) RAY CHARLES	36	2005
RAY CHARLES – LIVING LEGEND RAY CHARLES	48	1993
RAY MOORE – A PERSONAL CHOICE VARIOUS ARTISTS (BBC)	7	1989
RAY OF LIGHT MADONNA	1	1998
RAY SINGS BASIE SWINGS RAY CHARLES & COUNT BASIE ORCHESTRA	63	2006
RAYMOND LEFEVRE RAYMOND LEFEVRE	10	1967
RAYMOND LEFEVRE VOLUME 2 RAYMOND LEFEVRE	37	1968
RAZAMANAZ NAZARETH	11	1973
RAZORBLADE SUITCASE BUSH	4	1997
RAZORLIGHT RAZORLIGHT	1	2006
THE RAZOR'S EDGE AC/DC	4	1990
REACH FOR THE SKY SUTHERLAND BROTHERS & QUIVER	26	1976
REACH FOR THE SKY RATT	82	1988
REACH OUT FOUR TOPS	4	1967
REACH OUT BURT BACHARACH	52	1970
REACH THE BEACH FIXX	91	1983
REACHING TO THE CONVERTED BILLY BRAGG	41	1999
REACTIVATE 10 VARIOUS ARTISTS (REACT)	14	1995
REACTIVATE 11 – STINGER BEAT AND TECHNO RAYS VARIOUS ARTISTS (REACT)	14	1996
REACTIVATE 12 VARIOUS ARTISTS (REACT)	17	1997
REACTIVATE VOLUME 1 – THE BELGIAN TECHNO ANTHEMS VARIOUS ARTISTS (REACT)	13	1991
REACTIVATE VOLUME 2 – PHASERS ON FULL VARIOUS ARTISTS (REACT)	9	1991
REACTIVATE VOLUME 4 – TECHNOVATION VARIOUS ARTISTS (REACT)	16	1992
REACTIVATE VOLUME 5 – PURE TRANCE AND TECHNO VARIOUS ARTISTS (REACT)	18	1992
RE-AC-TOR NEIL YOUNG & CRAZY HORSE	69	1981
READ MY LIPS JIMMY SOMERVILLE	29	1989
READ MY LIPS SOPHIE ELLIS BEXTOR	2	2001
READING – THE INDIE ALBUM VARIOUS ARTISTS (POLYGRAM)	5	1992
READING WRITING AND ARITHMETIC SUNDAYS	4	1990
READY BLUES BAND	36	1980
READY 2 DIE (IMPORT) 2PAC	70	2005
READY AND WILLING WHITESNAKE	6	1980
READY FOR BATTLE ROCKSTEADY CREW	73	1984
READY FOR ROMANCE MODERN TALKING	76	1986
READY FOR THE STORM (FAVOURITE CUTS) KATHY MATTEA	61	1995
READY STEADY GO VARIOUS ARTISTS (DECCA)	20	1964
READY STEADY GO! – NUMBER ONE SIXTIES ALBUM (TELEVISION COMPILATION) TELEVISION AND RADIO COMPILATION	10	1997
READY STEADY GO! – SIXTIES MOTOWN SOUND (TELEVISION COMPILATION) TELEVISION AND RADIO COMPILATION	5	1998
READY TO RUN SINEAD QUINN	48	2003
REAL BELINDA CARLISLE	9	1993
REAL AS I WANNA BE CLIFF RICHARD	10	1998
THE REAL CHUCKEEBOO LOOSE ENDS	52	1988
A REAL DEAD ONE IRON MAIDEN	12	1993
REAL EIGHTIES – HITS PLUS EXTENDED MIXES VARIOUS ARTISTS (EMI)	8	2005
REAL GARAGE – MIXED LIVE BY MASTERSTEPZ VARIOUS ARTISTS (MINISTRY OF SOUND)	6	2001
REAL GIRL MUTYA BUENA	10	2007
THE REAL GLENN MILLER AND HIS ORCHESTRA PLAY THE ORIGINAL MUSIC OF THE FILM 'THE GLENN MILLER STORY' AND OTHER HITS (OST) GLENN MILLER & HIS ORCHESTRA	28	1971
REAL GONE TOM WAITS	16	2004
REAL LIFE MAGAZINE	29	1978
REAL LIFE SIMPLE MINDS	2	1991
REAL LIVE BOB DYLAN	54	1984
A REAL LIVE ONE IRON MAIDEN	3	1993
REAL LOVE LISA STANSFIELD	3	1991
REAL LOVE VARIOUS ARTISTS (UNIVERSAL)	1	2008
THE REAL PEOPLE REAL PEOPLE	59	1991
THE REAL RAMONA THROWING MUSES	26	1991
THE REAL SOUND OF AYIA NAPA VARIOUS ARTISTS (UNIVERSAL)	11	2000
REAL TALK FABOLOUS	66	2004
REAL THING REAL THING	34	1976
THE REAL THING FAITH NO MORE	30	1990
REAL THINGS 2 UNLIMITED	1	1994
REAL TO REEL MARILLION	8	1984
REALITY DAVID BOWIE	3	2003
REALITY EFFECT TOURISTS	23	1979
THE REALITY OF MY SURROUNDINGS FISHBONE	75	1991
REANIMATION LINKIN PARK	3	2002
REARVIEW MIRROR – GREATEST HITS '91-'03 PEARL JAM	58	2004
REASON MELANIE C	5	2003
THE REASON HOOBASTANK	41	2004
THE REASON LEMAR	41	2008

Title / Artist	Peak Position	Year of Release
REASON TO BELIEVE RITA MacNEIL	32	1990
REASON TO BELIEVE ALED JONES	15	2007
REASONS TO BE CHEERFUL – THE VERY BEST OF IAN DURY AND THE BLOCKHEADS IAN DURY & THE BLOCKHEADS	40	1999
REBEL JOHN MILES	9	1976
REBEL MUSIC BOB MARLEY & THE WAILERS	54	1986
REBEL MUSIC REBEL MC	18	1990
REBEL SOULS ASWAD	48	1984
REBEL YELL BILLY IDOL	36	1985
REBIRTH JENNIFER LOPEZ	8	2005
THE REBIRTH OF COOL III VARIOUS ARTISTS (FOURTH & BROADWAY)	9	1993
THE REBIRTH OF COOL, TOO VARIOUS ARTISTS (FOURTH & BROADWAY)	13	1992
RECITAL '70 NANA MOUSKOURI	68	1970
RECKLESS BRYAN ADAMS	7	1985
RECKONING R.E.M.	91	1984
RECONSIDER BABY ELVIS PRESLEY	92	1985
THE RECORD OF THE YEAR 2000 VARIOUS ARTISTS (TELSTAR)	16	2000
RECORD SHACK PRESENTS – VOLUME ONE VARIOUS ARTISTS (RECORD SHACK)	41	1984
RECORDED LIVE TEN YEARS AFTER	36	1973
RECORDS: THE BEST OF FOREIGNER FOREIGNER	58	1982
RECOVERING THE SATELLITES COUNTING CROWS	4	1996
RECURRENCE RAILWAY CHILDREN	96	1988
RECURRING SPACEMEN 3	46	1991
RECURRING DREAM – THE VERY BEST OF CROWDED HOUSE CROWDED HOUSE	1	1996
RECYCLER ZZ TOP	8	1990
RED KING CRIMSON	45	1974
RED BLACK UHURU	28	1981
RED COMMUNARDS	4	1987
RED GUILLEMOTS	9	2007
RED AND GOLD FAIRPORT CONVENTION	74	1989
RED BOOK TEXAS	16	2005
RED CARD STREETWALKERS	16	1976
RED CARPET MASSACRE DURAN DURAN	44	2007
RED DIRT GIRL EMMYLOU HARRIS	45	2000
RED HEAVEN THROWING MUSES	13	1992
RED HOT + DANCE VARIOUS ARTISTS (EPIC)	6	1992
RED HOT AND WHITE 2 VARIOUS ARTISTS (VITAL SOUNDS)	13	1992
RED HOT AND WHITE LABELS VARIOUS ARTISTS (VITAL SOUNDS)	17	1992
RED HOT HITS VARIOUS ARTISTS (SONY/BMG)	19	2005
RED HOT METAL – 18 ROCK CLASSICS VARIOUS ARTISTS (DOVER)	4	1991
RED HOT RHYTHM 'N' BLUES DIANA ROSS	47	1987
RED HOUSE PAINTERS RED HOUSE PAINTERS	63	1993
RED MEDICINE FUGAZI	18	1995
RED RIVER VALLEY SLIM WHITMAN	1	1977
RED ROSE SPEEDWAY PAUL McCARTNEY & WINGS	5	1973
RED ROSES FOR ME POGUES	89	1984
THE RED SHOES KATE BUSH	2	1993
RED STAR SHOWADDYWADDY	20	1977
RED WHITE & CRUE MOTLEY CRUE	67	2005
RED, HOT AND BLUE VARIOUS ARTISTS (CHRYSALIS)	6	1990
REDD HOTT SHARON REDD	59	1982
REEL LIFE BOY MEETS GIRL	74	1989
REELIN' IN THE YEARS – THE VERY BEST OF STEELY DAN STEELY DAN	43	1985
REFLECTION SHADOWS	5	1990
REFLECTIONS DIANA ROSS & THE SUPREMES	30	1968
REFLECTIONS ANDY WILLIAMS	2	1978
REFLECTIONS GEORGE HAMILTON IV	25	1979
REFLECTIONS VARIOUS ARTISTS (CBS)	4	1982
REFLECTIONS FOSTER & ALLEN	16	1987
REFLECTIONS PAUL YOUNG	64	1994
REFLECTIONS (A RETROSPECTIVE) MARY J. BLIGE	42	2006
REFLECTIONS – GREATEST HITS CARLY SIMON	25	2004
REFRIED ECTOPLASM (SWITCHED ON – VOLUME 2) STEREOLAB	30	1995
REFUGEES OF THE HEART STEVE WINWOOD	26	1990
REG STRIKES BACK ELTON JOHN	18	1988
REGENERATION DIVINE COMEDY	14	2001
REGGAE 93 VARIOUS ARTISTS (ISLAND)	5	1993
REGGAE CHARTBUSTERS 75 VARIOUS ARTISTS (CACTUS)	53	1976
REGGAE CHARTBUSTERS VOLUME 2 VARIOUS ARTISTS (TROJAN)	29	1971
REGGAE GROOVE VARIOUS ARTISTS (HIT LABEL)	12	1995
REGGAE HITS VOLUME 1 VARIOUS ARTISTS (JETSTAR)	32	1985
REGGAE HITS VOLUME 10 VARIOUS ARTISTS (JETSTAR)	6	1991
REGGAE HITS VOLUME 12 VARIOUS ARTISTS (JETSTAR)	5	1992
REGGAE HITS VOLUME 14 VARIOUS ARTISTS (JETSTAR)	13	1993
REGGAE HITS VOLUME 2 VARIOUS ARTISTS (JETSTAR)	86	1985
REGGAE HITS VOLUME 4 VARIOUS ARTISTS (JETSTAR)	56	1988
REGGAE HITS VOLUME 5 VARIOUS ARTISTS (JETSTAR)	96	1988
REGGAE HITS VOLUME 6 VARIOUS ARTISTS (JETSTAR)	13	1989
REGGAE HITS VOLUME 7 VARIOUS ARTISTS (JETSTAR)	13	1989
REGGAE HITS VOLUME 8 VARIOUS ARTISTS (JETSTAR)	7	1990
REGGAE LOVE SONGS VARIOUS ARTISTS (TROJAN)	4	2005
REGGAE LOVE SONGS: 50 JAMAICAN LOVERS CLASSICS VARIOUS ARTISTS (SANCTUARY)	2	2003
REGGAE MASSIVE VARIOUS ARTISTS (DINO)	19	1995
REGGAE OWES ME MONEY RAGGA TWINS	26	1991
REGGATTA DE BLANC POLICE	1	1979
REGULAR URBAN SURVIVORS TERRORVISION	8	1996
REGULATE...G FUNK ERA WARREN G	25	1994
REI MOMO DAVID BYRNE	52	1989
REIGN IN BLOOD SLAYER	47	1987
REILLY ACE OF THEMES (TELEVISION SOUNDTRACK) TELEVISION AND RADIO COMPILATION	54	1983
REINVENTING THE STEEL PANTERA	33	2000
REISE REISE RAMMSTEIN	37	2004
REJOICE ST. PAUL'S BOYS' CHOIR	36	1980
REJOICE KATHERINE JENKINS	3	2007
RELATIONSHIP OF COMMAND AT THE DRIVE IN	33	2000
RELAX MORE VARIOUS ARTISTS (CLASSIC FM)	7	2000
RELAX! THE ULTIMATE 80'S MIX VARIOUS ARTISTS (POLYGRAM)	4	1998
RELAX! THE ULTIMATE 80'S MIX – VOLUME 2 VARIOUS ARTISTS (POLYGRAM)	8	1999
RELAX... VARIOUS ARTISTS (CLASSIC FM)	11	1999
THE RELAXING ALBUM VARIOUS ARTISTS (SONY/BMG)	18	2005
RELAXING CLASSIC FM VARIOUS ARTISTS (CLASSIC FM)	12	2005
RELAXING SONGS VARIOUS ARTISTS (EMI)	16	2006
RELAXING SOUND OF BERT KAEMPFERT BERT KAEMPFERT & HIS ORCHESTRA	33	1967
RELAYER YES	4	1974
RELEASE DAVID KNOPFLER	82	1983
RELEASE PET SHOP BOYS	7	2002
RELEASE ME ENGELBERT HUMPERDINCK	6	1967
RELEASE SOME TENSION SWV	19	1997
RELEASE THE STARS RUFUS WAINWRIGHT	2	2007
RELEASE THERAPY LUDACRIS	69	2006
RELENTLESS JO O'MEARA	48	2005
RELICS PINK FLOYD	32	1971
RELISH JOAN OSBORNE	5	1996
RELOAD METALLICA	4	1997
RELOAD TOM JONES	1	1999
RELOADED VARIOUS ARTISTS (UNIVERSAL)	3	2000
RELOADED 2 VARIOUS ARTISTS (UNIVERSAL)	2	2001
RELOADED 3 VARIOUS ARTISTS (UNIVERSAL)	9	2001
RELOADED 4 VARIOUS ARTISTS (UNIVERSAL)	4	2002
REMAIN IN LIGHT TALKING HEADS	21	1980
REMAINS ALKALINE TRIO	68	2007
REMANUFACTURE – CLONING TECHNOLOGY FEAR FACTORY	22	1997
REMASTERED – THE BEST OF STEELY DAN STEELY DAN	42	1993
REMASTERS LED ZEPPELIN	10	1990
REMEDY BASEMENT JAXX	4	1999
REMEMBER CAT STEVENS – THE ULTIMATE COLLECTION CAT STEVENS	31	1999
REMEMBER ME THIS WAY GARY GLITTER	5	1974
REMEMBER THEN – 30 DOO-WOP GREATS VARIOUS ARTISTS (POLYGRAM)	10	1994
REMEMBER WHEN SINGERS COULD SING VARIOUS ARTISTS (HIT LABEL)	16	1992
REMEMBER YOU'RE A WOMBLE WOMBLES	18	1974
REMEMBER YOU'RE MINE FOSTER & ALLEN	16	1988
THE REMINDER FEIST	28	2007
REMINISCING BUDDY HOLLY	2	1963
REMINISCING FOSTER & ALLEN	11	1986
REMINISCING – THE HOWARD KEEL COLLECTION HOWARD KEEL	20	1985
THE REMIX ALBUM – DIAMONDS ARE FOREVER SHIRLEY BASSEY	62	2000
REMIXED INCOGNITO	56	1996
THE REMIXES GROOVE ARMADA	68	2000
THE REMIXES STONE ROSES	41	2000
THE REMIXES MARIAH CAREY	35	2003
REMIXES 81-04 DEPECHE MODE	24	2004
RE-MIXTURE VARIOUS ARTISTS (CHAMPAGNE)	32	1981
REMOTE CONTROL TUBES	40	1979
THE REMOTE PART IDLEWILD	3	2002
REMOTE/THE BITTER SUITE HUE & CRY	10	1988
RENAISSANCE RENAISSANCE	60	1970
RENAISSANCE ASWAD	52	1988
RENAISSANCE VARIOUS ARTISTS (SIX6)	9	1994
RENAISSANCE LIONEL RICHIE	6	2000
RENAISSANCE ANTHEMS VARIOUS ARTISTS (MINISTRY OF SOUND)	15	2008
RENAISSANCE – AWAKENING – DAVE SEAMAN VARIOUS ARTISTS (RENAISSANCE MUSIC)	18	2000
RENAISSANCE IBIZA 2001 VARIOUS ARTISTS (RENAISSANCE MUSIC)	2	2001
RENAISSANCE IBIZA – MIXED BY DEEP DISH VARIOUS ARTISTS (RENAISSANCE MUSIC)	20	2000
RENAISSANCE – MIX COLLECTION – PART 2 VARIOUS ARTISTS (NETWORK)	16	1996
RENAISSANCE – THE CLASSICS VARIOUS ARTISTS (RENAISSANCE)	2	2005
RENAISSANCE – THE CLASSICS PART 2 VARIOUS ARTISTS (RENAISSANCE MUSIC)	2	2006
RENAISSANCE THE MIX COLLECTION – PART 3 VARIOUS ARTISTS (SIX6)	12	1996
RENAISSANCE WORLDWIDE LONDON VARIOUS ARTISTS (RENAISSANCE MUSIC)	16	1997
RENDEZ-VOUS JEAN-MICHEL JARRE	9	1986
RENEGADE THIN LIZZY	38	1981

Title / Artist	Peak Position	Year of Release
RENEGADES BRASS CONSTRUCTION	94	1984
RENEGADES RAGE AGAINST THE MACHINE	71	2000
REPEAT OFFENDER RICHARD MARX	8	1989
REPEAT WHEN NECESSARY DAVE EDMUNDS	39	1979
REPLENISH REEF	9	1995
REPLICAS TUBEWAY ARMY	1	1979
REPRESS – 80'S CLUB CLASSICS VARIOUS ARTISTS (WARNER BROTHERS)	10	2003
RE-PRESS – THE 70'S SOUL REVIVAL VARIOUS ARTISTS (WARNER BROTHERS)	12	2003
REPRISE RUSSELL WATSON	13	2002
REPRODUCTION HUMAN LEAGUE	34	1981
REPTILE ERIC CLAPTON	7	2001
REPUBLIC NEW ORDER	1	1993
REPUBLICA REPUBLICA	4	1997
THE REPULSION BOX SONS & DAUGHTERS	70	2005
REPUTATION DUSTY SPRINGFIELD	18	1990
REQUESTS MERLE & ROY	74	1987
RESERECTION SAINT ETIENNE DAHO	50	1996
RESERVOIR DOGS FILM SOUNDTRACK	16	1993
RESIDENT – 2 YEARS OF OAKENFOLD AT CREAM VARIOUS ARTISTS (VIRGIN)	2	1999
RESIDENT ALIEN SPACEHOG	40	1997
RESIST KOSHEEN	8	2001
RESPECT VARIOUS ARTISTS (UNIVERSAL)	15	2000
RESPECT ME MISSY ELLIOTT	7	2006
RESPECT – THE VERY BEST OF ARETHA FRANKLIN	15	2002
RESPECT YOURSELF JOE COCKER	51	2002
RESPOND PACKAGE – LOVE THE REASON VARIOUS ARTISTS (RESPOND)	50	1983
REST INSIDE THE FLAMES 36 CRAZYFISTS	71	2006
RESTLESS XZIBIT	27	2001
RESTLESS AND WILD ACCEPT	98	1983
RESTLESS HEART DAVID COVERDALE & WHITESNAKE	34	1997
RESTLESS SOUL PROCLAIMERS	74	2005
RESULTS LIZA MINNELLI	6	1989
RESULTS MAY VARY LIMP BIZKIT	7	2003
RESURRECTION E-17	43	1998
RESURRECTION 2PAC	62	2003
RETRO LOU REED	29	1989
RETRO ACTIVE DEF LEPPARD	6	1993
RETRO DANCE MASTERS VARIOUS ARTISTS (VIRGIN)	10	2002
RETROSPECTACLE SUPERTRAMP	9	2005
A RETROSPECTIVE OF HOUSE '91-'95 – VOLUME 1 VARIOUS ARTISTS (SOUND DIMENSION)	10	1995
A RETROSPECTIVE OF HOUSE '91-'95 – VOLUME 2 VARIOUS ARTISTS (SOUND DIMENSION)	15	1996
A RETROSPECTIVE OF HOUSE '91-'96 – VOLUME 3: JAY/KELLY/ANDERSON VARIOUS ARTISTS (SOUND DIMENSION)	9	1996
A RETROSPECTIVE OF HOUSE '91-'96 – VOLUME 4 VARIOUS ARTISTS (SOUND DIMENSION)	7	1996
RETROSPECTIVE – THE BEST OF SUZANNE VEGA	27	2003
THE RETURN OF BRUNO BRUCE WILLIS	4	1987
RETURN OF DRAGON SISQO	22	2001
RETURN OF SATURN NO DOUBT	31	2000
THE RETURN OF SUPERBAD VARIOUS ARTISTS (K-TEL)	83	1988
RETURN OF THE CHAMPIONS QUEEN & PAUL RODGERS	12	2005
RETURN OF THE GLADIATORS (TELEVISION COMPILATION) TELEVISION AND RADIO COMPILATION	20	1993
RETURN OF THE JEDI (OST) JOHN WILLIAMS	85	1983
RETURN OF THE MACK MARK MORRISON	4	1996
THE RETURN OF THE SPACE COWBOY JAMIROQUAI	2	1994
THE RETURN OF THE SUPER 70'S VARIOUS ARTISTS (VIRGIN)	5	2003
RETURN TO FANTASY URIAH HEEP	7	1975
RETURN TO IBIZA – EUPHORIA VARIOUS ARTISTS (MINISTRY OF SOUND)	5	2007
RETURN TO THE CENTRE OF THE EARTH RICK WAKEMAN; LONDON SYMPHONY ORCHESTRA; ENGLISH CHAMBER CHOIR; NARRATED BY PATRICK STEWART	34	1999
RETURN TO THE LAST CHANCE SALOON BLUETONES	10	1998
RETURN TO THE VALLEY OF THE GO-GO'S GO-GO'S	52	1995
REUNION BLACK SABBATH	41	1998
REV IT UP VIXEN	20	1990
REVEAL R.E.M.	1	2001
REVELATION JOURNEY	68	2008
REVELATIONS KILLING JOKE	12	1982
REVELATIONS GENE	25	1999
REVELATIONS AUDIOSLAVE	12	2006
REVENGE EURYTHMICS	3	1986
REVENGE KISS	10	1992
REVENGE OF THE GOLDFISH INSPIRAL CARPETS	17	1992
REVERENCE FAITHLESS	26	1996
REVISITED EARTHA KITT	17	1961
REVOLT 3 COLOURS RED	17	1999
REVOLUTION THEATRE OF HATE	67	1984
THE REVOLUTION STARTS NOW STEVE EARLE	66	2004
THE REVOLUTION TONIGHT BLUE OYSTER CULT	95	1983
REVOLUTIONS JEAN-MICHEL JARRE	2	1988
REVOLUTIONS VARIOUS ARTISTS (SONY/BMG)	10	2005
REVOLVER BEATLES	1	1966
REWIND VARIOUS ARTISTS (UNIVERSAL)	7	2004
REWIND 1971-1984 (THE BEST OF THE ROLLING STONES) ROLLING STONES	23	1984
REWIND GARAGE CLASSICS VARIOUS ARTISTS (MINISTRY OF SOUND)	8	2004
REWIND – THE SOUND OF UK GARAGE VARIOUS ARTISTS (MINISTRY OF SOUND)	1	2000
REWIRED MIKE & THE MECHANICS	61	2004
REWIRED/THE HITS MIKE & THE MECHANICS	42	2004
RFTC ROCKET FROM THE CRYPT	63	1998
RHAPSODIES RICK WAKEMAN	25	1979
RHAPSODY AND BLUE CRUSADERS	40	1980
RHAPSODY IN BLACK LONDON SYMPHONY ORCHESTRA	34	1980
RHAPSODY IN WHITE LOVE UNLIMITED ORCHESTRA	50	1974
RHINESTONE COWBOY GLEN CAMPBELL	38	1975
RHINOS WINOS AND LUNATICS MAN	24	1974
RHUBARB ROOTJOOSE	58	1997
RHYDIAN RHYDIAN	3	2008
RHYMES AND REASONS CAROLE KING	40	1972
RHYMES AND REASONS JOHN DENVER	21	1973
RHYTHM AND CLASSICS LOUIS CLARK CONDUCTING THE ROYAL PHILHARMONIC ORCHESTRA	96	1988
RHYTHM AND STEALTH LEFTFIELD	1	1999
RHYTHM COUNTRY AND BLUES VARIOUS ARTISTS (MCA)	19	1994
THE RHYTHM DIVINE VARIOUS ARTISTS (DINO)	1	1991
THE RHYTHM DIVINE VOLUME 2 VARIOUS ARTISTS (DINO)	6	1991
RHYTHM KILLERS SLY & ROBBIE	35	1987
RHYTHM 'N' REGGAE VARIOUS ARTISTS (K-TEL)	42	1981
RHYTHM NATION 1814 JANET JACKSON	4	1989
RHYTHM OF LIFE PAUL HAIG	82	1983
RHYTHM OF LOVE KYLIE MINOGUE	9	1990
RHYTHM OF LOVE ANITA BAKER	14	1994
RHYTHM OF THE NIGHT DeBARGE	94	1985
RHYTHM OF THE NIGHT VARIOUS ARTISTS (K-TEL)	36	1987
THE RHYTHM OF THE NIGHT CORONA	18	1995
THE RHYTHM OF THE SAINTS PAUL SIMON	1	1990
RHYTHM OF THE SUN VARIOUS ARTISTS (TELSTAR)	12	1989
RHYTHM OF YOUTH MEN WITHOUT HATS	96	1983
A RHYTHM ROMANCE NILS LOFGREN	100	1982
RHYTHMEEN ZZ TOP	32	1996
RHYTHMS AND BALLADS OF BROADWAY JOHNNY MATHIS	6	1960
RHYTHMS DEL MUNDO – CUBA VARIOUS ARTISTS (HED KANDI)	5	2007
THE RHYTHMS OF A NATION VARIOUS ARTISTS (BMG)	20	2002
RIALTO RIALTO	21	1998
RICH AND POOR RANDY CRAWFORD	63	1989
RICHARD CHAMBERLAIN SINGS RICHARD CHAMBERLAIN	8	1963
RICHARD CLAYDERMAN – CHRISTMAS RICHARD CLAYDERMAN	53	1984
RICHARD D JAMES ALBUM APHEX TWIN	62	1996
RICHARD MARX RICHARD MARX	68	1988
RICHARD X PRESENTS HIS X-FACTOR VOLUME 1 RICHARD X	31	2003
RICKS ROAD TEXAS	18	1993
RICKY LEE JONES RICKIE LEE JONES	18	1979
RICKY MARTIN RICKY MARTIN	2	1999
RICOCHET TANGERINE DREAM	40	1975
RID OF ME PJ HARVEY	3	1993
THE RIDDLE NIK KERSHAW	8	1984
THE RIDE VARIOUS ARTISTS (MINISTRY OF SOUND)	3	2007
RIDE A ROCK HORSE ROGER DALTREY	14	1975
RIDE DA RIDDIMS VARIOUS ARTISTS (UNIVERSAL)	3	2003
RIDE DA RIDDIMS 2 VARIOUS ARTISTS (UNIVERSAL)	7	2004
RIDE ON A RAINBOW JOHNNY MATHIS	10	1960
RIDE THE LIGHTNING METALLICA	87	1984
RIDES REEF	3	1999
RIDICULOUS SQUEEZE	50	1995
RIDIN' HIGH ROBERT PALMER	32	1992
RIDING WITH THE KING B.B. KING & ERIC CLAPTON	15	2000
RIFFS STATUS QUO	44	2003
RIGHT HERE RIGHT NOW FIERCE	27	1999
THE RIGHT MOMENT BARBARA DICKSON	39	1986
THE RIGHT NIGHT AND BARRY WHITE BARRY WHITE	74	1987
RIGHT NOW ATOMIC KITTEN	1	2000
RIGHT NOW LEON JACKSON	4	2008
THE RIGHT STUFF 2 – NOTHING BUT A HOUSE PARTY VARIOUS ARTISTS (STYLUS)	2	1990
THE RIGHT STUFF – REMIX '89 VARIOUS ARTISTS (STYLUS)	2	1989
RING CONNELLS	36	1995
RING OF CHANGES BARCLAY JAMES HARVEST	36	1983
RING OF FIRE – THE LEGEND OF JOHNNY CASH JOHNNY CASH	11	2005
RING-A-DING-DING FRANK SINATRA	8	1961
RINGLEADER OF THE TORMENTORS MORRISSEY	1	2006
RINGO RINGO STARR	7	1973
RINGS AROUND THE WORLD SUPER FURRY ANIMALS	3	2001
RIO DURAN DURAN	2	1982
RIOT PARAMORE	24	2007
RIOT ACT PEARL JAM	34	2002

Title / Artist	Peak Position	Year of Release
RIOT CITY BLUES PRIMAL SCREAM	5	2006
RIOT ON AN EMPTY STREET KINGS OF CONVENIENCE	49	2004
RIP IT UP ORANGE JUICE	39	1982
RIPE BANDERAS	40	1991
RIPTIDE ROBERT PALMER	5	1985
RISE HERB ALPERT	37	1979
RISE GABRIELLE	1	1999
THE RISE AND FALL MADNESS	10	1982
THE RISE AND FALL OF RUBY WOO PUPPINI SISTERS	73	2007
THE RISE AND FALL OF ZIGGY STARDUST AND THE SPIDERS FROM MARS DAVID BOWIE	5	1972
RISE AND FALL RAGE AND GRACE OFFSPRING	39	2008
RISE AND SHINE ASWAD	38	1994
RISING DR. HOOK	44	1980
THE RISING BRUCE SPRINGSTEEN	1	2002
RISING FOR THE MOON FAIRPORT CONVENTION	52	1975
RISING FROM THE EAST BALLY SAGOO	63	1996
RISK MEGADETH	29	1999
RISOTTO FLUKE	45	1997
RISQUE CHIC	29	1979
RITCHIE BLACKMORE'S RAINBOW RITCHIE BLACKMORE'S RAINBOW	11	1975
RITMO JUDIE TZUKE	26	1983
THE RITUAL TESTAMENT	48	1992
RITUAL DE LO HABITUAL JANE'S ADDICTION	37	1990
RITUAL OF LOVE KARYN WHITE	31	1991
THE RIVER BRUCE SPRINGSTEEN	2	1980
RIVER DEEP – MOUNTAIN HIGH IKE & TINA TURNER	27	1966
RIVER OF DREAMS BILLY JOEL	3	1993
RIVER OF DREAMS: VERY BEST OF HAYLEY WESTENRA	24	2008
ROACHFORD ROACHFORD	11	1988
THE ROAD AND THE MILES MAX BOYCE	50	1978
THE ROAD GOES EVER ON MOUNTAIN	21	1972
THE ROAD GOES ON FOREVER ALLMAN BROTHERS BAND	54	1976
ROAD HAWKS HAWKWIND	34	1976
ROAD NOISE – THE OFFICIAL BOOTLEG JUDIE TZUKE	39	1982
ROAD SHOW HITS (21 YEARS OF RADIO 1 FM ROAD SHOW) VARIOUS ARTISTS (CONNOISSEUR COLLECTION)	18	1993
ROAD TESTED BONNIE RAITT	69	1995
THE ROAD TO ENSENADA LYLE LOVETT	62	1996
THE ROAD TO ESCONDIDO J.J. CALE & ERIC CLAPTON	50	2006
ROAD TO FREEDOM YOUNG DISCIPLES	21	1991
THE ROAD TO FREEDOM CHRIS DE BURGH	75	2004
THE ROAD TO HELL CHRIS REA	1	1989
THE ROAD TO HELL & BACK CHRIS REA	34	2006
THE ROAD TO HELL – PART 2 CHRIS REA	54	1999
ROAD TO REVOLUTION: LIVE AT MILTON KEYNES LINKIN PARK	58	2008
ROAD TO ROUEN SUPERGRASS	9	2005
ROAD TO RUIN RAMONES	32	1978
ROADRUNNER UNITED – ALL-STAR SESSIONS ROADRUNNER UNITED	45	2005
THE ROARING SILENCE MANFRED MANN'S EARTH BAND	10	1986
THE ROARING TWENTIES – SONGS FROM THE TV SERIES DOROTHY PROVINE	3	1961
ROBBERS & COWARDS COLD WAR KIDS	35	2007
ROBBIE ROBERTSON ROBBIE ROBERTSON	23	1987
THE ROBERT JOHNSON SONGBOOK PETER GREEN WITH NIGEL WATSON & THE SPLINTER GROUP	57	1998
ROBERT JOHNSON'S TOMBSTONE THUNDER	56	2006
ROBERTA FLACK AND DONNY HATHAWAY ROBERTA FLACK & DONNY HATHAWAY	31	1980
ROBERTA FLACK'S GREATEST HITS ROBERTA FLACK	35	1984
ROBIN HOOD: PRINCE OF THIEVES FILM SOUNDTRACK	3	1991
ROBIN TROWER LIVE ROBIN TROWER	15	1976
ROBSON & JEROME ROBSON & JEROME	1	1995
ROBYN ROBYN	13	2007
ROCK A LITTLE STEVIE NICKS	30	1985
ROCK ACTION MOGWAI	23	2001
ROCK AIN'T DEAD HEAVY PETTIN'	81	1985
ROCK & ROLL MUSIC TO THE WORLD TEN YEARS AFTER	27	1972
ROCK ANTHEMS VARIOUS ARTISTS (K-TEL)	10	1985
ROCK ANTHEMS VARIOUS ARTISTS (DINO)	3	1994
ROCK ANTHEMS – VOLUME 2 VARIOUS ARTISTS (K-TEL)	43	1986
ROCK ANTHEMS – VOLUME 2 VARIOUS ARTISTS (DINO)	10	1996
ROCK AROUND THE CLOCK BILL HALEY	2	1956
ROCK AROUND THE CLOCK BILL HALEY & HIS COMETS	34	1968
ROCK ART MAGNUM	57	1994
ROCK ART AND THE X-RAY STYLE JOE STRUMMER & THE MESCALEROS	71	1999
ROCK CHICKS VARIOUS ARTISTS (SONY)	3	2004
ROCK CITY NIGHT VARIOUS ARTISTS (VERTIGO)	3	1989
THE ROCK CONNECTION CLIFF RICHARD	43	1984
ROCK FOLLIES (TELEVISION SOUNDTRACK) TELEVISION AND RADIO COMPILATION	1	1976
ROCK GODDESS ROCK GODDESS	65	1983
ROCK GODZ VARIOUS ARTISTS (SONY/BMG)	9	2005
ROCK HOUSE VARIOUS ARTISTS (RONCO)	44	1981
ROCK IN RIO IRON MAIDEN	15	2002
A ROCK IN THE WEARY LAND WATERBOYS	47	2000
ROCK ISLAND JETHRO TULL	18	1989
ROCK LEGENDS VARIOUS ARTISTS (RONCO)	54	1979
ROCK LEGENDS VARIOUS ARTISTS (TELSTAR)	54	1986
ROCK MACHINE I LOVE YOU VARIOUS ARTISTS (CBS)	15	1969
THE ROCK MACHINE TURNS YOU ON VARIOUS ARTISTS (CBS)	18	1969
ROCK ME BABY DAVID CASSIDY	2	1973
ROCK ME TONIGHT FREDDIE JACKSON	27	1985
ROCK MONSTERS VARIOUS ARTISTS (UNIVERSAL)	9	2002
ROCK N ROLL RYAN ADAMS	41	2003
ROCK 'N' ROLL ELVIS PRESLEY	1	1956
ROCK 'N' ROLL JOHN LENNON	6	1975
ROCK 'N' ROLL MOTORHEAD	34	1987
ROCK 'N' ROLL ANIMAL LOU REED	26	1974
ROCK 'N' ROLL DUDES GLITTER BAND	17	1975
ROCK 'N' ROLL GYPSIES SPIDER	75	1982
ROCK N ROLL HEARTBEATS VARIOUS ARTISTS (TELSTAR)	13	1992
ROCK 'N' ROLL IS HERE TO STAY VARIOUS ARTISTS (DINO)	14	1992
ROCK N ROLL JESUS KID ROCK	4	2008
ROCK 'N' ROLL JUVENILE CLIFF RICHARD	3	1979
ROCK 'N' ROLL LOVE SONGS VARIOUS ARTISTS (DINO)	4	1990
ROCK 'N' ROLL LOVE SONGS VARIOUS ARTISTS (DECADANCE)	9	2004
ROCK 'N' ROLL MILLION SELLERS CONNIE FRANCIS	12	1960
ROCK 'N' ROLL MUSIC BEATLES	11	1976
ROCK 'N' ROLL NO.2 ELVIS PRESLEY	3	1957
ROCK 'N ROLL STAGE SHOWS BILL HALEY	1	1956
ROCK 'N' ROLL WITH THE MODERN LOVERS JONATHAN RICHMAN & THE MODERN LOVERS	50	1977
THE ROCK 'N' ROLL YEARS CLIFF RICHARD	32	1997
THE ROCK 'N' ROLL YEARS 1956-1959 (TELEVISION COMPILATION) TELEVISION AND RADIO COMPILATION	80	1987
THE ROCK 'N' ROLL YEARS 1960-1963 (TELEVISION COMPILATION) TELEVISION AND RADIO COMPILATION	84	1987
THE ROCK 'N' ROLL YEARS 1964-1967 (TELEVISION COMPILATION) TELEVISION AND RADIO COMPILATION	71	1987
THE ROCK 'N' ROLL YEARS 1968-1971 (TELEVISION COMPILATION) TELEVISION AND RADIO COMPILATION	77	1987
ROCK 'N' ROLLER DISCO VARIOUS ARTISTS (RONCO)	3	1979
ROCK 'N' ROLLING STONES ROLLING STONES	41	1972
ROCK 'N' SOUL (PART ONE) DARYL HALL & JOHN OATES	16	1983
ROCK OF AMERICA VARIOUS ARTISTS (TRAX)	7	1990
ROCK OF LIFE RICK SPRINGFIELD	80	1988
ROCK OF THE WESTIES ELTON JOHN	5	1975
ROCK ON DAVID ESSEX	7	1973
ROCK ON VARIOUS ARTISTS (ARCADE)	16	1977
ROCK PEBBLES AND SAND STANLEY CLARKE	42	1980
ROCK ROMANCE VARIOUS ARTISTS (ARCADE)	9	1993
ROCK RULES VARIOUS ARTISTS (K-TEL)	12	1978
ROCK STEADY NO DOUBT	43	2002
ROCK SWINGS PAUL ANKA	9	2005
ROCK THE DANCEFLOOR VARIOUS ARTISTS (ALL AROUND THE WORLD)	9	1998
ROCK THE DANCEFLOOR 2 VARIOUS ARTISTS (ALL AROUND THE WORLD)	7	1999
ROCK THE DANCEFLOOR 8 VARIOUS ARTISTS (ALL AROUND THE WORLD)	17	2003
ROCK THE DANCEFLOOR VOLUME 5 VARIOUS ARTISTS (ALL AROUND THE WORLD)	19	2001
ROCK THE HOUSE DJ JAZZY JEFF & THE FRESH PRINCE	97	1987
ROCK THE HOUSE 'LIVE' HEART	45	1991
ROCK THE JOINT BILL HALEY	5	1957
ROCK THE NATIONS SAXON	34	1986
ROCK THE WORLD FIVE STAR	17	1988
ROCK THE WORLD VARIOUS ARTISTS (GLOBAL TELEVISION)	9	1999
ROCK THERAPY VARIOUS ARTISTS (POLYGRAM)	9	1994
ROCK 'TIL YOU DROP STATUS QUO	10	1991
ROCK UNTIL YOU DROP RAVEN	63	1981
ROCK WILL NEVER DIE MICHAEL SCHENKER GROUP	24	1984
ROCK WITH ALVIN ALVIN STARDUST	52	1975
ROCK YOUR BABY GEORGE McCRAE	13	1974
ROCKABILLY PSYCHOS AND THE GARAGE DISEASE VARIOUS ARTISTS (BIG BEAT)	88	1984
ROCKABILLY REVIVAL VARIOUS ARTISTS (TELSTAR)	10	2003
ROCKBIRD DEBBIE HARRY	31	1986
ROCKET COTTAGE STEELEYE SPAN	41	1976
ROCKET MAN – THE DEFINITIVE HITS ELTON JOHN	2	2007
ROCKET TO RUSSIA RAMONES	60	1977
ROCKFERRY DUFFY	1	2008
ROCKIN' ALL OVER THE WORLD STATUS QUO	5	1977
ROCKIN' EVERY NIGHT GARY MOORE	99	1986
ROCKIN' ROLL BABY STYLISTICS	42	1974
ROCKIN' THE SUBURBS BEN FOLDS	73	2001
ROCKIN' WITH CURLY LEADS SHADOWS	45	1974
ROCKING ALL OVER THE YEARS STATUS QUO	2	1990
ROCKING AT THE FILLMORE HUMBLE PIE	32	1972

Title / Artist	Peak Position	Year of Release
ROCKS OFF VARIOUS ARTISTS (POLYGRAM)	4	1995
ROCKS THE HOUSE! JELLYBEAN	16	1988
ROCKS THE WORLD THIRD WORLD	37	1981
ROCKY III FILM SOUNDTRACK	42	1982
ROCKY IV FILM SOUNDTRACK	3	1986
THE ROCKY MOUNTAIN COLLECTION JOHN DENVER	19	1997
ROCKY MOUNTAIN HIGH JOHN DENVER	11	1973
ROCKY V FILM SOUNDTRACK	9	1991
ROD STEWART – GREATEST HITS VOL. 1 ROD STEWART	1	1979
ROD STEWART: LEAD VOCALIST ROD STEWART	3	1993
RODRIGO Y GABRIELA RODRIGO Y GABRIELA	53	2007
RODRIGO: CONCERTO DE ARANJUEZ JOHN WILLIAMS WITH THE ENGLISH CHAMBER ORCHESTRA CONDUCTED BY DANIEL BARENBOIM	20	1976
THE ROGER WHITTAKER ALBUM ROGER WHITTAKER	18	1981
ROGER WHITTAKER SINGS THE HITS ROGER WHITTAKER	52	1978
ROGUES GALLERY SLADE	60	1985
ROLL ON VARIOUS ARTISTS (POLYDOR)	3	1981
ROLL THE BONES RUSH	10	1991
ROLL WITH IT STEVE WINWOOD	4	1988
ROLLED GOLD + ROLLING STONES	26	2007
ROLLED GOLD – THE VERY BEST OF THE ROLLING STONES ROLLING STONES	7	1975
ROLLERCOASTER LET LOOSE	42	1996
ROLLIN' BAY CITY ROLLERS	1	1974
THE ROLLING STONES ROLLING STONES	1	1964
ROLLING STONES NUMBER 2 ROLLING STONES	1	1965
THE ROLLING STONES ROCK AND ROLL CIRCUS VARIOUS ARTISTS (ABKO)	12	1996
ROMANCE DAVID CASSIDY	20	1985
ROMANCE AND THE STAGE ELAINE PAIGE	71	1993
ROMANCE AT SHORT NOTICE DIRTY PRETTY THINGS	35	2008
ROMANCING THE SCREEN VARIOUS ARTISTS (EPIC)	5	1992
ROMANTIC CALLAS – THE BEST OF MARIA CALLAS	32	2001
ROMANTIC CLASSICS JULIO IGLESIAS	42	2006
ROMANTIC ELVIS – 20 LOVE SONGS/ ROCKIN' ELVIS – THE SIXTIES 20 GREAT TRACKS ELVIS PRESLEY	62	1982
ROMANTIC GUITAR PAUL BRETT	24	1980
ROMANTIC? HUMAN LEAGUE	24	1990
ROMANZA ANDREA BOCELLI	6	1997
ROMEO + JULIET FILM SOUNDTRACK	3	1997
RONAN RONAN KEATING	1	2000
ROOM ON FIRE STROKES	2	2003
ROOM ON THE 3RD FLOOR McFLY	1	2004
ROOM SERVICE BRYAN ADAMS	4	2004
ROOM TO ROAM WATERBOYS	5	1990
ROOSTER ROOSTER	3	2005
ROOT DOWN (EP) BEASTIE BOYS	23	1995
ROOTS SEPULTURA	4	1996
ROOTS & ECHOES CORAL	8	2007
ROOTS OF A LEGEND BOB MARLEY & THE WAILERS	51	2004
ROOTS REGGAE 'N' REGGAE ROCK VARIOUS ARTISTS (TELSTAR)	34	1983
ROOTS TO BRANCHES JETHRO TULL	20	1995
ROOTY BASEMENT JAXX	5	2001
ROPIN' THE WIND GARTH BROOKS	41	1992
RORY GALLAGHER RORY GALLAGHER	32	1971
THE ROSARY POPE JOHN PAUL II/FATHER COLM KILCOYNE	50	1994
THE ROSE BETTE MIDLER	68	1980
ROSE GARDEN LYNN ANDERSON	45	1971
ROSE MARIE SINGS JUST FOR YOU ROSE MARIE	30	1985
THE ROSE OF TRALEE AND OTHER IRISH FAVOURITES JAMES LAST	21	1984
ROSE ROYCE GREATEST HITS ROSE ROYCE	1	1980
ROSENROT RAMMSTEIN	29	2005
ROSES FROM THE SOUTH JAMES LAST	41	1981
ROSS DIANA ROSS	44	1983
ROTTEN APPLE LLOYD BANKS	40	2006
ROTTEN APPLES – THE GREATEST HITS SMASHING PUMPKINS	28	2001
ROTTERS CLUB HATFIELD & THE NORTH	43	1975
ROUGH AND READY VOL 1 SHABBA RANKS	71	1992
ROUGH DIAMONDS BAD COMPANY	15	1982
ROUGH JUSTICE SPIDER	96	1984
ROUGH MIX PETE TOWNSHEND & RONNIE LANE	44	1977
ROUND AMEN CORNER AMEN CORNER	26	1968
A ROUND AND A BOUT SQUEEZE	50	1990
ROUND MIDNIGHT ELKIE BROOKS	27	1993
ROUND MIDNIGHT VARIOUS ARTISTS (POLYGRAM)	16	1993
ROUND TRIP LIGHT OF THE WORLD	73	1981
ROUNDS FOUR TET	60	2003
ROUSTABOUT (OST) ELVIS PRESLEY	12	1965
ROXANNE ROXANNE (6 TRACK VERSION) U.T.F.O.	72	1985
ROXETTE HITS ROXETTE	22	2006
THE ROXY LONDON WC2 (JAN-APR 77) VARIOUS ARTISTS (HARVEST)	24	1977
ROXY MUSIC ROXY	10	1972
ROXY MUSIC – THE ATLANTIC YEARS (1973-1980) ROXY MUSIC	23	1983
ROY ORBISON'S GREATEST HITS ROY ORBISON	40	1967
ROYAL ALBERT HALL 2005 CREAM	61	2005
ROYAL MIX '89 MIRAGE	34	1989
ROYAL ROMANCE (ROYAL COMPILATION ALBUM) ROYAL COMPILATION ALBUM	84	1981
ROYAL SCAM STEELY DAN	11	1976
THE ROYAL SOCIETY EIGHTIES MATCHBOX B-LINE DISASTER	68	2004
ROYAL WEDDING (ROYAL COMPILATION ALBUM) ROYAL COMPILATION ALBUM	55	1986
RUBBER FACTORY BLACK KEYS	62	2004
RUBBER SOUL BEATLES	1	1965
RUBY WINTERS RUBY WINTERS	27	1978
RUBYCON TANGERINE DREAM	12	1975
RUDE BOY REVIVAL VARIOUS ARTISTS (TELSTAR)	4	2002
RUDEBOX ROBBIE WILLIAMS	1	2006
RUFUSIZED RUFUS	48	1975
RULE JA RULE	33	2004
RULE BRITANNIA VARIOUS ARTISTS (ARCADE)	56	1977
RUM, SODOMY AND THE LASH POGUES	13	1985
RUMOUR AND SIGH RICHARD THOMPSON	32	1991
RUMOURS FLEETWOOD MAC	1	1977
RUN COME SAVE ME ROOTS MANUVA	33	2001
RUN DEVIL RUN PAUL McCARTNEY	12	1999
RUN FOR COVER GARY MOORE	12	1985
RUN TO THE HILLS/THE NUMBER OF THE BEAST IRON MAIDEN	3	1990
RUN WITH THE PACK BAD COMPANY	4	1976
RUNAWAY HORSES BELINDA CARLISLE	4	1989
RUNNIN' WILD AIRBOURNE	62	2008
RUNNING FREE ALI CAMPBELL	9	2007
RUNNING FREE (LIVE)/RUN TO THE HILLS (LIVE) IRON MAIDEN	9	1990
RUNNING IN THE FAMILY LEVEL 42	2	1987
RUNNING ON EMPTY JACKSON BROWNE	28	1978
RUNNING/SANCTUARY IRON MAIDEN	10	1990
THE RUSH VARIOUS ARTISTS (MINISTRY OF SOUND)	8	2008
RUSH HOUR VARIOUS ARTISTS (UNIVERSAL)	2	2004
RUSH HOUR 2 VARIOUS ARTISTS (UNIVERSAL)	3	2005
RUSH HOUR 3 VARIOUS ARTISTS (UNIVERSAL)	5	2005
A RUSH OF BLOOD TO THE HEAD COLDPLAY	1	2002
RUSH STREET RICHARD MARX	7	1991
RUSS ABBOT'S MADHOUSE RUSS ABBOT	41	1983
RUSS CONWAY PRESENTS 24 PIANO GREATS RUSS CONWAY	25	1977
RUSSIAN ROULETTE ACCEPT	80	1986
RUSSIANS AND AMERICANS AL STEWART	83	1984
RUST IN PEACE MEGADETH	8	1990
RUST NEVER SLEEPS NEIL YOUNG & CRAZY HORSE	13	1979
THE RUTLES RUTLES	12	1978
RYANDAN RYANDAN	7	2007

S

Title / Artist	Peak Position	Year of Release
S AWFUL NICE RAY CONNIFF	13	1960
S CLUB S CLUB 7	2	1999
S WONDERFUL 'S MARVELLOUS RAY CONNIFF	18	1962
S&M METALLICA	33	1999
S*M*A*S*H S*M*A*S*H	28	1994
S.I.O.S.O.S. VOLUME 1 SPOOKS	25	2001
S.O.D. THE EPIC YEARS SPEAR OF DESTINY	53	1987
S.R.O. HERB ALPERT & THE TIJUANA BRASS	5	1967
SABBATH BLOODY SABBATH BLACK SABBATH	4	1973
SABOTAGE BLACK SABBATH	7	1975
SABRESONIC SABRES OF PARADISE	29	1993
SACHA DISTEL SACHA DISTEL	21	1970
SACRED ARIAS ANDREA BOCELLI	20	1999
SACRED ARIAS KATHERINE JENKINS	5	2008
SACRED HEART DIO	4	1985
SACRED HEART SHAKESPEARS SISTER	9	1989
SACRED LOVE STING	3	2003
SACRED SONGS HARRY SECOMBE	16	1962
SACRIFICE BLACK WIDOW	32	1970
SAD CAFÉ SAD CAFÉ	46	1980
SAD SONGS VARIOUS ARTISTS (VIRGIN)	1	2004
SAFE AS FUCK GOLDIE LOOKIN CHAIN	16	2005
SAFE TRIP HOME DIDO	2	2008
SAFINA ALESSANDRO SAFINA	27	2002
SAHB STORIES SENSATIONAL ALEX HARVEY BAND	11	1976
SAID AND DONE BOYZONE	1	1995
SAILING TO PHILADELPHIA MARK KNOPFLER	4	2000
THE SAINT FILM SOUNDTRACK	15	1997
ST JUDE COURTEENERS	4	2008
SAINT JULIAN JULIAN COPE	11	1987
SAINTS & SINNERS ALL SAINTS	1	2000
SAINTS 'N' SINNERS WHITESNAKE	9	1982
SALAD DAYS (ORIGINAL LONDON STAGE CAST RECORDING) STAGE CAST RECORDING	5	1956
SALSA FEVER! VARIOUS ARTISTS (GLOBAL TELEVISION)	12	1999
A SALT WITH A DEADLY PEPA SALT-N-PEPA	19	1988
A SALTY DOG PROCOL HARUM	27	1969
SALUTATION ROAD MARTIN STEPHENSON & THE DAINTEES	35	1990
SALVA NOS MEDIAEVAL BAEBES	62	1997
SAM SPARRO SAM SPARRO	4	2008
SAMANTHA FOX SAMANTHA FOX	22	1987
SAME AS IT EVER WAS HOUSE OF PAIN	8	1994
SAME OUL' TOWN SAW DOCTORS	6	1996
THE SAME SIDE LUCIE SILVAS	62	2007
THE SAME SKY HORSE	44	1990

Title / Artist	Peak Position	Year of Release
SAMMY DAVIS JR AT THE COCONUT GROVE SAMMY DAVIS JR	19	1963
SAMMY HAGAR SAMMY HAGAR	86	1987
SAM'S TOWN KILLERS	1	2006
SAMURAI GRAND PRIX	65	1983
SAN FRANCISCO AMERICAN MUSIC CLUB	72	1994
SAN FRANCISCO DAYS CHRIS ISAAK	12	1993
SANCTUARY SIMON WEBBE	7	2005
SANDIE SANDIE SHAW	3	1965
SANDINISTA CLASH	19	1980
SANDS OF TIME S.O.S. BAND	15	1986
SANDY JOHN TRAVOLTA	40	1978
SANTA MONICA '72 DAVID BOWIE	74	1994
SANTA SINGS SANTA/ELVES/CHILDREN'S CHOIR	49	2005
SANTANA SANTANA	26	1970
SANTANA III SANTANA	6	1971
SANTOGOLD SANTOGOLD	26	2008
SAPPHIRE JOHN MARTYN	57	1984
SASHA – IBIZA VARIOUS ARTISTS (GLOBAL UNDERGROUND)	12	1999
SASHA – INVOL2VER VARIOUS ARTISTS (GLOBAL UNDERGROUND)	19	2008
SASHA – SAN FRANCISCO VARIOUS ARTISTS (GLOBAL UNDERGROUND)	18	1998
SATAN LIVE ORBITAL	48	1997
SATCHMO PLAYS KING OLIVER LOUIS ARMSTRONG	20	1960
SATELLITE P.O.D.	16	2002
SATELLITES BIG DISH	43	1991
SATIN CITY VARIOUS ARTISTS (CBS)	10	1978
SATIN THE STEEL – WOMEN IN ROCK VARIOUS ARTISTS (POLYGRAM)	3	1994
SATISFACTION GUARANTEED: THE VERY BEST TEDDY PENDERGRASS	26	2004
SATISFY MY SOUL PAUL CARRACK	63	2000
SATURDAY NIGHT ZHANE	52	1997
SATURDAY NIGHT & SUNDAY MORNINGS COUNTING CROWS	12	2008
SATURDAY NIGHT FEVER FILM SOUNDTRACK	1	1978
SATURDAY NIGHT FEVER STAGE CAST RECORDING	17	1998
SATURDAY NIGHT SUNDAY MORNING RIVER DETECTIVES	51	1989
SATURDAY NIGHT WRIST DEFTONES	33	2006
THE SATURDAY SESSIONS – THE DERMOT O'LEARY SHOW VARIOUS ARTISTS (EMI)	11	2007
SATURNALIA WEDDING PRESENT	36	1996
SATURNALIA GUTTER TWINS	54	2008
SATURNZ RETURN GOLDIE	15	1998
SAUCERFUL OF SECRETS PINK FLOYD	9	1968
SAVAGE EURYTHMICS	7	1987
SAVAGE AMUSEMENT SCORPIONS	18	1988
SAVAGE GARDEN SAVAGE GARDEN	2	1998
SAVANE ALI FARKA TOURE	34	2006
SAVE THE LAST DANCE FILM SOUNDTRACK	5	2001
SAVE YOUR LOVE RENATO	26	1982
SAVE YOURSELF SPEEDWAY	42	2004
SAVED BOB DYLAN	3	1980
SAVED MY LIFE TODD EDWARDS	69	1996
SAWDUST KILLERS	7	2007
THE SAX ALBUM VARIOUS ARTISTS (POLYGRAM)	6	1996
SAX AT THE MOVIES STATE OF THE HEART	62	1996
SAX MOODS BLOWING FREE	6	1995
SAX MOODS – VOLUME 2 BLOWING FREE	70	1996
SAX-A-GO-GO CANDY DULFER	56	1993
SAXUALITY CANDY DULFER	27	1990
SAY HELLO TO SUNSHINE FINCH	48	2005
SAY IT AGAIN JERMAINE STEWART	32	1988
SAY SOMETHING GOOD RIVER CITY PEOPLE	23	1990
SAY WHAT! TROUBLE FUNK	75	1986
SAY YOU WILL FLEETWOOD MAC	6	2003
SCALLYWAG JAZ THOMAS LANG	92	1988
SCANDAL FILM SOUNDTRACK	13	1989
SCANDALOUS IMAGINATION	25	1983
SCARED TO DANCE SKIDS	19	1979
SCARLET AND OTHER STORIES ALL ABOUT EVE	9	1989
SCARLET, RED AND BLUE ZOE	67	1991
SCARLET'S WALK TORI AMOS	26	2002
SCARS ON BROADWAY SCARS ON BROADWAY	41	2008
SCARY MONSTERS AND SUPER CREEPS DAVID BOWIE	1	1980
SCATTERLINGS JULUKA	50	1983
SCENES FROM THE SECOND STORY GOD MACHINE	55	1993
SCENES FROM THE SOUTHSIDE BRUCE HORNBY & THE RANGE	18	1988
SCHINDLER'S LIST (OST) JOHN WILLIAMS	59	1994
SCHIZOPHONIC GERI HALLIWELL	4	1999
SCHIZOPHRENIC JC CHASEZ	46	2004
SCHOOL DISCO.COM VARIOUS ARTISTS (COLUMBIA)	9	2001
SCHOOL DISCO.COM – SPRING TERM VARIOUS ARTISTS (COLUMBIA)	1	2002
SCHOOL DISCO.COM – SUMMER HOLIDAY VARIOUS ARTISTS (COLUMBIA)	2	2002
SCHOOL REUNION – THE 80'S VARIOUS ARTISTS (VIRGIN)	4	2003
SCHOOL REUNION – THE DISCO VARIOUS ARTISTS (VIRGIN)	9	2004
SCHOOL REUNION – THE PARTY VARIOUS ARTISTS (EMI)	15	2005
SCHOOL REUNION – THE SMOOCHIES VARIOUS ARTISTS (VIRGIN)	2	2005
SCHOOL'S OUT ALICE COOPER	4	1972
SCHUBERT DIP EMF	3	1991
SCIENCE & NATURE BLUETONES	7	2000
SCIENCE OF THE GODS EAT STATIC	60	1997
THE SCIENCE OF THINGS BUSH	28	1999
SCI-FI LULLABIES SUEDE	9	1997
SCISSOR SISTERS SCISSOR SISTERS	1	2004
SCISSORS CUT ART GARFUNKEL	51	1981
THE SCORE FUGEES	2	1996
SCORPIO RISING DEATH IN VEGAS	19	2002
SCORPION EVE	22	2001
SCOTCH ON THE ROCKS BAND OF THE BLACK WATCH	11	1976
SCOTLAND ROCKS VARIOUS ARTISTS (VIRGIN)	20	2003
SCOTT SCOTT WALKER	3	1967
SCOTT 2 SCOTT WALKER	1	1968
SCOTT 3 SCOTT WALKER	3	1969
SCOTTISH LOVE SONGS CORRIES	46	1970
SCOUNDREL DAYS A-HA	2	1986
SCOUTING FOR GIRLS SCOUTING FOR GIRLS	1	2007
SCRATCH AND SNIFF SMITH & JONES	62	1986
THE SCREAM SIOUXSIE & THE BANSHEES	12	1978
SCREAM AIM FIRE BULLET FOR MY VALENTINE	5	2008
SCREAM DREAM TED NUGENT	37	1980
SCREAM IF YOU WANT TO GO FASTER GERI HALLIWELL	5	2001
SCREAM, DRACULA, SCREAM! ROCKET FROM THE CRYPT	41	1996
SCREAMADELICA PRIMAL SCREAM	8	1991
SCREAMING BLUE MURDER GIRLSCHOOL	27	1982
SCREAMING FOR VENGEANCE JUDAS PRIEST	11	1982
THE SCREEN BEHIND THE MIRROR ENIGMA	7	2000
SCREEN GEMS ELKIE BROOKS	35	1984
THE SCRIPT THE SCRIPT	1	2008
SCRIPT FOR A JESTER'S TEAR MARILLION	7	1983
SEA CHANGE BECK	20	2002
SEA MONSTERS WEDDING PRESENT	13	1991
THE SEA OF LOVE ADVENTURES	30	1988
SEA OF TRANQUILLITY PHIL COULTER	46	1984
SEAL SEAL	1	1991
SEAL II SEAL	1	1994
SEAN KINGSTON SEAN KINGSTON	8	2007
SEAN MAGUIRE SEAN MAGUIRE	75	1994
SEAN-NOS-NUA SINEAD O'CONNOR	52	2002
SEARCHING FOR THE HOWS AND WHYS GET CAPE WEAR CAPE FLY	30	2008
SEARCHING FOR THE YOUNG SOUL REBELS DEXYS MIDNIGHT RUNNERS	6	1980
SEARCHLIGHT RUNRIG	11	1989
SEASON OF GLASS YOKO ONO	47	1981
SEASONS MAGNA CARTA	55	1970
SEASONS BING CROSBY	25	1977
SEASONS SYNTHPHONIC VARIATIONS	84	1986
SEASON'S END MARILLION	7	1989
SEASONS IN THE ABYSS SLAYER	18	1990
THE SEBADOH SEBADOH	45	1999
SEBASTAPOL ROAD MEGA CITY FOUR	41	1992
SECOMBE'S PERSONAL CHOICE HARRY SECOMBE	6	1967
THE SECOND ALBUM SPENCER DAVIS GROUP	3	1966
THE SECOND ALBUM OF THE VERY BEST OF ROGER WHITTAKER ROGER WHITTAKER	27	1976
SECOND COMING STONE ROSES	4	1994
THE SECOND COMING TQ	32	2000
SECOND EDITION OF PIL PUBLIC IMAGE LTD	46	1980
SECOND FIRST IMPRESSION DANIEL BEDINGFIELD	8	2004
SECOND FLIGHT PILOT	48	1975
SECOND LIGHT DREADZONE	37	1995
SECOND NATURE KATHERINE JENKINS	16	2004
SECOND ROUND'S ON ME OBIE TRICE	46	2006
SECOND SIGHTING FREHLEY'S COMET	79	1988
SECOND SPRING MATTHEWS' SOUTHERN COMFORT	52	1970
THE SECOND TINDERSTICKS ALBUM TINDERSTICKS	13	1995
2ND TO NONE ELVIS PRESLEY	4	2003
SECOND TOUGHEST IN THE INFANTS UNDERWORLD	9	1996
2ND VERSE SO SOLID CREW	70	2003
SECOND WINTER JOHNNY WINTER	59	1970
SECONDHAND DAYLIGHT MAGAZINE	38	1979
SECONDS OF PLEASURE ROCKPILE	34	1980
SECONDS OF PLEASURE SILENCERS	52	1993
SECONDS OUT GENESIS	4	1977
SECRET COMBINATION RANDY CRAWFORD	2	1981
SECRET DREAMS AND FORBIDDEN FIRE BONNIE TYLER	24	1986
A SECRET HISTORY – THE BEST OF DIVINE COMEDY DIVINE COMEDY	3	1999
SECRET LOVERS VARIOUS ARTISTS (COLUMBIA)	8	1994
SECRET MESSAGES ELECTRIC LIGHT ORCHESTRA	4	1983
THE SECRET MIGRATION MERCURY REV	16	2005
THE SECRET OF ASSOCIATION PAUL YOUNG	1	1985
SECRET PEOPLE CAPERCAILLIE	40	1993
THE SECRET POLICEMAN'S BALL VARIOUS ARTISTS (ISLAND)	33	1980
THE SECRET POLICEMAN'S OTHER BALL VARIOUS ARTISTS (SPRINGTIME)	69	1981
THE SECRET POLICEMAN'S OTHER BALL (THE MUSIC) VARIOUS ARTISTS (SPRINGTIME)	29	1982
SECRET SAMADHI LIVE	31	1997
SECRET SECRETS JOAN ARMATRADING	14	1985
THE SECRET VALUE OF DAYDREAMING JULIAN LENNON	93	1986
SECRET WISH PROPAGANDA	16	1985
SECRET WORLD LIVE PETER GABRIEL	10	1994

Title / Artist	Peak Position	Year of Release
SECRETS ROBERT PALMER	54	1979
SECRETS WILTON FELDER FEATURING BOBBY WOMACK & INTRODUCING ALLTRINA GRAYSON	77	1985
SECRETS TONI BRAXTON	10	1996
SECRETS HUMAN LEAGUE	44	2001
SECRETS OF THE BEEHIVE DAVID SYLVIAN	37	1987
SEDUCED AND ABANDONED HUE & CRY	22	1987
SEDUCTION VARIOUS ARTISTS (K-TEL)	15	1989
SEE JUNGLE! SEE JUNGLE! GO JOIN YOUR GANG YEAH CITY ALL OVER! GO APE CRAZY BOW WOW WOW	26	1981
SEE THE LIGHT JEFF HEALEY BAND	58	1989
SEE THIS THROUGH AND LEAVE COOPER TEMPLE CLAUSE	27	2002
SEE YOU ON THE OTHER SIDE KORN	71	2005
THE SEEDS OF LOVE TEARS FOR FEARS	1	1989
SEEING DOUBLE S CLUB	17	2002
SEEING SOUNDS N*E*R*D	20	2008
THE SEEKERS SEEKERS	16	1965
SEEKERS – SEEN IN GREEN SEEKERS	15	1967
SEEKRET KLEEER	96	1983
THE SEER BIG COUNTRY	2	1986
SEIZE THE TIME FUN DA MENTAL	74	1994
THE SELDOM SEEN KID ELBOW	5	2008
SELECT KIM WILDE	19	1982
SELECTED AMBIENT WORKS VOLUME II APHEX TWIN	11	1994
SELF QUINTESSENCE	50	1972
SELF ABUSED S*M*A*S*H	59	1994
SELF CONTROL LAURA BRANIGAN	16	1984
SELF PORTRAIT BOB DYLAN	1	1970
SELLING ENGLAND BY THE POUND GENESIS	3	1973
SELMA SONGS BJORK	34	2000
SEMI-DETACHED THERAPY?	21	1998
SEMI-DETACHED SUBURBAN MANFRED MANN	9	1979
SEMINAL LIVE FALL	40	1989
SEND AWAY THE TIGERS MANIC STREET PREACHERS	2	2007
SENSATIONAL MICHELLE GAYLE	17	1997
SENSATIONAL ALEX HARVEY BAND LIVE SENSATIONAL ALEX HARVEY BAND	14	1975
SENSE LIGHTNING SEEDS	53	1992
SENSE AND SENSUALITY AU PAIRS	79	1982
A SENSE OF PURPOSE IN FLAMES	54	2008
A SENSE OF WONDER VAN MORRISON	25	1985
SENSES VARIOUS ARTISTS (POLYGRAM)	5	1994
SENSUAL CLASSICS VARIOUS ARTISTS (TELDEC)	19	1992
THE SENSUAL WORLD KATE BUSH	2	1989
SENTIMENTAL JOURNEY RINGO STARR	7	1970
SENTIMENTALLY YOURS ROSE MARIE	22	1987
SENTIMENTO ANDREA BOCELLI	7	2002
SENTINEL PALLAS	41	1984
SEPTEMBER MORN NEIL DIAMOND	14	1980
SERENADE NEIL DIAMOND	11	1974
SERENADE JUAN MARTIN WITH THE ROYAL PHILHARMONIC ORCHESTRA	21	1984
SERENADE KATHERINE JENKINS	5	2006
SERENITY CULTURE BEAT	13	1993
SERGEANT PEPPER KNEW MY FATHER VARIOUS ARTISTS (NME)	37	1988
SERIOUS CLUB HITS VARIOUS ARTISTS (UNIVERSAL)	17	2002
SERIOUS HIP-HOP 2 VARIOUS ARTISTS (SERIOUS)	95	1987
SERIOUS HITS...LIVE! PHIL COLLINS	2	1990
SERIOUSLY ORCHESTRA LOUIS CLARK CONDUCTING THE ROYAL PHILHARMONIC ORCHESTRA	31	1991
SERVE CHILLED VARIOUS ARTISTS (VIRGIN)	16	1995
SESSION EIGHT – TODD TERRY VARIOUS ARTISTS (MINISTRY OF SOUND)	11	1997
A SESSION WITH THE DAVE CLARK FIVE DAVE CLARK FIVE	3	1964
SESSIONS NINE – ERICK MORILLO VARIOUS ARTISTS (MINISTRY OF SOUND)	17	1998
SESSIONS SEVEN VARIOUS ARTISTS (MINISTRY OF SOUND)	4	1997
SESSIONS TEN – SUBLIMINAL SESSIONS VARIOUS ARTISTS (DEFECTED)	18	2000
SET THOMPSON TWINS	48	1982
SET THE CONTROLS FOR THE HEART OF THE BASS BASS-O-MATIC	57	1990
SET THE MOOD DAVID JORDAN	13	2008
SET THE TWILIGHT REELING LOU REED	26	1996
SETTING SONS JAM	4	1979
SEVEN JAMES	2	1992
7 S CLUB 7	1	2000
SEVEN ENRIQUE IGLESIAS	13	2003
SEVEN AGES OF ACKER MR ACKER BILK	6	1960
SEVEN AND THE RAGGED TIGER DURAN DURAN	1	1983
SEVEN BRIDES FOR SEVEN BROTHERS FILM SOUNDTRACK	6	1961
7 INCH HEROES – THE ORIGINAL 45S VARIOUS ARTISTS (UNIVERSAL)	14	2007
777 SYSTEM 7	30	1993
SEVEN SINGLES DEEP ICICLE WORKS	52	1986
SEVEN TEARS GOOMBAY DANCE BAND	16	1982
SEVEN THE HARD WAY PAT BENATAR	69	1985
SEVEN YEARS – TEN WEEKS DAVID SNEDDON	5	2003
SEVENS GARTH BROOKS	34	1997
17 SECONDS CURE	20	1980
THE SEVENTH ONE TOTO	73	1988
SEVENTH SOJOURN MOODY BLUES	5	1972
SEVENTH SON OF A SEVENTH SON IRON MAIDEN	1	1988
SEVENTH STAR BLACK SABBATH FEATURING TONY IOMMI	27	1986
SEVENTH TREE GOLDFRAPP	2	2008
THE SEVENTIES ALBUM VARIOUS ARTISTS (SANCTUARY)	9	2005
THE SEVENTIES COLLECTION ROD STEWART	20	2007
70'S DINNER PARTY VARIOUS ARTISTS (SONY BMG)	13	2008
70S HEART THROBS VARIOUS ARTISTS (SONY/BMG)	6	2007
SEVENTIES POWER BALLADS VARIOUS ARTISTS (EMI)	11	2008
70'S SOUL MIX VARIOUS ARTISTS (UNIVERSAL)	13	2003
7800O FAHRENHEIT BON JOVI	28	1985
SEX & JAZZ & ROCK & ROLL JOOLS HOLLAND & HIS R&B ORCHESTRA	38	1996
SEX AND RELIGION STEVE VAI	17	1993
SEX AND THE CITY TELEVISION AND RADIO COMPILATION	6	2004
SEX AND THE CITY FILM SOUNDTRACK	6	2008
SEX AND TRAVEL RIGHT SAID FRED	35	1993
SEX MACHINE – THE VERY BEST OF JAMES BROWN JAMES BROWN	19	1991
SEX PACKETS DIGITAL UNDERGROUND	59	1990
SEX SWEAT AND BLOOD VARIOUS ARTISTS (BEGGARS BANQUET)	88	1982
SEX, CHIPS & ROCK 'N' ROLL (TELEVISION SOUNDTRACK) TELEVISION AND RADIO COMPILATION	12	1999
SEXTET A CERTAIN RATIO	53	1982
SEXUAL HEALING VARIOUS ARTISTS (EMI)	7	1991
SEXY CRAZY COOL VARIOUS ARTISTS (UNIVERSAL)	5	2002
SGT PEPPER'S LONELY HEARTS CLUB BAND BEATLES	1	1967
SGT. PEPPER'S LONELY HEARTS CLUB BAND FILM SOUNDTRACK	38	1978
A SHADE OF RED REDHEAD KINGPIN & THE F.B.I.	35	1989
SHADES J.J. CALE	44	1981
SHADES SHADES OF RHYTHM	51	1991
SHADES OF GREEN FOSTER & ALLEN	55	1997
SHADES OF ROCK SHADOWS	30	1970
SHADES OF SOUL VARIOUS ARTISTS (GLOBAL TELEVISION)	9	1996
SHADOW DANCING ANDY GIBB	15	1978
SHADOW MUSIC SHADOWS	5	1966
SHADOW OF YOUR SMILE ANDY WILLIAMS	24	1966
THE SHADOWS SHADOWS	1	1961
SHADOWS 20 GOLDEN GREATS SHADOWS	1	1977
SHADOWS AND LIGHT JONI MITCHELL	63	1980
SHADOWS AND LIGHT WILSON PHILLIPS	6	1992
SHADOWS COLLIDE WITH PEOPLE JOHN FRUSCIANTE	53	2004
THE SHADOWS' GREATEST HITS SHADOWS	2	1963
SHADOWS IN THE NIGHT – 16 CLASSIC TRACKS SHADOWS	22	1993
SHADOWS ON THE WALL GORDON HASKELL	44	2002
SHAFT ISAAC HAYES	17	1971
SHAKA ZULU LADYSMITH BLACK MAMBAZO	34	1987
SHAKE RATTLE & ROLL VARIOUS ARTISTS (SANCTUARY)	13	2005
SHAKE YOU DOWN GREGORY ABBOTT	53	1987
SHAKE YOUR MONEY MAKER BLACK CROWES	36	1991
SHAKEN AND STIRRED DAVID ARNOLD	11	1997
SHAKEN 'N' STIRRED ROBERT PLANT	19	1985
SHAKESPEARE ALABAMA DIESEL PARK WEST	55	1989
SHAKIN' STEVENS SHAKIN' STEVENS	34	1981
SHAKIN' STEVENS GREATEST HITS SHAKIN' STEVENS	8	1984
SHAKING THE TREE – GOLDEN GREATS PETER GABRIEL	11	1990
SHAKY SHAKIN' STEVENS	1	1981
SHAMAN SANTANA	15	2002
SHAME BRAD	72	1993
SHAME AND SIN ROBERT CRAY BAND	48	1993
THE SHAMEN COLLECTION SHAMEN	26	1998
SHAMROCK DIARIES CHRIS REA	15	1985
SHAMROCKS AND SHENANIGANS VARIOUS ARTISTS (WARNER BROTHERS)	10	2003
SHANGO SANTANA	35	1982
SHANGRI-LA ANIMAL NIGHTLIFE	36	1985
SHANGRI-LA MARK KNOPFLER	11	2004
SHAPE UP AND DANCE FEATURING ANGELA RIPPON (VOLUME II) ANGELA RIPPON	8	1982
SHAPE UP AND DANCE WITH FELICITY KENDAL (VOLUME ONE) FELICITY KENDAL	29	1982
SHAPE UP AND DANCE WITH SUZANNE DANDO SUZANNE DANDO	87	1984
SHAPES DOMINIC MILLER	38	2003
SHAPESHIFTERS PRESENTS HOUSE GROOVES VARIOUS ARTISTS (VIRGIN)	13	2004
SHARE MY WORLD MARY J. BLIGE	8	1997
SHARK TALE FILM SOUNDTRACK	18	2004
SHARPE – OVER THE HILLS & FAR AWAY VARIOUS ARTISTS (VIRGIN)	14	1996
SHATTERPROOF IS NOT A CHALLENGE HUNDRED REASONS	20	2004
SHAVED FISH JOHN LENNON	8	1975
SHAVING PEACHES TERRORVISION	34	1998
SHAYNE WARD SHAYNE WARD	1	2006
SHE HARRY CONNICK JR.	21	1994
SHE WAS ONLY A GROCER'S DAUGHTER BLOW MONKEYS	20	1987
SHE WEARS MY RING SOLOMON KING	40	1968

Title / Artist	Peak Position	Year of Release
SHE WORKS HARD FOR THE MONEY DONNA SUMMER	28	1983
SHEER GREED GIRL	33	1980
SHEER HEART ATTACK QUEEN	2	1974
SHEER MAGIC MR ACKER BILK	5	1977
SHEET MUSIC 10 C.C.	9	1974
SHEIK YERBOUTI FRANK ZAPPA	32	1979
SHELTER LONE JUSTICE	84	1986
SHELTER BRAND NEW HEAVIES	5	1997
SHENANIGANS GREEN DAY	32	2002
SHEPHERD MOONS ENYA	1	1991
THE SHEPHERD'S DOG IRON AND WINE	74	2007
SHER-OO CILLA BLACK	7	1968
SHERRICK SHERRICK	27	1987
SHERRY FOUR SEASONS	20	1963
SHERYL CROW SHERYL CROW	5	1996
SHE'S A LADY TOM JONES	9	1971
SHE'S JUST AN OLD LOVE TURNED MEMORY CHARLEY PRIDE	34	1977
SHE'S SO UNUSUAL CYNDI LAUPER	16	1984
SHE'S THE BOSS MICK JAGGER	6	1985
SHE'S THE ONE (OST) TOM PETTY & HEARTBREAKERS	37	1996
SHIFT-WORK FALL	17	1991
SHINE AVERAGE WHITE BAND	14	1980
SHINE FRIDA	67	1984
SHINE DAVID HIRSCHFELDER	46	1997
SHINE MARY BLACK	33	1997
SHINE BOND	26	2002
SHINE JONI MITCHELL	36	2007
SHINE ESTELLE	6	2008
SHINE 10 VARIOUS ARTISTS (POLYGRAM)	10	1998
SHINE 2 VARIOUS ARTISTS (POLYGRAM)	3	1996
SHINE 3 VARIOUS ARTISTS (POLYGRAM)	13	1995
SHINE 5 VARIOUS ARTISTS (POLYGRAM)	2	1996
SHINE 6 VARIOUS ARTISTS (POLYGRAM)	2	1996
SHINE 7 VARIOUS ARTISTS (POLYGRAM)	13	1996
SHINE 8 VARIOUS ARTISTS (POLYGRAM)	6	1997
SHINE 9 VARIOUS ARTISTS (POLYGRAM)	7	1997
SHINE A LIGHT (OST) ROLLING STONES	2	2008
SHINE – BEST OF 97 VARIOUS ARTISTS (POLYGRAM)	20	1998
SHINE ON JET	13	2006
SHINE TOO VARIOUS ARTISTS (POLYGRAM)	4	1995
SHINE: 20 BRILLIANT INDIE HITS VARIOUS ARTISTS (POLYGRAM)	4	1995
SHIP ARRIVING TOO LATE TO SAVE A DROWNING WITCH FRANK ZAPPA	61	1982
SHIRLEY SHIRLEY BASSEY	9	1961
SHIRLEY BASSEY SHIRLEY BASSEY	14	1962
SHIRLEY BASSEY AT THE PIGALLE SHIRLEY BASSEY	15	1965
THE SHIRLEY BASSEY COLLECTION SHIRLEY BASSEY	37	1972
THE SHIRLEY BASSEY SINGLES ALBUM SHIRLEY BASSEY	2	1975
SHIRLEY BASSEY SINGS ANDREW LLOYD WEBBER SHIRLEY BASSEY	34	1993
SHIRLEY BASSEY SINGS THE MOVIES SHIRLEY BASSEY	24	1995
SHOGUN TRIVIUM	17	2008
SHOOT FROM THE HIP SOPHIE ELLIS BEXTOR	19	2003
SHOOT THE BOSS MONKEY MAFIA	69	1998
SHOOT THE MOON JUDIE TZUKE	19	1982
SHOOTENANNY EELS	35	2003
SHOOTING RUBBERBANDS AT THE STARS EDIE BRICKELL & THE NEW BOHEMIANS	25	1989
SHOOTING STAR ELKIE BROOKS	20	1978
SHOOTING STARS DOLLAR	36	1979
SHOPPING BAG PARTRIDGE FAMILY	28	1972
A SHORT ALBUM ABOUT LOVE DIVINE COMEDY	13	1997
SHORT BACK 'N' SIDES IAN HUNTER	79	1981
SHORT SHARP SHOCKED MICHELLE SHOCKED	33	1988
SHORT STORIES JON & VANGELIS	4	1980
SHOT OF LOVE BOB DYLAN	6	1981
SHOT TO HELL BLACK LABEL SOCIETY	69	2006
SHOTTER'S NATION BABYSHAMBLES	5	2007
SHOULD THE WORLD FAIL TO FALL APART PETER MURPHY	82	1986
THE SHOUTING STAGE JOAN ARMATRADING	28	1988
SHOVE IT CROSS	58	1988
SHOW ME LOVE ROBIN S	34	1993
THE SHOW MUST GO ON SHIRLEY BASSEY	47	1996
A SHOW OF HANDS RUSH	12	1989
SHOW PEOPLE MARI WILSON	24	1983
SHOW SOME EMOTION JOAN ARMATRADING	6	1977
THE SHOW THE AFTER-PARTY THE HOTEL JODECI	4	1995
SHOW YOUR BONES YEAH YEAH YEAHS	7	2006
SHOWADDYWADDY SHOWADDYWADDY	9	1974
SHOWBIZ CURE	29	1993
SHOWBIZ CUD	46	1994
SHOWBIZ MUSE	29	1999
SHOWBIZ KIDS – THE STEELY DAN STORY STEELY DAN	53	2005
SHOWBOAT (ORIGINAL STUDIO CAST RECORDING) STAGE CAST RECORDING	12	1960
SHOWDOWN ISLEY BROTHERS	50	1978
SHOWGIRL – HOMECOMING LIVE KYLIE MINOGUE	7	2007
SHOWSTOPPERS BARRY MANILOW	53	1991
SHOWTIME GEORGE MITCHELL MINSTRELS	26	1967
SHOWTIME DIZZEE RASCAL	8	2004
SHREK 2 FILM SOUNDTRACK	8	2004
SHUT UP KELLY OSBOURNE	31	2003
SHUT UP AND DANCE PAULA ABDUL	40	1990
SHUT UP AND DANCE VARIOUS ARTISTS (SHUT UP AND DANCE)	20	1992
SHUT UP AND DIE LIKE AN AVIATOR STEVE EARLE & THE DUKES	62	1991
SHUTTERED ROOM FIXX	54	1982
SIAMESE DREAM SMASHING PUMPKINS	4	1993
SID SINGS SID VICIOUS	30	1979
SIEMPRE IL DIVO	2	2006
SIGN 'O' THE TIMES PRINCE	4	1987
SIGN OF THE HAMMER MANOWAR	73	1984
SIGNALS RUSH	3	1982
THE SIGNATURE LP SWAY	51	2008
SIGNIFICANT OTHER LIMP BIZKIT	10	1999
SIGNING OFF UB40	2	1980
SIGNS OF LIFE PENGUIN CAFÉ ORCHESTRA	49	1987
S'IL SUFFISAIT D'AIMER CELINE DION	17	1998
SILENCE IS EASY STARSAILOR	2	2003
SILENT ALARM BLOC PARTY	3	2005
SILENT ALARM REMIXED BLOC PARTY	54	2005
SILENT CRY FEEDER	8	2008
THE SILENT HOURS OPEN	72	2004
SILK AND STEEL FIVE STAR	1	1986
SILK AND STEEL VARIOUS ARTISTS (POLYGRAM)	3	1995
SILK DEGREES BOZ SCAGGS	37	1977
SILK ELECTRIC DIANA ROSS	33	1982
SILKY SOUL MAZE FEATURING FRANKIE BEVERLY	43	1989
SILVER CLIFF RICHARD	7	1983
SILVER MOIST	49	1995
SILVER AND GOLD A.S.A.P	70	1989
SILVER AND GOLD NEIL YOUNG	10	2000
SILVER BIRD LEO SAYER	2	1974
SILVER CONVENTION: GREATEST HITS SILVER CONVENTION	34	1977
SILVER LINING NILS LOFGREN	61	1991
SILVER SIDE UP NICKELBACK	1	2002
SILVER SPOONS & BROKEN BONES STONE GODS	67	2008
SILVER SUN SILVER SUN	30	1997
SILVER TOWN MEN THEY COULDN'T HANG	39	1989
THE SIMON AND GARFUNKEL COLLECTION SIMON & GARFUNKEL	4	1981
SIMON BATES – OUR TUNE VARIOUS ARTISTS (POLYDOR)	58	1986
SIMON BATES – THE VERY BEST OF OUR TUNE VARIOUS ARTISTS (SONY/BMG)	6	2006
SIMON'S WAY SIMON MAY ORCHESTRA	59	1986
SIMPATICO CHARLATANS	10	2006
SIMPLE DREAMS LINDA RONSTADT	15	1977
SIMPLE GIFTS BRYN TERFEL	10	2005
SIMPLE PLAN SIMPLE PLAN	31	2008
SIMPLE PLEASURE TINDERSTICKS	36	1999
SIMPLE PLEASURES BOBBY McFERRIN	92	1988
SIMPLE THINGS ZERO 7	28	2001
SIMPLIFIED SIMPLY RED	3	2005
SIMPLY ACOUSTIC VARIOUS ARTISTS (UNIVERSAL)	5	2002
SIMPLY DEEP KELLY ROWLAND	1	2003
SIMPLY SHADOWS SHADOWS	11	1987
SIMPLY THE BEST TINA TURNER	2	1991
SIMPLY THE BEST VARIOUS ARTISTS (WARNER BROTHERS)	16	2007
SIMPLY THE BEST CLASSIC SOUL VARIOUS ARTISTS (WARNER BROTHERS)	7	1997
SIMPLY THE BEST CLASSICAL ANTHEMS VARIOUS ARTISTS (WARNER BROTHERS)	14	1998
SIMPLY THE BEST DISCO VARIOUS ARTISTS (WARNER BROTHERS)	9	1998
SIMPLY THE BEST LOVE SONGS VARIOUS ARTISTS (WARNER BROTHERS)	2	1997
SIMPLY THE BEST LOVE SONGS 2 VARIOUS ARTISTS (WARNER BROTHERS)	2	1998
SIMPLY THE BEST RADIO HITS VARIOUS ARTISTS (WARNER BROTHERS)	17	1998
SIMPLY THE BEST REGGAE ALBUM VARIOUS ARTISTS (WARNER BROTHERS)	12	2001
SIMPLY...LOVE VARIOUS ARTISTS (COLUMBIA)	3	1991
THE SIMPSONS SING THE BLUES SIMPSONS	6	1991
THE SIMPSONS – SONGS IN THE KEY OF SPRINGFIELD SIMPSONS	18	1998
SIN AFTER SIN JUDAS PRIEST	23	1977
THE SIN OF PRIDE UNDERTONES	43	1983
SINATRA 80TH – ALL THE BEST FRANK SINATRA	49	1995
SINATRA AND COMPANY FRANK SINATRA	9	1971
SINATRA AND STRINGS FRANK SINATRA	6	1962
SINATRA PLUS FRANK SINATRA	7	1961
SINATRA SOUVENIR FRANK SINATRA	18	1961
SINATRA SWINGS FRANK SINATRA	8	1961
SINATRA – THE MAIN EVENT LIVE FRANK SINATRA	30	1975
SINATRA WITH SWINGING BRASS FRANK SINATRA	14	1962
SINATRA-BASIE FRANK SINATRA & COUNT BASIE	2	1963
SINATRA'S SINATRA FRANK SINATRA	9	1963
SINATRA'S SWINGING SESSION!!! AND MORE FRANK SINATRA	6	1961
SINCE I LEFT YOU AVALANCHES	8	2001
SINCE YOU'VE BEEN GONE DAMAGE	16	2001
SINCERE MJ COLE	14	2000
SINCERELY CLIFF RICHARD	24	1969
SING A FAVOURITE SONG DES O'CONNOR	25	1972
SING ALONG WITH MAX MAX BYGRAVES	4	1972
SING ALONG WITH MAX VOLUME 2 MAX BYGRAVES	11	1972
SING BROTHER SING EDGAR BROUGHTON BAND	18	1970

Title / Artist	Peak Position	Year of Release
SING IT AGAIN ROD ROD STEWART	1	1973
SING LOFTY DON ESTELLE & WINDSOR DAVIES	10	1976
SING SOMETHING SIMPLE CLIFF ADAMS SINGERS	15	1960
SING SOMETHING SIMPLE '76 CLIFF ADAMS SINGERS	23	1976
SING THE IRVING BERLIN SONGBOOK GEORGE MITCHELL MINSTRELS	33	1968
SING THE NUMBER 1'S FOSTER & ALLEN	30	2005
SING THE SIXTIES FOSTER & ALLEN	31	2004
SING THE SORROW AFI	52	2003
SING WHEN YOU'RE WINNING ROBBIE WILLIAMS	1	2000
SINGALONGAMAX VOLUME 3 MAX BYGRAVES	5	1973
SINGALONGAMAX VOLUME 4 MAX BYGRAVES	7	1973
SINGALONGAWARYEARS MAX BYGRAVES	5	1989
SINGALONGAWARYEARS VOLUME 2 MAX BYGRAVES	33	1989
SINGALONGPARTY SONG MAX BYGRAVES	15	1973
SINGALONGXMAS MAX BYGRAVES	21	1974
THE SINGER LIZA MINNELLI	45	1973
SINGER VARIOUS ARTISTS (SONY BMG)	10	2008
SINGER AND THE SONG LABI SIFFRE	47	1971
THE SINGER AND THE SONG VARIOUS ARTISTS (STYLUS)	5	1989
THE SINGER AND THE SONG VARIOUS ARTISTS (VIRGIN)	5	1993
SINGIN' WITH THE BIG BANDS BARRY MANILOW	54	1994
SINGING TO MY BABY EDDIE COCHRAN	19	1960
THE SINGLE FACTOR CAMEL	57	1982
SINGLE LIFE CAMEO	66	1985
A SINGLE MAN ELTON JOHN	8	1978
THE SINGLES ROY WOOD	37	1982
THE SINGLES PRETENDERS	6	1987
SINGLES ALISON MOYET	1	1995
SINGLES SMITHS	5	1995
THE SINGLES INSPIRAL CARPETS	17	1995
THE SINGLES BLUETONES	14	2002
SINGLES SUEDE	31	2003
SINGLES TRAVIS	4	2004
SINGLES NEW ORDER	14	2005
THE SINGLES BASEMENT JAXX	1	2005
SINGLES DEACON BLUE	18	2006
THE SINGLES FEEDER	2	2006
THE SINGLES CLASH	13	2007
THE SINGLES DARYL HALL & JOHN OATES	29	2008
THE SINGLES 1969-1973 CARPENTERS	1	1974
THE SINGLES 1974-1978 CARPENTERS	2	1978
THE SINGLES 1992 – 2003 NO DOUBT	5	2003
SINGLES – 45'S AND UNDER SQUEEZE	3	1982
THE SINGLES 81-85 DEPECHE MODE	6	1985
THE SINGLES 81-85 DEPECHE MODE	6	1998
THE SINGLES 86-98 DEPECHE MODE	5	1998
SINGLES 93-03 CHEMICAL BROTHERS	9	2003
THE SINGLES ALBUM UB40	17	1982
THE SINGLES ALBUM JIMI HENDRIX	77	1983
THE SINGLES ALBUM SOFT CELL	58	1986
THE SINGLES ALBUM GLADYS KNIGHT & THE PIPS	12	1989
THE SINGLES COLLECTION SPANDAU BALLET	3	1985
THE SINGLES COLLECTION KOOL & THE GANG	28	1988
THE SINGLES COLLECTION CLASH	68	1991
THE SINGLES COLLECTION FOUR TOPS	11	1992
THE SINGLES COLLECTION CONNIE FRANCIS	12	1993
THE SINGLES COLLECTION DAVID BOWIE	9	1993
SINGLES COLLECTION CORAL	13	2008
THE SINGLES COLLECTION 1981-1993 KIM WILDE	11	1993
A SINGLES COLLECTION 1982-1992 MARILLION	27	1992
THE SINGLES COLLECTION 1984/1990 JIMMY SOMERVILLE	4	1990
SINGLES OF THE 90S ACE OF BASE	62	1999
THE SINGLES – THE FIRST TEN YEARS ABBA	1	1982
THE SINGLES – THE UA YEARS STRANGLERS	57	1989
SINGS GREATEST PALACE MUSIC BONNIE PRINCE BILLY	63	2004
SINGS THE HITS OF WET WET WET & SMILE MARTI PELLOW	34	2002
SINGS THE PEGGY LEE SONGBOOK BETTE MIDLER	41	2006
THE SINGULAR ADVENTURES OF THE STYLE COUNCIL GREATEST HITS VOLUME 1 STYLE COUNCIL	3	1989
SINITTA! SINITTA	34	1987
SINNER DROWNING POOL	70	2002
SIOGO BLACKFOOT	28	1983
SIREN ROXY	4	1975
SIREN HEATHER NOVA	55	1998
SIRIUS CLANNAD	34	1987
SISTER ACT FILM SOUNDTRACK	14	1993
SISTERS BLUEBELLS	22	1984
SISTERS ARE DOIN' IT VARIOUS ARTISTS (TOWERBELL)	27	1986
SISTERS OF AVALON CYNDI LAUPER	59	1997
SISTERS OF SWING VARIOUS ARTISTS (POLYGRAM)	1	1996
SISTERS OF SWING 2 VARIOUS ARTISTS (POLYGRAM)	4	1996
SISTERS OF SWING 98 VARIOUS ARTISTS (POLYGRAM)	5	1998
SISTERS OF SWING 99 VARIOUS ARTISTS (UNIVERSAL)	9	1999
SISTERS OF SWING III VARIOUS ARTISTS (POLYGRAM)	7	1997
SITTIN' ON TOP OF THE WORLD LEANN RIMES	11	1998
SITUATION: CRITICAL ULTRA NATE	17	1998
SIX MANSUN	6	1998
SIX WHEELS ON MY WAGON FLUKE	41	1993
THE SIX WIVES OF HENRY VIII RICK WAKEMAN	7	1973
SIXPENCE NONE THE RICHER SIXPENCE NONE THE RICHER	27	1999
16 DIFFERENT FLAVOURS OF HELL POP WILL EAT ITSELF	73	1993
16 HITS FROM 'STARS AND GARTERS' KATHY KIRBY	11	1964
16 LOVER'S LANE GO-BETWEENS	81	1988
16 ORIGINAL BIG HITS – VOLUME 4 VARIOUS ARTISTS (MOTOWN)	33	1967
SIXTEEN STONE BUSH	42	1996
THE SIXTIES VARIOUS ARTISTS (VIRGIN)	16	1999
THE SIXTIES ALBUM VARIOUS ARTISTS (SANCTUARY)	9	2004
SIXTIES BEAT VARIOUS ARTISTS (DINO)	1	1992
SIXTIES MANIA VARIOUS ARTISTS (TELSTAR)	19	1986
SIXTIES MIX 2 VARIOUS ARTISTS (STYLUS)	14	1988
SIXTIES MIX 3 VARIOUS ARTISTS (STYLUS)	4	1990
SIXTIES MIX – 60 SEQUENCED HITS FROM THE SIXTIES VARIOUS ARTISTS (STYLUS)	3	1987
SIXTIES PARTY MEGAMIX ALBUM VARIOUS ARTISTS (TELSTAR)	46	1987
SIXTIES POWER BALLADS VARIOUS ARTISTS (EMI)	10	2007
60'S SOUL MIX VARIOUS ARTISTS (UNIVERSAL)	3	2003
60'S SOUL MIX 2 VARIOUS ARTISTS (UNIVERSAL)	14	2004
60'S SOUL 90'S SOUL VARIOUS ARTISTS (PARLOPHONE)	6	1994
SIXTIES SUMMER LOVE VARIOUS ARTISTS (UNIVERSAL)	16	1999
SIXTIES SUMMER MIX VARIOUS ARTISTS (TELSTAR)	5	1997
SIXTIES SUMMER MIX 2 VARIOUS ARTISTS (TELSTAR)	19	1998
64-'95 LEMON JELLY	17	2005
60 NUMBER ONES OF THE SIXTIES VARIOUS ARTISTS (TELSTAR)	7	1990
60 NUMBER ONE'S OF THE 60'S VARIOUS ARTISTS (WARNER BROTHERS)	13	2000
SIXTY SIX TO TIMBUKTU ROBERT PLANT	27	2003
SIZE ISN'T EVERYTHING BEE GEES	23	1993
SK8ER ROCK VARIOUS ARTISTS (BMG)	8	2003
SKA MANIA VARIOUS ARTISTS (DINO)	4	1995
SKA 'N' B BAD MANNERS	34	1980
SKATE TO HELL VARIOUS ARTISTS (WARNER BROTHERS)	20	2003
SKELLERN PETER SKELLERN	48	1978
SKETCHES FOR MY SWEETHEART THE DRUNK JEFF BUCKLEY	7	1998
SKID SKID ROW	30	1970
SKID ROW SKID ROW	30	1989
SKIDIP EEK-A-MOUSE	61	1982
THE SKIFFLE SESSIONS – LIVE IN BELFAST VAN MORRISON/LONNIE DONEGAN/CHRIS BARBER	14	2000
SKIN SKIN	9	1994
SKIN AND BONES FOO FIGHTERS	35	2006
SKIN 'EM UP SHAKIN' PYRAMIDS	48	1981
SKIN MECHANIC GARY NUMAN	55	1989
SKINBEAT – THE FIRST TOUCH VARIOUS ARTISTS (POLYDOR)	6	1990
SKULL & BONES CYPRESS HILL	6	2000
SKUNKWORTHS BRUCE DICKINSON	41	1996
SKY SKY	9	1979
SKY 2 SKY	1	1980
SKY 3 SKY	3	1981
SKY 4 – FORTHCOMING SKY	7	1982
SKY BLUE SKY WILCO	39	2007
SKY FIVE LIVE SKY	14	1983
SKY HIGH TAVARES	22	1976
THE SKY IS TOO HIGH GRAHAM COXON	31	1998
SKYBOUND TOM BAXTER	12	2008
SKYDIVIN' DARREN STYLES	4	2008
SKYE BOAT SONG AND OTHER GREAT SONGS OF OUR ISLANDS ROGER WHITTAKER	89	1986
SKYLARKING XTC	90	1986
SKYNYRD'S FIRST AND LAST LYNYRD SKYNYRD	50	1978
THE SKY'S GONE OUT BAUHAUS	4	1982
SKYSCRAPER DAVID LEE ROTH	11	1988
SLADE ALIVE! SLADE	2	1972
SLADE IN FLAME (OST) SLADE	6	1974
SLADE ON STAGE SLADE	58	1982
SLADE SMASHES SLADE	21	1980
SLADE'S GREATZ SLADE	89	1984
SLADEST SLADE	1	1973
SLAIN BY URUSEI YATSURA	64	1998
SLAM DAN REED NETWORK	66	1989
SLAMMIN' VARIOUS ARTISTS (A&M)	1	1990
SLAMMIN' VINYL PRESENTS HARDCORE HEAVEN 2 VARIOUS ARTISTS (RESIST)	15	2005
SLANG DEF LEPPARD	5	1996
SLANTED AND ENCHANTED PAVEMENT	72	1992
SLAUGHTER ON TENTH AVENUE MICK RONSON	9	1974
SLAVE TO LOVE BRYAN FERRY	11	2000
SLAVE TO THE GRIND SKID ROW	5	1991
SLAVE TO THE RHYTHM GRACE JONES	12	1985
SLAVES AND MASTERS DEEP PURPLE	45	1990
SLAYED? SLADE	1	1972

Title / Artist	Peak Position	Year of Release
SLEEP NO MORE COMSAT ANGELS	51	1981
SLEEP THROUGH THE STATIC JACK JOHNSON	1	2008
SLEEPING IN THE NOTHING KELLY OSBOURNE	57	2005
SLEEPING WITH GHOSTS PLACEBO	11	2003
SLEEPING WITH THE PAST ELTON JOHN	1	1989
SLEEPLESS IN SEATTLE FILM SOUNDTRACK	10	1993
SLEEPLESS NIGHTS LINDISFARNE	59	1982
SLEEPOVER VARIOUS ARTISTS (SONY)	16	2004
SLEEPS WITH ANGELS NEIL YOUNG & CRAZY HORSE	2	1994
SLEEPWALKING GERRY RAFFERTY	39	1982
SLEEPWALKING MAGNUM	27	1992
SLEEPWALKING KINGMAKER	15	1993
SLEEPWALKING RAE & CHRISTIAN	57	2001
SLEEPY EYED BUFFALO TOM	31	1995
SLEIGHT OF HAND JOAN ARMATRADING	34	1986
SLICKER THAN YOUR AVERAGE CRAIG DAVID	4	2002
THE SLIDE AREA RY COODER	18	1982
SLIDE IT IN WHITESNAKE	9	1984
THE SLIDER T. REX	4	1972
SLIK SLIK	58	1976
SLIM SHADY EMINEM	10	1999
SLIM WHITMAN'S 20 GREATEST LOVE SONGS SLIM WHITMAN	18	1979
SLIME & REASON ROOTS MANUVA	22	2008
SLINKY MILLTOWN BROTHERS	27	1991
SLINKY FACTOR 3 VARIOUS ARTISTS (BEECHWOOD)	20	2000
SLINKY PRESENTS SUPERCLUB DJ'S – GUY ORNADEL VARIOUS ARTISTS (SLINKY MUSIC)	17	2001
SLINKY – TECH-NIQUE VARIOUS ARTISTS (BEECHWOOD)	10	2000
SLIP NINE INCH NAILS	25	2008
SLIP OF THE TONGUE WHITESNAKE	10	1989
SLIP STREAM VARIOUS ARTISTS (BEGGARS BANQUET)	72	1981
SLIPKNOT SLIPKNOT	37	1999
SLIPPERY WHEN WET BON JOVI	6	1986
SLIPSTREAM SUTHERLAND BROTHERS & QUIVER	49	1976
SLIPWAY FIRES RAZORLIGHT	4	2008
SLIVER FILM SOUNDTRACK	20	1993
SLIVER – THE BEST OF THE BOX NIRVANA	56	2005
SLOE GIN JOE BONAMASSA	50	2007
SLOW JAMS VARIOUS ARTISTS (PUMP)	10	1997
SLOW JAMZ VARIOUS ARTISTS (SONY/BMG)	4	2005
SLOW TRAIN COMING BOB DYLAN	2	1979
SLOWHAND ERIC CLAPTON	23	1977
SMALL CORNERS CLIFF RICHARD	33	1978
SMALL FACES SMALL FACES	3	1966
THE SMALL PRICE OF A BICYCLE ICICLE WORKS	55	1985
SMALL WORLD HUEY LEWIS & THE NEWS	12	1988
SMALL WORLD BIG BAND JOOLS HOLLAND	8	2001
SMALLCREEP'S DAY MIKE RUTHERFORD	13	1980
SMART SLEEPER	5	1995
SMART CASUAL KIDS IN GLASS HOUSES	29	2008
SMASH OFFSPRING	21	1995
SMASH HITS PARTY '88 VARIOUS ARTISTS (DOVER)	6	1988
SMASH HITS PARTY '89 – 30 SMASH HITS VARIOUS ARTISTS (DOVER)	1	1989
SMASH HITS JIMI HENDRIX EXPERIENCE	4	1968
SMASH HITS 1990 VARIOUS ARTISTS (DOVER)	2	1990
SMASH HITS 1991 VARIOUS ARTISTS (DOVER)	3	1991
SMASH HITS 2000 VARIOUS ARTISTS (VIRGIN)	8	1999
SMASH HITS 2001 VARIOUS ARTISTS (VIRGIN)	20	2000
SMASH HITS 2002 VARIOUS ARTISTS (EMI)	5	2001
SMASH HITS 2003 VARIOUS ARTISTS (EMI)	20	2003
SMASH HITS '71 ANONYMOUS COVER VERSIONS	21	1971
SMASH HITS '92 – 40 BIG HITS! SORTED! VARIOUS ARTISTS (DOVER)	5	1992
SMASH HITS '93 – 40 TOP CHARTIN' GROOVES VARIOUS ARTISTS (CHRYSALIS)	4	1993
SMASH HITS '94 VARIOUS ARTISTS (TELSTAR)	9	1994
SMASH HITS '95 – VOLUME 1 VARIOUS ARTISTS (TELSTAR)	1	1995
SMASH HITS '95 – VOLUME 2 VARIOUS ARTISTS (TELSTAR)	4	1995
SMASH HITS '98 VARIOUS ARTISTS (VIRGIN)	9	1997
SMASH HITS '99! VARIOUS ARTISTS (VIRGIN)	10	1998
SMASH HITS CHART SUMMER 2003 VARIOUS ARTISTS (VIRGIN)	5	2003
SMASH HITS COUNTRY STYLE ANONYMOUS COVER VERSIONS	38	1971
SMASH HITS – LET'S PARTY VARIOUS ARTISTS (EMI)	1	2002
SMASH HITS – LET'S PARTY ON VARIOUS ARTISTS (EMI)	8	2003
SMASH HITS – MASSIVE! VARIOUS ARTISTS (DOVER)	1	1991
SMASH HITS MIX '97 VARIOUS ARTISTS (VIRGIN)	8	1996
SMASH HITS – PARTY ON! VARIOUS ARTISTS (HIT LABEL)	9	1992
SMASH HITS – RAVE! VARIOUS ARTISTS (DOVER)	1	1990
SMASH HITS SUMMER 2000 VARIOUS ARTISTS (VIRGIN)	3	2000
SMASH HITS SUMMER 2001 VARIOUS ARTISTS (EMI)	2	2001
SMASH HITS SUMMER 2002 VARIOUS ARTISTS (VIRGIN)	1	2002
SMASH HITS – SUMMER '97 VARIOUS ARTISTS (VIRGIN)	1	1997
SMASH HITS – SUMMER '98 VARIOUS ARTISTS (VIRGIN)	2	1998
SMASH HITS – SUMMER '99 VARIOUS ARTISTS (VIRGIN)	3	1999
SMASH HITS SUPREMES STYLE ANONYMOUS COVER VERSIONS	36	1971
SMASH HITS – THE 80S VARIOUS ARTISTS (WARNER BROTHERS)	5	2008
SMASH HITS – THE REUNION VARIOUS ARTISTS (VIRGIN)	4	2003
SMASHES, THRASHES AND HITS KISS	62	1988
SMASHIE AND NICEY PRESENT LET'S ROCK! VARIOUS ARTISTS (EMI)	8	1992
SMELL OF FEMALE CRAMPS	74	1983
SMILE NEIL REID	47	1972
SMILE JAYHAWKS	60	2000
SMILE MARTI PELLOW	7	2001
SMILE CHARLIE LANDSBOROUGH	37	2003
SMILE BRIAN WILSON	7	2004
SMILE IT CONFUSES PEOPLE SANDI THOM	1	2006
SMILE JAMAICA VARIOUS ARTISTS (TELSTAR)	20	1998
SMILER ROD STEWART	1	1974
SMILEY SMILE BEACH BOYS	9	1967
THE SMITHS SMITHS	2	1984
SMOKE AND STRONG WHISKEY CHRISTY MOORE	49	1991
SMOKIN' HUMBLE PIE	28	1972
SMOOTH CLASSICS – DO NOT DISTURB VARIOUS ARTISTS (CLASSIC FM)	10	2003
SMOOTH JAZZ 2 VARIOUS ARTISTS (UNIVERSAL)	8	2003
SMOOTH SUMMER SOUL VARIOUS ARTISTS (SONY/BMG)	13	2005
SMOOVE PRESENTS STREET BEATS VARIOUS ARTISTS (MINISTRY OF SOUND)	16	2003
SMURF'S CHRISTMAS PARTY SMURFS	8	1996
THE SMURFS GO POP! SMURFS	2	1996
THE SMURFS HITS '97 – VOLUME 1 SMURFS	2	1997
SNAFU EAST OF EDEN	29	1970
THE SNAKE SHANE MacGOWAN & THE POPES	37	1994
SNAKES & ARROWS RUSH	13	2007
SNAKES AND LADDERS GERRY RAFFERTY	15	1980
SNAP JAM	2	1983
SNAP CRACKLE AND BOP JOHN COOPER CLARKE	26	1980
SNAP! JAM	8	2006
SNAP! ATTACK – THE BEST OF SNAP!/SNAP! ATTACK – THE REMIXES SNAP!	47	1996
SNAP! IT UP – MONSTER HITS 2 VARIOUS ARTISTS (CBS)	2	1990
SNATCH FILM SOUNDTRACK	11	2000
SNEAKIN' SUSPICION DR. FEELGOOD	10	1977
SNIVILISATION ORBITAL	4	1994
THE SNOW GOOSE CAMEL	22	1975
THE SNOW GOOSE SPIKE MILLIGAN WITH THE LONDON SYMPHONY ORCHESTRA	49	1976
SNOWFLAKE MIDNIGHT MERCURY REV	52	2008
SNOWFLAKES ARE DANCING TOMITA	17	1975
THE SNOWMAN HOWARD BLAKE CONDUCTING THE SINFONIA OF LONDON	54	1984
SNOWY WHITE SNOWY WHITE	88	1985
SO PETER GABRIEL	1	1986
SO AMAZIN' CHRISTINA MILIAN	67	2006
SO AMAZING DIONNE WARWICK	60	1983
SO CALLED CHAOS ALANIS MORISSETTE	8	2004
SO CLOSE DINA CARROLL	2	1993
SO FAR CROSBY, STILL, NASH & YOUNG	25	1974
SO FAR ALEX REECE	19	1996
SO FAR AWAY CHORDS	30	1980
SO FAR SO GOOD BRYAN ADAMS	1	1993
SO FAR, SO GOOD...SO WHAT! MEGADETH	18	1988
SO FAR...THE BEST OF SINEAD O'CONNOR SINEAD O'CONNOR	28	1997
SO GOOD MICA PARIS	6	1988
SO LUCKY ROSE MARIE	62	1986
SO MANY RIVERS BOBBY WOMACK	28	1985
SO MUCH FOR THE AFTERGLOW EVERCLEAR	63	1998
SO MUCH FOR THE CITY THRILLS	3	2003
SO NATURAL LISA STANSFIELD	6	1993
SO REAL – SONGS FROM JEFF BUCKLEY JEFF BUCKLEY	16	2007
SO RED THE ROSE ARCADIA	30	1985
SO SOLID CREW – FUCK IT VARIOUS ARTISTS (RELENTLESS)	3	2002
SO THIS IS GREAT BRITAIN HOLLOWAYS	54	2006
SO TONIGHT THAT I MIGHT SEE MAZZY STAR	68	1993
SO TOUGH SAINT ETIENNE	7	1993
SO WHERE ARE YOU? LOOSE ENDS	13	1985
SOAPSTAR SUPERSTAR 2007 VARIOUS ARTISTS (SONY/BMG)	8	2007
SOAPSTAR SUPERSTAR – THE ALBUM VARIOUS ARTISTS (EMI)	5	2006
SOCCER AM PRESENTS THE MUSIC VARIOUS ARTISTS (UNIVERSAL)	13	2006
THE SOFT BULLETIN FLAMING LIPS	39	1999
SOFT METAL VARIOUS ARTISTS (STYLUS)	7	1988
SOFT METAL BALLADS VARIOUS ARTISTS (ARCADE)	5	1991
SOFT REGGAE VARIOUS ARTISTS (GLOBAL TELEVISION)	2	1995
SOFT ROCK VARIOUS ARTISTS (TELSTAR)	15	1989
SOFT ROCK VARIOUS ARTISTS (POLYGRAM)	3	1996
SOFT ROCK ANTHEMS VARIOUS ARTISTS (SONY)	2	2005
SOFTLY AS I LEAVE YOU FRANK SINATRA	20	1965
SOFTLY WITH THESE SONGS – THE BEST OF ROBERTA FLACK ROBERTA FLACK	7	1994
SOGNO ANDREA BOCELLI	4	1999
SOIL FESTIVITIES VANGELIS	55	1984

Title / Artist	Peak Position	Year of Release
THE SOLAR SYSTEM VARIOUS ARTISTS (SOLAR)	70	1987
SOLARIZED IAN BROWN	7	2004
SOLD BOY GEORGE	29	1987
SOLDIER IGGY POP	62	1980
SOLDIER OF FORTUNE – THE BEST OF PHIL LYNOTT AND THIN LIZZY PHIL LYNOTT & THIN LIZZY	55	1987
SOLID GROUNDHOGS	31	1974
SOLID ASHFORD & SIMPSON	42	1985
SOLID BOND GRAHAM BOND	40	1970
SOLID BRONZE – GREAT HITS BEAUTIFUL SOUTH	10	2001
SOLID GOLD T. REX	51	1979
SOLID GOLD GANG OF FOUR	52	1981
SOLID GOLD HITS BEASTIE BOYS	71	2005
SOLID GOLD SOUL VARIOUS ARTISTS (ATLANTIC)	12	1966
SOLID GROUND RONNIE LAWS	100	1981
SOLID LOVE ROMEO	46	2002
SOLID ROCK TEMPTATIONS	34	1972
SOLID SENDERS SOLID SENDERS	42	1978
SOLID SOUL SENSATIONS VARIOUS ARTISTS (DISCO DEMAND)	30	1975
SOLITAIRE ANDY WILLIAMS	3	1973
SOLITUDE STANDING SUZANNE VEGA	2	1987
SOLITUDE/SOLITAIRE PETER CETERA	56	1986
SOLO FREDDIE MERCURY	13	2000
SOLO CONCERT BILLY CONNOLLY	8	1974
SOLO IN SOHO PHIL LYNOTT	28	1980
THE SOME BIZZARE ALBUM VARIOUS ARTISTS (SOME BIZZARE)	9	1981
SOME CITIES DOVES	1	2005
SOME DAY SOON KRISTIAN LEONTIOU	14	2004
SOME ENCHANTED EVENING BLUE OYSTER CULT	18	1978
SOME ENCHANTED EVENING BRYN TERFEL	49	2001
SOME FANTASTIC PLACE SQUEEZE	26	1993
SOME FRIENDLY CHARLATANS	1	1990
SOME GAVE ALL BILLY RAY CYRUS	9	1992
SOME GIRLS ROLLING STONES	2	1978
SOME GIRLS WANDER BY MISTAKE SISTERS OF MERCY	5	1992
SOME GREAT REWARD DEPECHE MODE	5	1984
SOME GUYS HAVE ALL THE LUCK ROD STEWART	19	2008
SOME LOUD THUNDER CLAP YOUR HANDS SAY YEAH	45	2007
SOME MORE OF ME POEMS AND SONGS PAM AYRES	23	1976
SOME NICE THINGS I'VE MISSED FRANK SINATRA	35	1974
SOME OF ME POEMS AND SONGS PAM AYRES	13	1976
SOME OF MY BEST FRIENDS ARE SONGS VAL DOONICAN	29	1977
SOME OTHER SUCKER'S PARADE DEL AMITRI	6	1997
SOME PEOPLE CAN DO WHAT THEY LIKE ROBERT PALMER	46	1976
SOME PEOPLE'S LIVES BETTE MIDLER	5	1991
SOME PRODUCT – CARRI ON SEX PISTOLS SEX PISTOLS	6	1979
SOME RAINY MORNING ROBERT CRAY	63	1995
SOME THINGS LASGO	30	2002
SOME THINGS NEVER CHANGE SUPERTRAMP	74	1997
SOMEBODY'S WATCHING ME ROCKWELL	52	1984
SOMEONE LOVES YOU HONEY CHARLEY PRIDE	48	1978
SOMEONE TO DRIVE YOU HOME LONG BLONDES	44	2006
SOMETHING SHIRLEY BASSEY	5	1970
SOMETHING ELSE SHIRLEY BASSEY	7	1971
SOMETHING ELSE BY THE KINKS KINKS	35	1967
SOMETHING FOR EVERYBODY ELVIS PRESLEY	2	1961
SOMETHING IN THE AIR VARIOUS ARTISTS (COLUMBIA)	10	1992
SOMETHING OLD, SOMETHING NEW SYD LAWRENCE	34	1972
SOMETHING SPECIAL KOOL & THE GANG	10	1981
SOMETHING SPECIAL – 100 GOLDEN LOVE SONGS FOSTER & ALLEN	46	1996
SOMETHING TO BE ROB THOMAS	11	2005
SOMETHING TO REMEMBER MADONNA	3	1995
SOMETHING UP MY SLEEVE SUZY BOGGUSS	69	1993
SOMETHING WICKED THIS WAY COMES HERBALISER	71	2002
SOMETHING WONDERFUL BRYN TERFEL	72	1996
SOMETHING'S GOIN' ON CLIFF RICHARD	7	2004
SOMETHING'S GOING ON FRIDA	18	1982
SOMETIME IN NEW YORK CITY JOHN AND YOKO LENNON WITH THE PLASTIC ONO BAND & ELEPHANT'S MEMORY	11	1972
SOMETIMES WHEN WE TOUCH CLEO LAINE & JAMES GALWAY	15	1980
SOMETIMES WHEN WE TOUCH VARIOUS ARTISTS (RONCO)	8	1984
SOMETIMES YOU WIN DR. HOOK	14	1979
SOMEWHERE EVA CASSIDY	4	2008
SOMEWHERE BACK IN TIME – THE BEST OF IRON MAIDEN	14	2008
SOMEWHERE ELSE MARILLION	24	2007
SOMEWHERE IN AFRIKA MANFRED MANN'S EARTH BAND	87	1983
SOMEWHERE IN ENGLAND GEORGE HARRISON	13	1981
SOMEWHERE IN TIME IRON MAIDEN	3	1986
SOMEWHERE IN TIME DONNY OSMOND	12	2002
SOMEWHERE MY LOVE RAY CONNIFF	34	1967
SOMEWHERE SOON HIGH	59	1990
SON OF SCHMILSSON NILSSON	41	1972
SONG AND DANCE (TELEVISION SOUNDTRACK) TELEVISION AND RADIO COMPILATION	46	1984
THE SONG AND DANCE MEN MAX BYGRAVES	67	1978
A SONG FOR ALL SEASONS RENAISSANCE	35	1978
A SONG FOR EUROTRASH VARIOUS ARTISTS (EMI)	19	1998
A SONG FOR ME FAMILY	4	1970
A SONG FOR YOU CARPENTERS	13	1972
A SONG FOR YOU JACK JONES	9	1972
SONG OF SEVEN JON ANDERSON	38	1980
THE SONG REMAINS THE SAME (OST) LED ZEPPELIN	1	1976
SONG REVIEW – A GREATEST HITS COLLECTION STEVIE WONDER	19	1996
SONG WITHOUT END FILM SOUNDTRACK	9	1961
SONGBIRD BARBRA STREISAND	50	1978
SONGBIRD RUBY WINTERS	31	1979
SONGBIRD EVA CASSIDY	1	2001
SONGBIRD VARIOUS ARTISTS (UNIVERSAL)	7	2004
SONGBIRD 2008 VARIOUS ARTISTS (UNIVERSAL)	6	2008
SONGBIRD – THE ULTIMATE COLLECTION KENNY G	24	2004
SONGBIRDS VARIOUS ARTISTS (WARNER BROTHERS)	4	2003
SONGBOOK – A LIFETIME OF MUSIC DAVID GATES	11	2002
SONGBOOK – THE SINGLES VOLUME 1 SUPER FURRY ANIMALS	18	2004
SONGS LUTHER VANDROSS	1	1994
THE SONGS VARIOUS ARTISTS (EMI)	7	2007
THE SONGS 1975 – 1990 BARRY MANILOW	13	1990
SONGS ABOUT GIRLS WILL.I.AM	68	2008
SONGS ABOUT JANE MAROON 5	1	2004
A SONG'S BEST FRIEND – THE VERY BEST OF JOHN DENVER	18	2004
SONGS BY TOM LEHRER TOM LEHRER	7	1958
SONGS FOR A TAILOR JACK BRUCE	6	1969
SONGS FOR A WINTER'S NIGHT GEORGE HAMILTON IV	94	1982
SONGS FOR BEGINNERS GRAHAM NASH	13	1971
SONGS FOR DRELLA LOU REED & JOHN CALE	22	1990
SONGS FOR SILVERMAN BEN FOLDS	65	2005
SONGS FOR SWINGIN' LOVERS FRANK SINATRA	1	1956
SONGS FOR SWINGING LOVERS FRANK SINATRA	63	1998
SONGS FOR SWINGING SELLERS PETER SELLERS	3	1959
SONGS FOR THE DEAF QUEENS OF THE STONE AGE	4	2002
SONGS FOR YOU, TRUTHS FOR ME JAMES MORRISON	3	2008
SONGS FROM A ROOM LEONARD COHEN	2	1969
SONGS FROM 'ALLY MCBEAL' VONDA SHEPARD	3	1998
SONGS FROM AN AMERICAN MOVIE VOLUME 1: LEARNING HOW TO SMILE EVERCLEAR	51	2000
SONGS FROM AN AMERICAN MOVIE VOLUME 2: GOOD TIME FOR A BAD ATTITUDE EVERCLEAR	69	2001
SONGS FROM DAWSON'S CREEK (TELEVISION SOUNDTRACK) TELEVISION AND RADIO COMPILATION	3	1999
SONGS FROM DAWSON'S CREEK – VOL 2 (TELEVISION SOUNDTRACK) TELEVISION AND RADIO COMPILATION	5	2000
SONGS FROM 'HEATHCLIFF' CLIFF RICHARD	15	1995
SONGS FROM HER TV SERIES NANA MOUSKOURI	29	1973
SONGS FROM HIS TV SERIES SCOTT WALKER	7	1969
SONGS FROM MY SKETCHBOOK VAL DOONICAN	33	1990
SONGS FROM NORTHERN BRITAIN TEENAGE FANCLUB	3	1997
SONGS FROM STAGE AND SCREEN MICHAEL CRAWFORD & THE LONDON SYMPHONY ORCHESTRA	12	1987
SONGS FROM SUN STREET SAW DOCTORS	24	1998
SONGS FROM THE BIG CHAIR TEARS FOR FEARS	2	1985
SONGS FROM THE CHILLOUT LOUNGE VARIOUS ARTISTS (TELSTAR)	20	2002
SONGS FROM THE FRONT ROW – THE BEST OF OCEAN COLOUR SCENE	16	2001
SONGS FROM THE LABYRINTH STING	24	2006
SONGS FROM THE LAST CENTURY GEORGE MICHAEL	2	1999
SONGS FROM THE MARDI GRAS FEARGAL SHARKEY	27	1991
SONGS FROM THE MIRROR FISH	46	1993
SONGS FROM THE OTHER SIDE CHARLATANS	55	2002
SONGS FROM THE RAIN HOTHOUSE FLOWERS	7	1993
SONGS FROM THE SPARKLE LOUNGE DEF LEPPARD	10	2008
SONGS FROM THE STUDENT PRINCE AND OTHER FAMOUS MELODIES MARIO LANZA	5	1956
SONGS FROM THE WEST COAST ELTON JOHN	2	2001
SONGS FROM THE WOOD JETHRO TULL	13	1977
SONGS FROM WHISTLE DOWN THE WIND VARIOUS ARTISTS (REALLY USEFUL)	3	1998
SONGS IN A MINOR ALICIA KEYS	6	2001

Title / Artist	Peak Position	Year of Release
SONGS IN A&E SPIRITUALIZED	15	2008
SONGS IN THE ATTIC BILLY JOEL	57	1981
SONGS IN THE KEY OF LIFE STEVIE WONDER	2	1976
SONGS IN THE KEY OF X VARIOUS ARTISTS (WARNER BROTHERS)	8	1996
SONGS OF A LIFETIME BING CROSBY	29	1979
THE SONGS OF BOB DYLAN VARIOUS ARTISTS (START)	13	1989
THE SONGS OF DISTANT EARTH MIKE OLDFIELD	24	1994
SONGS OF FAITH AND DEVOTION DEPECHE MODE	1	1993
SONGS OF FREEDOM BOB MARLEY	10	1992
SONGS OF INSPIRATION DANIEL O'DONNELL	11	1996
SONGS OF JOY PESTALOZZI CHILDREN'S CHOIR	65	1981
SONGS OF LEONARD COHEN LEONARD COHEN	13	1968
SONGS OF LOVE RICHARD CLAYDERMAN	19	1987
SONGS OF LOVE PLACIDO DOMINGO	53	2000
SONGS OF LOVE AND HATE LEONARD COHEN	4	1971
SONGS OF LOVE AND LAUGHTER FOSTER & ALLEN	50	2007
SONGS OF MASS DESTRUCTION ANNIE LENNOX	7	2007
SONGS OF OUR HERITAGE DUANE EDDY	13	1960
SONGS OF PRAISE VARIOUS ARTISTS (WARWICK)	31	1977
THE SONGS OF PRAISE ALBUM VARIOUS ARTISTS (UNIVERSAL)	15	2005
SONGS OF SANCTUARY ADIEMUS	35	1995
SONGS OF THE FREE GANG OF FOUR	61	1982
SONGS OF THE SEASHORE JAMES GALWAY	39	1979
SONGS OF THE VALLEYS LONDON WELSH MALE VOICE CHOIR	61	1981
THE SONGS THAT GOT AWAY SARAH BRIGHTMAN	48	1989
SONGS THAT WARM THE HEART VARIOUS ARTISTS (DMG TV)	16	2006
SONGS THAT WON THE WAR VARIOUS ARTISTS (DMG TV)	7	2005
SONGS TO LEARN AND SING ECHO & THE BUNNYMEN	6	1985
SONGS TO MAKE THE WHOLE WORLD SING BARRY MANILOW	20	1989
SONGS TO MAKE YOU FEEL GOOD - - 41 UPLIFTING CLASSICS VARIOUS ARTISTS (TELSTAR)	5	2002
SONGS TO REMEMBER SCRITTI POLITTI	12	1982
SONGS TO SING IN YOUR BATH RUSS CONWAY	8	1959
SONGS WE LOVE TO SING FOSTER & ALLEN	41	1994
SONGWRITER JUSTIN HAYWARD	28	1977
A SONGWRITERS TALE MIKE BATT	24	2008
SONIA SONIA	33	1991
SONIC ATTACK HAWKWIND	19	1981
SONIC FLOWER GROOVE PRIMAL SCREAM	62	1987
SONIC SYSTEM VARIOUS ARTISTS (TELSTAR)	17	1992
SONIC TEMPLE CULT	3	1989
SONNY SIDE OF CHER CHER	11	1966
SONS AND FASCINATIONS/SISTERS FEELINGS CALL SIMPLE MINDS	11	1981
SONS OF SOUL TONY! TONI! TONE!	66	1993
SOONER OR LATER BBMAK	16	2001
SOPHISTICATED BOOM BOOM DEAD OR ALIVE	29	1984
SOPHTWARE SLUMP GRANDADDY	36	2000
SOPRANO IN HOLLYWOOD LESLEY GARRETT	53	1996
SOPRANO IN RED LESLEY GARRETT	59	1995
A SOPRANO INSPIRED LESLEY GARRETT	48	1997
THE SOPRANO'S GREATEST HITS LESLEY GARRETT	53	1997
SORCERER (OST) TANGERINE DREAM	25	1977
SORTED VARIOUS ARTISTS (MINISTRY OF SOUND)	19	2002
SOUL VARIOUS ARTISTS (POLYGRAM)	10	1998
SOUL SEAL	12	2008
THE SOUL ALBUM OTIS REDDING	22	1966
THE SOUL ALBUM VARIOUS ARTISTS (VIRGIN)	1	1997
THE SOUL ALBUM II VARIOUS ARTISTS (VIRGIN)	3	1998
SOUL ALONE DARYL HALL	55	1993
SOUL BEAT VARIOUS ARTISTS (COOKIE JAR)	8	1993
THE SOUL BOX VARIOUS ARTISTS (DECADANCE)	12	2004
SOUL BROTHERS VARIOUS ARTISTS (WARNER BROTHERS)	9	2002
THE SOUL CAGES STING	1	1991
SOUL CITY VARIOUS ARTISTS (K-TEL)	12	1977
SOUL DAZE/SOUL NITES VARIOUS ARTISTS (RONCO)	25	1982
SOUL DECADE: THE SIXTIES VARIOUS ARTISTS (MOTOWN)	3	1990
SOUL DESTRUCTION ALMIGHTY	22	1991
SOUL DEVOTION VARIOUS ARTISTS (POLYGRAM)	1	1994
SOUL EMOTION VARIOUS ARTISTS (POLYGRAM)	1	1992
SOUL INSPIRATION VARIOUS ARTISTS (POLYGRAM)	4	1993
SOUL JOURNEY GILLIAN WELCH	65	2003
SOUL KISS OLIVIA NEWTON-JOHN	66	1986
SOUL LOVE VARIOUS ARTISTS (WARNER BROTHERS)	15	2005
SOUL MAN VARIOUS ARTISTS (SONY)	10	2004
SOUL MAN ANDY ABRAHAM	19	2006
SOUL MATE VARIOUS ARTISTS (DINO)	6	1994
SOUL MEN SAM & DAVE	32	1968
SOUL MINING THE THE	27	1983
SOUL MOODS VARIOUS ARTISTS (EMI)	4	1993
SOUL MOTION VARIOUS ARTISTS (K-TEL)	1	1976
SOUL NIGHTS VARIOUS ARTISTS (POLYGRAM)	3	1994
SOUL OF MANN MANFRED MANN	40	1967
THE SOUL OF SPAIN 101 STRINGS	17	1960
SOUL PROVIDER MICHAEL BOLTON	4	1990
SOUL REFLECTION VARIOUS ARTISTS (HEART & SOUL)	2	1991
SOUL SEARCHING VARIOUS ARTISTS (COLUMBIA)	6	1994
SOUL SEARCHING TIME AVERAGE WHITE BAND	60	1976
THE SOUL SESSIONS JOSS STONE	4	2004
SOUL SPEAK MICHAEL McDONALD	27	2008
SOUL SURVIVORS 2 VARIOUS ARTISTS (TELSTAR)	17	1998
SOUL SURVIVORS – 40 NORTHERN SOUL ANTHEMS VARIOUS ARTISTS (TELSTAR)	10	1997
SOULFLY SOULFLY	16	1998
SOULJACKER EELS	12	2001
SOUL'S CORE SHAWN MULLINS	60	1999
SOULS OF BLACK TESTAMENT	35	1990
SOULWAX – MOST OF THE REMIXES WE'VE MADE VARIOUS ARTISTS (PARLOPHONE)	16	2007
SOUND EFFECTS JAM	2	1980
THE SOUND INSIDE BREAKS CO-OP	55	2006
SOUND LOADED RICKY MARTIN	14	2000
THE SOUND OF JAM	3	2002
THE SOUND OF BASSLINE VARIOUS ARTISTS (MINISTRY OF SOUND)	2	2008
THE SOUND OF BREAD BREAD	1	1977
THE SOUND OF BREAD BREAD	18	2006
THE SOUND OF CLASSIC FM VARIOUS ARTISTS (CLASSIC FM)	16	2001
THE SOUND OF FURY BILLY FURY	18	1960
SOUND OF GLORY LONDON PHILHARMONIC CHOIR WITH THE NATIONAL PHILHARMONIC ORCHESTRA CONDUCTED BY JOHN ALDISS	10	1976
THE SOUND OF KISS 100FM VARIOUS ARTISTS (POLYGRAM)	1	1994
SOUND OF LIES JAYHAWKS	61	1997
THE SOUND OF LOVE VARIOUS ARTISTS (WARNER BROTHERS)	11	2007
THE SOUND OF MAGIC VARIOUS ARTISTS (UNIVERSAL)	10	1999
THE SOUND OF MAGIC LOVE VARIOUS ARTISTS (UNIVERSAL)	5	1999
THE SOUND OF MAGIC VOLUME 2 VARIOUS ARTISTS (UNIVERSAL)	9	2000
THE SOUND OF MCALMONT AND BUTLER McALMONT & BUTLER	33	1995
THE SOUND OF MUSIC STAGE CAST RECORDING	4	1961
THE SOUND OF MUSIC FILM SOUNDTRACK	1	1965
SOUND OF MUSIC ADICTS	99	1982
SOUND OF PIBROCH CORRIES	39	1972
THE SOUND OF REVENGE CHAMILLIONAIRE	22	2006
SOUND OF SILVER LCD SOUNDSYSTEM	28	2007
THE SOUND OF SKA VARIOUS ARTISTS (QUALITY TELEVISION)	4	1992
THE SOUND OF SMOOVE VARIOUS ARTISTS (MINISTRY OF SOUND)	19	2004
THE SOUND OF SPEED JESUS & MARY CHAIN	15	1993
THE SOUND OF SUPER K KENNY	56	1976
THE SOUND OF THE 70S VARIOUS ARTISTS (WARNER BROTHERS)	17	2007
THE SOUND OF THE CITY VARIOUS ARTISTS (COLUMBIA)	11	1992
THE SOUND OF – THE GREATEST HITS GIRLS ALOUD	1	2006
THE SOUND OF THE PIRATES VARIOUS ARTISTS (UNIVERSAL)	7	2006
THE SOUND OF THE SHADOWS SHADOWS	4	1965
THE SOUND OF THE SMITHS DELUXE EDITION SMITHS	21	2008
THE SOUND OF THE SUBURBS VARIOUS ARTISTS (COLUMBIA)	1	1991
SOUND OF THE UNDERGROUND GIRLS ALOUD	2	2003
SOUND OF THE WHITE NOISE ANTHRAX	14	1993
SOUND OF WATER SAINT ETIENNE	33	2000
THE SOUND OF YOUR CRY ELVIS PRESLEY	31	1982
SOUND ON SOUND BILL NELSON'S RED NOISE	33	1979
SOUND VENTURE GEORGIE FAME	9	1966
SOUND WAVES L'ORCHESTRE ELECTRONIQUE	75	1983
SOUNDBOY ROCK GROOVE ARMADA	10	2007
SOUNDCLASH RENEGADE SOUNDWAVE	74	1990
SOUNDS GENTLE VAL DOONICAN	22	1969
SOUNDS LIKE HERB ALPERT & THE TIJUANA BRASS	21	1967
SOUNDS LIKE THE SEARCHERS SEARCHERS	8	1965
SOUNDS OF SILENCE SIMON & GARFUNKEL	13	1966
SOUNDS OF SUMMER – THE VERY BEST OF BEACH BOYS	46	2006
SOUNDS OF THE SEVENTIES VARIOUS ARTISTS (GLOBAL TELEVISION)	11	1994
SOUNDS SENSATIONAL BERT KAEMPFERT & HIS ORCHESTRA	17	1980
SOUNDTRACK RECORDINGS FROM THE FILM 'JIMI HENDRIX' (OST) JIMI HENDRIX	37	1973
SOUNDTRACK TO THE WEEKEND VARIOUS ARTISTS (GLOBAL TELEVISION)	8	2000
SOUP BLIND MELON	48	1995
SOUP BEAUTIFUL SOUTH & THE HOUSEMARTINS	15	2007

Title / Artist	Peak Position	Year of Release
SOURCE TAGS AND CODES AND YOU WILL KNOW US BY THE TRAIL OF DEAD	73	2002
SOUTH OF HEAVEN SLAYER	25	1988
SOUTH PACIFIC FILM SOUNDTRACK	1	1958
SOUTH PACIFIC (ORIGINAL STUDIO CAST RECORDING) STAGE CAST RECORDING	5	1986
SOUTH PARK: BIGGER, LONGER & UNCUT FILM SOUNDTRACK	9	1999
SOUTHERN ACCENTS TOM PETTY & HEARTBREAKERS	23	1985
THE SOUTHERN DEATH CULT SOUTHERN DEATH CULT	43	1983
SOUTHERN FREEZ FREEEZ	17	1981
THE SOUTHERN HARMONY AND MUSICAL COMPANION BLACK CROWES	2	1992
SOUTHERN HUMMINGBIRD TWEET	15	2002
SOUTHERN KNIGHTS VARIOUS ARTISTS (KNIGHT)	13	1991
SOUTHERN NIGHTS GLEN CAMPBELL	51	1977
SOUTHPAW GRAMMAR MORRISSEY	4	1995
SOUTHSIDE TEXAS	3	1989
SOUVENIR SINGLES PACK MICHAEL JACKSON	91	1988
SOUVENIRS DEMIS ROUSSOS	25	1975
SOUVENIRS FOSTER & ALLEN	15	1990
SOUVLAKI SLOWDIVE	51	1993
SOWETO VARIOUS ARTISTS (ROUGH TRADE)	66	1982
SPACE VARIOUS ARTISTS (WARNER BROTHERS)	8	2000
SPACE BANDITS HAWKWIND	70	1990
A SPACE IN TIME TEN YEARS AFTER	36	1971
SPACE INVADERS VARIOUS ARTISTS (RONCO)	47	1980
SPACE JAM FILM SOUNDTRACK	5	1997
SPACE ODDITY DAVID BOWIE	17	1972
SPACE RITUAL ALIVE HAWKWIND	9	1973
THE SPAGHETTI INCIDENT? GUNS N' ROSES	2	1993
SPANISH HARLEM BEN E. KING	30	1967
SPANISH TRAIN AND OTHER STORIES CHRIS DE BURGH	78	1985
A SPANNER IN THE WORKS ROD STEWART	4	1995
SPANNERS BLACK DOG	30	1995
SPARKLE SPARKLE	57	1998
SPARKLE IN THE RAIN SIMPLE MINDS	1	1984
SPARTACUS VIENNA PHILHARMONIC ORCHESTRA CONDUCTED BY ARAM KHACHATURIAN	16	1972
SPARTACUS FARM	1	1991
SPARTACUS JEFF WAYNE	36	1992
SPAWN – THE ALBUM FILM SOUNDTRACK	18	1997
SPEAK AND SPELL DEPECHE MODE	10	1981
SPEAKERBOXXX/THE LOVE BELOW OUTKAST	8	2003
SPEAKING IN TONGUES TALKING HEADS	21	1983
SPEAKING WITH THE ANGEL MARY BLACK	61	1999
SPECIAL BEAT SERVICE BEAT	21	1982
SPECIAL FORCES ALICE COOPER	96	1981
SPECIAL OCCASION BOBBY	68	2007
SPECIAL OLYMPICS – A VERY SPECIAL CHRISTMAS VARIOUS ARTISTS (A&M)	19	1987
A SPECIAL PART OF ME JOHNNY MATHIS	45	1984
SPECIALS SPECIALS	4	1979
THE SPECIALS SINGLES SPECIALS	10	2001
SPECS APPEAL SHADOWS	30	1975
SPECTRAL MORNINGS STEVE HACKETT	22	1979
SPECTRES BLUE OYSTER CULT	60	1978
SPECTRUM SONIC BOOM	65	1990
SPEED BALLADS REPUBLICA	37	1998
SPEED GARAGE ANTHEMS VARIOUS ARTISTS (GLOBAL TELEVISION)	5	1997
SPEED GARAGE ANTHEMS 99 VARIOUS ARTISTS (GLOBAL TELEVISION)	13	1999
SPEED GARAGE ANTHEMS IN IBIZA VARIOUS ARTISTS (GLOBAL TELEVISION)	7	1998
SPEED GARAGE ANTHEMS – VOLUME 2 VARIOUS ARTISTS (GLOBAL TELEVISION)	5	1998
SPELLBOUND TYGERS OF PAN TANG	33	1981
SPELLBOUND PAULA ABDUL	4	1991
SPICE SPICE GIRLS	1	1996
SPICE GIRLS PRESENT THE BEST GIRL POWER ALBUM IN THE WORLD…EVER! VARIOUS ARTISTS (VIRGIN)	2	1997
SPICEWORLD SPICE GIRLS	1	1997
SPIDER-MAN FILM SOUNDTRACK	14	2002
SPIDER-MAN 2 FILM SOUNDTRACK	17	2004
SPIDERS SPACE	5	1996
SPIKE ELVIS COSTELLO	5	1989
SPILT MILK JELLYFISH	21	1993
SPIN DARREN HAYES	2	2002
SPINNER BRIAN ENO & JAH WOBBLE	71	1995
THE SPINNERS ARE IN TOWN SPINNERS	40	1970
SPINNERS LIVE PERFORMANCE SPINNERS	14	1971
SPIRIT JOHN DENVER	9	1976
THE SPIRIT MAGNUM	50	1991
SPIRIT SEAN MAGUIRE	43	1996
SPIRIT JEWEL	54	1998
SPIRIT LEONA LEWIS	1	2007
SPIRIT OF EDEN TALK TALK	19	1988
SPIRIT OF RELAXATION DREAMKEEPER	71	1997
SPIRIT OF ST LOUIS ELLEN FOLEY	57	1981
SPIRIT OF THE ANDES GHEORGHE ZAMFIR	31	2008
SPIRIT OF THE GLEN ROYAL SCOTS DRAGOON GUARDS	13	2007
SPIRIT OF THE GLEN – JOURNEY ROYAL SCOTS DRAGOON GUARDS	29	2008
SPIRIT OF THE IRISH DUBLINERS	19	2003
SPIRIT OF TRANQUILLITY HARMONIUM	25	1998
THE SPIRIT ROOM MICHELLE BRANCH	54	2002
SPIRIT – STALLION OF THE CIMARRON – OST BRYAN ADAMS	8	2002
SPIRITCHASER DEAD CAN DANCE	43	1996
SPIRITS DANCING IN THE FLESH SANTANA	68	1990
SPIRITS HAVING FLOWN BEE GEES	1	1979
SPIRITS OF NATURE VARIOUS ARTISTS (VIRGIN)	5	1996
SPIRITUALLY IBIZA VARIOUS ARTISTS (DINO)	17	1995
SPIT IN YOUR EAR SPITTING IMAGE	55	1986
SPITFIRE JEFFERSON STARSHIP	30	1976
SPLINTER OFFSPRING	27	2003
SPLINTER GROUP PETER GREEN	71	1997
SPLIT GROUNDHOGS	5	1971
SPLIT LUSH	19	1994
SPLIT SERIES – VOLUME 3 RANCID/NOFX	75	2002
SPLIT THE DIFFERENCE GOMEZ	35	2004
SPOOKY LUSH	7	1992
SPORTS HUEY LEWIS & THE NEWS	23	1985
SPORTS CAR JUDIE TZUKE	7	1980
THE SPOTLIGHT KID CAPTAIN BEEFHEART & HIS MAGIC BAND	44	1971
SPOTLIGHT ON NANA MOUSKOURI NANA MOUSKOURI	38	1974
SPOTLIGHT ON THE GEORGE MITCHELL MINST6RELS GEORGE MITCHELL MINSTRELS	6	1964
SPRING ANNUAL 2002 VARIOUS ARTISTS (MINISTRY OF SOUND)	3	2002
SPYBOY EMMYLOU HARRIS	57	1998
SPYGLASS GUEST GREENSLADE	34	1974
SQUARE THE CIRCLE JOAN ARMATRADING	34	1992
SQUEEZING OUT SPARKS GRAHAM PARKER & THE RUMOUR	18	1979
SSSSH TEN YEARS AFTER	4	1969
ST ANGER METALLICA	3	2003
ST ELSEWHERE GNARLS BARKLEY	1	2006
STACIE ORRICO STACIE ORRICO	37	2003
STACKED UP SENSER	4	1994
STADIUM ARCADIUM RED HOT CHILI PEPPERS	1	2006
THE STADIUM TECHNO EXPERIENCE SCOOTER	20	2003
STAGE DAVID BOWIE	5	1978
STAGE FRIGHT BAND	15	1970
STAGE HEROES COLM WILKINSON	27	1989
STAGE STRUCK RORY GALLAGHER	40	1980
STAGES ELAINE PAIGE	2	1983
STAGE-STRUCK DAVID ESSEX	31	1982
STAIN LIVING COLOUR	19	1993
STAINED CLASS JUDAS PRIEST	27	1978
STAINLESS STYLE NEON NEON	67	2008
STAKES IS HIGH DE LA SOUL	42	1996
STAMPEDE DOOBIE BROTHERS	14	1975
THE STAMPING GROUND RUNRIG	64	2001
STAND BY ME (THE ULTIMATE COLLECTION) BEN E. KING & THE DRIFTERS	14	1987
STAND BY YOUR MAN TAMMY WYNETTE	13	1975
STAND BY YOUR MAN – THE BEST OF TAMMY WYNETTE	23	2008
STAND STRONG STAND PROUD VICE SQUAD	47	1982
STAND UP JETHRO TULL	1	1969
STANDARDS ALARM	47	1990
STANDING HAMPTON SAMMY HAGAR	84	1982
STANDING IN THE LIGHT LEVEL 42	9	1983
STANDING IN THE WAY OF CONTROL GOSSIP	22	2007
STANDING ON A BEACH – THE SINGLES CURE	4	1986
STANDING ON THE SHOULDER OF GIANTS OASIS	1	2000
STANDING TALL CRUSADERS	47	1981
STANDING TALL KYM MARSH	9	2003
STANKONIA OUTKAST	10	2001
STANLEY ROAD PAUL WELLER	1	1995
STAR BELLY	2	1993
STAR FLEET PROJECT BRIAN MAY & FRIENDS	35	1983
A STAR IS BORN BARBRA STREISAND	1	1977
STAR PARTY VARIOUS ARTISTS (K-TEL)	4	1978
STAR PORTRAIT JOHNNY CASH	16	1972
STAR TRACKIN' 76 VARIOUS ARTISTS (RONCO)	9	1976
STAR TRACKS VARIOUS ARTISTS (K-TEL)	6	1980
STAR WARS (OST) JOHN WILLIAMS & THE LONDON SYMPHONY ORCHESTRA	21	1978
STAR WARS EPISODE II: ATTACK OF THE CLONES (OST) JOHN WILLIAMS & THE LONDON SYMPHONY ORCHESTRA	15	2002
STAR WARS EPISODE III – REVENGE OF THE SITH (OST) JOHN WILLIAMS	16	2005
STAR WARS – THE PHANTOM MENACE (OST) JOHN WILLIAMS & THE LONDON SYMPHONY ORCHESTRA	8	1999
STAR! FILM SOUNDTRACK	36	1968
STARDOM ROAD MARC ALMOND	53	2007
STARDUST PAT BOONE	10	1958
STARDUST MEMORIES PETER SKELLERN	50	1995
STARDUST – THE GREAT AMERICAN SONGBOOK VOLUME III ROD STEWART	3	2004
STARGAZERS VARIOUS ARTISTS (KASINO)	69	1985
STARING AT THE SUN LEVEL 42	2	1988
STARLESS AND BIBLE BLACK KING CRIMSON	28	1974
STARLIGHT EXPRESS STAGE CAST RECORDING	21	1984
STARRY EYED AND BOLLOCK NAKED CARTER – THE UNSTOPPABLE SEX MACHINE	22	1994
STARRY NIGHT JULIO IGLESIAS	27	1990
STARS SIMPLY RED	1	1991
STARS AND TOPSOIL – A COLLECTION 1982-1990 COCTEAU TWINS	63	2000
STARS CHARITY FANTASIA SAVE THE CHILDREN FUND VARIOUS ARTISTS (SCF)	6	1966
STARS CRASH DOWN HUE & CRY	10	1991

Title / Artist	Peak Position	Year of Release
STARS FROM STARS AND GARTERS (TELEVISION COMPILATION) TELEVISION AND RADIO COMPILATION	17	1964
STARS MEDLEY STARSOUND	94	1982
STARS OF '68 VARIOUS ARTISTS (MARBLE ARCH)	23	1968
STARS OF CCTV HARD-FI	1	2005
STARS ON 45 STARSOUND	1	1981
STARS ON 45 VOLUME 2 STARSOUND	18	1981
STARS ON SUNDAY BY REQUEST (TELEVISION COMPILATION) TELEVISION AND RADIO COMPILATION	65	1978
STARS – THE BEST OF 1992-2002 CRANBERRIES	20	2002
THE STARS WE ARE MARC ALMOND	41	1988
STARS: SPECIAL EDITION SIMPLY RED	31	2008
STARSKY AND HUTCH PRESENTS (TELEVISION COMPILATION) TELEVISION AND RADIO COMPILATION	13	1998
START SOMETHING LOSTPROPHETS	4	2004
START – THE BEST OF BRITISH VARIOUS ARTISTS (DINO)	13	1994
START WITH A STRONG AND PERSISTENT VEX RED	48	2002
STARTED A FIRE ONE NIGHT ONLY	10	2008
STARTRAX CLUB DISCO STARTRAX	26	1981
STATE OF EUPHORIA ANTHRAX	12	1988
STATE OF MIND HOLLY VALANCE	60	2003
STATE OF OUR UNION LONG RYDERS	66	1985
STATE OF THE WORLD ADDRESS BIOHAZARD	72	1994
THE STATE OF THINGS REVEREND & THE MAKERS	5	2007
STATELESS LENE LOVICH	35	1979
STATIC & SILENCE SUNDAYS	10	1997
STATION TO STATION DAVID BOWIE	5	1976
STATIONARY TRAVELLER CAMEL	57	1984
STATUES MOLOKO	18	2003
STATUS QUO – LIVE STATUS QUO	3	1977
STATUS QUO LIVE AT THE N.E.C. STATUS QUO	83	1984
STAY SIMPLY RED	4	2007
STAY HUNGRY TWISTED SISTER	34	1984
STAY ON THESE ROADS A-HA	2	1988
STAY POSITIVE HOLD STEADY	15	2008
STAY STICK! CRAMPS	62	1990
STAY WITH ME REGINA BELLE	62	1989
STAY WITH ME TONIGHT JEFFREY OSBORNE	56	1984
STAY WITH THE HOLLIES HOLLIES	2	1964
STAYING ALIVE FILM SOUNDTRACK	14	1983
STEADY DIET OF NOTHIMG FUGAZI	63	1991
STEAL THIS ALBUM SYSTEM OF A DOWN	56	2002
STEAL YOUR FACE GRATEFUL DEAD	42	1976
STEAM EAST 17	3	1994
STEAMIN' – HARDCORE '92 VARIOUS ARTISTS (COOKIE JAR)	3	1991
STEEL WHEELS ROLLING STONES	2	1989
STEELTOWN BIG COUNTRY	1	1984
STELLA YELLO	92	1985
STEP BY STEP JEFF LORBER	97	1985
STEP BY STEP NEW KIDS ON THE BLOCK	1	1990
STEP IN THE ARENA GANG STARR	36	1991
STEP ONE STEPS	2	1998
STEP TWO SHOWADDYWADDY	7	1975
STEP UP 2 – THE STREETS VARIOUS ARTISTS (ATLANTIC)	6	2008
STEPHEN MALKMUS STEPHEN MALKMUS	49	2001
STEPHEN STILLS STEPHEN STILLS	8	1970
STEPHEN STILLS 2 STEPHEN STILLS	22	1971
STEPPENWOLF STEPPENWOLF	59	1970
STEPPENWOLF LIVE STEPPENWOLF	16	1970
STEPPIN' TO THE SHADOWS SHADOWS	11	1989
STEPPING OUT – THE VERY BEST OF JOE JACKSON JOE JACKSON	7	1990
STEPS IN TIME KING	6	1985
STEPTACULAR STEPS	1	1999
STEPTOE AND SON WILFRED BRAMBELL & HARRY H. CORBETT	4	1964
STEREO '57 (ESSENTIAL ELVIS VOLUME 2) ELVIS PRESLEY	60	1989
STEREO MUSICALE SHOWCASE VARIOUS ARTISTS (POLYDOR)	26	1966
THE STEVE HOWE ALBUM STEVE HOWE	68	1979
STEVE MCQUEEN PREFAB SPROUT	21	1985
STEVE MILLER BAND LIVE! STEVE MILLER BAND	79	1983
STEVE WINWOOD STEVE WINWOOD	12	1977
STEVE WRIGHT'S ALL NEW SUNDAY LOVE SONGS VARIOUS ARTISTS (UNIVERSAL)	14	2005
STEVE WRIGHT'S CHOCOLATES AND CHAMPAGNE VARIOUS ARTISTS (UNIVERSAL)	2	2004
STEVE WRIGHT'S SUNDAY LOVE SONGS VARIOUS ARTISTS (UNIVERSAL)	6	2000
STEVE WRIGHT'S SUNDAY LOVE SONGS VOLUME 2 VARIOUS ARTISTS (UNIVERSAL)	12	2001
STEVEN HOUGHTON STEVEN HOUGHTON	21	1997
STEVEN SMITH AND FATHER AND 16 GREAT SONGS STEVEN SMITH AND FATHER	17	1972
STEVIE WONDER'S GREATEST HITS STEVIE WONDER	25	1968
STICK AROUND FOR JOY SUGARCUBES	16	1992
STICK TO ME GRAHAM PARKER & THE RUMOUR	19	1977
STICKS AND STONES NEW FOUND GLORY	10	2002
STICKY FINGERS ROLLING STONES	1	1971
STIFF UPPER LIP AC/DC	12	2000
STIFF'S LIVE STIFFS VARIOUS ARTISTS (STIFF)	28	1978
STIGMA EMF	19	1992
STILETTO LITA FORD	66	1990
STILL JOY DIVISION	5	1981
STILL BURNING MIKE SCOTT	34	1997
STILL CAN'T SAY GOODBYE CHARLIE LANDSBOROUGH	39	1999
STILL CLIMBING BROWNSTONE	19	1997
STILL CRAZY AFTER ALL THESE YEARS PAUL SIMON	6	1975
STILL GOT THE BLUES GARY MOORE	13	1990
STILL I RISE 2PAC & OUTLAWZ	75	2000
STILL IN THE GAME KEITH SWEAT	62	1998
STILL LIFE (AMERICAN CONCERTS 1981) ROLLING STONES	4	1982
STILL NOT BLACK ENOUGH W.A.S.P.	52	1995
STILL ON TOP – BEST OF VAN MORRISON	2	2007
STILL OUT OF ORDER INFA RIOT	42	1982
STILL SEXY – THE ALBUM ERROL BROWN	44	2001
STILL THE SAME...GREAT ROCK CLASSICS OF OUR TIME ROD STEWART	4	2006
STILL TOGETHER GLADYS KNIGHT & THE PIPS	42	1977
STILL WATERS BEE GEES	2	1997
STILL WATERS RUN DEEP FOUR TOPS	29	1970
STILLS STEPHEN STILLS	31	1975
THE STING (OST) MARVIN HAMLISCH	7	1974
STOCK/AITKEN/WATERMAN – GOLD VARIOUS ARTISTS (SONY/BMG)	12	2005
STOLEN MOMENTS JOHN HIATT	72	1990
STOMPIN' AT THE SAVOY RUFUS & CHAKA KHAN	64	1984
STOMPIN' PARTY VARIOUS ARTISTS (DINO)	10	1992
STONE AGE ROLLING STONES	4	1971
STONE GON' BARRY WHITE	18	1974
STONE KILLERS PRINCE CHARLES & THE CITY BEAT BAND	84	1983
STONE LOVE ANGIE STONE	56	2004
THE STONE ROSES STONE ROSES	9	1989
STONE ROSES – 10TH ANNIVERSARY EDITION STONE ROSES	26	1999
STONE SOUR STONE SOUR	41	2002
STONED AND DETHRONED JESUS & MARY CHAIN	13	1994
STONED RAIDERS CYPRESS HILL	71	2001
STONEDHENGE TEN YEARS AFTER	6	1969
STONES NEIL DIAMOND	17	1971
STONES IN THE ROAD MARY CHAPIN CARPENTER	26	1994
STONEY END BARBRA STREISAND	28	1971
STOOSH SKUNK ANANSIE	9	1996
STOP DROP AND ROLL FOXBORO HOT TUBS	37	2008
STOP MAKING SENSE TALKING HEADS	24	1984
STOP THAT TRAIN CLINT EASTWOOD & GENERAL SAINT	98	1983
STOP THE CLOCKS OASIS	2	2006
STOP THE WORLD BLACK, ROCK & RON	72	1989
STOP THE WORLD – I WANT TO GET OFF STAGE CAST RECORDING	8	1961
STOP! SAM BROWN	4	1989
STORIES FROM THE CITY STORIES FROM THE SEA PJ HARVEY	23	2000
STORIES OF JOHNNY MARC ALMOND	22	1985
STORM VANESSA-MAE	27	1997
STORM BRINGER DEEP PURPLE	6	1974
STORM FRONT BILLY JOEL	5	1989
A STORM IN HEAVEN VERVE	27	1993
THE STORM INSIDE LAURA MICHELLE KELLY	72	2006
STORM WATCH JETHRO TULL	27	1979
STORMS NANCI GRIFFITH	38	1989
STORMSVILLE JOHNNY & THE HURRICANES	18	1960
THE STORY BRANDI CARLILE	58	2008
THE STORY GOES CRAIG DAVID	5	2005
THE STORY OF A YOUNG HEART A FLOCK OF SEAGULLS	30	1984
THE STORY OF THE CLASH – VOLUME 1 CLASH	7	1988
STORY OF THE STONES ROLLING STONES	24	1982
THE STORY OF THE WHO WHO	2	1976
THE STORY SO FAR (SPUNGE)	48	2002
THE STORY SO FAR – THE VERY BEST OF ROD STEWART	7	2001
STORY SONGS VARIOUS ARTISTS (EMI)	16	2008
THE STORYMAN CHRIS DE BURGH	38	2006
STORYTELLER RAGHAV	36	2004
STORYTELLING BELLE & SEBASTIAN	26	2002
STORYVILLE ROBBIE ROBERTSON	30	1991
STR8 OFF THA STREETZ OF MUTHAPHUKKIN COMPTON EAZY-E	66	1996
STRAIGHT DOGS D'AMOUR	32	1990
STRAIGHT BETWEEN THE EYES RAINBOW	5	1982
STRAIGHT FROM THE HEART PATRICE RUSHEN	24	1982
STRAIGHT OUTTA CASHVILLE YOUNG BUCK	22	2004
STRAIGHT OUTTA COMPTON N.W.A.	35	1989
STRAIGHT SHOOTER BAD COMPANY	3	1975
STRANDED ROXY	1	1973
STRANGE AND BEAUTIFUL VARIOUS ARTISTS (WARNER BROTHERS)	11	2003
STRANGE ANGELS KRISTIN HERSH	64	1998
STRANGE BEHAVIOUR DURAN DURAN	70	1999
STRANGE BOUTIQUE MONOCHROME SET	62	1980
STRANGE BROTHERHOOD NEW MODEL ARMY	72	1998
STRANGE CHARM GARY NUMAN	59	1986
STRANGE FOLK KULA SHAKER	69	2007
STRANGE FREE WORLD KITCHENS OF DISTINCTION	45	1991
STRANGE FRONTIER ROGER TAYLOR	30	1984
STRANGE HOUSE HORRORS	37	2007
STRANGE KIND OF LOVE LOVE & MONEY	71	1988
STRANGE LITTLE GIRLS TORI AMOS	16	2001

Title / Artist	Peak Position	Year of Release
STRANGE REFLECTIONS SECOND IMAGE	100	1985
STRANGE TIMES CHAMELEON	44	1986
STRANGE WEATHER MARIANNE FAITHFULL	78	1987
STRANGEITUDE OZRIC TENTACLES	70	1991
STRANGELOVE STRANGELOVE	67	1997
THE STRANGER BILLY JOEL	25	1978
STRANGER IN MY OWN BACK YARD GILBERT O'SULLIVAN	9	1974
STRANGER IN THE CITY JOHN MILES	37	1977
STRANGER IN THIS TOWN RICHIE SAMBORA	20	1991
STRANGER IN TOWN BOB SEGER & THE SILVER BULLET BAND	31	1978
STRANGER ON THE SHORE MR ACKER BILK	6	1962
STRANGERS ED HARCOURT	57	2004
STRANGERS IN THE NIGHT BERT KAEMPFERT & HIS ORCHESTRA	13	1966
STRANGERS IN THE NIGHT FRANK SINATRA	4	1966
STRANGERS IN THE NIGHT UFO	8	1979
STRANGEWAYS, HERE WE COME SMITHS	2	1987
STRANGLERS IN THE NIGHT STRANGLERS	33	1992
STRANGLERS IV (RATTUS NORVEGICUS) STRANGLERS	4	1977
STRATOSFEAR TANGERINE DREAM	39	1976
THE STRAUSS FAMILY (OST) LONDON SYMPHONY ORCHESTRA CONDUCTED BY CYRIL ORNADEL	2	1972
STRAW DONKEY...THE SINGLES CARTER – THE UNSTOPPABLE SEX MACHINE	37	1995
STRAWBERRIES DAMNED	15	1982
STRAWBERRY SWITCHBLADE STRAWBERRY SWITCHBLADE	25	1985
STRAY AZTEC CAMERA	22	1990
STRAY CATS STRAY CATS	6	1981
STRAYS JANE'S ADDICTION	14	2003
STREET ANGEL STEVIE NICKS	16	1994
STREET BEATZ VARIOUS ARTISTS (SONY BMG)	9	2005
STREET DREAMS FABOLOUS	51	2003
STREET FIGHTING YEARS SIMPLE MINDS	1	1989
STREET JAMS VARIOUS ARTISTS (TELSTAR)	14	1998
STREET LEGAL BOB DYLAN	2	1978
STREET LEVEL VARIOUS ARTISTS (RONCO)	29	1980
STREET LIFE CRUSADERS	10	1979
STREET LIFE – 20 GREAT HITS BRYAN FERRY & ROXY MUSIC	1	1986
STREET MACHINE SAMMY HAGAR	38	1979
STREET MOVES TWENTY 4 SEVEN FEATURING CAPTAIN HOLLYWOOD	69	1991
STREET PARTY CHAS & DAVE	3	1995
STREET SOUL VARIOUS ARTISTS (VIRGIN)	2	1995
STREET SOUNDS 87 VOLUME 2 VARIOUS ARTISTS (STREET SOUNDS)	47	1987
STREET SOUNDS 88-1 VARIOUS ARTISTS (STREET SOUNDS)	73	1988
STREET SOUNDS ANTHEMS – VOLUME 1 VARIOUS ARTISTS (STREET SOUNDS)	61	1987
STREET SOUNDS CRUCIAL ELECTRO VARIOUS ARTISTS (STREET SOUNDS)	24	1984
STREET SOUNDS CRUCIAL ELECTRO 2 VARIOUS ARTISTS (STREET SOUNDS)	35	1984
STREET SOUNDS CRUCIAL ELECTRO 3 VARIOUS ARTISTS (STREET SOUNDS)	41	1987
STREET SOUNDS DANCE MUSIC '87 VARIOUS ARTISTS (STREET SOUNDS)	40	1987
STREET SOUNDS EDITION 10 VARIOUS ARTISTS (STREET SOUNDS)	24	1984
STREET SOUNDS EDITION 11 VARIOUS ARTISTS (STREET SOUNDS)	48	1984
STREET SOUNDS EDITION 12 VARIOUS ARTISTS (STREET SOUNDS)	23	1985
STREET SOUNDS EDITION 13 VARIOUS ARTISTS (STREET SOUNDS)	19	1985
STREET SOUNDS EDITION 14 VARIOUS ARTISTS (STREET SOUNDS)	43	1985
STREET SOUNDS EDITION 15 VARIOUS ARTISTS (STREET SOUNDS)	58	1985
STREET SOUNDS EDITION 16 VARIOUS ARTISTS (STREET SOUNDS)	17	1986
STREET SOUNDS EDITION 17 VARIOUS ARTISTS (STREET SOUNDS)	35	1986
STREET SOUNDS EDITION 18 VARIOUS ARTISTS (STREET SOUNDS)	20	1986
STREET SOUNDS EDITION 19 VARIOUS ARTISTS (STREET SOUNDS)	61	1986
STREET SOUNDS EDITION 2 VARIOUS ARTISTS (STREET SOUNDS)	35	1983
STREET SOUNDS EDITION 20 VARIOUS ARTISTS (STREET SOUNDS)	25	1987
STREET SOUNDS EDITION 3 VARIOUS ARTISTS (STREET SOUNDS)	21	1983
STREET SOUNDS EDITION 4 VARIOUS ARTISTS (STREET SOUNDS)	14	1983
STREET SOUNDS EDITION 5 VARIOUS ARTISTS (STREET SOUNDS)	16	1983
STREET SOUNDS EDITION 6 VARIOUS ARTISTS (STREET SOUNDS)	23	1983
STREET SOUNDS EDITION 7 VARIOUS ARTISTS (STREET SOUNDS)	48	1983
STREET SOUNDS EDITION 8 VARIOUS ARTISTS (STREET SOUNDS)	22	1984
STREET SOUNDS EDITION 9 VARIOUS ARTISTS (STREET SOUNDS)	22	1984
STREET SOUNDS ELECTRO 1 VARIOUS ARTISTS (STREET SOUNDS)	18	1983
STREET SOUNDS ELECTRO 10 VARIOUS ARTISTS (STREET SOUNDS)	72	1985
STREET SOUNDS ELECTRO 2 VARIOUS ARTISTS (STREET SOUNDS)	49	1984
STREET SOUNDS ELECTRO 3 VARIOUS ARTISTS (STREET SOUNDS)	25	1984
STREET SOUNDS ELECTRO 4 VARIOUS ARTISTS (STREET SOUNDS)	25	1984
STREET SOUNDS ELECTRO 5 VARIOUS ARTISTS (STREET SOUNDS)	17	1984
STREET SOUNDS ELECTRO 6 VARIOUS ARTISTS (STREET SOUNDS)	24	1985
STREET SOUNDS ELECTRO 7 VARIOUS ARTISTS (STREET SOUNDS)	12	1985
STREET SOUNDS ELECTRO 8 VARIOUS ARTISTS (STREET SOUNDS)	23	1985
STREET SOUNDS ELECTRO 9 VARIOUS ARTISTS (STREET SOUNDS)	18	1985
STREET SOUNDS HI-ENERGY NO 1 VARIOUS ARTISTS (STREET SOUNDS)	71	1984
STREET SOUNDS HIP-HOP 17 VARIOUS ARTISTS (STREET SOUNDS)	38	1987
STREET SOUNDS HIP-HOP 18 VARIOUS ARTISTS (STREET SOUNDS)	67	1987
STREET SOUNDS HIP-HOP 20 VARIOUS ARTISTS (STREET SOUNDS)	39	1988
STREET SOUNDS HIP-HOP 21 VARIOUS ARTISTS (STREET SOUNDS)	87	1988
STREET SOUNDS HIP-HOP ELECTRO 11 VARIOUS ARTISTS (STREET SOUNDS)	19	1986
STREET SOUNDS HIP-HOP ELECTRO 12 VARIOUS ARTISTS (STREET SOUNDS)	28	1986
STREET SOUNDS HIP-HOP ELECTRO 13 VARIOUS ARTISTS (STREET SOUNDS)	23	1986
STREET SOUNDS HIP-HOP ELECTRO 14 VARIOUS ARTISTS (STREET SOUNDS)	40	1986
STREET SOUNDS HIP-HOP ELECTRO 15 VARIOUS ARTISTS (STREET SOUNDS)	46	1986
STREET SOUNDS HIP-HOP ELECTRO 16 VARIOUS ARTISTS (STREET SOUNDS)	40	1987
STREET SOUNDS N.Y. VS L.A. BEATS VARIOUS ARTISTS (STREET SOUNDS)	65	1985
STREET SOUNDS UK ELECTRO VARIOUS ARTISTS (STREET SOUNDS)	60	1984
STREET SURVIVORS LYNYRD SKYNYRD	13	1977
STREET TALK STEVE PERRY	59	1984
STREET VIBES VARIOUS ARTISTS (GLOBAL TELEVISION)	6	1998
STREET VIBES 2 VARIOUS ARTISTS (GLOBAL TELEVISION)	5	1999
STREET VIBES 3 VARIOUS ARTISTS (GLOBAL TELEVISION)	6	1999
STREET VIBES 4 VARIOUS ARTISTS (GLOBAL TELEVISION)	4	2000
STREET VIBES 5 VARIOUS ARTISTS (GLOBAL TELEVISION)	2	2000
STREET VIBES 6 VARIOUS ARTISTS (BMG)	6	2000
STREET VIBES 7 VARIOUS ARTISTS (TELSTAR)	7	2001
STREET VIBES 8 VARIOUS ARTISTS (BMG)	4	2001
STREETCORE JOE STRUMMER & THE MESCALEROS	50	2003
STREETNOISE VOLUME 1 VARIOUS ARTISTS (STREET SOUNDS)	51	1982
STREETS RALPH McTELL	13	1975
STREETS DISCIPLE NAS	45	2004
STREETSCENE VARIOUS ARTISTS (K-TEL)	42	1982
STREETSOUL GURU'S JAZZMATAZZ	74	2000
STREISAND SUPERMAN BARBRA STREISAND	32	1977
STRENGTH ALARM	18	1985
STRENGTH ENUFF Z'NUFF	56	1991
STRENGTH IN NUMBERS MUSIC	19	2008
STRENGTH THROUGH OI! VARIOUS ARTISTS (DERAM)	51	1981
STRICTLY COME DANCING STRICTLY COME DANCING BAND	48	2008
STRICTLY COMMERCIAL – THE BEST OF FRANK ZAPPA FRANK ZAPPA	45	1995
STRICTLY DANCE FEVER VARIOUS ARTISTS (VIRGIN)	18	2005
STRICTLY FOR GROWN UPS PADDY ROBERTS	8	1959
STRICTLY RAGGA VARIOUS ARTISTS (VITAL SOUNDS)	12	1993
STRIKES AGAIN ROSE ROYCE	7	1978
STRING ALONG WITH NAT 'KING' COLE NAT 'KING' COLE	12	1961
STRING OF HITS SHADOWS	1	1979
A STRING OF PEARLS PETER SKELLERN	67	1982
A STRING OF TONY'S HITS TONY BENNETT	9	1966
STRING SWAY KNIGHTSBRIDGE STRINGS	20	1960
STRINGS OF SCOTLAND JOHN MASON	50	1975
STRIP ADAM ANT	20	1983
STRIP MINE JAMES	90	1988
STRIPPED ROLLING STONES	9	1995
STRIPPED CHRISTINA AGUILERA	2	2002
STRIVE TO SURVIVE CAUSING LEAST SUFFERING POSSIBLE A FLUX OF PINK INDIANS	79	1983
STRONG ARM OF THE LAW SAXON	11	1980
STRONG PERSUADER ROBERT CRAY BAND	34	1986
STRONGER CLIFF RICHARD	7	1989
STRONGER THAN PRIDE SADE	3	1988
STRONGER TOGETHER D-SIDE	62	2004
THE STUD FILM SOUNDTRACK	2	1978
STUDENT DAZE VARIOUS ARTISTS (SONY/ BMG)	17	2005
THE STUDENT PRINCE JOHN HANSON	17	1960
THE STUDENT PRINCE/THE GREAT CARUSO (OST) MARIO LANZA	4	1958
THE STUDENT PRINCE/THE VAGABOND KING JOHN HANSON	9	1961
STUDIO 1 ALL SAINTS	40	2006
STUDIO 150 PAUL WELLER	2	2004
STUDIO TWO CLASSICS VARIOUS ARTISTS (STUDIO TWO)	16	1971
STUMBLE INTO GRACE EMMYLOU HARRIS	52	2003

Title / Artist	Peak Position	Year of Release
THE STUN (CARROTT TELLS ALL) JASPER CARROTT	57	1983
STUNT BARENAKED LADIES	20	1999
STUPID STUPID STUPID BLACK GRAPE	11	1997
STUPIDITY DR. FEELGOOD	1	1976
STUTTER JAMES	68	1986
THE STYLE COUNCIL COLLECTION STYLE COUNCIL	60	1996
SU SU POLLARD	86	1986
SUBHUMAN RACE SKID ROW	8	1995
SUBJECT TO CHANGE VANESSA-MAE	58	2001
SUBSTANCE NEW ORDER	3	1987
SUDDENLY BILLY OCEAN	9	1984
SUE FRAZIER CHORUS	56	1989
SUEDE SUEDE	1	1993
SUGAR AND SPICE SEARCHERS	5	1963
SUGAR HITS! VARIOUS ARTISTS (POLYGRAM)	9	1997
SUGAR MOUNTAIN LIVE AT CANTERBURY HOUSE 1968 NEIL YOUNG	72	2008
SUGAR TAX ORCHESTRAL MANOEUVRES IN THE DARK	3	1991
SUICIDE PACT – YOU FIRST THERAPY?	61	1999
SUICIDE SEASON BRING ME THE HORIZON	47	2008
SUIT NELLY	8	2004
SUITED & BOOTED VARIOUS ARTISTS (V2)	4	2005
SUITS FISH	18	1994
SULK ASSOCIATES	10	1982
SULTANS OF SWING – THE VERY BEST OF DIRE STRAITS DIRE STRAITS	6	1998
SUM AND SUBSTANCE MISSION	49	1994
SUMDAY GRANDADDY	22	2003
SUMMER BREEZE VARIOUS ARTISTS (COLUMBIA)	14	2000
SUMMER BREEZE – GREATEST HITS ISLEY BROTHERS	69	2005
SUMMER CHART PARTY VARIOUS ARTISTS (TRAX)	9	1990
SUMMER CLUB HITS VARIOUS ARTISTS (UNIVERSAL)	4	2006
SUMMER COUNTRY – 41 CLASSIC COUNTRY HITS FOR A MODERN WORLD VARIOUS ARTISTS (TELSTAR)	16	2002
SUMMER CRUISING VARIOUS ARTISTS (K-TEL)	30	1976
SUMMER DANCE '98 VARIOUS ARTISTS (COLUMBIA)	12	1998
SUMMER DANCE ANTHEMS 99 VARIOUS ARTISTS (TELSTAR)	10	1999
SUMMER DANCE PARTY VARIOUS ARTISTS (GLOBAL TELEVISION)	2	1995
SUMMER DAYS (AND SUMMER NIGHTS) BEACH BOYS	4	1966
SUMMER DAYS, BOOGIE NIGHTS – 16 TRACKS VARIOUS ARTISTS (PORTRAIT)	40	1986
SUMMER DREAMS – 28 CLASSIC TRACKS BEACH BOYS	2	1990
SUMMER GROOVE VARIOUS ARTISTS (WARNER BROTHERS)	14	1997
SUMMER HAPPENING JAMES LAST	38	1971
SUMMER HITS '06 VARIOUS ARTISTS (WARNER BROTHERS)	12	2006
SUMMER HOLIDAY (OST) CLIFF RICHARD & THE SHADOWS	1	1963
SUMMER HOLIDAY DANCE CRAZE VARIOUS ARTISTS (V2)	5	2005
SUMMER HOLIDAY DANCE PARTY VARIOUS ARTISTS (INSPIRED)	12	2008
SUMMER HOLIDAY HITS VARIOUS ARTISTS (UNIVERSAL)	6	2006
SUMMER IN THE SIXTIES VARIOUS ARTISTS (VIRGIN)	9	2004
SUMMER OF '78 BARRY MANILOW	66	1996
THE SUMMER OF LOVE VARIOUS ARTISTS (DINO)	9	1990
THE SUMMER OF LOVE GOES ON – SIXTIES VARIOUS ARTISTS (POLYGRAM)	16	1998
THE SUMMER OF NINETY SIX – UP YER RONSON VARIOUS ARTISTS (HI-LIFE)	17	1996
SUMMER RIDDIMS 2004 VARIOUS ARTISTS (WARNER BROTHERS)	10	2004
SUMMER SWING VARIOUS ARTISTS (VIRGIN)	18	1995
SUMMER VYBES VARIOUS ARTISTS (POLYGRAM)	8	1996
SUMMERTEETH WILCO	38	1999
SUMMERTIME VARIOUS ARTISTS (UNIVERSAL)	15	2000
SUMMERTIME SOUL VARIOUS ARTISTS (POLYGRAM)	5	1995
THE SUMMIT VARIOUS ARTISTS (K-TEL)	17	1980
THE SUN IS OFTEN OUT LONGPIGS	26	1996
THE SUN IS SHINING BOB MARLEY VS FUNKSTAR DELUXE	40	1999
THE SUN YEARS ELVIS PRESLEY	31	1977
SUNBURN FILM SOUNDTRACK	45	1980
SUNBURST FINISH BE-BOP DELUXE	17	1976
SUNDANCE – CHAPTER ONE VARIOUS ARTISTS (TELSTAR)	9	1998
SUNDAY 8PM FAITHLESS	10	1998
SUNDAY AT DEVIL DIRT ISOBEL CAMPBELL & MARK LANEGAN	38	2008
SUNDAY MORNING SONGS VARIOUS ARTISTS (EMI)	18	2006
SUNDEW PARIS ANGELS	37	1991
SUNDISSENTIAL – HARDER FASTER VARIOUS ARTISTS (SUNDISSENTIAL)	16	2002
SUNDOWN GORDON LIGHTFOOT	45	1974
SUNDOWN S CLUB 8	13	2003
SUNFLOWER BEACH BOYS	29	1970
SUNLIGHT HERBIE HANCOCK	27	1978
SUNMACHINE DARIO G	26	1998
SUNNY AFTERNOON KINKS	9	1967
SUNNY AFTERNOON VARIOUS ARTISTS (IMPRESSION)	13	1983
SUNNY AFTERNOON VOLUME TWO VARIOUS ARTISTS (IMPRESSION)	90	1984
SUNNY AFTERNOONS VARIOUS ARTISTS (POLYGRAM)	6	1995
SUNSET BOULEVARD STAGE CAST RECORDING	11	1993
SUNSET IBIZA VARIOUS ARTISTS (UNIVERSAL)	7	2001
SUNSET TO SUNRISE VARIOUS ARTISTS (UNIVERSAL)	8	2008
SUNSETS ON EMPIRE FISH	42	1997
SUNSHINE FILM SOUNDTRACK	47	1974
SUNSHINE S CLUB 7	3	2001
SUNSHINE MIX VARIOUS ARTISTS (STYLUS)	9	1989
THE SUNSHINE OF YOUR SMILE MIKE BERRY	63	1981
SUNSHINE ON LEITH PROCLAIMERS	6	1988
SUNSHINE SUPERMAN DONOVAN	25	1967
SUPA FUNKY VARIOUS ARTISTS (UNIVERSAL)	6	2002
SUPER 60'S VARIOUS ARTISTS (VIRGIN)	16	2003
SUPER 70'S VARIOUS ARTISTS (VIRGIN)	5	2003
SUPER 70'S ROCK VARIOUS ARTISTS (VIRGIN)	10	2004
SUPER 70'S SUMMER VARIOUS ARTISTS (VIRGIN)	14	2004
SUPER CHARGED VARIOUS ARTISTS (UNIVERSAL)	5	2005
SUPER HITS 1 & 2 VARIOUS ARTISTS (RONCO)	2	1981
SUPER TARANTA GOGOL BORDELLO	67	2007
SUPER TROUPER ABBA	1	1980
SUPERABUNDANCE YOUNG KNIVES	28	2008
SUPERBAD VARIOUS ARTISTS (WARNER BROTHERS)	10	2004
SUPERBI BEAUTIFUL SOUTH	6	2006
SUPERCHARGED VARIOUS ARTISTS (UNIVERSAL)	1	2002
SUPERCHARGER MACHINE HEAD	34	2001
SUPERCHART '83 VARIOUS ARTISTS (TELSTAR)	22	1983
SUPERFLY CURTIS MAYFIELD	26	1973
SUPERFUNK VARIOUS ARTISTS (VIRGIN)	8	1994
SUPERGRASS SUPERGRASS	3	1999
SUPERGRASS IS 10 – THE BEST OF 94-04 SUPERGRASS	4	2004
SUPERGROUPS VARIOUS ARTISTS (RONCO)	57	1977
SUPERNATURAL DES'REE	16	1998
SUPERNATURAL SANTANA	1	1999
SUPERNATURAL FEELING JAMES TAYLOR QUARTET	36	1993
SUPERNATURE CERRONE	60	1978
SUPERNATURE GOLDFRAPP	2	2005
SUPERSONIC (TELEVISION COMPILATION) TELEVISION AND RADIO COMPILATION	21	1975
SUPERSTAR – THE HITS JAMELIA	55	2007
SUPERSTITION SIOUXSIE & THE BANSHEES	25	1991
SUPERUNKNOWN SOUNDGARDEN	4	1994
SUPERWOMAN VARIOUS ARTISTS (VIRGIN)	2	1998
SUPPOSED FORMER INFATUATION JUNKIE ALANIS MORISSETTE	3	1998
SUPREMES A GO-GO SUPREMES	15	1966
THE SUPREMES SING MOTOWN SUPREMES	15	1967
THE SUPREMES SING RODGERS AND HART SUPREMES	25	1967
SUR LA MER MOODY BLUES	21	1988
SURFACING SARAH McLACHLAN	47	1998
SURFER GIRL BEACH BOYS	13	1967
SURFIN' USA BEACH BOYS	17	1965
SURF'S UP BEACH BOYS	15	1971
SURPRISE PAUL SIMON	4	2006
SURPRISE SURPRISE MEZZOFORTE	23	1983
SURRENDER CHEMICAL BROTHERS	1	1999
SURRENDER JAVINE	73	2004
SURVIVAL BOB MARLEY & THE WAILERS	20	1979
SURVIVOR DESTINY'S CHILD	1	2001
SUZANNE VEGA SUZANNE VEGA	11	1985
SUZI QUATRO SUZI QUATRO	32	1973
SUZI QUATRO'S GREATEST HITS SUZI QUATRO	4	1980
SWAGGER BLUE AEROPLANES	54	1990
SWAGGER GUN	5	1994
SWALLOW THIS LIVE POISON	52	1991
SWAMP OPHELIA INDIGO GIRLS	66	1994
SWANSONG CARCASS	68	1996
SWEAT NELLY	11	2004
SWEAT & SUIT NELLY	41	2005
SWEENEY TODD – THE DEMON BARBER OF FLEET STREET STEPHEN SONDHEIM	38	2008
SWEET BABY JAMES JAMES TAYLOR	6	1970
SWEET DANNY WILSON DANNY WILSON	54	1991
SWEET DREAMS PATSY CLINE	18	1991
SWEET DREAMS (ARE MADE OF THIS) EURYTHMICS	3	1983
THE SWEET ESCAPE GWEN STEFANI	14	2006
SWEET FANNY ADAMS SWEET	27	1974
SWEET FREEDOM URIAH HEEP	18	1973
SWEET FREEDOM: BEST OF MICHAEL MCDONALD MICHAEL McDONALD	6	1986
SWEET INSPIRATION CILLA BLACK	42	1970
SWEET INSPIRATION INSPIRATIONAL CHOIR	59	1986
THE SWEET KEEPER TANITA TIKARAM	3	1990
SWEET KISSES JESSICA SIMPSON	36	2000
SWEET LOVE – THE VERY BEST OF ANITA BAKER ANITA BAKER	49	2002
SWEET SIXTEEN – IT'S IT'S...SWEET HITS SWEET	49	1984
SWEET SOUL HARMONIES VARIOUS ARTISTS (VIRGIN)	1	1994
SWEET SOUL HARMONIES 2 VARIOUS ARTISTS (VIRGIN)	10	1994
SWEET SOUL MUSIC – THE BEST OF VARIOUS ARTISTS (STAX)	20	2007

Title / Artist	Peak Position	Year of Release
SWEET SURRENDER JOHNNY MATHIS	55	1977
SWEET THINGS GEORGIE FAME	6	1966
SWEET WARRIOR RICHARD THOMPSON	39	2007
SWEETS FROM A STRANGER SQUEEZE	20	1982
SWEPT JULIA FORDHAM	33	1991
SWEPT AWAY DIANA ROSS	40	1984
SWIMMER BIG DISH	85	1986
SWING BATTA SWING K7	27	1994
SWING CLASSICS VARIOUS ARTISTS (WARNER BROTHERS)	9	2003
SWING EASY FRANK SINATRA	5	1960
SWING HITS VARIOUS ARTISTS (DINO)	19	1992
SWING MIX 96 VARIOUS ARTISTS (TELSTAR)	3	1996
THE SWING OF DELIGHT CARLOS SANTANA	65	1980
SWING SOFTLY JOHNNY MATHIS	10	1959
SWING STREET BARRY MANILOW	81	1988
SWING WHEN YOU'RE WINNING ROBBIE WILLIAMS	1	2001
A SWINGIN' AFFAIR! FRANK SINATRA	1	1957
A SWINGIN' SAFARI BERT KAEMPFERT & HIS ORCHESTRA	20	1966
SWINGIN' WITH RAYMOND CHUMBAWAMBA	70	1995
SWINGIN' WITH THE BIG BAND BIG BAND	62	2002
THE SWINGING CITY SPINNERS	20	1971
SWINGING SIXTIES VARIOUS ARTISTS (SONY/BMG)	16	2005
SWINGING THE BLUES DANCING THE SKA JOOLS HOLLAND & HIS R&B ORCHESTRA	36	2005
SWITCHED ON VARIOUS ARTISTS (TELSTAR)	13	2000
SWITCHED ON SWING KINGS OF SWING ORCHESTRA	28	1982
SWOON PREFAB SPROUT	22	1984
SWORDFISHTROMBONE TOM WAITS	62	1983
SYD LAWRENCE WITH THE GLENN MILLER SOUND SYD LAWRENCE	31	1971
SYMBOLS PRINCE & THE NEW POWER GENERATION	1	1992
SYMPHONIC ROCK ROYAL PHILHARMONIC ORCHESTRA	42	2004
SYMPHONIC ROCK WITH THE VIENNA SYMPHONY ORCHESTRA VIENNA SYMPHONY ORCHESTRA	43	1987
SYMPHONIES FOR THE SEVENTIES WALDO DE LOS RIOS	6	1971
SYMPHONY SARAH BRIGHTMAN	13	2008
SYMPHONY OR DAMN TERENCE TRENT D'ARBY	4	1993
SYNCHRO SYSTEM KING SUNNY ADE & HIS AFRICAN BEATS	93	1983
SYNCHRONICITY POLICE	1	1983
SYNKRONIZED JAMIROQUAI	1	1999
SYNTHESIZER 2 PROJECT D	25	1990
THE SYNTHESIZER ALBUM PROJECT D	13	1990
SYNTHESIZER GOLD ED STARINK	29	1993
SYNTHESIZER GREATEST ED STARINK	22	1990
SYSTEM SEAL	37	2007
THE SYSTEM HAS FAILED MEGADETH	60	2004
SYSTEMATIC CHAOS DREAM THEATER	25	2007

T

Title / Artist	Peak Position	Year of Release
T. REX T. REX	7	1971
T. REX IN CONCERT T. REX	35	1981
T.V. SKY YOUNG GODS	54	1992
TA-DAH SCISSOR SISTERS	1	2006
TADPOLES BONZO DOG DOO-DAH BAND	36	1969
TAILS LISA LOEB & NINE STORIES	39	1995
TAJA SEVELLE TAJA SEVELLE	48	1988
TAKE 2: OPERA FAVOURITES/ORCHESTRAL CLASSICS VARIOUS ARTISTS (MASTERWORKS)	18	1992
TAKE A BREAK VARIOUS ARTISTS (COLUMBIA)	10	1996
TAKE A LOOK NATALIE COLE	16	1993
TAKE A LOOK IN THE MIRROR KORN	53	2003
TAKE A LOOK OVER YOUR SHOULDER (REALITY) WARREN G	20	1997
TAKE A PAIR OF SPARKLING EYES JOSEF LOCKE	41	1992
TAKE DIS CREDIT TO THE NATION	20	1994
TAKE FAT AND PARTY ROY 'CHUBBY' BROWN	29	1995
TAKE FOUNTAIN WEDDING PRESENT	68	2005
TAKE GOOD CARE OF MY BABY BOBBY VEE	7	1962
TAKE GOOD CARE OF YOURSELF THREE DEGREES	6	1975
TAKE IT EASY WALKER BROTHERS	3	1965
TAKE IT HOME B.B. KING	60	1979
TAKE IT TO HEART MICHAEL McDONALD	35	1990
TAKE ME HIGH (OST) CLIFF RICHARD	41	1974
TAKE ME HIGHER DIANA ROSS	10	1995
TAKE ME TO GOD JAH WOBBLE'S INVADERS OF THE HEART	13	1994
TAKE MY BREATH AWAY – ULTIMATE MOVIE HITS VARIOUS ARTISTS (SONY BMG)	8	2008
TAKE MY TIME SHEENA EASTON	17	1981
TAKE OFF YOUR COLOURS YOU ME AT SIX	25	2008
TAKE OFF YOUR PANTS AND JACKET BLINK 182	4	2001
TAKE ONE! SHAKIN' STEVENS	62	1980
TAKE THAT AND PARTY TAKE THAT	2	1992
TAKE THE HEAT OFF ME BONEY M	40	1977
TAKE THEM ON ON YOUR OWN BLACK REBEL MOTORCYCLE CLUB	3	2003
TAKE TO THE SKIES ENTER SHIKARI	4	2007
TAKE TWO DIANE SOLOMON	26	1975
TAKE TWO ROBSON & JEROME	1	1996
TAKIN' IT TO THE STREETS DOOBIE BROTHERS	42	1976
TAKING CHANCES CELINE DION	5	2007
TAKING ON THE WORLD GUN	44	1989
TAKING THE LONG WAY DIXIE CHICKS	10	2006
TAKK SIGUR ROS	16	2005
A TALE OF TWO CITIES MR HUDSON & THE LIBRARY	69	2007
TALES DON'T TELL THEMSELVES FUNERAL FOR A FRIEND	3	2007
TALES FROM NEW YORK – THE VERY BEST OF SIMON & GARFUNKEL SIMON & GARFUNKEL	8	2000
TALES FROM THE CITY (TELEVISION COMPILATION) TELEVISION AND RADIO COMPILATION	17	1993
TALES FROM TOPOGRAPHIC OCEANS YES	1	1973
TALES FROM TURNPIKE HOUSE SAINT ETIENNE	72	2005
TALES OF A LIBRARIAN TORI AMOS	74	2003
TALES OF MYSTERY AND IMAGINATION ALAN PARSONS PROJECT	56	1976
TALK YES	20	1994
TALK IS CHEAP KEITH RICHARDS	37	1988
TALK OF THE DEVIL OZZY OSBOURNE	21	1982
TALK ON CORNERS CORRS	1	1997
TALK TALK TALK PSYCHEDELIC FURS	30	1981
TALKIE WALKIE AIR	2	2004
TALKIN LOUD TWO VARIOUS ARTISTS (TALKIN' LOUD)	6	1993
TALKING BACK TO THE NIGHT STEVE WINWOOD	6	1982
TALKING BOOK STEVIE WONDER	16	1973
TALKING HEADS '77 TALKING HEADS	60	1978
TALKING TIMBUKTU ALI FARKA TOURE & RY COODER	44	1994
TALKING WITH THE TAXMAN ABOUT POETRY BILLY BRAGG	8	1986
TALLER IN MORE WAYS SUGABABES	1	2005
TALLULAH GO-BETWEENS	91	1987
TAMING THE TIGER JONI MITCHELL	57	1998
TAMLA MOTOWN HITS VOLUME 5 VARIOUS ARTISTS (MOTOWN)	11	1967
TAMLA MOTOWN HITS VOLUME 6 VARIOUS ARTISTS (MOTOWN)	32	1968
TANGLED UP GIRLS ALOUD	4	2007
TANGO JULIO IGLESIAS	56	1996
TANGO IN THE NIGHT FLEETWOOD MAC	1	1987
TANGRAM TANGERINE DREAM	36	1980
TANTO TEMPO BEBEL GILBERTO	49	2002
TANX T. REX	4	1973
TAO RICK SPRINGFIELD	68	1985
TAP ROOT MANUSCRIPT NEIL DIAMOND	19	1971
TAPESTRY CAROLE KING	4	1971
TAPESTRY DON McLEAN	16	1972
TAPESTRY CAROLE KING	24	1998
A TAPESTRY OF DREAMS CHARLES AZNAVOUR	9	1974
THE TARANTINO COLLECTION VARIOUS ARTISTS (MCA)	18	1996
TARANTULA RIDE	21	1996
TARKUS EMERSON, LAKE & PALMER	1	1971
TASTE – LIVE AT THE ISLE OF WIGHT TASTE	41	1972
A TASTE OF HONEY MR ACKER BILK	17	1963
TASTY KELIS	11	2004
TATTOO RORY GALLAGHER	32	1973
TATTOO YOU ROLLING STONES	2	1981
TATTOOED BEAT MESSIAH ZODIAC MINDWARP & THE LOVE REACTION	20	1988
TATTOOED MILLIONAIRE BRUCE DICKINSON	14	1990
TAXI BRYAN FERRY	2	1993
TAXI FOR THESE ANIMAL MEN THESE ANIMAL MEN	64	1995
TEA FOR THE TILLERMAN CAT STEVENS	20	1970
TEACH THE WORLD TO LAUGH BARRON KNIGHTS	51	1979
TEAR DOWN THESE WALLS BILLY OCEAN	3	1988
TEARDROPS VARIOUS ARTISTS (RITZ)	37	1983
TEARS AND LAUGHTER JOHNNY MATHIS	1	1980
TEARS OF HAPPINESS KEN DODD	6	1965
TEARS OF STONE CHIEFTAINS	36	1999
TEARS ROLL DOWN (GREATEST HITS 1982-1992) TEARS FOR FEARS	2	1992
TEASE ME CHAKA DEMUS & PLIERS	1	1993
TEASER AND THE FIRECAT CAT STEVENS	3	1971
TEASES AND DARES KIM WILDE	66	1984
TEATRO TEATRO	43	2007
TECHNICAL ECSTASY BLACK SABBATH	13	1976
TECHNIQUE NEW ORDER	1	1989
TECHNO NIGHTS AMBIENT DAWN VARIOUS ARTISTS (EMI)	16	1995
TECHNOHEDZ – 20 FIRESTARTIN' TECHNO ANTHEMS VARIOUS ARTISTS (TELSTAR)	12	1996
TECHNOSTATE VARIOUS ARTISTS (COOKIE JAR)	2	1992
TED NUGENT TED NUGENT	56	1976
TEENAGE DEPRESSION EDDIE & THE HOT RODS	43	1976
TEENAGE DREAMS DANIEL O'DONNELL	10	2005
TEENAGE DRUG SULTANS OF PING	57	1994
TEENAGE KICKS VARIOUS ARTISTS (POLYGRAM)	8	1995
TEENAGE KICKS VARIOUS ARTISTS (UNIVERSAL)	20	2002
TEENAGE KICKS VARIOUS ARTISTS (SANCTUARY)	2	2005
TEENAGE KICKS – THE BEST OF UNDERTONES	35	2003

Title / Artist	Peak Position	Year of Release
TEENAGE MUTANT NINJA TURTLES FILM SOUNDTRACK	6	1990
TEENAGE WARNING ANGELIC UPSTARTS	29	1979
TEENAGER THRILLS	48	2007
TEENAGER OF THE YEAR FRANK BLACK	21	1994
TEENDREEM VARIOUS ARTISTS (WARNER BROTHERS)	19	2001
TELEKON GARY NUMAN	1	1980
TELL GOD I'M HERE HURRAH!	71	1987
TELL IT TO MY HEART TAYLOR DAYNE	24	1988
TELL ME IT'S NOT TRUE 'FROM THE MUSICAL BLOOD BROTHERS' BARBARA DICKSON	100	1983
TELL ME ON A SUNDAY MARTI WEBB	2	1980
TELL ME ON A SUNDAY DENISE VAN OUTEN	34	2003
TELL TALE SIGNS – THE BOOTLEG SERIES VOLUME 8 BOB DYLAN	9	2008
TELL US THE TRUTH SHAM 69	25	1978
TELLIN' STORIES CHARLATANS	1	1997
TELLY TELLY SAVALAS	12	1975
TELLYHITS – 16 TOP TV THEMES (TELEVISION COMPILATION) TELEVISION AND RADIO COMPILATION	34	1985
TELLYHITS 2 – 16 TOP TV THEMES (TELEVISION COMPILATION) TELEVISION AND RADIO COMPILATION	68	1986
TEMPERAMENTAL EVERYTHING BUT THE GIRL	16	1999
TEMPERANCE SEVEN 1961 TEMPERANCE SEVEN	8	1961
TEMPERANCE SEVEN PLUS ONE TEMPERANCE SEVEN	19	1961
TEMPTATION VARIOUS ARTISTS (QUALITY TELEVISION)	3	1992
TEMPTATIONS GREATEST HITS TEMPTATIONS	17	1967
THE TEMPTATIONS LIVE! TEMPTATIONS	20	1967
TEMPTATIONS WITH A LOT OF SOUL TEMPTATIONS	19	1967
TEMPTATIONS/FOUR TOPS: AT THEIR BEST VARIOUS ARTISTS (UNIVERSAL)	18	2002
TEMPTED VARIOUS ARTISTS (POLYGRAM)	10	1993
10 STRANGLERS	15	1990
TEN PEARL JAM	18	1992
10 WET WET WET	2	1997
10 LL COOL J	26	2002
10 C.C. 10 C.C.	36	1973
TEN FEET HIGH ANDREA CORR	38	2007
TEN GOOD REASONS JASON DONOVAN	1	1989
TEN MORE TURNIPS FROM THE TIP IAN DURY & THE BLOCKHEADS	60	2002
TEN NEW MESSAGES RAKES	38	2007
TEN NEW SONGS LEONARD COHEN	26	2001
TEN SHORT SONGS ABOUT LOVE GARY CLARK	25	1993
TEN SILVER DROPS SECRET MACHINES	43	2006
TEN SUMMONER'S TALES STING	2	1993
10,000 DAYS TOOL	4	2006
TEN THOUSAND FISTS DISTURBED	59	2005
10,000 HZ LEGEND AIR	7	2001
10 TO 23 JOSE FELICIANO	38	1970
TEN YEARS NON-STOP JUBILEE JAMES LAST	5	1975
10 YEARS OF HITS RONAN KEATING	1	2004
10 YEARS OF HITS – RADIO ONE VARIOUS ARTISTS (BBC)	39	1977
TEN YEARS TOGETHER PETER, PAUL & MARY	60	1970
TENACIOUS D TENACIOUS D	38	2002
TENDER LOVE – 17 ROMANTIC LOVE SONGS VARIOUS ARTISTS (EMI)	2	1992
TENDER PREY NICK CAVE & THE BAD SEEDS	67	1988
TENDERLY GEORGE BENSON	52	1989
TENEMENT SYMPHONY MARC ALMOND	39	1991
TENNESSEE MOON (THE NASHVILLE COLLECTION) NEIL DIAMOND	12	1996
TENNIS CHRIS REA	60	1980
TENOR AT THE MOVIES JONATHAN ANSELL	9	2008
THE TENSION AND THE SPARK DARREN HAYES	13	2004
TERENCE TRENT D'ARBY'S VIBRATOR TERENCE TRENT D'ARBY	11	1995
TERMINATOR 2 BRAD FIEDEL	26	1991
TERRAPIN STATION GRATEFUL DEAD	30	1977
TERROR TWILIGHT PAVEMENT	19	1999
TEST FOR ECHO RUSH	25	1996
TESTAMENT '93 INNER CITY	33	1993
TESTIFY PHIL COLLINS	15	2002
TESTIMONY DANA GLOVER	43	2003
TEXAS FEVER ORANGE JUICE	34	1984
THA BLUE CARPET TREATMENT SNOOP DOGG	47	2006
THA CARTER III LIL' WAYNE	23	2008
THA DOGGFATHER SNOOP DOGGY DOGG	15	1996
THA LAST MEAL SNOOP DOGG	62	2001
THANK CHRIST FOR THE BOMB GROUNDHOGS	9	1970
THANK GOD IT'S FRIDAY FILM SOUNDTRACK	40	1978
THANK YOU DURAN DURAN	12	1995
THANK YOU JAMELIA	4	2003
THANK YOU AND GOODNIGHT IT BITES	59	1991
THANK YOU BABY STYLISTICS	5	1975
THANK YOU FOR THE MUSIC ABBA	17	1983
THANK YOU FOR THE YEARS SHIRLEY BASSEY	19	2003
THANK YOU VERY MUCH – REUNION CONCERT AT THE LONDON PALLADIUM CLIFF RICHARD & THE SHADOWS	5	1979
THANKFUL KELLY CLARKSON	41	2003
THANKS BUT I'LL EAT IT HERE LOWELL GEORGE	71	1979
THANKS FOR THE MEMORY – THE GREAT AMERICAN SONGBOOK IV ROD STEWART	3	2005
THAT ALBUM BY OCEANIC OCEANIC	49	1992
THAT LOVING FEELING VINCE HILL	51	1978
THAT LOVING FEELING VARIOUS ARTISTS (DINO)	3	1989
THAT LOVING FEELING VARIOUS ARTISTS (WARNER BROTHERS)	7	2005
THAT LOVING FEELING VOLUME 2 VARIOUS ARTISTS (DINO)	5	1990
THAT LOVING FEELING VOLUME 3 VARIOUS ARTISTS (DINO)	1	1990
THAT LOVING FEELING VOLUME 4 VARIOUS ARTISTS (DINO)	3	1991
THAT LOVING FEELING VOLUME 5 VARIOUS ARTISTS (DINO)	2	1991
THAT LOVING FEELING VOLUME VI VARIOUS ARTISTS (DINO)	3	1993
THAT LOVING FEELING VOLUME VII VARIOUS ARTISTS (DINO)	4	1994
THAT LUCKY OLD SUN BRIAN WILSON	37	2008
THAT OLE DEVIL CALLED LOVE VARIOUS ARTISTS (UNIVERSAL)	5	2000
THAT SUMMER FILM SOUNDTRACK	36	1979
THAT WAS THE WEEK THAT WAS (TELEVISION SOUNDTRACK) TELEVISION AND RADIO COMPILATION	11	1963
THAT WHAT IS NOT PUBLIC IMAGE LTD	46	1992
THAT WONDERFUL SOUND OF LENA MARTELL LENA MARTELL	35	1974
THAT'LL BE THE DAY BUDDY HOLLY	5	1961
THAT'LL BE THE DAY VARIOUS ARTISTS (RONCO)	1	1973
THAT'S ALL BOBBY DARIN	15	1960
THAT'S CHRISTMAS VARIOUS ARTISTS (EMI)	10	1994
THAT'S COUNTRY VARIOUS ARTISTS (EMI)	11	1995
THAT'S LIFE FRANK SINATRA	22	1967
THAT'S LIFE SHAM 69	27	1978
THAT'S LIFE RUSSELL WATSON	4	2007
THAT'S RIGHT GEORGE BENSON	61	1996
THAT'S ROCK 'N' ROLL VARIOUS ARTISTS (EMI)	12	1995
THAT'S THE WAY IT IS (OST) ELVIS PRESLEY	12	1971
THAT'S WHAT FRIENDS ARE FOR JOHNNY MATHIS & DENIECE WILLIAMS	16	1978
THAT'S WHAT LIFE IS ALL ABOUT BING CROSBY	28	1975
THEATRE OF PAIN MOTLEY CRUE	36	1985
THEAUDIENCE THEAUDIENCE	22	1998
THEIR FIRST LP SPENCER DAVIS GROUP	6	1966
THEIR GREATEST HITS FOUR TOPS	47	1990
THEIR GREATEST HITS HOT CHOCOLATE	1	1993
THEIR GREATEST HITS 1971-1975 EAGLES	2	1976
THEIR GREATEST HITS – THE RECORD BEE GEES	5	2001
THEIR LAW – THE SINGLES 1990-2005 PRODIGY	1	2005
THEIR SATANIC MAJESTIES REQUEST ROLLING STONES	3	1967
THEM OR US FRANK ZAPPA	53	1984
THEMENINBLACK STRANGLERS	8	1981
THEMES VARIOUS ARTISTS (K-TEL)	6	1981
THEMES VANGELIS	11	1989
THE THEMES ALBUM VARIOUS ARTISTS (K-TEL)	43	1984
THEMES AND DREAMS SHADOWS	21	1991
THEMES AND DREAMS VARIOUS ARTISTS (GLOBAL TELEVISION)	11	1995
THEMES FOR DREAMS PIERRE BELMONDE	13	1980
THEN AND NOW DAVID CASSIDY	5	2001
THEN AND NOW WHO	5	2004
THEN & NOW – THE VERY BEST OF PETULA CLARK PETULA CLARK	17	2008
THEN CAME ROCK 'N' ROLL VARIOUS ARTISTS (EMI)	5	1984
THEN PLAY ON FLEETWOOD MAC	6	1969
THERE AND BACK JEFF BECK	38	1980
THERE GOES RHYMIN' SIMON PAUL SIMON	4	1973
THERE IS NOTHING LEFT TO LOSE FOO FIGHTERS	10	1999
THERE IS ONLY ONE ROY ORBISON ROY ORBISON	10	1965
THERE IT IS 911	8	1999
THERE MUST BE A WAY FRANKIE VAUGHAN	22	1967
THERE YOU'LL BE FAITH HILL	6	2001
THERE'S A POISON GOIN' ON... PUBLIC ENEMY	55	1999
THERE'S A RIOT GOIN' ON SLY & THE FAMILY STONE	31	1972
THERE'S NOTHING LIKE THIS OMAR	19	1990
THERE'S ONE IN EVERY CROWD ERIC CLAPTON	15	1975
THERE'S SOMETHING GOING ON BABYBIRD	28	1998
THERE'S THE RUB WISHBONE ASH	16	1974
THERE'S TWO KINDS OF MUSIC: ROCK 'N' ROLL! SHAKIN' STEVENS	65	1990
THESE ARE MY MOUNTAINS ALEXANDER BROTHERS	29	1966
THESE ARE MY SONGS PETULA CLARK	38	1967
THESE ARE MY SONGS MOIRA ANDERSON	50	1970
THESE ARE SPECIAL TIMES CELINE DION	20	1998
THESE ARE THE FACTS MILBURN	51	2007
THESE DAYS BON JOVI	1	1995
THESE DREAMS – GREATEST HITS HEART	33	1997
THESE FOOLISH THINGS BRYAN FERRY	5	1973
THESE STREETS PAOLO NUTINI	3	2006
THESE THINGS MOVE IN THREES MUMM-RA	42	2007
THEY DON'T KNOW SO SOLID CREW	6	2001
THEY NEVER SAW ME COMING TQ	27	1999
THEY SAID IT COULDN'T BE DONE GRANDMASTER FLASH	95	1985
THICK AS A BRICK JETHRO TULL	5	1972
THIEF (OST) TANGERINE DREAM	43	1981

Title / Artist	Peak Position	Year of Release
THE THIEVING MAGPIE MARILLION	25	1988
THIN ICE 2 – THE SECOND SHIVER VARIOUS ARTISTS (TELSTAR)	1	1991
THIN ICE – THE FIRST STEP VARIOUS ARTISTS (TELSTAR)	2	1991
A THING CALLED LOVE JOHNNY CASH	8	1972
THINGS TO MAKE AND DO MOLOKO	3	2000
THINK BEFORE YOU SPEAK GOOD SHOES	55	2007
THINK ON YOUR FEET JAIMESON	42	2004
THINK TANK BLUR	1	2003
THINKING ABOUT MYSELF COSMIC BABY	60	1994
THINKING IT OVER LIBERTY X	3	2002
THINKING OF YOU... VARIOUS ARTISTS (COLUMBIA)	1	1991
THIRD SOFT MACHINE	18	1970
THIRD PORTISHEAD	2	2008
THE THIRD CHAPTER VARIOUS ARTISTS (XL RECORDINGS)	6	1992
THIRD DEGREE 9 BELOW ZERO	38	1982
THIRD STAGE BOSTON	37	1986
THIRST FOR ROMANCE CHERRY GHOST	7	2007
THIRSTY WORK STATUS QUO	13	1994
THIRTEEN TEENAGE FANCLUB	14	1993
13 BLUR	1	1999
13 SMASH HITS TOM JONES	5	1967
THIRTEEN TALES FROM URBAN BOHEMIA DANDY WARHOLS	32	2000
THIRTEENTH STEP A PERFECT CIRCLE	37	2003
30TH ANNIVERSARY COLLECTION WHITESNAKE	38	2008
30 GOLDEN GREATS GEORGE MITCHELL MINSTRELS WITH THE JOE LOSS ORCHESTRA	10	1977
30 GREATEST GLADYS KNIGHT & THE PIPS	3	1977
3121 PRINCE	9	2006
30 SMASH HITS OF THE WAR YEARS BAND & CHORUS OF HER MAJESTY'S GUARDS DIVISION	38	1975
30 SOMETHING CARTER – THE UNSTOPPABLE SEX MACHINE	8	1991
THIRTY THOUSAND FEET OVER CHINA PASSIONS	92	1981
THIRTY THREE AND A THIRD GEORGE HARRISON	35	1976
33 REVOLUTIONS PER MINUTE MARXMAN	69	1993
32 MINUTES AND 17 SECONDS CLIFF RICHARD & THE SHADOWS	3	1962
32 ONES ON ONE – RADIO 1'S 25TH ANNIVERSARY VARIOUS ARTISTS (CONNOISSEUR COLLECTION)	8	1992
30 YEARS OF MAXIMUM R&B WHO	48	1994
THIS ARE TWO TONE VARIOUS ARTISTS (2 TONE)	51	1983
THIS DELICATE THING WE'VE MADE DARREN HAYES	14	2007
THIS DESERT LIFE COUNTING CROWS	19	1999
THIS FILM'S CRAP, LET'S SLASH THE SEATS DAVID HOLMES	51	1995
THIS FIRE PAULA COLE	60	1997
THIS GIFT SONS & DAUGHTERS	66	2008
THIS IS ...CLUB NATION VARIOUS ARTISTS (BEECHWOOD)	19	1997
THIS IS ...CLUB NATION 2 VARIOUS ARTISTS (BEECHWOOD)	19	1998
THIS IS ...HOUSE VARIOUS ARTISTS (BEECHWOOD)	18	1996
THIS IS ...IBIZA VARIOUS ARTISTS (BEECHWOOD)	13	1997
THIS IS ...IBIZA 2000 VARIOUS ARTISTS (BEECHWOOD)	17	1999
THIS IS ...IBIZA 98 VARIOUS ARTISTS (BEECHWOOD)	16	1998
THIS IS ...R&B VARIOUS ARTISTS (BEECHWOOD)	14	1999
THIS IS ...SPEED GARAGE VARIOUS ARTISTS (BEECHWOOD)	10	1998
THIS IS ...SWING VARIOUS ARTISTS (BEECHWOOD)	20	1996
THIS IS ...TRANCE VARIOUS ARTISTS (BEECHWOOD)	19	1999
THIS IS A FIX AUTOMATIC	44	2008
THIS IS ALPHABEAT ALPHABEAT	10	2008
THIS IS BIG AUDIO DYNAMITE BIG AUDIO DYNAMITE	27	1985
THIS IS CHAQUITO CHAQUITO & QUEDO BRASS	36	1968
THIS IS CULT FICTION VARIOUS ARTISTS (VIRGIN)	9	1995
THIS IS DARIN BOBBY DARIN	4	1960
THIS IS DESMOND DEKKER DESMOND DEKKER	27	1969
THIS IS ELVIS PRESLEY (OST) ELVIS PRESLEY	47	1981
THIS IS ENNIO MORRICONE ENNIO MORRICONE	23	1981
THIS IS FRANK SINATRA 1953-1957 FRANK SINATRA	56	1995
THIS IS GARAGE VARIOUS ARTISTS (COOLTEMPO)	18	1989
THIS IS HANCOCK TONY HANCOCK	2	1960
THIS IS HARDCORE PULP	1	1998
THIS IS HAZELVILLE CAPTAIN	23	2006
THIS IS HOPE MULL HISTORICAL SOCIETY	58	2004
THIS IS HOW WE DO IT MONTELL JORDAN	53	1995
THIS IS IT VARIOUS ARTISTS (CBS)	6	1979
THIS IS JAMES LAST JAMES LAST	6	1967
THIS IS MANUEL MANUEL & THE MUSIC OF THE MOUNTAINS	18	1971
THIS IS ME...THEN JENNIFER LOPEZ	13	2002
THIS IS MUSIC – THE SINGLES 92-98 VERVE	15	2004
THIS IS MY DEMO SWAY	45	2006
THIS IS MY LIFE – THE GREATEST HITS SHIRLEY BASSEY	54	2000
THIS IS MY TRUTH TELL ME YOURS MANIC STREET PREACHERS	1	1998
THIS IS NIECEY DENIECE WILLIAMS	31	1977
THIS IS NOIZE VARIOUS ARTISTS (COLUMBIA)	17	1999
THIS IS NOT A LOVE SONG OMAR	50	1997
THIS IS NOT A TEST MISSY ELLIOTT	47	2003
THIS IS NOT THE WORLD FUTUREHEADS	17	2008
THIS IS OUR ART SOUP DRAGONS	60	1988
THIS IS POURCEL FRANK POURCEL	8	1971
THIS IS SINATRA (VOLUME 2) FRANK SINATRA	3	1958
THIS IS SINATRA! FRANK SINATRA	1	1957
THIS IS SKA VARIOUS ARTISTS (TELSTAR)	6	1989
THIS IS SOUL VARIOUS ARTISTS (ATLANTIC)	16	1969
THIS IS THE DAY...THIS IS THE HOUR...THIS IS THIS? POP WILL EAT ITSELF	24	1989
THIS IS THE LIFE MATT MONRO	25	1966
THIS IS THE LIFE AMY MacDONALD	1	2007
THIS IS THE MODERN WORLD JAM	22	1977
THIS IS THE MODERN WORLD VARIOUS ARTISTS (UNIVERSAL)	9	2004
THIS IS THE MOMENT ADAM WATKISS	65	2001
THIS IS THE MOMENT DONNY OSMOND	10	2001
THIS IS THE MOODY BLUES MOODY BLUES	14	1974
THIS IS THE REMIX DESTINY'S CHILD	25	2002
THIS IS THE RETURN OF CULT FICTION VARIOUS ARTISTS (VIRGIN)	15	1996
THIS IS THE SEA WATERBOYS	37	1985
THIS IS THE STORY PROCLAIMERS	43	1987
THIS IS THE WORLD RIVER CITY PEOPLE	56	1991
THIS IS TOM JONES TOM JONES	2	1969
THIS IS TONGUE 'N' CHEEK TONGUE 'N' CHEEK	45	1990
THIS IS VAL DOONICAN VAL DOONICAN	40	1971
THIS IS WHAT YOU WANT...THIS IS WHAT YOU GET PUBLIC IMAGE LTD	56	1984
THIS IS WHERE I CAME IN BEE GEES	6	2001
THIS IS...TRANCELIFE VARIOUS ARTISTS (BEECHWOOD)	19	2000
THIS KIND OF LOVE PHIL FEARON & GALAXY	98	1985
THIS LAST NIGHT IN SODOM SOFT CELL	12	1984
THIS LEFT FEELS RIGHT BON JOVI	4	2003
THIS LOVE VARIOUS ARTISTS (SONY BMG)	4	2005
THIS MAN ALONE EDWARD WOODWARD	53	1970
THIS NATION'S SAVING GRACE FALL	54	1985
THIS NEW DAY EMBRACE	1	2006
THIS NOTE'S FOR YOU NEIL YOUNG & THE BLUE NOTES	56	1988
THIS OLD HEART OF MINE ISLEY BROTHERS	23	1968
THIS OLE HOUSE SHAKIN' STEVENS	2	1981
THIS SHOULD MOVE YA MANTRONIX	18	1990
THIS STRANGE ENGINE MARILLION	27	1997
THIS THING CALLED LOVE – THE GREATEST HITS OF ALEXANDER O'NEAL ALEXANDER O'NEAL	4	1992
THIS TIME ENGLAND WORLD CUP SQUAD	37	1982
THIS TIME MELANIE C	57	2007
THIS TIME AROUND HANSON	33	2000
THIS TIME I'M SWINGING DEAN MARTIN	18	1961
THIS TIME IT'S PERSONAL MICHAEL BALL	20	2000
THIS TIME THE FIRST FOUR YEARS CULTURE CLUB	8	1987
THIS WAS JETHRO TULL	10	1968
THIS WAY JEWEL	34	2002
THIS WAY UP CHRIS DE BURGH	5	1994
THIS WORLD AND BODY MARION	10	1996
THIS YEAR IN IBIZA VARIOUS ARTISTS (WARNER BROTHERS)	5	1999
THIS YEAR'S LOVE (WILL LAST FOREVER) XXX VARIOUS ARTISTS (SONY)	12	1996
THIS YEAR'S LOVE IS FOREVER VARIOUS ARTISTS (SONY)	4	1995
THIS YEAR'S MODEL ELVIS COSTELLO	4	1978
THOMPSON TWINS – THE GREATEST HITS THOMPSON TWINS	23	1990
THORNOGRAPHY CRADLE OF FILTH	46	2006
THE THORNS THORNS	68	2003
THOROUGHLY MODERN MILLIE FILM SOUNDTRACK	9	1967
THOSE THE BROKES MAGIC NUMBERS	11	2006
THOSE WERE THE DAYS DOLLY PARTON	35	2006
THOUGHT 'YA KNEW CE CE PENISTON	31	1994
THOUGHTS OF A PREDICATE FELON TONY YAYO	41	2005
THOUGHTS OF HOME DANIEL O'DONNELL	43	1989
THOUGHTS OF LOVE SHIRLEY BASSEY	15	1976
A THOUSAND LEAVES SONIC YOUTH	38	1998
A THOUSAND VOLTS OF HOLT JOHN HOLT	42	1975
THRAK KING CRIMSON	58	1995
3 SOULFLY	61	2002
THREE SUGABABES	3	2003
3 CAR GARAGE – INDIE RECORDINGS 95-96 HANSON	39	1998
THREE CHEERS FOR SWEET REVENGE MY CHEMICAL ROMANCE	34	2005
THREE CHORD OPERA NEIL DIAMOND	49	2001
3D THREE DEGREES	61	1979
3D TLC	45	2002
THREE DEGREES THREE DEGREES	12	1974
THREE DOLLAR BILL Y'ALL LIMP BIZKIT	50	2000
THE THREE E.P.'S BETA BAND	35	1998
3 FEET HIGH AND RISING DE LA SOUL	13	1989
THREE HEARTS IN THE HAPPY ENDING MACHINE DARYL HALL	26	1986
THREE IMAGINARY BOYS CURE	44	1979

Title / Artist	Peak Position	Year of Release
THREE LIGHT YEARS ELECTRIC LIGHT ORCHESTRA	38	1979
3LW 3LW	75	2001
THREE MINUTE HEROES VARIOUS ARTISTS (VIRGIN)	4	1992
THREE OF A PERFECT PAIR KING CRIMSON	30	1984
THREE SIDES LIVE GENESIS	2	1982
III SIDES TO EVERY STORY EXTREME	2	1992
THREE SNAKES AND ONE CHARM BLACK CROWES	17	1996
THREE STEPS TO HEAVEN – ROCK 'N' ROLL LEGENDS VARIOUS ARTISTS (QUALITY TELEVISION)	6	1992
THE THREE TENORS CHRISTMAS CARRERAS/ DOMINGO/PAVAROTTI FEATURING MEHTA	57	2000
THE THREE TENORS IN CONCERT 1994 CARRERAS DOMINGO PAVAROTTI WITH ORCHESTRA CONDUCTED BY ZUBIN MEHTA	1	1994
THE THREE TENORS PARIS 1998 CARRERAS DOMINGO PAVAROTTI WITH JAMES LEVINE	14	1998
3 YEARS, 5 MONTHS AND 2 DAYS IN THE LIFE OF... ARRESTED DEVELOPMENT	3	1992
THE THRILL OF IT ALL THUNDER	14	1997
THRILL TO THE SENSATIONAL SOUND OF SUPER STEREO VARIOUS ARTISTS (CBS)	20	1967
THRILLER EDDIE & THE HOT RODS	50	1979
THRILLER MICHAEL JACKSON	1	1982
THRILLER – 25TH ANNIVERSARY EDITION MICHAEL JACKSON	3	2008
THRILLER THEMES CHAQUITO ORCHESTRA	48	1972
THROUGH A BIG COUNTRY – GREATEST HITS BIG COUNTRY	2	1990
THROUGH THE BARRICADES SPANDAU BALLET	7	1986
THROUGH THE EVIL CLAYTOWN TROUPE	72	1989
THROUGH THE FIRE HAGAR, SCHON, AARONSON, SHRIEVE	92	1984
THROUGH THE LOOKING GLASS SIOUXSIE & THE BANSHEES	15	1987
THROUGH THE PAST DARKLY (BIG HITS VOLUME 2) ROLLING STONES	2	1969
THROUGH THE STORM ARETHA FRANKLIN	46	1989
THROUGH THE WINDOWPANE GUILLEMOTS	17	2006
THROUGH THE YEARS CILLA BLACK	41	1993
THROWIN' DOWN RICK JAMES	93	1982
THROWING COPPER LIVE	37	1995
THROWING MUSES THROWING MUSES	75	2003
THUNDER ANDY TAYLOR	61	1987
THUNDER AND CONSOLATION NEW MODEL ARMY	20	1989
THUNDER AND LIGHTNING THIN LIZZY	4	1983
THUNDER IN MY HEART LEO SAYER	8	1977
THUNDER LIGHTNING STRIKE THE GO! TEAM	48	2006
TI ADORO LUCIANO PAVAROTTI	21	2003
TI AMO – PUCCINI'S GREATEST LOVE SONGS LUCIANO PAVAROTTI	23	1993
TICAL 0 – THE PREQUEL METHOD MAN	29	2004
TICAL 2000: JUDGEMENT DAY METHOD MAN	49	1998
TICKET TO RIDE CARPENTERS	20	1972
TICKET TO RIDE CARPENTERS	35	1975
TIDY EUPHORIA VARIOUS ARTISTS (MINISTRY OF SOUND)	10	2005
TIESTO – IN SEARCH OF SUNRISE VARIOUS ARTISTS (BLACK HOLE)	12	2006
TIESTO – IN SEARCH OF SUNRISE 6 – IBIZA VARIOUS ARTISTS (BLACK HOLE)	12	2007
TIESTO – IN SEARCH OF SUNRISE 7 – ASIA VARIOUS ARTISTS (BLACK HOLE)	14	2008
TIFFANY TIFFANY	5	1988
TIGER BAY SAINT ETIENNE	8	1994
TIGERLILY NATALIE MERCHANT	39	1995
TIGERMILK BELLE & SEBASTIAN	13	1999
TIGHT FIT TIGHT FIT	87	1982
TIGHTEN UP VOLUME 1 LOOSE ENDS	40	1992
TIGHTEN UP VOLUME 4 VARIOUS ARTISTS (TROJAN)	20	1971
TIGHTEN UP VOLUME 88 BIG AUDIO DYNAMITE	33	1988
TILL DEAF US DO PART SLADE	68	1981
TILL DEATH DO US PART CYPRESS HILL	53	2004
TILL I LOVED YOU BARBRA STREISAND	29	1988
TILL THE SUN TURNS BLACK RAY LAMONTAGNE	35	2006
TILL WE HAVE FACES STEVE HACKETT	54	1984
TILT COZY POWELL	58	1981
TILT SCOTT WALKER	27	1995
TILT LIGHTNING SEEDS	46	1999
TIMBALAND PRESENTS SHOCK VALUE TIMBALAND	2	2007
TIME ELECTRIC LIGHT ORCHESTRA	1	1981
THE TIME BROS	4	1989
TIME FLEETWOOD MAC	47	1995
TIME PETER ANDRE	28	1997
TIME LIONEL RICHIE	31	1998
TIME AFTER TIME EVA CASSIDY	25	2000
TIME AND A WORD YES	45	1970
TIME AND TIDE SPLIT ENZ	71	1982
TIME AND TIDE BASIA	61	1988
TIME CHANGES EVERYTHING JOHN SQUIRE	17	2002
TIME FADES AWAY NEIL YOUNG	20	1973
TIME FOR HEROES: BEST OF LIBERTINES	23	2007
TIME FOR LOVE BILL TARMEY	28	1994
TIME FOR THE REST OF YOUR LIFE STRANGELOVE	69	1994
A TIME FOR US DONNY OSMOND	4	1973
TIME FURTHER OUT DAVE BRUBECK	12	1962
THE TIME HAS COME (EP) UNKLE	73	1995
TIME HONOURED GHOST BARCLAY JAMES HARVEST	32	1975
THE TIME IS NEAR KEEF HARTLEY BAND	41	1970
TIME LOVES A HERO LITTLE FEAT	8	1977
TIME MACHINE JOE SATRIANI	32	1993
TIME ON EARTH CROWDED HOUSE	3	2007
TIME OUT DAVE BRUBECK QUARTET	11	1960
TIME OUT OF MIND BOB DYLAN	10	1997
TIME PASSAGES AL STEWART	39	1978
TIME PIECES – THE BEST OF ERIC CLAPTON ERIC CLAPTON	20	1982
TIME SEX LOVE MARY CHAPIN CARPENTER	57	2001
TIME TELLS NO LIES PRAYING MANTIS	60	1981
TIME THE CONQUEROR JACKSON BROWNE	57	2008
TIME TO CELEBRATE RUSS CONWAY	3	1959
TIME TO GROW LEMAR	8	2004
TIME TO RELAX VARIOUS ARTISTS (CLASSIC FM)	9	2001
A TIME 2 LOVE STEVIE WONDER	24	2005
TIME WAS CURTIS STIGERS	34	1995
TIME, LOVE AND TENDERNESS MICHAEL BOLTON	2	1991
TIMELESS GOLDIE	7	1995
TIMELESS DANIEL O'DONNELL & MARY DUFF	13	1996
TIMELESS SARAH BRIGHTMAN	2	1997
TIMELESS VARIOUS ARTISTS (DECCA)	8	2003
TIMELESS SERGIO MENDES	15	2006
TIMELESS WET WET WET	41	2007
TIMELESS (THE CLASSICS) MICHAEL BOLTON	3	1992
TIMELESS FLIGHT STEVE HARLEY & COCKNEY REBEL	18	1976
TIMELESS – LIVE IN CONCERT BARBRA STREISAND	54	2000
TIMELESS – THE CLASSICS VOLUME 2 MICHAEL BOLTON	50	1999
TIMELESS – THE VERY BEST OF NEIL SEDAKA NEIL SEDAKA	10	1991
TIMES LIKE THESE FRIDAY HILL	67	2006
THE TIMES THEY ARE A-CHANGIN' BOB DYLAN	4	1964
TIME'S UP LIVING COLOUR	20	1990
TIMESPACE – THE BEST OF STEVIE NICKS STEVIE NICKS	15	1991
TIMING IS EVERYTHING CHRIS DE BURGH	41	2002
TIMO MAAS – CONNECTED VARIOUS ARTISTS (PERFECTO)	20	2001
TIM'S HOUSE KATE WALSH	75	2007
TIN DRUM JAPAN	12	1981
TIN MACHINE TIN MACHINE	3	1989
TIN MACHINE II TIN MACHINE	23	1991
TIN PLANET SPACE	3	1998
TINDERBOX SIOUXSIE & THE BANSHEES	13	1986
TINDERSTICKS TINDERSTICKS	56	1993
TINSEL TOWN REBELLION FRANK ZAPPA	55	1981
TINY MUSIC...MUSIC FROM THE VATICAN GIFT SHOP STONE TEMPLE PILOTS	31	1996
THE TIPPING POINT ROOTS	71	2004
TIRED OF HANGING AROUND ZUTONS	2	2006
TISSUES AND ISSUES CHARLOTTE CHURCH	5	2005
TITANIC (OST) JAMES HORNER	1	1998
TITANIC DAYS KIRSTY MacCOLL	46	1994
TITLE OF RECORD FILTER	75	1999
TITLE TK BREEDERS	51	2002
TITLES MICK KARN	74	1982
TO ALL NEW ARRIVALS FAITHLESS	30	2006
TO BRING YOU MY LOVE PJ HARVEY	12	1995
TO HAVE AND TO HOLD – THE WEDDING ALBUM VARIOUS ARTISTS (QUALITY TELEVISION)	7	1992
TO LOVE AGAIN DIANA ROSS	26	1981
TO LOVERS EVERYWHERE MANTOVANI & HIS ORCHESTRA	44	1972
TO MUM LOVE MOTOWN VARIOUS ARTISTS (MOTOWN)	2	2006
TO MUM WITH LOVE VARIOUS ARTISTS (UNIVERSAL)	1	2007
TO OUR CHILDREN'S CHILDREN'S CHILDREN MOODY BLUES	2	1969
TO RIDE, SHOOT STRAIGHT AND SPEAK THE TRUTH ENTOMBED	75	1997
TO SEE THE LIGHTS GENE	11	1996
TO SURVIVE JOAN AS POLICE WOMAN	56	2008
TO THE 5 BOROUGHS BEASTIE BOYS	2	2004
TO THE EXTREME VANILLA ICE	4	1990
TO THE FAITHFUL DEPARTED CRANBERRIES	2	1996
TO THE LIMIT JOAN ARMATRADING	13	1978
TO THE MAXXIMUM MAXX	66	1994
TO THE MOON CAPERCAILLIE	41	1995
TO THE NEXT LEVEL MN8	13	1995
TO THE TOP ASWAD	71	1986
TO VENUS AND BACK TORI AMOS	22	1999
TO WHOM IT MAY CONCERN PASADENAS	3	1988
TO WHOM IT MAY CONCERN LISA MARIE PRESLEY	52	2003
TOCA FRAGMA	19	2001
TOCSIN X MAL DEUTSCHLAND	86	1984
TODAY ELVIS PRESLEY	48	1975
TOGETHER DIANA ROSS & THE SUPREMES & THE TEMPTATIONS	28	1970
TOGETHER JACK JONES	8	1973
TOGETHER NEW SEEKERS	12	1974
TOGETHER VARIOUS ARTISTS (K-TEL)	20	1979
TOGETHER VARIOUS ARTISTS (POLYGRAM)	2	1995
TOGETHER LULU	4	2002
TOGETHER S CLUB JUNIORS	5	2002
TOGETHER VARIOUS ARTISTS (UNIVERSAL)	20	2002
TOGETHER SALVATION ARMY	20	2008
TOGETHER AGAIN ROSE MARIE	52	1988
TOGETHER AGAIN DANIEL O'DONNELL & MARY DUFF	6	2007

Title / Artist	Peak Position	Year of Release
TOGETHER ALONE CROWDED HOUSE	4	1993
TOGETHER AT LAST RICHARD CLAYDERMAN & JAMES LAST	14	1991
TOGETHER FOR THE CHILDREN OF BOSNIA LUCIANO PAVAROTTI	11	1996
TOGETHER FOREVER – GREATEST HITS 1983-1998 RUN D.M.C.	31	1998
TOGETHER – THE BEST OF REEF	52	2003
TOGETHER WE'RE HEAVY POLYPHONIC SPREE	61	2004
TOGETHER WITH CLIFF RICHARD CLIFF RICHARD	10	1991
TOKYO PROJECT PRESENTS THE COLLECTION VARIOUS ARTISTS (UNIVERSAL)	19	2005
TOM TOM JONES	4	1970
TOM JONES AND JOOLS HOLLAND TOM JONES & JOOLS HOLLAND	5	2004
TOM JONES LIVE IN LAS VEGAS TOM JONES	2	1969
TOM PETTY AND HEARTBREAKERS TOM PETTY & HEARTBREAKERS	24	1977
TOM TOM CLUB TOM TOM CLUB	78	1981
TOMB RAIDER FILM SOUNDTRACK	13	2001
TOMITA'S GREATEST HITS TOMITA	66	1980
TOMMY (OST) WHO	2	1969
TOMMY FILM SOUNDTRACK	21	1975
TOMMY WEDDING PRESENT	42	1988
TOMMY BOY GREATEST BEATS VARIOUS ARTISTS (TOMMY BOY)	44	1985
TOMMY STEELE STAGE SHOW TOMMY STEELE	5	1957
THE TOMMY STEELE STORY TOMMY STEELE	1	1957
TOMORROW BELONGS TO ME SENSATIONAL ALEX HARVEY BAND	9	1975
TOMORROW THE GREEN GRASS JAYHAWKS	41	1995
A TON OF HITS – THE BEST OF STOCK AITKEN WATERMAN VARIOUS ARTISTS (DOVER)	7	1990
TONGUES AND TAILS SOPHIE B HAWKINS	46	1992
TONI BRAXTON TONI BRAXTON	4	1994
TONIC FOR THE TROOPS BOOMTOWN RATS	8	1978
TONIGHT DAVID BOWIE	1	1984
TONIGHT I'M YOURS ROD STEWART	8	1981
TONIGHT'S THE NIGHT NEIL YOUNG	48	1975
TONY ANTHONY NEWLEY	5	1961
TONY CHRISTIE – LIVE TONY CHRISTIE	33	1975
TONY HADLEY TONY HADLEY	45	1997
TONY JOE TONY JOE WHITE	63	1970
TONY MAKES IT HAPPEN TONY BENNETT	31	1967
TONY MONOPOLY TONY MONOPOLY	25	1976
TONY'S GREATEST HITS TONY BENNETT	14	1967
TOO BLIND TO SEE IT KYM SIMS	39	1992
TOO HOT TO HANDLE HEATWAVE	46	1977
TOO LATE TO STOP NOW – THE VERY BEST OF DUBLINERS	54	2006
TOO LEGIT TO QUIT HAMMER	41	1991
TOO LONG IN EXILE VAN MORRISON	4	1993
TOO LOW FOR ZERO ELTON JOHN	7	1983
TOO MUCH PRESSURE SELECTER	5	1980
TOO OLD TO ROCK 'N' ROLL TOO YOUNG TO DIE JETHRO TULL	25	1976
TOO POSH TO MOSH, TOO GOOD TO LAST? LITTLE ANGELS	18	1994
TOO SUSSED? THESE ANIMAL MEN	39	1994
TOO TOUGH TO DIE RAMONES	63	1985
TOO WICKED ASWAD	51	1990
TOO YOUNG DONNY OSMOND	7	1972
TOO YOUNG TO DIE – THE SINGLES SAINT ETIENNE	17	1995
TOONAGE CARTOONS	17	1999
TOO-RYE-AY KEVIN ROWLAND & DEXY'S MIDNIGHT RUNNERS	2	1982
THE TOP CURE	10	1984
THE TOP 25 FROM YOUR 100 BEST TUNES VARIOUS ARTISTS (DECCA)	21	1975
TOP DOGG SNOOP DOGG	48	1999
TOP GEAR (TELEVISION COMPILATION) TELEVISION AND RADIO COMPILATION	3	1994
TOP GEAR 2 VARIOUS ARTISTS (COLUMBIA)	4	1995
TOP GEAR 3 (TELEVISION COMPILATION) TELEVISION AND RADIO COMPILATION	11	1996
TOP GEAR ANTHEMS VARIOUS ARTISTS (EMI)	1	2007
TOP GEAR ANTHEMS (TELEVISION COMPILATION) TELEVISION AND RADIO COMPILATION	6	1998
TOP GEAR ANTHEMS 2008 VARIOUS ARTISTS (EMI)	2	2008
TOP GEAR CLASSICS – TURBO CLASSICS (TELEVISION COMPILATION) TELEVISION AND RADIO COMPILATION	17	1995
TOP GEAR – ON THE ROAD AGAIN (TELEVISION COMPILATION) TELEVISION AND RADIO COMPILATION	12	1996
TOP GEAR SERIOUSLY COOL DRIVING MUSIC VARIOUS ARTISTS (EMI)	9	2007
TOP GEAR – SUB ZERO DRIVING ANTHEMS VARIOUS ARTISTS (UNIVERSAL)	13	2008
TOP GUN FILM SOUNDTRACK	4	1986
TOP KATZ – THE ALBUM PJ & DUNCAN	46	1995
TOP OF THE POPS 1 VARIOUS ARTISTS (COLUMBIA)	1	1995
TOP OF THE POPS 1998 – VOLUME 1 VARIOUS ARTISTS (POLYGRAM)	2	1998
TOP OF THE POPS 1998 – VOLUME 2 VARIOUS ARTISTS (POLYGRAM)	3	1998
TOP OF THE POPS 2 VARIOUS ARTISTS (COLUMBIA)	14	1995
TOP OF THE POPS 2 VARIOUS ARTISTS (UNIVERSAL)	15	2000
TOP OF THE POPS 2 – 70'S ROCK VARIOUS ARTISTS (UNIVERSAL)	10	2001
TOP OF THE POPS 2000 – VOL 3 VARIOUS ARTISTS (UNIVERSAL)	4	2000
TOP OF THE POPS 2000 VOLUME 1 VARIOUS ARTISTS (UNIVERSAL)	3	2000
TOP OF THE POPS 2000 VOLUME 2 VARIOUS ARTISTS (UNIVERSAL)	1	2000
TOP OF THE POPS 2001 – VOL 1 VARIOUS ARTISTS (UNIVERSAL)	4	2001
TOP OF THE POPS 2003 VARIOUS ARTISTS (UNIVERSAL)	14	2002
TOP OF THE POPS '99 – VOLUME ONE VARIOUS ARTISTS (UNIVERSAL)	2	1999
TOP OF THE POPS '99 – VOLUME TWO VARIOUS ARTISTS (UNIVERSAL)	1	1999
TOP OF THE POPS – AUTUMN 2001 VARIOUS ARTISTS (UNIVERSAL)	8	2001
TOP OF THE POPS – BEST OF 1998 VARIOUS ARTISTS (POLYGRAM)	11	1998
TOP OF THE POPS SPRING 2002 VARIOUS ARTISTS (UNIVERSAL)	4	2002
TOP OF THE POPS SPRING 2003 VARIOUS ARTISTS (UNIVERSAL	6	2003
TOP OF THE POPS – SUMMER 2001 VARIOUS ARTISTS (UNIVERSAL)	4	2001
TOP OF THE POPS SUMMER 2003 VARIOUS ARTISTS (UNIVERSAL)	11	2003
TOP OF THE POP'S – THE 80'S VARIOUS ARTISTS (EMI)	8	2008
TOP OF THE POPS – THE CUTTING EDGE VARIOUS ARTISTS (COLUMBIA)	10	1996
TOP OF THE POPS VOLUME 17 ANONYMOUS COVER VERSIONS	16	1971
TOP OF THE POPS VOLUME 18 ANONYMOUS COVER VERSIONS	1	1971
TOP OF THE POPS VOLUME 19 ANONYMOUS COVER VERSIONS	3	1971
TOP OF THE POPS VOLUME 20 ANONYMOUS COVER VERSIONS	1	1971
TOP PRIORITY RORY GALLAGHER	56	1979
TOP TV THEMES LONDON SYMPHONY ORCHESTRA	13	1972
TOPOL'S ISRAEL TOPOL	80	1985
TOPS WITH ME HELEN SHAPIRO	2	1962
TORMATO YES	8	1978
TORMENT AND TOREROS MARC & THE MAMBAS	28	1983
TORN BETWEEN TWO LOVERS MARY MacGREGOR	59	1977
TOS G-UNIT	39	2008
TOTAL CONTRAST TOTAL CONTRAST	66	1986
TOTAL SOUND VARIOUS ARTISTS (STUDIO TWO)	39	1971
TOTALLY HOT OLIVIA NEWTON-JOHN	30	1978
TOTALLY KROSSED OUT KRIS KROSS	31	1992
TOTALLY WICKED VARIOUS ARTISTS (WARNER BROTHERS)	4	1998
TOTALLY WICKED TOO! VARIOUS ARTISTS (WARNER BROTHERS)	7	1999
TOTO TOTO	37	1979
TOTO IV TOTO	4	1983
TOUCH SUPREMES	40	1971
TOUCH EURYTHMICS	1	1983
TOUCH AMERIE	28	2005
TOUCH DANCE EURYTHMICS	31	1984
TOUCH 'EM WITH LOVE BOBBIE GENTRY	21	1969
TOUCH ME GARY GLITTER	2	1973
TOUCH ME SAMANTHA FOX	17	1986
TOUCH ME IN THE MORNING DIANA ROSS	7	1973
A TOUCH MORE MAGIC BARRY MANILOW	10	1983
A TOUCH OF BLUE DAVID CASSIDY	61	2003
A TOUCH OF CLASS FILM SOUNDTRACK	32	1974
A TOUCH OF CLASS VARIOUS ARTISTS (TOPAZ)	57	1976
A TOUCH OF COUNTRY VARIOUS ARTISTS (TOPAZ)	7	1976
THE TOUCH OF LOVE GLADYS KNIGHT & THE PIPS	16	1980
A TOUCH OF MUSIC IN THE NIGHT MICHAEL CRAWFORD	12	1993
A TOUCH OF SADNESS JIM REEVES	15	1969
A TOUCH OF VELVET JIM REEVES	8	1964
TOUCH SENSITIVE BRUCE FOXTON	68	1984
TOUCHED BY JESUS ALL ABOUT EVE	17	1991
TOUCHING DOWN RONI SIZE	72	2002
TOUGH IT OUT FM	34	1989
TOUGHER THAN LEATHER RUN D.M.C.	13	1988
TOUGHER THAN LOVE DIANA KING	50	1995
TOUR DE FRANCE SOUNDTRACKS KRAFTWERK	21	2003
TOUR SOUVENIR PACK MICHAEL JACKSON	32	1992
TOURISM ROXETTE	2	1992
TOURIST ST. GERMAIN	73	2000
TOURIST ATHLETE	1	2005
THE TOURISTS TOURISTS	72	1979
TOXICITY SYSTEM OF A DOWN	13	2001
TOYAH! TOYAH! TOYAH! TOYAH	22	1981
TP 3 RELOADED R KELLY	23	2005
TP-2.COM R KELLY	21	2000
TRACK RECORD JOAN ARMATRADING	18	1983
TRACKS BRUCE SPRINGSTEEN	50	1998
TRACKS 'N' GROOVES CLIFF RICHARD	37	1970
TRACKS OF MY TEARS VARIOUS ARTISTS (TELSTAR)	27	1987
TRACKS OF MY TEARS (SMOKEY ROBINSON – WRITER AND PERFORMER) VARIOUS ARTISTS (DINO)	6	1991

Title / Artist	Peak Position	Year of Release
TRACKSPOTTING VARIOUS ARTISTS (POLYGRAM)	12	1997
TRACY CHAPMAN TRACY CHAPMAN	1	1988
TRADE VARIOUS ARTISTS (FEVERPITCH)	14	1995
TRADE – VOLUME FOUR VARIOUS ARTISTS (FEVERPITCH)	15	1997
TRADE – VOLUME THREE VARIOUS ARTISTS (FEVERPITCH)	19	1996
TRADE – VOLUME TWO VARIOUS ARTISTS (FEVERPITCH)	11	1996
TRADING SECRETS WITH THE MOON ADVENTURES	64	1990
TRADING SNAKEOIL FOR WOLFTICKETS GARY JULES	12	2004
TRADITIONAL PETER GRANT	29	2007
TRAFFIC TRAFFIC	9	1968
TRAFFIC – ON THE ROAD TRAFFIC	40	1973
TRAGIC KINGDOM NO DOUBT	3	1997
TRAILER PARK BETH ORTON	68	1996
TRAINS, BOATS AND PLANES FRANK & WALTERS	36	1992
TRAINSPOTTING FILM SOUNDTRACK	2	1996
TRAINSPOTTING #2 FILM SOUNDTRACK	11	1997
THE TRA-LA DAYS ARE OVER NEIL SEDAKA	13	1973
TRAMPIN' PATTI SMITH	70	2004
TRAMPOLINE MAVERICKS	10	1998
TRANCE VARIOUS ARTISTS (RUMOUR)	18	1992
TRANCE CLASSICS VARIOUS ARTISTS (MINISTRY OF SOUND)	9	2002
TRANCE DANCE VARIOUS ARTISTS (DINO)	7	1992
TRANCE EUROPE EXPRESS VARIOUS ARTISTS (VOLUME)	14	1993
TRANCE EUROPE EXPRESS 2 VARIOUS ARTISTS (VOLUME)	17	1994
TRANCE MASTERS VARIOUS ARTISTS (VIRGIN)	4	2002
TRANCE NATION VARIOUS ARTISTS (MINISTRY OF SOUND)	2	2002
TRANCE NATION 2: MIXED BY FERRY CORSTEN VARIOUS ARTISTS (MINISTRY OF SOUND)	1	1999
TRANCE NATION 2003 VARIOUS ARTISTS (MINISTRY OF SOUND)	18	2002
TRANCE NATION 3 VARIOUS ARTISTS (MINISTRY OF SOUND)	2	2000
TRANCE NATION 4 VARIOUS ARTISTS (MINISTRY OF SOUND)	1	2000
TRANCE NATION 5 VARIOUS ARTISTS (MINISTRY OF SOUND)	4	2001
TRANCE NATION ANTHEMS – JUDGE JULES VARIOUS ARTISTS (MINISTRY OF SOUND)	16	2003
TRANCE NATION DEEPER VARIOUS ARTISTS (MINISTRY OF SOUND)	8	2003
TRANCE NATION ELECTRIC – JUDGE JULE VARIOUS ARTISTS (MINISTRY OF SOUND)	13	2004
TRANCE NATION – FUTURE VARIOUS ARTISTS (MINISTRY OF SOUND)	3	2003
TRANCE NATION HARDER VARIOUS ARTISTS (MINISTRY OF SOUND)	4	2003
TRANCE NATION: MIXED BY SYSTEM F VARIOUS ARTISTS (MINISTRY OF SOUND)	1	1999
TRANCEFORMER VARIOUS ARTISTS (VIRGIN)	3	1999
TRANCEMIX 99 – A SPRITUA; JOURNEY THROUGH TIME AND SPACE VARIOUS ARTISTS (VIRGIN)	8	1999
TRANCENDENTAL EUPHORIA VARIOUS ARTISTS (TELSTAR)	6	2000
TRANQUILLITY MARY O'HARA	12	1979
TRANQUILLITY VARIOUS ARTISTS (EMI)	14	1994
TRANS NEIL YOUNG	29	1983
TRANS CANADA HIGHWAY BOARDS OF CANADA	63	2006
TRANSCENDENTAL BLUES STEVE EARLE	32	2000
TRANS-EUROPE EXPRESS KRAFTWERK	49	1982
TRANSFORMER LOU REED	13	1973
TRANSIENT RANDOM-NOISE BURSTS STEREOLAB	62	1993
TRANSMITTING LIVE RUNRIG	41	1994
TRANZOPHOBIA MEGA CITY FOUR	67	1989
TRASH ALICE COOPER	2	1989
TRASHED IN IBIZA VARIOUS ARTISTS (GLOBAL TELEVISION)	16	2000
THE TRAVELING WILBURYS VOLUME 1 TRAVELING WILBURYS	16	1988
THE TRAVELING WILBURYS VOLUME 3 TRAVELING WILBURYS	14	1990
TRAVELLING JOHN WILLIAMS	23	1978
TRAVELLING LIGHT LESLEY GARRETT	75	2001
TRAVELLING WITHOUT MOVING JAMIROQUAI	2	1996
TRAVELOGUE HUMAN LEAGUE	16	1980
TRB2 TOM ROBINSON BAND	18	1979
TREASURE COCTEAU TWINS	29	1984
TREASURE HAYLEY WESTENRA	9	2007
TREDDIN' ON THIN ICE WILEY	45	2004
TRESPASS GENESIS	98	1984
TREVOR NELSON'S RHYTHM NATION VARIOUS ARTISTS (INCREDIBLE)	9	2000
TRIAL OF FIRE – LIVE IN LENINGRAD YNGWIE J MALMSTEEN	65	1989
TRIBAL GATHERING '96 VARIOUS ARTISTS (UNIVERSE)	15	1996
TRIBES, VIBES AND SCRIBES INCOGNITO	41	1992
TRIBUTE OZZY OSBOURNE	13	1987
TRIBUTE YANNI	40	1998
TRIBUTE TO BOBBY HUCKNALL	18	2008
TRIBUTE TO MARTYRS STEEL PULSE	42	1979
A TRIBUTE TO THE CROONERS DES O'CONNOR	51	2001
TRIBUTE TO THE SMALL FACES – LONG AGOS/WORLDS APART VARIOUS ARTISTS (NICE)	20	1996
TRICK OF THE LIGHT MODERN ROMANCE	53	1983
A TRICK OF THE TRAIL GENESIS	3	1976
TRICK OR TREAT PAUL BRADY	62	1991
THE TRICK TO LIFE HOOSIERS	1	2007
TRIED AND TRUE – THE BEST OF SUZANNE VEGA SUZANNE VEGA	46	1998
TRIGGER HAPPY TV – SERIES 2 TELEVISION AND RADIO COMPILATION	15	2001
TRILENIUM SASH!	13	2000
TRILOGY EMERSON, LAKE & PALMER	2	1972
TRINI LOPEZ AT P.J.'S TRINI LOPEZ	7	1963
TRINI LOPEZ IN LONDON TRINI LOPEZ	6	1967
TRINITI TRINITI	28	2006
THE TRINITY SEAN PAUL	11	2005
TRIO DOLLY PARTON, LINDA RONSTADT & EMMYLOU HARRIS	60	1987
TRIP ON THIS – REMIXES TECHNOTRONIC & HI TEK 3	7	1990
TRIP THE LIGHT FANTASTIC SOPHIE ELLIS BEXTOR	7	2007
TRIPPING THE LIVE FANTASTIC PAUL McCARTNEY	17	1990
TRIPTOMATIC FAIRYTALES JAM & SPOON	71	1994
TRIUMPH JACKSONS	13	1980
TRIUMPH AND AGONY WARLOCK	54	1987
TRIVIAL PURSUIT – THE MUSIC MASTER GAME MISCELLANEOUS	20	1991
TROCADERO SHOWADDYWADDY	41	1976
TROGGLODYNAMITE TROGGS	10	1967
TROMPE LE MONDE PIXIES	7	1991
TROOPS OF TOMORROW EXPLOITED	17	1982
TROPICAL BRAINSTORM KIRSTY MacCOLL	39	2000
TROPICAL GANGSTERS KID CREOLE & THE COCONUTS	3	1982
TROPICO PAT BENATAR	31	1984
TROUBADOUR J.J. CALE	53	1976
TROUBLE SAILOR	45	1976
TROUBLE WHITESNAKE	50	1978
TROUBLE AKON	1	2005
TROUBLE RAY LAMONTAGNE	5	2006
TROUBLE IN SHANGRI-LA STEVIE NICKS	43	2001
TROUBLE OVER HERE, TROUBLE OVER THERE TROUBLE FUNK	54	1987
THE TROUBLE WITH BEING MYSELF MACY GRAY	17	2003
TROUBLEGUM THERAPY?	5	1994
TROUSER JAZZ MR. SCRUFF	29	2002
TROUT MASK REPLICA CAPTAIN BEEFHEART & HIS MAGIC BAND	21	1969
TRUANT ALIEN ANT FARM	68	2003
TRUE SPANDAU BALLET	1	1983
TRUE BALLADS TONY HADLEY	31	2003
TRUE BLUE MADONNA	1	1986
TRUE COLOURS SPLIT ENZ	42	1980
TRUE COLOURS LEVEL 42	14	1984
TRUE COLOURS CYNDI LAUPER	25	1986
TRUE CONFESSIONS BANANARAMA	46	1986
TRUE EUPHORIA VARIOUS ARTISTS (TELSTAR)	3	2001
TRUE HARDCORE 2 VARIOUS ARTISTS (GTV)	10	2008
TRUE HARDCORE – IT'S A WAY OF LIFE VARIOUS ARTISTS (GTV)	6	2007
TRUE LOVE VARIOUS ARTISTS (K-TEL)	38	1987
TRUE LOVE PAT BENATAR	40	1991
TRUE LOVE WAYS BUDDY HOLLY	8	1989
TRUE LOVE WAYS VARIOUS ARTISTS (COLUMBIA)	14	1994
TRUE SKIES SHINING	73	2002
TRUE SPIRIT CARLEEN ANDERSON	12	1994
TRUE STORIES TALKING HEADS	7	1986
TRUEBRIT VARIOUS ARTISTS (POLYGRAM)	7	1996
TRULY FOR YOU TEMPTATIONS	75	1984
TRULY MADLY COMPLETELY – THE BEST OF SAVAGE GARDEN	25	2005
TRULY – THE LOVE SONGS LIONEL RICHIE	5	1998
TRULY UNFORGETTABLE VARIOUS ARTISTS (EMI)	6	1990
TRUMPET A-GO-GO JAMES LAST	13	1969
TRUNK FUNK – THE BEST OF THE BRAND NEW HEAVIES BRAND NEW HEAVIES	13	1999
TRUST ELVIS COSTELLO & THE ATTRACTIONS	9	1981
TRUST BROTHER BEYOND	60	1989
TRUST ME CRAIG DAVID	18	2007
THE TRUTH ABOUT LOVE LEMAR	3	2006
TRUTH AND BEAUTY IAN McNABB	51	1993
TRUTH AND LOVE HUE & CRY	33	1992
TRUTH AND THE LIGHT: MUSIC FROM THE X-FILES MARK SNOW	42	1996
TRUTH BE TOLD SHED SEVEN	42	2001
TRUTHDARE DOUBLEDARE BRONSKI BEAT	18	1986
TRUTHFULLY SPEAKING TRUTH HURTS	61	2002
TRY A LITTLE KINDNESS GLEN CAMPBELL	37	1970
TRY THIS P!NK	3	2003
TRY WHISTLING THIS NEIL FINN	5	1998
TSOP – THE SOUND OF PHILADELPHIA VARIOUS ARTISTS (K-TEL)	26	1988
THE TUBE (TELEVISION COMPILATION) TELEVISION AND RADIO COMPILATION	30	1984
TUBEWAY ARMY TUBEWAY ARMY	14	1979
TUBTHUMPER CHUMBAWAMBA	19	1997
TUBULAR BELLS MIKE OLDFIELD	1	1973
TUBULAR BELLS 2003 MIKE OLDFIELD	51	2003
TUBULAR BELLS II MIKE OLDFIELD	1	1992
TUBULAR BELLS III MIKE OLDFIELD	4	1998
TUESDAY NIGHT MUSIC CLUB SHERYL CROW	8	1994
TUFF JAM PRESENTS UNDERGROUND FREQUENCIES – 1 VARIOUS ARTISTS (SATELLITE)	20	1997

Title / Artist	Peak Position	Year of Release
TUFF JAM PRESENTS UNDERGROUND FREQUENCIES – 2 VARIOUS ARTISTS (SATELLITE)	14	1998
TUG OF WAR PAUL McCARTNEY	1	1982
TUMBLEWEED CONNECTION ELTON JOHN	2	1971
TUNDE TUNDE	32	2004
A TUNE A DAY SUPERNATURALS	21	1998
TUNE IN-CHILL OUT VARIOUS ARTISTS (INSPIRED)	17	2002
THE TUNNEL MIXES VARIOUS ARTISTS (LIMBO)	17	1996
TUNNEL OF LOVE BRUCE SPRINGSTEEN	1	1987
TURBO JUDAS PRIEST	33	1986
TURBO TRAX VARIOUS ARTISTS (K-TEL)	17	1982
TURBULENT INDIGO JONI MITCHELL	53	1994
THE TURN ALISON MOYET	21	2007
TURN BACK THE CLOCK JOHNNY HATES JAZZ	1	1988
TURN IT ON RONAN KEATING	21	2003
TURN IT ON AGAIN – THE HITS GENESIS	4	1999
TURN IT UP – THE VERY BEST OF BUSTA RHYMES	44	2001
TURN IT UPSIDE DOWN SPIN DOCTORS	3	1994
THE TURN OF A FRIENDLY CARD ALAN PARSONS PROJECT	38	1980
TURN OF THE TIDE BARCLAY JAMES HARVEST	55	1981
TURN ON THE RADIO CHANGE	39	1985
TURN ON THE SUN NANA MOUSKOURI	16	1971
TURN OUT THE LIGHTS BERNIE TORME	50	1982
TURN THE DARK OFF HOWIE B	58	1997
TURN THE MUSIC UP PLAYERS ASSOCIATION	54	1979
TURN, TURN, TURN BYRDS	11	1966
TURNAROUND WESTLIFE	1	2003
THE TURNING POINT JOHN MAYALL	11	1969
TURNING POINT MARIO	8	2005
TURNING STONES JUDIE TZUKE	57	1989
TURNS INTO STONE STONE ROSES	32	1992
TURTLE SOUP MOCK TURTLES	54	1991
TUSK FLEETWOOD MAC	1	1979
TUTTI FRUTTI MAJESTICS	64	1987
TUTTO MOZART BRYN TERFEL	59	2006
TUTU MILES DAVIS	74	1986
TV 2000 VARIOUS ARTISTS (COLUMBIA)	16	2000
TV AD SONGS VARIOUS ARTISTS (EMI)	18	2008
THE TV HITS ALBUM (TELEVISION COMPILATION) TELEVISION AND RADIO COMPILATION	26	1985
THE TV HITS ALBUM TWO – 16 ORIGINAL HIT-TV THEMES (TELEVISION COMPILATION) TELEVISION AND RADIO COMPILATION	19	1986
TV SPECIAL ELVIS PRESLEY	50	1978
TV TUNES (TELEVISION COMPILATION) TELEVISION AND RADIO COMPILATION	17	1989
TWANGIN' DAVE EDMUNDS	37	1981
THE TWANG'S THE THANG DUANE EDDY	2	1960
TWANGY GUITAR – SILKY STRINGS DUANE EDDY	13	1962
TWELVE VARIOUS ARTISTS (WARNER BROTHERS)	10	1996
TWELVE PATTI SMITH	63	2007
THE TWELVE COMMANDMENTS OF DANCE LONDON BOYS	2	1989
TWELVE DEADLY CYNS...AND THEN SOME CYNDI LAUPER	2	1994
TWELVE DREAMS OF DR SARDONICUS SPIRIT	29	1971
12 GOLD BARS STATUS QUO	3	1980
12 GOLD BARS VOLUME TWO – (AND ONE) STATUS QUO	12	1984
12 GREATEST HITS VOLUME 2 NEIL DIAMOND	32	1982
12 INCH 80'S VARIOUS ARTISTS (FAMILY RECORDINGS)	5	2005
12 INCH 80S DANCE VARIOUS ARTISTS (FAMILY RECORDINGS)	4	2006
12 INCH 80S GROOVE VARIOUS ARTISTS (FAMILY)	2	2007
12 INCH 80S LOVE VARIOUS ARTISTS (FAMILY RECORDINGS)	9	2008
12 INCH 80'S POP VARIOUS ARTISTS (UNIVERSAL)	4	2007
12 INCH 80'S VOLUME 2 VARIOUS ARTISTS (EMI)	16	2005
THE 12" ALBUM HOWARD JONES	15	1984
TWELVE INCHES OF PLEASURE VARIOUS ARTISTS (PROTO)	100	1983
12 INCHES OF SNOW SNOW	41	1993
12 MEMORIES TRAVIS	3	2003
TWELVE MONTHS, ELEVEN DAYS GARY BARLOW	35	1999
TWELVE OF THOSE SONGS SHIRLEY BASSEY	38	1968
12 PLAY R KELLY	20	1993
12 SONGS NEIL DIAMOND	5	2006
TWELVE SONGS OF CHRISTMAS JIM REEVES	3	1964
TWELVE STOPS AND HOME THE FEELING	2	2006
12 X 12 MEGA MIXES VARIOUS ARTISTS (STARBLEND)	77	1985
THE 20TH ANNIVERSARY ALBUM VARIOUS ARTISTS (MOTOWN)	53	1980
TWENTIETH CENTURY BLUES VARIOUS ARTISTS (EMI)	14	1998
20 ALL TIME EUROVISION FAVOURITES NIGEL BROOKS SINGERS	44	1976
20 ALL TIME GREATEST PETULA CLARK	18	1977
20 ALL TIME GREATS CONNIE FRANCIS	1	1977
20 ALL TIME GREATS ROGER WHITTAKER	24	1979
20 ALL TIME GREATS OF THE 50'S VARIOUS ARTISTS (K-TEL)	1	1972
20 CLASSIC HITS PLATTERS	8	1978
20 COUNTRY CLASSICS TAMMY WYNETTE	3	1977
20 DYNAMIC HITS VARIOUS ARTISTS (K-TEL)	1	1972
20 FAMILY FAVOURITES VERA LYNN	25	1981
20 FANTASTIC HITS VARIOUS ARTISTS (ARCADE)	1	1972
20 FANTASTIC HITS VOLUME 2 VARIOUS ARTISTS (ARCADE)	2	1972
20 FANTASTIC HITS VOLUME 3 VARIOUS ARTISTS (ARCADE)	3	1973
25TH ANNIVERSARY BRENDA LEE	65	1984
25TH ANNIVERSARY ALBUM SHIRLEY BASSEY	3	1978
21ST CENTURY DISCO VARIOUS ARTISTS (MINISTRY OF SOUND)	3	2002
21ST CENTURY ROCK VARIOUS ARTISTS (VIRGIN)	9	1999
25 HARRY CONNICK JR.	35	1993
TWENTY FIVE GEORGE MICHAEL	1	2006
25 DYNAMIC HITS VOLUME 2 VARIOUS ARTISTS (K-TEL)	2	1972
25 GOLDEN GREATS BACHELORS	38	1979
25 ROCKIN' AND ROLLIN' GREATS VARIOUS ARTISTS (K-TEL)	1	1972
25 THUMPING GREAT HITS DAVE CLARK FIVE	7	1978
25 YEARS ON HAWKLORDS	48	1978
20 FLASHBACK GREATS OF THE SIXTIES VARIOUS ARTISTS (K-TEL)	1	1973
24 CARAT AL STEWART	55	1980
24 CARAT PURPLE DEEP PURPLE	14	1975
24 GOLDEN GREATS ADAM FAITH	61	1981
24 HOUR PARTY PEOPLE FILM SOUNDTRACK	15	2002
24 HOURS TOM JONES	32	2008
24 NIGHTS ERIC CLAPTON	17	1991
24 ORIGINAL HITS DRIFTERS	2	1975
TWENTY FOUR SEVEN TINA TURNER	9	1999
20 GIANT HITS NOLAN SISTERS	3	1978
20 GOLDEN GREATS BEACH BOYS	1	1976
20 GOLDEN GREATS GLEN CAMPBELL	1	1976
20 GOLDEN GREATS BUDDY HOLLY & THE CRICKETS	1	1978
20 GOLDEN GREATS FRANK SINATRA	4	1978
20 GOLDEN GREATS HOLLIES	2	1978
20 GOLDEN GREATS KINKS	19	1978
20 GOLDEN GREATS NAT 'KING' COLE	1	1978
20 GOLDEN GREATS NEIL DIAMOND	2	1978
20 GOLDEN GREATS DIANA ROSS	2	1979
20 GOLDEN GREATS DORIS DAY	12	1979
20 GOLDEN GREATS DION & THE BELMONTS	31	1980
20 GOLDEN GREATS AL JOLSON	18	1981
20 GOLDEN GREATS GILBERT O'SULLIVAN	98	1981
20 GOLDEN GREATS OF KEN DODD KEN DODD	8	1980
20 GREAT ITALIAN LOVE SONGS VARIOUS ARTISTS (TELSTAR)	28	1983
20 GREATEST HITS TOM JONES	1	1975
20 GREATEST HITS HERMAN'S HERMITS	37	1977
20 GREATEST HITS REAL THING	56	1980
20 GREATEST HITS BEATLES	10	1982
20 GREATEST HITS VOLUME 2 ELVIS PRESLEY	98	1985
20 GREATEST LOVE SONGS NAT 'KING' COLE	7	1982
20 HOLIDAY HITS VARIOUS ARTISTS (CREOLE)	48	1985
20 HOTTEST HITS HOT CHOCOLATE	3	1979
20 OF ANOTHER KIND VARIOUS ARTISTS (POLYDOR)	45	1979
21 OMARION	24	2007
TWENTY ONE MYSTERY JETS	50	2008
21 AT 33 ELTON JOHN	12	1980
20 ORIGINAL CHART HITS VARIOUS ARTISTS (PHILIPS)	9	1973
20 ORIGINAL DEAN MARTIN HITS DEAN MARTIN	7	1976
20 ORIGINAL GREATS CLIFF RICHARD	43	1984
20 REGGAE CLASSICS VARIOUS ARTISTS (TROJAN)	89	1984
26 MIXES FOR CASH APHEX TWIN	63	2003
20 SMASH DISCO HITS (THE BITCH) VARIOUS ARTISTS (WARWICK)	42	1979
20 SONGS OF JOY NIGEL BROOKS SINGERS	5	1975
20 STAR TRACKS VARIOUS ARTISTS (RONCO)	2	1972
23AM ROBERT MILES	42	1997
2300 JACKSON ST JACKSONS	39	1989
20/20 BEACH BOYS	3	1969
20/20 GEORGE BENSON	9	1985
22 DREAMS PAUL WELLER	1	2008
22 GOLDEN GUITAR GREATS BERT WEEDON	1	1976
22-20S 22-20S	40	2004
20 WITH A BULLET VARIOUS ARTISTS (EMI)	11	1982
20 WOMBLING GREATS WOMBLES	29	1977
20 Y.O. JANET JACKSON	63	2006
20 YEARS OF JETHRO TULL JETHRO TULL	78	1988
TWENTYSOMETHING JAMIE CULLUM	3	2003
TWICE AS KOOL KOOL & THE GANG	4	1983
TWICE AS NICE – ESSENTIAL GROOVES VARIOUS ARTISTS (WARNER BROTHERS)	9	2002
TWICE AS NICE IN AYIA NAPA – DJ SPOONY VARIOUS ARTISTS (REACT)	18	1999
TWICE AS NICE PRESENTS MOBO 2002 VARIOUS ARTISTS (WARNER BROTHERS)	3	2002
TWICE AS NICE PRESENTS URBAN FLAVAS VARIOUS ARTISTS (WARNER BROTHERS)	5	2002
TWICE AS NICE PRESENTS URBAN FLAVAS 2003 VARIOUS ARTISTS (WARNER BROTHERS)	8	2003
TWICE AS NICE – SEXY & STYLISH VARIOUS ARTISTS (WARNER BROTHERS)	5	2000
TWICE AS NICE – SEXY AND STYLISH VARIOUS ARTISTS (WARNER BROTHERS)	11	2001
TWICE AS NICE – SUMMER OF LOVE VARIOUS ARTISTS (WARNER BROTHERS)	6	2000

Title / Artist	Peak Position	Year of Release
TWICE AS NICE – THE ULTIMATE URBAN VARIOUS ARTISTS (UNIVERSAL)	8	2008
TWICE AS NICE – URBAN ANTHEMS VARIOUS ARTISTS (UNIVERSAL)	2	2007
TWICE AS NICE – URBAN CLUB CLASSICS VARIOUS ARTISTS (WARNER BROTHERS)	7	2005
TWICE AS NICE – WEEKENDER VARIOUS ARTISTS (WARNER BROTHERS)	4	2006
TWICE THE LOVE GEORGE BENSON	16	1988
TWICE UPON A TIME – THE SINGLES SIOUXSIE & THE BANSHEES	26	1992
TWIGGY TWIGGY	33	1976
TWILIGHT OF IDOLS FASHION	69	1984
TWILIGHT OF THE INNOCENTS ASH	32	2007
TWIN BARRELS BURNING WISHBONE ASH	22	1982
TWIST FAT LADY SINGS	50	1991
TWIST WITH CHUBBY CHECKER CHUBBY CHECKER	13	1962
TWISTED DEL AMITRI	3	1995
TWISTED ANGEL LEANN RIMES	14	2002
TWISTED DISCO 02.04 VARIOUS ARTISTS (HED KANDI)	16	2004
TWISTED DISCO 0205 VARIOUS ARTISTS (HED KANDI)	18	2005
TWISTED TENDERNESS ELECTRONIC	9	1999
TWISTIN' AND TWANGIN' DUANE EDDY	8	1962
II BOYZ II MEN	17	1994
II PRESIDENTS OF THE UNITED STATES OF AMERICA	36	1996
III GUY	55	2000
TWO CALLING	9	2004
TWO AGAINST NATURE STEELY DAN	11	2000
2.00 A.M. PARADISE CAFÉ BARRY MANILOW	28	1984
TWO BAD DJ CLINT EASTWOOD & GENERAL SAINT	99	1982
TWO CAN PLAY THAT GAME BOBBY BROWN	24	1995
TWO DAYS AWAY ELKIE BROOKS	16	1977
THE TWO FACES OF FAME GEORGIE FAME	22	1967
TWO FINGERS MY FRIENDS? POP WILL EAT ITSELF	25	1995
2 FUTURE 4 U ARMAND VAN HELDEN	22	1999
200 KHM IN THE WRONG LANE t.A.T.u.	20	2003
2 IN 3 ESTHER & ABI OFARIM	6	1968
2,000,000 VOICES ANGELIC UPSTARTS	32	1981
2 MINUTES TO MIDNIGHT/ACES HIGH IRON MAIDEN	11	1990
THE TWO OF US VARIOUS ARTISTS (K-TEL)	3	1983
TWO PAGES 4 HERO	38	1998
TWO ROOMS – CELEBRATING THE SONGS OF ELTON JOHN AND BERNIE TAUPIN VARIOUS ARTISTS (MERCURY)	1	1991
TWO SEVENS CLASH CULTURE	60	1978
TWO SIDES MOCK TURTLES	33	1991
TWO SIDES OF THE FOUR PENNIES FOUR PENNIES	13	1964
TWO STEPS FROM THE MOVE HANOI ROCKS	28	1984
2 STEPZ AHEAD OXIDE & NEUTRINO	28	2002
2001 DR. DRE	4	1999
2001 – A SPACE ODYSSEY FILM SOUNDTRACK	3	1969
THE 2000 BRIT AWARDS VARIOUS ARTISTS (COLUMBIA)	3	2000
2000 YEARS – THE MILLENNIUM CONCERT BILLY JOEL	68	2000
2 X 45 CABARET VOLTAIRE	98	1982
THE 2 TONE STORY VARIOUS ARTISTS (2 TONE)	16	1989
TWO'S COMPANY VARIOUS ARTISTS (TOWERBELL)	51	1986
TWO'S COMPANY – THE DUETS CLIFF RICHARD	8	2006
TYGER TANGERINE DREAM	88	1987
TYR BLACK SABBATH	24	1990
TYRANNOSAURUS HIVES HIVES	7	2004
TYRANNY FOR YOU FRONT 242	49	1991
TYRANNY OF SOULS BRUCE DICKINSON	50	2005

U

Title / Artist	Peak Position	Year of Release
U INCREDIBLE STRING BAND	34	1970
U GOT 2 KNOW CAPPELLA	10	1994
U.F. OFF – THE BEST OF ORB ORB	38	1998
U.F. ORB ORB	1	1992
U.K. U.K.	43	1978
U.S.A. UNION JOHN MAYALL	50	1970
U2 LIVE 'UNDER A BLOOD RED SKY' U2	2	1983
U218 SINGLES U2	4	2006
UB 44 UB40	4	1982
UB40 UB40	12	1988
UB40 LIVE UB40	44	1983
UGLY BEAUTIFUL BABYBIRD	9	1996
UH HUH HER PJ HARVEY	12	2004
UH! TEARS BABY (A TRASH ICON) WIN	51	1987
UH-HUH JOHN COUGAR MELLENCAMP	92	1984
UH-OH DAVID BYRNE	26	1992
UK BLAK CARON WHEELER	14	1990
UK GARAGE – THE ALBUM VARIOUS ARTISTS (MINISTRY OF SOUND)	9	2000
UKRAINSKI VISTUIP V JOHNA PEELA WEDDING PRESENT	22	1989
ULTIMATE DOLLY PARTON	17	2003
ULTIMATE TONI BRAXTON	23	2003
THE ULTIMATE AALIYAH	32	2005
THE ULTIMATE MATT MONRO	7	2005
ULTIMATE PRINCE	6	2006
THE ULTIMATE 60S COLLECTION VARIOUS ARTISTS (CASTLE COMMUNICATIONS)	4	1990
ULTIMATE 70'S POP VARIOUS ARTISTS (SONY/BMG)	7	2005
THE ULTIMATE 80'S BALLADS VARIOUS ARTISTS (POLYGRAM)	5	1994
ULTIMATE ACOUSTIC VARIOUS ARTISTS (SONY)	3	2004
ULTIMATE ACOUSTIC SONGBOOK VARIOUS ARTISTS (SONY/BMG)	18	2005
ULTIMATE ALL TIME CLASSIC TEARJERKERS VARIOUS ARTISTS (WARNER BROTHERS)	17	2004
ULTIMATE AYIA NAPA VARIOUS ARTISTS (INSPIRED)	7	2000
ULTIMATE BALLROOM DANCE CRAZE VARIOUS ARTISTS (V2)	15	2005
THE ULTIMATE BANDS – THE CLASSIC ANTHEMS VARIOUS ARTISTS (EMI)	13	2006
THE ULTIMATE BLUES COLLECTION VARIOUS ARTISTS (CASTLE COMMUNICATIONS)	14	1991
ULTIMATE BOY BANDS VARIOUS ARTISTS (UNIVERSAL)	6	2006
THE ULTIMATE CHEESE PARTY VARIOUS ARTISTS (WARNER BROTHERS)	12	2003
THE ULTIMATE CHICK FLICK LOVE SONGS VARIOUS ARTISTS (WARNER BROTHERS)	5	2003
THE ULTIMATE CHICK FLICK SOUNDTRACK VARIOUS ARTISTS (WARNER BROTHERS)	4	2002
THE ULTIMATE CHRISTMAS COLLECTION VARIOUS ARTISTS (POLYGRAM)	11	1998
ULTIMATE CLUB MIX VARIOUS ARTISTS (POLYGRAM)	1	1998
ULTIMATE CLUB MIX 2 VARIOUS ARTISTS (POLYGRAM)	5	1998
ULTIMATE CLUB MIX – 98 VARIOUS ARTISTS (POLYGRAM)	13	1998
THE ULTIMATE COLLECTION BRYAN FERRY & ROXY MUSIC	6	1988
THE ULTIMATE COLLECTION KINKS	32	1989
THE ULTIMATE COLLECTION MARC BOLAN & T. REX	4	1991
THE ULTIMATE COLLECTION LOUIS ARMSTRONG	48	1994
THE ULTIMATE COLLECTION JIM REEVES	17	1996
THE ULTIMATE COLLECTION NEIL DIAMOND	5	1996
THE ULTIMATE COLLECTION CLANNAD	46	1997
THE ULTIMATE COLLECTION LUCIANO PAVAROTTI	8	1997
THE ULTIMATE COLLECTION JANIS JOPLIN	26	1998
THE ULTIMATE COLLECTION SANTANA	12	1998
THE ULTIMATE COLLECTION EARTH WIND & FIRE	34	1999
THE ULTIMATE COLLECTION NAT 'KING' COLE	26	1999
THE ULTIMATE COLLECTION BILLY JOEL	4	2001
THE ULTIMATE COLLECTION CHRIS DE BURGH	19	2001
THE ULTIMATE COLLECTION ELECTRIC LIGHT ORCHESTRA	18	2001
THE ULTIMATE COLLECTION GENE PITNEY	40	2001
THE ULTIMATE COLLECTION LADYSMITH BLACK MAMBAZO	37	2001
THE ULTIMATE COLLECTION PETULA CLARK	18	2002
THE ULTIMATE COLLECTION WHO	17	2002
ULTIMATE COLLECTION OSMONDS	4	2003
ULTIMATE COLLECTION SMALL FACES	24	2003
THE ULTIMATE COLLECTION EMERSON, LAKE & PALMER	43	2004
THE ULTIMATE COLLECTION MICHAEL JACKSON	75	2004
ULTIMATE COLLECTION BILLY OCEAN	28	2004
THE ULTIMATE COLLECTION MARY DUFF	52	2005
THE ULTIMATE COLLECTION POGUES	15	2005
THE ULTIMATE COLLECTION RANDY CRAWFORD	31	2005
THE ULTIMATE COLLECTION SAMMY DAVIS JR	75	2005
ULTIMATE COLLECTION EURYTHMICS	5	2005
ULTIMATE COLLECTION M PEOPLE FEATURING HEATHER SMALL	17	2005
THE ULTIMATE COLLECTION CARPENTERS	53	2006
ULTIMATE COLLECTION WHITNEY HOUSTON	3	2007
THE ULTIMATE COLLECTION RICK ASTLEY	17	2008
THE ULTIMATE COUNTRY COLLECTION VARIOUS ARTISTS (COLUMBIA)	1	1992
ULTIMATE COUNTRY: 40 COUNTRY GREATS VARIOUS ARTISTS (TELSTAR)	8	1998
ULTIMATE DANCE CRAZE VARIOUS ARTISTS (V2)	7	2004
ULTIMATE DIRTY DANCING FILM SOUNDTRACK	1	2004
ULTIMATE DISCO MIX VARIOUS ARTISTS (POLYGRAM)	15	1998
ULTIMATE DISCO PARTY VARIOUS ARTISTS (SONY BMG)	10	2008
ULTIMATE DISNEY VARIOUS ARTISTS (WALT DISNEY)	8	2004
ULTIMATE DISNEY PRINCESS VARIOUS ARTISTS (WALT DISNEY)	5	2005
THE ULTIMATE EIGHTIES VARIOUS ARTISTS (POLYGRAM)	2	1994
ULTIMATE EUROVISION PARTY VARIOUS ARTISTS (SONY BMG)	12	2008
ULTIMATE FAME VARIOUS ARTISTS (BMG)	8	2004
ULTIMATE FEELGOOD ANTHEMS VARIOUS ARTISTS (SONY)	11	2004
THE ULTIMATE FUNK PARTY VARIOUS ARTISTS (WARNER BROTHERS)	8	2004
ULTIMATE GIRL GROUPS VARIOUS ARTISTS (UNIVERSAL)	7	2007
ULTIMATE GIRLS NIGHT IN VARIOUS ARTISTS (BMG)	11	2004

Title / Artist	Peak Position	Year of Release
THE ULTIMATE GLENN MILLER GLENN MILLER & HIS ORCHESTRA	11	1993
THE ULTIMATE GOLD COLLECTION VARIOUS ARTISTS (HIT LABEL)	12	1994
THE ULTIMATE GUITAR COLLECTION JULIAN BREAM	66	1996
THE ULTIMATE HARDCORE VARIOUS ARTISTS (TELSTAR)	1	1992
THE ULTIMATE HEN NIGHT PARTY ALBUM VARIOUS ARTISTS (WARNER BROTHERS)	8	2002
ULTIMATE HITS GARTH BROOKS	10	2007
THE ULTIMATE HITS ALBUM VARIOUS ARTISTS (TELSTAR)	11	1994
THE ULTIMATE HITS COLLECTION TOM JONES	26	1998
ULTIMATE HOLIDAY PARTY VARIOUS ARTISTS (SONY BMG)	9	2008
ULTIMATE IBIZA VARIOUS ARTISTS (INSPIRED)	14	2000
THE ULTIMATE JUNGLE COLLECTION VARIOUS ARTISTS (DINO)	17	1995
ULTIMATE KAOS ULTIMATE KAOS	51	1995
ULTIMATE KYLIE KYLIE MINOGUE	4	2004
THE ULTIMATE LINE DANCING ALBUM VARIOUS ARTISTS (GLOBAL TELEVISION)	7	1996
ULTIMATE LIVE BARRY MANILOW	51	2005
ULTIMATE LOVE VARIOUS ARTISTS (HIT LABEL)	13	1995
ULTIMATE LOVE COLLECTION VARIOUS ARTISTS (UNIVERSAL)	14	2007
THE ULTIMATE LUTHER VANDROSS LUTHER VANDROSS	10	2006
ULTIMATE MANILOW BARRY MANILOW	8	2004
THE ULTIMATE MOODS AL BUM VARIOUS ARTISTS (UNIVERSAL)	12	2005
THE ULTIMATE MOVIE ALBUM VARIOUS ARTISTS (DECCA)	16	2001
THE ULTIMATE NORTHERN SOUL ALBUM VARIOUS ARTISTS (DECADANCE)	7	2004
ULTIMATE NRG VARIOUS ARTISTS (ALL AROUND THE WORLD)	3	2006
ULTIMATE NRG 2 VARIOUS ARTISTS (UNIVERSAL)	5	2007
ULTIMATE NRG 3 VARIOUS ARTISTS (UNIVERSAL)	1	2008
THE ULTIMATE OLK SKOOL ALBUM VARIOUS ARTISTS (DECADANCE)	16	2003
THE ULTIMATE OPERA COLLECTION VARIOUS ARTISTS (ERATO)	14	1992
THE ULTIMATE PARTY ANIMAL VARIOUS ARTISTS (GLOBAL TELEVISION)	4	1996
THE ULTIMATE PARTY ANIMAL VARIOUS ARTISTS (UNIVERSAL)	20	2006
THE ULTIMATE PERFORMANCE ELVIS PRESLEY	45	1981
ULTIMATE R&B VARIOUS ARTISTS (UNIVERSAL)	6	2004
ULTIMATE R&B DANCE CRZE VARIOUS ARTISTS (V2)	19	2006
THE ULTIMATE RAVE VARIOUS ARTISTS (EMI)	1	1992
ULTIMATE REGGAE PARTY ALBUM! VARIOUS ARTISTS (TELSTAR)	14	1994
THE ULTIMATE RELAXATION ALBUM VARIOUS ARTISTS (VIRGIN)	16	2003
ULTIMATE SANTANA SANTANA	16	2007
THE ULTIMATE SIN OZZY OSBOURNE	8	1986
ULTIMATE SIXTIES COLLECTION VARIOUS ARTISTS (TELSTAR)	19	2000
THE ULTIMATE SMOOCHY ALBUM VARIOUS ARTISTS (WARNER BROTHERS)	7	2003
THE ULTIMATE SOUL COLLECTION VARIOUS ARTISTS (TELSTAR)	10	2001
THE ULTIMATE SOUL COLLECTION – 45 SOUL CLASSICS VARIOUS ARTISTS (WARNER BROTHERS)	4	1995
THE ULTIMATE SOUL COLLECTION – VOLUME 2 VARIOUS ARTISTS (WARNER BROTHERS)	11	1995
ULTIMATE STREETDANCE VARIOUS ARTISTS (SONY BMG)	3	2008
THE ULTIMATE SUMMER PARTY ALBUM VARIOUS ARTISTS (POLYGRAM)	7	1998
THE ULTIMATE SUMMER PARTY ANIMAL VARIOUS ARTISTS (GLOBAL TELEVISION)	2	1997
ULTIMATE TEARJERKERS VARIOUS ARTISTS (WARNER BROTHERS)	20	2006
ULTIMATE TRAX 3 – BATTLE OF THE DJS VARIOUS ARTISTS (CHAMPION)	69	1987
ULTIMATE TRAX VOLUME 1 VARIOUS ARTISTS (CHAMPION)	66	1986
ULTIMATE TRAX VOLUME 2 VARIOUS ARTISTS (CHAMPION)	50	1987
THE ULTIMATE YES – 35TH ANNIVERSARY YES	10	2003
ULTRA DEPECHE MODE	1	1997
ULTRA ULTRA	37	1999
ULTRA BEATDOWN DRAGONFORCE	18	2008
ULTRA OBSCENE BREAKBEAT ERA	31	1999
ULTRAVIOLET ALL ABOUT EVE	46	1992
ULTRAVIOLET ED ALLEYNE-JOHNSON	68	1994
UMMAGUMMA PINK FLOYD	5	1969
UNA MATTINA LUDOVICO EINAUDI	59	2004
THE UNAUTHORIZED BIOGRAPHY OF REINHOLD MESSNER BEN FOLDS FIVE	22	1999
UNBELIEVABLE VARIOUS ARTISTS (VIRGIN)	3	2001
UNBELIEVABLE TOO VARIOUS ARTISTS (VIRGIN)	20	2002
UNBREAKABLE BACKSTREET BOYS	21	2007
UNBREAKABLE – THE GREATEST HITS VOLUME 1 WESTLIFE	1	2002
UNCHAINED MELODIES VARIOUS ARTISTS (TELSTAR)	1	1991
UNCHAINED MELODIES – II VARIOUS ARTISTS (TELSTAR)	3	1991
UNCLE B N-DUBZ	11	2008
UNCLE DYSFUNKTIONAL HAPPY MONDAYS	73	2007
UNCOVERED VARIOUS ARTISTS (VIRGIN)	10	2001
UNCOVERED – THE VERY BEST OF SMOKIE SMOKIE	63	2001
UNDEAD TEN YEARS AFTER	26	1968
UNDER A RAGING MOON ROGER DALTREY	52	1985
UNDER A SUN WITNESS	62	2001
UNDER BLUE SKIES CHARLIE LANDSBOROUGH	73	2008
UNDER CONSTRUCTION MISSY ELLIOTT	23	2002
UNDER COVER OZZY OSBOURNE	67	2005
UNDER LATIN SKIES VARIOUS ARTISTS (GLOBAL TELEVISION)	14	1999
UNDER MY SKIN AVRIL LAVIGNE	1	2004
UNDER RUG SWEPT ALANIS MORISSETTE	2	2002
UNDER SPANISH SKIES VARIOUS ARTISTS (DINO)	5	1992
UNDER THE BLACKLIGHT RILO KILEY	34	2007
UNDER THE BLADE TWISTED SISTER	70	1982
UNDER THE COVERS VARIOUS ARTISTS (POLYGRAM)	11	1993
UNDER THE INFLUENCE STATUS QUO	26	1999
UNDER THE IRON SEA KEANE	1	2006
UNDER THE PINK TORI AMOS	1	1994
UNDER THE RADAR DANIEL POWTER	43	2008
UNDER THE RED SKY BOB DYLAN	13	1990
UNDER THE WATER-LINE TEN SHARP	46	1992
UNDER WRAPS JETHRO TULL	18	1984
UNDERCLASS HERO SUM 41	46	2007
UNDERCOVER ROLLING STONES	3	1983
UNDERGROUND EXPLOSION – THE REAL GARAGE MIX VARIOUS ARTISTS (VIRGIN)	10	2000
UNDERGROUND VOLUME 1 VARIOUS ARTISTS (COOKIE JAR)	6	1993
UNDERNEATH HANSON	49	2005
THE UNDERSTANDING ROYKSOPP	13	2005
THE UNDERTONES UNDERTONES	13	1979
UNDERWATER SUNLIGHT TANGERINE DREAM	97	1986
UNDISCOVERED JAMES MORRISON	1	2006
UNDISCOVERED SOUL RICHIE SAMBORA	24	1998
UNDISPUTED VARIOUS ARTISTS (POLYGRAM)	6	1998
UNDISPUTED ATTITUDE SLAYER	31	1996
UNEQUALLED EQUALS EQUALS	10	1967
THE UNEXPECTED GUEST DEMON	47	1982
THE UNEXPECTED SONGS – SURRENDER SARAH BRIGHTMAN	45	1995
UNFINISHED BUSINESS R KELLY & JAY-Z	61	2004
UNFINISHED MONKEY BUSINESS IAN BROWN	4	1998
UNFORGETTABLE VARIOUS ARTISTS (EMI)	5	1988
UNFORGETTABLE 2 VARIOUS ARTISTS (EMI)	1	1989
THE UNFORGETTABLE FIRE U2	1	1984
THE UNFORGETTABLE GLENN MILLER GLENN MILLER & HIS ORCHESTRA	4	1977
UNFORGETTABLE LOVESONGS VARIOUS ARTISTS (EMI)	9	2007
UNFORGETTABLE NAT 'KING' COLE NAT 'KING' COLE	11	1965
THE UNFORGETTABLE NAT 'KING' COLE NAT 'KING' COLE	23	1991
UNFORGETTABLE – WITH LOVE NATALIE COLE	11	1991
UNFORGETTABLE: A MUSICAL TRIBUTE TO NAT KING COLE JOHNNY MATHIS & NATALIE COLE	5	1983
UNHALFBRICKING FAIRPORT CONVENTION	12	1969
UNICORN TYRANNOSAURUS REX	12	1969
UNION TONI CHILDS	73	1989
UNION YES	7	1991
UNION GAP GARY PUCKETT & THE UNION GAP	24	1968
THE UNIQUE KLAUS WUNDERLICH SOUND KLAUS WUNDERLICH	28	1978
UNISON CELINE DION	55	1995
UNITED ABOMINATIONS MEGADETH	23	2007
UNITED DANCE PRESENTS ANTHEMS 2 – '88-'92 VARIOUS ARTISTS (UNITED DANCE)	17	1997
UNITED DANCE – VOLUME FOUR VARIOUS ARTISTS (4 BEAT)	17	1996
UNITED KINGDOMS ULTRAMARINE	49	1993
UNITED – VOLUME 3 VARIOUS ARTISTS (4 BEAT)	11	1996
UNITED – VOLUME 5 VARIOUS ARTISTS (4 BEAT)	20	1996
UNITED – VOLUME 6 VARIOUS ARTISTS (4 BEAT)	10	1997
UNIVERSAL K-KLASS	73	1994
UNIVERSAL ORCHESTRAL MANOEUVRES IN THE DARK	24	1996
UNIVERSAL HALL WATERBOYS	74	2003
UNIVERSAL MOTHER SINEAD O'CONNOR	19	1994
UNIVERSAL SOLDIER DONOVAN	5	1967
UNIVERSE PRESENTS THE TRIBAL GATHERING VARIOUS ARTISTS (UNIVERSE)	19	1995
UNIVERSE – WORLD TECHNO TRIBE VARIOUS ARTISTS (UNIVERSE)	13	1993
UNIVERSITY THROWING MUSES	10	1995
UNKNOWN PLEASURES JOY DIVISION	71	1980
UNKNOWN TERRITORY BOMB THE BASS	19	1991
UNLACED VARIOUS ARTISTS (EMI)	8	1995
UNLEASH THE DRAGON SISQO	15	2000
UNLEASHED IN THE EAST JUDAS PRIEST	10	1979
UN-LED-ED DREAD ZEPPELIN	71	1990
UNMASKED KISS	48	1980
UNMIXED FREEMASONS	58	2008
UNPLUGGED ERIC CLAPTON	2	1992
UNPLUGGED ARRESTED DEVELOPMENT	40	1993

Title / Artist	Peak Position	Year of Release
UNPLUGGED NEIL YOUNG	4	1993
UNPLUGGED BOB DYLAN	10	1995
UNPLUGGED BRYAN ADAMS	19	1997
UNPLUGGED CORRS	7	1999
UNPLUGGED ALICIA KEYS	52	2005
UNPLUGGED IN NEW YORK NIRVANA	1	1994
UNPLUGGED – THE OFFICIAL BOOTLEG PAUL McCARTNEY	7	1991
UNPLUGGED...AND SEATED 10,000 MANIACS	40	1993
UNPLUGGED...AND SEATED ROD STEWART	2	1993
UNPREDICTABLE JAMIE FOXX	9	2006
THE UNQUESTIONABLE TRUTH – PART 1 LIMP BIZKIT	71	2005
THE UNRECORDED JASPER CARROTT JASPER CARROTT	19	1979
UNRELEASED AND REVAMPED CYPRESS HILL	29	1996
UNTIL THE END OF TIME 2PAC	33	2001
UNTIL THE NEXT TIME DANIEL O'DONNELL	10	2006
UNTITLED BYRDS	11	1970
UNTITLED MARC & THE MAMBAS	42	1982
UNTITLED VARIOUS ARTISTS (GLOBAL TELEVISION)	6	1996
UNTITLED KORN	15	2007
UNTITLED 2 VARIOUS ARTISTS (GLOBAL TELEVISION)	6	1996
UNTITLED 3 VARIOUS ARTISTS (GLOBAL TELEVISION)	20	1996
THE UNTOUCHABLE ALVIN STARDUST	4	1974
UNTOUCHABLES KORN	4	2002
UNTRUE BURIAL	58	2008
UNUSUAL HEAT FOREIGNER	56	1991
UNWRITTEN NATASHA BEDINGFIELD	1	2004
UP ABC	58	1989
UP RIGHT SAID FRED	1	1992
UP R.E.M.	2	1998
UP PETER GABRIEL	11	2002
UP SHANIA TWAIN	4	2002
UP ALL NIGHT EAST 17	7	1995
UP ALL NIGHT VARIOUS ARTISTS (VIRGIN)	5	2003
UP ALL NIGHT RAZORLIGHT	3	2004
UP AT THE LAKE CHARLATANS	13	2004
THE UP ESCALATOR GRAHAM PARKER & THE RUMOUR	11	1980
UP ON THE ROOF – SONGS FROM THE BRILL BUILDING NEIL DIAMOND	28	1993
UP THE BRACKET LIBERTINES	35	2002
UP TO DATE PARTRIDGE FAMILY	46	1972
UP TO OUR HIPS CHARLATANS	8	1994
UPFRONT 1 – 14 DANCE TRACKS VARIOUS ARTISTS (SERIOUS)	17	1986
UPFRONT 2 – 14 DANCE TRACKS VARIOUS ARTISTS (SERIOUS)	27	1986
UPFRONT 3 VARIOUS ARTISTS (SERIOUS)	37	1986
UPFRONT 4 VARIOUS ARTISTS (SERIOUS)	21	1987
UPFRONT 5 VARIOUS ARTISTS (SERIOUS)	21	1987
UPFRONT 6 VARIOUS ARTISTS (SERIOUS)	22	1987
UPFRONT 7 VARIOUS ARTISTS (SERIOUS)	31	1987
UPFRONT 8 VARIOUS ARTISTS (SERIOUS)	22	1987
UPFRONT 9 VARIOUS ARTISTS (SERIOUS)	92	1987
UPFRONT 10 VARIOUS ARTISTS (SERIOUS)	45	1988
UPFRONT 89 VARIOUS ARTISTS (SERIOUS)	15	1989
UPRISING BOB MARLEY & THE WAILERS	6	1980
THE UPS AND DOWNS STEPHEN 'TIN TIN' DUFFY	35	1985
UPSTAIRS AT ERIC'S YAZOO	2	1982
URBAN ACID VARIOUS ARTISTS (URBAN)	51	1988
URBAN BEACHES CACTUS WORLD NEWS	56	1986
URBAN CHILL VARIOUS ARTISTS (UNIVERSAL)	15	2001
URBAN CLASSICS VARIOUS ARTISTS (URBAN)	96	1987
URBAN DANCE EXPLOSION VARIOUS ARTISTS (WARNER BROTHERS)	18	2005
URBAN EXPLOSION VARIOUS ARTISTS (WARNER BROTHERS)	5	2003
URBAN FUSION VARIOUS ARTISTS (UNIVERSAL)	15	2003
URBAN HEAT VARIOUS ARTISTS (UNIVERSAL)	15	2005
URBAN HYMNS VERVE	1	1997
URBAN KISS VARIOUS ARTISTS (UNIVERSAL)	5	2001
URBAN KISS 2002 VARIOUS ARTISTS (UNIVERSAL)	3	2002
URBAN KISS 2003 VARIOUS ARTISTS (UNIVERSAL)	6	2003
URBAN LICKS VARIOUS ARTISTS (VIRGIN)	7	2004
URBAN MUSIC FESTIVAL VARIOUS ARTISTS (WARNER BROTHERS)	8	2004
URBAN RENEWAL – SONGS OF PHIL COLLINS VARIOUS ARTISTS (WARNER BROTHERS)	16	2001
URBAN RHYMES VARIOUS ARTISTS (GLOBAL TELEVISION)	5	1998
URBAN VIBES VARIOUS ARTISTS (BMG)	13	2002
URBAN WEEKEND VARIOUS ARTISTS (UNIVERSAL)	4	2006
URIAH HEEP LIVE URIAH HEEP	23	1973
URUGUAY – DARREN EMERSON VARIOUS ARTISTS (GLOBAL UNDERGROUND)	20	2000
US PETER GABRIEL	2	1992
US MULL HISTORICAL SOCIETY	19	2003
US AND US ONLY CHARLATANS	2	1999
USE YOUR ILLUSION I GUNS N' ROSES	2	1991
USE YOUR ILLUSION II GUNS N' ROSES	1	1991
USE YOUR IMAGINATION MUD	33	1975
USELESS TRINKETS – B-SIDES SOUNDTRACKS EELS	69	2008
UTAH SAINTS UTAH SAINTS	10	1993
UTOPIA BANISHED NAPALM DEATH	58	1992
UTOPIA – CHILLED CLASSICS VARIOUS ARTISTS (PHILIPS)	10	2001
UTTER MADNESS MADNESS	29	1986
U-VOX ULTRAVOX	9	1986

Title / Artist	Peak Position	Year of Release
V DEEP BOOMTOWN RATS	64	1982
V.U. VELVET UNDERGROUND	47	1985
V2 VIBRATORS	33	1978
VACATION GO-GO'S	75	1982
VAGABOND HEART ROD STEWART	2	1991
VAL VAL DOONICAN	6	1968
VAL DOONICAN ROCKS BUT GENTLY VAL DOONICAN	1	1967
VALENTINE ROY HARPER	27	1974
VALENTYNE SUITE COLOSSEUM	15	1969
VALHALLA AVENUE FATIMA MANSIONS	52	1992
VALLEY OF THE DOLLS DIONNE WARWICK	10	1968
VALLEY OF THE DOLLS GENERATION X	51	1979
VALOTTE JULIAN LENNON	20	1984
VAMP OF THE ROARING TWENTIES DOROTHY PROVINE	9	1962
VAMPIRE WEEKEND VAMPIRE WEEKEND	15	2008
VAN HALEN VAN HALEN	34	1978
VAN HALEN 3 VAN HALEN	43	1998
VAN HALEN II VAN HALEN	23	1979
VAN MORRISON, HIS BAND AND THE STREET CHOIR VAN MORRISON	18	1971
VANESSA PARADIS VANESSA PARADIS	45	1992
VANGUARD FINLEY QUAYE	35	2000
VANILLA FUDGE VANILLA FUDGE	31	1967
VANISHING POINT PRIMAL SCREAM	2	1997
VAPOR TRAILS RUSH	38	2002
VARIATIONS ANDREW LLOYD WEBBER FEATURING CELLIST JULIAN LLOYD WEBBER	2	1978
VARIOUS POSITIONS LEONARD COHEN	52	1985
VAULT – THE GREATEST HITS 1980-1995 DEF LEPPARD	3	1995
THE VAULT...OLD FRIENDS 4 SALE PRINCE	47	1999
VAUXHALL AND I MORRISSEY	1	1994
VE DAY – THE ALBUM VARIOUS ARTISTS (VIRGIN)	6	2005
VEEDON FLEECE VAN MORRISON	41	1974
THE VEGETARIANS OF LOVE BOB GELDOF	21	1990
VEHICLES & ANIMALS ATHLETE	19	2003
VELOCIFERO LADYTRON	75	2008
THE VELVET ROPE JANET JACKSON	6	1997
VELVET UNDERGROUND AND NICO VELVET UNDERGROUND AND NICO	59	2002
VELVET WATERS VARIOUS ARTISTS (STYLUS)	54	1985
VELVETEEN TRANSVISION VAMP	1	1989
VENEER JOSE GONZALEZ	7	2006
VENGEANCE NEW MODEL ARMY	73	1984
VENICE IN PERIL RONDO VENEZIANO	34	1983
VENUS AND MARS WINGS	1	1975
VENUS DOOM H.I.M.	31	2007
VERDI ANDREA BOCELLI	17	2000
VERMIN IN ERMINE MARC ALMOND & THE WILLING SINNERS	36	1984
VERSION MARK RONSON	2	2007
VERSION 2.0 GARBAGE	1	1998
VERTICAL SMILES BLACKFOOT	82	1984
VERTIGO GROOVE ARMADA	23	1999
THE VERTIGO OF BLISS BIFFY CLYRO	48	2003
VERY PET SHOP BOYS	1	1993
THE VERY BEST CLUB ANTHEMS EVER VARIOUS ARTISTS (VIRGIN)	17	2004
THE VERY BEST EUPHORIC CHILLOUT MIXES VARIOUS ARTISTS (TELSTAR)	10	2001
THE VERY BEST EUPHORIC HOUSE BREAKDOWN VARIOUS ARTISTS (TELSTAR)	2	2003
VERY BEST EUPHORIC OLD SKOOL BREAKDOWN VARIOUS ARTISTS (TELSTAR)	4	2002
THE VERY BEST OF ENNIO MORRICONE	48	2000
THE VERY BEST OF OTIS REDDING	26	2000
THE VERY BEST OF BANANARAMA	43	2001
THE VERY BEST OF CHRIS REA	69	2001
THE VERY BEST OF DINA CARROLL	15	2001
THE VERY BEST OF EAGLES	3	2001
THE VERY BEST OF MICHAEL McDONALD	21	2001
THE VERY BEST OF MIDGE URE & ULTRAVOX	45	2001
THE VERY BEST OF POGUES	18	2001
THE VERY BEST OF SMITHS	30	2001
THE VERY BEST OF FLEETWOOD MAC	7	2002
THE VERY BEST OF MOODY BLUES	27	2002
THE VERY BEST OF SEARCHERS	11	2008
THE VERY BEST OF SOFT CELL	37	2002
THE VERY BEST OF STONE ROSES	19	2002
THE VERY BEST OF CHER	17	2003
THE VERY BEST OF HUMAN LEAGUE	24	2003
THE VERY BEST OF LIGHTHOUSE FAMILY	9	2003
THE VERY BEST OF LINDA RONSTADT	46	2003
THE VERY BEST OF SHERYL CROW	2	2003
THE VERY BEST OF ALAN JACKSON	47	2004
THE VERY BEST OF BAY CITY ROLLERS	11	2004
THE VERY BEST OF GRIMETHORPE COLLIERY BAND	59	2004
THE VERY BEST OF JACKSON BROWNE	53	2004
THE VERY BEST OF JACKSONS	7	2004
THE VERY BEST OF MACY GRAY	36	2004
THE VERY BEST OF MICHAEL CRAWFORD	54	2004
VERY BEST OF DEAN MARTIN	59	2004
THE VERY BEST OF EAST 17	34	2005
THE VERY BEST OF GIPSY KINGS	32	2005
THE VERY BEST OF MICHAEL BOLTON	18	2005
THE VERY BEST OF SANDIE SHAW	60	2005

Title / Artist	Peak Position	Year of Release
THE VERY BEST OF SLADE	39	2005
THE VERY BEST OF SWEET	72	2005
THE VERY BEST OF ADAM & THE ANTS	39	2006
THE VERY BEST OF AEROSMITH	19	2006
THE VERY BEST OF DRIFTERS	46	2006
THE VERY BEST OF GLORIA ESTEFAN	40	2006
THE VERY BEST OF JOHNNY MATHIS	6	2006
THE VERY BEST OF LIGHTNING SEEDS	33	2006
THE VERY BEST OF NINA SIMONE	6	2006
THE VERY BEST OF ROBERTA FLACK	50	2006
THE VERY BEST OF ROY ORBISON	20	2006
THE VERY BEST OF STRANGLERS	28	2006
THE VERY BEST OF BUCKS FIZZ	40	2007
THE VERY BEST OF DOLLY PARTON	8	2007
THE VERY BEST OF DOORS	15	2007
THE VERY BEST OF JOHN BARRY	64	2007
THE VERY BEST OF STYLISTICS	30	2007
THE VERY BEST OF BOBBY VEE	18	2008
THE VERY BEST OF DAVE DEE, DOZY, BEAKY, MICK & TICH	24	2008
THE VERY BEST OF DEEP PURPLE	43	2008
THE VERY BEST OF EDDIE COCHRAN	31	2008
THE VERY BEST OF OSMONDS	11	2008
THE VERY BEST OF PLATTERS	8	2008
THE VERY BEST OF VAL DOONICAN	33	2008
THE VERY BEST OF – THE GREATEST HITS OF GEORGE BENSON GEORGE BENSON	4	2003
THE VERY BEST OF (ARETHA FRANKLIN & OTIS REDDING) VARIOUS ARTISTS (WARNER BROTHERS)	10	2005
THE VERY BEST OF 10CC 10 C.C.	37	1997
THE VERY BEST OF – 1980-2000 UB40	7	2000
THE VERY BEST OF ADAM AND THE ANTS ADAM & THE ANTS	33	1999
THE VERY BEST OF ALL WOMAN VARIOUS ARTISTS (TELSTAR)	2	2002
THE VERY BEST OF ALL WOMAN VARIOUS ARTISTS (SONY)	4	2003
THE VERY BEST OF ALL WOMAN 2003 VARIOUS ARTISTS (TELSTAR)	3	2003
THE VERY BEST OF ALL WOMAN – PLATINUM VARIOUS ARTISTS (WARNER BROTHERS)	9	2005
THE VERY BEST OF ANDREW LLOYD WEBBER VARIOUS ARTISTS (REALLY USEFUL)	3	1994
THE VERY BEST OF ANDY WILLIAMS ANDY WILLIAMS	27	2000
THE VERY BEST OF ANNE MURRAY ANNE MURRAY	14	1981
THE VERY BEST OF ART GARFUNKEL – ACROSS AMERICA ART GARFUNKEL	35	1996
THE VERY BEST OF BACK TO THE MOVIES VARIOUS ARTISTS (EMI)	8	2006
THE VERY BEST OF BACK TO THE OLD SKOOL VARIOUS ARTISTS (MINISTRY OF SOUND)	10	2005
THE VERY BEST OF BARBARA DICKSON BARBARA DICKSON	78	1986
THE VERY BEST OF BEN E. KING & THE DRIFTERS BEN E. KING & THE DRIFTERS	15	1990
THE VERY BEST OF BEN E. KING & THE DRIFTERS BEN E. KING & THE DRIFTERS	41	1998
THE VERY BEST OF BLUES BROTHER SOUL SISTER VARIOUS ARTISTS (DINO)	11	1995
VERY BEST OF BLUES BROTHER SOUL SISTER VARIOUS ARTISTS (WARNER BROTHERS)	9	2005
THE VERY BEST OF BRASS VARIOUS ARTISTS (DINO)	18	1997
THE VERY BEST OF BRENDA LEE BRENDA LEE	16	1985
THE VERY BEST OF BRENDA LEE...WITH LOVE BRENDA LEE	20	1994
THE VERY BEST OF BUDDY HOLLY BUDDY HOLLY	24	1996
THE VERY BEST OF BUDDY HOLLY AND THE CRICKETS BUDDY HOLLY & THE CRICKETS	25	1999
THE VERY BEST OF CAJUN – 40 HOT CAJUN CLASSICS VARIOUS ARTISTS (DINO)	16	1996
THE VERY BEST OF CAT STEVENS CAT STEVENS	4	1990
THE VERY BEST OF CHARLIE LANDSBOROUGH CHARLIE LANDSBOROUGH	41	1998
THE VERY BEST OF CHILLED CLASSICS VARIOUS ARTISTS (UNIVERSAL)	18	2003
THE VERY BEST OF CHRIS DE BURGH CHRIS DE BURGH	6	1984
THE VERY BEST OF CILLA BLACK CILLA BLACK	20	1983
THE VERY BEST OF CLASSICAL CHILLOUT VARIOUS ARTISTS (VIRGIN)	15	2003
THE VERY BEST OF CLASSICAL CHILLOUT GOLD VARIOUS ARTISTS (DECADANCE)	13	2003
THE VERY BEST OF CLASSICAL EXPERIENCE VARIOUS ARTISTS (VIRGIN)	18	1999
THE VERY BEST OF COLD FEET TELEVISION AND RADIO COMPILATION	1	2003
THE VERY BEST OF – COOL & COLLECTED MILES DAVIS	69	2006
THE VERY BEST OF COUNTRY GOLD VARIOUS ARTISTS (DECADANCE)	6	2003
THE VERY BEST OF – CRAZY SEXY HITS TLC	57	2007
THE VERY BEST OF DANIEL O'DONNELL DANIEL O'DONNELL	34	1991
VERY BEST OF DAVE PEARCE DANCE ANTHEMS VARIOUS ARTISTS (TELSTAR)	4	2003
THE VERY BEST OF DAVID BOWIE DAVID BOWIE	3	1981
THE VERY BEST OF DAVID ESSEX DAVID ESSEX	37	1982
THE VERY BEST OF DEAN MARTIN – THE CAPITOL & REPRISE YEARS DEAN MARTIN	5	1999
VERY BEST OF DEEP PURPLE DEEP PURPLE	39	1998
THE VERY BEST OF DEXY'S MIDNIGHT RUNNERS DEXYS MIDNIGHT RUNNERS	12	1991
THE VERY BEST OF DIANA KRALL DIANA KRALL	35	2007
THE VERY BEST OF DISNEY VARIOUS ARTISTS (PICKWICK)	4	1993
THE VERY BEST OF DISNEY 2 VARIOUS ARTISTS (PICKWICK)	9	1994
THE VERY BEST OF DISNEY CHANNEL VARIOUS ARTISTS (WALT DISNEY)	6	2007
THE VERY BEST OF DOLLAR DOLLAR	31	1982
THE VERY BEST OF DON MCLEAN DON McLEAN	4	1980
THE VERY BEST OF DRIVE TIME VARIOUS ARTISTS (TELSTAR)	3	2003
THE VERY BEST OF DRIVETIME VARIOUS ARTISTS (INSPIRED)	8	2004
VERY BEST OF – EARLY DAYS AND LATTER DAYS LED ZEPPELIN	11	2003
THE VERY BEST OF EARTH WIND & FIRE EARTH WIND & FIRE	40	1992
VERY BEST OF EDDIE COCHRAN EDDIE COCHRAN	34	1970
VERY BEST OF EDDY GRANT EDDY GRANT	14	2008
THE VERY BEST OF ELKIE BROOKS ELKIE BROOKS	10	1986
THE VERY BEST OF ELTON JOHN ELTON JOHN	1	1980
THE VERY BEST OF ELVIS COSTELLO ELVIS COSTELLO	4	1999
THE VERY BEST OF ELVIS COSTELLO AND THE ATTRACTIONS ELVIS COSTELLO & THE ATTRACTIONS	57	1994
THE VERY BEST OF ENTERTAINMENT FROM THE U.S.A. VOLUME 2 (TELEVISION COMPILATION) TELEVISION AND RADIO COMPILATION	44	1986
THE VERY BEST OF EUPHORIA – MATT DAREY VARIOUS ARTISTS (TELSTAR)	3	2002
THE VERY BEST OF EUPHORIC DANCE VARIOUS ARTISTS (MINISTRY OF SOUND)	2	2006
VERY BEST OF EUPHORIC DANCE BREAKDOWN VARIOUS ARTISTS (TELSTAR)	4	2002
THE VERY BEST OF EUPHORIC DANCE BREAKDOWN VARIOUS ARTISTS (MINISTRY OF SOUND)	1	2008
THE VERY BEST OF EUPHORIC DANCE BREAKDOWN – SUMMER 2008 VARIOUS ARTISTS (MINISTRY OF SOUND)	4	2008
VERY BEST OF EUPHORIC DISCO BREAKDOWN VARIOUS ARTISTS (TELSTAR)	17	2004
THE VERY BEST OF EUPHORIC FUNKY HOUSE VARIOUS ARTISTS (MINISTRY OF SOUND)	3	2005
VERY BEST OF FATS DOMINO FATS DOMINO	56	1970
THE VERY BEST OF FOREIGNER FOREIGNER	19	1992
THE VERY BEST OF FOSTER AND ALLEN FOSTER & ALLEN	18	1984
THE VERY BEST OF FRANKIE LAINE FRANKIE LAINE	7	1977
THE VERY BEST OF FRANKIE VALLI AND THE FOUR SEASONS FRANKIE VALLI & THE FOUR SEASONS	7	1992
THE VERY BEST OF FREDDIE MERCURY SOLO FREDDIE MERCURY	6	2006
THE VERY BEST OF GREATEST LOVE VARIOUS ARTISTS (TELSTAR)	5	1990
VERY BEST OF HANK MARVIN AND THE SHADOWS – THE FIRST 40 YEARS HANK MARVIN & THE SHADOWS	56	1998
THE VERY BEST OF HEARTBEAT – THE ALBUM TELEVISION AND RADIO COMPILATION	14	2006
THE VERY BEST OF HERB ALPERT HERB ALPERT	34	1991
THE VERY BEST OF HOT CHOCOLATE HOT CHOCOLATE	1	1987
THE VERY BEST OF – IDOLIZE YOURSELF BILLY IDOL	37	2008
THE VERY BEST OF IVAN REBROFF IVAN REBROFF	57	1990
VERY BEST OF JAMES LAST JAMES LAST	45	1970
THE VERY BEST OF JAMES LAST AND HIS ORCHESTRA JAMES LAST	36	1995
THE VERY BEST OF – JERSEY'S BEST FRANKIE VALLI & THE FOUR SEASONS	25	2008
THE VERY BEST OF JIMMY SOMERVILLE BRONSKI BEAT AND THE COMMUNARDS JIMMY SOMERVILLE BRONSKI BEAT & THE COMMUNARDS	29	2001
THE VERY BEST OF JOAN ARMATRADING JOAN ARMATRADING	9	1991
THE VERY BEST OF JOE BROWN JOE BROWN	14	2008
THE VERY BEST OF JOE JACKSON JOE JACKSON	60	2007
THE VERY BEST OF KIKI DEE KIKI DEE	62	1994
THE VERY BEST OF KIM WILDE KIM WILDE	78	1985
THE VERY BEST OF LATIN JAZZ VARIOUS ARTISTS (DECADANCE)	15	2003
THE VERY BEST OF LATIN JAZZ VARIOUS ARTISTS (UNIVERSAL)	10	2007
THE VERY BEST OF LATIN JAZZ – 2 VARIOUS ARTISTS (GLOBAL TELEVISION)	15	1999
THE VERY BEST OF LEO SAYER LEO SAYER	1	1979
THE VERY BEST OF LEVEL 42 LEVEL 42	41	1998
THE VERY BEST OF LOUIS ARMSTRONG LOUIS ARMSTRONG	30	1982

Title / Artist	Peak Position	Year of Release
THE VERY BEST OF LOVE LEGENDS VARIOUS ARTISTS (EMI)	4	2006
THE VERY BEST OF MANFRED MANN'S EARTH BAND MANFRED MANN'S EARTH BAND	69	1994
THE VERY BEST OF MARVIN GAYE MARVIN GAYE	3	1994
THE VERY BEST OF MEAT LOAF MEAT LOAF	14	1998
THE VERY BEST OF MICHAEL BALL IN CONCERT AT THE ROYAL ALBERT HALL MICHAEL BALL	18	1999
THE VERY BEST OF MICK JAGGER MICK JAGGER	57	2007
THE VERY BEST OF MILES DAVIS MILES DAVIS	64	1996
THE VERY BEST OF – MORE SONGS TO LEARN ECHO & THE BUNNYMEN	47	2006
THE VERY BEST OF MOTOWN LOVE SONGS VARIOUS ARTISTS (TELSTAR)	10	1984
THE VERY BEST OF MTV UNPLUGGED VARIOUS ARTISTS (UNIVERSAL)	1	2002
THE VERY BEST OF MTV UNPLUGGED 2 VARIOUS ARTISTS (WARNER BROTHERS)	1	2003
THE VERY BEST OF NEIL DIAMOND NEIL DIAMOND	33	1983
THE VERY BEST OF NEIL SEDAKA NEIL SEDAKA	33	1999
THE VERY BEST OF NEW WOMAN VARIOUS ARTISTS (VIRGIN)	1	2004
THE VERY BEST OF NOW DANCE VARIOUS ARTISTS (VIRGIN)	2	2005
THE VERY BEST OF PATSY CLINE PATSY CLINE	21	1996
THE VERY BEST OF POWER BALLADS VARIOUS ARTISTS (EMI)	10	2005
THE VERY BEST OF PRINCE PRINCE	2	2001
THE VERY BEST OF PURE DANCEHALL VARIOUS ARTISTS (TELSTAR)	8	2003
THE VERY BEST OF PURE GARAGE VARIOUS ARTISTS (WARNER BROTHERS)	20	2009
THE VERY BEST OF PURE HIP HOP VARIOUS ARTISTS (TELSTAR)	14	2003
THE VERY BEST OF PURE R&B – SUMMER 2003 VARIOUS ARTISTS (TELSTAR)	2	2003
THE VERY BEST OF PURE R&B – THE SUMMER VARIOUS ARTISTS (TELSTAR)	1	2002
THE VERY BEST OF PURE R&B – THE WINTER VARIOUS ARTISTS (TELSTAR)	11	2002
THE VERY BEST OF PURE R&B – WINTER 2003 VARIOUS ARTISTS (TELSTAR)	3	2003
THE VERY BEST OF PURE SWING VARIOUS ARTISTS (PUMP)	17	1996
THE VERY BEST OF RANDY CRAWFORD RANDY CRAWFORD	8	1993
THE VERY BEST OF RELAXING CLASSICS VARIOUS ARTISTS (DECCA)	4	2003
THE VERY BEST OF RICHARD CLAYDERMAN RICHARD CLAYDERMAN WITH THE ROYAL PHILHARMONIC ORCHESTRA	47	1992
THE VERY BEST OF RITA COOLIDGE RITA COOLIDGE	6	1981
THE VERY BEST OF ROBERT PALMER ROBERT PALMER	4	1995
THE VERY BEST OF ROGER WHITTAKER ROGER WHITTAKER	5	1975
THE VERY BEST OF ROY ORBISON ROY ORBISON	18	1996
THE VERY BEST OF SCHOOLDISCO.COM VARIOUS ARTISTS (V2)	5	2004
THE VERY BEST OF SHOWADDYWADDY SHOWADDYWADDY	33	1981
THE VERY BEST OF SISTER SLEDGE 1973-1993 SISTER SLEDGE	19	1993
THE VERY BEST OF SLIM WHITMAN SLIM WHITMAN	1	1976
THE VERY BEST OF SLIM WHITMAN – 50TH ANNIVERSARY COLLECTION SLIM WHITMAN	54	1997
THE VERY BEST OF SMOKIE SMOKIE	23	1980
THE VERY BEST OF SMOOTH JAZZ VARIOUS ARTISTS (UNIVERSAL CLASSICS)	7	2002
THE VERY BEST OF SMOOTH JAZZ VARIOUS ARTISTS (UNIVERSAL)	11	2008
THE VERY BEST OF STING AND THE POLICE STING & THE POLICE	1	1997
THE VERY BEST OF STREET VIBES VARIOUS ARTISTS (TELSTAR)	4	2003
THE VERY BEST OF SUPERTRAMP SUPERTRAMP	8	1992
THE VERY BEST OF TALK TALK TALK TALK	54	1997
THE VERY BEST OF TALK TALK – NATURAL HISTORY TALK TALK	3	1990
THE VERY BEST OF THAT LOVING FEELING VARIOUS ARTISTS (DINO)	2	1993
THE VERY BEST OF THE BEACH BOYS BEACH BOYS	1	1983
THE VERY BEST OF THE BEACH BOYS BEACH BOYS	31	2001
THE VERY BEST OF THE BEE GEES BEE GEES	6	1990
THE VERY BEST OF THE COMMODORES COMMODORES	26	1995
THE VERY BEST OF THE COMMODORES – 16 CLASSIC TRACKS COMMODORES	25	1985
THE VERY BEST OF THE DRIFTERS DRIFTERS	24	1986
THE VERY BEST OF THE EAGLES EAGLES	4	1994
THE VERY BEST OF THE ELECTRIC LIGHT ORCHESTRA ELECTRIC LIGHT ORCHESTRA	4	1994
THE VERY BEST OF THE EVERLY BROTHERS EVERLY BROTHERS	43	1974
THE VERY BEST OF THE FANTASTIC 80'S VARIOUS ARTISTS (COLUMBIA)	7	2003
THE VERY BEST OF THE JAM JAM	9	1997
THE VERY BEST OF THE KINKS KINKS	42	1997
THE VERY BEST OF THE LOVE ALBUM VARIOUS ARTISTS (VIRGIN)	3	1998
THE VERY BEST OF THE MOODY BLUES MOODY BLUES	13	1996
THE VERY BEST OF THE OSMONDS OSMONDS	17	1996
THE VERY BEST OF THE PAN PIPES INSPIRATIONS	37	1996
THE VERY BEST OF THE RIGHTEOUS BROTHERS: UNCHAINED MELODY RIGHTEOUS BROTHERS	11	1990
THE VERY BEST OF – THE SHOW GOES ON NEIL SEDAKA	20	2006
THE VERY BEST OF TONY BENNETT – 20 GREATEST HITS TONY BENNETT	23	1977
VERY BEST OF TRIED AND TESTED EUPHORIA VARIOUS ARTISTS (MINISTRY OF SOUND)	15	2004
VERY BEST OF UPLIFTING HOUSE EUPHORIA VARIOUS ARTISTS (MINISTRY OF SOUND)	20	2005
THE VERY BEST OF VOLUME 2 DEAN MARTIN	40	2000
THE VERY BEST OF WHILE MY GUITAR GENTLY WEEPS VARIOUS ARTISTS (UNIVERSAL)	6	2008
THE VERY BEST OF/STRANGE TIMES MOODY BLUES	19	2000
THE VERY BEST POP ALBUM VARIOUS ARTISTS (TELSTAR)	18	2002
A VERY FINE LOVE DUSTY SPRINGFIELD	43	1995
A VERY MERRY DISCO SLEIGHRIDERS	100	1983
VERY NECESSARY SALT-N-PEPA	36	1994
VERY SPECIAL LOVE SONGS CHARLIE RICH	34	1974
A VERY SPECIAL SEASON DIANA ROSS	37	1994
VESPERTINE BJORK	8	2001
VH1 DIVAS LIVE VARIOUS ARTISTS (EPIC)	3	1998
VI: RETURN OF THE REAL ICE-T	26	1996
VIAGGIO ITALIANO ANDREA BOCELLI	24	1999
VIBRATE YOU KING ADORA	30	2001
VIC DAMONE SINGS THE GREAT SONGS VIC DAMONE	87	1983
VICES WAYSTED	78	1983
VICTIM OF LOVE ELTON JOHN	41	1979
VICTIMS OF CIRCUMSTANCES BARCLAY JAMES HARVEST	33	1984
VICTIMS OF THE FURY ROBIN TROWER	61	1980
VICTIMS OF THE FUTURE GARY MOORE	12	1984
VICTORIA BECKHAM VICTORIA BECKHAM	10	2001
VICTORIALAND COCTEAU TWINS	10	1986
VICTORY JACKSONS	3	1984
VICTORY AT SEA LONDON PHILHARMONIC ORCHESTRA	12	1961
VICTORY FOR THE COMIC MUSE DIVINE COMEDY	43	2006
VICTORY IN EUROPE – BROADCASTS AND REPORTS FROM BBC CORRESPONDENTS (RADIO SOUNDTRACK) TELEVISION AND RADIO COMPILATION	61	1985
VIDEO STARS VARIOUS ARTISTS (K-TEL)	5	1980
VIENNA ULTRAVOX	3	1980
VIGIL IN A WILDERNESS OF MIRRORS FISH	5	1990
VIGILANTE MAGNUM	24	1986
VILLIANS SAW DOCTORS	58	2001
VINTAGE MICHAEL BOLTON	23	2004
VINTAGE CHEESE VARIOUS ARTISTS (UNIVERSAL)	16	2005
VIOLATOR DEPECHE MODE	2	1990
THE VIOLIN PLAYER VANESSA-MAE	11	1995
VIOLINS IN LOVE JAMES LAST	60	1975
THE VIRGIN SUICIDES – OST AIR	14	2000
VIRGINS AND PHILISTINES COLOUR FIELD	12	1985
VIRTUAL XI IRON MAIDEN	16	1998
VIRTUOSO DAVID GARRETT	17	2008
VIRUS 100 – ALTERNATIVE TENTACLES VARIOUS ARTISTS (ALTERNATIVE TENTACLES)	15	1992
VISAGE VISAGE	13	1981
VISIBLE WORLD JAN GARBAREK	69	1996
VISION OF PEACE MONKS OF AMPLEFORTH ABBEY	73	1995
VISION THING SISTERS OF MERCY	11	1990
VISION VALLEY VINES	71	2006
VISIONS DON WILLIAMS	13	1977
VISIONS VARIOUS ARTISTS (K-TEL)	5	1983
VISIONS JAKATTA	12	2002
THE VISITORS ABBA	1	1981
VITAL IDOL BILLY IDOL	7	1985
VITALOGY PEARL JAM	4	1994
VIVA EL AMOR PRETENDERS	32	1999
VIVA ESPANA JAMES LAST	23	1992
VIVA! EUROPOP VARIOUS ARTISTS (WARNER BROTHERS)	4	1996
VIVA HATE MORRISSEY	1	1988
VIVA LA VIDA OR DEATH AND ALL HIS FRIENDS COLDPLAY	1	2008
VIVA! LATINO VARIOUS ARTISTS (COLUMBIA)	11	1999
VIVA! ROXY MUSIC ROXY	6	1976
VIVA! SANTANA – THE VERY BEST SANTANA	50	1986
VIVADIXIESUBMARINETRANSMISSIONPLOT SPARKLEHORSE	58	1996
VIVALDI: THE FOUR SEASONS NIGEL KENNEDY WITH THE ENGLISH CHAMBER ORCHESTRA	3	1989
VIVALDI'S THE FOUR SEASONS ACADEMY OF ANCIENT MUSIC (CONDUCTED BY CHRISTOPHER HOGWOOD)	85	1985
VIVE LE ROCK ADAM ANT	42	1985
VIVERE – GREATEST HITS ANDREA BOCELLI	4	2007
VIVERE – LIVE IN TUSCANY ANDREA BOCELLI	26	2008

Title / Artist	Peak Position	Year of Release
VIXEN VIXEN	66	1988
THE VOICE BRENDA COCHRANE	14	1990
THE VOICE RUSSELL WATSON	5	2000
VOICE ALISON MOYET	7	2004
VOICE OF A GENERATION BLITZ	27	1982
VOICE OF AN ANGEL CHARLOTTE CHURCH	4	1998
THE VOICE OF CHURCHILL SIR WINSTON CHURCHILL	6	1965
VOICE OF LOVE DIANA ROSS	42	1996
THE VOICE OF RICHARD DIMBLEBY RICHARD DIMBLEBY	14	1966
VOICE OF THE HEART CARPENTERS	6	1983
VOICE – THE BEST OF BEVERLEY KNIGHT	9	2006
THE VOICE – THE ULTIMATE COLLECTION RUSSELL WATSON	2	2006
VOICES KENNY THOMAS	3	1991
VOICES VANGELIS	58	1996
VOICES VARIOUS ARTISTS (DECCA)	6	2002
VOICES FROM THE FIFA WORLD CUP VARIOUS ARTISTS (SYCO MUSIC)	16	2006
VOICES FROM THE HOLY LAND ALED JONES WITH THE BBC WELSH CHORUS	6	1985
VOICES OF ANIMALS & MEN YOUNG KNIVES	21	2006
VOICES OF THE VALLEY FRON MALE VOICE CHOIR	9	2006
VOICES OF THE VALLEY – ENCORE FRON MALE VOICE CHOIR	11	2007
VOICES OF THE VALLEY – HOME FRON MALE VOICE CHOIR	14	2008
VOICES OF TRANQUILLITY HYPNOSIS	16	1996
VOICES OF TRANQUILLITY – VOLUME 2 HYPNOSIS	32	1997
VOLARE – THE VERY BEST OF THE GIPSY KINGS GIPSY KINGS	20	1999
VOLTA BJORK	7	2007
VOLUME 1 – SOUND MAGIC AFRO CELT SOUND SYSTEM	59	1996
VOLUME 2 – CULTURE CLASH SACRED SPIRIT	24	1997
VOLUME 2: RELEASE AFRO CELT SOUND SYSTEM	38	1999
VOLUME 3 (THE SUBLIMINAL VERSES) SLIPKNOT	5	2004
VOLUME 8 – THE THREAT IS REAL! ANTHRAX	73	1998
VOLUME FOUR VARIOUS ARTISTS (WORLDS END)	17	1992
VOLUME II (A NEW DECADE) SOUL II SOUL	1	1990
VOLUME III JUST RIGHT SOUL II SOUL	3	1992
VOLUME IV THE CLASSIC SINGLES 88-93 SOUL II SOUL	10	1993
VOLUME SIX VARIOUS ARTISTS (VOLUME)	19	1993
VOLUME V – BELIEVE SOUL II SOUL	13	1995
VOLUNTEERS JEFFERSON AIRPLANE	34	1970
VOODOO D'ANGELO	21	2000
VOODOO CHILD – THE COLLECTION JIMI HENDRIX	10	2002
VOODOO HIGHWAY BADLANDS	74	1991
VOODOO LOUNGE ROLLING STONES	1	1994
VOODOO PARTY JAMES LAST	45	1972
VOULEZ-VOUS ABBA	1	1979
VOYAGE VOYAGE	59	1978
VOYAGE OF THE ACOLYTE STEVE HACKETT	26	1975
VOYAGER MIKE OLDFIELD	12	1996
VOYAGEUR ENIGMA	46	2003
VS PEARL JAM	2	1993
VULGAR DISPLAYS OF POWER PANTERA	64	1992
VULTURE CULTURE ALAN PARSONS PROJECT	40	1985
VYBIN' 3 – NEW SOUL REBELS VARIOUS ARTISTS (GLOBAL TELEVISION)	2	1996
VYBIN' 4 VARIOUS ARTISTS (GLOBAL TELEVISION)	7	1996
VYBIN' – YOUNG SOUL REBELS VARIOUS ARTISTS (GLOBAL TELEVISION)	9	1996

W

Title / Artist	Peak Position	Year of Release
THE W WU-TANG CLAN	19	2000
W.A.S.P. W.A.S.P.	51	1984
W.O.W. WENDY O. WILLIAMS	100	1984
WAH WAH BRIAN ENO	11	1994
WAH WAH JAMES & BRIAN ENO	11	1994
WAIT FOR ME KENNY THOMAS	10	1993
WAIT FOR ME PIGEON DETECTIVES	3	2007
WAITING FUN BOY THREE	14	1983
WAITING FOR BONAPARTE MEN THEY COULDN'T HANG	41	1988
WAITING FOR COLUMBUS LITTLE FEAT	43	1978
WAITING FOR COUSTEAU JEAN-MICHEL JARRE	14	1990
WAITING FOR HERB POGUES	20	1993
WAITING FOR THE FLOODS ARMOURY SHOW	57	1985
WAITING FOR THE PUNCHLINE EXTREME	10	1995
WAITING FOR THE SIRENS' CALL NEW ORDER	5	2005
WAITING FOR THE SUN DOORS	16	1968
WAITING TO EXHALE FILM SOUNDTRACK	8	1996
THE WAKE IQ	72	1985
WAKE ME WHEN IT'S OVER FASTER PUSSYCAT	35	1989
WAKE UP AND SMELL THE COFFEE CRANBERRIES	61	2001
WAKE UP CALL JOHN MAYALL	61	1993
WAKE UP! BOO RADLEYS	1	1995
THE WAKING HOUR DALI'S CAR	84	1984
WAKING HOURS DEL AMITRI	6	1990
WAKING UP THE NEIGHBOURS BRYAN ADAMS	1	1991
WAKING UP WITH THE HOUSE ON FIRE CULTURE CLUB	2	1984
A WALK ACROSS THE ROOFTOPS BLUE NILE	80	1984
WALK INTO LIGHT IAN ANDERSON	78	1983
WALK OF LIFE BILLIE PIPER	14	2000
WALK ON BOSTON	56	1994
WALK ON JOHN HIATT	74	1995
WALK ON BY SYBIL	21	1990
WALK ON BY – THE VERY BEST OF DIONNE WARWICK	72	2006
WALK RIGHT BACK WITH THE EVERLYS EVERLY BROTHERS	10	1975
WALK THE LINE FILM SOUNDTRACK	8	2006
WALK UNDER LADDERS JOAN ARMATRADING	6	1981
WALK WITH ME JAMELIA	20	2006
WALKER BROTHERS' STORY WALKER BROTHERS	9	1967
WALKING BACK HOME DEACON BLUE	39	1999
WALKING INTO CLARKSDALE JIMMY PAGE & ROBERT PLANT	3	1998
WALKING ON SUNSHINE (THE VERY BEST OF EDDY GRANT) EDDY GRANT	20	1989
WALKING THE LINE – LEGENDARY SUN RECORDINGS JOHNNY CASH	25	2006
WALKING WITH A PANTHER LL COOL J	43	1989
WALKING WOUNDED EVERYTHING BUT THE GIRL	4	1996
THE WALL PINK FLOYD	3	1979
THE WALL – LIVE IN BERLIN ROGER WATERS & VARIOUS ARTISTS	27	1990
WALL OF HITS SLADE	34	1991
WALLS AND BRIDGES JOHN LENNON	6	1974
WALTERS ROOM BLACK SCIENCE ORCHESTRA	68	1996
WALTHAMSTOW EAST 17	1	1993
WALTZ DARLING MALCOLM McLAREN & THE BOOTZILLA ORCHESTRA	30	1989
THE WANDERER DONNA SUMMER	55	1980
THE WANDERER FREDDIE STARR	33	1990
THE WANDERERS FILM SOUNDTRACK	48	1980
WANDERING SPIRIT MICK JAGGER	12	1993
WANT TWO RUFUS WAINWRIGHT	21	2005
WANTED CLIFF RICHARD	11	2001
WANTED/WANTED – THE REMIXES YAZZ	3	1988
WAR U2	1	1983
WAR & PEACE – VOLUME II ICE CUBE	56	2000
WAR ALL THE TIME THURSDAY	62	2003
WAR CHILD JETHRO TULL	14	1974
WAR HEROES JIMI HENDRIX	23	1972
THE WAR OF THE WORLDS JEFF WAYNE	5	2005
WAR ON ERRORISM NOFX	48	2003
WAR STORIES UNKLE	58	2007
WAREHOUSE RAVES VARIOUS ARTISTS (RUMOUR)	15	1989
WAREHOUSE RAVES 3 VARIOUS ARTISTS (RUMOUR)	12	1990
WAREHOUSE RAVES 4 VARIOUS ARTISTS (RUMOUR)	13	1990
WAREHOUSE RAVES 5 VARIOUS ARTISTS (RUMOUR)	18	1991
WAREHOUSE RAVES 6 VARIOUS ARTISTS (RUMOUR)	16	1992
WAREHOUSE RAVES 7 VARIOUS ARTISTS (RUMOUR)	20	1992
WAREHOUSE: SONGS AND STORIES HUSKER DU	72	1987
WARE'S THE HOUSE? VARIOUS ARTISTS (STYLUS)	2	1989
WARM JOHNNY MATHIS	6	1958
WARM HERB ALPERT & THE TIJUANA BRASS	30	1969
WARM LEATHERETTE GRACE JONES	45	1980
THE WARNING QUEENSRYCHE	100	1984
WARNING GREEN DAY	4	2000
THE WARNING HOT CHIP	34	2006
WARNING! DANCE BOOM VARIOUS ARTISTS (TELSTAR)	2	1995
WARNING! DANCE BOOM 2 VARIOUS ARTISTS (TELSTAR)	7	1995
WARNINGS/PROMISES IDLEWILD	9	2005
WARPAINT BLACK CROWES	52	2008
WARRIOR ON THE EDGE OF TIME HAWKWIND	13	1975
WARRIOR ROCK – TOYAH ON TOUR TOYAH	20	1982
THE WARRIORS FILM SOUNDTRACK	53	1979
WARRIORS GARY NUMAN	12	1983
WARRIOZ M.O.P.	40	2001
WASHING MACHINE SONIC YOUTH	39	1995
WASHINGTON SQUARE SERENADE STEVE EARLE	55	2007
WASTED IN AMERICA LOVE/HATE	20	1992
WASTED YEARS/STRANGER IN A STRANGE LAND IRON MAIDEN	9	1990
WASTED YOUTH GIRL	92	1982
WATCH MANFRED MANN'S EARTH BAND	33	1978
WATCHING YOU, WATCHING ME BILL WITHERS	60	1985
WATER MARK ART GARFUNKEL	25	1978
WATER SIGN CHRIS REA	64	1983
WATERFRONT WATERFRONT	45	1989
WATERLOO ABBA	28	1974
WATERLOO TO ANYWHERE DIRTY PRETTY THINGS	3	2006
WATERMARK ENYA	5	1988
WATERSHED k.d. lang	35	2008
WATERSHED OPETH	34	2008
WATERTOWN FRANK SINATRA	14	1970
WATT TEN YEARS AFTER	5	1971
WATUSI WEDDING PRESENT	47	1994

Title / Artist	Peak Position	Year of Release
WAVE PATTI SMITH GROUP	41	1979
WAVELENGTH VAN MORRISON	27	1978
WAVES KATRINA & THE WAVES	70	1986
WAXWORKS – SOME SINGLES (1977-1982) XTC	54	1982
WAY BEYOND BLUE CATATONIA	32	1996
THE WAY I FEEL TODAY SIX BY SEVEN	69	2002
THE WAY IT IS BRUCE HORNBY & THE RANGE	16	1986
WAY OF TODAY VIKKI CARR	31	1967
WAY OUT WEST WAY OUT WEST	42	1997
WAY TO NORMAL BEN FOLDS	70	2008
THE WAY TO THE SKY NEIL DIAMOND	39	1981
THE WAY WE WERE ANDY WILLIAMS	7	1974
THE WAY WE WERE BARBRA STREISAND	49	1974
THE WAY WE WERE VARIOUS ARTISTS (SONY/BMG)	4	2005
WAYNE FONTANA AND THE MINDBENDERS WAYNE FONTANA & THE MINDBENDERS	18	1965
WAYNE'S WORLD FILM SOUNDTRACK	5	1992
WAYNE'S WORLD 2 FILM SOUNDTRACK	17	1994
WAYSTED WAYSTED	73	1984
WE ALL HAD DOCTOR'S PAPERS MAX BOYCE	1	1975
WE ARE FAMILY SISTER SLEDGE	7	1979
WE ARE IN LOVE HARRY CONNICK JR.	7	1990
WE ARE MOST AMUSED (THE BEST OF BRITISH COMEDY) VARIOUS ARTISTS (RONCO)	30	1981
WE ARE ONE MAZE FEATURING FRANKIE BEVERLY	38	1983
WE ARE SHAMPOO SHAMPOO	45	1994
WE ARE THE NIGHT CHEMICAL BROTHERS	1	2007
WE ARE THE PIPETTES PIPETTES	41	2006
WE ARE THE WORLD USA FOR AFRICA	31	1985
WE ARE...THE LEAGUE ANTI-NOWHERE LEAGUE	24	1982
WE CAN DO IT RUBETTES	41	1975
WE CAN MAKE IT PETERS & LEE	1	1973
WE CAN'T DANCE GENESIS	1	1991
WE CARE WHALE	42	1995
WE DON'T NEED TO WHISPER ANGELS & AIRWAVES	6	2006
WE GET LETTERS (VOL. 2) PERRY COMO	4	1958
WE HAVE ALL THE TIME IN THE WORLD – THE VERY BEST OF LOUIS ARMSTRONG LOUIS ARMSTRONG	10	1994
WE HAVE SOUND TOM VEK	73	2005
WE INVENTED THE REMIX P DIDDY & THE BAD BOY FAMILY	17	2002
WE LOVE GREASE VARIOUS ARTISTS (GTV)	15	2007
WE LOVE LIFE PULP	6	2001
WE LOVE LIFE VARIOUS ARTISTS (SONY/BMG)	13	2005
WE LOVE MAMBO VARIOUS ARTISTS (BMG)	11	2004
WE MADE IT HAPPEN ENGELBERT HUMPERDINCK	17	1970
WE MUST BELIEVE IN MAGIC CRYSTAL GAYLE	15	1978
WE ROCK HARD FREESTYLERS	33	1998
WE SHALL OVERCOME – THE SEEGER SESSIONS BRUCE SPRINGSTEEN	3	2006
WE SOLD OUR SOUL FOR ROCK 'N' ROLL BLACK SABBATH	35	1976
WE STARTED NOTHING TING TINGS	1	2008
WE THANK THEE JIM REEVES	17	1964
WE TOO ARE ONE EURYTHMICS	1	1989
WE WANT BILLY BILLY FURY	14	1963
WE WANT MOORE? GARY MOORE	32	1984
WE WERE DEAD BEFORE THE SHIP EVEN SANK MODEST MOUSE	47	2007
WE WILL BE DEAD TOMORROW RAGING SPEEDHORN	63	2002
WE WILL ROCK YOU VARIOUS ARTISTS (DINO)	3	1991
WE WISH YOU A MERRY CHRISTMAS RAY CONNIFF	12	1962
WEAPON IS MY LYRIC OVERLORD X	68	1989
WEASELS RIPPED MY FLESH MOTHERS OF INVENTION	28	1970
WEATHER REPORT WEATHER REPORT	88	1982
WEATHERED CREED	44	2001
WE'D LIKE TO TEACH THE WORLD TO SING NEW SEEKERS	2	1972
THE WEDDING DISCO VARIOUS ARTISTS (UNIVERSAL)	14	2006
THE WEDDING SINGER FILM SOUNDTRACK	15	1998
THE WEDGE PALLAS	70	1986
WEDNESDAY MORNING 3 A.M. SIMON & GARFUNKEL	24	1968
THE WEEKEND VARIOUS ARTISTS (UNIVERSAL)	4	2005
WEEKEND IN L.A. GEORGE BENSON	47	1978
A WEEKEND IN THE CITY BLOC PARTY	2	2007
THE WEEKEND STARTS HERE VARIOUS ARTISTS (EMI)	13	2008
THE WEEKEND VOLUME 2 VARIOUS ARTISTS (UNIVERSAL)	5	2006
WEEZER WEEZER	23	1995
WEEZER WEEZER	21	2008
WEIGHT ROLLINS BAND	22	1994
WEIRD SCENES INSIDE THE GOLD MINE DOORS	50	1972
WEIRD'S BAR AND GRILLS POP WILL EAT ITSELF	44	1993
WELCOME SANTANA	8	1973
WELCOME BACK MASE	68	2004
WELCOME BACK MY FRIENDS TO THE SHOW THAT NEVER ENDS – LADIES AND GENTLEMEN: EMERSON, LAKE AND PALMER EMERSON, LAKE & PALMER	5	1974
WELCOME TO JAMROCK DAMIAN JR GONG MARLEY	34	2005
WELCOME TO LOSERVILLE SON OF DORK	35	2005
WELCOME TO MY NIGHTMARE ALICE COOPER	19	1975
WELCOME TO MY WORLD DEAN MARTIN	39	1967
WELCOME TO MY WORLD ELVIS PRESLEY	7	1977
WELCOME TO MY WORLD DANIEL O'DONNELL	6	2004
WELCOME TO POPPY'S FUN LOVIN' CRIMINALS	20	2003
WELCOME TO REALITY ROSS COPPERMAN	59	2007
WELCOME TO THE BEAUTIFUL SOUTH BEAUTIFUL SOUTH	2	1989
WELCOME TO THE CLUB IAN HUNTER	61	1980
WELCOME TO THE CRUISE JUDIE TZUKE	14	1979
WELCOME TO THE MONKEYHOUSE DANDY WARHOLS	20	2003
WELCOME TO THE NEIGHBOURHOOD MEAT LOAF	3	1995
WELCOME TO THE NORTH MUSIC	8	2004
WELCOME TO THE PLEASUREDOME FRANKIE GOES TO HOLLYWOOD	1	1984
WELCOME TO THE REAL WORLD MR. MISTER	6	1986
WELCOME TO TOMORROW SNAP!	69	1994
WELCOME TO WHEREVER YOU ARE INXS	1	1992
WELD NEIL YOUNG & CRAZY HORSE	20	1991
WE'LL BRING THE HOUSE DOWN SLADE	25	1981
WE'LL KEEP A WELCOME BRYN TERFEL	33	2000
WELL KEPT SECRET JOHN MARTYN	20	1982
WE'LL LIVE AND DIE IN THESE TOWNS ENEMY	1	2007
WE'LL MEET AGAIN VERA LYNN	44	1989
WE'LL MEET AGAIN VARIOUS ARTISTS (VIRGIN)	16	2004
WELL PLEASED CHAS & DAVE	27	1984
WELL RESPECTED KINKS KINKS	5	1966
WELL WELL WELL MILBURN	32	2006
WELL, WELL SAID THE ROCKING CHAIR DEAN FRIEDMAN	21	1978
WELSH COLLECTION MAN	40	1976
WENDY AND LISA WENDY & LISA	84	1987
WENDY MOTEN WENDY MOTEN	42	1994
WE'RE ONLY IN IT FOR THE MONEY MOTHERS OF INVENTION	32	1968
WE'RE THE MINIPOPS MINIPOPS	54	1983
WEST LUCINDA WILLIAMS	30	2007
WEST SIDE STORY STAGE CAST RECORDING	3	1959
WEST SIDE STORY FILM SOUNDTRACK	1	1962
WEST SIDE STORY (ORIGINAL STUDIO CAST RECORDING) STAGE CAST RECORDING	11	1985
WESTING (BY MUSKET AND SEXTANT) PAVEMENT	30	1993
WESTLIFE WESTLIFE	2	1999
WESTWOOD VARIOUS ARTISTS (DEF JAM)	7	2001
WESTWOOD 2 VARIOUS ARTISTS (DEF JAM)	19	2002
WESTWOOD 3 VARIOUS ARTISTS (DEF JAM)	2	2002
WESTWOOD – HEAT VARIOUS ARTISTS (DEF JAM)	3	2005
WESTWOOD – PLATINUM EDITION VARIOUS ARTISTS (UNIVERSAL)	1	2003
WESTWOOD – RIDE WITH THE BIG DAWG VARIOUS ARTISTS (DEF JAM)	6	2006
WESTWOOD – THE BIG DAWG VARIOUS ARTISTS (DEF JAM)	3	2004
WESTWOOD – THE GREATEST – CLASSIC JOINTZ VARIOUS ARTISTS (DEF JAM)	6	2006
WESTWOOD – THE INVASION VARIOUS ARTISTS (DEF JAM)	2	2005
WESTWOOD – THE JUMP OFF VARIOUS ARTISTS (DEF JAM)	2	2004
WESTWOOD – THE TAKEOVER VARIOUS ARTISTS (DEF JAM)	2	2004
WESTWOOD X VARIOUS ARTISTS (DEF JAM)	4	2005
WESTWORLD THEATRE OF HATE	17	1982
WET BARBRA STREISAND	25	1979
WE'VE GOTTA GET OUT OF THIS PLACE ANGELIC UPSTARTS	54	1980
WHALER SOPHIE B HAWKINS	46	1994
WHALES AND NIGHTINGALES JUDY COLLINS	16	1971
WHAMMY! B-52'S	33	1983
WHA'PPEN BEAT	3	1981
WHAT A BUNCH OF SWEETIES PINK FAIRIES	48	1972
WHAT A FEELING VARIOUS ARTISTS (COLUMBIA)	4	1997
WHAT A FEELING VARIOUS ARTISTS (UNIVERSAL)	15	2003
WHAT A WONDERFUL WORLD LOUIS ARMSTRONG	37	1968
WHAT ABOUT ME? KENNY ROGERS	97	1984
WHAT ARE YOU GOING TO DO WITH YOUR LIFE? ECHO & THE BUNNYMEN	21	1999
WHAT DO YOU WANT FROM LIFE TUBES	38	1978
WHAT DOES ANYTHING MEAN? BASICALLY CHAMELEON	60	1985
WHAT GOES UP MIGHT COME DOWN DAVID GUNSON	92	1982
WHAT HITS!? RED HOT CHILI PEPPERS	23	1992
WHAT I MEANT TO SAY DONNY OSMOND	26	2004
WHAT IN THE WORLD'S COME OVER YOU JACK SCOTT	11	1960
WHAT IS BEAT? (THE BEST OF THE BEAT) BEAT	10	1983
WHAT I'VE GOT IN MIND BILLIE JO SPEARS	47	1976
WHAT MY HEART WANTS TO SAY GARETH GATES	2	2002
WHAT NOW MY LOVE HERB ALPERT & THE TIJUANA BRASS	18	1966
WHAT NOW MY LOVE SHIRLEY BASSEY	17	1971
WHAT PRICE PARADISE? CHINA CRISIS	63	1986
WHAT SILENCE KNOWS SHARA NELSON	22	1993

Title / Artist	Peak Position	Year of Release
WHAT SOUND LAMB	54	2001
WHAT UP DOG? WAS (NOT WAS)	47	1988
WHAT WERE ONCE VICES ARE NOW HABITS DOOBIE BROTHERS	19	1974
WHAT WILL THE NEIGHBOURS SAY GIRLS ALOUD	6	2004
WHAT YOU ARE RICKY ROSS	36	1996
WHAT YOU SEE IS WHAT YOU GET GLEN GOLDSMITH	14	1988
WHATEVER AIMEE MANN	39	1993
WHATEVER AND EVER AMEN BEN FOLDS FIVE	30	1997
WHATEVER GETS YOU THROUGH THE DAY LIGHTHOUSE FAMILY	7	2001
WHATEVER HAPPENED TO JUGULA? ROY HARPER & JIMMY PAGE	44	1985
WHATEVER HAPPENED TO ROMANCE VICTORIA HART	61	2007
WHATEVER PEOPLE SAY I AM, THAT'S WHAT I'M NOT ARCTIC MONKEYS	1	2006
WHATEVER WE WANNA LEANN RIMES	15	2006
WHATEVER YOU SAY, SAY NOTHING DEACON BLUE	4	1993
WHATEVER YOU WANT STATUS QUO	3	1979
WHATEVER YOU WANT – THE VERY BEST OF STATUS QUO STATUS QUO	13	1997
WHAT'S BIN DID AND WHAT'S BIN HID DONOVAN	3	1965
WHAT'S GOING ON? MARVIN GAYE	56	1999
WHAT'S INSIDE JOAN ARMATRADING	48	1995
WHAT'S LOVE GOT TO DO WITH IT (OST) TINA TURNER	1	1993
WHAT'S NEW LINDA RONSTADT WITH THE NELSON RIDDLE ORCHESTRA	31	1984
WHAT'S THAT NOISE COLDCUT	20	1989
WHAT'S THE 411? MARY J. BLIGE	53	1993
(WHAT'S THE STORY) MORNING GLORY? OASIS	1	1995
(WHAT'S THE STORY) MORNING GLORY? SINGLES BOX – GOLD OASIS	24	1996
WHAT'S THE TIME MR WOLF NOISETTES	75	2007
WHAT'S THIS FOR KILLING JOKE	42	1981
WHAT'S WORDS WORTH MOTORHEAD	71	1983
WHAT'S WRONG WITH THIS PICTURE VAN MORRISON	43	2003
WHEATUS WHEATUS	7	2001
WHEELS OF FIRE (DOUBLE: LIVE AND STUDIO) CREAM	3	1968
WHEELS OF FIRE (SINGLE: IN THE STUDIO) CREAM	7	1968
WHEELS OF STEEL SAXON	5	1980
WHEN A MAN LOVES A WOMAN VARIOUS ARTISTS (DINO)	7	1994
WHEN A MAN LOVES A WOMAN (THE ULTIMATE COLLECTION) PERCY SLEDGE	36	1987
WHEN DISASTER STRIKES BUSTA RHYMES	34	1997
WHEN I DREAM CRYSTAL GAYLE	25	1978
WHEN I FALL IN LOVE LESLEY GARRETT	11	2007
WHEN I LOOK IN YOUR EYES DIANA KRALL	72	1999
WHEN I WAS BORN FOR THE 7TH TIME CORNERSHOP	17	1997
WHEN I WAS CRUEL ELVIS COSTELLO	17	2002
WHEN IN SPAIN CLIFF RICHARD & THE SHADOWS	8	1963
WHEN IT FALLS ZERO 7	3	2004
WHEN THE BOYS MEET THE GIRLS SISTER SLEDGE	19	1985
WHEN THE EAGLE FLIES TRAFFIC	31	1974
WHEN THE PAWN HITS THE CONFLICTS FIONA APPLE	46	2000
WHEN THE WORLD KNOWS YOUR NAME DEACON BLUE	1	1989
WHEN WE WERE THE NEW BOYS ROD STEWART	2	1998
WHEN WILL I SEE YOU AGAIN JOHNNY MATHIS	13	1975
WHEN YOU WERE SWEET SIXTEEN FUREYS & DAVEY ARTHUR	99	1982
WHEN YOUR HEART STOPS BEATING PLUS 44	50	2006
WHEN YOUR LOVER HAS GONE FRANK SINATRA	6	1961
WHEN YOU'RE A BOY SUSANNA HOFFS	56	1991
WHENEVER WE WANTED JOHN MELLENCAMP	39	1991
WHENEVER YOU NEED SOMEBODY RICK ASTLEY	1	1987
WHERE AM I GOING? DUSTY SPRINGFIELD	40	1967
WHERE ARE YOU GONNA BE TONIGHT? WILLIE COLLINS	97	1986
WHERE ARE YOU? FRANK SINATRA	3	1958
WHERE E'ER YOU WALK ALED JONES	36	1986
WHERE I WANNA BE DONELL JONES	47	2000
WHERE MY HEART IS DANNY SEWARD	56	2005
WHERE THE ACTION IS WESTWORLD	49	1987
WHERE THE HUMANS EAT WILLY MASON	38	2005
WHERE WE BELONG BOYZONE	1	1998
WHERE YOU BEEN DINOSAUR JR	10	1993
WHERE YOU LIVE TRACY CHAPMAN	43	2005
WHERE YOU WANT TO BE TAKING BACK SUNDAY	71	2004
WHERE YOUR ROAD LEADS TRISHA YEARWOOD	36	1998
WHIGFIELD WHIGFIELD	13	1995
WHILE MY GUITAR GENTLY WEEPS VARIOUS ARTISTS (UNIVERSAL)	3	2002
WHILE MY GUITAR GENTLY WEEPS II VARIOUS ARTISTS (UNIVERSAL)	10	2003
WHILE MY GUITAR GENTLY WEEPS III VARIOUS ARTISTS (UNIVERSAL)	5	2005
WHILE THE CITY SLEEPS GEORGE BENSON	13	1986
WHIPLASH JAMES	9	1997
WHIPLASH SMILE BILLY IDOL	8	1986
WHIPPED CREAM AND OTHER DELIGHTS HERB ALPERT & THE TIJUANA BRASS	2	1966
WHIPPED! FASTER PUSSYCAT	58	1992
WHIRLPOOL CHAPTERHOUSE	23	1991
THE WHISPER DAVID ESSEX	67	1983
WHISPER A PRAYER MICA PARIS	20	1993
WHISPERING JACK JOHN FARNHAM	35	1987
WHITE BLOOD CELLS WHITE STRIPES	55	2001
WHITE BOY WITH A FEATHER JASON DOWNS	64	2001
WHITE BUTTERFLY INME	56	2005
WHITE CHALK PJ HARVEY	11	2007
WHITE CHRISTMAS NAT 'KING' COLE & DEAN MARTIN	45	1971
WHITE CHRISTMAS BING CROSBY	45	1974
WHITE CITY A NOVEL PETE TOWNSHEND	70	1985
WHITE EAGLE TANGERINE DREAM	57	1982
WHITE FEATHERS KAJAGOOGOO	5	1983
WHITE FLAMES SNOWY WHITE	21	1984
WHITE GOLD BARRY WHITE	37	2005
WHITE LABEL EUPHORIA – JOHN OO FLEMING VARIOUS ARTISTS (TELSTAR)	6	2002
WHITE LABEL EUPHORIA – LEVEL 2 VARIOUS ARTISTS (TELSTAR)	12	2003
WHITE LADDER DAVID GRAY	1	2000
WHITE LILIES ISLAND NATALIE IMBRUGLIA	15	2001
WHITE MAGIC FOR LOVERS DRUGSTORE	45	1998
WHITE MANSIONS (ORIGINAL STUDIO CAST RECORDING) STAGE CAST RECORDING	51	1978
WHITE MUSIC XTC	38	1978
WHITE NOISE – LIVE GARY NUMAN	29	1985
WHITE ON BLONDE TEXAS	1	1997
WHITE PONY DEFTONES	13	2000
WHITE ROCK RICK WAKEMAN	14	1977
THE WHITE ROOM KLF	3	1991
A WHITER SHADE OF PALE/A SALTY DOG PROCOL HARUM	26	1972
WHITESNAKE 1987 WHITESNAKE	8	1987
THE WHITEY ALBUM CICCONE YOUTH	63	1989
WHITEY FORD SINGS THE BLUES EVERLAST	65	1999
WHITNEY WHITNEY HOUSTON	1	1987
WHITNEY HOUSTON WHITNEY HOUSTON	2	1985
WHO ARE YOU WHO	6	1978
THE WHO BY NUMBERS WHO	7	1975
WHO CAME FIRST PETE TOWNSHEND	30	1972
WHO CAN YOU TRUST? MORCHEEBA	57	1997
WHO CARES A LOT? – THE GREATEST HITS FAITH NO MORE	37	1998
THE WHO COLLECTION WHO	44	1985
WHO DO WE THINK WE ARE DEEP PURPLE	4	1973
WHO ELSE? JEFF BECK	74	1999
WHO I AM BEVERLEY KNIGHT	7	2002
WHO IS JILL SCOTT – WORDS AND SOUNDS VOLUME 1 JILL SCOTT	69	2000
WHO KILLED THE ZUTONS? ZUTONS	6	2004
WHO LOVES YOU FOUR SEASONS	12	1976
WHO MADE WHO AC/DC	11	1986
WHO NEEDS ACTIONS WHEN YOU GOT WORDS PLAN B	30	2006
WHO NEEDS GUITARS ANYWAY ALICE DEEJAY	8	2000
WHO PAYS THE FERRYMAN YANNIS MARKOPOULOS	22	1978
THE WHO SELL-OUT WHO	13	1968
THE WHO SINGS MY GENERATION WHO	5	1965
WHO WILL SAVE THE WORLD GROUNDHOGS	8	1972
WHO YOU FIGHTING FOR UB40	20	2005
WHOA NELLY NELLY FURTADO	2	2001
A WHOLE LOTTA SHAKY SHAKIN' STEVENS	42	1988
A WHOLE NEW WORLD KATIE PRICE & PETER ANDRE	20	2006
THE WHOLE STORY KATE BUSH	1	1986
THE WHOLE STORY – HIS GREATEST HITS CLIFF RICHARD	6	2000
WHOOPS! THERE GOES THE NEIGHBOURHOOD BLOW MONKEYS	46	1989
(WHO'S AFRAID OF) THE ART OF NOISE ART OF NOISE	27	1984
WHO'S BETTER, WHO'S BEST WHO	10	1988
WHO'S LAST WHO	48	1984
WHO'S NEXT WHO	1	1971
WHO'S THAT GIRL FILM SOUNDTRACK	4	1987
WHO'S ZOOMIN' WHO? ARETHA FRANKLIN	49	1986
WHOSE SIDE ARE YOU ON MATT BIANCO	35	1984
WHY DO FOOLS FALL IN LOVE DIANA ROSS	17	1981
WHY THE LONG FACE BIG COUNTRY	48	1995
WHY TRY HARDER – THE GREATEST HITS FATBOY SLIM	2	2006
WICKED SINITTA	52	1989
WICKED GAME CHRIS ISAAK	3	1991
WICKED! VARIOUS ARTISTS (EMI)	2	1992
WIDE ANGLE HYBRID	45	1999
WIDE AWAKE IN AMERICA U2	11	1985
WIDE AWAKE IN DREAMLAND PAT BENATAR	11	1988
WIDE OPEN SPACES DIXIE CHICKS	26	1999
THE WIDE WORLD OVER CHIEFTAINS	37	2002
WIGGLE IT 2 IN A ROOM	73	1991
WILD & WICKED SHANIA TWAIN	62	2000
WILD AND LONELY ASSOCIATES	71	1990
WILD CAT TYGERS OF PAN TANG	18	1980
WILD CHILD UNTOUCHABLES	51	1985
WILD DOGS RODS	75	1982
WILD FRONTIER GARY MOORE	8	1987
THE WILD HEART STEVIE NICKS	28	1983
WILD HONEY BEACH BOYS	7	1968
WILD HORSES WILD HORSES	38	1980
WILD LIFE MOTT THE HOOPLE	44	1971
THE WILD LIFE SLAUGHTER	64	1992

Title / Artist	Peak Position	Year of Release
WILD MOOD SWINGS CURE	9	1996
THE WILD ONE VARIOUS ARTISTS (EMI)	8	1990
WILD ONE – THE VERY BEST OF THIN LIZZY THIN LIZZY	18	1996
WILD PLANET B-52'S	18	1980
THE WILD THE WILLING AND THE INNOCENT UFO	19	1981
WILD THINGS RUN FAST JONI MITCHELL	32	1982
WILD WOOD PAUL WELLER	2	1993
WILD! ERASURE	1	1989
THE WILD, THE INNOCENT AND THE E. STREET SHUFFLE BRUCE SPRINGSTEEN	33	1985
WILDER TEARDROP EXPLODES	29	1981
WILDERNESS IS PARADISE NOW MORNING RUNNER	25	2006
WILDEST DREAMS TINA TURNER	4	1996
WILDFLOWER SHERYL CROW	25	2005
WILDFLOWERS TOM PETTY & HEARTBREAKERS	36	1994
THE WILDHEARTS WILDHEARTS	55	2007
THE WILDHEARTS MUST BE DESTROYED WILDHEARTS	54	2003
WILL ANYTHING HAPPEN SHOP ASSISTANTS	100	1986
WILL DOWNING WILL DOWNING	20	1988
WILLENNIUM WILL SMITH	10	1999
WILLIAM BLOKE BILLY BRAGG	16	1996
WILLY AND THE POOR BOYS CREEDENCE CLEARWATER REVIVAL	10	1970
WILSON PHILLIPS WILSON PHILLIPS	7	1990
WIMOWEH KARL DENVER	7	1961
WINCING THE NIGHT AWAY SHINS	16	2007
THE WIND WARREN ZEVON	57	2003
WIND AND WUTHERING GENESIS	7	1977
THE WIND DOWN ZONE VARIOUS ARTISTS (ELEVATE)	17	1993
WIND OF CHANGE – CLASSIC ROCK LONDON SYMPHONY ORCHESTRA & THE ROYAL CHORAL SOCIETY	24	1992
WIND SONG JOHN DENVER	14	1975
WINDJAMMER II WINDJAMMER	82	1984
WINDOW IN THE JUNGLE 10 C.C.	70	1983
WINDSONG RANDY CRAWFORD	7	1982
WINELIGHT GROVER WASHINGTON JR.	34	1981
A WING AND A PRAYER GERRY RAFFERTY	73	1993
WINGS AT THE SPEED OF SOUND WINGS	2	1976
WINGS GREATEST HITS WINGS	5	1978
WINGS OF A DOVE ANTHONY WAY	69	1997
WINGS OF HEAVEN MAGNUM	5	1988
WINGS OF JOY CRANES	52	1991
WINGS OF LOVE VARIOUS ARTISTS (A&M)	1	1991
WINGS OF SONG JAMES GALWAY	45	2004
WINGS OVER AMERICA WINGS	8	1977
WINGS WILDLIFE WINGS	11	1971
WINGSPAN – HITS AND HISTORY PAUL McCARTNEY	5	2001
WINNER IN YOU PATTI LABELLE	30	1986
WINNERS BROTHERS JOHNSON	42	1981
WINNER'S CIRCLE VARIOUS ARTISTS (EXPANSION)	20	1993
WINNING DAYS VINES	29	2004
WIPEOUT – 20 INSTRUMENTAL GREATS VARIOUS ARTISTS (IMPRESSION)	37	1984
WIPEOUT 2097: THE SOUNDTRACK VARIOUS ARTISTS (VIRGIN)	16	1996
WIRED JEFF BECK	38	1976
WIRED VARIOUS ARTISTS (POLYGRAM)	2	1997
WIRED FOR CLUBS (CLUB TRACKS VOLUME 1) VARIOUS ARTISTS (MERCURY)	58	1983
WIRED FOR SOUND CLIFF RICHARD	4	1981
WIRED TO THE MOON CHRIS REA	35	1984
WISEBLOOD CORROSION OF CONFORMITY	43	1996
WISH CURE	1	1992
WISH YOU WERE HERE PINK FLOYD	1	1975
WISHBONE ASH WISHBONE ASH	29	1971
WISHBONE FOUR WISHBONE ASH	12	1973
WISHFUL THINKING PROPAGANDA	82	1985
WISHING MARTINE McCUTCHEON	25	2000
WITH A SONG IN MY HEART JOSE CARRERAS	73	1993
WITH LOVE DES O'CONNOR	40	1970
WITH LOVE BRENDAN SHINE	74	1984
WITH LOVE MICHAEL CRAWFORD	31	1989
...WITH LOVE RICHARD CLAYDERMAN	62	1999
WITH LOVE VARIOUS ARTISTS (SONY BMG)	8	2008
WITH LOVE AND SQUALOR WE ARE SCIENTISTS	43	2005
WITH LOVING FEELING TONY CHRISTIE	19	1973
WITH TEETH NINE INCH NAILS	3	2005
WITH THE BEATLES BEATLES	1	1963
WITH THE LIGHTS OUT NIRVANA	56	2004
WITH YOU IN MIND CHARLIE LANDSBOROUGH	49	1996
WITHOUT A SOUND DINOSAUR JR	24	1994
WITHOUT RESERVATIONS SIMON DUPREE & THE BIG SOUND	39	1967
WITHOUT THE AID OF A SAFETY NET (LIVE) BIG COUNTRY	35	1994
WITHOUT YOU I'M NOTHING PLACEBO	7	1998
WITHOUT YOUR LOVE DIONNE WARWICK	86	1985
WITNESS HALO JAMES	18	1990
WIZZARD BREW WIZZARD	29	1973
WOLF HUGH CORNWELL	98	1988
WOLFMOTHER WOLFMOTHER	25	2006
WOMAN VARIOUS ARTISTS (POLYGRAM)	5	1998
WOMAN 2 VARIOUS ARTISTS (UNIVERSAL)	4	1999
WOMAN 2 WOMAN TWO VARIOUS ARTISTS (POLYGRAM)	9	1994
WOMAN 3 VARIOUS ARTISTS (UNIVERSAL)	10	2000
A WOMAN AND A MAN BELINDA CARLISLE	12	1996
WOMAN IN ME LOUISE	5	1997
THE WOMAN IN ME SHANIA TWAIN	7	2000
WOMAN IN RED (OST) STEVIE WONDER & FEATURING DIONNE WARWICK	2	1984
WOMAN – THE COLLECTION 2007 VARIOUS ARTISTS (UNIVERSAL)	6	2007
WOMAN TO WOMAN VARIOUS ARTISTS (POLYGRAM)	5	1993
A WOMAN'S TOUCH VARIOUS ARTISTS (UNIVERSAL)	10	2002
WOMBLING SONGS WOMBLES	19	1974
WOMEN AND CAPTAIN FIRST CAPTAIN SENSIBLE	64	1982
WOMEN AND CHILDREN FIRST VAN HALEN	15	1980
WOMEN HOLD UP HALF THE SKY RUBY TURNER	47	1986
WOMEN IN UNIFORM/TWILIGHT ZONE IRON MAIDEN	10	1990
WONDER NO. 8 HONEYZ	33	1998
WONDERFUL ADAM ANT	24	1995
WONDERFUL MADNESS	17	1999
THE WONDERFUL AND FRIGHTENING WORLD OF... FALL	62	1984
WONDERFUL LIFE (OST) CLIFF RICHARD & THE SHADOWS	2	1964
WONDERFUL LIFE BLACK	3	1987
WONDERFUL WORLD VARIOUS ARTISTS (DINO)	8	1994
A WONDERFUL WORLD TONY BENNETT & K.D. LANG	33	2003
WONDERFUL WORLD EVA CASSIDY	11	2004
WONDERLAND ERASURE	71	1986
WONDERLAND CHARLATANS	2	2001
WONDERLAND McFLY	1	2005
WONDERWORLD URIAH HEEP	23	1974
THE WONDROUS WORLD OF SONNY AND CHER SONNY & CHER	15	1966
WOODEN FOOT COPS ON THE HIGHWAY WOODENTOPS	48	1988
WOODFACE CROWDED HOUSE	6	1991
WOODSTOCK FILM SOUNDTRACK	35	1970
WOODSTOCK JIMI HENDRIX	32	1994
THE WORD VARIOUS ARTISTS (ZOMBA)	86	1987
WORD GETS AROUND STEREOPHONICS	6	1997
WORD OF MOUF LUDACRIS	57	2002
WORD OF MOUTH TONI BASIL	15	1982
WORD OF MOUTH MIKE & THE MECHANICS	11	1991
WORD SALAD FISCHER-Z	66	1979
A WORD TO THE WISE GUY MIGHTY WAH!	28	1984
WORD UP CAMEO	7	1986
THE WORD VOLUME 2 VARIOUS ARTISTS (JIVE)	70	1988
WORDS F.R. DAVID	46	1983
WORDS TONY RICH PROJECT	27	1996
WORDS AND MUSIC BENNY HILL	9	1971
WORDS AND MUSIC BILLY CONNOLLY	34	1975
WORDS AND MUSIC HANK MARVIN	66	1982
WORDS OF LOVE BUDDY HOLLY & THE CRICKETS	1	1993
WORK 1989 – 2002 ORBITAL	36	2002
WORK IT VARIOUS ARTISTS (BMG)	6	2005
WORK IT 06 VARIOUS ARTISTS (SONY/BMG)	17	2006
WORK PARTY GRANDMASTER MELLE MEL & THE FURIOUS FIVE	45	1984
WORK THAT BODY JACKIE GENOVA	74	1983
WORK, LOVELIFE, MISCELLANEOUS DAVID DEVANT & HIS SPIRIT WIFE	70	1997
WORKERS PLAYTIME BILLY BRAGG	17	1988
WORKIN' OVERTIME DIANA ROSS	23	1989
WORKING CLASS HERO – THE DEFINITIVE JOHN LENNON	11	2005
WORKING NIGHTS WORKING WEEK	23	1985
WORKING WITH FIRE AND STEEL – POSSIBLE POP SONGS VOLUME 2 CHINA CRISIS	20	1983
WORKINGMAN'S DEAD GRATEFUL DEAD	69	1970
WORKS EMERSON, LAKE & PALMER	9	1977
THE WORKS QUEEN	2	1984
THE WORKS OF RICE AND LLOYD WEBBER LONDON SYMPHONY ORCHESTRA	55	1994
WORKS VOLUME 2 EMERSON, LAKE & PALMER	20	1977
WORLD D:REAM	5	1995
THE WORLD BEATERS SING THE WORLD BEATERS ENGLAND FOOTBALL WORLD CUP SQUAD 1970	4	1970
WORLD CLIQUE DEEE-LITE	14	1990
WORLD COMING DOWN TYPE O NEGATIVE	49	1999
WORLD DANCE – THE DRUM + BASS EXPERIENCE VARIOUS ARTISTS (FIRM)	10	1997
WORLD DEMISE OBITUARY	65	1994
WORLD GONE WRONG BOB DYLAN	35	1993
WORLD IN MOTION JACKSON BROWNE	39	1989
WORLD IN UNION UNION	17	1991
WORLD IN UNION 2003 VARIOUS ARTISTS (DECCA)	10	2003
WORLD IN UNION – ANTHEMS VARIOUS ARTISTS (POLYGRAM)	8	1995
WORLD IN UNION – RUGBY WORLD CUP 2007 VARIOUS ARTISTS (UNIVERSAL)	10	2007
THE WORLD IS FULL OF MARRIED MEN FILM SOUNDTRACK	25	1979
THE WORLD IS OUTSIDE GHOSTS	18	2007
THE WORLD IS YOURS IAN BROWN	4	2007
WORLD MACHINE LEVEL 42	3	1985
WORLD MOODS VARIOUS ARTISTS (VIRGIN)	17	1998
THE WORLD NEEDS A HERO MEGADETH	45	2001
THE WORLD OF BLUES POWER VARIOUS ARTISTS (DECCA)	24	1969

Title / Artist	Peak Position	Year of Release
THE WORLD OF BRASS BANDS VARIOUS ARTISTS (DECCA)	13	1969
THE WORLD OF CHARLIE KUNZ CHARLIE KUNZ	9	1969
THE WORLD OF CHRISTMAS CHOIR OF KING'S COLLEGE, CAMBRIDGE	38	1971
WORLD OF HIS OWN JOOLS HOLLAND	71	1990
THE WORLD OF HITS VOLUME 2 VARIOUS ARTISTS (DECCA)	7	1969
THE WORLD OF JOHNNY CASH JOHNNY CASH	5	1970
THE WORLD OF JOSEF LOCKE TODAY JOSEF LOCKE	29	1969
THE WORLD OF KENNETH MCKELLAR KENNETH McKELLAR	27	1969
WORLD OF MANN – THE VERY BEST OF MANFRED MANN	24	2006
THE WORLD OF MANTOVANI MANTOVANI & HIS ORCHESTRA	6	1969
THE WORLD OF MANTOVANI VOLUME 2 MANTOVANI & HIS ORCHESTRA	4	1969
WORLD OF MORRISSEY MORRISSEY	15	1995
THE WORLD OF NAT KING COLE NAT 'KING' COLE	51	2005
THE WORLD OF OLIVER STAGE CAST RECORDING	23	1969
A WORLD OF OUR OWN SEEKERS	5	1965
WORLD OF OUR OWN WESTLIFE	1	2001
THE WORLD OF PHASE 4 STEREO VARIOUS ARTISTS (DECCA)	29	1969
THE WORLD OF PROGRESSIVE MUSIC (WOWIE ZOWIE) VARIOUS ARTISTS (DECCA)	17	1969
WORLD OF THE BACHELORS BACHELORS	8	1969
WORLD OF THE BACHELORS VOLUME 2 BACHELORS	11	1969
THE WORLD OF VAL DOONICAN VAL DOONICAN	2	1969
THE WORLD OF YOUR 100 BEST TUNES VARIOUS ARTISTS (DECCA)	10	1971
THE WORLD OF YOUR 100 BEST TUNES VOLUME 10 VARIOUS ARTISTS (DECCA)	41	1975
THE WORLD OF YOUR 100 BEST TUNES VOLUME 2 VARIOUS ARTISTS (DECCA)	9	1971
WORLD OUTSIDE PSYCHEDELIC FURS	68	1991
THE WORLD OUTSIDE MACDONALD BROTHERS	41	2007
WORLD POWER SNAP!	10	1990
WORLD RADIO LEO SAYER	30	1982
WORLD SERVICE SPEAR OF DESTINY	11	1985
WORLD SHUT YOUR MOUTH JULIAN COPE	40	1984
WORLD WIDE EVERYTHING BUT THE GIRL	29	1991
WORLD WIDE LIVE SCORPIONS	18	1985
A WORLD WITHOUT DAVE CARTER – THE UNSTOPPABLE SEX MACHINE	73	1997
THE WORLD WITHOUT END MIGHTY LEMON DROPS	34	1988
WORLD WITHOUT TEARS LUCINDA WILLIAMS	48	2003
THE WORLD WON'T LISTEN SMITHS	2	1987
WORLD WRESTLING FEDERATION – THE MUSIC – VOLUME 4 JAMES A JOHNSTON	44	1999
WORLD WRESTLING FEDERATION – THE MUSIC – VOLUME 5 JAMES A JOHNSTON	11	2001
WORLDES BLYSSE MEDIAEVAL BAEBES	73	1998
WORLD'S BEST DAD VARIOUS ARTISTS (SONY/BMG)	2	2005
WORLD'S BEST DAD 2007 VARIOUS ARTISTS (SONY/BMG)	7	2007
WORLD'S BEST MUM VARIOUS ARTISTS (SONY/BMG)	1	2005
WORLD'S BEST MUM 2007 VARIOUS ARTISTS (SONY/BMG)	2	2007
THE WORLD'S GREATEST VARIOUS ARTISTS (BMG)	4	2004
THE WORLDS OF FOSTER AND ALLEN FOSTER & ALLEN	16	1988
THE WORLD'S WORST RECORD SHOW VARIOUS ARTISTS (K-TEL)	47	1978
WORLDWIDE 50 GOLD AWARD HITS VOLUME 1 – A TOUCH OF GOLD ELVIS PRESLEY	49	1970
WORRY BOMB CARTER – THE UNSTOPPABLE SEX MACHINE	9	1995
THE WORST ALBUM IN THE WORLD EVER... EVER! SHIREHORSES	22	1997
WOULD YA LIKE MORE SCRATCHIN' MALCOLM McLAREN & THE WORLD FAMOUS SUPREME TEAM SHOW	44	1984
WOULD YOU BELIEVE HOLLIES	16	1966
WOULDN'T YOU LIKE IT BAY CITY ROLLERS	3	1975
WOW! BANANARAMA	26	1987
WOW! – LET THE MUSIC LIFT YOU UP VARIOUS ARTISTS (ARCADE)	13	1994
WOW WHAT A PARTY VARIOUS ARTISTS (K-TEL)	97	1987
WOWEE ZOWEE PAVEMENT	18	1995
WOYAYA OSIBISA	11	1972
WRAP YOUR ARMS AROUND ME AGNETHA FALTSKOG	18	1983
WRECKIN' CREW METEORS	53	1983
WRECKING BALL EMMYLOU HARRIS	46	1995
WRECKLESS ERIC WRECKLESS ERIC	46	1978
WRESTLEMANIA – THE ALBUM WWF SUPERSTARS	10	1993
WRITER'S BLOCK PETER BJORN & JOHN	68	2007
THE WRITING ON THE WALL BUCKS FIZZ	89	1986
THE WRITING'S ON THE WALL DESTINY'S CHILD	10	1999
WRITTEN IN RED STRANGLERS	52	1997
WU-TANG FOREVER WU-TANG CLAN	1	1997
WWE ORIGINALS VARIOUS ARTISTS (COLUMBIA)	11	2004
WWE – WRECKLESS INTENT VARIOUS ARTISTS (COLUMBIA)	16	2006
WWF AGGRESSION VARIOUS ARTISTS (PRIORITY)	13	2000
WWF – FORCEABLE ENTRY VARIOUS ARTISTS (COLUMBIA)	6	2002

Title / Artist	Peak Position	Year of Release
X INXS	2	1990
X BELOVED	25	1996
X DEF LEPPARD	14	2002
X LIBERTY X	27	2005
X KYLIE MINOGUE	4	2007
X & Y COLDPLAY	1	2005
THE X FACTOR IRON MAIDEN	8	1995
THE X LIST VARIOUS ARTISTS (VIRGIN)	9	2003
X MARKS DESTINATION THE WHIP	75	2008
XANADU (OST) OLIVIA NEWTON-JOHN/ ELECTRIC LIGHT ORCHESTRA	2	1980
THE XENON CODEX HAWKWIND	79	1988
XL – 1 PETE SHELLEY	42	1983
XL RECORDINGS – THE SECOND CHAPTER VARIOUS ARTISTS (XL RECORDINGS)	5	1991
XPANDER (EP) SASHA	18	1999
XS ALL AREAS – THE GREATEST HITS STATUS QUO	16	2004
X-TRA NAKED SHABBA RANKS	38	1993
XXV SHADOWS	34	1983
XXX HIP HOP VARIOUS ARTISTS (UNIVERSAL)	12	2003

Title / Artist	Peak Position	Year of Release
Y		
YANG FISH	52	1995
YANKEE HOTEL FOXTROT WILCO	40	2002
YARDBIRDS YARDBIRDS	20	1966
YEAH WANNADIES	73	2000
YEAH DEF LEPPARD	52	2006
YEAH YEAH YEAH YEAH/OUR TROUBLED YOUTH BIKINI KILL/HUGGY BEAR	12	1989
YEAR OF THE CAT AL STEWART	38	1977
YEAR OF THE DOG AGAIN DMX	22	2006
YEAR OF THE GENTLEMAN NE-YO	2	2008
YEAR OF THE HORSE NEIL YOUNG & CRAZY HORSE	36	1997
YEAR ZERO NINE INCH NAILS	6	2007
YELLOW MOON DON WILLIAMS	52	1983
YELLOW SUBMARINE BEATLES	3	1969
YELLOW SUBMARINE SONGTRACK BEATLES	8	1999
YEMEN CUTTA CONNECTION BLACK STAR LINER	66	1996
YENTL BARBRA STREISAND	21	1983
YES DO ME BAD THINGS	68	2005
THE YES ALBUM YES	4	1971
...YES PLEASE! HAPPY MONDAYS	14	1992
YESSHOWS YES	22	1981
YESSONGS YES	7	1973
YESTERDAY ONCE MORE CARPENTERS	10	1984
YESTERDAY WENT TOO SOON FEEDER	8	1999
YESTERDAYS YES	27	1975
YESTERDAY'S DREAMS FOUR TOPS	37	1969
YESTERDAY'S MEMORIES JAMES LAST	17	1971
YESTERDAY'S MEMORIES DANIEL O'DONNELL	19	2002
YIELD PEARL JAM	7	1998
YIN FISH	58	1995
YOSHIMI BATTLES THE PINK ROBOTS FLAMING LIPS	13	2002
YOU AND ME BOTH YAZOO	1	1983
YOU ARE BEAUTIFUL STYLISTICS	26	1975
YOU ARE THE QUARRY MORRISSEY	2	2004
YOU ARE WHAT YOU IS FRANK ZAPPA	51	1981
YOU BELONG TO ME JANE McDONALD	21	2005
YOU BOYZ MAKE BIG NOIZE SLADE	98	1987
YOU BREAK MY HEART IN 17 PLACES TRACEY ULLMAN	14	1983
YOU CAN ALL JOIN IN VARIOUS ARTISTS (ISLAND)	18	1969
YOU CAN DANCE MADONNA	5	1987
YOU CAN DO ANYTHING ZUTONS	6	2008
YOU CAN'T ARGUE WITH A SICK MIND JOE WALSH	28	1976
YOU CAN'T HIDE YOUR LOVE FOREVER ORANGE JUICE	21	1982
YOU CAN'T STOP ROCK 'N' ROLL TWISTED SISTER	14	1983
YOU CAUGHT ME OUT TRACEY ULLMAN	92	1984
YOU COULD HAVE BEEN WITH ME SHEENA EASTON	33	1981
YOU COULD HAVE IT SO MUCH BETTER FRANZ FERDINAND	1	2005
YOU CROSS MY PATH CHARLATANS	39	2008
YOU DON'T BRING ME FLOWERS NEIL DIAMOND	15	1979
YOU DON'T KNOW ME – THE BEST OF ARMAND VAN HELDEN	41	2008
YOU GOTTA GO THERE TO COME BACK STEREOPHONICS	1	2003
YOU GOTTA SAY YES TO ANOTHER EXCESS YELLO	65	1983

	Peak Position	Year of Release
YOU GOTTA SIN TO GET SAVED MARIA McKEE	26	1993
YOU HAVE NO IDEA WHAT YOU'RE GETTING YOURSELF INTO DOES IT OFFEND YOU, YEAH?	48	2008
YOU KNOW IT'S ME BARBARA DICKSON	39	1981
YOU LIGHT UP MY LIFE JOHNNY MATHIS	3	1978
YOU MAKE ME FEEL LIKE SINGING A SONG MAX BYGRAVES	39	1974
YOU MIGHT BE SURPRISED ROY AYERS	91	1985
YOU MUST REMEMBER THIS... VARIOUS ARTISTS (HAPPY DAYS)	16	1995
YOU NEVER CAN TELL CHUCK BERRY	18	1964
YOU RAISE ME UP VARIOUS ARTISTS (UNIVERSAL)	3	2006
YOU RAISE ME UP 2008 VARIOUS ARTISTS (UNIVERSAL)	1	2008
YOU RAISE ME UP – THE BEST OF ALED JONES	63	2006
YOU SCARE ME TO DEATH MARC BOLAN	88	1981
YOU SEE COLOURS DELAYS	24	2006
YOU TAKE MY HEART AWAY SHIRLEY BASSEY	34	1977
YOU WANT IT, YOU GOT IT BRYAN ADAMS	78	1985
YOU WIN AGAIN VAN MORRISON/LINDA GAIL LEWIS	34	2000
YOU, ME & US MARTINE McCUTCHEON	2	1999
YOU, ME AND HE MTUME	85	1984
YOU? ME? US? RICHARD THOMPSON	32	1996
YOU'LL LOVE TO HATE THIS RICHARD BLACKWOOD	35	2000
YOU'LL NEVER KNOW RODNEY FRANKLIN	64	1980
YOU'LL NEVER WALK ALONE ELVIS PRESLEY	20	1971
YOU'LL NEVER WALK ALONE VARIOUS ARTISTS (V2)	18	1997
YOUNG AMERICANS DAVID BOWIE	2	1975
THE YOUNG AND THE HOPELESS GOOD CHARLOTTE	15	2003
YOUNG FOR ETERNITY SUBWAYS	32	2005
YOUNG GIFTED & BLACK VARIOUS ARTISTS (TROJAN)	6	2002
YOUNG GIFTED & BLACK 2 VARIOUS ARTISTS (TROJAN)	12	2004
YOUNG GODS LITTLE ANGELS	17	1991
YOUNG GUNS GO FOR IT VARIOUS ARTISTS (VIRGIN)	10	2000
YOUNG HEARTS RUN FREE CANDI STATON	34	1976
YOUNG LUST – THE ANTHOLOGY AEROSMITH	32	2001
THE YOUNG ONES (OST) CLIFF RICHARD & THE SHADOWS	1	1961
YOUNG TEAM MOGWAI	75	1997
YOUNG WARM AND WONDERFUL GENE PITNEY	39	1967
YOUNGER THAN YESTERDAY BYRDS	37	1967
YOUR ARSENAL MORRISSEY	4	1992
YOUR FAVOURITE HYMNS IAN TRACEY WITH THE LIVERPOOL CATHEDRALS' CHOIRS	62	1992
YOUR FILTHY LITTLE MOUTH DAVID LEE ROTH	28	1994
YOUR NEW FAVOURITE BAND HIVES	7	2002
YOUR SECRET LOVE LUTHER VANDROSS	14	1996
YOUR WOMAN SUNSHINE ANDERSON	39	2001
YOU'RE BEAUTIFUL – 40 INSPIRING SONGS VARIOUS ARTISTS (UNIVERSAL)	8	2007
YOU'RE GONNA GET IT TOM PETTY & HEARTBREAKERS	34	1978
YOU'RE MY BEST THING DON WILLIAMS	58	1978
YOU'RE NEVER ALONE WITH A SCHIZOPHRENIC IAN HUNTER	49	1979
YOU'RE THE INSPIRATION – 16 ROMANTIC LOVE SONGS VARIOUS ARTISTS (COLUMBIA)	10	1991
YOU'RE THE ONE PAUL SIMON	20	2000
YOU'RE UNDER ARREST MILES DAVIS	88	1985
YOURS SINCERELY HARRY SECOMBE	46	1991
YOURS SINCERELY PASADENAS	6	1992
YOURS TO KEEP ALBERT HAMMOND JR	74	2006
YOURS TRULY ANGRY MOB KAISER CHIEFS	1	2007
YOURSELF OR SOMEONE LIKE YOU MATCHBOX 20	50	1998
YOUTH AND YOUNG MANHOOD KINGS OF LEON	3	2003
YOUTH AND YOUNG MANHOOD/AHA SHAKE HEARTBREAK KINGS OF LEON	67	2008
THE YOUTH OF TODAY MUSICAL YOUTH	24	1982
YOUTHANASIA/HIDDEN TREASURE MEGADETH	6	1995
YOUTHQUAKE DEAD OR ALIVE	9	1985
YOU'VE COME A LONG WAY, BABY FATBOY SLIM	1	1998
YOU'VE GOT A FRIEND BARBARA WINDSOR	45	1999
YOU'VE GOT A FRIEND – THE BEST OF JAMES TAYLOR	4	2003
YOU'VE GOT THE POWER THIRD WORLD	87	1982
YOU'VE GOT TO LAUGH VARIOUS ARTISTS (TOWERBELL)	51	1986
YS JOANNA NEWSOM	41	2006

Z

	Peak Position	Year of Release
Z MY MORNING JACKET	74	2005
ZAGORA LOOSE ENDS	15	1986
ZAPPA IN NEW YORK FRANK ZAPPA	55	1978
ZARAGON JOHN MILES	43	1978
ZAZU ROSIE VELA	20	1987
ZEBOP! SANTANA	33	1981
ZEITGEIST LEVELLERS	1	1995
ZENYATTA MONDATTA POLICE	1	1980
ZERO SHE FLIES AL STEWART	40	1970
ZETGEIST SMASHING PUMPKINS	4	2007
ZIGGY STARDUST – THE MOTION PICTURE DAVID BOWIE	17	1983
ZINC ALLOY AND THE HIDDEN RIDERS OF TOMORROW MARC BOLAN & T. REX	12	1974
ZINGALAMDUNI ARRESTED DEVELOPMENT	16	1994
ZIP STYLE METHOD JOHN COOPER CLARKE	97	1982
ZOMBIES ALIENS VAMPIRES DINOSAURS HELLOGOODBYE	17	2007
THE ZOMBIES AND BEYOND ZOMBIES	43	2008
ZONES HAWKWIND	57	1983
ZOOLOOK JEAN-MICHEL JARRE	47	1984
ZOOM ELECTRIC LIGHT ORCHESTRA	34	2001
ZOOROPA U2	1	1993
ZOOT ZOOT MONEY & THE BIG ROLL BAND	23	1966
ZUCCHERO ZUCCHERO	29	1991
ZUMA NEIL YOUNG & CRAZY HORSE	44	1975